THE COLUMBIA-
VIKING DESK
ENCYCLOPEDIA

A – K

VOLUME ONE

THE COLUMBIA-
VIKING DESK
ENCYCLOPEDIA

Compiled and edited at Columbia University
by the staff of The Columbia Encyclopedia
WILLIAM BRIDGWATER, Editor-in-chief

A – K

VOLUME ONE

PUBLISHED BY THE VIKING PRESS

NEW YORK

PREFACE

The Columbia-Viking Desk Encyclopedia is a compact presentation of ready-to-use information in brief and portable form. It is derived from *The Columbia Encyclopedia*, specifically from the second edition of that standard reference book, published in 1950. Every effort has been made to keep the spirit of *The Columbia Encyclopedia* through careful pruning of the articles and elimination of headings. The present work has some 31,000 entries covered in about a million and a quarter words.

Like the parent volume, this book is an encyclopedia and makes no attempt to be a dictionary. Entries that would supply no more than dictionary information are excluded. The limited space has been given to specific headings that seem most useful to the ordinary reader. Articles on general topics, such as American literature, which could be covered only inadequately, have been disregarded, while articles giving directly useful facts, such as those on important figures in American literature, have been scrupulously retained. The book is not what is called in English an encyclopedic dictionary. It is rather a parallel in English to the compact hand encyclopedias issued on the Continent. It is designed to give as much finger-tip knowledge as can be offered in brief scope.

This is an American encyclopedia, and therefore stress has been laid on places and persons in the United States, Canada, and Latin America. The European tradition in Western culture has not been ignored. There are thousands of articles on European places, persons, and history, but the accent is American. This desk encyclopedia belongs primarily to the New World.

In preparing this much reduced form of an encyclopedia, the writers have used as many abbreviations as seemed feasible for the convenience of the ordinary reader.

Similarly, wherever the subject of a sentence is clear, that word has been omitted. These practices, however, have been limited to sentences where no ambiguity could occur. When full sentences are required for the ease of the reader, all the words appear. The seeming inconsistency has been adopted to save as much space as possible without cost to the reader's understanding. Shorter and more rapidly comprehensible articles are more abbreviated than the longer articles, which require longer concentration of the reader's attention.

In this book even more than in *The Columbia Encyclopedia* the cross references are of the utmost importance. To save space, the writers have avoided repeating the same information under different headings. The cross references within articles are indicated by the use of SMALL CAPITALS. These appear only when the reader will find under the other heading further information on the heading he is consulting. Learning to follow out such cross references will benefit the reader immeasurably.

These volumes contain a number of illustrations and maps for the convenience of the reader. The maps on the end papers and in the text are not intended to replace an atlas but may, like the articles, give information rapidly to the busy reader. The illustrations also present knowledge in brief compass.

Since *The Columbia Encyclopedia* appeared in 1950 the world has seen many events, and many new faces have appeared. *The Columbia-Viking Desk Encyclopedia* has taken these happenings and persons into account so far as the allowance of space would permit.

Figures for populations, for areas of countries, and for altitudes of mountains have also been brought up to date according to the latest official data available from various parts of the world. The populations given for places in the United States are those listed in the 1950 census. Elsewhere the latest complete census figures or official estimates have been inserted.

The articles are written for English-speaking readers, and English forms have been used throughout. The pronunciations given are those that are current among educated Americans. Wherever a foreign spelling, differing from the English form, would seem of use to the reader, that spelling is given in italics after the ordinary form.

The articles are capsules of information, too small to contain extended discussion. Therefore it has seemed to the editors of this work of the utmost importance to examine every line with the intention of eliminating any possible bias. Where it has proved misleading to avoid controversy, extra space has been taken to offer brief statements of both sides of the disagreement.

The spirit that has breathed life into the making of this work has come ultimately from the late Clarke Fisher Ansley, who planned and edited the first edition of *The Columbia Encyclopedia*. More directly the makers of these volumes are indebted to Elizabeth J. Sherwood, who was one of the two editors of the second edition and a shaper of the ideals that have guided the workers on *The Columbia-Viking Desk Encyclopedia*.

Though the publication of this book is an undertaking of The Viking Press, the work itself owes much to Columbia University. It would be impossible to list all those at the University who contributed to the creation of *The Columbia Encyclopedia* and to the abridged version.

The chief burden of creating these volumes fell upon the assistant editors whose names appear in small capitals in the staff list. They gave generously of their own time and vigor to make this book as useful as possible.

The staff of The Viking Press, having undertaken the hardships of producing a reference book, have borne with fortitude and patience the mishaps and delays that seem inevitable in such projects. Thanks are particularly due to Harold K. Guinzburg for his constructive thinking about all aspects of the problem; to Milton B. Glick, who gave the project its first impetus at The Viking Press and was responsible for design and production; and to Marshall A. Best, who undertook the task of reading all the copy and suggested many changes, always for the betterment of the book.

The book also owes much to Charles G. Proffitt, Director of Columbia University Press, and Henry H. Wiggins, Manager of the Publication Department.

WILLIAM BRIDGWATER
EDITOR-IN-CHIEF

April 20, 1953

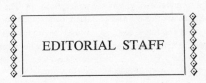

EDITORIAL STAFF

WILLIAM BRIDGWATER, Editor-in-chief

ELIZABETH E. ADAMS
BEATRICE ALDRICH
GWENDOLYN JONES
William F. Bernhardt
James T. Burns, Jr.
George L. Groman, Evelyn Merrin, Warren
Walter L. Sherry, Jr.

J. CHRISTOPHER HEROLD
SONO ROSENBERG
MILDRED M. MALKIN
Ida T. Hopper   Arthur J. Moore
Joan McQuary   Barbara Melissa Voorhis
William Paul, Philip L. Perl,

CONTRIBUTORS

Philip M. Bergovoy
Nelda Cassuto
Rollin P. Dickerson
Lily Edelman
Alida Fortier Gaewsky
Natalie Gurney
V. J. Harward
Glenn Hasselrooth
Elva D. Hoover
George M. Johnson

Marjorie P. Johnson
Annie Kessler
Matthew Lipman
Helene K. Marer
Dorothée Nolan
Henry Paolucci
Geraldine Pelles
Esther I. Persson
Julius Rabin

Hans R. Reinhardt
Henry B. Reuben
Maureen Rosenhaupt
David G. Rubin
Jean Rubin
Marie-Anne Phelps Seabury
Ann Smith
Helen E. Stroop
Elizabeth K. Valkenier
Peter Welgos

ILLUSTRATIONS

All illustrations especially designed for The Columbia-Viking Desk Encyclopedia

Research Editor: NATALIE RAYMOND; Technical drawings by I. N. STEINBERG and Associates

Continental maps drawn by JACK LUBOFF (*New York Herald Tribune*)
Consultant: GERARD L. ALEXANDER (*Map Division, New York Public Library*)
World maps by RICHARD EDES HARRISON

The following were among the advisers and contributors to
The Columbia Encyclopedia, Second Edition, of which this is a condensed version

EVELYN B. BOYCE
Adriaan J. Barnouw
Chung-Yuan Chang
Elliott Van Kirk Dobbie
Mary K. Dobbie
Clarissa P. Farrar
James Gilbert
Talbot Hamlin
William Robert Irwin
John Kepke

LEON E. SELTZER
William M. Mitchell
Robert Molloy
José Ferrater Mora
H. C. Nixon
Norma Pfeiffer
Bernard K. Sandwell
Carl T. Schmidt
Theodore Shabad

RAYMOND J. DIXON
William B. S. Smith
Peter Stern
Emerson H. Swift
William York Tindall
George L. Trager
James G. Van Derpool
Isabella Wakeham, M.D.
Ralph F. Weld
Henry H. Wiggins

SMALL CAPITALS = cross references.   Pronunciation key: pp. xiv and xv.   Abbreviations: p. 2.

vii

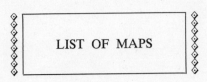

LIST OF MAPS

MAPS

As a rule the articles on places do not give cross references to maps; but countries, principal cities, large rivers, and many other geographic features may be located on the maps of their respective continents

WORLD MAPS

THE ATLANTIC WORLD   *Inside front cover of Volume I and Volume II*

THE PACIFIC WORLD   *Inside back cover of Volume I and Volume II*

CONTINENT MAPS

LIST OF ILLUSTRATIONS

Grouped under subject headings for convenient comparison of related material. A number of subjects have been included in the illustrations, though not in the text, when it was felt that a picture served the purpose better than words

TABLES AND LISTS

TABLES

The following data are arranged in tabular form

LISTS

Some of the ready-reference material in the text is located as follows

SMALL CAPITALS = cross references.   Pronunciation key: pp. xiv and xv.   Abbreviations: p. 2.

PRONUNCIATION KEY

NOTES

The purpose of the pronunciation symbols is to give at least one serviceable way in which the word in question may be pronounced when used by careful speakers of English.

In this work a pronunciation is ordinarily indicated for words printed in boldface when this pronunciation is not obvious to the English-speaking reader. Of two or more words or names in succession spelled and pronounced alike, a pronunciation is frequently indicated for the first occurrence only.

For names of localities in English-speaking areas the local pronunciation is preferred, provided it is acceptable to careful speakers.

For foreign words and names the speaker of English desires to use a pronunciation that will be acceptable to other speakers of English (unless he is speaking in a foreign language). In many cases (e.g., Paris) there is a traditional pronunciation that resembles little the current native pronunciation, and attempts to introduce into English conversation an approximation of the native form (something like pärē′) are regarded as an affectation. It is customary with foreign names that have no conventional English form to pronounce them with English sounds approximating the foreign ones. Such an approximation is indicated in this work, whenever there is no established usage to follow.

Actual good foreign-language pronunciations can be acquired only through imitation and study. Nevertheless, Englishmen and Americans have for many years made a practice of imitating roughly five French sounds: ã, ẽ, õ, ũ, and ü. A speaker of English can attain ã by saying äng without the closure at the back of the mouth necessary to make ng, breathing through nose and mouth as well; ẽ is similarly like the beginning of ăng, õ like that of ŏng, and ũ like that of ûng. To approximate ü say o͞o with vigor, then, keeping the lips rounded, change the sound quickly to ē.

For Latin words the venerable English tradition is followed [e.g., Caesar (sē′zŭr)], except where some other pronunciation is well established, as in ecclesiastical names [e.g., Salve Regina (säl′vä rājē′nú)]. The so-called classical pronunciation, which approximates the pronunciation Caesar used [e.g., Caesar (kī′sär)], is not given, as being not usual in English conversation.

Pronunciation Key

ā   fate (fāt), fail (fāl), vacation (vākā'shún)

â   care (kâr), Mary (mâ'rē)

ă   bat (băt), add (ăd), marry (mă'rē)

ä   father (fä'dhúr), marble (mär'búl)

ã   French tant (tã), Rouen (rōōã'), and similar sounds in some other languages

b   back (băk), cab (kăb)

ch   chap (chăp)

d   dock (dŏk), cod (kŏd)

dh   father (fä'dhúr), then (dhĕn). Compare with th.

ē   even (ē'vún), clearing (klēr'ĭng), obvious (ŏb'vēús)

ĕ   end (ĕnd), met (mĕt), merry (mĕ'rē)

ē̃   French vin (vē̃), bien (byē̃), and similar sounds in some other languages

f   fat (făt), Philip (fĭ'lĭp)

g   get (gĕt), tag (tăg)

h   hat (hăt). See also ch, dh, kh, sh, th, zh, and hw

hw   where (hwâr), what (hwŏt)

ī   fine (fīn), buyer (bī'úr)

ĭ   pin (pĭn), pit (pĭt), spirit (spĭr'ĭt), fated (fā'tĭd)

j   jam (jăm), edge (ĕj), ginger (jĭn'júr)

k   cook (kōōk), tackle (tă'kúl)

kh   loch (lŏkh), German Aachen (ä'khún), Licht (lĭkht), and similar sounds in some other languages

l   peal (pēl), pull (pōōl)

m   hammer (hă'múr)

n   dinner (dĭ'núr)

ng   singing (sĭng'ĭng), finger (fĭng'gúr), sang (săng), sank (săngk)

ō   hope (hōp), potato (pútā'tō)

ô   orbit (ôr'bĭt), fall (fôl)

ŏ   hot (hŏt), toddy (tŏ'dē), borrow (bŏ'rō)

õ   French dont (dõ), chanson (shäsõ'), and similar sounds in some other languages

oi   boil (boil), royal (roi'úl)

ōō   boot (bōōt), lose (lōōz)

ŏŏ   foot (fŏŏt), purely (pyŏŏr'lē), manipulate (múnĭ'pyŏŏlāt)

ou   scout (skout), crowd (kroud)

p   pipe (pīp), happy (hă'pē)

r   road (rōd), appeared (úpērd'), carpenter (kär'púntúr)

s   saw (sô), case (kās)

sh   shall (shăl), nation (nā'shún)

t   tight (tīt), rating (rā'tĭng)

th   thin (thĭn), myth (mĭth). Compare with dh.

ū   fume (fūm), euphemism (ū'fúmĭzm)

û   curl (kûrl), Hamburg (hăm'bûrg), French œuvre (û'vrú), peu (pû), German schön (shûn), Goethe (gû'tú), and similar sounds in some other languages

ŭ   butter (bŭ'túr), suds (sŭdz), hurry (hŭ'rē)

ú   affair (úfâr'), sofa (sō'fú), contravene (kŏntrúvēn'), monopoly (múnŏ'púlē), suburban (súbûr'bún), callous (kă'lús), rather (ră'dhúr)

ü   French Cluny (klünē') German Lübeck (lü'bĕk), and similar sounds in some other languages

ũ   French Melun (múlũ'), Chambrun (shäbrũ'), and similar sounds in some other languages

v   vest (vĕst), trivial (trĭ'vēúl)

w   wax (wăks)

y   you (yōō), bunion (bŭ'nyún)

z   zipper (zĭ'púr), ease (ēz), treads (trĕdz)

zh   pleasure (plĕ'zhúr), rouge (rōōzh)

'   main accent, written after accented vowel or syllable: Nebraska (núbră'skú), James Buchanan (jāmz' būkă'nún)

"   secondary accent: Mississippi (mĭ"sŭsĭ'pē)

–   dash, replacing obvious portion of pronunciation: hegemony (hĭjĕ'múnē, hē–, hē'jùmō"nē, hē'gú–)

-   hyphen, to prevent ambiguity: Erlanger (ûr'lăng-úr), dishearten (dĭs-här'tún)

THE COLUMBIA-
VIKING DESK
ENCYCLOPEDIA

A

A, chemical symbol of element ARGON.

Aa (ä), name of many small streams of N Europe and Switzerland. The word is derived from an Indo-European root meaning "water."

Aachen (ä′khůn) or **Aix-la-Chapelle** (āks′-lä-shůpĕl′), city (pop. 129,967), North Rhine-Westphalia, W Germany, near Dutch and Belgian borders, in a brown-coal dist. Machinery, rubber, textile mfg. Hot mineral baths in use since Roman times. Charlemagne built splendid palace, and founded cathedral (rebuilt 10th cent.; partly Byzantine, partly Gothic), which contains his tomb. German kings were crowned at Aachen until 1531. Free imperial city until annexed by France (1801); awarded to Prussia 1814. Except for cathedral, most of historic buildings were devastated in World War II, when U.S. troops captured Aachen after bitter fighting (Oct. 21, 1944). For treaties signed here 1668 and 1748, see AIX-LA-CHAPELLE, TREATY OF.

Aakjaer, Jeppe (yĕp′ů ôk′yâr), 1866–1930, Danish poet, author of *Songs of the Rye* (1906) and *Heimdal's Wanderings* (1924). Also wrote novels.

Aaland Islands, Finland: see ÅLAND ISLANDS.

Aalborg, Dan. *Ålborg* or *Aalborg* (all: ôl′bôrg), city (pop. 79,806), Denmark, in N Jutland; a port on S shore of Lim Fjord.

Aalesund, Norway: see ÅLESUND.

Aalst, Belgium: see ALOST.

Aalto, Alvar (ôl′vär äl′tō), 1899–, Finnish architect and furniture designer. Pioneered in evolving functional plywood furniture.

Aanrud, Hans (häns′ ôn′rŏŏd), 1863–, Norwegian writer of stories, plays, and books for children. Portrayed life in his home valley, Gudbrandsdal.

Aar (är), river, 183 mi. long, Switzerland, rising in Bernese Alps and flowing through L. Brienz and L. Thun, past Bern, Solothurn, and Aarau, into the Rhine.

Aarau (ä′rou), town (pop. 14,295), cap. of Aargau canton, N Switzerland, on the Aar. Mfg. shoes, scientific instruments.

aardvark (ärd′värk), nocturnal mammal, order Tubulidentata. Two species (genus *Orycteropus*), one in central, one in S Africa. Long snout, erect ears, naked or sparse hair on body; c.6 ft. long; long tail. Also called ant bear and earth pig.

Aargau (är′gou), canton (542 sq. mi.; pop. 300,442), N Switzerland; cap. Aarau. Traversed by fertile Aar valley. Swiss possession since 1415; canton since 1803. Pop. is Protestant. German-speaking.

Aarhus, Dan. *Århus* or *Aarhus* (all: ôr′hōōs), city (pop. 116,167), Denmark, in E Jutland, on Aarhus Bay, which opens on the Kattegat. Second largest Danish city; commercial and industrial center. An episcopal see since 13th cent., it has a medieval cathedral and many fine Renaissance houses.

Aaron (â′růn), in Bible, first high priest, brother of Moses and his spokesman in Egypt. Descendants were high priests and priests. Jehovah performed miracles through him (e.g., blossoming of Aaron's rod). Aaron made the golden calf and led worship of it. Ex. 4.14–16; 6.20; 7.1–12; 28–32; Num. 12; 17; 18; 20; 33.38,39; Deut. 10.6.

Aasen, Ivar Andreas (ē′vär ändrä′äs ô′sůn), 1813–96, Norwegian lexicographer. By standardizing the dialects of his people he created a speech (i.e., Landsmaal) which became the national language.

abacus, in mathematics, simple calculating device. One type is frame with movable counters on parallel rods or in grooves.

Abadan (äbädän′), city (pop. 39,739), E Iran, on Abadan isl., in delta of the Shatt-el-Arab at head of Persian Gulf. Site of huge oil refinery.

Abaddon (ůbăd′ůn) [Heb.,= destruction], Hebrew name of the destroying angel. See SATAN.

abalone (ăbůlō′nē), popular name in America of univalve mollusk, genus *Haliotis*, also called ear shell or sea ear. Common food on California coast.

Abana (ůbā′nů), river of Damascus. 2 Kings 5.12. It is probably the Barada, flowing near Damascus.

abandonment, in law, absolute relinquishment of property rights, accomplished in such a manner that another person may acquire them in an original (not derived) form. See also DESERTION.

Abano, Pietro d' (pyä′trō dä′bänō), 1250?–1316?, Italian physician and philosopher,

SMALL CAPITALS = cross references.   Pronunciation key: pp. xiv and xv.   Abbreviations: p. 2.

1

chief founder of Paduan school of medical learning.

Abarbanel, Isaac: see ABRAVANEL, ISAAC.

A battery: see BATTERY, ELECTRIC.

Abbadides (ă'bŭdīdz), Arabian dynasty in Spain; ruled emirate of SEVILLE 1023–91. Succeeding the caliphs of Córdoba as chief Moorish power in Spain, they were replaced in turn by the ALMORAVIDES.

Abbas (ă'bŭs, äbäs'), d. 652, uncle of Mohammed; ancestor of Abbasid caliphs.

Abbas I (Abbas the Great), 1557–1628, shah of Persia (1587–1628), of Safavid dynasty. Took large area from the Turks 1603–23; estab. order.

Abbas II (Abbas Hilmi), 1874–1944, khedive of Egypt (1892–1914), deposed by the British.

Abbasid (ŭbă'sĭd, ă'bŭsĭd) or **Abbaside** (–sīd, –sĭd), Arabic family, descended from Abbas (uncle of Mohammed), which held caliphate 749–1258. First caliph was ABU-L-ABBAS AS-SAFFAH; second was MANSUR. Early years of Abbasid rule were brilliant, especially under HARUN-AL-RASHID and MAMUN. Rival caliphs (see CALIPHATE) helped to weaken power of the Abbasid, who were finally overthrown 1258 by Hulagu Khan (grandson of Jenghiz Khan).

Abbe, Cleveland (ăb'ē), 1838–1916, American meteorologist. As Cincinnati Observatory director, he inaugurated daily weather forecasting based on telegraph reports. Influenced establishment of, and served in, government weather service.

Abbe, Ernst (ĕrnst ä'bŭ), 1840–1905, German physicist; owner of Zeiss optical works. Invented Abbe refractometer.

Abbeville (äbvēl'), city (pop. 16,098), Somme dept., N France, on Somme R. Textile mfg., especially linen. Here Louis IX made advantageous treaty with Henry III of England (1259). Gothic Church of St. Wolfram damaged in World War II.

Abbeville (ăb'ĕvĭl). **1** Town (pop. 9,338), S La., N of Vermilion Bay of Gulf of Mexico, in a rice-growing area. Grew around Roman Catholic chapel (1845). **2** City (pop. 5,395), NW S.C., near Savannah R. WNW of Columbia. Mfg. of textiles.

Abbey, Edwin Austin, 1852–1911, American artist, noted for book illustrations. Official painter of coronation of Edward VII.

abbey, autonomous monastic community, especially among Benedictine, Cistercian, Carthusian, and Cluniac orders. Generally a courtyard (ecclesiastical atrium) is surrounded by cloister; buildings center about church, and all are enclosed by a wall. In Benedictine expansion after 8th cent., abbeys were centers of peaceful arts in chaotic Europe.

Abbey Theatre, Irish theatrical group. Experiments with an Irish theater resulted in forming (1902) of Irish Natl. Theatre Society, whose playwright-directors included Yeats, A.E., Lady Gregory, Synge. The Abbey Theatre (donated for free use by Miss A. E. F. Horniman 1904) was purchased 1910. Building burned down 1951. First to present plays of such writers as Sean O'Casey and Paul Vincent Carroll.

Abbot, Charles Greeley, 1872–, American astrophysicist, authority on solar radiation. Associated with Smithsonian Institution from 1896.

Abbotsford, estate (1811–32) of Sir Walter Scott, Roxburghshire, Scotland. Contains relics of Scott.

Abbott, Grace, 1878–1939, American social worker, director of Child Labor Division of U.S. Children's Bureau. Her sister, **Edith Abbott,** 1876–, became (1924) dean of School of Social Service Administration, Univ. of Chicago.

Abbott, Jacob, 1803–79, American writer of over 180 books, including the *Rollo* series for boys. His son was **Lyman Abbott,** 1835–1922, American clergyman. Edited *Christian Union* (later *Outlook*) with Henry Ward Beecher. Succeeded him at Plymouth Church, Brooklyn, 1888; resigned 1899 for editorial duties. Leader in "social gospel" movement.

abbreviation, in writing, arbitrary shortening of a word, usually by cutting off letters from the end, e.g., U.S.A., Geo. (George). Contraction serves the same purpose but is understood strictly to be the shortening of a word by cutting out letters in the middle, the omission sometimes being indicated by an apostrophe. Many writers hold that a contraction (in which last letter of the word appears) should not be followed by a point, though an abbreviation should. Usage, however, differs widely. A period is never used when apostrophes appear. A select list of widely used abbreviations, including all used in this volume, follows:

LIST OF ABBREVIATIONS

a = are [100 sq. meters]
a.= acre, acres
AAA = Agricultural Adjustment Administration
A.A.A.= American Automobile Association
A.B.= Able-bodied Seaman; *Artium Baccalaureus* [Bachelor of Arts]
abbr. (*or* abbrev.) = abbreviation
Abp.= Archbishop
abr.= abridged
AC = alternating current
Acad.= Academy
acct.= account
A.D.= *anno Domini* [in the year

of the Lord] (often small capitals)
ad fin.= *ad finem* [to the end, at the end]
adj.= adjective
Adjt.= Adjutant
ad lib.= *ad libitum* [at pleasure]
Adm.= Admiral, Admiralty
adv.= adverb
ad val. (*or* adv.) = *ad valorem* [on the value]
advt. (*or* adv.) = advertisement
AEC = Atomic Energy Commission
A.E.F.= American Expeditionary Force

aet. (*or* aetat.) = *aetatis* [of age]
A.F. of L. (*or* A.F.L.) = American Federation of Labor
Afr.= Africa
agr.= agriculture, agricultural
agt.= agent
A.H.= *anno Hegirae* [in the year of the Hegira] (often small capitals)
A.I.A.= American Institute of Architects
A.L.A.= American Library Association
Ala.= Alabama
alt.= altitude
Alta.= Alberta
A.M.= *ante meridiem* [before

noon] (often small capitals); *anno mundi* [in the year of the world] (often small capitals); *Artium Magister* [Master of Arts]

A.M.A.= American Medical Association

A.M.D.G.= *ad majorem Dei gloriam* [to the greater glory of God]

Amer. (*or* Am.) = America, American

amp.= ampere, amperes

amt.= amount

anc.= ancient

ann.= annual, annals

anon.= anonymous

AP = Associated Press

A.P.A.= American Protective Association

app.= appendix, appointed

apt.= apartment

Ariz.= Arizona

Ark.= Arkansas

art.= article

A.S. (*or* AS) = Anglo-Saxon

ASCAP = American Society of Composers, Authors, and Publishers

assn.= association

ASSR = Autonomous Soviet Socialist Republic

asst.= assistant

atty.= attorney

at. wt.= atomic weight

A.U.C.= *ab urbe condita* [from the founding of the city] or *anno urbis conditae* [in the year of the founding of the city] (often small capitals)

Aug.= August

AUS = Army of the United States

AV = Authorized Version

Av. (*or* Ave.) = Avenue

av.= average, avoirdupois

AVC = American Veterans Committee

avdp. (*or* av.) = avoirdupois

Ave. (*or* Av.) = Avenue

AWOL = absent without leave

b.= born, born in

B.A.= Bachelor of Arts

bal.= balance

Bapt.= Baptist

B.Arch.= Bachelor of Architecture

Bart.= Baronet

B.B.C.= British Broadcasting Corporation

bbl.= barrel

B.C.= before Christ (often small capitals); British Columbia

B.D.= Bachelor of Divinity

bd.= board

bf = boldface

Bl.= Blessed

Bldg.= Building

B.Lit.= Bachelor of Literature

Blvd.= Boulevard

B.Mus.= Bachelor of Music

bor.= borough

Bp.= Bishop

B.P.O.E.= Benevolent Protective Order of Elks

Br. (*or* Brit.) = British

Brig. Gen.= Brigadier General

Brit. (*or* Br.) = British

bro.= brother

B.S.= Bachelor of Science

B.Sc.= Bachelor of Science

B.T.U.= British thermal unit

bu.= bushel, bushels

bul.= bulletin

Bulg.= Bulgarian

bur.= bureau

B.V.M.= Blessed Virgin Mary

C.= centigrade, Caius

c.= copyright

c. (*or* ca.) = *circa* [about]

ca = centare

cal.= calorie

Calif.= California

Can.= Canadian

can.= canon, canto

Cant.= Canticles (Song of Solomon)

Cantab.= *Cantabrigiensis* [of Cambridge]

cap.= capital, capital letter, capitulum [chapter]

Capt.= Captain

car. (*or* k.) = carat

CARE = Cooperative for American Remittances to Everywhere, Inc.

Cath.= Catholic

C.B.= Companion of the Order of the Bath

C.C.= Chamber of Commerce

c.c. (*or* cc.) = cubic centimeter

CCC = Civilian Conservation Corps, Commodity Credit Corporation

C.E.= Civil Engineer

cen.= central

cent.= century, centuries

cf.= *confer* [compare]

cgs = centimeter-gram-second

chap.= chapter

Chem.E.= Chemical Engineer

Chron.= Chronicles

Cia = *Compañia* [Company]

C.I.D.= Criminal Investigation Department

Cie = *Compagnie* [Company]

CINC = Commander in Chief

C.I.O.= Congress of Industrial Organizations

C.J.= Chief Justice

cm = centimeter, centimeters

Cn.= Cneius

Co.= Company

co.= county

C.O.D.= cash (also collect) on delivery

coed.= coeducational

Col.= College, Colonel, Colossians

col.= collector, column

Coll.= Collection

Colo.= Colorado

Comdr.= Commander

comp.= compiled, compiler

Cong.= Congregational, Congressional

conj.= conjunction

Conn.= Connecticut

cont.= continued

Cor.= Corinthians

cor.= corrected

Corp.= Corporal

corp.= corporation

CP = Communist party

c.p.= candle power

C.P.A.= Certified Public Accountant

CPO = Chief Petty Officer

Cr.= credit, creditor

C.S.= Christian Science

C.S.A.= Confederate States of America

cu.= cubic

CVA = Columbia Valley Authority

cwt.= hundredweight

C.Z.= Canal Zone

D.= Don or Doña (Span. address), Dom or Dona (Port. address); Decimus

d.= daughter; *denarius* [penny], *denarii* [pence]; died, died in

Dan.= Daniel, Danish

D.A.R.= Daughters of the American Revolution

DC = direct current

D.C.= District of Columbia

D.C.L.= Doctor of Civil Law

D.D.= Doctor of Divinity

D.D.S.= Doctor of Dental Surgery

DDT = Dichlorodiphenyltrichloroethane

Dec.= December

deg.= degree, degrees

Del.= Delaware

Dem.= Democrat, Democratic

dept.= department

Deut.= Deuteronomy

diam.= diameter

dict.= dictionary

dist.= district

div.= division

DM = Deutschemark

do.= ditto [the same]

doz.= dozen, dozens

DP = displaced person

Dr.= debtor, Doctor

dr.= dram, drams

D.S.C.= Distinguished Service Cross

D.Sc.= Doctor of Science

D.S.M.= Distinguished Service Medal

D.S.O.= Companion of the Distinguished Service Order

Du.= Dutch

D.V.= *Deo volente* [God willing]

dwt.= pennyweight

E = east

ECA = Economic Cooperation Administration

Eccles.= Ecclesiastes

Ecclus.= Ecclesiasticus

ed.= edited, edition, editor, educated

E.E.= Electrical Engineer

e.g.= *exempli gratia* [for example]

E.M.= Engineer of Mines

emf = electromotive force

ency. (*or* encyc.) = encyclopedia

ENE = east-northeast

Eng.= English

engr.= engraved

enl.= enlarged

Eph.= Ephesians

Epis. (*or* Episc.) = Episcopal

ERP = European Recovery Program

ESE = east-southeast

esp.= especially

Esq.= Esquire

est.= estimated

estab.= establish, established

et al.= *et alibi* [and elsewhere]; *et alii* [and others]

etc.= *et cetera* [and others, and so forth]

et seq.= *et sequens* [and the following]

et sqq.= *et sequentes, et sequentia* [and those following]

Eur.= Europe

Ex.= Exodus

ex.= example, except

Ezek.= Ezekiel

F.= Fahrenheit, Fellow

F. (*or* Fri.) = Friday

f.= and the following page

f. (*or* fem.) = feminine

fac.= facsimile

F.A.G.S.= Fellow of the American Geographical Society

F. and A.M.= Free and Accepted Masons

FAO = Food and Agriculture

Organization of the United Nations

FBI = Federal Bureau of Investigation

FCC = Federal Communications Commission

Feb.= February

fed.= federated, federation

fem. (or f.) = feminine

FEPC = Fair Employment Practices Committee

ff.= and the following pages

fig.= figure

fl.= *floruit* [flourished]

Fla.= Florida

fl. oz.= fluid ounce

fo.= folio

f.o.b.= free on board

Fr.= French, Father, Friar

fr.= franc

F.R.A.S.= Fellow of the Royal Astronomical Society

F.R.C.P.= Fellow of the Royal College of Physicians

F.R.C.S.= Fellow of the Royal College of Surgeons

F.R.G.S.= Fellow of the Royal Geographical Society

Fri. (or F.) = Friday

front.= frontispiece

F.R.S.= Fellow of the Royal Society

FSA = Federal Security Agency

ft.= foot, feet, fort

FTC = Federal Trade Commission

g = gram, grams

Ga.= Georgia

Gal.= Galatians

gal.= galley, gallon, gallons

Gall.= Gallery

G.A.R.= Grand Army of the Republic

G.C.= Knight Grand Cross; Knight Grand Commander (of various British orders, when followed by abbreviation designating the order)

G.C.B.= Knight Grand Cross of the Order of the Bath

Gen.= General, Genesis

Ger.= German

GHQ = General Headquarters

G.I.= general issue (term for common soldier); gastro-intestinal

gloss.= glossary

G.O.P.= Grand Old Party (Republican Party)

Gov.= Governor

govt.= government

Gr.= Greek

gr.= grain, grains

grad.= graduate, graduated, graduated at

ha = hectare

Hab.= Habakkuk

Hag.= Haggai

Heb.= Hebrew, Hebrews (NT)

hhd.= hogshead

H.M.S.= His (Her) Majesty's Ship; His (Her) Majesty's Service

Hon.= the Honorable

hp = horsepower

hq.= headquarters

H.R.= House of Representatives

hr.= hour, hours

H.R.H.= His (Her) Royal Highness

ht.= height

Hung.= Hungarian

ib. (or ibid.) = *ibidem* [in the same place]

ICAO = International Civil Aviation Organization

ICC = Interstate Commerce Commission

I.E. (or I-E or IE) = Indo-European

i.e.= *id est* [that is]

IHS = *Iesus Hominum Salvator* [Jesus, the Savior of men]; *in hoc signo* [in this sign] (originally three letters of the Greek for Jesus)

Ill.= Illinois

ill. (or illus.) = illustrated, illustration

ILO = International Labor Organization

in.= inch, inches

inc.= incorporated

incl.= including, inclusive

incog.= incognito [unknown, unrecognized]

Ind.= Indiana

ind.= index

inf.= infinitive, *infra* [below]

I.N.R.I.= *Iesus Nazarenus, Rex Iudaeorum* [Jesus of Nazareth, King of the Jews]

Inst.= Institute, Institution

inst.= instant [the present month]

int.= interest

internatl.= international

introd.= introduction

I.O.F.= Independent Order of Foresters

I.O.O.F.= Independent Order of Odd Fellows

I O U = I owe you

I.Q. (or IQ) = intelligence quotient

Ir.= Irish

IRO = International Refugee Organization

Isa.= Isaiah

isl.= island

Ital. (or It.) = Italian

ital = italic type

ITO = International Trade Organization

I.W.W.= Industrial Workers of the World

JAG = Judge Advocate General

Jan.= January

Jap.= Japanese

J.D.= *Juris Doctor* [Doctor of Laws]

Jer.= Jeremiah

jg = junior grade (in U.S. Navy)

jour.= journal

J.P.= Justice of the Peace

Jr.= Junior

J.U.D.= *Juris Utriusque Doctor* [Doctor of Both Civil and Canon Laws]

k. (or car.) = carat

K.C.= King's Counsel; Knight Commander (of various British orders, when followed by abbreviation designating the order)

K.C. (or K. of C.) = Knights of Columbus

kc = kilocycle, kilocycles

K.G.= Knight of the Order of the Garter

kg = kilogram, kilograms

K.K.K.= Ku Klux Klan

kl = kiloliter, kiloliters

km = kilometer, kilometers

K. of C. (or K.C.) = Knights of Columbus

K.P.= Knights of Pythias

K.T.= Knight Templar

Kt.= Knight

kw = kilowatt, kilowatts

kwh = kilowatt hour, kilowatt hours

Ky.= Kentucky

L.= Lake; Left (in stage directions); Lucius

£ = *libra* [pound]

l = liter, liters

l.= line

La.= Louisiana

Lab.= Labrador

Lam.= Lamentations

Lat.= Latin

lat.= latitude

lb.= *libra* [pound], *librae* [pounds]

l.c.= lower case [not capitalized]

Lev.= Leviticus

L.H.D.= *Litterarum Humaniorum Doctor* [Doctor of Humane Letters]

L.I.= Long Island

Lieut.= Lieutenant

Litt.B.= *Litterarum Baccalaureus* [Bachelor of Literature]

Litt.D.= *Litterarum Doctor* [Doctor of Literature]

ll.= lines

LL.B.= *Legum Baccalaureus* [Bachelor of Laws]

LL.D.= *Legum Doctor* [Doctor of Laws]

loc. cit.= *loco citato* [in the place cited]

log.= logarithm

long.= longitude

Lt.= Lieutenant

Ltd.= Limited

Luth.= Lutheran

M.= mark [German coin]; *meridies* [noon] (often small capitals); Monsieur [Mr., Sir]; Marcus

m = meter, meters

m.= married

m. (or masc.) = masculine

M.A.= Master of Arts

Mac.= Maccabees

Maj.= Major

Mal.= Malachi

Man.= Manitoba

masc. (or m.) = masculine

Mass.= Massachusetts

Mat.= Matthew

max.= maximum

M.D.= *Medicinae Doctor* [Doctor of Medicine]

Md.= Maryland

mdse.= merchandise

M.E.= Mechanical Engineer, Methodist Episcopal

M.E. (or ME or Mid. Eng.) = Middle English

memo.= memorandum

Messrs.= Messieurs [Gentlemen] (plural of Mr.)

Met. E.= Metallurgical Engineer

Meth.= Methodist

Mex.= Mexican

mfg.= manufacturing

M.F.H.= Master of Foxhounds

mg = milligram, milligrams

Mgr = Monsignor

mgr.= manager

M.H.G. (or MHG) = Middle High German

mi.= mile, miles

Mich.= Michigan

Mid. Eng. (or M.E. or ME) = Middle English

min.= minimum, minute, minutes

Minn.= Minnesota

misc.= miscellaneous

Miss.= Mississippi

ml = milliliter, milliliters

Mlle = Mademoiselle [Miss]
MM.= Messieurs [Gentlemen] (plural of M.)
mm = millimeter, millimeters
Mme = Madame
Mo.= Missouri
mo.= month
Mon.= Monday
Mont.= Montana
M.P.= Member of Parliament
mph = miles per hour
Mr.= Mister (always abbreviated)
Mrs.= Mistress (always abbreviated)
MS = manuscript
M.S. (or M.Sc.) = Master of Science
Msgr = Monsignor
MSS = manuscripts
mt.= mount, mountain
mus.= museum, music
Mus.B.= *Musicae Baccalaureus* [Bachelor of Music]
Mus.D.= *Musicae Doctor* [Doctor of Music]
MVA = Missouri Valley Authority
N = north
n.= *natus* [born], neuter, noun
n. (or nom.) = nominative
N.A.= National Academy, North America
N.A.M.= National Association of Manufacturers
natl.= national
NATO = North Atlantic Treaty Organization
N.B.= New Brunswick; *nota bene* [note well]
N.C.= North Carolina
NCO = Noncommissioned Officer
n.d.= no date
N.Dak.= North Dakota
NE = northeast
N.E.A.= National Educational Association
Nebr.= Nebraska
Neh.= Nehemiah
neut. (or n.) = neuter
Nev.= Nevada
N.F.= Newfoundland
N.H.= New Hampshire
N.J.= New Jersey
NLRB = National Labor Relations Board
N.Mex.= New Mexico
NNE = north-northeast
NNW = north-northwest
No., no.= *numero* [number]
Nor.= Norwegian
Nov.= November
N.P.= Notary Public
NRA = National Recovery Administration
NROTC = Naval Reserve Officers' Training Corps
N.S.= New Style, Nova Scotia
NT = New Testament
Num.= Numbers
NW = northwest
N.Y.= New York
NYA = National Youth Administration
ob.= *obiit* [died]
Obad.= Obadiah
obs.= obsolete
Oct.= October
O.E. (or OE) = Old English
O.F.M.= *Ordo Fratrum Minorum* [Order of Friars Minor] (Franciscan)
O.Fr. (or O.F. or OF) = Old French

O.H.G. (or OHG) = Old High German
O.Ir.= Old Irish
O.K. (or OK) = correct
Okla.= Oklahoma
O.M.= Order of Merit
O.N. (or ON) = Old Norse
Ont.= Ontario
O.P.= Order of Preachers (Dominicans)
op.= *opus* [work]
OPA = Office of Price Administration
op. cit.= *opere citato* [in the work cited]
opp.= opposite
O.S.= Old Style
O.S.B.= *Ordo Sancti Benedicti* [Order of St. Benedict] (Benedictines)
OSS = Office of Strategic Services
OT = Old Testament
Oxon.= *Oxoniensis* [of Oxford]
oz.= ounce, ounces
P.= Publius
p.= page
Pa.= Pennsylvania
Pat. Off.= Patent Office
p.c.= per cent
pd.= paid
Pd. D.= *Pedagogiae Doctor* [Doctor of Pedagogy]
P.E.= Protestant Episcopal
P.E.I.= Prince Edward Island
PFC (or Pfc) = Private First Class
Pg. (or Port.) = Portuguese
Ph.B.= *Philosophiae Baccalaureus* [Bachelor of Philosophy]
Ph.D.= *Philosophiae Doctor* [Doctor of Philosophy]
Philip.= Philippians
P.I.= Philippine Islands
pinx.= *pinxit* [he painted]
pk.= peck
pl.= plate
pl. (or plur.) = plural
plur. (or pl.) = plural
P.M.= Postmaster; *post meridiem* [afternoon] (often small capitals)
PO = Petty Officer
P.O.= post office
Pol.= Polish
pop.= population
Port. (or Pg.) = Portuguese
POW = prisoner of war
pp.= pages
P.R.= Puerto Rico
pref.= preface
prep.= preparatory, preposition
Pres.= President
Presb.= Presbyterian
pron.= pronoun, pronounced
Prot.= Protestant
pro tem.= *pro tempore* [temporarily]
Prov.= Proverbs
prov.= province
prox.= *proximo* [of the next month]
P.S.= *post scriptum* [postscript]
Ps.= Psalm
pseud.= pseudonym
Pss.= Psalms
pt.= part, pint, pints, point
pub.= published, publisher
Pvt.= Private
PWA = Public Works Administration
Q.= Quintus
Q.C.= Queen's Counsel
Q.E.D.= *quod erat demonstrandum* [which was to be demonstrated]

Q.E.F.= *quod erat faciendum* [which was to be done]
QM = Quartermaster
qq.v.= *quae vide* [which see] (plural)
qt.= quart, quarts
Que.= Quebec
q.v.= *quod vide* [which see]
R.= River; Réaumur; *Rex* [King]; *Regina* [Queen]; Right (stage direction)
R.A.= Royal Academician
RAF = Royal Air Force
R.C.= Red Cross, Roman Catholic
Rd.= Road
REA = Rural Electrification Administration
recd.= received
rect. (or rept.) = receipt
reestab.= reestablish, reestablished
Regt.= Regiment
Rep.= Republican, Representative
rept.= report
rept. (or rect.) = receipt
Ret.= Retired
Rev.= Revelations, the Reverend
rev.= revised
RFC = Reconstruction Finance Corporation
R.F.D.= rural free delivery
R.I.= Rhode Island
R.I.P.= *requiescat in pace* [may he rest in peace]
RM.= Reichsmark
R.N.= Registered Nurse, Royal Navy
Rom.= Romans
rom = roman type
ROTC = Reserve Officers' Training Corps
rpm.= revolutions per minute
RR = railroad
RSFSR = Russian Socialist Federated Soviet Republic
R.S.V.P.= *Répondez, s'il vous plaît* [An answer is requested]
Rt. Rev.= the Right Reverend
Rus.= Russian
RV = Revised Version
Ry.= railway
S = south
S.= *San, Santa, Santo,* or *São* [Saint]
S. (or Sun.) = Sunday
s.= *solidus* [shilling], *solidi* [shillings]
S.A.= Salvation Army; South America; *Sociedad Anónima, Société Anonyme* [Limited]
Sam.= Samuel
S.A.R.= Sons of the American Revolution
Sask.= Saskatchewan
Sat.= Saturday
S.C.= South Carolina
s.c.= small capitals
sc.= *scilicet* [namely]
Sc.D.= *Scientiae Doctor* [Doctor of Science]
S.Dak.= South Dakota
SE = southeast
SEC = Securities and Exchange Commission
sec.= second, seconds, section, sections
secy.= secretary
Sen.= Senator
Sept.= September
ser.= series
Sex.= Sextus
Sgt.= Sergeant

SHAEF = Supreme Headquarters, Allied Expeditionary Force
SHAPE = Supreme Headquarters, Allied Powers in Europe
sing.= singular
S.J.= *Societas Jesu* [Society of Jesus]
Skt.= Sanskrit
Soc.= society
SOS = distress signal (not a true abbreviation)
Span. (*or* Sp.) = Spanish
S.P.C.A.= Society for the Prevention of Cruelty to Animals
S.P.C.C.= Society for the Prevention of Cruelty to Children
sp. gr.= specific gravity
S.P.Q.R.= *Senatus Populusque Romanus* [the Senate and People of Rome]
sq.= *sequens* [the following]; square
sqq.= *sequentes, sequentia* [those following]
Sr.= Senior
SS.= Saints
S.S.= Steamship, Sunday School
SSE = south-southeast
SSR = Soviet Socialist Republic
SSW = south-southwest
St.= Saint, Street
S.T.D.= *Sacrae Theologiae Doctor* [Doctor of Sacred Theology]
Ste = *Sainte* [Saint, feminine]
Sun. (*or* S.) = Sunday
sup.= supplement, *supra* [above]
Supt.= Superintendent
s.v.= *sub verbo* (under the entry)
SW = southwest
Swed. (*or* Sw.) = Swedish
T.= Titus
Tenn.= Tennessee
T.H.= Territory of Hawaii

Th. (*or* Thurs.) = Thursday
Thess.= Thessalonians
Thurs. (*or* Th.) = Thursday
Ti.= Tiberius
Tim.= Timothy
TNEC = Temporary National Economic Committee
T.N.T. (*or* TNT) = trinitrotoluene, trinitrotoluol
tp.= township
t.p. (*or* t.-p.) = title page
tr.= transitive, translated, translation, translator, transpose
treas.= treasurer
Tu. (*or* Tues.) = Tuesday
TVA = Tennessee Valley Authority
U.C.V.= United Confederate Veterans
U.D.C.= United Daughters of the Confederacy
ult.= *ultimo* [of the last month]
UN = United Nations
UNESCO = United Nations Educational, Scientific, and Cultural Organization
uninc.= unincorporated
Unit.= Unitarian
Univ.= Universalist, University
UNRRA = United Nations Relief and Rehabilitation Administration
UP = United Press
U.S.= United States
USA = United States Army
U.S.A.= United States of America
USBGN = United States Board on Geographic Names
USCG = United States Coast Guard
USMC = United States Marine Corps
USN = United States Navy
USO = United Service Organizations
U.S.S.= United States Ship
USSR = Union of Soviet Socialist Republics

v.= *vide* [see]
v. (*or* vb.) = verb
v. (*or* vs.) = *versus* [against]
VA = Veterans' Administration
Va.= Virginia
V.C.= Victoria Cross
Ved.= Vedic
Ven.= the Venerable
V.I.= Virgin Islands
viz.= *videlicet* [namely]
vol.= volume, volunteer
vs.= verse, versus
Vt.= Vermont
W = west
W. (*or* Wed.) = Wednesday
WAC = Women's Army Corps
Wash.= Washington
WAVES = Women Accepted for Voluntary Emergency Service (United States Women's Naval Reserve)
W.C.T.U.= Woman's Christian Temperance Union
Wed. (*or* W.) = Wednesday
WHO = World Health Organization
W.I.= West Indies
Wis.= Wisconsin
wk.= week
WNW = west-northwest
WO = Warrant Officer
WPA = Work Projects Administration
WSW = west-southwest
wt.= weight
W.Va.= West Virginia
Wyo.= Wyoming
yd.= yard, yards
Y.M.C.A.= Young Men's Christian Association
Y.M.H.A.= Young Men's Hebrew Association
yr.= year
Y.W.C.A.= Young Women's Christian Association
Y.W.H.A.= Young Women's Hebrew Association
Zech.= Zechariah
Zeph.= Zephaniah

A.B.C. Powers, term applied to Argentina, Brazil, and Chile when acting in unison.

Abd al-Rahman. For Moslem rulers thus named, see ABDU-R-RAHMAN.

Abd-el-Krim (ăb″dĕl-krĭm′), 1882?–, leader of the Riffian tribes of Morocco. Defeated 1925 by a joint Franco-Spanish army and deported to Réunion isl. Escaped 1947 to Egypt, where he became a leader of the N African independence movement.

Abdera (ăbdēr′ů), Gr. *Avdera,* town (pop. 2,821), Greece, in SW Thrace. Agr. market. Founded c.650 B.C. Protagoras and Democritus lived here.

Abderhalden, Emil (ä′mēl äp′dùrhäl″dùn), 1877–, Swiss physiologist and biochemist. Worked on enzymes and food metabolism. Devised pregnancy test.

Abdias: see OBADIAH.

abdication, renunciation of high public office, usually by a monarch. Known from antiquity and in many lands, act may be voluntary (e.g., Emperor Charles V) or forced (many cases in China, including Hsüan T'ung in 1912). Forbidden in Great Britain since 1688 unless with consent of Parliament, as in the case of Edward VIII (1936).

abdomen, portion of trunk below diaphragm. Cavity, lined by membrane (peritoneum), contains stomach, intestines, liver, pancreas, spleen, kidneys; in lower part (called pelvis) are bladder, rectum, some of reproductive organs. See *ill.,* p. 763.

abduction, unlawful taking away of a person, especially of a woman under an age prescribed by law or of a married woman without consent of husband.

Abdu-l-Aziz IV (äb″dōōl-äzēz′), 1881?–1943, sultan of Morocco (1894–1908). French influence in Morocco was strengthened during his weak and unpopular reign. Deposed by his brother Abdu-l-Hafid.

Abdu-l-Aziz, 1830–76, Ottoman sultan (1861–76). During his reign Turkey became financially dependent on the West; Rumania, Serbia, Egypt gained virtual independence. Overthrown by MIDHAT PASHA, he died a few days later (probably, but not certainly, murdered).

Abdu-l-Hamid (–hämēd′), Ottoman sultans. **Abdu-l-Hamid I,** 1725–89, reigned 1774–89. Made peace with Russia in Treaty of KUCHUK-KAINARJI (1774); renewed war 1787. **Abdu-l-Hamid II,** 1842–1918, reigned 1876–1909. He suspended the constitution; disposed of MIDHAT PASHA. After Congress of BERLIN (1878), he began a pro-German policy. Called Red Sultan for his part in Armenian massacres (1894–96). Deposed by Young Turks 1909.

Abdu-l-Kadir (–kädēr'), 1808–83, Algerian leader, of Arab descent. As emir of Mascara, he extended his power over much of N Algeria (1832–39). In 1839 declared a holy war against the French. Driven by Gen. Bugeaud into Morocco, where he won the sultan's support. Defeated 1844 at Isly, surrendered 1847, imprisoned in France until 1852.

Abdullah (äbdŭ'lû, äbdōōlä), d. c.570, father of Mohammed.

Abdullah, 1882–1951, king of JORDAN (1946–51), b. Mecca. Lost Hejaz to Ibn Saud. Led British-trained Arab Legion against Israel in 1948. Assassinated 1951.

Abdu-l-Malik (äb"dōōl-mùlĭk'), c.646–705, the 5th OMAYYAD caliph (685–705). Overthrew rival caliphs and united Islam.

Abdu-l-Mejid (–mĕjēd'), 1823–61, Ottoman sultan (1839–61). Promoted reform. Revolt of MOHAMMED ALI was checked by Great Powers. CRIMEAN WAR and Congress of PARIS (1856) brought Turkey no gain. Decline of sultanate began.

Abdu-l-Mumin (–mōō'mĭn), 1094–1163, founder of the ALMOHADES. Conquered Morocco in the 1140s, became dominant in Spain in 1151, and extended his African domain as far east as Tripoli, 1158–59.

Abdu-r-Rahman (äb"dōōr-rä'män, –rämän') or **Abd al-Rahman** (äb"dōōl–), OMAYYAD rulers of Córdoba. **Abdu-r-Rahman I**, d. 788, fled Damascus, seized power in Córdoba (756), ruled as emir till his death. **Abdu-r-Rahman III**, 891–961, ruled as emir from 912, as caliph from 929. Under him Moslem Spain reached height of glory. Also ruled Moslem part of N Africa 939–47.

Abdu-r-Rahman or **Abd al-Rahman**, d. 732, Moslem governor in Spain. Defeated in battle of Tours or Poitiers by CHARLES MARTEL (732).

à Becket, Thomas: see THOMAS À BECKET, SAINT.

Abed-nego (ùbĕd'nēgō), one of THREE HOLY CHILDREN.

Abel, shepherd son of Adam and Eve, killed by Cain, his brother. Gen. 4.1–8.

Abel, Sir Frederick Augustus, 1826–1902, English chemist. Improved guncotton manufacture. Invented cordite (with Dewar) and Abel test for flash point of petroleum.

Abel, John Jacob, 1857–1938, American pharmacologist, associated with Johns Hopkins from 1893. He isolated epinephrine (adrenaline), crystalline form of insulin, and amino acids from blood.

Abel, Niels Henrik (nēls' hĕn'rēk" ä'bùl), 1802–29, Norwegian mathematician.

Abelard, Peter (ă'bùlärd), Fr. *Pierre Abélard*, 1079–1142, French scholastic. Regarded as founder of Univ. of Paris. His romance and secret marriage with his pupil Heloise, niece of Fulbert, a canon of Notre Dame, ended when Fulbert had him emasculated by hired ruffians. Abelard became monk at Saint-Denis; left in 1120 to teach. Hostility of St. Bernard of Clairvaux caused condemnation of certain of his doctrines at Council of Soissons (1121). Abelard built a hermitage near Troyes, adding a monastery, the Paraclete, to house students; later he gave it to Heloise, who became abbess of a sisterhood

there. To avoid condemnation at Council of Sens (1141), he made submission and retired to Cluny. Abelard applied logical methods to truths of faith; considered universals as existing only in thought but with basis in particulars (see SCHOLASTICISM). Chief work: *Sic et non* (collection of contradictory statements of Church Fathers). *Historia calamitatum* is autobiographical. Letters of Abelard and Heloise belong to world literature.

Abell, Kjeld (kyĕl' ä'bĕl), 1901–, Danish dramatist, an innovator in stage techniques. Among his plays on social problems are *Anna Sophie Hedvig* (1939) and *The Queen Walks Again* (1943).

Abercrombie, Lascelles (lăs'ùls äb'ùrkrŏmbi), 1881–1938, English poet and critic. Wrote long blank-verse poems.

Abercromby, Sir Ralph, 1734–1801, British general. Won major military reputation for campaigns against the French, especially in Flanders (1794–95) and W Indies. Killed in successful battle at Aboukir.

Aberdeen, George Hamilton-Gordon, 4th **earl of** (ă'bùrdēn'), 1784–1860, British statesman. By Treaty of Töplitz (1813) cemented Austria to anti-Napoleonic coalition. By Webster-Ashburton Treaty (1842) settled Northeast Boundary Dispute with U.S. Prime Minister (1852–55); he resigned after failure to stop British involvement in unpopular Crimean War.

Aberdeen, independent burgh (pop. 182,714), Aberdeenshire and Kincardine, Scotland, on North Sea at mouth of the Dee; chief port and largest city of NE Scotland. Called the Granite City. Univ. of Aberdeen includes King's Col. (1494) and Marischal Col. (1593).

Aberdeen. 1 Town (pop. 2,944), N Md., NE of Baltimore. Near by are Aberdeen Proving Ground and Army Chemical Center. **2** Cotton city (pop. 5,290), NE Miss., on Tombigbee R. and N of Columbus. **3** City (pop. 21,051), NE S.Dak., NW of Watertown; platted 1881. Rail and distribution center for agr. area. Has mfg. of farm machinery. **4** City (pop. 19,653), W Wash., port on Grays Harbor adjoining Hoquiam; settled c.1865. Has lumbering, mfg. of wood products, fishing, and canning.

Aberdeenshire, maritime county (1,971 sq. mi.; pop. 308,055), NE Scotland; cap. Aberdeen. Chief occupations agr., fishing, and cattle breeding. At Braemar is British royal residence, Balmoral Castle.

Aberhart, William (ä'bùrhärt), 1878–1943, Canadian statesman. Organizer of Social Credit party of Alberta; premier of Alberta (1935–43).

aberration, optics, blurring or loss of clearness in images produced by lenses or mirrors. It is spherical when rays of light from a point are not brought to a single focus, chromatic when image is blurred and fringes of color appear at its edges.

Abertawe, Glamorganshire, Wales: see SWANSEA.

Aberystwyth (ăbùrĭst'wĭth), municipal borough (pop. 9,323), Cardiganshire, Wales; summer resort on Cardigan Bay. Has a constituent college of Univ. of Wales and Natl. Library of Wales.

Abgar, Epistles of: see PSEUDEPIGRAPHA.

Abiathar (ŭbī'–), priest, son of Ahimelech. Escaped massacre by Doeg. 1 Sam. 22.9–23; 2 Sam. 15.17,29; 1 Kings 1.7; 2.27; Mark 2.26. Name sometimes exchanged with his father's.

Abigail (ăb'ŭgāl) [Heb.,= my father is joy]. 1 Wife of Nabal. After his death, she married David. 1 Sam. 25; 2 Sam. 3.13; 1 Chron. 3.1. 2 David's stepsister. 2 Sam. 17.25; 1 Chron. 2.16,17.

Abihu (ŭbī'hū), son of Aaron, destroyed for offering "strange" fire. Ex. 6.23; 24.1,9; 28.1; Lev. 10.1; Num. 3.2,4; 26.60,61; 1 Chron. 6.3; 24.1,21.

Abijah (ŭbī'jū), died c.911 B.C., king of Judah (c.914–c.911 B.C.); successor of Rehoboam. Jeroboam warred against him. 2 Chron. 13. Abijam: 1 Kings 15.1–8.

Abilene. 1 City (pop. 5,775), central Kansas, on Smoky Hill R. and W of Topeka; laid out 1860; wheat-shipping point. Was cow town and railhead for CHISHOLM TRAIL. Early home of Eisenhower. **2** City (pop. 45,570), W central Texas, WSW of Fort Worth; founded 1881. Distributing center for livestock, cotton, wheat, and dairy region. Refines oil. Seat of Hardin-Simmons Univ. (Baptist; 1891), Abilene Christian Col., and McMurry Col. (Methodist; 1923), all coed.

Abimelech (ŭbĭm'ŭlĕk). **1.** See AHIMELECH. **2** Son of Gideon. Slew his 70 brothers, except Jotham, and became "king." Judges 9.1–57; 2 Sam. 11.21.

Abinadab (ŭbin'ŭdăb). **1** Son of King Saul, killed at battle of Mt. Gilboa. 1 Sam. 31.2; 1 Chron. 10.2. **2** Keeper of ark for 20 years. 1 Sam. 7.1,2; 2 Sam. 6.3,4; 1 Chron. 13.7.

Abington, town (pop. 7,152), SE Mass., SSE of Boston. Mfg. of shoes.

Abiram (ŭbī'rŭm), rebel (with KORAH) against Moses.

Abishag (ăb'–), handmaid to David in his old age. Adonijah wanted to marry her after David's death, and thus incurred Solomon's wrath. 1 Kings 1;2.

Abitibi, Fort (ăbŭtĭb'ē), important Canadian fur-trading post, on Abitibi L., built 1686.

Abkhaz Autonomous Soviet Socialist Republic (äbkäz', Rus. ŭpkhäs') or **Abkhasia,** autonomous state (3,300 sq. mi.; pop. c.300,000) NW Georgian SSR; cap. Sukhum. Annexed by Russia from Turkey 1810. Abkhasians (30% of pop.) are largely Mohammedans.

ablative: see CASE.

ablaut (äp'lout), in inflection, the variation between vowels in related words (e.g., English, *ring, rang, rung*) indicating a corresponding modification of meaning. At an earlier unknown period the corresponding forms of the language had differences in accent, not differences in vowel.

Abner, head of Saul's army. Killed by Joab. 1 Sam. 9.1; 14.50,51; 17.55; 2 Sam. 2; 3.

Abo, Finland: see TURKU.

abolitionists, in U.S. history, especially 1830–60, advocates of compulsory freeing of Negro slaves, as distinguished from freesoilers, opposed only to extension of slavery. Active campaign had mainspring in religious revival in 1820s and reached crusading stage in 1830s led by T. D. Weld, Tappan brothers, and W. L. GARRISON. American Anti-Slavery Society, estab. 1833, flooded slave states with literature and lobbied in Washington. Writers such as J. G. Whittier and orators such as Wendell Phillips lent strength to cause. Despite unanimity on goal, there was division over methods, Garrison advocating moral suasion, others direct political action. Stringent fugitive slave laws in 1850 increased activity on UNDERGROUND RAILROAD. Harriet B. Stowe's *Uncle Tom's Cabin* and the Kansas question aroused both North and South, culminating in John Brown's raid on Harpers Ferry. Uncompromising temper of movement made war the only solution. See also SLAVERY.

abortion, expulsion of product of conception before fetus can survive. Spontaneous abortion popularly called miscarriage. Induced abortion criminal offense in U.S. except to save mother's life.

abortion, contagious: see BRUCELLOSIS.

Aboukir or **Abukir** (both: ä"boōkēr'), village, Egypt, on Aboukir Bay, SW of Rosetta mouth of the Nile. Nelson's victory here over the French fleet in 1798 restored British prestige in the Mediterranean. The battle is sometimes called the battle of the Nile.

abracadabra (ăb'rŭkŭdăb'rŭ), magic formula used by Gnostics in 2d cent. to invoke aid of benevolent spirits to ward off affliction; usually engraved on amulets as protective charm. The word gradually lost occult significance; now means any hocus-pocus.

Abraham [according to Gen. 17.5 = father of many] or **Abram** [Heb.,= the father is high], forefather of the Hebrews through his son Isaac and of the Arabs through his son Ishmael. Chiefly important as the founder of Judaism. He instituted circumcision and received God's word that his people would gain the promised land of Canaan. Revered by many faiths as a symbol of devotion to, and trust in, God (as shown in willingness to sacrifice Isaac, kindliness to his wayward nephew Lot). Gen. 11–25.

Abraham, Plains of, field adjoining upper part of Quebec city. Here the English under Wolfe defeated French under Montcalm (1759), ending FRENCH AND INDIAN WARS and deciding fate of Canada.

Abraham Lincoln National Historical Park: see NATIONAL PARKS AND MONUMENTS (table).

Abram: see ABRAHAM.

Abramovich, Sholem (or Solomon) Yakob: see MENDELE MOCHER SFORIM.

abrasive, material used in grinding, cutting, polishing. Natural forms include DIAMOND, CORUNDUM, emery, SAND, PUMICE, chalk. Alundum (see ALUMINA) and Carborundum (see SILICON CARBIDE) are artificial. For special purposes powdered abrasives are often mixed with oil or water, molded with cement into wheels or sticks, or glued on cloth or paper.

Abravanel or **Abarbanel, Isaac** (ŭbrä'vŭnĕl, –bärbū–), 1437–1508, Jewish theologian, a Portuguese government official. His writings upheld miracles against the rationalism of Maimonides.

Abruzzi, Luigi Amedeo, duca degli (äbroōt'sē),

1873–1933, Italian naval officer, mountain climber, and arctic explorer, b. Madrid. Duke of the Abruzzi was cousin of Victor Emmanuel III.

Abruzzi e Molise (–ā môlē′zĕ), region (5,883 sq. mi.; pop. 1,589,804), central Italy, in most rugged part of Apennines (Gran Sasso d'Italia); cap. Aquila. Vineyards, olives, sheep raising. Shared history of kingdom of NAPLES.

Absalom (ăb′sŭlŏm), beloved but treacherous son of David. He fled after murdering his brother Amnon. Forgiven by David but led abortive revolt and was slain. 2 Sam. 3.3; 13–19; 2 Chron. 11.20,21.

Absalon (äp′sälôn) or **Axel** (äk′sŭl), c.1128–1201, Danish churchman, archbishop of Lund. Held great political influence, warred against Wends, defeated Duke Bogislav of Pomerania in naval battle (1184). Patron of Saxo Grammaticus.

Absaroka Indians: see CROW INDIANS.

Absaroka Range (ăbsŭrō′kŭ), part of Rocky Mts., c.150 mi. long; in Yellowstone Natl. Park, NW Wyo., and S Mont.

absenteeism, originally system under which a person controls, and derives income from, land or capital in a region in which he does not live. Notable abuse in Ireland in 18th and 19th cent. and in E Europe until 20th cent. Recently term applied to concentrated control of wealth through corporate devices, shutting investor from conduct of business.

absinthe (ăb′sĭnth), a toxic green LIQUEUR distilled from wormwood and other aromatics. Excessive use may cause delirium and idiocy. Switzerland and France have banned manufacture and sale; importation forbidden by U.S. in 1912.

absolute, the (often with capital letter), in metaphysics, the unknowable, all-comprehensive principle underlying all reality; the opposite of relative. In various philosophic systems variously defined. In theology identified with God. See also HEGEL.

absolute zero: see TEMPERATURE.

absolutism, system of government with SOVEREIGNTY highly concentrated and in theory unchecked by portions of the body politic or by the people as a whole. In practice limited by existing law and custom, by danger of war and revolution. Tyrants of Greek cities were absolute. In Hellenic and Roman periods, some of the rulers were regarded as gods. In Renaissance, absolutism triumphed over feudalism in West. Absolute rule of Louis XIV of France was a standard example. In 20th cent. absolutism of DICTATOR or party rose with Fascism and Communism. See also DIVINE RIGHT.

absorption: see GAS; OSMOSIS; SPECTRUM.

abstract art, 20th cent. painting style stressing basic formalized structures and ignoring representation of objects. Cézanne is an example of the initial period; cubism and expressionism thrived later. Abstract art may be "pure" (e.g., geometric) or mixed with other styles. Also used in other arts.

Abu Bakr (ä′boō bă′kŭr) 573–634, 1st caliph, father of AYESHA, Mohammed's wife; most zealous convert, first outside Prophet's family. Mohammed's only companion on the Hegira. During his critical two-year caliphate

Arabian opposition was crushed; extension of Islam as world religion began.

Abu Hanifa (–hänē′fŭ), 699–767, Moslem jurist, founder of a system of Islamic jurisprudence.

Abu Khasim, Arabian physician: see ABULCASIS.

Abukir, Egypt: see ABOUKIR.

Abu-l-Abbas as-Saffah (ä′boōl-äbäs′äs-säfä′), d. 754, 1st ABBASID caliph (749–54). Took caliphate from the Omayyad with help of Abu Muslim.

Abu-l-Ala al-Maarri (–äl-mä-är-rē′), 973–1057, blind Arabic poet, a fatalistic freethinker. Discarded classicism for intellectual urbanity.

Abulcasis (ä′boōlkä′sĭs) or **Abu Khasim** (ä′boō kä′-sīm), fl. 11th cent., Arabian physician, author of influential text, *Tasrif,* on medicine and surgery.

Abu-l-Faraj Ali of Isfahan (ä′boōlfä′räj), 897–967, Arabic scholar. His *Book of Songs* is an annotated compilation of Arabic poems set to music.

Abu Muslim (ä′boō moō′slīm), c.728–755, Persian revolutionist. Won the caliphate for the Abbasid, who later killed him.

Abu Nuwas (–noōwäs′), d. c.810, Arabic poet. His poetry echoes extravagance of Baghdad court.

Abu Said ibn Abi-l-Khair (sä′id ä′bēl-khīr′), 967–1049, Persian poet, a Sufi dervish. First to write rubaiyat in Sufistic strain.

abutilon (ŭbū′tĭlŭn) or **flowering maple,** tropical shrubs (*Abutilon*), with yellow, white, or pink bell-shaped flowers, lobed leaves. House plant in North.

Abydos (ŭbī′dŭs), city of anc. Egypt, NW of Thebes; center of worship of Osiris.

Abydos, anc. Greek town, on the Hellespont. Near by Athenian fleet defeated Sparta (411 B.C.). Abydos was the scene of the story of Hero and Leander.

Abyssinia: see ETHIOPIA.

Ac, chemical symbol of the element ACTINIUM.

acacia (ŭkā′shŭ), leguminous, tropical or subtropical trees or shrubs of genus *Acacia,* with fluffy clusters of yellow or white flowers. Known as wattle in Australia. Yield GUM arabic, dyes, tanning aids, furniture wood, CATECHU, and SHITTIM WOOD mentioned in the Bible.

academic costume, dress required on stated occasions by educational institutions for faculty, students, degree candidates, degree holders. In U.S. style adopted 1895, revised 1932, accepted by over 700 institutions. Includes gown, showing academic rank (see DEGREE, ACADEMIC); hood, lined with color of institution giving degree; mortarboard, a skullcap supporting stiff square top with tassel.

academic freedom, right of scholars to teach, pursue research, and publish unrestrained by employing institution. A civil right in democratic countries, it usually includes right of tenure. Academic freedom is based on beliefs that open investigation best reveals truth and that scholars ought to pursue research regardless of personal opinion. The idea of completely free inquiry, evolving in the period of Enlightenment, was first accepted in Prussia and other German states. In England, Jeremy Bentham, Herbert

Spencer, Charles Darwin, and Thomas Huxley showed value of free investigation. In U.S. the Association of University Professors maintains standards of academic freedom and obligation.

Académie française: see FRENCH ACADEMY.

Academy, garden near Athens where PLATO taught (c.387 B.C.), and his followers met until banned by Justinian (A.D. 529).

Acadia (ŭkā'dēŭ), region and former French colony, E Canada, centered on Nova Scotia but including Prince Edward Isl. and mainland coast from Gulf of St. Lawrence S into Maine. First and chief town, Port Royal, was founded 1605. Attacked and taken by British 1710. In 1755 French settlers who refused to swear allegiance to Great Britain were deported. Exiles found refuge in many places. Longfellow's *Evangeline* tells of those in St. Martinville, La., where the Cajuns—as they are popularly called—maintain a separate folk culture. In 1762 a new mass deportation was thwarted, and gradually some exiles returned. Today in Canada, Acadian (French *Acadien*) means a French-speaking inhabitant of Maritime Provs.

Acadia National Park: see NATIONAL PARKS AND MONUMENTS (table).

Acadia University: see WOLFVILLE, N.S.

acanthus (ŭkăn'-), perennial herbs (*Acanthus*), with deeply cut leaves often copied in architectural motif (see CORINTHIAN ORDER).

Acapulco (äkäpōōl'kō), city (pop. 9,993), Guerrero, SW Mexico; Pacific port. Winter resort.

Acarya: see BHASCARA.

Accad: see AKKAD.

Accault, Michel, French explorer: see ACO.

accent, in language, emphasis given a particular sound. In English each independently spoken form has an accented vowel. The English accent is phonemic (or significant), for there are words different from each other only in their accent, e.g., *contract*, verb and noun. The so-called accents in French, acute (´), grave (`), and circumflex (^), are borrowed from Greek writing, where they probably showed differences in pitch. Some languages have significant variations of both pitch and loudness.

accessory, person somehow connected with a crime other than the principal perpetrator. The law usually distinguishes between one who in some way abets the committing of crime (before the fact) and who aids the criminal after the crime is committed (after the fact).

accordion, small portable musical instrument, consisting of rectangular bellows expanded and contracted between the hands. Buttons or keys operated by the player determine tones. Introduced in 1822; keyboard added in 1852. Similar to the concertina, which is smaller and has bellows attached to hexagonal blocks that have handles and buttons.

accounting, classifying, analyzing, interpreting of BOOKKEEPING records intended to show business operation in light of profit and loss. AUDITING is branch of accounting.

Accra (ŭkrä'), city (pop. 135,456), cap. of the Gold Coast, a port on Gulf of Guinea.

accusative: see CASE.

Aceldama (ŭsĕl'dŭmŭ), "field of blood," apparently place where Judas died. Money given him for betraying Jesus was used to buy this place for burial of strangers. Earlier it had been called "potter's field," hence term for paupers' burying ground. Mat. 27.3–10; Acts 1.16–19.

acetaldehyde: see ALDEHYDE.

acetic acid (ŭsē'tĭk), weak organic acid (constituent of vinegar), a colorless liquid with pungent odor; boils at 118.5°C. Miscible with water; heat evolved. Pure (99.5%) acid called glacial acetic acid. Its compounds used in plastics, medicines, lacquers, and as mordants.

acetone (ăs'ĭtōn), colorless, inflammable liquid with minty taste and odor; boils at 56.1°C. Used as a solvent for organic substances and in making celluloid, smokeless powders, and chloroform.

acetylene (ŭsĕt'ĭlēn), colorless gas, boiling at −84°C., with ethereal odor when pure. Forms explosive mixture with air; explosive when liquefied. Used as illuminant and for cutting and welding metals (see OXYACETYLENE FLAME).

Achaea (ŭkē'ŭ), region of anc. Greece, in N Peloponnesus, on Gulf of Corinth, the home of the **Achaeans,** powerful in Greece by 1300 B.C. Their cities were formed before 5th cent. B.C. in the first **Achaean League,** which lasted until it opposed Philip II of Macedon (338 B.C.) and was then dissolved. The second Achaean League was formed in 3d cent. B.C. and tried to liberate Greece from Macedonian rule but ran into opposition of Sparta. In 198 B.C. the league got Roman help and gained power. Later suspected by Rome of sympathy for Macedon, many Achaeans were deported (168 B.C.) to Italy. In 146 B.C. Achaeans waged suicidal war against Rome.

Achaemenidae (ăkĭmĕ'nĭdē) or **Achaemenids** (ăkĭmĕ'nĭdz), dynasty of ancient Persia, c.550–330 B.C., founded by CYRUS THE GREAT.

Ache, Caran d': see CARAN D'ACHE.

Achelous (ăkĭlō'ŭs), in Greek religion, river-god. The son of Oceanus and Tethys, he was father of the Sirens and other nymphs.

Achelous (ăkhĕlō'ôs), river, 137 mi. long, NW Greece, flowing from Pindus mts. S to the Ionian Sea. Also known as Aspropotamos.

Acheron (ă'kŭrŏn), in Greek religion, river of Hades.

Acheson, Dean (Gooderham) (ăch'ĭsun), 1893–, U.S. Secretary of State (1949–53). He was Asst. Secretary of State 1941–45, Undersecretary 1945–47.

Acheson, Edward Goodrich, 1856–1931, American inventor. Discovered carborundum; developed processes for producing silicon, aluminum, synthetic graphite.

Acheulian (ŭshōō'lĕŭn), phase of Paleolithic period named for Saint-Acheul, France, where typical implements were found.

Achilles (ŭkĭl'ēz), in Greek legend, hero of the *Iliad*, prominent Greek warrior in TROJAN WAR; son of Peleus and Thetis. His mother, hearing prophecy of his death at Troy, dipped him in river Styx to make him invulnerable, but the water did not touch the heel she held. She disguised him as a girl and hid him at Skyros. Odysseus persuaded him to join expedition against Troy. He quarreled with AGAMEMNON and sulked in his tent, but to avenge the death of his friend PATROCLUS, he fought again and slew Hector. He was killed by Paris, who wounded his heel.

Achitophel, variant of AHITHOPHEL.

acid, according to ionization theory (see ION), compound yielding hydrogen ions when dissolved in water. Properties result from presence of hydrogen ion: in aqueous solution acids taste sour, turn blue litmus red, react with bases and basic oxides (see NEUTRALIZATION) to form salts and water. Can conduct electricity. Most acids are solids, few are liquids, and very few are gases. Strong acids (e.g., nitric) are largely ionized in solution; weak acids (e.g., acetic) are little ionized. Classified also by number of replaceable hydrogen ions in molecule as monobasic (e.g., nitric), dibasic (e.g., sulphuric), tribasic (e.g., phosphoric). Carboxyl group (—COOH) characteristic of organic acids.

acidosis, reduction of the body's alkali reserve resulting from starvation, diabetes, nephritis, infectious diseases. It does not imply real acidity of the blood. Alkalosis is abnormal increase in alkali reserve.

Ackia Battleground National Monument: see NATIONAL PARKS AND MONUMENTS (table).

Acmeists (ăk'mēĭsts), school of Russian poets, started 1912 in reaction against symbolists. Strove after concreteness of image, clarity of expression. Leading Acmeists: Akhmatova, Gumilev, Mandelstam.

acne (ăk'nē), disease of sebaceous glands common during adolescence. Characterized by pink pimples (papules) surrounding blackheads, especially on face, back, and chest. Sometimes chronic.

Aco or **Accault, Michel** (äkō'), fl. 1680–1702, French explorer of region of upper Mississippi; R. lieutenant of La Salle.

Acoma or **Ácoma** (both: ä'kŭmŭ), Indian pueblo village (1948 pop. 1,482), W central N.Mex., W of Albuquerque, on mesa above reservation villages of Santa María de Ácoma and Acomita. Visited by Coronado's men (1540), Juan de Onate (1598), and Fray Juan Ramírez (1629). Scene of revolts against Spanish in 1599 and late 1600s. Language is Western Keresan. Farming and pottery-making. Holds festival to St. Stephen, Sept. 2.

Aconcagua (äkōnkä'gwä), peak, 22,835 ft. high, W Argentina, in Andes; considered highest peak in W Hemisphere.

aconite (ăk'–), **monkshood,** or **wolfsbane** (*Aconitum*), hardy plant with blue, purple, yellow, or white hooded flowers. Drug aconite, a sedative, contains poisonous alkaloid aconite. Winter aconite (*Eranthis*) has small, yellow flowers in spring.

Açores: see AZORES.

acorn: see OAK.

Acosta, Joaquín (hwäkēn' äkō'stä), 1799?– 1852, Colombian scientist. Fought in revolution. Wrote on Colombian geography, history, meteorology.

acoustics (ŭkōō'stĭks), science of sound, its production, transmission, and effects. Acoustical problems in buildings include reverberation (repeated reflection of sound waves from smooth surface in enclosed space) and

interference (from reflection of sound waves of different frequencies). Some reverberation avoids sound deadening; interference either reinforces or destroys sound.

acquittal, discharge of an indicted person. An acquittal-in-fact follows on a verdict of not guilty on the basis of facts and cannot be appealed. An acquittal-in-law results from the operation of the rules of law.

Acre (ä'kŭr, ä'kŭr), Arabic *Acca,* Heb. *Acco,* city (pop. 8,000), N Palestine, a port on Bay of Acre opposite Haifa. Biblical names are Accho and Ptolemais. Taken by Arabs 638, held by Crusaders 1104–87 and by Knights Hospitalers 1190–1291. Surrender to Saracens in 1291 marked decline of Latin Kingdom of Jerusalem and the Crusades. Held by Turkey 1517–1832, 1840–1918, by Egypt 1832–40, and by Great Britain 1918–48. Partition of Palestine in 1948 assigned Acre to Arabs, but Israeli forces captured it.

Acre (ä'krä), river rising at border of Peru and Brazil and flowing NE. Treaty of Petrópolis (1903) gave Brazil most of territory surrounding river, with large indemnity to Bolivia.

acre, land measure used by English-speaking peoples, now set at 160 sq. rods (4,840 sq. yd.; 43,560 sq. ft.; ⅟₆₄₀ sq. mi.). Local variations survive.

Acrocorinthus (ă″krōkŭrĭn'thŭs), rock, 1,886 ft. high, site of the Acropolis of Old CORINTH, Greece. On its summit stood temple of Aphrodite; below was fountain of Pirene, from which Pegasus drank.

Acropolis (ŭkrŏp'ŭlĭs), elevated, fortified section of ancient Greek cities. Athenian Acropolis, a hill c.260 ft. high, was adorned, chiefly during time of Cimon and Pericles, with some of world's greatest architectural works (PROPYLAEA, PARTHENON, ERECHTHEUM). See ELGIN MARBLES.

Actaeon (ăk-tē'ŭn), in Greek legend, a hunter. Because he saw Artemis bathing, she changed him into a stag, and his own dogs killed him.

actinic ray: see RAY; SPECTRUM.

actinium (ăktĭn'ēŭm), radioactive element of actinide series (symbol = Ac; see also ELEMENT, table). Occurs in minerals containing uranium; is disintegration product of protactinium; emits beta rays.

Actium (ăk'tēŭm, ăk'shēŭm), Gr. *Aktion,* promontory NW Greece. Here forces of Octavian (later AUGUSTUS) defeated Antony and Cleopatra (31 B.C.).

active: see VOICE.

act of God, accident caused by an extraordinary, unforeseeable, and unavoidable natural force. The injured party has in general no right to damages.

Acton, John Emerich Edward Dalberg Acton, 1st Baron, 1834–1902, English historian. Taught at Cambridge from 1895. Planned *Cambridge Modern History.* Notable as a liberal and a Roman Catholic. Wrote *History of Freedom* (1907), essays.

Acton, Sir John Francis Edward, 1736?–1811, Neapolitan statesman of British origin. Favorite of Marie Caroline. Chief minister 1779–1804.

Acts of the Apostles, book of Bible between Gospels and Epistles, only contemporary historical account of early expansion of Christianity. Written in Greek A.D. c.60–80. Traditional author is St. Luke. Three critical events are: descent of the Holy Ghost, martyrdom of St. Stephen, conversion of St. Paul.

actuary, originally, in England, registrar recording court acts or managing a joint stock company. Later managers of insurance companies only, now especially insurance statisticians who calculate probabilities (e.g., length of life, accident rate) to determine premium rates.

Acuña, Cristóbal de (krēstō′bäl dā äkōō′nyä), 1597–1676?, Spanish Jesuit missionary and explorer. Accompanied Teixeira on journey down Amazon (1638), wrote earliest firsthand description of river (1639).

Ada, city (pop. 15,995), S central Okla., near Canadian R. SE of Oklahoma City; settled 1889. Industrial center for oil and agr. area with mfg. of cement, machinery, and glass.

Adak (ä′däk), off W Alaska, one of ALEUTIAN ISLANDS. U.S. base in World War II, important in Aleutian campaign.

Adalbert, d. 1072, archbishop of Hamburg-Bremen, a diocese which included Scandinavia. Favorite of Emperor Henry III; guardian of Henry IV. Relentlessly ambitious, he helped to consolidate imperial authority despite opposition of nobles and clergy.

Adalia, Turkey: see ANTALYA.

Adam [Heb.,= mankind], in Bible, the first man. His story from creation to expulsion from Garden of Eden (with his wife EVE) is told in Gen. 1.26–5.5. To St. Paul, Adam represented earthly side of man (1 Cor. 15.20–22,42–58). Higher criticism compares Adam's story with Babylonian myths of creation. For examples of Judaic and Islamic legends stemming from biblical account, see LILITH; PSEUDEPIGRAPHA.

Adam, Adolphe (ädōlf′ ädä′), 1803–56, French composer of comic opera and other stage works, known for his ballet *Giselle* and the popular *Cantique de Noël.*

Adam, Robert (ăd′ŭm), 1728–92, and **James Adam,** 1730–94, Scottish architects, brothers. Chiefly inspired by classic architecture, they created a style of great elegance. Designed important buildings in England and Scotland. Also furniture (see *ill.,* p. 456).

Adam de la Halle (ädä′ dü lä äl′), 1237?–c.1285, French dramatist. Author of *Le Jeu de Robin et de Marion,* sometimes called earliest comic opera.

Adamic, Louis (ăd′ŭmĭk), 1899–1951, American author, b. Slovenia; in U.S. after 1913. Wrote on immigrants, racial tolerance; *The Native's Return* (1934) was popular. He died in mysterious circumstances.

Adams, family of distinguished Americans from Mass. **John Adams,** 1735–1826, was 2d President of the United States (1797–1801). A patriot leader who opposed British measures leading to American Revolution, he later served in both Continental Congresses and argued eloquently for the Declaration of Independence, which he signed. Served as Washington's Vice President (1789–97). His administration as President revealed his honest and stubborn integrity; though allied with the conservative Federalists, he was not dominated by them in their struggle against the Jeffersonians. By conciliation he prevented war with France; he had reservations about the ALIEN AND SEDITION ACTS. His wife, **Abigail (Smith) Adams,** 1744–1818, was one of the most distinguished and influential first ladies in U.S. history. Their son, **John Quincy Adams,** 1767–1848, was 6th President of the United States (1825–29). As U.S. Senator from Mass. (1803–8), he outraged his fellow Federalists by supporting Jeffersonian policies. Served in several ministerial positions. Best-known achievement as U.S. Secretary of State (1817–25) was MONROE DOCTRINE. Elected President in House of Representatives through support of Henry Clay, Adams had an unhappy, ineffective administration. Won new renown as U.S. Representative from Mass. (1831–48); eloquently attacked all measures expanding slavery. Promoted Smithsonian Inst. His diary is a valuable historical document. His son, **Charles Francis Adams,** 1807–86, was minister to Great Britain (1861–68). He won British respect for wisdom in upholding Northern cause, especially in *Trent* and *Alabama* incidents. Later represented U.S. in settlement of Alabama claims. His son, **Charles Francis Adams,** 1835–1915, American historian and railroad expert, was president of the Union Pacific (1884–90). Author of *Three Episodes of Massachusetts History* (1892). His brother, **Brooks Adams,** 1848–1927, was also an historian. He developed theory that civilization rose and fell according to growth and decline of commerce in *The Law of Civilization and Decay* (1895). His ideas influenced another brother, **Henry (Brooks) Adams,** 1838–1918, also an historian. In developing a basic philosophy of history he found a unifying principle in force or energy. Applied this theory in two books, *Mont-Saint-Michel and Chartres* (privately printed 1904, pub. 1913), and *The Education of Henry Adams* (privately printed 1906, pub. 1918). Also wrote study of administrations of Jefferson and Madison. **Charles Francis Adams,** 1866–, grandson of Charles Francis Adams (1807–86), was U.S. Secretary of the Navy (1929–33).

Adams, Franklin Pierce, pseud. **F. P. A.,** 1881–, American columnist ("The Conning Tower"). Humorous verse and light essays. Became member of "Information Please" radio program in 1938.

Adams, Henry (Brooks): see ADAMS, family.

Adams, Herbert, 1858–1945, American sculptor, a founder of the Natl. Sculpture Society.

Adams, James Truslow, 1878–1949, American historian. His books on the American scene include *The Epic of America* (1931), *The Adams Family* (1930), and *Henry Adams* (1933). Editor in chief of *Dictionary of American History, Atlas of American History,* and *Album of American History.*

Adams, John: see ADAMS, family.

Adams, John Couch, 1819–92, English astronomer. Calculated position of then unknown planet NEPTUNE.

Adams, John Quincy: see ADAMS, family.

Adams, Maude, 1872–, American actress, whose real name is Kiskadden. Famous in

Barrie plays, she starred in his *Little Minister* (1897), *Quality Street* (1901), *What Every Woman Knows* (1908), and *Peter Pan* (1905), role for which she is best known.

Adams, Roger, 1889–, American chemist. Developed methods of identification, preparation, and synthesis. Among first to synthesize the local anesthetics butyn and procaine.

Adams, Samuel, 1722–1803, American Revolutionary patriot, signer of Declaration of Independence; second cousin of John Adams. Leader of extremists in colonial resistance to British.

Adams, Walter Sydney, 1876–, American astronomer, authority on motions and spectroscopy of stars. Director (1923–46) of Mt. Wilson Observatory.

Adams, Will(iam), 1564?–1620, first Englishman to visit Japan. Settled there permanently as successful shipbuilder and trader.

Adams, town (pop. 12,034), NW Mass., in the Berkshires and on Hoosic R. Mfg. of textiles, paper. Calcium quarried. Birthplace of Susan B. Anthony.

Adams, Mount. 1 Peak, N.H.: see PRESIDENTIAL RANGE. **2** Peak (12,307 ft.), SW Wash., in Cascade Range.

Adana (ä′dänä), city (pop. 117,799), S Turkey, on Seyhan R. Once a Roman colony, it is now a commercial center.

Addams, Jane, 1860–1935, American social worker. Founded (1899, with Ellen G. Starr) noted social settlement, Hull House, in Chicago. Leader in woman-suffrage and peace movements. Awarded 1931 Nobel Peace Prize. Wrote *Twenty Years at Hull-House* (1910).

adder, poisonous snake of European viper family. Species also found in Asia, Africa, Australia. In U.S. name is applied to various harmless snakes.

adding machine: see CALCULATING MACHINE.

Addington, Henry: see SIDMOUTH, HENRY ADDINGTON, VISCOUNT.

Addis Ababa (ä′dĭs ä′bŭbŭ), city (pop. c.300–000), cap. of Ethiopia. Founded 1887 by Menelik II, who made it his cap. in 1889. It was cap. of Italian East Africa, 1936–41. Imperial palace is near by.

Addison, Joseph, 1672–1719, English essayist. First achieved notice with epic poem *The Campaign* (1704) and later wrote poems, dramas (e.g., tragedy, *Cato,* 1713) and criticism (notably on *Paradise Lost,* praising Milton), but he is best remembered for witty, urbane essays, some of the finest in English. He began in 1710 to contribute to Richard Steele's *Tatler* and later continued his essays in the *Spectator* (1711–12). His most popular papers were on the imaginary squire, Sir Roger de Coverley (invented by Steele), and his coterie. Addison held a seat in Parliament and government posts.

Addison, Thomas: see ADDISON'S DISEASE.

Addison, W.Va.: see WEBSTER SPRINGS.

Addison's disease, serious malady resulting from destruction of cortex of adrenal glands. First described by **Thomas Addison,** 1793–1860, English pathologist.

addition, a basic arithmetical operation using the symbol +. Properties important in higher algebra include associativity (of three numbers, sum of two may be added to third without affecting final sum), commutivity (of two numbers, either may be added to other without affecting sum), distributivity (result of multiplying sum of two numbers by third number same as multiplying each number alone and adding products). To add numerical quantities all must be converted to same denomination.

address, forms of. Both spoken and written salutations differ widely even in English-speaking countries. Monarchical traditions and hereditary titles give rise to great complexity; England has a multiplicity of forms and a strict code of address. The U.S. has fewer and simpler forms, which have grown out of custom and convenience rather than inheritance and are indicative, not of a man's birth or family, but of his professional or political position. However, in all official and diplomatic correspondence and in formal social intercourse, modes of addressing letters and invitations, as well as the manner of personal address, are of great importance. The President of the U.S. is addressed in speech as *Mr. President,* in writing as *The President, The White House, Washington.* The formal opening of a letter may be *Sir,* the informal opening *My Dear Mr. President.* Ambassadors, in speech, are *Your Excellency,* in writing *His Excellency the Ambassador of Great Britain.* A governor of a state is spoken of formally as *His Excellency the Governor of Ohio.* An invitation would read *The Honorable the Governor of New York.* The Vice President, heads of executive departments (cabinet members), justices of the higher courts, mayors of cities, American ministers, Senators and Representatives, and ex-Presidents are addressed as *The Honorable,* e.g., *The Honorable the Vice President of the United States, The Honorable the Secretary of State.* The secretary to the President, heads of independent boards and commissions, assistant secretaries of executive departments, are also addressed as *Honorable. Esquire* is used after the names of chief clerks and chiefs of the bureaus of executive departments, diplomatic officers below the rank of minister, consular officers, clerk of the Supreme Court and officers of other courts. *Reverend* or *Honorable* should be preceded by the word *the* and should not be abbreviated; letters after the heading should begin (this is known as the salutation) *Dear Mr. ———.* Professional titles precede the name, and professional abbreviations follow. Church dignitaries are addressed in writing thus: the pope, *His Holiness Pope Pius XII,* in the salutation *Your Holiness* or *Most Holy Father;* cardinals, *His Eminence the Cardinal Archbishop of New York* or (when not an archbishop) *His Eminence Cardinal ———,* salutation *Your Eminence;* archbishops, *His Grace the Archbishop of ———,* salutation *My Lord Archbishop* or *Your Grace;* bishops, *The Right Reverend Bishop ———* or *The Right Reverend Bishop of ———,* salutation *Dear Sir* or *My Lord;* Methodist Episcopal bishops, *The Reverend Bishop ——— ———,* salutation *Dear Sir;* deans, *The Very Reverend ———*

———, salutation *Very Reverend Sir.* English titles are numerous and complex. The king and the queen, in speech with intimates, are *Sir* and *Ma'am.* Addressed by letter, the king is *His Most Gracious Majesty the King;* the salutation of the letter is *Sire* or *Your Majesty.* The queen in writing is *Her Most Gracious Majesty the Queen,* salutation *Madame* or *Your Majesty.* A prince is in writing *His Royal Highness the Prince of* ———, a princess *Her Royal Highness the Princess Margaret Rose.* A duke is in writing *His Grace the Duke of* ———, salutation *My Lord Duke* or *Your Grace.* A countess is in writing *The Right Honourable the Countess of* ———, salutation *Madame* or *Your Ladyship.* An earl is in writing *The Right Honourable the Earl of* ———, salutation *My Lord* or *Your Lordship.* Members of Parliament add the letters M.P. to their address. A privy councilor is *The Right Honourable* ——— ———. In addressing invitations the full title is used except in the case of barons. The title *Right Honourable* belongs to all peers and is the right of members of the privy council and of cabinet ministers. Professional titles precede titles of rank as *Captain the Honourable John Blank.* The use of *Esquire,* formerly limited to lawyers, country gentlemen, and the eldest sons of knights, is now more general. The title *Honourable* is ignored in conversation and is never used on visiting cards.

Ade, George, 1866–1944, American journalist, humorist, dramatist, satirist of the Midwest. Notable book is *Fables in Slang* (1900). Also wrote comedies, comic operas, musical-comedy librettos.

Adelaide, empress: see OTTO I, emperor.

Adelaide, city (pop. 34,990; metropolitan pop. 382,454), cap. of South Australia, near Gulf St. Vincent. Founded 1836, it is the state's oldest city. Seat of Univ. of Adelaide. Has knitting mills and state-owned munitions plants.

Adelard of Bath (ă'dŭlärd), fl. 12th cent., English scholastic philosopher, noted for Arabic studies.

Adelheid, empress: see OTTO I, emperor.

Adélie Coast, region, Antarctica, in Australian quadrant, W of George V Coast and E of Wilkes Land. Heavily glaciated, has strongest winds in world. Discovered 1840.

Adelphi, the (ŭdĕl'fē), area in central London, devoloped by Adam brothers. Here many literary and theatrical great lived.

Adelphi College: see GARDEN CITY, N.Y.

Adelsberg, Yugoslavia: see POSTOJNA.

Aden (ā'dŭn, ä'–), British crown colony (80 sq. mi.; pop. 81,236, including PERIM), SW Arabia, on Gulf of Aden. Captured by Moslems 636; occupied by Turks almost continuously 1538–1630; under British administration as part of India 1839–1937. Town of Aden is a free port; important air base in World War II. British protectorate of Aden (c.112,000 sq. mi; pop. c.630,000) is bordered by Yemen and Saudi Arabia. Mostly mountainous or desert.

Aden, Gulf of, W arm of Arabian Sea, between Aden protectorate and Somaliland.

On trade route from Mediterranean Sea to Indian Ocean via Suez Canal.

adenoids, pharyngeal tonsils, masses of lymphoid tissue in upper part of throat. When unusually large, may interfere with normal breathing.

Adeste Fideles (ädĕs'tā fēdā'lĕs), Christian hymn, written in Latin in 17th or 18th cent. Best-known English version, beginning "O come, all ye faithful," by Frederick Oakeley (1802–80). Usual tune, *Portuguese Hymn,* is from collection of hymns called *Cantus Diversi;* author and composer are unknown.

adhesive, substance used for bonding surfaces. Animal glue, made from hides, hoofs, bones, probably was known to prehistoric man. In 19th cent. appeared many vegetable adhesives including gums, resins, mucilage, and starch. Other adhesives are made from casein, soybeans, rubber, cellulose, and synthetic substances.

Adige (ä'dējĕ), Ger. *Etsch,* river, 225 mi. long, N Italy. Flows from Alps, past Verona, to Adriatic.

Adighe, Caucasian people: see CIRCASSIA.

Adirondack Mountains (ădĭrŏn'dăk), NE N.Y., sometimes mistakenly included in Appalachian system; geologically a S extension of Laurentian Plateau. Its preCambrian metamorphic rock with intruded igneous rock has been uplifted and eroded through countless years. Group, bounded E by L. Champlain and L. George region, extends from foothills near St. Lawrence R. (N) to Mohawk valley (S). Rises to 5,344 ft. in Mt. Marcy, highest point in N.Y., where L. Tear of the Clouds is source of chief headstream of the Hudson. Another well-known peak is Whiteface (4,872 ft.), ski center with meteorological station on summit. Both are near L. Placid and Saranac Lakes. Much of region—noted for wild scenery, beautiful forests, many lakes—is in Adriondack Forest Preserve (2,177,701 acres) and includes many summer and winter resorts. Iron mining revived c.1938; much ore produced in World War II.

Adlai (ăd'lī, ăd'lā), father of Shaphat, one of David's officers. 1 Chron. 27.29.

Adler, Alfred (äd'lûr), 1870–1937, Austrian psychiatrist, founder of school of individual psychology. He rejected Freudian emphasis on sex and maintained that all personality difficulties or behavior disorders are over-compensation for deficiencies, environmental repressions, or feelings of inferiority. Later Adler lectured and practiced in U.S.

Adler, Cyrus, 1863–1940, founder of American Jewish Historical Society; an editor of the *Jewish Encyclopedia* and of the *American-Jewish Year Book.*

Adler, Dankmar, 1844–1900, American architect, b. Germany; associate of Louis SULLIVAN.

Adler, Felix, 1851–1933, American educator and founder of ETHICAL CULTURE MOVEMENT, b. Germany. Was professor of ethics, Columbia Univ., after 1902 and leader in social welfare activities.

Adler, Viktor, 1852–1918, Austrian politician, founder of Austrian Social Democratic party. His son, **Friedrich Adler,** 1879–, Socialist leader, shot Count STÜRGKH (1916); amnestied 1918.

Admetus (ădmē'tŭs), in Greek legend, Thessalian king, whom Apollo served. On condition that his life be spared, his wife, ALCESTIS, gave her life, but Hercules rescued her from Hades.

Admiralty Island (1,164 sq. mi.), off SE Alaska, in ALEXANDER ARCHIPELAGO and SW of Juneau. Separated from mainland by Stephens Passage. Has fish canning and lumbering.

Admiralty Islands, small volcanic group, area 800 sq. mi., SW Pacific, W of New Ireland, in BISMARCK ARCHIPELAGO. Japanese air base on Manus (main island) was taken 1944 by Allied forces.

Admiralty Range, N part of great mountain range in Victoria Land, W of Ross Sea, Antarctica. Its peaks reach 10,000 ft.

adolescence (ă"dŭlĕ'sŭns), physical stage between puberty and maturity lasting generally from ages of 12 to 21. Adolescent physiological changes strengthen heterosexual drives and strivings for independence. Typical emotional difficulties arise from conflicting biological changes and inability to express new needs in socially acceptable form.

Adolf of Nassau, d. 1298, German king (1292–98). Deposed by diet; defeated and slain by army of Albert I.

Adonai, another name for GOD.

Adonijah (ăd"nī'jŭ, ŭdŏn'ŭjŭ), son of David. He schemed for the throne, but David gave it to Solomon. 2 Sam. 3.4; 1 Kings 1; 2.1–25.

Adonis (ŭdō'nĭs), in Greek religion, young man loved by APHRODITE. When he was killed by a wild boar, Aphrodite persuaded the gods to let him live for six months of each year. Hence his death and resurrection were celebrated in midsummer festival Adonia, symbolizing yearly growth and decay.

adoptionism, heresy in Spain in 8th and 9th cent., holding old belief that Christ is a man adopted as Son of God by baptism.

Adour (ădŏōr'), river, 210 mi. long, SW France. Rises in Pyrenees, enters Bay of Biscay near Bayonne. Forms N limit of Basque country.

Adowa, Ethiopia: see ADUWA.

Adrammelech (ŭdrăm'–), in Bible, one of two men named as murderers of their father, Sennacherib; Sharezer was the other. 2 Kings 19.37 (= Isa. 37.38).

adrenal gland (ădrē'nŭl) or **suprarenal gland** (sōŏprŭrē'nŭl), one of two small, endocrine glands, one resting on upper part of each kidney. Outer layer (cortex) secretes hormone (cortin) influencing metabolism and sex function; inner portion (medulla) secretes hormone adrenaline.

adrenaline (ŭdrĕn'ŭlĭn) or **epinephrine** (ĕpĭnĕf'rĭn), hormone secreted by medulla of adrenal gland. Helps to maintain normal blood pressure. Takamine obtained it in pure form (1901). Synthesized 1904. Injections are used to cause contraction of capillaries.

Adria (ā'drĕŭ), ancient name of the Adriatic, extended to mean central Mediterranean in Acts 27.27.

Adrian, emperor: see HADRIAN.

Adrian I, d. 795, pope (772–95). Called on CHARLEMAGNE to repulse Lombard king, Desiderius. Increased papal lands through Donation of Charlemagne. Supported Empress IRENE against ICONOCLASM.

Adrian IV, d. 1159, pope (1154–59), an Englishman named Nicholas Breakspear. Driven from Rome by ARNOLD OF BRESCIA, he returned by 1155 and put down rebels with help of FREDERICK I, whom he crowned. Adrian had difficulties with William I of Sicily and Frederick. His donation of Ireland as fief to Henry II of England much disputed.

Adrian, Edgar Douglas, 1889–, English physiologist, authority on nervous system. Shared 1932 Nobel Prize in Physiology and Medicine for work on function of neuron.

Adrian, city (pop. 18,393), S Mich., SW of Detroit; settled 1835. Farm trade center with chrysanthemum culture and mfg. of metal and paper products.

Adrianople (ā"drēŭnō'pŭl) or **Edirne** (ĕdēr'nĕ), city (pop. 30,245), European Turkey, in Thrace. Commercial center; silk and cotton mfg. Founded by Emperor Hadrian A.D. c.125, it was the scene of a fateful Visigothic victory over Emperor VALENS in 378. Passed to the Turks 1361; residence of the sultans 1361–1453. Briefly held by Bulgaria in the Balkan Wars (1913), it was given to Greece in 1920 and restored to Turkey in 1923. Chief among landmarks is the Mosque of Selim I, built by Sinan.

Adrianople, Treaty of, 1829, ended Russo-Turkish War of 1828–29. Turkey ceded some territories on Black Sea to Russia, allowed Russian occupation of Moldavia and Walachia, and granted Russia exclusive protective rights over Palestinian holy places and over Christian subjects of sultan. Dardanelles opened to all commercial vessels; autonomy given to Serbia, and promised to Greece.

Adriatic Sea (ādrēă'tĭk), arm of the Mediterranean, between Italy and Balkan Peninsula; 500 mi. long, 60–140 mi. wide, max. depth 4,035 ft. Low W and N shores belong to Italy, rugged E shore to Yugoslavia and Albania. Chief ports: Trieste, Venice, Bari, Fiume.

adsorption, attraction and adhesion of molecules of one substance to surface of another; no chemical change. Certain solids (e.g., charcoal) readily adsorb gases. Particles in colloidal solution may adsorb much of the solvent. Adsorption used in removing colors from solutions, in photography, in hydrogenation of oils, and in gas analysis.

Adullam (ŭdŭl'–), town of Judah, SW of Jerusalem. David hid in Cave of Adullam when fleeing from Saul. 1 Sam. 22; 2 Sam. 23.13–17; 1 Chron. 11.15–19.

adult education, training of adults beyond school age. Usual forms are lecture, reading, discussion groups. Formal attempts to organize adult education in 19th cent. Europe gave rise to continuation schools in Switzerland and Germany, the FOLK SCHOOL in Denmark. In U.S. lectures of the LYCEUM and of the Lowell Institute of Boston long preceded the Chautauqua movement. Lectures supplemented by extension and correspondence courses offered by many colleges in 20th cent. Political and labor organs have promoted adult education, including VOCATIONAL TRAINING. Libraries have also advanced adult education groups, as has the Federal government. A separate program is that of the "great books" groups, which began meeting in 1947; the "great books" were published in a set in 1952. American Association for Adult Education was estab. (1926) to systematize philosophy and methods. In U.S., USSR, Mexico, and elsewhere adult-education schemes have successfully combated illiteracy.

Aduwa or **Adowa** (both: ä′důwä), town (pop. 6,000), N Ethiopia. Scene in 1896 of Menelik II's decisive victory over the Italian invaders.

Advent, four-week penitential season. In West, from Sunday nearest Nov. 30 (St. Andrew's) to Christmas. First season of church year.

Adventists, religious groups centering belief on second coming of Christ. William MILLER led Millerites or Second Adventists; Advent Christian Church (1861) was a branch. Seventh-Day Adventists adopted (1846) Saturday as Sabbath; divided on Ellen Gould White's prophecies. Church of God (organized c.1866) became (1888) Churches of God in Jesus Christ. There are other Adventist groups.

advertising, public notices, especially those designed to influence sales or use of the product made by the announcer (the advertiser). Major media are magazines, newspapers, television and radio, and such outdoor advertising as billboards and posters. Advertising agencies (becoming prominent in 1860s) have done much to put "salesmanship" into what had previously been merely "offers for sale."

Ady, Andrew (ŏ′dē), Hung. *Ady Endre,* 1877–1919, Hungarian modernist poet.

Adyge, Caucasian people: see CIRCASSIA.

Adzhar Autonomous Soviet Socialist Republic (ůjär′, ä′jär) or **Adzharistan** (ůjä′rĭstăn″), autonomous state (1,100 sq. mi.; pop. c.200,-000, largely Mohammedan), SW Georgian SSR; cap. BATUM. Annexed by Russia from Turkey 1829 and 1878.

A. E., poet: see RUSSELL, GEORGE WILLIAM.

Aeëtes, king of Colchis: see JASON; MEDEA.

Aegadian Isles (ēgā′dēŭn), Latin *Aegates,* small archipelago, Italy, in Mediterranean off W Sicily. Here Roman naval victory (241 B.C.) ended First Punic War.

Aegean civilization (ējē′ŭn), general term for cultures of pre-Hellenic Greece. MINOAN CIVILIZATION was a rich culture of Crete (late 4th millennium B.C.). MYCENAEAN CIVILIZATION occupied mainland of Greece later. Other centers at Troy and in Cyclades.

Aegean Sea, arm of Mediterranean, c.400 mi. long and c.200 mi. wide, between Greece and Asia Minor; connected by Dardanelles with the Sea of Marmara. Its ancient name, Archipelago, now applies to its numerous islands, which include EUBOEA, N and S SPORADES, CYCLADES, and DODECANESE.

Aegeus (ē′jěŭs, ē′jōōs), legendary king of Athens. Believing his son, Theseus, killed by the Minotaur, drowned himself in the sea (hence called Aegean).

Aegina (ējī′nů), Gr. *Aigina,* island (32 sq. mi.; pop. 10,052), off SE Greece, in the Gulf of Aegina (Saronic Gulf), an arm of the Aegean, near Athens; chief town Aegina (pop. 5,820), on NW shore. Agr.; sulphur springs. Influenced by MINOAN CIVILIZATION, island was conquered c.1000 B.C. by Dorian Greeks. It struck first Greek coins and rose to great commercial importance. Was sacked by Athens against whom it sided in Peloponnesian War (431 B.C.). AEGINETAN MARBLES discovered near by (1811).

Aegnieta, Paulus: see PAUL OF AEGINA.

Aeginetan marbles (ē″jĭnē′tŭn), Greek sculptures, probably of the 5th cent. B.C., discovered 1811 in Aegina. Depict story of Troy.

Aegisthus (ējĭs′thŭs), in Greek legend, lover of Clytemnestra. The lovers killed her husband, Agamemnon. In revenge her son, ORESTES, killed both.

Aegospotamos (ē″gŭspŏ′tůmŭs), river of anc. Thrace. At its mouth occurred the final battle of the PELOPONNESIAN WAR (405 B.C.) when Lysander of Sparta destroyed the Athenian fleet.

Ælfric (ăl′frĭk), c.955–1020, English churchman, author of homilies, saints' lives, free version of first seven books of the Bible.

Aemilian Way: see ROMAN ROADS.

Aeneas (ĭnē′ŭs), Trojan prince who escaped from Troy to Carthage (where he met Dido) and finally went to Italy, where his descendants founded Rome. The *Aeneid* (ĭnē′ĭd), a 12-book Latin epic by VERGIL, tells of his adventures.

Aeolia, ancient Greek region: see AEOLIS.

Aeolian Islands: see LIPARI ISLANDS.

Aeolis (ē′ŭlĭs), or **Aeolia** (ēō′lĕŭ), collective term for cities on W coast of Asia Minor planted by the Aeolians, a branch of the Hellenic peoples.

Aeolus (ē′ŭlŭs), in Greek mythology. 1 Wind-god, who kept winds in cave on Aeolia. 2 Son of Hellen and ancestor of Aeolian branch of Hellenic race.

aerial: see ANTENNA.

aerial photography, taking of still or moving-picture photographs from flying aircraft. Top military intelligence source in World War II. Photogrammetry is a map-making development.

aerodynamics: see FLIGHT.

aeroplane: see AIRPLANE.

Aeschines (ě′skĭnēs), c.389–314? B.C., Athenian orator, rival of Demosthenes.

Aeschylus (ěs′kĭlŭs, ěs–), 525–456 B.C., first of three great Greek poets of TRAGEDY. Added an actor and increased possibilities of the drama; won 13 first prizes. Author of perhaps 90 plays, seven in full extant: *The Suppliants, The Persians, The Seven against Thebes, Prometheus Bound,* and only extant ancient trilogy; the *Oresteia,* which contains the plays *Agamemnon, The Choëphoroe,* and *The Eumenides.*

Aesculapius: see ASCLEPIUS.

Aesir, Norse Olympian gods: see ASGARD.

Aesop (ē′sŭp, –sŏp), 6th cent. B.C., Greek fabulist, a slave of Samos (existence is doubtful). See FABLE.

aesthetics, philosophy of beauty and art. It studies the nature of beauty and laws governing its expression, as in the fine arts, as well as principles of artistic criticism. Some philosophers stress objectivity of nature of beauty, others claim that it is purely subjective.

Æthelbald (ĕ'thŭlbôld, ă'–), Anglo-Saxon kings. **Æthelbald,** d. 757, king of Mercia (716–57). A strong ruler, by 731 he controlled all England S of the Humber. Murdered by his bodyguard. **Æthelbald,** d. 860, king of Wessex, son of ÆTHELWULF and brother of ALFRED. Refused to allow his father to return to the kingdom after a pilgrimage to Rome. Married his father's widow, Judith of France, 858.

Æthelbert (–bûrt, –bûrt), Anglo-Saxon kings. **Æthelbert,** d. 616, king of Kent (560?–616), was strongest ruler S of the Humber. St. Augustine converted him to Christianity and made his cap., Canterbury, a great Christian center. His laws are earliest extant body of laws in any Germanic language. **Æthelbert,** d. 866, king of Wessex (860–66), was son of Æthelwulf and brother of Alfred.

Æthelflæd (–flĕd) or **Ethelfleda** (ĕthŭlflē'dŭ), d. 918, daughter of ALFRED. Reigned over Mercia alone from 911; was known as Lady of the Mercians. Her wise government made her known as one of English history's outstanding women.

Æthelfrith (–frĭth), d. 617, king of Northumbria; first great leader of N Angles. He forced his brother-in-law EDWIN (who pretended to throne) into exile. Killed in battle with Edwin's supporters near Nottingham.

Æthelred (–rĕd), Anglo-Saxon kings. **Æthelred,** d. 871, king of Wessex (866–71), son of ÆTHELWULF and brother of ALFRED. **Æthelred,** 965?–1016, king of England (978–1016), called Æthelred the Unready (Old Eng.= without counsel), son of Edgar and brother of EDWARD THE MARTYR. A weak king, he reigned at height of Danish power. He first levied DANEGELD 991. Danes returned in 997; stayed to plunder until 1000. He married (1002) Emma, sister of duke of Normandy, possibly to gain an ally. National navy built by 1009 was rendered useless by treason of its commanders. Danish king SWEYN was received by the DANELAW in 1013; London capitulated; Æthelred fled to Normandy. Restored on Sweyn's death (1014). Æthelred's son EDMUND IRONSIDE succeeded him (1016) and made treaty with CANUTE, son of Sweyn, who ruled England and married Æthelred's widow.

Æthelstan, English king: see ATHELSTAN.

Æthelwulf (–wŭlf), d. 858, king of Wessex (839–56), son of EGBERT and father of ÆTHELBALD, ÆTHELBERT, ÆTHELRED, and ALFRED. With Æthelbald won notable victory over Danes at Aclea (851). Married Judith of France in 856. A man of great piety, he learned while on pilgrimage in Rome that Æthelbald would resist his return; he left his son as king of Wessex and ruled in Kent and dependencies.

Aetius (āē'shĕŭs), c.396–454, Roman general. Defeated the Germans in Gaul. Repulsed Attila and the Huns at Châlons (451). Murdered by Valentinian III.

Aetna: see ETNA.

Aetolia (ētōl'yŭ), region of anc. Greece, N of Gulf of Corinth and Gulf of Calydon. Its people, the Aetolians, were farmers and shepherds. Cities of Aetolia joined in **Aetolian League** in 4th cent. B.C. to oppose Achaean League and the Macedonians. With Roman help it defeated Philip V of Macedon in 200 B.C. but then joined Antiochus III and went down with his defeat (189 B.C.).

Afanasyev, Aleksandr Nikolayevich (ŭlyĭksän'dŭr nyĭkŭlī'ŭvĭch ŭfŭnä'syŭf), 1826–71, Russian folklorist. His collections of popular tales introduced Russian folklore to world literature.

affidavit, written statement sworn to by a person making it and signed by him and by officer administering the oath. It is used whenever written attestation of facts is needed, but in court only when cross-examination is not necessary.

Afghan hound: see HOUND.

Afghanistan (ăfgă'nĭstăn"), kingdom (253,000 sq. mi.; pop. 12,000,000), SW Asia; cap. Kabul. Bounded on N by USSR, on W by Iran, and on S and E by Pakistan. Mostly mountainous, with ranges fanning out from the Hindu Kush. Wheat, rice, and fruits are grown in fertile valleys; chief export is karakul. Helmand is longest river, with Amu Darya R. marking part of boundary with USSR. To the N are Afghan Turkistan and highlands of Badakshan (noted for lapis lazuli). Communications are poor (there are no railroads), and industry is in stage of infancy. Diversified population comprises Afghans, Tazhiks, Hazaras, Turkmen, and Uzbeks; unifying factor is religion, for almost all are Moslem. Chief languages are Afghan or Pushtu and Iranian. Area was annexed 516 B.C. by Darius I and conquered 326 B.C. by Alexander the Great on his way to India. Kingdom of BACTRIA (fl. 3d cent.–2d cent. B.C.) fell to Parthians and rebellious tribes. Buddhism spread from the E but had brief survival; stable religion was provided by Moslem conquest, begun in 7th cent. Greatest of many Moslem states was that of Mahmud of Ghazni, who in 11th cent. conquered parts of Persia and India. Area was later conquered by Jenghiz Khan and Tamerlane, and in 16th cent. Baber used Kabul as base for conquest of India. Unified state covering most of present Afghanistan was estab. in 18th cent. by AHMED SHAH. Reigns of DOST MOHAMMED and SHERE ALI saw Afghan Wars (1839–42, 1878–81), resulting from rivalry between Britain and Russia for Afghan buffer state. Anglo-Russian agreement (1907) guaranteeing country's independence under British influence roused anti-British feeling and led to short war in 1919. Emirate was changed to a kingdom in 1926 under Amanullah, who was deposed in 1929 by fanatical Moslem subjects who resented his radical reforms. His successor, Mohammed Nadir Shah, was assassinated in 1933 for continuing the program of modernization. He was succeeded by his son, Mohammed Zahir Shah. Despite Afghan opposition, Pakistan in 1950 took over the vaguely defined lands of Pathan tribes within Durand line (boundary estab. 1893 by Sir Mortimer Durand between North-West Frontier Prov., India, and Afghanistan). In 1953 Afghanistan was still supporting Pathans' desire for independent state of Pushtunistan.

Afghan language (ăf'găn"), Iranian language of Indo-European family, also called Pushtu. See LANGUAGE (table).

A.F. of L.: see AMERICAN FEDERATION OF LABOR.

Afonso. For rulers thus named, see ALFONSO.

Africa, continent (with adjacent islands c.11,-500,000 sq. mi.; pop. c.200,000,000), joined to Asia by Sinai peninsula and facing Europe across Strait of Gibraltar. Mainly a plateau with its highest point at Mt. Kilimanjaro (19,565 ft.). In east is L. Victoria, its greatest lake. Vast river systems include the Nile, Niger, Congo, and Zambezi. The deserts, notably the Sahara, are edged by savannas. Jungles cover W equatorial Africa. In the civilization of Egypt (dating from before 3,000 B.C.) Africa may claim one of the world's most ancient settled cultures. The N African coast was colonized by Rome after the defeat of Carthage (149 B.C.). Islam was brought by the Arab invasion, 7th–11th cent. Moslem peoples (chiefly Moors) from N Africa launched a series of European invasions which ended in 15th cent. European exploration of the coast began in 15th cent. with Diaz's voyage around the Cape of Good Hope in 1488. The Portuguese were followed by Dutch, British, and French traders, 16th–17th cent. Explorations of interior revealed Africa's great wealth and led to large-scale colonization. By 1912 the European powers had partitioned Africa, with only Egypt, Ethiopia, and Liberia retaining a measure of independence. After World War I Germany lost her colonies to France and England (see BRITISH EMPIRE; FRENCH UNION). Other powers with lesser interests in Africa are Belgium, Portugal, and Spain. Italy after World War II was shorn by the UN of virtually all her African holdings. In World War II a series of major campaigns in NORTH AFRICA ended in 1943 with Axis defeat.

African Methodist Episcopal Church, American Negro denomination, founded (1794) by Richard ALLEN.

African Negro art, primarily the art of equatorial Africa. Known examples are mostly of recent origin, due to ravages of tropical climate. Style ranges from extreme naturalism to extreme formalism, from crudity to greatest refinement. Animism led to creation of ritual masks and fetishes. Highly prized ivories and bronzes of Benin, Nigeria, were produced 16th–17th cent. White domination brought rapid decline in production. Popular in Europe since 1905; vastly influenced abstract modern art.

African Negro music is highly rhythmic and polyphonic. Instruments are mainly percussive and wind. It was little studied until after invention of the phonograph. Extent of its influence on American Negro spirituals and jazz is subject of much debate.

Afrikaans (ä"frĭkäns', –känz'), standard language of the South African Dutch, a Germanic language of Indo-European family. See LANGUAGE (table).

afterbirth: see PLACENTA.

Afton, river of Ayrshire, Scotland. It is the "sweet Afton" of Burns's poem.

Ag, chemical symbol of the element SILVER.

Agade, ancient Mesopotamian city; see AKKAD.

Agadir (ägädēr'), town (pop. 12,438), French Morocco, a port on the Atlantic. Occupied and fortified by the Portuguese 1505–41. In 1911 when French troops were intervening in a Moroccan revolt, the German cruiser *Panther* appeared here, ostensibly to protect German property. The incident created a tense situation, later eased by agreements.

Agag (ā'găg), king of the Amalekites. Defeated and spared by Saul, he was killed by Samuel. I Sam. 15.

Aga Khan (ä'gä khän'), 1877–, Indian leader, the hereditary head of Mohammedan Ismaili sect. Sought Moslem support of British rule in India by founding All-India Moslem League in 1906. Represented India at League of Nations in 1930s. Famous for his wealth and for interest in horse racing.

Agamemnon (ă"gŭmĕm'nŏn), in Greek legend, leader of Greek armies in TROJAN WAR; brother of Menelaus. Quarrel with Achilles is a main theme of the *Iliad*. He married CLYTEMNESTRA, who bore him ELECTRA, ORESTES, and IPHIGENIA. Murdered by his wife and Aegisthus, he was avenged by his son, Orestes.

Agana (ägä'nyä), municipality, on Guam, near naval base at Apra Harbor. Before its destruction by the Japanese in 1945, it was Guam's largest town (1940 pop. 10,004; 1950 pop. 1,330).

Aganippe (ăg"ŭnĭp'ē), in Greek legend, nymph whose fountain on HELICON gives poetic inspiration to all who drink from it. Muses are often called Aganippides [Gr.,= daughters of Aganippe].

agar (ä'gär), or **agar-agar,** gelatinous product from red algae or seaweed, used as a laxative, sizing, food thickening, and culture medium for bacteria.

Agasias (ägä'shĕäs), name of two Greek sculptors of the 1st cent. B.C. The creator of the Borghese Warrior (Louvre) was the son of Dositheus; the other was the son of Menophilus.

Agassiz, (Jean) Louis (Rodolphe) (zhä' lwē rōdōlf' äg'ŭsē), 1807–73, Swiss-American zoologist, geologist. His research on fossil fish, exposition of glacial movement and deposit, and his teaching made Univ. of Neuchâtel a center of scientific study. As professor of zoology and geology at Lawrence Scientific School at Harvard he stimulated scientific study of nature in U.S. Agassiz's first wife died in Germany in 1848. His second wife **Elizabeth Cary Agassiz,** 1822–1907, was an author and educator. She accompanied her husband on expeditions to Brazil (1865–66) and along the E and W coasts of the Americas (1871–72). Influential in the founding of Radcliffe College, she served to 1903 as its first president. With her husband she wrote *A Journey in Brazil* (1868) and with her stepson Alexander, *Seaside Studies in Natural History* (1885). **Alexander Agassiz,** 1835–1910, son of Louis Agassiz, was from 1862 connected with Harvard and its Museum of Comparative Zoology. Much of the wealth he acquired from copper mines was used for scientific expeditions and research publication. Noted also as oceanographer.

Agassiz, Lake, former lake, c.700 mi. long, 250

CAPITAL CITIES are designated by CAPITAL AND SMALL CAPITAL type

mi. wide, of Pleistocene epoch, formed by melting of continental ice sheet, c.10,000 years ago over what are now NW Minn., NE N.Dak., S Manitoba. Named in 1879 for Louis Agassiz. Water drained N into Hudson Bay, left many smaller lakes and rich, deep soils.

agate, variety of QUARTZ banded in two or more colors. Used as semiprecious gem. Found in Brazil, India, Uruguay, and U.S.

Agatharchus (ăg″ŭthär′kŭs), 5th cent. B.C. Greek painter, credited with discoveries in perspective.

agave (ŭgä′vē, -gä′-), plant of genus *Agave* with long, stiff, fleshy leaves. Important in tropical America for fibers (e.g., SISAL HEMP), soap (see SOAP PLANT), food, and beverages (e.g., PULQUE and mescal). One species, century plant, used as house plant in North.

Agawam (ă′gŭwäm). **1** Town (pop. 10,166), SW Mass., on Connecticut R. below Springfield; settled 1635. Mfg. of woolens. **2** Former name of IPSWICH, Mass.

Ageladas (ăj″ŭlä′dŭs), c.540–c.460 B.C., Greek sculptor, famous for his statues of gods and athletes. Possibly taught Phidias and Myron.

Agen (äzhē′), city (pop. 26,051), cap. of Lot-et-Garonne dept., SW France, on the Garonne. Vineyards and orchards. Romanesque cathedral.

Agenor (ŭjē′–), Phoenician king; father of CADMUS and EUROPA.

ageratum (ăj″ŭrā′tŭm), popular annual (*Ageratum*), also called flossflower, with clustered lavender flowers. It is grown in borders and pots.

Agesander: see LAOCOÖN.

Agesilaus II (ŭjē″sĭlā′ŭs), c.444–360 B.C., king of Sparta; successor of Agis I. Though admired by Xenophon, he gave Greek cities to Persia by King's Peace (386) and, having excluded Thebes from a peace treaty, was defeated by Epaminondas at Leuctra (371 B.C.).

Agincourt (ă′jĭnkôrt), modern Fr. *Azincourt* (äzēkōōr′), village, Pas-de-Calais dept., N France. Here Henry V of England routed French Oct. 25, 1415.

Agis I (ā′jĭs), d. 398? B.C., king of Sparta, victor at Mantinea (418 B.C.).

Aglaia, one of the GRACES.

Agnes, Saint, 4th cent., noble Roman virgin martyred at 13 for rejecting pagan suitor. Feast: Jan. 21.

Agnes Scott College: see EMORY UNIVERSITY.

agnosticism, form of skepticism holding that reason cannot go beyond experience and that metaphysical beliefs (notably belief in God) cannot be definitely proved. Broadly, agnosticism includes teaching that metaphysical belief rests on faith alone (e.g., Kant) as well as materialistic systems (e.g., Comte, T. H. Huxley, Spencer).

Agnus Dei (än′yōōs dā′ē) [Latin,= Lamb of God, i.e., Jesus Christ], precommunion hymn in the Mass, so called from opening words; final number of sung Masses. The figure is of crucified Christ as sacrifice for mankind (sacrificial lamb).

Agoracritus (ăg″ōräk′rĭtŭs), fl. 5th cent. B.C., Greek sculptor, said to have been a pupil of

Phidias. Fragments of his colossal *Nemesis* survive.

Agoult, Marie (de Flavigny), comtesse d' (märē′ dù flävēnyē′ kōtĕs′ dägōō′), pseud. **Daniel Stern,** 1805–76, French author of autobiographical romances and social and political writings. Mistress of Liszt; mother of Cosima WAGNER.

agouti (ùgōō′tē), rodents of genera *Dasyprocta* and *Myoprocta* of Central and South America, West Indies. Length c.1½ ft.; coat speckled reddish to black; legs long, slender.

Agra (ä′grù), city (pop. 284,149), W Uttar Pradesh, India, on Jumna R. Founded 1566 by Akbar as cap. of Mogul empire. Outstanding among many splendid buildings are the TAJ MAHAL, Pearl Mosque, and Great Mosque. Important rail junction. Cotton spinning and carpet mfg. Seat of Agra Col.

Agra and Oudh, India: see UTTAR PRADESH.

Agram, Yugoslavia: see ZAGREB.

Agrapha of Jesus (ăg′rùfù) [Gr.,= not written], sayings attributed to Jesus not found in the four Gospels. There are quotations in the New Testament (e.g., Acts 20.35), and Agrapha from oral tradition appear in early Christian literature. Many are probably pseudepigrapha.

agrarian laws, in ancient Rome, regulated disposition of public lands. Patricians tended to gain (and hold) large areas, nominally as state tenants. Poorer classes' land hunger gave rise to laws, mostly ineffectual, beginning in 5th cent. B.C. Despite Licinian Rogations (367 B.C.), Sempronian Law (133 B.C.) and its revival (123 B.C.), and later large-scale reassignments, Domitian's edict (1st cent. A.D.) giving lands to their holders only confirmed long trend toward dependency of the poor upon the powerful.

Agricola (Cneius Julius Agricola) (ùgrĭ′kùlù), A.D. c.37–A.D. 93, Roman general, governor and pacifier of Britain; father-in-law of Tacitus.

Agricola, Georg (gä′ôrk), 1490?–1555, German physician and scientist, pioneer in scientific classification of minerals, and author of *De re metallica* (1556; Eng. tr. 1912).

Agricola, Johann or **Johannes** (yō′hän, yōhän′ùs), 1492–1566, German Protestant minister (family name Schnitter, originally Schneider). Broke with Luther by upholding antinomianism.

Agricultural Adjustment Administration (AAA), U.S. government agency estab. in Dept. of Agriculture (1933) as part of New Deal program. Designed to help farmers by cutting supplies of staple crops, thus raising farm prices and changing agr. pattern from overproduction of staple crops to more diversified farming. In 1936 Supreme Court declared important sections of act invalid for infringing on powers of the states. Soil Conservation and Domestic Allotment Act (1936) subsidized conservation. Agricultural Adjustment Act of 1938 estab. "ever-normal granary"; empowered AAA to store surplus crops and maintain balance of prices between years of low yield and years of high yield. Functions of AAA taken over in 1946 by Production and Marketing Administration.

agriculture, in its narrow sense, is tilling the

soil; more broadly, it includes stock raising, forestry, some mfg. (e.g., buttermaking). In prehistory, the change from hunting economy to tillage and domestication of beasts marked beginning of settlement, hence beginning of civilization. European agr. has long been mixed farming, much of it on subsistence level; in U.S., because of conquest of vast frontiers, increased growth of cities, and mechanization, farming tends to be on larger scale. Agr. colleges and government bureaus seek to increase productivity, improve depleted soil, and develop new plant and animal breeds.

Agriculture, United States Department of, division of U.S. government. Federal aid to agr. began modestly in 1839; Dept. of Agriculture, under a commissioner, was created 1862; Secretary of Agriculture became Cabinet member 1889. One of chief research, planning, service, and regulatory agencies of government; helps farmers with production, marketing, farm organization, land tenure, and land utilization problems, conducts huge research program, serves urban consumers, and issues many valuable publications.

Agrigento (ägrējěn'tō), city (pop. 27,785), S Sicily, Italy, on a height 2 mi. from sea; called Girgenti before 1927. Founded as Acragas c.580 B.C. by Greek colonists from Gela; one of most splendid cities of anc. Grecian world. Remains of Doric temples (6th–5th cent. B.C.). Birthplace of the Greek philosopher, Empedocles, for whom near-by Porto Empedocle is named.

agrimony (ăg'rĭmō"nē), perennial plant of genus *Agrimonia*. Grows wild in N temperate zone and is cultivated in herb gardens. It has aromatic leaves and yellow flowers, followed by top-shaped burs.

Agrippa, in Palestinian history: see HEROD.

Agrippa, Marcus Vipsanius (mär'kŭs vĭpsā'nēŭs ūgrī'pŭ), c.63 B.C.–c.12 B.C., Roman general, lieutenant and son-in-law of Augustus. Fought against Sextus Pompeius and against Antony at Actium.

Agrippina I (ă"grĭpī'nŭ), d. A.D. 33, Roman matron, daughter of Agrippa, granddaughter of Augustus, mother of Caligula. She accused Tiberius of having her husband Germanicus poisoned. Her daughter, **Agrippina II,** d. A.D. 59, was mother of NERO by her first marriage; after marriage to her uncle CLAUDIUS I she persuaded him to adopt Nero, then probably poisoned him to advance Nero, who had her murdered.

Agua (ä'gwä), inactive volcano, 12,310 ft. high, S Guatemala. In 1541 a flood from the mountain destroyed Ciudad Vieja, then cap. of Guatemala.

Aguascalientes (ä"gwäskälyän'tās), state (2,499 sq. mi.; pop. 188,104), N central Mexico, on central plateau; cap. Aguascalientes (pop. 82,234), founded 1575. State is rich in agr. produce and cattle; has mineral resources (largely unexploited) and warm mineral springs.

Aguinaldo, Emilio (ägwĭnäl'dō; āmē'lyō ägēnäl'dō), 1869?–, Philippine leader. Led insurrection in Spanish-American War; headed rebellion (1899–1901) against U.S. occupying forces until captured.

Aguirre, Lope de (lō'pä dä ägē'rä), c.1510–1561, Spanish rebel in colonial South America, noted for violence and cruelty. On expedition down Marañón and Amazon (1560), he killed Ursúa, the leader, laid waste Indian villages; held Margarita Isl. in terror (1561); and proclaimed rebellion against Spain. Surrounded at Barquisimeto, before he surrendered and was shot, he had his own daughter murdered.

Agulhas, Cape (ŭgŭ'lŭs), W Cape Prov., South Africa; most southerly point of Africa. On dividing line between Atlantic and Indian oceans.

Ahab (ā'hăb), d. c.853 B.C., king of Israel (c.874–c.853 B.C.), politically one of its greatest kings, religiously one of its wickedest; successor of Omri. He consolidated foreign relations by strategic marriages: his own to JEZEBEL of Tyre, his daughter Athaliah's to son of king of Judah. Bible account concerned chiefly with religious aspects of his reign. His foreign wife, with her Tyrian cults, led him into constant clashes with ELIJAH. He died in battle against Benhadad of Syria. 1 Kings 16.28–22.40.

Ahasuerus (ähăs"ūē'rŭs), Hebrew form of Xerxes used in Bible. In Esther probably Xerxes I; in Tobit 14.15 may be Cyaxares I, destroyer of Nineveh. Father of DARIUS THE MEDE given as Ahasuerus.

Ahaz (ā'hăz), d. c.727 B.C., king of Judah (c.731–727 B.C.). His reign marks end of Judah's real independence. Coalition of Israel and Syria attacked him and nearly took Jerusalem. He appealed to Assyrians, who defeated his enemies but demanded tribute, which he paid with Temple gold. Succeeded by Hezekiah. Isaiah was a contemporary of Ahaz. 2 Kings 16; 2 Chron. 28; Isa. 7; 38. Achaz: Mat. 1.9.

Ahaziah (āhúzī'ū). **1** Died c.852 B.C., king of Israel (c.853–852 B.C.), son of Ahab. 1 Kings 22.51–53; 2 Kings 1; 2 Chron. 20.35–37. **2** Died c.846 B.C., king of Judah (c.846 B.C.), son of Jehoram 2 and Athaliah. Killed in Jehu's coup d'état. His mother succeeded him. 2 Kings 8.25–29; 9; 2 Chron. 22.

Ahijah (ŭhī'jŭ) [Heb.,= brother of God], priest in Saul's time. May be same as AHIMELECH. 1 Sam. 14.3.

Ahimelech (ŭhĭm'ŭlĕk), priest, brother of (or perhaps same as) Ahijah. Saul had him killed for helping David. 1 Sam. 22.9–19. Abimelech: 1 Chron. 18.16.

Ahithophel (ŭhĭth'ŭfĕl), David's counselor. Plotted with Absalom; facing ruin, he killed himself. 2 Sam. 15.12; 16.20–17.23; 11.3; 23.34. Dryden's satire, *Absalom and Achitophel,* uses instead the Vulgate form of name.

Ahmadabad, India: see AHMEDABAD.

Ahmed IV (ä'mĕd), d. 1603, sultan of Morocco (1578–1603). Defeated the Portuguese at Alcazarquivir in 1578. Morocco prospered under his reign.

Ahmed, Ottoman sultans. **Ahmed I,** 1589–1617, reigned 1603–1617. Made peace with Austria (1606), recognizing Transylvanian independence. Lost Tabriz to ABBAS I. **Ahmed III,** 1673–1736, reigned 1703–30. Harbored CHARLES XII of Sweden. In war with Russia (1710–11) he recovered Azov. Defeated by the Austrians, he signed Treaty of PASSAROWITZ (1718). He was overthrown by the Janizaries.

Ahmed, 1898–1930, shah of Persia (1909–25), last of Kajar dynasty; deposed by Reza Shah Pahlevi.

Ahmedabad or **Ahmadabad** (both: ăm″ŭdŭbăd′), city (pop. 595,210), NW Bombay, India. Sacred to Gujarat sect of Jains. Cotton textile mills.

Ahmed Shah (ä′mĕd shä′), c.1723–1773, Afghan ruler, founder of Durani dynasty. Won Afghan rule by supporting Nadir Shah of Iran.

Ahriman: see ZOROASTRIANISM.

Ahura Mazdah: see ZOROASTRIANISM.

Ahvenanmaa, Finland: see ALAND ISLANDS.

aids, in feudalism, type of feudal due paid by a vassal to his suzerain or lord. Their exact nature is subject to controversy. In English-speaking countries, as specified in MAGNA CARTA of 1215, aids were due on knighting of lord's eldest son, on marriage of his eldest daughter, for ransom when lord was in captivity. In France aids were converted into a form of royal tax and continued to 1789. See also SCUTAGE; TALLAGE.

Aigues-Mortes (ĕg-môrt′), town (pop. 3,320), Gard dept., S France, near Mediterranean. Louis IX built port (now silted up). Medieval towers, ramparts.

Aijalon (ă′jŭ–, ī′jŭ–, ā′jŭ–), valley over which Joshua commanded moon to stand still. Joshua 10.12.

Aiken, Conrad (ā′kĭn), 1889–, American poet, novelist. Poems (e.g., *The Jig of Forslin,* 1916; *Preludes for Memnon,* 1931) show preoccupation with music. Novels (e.g., *Blue Voyage,* 1927) are psychological. Also wrote short stories, criticism, autobiography.

Aiken, city (pop. 7,083), W S.C., NE of Augusta, Ga. Resort, trade, and industrial center for farming and forest area.

ailanthus (ālăn′–) or **tree of heaven,** hardy deciduous tree (*Ailanthus*), with large compound leaves. Native to China, common in European and American cities. Is tolerant of smoke and other handicaps.

Ailly, Pierre d' (pyĕr′dāyē′), 1350–1420, French cardinal. Favored calling of general council to end Great Schism and was prominent in Council of Constance. His astronomical work, *Imago mundi,* studied by Columbus.

Ailsa Craig (āl′sŭ), conspicuous rocky island (1,114 ft. high) off SW Scotland, in Ayrshire.

Ain (ē), department (2,249 sq. mi.; pop. 306,778), E France, in Bresse; cap. Bourg-en-Bresse.

Aintab, Turkey: see GAZIANTEP.

Aintree, difficult and dangerous racecourse, Lancashire, England. The Grand National is run here.

Ainu (ī′nōō), aborigines of Japan. Forced by Japanese to retreat to N islands where they now live as hunters and food gatherers. Short, stocky, and hairy, they resemble Europeans more than Mongoloids. Their language is unrelated to any known speech.

air: see ATMOSPHERE; LIQUID AIR; VENTILATION.

air, law of the, law, both national and international, regulating civil aviation. Generally national legislation has been modeled in most countries on rules adopted in international conventions. The Paris meeting in 1919 drew up Paris Convention. In 1944 conference of 52 nations (not including the USSR) led to agreements and to founding of Internatl. Civil Aviation Organization. Question of national rights *vs.* freedom of the air not settled.

aircraft carrier, ship designed to store, launch, and land aircraft. Used experimentally in World War I; most important of capital ships in World War II battles.

Airedale terrier: see TERRIER.

airfoil, surface designed to react in particular way to moving air stream. Thus aircraft wing surfaces produce lift, movable aileron surfaces make possible rotation around longitudinal axis, and variable pitch propeller blades produce change in thrust. Autogiro rotor blades with suddenly changed pitch can jump craft into air.

air mail. Demonstrated in U.S. and England in 1911. Army pilots and aircraft began regular U.S. civilian service with New York-to-Washington flight May 15, 1918; continued by Post Office Dept. 1920–21. Coast-to-coast service (all by air) operated by Post Office Dept. 1924–27. Commercial contracts authorized in 1925. Service extends to most of world.

airplane or **aeroplane,** heavier-than-air craft developing propulsive power and sustained by air action on external surfaces. First man-carrying, power-driven, heavier-than-air flight was that of Wright brothers' biplane (Kitty Hawk, N.C., Dec. 17, 1903). Airplanes are usually monoplane (one wing). Main structures: fuselage (main body); one or more power plants (engines), each with propeller; landing gear; and movable control surfaces (ailerons for longitudinal control; rudder for vertical control; and elevator for horizontal control). See also JET PROPULSION. See *ill.,* p. 23.

air plant or **epiphyte,** plant, such as orchid and Spanish moss, not normally rooted in soil, but uses PARASITE, able to make its food by PHOTOSYNTHESIS. Grows on another plant or other support and gets water from atmosphere.

airport, land area with runways suitable for heavier aircraft. Provides taxiing and parking strips; hangars; repair and fueling facilities; traffic tower; radio and meteorological apparatus; passenger and cargo stations; beacons, floodlights, obstacle lights, other illumination. See also AIRWAY.

air power. Use of aircraft in World War I led some theorists (notably the American William Mitchell and the Italian Giulio Douhet) to develop the idea of predominance of air power—victory by aircraft alone. In World War II airplanes were used extensively, and Germans and Italians used aircraft effectively (as in capture of Crete). Similarly, loss of air supremacy locally (as in attacks on Britain, 1940–41) and generally in 1944–45 played a large part in defeat of the Axis. Aircraft carriers were prominent in the Pacific warfare. Yet the question of victory by air alone was not settled, and was complicated by introduction of atomic bombs and jet-propulsion.

airship, self-propelled, steerable (dirigible) balloon. Internal gas pressure shapes nonrigid

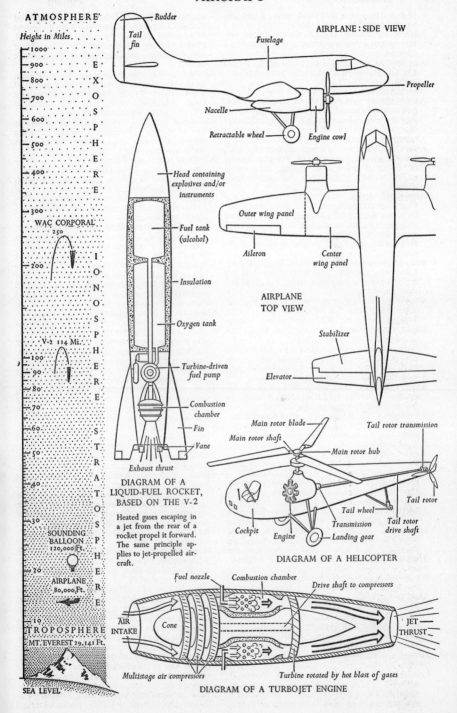

ATMOSPHERE

Height in Miles

EXOSPHERE

IONOSPHERE

WAC CORPORAL 250

V-2 114 Mi.

STRATOSPHERE

SOUNDING BALLOON 120,000 Ft.

AIRPLANE 80,000 Ft.

TROPOSPHERE

MT. EVEREST 29,141 Ft.

SEA LEVEL

Rudder

Tail fin

Fuselage

AIRPLANE: SIDE VIEW

Propeller

Nacelle

Retractable wheel

Engine cowl

Head containing explosives and/or instruments

Fuel tank (alcohol)

Outer wing panel

Aileron

Center wing panel

AIRPLANE TOP VIEW

Insulation

Oxygen tank

Stabilizer

Turbine-driven fuel pump

Elevator

Combustion chamber

Fin

Vane

Exhaust thrust

DIAGRAM OF A LIQUID-FUEL ROCKET, BASED ON THE V-2

Heated gases escaping in a jet from the rear of a rocket propel it forward. The same principle applies to jet-propelled aircraft.

Main rotor blade

Main rotor shaft

Tail rotor transmission

Main rotor hub

Tail rotor

Cockpit

Engine

Tail wheel

Transmission

Landing gear

Tail rotor drive shaft

DIAGRAM OF A HELICOPTER

Fuel nozzle

Combustion chamber

Drive shaft to compressors

AIR INTAKE

Cone

JET THRUST

Multistage air compressors

Turbine rotated by hot blast of gases

DIAGRAM OF A TURBOJET ENGINE

(e.g., blimp) and semirigid types. Rigid airships (largest type) are elongated, have rigid frame or latticework of aluminum or duraluminum compartmented for gas cells and covered by fabric. Engines inside drive propellers outside. Lift is provided by hydrogen gas (most buoyant) or helium (noninflammable).

airsickness, any disorder arising from flight at high altitudes or great speed. Similar to seasickness but caused by aircraft motion. Rapid ascent causes aeroembolism (circulation blocked by nitrogen bubbles released in blood by sudden change of atmospheric pressure). Anoxia (insufficient oxygen in cells), a form of altitude sickness induced by decrease of pressure and oxygen, may result in loss of muscular control and unconsciousness.

airway, air route between air traffic centers over terrain most suitable for emergency landings, spaced with landing fields equipped with air navigation and radio facilities. Civil Aeronautics Authority supervises U.S. airway traffic and facilities and enforces flight rules.

Airy, Sir George Biddell, 1801–92, English astronomer, authority on magnetism and on meteorology, astronomer royal (1835–81).

Aisha: see AYESHA.

Aisne (ān, Fr. ĕn), department (2,868 sq. mi.; pop. 453,411), NE France; cap. Laon. Towns: Soissons, Château-Thierry, Saint-Quentin. Aisne R., tributary of Oise, was important battle line in World War I.

Aitken, Robert Grant (āt'kĭn), 1864–1951, American astronomer, authority on double stars. Director (1930–35) Lick Observatory.

Aix-en-Provence (ĕks-ă-prôvãs', ĕk"sä–), city (pop. 32,076), Bouches-du-Rhône dept., SE France. Founded c.122 B.C. by Romans as Aquae Sextiae; scene of Marius' victory over Teutons (102 B.C.); cap. of Provence before 1789; center of medieval Provençal culture. University founded 1409, now partly in Marseilles.

Aix-la-Chapelle, Germany: see AACHEN.

Aix-la-Chapelle, Treaty of. 1 Compact of May 2, 1668, which ended War of DEVOLUTION. France kept most of its conquests in Flanders but returned Franche-Comté to Spain. Spanish possessions in Low Countries were guaranteed by TRIPLE ALLIANCE. **2** Treaty of 1748, ending War of the AUSTRIAN SUCCESSION. It generally restored the prewar map, but awarded Silesia to Prussia and conferred Parma, Piacenza, and Guastalla on the Spanish infante, Philip. PRAGMATIC SANCTION was confirmed.

Aix-les-Bains (ĕks'-lä-bĕ'), town (pop. 10,720), Savoie dept., E France, on Lake Bourget; spa.

Ajaccio (Fr. äzhäksyō', It. äyät'chô), city (pop. 27,536), cap. of Corsica, France; seaport. Birthplace of Napoleon I.

Ajanta (ŭjŭn'tŭ), village, NW Hyderabad, India. Has cave dwellings and shrines decorated with Buddhist art (200 B.C.–A.D. 600).

Ajax (ā'jăks), Gr. Aias, in Greek legend. **1** Hero of Trojan War, called Telemonian Ajax. A giant, slow of mind and speech. Rescued body of Achilles. When Achilles'

armor was given to Odysseus, he committed suicide. **2** Leader of Locrian forces in Trojan War, called the Locrian Ajax. Violated Cassandra. Rescued from shipwreck by Poseidon, he defied the lightning and was struck dead.

Ajmer (äjmēr'), state (2,400 sq. mi., pop. 583,-693), NW India. Comprises two detached areas surrounded by Rajasthan. **Ajmer,** city (pop. 147,258), state cap. was founded c.1100. Cotton mills, railroad shops.

Ajo (ä'hō), village (pop. 5,817), SW Ariz., SW of Phoenix. Health resort and smelting center in mining area. Organ Pipe Cactus Natl. Monument is S.

Ajodhya, India: see FYZABAD.

Akbar (äk'bär), 1542–1605, Mogul emperor of India (1556–1605), grandson of Baber. Enlarged his original domain in N central India to include Afghanistan and all of N India. Known for administrative reforms and religious tolerance.

Akeley, Carl Ethan (āk'lē), 1864–1926, American naturalist, sculptor. Noted for improved methods of mounting habitat groups, invention of cement gun and Akeley camera, and bronze works of sculpture of African wildlife and natives. Made numerous African expeditions for American museums. Author of *In Brightest Africa* (1923).

Akhenaton: see IKHNATON.

Akhmatova, Anna (ŭkhmä'tŭvŭ), pseud. of Anna Andreyevna Gorenko, 1888–, Russian poet, a leading Acmeist. Her poems of love and tragedy are sculptured in their simplicity yet rhythmic in the tradition of Pushkin. Long very popular in Soviet Russia, she was criticized in 1948 by the Communist party for "bourgeois aristocratic aestheticism."

Akiba ben Joseph (ŭkĭ'bŭ), A.D. c.50–c.132, Palestinian rabbi, one of first to systematize Hebrew oral laws. Aided revolt of Simon Bar Kochba against Rome.

Akihito (äke'hētō), 1933–, Japanese prince, son of Emperor Hirohito. Officially named heir apparent to Japanese throne in Nov., 1952.

Akkad (ă'kăd, ä'käd), northern part of Babylonia, in Mesopotamia; the southern part was Sumer. From the 4th millennium B.C. a Semitic people flourished and under Sargon (c.2800) became an imperial power. Under Hammurabi Akkad and Sumer were united as Babylonia. Also spelled Accad.

Akkerman: see BELGOROD-DNESTROVSKY, Ukraine.

Aklavik (äklä'vĭk), Royal Canadian Mounted Police post and public seaplane anchorage in Mackenzie dist., Northwest Territories, Canada, on Peel R.

Akron, city (pop. 274,605), NE Ohio, on Cuyahoga R. and SE of Cleveland; settled 1807. Its site was in the WESTERN RESERVE. Growth was spurred by opening (1827) of Ohio and Erie Canal. Hub of U.S. rubber industry and U.S. center for lighter-than-air craft, it has airport stadium, Zeppelin airdock (*Akron* and *Macon* dirigibles built here), and mfg. of cereals, machinery, and chemicals. **University of Akron** (city supported; coed.) was chartered 1870, opened 1872 as Buchtel Col., became (1913) Municipal Univ., renamed 1926; includes Guggenheim Airship Inst. and city testing laboratory.

Aksakov, Sergei Timofeyevich (syĭrgä′ tyĭmù-fyä′ùvĭch ŭksä′kúf), 1791–1859, Russian writer. Author of *The Family Chronicle* (1856; Eng. tr., 1916–24), a remarkable picture of life of landed gentry.

Aksum or **Axum** (both: äksōōm′), town (pop. 10,000), N Ethiopia. Was cap. of dynasty (1st–6th cent.) which ruled over parts of modern Ethiopia and the Sudan. A major center of Coptic Christianity.

Akte, Greek peninsula: see ATHOS.

Akureyri (ä′kürä″rē), port (pop. 7,017), N Iceland, on Eyja Fjord. Exports train oil, fish products, wool, sheepskins.

Al, chemical symbol of the element ALUMINUM.

Alabama (ălùbă′mù), state (51,609 sq. mi.; pop. 3,061,743), SE U.S.; admitted 1819 as 22d state (slaveholding); cap. MONTGOMERY. N part is on Cumberland Plateau; mineral-rich highlands; BIRMINGHAM is iron and steel center. Alluvial plains in S drained by Alabama and Tombigbee rivers. Extreme SW touches Gulf of Mexico; great port is MOBILE. Around Tennessee R. is industrial development of TENNESSEE VALLEY AUTHORITY. Long a "cotton" state, Ala. has usual problems following one-crop culture. Agr. now much diversified. Area first explored by Spanish (esp. De Soto 1540), first settled (1702) by French under BIENVILLE. Ceded to Great Britain 1763, to U.S. 1783. Settlement heavy after defeat (1814) of Creek Indians. Made territory in 1817. In Confederacy (seceded Jan. 11, 1861) in Civil War. Industrial development later.

Alabama, navigable river formed in central Ala. by confluence of Coosa and Tallapoosa rivers above Montgomery. Flows 318 mi. W, SW, then S to join Tombigbee R. and form Mobile R. c.30 mi. N of Mobile.

Alabama, ship: see CONFEDERATE CRUISERS.

Alabama, University of, mainly near Tuscaloosa; state supported, coed.; chartered 1820, opened 1831.

Alabama City, Ala.: see GADSDEN.

Alabama claims, damages sought by U.S. from Great Britain for losses to merchant marine caused by British-financed CONFEDERATE CRUISERS. Tribunal at Geneva (1871–72) awarded U.S. $15,500,000 for damage by *Florida, Alabama,* and *Shenandoah.*

Alabama College: see MONTEVALLO.

Alabama Polytechnic Institute: see AUBURN, Ala.

alabaster, (ăl′ùbăs″tùr), fine-grained, translucent variety of GYPSUM, white or streaked with reddish brown. Used for statues, decorations. Very soft, hence easily worked but subject to breaking and other damage. Alabaster of the ancients is marble.

Alacoque, Margaret Mary: see MARGARET MARY, SAINT.

Alagez, Mount: see ARAGATS, MOUNT.

Alameda (ălùmē′dù, –mä′dù), city (pop. 64,-430), W Calif., on island in E San Francisco Bay. Mfg. and shipping center with shipyards and U.S. naval installations. Bridges and tunnel to mainland.

Alamein (ălùmān′, ä–) or **El Alamein** (ĕl), town, N Egypt, on Mediterranean coast, 70 mi. W of Alexandria. Here in World War II British under Montgomery defeated Germans under Rommel (Nov. 1–2, 1942).

Alamo, the (ăl′ùmō) [Spanish,= cottonwood], building in San Antonio, Texas, "the cradle of Texas liberty." Heroic but hopeless defense of the fortified building in Feb., 1836, against Santa Anna's demands for surrender, roused fighting anger among Texans, who six weeks later defeated the Mexicans at San Jacinto, crying, "Remember the Alamo!"

Alamogordo (ăl″ùmùgôr′dō), town (pop. 6,783), S central N.Mex. Trade center in farm, timber, and resort area. First atomic bomb, made at Los Alamos, was exploded in desert region NW on July 16, 1945. White Sands Natl. Monument is near.

Alamo Heights, city (pop. 8,000), S central Texas, N suburb of San Antonio.

Alamosa (ălùmō′sù), city (pop. 5,354; alt., c.7,500 ft.), S Colo., on Rio Grande; founded 1878. Processing and shipping center for farm and ranch area. Great Sand Dunes Natl. Monument is NE.

Aland Islands (ä′lùnd, ô′–), Finnish *Ahvenanmaa,* Swed. *Ålandsöerna,* archipelago (572 sq. mi.; pop. 22,569), Finland, in Baltic Sea, strategically placed at entrance to Gulf of Bothnia; chief town Mariehamn. Pop. largely Swedish. Fishing, farming. Ceded by Sweden to Russia 1809; became part of independent Finland 1917. Finnish-Swedish dispute over islands was settled 1921 by League of Nations, which awarded islands to Finland (with autonomous status) and forbade remilitarization. Russo-Finnish demilitarization agreement (1940) was renewed after World War II. Also spelled Aaland.

Alarcón, Hernando de (ĕrnän′dō dä älärkōn′), fl. 1540, Spanish explorer in American Southwest, discovered Colorado R.

Alarcón, Pedro Antonio de (pād′rō äntō′nyō), 1833–91, Spanish writer. His short novels, such as *El final de Norma* (1855), *El sombrero de tres picos* (1874, Eng. tr. *The Three-cornered Hat,* 1891), and *El capitán Veneno* (1881), are popular.

Alarcón y Mendoza, Juan Ruiz de (hwän′ rōōeth′ dä älärkōn′ ē mändō′thä), d. 1639, Spanish dramatic poet of the Golden Age, b. Mexico. His comedies in the classical tradition are notable for characterization; perhaps best known is *La verdad sospechosa* [the suspicious truth].

Alaric I (ă′ lùrĭk), c.370–410, Visigothic king. Led his troops in rebellion after death of Theodosius I, devastated S Balkans until stopped by Stilicho. Invaded Italy (408); sacked Rome (410).

Alaric II, d. 507, Visigothic king of Spain and S Gaul (c.484–507). Issued BREVIARY OF ALARIC. Routed and slain by Clovis I at Vouillé.

Alaska, U.S. territory (571,065 sq. mi.: pop. 128,643), NW North America; admitted 1912; cap. JUNEAU. Bounded N by Arctic Ocean; W by Bering Sea; S by Pacific Ocean; E by Canada. Includes ALEUTIAN ISLANDS, PRIBILOF ISLANDS, KODIAK ISLAND, SAINT LAWRENCE ISLAND; other coastal islands. BROOKS RANGE separates interior lands from Barren Grounds of N. Coastal mountains and ALASKA RANGE (with Mt. McKinley) rim valleys in S (esp. the MATANUSKA VALLEY, with its metropolis, ANCHORAGE). Panhandle, with ALEXANDER ARCHIPELAGO, is most accessible, highly developed area. Fishing main industry (esp. Alaska salmon); mining (gold, coal, platinum, antimony, tin). Fur trade still important. Vitus BERING and Aleksandr Chirikov first reached Alaska from Russia 1741. Grigori SHELEKHOV founded first permanent settlement on Kodiak Isl. 1784; Aleksandr BARANOV estab. SITKA 1799. Purchased by U.S. 1867, mostly due to Secretary of State W. H. Seward. Development proceeded slowly. Boundaries set 1903; BERING SEA FUR-SEAL CONTROVERSY settled 1911. Gold strikes (NOME 1899; FAIRBANKS 1902) followed 1896 Yukon strike, drew prospectors, adventurers. Attempt of monopolies to take over was opposed by Theodore Roosevelt and Gifford Pinchot. World War II saw Alaska's emergence as strategic area. Japanese estab. foothold in Aleutians 1942-43. War also saw great boom, which has continued with present military, economic concern over area. Hopes for statehood shared by many in U.S.

Alaska, University of, at College, near Fairbanks; land grant and territorial, coed.; chartered 1917. Opened 1922 as Alaska Agricultural Col. and School of Mines; became university 1935. Has school of mines, geophysical observatory, and a seismograph. Cooperates in research with government and private institutions.

Alaska Highway, 1,527 mi. long, from Dawson Creek, B.C., Canada, to Fairbanks, Alaska, formerly called Alaska Military Highway, Alaska International Highway, and Alcan Highway. Noted engineering feat, built March–Oct., 1942, by U.S. troops to supply Alaskan forces. Haines Cutoff connects it with Alaska's Panhandle. Last stretch to Fairbanks uses previously built Richardson Highway. Canadian part of road transferred 1946 to Canadian control.

Alaska Range, S central Alaska, rising to 20,-270 ft. in Mt. McKinley, highest point in North America; Range divides S central Alaska from great interior plateau.

Alastor (ŭlă′stŭr), in Greek mythology, the spirit of vengeance.

Ala-Tau (ä′lä-tou′), six lofty mountain ranges of central Asia. Four of them rise to more than 16,000 ft. In general they are near L. Issyk Kul and belong to Tien Shan system.

Álava, Spain: see BASQUE PROVINCES.

Alba or **Alva, Fernando Álvarez de Toledo, duque de** (fĕrnän′dō äl′väräth dä tōlä′dhō dōōkä dä äl′vä), 1508–1582, duke of Alba, Spanish general. Succeeded (1567) Margaret of Parma as regent in Netherlands for Philip II. To suppress rebellion set up "Court of Blood" (18,000 executed, including EGMONT). Resigned 1573. Conquered Portugal (1580); seized Lisbon, permitted massacre there.

Albacete (älbäthä′tä), city (pop. 50,567), cap. of Albacete prov., SE Spain, in Murcia; agr. center.

Alba-Iulia (äl′bä-yōō′lyä), Hung. *Gyulafehér-vár,* Ger. *Karlsburg,* city (pop. 14,420), central Rumania, in a wine-growing region. Former seat of Transylvanian princes. Fortress built by Emperor Charles VI.

Alba Longa (äl′bŭ lông′gŭ), city of anc. Latium. In legend founded by son of Aeneas; birthplace of Romulus and Remus; destroyed by Roman king, Tullus Hostilius (c.600 B.C.?).

Albania (älbā′nyŭ), Albanian *Shqipnija* or *Shqiperia,* republic (10,629 sq. mi.; pop. 1,122,044), SE Europe, on Adriatic coast of Balkan Peninsula, between Yugoslavia and Greece; cap. Tirana. A rugged mountain country (except for a fertile coastal strip, with ports of DURAZZO and Valona), it has rich copper and coal deposits but is economically underdeveloped. The people are mainly hill tribes of very ancient stock; c.60% are Moslem, 20% Greek Orthodox, 10% Roman Catholic. Large Albanian minorities live in Yugoslavia and Greece. Including parts of ancient ILLYRIA and EPIRUS, Albania has known many masters (notably Macedon, Rome, Byzantium, and Turkey), but their domination was never effective among the inland mountain clans. Italian penetration began with ROBERT GUISCARD (11th cent.). It was continued by Naples and Venice, which held Durazzo until 1501, when the Turkish conquest, long delayed by SCANDERBEG, became final. Independence from Turkey was proclaimed 1912 during the first Balkan War. An international commission assigned large areas claimed by Albania to Montenegro, Serbia, and Greece (1913). A battleground and the scene of political chaos during and after the second Balkan War and World War I, Albania passed in turn under the kingship of WILLIAM, PRINCE OF WIED, the dictatorship of ESSAD PASHA, and the dictatorship (after 1928 kingship) of ZOG. It soon became a virtual Italian protectorate. In April, 1939, Italy occupied the country, set up a puppet government, and proclaimed Victor Emmanuel III king of Albania. The base for Italy's attack on Greece (1940), Albania again became a battleground in World War II. After the Allied landing (1944), the antifascist guerrilla leader Enver Hoxha seized control, and in 1946 set up a Communist dictatorship.

Albano, Lake (älbä′nô), crater lake, central Italy, in Alban Hills, SE of Rome; circumference 6 mi. Underground tunnel, built 4th cent. B.C., is still its only outlet. Alba Longa was near by.

Albany, dukes of: see STUART, ALEXANDER and ROBERT.

Albany, Louisa, countess of, 1752–1824, wife of Charles Edward STUART. Married in 1772, she left her dissolute husband after eight years. Was mistress of poet Vittorio Alfieri until his death (1803) and then mistress of French artist François Fabre.

Albany, ancient and literary name of Scotland.

Albany. 1 Residential city (pop. 17,590), W Calif., on San Francisco Bay adjoining Berkeley. **2** City (pop. 31,155), SW Ga., on Flint R.; founded 1836. Pecan and peanut market. Meat packing; mfg. of farm machinery and hosiery. Tourist center for near-by Radium Springs resort. **3** City (pop.

134,995), state cap. (since 1797), E N.Y., on W bank of the Hudson. Site visited by Henry Hudson, 1609; Dutch estab. Fort Nassau near by, 1614; Walloons began permanent settlement at Fort Orange (Albany after 1664) in 1623; chartered as city 1686. Was fur-trading center. Commerce grew after Erie Canal opened (1820s). A major shipping point, it has oil refineries, railroad shops, and mfg. of machinery, chemicals, and paper. Seat of N.Y. State Col. for Teachers and parts of Union Univ. 4 City (pop. 10,115), NW Oregon, on Willamette R. and S of Salem; founded 1848. Farm trade center.

Albany, river rising in W central Ont., Canada, and flowing c.610 mi. E and NE to James Bay.

Albany, Fort, fur-trading post, at mouth of Albany R. on James Bay, Ont., Canada. One of earliest Hudson's Bay Co. forts (before 1682). From 1697 to 1713 was only post in region in possession of British company.

Albany Congress, 1754, meeting at Albany, N.Y., in which treaty was concluded between seven British colonies and the Iroquois. Benjamin Franklin's Plan of Union for the colonies, though accepted favorably, was later rejected by colonial legislatures and the crown.

Albany Regency, informal group of leaders of Democratic party in N.Y. after 1820. Enforced party regularity and controlled elections, partly through SPOILS SYSTEM. Martin Van Buren was member. Slavery issue and quarrel between BARNBURNERS and HUNKERS led to decay; prestige dwindled after 1848.

albatross (ăl'bŭtrôs), sea bird, order of tube-nosed swimmers (includes petrels, shearwaters, fulmars), found chiefly in S Pacific. Wandering albatross (of Coleridge's *Rime of the Ancient Mariner*) has wingspread 10–12 ft.

Albemarle, George Monck or **Monk,** 1st **duke of:** see MONCK or MONK, GEORGE.

Albemarle, town (pop. 11,798), central N.C., ENE of Charlotte. Textile, lumber, cotton, hosiery, and flour mills.

Albemarle Sound, Atlantic Ocean arm, 5–15 mi. wide, NE N.C., extending inland c.50 mi. Fishing and boating resort. Bridged near Edenton.

Albéniz, Isaac (ēsäk' älbā'nēth), 1860–1909, Spanish pianist and composer; used Spanish folk themes in his music. Best known is his piano suite, *Iberia.*

Alberdi, Juan Bautista (hwän' boutē'stä älbĕr'dē), 1810–84, Argentine publicist, diplomat. Suggestions in his *Bases y puntos de partida para la organización política de la república argentina* were incorporated into 1853 constitution.

Alberni, city (pop. 3,323), on S central Vancouver Isl., B.C., Canada, adjoining PORT ALBERNI.

Alberoni, Giulio (jōō'lyō älbärō'nē), 1664–1752, Italian cardinal, chief minister to Philip V of Spain. His efforts to nullify Peace of Utrecht were stopped by Quadruple Alliance. Dismissed 1719.

Albert, rulers of Holy Roman Empire. **Albert I,** c.1250–1308, son of Rudolf I, was elected German king after his victory over ADOLF OF NASSAU (1298). Put down rebellion of Rhenish archbishops and of elector palatine (1300); secured crowns of Hungary and Bohemia for his son Rudolf (1306). Assassinated by conspirators. **Albert II,** 1397–1439, German king and king of Bohemia and Hungary (1438–39); son-in-law of Emperor Sigismund. Was unable to suppress revolt of Bohemia. With him began continuous HAPSBURG rule over empire.

Albert I, 1875–1934, king of the Belgians (1909–34). Led Belgian resistance to German invasion in World War I; improved social conditions in Belgium and Belgian Congo; won great popularity through his democratic ways. Died in rock-climbing accident. Married Queen ELIZABETH 1900.

Albert (Prince Albert), 1819–61, royal consort of VICTORIA of Great Britain; son of Ernest I of Saxe-Coburg-Gotha. Initial unpopularity was modified through his devotion to queen and responsible concern with public affairs. His insistence on moderate approach to Trent affair may have averted war with the U.S.

Albert, Eugen Francis Charles d' (däl'bĕr), 1864–1932, pianist and composer, b. Glasgow, of German-French origins. Known for operas *Tiefland* (1903) and *Die toten Augen* (1916).

Albert, Lake: see ALBERT NYANZA.

Alberta, province (c.248,800 sq. mi; with water surface 255,285 sq. mi.; pop. 939,501), W Canada; cap. EDMONTON. Other cities are CALGARY, LETHBRIDGE, MEDICINE HAT, and RED DEER. Westernmost of the Prairie Provs., it has grass-covered plains to S and woodlands to N. In the Rockies are Banff, Jasper, and Waterton Lakes national parks. Drained by Peace, Athabaska, Red Deer, St. Mary, and Milk rivers, and north and south branches of the Saskatchewan. Largest lakes are ATHABASKA and LESSER SLAVE. Population is centered in S and in wheatlands of Peace R. valley. Farming, supplemented by ranching and dairying, is basic industry. Province produces much of Canada's domestic supply of crude oil, natural gas, and coal. After exploration by fur traders in mid-18th cent., North West and Hudson's Bay companies estab. trading posts. Area ceded to Canada by Hudson's Bay Co. 1869 and incorporated into Northwest Territories. Became a district 1882, a province 1905. Canadian Pacific RR arrived 1883. During World War II Edmonton was important as S focal point of Alaska Highway traffic.

Alberta, University of, at Edmonton; provincially supported, coed.; chartered 1906, opened 1908. Affiliated are two men's colleges, St. Joseph's (R.C.) and St. Stephen's (United Church).

Albert Canal, waterway, 81 mi. long, Belgium, from Meuse R. at Liége to Scheldt R. at Antwerp. Inaugurated 1939. Its fortifications were quickly overrun by German forces in May, 1940.

Alberti, Domenico (älbĕr'tē), c.1710–c.1740, Venetian composer. Developed a type of broken-chord bass accompaniment, now called Alberti bass.

Alberti, Leone Battista (lāo'nä bät-tēs'tä),

1404–72, Italian architect. Wrote the first printed book on architecture; it helped spread appreciation for the classical Roman style.

Albertinelli, Mariotto (märyôt′tō älbĕr″tēnĕl′-lē), 1474–1515, Florentine painter, pupil of Piero di Cosimo. His masterpiece is the *Visitation* (Uffizi).

Albert Lea (lē), city (pop. 13,545), S Minn., near Iowa line S of Minneapolis; settled 1855. In a farm area, it has mfg. of oil burners and clothing.

Albert Nyanza (nīăn′zù), lake, area 2,064 sq. mi., central Africa, on Belgian Congo-Uganda border; alt. 2,018 ft. Also called L. Albert.

Albert of Brandenburg, 1490–1568, grand master of TEUTONIC KNIGHTS (1511–25), first duke of PRUSSIA (1525–68). Turned to Protestanism 1525 and transformed dominions of his order into hereditary duchy, under Polish suzerainty.

Albert the Bear, c.1100–1170, first margrave of Brandenburg (1150?–1170). A loyal follower of Lothair II and Conrad III, he temporarily held Austria and Saxony, but is most notable for obtaining, partly by peaceful methods, the Wendish territory of BRANDENBURG. He helped to Christianize NE Germany.

Albertus Magnus, Saint (Albert the Great) (älbûr′tùs măg′nùs), b. 1193 or 1206, d. 1280, scholastic philosopher, called the Universal Doctor, a Dominican, b. Swabia. Taught in Germany (esp. at Cologne) and in Paris. Tried in *Summa theologiae* to reconcile Aristotelianism and Christianity and to oppose the attempt of Averroës to reconcile them. Had great influence on his pupil, St. Thomas Aquinas. Interested, like Roger Bacon, in natural science, wrote on botany and metals. Feast: Nov. 15.

Albertville, city (pop. 5,397), NE Ala., NNW of Gadsden, in cotton and corn area. Lumber milling.

Albi (älbē′), city (pop. 27,185), cap. of Tarn dept., S France. Famous as former center of the ALBIGENSES and for well-preserved medieval architecture (mostly in red brick), including Gothic cathedral, episcopal palace, 11th-cent. bridge.

Albigenses (älbĭjĕn′sēz), religious group of S France, strong in 12th and 13th cent. Officially called heretics, they were actually non-Christian Cathari who believed in absolute Manichaean dualism of good and evil and held that Jesus lived only in semblance. An ascetic, enthusiastic sect, the Albigenses had powerful preachers and gained protectors—notably RAYMOND VI of Toulouse (backed by the Catholic Peter II of Aragon). St. Bernard of Clairvaux tried to convert them, as did the Dominicans. Murder of a Cistercian set off the **Albigensian Crusade,** proclaimed by Pope Innocent III (1208). Troops led by Simon de Montfort in interests of France turned this into a political affair and victory at Muret (1213) paved the way for Louis IX of France to get Toulouse (1229) from Raymond VII, son of Raymond VI. Use of the Inquisition and ardent preaching converted Albigensians slowly.

albino (älbī′nō), animal or plant lacking normal pigmentation. In animals the absence of pigment is observed in the body covering (skin, hair, and feathers) and in the iris of the eye. Blood vessels of the iris show through, giving it a pinkish color, and eyes are very sensitive to light. Albinism is inherited as a Mendelian recessive character.

Albion, ancient and literary name of Britain.

Albion (ăl′bĕùn). **1** City (pop. 2,287), SE Ill., W of Mt. Carmel; founded 1818 by Englishmen led by Morris Birkbeck, George Flower. **2** City (pop. 10,406), S Mich., on Kalamazoo R. and S of Lansing; settled 1833. Mfg. of trucks. Seat of Albion Col. (Methodist; coed.; 1835).

Alboin (ăl′boin), d. 572?, Lombard chieftain. Conquered most of N and central Italy (568–72); crowned first Lombard king 569. See also ROSAMOND.

Alborg, Denmark: see AALBORG.

Albornoz, Gil Álvarez Carrillo de (hēl′ äl′värāth kärē′lyō dä älbôrnōth′), 1310?–1367, cardinal, Spanish and papal statesman and general. Sent (1353) by pope (then at Avignon) as legate to Papal States and entered Rome with RIENZI. Temporarily restored papal authority in Marches and Romagna.

Albrecht. For rulers thus named, see ALBERT.

Albret, Jeanne d′: see JEANNE D′ALBRET.

Albret (älbrā′), former fief, SW France, in the Landes of Gascony. By his marriage (1494) with the heiress of FOIX, Lord Jean d′Albret acquired Navarre, Foix, and Béarn. His son, Henri d′Albret, married (1527) Margaret of Navarre, who had inherited Armagnac from her first husband. In 1550 Albret was made a duchy. Henry IV of France, son of JEANNE D′ALBRET, added duchy to royal domain (1607).

Albright, Ivan Le Lorraine, 1897–, American painter. His paintings, meticulously executed, are macabre and symbolic. His twin brother, **Malvin Albright,** also a painter, is called Zsissly.

Albuquerque, Afonso de (äfô′zō dù äl″bùkĕr′kù), 1453–1515, Portuguese admiral, founder of Portuguese Empire in East. Succeeded Almeida in India; took Goa (1510), Malacca (1511), also Socotra Isl. and Hormuz. Died off Goa after his dismissal.

Albuquerque (ăl′bùkûr″kē), city (pop. 96,815), W central N.Mex., on upper Rio Grande and SW of Santa Fe, in mountain region. State's largest city, it is a commercial, industrial, rail, and air center. Area is rich in timber, mineral (coal), farm, and livestock area. Health resort. Has rail shops, lumber mills, wool warehouses, metal works, food-processing plants (meat, dairy products, fruit), and Indian handicraft. Old town was founded 1706, new town platted 1880. Here are Church of San Felipe de Neri (1706), old-town plaza, U.S. school for Indians, near-by Indian pueblos, United Pueblos Agency, Kirtland Air Force Base, and Sandia Base (guided-missiles experiment station). Seat of Univ. of New Mexico (state supported; coed.; chartered 1889, opened 1892).

Alcaeus (ălsē′ùs), d. c.580 B.C., Greek lyric poet, associate of Sappho. His Alcaic strophe (ălkā′ĭk) was widely imitated by the Greeks and by Horace.

Alcalá de Henares (älkälä′ dä änä′räs), city (pop. 18,013), central Spain, in New Castile. Great univ. (1508–1836). Birthplace of Cervantes.

Alcalá Zamora, Niceto (nēthä′tō älkälä′ thämō′rä), 1877–1949, president of Spain (1931–36), a liberal.

Alcamenes (äl″kùmē′nēz), 5th cent. B.C. Athenian sculptor. His *Aphrodite of the Gardens* was one of the great masterpieces of antiquity.

Alcántara (älkän′tärä), town (pop. 4,404), W Spain, in Estremadura. Military religious Order of Alcántara founded here in 13th cent. Roman bridge (see *ill.*, p. 167) and ruins of order's church and convent.

Alcatraz (äl′kùträz″), island in San Francisco Bay, W Calif. Fortified by Spanish and used after 1859 as U.S. military prison and after 1933 as Federal prison.

Alcazarquivir (älkäsär′kēvēr′), city (pop. 35,-786), W Spanish Morocco. Here in 1578 Ahmed IV's Moroccan army decisively defeated the Portuguese forces led by King Sebastian, who was killed.

Alcestis (älse′stĭs), in Greek mythology, daughter of Pelias. She married ADMETUS, who met her father's demand that suitor come for her in chariot drawn by wild animals. Her wifely devotion led her to sacrifice herself in place of her husband.

alchemy (äl′kùmē), learning, originating either in anc. Egypt or China, and dealing with attempts to change one substance into another (notably to turn base metals into gold). The alchemical belief in a miraculous philosopher's stone may have originated in Alexandria. Alchemy was influenced by Hellenistic philosophy, later (probably after 8th cent.) by Moslems. In 12th cent. it reached Europe through the Arabs. There the art, though symbolic and cryptic, gave rise gradually to modern chemistry. The TRANSMUTATION OF ELEMENTS has now been accomplished. Alchemy long a sister science of astrology.

Alcibiades (älsĭbī′ùdēz), c.450–404 B.C., Athenian statesman. Leader in the struggle against Sparta in the PELOPONNESIAN WAR, he was defeated at Mantinea (418 B.C.). Promoted Sicilian campaign (415), but was accused (probably falsely) of sacrilege and was called home for trial. Instead he fled to Sparta (where he counseled Agis I), then to Persian lands. Back in Athens after 411, he won a naval victory (410), but Athenian forces were defeated at Notium (406) by Lysander, who procured the murder of Alcibiades (then in exile).

Alcinoüs (älsĭ′nōüs), in Greek legend, father of Nausicaä, host to Odysseus and to Jason and Medea.

Alciphron (äl′sĭfrŏn), fl. A.D. c.200?, Greek satirist. Wrote imaginary letters, supposedly by Athenians of 4th cent. B.C.

Alcmaeon (älkmē′ùn), in Greek legend, one of the EPIGONI. Having killed his mother, Eriphyle, for the murder of his father, he was pursued by the Furies. Later, for his wife Callirrhoë, he tried to get the robe and necklace of Harmonia from his former wife, Arsinoë, but was killed.

Alcmaeonidae (älk″mēŏ′nĭdē), powerful Athenian family, 7th–5th cent. B.C. Members were CLEISTHENES, PERICLES, and ALCIBIADES.

Alcmene (älkmē′nē), in Greek legend, wife of AMPHITRYON; mother of Hercules by Zeus.

Alcoa (älkō′ù), city (pop. 6,355), E Tenn., S of Knoxville. Aluminum reduction plants.

Alcobaça (älkōōbä′sù), town (pop. 4,016), Estremadura, W central Portugal, near Leiria. Cistercian abbey (building begun 1152), greatest of medieval Portugal, ís burial place of early kings.

alcohol, organic compound of carbon and hydrogen with one or more hydroxyl radicals (see HYDROXIDE) on each molecule. Alcohol popularly used to mean ETHYL ALCOHOL. Classes (by number of hydroxyl groups in molecule): monohydric (one group), e.g., methyl; dihydric (two groups), e.g., glycol; trihydric (three groups), e.g., glycerin.

alcoholism, abnormal and persistent desire to drink excessive amounts of ethyl alcohol; also, the condition resulting from that drinking. Acute form connected with action of alcohol on central nervous system. Chronic alcoholism is generally considered a symptom of psychic instability. It may produce psychological and structural changes. Problem attacked through scientific studies, clinics for inebriates, organizations such as Alcoholics Anonymous (founded 1934), and Research Council on Problems of Alcohol (organized 1937).

Alcott, (Amos) Bronson (ôl′kùt), 1799–1888, American educational reformer, transcendentalist philosopher; father of Louisa May Alcott. Founded Temple School (Boston, 1834), "Fruitlands" community (1843). Both failed, but ideas gained notice.

Alcott, Louisa May, 1832–88, American writer of juvenile stories; daughter of Bronson Alcott. *Little Women* (1868–69) is her beloved classic of girls' literature. Among other works (many in series) are *Little Men* (1871), *Eight Cousins* (1875), *Rose in Bloom* (1876), *Under the Lilacs* (1878), *Jo's Boys* (1886).

Alcuin (äl′kwĭn), 735?–804, English churchman, scholar at court of Charlemagne, center of Carolingian renaissance; founder of schools at Tours and Aix-la-Chapelle.

Aldan (ŭldän′), city (1939 pop. over 10,000), Yakut ASSR, RSFSR, in E Siberia. Gold mining.

Aldanov, Mark (ŭldä′nùf), pseud. of Mark Aleksandrovich Landau, 1886–, Russian novist. Emigrated to France after 1917, to America in 1941; became U.S. citizen. Among his works are the tetralogy *The Thinker* (4 vols., 1921–1927; on the Napoleonic era), *The Fifth Seal* (1939), and *The Escape* (1950; both on Bolshevism).

Aldegrever, Heinrich (hīn′rĭkh äl′dùgrävùr), b. 1502, d. after 1555, painter and engraver, one of German Little Masters.

aldehyde (äl′dĭhīd), organic compound with a carbon-hydrogen-oxygen (CHO) group. Used in synthetic resins and dyestuffs. Aldehyde is often used to mean acetaldehyde, prepared from oxidation of ethyl alcohol; oxidizes to acetic acid. FORMALDEHYDE is simplest aldehyde. See also FURFURAL.

Alden, John, c. 1599–1687, Puritan settler in

Plymouth Colony. Legendary romance with Priscilla Mullens made familiar by Longfellow's poem, *The Courtship of Miles Standish.*

Alder, Kurt (äl'dùr), 1902–, German chemist. Shared 1950 Nobel Prize for work on methods of synthesizing complex compounds.

alder, deciduous tree and shrub of genus *Alnus,* with conelike fruits, widely found in N Hemisphere. Bark of black alder is used for dyes and tanning, wood of Western red alder for furniture.

Alderney: see CHANNEL ISLANDS.

Aldershot, municipal borough (pop. 36,184), Hampshire, England; site of largest and most complete military training center (estab. 1854) in United Kingdom.

Aldington, Richard (ôl'–), 1892–, English poet. Once a leader of IMAGISTS, he later opposed them. Also a novelist, biographer (e.g., of Wellington), critic, editor, translator.

Aldrich, Nelson Wilmarth, 1841–1915, U.S. Senator from R.I. (1881–1911). Spokesman of big business in Republican party. Coauthor of Payne-Aldrich Tariff Act (1909). Concerned with monetary problems.

Aldrich, Thomas Bailey, 1836–1907, American author, editor. His *Story of a Bad Boy* (1870) is based on his Portsmouth (N.H.) boyhood. Wrote poems, short stories (*Marjorie Daw and Other People,* 1873), edited (1881–90) *Atlantic Monthly.*

Aldus Manutius (mùnū'shùs), 1450–1515, Venetian printer, humanist. Through Aldine Press (with dolphin and anchor mark), made classical manuscripts available to scholars. Had *italic* type designed (1501).

ale: see BEER.

Alegría, Ciro (sē'rō älägrē'ä), 1909–, Peruvian novelist. Wrote novels of social protest, e.g., *El mundo es ancho y ajeno* (Latin American Novel Prize, 1941; Eng. tr., *Broad and Alien Is the World,* 1941).

Aleichem, Sholom (shō'lùm älä'khùm) [Heb., = Peace be upon you! (a Yiddish greeting)], 1859–1916, author of tragicomic Yiddish tales about late 19th-cent. Russian Jewry. Real name Rabinowitz.

Aleijadinho (ùlā"zhùdē'nyō), 1730–1814, Brazilian sculptor, b. Minas Gerais. Though crippled, he created fine Churrigueresque church sculpture.

Alekhine, Alexander (ùlyĕkh'ēn), 1892–1946, Russian-French chess player. He was world champion 1927–35, 1937–46.

Aleksandrovsk-Sakhalinski (ùlyĭksän'drùfsk-sùkhùlyēn'skē), city (pop., with environs, c.100,000), Far Eastern RSFSR, on N Sakhalin; a port on Tatar Strait. Coal mining.

Alemán, Mateo (mätä'ō älämän'), 1547–1614?, Spanish novelist, author of picaresque *Guzmán de Alfarache* (two parts, 1599, 1604).

Alemán, Miguel (mēgĕl' älämän'), 1902–, president of Mexico (1946–52).

Alemanni (ălĭmä'nī), Germanic tribe which occupied territories along the Rhine (present Alsace, Baden, and NE Switzerland) in 5th cent. A.D. Defeated by Franks under Clovis I in 496, they retired into Rhaetia, and in 536 passed under Frankish rule. High German dialects of SW Germany and Switzerland are called Alemannic. See also GERMANS.

Alembert, Jean le Rond d' (zhä' lù rō' däläbär'), 1717–83, French mathematician and philosopher. As coeditor of Diderot's ENCYCLOPÉDIE he wrote its remarkable "Preliminary discourse." For his work in dynamics, see D'ALEMBERT'S PRINCIPLE.

Alemtejo, Portugal: see ALENTEJO.

Alençon, François, duc d': see FRANCIS, duke of Alençon and Anjou.

Alençon (äläsō'), town (pop. 16,692), cap. of Orne dept., N France, on Sarthe R.; famous for its lace.

Alentejo (äläntä'zhō), historic province, SE Portugal, now divided into Upper Alentejo (4,888 sq. mi.; pop. 375,511; cap. Évora) and Lower Alentejo (5,318 sq. mi.; pop. 355,771; cap. Beja). "Granary of Portugal." Also livestock, wine, olives, fruit. Formerly spelled Alemtejo.

Alep (ùlĕp') or **Aleppo** (ùlĕ'pō), city (pop. c.320,000), NW Syria. Was the Greek and biblical Beroea or Berea. Ancient city on main caravan route across Syria to Baghdad, center of a Hittite kingdom before 1000 B.C. Flourished as city of Byzantine Empire. Taken by Arabs in 7th cent. and by Seljuk Turks in 11th cent. Crusaders besieged it unsuccessfully 1124, Saladin took it 1183. Mongols seized Alep in 1260 and 1401. Held by the Turks (1517–1832, 1840–1920) and by Egypt (1832–40). Produces silk and cotton textiles; trades in wool, hides, and fruit.

Alesia (ùlē'zhù), town in anc. Gaul, held by Vercingetorix, besieged by Caesar (52 B.C.). Its surrender because of starvation marked the end of Gallic resistance.

Alesius, Alexander (ù-lē'shùs), 1500–1565, Scottish Protestant theologian, early preacher of Lutheranism in England and Germany.

Alessandria (älĕs-sän'drēä), city (pop. 51,949), Piedmont, N Italy. Felt hats, commerce. Founded 1168 by Pope Alexander III.

Alesund or **Aalesund,** Nor. *Ålesund* (all: ô'lùsōōn), city (pop. 18,143), W Norway, on three small islands at mouth of Stor Fjord. Largest Norwegian fishing harbor; whaling base.

Aletsch (ä'lĕch), largest glacier (66 sq. mi.) of Swiss Alps, between Jungfrau and Aletschhorn, in Bernese Alps.

Aleutian Islands (ùlōō'shùn), chain of volcanic islands SW from tip of Alaska Peninsula and approaching Russian Komandorski Isls. Partially submerged, they are a continuation of Aleutian Range dividing the Bering Sea from the Pacific. There are four main groups. Fox Isls. nearest Alaska include Unimak, Unalaska (with Dutch Harbor on small Amaknak Isl.) and Umnak. Andreanof Isls. are many, including Adak. Important in Rat Isls. are Amchitka and Kiska. Near Isls., farthest W and smallest group of all, include Attu. Islands are generally rugged, of volcanic action, and have few good harbors, owing to reefs. Temperature is relatively moderate, but fog is constant. They are almost completely treeless with dense vegetation. Vitus BERING discovered islands 1741. Russian fur traders exploited native Aleuts. Fishing and fur hunting are now state controlled. Dutch Harbor became transshipping point for Nome 1900, and U.S. Naval Base 1940. Japanese occupied Attu and Kiska 1942–43; withdrawal forced by bitter U.S. fighting.

Aleutian Range, mountain chain, SW Alaska, extending along entire Alaska Peninsula and continuing, partly submerged, in Aleutian Isls. Recent volcanic activity was notable at Katmai (Valley of Ten Thousand Smokes), one of world's largest volcanoes.

Alexander III, d. 1181, pope (1159–81), a Sienese named Rolando Bandinelli. A learned canon lawyer, he issued many legal rules for governing church. Backed Lombard League in opposing Emperor Frederick I, who exiled him to France. His rule contested by antipopes until 1178. Convened Third LATERAN COUNCIL.

Alexander VI, 1431–1503, pope (1492–1503), a Spaniard named Rodrigo de Borja (of BORGIA family). Notorious in following centuries as corrupt and worldly Renaissance pope, he showered money and favors on his children by a Roman woman, Cesare and Lucrezia Borgia. Opposed Charles VIII of France, who invaded Italy. Proclaimed the line of demarcation between Spanish and Portuguese colonial spheres (1494).

Alexander, emperors of Russia. **Alexander I,** 1777–1825? (reigned 1801–25), succeeded his father, PAUL I, in whose murder he may have had indirect part. His early liberalism did not lead to internal reform. Alexander joined coalition against NAPOLEON I (1805); was defeated at Austerlitz, Friedland; made peace at TILSIT 1807. After repulsing French invasion (1812), led allies into Paris (1814) and attended Congress of VIENNA. Under influence of Metternich and Julie de KRÜDENER he turned to extreme reaction and promoted HOLY ALLIANCE. Officially, he died at Taganrog; according to popular belief—shared by some historians—he retired to live in penitence as a hermit. His tomb, opened 1926, was empty. His brother, Nicholas I, succeeded him. **Alexander II,** 1818–81, son of Nicholas I, reigned 1855–81. A liberal reformer, he abolished serfdom (1861; see EMANCIPATION, EDICT OF), introduced ZEMSTVO system of local government and new judicial system (1864). Reforms did not satisfy the radicals. Terrorism and NIHILISM increased; led to Alexander's assassination. Other events of reign: end of CRIMEAN WAR; Russian expansion in Asia; and Russo-Turkish War of 1877–78. Succeeded by his son, **Alexander III,** 1845–94 (reigned 1881–94), a fanatic reactionary. Fostered persecution of Jews and forcible Russification of minorities. Suppressed liberal thought, but promoted peace policy and industrial development. Nicholas II succeeded him.

Alexander, 1893–1920, king of the Hellenes (1917–20). Succeeded his deposed father, Constantine, with aid of Allies, who favored him over his elder brother (later King George II).

Alexander, kings of Scotland. **Alexander I,** 1078?–1124, ruled 1107–24. He opposed English efforts to rule church in Scotland. Estab. abbeys at Inchcolm and Scone. **Alexander II,** 1198–1249, ruled 1214–49. **Alexander III,** 1241–86, ruled 1249–86. Acquired for Scotland Western Isles and Isle of Man, already claimed from Norway. After his death struggle between ROBERT I and John de BALIOL (1249–1315) began.

Alexander, rulers of Serbia and Yugoslavia. **Alexander** (Alexander Karageorgevich), 1806–85, prince of Serbia (1842–58); son of KARAGEORGE. Deposed. **Alexander** (Alexander Obrenovich), 1876–1903, king of Serbia (1889–1903); son and successor of MILAN. Abolished liberal constitution 1894. His marriage in 1900 to Draga Mashin, a lady of scandalous past, aggravated the opposition. Royal couple was assassinated by an army clique, the Obrenovich dynasty deposed, and Peter I made king. **Alexander,** 1888–1934, king of Yugoslavia (1921–34); son and successor of Peter I. Became regent of kingdom of Serbs, Croats, and Slovenes 1918; ruled dictatorially 1929–31 to unify kingdom, which he renamed Yugoslavia. Antagonized Croatian and Macedonian separatists. In foreign policy he was loyal to French alliance and LITTLE ENTENTE. Assassinated with Louis BARTHOU, by Yugoslav terrorist at Marseilles, France.

Alexander (Alexander of BATTENBERG), 1857–93, prince of Bulgaria (1879–86). He was elected with Russian support and ruled under Turkish overlordship. His annexation of E RUMELIA (1885) antagonized Russia and caused Serbia to declare war. Though victorious, he was deposed by a pro-Russian faction.

Alexander, in Greek legend, another name for PARIS.

Alexander, Harold Rupert Leofric George, Earl Alexander of Tunis, 1891–, British field marshal. In World War II commanded retreats of Dunkirk and Burma and triumphs in N Africa and Sicily. Governor general of Canada 1945–52. Made defense minister in Churchill cabinet 1952.

Alexander, John White, 1856–1915, American painter, best remembered for his graceful studies of women.

Alexander, Samuel, 1859–1938, British naturalist philosopher. He held that space-time was ultimate principle of all existence.

Alexander, Sir William, d. 1640: see STIRLING, WILLIAM ALEXANDER, EARL OF.

Alexander Archipelago, just off SE Alaska. It and mountainous coast make up Panhandle of Alaska, Territory's most populous area. A submerged mountain system, the islands rise steeply from sea. Deep channels separate them, cut them from the mainland, making part of the Inside Passage from Seattle to Alaska. Included are CHICAGOF ISLAND, ADMIRALTY ISLAND, BARANOF ISLAND (with Sitka), WRANGEL ISLAND (with Wrangel), REVILLAGIGEDO ISLAND (with Ketchikan), and PRINCE OF WALES ISLAND.

Alexander Balas (bā′–), d. 145 B.C., ruler of Syria. Seized power from his uncle Demetrius I. Jonathan the Maccabee supported him. Eventually defeated by Ptolemy Philometor. 1 Mac. 10–11.

Alexander City, city (pop. 6,430), E central Ala., SE of Birmingham, near Martin L. Textiles.

Alexander Nevski, Saint (nĕv′skē), 1220?–

1263, grand duke of Vladimir-Suzdal; Russian national hero. Defeated Swedes on the Neva (1240) and Livonian Knights near Lake Peipus (1242).

Alexander of Hales (hālz), d. 1245, English scholastic philosopher, called the Unanswerable Doctor, a Franciscan who taught at Univ. of Paris. Introduced Aristotle as authority in systematic exposition of Christian doctrine.

Alexander Severus (Marcus Aurelius Alexander Severus) (sĭvēr′ŭs), d. 234, Roman emperor (222–35).

Alexander the Great (Alexander III), 356–323 B.C., king of Macedon (336–323); son of PHILIP II. He put down rebellion in Greece, and in 334 he undertook what was to be the widest conquest of ancient times. Victories at the Granicus (334), the Issus (333), and Gaugamela (or Arbela, 331) punctuated his seizure of Asia Minor, peaceful occupation of Egypt, and overthrow of the Persian Empire of Darius III. He pushed on through Bactria and into India. There his men refused to go farther. A fleet was sent back under Nearchus, but Alexander led his men back across deserts, reaching Susa in 324. Married Roxana, a Bactrian princess, and adopted Persian ways. Died of a fever at 33. One of the greatest generals of all time, he was also one of the most romantic figures of antiquity. His great empire was broken by wars of the DIADOCHI.

Alexandra, 1844–1925, queen consort of Edward VII of Great Britain; daughter of Christian IX of Denmark. Married Edward 1863.

Alexandra, Mount: see RUWENZORI.

Alexandra Feodorovna (fêô″dŭrŏv′nŭ), 1872–1918, Russian empress, consort of NICHOLAS II; a Hessian princess, granddaughter of Queen Victoria. Under influence of RASPUTIN, she encouraged tsar's reactionary policies. Shot by Bolsheviks 1918.

Alexandretta or **Alexandrette,** Turkish seaport: see ISKENDERUN.

Alexandretta, sanjak of (sän″jăk′, ä″lĭgzăndrĕ′tŭ), former name of Hatay prov. (2,141 sq. mi.; pop. 245,141), S Turkey, comprising cities of Antioch and its port Alexandretta (now Iskenderun). Awarded 1920 to Syria, given autonomous status 1937. Turkish-Arab riots resulted 1938 in joint military control by France and Turkey. Transferred to Turkey 1939.

Alexandria, Arabic *Al Iskandariya*, city (pop. 928,237), N Egypt, port on Mediterranean. Founded 332 B.C. by Alexander the Great. Cap. of the Ptolemies (304–30 B.C.), it received much Mediterranean trade and soon outgrew Carthage to become largest city in West. The great center of Hellenistic and Jewish culture. Became part of Roman Empire (30 B.C.) and was greatest provincial cap. with free population of 300,000. In 642 fell to the Arabs who moved the cap. to modern Cairo. Today handles most of Egypt's foreign trade.

Alexandria. 1 City (pop. 5,147), E central Ind., NE of Indianapolis. Produces rock wool and limestone. **2** City (pop. 34,913), central La., on Red R. opposite PINEVILLE; laid out 1810. Processes cotton, foodstuffs, and lumber, and

has chemical and metal works. Has cathedral (R.C.; 1898). **3** City (pop. 6,319), W Minn., SE of Fergus Falls, in resort and agr. region. KENSINGTON RUNE STONE is here. **4** City (pop. 61,787), N Va., S of Washington, D.C., port on Potomac R. Permanently settled in early 18th cent., it was once a part of D.C. (1789–1847). A rail center, it has mfg. of fertilizers, concrete and metal products. Points of interest (many associated with George Washington) include Gadsby's Tavern (1752), Carlyle House (1752), Christ Church (1767–73), and Ramsay House (1749–51). George Washington Natl. Memorial Temple houses Washington mementoes. Near-by Woodlawn, Washington family estate, was made national shrine in 1949.

Alexandria Bay, resort village (pop. 1,688), N N.Y., on the St. Lawrence and N of Watertown. Near by is Thousand Isls. Internatl. Bridge to Canada.

alexandrine, in poetry, a line of 12 or 13 syllables. Considered an iambic hexameter, the last foot has a final unstressed syllable if the line has 13 syllables. Name probably derives from a medieval romance on Alexander. Rhyming alexandrine couplets are the classic form for French serious poetry (works of Ronsard, Racine, Corneille). The Spenserian stanza ends with an alexandrine.

Alexis, 1629–76, tsar of Russia (1645–76), successor of Michael Romanov. He acquired part of Ukraine, began a schism by deposing Patriarch NIKON, suppressed Stenka RAZIN rebellion, and promulgated law code of 1648, which favored middle class, but tied peasants to soil. His son Feodor III succeeded him. Peter the Great was his son by a second marriage.

Alexishafen, (ŭlĕk′sĭs-hä″fŭn), harbor, E New Guinea, in Territory of New Guinea. Japanese air base here was taken 1944 by Allied forces.

Alexius (ŭlĕk′sēŭs), Byzantine emperors. **Alexius I** (Comnenus), 1048–1118; nephew of Isaac I. Gained throne by overthrowing Nicephorus III (1081). Withstood Norman invasions under ROBERT GUISCARD and BOHEMOND; defeated Petchenegs (1091) and Cumans (1095). In the First Crusade he persuaded leaders to pledge their conquests to him, later forced Bohemond to recognize his suzerainty over Antioch. His last years brought struggle with the Turks and intrigues of his daughter ANNA COMNENA against his son John II. Restored Byzantine prestige. **Alexius III** (Angelus), d. after 1210. Gained throne by deposing his brother ISAAC II (1195). This gave the leaders of the Fourth Crusade a pretext for attacking Constantinople (1203). Alexius III fled; Isaac was restored, with his son **Alexius IV** (d. 1204) as joint emperor. In 1204 **Alexius V** (Ducas Mourtzouphlos), son-in-law of Alexius III, led the Byzantine national party in the overthrow of Isaac and Alexius IV. This act brought the sack of Constantinople by the Crusaders, who had Alexius V executed (1204) and set up the Latin Empire of Constantinople.

alfalfa (ălfăl′fŭ), a perennial (*Medicago sativa*), also called lucerne, native to Europe, with usually blue or purple flowers; North

America's chief leguminous forage plant. Adaptable to diverse conditions, it can be mowed two to six times yearly, enriches soil, and is high in protein. See *ill.,* p. 999.

Alfieri, Vittorio, Conte (vēt-tŏ'rēō kōn'tä älfyä'rē), 1749–1803, Italian tragic poet, b. Piedmont. After a dissipated youth, he became a poet and poured his hatred of tyranny into tragedies, intentionally harsh and unornamented—*Saul* (1782), *Antigone* (1783), *Maria Stuart* (1804). Also wrote comedies, satires, political tracts, autobiography. Allied with Louisa, countess of Albany.

Alfonsine tables, improved revision of Ptolemaic planetary tables, made at Toledo by astronomers assembled by Alfonso X of Spain. Completed c.1252; printed 1483 in Venice.

Alfonso, kings of Aragon. **Alfonso I,** d. 1134, king of Aragon and Navarre (1104–34), husband of URRACA of Castile. Took Saragossa and Calatayud from Moors. **Alfonso II,** 1152–96, king of Aragon (1164–96), count of Barcelona (1162–96). Inherited Provence (1166); Roussillon (1172). Wrote Provençal poetry. **Alfonso V** (the Magnanimous), 1396–1458, king of Aragon and Sicily (1416–58), became king of Naples (1443–58) after defeating René of Anjou. His splendid court at Naples was center of arts and letters.

Alfonso, kings of Portugal. **Alfonso I** (Port. *Afonso Henriques*), 1111?–1185, became first king of Portugal (1139), took Santarém and Lisbon (1147). **Alfonso II** (the Fat), 1185–1223, reigned 1211–23. **Alfonso III** (Port. *Afonso o Bolonhez*), 1210–79, reigned 1248–79. Completed reconquest of Portugal from Moors; quarreled with Alfonso X of Castile over Algarve, and with Church; and called Cortes of Leiria (1254; first to include commoners). Fostered commerce and cultural revival. **Alfonso IV,** 1291–1357, reigned 1325–57. Approved murder of Inés de CASTRO. **Alfonso V** (the African), 1432–81, reigned 1438–81. Took Tangier (1471). His marriage with Juana la Beltraneja led to unsuccessful war with Ferdinand and Isabella. **Alfonso VI** (the Victorious), 1643–83, reigned 1656–67. Physically and mentally defective, he yet ousted his mother from regency with aid of count of Castelho Melhor, who took over the government and repulsed the Spanish in 1663. Alfonso's wife, Marie Françoise of Savoy, and his brother (later Peter II) forced him to abdicate. After having her marriage annulled, the queen married Peter, who ruled as regent.

Alfonso, Spanish kings. **Alfonso I** (the Catholic), 693?–757, king of Asturias (739–57), conquered parts of Galicia, Leon, and Santander from Moors. **Alfonso III** (the Great), 838?–910?, king of Asturias (866–909), consolidated kingdom. **Alfonso V** (the Noble), 994?–1027, king of Asturias and Leon (999–1027), gave Leon its *fuero* [code of laws]. **Alfonso VI,** 1030–1109, king of Leon (1065–1109) and Castile (1072–1109), took Galicia from his brother García (1073), and Toledo from Moors (1085). His court at Toledo was meeting place of Christian and Moorish cultures. **Alfonso VII** (the Emperor), 1104–57, king of Castile and Leon (1126–57). Recovered places lost by

his mother, URRACA, to her second husband; had himself crowned emperor in Leon (1135); and took Almería from Moors. **Alfonso VIII** (the Noble), 1155–1214, king of Castile (1158–1214), won great victory of Navas de Tolosa (1212) over Moors. **Alfonso X** (the Wise), 1221–84, king of Castile and Leon (1252–84), grandson of Emperor Philip of Swabia, was elected German king (1256) by faction of German princes, but renounced claim in 1275. Took Cádiz from Moors (1262). Patron of learning; largely responsible for great legal compilation, *Siete partidas,* and ALFONSINE TABLES. **Alfonso XI,** 1311–50, king of Castile and Leon (1312–50), defeated Moors at Tarifa (1340), took Algeciras (1344), died in siege of Gibraltar. **Alfonso XII,** 1857–85, king of Spain (1870–85), son of Isabella II, lived in exile (1868–75) during Carlist revolt. Proclaimed king 1874; returned to Madrid 1875 and restored order. **Alfonso XIII,** 1886–1941, king of Spain (1886–1931), supported dictatorship of Primo de Rivera (1923–30). Went into exile when republicans won election (1931).

Alfred [Old Eng. Ælfred], 849–899?, overking of England; one of best-loved figures of English history. Victory over Danes at Ashdown being followed by defeats, he decided, in face of their threat to overrun England, to make them payments. His flight to fens of Somerset (878) gave basis for legend of Alfred and the cakes. Victory over Danes at Ethandun (Edington) led to program of reform and to code of laws combining Christian doctrine with strong centralized monarchy. His greatest achievements were creation of a navy, revival of learning among the clergy, education for youths and nobles at court, the establishment of old English literary prose, his own English translation of Latin works, and his influence on extant form of ANGLO-SAXON CHRONICLE. Many heroic legends later embroidered his career. See editions of his own works and contemporary biography by Bishop Asser, *Life of King Alfred* (1906).

Alfred University, at Alfred village (pop. 2,053), N.Y., SW of Hornell; nonsectarian, with state and private support, coed.; opened as school 1836, chartered as univ. 1857. Includes state college of ceramics.

Alfsborg, county, Sweden: see ALVSBORG.

algae (ăl'jē), primitive plants lacking true roots, stems, leaves, and flowers, but having chlorophyll. Chief aquatic plants in fresh and salt water (including pond scum and SEAWEED) are algae, ranging from microscopic size to 100 ft. long (e.g., kelp). See also DIATOM; GULFWEED; IRISH MOSS. See *ill.,* p. 813.

Algardi, Alessandro (äläs-sän'drō älgär'dē), 1602–54, Italian architect and sculptor, pupil of Lodovico Carracci. Designed the Villa Doria Pamphili.

Algarve (älgär'vù), southernmost province (1,958 sq. mi.; pop. 317,628), Portugal; cap. Faro.

Al-Gazel (ăl-gùzĕl') or **Al-Ghazali** (gäzä'lē), 1058–1111, Arabian mystical philosopher.

algebra, branch of mathematics which generalizes arithmetic operations. Elementary algebra achieves this by use of letters to represent numbers. Product of several numbers and letters, e.g., a term such as 6xy³ depends on values of unknowns x and y; number 6 is a coefficient; number ³ (written above, to right of y) is an exponent. There are rules for addition, subtraction, multiplication, and division of such expressions and for simplifying resulting expressions, often involving factoring, combining like terms, canceling, removing parentheses (grouping symbols). Algebra is used in most mathematics branches (geometry, trigonometry, calculus) and in other fields, e.g., physics, statistics; in these it is usually needed to solve equations expressing the relation of unknown to known quantities. Modern abstract algebra generalizes not only numbers but also operations.

Algeciras (ăljŭsēr′ŭs, Span. älhäthē′räs), city (pop. 20,226), S Spain, in Andalusia; Mediterranean port on Bay of Algeciras opposite Gibraltar. British victory (1801) over French-Spanish fleet.

Algeciras Conference: see MOROCCO.

Alger, Horatio (ăl′jŭr), 1834–99, American writer of boys' stories. His more than 100 books show success gained by exemplary living, heroic deeds, struggle against odds.

Algeria (ăljēr′ēŭ), French government general (847,552 sq. mi.; pop. 7,234,684) of the FRENCH UNION, N Africa; cap. ALGIERS. The Atlas Mts. are between the long Mediterranean coastal strip and the grain-producing TELL. In interior are semiarid plateaus and the great Sahara. Natives are of mixed Berber and Arab stock. Carthage was the first to dominate area. The richness of the Tell attracted the Roman conquerors, who subjugated NUMIDIA and MAURETANIA. In the Christian days of the empire, St. Augustine was bishop of Hippo Regius (now Bône). The declining civilization was conquered by Vandals (430–31) and by Byzantines (534). Arab invasion (7th cent.) brought Islam, which profoundly affected Algerian culture. In the 16th cent. the Turks estab. their control over the coast, which became a stronghold for pirates (see BARBARY STATES). In 1847 France won complete control over Algeria, except for the Saharan area (subdued 1900–1909). New crops (esp. grapes and tobacco) were introduced, and the exploration of mineral resources was begun. Algeria played a vital part in World War II (see NORTH AFRICA, CAMPAIGNS IN).

Algerine War: see DECATUR, STEPHEN; TRIPOLITAN WAR.

Algiers (ăljērz′), Fr. *Alger*, city (pop. 266,-165), N Algeria, cap. of Algeria; a major port of N Africa. Founded in late 10th cent. by the Berbers on site of the Roman Icosium. Became important after establishment of Turkish rule by Barbarossa in 1518. A base for Barbary pirates, it was visited by several European punitive expeditions. Occupied in 1830 by the French, who later built modern city along the harbor. The 16th-cent. Casbah (fortress), surmounting a height, gives its name to whole of old quarter. In World War II, after capture by Allies in Nov., 1942, it became hq. of Gen. de Gaulle's government.

Algona (ălgō′nŭ), city (pop. 5,415), N Iowa,

N of Fort Dodge on Des Moines R., in farm area.

Algonquian (ălgŏng′kwēŭn, –kēun), linguistic family of North America, a widespread stock of Canadian and U.S. Indians. See LANGUAGE, table.

Algonquin Indians (ălgŏng′kwĭn, –kŭn), North American Indian people in Canada, of Algonquian linguistic stock. Friendly to the French, they were dispersed by Iroquois in 17th cent.

Algonquin Provincial Park, 2,741 sq. mi., S Ont., Canada; estab. 1893 as game preserve and recreation area.

algum: see ALMUG.

Alhambra (ălhăm′brŭ), city (pop. 51,359), S Calif., NE of Los Angeles; founded 1881. Mfg. of aircraft and oil-refining machinery.

Alhambra [Arabic,= the red], group of Moorish buildings on a hill overlooking Granada, Spain. Comprises citadel remains, palace of kings, and quarters of nobles and officials. Halls and chambers, with intricate geometric ornament and honeycomb vaulting, surround a series of open courts with fountains and gardens. Built 1248–1354, it was mutilated after expulsion of the Moors in 1492 and extensively restored after 1828.

Ali (ä′lē, älē′), 602?–661, 4th caliph (656–61); first cousin and faithful follower of Mohammed, husband of Fatima. Caliphate opposed by Ayesha and Muawiya. Shiite-Sunnite division in Islam stems from this period. Ali and his son HUSEIN major Shiite saints.

Alicante (älēkän′tā), city (pop. 83,140), cap. of Alicante prov., SE Spain, in Valencia; Mediterranean port.

Alice, city (pop. 16,449), S Texas, W of Corpus Christi. Cattle and oil center with mfg. of dairy and cotton products.

Alice in Wonderland: see CARROLL, LEWIS.

Alice Springs, town (pop. 1,871), Northern Territory, Australia, at terminus of Central Australian RR. Formerly called Stuart, it was cap. of Central Australia 1926–31. Opal mining.

Alien and Sedition Acts, 1798, passed by U.S. Congress when warfare with France threatened (see XYZ AFFAIR). Empowered President to expel "dangerous" aliens; provided for indictment of those who should "unlawfully combine or conspire" against the administration or should write or speak "with intent to defame" the government, the Congress, or the President. Acts provoked KENTUCKY AND VIRGINIA RESOLUTIONS.

Aligarh (ŭlēgŭr′), city (pop. 112,655) W Uttar Pradesh, India; trade center. Moslem university.

alimentary canal, tubular passage (c.30 ft. long) from mouth to anus functioning in DIGESTION and absorption of food. Includes pharynx, esophagus, STOMACH, INTESTINE, and rectum. See *ill.,* p. 763.

alimony, allowance which by court order a husband pays to wife not living with him. Temporary alimony is allowed pending a suit for separation, divorce, or nullity of marriage; permanent alimony, only after a decree has been rendered.

Ali Pasha (ä′lē päshä′), 1741?–1822, Turkish governor of Yannina (1787–1820); called the Lion of Yannina. Originally an Albanian brigand chief, he ruled as quasi-independent despot over most of Albania and Epirus. Ordered deposed for his ambitious plans (1820), he rebelled and resisted Turkish troops (badly needed in fight against Greek insurrection) until his assassination by a Turkish agent. Byron described his rugged court in *Childe Harold*.

Aliquippa (ălĭkwĭp'ủ), borough (pop. 26,132), W Pa., on Ohio R. and NW of Pittsburgh. Has steel mills.

Alisal, village (pop. 16,714), W Calif., near Salinas.

Aljubarrota (älzhŏŏbŭrô'tủ), village, Estremadura, W central Portugal. Here Portuguese, aided by English, defeated Spanish, kept independence (1385).

alkali (ăl'kủlī), in chemistry, a strong BASE, e.g., sodium hydroxide (see LYE). Has properties of bases: soluble in water, and neutralizes acids. Strongly CAUSTIC. Used to make soap, cotton goods, paper. **Alkali metals** are cesium, rubidium, potassium, sodium, and lithium. Oxides of barium, strontium, calcium, and sometimes magnesium called **alkaline earths** because they act like alkalis.

alkali soils contain an excess of soluble salts: in white alkali soils, chiefly sulphates of sodium, magnesium, potassium; in black alkali soils, sodium carbonate. Such soils may be improved by adding lime or gypsum, cultivating thoroughly, and growing alkali-tolerant plants; flooding and then underdraining actually removes some alkali.

alkaloid, organic compound composed of carbon, hydrogen, nitrogen, and usually oxygen. Derived from plants; name indicates properties of a BASE. Examples: ATROPINE, CAFFEINE, COCAINE, MORPHINE, NICOTINE, QUININE, STRYCHNINE, codeine.

Al-Khowarizmi (äl-khŏwärēz'mē), fl. 820, Arabian mathematician, noted for treatises on Hindu arithmetic and algebra. He is said to have given algebra its name. Latin translations of his works were a major source of knowledge in medieval Europe.

Al-Kindi, Arabian philosopher: see KINDI.

Alkmaar (älk'mär), municipality (pop. 37,-837) and town, North Holland prov., NW Netherlands. Market center; iron foundries. Weekly cheese market in front of ancient weighhouse is famous.

Allah (ă'lủ, ä'lủ), Arabic name for God, used in Islam and Arabic-speaking Christian countries.

Allahabad (ăl''ủhủbăd'), city (pop. 260,630), S Uttar Pradesh, India. On site of Prayag, ancient Aryan holy city, at junction of the sacred Jumna and Ganges rivers. Trade center.

All-American Canal, SE Calif., largest irrigation canal in U.S.; built 1934–40 by Bureau of Reclamation. Taps Colorado R. at Imperial Dam, N of Yuma, Ariz., and runs 80 mi. W, past Calexico, Calif. Serves IMPERIAL VALLEY and Coachella Valley.

Allan, Sir Hugh, 1810–82, Canadian financier and shipowner, b. Scotland. Involved in PACIFIC SCANDAL over construction of Canadian Pacific Ry.

Allbutt, Sir Thomas Clifford (ôl'bŭt), 1836–1925, English physician, authority on dis-

eases of circulatory and nervous systems. Wrote on history of medicine.

Allegany (ăl'ủgã''nē), village (pop. 1,738), W N.Y., on Allegheny R. and W of Olean. Near by is St. Bonaventure Univ. (Catholic; for men; 1859).

Alleghany, variant spelling: see ALLEGHENY.

Allegheny (ă'lủgã''nē), river rising in N Pa., and flowing NW to N.Y., then SW into Pa., joining the Monongahela at Pittsburgh to form the Ohio; 325 mi. long. Transports some freight.

Allegheny College: see MEADVILLE, Pa.

Allegheny Mountains, a W part of Appalachian Mts., extending SW from N Pa. through Md., W.VA., and Va., and rising to 4,860 ft. in Spruce Knob, W.Va. E portion has Allegheny Front, a steep escarpment; W portion is plateau reaching into E Ohio and Ky. Allegheny upland largely formed by folding of sedimentary rock. Much erosion and leveling followed. Range is rich in coal and contains iron, oil, and gas.

allegory (ăl'ĭgôr''ē), literary work expressing through elaborate symbols a commentary or account of social, political, or artistic ideas. Characters are types or personifications. Spenser's *Faerie Queene* and Bunyan's *Pilgrim's Progress* are famous examples.

Allegri, Gregorio (grägō'rēō äl-lā'grē), 1582–1652, Italian composer of a nine-part *Miserere* sung annually during Holy Week in the Sistine Chapel.

Alleluia, Latin form of HALLELUJAH.

Allen, Ethan, 1738–89, hero of American Revolution, leader of GREEN MOUNTAIN Boys. Helped capture Ticonderoga (1775). Captured by British on expedition against Canada (1775). Promoted independence and statehood of Vt. His brother, Ira Allen, 1751–1814, was a political leader in early Vt.

Allen, Hervey, 1889–1949, American author. After World War I he taught at Charleston, S.C., where with DuBose Heyward he wrote poems in *Carolina Chansons* (1922). He is best known for his historical novels, which include *Anthony Adverse* (1933) and three volumes of an unfinished series (begun with *The Forest and the Fort,* 1943).

Allen, Horatio, 1802–90, American civil and mechanical engineer. Operated first steam locomotive (English-built) to run on rails in U.S.; designed steamboats.

Allen, Ira: see ALLEN, ETHAN.

Allen, James Lane, 1849–1925, American novelist. Wrote stories, poems on Ky. Novels include *A Kentucky Cardinal* (1894), *The Choir Invisible* (1897).

Allen, Richard, 1760–1831, founder of the African Methodist Episcopal Church (1794). He was born a slave in Philadelphia.

Allenby, Edmund Henry Hynman Allenby, 1st **Viscount** (ă'lủnbē), 1861–1936, British field marshal. Invaded Palestine and ended Turkish resistance (1918). British high commissioner for Egypt 1919–25.

Allen Park, village (pop. 12,329), SE Mich., W suburb of Detroit; settled 1776.

Allenstein (ä'lủnshtīn), Pol. *Olsztyn,* city (pop. 29,053), S East Prussia; under Polish administration since 1945. Trade and railroad center. Founded 1348 by Teutonic

Knights, who built its impressive castle. Resettled by Poles after World War II.

Allentown, industrial city (pop. 106,756), E Pa., on Lehigh R. and NNW of Philadelphia, in Pennsylvania Dutch region; settled by German religious groups, laid out c. 1752. Has metal and textile industries. Liberty Bell brought here (1777) for safekeeping; munitions center for Continental Army. Seat of Cedar Crest Col. and Muhlenberg Col. (Lutheran; for men; 1848).

allergy, excessive sensitivity to a usually harmless substance. Agents (known as allergens) include air-borne substances, vegetable oils, bacteria, various proteins, and physical agents, e.g., light, cold. Allergens produce antibodies in blood stream; said to cause tissues to produce histamine.

Allia (ă'lĕû), river, Latium, Italy, tributary of Tiber. Gauls defeated Romans on Allia 390 B.C.

Alliance. 1 City (pop. 7,891), NW Nebr., in Great Plains region. Ships grain, seed potatoes, and livestock. Has railroad repair shops. **2** City (pop. 26,161), NE Ohio, NE of Canton and SE of Akron, on Mahoning R.; laid out 1838. Mfg. (esp. steel, aircraft, machinery), distributing, and rail center. Seat of Mt. Union Col. (Methodist; coed.; 1846), with Clarke Observatory.

Allier (älyā'), department (2,850 sq. mi.; pop. 373,381), central France, in Bourbonnais; cap. Moulins. Traversed by Allier R. (tributary of Loire).

alligator, large reptile (order Crocodilia) similar to CROCODILE. American alligator, c.12 to 14 ft. long, ranges N Carolina to Florida, Gulf states. Adults black, young dark brown or black with yellow bands. Eats water life.

alligator pear: see AVOCADO.

Allori, Alessandro (älĕs-sän'drō äl-lō'rē), 1535–1607, Florentine painter, pupil and foster son of Il Bronzino; known also as Alessandro Bronzino. Many portraits in the Uffizzi, Florence. His son and pupil, **Cristofano Allori** (krēstōfä'nō), 1577–1621, was also a portraitist.

allotropy (ŭlŏt'rŭpē), occurrence of chemical element in two or more forms differing in atomic arrangement and physical properties but alike in chemical properties. Among elements showing allotropy: arsenic, carbon, oxygen, phosphorus, sulphur.

Allouez, Claude Jean (klōd' zhä' älwä'), 1622–89, French Jesuit missionary in Canada and Old Northwest. Founded missions in present Wis.

Alloway (ăl'–), hamlet, Ayrshire, Scotland; birthplace of Robert Burns.

alloy (ăl'oi), combination of metal with metallic or nonmetallic elements to form mixture or compound having metallic properties suitable for special purposes. May be heterogeneous (composed of crystals embedded in a matrix or of interlocking crystals of several types) or homogeneous (solid solution with uniform physical properties). See also BRASS; BRONZE; GOLD; STEEL.

All Souls College: see OXFORD UNIVERSITY.

allspice, dried green berry from tropical pimento or allspice tree (*Pimenta officinalis*), used in medicine and food seasoning. Carolina allspice is *Calycanthus.*

Allston, Washington, 1779–1843, American painter, a pupil of Benjamin West. His work is usually biblical or classical in subject.

alluvium (ůlōō'vēům), land built up of sediments deposited by running water. Common forms are alluvial fans and cones, river deltas, and flood plains.

Alma, city (pop. 8,341), S Mich., N of Lansing. Beet-sugar and oil refineries. Seat of Alma Col.

Alma-Ata (äl'mú-ä'tä, Rus. ŭlmä"-ŭtä'), city (pop. 230,528), cap. of Kazakh SSR, on Turk.-Sib. RR. Processes cotton, fruit, meat, tobacco.

Almadén (älmädhän'), city (pop. 12,468), central Spain, in New Castile. Center of rich mercury mines exploited since Roman times.

Almagest: see PTOLEMY (Claudius).

Almagro, Diego de (dyä'gō dä älmä'grō), c.1475–1538, Spanish conquistador, a leader with Pizarros in conquest of Peru. Led expedition into Chile 1535.

Al-Mansur: see MANSUR.

Almeida, Francisco de (fränsēsh'kō dù älmä'dù), c.1450–1510, Portuguese admiral. Became (1505) viceroy of Portuguese India and fortified E coast of Africa. Routed Egyptians and their Indian allies off Diu (1509). Sought Portuguese supremacy on seas. Killed by Hottentots on way home.

Almeida Garrett, João Batista de (zhwäō' bútēsh'tù dù älmä'dù gúrĕt'), 1799–1854, Portuguese romantic dramatist and poet. Notable are plays *Alfageme de Santarém* and *Frei Luis de Sousa,* and long poems *Camões* and *Dona Branca.*

Almería (älmārē'ä), city (pop. 69,824), cap. of Almería prov., S Spain, in Andalusia; Mediterranean port. Ships fruits, esparto, minerals. Probably founded by Phoenicians. Flourished (13th–15th cent.) under Moors. Gothic cathedral.

Almohades (ăl'mûhādz, –hădz) or **Almohads** (–hădz), Berber Moslem dynasty, 12th–13th cent. of Morocco and Spain. Puritanical anti-ALMORAVIDES sect founded by Mohammed ibn Tumart c.1120. His successors conquered Morocco, Moslem Spain, displacing Almoravides by 1174. Defeated by Spanish and Portuguese 1212; by Merenide dynasty in Morocco 1269.

almond, fruit kernel of an orchard tree (*Prunus amygdalus*), resembling the peach and bearing single or double spring blossoms, pink in sweet, white in bitter. Both yield almond oil, and the bitter yields also amygdalin, which on decomposing gives prussic acid. Sweet almond nut used in confections. Flowering almonds are ornamental shrubs of other *Prunus* species.

Almoravides (ălmō' rùvĭdz, –vĭdz) or **Almoravids** (–vĭdz), Berber Moslem dynasty, 11th–12th cent., of Morocco and Spain; militant puritanical reform sect founded by Abdullah ibn Yasin (d. 1059). His successors founded Marrakesh (1062), helped Spanish Moors stem Christian reconquest (1086), then took over Moslem Spain. Overthrown by ALMOHADES by 1174.

Almquist, Carl Jonas Love (kärl' yōō'näs lōō'vú älm'kvĭst), 1793–1866, Swedish writer. Novels, plays, poems, and short stories are in *The Book of the Thorn Rose* (14 vols., 1832–51).

almug or **algum,** precious wood, mentioned in Bible, used in the Temple and Solomon's palace. 2 Chron. 2.8; 9.10, 11. Perhaps a red sandalwood.

aloe (ăl′ō), perennial of genus *Aloe* (ăl′ōē), with stiff, fleshy leaf clusters, red or yellow flowers. Some are a few inches high, others tree size. Native to South Africa; tub plant elsewhere. Yields drugs and fibers (for cords and nets).

Alost (ălôst′), Flemish *Aalst,* town (pop. 42,-193), East Flanders, Belgium. Textile mfg.

alpaca (ălpăk′ủ), partially domesticated South American hoofed mammal of camel family. Of same genus (*Lama*) as wild guanaco (probably descended from it) and vicuña. Bred chiefly for long, lustrous wool (black through shades of brown to white) by Indians in highlands of Peru, Chile, Bolivia.

Alp Arslan (älp ärslän′), 1029–72, Seljuk sultan of Persia (1063–72). Vigorous conqueror of Christians; victor of MANZIKERT.

Alpena, resort city (pop. 13,135), N Mich., on Thunder Bay of L. Huron; laid out 1856. Has fisheries, limestone quarries, and cement and paper plants.

Alpes-Maritimes (älp′-märētēm′), department (1,644 sq. mi.; pop. c.453,000—incl. BRIGUE AND TENDE), SE France, on French RIVIERA; cap. Nice.

alphabet, type of writing, theoretically having a one-for-one relation between character (or letter) and phoneme (see PHONETICS). Few alphabets have achieved the ideal exactness. An alphabet is called a syllabary when one character represents a syllable rather than a phoneme (e.g., kana of Japan). The modern Western European alphabet is that of Rome (developed from Greek), the base of most alphabets used for newly written languages of Africa and America. The Cyrillic alphabet, an augmented Greek alphabet, is used for Russian, Serbian, Bulgarian, and many languages of the USSR. Greek (developed from Phoenician), Hebrew, Arabic, and Devanagari of India (with syllabic features) all have their own alphabets, based ultimately on Egyptian HIEROGLYPHIC writing. This, though not alphabetic, bore the germ of phonemic writing in the phonogram. A similar development created Persian CUNEIFORM syllabary.

alpha particle and **alpha ray:** see RADIOACTIVITY; RADIUM; RAY.

Alpheus (ălfē′ủs), Gr. *Alpheios,* river, 69 mi. long, S Greece, flowing from Taygetus mts. NW through Peloponnesus to the Ionian Sea. In mythology its waters were said to pass under the sea and emerge as fountain of Arethusa at Syracuse. Hercules turned the river through Augeas' stables to clean them. It is the river Alph of Coleridge's *Kubla Khan.*

Alphonso. For rulers thus named, see ALFONSO.

Alphonsus Liguori, Saint (ălfŏn′sủs līgwō′rē), 1696–1787, Italian Catholic churchman, Doctor of the Church, founder of Redemptorist order. Wrote many hymns. Original name Alfonso Maria de' Liguori. Feast: Aug. 2.

Alpine (ăl′pīn), resort town (pop. 5,261), W Texas, in mountains N of Big Bend of Rio Grande. Rail junction, it ships cattle and sheep. Big Bend Natl. Park is near by.

Alps, mountain system, S central Europe, forming great arc from Mediterranean coast between France and Italy to Adriatic coast of Yugoslavia. Covering most of Switzerland and Austria, the Alps separate Po plain (N Italy) from France (W), Germany (N), and Danubian plain (E). Many rivers (Rhine, Rhone, Po) originate in the Alpine watershed. Cattle raising, dairying are common in high Alps; agr., orchards, vineyards in valleys. Hydroelectric plants. Beautiful, varied scenery attracts many tourists. Towering peaks, covered by glaciers and perpetual snow, rise above the relatively low base level (3,000–4,000 ft.) and the many fine lakes, e.g., Geneva, Lucerne, Como, Garda, Maggiore. Best-known peaks include Mont Blanc (15,781 ft.; highest of chain), Monte Rosa, Matterhorn (all in W Alps); Jungfrau, Finsteraarhorn, Piz Bernina (Central Alps, in Bernese Oberland and Engadine); Ortles, Grossglockner, Zugspitze (E Alps, including Dolomites, Hohe Tauern, Bavarian Alps). Principal tunnels and highway passes: Mont CENIS, SIMPLON, SAINT GOTTHARD, ARLBERG, BRENNER PASS, Great and Little SAINT BERNARD, FURKA, MALOJA, STELVIO PASS.

Als (äls), Ger. *Alsen,* island (121 sq. mi.; pop. 34,294), Denmark, in the Little Belt, separated from S Jutland by narrow Als Sound; chief city Sonderborg. Agr., fruitgrowing. Held by Prussia 1864–1920.

Alsace (ăl′sãs, ăl′săs, Fr. älzäs′), Ger. *Elsass* (ĕl′zäs), region and former province, E France, along Rhine border with Germany; crossed by Vosges mts. Comprises Bas-Rhin, Haut-Rhin, and Territory of Belfort depts. Chief cities: Strasbourg, Colmar, Mulhouse. Bilingual (French, German), 25% of pop. is Protestant. Agr., vineyards, cotton mfg., and potash mines. Included in East Frankish (later German) kingdom (870); Peace of Westphalia (1648) and annexations by Louis XIV (1680–97) gave most of Alsace to France; rest annexed in French Revolution. Ceded (except Belfort) to Germany with part of Lorraine (1871), but recovered by France (1918). Occupied by Germany (1939–44).

alsike: see CLOVER.

Altai or **Altay** (ăl′tī, ältī′), mountain system of SW Siberia, RSFSR and Kazakh SSR, and of W Mongolia. Highest peak (15,266 ft.) is in Mongolia. Forests, meadows, rich mineral deposits (lead, zinc, silver, wolfram, copper, mercury, gold). Larger part of mountains is administratively included in **Altai Territory** (101,000 sq. mi.; pop. c.2,400,000), RSFSR, which also has some of richest black-earth area of Siberia; cap. Barnaul. Drained by Ob R. Population is largely Russian; in mountains Altai-speaking Oirats or Oirots predominate. Oirats were seminomadic until recent settlement on collective farms.

Altamira (äl″tämē′rä) site of the caverns in N Spain, near Santander, where famous examples of CAVE ART were discovered in 1879.

Altamirano, Ignacio Manuel (ēgnä′syō mänwĕl′ ältämērä′nō), 1834–93, Mexican novelist, of pure Indian blood. Key figure in reconstruction of republic after collapse of Maximilian's empire. Wrote novels *Clemencia* and *La navidad en las montañas*.

Altay: see ALTAI.

Altdorf (ält'dôrf), town (pop. 5,692), cap. of Uri, Switzerland. Scene of William Tell's exploits.

Altdorfer, Albrecht (äl'brĕkht ältdôr'fûr), 1480–1538, German painter and engraver, follower of Dürer. Painted landscapes in a romantic vein.

Altenburg, Germany: see SAXE-ALTENBURG.

alternating current: see ELECTRICITY; GENERATOR.

Altgeld, John Peter (ält'gĕlt), 1847–1902, governor of Ill. (1892–96), b. Germany. A Democrat and sturdy champion of human rights, he pardoned the men convicted for Haymarket riots and opposed sending of Federal troops when there was a strike at PULLMAN (1894).

Althing (äl'thĭng), parliament of Iceland. Oldest assembly in Europe, first convened 930. Dissolved 1800, revived as advisory body 1843, restored 1874.

Altichiero da Zevio (ältēkyä'rō dä tsäv'yō), c.1330–c.1395, Italian painter, follower of Giotto, founder of school of Verona.

altimeter (ältĭm'ĭtûr, äl'tĭmē''tûr), altitude-measuring device for aircraft, usually a BAROMETER indicating altitude above sea level only. Newer type uses radio waves and shows actual distance.

altitude sickness: see AIRSICKNESS.

Alto Adige, Italy: see TRENTINO-ALTO ADIGE.

Alton (âl'tŭn), city (pop. 32,550), SW Ill., on the Mississippi and N of St. Louis; laid out 1817. Shipping center with mfg. of flour, metal products, and glass. Has monument to E. P. LOVEJOY, and tablet marking scene of a Lincoln-Douglas debate (1858). The Principia (coed. college; Christian Scientist; chartered 1921) is near by.

Altona, Germany: see HAMBURG.

Altoona, industrial city (pop. 77,177), central Pa., E of Pittsburgh, in bituminous coal region; settled c.1769. Has railroad shops and mfg. of textiles, automobile parts, and metal products. Horseshoe Curve of Pennsylvania RR is W.

Altus (äl'tŭs), city (pop. 9,735), SW Okla., between Wichita Mts. and Red R. Produces cotton and food products. Main city of W. C. Austin (formerly Altus) project (1941; irrigation).

alum (äl'ŭm), double crystalline salt, a sulphate of a univalent and a trivalent cation (positively charged atom or radical). Alum in popular use means double sulphate of potassium and aluminum, i.e., potassium alum or potash alum.

alumina (úlōō'mĭnú) or **aluminum oxide,** occurs nearly pure as CORUNDUM and is combined with silica in clay. Corundum and emery (an impure form) are among the hardest of abrasives. Alundum is an artificial form used as an abrasive. Alumina from BAUXITE is important source of metallic aluminum.

aluminum, silvery-white metallic element (symbol = Al; see also ELEMENT, table). Ductile and malleable; resists corrosion; excellent conductor of heat and electricity; very light. Used in dirigibles, airplanes, autos, kitchen utensils, wrapping foil, paints, high-tension wires. Main source is BAUXITE.

alundum: see ALUMINA.

Alva, Fernando de: see ALBA.

Alva, city (pop. 6,505), NW Okla., on Salt Lake Fork of Arkansas R. Center of wheat-growing area.

Alvarado, Juan Bautista (hwän' boutēs'tä älvärä'dhō), 1809–82, governor of Alta California (present California) 1836–42. Local rivalries and immigration of U.S. citizens brought about recurrent disturbances.

Alvarado, Pedro de (pä'dhrō dä), 1485?–1541, Spanish conquistador. Served under Hernán Cortés in conquest of Mexico. Sent out by Cortés, he conquered Guatemala and Salvador (1523). Governor of Guatemala until his death; his wife, Beatriz de la Cueva, succeeded him. Led expedition to Ecuador (1534–35) but was defeated. Killed in Mixtón War.

Álvarez Quintero, Serafín (säräfēn' äl'väräth kēntä'rō), 1871–1938, and **Joaquín Álvarez Quintero** (hwäkēn'), 1873–1944, Spanish dramatists; brothers. Collaborated on plays, notably comedies of Andalusian middle-class life.

Alvsborg, Swed. *Älvsborgs län* (ĕlfs'bôr''yús lĕn'), county (4,919 sq. mi.; pop. 358,506), SW Sweden; cap. Vanersborg. N section, W of Vanern lake, is agr. and lumbering district; important textile plants in S; large power works at TROLLHATTAN. Alfsborg and Elfsborg are former spellings.

alyssum (–lĭs'–), plant of genus *Alyssum,* low perennials with yellow flowers, used in borders and rock gardens. **Sweet alyssum** is an annual species of *Lobularia* with fragrant white or lavender flowers.

Am, chemical symbol of the element AMERICIUM.

Amadeus VIII (ămûdē'ús), 1383–1451, duke of Savoy, antipope (1439–49), as Felix V. Had few supporters and yielded to Nicholas V.

Amadeus, 1845–90, king of Spain (1870–73), duke of Aosta, son of Victor Emmanuel II of Italy. Elected king after expulsion of Isabella II. His difficulties with his own government, and with the rebel CARLISTS, compelled him to abdicate.

Amadis of Gaul (ă'mûdĭs), romance of chivalry, first composed in Spain or Portugal (13th or 14th cent.), probably based on French sources. Often rewritten and translated, it gives ideal of perfect knight.

Amado, Jorge (zhôr'zhù úmä'dō), 1912–, Brazilian novelist. Wrote with grim realism of Brazilian life, especially of the economically oppressed.

Amagasaki (ä'mägäsä'kē), industrial city (pop. 233,183), S Honshu, Japan; a port on Osaka Bay.

Amager (ä'mägûr), island (25 sq. mi.; pop. 150,775), Denmark, in the Oresund. N end is occupied by part of Copenhagen.

Amalasuntha (ä''mùlùsùn'thù), d. 535, Ostrogothic queen in Italy, daughter of Theodoric the Great. Regent for son Athalaric (526–34); ruled after his death till murdered by order of her husband.

Amalek (ăm'ŭlĕk), people of Canaan, descendants of Esau, hereditary enemies of Hebrews until dispersed by Saul. Gen. 14.7; Ex. 17.8–16; Gen. 36.12,16; Num. 13.29; 14.25,45; 24.20; Judges 3.13; 6.3,33; 7.12; 1 Sam. 15.5–8; 30.1–20; 1 Chron. 1.36; 4.43.

Amalfi (ämäl'fē), town (pop. 4,259), Campania, S Italy, on Gulf of Salerno. First Italian maritime republic (9th cent.); duchy from 953 until fall to Normans (1131). Cathedral in Sicilian-Arabic style was begun in the 10th cent.

amalgam, ALLOY of mercury with any metal except platinum or iron. Most are made artificially. Amalgamation process extracts gold and silver, which are dissolved from ores.

Amalric (ŭmăl'rĭk) or **Amaury** (ŭmô'rē), Latin kings of Jerusalem. **Amalric I,** c.1135–74, reigned 1163–74. Lost suzerainty of Egypt to NUREDDIN. **Amalric II,** d. 1205, gained the title in 1197 through marriage to Isabella, eldest daughter of Amalric I. Succeeded his brother Guy of Lusignan as king of Cyprus in 1194.

Amalthaea (ămŭlthē'ŭ), nurse of Zeus, often represented as a goat with wonderful horns; one horn became the CORNUCOPIA.

Amana Society (ŭmăn'ŭ), corporate name of seven villages, E central Iowa, grouped around Iowa R. WNW of Iowa City; settled 1855 by members of Community of True Inspiration. Community originated in 17th cent. German religious sect. Fled to U.S. 1843 under Christian Metz to escape persecution. Settled first near Buffalo, N.Y. One of most successful U.S. communal communities. Made cooperative corporation with separation of religious and economic administration, 1932. Wool and wood handicrafts prominent.

amaranth (ăm'–), coarse annual plant (*Amaranthus*), with colorful foliage and chaffy flower spikes. Garden kinds include love-lies-bleeding or tassel flower, Joseph's coat. Some species are weeds, e.g., pigweed, TUMBLEWEED.

Amarapura (ŭ"mŭräpōō'rä), town, Upper Burma, on Irrawaddy R. Was cap. of Burma 1783–1823, 1837–60.

Amarillo (ămŭrĭl'ō), city (pop. 74,246), N Texas; settled c.1887 (though spot known to Indians, hunters, and cowboys before). A former cow town, it now processes meat, zinc, oil, and flour and produces machinery and farm and dairy products. Main city of Panhandle, it has VA hospital, symphony orchestra, and annual music festival.

amaryllis (ăm"ŭrĭl'ĭs), South African bulbous plant (*Amaryllis belladonna*), the belladonna lily, often cultivated for its rose-red, fragrant flowers. Name used for related plants, especially for those of the genus *Hippeastrum*, whose heavy stalks bear clusters of vivid lilylike flowers.

Amasa (ăm'ŭsŭ), cousin of Absalom with whom he revolted. 2 Sam. 17.25; 19.13; 20.4–13; 1 Kings 2.5.

Amasis I (ŭmā'sĭs) (Ahmose), d. c.1557 B.C., king of Egypt. Founded XVIII dynasty and drove out HYKSOS.

Amati (ämä'tē), family of violinmakers of Cremona, beginning with Andrea Amati (fl. 1535–80). Niccolò Amati (1596–1684)

brought the Amati violin to its peak. Antonio Stradivari was his pupil.

Amaury. For persons thus named, see AMALRIC.

Amaziah (ăm"ŭzī'ŭ), died c.775 B.C., king of Judah (c.802–c.775 B.C.), successor of Jehoash of Judah. Two events of reign were conquest of Edom and unprovoked attack on King Jehoash of Israel. Jehoash took Amaziah prisoner, entered Jerusalem, sacked the Temple. Amaziah was killed. 2 Kings 14; 2 Chron. 25.

Amazon (ă'mŭzŏn), in Greek legend, one of tribe of women who spent time in hunting and warfare. One of Hercules' 12 labors was to steal girdle of Queen Hippolyte. In Trojan War they fought against Greeks, and their leader, Penthesilea, was slain by Achilles.

Amazon, Port. *Amazonas* (ämŭzō'nŭsh), river rising in Peruvian Andes in two major headstreams, MARAÑÓN and Ucayali, and flowing across Brazil to Atlantic. Carries more water than any other river. Length is 3,000 mi. with Marañón or 4,000 with Ucayali. Extremely low gradient and enormous drainage basin. In lowlands E of Andes is world's largest rain forest. Principal tributaries from N are NEGRO, NAPO, PUTUMAYO, Caquetá; from S are JURUÁ, PURUS, MADEIRA, XINGÚ, TAPAJÓS, TOCANTINS. Below Xingú, Amazon reaches delta and divides around MARAJÓ isl.; S stream called Pará. Basin sparsely peopled, mostly by Indians. Early explorers include Vicente Yañez Pinzón (lower part, 1500), ORELLANA (from Napo, 1540–41; his fanciful story of female warriors gave Amazon its name), Pedro de Ursúa (1559), TEIXEIRA (1637–39). Resources of basin are principally wild rubber (important in early 20th cent.), cacao, woods, jute. Brazilian government in 1940s undertook development of area and estab. health service.

ambassador: see DIPLOMATIC SERVICE.

Ambato (ämbä'tō), city (pop. 33,908), central Ecuador, a commercial town in high Andean basin.

amber, fossil resin exuded as gum by coniferous trees in past geologic time. It is either transparent or cloudy and is used in making beads, mouthpieces, and small ornaments. Ancient Greeks knew that rubbing it with fur produced static electricity.

ambergris (ăm'bŭrgrēs), waxlike substance produced by abnormal conditions in sperm whale's digestive tract. Floats in tropical seas as yellow, gray, black, or variegated mass. Perfume fixative.

Ambiorix (ămbī'ŭrĭks), fl. 54 B.C., Gallic chieftain. Though earlier in Roman favor, he joined in attacking Caesar's legates. When Caesar approached, he fled across the Rhine and disappeared from history.

Ambleside, village, Westmorland, England; Lake District tourist center. Church has stained glass window given by admirers of Wordsworth.

Amboina (ămboi'nŭ), island (314 sq. mi.; pop. 66,821), Moluccas, Indonesia. Produces nutmeg, cloves, rice, and sugar. Discovered 1512 by the Portuguese, taken 1600 by the Dutch. Port town of Amboina (pop. 17,334) was allied naval base in early phase of World War II.

Amboise, Georges d' (zhôrzh′ däbwäz′), 1460–1510, cardinal, French statesman. Chief minister of Louis XII; patron of arts and letters.

Amboise (äbwäz′), town (pop. 4,224), Indre-et-Loire dept., central France, on the Loire. Famous castle was royal residence 15th–16th cent.

Amboise, conspiracy of, 1560, unsuccessful plot of French Huguenots and others to abduct Francis II from Amboise and to arrest Charles and François de Guise. The rebels were massacred.

Ambridge, borough (pop. 16,429), W Pa., on Ohio R. and NW of Pittsburgh: HARMONY SOCIETY estab. communistic settlement Economy here 1825–1906. Mfg. of steel, metal products, and electrical machinery.

Ambrose, Saint, 339?–397, bishop of Milan, Doctor of the Church, b. Trier. As governor in NW Italy, he won much esteem; the people insisted on his being made bishop (371). He administered the diocese ably, refusing to bow to the emperors: he opposed the Arianism favored by Valentinian II, persuaded Gratian to outlaw heresy, and made Theodosius I do penance for a massacre of rebellious citizens of Salonica. His brilliant religious writing molded classic learning in a Christian context. His name is also associated with the type of plain song called Ambrosian chant, and he wrote hymns (many ascribed to him are spurious). He was one of the chief "founders" of the Middle Ages. Feast: Dec. 7.

Ambrosian Library, public library (founded c.1609), Milan, rich in Greek and Latin texts and incunabula.

Amchitka (ămchĭt′kủ), island, 40 mi. long, off W Alaska, one of ALEUTIAN ISLANDS. Had U.S. air base in World War II.

amendment, in law, alteration of provisions of legal document (STATUTE or CONSTITUTION). In parliamentary law also, proposed changes of bill or motion. In judicial procedure, correction of errors. Amendment to Constitution of the United States requires approval of two thirds of each house of Congress, ratification by three quarters of states.

Amenemhet (ä″měněm′hĕt, ä″), kings of anc. Egypt of the XII dynasty. **Amenemhet I,** d. 1970 B.C., seized throne, centralized government, and humbled nobles. **Amenemhet III,** d. 1801 B.C., son and successor of Sesostris III, reclaimed the Fayum.

Amenhotep (ä″měnhō′tĕp, ä″–), or **Amenophis** (ä″měnō′fĭs), kings of anc. Egypt of the XVIII dynasty. **Amenhotep I,** fl. 1557 B.C., successor to his father, Amasis I, pushed S boundary to second Nile cataract and invaded Syria. **Amenhotep II** succeeded his father, Thutmose III (1448 B.C.), kept conquests already made. **Amenhotep III** succeeded his father, Thutmose IV (c.1411 B.C.). His was an age of splendor and comparative peace. His son and successor was IKHNATON.

America [for Amerigo VESPUCCI], the lands of the Western Hemisphere—North America, Central America (sometimes Middle America), and South America. In English, Amer-

ica and American are often used to refer only to U.S. Martin WALDSEEMÜLLER first used the name.

America, patriotic hymn of the U.S., beginning, "My country, 'tis of thee." Words written in 1832 by Samuel F. Smith to a tune found in book of German school songs. Only later did he discover he had used tune of *God Save the King.*

American, river rising in N central Calif. and flowing W and SW to Sacramento R. at Sacramento. Gold discovered along its banks (1848) brought great gold rush.

Americana, all that has been printed in and about the Americas or written by Americans; usually restricted to formative period in history of the two continents. Earliest-known example is Columbus letter (1493), on discovery of West Indies. Some early American books were printed by Juan Pablos, Stephen Daye and William Bradford.

American Academy in Rome, founded 1894 as the American School of Architecture in Rome, chartered by New York state 1897, inc. under its present name by act of Congress 1905. Comprises schools of fine arts and classical studies. Annual awards include residence in Rome, travel allowance, and yearly stipend for U.S. citizens under 30. Only men are eligible for the fine arts fellowships.

American Colonization Society, organized Dec., 1816–Jan., 1817, at Washington, D.C., to transport free Negroes from U.S. and settle them in Africa. Purchase of land in Africa in 1822 led to foundation of LIBERIA. Colonization movement attacked by abolitionists, who charged that removal of free Negroes strengthened slavery in the South. Society declined after 1840.

American Expeditionary Force: see WORLD WAR I.

American Falls, city (pop. 1,874), SE Idaho, on Snake R. and SW of Pocatello. Oregon Trail camps were near actual falls. City moved ½ mi. after dam was built (1925–27) on former site; 25-mi. reservoir serves MINIDOKA PROJECT. Wheat center.

American Federation of Labor (A.F. of L.), federation of trade unions in the U.S. and Canada; formed 1881, present name adopted 1886. A fairly loose combination of craft unions, the A.F. of L. opposes organization by industry. Under leadership of Samuel Gompers and, after 1924, of William Green, the A.F. of L. has become the largest American labor federation. The CONGRESS OF INDUSTRIAL ORGANIZATIONS and the UNITED MINE WORKERS OF AMERICA split with the A.F. of L.

American Fork, city (pop. 5,126), N central Utah, S of Salt Lake City. Resort and poultry-raising center served by Provo river project.

American Fur Company, chartered 1808 by John Jacob Astor (1763–1848) as rival to companies in Canada. Company maintained virtual monopoly, expanded from Lakes region W to Rocky Mts.

Americanization, term used to describe cultural process by which the immigrant to U.S. assimilates American speech, ideals, traditions, ways of life. Name also given to the movement fostering assimilation, which grew to crusading proportions in first quarter of 20th cent. as result of great immigation from E and S Europe from 1880 to World War I (see IMMIGRATION). Federal bureaus of education and of naturalization joined crusade and aided private Americanization groups. Passage of immigrant education legislation by states plus return of "normalcy" after World War I and, more especially, coming of the quota system of immigration caused Americanization move to subside.

American Labor party, organized in N.Y. by labor leaders and liberals in 1936, primarily to support the New Deal. Pro-Soviet faction caused internal strife after 1939. Right-wing dissenters formed Liberal party 1944.

American Legion, national association of veterans of First and Second World Wars, founded in Paris in 1919. Largest of veterans' associations, it exerts considerable influence on national life. Has done much work in social welfare, particularly child care; obtained benefits for veterans; attacked "subversive" or "anti-American" teachings and organizations.

American Museum of Natural History, incorporated (1869) in New York city to promote study of natural science and related subjects. Buildings on present site opened 1877; Hayden Planetarium (1935) and Roosevelt Memorial building (1936) added since.

American party: see KNOW-NOTHING MOVEMENT.

American Red Cross: see RED CROSS.

American Revolution, 1775–83, struggle by which the THIRTEEN COLONIES on Atlantic seaboard of North America won independence from Great Britain. By middle of 18th cent., differences in thought and interests had developed between colonies and mother country. STAMP ACT (1765) aroused colonial resistance as act of taxation without representation. TOWNSHEND ACTS (1767) led to such incidents as BOSTON MASSACRE (1770), burning of the GASPEE (1772), and BOSTON TEA PARTY (1773). Parliament replied with the INTOLERABLE ACTS. At CONTINENTAL CONGRESS (1774) grievances were listed in petitions to the king. Fighting began at Lexington and Concord on April 19, 1775, followed by capture of Ticonderoga from British and battle of Bunker Hill. QUEBEC CAMPAIGN (1775–76) was disastrous. DECLARATION OF INDEPENDENCE was adopted on July 4, 1776, but many colonists remained pro-British LOYALISTS. SARATOGA CAMPAIGN (1777), successful for colonists, was followed by harsh winter at Valley Forge. Aid from France helped patriot cause. In West, George Rogers CLARK estab. patriot hold on frontier. CAROLINA CAMPAIGN (1780–81) led into YORKTOWN CAMPAIGN. Surrender of Cornwallis at Yorktown in Oct., 1781, ended fighting. Treaty of Paris (1783) formally recognized U.S. as nation.

American Samoa: see SAMOA.

American University: see WASHINGTON, D.C.

American Veterans Committee (AVC), organization of veterans of World War II,

founded Jan., 1943. Opposed special privileges for veterans.

American Veterans of World War II (Amvets), organization of veterans of World War II, founded Dec., 1944; chartered 1947.

americium (ămûrĭ'shēŭm), radioactive element (symbol = Am; atomic no.= 95) of the actinide series. Was first produced from plutonium in cyclotron.

Americus (ûmĕr'ĭkŭs), city (pop. 11,389), SW Ga., SE of Columbus, in farm and lumber area. Food canning, peanut processing, and clothing mfg. Near-by national cemetery contains graves of over 13,000 Union soldiers, most of whom died (1864–65) in Andersonville Prison.

Ames, Fisher, 1758–1808, American political leader from Mass. U.S. Congressman (1789–97), a staunch Federalist and violent attacker of Jefferson.

Ames, James Barr, 1846–1910, American jurist, dean of Harvard Law School after 1895. Helped make case method popular in law study.

Ames, Joseph, 1689–1759, English bibliographer. Compiled list of English books printed before 1600.

Ames, Oakes, 1804–73, American manufacturer, railroad promoter, and politician. U.S. Congressman (1863–73). Involved in CRÉDIT MOBILIER scandal.

Ames, Winthrop, 1871–1937, American theatrical producer. Encouraged noncommercial experimentation.

Ames, city (pop. 22,898), central Iowa, N of Des Moines; laid out 1864. Mfg. of apparel and metal products. Has atomic-energy laboratory. IOWA STATE COLLEGE OF AGRICULTURE AND MECHANIC ARTS is near by.

Amesbury, town (pop. 10,851), including Amesbury village (pop. 9,711), NE Mass., on Merrimack R.; settled 1654. Mfg. of metal goods, hats, and boats. Whittier lived here.

amethyst (ăm'ŭthĭst), variety of QUARTZ, violet to purple in color. Valued as a semiprecious gem.

Amharic (ämhä'rĭk), standard language of Ethiopia, belonging to Ethiopic group of Semitic languages. See LANGUAGE (table).

Amherst, Jeffrey Amherst, Baron (ăm'ûrst), 1717–97, British army officer. Commanded British forces in French and Indian War; captured Louisburg (1758) and Montreal 1760). Amherst, Mass., named for him.

Amherst, town (pop. 9,870), N N.S., Canada, NW of Truro. Has iron foundries, woolen mills, and mfg. of railroad cars and machinery. Near by are ruins of Fort Lawrence and Fort Beausejour.

Amherst, town (pop. 10,856), including Amherst village (pop. 7,900), W Mass., NE of Northampton; settled 1703; named for Lord Amherst. Emily Dickinson and Noah Webster lived here. Seat of Univ. of Massachusetts (land-grant, state supported; coed.; chartered 1863, opened 1867; called Massachusetts Agr. Col. to 1931, Massachusetts State Col. to 1947) and Amherst Col. (nonsectarian; for men; opened 1821, chartered 1825 by Congregationalists), which holds in trust Folger Shakespeare Memorial Library.

Amherstburg, town (pop. 3,638), S Ont., Canada, on Detroit R. at entrance to L. Erie. Fort Malden built here 1796. Was British garrison town and naval station in War of 1812. Held by Americans at end of war.

Amherst College: see AMHERST, MASS.

Amicis, Edmondo de: see DE AMICIS, EDMONDO.

Amiel, Henri Frédéric (ärē′ frädärēk′ ämyĕl), 1821–81, Swiss critic. His introspective *Journal intime*, published posthumously, reveals a personality seeking to explain and justify his lifelong inactivity (partial Eng. tr., 1936).

Amiens (ämyĕ′), city (pop. 79,807), cap. of Somme dept., N France, on Somme R.; historic cap. of Picardy. Old textile industry. Fought over in World War I, half destroyed in World War II. Cathedral (begun 1220), largest and among finest French Gothic cathedrals, escaped damage.

Amiens, Treaty of, 1802, made by England with France, Spain, Batavian Republic. France agreed to evacuate Naples; England to give up most conquests made in French Revolutionary Wars.

Amiot, Joseph: see AMYOT, JOSEPH.

Amish Church: see MENNONITES.

Amityville, residential and resort village (pop. 6,164) SE N.Y., on S shore of Long Isl.; settled 1780.

Amman, Jost (yōst′ äm′än), 1539–91, Swiss engraver, noted for Bible illustrations.

Amman (ämän′), city (pop. c.90,000), N Jordan, cap. and royal residence, on Wadi Zerka (Jabbok R.), on Hejaz RR, and ENE of Jerusalem. Industrial and commercial center. Was biblical Rabbah (răb′ù) or Rabbath, cap. of Ammonites. Rebuilt as Philadelphia; has noted Roman ruins.

Ammanati, Bartolomeo (bärtōlōmä′ō ämmänä′tē), 1511–92, Italian architect and sculptor. Collaborated with Vignola and Vasari on villa of Pope Julius III. As architect to Cosimo de′ Medici, he designed court façade of Pitti Palace (Florence).

Ammann, Othmar Hermann (ôt′mär, ŏ′mŏn), 1879–, American civil engineer. Engaged in major bridge-building projects in New York city and San Francisco (Golden Gate Bridge).

ammeter: see GALVANOMETER.

Ammi (ăm′ī) [Heb.,= my people], figurative name of Israel after reconciliation with God. Hosea 2.1. Cf. LOAMMI.

Ammon (ăm′ŭn), in Bible, marauding, nomadic people living E of Dead Sea, relentlessly hostile to Hebrews. Gen. 19.38; Deut. 2.19,20,37; 23.3,4; Judges 3.13; 1 Sam. 11; 2 Sam. 10–12; 2 Chron. 20; Neh. 2.10; 4.7; Jer. 49.1–6.

Ammon, Egyptian god: see AMON.

ammonia, compound of nitrogen and hydrogen in proportion of one to three. Colorless gas with penetrating odor. Very soluble in water (household ammonia is aqueous solution); solution basic. Easily liquefied with pressure. Forms salts with acids. Used to make SAL AMMONIAC, nitric acid, soda; in REFRIGERATION; in medicine. Prepared by destructive distillation of coal, by HABER PROCESS, by treating calcium carbide with nitrogen. Occurs in air, in plant and animal decomposition products, in animal excretions. Amides are derivatives formed by replacing

one or more hydrogen atoms of ammonia by organic acid radicals; amines by replacing them with alkyl groups (chains of carbon and hydrogen atoms) or aryl groups (rings of the same).

amnesia, temporary or prolonged loss of memory of events before or after the causative shock, injury, illness, or mental disease. It is usually cured by establishment of associations with the past by suggestion or hypnotism. It is distinct from aphasia, the loss of verbal usages.

Amnon [Heb.,= faithful], David′s eldest son. He ravished his half sister Tamar and was killed by her brother Absalom in revenge. 2 Sam. 3.2; 13.

amoeba (ùmē′bù), member of genus (*Amoeba*) of PROTOZOA. *A. proteus* (common species) of fresh waters is c.¹⁄₁₀₀ in. long. Amoeba, a single cell, has oval nucleus surrounded by granular mass, in turn surrounded by outer clear layer. Locomotion is by false feet or pseudopods formed by outpushing of clear layer with granular mass flowing into outpushings. Pseudopods also engulf food (minute animals, plants) in water; food circulates through protoplasm until digested. Sensitive to light, heat, food. See *ill.*, p. 813.

Amon (ä′mŏn), d. c.641 B.C., idolatrous king of Judah (c.643–c.641 B.C.). He was murdered by servants and succeeded by Josiah. Jeremiah was a contemporary. 2 Kings 21.19 –26; 2 Chron. 33.20–25.

Amon (ä′mùn, ä′–) or **Ammon** (ă′mùn), ancient Egyptian deity, originally local god of Thebes. He was early represented as a ram or as a man with ram′s head. The principal temple to him was in Libyan desert. Identified by Greeks with Zeus and by Romans with Jupiter. See EGYPTIAN RELIGION.

amontillado (ùmŏn″tĭlä′dō), dry sherry noted for delicate bouquet. It resembles the wine produced in Montilla, Spain, from which it derives its name.

Amor, Roman god of love: see CUPID; EROS.

amortization, reduction, liquidation, or satisfaction of a debt or the sum used for this purpose. In security investment, amortization is charging off premium or discount to bring value of security to par at maturity. Other forms of amortization: paying off mortgage, paying off debt by sinking fund, and paying off public corporation bonds annually.

Amos (ä′mùs), book of Old Testament, written by a shepherd-prophet in time of Jeroboam II. The book falls into 3 parts: God′s judgment on Gentile nations, finally on Israel; three sermons on doom of Israel; five visions of destruction, the last promising redemption.

Amoskeag Falls: see MANCHESTER, N.H.

Amoy (ùmoi′), commercial city (pop. 158,-271), Fukien prov., China; port on Amoy Isl. in inlet of Formosa Strait. Treaty port, opened 1842. Exports sugar, tobacco, and tea. Seat of a university.

ampelopsis (ăm″pĭlŏp′–), woody vines of genus *Ampelopsis*, including pepper vine of S U.S. Berries are blue, purple, yellow, or orange in various species.

Ampère, André Marie (ăm′pēr; ädrä′ märē äpēr′), 1775–1836, French physicist, mathematician, natural philosopher. Worked in electrodynamics, derived Ampère's law, studied relationship of electricity and magnetism.

ampere [for A. M. Ampère], electrical unit of current strength and measurement unit of rate of current flow. Current intensity (in amperes) determined by dividing volts (electromotive force) by ohms (resistance).

amphibian (ămfĭ′bēŭn), cold-blooded vertebrate animal of class Amphibia, intermediate between fish and reptiles. Characteristic metamorphosis is from aquatic to partially terrestrial form. See FROG; NEWT; SALAMANDER; TOAD.

amphibious warfare (ămfĭ′bēŭs), the combined use of land and sea forces in warfare. Known from the time of the ancient Greeks, it is in modern war also supported by air power. In World War II, many special vessels were made for landing tanks, supplies, and men in shallow water. Warfare in the Pacific and the invasion of Europe used amphibious warfare extensively.

Amphilochus (ămfĭ′lŭkŭs), in Greek legend, son of Amphiaraüs and Eriphyle. He was one of the EPIGONI, and fought in Trojan War.

Amphitheater, suburb (pop. 12,664) of Tucson, Ariz.

Amphitrite (ămfĭtrī′tē), in Greek religion, queen of the sea; wife of Poseidon and mother of Triton.

Amphitryon (ămfĭ′trēŭn, -ŏn″), in Greek legend, husband of Alcmene. In Amphitryon's absence, Zeus assumed his form and visited Alcmene; she bore him Hercules, whom Amphitryon accepted as his son.

Amram ben Scheschna (shĕsh′nä), or **Amram Gaon** (gä′ōn), d. 875, author of *Siddur Rab Amram,* a prayer book, the basis for Orthodox Jewish religious rites.

Amritsar (ŭmrĭt′sŭr), city (pop. 391,010), NW Punjab, India. Founded 1577 by Ram Das, 4th guru [Hindustani = teacher], it is center of Sikh religion. Mfg. of silks and carpets. At open-air meeting, April 13, 1919, many Gandhi followers were killed or wounded by British forces.

Amru-l-Kais (kīs′), 6th cent., Arabian poet. Subjective, formally perfect verse is esteemed by Arabs as model for erotic poetry. Included in MUALLAQAT.

Amsterdam (ăm′stŭrdăm″, Dutch ämstŭr-däm′), municipality (pop. 803,847), and city, constitutional cap. and largest city of the Netherlands, in North Holland. Situated mainly on S bank of the IJ and connected by canals with the North Sea and the Rhine delta, it is a major port and a great commercial, intellectual, and artistic center. Stock exchange and diamond-cutting industry are important. Amsterdam is built on wooden piles; some 400 bridges cross numerous concentric and radial canals. Chartered in 1300, it joined the Hanseatic League in 1369 and the United Provs. in 1578. Large influx of refugees from all nations (notably French Protestants and Spanish and Portuguese Jews) contributed to rapid growth after late 16th cent. Birthplace of Spinoza and residence of Rembrandt, Amsterdam reached apex as cultural center in 17th cent. It was taken by the French in

1795; served as cap. of kingdom of Netherlands under Louis Bonaparte; was declared cap. under 1814 constitution. Actually, the government is at The Hague; sovereigns are merely sworn in at Amsterdam. German occupation (1940–45) in World War II brought severe hardship. Of the large Jewish population only a few survived. Points of interest include Oude Kerk [old church], built c.1300; weighhouse (15th cent.); city hall (16th cent.); Rijks Mus. (has Dutch masters); Univ. of Amsterdam (1632; reorganized 1876).

Amsterdam, industrial city (pop. 32,240), E central N.Y., on Mohawk R. and NW of Albany. Center for rug and carpet mfg. Fort Johnson, home of Sir William Johnson, is near.

Amu Darya (ä′moō där′yŭ), river, 1,577 mi. long, central Asia. Ancient name is Oxus.

amulet, object worn as charm to ward off evil influences. Reliance on such devices is common to many cultures. Egyptians wore many amulets; Hebrews wore phylacteries containing scriptural texts; Christians of 4th cent. wore crosses and amulets enclosing sacred objects and scriptural verses. Materials of amulets vary from teeth of animals to precious stones and may bear engravings of symbols, such as wheel of sun-god or a swastika.

Amundsen, Roald (rō′äl ä′moōnsŭn), 1872–1928, Norwegian polar explorer. Commanded first negotiation of Northwest Passage (1903–6). First to reach South Pole (1911). Flew over North Pole with Lincoln Ellsworth (1926). Died in attempt to rescue a former associate, Umberto Nobile.

Amur (ämoōr′), Chinese *Hei-lung-kiang* (hā′loōng′-jëäng′), river, 1,767 mi. long, NE Asia. Formed by junction of Shilka and Argun at Russo-Manchurian border; follows border for 1,100 mi.; turns NE near Khabarovsk and empties into Tatar Strait opposite Sakhalin isl. Important transport artery during ice-free summer months.

Amurath: see MURAD.

amylase: see DIASTASE.

Amyot, Jacques (zhäk′ ämyō′), 1513–93, French humanist, translator of Plutarch's *Lives* (1559).

Amyot or **Amiot, Joseph** (zhôzĕf′ ämyō′), 1718–1794?, French Jesuit missionary in China. He was one of first Europeans to make Chinese literature, antiquities, and customs known to Europe and also was an early authority on Manchu language.

Anabaptists [from Gr.,= rebaptizers], Protestant sects insisting on rebaptism for believers only. Persecuted for preaching separation of Church and state, they were disunited. Luther opposed them. Chief leaders were Thomas Münzer and John of Leiden. Group under Menno Simons became MENNONITES. Descendants of Jacob Hutter estab. HUTTERISCHE COMMUNITY (1874) in S.Dak.

Anabasis (ŭnă′bŭsĭs) [Gr.,= going up, i.e., to the sea], famed Greek prose history by XENOPHON of retreat of the Ten Thousand from Persia (c.399 B.C.).

Anacharsis (ănŭkär′sĭs), 6th cent. B.C., Scythian prince supposed to have toured Greece; in legend a very witty, wise man.

Anacletus, Saint: see CLETUS, SAINT.

Anaconda (ănŭkŏn'dŭ), city (pop. 11,254), SW Mont., NW of Butte; laid out 1883. Chosen by Marcus DALY for smelter of Anaconda Copper Mining Co. City, dominated by smelter, also has by-product plants (arsenic, sulphuric acid, phosphate fertilizer).

anaconda, nonvenomous South American snake, mostly aquatic, partially arboreal, related to boa constrictor, python. Largest is water boa (to 30 ft.).

Anacortes (ănŭkôr'tĕz), port city (pop. 6,919), NW Wash., S of Bellingham. Processes and ships lumber, fish, and food.

Anacostia (ănŭkŏs'tĕŭ), river rising near Bladensburg, Md., and flowing into Potomac R. at Washington, D.C. Naval installations on shores.

Anacreon (ŭnăk'rēŭn, –ŏn), fl. c.521 B.C., Greek lyric poet, author of drinking and love songs.

Anadarko (ănŭdär'kō), city (pop. 6,184), SW Okla., on Washita R. and SW of Oklahoma City. Center of cotton, grain, livestock, and oil area. Has remnants of Delaware Indians. Annual Indian exposition.

Anadyr (ŭnŭdīr'), river, 700 mi. long, RSFSR. Flows from extreme NE Siberia into Bering Sea. Coal and gold deposits along shores.

anae-, for words beginning thus: see ANE-.

Anaheim (ăn'ŭhīm), city (pop. 14,556), S Calif., SE of Los Angeles; founded 1857. Has mfg. of canning equipment and plants to pack and process food.

Anáhuac (änä'wäk) [Aztec,= near the water], geographical term in Mexico, today referring specifically to part of central plateau comprising Pánuco and Lerma river systems and lake basin of Valley of Mexico.

Anakim (ăn'ŭkĭm) or **Anakims,** in Bible, a race of giants inhabiting Hebron at time of conquest of Canaan. Practically extirpated by Joshua and Caleb. Num. 13.22,28,33; Deut. 1.28; 9.2; Joshua 11.21; 14.15; 15.13,14; 21.11; Judges 1.20.

Anamosa (ănŭmō'sŭ), city (pop. 3,910), E central Iowa, NE of Cedar Rapids. Birthplace of Grant Wood is near by.

Ananias (ăn'ŭnī'ŭs). **1** Man who, with his wife Sapphira, kept back part of gift to church and lied about it. He was rebuked by Peter and fell dead. Acts 5.1–11. Name became term for a liar. **2** High priest at Jerusalem, Roman sympathizer. Acts 23.2–5. **3** Christian who took care of the newly converted Paul. Acts 19.10–22. **4** One of THREE HOLY CHILDREN.

anarchism (ăn'ŭrkĭzŭm), theory that the state should be abolished and replaced by free association of groups (no private property). Differs from SOCIALISM in considering the state an intrinsic evil. Philosophic and literary anarchy appeared early (e.g., Zeno of Citium, medieval religious groups), political later (e.g., Anabaptists, Levelers). Modern anarchism outlined by William GODWIN and P. J. PROUDHON. Violent tone introduced by BAKUNIN, resisted by KROPOTKIN. Anarchism suppressed in Russia by Soviets. Violent doctrines brought from Europe to U.S. The Haymarket riot and the assassination of McKinley brought a law to keep anarchists from country. The Sacco and Vanzetti Case was linked to fear of anarchism.

Anatolia, the Asiatic part of TURKEY. A mountainous peninsula between the Black Sea (N), Aegean Sea (W), and Mediterranean (S), it comprises 97% (287,117 sq. mi.; pop. 12,308,441) of all Turkey. The name sometimes designates all ASIA MINOR.

anatomy, study of body structure and structural relationships. Includes study of body tissues (histology), of structure of various animal forms (comparative anatomy), and of prenatal development (embryology). International nomenclature estab. 1895. See *ill.,* p. 763.

Anaxagoras (ăn'ŭksă'gŭrŭs), c.500–c.428 B.C., Greek philosopher. Held that an all-pervading mind (*nous*) initiated motion and order by combining mass of particles into actual objects.

Anaximander (ŭnăk"sĭmăn'dŭr), c.611–c.547 B.C., Greek philosopher. Thought that the primary source of all things was "the boundless," which by constant motion caused the physical world to emerge. He had a crude theory of evolution.

Anaximenes (ăn"ŭksĭm'ĭnēz), 6th cent. B.C., Greek philosopher, who taught that air was basic universal substance.

Anchieta, José de (zhōōzā' dŭ änshēä'tŭ), 1530–97, Portuguese missionary in Brazil, a Jesuit, called first Brazilian writer.

Anchises (ăn-kī'sēz, ăngkī'sēz), in Greek Legend, Trojan hero; father of Aeneas by Aphrodite.

Anchorage (ăng'kŭrĭj), city (pop. 11,254), S central Alaska, at head of Cook Inlet; founded 1915 as hq. of Alaska RR. Alaska's largest city, it is important in defense and as a commercial, communications, and distribution center for agr., mining, and lumbering area. It has fisheries, sawmills, and railroad shops. Connected with Alaska Highway.

anchovy (ăn'chōvē), small fish of herring family. Spanish and Italian anchovies (*Engraulis encrasicholus*) cured by using fermentation; Norwegian or Swedish sprats or brislings (genus *Clupea*) without it.

Ancon (ăng'kŏn, Span. ängkōn'), town (pop. 1,695), Panama Canal Zone, near Pacific end of canal and just NW of Panama city. Residential and medical center on transisthmian railroad.

Ancona (ängkō'nä), city (pop. 57,100), cap. of the Marches, central Italy; Adriatic port. Settled by Syracusan Greeks 4th cent. B.C.; medieval maritime republic; passed under direct papal rule 1532. Byzantine-Romanesque cathedral (11th–13th cent.; damaged in World War II); Arch of Trajan.

Ancren Riwle (äng'krŭn rē'ōōlŭ, rōōl', äng'krŭn) [Mid. Eng.,= anchoresses' rule], anonymous tract written (c.1200) for three ladies about to enter hermitage. Rare example of Middle English prose.

Ancyra: see ANKARA, Turkey.

Andalusia (ăndŭlōō'zhŭ, –shŭ), Span. *Andalucía,* southernmost region (33,675 sq. mi.; pop. 5,219,362), Spain, crossed by Sierra Nevada and Sierra Morena and by Guadalquivir R. Cities: Seville, Granada, Cordoba, Cádiz, Málaga, Huelva. The climate is subtropical, the soil partly very fertile, producing cereals, fruit, olives. Cattle and horse raising. Copper, iron, zinc, and lead mines have been exploited since anc. times. Settled by Phoenicians (11th cent. B.C.), then by Greeks, Carthaginians, Romans, Andalusia was conquered by the Moors (A.D. 711), under whom it reached greatest prosperity. It was reconquered by Castile in 13th cent., except GRANADA, which fell in 1492.

Andalusia (ăn″dŭloō′zhŭ), city (pop. 9,162), S Ala., S of Montgomery, near Fla. line. Processing center in area yielding cotton, peanuts, cattle, pine.

Andaman and Nicobar Islands (ăn′dŭmŭn, nĭkōbär′), state (3,143 sq. mi.; pop. 30,963), India, in Bay of Bengal; cap. Port Blair. Lumber and copra.

Andersen, Hans Christian, 1805–75, Danish writer of fairy tales. After poverty-ridden, unhappy early years and failure of early writings, he gained success with a novel *Improvisatoren* (1835). In same year appeared *Eventyr,* first of many volumes of fairy tales that were to make him revered and beloved all over the world. Among stories are "The Ugly Duckling," "The Brave Tin Soldier," "The Little Mermaid," "The Red Shoes."

Andersen Nexo, Martin, Dan. *Nexø,* 1869–, Danish novelist. His proletarian novels (eg., *Pelle the Conqueror,* 4 vols., 1906–10) did much to improve social conditions in Denmark. In his later years lived much in Russia.

Anderson, Alexander, 1775–1870, American engraver, first successful wood engraver in America.

Anderson, Carl David, 1905–, American physicist. Shared 1936 Nobel Prize for discovery of POSITRON. Co-discoverer of MESON.

Anderson, Elizabeth Garrett, 1836–1917, English physician. Opened hospital, first in England to be staffed by women physicians. Her efforts led to opening of British medical examinations to women.

Anderson, Marian, 1907?–, American Negro contralto. Her first great successes were in Europe. After her return to the U.S. in 1935 she became one of the best loved of American concert singers.

Anderson, Mary Antoinette, later **Madame de Navarro,** 1859–1940, American actress, popular in U.S. and England as Desdemona, Rosalind, and Lady Macbeth. Married and retired to England 1890.

Anderson, Maxwell, 1888–, American dramatist. Was a journalist until the success of play written with Lawrence Stallings, *What Price Glory* (1924). Among plays (some in blank verse): *Saturday's Children* (1927), *Elizabeth the Queen* (1930), *Both Your Houses* (1933), *Winterset* (1935), *High Tor* (1937), *Joan of Lorraine* (1946).

Anderson, Robert, 1805–71, American army officer, defender of Fort SUMTER.

Anderson, Sherwood, 1876–1941, American author, b. Ohio. Starting work at 12, he had varied experience in advertising and commerce. His novels—e.g., *Windy McPherson's Son* (1916), *Poor White* (1920), *Dark Laughter* (1925), *Kit Brandon* (1936)—and short stories (e.g., in *Winesburg, Ohio,* 1919) are strongly American and Midwest in subject and feeling.

Anderson. **1** Industrial city (pop. 46,820), E central Ind., on White R. and NE of Indianapolis; platted 1823. Mfg. of machinery, metal and glass products. Mounds State Park has Indian mounds and museum. Moravian Indian mission was near by (1801–6). **2** City (pop. 19,770), NW S.C., SW of Greenville; laid out 1827. Has textile mills, foundries, and beverage plants.

Andersonville Prison: see AMERICUS, Ga.

Andes (ăn′dēz), mountain system, over 4,000 mi. long, South America, paralleling Pacific coast. Stretching from Tierra del Fuego N to VENEZUELA, Andes form one of world's great mountain masses, only Himalayas exceeding them in height. On border between ARGENTINA and CHILE, in Patagonia, are high glacier-fed lakes with noted resorts. Farther N lies highest range, with ACONCAGUA and Tupungato separated by USPALLATA PASS. Central Andes broaden in BOLIVIA and PERU, and on plateau and in valleys Inca civilization had its home. Lake Titicaca and volcanoes here. Ranges narrow again in ECUADOR, then divide in COLOMBIA —W range running along coast, E range into Venezuela. Andes influence communication, climate, weather, and life of all South America. Copper, silver, tin are mined in several areas.

Andorra (ăndô′rù), small state (191 sq. mi.; pop. 5,231), SW Europe, in E Pyrenees between France and Spain; cap. Andorra la Vella. Catalan-speaking population engages in sheep raising and smuggling. Nominally, Andorra has been under the joint suzerainty of the Spanish bishops of Urgel and the rulers of France since the Middle Ages, but actually it is governed by a council and a syndic.

Andover, town (pop. 12,437), NE Mass., S of Lawrence; settled 1643. Mfg. of woolens, soap, and rubber goods. Harriet Beecher Stowe buried here. Seat of Phillips Acad. (nonsectarian, for boys; opened 1778, chartered 1780 by Samuel Phillips); often called Andover or Phillips Andover.

Andrade, Olegario Víctor (ōlägä′ryō vēk′tōr ändrä′dhä), 1839?–1882, Argentine romantic poet, journalist, called national poet because of patriotism.

Andrassy, Julius, Count (ŏn′dräsh-shē), Hung. *Andrássy Gyula,* 1823–90, Hungarian statesman. Leading figure in revolution of 1848–49; returned from exile 1858; negotiated creation of AUSTRO-HUNGARIAN MONARCHY 1867. As prime minister of Hungary he fostered Magyar supremacy over Slavic and other minorities. As foreign minister of Austria-Hungary (1871–79) he signed alliance with Germany (1879). His son, **Count Julius Andrassy,** 1860–1929, Austro-Hungarian foreign minister in 1918, tried unsuccessfully to secure separate peace with Allies. Later led Hungarian royalists.

André, John (ăn′drē), 1751–80, British spy in American Revolution. Hanged after negotiating with Benedict ARNOLD for betrayal of West Point.

Andrea del Sarto: see SARTO, ANDREA DEL.

Andreanof Islands: see ALEUTIAN ISLANDS.

Andree, Salomon August (ändrā′), 1854–97, Swedish polar explorer. Aeronautical engineer, first to attempt arctic exploration by balloon. Entire expedition lost.

Andreev, Leonid Nikolayevich: see ANDREYEV.

Andreini (ändräē′nē), family of Italian actors, celebrated in COMMEDIA DELL' ARTE. **Francesco Andreini,** 1548–1624, was less famous than his celebrated wife, **Isabella Andreini,** 1562–1604, player in his troupe, the Gelosi, and author of poems and a pastoral. Her son, **Giovanni Battista** or **Giambattista Andreini** (jämbät-tēs′tä), 1579?–1654, managed the Fidele troupe. **Virginia Andreini,** 1583–c.1628, his wife, was noted both for acting and beauty.

Andrew, Saint [Gr.,= manly], one of Twelve Disciples; brother of Peter. Mat. 4.18; 10.2; Mark 3.16; 13.3; Luke 6.14; John 1.40–42; 6.8,9; 12.22; Acts 1.13. Traditionally a missionary in Asia Minor, Macedonia, S Russia. When martyred, he is said to have died on X-shaped cross (St. Andrew's cross). Andrew is patron of Russia and of Scotland (Union Jack has white St. Andrew's cross on blue field). Feast day: Nov. 30.

Andrew II, d. 1235, king of Hungary (1205–35). Signed Golden Bull, the "Magna Carta of Hungary" (1222; expanded 1231). Father of St. Elizabeth of Hungary and of Bela IV.

Andrewes, Lancelot, 1555–1626, Anglican bishop of Chichester, Ely, and Winchester. A learned preacher, he helped translate Authorized version of Bible and led High Church party opposed to Puritanism.

Andrew Johnson National Monument: see NATIONAL PARKS AND MONUMENTS (table).

Andrews, Roy Chapman, 1884–, American naturalist and explorer, director of American Mus. of Natural History (1935–41). Specialist in water mammals of Alaska, Malayan seas, and Asiatic coast, he also led expeditions to study fossil and living animals and plants in central Asia.

Andreyev or **Andreev, Leonid Nikolayevich** (lyŭnyēt′ nyĭkŭlī′úvĭch ŭndrä′úf), 1871–1919, Russian author. A revolutionist and friend of Gorki, he turned against Bolshevism in 1917 and died in Finland. *The Seven Who Were Hanged* (1908; Eng. tr., 1909) is a story of idealistic revolutionists. Other works reflect a morbid, negative view of society, as the short novel *The Red Laugh* (1905; Eng. tr., 1905) and the dramas *King Hunger* (1907; Eng. tr., 1911) and *He Who Gets Slapped* (1916; Eng. tr., 1921).

Andromache (ăndrŏ′múkē), in Greek legend, Trojan wife of Hector and mother of Astyanax. After Trojan War she was abducted by Neoptolemus and later married Hector's brother Helenus.

Andromeda (ăndrŏ′múdú), in Greek religion, Ethiopian princess; daughter of Cepheus and Cassiopeia. Poseidon, angered by claim that she was more beautiful than Nereids, sent sea monster appeasable only by sacrifice of king's daughter. She was rescued by Perseus, who married her.

Andronicus, Livius: see LIVIUS ANDRONICUS.

Andros, Sir Edmund, 1637–1714, British colonial governor in America. Bitterly criticized as governor of N.Y. (1674–81) for high-handed methods. Deposed as governor of Dominion of New England in 1689. Governor of Va. (1692–97).

Andros (ăn′drŏs), Aegean island (145 sq. mi pop. 17,926), off Greece, second largest an northernmost of CYCLADES, chief town an port Andros (pop. 3,028). Silk, fruits, wine manganese.

Androscoggin (ăndrŭskŏg′ĭn), river formed i NE N.H. Flows E and S through W Main to join Kennebec R. near Bath. Used fc power and logging.

Androuet du Cerceau (ädrōō-ā′ dü sĕrsō′) family of French architects. Founded b **Jacques Androuet** (zhäk), c.1510–c.1584, leader in introducing Italian Renaissanc style into France. His son **Baptiste Androue du Cerceau** (bätēst′), c.1544–1602, designe Pont-Neuf (Paris). Another son **Jacque Andouet du Cerceau,** d. 1614, worked o Tuileries. Both worked on Louvre.

Andrusov, Treaty of, 1667, peace treaty be tween Russia and Poland. Smolensk an Ukraine E of Dnieper (incl. Kiev) passe to Russia.

anemia, condition resulting from reduction i number or in hemoglobin content of re blood corpuscles. Causes include loss c blood, excessive destruction of red corpus cles, or inadequate blood formation owin to deficiency of iron or of antianemic factc of liver or to bone marrow malfunction.

anemometer: see WIND.

anemone (úněm′únē) or **windflower,** perenni plant of genus *Anemone.* Some have show flowers, e.g., the poppy anemone of florist and the PASQUEFLOWER and fall Japanes anemone of gardens. Among wild kinds spring-flowering wood anemone. Rue anem one is *Anemonella thalictroides.*

aneroid barometer: see BAROMETER.

anesthesia (ănĭsthē′zhú), loss of sensation ir duced by drugs. General anesthesia cause unconsciousness; produced by inhalation c anesthetic. Local anesthesia affects are about site of application. Spinal anesthesi produced by injection beneath spinal cor membranes; caudal, by injection into cauda canal. Anesthesia pioneers include Horac WELLS, C. W. LONG, W. T. G. MORTON, S J. Y. SIMPSON.

Aneto, Pico de (pē′kō dä änä′tō), Fr. *Pic a Néthou* or *Pic d'Anethou,* peak, 11,168 f high, NE Spain, near French border; highe of Pyrenees.

angel [Gr.,= messenger], bodiless, immorta spirit, limited in knowledge and power. I traditional belief of Judaism, Christianity and Islam, good angels are accepted as inte mediate beings between God and man, li ing in heaven, able to visit earth in visibl or invisible form—sometimes depicted wit wings. Hierarchy given in three choirs i descending order: seraphim, cherubin thrones; dominions, virtues, powers; prin cipalities, archangels, angels. The Bible tel of guardian angels protecting nations or in dividuals (Dan. 10.13,20; Mat. 18.10), concept popular in Western Christendon Angels of hell, dark angels, or devils, are th evil counterpart of heavenly host; they lea man into evil ways and are headed by SATA (or Lucifer). Famous literary depictions ar in Milton's *Paradise Lost* and Dante's *Divir Comedy.* See also ARCHANGEL; CHERUB SERAPH.

angelica (ănjĕl'ĭkŭ), perennial herb (*Angelica*). Compound leaves effective in herb gardens. Roots and fruits yield oil used in perfume and liqueurs.

Angelico, Fra (frä änjĕl'ĭkō), 1387–1455, Florentine painter of religious subjects, b. Tuscany. In 1407 entered Dominican convent at Fiesole where he executed some of his best work. Lovely color and gentleness of spirit mark his 200 to 300 extant works, which include frescoes in convent of St. Mark's (Florence) and scenes from lives of St. Stephen and St. Lawrence in Vatican.

Angel Island, W Calif., largest island in San Francisco Bay. U.S. army base, 1863–1946.

Angell, James Burrill, 1829–1916, American educator, editor, and diplomat. Left teaching in 1860 to edit Providence *Journal,* but returned to education to be president of the Univ. of Vermont (1866–71) and the Univ. of Michigan (1871–1909). Minister to China (1880–81) and to Turkey (1897–98). His son, **James Rowland Angell,** 1869–1949, was educator and psychologist. Taught psychology at Univ. of Chicago (1894–1920) and was dean (1911–18) and acting president (1918–19). President of Yale Univ. 1921–37. After 1937 he was educational counselor to the National Broadcasting Company.

Angell, Sir Norman, 1874–, British internationalist, valiant fighter for peace. Gained fame with *The Great Illusion* (1910), arguing futility of war because of economic interests of nations. Many later books. Received 1933 Nobel Peace Prize. Original name was Ralph Norman Angell Lane.

Angels Camp, city (pop. 1,147), central Calif., E of Stockton; founded 1848 after gold discovery. Annual Jumping Frog Jubilee honors Mark Twain's story.

Angelus (ăn'jŭlŭs), family name of ISAAC II, ALEXIUS III, and ALEXIUS IV, Byzantine emperors.

Angelus Silesius (ăn'jŭlŭs sīlē'zhŭs), pseud. of **Johannes Scheffler** (yōhän'ŭs), 1624–77, German poet. After conversion to Catholicism he wrote deeply mystical poems, the best of their period.

Angerman, Swed. *Ångermanälven* (ông'ŭrmänĕl'vŭn), river, 280 mi. long, rising in N central Sweden and flowing into Gulf of Bothnia at Harnosand. It is a main logging artery.

Angermanland, Swed. *Ångermanland,* historic province, NE Sweden. Now divided between Vasternorrland and Vasterbotten counties.

Angers (äzhā'), city (pop. 86,083), cap. of Maine-et-Loire dept., W France, on Maine R., historic cap. of Anjou. Dates from pre-Roman times. Cathedral (12th–13th cent.), medieval castle, museum.

Angevin (ăn'jŭvĭn), name of two medieval dynasties and their several branches.
First Angevin dynasty, originated 10th cent. with counts of ANJOU. Geoffrey Plantagenet (see GEOFFREY) conquered NORMANDY 1144. His son became king of England as Henry II and founded Angevin or Plantagenet dynasty of English kings (see list of kings at end of article ENGLAND). Count Fulk V of Anjou (see FULK) also became king of Jerusalem, which passed to his younger son, Baldwin III, and to Baldwin's

heirs (see JERUSALEM, LATIN KINGDOM OF).
Second Angevin dynasty, main line, collateral branch of Capetian dynasty; originated 1246 when Louis IX granted Anjou in appanage to younger brother Charles (see CHARLES I of Naples); ruled PROVENCE from 1246 and kingdom of NAPLES from 1266 until deposition of JOANNA I (1381).
Second Angevin dynasty, collateral lines. In Naples: CHARLES III, LANCELOT, and JOANNA II, lineal descendants of Charles II of Naples through a younger son, ruled 1381–1435. Succession was contested by Duke Louis of Anjou and his heirs (see LOUIS, kings of Naples; RENÉ). They made good their claim to Provence but not to Naples, which eventually was seized by Alfonso V of Aragon (1442). Their extinction (1486) left the French crown their heir. In Hungary and Poland: see CHARLES I of Hungary; LOUIS I of Hungary and Poland.

Anghiera, Pietro Martire d' (märtē'rä dänggyä'rä), 1457?–1526, Italian geographer and historian. Moved to Spain in 1487. From explorers and navigators (esp. Columbus, Vespucci, Magellan) he learned latest information about explorations in his time. Wrote *De orbe decades octo* (1530).

angina pectoris (ănji'nŭ pĕk'tŭrĭs), disease marked by chest pain. Caused by obstruction of coronary arteries, resulting in lack of oxygen to heart muscle.

Angkor Thom (ăng'kôr tôm'), ruined cap. of KHMER EMPIRE, W Cambodia, Indo-China. Among ruins of temples and royal palace are rows of huge seated stone figures. Most ornate carvings are those on the Bayon, temple of Siva or, more probably, of Lokesvara.

Angkor Wat, great temple of anc. Khmer Empire, Cambodia. Comparable as architectural entity to Taj Mahal. The moat-surrounded, richly carved temple contains a shrine of Vishnu.

angle, in plane geometry, figure formed by meeting of two straight lines. Meeting point called vertex; lines called sides. In solid geometry, two or more planes meeting form angle; two-plane-intersection line forms dihedral angle; three-plane-intersection angle called trihedral. In trigonometry the plane angle is defined as the degree one (initial) side must rotate about its vertex to reach the position of the other (terminal) side.

Angles: see ANGLO-SAXONS; EAST ANGLIA; MERCIA; NORTHUMBRIA.

Anglesey or **Anglesea** (both: ăng'gŭlsē), island county (276 sq. mi.; pop. 50,637), NW Wales. Shows traces of prehistoric occupation. Chief occupations are agr., sheep-raising, and fishing. Holyhead is terminus of packet service to Dublin.

Anglican Communion, body of churches in communion with Church of England, including Protestant Episcopal Church of America, Scottish Episcopal Church, and Church of Ireland.

Anglin, Margaret (Mary), 1876–, American actress, b. Canada. Won fame (1898) as Roxane in *Cyrano de Bergerac* and appeared (1903–4) with Henry Miller in *Camille* and *The Devil's Disciple.* Especially noted in *Antigone, Electra,* and *Medea.*

Anglo-Egyptian Sudan (sōōdăn'), condominium (967,500 sq. mi.; est. pop. 8,053,669), NE Africa, on Red Sea; cap. Khartoum. Comprises most of the SUDAN. E section is watered by the Nile; Nubia (N half) is mainly desert, inhabited by pastoral nomads. Negroes inhabit the south, which is largely jungle. Ancient Egypt colonized Nubia before 1500 B.C. In 6th cent. the Nubians embraced Coptic Christianity but were converted to Islam in 15th cent. by Arab conquerors. Unification of area began in early 19th cent. with conquest by Mohammed Ali. In 1870s Anglo-Egyptian armies under Sir Samuel Baker and Gen. Charles Gordon suppressed the slave trade and set up military posts on the upper Nile. MAHDISTS, who began their revolt in 1881, were defeated in 1898 by Lord Kitchener's Anglo-Egyptian army. Anglo-Egyptian condominium set up by 1899 convention was reaffirmed by treaty in 1936, but in 1951 Egypt declared full sovereignty over area. Anglo-Egyptian agreement of 1953 provided for Sudanese freedom within three years.

Anglo-Saxon Chronicle, annals of the English until 1154. Extant form probably begun c.892 by Winchester monks under supervision of Alfred the Great.

Anglo-Saxon literature, literary writings in Old English. Many early poems, though recorded after English conversion to Christianity, retain paganism, materials, or somber tone of old Germanic tradition (e.g., the epic BEOWULF; WIDSITH; and *Deor,* earliest English lyric). Hymn of CÆDMON first religious poem; later poets often paraphrased parts of Bible to produce stirring poems like epic fragment *Judith.* CYNEWULF and his school adapted saints' lives and homilies. "The Dream of the Rood" notable for vividness and religious intensity. Usual metrical form is alliterative, four-stress line broken into two half-lines and end-stopped. Literary prose began with translations from Latin by King ALFRED, who probably also directed ANGLO-SAXON CHRONICLE. Finest original prose in homilies of ÆLFRIC. Much contemporary writing was in Latin.

Anglo-Saxons, name given Germanic-speaking people who settled in England at end of Roman rule. Angles probably came from Schleswig late 5th cent. and formed foundations for kingdoms of East Anglia, Mercia, and Northumbria. Saxons, a Germanic tribe, settled in England at same time; kingdoms of Sussex, Wessex, and Essex were outgrowths of their settlements. Jutes, probably from area at mouth of the Rhine, settled in Kent and Isle of Wight. Term "Anglo-Saxons," denoting non-Celtic settlers of England, dates from 16th cent. Now more loosely used to denote any people (or their descendants) of British Isles, including Danes and Normans.

Angmagsalik (ängmäg'sälĭk), trading post, E Greenland coast, S of Arctic Circle. Strategic radio meteorological station estab. 1925.

Angola (ăng-gō'lŭ) or **Portuguese West Africa,** colony (with CABINDA 481,351 sq. mi.; pop. 3,378,010), W Africa, on Atlantic Ocean; cap. Luanda. Mostly desert or savanna land, except for narrow coastal strip and jungle in NE. Sugar, coffee, and palm oil are main ex-

ports. The Portuguese first settled here in 15th cent. Angola supplied most of the slaves sent to Brazil in 19th cent.

Angola (ăng"gōl'ù), resort city (pop. 5,081), NE Ind., NE of Fort Wayne, in hilly lake region.

Angora, Turkey: see ANKARA.

Angostura, Venezuela: see CIUDAD BOLÍVAR.

angostura bark (ăng"gústū'rù), bitter bark of a South American tree, *Cusparia.* It is used in **angostura bitters** to flavor cocktails.

Angoulême, Louis Antoine de Bourbon, duc d' (lwē' ātwän' dù bōōrbō' dük' dăgōōlĕm'), 1775–1844, last dauphin of France, son of Charles X. Renounced his claim in favor of Henri, comte de Chambord (1830).

Angoulême, Margaret of or **Marguerite d':** see MARGARET OF NAVARRE.

Angoulême (ägōōlĕm'), city (pop. 39,987), cap. of Charente dept., W France, on Charente R. Brandy distilleries. Seat of counts of Angoulême, 9th–16th cent.; cap. of Angoumois prov. till 1789.

Angstrom, Anders Jons (än'dùrs yûns' ōng'strûm), 1814–74, Swedish physicist. Studied light, spectrum analysis. His son **Knut Johan Angstrom** (knūt yōō'hän), 1857–1910, worked on solar radiation.

angstrom unit (ăng'strùm) [for A. J. Angstrom], length unit (1⁄100,000,000 cm) for wave lengths of light.

Anguier, François (fräswä' āgyä'), 1604–69, French sculptor. With his brother, **Michel Anguier** (mēshĕl'), 1614–86, considered among best sculptors of 17th cent. Another brother, **Guillaume Anguier** (gēyōm'), 1628–1708, was a painter.

Angus, earls of: see DOUGLAS, ARCHIBALD.

Angus, maritime county (874 sq. mi.; pop 274,870), E Scotland; co. town Forfar Mainly agr., also has jute and linen milling Historic remains include Glamis Castle. Formerly called Forfarshire.

Anhalt (än'hält), former German state (89 sq. mi.; 1939 pop. 432,289), central Germany, included since 1949 in state of Saxony-Anhalt, [East] German Democratic Republic; cap. Dessau. Minerals (salt, lignite copper, zinc); chemical and textile industries; agr. (sugar beets, grain, cattle). Ruled until 1918 by princely house descended from Albert the Bear. Joined German Empir 1871.

Anhwei or **An-hui** (both: än'hwä'), province (54,000 sq. mi.; pop. 25,000,000), E China Since 1949 divided into North Anhwei (cap Hofei) and South Anhwei (cap. Wuhu) Zone of transition between S Yangtze hill and N China plain. Produces c.60% o China's tea. Coal, iron, and copper mines Occupied by the Japanese 1938–45.

anhydride (ănhī'drĭd), nonmetallic oxide whic forms acid with water. Also refers to metal lic oxide which forms base with water.

Aniakchak (ănēăk'chăk), volcano, W Alaska in Aleutian Range, on Alaska Peninsula crater 6 mi. in diameter. Erupted 1931.

aniline (ăn'ùlĭn), colorless, oily liquid, com pound of carbon, hydrogen, nitrogen; a ba sic amine. Used as starting substance an aid in making dyes. Prepared by reductic of nitrobenzene.

animal, member of animal (as distinct fro

plant) kingdom. Animals require organized food; green plants can manufacture food from inorganic substances (see PHOTOSYNTHESIS). Animals have more highly developed nervous systems, sense organs, locomotion; adapted for securing, ingesting, digesting food. Classification of some microscopic forms disputed. See also INVERTEBRATE; VERTEBRATE; ZOOLOGY.

animated cartoon, form of moving picture in which a series of static drawings are photographed and synchronized with sound. Emile Cohl pioneered with animated puppets 1905, was first to use animated drawings 1907. Paper cut-outs also were used. Walt DISNEY has been a notable figure in the field.

animism, belief that all objects in world have consciousness and some personality. These "spirits" must be propitiated or outwitted. They may include spirits of the dead, leading to ancestor worship; or there may be a general, nonpersonalized spirit akin to the manito of the American Indian. Animism, prevalent in early cultures, has tended to disappear with growth of organized religions, but remains part of Japanese Shinto. See IDOL; SHAMAN.

anise (ăn'ĭs), annual plant, *Pimpinella anisum.* Flower clusters yield aniseed of commerce. Oil from leaves and seeds used as perfume and flavoring. **Anisette** is anise-flavored liqueur.

Anjou (ăn'jōō, Fr. äzhōō'), region and former duchy, W France, roughly coextensive with Maine-et-Loire dept.; historic cap. Angers. Drained by Loire, it is fertile and has excellent vineyards. Early counts of Anjou (see ANGEVIN dynasty) acquired Saumur, Touraine, Maine, Normandy and acceded to English throne with Henry II (1154). Anjou was confiscated (1204) by Philip II of France; became appanage of royal house; was raised to duchy 1360.

Ankara (ăng'kärä), city (pop. 286,781), cap. of Turkey, central Anatolia; known anciently as Ancyra, later as Angora. An important town from Hittite times and a provincial cap. under the Romans, it later sank into insignificance until it replaced Constantinople as Turkish cap. in 1923. Except for its old citadel it is a completely modern city. Its university was founded 1925. Ankara was the scene of Tamerlane's victory over BAJAZET I (1402). The region is famed for its long-haired goats and the production of Angora wool or mohair.

Anking (ăn'chĭng), commercial city (pop. 121,379), S Anhwei prov., China, on Yangtze R. Became treaty port 1902. Called Hwaining from 1912 to 1949.

Ann, Cape, NE Mass., N of Mass. Bay. Noted for old fishing villages, resorts, and artists' colonies (esp. GLOUCESTER and ROCKPORT).

Anna (Anna Ivanovna), 1693–1740, empress of Russia (1730–40), cousin and successor of Peter II. Ruled autocratically through her German favorites. Intervened in War of POLISH SUCCESSION; campaigned against Turkey (1736–39). Ivan VI succeeded her.

Anna [Gr.,= Heb. HANNAH]. 1 Aged prophetess who hailed Jesus' presentation at the Temple. Luke 2.36–38. 2 In Tobit, the mother of young Tobias.

Anna Comnena (kŏmnē'nù), b. 1083, d. after 1148, Byzantine princess and historian; daughter of Alexius I. Plotted against her brother JOHN II, seeking to put her husband on the throne. Discovered, she was pardoned and retired to a convent to write the *Alexiad,* a history covering the reign of Alexius I and the First Crusade.

Anna Ivanovna: see ANNA, empress of Russia.

Annam (ùnăm'), state (c.57,000 sq. mi.; pop. c.7,200,000), E. Indo-China; cap. Hué. Between Tonkin (N) and Cochin China (S). Its 800-mi. coast is on China Sea. Crops include rice (insufficient for Annam's needs), cinnamon, cocoa, and cotton. Even before Chinese invasion of Annam (c.214 B.C.), the Annamese had been under influence of Chinese culture for c.2000 years. Chinese rule lasted until 1428, when the Annamese estab. independent kingdom. After 1558 Annam was split between two dynasties of Hué and Tonkin; united again 1802 under the Hué. Maltreatment of French missionaries by native officials led to France's military campaigns (begun 1858), resulting in establishment of French protectorate over Annam in 1884. Under regime of Bao Dai, Annam forms part of VIET NAM.

Annandale-on-Hudson (ăn'ùndāl–), village, SE N.Y., on E bank of the Hudson S of Hudson. Seat of Bard Col. (coed.; 1860; affiliated 1928–44 with Columbia Univ.).

Annapolis (ùnăp'ùlĭs), city (pop. 10,047), state cap., central Md., on Severn R. near its mouth on Chesapeake Bay S of Baltimore. Trade center of agr. area, it has boatyards and seafood industry. Settled c.1648 as Providence by Va. Puritans, and later called Anne Arundel, it became provincial cap. in 1694 and was named Annapolis. Was social and commercial center in colonial days. Annapolis convention (1786) led to Federal Constitutional Convention. Seat of UNITED STATES NAVAL ACADEMY and of Saint John's Col. (nonsectarian, for men; opened 1789 as successor to King William's School, estab. 1696), which since 1937 has had nonelective curriculum based on "great books" plan. Points of interest are statehouse (1772), meeting place of Congress (1783) where Washington resigned as commander in chief of Continental army; Old Treasury (c.1695); and library (1737).

Annapolis, river, N.S., Canada, rising NE of Annapolis Royal in a valley noted for apple orchards. Flows c.75 mi. into **Annapolis Basin,** tidal arm of Bay of Fundy (c.10 mi. long, 3–5 mi. wide).

Annapolis Royal, town (pop. 784), W N.S., Canada, on Annapolis R. Founded as Port Royal by de Monts (1605), it was destroyed by Samuel Argall in 1614 and later rebuilt by the French. Changed hands between French and English until 1710, when it was captured by New Englanders under Francis Nicholson. Cap. of N.S. to 1749. Ruins of fort in Fort Anne Natl. Park (c.31 acres; estab. 1917).

Annapurna (ŭn-nŭpōōr'nù), mountain, Nepal in Himalayas; highest mountain climbed by man. Annapurna I (26,502 ft.), the higher of its two peaks, was climbed 1950 by French expedition led by Maurice Herzog. Annapurna II is 26,041 ft. high.

Ann Arbor, city (pop. 48,251), S Mich., on Huron R. and W of Detroit, in fruitgrowing area; laid out 1824. Mfg. of tools and metal products. Here are famous Nichols Arboretum, hq. of Michigan Municipal League, and Univ. of MICHIGAN.

Annas, Jewish high priest, who questioned Jesus. Non-Bible sources call him retired high priest. Was Caiaphas' father-in-law. John 18.13,24; Acts 4.6–22.

Anne, Saint [from Heb. Hannah], in tradition, mother of the Virgin, wife of St. Joachim. She is not mentioned in Scripture. Patroness of Quebec (Ste Anne de Beaupré) and Brittany (Sainte-Anne-d'Auray). Feast: July 26.

Anne, 1665–1714, queen of England, Scotland, and Ireland (1702–7), later first queen of Great Britain (1707–14); last Stuart ruler. Her reign, one of transition to parliamentary government, dominated by War of SPANISH SUCCESSION (1702–13). Many victories won by duke of MARLBOROUGH (whose wife was long favorite of the queen), but high cost of war source of friction between Tories and Whigs. None of Anne's children survived her and, by Act of Settlement (1701), George I succeeded to the throne. Despite personal mediocrity, her reign was marked by intellectual awakening, popularization of Palladian architecture, and by growth of empire and constitution and of the political power of the press.

Annecy (änsē'), city (pop. 24,414), cap. of Haute-Savoie dept., E France, on scenic Lake Annecy. Seat of bishops of Geneva after 1535; birthplace of St. Francis of Sales. Picturesque old city crossed by canals; medieval castle of counts of Geneva.

Anne de Beaujeu (dù bōzhû'), c.1460–1522, regent of France for her brother, Charles VIII, after death of Louis XI (1483). Arranged Charles's marriage with Anne of Brittany.

Anne of Austria, 1601–66, queen of France, daughter of Philip III of Spain; married Louis XIII (1615). Neglected by husband; persecuted by Richelieu. Her regency (1643–61) for her son, Louis XIV, was dominated by MAZARIN, disturbed by Fronde.

Anne of Brittany, 1477–1514, queen of France as wife of Charles VIII (1491–98) and of Louis XII (1499–1514); duchess of Brittany (1488–1514). Struggling to keep Brittany independent from invading French, she married by proxy (1490) Maximilian of Austria (later Emperor Maximilian I). Maximilian's dilatoriness and the use of force by France forced her to annul marriage. Her two subsequent marriages led to union of France and Brittany.

Anne of Cleves (klēvz), 1515–57, queen of England, fourth wife of Henry VIII. Henry married her (1540) for political purposes under influence of Thomas CROMWELL, but had marriage nullified same year.

Anne of Denmark, 1574–1619, queen consort of James I of England.

annexation, formal act asserting a state's sovereignty over newly incorporated territory (generally areas not inhabited by civilized peoples, areas settled by nationals of annexing power, areas already under protectorates, or conquered territory). The governing body of annexing power must ratify the act. Consent of all interested powers necessary for recognition in international law.

Anniston, city (pop. 31,066), NE Ala., ENE of Birmingham, in mining region of Appalachian foothills; founded 1872. Mfg. of iron, steel, textile, chemical products. U.S. Fort McClellan is near.

annual, plant which germinates, flowers, seeds, and dies within one year (e.g., marigold and zinnia), as distinguished from BIENNIAL and PERENNIAL plants.

Annunzio, Gabriele D': see D'ANNUNZIO, GABRIELE.

anode: see ELECTRODE and ELECTROLYSIS.

Anoka (ùnō'kù), city (pop. 7,396), E Minn., on the Mississippi at junction with Rum R. and NW of Minneapolis. Farm trade center and resort.

Ansbach (äns'bäkh), city (pop. 33,134), cap. of Middle Franconia, W Bavaria. Produces cars, motors, chemicals. Grew around 8th-cent. Abbey; residence from 1331 of Franconian branch of the HOHENZOLLERN dynasty. To Prussia 1791; to Bavaria 1806. Has Romanesque church (12th–15th cent.).

Anschluss (än'shlōōs) [Ger.,= junction], term applied to the project of union between Austria and Germany. Though forbidden by the peace treaties of 1919, it was advocated in Austria by both Socialists and National Socialists and became a reality when Hitler annexed Austria to Germany (1938–45).

Anselm, Saint (ăn'sĕlm), 1034?–1109, archbishop of Canterbury (1093–1109), Doctor of the Church, b. Italy. As abbot of Bec in Normandy, he gained wide reputation before succeeding his friend and master Lanfranc as archbishop. He stoutly upheld the papal claims in the quarrel over power to appoint bishops (see INVESTITURE) and had long quarrels with Kings William II and Henry I. His theological writings (e.g. *Monologium* and *Cur Deus homo?*) were influential. Offered ontological proof of existence of God—that the fact that the human mind can conceive of an Infinite Being necessarily means that such a Being must exist. Feast: April 21.

Anshan (än'shän'), city (pop. 219,715), Manchuria, on branch of South Manchurian RR; major steel center.

Anson, Adrian Constantine (Cap Anson), 1852–1922, American baseball player-manager. Four times National League batting champion.

Anson, George Anson, Baron, 1697–1762, British admiral. Sailed around world to attack Spanish possessions in South America. As first lord of the admiralty he estab. corps of marines (1755).

Anson, city (pop. 2,708), W central Texas NW of Abilene. Has annual Cowboy' Christmas Ball.

Ansonia, city (pop. 18,706), SW Conn., on Naugatuck R. and NW of New Haven; settled 1651. Metals center.

ant, cosmopolitan social insect, order Hymenoptera. Three body sections; narrow constriction between thorax and abdomen; usually black or various shades of brown, red

Antaeus   51   anthrax

yellow. Majority nest underground, others in decaying trees or plants; some make paper nests. Colonies (dozens to hundred thousands) usually include one or more queens (egg-laying, usually winged females); female wingless workers, usually sterile; and fertile males, usually winged. Males and females swarm in nuptial flight; males die; female sheds wings, and for rest of life (up to 15 years) can lay fertilized eggs. Workers live 4 to 7 years. Adult ants eat chiefly liquids of plants and animals; colonies often have parasites, sometimes enslave other species. TERMITE is miscalled white ant. See *ill.*, p. 601.

Antaeus (ăntē′ŭs), in Greek mythology, giant; son of Poseidon. He became stronger when touching earth (his mother, Gaea). Hercules overcame him by lifting him into the air.

Antakya, Turkey: see ANTIOCH.

Antalya (äntälyä′), city (pop. 27,478), SW Turkey; a Mediterranean seaport. Silk mfg.; chrome and manganese deposits near by. Known anciently as Attaleia or Attalia; in Middle Ages as Satalia or Satalieh; more recently as Adalia.

Antar (äntär′), fl. 600, Arabian warrior and poet. Rose from slave to tribal chief. Represented in MUALLAQAT. Hero of popular Arabic romance *Antar*.

Antarctica, continent of 5,000,000–6,000,000 sq. mi. surrounding South Pole. Encircling waters, sometimes called Antarctic Ocean, challenge navigation. Roughly circular outline broken by Ross and Weddell seas and Palmer Peninsula, c.600 mi. from South America, the only relatively near land. Coasts circled by pack ice hundreds of miles wide ending in sheer ice cliffs. Giant mountain ranges (peaks over 15,000 ft.) surround perpetually ice-capped central plateau. Highest average altitude and severest climate of any continent. Discovered by whalers, explored by 19th-cent. voyages of Palmer, Biscoe, Weddell, Ross, and others. Exploration impeded until 20th cent. technology made possible Amundsen, Scott, and U.S. naval expeditions (led by Byrd). Conflicting national claims nullified by impossibility of colonization. Antarctic regions, extending beyond Antarctic Circle (lat. 23° 30′S to lat. 50°S), are inimical to human life; have only mosses, lichens, algae, and support no year-round animal life except small wingless insects, microscopic organisms, and penguins. In summer, whales, seals, birds, and other penguins inhabit coast and sea. Once temperate or tropical, continent may again be habitable in millions of years, say some scientists.

anteater, name for sundry insect-eating animals; more accurately applied to a toothless group, order Edentata, of Central and South America. Great anteater or ant bear (*Myrmecophaga*) has long, nearly round head and snout, sticky tongue, coarse-haired body (c.4 ft. long), sharp claws, and long broad tail. Collared or lesser anteater (*Tamandua*) is half as large, short-haired, yellowish and black, and arboreal. Two-toed (*Cyclopes*) is squirrel-sized with silky yellow fur. See also PANGOLIN.

antelope, hoofed ruminant mammal, order Artiodactyla, family Bovidae or, in some classifications, family Antilopidae. True antelopes confined to Asia and Africa. African include bushbuck, waterbuck, lechwe, marshbuck, impala or palla, kudu, nyala, springbuck, bongo, dik-dik, klipspringer, ELAND, GNU. Nilgai or blue bull, four-horned antelope, and black buck in India. See also GAZELLE; PRONGHORN; ROCKY MOUNTAIN GOAT.

antenna (ăntĕn′ŭ) or **aerial** (âr′ēŭl), in radio, system of wires or metal bars to project or intercept radio waves. Frequency characteristic is based on wire length which is inherently tuned to radio wave of same length or simple fraction of it. Because of property of directivity of antenna arrays (except vertical conductors), more efficient transmission obtained by concentrating signal in desired area. Specially built antenna are needed for specific circuit requirements of television.

Antenor (ăntē′nŭr), fl. last half of 6th cent. B.C., Greek sculptor. Did bronze statues of Harmodius and Aristogiton.

anthem, short sacred choral composition. Arose in the Anglican church as English counterpart of the Latin motet. Important names in its history are Thomas Tallis, William Byrd, Henry Purcell, Handel, and Mendelssohn. Term also used for any hymn of praise or jubilation; hence, "national anthem."

Anthemius of Tralles (ănthē′mēŭs, trāl′ĕz), 6th cent., Greek architect and mathematician. With Isidorus of Miletus he built the church of HAGIA SOPHIA in Constantinople, A.D. 532–37.

Anthony, Saint (ăn′tūnē, –thŭnē), 251?–c.350, Egyptian hermit. In the desert he resisted temptations of devil. Colony of hermits grew about his retreat. Feast: Jan. 17.

Anthony, Marc, Roman soldier: see ANTONY.

Anthony, Susan B(rownell) (ăn′thŭnē), 1820–1906, American reformer, leader of woman-suffrage movement. Founder of Daughters of Temperance. Coorganizer (1863) of Women's Loyal League to support Lincoln's government, especially emancipation policy. With Elizabeth Cady Stanton she secured first laws in N.Y. giving women rights over their children and property, and with Mrs. Stanton organized Natl. Woman Suffrage Association. She helped compile a history of the woman-suffrage movement and was president (1892–1900) of the Natl. American Woman Suffrage Association.

Anthony of Padua, Saint, 1195–1231, Portuguese Franciscan. In a vision he received the child Jesus in his arms, and is usually so depicted in art. Canonized 1232. Invoked to find lost articles. Feast: June 13.

anthracene (ăn′thrŭsēn), colorless, crystalline solid with blue fluorescence, melting at 217°C. and boiling at c.350°C. Molecule has 14 carbon and 10 hydrogen atoms; carbons are arranged in three benzene rings set side by side and interlocking, with hydrogen atoms attached at each corner. Is obtained from coal tar and its derivatives are used in producing certain dyes. It is first member of anthracene series of aromatic hydrocarbons.

anthrax, infectious bacterial disease of animals transmissible to man by contact. Causative bacillus may exist as spore for years. Koch proved relation of bacillus to the disease; Pasteur developed method of vaccinating sheep and cattle against it. See *ill.*, p. 813.

anthropology (ănthrŭpŏl'ŭjē), science of man and his works. Concerned with the origin, development, and varieties of mankind and CULTURE, emphasizing data from nonliterate peoples. Physical and cultural anthropology are the two major divisions. Cultural anthropology includes ARCHAEOLOGY, the study of extinct cultures; ethnology, the study of living cultures; and linguistics.

anthropometry (ănthrŭpŏm'ŭtrē), measurement of human body and its parts for studies in race classification, growth, and human paleontology.

Antibes (ătēb'), town (pop. 13,778), Alpes-Maritime dept., SE France; a Mediterranean port. Near-by Cap d'Antibes is a fashionable resort.

antibiotic substances (ăn"tēbīŏ'tĭk), substances obtained from living organisms and inhibiting growth of or destroying certain microorganisms. Used in treatment of human diseases are PENICILLIN; streptomycin, discovered by S. A. Waksman and associate (1943); chloromycetin; and aureomycin. R. J. Dubos isolated (1939) first antibiotic substance (composed of gramicidin and tyrocidine) from soil bacteria.

antibody, specific substance produced by tissues when stimulated by an antigen (e.g., bacteria, toxins, foreign proteins) and capable of neutralizing or giving immunity against a specific antigen.

Antichrist, in Christian belief, person who will lead forces of evil on earth against ultimately victorious forces of good. 1 John 2.18–22; 4.3; 2 John 7. Often identified with Beast of Revelation; wrongly linked to Satan. Christians have tended to call opponents of their particular beliefs the Antichrist.

Anti-Comintern Pact: see COMINTERN and AXIS.

Anti-Corn-Law League, organization formed 1839 to work for repeal of English CORN LAWS. Its leading figures were Richard COBDEN and John BRIGHT.

Anticosti, island (pop. 424), 140 mi. long, 30 mi. wide, E Que., Canada, at mouth of St. Lawrence R. Lumbering is main industry. Discovered by Cartier 1534. Granted to Jolliet and long held by his heirs. Now belongs to paper interests.

Antietam campaign (ăntē'tŭm), Sept., 1862, of Civil War. In invasion of Md. and Pa., R. E. Lee sent Stonewall Jackson to take Harpers Ferry and moved toward Hagerstown. Harpers Ferry taken Sept. 15, but Gen. G. B. McClellan on Sept. 14 stopped Lee, who fell back to Sharpsburg (c.9 mi. W of South Mt.), behind Antietam Creek. Sept. 17 was bloodiest day of war, a Union victory only in that Lee was stopped.

antifreezing solution, aqueous solution with freezing point below that of water used in automobile cooling systems. Solutions include alcohol (evaporates rapidly); salt (formerly used; highly corrosive); glycerin or glycerol (sluggish at low temperatures); and ethylene glycol (acts upon rubber).

antifriction metal, ALLOY used to line machinery bearings when ball bearings are not used. Consists of soft matrix in which hard particles are embedded. See also BABBITT METAL.

antigen: see ANTIBODY.

Antigo (ăn'tĭgō), city (pop. 9,902), NE Wis., NE of Wausau. Produces dairy and wood products.

Antigone (ăntĭ'gŭnē), in Greek legend, daughter of Oedipus. When CREON forbade burial of her brother POLYNICES, she defied him and performed the funeral rites. Creon buried her alive.

Antigonish (ăn"tĭgōnĭsh'), town (pop. 3,196), NE N.S., Canada, on West R. and NE of Truro. Seat of St. Francis Xavier Univ. (R.C.; for men and women; 1853) which has promoted a noted cooperative here.

Antigonus (ăntĭ'gŭnŭs), rulers of anc. Macedon. **Antigonus I** (Cyclops), 382?–301 B.C., general of Alexander the Great and ruler in Asia. He tried to rebuild the entire empire, but in the wars of the DIADOCHI he was defeated and killed at Ipsus (301). His son, Demetrius I, conquered Macedonia. Demetrius' son, **Antigonus II** (Gonatas), c.320–239 B.C., took Macedon 276, rebuilt the state and amid much warfare briefly united Greece. Succeeded by Demetrius II. **Antigonus III** (Doson), d. 221 B.C., was regent for Demetrius' son, PHILIP V, but proclaimed himself king (227). Aided the Achaean League against Cleomenes and rebuilt power in Greece.

Antigua (ăntē'gwŭ), city (pop. 10,691), S central Guatemala, a commercial and tourist center. Founded 1542 to succeed Ciudad Vieja as cap. In 18th cent. had much splendor. Earthquakes caused removal of cap. to Guatemala City (1776).

Antigua (ăntē'gwŭ), island, area 108 sq. mi. British West Indies, chief island of Antigua presidency (pop. 40,778) in LEEWARD ISLANDS; cap. SAINT JOHN'S. Discovered by Columbus 1493, settled by British 1632.

Anti-Lebanon, mountain range between Syria and Lebanon, rising to Mt. HERMON.

Antilles: see WEST INDIES.

Anti-Masonic party, American political organization which rose after the disappearance in W N.Y. in 1826 of William Morgan. The Masons were said, without proof, to have murdered him, and in reaction local organizations arose to refuse support to Masons for public office. At Baltimore, in 1831 Anti-Masons held first national nominating convention of any party and issued first writ ten party platform. Helped in 1834 to form Whig party.

antimony (ăn'tĭmō"nē), silver-white crystalline element (symbol = Sb [L. *stibium*]; see also ELEMENT, table), with properties of metal and nonmetal. Forms stibine, a poison gas with hydrogen; combines readily with oxygen, sulphur, phosphorus, and the halogens. Used in making BABBITT METAL, BRITANNIA METAL, TYPE METAL, castings, batteries, and medicines. Chief ore is STIBNITE. Detected by MARSH'S TEST.

antinomianism (ăntĭnō'mēŭnĭzŭm) [Gr.,= against law], belief in Christianity that Christians, redeemed by Christ and justified by faith, need not follow the moral law (esp. that of the Old Testament). Considered heretical by majority from early Christian days to accusation of Anne Hutchinson in colonial Mass. Only large sect to hold the doctrine was that of ANABAPTISTS.

Antinoüs (ăntī′nōŭs), c.110–130, favorite of Emperor Hadrian, b. Bithynia. Notable for his youthful beauty, he was drowned in the Nile. Hadrian honored his memory by naming cities after him and having him deified.

Antioch or **Antakya** (äntäkyä′), town (pop. 30,385), S Turkey, on Orontes R., at foot of Mt. Silpius. Founded c.300 B.C. by Seleucus I. At crossing of routes from the Euphrates to the sea and from El Bika to Asia Minor, it soon became one of world's largest trade centers. Here followers of Jesus were first called Christians. City is one of three ancient patriarchates: seat of a Melchite, a Maronite, and a Jacobite patriarch. Fell to Persians 538 and to Arabs 637. Was under Byzantine Empire 969–1085 and under Seljuk Turks 1085–98. Taken 1098 by Crusaders, it became virtually independent fief of Latin Kingdom of Jerusalem under BOHEMOND I and successors. Fell to Mamelukes of Egypt 1268 and to Ottoman Turks 1516. Transferred to Syria 1920 but restored to Turkey 1939. Modern Antioch occupies mere fraction of ancient city, remains of whose walls, aqueduct, theater, and castle survive. Excavations here and at near-by Daphne have yielded splendid mosaics. An early find was Great Chalice of Antioch, held by many to be Holy Grail.

Antioch, town (pop. 11,051), W Calif., on San Joaquin R.; founded 1849–50. Central Valley project power plant is here.

Antioch College, at Yellow Springs, Ohio; nonsectarian, coed.; opened 1853, with Horace Mann as president. Pioneered in plan by which students alternate study with full-time work.

Antiochus (ăntī′ŭkŭs), kings of anc. Syria. **Antiochus I** (Soter), d. c.261 B.C. (reigned 280–c.261 B.C.), was son of Seleucus I. **Antiochus II** (Theos), d. 247 B.C. (reigned c.261–247 B.C.). Rivalry with PTOLEMY II ended with marriage to Ptolemy's daughter Berenice, but warfare followed his death. **Antiochus III** (the Great), d. 187 B.C. (reigned 223–187 B.C.), son of Seleucus II, tried to restore crumbling Seleucid empire. An ally of Philip V, he won much territory, but was crushed by the Romans at Thermopylae (191) and Magnesia (190). **Antiochus IV** (Epiphanes), d. 163 B.C. (reigned 175–163 B.C.), son of Antiochus III, successor of his brother, Seleucus IV. Attempted to Hellenize Judaea, arousing MACCABEES. His invasion of Egypt was thwarted by the Romans.

Antiope (ăntī′ŭpē), in Greek legend. **1** Daughter of king of Boeotia. Visited by Zeus in form of satyr, she bore him Amphion and Zethus. **2** Sister of Hippolyte, queen of the Amazons. In one legend, she is mother of Hippolytus by Theseus.

Antipas: see HEROD.

Antipater (ăntī′pŭtŭr), d. 319 B.C., Macedonian general under Alexander the Great, regent in Macedon (334–323 B.C.). Opposed PERDICCAS and later held the kingdom to-

gether. After his death came wars of the DIADOCHI.

Antipater, in Bible: see HEROD.

Antiphilus (ăntĭf′ĭlŭs), fl. 4th cent. B.C., Greek artist, of Egyptian origin. Painted portraits of Philip of Macedon and Alexander the Great.

antipope, one supposed to be pope but not subsequently recognized by Holy See. See, e.g., GUIBERT OF RAVENNA; LUNA, PEDRO DE; COSSA, BALDASSARRE.

Anti-Saloon League, U.S. organization working for prohibition of sale of alcoholic liquors. Founded in Ohio 1893. Wielded great political influence.

anti-Semitism, sentiment against the JEWS. Pre-19th-cent. anti-Semitism, largely religious, was expressed in persecutions, expulsions, and restrictions (see GHETTO). The Jews were limited to such means of living as usury, and anti-Semitism became economic. After the 19th-cent. emancipation of Jews, "race" feeling, allied with rising nationalism, developed. All evils were blamed on the Jews, either by demagogues or by governments (as in Russia) to divert popular discontent. The "Protocols of the Wise Men of Zion," a spurious document purporting to outline a Jewish plan for world domination, appeared in early 20th-cent. Russia. The teachings of Gobineau and Houston Stewart Chamberlain were climaxed by pseudo-scientific doctrine of "Aryan" superiority in NATIONAL SOCIALISM. Hitler exterminated an estimated 6,000,000 European Jews between 1939 and 1945.

antiseptic, agent inhibiting growth of or destroying microorganisms. Influenced by Pasteur's theory that microorganisms cause infection, LISTER was first to use antiseptic in surgery. Modern techniques founded on asepsis (absence of pathogenic organisms).

antislavery movement: see SLAVERY; ABOLITIONISTS.

Anti-Taurus, Turkish mountain range: see TAURUS.

antitoxin: see TOXIN.

Anti-Trust Act: see CLAYTON ANTI-TRUST ACT; SHERMAN ANTI-TRUST ACT.

Antium, Italy: see ANZIO.

Antofagasta (äntōfägä′stä), city (pop. 43,318), N Chile; a Pacific port. Its founding by Chileans (1870) in Bolivian territory was a cause of war (see PACIFIC, WAR OF THE). Nitrates and copper are chief exports.

Antoine, André (ädrä′ ätwän′), 1858–1943, French theatrical manager. Formed Théâtre Libre company 1887 and presented works of naturalist school. His work became a model for European and American experimental theaters.

Antonello da Messina (äntōnĕl′lō dä mäs-sē′nä), c.1430–c.1479, one of the first Italian painters to utilize Flemish technique of oil painting.

Antonescu, Ion (yôn äntônĕ′skŏo), 1882–1946, Rumanian marshal and dictator. Appointed premier 1940; forced abdication of Carol II in favor of King MICHAEL; brought Rumania into AXIS camp; gave Hitler virtual control of country. Arrested 1944; executed.

Antonines (ăn′tŭnīnz), name used for several 2d-cent. Roman emperors including Antonius Pius, Marcus Aurelius, and Commodus.

Antoninus, Wall of, ancient Roman wall built across N Britain in reign of Antoninus Pius —probably A.D. 140–42. It was 37 mi. long.

Antoninus Pius (ăntōnī′nŭs pī′ŭs), A.D. 86– A.D. 161, Roman emperor (138–161). Adopted by HADRIAN, he succeeded and administered the empire well. Succeeded by his adopted son, MARCUS AURELIUS.

Antony or Marc Antony, Latin *Marcus Antonius,* c.83 B.C.–30 B.C., Roman political leader and general. A dashing young soldier of good family, he became a protégé of Julius Caesar, and as tribune he (with Cassius) vetoed the bill to strip Caesar of his army. After serving as Caesar's lieutenant in the Civil War against Pompey, he gained power from the victory. Caesar was assassinated in 44 B.C., and Antony roused the people against the conspirators responsible. He formed an uneasy alliance with Octavian (later AUGUSTUS), was embroiled in trouble trying to gain the province of Gaul assigned to him, and was a member of the Second Triumvirate (Octavian, Lepidus, Antony). He and Octavian defeated the republicans at Philippi (42 B.C.), and in the proscription that followed Antony brought about the death of his enemy Cicero. Antony undertook to rule Asia. In Rome his wife, Fulvia, intrigued against Octavian, but she died, and Antony married Octavian's sister, Octavia. The alliance went on. Antony had, however, already met Cleopatra and fallen under her sway; he ruled from Alexandria in great luxury. Octavian grew impatient, and Antony was deprived of power. Civil war followed. Antony and Cleopatra were defeated in the naval battle at Actium (31 B.C.) and fled to Alexandria. When Octavian approached, Antony committed suicide. He is known to English-speaking people largely through Shakspere's *Julius Caesar* and *Antony and Cleopatra.* Also Marc or Mark Anthony.

Antrim, maritime county (1,098 sq. mi; pop. 231,099, excluding Belfast), Ulster prov., Northern Ireland. County town is BELFAST, a major British port and chief industrial center of Ireland. Region mainly agr. with fishing and cattle breeding. E part of county mountainous. N coast has formation known as GIANT'S CAUSEWAY.

Antung (än′tŏong), industrial city (pop. 271,- 115), cap. Liaotung prov., Manchuria; port at mouth of Yalu R. Opened to foreign trade 1907.

Antwerp (ăn′twûrp), Flemish *Antwerpen,* Fr. *Anvers,* province (1,104 sq. mi.; pop. 1,296,- 687), N Belgium. It is a cultivated plain drained by Scheldt R. and Albert Canal. Population is largely Flemish-speaking. The province was part of the duchy of BRABANT. Its cap. is **Antwerp** (pop. 266,636; with suburbs 599,240), on the Scheldt. Rivaled only by Rotterdam as largest sea and transit port of continental Europe, Antwerp is also a world center of the diamond trade and industry and the seat of the oldest stock exchange (founded 1460). It has oil refineries, automobile plants, flour mills. Its churches and museums contain treasures of Flemish art. Rising into prominence with the decline

of Bruges and Ghent, Antwerp was by the 16th cent. the commercial and financial hub of Europe. Its prosperity suffered a fatal blow when it was sacked by mutinous Spanish troops (the "Spanish Fury," 1576), but it resisted for 14 months before surrendering to the Spanish under Alexander Farnese (1584–85). The Peace of Westphalia (1648) closed the Scheldt to navigation. Antwerp was reduced to insignificance until 1863, when Belgium redeemed from the Dutch the right to collect a toll on Scheldt shipping. The city suffered in both world wars. Captured by British troops in Aug., 1944, it became a vital Allied supply base and was heavily damaged by German rocket weapons. Antwerp was the home of Rubens and the birthplace of Sir Anthony Van Dyck. Among its many splendid buildings are the Gothic Cathedral of Notre Dame and the old guild houses on the Groote Market [market place]. The zoological garden has long been world famous.

Anuradhapura (ûnŏō′rädùpŏō′rû), town (pop. 12,287), N Ceylon. On the site of an ancient cap. (4th cent. B.C.–8th cent. A.D.) of Ceylon. A great Buddhist center, it has ruins of large stupas and the Brazen Palace. Buddhist pilgrims visit bo tree, grown from slip of tree at Buddh Gaya.

Anville, Jean Baptiste Bourguignon d' (bŏōr- gēnyŏ′ dävēl′), 1697–1782, French geographer and cartographer. Noted for accurate maps of ancient geography; had largest collection of maps, atlases, and geographic material in France.

Anyox (ă′nĕŏks″), village, W B.C., Canada, NNE of Prince Rupert. Center for copper mining and smelting, with large pyrite smelter.

Anza, Juan Bautista de (hwän′boutēs′tä dä än′sä), 1735–88, Spanish explorer and official in Southwest and Far West, founder of San Francisco. b. Mexico. Governor of New Mexico 1777–88.

Anzengruber, Ludwig (lŏōt′vīkh än′tsüngrŏō″- bûr), 1839–89, Austrian author of successful folk plays. *Das vierte Gebot* [the fourth commandment] is considered one of first naturalistic plays.

Anzio (än′tsyō), Latin *Antium,* town (pop. 5,989), Latium, central Italy, on Tyrrhenian Sea. Bathing resort since Roman times; important Roman ruins. Scene of fierce fighting between Allied beachhead forces and Germans, Jan.–May, 1944.

Aomori (äōmô′rē), city (pop. 90,828), extreme N Honshu, Japan; chief port of N Honshu.

Aosta, Val d' (väldäō′stä), autonomous region (1,260 sq. mi.; pop. 83,455), NW Italy, on French and Swiss borders. Includes Gran Paradiso and Italian slopes of Mont Blanc, Matterhorn, Monte Rosa; many resorts. Most of pop. speaks French dialect. The capital is **Aosta** (pop. 13,466), near junction of Great and Little St. Bernard roads.

Apache Indians (ùpäch′ē), Indian people of U.S. Southwest, speaking Athapascan languages (see LANGUAGE, table). Divided into many groups. Chiefly known for fierce opposition (late 19th cent.) to white intrusion into N.Mex. and Ariz. Notable leaders were Geronimo and Cochise.

Apalachee Bay (ăpǔlăch'ē), a Gulf of Mexico arm (c.30 mi. wide), NW Fla., S of Tallahassee.

Apalachicola (ăp″ŭlăchĭkō'lǔ), city (pop. 3,222), NW Fla., SW of Tallahassee, on Apalachicola Bay (bridged 1935); founded c.1820. Seafood (oysters, shrimp). Its important cotton-shipping activities (after 1830) were adversely affected by Civil War blockade. City is at mouth of the **Apalachicola**, navigable river formed by junction of Chattahoochee and Flint rivers at Ga. line and flowing 112 mi. S to the bay.

apatite (ăp'ǔtīt), calcium phosphate mineral containing fluorine, chlorine, or both. Colorless when pure; impure colored types sometimes cut as gem stones. Used in making phosphorus fertilizers.

ape, usually name for primates most closely resembling man (GORILLA, CHIMPANZEE, ORANGUTAN, GIBBON). These lack external tails, cheek pouches, ischial callosites (except gibbon); stand semierectly. Brain structure similar to man. Name was once used for tailless monkeys or as synonym for monkey.

Apeldoorn (ä'pǔldōrn), municipality (pop. 62,876), and town, Gelderland prov., E central Netherlands. Produces pharmaceuticals, refrigerators, papers. Royal summer palace of Het Loo is near by.

Apelles (ǔpěl'ēz), fl. 4th cent. B.C., Greek painter, the most celebrated of antiquity, but now known only through descriptions of his works. Court painter to Philip and Alexander.

Apennines (ă'pǔnīnz), mountain system traversing entire Italian peninsula. Mts. of Sicily are a continuation. Highest peak (9,560 ft.) in Gran Sasso d'Italia group. Extensive pastures. Forests (chestnut, birch, oak, pine) much reduced by erosion.

aphid (ē'fĭd, ăf'ĭd) or **plant louse,** parasitic insect, also called green fly and blight. Injures vegetation. Species seen on field plants is soft-bodied, green, with long legs, antennae, two pairs membranous wings (some wingless). Reproductive cycle varies with species; many lay fertilized eggs in fall which hatch in spring or summer into stem mothers. These produce several generations by PARTHENOGENESIS. Winged descendants migrate to other host plants to continue cycle. Numbers reduced by other insects, fungi, damp weather. See also GALL.

Aphrodite (ăfrǔdī'tē), in Greek religion. Olympian goddess of love, beauty, and fertility; wife of Hephaestus. Daughter of Zeus and Dione or of the sea into which blood of Uranus fell. Mother of Eros by Ares, of Aeneas by Anchises, and of Priapus by Dionysus. As goddess of fertility she is closely linked with ADONIS. Known also as Aphrodite Urania; her worship may have been imported from Orient, and she is akin to Astarte or Ishtar. Identified with Roman Venus. By awarding Aphrodite APPLE OF DISCORD, Paris won Helen and thus caused Trojan War.

Apo, Mount (ä'pō), active volcano, 9,690 ft.

high, on S Mindanao; highest peak of the Philippines.

apocalypse (ǔpŏk'ǔlĭps) [Gr.,= uncovering], type of ancient Hebrew and Christian prophetic literature, usually written in veiled symbolism and inspired by visions (e.g., FOUR HORSEMEN OF THE APOCALYPSE). The biblical REVELATION is often called simply the Apocalypse.

Apocrypha (ǔpŏk'rĭfǔ) [Gr.,= hidden things], appendix to Authorized Version of Old Testament containing following books or parts of books: 1 and 2 ESDRAS; TOBIT; JUDITH; ESTHER 10.4–16; WISDOM; ECCLESIASTICUS; BARUCH; Dan. 3.24–90 (see DANIEL and THREE HOLY CHILDREN); Dan. 13 (see SUSANNA); Dan. 14 (see BEL AND THE DRAGON); Prayer of Manasses (see MANASSEH 2); 1 and 2 MACCABEES. All but Prayer of Manasses, 1 and 2 Esdras considered canonical by Roman Catholics (Council of Trent, 1546). Protestants regard Apocrypha valuable for instruction but not canonical (see OLD TESTAMENT). For Jewish and Christian works resembling biblical books but not included in Western or Hebrew canon, see PSEUDEPIGRAPHA.

Apodaca, Juan Ruiz de (hwän' rōōēth' dä äpōdhä'kä), 1754–1835, last viceroy of New Spain (1816–21).

Apollinaire, Guillaume (gēyōm' äpōlēnär'), 1880–1918, French poet, b. Rome. Of illegitimate birth, he was christened Wilhelm Apollinaris de Kostrowitzky. His bizarre, exquisite poems (*Alcools,* 1913; *Calligrammes,* 1918) and his surrealistic drama, *Les Mamelles de Tirésias* (1918), were influential experiments. His art criticism promoted cubism.

Apollinarianism (ǔpŏlĭnâ'rēŭīzǔm), popular heretical doctrine of Apollinaris or Apollinarius (c.315–c.390) of Laodicea. Taught Christ possessed Logos in place of human mind. Anticipated MONOPHYSITISM.

Apollo (ǔpŏ'lō) or **Phoebus Apollo** (fē'bǔs), in Greek religion, Olympian god of light, music, poetry, pastoral pursuits, and prophecy. As god of music, the lyre was sacred to him (he was father of ORPHEUS). He was also god of healing and father of Asclepius. Identified with Helios as the sun-god. Son of Zeus and Leto, he (with twin sister ARTEMIS) was born in DELOS. At his temple in DELPHI, he was god of prophecy. Later he was best known as god of music and poetry, attended by MUSES. The **Apollo Belvedere** (běl″vīdēr'), a marble figure in the Vatican, Roman copy of Greek original in bronze, is best-known statue of him.

Apollodorus (ǔpŏl″ōdôr'ǔs), fl. c.415 B.C., Athenian painter, reputedly first to use light and shadow.

Apollonius of Perga, fl. 247–205 B.C., Greek mathematician of Alexandrian school. Treatise on conic sections included work of Euclid and others.

Apollonius of Tralles: see FARNESE BULL.

Apollonius Rhodius (rō'dēǔs), 3d cent. B.C., epic poet, librarian at Alexandria, author of *Argonautica.*

Apollyon (ǔpŏl'yǔn), Greek name of the destroying angel. Rev. 9.11. See SATAN and HELL.

Apopka, Lake (ŭpŏp'kû), central Fla.; fishing. Winter Garden is on S shore.

apoplexy or **stroke,** result of cerebral hemorrhage. Often accompanied by coma and followed by partial paralysis abating as blood clot is resorbed.

apostle (ûpŏs'ûl) [Gr.,= envoy], one of prime missionaries of Christendom. The chief 12: PETER, ANDREW, JAMES (the Greater), JOHN, THOMAS, JAMES (the Less), JUDE (or Thaddeus), PHILIP, BARTHOLOMEW (may be same as Nathanael), MATTHEW, SIMON, and MATTHIAS (replacing JUDAS ISCARIOT). Traditional list of Twelve Disciples includes Judas and not Matthias, list of Twelve Apostles includes Matthias and not Judas. Number originally symbolic of 12 tribes of Israel. St. PAUL is always classed a chief apostle though not of the 12. Name also given to others such as St. BARNABAS. For Apostles' Creed, see CREED; see also DIDACHE.

Apostle Islands, group of over 20 islands, off N Wis., in SW L. Superior. Connected with Wis. mainland by boat. Have noted waveeroded cliffs. Madeline, the largest, includes LA POINTE town.

Apostolic Constitutions: see CONSTITUTIONS, APOSTOLIC.

apostolic succession, in some Christian churches, belief that the position of the apostles of Christ has been transmitted from generation to generation in unbroken succession so that the bishops of today are the true inheritors of the power of the apostles. This is stoutly denied in churches that do not recognize any episcopacy. The apostolic succession is to be distinguished from the doctrine of Petrine supremacy (see PAPACY).

Apoxyomenus (ûpŏk"sēŏm'ĭnŭs) [Gr.,= scraping one's self], Roman copy in marble of a bronze statue by LYSIPPUS. Represents an athlete.

Appalachian Mountains (ăpûlá'chŭn), great mountain system of E North America, extending SW from St. Lawrence valley in Quebec prov., Canada, to Gulf Coast plain in Ala., and rising to 6,684 ft. in Mt. MITCHELL. They include WHITE MOUNTAINS, GREEN MOUNTAINS, CATSKILL MOUNTAINS, ALLEGHENY MOUNTAINS, BLUE RIDGE, GREAT SMOKY MOUNTAINS, and other ranges. Mainly formed by folding (see MOUNTAIN), they consist largely of sedimentary rocks and are much eroded. W portions, less rugged than E portions, are largely plateau formations of horizontal rock structure. System has deposits of coal, iron, oil, and gas. With few passes, they barred early expansion W. Remote settlements in mountain valleys have preserved old ways of life more than any other U.S. region. Beautiful scenery and many resorts line system.

Appalachian Trail, for hikers, extending 2,050 mi. along ridges of Appalachian Mt. system from Mt. Katahdin, Maine, to Mt. Oglethorpe, N Ga.

appeal, process by which a superior court reviews errors allegedly committed by a lower court. If case had a jury trial only errors of law (i.e., in legal rules) may be reviewed; if trial had no jury, errors both of law and of fact (erroneous interpretation of evidence) may be reviewed.

appendix, vermiform, tubular outgrowth (c.3 in. long) of large intestine, in lower right abdomen, probably vestigial remnant. Infection may result in **appendicitis,** usually making imperative the removal of appendix; use of cathartics entails risk of rupture of appendix and spread of infection (see PERITONITIS).

Appenzell (ä'pûntsĕl), canton, E Switzerland. Mostly meadowland; textile mfg. Ruled by abbots of St. Gall after 11th cent., rebelled 1403; joined Swiss Confederation 1513. In 1597 Appenzell split into two independent half-cantons. Ausser-Rhoden (94 sq. mi.; pop. 48,026; cap. Herisau) accepted Reformation. Inner-Rhoden (67 sq. mi.; pop. 13,448) remained Catholic; its cap., Appenzell (pop. 4,983), has noted embroidery mfg.

Appian (ă'pēûn), fl. 2d cent., Roman historian. His history of Roman conquests reproduces documents and sources otherwise lost. Of 24 books, in Greek, only VI–VII and XI–XVII are fully preserved.

Appian Way, Latin *Via Appia,* road built under Appius Claudius Caecus (312 B.C.). Connecting Rome with Brundisium, it was chief highway to Greece and the provinces in Asia.

apple, best known and commercially most important fruit of temperate zones and its tree, *Malus sylvestris,* member of rose family. Cultivated from prehistoric times. Long lived and easy to grow. North America leads in apple production. See also CRAB APPLE.

Appleby, county town (pop. 1,704), Westmorland, England; site of historic Appleby Castle.

applejack, brandy made from hard cider or fermented apple pomace, the residue from cider making.

apple of discord, in Greek mythology, a golden apple inscribed "for the fairest," thrown by uninvited ERIS among guests at wedding of Peleus and Thetis. It was claimed by Aphrodite, Athena, and Hera. Paris, selected to decide, chose Aphrodite, who offered him the fairest of women, Helen. His abduction of Helen caused TROJAN WAR.

Appleseed, Johnny: see CHAPMAN, JOHN.

Appleton, Daniel, 1785–1849, American publisher, founder of a large publishing house.

Appleton, Sir Edward Victor, 1892–, English physicist. Won 1947 Nobel Prize for studies of ionosphere which led to development of radar.

Appleton, city (pop. 34,010), E Wis., on Fox R., near its exit from L. Winnebago, in dairying and stock-raising region; settled before 1850. Mfg. of paper, wool, and wood products. Had first U.S. hydroelectric plant. Seat of Lawrence Col. of Wisconsin (nonsectarian, coed. [pioneer]; chartered 1847, opened 1849 with grant from A. A. Lawrence), with affiliated Inst. of Paper Chemistry.

Appomattox (ăpŭmă'tûks), town (pop. 1,094), central Va., E of Lynchburg, near source of Appomattox R. R. E. Lee surrendered to U. S. Grant at near-by **Appomattox Courthouse,** April 9, 1865. Retreating from Petersburg and Richmond, Lee was cut off here by P. H. Sheridan and yielded. This was end of war, as other Southern armies followed suit.

apprenticeship, system of learning a trade by paying with years of work for instruction from one skilled in the trade. Known in ancient world, the system was also part of medieval guild system. Apprenticeship less widespread after Industrial Revolution, but it survives in highly skilled trades. Typically apprentice becomes journeyman (working for master for wages), finally master.

APRA: see HAYA DE LA TORRE, VÍCTOR RAÚL; PERU.

Apra Harbor (ä'prä) or **Port Apra,** in Sumay town, W Guam; U.S. naval base. Port is closed to foreign vessels except by permit.

apricot, a tree, *Prunus armeniaca,* and its orange-colored fruit. It is a commercial crop in California.

Apries (ā'prē-ēz), king of anc. Egypt (588–569 B.C.), of the XXVI dynasty. Succeeded Psamtik II and sought to recover Syria and Palestine from NEBUCHADNEZZAR. Murdered by Amasis II.

April: see MONTH.

Apsheron, Azerbaijan SSR: see BAKU.

Apuleius, Lucius (ă"pyōōlē'ŭs), fl. 2d cent., Latin writer. His novel, *Golden Ass* or *Metamorphoses,* strongly influenced the later novel.

Apulia (ŭpū'lēŭ), Ital. *Puglia* (pōō'lyä), region (7,469 sq. mi.; pop. 2,642,076), S Italy, occupying southernmost third of Italian E coast; cap. Bari. In anc. times only N part of region was called Apulia. Cities: Bari, Brindisi, Foggia, Taranto, Lecce. Wine, olives, almonds, corn are grown despite scarcity of water. Sheep and goat raising. Conquered (11th–12th cent.) from Byzantines by Normans, who made it a powerful duchy, it later became part of kingdom of Naples.

Aquae Sextiae: see AIX-EN-PROVENCE.

aquamarine, transparent BERYL with blue to blue-green tint. Found in Brazil, Ceylon, Germany, Siberia, and U.S. Similar to emerald save for color.

aquarium, tank, bowl, artificial pond, or museum for aquatic animals and plants, preferably rectangular, with no copper, brass, zinc, or galvanized iron in contact with water. Tanks with new wood or concrete should be filled with water and changed at intervals for several weeks before putting in fish. Green aquarium plants are valuable oxygenators. A properly set up and unpolluted aquarium rarely needs complete change of water, only replacement of loss by evaporation.

Aquarius [Lat.,= water bearer], 11th sign of ZODIAC.

aqueduct (ă'kwŭdŭkt), channel or trough conveying water, usually fresh water to a city. First used probably in Mesopotamia; greatly developed later by Romans. Aqueduct to present Mexico city built by Mayas before Spanish Conquest. Aqueducts carry water to many large U.S. cities from great distances.

Aquidneck (ŭkwĭd'nĭk), Indian and early colonial name of Rhode Island (the isl. in Narragansett Bay).

Aquila or **Aquila degli Abruzzi** (ä'kwēlä dā'lyē äbrōōt'sē), city (pop. 20,573), cap. of Abruzzi e Molise region, S central Italy, below Gran Sasso d'Italia; medieval architecture.

Aquila Ponticus (pŏn'tĭkŭs), 2d cent., Jewish translator of Old Testament from Hebrew into Greek. Much used by Jews. No complete specimen exists.

Aquilegia: see COLUMBINE.

Aquileia (äkwēlä'yä), town (pop. 1,116), Friuli-Venezia Giulia, NE Italy, near Adriatic. Founded 181 B.C.; important Roman stronghold; see of patriarchate, 6th–18th cent. Early Romanesque basilica has splendid mosaic floor. Grado, on near-by island, is a bathing resort.

Aquinas, Saint Thomas: see THOMAS AQUINAS, SAINT.

Aquitaine (ăk'wĭtān), former duchy, SW France; historic cap., Bordeaux. Frontiers shifted often. A Roman prov., it passed to Visigoths (5th cent.), then to Franks (507), and was a kingdom (781–838) under Charlemagne's son Louis, and grandson Pepin. Late in 9th cent. it emerged as duchy, enfeoffed to French crown. It grew powerful and came to include most of SW and S central France. Second marriage (1152) of ELEANOR OF AQUITAINE started French-English struggle over duchy; Hundred Years War gave France victory. See also GUIENNE; GASCONY.

Arabia, peninsula (c.1,000,000 sq. mi.; pop. 12,000,000), SW Asia, between Red Sea and Gulf of Aqaba on W and Persian Gulf and Gulf of Oman on E. Bounded on S by Arabian Sea and Gulf of Aden. Occupied by SAUDI ARABIA, YEMEN, British protectorates of Aden, Bahrein, Kuwait, Oman, Qatar, and Trucial Oman, and British colony of Aden. Mainly desert; more habitable areas in HEJAZ, NEJD, and the SW (only section fit for extensive agriculture). Pastoral nomads raise goats and sheep. Rich oil fields (exploited by European and American firms) are in E. Much of ancient Arabia was divided between domains of Ma'in and SHEBA. Ethiopia twice held S coast (HADRAMAUT) and Yemen (300–378, 525–70). In 7th cent. dynamic faith of MOHAMMED the Prophet unified Arab tribes, inspiring them to conquer neighboring states. OMAYYAD caliphate conquered Persia but was checked in E by Byzantines and in W by defeat in battle of Tours, France (732). After removal of seat of caliphate from Medina to Damascus, Arabia again lost political cohesion. Nominally ruled after 1517 by Ottoman Turks, harassed 18th–19th cent. by WAHABI movement. Turkish rule was broken during World War I by IBN SAUD and HUSEIN IBN ALI.

Arabian art and architecture: see MOSLEM ART AND ARCHITECTURE.

Arabian music, term used popularly to include the music of all Islamic peoples. It is related to Greek, Hebrew, and Hindu music. Present-day scale has 17 notes. Rhythms are provided by the meters of poetry. Its principal form is the *nuba,* which is a sort of cantata, in nine parts, some of which are instrumental, some vocal. Chief instruments are a long lute and a short lute; influence of Arabian music on that of Europe lies mainly in the introduction of the lute by the Moors in Spain.

Arabian Nights: see THOUSAND AND ONE NIGHTS.

Arabian Sea, NW part of Indian Ocean, lying between Arabia and India.

Arabic language, Semitic language, one of most widely spoken languages in the world. See LANGUAGE (table).

Arabic literature. Golden age of lyric poets (Amru-l-Kais, Antar, Zuhair) lasted from 4th to 7th cent. It was marked by personal odes about love, fighting, and hunting, with references to power of God. These survive only in the collections MUALLAQAT, HAMASA, and MOFADDALIYAT. KORAN supplanted poetry (decried by Mohammed) until Arabic-Persian cultural renascence under Abbasids at Baghdad (8th–9th cent). New court poetry of Abu-l-Atahiya and Abu Nuwas soon became precious, as in poetry of Hariri (11th cent.). Prose romances, notably THOUSAND AND ONE NIGHTS, superseded poetry. They show Hindu and Persian influence but are essentially Arabic in form. Bukhari, Tabari, Masudi, Ibn Khaldun, and Ibn Batuta are noted for historical and geographical writing. Omayyad Spain fostered vigorous Arabic literature; its great philosophers were Avempace, Averroës, and Ibn Tufail. Since 1300 there has been little Arabic literature of wide interest.

Arab League, association of countries predominantly Arabic in descent. Protocol calling for it was signed 1944 at Alexandria. Constitution drafted 1945 at Cairo was accepted by Egypt, Syria, Lebanon, Trans-Jordan, Iraq, Saudi Arabia, and Yemen. A representative of Palestinian Arabs also has a vote in the League. Charter provides for coordination on domestic and foreign policies and forbids use of force to settle disputes among members. League countries joined in unsuccessful attack on new state of Israel in 1948.

Arachne (ŭrăk′nē) [Gr.,= spider], in Greek legend, girl who challenged Athena to a trial of skill in weaving. The goddess changed her into a spider.

Arad (äräd′), city (pop. 87,291), W Rumania, on Mures R. and near Hungarian border. Commercial and mfg. center (flour, leather, machinery). Population c.40% Hungarian.

Aradus (ăr′ŭdŭs), islet and town of anc. Phoenicia, the modern Ruad, N of Tripoli off Syrian coast, most important of N Phoenician centers. Called Arvad in Old Testament.

Arafat (äräfät′), granite hill, Saudi Arabia, near Mecca. Mohammed's stop here on his flight from Mecca to Medina is commemorated by pilgrims.

Arafura Sea (ärŭfoō′rŭ), part of the Pacific between Australia and New Guinea.

Aragats, Mount (ärŭgăts′), or **Mount Alagez** (ŭlŭgyôs′), extinct volcano, 13,435 ft. high, Armenian SSR. Astrophysical research center.

Aragon, Louis (lwē′ ärägō′), 1897–, French poet and novelist. Onetime Dadaist and surrealist and later a Communist and leader of wartime resistance. Le Crève-Cœur (1941) is among his best poetry.

Aragon (ă′rŭgŏn), Span. Aragón (ärägōn′), region (18,382 sq. mi.; pop. 1,058,806) and former kingdom, NE Spain, in E Pyrenees and Ebro plain; historic cap. Saragossa. Other cities: Huesca, Teruel. Region is arid and sparsely populated, but irrigated areas yield cereals, wine, olives, sugar beets. Sheep and cattle raising. Kingdom was created (1035) out of W part of Navarre for Ramiro I. It grew at expense of emirate of SARAGOSSA and was united, by personal union, with Catalonia after 1137. Union of Aragon with Castile began in 1469 through marriage of Ferdinand and Isabella.

Aragon, house of, family which ruled in Aragon, CATALONIA, MAJORCA, SICILY, the kingdom of NAPLES, SARDINIA, ROUSSILLON, ATHENS, and other lands in Middle Ages; founded by RAMIRO I. Aragon and Catalonia were in personal union after 1137, but the other territories were generally ruled separately by branches of the house. Alfonso V, who conquered Naples in 1442, temporarily united all Aragonese dominions. The marriage of Ferdinand II of Aragon with Isabella of Castile led to union of the two kingdoms. In their grandson, Emperor CHARLES V, the houses of Aragon and Castile were merged with that of Hapsburg.

Arakan (ărŭkăn′), division (14,194 sq. mi.; pop. 1,152,733) of Lower Burma, on Bay of Bengal; cap. Akyab. Area was annexed 1784 by Burma, ceded 1826 to the British.

Arakcheyev, Aleksey Andreyevich (ŭlyĭksyä′ ŭndrä′yĭvĭch äräkchā′ĕf), 1769–1834, Russian general, minister of war under Alexander I. An extreme reactionary who greatly influenced his period.

Aral Sea (ä′rŭl, Rus. ŭräl′), inland sea (24,635 sq. mi.), USSR, in Kazakh SSR and Kara-Kalpak ASSR. Fed by Amu and Darya and Syr Darya rivers, it has no outlet, and is shallow, slightly saline. Fisheries.

Aram (ā′răm), an anc. people and their country, roughly identified with Syria. Their language a form of Aramaic. Bible records constant contacts between Hebrews and Aram.

Aram, Eugene, 1704–59, English philologist, hanged after discovery that he had murdered (1745) his friend Daniel Clark. This story was used for a poem by Thomas Hood, a novel by Bulwer-Lytton.

Aramaic (ărŭmā′ĭk), Semitic languages of Syria, flourishing in the centuries before and after Christ. See LANGUAGE (table).

Aranha, Oswaldo (ŭzhväl′dō ŭrä′nyù), 1894–, Brazilian statesman, ambassador to U.S. (1934–38), foreign minister (1938–44), president of General Assembly, United Nations (1947).

Aran Islands or **Arran Islands** (both: ăr′ŭn), in Galway Bay, Co. Galway, Ireland. The three islands are Inishmore, Inisheer, and Inishmaan. They are barren, and living conditions are primitive.

Aranjuez (äränghwäth′) town (pop. 21,771), central Spain, in New Castile, near the Tagus. Its palace, a royal residence since 16th cent., rebuilt 1727.

Aransas Pass (ŭrăn′zùs), city (pop. 5,396), S Texas, on Aransas Bay and NE of Corpus Christi. Port on deep-water ship channel passing through Harbor Isl., between St. Joseph and Mustang islands (Port Aransas) and emptying into Gulf of Mexico. Ships oil. Has carbon-black plant and fisheries.

Arany, John (ŏ'rŏnyŭ), Hung. *Arany János*, 1817–82, Hungarian epic poet, author of *Toldi* (1846).

Arapahoe Peak: see FRONT RANGE.

Arapaho Indians (ŭrăp'ŭhō), North American people, of Algonquian linguistic stock. Three main divisions are Gros Ventre (allied with Blackfoot), Southern Arapaho (allied with Cheyenne), and Northern Arapaho (considered the parent group). Ceremonial societies for different age groups are notable.

Ararat (ă'rŭrăt), region, W Turkey and E Armenian SSR, called Massis in Armenian, Aghri (or Egri) Dagh in Turkish, Koh-i-nuh in Persian. Identical with Armenia in many ancient records; Assyrians called it Urartu. Mt. Ararat (16,946 ft.) highest peak in Turkey; in the Bible, the landing place of Noah's ark.

Araucanian Indians (ä"rôkä'nëŭn, ä"rŭ-), South American people occupying much of present Chile at time of Spanish Conquest (1540). Opposition to Spanish under Pedro de VALDIVIA gave Araucanian leaders, Lautaro and CAUPOLICÁN, fame immortalized in epic of ERCILLA Y ZÚÑIGA. Resistance to whites ended in Chile in war of 1880–81. Araucanians who fled earlier to Argentina were subjugated 1883. Chief language: Mapuche.

Araunah (ârō'nŭ), man who sold his threshing floor to David who erected altar there. Site, on Mt. Moriah, later used for Temple. 2 Sam. 24.15–25. Ornan: 1 Chron. 21.14–30; 2 Chron. 3.1.

Arbela (ärbē'lŭ), town, anc. Assyria (modern Erbil). Near here (at Gaugamela) Alexander the Great defeated Darius III (331 B.C.).

Arblay, Madame d': see BURNEY, FRANCES.

Arbogast (är'bŭgăst), d. 394, Frankish general in Roman service. After murder of VALENTINIAN II (392), he set up puppet emperor, Eugenius, but both were defeated by THEODOSIUS (394).

arborvitae (är"bŭrvī'tē), evergreen tree or shrub (*Thuja*), with scalelike leaves, fanlike branchlets, and small cones. There are many garden forms of American arborvitae or northern white cedar (*Thuja occidentalis*), and less hardy Oriental species (*T. orientalis*). Wood of western red cedar (*T. plicata*) used in interiors and to make shingles and doors.

Arbuckle Mountains, low range, S Okla., average height 700 ft. Have geological formations. Platt Natl. Park is near.

Arbuthnot, John (ärbŭth'–, är'–), 1667–1735, English satirical writer, court physician to Queen Anne; a friend of Swift, Pope, and Gay.

Arc, Joan of: see JOAN OF ARC.

arc, in electricity, highly luminous, intensely hot path formed when two charcoal rods, originally touching and transmitting electric current, are pulled a short distance apart and current still flows between them. Formerly used for LIGHTING. Principle is used in WELDING and to generate heat in electric furnaces. For mercury-arc lamp see MERCURY; for oscillating arc, see OSCILLATOR.

arc, in geometry, a curved line or any part of it, in particular a portion of the circumference of a circle.

Arcadia (ärkā'dĕŭ), region of anc. Greece in mid-Peloponnesus, inhabited by a pastoral people.

Arcadia, city (pop. 28,733), S Calif., E of Pasadena, in agr. (oranges, walnuts, truck) and poultry area. Santa Anita race track is here.

Arcadius (ärkā'dĕŭs), c.377–408, Roman emperor of the East (395–408), son and successor of Theodosius I. His brother Honorius inherited the West. During his reign ALARIC I invaded Greece and was expelled (395–96) by Stilicho.

Arcagnolo: see ORCAGNA.

Arc de Triomphe de l'Étoile (ärk' dù trēôf' dù lätwäl'), triumphal arch in Paris at end of the Avenue des Champs Élysées and in center of the Place de l'Étoile. Commemorates Napoleon's victories. Built 1806–36 mainly on designs by J. F. Chalgrin, it is 160 ft. high, c.150 ft. wide, and 72 ft. deep, with colossal groups flanking the arch. In 1920 a French unknown soldier was buried beneath it.

Arce, Manuel José (mänwĕl' hōsā' är'sā), d. 1847, first president of Central American Federation (1825–29). Ruled arbitrarily.

archaeology (ärkēō'lŭjĕ), scientific study of the relics of man found in deposits and ruins. To find, interpret, and preserve materials which delineate prehistoric life and supplement the documentary material of historic eras, modern archaeologists work with various experts and technicians and are often sponsored by museums, organizations, and societies which publish and maintain collections of their findings. Such materials had long been collected, but excavations at HERCULANEUM and POMPEII in the 18th cent., and the discovery of the ROSETTA STONE, inspired systematic research into the historic past. In 1832 C. J. Thomsen showed that cultural stages may be defined according to principal materials used for weapons and implements. These stages, the PALEOLITHIC PERIOD, NEOLITHIC PERIOD, BRONZE AGE, and IRON AGE, indicate the condition of a people, rather than divisions of time. Study of such prehistoric finds as at LA TÈNE and of remains of barrow, KITCHEN MIDDEN, LAKE DWELLING, various mounds, and MEGALITHIC MONUMENTS, have been enhanced by the study of existent aboriginal groups. See GEOLOGY, table.

archaeopteryx (är"kēŏp'tŭrĭks), ancient bird. Fossil remains indicate it to be link between reptiles and birds.

Archaeozoic era: see ARCHEOZOIC ERA.

Archangel (ärk'–), Rus. *Arkhangelsk* (ŭrkhän'gĭlsk), city (pop. 281,091), RSFSR, on mouth of Northern Dvina; major White Sea port (ice-free July–Sept.). Chief sawmilling center of USSR. Founded 1583 as Novo-Kholmogory after CHANCELLOR had landed here; renamed 1716. Major supply port in both World Wars; occupied 1918–20 by Allies and White Army.

archangel (ärk'–), chief ANGEL, differing from other angels only in importance. Best known are MICHAEL, GABRIEL, RAPHAEL.

Archbald, mining and industrial borough (pop. 6,304), NE Pa., on Lackawanna R. and NE of Scranton.

Archeozoic era (är″keūzō′ĭk), first grand division of geologic time, marked by formation of oldest rocks. One large exposed area is the Canadian Shield (see LAURENTIAN PLATEAU), mainly of gneiss, granite, and schist. Earliest named rock system is the Keewatin, consisting of intermingled lava layers and sediments. No fossils yet discovered have been definitely proved of Archeozoic origin. See GEOLOGY, table.

Archer, William, 1856–1924, English critic. Translated Ibsen; helped G. B. Shaw; wrote popular play *The Green Goddess* (1921); was influential as London *World* dramatic critic.

Archer, the, in astronomy: see ZODIAC.

archery. An important military skill in ancient and medieval times, shooting with bow and arrow was revived as sport (c.1675) by Charles II of England. Archers try to hit inner circle (or "bull's eye") of target composed of concentric circles.

Arches National Monument: see NATIONAL PARKS AND MONUMENTS (table).

Archimedes (ärkĭmē′dēz), 287–212 B.C., Greek mathematician, physicist, inventor. Nine of his famous treatises on geometry and hydrostatics survive. **Archimedes' principle:** a solid body immersed in liquid is buoyed up by a force equal to weight of liquid it displaces. Used in determining ship displacement and specific gravity of substances. Applies also to gases, e.g., "lifting" force of balloons. Attributed to Archimedes also is machine known as **Archimedes' screw,** a cylinder inside which a continuous screw extends full length to form spiral chamber. By placing lower end in water and revolving screw, water is raised. Principle applied also in spiral conveyors and some highspeed tools. See *ill.,* p. 793.

Archipelago (ärkĭpĕ′lŭgō), ancient name of AEGEAN SEA, later applied to its numerous islands, and finally to any cluster of islands.

Archipenko, Aleksandr (ŭlyĭksändr′ ärkĭpĕng′kō), 1887–, Russian sculptor in America. Known for abstract figures, often based on the female nude.

archons (är′kŏnz, –kŭnz) [Gr.,= leaders], in anc. Greek cities; officers of state. In Athens there were nine; after serving they entered the AREOPAGUS. After 487 B.C. they were chosen by lot.

Arciniegas, Germán (hĕrmän′ ärsēnyä′gäs), 1900–, Colombian historian and diplomat. His works publicized Latin American history in U.S.

Arco, resort village (pop. 961), SE central Idaho, NW of Pocatello. Hq. for Craters of the Moon Natl. Monument. Lost River atomic-energy reactor testing station (1949) near.

Arcole (är′kōlä), village, NE Italy, SE of Verona. Here Bonaparte defeated Austrians 1796.

Arcot (ärkŏt′), town (pop. 16,583), E central Madras, India. A major prize in British-French struggle for S India in 18th cent.

Arctic Archipelago, large Canadian islands in Arctic Ocean, Franklin dist., Northwest Territories.

Arctic Ocean, sea, roughly circular, from North Pole to lat. c.70°N, nearly landlocked (by Greenland, Canada, Alaska, USSR, Norway), c.5,400,000 sq. mi. Has many islands, fringe of small seas and bays. Communicates widely with Atlantic, with Pacific only through Bering Strait. Deepest (14,070 ft.) near pole on Bering Strait side. Ice drifts S and W into northernmost Atlantic shipping lanes, but more seriously from W Greenland fjords. Arctic currents give NE shores of North America and Asia much colder climate than NW shores of Europe and North America (warmed by North Atlantic Drift, Gulf Stream, Japan Current). Aerial study has increased knowledge of drifts, ice floes, water depths, and ocean floor. Observation reveals warming of Arctic.

arctic regions, northernmost area of earth, centered about North Pole and Arctic Ocean. Extends more than one third way to equator. Weather boundary varies seasonally, set arbitrarily at Arctic Circle (lat. 66°17′N). Under "midnight sun" temperatures mount, vegetation appears. Abundant animal life (including seal, walrus, whale, many fish, water fowl, sea birds) supports ESKIMO tribes. Viking explorers were followed by those seeking NORTHWEST PASSAGE and NORTHEAST PASSAGE (16th, 17th cent.). Hardships, negative results discouraged exploration until late 18th cent. North Pole first reached by Robert Peary 1909. Discovery that shortest air routes ("great circle") between capitals and commercial centers of N Hemisphere lie over Arctic Ocean replaced individual exploration with cooperative enterprise. Natural resources and strategic military value led to national settlement and exploitation in which USSR has been most consistently active.

Arcturus (ärktyōōr′ús), orange-colored first magnitude star of constellation Boötes, also called Alpha Boötis. Diameter c.18,000,000 mi.; c.32.6 light years from earth.

Ardashir I (ärdäsher′), d. 240, king of Persia (226?–240). Reunited Persia and founded Sassanian dynasty (see SASSANIDAE). Name another form of Artaxerxes.

Ardebil (ärdübēl′), city (pop. 63,406), NW Iran. Cap. of Azerbaijan c.700–c.1100. Russians took city 1828; removed fine library to St. Petersburg.

Ardèche (ärdĕsh′), department (2,145 sq. mi.; pop. 254,598) S France, in Vivarais; cap. Privas.

Arden, Forest of, N Warwickshire, England. Most of Shakspere's *As You Like It* is laid here.

Ardennes (ärdĕn′), department (2,078 sq. mi.; pop. 245,335), NE France; cap. Mézières.

Ardennes, wooded plateau, 1,600–2,300 ft. high, N France, SE Belgium, N Luxembourg, E and S of Meuse R. Wild, craggy landscape. Agr., cattle raising. Population mostly Walloons. Cities: Liége, Namur, Verviers, Spa. Traditional battleground; BATTLE OF THE BULGE fought here in World War II.

Ardmore. 1 City (pop. 17,890), S Okla., S of Oklahoma City; settled 1887. Center of agr., livestock, oil, and asphalt area, it processes

ENTABLATURE

Cornice
Frieze
Architrave

COLUMN

Capital

Shaft

TUSCAN

Base

PEDESTAL

Cap
Die

Base

DORIC

IONIC

CORINTHIAN

COMPOSITE

THE FIVE ORDERS

Springer — Keystone — Extrados
Voussoir — Intrados — Voussoir
Rise
Impost
Semicircular
Pier

Lancet   Ogee   Cinquefoil   Moorish multifoil

ARCHES

BASILICA

AISLE
ATRIUM   Narthex   NAVE   BEMA   APSE
AISLE

VAULTING

Groined

Ribbed

CATHEDRAL

Baptistery
AISLE
Chapels
NAVE   TRANSEPTS   CHOIR   APSE
AISLE
Chapels   Sacristy

N
W   E
S

Interior

Wall

Flying buttress

FLYING BUTTRESS

cotton products, oil, and flour and has mfg. of machinery. Has U.S. Indian school. 2 Village (pop. 9,015), E Pa., W of Philadelphia. Mfg. of motor vehicles.

area, in geometry, extent of surface measured in some unit (e.g., square feet or acres). Formulae for simple plane figures and simple solids (a = altitude; b = base; s = side; r = radius; l = slant height):

Plane figures	Area
triangle	$ab/2$
parallelogram	ab
rectangle	ab
square	s^2
circle	πr^2

Solids	Total area
right circular cylinder	$2\pi r(r+a)$
right circular cone	$\pi r(r+l)$
sphere	$4\pi r^2$

Areopagite: see DIONYSIUS THE AREOPAGITE, SAINT.

Areopagus (ărēŏ′pŭgŭs), rocky hill NW of the Acropolis of Athens, sacred meeting place of prime council of Athens, the **Areopagus,** which arose out of countil of elders and had judicial and legislative functions. Declined after 487 B.C.

Arequipa (ärākē′pä), city (pop. 79,185), S Peru; founded by Francisco Pizarro 1540. Commercial hub of S Peru and N Bolivia, it also draws tourists.

Ares (â′rēz), in Greek mythology, Olympian god of war; son of Zeus and Hera; either husband or lover of Aphrodite. He favored the Trojans in the Trojan War. Identified with Roman Mars.

Arethusa (ărĭthū′sŭ), in Greek mythology, nymph loved by Alpheus. She fled from him and was changed into a fountain, but he caught her; hence the story that Alpheus river flows beneath sea from Greece to reappear in fountain of Arethusa in harbor of Syracuse.

Aretinian syllables: see GUIDO D'AREZZO.

Aretino, Pietro (pyā′trō ärātē′nō), 1492–1556?, Italian satirist, adventurer who wrote for hire, called by Ariosto the "scourge of princes."

Arezzo (ärāt′tsō), city (pop. 24,411), Tuscany, central Italy. An Etruscan, later a Roman, town (famous for red-clay Arretine vases), Arezzo became a cultural center in late Middle Ages. Birthplace of Guido d'Arezzo, Petrarch, Aretino, Vasari. Much medieval and Renaissance architecture.

Argand burner (är′gănd), introduced principle of admitting air to interior of flame. Modern gas and oil burners based on this principle.

Argelander, Friedrich Wilhelm August (frē′drĭkh vĭl′hĕlm ou′gŏŏst är′gŭländŭr), 1799–1875, German astronomer, noted for star catalogue, *Bonn Durchmusterung* (1862).

Argenson (ärzhäsō′), French noble family, prominent in the public service in the 18th cent. Among them were **René Louis de Voyer de Paulmy, marquis d'Argenson** (rŭnā′ lwē dŭ vwäyä′ dŭ pōlmē′, märkē′), 1694–1757, foreign minister (1744–47), and his brother, **Marc Pierre de Voyer de Paulmy, comte d'Argenson** (märk′ pyĕr′, kōt′), 1696–1764, who as secretary of war

(1743–57) reformed the army and founded the École militaire. Both brothers were friends of Voltaire and the Encyclopedists.

Argenteuil (ärzhätû′ĕ), town (pop. 53,513), Seine-et-Oise dept., N France, on the Seine; industrial suburb of Paris. Convent where Heloise was prioress destroyed in French Revolution.

Argentia, N.F.: see PLACENTIA BAY.

Argentina, La, d. 1936, Spanish dancer, whose real name was Antonia Mercé. Revived interest in Spanish classical dance by performances in U.S. 1928.

Argentina (ärjŭntē′nù), republic (1,073,699 sq. mi.; pop. 15,893,827), S South America, between Andes and Atlantic; cap. BUENOS AIRES. Second largest South American nation, stretches from subtropics 2,000 mi. S to TIERRA DEL FUEGO. Argentina claims FALKLAND ISLANDS, which are held by British. Towering Andes (crossed by TRANS-ANDINE RAILWAY; highest peak ACONCAGUA; snow-topped volcanoes) are W border with Chile. Arid Andean highlands and CHACO border Bolivia in NW. Rivers of Río de la PLATA system form boundaries across N: Pilcomayo, Paraguay, Paraná, with Paraguay; Uruguay, with Uruguay and Brazil. In extreme NE, Argentina meets Brazil and Paraguay in Brazilian highlands at IGUASSÚ FALLS. N Argentina, mostly plain, yields QUEBRACHO, MATE, agr. produce. To the S, vast plain of the PAMPA (once the wild home of the GAUCHO; tamed in 19th cent. by Italian immigrants) provides from farms and ranches the basic wealth of Argentina. Chief cities here are Buenos Aires, on Río de la Plata estuary, one of great ports of world; LA PLATA; ROSARIO; SANTA FE; MAR DEL PLATA; BAHÍA BLANCA. On W edge of Pampa is CÓRDOBA. MENDOZA, SAN JUAN, TUCUMÁN, and SALTA are productive oases in arid Andean foothills. In S is PATAGONIA (with COMODORO RIVADAVIA and other oil fields), producing 70% of nation's oil. Argentine pop. is overwhelmingly of European descent (with native Indians in far N and Andean areas only). First European explorers: VESPUCCI (1502), Juan Díaz de SOLÍS (1516), MAGELLAN (1520), Sebastian CABOT. Buenos Aires first founded (1536) by Pedro de MENDOZA, abandoned after Indian attacks, refounded (1580) from Asunción by GARAY. It was finally (1776) made cap. of Spanish vice-royalty. From 1810 to 1816, successful struggle for Argentine independence led by patriot generals BELGRANO, Moreno, PUEYRREDÓN, and (most distinguished) SAN MARTÍN. Civil war lasted until harsh dictatorship (1829–32, 1835–52) of Juan Manuel de ROSAS, who was opposed by intellectuals (e.g., SARMIENTO, ALBERDI), defeated by URQUIZA. New constitution in 1853. Under MITRE, Sarmiento, and Nicolás Avellaneda schools were built, liberal reforms started. In 1880 long struggle between centralism and federalism settled in favor of federal system. Conquest (1878–79) of Indians by Roca opened S and SW to European immigration. Argentina became one of world's granaries, and industry developed, aided by British. Refrigerating plants for meat forwarded commerce. Argentine-Chilean boundary dispute settled 1902; perpetual peace symbolized by CHRIST OF THE ANDES. Politics showed military tradition and conflict. In 1946 Juan D. PERÓN established a new type of Latin American dictatorship, supported by workers, nationalists, reactionaries, clericals, army. Argentina remained neutral in World War I, belatedly entered World War II on side of Allies, and became (1945) member of UN.

Arginusae, battle of (ärjĭnū′sē), 406 B.C., last Athenian naval victory in the PELOPONNESIAN WAR, off the Arginusae Isls., near Asia Minor. A storm caused six Athenian ships to founder. The commanders' failure to rescue the crews was used as a pretext by their political enemies to have them executed. A son of Pericles was among the victims.

Argo (är′gō), in Greek mythology, ship in which the Arognauts sailed to find the GOLDEN FLEECE.

argol: see TARTAR.

Argolis (är′gŭlĭs), region of anc. Greece, in NE Peloponnesus, around Argive plain; dominated by city of Argos.

argon (är′gŏn), colorless, odorless, tasteless, inert gaseous element (symbol = A; see also ELEMENT, table). Occurs in air and some volcanic gases. Used in electric-light bulbs, electric signs.

Argonaut (är′gŭnôt″) [Gr.,= sailor on Argo], in Greek mythology, one of band led by JASON who went to Colchis in quest of GOLDEN FLEECE. Among the voyagers were Argus, Orpheus, Hercules, and the huntress Atalanta. Voyage was interrupted for a year while they tarried on Lemnos. The ship safely passed the Symplegades (floating cliffs) and also SCYLLA and CHARYBDIS, and the mariners escaped the wiles of the Sirens' singing.

Argonne (är′gŏn, Fr. ärgôn′), hilly and wooded region, NE France, in Champagne and Lorraine. French repulsed Prussians here at Valmy 1792. In World War I, the Meuse-Argonne sector was carried by U.S. troops Sept.–Nov., 1918.

Argos, in Greek legend: see ARGUS.

Argos (är′gŏs, –gŭs), city of anc. Greece, NE Peloponnesus, near modern Nauplia. Center of Argolis, it struggled with Sparta and rivaled Athens and Corinth. Taken by Sparta (c.494 B.C.). Flourished under Rome after 146 B.C.

Arguedas, Alcides (älsē′däs ärgä′däs), 1879–, Bolivian novelist. Deep interest in Bolivian social ills expressed in *Un pueblo enferno* (1910).

Argun (ärgōōn′), river, 980 mi. long, NE Asia, a headstream of the Amur. Forms part of border between USSR and Manchuria.

Argus (är′gŭs) or **Argos** (är′gŏs, –gŭs), in Greek myth. 1 The hundred-eyed guardian of Io, ancestor of people of Argos. 2 Son of Phrixus. Builder of the ARGO and an Argonaut. 3 Dog of Odysseus, first creature to welcome him home.

Argyll, dukes of, earls of, and **marquesses of,** Scottish nobles: see the family name, CAMPBELL.

Argyllshire (ärgīl′shĭr) or **Argyll,** maritime county (3,110 sq. mi.; pop. 63,270), W Scotland; co. town Inverary. Includes numerous islands of Inner Hebrides. Wild and mountainous, has agr. on coast only. One of chief sheep-raising areas of British Isles. Iona has remains of ancient monastic center.

Argyrokastron (äryērô′kästrôn), Albanian *Argirokastra,* city (pop. 10,910), S Albania, above Drin R. Its old castle was rebuilt (19th cent.) by Ali Pasha. Held by Greeks 1940–41 during World War II.

Arhus, Denmark: see AARHUS.

aria, air or melody, especially an accompanied solo in an opera, oratoria, or cantata. The *aria da capo* has a contrasting, usually shorter, middle section followed by a repetition of the first section.

Ariadne (ărēăd′nē), in Greek legend, Cretan princess, daughter of Minos and Pasiphaë. Gave THESEUS thread to guide him out of Labyrinth after he slew Minotaur. He took her away with him but deserted her.

Arianism, heretical movement arising from teaching of Arius (c.256–336), a Libyan theologian, priest in Alexandria. He advanced the doctrine that before the general creation God had created and begotten a Son, the first creature, but neither eternal nor equal with the Father. This idea spread, and the unity of Christendom was threatened by the resultant conflict. Emperor Constantine called the First Council of NICAEA, where ATHANASIUS vigorously opposed Arius and won a victory. Arianism was condemned, but the matter had become political as well as religious. Arius, condemned locally in 321 and anathematized by the council, was brought back from exile (335). The conflict went on, with whole groups of bishops being exiled by emperors favoring one or the other party. The Arians split into three groups, mutually antagonistic. Finally the doctrines favored by Athanasius and Rome triumphed. Theodosius made Catholicism the state religion. Arianism had, however, been carried to the Goths and Vandals, and it survived in Africa until the 6th cent., in Visigothic Spain until the 7th. Contrary to popular belief, Arianism had nothing to do with the split between Eastern and Western Churches or with Protestantism.

Arias de Ávila, Pedro, (pä′dhrō ä′ryäs dä ä′vēlä), known as **Pedrarias** (pädhrä′ryäs), c.1440–1531?, Spanish colonial administrator. Sent (1514) as governor of Darien, he had BALBOA executed, was notoriously cruel. Extended Spanish dominions; founded Panama city (1519). Went to Nicaragua (1526) and held power until death.

Arias de Saavedra, Hernando (ĕrnän′dō ä′ryäs dä sävä′drä), known as **Hernandarias** (ĕrnändä′ryäs), 1561–1634, b. Asunción. First American-born governor of Río de la Plata prov., he was able administrator.

Arica (ärē′kä), city (pop. 14,064), N Chile, Pacific port won from Peru in War of the Pacific (1879–84). In settlement of Tacna-Arica controversy (1929), Chile was required to furnish port facilties to Peru. Subject to earthquake.

Ariège (äryĕzh′), department (1,893 sq. mi.; pop. 145,956), SW France, in Pyrenees; cap. Foix.

Aries [Lat.,= ram], first sign of ZODIAC.

Arikara Indians (ŭrĭ′kŭrŭ), North American

tribe, formerly on Missouri R., of Caddoan linguistic stock. Semisedentary, they hunted buffalo and grew maize.

Ariminium: see RIMINI, Italy.

Arion (ŭrī'ŭn), legendary Greek poet, inventor of the DITHYRAMB (supposedly 7th cent. B.C.).

Ariosto, Ludovico (lōōdōvē'kō äryōs'tō), 1474–1533, Italian epic and lyric poet, famous for his *Orlando Furioso* (1532), epic treatment of the Roland story, a sequel to the unfinished poem of BOIARDO. Written for his patrons, the Este family, *Orlando Furioso* combines irony and grandeur and is called the greatest Renaissance poem.

Ariovistus (â"rēōvī'stŭs), fl. 58 B.C., Germanic chieftain, leader of the Suebi. Came to dominate much of GAUL, and in 60 B.C. became a friend and ally of Rome, but his power threatened Roman rule in Gaul, and Caesar defeated and drove him out (58).

Aristarchus of Samos (ăr"ĭstär'kŭs, sā'mōs), 3d cent. B.C. Greek astronomer of Alexandrian school. One of first to conclude that earth moves around sun and to state causes of day and night and of change of seasons.

Aristides (ărĭstī'dēz), d. c.468 B.C., Athenian statesman and general. Ostracized by Themistocles, he was recalled and commanded the fleet in victory over the Persians at Plataea (479 B.C.). Later organized Delian League. Called Aristides the Just.

Aristides, probably two Greek painters, often confused. One was of the 5th cent. B.C., the other of the 4th cent. B.C.

aristocracy (ăr"ĭstŏk'rŭsē), in political science, government by best in interest of all. All governments contain an aristocratic element since rulers are thought best fitted for rule. Aristocracy usually based on landed possessions (flourishing chiefly within monarchy), sometimes on wealth (e.g., medieval Venice).

Aristogiton: see HARMODIUS AND ARISTOGITON.

Aristophanes (ăr"ĭstŏf'ŭnēz), b. c.448, d. after 388 B.C., greatest Greek poet of COMEDY. His plays, only full samples of the Greek Old Comedy, mix political, social, and literary satire. Among surviving eleven plays are: *The Clouds, The Wasps, The Birds, Lysistrata,* and *The Frogs.*

Aristotle (ăr"ĭstŏt'ŭl), 384–322 B.C., Greek philosopher, b. Stagira (hence the Stagirite). Studied under Plato (366–347 B.C.), later tutored Alexander the Great (343–336 B.C.), and finally founded Peripatetic school in the Lyceum at Athens. His extant works are *Organon* (six treatises on logic), *Metaphysics, Physics, On the Heavens, History of Animals, On the Parts of Animals, On the Soul, Politics, Nichomachean Ethics, Rhetoric,* and *Poetics.* Like Plato, Aristotle saw the universe as an ideal world, but they differed as to the relation of form and matter, Aristotle arguing that these were inseparable. This union became a principle by which he explained all growth, all movement. Motion and change are the realization of form in matter. In scientific works he differed from Plato in using close observation and accurate classification of nature. His analysis of nature into four elements, earth, air, fire, and water, perpetuated a common Greek error. His ethics argue that the goodness of a

thing lies in realization of its specific nature, and for man this consisted of the exercise of man's rational faculty through agency of the golden mean. The *Poetics* (which, like all his works, was revered by many later generations) explained the imitative and cathartic nature of tragic poetry and set the unities as formal elements of tragedy.

arithmetic, elementary and anc. branch of mathematics. Includes calculation (concrete, practical, or elementary arithmetic) and theory of numbers (abstract, theoretical, or higher arithmetic). Both deal with number behavior in four basic operations: ADDITION, SUBTRACTION, MULTIPLICATION, DIVISION; and operations of involution, evolution. Higher arithmetic generalizes number concept to include complex numbers, quaternions, tensors, abstract entities.

Arius, theologian: see ARIANISM.

Arizona, state (113,580 sq. mi.; pop. 749,587), SW U.S.; admitted 1912 as 48th state; cap. PHOENIX. TUCSON other main city. In COLORADO R. drainage basin; river forms most of W boundary. Has mountains, plateaus, chasms (GRAND CANYON), deserts (PAINTED DESERT), scenic wonders (Petrified Forest), Indian ruins. Mining (copper, gold, silver, lead, zinc), farming, cattle raising. Lack of rainfall necessitates irrigation projects. Main industry is mining and processing of copper. Spanish first came 1539–40. Missions founded by Eusebio KINO in 1690s. Became part of U.S. by Treaty of GUADALUPE HIDALGO (1848) and GADSDEN PURCHASE (1853); made a territory in 1863. Warfare with the Apache troubled region (1861–86). Tourist trade has become quite important.

Arizona, University of: see TUCSON.

ark, in Bible. **1** Boat built by NOAH to save his family and some animals from Deluge. Gen. 6–9; Luke 17.27; Heb. 11.7; 1 Peter 3.20. **2** Wooden chest, overlaid with gold, known as Ark of the Covenant, sacred symbol of early Hebrews, representative of God. Touching it was a desecration punishable by death. Its presence implied victory, so was carried into battle by poles thrust through rings on its sides. Taken by Philistines, it brought them disaster and was sent back to Israel. Brought by David to Jerusalem, placed in Temple by Solomon. Since lost from view. Possibly held tables of Ten Commandments. Ex. 25.10–21; Num. 10.33–36; Deut. 10.1–5; Joshua 3–6; 1 Sam. 4–7; 2 Sam. 6; 15.24,29; 1 Kings 8.3,9; 1 Chron. 13; 15–16.6; 2 Chron. 5; Jer. 3.16; Heb. 9.4.

Arkadelphia (ärkŭdĕl'fēŭ), city (pop. 6,819), SW Ark., on Ouachita R, in timber and agr. area. Seat of Ouachita Col.

Arkansas (är'kŭnsô"), state (52,725 sq. mi.; pop. 1,909,511), S central U.S., admitted 1836 as 25th state (slaveholding); cap. LITTLE ROCK. Other major cities are FORT SMITH, PINE BLUFF, HOT SPRINGS, TEXARKANA. Bounded on E by Mississippi R. Mississippi alluvial plains S and E; OZARK MOUNTAINS in NW. Has ARKANSAS R., SAINT FRANCIS R., WHITE RIVER, OUACHITA R., RED RIVER. Produces cotton, corn, rice, grains, truck, livestock, timber, petroleum, bauxite, coal. Industries based on processing of raw materials. QUAPAW INDIANS lived here. Hernando De Soto led first white men into region in 1541–42. Trading center at Arkansas Post estab. by French 1686. Part of French territory, region was ceded to Spain (1762) and back to France before going to U.S. in Louisiana Purchase. 1818 cotton boom brought many settlers. Became territory 1819. Joined Confederacy 1861. State not readmitted to Union until 1868. Reconstruction turbulent. Depression of 1930s hit cotton economy hard, causing much migration (esp. to Calif.). World War II caused further population loss, also boomed new industries (esp. aluminum). Has growing tourist trade.

Arkansas (ärkăn′zŭs, är′kŭnsô″), river rising in the Rockies of central Colo. and flowing c.1,500 mi. SE, across Colo., Kansas, Okla., and Ark., to the Mississippi between Memphis, Tenn., and Vicksburg, Miss. Bridged at Royal Gorge canyon (granite walls rise sharply to over 1,000 ft.), Colo. Receives Cimarron and Canadian rivers in Okla. Passes through Wichita (Kansas), Tulsa (Okla.), and Little Rock (Ark.). Flood-control, irrigation, and power project on river and its tributaries includes John Martin Dam (153 ft. high, 13,946 ft. long, completed 1948), Colo., and others. Cotton, rice, wheat, sugar beets, and fruit are grown in river's valley. There are also oil refining and coal mining.

Arkansas, University of: see FAYETTEVILLE.

Arkansas City, city (pop. 12,903), S Kansas, SSE of Wichita at junction of Arkansas and Walnut rivers; laid out 1870. Refines and ships oil.

Arkansas Post, community, SE Ark., on Arkansas R. and SE of Little Rock; founded 1686 by French; oldest white settlement in state. Confederate stronghold until captured by Gen. McClernand (1863).

Arkhangelsk, RSFSR: see ARCHANGEL.

Ark of the Covenant: see ARK.

Arkwright, Sir Richard, 1732–92, English inventor. His construction of a spinning machine (patented 1769) an early step in the INDUSTRIAL REVOLUTION.

Arlberg (ärl′bĕrk), pass, 5,910 ft. high, W Austria, near Arlberg peak. Arlberg Tunnel is 6½ mi. long.

Arles (ärl), city (pop. 20,138), Bouches-du-Rhône dept., SE France, in Provence, on Rhone delta. Silk mfg., wine trade. A flourishing Roman town (Arelas) and the metropolis of Gaul under late empire, it became the cap. of medieval kingdom of Arles and was the site of many Church councils and a center of Provençal culture. Roman remains include huge arena, theater. Church of St. Trophime was begun 11th cent. Arles was damaged in World War II.

Arles, kingdom of, formed 933 when Rudolph II united his kingdom of Transjurane BURGUNDY with the kingdom of PROVENCE or Cisjurane Burgundy. Emperor Conrad II joined it to Holy Roman Empire in 1033. Government by imperial vicars was nominal; France, Savoy, Switzerland, and Burgundy held actual control over component territories. After the dauphin (later Charles VI of France) was made vicar in 1378, the kingdom survived only in theory.

Arlington, Henry Bennet, 1st earl of, 1618–85, English courtier. Under Charles II was a secretary of state and member of unscrupulous CABAL ministry.

Arlington. 1 Residential town (pop. 44,353), E Mass., NW suburb of Boston; settled c.1630. **2** See POUGHKEEPSIE, N.Y. **3** Village (pop. 5,085), S N.C., W of Gastonia. **4** City (pop. 7,692), N Texas, E of Fort Worth. Market and industrial center of agr. area. Seat of North Texas Agricultural Col. (branch of Agricultural and Mechanical Col. of Texas). **5** Uninc. town, N Va., on Potomac R. (bridged) opposite Washington, D.C. Here are government offices, ARLINGTON NATIONAL CEMETERY, and Lee Mansion National Memorial.

Arlington Heights, residential village (pop. 8,768), NE Ill., just NW of Chicago. Has race track.

Arlington National Cemetery, 408 acres, N Va., on Potomac R. opposite Washington, D.C.; estab. 1864, extended 1889 and 1897. Here are graves of c.60,000 war dead, tomb of Unknown Soldier, and marble amphitheatre. Cemetery is part of "Arlington," former estate of Custis and Lee families.

Arliss, George, 1868–1946, English stage and film actor. Had his first great success (1911) in the title role of *Disraeli.* Later appeared in such plays as *The Green Goddess* and *Old English.* Repeated many of his stage triumphs in moving pictures.

Armada, Spanish (ärmä′dù), 1588, fleet launched by Philip II of Spain against England; called also Invincible Armada. Consisting of c.130 ships and 30,000 men, and commanded by duke of Medina Sidonia, it was to go to Flanders and from there convoy the army of Alessandro Farnese to invade England and seize the throne for Philip. The Armada set out from Lisbon in May, was delayed at Coruña, and in July, at Plymouth, found the English fleet, under Charles Howard (later earl of Nottingham). Among the English captains were Sir Francis Drake, Sir John Hawkins, and Sir Martin Frobisher. Forced up the English Channel, the Armada suffered losses in several engagements, but escaped north with favorable wind. Only half the fleet reached home; the rest was dispersed by storms off Ireland and its crews killed or captured by the Irish.

armadillo (ärmŭdĭl′ō), mammal of order Edentata, found from Patagonia northward to parts of S and SW U.S. Armor of bone and horny material almost covers head and body; tail has bony rings. Is omnivorous but eats chiefly insects. Nine-banded armadillo (*Dasypus*), only U.S. species. Flesh palatable.

Armageddon (–gĕd′ùn), great battlefield, to be site of final conflict between powers of good and evil. Rev. 16.16. Name may come from MEGIDDO.

Armagh (ärmä′), inland county (449 sq. mi.; pop. 114,226), N. Ireland. Mainly a farming region, also noted for its linen. County town is **Armagh,** urban district (pop. 9,279), religious center of Ireland. St. Patrick was bishop here 5th cent. Seat of Roman Catholic and Protestant archbishoprics.

Armagnac (ärmänyäk′), region and former

county, SW France, in Gascony; historic cap. Auch. Produces brandy. Added to royal domain 1607.

Armagnacs and Burgundians, opposing factions in 15th-cent. France. Their struggle arose out of rivalry of Louis d'ORLÉANS and JOHN THE FEARLESS of Burgundy. After Louis's murder (1407) his followers were led by BERNARD VII, count of Armagnac—hence their nickname. The Burgundians—followers of John the Fearless—were strong in Paris, where the radical CABOCHIENS supported them. Civil war broke out (1411) and merged after 1415 with the HUNDRED YEARS WAR. In 1418 the Burgundians seized Paris and massacred the Armagnacs; in 1419 the Armagnacs murdered John the Fearless. The Burgundians now became full allies of England, while the Armagnacs, led by the dauphin (later Charles VII), represented the national party.

armature. 1 Part of electric GENERATOR and MOTOR. Coil of wire that rotates in magnetic field between opposite magnetic poles and cuts magnetic lines of force between them, generating current in coil. **2** Piece of iron or steel, called a keeper, placed between or across poles of magnet to prevent decrease in magnetic property.

Armenia (ärmē'nēū), region and former kingdom of Asia Minor. Roughly includes E Turkey and ARMENIAN SOVIET SOCIALIST REPUBLIC. Tradition says kingdom was founded in region of Lake Van by Haig or Haik, descendant of Noah. A battleground of Assyrians, Medes, and Persians, it became a Persian satrapy c.6th cent. B.C. Conquered 4th cent. B.C. by Alexander the Great; later ruled by Seleucus I. Was independent kingdom from 189 B.C. to 69 B.C., when it fell to Rome. Armenia is oldest Christian state. After 3d cent., when region was under Persian rule, Armenian Christians suffered much persecution. Enjoyed autonomy 885–1046 under the native Bagratids. Reconquered 1046 by the Byzantines, who were ousted by Seljuk Turks. Pushed westward, an Armenian group estab. kingdom of Little Armenia in CILICIA. Greater Armenia was occupied 1386–94 by Tamerlane. All Armenia was under Turkish rule by 16th cent., but E Armenia was claimed also by Persia, who lost it to Russia in 1828. Congress of Berlin (1878) gave some Armenian territory to Russia, but much of it was restored 1921 to Turkey. Armenians were sporadically massacred by the Turks 1894–1915. Treaty of Brest-Litovsk (1918), which made Russian Armenia independent under German auspices, was superseded by Treaty of Sèvres (1920) which created independent Greater Armenia (comprising Turkish and Russian parts), but in same year Communists proclaimed Russian Armenia a Soviet Republic. With Russo-Turkish treaty (1921) marking present boundaries Armenian independence was ended.

Armenian Church, group that split from the orthodox Christians in 4th cent. and accepted (5th cent.) some doctrines of MONOPHYSITISM. Liturgical language is Classical Armenian. In 1198 the Cilician Armenians reunited with the Holy See but have kept close relations with Armenian Church to the present.

Armenian language, subfamily of Indo-European languages. See LANGUAGE (table).

Armenian literature. First work (c.5th cent.), a translation of Bible, became standard of Classical Armenian. Armenian Church fostered literature, mostly saints' lives and histories. Among secular works were translations of Aristotle and the romance of Alexander. History of Moses of Khorni is main source on pre-Christain Armenia. Catholicos Narses IV, 12th cent. prelate and poet, had unexcelled literary style. In 12th cent. vernacular came into use for contemporary topics. In 18th cent. Mechitar, Catholic Armenian monk, founded monastic literary community at Constantinople. The Mechitarists, now centered at Venice, publish works in Armenian.

Armenian Soviet Socialist Republic, constituent republic (11,500 sq. mi.; pop. c.1,345,000), USSR, in S Transcaucasia, bordering on Turkey and Iran; cap. Erivan. Mountainous (Mt. Aragats, 13,435 ft., is highest peak), it has good pastures. Valleys are artifically irrigated. Main products are wine, cotton, wool, copper. Hydroelectric power from L. Sevan. A part of ancient ARMENIA, territory was taken by Russia from Persia in 1828.

Armentières (ärmŭntērz', Fr. ärmätyĕr'), town (pop. 18,691), Nord dept., N France, on Lys R. Famous for World War I song, *Mademoiselle from Armentières.*

Arminius (ärmĭ'nēŭs), d. A.D. 21?, leader of the Germans. When Romans pushed E from the Rhine, Arminius, ex-Roman citizen and soldier, gathered a great force and destroyed the army of P. Quintilius VARUS. Rome never again tried to conquer E of Rhine. In German he is Hermann.

Arminius, Jacobus, 1560–1609, Dutch Reformed theologian (originally Jacob Harmensen), professor at Leiden after 1603. Arminianism, as fully formulated later by Simon Episcopius, opposed predestination and was in favor of election and doctrine of the Wesleys and Methodist Church.

Armitage, Edward, 1817–96, English historical and religious painter.

armor, protective covering in warfare for persons, horses, vehicles, naval vessels, and aircraft. Body armor was known to many peoples, and metal armor became elaborate in the Middle Ages. Increased emphasis on mobile warfare and introduction of firearms (16th cent.) reduced importance of armor almost to zero, but in 20th cent. steel helmet was reintroduced, and the TANK and armor plate for ships and aircraft became important. Many experiments were made in World War II in personal armor. See *ill.,* p. 67.

Armorica: see BRITTANY.

Armour Institute of Technology: see CHICAGO, Ill.

Arms, John Taylor, 1887–, American etcher, noted for studies of medieval architecture.

Armstrong, Edwin Howard, 1890–, American engineer. Radio contributions include regenerative circuit; superheterodyne circuit (basis for design of most receivers); super-

15th CENTURY — Helmet { Visor, Beaver }, Gorget, Habergeon (type of coat of mail), Cubitiere, Skirt of tasses, Cuisse, Jamb, Solleret, Epaulière, Brassart, Breastplate, Gauntlet, Genouillière, Rowel spurs

The Golden Age of armor. "Gothic" armor, with flexibly jointed steel plates.

GREEK — Helmet, Horsehair crest, Bronze corselet, Chiton, Leather or bronze greaves

ROMAN — Bronze helmet

12th CENTURY — Iron helmet and visor, Leather armor covered with iron rings, Two-edged sword, Leather-covered wooden shield

13th CENTURY — Pike, Coat of mail, Surcoat

14th CENTURY — Basinet, Coat of mail, Shield, Gauntlet, Jamb, Solleret

Metal plates were added for protection at vital spots.

16th CENTURY

Gunpowder, introduced in the 14th century, outdated armor, which became increasingly elaborate, decorative, and nonfunctional.

17th-CENTURY PIKEMAN — Steel cap, Corselet, Tasses

Even these remnants of steel plate disappeared by the end of the century.

regenerative circuit; development of "wide-swing" frequency modulation.

Armstrong, John, 1758–1843, American army officer, U.S. Secretary of War (1813–14). Held responsible for disasters in War of 1812; resigned in disfavor.

Armstrong, Samuel Chapman, 1839–93, American educator and philanthropist. A major general of the Union army, he later helped found (1868) and was head of Hampton Normal and Agricultural Inst. (now Hampton Inst.).

Armstrong, William George, 1810–1900, English inventor of a breech-loading gun with rifle-bored barrel. His firm became Vickers, Armstrong, Ltd.

army worm, striped green, brown, and yellow larva of a noctuid moth; in North America, found E of Rocky Mts. Moving in hordes, they ravage crops; controlled by poisoning and trapping in ditches.

Arnaud, Henri (ärē′ ärnō′), 1641–1721, Savoyard pastor, leader of WALDENSES at home and in exile.

Arnauld (ärnō′), French family involved in JANSENISM. Also Arnaut, Arnault. **(Marie) Angélique (de Sainte Madeleine)** (äzhälēk′), 1591–1661, was abbess of PORT-ROYAL. Under the influence of St. Francis de Sales, she reformed her abbey. Later DUVERGIER DE HAURANNE led her to adopt Jansenist ideas. Her younger brother, **Antoine Arnauld** (ätwän′), 1612–94, was a Jansenist controversialist, author of *De la fréquente communion* (1643), collaborator in famous Port-Royal textbooks. His older brother, **Robert Arnauld d'Andilly** (rōbĕr′, dädēyē′), 1588–1674, translated religious writings and wrote poetry.

Arnhem (är′nŭm), municipality (pop. 97,350) and city, cap. of Gelderland prov., E Netherlands; a port on the Lower Rhine. Industrial center. In Sept., 1944, British troops landed here in a huge Allied airborne operation; isolated, they made a heroic stand and lost two thirds of their strength before they were evacuated.

Arnhem Land, aboriginal reservation, area 31,200 sq. mi., Northern Territory, Australia, on a peninsula W of Gulf of Carpentaria.

Arnim, Achim von (äkh′ïm fŭn är′nïm), 1781–1831, German romantic writer. Published, with brother-in-law Clemens BRENTANO, collection of folk songs, *Des Knaben Wunderhorn* [the boy's magic horn] (1806–8). *Isabella von Ägypten* (1812; Eng. tr., 1927), a short novel, is his best-known work. His wife, **Bettina von Arnim** (bĕtē′nä), 1785–1859, is also known under her maiden name, Elisabeth Brentano. A friend of Beethoven and, supposedly, of Goethe, she wrote the unreliable *Goethe's Correspondence with a Child* (1835; Eng. tr., 1837).

Arno (är′nō), river, 150 mi. long, central Italy. Flows past Florence, Pisa into Tyrrhenian Sea.

Arnold, Benedict, 1741–1801, American Revolutionary general and traitor. Took part in QUEBEC CAMPAIGN and SARATOGA CAMPAIGN. Plot to betray West Point to British failed with capture of John ANDRÉ. Arnold escaped and fought for British.

Arnold, Sir Edwin, 1832–1904, English poet,

author of a long blank-verse epic on Buddha, *The Light of Asia* (1879).

Arnold, H(enry) H(arley), 1886–1950, American general, chief of Army Air Forces (1941–46). Called Hap or Happy Arnold.

Arnold, Matthew, 1822–88, English poet and critic; son of Thomas Arnold. Inspector of elementary schools 1851–86, he became (1857) professor of poetry at Oxford. Believed poetry should be objective, but his own poetry showed romantic pessimism (e.g., "Dover Beach"; elegy for A. H. Clough, "Thyrsis"; "The Scholar Gypsy"). Also wrote "Rugby Chapel" (on his father), long narratives (e.g., "Sohrab and Rustum"), and many lyrics. His criticism, based on classical standards, was mostly directed against "Barbarians" (the aristocracy) and "Philistines" (the bourgeoisie); he was the apostle of "culture."

Arnold, Thomas, 1795–1842, English educator; father of Matthew Arnold, grandfather of Mrs. Humphry Ward. As headmaster at Rugby (1827–42) he gave new life to whole English public school system by reforms (adding mathematics, modern languages to course of study; introducing monitorial system; encouraging independent thought). Also classical scholar and historian, and an eloquent, effective preacher.

Arnold, borough (pop. 10,263), SW Pa., on the Allegheny and NE of Pittsburgh. Mfg. of glass.

Arnold of Brescia (brĕ′shù), c.1090–1155, Italian reformer. A priest and a pupil of Abelard, he criticized the Church for owning any property at all. This idea was condemned at the Synod of Sens (1140). In Rome after 1145, he took the part of the commune, pleading for liberty and democracy. Excommunicated in 1148, he was forced from power by Adrian IV (1155) and executed as a political rebel.

Arnoldson, Klas Pontus (kläs′ pôn′tùs är′nōldsōn), 1844–1916, Swedish journalist and pacifist. Shared 1908 Nobel Peace Prize with Fredrik Bajer.

Arnold von Winkelried: see WINKELRIED.

Arnolfo di Cambio (ärnōl′fō dē käm′byō), c.1232–c.1310, Italian architect and sculptor. Designed the Baptistry, Palazzo Vecchio, and the basic portion of Santa Maria del Fiore in Florence.

Arnulf (är′nŭlf), c.850–899, last Carolingian emperor (896–99); natural son of Carloman of Bavaria. Was proclaimed king of East Franks (887) after leading rebellion which deposed his uncle Charles III. Defeated Normans 891. Invaded Italy 894 and 895 on request of Pope Formosus, who crowned him emperor at Rome (896).

Aroostook (ùrōōs′tŏŏk), river, c.140 mi. long, rising in N Maine and winding E to St. John R. in N.B. Gives name to a county famous for potatoes.

Aroostook War, brief conflict, 1838–39, between Maine and New Brunswick over disputed U.S.–Canadian border. Full-scale war averted through agreement reached in March, 1839. Boundary settled by WEBSTER-ASHBURTON TREATY.

Arpad (ör′päd), c.840–907?, chief of the

MAGYARS, whom he led into Hungary in 895. His descendants ruled Hungary till 1301.

arrack, spirits distilled chiefly in Far East from fermented juices (e.g., palm toddy) or grains.

Arran, earls of: see HAMILTON, JAMES; STUART, JAMES.

Arran, wild rocky island (165 sq. mi.; pop. 4,506), Buteshire, Scotland; hunting and fishing resort.

Arran Islands, Ireland: see ARAN ISLANDS.

Arras (äräs′), city (pop. 30,065), cap. of Pas-de-Calais dept., N France; historic cap. of Artois. Flourished in late Middle Ages (famed for TAPESTRY). Heavy damage in both World Wars. Renaissance city hall; cathedral (18th cent.); Abbey of St. Vaast (18th cent.; now museum); 17th-cent. citadel.

Arras, Treaty of. 1 Treaty, 1435, by which Charles VII of France, at heavy costs, secured the alliance of Philip the Good of Burgundy against England. **2** Treaty, 1482, between Louis XI of France and representatives of the Netherlands, regarding succession to MARY OF BURGUNDY; ratified 1483 by Mary's widower, Archduke Maximilian (later Emperor Maximilian I). Margaret of Austria, Maximilian's daughter, was promised in marriage to the dauphin (later Charles VIII), with Artois and Franche-Comté as dowry. Charles VIII eventually married Anne of Brittany instead, and treaty became void.

Arreboe, Anders (än′ûrs ä′rûbō), 1587–1637, Danish poet, a bishop of Trondheim, author of the *Hexaemeron* (1661), narrative poem in alexandrines.

arrest, seizure and detention of a person according to civil or criminal law. Civil arrest, used mostly in cases of contempt of court, always requires a warrant. Criminal arrest may be made without a warrant by any person present when a crime is committed or by an officer who reasonably suspects someone of having recently committed a felony. In some cases, release may be through habeas corpus; otherwise release usually can be obtained through bail. Diplomatic personnel and members of legislature (during sessions only) are exempt from arrest.

Arrhenius, Svante August (sfän′tû ou′gŭst ärä′nēŭs), 1859–1927, Swedish chemist. Won 1903 Nobel Prize for ionization theory; worked on osmosis, toxins.

arrowhead, aquatic plant (*Sagittaria*), having white flowers and leaves that are shaped like arrowheads. Grown in aquariums, ponds, and bogs.

arrowroot, edible, easily digested starch extracted from certain plants. True or West Indian arrowroot from a maranta (*Maranta arundinacea*), often grown as house plant for its decorative foliage. See also TAPIOCA.

Arsaces (är′sûsēz), fl. 250 B.C., founder of the Parthian dynasty, the **Arsacidae** (–sā′sĭdē″), which ruled Persia c.250 B.C.–A.D. 226.

arsenic (är′sûnĭk), chemical element (symbol = As; see also ELEMENT, table). Known in three forms (see ALLOTROPY): silver-gray crystalline, metallike, brittle solid; black, amorphous form; yellow, crystalline solid. Related to nitrogen and phosphorus. Used in making pigments, weed killers, insecticides (PARIS GREEN), poison gas; in dyeing textiles, in tanning, and in medicine. It is a strong poison. Its presence in compounds is detected by MARSH'S TEST.

arsenopyrite (är″sĭnōpī′rīt), silvery to steel-gray PYRITE. Important source of arsenic.

Arsonval, Arsène d' (ärsén′ därsōväl′), 1851–1940, French physicist, physician. Pioneer in electrotherapy; originated term *diathermy*.

Artaxerxes (är″tûzûrk′sēz), Persian *Ardashir*, kings of the Achaemenid dynasty of anc. Persia. **Artaxerxes I,** d. 425 B.C. (reigned 465–425 B.C.), succeeded his father, XERXES I. Because of trouble in Egypt and Bactria and warfare with Greeks weakness of Persia said to appear in his reign. Judaism revived in his time. **Artaxerxes II,** d. 358 B.C. (reigned 404–358 B.C.), son and successor of Darius II. CYRUS THE YOUNGER tried to seize the throne but was killed at Cunaxa (401). A revolt of satraps was put down. The cult of MITHRA was revived. **Artaxerxes III,** d. 338 B.C. (reigned 358–338 B.C.), son of Artaxerxes II. Gained throne by general massacre of the family, and continued policy of terror, destroying Sidon and reducing Egypt. He was finally poisoned.

Artemis (är′tûmĭs), in Greek legend, goddess (Roman Diana), virgin huntress with virgin attendants; daughter of Zeus and Leto, twin sister of APOLLO. She was goddess of the wild. By loosing a boar she caused CALYDONIAN HUNT. She visited punishments on Actaeon, Agamemnon, and Niobe. She was also a protector of women (temple at Ephesus was center of this cult). Complementary to Apollo, she was the goddess of the moon and the night.

artemisia: see WORMWOOD.

arteriosclerosis, hardening and thickening of arterial walls. Loss of elasticity of vessel walls may result in high blood pressure.

artery, vessel carrying blood from heart to body tissues in CIRCULATION OF THE BLOOD.

Artesia (ärtē′zhû), city (pop. 8,244), SE N.Mex., W of Pecos R. and N of Carlsbad, in a livestock, oil, cotton, alfalfa area, watered by artesian wells.

artesian well (ärtē′zhûn), in the strictest sense, a well made by drilling into a porous, water-bearing layer between two impervious strata. The water rises as a result of hydrostatic pressure dependent on the slope and rainfall. However, the term artesian is usually applied to any deep, drilled well from which water can be pumped.

Artevelde, Jacob van (yä′kôp vän är′tûvĕldû), c.1290–1345, Flemish statesman. Caught in the conflict between EDWARD III of England and PHILIP VI of France, Artevelde, as head of the city government of Ghent, negotiated a commercial treaty with England (1338) and obtained recognition of Flemish neutrality. In 1340 he secured support of Flemish towns for Edward. He was killed in a riot. His son, **Philip van Artevelde,** 1340–82, led the weavers' rebellion against the count of Flanders (1381), captured most of Flanders, but was defeated and slain by the French at Roosebeke.

arthritis (ärthrī′tĭs), inflammation of a joint. Classes of chronic arthritis: atrophic, marked by degenerative changes in joint structure;

hypertrophic, marked also by bony spicules in joint.

arthropod (är'thrŭpŏd"), member of phylum of invertebrate animals called Arthropoda (more species than all other animal groups combined). Includes CRUSTACEAN; SPIDER and relatives; CENTIPEDE; MILLIPEDE; INSECT; and extinct TRILOBITE. They have segmented bodies, jointed appendages, horny outer skeleton. Respiratory organs are gills or trachea.

Arthur: see ARTHURIAN LEGEND.

Arthur, dukes of Brittany. **Arthur I,** 1187–1203, posthumous son of Geoffrey, second son of Henry II of England. Succeeded his mother, duchess Constance, 1196. His claim to England was passed over (1199) in favor of his uncle JOHN, but he was invested by Philip II of France with all the French fiefs of the deceased Richard Cœur de Lion. In the ensuing warfare with John, Arthur was captured (1202), imprisoned at Rouen, and probably murdered. His brother-in-law succeeded him in Brittany as Peter I. **Arthur III,** 1393–1458, was known as comte de Richemont before his accession in 1457. As constable of France in the Hundred Years War, he captured Paris from the English (1436); led in reconquest of Normandy.

Arthur, Chester Alan, 1830–86, 21st President of the United States (1881–85). Collector of the port of New York (1871–78); his removal by Pres. Hayes defied the Conkling machine. His nomination for Vice President placated that group. Succeeding to the presidency after Garfield's assassination, Arthur had an honest, efficient, dignified administration. Supported civil service reform act of 1883; vetoed Chinese exclusion bill violating a treaty with China; prosecuted STAR ROUTE trials.

Arthurian legend, vast body of medieval story centering about King Arthur of Britain. First references to him, early as c.600, indicate that Arthur was historically a British leader in the Anglo-Saxon invasion, but *Historia* (1137) of GEOFFREY OF MONMOUTH makes him head of magnificent court and master of Europe. Meanwhile the legend had developed, with traditional Irish hero stories joining those of Welsh (see MABINOGION), Cornish, and North Britons. The expanded stories of Arthur were transmitted (before the year 1000) to the Bretons, who spread the tales over Western Europe. After Geoffrey came the chronicles of WACE, then of English LAYAMON. More important, the romances *Perceval* by CHRESTIEN DE TROYES and *Parzifal* by WOLFRAM VON ESCHENBACH became sources of PARSIFAL story. Early in the 13th cent. GOTTFRIED VON STRASSBURG composed his *Tristan,* first great version of TRISTRAM AND ISOLDE romance, which became attached to Arthurian legend. The third main theme, the knightly quest for Holy GRAIL, also developed. In England, Arthurian legend flourished in *Sir Gawain and the Green Knight* (see PEARL, THE) and the *Morte d'Arthur* of Sir Thomas MALORY. The full, later legend has Arthur, King Uther Pendragon's illegitimate son, show his royal blood by drawing a sword from a stone. His own sword, Excalibur, is given him by

the Lady of the Lake; he keeps grand court with knights around honored Round Table at Camelot. When fatally wounded by his treacherous nephew (or son) Sir Mordred, Arthur is taken by three queens to the isle Avalon, whence he will return to save his people. Other characters in the legends are: Sir Launcelot of the Lake, gallant but faithless knight, lover of Arthur's queen; Elaine of Astolat, hopelessly in love with Launcelot; Elaine, daughter of Pelles, mother (by Launcelot) of the pure Sir Galahad, leader of Grail quest; Sir Gawain, Arthur's nephew, an ideal knight; Guinevere, Arthur's faithless queen, mistress of Launcelot; Sir Kay, churlish foster brother of Arthur; Merlin, great court magician; Morgan le Fay, Arthur's sister, an enchantress; and Sir Percivale (Parsifal).

artichoke, name for two different edible plants. Fleshy base of flower head and scales of the globe (or French) artichoke (*Cynara scolymus*) are eaten as salad or vegetable. It is a commercial crop in California. **Jerusalem artichoke** (*Helianthus tuberosus*) is a perennial sunflower with tuberous roots, potatolike but starchless, and grown for human food, stock feed, and as a source of inulin which yields levulose sugar.

artificial respiration, maintenance of breathing by artificial means. Mechanical devices are iron lung, respirator, pulmotor. Common hand method is Schafer (Schäfer, Shaefer) prone pressure method in which victim lies on stomach and operator presses and releases pressure on back 12–14 times per minute. More recently introduced is the back pressure arm lift method.

Artigas, José Gervasio (hōsā' hĕrvä'syō ärtē'gäs), 1764–1850, national hero of Uruguay. Typical gaucho of BANDA ORIENTAL, he championed Uruguayan independence from Spain, from Buenos Aires, and from Brazil. Exiled after annexation by Brazil (1820).

artillery, term originally applied to all projectiles employed in war, but later limited to certain types of heavy guns and the troops serving them. Small guns are said to have been used at Crécy (1346). The use of artillery against fortifications put an end to the security of the medieval castle. Artillery may be fixed or mobile. Artillery is now almost entirely mechanized (i.e., drawn by tractors or mounted on self-propelled trucks).

Art Institute of Chicago, museum and art school, inc. 1879 as Chicago Acad. of Fine Arts. It has galleries of paintings and sculpture; departments of textiles, prints, furniture, and Oriental art; the Ryerson Library; and a school of drama.

Artois (ärtwä'), region and former province, N France, in Pas-de-Calais dept.; historic cap., Arras. Agr., coal mines, and textile mfg. Annexed from Flanders to France (12th cent.), it passed to Burgundy (14th cent.) and to Hapsburgs (1493). It was conquered by France in 1640 and formally ceded by Spain to France in 1659. A battleground in many wars, particularly World War I.

Art Students League of New York, art school, founded 1875 in New York city by a group of students; self-governing. A board of control elected annually by members selects noted artists to serve as teachers.

Artzybashev, Mikhail Petrovich (mēkhŭyēl' pĕtrô'vĭch ärtsĭbä'shĕf), 1878–1927, Russian author. He leaped into fame with the sensational novel *Sanine* (1903; Eng. tr., 1914). Emigrated after October Revolution. Father of **Boris Artzybasheff**, 1899–, American illustrator of books and periodicals.

Aruba, Dutch West Indies: see CURAÇAO.

Arundel, Henry Fitzalan, 12th **earl of** (ă'rŭndŭl), c.1518–80, English statesman. Powerful Catholic noble, he helped bring Mary to the throne.

Arundel, Thomas Howard, 2d **earl of** c.1586–1646, first great English art collector. First a privy councilor, later earl marshal of England. **Arundel Marbles** are his collection of ancient sculptures donated 1667 to Oxford Univ. *Arundel Collection* of manuscripts are in British Mus. **Arundel Society** (1849–97) reproduced works of famous artists. **Arundel Club** founded 1904, reproduces in photogravure privately owned art works.

Arundel (ă'rŭndŭl), municipal borough (pop. 2,680), Sussex W, England. Arundel Castle (12th cent.), seat of dukes of Norfolk, overlooks town.

Arval Brothers (är'vŭl), in Roman religion, organization of 12 priests, with the emperor always a member. Their festival in May was a blessing of fields.

Arvida (ärvē'dŭ), city (pop. 11,078), S Que., Canada, on Saguenay R. and W of Chicoutimi. Has large aluminum and bauxite-reduction plants.

Aryabhatta (är"yŭbhŭt'ŭ), fl. 5th cent., Hindu mathematician, astronomer. One of first known users of algebra. Writings include rules of arithmetic, plane and spherical trigonometry; solutions of quadratic equations.

Aryan, name used by Hindus to designate themselves and other speakers of Indo-Iranian languages. Came to be used also for other Indo-European languages. Was favorite term of unscientific racism.

As, chemical symbol of the element ARSENIC.

Asa (ā'sŭ) [Heb.,= physician], d. c.870 B.C., king of Judah (c.911–c.870 B.C.); a "good" king, zealous in abolishing idols. Succeeded by Jehoshaphat. 1 Kings 15.8–24; 2 Chron. 14–16.

Asama, Mount (äsä'mä), active volcano, c.8,200 ft. high, central Honshu, Japan.

Asbestos, town (pop. 8,190), SE Que., Canada, NNW of Sherbrooke. Asbestos mining and mfg. center.

asbestos, any magnesium silicate mineral fibrous in structure and resistant to acid and fire. Often forms veins in other rock; probably results from metamorphism. Found in Canada, South Africa, U.S. It can be ground to make cement, woven into cloth, pressed into plasterboard. Used in pipe covering, fire-fighting equipment, shingles, etc.

Asbjørnsen, Peter Christian (äs'byŭrnsŭn), Nor. *Asbjørnsen*, 1812–85, Norwegian folklorist.

Asbury, Francis, 1745–1816, American Methodist bishop, b. England. As missionary (1771) he promoted circuit rider system. Became bishop 1784.

Asbury Park, Atlantic resort city (pop. 17,094), E N.J., SE of New Brunswick; founded 1869.

Ascalon (ăs'kŭ–), variant of ASHKELON.

Ascension, island in the S Atlantic, part of the British St. Helena Colony. A small island with few inhabitants, it is a naval station and had U.S. airfield World War II.

Asch, Sholem or **Shalom** (shō'lŭm ăsh', shä'lŭm), 1880–, Yiddish novelist and playwright, b. Poland, naturalized in U.S. 1920. Among novels are *The Nazarene* (1939), *The Apostle* (1943), *Mary* (1949).

Aschaffenburg (äshä'fŭnbŏŏrk), city (pop. 44,919), Lower Franconia, NW Bavaria, on Main R. Textile and paper mfg. Anc. Roman garrison city; summer residence of archbishops of Mainz after 9th cent. Heavily damaged in World War II.

Ascham, Roger (ăs'kŭm), 1515–68, English humanist, an outstanding scholar in Latin and Greek. Served as tutor (1548–50) to Princess Elizabeth and Latin secretary to Queen Mary (1553–58). Wrote *Toxophilus* (1545; on archery) and *The Scholemaster* (1570; a treatise on teaching Latin).

Asclepiades of Bithynia (ŭsklēpēăd'ēz, bĭthĭn'ēŭ), c.124 B.C.–40 B.C., Greek founder of influential school of medicine in Rome.

Asclepius (ăsklē'pēŭs), Latin *Aesculapius*, legendary Greek physician and god of medicine; son of Apollo and Coronis. Sick treated at his temples. Serpent and cock sacred to him.

Ascot, village, Berkshire, England. Near-by Ascot Heath has annual horse races held since 1711.

Asenath (ăs'ŭnăth), Egyptian wife of Joseph. Gen. 41.45,50–52; 46.20. Their marriage is subject of story of Joseph and Asenath, one of PSEUDEPIGRAPHA.

Asgard (ăs'gärd) [Norse,= home of gods], Norse Olympus, home of 12 chief gods (Aesir).

ash, any tree or shrub of genus *Fraxinus*, e.g., white ash (*Fraxinus americana*), a valuable American timber tree with strong wood, black ash (*F. nigra*), and blue ash (*F. quadrangulata*). Mountain ash and prickly ash are not true ashes.

Ashanti (ŭshän'tē), British protectorate (24,560 sq. mi.; pop. 823,672), Gold Coast, W Africa; cap. Kumasi. Formerly a strong native kingdom, founded 1697. Under British protection since 1896.

Ashby-de-la-Zouch (–zōōch', –zōōsh'), urban district (pop. 6,406), Leicestershire, England. Figures in Scott's *Ivanhoe*. Mary Queen of Scots held in Ashby Castle 1569.

Ashdod, ancient city of Philistines, between Jaffa and Gaza, of military importance in wars between Egypt and countries to N. Seat of the worship of Dagon, it was destroyed by the Maccabees. Now a village called Esdud. 1 Sam. 5.1; Joshua 15.47; 2 Chron. 26.6; Neh. 4.7; 13.23; Isa. 20.1; Jer. 25.20.

Asheboro (ăsh'bŭrŭ), town (pop. 7,701), central N.C., in piedmont S of Greensboro. Produces hosiery, textiles, furniture, and flour. Near-by prehistoric Keyauwee Indian burial ground excavated 1936.

Asher (ăsh'ŭr), son of Jacob, ancestor of one (Asher) of 12 tribes of Israel. Tribe occupied NW Palestine. Gen. 30; Deut. 33.24; Joshua 19.24–31; Judges 5.17,18. Aser: Luke 2.36; Rev. 7.6.

Asheville, city (pop. 53,000), W N.C., on French Broad R., on plateau in Blue Ridge, founded after 1791. Resort and financial, transportation, and commercial center of W N.C., it is near Great Smoky Mountains Natl. Park, Pisgah Natl. Forest, and Mt. Mitchell (6,684 ft.). Mfg. of textiles, leather goods, and furniture. Birthplace of Thomas Wolfe. "Biltmore," the Vanderbilt estate, is showplace.

Ashkelon (ăsh'kŭ–) or **Ascalon** (ăs'–), ancient city of Philistines on Mediterranean coast, between Jaffa and Gaza; center of worship of goddess Astarte. Played important role in Crusades. Also in Bible, Askelon, Eshkalon.

Ashkenazim (–năz'–), term referring to the German Jews as distinguished from Sephardim, the Jews of Spain and Portugal.

Ashkhabad (ŭshkhŭbät'), city (pop. 126,580), cap. of Turkmen SSR, on Trans-Caspian RR, near Iranian border. Cotton and silk mills.

Ashland. 1 City (pop. 31,131), E Ky., on Ohio R. near influx of Big Sandy R. and NW of Huntington, W.Va.; settled 1815. Air, rail, and river shipping center in coal, oil, gas, and lumber region, it processes iron, steel, coke, oil, chemicals, leather, and brick. "Traipsin' Woman's Cabin," scene of annual American Folk Song Festival, is near by. **2** City (pop. 14,287), N Ohio, NE of Mansfield; laid out 1815. Mfg. of machinery, hardware, and rubber goods. Seat of Ashland Col. **3** City (pop. 7,739), SW Oregon, W of Klamath Falls, near Calif. line. Lumber, fruit, grain center. Resort near mountains. Holds annual Shakspere festival. **4** Borough (pop. 6,192), E Pa., near Pottsville. Produces coal, metal products, textiles. **5** Town (pop. 2,610), central Va., N of Richmond. Seat of RANDOLPH-MACON COLLEGE. Birthplaces of Patrick Henry and Henry Clay and girlhood home of Dolly Madison are near by. **6** City (pop. 10,640), N Wis., port on Chequamegon Bay of L. Superior; settled 1854 near site of Father Allouez's mission (1665). Industrial and shipping center with woodworking and paper plants and ironworks. Apostle Isls. to N.

Ashley, Anthony Ashley Cooper, Baron: see SHAFTESBURY, ANTHONY ASHLEY COOPER, 1ST EARL OF.

Ashley, William Henry, c.1778–1838, American fur trader, U.S. Representative from Mo. (1831–37). After 1821 he sent expeditions to upper Missouri R. region and into Green R. valley.

Ashley, borough (pop. 5,243), NE Pa., near Wilkes-Barre. Produces anthracite and metal products.

Ashley, river: see CHARLESTON, S.C.

Ashmead, William Harris, 1855–1908, American entomologist who described 607 new genera and 3,100 new species.

Ashokan Reservoir, N.Y.: see CATSKILL AQUEDUCT.

Ashtabula (ăsh"tŭbū'lŭ), city (pop. 23,696), NE Ohio, on L. Erie; settled c.1801. Receiving port for ore. Mfg. of metal products,

leather goods, and chemicals. Hothouse vegetables grown.

Ashtaroth (ăsh'tŭrŏth), Hebrew form of ASTARTE. A city of Bashan was named Ashtaroth. Joshua 9.10; 12.4; 13.12,31; 1 Chron. 6.71.

Ashtoreth (ăsh'tŏrĕth), Hebrew form of ASTARTE.

Ashur, anc. Assyrian city: see ASSYRIA.

Ashur-bani-pal, Assyrian king: see ASSUR-BANI-PAL.

Ashurnasirpal III (ä"shōōrnä'zîrpäl), d. 860? B.C., king of anc. Assyria (884–860? B.C.). Conquered westward to the Mediterranean and estab. administration of empire.

Ash Wednesday: see LENT.

Asia, world's largest continent. Forms with Europe the Eurasian land mass. Its boundary with Europe lies along Ural Mts., Ural R., and Greater Caucasus. Thus defined, Asia has area of c.16,000,000 sq. mi. and pop. of c.1,050,000,000. In W separated from Europe by the Bosporus, Dardanelles, and Aegean Sea, in NE separated from N America by Bering Strait. Suez Canal (between Mediterranean and Red Sea) breaks Asia's connection with Africa. Washed on S by Arabian Sea, on E by China Sea, Yellow Sea, Sea of Japan, Sea of Okhotsk, and Bering Sea, and on N by Arctic Ocean. Westernmost part of Asia is ASIA MINOR (major part of Turkey). To SE is peninsula of Arabia, N of which are Syria, Lebanon, Israel, Jordan, Iraq. Farther E are Iran, Afghanistan, India, and Pakistan. On SE peninsula are Burma, Malaya, Thailand, and Indo-China. Much of SE and central Asia belongs to China, bordered by Mongolian People's Republic, Tibet, and Korea. A major part of Asia is occupied by USSR.

Asia Minor, peninsula, extreme W Asia; called also Anatolia. It is bounded by the Black Sea, the Bosporus, the Sea of Marmara, and the Dardanelles (N); the Mediterranean (S); and the Aegean Sea (W). A high plateau, it is crossed by mountains, notably the TAURUS near the S coast, and is roughly identical with Asiatic TURKEY. Asia Minor, in close touch with Greece and Mesopotamia, was the chief meeting place of the ancient Orient and Occident. After the decline of the Hittites, the Greeks colonized coastal Ionia, coming in contact with Lydia, Phrygia, and more especially Troy. Conquest of Asia Minor by the Persians led to the Persian Wars. Divided into several small rival states in Hellenistic times, it was reintegrated by the Romans, but was subject to almost constant invasions under the Byzantine Empire and finally fell to the Ottomans in the 13th–15th cent.

Asiatic cholera: see CHOLERA.

Aske, Robert (ăsk), d. 1537, English revolutionist, leader of PILGRIMAGE OF GRACE. He was executed.

Askelon (ăs'kŭ–), variant of ASHKELON.

Asmara (äsmä'rä), city (pop. c.95,000), cap. of Eritrea; alt. c.7,700 ft. In 1897 it succeeded Massawa as cap. of Eritrea.

Asmodeus (ăs"mōdē'ŭs), demon of Hebrew story, important in book of Tobit (3.6; 8).

Asmoneans: see MACCABEES.

Asoka (ŭsō'kŭ), d. c.237 B.C., emperor

CAPITAL CITIES are designated by CAPITAL AND SMALL CAPITAL type

(c.255–c.237 B.C.) of MAURYA empire. Domain included most of India and Afghanistan. Converted to Buddhism c.257. Pillars inscribed with his pious sayings survive.

Aso-san (ä′sō-sän), group of five volcanic cones, central Kyushu, Japan. Only the central cone is active. Crater floor is 37.2 mi. in circumferance.

asp, popular name of poisonous snake (probably either Egyptian cobra or horned viper), known as instrument in story of Cleopatra's suicide.

Aspadana: see ISFAHAN, Iran.

asparagus (ùspăr′ù–), perennial garden vegetable (*Asparagus officinalis*). Its tender shoots are eaten in spring. Feathery foliage sometimes used by florists but more popular decorative species include SMILAX and asparagus fern.

Aspasia (ăspā′zhù), 5th cent. B.C., Greek courtesan; beautiful, learned mistress of Pericles.

Aspen, city (pop. 916; alt. 7,850 ft.), W central Colo., W of Leadville. Once a rich silver camp, it is now a resort. Had Goethe festival, 1949.

aspen, name for several species of POPLAR, e.g., quaking aspen (*Populus tremuloides*) and large-toothed aspen (*P. grandidentata*). The long leafstalks cause their broad leaves to tremble in even the faintest breeze.

Aspern (äs′pùrn), eastern suburb of Vienna, Austria. Scene of Austrian victory over Napoleon I (1809).

asphalt (ăs′fôlt), brownish-black natural mixture of hydrocarbons used in road making, roofing, waterproofing, in making paints and varnishes. Varies from solid to semisolid, has great tenacity, melts when heated.

asphodel (ăs′fùděl″), hardy stemless plant (*Asphodelus*) with showy flower spikes. The ancient asphodel sacred to Persephone belongs to the genus *Asphodeline*.

Aspropotamos, Greek river: see ACHELOUS.

Asquith, Herbert Henry: see OXFORD AND ASQUITH, HERBERT HENRY ASQUITH, 1st EARL OF.

ass, smaller animal of HORSE genus, known in domesticated state as the donkey; male is called a jack or jackass, female a jennet or jenny. Hardy and sure-footed, it has large head, small hoofs, short mane and tail, long ears. The diminutive burro is common pack animal in W U.S., Mexico. Ass was probably domesticated by c.4000 B.C. in Mesopotamia and Egypt. Several breeds have been used to breed the MULE.

Assam (ăsăm′), state (54,084 sq. mi.; pop. 9,129,442), NE India; cap. Shillong. Rugged terrain with fertile valleys of the Brahmaputra and Surma. Cherrapunji village in SW reputedly has world's heaviest rainfall (c.500 in. annually). Crops include rice, citrus fruits, sugar cane, tea, cotton, and jute. Lumbering is important. Suffered Burmese invasions from 13th to early 19th cent. Became part of British India in 1826. Japan held S area in 1944. A SW section was included 1947 in E Pakistan.

Assandum, battle of (ă′sùndùn), victory (1016) of the Danes under CANUTE over the English.

Assassin (ùsă′sĭn) [Arabic,= under the influ-

ence of hashish], European name for member of secret order of SHIITES, which ruthlessly murdered enemies. Founded c.1090, flourished in Syria and Persia. Grand master, Sheikh al Jabal, known in W Europe as Old Man of the Mountain, was absolute ruler.

assault, any unlawful attempt to use violence to cause bodily harm. If successful, the offense becomes BATTERY. Every criminal assault entitles the victim to sue for damages. Simple assault is a misdemeanor; aggravated assault (e.g., with intent to kill) a felony.

assaying, in metallurgy, process of determining content of a specific metal in an ore or alloy. To obtain representative sample, often several samples are crushed and mixed. "Wet" assay (using liquid reagents) determines weight of metal; "dry" or fire assay yields metal in pure state.

Asser, Tobias Michael Carel (tōbē′äs mē′khäl kä′rùl äs′ùr), 1838–1913, Dutch statesman and jurist. For his work in international arbitration, he shared 1911 Nobel Peace Prize with Alfred Fried.

Assideans: see HASIDIM.

Assiniboine (ùsĭn′ùboin), river, c.600 mi. long, rising in E Sask., Canada, and flowing SE into SW Man. to join Qu'Appelle R., then SE and E to Red R. at Winnipeg. Valley is a leading wheat area. Discovered 1736 by the Vérendryes, it became route of fur traders and settlers westward.

Assiniboine, Mount, 11,870 ft. high, on Alta.–B.C. line, Canada, in Rocky Mts. and S of Banff.

Assisi (äs-sē′zē), town (pop. 4,686), Umbria, central Italy; birthplace of St. Francis. Above saint's tomb are two superimposed Gothic churches, with frescoes by Cimabue and Giotto. Medieval in atmosphere, Assisi has many churches, including cathedral and (outside town) Santa Maria degli Angeli, built around Porziuncola chapel.

association, psychological tendency to link words and ideas consciously or unconsciously. In free association, a basic psychoanalytic technique, the patient voices all thoughts, however apparently trivial or disconnected, to reveal conflict areas, repressed desires, traumatic events; psychoanalyst observes manifest content and accompanying somatic reactions which expose attempted suppression of material.

Assuan, Egypt: see ASWAN.

Assur, anc. Assyrian city: see ASSYRIA.

Assur-bani-pal (ä″sōō-bä′nē-päl) or **Ashur-bani-pal** (ä″shōōr–), d. 626 B.C.?, king of anc. Assyria (669?–626? B.C.), son and successor of Esar-Haddon. Under him Assyria reached height of glory in riches, art, and learning (his library was famous). He conquered Egypt and set Necho in power but later lost power there to Necho's son, Psamtik I. Put down revolt led by his brother, but power of empire was fading. Identified with Osnapper or Asnappar of Bible, Sardanapalus of Greeks.

Assyria (ùsĭ′rēù), anc. empire of W Asia, originating around city of Ashur or Assur on upper Tigris R., with cap. later at Calah and resplendent Nineveh. Nucleus of a struggling Semitic city-state, it was overshadowed by Babylonia, but in 12th cent.

B.C. rose to transitory greatness under TIGLATH-PILESER I. Real importance began in 9th cent. with conquests of ASHURNASIR-PAL III, who set up an imperial administration. Later kings (SHALMANESER III, TIGLATH-PILESER III, and SARGON) gained hegemony in the Middle East. SENNACHERIB consolidated the holdings, and ESAR-HADDON (reigned 681–668 B.C.) defeated the Chaldeans and won power in Egypt. Under his successor, ASSUR-BANI-PAL (reigned 669?–626? B.C.), Assyria reached its height of learning, art, and splendor. Yet Egypt broke away, and decline was rapid. Soon after his death Nineveh was sacked (612 B.C.). The Babylonian empire returned briefly to power, and the Persian Empire was founded.

Assyrian language, Semitic language of anc. times, in Akkadian group. See LANGUAGE (table).

Astaroth (ăs′tŭrŏth), Hebrew form of Astarte.

Astarte (ăstär′tē), Semitic goddess of fertility, beauty, and love. She was the most important Phoenician goddess, corresponding to Ishtar (also to APHRODITE), and was sometimes regarded as goddess of moon. The Bible refers to her as Ashtaroth or Ashtoreth.

astatine (ăs′tŭtēn), chemical element (symbol = At; atomic no.= 85). Discovery was announced in 1931; was at first called alabamine. In 1940 was produced in cyclotron at Univ. of California.

Astell, Mary (ăs′tŭl), 1666–1731, English author and feminist. Advocated a woman's college in *Serious Proposal to the Ladies* (1694–97).

aster, perennial plant (often called wild aster) of genus *Aster,* with small daisylike flowers. Most important garden varieties derived from North American fall-blooming species and grown in Europe as Michaelmas daisies. China aster (*Callistephus*) is a popular garden annual with larger heads of ray flowers, ranging from white and pink to purple.

asteroid or **planetoid,** minor planet revolving around sun. Over 1,500 recognized; orbits of most lie between Mars and Jupiter. Ceres (diameter c.480 mi.), largest and first known, discovered Jan. 1, 1801, by Piazzi.

asthma, condition marked by labored breathing. Allergy probable cause; specific agent determinable by skin tests.

Asti (äs′tē), city (pop. 26,476), Piedmont, NW Italy; famous sparkling wine.

Astolat, in ARTHURIAN LEGEND: see GUILDFORD.

Aston, Francis William, 1877–1945, English chemist. Won 1922 Nobel Prize for discovery of a number of isotopes in nonradioactive elements.

Astor, John Jacob, 1763–1848, American merchant, b. Germany. Chartered AMERICAN FUR COMPANY. Richest man in U.S. at death; left fortune that has kept family name prominent. His great-grandson, **William Waldorf Astor, 1st Viscount Astor,** 1848–1919, American-British capitalist, moved to England in 1890. Contributed huge sums to public causes. His elder son, Waldorf Astor, married **Nancy Witcher (Langhorne) Astor, Viscountess Astor,** 1879–, British political leader, b. Va. As Conservative, the first woman to sit in Parliament. In late 1930s be-

gan with her husband to take a large part in politics through the "Cliveden set"—named after Astor country home.

Astoria (ăstôr′ēŭ), city (pop. 12,331), NW Oregon, on S bank of Columbia R. near its mouth. American fur-trading post estab. here in 1811 under John Jacob Astor. Trade in British hands after 1813. Refounded 1843 by overlanders; grew as port of entry.

Astrakhan (ă′strŭkăn″), city (pop. 253,655), SE European RSFSR; Caspian port on Volga delta. Fishing, caviar processing; transshipment point for Baku oil. Cap. of a Tatar khanate until 1557, when Ivan IV conquered it. Oriental in character, city has kept old kremlin, with cathedral, monastery, and palace.

astrolabe (ăs′trŭlāb), instrument formerly used to determine positions of heavenly bodies. Simple astrolabe had suspended disk with degrees marked on circumference and movable pointer at center. In navigation superseded by sextant (18th cent.).

astrology [Gr.,= science of stars], method of DIVINATION based on theory that stars influence human affairs. Its lore is very old and was basis for ancient knowledge of astronomy. In Middle Ages it was associated with alchemy and occult sciences. After Copernicus, astrology and astronomy diverged. In astrology a horoscope is a map of the heavens at time of birth, using chart of the zodiac; the "house" or sign in the ascendant at time of one's birth is said to determine his temperament, tendencies to disease, and liability to certain fortunes or calamities.

astronomy, scientific study of the heavenly bodies. Arose from need for designating time intervals; was early associated with astrology. Theoretical contributions stem from Greeks including Thales, Pythagoras, Eratosthenes, and Aristarchus of Samos. Earth-centered view of HIPPARCHUS and other Alexandrian Greeks, preserved in *Almagest* of Claudius PTOLEMY, was displaced in 16th cent. by sun-centered view of COPERNICUS, which was supported by observations of GALILEO, Tycho BRAHE, and KEPLER. Astronomical knowledge was advanced by scientists including Edmund Halley, Sir William and Sir J. F. W. Herschel, C. G. Abbot, Einstein, G. E. Hale, Sir James Jeans, Sir A. S. Eddington, Harlow Shapley, and Otto Struve and also by application of physics (astrophysics) in studies of radiation, light, and composition of heavenly bodies. See also ASTEROID; COMET; COSMOGONY; METEOR; MOON; PLANET; STAR; SUN. See *ill.,* p. 1187.

Asturias (ästōō′ryäs), region (4,207 sq. mi.; pop. 836,642), NW Spain, on Bay of Biscay, crossed by Cantabrian Mts.; historic cap. Oviedo. Coal, iron, zinc mines, steel mills; cattle raising; fishing. Chief port: Gijón. Reconquest of Spain from Moors was begun by Christian nobles who had held out in Asturian mountains. Kingdom of Asturias was joined with Leon in 10th cent.

Astyages (ăstī′ŭjēz), 6th cent. B.C., semilegendary king of the Medes. His grandson, CYRUS THE GREAT, is supposed to have overthrown him to found greatness of Persian Empire.

Astyanax (ŭstī′ŭnăks), in Greek legend, son

of Hector and Andromache. Slain by Greeks at Troy.

Asunción (äsōōnsyōn'), city (pop. 113,598; with suburbs, 144,327), cap. of Paraguay, on Paraguay R.; port and commercial center. Has many small industries. Founded in 1536 or 1537, Asunción was most important town in Río de la Plata region until rise of Buenos Aires.

Aswan or **Assuan** (both: äswän'), city (pop. 25,397), Upper Egypt, at First Cataract of the Nile. Near by is the great **Aswan Dam** (built 1902), 1¼ mi. long, 176½ ft. high.

Asyut (äsūt'), anc. *Lycopolis*, largest city (pop. 88,730) of Upper Egypt; trade center in Nile valley. Near by is Asyut barrage (for irrigation).

At, chemical symbol of the element ASTATINE.

Atacama, Desert of (ätäkä'mä), arid region, c.600 mi. long, N Chile, c.2,000 ft. above sea level, between Pacific coastal range and Andes. Has no vegetation, but is rich in nitrate and copper. ALMAGRO was first European to cross it (1537). Passed from Bolivia to Chile in War of the Pacific.

Atahualpa (ätäwäl'pä), d. 1533, last Inca of Peru. Successfully rebelled against HUÁSCAR (who shared rule with him), took whole empire. Francisco Pizarro imprisoned Atahualpa (1532) and in spite of offer of a roomful of gold as ransom had him put to death.

Atalanta (ätŭlăn'tŭ), in Greek legend, huntress who joined Calydonian hunt and Argonaut voyage. She ran a race with each suitor, on condition that winner should marry her but loser should die. Hippomenes (hĭpŏ'mĭnēz) won by dropping three apples; Atalanta paused to pick them up.

Ataturk, Kemal (kĕmäl' ätätürk'), 1880–1938, Turkish leader, founder of Modern Turkey; known before 1934 as Mustafa Kemal or Kemal Pasha. An army officer, he took part in the Young Turk revolution of 1908, distinguished himself in World War I, and after Turkey's collapse organized the Nationalist party and army in E Anatolia. After the Greek landing at SMYRNA (1919), he convoked Nationalist congresses at Erzerum and Sivas, was outlawed by the Allied-controlled government at Constantinople, and set up a rival government at Ankara. The signing of the Treaty of SÈVRES by the Constantinople government made the split with Ankara final. Kemal expelled the Greeks from Anatolia in a brilliant campaign (1921–22), which earned him the title Ghazi [victorious]; abolished the sultanate (1922); secured honorable peace at the LAUSANNE CONFERENCE (1923); and served as president of the Turkish republic for five terms (1927–35). Ruling dictatorially, he carried out a drastic program of Westernization and reform which changed the face of TURKEY.

Ataulf (ă'täŭlf), d. 415, Visigothic king (410–15). Led VISIGOTHS from Italy into S Gaul (412), later into N Spain. Married GALLA PLACIDIA.

Atchafalaya (ŭchä'fŭlī"ŭ), river branching in E La. from Red R. near its junction with the Mississippi, and flowing c.170 mi. S through several lakes to Atchafalaya Bay of Gulf of Mexico. Navigable.

Atchison, city (pop. 12,792), NE Kansas, on the Missouri; settled 1854. Grew as river port, rail terminus, and supply point for westward travel. Trade center for grain, livestock, and apple area, it mills flour and has mfg. of steel products. Seat of Mt. St. Scholastica Col. (R.C.; for women; 1863).

Ate (ā'tē) [Gr.,= folly], in Greek religion, personification of rash temper leading to folly.

Athabaska, Lake, 3,058 sq. mi., c.200 mi. long, 5–35 mi. wide, NE Alta. and NW Sask., Canada. Receives Athabaska and Peace rivers in SW, drains NW into Great Slave R., thence via Mackenzie R. into Arctic Ocean. On edge of Laurentian Plateau, it is connected to Churchill R. by canoe route. Fort Chipewyan, at W end of lake, built 1788. Lake surveyed and mapped by Philip Turnor 1790–92.

Athabaska, Mount, 11,452 ft. high, W Alta., Canada, on edge of Columbia Icefield and surrounded by Athabaska and Saskatchewan glaciers.

Athabaska Pass, 5,736 ft. high, W Alta. and E B.C., Canada, from headwaters of Athabaska R. across Continental Divide to Columbia R. Discovered c.1811, it became route to Columbia R. country.

Athaliah (äth"ŭlī'ŭ), died c.841 B.C., queen of Judah (c.846–c.841 B.C.); daughter of Ahab and Jezebel, wife of Jehoram of Judah. She succeeded her murdered son, Ahaziah of Judah. Killed in coup d'état in favor of JEHOASH 2. She is subject of Racine's ATHALIE. 2 Kings 11; 2 Chron. 22–23.

Athanagild (ŭthä'nŭgĭld), d. 567, Visigothic king of Spain (554–67). Helped into power by Byzantines, to whom he ceded part of S Spain. Later fought Byzantines, Franks, Basques. Held splendid court at Toledo. Father of Brunhilda and Galswintha.

Athanasius, Saint (äthŭnā'zhŭs), 295–373, patriarch of Alexandria, Doctor of the Church. Distinguished himself at First Council of NICAEA by eloquent opposition to ARIANISM and fought it later steadfastly. He was exiled five times. When he fled to Rome, he gained the aid of Pope Julius I. A vigorous administrator in his patriarchate, he was also a gifted writer against Arianism and helped to shape the statement of Catholic doctrine. Feast: May 2. The **Athanasian Creed** was not by him but by a Western writer of the 6th cent. It is an exact statement of Catholic belief on the Trinity and the Incarnation. Sometimes called QUICUNQUE VULT.

Athapascan (äthŭpäs'kŭn), linguistic stock of North America, widely distributed among Indian tribes of W Canada and W U.S. See LANGUAGE, table.

atheism, doctrine that there is no supernatural being. Through history many nonatheists have been accused of atheism because they held unorthodox views (e.g., Socrates, Spinoza, the deists). Atheism is related to, and often confused with, AGNOSTICISM.

Athelstan or **Æthelstan** (both: äth'ŭlstŭn, –stän"), d. 940, king of the English (924–40). Grandchild of ALFRED, built up state on foundations laid by him. Issued laws that attempted to impose royal authority on customary law.

Athena (ŭthē'nŭ) or **Pallas Athena** (pă'lŭs),

Olympian goddess of wisdom, patron of arts of peace and war, ruler of storms, and guardian of Athens, a virgin goddess, sprung from the forehead of Zeus. She is usually shown wearing helmet and aegis with head of MEDUSA. Parthenon was her temple, Panathenaea her festival. Identified with Roman Minerva.

Athena Parthenos, a gold and ivory statue by PHIDIAS, dedicated c.438 B.C. in the Parthenon. It was the chief treasure of Athens.

Athenodorus: see LAOCOÖN.

Athens (ăth'ĭnz), Gr. *Athenai,* city (pop. 559,250; greater Athens, with port PIRAEUS and other cities, 1,368,142), cap. of Greece, on the plain of Attica. It is cultural, religious (focus of Greek Orthodox Church), and industrial (textiles, machine-tool plants, utilities) center of country. Many tourists come to view remains in city that was fountainhead of Western civilization. Early history is mixed with legend (e.g., story of Theseus as consolidator of cities of Attica, account of early kings). Aristocratic archons held power when Solon presumably began reforms in 594 B.C. A period of tyrants under Pisistratus and his sons Hippias and Hipparchus lasted until 510 B.C., when CLEISTHENES founded the democracy that was to persist in the period of greatness. In the period of the PERSIAN WARS (500–449 B.C.) small Athens emerged, under hero leaders such as MILTIADES, THEMISTOCLES, and CIMON, as a great naval power, and the DELIAN LEAGUE became practically an Athenian empire. Architecture, art, and literature rose to astonishing height in the Golden Age under Pericles (5th cent. B.C.). The Parthenon was built; SOCRATES spoke his philosophy; Greek drama was founded with AESCHYLUS, SOPHOCLES, and EURIPIDES. In later decline this glory went on with PLATO and ARISTOTLE, ARISTOPHANES and the orator DEMOSTHENES. In the long-drawn PELOPONNESIAN WAR Athens was finally conquered by SPARTA. Recovery after defeat in 404 B.C. was rapid but transitory, and in the 4th cent. Athens was subjected by PHILIP II of Macedon and his son, ALEXANDER THE GREAT. When Roman greatness grew Athens became a provincial cap., and attempts to regain power resulted in humiliation (notably the sack by Sulla, 86 B.C.). Yet the tradition of Athens affected Rome and even more affected the Byzantine Empire, under which it fell. With the fall of that empire Athens passed (1205) to a French nobleman and became a duchy, later prosperous in Catalan hands (under house of Aragon). A brief renascence under the rule of Florentine nobles, the Acciajuoli, in the late 14th and early 15th cent. was followed by decline under Ottoman rule after 1458. When Greece was freed, Athens became the cap. of independent Greece and gradually grew to its present position. It retains relics of the past. On the ACROPOLIS are the Parthenon, the Propylaea, and the Erechtheum. Elsewhere about the city are fine Greek and Roman remains.

Athens. 1 City (pop. 6,309), N Ala., near Tenn. line, N of Birmingham, in cotton area. Hosiery and lumber mills. Sacked and occupied by Federals (1862), recaptured by N. B. Forrest (1864). **2** City (pop. 28,180), NE Ga., on Oconee R. and ENE of Atlanta. Founded 1801 as site of Univ. of GEORGIA. Cotton market and mfg. center (textiles, tire cord, cottonseed oil). Has many fine classic revival homes. **3** City (pop. 11,660), SE Ohio, W of Marietta. Surveyed 1795–96 by Ohio Co. of Associates as university site, its settlement soon followed. Has printing and mfg. of meat products and machinery. Seat of Ohio Univ. (state controlled; coed.; chartered 1804, opened 1809, oldest college in the Old Northwest). **4** City (pop. 8,618), E Tenn., NE of Chattanooga. Trade center of agr. and timber area with mfg. of clothing and furniture. **5** City (pop. 5,194), E Texas, WSW of Tyler. Shipping center of oil and agr. area with mfg. of clay products.

athlete's foot: see RINGWORM.

Athlone, Godart van Ginkel, 1st earl of: see GINKEL.

Athlone (ăthlōn'), urban district (pop. 8,379), Co. Westmeath, Ireland, on Shannon R. Athlone Castle was of strategic value in early Irish history.

Athol (ă'thŏl), town (pop. 11,554), including Athol village (pop. 9,708), N Mass., W of Fitchburg. Mfg. of machinery and tools.

Atholl or **Athole** (both: ăth'ŭl), mountainous district, 450 sq. mi., N Perthshire, Scotland.

Athos (ăth'ŏs) or **Akte** (äk'tā), easternmost peninsula of CHALCIDICE, NE Greece; c.30 mi. long, 1½–7 mi. wide. It forms the autonomous state of the Greek Orthodox monks of **Mount Athos,** or Hagion Oros [Holy Mountain], rising c.6,000 ft. at S tip of peninsula. The community, founded 10th cent., consists of 20 convents. Under direct rule of the patriarch of Constantinople, it has always enjoyed virtual independence. No female, human or animal, is admitted. Libraries contain a wealth of Byzantine manuscripts.

Atkinson, Henry, 1782–1842, American army officer, general commander in BLACK HAWK WAR.

Atlanta, city (pop. 331,314), state cap. (since 1868), NW Ga., near Chattahoochee R. Largest city in state. Chief rail center of the South and one of its principal distributing, industrial, commercial, and cultural centers. Mfg. of textiles, furniture, cottonseed oil, machinery, electrical goods, shoes, and pharmaceuticals. Hardy Ivy settled here in 1833. Town founded 1837 as Terminus (end of a rail line) and renamed 1845. Important as a Confederate supply and communications center, it fell to W. T. SHERMAN on Sept. 2, 1864 (see ATLANTA CAMPAIGN). He burned it (Nov. 15) before his march to the sea. Conventions and expositions in 19th and 20th cent. drew attention to city's strategic distributory position. Federal penitentiary (1899) here is widely known. Here are High Mus. of Art, state archives building, co-cathedral of Christ the King (R.C.), building with *Cyclorama of the Battle of Atlanta,* stockyards, farmers' market, and Fort McPherson. Seat of GEORGIA INSTITUTE OF TECHNOLOGY, Oglethorpe Univ. (coed.; 1916), and Morris Brown Col. (Negro; Methodist; coed.; 1885). EMORY

UNIVERSITY is near. Atlanta Univ. System (Negro; 1929) has four affiliated schools with adjacent campuses and some common facilities: Atlanta Univ. (coed.; grad.; opened 1865), Atlanta Univ. School of Social Work (coed.; 1920; joined 1938), Morehouse Col. (for men; 1867), Spelman Col. (for women; 1881). Clark Col. (Negro; Methodist; coed.; opened 1870) cooperates with Atlanta Univ. System.

Atlanta campaign, May–Sept., 1864, of Civil War. W. T. Sherman gathered Union armies near Chattanooga with two aims—to destroy J. E. Johnston's army and to capture Atlanta. By flanking actions he forced Johnston from successive positions to Chattahoochee R. Here J. B. Hood counterattacked but failed to stop advance, and retired to Atlanta. After Union army cut communications, Confederates abandoned city Sept. 1. Sherman occupied it Sept. 2.

Atlanta University System: see ATLANTA, Ga.

Atlantic, city (pop. 6,480), SW Iowa, ENE of Council Bluffs. Trade and processing center in a farming area.

Atlantic Charter, program of peace aims, jointly enunciated by Prime Minister Winston Churchill of Great Britain and Pres. F. D. Roosevelt of U.S. on Aug. 14, 1941. Aims incorporated in UN declaration of 1942.

Atlantic City, seaside resort and convention city (pop. 61,657), SE N.J., c.60 mi. SE of Philadelphia, c.100 mi. SW of New York. Boardwalk built 1870; present boardwalk lined with shops and hotels. Has large municipal auditorium, six amusement piers.

Atlantic Highlands, resort borough (pop. 3,083), NE N.J., on Sandy Hook Bay near Navesink Highlands, one of highest (c.276 ft.) U.S. Atlantic coastal ridges.

Atlantic Ocean, second largest ocean, est. area 31,830,000 sq. mi., extends in S-shape from arctic to antarctic regions between the Americas, Europe, and Africa. Connected with the Pacific by Panama Canal, and (through Mediterranean) with Red Sea by Suez Canal. Chief western arms: Hudson and Baffin bays, Gulf of Mexico, Caribbean Sea. Chief eastern arms: Baltic and North seas, Bay of Biscay, the Mediterranean, Gulf of Guinea. Shortest trans-Atlantic distance is between Dakar, Africa, and bulge of Brazil. More large rivers drain into it than into any other ocean. Surface waters of trade-wind belts attain highest oceanic salinity known. Chief currents: North and South Equatorial, Brazil, Guinea, and GULF STREAM, which meets Labrador Current in Grand Banks off Newfoundland, forming heavy fogs. Gulf Stream then bends eastward to form part of NORTH ATLANTIC DRIFT. This area, part of busiest shipping lane in world, is patrolled for icebergs by U.S. coast guard. A submarine ridge extends from E Greenland to N Scotland, bearing telegraph cable network. Mid-Atlantic ridge, 300–600 mi. wide, from Iceland almost to Antarctic Circle, rises to average height of c.10,000 ft. It is center of volcanic activity and earthquakes; a few of its peaks emerge as islands. Chief Atlantic deeps are Milwaukee Depth (30,246 ft.) near the Bahamas and Nares Deep (27,972 ft.) near Puerto Rico. Discovery of an 800-mile

canyon in floor of the Atlantic midway between Bermuda and the Azores was reported in 1952.

Atlantis, in Greek legend, large island in western sea. Plato, who describes it as a Utopia, tells of high civilization there until its destruction by earthquake. Question of its actual existence has provoked much speculation.

Atlas (ăt'lŭs), in Greek religion, Titan. After the downfall of the Titans he was condemned to hold up the sky on his head and hands.

Atlas Mountains, mountain system of NW Africa, extending c.1500 mi. NE from Morocco through Algeria to Cape Bon in Tunisia.

Atlin Lake, 308 sq. mi., 66 mi. long, 2–6 mi. wide, NW B.C. and S Yukon, Canada. On E shore is Atlin village, hq. of gold-mining region.

atmosphere, gaseous envelope around earth, probably extending at least 600 mi. Lower layer (troposphere) extends to limiting boundary (tropopause) and decreases in height from c.10 mi. at equator to c.5 mi. at poles; above lies stratosphere, first reached by Auguste Piccard in balloon ascent (1931). Within troposphere, air is mixed by ascending and descending currents; temperature decreases c.1°C. per 500-ft. altitude increase; air is composed of nitrogen (78.09%), oxygen (20.95%), and small amounts of argon, carbon dioxide, and other gases, and also containing water vapor and dusts. Air pressure decreases with altitude (see BAROMETER); standard pressure at sea level is 14.7 lb. per sq. in. (called an atmosphere); c.%10 of mass of atmosphere is within 10 mi. above sea level. See also IONOSPHERE. See *ill.*, p. 23.

atoll: see CORAL.

atom, according to atomic theory, minute particle of matter. Formerly considered indivisible unit of matter. Now believed to consist of protons (positively charged [+] particles), electrons (negatively charged [−] particles), and neutrons (neutral particles). Central nucleus contains protons and neutrons, has + charge. Because extranuclear electrons are equal in number to nuclear protons, atom is neutral. Ions are atoms or groups of atoms with electrical charge. Atoms of different elements differ in weight (ATOMIC WEIGHT) and in number of protons and electrons (this number indicated by atomic number; see PERIODIC LAW). Electron arrangement varies in different elements. Chemically, atoms of an element react the same; sometimes differ in mass (see ISOTOPE). Atoms of elements joined in MOLECULE. Discovery of ELECTRON and RADIOACTIVITY essential to modern concept of atom. Among contributors to knowledge of atom: N. H. D. BOHR, Sir W. H. BRAGG, W. L. BRAGG, James CHADWICK, John DALTON, Albert EINSTEIN, Enrico FERMI, Otto HAHN, Werner HEISENBERG, Irving LANGMUIR, Max von LAUE, Lise MEITNER, R. A. MILLIKAN, H. G. MOSELEY, Max PLANCK, 1st Baron RUTHERFORD. See also ATOMIC BOMB; ATOMIC ENERGY. See *ill.*, p. 989.

atomic bomb, weapon deriving explosive force from release of atomic energy. Reported splitting of uranium nucleus in Germany led in 1940 to organized research in U.S. First bombs produced at Los Alamos, used on HIROSHIMA and NAGASAKI in World War II.

atomic energy is derived from fission (splitting) of nucleus of atom. Experimenting with CYCLOTRON, U.S. scientists (1939) confirmed the splitting of uranium nucleus by Germany. Roosevelt named committee to investigate military uses of atomic energy. In 1942, a group under Fermi achieved, in a "pile" of graphite and uranium, first nuclear chain reaction (uranium nucleus splits as result of capture of a bombarding neutron, releases other neutrons causing more nuclear fissions). U-235 (uranium isotope, atomic wt. 235) by capturing a neutron becomes unstable and splits in two. When nucleus of U-238, the most abundant isotope in uranium ore, captures a neutron, neptunium (atomic no. 93) is produced. Neptunium yields plutonium (new element; atomic no. 94). Plutonium and U-235 both yield some 200,-000,000 electron volts during fission. To produce explosion must set up chain reaction that results in many fissions; such a chain-reacting system later called a reactor. Use of atomic energy as power source and in biology and medicine among peacetime research projects. UN devised plan for international control of research and production independent of Security Council. This was favored by Western powers; opposed by USSR, which wanted prohibition and destruction of existing bombs, then control by group with limited powers, regulated by Security Council. Negotiations became deadlocked. See *ill.*, p. 989.

atomic number: see PERIODIC LAW.

atomic theory, holds that matter is made up of minute particles, atoms. John Dalton (19th cent.) revived ancient (5th cent. B.C.) theory of atom, accepted early idea of indivisibility (no longer held), and believed that atoms of any element are same in size and weight and unite chemically in simple numerical ratios to form compounds. Mendelejeff and Arrhenius contributed to theory. Modern theory based on discovery of ELECTRON and RADIOACTIVITY.

atomic weight, ratio of weight of atom of element to weight of atom of standard element. Hydrogen once used as standard. Later oxygen ($O = 16$) used, since it forms more compounds than hydrogen. Atomic weight determined by quantitative analysis of compounds; specific-heat method used to determine that of elements forming no stable gaseous compounds. Atomic weight of elements having atoms of different weights (see ISOTOPE) is an average.

atonality, in music, the absence of TONALITY. Term often applied to any 20th-cent. music which does not observe the principles of harmonic relationship of the 18th or 19th cent. From time of Rameau the seven tones of the diatonic scale were felt to bear certain definite relations to one another. The five additional chromatic tones were available as auxiliary tones. Increased use of auxiliary tones by 19th-cent. composers reached a peak in the chromaticism of Wagner. In his and in Debussy's music the feeling of tonality began to break down. Polytonality,

in which several different keys were used simultaneously, contributed to the process. Finally all 12 tones were regarded as equal, bearing no fixed relations to one another. The 12-tone technique, which Schönberg arrived at in 1914, is a specific system to give form to this new concept. The composer arranges the 12 chromatic tones into a tone row, in which the tones may be used in any order but none may be repeated until all 12 have been used. This tone row is the basis of the composition. It may be transposed, inverted, used backward, used to form chords, or used in counterpoint with itself—transformations which the uninitiated ear finds difficult to follow. System yet in its infancy; its significance yet to be determined. Among Schönberg's disciples were Alban Berg and Ernst KRENEK.

Atonement, Day of, Heb. *Yom Kippur,* the most sacred Hebrew holy day, in late September or early October (the 10th day of the 7th month), a day of fasting and prayer for forgiveness of sins.

Atreus (ā'trēŭs), in Greek legend, king of Mycenae; father of Agamemnon and Menelaus. He slew three sons of his brother Thyestes and served them to him at a feast. The fourth son of Thyestes killed him.

atropine (ăt'rŭpēn, –pĭn), poisonous alkaloid discovered in belladonna (deadly nightshade) by P. L. Geiger (1833). Used to dilate pupil of eye and as antispasmodic, narcotic, and pain reliever.

Atropos, one of the FATES.

Attalla (ùtăl'ù), railroad city (pop. 7,537), NE Ala., W of Gadsden, in iron, cotton area. Foundries.

Attica (ăt'tĭkù), region of E central anc. Greece, around ATHENS. According to legend its four tribes founded by Ion and combined as a state by Theseus.

Attila (ăt'tĭlù), d. 453, king of the HUNS (c.433–53), called the Scourge of God. He extorted tribute from Rome, but in 450 emperors Marcian and Valentinian III refused to pay. In the same year Valentinian's sister Grata secretly offered herself in marriage to Attila, who demanded half the Western Empire as dowry. Turned down, he invaded Gaul but was defeated by AETIUS at Chalons (451). In 452 he invaded N Italy but abandoned his plan to take Rome, according to some because of the plea of Pope LEO I, but more probably because of a shortage of supplies. Accounts of his savagery, though based on fact, are probably exaggerated.

Attis (ă'tĭs), or **Atys** (ā'tĭs), Phrygian fertility god. Like Adonis, he died and was resurrected yearly.

Attleboro, city (pop. 23,809), SE Mass., NE of Providence, R.I.; settled 1634. Mfg. of jewelry, tools, and paper and metal specialties.

Attlee, Clement R(ichard) (ăt'lē), 1883–, British statesman and LABOUR PARTY leader. A former social service worker, held posts in 1924 and 1929 Labour governments. Became party leader 1935. Was deputy prime minister (1942–45) in Churchill's wartime coalition cabinet. Made prime minister (1945) while attending POTSDAM CONFER-

ENCE. His government nationalized much industry, began national health service, ended Palestine mandate and control of India, and strengthened ties with U.S. Stress on rearmament caused opposition, headed by Aneurin BEVAN, within Labour party. After loss to Conservatives in 1951 elections Attlee became opposition leader.

Attu (ä'tōō), island, 30 mi. long, off W Alaska, westernmost of ALEUTIAN ISLANDS. Very rugged, it rises above 4,000 ft. Japanese occupied it 1942 and removed inhabitants to Japan. U.S. forces landed May 11, 1943, retook island in three weeks of bloody fighting, and estab. air base.

Atys: see ATTIS.

Au, chemical symbol of the element GOLD.

Aube (ōb), department (2,327 sq. mi.; pop. 235,237), NE France, in arid part of Champagne; cap. Troyes.

Auber, Daniel François (fräswä' ōbĕr'), 1782–1871, French composer, known chiefly for his comic opera. Among his works are *Fra Diavolo, Le Domino Noir,* and *La Muette de Portici* (also called *Masaniello*).

Aubigné, Théodore Agrippa d' (tāōdôr' ägrēpä' dōbēnyä'), 1552–1630, French poet and Huguenot soldier. His reputation rests on *Les Tragiques,* a powerful, partly satirical, partly epical poem.

Aubrey, John, 1627–97, English biographer, author of *Lives of Eminent Men* (pub. 1813; later called *Brief Lives*).

Auburn or **Lissoy,** village, Co. Westmeath, Ireland; scene of Goldsmith's *Deserted Village.*

Auburn. 1 City (pop. 12,939), E Ala., ENE of Montgomery. Seat of Alabama Polytechnic Inst. (land-grant, state supported; coed.; chartered and opened 1872 as Alabama Agricultural and Mechanical Col., renamed 1899). **2** Resort city (pop. 4,653), N central Calif., NE of Sacramento; settled 1848 after gold discovery. *Placer Herald* published here since 1852. Old New Orleans Hotel was chronicled by Bret Harte. **3** City (pop. 5,879), NE Ind., N of Fort Wayne. Mfg. of metal products. **4** City (pop. 23,134), SW Maine, on Androscoggin R. (bridged) opposite Lewiston; settled c.1786. Mfg. of shoes (since c.1835). **5** Town (pop. 8,840), S central Mass., S of Worcester; settled 1714. Concrete and metal products. **6** City (pop. 36,772), W central N.Y., in Finger Lakes region, on outlet of Owasco L. and SW of Syracuse; settled 1793. Mfg. of metal and food products and clothing. Here are Auburn State Prison and home and grave of W. H. Seward. **7** City (pop. 6,497), W Wash., between Seattle and Tacoma. Agr. center and rail junction.

Aubusson, Pierre d' (pyĕr' dōbüsō'), 1423–1503, French cardinal, grand master of Knights Hospitalers. Defended Rhodes heroically against Turks (1480).

Aubusson (ōbüsō'), town (pop. 4,935), Creuse dept., central France. famous tapestry and carpet manufacture dates from 15th cent.

Aucassin et Nicolette (ōkäsē' ĕ nēkōlĕt') medieval French love story in prose and verse (probably 13th cent.). The original music, to which verses were to be sung, has been preserved. The simplicity of the story is its charm. Many English translations.

Auch (ōsh), city (pop. 11,489), cap. of Gers dept., S France; wine, brandy trade. Archiepiscopal see from 9th cent.; was cap. of Armagnac and of Gascony. Cathedral contains magnificent stained glass.

Auckland (ôk'lŭnd), city (pop. 123,457, metropolitan pop. 263,370), N North Isl., New Zealand, in hot-springs area; founded 1841. Former cap. (1841–65) and chief port of dominion. Exports dairy products, hides, and timber. Has shipyards, ammunition plants, and canneries. Seat of Auckland Univ. Col., and. museum with collection of Maori art.

Aude (ōd), department (2,449 sq. mi.; pop. 268,889), SE France, in Languedoc; cap. Carcassonne.

Auden, W(ystan) H(ugh) (ô'dŭn), 1907–, Anglo-American poet, b. England. Leader of left-wing literary group at Oxford, he wrote (with Isherwood) verse plays: *The Dog beneath the Skin* (1935), *The Ascent of F 6* (1936), *On the Frontier* (1938). Perhaps better known are lyrics such as those in *Collected Poetry* (1945).

Audenarde, Belgium: see OUDENARDE.

audio frequency: see VIBRATION.

auditing, examination and checking of accounts and related documents by persons unconnected with their preparation. System became common in 19th cent. as increasingly complex businesses required licensed experts to conduct annual audits. The accountant records the facts of a business; the auditor determines whether such recording has been accurately done.

Audubon, John James (ô'dŭbŏn), d. 1851, American ornithologist. Birth date and place disputed (New Orleans, 1780, or Aux Cayes, Haiti, 1785). Came to U.S. in 1803. His birdbanding experiments near Philadelphia (c.1803) were first in America. Married Lucy Bakewell (1808); lived mostly in Henderson, Ky., during 1808–20, changing occupation frequently, observing birds. Taught drawing in New Orleans. On 1826 trip to England he secured publication of *The Birds of America* and *Ornithological Biography* (with William MacGillivray). Later, in New York he began with John Bachman *The Viviparous Quadrupeds of North America* completed by his sons, Victor Gifford Audubon and John Woodhouse Audubon. National Association of Audubon Societies devoted to preserving and studying American wildlife publishes *Audubon Magazine.*

Aue, Hartmann von: see HARTMANN VON AUE.

Auenbrugger, Leopold (lā'ōpôlt ou'ŭnbrōōg"ŭr), 1722–1809, Viennese physician, pioneer in use of percussion in diagnosing chest diseases.

Auerbach, Berthold (bĕrt'hōlt ou'ŭrbäkh), 1812–82, German novelist. Virtual founder of peasant-story genre in German. *Village Tales from the Black Forest* (1843; Eng. tr., 1846–47), somewhat stylized pictures of peasant life, were much imitated.

Auerstedt (ou'ŭrshtĕt), village, central Germany, NE of Weimar. Here the French Marshal Davout defeated Prussians on same day that Napoleon I triumphed at Jena (Oct. 14, 1806).

Augeas (ôjē'ŭs), in Greek legend, king who

owned 3,000 oxen. Hercules, commanded to clean in one day the Augean stables, untouched for 30 years, did so by turning rivers Peneus and Alpheus through them.

Augier, Émile (āmēl′ ōzhyā′), 1820–89, French dramatist and satirist. Best-known comedy is *Le Gendre de M. Poirier* (1854), written with J. Sandeau.

Augsburg (ouks′bŏŏrk), city (pop. 184,712), cap. of Swabia, W Bavaria, on Lech R. Textile center of S Germany. Founded by Augustus 15 B.C. as Augusta Vindelicorum; free imperial city 1276; prominent member of Swabian League (1488–1534). Home of Fugger family and birthplace of Holbein, it was a major commercial, banking, and cultural center in 15th–16th cent. Its architectural treasures were heavily damaged in World War II.

Augsburg, League of, defensive alliance formed 1686 against Louis XIV of France by Emperor Leopold I with Sweden, Spain, Bavaria, Palatinate, and other German states. Transformed into GRAND ALLIANCE (1689) after adherence of Holland, England, Savoy.

Augsburg, Peace of, 1555, temporary settlement within Holy Roman Empire of conflicts arising from the Reformation. Chief principle: *Cuius regio, eius religio*—i.e., each prince was to determine whether Lutheranism or Catholicism was to prevail in his lands. All Church property held by abbots or bishops who had changed their faith after 1552 was to be forfeited by them.

Augsburg Confession: see CREED.

Augsburg Interim: see REFORMATION.

August: see MONTH.

Augusta. 1 City (pop. 71,508), E Ga., at head of navigation on Savannah R. (levees). Cotton market, it has mfg. of cotton products, brick, tile, fertilizer, lumber, and chemicals and food processing. Winter resort with mild climate. Laid out 1735 as trading post by Oglethorpe. Finally fell in 1781 to Continentals under Andrew Pickens and Light-Horse Harry Lee. Cap. of Ga. 1785–95. Site of largest Confederate powder works in Civil War. Here are Paine Col. (Negro; Methodist; coed.; 1883), Univ. of Ga. School of Medicine, a U.S. arsenal (1819), boyhood home of Woodrow Wilson, and many old Georgian and classic revival homes. **2** City (pop. 20,913), state cap., SW Maine, at head of navigation on Kennebec R. and NE of Portland. Trading post estab. here by Plymouth Co. in 1628. After founding of Fort Western (1754) the town grew as a river port. A dam (1837) stimulated industry. Mfg. of wood products, shoes, paper, and textiles. James G. Blaine's home is now governor's mansion. Has airport and U.S. arsenal.

Augustana College and Theological Seminary: see ROCK ISLAND, Ill.

Augustine, Saint (ô′gústēn, –tĭn; ôgǔ′stĭn), 354–430, Doctor of the Church, b. Tagaste, N Africa. Though reared as a Christian by his mother, St. Monica, he became a Manichaean. In Milan as a teacher of rhetoric, he was attracted by the teachings of St. Ambrose and again became a Christian (387). Returned to Tagaste, became a hermit, was later (396) made bishop of Hippo. Brought immense learning to bear on exposition of Christian doctrine and in arguments against Manichaeism, Donatism, and Pelagianism. Theologians, both Catholic and Protestant, have drawn on his works heavily and considered him master of theology. Among lay readers his autobiographical *Confessions* and his *City of God* (a profound view of the actual and the ideal in Christian society) are still very popular. Feast: Aug. 28.

Augustine of Canterbury, Saint, d. c.605, first archbishop of Canterbury. A Roman Benedictine sent with some monks to England by Pope Gregory I, he gained the favor of King Æthelbert of Kent. Introduced to England Roman rites and calendar which later triumphed over Celtic forms introduced in the N. The "apostle of England." Feast: May 28 or (in England) May 26.

Augustinians, Roman Catholic religious orders. The canons regular (Augustinians, or Austin canons) use an old rule of St. Augustine. Austin friars are a different group dating from 13th cent.

Augustus, 63 B.C.–A.D. 14, first Roman emperor. Grandnephew of Julius CAESAR, he was adopted and made heir by Caesar, without his knowledge. Originally Octavius (Caius Octavius), he became on adoption Octavian (Caius Julius Caesar Octavianus). After Caesar was assassinated he gained power in Rome and allied himself with Antony and Lepidus in the Second Triumvirate. He and Antony defeated the republicans under Brutus and Cassius at Philippi (42 B.C.). He and his lieutenant, Agrippa, drove the pirate forces of Sextus Pompeius from the sea, then after differences with Antony (see ANTONY) defeated that general and Cleopatra at Actium (31 B.C.). Augustus then was master of the Roman world. The senate showered titles on him, including *imperator* [general; from it comes word *emperor*] and *augustus* [revered]. He reformed administration, solidified Roman holdings (his only reverse was defeat of his general Varus by German leader Arminius), and beautified the city (he is said to have claimed that he found Rome of brick and left it of marble). Roman roads were extended and improved. Architecture flourished, and he was a patron of Vergil, Ovid, Livy, and Horace in the age of literature called Augustan. He imposed the Pax Romana [Roman peace] on the known civilized world. His stepson, Tiberius, succeeded him.

Augustus, kings of Poland. **Augustus I:** see SIGISMUND II (Sigismund Augustus). **Augustus II** (the Strong), 1670–1733, as Frederick Augustus I, elector of Saxony (1694–1733), was elected to succeed John III on the Polish throne (1697). Opportunistic, he became a Catholic, granted the Polish nobility unprecedented privileges, and allied himself with Russia and Denmark against CHARLES XII of Sweden (see NORTHERN WAR). Charles forced him to renounce the Polish crown in favor of STANISLAUS I (1706), but after Charles's defeat at Poltava (1709) Augustus recovered Poland (1716). Among his innumerable mistresses and illegitimate offspring were Maria Aurora von KÖNIGSMARK and her son, Maurice de

Saxe. His son **Augustus III,** 1696–1763, succeeded him as elector of Saxony as Frederick Augustus II and claimed Poland from Stanislaus I, who had been reelected on Augustus II's death. After The War of the POLISH SUCCESSION he was elected Polish king (1736). As son-in-law of Emperor Joseph I, he claimed the Hapsburg lands in the War of the AUSTRIAN SUCCESSION, but he changed sides in 1742. In the SEVEN YEARS WAR (1756–63) he fled Saxony and took residence in Poland. Indolent, he left the government to Count BRÜHL.

auk (ôk), swimming, diving bird of N Atlantic, Pacific; related to puffin. Legs set far back on body. Auk is clumsy on land, where it nests. Flightless great auks, largest species, once abundant in N Atlantic, were killed off (c.1844) for flesh, feathers, oil. Least auklet (c.6½ in.), common in Bering Sea, is smallest. Largest surviving (16–18 in.) is razor-billed auk.

Aulis (ô′lĭs), small port of ancient Greece, in Boeotia. Here Greek fleet was becalmed on way to Troy; resumed sail after sacrifice of IPHIGENIA.

Aurangzeb (ôr′ŭngzĕb″), 1618–1707, Mogul emperor (1658–1707), son of Shah Jehan. Won throne by defeating his brothers and imprisoning his father. Brought empire to greatest extent by military conquests. Intensely devoted to Islam.

Auray (ôrā′), town (pop. 8,038), Morbihan dept., NW France, in Brittany. Famous pilgrimage shrine of Sainte-Anne-d'Auray is 4 mi. N.

Aurelian (ôrē′lēŭn), c.212–275, Roman emperor (270–75). After succeeding Claudius II, he defended the empire vigorously against barbarians and ambitious rulers (notably Zenobia of Palmyra); consolidated rule once again in Britain, Gaul, Spain, Egypt, Syria, and Mesopotamia; and revived the glory of Rome.

aureomycin: see ANTIBIOTIC SUBSTANCES.

Auriesville, village, E central N.Y., near Amsterdam. Site of Roman Catholic shrine to St. Isaac Jogues and other Jesuit Martyrs of North America, killed by Iroquois.

Aurignac (ôrēnyäk′), village, S France, SW of Toulouse. Its caves contain relics of prehistoric man (Aurignacian period; see PALEOLITHIC PERIOD.)

Auriol, Vincent (vēsä′ ôryôl′), 1884–, president of French republic (1947–); a moderate Socialist.

aurochs (ôr′ŏks), name for now extinct European wild ox or urus (*Bos primigenius*), large, blackish-brown, and believed ancestor of European domestic cattle. European bison often called aurochs.

Aurora (ûrô′rŭ, ôrô′–), in Roman religion, goddess of dawn, identified with Greek Eos.

Aurora. 1 Residential city (pop. 11,421), N central Colo., just E of Denver, in metropolitan area. **2** City (pop. 50,576), NE Ill., W of Chicago and on Fox R. Has railroad shops and mfg. of metal products, textiles, and office supplies. **3** Village (pop. 711), W central N.Y., on Cayuga L. Seat of Wells Col. (for women; 1868).

aurora borealis (bō″rēä′lĭs, –ā′lĭs) and **aurora australis** (ôsträ′lĭs), luminous displays of N

and S Hemispheres respectively, called also northern and southern lights. Visible in a variety of colors and forms over areas near geomagnetic poles, they extend to altitudes from c.35 to c.600 mi. Believed to result from collisions of charged particles from sun with gases of upper atmosphere. Occurrence correlated with sunspot activity and magnetic storms.

Au Sable (ôsä′bŭl –sä′–), river rising in several branches in N Mich. and flowing swiftly c.80 mi. SE to L. Huron N of mouth of Saginaw Bay. Once important for log driving.

Ausable, river, NE N.Y., formed by E and W branches (rise in the Adirondacks) at Au Sable Forks village and flowing c.20 mi. NE to L. Champlain S of Plattsburg. Above Keeseville (1842 bridge) is **Ausable Chasm,** with waterfalls, rapids, odd rock formations.

Auschwitz, Poland: see OSWIECIM.

Ausonius (Decimus Magnus Ausonius) (ôsō′nēŭs dēs′imŭs), c.310–c.393, Latin poet, a prefect of Gaul and consul (379). He pictures contemporary society.

Aussig, Czechoslovakia: see USTI NAD LABEM.

Austen, Jane, 1775–1817, English novelist. A clergyman's daughter, she lived a quiet life, and her novels of social comedy have a small stage, though they are made masterpieces by her observation, witty characterization, and sparkling, polished style. Published in her lifetime were *Sense and Sensibility* (1811), *Pride and Prejudice* (1813), *Mansfield Park* (1814), *Emma* (1816). *Northanger Abbey* (satire on the romances of Mrs. Radcliffe), written early, appeared with *Persuasion* in 1818. Little known in her day, Jane Austen later became one of the best-known and best-loved English novelists.

Austerlitz (ô′stŭrlĭts, ou′–), Czech *Slavkov u Brna,* small town, Czechoslovakia, E of Brno. Here, on Dec. 2, 1805, Napoleon I won the most brilliant victory of his career over the Russians and Austrians under emperors Alexander I and Francis I ("battle of the three emperors"), thus forcing Austria out of the war.

Austin, John, 1790–1859, English jurist, who argued that will of authority, not ethics, was basis of law.

Austin, Mary (Hunter), 1868–1934, American author. Long lived in Calif. and N. Mex.; did much to introduce Indian and Spanish elements of U.S. culture into American literature.

Austin, Moses, 1761–1821, American pioneer. Secured grant from Spanish to settle 300 families in Texas. His son, **Stephen Fuller Austin,** 1793–1836, took up plans when his father died and estab. settlements between Brazos and Colorado rivers. Opposed SANTA ANNA and thus forwarded Texas Revolution.

Austin, Warren R(obinson), 1877–, U.S. representative at the United Nations (1946–52).

Austin. 1 City (pop. 23,100), SE Minn., on Cedar R. near Iowa line; settled 1853. Rail center of agr. area with meat packing plants and railroad shops. **2** City [named for S. F. Austin] (pop. 132,459), state cap., S central Texas, on Colorado R. Laid out 1838, voted cap. 1839. Temporary cap. after annexation to U.S.; made permanent 1870. Grew to industrial city through power and flood-control projects on Colorado R. and urgencies of World War II. Mfg. of clay and food products, metalwork, and machinery. Has capitol (1885) and other state buildings. Seat of Univ. of TEXAS, Samuel Huston and Tillotson Cols. (Negro), and Texas Southern Univ. (Negro). Has O. Henry's house, Elizabeth Ney's studio (both museums), and old French embassy. Near pleasure spots (esp. Barton Springs).

Austin canons: see AUGUSTINIANS.

Australia, island continent between Indian and Pacific oceans. Nearly as large as continental U.S., it spans c.2,400 mi. from E to W and c.2,000 mi. from N to S. With the island state of TASMANIA, it forms the Commonwealth of Australia, a British dominion (2,974,581 sq. mi.; pop. 7,580,820, excluding aboriginals). The five continental states are QUEENSLAND, NEW SOUTH WALES, VICTORIA, SOUTH AUSTRALIA, and WESTERN AUSTRALIA. NORTHERN TERRITORY and AUSTRALIAN CAPITAL TERRITORY (containing Canberra, the federal cap.) are areas under direct federal control. Australia owns Territory of Papua (see PAPUA, TERRITORY OF), Norfolk Isl., and Australian Antarctic Territory; holds under UN trusteeship the Territory of New Guinea (see NEW GUINEA, TERRITORY OF) and NAURU (jointly with the United Kingdom and New Zealand). The W half of the Australian continent is an arid plateau (important mainly for large gold fields) while the extreme N areas are wet jungle. In the east are the Great Dividing Range and the Murray R. The main coal-mining state is New South Wales. Staple products are wool and grain. Australia is noted for its distinctive animal life which includes the kangaroo and the platypus. The continent was first sighted in the early 17th cent. by the Portuguese and the Spaniards. In 1770 Capt. James Cook claimed the E coast for Great Britain, and in 1829 the whole continent was brought under British rule. Federation of the former Australian colonies was achieved in 1901. Executive power is vested in a governor-general (representing the British crown) and a cabinet headed by a prime minister. Parliament consists of a Senate and a House of Representatives. See map, p. 85.

Australian Alps, mountain ranges, SE Australia, comprising S part of Great Dividing Range. Mt. Kosciusko (7,305 ft.) is highest peak in Australia.

Australian Antarctic Territory, comprising the islands and territory (except Adélie Land) between long. 45°E and 160°E and below lat. 60°S. Claimed in 1933 by Australia.

Australian Capital Territory (911 sq. mi.; pop. 16,905), SE Australia within New South Wales; contains Canberra cap. of Commonwealth of Australia. Ceded 1911 by state to commonwealth. Area was called Federal Capital Territory until 1938.

Austral Islands: see TUBUAI ISLANDS.

Austrasia (ôstrā′zhǔ), Frankish kingdom (6th–8th cent.), comprising E France, W Germany, Netherlands; cap. Metz. For history, see MEROVINGIANS.

Austria, Ger. *Osterreich,* federal republic (32,-375 sq. mi.; pop. 6,918,959), central Europe, traversed by the Danube, bounded by Yugoslavia and Italy (S), Switzerland and Liechtenstein (W), Bavaria and Czechoslovakia (N), and Hungary (E); cap. Vienna. Its nine provinces—VORARLBERG, TYROL, SALZBURG, CARINTHIA, STYRIA, UPPER AUSTRIA, LOWER AUSTRIA, BURGENLAND, and VIENNA —are largely self-governing and are represented in the upper chamber of the federal bicameral parliament. Population is predominantly Roman Catholic and German-speaking. The ALPS, covering three quarters of the country, rise to 12,460 ft. in the HOHE TAUERN. Largely agricultural—yet not self-sufficient in major food staples—Austria also has industries (metallurgy, machinery, chemicals, textiles), concentrated mainly in the Vienna basin and at LINZ, STEYR, and GRAZ. Mineral resources include iron, manganese, copper, lead, zinc, petroleum (at Zistersdorf), and salt. The area of present Austria was inhabited by Celts when it was conquered by Rome (15 B.C.–10 A.D.). It was overrun after the 5th cent. by Huns, Goths, Lombards, and Bavarians; conquered 788 by Charlemagne; reconquered 955 from the Magyars by Otto I; and attached as Eastern March to Bavaria 955–76. In subsequent history, the word *Austria* has four distinct meanings: (1) Austria proper, i.e., Upper and Lower Austria, including Vienna. This was ruled from 976 as margraviate (after 1156, duchy) by the house of Babenberg, and acquired in 1251 by OTTOCAR II of Bohemia. In 1276 Ottocar had to cede Austria, along with Styria, Carinthia, and CARNIOLA, to RUDOLF I of Hapsburg, in whose family it remained until 1918 (raised to archduchy 1453). (2) With the rise of Hapsburg greatness, the term *Austria* came to designate the house of Hapsburg or Austria, which ruled the HOLY ROMAN EMPIRE from 1438 to 1806 and at one time held an hereditary empire which embraced the world (see HAPSBURG). The chief historic importance of Austria proper in that period was as bulwark against Turkish onslaughts, which culminated and ended with the siege of Vienna in 1683. The house of Austria lost its primacy in German affairs in the THIRTY YEARS WAR and the wars of the 18th cent. As a result, it concentrated, especially under MARIA THERESA and JOSEPH II, on internal consolidation of its hereditary lands and on eastward expansion (esp. in POLAND and Balkans). Thrice defeated in the French Revolutionary and Napoleonic Wars (see FRANCIS II, emperor), it nevertheless emerged in 1815 from the CONGRESS OF VIENNA as leader of the GERMAN CONFEDERATION. (3) Shortly before the dissolution of the Holy Roman Empire, Francis II assumed the title "Francis I, emperor of Austria." The Austrian Empire, which is the third meaning of the term, consisted after 1815 of, roughly, German-speaking Austria, Bohemia, Moravia, S Poland, Lombardy, Venetia, Carniola, Istria, Dalmatia, and the separate kingdom of Hungary, with Croatia and Slavonia. The Revolution of 1848 drove METTERNICH from power but Emperor

FRANCIS JOSEPH soon restored absolutism. In the Italian War of 1859 Austria lost Lombardy; the AUSTRO-PRUSSIAN WAR of 1866 cost it Venetia and eliminated it from German affairs. In 1867 a general reorganization of the empire resulted in the creation of the AUSTRO-HUNGARIAN MONARCHY, which collapsed at the end of World War I. (4) In Nov., 1918, German Austria was proclaimed a republic. The Treaty of SAINT-GERMAIN (1919) fixed the boundaries of present Austria—i.e., the German-speaking remnant of the Austrian Empire—a small country of 6,000,000 people (a third of whom lived in the capital), stripped of its former raw materials, food, and markets. Chronic bankruptcy, unemployment, and political unrest resulted. The three-cornered struggle among Socialists, clerico-fascists, and National Socialists led to the establishment in 1934 of a corporative, authoritarian regime under Chancellor DOLLFUSS and his successor, SCHUSCHNIGG. The growth of local Nazism, German pressure, and Western appeasement resulted in the occupation of Austria by Germany in 1938. It was fully incorporated into the Reich in 1940. Conquered in 1945 by American and Russian troops, Austria was restored as a republic and divided into five zones of occupation—Vorarlberg and Tyrol (French); Salzburg and W Upper Austria (U.S.); E Upper Austria, Lower Austria, and Burgenland (Russian); Carinthia and Styria (British); and Vienna (joint four-power occupation). Though Austria was formally recognized in 1946, no peace treaty was signed, largely because of basic disagreements between Russia and the West on the reparations question. As of 1952, a Catholic-Socialist coalition cabinet is in power.

Austrian Succession, War of the, 1740–48, European war precipitated by succession of MARIA THERESA of Austria to the Hapsburg lands by virtue of PRAGMATIC SANCTION. Her succession was challenged by the elector of Bavaria (later Emperor CHARLES VII), PHILIP V of Spain, and AUGUSTUS III of Poland and Saxony, while FREDERICK II of Prussia claimed part of SILESIA. Prussia opened war by invading Silesia, was joined (1741) by France, Spain, Bavaria, Saxony; made separate peace 1742; reentered war 1744; made final separate peace 1745 (Treaty of Dresden). England, then at war with Spain (see JENKINS'S EAR, WAR OF) supported Austria, as did Holland and Sardinia. Saxony went over to Austrian side 1743. Bavaria withdrew from war at death of Charles VII (1745). Notable military events up to 1745: Prussian victory at MOLLWITZ (1741); capture of Prague by Franco-Bavarians (1742); occupation of Bavaria and recapture of Prague by Austrians (1742); English victory at DETTINGEN (1743); French victory at FONTENOY (1745); Prussian victory at HOHENFRIEDBERG (1745). By Treaty of Dresden Prussia obtained most of Silesia but promised to support election of Maria Theresa's husband as emperor (Francis I). The remaining belligerents fought on inconclusively in N Italy, Low Countries, America (see FRENCH AND INDIAN WARS), and India until Treaty of AIX-LA-CHAPELLE of 1748.

Austro-Hungarian Monarchy or **Dual Monarchy,** the Hapsburg empire from the constitutional compromise (*Ausgleich*) of 1867 between AUSTRIA and HUNGARY until its fall in 1918. Rulers: FRANCIS JOSEPH (1867–1916), CHARLES I (1916–18). Empire was divided into Cisleithania (lands W of Leitha R.), including Austria proper, Bohemia, Moravia, Austrian Silesia, and Austrian Poland; and Transleithania, including Hungary, Transylvania, CROATIA, Slovenia, and part of Dalmatia. Cisleithania was ruled by emperor of Austria, Transleithania by king of Hungary (both dignities being united in the same monarch); each elected its own parliament and had its own cabinet and customs regime. A three-man common cabinet governed foreign policy, defense, imperial finances. Economically an organic whole, empire was torn and eventually broken up by nationalist aspirations of its many minorities, notably Czechs, Poles, Serbs, Italians, Rumanians. Threatened by pan-Slavism (spearheaded by Serbia and supported by Russia), Austria-Hungary concluded alliance with Germany (1879), joined also by Italy (1882; see TRIPLE ALLIANCE AND TRIPLE ENTENTE). The annexation of BOSNIA AND HERCEGOVINA (1908) envenomed relations with Serbia and Russia. The assassination of Archduke FRANCIS FERDINAND precipitated WORLD WAR I (1914), Austria-Hungary surrendered Nov. 3, 1918. The Treaties of Versailles, Trianon, and Saint-Germain fixed boundaries of successor states.

Austro-Prussian War or **Seven Weeks War,** June 15–Aug. 23, 1866, between Prussia, allied with Italy, and Austria, seconded by Bavaria, Württemberg, Saxony, Hanover, Baden, and several smaller German states. Provoked by BISMARCK with object of expelling Austria from GERMAN CONFEDERATION. Austro-Prussian dispute over administration of SCHLESWIG-HOLSTEIN served as pretext. Prussia quickly overran German states, crushed Austrians at SADOWA. Austrian victories over Italians at Custozza and Lissa proved useless at Peace of Prague (Aug. 23, 1866): Austria had to cede Venetia to Italy. Prussia demanded no territory from Austria but annexed Hesse-Kassel, Hanover, Frankfurt. New NORTH GERMAN CONFEDERATION was estab. under Prussian leadership. War paved way for founding of German Empire in 1871.

Auteuil (ōtû′ē), section of Paris, France, near Bois de Boulogne. Famous racecourse.

authentic modes, in music: see MODE.

autogiro (ô′tōjī′rō) or **gyroplane** (jī′rŭplän), first aircraft to depart from Wright brothers type. Overhead airfoils, rotated by aerodynamic forces arising from craft's propulsion by ordinary engine and propeller, provide principal lift; wing area much reduced. Inventor, Juan de la CIERVA. Generally superseded by HELICOPTER.

automaton: see ROBOT.

automobile. Probably the first self-propelled vehicle was a steam-driven, three-wheeled carriage introduced 1769 in Paris by Nicolas Joseph Cugnot. In early 19th cent. attempts to operate steam road carriages failed in England because of excessive tolls and re-

AUSTRALIA

85

CAPITAL CITIES are designated by CAPITAL AND SMALL CAPITAL type

strictive legislation (e.g., the Red Flag Act). In Germany, INTERNAL-COMBUSTION ENGINE was used in 1885 by Karl Benz to operate vehicle; improved engine built by Gottlieb Daimler c.1885. Internal-combustion models manufactured in U.S. during 1890s by Charles Duryea, J. Frank Duryea, Elwood Haynes, Henry Ford, Ransom E. Olds, and Alexander Winton. By 1903 Detroit was becoming U.S. automotive center. Free growth of the industry was threatened by patent granted (1895) to George Selden for gasoline car. Manufacturers licensed by Selden formed association (1903) to control manufacture. Independents, led by Henry Ford, opposed this; U.S. Circuit Court of Appeals ruled (1911) Selden's patent valid but applicable to two-cycle engines only. Steam-driven cars thereafter were rapidly displaced by gasoline models; electric models retain limited use for local delivery trucks.

automobile racing, sport in which specially constructed, high-speed automobiles race on outdoor or indoor tracks. Started 1894 in France, 1895 in U.S. Indianapolis Speedway meet first held 1911. Famous drivers include William K. Vanderbilt, Barney Oldfield, Edward V. Rickenbacker, Wilbur Shaw.

autonomy (ôtŏn′ümē), in political sense, limited self-government, short of independence. The objective test of autonomy is recognition that the group may legislate for itself. The right may be delegated or permitted by the state. Situation of the autonomous border regions of USSR today is peculiar because one object of autonomy is to attract others into the Russian orbit.

Autun (ōtŭ′), city (pop. 11,767), Saône-et-Loire dept., E central France. Early medieval center of learning. Roman ruins; 12th-cent. cathedral.

Auvergne (ōvĕr′nyü), region and former province, central France, in the Massif Central, in Cantal, Puy-de-Dôme, Haute-Loire depts.; historic cap., Clermont (now Clermont-Ferrand). Auvergne mts. culminate in Mont-Dore and Puy de Dôme. Stock raising, dairying in mountains; agr. in valleys. Mineral springs and spas. Auvergnats descend from Celtic Arverni, whose leader Vercingetorix led Gallic revolt against Caesar. Region passed to English (1154) as part of Aquitaine; later was incorporated in several stages into French royal domain.

Auxerre (ōsĕr′), town (pop. 20,809), cap. of Yonne dept., E central France; trading center for Chablis wines. Fine medieval architecture: Church and Abbey of St. Germain; Gothic cathedral.

AV, the Authorized Version or King James Version of the Bible. See also OLD TESTAMENT.

Avalon (ăv′ülŏn), in Celtic mythology, island of the happy otherworld. See ARTHURIAN LEGEND.

Avalon. 1 See SANTA BARBARA ISLANDS, Calif. **2** Residential borough (pop. 6,463), SW Pa., NW suburb of Pittsburgh.

Avalon Peninsula, 3,579 sq. mi., SE N.F., Canada, most densely populated part of the province. Deeply indented at center by Conception Bay (N) and St. Mary's Bay (S).

Aveiro (ävā′rō), city (pop. 11,247), Beira Litoral, NW Portugal. Notable fishing port since 16th cent. Partially built over water: "Portuguese Venice."

Avellaneda (äväyänä′dhä), city (pop. 278,-621), Buenos Aires prov., Argentina; industrial city, usually considered part of greater Buenos Aires.

Ave Maria (ä′vä märē′ä) [Latin,= hail, Mary], Roman Catholic prayer in Latin to the Virgin. Much set to music (notably by Schubert, Gounod). The English version, *Hail, Mary,* one of the most common of Catholic prayers.

Avempace (ä′vümpäs, ä″vĕmpä′thä), Arabic *Ibn Bajja,* d. 1138, Spanish-Arabian Aristotelian philosopher.

Avenches (äväsh′), Latin *Aventicum,* small town, Vaud canton, W Switzerland. Flourished 1st cent. B.C.–2d cent. A.D. as chief town (pop. c.80,000) of Helvetia. Numerous Roman remains.

Avenzoar (ăv″ünzō′ûr, –zōär′) or **Ibn Zohr** (ĭb′n zōr′), c.1090?–1162, Arabian physician, pioneer in experimental medicine.

average, statistical measure expressing numerically the characteristics of a group of figures. See MEAN; MEDIAN; MODE.

Avernus (üvûr′nüs), Ital. *Averno,* small crater lake, Campania, S Italy, near Cuma. For its sulphuric vapors and gloomy aspect, it was regarded by Romans as entrance to hell; later the name was used for hell itself.

Averroës (üvĕr′ōēz), 1126–98, Moorish philosopher. In his study of Aristotle, he sought to reconcile philosophy with religion, holding religion to be a symbolic expression of philosophical truth.

Avery Island, S La., in sea marshes and swamps, SW of New Iberia. Has bird (esp. egret) sanctuary and Jungle Gardens (rare plants). Rock salt has been mined since 1791. Has yielded prehistoric relics.

Aveyron (ävärō′), department (3,386 sq. mi.; pop. 307,717), S central France, in Rouergue; cap. Rodez.

aviation, term applied broadly to all activities, facilities, and enterprises related to flying. Leonardo da Vinci first studied flight scientifically. Flight first achieved (1783) in lighter-than-air craft (see BALLOON). Among pioneers in heavier-than-air flight: Sir George Cayley (mechanics-of-flight analysis, 1809–10); W. S. Henson (foreshadowed modern monoplane, 1842); John Stringfellow (power-driven model plane, said to be first to fly); F. H. Wenham (devised wind tunnel, 1866); Alphonse Penaud (with Paul Gauchot designed amphibian monoplane, 1878); Clément Ader (his bat-fashioned monoplane flew, 1890); Sir Hiram S. Maxim (steam-driven plane with crew rose into air, 1894); and Americans, S. P. LANGLEY, Octave CHANUTE, and Otto LILIENTHAL. First man-carrying, motor-driven airplane flight was by Orville Wright, repeated by Wilbur Wright (Dec. 17, 1903, Kitty Hawk, N.C.). Louis BLÉRIOT flew English Channel (1909). Glenn Curtis built first flying boat (1912). After World War I, aviation grew in importance. First N Atlantic crossing was by A. C. Read in U.S. Navy flying boat (May, 1919). John Alcock and A. W. Brown

flew Newfoundland–Ireland (1919); Ross
Smith London–Australia (1919). Richard
E. Byrd and Floyd Bennett flew Spitsbergen–
North Pole (1926). Charles A. Lindbergh
flew the Atlantic solo (1927). Hermann
Köhl, J. C. Fitzmaurice, and G. von Hüne-
feld flew Ireland–Newfoundland (1928).
Charles Kingsford-Smith was first to fly
Pacific (1928), San Francisco–Australia
with two stops. Clyde E. Pangborn and
Hugh Herndon flew from Japan to Washington state nonstop (1931). Wiley Post and
Harold Gatty flew round the world (1931).
Post circled world solo (1933). Howard
Hughes and four companions circled world
(1938). Amelia Earhart Putnam was first
woman to fly Atlantic as passenger (1928)
and solo (1932). U.S. air transport chiefly
of mail until, after 1930, passenger carrying
became profitable. Pan American Airways
(later Pan American World Airways) began
transpacific air-mail service in 1934; added
passenger service with San Francisco-to-
Manila China Clipper. World War II saw
Army Air Transport Command and Navy
Air Transport Service pioneer in global air
routes. See also AERIAL PHOTOGRAPHY; AIR,
LAW OF THE; AIRPLANE; AIR POWER; AIRSHIP.
See *ill.*, p. 23.

Avicebron: see IBN GABIROL, SOLOMON BEN
JUDAH.

Avicenna (ăvĭsĕn'ù), Arabic *Ibn Sina*, 980–
1037, Arabian philosopher. Interpreted
Aristotle in Neoplatonic fashion, but was
known in West chiefly as a writer on medicine and other sciences.

Avignon (ävēnyō'), city (pop. 47,040), cap.
of Vaucluse dept., SE France, in Provence.
Wine trade, silk mfg. See of popes during
"Babylonian captivity," 1309–78, and of several antipopes during Great Schism, 1378–
1408. City was bought (1348) by Clement
VI from countess of Provence; remained
papal property until annexed by France
(1791). Landmarks: 14th-cent. papal palace, Basilica of St. Peter, fragment of 12th-
cent. bridge.

Ávila, Gil González de: see GONZÁLEZ DE
ÁVILA.

Ávila (ä'vēlä), city (pop. 19,590), cap. of
Ávila prov., central Spain, in Old Castile;
birthplace of St. Theresa. Medieval walls;
cathedral.

Ávila Camacho, Manuel (mänwĕl' ä'vēlä
kämä'chō), 1897–, president of Mexico
(1940–46).

Aviz, Port. *Avis* (both: ùvēsh'), village, central Portugal. Granted (c.1162) to branch
of Knights of Calatrava, which became the
separate Order of Aviz. Master of order became King John I of Portugal, establishing
dynasty of Aviz (1383–1580).

Avoca or **Ovoca** (both: ùvō'kù), river of Co.
Wicklow, Ireland, formed by union of Avon-
more R. and Avonbeg R. (Thomas Moore's
"Meeting of the Waters").

avocado (äv"ùkä'dō), broad-leaved evergreen
tree (*Persea*), grown in Calif. and Fla. for
pear-shaped, oil-rich fruit (alligator pear)
often used in salads.

avocet (ăv'ùsĕt), wading bird (c.15–18 in.
long) related to snipe and stilt. North and
South America, Europe, and Australia each

have one species. North American "blue
shanks," hunted for food, are rare E of
Mississippi. See *ill.*, p. 135.

Avogadro, Amadeo (ämädä'ō ävōgä'drō),
1776–1856, Italian physicist, a count. Avogadro's law: equal volumes of gases under
same pressure and temperature have same
number of molecules. Avogadro's number
(6.02×10^{23}): number of molecules in gram
molecular volume of gas.

Avon (ä'vùn, ăv'ùn) [Celtic,= river], name of
several rivers in England. **1 Bristol Avon** or
Lower Avon rises in Gloucestershire and
flows 75 mi. through Wiltshire and Somerset,
past Bath and Bristol, to the Severn. **2 East
Avon,** in Wiltshire and Hampshire, flows 48
mi. past Salisbury to the English Channel.
3 Upper Avon, in Northamptonshire,
Leicestershire, Warwickshire, and Worcestershire is most famous. Flows 96 mi. past
Rugby, Warwick, and Stratford-on-Avon to
the Severn.

ax or **axe,** tool used since prehistoric times for
felling trees, working wood, preparing soil,
and as a weapon. It was a major item in
equipment of American pioneers. Related
tools are hatchet (short-handled ax with
hammer head) and hammer. Double-bitted
ax was religious emblem in Crete and elsewhere.

Axel: see ABSALON.

Axis, coalition of states headed by Germany,
Italy, and Japan, 1936–45 (see WORLD WAR
II). Original Italo-German accord of 1936
became full alliance 1939 and was acceded
to by Japan in Berlin Pact of 1940, to which
Hungary, Rumania, Bulgaria, Slovakia, and
Croatia adhered later. The related Anti-
Comintern Pact of 1936 (see COMINTERN),
between Germany and Japan, later included
Berlin Pact nations, Spain, Finland, and
others.

Axminster, urban district (pop. 2,673), Devonshire, England. Its famous carpets now made
at Wilton.

Axum, Ethiopia: see AKSUM.

Ayacucho (äyäkōō'chō), city (pop. 18,275),
S Peru. Defeat of Spanish by Sucre here
(1824) secured Peruvian independence,
marked triumph of revolution in South
America and guaranteed independence from
Spain.

Ayala, Ramón Pérez de: see PÉREZ DE AYALA.

Ayer (âr), town (pop. 5,740), N Mass., ESE
of Fitchburg. U.S. Fort Devens is near by.

Ayesha (Aisha) (ī'shù, ä'īshä"), d. 678, Mohammed's favorite wife; Abu Bakr's daughter. Fomented unsuccessful revolt during
caliphate of ALI.

Aylesbury (ālz'bùrē), county town (pop. 21,-
054) of Buckinghamshire, England; agr.
market for upper Thames valley famed for
its ducks.

Aymara (īmärä'), South American Indians inhabiting L. Titicaca basin. Although subjugated by the Inca in 15th cent. and by Pizarro
brothers (1538), they continue to dominate
region.

Aymer of Valence (ā'mùr, vùlĕns', välās'), d.
1260, bishop of Winchester. Half brother of
King Henry III of England, he was elected
at the king's order. Hostility towards him
important factor in BARONS' WAR.

Ayodhya, India: see FYZABAD.

Ayolas, Juan de (hwän'dä äyō'läs), d. 1537?, Spanish conquistador, explorer of Río de la Plata region (esp. Paraguay); lieutenant of Pedro de MENDOZA.

Ayrshire (âr'shĭr) or **Ayr,** maritime county (1,132 sq. mi.; pop. 321,184), SW Scotland. Has pleasant terrain and is primarily agr. and pastoral. Ayr cows are famous. Country of Robert Bruce, Burns, and Boswell. The county town, **Ayr** (âr), burgh (pop. 43,011), on the Firth of Clyde, is heart of the Burns country and has Burns memorials. Alloway, his birthplace, is a suburb.

Ayuthia or **Ayutthaya** (both: äyōōt'hīä), town (pop. 15,821), S Thailand, on Menam R.; trade center. Was Siamese cap. (c.1350–1767).

azalea: see RHODODENDRON.

Azaña, Manuel (mänwäl' äthä'nyä), 1880–1940, Spanish republican statesman. As premier (1931–33, 1936), he pressed for social reforms. President of Spain 1936–39. Fled to France near end of Civil War.

Azariah (ăzŭrī'ŭ), one of THREE HOLY CHILDREN. Greek form is Azarias.

Azerbaijan (ä"zürbĭjän'), region (41,160 sq. mi.; pop. 2,734,973), extreme NW Iran. Aras R. in N separates it from Azerbaijan SSR. Mainly mountainous with fertile lowlands yielding grain and fruit. Chief city is TABRIZ. In remote times region was dominated by kings of Van and Urartu (in Armenia). Settled by Medes before 8th cent. B.C.; became a province in Persian empire. Supposedly birthplace of Zoroaster. Persian Atropates estab. himself as independent king here after 328 B.C. Region again became part of Persia in 3d cent. A.D. Converted to Islam in 7th cent. by Arabs, who brought it under caliphate. Dominated by Seljuk Turks 11th–12th cent., conquered in 14th cent. by Tamerlane. Ruled by shahs from early 17th to early 19th cent., when N part was ceded to Russia. Remainder was organized as a Persian province, which was divided 1938 into Third and Fourth provs.

Azerbaijan (ä"sürbĭjän'), constituent republic (33,100 sq. mi.; pop. c.3,100,000), USSR, bordering Iranian Azerbaijan in E; cap. BAKU. Includes E ranges of Greater and Lesser Caucasus; hot, arid Kura valley; subtropical Lenkoran lowland and oil-rich Apsheron peninsula on Caspian coast. Chief products: oil, cotton, grapes, tea, fruit, tobacco. Sheep raising in mountains. Population largely Turkic Azers or Azerbaijani—

Shiite Moslems of Persian culture. Region ceded by Persia to Russia (1813, 1828). For earlier history, see preceding article.

Azores (ùzôrz', ä'zôrz), Port. *Açores* (ùsô'rïsh), islands (888 sq. mi; pop. 318,686), in N Atlantic, administratively part of Portugal. São Miguel is largest island. Chief cities: Ponta Delgada (on São Miguel), Angra do Heroísmo (Terceira isl.), Horta (Fayal isl.). Products: grain, fruit, wine. Islands were known by 1351; colonized by Portuguese in 1445.

Azorín: see MARTÍNEZ RUIZ, JOSÉ.

Azov (ä'zŏv, Rus. ŭzôf'), city (pop. 17,545), S European RSFSR; fishing port near mouth of Don and Sea of Azov. Strategic fortress until late 18th cent. Peter the Great took it from khan of Crimea 1696, had to return it 1711. Definitively secured by Russia 1774. Ancient Greek colony of Tanais was near by. The **Sea of Azov,** Latin *Palus Maeotis,* is a N arm (c.14,000 sq. mi.) of the Black Sea, with which it is connected by the Kerch Strait. Fed by the Don and Kuban, it has important fisheries. Rostov-on-Don, Taganrog, Kerch are chief ports. SIVASH SEA is a W branch.

Aztec (ăz'tĕk"), Indian people dominating central Mexico at time of Spanish Conquest. Arrived in Valley of Mexico from N in 12th cent.; nomadic until founding of their cap., TENOCHTITLÁN (c.1325; present Mexico city). Created a composite civilization based on TOLTEC and Mixteca-Puebla heritage. Among their accomplishments were a stone wheel or calendar stone, weaving, sculpture, engineering, metalwork, music, picture writing. Agr. well advanced; education almost universal. Political and social life based on caste system (nobility; priesthood; military and merchant). Civilization fell before Spanish under Hernán CORTÉS. See also MONTEZUMA; CUAHTEMOC.

Aztec Ruins National Monument: see NATIONAL PARKS AND MONUMENTS (table).

Azuela, Mariano (märyä'nō äswä'lä), 1873–1952, Mexican novelist. Experiences with Villa's revolutionary forces gave material for *Los de abajo* (1915).

azurite (äzh'ùrīt), mineral, the blue basic carbonate of copper, an important copper ore. Occurs in monoclinic crystals and in masses. Crystals used for ornament are found in SW U.S. and in France.

Azusa (ùzōō'sù), city (pop. 11,042), S Calif., E of Pasadena; founded 1887. Ships citrus fruit.

B

B, chemical symbol of element BORON.

Ba, chemical symbol of element BARIUM.

Baal (bā'ŭl), plural **Baalim** (bā'ŭlĭm) [Semitic, = possessor], term used in Old Testament for the gods of Canaan. Each locality had its own Baal who either had his own name, as Melkart of Tyre, or a name formed by adding the name of a place or special attribute to the word Baal, e.g., Baal-peor [Heb.,= Baal of Peor] or Baal-hanan [Heb., = Baal is gracious]. Baal worship was usually characterized by fertility rites and human sacrifice. At first Hebrews adopted the term for their God, but as struggle between Canaanite polytheism and Hebrew monotheism grew, name became synonymous with evil—hence Beelzebub (see SATAN), probably from Baal-zebub, god of Ekron. Other forms of Baal: Bel (in Babylonian religion); endings in Tyrian names (e.g., Jezebel, Hannibal).

Baalbek (bäl'bĕk), town, Lebanon, N of Damascus. Has ruins of great ancient city devoted to worship of Baal or Bel, the sun-god, hence called in Greek Heliopolis [city of the sun]; notable in Roman days.

Baal-peor (-pē'ôr), local god of Peor. Practices of his worship were especially abominable to the Hebrews, hence his name became a symbol of all shameful cults. Num. 25; Deut. 4.3; Ps. 106.28; Hosea 9.10. Under form of Belphegor, this was name of a devil in Middle Ages; Machiavelli used it in his *Belfagor.*

Baal-Schem-Tov (bäl-shĕm'-tōv') [Heb.,= man with a reputation], 1700–1760, first leader of the modern Hasidim, b. Russia; real name Israel ben Eliezer. Gained fame as a miracle worker. Taught that man reaches God through joy rather than sorrow, that learning is not necessary for prayer, and that repentance is always possible.

Baal-zebub: see BAAL and SATAN.

Baasha (bā'äshù), d. c.886 B.C., king of Israel (c.909–c.886 B.C.). Murdered Nadab and royal family to make himself king. 1 Kings 15.27–16.7; 2 Chron. 16.

Babar: see BABER.

Babbitt, Irving, 1865–1933, American teacher, humanist, vigorous critic of romanticism.

Babbitt metal, silver-white ANTIFRICTION METAL alloy, originally of tin, antimony, and copper, later also of varying composition. Developed by Isaac Babbitt (1799–1862), American inventor.

Babcock, Stephen Moulton, 1843–1931, American agr. chemist. Babcock test (1890) for percentage of butterfat in milk advanced the dairy industry.

Babel, Isaac Emmanuelovich (ē'säk úmänōōä'lúvich bä'bùl), 1894–, Russian author. One of the "fellow travelers," he won fame with his concise, realistic stories of the ghetto and the revolution, notably *Odessa Tales* (1923–24), *Red Cavalry* (1926; Eng. tr., 1929), *Benia Krik* (1927; Eng. tr., 1935).

Babel (bā'bùl), city where Noah's descendants (who spoke one language) tried to build tower to heaven. For this presumption they lost ability to speak intelligibly to each other. Gen. 11.1–9. Some see in this an explanation of world's many languages.

Baber or **Babar** (both: bä'bùr), popular name of Zahir-ud-din Mohammed, 1480–1530, founder of Mogul empire of India; descendant of Tamerlane. Invaded India from Afghanistan, conquering nearly all N India (1525–26). Autobiography is greatest of his literary works. Was also an excellent musician.

Babeuf, François Noël (fräswä' nôĕl' bäbûf'), 1760–97, French revolutionist. Argued for economic and social as well as political equality. After brief imprisonment he formed a group to forward economic equality and communism. After the Directory banned the group, a plot (the Conspiracy of the Equals) was made to overthrow the government. It was betrayed, and Babeuf was executed.

Babington, Anthony (bă'bĭngtùn), 1561–86, English conspirator. Plotted murder of Queen Elizabeth and freeing of MARY QUEEN OF SCOTS. Proof against him was used to bring about Mary's execution.

Babism (bä'bĭzùm), religion of 19th-cent. Persian sect, founded 1843, when Mirza Ali Mohammed of Shiraz proclaimed himself Bab ed-Din [gate of faith], successor to Moses, Sufism, Christ, and Mohammed. Doctrines from Sufism, Gnosticism, Shiite Islam. The sect rebelled unsuccessfully 1848; the Bab was executed 1850. Babism supplanted by Bahaism.

baboon, large, chiefly terrestrial monkey (genus *Papio*) of Africa, Arabia. Face doglike, canine teeth large, limbs powerful; medium tail is carried arched. Travels in packs; eats scorpions, insects, other animals, plant food. Most are yellowish or brown. MANDRILL and chacma are large baboons.

Babson, Roger Ward, 1875–, American statistician. Founded Babson Statistical Organization (1904), which publishes business statistics. Founded Babson Institute (1919) to train business executives.

baby: see INFANT.

Babylon (bă'bĭlùn), city of anc. Mesopotamia, on the Euphrates; center of Babylonia. HAMMURABI founded its greatness, which was destroyed by SENNACHERIB but revived in later period. Under NEBUCHADNEZZAR (d. 562 B.C.) it reached a height of luxury that made it fabulous; its Hanging Gardens were considered one of the wonders of the world.

SMALL CAPITALS = cross references.   Pronunciation key: pp. xiv and xv.   Abbreviations: p. 2.

89

After capture by Persians (538 B.C.) it declined.

Babylon, residential and resort village (pop. 6,015), SE N.Y., on S shore (Great South Bay) of Long Isl.

Babylonia (băbĭlō'nĕú), anc. Mesopotamian empire, centered on Babylon. Name sometimes used to include all S Mesopotamia with city-states (Lagash, Akkad, Erech, Ur) that flourished 3d millennium B.C., but more often limited to Semitic civilization founded by SARGON and brought to a peak by HAMMURABI (c.2100 B.C.). Learning (with cuneiform writing), commerce, and architecture flourished. Attacks by Hittites and nomadic Kassites (18th cent. B.C.) caused decline, but Babylonia again flowered under the Assyrian empire. A revolt was put down by SENNACHERIB (late 8th cent. B.C.), but later Nabopolassar estab. (625 B.C.) Babylonian independence, and the empire grew to new and greater splendor under NEBUCHADNEZZAR. After conquest by Persians under Cyrus the Great (538 B.C.) Babylonia declined. Its contributions to art, science, and other aspects of civilization were incalculable.

Babylonian captivity: see CAPTIVITY and PAPACY.

Babylonian religion. The religion of the whole Tigris-Euphrates valley was really one, with many local gods. Dominant gods were determined by dominant cities (e.g., when Babylon was paramount, Marduk, or Bel or BAAL, was king of gods). Priests were very powerful. The rich mythology of Babylon, further elaborated by Assyria, was preserved in cuneiform writing on clay tablets. It included stories of creation of world, of flood covering whole world, journey of Ishtar to underworld, and legends of gods and heroes. Babylon was indebted to Sumerian culture for its religion, and its great towers (suggesting BABEL) were reminiscent of Sumerian worship of high places.

baby's-breath, garden perennial, *Gypsophila paniculata,* marked by delicate panicles of small white blooms.

Bacchae (bă'kē) or **Bacchantes** (bŭkăn'tēz, bŭkănts', bă'kŭnts), in Greek and Roman religion, female worshipers of DIONYSUS or BACCHUS. Their secret rites, performed in frenzied ecstasy, involved the thyrsus, the myrtle, drinking, and sweet wild music. Also called Maenads.

Bacchanalia (băkŭnā'lĕú) [Latin], in Roman religion, festival in honor of BACCHUS. Originally religious, it became a drunken orgy and was outlawed.

Bacchantes: see BACCHAE.

Bacchus (bă'kŭs), in Greek and Roman mythology, god of wine, identified with DIONYSUS; also god of vegetation and fertility. His rites were orgiastic.

Bacchylides (băkĭ'lĭdēz), fl. c.470 B.C., Greek lyric poet, b. Ceos; contemporary of Pindar.

Bach (bäkh), German family of distinguished musicians beginning with Hans Bach, c.1580-1626, a Thuringian violinist who was called The Player. Two of his grandsons were Johann Christoph Bach, 1642-1703, a composer and organist at Eisenach, and Johann Ambrosius Bach, 1645-95, a violinist at Eisenach and father of Johann Sebastian

Bach (see separate article). The eldest son of Johann Ambrosius was **Johann Christoph Bach,** 1671-1721, an organist. When his parents died he took his younger brother, Johann Sebastian, into his home and became his teacher. Of Johann Sebastian's 20 children, several became outstanding musicians. **Wilhelm Friedeman Bach** (frē'důmän), 1710-84, was an organist, composer, and musical director at Halle. **Carl Philipp Emanuel Bach,** 1714-88, wrote cantatas, oratorios, symphonies, Passion music, and two volumes of sonatas; also a treatise on clavier playing. **Johann Christian Bach,** 1735-82, lived in Italy and England. He became a Roman Catholic and wrote Masses and church music, operas, and sonatas and concertos for clavier.

Bach, Alexander, 1813-93, Austrian statesman; created baron 1854. Minister of interior 1849-59. Instituted reactionary "Bach system" of bureaucratic control, centralization, and Germanization of Hapsburg empire, along with beneficial reforms, e.g., abolition of internal tariff barriers.

Bach, Johann Sebastian, 1685-1750, German composer, b. Eisenach. Became organist at Arnstadt (1703) and at Mülhausen (1707); court organist and chamber musician at Weimar (1708), musical director (1714); musical director at Cöthen (1717); cantor at Leipzig (1723) until his death. Few of Bach's works were published during his lifetime, hence exact dates cannot be fixed for all of them, but most of them can be placed in their proper period. At Arnstadt and Mülhausen he began a series of organ works which culminated in the great works of Weimar period—the Passacaglia and Fugue in C minor, most of the noted preludes and fugues, the 45 chorale-preludes of *Das Orgelbüchlein.* At Cöthen he produced instrumental works, e.g., the English and French Suites, the Two-Part and Three-Part Inventions, *The Well-tempered Clavier,* Book I, the unaccompanied violin sonatas, and the Brandenburg concertos. Great works of the Leipzig period include the St. John Passion, the Magnificat, the St. Matthew Passion, the Mass in B Minor, *The Well-tempered Clavier,* Book II, and the *Clavierübung* (including the Six Partitas, the Italian Concerto, and the Goldberg variations). His last work was *The Art of the Fugue* (1749). Despite his many secular compositions, Bach is regarded primarily as a church composer.

Bach Choir, name of choral organizations producing music of J. S. Bach. Outstanding are the Bach Choir of London, founded 1875, and the Bach Choir of Bethlehem, Pa., founded 1900.

Bache, Benjamin Franklin (bāch), 1769-98, American journalist; grandson of Benjamin Franklin. Founded Philadelphia *General Advertiser* (later the *Aurora*) in 1790. Denounced Federalists; arrested under Sedition Act; released on parole. His son, **Franklin Bache,** 1792-1864, physician and chemist, prepared (with G. B. Wood) the first 11 editions of *The Dispensatory of the United States* (1st ed., 1833). His cousin, **Alexander Dallas Bache,** 1806-67, was an educator and physicist. He influenced development of free education in Philadelphia. Estab. (1839) first magnetic observatory in North America; reorganized U.S. Coast Survey; founded Natl. Acad. of Sciences.

Bache, Jules Semon, 1861–1944, American financier and art collector. His collection, which includes works by Raphael and Titian, is in the Metropolitan Mus.

bachelor's button: see CORNFLOWER.

bacillus: see BACTERIA.

Back, Sir George, 1796–1878, British explorer in N Canada. Explored Great Fish R. (now Back R.) in Northwest Territories (1833–35). Explored the arctic coast of Canada (1836–37).

backbone: see SPINAL COLUMN.

Backbone Mountain, ridge of the Alleghenies, NW Md., rises to 3,360 ft., highest elevation in state.

Bacon, Delia Salter: see BACON, LEONARD.

Bacon, Francis, 1561–1626, English philosopher and statesman. Advanced slowly under Elizabeth but swiftly under James I from knight (1603) to lord chancellor (1621). Pleaded guilty 1621 to accepting bribes, was barred from office, and spent the rest of his life in retirement. His shrewd, concentrated *Essays* (1597) are his most popular works. Inductive method of modern experimental science was his tremendous contribution to philosophy. Of his projected reorganization of all human knowledge, *Instauratio Magna,* he completed two parts, *The Advancement of Learning* (1605) and *Novum Organum* (1620). *The New Atlantis* (1627) describes a utopia established on scientific principles.

Bacon, Henry, 1866–1924, American architect. Designed Lincoln Memorial, Washington, D.C.

Bacon, Leonard, 1802–81, American Congregational minister, pastor for 41 years of First Church of New Haven, and noted antislavery leader. His sister, **Delia Salter Bacon,** 1811–59, was an author. She held that Shakspere's plays were written by group including Francis Bacon.

Bacon, Nathaniel, 1647–76, leader of Bacon's Rebellion, 1676, popular revolt in colonial Va. Uprising precipitated by failure of governor, Sir William BERKELEY, to defend frontier against Indian attacks. Underlying cause was economic exploitation of small farmers by England and tidewater aristocracy. Rebellion collapsed after Bacon's death.

Bacon, Peggy, 1895–, American illustrator and etcher, best known for satirical etchings and dry points.

Bacon, Roger, c.1214–1294?, English scholastic philosopher, a Franciscan, called the Admirable Doctor. A learned teacher at Oxford, he pugnaciously entered into many quarrels with other learned men and was in constant trouble. In modern times Friar Bacon has been celebrated chiefly for his interest in natural science, experiments, and direct observation. He considered science as complementary to, not opposed to, faith. His best-known works are the *Opus majus, Opus minor,* and *Opus tertium.* Because he wrote works on alchemy, many others on alchemy and magic have been attributed to him. The claim that he invented gunpowder is false,

and the idea that he had a telescope or microscope is highly improbable.

Bacon's Rebellion: see BACON, NATHANIEL.

bacteria, minute unicellular organisms, usually classified as plants (class Schizomycetes) of division of thallophytes called fungi. Sometimes classified with blue-green algae as separate division of plant kingdom. Rod-shaped (bacillus), round (coccus), spiral (spirillum) are typical forms; range from c.$\frac{1}{250,000}$ in. to $\frac{1}{250}$ in. long; reproduce chiefly by transverse fission. Parasitic (or pathogenic) bacteria cause such diseases as tuberculosis, diphtheria, cholera, typhoid fever, pneumonia, tetanus, gangrene, anthrax, tularemia. Some bacteria attack tissues directly; some produce poisonous toxins. Vaccination induces immunity to some diseases. Useful bacteria outnumber harmful; NITROGEN-FIXING BACTERIA and NITRIFYING BACTERIA help enrich soil, as do decay bacteria. See *ill.*, p. 813.

bacteriophage (băktēr'ēŭfāj). Believed to be composed of ultramicroscopic particles destructive to bacteria. F. H. d'Herelle and followers believe it resembles virus, acts as parasite; others think it similar to enzyme. Several bacteriophages recognized; each acts only on specific bacteria.

Bactria (băk'trēŭ), ancient Greek kingdom of central Asia (now N Afghanistan and E Iran); cap. was Bactra (modern BALKH). As satrapy of Persian Empire, it was taken 328 B.C. by Alexander the Great. Later under Seleucidae. Declared independence in 240 B.C. and became powerful Greco-Bactrian state. Fell c.130 B.C., to nomadic Sakas.

Badajoz (bädähōth'), city (pop. 32,604), cap. of Badajoz prov., W Spain, in Estremadura, on Guadiana R. Seat of a Moorish emirate (1022–94), reconquered by the Christians 1228. In Peninsular War it resisted French siege (1808–9), fell to French 1811, was liberated by Wellington 1812. Large 13th-cent. cathedral; ruins of Moorish citadel.

Badakhshan, USSR: see MOUNTAIN-BADAKH-SHAN.

Bad Ems, Germany: see EMS.

Baden (bä'dŭn), former German state, SW Germany, on right bank of the Rhine from the Main to Lake Constance; former cap. Karlsruhe. After World War II its S part became the French-occupied state of Baden (3,842 sq. mi.; pop. 1,335,458; cap. Freiburg); N part (1,984 sq. mi.; pop. 1,467,-316), including Karlsruhe, Mannheim, and Heidelberg, was incorporated into American-occupied state of WÜRTTEMBERG-BADEN. Landscape, notably NECKAR valley and BLACK FOREST, is famed for its beauty. Agr., wine growing; industries in N. Until French Revolution Baden had no political unity, consisting of several petty margraviates; the bishoprics of Mainz, Speyer, Strasbourg, and Constance; the Mannheim-Heidelberg dists. of Rhenish PALATINATE; and the BREISGAU, under Hapsburg rule. In 1771 the margraviates of Baden-Baden and Baden-Durlach were united under the same branch of the old house of ZÄHRINGEN. Margrave Charles Frederick, an ally of Napoleon, was raised to grand duke (1806) and by 1810 had acquired the entire state. Prussian troops helped to suppress Revolution of 1848. Baden sided with Austria in Austro-Prussian War (1866); joined German Empire 1871; became republic 1918.

Baden or **Baden-bei-Wien** (-bī-vēn'), city (pop. 20,528), Lower Austria. Hot sulphur springs; resort.

Baden, town (pop. 11,595), Aargau, N Switzerland, on the Limmat. Noted for sulphur baths since antiquity. Meeting place of Swiss diet 1424–1712. For treaty signed here 1714, see UTRECHT, PEACE OF.

Baden-Baden, city (pop. 37,007), S Baden, SW Germany, in Black Forest. Fashionable spa.

Baden-bei-Wien: see BADEN, Lower Austria.

Baden-Powell of Gilwell, Robert Stephenson Smyth Baden-Powell, 1st Baron (bā'dǔn-pōul), 1857–1941, British soldier, founder (1908) of the Boy Scouts.

badger, carnivorous mammal of family Mustelidae. Broad, heavy body; rather long snout; sharp claws; shaggy fur, usually gray and brownish with black and white markings. Include *Meles* of Europe and Asia; *Taxidea* of America; ferret badger (*Helictis*) and sand or hog badger (*Arctonyx*) of Asia.

Bad Godesberg (bät' gö'dúsbĕrk), town (pop. 44,536), North Rhine-Westphalia, NW Germany, idyllically situated on a height above Bonn on the Rhine. Radioactive spa. Ruined castle (built 1210). Scene of meeting between Hitler and Neville Chamberlain in 1938 (see MUNICH PACT).

Bad Ischl, Austria: see ISCHL.

Badlands, arid plateau, c.120 mi. long and 30–50 mi. wide, SW S.Dak., E of the Black Hills. Has fantastic scenery and deposits of prehistoric fossils. The Badlands Natl. Monument occupies part of region.

badminton (băd'mĭntùn), game played by two or four persons, in which a shuttlecock—small, cork hemisphere with feathers attached—is volleyed over a net. Light, gutstring rackets are used. Probably originated in India. Popular in England in 1870s, taking name from seat of duke of Beaufort.

Bad Nauheim (bät' nou'hīm), town (pop. 11,896), Hesse, W Germany, in Taunus Mts. World-famous health resort for heart diseases.

Badoglio, Pietro (pyä'trō bädō'lyō), 1871–, Italian field marshal. Completed conquest of Ethiopia (1936); succeeded Mussolini as premier (1943–44); signed armistice with Allies (1943).

Bad Pyrmont, Germany: see PYRMONT.

Baduila, king of Ostrogoths: see TOTILA.

Baeda: see BEDE.

Baedeker, Karl (bā'dúkúr), 1801–59, German publisher, founder of Baedeker guidebooks.

Baer, Karl Ernst von, 1792–1876, Estonian biologist. Considered a founder of modern embryology. He discovered mammalian ovum in 1827 and originated theory of embryonic germ layers.

Baeyer, Adolf von (ä'dôlf fŭn bā'yùr), 1835–1917, German chemist. Won 1905 Nobel Prize for work on organic dyes and hydroaromatic compounds. Discovered molecular structure of indigo, cerulein, eosin.

Baffin, William, c.1584–1622, British arctic explorer. Failed to find Northwest Passage but discovered Baffin Bay and Baffin Isl.

Baffin Bay, arm of Arctic Ocean between Greenland and Arctic Archipelago. Connects with the Arctic by Smith Sound and with the Atlantic by Davis Strait. Labrador Current brings many icebergs, making navigation hazardous.

Baffin Island, 197,754 sq. mi., largest and most easterly of the Arctic Archipelago, in Arctic Ocean. Formerly considered Baffin Land, it is geographically a N continuation of Labrador, separated from mainland by Hudson Strait. Interior has fresh-water lakes; mountains in E. Population largely Eskimo. Trading posts generally have Royal Canadian Police posts and mission schools. First visited by Frobisher 1576–78.

Bagdad, Iraq: see BAGHDAD.

Bagehot, Walter (băj'ùt), 1826–77, English social scientist and critic. Among his books are *The English Constitution* (1867), *Lombard Street* (1873; on banking), *Physics and Politics* (1875; pioneer analysis of relations of natural and social sciences), and *Literary Studies* (1879).

Baghdad or **Bagdad** (both: băg'dăd, bägdäd'), city, (pop. 364,049), cap. of Iraq, on the Tigris and 25 mi. N of the Euphrates. From Sumerian times site was center for desert travel and trade. Founded A.D. 762 by MANSUR, city became great commercial center, reaching its height under HARUN-AL-RASHID. Its glory is reflected in many tales of *Thousand and One Nights.* City declined after Harun's death and temporary removal of caliphate to Samarra. Sacked by Mongols (1258) and destroyed by Tamerlane (1400) and by Ismail (1524). Later fell prey to warring Turks and Persians. By 1638, when it became part of Ottoman Empire, city had only c.14,000 people. Few antiquities remain, but city is still partly enclosed by ancient wall. Captured 1917 by British forces. Became cap. of Iraq 1920. City is major rail and air terminus.

Baghdad Railway, connecting Haidarpasha (opposite Istanbul), Turkey, with Basra, Iraq. Branch lines to N Iran, USSR, and Palestine. Begun with German capital (1896), it aroused protests of England (which saw in it a threat to its Indian Empire) and others. Work was suspended and then resumed (1911) when the line became a factor leading to World War I. Last link between Mosul and Samarra completed 1940 with British funds.

Bagnell Dam, central Mo., in Osage R.; built 1929–31. State's largest power dam (2,543 ft. long, 148 ft. high), it forms L. of the OZARKS.

bagpipe, musical instrument of anc. origin. Called the musette in 18th-cent. France. Now chiefly associated with Scotland. Consists of a leathern bag with either bellows or tube to inflate it: chanters or chaunters (melody pipes having finger holes); and drones, each of which produces one sustained tone.

Bagration, Piotr Ivanovich, Prince (pyô'tùr ēvä'nùvĭch bägrätēōn'), 1765–1812, Russian general. Commanded an army at BORODINO; mortally wounded.

Baguio (bä'gēō), city (pop. 29,262; alt. c.5,000 ft.), on W Luzon, Philippines; summer cap. of the republic. A resort and gold-mining center. Severely damaged in World War II.

bagworm, larva of moth family including species destructive to forest and shade trees in E U.S. Growing larva travels in silken covering; passes pupa stage in this bag (sometimes leaf-covered) fastened to twig. Adult female emerges partly, male fertilizes eggs. Female lays eggs inside; dies.

Bahaism (bä'hä̈izům bůhä'–), religion founded 1862, when Baha Ullah (a Persian originally named Mirza Hussein Ali), announced himself prophet succeeding the Bab (see BABISM). Bahaists believe in simple living, universal education, unity of all religions, world peace, equality of men and women. Religion spread in 20th cent. (U.S. center Wilmette, Ill.).

Bahama Islands or **Bahamas** (bůhä'můz), archipelago (4,403 sq. mi.; pop. 68,846) c.700 islands and islets, beginning c.50 mi. off SE Florida and extending c.750 mi. SE almost to Haiti. Governed as British crown colony; cap. NASSAU on New Providence Isl. Winter resort. Spanish visited islands, but English settled them in 17th cent. and imported Negroes. Islands were haunt of pirates (17th–18th cents.), notably Blackbeard; of blockade runners in Civil War; of rum runners during prohibition era in U.S. Used as U.S. military bases in World War II.

Bahawalpur (bůhä'wůlpōŏr"), princely state (17,494 sq. mi.; pop. 1,341,209), W Pakistan; cap. Bahawalpur (pop. 40,015). Mostly a sandy waste. Grain, dates, and cotton are grown in irrigated area.

Bahia or **Baía** (both: bäë'ů), state (217,688 sq. mi.; pop. 4,900,419), E Brazil; cap. SALVADOR, port on Todos os Santos Bay, once chief city of Brazil. SE Bahia is one of great cacao-growing regions of world. State formerly sugar-growing.

Bahía Blanca (bäë'ä bläng'kä), city (pop. 122,-059), SE Argentina, Atlantic port. Offers access to S Pampa, oilfields of Neuquén, Patagonian lakes.

Bahrein Islands (bärän'), archipelago (c.200 sq. mi.; pop. c.120,000), off Arabia, in Persian Gulf. Ruled by Arab sheik; under British protection since 1861. Chief port and cap. is Manamah on Bahrein or Aval isl. Oil discovered here 1932.

Bahr el-Huleh (bär' ĕl-hōŏ'lä), lake, NE Palestine. Jordan R. headwaters flows through it. May be same as Waters of Merom (site of great victory). Joshua 11.

Baía, Brazil: see BAHIA.

Baia (bī'ä), Latin *Baiae,* village, Campania, S Italy, on Bay of Naples. Celebrated resort in ancient times. Remains of Roman baths.

Baïf, Antoine de (ätwän' dů bäëf'), 1532–89, French poet; one of the PLÉIADE.

Baikal (bīkäl'), lake, area 13,180 sq. mi.; RSFSR, in SE Siberia; largest fresh-water lake of Asia, deepest lake in world (5,710 ft.).

Baikie, William Balfour (bä'kē), 1825–64, Scottish explorer in W Africa, a philologist. Opened Niger R. to trade and translated Scriptures into Hausa.

bail, release from prison of a person awaiting trial, on the deposit of a security, which is to be forfeited in case of failure of the accused to surrender at an appointed time.

Bail is usually granted in all civil arrests, but is sometimes refused in criminal cases (e.g., that of a murder charge).

Baile Átha Cliath, Ireland: see DUBLIN.

Bailén (bīlän'), city (pop. 9,727), S Spain, in Andalusia; scene of French defeat (1808) by Spanish.

Bailey, Liberty Hyde, 1858–, American botanist and horticulturist, noted for clarifying plant classifications. He edited cyclopedias of agr. and horticulture, compiled *Hortus* and *Hortus Second* (1941).

Baillie, Matthew, 1761–1823, English physician, an authority on pathology and morbid anatomy.

Bailly, Jean Sylvain (zhä' sĕlvē' bäyē'), 1736–93, French astronomer and politician. Won distinction as scientist before his election as president of National Assembly (1789); mayor of Paris 1789–91. Permitted National Guard to fire upon demonstrators (July 17, 1791). Arrested 1793; guillotined.

Bain, Alexander, 1818–1903, Scottish philosopher. Helped to found modern psychology by eliminating metaphysics and stressing physiology. Long associated with the Univ. of Aberdeen.

Bainbridge, William, 1774–1833, American naval officer. As commander of U.S. vessel, insult offered him by dey of Algiers contributed greatly to American declaration of war against BARBARY STATES.

Bainbridge, city (pop. 7,562), SW Ga., on Flint R. Trade center for farm and timber area. Mfg. of wood products and peanut shelling.

Baird, John Logie, 1888–1946, Scottish inventor. First to demonstrate true television (1926), and, in 1928, transatlantic and color television.

Baird, Spencer Fullerton, 1823–87, American zoologist known for pioneer studies of North American fauna. Secretary of Smithsonian Institution (from 1878); influenced establishing of U.S. Bureau of Fisheries and marine biological station (Woods Hole, Mass.).

Bairnsfather, Bruce, 1888–, English illustrator and author. Created the character "Old Bill," who typified the British infantryman in World War I.

Baja California: see LOWER CALIFORNIA.

Bajazet (băjůzĕt'), Ottoman sultans; also spelled Bayazit, Bayazid. **Bajazet I,** 1347–1403, reigned 1389–1402. Conquered E Anatolia; defeated Christian army at NIKOPOL (1396). His siege of Constantinople (1402) was interrupted by the invasion of TAMERLANE, who defeated him at Ankara (1402) and reputedly carried him in an iron cage (really a palanquin). **Bajazet II,** 1447–1513, reigned 1481–1512; put down the revolt of his brother Djem, who fled and eventually died in custody of Charles VIII of France (1495). The sultan lost Cilicia to the Egyptian Mamelukes (1491) and warred unsuccessfully against Venice (1499–1503), but he furthered Ottoman culture and rebuilt Constantinople after an earthquake (1509).

Bajer, Fredrik (frädh'rĭk bī'ůr), 1837–1922, Danish pacifist and writer. Helped to found Internatl. Peace Bureau at Berne (1891). Shared 1908 Nobel Peace Prize with K. P. Arnoldson.

Bakacs, Thomas: see BAKOCZ, THOMAS.

Bakelite (bā'kŭlīt), trade name for synthetic resin (amber or colorless unless dyed) made by heating under pressure the product of reaction between phenol and formaldehyde. Used in making many small molded articles (e.g., drinking glasses) and for many purposes. Invented by Leo Hendrik Baekeland (1863–1944).

Baker, Sir Benjamin, 1840–1907, English civil engineer of metropolitan railway systems.

Baker, George Pierce, 1866–1935, American educator (Harvard, 1888–1924; Yale, 1925–33). At Harvard instituted the 47 Workshop, a laboratory of the drama. O'Neill, Sidney Howard, R. E. Jones, and others studied there. Works include *Dramatic Technique.*

Baker, Newton D(iehl), 1871–1937, U.S. Secretary of War (1916–21). Much criticized at first, he was later praised for his direction of World War I.

Baker, Ray Stannard, pseud. **David Grayson,** 1870–1946, American author. A Chicago journalist, he became a muckraker for *McClure's.* As "David Grayson" he wrote gentle essays (e.g., *Adventures in Contentment,* 1907). Intimate of Pres. Wilson, Baker went to Europe (1918) as his special agent. Wrote *Woodrow Wilson and World Settlement* (3 vols., 1922), edited Wilson's papers, and wrote a biography.

Baker, city (pop. 9,471), NE Oregon, SE of Pendleton and on Powder R.; laid out 1865. Trade center in farm, stock, lumber, and mine region.

Baker Island, coral islet, area 1 sq. mi., central Pacific near the equator. Claimed 1857 by U.S., colonized 1935 by Americans from Hawaii, placed under Dept. of the Interior 1936. Held by the Japanese 1942–44. Now a naval station.

Baker Lake, 1,029 sq. mi., Keewatin dist., Northwest Territories, Canada, near Chesterfield Inlet. At W end is Royal Canadian Mounted Police post.

Bakersfield, city (pop. 34,784), S central Calif., on Kern R. and N of Los Angeles; laid out 1869. Center for oil area with refineries and mfg. of oil tools. Paint and chemical plants.

Baker University: see BALDWIN CITY, Kansas.

Bakhchisarai (bākh″chēsŭrī′), city (pop. c.10,-000), RSFSR, in S Crimea; historic cap. of khanate of Crimea (15th cent.–1783). Celebrated for palace of khans, built 16th cent.

Bakhtiari (bākh″tēä′rē), mountainous region of SW Iran. Chief home of nomadic Bakhtiari tribe, famed for warlike behavior. Region became important with discovery of oil in late 19th cent. Tribe played decisive part in revolution of 1908 9.

baking powder, mixture containing baking soda (sodium bicarbonate) and one or more acid-producing ingredients and used in making quick breads, cakes, and pastry. Acted upon by moisture (and by oven heat if "double-acting" type), produces carbon dioxide, thus leavening dough more rapidly than yeast.

baking soda: see SODA.

Bakocz or **Bakacs, Thomas** (bŏ′kôts, bŏ′kŏch), Hung. *Bakócz* or *Bakács Tamás,* c.1442–1521, Hungarian statesman and cardinal. Of unbounded ambition, he rose from servile origin to chancellor and archprimate of Hungary. In 1514 he suppressed, with help

of John Zapolya, a peasant rebellion; peasants were reduced to serfdom. He died enormously rich.

Bakst, Lev Nikolayevich (lyĕf′ nyīkŭlī′ŭvĭch bäkst′), 1866?–1924, Russian painter. Created settings and costumes for Diaghilev's ballet company.

Baku (bäkōō′), cap. of Azerbaijan, USSR, on Caspian Sea. Greater Baku (pop. 809,347) includes entire Apsheron peninsula, which extends c.40 mi. into Caspian Sea and contains 15% of world's petroleum reserves. The chief oil center of USSR, Baku also has a large port and many cultural institutions. First mentioned 5th cent. A.D., it had Zoroastrian shrines of constantly burning fires (from oil and gas wells). Ceded by Persia to Russia 1813. Oil industry began late 19th cent.

Bakunin, Mikhail (mēkhĕyēl′ běkōō′nyĭn), 1814–76, Russian anarchist. Young aristocrat turned revolutionist, he was exiled (1849) to Siberia, but escaped. In First International after 1868 he was opposed by Marxists, who expelled him (1872). He believed "anarchism, collectivism, and atheism" would give man complete freedom and advocated violent revolution.

Balaam (bā′lŭm), prophet hired by King of Moab to curse the Hebrews. By order of God he was forced to bless them instead. Num. 22–24; 31.8, 16; Micah 6.5; 2 Peter 2.15, 16; Jude 11; Rev. 2.14.

Balak (bā′lăk), King of Moab who hired Balaam to curse the Hebrews. Num. 22–24.

Balakirev, Mili (Alekseyevich) (mē′lyī bŭlä′kyĭrĭf), 1837–1910, Russian composer and conductor. With Borodin, Moussorgsky, Rimsky-Korsakov, and Cui he formed a group of highly nationalistic composers known as the Russian Five. Best-known works are piano fantasy *Islamey* and the incidental music for *King Lear.*

Balaklava (bä″lŭklä′vŭ), city (pop. 2,323), RSFSR, in S Crimea, near Sevastopol; fishing port and resort on Black Sea. Famous for allied victory (1854) in Crimean War and for suicidal charge of an English light-cavalry brigade, celebrated by Tennyson.

balalaika: see STRINGED INSTRUMENTS.

Balance, the, in astronomy: see ZODIAC.

balance, instrument to measure MASS or weight. Equal-arm (beam) balance simplest; based on LEVER principle. Beam is suspended at its center on knife-edge at right angles to it; pans of equal weight are suspended at each end, equidistant from fulcrum (point of support). Pointer is at zero when beam is in equilibrium. Object to be weighed is put in one pan, standard weights in other until balanced. Platform balances may be equal- or unequal-arm types. Spring balance (from which object is suspended) measures force of gravity at certain point on earth's surface. TORSION BALANCE not strictly a balance. See also SCALES.

balance of trade, difference between exports and imports of a country. Mercantilists believed that a country should have a "favorable" balance of trade—an excess of exports over imports; though refuted by Adam Smith and David Hume, this idea is still widely held, notably in nations seeking "autarchy."

Balanchine, George, 1904–, Russian-American choreographer and ballet dancer. Performed in Russia 1921–24 and with Diaghilev troupe in Paris 1924–28. In U.S. since 1933; founded School of American Ballet 1934. Directed Metropolitan Opera ballet 1934–37 and New York City ballet 1948–.

Balard, Antoine Jérôme (ätwän′ zhärõm′ bälär′), 1802–76, French chemist. Discovered bromine; extracted sodium sulphate from sea water.

Balassa, Baron Balint (bä′lĭnt bŭlăs′ŭ, bŏ′lŏsh-shŏ), 1551–94, Hungarian poet, regarded as the creator of Hungarian lyric poetry.

Balaton (bä′lŭtŏn, Hung. bŏ′lŏtôn), Ger. *Plattensee,* lake 231 sq. mi.), W Hungary, largest in Central Europe. Fisheries; vineyards; resorts.

Balbo, Italo (ē′tälō bäl′bō), 1896–1940, Italian Fascist leader and aviator. Took part in March on Rome (1922); became minister of aviation 1929, governor of Libya 1933. Died in plane accident.

Balboa, Vasco Núñez de (vä′skō nōō′nyäth dä bälbō′ä) c.1475–1519?, Spanish conquistador, discoverer of Pacific. After reaching DARIEN (1510), he won friendship of Indians, who accompanied him on epic march across isthmus (1513). Claimed Pacific and all shores washed by it for Spain. Pedrarias had him beheaded for treason.

Balboa, town (pop. 4,168), Panama Canal Zone, Pacific port. Has administration hq. of Zone and canal. Balboa dist. comprises Pacific half of Zone.

Balch, Emily Greene, 1867–, American economist and sociologist. She shared the 1946 Nobel Peace Prize with John R. Mott.

Balchen, Bernt (bäl′kŭn), 1899–, Norwegian-American aviator. Headed arctic search for Amundsen and Ellsworth (1925) and joined their 1926 expedition. Chief pilot of Byrd's antarctic expedition, 1928–30. World War II colonel in U.S. Army Air Forces, recalled (1948) to active service.

Balder (bôl′dŭr), Norse god of light; son of Odin and Frigg. One legend says that, invulnerable to everything but mistletoe, he was killed by a mistletoe dart made by Loki.

Baldoon, locality, S Ont., Canada, near Chatham. Failure of settlement here led Lord Selkirk to sponsor Red River Settlement.

Baldovinetti, Alessio (äläs′syō bäldō vēnĕt′tē), c.1425–1499, Italian painter, one of the first Florentine artists to experiment with oil painting. Taught Ghirlandaio.

Baldung, Hans (häns′ bäl′dŏong), 1480–1545, German religious and mythological painter, surnamed Grien or Grün because of his predilection for green.

Baldwin, Latin emperors of Constantinople (see CONSTANTINOPLE, LATIN EMPIRE OF). **Baldwin I,** 1171–1205, count of Flanders and a leader of the Fourth Crusade, was elected emperor in 1204. Captured in battle with the Bulgarians (1205), he died in captivity. Succeeded by his brother, Henry of Flanders. **Baldwin II,** 1217–73, succeeded his brother ROBERT OF COURTENAY (1228). JOHN OF BRIENNE was regent till 1237. He sold part of the True Cross to Louis IX of France and

pawned his son with the Venetians to get funds for his tottering throne, but in 1261 MICHAEL VIII stormed Constantinople and Baldwin fled.

Baldwin, kings of Jerusalem. **Baldwin I,** 1058?–1118, brother of GODFREY OF BOUILLON, whom he accompanied on First Crusade. Took title king 1100; consolidated the Latin states; gained the chief ports of Palestine. His cousin and successor, **Baldwin II** (Baldwin du Bourg), d. 1131, fought the Turks in N Syria and made Tyre and Antioch dependent on his crown. **Baldwin III,** 1130–63, son of FULK of Anjou, reigned 1143–63. The decay of Latin power in the East had begun. Edessa fell to the Moslems (1144); the Second Crusade failed; and Sultan NUREDDIN seized N Syria (1154). His nephew, **Baldwin IV** (the Leper), c.1161–85, spent his whole reign (1174–85) defending the kingdom against SALADIN. Disabled by leprosy, he made Guy of LUSIGNAN his lieutenant, but withdrew the commission and had his five-year-old nephew crowned (1183) as **Baldwin V** (d. 1186), with RAYMOND, count of Tripoli, as regent.

Baldwin, Abraham, 1754–1807, American statesman. U.S. Representative from Ga. (1789–99); U.S. Senator (1799–1807). A founder of present Univ. of Georgia.

Baldwin, Loammi (lōă′mī), 1740–1807, American civil engineer, builder of Middlesex Canal. Developed Baldwin apple. His son, **Loammi Baldwin,** 1780–1838, engineer of Union Canal and dry-dock builder.

Baldwin, Matthias William, 1795–1866, American industrialist, founder of Baldwin Locomotive Works.

Baldwin, Robert, 1804–58, Canadian statesman, leader of movement for representative government in Canada. In the assembly he led opposition group and effected alliance with French in Lower Canada. In 1842 he joined with Louis H. LaFONTAINE to form a coalition government. Second Baldwin-La Fontaine ministry (1848–51), often called the "great ministry," accomplished reform of local government in Ontario, promoted judicial and educational reforms.

Baldwin, Stanley, 1867–1947, British statesman. Conservative party leader 1923–37, he was three times prime minister. Broke 1926 general strike. League of Nations declined, Fascist powers rose, and Edward VIII abdicated during his third government (1935–37).

Baldwin City, city (pop. 1,741), NE Kansas, SE of Topeka. Seat of Baker Univ. (Methodist; coed.; 1858).

Baldwyn, town (pop. 1,567), NE Miss., N of Tupelo. Brices Cross Roads Natl. Battlefield Site, where Gen. N. B. Forrest routed Union force June 10, 1864, is near by.

Bâle, Switzerland: see BASEL.

Balearic Islands (bălēä′rĭk), Span. *Baleares,* archipelago in W Mediterranean, forming a province (1,936 sq. mi.; pop. 407,497) of Spain; cap. Palma. Chief islands: Majorca, Minorca, Iviza. Agr., fishing, tourist trade. Export of majolica ware, silver filigree. Inhabited since prehistoric times, the islands were occupied by Iberians, Phoenicians, Greeks, Carthaginians, Romans, Byzantines; conquered by Moors 8th cent. A.D.; made a kingdom 11th cent.; conquered by Aragonese 13th cent. See also MAJORCA.

Balfour, Arthur James (băl'fŏŏr), 1848–1930, British statesman. Held many posts. As foreign secretary, issued (1917) Balfour Declaration pledging British support for a Jewish national home in Palestine. Devoted to cause of international peace.

Bali (bä'lē), island (2,533 sq. mi.; pop. 1,074,-925), Lesser Sundas, Indonesia, separated from Java by Bali Strait. Culturally and economically one of the most important islands of Indonesia. Chief products are copra, rice, coffee, and teakwood. Hinduism has been dominant here since 7th cent. The Dutch first landed here in 1597.

Balieff, Nikita (bä'lyĕf), 1877–1936, Russian impresario. Founded and acted as master of ceremonies in the *Chauve-Souris* revue.

Balikesir (bä"lĭkĕsēr'), city (pop. 36,001), NW Turkey. Rail junction; agr. center. Has a large annual fair.

Balinese music, chiefly a survival of pre-Islamic music of Java, using the tonal systems of JAVANESE MUSIC. The orchestra of tuned percussion instruments is called a *gamelan.* Each type of dance or drama has its own *gamelan.* Basic instruments include bronze or bamboo xylophones, gongs, flutes, fiddles, rattles, and cymbals. Little use is made of notation; compositions are learned by rote.

Baliol, John de (bä'lēŭl), d. 1269, English baron, founder of Balliol Col., Oxford. A regent for Alexander III of Scotland, he was removed from office for treason. His third son, **John de Baliol,** 1249–1315, king of Scotland (1292–96), claimed the throne at the death of MARGARET MAID OF NORWAY. EDWARD I of England supported him, over ROBERT I, in return for feudal overlordship and he was crowned. Renounced (1296) his oath of fealty, was defeated, and surrendered to Edward. Retired to France 1299. His son, **Edward de Baliol,** d. 1363, king of Scotland, invaded Scotland (1332) with aid of Edward III and defeated supporters of DAVID II. After David's return from France (1341), he never held power.

Balkan Peninsula, SE Europe, extending S from Danube and Sava rivers. Bounded by Black Sea (E); Bosporus, Sea of Marmara, Dardanelles, Aegean Sea (S); Ionian and Adriatic seas (W). Comprises ALBANIA, BULGARIA, continental GREECE, SE RUMANIA, European TURKEY, most of YUGOSLAVIA. Very mountainous, it contains the DINARIC ALPS, the RHODOPE mts., and the **Balkans,** a range of N Bulgaria, culminating at 7,785 ft. in Yumrukchal and crossed by Shipka Pass.

Balkan Wars, 1912–13, two short wars for possession of European Turkey. In the first war Serbia, Bulgaria, Greece, and Montenegro expelled the Turks from all their European holdings except Constantinople (1912). The territorial settlement made by the Great Powers in 1913 disappointed Serbia, which was cut off from the Adriatic by the creation of independent Albania. Serbia now demanded Bulgaria cede the larger part of Macedonia, thus precipitating the Second Balkan War. Rumania, Greece, and Turkey joined Serbia against Bulgaria, which was

defeated and lost territory to all its enemies in the Treaty of Bucharest (1913). Balkan Wars heightened nationalism and prepared way for World War I.

Balkh (bälkh), town (pop. 10,000), N Afghanistan. Was cap. of ancient BACTRIA. Taken 653 by Arabs, sacked 1221 by Jenghiz Khan.

Balkhash (bŭl-khäsh'), city (pop. c.70,000), SE Kazakh SSR, on N shore of Lake Balkhash; founded 1929. Railroad terminus; port; copper smelting. The saline **Lake Balkhash** (6,680 sq. mi.) stretches for 375 mi. between Kazakh Hills (N) and desert (S). Fed by Ili R., has no outlet.

Balkis, name given in Koran to the queen of Sheba.

Ball, John, d. 1381, English priest; an instigator of the Peasants' Revolt under Wat TYLER.

ballad (bă'lŭd), narrative poem of unknown authorship, intended to be sung, preserved by oral tradition among people culturally homogeneous. Objective, impersonal, abounding in set phrases. Francis Child made definitive collection, *English and Scottish Popular Ballads* (5 vols., 1883–98). Word *ballad* popularly used for any narrative poem. In music *ballad* refers to simple, often sentimental type of song (not folk song).

Ballarat (băl'ŭrăt'), city (pop. 38,140; metropolitan pop. 40,181), Victoria, Australia; founded 1851. Once a noted mining center. Woolen mills.

ball bearings: see BEARINGS.

ballet (bă'lā, bălā'), solo or ensemble dancing of drama set to music. First appeared as part of opera. Ballet, though known in 15th-cent. Italy, was first seen as a coordinated whole in the Ballet comique de la Reine (Paris, 1581). The five absolute ballet positions were set down by Rameau (1725). Ballet flourished in early 19th-cent. Italy and reached a zenith in mid-19th-cent. Russia. Such Russians as FOKINE and DIAGHILEV (aided by such dancers as Nijinsky and Pavlova) extended Russian influence to Europe in early 20th cent. The dawning of a non-Russian ballet followed, aided by such groups as Jooss Ballet (Germany), Sadler's Wells (England), Ballet Theatre (U.S.), and such artists as Anthony Tudor (England) and Agnes de Mille (U.S.).

Ballinger, Richard Achilles (băl'ĭnjŭr), 1858–1922, U.S. Secretary of the Interior (1909–11). Center of controversy over handling of natural resources.

Ballinger, city (pop. 5,302), W central Texas, on Colorado R. at mouth of Elm Creek and SSW of Abilene. Processing center in livestock and agr. area. Reservoir on Elm Creek is unit of Colorado River project.

Balliol College: see OXFORD UNIVERSITY.

ballistics (bŭlĭ'stĭks), science of projectile propulsion and motion. Includes interior ballistics (processes and motion of projectile within gun) and exterior ballistics (projectile's motion outside gun, or its trajectory).

balloon, aircraft lacking propulsive system, obtaining lift from lighter-than-air gas in containers. J. M. and J. É. Montgolfier of France credited with invention (1783). Pilâtre de Rozier, using hot-air-filled balloon attached to ground, first man to make balloon ascent (1783). Also in 1783 Robert brothers and J. A. C. Charles ascended and traveled 27 mi. in hydrogen-filled balloon. Balloons carried messages in siege of Paris (1870). Observation balloons used in World War I; in World War II balloons held by cables used in air defense. In sport, James Gordon Bennett Cup prize for international race. Altitude record 72,395 ft. by A. W. Stevens and O. A. Anderson in 1935.

balm: see LEMON BALM; for bee balm, see OSWEGO TEA.

balm of Gilead, name for several unrelated plants: historic Old World *Commiphora meccanensis,* a small evergreen tree (referred to in Jer. 8.22), and the source of commercial balm of Gilead; American balm of Gilead, a poplar (*Populus candicans*); and Canary balm, *Cedronella canariensis,* a small shrub.

Balmoral Castle (bălmŏr′ŭl), royal residence in Braemar, Aberdeenshire, Scotland. Built by Queen Victoria 1854.

balsa, deciduous tree (*Ochroma*), native to tropical America. Its very light wood (also called corkwood) is used in airplane construction, in life preservers and floats, and for insulating purposes.

balsam, resin of various trees, including commercial and tolu balsam of South America, Mecca balsam or BALM OF GILEAD, copaiba, and CANADA BALSAM. For the herbaceous balsam plant, see IMPATIENS.

balsam fir or **balsam,** a fir (*Abies balsamea*) of Canada and NE U.S. Valuable for CANADA BALSAM contained in its bark. Much used as a Christmas tree.

Balthazar: see WISE MEN OF THE EAST.

Baltic provinces and **Baltic states,** countries bordering on extreme E coast of Baltic Sea. See COURLAND; LIVONIA; ESTONIA; LATVIA; LITHUANIA.

Baltic Sea, arm of Atlantic Ocean, indenting N Europe, surrounded by Sweden, Finland, USSR (incl. Baltic states), Poland, Germany, and Denmark. Area c.160,000 sq. mi. (incl. gulfs of Bothnia, Finland, and Riga). Many islands (see DENMARK). Connected with North Sea by ORESUND and Great and Little BELT by way of Kattegat and Skagerrak); KIEL CANAL is a more direct connection. Other canal systems link it with White Sea and Volga R. Generally shallow; important fisheries. Chief ports: Copenhagen, Stettin, Gdynia, Danzig, Leningrad, Helsinki, Stockholm.

Baltimore, Charles Calvert, 3d **Baron:** see CALVERT, GEORGE.

Baltimore, George Calvert, 1st **Baron:** see CALVERT, GEORGE.

Baltimore (bôl′tĭmôr), city (pop. 949,708), N Md., on Patapsco R. near Chesapeake Bay. State's largest city and sixth largest in U.S., it is cultural, commercial, and industrial center and main port for importing iron and other ores. Among diverse industries are shipbuilding, meat packing, food processing, sugar, petroleum, and copper refining, printing and publishing, and mfg. of tin cans, machinery, autos, and tractors. Area settled in early 17th cent.; royal governor authorized building of Baltimore 1729. Fine harbor encouraged shipping; extensive rail lines, beginning with Baltimore & Ohio RR (1830), later

fed town. Shipbuilding thrived and brought fame with clipper ships of early 1800s. Continental Congress met here in 1776–77. In 1814 F. S. Key wrote STAR-SPANGLED BANNER during defense of Fort McHENRY here. Although a Union supply base during the Civil War, city held divided loyalties. Was shipbuilding and supply point in both world wars. Seat of JOHNS HOPKINS UNIVERSITY, Loyola Col., Morgan State Col., and Col. of Notre Dame of Maryland. Points of interest include Washington Monument, first Roman Catholic cathedral in U.S. (built 1806–21), Walters Art Gall., Enoch Pratt Free Library, Maryland Inst. of Art, Peabody Inst., Westminster Churchyard (with grave of E. A. Poe), Baltimore Mus. of Art, and Pimlico race track.

Baltimore & Ohio Railroad, first railroad in U.S. open for public traffic (1830). Rapid decline of Baltimore after trans-Allegheny traffic had gravitated toward Erie Canal in N.Y. led to its construction. Successful trial in 1830 of the *Tom Thumb,* built by Peter Cooper, brought introduction of steam locomotives. Railroad was important life line in Civil War. Centrally located route maintains prominence of railroad.

Baltimore oriole: see ORIOLE.

Baluchi (bŭlōō′chē), Eastern Iranian language of Indo-Iranian subfamily of Indo-European languages. See LANGUAGE (table).

Baluchistan (bŭlōō′chĭstăn), arid region in SE Iran and W Pakistan. Iranian section was formerly a separate province; since 1938 a part of Kerman Prov. Pakistani region (134,139 sq. mi.; pop. 1,178,000) was added 1946–47 to Pakistan. Comprises Baluchistan proper and several princely states.

baluchitherium (bŭlōō′chĭthēr′ēŭm), extinct primitive, rhinoceros of Miocene period. Fossilized bones found in central Asia. Believed largest of land mammals; estimated height 18 ft., weight 10 tons.

Balue, Jean (zhä′bälü′), c.1421–1491, French cardinal and statesman, adviser to Louis XI. Conspired with Charles the Bold of Burgundy against Louis, who had him imprisoned in an iron cage (1469–80). Freed by papal intervention.

Balzac Honoré de (ônôrä′ dü bälzäk′), 1799–1850, French novelist. His greatest work, "La Comédie humaine," is a vast edifice of partly interconnected novels and short novels, recreating French society of his time and picturing in precise detail individuals of every class and profession. Among best-known novels are *Eugénie Grandet* (1833), *Le Père Goriot* (1835), *La Cousine Bette* (1847), *Le Cousin Pons* (1847). Balzac wrote some masterly short stories but failed in his attempts at drama.

Balzac, Jean Louis Guez de (zhä′ lwē′ gā′), 1597?–1654, French writer, influential in reforming French prose style.

Bamberg (bäm′bĕrk), city (pop. 75,830), Upper Franconia, NE Bavaria, on Regnitz R. Cotton mfg. Now an archiepiscopal see, it was the cap. of a powerful prince-bishopric until 1802. Splendid 13th-cent. cathedral contains tombs of Emperor Henry VI, his wife St. Kunigunde, and Pope Clement II. Episcopal palaces date from 16th and 18th cent.

bamboo, a woody perennial grass of warm and tropical regions. It has rounded, hollow, jointed stalks, is usually treelike but occasionally low or climbing. Wood used for construction, furniture, utensils, and paper. Chief commercial species is *Bambusa arundinacea.* A few species are native to the S U.S., e.g., cane or cane reed, *Arundinaria gigantea.*

banana, tropical palmlike plant (*Musa*) and its long, fleshy fruit, usually yellow or red skinned. An important commercial crop. Fruit is edible raw or cooked and is rich in carbohydrates. Other banana species are plantain, the fruit of which is cooked as a vegetable in the tropics, and MANILA HEMP.

Banat (bä'nät'), term originally used for several military frontier provs. of Hungary and Croatia; governors had title *ban.* The former **Banat of Temesvar** (tĕ'mĕshvär), a fertile plain between Danube, Theiss, and Mures rivers, was an integral part of Hungary; chief city Temesvar (see TIMISOARA). Partitioned 1920 between Yugoslavia and Rumania.

Banbury, municipal borough (pop. 18,917), Oxfordshire, England. Still produces famous cakes. Banbury Cross of the nursery rhyme destroyed in 1602; new one built in 19th cent.

Bancroft, Edward, 1744–1821, American Revolutionary spy. Operated as secret agent to American commissioners in France, but also reported their movements to British.

Bancroft, George, 1800–1891, American historian and statesman, author of monumental *History of the United States* (10 vols. 1834–74). As Secretary of the Navy, he estab. U.S. Naval Academy at Annapolis. Minister to Britain 1846–49. An antislavery Democrat, he supported Lincoln in Civil War. Minister to Prussia 1867–74. Revised and extended editions of the *History* (6 vols.; 1876, 1883–85) won high praise.

Bancroft, Hubert Howe, 1832–1918, American publisher and historian. Collected materials on all W America, culminating in Bancroft Library of Univ. of California. Collection has some 60,000 volumes of books, manuscripts, transcripts, and personal narratives. He edited and published a history (39 vols., 1874–90), and reissued (1882–90) as *The Works of Hubert Howe Bancroft.*

band, in music, a group of musicians playing chiefly upon wind instruments. Present-day band originated from military ensembles used for marches. First significant band in America was the U.S. Marine Band, founded 1798. In 1854 the concert band developed. The bands and band music of Sousa and Franko Goldman have been most important in the U.S. Modern bands usually include the chief brass, wood-wind, and percussion instruments, while concert bands and jazz bands may employ strings and harp.

Banda Oriental (bän'dä ōryäntäl') [Span.,= eastern shore, i.e., of the Río de la Plata], region, S Uruguay. Term applied to Uruguay in Spanish colonial period. Most of Uruguayan population concentrated here.

Bandar, India: see MASULIPATAM.

Banda Sea (bän'dä), part of Pacific Ocean, bounded by S Moluccan isls. of Indonesia.

Bandelier, Adolph Francis Alphonse, 1840–

1914, American archaeologist, b. Switzerland. Carried on field researches in N.Mex. (1880–89) and explored Peru and Bolivia (1892–1902).

Bandelier National Monument: see NATIONAL PARKS AND MONUMENTS (table).

Bandello, Matteo (mät-tā'ō bändĕl'lō), c.1480–1562, Italian novelist, a priest, author of *novelle.*

Bandera (bändâ'rü), village (pop. 1,036), SW Texas, on Medina R. and SW of San Antonio; founded 1854 by Mormons (later Polish settlement). Tourist trade.

Bandung (bän'dōōng), town (pop. 166,815), W Java, Indonesia. Produces textiles and quinine.

baneberry, perennial plant (*Actaea*), with compound leaves, clusters of small white flowers, and poisonous but handsome white, red, or black berrylike fruits. Also called cohosh.

Banér, Johan (yōō'hän bänâr'), 1596–1641, Swedish general in Thirty Years War. Succeeded Gustavus Adolphus in command of Swedish forces in Germany (1632). Routed at Nördlingen 1634. Restored Swedish prestige by victory at Wittstock (1636) and reconquest of Pomerania and Mecklenburg (1638).

Banff (bämf), famous summer and winter resort town (1946 pop. 2,081), SW Alta., Canada, on Bow R. in the Rocky Mts. Here is Canadian Pacific RR station for Banff Natl. Park (2,564 sq. mi.; estab. 1887). Has annual winter carnival. Park has hot sulphur springs.

Banffshire or **Banff,** county (630 sq. mi.; pop. 50,135), NE Scotland; co. town Banff. Largely agr., it has fishing villages along the rolling fertile coast. Fine whisky distilled. Scene of many battles between Scots and Norse invaders, it was later torn by religious strife after the Reformation.

Bangalore (bän-gûlôr'), city (pop. 407,760), SE Mysore, India; cap. and commercial center of Mysore. Has remains of Tippoo Sahib's palace. Rail hub and textile center. Seat of Mysore Univ.

Bangka (bäng'kä), island (4,611 sq. mi.; pop. 205,363), Indonesia, in Java Sea SE of Sumatra. Major tin producer since c.1710.

Bangkok (bäng'kŏk"), city (pop. 688,832), cap. of Thailand, on Menam R., near Gulf of Siam. Industrial center, chief port of Thailand. Exports rice, tin, teak, and rubber. Rice mills, oil refineries, sawmills. In 1782 succeeded Ayuthia as Thai cap.

Bangor (bäng'gûr), municipal borough (pop. 20,615), Co. Down, N. Ireland. Scene of annual yachting regatta. Has remains of an abbey founded c.555.

Bangor (bäng'gôr). **1** City (pop. 31,558), S Maine, at head of navigation on Penobscot R. opposite Brewer; settled 1769. Commercial center and gateway to resort area. Once-dominant lumbering and paper milling industries are now supplemented by mfg. of shoes, dental supplies, and machinery. **2** Borough (pop. 6,050), E Pa., N of Easton. Has slate quarrying and mfg. of textiles.

Bangor (bäng'gôr), municipal borough (pop. 12,822), Caernarvonshire, Wales. Seat of Univ. Col. of North Wales. Cathedral dates from 15th–16th cent.

Bangorian Controversy, in Church of England. Bishop Benjamin Hoadly, of Bangor, Wales, denied (1717) that Christ delegated authority to church. Opposed by William Law and some 50 writers in 200 pamphlets.

Bang's disease: see BRUCELLOSIS.

Bangweulu (bängwāōō′lōō), lake, 60 mi. long 25 mi. wide, in Northern Rhodesia. Discovered 1868 by David Livingstone.

Banja Luka (bän′jä lōō′kä), city (pop. 33,191), Bosnia, N Yugoslavia; seat of pashas 1580–1640. Orthodox cathedral, 16th-cent. mosque, ruins of Roman baths.

banjo: see STRINGED INSTRUMENTS.

Bankhead, Tallulah (Brockman), 1903–, American actress. Since her debut in 1918, her flamboyant personality has won her fame in England and U.S. in plays (e.g., *The Little Foxes*), films (e.g., *Lifeboat*), and on radio and television.

banking, financial transactions through institutions primarily devoted to accepting deposits and making loans. Practiced in ancient Egypt and Greece and developed by the Romans, banking during the Middle Ages came to be largely dominated by Jews because of Christian prejudice against interest. Modern banking developed in 18th and 19th cent. In U.S. first bank was founded at Philadelphia 1781. The BANK OF THE UNITED STATES was the subject of political controversy. An act in 1863 set up the national banks, but banks of deposit continued under state charters and grew in number. In 1913 the FEDERAL RESERVE SYSTEM was set up.

Bank of England, popularly known as the Old Lady of Threadneedle Street, founded (1694) by William Paterson as commercial bank. Bank Charter Act of 1842 set up present system. Issue department issues bank notes; banking department handles other functions (e.g., national debt). Nationalized 1945.

Bank of the United States. Against opposition of the Jeffersonian party the Federalists under Alexander HAMILTON estab. a central bank, the Bank of the United States (1791–1811). Its conservative policies were unpopular, and it was not rechartered, but after financial difficulties in the War of 1812, the second Bank of the United States was given (1816) a 20-year charter. Under Nicholas BIDDLE it prospered, but was viewed as a tool of Eastern moneyed interests by the followers of Andrew JACKSON. It was a chief issue of the 1832 election and Jackson, successful, took government deposits from it in 1833.

bankruptcy, settlement of liabilities of a debtor wholly or partially unable to meet his obligations. Bankruptcy laws intended to distribute the bankrupt's assets equitably among his creditors and to discharge him from liability. Present U.S. bankruptcy act that of 1898, with amendments.

Banks, Sir Joseph, 1743–1820, British naturalist. Collected (on round-the-world voyage with Capt. Cook and other travels) many previously unknown plants. Long influential in activities of Kew Gardens and Royal Society.

Banks, Nathaniel Prentiss, 1816–94, American politician and Union general in Civil War. U.S. Congressman before and after war. Governor of Mass. 1858–60. Helped Grant open the Mississippi by capture of PORT HUDSON, July, 1863.

Banksia [for Sir Joseph Banks], genus of Australian trees and shrubs with yellow, honey-bearing blooms.

Bankside, locality by the Thames, in Southwark metropolitan borough, London, England. Amusement center 16th–17th cent.; Globe Theatre and other places associated with Shakspere were here. Palace of bishop of Winchester and the CLINK were also here.

Bannack, ghost town, SW Mont., SW of Butte; founded 1862 with discovery of gold. First town in Mont., it was territorial cap. 1864–65. Declined when richer Virginia City fields attracted miners.

Banning, city (pop. 7,034), S Calif., E of Riverside; laid out 1883. Health resort.

Bannockburn, field on Bannock R., Stirlingshire, Scotland. Site of Battle of Bannockburn June 23–24, 1314, in which Robert the Bruce defeated the English under Edward II and estab. himself on the Scottish throne.

Bantam fowl: see POULTRY.

Banting, Sir Frederick Grant, 1891–1941, Canadian physician, noted for research. Shared 1923 Nobel Prize in Physiology and Medicine for isolating INSULIN.

Bantry Bay, inlet of the Atlantic, 21 mi. long and 4 mi. wide, in Co. Cork, Ireland; one of Europe's best natural anchorages.

Bantu (bän′tōō″), ethnic and (principally) linguistic group of Africa, numbering c.40,000,000. They are a Negro people inhabiting all the continent S of the Congo except extreme SW. There are several hundred Bantu languages and dialects, including Kafir, Zulu, and Swahili. Highly developed Bantu states included Buganda. In 19th cent. several additional confederations developed, e.g., Zulu and Basuto. Matabele is also a well-known Bantu tribe.

Banville, Théodore de (tāōdôr′ dù bävēl′), 1823–91, French poet; one of PARNASSIANS. His volumes of verse include *Odes funambulesques* (1857) and *Occidentales* (1869).

banyan (băn′yùn), tree (*Ficus benghalensis*) of fig genus, native to India. Its branches put forth numerous aerial roots, which on reaching the ground, enlarge to form many trunks.

baobab (bā′ō–), gigantic tree (*Adansonia digitata*) of Senegal. Its fruit is edible and the bark yields rope and cloth.

baptism: see SACRAMENT.

Baptists, denomination of Christians who hold that baptism is only for believers and only by immersion. Separatists under John Smyth formed (c.1608) in Amsterdam first English Baptist congregation. First group in London estab. 1611. First American church founded (1639) by Roger Williams in Providence, R.I. Baptist churches are congregational, with nongoverning general associations—American Baptist Convention, Southern Baptist Convention, Natl. Baptist Convention, U.S.A., and many other associations and independent bodies.

bar, the, court or system of courts. Persons authorized to conduct court trials also known collectively as the bar; hence lawyers collectively. The distinction between the pleader before the court (barrister, advocate, counselor at law) and the agent merely advising the client (solicitor, attorney) has disappeared in U.S., while it is retained in England.

Barabbas (bŭrăb'ŭs), notorious bandit whom mob demanded be released from punishment, demanding instead the death of Jesus. Mat. 27.15–18; Mark 15.6–14; Luke 23.13–25; John 18.39,40.

Baraboo (băr'ŭbōō), city (pop. 7,264), central Wis., on Baraboo R. and NW of Madison. Farm trade center. Ringling Brothers' circus began here. Dells of the Wisconsin near by.

Barak (bā'răk) [Heb.,= lightning], leader who joined Deborah in fighting Jabin and Sisera. Judges 4–5.

Baranof Island (bă'rŭnôf), off SE Alaska, in ALEXANDER ARCHIPELAGO; over 100 mi. long, 1,607 sq. mi. in area. Was named for Aleksandr Baranov. On it is SITKA, center of fur trade and administration during Russian ownership.

Baranov, Aleksandr Andreyevich (bŭrä'nôf), 1746–1819, Russian trader, chief figure during Russian control in Alaska. Virtual governor of Russian activities in North America (1799–1817).

Barany, Robert (rō'bert bä'ränē), 1876–1936, Austrian physician. Won 1914 Nobel Prize in Physiology and Medicine for work on vestibular apparatus of ear.

Barataria Bay (bărŭtăr'ēŭ), SE La., S of New Orleans, cut off from Gulf of Mexico by islands. Was base of pirates under Jean LAFITTE.

Barbados (bärbā'dōz), island (166 sq. mi.; pop. 192,841) British West Indies, and colony; cap. Bridgetown. Winter resort. Claimed by British from 1605. Produces sugar, rum, cotton.

Barbara, Saint, 3d or 4th cent., virgin martyr, supposed to have been killed by her father for being a Christian. Feast: Dec. 4.

Barbarossa (bärbŭrŏs'ŭ), surname of Algerian corsair Khair ad-Din (c.1483–1546). His brother, Koruk, or Aruj (c.1474–1518), seized Algiers from the Spanish (1518), and Barbarossa put Algeria under Turkish suzerainty. As admiral of the Turkish fleet, he twice defeated Andrea Doria and ravaged the coast of S Europe (1533–44).

Barbarossa, Frederick: see FREDERICK I, emperor.

Barbary Coast, former (till 1917) waterfront area of San Francisco, Calif. After 1849 gold rush its open gambling, prostitution, and gangsterism had world notoriety.

Barbary States, term used for the N African states of TRIPOLITANIA, TUNISIA, and ALGERIA (and usually also MOROCCO), which were semi-independent under Turkish rule from 16th cent. onward. Rulers derived revenue from large-scale piracy on Mediterranean shipping. European powers launched punitive expeditions against them but generally relied on payment of tribute as a means of protection. The U.S. joined in this system. The insult offered by the dey of Algiers to William BAINBRIDGE, taking U.S. tribute to Algiers, led to the TRIPOLITAN WAR. French capture of Algiers (1830) marked the end of piracy in the region.

Barbauld, Anna Laetitia (Aikin) (bär'bôld), 1743–1825, English author of didactic works for children, *Hymns in Prose* and *Early Lessons* (both 1781).

barbecue (bär'bŭkū), in U.S., open-air political or social gathering, where carcass or large joints of meat are roasted whole. Barbecued meat may also be smaller cuts, basted with spicy sauce.

Barber, Samuel, 1910–, American composer. Despite experimentation with modern techniques, his music is conservative. Among his works are a setting for Matthew Arnold's "Dover Beach"; two *Essays for Orchestra*; *Adagio for Strings*; a ballet, *Medea*; two symphonies.

Barberini vase: see PORTLAND VASE.

barberry, spiny shrub (*Berberis*), used for hedges. Some have bright autumn foliage; others, less hardy, are evergreen. Berries are red or black. Common barberry (*Berberis vulgaris*) is a wheat rust host.

Barberton, city (pop. 27,820), NE Ohio, SW of Akron; laid out 1891. Mfg. of metal and rubber products and chemicals.

Barbey d'Aurevilly, Jules (zhül' bärbā' dōrvēyē'), 1809–89, French author. His novels and short novels (notably *Les Diaboliques*, 1874), laid in his native Normandy, are remarkable for vigorous style, psychological realism, and morbid imagination. He also was an intransigeant critic and polemicist.

Barbizon school, informal school of French landscape painting which flourished c.1830–1870. Barbizon village, near the forest of Fontainebleau, was a favorite resort of a group of painters who, by painting from nature in rebellion against the prevalent classical tradition, helped pave the way for the later realists and impressionists. The group (called the "Men of Thirty") included Theodore Rousseau, Corot, and Millet.

Barbon, Praise-God: see BAREBONE, PRAISE-GOD.

Barbosa, Ruy or **Rui** (both: rōō'ē bŭrbô'sŭ), 1849–1923, Brazilian philosopher of law, noted jurist, member of World Court.

Barbour, John, c.1320–1395, Scottish poet and churchman. *The Bruce* (1375) chronicles deeds of ROBERT I.

barbourville, city (pop. 2,926), S Ky., in Cumberland R. valley NW of Middlesboro. Seat of Union Col. (Methodist; coed.; 1880). Near state park with cabin of first white people in Ky. (replica).

Barbusse, Henri (ārē' bärbüs'), 1873–1935, French author. Best known for *Under Fire* (1916; Eng. tr., 1917), a realistic story of World War I.

Barca, surname of Carthaginian family, which included HANNIBAL.

Barcelona (bärthälō'nä), city (pop. 1,076,601), cap. of Barcelona prov. and of Catalonia, NE Spain, on Mediterranean. Second-largest city, largest port, chief commercial and industrial center of Spain. Machinery mfg. Flourished under Romans and Visigoths, fell to Moors (8th cent.) and to Charlemagne (801). Counts of Barcelona acquired all CATALONIA and parts of S France. Marriage of Count Raymond Berengar IV with heiress of Aragon united Catalonia and Aragon (1137). Barcelona became royal residence, powerful trade and banking center. Univ. founded 1450. City declined after unification of Spain, was center of Catalan separatism and various radical movements. A modern city, Barcelona also has medieval landmarks: Gothic cathedral, city hall, exchange, Church of Santa María del Mar.

Barclay de Tolly, Mikhail, Prince (mēkhŭyēl', bŭrklī' dù tô'lyē), 1761–1818, Russian field marshal, of Scottish descent. Commanded Russian forces against Napoleon (1812), adopted strategy of retreat into heart of Russia. Replaced by Kutuzov after defeat at Smolensk (August) but resumed command 1813.

Bar Cochba, Simon: see BAR KOKBA, SIMON.

Bard, Samuel, 1742–1821, American physician, active in developing institution which became medical school of Columbia Univ. Writings include midwifery text, works on pathology and medical education.

bard, in Wales, a minstrel and poet who served as a national chronicler and enjoyed many noble privileges, regardless of birth. The order (estab. 940) became hereditary. After their power was broken by Edward I, they became professional poets and singers. The poets in Ireland are similar.

Bard College: see ANNANDALE-ON-HUDSON, N.Y.

Bardstown, city (pop. 4,154), central Ky., SSE of Louisville in farm area; settled 1778. Center of early missionary work in Mississippi valley and of institutions founded by Bishop J. B. M. David. Taken in Civil War (Sept., 1862) by Bragg's Confederates. Has several old structures (Foster may have written *My Old Kentucky Home* in one house).

Barebone or **Barbon, Praise-God** (both: bär'-bŏn), 1596?–1679, English lay preacher, member of Cromwell's nominated parliament (1653). This called Barebone's Parliament, though his part was insignificant.

Bareilly (bŭrā'lē), city (pop. 192,688), N central Uttar Pradesh, India; founded 1537; a commercial center.

Barents Island: see SPITSBERGEN.

Barents Sea, arm of Arctic Ocean, N of Norway and European RSFSR. Shallow, it is warmed by remnants of North Atlantic Drift.

Barentz or **Barents, Willem,** d. 1597, Dutch navigator. Noted for extent of exploration and accuracy of charts in search for Northwest Passage.

Barge Canal: see NEW YORK STATE BARGE CANAL.

Bargello (bärjĕl'lō), 13th-cent. palace in Florence, Italy, which houses the national museum. Once used by the chief of police (*bargello*). Its treasures include Giotto's frescoes and Michelangelo's *David*.

Barham, Richard Harris (bär'm), pseud. **Thomas Ingoldsby** (ĭn'glŭlzbē), 1788–1845, English humorist, a clergyman, author of *The Ingoldsby Legends* (prose tales, verse, modern satire).

Bar Harbor, town (pop. 3,864), on Mt. Desert Isl., S Maine, SE of Bangor. A famous summer resort of New England coast, it developed in mid-1800s.

Bar-Hebraeus, Gregorius (bär-hēbrē'ùs), 1226–86, Syrian scholar, catholicos of Jacobite church. Noted for Syriac chronicle of the

world since Adam and for commentaries on Aristotle.

Bari or **Bari delle Puglie** (bä'rē dĕl'lĕ pōō'lyĕ), city (pop. 162,238), cap. of Apulia, S Italy; Adriatic seaport. Center of fertile agr. area. Founded by Romans; conquered from Byzantines by Normans 1071; port of embarkation during Crusades. Has Romanesque Basilica of St. NICHOLAS of Bari (shrine of pilgrimage), cathedral, medieval castle. University founded 1924. Port bombarded in World War II.

Baring-Gould, S(abine) (bā'rĭng-gōōld'), 1834–1924, English novelist, folklorist, hymn writer, a clergyman, best known for words of hymn *Onward, Christian Soldiers* (1865).

barite (bâ'rīt), **barytes** (bŭrī'tēz), or **heavy spar,** natural mineral, barium sulphate. Almost insoluble. Used to test for SULPHATE, as source of barium, and to make paint and lithopone (white pigment).

Barito (bärē'tō), river, c.550 mi. long, in S Borneo; flows to Java Sea.

barium (bâ'–), silvery-white active, poisonous metallic element (symbol = Ba; see also ELEMENT, table). Divalent, alkaline earth; resembles calcium. Oxidizes in air; ionizes in solution; with water, forms hydroxide, liberates hydrogen. Forms many compounds used in ceramic industry, medicine, etc. Barium carbonate and sulphate found in nature; metal obtained by hydrolysis of chloride. Gives green FLAME test in Bunsen burner.

barium sulphate: see BARITE.

Bar-jesus or **Elymas** (ĕl'ĭmăs), sorcerer who tried to mislead a prospective Christian. Acts 13.4–12.

Bar-jona (-jō'–) [Aramaic,= son of Jonah], patronymic of St. Peter. Mat. 16.17.

bark, covering of stems and roots, best developed in woody plants. Outer portion is cork layer and inner (see BAST) is separated from wood by cambium. Bark yields TANNIN, latex (a source of rubber), dyes, and cork (see CORK OAK).

bark (bärk), three-masted sailing vessel with fore- and mainmasts square-rigged and mizzenmast fore-and-aft-rigged. Modern bark may be as large as 6,000 tons. A four-master bark has its aftermast fore-and-aft-rigged. A barkentine has three masts, with foremast square-rigged, others fore-and-aft-rigged.

bark cloth, primitive fabric made by many peoples from soft inner bark of certain tropical and subtropical trees. It is often elaborately decorated. Tapa cloth is a fine kind made in Pacific isls.

Barker, Harley Granville-: see GRANVILLE-BARKER.

Barkla, Charles Glover (bär'klù), 1877–1944, English physicist. Won 1917 Nobel Prize for discovery of characteristic X rays of elements.

Barkley, Alben W(illiam), 1877–, Vice President of the United States (1949–53). Earlier was Democratic Representative (1913–27) and Senator (1927–49) from Ky.

Bar Kokba, Simon, or **Simon Bar Cochba** (kŏk'bù) [Heb.,= son of the stars], d. 135, Hebrew leader of revolt against Rome (131–135), a self-proclaimed Messiah. The revolt failed disastrously.

Barlaam and Josaphat (bär'läŭm, jō'sú̇făt), popular romance found in many languages. A Christianized version of the Buddha legend (c.980) by Euthymius, a Georgian monk, and later elaborated, it tells of the conversion to Christianity of a young Indian prince, Barlaam, by the hermit Josaphat.

Barlach, Ernst (ĕrnst' bär'läkh), 1870–1938, German sculptor. Illustrated his own poems and plays.

Bar-le-Duc (bär-lù-dük'), town (pop. 14,015), cap. of Meuse dept., NE France; historic cap. of county (later duchy) of Bar (united with Lorraine in 15th cent.). Exports famed preserves, jellies.

barley, cereal grass (*Hordeum vulgare*), probably one of earliest cereals cultivated by man. Matures quickly, hence has a wide range, including high altitudes. Used for stock feed, malting, flour; until 16th cent., was chief breadstuff of Europe.

Barlow, Joel, 1754–1812, American poet and diplomat, one of the Connecticut Wits. His best-known poetic works are the epic *The Vision of Columbus* (1787; rev. ed., *The Columbiad,* 1807) and the mock eulogy *The Hasty-Pudding* (written 1793). Wrote *Advice to the Privileged Orders* (1792), a prose tract for democracy, and also an able critique of the French constitution of 1791. Sent to Europe as agent for an ill-fated Ohio land company, he remained abroad 17 years and was for a time U.S. consul in Algiers. Died of exposure on a diplomatic mission to Napoleon at time of retreat from Moscow.

Barmecides: see HARUN-AL-RASHID.

Barmen, Germany: see WUPPERTAL.

Barnabas, Saint (bär'nú̇bù̇s), apostle, missionary, companion of Paul and Mark. Acts 4.36,37; 9.27; 11.22–15.41; 1 Cor. 9.6; Gal. 2.1,9,13; Col. 4.10. Among Christian PSEUDEPIGRAPHA is an epistle attributed to him. Named in Canon of Mass. Feast: June 11.

barnacle, marine crustacean usually attached to rocks, stones, seaweed, wharf piles, ships, and marine animals. Shell-like plates cover adult's body. Usually has six pairs of plumelike legs, which are plied to draw food to mouth.

Barnard, Edward Emerson (bär'nù̇rd), 1857–1923, American astronomer, pioneer in astronomical photography. Discoverer of Jupiter's fifth satellite and 16 comets.

Barnard, Frederick Augustus Porter, 1809–89, American educator, a mathematician. Professor, Univ. of Alabama (1837–54); professor, Univ. of Mississippi (1854–61), president (1856–58), chancellor (1858–61). As president of Columbia Col. (1864–89) he expanded the curriculum, supported sciences, extended elective system, fostered School of Mines. Advocated equal educational privileges for men and women; Barnard Col. named for him.

Barnard, George Grey, 1863–1938, American sculptor. His realistic statue of Lincoln caused heated controversy in 1917. His collection of Gothic art is in the CLOISTERS in New York city.

Barnard, Henry, 1811–1900, American educator, a leader in reform of common schools in Conn. and R.I. Chancellor of the Univ. of Wisconsin (1858–60), president of St.

John's Col., Annapolis (1866–67), and first U.S. commissioner of education (1867–70).

Barnard College: see COLUMBIA UNIVERSITY.

Barnato, Barnett (bärnä'tō), 1852–97, South African financier, b. London; originally named Barney Isaacs. Made a fortune by buying up and exploiting worked-out Kimberley diamond mines. Later combined his interests with those of Cecil Rhodes.

Barnave, Joseph (zhō̆zĕf' bärnäv'), 1761–93, French revolutionist. An extremist, he was sent in 1791 to bring fugitive royal family back from Varennes and turned monarchist. He supported Mirabeau, led FEUILLANTS, and was guillotined.

Barnburners, radical element of Democratic party in N.Y. (1843–48), opposed to HUNKERS. Name arose from story of Dutchman who burned his barn to get rid of rats, implying that Barnburners would destroy corporations and public works to do away with their abuses. Group also opposed extension of slavery. United with FREE-SOIL PARTY in 1848.

Barnegat Bay (bär'nú̇găt), Atlantic arm, c.30 mi. long, E N.J., entered via inlet between Long Beach isl. and Island Beach peninsula. Lighthouse built 1858; replaced 1930 by lightship.

Barnes, Juliana: see BERNERS, JULIANA.

Barnes, William, 1801–86, English writer, author of poems in Dorset dialect.

Barneveldt, Jan van Olden: see OLDENBARNEVELDT.

Barnstable (bärn'stù̇bù̇l), resort town (pop. 10,480), SE Mass., on Cape Cod; settled 1639. Includes Hyannis resort (pop. 4,235), with Massachusetts Maritime Acad., and Cotuit village, noted for oysters.

Barnum, Phineas Taylor, 1810–91, American showman. Gained fame (1842) with his American Museum in N.Y., publicized by extravagant advertising and exhibits such as a bearded lady. Major attractions included "Gen. TOM THUMB." Managed U.S. tour of singer Jenny LIND. His circus ("The Greatest Show on Earth"), soon an American institution, opened 1871. Merged (1881) with J. A. Bailey's, circus continued under name Barnum and Bailey.

Baroda (bù̇rō'dù̇), former princely state; since 1949 part of Bombay state, India. Became independent Mahratta kingdom in 18th cent. under the Gaekwars. Its former cap. Baroda (pop. 153,301) has a palace and several colleges; cotton-milling center.

Baroja (y Nessi), Pío (pē'ō bärō'hä ē nĕ'sē), 1879–, Spanish novelist of Basque origin, prominent in the literary group, Generation of 1898. Best known of his trilogies is *La lucha por la vida* [the struggle for existence] (1904). *Memorias de un hombre de acción* [memoirs of a man of action] is cycle of historical novels.

barometer (bù̇rŏm'ù̇tù̇r), instrument for measuring atmospheric pressure. Torricelli mercurial barometer uses 3-ft. mercury-filled glass tube (sealed at one end) supported vertically with open end under surface of mercury in container exposed to atmospheric pressure. Standard pressure at sea level holds mercury in tube to height of 29.92 in., 76 cm., or 1013.2 millibars (space above mercury is vacuum). Height of column varies with changes in air pressure; slight changes occur continually. Air pressure diminishes with altitude, the barometer reading dropping roughly one inch per 1,000 ft. until at c.3.5 mi. above earth's surface air pressure is about one half that at sea level; at c.10 mi. above earth pressure is c.10% that at sea level and it diminishes ultimately to zero. **Aneroid barometer** is metal box partially exhausted of air, its surface reacting to outside air pressure which registers on dial face.

Baronius, Caesar (bûrō'nēús), 1538–1607, Italian cardinal, author of an erudite history of the Roman Catholic Church to 1198. A librarian of the Vatican, he was largely responsible for the Roman Martyrology.

Barons' War, 1263–67, phase of the English struggle between king and barons. Henry III reasserted his power in 1261. Barons led by Simon de MONTFORT resorted to arms. Failed to estab. power of the nobles but helped prepare for constitutional developments of reign of EDWARD I.

baroque (bùrōk'), in architecture and decoration, a grandiose, richly ornamented, often extravagant style which originated in Italy in late 16th cent. as reaction against classicism. Reaching its height throughout Europe a century later, it was dethroned by 18th-cent. classic revival. Epitomized in Rome in Bernini's colonnades in St. Peter's Square and in works by Borromini and Vignola. In France the style culminated under Louis XIV and gave way to ROCOCO under Louis XV. It flourished in Germany and Austria, and reached extremes in Spain in work of Churriguera.

baroque, in music, a style which extends from 1600, the date of production of the first extant opera music, to 1750, the year of Bach's death. It grew from the late 16th-cent. revolt against POLYPHONY. Baroque music is romantic with emotional extremes. Major and minor scales replaced church modes (see MODE). The individual character and capacities of instruments and voices were now considered. Principal forms: vocal—opera, oratorio, and cantata; instrumental—fugue, sonata, concerto, and overture.

Barotseland: see NORTHERN RHODESIA.

Barquisimeto (bärkēsēmä'tō), city (pop. 105,-080) NW Venezuela; founded 1552. A commercial center on Pan American Highway, it ships cattle.

barracuda (bärúkōō'dú), elongated fish of tropical and subtropical seas. It has a long snout, large sharp-edged teeth, projecting lower jaw. Swift and voracious, it kills other fish and is often a hazard to human bathers.

Barranquilla (bärängkē'yä), city (pop. 150,-395), N Colombia, Caribbean port, near mouth of Magdalena; founded 1629. It has small industries.

Barras, Paul, vicomte de (pōl' vēkōt' dù bäräs'), 1755–1829, French revolutionist. At first a Jacobin, he turned against Robespierre on 9 THERMIDOR; led in Thermidorian reaction. Was chief member of DIRECTORY; supported Bonaparte on 18 Brumaire (1799). Notoriously corrupt and immoral.

Barre (bä'rē), city (pop. 10,922), central Vt., surrounded by Barre town and near Mont-

pelier. Granite quarries were developed after War of 1812. Goddard Col. is at near-by Plainfield.

Barre des Écrins (bär' dāzäkrē'), peak, 13,461 ft. high, SE France; highest of Dauphiné Alps.

barren grounds, arctic prairie region of NW Canada, NW of Hudson Bay and E of the Mackenzie basin. Geologically part of the LAURENTIAN PLATEAU, it has large areas of bare rock, few trees, and limited vegetation. The many lakes and streams contain fish, and musk oxen are found in the N. Vast herds of caribou cross the area seasonally. Barren grounds first crossed by Samuel Hearne 1770–71.

Barrès, Maurice (mōrēs' bärĕs'), 1862–1923, French novelist. From his early advocacy of egoism, expressed in the trilogy *Le Culte du moi* (1888–91), he turned to ardent nationalism and royalism. *Les Déracinés* [the uprooted] (1897), his best-known work, is typical of his lucid, powerful style.

Barrett, Elizabeth: see BROWNING, ELIZABETH.

Barrie, Sir J(ames) M(atthew) (bă'rē), 1860–1927, British novelist and playwright. Novels laid in his native Scotland (e.g., *The Little Minister,* 1891; *Sentimental Tommy,* 1896) were followed by whimsical, sentimental plays (e.g., *Quality Street,* 1901; *The Admirable Crichton,* 1902; *Peter Pan,* 1904; *What Every Woman Knows,* 1908; *Dear Brutus,* 1917).

Barrie, town (pop. 12,514), S Ont., Canada, on arm of L. Simcoe. Resort in farming and dairying region. Has meat packing and flour milling.

Barrier Reef, Australia: see GREAT BARRIER REEF.

Barrington, residential and resort town (pop. 8,246), E R.I., SE of Providence; settled c.1670. Mfg. of brick and textiles; shipbuilding; shellfishing.

Barron, James, 1769–1851, U.S. naval officer. Court-martialed as commander of CHESAPEAKE, frigate involved in famous incident in 1807. Mortally wounded Stephen Decatur in duel in 1820.

Barrow, Sir John, 1764–1848, British geographer, promoter of arctic exploration. Founder of Royal Geographical Society (1830).

Barrow, river of Ireland, rising in the Slieve Bloom mts. and flowing 119 mi. to Waterford Harbour.

Barrow, Point, Alaska: see POINT BARROW.

Barrow-in-Furness (-fûr'nús), county borough (pop. 67,473), on SW coast of FURNESS peninsula, Lancashire, England; one of Britain's chief steel producing cities. Also has shipbuilding and armaments mfg. Near-by Walney Isl. connected by bridge.

Barry, Sir Charles, 1795–1860, English architect, best known for Westminster Palace, London.

Barry, John, 1745–1803, U.S. naval officer and hero in American Revolution, b. Ireland.

Barry, Philip, 1896–1949, American dramatist. Studied under George Pierce Baker. His gently satirical comedies of manners were popular, notably *Paris Bound* (1927), *Holiday* (1928), and *The Philadelphia Story* (1939). Also wrote symbolic philosophical dramas such as *White Wings* (1926), *Hotel Universe* (1930), and *Here Come the Clowns* (1938).

Barry, municipal borough (pop. 40,979), Glamorganshire, Wales; a great coal exporting port of Britain.

Barrymore, family of actors. The first, **Maurice Barrymore** (real name Herbert Blythe), 1847–1905, was English. In U.S. (1875), joined Augustin Daly's stock company. Acted in Modjeska's company with his wife, **Georgiana Drew Barrymore,** 1856–93, American actress, one of the great comediennes of her day. Her oldest son, **Lionel Barrymore,** 1878–, appeared in such plays as *Peter Ibbetson;* won acclaim in *Macbeth.* Among first distinguished actors to star in films, he is also famed for radio appearances in Dickens's *Christmas Carol.* His sister, **Ethel Barrymore,** 1879–, actress of great depth, has been on stage since 1894 (e.g., in *The Silver Box, The Corn Is Green*) and also in films. Her brother, **John Barrymore,** 1882–1942, attempted painting, but turned to stage to give distinguished performances, e.g., in *Peter Ibbetson, Richard III,* and as a notable *Hamlet.* Films include *Grand Hotel* and *Dinner at Eight.*

Barsabas: see JOSEPH BARSABAS.

Barsetshire: see TROLLOPE, ANTHONY.

Barstow, city (pop. 6,135), SE Calif., on dry Mojave R. Railroad division point. Outfitting point for Death Valley expeditions.

Bart, Jean (zhä′ bär′), 1650–1702, French naval hero. A privateer from 1672, he was ennobled and created rear admiral (1696) by Louis XIV, as reward for spectacular exploits in War of the Grand Alliance. Noted for his naïve bluntness.

Bartas, Guillaume de Salluste du: see DU BARTAS.

Barth, Karl, 1886–, Swiss Protestant Reformed theologian. Argues for revelation by faith—a return to doctrine of predestination.

Bartholdi, Frédéric Auguste (frädärēk′ ōgüst′ bärtōldē′), 1834–1904, French sculptor. Best-known works are *Lion of Belfort* and Statue of LIBERTY.

Bartholomew, Saint (–thŏl′ûmū), one of the Twelve Apostles. May be same as Nathanael (Nathanael given name, Bartholomew patronymic). Mat. 10.3; Mark 3.18; Luke 6.14; Acts 1.13. Feast: Aug. 24.

Barthou, Louis (lwē′ bärtōō′), 1862–1934, French foreign minister (1934). Assassinated with King ALEXANDER of Yugoslavia.

Bartimaeus (–mē′ûs), blind man cured by Jesus. Mat. 22.29–34, Mark 10.46–52, Luke 18.35–43.

Bartlesville, city (pop. 19,228), NE Okla., on Caney R. and N of Tulsa; founded c.1877 on trading-post site. Distributes food stuffs, oil. Has hq. for oil firms and a U.S. Bureau of Mines experiment station. Oil refining and zinc smelting.

Bartlett, John, 1820–1905, American compiler of *Familiar Quotations,* first published in 1855. Also compiled a Shakspere concordance.

Bartlett, Robert Abram (Captain Bob), 1875–1946, American arctic explorer, b. Newfoundland. Noted especially for exploring

and scientific work in Greenland. Made annual arctic cruises from 1925 to 1941.

Bartok, Bela (bä′lû bär′tôk), 1881–1945, Hungarian composer, pianist, collector of folk music (which greatly influenced his own compositions). He played and lectured in Europe and America. Among his principal works: six string quartets; three orchestral suites; a set of progressive piano studies, *Mikrokosmos;* Music for Two Pianos and Percussion; and concertos and rhapsodies for violin and for piano. His music, harsh and vigorous, sometimes combines four melodies in different keys.

Bartolomeo, Fra (frä′ bärtōlōmä′ō), 1472?–1517, Florentine painter of religious subjects; also called Baccio della Porta. Became a Dominican in 1500. Influenced by Raphael, Bellini, and Giorgione; collaborated on several pictures with Albertinelli.

Barton, Clara, 1821–1912, American humanitarian. Nurse to Civil War soldiers. Organized American Natl. Committee (1877), which later became American Red Cross; served as its president until 1904.

Barton, Elizabeth, 1506?–1534, English prophetess, called the Maid of Kent or the Nun of Kent. After prophecies against Henry VIII's divorce, she was tried, induced to confess, and executed for treason.

Bartow, city (pop. 8,694), central Fla., E of Tampa and W of L. Kissimmee. Processes and ships phosphates, citrus fruit, and truck.

Bartram, John, 1699–1777, pioneer American botanist. In 1728, in Philadelphia, he established the first botanical garden in U.S. His son, **William Bartram,** 1739–1823, was a naturalist. His *Travels* (1791) written after he explored SE U.S. served Wordsworth, Coleridge, and others as a source of descriptions of the American wilderness.

Baruch (bā′rûk) [Heb.,= blessed], Jeremiah's scribe for whom book of Baruch is named.

Baruch, Bernard M(annes) (bûrōōk′), 1870–, U.S. government adviser on economics.

Baruch, in Western canon, book of Old Testament; placed in Apocrypha in AV. Named for Jewish prince Baruch (fl. 600 B.C.), faithful scribe of Jeremiah. Jer. 32.12–16; 36; 43.3,6; 45. Book contains: message from exiled Jews to those at home; well-known Messianic allusion (3.37); words of consolation; letter of Jeremiah (sometimes called Epistle of Jeremy). For Apocrypha of Baruch, see PSEUDEPIGRAPHA.

Barye, Antoine Louis (ätwän′ lwē′ bärē′), 1796–1875, French animal sculptor, popular for his small studies designed for commercial reproduction.

barytes: see BARITE.

Barzun, Jacques (zhäk′ bär′zùn), 1907–, American historian and teacher, b. France. He began (1928) teaching history in Columbia Col., becoming professor of history in 1945. He is also known as a critic of literature and the arts (esp. music).

basalt (bùsôlt′), common fine-grained extrusive lava, dark gray to black. The Deccan trap, Columbia R. plateau, and Iceland flows are of basalt.

base, chemical compound that, by theory of ION, yields hydroxyl (OH) ions in aqueous solution. Described also as HYDROXIDE o metal or of positive RADICAL. OH ion has a negative charge, tastes bitter, feels soapy, turns red litmus blue. In solution bases conduct electricity, react with acids (NEUTRALIZATION); strong bases (alkalis) ionize freely.

baseball, "national game" of U.S. Derived from English cricket and rounders. Commission headed by A. G. Mills reported (1907) that Abner Doubleday created the modern game at Cooperstown, N.Y., in 1839, though the question has been hotly disputed. Professional baseball's two major leagues (eight teams each) are the National (organized 1876) and the American (organized 1901). Since 1903, winners of these leagues have met in the World Series. The sport's greatest stars have been elected to Natl. Baseball Hall of Fame and Mus., built at Cooperstown 1939.

Basedow, Johann Bernhard (yōhän' běrn'härt bä'zŭdō), 1723–90, German educator. Emphasized realistic teaching, including physical education, manual training, nature study.

Basel (bä'zŭl), Fr. *Bâle*, canton, N Switzerland, bordering on France and Germany; in English also spelled Basle. Crossed by Rhine R. (navigable from here) and by Jura mts. Population is Protestant, German-speaking. Canton has been divided since 1833 into two independent half cantons—Basel-Land (165 sq. mi.; pop. 107,393), with cap. at Liestal, and Basel-Stadt, coextensive with city of Basel and suburbs (14 sq. mi.; pop. 196,658), on the Rhine. A commercial, industrial, and intellectual center, it is the seat of the Bank for International Settlements, the Swiss Industries Fair, and of important chemical and other industries. Univ. was founded 1460. A Roman colony, Basel became a bishopric in 7th cent. A free imperial city from 11th cent., it joined the Swiss Confederation in 1501 and in 1523 accepted the Reformation. (The prince-bishops of Basel, expelled from the city, continued to rule their vast territory from DELÉMONT until 1792.) The oppressive regime of the city patriciate led to civil troubles (1831–33) and the secession of Basel-Land. Among notable buildings are the cathedral (founded 1019) and the 16th-cent. city hall, with a Holbein collection. Erasmus and Holbein the Younger lived here; Euler and the Bernoulli family were born here.

Basel, Council of, 1431–49, council of Roman Catholic Church. A primary reason for its being summoned was trouble with the Hussites, and an agreement called the Compactata was drawn up (1433) and later split the Hussites (with the Utraquists rejoining the Church). The council is, however, remarkable chiefly for trying to put in practice the conciliar theory already advanced at the Council of Constance—the theory that ultimate authority resides in the general council, not the pope. Pope EUGENE IV early ordered it dissolved, but tried to compromise with the council, which instituted a process against the pope. He denounced the council in a bull (*Doctoris gentium,* 1437). The council deposed him and elected AMADEUS VIII of Savoy (antipope Felix V), Eugene, who summoned the Council of FERRARA-FLORENCE, had the support of most rulers. Though the French adopted many ideas of

the council and many reforms proposed were adopted by the Church, the council failed. Felix V resigned in favor of Eugene's successor, Nicholas V, and the conciliar theory died with the council.

Bashan (bā'-), in Bible, region E of Jordan R., known for cattle and sheep. Num. 21.33; Deut. 3; 2 Kings 10.33; Ps. 22.12; 68.15; Amos 4.1.

Bashkir Autonomous Soviet Socialist Republic (bŭshkēr'), autonomous state (55,400 sq. mi.; pop. 3,144,713), E European RSFSR, partly in S Urals; cap. Ufa. Agr., timber, minerals (iron, copper, manganese, gold, chromium, lead, bauxite, petroleum). Bashkirs (24% of pop.) are Moslem, Turkic-speaking people, tributary to Russia since 1556; rest of population mainly Russians (40%) and Turko-Tatars.

Bashkirtsev, Marie (bäsh'kûrtsĕf), 1860–84, French diarist and painter, b. Russia. Famous for her journal (published posthumously), a frank record of a precocious child avid for fame.

Basil, Saint: see BASIL THE GREAT, SAINT.

Basil, Byzantine emperors. Basil I (the Macedonian), c.813–86. Boon companion of Emperor MICHAEL III, whom he persuaded to make him coemperor (866) and whom he ordered slain (867). Capable, he reformed finances and the law code, and restored Byzantine military prestige. He strove vainly to prevent a schism of E and W churches and restored IGNATIUS OF CONSTANTINOPLE to the patriarchate (867). **Basil II,** c.958–1025, was co-ruler with his brother Constantine VIII after the reigns of usurpers NICEPHORUS II (963–67) and JOHN I (967–76). He suppressed the revolts of the landowners, revived laws of ROMANUS I, annexed Bulgaria (1018), and extended his empire to Caucasus. Called Bulgaroktonos, "Bulgar slayer."

Basil III, grand duke of Moscow: see VASILY III.

basil (băz'ŭl), tender herb or shrub of genus *Ocimum.* Cultivated for aromatic leaves used as seasoning.

Basilian monks (bŭzĭ'lĕŭn), monks of the Eastern Church, following the rule of St. BASIL THE GREAT. They live in collections of small cells without central government. The reformation by St. THEODORE OF STUDIUM (9th cent.) revitalized the order. Noted monasteries (hermitages) are at Mt. Athos and Mt. Sinai.

Basilicata (bäzēlēkä'tä), region (3,856 sq. mi.; pop. 543,262), S Italy; cap. Potenza. Other cities: MELFI, Matera. Poor, arid soil. Sheep and goat raising. Comprising parts of anc. Lucania and Samnium, region fell to Lombards, Byzantines; annexed (11th cent.) to Norman duchy of Apulia.

Basilius Valentinus (bŭsil'ēŭs văl'ŭntī'nŭs), believed pseudonym of Johannes Thölde. Wrote on chemistry, use of antimony in fevers (1604).

Basil the Great, Saint (bă'zĭl, bā'-), c.330–379, Greek churchman, one of the Greek Fathers, Doctor of the Church, bishop of Caesarea in Cappadocia; brother of St. Gregory of Nyssa. He wrote most of the two rules for the Basilian monks. As aid and successor to

Eusebius, he helped estab. orthodoxy over ARIANISM.

Baskerville, John, 1706–75, English type designer, printer for Cambridge Univ. after 1758. Introduced influential "modern" type faces. His books are large, with wide margins and excellent paper and ink.

basketball. Played by two opposing teams of five players each on regulation court 94 ft. long, 50 ft. wide. Originated (1891) in U.S. by James Naismith, physical director of Y.M.C.A. college, Springfield, Mass.

Basket Makers, early Indian people of U.S. Southwest, dating possibly from c.1500 B.C. Had great skill in making baskets; developed from nomadic hunters to farmers; lived in pit houses. Succeeded by ancestors of Pueblo Indians.

Basle, Switzerland: see BASEL.

Basque Provinces (băsk), Basque *Euzkadi,* Span. *Vascongadas,* region (2,803 sq. mi.; pop. 955,764), N Spain, S of Bay of Biscay, consisting of Álava, Guipúzcoa, and Vizcaya provs. Chief cities: Bilbao, Vitoria, San Sebastián. Iron, lead, copper mines; shipyards; fisheries. Majority of pop. are **Basques,** a stoutly Catholic people of peasants, shepherds, and fishermen. There are c.1,550,000 Basques in Spanish Navarre and Basque Provs.; c.200,000 in SW France (Labourd, Soule, and Lower Navarre dists.); c.250,000 in S America and rest of world. Possibly descended from Cro-Magnon man, they antedate anc. Iberian tribes of Spain. Their language is related to no other. Before Roman conquest of Spain and Gaul, Basque pop. extended further N and S than now. Core of Basque country fought off Romans, Visigoths, Moors, and Franks. Basque victory at RONCESVALLES threw off short-lived overlordship of Charlemagne (778). In GASCONY the duchy set up by Basques in 601 fell apart in 9th cent., but in 824 the Basque kingdom of NAVARRE was founded; under SANCHO III it united nearly all Basques (1000–1035). Basques lost independence as Castile acquired Guipúzcoa (1200), Álava (1332), Vizcaya (1370), and most of Navarre (1512), but they retained their old democratic rights. Their assemblies at GUERNICA remain famous. In 1873 Basque privileges were abolished after Basques' pro-Carlist stand in Carlist wars. The three Basque Provs. were granted autonomy in 1936. They stoutly resisted Franco, who revoked autonomy after conquering them in 1937.

Basra (bŭs′rü), city (pop. 206,302), SE Iraq, port on the Shatt el Arab, 75 mi. from Persian Gulf. Founded A.D. 636 by Caliph Omar, declined during Abbasid caliphate. Railroad link to Baghdad revived its importance. Exports dates, barley, and wool.

Bas-Rhin (bä-rĕ′), department (1,848 sq. mi.; pop. 673,281), E France, in Alsace; cap. Strasbourg.

Bass, Sam (băs), 1851–78, American desperado. Train robber in S.Dak. and Texas. Career provided material for frontier ballads.

bass, name for various food and game fish, chiefly seabass family (Serranidae) and sunfish family (Centrarchidae). Common sea bass (*Centropristes striatus*) along U.S. coast from Massachusetts to N Florida. Sometimes classed as sea bass and sometimes as separate family (Moronidae) are striped bass or rockfish (*Roccus saxatilis* or *R. lineatus*); white bass (*R. chrysops*); yellow bass (*Morone interrupta*); white or silver perch (*M. americana*). *M. labrax* found on coast SW Europe and Mediterranean.

Bassano, Jacopo (yäkō′pō bäs-sä′nō), 1510–92, Venetian painter, b. Bassano. His real name was Da Ponte. Perhaps the first Italian genre artist. His son and follower was **Leandro Bassano** (lään′drō), 1558–1623.

Bassano, town (pop. 624), E Alta., Canada, ESE of Calgary. Bassano or Horseshoe Bend Dam near by on Bow R. is one of world's longest.

Bassano (bäs-sä′nō), city (pop. 11,774), Venetia, NE Italy, on Brenta R. Free commune in Middle Ages; under Venice 1402–1797. Home of Da Ponte family of painters (surnamed BASSANO) and of famous Remondini printing plant (17th–18th cent.) Palaces and churches recall past glory. Scene of Bonaparte's victory over Austrians 1796.

Basses-Alpes (bäs-zälp′), department (2,698 sq. mi.; pop. 83,354), SE France, in Provence; cap. Digne.

Basses-Pyrénées (bäs″-pērānä′), department (2,978 sq. mi.; pop. 415,797), SW France; cap. Pau.

Basse-Terre (bästĕr′), port (pop. 10,086), cap. of Guadeloupe dept., French West Indies.

Basseterre, town (pop. 12,194), SAINT KITTS, cap. of St. Kitts-Nevis presidency, British West Indies.

Bassett, John Spencer, 1867–1928, American historian. Founder (1902) of *South Atlantic Quarterly.* His many works on American history include *The Federalist System, 1789–1801* (1906) and *The Life of Andrew Jackson* (1911).

Bassompierre, François, baron de (fräswä′ bärō′ dü bäsōpyĕr′), 1579–1646, marshal of France. Served under Henry IV; later fought Huguenots (1621–22, 1627–28). His opposition to Richelieu caused his imprisonment in Bastille (1631–43). Wrote memoirs.

bassoon: see WIND INSTRUMENTS.

Bass Strait (băs), channel, 80–150 mi. wide between Tasmania and Victoria, Australia. Its discovery by George Bass in 1798 destroyed belief that Tasmania was part of Australian continent.

basswood: see LINDEN.

bast, inner bark of plant stems which is phloem or food-conducting tissue. Source of valuable fibers in such plants as hemp, flax, jute, ramie, sunn hemp.

bastard, person born out of wedlock, illegitimate child. It is legally presumed that an child born to a married woman is the child of her husband. The latter has the burden of proof if he contests his paternity on the ground of physical impossibility. Attitude toward illegitimacy have varied greatly under different social conditions. Under English common law illegitimate children had few rights. Rights now given by statutes. In U.S. state laws on illegitimacy vary greatly; generally subsequent marriage of parents legitimizes child, and some states provide special judicial proceedings for legitimation.

Bastard of Orléans, French general: see DUNOIS, JEAN, COMTE DE.

Bastia (bästē'ä), town (pop. 37,122), NE Corsica, France; seaport. The chief commercial center of Corsica, Bastia was its cap. till 1791. Citadel.

Bastian, Adolf (ä'dôlf bäs'tyän), 1826–1905, German anthropologist. His concept of "elemental ideas" as common to all mankind, foreshadowed culture-area theory.

Bastidas, Rodrigo de (rôdhrē'gō dä bästē'dhäs), c.1460–1526, Spanish conquistador in Colombia. Discovered mouth of Magdalena (1501), founded Santa Marta (1525).

Bastien-Lepage, Jules (zhül' bästyē'-lúpäzh'), 1848–84, French painter of figures in the open air.

Bastille (bästēl'), former state prison in Paris, France. Begun as fortress c.1369; demolished 1789. Fouquet, Man with the Iron Mask, and Voltaire were imprisoned here. Despite horror stories, most political prisoners were treated mildly. On July 14, 1789, a Parisian mob, protesting Necker's dismissal, stormed Bastille. The date, marking outbreak of French Revolution, became national holiday of republican France.

Bastogne (bästô'nyù), town (pop. 4,717), Luxembourg prov., SE Belgium, in Ardennes. During BATTLE OF THE BULGE, U.S. troops under Gen. Anthony McAuliffe held encircled town until relieved by U.S. 3d Army (Dec. 20–26, 1944). McAuliffe's supposed reply when invited to surrender: "Nuts!"

Bastrop, town (pop. 12,769), NE La., NNE of Monroe; founded c.1845. Processes paper, carbon, and brick.

Basutoland (bùsōō'tōländ''), British territory (11,716 sq. mi.; pop. 624,605), enclave in Union of South Africa, administered directly by the crown; cap. Maseru. Basuto nation was formed (1815–31) from tribal remnants left in the wake of Zulu and Matabele raids. Under British rule since 1868.

bat, mammal of order Chiroptera. Found in most temperate and tropical regions, it is only mammal with power of true flight. Wing is membrane stretched between elongated bones of four fingers, extending in most bats along body from forelimbs to hind limbs to tail. Thumb is small, clawed, free of membrane. Chiefly nocturnal, they have some sight; avoid collision in flight mostly by keen senses of hearing, touch. In temperate climates, some bats hibernate in caves in winter; some migrate.

Bataan (bătän', bätä-än'), peninsula and province (157 sq. mi.; pop. 92,901), W Luzon, Philippines. Forms W shore of Manila Bay. After fall of Manila in World War II, U.S. troops (first led by Gen. MacArthur and later by Lt. Gen. Wainwright) made a gallant stand here Jan.–April, 1942.

Bataille, Henry (ärē' bätä'yù'), 1872–1922, French dramatist. His plays are based on morbid psychology. *Maman Colibri* (1904) and *La Vierge folle* [the foolish virgin] (1910) were most successful.

Batalha (bùtä'lyù), town, Estremadura, W central Portugal, S of Leiria. John I built its famous Dominican monastery and church to commemorate victory of Aljubarrota (1385).

Batavia, Indonesia: see JAKARTA.

Batavia. 1 City (pop. 5,838), NE Ill., W of Chicago. Mfg. of machines and cosmetics. **2** City (17,799), W N.Y., SW of Rochester. Settled 1801 by a HOLLAND LAND COMPANY agent. Mfg. of shoes, paper and metal products. Has U.S. veterans' hospital.

Batavian Republic, 1795–1806. The United Provs. of the Netherlands, occupied by French in the French Revolutionary Wars, were reconstituted as the Batavian Republic in 1795, remaining under French tutelage. In 1806 Napoleon made it into kingdom of Holland for his brother Louis.

Bates, Henry Walter, 1825–92, English naturalist, explorer of upper Amazon with A. R. Wallace. In 1859 returned with 8,000 new species of animals. First to state plausible theory of mimicry.

Bates College: see LEWISTON, Maine.

Batesville, city (pop. 6,414), N central Ark., on White R. in the Ozarks. Processing center of area yielding cotton, fruit, poultry, milk, corn, lumber, manganese, and marble.

Bath, county borough (pop. 79,275) and city, Somerset, England, on the Avon. Romans discovered warm springs here 1st cent. A.D.; built elaborate walls and baths. In Chaucer's time, it had become wool and cloth town. Became famous spa in 18th cent., with Beau Nash as social arbiter. John WOOD and his son planned streets and buildings such as the Royal Crescent, Assembly Rooms (destroyed in 1942 air raid), and Circus. Now residential and resort town with mfg. and quarrying. Has 17th-cent. abbey.

Bath. 1 City (pop. 10,644), SW Maine, on lower Kennebec R. (bridged 1927); settled c.1670. Longtime shipbuilding center. Has Davenport Memorial, with marine exhibits. **2** Village (pop. 5,416), S N.Y., NW of Elmira, in farm area; settled 1793. Has U.S. veterans' administration center (1878). **3** Town, E N.C., on Pamlico R. and SE of Washington; settled 1690 on Indian village site. State's oldest town, was cap. of province of N.C. **4** See BERKELEY SPRINGS, W.Va.

Bath, Order of the, British order of knighthood. Estab. 1725 as military order, in 1847 opened also to civilians. Ranks second to Order of the Garter.

Bathory (bä'tôrē), Hung. *Báthory,* Pol. *Batory,* Hungarian noble family. **Stephen Bathory,** 1477–1534, voivode of Transylvania (1529–34) was the father of STEPHEN BATHORY, king of Poland, and of **Christopher Bathory,** 1530–81, prince of Transylvania (1575–81). Christopher's son **Sigismund Bathory,** 1572–1613, was recognized as hereditary prince of Transylvania by Rudolf II (1594). Probably insane, he abdicated 1596, but soon afterward returned to power, with Bocskay's help, as vassal of the sultan. He briefly abdicated again in 1599, and definitively in 1601 (in favor of Rudolf). Other members of the family include **Elizabeth Bathory,** d. 1614, celebrated as a werewolf (she is said to have slaughtered 600 virgins to renew her youth by bathing in their blood), who died in prison, and **Gabriel Bathory,** 1589–1613, prince of Transylvania (1608–13), murdered by rebellious nobles.

Bath-sheba (băth-shē'bù), wife of Uriah the Hittite. David caused Uriah's death and married her. She bore him Solomon. 2 Sam. 11; 12; 1 Kings 1; 2; Mat. 1.6.

Bathurst, town (pop. 4,453), NE N.B., Canada, on arm of Chaleur Bay; fishing and resort center.

bathysphere: see DIVING.

Batista (y Zaldívar), Fulgencio (fōōlhĕn′sēō bätē′stä ē söldē′vär), 1901–, president of Cuba (1940–44), "strong man" (1933–44). After exile in U.S. (1945–49), led successful coup in Cuba 1952.

Batoche (bătŏsh′), village, central Sask., Canada, S of Prince Albert. Hq. of Louis RIEL in Riel's Rebellion.

Baton Rouge (băt′ŭn rōōzh″), city (pop. 125-629), state cap., SE La., NW of New Orleans, on E bank of Mississippi R.; settled 1719 by French. Taken by Farragut in Civil War (May, 1862). Major distributing and commercial center, it has one of world's largest oil refineries; also food-processing, woodworking, chemical plants. Seat of LOUISIANA STATE UNIVERSITY AND AGRICULTURAL AND MECHANICAL COLLEGE. Southern Univ. and Agricultural and Mechanical Col. (Negro; land grant; coed.; 1880) is near.

Batory: see BÁTHORY.

Battenberg (bä′tŭnbûrg), princely family issued from morganatic marriage of Alexander, younger son of Louis II of Hesse-Darmstadt, and countess Julia von Hauke, created princess of Battenberg 1858. Their oldest son, Louis, an admiral in British service, was created marquess of Milford Haven, married a granddaughter of Queen Victoria, changed his name to Mountbatten in World War I; father of Earl MOUNTBATTEN and grandfather of duke of EDINBURGH. Alexander's second son was Prince ALEXANDER of Bulgaria. A third son, Henry, married Beatrice, daughter of Queen Victoria; their daughter, Victoria Eugenie, married Alfonso XIII of Spain.

Battersea, metropolitan borough (pop. 117,130) of SW London, England, on S bank of the Thames. Chiefly workingmen's residences, suffered much air raid damage 1940–41. Has 200 acre Battersea Park.

Battery, the, park at S tip of Manhattan isl., New York city. Castle Clinton fort (built here c.1807, razed 1941) later became, in turn, Castle Garden amusement hall (scene of Jenny Lind's American debut 1850), immigration station (1855–92), and municipal aquarium (1896–1941); it was designated a national monument in 1950.

battery, unlawful touching by an aggressor— directly or indirectly, intentionally or negligently—of any part of another person. Intentional battery justifies a claim for damages regardless of physical injury. "Assault and battery" presupposes such injury, however slight.

battery, electric, commonly describes electric CELL; more correctly means group of cells used as source of electric current. A or filament battery provides current to heat FILAMENT in vacuum tube of radio. B battery is the source of current in plate circuit; produces needed voltage on plates of vacuum tubes. Usually consists of small dry cells connected in series; also may be of storage type. C battery is used in grid circuit of tube

(see TUBE, VACUUM) to create bias (usually negative) on grid of tube. Storage battery is a much used current source, e.g., in automobile; has electric cells in series (see ELECTRIC CIRCUIT; *ill.*, p. 377).

Battle, former urban district (pop. 3,491), Sussex E., England, NW of Hastings. Scene of 1066 battle which resulted in death of Harold and elevation of Norman conqueror as WILLIAM I of England. Has ruins of **Battle Abbey**, founded by William after his victory. **Battle Abbey Roll**, which was kept here, supposedly listed William's noble battle companions. Its authenticity is doubtful.

battle, in war, single conflict or, more broadly, prolonged combat over extended area. Sir E. S. Creasy's list of 15 decisive battles of the world, 490 B.C.–1815, nominates Marathon (490 B.C.), Syracuse (413 B.C.), Arbela (331 B.C.), Metaurus (207 B.C.), the Teutoburg Forest (A.D. 9), Chalons-sur-Marne or Catalaunian Fields (451), Tour or Poitiers (732), Hastings or Senlac (1066), Orléans (1429), victory over Spanish Armada (1588), Blenheim (1704), Poltava (1709), Saratoga (1777), Valmy (1792), and Waterloo (1815). Others are Salamis (480 B.C.), Issus (333 B.C.), Cannae (216 B.C.), Zama (202 B.C.), Pharsala (48 B.C.), Philippi (42 B.C.), Actium (31 B.C.), Adrianople (A.D. 378), Lechfeld (955), Bouvines (1214), Sluis (1340), Crécy (1346), Nikopol (1396), Agincourt (1415), Constantinople (1453), Pavia (1525), Mohacs (1526), Mühlberg (1547), Lepanto (1571), White Mt. (1620), Lützen (1632), Rossbach (1757), Plassey (1757), Kings Mt. (1780), Yorktown (1781), Aboukir Bay or battle of the Nile (1798), Austerlitz (1805), Trafalgar (1805), Leipzig (1813), Ayacucho (1824), Solferino (1859), Vicksburg (1863), Gettysburg (1863), Sedan (1870), Manila Bay (1898), Tsushima (1905), two battles of the Marne (1914, 1918), Jutland (1916), Verdun (1916), Coral Sea and Midway (1942), Alamein (1942), and Stalingrad (1942–43).

Battle Abbey and **Battle Abbey Roll:** see BATTLE.

Battle above the Clouds: see CHATTANOOGA CAMPAIGN.

Battle Creek, city (pop. 48,666), S Mich., SW of Lansing, at junction of Kalamazoo R. and the Battle Creek; settled 1831. Farm trade center and health resort, known for mfg. of cereal foods, it also has mfg. of auto parts, farm equipment, and ink. Here are Battle Creek Sanitarium, hq. of W. K. Kellogg Foundation (child welfare), and an army hospital. U.S. VA center is at near-by Fort Custer.

Battleford, town (pop. 1,319), W Sask., Canada, on North Saskatchewan R. at mouth of Battle R. NW of Saskatoon. Cap. of North west Territories 1876–83. Prominent in Riel Rebellion.

Battle Hymn of the Republic, The: see HOWE, JULIA WARD.

Battle of the Bulge, popular name given World War II to last German offensive on Western Front (Dec., 1944–Jan., 1945). On Dec. 16 Germans under von Rundstedt's surprise attack broke through American front in Belgian Ardennes, creating a "bulge in Allied lines. Allied counterthrusts turned German offensive into rout by mid-January. U.S. troops suffered heavy casualties. Defense of BASTOGNE was a notable episode.

Battle of the Spurs. 1 Victory, 1302, near Courtrai, Belgium, of Flemish towns over French army sent by Philip IV; so called for trophy formed by spurs of fallen French. **2** Victory, 1513, at GUINEGATE, of Henry VIII of England over French; possibly so-called for speedy flight of French cavalry.

Batu Khan (bä′tōō kän′), d. 1255, Mongol commander of GOLDEN HORDE; grandson of Jenghiz Khan. Conquered Russia, Hungary, and Poland.

Batum (bŭtōōm′), city (pop. 70,807), cap. of Adzhar ASSR, Georgian SSR, on Black Sea. Connected by pipe lines with Baku; major oil-refining and -shipping center. Ceded by Turkey to Russia 1878.

Baucis: see PHILEMON AND BAUCIS.

Baudelaire, Charles (shärl′ bōdlâr′), 1821–67, French poet. His neurotic, eccentric personality led him along a road of poverty, misunderstanding, excesses, and disease. A perfectionist, he labored for years on his one volume of verse, *Les Fleurs du Mal* [flowers of evil] (1857), six poems of which were condemned as obscene by a court. Baudelaire never recovered fully from that blow. His other work includes remarkable literary and art criticism and exceptionally fine translations of Poe, to whom he felt great affinity. His influence on all subsequent poetry is immeasurable. There are several English translations of his poems.

Baudouin (bōdōōē′), 1930–, king of the Belgians (1951–); son and successor of LEOPOLD III.

Bauer, Louis Agricola, 1865–1932, American magnetician. Influential in international coordination of work in terrestrial magnetism. Founded and edited *Terrestrial Magnetism and Atmospheric Electricity.*

Bauhaus (bou′hous), art school in Germany. It revolutionized art training by combining the teaching of pure arts with the study of crafts. Founded in 1919 at Weimar with Walter GROPIUS as director, it stressed functional craftsmanship in every field with a realization of the industrial problems of mass production. Bauhaus met vigorous opposition which forced its removal to Dessau and later to Berlin. Finally closed in 1933 by the German government, but Bauhaus ideas concerning architecture and many industrial fields found wide acclaim. The Chicago Inst. of Design carried on its teaching plan.

Bauhin, Gaspard (gäspär′ bōē′), 1560–1624, Swiss botanist. He classified plants by genus and species, anticipating the binomial system of Linnaeus.

Baum, L(yman) Frank (bôm), 1856–1919, American author of juvenile books laid in imaginary magic land of Oz (e.g., *The Wonderful Wizard of Oz,* 1900).

Baumé, Antoine (ätwän′ bōmä′), 1728–1804, French chemist. Invented a graduated hydrometer, discovered various important industrial processes.

Bausch, Edward (boush), 1854–1944, American inventor. Worked on kinetoscope, camera, microscope.

Bautzen (bou′tsůn), city (pop. 38,524), Saxony, SE Germany, in Upper Lusatia, on the Spree. Machine and textile mfg. Napoleon I defeated Russo-Prussian forces near by (1813).

Baux, Les (lä bō′), ruined medieval town near Arles, SE France. Was seat of powerful feudal family. Impressive ruins. Bauxite, first discovered here, is named for Les Baux.

bauxite, hydrate of ALUMINA, with other oxides. A claylike, earthy mineral, white to red or brown. Chief source of aluminum and its compounds.

Bavaria, Ger. *Bayern,* state (27,119 sq. mi.; pop. 9,118,635), S Germany; cap. MUNICH. Rises in S to Bavarian Alps (highest peak ZUGSPITZE) along Austrian frontier; BOHEMIAN FOREST forms E frontier with Czechoslovakia. Danube and Main are chief rivers. State consists of Bavaria proper, i.e., Upper Bavaria (cap. Munich) and Lower Bavaria (cap. Landshut) in S; of Upper, Middle, and Lower FRANCONIA (with BAYREUTH, BAMBERG, NUREMBERG, WÜRZBURG) in N; of SWABIA (cap. AUGSBURG) in W; and of the Upper PALATINATE (cap. REGENSBURG) in NE. Rich in agr. and forests, Bavaria also has mfg. (machinery, textiles, beer, toys), resorts and spas for tourists. Roman Catholicism is predominant except in N. Until early 19th cent. Bavaria did not include Franconia and Swabia, which have separate histories. Conquered by Romans 15 B.C., the region was made a duchy 6th cent. A.D. by an invading Germanic tribe (Baiuoarii). Under Carolingians 788–911; under GUELPHS 1070–1180 (with interruptions); under WITTELSBACH dynasty 1180–1918. Austria, Carinthia, and Upper Palatinate were detached (976) from original duchy to curb power of dukes. Wittelsbach fiefs (incl. Rhenish PALATINATE) were long divided among various branches of family, fully united only in 1799. Duke MAXIMILIAN I received Upper Palatinate and electoral rank (1623; see ELECTORS). Enlarged and raised to kingdom (1806), Bavaria emerged from Congress of Vienna with present territory and Rhenish Palatinate (1815). Sided with Austria in Austro-Prussian War (1866), with Prussia in Franco-Prussian War (1870–71); joined German Empire 1871. As chief German state after Prussia, it retained special position and separatist tendencies. Republic set up Nov., 1918; joined Weimar Republic after unsuccessful Communist revolution (1919). All Bavaria under U.S. occupation after 1945, except for Rhenish Palatinate and LINDAU dist., which were detached and occupied by France. New constitution adopted 1946. Joined Federal Republic of [Western] Germany 1949. Kings of Bavaria: MAXIMILIAN I, LOUIS I, MAXIMILIAN II, LOUIS II, OTTO I, LOUIS III.

Bavarian Succession, War of the, 1778–79. Elector Maximilian III having died childless in 1777, Bavaria passed to the elector palatine, Charles Theodore, who in return for certain concessions ceded Bavaria to Austria. Prussia protested the transfer. The ensuing campaign, spent entirely in provisioning the armies, has been called the Potato War. At the Congress of Teschen (1779) Austria renounced its claims.

Bax, Sir Arnold, 1883–, English composer. His

works, which reflect Wagner and Debussy, include several tone poems, e.g., *The Garden of Fand;* seven symphonies; instrumental and vocal compositions.

Baxter, Richard, 1615–91, English nonconformist clergyman. A supporter of Cromwell, yet a moderate, he sought under Charles II to keep dissenters in Church; after Act of Uniformity (1662) withdrew from Church of England, but continued preaching despite persecution. Wrote *The Saints' Everlasting Rest* (1650).

bay or **sweet bay:** see LAUREL.

Bayard, Pierre du Terrail, seigneur de (bā´ůrd, Fr. pyĕr´ dü tĕrī´yů sānyûr´ dů bäyär´), c.1474–1524, French hero, *le chevalier sans peur et sans reproche* [the knight without fear or blame]. Fought in Italian Wars; fell in battle.

Bayazid or **Bayazit:** see BAJAZET.

bayberry, American shrub (*Myrica pennsylvanica*), native to the eastern seacoast of U.S. It is often cultivated for its handsome aromatic foliage. Its gray, waxy berries are used in winter bouquets and in making candles. California bayberry (*Myrica californica*) is evergreen and treelike.

Bay City. 1 City (pop. 52,523), S Mich., on Saginaw R. near its mouth on Saginaw Bay; settled c.1831. Port for Great Lakes and ocean shipping, it has shipbuilding and fishing. Mfg. of auto parts, machinery, and metal and chemical products. Coal mines in area. **2** Town (pop. 9,427), S Texas, SW of Houston near Colorado R. Shipping and industrial center for oil and farm area.

Bayer, Johann (yō´hän bī´ůr), 1572–1625, German astronomer, known for system of designating stars of a CONSTELLATION (using Greek letters with constellation names) and for star chart, *Uranometria* (1603).

Bayeux (bäyû´), town (pop. 8,744), Calvados dept., N France, in Normandy. First French town liberated (June 8, 1944) by Allies in World War II. Fine Gothic cathedral. In Bayeux Mus. is the **Bayeux tapestry,** an embroidery chronicling the Norman conquest of England in 1066; it is worked on coarse linen, 230 ft. by 20 in. Its date is disputed.

Bay Islands, archipelago, off N coast of Honduras, in Caribbean. Held by British for years after 1848.

Bayle, Pierre (bāl), 1647–1706, French rationalist philosopher. Through his works (among them *Dictionnaire historique et critique,* 1697) he influenced the philosophers of the Enlightenment in France and the deists in England.

Bayley, Richard, 1745–1801, American physician, known for scientific account of yellow fever epidemic of 1795 in New York city.

Bayliss, Sir William Maddock (bā´lĭs), 1860–1924, English physiologist, pioneer (with Starling) in evolving theory of hormone action after discovering secretion.

Baylor University, mainly at Waco, Texas; chartered, opened 1845 by Baptists at Independence; moved and absorbed Waco Univ. 1886. Medical college at Houston, dental college and nursing school at Dallas. Fine Robert Browning collection. Connected with Mary Hardin-Baylor Col. at BELTON.

Bayonne (bäyôn´), city (pop. 28,110), Basses-Pyrénées dept., SW France, in Basque country, on Adour R. near Bay of Biscay; fortified seaport. Bayonet invented here in 17th cent. Gothic cathedral; museums of fine arts and of Basque folklore.

Bayonne (bāyōn´), city (pop. 77,203), NE N.J. on peninsula S of Jersey City, between New York harbor (bridged 1931 to Staten Isl.) and Newark Bay; settled by Dutch c.1650, taken by British 1664. Oil refineries (receives pipe line from SW), U.S. naval dry dock. Mfg. of chemicals, clothing, machinery.

Bay Psalm Book, hymnal used in Mass. Bay colony, appearing as *The Whole Book of Psalms Faithfully Translated into English,* first book published (1640) in Thirteen Colonies.

Bayreuth (bīroit´), city (pop. 58,630), cap. of Upper Franconia, NE Bavaria. Textile, metal, and food mfg. Founded 1194; under HOHENZOLLERN family 1248–1807. Residence of Richard WAGNER 1872–83; celebrated for annual music festivals. Wagner and Liszt are buried here. Wagner's house, "Villa Wahnfried," destroyed in World War II.

Bay Shore, village (pop. 9,665), SE N.Y., on S shore (Great South Bay) of Long Isl. Center for fishing and duck hunting. Ferry to Fire Isl.

Baytown, city (pop. 22,983), S Texas, on Galveston Bay SE of Houston. Formed 1947 by combining Goose Creek, Pelly, and Baytown. Oil port, it has refineries and chemical plants.

Bay Village, city (pop. 6,917) NE Ohio, W suburb of Cleveland.

Bazaine, Achille (äshēl´ bäzĕn´), 1811–88, marshal of France. In Franco-Prussian War he allowed Germans to lock up his army at Metz and eventually capitulated (1870). MacMahon's attempt to relieve Metz led to disaster of Sedan. Condemned for treason (1873), Bazaine escaped abroad.

Bazán, Emilia Pardo: see PARDO BAZÁN.

Bazargic, Bulgaria: see TOLBUKHIN.

B battery: see BATTERY, ELECTRIC.

Be, chemical symbol of the element BERYLLIUM.

Beach, Chester, 1881–, American sculptor, b. San Francisco. Works include many portrait busts.

Beach, Moses Yale, 1800–1868, American journalist. After buying the New York *Sun* (1838) from his brother-in-law, Benjamin Day, he rivaled James Gordon Bennett in hustling for news, speeding transmission, widening coverage. Helped found the New York Associated Press and was first to have European edition of a U.S. paper and to syndicate articles.

beach grass or **marram grass,** perennial grass of genus *Ammophila.* Helps to control shifting sands.

Beacon, city (pop. 14,012), SE N.Y., on E bank of the Hudson opposite Newburgh; formed (1913) with union of Fishkill Landing and Matteawan. Has Matteawan State Hospital for insane criminals.

Beaconsfield, Benjamin Disraeli, 1st earl of: see DISRAELI, BENJAMIN.

beagle: see HOUND.

Bean, Roy, c.1825–1903, American frontiersman. Justice of the peace—self-styled "law west of the Pecos"—at Vinegaroon (later renamed Langtry), Texas. Meted out justice in his saloon, the "Jersey Lily," named for actress Lillie Langtry.

Bean, Tarleton Hoffman, 1846–1916, American ichthyologist. His fish-propagation methods widely used.

bean, name for various genera and species of the legume family. Prolific, adaptable, and easily grown, beans have been from prehistoric times an important food crop for humans and cattle. Some are grown for forage and cover crops. Both pods and seeds of snap or string beans are edible while only seeds of kidney and lima beans are eaten. Scarlet runner bean is an ornamental. See also CAROB; FRIJOLE; SOYBEAN.

Bear, river rising in NE Utah in Uinta Mts., flowing 350 mi. in long loop N, NW through Wyo., around Bear L. in Idaho, S into Utah to Great Salt L.

bear, mammal of family Ursidae of order Carnivora, found almost exclusively in N hemisphere. Feet are plantigrade, claws nonretractile, fur thick and shaggy, tail very short, and body clumsy appearing. Some run at 25–30 mi. an hour speed; excepting heavy grizzly bears, most climb trees. Bears eat fruits, roots, honey, insects, fish, carrion, and infrequently mammals. Where winters are cold they hibernate. Young, usually twins, are born during winter in undeveloped state.

bear, in speculative markets: see BULLS AND BEARS.

bearberry, trailing woody plant (*Arctostaphylos uvaursi*) of N Hemisphere. Evergreen, astringent leaves and red berries. Often used as ground cover.

Beard, Charles A(ustin), 1874–1948, American historian. As professor (1904–17) at Columbia Univ., he broadened history teaching to embrace civilization. Helped found New School for Social Research. Widely known for *The Rise of American Civilization* (2 vols., 1927), *America in Midpassage* (1939), and *The American Spirit* (1943). These were written in collaboration with his wife, **Mary (Ritter) Beard**, 1876–.

Beard, Daniel Carter, 1850–1941, American illustrator and naturalist, a founder of the Boy Scouts of America (1910).

Beardsley, Aubrey (Vincent), 1872–98, celebrated English black-and-white illustrator. Art editor of the *Yellow Book*, 1894–96.

Beardstown, city (pop. 6,080), W central Ill., WNW of Springfield and on Illinois R., in agr. area. Has rail shops and commercial fisheries.

beardtongue or **penstemon,** any herb or shrub of genus *Penstemon* with showy tubular flowers. Most species native to W U.S. and Canada.

bearings, in general, machine parts supporting a shaft, and intended to minimize FRICTION. Generally made of ANTIFRICTION METAL, such as BABBITT METAL. Since friction generates heat, bearing efficiency depends largely upon lubrication. High-speed machinery usually fitted with ball bearings (these and roller bearings known as antifriction bearings). Bearings should fit so shaft turns freely but cannot otherwise move to set up vibration. Thrust bearings designed to resist forces in shaft along direction of its length, as in a ship's propeller shaft.

Bear Island: see SPITSBERGEN.

Bear Lake, c.20 mi. long, N Utah and SE Idaho.

Bear Mountain, peak, 1,314 ft. high, SE N.Y., in Palisades Interstate Park, overlooking the Hudson (bridged 1924) S of Newburgh.

Béarn (bäärn'), region and former province, SW France, in Basses-Pyrénées dept.; historic cap. Orthez, later Pau. Agr., cattle breeding. Viscounty of Béarn passed (13th cent.) to counts of FOIX, thence, along with Navarre, to houses of Albret (1494) and Bourbon (1572); inc. into France 1620.

beatification: see CANONIZATION.

Beatitudes (bēăt'-) [Latin,= blessing], blessings spoken by Jesus at opening of Sermon on Mount. Mat. 5.3–12. Luke 6.20–26.

Beaton, Cecil (Walter Hardy), 1904–, English photographer and stage designer.

Beaton or **Bethune, David** (both: bē'tùn), 1494–1546, Scottish churchman, cardinal of the Roman Church. Arranged marriage of James V and Mary of Guise. Failed to gain regency for Mary Queen of Scots. Murdered for execution of George WISHART.

Beatrice (bēăt'rĭs), city (pop. 11,813), SE Nebr., on Big Blue R. and S of Lincoln; founded 1857 on old Oregon Trail. Trade center for grain, dairy, and livestock area. Mfg. of farm equipment. Homestead Natl. Monument of America is near.

Beatrice Portinari (bē'ŭtrĭs; bäätrē'chā pōrtēnä'rē), 1266–90, Florentine lady believed to be the Beatrice named in the writings of Dante.

Beatty, David Beatty, 1st Earl (bē'tē), 1871–1936, British admiral. Aided in defeat of German fleet at Jutland 1916. Commanded British fleet 1916–19 and was first sea lord 1919–27.

Beauce (bōs), flat region, N France, SW of Paris; chief city Chartres. The "granary of France," it is covered with wheat fields.

Beauchamp, English noble family: see WARWICK, GUY DE BEAUCHAMP, EARL OF.

Beaufort, Edmund: see SOMERSET, EDMUND BEAUFORT, 2d DUKE OF.

Beaufort, Henry (bō'fùrt), c.1377–1447, English prelate and statesman; half brother of Henry IV. Chancellor 1403–4; fell when Prince Henry lost power. Again made chancellor when prince became Henvy V. Swung English influence (1417) to elect Pope Martin V. Was chancellor (1424–26) in regency for Henry VI. Became a cardinal in 1426 and was a papal legate. Crowned Henry VI in Paris, 1431.

Beaufort, Margaret, countess of Richmond and Derby, 1443–1509, English noblewoman; mother of Henry VII. Founded Christ's Col. and St. John's Col., Cambridge. Patron of Caxton.

Beaufort (bū'fùrt), resort city (pop. 5,081), on Port Royal Isl., S S.C., SW of Charleston; founded 1711. State's second oldest town, it has old buildings, national cemetery, and arsenal. Has good harbor. Shipping and canneries for agr. and fishing area. Held by North in most of Civil War.

Beaufort Sea (bō'fùrt), part of Arctic Ocean, between N Alaska and Arctic Archipelago of Canada.

Beauharnais, Alexandre, vicomte de (älĕksä'drù vēkōt' dù bōärnä'), 1760–94, French general in American Revolution and in French Revolutionary Wars. Guillotined in Reign of Terror. His widow, **Josephine de Beauharnais**, married Napoleon I (see JOSEPHINE). Alexandre's and Josephine's son, **Eugène de Beauharnais** (ûzhĕn'), 1781–1824, served as general under Napoleon, who made him viceroy of Italy in 1805. Capable administrator. Retired to Munich after Napoleon's downfall. His sister, **Hortense de Beauharnais** (ôrtäs'), 1783–1837, married Louis BONAPARTE, whom Napoleon made king of Holland (1806–10); mother of Napoleon III and the duc de Morny.

Beauharnois (bōhär'nwä), town (pop. 5,694), S Que., Canada, on S shore of L. St. Louis, SW of Montreal. **Beauharnois Canal**, opened 1843 on S side of St. Lawrence R. to bypass rapids, was superseded by Soulange Canal on N side in 1899. New Beauharnois Canal, begun 1930 for power development, was subject of political scandal. Province bought plant as public-ownership enterprise in 1945.

Beaujeu, Anne de: see ANNE DE BEAUJEU.

Beaujolais (bōjôlā'), hilly region, Rhône dept., E central France; famous for light red wine. Once the fief of lords of Beaujeu.

Beaumarchais, Pierre Augustin Caron de (pyĕr' ōgüstĕ' kärō' dú bōmärshā'), 1732–99, French dramatist, at first a watchmaker by trade. His sparkling comedies, *Le Barbier de Séville* (1775) and *Le Mariage de Figaro* (1784) are famous in their own right and as sources for operas by Rossini and Mozart. Beaumarchais was chronically engaged in litigation, about which he wrote many witty pamphlets, and also was in the secret service of the monarchy. His dealings with Silas DEANE and Arthur LEE led to the estab. of his mock firm, Hortalès & Cie, which furnished arms to the American revolutionists (1776–77). Repayment was delayed until 1835, when the U.S. Congress made a grant to his heirs. Another costly venture was a 70-vol. edition of Voltaire (1784–90).

Beaumont, Francis (bō'mŏnt), 1584?–1616, English dramatist. *The Woman Hater* (1606) and *The Knight of the Burning Pestle* (c.1608) show traces of John FLETCHER, with whom he began collaborating by 1610 to produce *Philaster* (1608?–1610?), *A King and No King* (1611), and other romantic tragicomedies.

Beaumont, William, 1785–1853, American physician, author of work (1833) which revolutionized knowledge of digestive process. Observations based on case of Alexis St. Martin, victim of stomach wound leaving an opening to exterior of body.

Beaumont, city (pop. 94,014), SE Texas, on Neches R. (arm of Sabine-Neches Waterway) and ENE of Houston; settled before 1835. Industrial and transportation center of oil and agr. area, it has refineries, rice mills, mfg. of paper, synthetic rubber, and metal products, and shipbuilding. Deepwater channel to city completed 1916.

Beaune (bōn), town (pop. 11,022), Côte-d'Or dept., E France, in Burgundy. Wine center. Once a residence of dukes of Burgundy. The Hôtel Dieu hospital (founded 1443) contains Roger van der Weyden's *Last Judgment*.

Romanesque church with Flemish tapestries; Hôtel de la Rochepot (c.1501).

Beauport, town (pop. 5,390), S Que., Canada, on St. Lawrence R. and NE of Quebec. One of oldest communities in Canada, settled 1634. French repulsed Wolfe's attacks here (1759) in Quebec campaign.

Beauregard, Pierre Gustave Toutant, 1818–93, Confederate general. Commander in NE Va., second in command at first battle of Bull Run. Defended coast of S.C. and Ga., and supported R. E. Lee in Va., especially at Petersburg. Stronger as engineer than as field commander.

Beauséjour, Fort, national park in SE N.B., Canada, (81 acres; estab. 1926), WNW of Amherst, N.S. Built 1751–55 by French; captured in 1755 by British and American troops under Gen. Monckton.

Beauvais (bōvā'), city (pop. 20,910), cap. of Oise dept., N France. Famous until World War II as tapestry mfg. center. War damage virtually wiped out center of city, a gem of medieval architecture. Famous cathedral (partly damaged) was begun 1227 as highest building in Christendom; choir vault (154 ft.; highest of Gothic vaults) fell 1284 but was reinforced; nave uncompleted.

Beaux-Arts, École des: see ÉCOLE DES BEAUX-ARTS.

Beaver. 1 Town (pop. 1,495), NW Okla., on North Canadian R. in Panhandle. Was cap. (1887) of Territory of CIMARRON. **2** Residential borough (pop. 6,360), W Pa., NW of Pittsburgh. Site of Fort McIntosh (1778), first U.S. military post N of the Ohio.

beaver, rodent, family Castoridae, of Europe, North America. Has thick fur, round head, small ears, scaly, flattened tail (c.10 in. long, c.6 in. wide), webbed hind feet, and body c.30 in. long. Weighs 40–50 lb. Tail is used as rudder when swimming, for support while gnawing tree, or to slap water to warn other beavers of danger. American beaver *Castor canadensis* usually builds twig and mud "lodges" with underwater entrances. If water is too shallow, makes dam of tree trunks or mud. *C. fiber* found in small numbers in parts of Europe.

Beaverbrook, William Maxwell Aitken, 1st Baron, 1879–, British statesman and newspaper owner. A Canadian, he amassed a fortune before going to England. Since 1917 his newspapers (*Daily Express, Sunday Express,* and *Evening Standard*) have thundered out his Imperialist views. Held several posts in Churchill's wartime cabinet 1940–45.

Beaver Dam, locality, S Ont., Canada, S of St. Catherines. Scene of a British victory, June 24, 1813, in War of 1812.

Beaver Dam, city (pop. 11,867), central Wis., SW of Fond du Lac and on Beaverdam L.; settled 1841. Mfg. of shoes and stoves.

Beaver Falls, city (pop. 17,375), W Pa., on Beaver R. and NW of Pittsburgh; settled c.1793. Chinaware and metal and cork products. Seat of Geneva Col. (Reformed Presbyterian; coed.; 1848).

Beaver Island, 13 mi. long, c.3–6 mi. wide, off N Mich., in L. Michigan NNW of Charlevoix (connected by ferry and plane). Largest of Beaver Archipelago; has lakes, beaches, and a harbor at St. James village. Inhabitants mainly fishermen. J. STRANG had Mormon settlement here 1847–56.

Bebel, August (ou'gōost bā'bŭl), 1840–1913, German Socialist. Helped found German Social Democratic party (1869); promoted its union with Lassallean socialists (1875).

Bec (bĕk), former Benedictine abbey, N France, in Normandy, S of Rouen. Founded 11th cent. Lanfranc taught here, Anselm was abbot. Fell into ruin after suppression in French Revolution.

Beccafumi, Domenico di Pace (dōmā'nēkō dē pä'chä bĕk-käfōō'mē), 1486–1551, Italian artist. Designed famous pavement of Siena cathedral 1517–46.

Beccaria, Cesare Bonesana, marchese di (chä'zärä bōnäzä'nä märkā'zä dē bĕk-kärē'ä), 1738–94, Italian economist, jurist, and criminologist. Brought about local economic reforms, but his notable contribution was bringing about penal reform throughout Europe. Also applied mathematics to economics.

Béchamp, Pierre Jacques Antoine (pyĕr' zhäk' ätwän' bäshä'), 1816–1908, French chemist, first to prepare aniline from nitrobenzene.

Becher, Johann Joachim (yō'hän yō'äkhĭm bā'khŭr), 1635–82, German chemist, cofounder of PHLOGISTON THEORY.

Bechuanaland (bĕchōōä'nŭlănd"), British protectorate (c.275,000 sq. mi.; pop. 296,883), S Africa; administered from Mafeking. Bounded on S by South Africa. Stock raising is main occupation. Nearly whole area is a native reservation. Under British protection since 1885.

Beck, Theodric (or Theodoric) Romeyn, 1791–1855, American physician, author of standard work (1823) on medical jurisprudence.

Becker, Carl Lotus, 1873–1945, American historian. Professor (1917–41) at Cornell Univ. Books include *The Eve of the Revolution* (1918) and *The Heavenly City of the Eighteenth-Century Philosophers* (1932).

Becket, Thomas: see THOMAS À BECKET, SAINT.

Beckford, William, 1760–1844, English author of an Oriental romance, *Vathek* (written in French; pub. in English, 1784). His spendthrift, dissolute life caused much scandal.

Beckley, city (pop. 19,397), W.Va., N of Bluefield, in coal area; chartered 1838.

Becknell, William: see SANTA FE TRAIL.

Beckwith, James Carroll, 1852–1917, American painter, best known for portraits.

Becque, Henry (ãrē' bĕk'), 1837–99, French dramatist. *The Vultures* (1882; Eng. tr., 1913) and *The Woman of Paris* (1885; Eng. tr., 1913) are mordant portraits of French bourgeois life.

Bécquer, Gustavo Adolfo (gōōstä'vō ädôl'fō bā'kĕr), 1836–70, Spanish lyric poet. Wrote subtle, dreamlike *Rimas.* Also prose *leyendas.*

Becquerel, Antoine César (ätwän' sāzär' bĕkûrĕl'), 1788–1878, French physicist. Pioneer in electrochemistry; studied telegraphy, magnetism. His son **Alexandre Edmond Becquerel** (älĕksä'drü ĕdmō'), 1820–91, also a physicist, professor at the Muséum d'Histoire naturelle, studied light, photochemistry, phosphorescence; invented phosphoroscope. **Antoine Henri Becquerel,** 1852–1908, son of Alexandre Edmond, discovered radioactivity in uranium and shared with the Curies the 1903 Nobel Prize in Physics.

bedbug, bug of order Hemiptera found over most of world. Common species *Cimex lectularius* is flat, reddish-brown, c.⅕ in. long; unpleasant odor; eats only blood. Attacks man, other mammals, poultry.

Beddoes, Thomas Lovell, 1803–49, English poet. Grotesque contrasted with delicate lyricism in poems (*The Improvisatore,* 1821; *The Bride's Tragedy,* 1822), play (*Death's Jest-Book; or, The Fool's Tragedy,* 1850).

Bede (bēd) or **Baeda** (bē'dŭ), 673?–735, English historian; Benedictine monk called Venerable Bede and St. Bede. Writings are summary of learning of his time. Best known for *Ecclesiastical History of the English Nation,* in Latin, often translated.

Bedford, dukes and earls of: see RUSSELL, family; JOHN OF LANCASTER.

Bedford, England: see BEDFORDSHIRE.

Bedford. 1 City (pop. 12,562), S Ind., near East Fork of White R. SSE of Bloomington; laid out 1826. Limestone-quarrying center. **2** Town (pop. 5,234), E Mass., NW of Boston. **3** Residential city (pop. 9,105), NE Ohio, SE of Cleveland. **4** Borough (pop. 3,521), S Pa., SE of Johnstown. Colonial fort (built c.1757) was Washington's hq. (1794) in Whisky Rebellion. Some colonial buildings remain.

Bedfordshire or **Bedford,** county (473 sq. mi.; pop. 311,844), S central England. More than four fifths of flat fertile area cultivated, mainly in market gardening. Luton, largest town, known for lace and straw plait mfg. Part of ancient kingdom of Mercia, region laid waste by King Canute. County town is **Bedford,** municipal borough (pop. 53,065), a market center on Ouse R. Has memorial chapel to John Bunyan, who preached here. Bedford School (estab. 1552) one of England's largest public schools.

Bédier, Joseph (zhōsĕf' bädyä'), 1864–1938, French authority on medieval literature. *Les Légendes épiques* (4 vols., 1908–13) developed a new theory of the origin of the great medieval romances.

Bedlam [i.e., Bethlehem], oldest English insane asylum, estab. c.1400 in Lambeth borough (London); after 1930 near Croydon.

Bedlington terrier: see TERRIER.

Bedloe's Island, N.Y.: see LIBERTY, STATUE OF.

Bedouin (bĕ'dōōĭn) nomad peoples of interior Arabia of Semitic stock. Devout believers in Islam. Economy based on cattle breeding.

bee, insect of the order Hymenoptera. There are several kinds of solitary bees. Best known of the social bees are the honeybee, especially *Apis mellifera* (or *mellifica*), of Old World origin, and the bumblebee, of the genus *Bombus.* Honeybees are invaluable agents of pollination and producers of HONEY and beeswax. Honeybee colony has a single queen (who mates once in her lifetime and lays countless eggs), thousands of sexually undeveloped workers, and a few hundred males (drones). Workers build wax cells, make honey, clean and defend hive, feed queen and larvae; life span is only about six weeks during active season. Use of bee's lancet (sting) on a human or animal usually kills insect. Stingless bees live in tropics. See *ill.*, p. 601.

bee balm: see OSWEGO TEA and LEMON BALM.

Beebe, William (bē'bē), 1877–, American scientist, explorer, author. Noted as curator of ornithology at New York Zoological Society and for underwater explorations in a bathysphere.

beech, large, deciduous tree (*Fagus*) of N Hemisphere. Edible nuts and smooth gray bark. Valued for timber and for landscaping (especially copper and purple varieties of European beech). American and European beeches are dominant forest trees.

Beecham, Sir Thomas, 1879–, English conductor. He introduced the operas of Richard Strauss into England and was a champion of the music of Delius.

Beecher, Lyman, 1775–1863, American Protestant minister in N.Y., Conn., and Mass. President (1832–52) of Lane Theological Seminary, Cincinnati. A founder (1816) of the American Bible Society and preacher of temperance. One daughter was Harriet Beecher STOWE. Another was **Catharine Esther Beecher,** 1800–1878, who promoted liberal education for women. One of Lyman's sons was **Henry Ward Beecher,** 1813–87, American Congregational minister, one of the great speakers of his time; pastor after 1847 of Plymouth Church, Brooklyn. Championed reforms (antislavery, woman suffrage). He was the center of a trial resulting from Theodore Tilton's accusing Beecher of adultery; the jury disagreed.

Beech Grove, suburban town (pop. 5,685), central Ind., near Indianapolis. Has railroad shops.

beef, flesh of CATTLE, prepared for food. In U.S. a chief product of MEAT PACKING industry. It is sold fresh (chilled), frozen, or cured. Finest carcasses go to retail butchers for cutting into consumers' portions; others yield such products as sausage, beef extract, pickled or corned beef, and potted and canned products.

Beefeaters, popular name for YEOMEN OF THE GUARD and for Tower of London warders. They both wear colorful Elizabethan uniforms.

Beelzebub (bēĕl'zĭbŭb), in Bible: see SATAN.

beer, one of oldest known alcoholic beverages. Brewing processes are similar in various countries but beer varies in color, flavor, alcoholic content (usually 3–6%). Mash of crushed malt (usually barley) and cereal adjuncts is heated and agitated, then the liquid is boiled with hops, cooled, liquid yeast is added, and fermentation is allowed to take place. Ale, in England, means any light-colored beer; in U.S. it is a pale, strongly hopped beverage. Porter is a strong, dark ale; stout is darker, stronger, and maltier than porter.

Beerbohm, Sir Max, 1872–, English satirist, caricaturist. Contributed to *Yellow Book,* was dramatic critic of the *Saturday Review.* Mordant satire shown in caricatures, in novel *Zuleika Dobson* (1911), and in sketches, literary and graphic.

Beer-Hofmann, Richard (rīkh'ärt bâr-hôf'-män), 1866–1945, Austrian poet and dramatist. Among his poems is *Schlaflied für*

Mirjam [cradle song for Miriam] (1898). *Der Graf von Charolais* (1904) is his first and best-known play. Lived in U.S. after 1939.

Beernaert, Auguste (ōgüst' bârnärt', bâr'närt), 1829–1912, Belgian statesman, prominent in Hague Peace Conferences of 1899 and 1907. Shared 1909 Nobel Peace Prize with Estournelles de Constant.

Beers, Clifford W(hittingham), 1876–1943, American founder of mental hygiene movement. Wrote autobiographical *A Mind That Found Itself* (1908).

Beersheba (bērshē'bù), town, S Israel, SW of Jerusalem. In Bible times Beersheba was S extremity of Palestine, Dan was N extremity; hence expression "from Dan to Beersheba." Especially associated with Abraham, Hagar, Isaac, and Elijah. Gen. 21.31; 26.33; Joshua 19.1,2; Judges 20.1; 1 Chron. 21.2; 2 Kings 23.8; 2 Chron. 19.4; Neh. 11.30.

beet, vegetable (*Beta vulgaris*), cultivated for its edible roots. Other varieties grown for edible leaves (e.g., Swiss chard), for cattle feed (e.g., mangelwurzel), and one, sugar beet, for beet sugar.

Beethoven, Ludwig van (bā'tōvùn), 1770–1827, German composer, b. Bonn. Among his teachers were Mozart and Haydn. He appeared as a solo pianist, but his growing deafness made a career as a virtuoso impossible. Most critics divide his compositions into three periods: the early years, lasting until 1801, when he was still mostly writing in the classic tradition; the middle period, lasting until 1814, when, although already beset with deafness, he wrote some of his greatest music, e.g., the Third (or Eroica) Symphony, the Fifth Symphony, the Sixth (or Pastoral) Symphony, the Fifth (or Emperor) Piano Concerto, and his one opera *Fidelio;* and the last years, beginning in 1817, when most of his music was composed in total deafness. Belonging to this final period are the Ninth Symphony, the *Missa Solemnis,* and the last five string quartets. Beethoven wrote much chamber music—16 string quartets; 10 sonatas for violin and piano, including the Ninth (or Kreutzer) Sonata; and 32 sonatas for piano. His orchestral compositions include a violin concerto, five piano concertos, and nine symphonies. The "Jena" symphony, attributed to him, is an early work and not counted among the nine. Beethoven is regarded as the last of the classic and the first of the romantic composers.

beetle, insect of order Coleoptera (includes c.180,000 species). North America has c.22,000 species. Most have two pairs of wings; modified front wings form thickened wing covers protecting body and membranous hind wings. Metamorphosis is complete; larva usually called a grub. Majority are terrestrial; few families aquatic. See BOLL WEEVIL; COLORADO POTATO BEETLE; FIREFLY; JAPANESE BEETLE; JUNE BEETLE; LADYBIRD; SCARAB; TUMBLEBUG; WIREWORM; WEEVIL. See also *ill.*, p. 601.

Beeville, city (pop. 9,348), S Texas, NW of Corpus Christi. Former cowtown, it is center of oil, cattle, and agr. area.

Begas, Karl Joseph (kärl' yō'zĕf bā'gäs), 1794–1854, German historical and portrait painter.

Beggars of the Sea: see GUEUX.

Beggar's Opera, The: see GAY, JOHN.

beggarweed, leguminous plant (*Desmodium purpureum*), grown in S U.S. for forage and for green manure.

Beghards (bĕg'ûrdz), religious associations of men, first known (1220) at Louvain, later widespread in Netherlands, Germany, France, and Italy. Organization was like that of BEGUINES. Charged by Council of Vienne (1311) with teaching that a man may attain such perfection that no later action of his may be considered sinful. Beghards lasted until 15th cent.

begonia, tropical perennial of genus *Begonia*. Showy single or double flowers (e.g., wax and tuberous types), succulent stems and leaves, often richly colored (e.g., rex begonias). Grown in beds and pots.

Beguines (bāgēn'), religious associations of women estab. in the Low Countries in 12th cent. They took no vows and lived by no rule, but did charitable work. In 13th and 14th cent. their communities (beguinages) came into disrepute and most were dissolved. Those remaining are almshouses (esp. for spinsters). See also BEGHARDS.

Beham (bā'häm), **Behem** (–hĕm), or **Peham** (pā'–), name of two engravers, among most famous of German Little Masters. Both banished 1525 from Nuremberg for free-thinking. **Hans Sebald Beham** (sā'bält), 1500–1550, was a pupil of Dürer. Best work depicted daily life. His brother, **Barthel Beham** (bär'tûl), 1502–40, was painter to Duke William of Bavaria.

behaviorism, explanation of human behavior entirely as physiological response to environmental stimuli. Introduced by J. B. Watson, 1912; based on mechanistic concepts of Democritus, Epicurus, and Thomas Hobbes; supported by conditioned-reflex experiments of Pavlov and Bekhterev. Watson denied value of introspection and consciousness as unscientific concepts, saw all mental processes as bodily movements. Influential in U.S. between World Wars.

Behem, artists: see BEHAM.

behemoth (bē'hǐmŏth) [Heb.,= plural of *beast*], animal mentioned in Job 40.15–24, possibly the hippopotamus (there are various theories).

Behistun (bähǐstōōn') or **Bisuntun** (bĕsōōtōōn'), village, W Iran, E of Kermanshah. Near by is mountainous rock with cuneiform inscriptions and bas-relief depicting Darius I. In 1835 Sir Henry Rawlinson scaled rock and copied writings, thus making it possible to decipher the Assyrian text and provide key for study of ancient Mesopotamia.

Behm, Ernst (bām'), 1830–84, German geographer and statistician of *Almanach de Gotha* (1876–84).

Behn, Aphra (bān, bĕn), 1640–89, English writer, supposedly b. Surinam. Her works, witty, coarse, and vigorous, include comedy *The Lucky Chance* (1686) and novel *Oroonoko* (1688).

Behrens, Peter (pā'tûr bā'rûns), 1868–1940, German architect, influential in the evolution of modern architectural style. Emphasized utilitarian aspect of design in his buildings in Vienna. Taught Le Corbusier and Walter Gropius.

Behring, Emil Adolph von (ā'mil ä'dôlf fûn bâr'ing), 1854–1917, German physician, pioneer in serum therapy. Won 1901 Nobel Prize in Physiology and Medicine for demonstrating immunization against diphtheria (1890) and tetanus (1892) by antitoxin injections.

Behrman, S(amuel) N(athaniel) (bâr'mûn), 1893–, American dramatist. Studied with George Pierce Baker. Among his plays, notable for literate and subtle dialogue, are *The Second Man* (1927), *Biography* (1932), and *No Time for Comedy* (1939).

Beira (bā'rû, bā'ĭrû), historic province, N central Portugal, S of the Douro; cap. Coimbra. It is now occupied by the provinces of Beira Alta (3,682 sq. mi.; pop. 662,616; cap. Viseu), Beira Baixa (2,897 sq. mi.; pop. 334,788; cap. Castelo Branco), and part of Beira Litoral (2,908 sq. mi.; pop. 896,719; cap. Coimbra). Largely mountainous, it has agr., vineyards, and olive groves. Was long contested between Portugal and Castile.

Beirut or **Beyrouth** (both: bārōōt'), anc. *Berytus*, city (pop. 181,271), cap. of Lebanon; port on Mediterranean at foot of Lebanon range. Ancient Phoenician trade center. Flourished under Seleucids, Romans, and Byzantines. Captured 635 by Arabs. Taken 1110 by Crusaders, it remained part of Latin Kingdom of Jerusalem until 1291. Controlled by Druses under Ottoman Empire. In 19th cent. it was a storm center of revolt of Mohammed Ali of Egypt. Seat of important American university.

Beisan (bāsän'), village, NE Israel, in Jordan valley, 322 ft. below sea level. Site of biblical BETH-SHAN. Has ruins dating from c.1500 B.C.

Bejapur, India: see BIJAPUR.

Béjart or **Béjard** (both: bāzhär'), French family of actors, a successful troupe associated (after 1643) with MOLIÈRE. Included Joseph (c.1616–1659), sisters Madeleine (1618–72; Molière's mistress) and Geneviève (1624–75), brother Louis (1630–78), and Madeleine's sister or daughter, Armande Grésinde (Molière's wife 1662; d. 1700). Absorption of two rival troupes resulted (1680) in COMÉDIE FRANÇAISE.

Beke, Charles Tilstone (bēk), 1800–1874, English traveler and author. Mapped much of Ethiopia, compiled vocabularies of 14 languages or dialects.

Bekescsaba or **Csaba,** Hung. *Békéscsaba* (bā'kĕshchŏ'bŏ), city (pop. 52,404), SE Hungary, in a silk-raising and tobacco-growing dist. Textile mfg.

Bekhterev, Vladimir Mikhailovich (vlŭdyē'mir mēkhī'lŭvĭch byĕkh' tyĭrîf), 1857–1927, Russian neurologist, psychologist. He studied localization of functions in brain areas and applied his study of conditioned reflexes in dogs to interpretation of human behavior. His emphasis on physiological nature of psychic phenomena influenced behaviorists.

Bel, deity of BABYLONIAN RELIGION; a form of BAAL. For Bel in Bible, see BEL AND THE DRAGON.

Bela IV (bē'lŭ, bā'lŭ), 1206–70, king of Hungary (1235–70). Defeated by Mongols at

Mohi 1241; invited foreigners to settle de-populated country after Mongols withdrew. His last years disturbed by rebellion of son, later King Stephen V.

Bel and the Dragon, name given to Daniel 14 in Western canon, a chapter placed in the Apocrypha in AV. Verses 1–22 tell how Daniel brilliantly outwitted the priests of the idol Bel. Verses 23–42 tell of a dragon or great beast who was worshiped as a god. Daniel killed the dragon and was thrown into the lions' den but was protected by God.

Belasco, David, 1853–1931, American actor, playwright, manager. Acted in plays ranging from *Hamlet* to *Uncle Tom's Cabin.* Prolific playwright, he excelled in collaboration with James HERNE, J. L. Long, H. C. De Mille, and others. As independent producer was famous for lighting and scenic effects. Built Stuyvesant, later Belasco, Theatre 1907.

Belém (búlãn'), city (pop. 230,181), cap. of Pará state, NE Brazil, on the Pará, chief port and metropolis of Amazon basin. Founded in 17th cent., city reached peak of prosperity in wild-rubber boom of early 20th cent. Sometimes called Pará.

Belfast, county borough (pop. 443,670), cap. of N. Ireland, in Co. Antrim and Co. Down. Has 8½-mi.-long harbor navigable to largest ships and great shipyards. Center of Irish linen industry, stimulated by French Hugue-nots. Had heavy air raids 1941. Seat of Queen's Univ. and Protestant cathedral. Parliament House at Stormont, a suburb.

Belfast, resort city (pop. 5,960), S Maine, on Penobscot Bay opposite Castine; settled 1770. Sacked by British, 1779 and 1814. Shipping center in 19th cent. Now has mfg. of marine supplies and shoes.

Belfort (búfôr', bĕ-, bĕl-), town (pop. 35,952), cap. of Territory of Belfort (235 sq. mi.; pop. 86,648), E France. Strategic fortress commanding Belfort Gap between Vosges and Jura mts. Huge statue, *Lion of Belfort,* by Bartholdi, commemorates resistance to siege (1870–71) in Franco-Prussian War. Belfort remained French when rest of Alsace went to Germany (1871).

Belgae: see GAUL.

Belgian Congo, colony (904,754 sq. mi.; pop. 10,962,799), equatorial Africa; cap. Leopold-ville. Belgium's only colony, it includes the UN trust territory RUANDA-URUNDI. Bordered on W by French Equatorial Africa along CONGO R. and on E by Tanganyika. Export-able wealth includes copper, uranium ore, diamonds, gold, and tin, with Katanga prov. as leading mining area. Main centers include Leopoldville, Stanleyville, and Elizabethville. Population consists mainly of Bantu tribes and Pygmies. In 1878 Henry STANLEY was commissioned by Leopold II of Belgium to make surveys of the area and conclude trea-ties with native rulers. Congo Free State was organized in 1885 (with Leopold as mon-arch). International protest against harsh treatment of natives led to area's annexation by Belgium in 1908.

Belgium (bĕl'jùm), Flemish *België,* Fr. *Bel-gique,* kingdom (11,779 sq. mi.; pop. 8,512,-195), NW Europe, bounded by North Sea and Netherlands (N), Germany and grand duchy of Luxembourg (E); and France (W); cap. Brussels. Constitutional mon-archy; bicameral legislature. Its nine prov-inces—Antwerp, Brabant, East Flanders, West Flanders, Hainaut, Liége, Limburg, Luxembourg, Namur—are partly self-gov-erning. BELGIAN CONGO is a valuable colony. Low-lying, except for ARDENNES plateau in S, Belgium is crossed by the MEUSE and SCHELDT rivers and by a dense network of canals and railroads. Truck farming and cattle raising are important, but Belgium is one of the world's most intensely industrial-ized countries. Mining (coal, zinc, iron) and steel and chemical industries are concen-trated in Sambre and Meuse valleys, at MONS, CHARLEROI, NAMUR, and LIÉGE. West Flanders and Hainaut have a huge textile industry, notably at Courtrai and Tournai. BRUSSELS, BRUGES, and MALINES are famed for their lace. ANTWERP and GHENT are major ports. Belgium is a leading nation in shipping and transit trade. Despite indus-trialization, the old cities of Belgium have retained many treasures of medieval archi-tecture and art. A language border running, roughly, E-W through Brussels divides the Flemish-speaking north from the French-speaking south (see also WALLOONS); Ger-man is spoken in EUPEN and MALMÉDY dists. The Church, with the archbishop of Malines as primate, plays a leading role in over-whelmingly Catholic Belgium. As sovereign state, Belgium dates only from 1831. It is named after the Belgae, a people of ancient GAUL. The cradle of the Carolingian dynasty, the region (except Flanders) was comprised in LOTHARINGIA and later in the duchy of Lower Lorraine, which by the 12th cent. had broken up into the duchies of BRABANT and LUXEMBOURG, the county of HAINAUT, and lesser feudal states. The history of these and of FLANDERS constitute the medieval history of Belgium. By the 15th cent. all of present Belgium had passed to the dukes of BUR-GUNDY. The death of MARY OF BURGUNDY (1482) opened three centuries of Hapsburg rule (see NETHERLANDS, AUSTRIAN AND SPANISH). In 1797 the area was annexed by France. The Treaty of Paris (1815) gave it to the Netherlands, but in 1830 Belgium rose against WILLIAM I and proclaimed its inde-pendence. LEOPOLD I, of the house of Saxe-Coburg-Gotha, was chosen king (1831); Anglo-French intervention stopped warfare with the Dutch (1832); peace was signed in 1839. Rapid industrialization under LEOPOLD II brought grave social problems. Belgian neutrality was violated by Germany in both world wars. In World War I Belgian forces under ALBERT I fought alongside the Allies even though Belgium was occupied by the Germans (1914–18). In World War II LEO-POLD III surrendered Belgium on May 28, 1940, after a disastrous two-week campaign; the Belgian government continued the fight from London as one of United Nations. Ger-man occupation brought a reign of terror. Liberated by the Allies and by Belgian under-ground fighters (Sept., 1944), war-scarred Belgium recovered quickly. The king's fitness to govern was a burning issue until Leopold abdicated in favor of his son BAUDOUIN (1951). In 1947 Belgium, the Netherlands and Luxembourg joined to form a customs union, the "Benelux" bloc, which entered a Five-Power-Pact with England and France (1948), took part in the European Recovery Program, and joined in the North Atlantic Treaty (1949).

Belgorod-Dnestrovsky (byĕl'gŭrŭd-dŭnyĕstrôf'-skē), Rumanian *Cetatea-Alba*, Turkish *Akkerman*, city (1930 pop. 20,907), S Ukraine, in Bessarabia. Port on mouth of Dniester. Founded as Tyras by Greek colonists 7th cent. B.C. Under Turks 1484–1812.

Belgrade, town (pop. 1,099), SW Maine, SW of Waterville. Hq. for Belgrade Lakes resort area.

Belgrade (bĕl'grād), Serbo-Croatian *Beograd*, city (pop. 388,246), cap. of Yugoslavia and of Serbia, on the Danube and the Sava. Seat of univ. (founded 1863), of Orthodox patriarch, and of archbishop (R.C.). The "key to the Balkans," it has been a strategic fortress since Roman times. Became cap. of Serbia in 12th cent.; repulsed Turks 1456; fell to Turks 1521; was stormed 1688, 1717, and 1789 by Austrians, who held it briefly (1717–39). Turkish garrison withdrew 1867. Occupied by Austrians in World War I, by Germans in World War II, when it was heavily damaged and suffered great hardship.

Belgrano, Manuel (mänwäl' bĕlgrä'nō), 1770–1820, Argentine revolutionist, member of first patriot governing junta (1810). Commander of Army of the North (1812–14; 1816–19), he was succeeded by San Martín.

Belgravia, fashionable section of London. Touches Buckingham Palace gardens and Hyde Park.

Belial (bē'lĕúl), name applied to SATAN.

Belinsky, Vissarion Grigoryevich (vĭsŭryôn' grĭgôr'yŭvĭch byĭlyĭn'skē), 1810–48, Russian writer. The founder of modern Russian literary criticism and a liberal, he championed Dostoyevsky and Turgeniev.

Belisarius (bĕlĭsâr'ēús), c.505–565, Byzantine general under Justinian I. Suppressed *Nika* rebellion (532). Defeated Vandals of Africa (533–34). Led expedition to recover Italy from Ostrogoths (535–40; 544–48); took Naples, Rome, Milan, Ravenna. Handicapped by political intrigue; replaced by NARSES 548. Drove Bulgarians from Constantinople (559). Briefly disgraced and imprisoned (562).

Belize (bŭlēz'), city (pop. 21,884), cap. and chief port of British Honduras, at mouth of Belize R.

Belknap, William Worth, 1829–90, U.S. Secretary of War (1869–76). Evidence that he had indirectly taken bribes led to his resignation; impeachment attempt failed.

Bell, Alexander Graham, 1847–1922, American scientist, inventor of telephone. Improved education for deaf, carrying forward the work of his father, Alexander Melville Bell. In 1865 conceived idea of transmitting speech by electric waves; developed principle in 1875 and transmitted first sentence 1876. Organized Bell Telephone Co. in 1877. Estab. Volta Laboratory, where first successful phonograph record was produced. Invented photophone to transmit speech by light waves, audiometer, induction balance to locate metallic objects in body, wax recorders

for phonographs, and tetrahedral kite. Influenced founding of *Science* (1880). Estab. Astrophysical Observatory at Smithsonian Institution and founded Aerial Experiment Association.

Bell, Andrew, 1753–1832, British educator. In Madras, India, he devised MONITORIAL SYSTEM.

Bell, Sir Charles, 1774–1842, Scottish anatomist and surgeon, first to distinguish between motor and sensory functions of nerves. His brother John Bell, 1763–1820, was a founder of modern blood vessel surgery.

Bell, Gertrude Margaret Lowthian, 1868–1926, English expert on Near East, traveler, author. Invaluable as liaison officer of Arab Bureau in Iraq and assistant political officer, largely responsible for selection of Feisal I as king.

Bell, Henry, 1767–1830, British ship designer, pioneer steamship builder. Introduced practical steam river navigation in Europe (1812).

Bell, John, surgeon: see BELL, SIR CHARLES.

Bell, John, 1797–1869, American statesman. U.S. Representative from Tenn. (1827–41); U.S. Senator (1847–59). Leader of conservative Southern element. Presidential candidate of CONSTITUTIONAL UNION PARTY 1860, he unintentionally helped elect Lincoln.

Bell, city (pop. 15,430), S Calif., near Los Angeles. Mfg. of steel and iron products.

bell, in music, a percussion instrument consisting of a hollow vessel usually cup-shaped, set into vibration by a blow from a clapper within or from a hammer without. A set of bells tuned to the intervals of the major scale is called a chime. A set with chromatic intervals is called a carillon. The bells of a carillon are stationary, are struck from without by a hammer, and are played from a keyboard. Carillon making developed in the Low Countries, reached its peak in the 18th cent., declined, revived at end of 19th cent., when English bellmakers rediscovered the tuning secrets used by 17th cent. craftsmen. In England, carillon playing was less popular than change ringing. In this practice a group of ringers, using a set of bells tuned to the diatonic scale, ring the bells by swinging them in full circle in various stated orders. Bells are of ancient origin and have been used in all major religions except Islam.

belladonna, Old World perennial (*Atropa belladonna*), in NIGHTSHADE family. Grown for narcotic poison (ATROPINE) used medicinally. See *ill.*, p. 999.

Bellaire. 1 City (pop. 12,573), E Ohio, on Ohio R. below Wheeling, W.Va.; settled c.1802. Has coal mining and mfg. of enamelware and glass products. **2** Suburb, S Texas, SW residential section (pop. 10,173) of Houston, absorbed 1948.

Bellamy, Edward (bĕ'lŭmĭ), 1850–98, American writer of novels and short stories, now known chiefly for *Looking Backward, 2000–1887* (1888). This utopian romance, representing the triumphantly socialistic state of A.D. 2000, had great influence immediately and later. "Nationalist" clubs, a monthly (1889–91) and a weekly periodical (1891–94) forwarded his socialist ideas.

Bellarmine (bĕlär'mĭn), 1542–1621, Italian cardinal, originally named Roberto Francesco Romolo Bellarmino; a Jesuit. His polemical works setting forth Catholic views against the Protestants and popular devotional works made him widely known. He greatly influenced the Catholic Reform.

Bellay, Joachim du: see DU BELLAY, JOACHIM.

Belle-Alliance (bĕl′-älyäs′), village near Waterloo, Belgium: see WATERLOO CAMPAIGN.

Belleau, Remy (rümē′ bĕlō′), 1528–77, French poet; one of the PLÉIADE.

Belleau Wood (bĕ′lō, bĕlō′), forested area, N France, E of Château-Thierry. Here U.S. troops stopped German advance in World War I (June, 1918).

Bellefontaine (bĕlfoun′tĭn), city (pop. 10,232), W central Ohio, N of Springfield; laid out 1820. Trade and rail center for farm area.

Bellefonte, borough (pop. 5,651), central Pa., NE of Altoona. Resort and farm trade town.

Belle Fourche, river, rising in NE Wyo., flowing N of Black Hills to Cheyenne R. in W central S.Dak. U.S. project uses Belle Fourche Dam and Keyhole Dam.

Belle Glade, town (pop. 7,219), S central Fla., W of Palm Beach near S tip of L. Okeechobee; founded c.1925. Trade center for truck area. Devastated by hurricane in 1928.

Belle-Isle, Charles Fouquet, duc de (shärl′ fōōkä′ dük′ dü bĕl-ēl′), 1684–1761, marshal of France. Noted for epic retreat from Prague (1742) in War of the Austrian Succession.

Belle Isle, Strait of, 10–15 mi. wide, 60 mi. long, between N.F. and Lab., Canada, N entrance to Gulf of St. Lawrence.

Bellerophon (bŭlĕ′rŭfŏn″, –fŭn), in Greek legend, hero who slew the CHIMERA. He accomplished this task with aid of winged horse Pegasus. Grown proud, he tried to fly to heaven on Pegasus, but was thrown and blinded—according to one legend, killed.

Belleville, city (pop. 19,519), S Ont., Canada, on Bay of Quinte. Port with mfg. of machinery and optical equipment. Seat of Albert Col.

Belleville. 1 City (pop. 32,721), SW Ill., adjoining East St. Louis, in coal, clay, sand area; platted 1815. Mfg. of stoves, clay products, and clothing. Scott Air Force Base near by. **2** Town (pop. 32,019), NE N.J., on Passaic R. just N of Newark; settled c.1680. Mfg. of machinery, chemicals, and leather.

Bellevue. 1 City (pop. 9,040), N Ky., near Ohio R., suburb of Covington and Cincinnati. **2** Village (pop. 3,858), E Nebr., on the Missouri and S of Omaha. Oldest town in state, it was estab. c.1823 as trading post. Site of a Presbyterian Indian mission (1848). **3** City (pop. 6,906), N Ohio, SW of Sandusky. Rail center in farm area. **4** Residential borough (pop. 11,604), SW Pa., near Pittsburgh; settled 1802.

bellflower or **campanula** (kămpăn′ūlù), plant of genus *Campanula* with bell- or star-shaped flowers, often blue. Species for rock gardens and borders include Canterbury bells, a biennial; HAREBELL; and the edible rampion.

Bellingham, port city (pop. 34,112), NW Wash., on Bellingham Bay, near Canada; settled 1852. Shipping and processing center for truck, fruit, salmon, coal, lumber, dairy products, and poultry. Gateway to recreational area.

Bellini (bĕl-lē′nē), family of Venetian painters of the Early Renaissance. **Jacopo Bellini** (yä′kōpō), c.1400–c.1464, was father and teacher of Giovanni and Gentile. **Giovanni Bellini** (jōvän′nē), c.1426–1516, became teacher of Giorgione and Titian. Serenity, majesty, and luminous color characterize his works, which include altarpieces in the Frari and San Zaccaría, Venice; *Feast of the Gods* (Natl. Gall., Washington, D.C.); *St. Francis* (Frick Coll., New York). **Gentile Bellini** (jäntē′lä), c.1427–c.1507, painted contemporary Venetian life and used Turkish subjects after visit to Constantinople.

Bellini, Vincenzo (vēnchän′tsō bĕl-lē′nē), 1801–35, Italian operatic composer. Among his operas are *Norma* and *La sonnambula* (both 1831).

Bellinzona (bĕl-lēntsō′nä), town (pop. 12,073), cap. of Ticino, S Switzerland, on Ticino R. Has several churches and castles dating from 15th–16th cent.

Bell Island (11 sq. mi.; pop. c.8,167), SE N.F., Canada, in Conception Bay. Bell Island town is oldest industrial center in N.F.

Bellman, Carl Michael, 1740–95, Swedish writer of drinking songs, pastorals, and comic songs.

Bellmawr (bĕl′mär′), residential borough (pop. 5,213), SW N.J., near Camden.

bell metal: see BRONZE.

Bello, Andrés (ändräs′ bä′yō), 1781–1865, South American intellectual leader, b. Venezuela. After 19 years in London (1810–29), he went to Chile, became leader in education. Wrote poems, works on grammar and law; forwarded American intellectual freedom.

Belloc, Hilaire (bĕl′ŏk), 1870–, British author, b. France. A poet, essayist, and biographer, he wrote many works, some of Roman Catholic apologetics.

Bellona (bŭlō′nù), in Roman religion, goddess of war. She was associated with Mars, and her temple stood in Campus Martius.

Bellows, George (Wesley), 1882–1925, American painter and lithographer. His work is marked by a direct, unself-conscious realism.

Bellows Falls, Vt.: see ROCKINGHAM.

Bellwood, residential village (pop. 8,746), NE Ill., near Chicago. Metal products plants.

Belmar, resort borough (pop. 4,636), E N.J., on the Atlantic S of Asbury Park.

Belmont. 1 City (pop. 5,567), W Calif., SE of San Francisco. Ships flowers. **2** Residential town (pop. 27,381), E Mass., NW suburb of Boston; settled 1636. **3** Town (pop. 5,330), W central N.C., on Catawba R. and W of Charlotte. In agr. piedmont region, it has textile mills and dye works.

Belmonte, Juan (hwän′ bĕlmōn′tä), 1892–, Spanish bullfighter.

Belo Horizonte (bĕl′ ōrēzŏnt′), city (pop. 346,207), cap. of Minas Gerais, E Brazil. A planned city built to replace Ouro Prêto as state cap. (1895), it handles minerals, cattle, agr. produce. Opening of hydroelectric plant (1946) speeded growth of industries.

Beloit (bĭloit′), city (pop. 29,590), S Wis., on Rock R. at Ill. line; founded c.1837. Mfg. of paper and metal products. Winter sports. Seat of **Beloit College** (non-sectarian; coed.), chartered 1846, organized 1847 by Congregationalists and Presbyterians; noted for anthropology courses.

Belorussia (byĕ″lŭrōō′sĕŭ) or **White Russia,** constituent republic (80,150 sq. mi.; pop. c.7,220,000), W European USSR; cap. Minsk. Largely a lowland, drained by Dnieper, Western Dvina, Niemen. PRIPET MARSHES in S. Agr., with chemical, textile, machinery industries. Population is 80% Belorussian, a Slavic group, influenced by Polish culture, partly Roman Catholic, partly Russian Orthodox. Region was part of Kievan Russia from 9th cent.; conquered by LITHUANIA 14th cent.; passed to Russia through Polish partitions of 1772–95. Treaty of Riga (1921) gave part to Poland. Belorussian SSR, founded 1919, joined USSR 1922, was nearly doubled in Polish partition of 1939. Joined U.N. 1945. Devastated in World War II. Also spelled Bielorussia, Byelorussia.

Belsen (bĕl′zùn), village, Lower Saxony, NW Germany, near Celle. Site of notorious concentration camp during Hitler regime.

Belshazzar (bĕlshăz′ûr), in Bible, son of Nebuchadnezzar, last king of Babylon. At his riotous feast, handwriting appeared on the wall and was interpreted by Daniel as sign of doom. That night Babylon fell to Cyrus. Dan. 5. Identity of Belshazzar uncertain. May be same as Nabonidus (last king of Babylon but unrelated to Nebuchadnezzar) or possibly Belshar-uzur (royal governor but not a king).

Belt, Great, and **Little Belt,** shallow straits connecting Kattegat with Baltic Sea. Great Belt, c.10 mi. wide, separates Zealand and Fyn isls., Denmark. Little Belt, ½–c.20 mi. wide, between Fyn and Jutland, is crossed by railroad and road bridge.

Belteshazzar (–shăz′–), Babylonian name of DANIEL.

Belton, city (pop. 6,246), central Texas, W of Temple. Farming market center. Seat of Mary Hardin-Baylor Col. (Baptist; women; 1845; connected with Baylor Univ.). Prehistoric skeletons and artifacts have been found near by.

Belvedere (bĕl′vŭdēr), a gallery and court of the Vatican, Rome, containing the *Apollo Belvedere* and the *Laocoön;* built 1490. A palace by this name in Vienna houses the Mus. of History and Art.

Belvidere, city (pop. 9,422), N Ill., E of Rockford. Trade center of agr. area, it has mfg. of food and metal products.

Bely, Andrei (ŭndrā′ byĕ′lē), pseud. of Boris Nikolayevich Bugayev, 1880–1934, Russian poet, a leading symbolist. Besides poetry (collected in *Symphonies,* 4 vols., 1901–8), he wrote rich, masterful novels, notably *The Silver Dove* (1910) and *Petersburg* (1912).

Bembo, Pietro (pyä′trō bĕm′bō), 1470–1547, Italian humanist, cardinal of the Roman Church, secretary of Leo X. Arbiter of literary taste, he insisted on preserving classic traditions.

Bemidji (bùmĭj′ē), city (pop. 10,001), N central Minn., on Bemidji L.; settled c.1892. The Mississippi flows through lake. Resort and farm trade center in lake and forest region.

Bemis Heights, battle of: see SARATOGA CAMPAIGN.

Benaiah (bēnā′yù), heroic warrior, loyal follower of David and Solomon. 2 Sam. 8.18; 20.23; 23.20–23; 1 Kings 1; 2; 1 Chron. 11.22–25; 18.17; 27.5,6.

Benalcázar, Sebastián de (sāvästyän′ dā bānälkä′thär), c.1479–1551, Spanish conquistador. Accompanied Columbus on third voyage (1498), served in Darien and Nicaragua, then joined Pizarros in conquest of Peru (1532). From 1533 to 1550 was active in conquest of present Ecuador and Colombia.

Benares (bùnä′rĭz), city (pop. 263,100), SE Uttar Pradesh, India, on Ganges R. Great Hindu center since 6th cent. B.C. Also sacred to Buddhists and Jains. Annually c.1,000,000 pilgrims visit numerous ghats and shrines stretching 4 mi. along Ganges R. Site of Golden Temple (1777) and Aurangzeb's mosque. Rail and trade center. Textiles, brassware, jewelry industries. Hindu university.

Benavente (y Martínez), Jacinto (häthēn′tō bā″nävän′tä ē märtē′nĕth), 1866–, Spanish dramatist. Notable works are the farce *Los intereses creados* (1907; Eng. tr., *Bonds of Interest,* 1917) and the rural drama *La malquerida* (1913). Awarded 1922 Nobel Prize in Literature.

Benbow, William, fl. 1825–40, English pamphleteer. Introduced theory of the general strike.

Benchley, Robert (Charles), 1889–1945, American humorist. Long the dramatic critic of *Life* (1920–29) and the *New Yorker* (1929–40), he is better known for gently sardonic short pieces, collected in such volumes as *Of All Things* (1921) and *My Ten Years in a Quandary* (1936). He wrote, directed, and acted in humorous film shorts.

Bend, city (pop. 11,409), W central Oregon, on Deschutes R. just E of Cascade Range. Trade center for lumber, irrigated-farm, and resort area.

Benda, Julien (zhülye′ bādä′), 1867–, French novelist and critic. A humanist, he attacked the aesthetic philosophy of Bergson. *The Yoke of Pity* (1912; Eng. tr., 1913), a novel, won immediate recognition. *The Treason of the Intellectuals* (1927; Eng. tr., 1928) stated the theory that the thinker in pursuit of truth should disregard practical consequences.

Bendemann, Eduard Julius Friedrich (ā′dōōärd″ yōō′lyōōs frēd′rĭkh bĕn′dùmän), 1811–89, German Jewish historical and portrait painter.

Bender (bĕn′dùr), Rumanian *Tighina,* Rus. *Bendery,* city (1930 pop. 31,384), S Moldavian SSR, in Bessarabia. Conquered by Turks 1538. Residence of CHARLES XII of Sweden 1709–13.

Bendigo (bĕn′dĭgō), municipality (pop. 26,739; metropolitan pop. 30,779), Victoria, Australia; founded 1851. Formerly an important mining town, now a wheat-trading center.

Bendix, N.J.: see TETERBORO.

bends: see CAISSON DISEASE.

Benedetti, Vincent, Comte (vēsā′ kōt′ bānādĕt′tē), 1817–1900, French ambassador to Prussia (1864–70). His interview with William I at Ems was published by Bismarck in an altered version (see EMS DISPATCH) which precipitated Franco-Prussian War.

Benedetto da Majano (bānādĕt′tō dā mäyä′nō), 1442–97, Florentine sculptor. Chief work is altarpiece in Church of Monte Oliveto at Naples.

Benedict, Saint, d. c.547, Italian monk, founder of the Benedictines, b. Norcia (or Nursia). Became a hermit at Subiaco, where monks gathered around him. Later founded first Benedictine monastery, at MONTE CASSINO, and created the Rule of St. Benedict, the chief rule of Western monasticism. Feast: March 21.

Benedict XIII, antipope: see LUNA, PEDRO DE.

Benedict XIV, 1675–1758, pope (1740–58), b. Bologna; originally named Prospero Lambertini. He was renowned for learning, for patronizing art, and for protecting Eastern Catholic rites from Latinization.

Benedict XV, 1854–1922, pope (1914–22), b. Genoa; originally named Giacomo della Chiesa. In World War I, he kept the Vatican neutral and strenuously tried to restore peace.

Benedict, Ruth (Fulton), 1887–1948, American anthropologist. Student and colleague of Franz Boas at Columbia Univ. Contributed to enlarging scope of anthropology through work on concept of culture motif and relation of personality to culture. Her works include *Patterns of Culture* (1934).

benedictine (bĕnŭdĭk'tēn), sweet, brown LIQUEUR originated in 1510 by Benedictine monks in France.

Benedictines, monks of the Roman Catholic Church, estab. at MONTE CASSINO by St. BENEDICT, whose rule they follow. Unlike earlier groups they stress communal living, and their abbeys are like homes of Christian families with abbots as fathers. Their waking hours are devoted principally to worship and work—chiefly manual work, though the Benedictines did much to preserve learning through the early Middle Ages. Many notable missionaries were Benedictines (e.g., St. Augustine of Canterbury, St. Boniface), and with urging of Pope Gregory I (a Benedictine himself) and others, the abbeys were spread across Europe as outposts of civilization. Among these were St. Gall, Fulda, Solesmes, Monserrat, and St. Albans. Later reforms created new orders within the general Benedictine family—the CLUNIAC ORDER, the CISTERCIANS, and the TRAPPISTS (Cistercians of the Stricter Observance).

benefice, in feudal law, an estate held for life, a non-hereditary fief. The term early became restricted to ecclesiastical holdings—usually an income attached to an office or a position or to a particular parish or cure. Since the benefice was usually granted by a layman, it posed serious problems of lay control in the Church and led to many abuses in the late Middle Ages. The Council of Trent disestablished them in the Roman Catholic Church. Benefices continue in England for the holding of rectories, vicarages, and the like (not for simple offices).

Bene Israel or **Beni Israel** (both: bā'nē) [Heb.,= sons of Israel], Jewish community (c.15,000) of Bombay. India, possibly dating from 2d cent. A.D. In the last 200 years, a program of Jewish education has greatly changed the once Hindulike customs of this group.

Benelux, name of the customs union of Belgium, the Netherlands, and Luxembourg, estab. 1947 and in force after 1948.

Benes, Eduard, Czech Beneš (bĕ'nĕsh), 1887–1948, Czech statesman. Chief collaborator of T. G. Masaryk, he was foreign minister (1918–35), premier (1921–22), president of the republic (1935–38; 1945–48), and leader of the National Socialist (i.e., liberal) party. The Franco-Czech alliance and LITTLE ENTENTE were mainly his work. Exiled after the MUNICH PACT, he headed the Czech provisional government at London during World War II; was reelected president of liberated Czechoslovakia; resigned after Communist coup d'état of 1948.

Benét, Stephen Vincent (bĕnā'), 1898–1943, American poet, novelist, and short-story writer. He is especially noted for his vigorous use of American historical and folk materials as in his long Civil War poem, *John Brown's Body* (1928); poems for children in *A Book of Americans* (1933 with his wife, Rosemary Benét); his unfinished epic *Western Star* (1943); and notable short stories such as "Johnny Pye and the Fool-Killer" and "The Devil and Daniel Webster." His brother, **William Rose Benét,** 1886–1950, was also a poet, author of many romantic lyrics and ballads and other narrative poems. He was an editor of *Century Magazine,* the *Saturday Review of Literature* (which he helped found 1924), and a volume called *The Reader's Encyclopedia* (1948). *The Dust Which Is God* (1941) is verse autobiography. Also wrote essays and novels. Elinor Wylie was his second wife.

Benevento (bĕnŭvĕn'tō), city (pop. 26,692), Campania, S Italy. Was important Roman town on Appian Way; cap. of powerful Lombard duchy (6th–11th cent.); later under papal rule. Many Roman remains. Church of Santa Sofia (8th cent.). Heavy damage in World War II.

Ben Ezra: see IBN EZRA, ABRAHAM BEN MEIR.

Bengal (bĕng-gôl'), region in NE India and E Pakistan, on Bay of Bengal. Mostly in Ganges-Brahmaputra delta between Bihar and Assam. Himalayan forests in N., Sundarban jungles in S. The British took Bengal from Mogul empire in 1764. Divided 1947 between India and Pakistan. **East Bengal,** province (54,501 sq. mi.; pop. 42,119,000), is coextensive with E Pakistan; cap. Dacca. Includes large jute-growing area. **West Bengal,** state (29,476 sq. mi.; pop. 24,786,683) of India; cap. Calcutta. Includes former native state of Cooch Behar. Contains industrial area and large coal fields.

Bengal, Bay of, arm, c.1,300 mi. long and c.1,000 mi. wide, of Indian Ocean, with India on W and Burma and Malaya on E.

Bengali (bĕngäl'ē), Indo-European language. See LANGUAGE (table).

Bengasi or **Benghazi** (both: bĕngä'zē), city (pop. 56,325), Cyrenaica, Libya; Mediterranean port. In World War II it was captured and held by the British in Dec., 1942.

Ben-Gurion, David (bĕn-gōō'rĭŏn), 1886–, Israeli statesman, prime minister of Israel (1948–), b. Poland. Fled to Palestine after pogroms of 1905. Exiled by Turks for Zionist and pro-British activity in World War I. Helped organize Jewish Legion which fought on British side in Palestine and was later a Jewish leader there. First prime minister of Israel (1948), he again won the post in 1952.

Benhadad (–hā′dăd), kings of Damascus. **1** Fl. 890 B.C., ally of Asa of Judah against Baasha of Israel. 1 Kings 15.17–20. **2** Fl. 854 B.C., continued traditional enmity with Israel and defeated Ahab and Jehoshaphat. Murdered and suceeded by Hazael. 1 Kings 20; 22; 2 Kings 8.15. **3** Fl. 800 B.C., son of Hazael. Defeated Jehoash of Israel. 2 Kings 13.25; Amos 1.4.

Benicia (bŭnī′shù), city (pop. 7,284), W Calif., port on Carquinez Strait NE of Oakland. U.S. army ordnance depot and arsenal are here.

Beni Hassan (bĕ′nē hä′sän), village, central Egypt, on the Nile. Has 39 rock-cut tombs of XII dynasty of ancient Egypt.

Beni Israel: see BENE ISRAEL.

Benjamin, youngest son of Jacob and Rachel, eponymous ancestor of one of 12 tribes of Israel. Tribe occupied E central Palestine. Tribesmen were noted archers. Famous son of house of Benjamin was Saul. Gen. 35.18; 42–46; 49.27; Num. 1.36; 13.9; 26.38–41; 34.21; Deut. 33.12; Joshua 18.11–28; Judges 3.15; 20–21; 1 Chron. 8.40; 12.2; 2 Chron. 14.8; 17.17.

Benjamin, Asher, 1773–1845, American architect. Books popularized details of Late Colonial style.

Benjamin, Judah Philip, 1811–84, Confederate statesman and British barrister, b. Virgin Isls. Ably defended Southern policy as U.S. Senator (1853–61). In Southern government he was successively attorney general, secretary of war, and secretary of state. Known in North as "the brains of the Confederacy." On its collapse in 1865, he escaped to England, where he became prominent lawyer.

Benjamin of Tudela (tōōdā′lä), d. 1173, Spanish rabbi, author of an account of a journey to China (Eng. tr., *Itinerary of Benjamin of Tudela*).

Ben Macdhui or **Ben Muich-Dhui** (măkdōō′ē), peak, 4,296 ft. high, Aberdeenshire, Scotland; second highest peak in Scotland.

Bennet, Henry: see ARLINGTON, HENRY BENNET, 1st EARL OF.

Bennett, (Enoch) Arnold, 1867–1931, English naturalistic novelist. Among his many novels, *The Old Wives' Tale* (1908), and a trilogy of life in the "Five Towns."

Bennett, Floyd, 1890–1928, American aviator. In 1926, with Byrd, flew nonstop Spitsbergen to North Pole and return, first flight over either pole. Appointed second in command of Byrd's antarctic expedition, but died of pneumonia contracted on *Bremen* rescue flight.

Bennett, James Gordon, 1795–1872, American journalist, b. Scotland. Coming to the U.S. in 1819, he won fame as a reporter. He founded (1835) the New York *Herald*, which he made a phenomenal popular success, increasing the field of news (e.g., with financial news, with reports of foreign correspondents, with accent on detailed accounts of crimes and sensations), using the telegraph and other means to speed reporting, and employing illustrations. In 1867 he relinquished control of the *Herald* to his son,

James Gordon Bennett, 1841–1918, who also founded the *Evening Telegram* and London and Paris daily editions of the *Herald*. He stressed international news and attention-getting "stunts" (e.g., financing Stanley's expedition to Africa in order to find David Livingstone and G. W. De Long's Arctic expedition). He helped found Commercial Cable Co. Was also a yachtsman and gave a trophy for international yacht races.

Bennett, Richard Bedford, 1870–1947, Canadian prime minister (1930–35), leader of Conservative party. Urged preferential tariff for the empire, and saw policy adopted 1932.

Bennettsville, town (pop. 5,140), NE S.C., NE of Columbia. Trade and processing center in agr. area. Mfg. of aircraft parts.

Ben Nevis (nĕ′vĭs, nĕv′ĭs), peak, 4,406 ft. high, Inverness-shire, Scotland; highest peak in Great Britain. NE side has precipice of more than 1,450 ft.

Bennington, town (pop. 12,411), SW Vt., NE of Albany, N.Y.; chartered 1749 as a N.H. town (first W of Connecticut R.); settled 1761. Includes industrial Bennington village (pop. 8,002; textiles, paper); North Bennington village (pop. 1,327), seat of **Bennington College** (nonsectarian; for women; chartered 1925, opened 1932), a leading experimental col. with program of self-dependent education and a noted summer school of modern dance; and historic Old Bennington village (pop. 198), now a resort. Has shaft commemorating battle of Bennington (see SARATOGA CAMPAIGN); marked site of Catamount Tavern, rendezvous of Green Mountain Boys; and Old First Church (1806; restored 1937 as state monument). Prized stoneware was made at Bennington from late 18th to late 19th cent.

Benois, Aleksandr Nikolayevich (bĕnōōä′), 1870–, Russian painter. Did scenery for Diaghilev's ballet productions, notably *Petrouchka*.

Benoît de Sainte-More or **Benoît de Sainte-Maure** (bùnwä′ dù sĕt-môr′), fl. 1175, French TROUVÈRE. His *Roman de Troie*, a romance based on Dares and Dictys, became source of medieval version of the Trojan legend, notably of TROILUS AND CRESSIDA.

Benson, Ezra Taft, 1899–, U.S. Secretary of Agriculture (1953–). Marketing specialist; executive secretary of Natl. Council of Farmer Cooperatives (1939–44). Official in Mormon Church.

Bent, Charles, 1799–1847, American frontiersman. Led expeditions on Santa Fe Trail. Member of famous trading firm. His brother, **William Bent,** 1809–69, also a trader and frontiersman, was long the manager of BENT'S FORT.

bent grass, any species of genus *Agrostis*, slender, delicate grasses. Grown for pasture, hay, lawn (e.g., creeping bent, established by planting stolons).

Bentham, George (bĕn′thùm), 1800–1884, English botanist, a great systematist.

Bentham, Jeremy, 1748–1832, English philosopher, founder of utilitarianism, which holds that the goal of social ethics is to achieve the greatest good (i.e., pleasure) of the greatest number. In his influential studies of political theory he urged that political institutions and laws should serve social ethics. He argued for political democracy but not for the economic equality of all. Wrote *Principles of Morals and Legislation* (1789; second part, *The Limits of Jurisprudence Defined,* pub. 1945).

Bentinck, William: see PORTLAND, WILLIAM BENTINCK, 1st EARL OF.

Bentley, Richard, 1662–1742, English philologist, generally considered greatest of English classical scholars. His exposure of a 2d-cent. forgery, *The Epistles of Phalaris,* gained notice.

Benton, Thomas Hart, 1782–1858, American statesman. U.S. Senator from Mo. (1821–51) and U.S. Representative (1853–55). Supported currency measures to benefit common man; drew up Pres. Jackson's Specie Circular (1836). Supported all legislation favoring Western development and aiding settlers. Opposed extension of slavery. His grandnephew is **Thomas Hart Benton,** 1889–, American painter. Dramatized American themes (notably in his murals) with characterizations of popular types.

Benton. 1 City (pop. 6,277), central Ark., SW of Little Rock. Mfg. of furniture and pottery. Bauxite mines. **2** City (pop. 7,848), S Ill. S of Mount Vernon. Agr. and coal-mining center. **3** Town (pop. 1,980), SW Ky., SE of Paducah. Has annual Southern Harmony Singing Festival (since 1884) and "Tater Day" (potatoes).

Benton Harbor, city (pop. 18,769), SW Mich., on L. Michigan at mouth of St. Joseph R. opposite St. Joseph city; settled c.1840. In rich fruitgrowing area, it is a resort with mineral springs. Municipal fruit market here said to be nation's largest. Has mfg. of metal products. Religious colony, House of David (founded 1903), has business and farm holdings here; its rival, Israelite City of David, is near by. Annual Blossom Festival held with St. Joseph.

bentonite: see CLAY.

Bent's Fort, noted trading post of the American West, on Arkansas R. in present SE Colo., E of La Junta. The successful trading company headed by Charles Bent and Ceran St. Vrain estab. post here in 1828 after founding it near by in 1826. Fort (often called Bent's Old Fort) completed 1832. On the mountain branch of Santa Fe Trail, it dominated trade with Indians, Mexicans, Americans. Kit Carson hunted here 1831–42. American troops used it briefly in Mexican War. Tradition says that manager William Bent blew it up. He built Bent's New Fort further downstream in 1852 or 1853, leased it to U.S. in 1859. Fort destroyed by flood shortly thereafter and replaced by new army fort.

Benzedrine, drug used to stimulate higher nerve centers. Should be used only on prescription.

benzene (běn'zēn) or **benzol** (běn'zōl), colorless liquid, aromatic odor, boils at 80.1°C., solidifies at 5.48°C. Molecule has six carbons arranged in ring, with one hydrogen attached to each. First in series of aromatic hydrocarbons, **benzene series;** all from coal tar. Used to make dyes, explosives, synthetic drugs, perfumes, lacquers, and as organic solvent. Derivatives are carbolic acid, picric acid, nitrobenzene, and aniline.

benzine (běn'zēn), colorless inflammable liquid mixture of hydrocarbons chiefly of methane (not benzene) series; obtained from petroleum by fractional distillation. Used as cleaning agent, organic solvent; used in some dyes and paints.

benzoate of soda: see SODIUM BENZOATE.

benzoic acid (běnzō'ĭk), solid, crystalline, organic acid. Used as antiseptic, as starting point for organic syntheses, in making dyes.

benzoin (běn'zoin), balsamic RESIN, dried exudate from pierced bark of benzoin tree (*Styrax*). Used in perfumery, incense, and in medicine.

benzol: see BENZENE.

Ben-Zvi, Itzhak (yĭts'häk běn-tsvē'), 1884–, Israeli statesman and Orientalist, second president of Israel, b. Russia. An active Zionist, he emigrated 1907 to Palestine, where he worked closely with Ben-Gurion. Succeeded Chaim Weizman as president of Israel, 1952.

Beograd, Yugoslavia: see BELGRADE.

Beowulf (bā'ŭwŏŏlf), oldest English epic, probably composed early 8th cent. by Anglian bard in the vicinity of Northumbria. Materials for the poem mainly from Scandinavian history, folk tale, mythology, and the events take place in Denmark and Sweden. In the first part the young hero kills water monster Grendel and Grendel's mother; in second, at end of long life of honor, he conquers a dragon and dies. Written in strongly accentual, alliterative verse.

Béranger, Pierre Jean de (pyěr' zhä' dü bārāzhä'), 1780–1857, French poet, author of many popular songs. Like Burns he fitted his verse to existing melodies. Many of his songs helped to further the Napoleonic legend.

Berar, India: see MADHYA PRADESH.

Berat (běrät'), town (pop. 11,872), S central Albania, probably on site of anc. Antipatrea. Has 13th-cent. Byzantine citadel, 15th-cent. mosque.

Berbers, aboriginal peoples of N Africa. Moslems, they speak Arabic and Hamitic tongues. Economy is based on agr.

Berceo, Gonzalo de (gônthä'lō dā běrthä'ō), 1180?–1247?, Spanish poet, Benedictine monk. His are the earliest-known poems in vernacular.

Berchtesgaden (běrkh'tùsgä"dùn), winter and summer resort, S Bavaria, in Bavarian Alps. Favorite residence of Hitler, who built a retreat on the Obersalzberg.

Berchtold, Leopold, Graf von (lā'ōpôlt gräf fün běrkh'tôlt), 1863–1942, Austro-Hungarian foreign minister (1912–15). Directed the policy which precipitated WORLD WAR I after assassination of Archduke FRANCIS FERDINAND.

Berdyaev, Nicholas (běrdyī'ùf), 1874–1948, Russian Orthodox religious philosopher, in exile from Russia after 1922. Early a Marxist, he later stressed the need for spiritual meaning and direction in individual life and in history.

Berea or **Beroea** (both: bērēù'), Greek name of three places in Bible. **1** Syrian camp. **2** Mac. 9.4. **2** See VEROIA, Macedonia. **3** See ALEP, Syria.

Berea (bùrē'ù). **1** Town (pop. 3,372), central Ky., SSE of Lexington. Seat of Berea Col. (nonsectarian; coed.); opened 1855 by J. G.

FEE, chartered 1866, became college 1869. Town utilities and other businesses are owned by school and operated by students. Products of crafts classes are sold. Has extension services, schools for mountain people, and land holdings. **2** City (pop. 12,051), NE Ohio, SW of Cleveland; settled 1809. Seat of Baldwin-Wallace Col.

Berengar II (bĕ'rĭng-gŭr), d. 966, marquis of Ivrea. Made himself king of Italy in 950. His designs on Adelaide led to intervention of Emperor OTTO I. He swore fealty to Otto (952) but continued his intrigues until Otto imprisoned him (963).

Berengar of Tours, c.1000–1088, French theologian, head of the cathedral school at Tours. He was widely known as a dialectician, but his views on the Eucharist were considered radical and suspect by some theologians though approved by others (Leo IX and Gregory VII early defended him). A very bitter quarrel with LANFRANC led Berengar to an angry reply rejecting authority. This was condemned, and Berengar was declared a heretic. Also Bérenger, Berengarius.

Berenice (bĕrŭnī'sē), members of royal family of Egypt. **1** Born c.340 B.C., consort and half sister of Ptolemy I. **2** Died 246 B.C., daughter of Ptolemy II, wife of ANTIOCHUS II. After the death of her husband, she and her infant son were murdered by Seleucus II before her brother, Ptolemy III, arrived with aid. **3** Died 221? B.C., a Cyrenian, wife of Ptolemy III; joint ruler with her son Ptolemy IV, who had her murdered. The constellation Berenice's Hair is named for her.

Berenice, Jewish princesses. **1** Late 1st cent. B.C., sister of Herod the Great, wife of her nephew Aristobulus, whom she supposedly had killed. Her second husband was put to death for a plot against Herod. She married a third time and settled in Rome. **2** Born A.D. c.28, granddaughter of Berenice **1.** Her devotion to her brother, Herod Agrippa II, was greater than her love of her husbands. Titus apparently planned to marry her but could not because of unpopularity of Jews in Rome.

Berenson, Bernard (bĕ'rŭnsŭn), 1865–; American art critic, b. Lithuania, grad. Harvard, 1887. Authority on Italian art, especially of the Renaissance.

Berezina (bĕrĕzē'nŭ), river, 365 mi. long, Belorussia; tributary of Dnieper. Scene of heroic, costly crossing of Napoleon's fleeing army (Nov., 1812).

Berg, Alban (bĕrk), 1885–1936, Austrian composer. He used the 12-tone technique invented by his teacher, Arnold Schönberg. Although he met violent opposition, his opera *Wozzeck* (1925) attained considerable success. Among other compositions are a *Lyric Suite* (1926) for string quartet; a violin concerto (1936); an unfinished opera, *Lulu.*

Berg, former duchy (before 1380, county), NW Germany; chief city Düsseldorf. Under dukes of JÜLICH 1348–1524; under dukes of CLEVES 1524–1609; under Wittelsbachs (Palatinate line) 1666–1806. Raised to grand duchy (1806) by Napoleon I in favor of Joachim Murat. To Prussia 1815.

Bergamo (bĕr'gämō), city (pop. 73,534), Lombardy, N Italy. Textile mfg. Ruled by Venice

1427–1797. Romanesque cathedral; baptistery; Renaissance Colleoni chapel. Birthplace of Donizetti.

bergamot (bûr'gŭmŏt), citrus tree (*Citrus bergamia*). Fruit, an orange, yields oil for perfumes and eau de Cologne. Wild bergamot is related to OSWEGO TEA.

Bergen (bûr'gŭn, Nor. bĕr'gŭn), city (pop. 110,424), SW Norway, on the Vagen and the Pudde Fjord—both inlets of North Sea. Main shipping center and second largest city of Norway. Founded c.1070, it was the chief city and royal residence of medieval Norway, an episcopal see, and a cultural center. HANSEATIC LEAGUE created c.1350 one of its four great foreign establishments here and dominated the city until 1560. In World War II the German naval installations were heavily bombed. Ancient buildings (mostly restorations) include Haakon's Hall, a 12th-century palace; cathedral (13th cent.); Rosenkrantz Tower (16th cent.). Bergen has a university. Its theater gained international importance in 19th cent. through association with Ibsen and Bjornson.

Bergen, N.J.: see JERSEY CITY.

Bergenfield, residential borough (pop. 17,647), NE N.J., NE of Hackensack. Mfg. of machinery, cutlery, knitware, and wood products.

Bergen op Zoom (bĕr'gŭn ôp zōm'), municipality (pop. 26,642) and town, North Brabant prov., SW Netherlands; a North Sea port on the Eastern Scheldt. Once strongly fortified, it was often besieged in the wars of the 16th–18th cent.

Berger, Victor Louis, 1860–1929, American Socialist leader and Congressman, b. Austria-Hungary. First Socialist member of Congress (1911–13). Sentenced to 20-year prison term for sedition; decision reversed by U.S. Supreme Court in 1921.

Bergerac, Cyrano de: see CYRANO DE BERGERAC.

Bergh, Henry, 1811–88, American philanthropist. Founded American Society for the Prevention of Cruelty to Animals (1866) and helped Elbridge T. Gerry estab. Society for the Prevention of Cruelty to Children (1875).

Bergius, Friedrich (frēd'rĭkh bĕr'gēŏōs), 1884–1949, German chemist. Transformed coal into liquid fuel, wood into sugar. Shared 1931 Nobel Prize.

Bergman, Torbern Olof (tŏōr'bûrn ŏō'lôv bĕr'yūmän), 1735–84, Swedish chemist, physicist, naturalist. Developed theory of chemical affinity, improved chemical analysis and rock classification, worked in crystallography.

Bergmann, Ernst von (ĕrnst fûn bĕrg'män), 1836–1907, German surgeon, introducer (1886) of steam sterilization of instruments and dressings.

Bergson, Henri (ärē' bĕrgsō'), 1859–1941, French philosopher, long a professor at the Collège de France. He opposed prevailing positivistic thought by accenting the dualism between the dynamic *élan vital* [life force] and resistant matter. Man knows matter through intellect, but, more important, knows through intuition how the *élan vital* operates and also discovers the true nature of time, which is duration in terms of life experience, not a mathematically clocked measurement.

Berhampore (bûr'ŭmpôr'), town (pop. 41,558), N West Bengal, India. Scene of first uprising of Sepoy Rebellion (1857).

Beria, Lavrenti Pavlovich (bĕ'ryä), 1899?–, Russian Communist leader. Head of the NKVD (Russian secret police; now MVD) from 1938; deputy premier in charge of ministries of state control and interior.

beriberi (bĕ'rēbĕ'rē), disease affecting nervous system and resulting from unbalanced diet low in vitamin B. Common among Orientals subsisting on polished rice.

Bering, Vitus Jonassen (vē'tōōs yō'näsùn bā'rĭng), 1681–1741. Danish explorer in Russian employ. Planned and carried out with government support notable expedition to map Siberian arctic regions. Died on Bering Isl. after leading expedition to Alaska.

Bering Island, off Kamchatka, extreme NE Asiatic RSFSR, in Bering Sea, largest of KOMANDORSKI ISLANDS. Here Vitus Bering was wrecked and died.

Bering Sea, northward extension of Pacific between Siberia and Alaska, c.878,000 sq. mi. Screened from Pacific by Aleutian Isls., navigable only after late May; connected with Arctic Ocean by Bering Strait, navigable only after late June. Contains several islands owned by U.S. and USSR. Bering voyages revealed fur-seal wealth, and from mid-18th cent. unregulated slaughter threatened their extinction. Protection of seals became subject of **Bering Sea Fur-Seal Controversy** (1886), international dispute over pelagic (open sea) sealing. Court of arbitration in 1893 declared against U.S. claim to control all of Bering Sea, and damages were paid to seized Canadian vessels. In 1911 international agreement gave U.S. supervision of seal summering places in Pribilof Isls., prohibited pelagic sealing, and forbade altogether the killing of sea otters.

Bering Strait, waterway between NE Asia and NW North America. Connects Arctic Ocean and Bering Sea. Narrowness (c.50 mi.) makes it plausible place of American Indian entry into America.

Berkeley, George (bär'klē), 1685–1753, British philosopher, b. Ireland; bishop of Cloyne after 1734. Going beyond the teachings of Locke, he argued for what has been called subjective idealism—the theory that all qualities are known only in the mind, that matter does not exist apart from its being perceived, and that the observing mind of God makes possible the continued apparent existence of material objects. Tried unsuccessfully to found a college for converting American Indians to Christianity. Among his works are his *New Theory of Vision* (1709), *Treatise concerning the Principles of Human Knowledge* (1710), *Dialogues* (1713).

Berkeley, Sir William, 1606–77, British colonial governor of Va. A tyrant, his negligence brought on rebellion led by Nathaniel BACON. Removed from office after exacting bloody vengeance.

Berkeley (bûrk'lē). **1** City (pop. 113,805), W Calif., on E shore of San Francisco Bay. Originally part of Peralta family's Rancho San Antonio (granted 1820); bought 1853 by Americans. Suburban and educational center, it is seat of Univ. of CALIFORNIA.

Has aquatic park and yacht harbor. **2** City (pop. 5,268), E Mo., W suburb of St. Louis.

Berkeley Springs, town (pop. 1,213), W.Va., in E Panhandle, NW of Martinsburg; chartered 1776 as Bath, still its official name. Warm springs have made town a health resort from colonial days.

Berkhampstead or **Berkhamstead,** Hertfordshire, England: see GREAT BERKHAMPSTEAD.

Berkley, city (pop. 17,931), SE Mich., NW suburb of Detroit.

Berkman, Alexander, 1870?–1936, anarchist, b. Vilna, came to U.S. c.1887. Unsuccessful attempt to kill Henry Clay Frick (1892) caused 14 years of imprisonment. He and Emma GOLDMAN long associated, were arrested for obstructing the draft (1917) and deported to Russia (1919). Disappointed with USSR, he left and later committed suicide.

Berkshire (bärk'shĭr, –shûr, bûrk'–) or **Berks,** inland county (725 sq. mi.; pop. 402,939) in Thames R. basin, England; co. town Reading. Largely agr., has dairying and hog raising. At Windsor is famous royal castle.

Berkshire Hills (bûrk'shēr), W Mass., region of wooded hills with many streams, small lakes, resorts, and country homes. Name is sometimes restricted to Mass. part of TACONIC MOUNTAINS, but is generally applied to all highlands in W Mass. Rise to 3,491 ft. in Mt. Greylock, highest point in state, SW of North Adams. Pittsfield, Great Barrington, Lenox, and Stockbridge are here. Chief rivers: Housatonic, Westfield.

Berkshire Symphonic Festival, summer music festival, featuring the Boston Symphony Orchestra, held since 1937 at "Tanglewood" near Lenox, Mass., but mostly in adjoining Stockbridge town. In 1940 a summer school, the Berkshire Music Center, was begun in combination with the festival.

Berle, Adolf A(ugustus), Jr. (bûr'lē), 1895–, U.S. Assistant Secretary of State (1938–44).

Berlichingen, Götz von (gûts fŭn bĕr'lĭkhĭngùn), c.1480–1562, German knight, adventurer. Led rebellious peasants in PEASANTS' WAR. His memoirs inspired Goethe's drama, *Götz von Berlichingen* (1773).

Berlin, Irving, 1888–, American composer of over 1,000 popular songs, b. Russia. His songs are of many types, e.g., the jazzy *Alexander's Ragtime Band* (his first great success, 1911); the nostalgic *White Christmas;* the patriotic *God Bless America.* He has written music for many musical comedies and films.

Berlin, Ont.: see KITCHENER.

Berlin (bûr''lĭn', Ger. bĕrlēn'), city (pop. c.3,-336,000), former cap. of Germany and of Prussia; N Germany, in Brandenburg (from which it is administratively separate), on the Spree and Havel rivers. City area (344 sq. mi.) includes large forests and lakes. Until its virtual destruction in World War II Berlin was second largest city of Europe; political, economic, cultural center of Germany. It remains a major inland port and communications center (six railroad stations; several airfields, notably Tempelhof) and has much mfg. (textiles, chemicals, electrical machinery). Originating in two Wendish villages, Berlin and Kölln (merged 1307), city rose as member of Hanseatic League; became cap. of Brandenburg (15th cent.) and of Prussia (1701); underwent phenomenal growth after becoming cap. of Germany (1871). Has been occupied by Russo-Austrian forces (1760); by the French (1805); and by the Allies (1945–). Much bombed in World War II, it was most severely damaged by artillery during capture by Russians under Marshal Zhukov (April 28, 1945). Berlin was divided at POTSDAM CONFERENCE into four occupation zones, under joint Allied *Kommandatura.* Mounting friction between Russia and Western Allies resulted in 1948 in withdrawal of Russians from *Kommandatura* and in split of Berlin into two separate cities: "West Berlin," i.e., the combined American, English, and French sectors (188 sq. mi.; pop. c.2,142,000), which in 1949 became a member state of the Federal Republic of Germany; and the "Soviet sector" (pop. c.1,194,000), which in 1949 became the cap. of the [East] German Democratic Republic. Introduction of West German currency into Berlin was the ostensible cause of Russian blockade of West Berlin (June, 1948–May, 1949), during which Allies supplied the city by a constant stream of aircraft—the historic "airlift." Though Russia lifted the blockade, lesser incidents continued. Despite physical destruction and constant tension, Berlin experienced a vigorous intellectual and artistic revival in postwar period. Beside Humboldt Univ. (founded 1810), there is the Free Univ. (founded 1948), in Western sector.

Berlin (bûr'lĭn). **1** Town (pop. 7,470), central Conn., SSW of Hartford; settled 1686. Metal goods. **2** Town (pop. 2,001), Eastern Shore, Md., SE of Salisbury. The racehorse War Admiral was trained on near-by training grounds. Birthplace of Stephen Decatur. **3** City (pop. 16,615), NE N.H., at N edge of White Mts. at falls of Androscoggin R.; settled 1821. Pulp and paper mills. Winter sports center, with first ski club organized in U.S.

Berlin, Congress of, 1878, called by signatories of Treaty of Paris of 1856 to revise Treaty of SAN STEFANO, which Russia had forced on Turkey. Bismarck, acting as "honest broker," was chairman. Other outstanding figures were Disraeli, A. M. Gorchakov, Andrassy. Principal decisions included recognition of Serbia, Montenegro, and Rumania as independent states; threefold division of BULGARIA; assignment of BOSNIA AND HERCEGOVINA to Austro-Hungarian administration; revision of Greco-Turkish boundary.

Berlin Decree, issued in Berlin, Nov. 21,1806, by Napoleon I in answer to British blockade of commercial ports. Declared British Isles under blockade; initiated CONTINENTAL SYSTEM.

Berliner, Emile (bûr'lĭnŭr), 1851–1929, American inventor of loose-contact telephone transmitter, disk record, method for quantity duplication of records. Worked on helicopter. Started program to publicize dangers of raw milk.

Berlin Pact: see AXIS.

Berlioz, Hector (bĕrlēōs'), 1803–69, French romantic composer, whose ideas of orchestral coloring influenced many later composers. His first important work was the *Symphonie*

fantastique (1830). In next decade he wrote the symphonies *Harold in Italy* and *Romeo and Juliet.* His outstanding dramatic works are *The Damnation of Faust, The Trojans.*

Bermuda (bûrmū'dù), British crown colony (21 sq. mi.; pop. 35,560), comprising some 300 coral islands (c.20 inhabited), c.650 mi. SE of N. Carolina; cap. HAMILTON, on largest island, Bermuda. Year-round resort. Discovered by Spaniard, Juan de Bermúdez (1515), it was uninhabited until colonists under Sir George Somers were wrecked there (1609).

Bermuda grass, a grass (*Cynodon dactylon*) used for pasture and lawn in the S U.S. It is resistant to heat and drought.

Bern (bûrn, Ger. bĕrn) or **Berne** (Fr. bĕrn), most populous canton (2,658 sq. mi.; pop. 798,264) of Switzerland. Comprises Bernese Alps or Oberland, with JUNGFRAU and other peaks; Mittelland [midlands], in N foothills of Alps; and Seeland [lake country], in the NW, including Biel and Bernese Jura. Agr., dairying, tourist trade in Oberland and Mittelland; watchmaking in Seeland. Pop. mostly Protestant and—except in Jura—German-speaking. History of canton is largely that of its cap., **Bern** or **Berne** (pop. 145,740), since 1848 also the cap. of Switzerland, on Aar R. Founded 1191; became free imperial city 1218; joined Swiss Confederation 1353; soon became its leading member; conquered AARGAU (1415) and VAUD (1536); accepted the Reformation (1528). Autocratic urban aristocracy governed until 1798, when French revolutionary armies sacked city and dismembered Bernese state. At Congress of Vienna (1815) Bern did not recover Aargau and Vaud but received Bernese Jura (former bishopric of Basel). Liberal cantonal constitution adopted 1831. Largely medieval in architecture, Bern has 15th-cent. cathedral, quaint arcaded streets, fountains. Modern buildings include federal palace, museums, univ. (founded 1834). Seat of Universal Postal Union, International Copyright Union, and other international agencies.

Bernadette, Saint (bûrnŭdĕt'), 1843–79, French saint, whose visions of the Virgin in a grotto caused Lourdes to become a major Roman Catholic shrine. A poor and unlettered girl (Bernadette Soubirous), she was severely challenged by the skeptical both within the Church and outside before she was allowed to retreat to a quiet convent at Nevers. Canonized 1933. Feast: April 16.

Bernadotte, Count Folke (fôl'kù bĕrnädôt'), 1895–1948, Swedish internationalist; nephew of King Gustavus V. Appointed UN mediator in Palestine (1948), he was assassinated by a Jewish extremist in Jerusalem. Ralph Bunche succeeded him.

Bernadotte, Jean Baptiste Jules: see CHARLES XIV, king of Sweden.

Bernanos, Georges (zhôrzh' bĕrnänôs'), 1888–1948, French author. His novels, such as *Sous le soleil de Satan* (1926; Eng. tr., *The Star of Satan*) and *Journal d'un curé de campagne* (1936; Eng. tr., *The Diary of a Country Priest*), reflect deep mysticism. Though a monarchist and Catholic, Bernanos wrote eloquently against the Insurgents of the Spanish civil war in *Les Grands Cime-*

tières sous la lune (1938; Eng. tr., *A Diary of My Times*).

Bernard, Saint: see BERNARD OF CLAIRVAUX, SAINT, and BERNARD OF MENTHON, SAINT. For the two Alpine passes, see SAINT BERNARD.

Bernard VII, d. 1418, count of Armagnac, constable of France; father-in-law of Charles d'ORLÉANS. Led Armagnac faction (named for him) after Charles's capture in 1415. Killed in Paris massacre (see ARMAGNACS AND BURGUNDIANS).

Bernard, Claude (klōd bĕrnär'), 1813–78, French physiologist, a founder of experimental medicine through work on digestive process and vasomotor mechanism.

Bernard, Joseph Antoine (zhōzĕf' ätwän' bĕrnär'), 1866–1931, French sculptor, b. Vienna.

Bernardin de Saint-Pierre, Jacques Henri (zhäk' ārĕ' bĕrnärdĕ' dù sĕ-pyĕr'), 1737–1814, French author. Strongly influenced by Rousseau, he is best known for the charming prose idyl *Paul et Virginie* (1788).

Bernardo del Carpio (bĕrnär'dō dĕl kär'pyō), hero of medieval Spanish legend, counterpart of French Roland; supposedly nephew of Alfonso II.

Bernard of Clairvaux, Saint (bûr'nùrd, bûrnärd', klârvō'), 1090?–1153, French churchman, Doctor of the Church. In 1115 he founded a Cistercian monastery at CLAIRVAUX, where he remained as abbot the rest of his life, refusing high church offices. Nevertheless, holiness of life, immense capacity of mind, force of character, and burning eloquence made him the most powerful figure of his day. He sought peace among the rulers of Western Europe and had a hand in many political affairs. He led the successful fight to seat Pope INNOCENT II and was the adviser of Pope Eugene III. His vigorous attacks brought condemnations of ABELARD and ARNOLD OF BRESCIA. His preaching launched the Second Crusade. Bernard was notable also for his charity and his protection of the weak (e.g., the Jews of the Rhineland) from the powerful. Today his greatest importance lies perhaps in his writings, which include many superb sermons and profound and well-written treatises on the Christian life, theology, and mysticism (e.g., *On the Steps of Humility and Pride; On the Love of God; On Grace and Free Will; On Conversion; On Consideration;* and a life of St. Malachy). He probably did not write the hymn, *Jesu, dulcis memoriae,* sometimes attributed to him. Feast: Aug. 20.

Bernard of Menthon, Saint (mätō'), 11th cent., Savoyard churchman, founder of the Alpine hospices in both of the SAINT BERNARD passes. Feast: May 28.

Bern Convention: see COPYRIGHT.

Berne, Switzerland: see BERN.

Berners or Barnes, Juliana (bûr'nùrz, bärnz), fl. early 15th cent.?, supposed English author of treatise on hunting in *The Book of St. Albans.*

Bernese Alps, Switzerland: see BERN, canton.

Bernhard of Saxe-Weimar, 1604–39, Protestant general in THIRTY YEARS WAR. Captured Regensburg 1633; was routed at Nördlingen 1634; entered French pay 1635; defeated imperials at Breisach (1638).

Bernhardt, Sarah (bûrn'härt, Fr. bĕrnär'), 1844–1923, stage name of Rosine Bernard, French actress. Superb portrayals, e.g., in *King Lear* (1867), *Ruy Blas* (1867), *Phèdre* (1874), *Hernani* (1877), earned her the title "divine Sarah." She appeared also in Sardou and Rostand plays, toured Europe and U.S. (after 1880), and managed the Théâtre Sarah Bernhardt (1895) where she did *L'Aiglon* and played Hamlet. She made two silent films (1912) and continued acting even after a leg amputation in 1915.

Berni, Francesco (fränchä'skō bĕr'nē), 1497?–1535, Italian humorous poet, a priest, author of revision of the *Orlando Innamorato* of Boiardo.

Bernina (bĕrnē'nä), Alpine mountain group on Swiss-Italian border, culminating in the Piz Bernina at 13,304 ft. The Bernina pass, 7,645 ft. high, is crossed by a road and a railroad.

Bernini, Giovanni Lorenzo (jōvän'nē lōrĕn'tsō bĕrnē'nē), 1598–1680, Italian baroque sculptor and architect. Carved the graceful Apollo and Daphne (Borghese Gall., Rome). Other works include royal staircase in Vatican, colonnades of elliptical plaza before St. Peter's Church, and the bronze baldachin beneath its dome.

Bernoulli or Bernouilli (both: bĕrnōōyē'), name of family distinguished in mathematics and other sciences. After leaving Antwerp the family settled in Basel, Switzerland. **Jacob, Jacques, or James Bernoulli** (zhäk), 1654–1705, wrote treatise on theory of probability (1713), discovered Bernoulli's numbers. A professor at Basel, he was succeeded by his brother **Jean, Johann, or John Bernoulli** (zhä, yō'hän), 1667–1748, known for work in integral and exponential calculus. His son **Daniel Bernoulli** (dänyel'), 1700–1782, a mathematician and physician, solved equation known as Bernoulli's equation and advanced the kinetic theory of gases and fluids.

Bernstein, Eduard (ā'dōōärt bĕrn'shtīn), 1850–1932, German socialist. In Social Democratic party after 1872, he was exiled in 1878 (returned to Germany 1901). Criticized Marxist theories, denying inevitability of world revolution, and became leader of "revisionism."

Bernstein, Henri (ārē' bĕrnstīn'), 1876–, French dramatist, author of many sophisticated comedies. *The Thief* (1906; Eng. tr., 1907) was most successful among his plays performed in America.

Bernstorff, Johann Hartwig Ernst (yohän' härt'-vīkh, bĕrns'tôrff), 1712–72, Danish statesman, of German origin. As foreign minister (1751–70) he kept Denmark at peace, negotiated exchange of Oldenburg for ducal Holstein with Russia. Dismissed through influence of STRUENSEE. His nephew, **Andreas Peter Bernstorff,** 1735–97, was Danish foreign minister (1773–80) and chief minister (1784–97). Kept Denmark neutral in French Revolutionary Wars; undertook social, economic, and educational reforms.

Beroea (bērē'ù), the same as BEREA.

Berruguete, Alonso (älōn'sō bĕr-rōōgä'tä), c.1480–1561, Spanish court artist to Charles V. Studied with Michelangelo. Known for carved altar screens and other church furniture.

Berry, Charles, duc de (shärl′ dük′ dù bĕrē′), 1778–1820, younger son of Charles X of France. Fought with Condé against French Revolution. His assassination caused reaction against liberals. His wife, **Caroline Fernande Louise, duchesse de Berry** (kärōlēn′ fĕrnäd′ lwēz′ düshĕs′), 1798–1870, attempted in 1832 to win French throne for her son, later known as Henri, comte de Chambord. Temporarily imprisoned.

Berry, Martha McChesney, 1866–1942, American educator, founder of school for underprivileged mountain children at Mt. Berry, Ga., in 1902.

Berry (bĕrē′), region and former province, central France; historic cap. Bourges. Dry plateau (cattle raising), except fertile Indre and Cher valleys. Bought by French crown c.1100; duchy-appanage of various princes of the blood 1360–1601.

Bertha of the Big Foot, d. 783, Frankish queen, mother of Charlemagne.

Berthelot, Pierre Eugène Marcelin (pyĕr′ ûzhĕn′ märsùlĕ′ bĕrtúlō′), 1827–1907, French chemist. A founder of modern organic chemistry, he pioneered in producing synthetic organic compounds; also worked in thermochemistry and explosives.

Berthier, Louis Alexandre (lwē′ älĕksä′drù bĕrtyä′), 1753–1815, marshal of France. Served in American Revolution and as chief of staff under Napoleon I. Was created prince of Neuchâtel and Wagram. Welcomed return of Bourbons. Committed suicide (or was killed) when Napoleon debarked from Elba.

Berthollet, Claude Louis, Comte (klōd′ lwē′ kōt′ bĕrtōlā′), 1748–1822, French chemist. Stated theories of chemical equilibrium and of double decomposition of salts; analyzed ammonia. Discovered that chlorine is a bleach, carbon purifies water, and potassium chlorate has detonating properties.

Bertillon system (bûrtĭl′yùn), first scientific method of criminal identification, developed by Alphonse Bertillon (1853–1914), based on classification of body measurements.

Bertrand, Henri Gratien, Comte (ärē′ gräsyē′ kōt′ bĕrträ′), 1773–1844, French general. Followed Napoleon I to St. Helena. His memoirs, *Napoleon at St. Helena,* appeared in English 1952.

Bertrand de Born or **Bertram de Born,** c.1140–c.1214, French troubadour of Limousin. Some of his 40 surviving poems commemorate his part in the struggles between Henry II of England and his sons.

Berwick, James Fitz-James, duke of (bĕr′ĭk), 1670–1734, marshal of France; illegitimate son of James II of England and Arabella Churchill (Marlborough's sister). Fought at the BOYNE and in War of Spanish Succession (took Barcelona 1714). Killed in War of Polish Succession. Author of memoirs.

Berwick (bĕr′ĭk) or **Berwickshire** (bĕr′ĭkshĭr), agr. maritime county (457 sq. mi.; pop. 25,060), SE Scotland; co. town Duns. Separated from England by the Tweed, was long scene of border strife.

Berwick (bûr′wĭk), borough (pop. 14,010), E Pa., on the Susquehanna and SW of Wilkes-Barre; settled 1783. Mfg. of silk, railway cars, and clothing. Site of Fort Jenkins (1777).

Berwick-on-Tweed (bĕr′ĭk) or **Berwick-upon-Tweed,** municipal borough (pop. 12,550), Northumberland, England, on N side of mouth of Tweed R. As leading border town, contested by England and Scotland until made part of Northumberland 1885.

Berwyn, city (pop. 51,280), NE Ill., W suburb of Chicago; founded 1890.

beryl (bĕr′ĭl), very hard silicate of beryllium and aluminum. Most valued variety is emerald.

beryllium (bùrĭ′lēùm) or **glucinum** (glōōsī′nùm), rare, steel-white, metallic element (symbol = Be, sometimes Gl; see also ELEMENT, table). Resembles magnesium; forms some compounds. Cost of extraction from ore limits use; alloyed with other metals to add hardness, strength, and lightness.

Berzelius, Jons Jakob, Baron (bùrzē′lēùs), 1779–1848, Swedish chemist. Developed modern chemical symbols; prepared table of atomic weights; analyzed many compounds; discovered selenium, thorium, cerium.

Besançon (bùzäsō′), city (pop. 51,939), cap. of Doubs dept., E France, in Franche-Comté. Watch mfg. Archiepiscopal see. Free imperial city until incorporation (1648) into Franche-Comté (then Spanish). After French annexation the cap. of Franche-Comté and a university were transferred from DÔLE to Besançon (1676). Medieval and Renaissance architecture. Birthplace of Victor Hugo.

Besant, Annie (Wood) (bē′zùnt), 1847–1933, English theosophist and social reformer. Advocated free thought, Socialism. She and Charles Bradlaugh edited the *National Reformer* and for publishing a pamphlet on birth control (1877) were tried on charges of immorality and acquitted. In 1889 she became a disciple of Mme Blavatsky. She lived in India and furthered the Indian nationalist cause. President of the Theosophical Society after 1907, she wrote much on religion. In 1926–27 she introduced her protégé, Jiddu Krishnamurti, in England and America as the new Messiah (he later declined the honor).

Besant, Sir Walter (bĭzănt′), 1836–1901, English writer and reformer, author of novels on social problems, criticism, biographies, works on London.

Beskids, range of Carpathians, along Polish-Czech border. Highest peak at 5,658 ft.

Besnard, Paul Albert (pôl′ älbĕr′ bänär′), 1849–1934, French academic painter, known for his murals.

Bessarabia (bĕsùrä′bēù), region of SE Europe, bounded by the Dniester, Danube and Pruth rivers and the Black Sea. Cities: Kichenev, Izmail, Belgorod-Dnestrovsky. Largely a fertile agr. steppe and grazing land (grain, tobacco, fruit, wool). Always a border country, it was part of Roman Dacia; was invaded by Goths, Petchenegs, Cumans, Mongols; fell to Moldavia 14th cent.; to Turks 15th cent.; to Russia 1812. Congress of Paris (1856) gave S Bessarabia to Moldavia; Congress of Berlin (1878) restored it to Russia. Rumania annexed the entire prov. 1918, was forced to return it to Russia 1940, reoccupied it 1941–44, ceded it formally 1947. Larger part now incorporated with Moldavian SSR, except for S part, which was added to Ukraine.

Bessarion (bĕsä'rēûn), 1395?–1472, Byzantine humanist in Renaissance Italy; made a cardinal 1439, patriarch of Constantinople 1463. Notable for his learning, he translated many Greek works into Latin.

Bessel, Friedrich Wilhelm (frēd'rĭkh vĭl'hĕlm bĕs'ûl), 1784–1846, German astronomer. Made first authenticated measurement of distance of a star (1841).

Bessemer, Sir Henry: see BESSEMER PROCESS.

Bessemer, industrial city (pop. 28,445), central Ala., near Birmingham; founded 1887. Processes iron, steel, chemicals.

Bessemer process (bĕs'ûmûr), industrial process for making steel from cast iron (pig iron). Oxygen of air blown through molten iron oxidizes impurities in it, oxidation heat raising temperature of mass and keeping it molten during operation. Efficiency of process depends upon large steel container (Bessemer converter) lined with silica and clay or with dolomite. To make steel of desired properties, another substance, often spiegeleisen, is usually added to molten metal once oxidation is complete. Basic principle of process invented by **Sir Henry Bessemer,** 1813–98, who erected Bessemer Steel Works at Sheffield, England.

Bessenyei, George (bĕ'shĕnyä), 1747–1811, Hungarian dramatist and writer. Helped make Hungarian a modern literary language.

Best, Charles Herbert, 1899–, Canadian physiologist, developer with Banting of insulin treatment of diabetes. Author of works on physiology.

betatron (bā'tûtrŏn), electron-accelerating machine first developed by D. W. Kerst in 1941. The accelerated electrons are either released as a beam or are directed at a metal target to generate X rays; mesons and other subatomic particles can be produced from the X rays. Betatron is used in study of cosmic rays and in medical and industrial research.

betel nut (bē'–), fruit of a palm (*Areca catechu*). Chewed with leaf of betel pepper smeared with lime, it is narcotic stimulant for many Eastern peoples.

Bethabara (–äb'ûrû), place on Jordan R., near Dead Sea, where John was baptizing when Jesus came to him. Called Bethany in RV. John 1.28.

Bethany (bĕth'ûnē). 1 Village at SW foot of Mt. Olivet, E of Jerusalem. Home of Lazarus, Martha, and Mary, and often visited by Jesus. Ascension took place near by. Mark 11.1,11; John 11; Mat. 21.17; 26.6; Mark 14.3; Luke 19.29; 24.50. 2 See BETHABARA.

Bethany. 1 City (pop. 5,705), central Okla., near Oklahoma City. Members of Nazarene sect, who predominate, have college. **2** Town (pop. 1,063), N W.Va., NNE of Wheeling near Pa. line. Seat of **Bethany College** (coed.; chartered 1840, opened 1841 by Alexander Campbell).

Bethe, Hans Albrecht (bā'tù), 1906–, American physicist. Developed theories on atomic properties and on origin of solar and stellar energy. Directed theoretical physics division, Los Alamos Atomic Bomb Project, 1943–46.

Bethel (bĕth'ûl) [Heb.,= house of God], ancient city, N of Jerusalem. Here Abraham built altar, Jacob had vision of ladder reaching to heaven, and Samuel often visited. Jeroboam tried to make it a religious capital to rival Jerusalem and set up a golden calf for worship. Bethel became associated with idolatry and was denounced by later prophets. Gen. 12.8; 35.1–15; Judges 20.26, 27; 1 Kings 12.26–33; Amos 3.14. Bible says name originally Luz; modern town called Beitin.

Bethel, town (pop. 5,104), SW Conn., near Danbury. Hat mfg. since c.1800.

Bethesda (–thĕz'–), pool in Jerusalem said to have miraculous healing powers. John 5.2–9. May be same as pool recently discovered in NE corner of city.

Bethesda (bĭthĕz'dû), uninc. town, central Md., NW suburb of Washington, D.C. Here are Natl. Cancer Inst. research center, Naval Medical Center, and Natl. Institutes of Health.

Beth-horon (–hō'–), name of two neighboring towns between Lydda and Jerusalem. Scene of 2 historic victories—one by Joshua and one by Judas Maccabaeus.

Bethlehem (bĕth'lēûm) [Heb.,= house of bread or house of Lahmu, a goddess], Arabic *Beit Lahm,* town (pop. 6,814), S central Palestine, just S of Jerusalem, birthplace of Jesus and one of world's great shrines, now in republic of Israel. Inhabitants, largely Christian, depend on pilgrims for livelihood. In Old Testament, scene of book of Ruth and home of David. In A.D. 330 Constantine erected basilica on traditional site of the Nativity. Church standing there today is shared by monks of Greek, Latin, and Armenian rites. Manger where Jesus was born is said to have been in grotto under church. Bethlehem's older name was Ephrath or Ephratah. Gen. 35.16–20; 48.7; 1 Sam. 16; 17; 2 Sam. 23.13–17; 1 Chron. 15–19.

Bethlehem. 1 Town (pop. 882), NW N.H., in White Mts. and SW of Whitefield. Health resort. **2** City (pop. 66,340), E Pa., on Lehigh R. and N of Philadelphia; settled 1787 by Moravians. Steel products, site of Bethlehem Steel Corp. Seat of LEHIGH UNIVERSITY, Moravian Col. (for men; 1807), and Moravian Col. for Women (1742). Has annual music festival in May with Bach Choir.

Bethlen, Gabriel (bĕth'lùn, bĕt'lĕn), Hung. *Bethlen Gábor,* 1580–1629, prince of Transylvania (1613–29). A Protestant, he allied himself with FREDERICK THE WINTER KING and invaded Hungary, of which he was elected king (1620). After Frederick's defeat he made peace with Emperor Ferdinand II and renounced the royal title (1621). He ruled Transylvania wisely, encouraged law and learning.

Bethlen, Count Stephen, Hung. *Bethlen István,* 1874–1950?, Hungarian premier (1921–31). Though a royalist, he prevented the return of King Charles (Emperor CHARLES I) to avoid military intervention of Little Entente. Sought revision of Treaty of Trianon. His death in a Russian prison was reported but not confirmed.

Bethmann-Hollweg, Theobald von (tā'ōbält fün bät'män-hôl'väk), 1856–1921, chancellor of Germany (1909–17). Famed for calling guarantee of Belgian neutrality a "scrap of paper" (1914). Overthrown in 1917 for his efforts to negotiate peace.

Bethsaida (-sā'ĭdù) [Heb.,= house of fish], birthplace of Peter, Andrew, and John. Near, or on, Sea of Galilee, exact location uncertain. Mat. 11.21; Mark 6.45; 8.22; Luke 10.13; John 1.44; 12.21.

Beth-shan (-shăn') or **Beth-shean** (-shē'ŭn), anc. fortress in Jordan valley, principal strategic point of E Palestine. Modern name: Beisan.

Bethulia (bĕthū'lēù), city, Palestine, apparently NE of Samaria. Scene of book of JUDITH. Sometimes identified with Jerusalem.

Bethune, David: see BEATON, DAVID.

Bethune, Mary McLeod (mŭkloud' bùthūn'), 1875–, American Negro educator. Founded (1904) Daytona Normal and Industrial Inst. for Negro Girls (now Bethune-Cookman Col.) and was president 1904–42.

Bethune-Cookman College: see DAYTONA BEACH, Fla.

Bettendorf, city (pop. 5,132), E Iowa, suburb of Davenport, on Mississippi R. Mfg. of industrial gases and machinery.

Betterton, Thomas, 1635?–1710, English actor, manager. In William D'Avenant's company (1661–68) became leading actor of his day. A great Hamlet, Mercutio, and Macbeth, he played many roles in Shakspere adaptations by Dryden, Shadwell, and himself. As actor-manager, opened Haymarket Theatre 1705.

Beulah, allegorical name for Israel. Isa. 62.4,5.

Beuthen (boi'tùn), Pol. *Bytom,* city (pop. 93,179), Upper Silesia; since 1945 under Polish administration. Mfg. center in Katowice mining region.

Bevan, Aneurin (ùnī'rĭn bĕ'vùn), 1897–, British political leader. Former coal miner and a trade unionist, became minister of health (1945) for Labour government's system of socialized medicine. On return of Churchill government (1951) became chief left-wing opponent of ATTLEE within LABOUR PARTY.

Beveland, North, and **South Beveland** (bā'vùlänt), two islands (combined area 170 sq. mi.), Zeeland prov., SW Netherlands, in the Scheldt estuary. Connected by railroad with mainland and with Walcheren. Agr., livestock raising. British dislodged Germans from islands after heavy fighting late in 1944.

Beveridge, Albert J(eremiah), 1862–1927, U.S. Senator (1899–1911) and historian. Supported policies of Theodore Roosevelt. Wrote biographies of John Marshall and Lincoln.

Beveridge, William Henry, 1879–, British economist. In government service 1908–19, set up labor exchanges and devised wartime food rationing. Was director of London School of Economics 1919–37 and master of Univ. Col., Oxford, 1937–45. In noted government reports, proposed full social security system for all citizens (1942) and planned spending to insure full employment (1944).

Beverley, municipal borough (pop. 15,499), cap. of E. Riding of Yorkshire, England. Famous 13th-cent. minster contains "chair of peace" which gave right of sanctuary.

Beverly. 1 City (pop. 28,884), NE Mass., on coast just N of Salem; settled before 1630.

Mfg. of shoes and clothing. Had New England's first successful cotton-weaving mill (1789). O. W. Holmes and his son had summer home here. **2** City (pop. 3,084), SW N.J., on Delaware R. below Burlington. Has natl. cemetery.

Beverly Hills, city (pop. 29,032), S Calif.; planned 1906. A Los Angeles suburb, it is the home of many screen stars.

Bevin, Ernest (bĕ'vùn), 1881–1951, British trade-union and political leader. Merged unions to make powerful Transport and General Workers' Union. Was minister of labor in wartime cabinet 1940–45. As Labour government foreign minister (1945 until his death) his policy toward USSR was uncompromising. His Palestine policy criticized by Arabs and Jews.

Bewick, Thomas (bū'ĭk), 1753–1828, English wood engraver, noted for illustrations of Beilby's *History of British Birds.*

Bexley, residential city (pop. 12,378), central Ohio, near Columbus. Capital Univ. is here.

Beyle, Henri: see STENDHAL.

Beyrouth: see BEIRUT.

Beza, Theodore (bĕ'zù), Fr. *Théodore de Bèze* (tão-dôr' dù bĕz'), 1519–1605, French reformer and Calvinist theologian, friend and aid of Calvin.

Bezer (bĕ'zùr), town, E of the Jordan. One of the cities of refuge. Deut. 4.43; Joshua 20.8; 21.36.

Béziers (bāzyā'), city (pop. 59,894), Hérault dept., S France. Wine and spirits trade. Population was massacred (1209) after Simon de Montfort captured city in Albigensian Crusade.

Bezruc, Petr, Czech *Bezruč* (pĕt'ùr bĕz'rŏŏch), pseud. of Vladimir Vasek, 1867–, Czech poet, author of nationalistic *Silesian Songs* (1903; latest ed., 1944).

Bezwada (bāzwä'dù), officially *Vizayawada,* city (pop. 86,184), NE Madras, India, on Kistna R. Trade center. Headworks of irrigation-canal system.

Bhagavad-Gita (bŭg'ùvùd-gē'tù), Sanskrit philosophical poem in MAHABHARATA. Important, widely translated expression of Hinduism.

Bhascara (bŭs'kùrù), called **Acarya** (ùchär'yù), b. 1114, Hindu mathematician, astronomer, first to give systematic exposition of decimal system.

Bhatpara (bùtpä'rù), city (pop. 117,044), S West Bengal, India; anc. seat of Sanskrit learning.

Bhils (bēlz), people (more than 1,000,000) who inhabit parts of W central India, esp. S Rajputana and N Bombay state. Speak Bhili, an Indo-European language (see LANGUAGE, table); their culture is affected by, but not absorbed into, Hinduism.

Bhopal (bō'päl), state (6,921 sq. mi.; pop. 838,107), central India. At Sanchi is a 54-ft.-high Buddhist stupa (c.300 B.C.). Bhopal (pop. 75,228) is state cap.; trade center with textile mfg.

Bhubaneswar, India: see BHUVANESWAR.

Bhutan (bōŏtän'), Indian protectorate (c.18-000 sq. mi.; pop. c.300,000), in E Himalayas, between India and Tibet; cap. Punaka. Formerly under dual control of a spiritual and a temporal ruler; since 1907 under a maharaja. Lamaism is main religion. Largely mountainous and forested. In 1949 India assumed Britain's former role in subsidizing Bhutan and directing its foreign affairs.

Bhuvaneswar (boōvänĕ'swär) or **Bhubaneswar** (boōbä–), cap. of Orissa, India. Was center of Sivaism and cap. of Kesaris dynasty from 5th to 10th cent. Has remains of c.500 shrines.

Bi, chemical symbol of the element BISMUTH.

Bialik, Hayyim Nahman (byä'lĕk), 1873–1934, Hebrew poet and translator, b. Russia.

Bialowieza, Pol. *Białowieza* (byäwôvyĕ'zhä), large forest, E Poland. Favorite royal hunting preserve; national park since 1921. Has aurochs, boar, deer.

Bialystok, Pol. *Białystok* (byäwïs'tôk), city (pop. 65,800), NE Poland. Textile center.

Biard, Pierre (byär), c.1567–1622, French Jesuit missionary in North America. Headed first Jesuit mission to Canada (1611). His *Relation de la Nouvelle France* (1616) has much historical value.

Biarritz (bē'ürïts, Fr. byärēts') town (pop. 20,447), Basses-Pyrénées dept., SW France, on Bay of Biscay near Spanish border. Fashionable resort.

Bibiena or **Bibbiena, Galli da** (gäl'lē dä bēbyä'nä), family of Italian artists of 17th and 18th cent. Founder, **Giovanni Maria Galli da Bibiena** (jōvän'nē), 1625–65, painted altarpieces for churches in Bologna. A son, **Ferdinando Galli Bibiena** (fĕrdēnän'dō), 1657–1743, most famous of family, was known throughout Europe for architectural views, theatrical designs, and decorations for court festivities. Rest of family noted also as decorative artists.

Bible [Gr.,= the books], name used by Christians for their Scriptures, for them a holy guide of faith and conduct. For composition and canon of the Bible, see OLD TESTAMENT; NEW TESTAMENT; APOCRYPHA; PSEUDEPIGRAPHA; articles on individual books. Traditional Christian view is that the Bible was written under the guidance of God and is, therefore, all true, literally or under the veil of allegory. Interpretation of the Bible is one of the chief points of difference between Protestantism, which believes that individuals have the right to interpret the Bible for themselves, and Roman Catholicism, which teaches that individuals may read the Bible only in accord with interpretation of the Church. Among extant manuscripts of the Bible are the Codex Vaticanus (Greek, 4th cent.), at the Vatican; Codex Sinaiticus (Greek, 4th cent.) and Codex Alexandrinus (Greek, 5th cent.), at the British Mus.; and Codex Bezae (Greek and Latin, 6th cent.) at Cambridge, England. First great translation of the whole Bible into Latin was the Vulgate of St. Jerome. The Bible, with Latin text, was the first book to be printed on the press of Johann GUTENBERG. In England there were from Anglo-Saxon times vernacular versions of parts of the Bible, mostly the four Gospels and the Psalms. Great names in the history of the English Bible are: John Wyclif (d. 1384), whose name is borne by two translated versions; William Tyndale (d. 1536), whose New Testament (1525–26) was the first English translation to be printed; Miles Coverdale (d. 1569), who was respon-

sible for the Great Bible (1539), the first to be issued by the crown (in the name of Henry VIII). Greatest of all English translations was the Authorized (AV) or King James Version (1611), made by a committee of churchmen led by Lancelot Andrewes. The Douay, or Rheims-Douay, Version was published by Roman Catholic scholars at Rheims (New Testament, 1582) and Douai, France (Old Testament, 1610), since extensively revised. In the 19th cent., the Authorized Version was revised from the original tongues by the Church of England and appeared as the English Revised Version and American Revised Version (both: RV). English translations begun in the 20th cent. include the Revised Standard Version (Protestant; pub. 1952) and the American Roman Catholic Confraternity of Christian Doctrine (New Testament pub. 1941). Translations have been important in the histories of other literature besides English (e.g., Luther's translation, which had much to do with shaping the modern German language).

Bible school, usual term for nondenominational institution giving daily vacation Bible study to children. First founded (1901) in New York city.

Bible societies, nonsectarian Protestant groups for printing and dissemination of Scriptures. Canstein Bible Society estab. 1710 in Germany. In England societies formed 1780 and 1804. In U.S., American Bible Society estab. 1816. Group called Gideons, International (estab. 1898) places Bibles in hotel rooms. In 1946 United Bible Societies united more than 20 national groups.

Biblical Antiquities, Book of: see PSEUDEPIGRAPHA.

bibliography, The listing of books is of ancient origin. Lists of clay tablets have been found at Nineveh. Library at Alexandria had subject lists of its books. Modern bibliography began with invention of printing. Efforts at universal bibliography resulted in Konrad von Gesner's *Bibliotheca universalis* in 1545. There are lists of publications of publishing houses (e.g., *Trade List Annual,* British *Reference Catalogue of Current Literature*); subject bibliographies (e.g., Sabin's *Dictionary of Books Relating to America*); lists of works of individual authors; monthly lists of books in English (*The Cumulative Book Index*); and many special bibliographies (e.g., *The Cambridge Bibliography of English Literature* and *Literary History of the United States*).

Bibliothèque nationale (bēblēōtĕk' näsyônäl'), national library of France (with c.5,000,000 books), in Paris. Originated when early French kings made collections of writings. Building erected 1854–75 under direction of Henri Labrouste; remodeling was done 1932–39.

Bibracte (bïbräk'tē), town in Gaul, cap. of the Aedui. Here Caesar defeated the Helvetii (58 B.C.). Autun was built not far away to replace it.

bicarbonate: see CARBONATE.

bicarbonate of soda: see SODA.

Bichat, Marie François (märē' fräswä' bēshä'), 1771–1802, French anatomist and physiologist. His study of tissues was basis of modern histology.

Bickerstaff, Isaac, pseudonym used by Jonathan Swift, and later by Richard Steele in the *Tatler*.

bicycle, two-wheeled vehicle propelled by pedals. Developed in Scotland c.1839 from earlier machines operated by thrust of rider's feet upon ground. By the 1880s developments included larger front wheel, hollowsteel frame, ball bearings, tangential metal spokes. Safety bicycle, with equal-sized wheels and sprocket chain drive, was first manufactured c.1885 in England; it displaced other models following introduction of pneumatic tire (c.1888). Later improvements include freewheel, coaster brake, and hand brake. Cycling fad in '80s and '90s stimulated road construction.

Biddeford (bĭd'ĭfûrd), city (pop. 20,836), SW Maine, at Saco R. falls (water power) opposite Saco. Mfg. of textiles, textile machinery, lumber products.

Biddle, well-known family of Philadelphia. **James Biddle,** 1783–1848, U.S. naval officer, was commander of *Ontario* and took formal possession of Oregon country for U.S. in 1818. **Nicholas Biddle,** 1786–1844, as president of BANK OF THE UNITED STATES (1822–36), was a chief target of Jacksonians. **George Biddle,** 1885–, American painter, did notable frescoes in Dept. of Justice Building, Washington, D.C.

Biddle, John, 1615–62, founder of English Unitarianism. Persecuted for his *Twelve Arguments Drawn Out of Scripture* (c.1645) and *Two-fold Catechism* (1654).

Biedermeier (bē'dûrmīûr), a style of furniture and decorations originating in Germany in the early 19th cent.; named for a humorous character in verses by Ludwig Eichrodt. A simplified and less expensive form of French Empire, Directoire, and 18th-cent. English styles. Cabinets are severe in line and surface, while chairs and sofas have curved lines.

Biel (bēl) or **Bienne** (byĕn), town (pop. 48,-401), Bern canton, W Switzerland, on L. of Biel. Watchmaking center. Museum has relics of lake dwellings found in **Lake of Biel,** at foot of Jura mts. Contains Isle of St. Pierre (now a peninsula), made famous because of association with J. J. Rousseau.

Biel-. For Russian names beginning thus, see BEL-.

Bielefeld (bē'lŭfĕlt), city (pop. 153,111), North Rhine-Westphalia, NW Germany. Mfg. of linen, silk, glassware, sewing machines. Damaged in World War II.

Bien, Jules (bēn), 1826–1909, American map engraver, b. Germany. Engraved maps for many official publications.

Bienne, Switzerland: see BIEL.

biennial, plant normally living but two years. Produces leaves and roots first year, flowers and seeds second. Some ANNUAL and PERENNIAL plants behave as biennials, while certain biennials act as perennials. Canterbury bells, hollyhock, and foxglove are biennials.

Bienville, Jean Baptiste le Moyne, sieur de (zhä' bätēst' lù mwän' syûr' dù byēvēl'), 1680–1768, colonizer and governor of Louisiana for France, b. Canada. Aided colonizing

plans of brother, sieur d'IBERVILLE. Founded Mobile in 1710 and New Orleans in 1718.

Bierce, Ambrose (Gwinett), 1842–1914?, American author, b. Ohio. After service in the Union army in the Civil War, he settled in San Francisco where he was a journalist (except for years of intense literary productivity in London, 1872–76) until 1896, becoming the literary arbiter of the West Coast. Later he was a Washington correspondent. He was a strong advocate of "pure" and correct (i.e., long-established) usages in English, and his own work is notable for its terse and brilliant vigor, whether in short stories (as in collections *Tales of Soldiers and Civilians*, 1891, and *Can Such Things Be?*, 1893), literary essays, or bitter satires (as in *Fantastic Fables*, 1899). Fascinated by the macabre, he wrote some of the finest of horror stories. In 1913 he went to Mexico, where he disappeared without trace.

Bierstadt, Albert (bēr'stät), 1830–1902, American painter of Western scenes, b. Germany.

Big Ben, bell in Parliament tower (Westminster Palace), London. Name also given huge tower clock.

Big Bend National Park: see NATIONAL PARKS AND MONUMENTS (table).

Big Bethel, locality near Fort Monroe, Va., scene of early battle of Civil War, June 10, 1861. E. W. Pierce led Union brigade against J. B. Magruder's Confederate encampment and was repulsed.

Big Black Mountain, 4,150 ft. high, E Ky., in Cumberlands near Lynch. State's highest peak.

Bigelow, John, 1817–1911, American author and diplomat. Noted for diplomatic service in France during Civil War, preventing her recognition of Confederacy. Author of life of Benjamin Franklin.

Biggs, E(dward) Power, 1906–, English-American organist. Through recitals, broadcasts, and recordings, he has done much to make great organ music familiar to the American public.

Biggs, Hermann Michael, 1859–1923, American physician, noted as public health administrator.

Big Hole Battlefield National Monument: see NATIONAL PARKS AND MONUMENTS (table).

Bighorn, river, 461 mi. long, formed at Riverton, W central Wyo., by confluence of Wind and Popo Agie rivers. Flows N between Absaroka Range and Bighorn Mts. into Mont., where it receives Little Bighorn R. and flows NE to Yellowstone R. MISSOURI RIVER BASIN PROJECT plans provide for Hardin and Boysen projects on Bighorn R. In Bighorn basin are Riverton project and SHOSHONE PROJECT.

bighorn or **Rocky Mountain sheep,** wild sheep (*Ovis canadensis*) of W North America, once plentiful. Grayish-brown, with whitish patch on hindquarters, it is a heavy animal, with curling horns on male, short spikes on female. Alaskan forms are Dall's or white sheep (*O. dalli*) and Stone's or black sheep.

Bighorn Mountains, range of Rocky Mts., c.120 mi. long, in N Wyo. and S Mont., E of Bighorn R. Rises to 13,165 ft. in Cloud Peak, Wyo.

Big Manitou Falls (măn'ĭtoō), 165 ft. high, NW Wis., in Black R. Highest falls in Wis.

Bignonia (bĭgnō'nĕŭ), genus of woody vines, especially cross vine or trumpet flower (*Bignonia capreolata*), which has orange-red trumpet-shaped blossoms and compound leaves. Native to the S U.S., it is grown in greenhouses in the North and in milder areas out-of-doors.

Bigod, Hugh: see NORFOLK, HUGH BIGOD, 1ST EARL OF.

Bigot, François (bēgō'), d. after 1760, intendant of New France (1748–59), b. France. His corrupt administration paved way for English conquest.

Big Rapids, resort city (pop. 6,736), N Mich., at falls of Muskegon R. NE of Grand Rapids. Has large gas field and mfg. of machinery and tools.

Big River: see FORT GEORGE, river, Que.

Big Sandy, river rising in W Tenn., N of Lexington, and flowing c.65 mi. NNE to Kentucky Reservoir of Tennessee R.

Big Sandy River, formed by junction of Tug and Levisa forks at Louisa, Ky., and flowing 27 mi. N to the Ohio, forming part of Ky.–W.Va. line.

Big Sioux (soō), river rising in NE S. Dak. and flowing 420 mi. S to Missouri R. at Sioux City, Iowa.

Big Spring, city (pop. 17,286), W Texas, SW of Sweetwater; founded 1881. Spring, now dry, long known. Industrial center of oil and agr. area with rail shops and mfg. of cottonseed, food, and clay products.

Big Stone Gap, town (pop. 5,173), SW Va., near Ky. line. Mountain resort with coal mining and mfg. of dairy products. Southwest Virginia Mus. has regional collections. Natl. Tunnel, which is c.900 ft. long, is to S.

Big Stone Lake, long narrow lake, W Minn. and NE S. Dak., once a S outlet of glacial L. AGASSIZ.

Bihar (bēhär'), state (70,368 sq. mi.; pop. 36,-545,575), NE India; cap. Patna. Agr. area in N is drained by the Ganges. Chief crops are rice, maize, wheat, sugar cane, jute, and tobacco. Major source of India's mineral wealth (mica, copper, coal, iron). In 6th cent. B.C. Bihar was heart of Magadha empire and scene of early development of Buddhism and Jainism. Its history after 17th cent. is linked with that of Bengal.

Bihari (bēhär'ē), Indo-European language. See LANGUAGE (table).

Bijapur or **Bejapur** (both: bĭjä'pŏŏr), town (pop. 48,968) SE Bombay, India. Cap. of Deccan kingdom of Bijapur (1490–1686). Cotton ginning.

Bijns, Anna (bīns), c.1494–1575?, Flemish religious poet. Also wrote robust satires.

Bika, El: see LEBANON.

Bikaner: see RAJASTHAN.

Bikini (bēkē'nē), uninhabited atoll comprising 36 islets, central Pacific, one of the Marshall Isls. U.S. atom-bomb tests were made here in 1946.

Bilaspur (bēläs"pŏŏr'), state (453 sq. mi.; pop. 127,566), NW India, in W Himalayas; cap. Bilaspur. Site of projected dam across Sutlej R.

Bilbao (bēlbä'ō), city (pop. 183,200), cap. of Vizcaya prov., N Spain, near Bay of Biscay. Chief city of Basque Provinces, second-largest port of Spain. Steel mills, shipyards. Iron mines near by.

Bildad, second and least consoling of Job's comforters. Job 8; 18; 25; 42.9.

Bilderdijk, Willem (bĭl'dürdīk), 1756–1831, Dutch poet. In exile (1795–1806), he returned to the Netherlands under Louis Bonaparte (whom he tutored in Dutch). His poetry is uneven but at its best of a high order.

bile, alkaline fluid formed in liver. In man, stored in gall bladder (pear-shaped sac under liver), then passes through bile ducts into small intestine. Aids in emulsification, digestion, and absorption of fats and in carrying off bile pigments and other excretions. Obstruction of flow may result in digestive disturbances and JAUNDICE.

Bilhah (bĭl'hú), Rachel's maid, Jacob's concubine, mother of Dan and Naphtali. Gen. 29.29; 30.1–8; 35.22,25; 46.25; 49.4; 1 Chron. 7.13.

Billaud-Varenne, Jean Nicolas (zhä' nēkōlä' bēyō'-värĕn'), 1756–1819, French revolutionist, member of Committee of Public Safety. Deported to French Guiana after Robespierre's fall; refused amnesty from Napoleon. Fled to Haiti 1816.

Billerica (bĭl'rĭkú), town (pop. 11,101), NE Mass., S of Lowell; settled 1637. Mfg. of woolen and asbestos products.

billiards, game played with tapered, leather-tipped stick (cue) and usually three ivory balls on oblong, cloth-covered slate table with raised and cushioned edges. In England table is 6 ft. by 12 ft. with six pockets; in U.S. table is 5 ft. by 10 ft., pocketless. Pool is played on a table with pockets (usually six), and with 15 balls and a cue ball. Variants of billiards were popular in France in 16th cent., similar game played earlier. Willie Hoppe considered world's greatest player.

Billings, John Shaw, 1838–1913, American surgeon and librarian. Medical inspector in Civil War. Began *Index Catalogue* and *Index Medicus.* Helped to create New York Public Library.

Billings, Josh, pseud. of Henry Wheeler Shaw, 1818–85, American author of humorous sketches in exaggerated New England and N.Y. rural dialect; also a popular lecturer.

Billings, William, 1746–1800, American composer, first American professional musician, b. Boston. He chiefly composed hymns and other church music.

Billings, city (pop. 31,834), S Mont., on Yellowstone R. Founded 1882 by Northern Pacific RR, it is a shipping center with oil and sugar refineries and meat processing. Served by Huntley irrigation project. Seat of Rocky Mountain Col. (interdenominational; coed.; formed 1947 by merger of Billings Polytechnic Inst. and Intermountain Union Col.).

Billingsgate, wharf and fish market district of central London, named for old city gate. Also name given coarse language used here and in similar districts.

Bill of Rights, 1689, in British history, a great instrument of the constitution. Accepted by William and Mary, it recognized results of struggle against Stuart kings. Gave inviolable civil and political rights to people and political supremacy to Parliament. Act of SETTLEMENT supplemented it 1701.

Bill of Rights, in U.S. history: see CONSTITUTION.

Billy the Kid, 1859–81, American outlaw, cattle rustler in N. Mex. Real name was William H. Bonney. Shot by a sheriff.

Biloxi (bĭlŭk′sē), city (pop. 37,425), SE Miss., on peninsula between Mississippi Sound and Biloxi Bay. First white settlement in lower Mississippi valley, estab. 1699 by French under IBERVILLE across bay at Old Biloxi (now Ocean Springs). Present city, founded 1719, was cap. of La. until 1722. Resort with fishing, boatbuilding, and seafood processing. Has several U.S. military installations. Near by is "Beauvoir," Jefferson Davis's last home, now state Confederate veterans' home. Ship Isl. is sandy bar off coast.

Biloxi Bay, arm of Mississippi Sound, c.17 mi. long, 1–3 mi. wide, SE Miss. Receives Biloxi R. Bridged from Biloxi to Ocean Springs.

bimetallism, monetary system in which gold and silver are used as a standard and coined at a fixed ratio (as 16 to 1, meaning that 16 oz. of silver = 1 oz. of gold). Bimetallism usual in Western countries until Britain adopted gold standard by acts of 1798 and 1816; new German Empire adopted it 1873. In U.S. political battle on question strong from Civil War to 1910. Gold standard triumphed in most countries, but was dropped in many in 1930s.

Biminis (bĭ′mĭnēz), island group, part of Bahama Isls. Good fishing in near-by waters.

Binet, Alfred (älfrĕd′ bēnā′), 1857–1911, French psychologist. With Théodore Simon, he devised (1905–11) tests for human intelligence, revised by others and widely used.

Bingen (bĭng′ŭn), city (pop. 16,727), Rhineland-Palatinate, W Germany, on the Rhine. Center of famous wine district. Fortified by Romans 1st cent. B.C. Member of Hanseatic League from 1254. Near by, on rock in the Rhine, is the Mäuseturm, where according to legend Archbishop Hatto of Mainz was devoured by mice for his evil deeds.

Bingham, George Caleb, 1811–79, American genre painter. Active in Missouri politics.

Bingham, Hiram, 1789–1869, American Congregational missionary, b. Vt. Went (1819) to Hawaiian Isls. Developed writing from Hawaiian language. His son, **Hiram Bingham,** 1831–1908, b. Honolulu, was missionary (1857–64) in Gilbert Isls. His son, **Hiram Bingham,** 1875–, became an archaeologist and statesman. U.S. Senator from Conn. 1925–33. Discovered "lost" Inca cities of Vitcos and Machu Picchu.

Bingham Canyon or **Bingham,** mining town (pop. 2,569; alt. 6,100 ft.), N central Utah, SW of Salt Lake City. A Mormon farm (1848) became boom town (gold, silver, lead) in 1860s. Open-pit copper mine is an attraction for tourists.

Binghamton, industrial city (pop. 80,674) S N.Y., at junction of Chenango and Susquehanna rivers; laid out 1800. Largest of the Triple Cities (others are Endicott and Johnson City), which are famous for shoes. Also has mfg. of books, metal products, and textiles.

Binyon, Laurence, 1869–1943, English poet and authority on Oriental art.

Bío-Bío (bē′ō-bē′ō), river, c.240 mi. long, rising in Andes of central Chile and flowing NW to Pacific.

biochemistry, science concerned with chemical processes in living organisms and with their organic products, also called biological or physiological chemistry. Includes studies of photosynthesis, metabolism, digestion, absorption, biological oxidation. Deals also with chemistry of proteins, carbohydrates, fats, vitamins, hormones, enzymes, blood.

biology, science of living things. Broadly divided into BOTANY and ZOOLOGY, it includes plant and animal cytology (cell study), histology (tissue study), anatomy or morphology, physiology, embryology, ecology, genetics, evolution, paleontology, and systematics. Microbiology is the scientific study of microscopic forms of life, including protozoa, bacteria, algae, fungi, and viruses.

Bion (bī′ŭn), fl. 2d cent.? B.C., Greek bucolic poet, an imitator of Theocritus.

biophysics: see PHYSICS.

Birch, Reginald (Bathurst), 1856–1943, American illustrator of children's books, notably *Little Lord Fauntleroy.*

birch, deciduous tree or shrub of genus *Betula,* widely found in N Hemisphere. Paper or canoe birch (*Betula papyrifera*) and gray birch (*B. populifolia*) are native American trees with white bark. Yellow birch (*B. lutea*) important for timber in NE U.S. Others yield oil of wintergreen, birch beer extract.

Bird, Robert Montgomery, 1806–54, American romantic playwright and novelist. His verse plays for Edwin Forrest (including *The Gladiator* and *The Broker of Bogota*) won a success halted by a quarrel with Forrest. Bird turned to prose romances. Notable are two novels with a Mexico scene (*Calavar,* 1834; *The Infidel,* 1835) and two laid in the U.S. (*The Hawks of Hawk-Hollow,* 1835; *Nick of the Woods,* 1837, which was a tremendous popular success).

Bird, William: see BYRD, WILLIAM (b. 1542 or 1543).

bird, warm-blooded, egg-laying, vertebrate animal covered with FEATHERS, forelimbs modified into WINGS. Four-chambered heart like mammals; body temperature 2° to 14° higher; relatively large brain; keen sight; acute hearing; little sense of smell; believed evolved from reptiles. Adapted for FLIGHT—body weight reduced by horny bill instead of jaws and air sacs in hollow bones; heavy parts located for balanced flight. Feathers renewed in MOLTING; males more vividly colored, aggressor in courtship, superior singer. Most birds build NEST for eggs. Birds valued for insect, weed seed destruction; many scavenge. Bills adapted to food habits. See also MIGRATION OF ANIMALS. See *ill.,* p. 135.

bird of paradise, any of several birds of New Guinea and adjacent islands. Male has bright plumage, elongated tail feathers, ruffs on wings and neck.

bird sanctuary: see WILDLIFE REFUGE.

Bird Woman: see SACAJAWEA.

Birkbeck, Morris, 1764–1825, English pioneer in U.S. Undertook, with George Flower, scheme to create a settlement in Ill. which led to founding of Albion.

Birkeland, Olaf Christian (ō'läv krĭs'tyän bēr'kŭlän), 1867–1917, Norwegian physicist. Developed (with Samuel Eyde) electric-arc process for nitrogen fixation; worked on magnetics.

Birkenhead, county borough (pop. 142,392), Cheshire, England; port opposite Liverpool at mouth of the Mersey. Has grain milling, steel mfg., and shipbuilding. Heavily bombed 1941.

Birkhoff, George David (bûrk'hôf), 1884–1944, American mathematician. Research in dynamics and relativity; conceptual theory of atomic structure.

Birmingham (bûr'mĭng-ùm), second largest English city (pop. 1,112,340), Warwickshire; a great industrial center. Covers 80 sq. mi. Has iron and coal near by and is noted for metal mfg. Most of Britain's brass and bronze coins minted here. Utilities and a bank are city owned. Has noted city orchestra. Site of Anglican and Roman Catholic cathedrals and Univ. of Birmingham. Heavily bombed World War II.

Birmingham. 1 City (pop. 326,037), N central Ala., near S tip of Appalachian system; founded 1871. Largest city in state, leading iron and steel center of the South. Iron, coal, limestone from vicinity supply its mills and foundries. Mfg. of textiles, chemicals, construction materials; meat-packing plants. Important rail, air terminus. Grew with development of its metals industry by men like H. F. DE BARDELEBEN. Seat of Howard Col. (Baptist; coed.; 1841); Miles Col. (Negro; coed.; 1907); **Birmingham–Southern College** (coed.), formed 1918 by merging Southern Univ. (chartered 1856) and Birmingham Col. (1898), and with which Birmingham Conservatory of Music became affiliated, 1940. **2** City (pop. 15,467), SE Mich., on River Rouge, NW residential suburb of Detroit, in farm area; settled 1819.

Birnam, village, Perthshire, Scotland. Near-by Birnam Hill once covered by Birnam Wood of witches' prophecy in *Macbeth.*

Birney, James Gillespie, 1792–1857, American abolitionist. Edited the *Philanthropist.* Advocated political action and was leader in LIBERTY PARTY, which nominated him for presidency in 1840 and 1844.

Birobidzhan (bē″rūbējän') or **Jewish Autonomous Oblast,** district (13,820 sq. mi.; pop. 108,419), RSFSR, in SE Siberia, on Manchurian border; cap. Birobidzhan (pop. 29,654). Agr., timber, gold, iron. *Oblast* [district] was formed 1934 for colonization, with government aid, by Jews from Russia and elsewhere. By 1948 25–50% of population was Jewish.

birth or **labor,** process by which offspring is delivered from mother. Contractions of uterine muscle occur at first every 15–30 min. and later every 2 or 3 min. Average duration is c.18 hr. for woman having first child and under 12 hr. in subsequent births. PLACENTA is expelled c.15–30 min. after birth of child.

birth control, methods of voluntarily limiting births. Limitation of sexual intercourse and mechanical and chemical contraceptives are included. Organized birth-control movement began in England where the writings of Malthus stirred interest in overpopulation. Clinics were opened in the U.S. through efforts of Dr. Marie Stopes and Margaret Sanger. Movement much opposed by church groups, particularly the Roman Catholic Church, as violation of the order of nature. Nevertheless contraception became much more widespread in Western countries in 20th cent.

Bisayas, Philippine Islands: see VISAYAN ISLANDS.

Bisbee (bĭz'bē), city (pop. 3,801), SE Ariz., near Mexican border. Copper mining. City is spectacularly situated in two steep canyons.

Biscay, Bay of, arm of the Atlantic, indenting coast of W Europe from Ushant isl., off Brittany, France, to Cape Ortegal, NW Spain. Chief ports: Brest, Nantes, Bordeaux, Bilbao, Santander.

Bischoff, Theodor Ludwig Wilhelm (tā'ōdōr lōōt'vĭkh vĭl'hĕlm bĭ'shôf), 1807–82, German physiologist. Authority on blood and embryology.

Biscoe, John, d. 1848, British navigator. Discovered ENDERBY LAND (1831–32); voyage was chief basis for British claims to Antarctica.

Bishop, resort town (pop. 2,891), E Calif., in Owens R. valley, in livestock and mineral area.

Bishop Hill, village (pop. 202), NW Ill., NE of Galesburg; founded 1846 by Swedish religious dissenters under Eric JANSON. Had communistic organization. Failed due to poor management.

Bishop's College, University of: see LENNOXVILLE.

Bishops' Wars, two brief campaigns of the Scots against Charles I of England, 1639–40. Opposing his attempt to impose episcopacy, COVENANTERS pledged return to Presbyterianism. Resisting Charles's armies, they invaded England and forced him to sign Treaty of Ripon. See PURITAN REVOLUTION.

Biskra (bēskrä'), anc. *Vescera,* town (pop. 36-347), Algeria, in an oasis. Modern Biskra was founded 1844 as a French military post.

Bismarck, Otto, Fürst von (bĭz'märk, Ger. ô'tō fürst' fŭn bĭs'märk), 1815–98, German statesman. Creator of the German Empire; premier of Prussia 1862–90; chancellor of Germany 1871–90; called the "iron chancellor." After dissolving parliament for opposing his armaments budget (1862), he used the SCHLESWIG-HOLSTEIN question as pretext for war on Denmark (1864). Friction with Austria over administration of conquered Danish territories enabled him in turn to eliminate Austria from German affairs through the AUSTRO-PRUSSIAN WAR (1866) and to reorganize Germany under Prussian leadership in the NORTH GERMAN CONFEDERATION. Bismarck deliberately provoked the FRANCO-PRUSSIAN WAR (1870–71) by publishing the EMS DISPATCH. In Jan., 1871, WILLIAM I of Prussia was proclaimed emperor of GERMANY. Having achieved unification by war, Bismarck sought to consolidate it by peace. In complete control of domestic and foreign policy, he allied Germany with Austria (1879) and Italy (1882), conciliated

Upper wing coverts
Bastard wing
Scapulars
Crown
Forehead
Primaries
Breast
Secondaries
Abdomen
Tail feathers
Under tail coverts

Clinging to a vertical surface (SWIFT)

Climbing (WOODPECKER)

Scratching (FOWL)

Perching (FINCH)

Seizing prey (HAWK)

Running (RHEA)

Swimming (DUCK)

Wading (STORK)

Swimming and diving (GREBE)

FEET, SHOWING THEIR ADAPTATION TO BIRDS' HABITS

Walking and swimming (PELICAN)

FINCH

CROSSBILL

FALCON

PARROT

TOUCAN

FLAMINGO

CURLEW

AVOCET

SHOEBILL

SPOONBILL

PELICAN

SOME TYPES OF BILLS

Resting in the fork of a branch (GOLDFINCH)

Attached to a branch (RED-EYED VIREO)

In the hollow of a tree trunk (WOODPECKER)

Hanging from a branch (BALTIMORE ORIOLE)

Built of mud and grass (BARN SWALLOW)

Lying loosely among rushes (BITTERN)

SOME TYPES OF NESTS

Russia, acted as arbiter of Europe. In his struggle against the Church (see KULTUR-KAMPF) he failed. In 1883 he replaced his stringent but unsuccessful antisocialist legislation with a series of pioneering social security and labor laws, designed to weaken the appeal of socialism. German commerce, industry, and colonies expanded rapidly. WILLIAM II, who acceded in 1888, resented Bismarck's supremacy and eventually dismissed him. In retirement, Bismarck vigorously criticized William's policies. Wrote reminiscences (Eng. tr., 1898).

Bismarck, city (pop. 18,640), state cap., S central N.Dak., on hills overlooking Missouri R.; settled 1871–72. Lewis and Clark camped near by, 1804–5. Boomed as river and rail center and also as supply point for Black Hills gold mines (1874). Became territorial cap. 1883. Distributing center for large spring-wheat and dairying area, with coal mining. Capitol (1932) is skyscraper.

Bismarck Archipelago, volcanic group, area 19,200 sq. mi., SW Pacific, part of Territory of New Guinea (see NEW GUINEA, TERRITORY OF). Includes NEW BRITAIN (largest island), NEW IRELAND, LAVONGAI, ADMIRALTY ISLANDS, Duke of York Isls., and Vitu Isls. Became a German protectorate in 1884, mandated to Australia in 1920.

Bismarck Sea, SW arm of Pacific Ocean, NE of New Guinea. In 1943 a Japanese naval force was destroyed here by U.S. aircraft.

bismuth (bĭz′mùth), silvery-white, reddish-tinged, crystalline, brittle element (symbol = Bi; see also ELEMENT, table). Grouped with nitrogen, phosphorus, etc., in periodic system; more strongly metallic than others. Expands on solidification. Used in low-melting-point alloys (e.g., Wood's metal, casting alloys), in cotton printing, cosmetic manufacture; insoluble compounds used in medicine and fluoroscopy.

bison, hoofed short-horned mammal related to domestic cattle, with heavily mantled shoulders sloping to hindquarters. Two species of genus *Bison:* European or wisent (miscalled aurochs; reduced by 1948 to 97 known purebred specimens); American bison (buffalo), now protected on national and state refuges.

Bisschop, Simon: see EPISCOPIUS, SIMON.

Bisutun: see BEHISTUN.

Bithynia (bĭthĭ′nĕù), anc. country of NW Asia, in present Turkey. Independent Thracian state became autonomous part of Persian Empire and after the death of Alexander the Great was independent kingdom (3d–1st cent. B.C.), warring against Seleucids and others until King Nicomedus III (or IV) willed it to Rome (74 B.C.). Long joined with Pontus as a colony, Bithynia declined after the time of Hadrian.

Bitolj (bē′tôlyù), Macedonian *Bitola,* formerly *Monastir,* city (pop. 31,131), Macedonia, S Yugoslavia. Became bishopric 11th cent.; conquered by Turks 1382; developed into military and commercial center. Noted for its many mosques, churches, and bazaar.

bittern, migratory marsh bird, heron family. American species (called "stake driver" for booming call) is widespread in E North America. Mostly nocturnal, it eats frogs, fish,

insects. Is 2–3 ft. tall, brown and yellow, with striped foreneck. See *ill.,* p. 135.

bitterroot, low perennial (*Lewisia rediviva*), native to W North America. Its large pink or white blossom is Montana state flower. Rock garden plant.

Bitterroot Range, part of Rocky Mts., on Idaho-Mont. line, running NW-SE. Highest peak is Mt. Garfield (10,961 ft.) in range's SE spur, Beaverhead Mts.

bitters, spirituous liquor (to 40% alcohol) containing bitter principles, e.g., angostura bark; used as flavoring (as in cocktails), and as appetizers and digestives.

bittersweet, name for two vines: *Celastrus scandens,* native to North America, which bears clusters of orange-red fruits; and bitter or woody nightshade (*Solanum dulcamara*), a native of the Old World, which has scarlet berries.

Bitzius, Albert: see GOTTHELF, JEREMIAS.

Biwa (bē′wä), lake, c.40 mi. long, 2–12 mi. wide, largest in Japan, in S Honshu.

Bizerta (bĭzûr′tù), Fr. *Bizerte,* city (pop. 39,-327), Tunisia. Its port and naval base are on the Mediterranean and on the lagoon Lake of Bizerte (42 sq. mi.). Anciently a colony of Tyre, it was successively held by the Romans, Vandals, Arabs, Moors, Spaniards, and Barbary pirates. In 1881 occupied by the French who improved and fortified the harbor. A German base in World War II, it was heavily damaged by bombs in 1943 by the Allies.

Bizet, Georges (zhôrzh′ bēzā′), 1838–75, French composer. His opera, *Carmen* (based on a story by Mérimée), became immensely popular though not successful when first performed. He also composed other operas: *Les Pêcheurs de perles* and *La Jolie Fille de Perth.* Among non-operatic compositions are suites for Daudet's *Arlésienne,* a Symphony in C.

Bjerknes, Vilhelm Friman Koren (byĕrk′nĕs), 1862–1951, Norwegian physicist. His work in meteorology and on electric waves helped develop wireless telegraphy. Evolved polar-front theory of cyclones with his son, **Jakob Aall Bonnevie Bjerknes** (ôl′ bô′nùvē), 1897–, U.S. citizen in 1946. Professor of meteorology, Univ. of California (1940–).

Bjornson, Bjornstjerne (byûrn′styĕrnù byûrn′-sōn), Nor. *Bjørnstjerne Bjørnson,* 1832–1910, Norwegian writer. His dramas, novels (many of peasant life), and epic poetry won him repute as foremost Norwegian poet and novelist, second as dramatist only to Ibsen. Among his novels are *Arne* (1859) and *The Fisher Girl* (1868). Among his dramas are *Sigurd Slembe* (1862) and *The Bankrupt* (1875). Awarded 1903 Nobel Prize in Literature.

Black, Greene Vardiman, 1836–1915, American dentist, noted as teacher, author, and originator of methods and instruments.

Black, Hugo LaFayette, 1886–, Associate Justice of U.S. Supreme Court (1937–).

Black, Jeremiah Sullivan, 1810–83, U.S. Attorney General (1857–60) and U.S. Secretary of State (1860–61). Persuaded Pres. Buchanan to send supplies to Fort Sumter.

Black, Joseph, 1728–99, Scottish chemist, physician. Discovered carbon dioxide, studied latent heat. Taught medicine at Glasgow (1756–66) and Edinburgh (from 1766).

black Angus: see CATTLE.

Blackbeard, d. 1718, English pirate whose real name was probably Edward Teach or Thatch. Probably originally a privateer, preyed on West Indies and Atlantic coast 1716–18. Killed by British.

Black Belt, term loosely applied to belt across central S.C. and Ga., and also to black-soil areas in Ala., Miss., and other states.

blackberry, thorny plant (*Rubus*) with juicy, black fruits, eaten raw or used in jams or preserves.

blackbird, in North America a perching bird allied to bobolink, meadow lark, grackle, oriole. Red-winged blackbird common in E U.S.; yellow-headed, tricolored red-winged, Brewer's blackbird known to West; rusty blackbird winters in U.S. European blackbird is a thrush.

Blackburn, Joseph, b. c.1700, d. after 1765, American artist. Painted portraits of members of distinguished New England families.

Blackburn, county borough (pop. 111,217), Lancashire, England; a cotton-weaving center. James Hargreaves invented the spinning jenny here (1764).

Black Canyon of the Gunnison National Monument: see NATIONAL PARKS AND MONUMENTS (table).

black codes: see RECONSTRUCTION.

Black Country, highly industrialized region, mostly in Staffordshire, but also in Worcestershire and Warwickshire, England. Produces coal, iron, and steel. Birmingham is the principal city.

Black Death: see PLAGUE.

Blackett, Patrick Maynard Stuart (blă′kĭt), 1897–, English physicist. Won 1948 Nobel Prize for work in improving and extending use of Wilson cloud chamber and for discoveries concerning cosmic rays.

black-eyed Susan, North American wild herb (*Rudbeckia hirta*), having yellow daisylike blossoms with dark brown centers. Maryland state flower.

Blackfeet Indians: see BLACKFOOT INDIANS.

black fly, small vicious-biting fly with gauzy wings, short legs, humped back. Most attach eggs to underwater plants or rocks; larvae live in flowing water; adult emerges from water in air bubble.

Blackfoot, city (pop. 5,180), SE Idaho, N of Pocatello, between Blackfoot R. and Snake R. near their confluence; founded 1878. Irrigated area produces sugar beets, dairy products, and grain.

Blackfoot Indians, tribes formerly around upper Missouri and Saskatchewan rivers and W to the Rockies, of Algonquian linguistic stock. Three main branches (Siksika or Blackfoot proper, Piegan, and Blood) were united only by sense of being one people. Allied with Gros Ventre and Sarsi Indians, hostile to other groups and whites. They gained wealth from fur trade, but their nomadic Plains culture was destroyed with disappearance of buffalo. Elaborate rituals include the sun dance and the vision quest. Also called Blackfeet.

Black Forest, Ger. *Schwarzwald,* mountain range in S Baden and Württemberg, SW Germany. Covered by dark pine forests; rises to 4,903 ft. in Feldberg. Chief resorts: Baden-Baden and Wildbad. Clock and toy industries.

Black Friday. In 1868 a small group of American financial speculators, including Jay GOULD and James FISK, sought support of Federal officials in drive to corner gold market. Attempt failed when government gold was released for sale. Drive culminated in day of panic when thousands were ruined— Friday, Sept. 24, 1869, popularly called Black Friday.

black gum, sour gum, or **pepperidge,** ornamental tree (*Nyssa sylvatica*), of E North America. In autumn the foliage is bright red. This and other *Nyssa* species are also called tupelo.

Black Hand, name and symbol used by criminal or terrorist groups. Flourished in Sicily in late 19th cent.; carried to U.S. See also CAMORRA.

black haw, a VIBURNUM (*Viburnum prunifolium*), native to E North America. Bluish-black, edible berries.

Black Hawk War. 1 Conflict between Sac and Fox Indians and U.S. in 1832. Treaty imposed on Indians in 1831 compelled removal from Ill. Return in April, 1832, of an Indian group under Black Hawk (1767–1838) resulted in armed conflict; most of Black Hawk's party destroyed by force under command of Henry Atkinson. **2** Conflict between Indians and whites in Utah 1865–68. Treaty signers in 1868 included Black Hawk (d. 1870), Ute chief.

Black Hills, mountains, SW S.Dak. and NE Wyo. They cover c.6,000 sq. mi. between Belle Fourche R. and Cheyenne R., rising amid semiarid plains to altitudes of 5,000 ft. and over. Forests of yellow pine, black from a distance, gave hills their name. Preserved features include Wind Cave, Jewel Cave, Fossil Cycad, and Mt. Rushmore. White settlement and mining were vigorous after 1874 gold discovery. Found here also are silver, tungsten, mica, coal, and oil. Harney Peak (7,242 ft.) is the highest point.

Black Hole of Calcutta: see CALCUTTA.

Blackmore, Richard Doddridge, 1825–1900, English novelist, author of *Lorna Doone* (1869).

Black Mountain, resort town (pop. 1,174), W N.C., in Blue Ridge E of Asheville. Near by are Y.M.C.A. and Presbyterian assembly areas and **Black Mountain College** (nonsectarian; coed.; 1933), experimental school, integrating college-community life with student needs. Students are self-responsible.

Black Mountains, part of Appalachian system, W N.C., rising to 6,684 ft. in Mt. MITCHELL.

Blackmur, R(ichard) P., 1904–, American critic and poet. His critical writings include *The Double Agent* (1935) and *Language as Gesture* (1952).

Blackpool, county borough (pop. 147,131), Lancashire, England; resort on the Irish Sea.

Black Prince: see EDWARD THE BLACK PRINCE.

Black River. 1 Tributary of White R. (Ark.), rising in SE Mo. and flowing c.300 mi. SW to White R. near Newport, Ark. Partly navigable. Clearwater Dam (flood control) completed 1948. **2** River, NE La., formed after

Tensas R. joins Ouachita R. Flows 57 mi. into Red R. **3** River, N N.Y., rising in the Adirondacks and flowing c.120 mi. SW, NNW, and WSW to an inlet of L. Ontario W of Watertown. Falls provide power (esp. for paper mills).

Blacksburg, town (pop. 3,358), SW Va., W of Roanoke. Seat of Virginia Polytechnic Inst. (land-grant and state supported; coed; opened 1872; woman's division at Radford consolidated with V.P.I. in 1944). Mountain Lake, a resort village, is near.

Black Sea, anc. *Pontus Euxinus,* inland sea (c.160,000 sq. mi.; max. depth c.7,360 ft.), connected with Mediterranean by Bosporus, Sea of Marmara, and DARDANELLES. Enclosed by Bulgaria, Rumania, USSR, Turkey. Chief ports: Odessa, Batum, Constanta. Receives Danube, Dnieper, Don rivers. The Sea of Azov is one of its arms.

black snake, nonpoisonous snake of E U.S. Adults dull black, 5–6 ft. long. Seizes prey (small animals) in mouth, pressing it to ground to kill. Pilot black snake of NE U.S. has shiny black scales.

Blackstone, Sir William, 1723–80, English jurist. His *Commentaries on the Law of England* (1765–69) influential in England and the U.S.; long used as authority.

Blackstone, river rising in central Mass, and flowing c.50 mi. SSE, past Worcester, Mass., Woonsocket and Pawtucket, R.I. (below which it is now called Seekonk R.), to Providence R. at Providence.

blackthorn or **sloe,** thorny plum tree (*Prunus spinosa*), of Europe, Asia, N. Africa. Blue fruits used in brandy, sloe gin. Limbs used for canes in Ireland.

Black Tom, part of Jersey City, N.J., called also Black Tom Isl. Here, in Aug., 1916, German saboteurs demolished a munitions plant.

Black Warrior, navigable river, W Ala., formed by forks W of Birmingham and flowing 178 mi. SW to Tombigbee R. at Demopolis.

Black Watch or **Royal Highlanders,** Scottish infantry regiment. Name comes from their dark kilts. Formed 1735 to watch Scottish rebels and keep peace.

Blackwell, Elizabeth, 1821–1910, American physician, b. England; first woman in U.S. to be granted medical degree (1849). Helped to found (1857) New York Infirmary and Col. for Women, first nurses' school in U.S., and London School of Medicine for Women. Her brother, **Henry Brown Blackwell,** 1825–1909, was an abolitionist and, with his wife, Lucy STONE, worked for woman suffrage. Their daughter, **Alice Stone Blackwell,** 1857–1950, edited (1881–1917) the *Woman's Journal,* suffrage organ. **Antoinette Louisa (Brown) Blackwell,** 1825–1921, sister-in-law of Elizabeth Blackwell and H. B. Blackwell, was a Unitarian minister and a worker for woman suffrage.

Blackwell, city (pop. 9,199), N Okla., NE of Enid, in wheat and oil area. Has oil refineries, zinc smelters, and glass plants.

bladder, urinary, muscular sac in pelvis. Urine secreted by kidneys enters bladder by two tubes (ureters) and is conveyed out of body by another tube (urethra).

bladderwort, carnivorous aquatic or bog plant

(*Utricularia* and related genera), equipped with small bladderlike organs to trap minute animal life.

Bladensburg, town (pop. 2,899), W central Md., on Anacostia R., near Washington, D.C. Here British defeated Americans (Aug. 24, 1814) before entering Washington. Stephen Decatur was mortally wounded in duel here.

Blaeu, Willem Janszoon (vĭ′lùm yän′sōn blou′), 1571–1638, Dutch cartographer, printer. Founded unusually fine printing establishment in Amsterdam.

Blagoveshchensk (blŭgùvyĕsh′chĭnsk), city (pop. 58,761), RSFSR, in extreme E Siberia, on Amur R. and on spur of Trans-Siberian RR. Agr. center.

Blaine, James G(illespie), 1830–93, American politician. U.S. Representative from Maine (1863–76); speaker of House (1869–75). U.S. Senator (1876–81). U.S. Secretary of State (1881, 1889–92). First called "plumed knight" in 1876 Republican convention, where improper influence he had used in case of a railroad in Ark. prevented his nomination. Nominated in 1884, he was largely defeated for President by "rum, Romanism, and rebellion" epithet used to characterize Democrats by New York minister supporting him. As Secretary of State, he fostered closer U.S.–Latin American relations, brought about first Pan American Congress (see PAN-AMERICANISM).

Blaine, tourist city (pop. 1,693), NW Wash. Site of Peace Arch on Canadian border.

Blair, Francis Preston, 1791–1876, American journalist and politician. Founder (1830) of Washington *Globe.* A leader in KITCHEN CABINET. Helped found Republican party; adviser to Pres. Lincoln. Blair House, his Washington residence, is now government property. His son, **Francis Preston Blair,** 1821–75, was a political leader in Mo. and a Union general in Civil War. His regiment of "Wide Awakes" helped keep Mo. loyal to Union. Served with distinction in Vicksburg, Chattanooga, and Atlanta campaigns. U.S. Senator (1871–73). An older brother, **Montgomery Blair,** 1813–83, was U.S. Postmaster General (1861–64). As first U.S. solicitor in Court of Claims (1855–57) he was counsel for Scott in Dred Scott Case.

Blair, James, 1656–1743, Church of England clergyman in Va., b. Scotland, founder (1693) of College of William and Mary.

Blair, Montgomery: see BLAIR, FRANCIS PRESTON.

Blairsville, borough (pop. 5,000), SW Pa., on Conemaugh R. and E of Pittsburgh, in coal and clay area.

Blake, Robert, 1599–1657, English admiral. Without naval training, had brilliant career after 1649. Estab. British power in Mediterranean 1654. Helped develop Commonwealth Navy.

Blake, William, 1757–1827, English artist and poet. An engraver, he (with the assistance of his wife, Catherine Boucher) engraved powerful illustrations for editions of various authors (Edward Young, Cowper, Dante, Thomas Gray, the book of Job) and for all his own volumes of poetry except *Poetical Sketches* (1783). His poems show the same fusing of metaphysical vision and strong, simple line as his engravings. *Songs of Innocence* (1789) and *Songs of Experience* (1794) have many haunting and familiar short poems (e.g., "Piping down the Valleys Wild," "The Tiger"). Except for lyric bits, the "Prophetic Books" (*The Book of Thel,* 1789; *America,* 1793; *The Book of Urizen,* 1794; *The Book of Los,* 1795; *Milton,* 1804; *Jerusalem,* 1804) are less familiar to ordinary readers; in them he developed his own mythology and religion.

Blakelock, Ralph Albert, 1847–1919, American landscape painter, known for melancholy effects.

Blakely, residential borough (pop. 6,828), NE Pa., near Scranton.

Blakeslee, Albert Francis, 1874–, American botanist. Discovered sexual reproduction in bread molds. Work on inheritance and geographic distribution of Jimson weed (*Datura*) yielded information on chromosome action, genic balance, evolution. Used colchicine, an alkaloid, to produce polyploid plants.

Blanc, Louis (lwĕ′ blä′), 1811–82, French socialist. His *Organisation du travail* (1840) outlined social order based on principle, "From each according to his abilities, to each according to his needs." Leader in the revolution of 1848, he was disappointed when his plan for social workshops was sabotaged; fomented unsuccessful workers' uprising; fled to England, staying until 1871.

Blanc, Mont: see MONT BLANC.

Blanca Peak: see SANGRE DE CRISTO MOUNTAINS.

Blanchard, Jean Pierre (zhä′ pyĕr′ blä̈shär′), or François Blanchard (frä̈swä′), 1753–1809, French balloonist. Reputed inventor of parachute (1785). With Dr. John Jeffries, he made (1785) first English Channel crossing by air.

Blanche of Castile (kästēl′), 1185?–1252, queen of Louis VIII of France, regent during minority of her son Louis IX and after his departure on Crusade (1248). Capable and authoritarian.

Blanco Fombona, Rufino (rōōfē′nō blä̈ng′kō fōmbō′nä), 1874–1944, Venezuelan poet, essayist, novelist, a leader of *modernismo,* active in political affairs.

Bland-Allison Act, 1878, passed by U.S. Congress to provide for freer coinage of silver. Original bill offered by Rep. Richard P. Bland met Western demands for free, unlimited coinage of silver. Sen. William B. Allison offered amended version. Act required U.S. treasury to purchase $2,000,000–$4,000,000 worth of silver bullion each month at market prices for coinage into silver dollars, which were made legal tender for all debts. Neither free-silver nor goldstandard forces were satisfied, but act remained law until passage of SHERMAN SILVER PURCHASE ACT of 1890.

Blanding, town (pop. 1,177), SE Utah, N of San Juan R. Natural Bridges and Hovenweep national monuments are near.

Blane, Sir Gilbert, 1749–1834, Scottish physician, known for introducing lime juice to prevent scurvy and advancing sanitary measures in British navy.

blank verse: see PENTAMETER.

Blanqui, Louis Auguste (lwĕ′ ōgüst′ blä̈kē′), 1805–81, French revolutionist and radical thinker. A leader in February Revolution of 1848. Exiled (1864–70) in Brussels, he opposed Napoleon III, and was instrumental in his deposition. The Commune of Paris of 1871 was largely his creation, though Thiers had him arrested shortly before its proclamation. Freed in 1879. His social theories influenced Marx. Chief work: *Critique sociale* (1869).

Blarney, village, Co. Cork, Ireland. Castle (15th-cent.) contains Blarney stone, supposed to bestow persuasive powers on those who kiss it.

Blasco Ibáñez, Vicente (vēthän′tä blä′skō ēbä′nyäth), 1867–1928, Spanish novelist, b. Valencia, best known for *The Four Horsemen of the Apocalypse* (1916), a novel of World War I.

Blashfield, Edwin Howland, 1848–1936, American mural and genre painter.

Blasket Islands, group of rocky islets off Co. Kerry, SW Ireland. Only one is inhabited. Stronghold of last Irish chieftain to surrender to Cromwell.

blast furnace, structure for smelting, i.e., for extracting metals from ores. Principle involves removing oxygen from metal oxide to obtain metal. Furnace for iron is chimneylike, narrowing at top and bottom. Ore, coke, and flux are fed into top; hot air piped into bottom passes up through the mass. Coke oxidizes to carbon dioxide, which great heat changes to carbon monoxide; this reduces the ore, taking on oxygen and forming carbon dioxide, which is piped off. Molten iron descends to crucible at bottom of furnace and is separated from slag.

blasting, fragmentizing of rock or other material by explosive discharged within it or against it. Four steps in modern blasting: drilling holes to receive charge, placing charge, tamping hole, and igniting or detonating charge. Explosives used include black powder, dynamite, and ammonium nitrate.

Blavatsky, Helena Petrovna (blŭvät′skē), 1831–91, Russian theosophist and occultist. After traveling widely, she went (1873) to New York where she founded (1875) the Theosophical Society and wrote (1877) *Isis Unveiled.* After 1879 she made her hq. at Madras, India. She was the chief founder of theosophy.

blazing star or **gay-feather,** a North American perennial (*Liatris* or *Lacinaria*), with racemes of purple or white feathery flowers.

bleaching, process of whitening by chemicals or sunlight, commonly applied to textiles, paper pulp, flour, fats, hair, feathers, wood, and other materials. Chemical methods include oxidation, reduction, and adsorption; textiles have long been sun bleached. Chloride of lime, invented 1799, was first of modern chemical bleaches. Javelle water and other chlorine mixtures are common domestic bleaches.

Bled, resort town, Slovenia, N Yugoslavia, in the Julian Alps. Former royal castle is near by.

bleeding: see HEMOPHILIA; HEMORRHAGE.

bleeding heart, perennial (*Dicentra spectabilis*), native to Japan. A spring-flowering garden plant with drooping, deep pink heart-shaped blooms.

Blekinge, Swed. *Blekinge län* (blä'kĭng-ù lĕn'), county (1,173 sq. mi.; pop. 145,909) and historic province, SE Sweden, on the Baltic coast; cap. Karlskrona. Cultivated valleys make it "the garden of Sweden." Conquered from Denmark in 1658.

Blenheim (blĕn'ŭm), Ger. *Blindheim,* village, W Bavaria, on the Danube E of Ulm. Between Blenheim and near-by Höchstädt Marlborough and Prince Eugene defeated French and Bavarians under Tallard in major battle of War of Spanish Succession (1704).

Blenheim Park, estate, Oxfordshire, England; seat of duke of Marlborough. Government provided estate and castle for victor of the battle of Blenheim.

Blennerhassett, Harman, 1765–1831, Anglo-Irish pioneer in America, an associate of Aaron Burr. Advanced money to Burr for Western schemes. Taken into custody after Burr's arrest, but released. In 1798 he bought part of **Blennerhassett Island,** in the Ohio, near Parkersburg, W.Va., and Belpre, Ohio. Here he built mansion and laboratory.

Blériot, Louis (lwē' blärēō'), 1872–1936, French aviator and inventor. First to fly English Channel in heavier-than-air machine (July 25, 1909).

Blessington, Marguerite, countess of, 1789–1849, Irish beauty and intellectual who set up a briliant salon in Kensington (1822). Wrote novels.

Blest Gana, Alberto (älbĕr'tō blĕst' gä'nä), 1830–1920, Chilean novelist, generally considered greatest of 19th-cent. Spanish American realists. His masterpiece is *Martín Rivas* (1862).

Blicher, Steen Steensen (stän' stän'sùn blē'kùr), 1782–1848, Danish realistic novelist, author of *The Diary of a Parish Clerk* (1824). Also wrote poetry.

Bligh, William, 1754–1817, British admiral. Chiefly remembered for mutiny on his ship, the BOUNTY, 1789. Was governor of New South Wales 1805–8.

blindness, lack or loss of sight. May result from injury or certain diseases including cataract, glaucoma. See also COLOR BLINDNESS; BRAILLE SYSTEM.

Bliss, Eleanor Albert, 1899–, American bacteriologist, authority on sulfa drugs.

Bliss, Philip Paul, 1838–76, American evangelist and writer of gospel songs. Among his songs are *Let the Lower Lights Be Burning* and *Jesus Loves Me.*

Bliss, Porter Cornelius, 1833–85, American explorer and adventurer. Explored Gran Chaco for Argentine government. Imprisoned as suspected spy in Paraguay, released on demand of U.S.

Bliss, Tasker Howard, 1853–1930, American army officer and statesman. Appointed chief of staff of U.S. army (1917), he helped work out mobilization plans. Delegate to Paris Peace Conference.

blister rust or **white-pine blister rust,** European disease of white pine, now common in North America. Currant and gooseberry are alternate hosts.

Blixen, Karen, Baroness: see DINESEN, ISAK.

Bloch, Ernest (blŏk), 1880–, Swiss-American composer. Most work filled with intense Hebraic feeling, (e.g., the Hebrew rhapsody *Schelomo,* 1916). Among other works are an opera, *Macbeth;* a *concerto grosso* for string orchestra and piano.

Bloch, Felix, 1905–, American physicist, b. Switzerland. Shared 1952 Nobel Prize for developing method of measuring magnetic fields in atomic nuclei.

blockade, use of naval vessels to cut off access to a coast, usually to prevent neutral shipping from trade with the enemy. The Declaration of Paris (1856) provided that blockades be announced to all affected parties and be legal only if effective and enforced against all neutrals.

block book, book with each page printed from a separate wood block. European examples (after middle of 15th cent.) were crude, inexpensive (e.g., *Biblia pauperum*). Chinese examples (earliest in 8th cent.) often beautiful.

blockhouse, small fortification, usually temporary, serving as a post for a small garrison. Its use dates probably from the 15th cent. Typical structure in U.S. came to be one of two stories, the second story overhanging.

Block Island, 7 mi. long and 3½ mi. wide, off S R.I., at E entrance to Long Isl. Sound between Point Judith, R.I., and Montauk Point, N.Y.; coextensive with New Shoreham town (pop. 732). Visited by Adriaen Block in 1614, settled 1661. Glaciated surface has low hills, many ponds, peat deposits. Has two lighthouses. Popular summer resort.

Blocksberg, Germany: see BROCKEN.

Blodgett, Katharine Burr, 1898–, American chemist. Worked on tungsten filaments, monomolecular layers. Made nonreflecting glass by coating glass with layers of barium stearate.

Bloemfontein (blōōm'fŏntän"), city (pop. 67,-196), cap. of Orange Free State, South Africa. Seat of Appellate Division of Supreme Court.

Blois (blwä), city (pop. 21,666), cap. of Loir-et-Cher dept., central France, on the Loire. Thibaut the Cheat, 1st count of Blois, acquired Chartres and Touraine (10th cent.); successors added Champagne and Brie. Blois itself was assigned to cadet branch of family, sold to duke of Orleans 1397, incorporated into royal domain 1498. Famous Renaissance château was residence of Francis I, Mary Queen of Scots, Catherine de' Medici; scene of murder of Henri de Guise 1588. The Treaties of Blois (1504–5) were a temporary settlement of the ITALIAN WARS.

Blok, Aleksandr Aleksandrovich (ŭlyĭksän'dùr ŭlyĭksän'drŭvĭch blŏk'), 1880–1921, greatest of Russian symbolist poets. He achieved fame through the cycle *Beautiful Lady* (1904). Embracing the Revolution of 1917, he wrote *The Twelve* (1918; Eng. tr., 1920), a powerful epic.

Blomfield, Sir Reginald, 1856–1942, English architect who specialized in Renaissance and Georgian styles. His books are standard reference works.

Blondel, François (fräswä' blōdĕl'), 1617–86, French architect. Designed triumphal arch, Porte Saint-Denis, Paris. His nephew,

Jacques François Blondel, 1705–74, was also an eminent architect.

Blondel de Nesle (Fr. blōdĕl' dû nĕl'), fl. late 12th cent., French troubadour, a favorite of Richard I. According to legend, found Richard in prison by singing song known only to two of them and was able to effect his rescue.

blood, circulating fluid which brings food and oxygen to body tissues and carries off carbon dioxide and other wastes. In man, consists of fluid plasma containing substances essential for CLOTTING OF BLOOD, hormones, and several types of cells including red and white CORPUSCLES. Recognition of four blood groups and RH FACTOR important in BLOOD TRANSFUSION. See also CIRCULATION OF THE BLOOD. See *ills.*, pp. 763, 813.

blood clotting: see CLOTTING OF BLOOD.

bloodhound: see HOUND.

blood poisoning: see SEPTICEMIA.

blood pressure, pressure of blood on walls of blood vessels, especially arteries. Depends on heart action, arterial elasticity, capillary resistance, and volume and viscous quality of blood. Max. pressure during contraction of heart (systole); min. during relaxation (diastole). Normal systolic range 100–140. Persistent high pressure (hypertension) is often associated with obesity, arteriosclerosis, and kidney inflammations.

bloodroot, North American woodland wild flower (*Sanguinaria canadensis*). White blossoms (1–3 in. across, usually borne singly), open in early spring.

blood transfusion, transfer of blood from one person or animal to another. For safe transfusion blood of donor and recipient must belong to groups which when mixed do not cause clumping or agglutination of red blood cells. Classification of human blood based on agglutinating substances present. Four major groups designated by Karl LANDSTEINER as O, A, B, AB; in Jansky systems as I, II, III, IV. In Moss system group IV corresponds to O, group I to AB. People in O group called universal donors, in AB group, universal recipients. Blood should be tested also for RH FACTOR.

Bloody Assizes: see JEFFREYS, GEORGE, 1ST BARON JEFFREYS OF WEM.

Bloomer, Amelia Jenks, 1818–94, American reformer. Edited (1848–54) *Lily*, a reform organ. In 1851 adopted dress now known as Bloomer costume.

Bloomfield, Leonard, 1887–1949, American linguist. His masterpiece, *Language* (1933), a standard text, is a clear statement of linguistic principles which are now axiomatic, notably that language study must always be centered in the spoken language, that definitions used in grammar should be based on forms of the language, and that a given language at a given time is a complete system of sounds and forms which exist independently of the past.

Bloomfield. 1 Town (pop. 5,746), N Conn., near Hartford. **2** Town (pop. 49,307), NE N.J., adjoining NW Newark. Mfg. of metal products and chemicals.

Bloomgarden or **Blumengarten, Solomon,** pseud. **Yehoash** (yĕhō'äsh), 1870–1927, American writer of Yiddish poetry. Trans-lated Old Testament from Hebrew into Yiddish.

Bloomington. 1 City (pop. 34,163), central Ill., SE of Peoria; settled 1822. Rail, commercial, industrial center in agr. area; coal fields near. Lincoln made famous "lost speech" to first Republican state convention here 1856. Seat of Illinois Wesleyan Univ. (1854). Annual Passion play. **2** City (pop. 28,163), S central Ind., SW of Indianapolis; settled 1818. Mfg. of wood, limestone (quarries near), and glass products. Seat of INDIANA UNIVERSITY.

Bloomsburg, town (pop. 10,633), E Pa., on Susquehanna R. and SW of Wilkes-Barre; settled 1772. Mfg. of carpets, clothing, and rayon.

Bloomsbury, residential district, central London, England. Has British Mus., Univ. of London, and many squares (e.g., Bedford, Russell, Bloomsbury). Many artists, writers, and students live here.

Blount, William, 1749–1800, American statesman. Governor of Territory South of the River Ohio (present Tenn.) 1790–96. Involved in plan to help British conquer West Florida.

Blow, John, c.1648–1708, English composer, organist at Westminster Abbey, chiefly remembered for his church music and for his masque *Venus and Adonis.* Henry Purcell was his pupil.

Blow, Susan Elizabeth, 1843–1916, American educator, follower of Froebel. Opened first successful public kindergarten (1873) in U.S.

Bloy, Léon (lāō' blwä'), 1846–1917, French author. A Roman Catholic and social reformer, he savagely attacked existing society. His novels *Le Désespéré* [the hopeless one] (1886) and *The Woman Who Was Poor* (1897; Eng. tr., 1939) are autobiographical. His correspondence forms a major part of his work.

Blücher, Gebhard Leberecht (blōō'kŭr, Ger. gĕp'härt lā'bûrĕkht fŭn blü'khŭr), 1742–1819, Prussian general in Napoleonic Wars. Played crucial part in allied victory at Leipzig (1813) and in WATERLOO CAMPAIGN. Created prince of Wahlstatt 1814.

Bluebeard, nickname of the chevalier Raoul in a story by Charles Perrault. Bluebeard's seventh wife opens a locked door and finds the bodies of his former wives. She is saved from death at Bluebeard's hands by the arrival of her brothers.

bluebell: see HAREBELL; VIRGINIA COWSLIP; SQUILL.

blueberry, hardy shrub of genus *Vaccinium*. Varieties of low-bush blueberry (*Vaccinium angustifolium*) cultivated commercially for blue or black edible berries. High-bush blueberry or whortleberry (*V. corymbosum*) valued for brilliant autumn foliage. Blueberries need acid soil.

bluebird, migratory bird of North America, a thrush. In East male is c.7 in. long; blue upper plumage, cinnamon-red breast, white underneath. Related are mountain, Western, azure, and chestnut-backed bluebirds. Symbol of elusive happiness in Maeterlinck's *Blue Bird.*

bluebonnet, spring-blooming LUPINE (*Lupinus subcarnosus*), with blue flowers. State flower of Texas.

Blue Cross plans: see HEALTH INSURANCE.

Bluefield, city (pop. 21,506), S W.Va., and adjoining town (pop. 4,212) in Va., settled 1777. Shipping point for coal area with textile and flour milling and mfg. of mining supplies and equipment.

Bluefields, Caribbean port (pop. 7,463), SE Nicaragua, on Bluefields Bay. An early pirate resort, it became cap. of British protectorate over MOSQUITO COAST (1678). Nominally returned to Nicaragua (1850), it was finally annexed (1894) by Zelaya.

bluefish, stout-bodied, delicately flavored food fish (*Pomatomus saltatrix*), of warm waters of Atlantic and Indian oceans. Adults weigh 10 to 25 lb. Deep bluish, tinged with green above, silver below.

bluegrass, a grass species of genus *Poa* with bluish-green leaves. Used for pasture, hay, and lawns. Best known is Kentucky bluegrass (*Poa pratensis*), in region noted for racehorses.

Blue Island, city (pop. 17,622), NE Ill., just S of Chicago; settled 1835. Has railroad shops. Mfg. of clay and metal products.

blue jay, bird of central and E North America, allied to crow, raven, magpie. Grayish violet-blue upper parts and crest; blue wings and tail, black and white markings; black-collared neck; gray to white under parts; raucous cry, also musical notes.

blue laws, legislation aimed at rigid, minute control of public and private morals. Term originated with Loyalist clergyman, Samuel A. Peters, who in 1781 described "Blue Laws" of Conn. with exaggeration but some truth. Strict laws against Sabbath breaking, drunkenness, sex misconduct common in American colonies. Many blue laws revived in 19th and 20th cent.; now generally disregarded.

Blue Nile, river c.950 mi. long, in the Anglo-Egyptian Sudan. Rises in L. Tana in NW Ethiopia, joins the White Nile at Khartoum to form the NILE.

Blue Point, village (pop. 1,613), SE N.Y., on S shore of Long Isl. Gives name to blue-point oysters.

blueprint. Plans drawn to scale on translucent material, then placed on paper treated with mixture of ferric salts and exposed to strong light. Ferric salts unprotected by drawing react to give blue color; salts under drawing wash away in water, leaving white lines.

Blue Ridge, range of Appalachian system, W of the piedmont, extending from NW Md. just above Harpers Ferry, W.Va., SW through Va. and N.C. into N Ga. Rises to c.5,000 ft. in S. Famous for scenery. Remote valleys (esp. to S) shelter people who preserve old ways of life and speech.

blues, type of song with melancholy text set to mournful tune. Grew from Negro work songs and spirituals. Typical blues song is W. C. Handy's *St. Louis Blues* (1914).

Blues and Greens [names derived from colors of circus charioteers], political factions in the Byzantine Empire in 6th cent. The Greens usually upheld MONOPHYSITISM; the Blues, orthodoxy. Both joined in the *Nika* sedition against Justinian I and Theodora (532). The empress saved the day by ordering Belisarius

to put the rebels down by force; 30,000 were killed.

bluestocking [said by Samuel Johnson to have come from blue rather than formal stockings worn by a man at meetings], member of 18th-cent. English "conversation groups" of intellectuals; later only a woman of the groups, hence an intellectual woman. Famous early bluestockings were Elizabeth Montagu, Elizabeth Carter, Hannah More.

bluestone: see BLUE VITRIOL.

bluet or **quaker-ladies,** small North American wild flower (*Houstonia caerulea*), with blue, yellow-eyed blooms.

blue vitriol or **bluestone,** common blue crystalline hydrous copper salt (cupric sulphate or copper sulphate). Produced when white anhydrous salt crystallizes from aqueous solution. Occurs in nature in chalcanthite. Used in copperplating; as dye mordant.

Bluffton. 1 City (pop. 6,076), NE Ind., on Wabash R. and S of Fort Wayne. Dairying center. **2** Village (pop. 2,423), NW Ohio, NE of Lima. Has large Mennonite population and a Mennonite school.

Blum, Léon (läō′ blŏōm′), 1872–1950, French Socialist statesman. Headed first Popular Front government (1936–37; coalition of Socialists, Radical Socialists, Communists); passed important labor reforms. Arrested by Vichy govt. 1940; defended himself courageously at RIOM trial; held prisoner by Germans until 1945. Briefly headed Socialist cabinet 1946–47. A moderate in his later years.

Blume, Peter (blŏŏm), 1906–, American painter, b. Russia. Variously classified as expressionist or surrealist.

Blumenbach, Johann Friedrich (yōhän′ frē′drĭkh blŏŏ′mŭnbäkh), 1752–1840, German comparative anatomist and physical anthropologist. Notable craniometric studies. Proposed fivefold scheme of race classification.

Blumengarten, Solomon: see BLOOMGARDEN, SOLOMON.

Blunden, Edmund (Charles), 1896–, English poet and critic. Author of poetry of rural England. He is also a scholarly critic, biographer, and editor.

Blunt, Wilfrid Scawen (skō′ĭn), 1840–1922, English poet, author of *The Love Sonnets of Proteus* (1881). Advocated Irish, Indian, and Egyptian home rule.

Blytheville, city (pop. 16,234), NE Ark., near Mississippi R.; settled c.1853. Market and industrial center for state's richest cotton area, where soybeans and feed crops are also produced.

Boabdil (bōŭbdēl′), d. 1538, last Moorish king of Granada in Spain (1482–92). Defeated by Ferdinand and Isabella; fled to Morocco.

boa constrictor (bō′ŭ kŭnstrĭk′tŭr), nonpoisonous constrictor snake in South America; of anaconda and python family. Rarely over 12 ft. long. Agile climber.

Boadicea (bō″ŭdĭse′ŭ), d. A.D. 62, British queen of the Iceni (of Norfolk). Led revolt against the Romans. On defeat she took poison.

Boanerges (bō′ŭnûr′jēz) [Gr.,= sons of thunder], name given by Jesus to James and John. Mark 3.17.

Boardman, Thomas Danforth, 1784–1873,

American maker of pewter ware, now prized by collectors.

Boas, Franz (bō'ăz), 1858–1942, American anthropologist. Taught at Columbia Univ. (1896–1936). His approach was independent of theoretical preconceptions and was marked by a rigorous methodology. He did significant work in physical and cultural anthropology and in linguistics. His teachings had lasting influence on other anthropologists.

Boaz (bō'ăz), Ruth's husband, ancestor of David. Ruth 2; 3; 4; Booz: Mat. 1.5; Luke 3.32.

Bobbio (bôb'bēō), small town, Emilia e Romagna, N central Italy, SW of Piacenza. Monastery founded here by St. Columban in 612 was oldest in N Italy, flourished as cultural center 9th–12th cent.

bobcat, small lynx (*Lynx rufus*) of U.S., S Canada, parts of Mexico. Powerful, usually nocturnal hunter. Known also as bay lynx, red lynx, wildcat.

bobolink, in N U.S. and Canada name of American songbird related to blackbird, oriole. Called reed bird and rice bird in South. In autumn, male spring plumage (black with shoulders and lower back white, buff nape) is yellowish-brown, dark stripes on upper parts. Winters in South America.

bobwhite, American game bird of same family as pheasant and partridge. Eastern bobwhite c.10 in. long; male plumage brown, black, white; female brown, buff. Eats insects, weed seeds. Male whistles "bob-white" to attract female.

Boccaccio, Giovanni (jōvän'nē bōk-kät'chō), 1313–75, Italian poet and novelist, b. Paris. He spent his youth at Certaldo, near Florence, went to Naples (c.1330), where he won Petrarch's friendship, and returned to Tuscany 1341, spending his last years in Florence. His chief work is the DECAMERON, one of the world's great books. Other works include a biography of Dante; *Filocolo* (c.1340) and *La Fiammetta* (c.1344), prose romances; *Filostrato,* upon which Chaucer drew for his *Troilus and Criseyde;* and the *Corbaccio,* a verse satire on women.

Boccherini, Luigi (bôk-kěrē'nē), 1743–1805, Italian composer. Perhaps most popular of his works is the *Minuet* from his String Quintet in E Minor.

Bochum (bō'khŏŏm), city (pop. 290,406), North Rhine-Westphalia, NW Germany; a center of RUHR dist.

Bocskay, Stephen (bôch'kī), Hung. *Bocskay István,* 1557?–1606, Hungarian noble, prince of Transylvania (1604–6). His chief aim was to secure Transylvanian independence from both Austria and Turkey. In 1604 he led a revolt, supported by Turkey, against Emperor Rudolf II's attempt to reimpose Catholicism on Hungary. The Treaty of Vienna (1606), which he negotiated, guaranteed religious freedom and legalized the threefold partition of HUNGARY (confirmed by Treaty of Szitvatorok between Austria and Turkey).

Bode, Johann Elert (yō'hän ā'lĕrt bō'dŭ), 1747–1826, German astronomer. Compiler of *Uranographia* (1801; star maps and catalogue of stars and nebulae).

Bodel, Jehan (zhä' bōdĕl'), b. c.1165, French trouvère. *Le Jeu de Saint-Nicolas,* a mystery,

is first long play entirely in French. He died a leper.

Bodensee: see CONSTANCE, LAKE OF.

Bodenstein, Andreas Rudolf: see CARLSTADT.

Bodh Gaya, India: see BUDDH GAYA.

Bodin, Jean (zhä' bōdē'), 1530–96, French social and political philosopher. His *Les Six Livres de la république* (1576; Eng. tr., 1606) was first attempt to formulate scientific philosophy of history.

Bodleian Library (bŏd'lēûn), at Oxford Univ. Original library destroyed; replaced in 17th cent. through efforts of Sir Thomas Bodley, who left a fund for its maintenance. Receives a copy of every book published in Great Britain.

Bodley, George Frederick (bŏd'lē), 1827–1907, English architect of ecclesiastical buildings, an adherent of the Victorian Gothic revival.

Bodley, Sir Thomas, 1545–1613, English scholar and diplomat, organizer of the BODLEIAN LIBRARY.

Bodmer, Johann Jakob (yō'hän yä'kôp bōd'mûr), 1698–1783, Swiss critic. Founded with Johann Jakob Breitinger the critical journal *Diskurse der Mahlern,* which attacked French classicism and paved the way for Klopstock, Goethe, and Schiller. Translated *Paradise Lost;* edited *Nibelungenlied.*

Bodoni, Giambattista (jämbät-tē'stä bōdō'nē), 1740–1813, Italian printer. Like Baskerville and Didot a leader in producing "modern" type faces. Indifferent to quality of text, editing, and proofreading, Bodoni produced stately quartos and folios of impressive appearance.

body snatching, stealing dead bodies. Before legal provision for supplying needs of medical schools, traffic in cadavers was profitable. Snatchers known as resurrectionists; their activities in 18th and early 19th cent. increased public opposition to dissection and led to violence.

Boehler, Peter (bû'lûr), 1712–75, German-born missionary of the Moravian Church in America (1738–42, 1753–64). Worked in Ga.; later founded Nazareth and Bethlehem, Pa., and other settlements. In England (1747–53) he was made bishop.

Boehm, Sir Joseph Edgar (bām), 1834–90, English portrait sculptor, b. Vienna.

Boehm, Martin (bām), 1725–1812, American evangelical preacher, b. Pa. Became (1759) Mennonite bishop, but later with P. W. OTTERBEIN founded United Brethren in Christ and was elected bishop (1800).

Boehme or **Böhme Jakob** (bē'mŭ, Ger. bû'mŭ), 1575–1624, German mystic. His religious teaching, based on the belief that God is manifest in all aspects of creation and that evil results when one aspect (e.g., man) attempts to become the whole, was highly influential in England and the Continent.

Boeotia (bēō'shù), region of anc. Greece, N of the Gulf of Corinth; cap. THEBES. A confederacy of cities was cemented in the Boeotian League (7th cent. B.C.), dominated by Thebes until Athens after many battles broke up the confederacy in 457 B.C. Shortly afterward Thebes returned to power with Epaminondas' victory over Sparta at Leuctra (371 B.C.), and all Boeotia shared with Thebes the defeats by Philip II and Alexander the Great. Athenians generally considered Boeotians dull-witted clods, though Hesiod and Pindar belonged to the region.

Boer (bôr, bōōr) [Dutch,= farmer], inhabitant of South Africa of Dutch descent. The Boer language is Afrikaans (see LANGUAGE, table).

Boerhaave, Hermann (bōōr'hävŭ), 1668–1738, Dutch physician and chemist, introducer of clinical teaching at Univ. of Leiden.

Boer War: see SOUTH AFRICAN WAR.

Boethius, Anicius Manlius Severinus (bōē'thēŭs), c.475–525, Roman philosopher. A consul and a minister of Theodoric, he was accused of treason. While in prison awaiting death he wrote *De consolatione philosophiae* [the consolation of philosophy], which has been highly regarded by thoughtful readers from his time to this. Also wrote an influential treatise on music.

Boethus (bōē'thŭs), fl. 1st half of 2d cent. B.C., Greek sculptor, believed to have been the creator of the original SPINARIO.

bog, very old lake without inlet or outlet which becomes overgrown with vegetation. SPHAGNUM and PEAT obtained from bogs. Acid medium of bogs forms natural preservative for remains of animals and plants of earlier times. Typical bog plants are orchids, cranberry, pitcher plant, and sun dew.

Bogalusa (bōgŭlōō'sŭ), city (pop. 17,798), SE La., near Pearl R., in lumbering area; founded 1906. Mfg. of paper, furniture, and tung oil products.

Bogdanov, A. (bŭgdä'nŭf), pseud. of **Aleksandr Aleksandrovich Malinovski,** 1873–1928, Russian social philosopher, an active revolutionist after 1905. Led "proletarian culture" movement under Soviet regime.

Bogert, Marston Taylor, 1868–, American chemist. Synthesized aromatic organic compounds.

Boghazkeui (bō″gäzkû'ē), village, N central Asiatic Turkey, where Hugo Winckler discovered (1906–7) Hittite inscriptions. Name also spelled Boghazkoy.

bog iron ore: see LIMONITE.

Bogomils (bō'gōmĭlz), earliest (10th cent.) group of the CATHARI. Flourishing in Bulgaria and the Balkans, they were distinguished not only by dualistic religious beliefs but also by political nationalism and resentment of Byzantine culture. Various subgroups were called Babuns, Phundaits, and Patarenes. They spread to Italy and converted the ALBIGENSES. Opposition of Christian churches weakened the Bogomils, who were wiped out by the triumph of Islam (15th cent.).

Bogotá (bōgōtä'), city (pop. 325,658; alt. 8,660 ft.) central Colombia; cap. and largest city of country. Founded (1538) by Jiménez de Quesada to succeed center of Chibcha culture. In a broad valley of E Andes, it was difficult of access before air transportation. Called by Alexander von Humboldt (1801) the Athens of America. After independence from Spain, Bogotá was cap. of Greater Colombia until dissolution of union (1830). Organization of American states founded here 1948.

Bogota (bŭgō'tŭ), borough (pop. 7,662), NE NJ., on Hackensack R. Mfg. of paper and metal products.

Bohemia, Czech *Čechy,* historic province (20,-102 sq. mi.; pop. 5,490,000), W Czechoslovakia; cap. PRAGUE. Separated from Bavaria by the BOHEMIAN FOREST, from Saxony by the ERZGEBIRGE, and from Silesia by the SUDETES, it is a fertile, hilly region, drained by the Elbe and Moldau rivers. Industries include mining (coal, silver, copper, lead, radium, uranium), especially in the Erzgebirge; textile and glass mfg.; heavy industries (centered in Prague region); brewing (notably at Pilsen). Many resorts (e.g., Carlsbad, Marienbad). Since the expulsion, after 1945, of most of German-speaking minority, population is overwhelmingly Czech. Bohemia takes its name from the probably Celtic Boii, whom Czech settlers displaced during 1st–5th cent. A.D. Temporarily subjugated by the Avars and later by MORAVIA, and Christianized by SS. CYRIL AND METHODIUS, it became a duchy of the Holy Roman Empire under St. WENCESLAUS (d. 935). Later dukes of the PREMYSL dynasty acquired Moravia and most of SILESIA, and in 1198 OTTOCAR I took the title king. The vast conquests of OTTOCAR II proved ephemeral, and in 1306 the Premyslide line became extinct. Under the Luxembourg dynasty, particularly under Emperor CHARLES IV, Bohemia had its golden age. Charles's Golden Bull (1356) gave the kings of Bohemia the rank of ELECTORS. In the 15th cent. the HUSSITE WARS brought Bohemia into chaos. GEORGE OF PODEBRAD (d. 1471) restored peace, but he was the last native ruler. The crown passed first to the kings of Hungary (see JAGIELLO), and in 1526 to the house of HAPSBURG, which ruled it until 1918. Religious tension continued. When in 1618 Emperor Matthias abrogated religious freedom (granted 1609), the Bohemian diet in defiance deposed their Hapsburg king (later Emperor FERDINAND II) and elected FREDERICK THE WINTER KING. These events led directly to the THIRTY YEARS WAR (1618–48). The Protestant defeat at the WHITE MOUNTAIN (1620) ended Czech freedom. Bohemia became a Hapsburg crownland (1627) and was subjected to rigorous Germanization. Czech nationalism flared up in the Revolution of 1848, but was crushed in 1849. Later concessions to Czech demands for equal status in the AUSTRO-HUNGARIAN MONARCHY were insufficient, and Czech disaffection was one of the causes of Austria's defeat in World War I. With the realization of Czech independence in 1918, the history of Bohemia became that of CZECHOSLOVAKIA.

Bohemian Forest, Czech *Česky Les,* Ger. *Böhmerwald,* thickly wooded mountain range along border of Bohemia, Czechoslovakia, and Bavaria, Germany. S section called *Šumava* in Czech. Highest point, Arber (4,780 ft.), is in Bavaria.

Bohemond I (bō'hŭmŏnd), c.1056–1111, prince of Antioch (1099–1111), a leader in First Crusade; son of ROBERT GUISCARD. Swore fealty to ALEXIUS I but, upon capturing Antioch, made himself prince (1098). Defeated by Alexius (1108), he acknowledged him as overlord but retired and made TANCRED regent.

Bohm, Max (bōm), 1868–1923, American marine, figure, and mural painter.

Böhme, Jakob: see BOEHME, JAKOB.

Böhmerwald: see BOHEMIAN FOREST.

Bohol (bôhôl′), island (1,491 sq. mi.; pop. 449,549), Philippines, N of Mindanao and between Cebu and Leyte. Produces rice, hemp, and manganese.

Bohr, Niels Henrik David (nēls′ hăn′rēk dä′vēdh bōr), 1885–, Danish physicist. Won 1922 Nobel Prize for concept of structure of atom; reconciled this with quantum theory. Assisted in atomic-bomb research in U.S. (1938–39; 1943–45). Instrumental in founding Inst. of Theoretical physics, Copenhagen.

Bohun (bōōn), English noblemen of Norman descent. **Henry de Bohun, 1st earl of Hereford,** 1176–1220, was one of barons who forced King John to accept Magna Carta (1215). **Humphrey V de Bohun, 2d earl of Hereford** and 1st earl of Essex, d. 1274, led barons of Welsh Marches who returned (1263) to side of Henry III in BARONS′ WAR. **Humphrey VII de Bohun, 3d earl of Hereford** and 2d earl of Essex, d. 1298, was constable of England and a leader of barons who forced Edward I to sign confirmation of the charters 1297. **Humphrey VIII de Bohun, 4th earl of Hereford** and 3d earl of Essex, 1276–1322, was one of lord ordainers attempting to curb Edward II in 1310. Aided in execution of Piers GAVESTON.

Bohuslän, Swed. *Bohuslän* (bōō′hüslĕn), historic province, SW Sweden, conquered from Denmark 1658.

Boiardo or **Bojardo, Matteo Maria** (mät-tā′ō mä-rē′ä bōyär′dō), c.1434–1494, Italian poet, count of Scandiano. Wrote the unfinished *Orlando Innamorato,* based on the Roland story. The poem was revised satirically by Francesco Berni, and the story was continued by ARIOSTO in *Orlando Furioso.*

Boieldieu, François Adrien (bwäldyû′), 1775–1834, French composer, master of *opéra comique,* composer of *Le Calife de Bagdad, La Dame blanche.*

Boileau, Nicolas (nēkôlä′ bwälō), 1636–1711, French critic and poet. His verse treatise on poetics (1674) made him foremost spokesman of CLASSICISM. His poetic repute rests on *Le Lutrin* (1683), a mock epic, and on his *Satires* and *Épîtres.* Full surname Boileau-Despréaux.

boiler, steam-generating device consisting of fire box (furnace to burn fuel) and boiler proper (enclosed vessel where heated water becomes steam). Common types: fire-tube boiler (hot gases in tubes heat outside water) and water-tube boiler (water in tubes heated by outside gases). Safety valve prevents explosions.

boiling point, temperature at which substance changes from liquid to gas with bubbling called "boiling." Under constant pressure each substance has specific boiling point; lowering pressure lowers boiling point, and vice versa. When substance is at boiling point, there is no increase in temperature until VAPORIZATION is complete.

Boisbrûlés (bwäbrülä′) [from Fr.= burnt wood], name given part-Indian descendants of fur traders in W Canada. Important group in Red River Settlement and in Riel's Rebellion.

Boise (boi′sē, –zē), city (pop. 34,393), state cap., SW Idaho, largest city of state, on Boise R.; founded 1863 near gold fields and military post. Became territorial cap. 1864. Grew as mining center, but with building of near-by Arrowrock Dam (1911–15), became trade and processing center for orchards, grain and potato fields, and dairies in BOISE PROJECT. Mineral springs near.

Boise, river, SW Idaho, rising in three forks in mountains E of Boise. Flows NW, past Boise and Caldwell, to Snake R. at Oregon line. First explored by W. P. Hunt in 1811; called Reed's R. in early days for John Reed, fur trader from Astoria, who, near river's mouth, estab. post where he was killed, 1814. Used today in BOISE PROJECT.

Boise, Fort, fur-trading post, SW Idaho. Founded 1834 on Boise R. by Hudson's Bay Co. to rival Fort HALL. Moved 1838 to Snake R. near Boise R. mouth. Abandoned 1855.

Boise project, SW Idaho and E Oregon, in the Boise, Payette, and Snake river valleys, irrigating c.400,000 acres. Arrowrock division, between Boise and Snake rivers, is served by Arrowrock Dam in Boise R., three Deer Flat Dams that create L. Lowell with canal from Boise R., and Anderson Ranch Dam in South Fork of Boise R. Notus division is N of Boise R., between Caldwell and Notus. Payette division, between Boise and Payette rivers and E of Snake R., is served by Black Canyon Diversion Dam in Payette R., Deadwood Dam in Deadwood R., and Cascade Dam in North Fork of Payette R. Some of Black Canyon power goes to MINIDOKA PROJECT and OWYHEE PROJECT.

Boisguilbert, Pierre le Pesant, sieur de (pyĕr′ lù pùzä′ syûr′ dù bwägēlbĕr′), 1646–1714, French economist. Argued that mass consumption was as important as mass production, and urged income tax.

Bois-le-Duc, Netherlands: see 's HERTOGEN-BOSCH.

Boito, Arrigo (är′rēgō bō′ētō), 1842–1918, Italian composer and librettist. His only significant opera is *Mefistofele.* More important are his librettos for Verdi's *Otello* and *Falstaff.*

Bojardo, Matteo Maria: see BOIARDO.

Bojer, Johan (yō′hän boi′ùr), 1872–, Norwegian novelist and dramatist, noted for portrayal of Norwegian contemporary life, as in *The Power of a Lie* (1896), *The Great Hunger* (1903), *The Last of the Vikings* (1921).

Bok, Edward (William), 1863–1930, American writer, b. Netherlands; editor of the *Ladies′ Home Journal* (1889–1919). His limpid style is at its best in autobiography, *The Americanization of Edward Bok* (1920). He financed the Singing Tower at Iron Mt., Fla. He is buried at its base.

Bokhara, Uzbek SSR: see BUKHARA.

Bolan Pass (bōlän′), NE central Baluchistan, W Pakistan; rises to c.5,580 ft. Used by railroad and highway. Historical route for invading India.

Boldini, Giovanni (jōvän′nē bōldē′nē), 1845–1931, Italian painter, known for portraits of women.

Boleslaus (bō′lùslôs), kings of Poland. **Boleslaus I** (the Brave), Pol. *Bolesław Chrobry,* c.966–1025 (reigned 992–1025), was the first Polish ruler to call himself king. He campaigned successfully against Germany, Bohemia, and Kiev but failed to unite all N Slavs under Polish rule. **Boleslaus III,** 1085–1138 (reigned 1102–38), reunited Poland by conquering his brother's share. By a treaty with Emperor Lothair II he was invested with Pomerania and Rügen as fiefs of Holy Roman Empire (1135).

Boleyn, Anne, 1507?–1536, queen consort of Henry VIII; his second wife and mother of Elizabeth. Henry divorced Katharine of Aragon to marry her. The marriage was generally unpopular; his ardor cooled; and she was executed for alleged adultery.

Bolgari: see BULGARS, EASTERN.

Bolingbroke, Henry of: see HENRY IV (England).

Bolingbroke, Henry St. John, Viscount: see ST. JOHN, HENRY.

Bolívar, Simón (sēmōn' bōlē'vär), 1783–1830, South American revolutionist, called the Liberator, b. Caracas. Participating in revolution against Spain from 1810, he was defeated (1812, 1815) but had liberated the N (Colombia, Venezuela, Ecuador, Panama) by 1822. Met in secret with SAN MARTÍN at Guayaquil (1822); San Martín withdrew from W campaign leaving Bolívar in command of army that won final triumph over royalist forces at Ayacucho (1824). Elected president of Venezuela (1819), he became (1919) president of Greater Colombia (present Colombia, Venezuela, Ecuador, Panama). He also organized government for liberated Peru and Bolivia. At the meeting he called at Panama (1826) to promote a united Spanish America, little was accomplished, but the meeting was beginning of Pan-Americanism. He resigned the presidency in 1830 and died of tuberculosis shortly thereafter. Hated by many during his lifetime for his tyrannical dictatorship, he is today revered as greatest of Latin American heroes.

Bolivia (bōlĭ'vēŭ, Span. bōlē'vyä), republic (412,777 sq. mi.; pop. c.3,990,200), W South America, an inland country. Legal cap. is SUCRE, but LA PAZ is political, financial and commercial center. The E section is tropical, N portion lying in rain forests drained by rivers of Amazon basin, S part merging into the CHACO. The W section is Andean; one cordillera traces border of Chile, the other runs N-S through the center of Bolivia. In the SW is an extensive salt plain, and in the NW the great basin of L. Titicaca. On the high windswept plateau (Altiplano) between mountain ranges and in mountain valleys are the chief centers of population, industries, and transportation. Bolivia has some of the richest mines in the world—tin, silver, copper, wolframite, bismuth, antimony, zinc, lead, gold. Important mining towns are POTOSÍ and ORURIO, and COCHABAMBA and TARIJA are agr. and commercial centers. There were Indian civilizations on the plateau long before the Inca became dominant, and today a large percentage of the Bolivian people are pure Indian. Spanish conquest began in 1538, when Gonzalo and Hernando Pizarro came in successful search for mineral wealth. Spanish poured in and developed mines, textile mills, and great landed estates,

all with Indian labor. As part of the *audiencia* of Charcas, it was attached to viceroyalty of Peru until 1776, then to that of La Plata. Revolution against Spain began in 1809, but independence was gained only by victory of Sucre at Ayacucho (1824). Bolívar drew up a constitution; Upper Peru became Bolivia, Chuquisaca became Sucre. Because the boundaries of the *audiencia* of Charcas were vague and because all the republics were ambitious, Bolivian history has been plagued by disastrous border wars; a Bolivian attempt to reunite Peru and Bolivia failed in 1839; war with Chile (1879–84; see PACIFIC, WAR OF THE) cost Bolivia the nitrate-rich coastal province of Atacama; trouble with Brazil over the Acre region led to Brazil's getting valuable wild-rubber forests (1903); a long-drawn-out dispute over the Chaco led to war (1932–35), in which Paraguay was the victor and Bolivia had to give up large claims. Minerals continued to be the chief basis of Bolivia's international trade, and petroleum found in SE Bolivia brought new railroad development. Demand for tin and wolfram made World War II a boon. Bolivia declared war on the Axis (1943) and became a member of the UN (1945). Recently efforts have been made to improve the lot of the Indians and increase agr. production.

Bollandists (bŏl'ŭndĭsts), group of Jesuits in Belgium, formed by Jean Bolland (17th cent.) and famous for compiling the *Acta sanctorum*, still being brought up to date.

Bolley, Henry Luke, 1865–, American plant pathologist. He discovered cause of potato scab, methods of preventing oak smut, bunt of wheat, and other diseases, and developed rust-resistant wheat and wilt-resistant flax.

boll weevil, snout beetle whose fiber-eating larvae cause losses up to $200,000,000 yearly to U.S. cotton crop. Combatted by dusting with chemicals, early planting, and destroying infected plants in the autumn.

bollworm, name for two cotton pests, both larvae of noctuid moths: pink bollworm, a feeder on blossoms, fiber, and seeds; and cotton bollworm (corn-ear worm), which burrows in the bolls and also attacks corn, tomatoes, and tobacco.

Bologna, Giovanni da (jōvän'nē dä bōlō'nyä), 1524–1608, Flemish sculptor whose real name was Jean Bologne or Boulogne. Identified chiefly with the Italian Renaissance. Famous for his *Flying Mercury* and *The Rape of the Sabines* (Florence).

Bologna (bōlō'nyä), city (pop. 226,771), cap. of Emilia-Romagna, N central Italy. Cultural and commercial center. Of pre-Roman origin, city passed (8th cent.) under papal rule, but a strong free commune was estab. in 12th cent. Guelph-Ghibelline strife enabled several familes to seize power over city in 14th–15th cent., Bentivoglio family being most notable. Papal rule, restored 1506, lasted (except during 1797–1815) until unification of Italy (1860). The famous Univ. of Bologna originated (11th cent.) with Roman law school and made city into one of main centers of medieval learning. Painting flourished 15th–17th cent. with Francia, the Carracci, Guido Reni. Seriously damaged in World War II, Bologna retains many fine medieval palaces and churches. Its two leaning towers and its arcaded streets are characteristic.

Bolsena (bôlsä'nä), village, Latium, central Italy, near site of second VOLSINII, on a crater lake. Here occurred c.1265 a famous reputed miracle: a doubting priest saw blood flow from Host at Mass.

Bolshevism and Menshevism (bōl'shŭvĭzŭm, bŏl'-, mĕn'-shŭvĭzŭm), the two main branches of Marxist SOCIALISM in Russia from 1903 to 1918. In 1903 the Russian Social Democratic party split into two wings. The *Bolsheviki* [majority members], led by LENIN, advocated immediate revolution and establishment of dictatorship of the proletariat. The *Mensheviki* [minority members], led by PLEKHANOV, held that before reaching socialism Russia must pass through an intermediary democratic or bourgeois regime, like the rest of Europe. Bolsheviks favored a small, disciplined party; Mensheviks sought to appeal to masses and to cooperate with "bourgeois" parties. Within the Social Democratic party, which in theory remained united, the Bolsheviks soon lost their numerical superiority. In the RUSSIAN REVOLUTION of 1917 the Mensheviks cooperated with the Kerensky regime, which the Bolsheviks overthrew in Nov., 1917. The Communist party, formed 1918, absorbed or "liquidated" the remaining Mensheviks.

Bolton or **Bolton-le-Moors** (-lŭ-mōōrz'), county borough (pop. 167,162), Lancashire, England; textile center. Connected with Manchester by canal.

Boltwood, Bertram Borden, 1870–1927, American chemist, physicist. Discovered that radium is disintegration product of uranium, intermediate is ionium, and ultimate product is lead. Developed theories that led to discovery of isotopes and had bearings on origin of elements. Taught at Yale.

Bolzano (bōltsä'nō), Ger. *Bozen* (bō'tsŭn), city (pop. 41,722), Trentino-Alto Adige, N Italy, in S Tyrol. Tourist and health resort. Its position on Brenner road made it important medieval trade center. Pop. largely German-speaking.

Bombay (bŏmbā'), state (115,570 sq. mi.; pop. 35,943,559) W India, on Arabian Sea. India's leading commercial and industrial area. Fertile coastal strip (edged by W Ghats) is major rice belt. In 3d cent. B.C. Bombay was part of Maurya-empire. Akbar annexed N section, but after 17th cent. Mahrattas were dominant until defeated by the British in 19th cent. Baroda and Kolhapur were largest of several former native states absorbed 1947. Its cap. **Bombay** (pop. 1,489,-883) is a major port and mfg. center. Was hq. of British East India Co. 1668–1858. Cotton-textile industry.

Bomoseen, Lake (bō'mŭzēn), 7½ mi. long and 1½ mi. wide, W Vt., W of Rutland; resort.

Bon, Cape (bŏn), headland, NE Tunisia, jutting into the Mediterranean. German forces in N Africa surrendered here to Allies in May, 1943.

Bona Dea (bō'nŭ dē'ù) [Latin,= good goddess], Roman earth and mother goddess.

Bonanza Creek, stream of the Yukon flowing into Klondike R. at Dawson. Famous in gold-rush days.

Bonaparte (bō'nŭpärt), Ital. *Buonaparte* (bwōnäpär'tä), family name of NAPOLEON I. His father, **Carlo Buonaparte,** 1746–85, a lawyer in Ajaccio, led pro-French party in Corsica. His mother, **Letizia** or **Laetitia Ramolino Bonaparte,** 1750–1836, "Madame Mère," was noted for her stoic virtues. She retired to Rome after Napoleon's fall. Their eldest son, **Joseph Bonaparte,** 1768–1844, was king of Naples (1806–8) and of Spain 1808–13); inefficient on both thrones. Lived mainly at Bordentown, N.J., from 1815–1841; died in Italy. His brother **Lucien Bonaparte,** 1775–1840, helped Napoleon in coup d'état of 18 BRUMAIRE but opposed establishment of empire. Retired to Rome; created prince of Canino by pope. His sister **Elisa Bonaparte,** 1777–1820, married Felice Bacciochi (an infantry captain). Napoleon made her princess of Lucca (1805), grand duchess of Tuscany (1809). Intelligent administrator. Another brother, **Louis Bonaparte,** 1778–1846, king of Holland (1806–10), married Hortense de BEAUHARNAIS. Deposed by Napoleon for defying Continental System. Died in Italy. **Pauline Bonaparte,** 1780–1825, Napoleon's favorite sister, was beautiful but frivolous. Accompanied her first husband, Gen. Leclerc, to Haiti; married Camillo Borghese, a Roman noble, 1803; was made princess of Guastalla 1806. Another sister, **Caroline Bonaparte,** 1782–1839, married Joachim MURAT, was queen of Naples (1808–14), intrigued against Napoleon. Fled to Austria after Murat's execution. Youngest brother, **Jérôme Bonaparte,** 1784–1860, king of Westphalia (1807–13), was extravagant and irresponsible. Early marriage (1803) with Elizabeth PATTERSON, on a visit to U.S., was annulled on pressure by Napoleon. Later married a princess of Württemberg. Returned to France 1847, lived at court of Napoleon III. Among second generation of family, NAPOLEON II (duke of Reichstadt) and NAPOLEON III were most important. Other members also gained prominence. **Charles Lucien Bonaparte,** 1803–57, prince of Canino, son of Lucien, noted ornithologist, lived in U.S. 1824–33, wrote *American Ornithology* (4 vols., 1825–33). **Pierre Napoléon Bonaparte,** 1815–81, another son of Lucien, entered French politics, supported Napoleon III, and killed a journalist during a quarrel (1870) but was acquitted of murder. Notoriously immoral. **Napoléon Joseph Charles Paul Bonaparte,** 1822–91, son of Jérôme, was known as Prince Napoleon or, familiarly, Plon-Plon. At the court of Napoleon III he advocated a liberal policy. His sister, **Mathilde Bonaparte,** 1820–1904, was prominent at Napoleon III's court. Napoleon III's only son, **Napoléon Eugène Louis Jean Joseph Bonaparte,** 1856–79, the Prince Imperial, was killed fighting the Zulus as a member of the British army. The claim to the Bonapartist succession passed to the descendants of Jérôme by his second marriage. From Jérôme's marriage with Elizabeth Patterson the American branch of the family is issued: **Jerome Napoleon Bonaparte,** 1805–70, and his son, **Charles Joseph Bonaparte,**

1851–1921, U.S. Secretary of the Navy (1905–6) and Attorney General (1906–9). He was active in antitrust suits and was among founders of National Municipal League.

Bonar Law, Andrew: see LAW, ANDREW BONAR.

Bonaventure (bŏnŭvĕn'chŭr) or **Bonaventura, Saint** (bōnäväntōō'rä), 1221–74, Italian-French scholastic theologian, a cardinal, Doctor of the Church, called the Seraphic Doctor, b. near Viterbo. At Univ. of Paris he studied under Alexander of Hales, then taught until he was made general of the Franciscans (1257) and archbishop of Paris (1265). Early works in theology and philosophy were largely devoted to reconciling Aristotelian learning with Augustinian Christianity. Later writings are guides to mysticism, bringing the mystical tradition of St. Bernard of Clairvaux to full flower. Feast: July 14.

Bonaventure Island, 2½ mi. long and ¾ mi. wide, E Que., Canada, in Gulf of St. Lawrence N of Percé Rock. Largest bird sanctuary on N Atlantic coast.

Bonavista Bay, NE N.F., Canada. Irregular bay filled with islands; has many fishing villages on its shores. Bonavista Peninsula (S) ends in Cape Bonavista (S entrance to bay), reputed landfall of Cabot in 1497. Bonavista town is on S shore.

Bond, Carrie Jacobs, 1862–1946, American song writer. The popularity of such songs as *I Love You Truly, Just a-Wearyin' for You,* and *A Perfect Day* earned her a fortune.

Bond, William Cranch, 1789–1859, and a son **George Phillips Bond,** 1825–65, American astronomers, pioneers in celestial photography. Both were associated with Harvard Observatory.

Bond Street, street in London noted for elegant shops. Fashionable residential street 18th–early 19th cent.

Bone, Henry, 1755–1834, English enamel painter.

Bône (bōn), city (pop. 77,675), NE Algeria, a Mediterranean port. Exports iron and phosphates. Once a Carthaginian colony and cap. of Numidian kings. Flourished as Hippo Regius in Roman times and was episcopal see of St. Augustine.

bone, hard tissue composing SKELETON of most adult vertebrates. Permeated with microscopic canals and sheathed by fibrous membrane. Long bones contain marrow, important in forming blood corpuscles.

bone black: see CHARCOAL.

bone implements, first found in Aurignacian phase of Paleolithic. Making of bone awls, needles, fishhooks, knives, dart points, etc., presupposed advanced stone tools. Modern Eskimos work in bone.

bone meal, ground bone used (because of phosphorus and nitrogen content) as fertilizer and feed.

boneset or **thoroughwort,** perennial North American herb (*Eupatorium perfoliatum*), with terminal clusters of small, white flowers in late summer.

Bonham (bŏn'ŭm), city (pop. 7,049), E Texas, NE of Dallas. Processes and ships cheese, cotton, and truck. Replica of Fort Inglish near by.

Bonheur, Rosa (bŭnûr'), 1822–99, French painter of animals.

Bon Homme Richard: see JONES, JOHN PAUL.

Boniface, Saint (bŏn'ĭfŭs, –fās), c.675–754? English missionary called the Apostle of Germany, a monk originally named Winfrid. Leaving England in 718, he soon devoted himself to the task of converting pagan Germany, which he and his companions almost completed in his lifetime. He founded many bishoprics and many abbeys (including Fulda). He was made bishop (722), missionary archbishop (732), and archbishop of Mainz (745). He was killed by pagans in Friesland. Feast: June 5.

Boniface VIII, 1235–1303, pope (1294–1303); originally named Benedetto Caetani; successor of Celestine V. Boniface tried to assert papal authority but was not successful. He interfered unsuccessfully in Sicily, further muddied the waters of the quarrel of GUELPHS AND GHIBELLINES, and was involved in a bitter struggle with PHILIP IV of France. Boniface tried to stop Philip from collecting illegal taxes from the clergy, issuing the bull *Clericis laicos* (1296), but he was forced to agree with Philip. New trouble caused the pope to thunder forth in the bulls *Ausculta fili* (1301) and *Unam sanctam* (1302; the most extreme statement ever made of the duty of princes to be subject to the pope), but the king sent a deputation to depose Boniface. After Sciarra Colonna, one of the deputies, struck Boniface, the enraged people of Anagni drove the French out. Boniface died soon afterward. Philip forced Pope CLEMENT V to repudiate the acts of Boniface. Boniface, an able canon lawyer, issued a code called the *Sext.*

Boniface (bŏn'ŭfās), d. 432, Roman general, governor and count of Africa. His refusal to obey his recall (427) led to warfare with imperial government. Made truce with Rome when Vandals under Gaiseric invaded Africa. Defeated by Vandals at Hippo (430), he was recalled to Italy by Galla Placidia to help her against AETIUS. Boniface defeated Aetius but died of wounds.

Bonifacio, José (zhōōzā' bōnīfä'tsēō), 1763?–1838, Brazilian statesman, scientist, author, whose full name was José Bonifacio de Andrade e Silva. Returning to Brazil in 1819 after studying in Europe, he became leader of the movement for the independence of Brazil from Portugal.

Bonington, Richard Parks (bŏn'–), 1801–28, English painter. Helped to bring influence of Constable and Turner to new school of French romanticists.

Bonin Islands (bō'nĭn), Jap. *Ogasawara-gunto,* volcanic island group (40 sq. mi.; 1940 pop. 7,361), N Pacific, c.600 mi. S of Tokyo. Largest is Chichi-jima. Discovered 1543 by Spaniards, claimed 1875 by Japan. Under U.S. control since 1945.

Bonivard, François de: see BONNIVARD, FRANÇOIS DE.

Bonn (bôn), city (pop. 111,287), North Rhine-Westphalia, NW Germany, on the Rhine; since 1949 temporary cap. of Federal Republic of Germany. Dates from Roman times. Residence of electors of Cologne 1263–1794. Passed to France 1801, to Prussia 1815.

Univ. founded 1784. The minster (11th–13th cent.) and electoral palace were gutted in World War II; house where Beethoven was born still stands.

Bonnard, Pierre (pyĕr bônär'), 1867–1947, French painter and lithographer, a post-impressionist known for his luminous and decorative use of color. Notable are his intimate interiors in oil.

Bonneville, Benjamin Louis Eulalie de (bŏn'-vĭl), 1796–1878, American army officer, trader in Far West, b. France. Colorful figure who failed as fur trader but helped open Rocky Mt. country.

Bonneville Dam, NW Oregon and SW Wash., in Columbia R., c.40 mi. E of Portland; built 1933–37 for power, flood control, navigation. Bradford Isl. divides river. Spillway in N channel is 1,450 ft. long, averages 170 ft. high; ladders aid fish migration. In S channel are powerhouse and lock.

Bonnie Prince Charlie: see STUART, CHARLES EDWARD.

Bonnivard or **Bonivard, François de** (fräswä' dù bônēvär'), c.1493–1570, Swiss hero of Byron's "The Prisoner of Chillon." Supported Geneva's revolt against Charles III of Savoy, who imprisoned him twice (1519–21, 1530–36). Freed when Bernese stormed CHILLON castle. Wrote chronicle of Geneva (published 1831).

Bonpland, Aimé Jacques Alexandre (ämä'zhäk' älĕksä'drù bōplä'), 1773–1858, French naturalist and author of works on Mexican and South American plants collected on travels with Humboldt.

Bonsels, Waldemar (väl'dùmär bōn'zĕls), 1881–, German author. *The Adventures of Maya, the Bee* (1912) is a juvenile classic, and a novel *The Adventures of Mario* (1927) was popular.

book, collection of written material, usually considered to have some sort of unity of thought in the contents (e.g., the divisions of anc. manuscripts); primarily today a written work of substantial proportions, printed and bound in a unit of one or more volumes. Volumes are still commonly graded by sizes with names derived from the number of times the original sheet on which the type is printed has been folded—folio, quarto, octavo (very popular modern size) and duodecimo. Papyrus fragments in Egypt preceded the regular organized manuscript book. The Greeks and Romans wrote books mainly on large papyrus rolls of varying size, though in the later period parchment was also used. The method of making books by binding collections of leaves came in the 2d cent. A.D. Vellum, a type of parchment, was popular with the monks who copied and produced the medieval books (some of these made very beautiful by illumination). Many manuscript books were made, but it was the introduction to Europe of PRINTING in the 15th cent. that made large-scale production possible. The development of books and printing thereafter was rapid and diverse. The book has been the primary dispenser of human knowledge. Making and selling of books today involves many specialized skills (editing, designing, printing, selling).

bookbinding, the art and skill of encasing a book (either manuscript or printed) in protective covering. The protective covering of ancient parchment rolls, unattached to the rolls, is not considered as bookbinding, which first arose in the Middle Ages, when boards were used to protect vellum sheets. Some medieval bindings are exquisite. After the coming of printing to Europe and adoption of the practice of folding printed sheets and sewing pages in small groups, the basic skills of bookbinding developed rapidly. They remain the same today, although machine binding has replaced hand binding to a large degree. The sheets are normally sewed together, and the covering is fastened on. In fine hand binding, the covering is made partly on the book itself; in machine binding it is completed separately and glued on. Popular covering materials are heavy paper, boards covered with cloth or paper, vellum, leather (esp. morocco and calfskin), and imitation leather. With the development of mass-production processes and new materials, new methods of binding have recently become popular. "Perfect" binding uses glue without sewing. In other cases holes are punched through the pages and plastic fasteners (usually hinged) or spiral wire bindings are inserted.

bookkeeping, the keeping of systematic records of money transactions. Proper records reveal losses and profits, assets and liabilities, and the net worth of the business. Commonly two sets of columns are used on a page—one for assets, the other for liabilities; this is double-entry method as opposed to single-entry method, in which debits and credits are entered in one set of columns. "Tabular" bookkeeping uses many columns for entries.

Book of Common Prayer, service book of Church of England and other Anglican churches. Derived from breviary and missal, the first was published 1549; Thomas Cranmer's revision incorporated 1552. Suppressed under Queen Mary, restored under Elizabeth, suppressed (1645–60) under Commonwealth and Protectorate, it was again made official and compulsory by Act of Uniformity (1662). Protestant Episcopal Church adopted first U.S. revised version in 1789.

Book of Concord, collection of authoritative confessions of faith of Lutheran Church, published 1580.

Book of the Dead, Egyptian religious text, probably estab. in final form in 7th-6th cent. B.C., though charms, formulas, and other parts may be found in inscriptions as early as 16th cent. B.C.

boomerang (bōō'mùrăng), missile in the form of a curved club used as a weapon. The small boomerang (1½ to 2 ft. long), used only for sport, describes a circle of c.50 ft. diameter and returns to the thrower. The larger or war boomerang does not return. Though best known as an Australian implement, the boomerang has been used, in various forms, in numerous civilizations.

Boone, Daniel, 1734–1820, American frontiersman, b. near Reading, Pa. In March, 1775, as advance agent for Transylvania Co., he blazed WILDERNESS ROAD and founded Boonesboro (or Boonesborough) on Kentucky R. Captured by Indians in 1778 but escaped. Moved to Missouri after land titles in Ky. were invalidated. His adventures became well known through so-called autobiographical account by John FILSON.

Boone, city (pop. 12,164), central Iowa, N of Des Moines and on Des Moines R.; laid out 1865. Rail and mining center; coal, clay, and gravel deposits.

Boonesboro, locality, central Ky., on Kentucky R. and SE of Lexington. Named for Daniel BOONE who built fort here 1775 for TRANSYLVANIA COMPANY. Was Transylvania cap. for time; had Indian attacks.

Boonton, town (pop. 7,163), N N.J., NNE of Morristown. Mfg. of radio equipment and plastics.

Boonville. 1 City (pop. 5,092), SW Ind., NE of Evansville. Trade center for coal-mining and agr. area. Has mfg. of underwear and food products. **2** City (pop. 6,686), central Mo., on Missouri R. and W of Columbia, in agr. area. Mfg. of corncob pipes. Civil War battle near here won by Union troops, June 17, 1861.

Booth, name of English family prominent in SALVATION ARMY. **William Booth,** 1829–1912, was an evangelist in London. There he and his wife, Catherine Mumford Booth (1829–90), estab. the Christian Mission which became (1878) the Salvation Army. A son, **Bramwell Booth,** 1856–1929, succeeded his father as general in 1912. Another son, **Ballington Booth,** 1859–1940, was commander in Australia and then in U.S. (1887–96). In 1896 with his wife he withdrew to found VOLUNTEERS OF AMERICA. A daughter of William Booth, **Emma Moss Booth-Tucker,** 1860–1903, with her husband jointly commanded the Army in U.S. (1896–1903). Another daughter, **Evangeline Cory Booth,** 1865–1950, was commander in Canada (1895–1904), commander in U.S. (1904–34), and general (1934–39).

Booth, Charles, 1840–1916, English social investigator, pioneer in social survey method. Headed group making exhaustive statistical study of London poverty (*Life and Labour of the People in London,* 17 vols., 1891–1903).

Booth, Edwin: see BOOTH, JUNIUS BRUTUS.

Booth, Evangeline Cory: see BOOTH, family.

Booth, Junius Brutus, 1796–1852, English actor of Shaksperian roles; one of the great figures of 19th-cent. theater. After 1821 he was in U.S. He was surpassed by his son, **Edwin Booth,** 1833–93, first great American tragedian. Gentle actor of grace and rare restraint, his roles included Richard III, Lear, Richelieu, Shylock. Toured extensively and built the Booth Theatre (N.Y., 1869), presenting Shakspere there until his bankruptcy in 1873. Also founded the Players Club. Appeared last in Hamlet in 1891. His career temporarily ceased (1865) when his brother, **John Wilkes Booth,** 1838–65, assassinated Abraham LINCOLN. A Confederate sympathizer, unlike his family, Booth first plotted to abduct Lincoln, a plan which failed. On Good Friday, April 14, 1865, learning Lincoln would attend that evening's performance of *Our American Cousin* in Washington, he plotted (with accomplices) simultaneous assassination of Lincoln, Vice Pres. Johnson,

and Secretary of State Seward. Seward was seriously wounded, while Johnson was spared. Booth entered the presidential box in Ford's Theater, shot Lincoln, vaulted to the stage (breaking his leg), and escaped on horseback. Found in a barn after two weeks' hysterical searching, Booth was shot (either by himself or his pursuers) and the barn was burned. See also M. E. SURRATT.

Booth, Shirley, 1907–, American actress, whose real name is Thelma Booth Ford. An actress of great range, since her New York debut in 1925 she has been notable in such varied plays as *My Sister Eileen, Come Back, Little Sheba,* and *The Time of the Cuckoo.*

Booth, William: see BOOTH, family.

Boothbay, town (pop. 1,559), S Maine, S of Wiscasset; settled 1630. Resort and artists' colony; boatbuilding and fishing center. Adjacent **Boothbay Harbor,** resort town (pop. 2,290), has summer theater.

Boothia Peninsula, northernmost tip of N Canada, Franklin dist., Northwest territories, connected with mainland by Isthmus of Boothia. Discovered and explored by Sir John Ross (1829–33) who estab. N magnetic pole here 1831. Later explored by Sir John Franklin (1847–48) and Roald Amundsen (1903–05).

Booth-Tucker, Emma Moss: see BOOTH, family.

Bootle, county borough (pop. 74,302), Lancashire, England; port adjacent to Liverpool. Has tanning, engineering, and flour milling.

Booz (bō′ŏz), same as BOAZ.

Bopp, Franz (fränts′ bôp′) 1791–1867, German philologist, who demonstrated relationship of Indo-European languages in his *Vergleichende Grammatik* [comparative grammar] (1833–52).

Bora, Katharina von: see LUTHER, MARTIN.

boracic acid: see BORIC ACID.

Borah, William Edgar, 1865–1940, U.S. Senator from Idaho (1907–40), Republican. Notable for independent stands; major interest in foreign policy. Opposed League of Nations, but advocated disarmament. Opposed both economic monopoly and extension of governmental powers.

Borah, Mount, or **Borah Peak** [for W. E. Borah], 12,655 ft. high, central Idaho, in Lost River Mts. Highest point in state.

borax, hydrated crystalline salt of sodium, boron, oxygen. Used as antiseptic, for cleaning textiles and metal surfaces, and in making glass, enamels, shellacs, ceramic glazes. In large doses it is toxic. In **borax bead test,** borax heated on loop to form "bead," then dipped in substance to be analyzed and reheated. Metals give bead different colors, e.g., cobalt, blue; copper, blue or green.

Bordeaux, Henri, duc de: see CHAMBORD, HENRI, COMTE DE.

Bordeaux, Henry (ärē′ bôrdō′), 1870–, French novelist. Wrote witty, popular stories propagating virtues of family life. *Les Rocquevillard* (1902; Eng. tr., *The Will to Live*) is typical.

Bordeaux (bôrdō′), city (pop. 238,653), cap. of Gironde dept., SW France, on the Garonne; historic cap. of Aquitaine and Guienne. Seaport (accessible from Atlantic through the Gironde); export center for wines from Bordeaux region. University founded 1441. As Burdigala, was provincial cap. under Romans; became archiepiscopal see in 4th cent. Under English rule 1152–1453. Temporary cap. of France 1914, 1940. Handsome 18th-cent. architecture partly damaged in World War II. Montaigne and Montesquieu were magistrates in Bordeaux.

Bordeaux mixture, a FUNGICIDE, containing copper sulphate and lime and used as a spray or as a dust.

Borden, Gail, 1801–74, American inventor and surveyor. He patented (1856) a process for evaporating milk. Superintended Texas land surveys before 1851.

Borden, Lizzie Andrew, 1860–1927, New England spinster, accused of killing father and stepmother (1892). Trial ended with verdict of not guilty.

Borden, Sir Robert Laird, 1854–1937, Canadian prime minister (1911–20). Led Canada through World War I. Helped define new status of self-governing dominions in British Empire.

Bordentown, city (pop. 5,497), W N.J., on Delaware R. below Trenton, and at W end of old Delaware and Raritan Canal; settled 1682. Partly destroyed by British 1778. Clara Barton's school (1739) is Red Cross memorial.

Border, the, in British history, region about the boundary between England and Scotland, former scene of much strife. The wild country figures in legends, folklore, and the Border ballads.

Bordet, Jules (zhül bôrdā′), 1870–, Belgian serologist and immunologist. Shared in devising complement fixation technique (1900) later used in Wassermann test and discovered whooping cough bacillus (1906). Won 1919 Nobel Prize in Physiology and Medicine for work in immunity.

Bordone, Paris (pä′rēs bôrdō′nä), 1500–1571?, Venetian painter of portraits and of religious and mythological scenes; pupil of Titian.

Boreas (bō′rēŭs), in Greek legend, north wind; son of Astraeus and Eos.

Borel, Félix Édouard Émile (fālēks′ ādwär′ āmēl′ bôrĕl′), 1871–, French mathematician. Noted for work in infinitesimal calculus, calculus of probabilities.

Borger, city (pop. 18,059), N Texas, NE of Amarillo near Canadian R., in Panhandle. Has oil refineries and carbon-black, synthetic rubber, and metal products plants.

Borgese, Giuseppe Antonio (jōōzĕp′pä äntō′nyō bōrjä′zä), 1882–1952, Italian-American author, b. near Palermo. Opponent of Fascism, he came to U.S. in 1931, taught at Smith College (1932–35) and the Univ. of Chicago (from 1936). One of his political works is *Goliath: the March of Fascism* (1937).

Borghese (bôrgā′zā), Roman noble family. Among its members were Pope PAUL V, several cardinals, and many prominent citizens.

Borghese, Villa (vēl′lä bōrgā′zä), summer palace in Rome, built by Scipione Cardinal Borghese. Now a repository for paintings.

Borghese Warrior, Greek statue of the 1st cent. B.C. by Agasias. Represents warrior attacking mounted foe. Formerly in Villa Borghese, now in Louvre.

Borgia (bôr′jä), Span. *Borja* (bôr′hä), Spanish-Italian noble family. Among members were Pope CALIXTUS III, Pope ALEXANDER VI, and St. FRANCIS BORGIA. **Cesare Borgia** (chā′zärā), c.1476–1507, younger son of Alexander VI, was an outstanding figure of Renaissance. Cardinal at 17, he resigned after murder of his elder brother (in which he probably took part); entered politics. Allied himself with Louis XII of France, who created him duke of Valentinois, and with his father's encouragement made himself master of Romagna, duchy of Urbino, and other places (1499–1502). He then lured his chief enemies to castle of Sinigaglia, where he had them strangled (1502). His father's death (1503) and Julius II's election to papacy ruined his ambitions. Julius forced him to restore his possessions to the Papal States, and Louis XII turned against him. He found asylum with his brother-in-law, the king of Navarre, in whose service he died fighting. Vicious, ruthless, but of superior intelligence and vision, he was the model for Machiavelli's *Prince*. His sister was **Lucrezia Borgia** (lōōkrā′tsyä), 1480–1519. Her first marriage (1492–97) ended in annulment; her second husband, Alfonso of Aragon (a natural son of Alfonso II of Naples) was murdered by her brother Cesare in 1500. In 1501 she was married to Alfonso d'Este, who became duke of Ferrara in 1505. Once removed from family influence, Lucrezia won wide esteem through her beauty, kindness, piety, despite unfounded rumors of her crimes and vices. Her brilliant court included Ariosto.

Borglum, Gutzon (John Gutzon de la Mothe Borglum) (bôr′glŭm), 1867–1941, American sculptor. The gigantic Mt. Rushmore Natl. Memorial in S.Dak. is his best-known work.

boric acid or **boracic acid,** white, crystalline, weakly acidic compound of boron, hydrogen, oxygen. Used as antiseptic (in solution), in pottery glazing, as fireproofing agent, and in making enamels. Poisonous if taken internally.

Borinage (bôrēnäzh′), region, S Hainaut, Belgium, surrounding Mons and extending W to French border. Important coal-mining district.

Boris, rulers of Bulgaria. **Boris I,** d. 903, ruled as khan 853–88. Baptized 865, he introduced Christianity of Greek rite among Bulgarians. **Boris III,** 1894–1943, tsar (1918–43), son and successor of Tsar FERDINAND. Set up royal dictatorship (1935); forced Rumania to restore S DOBRUJA (1940); joined Berlin Pact (1941; see AXIS). Died mysteriously soon after visiting Hitler. Succeeded by small son, Simeon II.

Boris Godunov: see GODUNOV, BORIS.

Born, Bertrand de: see BERTRAND DE BORN.

Börne, Ludwig (lōōd′vĭkh bûr′nŭ), 1786–1837, German journalist whose real name was Löb Baruch. With a generally satirical tone, he attacked censorship and encouraged liberalism. He and Heine are considered initiators of the Young Germany movement.

Borneo, island (286,969 sq. mi.; pop. c.3,080,-000), SW of the Philippines; largest of Malay Archipelago and third largest in world. Largely jungle and mountainous. Iron, copper, and coal are mined, and there are great oil fields. Interior is inhabited mainly by Dyaks; the coastal areas by Malays, Javanese, and Chinese. The Portuguese visited Borneo in 1521, preceding the Dutch and the English. In 19th cent. the Dutch established their control over W, S, and E Borneo. These Dutch territories (208,285 sq. mi.; pop. 2,168,661), comprising over two thirds of Borneo, became part of Indonesia in 1949. The British still control the N and NW in BRUNEI, SARAWAK, and NORTH BORNEO.

Bornholm (bôrn'hôlm), island (227 sq. mi.; pop. 48,134), Denmark, in Baltic Sea, 24 mi. off Swedish coast. Low tableland, rocky and steep on N and W coasts. Agr., fishing; granite, kaolin. Chief town and port is Ronne.

Borobudur or **Boroboedoer** (both: bō'rōbŏōdŏōr'), ruins of a Buddhist monument, Java, Indonesia. Within intricately carved truncated pyramid is a seated Buddha. Dates from 8th and 9th cent.

Borodin, Aleksandr (Porfirevich) (ŭlyĭksän'dŭr bôrôdēn'), 1833–87, Russian composer. A member of the Russian Five (see BALAKIREV). His chief works are two symphonies; a tone poem, *In the Steppes of Central Asia;* an opera, *Prince Igor.*

Borodino (bŭrŭdyĭnô'), village, RSFSR, W of Mozhaisk. Here in 1812 Russians under Kutuzov made heroic stand against Napoleon's advance on Moscow. Battle cost c.80,000 casualties.

Boroimhe, Brian: see BRIAN BORU.

boron (bō'rŏn), chemical element (symbol = B; see also ELEMENT, table), a brownish to yellow crystalline solid or an amorphous powder. Forms organic and inorganic compounds. Not found free in nature.

Borotra, Jean (zhä' bôrôträ'), 1898–, French tennis player. Member French Davis Cup team that defeated U.S. in 1927 and held the cup until 1933.

Borough, Stephen, 1525–84, English navigator. Master of first ship to round North Cape (1553) and reach Russia by arctic route. Thus direct trade relations became possible.

borough-English, a rule or custom in parts of England whereby land descended to the youngest son in preference to his older brothers. Abolished 1925.

Borromean Islands, Italy: see MAGGIORE, LAGO.

Borromeo, Charles: see CHARLES BORROMEO, SAINT.

Borromini, Francesco (fränchä'skō bōr-rōmē'nē), 1599–1667, Italian baroque architect. Official architect of Rome 1644–55. Collaborated in decoration of St. Peter's, designed façade of Sant' Agnese.

Borrow, George Henry, 1803–81, English writer. A wide wanderer, he distributed Bibles on the Continent and became a friend of the gypsies. Among his extraordinary books are *The Bible in Spain* (1843), *Lavengro* (1851), and *The Romany Rye* (1857).

Borstal system, method intended to rehabilitate delinquents (between ages of 16 and 21) by stressing good conditions, physical and vocational training. Originated 1902 at Borstal Prison, Kent, England.

Boru, Brian: see BRIAN BORU.

Borysthenes: see DNIEPER, river of USSR.

borzoi: see HOUND.

Bos, Jerom: see BOSCH, HIERONYMUS.

Bosanquet, Bernard (bō'zŭnkĭt), 1848–1923, British idealistic philosopher.

Bosch, Carl (bôsh), 1874–1940, German chemist. Shared 1931 Nobel Prize for adapting HABER PROCESS to achieve mass production.

Bosch, Hieronymus (hērôn'ĭmŭs bôs') or **Jerom Bos** (yä'rôm bôs'), c.1460–1516, Flemish painter. Treated such themes as the temptation of St. Anthony and the Last Judgment as fantasies peopled with diabolical little figures. A favorite with Philip II of Spain, some of best work is still in Madrid and the Escorial.

Boscoreale (bôs'kōrä-älä), small town, Campania, S Italy, at foot of Vesuvius. Celebrated collection of silverwork (1st cent. A.D.) unearthed here in 1895; now in Louvre, Paris.

Bose, Sir Jagadis Chandra (jŭgä'dēs chŭn'drŭ bōs), 1858–1937, Indian physicist noted for research in plant life. He invented the crescograph, a device for measuring plant growth.

Bosio, François Joseph, Baron (fräswä' zhôzĕf' bärô' bôsyô'), 1769?–1845, French sculptor, imperial portraitist to Napoleon I.

Bosnia and Hercegovina (bŏz'nĕŭ, hĕrtsùgōvē'nŭ), autonomous republic (19,909 sq. mi.; pop. 2,561,961), N Yugoslavia; cap. Sarajevo. Consists of Bosnia (N), with Sarajevo, and Hercegovina (S), with Mostar. Crossed by Dinaric Alps and Sava R., it is largely forested and agr. Inhabitants are Serbs and Croats of Catholic, Moslem, and Orthodox faiths. Settled by Serbs in 7th cent., Bosnia appeared as kingdom in 12th cent.; occasionally acknowledged kings of Hungary as overlords; annexed Hercegovina from Serbia late 14th cent.; fell to Turkey 1463. Peasants, held in serfdom by Moslem landlords, rebelled 1875. Serbia and Russia intervened in their favor (see RUSSO-TURKISH WARS). Congress of Berlin (1878) placed Bosnia and Hercegovina under Austro-Hungarian administration but left it, in theory, under Turkish overlordship. Full annexation by Austria-Hungary (1908) nearly brought war with Serbia and Russia, but German mediation in 1909 ended the crisis to Austria's satisfaction. Archduke Francis Ferdinand's assassination at Sarajevo precipitated World War I. Annexed by Serbia 1918, region became one of Yugoslavia's constituent republics 1946.

Bosporus (bŏs'pùrùs), strait, 20 mi. long, 1,800 ft. wide at its narrowest, separating European and Asiatic Turkey and joining Black Sea with Sea of Marmara. Istanbul lies on both shores. See also DARDANELLES.

Bossier City (bōzhùr), town (pop. 15,470), NW La., on Red R. opposite Shreveport. Processes oil, cotton, and chemicals; railroad shops. Has ruins of Confederate Fort Smith.

Bossuet, Jacques Bénigne (bôsüä'), 1627–1704, French preacher and writer. A canon at Metz, then long tutor to the son of Louis XIV at court (1670–81), and finally bishop of Meaux, he was one of the most celebrated of all French preachers, his panegyric sermons and his funeral orations for the great being particularly notable. He wrote religious polemics in favor of Gallicanism, against the

Protestants, and against the quietism of Fénelon. His *Discourse on Universal History* (1681) is a study of the hand of God in human history. His literary style is noted for vigorous purity, simplicity, and flashing eloquence.

Boston, municipal borough (pop. 24,453), Lincolnshire, England. Once an important port, now fishing center. John COTTON and other founders of Massachusetts Bay Colony sailed from here 1633.

Boston, city (pop. 801,444), state cap., E Mass., on Boston Bay; settled 1630 as main colony of MASSACHUSETTS BAY COMPANY. Largest city of New England and 10th largest of U.S., it is a major commercial, financial, industrial, and cultural center and a leading U.S. port. Important market for fish and wool, it has mfg. (textiles, leather and rubber goods, machinery, food products, chemicals), shipbuilding, and publishing. Early center of Puritanism, with vigorous intellectual life, it printed first newspaper in the colonies, *News-Letter* (1704). Important in prelude to Revolution (see BOSTON MASSACRE; BOSTON TEA PARTY; FANEUIL HALL; ADAMS, SAMUEL; REVERE, PAUL). Battle of BUNKER HILL was fought here, June 17, 1775, and city was besieged until March, 1776. After Revolution Boston prospered through world shipping and textile and shoe mfg. on New England rivers. Influence of rich and conservative Beacon Hill and Back Bay (patronized arts and letters, backed reformers) persisted long after industrial growth brought many immigrants (mostly Irish at first). City annexed adjacent towns, e.g., West Roxbury (with BROOK FARM) and CHARLESTOWN. Landmarks of the past include Old North Church, old statehouse (now museum), and Boston Common. Has Boston Symphony Orchestra (1881) and Mus. of Fine Arts. Seat of Simmons Col. (nonsectarian; for women; chartered 1899, opened 1902; first to combine liberal and professional instruction for women), Boston Univ. (nonsectarian; private; coed.; chartered 1869, opened 1871), Boston Public Latin School for boys (opened 1635; one of oldest free public schools in U.S.), New England Conservatory of Music (1867), New England Medical Center, and Harvard Medical School. HARVARD UNIVERSITY is at near-by Cambridge and Boston Col. mainly at CHESTNUT HILL.

Boston fern, house FERN (*Nephrolepis exaltata bostoniensis*), with graceful, drooping fronds.

Boston ivy or **Japanese ivy,** woody vine (*Parthenocissus tricuspidata*), popular for wall coverings. Its three-lobed leaves turn vivid red in the autumn.

Boston Massacre, 1770, pre-Revolutionary incident in which five members of rioting crowd were killed by British soldiers sent to Boston to maintain order and enforce TOWNSHEND ACTS.

Boston Mountains, E Okla. and NW Ark., most rugged section of the Ozarks, rising to c.2,345 ft. White R. rises here.

Boston Museum of Fine Arts: see MUSEUM OF FINE ARTS, at Boston, Mass.

Boston Public Latin School: see BOSTON.

Boston Public Library, founded 1852, chiefly through gift of Joshua Bates. Present building (1895) on Copley Square has murals by Puvis de Chavannes, Edwin Abbey, and John S. Sargent; libraries of John Adams and Nathaniel Bowditch; special collections.

Boston Symphony Orchestra, founded 1881 by Henry Lee Higginson. Among its outstanding conductors have been Pierre Monteux (1919–24), Serge Koussevitsky (1924–49), and Charles Münch (1949–).

Boston Tea Party, 1773, caused by retention of tea tax after repeal of TOWNSHEND ACTS. Group of indignant colonists, disguised as Indians, threw tea from three ships into Boston harbor.

Boston terrier, small, smooth-haired, nonsporting dog, developed in Boston, Mass., from crosses between bull terrier and bulldog. Usually brindle with white markings; body weight 15–25 lb.; erect ears; short tail.

Boston University: see BOSTON.

Bostwick, Arthur Elmore, 1860–1942, American librarian. Wrote *The American Public Library.*

Boswell, James (bŏz'wŭl), 1740–95, British biographer, b. Scotland, author of *The Life of Samuel Johnson, LL.D.* (1791), one of the most celebrated biographies of all time. A Scottish lawyer, he traveled widely on the Continent and spent much time in London. He met Johnson in 1763, became a member of the Johnson circle, and in his biography noted minutely all the doings and sayings of the literary dictator. Among Boswell's other works are his *Account of Corsica* (1768) and *The Journal of a Tour in the Hebrides with Samuel Johnson, LL.D.* (1785; complete ed., 1936). His papers, recovered in 20th cent. by Col. Ralph H. Isham, have yielded in published form *Private Papers* (18 vols., 1928–34), *Boswell's London Journal, 1762–1763* (1950), *Boswell in Holland, 1763–1764* (1952), and other volumes.

Bosworth Field, Leicestershire, England. Scene of battle (1485) in which Richard III was killed and the crown passed to his victor, Henry VII.

botanic garden, place in which plants are grown for display and scientific study. Performs diversified functions, e.g., plant breeding, maintenance of libraries and herbariums, administration of educational programs. Botanic gardens are found in or near most large cities.

botany, scientific study of plant life. Botany and zoology together comprise science of BIOLOGY. Beginnings of plant classification found in work of Aristotle but system of binomial nomenclature established by Linnaeus marked greatest progress in systematics. Among those who contributed to the growth of botany: Robert Brown, A. P. de Candolle, Hugo de Vries, Asa Gray, Nehemiah Grew, John Ray, Lamarck, Mendel, Hugo von Mohl, Julius von Sachs. See *ill.*, plant forms, p. 999.

Botany Bay, inlet, New South Wales, Australia, just S of Sydney. Named by Capt. Cook and the botanist Sir Joseph Banks. Though Australia's first penal colony was often called Botany Bay, its actual site was Sydney.

Botev, Khristo (khrĭ'stō bô'tĕf), 1848–76, Bulgarian poet and patriot, a leader of the revolution against Turkey (in which he was killed).

botfly, hairy fly with parasitic larvae. Horse botfly eggs, laid on horse, mule, donkey hair, are carried by tongue or lips, to mouth, and migrate to stomach, attaching to lining. Ox warble flies (heel fly; bomb fly) lay eggs on cattle, other animals; larvae migrate through skin, cause swellings (warbles). Sheep botfly or gadfly attacks sheep, goats, deer, sometimes man. Mosquitoes and other insects carry eggs of one species to humans.

Both, Andries (än'drēēs bōt'), c.1608–c.1640, and **Jan Both** (yän), c.1618–1652, Flemish painters and etchers; brothers. Jan painted Italian landscapes; Andries did animals and figures.

Botha, Louis (bō'tû), 1862–1919, South African soldier and statesman. Led Boers in South African War, but after 1902 favored working with the British. Premier of the Transvaal, 1907–10, and of Union of South Africa, 1910–19. In World War I he led forces which took German South-West Africa.

Bothnia, Gulf of, northernmost portion of Baltic Sea, between Finland and Sweden.

Bothwell, James Hepburn, 4th earl of, c.1536–1578, Scottish nobleman; third husband of MARY QUEEN OF SCOTS. After murder of RIZZIO (1566), Mary trusted only Bothwell. Accused of murdering her husband, LORD DARNLEY, Bothwell was acquitted in rigged trial and married Mary, 1567. Scottish aristocracy attacked him and forced Mary to give him up. Fled to Denmark, was imprisoned, and died insane.

bo tree or **pipal,** fig tree (*Ficus religiosa*) of India, sacred to Buddhists. An ancient specimen grows at Anuradhapura.

Böttger, Johann Friedrich (yö'hän frē'drĭckh bût'khûr), 1682–1719, German chemist, originator of Dresden china. Developed various glazes and perfected white porcelain.

Botticelli, Sandro (sän'drō bôt'tĭchĕl'lē), c.1444–1510, Florentine painter of the Renaissance; a pupil of Fra Filippo Lippi. A master of color and rhythmic line. Famous for such paintings as *Spring, Venus,* and *Allegory of Calumny* and for illustrations (in silverpoint and pen) of *Divine Comedy.* Painted religious themes in his last years.

botulism (bŏt'ŭlĭzŭm), food poisoning caused by toxin produced by a bacillus (*Clostridium botulinum*). Toxin attacks nervous system; fatal respiratory paralysis common sequel unless antitoxin serum is given.

Botwood, town (pop. c.2,744), NE central N.F., Canada, at mouth of Exploits R. Final refueling base for planes on N route to Ireland. Site of seaplane base. In World War II was base of North Atlantic air patrol. Airport estab. 1939.

Bouchard, Henry (ärē' bōōshär'), 1875–, French sculptor. His work often represents workers, in action or at rest.

Bouché, Louis (bōōshā'), 1896–, American painter of realistic and abstract pictures. Noted for murals.

Boucher, François (fräswä' bōōshā'), 1703–70, French painter. Famous for boudoir decorations, he was the most fashionable painter of his day. Became director of Gobelins factory.

Bouches-du-Rhône (bōōsh'-dü-rōn'), department (2,026 sq. mi.; pop. 976,241), SE France, in Provence; cap. Marseilles. Includes Rhone delta, CAMARGUE.

Boucicault, Dion (bōō'sĭkō), 1822?–1890, British playwright, actor; in U.S. after 1853. Among his more than 300 plays and adaptations (in many of which he acted) are *The Octoroon* (1859), *The Colleen Bawn* (1860), and *Rip Van Winkle* (1865).

Boucicaut (bōōsēkō'), c.1366–1421, marshal of France; real name: Jean Le Meingre. Captured by Turks at NIKOPOL 1396. Ransomed, he helped in defense of Constantinople 1399. Governor of Genoa 1401–7. Died in England after capture at Agincourt (1415). Wrote ballads, other poems.

Boudin, Eugène Louis (ûzhĕn' lwē' bōōdē'), 1824–98, French landscape and marine painter.

Boudinot, Elias (bōō'dĭnŏt), 1740–1821, American Revolutionary statesman. Member of Continental Congress (1777–78, 1781–84). Supported the Constitution. Director, U.S. mint (1795–1805).

Bougainville, Louis Antoine de (lwē' ätwän' dù bōōgēvēl'), 1729–1811, French navigator. Made voyage around the world (1767–69), rediscovering Solomon Isls., largest of which is named for him. In American Revolution fought Hood at Martinique. Wrote *Description d'un voyage autour du monde.*

Bougainville (bōō'gûnvĭl), volcanic island (3,880 sq. mi.; pop. 50,000), S Pacific, largest of SOLOMON ISLANDS. Visited 1768 by Bougainville. Became a German possession in 1884. Governed since 1920 as part of Territory of New Guinea (see NEW GUINEA, TERRITORY OF). In World War II it was last major Japanese stronghold in Solomons.

bougainvillea (bōō'gûnvĭl'ēù), woody vine (*Bougainvillea*) of tropical America, cultivated in U.S. for showy red or purple bracts that enclose flowers.

Bouguereau, Adolphe William (ädôlf' bōōgûrō'), 1825–1905, French academic and sentimental painter.

Bouillon, Godfrey of: see GODFREY OF BOUILLON.

Bouillon, Henri de la Tour d'Auvergne, vicomte de Turenne, duc de (ärē' dù lä tōōr' dōvĕr'nyù, vēkōt' dù türĕn' dük dù bōōyō'), 1555–1623, marshal of France and Protestant leader; a grandson of Anne de Montmorency. Acquired duchy of Bouillon by marriage. Briefly a member of regency council under Marie de' Medici, he retired to his duchy after quarrel with queen. His older son, **Frédéric Maurice de la Tour d'Auvergne, duc de Bouillon** (frädārĕk' mōrēs'), c.1605–1652, French general, took part in the CINQ MARS conspiracy but was pardoned. He espoused Catholicism, sided with the princes during Fronde, lost his principality of Sedan to France. TURENNE was his brother.

Bouillon, town (pop. 2,830), Luxembourg prov., S Belgium, in the Ardennes. Its ancient castle belonged to Godfrey of Bouillon, who sold it to bishop of Liége 1095. In 15th cent. town and environs passed to William de la Marck, whose heirs assumed titles duke of Bouillon and prince of Sedan. Bouillon was annexed to France 1678–1815.

Boulanger, Georges (zhôrzh′ boōläzhä′), 1837–91, French general, "the man on horseback." Minister of war, 1886–87; leader of nationalist reactionary movement—Boulangism—which foreshadowed fascism. Won overwhelming victory at polls 1889. A military coup d'état seemed imminent, but Boulanger lost his nerve, fled to Belgium, and killed himself.

Boulanger, Gustave Rodolphe Clarence (güstäv′ rôdôlf′ klärãs′), 1824–88, French painter of Oriental scenes.

Boulanger, Nadia, 1887–, French teacher of composition, professor at the Paris Conservatoire after 1945. Many American composers studied under her (e.g., Aaron Copland, Virgil Thomson).

Boulder, city (pop. 19,999; alt. c.5,350 ft.), N central Colo., NW of Denver; laid out 1859. Health resort, with mild, dry climate and mineral springs. Rail and trade center for mines and farms. Seat of Univ. of COLORADO. U.S. atomic energy plant begun near by in 1951.

boulder, any large rock fragment, either formed from bedrock below or transported by water or ice.

Boulder City, town (pop. 3,903), S Nev., just W of Hoover Dam. Year-round tourist center.

boulder clay, unstratified mixture of clay, sand, gravel, and boulders left by retreating glacier.

Boulder Dam: see HOOVER DAM.

Boulle or **Buhl, André Charles** (both: ädrä′ shärl′ boōl′), 1642–1732, French cabinetmaker who created a distinctive furniture style roughly similar to Louis XIV and Regence design. Excelled in marquetry.

Boulogne-sur-Mer (boōlô′nyü-sür-mĕr′), city (pop. 34,389), Pas-de-Calais dept., N France; port on English Channel. From here the Romans sailed A.D. 43 to conquer Britain. Heavily damaged in World War II. Statue of Our Lady of Boulogne, in cathedral, is object of pilgrimages.

Boulton, Matthew (bōl′tŭn), 1728–1809, English engineer and manufacturer, partner from 1775 of James Watt in production of steam engines. New British copper coinage estab. 1797 by Boulton.

bouncing Bet: see SOAPWORT.

Boundary Peak, 13,145 ft. high, SW Nev., in White Mts. near Calif. line. Highest point in Nev.

Bound Brook, borough (pop. 8,374), N central N.J., on Raritan R. and NW of New Brunswick; settled 1681. Mfg. of chemicals and textiles. Has flower nurseries. Site of a Cornwallis victory (1777).

Bountiful, city (pop. 6,004), N central Utah; N of Salt Lake City. Early Mormon chapel survives.

Bounty, British naval ship, scene of noted mutiny (1789) while on long trading voyage in the Pacific. Capt. William BLIGH and 18 of crew were set adrift in small boat; sailed c.4,000 mi. to Timor. Some mutineers settled on PITCAIRN ISLAND.

bounty, premium paid by the state for the production or export of certain goods. Unlike SUBSIDY, it involves payment per unit of the product. Used to encourage production or export of favored goods and as substitute for protective tariff. Money payments formerly made to induce army enlistment and rewards for killing destructive animals also called bounty.

Bourassa, Henri (boōräsä′), 1868–1952, Canadian political leader; grandson of Louis Joseph Papineau. Led powerful opposition (Nationalist) party in Quebec. Opposed diplomatic entanglements with U.S. and Great Britain; also against participation in World War I.

Bourbon (boōrbō′), royal family which ruled in France, Spain, the Two Sicilies, and Parma; a cadet branch of the Capetians. Takes its name from castle in Bourbonnais (now Allier dept.), whose first lord was Adhémar, a 9th-cent. noble. In 1272 Robert of Clermont, sixth son of Louis IX of France, married the heiress of Bourbon. His son Louis was 1st duke of Bourbon. His descendant, **Charles, duc de Bourbon** (shärl′, dük′ dü), 1490–1527, constable of France, treacherously went over to Emperor Charles V (1523); was killed while leading imperial troops in sack of Rome. His lands were confiscated; his title discontinued. A younger son of the 1st duke founded line of Bourbon-Vendôme. **Antoine de Bourbon** (ätwän′), 1518–62, duke of Vendôme, became king of Navarre by marrying JEANNE D'ALBRET. From his brother Louis descend the houses of CONDÉ and CONTI. Antoine's son became (1589) the first Bourbon king of France as HENRY IV. His direct descendants ruled FRANCE (except from 1792 to 1814) until 1830, when Charles X was deposed, and died out in 1883 with Henri, comte de CHAMBORD. The younger branch of Bourbon-Orléans (see ORLÉANS, family) gave France King Louis Philippe and inherited claim to throne. The house of **Bourbon-Spain,** Span. *Borbón,* began in 1700 with accession of Louis XIV's grandson, PHILIP V, on Spanish throne. The succession in SPAIN was contested (19th cent.) by CARLISTS against ISABELLA II. Alfonso XIII was deposed in 1931. The house of **Bourbon-Sicily,** sprung from the Spanish line, was founded (1759) by FERDINAND I of the TWO SICILIES and ceased to rule when Francis II abdicated (1861). The house of **Bourbon-Parma** was founded (1748) by a younger son of Philip V of Spain. Robert (1848–1907), 5th duke of PARMA and Piacenza, was deposed in 1860. He had 18 children, among them Empress ZITA of Austria and Sixtus of BOURBON-PARMA.

Bourbonnais (boōrbônä′), region and former province, central France, in Allier and Cher depts.; historic cap. Moulins. Other towns: Vichy, Montluçon. Appanage of dukes of BOURBON until 1527.

Bourbon-Parma, Bourbon-Sicily, and **Bourbon-Spain:** see BOURBON, family.

Bourdelle, Émile Antoine (ämēl′ ätwän′ boōrdĕl′), 1861–1929, French sculptor. Studied under Rodin. Recognized as one of the greatest modern sculptors, he achieved his greatest success in heroic and monumental works.

Bourg-en-Bresse or **Bourg** (boōrk-ä-brĕs′), town (pop. 21,169), cap. of Ain dept., E France, chief town of Bresse; a gastronomic mecca.

Bourgeois, Léon (lãō′ boōrzhwä′), 1851–1925,

French statesman, social philosopher. Premier 1895–96. Early advocate of League of Nations; won 1920 Nobel Peace Prize. Chief work: *Solidarité* (1896).

bourgeoisie (bŏŏrshwäzē′), name applied to citizens of French towns and subsequently to middle class in all nations. Known in feudal times as Third Estate. If defined as mercantile or trading class, bourgeoisie has existed since earliest history and was powerful in ancient Rome. In eclipse in early Middle Ages, merchants later won contest with nobles. They turned increasingly to principles of constitutionality and natural rights against claims of divine right and promoted English, French, and American revolutions. In 19th cent. position of the bourgeoisie became more insecure due to wars, economic crises, and rising socialist and communist criticism. While concept of bourgeoisie has less relevance to U.S. than to Europe, the influence of the middle class in American affairs has usually predominated.

Bourges (bŏŏrzh), city (pop. 41,597), cap. of Cher dept., central France; historic cap. of Berry. Arms and clothes mfg. Important in Roman times; early archiepiscopal see. University founded 1463, abolished in French Revolution. Cathedral and house of Jacques Cœur are glorious examples of French Gothic. See also PRAGMATIC SANCTION OF BOURGES.

Bourget, Paul (pôl′ bŏŏrzhä′), 1852–1935, French novelist. Catholic and conservative, he is noted for works of psychological analysis, as *Le Disciple* (1889), *Le Démon de midi* [the noonday demon] (1914).

Bourget, Le (lù), suburb of Paris, France; one of city's airports. Lindbergh landed here 1927.

Bourget, lake, c.11 mi. long, Savoie dept., E France. Aix-les-Bains is on its scenic shore.

Bourinot, Sir John George (bŏŏ′rĭnō″), 1837–1902, Canadian historian, known for standard works on the Canadian government.

Bourne, Francis (bôrn), 1861–1935, English Roman Catholic churchman, archbishop of Westminster (1903–35); made a cardinal 1911.

Bourne, Hugh (bŏŏrn), 1772–1852, English evangelist. Held outdoor revivals despite ban by Wesleyan Conference. Estab. Primitive Methodists 1810.

Bourne, Randolph (Silliman) (bôrn), 1886–1918, American writer. His liberal interests led to vigorous advocacy of many causes, notably progressive education, pacifism, and political and social reform. His ideas, though adopted only in a small group in his life, have had great influence. Crippled and frail, he succumbed to the 1918 influenza epidemic.

Bourne, resort town (pop. 4,720), SE Mass., crossed by Cape Cod Canal. Includes BUZZARDS BAY resort.

Bournemouth (bôrn′mùth), county borough (pop. 144,276), Hampshire, England; fashionable resort and art center on Poole Bay.

Boutens, Pieter Cornelis (bou′tùns), 1870–1943, Dutch lyric poet.

Bouts, Dierick or **Thierry** (dē′rĭk bouts′, tyĕ′rē), c.1410–1475, Netherlands painter, famous for landscape backgrounds of his altarpiece panels.

Boutwell, George Sewall (bout′–), 1818–1905, U.S. Secretary of the Treasury (1869–73). His preoccupation with reduction of the national debt led to neglect of more important problems.

Bouvier, John (bŏŏvēr′), 1787–1851, American jurist, b. France. His *Law Dictionary* (1839), often revised, is still standard in U.S.

Bouvines (bŏŏvēn′), village, Nord dept., N France, near Lille. Scene of victory (1214) of Philip II of France over King John of England, Emperor Otto IV, and count of Flanders.

Bow (bō), river of S Alta., Canada. Rises on E slope of the Rockies and flows 315 mi. SE through superb mountain scenery of Banff Natl. Park, past Calgary, to join Oldman R., forming South Saskatchewan R.

Bow Bells (bō), in church of St. Mary-le-Bow in mid-London. Traditionally only a person born in sound of Bow Bells is a true Londoner, a "cockney."

Bowditch, Nathaniel, 1773–1838, American navigator, mathematician. Corrected some 8,000 errors in Moore's *Practical Navigator*; new edition (*The New American Practical Navigator*) appeared under his name. His son **Henry Ingersoll Bowditch**, 1808–92, was a physician noted as authority on public health and on chest diseases. **Henry Pickering Bowditch**, 1840–1911, grandson of Nathaniel Bowditch, was known for work at Harvard Univ. in experimental physiology and medical education.

Bowdler, Thomas (boud′lùr, bŏd′–), 1754–1825, English editor. His prudish textual expurgations (especially of Shakspere) gave rise to term *bowdlerize*.

Bowdoin College: see BRUNSWICK, Maine.

Bowen, Elizabeth, 1899–, Anglo-Irish writer, author of novels of upper-class life (e.g., *The Hotel*, 1927; *The Death of the Heart*, 1938) and short stories (e.g., collection *Look at All These Roses*, 1941).

bower bird, any of several species of birds native to Australia and New Guinea. Build stick-grass bower or arbor for play, courtship display. Gardener bower bird makes lawn around bower and decorates with bright objects. Nests are outside bowers.

Bowery, the (bou′ùrē), section and street of lower Manhattan, New York city, between Chatham Square and Astor Place E of Broadway. Street was once a road to farm of Gov. Stuyvesant (buried at St. Mark's-in-the-Bouwerie). By 1860s section had many fine theatres; later became notorious for saloons and dives, and finally for derelicts.

Bowie, James (bŏŏ′ē), 1799–1836, hero of Texas revolution who died at the ALAMO. Legend says bowie knife was named after him or brother, Rezin Bowie.

bowlegs (*genu varum*), deforming curvature of legs, generally the result of rickets in early life.

Bowles, Samuel, 1797–1851, American newspaper proprietor; founded Springfield (Mass.) weekly *Republican*. His son, **Samuel Bowles**, 1826–78, who joined paper at 17 and took control at 25, made it (1845) a morning daily. He and an exceptional staff made the *Republican* one of the country's most influential newspapers. His son, **Samuel**

Bowles, 1851–1915, gave close editorial direction to the paper, but wrote little himself. **Chester B(liss) Bowles,** 1901–, grandson of Samuel Bowles (1826–78), was governer of Conn. (1949–51), U.S. ambassador to India (1951–53).

bowling, sport played by rolling heavy ball to knockdown bottle-like pin on indoor alley. Originated in Germany, probably as Christian rite. Dutch introduced game in America, where it became popular in 19th cent. Standardized as 10-pin game in 1895, when American Bowling Congress was founded.

Bowling Green. 1 City (pop. 18,347), S Ky., on Barren R. and SSW of Louisville; founded 1780. Shipping and marketing center of agr. area, it handles tobacco, oil, and livestock and has mfg. of metal and food products. Taken by Federals under Grant and Buell 1862. Near by are Lost River Cave, reputed hideout of James brothers and Gen. J. H. Morgan, and ruins of a Shaker settlement (1800). **2** City (pop. 12,005), NW Ohio, S of Toledo, in farm area; settled 1833. Seat of **Bowling Green State University** (state supported; coed.); chartered 1910, opened 1914 as normal school; became college 1929 and university 1935.

Bowman, Isaiah, 1878–1950, American geographer, b. Ontario. Led expeditions to South America. Territorial adviser to Pres. Wilson at Versailles conference, to Dept. of State in World War II. President of Johns Hopkins Univ. 1935–48.

Bowmanville, town (pop. 5,430), S Ont., Canada, on L. Ontario NE of Toronto. Port and mfg. center.

Bowne, Borden Parker (boun), 1847–1910, American philosopher, exponent of personalism, which emphasizes freedom and importance of the self.

Bowring, Sir John, 1792–1872, British statesman and linguist. Governor of Hong Kong (1854), where he precipitated war with China. Known for translations from many languages.

box, evergreen shrub of genus *Buxus* of Asia and Europe. Common box (*Buxus sempervirens*), slow growing, prized for clipped hedges in S U.S.

boxer: see BULLDOG.

Boxer Rebellion, Chinese revolt (1899–1900), caused by resentment against widening interests of the Western powers and Japan in China. Staged by military group called I Ho Ch'üan [righteous, harmonious fists] or the Boxers, with encouragement of dowager empress Tz'u Hsi. Revolt was crushed by composite force of British, French, Italian, German, Austrian, Russian, American, and Japanese troops. China was forced in 1901 to agree to payment of huge indemnity and to permit stationing of foreign troops in Peking and approach to it from the sea. Also called Boxer Rising or Uprising.

boxing, sport of fighting with the fists, an ancient sport, included in original Olympic games. Marquess of Queensberry's rules (introduced 1865) became standard by 1889. Boxers today fight in a ring, a roped-off area about 20 ft. square. Professional boxing in U.S. largely controlled by rulings of National Boxing Association and N.Y. State Athletic Commission.

Boyacá (bōyäkä′), locality, N central Colombia, where Bolívar defeated the Spanish (1819).

Boyce, William, 1710–79, English organist, composer. Compiled *Cathedral Music* (3 vols., 1760–78).

Boyce Thompson Institute for Plant Research, estab. 1924 at Yonkers, N.Y. through gifts of William Boyce Thompson. Institute is known for research in many branches of botany; fine library; arboretum.

boycott [from Irish land agent, Capt. Charles C. Boycott], concerted economic or social ostracism of an offender (individual, group, nation, or product) to express disapproval or effect coercion. Used in labor disputes and as a weapon in political and racial issues.

Boyd, Belle, 1843–1900, Confederate spy in Civil War. Operated in Shenandoah Valley (1862).

Boyd, Ernest, 1887–1946, American writer and critic, b. Ireland; in New York after 1920. His criticism of German, French, Irish, English, and American authors widened the American literary horizon. Translated the works of Maupassant and others.

Boyd, James, 1884–1944, American author. After World War I service, he lived in N.C. Among his novels of American history are *Drums* (1925), *Long Hunt* (1930), *Roll River* (1935), *Bitter Creek* (1939).

Boyd, Louise Arner, 1887–, American arctic explorer. She led series of explorations for scientific study of E coast of Greenland.

Boyden, Seth, 1788–1870, American inventor. Built locomotives and steam engines incorporating first automatic "cut-off" governor. Initiated U.S. manufacture of patent leather and malleable cast iron.

Boyle, Richard, 1st earl of Cork, 1566–1643, Irish statesman. Improved land, estab. ironworks, founded towns, created trade. As lord high treasurer of Ireland (1631) his opposition to Irish program of earl of STRAFFORD was a major cause of latter's downfall. His son, **Roger Boyle, 1st earl of Orrery,** 1621–79, was a statesman and writer who attempted to keep peace by supporting regime able to govern. Royalist until 1647, served Puritans until restoration of Charles II. Author of rhymed-verse tragedies. His brother **Robert Boyle,** 1627–91, a British chemist, was the first to distinguish between element and compound. He defined chemical reaction and analysis. Boyle's law: at constant temperature, volume of confined gas decreases in proportion to increase in pressure.

Boylston, Zabdiel, 1679–1766, American physician. He introduced in U.S. inoculation against smallpox during Boston epidemic of 1721.

Boyne, river of Ireland, flows 70 mi. NE through Co. Kildare and Co. Meath to the Irish Sea near Drogheda. William III defeated James II in the battle of the Boyne, July 1, 1690.

Boy Scouts, world-wide, nonmilitary organization of boys over 11 years old; founded 1908 by Sir Robert Baden-Powell; inc. in U.S. 1910. Similar movements in U.S. led by Dan Beard and Ernest Thompson Seton. Program designed to better mental, moral, physical development, increase knowledge of outdoors, train for citizenship.

Boys Town, village (pop. 975), E Nebr., founded by Mgr Edward J. Flanagan as community for homeless and abandoned boys.

Bozeman, John M. (bōz'mŭn), 1835–67, American pioneer. Found short route in 1862–63 from Bannack, Mont., to Colo., lying E of Bighorn Mts., known as **Bozeman Trail.** In 1865–66 U.S. government estab. forts to guard it; after FETTERMAN MASSACRE part of trail was abandoned.

Bozeman, city (pop. 11,325), SW Mont., SE of Butte and in Gallatin valley; founded 1864 by J. M. Bozeman. Farm and livestock center, it is also a gateway to Yellowstone Natl. Park. Seat of Montana State Col., a part of Univ. of MONTANA.

Bozeman Trail: see BOZEMAN, JOHN M.

Bozen, Italy: see BOLZANO.

Bozzaris, Marco or **Markos** (bôt'sārēs), c.1788–1823, Greek hero in War of Independence. Defended Missolonghi against Turks (1822–23); defeated superior Turkish army at Karpenisi but fell in battle.

Br, chemical symbol of the element BROMINE.

Brabant (brŭbănt'), former duchy, now divided among the Belgian provs. of ANTWERP and of Brabant (1,268 sq. mi.; pop. 1,811,330; cap. Brussels) and the Dutch prov. of NORTH BRABANT. The duchy emerged from the duchy of Lower Lorraine (12th cent.). Louvain was its cap. until Brussels superseded it (15th cent.). The textile industries and commercial enterprise of its cities gave medieval Brabant extraordinary prosperity. The cities were granted virtual self-government by the dukes, who in 1356 granted a charter, known as *Joyeuse Entrée,* which forbade the dukes to declare war, conclude alliances, or coin money without consent of an assembly or estates (in force until 1789). Brabant passed to the dukes of Burgundy in 1430. For its history after 1477, see NETHERLANDS, AUSTRIAN AND SPANISH.

Brac, Serbo-Croatian *Brač* (bräch), Ital. *Brazza,* Adriatic island (152 sq. mi.), Croatia, NW Yugoslavia; chief town Supetar (San Pietro).

bracken or **brake,** tall, coarse FERN (*Pteridium*) of wide distribution. Often becomes weedy.

Brackenridge, Hugh Henry, 1748–1816, American author, b. Scotland. His satirical and picaresque novel, *Modern Chivalry* (1792–97; with additions, 1813) pictures backwoods life and expresses moderate democratic views.

Brackenridge, borough (pop. 6,178), SW Pa., on the Allegheny and NE of Pittsburgh. Produces coal, coke, stainless steel, and glass.

Bracquemond, Félix (bräkmō'), 1833–1914, French engraver, painter, and decorator of ceramics.

Bracton, Henry de, d. 1268, English jurist, author of *De legibus et consuetudinibus Angliae* [on the laws and customs of England].

Braddock, Edward, 1695–1755, British general in French and Indian Wars. Mortally wounded in disastrous expedition to capture Fort Duquesne from French; more than half his force was lost.

Braddock, borough (pop. 16,488), W Pa. on Monongahela R. and SE of Pittsburgh; settled 1742. Gen. Edward Braddock was defeated here 1755. Was (1794) a center of Whisky Rebellion. Mfg. of machinery and steel (Carnegie Steel Co.).

Bradenton (brā'dŭntŭn), city (pop. 13,604), SW Fla., fishing port on Manatee R. near its mouth on Tampa Bay; founded 1878. Resort. Processes and ships truck and fruit. Dolomite and limestone quarries. Gamble Mansion, post-war refuge of J. P. Benjamin, Confederate Secretary of State, is near.

Bradford, Andrew: see BRADFORD, WILLIAM (1663–1752).

Bradford, Gamaliel (gŭmā'lēŭl), 1863–1932, American biographer, noted for "psychographs" (short psychological portraits), collected in volumes such as *Confederate Portraits* (1914), *Union Portraits* (1916), and *Damaged Souls* (1923). His autobiography is *Life and I* (1928).

Bradford, John, 1749–1830, pioneer printer of Ky. Founded *Kentucky Gazette* (1787), first Ky. newspaper. Helped found Transylvania Univ.

Bradford, Roark, 1896–1948, American writer, b. Tenn. Biblical stories seen through Negro eyes in *Ol' Man Adam an' His Chillun* (1928) were the source of Marc Connelly's play *The Green Pastures* (1930).

Bradford, William, 1590–1657, governor of Plymouth Colony, b. England. Reelected governor 30 times, he struggled hard to establish colony and discharge debts to London backers.

Bradford, William, 1663–1752, British printer in the American colonies. Set up the first press in Philadelphia and helped found first colonial paper mill (1690). Estab. first New York city newspaper, the *Gazette* (1725). His son, **Andrew Bradford,** 1686–1742, founded the *American Weekly Mercury,* first Pa. newspaper (1719). Imprisoned for criticism of council and assembly, he creditably defended own case for freedom of press. His nephew, **William Bradford,** 1722–91, estab. the Philadelphia *Weekly Advertiser.* A patriot in the American Revolution, he was printer to First Continental Congress and as a major was so badly wounded at Princeton that he did not regain health.

Bradford, county borough (pop. 292,394), Yorkshire, England. A center of the worsted-milling industry, it also has varied mfg.

Bradford, city (pop. 17,354), NW Pa., SE of Jamestown, N.Y. settled c.1823. Oil discovered 1871. Has refineries and mfg. of metal and clay products and chemicals.

Bradlaugh, Charles (brăd'lō), 1833–91, English social reformer, champion of woman suffrage, birth control, and trade unionism.

Bradley, Francis Herbert, 1846–1924, English philosopher, a fellow at Merton Col., Oxford. An absolute idealist, he challenged contemporary metaphysical theories with the assertion that true reality is perfect and changeless (as in *Appearance and Reality,* 1893).

Bradley, James, 1693–1762, English astronomer. Discovered aberration of light and nutation (nodding) of earth's axis. Astronomer royal from 1742.

Bradley, Omar (Nelson), 1893–, U.S. general. Led U.S. 1st Army in invasion of Normandy (1944); vastly aided defeat of Germany in World War II. Chairman of joint chiefs of staff (1949–).

Bradley, village (pop. 5,699), E Ill., just N of Kankakee, in agr. area. Mfg. of wood products.

Bradley University: see PEORIA, Ill.

Bradshaw, George, 1801–53, English map engraver and the originator of railway guides.

Bradstreet, Anne (Dudley), c.1612–1672, American poet, b. England; daughter of Thomas Dudley. First American woman to devote herself to writing. Early poems in *The Tenth Muse Lately Sprung up in America* (1650). Her husband, **Simon Bradstreet,** 1603–97, b. England, was colonial governor of Mass. (1679–86, 1689–92).

Brady, James Buchanan, 1856–1917, American financier and philanthropist, called "Diamond Jim" Brady. Had massive collection of jewelry. Funds he gave founded Urological Institute at Johns Hopkins Hospital, Baltimore.

Brady, Mathew B., 1823–96, American pioneer photographer. Known for his many photographs of Lincoln and for his photographic record of the Civil War. *Gallery of Illustrious Americans* published 1850.

Brady, city (pop. 5,944), central Texas, ESE of San Angelo. Ships turkeys, cotton, wool, and mohair, and has dairying.

Braga, Teófilo (tēō'fīlō brä'gù), 1843–1924, Portuguese intellectual and political leader, influential through his literary criticism and his teaching. A republican and anticlericalist, he served as first president of Portuguese republic (1910–11).

Braga, city (pop. 29,875), Minho prov., NW Portugal. Flourished in Middle Ages as see of powerful bishops. Old cathedral.

Bragança or **Braganza** (both: brùgän'zù), town (pop. 6,977), Tras-os-Montes prov., NE Portugal. Castle was seat of royal family of Braganza.

Braganza (brùgän'zù), royal house that ruled PORTUGAL from 1640 to 1910 and BRAZIL (as independent empire) from 1822 to 1889. Line founded by 1st duke of Braganza, a natural son of John I of Portugal. In 1640 his descendant expelled Spanish and became king as John IV.

Bragg, Braxton, 1817–76, Confederate general. Led A. S. Johnston's 2d Corps in battle of Shiloh. Unsuccessfully invaded Ky. (1862). In CHATTANOOGA CAMPAIGN he won at Chickamauga, but was thoroughly defeated by Grant in Nov., 1863.

Bragg, Sir William Henry, 1862–1942, English physicist. For studies, using X-ray spectrometer, of X-ray spectra and crystal structure, he shared 1915 Nobel Prize with his son, **Sir William Lawrence Bragg,** 1890–, who in 1938 became director of Cavendish Laboratory, Cambridge.

Bragg, Fort: see FAYETTEVILLE, N.C.

Brahe, Tycho (tī'kō brä), 1546–1601, Danish astronomer. By improving instruments and making exact observations of planets and stars, he paved way for discoveries of Kepler and other astronomers. On island of Ven built famed castle, Uranienborg, and observatory, Stjarneborg.

Brahma, supreme deity: see HINDUISM.

Brahman or **Brahmin:** see HINDUISM.

Brahmaputra (brämùpoo'trù), sacred river, c.1,800 mi. long, rising in SW Tibet and flowing through India and Pakistan. Lower course called Jamuna.

Brahms, Johannes (yōhän'ùs brämz'), 1833–97, German composer, b. Hamburg. Among his closest friends were Robert and Clara Schumann. By 1863 he was earning his living as a composer and settled in Vienna. He wrote in every form except opera. Among his works are: sonatas and short pieces for the piano; the popular Hungarian Dances; chamber music; many lieder; the *Academic Festival Overture;* the *German Requiem;* and four concertos—two for piano, one for violin, and a double concerto for violin and cello. Brahms's profound admiration of Beethoven made him hesitate to attempt a symphony, but he finally produced his first symphony— the C minor—in 1876. The others soon followed: the Second (1877), the Third (1883), and the Fourth (1884–85). Much of his music, which is increasingly popular, is highly romantic in content.

Braila (brùě'lä), city (pop. 95,514), SE Rumania, in Walachia, on lower Danube. Exports grain.

Braille, Louis (brāl', Fr. lwē' brī'yù), 1809?– 1852, French inventor of printing and writing system for the blind. Blinded after he was three, he studied and taught at the Institution nationale des Jeunes Aveugles, Paris. The **Braille system,** evolved from Charles Barbier's method, has 63 combinations of six raised points.

brain, mass of nerve tissue in skull. In man, includes cerebrum, the center of consciousness, sensation, and voluntary actions; cerebellum, important in coordination and regulation of muscles; medulla oblongata, pathway from brain to spinal cord. See *ill.,* p. 763.

Brainerd, Ezra, 1844–1924, American botanist, known for work in plant hybridization (esp. violets).

Brainerd, city (pop. 12,637), central Minn., on the Mississippi near Cuyuna iron range; settled 1870. Shipping and industrial center in lumbering and lake resort area.

Braintree, town (pop. 23,161), E Mass., SSE of Boston; settled 1634. Shoes, rubber and petroleum products. Holdup and murders of April 15, 1920, for which Sacco and Vanzetti were executed, occurred here.

Brain Trust, designation for academic group, advisers to F. D. Roosevelt as governor of N.Y. and in first years as President.

brake, in botany: see BRACKEN.

brake, device to retard or stop motion of mechanical body. Friction used to resist motion, changing kinetic to heat energy. Simple types are wood or shoe pressed against wheel rim with force applied through pedal and multiplied by levers; rope wound around axle and pulled taut to brake; metal bands fitted around drum attached to wheel and controlled by levers. Mechanical automobile foot brake regulates bands of metal around outside of drum attached to axle; emergency brake attached to shoes that press outward from inside of drum. Force applied to pedals transmitted by levers, cables, or hydraulic cylinder and piston arrangement. Hydraulic brakes generally used on automobiles; air brakes on railroad cars, busses, and trucks. Electric motor often used to brake electric machines.

Brakelond, Jocelin de: see JOCELIN DE BRAKELOND.

Bramah, Joseph (brăm'ŭ, brä'–), 1748–1814, English mechanician and inventor, who patented a safety lock (1784) and the HYDRAULIC PRESS (1795).

Bramante, Donato d'Agnolo (dōnä'tō dä'nyōlō brämän'-tä), 1444?–1514, Italian architect of the High Renaissance. Cancelleria Palace and circular Tempietto in courtyard of San Pietro in Montorio, both in Rome, reflect his study of classical remains. His original plans for the new St. Peter's were altered by later architects who worked on church.

Bramantino (brämäntē'nō), c.1455–c.1535, Lombard painter, architect; pupil and imitator of Bramante.

Brampton, town (pop. 8,389), S Ont., Canada, NW of Toronto. Flower-growing center with tanneries.

bran: see GRAIN.

Branch, Anna Hempstead, 1875–1934, American lyric poet, a social worker associated with Christodora House, New York.

Brancusi, Constantin (brän'kōōsh), 1876–, Rumanian sculptor. His abstract and frequently symbolic work has led to much controversy. Won lawsuit 1927 against U.S. customs authorities of Port of New York which led to lifting of duty on abstract art.

Brand, Sebastian: see BRANT, SEBASTIAN.

Brandeis, Louis Dembitz (brän'dīs), 1856–1941, Associate Justice of U.S. Supreme Court (1916–39), known for judicial liberalism.

Brandeis University: see WALTHAM, Mass.

Brandenburg (Ger. brän'dŭnbŏŏrk), former province (14,779 sq. mi.; 1939 pop. 3,007,-933) of Prussia, N Germany; since 1949 a member state (10,415 sq. mi.; pop. 2,527,-492) of [East] German Democratic Republic; cap. Potsdam. Flat, sandy region, drained by Havel, Spree, and Oder rivers. Berlin is geographically but not administratively part of Brandenburg. Other cities: Frankfurt-ander-Oder, Brandenburg, Cottbus. SPREE FOREST, in Lower LUSATIA, is inhabited by WENDS, remnants of Slavic people which held the region until its colonization and Christianization by Germans. ALBERT THE BEAR, made first margrave in 1134, became effective ruler after last Wendish prince made him his heir. His descendants (the Ascanians) ruled until 1320; various princes succeeded them until in 1415 the margraviate was given to the house of HOHENZOLLERN. Margraves also held rank of ELECTORS. Reformation was introduced in 1539. In the 17th cent. Brandenburg gained much territory (notably CLEVES, duchy of PRUSSIA, E POMERANIA) and rose in prestige under FREDERICK WILLIAM, the Great Elector, whose son in 1701 took the title king of Prussia as FREDERICK I. Brandenburg shared the history of Prussia until the Potsdam Conference of 1945, when all terri-

tory E of the Oder was placed under Polish administration pending final peace settlement.

Brandenburg, city (pop. 70,632), Brandenburg, N Germany, on Havel R. Has mfg. (trucks, textiles, machinery). The Slavic Brennabor, it was conquered 12th cent. by Albert the Bear and gave its name to his margraviate.

Brandes, Georg (Morris Cohen) (brän'dŭs), 1842–1927, Danish literary critic. Exerted an invigorating influence on Danish thought. Wrote widely on various literatures. His brother **Carl (Edvard Cohen) Brandes,** 1847–1931, was also a vigorous critic and an able dramatist.

Brandon, Charles: see SUFFOLK, CHARLES BRANDON, 1ST DUKE OF.

Brandon, city (pop. 20,598), SW Man., Canada, on Assiniboine R. and W of Winnipeg. Center of wheat-raising area, it has oil refining, meat packing, and mfg. of metal products. Here are dominion experimental farm and Brandon Col. (Baptist; 1899).

Brandt, Sebastian: see BRANT, SEBASTIAN.

brandy, strong alcoholic spirit distilled from wine or from marc, the residue of the wine press, which yields strong but inferior product. Made in many lands; most noted, called cognac, made from white grapes in Charente district of France. Brandy is also made from fruits (e.g., peach brandy), grains, and fermented sugar cane.

Brandy Station, trading center, NE of Culpeper, Va., scene of greatest cavalry battle in Civil War, June 9, 1863. First clash of Gettysburg campaign.

Brandywine, battle of, in American Revolution, fought Sept. 11, 1777, along Brandywine Creek, near Chadds Ford, SE Pa. British under Sir William Howe defeated Washington and continued advance on Philadelphia.

Branford, borough (pop. 2,552) in Branford town (pop. 10,944), S Conn., on Long Isl. Sound E of New Haven; settled 1644. Metal goods.

Brangwyn, Sir Frank (brăng'wĭn), 1867–, British painter. Decorative murals and etchings.

Brannan, Sam(uel), 1819–89, pioneer in Calif. Founded first Calif. newspaper (1847). Organizer and first president (1851) of Committee of Vigilance.

Branner, John Casper, 1850–1922, American geologist. Created model department of geology for Ark. Long associated with Stanford Univ. as professor, vice president, president.

Brant, Joseph, 1742–1807, war chief of Mohawk Indians. Aided British in American Revolution. Led Indian forces in Cherry Valley massacre (1778).

Brant, Brandt, or **Brand, Sebastian** (säbäs'tyän bränt'), 1458–1521, German poet. His chief work is *Das Narrenschiff* [the ship of fools], a series of satirical and moralizing poems (Eng. tr., 1944).

brant or **brant goose,** wild sea goose. American brant breeds in arctic regions, winters along Atlantic coast, rarely inland; black head, neck, tail; brownish gray back; grayish white under parts; eats eelgrass. Black brant migrates to Pacific coast. White brant is snow goose; prairie brant is American white-fronted goose.

Brantford, city (pop. 36,727), S Ont., Canada, on Grand R., WSW of Hamilton. Has mfg.

of farm and electrical equipment, machinery, furniture, and paper. Named for Joseph Brant. Hq. of the Six Nations and seat of Indian Inst.

Branting, Hjalmar (yäl'mär brän'tǐng), 1860–1925, Swedish statesman and Social Democratic leader, three times premier (1920, 1921–23, 1924–25). Shared 1921 Nobel Peace Prize with C. L. Lange.

Brantôme, Pierre de Bourdeilles, seigneur de (pyĕr' dù bōōrdā'yù sānyûr' dù brätōm'), 1535?–1614, French author, a courtier and soldier of fortune. His *Vies des hommes illustres et grands capitaines* and *Livre des dames* (Eng. tr., *Lives of Fair & Gallant Ladies*, 1933) form a racy account of his time.

Braque, Georges (zhôrzh' bräk'), 1881–, French painter. In 1905 joined the fauvists, in 1908 with Picasso launched cubism. His painting since has been consistently abstract, restrained and subtle in color and design. Best known for still lifes.

Bras d'Or Lakes (brä dôr'), arm of the Atlantic (360 sq. mi.; 44 mi. long, up to 20 mi. wide), extending into Cape Breton Isl., N.S., Canada. Area was scene of early aviation experiments.

Brasenose College: see OXFORD UNIVERSITY.

Brasidas (bră'sǐdùs), d. 422 B.C., Spartan general. Won victories over Athens in Peloponnesian War, including that at Amphipolis, in which he was killed.

Brasov (bräshôv'), Ger. *Kronstadt*, Hung. *Brassó*, city (pop. 82,984; c.30% Hungarian and German), central Rumania, in Transylvania. Food, textile, machinery mfg.; lumber. Founded 13th cent. by Teutonic Knights. Has Gothic cathedral (14th cent.), remains of medieval city wall, 17th-cent. citadel.

brass, name for various alloys of copper (60%–90%) and zinc (10%–40%). Properties vary with proportion of two metals; hardness varies with amount of zinc. Can be beaten, rolled into sheets, drawn into wires, machined, cast.

Brasso, Rumania: see BRASOV.

Brasstown Bald, peak, 4,784 ft. high, N Ga., in the Blue Ridge of the Appalachians near N.C. line; highest point in Ga.

brass wind instruments: see WIND INSTRUMENTS.

Bratianu, John (brútĭä'nōō), 1864–1927, Rumanian premier (1909–11, 1914–18, 1922–27). Governed dictatorially; prevented accession of Carol II (1927).

Bratislava (brä'těslä'vä), Ger. *Pressburg*, Hung. *Pozsony*, city (pop. 132,509), cap. of Slovakia, Czechoslovakia, on the Danube, near Austrian and Hungarian borders. Large river port; varied industries; univ. (founded 1919). Dates from Roman times; chartered 1291. Usual meeting place of Hungarian diet 1526–1848. To Czechoslovakia 1918. Rich in historical buildings, notably 13th-cent. castle and cathedral, 18th-cent. palace of archbishops (now city hall). Diversified pop. (Slovaks, Magyars, Jews, Czechs, Austrians). Treaty of PRESSBURG signed here 1805.

Brattleboro, town (pop. 11,522), including Brattleboro village (pop. 9,606), SE Vt., on Connecticut R. and E of Bennington; chartered 1753. Winter sports center. Mfg. of pipe organs (Estey's organ works date from c.1850), wood products, and textiles. Hq. of Holstein-Friesian cattle breeders' association. "Naulahka," N of village, was home of Rudyard Kipling.

Braun, Carl Ferdinand (kärl fĕr'dēnänt broun), 1850–1918, German physicist. Shared with Marconi the 1909 Nobel Prize for work on wireless telegraphy.

Braunschweig, Germany: see BRUNSWICK.

Brauwer, Adriaen: see BROUWER, ADRIAEN.

Brawley, city (pop. 11,922), SE Calif. Largest city in IMPERIAL VALLEY.

Bray, Thomas, 1656–1730, English clergyman. He founded Anglican church in Md. and served there and in England. Founded (1701) Society for the Propagation of the Gospel in Foreign Parts.

Bray, parish, Berkshire, England, on Thames R. Ballad about the vicar of Bray often supposed to describe Simon Aleyn, vicar of Bray 1540 to 1588.

Brazil (brùzĭl'), Port. *Brasil* (bräzēl'), republic (3,287,842 sq. mi.; pop. 52,645,479), E South America; full name the United States of Brazil; cap. RIO DE JANEIRO. By far the largest of South American countries, it occupies nearly half of the continent. In the N is the enormous basin of the AMAZON (mostly in States of Amazonas and PARÁ), with vast tropical rain forests, once famous for wild rubber, now yielding other forest products. The great inland port is MANAUS. The river near its mouth divides around MARAJÓ isl. On S arm (the Pará) is part of BELÉM. To the E Brazil thrusts far out toward Africa. This section, the Northeast, includes states of MARANHÃO, PIAUÍ, CEARÁ, RIO GRANDE DO NORTE, PARAÍBA, and Alagoas, with neighboring Sergipe and BAHIA. This area was the center of sugar plantations that for centuries produced great wealth and dominated the country. Many Negroes were imported to work as slaves here. Today on the coastal plains sugar, cotton, rice, and tobacco are raised, while drought-ridden interior regions (*sertões*) have been largely abandoned by farmers to ranchers. Important cities are: PARNAÍBA, TERESINA, FORTALEZA, NATAL, JOÃO PESSOA, RECIFE, MACEIÓ, and SALVADOR. The FERNANDO DA NORONHA isls. lie far out in the Atlantic. S of the "bulge" an irregular coastal plain, bordered on the W by an escarpment marking the edge of the great plateau of Brazil, has good harbors—VITÓRIA, NITERÓI, FLORIANÓPOLIS, and PÔRTO ALEGRE; Rio de Janeiro and SANTOS. In the SE and E sections of Brazil stretching far to the N on the plateau and to the S border with Argentina and Paraguay, population, agr., and industry are concentrated. The states on the S coast and inland are Espírito Santo, MINAS GERAIS, RIO DE JANEIRO, SÃO PAULO, PARANÁ, SANTA CATARINA, and RIO GRANDE DO SUL (where plateau ends in Río de la Plata plains). Great influx of Europeans in late 19th and 20th cent. helped build the coffee economy of São Paulo (Brazil is world's largest coffee producer) and later diverse industries especially around the cities of SÃO PAULO and Rio. On the plateau in the center of Brazil is the largely undeveloped state of GOLÁS, and in the NW is the developing frontier of

MATO GROSSO. Brazilians are proud of their "race" (an amalgamation of Indian, Negro, and various white strains). Portuguese is the official language, and although Vicente Yáñez PINZÓN and possibly others had visited the coast earlier, the Portuguese CABRAL is usually considered the "discoverer" (1500). The first permanent settlement was at São Vicente in São Paulo state (1532). Portuguese settlement was slow even after the coming of Martin Alfonso de SOUSA as governor. French Huguenots had to be driven from Rio de Janeiro harbor (1567), and the Dutch held the Northeast for years before they were driven out in 1654. Portuguese tried unsuccessfully to press claims in the S to prevent Uruguay and Paraguay. With the Napoleonic invasion of Portugal, King John VI fled (1807–8) to Rio de Janeiro, which became the cap. of the Portuguese Empire. After Napoleon's defeat, John returned to Portugal, leaving his son as regent in Brazil. In 1822 that son proclaimed Brazil independent (at Ipiranga) and became Emperor Pedro I. He had to abdicate in favor of his son, Pedro II, who reigned 1831–89. Brazil grew as a modern nation, though wars with Argentina and with Paraguay (see TRIPLE ALLIANCE, WAR OF THE) brought little benefit to Brazil. The abolition of slavery (1888) helped bring on the bloodless revolution that made Brazil a republic (1889). Immigration, the expanding coffee market, and the short wild-rubber boom (which caused trouble with neighbors, e.g., in ACRE) brought wealth to Brazil in late 19th and early 20th cent. Later, particularly under the presidency of Getulio VARGAS (1930–45, 1951–), great stress was laid on industrial expansion. The republic joined the Allies in World War I and World War II and became a member of the UN (1945).

Brazil, city (pop. 8,434), W Ind., near Terre Haute. Rail center in coal and agr. region.

Brazil nut, seed of a tall tree (*Bertholletia excelsa*) of tropical America. Borne in large pod, the nuts have a hard brown shell and sweet white meat.

brazilwood, bright red wood of tropical trees of genus *Caesalpinia*. It is used for cabinetwork.

brazing: see SOLDER.

Brazoria (brŭzôr'ēŭ), town (pop. 776), S Texas, on Brazos R. and SSW of Houston. Founded in 1820s, it was a thriving port in S. P. Austin's colony, then a center for plantations. Town was ruined by time and a hurricane; new town built near by.

Brazos (brăz'ŭs), river, formed in NW Texas by union of Double Mountain and Salt forks, joined by Clear Fork, and flowing more than 800 mi. SE through Waco to Freeport on Gulf of Mexico. Brazos water is used for city reservoirs, irrigation, flood control, and power, notably from Possum Kingdom Dam near Graham and Whitney Dam near Hillsboro.

Brazza, Pierre Paul François Camille Savorgnan de (sävôrnyä' dü brăzä'), 1852–1905, Franco-Italian explorer. Naturalized in France (1875) and sent by foreign office to establish French influence in Equatoria.

Founded Brazzaville (1880). Estab. French protectorate over Bateke territory.

Brazza, Adriatic island: see BRAC, Yugoslavia.

Brazzaville (brä'zŭvĭl), city (pop. 83,400), cap. of French Equatorial Africa, opposite Leopoldville on Stanley Pool of Congo R. Founded 1880 by the French explorer Brazza.

bread, universal article of food made by mixing crushed or ground grain or other seeds with liquids, then baking. Known in both leavened and unleavened forms since earliest history. In Western countries staple product contains white or whole-grain wheat flour, liquid yeast, shortening, sugar, salt. Other flours may be partly or entirely used: rye, barley, maize, buckwheat, sorghum, millet, potato, soybean, cassava, or rice. Quick breads (e.g., hot biscuits) generally leavened by BAKING POWDER.

Breadalbane, John Campbell, 1st earl of: see CAMPBELL, JOHN, 1ST EARL OF BREADALBANE.

breadfruit, tropical tree (*Artocarpis communis*) and its fruit, a staple food in tropics. When baked, the fruit resembles bread.

Bread Loaf Mountain, 3,823 ft. high. W Vt., E of Middlebury. Middlebury Col. holds summer session in writing and languages near by.

breadroot or **Indian breadroot,** perennial pealike plant (*Psoralea esculenta*), of North American prairies. Valued by Indians for edible, starchy roots.

Breakspear, Nicholas: see ADRIAN IV.

breakwater, structure protecting harbor from full force of waves and providing quieter ship anchorage. Artificial breakwaters may be rock or concrete-block mound, rock foundation and masonry superstructure, or superstructure from sea floor.

breast, frontal portion of chest in which mammary glands exist in most mammals. Gland tissue develops at onset of puberty; composed of lobes, each resembling grape cluster, from which ducts lead to nipple. In females, milk secretion follows birth of young.

Breasted, James Henry, 1865–1935, American Egyptologist. Taught (1894–1933) at Univ. of Chicago; director Haskell Oriental Mus. and Oriental Inst. of Univ. of Chicago. His important archaeological research in Egypt and Mesopotamia was basis for many publications.

breathing: see RESPIRATION.

Brébeuf, Jean de (zhä' dü brābûf'), 1593–1649, French Jesuit missionary and martyr in North America. Canonized in 1930.

Brecht, Bert (Bertold Brecht) (bĕrt' brĕkht'), 1898–, German author, a leading Communist propagandist. His *Dreigroschenoper* (with music by Kurt Weill, 1928), an adaptation of *The Beggars' Opera*, was an immediate success and was in turn adapted into English (*The Three-Penny Opera*, 1933). Among his books of ballads is *Hauspostille* (1927).

Breckenridge, Hugh Henry, 1870–1937, American painter, a noted teacher of art.

Breckenridge, city (pop. 6,610), N Texas, W of Fort Worth. Processing center for ranch and farm area with oil and gas industries.

Breckinridge, John, 1760–1806, American statesman. Advised Pres. Jefferson on KENTUCKY AND VIRGINIA RESOLUTIONS. Spokesman of Western interests in Senate (1801–5). His grandson, **John Cabell Breckenridge,** 1821–75, was Vice President of the United States (1857–61). Presidential candidate of Southern Democratic faction (1860) and a Confederate general in Civil War.

Brecknockshire (brĕk'nŏkshĭr) or **Brecon** (brĕk'ŭn), inland county (733 sq. mi.; pop. 56,484), S Wales. Mountainous region, rising to 2,910 ft. in Brecon Beacons. Chief occupations are sheep grazing and dairy farming; there is also coal and iron mining, and woolen mfg. County town, **Brecknock** (pop. 6,466), has cathedral dating from 11th cent.

Breda (brādä'), municipality (pop. 81,873) and town, North Brabant prov., SW Netherlands. Machine plants; rayon mfg. Surrender of Breda's heroic garrison to Spanish under Spinola (1625) was painted by Velázquez.

Breda, Compromise of, 1566: see GUEUX.

Breda, Declaration of, 1660: see CHARLES II, king of England.

Breda, Treaty of, 1667: see DUTCH WARS.

breeding of plants and animals to improve the breed, variety, or strain probably began soon after start of DOMESTICATION, as selective breeding—propagation of specimens with desirable qualities. Scientific breeding arose after Gregor Mendel's promulgation of laws of inheritance. Pure lines (in plants) and pure-bred animals show virtual uniformity. Plant hybrids—e.g., hybrid corn—are products of crosses between two strains of a pure line. Vigor of animal breeds is maintained by crossing strains and sometimes by crossing certain breeds. New breeds and varieties are chiefly hybrids and the product of breeding individuals in which mutations have occurred. See also GENETICS; HEREDITY.

Breed's Hill: see BUNKER HILL, BATTLE OF.

Breisgau (brīs'gou), region, S Baden, SW Germany; chief city Freiburg. Held by Hapsburgs 1368–1805.

Breitenfeld (brī'tŭnfĕlt"), village, Saxony, SE Germany, near Leipzig. Scene of victory of imperials over Swedes (1631) and of Swedes over imperials (1642) in Thirty Years War.

Breitmann, Hans (brīt'män), pseud. of Charles Godfrey Leland, 1824–1903, American author of poems in German dialect, originally in magazines (collected first in *Hans Breitmann's Ballads,* 1869). Leland edited *Graham's Magazine* and the *Continental Monthly* and wrote many works under his own name.

Bremen (brĕ'mŭn, Ger. brā'mŭn), state (156 sq. mi.; pop. 568,335), N Germany, on North Sea about the mouth of Weser R. Its fortunes are those of its cap., the free Hansa city of **Bremen** (pop. 444,196), second largest German port and an industrial and commercial center. Created in 845, the archdiocese of Bremen originally included all Scandinavia, Iceland, Greenland. City of Bremen itself was virtually independent from archbishops as its importance grew. Entered HANSEATIC LEAGUE 1358; accepted the Reformation; became free imperial city 1646. Trade was spurred by founding of BREMERHAVEN (1827). "Republic and Hansa city" of Bremen joined German Empire (1871), Weimar Republic (1919), and Federal Republic of [Western] Germany (1949).

Heavily damaged by air raids in World War II; under U.S. occupation from 1945. Gothic city hall, with statue of Roland (erected 1404 as symbol of city's freedom) and Cathedral of Sankt Petri (begun 1043) still stand.

Bremer, Fredrika, 1801–65, Swedish writer and feminist, b. Finland, author of *Homes in the New World* (1853; impressions of travel in America).

Bremerhaven (brā'mŭrhä"fŭn), city (pop. 113,925) Bremen, N Germany; North Sea port on mouth of Weser R. Founded 1827 as transatlantic port.

Bremerton (brĕm'ŭrtŭn), port city (pop. 27,-678), NW Wash., on arm of Puget Sound; founded 1891. Seat of Puget Sound navy yard.

Brenham (brĕn'ŭm), city (pop. 6,941), S central Texas, NW of Houston, center of agr. area. Processes cotton and cotton products. Oil fields near.

Brenner Pass (brĕ'nŭr), Ital. *Brennero* (brĕn'-närō), in Tyrolean Alps, 4,495 ft. high, on Austro-Italian border. Highway built 1772; railroad 1867.

Brent, Margaret, 1600–1671?, American feminist. First woman in Maryland to hold land in her own right, she was executrix of Gov. Calvert's estates and acted as attorney for Lord Baltimore.

Brentano, Clemens (brĕntä'nō), 1778–1842, German romantic poet; brother of Bettina von Arnim. Author of fairy tales and stories such as *Geschichte vom bravem Kasperl und dem schönen Annerl* (1817; Eng. tr., *Honor,* 1847), but best-known for collaboration with Achim von ARNIM on folk-song collection *Des Knaben Wunderhorn* (1806–8).

Brentano, Elisabeth: see ARNIM, BETTINA VON.

Brentano, Franz, 1838–1917, German psychologist, professor of philosophy at Vienna (1874–1880). Set out to estab. psychology as a distinct science based on empirical findings.

Brentford and Chiswick (chĭz'ĭk), municipal borough (pop. 59,354), Middlesex, England, a suburb of London at terminus of Grand Junction Canal. Has mfg. of electrical equipment, pharmaceuticals, and tires. Grave of Hogarth at Chiswick.

Brentwood. 1 City (pop. 7,504), E Mo., W suburb of St. Louis. **2** Residential borough (pop. 12, 535), W Pa., S of, and near, Pittsburgh.

Brescia (brā'shä), city (pop. 92,583), Lombardy, N Italy. Industrial center (steel, machinery). Of pre-Roman origin; independent commune in Middle Ages. Had flourishing school of painters in 16th cent. (G. B. Moroni, Moretto). Roman remains; medieval, Renaissance, and baroque churches and palaces.

Breslau (brĕs'lou), Pol. *Wrocław,* city (1950 pop. c.340,000), former cap. of Lower Silesia, on Oder; under Polish administration since 1945. Became episcopal see in 1000; cap. of duchy of SILESIA, under Piast dynasty, in 1163. Sacked by Mongols 1241. To Bohemia 1335; under Hapsburgs 1526–1742. Grew into major commercial and industrial center in 19th cent., with metal, textile, and food industries. Had two large annual fairs. Heavily damaged in World War II. City very large (pre-war pop. 615,000) until expulsion of Germans and resettlement by Poles after 1945. Has univ. (founded 1702); archiepiscopal see.

Bresse (brĕs), region, E France, between Saône and Ain, in Ain dept.; chief town Bourg-en-Bresse. Agr., poultry, wine. Pond-dotted Dombes dist. is being drained. Ceded to France by Savoy (1601) and incorporated into Burgundy prov.

Brest, town (pop. 62,707), Finistère dept., NW France, on an inlet of Atlantic into tip of Brittany. Chief French naval station. Harbor created 1631 by Richelieu. German submarine base in World War II, heavily bombed by Allies.

Brest, formerly **Brest-Litovsk** (brĕst'-lĭtôfsk'), city (1931 pop. 48,435), Belorussia, on Western Bug R. Rail and water transportation center; strategic fortress. Passed to Russia in third Polish partition (1795); fortified 1831; held by Germans in both World Wars; to Poland 1921; to USSR 1945. Union of Polish Orthodox and Roman Catholic churches (1596) and Treaty of BREST-LITOVSK (1918) were signed here.

Brest-Litovsk, Treaty of (-lĭtôfsk'), March 1918, separate peace treaty signed by Soviet Russia and the Central Powers at BREST, USSR, following armistice of Dec., 1917. Trotsky was chief Russian negotiator. Russia recognized independence of Poland, Baltic states, Georgia, Ukraine; permitted German occupation of Belorussia; ceded Kars, Ardahan, Batum to Turkey; promised large indemnity. General armistice of Nov., 1918, nullified this treaty.

Brétigny, Treaty of (brātēnyē'), 1360, short-lived truce between England and France in HUNDRED YEARS WAR; signed at Brétigny near Chartres. John II of France paid English 3,000,000 gold crowns for his ransom and ceded nearly half of France.

Breton, André (ädrä' brütō), 1896–, French poet, novelist, critic. First a Dadaist, he was later a leading surrealist.

Breton, Nicholas (brĕt'ŭn), 1551?–c.1623, prolific English poet and miscellaneous writer. *The Passionate Shepherd* (1604) his best-known work.

Bretón de los Herreros, Manuel (mänwäl' brätôn' dā lōs ĕr-rā'rôs), 1796–1873, Spanish author of satiric and lyric poems and plays.

Breton literature (brĕ'tŭn), in the Celtic language of Brittany, until the 19th cent. consisted mainly of popular plays (some dating back to c.1500), songs, and stories. Collection of these, as well as a cultivated literature, began mid-19th cent. Outstanding Breton poets include Auguste Brizeux (1803–58), author of collection *Telen Arvor* [the harp of Armorica] (1844), and Jean Pierre Calloc'h (1888–1917), whose poems show piety, love of the sea, and fascination with death. The 20th cent. has seen a revival and expansion of the Breton language.

Bretonneau, Pierre (pyĕr' brütônō), 1778–1862, French physician. His treatise on diphtheria established its identity; he performed first successful tracheotomy for diphtheria 1825. Stated germ theory of disease later established by Pasteur.

Breton Succession, War of the, 1341–64. Duke John III of Brittany having died childless,

the succession was contested by his brother, Jean de Montfort, who was backed by England, and by CHARLES OF BLOIS, who had married a niece of the late duke and was backed by France. Charles's death at the battle of Auray (1364) decided the issue, which had merged with the Hundred Years War.

Bretton Woods Conference, name commonly given to United Nations Monetary and Financial Conference, held in July, 1944, at Bretton Woods, N.H. Conference resulted in creation of International Monetary Fund, to promote monetary cooperation, and of International Bank for Reconstruction and Development.

Breuer, Josef (yō'zĕf broi'ŭr), 1842–1925, Austrian physician, whose therapy and theory, developed by Freud, became psychoanalysis.

Breuer, Marcel Lajos (broi'ŭr), 1902–, architect, b. Hungary. Associated with Bauhaus group. Partner of Walter Gropius 1937–42.

Breughel, family of painters: see BRUEGEL.

Breviary of Alaric (ă'lŭrĭk), Visigothic code of Roman law issued (506) by Alaric II for his Roman subjects in Spain and S Gaul.

Brewer, city (pop. 6,862), S Maine, on Penobscot R. opposite Bangor. Pulp and paper mills.

Brewster, Sir David, 1781–1868, Scottish physicist. Notable research on polarization of light. Invented dioptric system of improved lighthouse illumination; said to have invented kaleidoscope.

Brewster, William, 1567–1644, English separatist and religious leader of Plymouth Colony.

Brewton, city (pop. 5,146), S Ala., near Fla. line, NE of Mobile, in cotton, livestock, lumber area.

Brian Boru or **Brian Boroimhe** (both: brī'ŭn or brēn', bŭrōō' or bŭrō'), 962?–1014, high king of Ireland. A local king, he subjugated all Ireland. Annihilated coalition of Norse and his Irish enemies at Clontarf in 1014, but was murdered soon after. His victory broke Norse power in Ireland, but destroyed unity he had achieved.

Briand, Aristide (ärēstēd' brēä'), 1862–1932, French statesman, 11 times premier between 1909 and 1921. Originally a Socialist, he later was attacked by left and right for his liberalism. As foreign minister (1925–32) he was chief architect of LOCARNO PACT and KELLOGG-BRIAND PACT. Advocated international cooperation and United States of Europe. Shared 1926 Nobel Peace Prize with Stresemann.

Briareus (brīâ'rēŭs), in Greek religion, hundred-handed monster, who warred against the gods.

bribery, corrupt tendering or receiving of anything of value in return for official action. At common law a misdemeanor, but made a felony in many U.S. jurisdictions. More loosely bribery includes corrupt influencing of nonofficials (e.g., voters).

bridal wreath: see SPIRAEA.

Bride, Saint: see BRIDGET, SAINT.

Bridewell, parish of central London, England. Bridewell house of correction here until 1864.

bridge, roadway spanning body of water. Developed from primitive log or vine across stream to arched stone structures of 2000 to 4000 B.C., the longer Roman arches, and modern steel bridges. Beginning in mid-19th cent., wooden bridges of early U.S. were largely superseded by cast and wrought iron bridges. Development of Bessemer process of converting cast iron into steel revolutionized bridgebuilding. Use of TRUSS led to vast modern structures including panel-truss bridge (braced parallel trusses supporting road on transverse beams); center-swing bridge (revolves on pier midstream to permit passage of tall ships); cantilever (long spans, usually supported by two piers and two abutments); suspension bridge (a roadway suspended by cables anchored to piers on each bank); vertical lift (truss-type span suspended between steel towers by wire ropes); and bascule or quadrant bridge (rigid, truss-type bridge resting free on one bank and mounted on heavy quadrant on other, to permit lifting clear of water). See also DRAW-BRIDGE; PONTOON; VIADUCT. See *ill.,* p. 167.

bridge, card game, developed from whist, played with 52 cards by four players paired as partners. An old form of bridge was played in Middle East in 19th cent. The term *bridge* now usually means contract bridge, a form developed by Harold S. Vanderbilt of New York in 1925.

Bridgeburg, Ont.: see FORT ERIE.

Bridge of Sighs, covered stone bridge in Venice, Italy, built in 16th cent. to connect ducal palace with prison. Prisoners were led over bridge after trial in palace.

Bridgeport. 1 City (pop. 158,709), SW Conn., on harbor on Long Isl. Sound at Poquonock R. mouth; settled 1639. State's chief industrial city (metal goods, machinery). Seaside Park and Barnum Inst. of Science and History commemorate the showman who lived here. "Gen. Tom Thumb" born here. Has Univ. of Bridgeport. Socialist city government since 1933. **2** Borough (pop. 5,827), SE Pa., NW of Philadelphia. Produces coke, iron, and textiles. Dolomite is mined.

Bridger, James, 1804–81, American fur trader, one of most famous of MOUNTAIN MEN. Guided many expeditions in Northwest. Founded Fort Bridger on Oregon Trail in 1843.

Bridger, Fort: see FORT BRIDGER STATE PARK.

Bridges, Calvin Blackman, 1889–1938, American geneticist. Proved chromosome theory of heredity; formulated theory of genic balance; studied gene positions in salivary chromosomes of *Drosophila* (fruit fly or vinegar fly).

Bridges, Harry (Alfred Renton Bridges), 1900–, American labor leader in maritime industry, b. Australia. Sentenced 1950 to five-year prison term for swearing falsely in 1945 that he had never been Communist party member.

Bridges, Robert (Seymour), 1844–1930, English poet laureate after 1913. Wrote lyrics, long poems (e.g., *The Testament of Beauty,* 1929), verse dramas, criticism; published poetry of Gerard Manley Hopkins.

Bridget, Saint, 453?–523?, Irish holy woman. Little is known of her except that she founded a monastery at Kildare and that she is buried at Downpatrick with fellow patrons of Ireland, Patrick and Columba. Also Brigid and Bride. Feast: Feb. 1.

Bridget of Sweden, Saint, c.1300–1375, Swedish nun. A noblewoman and a mother of eight children, she retired to become a nun after the death of her husband. She had celebrated visions, and as a result of one of them founded a new order (the Bridgettines). She lived her last years in Rome (except for pilgrimage to Palestine) and was adviser to popes. Also Birgitta. Feast: Oct. 8.

Bridgeton, city (pop. 18,378), S N.J., S of Philadelphia; settled 1686. Shipping center for agr. region. Has canneries and glassworks.

Bridgetown, city (pop. 68,924), cap. of Barbados, British West Indies. Tourist resort.

Bridgeville, borough (pop. 5,650), SW Pa., SW of Pittsburgh. Mfg. of chemicals and metal products.

Bridgewater, town (pop. 9,512), SE Mass., S of Boston. Shoes, metal products, grain feed.

Bridgman, Laura, 1829–89, New England teacher of sewing, first blind deaf-mute to be successfully educated (by Dr. S. G. Howe of Perkins Inst.).

Bridgman, Percy Williams, 1882–, American physicist. Won 1946 Nobel Prize for work in high pressures.

Brie (brē), region, Marne and Seine-et-Marne depts., N France, E of Paris; chief city Meaux. Rich farm district, famous for cheese.

Brieg (brēk), Pol. *Brzeg,* city (pop. 7,744; 1939 pop. 31,419), Lower Silesia; under Polish administration since 1945. Seat of a principality under PIAST dynasty 1311–1675. Old castle and Renaissance city hall damaged in World War II.

Brienne, Étienne Charles Loménie de: see LOMÉNIE DE BRIENNE, ÉTIENNE CHARLES.

Brienz (brēĕnts'), village, Bern canton, Switzerland, on L. of Brienz. Woodcarving industry.

Brieux, Eugène (ûzhĕn' brēû'), 1858–1932, French dramatist. Wrote on family life and social themes. Well-known plays are *La Robe rouge* (1900) and *Les Avariés* (1901; produced in U.S. as *Damaged Goods*).

Briey (brēā'), town (pop. 2,539), Meurthe-et-Moselle dept., NE France. Center of Lorraine iron-ore basin.

brig, two-masted, square-rigged, sailing vessel, once popular in coastal trade. Length varies from 100 to 115 ft.; tonnages go up to 350. Smaller brigantine has a fore-and-aft mainsail and square topsail on the mainmast. See *ill.,* sailing craft, p. 1109.

Briga: see BRIGUE AND TENDE.

brigandage, robbery, blackmail, kidnaping, and plundering by armed bands. Arises from bad economic, political, or social conditions or in a chaotic society as after war or in frontier settlements. Many brigands are romantic figures, as Dick Turpin, Robin Hood, Hereward the Wake, Stenka Razin, Fra Diavolo, and Jesse James of U.S.

Briggs, Le Baron Russell, 1855–1934, American educator. A professor of English at Harvard, he was later dean of Harvard Col. (1891–1902) and president of Radcliffe Col. (1902–23).

Brigham, Albert Perry, 1855–1932. American

geographer. Became professor of geology, Colgate Univ., in 1892. His *Geographic Influences in American History* (1903) had wide influence.

Brigham City, city (pop. 6,790), N Utah, N of Ogden; founded 1851. Food-processing center for area (extensive peach culture) served by Ogden R. project.

Brigham Young University, at Provo, Utah; Latter-Day Saints, coed.; opened 1875 as academy, renamed 1903.

Bright, Sir Charles Tilston, 1832–88, English engineer. Among cables he laid were first from Ireland to Scotland (1853) and Ireland to Newfoundland (1858).

Bright, John, 1811–89, English statesman and orator; son of Quaker cotton miller. He and Richard COBDEN were greatest 19th-cent. champions of the middle class. Noted for laissez-faire views, support of FREE TRADE, and fight for repeal of CORN LAWS.

Bright, Richard: see BRIGHT'S DISEASE.

Brighton, county borough (pop. 156,440), Sussex East, England, on English Channel. Became fashionable resort under patronage of prince of Wales (later George IV), who built the Royal Pavilion.

Bright's disease, any of several forms of kidney inflammation. Symptoms include albumin in urine, dropsy, high blood pressure. Described 1827 by **Richard Bright,** 1789–1858, English physician noted for clinical observations.

Brigue and Tende (brēg, täd), Ital. *Briga* and *Tenda,* small districts (202 sq. mi.; 1936 pop. 4,274), Alpes-Maritimes dept., SE France. Ceded to France by Italy in Treaty of Paris of 1947.

Brill or **Bril,** two Flemish artists, brothers. **Mattys Brill** (mä'tīs), 1550–83, and **Paul Brill,** 1554–1626, both worked in Rome. The latter was important in the developing of landscape painting.

Brill, A(braham) A(rden), 1874–1948, American psychiatrist, b. Austria. One of the earliest, most active exponents of psychoanalysis in practice, teaching, and writing, he was first translator of many major works of Freud and Jung.

Brillat-Savarin, Anthelme (ätĕlm' brēyä'-sävä-rē'), 1755–1826, French lawyer, economist, and gastronomist, famous for *La Physiologie du goût* (1825), published in English as *The Physiology of Taste.*

Brill's disease, mild type of typhus fever. First described, though not identified, by Nathan Edwin Brill, 1860–1925, American physician.

Brindaban (brĭn"dùbŭn'), town (pop. 20,718), W Uttar Pradesh, India. Traditionally associated with the youth of the Hindu god Krishna.

Brindisi (brēn'dēzē), Latin *Brundisium,* city (pop. 35,984), Apulia, S Italy; Adriatic port. Important Roman naval station; embarkation port for Crusaders. One of two columns marking end of Appian Way still stands. Vergil died here.

Brinton, Daniel Garrison, 1837–99, American anthropologist, authority on American Indians.

Brinvilliers, Marie Madeleine d'Aubray, marquise de: see POISON AFFAIR.

Brion, Admiral de: see CHABOT, PHILIPPE DE.

Brisbane, Albert (brĭz'bän), 1809–90, American social theorist. An advocate of the ideas of Charles FOURIER, he was instrumental in founding of Fourierist communities at BROOK FARM and Red Bank, N.J.

Brisbane (brĭz'bùn), city (pop. 21,391; metropolitan pop. 402,030), cap. of Queensland, Australia; port on Brisbane R. above its mouth on Moreton Bay. Area was settled 1824 as a penal colony. Seat of Univ. of Queensland (1909). Exports textiles, wool, meat, gold, and sugar.

Briseis (brīsē'ĭs), maiden in the *Iliad* captured by Achilles, whose wrath was aroused when Agamemnon took her. See also CHRYSEIS.

Brissot de Warville, Jacques Pierre (zhäk' pyĕr' brēsō' dù värvēl'), 1754–93, French revolutionist and pamphleteer, leader of the GIRONDISTS. Also wrote on French-U.S. relations, founded abolitionist society, and originated phrase later made famous by Proudhon: "Property is theft." Guillotined.

Bristol, John Digby, 1st earl of, 1580–1653, English diplomat. Ambassador to Spain 1611–24; offended Charles I and was imprisoned 1626–28. Released by Parliament, he became a moderate leader. As such, was increasingly unpopular and again jailed, 1642. Was royalist in civil war and died in exile. His son, **George Digby, 2d earl of Bristol,** 1612–77, was secretary of state to Charles I in exile and returned to England after Restoration.

Bristol, county borough (pop. 442,281), Gloucestershire, England, on the Avon near mouth of the Severn. A major world port, with extensive trade with North America and Ireland, it is also an industrial center (mfg. of flour, chemicals, paper, biscuits, tiles, and leather goods, and notably of airplanes since 1910). Railroad tunnel under Severn leads to Wales. Early transatlantic steamship built here 1838. The Cabots sailed (1497) from Bristol for American discoveries. Birthplace of Thomas Chatterton and Robert Southey.

Bristol. 1 City (pop. 35,961), central Conn., SW of Hartford; settled 1727. Mfg. of clocks (since 1790) and metal goods. **2** Fishing and resort town (pop. 1,476), S Maine, E of Bath. Includes Pemaquid peninsula, with reproduction of tower of Fort William Henry (built here 1692). MONHEGAN island is near. **3** Borough (pop. 12,710), SE Pa., on Delaware, NE of Philadelphia; settled c.1681. Mfg. of paper, machinery, and textiles. Has old Friends Meetinghouse (c.1710). **4** Town (pop. 12,320), including Bristol village (pop. 10,335), E R.I., on Narragansett Bay SE of Providence; connected with Portsmouth by Mt. Hope Bridge; passed to R.I. from Plymouth Colony, 1746. Yachts, coastwise fishing boats use Bristol Harbor. Boat works (estab. 1863); textile mills. Near-by monument marks place where King Philip fell. **5** City (Tenn. pop., 16771; Va. pop., 15,954), on Tenn.-Va. line in mountains; settled 1749. Separate municipalities united economically; rail and industrial center in timber, farm, coal, and iron region with mfg. of textiles.

Bristol Avon: see AVON 1, river, England.

Bristol Channel, inlet (length 85 mi.; max. width 43 mi.) of the Atlantic separating Wales and SW England. It is approach, via the Severn, to Bristol.

FOOTBRIDGE (*Cables are made of bamboo fibers*)
Min River, Szechwan Province, China

PONTOON BRIDGE
Tigris River, Mosul, Iraq

ROMAN ARCH BRIDGE
Pons Trajan, Alcántara, Spain, 98 A.D.

STEEL ARCH BRIDGE
Sydney Harbor, Australia, 1932

STEEL TRUSS BRIDGE
Little Belt Bridge, Denmark, 1935

CANTILEVER BRIDGE
Quebec, Canada, 1917

SUSPENSION BRIDGE
Golden Gate Bridge, San Francisco, 1937

SWING BRIDGE
Kincardine-on-Forth, Scotland, 1936

BASCULE: ROLLING LIFT BRIDGE
Terminal Railway, Chicago, 1901

VERTICAL-LIFT BRIDGE
Hawthorne Avenue, Portland, Oregon, 1911

Bristow, city (pop. 5,400), E central Okla., SW of Tulsa, in oil and farm region.

Britain, conventional name of Great Britain before Germanic invasions of 5th–6th cent. It then became ENGLAND, WALES, and SCOTLAND. Successive waves of migration or invasion were mainly from S and E to N and W. Before 6th cent. B.C. Celtic invasions from continent brought Iron Age culture to British Bronze Age settlements. Brisk trade with Continent developed. Last Celtic invaders (c.75 B.C.) introduced the deep plough and coining of money. First Roman invaders under Julius CAESAR (55 B.C.) found Celtic tribal organization as in Gaul, including DRUIDS. By A.D. 85 Emperor Claudius and his successors had conquered Britain S of the Clyde despite such resistance as revolt of BOADICEA. Risings in N caused building of HADRIAN'S WALL (122 A.D.) and Wall of ANTONINUS (142 A.D.). Former became N frontier. First half of 3d cent. was Roman heyday in Britain, with number of towns whose gridiron plan and architecture were Roman and whose language was probably Latin. ROMAN ROADS, mainly military, radiated from Londinium (London). Decline of Rome and three-sided invasions by Saxons and Irish progressively weakened defense until Honorius supposedly gave Romano-Britons self-rule c.410. A final appeal to Rome for help failed 446 and warring tribal kings gradually took over. Christianization lessened invasion pressure in N and W, but Saxon raids in E were heavier. ANGLO-SAXONS and Jutes began to settle in England and Celtic tribal culture revived. Residue of Roman influence remained in place names, architectural ruins, and in force of tradition.

britannia metal, silvery-white alloy of tin, copper, antimony; sometimes also with bismuth, lead, zinc.

Britannicus (brĭtăʹnĭkŭs), A.D. 41?–A.D. 55, Roman prince, son of Claudius I and Messalina. Set aside in favor of Nero, son of his stepmother, Agrippina, he was apparently poisoned later.

British Cameroons: see NIGERIA and CAMEROONS.

British Columbia, province (359,279 sq. mi.; with water surface 366,255 sq. mi.; pop. 1,165,210), W Canada; cap. VICTORIA. Many islands (e.g. Vancouver and Queen Charlotte) lie off the indented W Pacific coastline. VANCOUVER is largest city and chief port. Other cities are NEW WESTMINSTER, NORTH VANCOUVER, and TRAIL. Province is mountainous with interior broken by numerous lakes and rivers. Drained by FRASER, COLUMBIA, KOOTENAY, PEACE, and SKEENA rivers. Population is centered in S and on Vancouver Isl. Lumbering is major industry, supplemented by truck and poultry farming and mining (copper, lead, zinc, silver). Tourist trade is growing. Area first explored by white men (Pérez, Heceta and Quadra, Cook, Meares) in late 18th cent. England gained control when Spanish claims were relinquished in Nootka Convention (1790). Capt. George Vancouver charted coast 1792–94, and Sir Alexander Mackenzie reached Pacific coast by land 1793. Trading posts estab. by North West Co. and Hudson's Bay Co.

Boundaries defined with Alaska (1825, 1903) and the U.S. (1846). Crown colonies on Vancouver Isl. (1849) and the mainland (1858) were united 1866 and became province 1871. Gold strikes brought scattered settlement which greatly increased after Canadian Pacific RR reached Vancouver. In recent years there has been considerable immigration from the Prairie Provs.

British Columbia, University of: see VANCOUVER.

British Commonwealth of Nations: see BRITISH EMPIRE.

British East Africa, inclusive term for KENYA, UGANDA, TANGANYIKA, and ZANZIBAR.

British East India Company: see EAST INDIA COMPANY, BRITISH.

British Empire, at its height (late 19th-early 20th cent.) greatest empire of the world. First colony was Newfoundland (1583). Foundations of empire laid in early 17th cent. by formation of EAST INDIA COMPANY. Desire for trade and to settle overseas led to scattered settlements by various groups. These were consolidated into colonies (by agreement or conquest) under London colonial office, with Parliament imposing taxes. Theories of MERCANTILISM were implanted by NAVIGATION ACTS. Refusal of colonists' demands for freedom in government and trade resulted in loss of the Thirteen Colonies in American Revolution (1775–83). Conquests of Ceylon, Malta, Cape of Good Hope increased British sea power. After change in attitude shown by Reform Bill (1832), abolition of slave trade (1833), and free trade policy (1842–46), trend to self-government of settled colonists led to Canada becoming first dominion, 1867. Emigration to Australia and New Zealand was for development, not exploitation. Queen Victoria proclaimed empress of India 1877; Burma added 1885. In late 19th-cent. European colonial race, British enlarged holdings in Africa, gained power in Egypt, and acquired Malaya, Borneo, part of New Guinea, and many Pacific islands. By 20th cent. Britain controlled nearly one quarter of world. New dominions were Australia, New Zealand (1907), Union of South Africa (1910). IMPERIAL CONFERENCE held this loose association together through World War I. Egypt again made independent in 1923, with British given control of Suez Canal and mandates over TANGANYIKA, PALESTINE, IRAQ. Dominion status given Irish Free State in 1921. Statute of Westminster (1931) created British Commonwealth of Nations; made dominions independent except for allegiance to the crown. In 1948 Palestine mandate given up; India, Pakistan, Ceylon became dominions; independent republic of Union of Burma set up India became republic within commonwealth, and Ireland withdrew in 1949. Today United Kingdom dependencies under colonial office are: in Mediterranean—Cyprus, Gibraltar Malta; in Africa—Kenya, Tanganyika, Uganda, British Somaliland, Zanzibar Northern Rhodesia, Nyasaland, Gambia Gold Coast, Nigeria, Sierra Leone; in Far East—Brunei, Hong Kong, Malaya, North Borneo, Sarawak, Singapore; in Indian Ocean—Aden, Mauritius, the Seychelles

Maldive Isls.; in Pacific Ocean—British Solomon Isls., Fiji, the Gilbert and Ellice Isls., Tonga, Pitcairn Isl.; in Atlantic Ocean—Bermuda, British West Indies, British Guiana, British Honduras, Falkland Isls., St. Helena. System of governments differs widely as attempt is made to use native traditions. Southern Rhodesia largely self-governing. Commonwealth relations office administers three high-commission territories in Africa—Basutoland, Bechuanaland, Swaziland. Mandates in Tanganyika, Togoland, Cameroons in W Africa placed under UN trusteeship with colonial office administration, 1946. Great Britain administers Anglo-Egyptian Sudan jointly with Egypt, New Hebrides with France, Canton and Enderbury Isls. with U.S. Population of commonwealth is over 500,000,000 in an area of nearly 16,000,000 sq. mi.

British Guiana: see GUIANA.

British Honduras (hŏndōō'rŭs), British crown colony (8,867 sq. mi.; pop. 59,220), Central America; cap. Belize. The region was probably entered by Cortés in 1524, but the founding of Belize is credited to British buccaneers (17th cent.), and logwood cutters were early settlers. Woods still a main product. Spain contested British ownership, which is now disputed by Guatemala.

British Isles: see GREAT BRITAIN and IRELAND.

British Museum, national repository, London, for treasures in literature, science, and art; opened 1759, estab. by act of Parliament 1853. It has collections of Sir Robert Bruce COTTON and Sir Hans SLOANE; HARLEIAN LIBRARY; royal libraries of George II and George III; Egyptian basalt slab (ROSETTA STONE); and the ELGIN MARBLES. Sir Anthony PANIZZI began printing of the library's catalogue. In World War II most treasures stored in coal mine in Wales.

British New Guinea: see PAPUA, TERRITORY OF.

British North America Act, constitution of dominion of Canada, sketched at Quebec Conference of 1864, passed by British Parliament in 1867 to take effect July 1, 1867. Gives enumerated powers to local (provincial) legislatures with residual powers left to the dominion. Interpretation by privy council has extended scope of provincial power of "property and civil rights," and a doctrine of "emergency powers" was invented for dominion use in time of war. Power of amendment is nominally vested in British Parliament which, in practice, acts only on request of Canadian Parliament. Act makes both French and English official languages in Quebec, in Parliament, and in courts; and guarantees separate tax-supported schools for Catholics and non-Catholics in Quebec and some other provinces.

British North Borneo: see NORTH BORNEO.

British Somaliland: see SOMALILAND.

British thermal unit (B.T.U.), amount of heat required to raise temperature of 1 lb. of water at maximum density 1°F. One B.T.U. equals: 251.9 calories; 777.9 foot-pounds; 1055 joules; 107.5 kilogram-meters; 0.0002928 kilowatt-hours.

British Togoland: see TOGOLAND.

British West Africa, inclusive term for British CAMEROONS, British TOGOLAND, GAMBIA, GOLD COAST, NIGERIA, and SIERRA LEONE.

British West Indies: see WEST INDIES.

Brittany (brĭt'ŭnē), Fr. *Bretagne,* region and former province, NW France, a peninsula between English Channel and Bay of Biscay, comprising Ille-et-Vilaine, Côtes-du-Nord, Finistère, Morbihan, and Loire-Inférieure depts. Irregular, rocky coast; hilly interior. Agr., fishing, sailing are main occupations. Excepting Rennes, the historic cap., all chief towns are ports: Nantes (on Loire R.), Saint-Nazaire, Brest, Saint-Malo, Lorient. A part of ancient Armorica, region was conquered by Caesar, received its modern name when settled by fugitive Britons (c.500). Breton still spoken in Lower (i.e., western) Brittany. Breton history was a long struggle for independence—first from Franks (5th–9th cent.), then from dukes of Normandy and counts of Anjou (10th–12th cent.), finally from England and France. ARTHUR I, an ANGEVIN, was recognized as duke 1196; after his murder, PETER I succeeded. Extinction of direct line led to War of the BRETON SUCCESSION. The marriages of ANNE OF BRITTANY led to personal union (1491) and formal incorporation (1532) with France. Breton autonomism revived in 19th cent. Local traditions have been kept alive.

Britten, Benjamin, 1913–, English composer. His works include choral music, e.g., *A Ceremony of Carols;* operas *Peter Grimes* and *Billy Budd;* songs; chamber music; and concertos.

Britton, John, 1771–1857, English antiquary and topographer. Wrote famous descriptions of landscapes and buildings. Influential in movement to preserve ancient monuments.

Britton, Nathaniel Lord, 1859–1934, American botanist, was first director of New York Botanical Garden.

Brixham (brĭk'sŭm), urban district (pop. 8,761), Devonshire, England; seaport. William III landed here 1688.

Brizeux, Auguste: see BRETON LITERATURE.

Brno (bŭr'nô), Ger. *Brünn,* city (pop. 133,-637), cap. of Moravia, Czechoslovakia. Major mfg. center (textiles, machinery, arms). Seat of Czechoslovak supreme court and of univ. (founded 1919). Large German-speaking pop. expelled 1945. Brno's charter, granted 1229, was a model of medieval liberal town government. Battle of AUSTERLITZ fought near by 1805. Old city includes cathedral (15th cent.), Spielberg fortress (long a celebrated political prison), many fine Gothic and baroque churches and public buildings. Heavily damaged in World War II.

broadcasting, public transmission by radio and television of sound and pictures. Radio broadcasting dates in U.S. from 1920; advertising "time" first sold in 1922; tentative network coast-to-coast hookup in 1924. By 1927 the two major networks had stations so numerous as to cause traffic problems and need for legislation (see FEDERAL COMMUNICATIONS COMMISSION). See also FREQUENCY MODULATION; TELEVISION.

Broad River, rising in W N.C., S of Asheville, and flowing 143 mi. SE, then S through S.C. to the Saluda, forming the Congaree near Columbia.

Broads, the, region of lakes and lagoons connected by rivers, in Suffolk and Norfolk, England; notable as yachting center.

Broadview, village (pop. 5,196), NE Ill., residential suburb of Chicago.

Broadway, famous street (longest in the world), extending 150 mi. N from Bowling Green near foot of Manhattan isl. to Albany, N.Y. Chiefly commercial in New York city where it is a main traffic artery: runs through nation's financial center at Wall St.; enters theater district at Times Square (42d St.) where it becomes the "Great White Way," illuminated by garish electric signs. Points of interest along it include Trinity Church, St. Paul's Chapel, Woolworth and Flatiron buildings, Columbia Univ., and Columbia-Presbyterian Medical Center.

Broca, Paul (pôl brôkä), 1824–80, French pathologist, anthropologist, and neurosurgeon. Localized center for articulate speech in left frontal lobe of brain. Originated methods of classifying hair and skin color and establishing ratio of brain to skull.

brocade, decorative fabric whose embossed patterns give effect of embroidery. Ground fabric usually silk; design may be of silk, silver, or gold thread. Made since antiquity in Orient; art came to Europe with Moors. Jacquard loom, perfected c.1804, improved modern weaving of intricate designs.

broccoli (brŏk′ûlē), garden vegetable with loose, green, leafy, edible flower panicles.

Brocéliande, Forest of (brōsālēäd′), in Arthurian legend, the home of Merlin in Brittany, France. Forest of Paimpont, SW of Rennes, is a remnant.

Brock, Sir Isaac, 1769–1812, British general, Canadian hero of War of 1812. Upon outbreak of war joined forces with Tecumseh, captured post at Detroit and gained control of upper lakes, thereby earning name of "hero of Upper Canada." Successfully defended Queenston Heights, where he was mortally wounded.

Brocken (brôk′ûn) or **Blocksberg** (blôks′bĕrk), peak, 3,747 ft. high, Saxony-Anhalt, central Germany; highest peak of Harz mts. Legend makes it meeting place of Walpurgis Night or Witches' Sabbath.

Brockton, city (pop. 62,860), SE Mass., S of Boston; settled c.1700. Mfg. of shoes.

Brockville, city (pop. 12,301), S Ont., Canada, on St. Lawrence R. and S of Ottawa, in dairy region. River port and summer resort, with mfg. of electrical equipment and hardware.

Brockway, Zebulon Reed, 1827–1920, American penologist, advocate of prison reforms, superintendent (1876–1900) of pioneer reformatory at Elmira, N.Y.

Broderick, David Colbreth, 1820–59, American politician. Fought with William M. GWINN for Democratic party control in Calif. Killed in famous duel.

Brodie, Sir Benjamin Collins (brō′dē), 1783–1862, English surgeon, authority on joint diseases.

Broglie (broi), French noble family of Piedmontese origin. **François Marie, duc de Broglie** (fräswä′ märē′, dük dù), 1671–1745, marshal of France, received ducal title from Louis XV. His son, **Victor François, duc de Broglie** (vēktôr′), 1718–1804, marshal of

France, distinguished himself in Seven Years War; was created a prince of Holy Roman Empire. In 1792 he commanded émigré forces against revolutionary France. His great-grandson, **Albert, duc de Broglie** (äl-bĕr′), 1821–1901, was French premier (1873–74; 1877); wrote important historical works on 18th cent. Two of his grandsons became distinguished physicists: **Maurice, duc de Broglie** (mōrēs′), 1875–, noted for work on X rays and atomic physics; and **Louis Victor, prince de Broglie** (lwē′, prēs′), 1892–, who won the 1929 Nobel Prize for his theory of the wave character of electrons.

Broken Hill, municipality (pop. 27,054), New South Wales, Australia; since 1884 the chief silver-lead mining center in Australia.

Bromberg, Poland: see BYDGOSZCZ.

brome grass, large, coarse grass of genus *Bromus.* Smooth brome (also called Hungarian or awnless brome) and rescue grass are used for forage and pasture. Many species have barbed fruits.

bromide (brō′mīd), compound of bromine and another element (except oxygen), salt of hydrobromic acid. Widely distributed in nature. Sodium and potassium bromides used as sedatives; silver bromide used in photography. In aqueous solution, hydrogen bromide is hydrobromic acid.

bromine (brō′mēn), active, nonmetallic element (symbol = Br; see also ELEMENT, table). Brownish-red liquid; vapor has suffocating odor. Member of HALOGEN family; less active than fluorine or chlorine, more active than iodine. Corrosive. Compounds occur in sea water, mineral springs, common salt deposits. Solidifies at −7°C.; boils at 58.8°C.

bronchitis (brŏng-kī′tis), inflammation in a bronchus (one of two air passages from windpipe to lung) or its branches caused by bacterial infection or by irritation.

bronco: see MUSTANG.

Brontë, Charlotte (brŏn′të), 1816–55, **Emily Jane Brontë,** 1818–48, and **Anne Brontë,** 1820–49, English novelists and poets. Life in the parsonage in Haworth, Yorks., caused them to live in an imaginary world and write imaginative literature as children. Later the three sisters produced *Poems* (1846) under pseudonyms of Currer, Ellis, and Acton Bell. Emily's poems were particularly notable, as was her novel, *Wuthering Heights* (1847). Anne wrote novels *Agnes Gray* (1847), *The Tenant of Wildfell Hall* (1848). Generally best known was Charlotte, whose novels— *Jane Eyre* (1847), *Shirley* (1849), *Villette* (1853) and *The Professor* (1857, but earliest written) won her fame that gladdened last year of her life as wife of Arthur Bell Nicholls.

Brontosaurus (brŏntûsô′rùs), largest vegetarian dinosaur, probably semiaquatic, length c.70 ft., weight over 30 tons; long neck and tail.

Bronx, the, northernmost borough (land area 41 sq. mi.; pop. 1,451,277) of NEW YORK city, SE N.Y. Settled 1641 under Dutch West India Co., became a New York city borough in 1898 and a co. of N.Y. state in 1914. On peninsula NE of Manhattan and S of Westchester co.; bounded on W by Hudson R. SW by Spuyten Duyvil Creek and Harlem R., S by East R., and E by Long Isl. Sound

Many bridge and tunnel connections to Manhattan and Queens. Mainly residential, though industrialized along Harlem R. Numerous parks include Bronx (zoo, botanic gardens), Van Cortlandt, and Pelham Bay. Seat of FORDHAM UNIVERSITY, Manhattan Col. (R.C., Christian Brothers; for men; opened as academy 1849, chartered as college 1863); parts of NEW YORK UNIVERSITY, and Hunter Col. (see New York, COLLEGE OF THE CITY OF). Has Yankee Stadium and Poe cottage.

Bronxville, N.Y.: see EASTCHESTER.

bronze, alloy of copper and tin or copper and certain other metals. Sometimes silver, aluminum, zinc, or lead added for brilliance or hardness. Harder and more resistant than brass, zinc, and copper. Used for gun metal and bell metal; also for machine bearings, valves, roofs, cornices, ornaments, and funerary urns and caskets. Ideal for casting art works, engraving, and repoussé work. Used by Egyptians, Greeks, Etruscans, Romans. Renaissance Italy noted for bronze doors of Ghiberti and others; 18th-cent. France for furniture mounts.

Bronze Age, prehistoric period, characterized by use of bronze for tools and artifacts. It followed the Neolithic and preceded the Iron Age, but did not reach all places at the same time. Egypt and SW Asia were in the Bronze Age by 2500 B.C.; Britain c.2000 B.C. The W Hemisphere had no true Bronze Age. Copper was known before bronze, and that period is sometimes termed the Copper Age. Horses and cattle were first used as draft animals in the Bronze Age. Important inventions—arch, wheel, potter's wheel.

Bronzino, Il (ēl brōntsē'nō), 1502?–1572, Florentine painter, whose real name was Agnolo di Cosimo Allori. Portraitist of many celebrated figures, including Cosimo I de' Medici, Dante, Boccaccio, Petrarch.

Bronzino, Alessandro: see ALLORI, ALESSANDRO.

Brook, Alexander, 1898–, American painter. His realistic style is marked by subtle color.

Brooke, Alan Francis, 1st Viscount Alanbrooke, 1883–, British field marshal. Was commander-in-chief of British Home Forces 1940–41 and chief of imperial general staff 1941–46.

Brooke, Sir Charles Johnson: see BROOKE, SIR JAMES.

Brooke, Sir Charles Vyner: see BROOKE, SIR JAMES.

Brooke, Fulke Greville, 1st Baron, 1554–1628, English poet, patron of letters, and statesman, author (as Fulke Greville) of philosophical poems and *Life of the Renowned Sir Philip Sidney* (1652).

Brooke, Sir James, 1803–68, English rajah of Sarawak on Borneo. After aiding local sultan to suppress rebel tribes he was made rajah (1841). Succeeded by his nephew, **Sir Charles Johnson Brooke,** 1829–1917, who abolished slavery and aided prosperity. His son, **Sir Charles Vyner Brooke,** 1874–, ceded Sarawak to Great Britain as a crown colony 1946.

Brooke, Rupert, 1887–1915, English poet. His poetry, *Poems* (1911) and *1914 and Other Poems* (1915), shows the dashing romanticism that made Brooke a legendary figure.

Died of blood poisoning on Skyros in World War I.

Brook Farm, experimental community on a 192-acre farm at West Roxbury, Mass. Founded 1841 by transcendentalists George and Sophia Ripley to combine "plain living and high thinking." The members shared manual labor and intellectual life. Nathaniel Hawthorne was a member, R. W. Emerson and Margaret Fuller visitors. Brook Farm was made into a Fourierist community under the aegis of Albert Brisbane in 1845, disbanded 1847.

Brookfield. 1 Village (pop. 15,472), NE Ill., W suburb of Chicago. **2** City (pop. 5,810), N central Mo., SW of Kirksville. Rail shipping point in farm and coal area. Gen. Pershing's boyhood home is near.

Brookhaven. 1 City (pop. 7,801), SW Miss., SSW of Jackson; center of dairy and timber area. **2** Resort village, SE N.Y., on S shore of Long Isl. E of Patchogue. Brookhaven Natl. Laboratory for atomic research is near by.

Brookings, city (pop. 7,764), E S.Dak., N of Sioux Falls and near Big Sioux R. Farm trade center. Seat of South Dakota State Col. of Agriculture and Mechanic Arts (land-grant support; coed; chartered 1881, opened 1884).

Brookings Institution, at Washington, D.C.; founded by Robert S. Brookings for research and education in social sciences; chartered 1927.

Brookline (brŏŏk'lĭn), beautiful suburban town (pop. 57,589), E Mass., just W of Boston.

Brooklyn. 1 Village (pop. 2,568), SW Ill., on the Mississippi above East St. Louis. An all-Negro town. Post office is Lovejoy. **2** Borough (land area 71 sq. mi.; pop. 2,738,175), of NEW YORK city, SE N.Y., on SW end of Long Isl. adjoining Queens borough. Settled 1636–37 by Walloons and Hollanders; hamlet of Breuckelen estab. c.1645; absorbed various settlements (e.g., Flatbush, a 17th-cent. Dutch village, now a residential section) until it became coextensive with Kings Co. (estab. 1683); became a New York city borough 1898. Separated from downtown Manhattan by East R. (many bridges, e.g., BROOKLYN BRIDGE, and tunnels), from Staten Isl. by the Narrows of New York Bay. Though largely residential, borough has important port facilities—New York Naval Shipyard (commonly Brooklyn Navy Yard), Bush Terminal—and industrial establishments (machinery, textiles, paper, chemicals, shoes, processed foods). Seat of Brooklyn Col. (see NEW YORK, COLLEGE OF THE CITY OF); PRATT INSTITUTE; Long Isl. Univ. (nonsectarian; coed; chartered 1926, opened 1927); St. John's Univ. (R.C., Vincentian; partly coed; opened 1870, chartered 1871); BROOKLYN INSTITUTE OF ARTS AND SCIENCES; and Long Isl. Historical Society. Here are Prospect Park (see LONG ISLAND, BATTLE OF); Ebbets Field (home of Brooklyn Dodgers); Coney Isl., famed beach resort and amusement center; and many noted churches. **3** City (pop. 6,317), NE Ohio, a S suburb of Cleveland.

Brooklyn Bridge, SE N.Y., bridge (1,595 ft.; suspension) across East R. between Manhattan and Brooklyn. Built (1869–83) by Roebling and son.

Brooklyn College: see NEW YORK, COLLEGE OF THE CITY OF.

Brooklyn Institute of Arts and Sciences, founded 1824. Includes Brooklyn Mus., Children's Mus., Brooklyn Acad. of Music, and a 42-acre botanical garden. The museum collections include water colors by Sargent and sculptures by Barye. Courses in the arts and the physical and social sciences are given.

Brooks, Phillips, 1835–93, American Episcopalian clergyman. Influential as preacher at Trinity Church, Boston, 1869–91. Made bishop of Mass. 1891. Wrote *O Little Town of Bethlehem.*

Brooks, Van Wyck (wĭk), 1886–, American critic. Wrote critical biographies (e.g., *The Ordeal of Mark Twain,* 1920) and works on the force of Puritanism in American thought. His series "Makers and Finders: a History of the Writer in America, 1800–1915," begun with *The Flowering of New England* (1936), stressed need for finding a "usable past."

Brooks Range, N Alaska, separating Yukon R. basin from watershed of Arctic Ocean. Embraces many mountain chains; height averages 5,500–6,500 ft. Area thinly settled. Transportation mainly by air.

Brooksville, city (pop. 1,818), W central Fla., N of Tampa. Near by are Devil's Punch Bowl, an arid sink, and Weekiwachee Spring, emptying 100,000 gal. a minute to form river flowing to Gulf of Mexico.

broom, shrubs of two related genera, *Cytisus* and *Genista.* Yellow or white (in *Cytisus,* purple also), pealike flowers. Common or Scotch broom is *Cytisus scoparius.* Florists' genista is *C. canariensis.*

broomcorn: see SORGHUM.

Brosse, Salomon de (sälōmō′ dü brôs′), 1565–1626, French architect of Luxembourg Palace. Built hunting chateau which was later to become nucleus of Versailles palace.

Broun, Heywood (Campbell) (bro͞on), 1888–1939, American newspaper columnist. Wrote for several New York papers, attacking social injustices and championing the weak. Founded American 'Newspaper Guild. Column ("It Seems to Me") syndicated.

Broussais, François Joseph Victor (fränswä′ zhôzĕf′ vĕktôr′ bro͞osä′), 1772–1838, French physician. Advocate of treatment by starvation and use of leeches.

Brouwer or **Brauwer, Adriaen** (äd″rēän′ brou′-wûr), c.1605–1638, Flemish painter of spirited genre and rustic scenes. Studied with Frans Hals.

Browder, Earl Russell, 1891–, American Communist leader. Opposition to his policies resulted in his removal from Communist party (1946).

Brown, family of bankers in U.S. **Alexander Brown,** 1764–1834, b. Ireland, became wealthy in Baltimore as an international banker. Took sons into partnership. Firm was for a generation leading institution of its kind in U.S. One son, **George Brown,** 1787–1859, helped found Baltimore & Ohio R.R.

Brown, Alice, 1857–1948, American author of New England short stories (e.g., *Meadow-Grass,* 1895; *Tiverton Tales,* 1899). Also

wrote novels and a play *Children of Earth* (1915).

Brown, Charles Brockden, 1771–1810, first professional American novelist. His interest in character development and abnormal behavior foreshadowed the psychological novel. *Wieland* (1798) was his most popular novel. Others were *Edgar Huntly* (1799), *Arthur Mervyn* (1799–1800), and *Ormond* (1799).

Brown, Elmer Ellsworth, 1861–1934, American educator. A teacher of education in Mich. and Calif., he became U.S. commissioner of education (1906–11). Chancellor of New York Univ. (1911–33).

Brown, Ford Madox, 1821–93, English historical painter, closely affiliated with the Pre-Raphaelites.

Brown, George, U.S. banker: see BROWN, family.

Brown, George, 1818–80, Canadian journalist and statesman, b. Scotland. Founded Toronto *Globe* (1844) which became most powerful political journal in Upper Canada. Elected to the assembly (1851), he led "Clear Grits" faction, which opposed influence of French Canadians in that body. Played important role in movement for confederation.

Brown, John, 1800–1859, American abolitionist. Following sack of LAWRENCE, Kansas (1856), he led retaliatory slaughter of five proslavery men on banks of Pottawatamie R. As step preliminary to liberating Southern slaves he captured U.S. arsenal at Harpers Ferry, Va. (now W.Va.) on Oct. 16, 1859. Arsenal was retaken and Brown was hanged.

Brown, John Carter, 1797–1874, American book collector and philanthropist. Donated library of early Americana to Brown Univ. (named for his father).

Brown, Lancelot, 1715–83, English landscape gardener and architect. Founder of English naturalistic school of landscape design.

Brown, Mather, 1761–1831, American portrait and historical painter, pupil of Benjamin West.

Brown, Moses, 1738–1836, American manufacturer. Estab. first water-powered cotton mill in America (1790) with Samuel Slater.

Brown, Robert, 1773–1858, Scottish botanist and botanical explorer. He collected plants in Australia. In 1827 he observed BROWNIAN MOVEMENT and in 1831 he discovered the cell nucleus.

Brown, William Hill, 1765–93, American writer, probable author of a novel, *The Power of Sympathy* (1789), long ascribed to Sarah Wentworth Morton.

brown coal: see LIGNITE.

Browne, Hablot Knight, pseud. **Phiz,** 1815–82, English illustrator of many of the novels of Charles Dickens.

Browne, Robert, c.1550–c.1633, English clergyman, leader of separatists called Brownists. He preached nonconformity, and his treatise are regarded as first expression of CONGREGATIONALISM.

Browne, Sir Thomas, 1605–82, English author, a physician. His *Religio Medici* (written c.1635), a private confession of faith, and *Hydrotaphia, Urne-Buriall* (1658), reflec tions on death and immortality, show his convolute, inimitably fine prose style.

Brownell, Herbert, Jr., 1904–, U.S. Attorney General (1953–). Chairman of Republican Natl. Committee (1944–46). Managed Thomas E. Dewey's 1948 presidential campaign.

Brownell, W(illiam) C(rary), 1851–1928, American literary critic, long a literary adviser to Charles Scribner's Sons, advocate of modern humanism, author of books of art, literary, and social criticism.

Brownfield, town (pop. 6,161), NW Texas, SW of Lubbock on Llano Estacado. Trading, processing center in cattle and agr. region. Has chemical plants.

brown hematite: see LIMONITE.

Brownian movement, irregular movement shown by minute solid particles suspended in fluid; continuous, vibratory, unrelated to outside disturbances. Estab. by Robert Brown. Upholds kinetic molecular theory that matter is composed of particles (see MOLECULE) in constant vibratory motion. Suspended particles are buffeted by molecules of liquid.

Browning, Elizabeth Barrett, 1806–61, English poet, wife of Robert BROWNING. She defied her own invalidism and her tyrannical father to marry him (1846) and go to Italy. Already known as a poet, she later produced *Sonnets from the Portuguese* (1850); *Casa Guidi Windows* (1851), and *Aurora Leigh* (novel in verse, 1856).

Browning, John Moses, 1855–1926, American inventor of an automatic pistol, a machine gun, and an automatic rifle.

Browning, Robert, 1812–89, English poet. His many long narrative poems (*Pauline,* 1833; *Sordello,* 1840, and his masterpiece, *The Ring and the Book,* 1868–69) show the same psychological insight apparent in his dramatic monologues, "Fra Lippo Lippi," "Andrea del Sarto," "The Bishop Orders His Tomb at St. Praxed's Church," "My Last Duchess," and "Soliloquy of the Spanish Cloister." The long poems include lyrics, and he wrote many others. Also wrote poetic dramas (*Strafford,* 1837, *A Blot in the 'Scutcheon,* 1843). His romance with Elizabeth Barrett ended in marriage and happy life in Italy.

Browning, town (pop. 1,691), NW Mont., near Glacier Natl. Park. Hq. of Blackfeet Indian Reservation.

Brownists, followers of Robert BROWNE.

Brownlow, William Gannaway (broun′lō), 1805–77, itinerant Methodist preacher, known as the "fighting parson," governor of Tenn. (1865–69), a union sympathizer. His harsh Reconstruction program left Tenn. broken and impoverished.

Brown-Séquard, Charles Édouard (broun′-sākär′), 1817–94, Franco-American physiologist, pioneer in study of internal secretions and rejuvenation.

Brownson, Orestes (Augustus), 1803–76, American reformer, b. Vt. A vigorous writer on social and religious questions, he went through several phases of religion. At first a Presbyterian, he later became a Universalist, a Unitarian minister, head of a church he founded, finally a Roman Catholic. He agi-

tated for the rights of workingmen and fought social evils. Wrote many works (including novels) and edited magazines to promote these causes.

Browns Valley, village (pop. 1,117), W Minn., on S.Dak. line. Controversial skeleton ("Browns Valley man") discovered near by, 1934.

Brownsville. 1 Borough (pop. 7,643), SW Pa., on the Monongahela and SSE of Pittsburgh. Has distilleries and railroad shops. **2** City (pop. 36,066), S Texas, on Rio Grande. Fort Taylor founded here 1846 by Gen. Zachary Taylor, who fought battles of Palo Alto and Resaca de la Palma coming to its aid. Renamed (1846) for defender, Major Jacob Brown. Fort Brown, held briefly by Union in Civil War and prominent in Mexican border disturbances, was active until 1944. Brownsville, laid out 1848, is an important port of entry across river from Matamoras, Mex. Center of rich region, it is ocean port (channel finished 1936) with oil and natural gas industries.

brown thrush: see THRASHER.

Brown University, at Providence, R.I.; nonsectarian, for men; chartered 1764 as Rhode Island Col. by Baptists at Warren, opened 1765, moved to Providence in 1770, renamed for Nicholas Brown, 1804. John Carter BROWN Library has notable collection of Americana. Brown Univ. has long led in academic freedom and curriculum reform. Pembroke Col. for women undergraduates, organized 1891, has own campus.

Brownwood, city (pop. 20,181), central Texas, WNW of Waco; settled 1856. Industrial and distribution center of agr. area with oil and gas wells. Mfg. of petroleum products, cottonseed oil, bricks, and clothing. Near-by L. Brownwood used for irrigation and recreation.

Bruce, celebrated Scottish family. Descended from 11th-cent. Norman duke, Robert de Brus, who aided William I in conquest of England. In struggle following death of MARGARET MAID OF NORWAY, Bruces claimed succession to the throne. Robert the Bruce was claimant to throne in 1290, rivaled by John de BALIOL. His grandson was famous Robert the Bruce, ROBERT I of Scotland. Edward Bruce, brother of Robert I, was crowned king of Ireland in 1316. Youngest son of Robert I succeeded him as DAVID II. Succeeded by his nephew ROBERT II, first STUART king.

Bruce, earls of Elgin: see ELGIN, THOMAS BRUCE, 7TH EARL OF.

Bruce, Sir David, 1855–1931, British bacteriologist, authority on cause of undulant fever and African sleeping sickness.

Bruce, Stanley Melbourne, 1st Viscount Bruce of Melbourne, 1883–, Australian statesman. As prime minister (1923–29) promoted relations with the empire. Was Australian delegate to League of Nations. High commissioner for Australia in London 1933–45.

Bruce, William Speirs, 1867–1921, Scottish explorer, authority on polar regions. Led Scottish Natl. Antarctic Expedition (1902–4); discovered Coats Land.

brucellosis (brōōsĭlō′sĭs), **undulant fever** (ŭn′-dyōōlŭnt), or **Malta fever,** disease caused by bacteria (certain brucella organisms). It is transmitted to man by infected food or fluids (esp. milk), or by contact with infected animals or tissues; may cause long disability from remittent fever. In animals it is known as contagious abortion (Bang's disease); it spreads through intake of feed or water containing the germs.

Bruch, Max (brōōkh'), 1838–1920, German composer, known for his Violin Concerto in G Minor and his variations on *Kol Nidre* for cello and orchestra.

Bruckner, Anton (brōōk'nûr), 1824–96, Austrian romantic composer. He wrote nine symphonies, several Masses and a *Te Deum*, and one string quartet.

Brudenell, James Thomas: see CARDIGAN.

Bruegel, Brueghel, or **Breughel** (all: brû'gŭl), family of Flemish genre and landscape painters. The foremost, **Pieter Bruegel** (pē'-tûr), c.1525–69, portrayed in vibrant colors the whole living world of field and forest in which gay, robust peasants are at work and play, as in *The Harvesters* (Metropolitan Mus.). In his *Carrying the Cross* (Vienna) and *Massacre of the Innocents* (Brussels) he showed horrors of the Inquisition in a Flemish village. A son, **Pieter Bruegel,** the younger, 1564–1637, was known as Hell Bruegel for his pictures of the infernal regions. His brother, **Jan Bruegel** (yän), 1568–1625, called Velvet Bruegel, painted landscapes and flowers. Shared his father's popularity.

Bruges (brōōzh, Fr. brüzh), Flemish *Brugge*, city (pop. 52,984), cap. of West Flanders, NW Belgium; connected by canal with ZEEBRUGGE. Once the greatest port of N Europe, it is now a quiet city, famed for its medieval architecture, quaint canals, bridges, convents, and churches. It has lace and beer mfg. and a printing industry. An early and typical Flemish commune, Bruges became (late 12th cent.) the chief port and a major wool-mfg. center of Flanders. It held extensive poiltical privileges, and its government passed gradually from the patricians to the chief guilds—weavers, fullers, shearers, dyers. Leading the Flemish rebellion against Philip IV of France, Bruges defeated the French in the BATTLE OF THE SPURS (1302). It became the chief warehouse of the HANSEATIC LEAGUE, reached its height as international port in the 14th cent., but foreign competition to the Flemish wool industry and the rise of Antwerp soon caused its decline (15th cent.), and its ports silted up. Bruges was the cradle and remains a treasure house of Flemish art. Among its many Gothic buildings are the Cloth Hall, with a famous belfry and carillon; the city hall; the cathedral; the Church of Notre Dame, with the tomb of Charles the Bold; and the Chapel of the Precious Blood, a major place of pilgrimage. The Hospital of St. John (12th cent.) contains masterpieces of Hans Memling.

Brugsch, Heinrich Karl (hīn'rīkh kärl' brōōksh'), 1827–94, German Egyptologist. Deciphered demotic and compiled a demotic-hieroglyphic dictionary.

Brühl, Heinrich, Graf von (hīn'rīkh gräf' fŭn brül'), 1700–1763, Saxon statesman; chief minister to AUGUSTUS III of Poland and Saxony. Dictated disastrous policy in Seven Years War; amassed huge fortune through fraud.

Brumaire (brümâr'), second month of FRENCH REVOLUTIONARY CALENDAR. Coup d'état of 18 Brumaire (Nov. 9–10, 1799), overthrew DIRECTORY and established CONSULATE under Napoleon.

Brummagem (brŭ'mŭjŭm) [colloquial form of Birmingham, England], name given counterfeit coin first made in Birmingham 17th cent. Applied to anything not genuine, as "sham Protestants" supporting Exclusion Bill of 1680.

Brummell, George Bryan (Beau Brummell), 1778–1840, wealthy Englishman; noted for fine clothes. Intimate of the prince regent (later George IV).

Brundisium: see BRINDISI.

Brunehaut, Frankish queen: see BRUNHILDA.

Brunei (brōōnī'), sultanate (c.2,225 sq. mi.; pop. 40,670), NW BORNEO, under British protection since 1888. Bordered by Sarawak.

Brunel, Sir Marc Isambard (brōōnĕl'), 1769–1849, English engineer and inventor of machinery. Constructed Thames tunnel, assisted by his son, **Isambard Kingdom Brunel,** 1806–59, English engineer and authority on railway traction and steam navigation, and designer and constructor of ocean steamships.

Brunelleschi, Filippo (fēlēp'pō brōōnĕl-lĕs'kē), 1377–1446, first great architect of the Italian Renaissance, a Florentine. In competition (1401) for bronze doors for Florence baptistry his design placed second to that of Ghiberti. Most famous work is octagonal ribbed dome of Florence cathedral. Other works include Pazzi chapel, churches of San Lorenzo and Santo Spirito, and Pitti Palace (all: Florence).

Brunetière, Ferdinand (fĕrdēnä' brünütyĕr'), 1849–1906, French literary critic, opponent of naturalism. His *Manuel de l'histoire de la littérature française* (1897) is his masterpiece.

Brunhild (brōōn'hĭld), **Brünnehilde** (brün''-ühïl'dü), or **Brynhild** (brĭn'hĭld), in Germanic mythology, mighty female warrior. In the NIBELUNGENLIED, as queen of Iceland, she is defeated by SIEGFRIED, whose death she contrives. In the VOLSUNGASAGA, as Brynhild, chief of the Valkyries, she is loved by Sigurd, but when he deserts her, she contrives his death and destroys herself on his funeral pyre. In Wagner's *Ring of the Nibelungs,* she is Brünnehilde, a Valkyrie (see NIBELUNGEN).

Brunhilda (brŭnhĭl'dü) or **Brunehaut** (brünō'), 534?–613, Frankish queen, wife of SIGEBERT I of Austrasia. Played leading part in the bloody war (567–613) against Neustria following the murder of her sister Galswintha by CHILPERIC I of Neustria. Put to horrible death by Clotaire II of Neustria.

Brüning, Heinrich (hīn'rīkh brü'nĭng), 1885–, German chancellor (1930–32), leader of Catholic Center party. Passed drastic, unpopular financial decrees; dissolved Hitler's storm troops (1932). Pres. Hindenburg dismissed him abruptly and appointed Papen his successor. Brüning left Germany 1934, became professor at Harvard Univ. 1937.

Brünn, Czechoslovakia: see BRNO.

Brünnehilde, another spelling for BRUNHILD.

Brunner, Emil (ä'mĕl brŏon'ŭr), 1889–, Swiss Protestant theologian, professor of theology at Univ. of Zurich. His theological position is associated with that of Karl BARTH, with some disagreement.

Bruno, Saint (brŏo'nō), c.1030–1101, German monk; founder (1084) of CARTHUSIANS at Grande Chartreuse. Feast: Oct. 6.

Bruno, Giordano (jōrdä'nō brŏo'nō), 1548–1600, Italian philosopher. A Dominican, he was accused of heresy and left the order to become a wandering scholar and teacher. In his metaphysical works he challenged all dogmatic authority, maintaining that each man's view of the world is relative to his position, that any absolute truth is beyond statement, and that possible knowledge is unlimited. He believed that the world is composed of irreducible elements (monads), which operate under laws of relationship governed by a pantheistic principle. He returned to Venice, where he was convicted of heresy and burned at the stake—a martyr for freedom of thought.

Brunswick, dukes of: see CHARLES WILLIAM FERDINAND; FREDERICK WILLIAM.

Brunswick (brŭnz'wĭk), Ger. *Braunschweig,* former state (1,379 sq. mi.; 1939 pop. 602,873), central Germany. It consisted of several enclaves surrounded by Prussian territory. After World War II the larger part (1,182 sq. mi.; pop. 870,291) was incorporated into British-occupied LOWER SAXONY; the rest, into Russian-occupied Saxony-Anhalt. Agr.; mining in N foothills of Harz (silver, copper, lead, iron). Duchy of Brunswick emerged 14th cent. from remnants of domains of HENRY THE LION, who retained only the territories of Brunswick and Lüneburg (roughly, modern Brunswick and Hanover). The Guelphic house repeatedly divided into several branches, notably those of Brunswick-Lüneburg (after 1692 electors of HANOVER) and of Brunswick-Wolffenbüttel, or Brunswick proper. Duchy was part of the kingdom of Westphalia under Jérôme Bonaparte (1807–13); joined German Empire 1871; became republic 1918; joined Weimar Republic 1919. Its early cap., Wolfenbüttel, was replaced in 1753 by **Brunswick** city (pop. 223,263), now in Lower Saxony, on the Oker, a commercial and mfg. center (machinery, beer). Chartered 12th cent., it later joined the Hanseatic League. The picturesque old city suffered severely in World War II. Notable landmarks (all more or less damaged) include the 12th-cent. cathedral, with Henry the Lion's tomb, and the famous 15th-cent. fountain named for Till Eulenspiegel, who lived here. Former Richmond Palace has fine art museum.

Brunswick. 1 City (pop. 17,954), SE Ga., on the Atlantic; founded 1771–72. Shipping center, with shrimp and crab processing plants, shipyards, creosoting works. Mfg. of lumber, naval stores, clothing, paint. National quarantine station. Sea Islands are offshore. Fort Frederica Natl. Monument is near. **2** Town (pop. 10,996), including Brunswick village (pop. 7,342), S Maine, on Androscoggin R. and W of Bath; settled

1628. Has canneries, textile and paper mills. Trade center for resort area. Harriet Beecher Stowe wrote *Uncle Tom's Cabin* here. Seat of Bowdoin Col. (nonsectarian; for men; opened 1802); Hawthorne and Longfellow were alumni.

Brusa, Turkey: see BURSA.

Brush, George de Forest, 1855–1941, American painter, known for paintings of American Indians.

Brussa, Turkey: see BURSA.

Brussels (brŭ'sŭlz), Flemish *Brussel,* Fr. *Bruxelles,* city (centered about Brussels commune, pop. 185,112; pop. of greater Brussels 960,740), cap. of Belgium and of Brabant prov. It is a major commercial, industrial, and cultural center. Lace is its oldest and best-known industry. Dating from 10th cent., Brussels replaced Louvain as cap. of Brabant in 15th cent. and was the seat of the Spanish, later Austrian, governors of the Netherlands (16th–18th cent.). Frequently besieged in the wars of that period, Brussels twice fell to the French in the French Revolutionary Wars (1792, 1794), was Wellington's hq. in the Waterloo campaign (1815), and became the cap. of independent Belgium in 1830. It was occupied by the Germans in both world wars (1914–18, 1940–44) but suffered no physical damage. On its historic center, the Grand' Place, are the city hall (14th–17th cent.); the Renaissance Maison du Roi or Broodhuis, meeting place of the old States-General; and the 18th-cent. royal palace and parliament building. Other notable buildings include the Gothic Church of St. Gudule. The general aspect, however, is modern. The Univ. of Brussels was founded 1834.

Brussels sprouts, variety of CABBAGE with small, edible heads or sprouts along the stem.

Brut, Brute, or **Brutus,** a Trojan, legendary first king of Britain, descendant of Aeneas. His name gave title to long poems by Wace and Layamon.

Bruttium (brŭ'tēûm), anc. region of S Italy, roughly present Calabria (the "toe" of the "boot"), inhabited in 8th cent. B.C. by native Brutii and Lucani and by Greek colonists. Sybaris and Crotona became important cities of Magna Graecia. After Roman conquest (3d cent. B.C.), Rhegium was favored.

Brutus, surname of anc. Roman family. The semilegendary **Lucius Junius Brutus,** fl. 510 B.C., was the brother of Lucrece and helped to end the TARQUIN dynasty. He is said to have killed his sons for plotting a restoration of the Tarquins and was honored as founder of the republic. Centuries later **Marcus Junius Brutus,** 85 B.C.–42 B.C., was the principal assassin of Julius Caesar. A partisan of Pompey, he was pardoned by Caesar after the battle of Pharsala and held high office, but joined Cassius in the successful plot to murder Caesar (44 B.C.). Antony fulminated against him and, with Octavian (later Augustus), defeated him at Philippi (42 B.C.). Brutus committed suicide. His character has been much disputed from that day to this. A kinsman, **Decimus Junius Brutus,** d. 43 B.C., also a member of the conspiracy, was besieged and killed by Antony.

Bry, Théodore de (täōdôr' dŭ brē', brī'), 1528–98, Flemish engraver and publisher. His son,

John Théodore de Bry, 1561–1623, assisted him.

Bryan, William Jennings, 1860–1925, American political leader. U.S. Representative from Nebr. (1891–95). Advocated free coinage of silver. Famous "Cross of Gold" speech led to Democratic presidential nomination in 1896. Nominee again in 1900 and 1908. As Secretary of State under Pres. Wilson (1913–15), he aided in passing reform measures. In later years Bryan diligently defended religious FUNDAMENTALISM, especially in famous SCOPES TRIAL. A man of integrity, a masterful orator of imposing appearance, he was idolized by the masses (esp. in West).

Bryan. 1 City (pop. 6,365), NW Ohio, NNW of Defiance. Mfg. of metal and wood products. 2 City (pop. 18,102), E central Texas, NW of Houston; founded 1865. Center of farm district, it processes cotton and lumber and makes insecticides. Agricultural and Mechanical Col. of Texas near by.

Bryansk (brēänsk′), city (pop. 87,473), W European RSFSR, on Desna R. Transportation center; ironworks; sawmills. In World War II Bryansk and Vyazma were anchor points of huge German "pincer movement" (Oct., 1941); retaken by Russians 1943.

Bryant, William Cullen, 1794–1878, American romantic poet, b. Mass. Famed when he was a youth for poetry (e.g., "Thanatopsis" and "To a Waterfowl"), he was a lawyer until he became after 1825 a journalist in New York—associate editor, later editor and part owner of free-trade, antislavery *Evening Post.* Among later nature poems are such familiar and widely loved verses as "The Death of the Flowers" and "To the Fringed Gentian." He also translated the *Iliad* and the *Odyssey* in blank verse.

Bryaxis (briăk′sĭs), 4th cent. B.C., Greek sculptor. Helped decorate the Mausoleum of Halicarnassus.

Bryce, David, 1803–76, Scottish architect. Used a modified Gothic style, named Scottish Baronial.

Bryce, James Bryce, Viscount, 1838–1922, English historian, statesman, diplomat, and jurist. Noted for wide knowledge and ability to combine deeply scholarly writing with full, active life. Well known are his *History of the Holy Roman Empire* (1864) and his commentary, *The American Commonwealth* (1888), a classic interpretation of American way of life. Ambassador to U.S. 1907–13. In law, his *Studies in History and Jurisprudence* (1901) is major work because of its wide view of liberal principle.

Bryce Canyon National Park: see NATIONAL PARKS AND MONUMENTS (table).

Brynhild, another spelling for BRUNHILD.

Bryn Mawr (brĭnmär′), uninc. village, SE Pa., residential suburb of Philadelphia. Seat of **Bryn Mawr College** (nonsectarian; for women; chartered 1880) opened by Friends 1885. Has group curriculum plan modeled on Johns Hopkins, and pioneer graduate school for women. Social studies are stressed.

Bryson, Lyman, 1888–, American educator, leader in adult education, professor at Teachers College, Columbia Univ. after 1934.

Brythonic (brĭthŏ′nĭk), group of Celtic languages of Indo-European family, including Welsh, Breton, and Cornish (now extinct). See LANGUAGE (table).

Buber, Martin (bōō′bĕr), 1878–, Jewish philosopher, b. Vienna. His mystic and theological writings, many of them on the teachings of the Hasidim, have had influence in and outside Judaism. A militant Zionist, he became a professor at the Hebrew Univ. in Jerusalem in 1938.

bubonic plague: see PLAGUE.

Bucaramanga (bōō″kärämän′gä), city (pop. 41,714), N central Colombia, in E Andes; founded 1622. Became after 1880 a coffee center.

buccaneer: see PIRACY.

Bucephalus (būsĕ′fŭlŭs), horse of Alexander the Great, hence, any horse noted for fire and speed.

Bucer or **Butzer, Martin** (bū′sûr, bōōt′sûr), 1491–1551, German Protestant reformer. Influenced by Luther's preaching, he joined (1523) Reformation movement at Strasbourg. Promoted Protestant education, brought about (1536) Wittenberg Concord on doctrine of the Eucharist.

Buchan, Alexander (bŭ′kŭn, –khŭn), 1829–1907, Scottish meteorologist. Curator, Royal Society of Edinburgh library and museum. Responsible for founding Ben Nevis observatory (1883).

Buchan, John, 1st Baron Tweedsmuir (twēdz-mūr), 1875–1940, Scottish author and statesman. Wrote many adventure novels (e.g., *The Thirty-nine Steps,* 1915; *Greenmantle,* 1916; *The Three Hostages,* 1924). Was governor general of Canada 1935–40.

Buchanan, Franklin (būkă′nŭn), 1800–1874, American naval officer. First superintendent (1845–47) U.S. Naval Academy. Joined Confederate navy; became ranking officer. Defeated by David G. FARRAGUT at Mobile Bay (Aug. 5, 1864).

Buchanan, George, 1506–82, Scottish humanist.

Buchanan, James, 1791–1868, 15th President of the United States (1857–61), b. Pa. Only bachelor to be President. U.S. Congressman from Pa. (1821–31); U.S. Senator (1834–45); Secretary of State (1845–49). As minister to Great Britain (1853–56) he helped draw up OSTEND MANIFESTO. As President (Democrat), he attempted to keep proslavery and antislavery factions in balance, was opposed by extremists on both sides. In 1860 he maintained that no state had the right to secede, but that he had no power to coerce seceding states; his view that the Federal government could use force in protecting Federal property made Federal forts in Southern states of paramount importance. Many recent historians consider Buchanan's constitutional views sound; all admire his valiant efforts for peace.

Buchanan, city (pop. 5,224), SW Mich., near Ind. line. Mfg. of auto parts. Indian village sites and mounds near by.

Bucharest (bōō′kûrĕst) or **Bucuresti** (bōōkōō-rĕsht′), city (pop. 886,110), cap. and chief commercial and mfg. center of Rumania, in Walachia. Seat of patriarch of Rumanian Orthodox Church. Univ. (founded 1864). Became residence of Walachian princes 14th cent. Famous until World War II for contrast between palatial buildings and hovels.

Buchenwald (bōō'khŭnvält"), forest near Weimar, Thuringia, central Germany. Site of notorious concentration camp during Hitler regime.

Buchman, Frank (Nathan Daniel) (bŏŏk'mŭn), 1878–, American evangelist, leader of Oxford Group (Buchmanites). In 1921 he preached "world-changing through life-changing" at Oxford Univ. Initiated (1938) Moral Rearmament (MRA) movement.

Buchner, Eduard (ā'dōōärt bŏŏkh'nŭr), 1860–1917, German chemist. Won 1907 Nobel Prize for establishing yeast enzymes as cause of alcoholic fermentation and discovering zymase (part of yeast enzyme system).

Büchner, Georg (gā'ôrk bükh'nŭr), 1813–37, German author, a medical student and radical agitator. In his brief life he produced several bold, powerful works—a drama, *Danton's Death* (1835; Eng. tr., 1928); a comedy, *Leonce and Lena* (1879; Eng. tr., 1928); the fragments of a tragedy, *Wozzeck* (1879; Eng. tr., 1928), from which Alban Berg derived his opera; and a short novel, *Lenz*. His brother was **Ludwig Büchner** (lōōt'vĭkh), 1824–99, German philosopher. He protested against idealist metaphysics with a philosophy of extreme materialism.

Buck, Leffert Lefferts, 1837–1909, American civil engineer. Designed Williamsburg Bridge (New York city), Columbia river railroad bridge (Pasco, Wash.), and many others.

Buck, Pearl S(ydenstricker), 1892–, American novelist. Like her parents and her first husband (John Lossing Buck, from whom she was divorced) she was long a missionary in China. She devoted her great talents to promoting understanding between the East and the West. Most of her novels picture Chinese life, notably *The Good Earth* (1931). Awarded the 1938 Nobel Prize in Literature.

buckeye, tree or shrub of genus *Aesculus* of N Hemisphere. It bears clusters of red, white, or yellow flowers in late spring and large spiny fruits. Ohio is called Buckeye State after Ohio buckeye.

Buckhannon, city (pop. 6,016), N W.Va., on Buckhannon R. and S of Clarksburg. Seat of West Virginia Wesleyan Col. Trade center for agr. area.

Buckingham, dukes of (Stafford line): see STAFFORD.

Buckingham, George Nugent Temple Grenville, 1st marquess of: see GRENVILLE.

Buckingham, George Villiers, 1st duke of (vĭl'yŭrz), 1592–1628, English nobleman, a royal favorite. Arrived at English court in 1614 as James I was tiring of Robert Carr. Rose rapidly and by 1620 was dispensing king's patronage. Received credit for preventing unpopular marriage of Charles I to Spanish Infanta. Urged war with Spain and promoted Charles's marriage to Henrietta Maria of France. Remained favorite after Charles came to throne. After failure of several expeditions, he was increasingly unpopular. King dissolved Parliament to prevent action against duke. Killed by a discontented naval officer. His son, **George Villiers, 2d duke of Buckingham**, 1628–87, was strong royalist in civil war. Served Charles II in exile but intrigues and his marriage to Mary Fairfax, daughter of Puritan lord, caused estrange-

ment. Regained favor after Restoration and became one of most powerful courtiers. His temper, recklessness, and dissoluteness kept his career stormy. Was member of the cabal. Dismissed 1674, regained favor 1684 in spite of earlier opposition to James II. Patronized science and learning and had refined taste. Wrote poetry, religious tracts, and plays (including *The Rehearsal*, 1671).

Buckingham, town (pop. 6,129), SW Que., Canada, E of Ottawa. Has lumber and paper mills.

Buckingham Palace, London residence of British sovereigns since 1837. It was originally built by the duke of Buckingham in 1703. Damaged by air raids in World War II.

Buckinghamshire (bŭ'kĭng-ŭmshĭr), **Buckingham**, or **Bucks**, inland county (749 sq. mi.; pop. 386,164), S central England; co. town, Aylesbury. Region includes chalky Chiltern Hills and richly agr. Vale of Aylesbury. Southern boundary is the Thames. County has Roman and pre-Roman remains.

Buckle, Henry Thomas, 1821–62, English historian. Projected panoramic history of civilization. Two volumes, *History of Civilization in England* (1857–61), caused sensation. His scientific method and broad approach influenced later historiography.

Bucknell University: see LEWISBURG, Pa.

Buckner, Simon Bolivar, 1823–1914, Confederate general. Surrendered Fort Donelson to Grant (1862). Later commanded in Ky., Tenn., and La.

Bucks, England: see BUCKINGHAMSHIRE.

buckthorn, thorny shrub or small tree (*Rhamnus*). Common buckthorn (*Ramnus cathartica*) used for hedges. Cascara sagrada comes from *R. purshiana*.

buckwheat, annual plant (*Fagopyrum sagittatum*), widely grown for its three-cornered fruit, valued for buckwheat flour. Also used as poultry and stock feed.

Bucuresti, Rumania: see BUCHAREST.

Bucyrus (būsī'rŭs), city (pop. 10,327), N central Ohio, on Sandusky R. and NE of Marion; settled 1819. Has mfg. of metal and rubber products.

bud, in lower plants and animals a protuberance from which a new organism develops. In seed plants, a growing point containing rudiments of flowers, leaves, and shoots. See also BUDDING and CUTTING.

Budaeus: see BUDÉ, GUILLAUME.

Budapest (bōō'dŭpĕst"), city (pop, 1,164,963), cap. of Hungary, on both banks of the Danube; formed 1873 by union of Buda and Obuda (right bank) with Pest (left bank). Obuda and Pest stand near site of two Roman towns, destroyed by Mongols 1241. Buda was founded as a fortress (13th cent.), became a royal residence (14th cent.), flourished as intellectual center under Matthias Corvinus. All three cities declined under Turkish occupation (1541–1686), but Buda revived through royal favors in 18th cent. The univ. founded 1635 at Trnava by Peter Pazmany was transferred to Buda 1777, to Pest 1784. Pest, rebuilt along modern lines in 19th cent., became a leading commercial and artistic center and was, until World War I, the leading grain market of Europe. Machine, textile, and chemical mfg. developed

after World War I. One of the finest cities of
Europe, Budapest was 70% destroyed during
a 14-week siege by the Russians in World
War II (1944–45).

Buddha (bŏŏ'dů) [Sanskrit,= the enlightened
one], title of Siddhartha Gautama, c.563–483
B.C., Indian religious leader, founder of
Buddhism. Son of a ruler of area N of
Benares, he at the age of 29 renounced
luxury, became an ascetic. "The great en-
lightenment" gave him principles of religion.
He and disciples spread the faith.

Buddh Gaya or **Bodh Gaya** (both: bŏŏd' gä'-
yä), village, Bihar, India. Here Buddha
achieved enlightenment under a bo tree.
Relics of Buddhist art.

Buddhism (bŏŏd'ĭzům), system of philosophy
and ethics founded by Buddha; one of the
great religions of the world. Its beliefs were
in origin closely related to Brahmanism (see
HINDUISM), but had less formalism and a
greater emphasis on self-denial and compassion. The "four noble truths" of Buddha are:
existence is suffering; the origin of suffering
is desire; suffering ceases when desire ceases;
the way to reach the end of desire is by
following the "noble eightfold path." This
path comprises right belief, right resolve (to
renounce carnal pleasure, harm no living
creature, and the like), right speech, right
conduct, right occupation or living, right
effort, right contemplation or right minded-
ness, and right ecstasy. The final goal of the
religious man is to escape from existence
into blissful nonexistence—nirvana [Sanskrit,
= annihilation]. Individual man is made up
of elements that existed before him, that
separate at his death, and that may be re-
combined in a somewhat similar fashion. It
is from this chain of being that man seeks to
escape by religious living. These "salvation"
doctrines were spread rapidly by Buddhist
monks and for a short time Buddhism
reached a great height in India under Asoka
(3d cent. B.C.). It later died out in India,
but persisted in Ceylon and in Burma in its
simpler, "purer" form (Hinayana). It entered China in the 1st cent. A.D. and later
spread from China to Japan through Korea.
Here it developed into Mahayana, which accepts a number of divine beings and has incorporated many aspects of local religion. In
Tibet Buddhism became LAMAISM. Various
sects and movements have arisen in Buddhism, one being ZEN BUDDHISM, which
grew very strong in Japan.

budding, a form of GRAFTING in which scion is
a bud. Used chiefly for roses and some fruits.

Budé, Guillaume (gēyŏm' büdä'), 1467–1540,
French scholar, known also as Budaeus. One
of greatest French humanists and scholars,
he was a towering figure of the Renaissance.
He persuaded Francis I to found Collège de
France, used textual criticism in study of
Roman law, and helped to establish philology. He fostered Greek learning in France
and wrote on various classical subjects.

Budejovice, Czechoslovakia: see BUDWEIS.

Budge, (John) Don(ald), 1915–, American tennis player. In 1938 won American, Australian, French, British singles championships.

Budge, Sir Ernest Alfred Wallis, 1857–1934,

English archaeologist, an authority on ancient Egypt and Assyria.

Budweis (Ger. bŏŏt'vīs), Czech České Budě-
jovice, city (pop. 38,194), SW Bohemia,
Czechoslovakia, on the Moldau. Produces
beer, pencils, enamelware. Has fine medieval
and baroque architecture.

Buell, Abel (bū'ůl), 1742–1822, American silversmith and engraver of maps; cast first
font of native-made American type (1769).

Buell, Don Carlos, 1818–98, Union general in
Civil War. Supported Grant in Tenn.; saved
the day at Shiloh. Forced Braxton Bragg to
leave Ky. Criticized and removed from command, he withdrew entirely from the war.

Buena Park (bwā'nů), village (pop. 5,483), S
Calif., just W of Fullerton, in oil, citrus,
truck area.

Buenaventura (bwā"näväntŏŏ'rä), city (pop.
14,515), W Colombia, Pacific port; founded
c.1540. Original town was burned by Indians
and resettled on island in bay. Exports coffee,
platinum, gold, and hides.

Buena Vista (bū'nů vĭs'tů), city (pop. 5,214),
western Va., E of Lexington. Mfg. of paper
and textiles.

Buenos Aires (bwā'nůs ī'rēz), city (pop. 2,982,-
580); cap. of Argentina, in federal district,
N Argentina, on right bank of Río de la
Plata. A metropolis of Latin America, Buenos Aires is the chief port and financial, industrial, and social center of Argentina.
Founded by Pedro de Mendoza (1536), it
was abandoned (1541) because of hostility
of Indians and resettled (1580) by Juan de
Garay. It became cap. of viceroyalty of Río
de la Plata in 1776. British invasions in 1806–
7 were repulsed by LINIERS. The cabildo deposed the viceroy and established junta
(1810). Centralist-federalist struggle in Argentina ended by making Buenos Aires paramount. The city was detached from its province and was federalized (1880). Near-by
Buenos Aires prov. (cap. LA PLATA) is rich
in cattle and grain.

Buffalo. 1 City (pop. 580,132), W N.Y., on L.
Erie and Niagara R.; laid out 1803 under
HOLLAND LAND COMPANY. State's second
largest city. It is a major Great Lakes port,
industrial center, and rail hub. Products are
iron, steel, flour, rubber, linseed oil, gypsum
and wood products, airplanes, autos, machinery, and packed meat. Burned by British
in War of 1812. Commercial and industrial
growth was rapid after completion of Erie
Canal (1825). Pres. McKinley was assassinated and Theodore Roosevelt took presidential oath here in 1901 during Pan-
American Exposition. Presidents Cleveland
(became mayor 1881) and Fillmore lived
here. Seat of Univ. of Buffalo (nonsectarian;
private; coed.; 1846) and Canisius Col.
(Jesuit; mainly for men; 1870). Has buildings by Louis Sullivan and F. L. Wright.
2 City (pop. 2,674), N Wyo., SSE of Sheridan. Trade center in resort area. L. De Smet
is N.

buffalo, common name for American bison,
but accurately applied only to certain related
oxlike mammals of Asia, Africa. Asiatic
water buffalo (*Bubalis*) or Indian buffalo
stands c.5 ft. at shoulder, with spreading,
backward-curving horns. Pygmy buffalo

(*Anoa*) is wild ox of Celebes. Cape buffalo (*Syncerus*) is in S Africa.

Buffalo, University of: see BUFFALO, N.Y.

buffalo berry, hardy North American shrub (*Shepherdia argentea*). Silvery foliage; female plant bears edible, yellow or scarlet berries.

Buffalo Bill, 1846–1917, American plainsman, scout, and showman; real name William Frederick Cody. Organized Buffalo Bill's Wild West Show in 1883; toured with it for many years.

buffalo fish, name for several fish of sucker family, chiefly in Mississippi valley rivers and lakes. Flesh bony and coarse, but commercially important as food.

buffalo grass, important range grass (*Buchloe dactyloides*) of plains regions. It is sod forming.

Buffon, Georges Louis Leclerc, comte de (zhôrzh' lwĕ' lûklĕrk' kôt' dü büfô'), 1707–88, French naturalist, author. Devoted life to *Histoire naturelle* (44 vols., 1749–1804).

Bug (boog), river, 487 mi. long, E Europe. Rises E of Lvov, flows N along Polish-Ukrainian border, then NW into the Narew. Canal connection with Dnieper. Also called Western Bug.

Bug or **Southern Bug,** Rus. *Yuzhny Bug,* river, 520 mi. long, Ukraine. Flows SE into Black Sea. Used for grain transport March–Dec.

bug, accurately only insect of order Hemiptera. Head has structure for piercing and sucking. Those with wings have two pairs. See *ill.,* p. 601.

Buganda: see UGANDA.

Bugayev, Boris Nikolayevich: see BELY, ANDREI.

Bugge, Sophus (so'foos boo'gü), 1833–1907, Norwegian philologist. Edited Norse runes and poems of the *Eddas* (1881–89; 2d series, 1896).

bugle, brass wind musical instrument, consisting of a conical tube coiled once upon itself. Chiefly used for military bugle calls, such as taps or reveille. Key and valve bugles developed in 19th cent.

Buhl, André Charles: see BOULLE, ANDRÉ CHARLES.

Buisson, Ferdinand Édouard (fĕrdēnā' ädwär' büēsô'), 1841–1932, French educator. He became professor of pedagogy at the Sorbonne in 1886 and was a member of chamber of deputies 1902–14 and 1919–24. An ardent pacifist, he attended (1867) first congress of International Peace League. With Ludwig Quidde he received 1927 Nobel Peace Prize.

Buitenzorg (boi'tünzôrkh), Malay *Bogor,* town (pop. 65,431), W Java, Indonesia. Summer resort at foot of two volcanoes. Notable botanical gardens.

Bukhara (bükä'rü), city (pop. 50,382), W Uzbek SSR; also spelled Bokhara. Karakul and silk processing. Bokhara rugs originally named after city. One of oldest cities of TURKISTAN and long a center of Islamic culture, it was the cap. of the emirate of Bukhara, which comprised parts of Uzbekistan, Tadzhikistan, and Turkmenistan. Ruled by despotic Uzbek princes after 16th cent., emirate was forced to accept Russian suzerainty in 1868. Last emir deposed 1920. City

has splendid mosques and palaces (9th–17th cent.).

Bukhari (bookhärĕ'), d. 870, Arabic scholar and Moslem saint, whose collection of traditional sayings of Mohammed is highly respected in Islam.

Bukharin, Nikolai Ivanovich (nyĭkûlī' ēvä'növĭch bookhä'rēn), 1888–1938, Russian Communist. Chief party theoretician after Lenin's death. Purged and executed in treason trials of 1936–38.

Bukovina (bookŭvē'nü), region, E Europe, in W Ukraine and NE Rumania; chief town Chernovtsy (Ukraine). Traversed by Carpathians and by upper Pruth R., it produces timber, grain, livestock. Mixed pop. includes Rumanians, Ukrainians, Russians, Jews, Magyars. Region was the nucleus of the old principality of Moldavia. Ceded by Turkey to Austria 1775; to Rumania 1919. N part (c.2,000 sq. mi.; pop. c.460,000) ceded to USSR 1940; reoccupied by Rumania 1941–44; formally ceded to USSR 1947. S part (c.2,000 sq. mi.; pop. c.300,000) forms a historic prov. of Rumania.

bulb, thickened fleshy plant bud, usually formed under soil. Carries plant over from one season to another. Examples are tulip, hyacinth, lily. The CORM, TUBER, and RHIZOME are not true bulbs. See *ill.,* p. 999.

bulbul (bool'bool), name for a number of species of thrushlike birds of Africa and Asia. The bulbul of Persian poetry was probably a nightingale.

Bulfinch, Charles, 1763–1844, American architect. Elegance of his structures in Boston places them among best of early American architecture. Designed Boston statehouse (1799); University Hall, Harvard Univ. (1815); First Church of Christ, Lancaster, Mass. (1816–17); and Mass. General Hospital (1820). Worked on Capitol at Washington, 1818–30.

Bulfinch, Thomas, 1796–1867, American author, popularizer of mythology in *The Age of Fable* (1855).

Bulganin, Nikolai Aleksandrovich (nyĭkûlī' ŭlyĭksän'drůvĭch bŏolgä'nĭn), 1895?–, Russian Communist leader. Helped plan defense of Moscow 1941; later was given rank of marshal; minister of armed forces 1947–49; vice premier of USSR from 1949.

Bulgari: see BULGARS, EASTERN.

Bulgaria (bŭlgâ'rēü), republic (42,796 sq. mi.; pop. 7,022,206), SE Europe, on Balkan Peninsula, bounded by the Black Sea (E), European Turkey and Greece (S), Yugoslavia (W), and Rumania (N); cap. Sofia. Stalin (formerly Varna) is chief port. Crossed by Balkan mts. and drained by Danube, Struma, and Maritsa rivers, Bulgaria is largely agr. Chief products: cotton textiles, tobacco, attar of roses. Population is mainly Greek Orthodox, with some Moslems. Expulsion of Turkish minority (c.250,000) began 1950. Occupying ancient THRACE and MOESIA, country was conquered A.D. 660 by a group of Eastern BULGARS, who later merged with older Slavic settlers and adopted their language. Their khan Krum exacted tribute from Byzantine Empire (9th cent.); BORIS I introduced Christianity; SIMEON I enlarged territory, took title tsar.

Subjugated by Byzantium 1018–1186, Bulgaria again became an empire (with cap. at Trnovo) under Ivan I; reached its height under IVAN II; became tributary to Serbia 1330; was annexed by Turkey after defeats at Kossovo (1389) and Nikopol (1396). Cruel repression of revolt under Stefan STAMBULOV (1875; "Bulgarian atrocities") gave Russia an excuse for war on Turkey (1877–78). Greater Bulgaria, set up by Treaty of SAN STEFANO, was reduced by Congress of BERLIN and divided into three parts: N Bulgaria, as principality under nominal Turkish overlordship; E RUMELIA, as Turkish province with autonomous rights; and MACEDONIA, under direct Turkish rule. ALEXANDER of Battenberg, first prince of Bulgaria, annexed E Rumelia 1885; his successor, FERDINAND of Saxe-Coburg-Gotha, proclaimed full independence 1908, took title tsar. Bulgarian claims to Macedonia led to BALKAN WARS of 1912–13, in which Bulgaria first won, then lost, much territory. One of Central Powers in World War I, it lost S DOBRUJA and outlet to Aegean Sea by Treaty of NEUILLY. The regime of Premier STAMBULISKI was followed by two military dictatorships (1923–26, 1934–35) and a royal dictatorship under BORIS III (1935–43). In World War II, Bulgaria joined the AXIS (1941) and occupied parts of Yugoslavia and Greece. In Sept., 1944, Russia declared war and invaded Bulgaria. A pro-Russian coalition cabinet took power but was soon replaced by a Communist regime. The monarchy was abolished, Tsar Simeon II deposed (1946). By 1948 all opposition was suppressed. Bulgarian peace treaty (ratified 1947) allowed Bulgaria to keep S Dobruja (ceded by Rumania 1940).

Bulgarian, language of Slavic subfamily of Indo-European languages. See LANGUAGE (table).

Bulgars, Eastern, people, probably speaking a Finnic language, who had a powerful state in E European Russia, along Middle Volga (8th–13th cent.). Their cap., Bulgari or Bolgari, was near Kazan. Conquered by Mongols 1236. A branch of the people moved west and merged with Slavs in Bulgaria.

Bulge, Battle of the: see BATTLE OF THE BULGE.

Bull, Ole (ō'lù), 1810–80, Norwegian violinist. He toured Europe and America, playing mostly his own compositions and Norwegian folk music.

Bull, the, in astronomy: see ZODIAC.

bull [Latin *bulla* = leaden seal], solemn official pronouncement of the pope, more solemn than an encyclical (letter to all the bishops) and a brief (short letter). Among well-known bulls are *Clericis laicos* (1296) and *Unam sanctum* (1302; both by Boniface VIII); the bull of demarcation for discoveries (1493, by Alexander VI); *Exsurge Domine* (1520, by Leo X); *Unigenitus* (1713, by Clement XI); *Mirari vos* (1832, by Gregory XVI); *Quanta cura* (1864, by Pius IX); *Pastor aeternus* (1871, of Pius IX); *Aeterni patris* (1879) and *Rerum novarum* (1891; both by Leo XIII); *Quadragesimo anno* (1931, by Pius XI). Pius XI issued two bulls not in Latin— *Non abbiamo bisogno* (1931, against Fascism) and *Mit brennender Sorge* (1937,

against Nazism). In recent years the encyclical has been employed much more than the bull. The term *bull* was formerly used for some nonpapal documents (e.g., Golden Bull).

bull bat: see NIGHTHAWK.

bulldog, smooth-haired dog. The English bulldog has a heavy, low-slung body, broad chest, undershot jaw, and wrinkled face, with front legs (appearing bowed) shorter than the hind legs. Once bred for bullbaiting, it is now generally good-natured and courageous. The French bulldog is smaller and usually darker. Outstanding are its "bat ears"—wide at the base, tapering to a rounded point, and held erect. Descended from numerous breeds of bulldogs is the boxer, a sleek, muscular, and rather stocky dog developed chiefly in Germany in the 19th cent. It is usually some shade of fawn or brindle; small erect ears and a protruding lower jaw are other characteristics. See also BOSTON TERRIER.

bullfighting, national sport of Spain, also popular in Latin America. Conducted in arena, or *plaza de toros.* The matador, who kills the bull, is assisted by *banderilleros,* who enrage bulls by stabbing them with darts, *picadores,* who jab bulls with lances, and *toreros,* who distract bulls by waving red flags.

bullfinch, any of several European songbirds of finch family, often caged. Common species is woodland bird; blue-gray upper plumage, tile red below.

bullfrog, largest North American frog; aquatic with fully webbed toes. Common bullfrog (*Rana catesbiana*) E of Rocky Mts. Deep bass cry or croaking.

bullhead, name for several species of genus *Ameiurus* of catfish family, found in sluggish waters. Commonest is brown bullhead or horned pout (12 to 18 in. long); others are black and yellow bullheads. Name also for some species of sculpin family (large-headed, toothed fish).

Bullitt, William C(hristian) (bōol'ĭt), 1891–, American diplomat; first U.S. ambassador to USSR (1933–36); ambassador to France (1936–41).

Bull Moose party: see PROGRESSIVE PARTY.

Bull Run, small stream, NE Va., c.30 mi. SW of Washington, D.C., scene of two important Civil War battles, July 21, 1861, and Aug. 29–30, 1862. In **first battle of Bull Run,** first major clash of war, Federals under Irvin McDowell attacked Confederates under P. G. T. Beauregard. They met resistance of T. J. Jackson standing "like a stone wall," and were forced into retreat, a rout ending only at defenses of Washington. Victory cheered South, and spurred North to greater efforts. **Second battle of Bull Run,** also a victory for Confederates, was culmination of R. E. Lee's strategy to prevent reinforcement of John Pope's army by G. B. McClellan along Rappahannock R., where Stonewall Jackson had driven it. James Longstreet, after attack by Pope, counterattacked and drove Federals back across Bull Run. In pursuit Jackson was stopped at Chantilly, Sept. 1, 1862, and Pope withdrew to Washington.

bulls and bears. In speculative markets, a "bear" is a speculator who sells what he does not own in the hope that, before he has to deliver, he will be able to buy back at a lower price. A "bull" is the opposite of a bear; he tries to force prices up rather than down.

bull terrier: see TERRIER.

Bülow, Bernhard, Fürst von (bĕrn'härt fürst' fŭn bü'lō), 1849–1929, chancellor of Germany (1900–1909). His aggressive policies (notably in Morocco) isolated Germany and paved way for World War I.

Bülow, Hans von, 1830–94, German pianist, first of modern virtuoso conductors. In 1857 he married Liszt's daughter Cosima, who left him in 1869 and later married Wagner. He was the first to call Bach, Beethoven, and Brahms the three B's of music.

bulrush, sedge of genus *Scirpus,* often with grasslike leaves. Grown in aquatic or bog gardens. Bulrush in which Moses was hidden (Ex. 2.3) was papyrus.

Bulwer-Lytton, Edward George Earle Lytton, 1st Baron Lytton, 1803–73, English novelist and playright. Among his many popular novels (some historical) are *Eugene Aram* (1832), *The Last Days of Pompeii* (1834), *Rienzi* (1835). Particularly well known among his plays are *The Lady of Lyons* (1838), *Richelieu* (1838). The son born to his unhappy marriage was **Edward Robert Bulwer-Lytton, 1st earl of Lytton,** 1831–91, who wrote under the pseud. *Owen Meredith.* A diplomat and statesman, viceroy of India, he is best remembered for his verse, notably *Lucile* (1880).

Buna rubber: see RUBBER, SYNTHETIC.

Bunau-Varilla, Philippe Jean (fēlēp' zhä' bünō-värēyä'), 1859–1940, French engineer, prominent in PANAMA CANAL controversy. Organized second French canal-building company; sold it to U.S.; then engineered PANAMA revolution of 1903. As minister of Panama to U.S. negotiated Hay-Bunau-Varilla Treaty, which gave control of Canal Zone to U.S.

bunchberry or **dwarf cornel,** low North American and Asiatic perennial (*Cornus canadensis*), related to dogwood. White-bracted flowers and red berries.

Bunche, Ralph (Johnson), 1904–, American internationalist, a Negro. Director, UN Trusteeship Division (1946–). Awarded 1950 Nobel Peace Prize.

Bunin, Ivan Alekseyevich (ēvän' ŭlyĭksyä'yĭvĭch bōō'nyĭn), 1870–, Russian author. A poet of distinction, he is best known for his short stories, especially *The Man* (or *The Gentleman*) *from San Francisco* (1916), and the autobiographical novel *The Well of Days* (1930; Eng. tr., 1933). Resided abroad after 1919. Awarded 1933 Nobel Prize in Literature.

Bunker Hill, battle of, in American Revolution, June 17, 1775, actually fought on neighboring Breed's Hill, Charlestown, Mass. British victory failed to break the triumphant ring of patriots besieging Boston.

Bunner, H(enry) C(uyler), 1855–96, American journalist; author of light verse (as in *Airs from Arcady and Elsewhere,* 1884) and humorous stories (as in *Short Sixes,* 1891); editor of *Puck,* 1877–96.

Bunsen, Robert Wilhelm (bŭn'sùn), 1811–99, German scientist. Studied organic arsenic compounds, photochemistry. Evolved method of gas analysis; with Kirchhoff discovered cesium and rubidium, using spectroscope; invented Bunsen electric cell. Known for **Bunsen burner:** hollow tube fitted around flame, with base opening to admit air; produces smokeless, nonluminous, high-temperature flame.

bunting, small, plump bird of finch family. American buntings include INDIGO BUNTING; painted bunting or nonpareil; snow bunting; dickcissel. Baywinged bunting is really vesper sparrow.

Buntline, Ned, pseud. of **Edward Zane Carroll Judson,** b. 1822 or 1823, d. 1886, American adventurer, editor of sensational magazine (*Ned Buntline's Own*), author of trashy novels that preceded dime novel. Lynched for murder (1846), he was cut down alive. Introduced Buffalo Bill to the stage.

bunya-bunya (bŭn'yù), large Australian tree (*Araucaria bidwillii*). Its seeds provide a staple food of native tribes.

Bunyan, John, 1628–88, English author, notable for his *Pilgrim's Progress from This World to That Which Is to Come* (1678). A Baptist lay preacher, he wrote many spiritual works, including *Grace Abounding to the Chief of Sinners* (1666; a spiritual autobiography) and *The Life and Death of Mr. Badman* (1680), but it was his allegory of Christian life, *Pilgrim's Progress,* that held the imagination of many generations.

Bunyan, Paul, Gargantuan hero of "tall tales" of American lumber camps from Mich. to the West Coast. He was aided in his feats by Babe, the Blue Ox.

Buonaparte: see BONAPARTE and NAPOLEON I.

Buoninsegna, Duccio di: see DUCCIO.

Burbage, James (bûr'bĭj), d. 1597, English actor. Built London's first permanent theater 1576; moved to Bankside (c.1598), it became the GLOBE THEATRE. Built Blackfriars Theatre also. His son, **Richard Burbage,** 1567?–1619, was leading actor of his day. Appeared in original productions of many plays by Shakspere and Ben Jonson. Noted as Hamlet, Lear, Othello, and Richard III.

Burbank, Luther, 1849–1926, American plant breeder. He developed the Burbank potato, Shasta daisy, and many other new plant varieties.

Burbank, city (pop. 78,577), S Calif., N of Los Angeles; laid out 1887. Industries include moving-picture and aircraft production.

Burchell, William John (bûr'chŭl), 1782?–1863, English explorer and scientist. Made vast collections in Africa of natural and meteorological objects. Discovered many animal and plant species.

Burchfield, Charles, 1893–, American painter, widely known as a painter of Victorian mansions, false-front stores, and other relics of the late 19th cent. His work is marked by subtlety of color and a slightly ironic realism.

Burckhardt, Jacob Christoph (yä'kôp krĭs'tôf bōōrk'härt), 1818–97, Swiss historian, a founder of cultural history. His works include the classic *Die Kultur der Renaissance in Italien* (1860).

Burckhardt, John Lewis (bûrk'härt), 1784–1817, explorer, b. Switzerland. Sponsored by

English association promoting African discovery. Posing as learned Moslem, was first Christian to reach Medina.

burdock, coarse, weedy biennial (*Arctium*), naturalized in North America. Rounded, many-seeded burs.

Burdwan (bûrdwän'), city (pop. 62,910) S West Bengal, India. A group of 108 Siva linga temples (1788) is near by. Cutlery mfg.

Burgas (bŏŏr'gäs), city (pop. 43,684), E Bulgaria; a Black Sea port.

Burgenland (Ger. bŏŏr'gŭnlänt), province (1,576 sq. mi.; pop. 275,911), E Austria, bordering on Hungary; cap. Eisenstadt. Hilly region, indented by Neusiedler L. Wine growing. Territory transferred from Hungary to Austria by treaties of 1919 and 1920. SOPRON, its leading town, was returned to Hungary by plebiscite (1921).

Bürger, Gottfried August (gôt'frēt ou'gŏŏst bür'gŭr), 1747–94, German poet. Credited with reviving the German ballad, he is best known for "Lenore" (1773), widely translated and highly influential.

Burgess, (Frank) Gelett, 1866–1951, American humorist, illustrator of his own stories and articles; best known for quatrain "The Purple Cow" and for originating the terms *goop* and *bromide.*

Burgess, John William, 1844–1931, American political scientist; educ. at Amherst and in Germany. Helped create faculty of political science at Columbia Univ. Wrote much on political science and U.S. history.

Burgh, Hubert de: see HUBERT DE BURGH.

Burghley or **Burleigh, William Cecil, 1st Baron,** 1520–98, English statesman, chief adviser of Queen Elizabeth. Rose to power 1548, but was not in favor with Mary I. Reappointed by Elizabeth; served her for 40 years. Responsible for execution of Mary Queen of Scots and solidification of Protestantism. His policy helped growing industry and commerce.

burglary, at common law, breaking and entering a dwelling house at night with intent to commit a felony; by statutes in many states of U.S. extended to mean all breaking and entering. Breaking involves only a slight use of force (e.g., turning a key) or by entry through fraud, threat, or conspiracy.

Bürglen (bürk'lŭn), village, Uri canton, Switzerland. Alleged birthplace of William Tell.

Burgos (bŏŏr'gōs), city (pop. 51,177), cap. of Burgos prov., N Spain, in Old Castile. Cap. of Castile until 1087, when Toledo replaced it. Gothic cathedral, founded 1221, among finest in S Europe.

Burgoyne, John (bûrgoin'), 1722–92, British general. Helped plan SARATOGA CAMPAIGN, but led poorly equipped army, untrained for frontier fighting. Surrendered at Saratoga, Oct. 17, 1777.

Burgundians, in French medieval history: see ARMAGNACS AND BURGUNDIANS.

Burgundy (bûr'gŭndē), Fr. *Bourgogne,* region and former province, E France, in Yonne, Côte-d'Or, Saône-et-Loire, and Ain depts.; historic cap., Dijon. Gay; wine growing (particularly in Chablis region and Côte-d'Or). Cities: Dijon, Beaune, Auxerre, Chalon-sur-Saône, Mâcon. In history, the term "Bur-gundy" often designated much wider areas. A part of Roman Gaul, it was peacefully settled (5th cent. A.D.) by the Germanic Burgundii, who founded the **First Kingdom of Burgundy.** This comprised SE France and W Switzerland. Conquered by the Franks (534), it was repeatedly partitioned under the Merovingians and Carolingians, though it survived in name. Two kingdoms emerged in the 9th cent.: Cisjurane Burgundy or PROVENCE in the south; Transjurane Burgundy in the north. These were united (933) in the kingdom of Arles or **Second Kingdom of Burgundy** (see ARLES, KINGDOM OF). A smaller area (roughly, present Burgundy) was created (877) as the **duchy of Burgundy,** which from the 11th cent. was ruled mostly by princes of the French royal house. In the 14th and 15th cent., Burgundy had its golden age under dukes PHILIP THE BOLD, JOHN THE FEARLESS, PHILIP THE GOOD, and CHARLES THE BOLD, who acquired the Low Countries, FRANCHE-COMTÉ, and other territories. The wealthiest state of W Europe and one of the great powers, Burgundy also was a center of art and culture. In the Hundred Years War Burgundy sided with England against France from 1415 until 1435, when its alliance with France turned the tide. (See also ARMAGNACS AND BURGUNDIANS.) The defeat and death (1477) of Charles the Bold left MARY OF BURGUNDY the heir. Through her, the Low Countries passed to the Hapsburgs (see NETHERLANDS, AUSTRIAN AND SPANISH), but the duchy itself was seized by Louis XI, who made it into a French prov.

Buriat-Mongolia, RSFSR: see BURYAT-MONGOL AUTONOMOUS SOVIET SOCIALIST REPUBLIC.

Buridan, Jean (byŏŏ'rĭdŭn, Fr. bürēdä'), fl. 1328, French scholastic philosopher, rector of the Univ. of Paris. A follower of William of Occam, he held man's will enables him to choose the greater good and to suspend choice in order to reconsider. He is credited (probably falsely) with using the figure of "Buridan's ass"—an unfortunate animal midway between identical bundles of hay and starving to death because he cannot decide which bundle to eat.

Burke, Edmund, 1729–97, British statesman and political writer, b. Dublin. Was a member of Dr. Johnson's circle. Strong Whig opponent of William Pitt, in famous speeches he advocated wiser policy in America. Exposed injustices in India by instigating long trial of Warren HASTINGS 1785–94. His opposition to French Revolution led to break with Whigs 1791. Advocate of many practical reforms, he feared political reform.

Burke, John, 1787–1848, Irish genealogist. Issued a publication which became British annual, *Burke's Peerage,* edited by his son, **Sir John Bernard Burke,** 1814–92, also publisher of *Burke's Landed Gentry.*

Burke, Robert O'Hara, 1820–61, Irish explorer of Australia. Crossed continent from Menindee to Gulf of Carpentaria; died from famine on return.

Burleigh, Harry T(hacker) (bûr'lē), 1866–1949, American Negro baritone and composer; soloist at St. George's Church, New York, 1894–1946, and at Temple Emanu-El for 25 years. His concert arrangements of Negro spirituals, such as *Deep River,* are well known.

Burleigh, William Cecil, 1st Baron: see BURGHLEY.

Burleson, Albert Sidney (bûr'lùsùn), 1863–1937, U.S. Postmaster General (1913–21). His strict control of communications in World War I aroused the ire of businessmen, labor unions, liberals.

Burley, city (pop. 5,924), S Idaho, on Snake R. It is a MINIDOKA PROJECT farm center, with beet-sugar, alfalfa-meal, and potato-flour mills.

Burlingame, Anson (bûr'lǐng-gām), 1820–70, American diplomat who contracted **Burlingame Treaty** (1868), a pact of friendship between China and U.S. based on Western principles of international law. One clause encouraged Chinese immigration; resulting friction led to policy of CHINESE EXCLUSION.

Burlingame, residential city (pop. 19,886), W Calif., on San Francisco Bay; founded 1868.

Burlingame Treaty: see BURLINGAME, ANSON.

Burlington, town (pop. 6,017), S Ont., Canada, on L. Ontario NE of Hamilton, in fruit-growing area.

Burlington. 1 City (pop. 30,613), SE Iowa, on four hills overlooking the Mississippi; platted 1833 on sites of Indian village and trading post. Temporary cap. of Wisconsin Territory (1837) and Iowa Territory (1838–40). With railroad shops and docks, it has mfg. of metal and wood products, fertilizer, and clothing. Munitions plant built in World War II. **2** City (pop. 12,051), W N.J., on Delaware R. between Trenton and Camden; settled 1677 by Friends. Early important port, now shipping center for agr. area, it makes textiles. Cap. of West Jersey 1681–1702, alternate cap. with Perth Amboy of united Jerseys 1702–90. Franklin printed first colonial money here 1726; first N.J. newspaper printed here 1777. Has Friends' school (1792) and meetinghouse (1784). **3** City (pop. 24,560), N N.C., E of Greensboro, near Haw R. Mfg. of hosiery, textiles, and wood products. Tobacco warehouses. **4** City (pop. 33,155), NW Vt., overlooking L. Champlain just below Winooski R. mouth; chartered by N.H. 1763, settled 1773. Largest Vt. city. Became important lake port (lumber, potash) after Revolution. Now has mfg. of textiles, wood and metal products; processing of maple syrup, and other food products. State's first Unitarian church organized here 1810; first Roman Catholic church built here 1831. Has birthplace of John Dewey and grave of Ethan Allen. Seat of Trinity Col. (R.C.; for women) and Univ. of Vermont and State Agricultural Col. (land-grant, state, and private support; coed.); founded by Ira ALLEN, chartered 1791, opened 1800; col. of agr. (chartered 1864) joined the univ. 1865; library, designed by H. H. Richardson, holds state's largest book collection.

Burma, Union of, republic (261,757 sq. mi.; pop. 16,823,798), SE Asia, on Indo-Chinese peninsula; cap. RANGOON. Densely populated valley of Irrawaddy R. is surrounded by mountains stemming from E Himalayas; its delta forms a great rice-growing area. Rich mineral resources include oil, tungsten, tin, silver, lead, and jade. Rice, teak, and oil are chief exports. Population comprises various Mongoloid groups, including the KARENS, Chins, Shans, and Mons. The Burmese proper, who live mainly in region around MANDALAY, moved down from Tibet before 9th cent. and were unified in 11th cent. by Anawratha, who estab. his cap. at Pagan. He introduced Buddhism, today the main religion. After his successors were crushed by Kublai Khan in 1287, Burma split into petty states ruled by Shan chieftains until 16th cent., when a Burmese dynasty, the Toungoo, became dominant. In 18th cent. the rising Mons were crushed by the Burmese under Alaungpaya, who later raided India and greatly enlarged his domain. European trade had been initiated by the Portuguese in 16th cent., but there were no clashes with Europeans until the Anglo-Burmese wars (1824–26, 1852, 1885), which resulted in annexation of Burma to British India. In 1937 Burma was given quasi-dominion status. In World War II Burma was occupied early 1942–1945 by the Japanese. After the war it became a sovereign republic (Jan. 4, 1948). However, it was soon beset by internal strife, aggravated by presence of many Chinese Nationalist troops who had moved into the area in 1949. Country is divided into Lower Burma, with divisions of ARAKAN, PEGU, TENASSERIM, and Irrawaddy, and Upper Burma, including semiautonomous CHIN HILLS, constituent units of SHAN, KACHIN, and KARENNI states.

Burman or **Burmese,** Indo-Chinese language. See LANGUAGE (table).

bur marigold, weedy plant (*Bidens*), of daisy family. Burlike fruits. Also called tickseed, beggar-ticks.

Burma Road, from Lashio, Burma, to Kunming, Yunnan prov., China; c.700 mi. long. Construction began 1937, completed 1938. Until Japanese occupation of Burma in 1942, it carried war supplies landed at Rangoon and shipped by rail to Lashio. In Jan., 1945 it was joined to Ledo (Stilwell) Road from Ledo, India, to Myitkyina, and was again a vital supply route. War's end reduced its importance.

Burmese or **Burman,** Indo-Chinese language. See LANGUAGE (table).

Burne-Jones, Sir Edward, 1833–98, English painter and decorator, an eminent exponent of Pre-Raphaelitism. Drew his material from the medieval period. His designs for stained glass were executed by the firm of William Morris.

Burnet, David Gouverneur (bûr'nǐt, bùrnět'), 1788–1870, provisional president of Texas (1836). Drew up Texas declaration of independence from Mexico.

burnet (bûr'nǐt), hardy perennial herb (*Sanguisorba*). White or greenish flowers. Leaves used in salads.

Burnett, Frances (Eliza) Hodgson, 1849–1924, American author, b. England, in U.S. after 1865. Among her children's books are *Little Lord Fauntleroy* (1886), *Sara Crewe* (1888), *The Secret Garden* (1909).

Burney, Frances (Fanny), later **Madame D'Arblay,** 1752–1840, English novelist, daughter of Dr. Charles Burney, member of the Samuel Johnson circle. Her acute novels of society include *Evelina; or, The History of a Young Lady's Entrance into the World* (1778), *Cecilia* (1782), and *Camilla* (1796).

Burnham, Daniel Hudson, 1846–1912, American architect and city planner. With his partner John W. Root he designed the 20-story Masonic Temple Building (first important skeleton skyscraper) in Chicago. Their general plan for the Columbia Exposition at Chicago (1893) had an enormous influence on contemporary civic design. Planned Baguio in the Philippines.

Burnham, Sherburne Wesley, 1838–1921, American astronomer, authority on double stars.

burning bush or **wahoo,** handsome North American deciduous shrub (*Euonymus atropurpureus*). Yellow autumn foliage and purple pods with scarlet seeds. Scriptural burning bush (Ex. 3.2) was a thorn.

Burns, John, 1858–1943, British socialist. With Ben Tillett and Tom Mann, led 1889 London dock strike.

Burns, Robert, 1759–96, Scottish lyric, descriptive, and narrative poet, one of the greatest of the romantics. Son of a poor farmer, he gained some education. The jaunty gaiety of some poems reflects his dissolute life, but his love poems have a simple sweetness that make them live. Some songs (e.g., "Flow Gently, Sweet Afton," "John Anderson My Jo," "Auld Lang Syne," "Coming thro' the Rye") are beloved in all English-speaking lands. He first published *Poems, Chiefly in the Scottish Dialect* (1786; 2d ed., 1787) to finance emigration to Jamaica after projected marriage to Mary Campbell. She died, and plan fell through; he later married Jean Armour (who had borne him four children). Briefly lionized in Edinburgh, he died poor. Faithful pictures of Scottish life (e.g., "The Cotter's Saturday Night"), boisterous humor, sincere sentiment, the use of dialect—all contributed to make his poetry distinctive.

burns and scalds. Classified according to depth of tissue damage as first-, second-, third-degree (most severe). Systemic reactions include shock, flow of fluid from blood into injured area, loss of body heat. Scalds are burns caused by moist heat.

Burnside, Ambrose Everett, 1824–81, Union general in Civil War. Won prestige by N.C. coastal campaign. Commanded Army of Potomac until defeat at Fredericksburg. Transferred to Dept. of the Ohio (1863); in 1864 commanded under Meade and Grant in Va.

Burr, Aaron, 1756–1836, American political leader. U.S. Senator (1791–97). Tied with Thomas Jefferson in election of 1800 for presidency; elected Vice President by House of Representatives. Killed Alexander HAMILTON in duel in 1804. Burr's plan for colonization in the Southwest led to his trial for treason in 1807; acquitted, he left for England, but after 1812 practiced law in N.Y.

Burr, William Hubert, 1851–1934, American civil engineer. Served on engineering commissions, e.g., Panama Canal and Port of New York Authority.

Burrillville, town (pop. 8,774), NW R.I., NW of Providence. Mfg. of woolens (since c.1800).

Burritt, Elihu, 1810–79, American worker for world peace, "the learned blacksmith." Supported William LADD in plans for international organization.

burro: see ASS.

Burroughs, John, 1837–1921, American naturalist. He ranged far from his farm at Esopus, N.Y. (from which he was called the Sage of Slabsides) to Alaska and the West Indies to gather material for his smooth philosophic nature essays (as in the books *Wake Robin,* 1871; *Locusts and Wild Honey,* 1879). Later books (e.g., *Time and Change,* 1912; *The Breath of Life,* 1915) are more weightily philosophical. Also wrote poems and early work (1867) on his friend Walt Whitman.

Bursa (bōōr'sä), city (pop. 100,007) NW Turkey, near the Sea of Marmara; also known as Brusa or Brussa. Silk and carpet mfg. Ancient Prusa was a flourishing city of Bithynia. Captured by Orkhan 1326; cap. of Ottoman Turks 1326–1423; sacked by Tamerlane 1402. Has fine mosques, tombs of early sultans.

Burton, Sir Richard Francis, 1821–90, English explorer, writer, linguist. Journeyed in various Moslem disguises to Mecca and Medina (1853), in Arabic guise to Harar, Ethiopia (1856). Explored in Africa and Brazil. Wrote accounts of his travels, translated *Arabian Nights* (16 vols., 1885–88).

Burton, Robert, 1577–1640, English clergyman, author of *The Anatomy of Melancholy* (1621; several times enlarged), a vast, wide-ranging treatise.

Burton-Opitz, Russell (–ō'pĭts), 1875–, American physiologist, authority on blood and circulatory system.

Bury, John Bagnell (byōō'rē), 1861–1927, Irish historian, authority on East Roman Empire. His chief works treat Greek, late Roman, and Byzantine history. He also edited Gibbon's *Decline and Fall.*

Bury, Richard de: see RICHARD DE BURY.

Buryat-Mongol Autonomous Soviet Socialist Republic (bōōryät'-mŏng'gŏl), autonomous state (135,700 sq. mi.; pop. 542,170), RSFSR, in S Siberia; cap. ULAN-UDE. Mountainous, heavily forested, rich in metals (tungsten, molybdenum, gold, tin, mercury, iron). Population is c.50% Buryat-Mongols (see MONGOLS), mostly herdsmen. Annexed by Russia 17th cent. Also known as Buriat-Mongolia.

bus, public road conveyance. Horse-drawn type introduced 1662 in Paris was operated for a few years. It was reintroduced in Bordeaux (c.1812), Paris (c.1827), London (1829), New York (1830). Busses were motorized in early 20th cent. First motorbus service from Los Angeles to New York estab. 1928.

Busch, Adolf (bōōsh'), 1891–1952, German-Swiss violinist. He organized the Busch string quartet and the Busch Chamber Players, both outstanding in the performance of chamber music. His brother, **Fritz Busch,** 1890–1951, was a conductor of opera and symphony and led the Glyndebourne Festivals in England.

Busch, Wilhelm (vĭl'hĕlm bōōsh'), 1832–1908, German cartoonist, author of humorous, illustrated poems for children.

Büsching, Anton Friedrich (büsh'ĭng), 1724–93, German geographer, educator. Noted for *Neue Erdbeschreibung* (10 vols., 1754–92); six volumes translated into English as *A New System of Geography* (1762).

Bush, Vannevar, 1890–, American electrical engineer, physicist, and administrator. In 1939 he became president of Carnegie Institution and in 1941 director of the wartime Office of Scientific Research and Development. He designed calculating devices including a differential analyzer. He is author of works on technical subjects and on the significance of research.

bushido (bōōshēdō′) [way of the warrior], code of honor of feudal Japan which governed the general conduct of the SAMURAI. Codified in 17th–18th cent.; stresses loyalty and self-sacrifice for one's superior and one's honor.

bushmaster, largest New World venomous snake, of pit viper family. Found in Central and South America.

Bushmen, a people of southern Africa related to Pygmies. Nomadic hunters and cave dwellers. Their complex language resembles that of Hottentots.

Bushnell, Horace, 1802–76, American Congregational minister. Minister at North Church, Hartford, Conn., 1833–59. His works helped shape modern religious thought.

Bushrangers, gangs of escaped convicts and adventurers who terrorized rural areas of Australia in 19th cent. Later groups attacked gold convoys.

Busoni, Feruccio (fär-rōōt′chō bōōzō′nē), 1866–1924, Italian pianist and composer. He transcribed for piano much of Bach's organ music.

Bustamante, Antonio Sánchez de (äntō′nyō sän′chäs dä), 1865–1951, Cuban authority on international law. Drew up a code of international private law.

Butades of Sicyon (bū′tŭdēz, sĭ′shēŏn), c.600 B.C., Greek sculptor, reputedly first to model in clay.

butcher bird: see SHRIKE.

Bute, John Stuart, 3d earl of, 1713–92, English Tory prime minister (1761–63). Confidant of George III, endorsed his aims of supremacy of monarchy, destruction of Whig monopoly, end of war with France. Unpopular Treaty of Paris after declaration of war on Spain (1762) led to his resignation.

Bute, island and county, Scotland: see BUTESHIRE.

Butenandt, Adolf (ä′dôlf bōō′tŭnänt), 1903–, German biochemist. Determined structure of progestin, female sex hormone; isolated and named androsterone, male sex hormone. Declined 1939 Nobel Prize because of Nazi doctrines.

Buteshire (būt′shĭr) or **Bute,** insular county (218 sq. mi.; pop. 19,285), in the Firth of Clyde, W Scotland; co. town Rothesay. ARRAN and Bute largest islands. Agr. chief occupation; cattle and sheep raised; fishing. Scenery attracts tourists.

Butler, Irish noble family. **Thomas Butler, 10th earl of Ormonde,** 1532–1614, was first of family to become Protestant. Supported movement against Shane O'Neill and had bitter quarrel with earl of Desmond. Made lieutenant governor of Ireland 1597. **James Butler, 12th earl and 1st duke of Ormonde,** 1610–88, was most powerful royalist influence in Ireland during Puritan Revolution. Succeeded earl of Strafford in command of army in Ireland and defeated rebels. Made lord lieuten-

ant 1643. Gave up office after concluding peace with Parliament 1647. Proclaimed Charles II as king of Ireland 1649. After 1660 was again lord lieutenant. Attacked by duke of Buckingham and then earl of Shaftesbury, he was removed from office by intrigue 1684. His son, **Thomas Butler, earl of Ossory,** 1634–80, distinguished himself in naval battles with the Dutch 1665, 1672. Was lieutenant general in Ireland after 1665. His son, **James Butler, 2d duke of Ormonde,** 1665–1745, supported William III and fought at battle of the Boyne. Was lord lieutenant of Ireland (1703–06, 1710–13) and commander in chief of army. Involved in plot to prevent accession of George I, he was impeached 1715. Fled to France, took part in Jacobite rising 1715, and spent rest of his life in exile.

Butler, Benjamin Franklin, 1818–93, American politician and Union general in Civil War. Commander in capture of New Orleans and military governor of city (1862), unpopular with Southerners. In U.S. Congress (1867–75), as radical Republican, was supporter of Reconstruction policy and a leader in impeachment of Pres. Johnson.

Butler, Ellis Parker, 1869–1937, American humorist, best known for sketch *Pigs Is Pigs* (1906).

Butler, Howard Crosby, 1872–1922, American archaeologist. Engaged in excavations at Sardis, in archaeological investigations in Syria.

Butler, James: see BUTLER, family.

Butler, John, 1728–96, Loyalist commander in American Revolution. Organized troop called Butler's Rangers. Defeated Zebulon Butler in Wyoming Valley (1778); Indian allies perpetrated Wyoming Valley massacre. His son, **Walter Butler,** 1752?–1781, also a Loyalist, fought with his father and led Cherry Valley massacre (1778).

Butler, Joseph, 1692–1752, English theologian, bishop of Bristol and later of Durham. His *Analogy of Religion, Natural and Revealed, to the Constitution and Course of Nature* (1736) was written to combat deism in England.

Butler, Nicholas Murray, 1862–1947, American educator, president of COLUMBIA UNIVERSITY (1902–45). Largely responsible for expansion of Columbia Col. into Columbia Univ. His efforts in behalf of international peace won him world-wide prestige.

Butler, Samuel, 1612–80, English satiric poet, author of mock romance *Hudibras* (1663–78; against Puritan hypocrisy).

Butler, Samuel, 1835–1902, English author. Spent some years in New Zealand, and New Zealand scenery appears in his utopian *Erewhon; or, Over the Range* (1872) and *Erewhon Revisited* (1901) [anagram of nowhere]. His novel, *The Way of All Flesh* (1903), is an astringent attack on Victorian family life. His notebooks, bitter and overfrank notations, have been until the present time only partially published.

Butler, Thomas: see BUTLER, family.

Butler, Walter: see BUTLER, JOHN.

Butler, Zebulon, 1731–95, American colonial leader. Military leader of Conn. settlers in Wyoming Valley. Defeated by Loyalists under John Butler in 1778.

Butler, city (pop. 23,482), W Pa., N of Pittsburgh, in coal, oil, and limestone area; settled c.1800. Makes glass and metal products and auto trailers.

Butler University: see INDIANAPOLIS, Ind.

Butte (būt), city (pop. 33,251; alt. 5,775 ft.), SW Mont., SSW of Helena; founded 1864. First a gold, then a silver town, it developed further with copper discovery (c.1880) and paralleled growth of Anaconda Copper Mining Co. Now state's second largest city and a leading U.S. copper center, with by-product (lead, arsenic, fertilizer) and smelting plants, it also mines zinc and manganese. Seat of Montana School of Mines (see Univ. of MONTANA).

butte, isolated hill, steep-sided and flat-topped, a remnant of erosion. Common in W U.S., Badlands.

butter, nourishing dairy product made by agitating cream or milk to unite the fat globules. Cows' milk is generally the basis, but that of goats, sheep, and mares has been used. Exclusively farm made until c.1850, it has become increasingly a factory product. The use of a starter culture of bacteria has generally replaced natural fermentation of cream; sweet (unsalted) butter is made of sweet cream. Clarified butter (called ghee in India) is much used in Eastern lands.

butter-and-eggs or **toadflax,** weedy perennial (*Linaria vulgaris*) introduced to U.S. from Eurasia. Yellow and orange flowers resemble small snapdragons.

buttercup or **crowfoot,** any *Ranunculus* species with yellow flowers and deeply cut foliage. Often weedy, but a few, e.g., florists' ranunculus and creeping buttercup, are grown for cutting and in gardens.

butterfly, insect of group comprising, with moths, order Lepidoptera. Broad membranous scaled wings. Four-stage life cycle: egg, larva, pupa, adult. Bodies more slender and smoother than in moths, antennae enlarged at tip (in moths, often feathery, rarely knobbed), when at rest wings held vertically (in moths horizontally), chiefly diurnal (moth largely nocturnal).

butterfly flower or **poor-man's-orchid,** showy annual (*Schizanthus*). Grown in greenhouse or garden.

butterfly weed or **pleurisy root,** handsome MILKWEED (*Asclepias tuberosa*) of U.S. Often cultivated for its terminal clusters of bright orange flowers.

butternut, deciduous North American tree (*Juglans cinerea*), also called white walnut, and its fruit, an edible nut. Dye from nut husks used by early settlers.

Butterworth, Hezekiah, 1839–1905, American author of juvenile stories, editor (1870–94) of the *Youth's Companion.*

buttons, knoblike appendages on clothing, either for ornament or fastening. First became important in 10th cent., though used occasionally in Greece and Rome. In 16th cent. their increasing magnificence led many Puritans to use hook-and-eye fastenings in protest. Innumerable materials, from wood, metal, shell, and bone to gems and coins, have been used.

buttonwood: see PLANE TREE.

Butyl rubber: see RUBBER, SYNTHETIC.

Butzer, Martin: see BUCER, MARTIN.

Buxar (bŭksär′), village, W Bihar, India. British won Bengal by defeat of Nawab of Oudh here (1764).

Buxtehude, Dietrich (dē′trĭkh bŏŏks″tŭhōō′- dŭ), 1637–1707, Swedish organist at Lübeck. Chiefly composed choral preludes, passacaglias, and fugues for organ.

Buxton, Sir Thomas Fowell, 1786–1845, English reformer. As member of Parliament led in abolishing (1833) slavery in British colonies.

Buys-Ballot, Christoph Heinrich Diedrich (bois′-bälō′), 1817–90, Dutch meteorologist. Strove to organize standard system for representing meteorological findings. Formulated Buys-Ballot's law: if one stands with his back to wind, low pressure area is to his left. Reverse is true in S Hemisphere.

Buzau (bŏŏzû′ŏŏ), town (pop. 43,365), SE Rumania. Oil refineries, foundries, flour mills.

buzzard, name for certain hawks and vultures. In S U.S. are turkey VULTURE or turkey buzzard, black vulture or black buzzard. Red-tailed, red-shouldered, broad-wing hawks called buzzards.

Buzzards Bay, inlet of the Atlantic, 30 mi. long and 5–10 mi. wide, SE Mass., connected with Cape Cod Bay by Cape Cod Canal and bounded on SE by Elizabeth Isls. **Buzzards Bay,** village (pop. 1,459), seat of Cape Cod Canal Administration, is in Bourne town.

Byblos (bĭb′lŭs), city of anc. Phoenicia, a port near present Beyrouth, Lebanon; biblical Gebal (modern Jebail). It was a center for worship of Adonis. Because of its papyri, it was the source of the Greek word for book (and English words such as Bible, bibliography).

Bydgoszcz (bĭd′gôshch), Ger. *Bromberg,* city (pop. 134,614), NW Poland, on Bydgoszcz Canal (part of Oder-Vistula waterway). Trade center. Passed to Prussia 1772; restored to Poland 1919. Lignite and salt deposits near by.

Byel-. For Russian names beginning thus, see BEL-.

bylini (bĭlē′nē), Russian narrative and heroic poems which were handed down by word of mouth from 11th cent. and began to be collected and studied in 18th cent. The largest cycle has Prince Vladimir of Kiev and the fabulous warrior Ilya of Murom as central figures. Among other cycles, that of Novgorod is most important.

Byng, George: see TORRINGTON, GEORGE BYNG, VISCOUNT.

Byng, John, 1704–57, British admiral; son of Viscount Torrington. Was shot for abandoning his task after defeat by French while attempting to relieve Minorca (1756). Sentence caused much indignation.

Byng, Julian Hedworth George, 1st Viscount Byng of Vimy, 1862–1935, British general. In World War I Canadian troops under his command stormed (1917) Vimy Ridge. He served as governor general of Canada 1921–26.

Byrd, Richard Evelyn (bûrd), 1888–, American aviator and polar explorer. Took part in notable polar and transatlantic flights from 1925. Led expeditions to Antarctica (1929,

1933). From base at LITTLE AMERICA he moved 123 mi. closer to South Pole to spend several winter months alone making observations (1933). Led government expeditions to Antarctic (1939–40, 1946–47). He has published records of his various experiences. His brother, **Harry Flood Byrd**, 1887–, is U.S. Senator from Va. (1933–). A conservative Democrat, he opposed New Deal and Truman administration.

Byrd, William, b. 1542 or 1543, d. 1623, English composer and organist. He composed both Anglican and Roman Catholic church music; also music for the virginal and other instruments. Also Bird, Byrde.

Byrd, William, 1674–1744, American colonial writer, planter, government official in Va. Owned extensive lands. Such writings as *A History of the Dividing Line* and *A Journey to the Land of Eden* are much admired for style and wit.

Byrne, Donn (bûrn), 1889–1928, Irish-American author, b. Brooklyn, N.Y., studied in Ireland. Among his tales are *Messer Marco Polo* (1921), *Blind Raftery* (1924). Full real name Brian Oswald Donn-Byrne.

Byrnes, James F(rancis), 1879–, U.S. Secretary of State (1945–47). Governor of S.C. (1951–).

Byron, George Gordon Noel Byron, 6th Baron (bī'rŭn), 1788–1824, English romantic poet, epitome of the romantic in his irregular life and his emotion-charged poetry. Lame from birth, left fatherless in 1791, he grew to be a dark, handsome man, beloved by and contemptuous of women. Lord Byron's name was linked with those of various women before and after his ill-fated marriage (1815–16) to Anne Isabella Milbanke. In 1819 he formed a liaison with Countess Teresa Guiccioli. Restlessly wandering about the Continent, he was fired by various causes and died while working for Greek independence. He wrote long romances and stories in verse such as *Childe Harold* (1812–18), *The Giaour* (1813), *The Bride of Abydos* (1813), *Manfred* (1817), *Mazeppa* (1819), and *Cain* (1821; much criticized for skepticism toward religion). He was also a master of satire, as in *English Bards and Scotch Reviewers* (1809), *The Vision of Judgment* (1822), and his masterpiece, *Don Juan* (1819–24). Shorter pieces (e.g., *The Prisoner of Chillon*) and lyrics are familiar works today.

Bytom, Upper Silesia: see BEUTHEN.

Bytown, Ont.: see OTTAWA.

Byzantine architecture (bĭ'zŭntēn, –tĭn, bĭzăn'-tĭn), style of building which developed after Byzantium (Constantinople) had been made cap. of the Roman Empire (A.D. 330). It crystallized in Ravenna and Constantinople and spread through Greece and the Balkans to Asia Minor, and ultimately to Russia. The style was the product of Roman methods of construction modified by the use of colorful materials and adornments. Under Justinian (527–65) it achieved its first definitive expression in the Church of San Vitale at Ravenna and the renowned HAGIA SOPHIA. The second phase of the style, in which Eastern influences became apparent, is represented by SAINT MARK'S CHURCH at Venice. In its later

phases, Byzantine architecture became more ornate in design and decoration, as in Moscow cathedral.

Byzantine art, an art blended of Hellenistic and Oriental traditions which flourished under the Byzantine Empire. It began to develop in the 2d cent. A.D., reaching its first Golden Age c.330. Except for the interruption caused by iconoclasm, the style persisted until the fall of Constantinople in 1453. It emphasized decorativeness, neglecting plasticity in favor of flat-line harmony. Sculpture was characterized by flat, even relief, with delicate, lacy designs. Mosaics reached a high point in the 6th-cent. cathedrals at Ravenna.

Byzantine Empire, successor state to the Roman Empire (see ROME), also called Eastern or East Roman Empire; named for its cap., CONSTANTINOPLE, the anc. Byzantium. The division of the Roman Empire into East and West became permanent in 395, although after the fall of West Rome (476) the Eastern emperors claimed succession to the entire Roman world. The core of the Byzantine Empire was Asia Minor and the S Balkan Peninsula. Throughout its 1,000 years of existence, the empire was beset by foreign invaders—Goths, Huns, Avars, Persians, Bulgars, Slavs, Arabs, Normans, Seljuk Turks, Serbs, the French, Italians, and Ottoman Turks. Its boundaries shifted according to military fortunes and to the vigor of central authority. Religious controversy played a major part in Byzantine history and was frequently interwoven with party strife (see BLUES AND GREENS; NESTORIANISM; MONOPHYSITISM; MONOTHELETISM, ICONOCLASM; PHOTIUS; ORTHODOX EASTERN CHURCH). With all its weaknesses, dissensions, court intrigues, and corruption, the empire possessed astonishing powers of recuperation and survival; it carried on the Graeco-Roman civilization, blended with Oriental influences, at a time when the West was in chaos. The first era of recuperation came under JUSTINIAN I, who recovered Italy and Africa, codified ROMAN LAW, and encouraged Hellenism. Byzantine art and architecture entered their most glorious period (6th cent.). His successors lost most of ITALY to the Lombards, and Syria, Palestine, Egypt, Africa, and Sicily to the Arabs. The reign of IRENE saw the coronation of Charlemagne as emperor of the West (800), and the schism between the Roman and the Eastern Church followed soon afterward, effectually destroying Roman universality. A new period of splendor and vigorous government was inaugurated by BASIL I (9th cent.) but ended with the Turkish victory at MANZIKERT (1071). After a brief resurgence under ALEXIUS I, a century of decay ended with the breakup of the empire under the impact of the Fourth Crusade (1204; see CRUSADES). However, the Latin Empire of CONSTANTINOPLE proved even less stable than the surviving Byzantine splinter states of NICAEA, TREBIZOND, and EPIRUS; in 1261 MICHAEL VIII of Nicaea recaptured Constantinople and restored the empire. For two centuries the ever-shrinking state held out against the Ottoman Turks, vainly begging the West for aid. At last, after a desperate defense under

CONSTANTINE XI, Constantinople fell to Mohammed II (1453), and Turkey fell heir to Byzantium. The modern era is generally reckoned from that day.

Byzantine music, now regarded as an independent musical culture that flourished between the 4th and 15th cent., reached its golden age in the 7th cent. Although some Greek instruments were used, the organ was most important. Almost all extant Byzantine music is liturgical. Its principal form was the hymn; texts were usually biblical. Byzantine chant attempted to depict melodical meaning of the words. Notation was originally only a series of symbols serving to remind the singer of a melody he already knew. Later a staffless notation indicating starting note and subsequent intervals of a melody was used.

Byzantium (bĭzăn′shĕŭm), anc. city, on site of present Istanbul; trade center founded by Greeks 658 B.C. Taken by Rome (A.D. 196), it was chosen by Constantine I (330) as site for CONSTANTINOPLE, later cap. of Byzantine Empire.

C, chemical symbol of the element CARBON.

Ca, chemical symbol of the element CALCIUM.

Caaba: see KAABA.

Cabal (kŭbăl′), secret group of advisers of Charles II of England (hence, any secret, conniving clique). Their initials form the word—Clifford of Chudleigh, Ashley (Lord Shaftesbury), Buckingham (George Villiers), Arlington (Henry Bennet), and Lauderdale (John Maitland).

cabala or **cabbala** (both: kǎ′bŭlů) [Heb.,= the received], a system of interpretation of the Scriptures based on the assumption that every word and letter in them has an occult meaning. It arose in the 7th cent. and lasted into the 18th. This attempt to spiritualize formal Judaism grew in an era of severe persecution. It held that all originates in God, that evil is the result of distance from God, that man's soul exists from eternity, and that if pure, the soul overcomes evil. The names of God were thought to have magical powers. Cabala supposedly contained Christian doctrines, and was taken up by Christians at various times. The principal sources of cabala are the *Sefer Yezirah* (Eng. tr., *Book of Creation*), which sets forth a system of numerical interpretation and the doctrine of emanation, and the *Zohar* [Heb.,= splendor], which develops these ideas further. Written by Moses de Leon (13th cent.), the *Zohar* is attributed by him to Simon ben Yohai (2d cent.).

cabbage, leafy garden vegetable (*Brassica oleracea capitata*) with white, green, or red leaves. It is derived from wild cabbage and allied to KALE, BRUSSELS SPROUTS, CAULIFLOWER, and BROCCOLI.

cabbage palm, popular name for several palm species with central edible buds (see PALMETTO PALM).

cabbala: see CABALA.

Cabell, James Branch (kǎ′bůl), 1879–, American novelist. Some novels (notably *Jurgen,* 1919) are set in imaginary medieval land (Poictesme). Also author of critical essays. Wrote both as Branch Cabell and James Branch Cabell.

Cabet, Étienne (ātyĕn′ käbā′), 1788–1856, French utopian socialist and reformer. In exile (1834–39) in England, he wrote description of ideal society, *Voyage en Icarie* (1840). Urged state control of all economy and social life. Founded several communistic settlements in U.S. Settlers called Icarians.

Cabeza de Vaca, Álvar Núñez (äl′vär nŏŏ′nyäth käbā′thä dä vä′kä), c.1490–c.1557, Spanish explorer. Wandered through American Southwest (1534–36) after shipwreck off Texas coast. Deposed as governor of colony in Paraguay (1544).

Cabinda (kůbĭn′dů), autonomous district (c.2,-800 sq. mi.; pop. 46,277) of ANGOLA, separated from Angola proper by a strip belonging to Belgian Congo.

Cabiri (kůbī′rī), Greek fertility gods, worshiped with mysteries at Samothrace.

Cable, George Washington, 1844–1925, American author of romantic novels, stories of La. (as in collection, *Old Creole Days,* 1879); novel (*The Grandissimes,* 1880).

cable. Once a term for fibrous rope and now applied to transoceanic telegraph message; to telephone-telegraph line of intertwisted strands in insulating sheath; to chain, heavy rope, or plaited wire used to anchor, moor, or tow ships; to twisted wire rope with many engineering uses; to wire conveying electricity from source to consumer; and to intercity coaxial telephone, telegraph, and television line. The coaxial cable (which permits simultaneous transmission of many signals) consists of a copper tube through the center of which extends a copper wire held in place by insulating disks; a number of such units are enclosed in insulating material.

Cabochiens (käbōshyĕ′), popular faction in Paris in early 15th cent. Mostly tradespeople chafing at heavy taxation, they sided with Burgundians in civil war between ARMA-

GNACS AND BURGUNDIANS, seized control of Paris in 1413, passed radical reforms (*ordonnance cabochienne*). Suppressed by Armagnacs 1413.

Cabot, John, fl. 1461–98, English explorer, probably b. Genoa, Italy. Under patent granted by Henry VII, he sailed W from Bristol (1497), presumably seeking access to riches of Far East, and reached North American coast. He set out on second exploratory expedition (1498) whose fate is unknown. English claims in North America were based on his discovery. His son, **Sebastian Cabot**, b. 1483–86?, d. 1557?, was explorer in Spanish service (1512–48). Explored (1526–30) Río de la Plata country; later reentered English service; as governor of Muscovy Co. was responsible for commercial treaty with Russia.

Cabral, Pedro Alvares (äl'vŭrĭsh käbräl'), c.1460–1526?, Portuguese navigator. Commanded fleet destined for India (1500), went far west of his course, reached coast of Brazil which he claimed for Portugal. Finally reached Calicut but roused native ire by highhanded practices in trade and religion. His landing in Brazil, accidental or prearranged, was not the first European visit to Brazil, though the question of discovery is still argued.

Cabrillo, Juan Rodríguez (hwän rōdhrē'gäth käbrē'lyō), d. 1543, Spanish conquistador, discoverer of California (1542), b. Portugal.

Cabrillo National Monument: see NATIONAL PARKS AND MONUMENTS (table).

Cabrini, Saint Frances Xavier (kŭbrē'nē), 1850–1917, American nun, b. Italy; first U.S. citizen to be canonized (1946). Founded Missionary Sisters of the Sacred Heart of Jesus, and after coming to the U.S. (1889) worked with the poor and the sick. Feast: Dec. 22.

cacao (kŭkā'ō), tropical American tree (*Theobroma cacao*), bearing pods containing cocoa beans of commerce. After drying, the seeds are screened, roasted, and skinned, resulting in clean kernels known as cocoa nibs, which are made into various products, e.g., edible CHOCOLATE and cocoa, and cocoa butter, used medicinally and in cosmetics. Exported mainly from South and Central America, British West Africa, and West Indies.

Caccini, Giulio (jōō'lyō kät-chē'nē), c.1558–c.1618, Italian composer. With Peri, he composed *Dafne* (c.1597), the first actual opera on record.

Cáceres (kä'thäräs), city (27,463), cap. of Cáceres prov., W Spain, in Estremadura. Cork mfg. Roman and Moorish walls and towers.

cactus, succulent plant, either small or treelike, of family Cactaceae, native to New World. It is characterized by fleshy green stem (leaves inconspicuous or absent), showy flowers, and colorful fruit, often edible (e.g., PRICKLY PEAR) and is adapted to high temperatures and arid regions. Among the cacti are NIGHT-BLOOMING CEREUS, cholla, PEYOTE, and Christmas cactus.

Cadamosto or **Cada Mosto, Luigi da** (lwē'jē dä kädämō'stō), 1432?–1480?, Venetian navigator in Portuguese service, from about 1454. Left a valuable record of Portuguese

activity in Canary Isls., and may have been discoverer of Cape Verde Isls. (1456 or 1457).

Caddoan (kă'dōŭn), linguistic family of North America, embracing many Indian tribes in the West and the South. See LANGUAGE, table.

Cade, Jack, d. 1450, English rebel, leader of uprising in S England in 1450. Grievances were mainly political. Rebels defeated royal army and entered London. Government pardoned (and so dispersed) Cade's men, but executed him.

Cadillac, Antoine de la Mothe (kä'dĭlăk, Fr. ätwän' dù lä môt' kädēyäk'), c.1658–1730, French colonial governor of territory of Louisiana (1713–16), founder of Detroit (1701).

Cadillac, resort city (pop. 10,425), N Mich., SE of Traverse City and on L. Cadillac, in agr. area; settled c.1871. Trading post was estab. by Cadillac. Mfg. of vehicle parts. Indian mounds and winter sports area near by.

Cádiz (Sp. kä'dēth), city (pop. 87,630), cap. of Cádiz prov., SW Spain, in Andalusia; Atlantic port and fortified naval base. Founded c.1100 B.C. by Phoenicians as Gadir, taken by Carthage c.500 B.C. Continued to flourish under Romans, who took it 3d cent. B.C. and called it Gades. Reconquered from Moors by Castile (1262), it prospered again after discovery of America. In 1587 Drake burned Spanish fleet in Cádiz harbor; in 1596 Essex devastated the city. During Peninsular War Cádiz successfully resisted French siege 1810–1812, was seat of Spanish Cortes.

Cadman, Charles Wakefield, 1881–1946, American composer, best known for the songs *From the Land of the Sky-blue Water* and *At Dawning*. Among his other works are the operas *Shanewis* and *A Witch of Salem*.

cadmium (kăd'mēŭm), metallic element (symbol = Cd; see also ELEMENT, table). White, lustrous, very malleable and ductile; like tin in physical properties, zinc in chemical. Forms oxide, hydroxide, carbonate, chloride, sulphide. Occurs in nature in compounds. Used to make low-melting-point alloys.

Cadmus, in Greek legend, son of Agenor and founder of Thebes; honored as inventor of alphabet.

Cadogan, William Cadogan, 1st Earl, 1675–1726, British general, diplomat. Friend of duke of MARLBOROUGH, aided him in War of the SPANISH SUCCESSION.

Cadorna, Luigi (lwē'jē kädôr'nä), 1850–1928, Italian field marshal in World War I. Took Gorizia 1916. Routed at Caporetto 1917.

Cadoudal, Georges (zhôrzh' kädōōdäl'), 1771–1804, French royalist conspirator. Leader of counterrevolutionists in Vendée and of plot (1803) to oust Bonaparte. Cadoudal was executed, as was the duc d'ENGHIEN, who was unjustly linked to the plot.

caduceus (kŭdū'sēŭs), wing-topped staff, with two snakes winding about it, carried by Hermes. As symbol of fertility, wisdom, and healing, it appeared early in Babylonia. Hermes' staff was carried by Greek heralds and ambassadors and became a Roman symbol of truce and neutrality. Since 16th cent. it has replaced one-snake symbol of Asclepius for medicine. By regulation, it has since 1902 been insignia of medical branch of U.S. Army.

Cadwaladr or **Cadwallader** (both: kădwä'-lŭdŭr), semi-legendary British king, leader against Anglo-Saxons in 7th cent.

Cædmon (kăd'mŭn), fl. 670, first English Christian poet and first English poet known by name. BEDE, *Ecclesiastical History*, tells how Cædmon, lay brother in abbey of Whitby, was divinely inspired to compose his first work, a brief hymn, and gives Latin version. Other poems described by Bede not extant.

Caen (kä), town (pop. 47,835), cap. of Calvados dept., N France, in Normandy. Textile and lace mfg. Favorite residence of William the Conqueror. Center of heavy fighting (June-July, 1944) in World War II. William's castle and the university (founded 1432) were destroyed, but the famous Abbaye aux Hommes [men's abbey], with William's tomb, the Abbaye aux Dames [ladies' abbey], and the Church of St. Nicholas were preserved. All three are gems of 11th-cent. Norman architecture.

Caerleon (kärlē'ŭn), urban district (pop. 4,711), Monmouthshire, England. Has extensive remains of Roman fortress Isca. Village often identified with Camelot of Arthurian legend.

Caermarthenshire or **Carmarthenshire** (both: kŭrmär'dhŭnshĭr), maritime county (920 sq. mi.; pop. 171,742), S Wales. Largest of Welsh counties, it is mostly hilly. Chief occupations agr. and grazing, but industrial S Wales coal fields extend into SE corner. Iron, copper, and lead also mined. The county town, **Caermarthen** or **Carmarthen** (pop. 12,121), has castle once headquarters of Welsh chieftains.

Caernarvonshire or **Carnarvonshire** (both: kŭrnär'vŭnshĭr, kär-), maritime county (569 sq. mi.; pop. 124,074), NW Wales. Region is largely mountainous; Snowden (3,560 ft.) highest peak in England and Wales. Sheep farming, quarrying, and mining (lead, zinc, and manganese) are the chief industries. County town is **Caernarvon** or **Carnarvon** (pop. 9,255), where the prince of Wales is invested. Its castle is fine example of a medieval fortress.

Caesalpinus, Andreas (ăn'drĕŭs sĕsălpī'nŭs), Latinized from **Andrea Cesalpino**, 1519–1603, Italian botanist and physiologist. He described in part the circulation of blood and developed the first classification of plants according to their fruits.

Caesar (sē'zŭr), name used by a patrician family of Rome. The careers of Julius Caesar and the adopted Augustus led to giving the name an imperial character. It was in the later Roman empire the title given to the subemperor, who would presumably later become the emperor. The title reappeared later as the German *Kaiser* and the Russian *Czar* or *Tsar*.

Caesar, (Caius) Julius, 102? B.C.–44 B.C., Roman statesman, one of the most renowned military commanders in world history. He came of a noble family and married Cornelia, the daughter of Cinna, colleague of Caesar's uncle by marriage, MARIUS, whose party he joined. In the hour of Sulla's triumph Caesar was proscribed. On Sulla's death he began his political career in earnest, becoming the champion of the people against the senate. As pontifex maximus he instituted important reforms in the calendar, creating the Julian calendar. He divorced his second wife, Pompeia, who was involved in a scandal with Clodius, and said "Caesar's wife must be above suspicion." He later married Calpurnia. After service in Spain he returned to Rome (60 B.C.) and organized the First Triumvirate, with POMPEY and CRASSUS. He mediated between his colleagues and himself took command in Gaul, where his prosecution of the GALLIC WARS (58 B.C.–49 B.C.) estab. his reputation as one of the great military commanders of all time. He ended by a journey of conquest in Britain, where he planted Roman power. Again in Gaul, he put down the uprising led by Vercingetorix and made Roman power secure. In 54 B.C. his daughter Julia, wife of Pompey, died, and from that time on rivalry between Pompey, who became the champion of the senatorial party, and Caesar, the popular leader, grew. The death of Crassus set the two face to face (53 B.C.). The senate, fearing Caesar's power, moved to take away his army command. He agreed to submit if Pompey would surrender his. This reply caused the senate to demand (quite illegally) that he disband his army immediately. Two tribunes, Marc ANTONY and CASSIUS, vetoed the bill and fled to Caesar. He made the fateful decision to defy the senate and signalized it by leading his army across the small river Rubicon (49 B.C.). Civil war began. Caesar marched triumphantly to Rome, then pursued Pompey until he conquered him on the plain of Pharsala in Greece (48 B.C.). He followed the defeated Pompey to Egypt and there had a love affair with Cleopatra. From Egypt he went to Pontus and defeated Pharnaces II with an easy victory recorded in his words "Veni, vidi, vici" [I came, I saw, I conquered]. Returning to Rome, he exercised the dictatorial powers granted him, though he refused the title of king, preferring to remain only consul, dictator, and general (44 B.C.). His social reforms won popular support, but his enemies and some of his followers resented his autocratic rule. A conspiracy was formed against him, largely by men he had befriended, most notably M. Junius BRUTUS, Cassius, Casca, and Cimber. Just as he was preparing to leave to conduct war against Parthia, he was stabbed to death in the senate on the Ides of March (March 15), 44 B.C. His will left his money and power to his grandnephew Octavius, who was to become Emperor Augustus after he and Marc Antony had avenged Caesar's murder. The character and achievements of Julius Caesar are still hotly debated by scholars. His military and literary gifts (his *Gallic Wars* and *Civil War* are masterpieces) are unquestioned, but whether he was a purely self-seeking opportunistic lover of power, a man dedicated to the redemption of the poor and rejected, the patriot restoring the glory of Rome, or something else is still an open question.

Caesarea (sĕsûrē'ù), name given to various anc. cities to honor the Roman Caesars. Among the most important were: Caesarea in Mauretania, a flourishing trade center (on the site of present Cherchel, Algeria) until sacked by the Vandals in the 5th cent.; Caesarea Mazaca or Caesarea of Cappadocia (on the site of present Kayseri, Turkey), a trade center and residence of Cappadocian kings; Caesarea Palestinae, in S. Palestine, the capital of Herod the Great and scene of massacre of Jewish citizens by Romans (A.D. 66); and Caesarea Philippi, in N Palestine, at foot of Mt. Hermon, built by Philip the Tetrarch, visited by Jesus.

Caesarean section or **Cesarean section** (both: sēzâ'rēùn), removal of child from uterus through abdominal incision; so named because of legend that Julius Caesar was delivered thus. Can be performed more than once.

Caesarion: see PTOLEMY XIV.

Caffa, RSFSR: see FEODOSIYA.

caffeine, alkaloid in coffee, tea, kola nut, cocoa. Acts as a stimulant and diuretic. In tea, known as theine. Can be synthesized from uric acid.

Cagayan (kägī'ùn) or **Rio Grande de Cagayan,** river, 220 mi. long, in central Luzon, Philippines.

Cagliari (kä'lyärē), city (pop. 78,632), cap. of Sardinia, Italy; Mediterranean port. Roman remains; medieval castle.

Cagliostro, Alessandro, Conte (älĕs-sän'drō kōn'tä kälyō'strō), 1743–95, Italian adventurer; real name Giuseppe Balsamo. Traveled all over Europe posing as physician, magician, alchemist. Popular at Louis XVI's court. Implicated in Affair of the DIAMOND NECKLACE; acquitted but banished from France. Condemned by Roman Inquisition as heretic and sorcerer (1789); died in prison.

Cahaba (kùhô'bù), deserted village, SW central Ala., SW of Selma. State cap. 1819–26.

Cahaba, river flowing from mountains NE of Birmingham c.200 mi. SW and S to Alabama R. near Selma.

Cahan, Abraham (kän), 1860–1951, Jewish-American journalist and socialist leader, b. Vilna, a founder and editor in chief of the Jewish *Daily Forward.*

Cahokia (kùhō'kēù), village (pop. 794), SW Ill., on the Mississippi just below East St. Louis. First permanent settlement in Ill., it was named for a tribe of ILLINOIS INDIANS served by French mission estab. here 1699. Became one of chief French centers in upper Mississippi valley; taken by British 1765 and by Americans under Clark 1778. Has several 18th cent. buildings.

Cahors (käôr'), city (pop. 12,706), cap. of Lot dept., S central France, on Lot R.; historic cap. of Quercy. Major medieval banking center; Cahorsin moneylenders rivaled Lombards and Jews. Old town contains medieval cathedral, palaces, and fortifications.

Caiaphas (kā'yùfùs), high priest who presided at council that condemned Jesus to death. Also at trial of Peter and John. Mat. 26.57–

68; John 11.47–54; 18.24; Acts 4.6; Mark 14.53–65; Luke 22.66–71.

Caicos Islands: see TURKS AND CAICOS ISLANDS.

Caillaux, Joseph (zhôzĕf' kāyō'), 1863–1944, French minister of finance (1899, 1906, 1913–14, 1925, 1926) and premier (1911–12). Introduced income tax (1906); reached peaceful settlement of Morocco crisis with Germany (1911), unpopular with nationalists; resigned 1914 after his wife murdered Gaston Calmette, a journalist who had attacked his private life. (She was acquitted.) Caillaux's pacifist sentiments led to his arrest (1917) and imprisonment (1920) for correspondence with the enemy. Restored to citizenship 1924; later served as senator.

Cain, farmer son of Adam and Eve. Known as world's first murderer for killing of brother Abel. Gen. 4.

Cairngorm, group of mountains (includes Ben Macdhui, Braeriach, and Cairngorm, peaks all over 4,000 ft.), forming part of the Grampians, Scotland. Name also given yellow or brown quartz found here.

Cairns, city (pop. 16,644), Queensland, Australia, on Trinity Bay. Chief sugar port of Australia.

Cairo (kī'rō), Arabic *El Kahirah* [the victorious], city (pop. 2,100,486), cap. of Egypt and largest city of Africa, at head of Nile delta. Commercial and mfg. center of Egypt. Near its site was the ancient Roman city of Babylon, and across the river was Memphis, cap. of ancient Egypt. Founded 969 by the Fatimite general Jauhar. Unsuccessfully attacked by Crusaders in 12th cent. Ruled by the Mamelukes from the 13th to early 16th cent. and by the Ottoman Turks, 1517–1798. Occupied by Napoleon, 1798–1801, and by the British, 1882–1936. Mosque of El Azhar houses world's most important Moslem university, founded 972. Seat of Mus. of Antiquities and Royal Library. The great citadel was built c.1179 by Saladin.

Cairo (kā'rō, kâ'rō). **1** City (pop. 5,577), SW Ga., W of Thomasville. Ships sugar cane and syrup. Processes pecans, peanuts, and lumber. **2** City (pop. 12,123), extreme S Ill., on levee-protected tongue of land between Mississippi R. (bridged to Mo.) and Ohio R. (bridged to Ky.). Shipping center for agr. area (esp. cotton), it has mfg. of cottonseed, soybean, and lumber products. Federal depot in Civil War; MOUND CITY, 5 mi. N, was naval base.

Cairo Conference, Nov. 22–25, 1943, meeting of U.S. Pres. Roosevelt, British Prime Minister Churchill, and Chinese Generalissimo Chiang Kai-shek at Cairo, Egypt. They pledged war against Japan until her unconditional surrender, foreswore territorial gains, and promised freedom of territory gained by her since 1895, notably Korea.

caisson (kā'sùn, –sŏn), in engineering, a chamber of steel, wood, or concrete used in constructing foundations or piers in or near water. Types of caissons include open (sunk, and then filled with concrete), pneumatic (air pressure prevents entry of water at cutting edge below, and airtight deck of chamber above is high enough to permit workers under it), and camel (water-filled chamber attached to sunken ship and emptied by compressed air or pump).

caisson disease, disturbances (also known as the bends), owing to tissue injury by nitrogen gas bubbles released from solution by rapid change from high to low pressure. Attacks men who work underwater or in underground chambers.

Caithness (kāth′nĕs), county (686 sq. mi.; pop. 22,705), N Scotland. Coastline is rocky, and much of the county treeless moorland. The county town, Wick, an important herring fishing center.

Caius, John (kēz), 1510–73, English physician who endowed Gonville Hall, renaming it Gonville and Caius College, Cambridge.

Cajal, Santiago Ramón y: see RAMÓN Y CAJAL.

Cajamarca (kähämär′kä), city (pop. 15,553; alt. 9,022 ft.), N Peru. Here Francisco Pizarro captured Atahualpa.

Cajetan (kä′jútăn) [Latin,= from Gaeta], 1470–1534, Italian churchman; originally named Giacomo de Vio. Made the general of the Dominicans (1508), he became a cardinal (1517). He tried to keep Luther in the Church and opposed the divorce of Henry VIII from Katharine of Aragon. Noted as a scholar.

Cajuns: see ACADIA.

Calabria (kälä′brēä), region (5,828 sq. mi.; pop. 1,771,651), S Italy, forming "toe" of Italian boot; cap. Reggio di Calabria. Mountainous, arid, economically backward. Agr., grazing, fruit growing, sericulture. Anc. BRUTTIUM, the region was renamed Calabria in Middle Ages. Conquered by Normans in 11th cent.; later shared history of kingdom of NAPLES.

caladium (kúlä′dēúm), tropical American plant (*Caladium*). Colorful foliage marked with white, purple, or rose. Popular summer bedding and pot plant.

Calais (Fr. kälā′), city (pop. 41,536), Pas-de-Calais dept., N France; a Channel port on Strait of Dover. Held by England 1347–1558. Edward III, who captured it in 1347, promised to spare the town if six prominent citizens offered their lives. The mayor and five others volunteered; the king relented. Monument by Rodin commemorates the event. City partly destroyed in World War II.

Calais (kăl′ĭs), city (pop. 4,589), SE Maine, on St. Croix R. opposite St. Stephen, N.B. On St. Croix Isl. in the river below Calais the sieur de Monts and Champlain planted a settlement, 1604.

calamander wood: see EBONY.

Calamatta, Luigi (lwē′jē kälämät′tä), 1802–69, Italian engraver. A pupil of Ingres, he became one of the leading engravers in France.

Calamian Islands (kälämyän′), group (c.600 sq. mi.; pop. 16,445), between Mindoro and Palawan. Produces rice and manganese.

Calamis (kä′lümĭs), 5th cent. B.C., Greek sculptor.

Calamity Jane, c. 1852–1903, American frontier character. Maiden name was Martha Jane Canary; origin of nickname is obscure. Lived in Deadwood, S.Dak. Went into show business.

Calamy, Edmund, 1600–1666, English Presbyterian preacher, a leader of Puritan thought.

Ejected from ministry by Act of Uniformity (1662).

Calatrava (käläträ′vä), ruined village, central Spain, near Ciudad Real. Original seat of powerful military religious order of **Knights of Calatrava,** founded 1158 by Cistercians as defense against Moors. Order declined after 13th cent.

Calcasieu (kăl′kùsoo″), river rising in W central La. and flowing c.215 mi. S through L. Charles and Calcasieu L. (20 mi. long) to Gulf of Mexico. Partly navigable; connects with Intracoastal Waterway.

calceolaria (kăl″sēōlâr′ĕú) or **slipperwort,** herbaceous or shrubby plant (*Calceolaria*), with showy pouch-shaped flowers. Most species South American.

calcit (kăl′sĭt), common mineral (calcium carbonate), usually white; its hexagonal crystals show perfect cleavage. Some forms of calcite are CHALK, LIMESTONE, MARBLE, MARL, and STALACTITE.

calcium (kăl′sēúm), silvery-white, relatively soft, active metallic element (symbol = Ca; see also ELEMENT, table). Classed with strontium and barium as metal of alkaline earths. Reacts with water and several elements, forming many compounds. Occurs in nature in widely distributed compounds. Is constituent of most plant and animal matter. Essential for strong bones and teeth; functions in regulation of heart beat and in blood clotting.

calculating machine, device to perform mathematical processes. Simple calculators include SLIDE RULE, ABACUS, and counting rods of John NAPIER. Probably the first adding machine using geared wheels was made by Blaise Pascal 1642. G. W. von Leibniz mechanism multiplied by repeated addition, using stepped wheel (c.1672); commercial version to add, subtract, multiply, and divide, was devised by C. X. Thomas 1820. Later in 19th cent. F. S. Baldwin in U.S. patented type more compact than stepped drum; later it was redesigned by W. J. R. Monroe. Key-driven machine was patented in 1850. D. E. Felt patented key-driven calculator (later developed into comptometer) in 1887. W. S. Burroughs patented key-set adding machine with crank 1888. Charles Babbage designed calculating machine in 1830s, but skills and materials to complete it were unavailable until 20th cent. Vannevar Bush completed mechanical differential analyzer in 1930; later one (1942) operated mechanically or electrically. Complex Computer (1940) embodied telephone-switchboard principle, a prototype of others for government in World War II. Many complex electronic computers developed in subsequent years.

calculus (kăl′kyulús), in higher mathematics, any advanced method, using a notation system peculiar to itself, to solve problems. Familiar calculi are the differential and integral, which together are often called infinitesimal calculus. Differential provides a means of computing the rate of change of a function relative to its independent variable; the difference between two succeeding values is called the increment. When the increment of the variable approaches zero, the ratio of the increment of the function to the increment of the variable approaches a constant figure, called the derivative of the function; the process is called differentiation. Integral calculus starts with given derivative and finds its function (integral).

calculus or **stone**, in medicine, deposit of mineral salts as a hard concretion of stone in body. Common sites are gall and urinary bladders, kidney, joints, and salivary ducts.

Calcutta (kălkŭ′tủ), city (pop. 2,070,619), cap. of West Bengal, India. India's largest city and chief commercial port. Founded by the British in 1690, it was captured 1756 by nawab of Bengal, who killed most of garrison by imprisoning it overnight in a small, stifling room, the notorious "black hole." Retaken 1757 by Clive. Cap. of India, 1833–1912. Industrial center with jute and textile mills. Exports include jute, tea, and mica. Seat of Univ. of Calcutta and Indian Mus.

Calder, Alexander Stirling (kôl′dủr), 1870–1945, American sculptor. His son, **Alexander Calder**, 1898–, is an abstract sculptor, best known for his "mobiles" and "stabiles."

Calderón Bridge (kăldārōn′), over Lerma R., E. of Guadalajara, Mexico, scene of battle 1811) in Mexican revolution against Spain.

Calderón (de la Barca), Pedro (pā′dhrō kăldārōnʹ dā lä bärʹkä), 1600–1681, Spanish dramatist, last great figure of the Golden Age. Wrote cape-and-sword plays, one-act religious plays, and philosophical dramas including the masterpiece, *La vida es sueño* [life is a dream]. Became a priest 1651.

Caldwell, Erskine 1903–, American author of realistic stories and novels, especially about the rural South as in *Tobacco Road* (1932; successfully dramatized) and *God's Little Acre* (1933).

Caldwell. 1 City (pop. 10,487), SW Idaho, on Boise R. and W. of Boise; founded 1883 on Oregon Trail. Ships farm, dairy, livestock products of BOISE PROJECT. Has noted cooperatives. Seat of Col. of Idaho (1891). 2 Borough (pop. 6,270), NE N.J., near Montclair. Mfg. of airplane propellers, clothing, and plastics. Birthplace of Grover Cleveland.

Caleb, warrior-champion of Israel's God and chief spy sent into Canaan. When given his choice of land, Caleb, though past 80, chose region still strongly fortified by Canaanites and drove them out. Num. 13.6; 14; 32,12; Joshua 14.6–14. Name associated with tribe in S Palestine. 1 Sam. 30.14; 1 Chron. 2.18, 19,42,46,48,49.

Caledonia (kă″lĭdō′nẻủ), Roman name for part of Britain lying N of the Firths of Clyde and Forth. Modern rhetorical use usually refers to all of Scotland.

Caledonian Canal, waterway (length 60½ mi.), running from Moray Firth to Loch Linnhe, Scotland. Opened in 1847, it is little used now.

calendar, system of reckoning time, usually based on recurrent natural cycle, e.g., seasons and moon's phases. Since length of solar year is 365 days 5 hr. 48 min. 46 sec. and of lunar year (12 months of 29½ days) is 354 days 8 hr. 48 min., solar and lunar reckonings must be harmonized. Because the year is not exactly divisible by months and days, practice arose of making arbitrary divisions

and inserting (intercalating) extra days or months. Gregorian calendar widely used today evolved from Roman calendar as reformed (45 B.C.) by Julius Caesar. In Julian calendar April, June, September, and November had 30 days; February, 28 days (29 days every fourth year, leap year); and other months, 31 days. In computation of month, days were counted backward from the Kalends (first day), the Ides (fifteenth day of March, May, July, October and thirteenth day of other months), and the Nones (eighth day before the Ides); hence Jan. 10 was fourth of Ides of January. Since Julian year of 365 days 6 hr. was too long, by the 16th cent. the vernal equinox was displaced from March 21 to March 11. Gregory XIII ordained that 10 days be dropped in 1582 and years ending in hundreds be leap years only if divisible by 400. The non-Roman Catholic countries were slow in accepting the Gregorian (New Style) calendar; it was adopted in England in 1752 and by the Eastern Church in the 20th cent. Christian ecclesiastical calendar was based on the belief that Jesus' resurrection was on a Sunday, hence Easter should fall on Sunday. First Council of Nicaea (325) decreed that Easter be the Sunday following the first full moon after the vernal equinox; today date varies from astronomical reckoning because certain factors of lunar period were not considered. Chronology is a major problem in ancient and medieval history because years were commonly identified by rulers. Era system of computing years from fixed date, e.g., birth of Christ, simplifies chronology. Calendars used today include Jewish calendar (12 months plus intercalary month seven times in 19 years) and Moslem lunar calendar with c.33 years to every 32 in Gregorian calendar. See also FRENCH REVOLUTIONARY CALENDAR.

calendula (kủlĕn′dủlủ), annual plant (*Calendula*), also called pot marigold. Has yellow to orange flower heads. The marigold of Shakspere's time.

Calexico (kủlĕk′sĭkō), city (pop. 6,433), SE Calif., in Imperial Valley and opposite Mexicali, Mexico.

calf, golden, idol erected by Israelites on several occasions (e.g., Aaron made one during absence of Moses); Jeroboam placed one at Bethel and one at Dan. Ex. 32; 1 Kings 12.26–32. Calf (or bull) worship recalls cults of Apis in Egypt, Minotaur in Crete.

Calgary (kăl′gủrē), city (pop. 129,060), S. Alta., Canada, on Bow R. near foothills of Rocky Mts. A trade, rail, and industrial center of S. Alta., it has oil refineries, meatpacking plants, and grain elevators. The city began 1875 as a fort of the Northwest Mounted Police.

Calhoun, John Caldwell (kăl″hōōn′), 1782–1850, American statesman and political philosopher. A "war hawk" as U.S. Representative from S.C. (1811–17). U.S. Secretary of War (1817–25); Vice President of U.S. (1825–32). Directed passage of S.C. ordinance of nullification (1832). U.S. Senator (1832–43, 1845–50); U.S. Secretary of State (1844–45). Leading defender of minority Southern cause against commercial, industrial North. Calhoun held that the Constitution estab. a government of concurrent majorities composed of the state governments and the Federal government, with states enjoying rights of veto (or nullification) and secession.

Calhoun, city (pop. 3,231), NW Ga., NNW of Atlanta. New Echota Marker Natl. Memorial, site of Cherokee's last cap. in Ga., is near.

Cali (kä′lē), city (pop. 88,366), W. Colombia; founded 1536 by Benalcázar; important commercial center.

calico, name for plain-weave, cheap cotton cloth, usually printed; derived from Calicut cloth, fabric first imported into England from India, c.1830.

Calicut (kă′lĭkŭt″), city (pop. 126,352), SW Madras, India; port on Arabian Sea. Visited 1498 by Vasco da Gama. Once famed for calico.

California, state (156,803 sq. mi.; pop. 10,586,-223), W U.S.; admitted 1850 as 31st state (free under COMPROMISE OF 1850); cap. SACRAMENTO. Second largest state in area and population. Bordered on S by Mexico, W by the Pacific (1,200-mi. coast), SE by Colorado R. Major ports (largest cities) are LOS ANGELES, SAN FRANCISCO, OAKLAND, SAN DIEGO, LONG BEACH. Calif. has amazing topographical, climatic contrasts. Central Valley is walled on W by COAST RANGES, E by SIERRA NEVADA (highest U.S. elevation is Mt. Whitney; lowest is near Death Valley). In E and SE are vast wastes (e.g., MOJAVE DESERT), with, in contrast, reclaimed IMPERIAL VALLEY. Water supply and control are acute problems (extensive irrigation). Chief industries: petroleum, natural gas, food processing, aircraft, metalworking, textile, movie, fishing, resort. Agr. highly diversified (e.g., fruit, truck, hardy grains). Many minerals produced commercially (e.g., gold, copper). State has several national parks and monuments. Early exploration included voyages of Juan R. CABRILLO (1542), Sir Francis DRAKE (1579), Sebastián VIZCAÍNO (1602). Spanish colonizing began 1769. Control passed to Mexico in 1822. Gradually outsiders such as J. A. SUTTER came by sea and across mountains. Calif. briefly asserted independence in 1836; republic set up at Sonoma under influence of J. C. Frémont (1846). Area finally ceded to U.S. by Treaty of Guadalupe Hidalgo (1848). Gold strike of 1848 and completion of first transcontinental railroad (1869) brought settlers. Population increased sevenfold in 20th cent. due largely to industrial development of S Calif., real-estate boom in 1920s, exodus from Dust Bowl (1936–38), and influx of workers and service personnel in World War II.

California, Gulf of, arm of Pacific, c.700 mi. long, c.100 mi. wide, NW Mexico. Separates peninsula of Lower California from Sonora and Sinaloa. Pearl diving and deep-sea fishing are important.

California, University of, mainly at Berkeley and Los Angeles, with branches at San Francisco and elsewhere; land-grant and state supported, coed. Chartered 1868 and opened 1869 to succeed private Col. of California. Univ. of California at Los Angeles

(UCLA), founded 1881 as normal school, was incorporated 1919. California School of Fine Arts at San Francisco is affiliated. Operates Lick Observatory and Scripps Inst. of Oceanography. Library has Western American history collection of H. H. BANCROFT.

California Institute of Technology: see PASADENA.

California laurel, beautiful evergreen tree (*Umbellularia californica*), native to California and Oregon and known also as Oregon myrtle, pepperwood, and California bay. It has fragrant flowers and aromatic foliage. It yields a volatile oil and the wood is used in boat building.

California poppy, annual or perennial wild flower (*Eschscholtzia californica*) with finely cut gray-green foliage and bright yellow blossoms. Native to the W Coast, it is the state flower of California.

californium, highly radioactive chemical element (symbol = Cf; atomic no.= 98), first produced (1950) in the cyclotron at the Univ. of California.

Caligula (kŭlĭg′yōōlŭ) [little boots], nickname of Caius Caesar Germanicus, A.D. 12–A.D. 41, Roman emperor (A.D. 37–A.D. 41). The son of Germanicus, he got his name from wearing military boots when he was a small boy with his father on the Rhine. He succeeded Tiberius as emperor. An illness had apparently affected his mind, and his rule was one of senseless cruelty and despotism. He is reputed to have expressed regret that all the people did not have a single neck, to be severed with one blow. Also said to have made his horse a consul. He was finally assassinated, and Claudius I succeeded him.

caliphate (kă′lĭfāt), in Islam the office of the caliph (kā′lĭf), head of the theocratic organization as the agent of God. When Mohammed the Prophet died, Abu Bakr was chosen as first caliph. He was succeeded by Omar, Othman, and Ali (the Orthodox caliphs). After Ali's death, Islam split. The Omayyad family became caliphs at Damascus, but were not recognized by the Shiites, who in 750 won the caliphate for the descendants of Ali (the Abbasid family), who ruled from Baghdad. One Omayyad escaped to Spain, where later the Western Caliphate or Caliphate of Córdoba was set up, to last until 1031. A third rival line was supported by the Fatimites in Africa from 909 to 1171. When the Mongols took Baghdad (1258), the Abbasids fled to Egypt, where they nominally continued the caliphate until the Ottomans took Egypt (1517) and Selim I appropriated the title of caliph. This title was used by the Ottoman rulers of Turkey until it was abolished in 1924. See also IMAM.

Calixtines, another name for UTRAQUISTS.

Calixtus I, Saint (kŭlĭk′stŭs), c.160–c.222, pope (c.217–222). Rejected Montanism. Supposedly martyred. Also Callixtus, Callistus. Feast: Oct. 14.

Calixtus II, d. 1124, pope (1119–24). As archbishop of Vienne, he convened a synod (1112) to excommunicate Emperor Henry V. Calixtus triumphed over Henry's antipope Gregory VIII, came to an agreement with

Henry in the Concordat of Worms (1122), and called the First Lateran Council.

Calixtus III, 1378–1458, pope (1455–58), a Spaniard named Alonso de Borja. Aided John Hunyadi in his fight against the Turks and tried to organize a crusade against them. He struggled with Alfonso V of Aragon. Estab. Borgia family in power in Italy.

Call, Richard Keith, 1791–1862, territorial govevnor of Fla. (1836–39, 1841–44). Led campaign against SEMINOLE INDIANS.

calla (kăl'ŭ), South African fleshy-rooted perennial (*Zantedeschia*). It has small flowers in a showy spathe; white in common calla lily, yellow or pink in others. Wild calla (*Calla palustris*) is bog plant of N Temperate Zone.

Callao (käyou'), port (pop. 71,217), W. Peru, just W of Lima; notable Pacific port.

Calleja del Rey, Félix María (fä'lĕks märē'ä kälyä'hä dĕl rā'), 1750–1828?, Spanish general, viceroy of New Spain (1813–16), conde de Calderón. Successfully repressed beginning of revolution against Spain led by Hidalgo y Costilla.

Calles, Plutarco Elías (plōōtär'kō ālē'äs kä'yäs), 1877–1945, Mexican statesman, president (1924–28). Many objectives of revolution of 1910 were consolidated in his administration—agrarian and educational reforms, public works, army reorganization. Later became a conservative and opposed reforms of Lázaro Cárdenas.

Callias (kă'lēŭs), fl. 449 B.C., Athenian statesman. Supposed to have negotiated the Peace of Callias, an agreement which set up "spheres of influence" for Persia and Athens. Peace between the two lasted a half century.

Callicrates (kŭlĭ'krŭtēz), 5th cent. B.C. Greek architect. Helped build Parthenon (447–432 B.C.).

Callimachus (kŭlĭm'ŭkŭs), 2d half of 5th cent. B.C. Greek sculptor who reputedly originated the Corinthian capital.

Callimachus, b. 330? B.C., Hellenistic poet, critic. Among his more than 800 works are a literary catalogue and *Actia*, a collection of legends.

Calliope (kŭlī'ōpē) [Gr.,= beautiful of voice], in Greek mythology, greatest of MUSES, patron of epic poetry and eloquence; mother of ORPHEUS by Apollo.

calliopsis: see COREOPSIS.

Callirrhoë (kŭlĭr'ōē), wife of ALCMAEON.

Callisto (kŭlĭ'stō), in Greek legend, virgin attendant of Artemis. She bore a son, Arcas, to Zeus. As punishment she was transformed into a bear. Zeus later transferred them both to heaven, where she became Ursa Major and Arcas became Arcturus.

Calloc'h, Jean Pierre: see BRETON LITERATURE.

Callot, Jacques (zhäk' kälō'), 1592–1635, French engraver and etcher. Studied in Rome. Famous for ability to group crowds in a small space, as in the splendid series *Miseries of War*.

Calmar, Sweden: see KALMAR.

Calonne, Charles Alexandre de (shärl' älĕksä'drŭ dŭ kälōn'), 1734–1802, French statesman; controller general of finances (1783–87). His spending policy, designed to restore public credit, ended in disaster and hastened FRENCH REVOLUTION.

calorie, metric unit of heat measurement. Small calorie (gram-calorie or therm): heat required to raise temperature of 1 gm. of water at maximum density 1°C. Large or kilogram-calorie; heat required to raise temperature of 1 kg. of water at maximum desity 1°C. Specific heat is number of calories needed to raise temperature of 1 gm. of any substance 1°C. In physics and chemistry term *calorie* usually means small calorie; in dietetics large calorie used to indicate amount of heat energy food can yield. **Calorimeter** determines number of calories given off by substance in combustion or other chemical reaction, measured by rise in temperature of given quantity of water.

Calpurnia (kălpûr'nēŭ), d. after 44 B.C., third wife of Julius Caesar, to whom she was married in 59 B.C. In story she is the model of the faithful, long-suffering wife.

Calumet, resort village (pop. 1,256), on Keweenaw Peninsula, extreme N Mich. Grew mainly after development of Calumet and Hecla copper mine.

Calumet City, city (pop. 15,799), NE Ill., S suburb of Chicago near Ind. line, in industrial area. Name changed from West Hammond 1924. L. Calumet, just N, connects with L. Michigan.

Calvados (kälvädôs'), department (2,198 sq. mi.; pop. 400,026), N France, in Normandy; cap. Caen. Gives name to strong apple brandy.

Calvary (kăl'vŭrē) [Latin,= a skull] or **Golgotha** (gŏl'gŭthŭ) [Heb.= a skull], place outside wall of Jerusalem where Jesus was crucified. Mat. 27.33; Mark 15.22; Luke 23.33; John 19.17–20. Church of the Holy Sepulchre now stands on traditional site, but scholars disagree as to exact location.

Calvé, Emma (kälvä'), 1866–1942, French operatic soprano. Sang at the Metropolitan Opera, New York, 1893–1904. Carmen was one of her famous roles.

Calvert, George, 1st Baron Baltimore, c.1580–1632, British colonizer. In 1632 he was granted territory N of Potomac R. which became province of MARYLAND. His grandson, **Charles Calvert, 3d Baron Baltimore,** 1637–1715, succeeded to proprietorship in 1675. His arbitrary rule was overthrown by revolt in 1689.

Calvin, John, 1509–64, French Protestant theologian of Reformation, b. Noyon. A man learned in theology and law, he experienced (1533) "sudden conversion"; leaving Catholicism, he became a hunted Protestant leader. In 1536 began work at Geneva. Banished in 1538, he preached at Basel and Strasbourg until welcomed back to Geneva in 1541. His monumental *Institutes of the Christian Religion* (written after 1531) sets forth basic Calvinist theology. This diverged from Catholic doctrine in such fundamental ways as rejecting papal authority, accepting justification by faith alone, and systematizing the doctrine of predestination. Calvin held that the Bible is sole source of God's law, and man's duty is to interpret it and preserve order in the world: this aim he set out to realize in Geneva by founding the government solely on religious law. From his teachings grew one of the most important of Christian religious systems, **Calvinism.** Broadly, Calvinism is the system in the Protestant "Reformed churches" (see PRESBYTERIANISM) as distinct from those professing Lutheran doctrines; the chief distinction is in the doctrine of predestination. Calvinism differs from Catholicism fundamentally in holding that redemption is for elect alone, the free gift of God not to be won by good works. Calvinism characterized the Covenanters in Scotland, the Puritans in England and in New England, and the Huguenots in France.

Calvinistic Methodist Church, Protestant denomination. Originated (1735–36) in Wales, where it kept strong as a movement. Separated from Established Church 1811; adopted confession of faith 1823. In U.S. united (1920) with Presbyterian Church.

Calvo, Carlos (kär′lōs käl′vō), 1824–1906, Argentine diplomat and historian, writer on international law. Principle known as **Calvo Doctrine** would prohibit diplomatic intervention to enforce private claims before local remedies have been exhausted. **Calvo Clause,** found in constitutions, treaties, statutes, and contracts, is concrete application of his doctrine.

Calydon (kăl′ĭdŭn), ancient city of S Aetolia, Greece. It was scene of legendary **Calydonian hunt,** successfully led by Meleager, prince of Calydon, against a wild boar loosed by Artemis to destroy city for neglect of a sacrifice. Among the hunters were Jason, Castor and Pollux, Theseus, and Atalanta.

Calymna, Greek island: see DODECANESE.

Calypso (kŭlĭp′sō), nymph in the *Odyssey.* Lived on isl. of Ogygia, where Odysseus stayed seven years.

calyx (kā′lĭks), outer ring of typical FLOWER parts, made up of sepals which are usually green and leaflike or united into a tube. Often colored if COROLLA is absent (e.g., buttercup). See *ill.,* p. 999.

Cam or **Granta,** river of England rising in Essex and flowing NE past Cambridge to the Ouse.

Camacho, Manuel Ávila: see ÁVILA CAMACHO.

Camagüey (kämägwä′), city (pop. 80,509), E central Cuba; commercial center of agricultural region producing cattle and sugar.

Camargue (kämärg′), island, SE France, in the Rhone delta. Intensive cattle ranching.

camass or **camas** (kăm′ŭs), hardy bulbous plant (*Camassia*), with spikes of dark blue or white flowers. Native to W North America, found in moist soils. Some species grown in gardens.

Cambacérès, Jean Jacques de (zhä′ zhäk′ dŭ kōbäsärĕs′), 1753–1824, French revolutionist and legislator. Second consul (1799–1804); archchancellor of the empire under Napoleon I. Created duke of Parma 1808. Prepared CODE NAPOLÉON.

Cambay, Gulf of, inlet of the Arabian Sea, between Bombay and Saurashtra states.

Camberwell, metropolitan borough (pop. 179,-729), S London, England; residential and park section.

Cambio, Arnolfo di: see ARNOLFO DI CAMBIO.

cambium (kăm′bēŭm), thin layer of tissue between bark and wood of stem, most developed in trees. It is the growth area that causes increase in diameter of stems.

Cambodia (kămbō′dēŭ), state (c.69,900 sq.

mi.; pop. c.3,700,000), Indo-China; cap. Pnom Penh. On saucer-shaped plain drained by Mekong R. and surrounded by mountain ranges. Climate is tropical. TONLE SAP is important for fisheries. Rice-growing area in S. Sericulture and weaving are only industries. Prominent during era of KHMER EMPIRE, Cambodia became prey of Siam and Annam 15th–19th cent. King of Cambodia appealed 1854 for French intervention; French protectorate estab. 1863. French-Siamese treaty (1907) restored Cambodia's W provinces. After World War II France gave Cambodia more self-government within French Union.

Cambodian art. Pre-Khmer (pre-7th cent.) art, such as the *Harihara* of Andet and shrines at Sambor and Kornpong Thom, was influenced by Indian Gupta art. Classical period (8th–13th cent.) of Cambodian art of Khmer Empire evolved from Hindu and Buddhist iconography. Step-pyramid plan and profuse sculpture of great temple complexes at Angkor Wat and Angkor Thom were involved in symbolization of "world mountain." Modeled with sensuous subtlety, cult images had closed or half-closed eyes, full lips set in sweet smile. Cambodian culture merged with that of Siam after 14th cent., but distinctive forms survived in music and dance.

Cambon, Paul (pôl′ käbō′), 1843–1924, French ambassador to England (1898–1920). One of chief framers of Triple Entente. His brother, **Jules Cambon** (zhül), 1845–1935, was made ambassador to U.S. 1897; mediated peace preliminaries of Spanish-American War. Ambassador to Germany 1907–14.

Cambrai (käbrä′), city (pop. 24,558), Nord dept., N France, on Escaut (Scheldt) R. Old textile center; cambric first manufactured here. Ruled by bishops until seized by Spain (1595); to France 1677. Damaged in both world wars.

Cambrai, League of, 1508–10, alliance of Emperor Maximilian I, Pope Julius II, Louis XII of France, Ferdinand V of Aragon, and several Italian states against Venice. French routed Venetians at Agnadello (1509), but in 1510 Julius II made peace with Venice and formed HOLY LEAGUE against France.

Cambrai, Treaty of, called the **Ladies' Peace,** treaty signed 1529 by Louise of Savoy and Margaret of Austria, representing FRANCIS I of France and Emperor Charles V respectively. It renewed Treaty of Madrid but left Burgundy to France.

Cambria (kăm′brēŭ) [from Welsh *Cymry* = Welshmen], ancient name of Wales.

Cambrian Mountains, a name for mountains of Wales.

Cambrian period (kăm′brēŭn, kăm′-), first period of PALEOZOIC ERA. Large continental areas lay under shallow seas; thus Cambrian rocks are mostly sedimentary with thickness up to 13,000 ft. in Appalachian region. For the first time fossils of marine invertebrates were abundant—TRILOBITE, brachiopods, snails, sponges. No vertebrate fossils yet discovered, but possibility is not excluded. See GEOLOGY, table.

Cambridge (kām′-), municipal borough (pop. 81,463), co. town of Cambridgeshire, England, on Cam R. The seat of CAMBRIDGE UNIVERSITY, it is an ancient market town retaining much medieval atmosphere. Has many old churches, including St. Benedict's (10th cent.), St. Edward's (13th cent.), and Church of the Holy Sepulchre, one of four Norman round churches in England.

Cambridge. 1 Town (pop. 10,351), Eastern shore, Md., on Choptank R., SE of Annapolis; founded 1684. Fishing and yachting port, it has seafood industry and processing of foodstuffs. **2** City (pop. 120,740), E Mass., on Charles R. and NW of Boston; settled 1630. Seat of HARVARD UNIVERSITY, Radcliffe Col., MASSACHUSETTS INSTITUTE OF TECHNOLOGY. Washington took command of troops here, July 3, 1775. Stephen Daye estab. first printing press in America here. Longfellow's home is memorial. He and J. R. Lowell are buried in Mt. Auburn Cemetery. Mfg. of metal products, rubber goods, clothing, building supplies, and soap. **3** City (pop. 14,739), E Ohio, NE of Zanesville; settled 1798. Center of agr. and coal area with mfg. of glass, furniture, and pottery.

Cambridge Bay, government post and U.S.-Canadian weather station, SE shore of Victoria Isl., Northwest Territories, Canada.

Cambridge Platform, constitution for government and discipline in Congregational churches; adopted (1648) by synod at Cambridge, Mass. Group in Conn. adopted (1708) new centralizing Saybrook Platform. See also CONGREGATIONALISM.

Cambridge Platonists, school of philosophy at Cambridge Univ. in the late 17th cent. Reacting to mechanism of Thomas Hobbes, the Platonists revived idealism. Among them were Robert Grenville, Ralph Cudworth, Henry More, and John Norris.

Cambridgeshire or **Cambridge,** inland county (864 sq. mi.; pop. 255,901), E England; co. town Cambridge. Isle of Ely, northern section of county, is separate administrative unit. Area is mostly fenland, with chalky East Anglian range (including Gogmagog Hills) in south. Efforts to reclaim the fens, dating back to Romans, completed by vast drainage project 1653. Region has since been agr. Ely, with its famous cathedral, has been an important ecclesiastical center since Anglo-Saxon days.

Cambridge University, Cambridge, England, one of two anc. English universities. Probably had beginnings in 12th cent. Residences or colleges, estab. by end of 13th cent., named for church to which they were attached or for saint to whom dedicated. They are Peterhouse or St. Peter's (1284), Clare (1326), Pembroke (1347), Gonville and Caius (1348), Trinity Hall (1350), Corpus Christi (1352), King's (1441), Queens' (1448), St. Catharine's (1473), Jesus (1496), Christ's (1505), St. John's (1511) Magdalene (1542; pronounced môd'lin), Trinity (1546), Emmanuel (1584), Sidney Sussex (1596), and modern colleges, Downing (1800) and Selwyn (1882). Girton (1869) and Newnham (1873) are women's colleges; women admitted to full degree only in 1948. University, which has 19 faculties, has led in science and modern literature. James Chadwick discovered the neutron at famed Cavendish

Laboratory here. Univ. Library, Fitzwilliam Mus., and botanic gardens are noteworthy. Cambridge Univ. Press dates from 16th cent. As at OXFORD UNIVERSITY, instruction is by lecturers and tutors (called supervisors). B.A. degree is awarded on passing tripos exam (honors exam at Oxford) after nine terms of continuous residence. Initials of a degree usually followed by Cantab. from Cantabrigia, Latin name of Cambridge.

Cambronne, Pierre (pyěr' kābrôn'), 1770–1842, French general. Commanded Old Guard at Waterloo. Replied to British invitation to surrender with a brisk vulgarism, thus gaining immortality.

Cambyses (kămbī'sēz), d. 521 B.C., king of Persia, son and successor of Cyrus the Great. He disposed of his brother Smerdis, but later a false Smerdis rose to haunt him just after an excursion to pacify Egypt. He died, possibly by suicide.

Camden, Charles Pratt, 1st Earl: see PRATT, CHARLES.

Camden. 1 City (pop. 11,372), S Ark., on Ouachita R.; settled 1824. Shipping point for cotton, corn, and poultry. Mfg. of furniture, paper, and pottery. **2** City (pop. 124,555), W N.J. on Delaware R. (bridged 1926 to Philadelphia); settled 1681. City grew as commercial and mfg. center after coming of railroad 1834. Mfg. of textiles, chemicals, electronic and television products, phonographs, radios, and pens. Has canneries, oil refineries, railroad shops, and marine terminals. Here are home and grave of Walt Whitman. **3** City (pop. 6,986), N central S.C., near Wateree R. NE of Columbia. Trade and processing center in pine and farm area with textile and lumber mills. Winter resort. Battles of Camden (Aug. 16, 1780) and Hobkirks Hill (April 25, 1781) fought near by in CAROLINA CAMPAIGN of American Revolution. Fired in British evacuation of May 8, 1781. Taken and partly burned (Feb. 24, 1865) by part of Sherman's army in Civil War.

camel, hoofed mammal of family Camelidae, which includes true camels (Asian genus *Camelus*) and South American genus *Lama* (wild guanaco, vicuña, domesticated alpaca, llama). Arabian camel or dromedary (*Camelus dromedarius*) has one hump; Bactrian camel (*C. bactrianus*) of central Asia has two humps. Fat is stored in humps. Color varies from dirty white to dark brown; the neck is long; the ears are small, and the teeth strong. Can carry heavy loads (500–600 lb., more for Bactrian camel) and survive without water for several days (longer if juicy plants are available).

camellia (–měl'–, –mē'–), Asiatic evergreen tree or shrub (*Camellia*), allied to the tea plant. Grown under glass or outdoors in warm regions for its beautiful flowers, single or double, in white or red shades. Leaves are glossy dark green.

Camelot (kăm'ŭlŏt), the seat of King Arthur's court in the ARTHURIAN LEGEND.

Camembert cheese (kă'mŭmbâr), a mold-ripened CHEESE.

camera, light-proof container with lens that focuses image of object on photographic plate or film (see PHOTOGRAPHY). When shutter is open, film is exposed. Many variations in parts and attachments. **Camera lucida** (lōō'sĭdú), optical instrument that extends virtual image of object on plane surface so outline can be traced; usually attached to eyepiece of microscope. **Camera obscura** (ŏbskyōō'rú), light-tight box with convex lens at one end and screen for image at other; used to make drawings.

Camerarius, Rudolph Jacob (kămûrâ'rēŭs), 1665–1721, German physician and botanist, first to present definite facts concerning sex in plants.

Cameron, Richard, d. 1680, Scottish leader of Covenanters. Opposed reestablishment of episcopacy in Scotland after Restoration. He was killed by royal troops, but Cameronian sect grew strong, forming a presbytery (1743) as Reformed Presbyterians. Most joined Free Church of Scotland (1876).

Cameron, Simon, 1799–1889, American politician. U.S. Senator from Pa. (1845–49, 1857–61, 1867–77). Notoriously corrupt U.S. Secretary of War (1861–62). Machine he created so dominated Pa. that it was not until 1936 that Democrats carried state in a national election. Definition of an "honest politician" as one who "when bought, stays bought" is attributed to Cameron.

Cameron, city (pop. 5,052), E central Texas, S of Waco, in farm area.

Cameroons, former German colony, W Africa, between Gulf of Guinea and L. Chad. German possession of area was recognized in 1902. In 1911 parts of French Equatorial Africa were added, but these were restored in 1919, when original colony was divided into French and British mandates under League of Nations. In 1946 they became UN trust territories. **British Cameroons** (34,081 sq. mi.; pop. 1,027,500) comprises two detached sections on E border of Nigeria; governed with NIGERIA. **French Cameroons** (166,489 sq. mi.; pop. 3,003,200) fronts on Gulf of Guinea; governed as separate territory by a high commissioner at Yaoundé.

Camille: see DUMAS, ALEXANDRE (fils).

Camillus (Marcus Furius Camillus) (kŭmĭ'lŭs), d. 365? B.C., Roman hero. Elected dictator five times (396–67 B.C.), he each time won a signal victory.

Camisards (kämēsär'), Protestant peasants of the Cévennes, France, who rebelled against religious persecution (1702–10). Successfully used guerrilla methods against superior forces. After defection of their leader Jean CAVALIER they fought on under Roland Laporte but were slowly forced into submission.

Cammaerts, Émile (ämēl' kä'märts), 1878–, Belgian poet and dramatist, noted for poems of World War I.

Camões or **Camoens, Luís de** (both: lōōĕsh' dù kŭmō'ĭsh), 1524?–1580, Portuguese epic poet, greatest figure of Portuguese literature. Vasco da Gama's voyage is the main theme of his epic *The Lusiads* (Port. *Os Lusíadas* = sons of Lusus, i.e., the Portuguese), which is modeled on Vergil and influenced by Ariosto, but is an original epic of world literature. Also wrote sonnets and other lyrics.

camomile or **chamomile** (kăm'ûmīl), perennial plant (*Anthemis nobilis*), with daisylike white or yellow flowers and aromatic, finely cut foliage. Dried flowers are source of camomile tea.

Camorra (kùmô'rù), Italian criminal association in Naples and Sicily. First appeared c.1830, grew all-powerful through intimidation, blackmail, bribery; extended terror to Italian immigrants in U.S. Action by citizens of Naples secured its dissolution (1911).

camouflage (kă'mûfläzh), in warfare, disguising of objects to deceive the observer as to their location and so protect them from attack. The principle is very old, a simple form being the wearing or white or light-colored clothing by warriors crossing a snowy waste or a sandy desert. Development of large-scale scientific camouflage came with World War I, when ships were dazzle-painted and false landscapes were created to conceal forts and factories. With the heavy air bombardments of World War II, the use of camouflage to deceive air observers grew very elaborate with the construction of dummy towns and factories to lure bombers as well as with concealing devices for real strategic points.

Camp, Walter (Chauncey), 1859–1925, American football expert, long coach at Yale.

Campagna di Roma (kämpä'nyä dē rō'mä), plain surrounding Rome, Italy. Malarial and arid until reclamation work of 19th and 20th cent. Flocks of grazing sheep and ruins of Roman aqueducts and tombs give landscape a special charm.

Campanella, Tommaso (tōm-mä'zō kämpänĕl'lä), 1568–1639, Italian Renaissance philosopher and poet, a Dominican. *The City of the Sun* is an account of a utopian society, recalling Plato's *Republic*. Insisted on the preeminence of faith, but foreshadowed scientific empiricism.

Campania (kämpä'nyä), region (5,250 sq. mi.; pop. 3,696,632), S Italy, between Apennines and Tyrrhenian Sea; cap. Naples. Other cities: Benevento, Salerno, Caserta. Fertile plains and hills covered with vineyards, orchards, olive groves. Conquered by Rome 4th–2d cent. B.C. In Middle Ages it was held, successively, by Goths, Byzantines, Lombards, Normans. From 1282 it shared history of kingdom of NAPLES.

campanula: see BELLFLOWER.

Campbell, Scottish noble family. **Archibald Campbell,** 5th **earl of Argyll,** 1530–73, fluctuated in support of Elizabeth and Mary Queen of Scots. Was lord chancellor under James VI. **Archibald Campbell,** 8th **earl of Argyll** and 1st **marquess of Argyll,** 1607–61, was a powerful Presbyterian statesman. After surrender of Charles I to Scots, he tried to secure Presbyterian settlement in England; crowned Charles II in Scotland. Executed for treason at Restoration. His son, **Archibald Campbell,** 9th **earl of Argyll,** 1629?–1685, both royalist and Protestant, opposed extreme measures against the COVENANTERS. Was beheaded after leading rebellion in aid of duke of MONMOUTH. His son, **Archibald Campbell,** 1st **duke of Argyll,** d. 1703, was partly responsible for massacre of the Macdonalds at Glencoe (1692). **John Campbell,** 2d **duke of Argyll** and **duke of Greenwich,** 1678–1743, Scottish general, supported union with England. Put down rebellion of

JACOBITES 1715. His brother, **Archibald Campbell, 3d duke of Argyll,** 1682–1761, commissioner for the union (1706), served as Scottish peer in the united Parliament. Supported Robert Walpole.

Campbell, Alexander, 1788–1866, American clergyman, b. Ireland. His father, **Thomas Campbell,** 1763–1854, settled in W Pa., where he and his congregation withdrew from Presbyterian Church. Alexander came to U.S. in 1809. Became leader of group, for a time (1813–20) joined to Baptists, later to be DISCIPLES OF CHRIST. Advocated return to early Christian simplicity. Founded (1840) Bethany Col. (W.Va.).

Campbell, John, 1st earl of Breadalbane, c.1635–1717, Scottish chieftain. Aided the Restoration. Brutally massacred Macdonald clan at Glencoe (1692) for unavoidable delay in taking oath of submission to William III. Joined in Jacobite rebellion (1715).

Campbell, John Archibald, 1811–89, American jurist. Associate Justice of U.S. Supreme Court (1853–62). Sought to avoid war by mediation.

Campbell, Sir Malcolm, 1885–1949, English racing enthusiast. Set speed records driving motorcycles, airplanes, automobiles, speedboats.

Campbell, Mrs. Patrick, 1865–1940, English actress, whose maiden name was Beatrice Stella Tanner. Won fame in Pinero's *Second Mrs. Tanqueray* 1893. A friend of Shaw's, she created part of Eliza Doolittle in his *Pygmalion* in 1912.

Campbell, Robert: see ROB ROY.

Campbell, Robert, 1808–94, Canadian fur trader and explorer, b. Scotland. Discovered Pelly R. 1840. Descended in it in 1843 to its confluence with Lewes R. and here estab. Fort Selkirk.

Campbell, Thomas, 1763–1854: see CAMPBELL, ALEXANDER.

Campbell, Thomas, 1777–1844, Scottish narrative and lyric poet. Wrote long didactic (*The Pleasures of Hope,* 1799) and narrative (*Gertrude of Wyoming,* 1809; *Theodric,* 1824) poems, but is best remembered for patriotic verses, "Hohenlinden," "Ye Mariners of England" and particular lines (e.g., "Coming events cast their shadows before," in "Lochiel's Warning").

Campbell, (William) Wilfred, 1861?–1918, Canadian author. Known for *Lake Lyrics* (1889), volume of nature poetry. *Collected Poems* appeared 1905.

Campbell, city (pop. 12,882), NE Ohio, near Youngstown, on Mahoning R.; called East Youngstown until 1926. Has steel mills.

Campbell-Bannerman, Sir Henry, 1836–1908, British statesman. As prime minister (1905–08), furthered Liberal measures and autonomy for Transvaal and Orange Free State.

Campbellites: see DISCIPLES OF CHRIST.

Campbellton, town (pop. 7,754), N N.B., Canada, on Restigouche R. and W of Dalhousie; a port. Lumbering center and outfitting point for sportsmen.

Camp Borden (20,000 acres), largest military training center in Canada, S Ont., NNW of Toronto.

Campeche (kämpā′chä), state (19,672 sq. mi.; pop. 121,411), SE Mexico, on Gulf of Cam-

peche. Comprises most of W half of Yucatan peninsula. Principal ports Carmen (pop. 7,-687) and Campeche (pop. 23,277; also cap.).

Camperdown (kăm′pûrdoun″), Dutch *Kamperduin,* locality near village of Kamp, NW Netherlands, on North Sea. Scene of British naval victory over Dutch (1797).

Camp Fire Girls, American organization for girls 7 to 18 years old; founded 1910 by Luther H. Gulick and others. Object is "to perpetuate the spiritual ideals of the home" and to develop health and character.

Camp Hill, residential borough (pop. 5,934), S Pa., across Susquehanna R. from Harrisburg.

camphor, volatile oil, solid at ordinary temperatures. Commercial camphor, or camphor gum, is white, crystalline, and translucent, and has a penerating odor. Natural camphor is obtained by steam distillation of wood of the camphor tree (*Cinnamomum camphora*) native to China, Japan, and Formosa, but introduced elsewhere. Much camphor is made synthetically from a turpentine derivative. It is used especially in making celluloid, explosives, and moth preventives, and in medicine and perfumery.

Camphuysen, Dirk Rafelszoon (dĭrk′ rä′fĕlsōn kämphoi′zŭn), 1586–1627, Dutch painter, author of short religious poems. Most of small interiors and landscapes once ascribed to him are now attributed to his nephew, **Raphael Camphuysen** (rä′fäĕl), 1598–1657, and his son, **Govert Camphuysen** (gō′vŭrt), 1624–c.1674.

Campi, Giulio (jōō′lyō käm′pē), c.1500–c.1572, Italian painter and architect, founder of school of painters at Cremona. Did altarpieces and frescoes. His pupils included his brothers, **Cavaliere Antonio Campi** (kävälyä′rä), b. before 1536, d. 1591, and **Vincenzo Campi** (vĕnchän′tsō), 1532-91, portrait and still-life painter. Another brother, **Bernardino Campi,** 1522–c.1590, did colossal biblical frescoes in cupola of San Sigismundo (Cremona).

Campian, Thomas: see CAMPION, THOMAS.

Campin, Robert (käm′pĭn), 1375–1444, Flemish artist, identified with the Master of Flémalle who did *Annunciation* (Brussels). Taught Roger van der Weyden.

Campinas (kämpē′nŭsh), city (pop. 101,746), E São Paulo, Brazil. Once a coffee-growing area, it suffered from depletion of soil and falling price of coffee. Now has diversified farming.

Campion, Edmund, c.1540–1581, English Jesuit martyr. At Oxford he was a favorite of Queen Elizabeth I, but in 1571 he fled to the Continent and later became a Jesuit. In 1580 he and Robert Persons came as missionaries to England. He converted many but was taken, tortured, and executed.

Campion or Campian, Thomas, 1567–1620, English poet, composer, and lutanist. He wrote Latin poetry and masques, but is most important for his lute songs.

camp meeting, outdoor religious gathering, held in summer over period of days, typical of frontier U.S. Originated c.1800 in Ky. under preaching of James McGready and spread rapidly with revival movement. Camp meetings were held by evangelical sects and were characterized by emotional fervor attendant upon "conversion."

Campoamor, Ramón de (rämōn' dā kämpōä-mōr'), 1817–1901, Spanish lyric poet.

Campobello, island (pop. 1,181), 9 mi. long, 3 mi. wide, in Passamaquoddy Bay, between Maine and N.B., Canada. Campobello village is on W coast. Summer resort and fishing base. Passed to Canada in Convention of 1817. Summer home of Pres. F. D. Roosevelt was here.

Campo Formio, Treaty of (käm'pō fōr'myō), Oct., 1797, French-Austrian peace treaty at end of Bonaparte's Italian campaign. Austria ceded Austrian Netherlands to France, secretly promised France left bank of Rhine. Venetian republic, despite neutrality, was dissolved: most of it (including Dalmatia) went to Austria; the Ionian Isls. to France; the rest to CISALPINE REPUBLIC.

Campos, Arsenio Martínez de: see MARTÍNEZ DE CAMPOS, ARSENIO.

Campos (käm'pôsh), city (pop. 63,384), NE Rio de Janeiro state, Brazil, on the Paraíba near mouth; commercial center of rich agr. region.

Camrose, town (pop. 4,131), central Alta., Canada, SE of Edmonton. Has Scandinavian Lutheran college.

Camulodunum: see COLCHESTER, England.

Camus, Albert (älbër' kämü'), 1913–, French author. Close in mood to existentialism, he stresses the gloomy absurdity of life in such novels as *The Stranger* (1942; Eng. tr., 1946) and *The Plague* (1947; Eng. tr., 1948).

Cana (kā'nů), ancient town of Galilee where Jesus performed His first miracle by turning water into wine at a wedding. John 2.1,11; 4.46,54; 21.2.

Canaan (kā'nůn). **1** Son of Ham, ancestor of the Canaanites. Gen. 9.20–27; 10.6,15,19. **2** Name given by Israelites to Palestine before they occupied it. To them it was the land promised them by God and goal of their wanderings after leaving Egypt. Gen. 12.5; Ex. 3.8; Num. 13.17,29; 14.45; 21.3; Joshua 22.11,32; Judges 1.

Canachus (kă'nůkůs), fl. 6th cent. B.C., Greek sculptor, known for his great statues of Apollo.

Canada, nation (3,847,597 sq. mi. including inland waters; pop. 14,009,429), N North America, N of U.S.; member of British Commonwealth of Nations; cap. OTTAWA. Consists of ten provinces (NEWFOUNDLAND, NOVA SCOTIA, NEW BRUNSWICK, PRINCE EDWARD ISLAND, QUEBEC, ONTARIO, MANITOBA, SASKATCHEWAN, ALBERTA, BRITISH COLUMBIA), the NORTHWEST TERRITORIES, and YUKON territory. Separated from U.S. by a 3,-986.9 mi. land border and the Great Lakes. N it fronts on Arctic Ocean where Boothia Peninsula and ARCTIC ARCHIPELAGO thrust far into the Arctic. Hudson and James bays cut deeply into NE coast. Atlantic coast, broken by Gulf of St. Lawrence, is swept by Labrador Current from N and Gulf Stream from S. Pacific coast is deeply indented with many islands offshore. The LAURENTIAN PLATEAU, a rolling wooded area rich in minerals, covers c.50% of the nation. Major mountains are Canadian Rockies between Alta. and B.C. and Coast Mts. of W B.C. River and lake country is general in N Que. and Ont., the N Prairie Provs., and the N.W.T. Fertile lowlands adjoin Great Lakes and highly productive plains cover S Prairie Provs. Agr. is major industry, followed by ranching, dairying, and lumbering. Although extensive mineral resources remain untouched, there is important mining of gold, copper, coal, nickel, pitchblende, petroleum, and uranium. Fishing and trapping are traditionally important occupations. Water resources have been developed to power Canadian industries. Ont. and Que. are leading industrial provinces. In general population is centered in Maritime Provs. and the S areas of Que., Ont., the Prairie Provs., and B.C. Many groups are represented, notably French (esp. in Que., where French is accepted language), English, Scottish, Irish, and German. John Cabot explored E Canadian coast 1497 and estab. English claims. In 1534 the Frenchman, Jacques Cartier, planted a cross on Gaspé Peninsula. Quebec was estab. 1608 by CHAMPLAIN. The St. Lawrence became gateway to new French empire. Settlements were bases for fur traders, explorers, missionaries, and empire builders, among them LA SALLE, LAVAL, FRONTENAC, MARQUETTE, JOLLIET, and VÉRENDRYE. British opposition to New France centered in ACADIA. Meanwhile HUDSON'S BAY COMPANY was building fur-trading empire in NW. Imperial contest closed with defeat of French under MONTCALM on Plains of Abraham (1759); British gained Canada by Treaty of Paris (1763). Exploration opened up land in W. UNITED EMPIRE LOYALISTS advanced Canada. Fight for responsible government, including separate futile rebellions in 1837–38 led by W. L. MACKENZIE in Upper Canada and Louis PAPINEAU in Lower Canada, resulted in victory for democratic groups over entrenched FAMILY COMPACT. Movement for confederation resulted in the BRITISH NORTH AMERICA ACT. Territory was added as RUPERT'S LAND was purchased from Hudson's Bay Co. (1869) and B.C. joined the Union in 1871, P.E.I. in 1873, and Newfoundland in 1949. Man. became a province in 1870, and Sask. and Alta. in 1905. Mining operations developed rapidly after KLONDIKE gold rush in 1896. Organization of cooperatives (in N.S. and Prairie Provs.) and of SOCIAL CREDIT and COOPERATIVE COMMONWEALTH FEDERATION originated new forms to meet economic and political problems. Canada made valuable contributions to both World Wars in man power, goods, and in providing air and naval bases.

Canada, Lower: see QUEBEC, province.

Canada balsam, yellow, oily turpentine from BALSAM FIR. Used in preparation of slides for microscopic work, and in paints and polishes.

Canada Company, founded by John GALT, chartered in England 1826 for purpose of making setlements. Held lands on L. Huron side of S Ont., Canada, with hq. at GUELPH. Built first road from L. Ontario to L. Huron. Successful colonizing venture.

Canada First movement, party in Canada formed soon ofter confederation (1867) to encourage growth of nonpartisan loyalty to new dominion. Although short-lived, its ideals influenced Canadian writers and older political parties.

Canada jay: see JAY.

Canadian, river rising in E N.Mex. and flowing 906 mi. E across Texas Panhandle and most of Okla. Here, joined by North Canadian R., it enters Arkansas R. SE of Muskogee.

Canadian literature, English. Until after 1800 only notable works were recorded travels of explorers. First novelist was John Richardson, whose *Wacousta* (1832) popularized genre of national historical novel. In *The Clockmaker* (1836) T. C. Haliburton began humorous series on Sam Slick, Yankee peddler. Important novelists writing c.1900 include William Kirby, Sir Gilbert Parker, and L. M. Montgomery. Since 1900 Canadian novels have tended toward stricter realism but have remained predominantly regional. Well-known authors are Mazo de la Roche and Hugh MacLennan. Humorous essays of Stephen Leacock remain perennial favorites. Canadian poetry was late in developing. The long poetic drama, *Saul* (1857), by Charles Heavysege, achieved recognition. Beginning c.1880 the "Confederation school"—C. G. D. Roberts, Archibald Lampman, Bliss Carman, and Duncan Campbell Scott—began producing large body of romantic poetry. After her death Isabella V. Crawford was recognized as a genuine poet. Other poets of early 20th cent. include W. H. Drummond, John McCrae, and Robert W. Service. Well-known modern poet is Edwin J. Pratt, who began writing his imaginative, heroic poems in 1926.

Canadian literature, French. The inspiration of almost all Canadian writing in French has been the passionate concern of French Canadians to preserve their identity. Its themes have been found in nationalism, simple lives and folkways of the habitants (French Canadian farmers), devotion to the Catholic Church, and the tie to mother France. First artistic expression of this "racial" impulse was F. X. Garneau's *Histoire du Canada* (1845–48). This classic of French Canadian nationalism inspired first nationalist poet, Octave Crémazie, and the Quebec school of writers—among them L. H. Fréchette, H. R. Casgrain, and Antoine Gérin-Lajoie. Louis Hémon's *Maria Chapdelaine* (1913) gave impetus to more realistic fiction, and there has followed a stream of works on habitant life of backwoods, farms, and villages.

Canadian Mounted Police: see ROYAL CANADIAN MOUNTED POLICE.

Canadian National Railways, government owned and operated transportation system in Canada extending from coast to coast with many branch lines in each province; unified 1923. Amalgamation of several separate private and government lines.

Canadian Pacific Railway, transcontinental transportation system in Canada, extending into U.S., privately owned and operated in competition with Canadian National Railways. Line completed to Pacific coast 1885, after PACIFIC SCANDAL.

canal. Irrigation canals are extremely ancient. Transportation canals (level or with inclines for hauling vessels to each level) came later. Modern canals use locks (see LOCK, CANAL). Canals connect inland waterways and seas to great economic advantage. Used also to avoid falls and shoals, to reclaim land (drainage canals).

Canaletto (känälät′tō), 1697–1768, Venetian painter, whose real name was Antonio Canale or Canal. Known for his Venetian scenes. His nephew and pupil, Bernardo Bellotto (c.1724–80), architectural and landscape painter, was also called Canaletto.

Canal Zone: see PANAMA CANAL ZONE.

Canandaigua (kănŭndā′gwŭ), city (pop. 8,-332), W central N.Y., at N end of Canandaigua L. and SE of Rochester; settled 1789. FINGER LAKES resort and farm trade center. Pickering treaty with the Six Nations signed here, 1794. Courthouse was scene of Susan B. Anthony's trial for voting, 1873.

canary, bird of finch family, a descendant either of wild serin finch or similar wild canary of Canary Isls., Madeira, Azores. Wild birds mostly gray or green, breeders developed both plain and variegated birds of yelow, buff, or greenish. Breed readily in captivity. Finest singers (Harz mt. and St. Andreasberg canaries) originated in Germany.

Canary Islands, group of seven islands (2,912 sq. mi.; pop. 680, 294), off NW Africa, in the Atlantic. Comprise two provinces of Spain: Santa Cruz de Tenerife (including Tenerife, largest island) and Las Palmas (including Grand Canary, most important and populous). Conquered in 15th cent. by Spain. In French Revolutionary Wars, Nelson was repulsed in 1797 at Santa Cruz. Produce tropical fruit and canned fish.

canasta: see RUMMY.

Canaveral, Cape (kŭnăv′ŭrŭl), E Fla., on Atlantic coast, SE of Titusville. Has lighthouse. It is a guided missiles proving ground.

Canberra (kăn′bŭrŭ), city (pop. 15,156), cap. of Commonwealth of Australia, in Australian Capital Territory. Site chosen 1908, city founded 1913. Succeeded Melbourne as federal cap. in 1927. Seat of Duntroon Military Col., Canberra Univ. Col. (1929), and Natl. Mus. of Australian Zoology.

Cancer [Lat.,= crab], in astronomy, fourth sign of ZODIAC.

cancer or **carcinoma** (kärsĭnō′mŭ), malignant growth or tumor of unknown cause. Wildly growing epithelial cells invade surrounding tissues. Characteristic of malignancy is metastasis, the separation of malignant cells from the original growth and their distribution by way of lymphatics and blood to other parts of body. Any lump, ulcer, or unusual bleeding from body orifice warrants examination by physician. Information offered by American Society for the Prevention of Cancer.

Candia (kăn′dēŭ), Gr. *Herakleion,* largest city (pop. 53,541) of Crete, Greece; a port on the Gulf of Candia. Heavily damaged in World War II. Has unique museum of Minoan antiquities discovered at ancient Cnossus near by.

Candish, Thomas: see CAVENDISH, THOMAS.

candle, mass of wax, tallow, paraffin, spermaceti or similar material surrounding a wick. Date of origin uncertain; in ancient writings words translated as "candle" may have meant torch or lamp. Formerly made by repeated dipping in melted material or by pouring material into molds; now are usually machine-molded. Used symbolically especially in Roman Catholic rites; blessed on Candlemas Day.

candlefish, fish of smelt family of Pacific coast from Oregon to Alaska. Flesh delicately flavored. Its oily body, if dried and supplied with a wick, will burn, hence its name. An alternative name is eulachon.

Candlemas, Feb. 2, the feast of the Purification of the Blessed Virgin. There is a procession of candles to celebrate the day, and in the Roman Catholic Church candles are blessed. In America this is "groundhog day" (see WOODCHUCK).

candle power: see PHOTOMETRY.

Candlewood, Lake, reservoir, W Conn., N of Danbury. Made (1926) by power dam in tributary of Housatonic R., it is 15 mi. long and covers 6,000 acres.

Candolle, Augustin Pyramus de (ōgüstē′ pērä-müs′ dù kädôl′), 1778–1841, Swiss botanist who advanced the natural system of plant classification.

Candy, Ceylon: see KANDY.

candytuft, low-growing annual or shrubby perennial plant (*Iberis*), with flower clusters of various colors. It is used in borders and rock gardens.

cane: see BAMBOO; RATTAN; SUGAR CANE.

Canea (kûnē′ù), anc. Gr. *Cydonia,* modern Gr. *Khania,* city (pop. 33,837), cap. of Crete, Greece, on the Gulf of Canea. Suffered air and naval attacks in World War II. Landmarks are cathedral, mosques, and old Venetian arsenal.

canella (kûnĕl′ù), small evergreen tree (*Canella winterana*) of S Florida and West Indies; it is also known as wild cinnamon. Its dried inner bark is the canella of commerce which has stimulant qualities.

cane sugar: see SUCROSE.

Canfield, Dorothy: see FISHER, DOROTHY CANFIELD.

Canfield, Richard Albert, 1855–1914, American gambler. His famous gambling house in New York city was closed in 1904. Solitaire game named for him.

Can Grande della Scala: See SCALA, CAN FRANCESCO DELLA.

Canisius College: see BUFFALO, N.Y.

cankerworm, name for destructive larvae (also called measuring worms) of two geometrid moths. Both fall and spring species pupate in ground. Wingless females lay eggs on bark of trees; larvae feed on leaves.

Canlaon, Mount (känläōn′), or **Malaspina** (mäläspē′nä), active volcano, 8,088 ft. high, on Negros isl., Philippines.

canna, tropical perennial (*Canna*) with large leaves and spikes of red or yellow flowers. Planted in parks and formal beds in temperate regions.

cannabis: see HEMP; MARIJUANA.

Cannae (kăn′ē), anc. village, Apulia, S Italy. Hannibal defeated the Romans here in 216 B.C.

Cannes (kän), town (pop. 36,647), Alpes-Maritimes dept., SE France. Fashionable resort on Riviera.

cannibalism, human consumption of human flesh. Practice, known since dawn of history and in many lands (e.g., among Negroes in Africa, Indians of Pacific coast) has been primarily ritual, intended as sympathetic magic. In Western civilization cannibalism considered peculiarly horrible even in time of starvation (e.g., Donner party).

Canning, Elizabeth, 1734–73, London servant girl, subject of a famous mystery. Disappeared for 28 days in 1753. Claimed to have been held in a garret. A gypsy woman was arrested and sentenced to hang but at second trial Elizabeth was accused of perjury and banished to America.

Canning, George, 1770–1827, English Tory statesman. As foreign minister (1807–9) planned seizure of Danish fleet (1807). After suicide of CASTLEREAGH (1822) was again foreign minister. Opposed decisions of Congress of Verona. Aided MONROE DOCTRINE by recognizing independence of Spanish colonies in America. Arranged French-Russian-British agreement resulting in Greek independence. Favored Catholic Emancipation, free trade. Prime minister 1827. His third son, **Charles John Canning, Earl Canning,** 1812–62, was noted for clemency as governor general of India in SEPOY REBELLION. Was first viceroy of India 1858–62.

Canning, Stratford: see STRATFORD DE REDCLIFFE, STRATFORD CANNING, VISCOUNT.

canning, the process of hermetically sealing cooked food for future use, was put into use in France at beginning of 19th cent. and first patented in U.S. c.1815. Glass jars were largely supplanted (except in home canning) by tin cans, patented 1810 in England, 1825 in U.S.; tin-plated steel cans have been mass produced in U.S. since 1847 and are today the basis of a huge industry. Home and commercial processes alike depend on rapid handling of sound raw materials to prevent vitamin loss, bacterial spoilage, and enzyme changes, and on sealing and cooking in containers to kill microorganisms.

Cannizzaro, Stanislao (stänēslä′ō kän-nēt-tsä′rō), 1826–1910, Italian chemist. He discovered cyanamide, worked to differentiate molecular from atomic weights, and obtained alcohols from aldehydes (Cannizzaro's reaction).

Cannon, Annie Jump, 1863–1941, American astronomer, especially noted for her work on Harvard College Observatory's catalogue of stellar spectra.

Cannon, Joseph G(urney), 1836–1926, speaker of U.S. House of Representatives (1903–11). "Uncle Joe" ruled House dictatorially in interest of "Old Guard" Republicans until bill reforming House rules broke his power.

Cannon, Walter Bradford, 1871–1945, American professor of physiology and author of works in the field. He was an authority on digestion and hormones.

Cano, Alonso (älōn′sō kä′nō), 1601–67, Spanish artist. Carved and painted monumental altarpieces; designed façade of Granada cathedral.

Cano, Juan Sebastián del, d. 1526, Spanish navigator, first to circumnavigate the globe. Set out under Magellan, but at Magellan's death took command of the expedition.

canoe (kŭnōō'), simple type of watercraft, long and narrow, shaped into sharp ends for guiding and propelled by a paddle or paddles. Known among peoples of low material culture all over the world, the canoe has been made of various materials and in various forms. Among North American Indians, the hollowed-out log or dugout was highly developed on the N Pacific coast, the birchbark canoe was much used in the N woods, and the skin or hide canoe was known in the Plains. The Eskimo developed the kayak, made of sealskin stretched over a driftwood or whalebone frame; the paddler sits in the "manhole" and wears a waterproof skin shirt that fits down over the "manhole" making the whole craft waterproof. In the S Pacific natives developed large, seagoing canoes for interisland journeys; some were elaborately carved. In many parts of the world the canoe survives as a working craft. In the U.S. it is primarily used for sport. Canoeing clubs were popular in the late 19th and early 20th cent., and summer campers use canoes extensively.

canon (kă'nŭn), in Christendom, term with several meanings: decree of church council (hence body of such decrees, when ratified, contribute to canon law); official list of saints (hence canonization); list of books recognized or accepted in the Bible (the canonical books, as in the Western canon); the principal part of the MASS; one of certain church officials (canons regular, uncloistered monks; canons attached to a cathedral).

canon, in music, a type of counterpoint in which all voices have the same melody but begin at different times. In the crab canon, the second voice consists of the melody turned backwards. In mensuration canons, each voice has the same melodic patterns but written in different note values. A simple, popular type of canon is the round.

Canon City (kă'nyŭn) city (pop. 6,345), S central Colo., on ARKANSAS R. at end of Royal Gorge and WNW of Pueblo. Laid out 1859 on site of Z. M. Pike blockhouse (1807). Trade center for fruitgrowing and mining area.

canonization, in the Roman Catholic Church, process by which a person is officially enrolled among the saints. The method of canonization was set by Urban VIII in acts that came in force in 1634. At a "trial" in Rome, a prosecutor (popularly called *advocatus diaboli* or devil's advocate) attacks the claims proposed by his opponent (*advocatus Dei* or God's advocate) that the proposed saint had lived a holy life and was responsible for at least four miracles. To secure beatification (frequently a step toward canonization) proof of two miracles is offered. The miracles are considered pious belief, but a Catholic is not required to believe in them. A holy person may be considered a saint without formal canonization, as indeed many of the earliest and greatest saints are.

canon law, in the Roman Catholic Church, law of the church courts, based on legislation of councils, popes, and bishops (in local matters). The present great code was promulgated in 1917. It is the culmination of long development, begun with early letters of the bishops of Rome. These and later letters and pronouncements are the decretals, gathered into collections (sometimes spurious, as in the False Decretals). The greatest figure in canon law was GRATIAN, whose compilation was the basis of all later collections. Gregory IX, Boniface VIII, and John XXII issued further collections of decretals (later gathered in *Extravagantes communes*). The Council of Trent (1545–63) added much to canon law, which deals primarily with governance of the clergy and the Church, including administration of the sacraments (notably holy orders and matrimony).

Canonsburg, borough (pop. 12,072), SW Pa., SW of Pittsburgh; settled 1773. Has coal mining and mfg. of metal products. Whisky Rebellion began here 1794. Seat of Log Academy, oldest school building (1780) W of Alleghenies.

Canossa (känôs'sä), hamlet, N central Italy, near Reggio nell' Emilia. The lords of its castle (now in ruins) ruled much of Tuscany and Emilia in 10th–11th cent. Countess MATILDA was last of line. In Jan., 1077, castle was scene of penance by Emperor HENRY IV, who supposedly waited barefoot in the snow for three days before Pope Gregory VII, who was Matilda's guest, lifted excommunication.

Canova, Antonio (äntō'nyō känō'vä), 1775–1822, Italian sculptor, leader of the classical revival in Italy. Did statues of Napoleon and his family.

Cantrabrian Mountains (käntä'brēŭn), N Spain, along Bay of Biscay from Pyrenees to Cape Finisterre. Highest peak is Peña de Cerredo (8,687 ft.). Rich in coal and iron.

Cantabrigia: see CAMBRIDGE UNIVERSITY.

Cantacuzene, John: see JOHN VI, emperor.

Cantal (kätäl'), department (2,231 sq. mi.; pop. 186,843). S central France, in Auvergne; cap. Aurillac. **Plomb du Cantal** (plô"dü), 6,096 ft. high, an extinct volcano, is highest peak of Cantal mts.

cantaloupe: see MELON.

Cantata, musical form developed in Italy in the baroque era. It was a short dramatic piece which in the 17th cent. took on the form of recitative and aria. In France and Italy the secular cantata prevailed; in Germany the church cantata, with choral and instrumental parts, was adopted by J. S. Bach.

Canterbury, county borough (pop. 27,778), on Stour R. at foot of N Downs, Kent, England; spiritual center of England. St. Augustine came from Rome 597 to convert English to Christianity, founded abbey here, and became first archbishop of Canterbury. Town famous in Europe as object of pilgrimage after murder of THOMAS À BECKET. Chaucer's *Canterbury Tales* based upon stories of these travelers. Magnificent cathedral embodies work of several periods and various men (notably Lanfranc and Anselm). Bombed 1942, but cathedral not directly hit. City also site of St. Martin's (Mother Church of England), St. Augustine's Abbey, and other old buildings.

Canterbury bells: see BELLFLOWER.

cantharides (känthä'rŭdēz) or **Spanish fly,** bright green or bluish beetle, *Lytta* (formerly *Cantharis) vesicatoria*, chiefly of S Europe. This and others of same family often called blister beetles because of irritating effect on skin. Poisonous drug **canthari-din** obtained from dried crushed bodies.

Canticles, another name for the SONG OF SOLOMON.

cantilever (kăn'tŭlēvûr), beam supported rigidly at one end to carry load along free arm or at free end. Principle used widely in construction. See *ill.,* p. 167.

Cantire, Argyllshire, Scotland: see KINTYRE.

Canton (kăn"tŏn'), Mandarin *Kuang-chou,* city (pop. 1,413,460), cap. of Kwangtung prov., China; port on Canton R. Major commercial center at terminus of Canton-Hankow RR. Visited by Arab traders in 10th cent. In 1511 Portugal won trade monopoly, which made her first European power to have commercial contact with China. Treaty ending Opium War (1839–42) made Canton a treaty port. After occupation by British and French forces in 1856, Shameen Isl. was made a foreign concession (restored 1946 to China). City was seat of revolutionary movement in 1911. Held 1938–45 by Japan, fell 1949 to Communists.

Canton. 1 City (pop. 11,927), W central Ill., SW of Peoria; founded 1825. Trade and industrial center for agr. (esp. corn) and coal area. **2** Town (pop. 7,465), E Mass., SSW of Boston. Mfg. of textiles. Paul Revere had foundry here. **3** City (pop. 7,048), W central Miss., NNE of Jackson. Trade and processing center of cotton, truck, and timber area. **4** City (pop. 2,490), NE Mo., on the Mississippi above Hannibal. Seat of CULVER-STOCKTON COLLEGE. **5** Village (pop. 4,379), N N.Y., SE of Ogdensburg. Seat of St. Lawrence Univ. (coed.; 1856) and of a state agr. school. **6** City (pop. 116,912), NE Ohio, SE of Akron; laid out 1806. Has important iron and steel works, an oil refinery, and mfg. of roller bearings and engines. William McKinley lived and was buried here.

Canton or **Pearl,** river, 110 mi. long, Kwangtung prov., S China; main navigation channel linking Canton to Hong Kong. Mouth of river channel called Boca Tigris. Chinese names: Yueh Kiang, Chu Kiang.

Canton Island, atoll (3.5 sq. mi.; pop. 81), central Pacific, one of Phoenix Isls. Important transoceanic air base. Claimed in 1856 by U.S. and in 1937 by Great Britain; agreement was made 1939 for joint control of Canton and near-by ENDERBURY ISLAND for 50 years.

Cantor, Georg (gā'ôrk kän'tôr), 1845–1918, German mathematician known for work on theory of numbers and for introducing term "transfinite numbers."

Canute (kŭnōot', kŭnūt'), c.995–1035, king of England, Norway, and Denmark, younger son of SWEYN of Denmark. Invaded England with his father in 1013. On Sweyn's death he withdrew to Denmark. Invaded England 1015. Divided country with EDMUND IRONSIDE after battle of Assandun. On death of Edmund (1016), Canute was accepted as sole king. Gave England peace, restored Church to high place, and codified English law. Married Emma, widow of Æthelred. Succeeded to throne of Denmark

1018. After several expeditions to Norway drove out Olaf II in 1028, thus becoming ruler of three kingdoms. He made his son Harthacanute king of Denmark, and his son Sweyn king of Norway. Canute estab. friendly relations with the Holy Roman Empire.

Canute the Saint, d. 1086, king (1080–86) and patron saint of Denmark. Feast Day: Jan. 19.

canvasback: see DUCK.

Canyon, city (pop. 4,364), N Texas, S of Amarillo in Panhandle. Prairie Dog Fork of Red R. is formed near by above Palo Duro Canyon, which draws many visitors. Buffalo L. (SW) is recreational.

Canyon de Chelly National Monument: see NATIONAL PARKS and MONUMENTS (table).

Capablanca, José Raoul (hōsā' räōōl' käpäbläng'kä), 1888–1942, Cuban chess player, world champion 1921–27.

Cap de la Madeleine (käp' dù lä mädlĕn'), city (pop. 18,667), S Que., Canada, on St. Lawrence R. opposite Trois Rivières. Has paper and silk mills and mfg. of aluminum foil.

Cape Breton Island, 3,975 sq. mi., forming NE part of N.S., Canada, bounded by the Atlantic (S and E) and the Gulf of St. Lawrence (W). BRAS D'OR salt lakes occupy center of island. There are many summer lake resorts and coastal fishing villages. SYDNEY and GLACE BAY coal fields feed important steelworks. Cabot Trail is a motor road which circles the center and W part of island, commemorating its discovery by John Cabot (1497). By Peace of Utrecht (1713–14) French retained island (named Île Royale with cap. at LOUISBURG) and some Acadians migrated here. Cape Breton was attached to N.S. in 1763. Was independent with cap. at Sydney 1784–1820.

Cape Charles, town (pop. 2,427), E Va., port on Chesapeake Bay near tip of Eastern Shore peninsula. Has ferries to Old Point Comfort and Norfolk. Occupied by Union forces in Civil War.

Cape Coast, town (pop. 23,061), cap. of the Gold Coast colony, a port on Gulf of Guinea.

Cape Cod, low sandy peninsula of glacial origin, 65 mi. long and 1–20 mi. wide, SE Mass.; bounded by Cape Cod Bay (N and W), the Atlantic (E), Nantucket and Vineyard sounds (S), and Buzzards Bay (SW). Name attributed to Gosnold, who visited here 1602. Known for its summer resorts and fishing towns, e.g., Provincetown (on site where Pilgrims put in, 1620), Barnstable, and Falmouth. Has large cranberry production. Cape Cod Canal (built 1909–14, improved 1927), c.8 mi. long, connects Cape Cod and Buzzards bays, crossing Bourne town.

Cape Colony: see CAPE PROVINCE.

Cape Fear River, formed in central N.C., flows c.200 mi. SE across piedmont and coastal plains to Atlantic Ocean just N of Cape Fear. Wilmington is at head of estuary, Southport at mouth; Elizabethtown and Fayetteville on banks.

Cape Girardeau (jĭrär'dō), city (pop. 21,578), SE Mo., SSE of St. Louis and on the Mississippi; founded 1793 as trading post. Important as a port, it was later a fort in Civil

War. Produces shoes, cement, and wood and tobacco products.

Cape jasmine: see GARDENIA.

Capek, Josef, Czech *Čapek* (chä′pĕk), 1887–1945, Czech author and primitivist painter. With his brother Karel he collaborated on *The Insect Play* (1921; Eng. tr., 1923), a satire produced in U.S. as *The World We Live In*. *Poems from a Concentration Camp* (1946) appeared after his death at Belsen. His brother **Karel Capek,** 1890–1938, won international fame with his satirical play *R.U.R.* (*Rossum's Universal Robots,* 1921; Eng. tr., 1923), which introduced the word *robot* into English. Among other works are the play *The Makropoulos Secret* (1923; Eng. tr., 1925), a novel *Krakatit* (1924; Eng. tr., 1925), and three vols. of conversations with T. G. Masaryk.

Capella, Martianus (märshēä′nŭs kŭpĕ′lŭ), fl. 5th cent.?, Latin writer. Long allegory, *The Marriage of Mercury and Philology,* popular in Middle Ages.

Capello, Bianca (byäng′kä käpĕl′lō), 1548–87, Italian adventuress. Became grand duchess of Tuscany by marrying Francesco de' Medici (1579). Died suddenly with her husband; presumably poisoned.

Cape May, Atlantic resort city (pop. 3,607), at end of Cape May peninsula, S extremity of N.J. Peninsula has lighthouse at Delaware Bay entrance. Canal (built by Federal government 1942–43; part of N.J. section of Intracoastal Waterway) bisects the cape c.3 mi. above its S point. **Cape May Court House** (pop. 1,093) is NNE of Cape May city.

Cape Province, officially **Cape of Good Hope Province** (277,169 sq. mi.; pop. 4,053,848), South Africa, on Atlantic and Indian oceans; cap. Capetown. Occupies S tip of Africa. Crops include grains, tobacco, citrus fruit, and grapes (for wine). Diamonds, copper, and coal are mined. The 15th-cent. Portuguese navigator Diaz was first to round Cape of Good Hope, but the Dutch were first to settle the area, founding Capetown in 1652. The late 17th cent. saw influx of French Huguenots. In 1806 the British annexed area as Cape Colony, and British settlers arrived in 1820. Opposition to British rule led many of the Boer farmers to migrate north (see TREK). In South African War fierce battles were fought at Mafeking and Kimberley. With founding of Union of South Africa in 1910, the colony became a province.

caper, white-flowered shrub (*Capparis spinosa*) of Mediterranean region. Its pickled buds, called capers, are used for flavoring.

Capernaum (kŭpûr′nāŭm) or **Capharnaum** (kŭfär′–), town, NE Palestine, associated with Jesus' ministry. John 2.12; 6.59; Mat. 11.23; 8; 9; Mark 1; 2; Luke 4; 5.

Capetians (kŭpē′shŭnz), royal house of FRANCE, named for HUGH CAPET, who became king in 987. His direct descendants ruled until death of Charles IV (1328), throne passed to collateral branch of VALOIS.

Capetown or **Cape Town,** city (pop. 383,891), cap. of Cape Prov., legislative cap. of Union of South Africa; a large port on the Atlantic. Scenically located at foot of Table Mt. and overlooking Table Bay. Here are Houses of Parliament (1886) and Univ. of Cape Town (1916). Founded 1652 by the Dutch, taken 1806 by the British.

Cape Verde Islands (vûrd), archipelago and Portuguese colony (1,557 sq. mi.; pop. 147,-097), in the Atlantic, c.375 mi. W of Dakar; cap. Praia (on São Tiago Isl.). Under Portuguese rule since late 15th cent. Important stopover point on transatlantic route between Africa and South America.

Cape Vincent, village (pop. 812), N N.Y., on St. Lawrence R. and NW of Watertown; a center for Thousand Isls. resort area.

Cape York Peninsula, N Queensland, Australia, between Gulf of Carpentaria and Coral Sea.

Cap-Haïtien (kăp′′-hä′shŭn), city (pop. 24,-957), N Haiti. Founded by French 1670, it was cap. of colonial Haiti until 1770.

Capharnaum, same as CAPERNAUM.

capillarity causes part of surface of liquid in contact with solid (e.g., a glass jar) to be elevated above or depressed below rest of surface. Named for behavior of liquids in capillary tube placed perpendicularly in liquid: water rises in tube to level above that outside; mercury is depressed. Forces operating are adhesion, cohesion, surface tension.

capillary, minute vessel connecting arterial and venous systems in CIRCULATION OF THE BLOOD.

Capistrano, John of: see JOHN CAPISTRAN, SAINT.

capitalism, economic system characterized by private ownership of property, production of goods for profit, and the institution of bank credit. Its modern importance dates from Industrial Revolution. Capitalism stresses freedom of individual economic enterprise, although ultimate right of state to regulate industry has seldom been questioned. In the 20th cent. the capitalist structure, grown to enormous proportions through quest for profits, has been restricted by social reforms and by totalitarianism.

capital punishment, putting to death by the state. Once imposed even for petty crimes, its use has decreased since 18th cent., because of efforts of such men as Beccaria. Modern methods include hanging, electrocution, gassing, shooting, and guillotining.

Capitol, building, Washington, D.C., over 725 ft. long and c.185 ft. wide; seat of U.S. government. Elevated site chosen by George Washington in consultation with Major L'ENFANT. Building begun in 1793; first architect was William THORNTON. Burned by British in 1814. Charles BULFINCH brought design to completion in 1830. T. U. Walter added extensive wings and dome (c.288 ft. in height) during period 1851–65.

Capitoline Hill or **Capitol,** highest of the seven hills of anc. Rome, historic and religious center of the city. On it were the great temple of Jupiter Capitolinus, the citadel (arx), and the senatorial palace. The temple, twice destroyed by fire, was last rebuilt by Domitian.

Capitol Reef National Monument: see NATIONAL PARKS AND MONUMENTS (table).

capitularies, decrees and written commands of the Merovingian and Carolingian kings of the Franks. Most important were those addressed by Charlemagne to his officers, the *missi dominici*, for administration of the empire and carrying out reforms.

Capiz (kä'pĕs), municipality (pop. 32,353), N Panay isl., Philippines. Has rice and sugar mills.

Capo d'Istria, Giovanni Antonio, Count (kä"pō dĕ'strēä), 1776–1831, Greek and Russian statesman, b. Corfu. Entered Russian service 1809; as Russian foreign minister (1820–22) he helped Greek uprising in 1821. Elected president of Greece 1827, but was unpopular because of aristocratic and pro-Russian leanings. Assassinated.

Capone, Al(fonso) (kŭpō'nē), 1899–1947, American gang leader, b. Italy. His crime syndicate terrorized Chicago in 1920s.

Caporetto (käpōrāt'tō), village of Slovenia, NW Yugoslavia, on Isonzo R; in Italy until 1945. Scene of Italian rout by Austrians in 1917.

Capote, Truman (käpō'tē), 1924–, American author. His works combine a delicate style with bizarre subject matter and Southern scenes. Among his novels are *Other Voices, Other Rooms* (1948) and *The Grass Harp* (1951; he later made this into a play). Some short stories are in *Tree of Night and Other Stories* (1949).

Cappadocia (kăpŭdō'shŭ), anc. region of Asia Minor, now in Turkey; term is used for varying territory. The inhabitants kept some independence even under Alexander the Great, and it became a kingdom in the 3d cent. B.C. Pontus split off from it. Cappadocia became a prosperous Roman province, and the name appears in the Bible.

Cappel, Switzerland: see KAPPEL.

Capper, Arthur, 1865–1951, American journalist and political leader. Published Topeka *Daily Capital* and several farm journals. U.S. Senator from Kansas (1919–49); led farm bloc, staunch isolationist.

Capri (kä'prē), small rocky island (pop. 7,-984), S Italy, near entrance to Bay of Naples. Striking scenery, pleasant climate make it a tourist center. Two small towns: Capri, Anacapri. Ruins of villas of emperors Augustus and Tiberius.

Capricornus [Lat.,= goat horn], 10th sign of ZODIAC.

Caprivi, Leo, Graf von (lä'ō gräf fŭn käprē'vē), 1831–99, chancellor of Germany (1890–94). Succeeded Bismarck. Favored industrial interests.

Captivity, Exile, or **Babylonian captivity,** in history of Israel, period from fall of Jerusalem (586 B.C.) to rebuilding of Temple (516 B.C.) thus lasting the 70 years prophesied for captivity. Jer. 25.11; Dan. 9.2; Zech. 7.5. After capture of city, thousands were deported to Mesopotamia; exiles kept close contact with kinsmen at home. In 538 B.C., Cyrus decreed that worship be restored at Jerusalem and that Jews might return home. The following century was a period of reintegration into a national and religious unit. See books of Ezekiel, Ezra, and Nehemiah. For "Babylonian captivity" of popes, see PAPACY.

Capua (kä'pūŭ), ancient city, Campania, S Italy, strategically situated on Appian Way. Opened its gates to Hannibal 216 B.C. Retaken by Romans, it became chief center of

S Italy. After its destruction by the Arabs (A.D. 841), the inhabitants fled to near-by Casilinum and founded modern Capua (pop. 10,218).

Capuchins (kă'pūchĭnz) [Ital.,= hooded ones], independent order of the Franciscans, officially Friars Minor Capuchin; founded 1525–28. Devoted to preaching and missions, they did much to forward the Catholic Reform.

Capulin Mountain National Monument: see NATIONAL PARKS AND MONUMENTS (table).

capybara (kăpĭbä'rŭ), mammal (*Hydrochoerus capybara*) of Central and much of South America. Also called water hog and carpincho. Largest living rodent (up to 4 ft. long, 75–100 lb.), it has brownish, yellow-flecked hair, no tail, partially webbed feet, and is semi-aquatic. It eats vegetation. Is a source of food, glove leather, and bristles.

caracal (kă'rŭkŭl) or **Persian lynx,** mammal of cat family, native to Asia, Africa. It is reddish brown with black-tufted ears, and c.3¼ ft. from nose to tip of tail. Preys on small deer, hares, birds.

Caracalla (kărŭkä'lŭ), 188–217, Roman emperor (211–17), son of Septimius SEVERUS. Called Caracalla after his Gallic tunic; real name Marcus Aurelius Antoninus. Had to share rule with his brother Geta, but murdered him and his followers (212). Extended citizenship to all free inhabitants of the empire, presumably to increase his income. He was murdered by Macrinus, who took the imperial rule, only to be replaced by Heliogabalus.

Caracas (kŭrä'kŭs), city (pop. 376,111; alt. c.3,100 ft.), N Venezuela, cap. and largest city of country. Independence declared here 1811. Earthquake of 1812 hurt patriot cause.

Caracci, family of Italian painters; see CARRACCI.

Caracciolo, Francesco (fränchä'skō kärät'chōlō), 1752–99, Neapolitan admiral. Commanded fleet of PARTHENOPEAN REPUBLIC (1799). Summarily executed by order of Lord Nelson.

Caractacus (kŭrăk'tŭkŭs) or **Caradoc** (kŭrä'dŭk), fl. A.D. 50, British chieftain, son of Cymbeline. Fought for nine years against Romans, was captured and taken to Rome. Claudius spared his life.

Caraman, Turkey: see KARAMAN.

Caran d'Ache (kärä'däsh'), pseud. of **Emmanuel Poiré** (ĕmänüĕl' pwärä'), 1858–1909, French caricaturist and illustrator.

Carausius (kŭrô'shēŭs), d. 293, Gallo-Roman commander. Condemned by Maximian, he fled to Britain and estab. rule. Diocletian and Maximian recognized him as coemperor. Defeated by Constantius and murdered.

Caravaggio, Michelangelo Amerighi da (mēkälän'jälō ämärē'gē dä kärävä'djō), 1565–1609, Italian painter; founder of naturalist school in Rome. One of earliest masters of dramatic light and shade. In genre and religious pictures he abandoned idealization for emphasis on the character of his lowly models.

caravan, group of travelers or merchants united for mutual assistance and defense on long journeys through dangerous country. Caravan trade preceded sea commerce in Near

East, existing from earliest recorded history, since fertile regions were divided by deserts and marauding tribes were a menace. Camels were chief beasts of burden but donkeys were used in Asia Minor. Caravan routes caused ancient wars. Cities rose and fell with trade volume on near-by routes; empires estab. caravansaries to accommodate travelers along the way. Trade continued in this fashion until use of motor trucks and planes. Advent of Islam led to pilgrim caravans to Mecca. Wagon-train commerce over Santa Fe Trail in New World was not unlike caravan trade.

caravel (kă′rŭvĕl″), three-masted, usually square-rigged, sailing ship. It had a roundish hull with high bow and stern and was a light ship with small displacement. Its advantage over bulkier ships was important in enabling the Portuguese to open the African coast in the 15th cent. Columbus' flagship, the *Santa Maria*, was a typical caravel.

caraway, biennial herb (*Carum carvi*) native to Europe. Small seeds are used medicinally and for seasoning pastries and liqueurs (e.g., kümmel).

carbide, compound of carbon and one other element, not hydrogen or oxygen. Generally produced in electric furnace. Many carbides are decomposed by water to yield a gas.

carbohydrate, any organic compound of carbon, hydrogen, oxygen (with hydrogen and oxygen in ratio of 2:1). Important group of heat-energy supplying foods, involved in fat production. Three groups are monosaccharides, e.g., GLUCOSE; disaccharides, e.g., LACTOSE; polysaccharides, e.g., CELLULOSE, STARCH.

carbolic acid or **phenol** (fē′–), colorless, crystalline solid compound of carbon, hydrogen, and hydroxyl radical (OH). Like alcohols in structure; has properties of weak acid. Corrosive and poisonous. Used as antiseptic, disinfectant, and to make resins, explosives, and dyes.

carboloy (kär′bŭloi), alloy of cobalt, tungsten, carbon. Harder than steel; used for cutting.

carbon, abundant, nonmetallic element (symbol = C; see also ELEMENT, table), found in all organic matter. Forms HYDROCARBON and CARBOHYDRATE compounds. Carbon is in perfumes, drugs, animal and plant secretions, foods, textiles, wood, paper, coal, gaseous fuels, etc. Carbonates are important (e.g., limestone). DIAMOND and GRAPHITE are crystalline forms. Steel contains iron and carbon.

Carbon, Mount: see ELK MOUNTAINS.

Carbonari (kärbōnä′rē), secret revolutionary society in SW Europe in early 19th cent. Active in revolts in Spain, Naples, Piedmont (1820–21).

carbonate, a salt or an ester (in the case of organic carbonates) of carbonic acid. Carbonate RADICAL is –CO₃. Carbonates, except for ammonium, potassium, and sodium, are insoluble in water. Most decompose with heat, yielding carbon dioxide and metallic oxide. Form bicarbonates with carbonic acid. Calcium carbonate occurs in animal shells and as ICELAND SPAR, LIMESTONE, MARBLE, and STALACTITE and STALAGMITE formations. Iron carbonate (siderite) is important iron

source. Potassium carbonate is POTASH; sodium, SODA. Calcium bicarbonate causes "hardness" in water .

Carbondale. 1 City (pop. 10,921), S Ill., N of Cairo, in coal and agr. area; founded 1852. Has railroad shops. **2** City (pop. 16,296), NE Pa., on Lackawanna R., NE of Scranton. Anthracite mining and mfg. of textile and metal products.

carbon dioxide, colorless, almost odorless, gaseous compound of carbon and oxygen; formula CO₂. Heavier than air; neither burns nor supports combustion; soluble in water; can be liquefied under pressure. Occurs in ATMOSPHERE. Results from burning of carbon, hydrocarbons, and from decomposition of carbonate. Product of respiration; given off in FERMENTATION, used in photosynthesis. Causes dough to rise when formed by BAKING POWDER; gives effervescence to water when dissolved under pressure; used in fire extinguishers. Also called carbonic acid gas because aqueous solution is weak acid. Dry ice is solid CO₂.

carbonic acid, weak acid known only in solution; formed when carbon dioxide is dissolved in water. Used in carbonated beverages.

carbonic acid gas: see CARBON DIOXIDE.

Carboniferous period (kärbŭnĭ′fŭrŭs), fifth period of PALEOZOIC ERA, marked by COAL formation. In North America it is divided into Lower Carboniferous or Mississippian and Upper Carboniferous or Pennsylvanian. The Mississippian was a period of repeated submergence and rising, with vast sediment deposits, mountain making, and volcanic activity. During the Pennsylvanian warm humid climate and extensive marshes favored rapid growth of the vegetation which later became coal. As in the Mississippian crustal disturbances took place on a huge scale. Land animals included primtive amphibians and reptiles, spiders, snails, scorpions, huge dragonflies. See GEOLOGY, table.

carbon monoxide, colorless, odorless, tasteless gaseous compound of carbon and oxygen; formula CO. May cause fatal poisoning if inhaled. Lighter than air; almost insoluble in water. Used as fuel (in PRODUCER GAS, WATER GAS), and as reducing agent (oxygen remover) in obtaining certain metals from ores. Formed by incomplete combustion of carbon. Present in exhaust of gasoline engines, in illuminating gas, in furnaces when there is insufficient air.

Carborundum: see SILICON CARBIDE.

carburetor (kär′byŭrātŭr). **1** Gasoline-engine device for vaporizing liquid fuel before combustion. Spray type has float chamber (regulates gasoline entry) and mixing chamber (vaporizes fuel spray), with vapor and air passing over throttle valve into cylinder intake manifold. **2** Device to enrich coal or water gas, increasing illuminative power.

Carcassonne (kärkäsôn′), city (pop. 31,752), cap. of Aude dept., S France, on Aude R. Medieval walled city was entirely restored by Viollet-le-Duc (19th cent.). "New city" (13th cent.) lies across Aude.

Carchemish (kär′kĭmĭsh, kärkē′mĭsh), city of anc. Syria; southern city of the HITTITES, taken by Egypt (15th cent. B.C.). Also Char-chemish.

carcinoma: see CANCER.

cardamom (kär′dŭmŏm″), plant (*Elettaria cardamomum*), native to India and Ceylon, grown for its aromatic seeds which are used medicinally and in spices.

Cardano, Geronimo (järō′nēmō kärdä′nō), 1501–76, Italian mathematician and physician. Works include treatises on arithmetic and algebra.

Cárdenas, García López de (gärthē′ä lō′pĕth dä kär′dänäs), fl. 1540, Spanish explorer in American Southwest, discoverer of Grand Canyon.

Cárdenas, Lázaro (lä′särō kär′dänäs), 1895–, president of Mexico (1934–40). His reform program included redistribution of land on EJIDO system; expropriation of foreign-owned properties; modernization of Mexico.

Cardiff (kär′dĭf), county borough (pop. 243,-627), co. seat of Glamorganshire, Wales, on the Taff near its mouth on Bristol Channel; one of world's great coal shipping ports. There are also large iron and steel works, flour mills, and a fishing industry. Cardiff Castle built 1090 on site of a Roman fort. Welsh Natl. Mus. and University Col. of S Wales and Monmouthshire are in Cathays Park. City and suburbs suffered severe air raid damage in 1941.

Cardigan, James Thomas Brudenell, 7th earl of (kär′dĭgŭn), 1797–1868, British general. In Crimean War led disastrous cavalry charge (1854) immortalized by Tennyson in *The Charge of the Light Brigade.* Cardigan jacket named for him.

Cardiganshire (kär′dĭgŭnshŭr) or **Cardigan,** maritime county (677 sq. mi.; pop. 53,267), on Cardigan Bay, S Wales; co. town Cardigan. Region is largely hilly, with fertile agr. valleys. Chief industries mfg. of woolen goods and lead mining. Welsh language and customs preserved here to a large degree.

cardinal, member of the highest body of the ROMAN CATHOLIC CHURCH below the pope—the college of cardinals, having (since 1059) the duty of electing the pope and all the duties of a privy council to him. The institution grew out of the council of clerics in and around Rome who advised the pope, and the titles of cardinals still reflect this: cardinal bishops (of the sees immediately around Rome), cardinal priests and cardinal deacons (with titles from the church in Rome itself); hence the title "Cardinal of the Roman Church"). The dignity of being a cardinal is quite separate from offices in the Church hierarchy; thus the term *cardinal archbishop* means only that a man is both a cardinal and an archbishop. The rarely attained maximum number of cardinals is 70 (set by Sixtus V). After the death (or in very rare instances resignation) of the pontiff, the cardinals must meet in not less than 15 nor more than 18 days to elect a new pope; they remain closeted until a candidate has been chosen and has accepted the office. Most of the cardinals have separate church offices over the world (usually archbishoprics); the remainder direct the affairs of the papal administration, the Curia Romana. Groups of them (with staffs) constitute the congrega-

tions for management of specific affairs—e.g., the Congregation of the Holy Office (see INQUISITION 3) and Congregation of the Propagation of the Faith (the Propaganda; in charge of missions). A cardinal heads each of the tribunals, the highest ecclesiastic courts. The secretariats, for handling of papal affairs, are also headed by cardinals (e.g., the papal secretary of state). The distinctive badge of a cardinal is a red hat, given him by the pope but never worn thereafter. Cardinals are styled "Eminence." See also PAPACY.

cardinal or **redbird,** North American songbird of finch family. The male eastern cardinal is scarlet with black throat and face, the female brown with red patches. Southern forms are the Arizona, gray-tailed, Louisiana, and San Lucas cardinals.

cardinal flower: see LOBELIA.

Cardozo, Benjamin Nathan (kärdō′zō), 1870–1938, Associate Justice of U.S. Supreme Court (1932–38). Interpreted law according to effects on society.

cards, playing: see PLAYING CARDS.

Cardston, town (pop. 2,487), SW Alta., Canada, SW of Lethbridge. Founded in mid-19th cent. by Mormons. Chief Mormon temple in Canada is here.

Carducci, Giosuè (jōzōōä′ kärdōōt′chē), 1835–1907, Italian poet, professor at Bologna (1860–1904). Works include rebellious *Inno a Satana* [hymn to Satan] (1865), *Rime nuove,* and *Odi Barbare* (1877, 1882, 1889). Critical writings helped form literary taste of his age.

Carew, Thomas (kûrōō′), 1595?–1639?, English lyric poet, one of the Cavalier poets, now best remembered for courtly verses on love (e.g., "Ask me no more where Jove bestows," "He that loves a rosy cheek").

Carey, Henry, c.1690–1743, English poet, musician, author-composer of song *Sally in Our Alley.*

Carey, Mathew, 1760–1839, American publisher, bookseller, economist, b. Dublin; in U.S. after 1784. Edited magazines (notably *American Museum*), stimulated American letters. Argued for protective tariffs. His son, **Henry Charles Carey,** 1783–1879, was a leader in developing economic nationalism. He opposed "pessimism" of Ricardo and Malthus.

Carey Land Act, written by Sen. Joseph M. Carey, passed by U.S. Congress in 1894. Provided for donation of U.S.-owned desert lands to Western states on condition they be irrigated.

Caribbean Sea (kă″rĭbē′ŭn, kŭrĭ′bēŭn), part of Atlantic. Central and South America lie to W and S; Yucatan peninsula and West Indies to N and E.

Carib Indians (kă′rĭb), native people originally inhabiting Lesser Antilles.

Cariboo Mountains (kă′rĭbōō), range, 200 mi. long, S central and E B.C., Canada. It is roughly parallel to the Rockies, extending between upper North Thompson R. and N apex of Fraser R. Mt. Titan is believed to be highest peak (c.11,750 ft.). In W foothills is Cariboo dist., scene of 1860 gold rush. Cariboo Road (built 1862–65) aided settlement of region. After extensive development, gold mining declined and was superseded by ranching and farming.

Caribou, town (pop. 9,923), NE Maine, on Aroostook R. and N of Presque Isle. A center for winter sports. Ships potatoes.

caribou (kă′rĭbōō), American name for mammal of deer family in arctic and subarctic regions. It is of same genus (*Rangifer*) as Old World REINDEER. Two main North American types: barren-ground caribou of Alaska, N Canada; woodland caribou in coniferous forests and bogs in parts of Canada.

Carignan-Salières regiment (kärēnyä-sälyĕr′), largest body of French troops ever sent to New France. Arrived in Canada 1665, over 1,000 strong, to render lower St. Lawrence valley safe from Indian raids. About half the regiment remained as settlers near Montreal.

carillon: see BELL.

Carinthia (kŭrĭn′thĕŭ), Ger. *Kärnten* (3,681 sq. mi.; pop. 482,886), S Austria; cap. Klagenfurt. Predominantly mountainous; the GROSSGLOCKNER is Austria's highest point. Mining (lead, iron, zinc); agr. in fertile Drava Valley. Tourist trade. In 976 Carinthia (which then included ISTRIA, CARNIOLA, and STYRIA) was detached from Bavaria and created an independent duchy. It was acquired by Ottocar II of Bohemia 1269; fell to Rudolf I of Hapsburg 1276; became Austrian crownland. After 1919 it lost minor territories to Italy and Yugoslavia.

Carleton, Guy, 1st **Baron Dorchester,** 1724–1808, governor of Quebec and British commander in American Revolution. Repulsed attack on Quebec in 1775; captured Crown Point in 1776.

Carleton College: see NORTHFIELD, Minn.

Carlinville, city (pop. 5,116), S central Ill., SW of Springfield, in coal, natural-gas, agr. area.

Carlisle, earls of: see HOWARD, family.

Carlisle, John Griffin (kärlīl′), 1835–1910, American statesman. U.S. Representative from Ky. (1877–90), speaker of House (1883–89). U.S. Senator (1890–93). U.S. Secretary of the Treasury (1893–97).

Carlisle (kärlīl′), county borough (pop. 67,-894), Cumberland, England, near Scottish border; an important rail center. Carlisle Castle, built by William Rufus in 1092, withstood many sieges, is now used as barracks. There is a 12th-cent. cathedral.

Carlisle, borough (pop. 16,812), S Pa., SW of Harrisburg; laid out c.1751. Has mfg. of textiles, clothing, and leather goods. French and Indian War expeditions (1758, 1763) were organized here. Was munitions depot in Revolution and Washington's hq. in Whiskey Rebellion. Was on Underground Railroad and attacked by Confederates 1863. Seat of Dickinson Col. (coed., opened 1773). From 1879 to 1918 Carlisle Indian School (Federal) was here.

Carlists, partisans of Don Carlos (1788–1855), second son of Charles IV of Spain, and of his successors, who claimed the Spanish throne under the SALIC LAW. Carlos's brother, Ferdinand VII, had abrogated the law of male succession in favor of his daughter, ISABELLA II. In the bloody civil war of 1836–39 Isabella's forces defeated the Carlists. Carlos's son, Don Carlos, conde de Montemolin (1818–61), and the latter's

nephew, Don Carlos, duque de Madrid (1848–1909), led unsuccessful uprisings in 1860, 1869, and 1872. In 1873 full-scale civil war broke out again. The Carlists held the Basque Provinces, Catalonia, and other parts of Spain but were completely defeated by 1876. Ultrareactionaries, the Carlists supported Franco in the civil war of 1936–39.

Carloman, 751–71, younger brother of CHARLEMAGNE.

Carloman, d. 880, German king of Bavaria, Pannonia, and Moravia (876–79), king of Italy (877–79); son of Louis the German and father of Arnulf.

Carloman, d. 884, French king (879–84). Ruled jointly with his brother Louis III till 882. Checked Norman invasion at Aisne R.

Carlos. For kings thus named, see CHARLES.

Carlos, 1545–68, Spanish prince; son of Philip II by Maria of Portugal. Mentally unbalanced. Arrested by Philip's order on eve of projected flight to Netherlands; died in prison soon afterward. Hero of Schiller's tragedy *Don Carlos.*

Carlos, name of three Spanish pretenders: see CARLISTS.

Carlotta (kärlō′tù), 1840–1927, empress of Mexico, daughter of Leopold I of Belgium. See MAXIMILIAN.

Carlow (kär′lō), inland county (346 sq. mi.; pop. 34,081), Leinster province, Ireland; co. town Carlow. A mostly fertile region, cattle raising, farming, and dairying are chief occupations.

Carlsbad or **Karlsbad** (kärlz′băd), Czech *Karlovy Vary,* city (pop. 17,187), NW Bohemia, Czechoslovakia; famous spa. Hot mineral water taken for digestive diseases.

Carlsbad, city (pop. 17,975), SE N.Mex., on Pecos R.; settled 1888. Grazing lands and irrigated farms (cotton, alfalfa) in region. Mining and refining of potash. Served by Carlsbad project. Carlsbad Caverns Natl. Park is near.

Carlsbad Caverns National Park: see NATIONAL PARKS AND MONUMENTS (table).

Carlsbad Decrees, 1819, resolutions of a conference of ministers of German states, convened by Metternich after murder of KOTZEBUE. Provided for press censorship, supervision of universities, suppression of liberal agitation. In force until 1848.

Carlsruhe, Germany: see KARLSRUHE.

Carlstadt or **Karlstadt** (both: kärl′shtät), c.1480–1541, German Protestant reformer, whose original name was Andreas Rudolf Bodenstein. Fervent reformer and follower of Luther, he led in Wittenberg in Luther's retirement but was criticized for abolishing old church practices.

Carlstadt (kärl′stät), borough (pop. 5,591), NE N.J., NE of Newark. Chemicals, clothing, textiles.

Carlyle, Thomas, 1795–1851, British man of letters, b. Ecclefechan, Scotland. After earning a precarious living chiefly as teacher and tutor he became the interpreter of German romanticism in his *Life of Schiller* (in *London Magazine* 1823–24) and translation of Goethe's *Wilhelm Meister* (1824). A trenchant critic of British society, he expressed his views in a sort of spiritual autobiography, *Sartor Resartus* (in *Frazer's Magazine,* 1833–

34), and in his interpretative rather than historical *French Revolution* (1837). His belief that the people could be saved from their woes by great men ("heroes") was put forth in *On Heroes, Hero-Worship, and the Heroic in History* (1841), an edition of the letters and speeches of Oliver Cromwell (1845), and a massive biography of Frederick the Great. *Past and Present* (1843) contrasts 12th-cent. England of Jocelyn de Brakelond with modern chaos. Had great influence on the literary world of his day. That influence was shared by his wife, **Jane (Baillie) Welsh Carlyle**, 1801–66, who was also notable as a letter writer.

Carman, Bliss, 1861–1929, Canadian poet. Friend of Richard Hovey, with whom he published the series *Songs from Vagabondia* (1894, 1896, 1901). Reputation rests on melodic quality of his verse and his sensuous pleasure in nature.

Carmarthen, Wales: see CAERMARTHEN.

Carmathians: see KARMATHIANS.

Carmel, Mount [Heb.,= garden land], mountain, NW Israel. Extends c.12 mi. NW from plain of Esdraelon to Mediterranean Sea, ending in promontory marking S limit of Bay of Acre. Associated with prophets Elijah and Elisha. On slopes are vineyards, a Carmelite monastery, and a Bahaist garden shrine.

Carmel-by-the-Sea or **Carmel** (kärmĕl'), city (pop. 4,351), W Calif., on Carmel Bay and S of Monterey. Art, literary, and recreation center. Father Junípero SERRA is buried at near-by mission.

Carmelites (kär'mŭlīts), Roman Catholic order of mendicant friars, originating apparently as hermits on Mt. Carmel, Palestine, made into a Western European order by St. Simon Stock (d. 1265). An enclosed order of Carmelite nuns was also estab. and became particularly important after the Carmelites were reformed by the Spanish mystics St. THERESA (of Ávila) and ST. JOHN OF THE CROSS.

Carmen Sylva: see ELIZABETH, queen of Rumania.

Carmi (kär'mī), city (pop. 5,574), SE Ill., NE of Harrisburg. Rail and trade center in agr. area.

Carmona, Antonio Oscar de Fragoso (äntŏ'nyŏ ùshkär' dù frägŏ'sŏ kärmŏ'nù), 1868–1951, Portuguese general and statesman. Interim president (1926–28) and president (1928–51) of Portugal. His regime was dictatorial, dominated after 1928 by SALAZAR.

Carnac (kärnäk'), village, NW France, near Auray, in Brittany. Site of remarkable MEGALITHIC MONUMENTS, especially menhirs.

Carnarvon, George Edward Stanhope Molyneux Herbert, 5th **earl of** (kärnär'vùn), 1866–1923, English Egyptologist. His most famous discovery in excavating in the Valley of the Kings from 1906 to 1923 (with Howward Carter) was the tomb of Tut-ankh-amen.

Carnarvon, Wales: see CAERNARVON.

Carnatic (kärnä'tĭk), region, SE Madras, India. In 18th cent. it was arena of British-French struggle for supremacy in India.

Carnation, perennial PINK (*Dianthus caryophyllus*), with double spice-scented flowers in white or shades of red. It is an important

greenhouse crop in cold regions and a garden flower where winters are mild.

Carnegie, Andrew (kärnä'gē), 1835–1919, American industrialist, philanthropist, b. Scotland. Concentrated on steel production after 1873; by 1900 the Carnegie Steel Co. produced one quarter of all U.S. steel. His benefactions, totaling about $350,000,000, include Carnegie Hall (1891) in New York city, and over 2,800 libraries.

Carnegie, industrial borough (pop. 12,105), SW Pa., SW of Pittsburgh. Mfg. of steel and metal products. Named for Andrew Carnegie.

Carnegie Corporation, foundation making grants to educational institutions and libraries, and occasionally to other worthy causes; estab. 1911 as chief repository of Andrew Carnegie's wealth.

Carnegie Endowment for International Peace, foundation to promote peace by publicity, support of organizations, and the like; estab. 1910 by gift of $10,000,000 from Andrew Carnegie.

Carnegie Foundation for the Advancement of Teaching, estab. 1905 by gift of $10,000,000; chartered by Congress 1905; further endowed with $17,000,000.

Carnegie Institute of Technology, at Pittsburgh; nonsectarian, partly coed.; opened 1905 with funds from Andrew Carnegie, chartered 1912. Had first collegiate department of drama (1914).

Carnegie Institution of Washington, D.C., chartered 1902 and 1904, organized 1904, endowed by Andrew Carnegie and Carnegie Corp. Projects include astronomy, terrestrial and biological sciences, historical research.

Carniola (kärnēō'lù), Croatian *Kranj*, Ger. *Krain*, mountainous region, Slovenia, NW Yugoslavia; historic cap. Ljubljana. Passed to Hapsburgs 13th cent.; Austrian crownland until 1918. Divided between Italy and Yugoslavia after World War I; to Yugoslavia 1947. Population mostly Slovenian.

carnivorous plants: see BLADDERWORT; PITCHER PLANT; VENUS'S-FLYTRAP.

Carnot, Lazare (läzär' kärnŏ'), 1753–1823, French revolutionist, the "architect of victory." Trained as military engineer. Organized the republican armies and masterminded strategy in French Revolutionary Wars. Member of Directory. Later held high posts under Napoleon. Exiled 1815. His son, **Nicolas Léonard Sadi Carnot** (nēkôlä' läô-när' sädē'), 1796–1832, a physicist, was a founder of modern thermodynamics. His work on relation between heat and mechanical energy anticipated that of Joule, Kelvin, and others. Another son, **Hippolyte Carnot** (ēpôlēt'), 1801–88, took part in Revolution of 1848, was minister of education in provisional government. His son, **Sadi Carnot**, 1837–94, president of France (1887–94), was assassinated by an Italian anarchist.

Caro or **Karo, Joseph ben Ephraim**, 1488–1575, Jewish legist, b. Toledo, Spain, d. Safed, Palestine, compiler of *Shulhan Aruk* [the table set], a basic legal and religious code of orthodox Judaism.

carob (kă'rùb), leguminous evergreen tree (*Ceratonia siliqua*) native to Mediterranean region, cultivated in other warm areas. It has edible red pods. Called St.-John's-bread from belief it was "locust" eaten by St. John in the wilderness (Mark 1.6).

Carol, kings of Rumania. **Carol I,** 1839–1914, a prince of the house of Hohenzollern-Sigmaringen, was elected prince of Rumania 1866, took title king 1881. Siding with Russia in war against Turkey (1877–78), he obtained at Congress of BERLIN full independence for Rumania. Married Elizabeth of Wied (Carmen Sylva). **Carol II,** 1893–1953, had to renounce right to succession (1925). In 1930 he proclaimed himself king, dethroning his son MICHAEL. Instituted personal dictatorship 1938. Was deposed in 1940 by Ion ANTONESCU and fled abroad with Magda Lupescu, whom he married in 1947.

carol, popular hymn, of joyful nature, especially associated with Christmas. The earliest date from the 15th cent.; many may be from pagan sources. Oldest printed carol is *Boar's Head Carol* (1521). Carols of French origin are also called noels.

Carolina campaign, 1780–81, of American Revolution. After capture of Charleston, British force under Cornwallis swept N, capping success at battle of Camden, Aug. 16, 1780. Patriot defense was broken in Carolinas except for guerrilla bands. American victory at Kings Mt., Oct. 7, 1780, prefaced campaign led by Gen. Nathanael Greene which freed both Carolinas of British and set stage for YORKTOWN CAMPAIGN.

Caroline Affair. In 1837 a small steamer, the *Caroline,* owned by U.S. citizens, carried men and supplies to Canadian rebels under W. L. MACKENZIE on Navy Isl. just above Niagara Falls. On Dec. 29, 1837, British and Canadian loyalists set fire to the ship and sent her over the falls. One American was killed. Affair caused tension in U.S.–British relations but was smoothed over.

Caroline Islands, group (525 sq. mi.; pop. 35,190), W Pacific; included 1947 in U.S. Trust Territory of the Pacific Isls. under UN trusteeship. Group includes two volcanic islands (Kusaie and Ponape), three major island groups (PALAU, TRUK, YAP), and many atolls and islets. Coconuts and sugar cane are produced. Discovered 1526 by Spaniards; was under Spanish rule 1886–99. Sold 1899 to Germany, occupied 1914 by Japan who received mandate over group in 1922. In World War II Palau and Ulithi were taken 1944 by U.S. forces.

Caroline of Anspach, 1683–1737, queen consort of George II of England. Supported Robert Walpole.

Caroline of Brunswick, 1768–1821, consort of George IV of England. Their marriage(1795) forced George, then prince of Wales, to put away his first wife, Mrs. Fitzherbert. Caroline was separated from George in 1796 but in 1820 refused to give up rights as queen. King instituted divorce proceedings, but these were later dropped.

Carolingians, dynasty of Frankish rulers, founded 7th cent. by PEPIN OF LANDEN. Ruled as mayors of the palace under MEROVINGIANS until PEPIN THE SHORT made himself king (751). His son, CHARLEMAGNE, crowned emperor in 800, brought dynasty to its zenith. After death of his son, LOUIS I, Carolingian empire was split by Treaty of VERDUN (843) among Louis's sons: LOTHARINGIA to LOTHAIR I; Germany to LOUIS THE GERMAN; France to CHARLES II. In 870 Lotharingia was divided between Louis and Charles. Arnulf was the last Carolingian emperor (d. 899); Louis the Child, the last Carolingian king in Germany (d. 911); Louis V, the last Carolingian king in France (d. 987).

Carolus-Duran (kärôlûs′-dürä′), 1838?–1917, French portrait and genre painter, teacher of many famous painters.

Carondelet, Francisco Luis Hector, barón de (kûrŏndûlĕt′), c. 1748–1807, governor of Louisiana and West Florida (1791–97), b. Flanders. Severely taxed relations between Spain and U.S. by intriguing with Indians and Ky. frontiersmen.

carp, fresh-water fish native to Asia, introduced into Europe and America. *Cyprinus carpio,* common in America, is European carp of varied form and color. It has four barbels around the mouth and a greenish or brown thick-scaled body (sometimes yellowish or silvery) with red on fins. Sometimes grows to 3 ft., 25 lb. Raised in ponds in Europe.

Carpaccio, Vittore (vēt-tō′rä kärpät′chō), c.-1450–c.1522, Venetian painter, follower of Giovanni Bellini. Depicted pageantry of 15th-cent. Venice.

Carpathian Russia: see RUTHENIA.

Carpathians (kärpā′thēŭnz), or **Carpathian Mountains,** chain of Central Europe, in E Czechoslovakia, S Poland, W Ukraine, and N Rumania. Forming an arc c.900 mi. long, they enclose the Danubian plain in N and E. The TATRA group in the N and the Transylvanian Alps (see TRANSYLVANIA) in the S rise to 8,737 ft. and 8,361 ft. respectively. Rich in timber, minerals, mineral spas.

Carpathian Ukraine: see RUTHENIA.

Carpathus, Greek island: see DODECANESE.

Carpeaux, Jean Baptiste (zhä′ bätēst′ kärpō′), 1827–75, French sculptor, a favorite of the Second Empire.

Carpentaria, Gulf of (kärpûntä′rêŭ), arm of Arafura Sea, indenting the N coast of Australia.

Carpenter, John Alden, 1876–1951, American composer. His music often depicts scenes of American life (e.g., orchestral suite *Adventures in a Perambulator,* ballet, *Skyscrapers*). He also wrote songs, symphonies, and chamber music.

carpet and **rugs** were used in anc. Nineveh, and in Egypt by c.2500 B.C. Today, types include antique Orientals, European hand-woven (e.g., Aubusson, Savonnerie), Brussels, Wilton, velvet, Axminster (Oriental type), chenille or chenille Axminster, ingrain carpeting (now little used), rag and hooked rugs (often made in households), many kinds of straw and fiber mattings. Handmade Orientals have wool pile knotted by hand (up to 1,000 knots per sq. in.). European industry depended on hand looms until Erastus Bigelow's introduction of power loom, 1841. U.S. rugmaking began in colonial days.

carpetbaggers, epithet used in the South after Civil War to describe Northern adventurers who flocked S to make money and seize political power in RECONSTRUCTION period. Carpetbags held their possessions. Some came as agents of the FREEDMEN'S BUREAU. Most engaged in large-scale political corruption.

Carpini, Giovanni de Piano (jōvän'nē dä pyä'nō kärpē'nē), 13th cent. Italian traveler, Franciscan monk. Sent in 1245 by Pope Innocent IV to the Tartary court, he crossed Russia and central Asia to Karakorum, Mongolia, on horseback in c.100 days. Brought back important accounts of peoples and places.

Carpocrates (kärpŏk'rŭtēz), fl. c.130–c.150, Alexandrian philosopher. He and his son Epiphanes created a sect that advocated communal ownership of property, including women. The Carpocratians, related to the Gnostics, believed that corrupt man could be restored to union with the Absolute (God) by despising all created things.

Carr, Robert: see SOMERSET, ROBERT CARR, EARL OF.

Carracci or **Caracci** (kärät'chē), family of Italian painters of Bolognese school, founders of Eclectic school. **Lodovico Carracci** (lōdōvē'kō), 1555–1619, was influenced by the Venetians. With his nephews, Agostino and Annibale, and with Anthony de la Tour, he established in Bologna an academy which tried to unite in one system the best characteristics of each of the great masters. Noted pupils included Guido Reni and Domenichino.

Carrantuohill (kä"rŭntōō'ŭl), mountain (height, 3,414 ft.), Co. Kerry; highest peak in Ireland.

Carranza, Venustiano (vānōōstyä'nō kärän'sä), 1859–1920, Mexican statesman. Active in political life of Mexico after overthrow of Díaz (1911), he acted as president (1914–20) and contested leadership of nation with Huerta, Villa, Zapata, and Obregón. Dominant features of his reform program were incorporated in constitution of 1917: national ownership of subsoil deposits, restoration of EJIDO system, church and labor reforms. Constitution was never actually in force.

Carrara (kär-rä'rä), city (pop. 25,259), Tuscany, central Italy. Center of Italian marble industry; over 400 quarries. Constituted a duchy with MASSA. Cathedral (12th cent.); ducal palace.

Carrel, Alexis (kä'rŭl), 1873–1944, American surgeon and experimental biologist, b. France. Won 1912 Nobel Prize in Physiology and Medicine for work in suturing blood vessels, transfusion, and transplantation of organs. With Charles A. Lindbergh invented mechanical heart. Carrel devised methods of keeping tissues and organs alive in nutritive solutions. Wrote *Man, the Unknown* (1935).

Carrera, Rafael (räfäēl' kär'rä'rä), 1814–65, president of Guatemala, a *caudillo*. Led revolt against anticlerical liberal government (1840), restored power of Church in Guatemala. Helped destroy Central American Federation and aided conservative governments in other Central American countries.

Carrera Andrade, Jorge (hôr'hä kärä'rä ändrä'dhä), 1903–, Ecuadorian lyric poet.

carriage, wheeled vehicle, usually horse-drawn, dating from Bronze Age. Early forms include CHARIOT and four-wheel goods wagon. During Middle Ages in Europe wheeled vehicles were largely superseded by litters because of poor roads. Cart and wagon introduced anew c.12th cent. Use of coach spread among nobility in 16th cent. Forms developed in 18th cent. include landau, barouche, phaeton; in 19th cent., hansom cab, brougham, victoria. U.S. carriage-building trade well estab. after 1812; four-wheel buggy with open sides and folding top was popular. See *ill.*, vehicles.

Carriera, Rosalba (rōzäl'bä kär-rēä'rä), 1675–1757, Italian portrait and miniature painter. Her works are delicate in color and vivacious.

Carroll, Charles, 1727–1832, American Revolutionary patriot, signer of Declaration of Independence. Known as Charles Carroll of Carrollton.

Carroll, John, 1735–1815, American Roman Catholic churchman, a Jesuit, b. Md.; educ. in Europe. A friend of Benjamin Franklin and an ardent patriot in the American Revolution, he is notable for his successful efforts to gain toleration for Catholics in the U.S. and to assure Catholicism a place in the republic. He was bishop (1790–1808) and archbishop (1808–15) of Baltimore.

Carroll, Lewis, pseud. of **Charles Lutwidge Dodgson,** 1832–98, English writer. An able mathematician, he developed from stories told to children of Dean Liddell (one of them named Alice) *Alice's Adventures in Wonderland* (1865) and *Through the Looking-Glass and What Alice Found There* (1872). Mingling of fantastic absurdity and shrewd observation has given delight to generations of children and adults. Also wrote humorous verse (e.g., *The Hunting of the Snark,* 1876).

Carroll, 1 City (pop. 6,231), W Iowa, W of Boone. Mfg. of farm equipment. **2** Town (pop. 359), N central N.H., NW of Crawford Notch in White Mts. Includes Twin Mountain, Fabyan House, and Bretton Woods resorts.

Carrollton, city (pop. 7,753), NW Ga., WSW of Atlanta. Farm trade center, with textile mills.

carrot, biennial plant (*Daucus carota*) with edible thickened root, rich in sugar, mineral salts, and vitamins. Cultivated for over 2,000 years.

Carryl, Guy Wetmore, 1873–1904, American humorist. His volumes of light verse include *Fables for the Frivolous* (1898) and *Mother Goose for Grown-Ups* (1900).

Carso, Yugoslavia: see KARST.

Carson, Edward Henry Carson, Baron, 1854–1935, North Irish politician. Opponent of Irish home rule, he denounced creation of Irish Free State (1921) but approved new government of N. Ireland.

Carson, Kit, 1809–68, American frontiersman and guide. Acted as guide for J. C. Frémont's Western expedition of 1842, 1843–44, 1845; led Gen. Stephen Kearny's troops in trek from N.Mex. to Calif. in 1846. Noted Indian fighter.

Carson City [for Kit Carson], mining and resort city (pop. 3,082), state cap., W Nev., in Carson valley S of Reno. Laid out 1858 on site of a trading post (1851), it grew with discovery in 1859 of COMSTOCK LODE. Later it was a rail shipping point for ore. Became territorial cap. 1861.

Carson-Newman College: see JEFFERSON CITY, Tenn.

Carson Sink, swampy area, c.100 sq. mi., W Nev., NE of Fallon. Remnant of old L. Lahontan. Carson R. disperses here. Lahontan Dam, completed 1915, saves most of river's flow for NEWLANDS PROJECT.

Carstares or **Carstairs, William,** 1649–1715, Scottish statesman and divine. Friend and chaplain of WILLIAM III, powerful in efforts to reconcile him with Scottish church. Under Queen Anne promoted union with England.

Carstensz, Mount (kär'stŭnz), group of peaks, W central New Guinea, in Netherlands New Guinea. Highest peak, c.16,400 ft., is highest on island.

Cartagena (kärtähä'nä), city (pop. 73,190), N Colombia, Caribbean port; founded 1533. A treasure city of Spanish Main, it was attacked by buccaneers. Declared independence from Spain 1811. Now oil port.

Cartagena, city (pop. 43,104), Murcia prov., SE Spain; Mediterranean port and naval base. Lead, iron, zinc mines near by. Founded c.225 B.C. by Hasdrubal; chief Carthaginian base in Spain; taken by Romans 209 B.C.; sacked by Drake 1585.

Cartago (kärtä'gō), city (pop. 100,725), central Costa Rica; founded 1563. Was political center of country until SAN JOSÉ was made cap. (1821).

Carte, Richard D'Oyly (doi'lē kärt'), 1844–1901, English impresario of Gilbert and Sullivan operas.

cartel, national or international organization of manufacturers or traders allied by agreement to fix prices, limit supply, or divide markets among the member firms. Since it may have international scope, it is broader than the TRUST. Cartels arose in Germany in 1870s. Classic theories of economic competition oppose them, and they are outlawed in some countries.

Carter, Howard, 1873–1939, English Egyptologist. Associate of 5th earl of CARNARVON.

Carter, Mrs. Leslie, 1862–1937, American actress, whose maiden name was Caroline Louise Dudley. Associated with Belasco, she starred in several of his plays 1890–1906.

Carter, Nick, fictional detective character in 19th-cent. melodramatic fiction, probably created by J. R. Coryell, used by F. V. R. Dey and others. Also used as pseudonym.

Carteret, Sir George (kär'tŭrĭt, –rĕt), c.1610–1680, British proprietor of East Jersey, part of present NEW JERSEY. His cousin, **Philip Carteret,** 1639–82, was first governor of the colony.

Carteret, John: see GRANVILLE, JOHN CARTERET, 1ST EARL OF.

Carteret, Philip: see CARTERET, SIR GEORGE.

Carteret, borough (pop. 13,030), NE N.J., on Arthur Kill opposite Staten Isl. Mfg. of machinery, metal products, chemicals, and textiles.

Cartersville, city (pop. 7,270), NW Ga., NW of Atlanta and on Etowah R. near Allatoona

Dam. Mines barite, ochre, manganese, limestone, and marble. Mfg. of textile goods.

Cartesian coordinates (kärtē'zhŭn) [for René Descartes], values representing the location of a point in relation to two straight lines (called axes). One axis is horizontal, the other vertical; the point is located by measuring its distance from each line along a parallel to the other line. Descartes advanced generality in mathematics by showing that an infinite number of curves are referable to one system of coordinates.

Carthage (kär'thĭj), anc. city of N Africa, on the Bay of Tunis; founded (traditionally by DIDO) by Phoenicians from Tyre in 9th cent. B.C. Grew to be a mercantile city-state under an oligarchy, with explorers (e.g., Hanno) going far and wide to gather trade. Leading families contended for control. The attempt to conquer Sicily in the 5th cent. was set back by the victory of Gelon of Syracuse at Himera (480 B.C.). Later Carthaginian excursions into Sicily led to the PUNIC WARS [from Poeni, the Roman name for Carthaginians, i.e., Phoenicians]. The contest between Rome and Carthage was hotly pursued, and the greatest general involved was a Carthaginian, HANNIBAL. Nevertheless, Carthage was finally defeated in the battle of Zama (202 B.C.), and the Carthaginian commercial empire fell. The city itself was destroyed by Scipio Africanus Minor (146 B.C.). A new city was later built and was the Vandal capital (A.D. 439–533), but it was virtually destroyed by the Arabs in 698. Louis IX of France died here on crusade.

Carthage. 1 City (pop. 3,214), W Ill., near the Mississippi and E of Keokuk, Iowa. Joseph Smith, Mormon leader, and brother killed in city jail (now Mormon shrine) by mob 1844. **2** City (pop. 11,188), SW Mo., NE of Joplin; founded 1842. Trade and mfg. center for farms, quarries, and mines (lead, zinc). Scene of a Confederate victory (1861) in Civil War. G. W. Carver was born near by.

Carthusians (kärthū'zhŭnz), Roman Catholic order of monks, noted for austerity, contemplation, and hermit life, founded by St. Bruno at La Grande CHARTREUSE. The Charterhouse in London and the Certosa at Pavia were Carthusian foundations, and their manufacture gave the name to the liqueur chartreuse.

Cartier, Sir George Étienne (kärtyā'), 1814–73, Canadian statesman. Elected to legislative assembly in 1848, he became leader of the French Canadians. Joined John A. Macdonald to form Macdonald-Cartier ministry (1857–62). Leading French Canadian advocate of confederation.

Cartier, Jacques, 1491–1557, French navigator, first explorer of Gulf of St. Lawrence and discoverer of St. Lawrence R.

Cartwright, John, 1740–1824, English reformer and pamphleteer. Had early naval career. Refused to fight American colonists; wrote *American Independence: the Glory and Interest of Great Britain* (1774). Called father of reform for advocacy of vote by ballot, abolition of slavery, and other reforms. His brother, **Edmund Cartwright,** 1743–1823, was the inventor of the power loom (1785) and other machines. Cooperated with Fulton in steam navigation experiments.

Caruso, Enrico (kŭrōō'sō), 1873–1921, Italian operatic tenor, considered by many the greatest of all time. Made his New York debut in 1903 as the duke in *Rigoletto*. He also appeared in *La Bohème, Pagliacci*, and in many roles.

Caruthersville, city (pop. 8,614), extreme SE Mo., on the Mississippi. Has cotton ginning and mfg. of shoes.

Carvajal, Francisco de (fränthē'skō dä kärvä-häl'), 1464?–1548, Spanish conquistador in Mexico and Peru. Executed for opposing New Laws.

Carver, George Washington, 1864?–1943, American Negro agricultural chemist. Worked to improve economy of South; taught soil improvement, crop diversity; discovered many uses for peanuts, sweet potatoes, soybeans; devised products from cotton wastes.

Carver, John, c.1576–1621, first governor of Plymouth Colony (1620–21), b. England.

Carver, Jonathan, 1710–80, American explorer of the upper Great Lakes and Mississippi region. Hired by Robert ROGERS to seek "Western Ocean."

Carville, town, SE La., on Mississippi R. SSE of Baton Rouge. Has Natl. Leprosarium.

Cary, Alice, 1820–71, and **Phoebe Cary,** 1824–71, American poets, sisters. Phoebe wrote the hymn "One Sweetly Solemn Thought."

Cary, (Arthur) Joyce (Lunel), 1888–, English author. His novels, notable for brilliant characterization, include the comic trilogy made up of *Herself Surprised* (1941), *To Be a Pilgrim* (1942), and *The Horse's Mouth,* (1944).

Cary, Phoebe: see CARY, ALICE.

Casa, Giovanni della (dĕl'lä kä'zä), 1503–56, Italian author of *Galateo* (1560), a treatise on manners.

Casabianca, Louis (kä"sŭbëäng'kŭ), d. 1798, French naval officer, b. Corsica. At Aboukir Bay he commanded the *Orient,* which caught fire. He refused to quit his ship, and his young son refused to desert him. Their heroic death is subject of poem by Felicia Hemans.

Casablanca (kä"sŭblăng'kŭ), city (pop. 551,-322), French Morocco, a port on the Atlantic. On site of ancient Anfa. Destroyed 1468 and resettled 1515 by the Portuguese. Rebuilt by Mohammed XVI after 1755 earthquake. Under French rule since 1907, it is Morocco's chief commercial and industrial center and has large exports of phosphates. In World War II it was scene of major Allied landing (Nov., 1942) and of Roosevelt-Churchill meeting (Jan., 1943).

Casablanca Conference, Jan. 14–26, 1943, meeting of U.S. Pres. Roosevelt and British Prime Minister Churchill at Casablanca, French Morocco. War pledged against Axis states until their unconditional surrender. Mediation united rival French forces.

Casadesus, Robert (käsädäsüs'), 1899–, French pianist, known especially for his playing of French music. He has frequently toured the U.S., often playing his own compositions.

Casa Grande National Monument: see NATIONAL PARKS AND MONUMENTS (table).

Casale or **Casale Monferrato** (käzä'lä mōnfär-rä'tō), city (pop. 25,485), Piedmont, NW Italy, on the Po. Cap. of MONTFERRAT from 1435; to Savoy 1703. Long an important fortress.

Casals, Pablo (pä'blō käsäls'), 1876–, Spanish cellist and conductor. He played many concerts in the U.S. In 1950 he emerged from retirement to play and direct at the Prades Music Festivals in S France.

Casanova de Seingalt, Giovanni Giacomo (jō-vän'nē jä'kōmō käzänō'vä dä sängält'), 1725–98, Venetian adventurer and author, an international gambler and spy. Imprisoned in Venice (1755–56), escaped and lived in Paris till 1774; became librarian to Count Waldstein at Dux, Bohemia. Wrote brilliantly on subjects ranging from poetry to theology. His remarkable memoirs (in French) stress his innumerable, perhaps partly mythical, feminine conquests.

Casas, Bartolomé de las: see LAS CASAS.

Casca (Publius Servilius Casca Longus) (käs'-kù), d. c.42 B.C., one of the conspirators against Julius Caesar, first to stab him. Said to have committed suicide after defeat at Philippi.

Cascade, village (pop. 943), W Idaho, on North Fork of Payette R., near Cascade Dam in BOISE PROJECT.

Cascade Range, N continuation of the Sierra Nevada extending over 700 mi. through N Calif., Oregon, and Wash. into British Columbia. Parallels Pacific coast c.100–150 mi. inland. Snow covers highest summits and much glaciation is present. Chief peaks are Mt. Shasta (Calif.), Mt. Hood (Oregon), and Mt. Rainier (highest, 14,408 ft., Wash.). Fir, pine, and cedar forests occur (many in national reserves). Klamath and Columbia rivers cut E–W through range.

Casco Bay, inlet of the Atlantic, SW Maine, with principal harbor at Portland. Wooded shores and islands have many summer estates and resorts.

case, in Latin INFLECTION, one of several possible forms of a given noun or adjective, the form being essential to the meaning of the word in context. In the theory of some grammarians case forms represent a fixed relationship of the word to other words in a sentence or to the speaker. The cases (in conventional order with conventional significance) are: nominative [Latin,= for naming], referring to a person performing an action; genitive [Latin,= genetic], indicating a possessor (commonly equated with English possessive); dative [Latin,= for giving], indicating the secondary recipient of an action (indirect object); accusative [Latin,= for accusing], direct recipient of an action (equated with English objective); and ablative [Latin, = for carrying off], indicating separation, cause, instrument, and location of place and time. All these have both singular and plural forms (see NUMBER); adjectives agree in case with corresponding nouns. A sixth case, the vocative [Latin,= for calling], occurs only in singular to refer to a person addressed. In many usages cases do not adhere to these conventional references (e.g., some verbs take genitive instead of accusative). The term *case* is used for noun, pronoun, and adjective inflections in other languages, some having many more cases (e.g., locative [Latin,= for placing], as in Sanskrit; instrumental, in many early and some present Indo-European languages including Russian). Cases called in English by the same name do not necessarily correspond in different languages. The case system in English is simple and shows best in personal pronouns (e.g., *he*, nominative; *his*, possessive; *him*, objective).

casein (kā'sēn), complex PROTEIN and phosphorous compound. Forms c.80% of total protein in milk; enzyme rennin turns it to curds. Important in cheese making. Used in making paints, glues, plastics, and wool.

Case Institute of Technology: see CLEVELAND, Ohio.

Casella, Alfredo (käsĕl'lä), 1883–1947, Italian composer, pianist, conductor, and writer on music. His best-known compositions are the ballets *Il convento veneziano* and *La Giara.* Did much to promote the recognition of contemporary music.

Casement, Roger David, 1864–1916, Irish rebel. Knighted for work in British consular service. Attempted to obtain German aid for 1916 Irish rebellion. Returned in German submarine, captured, and hanged for treason. Irish regard him as martyr patriot.

Caserta (käzĕr'tä), city (pop. 30,910), Campania, S Italy. Sumptuous 18th-cent. palace was residence of kings of Naples. Surrender of German forces in Italy to Allies signed here April 29, 1945.

Casgrain, Henri Raymond (käzgrē'), 1831–1904, French Canadian historian. His writings were inspired by French Canadian nationalism and by French romanticism.

cashew (kŭshoō', kăsh'oō), tropical American tree (*Anacardium occidentale*), valued for kidney-shaped cashew nut of commerce. Nuts are borne on end of fleshy stalk called cashew apple.

Cashmere, India: see KASHMIR.

cashmere, soft under wool of Tibetan or Kashmir goat, used for fine sweaters and cloth.

Casilear, John William (käs"lēr'), 1811–93, American engraver and landscape painter.

Casimir (kă'sŭmēr), Polish rulers. **Casimir II,** 1138–94, duke of Cracow (1177–94). Granted privileges to nobles, who in return vested hereditary rights as rulers of Cracow in his descendants (see PIAST). **Casimir III** (the Great), 1310–70, king of Poland (1333–70). During his relatively peaceful reign he acquired most of duchy of GALICH; codified Polish law; improved the lot of the peasants and the Jews; strengthened royal power at expense of nobles; founded Univ. of Cracow. Last Polish king of Piast dynasty, he recognized overlordship of Bohemia over Silesian branch of Piasts (1335). **Casimir IV,** 1427–92, ruled Poland and Lithuania 1447–92. Placed the two nations on equal footing; successfully ended war with Teutonic Knights by Second Peace of TORUN (1466).

Casimir-Perier, Jean Paul Pierre (zhä' pôl' pyĕr' käzēmēr'-pĕryä'), 1847–1907, president of France (1894–95); grandson of Casimir Périer.

Caslon, William, 1692–1766, English type founder. His "old-style" types combine well into legible words and pages without distracting details or "color" variations. Hence printers' maxim, "When in doubt, use Caslon."

Caspar: see WISE MEN OF THE EAST.

Casper, city (pop. 23,673), E central Wyo., on North Platte R.; founded 1888 on site of Oregon Trail ferry crossing (1847). Rail, distributing, processing center in an oil, livestock, and wool area. A city of oil booms, it taps Salty Creek (1890), Big Muddy, Teapot Dome, and Lost Soldier (1948) fields. Near by are Hell's Half Acre, Independence Rock, site of Old Fort Caspar, and Casper Mt. (recreation area). Region served by Kendrick project (Seminoe and Alcova dams), NORTH PLATTE PROJECT, and MISSOURI RIVER BASIN PROJECT (Kortes Dam).

Caspian dialects, related Western Iranian dialects of Indo-Iranian subfamily of Indo-European languages. See LANGUAGE (table).

Caspian Gates: see DERBENT, RSFSR.

Caspian Sea, salt lake (c.163,800 sq. mi.), USSR and Iran, between Europe and Asia, at 92 ft. below ocean level; world's largest inland body of water. Max. depth c.3,200 ft.; in S. Elburz mts. rise from S (Iranian) coast; Caucasus from SW coast. Fed by Volga, Ural, Kura, Terek rivers, sea has no outlet but a high evaporation rate. Large salt deposits. Fisheries, sealeries. Chief source of black caviar. BAKU and ASTRAKHAN are main ports. Project is under way to raise sea level, which has sunk 7 ft. since 1936.

Cass, Lewis, 1782–1866, American statesman. Governor of Michigan Territory (1813–31); U.S. Senator from Mich. (1845–48, 1849–57). Resigned in 1860 as Pres. Buchanan's Secretary of State, protesting decision not to reinforce Charleston, S.C., forts.

Cassaba, Turkey: see KASSABA.

Cassander (kŭsăn'dŭr), 354?–297 B.C., king of Macedon, one of the DIADOCHI; son of Antipater. He managed to defeat Alexander the Great's mother, Olympias (316 B.C.), and murdered Alexander's widow, Roxana, and infant son. Cassander became the ruler in Macedonia and Greece and helped defeat Antigonus I at Ipsus (301 B.C.).

Cassandra, in Greek legend, Trojan princess; daughter of Priam and Hecuba. She learned art of prophecy from Apollo, but was never believed. As Agamemnon's slave, she was slain by Clytemnestra.

Cassano d'Adda (käs-sä'nō däd'dä), village near Milan, N Italy. Scene of two French victories: 1705, of Vendôme over Eugene of Savoy; 1799, of Moreau over Suvarov.

Cassatt, Mary (kŭsăt'), 1845–1926, American painter and etcher. Spent most of her life in France. Greatly influenced by Manet and Degas; early allied herself with the impressionists.

cassava (kŭsä'vü) or **manioc** (mă'nēŏk), tropical American plant (*Manihot esculenta*). Its roots yield cassava starch, a staple food in South America, used elsewhere in the form of TAPIOCA.

Cassel (käsĕl'), small town, N France, near Dunkirk. Scene of French victories over Flemings (1328; see PHILIP VI) and over Dutch (1677; see DUTCH WARS).

Cassel, Germany: see KASSEL.

cassia: see CINNAMON.

Cassini (käs-sē'nē), family of French astronomers and topographers, of Italian origin. Four generations successively headed observatory at Paris. **Giovanni Domenico Cassini** (jōvän'nē dōmā'nēkō), 1625–1712, organized the observatory. He discovered four satellites of Saturn and division in its ring, and determined Mars' rotation period. His son, **Jacques Cassini** (zhäk), 1677–1756, continued his work and advanced the science of earth measurement. His son, **César François Cassini** (sāzär' fräswä'), 1714–84, and grandson, **Jacques Dominique, comte de Cassini** (dōmēnēk' kōt' dü), 1748–1845, constructed a great topographical map of France.

Cassino (käs-sē'nō), town (pop. 9,208), Latium, central Italy, in Appenines, on Rapido R. In World War II Germans blocked Allied advance to Rome at Cassino and near-by abbey of MONTE CASSINO, resisting concentrated air and ground attacks (late 1943 to May 18, 1944). Town was virtually destroyed.

Cassiodorus (kāshōdō'rús), c.480–c.575, Roman statesman and author. Held high office under Theodoric the Great. Made a collection of state papers (*Variae epistolae*); wrote *History of the Goths*.

Cassiopeia (kă"sēōpē'ù), in Greek legend, mother of ANDROMEDA. She was transferred to heaven, becoming the constellation Cassiopeia (five stars in it form a rough W, called Cassiopeia's Chair).

Cassirer, Ernst (käsēr'úr), 1874–1945, German philosopher, professor at Hamburg (1919–33), later lecturer at Oxford. His profound studies in the relationship of science and philosophy had a stimulating effect over the Western world, and his writings on the nature of the state, on aesthetics, and on the nature of meaning are influential today.

Cassius (kă'shús), Roman family. One member, **Quintus Cassius Longinus**, d. 45 B.C., won a reputation for greed and corruption when quaestor in Spain. He and Marc Antony vetoed the rule of the senate intended to compel Julius Caesar to surrender his army. Made an official in Spain after Caesar's triumph, he was faced with a rebellion that Caesar had to quell. Another member was **Caius Cassius Longinus**, d. 42 B.C., the Cassius of Shakspere's *Julius Caesar*. A supporter of Pompey, he was pardoned by Caesar but was a chief figure in the successful plot to assassinate Caesar. When Antony roused the people against the conspirators, he took part with Brutus in the battle of Philippi and there committed suicide.

Cassivellaunus (kă"sĭvĭlô'nús), fl. 54 B.C., British chief, leader against invasion of Julius Caesar, 54 B.C. Defeated, he sued for peace.

cassowary (kăs'ùwâr"ē), flightless, swift-running, pugnacious forest bird of Australia and Malay Archipelago. Smaller than the related ostrich and emu, it has dark, glossy plumage and vivid-colored, wattled neck.

Castagno, Andrea del (ändrā'ä dĕl kästä'nyō), d. c.1457, Florentine painter, a master of realism. Frescoes in Sant' Apollonia monastery, Florence.

Castaigne, André (ädrā' kästän'), 1861–, French illustrator and painter.

Castalia (kästā'lyù), spring near Delphi, Greece, on Mt. Parnassus, sacred to Apollo and the Muses.

Castalion or Castellio, Sébastien (kästāl'yùn, kästĕl'yō), 1515–63, French Protestant theologian, known for his defense of religious toleration in preface to his Latin translation of Bible (1551). His name also appears as Castellion and Châtillon.

caste, hereditary social class. Members restricted in choice of occupation and range of social participation. Marriage outside the caste prohibited. Social status determined by caste of one's birth. In India, four chief castes (with many subdivisions): Brahmans (priests), Kshatriyas (the military), Vaisyas (farmers and merchants), Sudras (laborers). Lowest social group, the pariahs or "untouchables" are outside caste system.

Castel Gandolfo (kästĕl' gändōl'fō), village, Latium, central Italy, near Rome; possibly on site of anc. Alba Longa. Summer residence of pope.

Castellammare di Stabia (kästĕl"lämä'rä dē stä'byä), city (pop. 36,469), Campania, S Italy, on Bay of Naples. Navy yards. Anc. Stabiae, near here, was Roman resort; buried A.D. 79 in eruption of Vesuvius.

Castellani, Aldo, 1877–, British-Italian bacteriologist, authority on tropical medicine, and known in this field for research (esp. on sleeping sickness), writing, and organization of schools.

Castellio or Castellion, Sébastien: see CASTALION, SÉBASTIEN.

Castello or Castelli, Bernardo (bĕrnär'dō kästĕl'lō, –tĕl'lē), 1557–1629, Italian painter of Genoese school. Made the designs for Tasso's *Jerusalem Delivered*. His son, **Valerio Castello**, 1625–1659, was a historical painter, whose best-known work is *The Rape of the Sabines* (Palazzo Brignole, Genoa.)

Castellón de la Plana (kästĕlyōn' dä lä plä'nä), city (pop. 42,324), cap. of Castellón de la Plana prov., E Spain, in Valencia, near Mediterranean. Its port, Grao, ships oranges, lemons, wine.

Castel Sant' Angelo (kästĕl' säntän'jälō) or Hadrian's Mole, landmark of Rome, on right bank of Tiber. Built A.D. 135–39 by Hadrian as imperial mausoleum; later converted into fortress; used as prison till 1870. Connected by secret passage with Vatican.

Castiglione, Baldassare, Conte (bäldäs-sä'rä kōn'tä kästēlyō'nä), 1478–1529, Italian author of *Libro del Cortegiano* (1518; Eng. tr., *The Courtier*, 1561), lively dialogues on Renaissance courtly ideals.

Castiglione, Giovanni Benedetto (jōvän'nē bānädĕt'tō), 1616–70, Italian painter and engraver of Genoese school. Excelled at painting animals.

Castiglione delle Stiviere (dĕl'lä stēvyä'rä), small town, N Italy, NW of Mantua. Scene of Bonaparte's victory over Austrians 1796.

Castile (kästēl'), Span. *Castilla*, former kingdom, central and N Spain. Traditionally divided into two regions: Old Castile (19,390 sq. mi.; pop. 1,577,135), in the north, with cities of Burgos, Santander, Segovia; and New Castile (27,933 sq. mi.; pop. 3,129,170), in the south, with Madrid, Toledo, Cuenca. Castile contains most of the high, arid plateau of central Spain. The upper Duero, Tagus, and Guadiana rivers form the chief basins. Agr., sheep grazing; much erosion. Mineral resources include mercury at Almadén. Few industries. Old Castile, at first a county of kingdom of LEON, became virtually independent by 10th cent. Sancho III of Navarre acquired it 1028, made it into separate kingdom for his son FERDINAND I. Later kings expanded territory at expense of Moors (New Castile); achieved permanent union with Leon (1230); estab. authority over rebellious nobles. Marriage of ISABELLA I of Castile with Ferdinand II of Aragon (Ferdinand V of Castile) resulted in personal union of the two kingdoms (1479). Union made permanent 1516 through accession of Charles I (later Emperor CHARLES V), who suppressed *comunidades* uprisings of 1519–21. Later history is that of Spain.

Castillo de San Marcos National Monument: see NATIONAL PARKS AND MONUMENTS (table).

Castine (kăstēn'), town (pop. 793), S Maine, on peninsula in Penobscot Bay. Plymouth Colony estab. trading post near by, 1626. Town later changed hands several times among French, British, Dutch, Americans. Baron J. V. St. Castin began his "rule" 1667. British held it in Revolution and War of 1812. Has Fort George (1779; British-built) and Fort Madison (1811; rebuilt in Civil War).

casting: see FOUNDING.

cast iron: see IRON.

Castle, Vernon, 1887–1918, English dancer and aviator, whose real name was Vernon Castle Blythe. Introduced many dances (e.g., "Castle walk") with his wife, **Irene (Foote) Castle,** 1893–. She popularized bobbed hair and boyish figure. He was killed in an airplane accident in World War I.

Castle Garden: see BATTERY, THE, New York city.

Castle Peak: see ELK MOUNTAINS.

Castle Pinckney National Monument: see NATIONAL PARKS AND MONUMENTS (table).

Castlereagh, Robert Stewart, 2d Viscount (kä'sŭlrā), 1769–1822, British statesman, b. Dublin. As chief secretary for Ireland, was responsible for suppressing French-aided rebellion in 1798. Secretary of war (1805, 1807–9) during struggle with Napoleon I; planned Peninsular War, coordinated land and sea power, and backed duke of Wellington. Resigned after political betrayal by George CANNING (with whom he fought a duel). As foreign secretary (1812-22), helped organize "concert of Europe" against Napoleon, later confirmed by QUADRUPLE ALLIANCE (1815). Advocate of moderate terms for France at Paris peace conference and Congress of VIENNA, favored policy of balance of power and ascendancy of conservative governments. Committed suicide.

Castle Shannon, borough (pop. 5,459), SW Pa., S suburb of Pittsburgh.

Castor and Pollux, in Greek and Roman religion, twin heroes called Dioscuri [Gr.,= youths of Zeus]. Sons of Leda by Zeus or by Tyndareus. They were giants, gifted in battle, and joined Calydonian hunt and Argonaut expedition. When Castor was slain, Zeus made the brothers into the constellation GEMINI. They were highly honored in Rome. Castor was notable as a horse trainer, Pollux as a boxer. Together they were patrons of sailors. Phenomenon of St. Elmo's fire is still called Castor and Pollux.

castor oil, oil extracted from seed of castor-bean or castor-oil plant (*Ricinus communis*). Used as purgative, lubricant, leather-softener, and in brake fluids, paints, and other materials.

Castracani, Castruccio (kästroōt'chō kästräkä'-nē), 1281–1328, Italian Ghibelline leader. Made duke of Lucca (1327) by Emperor Louis IV, he sought hegemony over Tuscany and was about to conquer Florence when he died and his principality went to pieces.

Castries (kä'strēz), town (pop. c.16,579), cap. of Saint Lucia, British West Indies. Has fine harbor.

Castriota, George: see SCANDERBEG.

Castro, Inés de (ī'nĕz dù kä'strō), d. 1355, Galician noblewoman, mistress of Dom Pedro of Portugal (later PETER I), to whom she probably was secretly married. Pedro's father, Alfonso IV, feared her influence and had her murdered. When Pedro became king he had two of her murderers put to cruel death. The tradition that he had Inés disinterred and crowned is probably untrue. Name is also spelled Inez.

Castrogiovanni, Italy: see ENNA.

Castro y Bellvís, Guillén de (gēlyän' dā käs'trō ē bĕlvēs'), 1569–1631, Spanish dramatist, author of *Las mocedades del Cid,* which inspired Corneille's *Le Cid.*

cat, small domestic carnivorous mammal related to lion, tiger, leopard, jaguar, puma. It has retractile claws and acute senses (good eyesight in dim light). Long-haired breeds include Persian (now generally includes Angora because of interbreeding), the sacred cat of Burma, and the Tibetan temple cat. Among short-haired cats are the common short-haired, Manx (tailless), Siamese, and Abyssinian. All are genus *Felis.*

catacombs, burial places of the early Christians, arranged in extensive subterranean vaults and galleries; also used incidentally for refuge from persecution and for religious services. Those at Rome lie outside the city gates, are 22 to 65 ft. below the ground, cover an area of c.600 acres, and were built in the first five centuries. Tombs were cut into walls of narrow plastered passages, which were covered with frescoes. Most bodies were removed to churches by 8th cent. Other catacombs were in Naples, Syracuse, Paris, Alexandria, and Sousse.

Catalan art. Although Catalonia still produces many fine artists, Catalan art as such (the religious art of Middle Ages and Renaissance) ended with 15th cent. Elaborately painted churches, architectural sculpture, and illuminated manuscripts (notably the Bible from Farfa abbey) were in international Romanesque style. Works of more distinctly regional character culminated in gorgeous 15th-cent. religious painting (esp. of Jaime Huguet and of Jaime, Rafael, and Pablo Vergós).

Catalan language, Romanic language of Italic subfamily of Indo-European languages. See LANGUAGE (table).

catalepsy (kă′tŭlĕpsē), psychogenic fit, neurotically or hypnotically induced. Voluntary motion and sensibility are suspended, muscles are rigid, body is cold and pale, and pulse and respiration are slow. Duration varies from minutes to days.

Catalina Island: see SANTA BARBARA ISLANDS.

catalogue, descriptive list of names or items, such as an alphabetical list on cards or in a book of the books in a library. Assur-banipal's library at Nineveh was catalogued on shelves of slate. First known subject catalogue compiled by Callimachus at the Alexandrian Library in 3d cent. B.C. Sir Anthony PANIZZI began printing of British Museum catalogue of printed books, and Charles A. CUTTER devised modern dictionary catalogue (author, title, and subject in one alphabet). In 1901 Library of Congress began printing catalogue on 3″x5″ cards.

Catalonia (kătŭlō′nėŭ), Span. *Cataluña*, region (12,332 sq mi.; pop. 2,890,974), NE Spain, stretching from Pyrenees southward along Mediterranean; historic cap. Barcelona. Other cities: Gerona, Lérida, Tarragona. Agr.; wine; olive oil. Hydroelectric power furnished by Ebro, Segre, and Cinca rivers has favored industries (textiles, machinery). Both Spanish and Catalan (akin to Provençal) are spoken. Part of the Spanish March founded by Charlemagne, medieval Catalonia was ruled by the counts of BARCELONA. Despite its dynastic union with Aragon from 1137 and with Castile from 1479, it kept its own laws and cortes until 18th cent. Peak of commercial prosperity came in 13th–15th cent., when Catalan merchants and adventurers helped the expansion of the house of ARAGON throughout the Mediterranean. Traditionally rebellious against central government, Catalonia obtained self-government in 1932–34 and in 1936–39; in the civil war it resisted Franco, who abolished its autonomy.

catalpa (kŭtăl′pŭ), ornamental tree of genus *Catalpa*, with large, heart-shaped leaves, large clusters of white flowers, and long beanlike pods. Species in North America, India, and Asia.

catalysis (kŭtă′lŭsĭs), changing speed of chemical reaction by introducing a **catalyst.** Positive catalysts increase speed of reaction; negative, decrease. Catalyst takes some part in reaction, but can be recovered unchanged chemically. Water acts as catalyst since many compounds react only in solution. Enzymes act as catalysts in metabolic processes.

Catania (kätä′nyä), city (pop. 241,462) and seaport, E. Sicily, Italy, in fertile plain at foot of Mt. Etna. Founded 8th cent. B.C. by Greek colonists; flourishing commercial center ever since. Suffered from repeated earthquakes, volcanic eruptions. Damaged in World War II. Cathedral dates partly from 12th cent. Univ. founded 1444.

catapult (kă′tŭpŭlt), machine commonly used in medieval warfare; in effect, a giant crossbow operated by a windlass and designed to throw large stones (also arrows and other objects). Used in siege warfare from the 5th cent. B.C. to the 15th cent. A.D., when gunpowder and artillery grew common.

cataract, in medicine, opacity of lens of eye or its capsule. Causes include faulty development, injuries, infections, toxic states, and senility.

catastrophism (kŭtăs′trŭfĭzŭm), doctrine that at intervals all living things have been destroyed by cataclysms and replaced by forms wholly different. This theory was attacked in 18th cent. by James Hutton, precursor of doctrine of UNIFORMISM.

Catawba, river: see WATEREE, river.

catbird, North American songbird and mimic related to mockingbird. It is slate gray, with black on the crown and tail and chestnut under tail coverts. It eats fruits and insects.

catchment area or **drainage basin,** area drained by a stream or other water body. Amount of water reaching stream or reservoir depends on size of catchment area, precipitation, and loss from evaporation and through absorption by soil and vegetation.

Cateau, Le (lŭ kätō′), town (pop. 7,682), Nord dept., N France; formerly Le Cateau-Cambrésis. Scene of heavy fighting (1914, 1918) in World War I.

Cateau-Cambrésis, Treaty of (kābrāzē′), 1559, peace treaty among Spain, France and England, signed at Le Cateau. From its 60-year struggle with France over hegemony in Italy, Spain emerged triumphant, winning Naples, Sicily, Milan. France restored Savoy to its duke. England, though technically allied with Spain, confirmed Calais in French possession.

catechism [Gr.,= oral instruction], series of questions and answers used in teaching a religious system. Martin Luther's date from 1520 and 1529. Reformed Churches revere Heidelberg Catechism (1563). Presbyterians adopted Longer and Shorter Catechisms (1647, 1648). A section of Book of Common Prayer is an Anglican catechism. Peter Canisius drew up a famous Catholic catechism (1556).

catechu (kă′tŭchōō), extract, also called cutch and black catechu, from *Acacia catechu*, tree of India and Burma. It and pale catechu, obtained from Malayan plant (*Uncaria gambier*), are used in dyeing, tanning, and medically as an astringent.

categorical imperative: see KANT, IMMANUEL.

Catena, Vincenzo di Biagio (vĕnchän′tsō dē byä′jō kätä′nä), c.1470–1531, Venetian painter. With Giorgione and Titian, ranked by contemporaries as one of three great painters of the day.

catfish, scavenger fish with barbels about mouth, adipose fin, tough scaleless skin (some South American forms contain bony plates). Most larger species are palatable. The blue or Mississippi catfish weighs c.20–150 lb. The mad tom and stone catfishes have pectoral spine with poison gland.

Cathari (kă′thŭrī), name given to various groups of a religious movement that began with the Bogomils in the Balkans (10th cent.) and included the ALBIGENSES. The fundamental ideas of the Cathari were belief in a dualism (God versus Satan, good versus evil) and practice of extreme asceticism. They did not accept the Christian idea of

God and rejected sacraments and the priestly hierarchy. There were two classes: the Prefect and the believers. Doctrines apparently descended from Gnosticism and Manichaeism to the Cathari through the Paulicians.

Cathay (kăthā'), medieval European name for China, popularized by Marco Polo.

Cather, Willa (Sibert), 1876–1947, American novelist. Wrote novels and short stories of the Midwest (*O Pioneers!,* 1913; *My Antonia,* 1918; *A Lost Lady,* 1923) and of historic past (*Death Comes for the Archbishop,* 1927; *Shadows on the Rock,* 1931).

Catherine: see KATHARINE. Other spellings include Catharine, Katherine, and Kathryn.

Catherine, Saint, 4th cent.?, Alexandrian virgin martyr, traditionally supposed to have miraculously escaped dying on the wheel, only to be beheaded later. Her principal shrine is on Mt. Sinai, her attributes sword, crown, palm, wheel, and book. Her mystical marriage with Christ was popular as a subject of Renaissance art. Feast: Nov. 25.

Catherine, empresses of Russia. **Catherine I** (Martha Skavronskaya), 1684?–1727, a Livonian servant girl, was a mistress of Peter the Great before he took her as second wife (1711). Chosen his successor (1725), she ruled ably. **Catherine II** or **Catherine the Great** (Princess Sophie of Anhalt-Zerbst), 1729–96, of German birth, married the future PETER III in 1744. His worthlessness soon estranged her. She became thoroughly Russian and very popular. In June, 1762, a group of conspirators, headed by her lover Grigori ORLOV, deposed Peter and proclaimed her empress. Influenced by the Enlightenment, she planned vast reforms, but the PUGACHEV rebellion and the French Revolution drove her into reaction. A liberal law code remained a project; her charter to the nobility (1785) completed the enslavement of the serfs. Her foreign policy was imperialistic. Through her favorite, STANISLAUS II, she made Poland a Russian protectorate, then secured the major share in the Polish partitions of 1772, 1793, and 1795. She annexed the Crimea (1783) and in two wars against Turkey (1768–74, 1787–92) made Russia dominant in Near East. She began the colonization of Alaska. With her main interests in the East she remained neutral in American and French revolutionary wars. Of versatile gifts, she wrote memoirs, comedies, stories, in French and in Russian, and encouraged birth of modern Russian literature. Among her many lovers, only Orlov and POTEMKIN were of consequence. Her son, Paul I, succeeded her.

Catherine de' Medici (dĭ mĕd'ĭchē), 1519–89, queen of Henry II of France; daughter of Lorenzo II de' Medici. Regent for her son CHARLES IX (1560–63). Sought to conciliate Protestants but later sided with Catholics. Plotted massacre of SAINT BARTHOLOMEW'S DAY (1572).

Catherine of Braganza, 1638–1705, queen consort of Charles II of England, daughter of John IV of Portugal. Dowry included Bombay and Tangier. Lived apart from court. Accused by Titus OATES of plot to poison the king (1678), but Charles protected her.

Catherine of Siena, Saint (sēē'nŭ), 1347–80, Italian Dominican nun. She early began to have visions that were to result in her *Dialogue* and *A Treatise of Divine Providence* and make her one of the greatest of Catholic mystics. Her life was one of great pain cheerfully borne, and her charitable love of mankind matched her love of God. In response to a vision, she went to Avignon and persuaded Gregory XI to end the "Babylonian Captivity" of the papacy, and later her influence was great in supporting the Roman claimant in the Great Schism. Her works were dictated for she never learned to write. Feast: April 30.

Catherine of Valois (văl'wä), 1401–37, queen consort of Henry V of England, daughter of Charles VI of France. Later married Owen TUDOR. Tudor kings descended from them.

Catherine Tekakwitha (tĕk"äkwĭth'ŭ), 1656–80, American Indian girl of the Mohawk tribe, a Roman Catholic noted for her austere piety.

Catherine the Great: see CATHERINE II, empress.

cathode: see ELECTRODE.

cathode ray: see ELECTRON and X RAY.

Catholic Apostolic Church, religious community founded in England (c.1831) under Edward IRVING (hence its members are called Irvingites). Symbolism, mystery, and stress on second coming of Christ characterize the church.

Catholic Church, term meaning the universal church, adopted by many Christian sects. Generally in English when referring to the time before the Reformation it means the orthodox faith as opposed to movements pronounced heretical; when referring to the time since the Reformation, it usually means the Roman Catholic Church (sometimes also the Orthodox Eastern Church).

Catholic Emancipation, term applied to process by which Roman Catholics in the British Isles were relieved of civil disabilities dating back to Henry VIII. First concessions produced Gordon riots (1780). Most disabilities removed in 1791 for those in Great Britain who took a loyalty oath. Attempts of William Pitt and Pope Pius VII to get general repeal of the PENAL LAWS failed. In Ireland (see IRISH LAND QUESTION) agitation which forced repeal of restrictions (e.g., POYNINGS's LAW) seemed a threat to Protestant domination. Act of Union (1800) destroyed Irish Parliament; gave Ireland representation in English Parliament. After repeal of the TEST ACT (1828), growing agitation in Ireland, headed by Daniel O'CONNELL, led to Catholic Emancipation Bill (1829) sponsored by Sir Robert PEEL. Most remaining restrictions removed in 1866, 1891, and 1926. Act of SETTLEMENT still excludes Catholics from the throne, from certain civil and religious offices, and from a few university places.

Catholic League, in French history: see LEAGUE.

Catholic University of America, at Washington, D.C.; controlled by Catholic hierarchy, the only U.S. pontifical university; for men and women; chartered 1887, opened 1889. Supported by contributions from all parishes.

Catiline (Lucius Sergius Catilina) (kă'tĭlīn),

c.108 B.C.–62 B.C., Roman politician. A partisan of Sulla, he was made praetor and governor of Africa. In 66 B.C. he was barred from candidacy for the consulship because he was accused of misconduct (falsely, as it turned out). Disgruntled he got up an abortive plot to murder the consuls; he and his confederates were acquitted. Running for consul in 63 B.C. he was opposed by Cicero and the conservatives and was defeated. Thereupon he concocted a conspiracy to gain power. Cicero, acting on information from Catiline's mistress, exposed the conspiracy in the first of perhaps the most famous series of orations ever delivered—the orations against Catiline. The conspirators, who even approached the ambassadors of the Allobroges, were arrested and condemned to death, though Julius Caesar urged moderation. Catiline did not surrender and was killed in battle. The question of Catiline's character and guilt is unsettled, since the only sources on him—Cicero and Sallust—are hostile.

Catlettsburg, city (pop. 4,750), E Ky., on Ohio R. at mouth of Big Sandy R. near Ashland. Scene of American Folk Song Festival near by.

Catlin, George, 1796–1872, American artist and traveler. Went over the West and later through Central and South America to paint Indian portraits and scenes. Many pictures in National Mus. Wrote *Manners, Customs, and Condition of the North American Indians* (2 vols., 1841) and other works.

catlinite: see PIPESTONE.

catnip or catmint, perennial mint (*Nepeta cataria*), with aromatic leaves often made into tea. Catnip is attractive to cats.

Catoctin Mountain, E prong of the Blue Ridge in Md., extending SSW from just S of Pa. line. "Shangri-La," President Roosevelt's retreat and scene of important World War II conferences, is here.

Cato Street Conspiracy: see THISTLEWOOD, ARTHUR.

Cato the Elder or Cato the Censor (Marcus Porcius Cato) (kā′tō), 234–149 B.C., Roman statesman. He spoke much of the austere virtues of old Rome and decried luxury, extravagance, and innovations. He had fought in the Second Punic War, and, when sent in old age to Carthage, returned to insist sternly, "Carthage must be destroyed!" He thus helped to bring on the Third Punic War, in which Carthage was destroyed. A man of great wealth, he was noted for cruelty to his servants and for niggardliness. His history of Rome is now lost, and of his extant works a treatise on farming is the best known. Also Cato Major. His great-grandson, **Cato the Younger or Cato Minor,** 95 B.C.–46 B.C., was also named Marcus Porcius Cato. He was known particularly for incorruptible honesty, supported by Stoicism. He opposed Julius Caesar and denounced Catiline. A supporter of Pompey, he continued the struggle against Caesar after the defeat at Pharsala and held Utica. After the crushing defeat at Thapsus, he committed suicide. Also Cato of Utica.

cat's-eye, name for two green gems which show a line of light caused by reflection from parallel fibers. The more valuable is a form of chrysoberyl; the less valuable is a variety of quartz.

Catskill, village (pop. 5,392), SE N.Y., on Hudson R. (Rip Van Winkle Bridge) and S of Albany. Gateway to resorts in Catskill Mts. Farm (dairy, fruit, truck) trade center.

Catskill Aqueduct, SE N.Y., a main unit of New York city water-supply system; planned 1905. Schoharie Reservoir water sent via 18-mi. Shandaken tunnel (opened 1924) to Esopus Creek, which is dammed c.15 mi. downstream to form Ashokan Reservoir (area c.13 sq. mi.; 1916) W of Kingston. After aeration here, Catskill Aqueduct carries the water 92 mi. S, passing for 1,114 ft. under the Hudson at Storm King, to Kensico Reservoir in Bronx R. near White Plains, thence to Hillview Reservoir in Yonkers. (Kensico and Hillview reservoirs also receive water from Delaware R. project, begun 1937 and placed in partial emergency use in 1944.) From Hillview Reservoir tunnels take water to New York city (steel pipe across the Narrows to Staten Isl.).

Catskill Mountains, range of the Appalachians, SE N.Y., W of the Hudson and S of Mohawk Valley, rising to 4,204 ft. in Slide Mt. They are a dissected and glaciated part of the Allegheny Plateau, well wooded and rolling, with deep gorges and many waterfalls. Popular summer and winter resort. Delaware R. headstreams and Esopus, Schoharie, and Catskill creeks are a source of New York city water supply through Catskill and Delaware aqueducts. Catskill Forest Preserve includes region of the Rip Van Winkle legend.

Catt, Carrie (Lane) Chapman, 1859–1947, American suffragist. President of Natl. American Woman Suffrage Association. Led campaign for Federal suffrage amendment. Organized League of Women Voters. After 1923 she devoted efforts to peace movement.

cattail or reed mace, marsh perennial of genus *Typha*, with long, narrow leaves and a brown cylindrical spike of flowers used in winter bouquets.

Cattaro, Yugoslavia: see KOTOR.

Cattell, James McKeen (kŭtĕl′), 1860–1944, American psychologist, pioneer in psychological research. His dismissal from Columbia Univ. teaching staff (1917) for alleged unpatriotic statements was widely protested. A prolific author, he also established and edited several scientific periodicals.

cattle, domestic animals of bovine genus, probably descended from the AUROCHS; closely related to the buffalo, bison, and yak. First cattle came to W Hemisphere on Columbus' second voyage. Since mid-18th cent., have been improved by selective and scientific breeding. Chief beef breeds are the Aberdeen Angus (black Angus) and Hereford (red, with white face); for dairying, Ayrshire (red and white or brown and white), brown Swiss, Dutch Belted (black, with white midriff), Guernsey (fawn and white), Holstein-Friesian (black and white), Jersey (tan, brown, gray, or cream; sometimes varicolored); for both purposes, Devon (red to chestnut), red polled (cherry red), and shorthorn (or Durham) and the related polled (hornless) shorthorn (red, red and white, or white and roan).

cattle plague: see RINDERPEST.

Catullus (Caius Valerius Catullus) (kûtŭ'lŭs), 84?–54? B.C., Latin poet, one of greatest lyricists. Poems ascribed to him (116 extant) include many satires and epigrams as well as exquisite lyrics on his beloved (probably Clodia), called Lesbia.

Catulus (kă'chŏōlŭs), family of anc. Rome. An early member was **Caius Lutatius Catulus,** consul in 242 B.C., victor in the naval engagement with Carthage off the Aegates that ended the First Punic War. Another was **Quintus Lutatius Catulus,** d. 87 B.C., consul in 102 B.C. with Marius. Helped defeat the Cimbri, later opposed Marius, favoring Sulla. In the hour of Marius' triumph he committed suicide or was killed. His son, **Quintus Lutatius Catulus,** d. c.60 B.C., was consul 78 B.C. and leader of archconservatives. He and Claudius put down the revolt of Lepidus. Later he violently opposed Julius Caesar.

Cauca (kou'kä), river, c.600 mi. long, rising in W Colombia and flowing N through Andes to the Magdalena.

Caucasian Gates: see DARYAL, Georgian SSR.

Caucasus (kô'kŭsŭs), mountain system, USSR, between Europe and Asia, extending c.750 mi. from Black Sea SE to Caspian Sea. Main range, the Greater Caucasus, is a majestic chain of snow-capped peaks, culminating in Mt. ELBRUS at 18,481 ft. Pierced by MAMISON, DARYAL, and other passes, it divides N Caucasia, which slopes down to Kuban steppe, from Transcaucasia. The Lesser Caucasus, S of KURA R., is extension of Iranian plateau. Pastures, forests in uplands; agr., orchards, vineyards in valleys. Many health resorts (e.g., Pyatigorsk, Kizlovodsk). Mineral resources include rich oil fields at BAKU, GROZNY, MAIKOP, manganese at Chiatura. Caucasus was known to ancient Greeks: here Prometheus was chained, Jason sought Golden Fleece. Centuries of invasions and migrations left complex ethnical structure. N Caucasia, including historic CIRCASSIA, is part of RSFSR. Transcaucasia is divided into GEORGIAN SSR, AZERBAIJAN SSR, ARMENIAN SSR. Russian penetration in 19th cent. was resisted by Moslem elements until collapse of SHAMYL uprising (1859).

Cauchon, Pierre (pyĕr' kôshô'), d. 1442, Bishop of Beauvais, France. President of court that convicted JOAN OF ARC.

Cauchy, Augustin Louis, Baron (ōgüstē' lwē' bärō' kōshē'), 1789–1857, French mathematician, influential in every mathematics branch (especially theory of functions, integral and differential calculus, algebraic analysis) and also in astronomy, optics, and other fields.

caucus, political party gathering or standing party organization. In the U.S., legislative caucuses once nominated presidential candidates, and are still used in Congress to aid in party policy formation. In Great Britain the term usually used to condemn groups.

caudillo (koudhē'yō), type of Hispanic American political leader who arose with wars of independence. Typical caudillo is usually mestizo with strong appeal to Indian and mestizo masses; has military ability; begins by championing rights of masses against wealthy white classes; later becomes oligarch himself. Famous caudillos: Rosas of Argentina, Carrera of Guatemala, Díaz of Mexico, Juan Vicente Gómez of Venezuela.

Caudine Forks (kô'dīn), narrow passes in Apennines, S Italy. Here in 321 B.C. Samnites routed Roman army, forced it to pass under yoke.

Caughnawaga (kä'näwä"gù), village, S Que., Canada, on St. Lawrence R. opposite Lachine. Founded 1667 as refuge for Iroquois Christian converts.

Caulaincourt, Louis, marquis de (lwē' märkē' dù kōlēkōōr'), b. 1772 or 1773, d. 1827, French general. Ambassador to Russia (1807–11); aide-de-camp to Napoleon on Russian campaign; foreign minister during Hundred Days. Left remarkable memoirs of years 1812–15, first published 1933 (Eng. tr., 1935–36).

cauliflower (kô'lĭ–), variety of cabbage, with edible white head of flowers and flower stems.

Caupolicán (koupōlēkän'), d. 1558, leader of ARAUCANIAN INDIANS who fiercely resisted Spanish Conquest of Chile.

caustic, substance that burns or corrodes organic matter. Caustic SODA is an alkali.

Cauvery or **Kaveri** (kô'vùrē), river, S India; flows c.475 mi. from W Ghats to Bay of Bengal. Sacred to Hindus. Irrigation-canal system at delta.

Cavaignac, Louis Eugène (lwē' ûzhĕn' kävänyäk'), 1802–57, French general. Fought in Algeria. As minister of war suppressed workingmen's rising in JUNE DAYS of 1848.

Cavalier, Jean (zhä' kävälyä'), 1679?–1740, French Protestant leader. Led uprising of CAMISARDS but made separate peace with government in 1704.

cavalier, in general, an armed horseman. In English civil war, Cavaliers were followers of Charles I, as against Roundheads, supporters of Parliament. Term for royalists until it was replaced by Tory.

Cavalier poets, literary group at court of Charles I of England, notable for the grace and wit of polished lyrics on love, fleeting youth and beauty. Included Herrick, Lovelace, Suckling, Carew.

Cavallini, Pietro (pyä'trō kävăl-lē'nē), c.1250–c.1330, Italian painter and mosaicist, who influenced Cimabue and Giotto.

cavalry, mounted troops trained to fight from horseback. Used among the anc. Egyptians, cavalry groups were much more commonly used by the Assyrians and the Persians. Speed gave them an advantage, but this was offset by the lack of saddles (until the time of Constantine I), and Greek and Roman victories were won by well-disciplined foot troops. Cavalry was first triumphant when used by Huns, Avars, Magyars, and Mongols in invading Europe. The typical soldierly figure of the Middle Ages was the mounted, armored knight. Reintroduction of mass warfare (e.g., the companies of English bowmen at Crécy, 1346) and the use of gunpowder made the infantry prominent again, but cavalry was extensively used, particularly for mobile striking forces and for scouting. Wherever warfare was open the cavalry shone, and cavalrymen were the elite of soldiery through the time of the American Civil War. In World War I and much more in World War II development of mechanized, motorized, and armored vehicles made horse cavalry obsolete except for very special missions (as in rough mountain terrain). In 1946 the U.S. army abolished cavalry as a separate army.

Cavan (kǎ'vừn), inland county (730 sq. mi.; pop. 70,355), Ulster prov., Ireland; co. town Cavan. It is a hilly region of lakes and bogs with cool damp climate. Agr. chief occupation, but only a third of area is cultivated.

cave, a hollow in earth or rock. Formed usually by chemical or mechanical action of water. Ground water dissolves or wears rock; dashing waves cut into rocky shores. Most caves are in limestone, owing to its solubility; many are famous for STALACTITE AND STALAGMITE formations. Caves of Iceland and Hawaii were caused by volcanic action.

cave art, paintings and engravings found on interior cave walls. Earliest examples date from Paleolithic times, the Magdalenian phase showing most highly developed technique. Subject matter of paintings suggests they had magical intent. Famous examples are those of lower Italy, ALTAMIRA (Spain), the Dordogne, and the central Pyrenees.

Cave City, town (pop. 1,119), S Ky., NE of Bowling Green. Center of cave region (Mammoth Cave, Diamond Caverns, and others); tourist center.

Cavell, Edith (kǎ'vǔl), 1865–1915, British nurse. Matron at Brussels hospital in World War I, she was shot by the Germans for aid to Allied prisoners.

Cavendish, Henry, 1731–1810, English physicist, chemist. Determined specific heats for certain substances. Did research on properties of "inflammable air" (hydrogen) that he isolated and described, on composition of air, electricity, density of earth.

Cavendish or **Candish, Thomas,** 1555?–1592, English navigator. Commanded third voyage around the world (1586–88), ravaging Spanish towns and shipping on W coast of South America. Died during disastrous second attempt at circumnavigation.

Cavendish, William: see NEWCASTLE, WILLIAM CAVENDISH, DUKE OF.

Cavendish Laboratory: see CAMBRIDGE UNIVERSITY.

caviar or **caviare** (kǎ'vēär), roe (eggs) of sturgeon prepared, mainly in Russia, as table delicacy. The eggs are black, green, brown, or yellow ("gray"), and vary in size from tiny grains to pea size.

Cavite (kävē'tä), city (pop. 35,052), SW Luzon, Philippines, on small peninsula in Manila Bay. Naval base (1898) at Sangley Point (opposite city proper) is held by U.S. as limited operational area.

Cavour, Camillo Benso, conte di (kämēl'lō bän'sō kōn'tä dē kävōōr'), 1810–61, Italian statesman, premier of Sardinia (1852–59, 1860–61). Chief architect of Italian unification under Victor Emmanuel II (see RISORGIMENTO).

cavy (kǎ'vē), name of GUINEA PIG and number of related South American rodents. Wild

cavy is usually brown and has no tail. Forms include Patagonian cavy, Bolivian cavy, Peruvian cavy, restless cavy of Brazil, and CAPYBARA.

Cawdor (kô'dừr), parish, Nairnshire, Scotland. Cawdor Castle represented by Shakspere as scene of the slaying of Duncan by Macbeth 1040.

Cawnpore or **Kanpur** (both: kôn'pôr"), city (pop. 487,324), S Uttar Pradesh, India, on Ganges R. Nana Sahib wiped out British garrison here in Sepoy Rebellion of 1857. Major trade and mfg. center.

Caxton, William, c.1421–1491, English printer. A mercer, he learned printing at Cologne. With Colard Mansion printed first book in English, *The Recuyell of the Historyes of Troye* (Bruges, 1475). He also issued first dated book printed in England, *Dictes or Sayengis of the Philosophres* (Westminster, 1477). He translated works and wrote prologues, epilogues, and additions.

Cayenne (kīěn'), city (pop. 10,961), cap. of French Guiana, on island at mouth of Cayenne R. Cayenne pepper originally came from here.

Cayman Islands (kā'mừn), archipelago (c.92 sq. mi.; pop. 9,625), dependency in British West Indies, NW of Jamaica.

Cayuga Indians: see IROQUOIS CONFEDERACY.

Cayuga Lake, N.Y.: see FINGER LAKES.

Cazin, Jean Charles (zhä' shärl' käzē'), 1841–1901, French painter of figure compositions in landscape.

Cb, symbol of columbium (see NIOBIUM).

C battery: see BATTERY, ELECTRIC.

Cd, chemical symbol of the element CADMIUM.

Ce, chemical symbol of the element CERIUM.

Ceara (seura'), state (59,168 sq. mi.; pop. 2,735,702), NE Brazil; cap. FORTALEZA. Atlantic coastal plain produces cotton, sugar, coffee. Semiarid uplands are used for cattle and goat raising. Suffered severely from droughts.

Cebu (sāboō'), island (1,702 sq. mi.; pop. 947,309), one of Visayan Isls., Philippines. Cap. and chief port is Cebu (pop. 167,503) on E coast, with harbor sheltered by Mactan isl. Founded 1565 by López de Legaspi; cap. of Philippine Isls. until 1571. Exports hemp and copra.

Cech, Svatopluk, Czech *Čech* (svä'tôploŏk chěkh'), 1846–1908, Czech poet and novelist. An ardent pan-Slavist, he wrote lyrics and epics based on Czech history (*Zizka,* 1879; *Vaclav of Michalovce,* 1880) and country life (*The Smith of Lesetin,* 1889).

Cecil, Edgar Algernon Robert, 1st Viscount Cecil of Chelwood (sǐ'sừl), 1864–, British statesman. Collaborated in draft of League of Nations Covenant. Won 1937 Nobel Peace Prize.

Cecil, Robert: see SALISBURY, ROBERT CECIL, 1ST EARL OF.

Cecil, Robert Arthur Talbot Gascoyne-: see SALISBURY, ROBERT ARTHUR TALBOT GASCOYNE-CECIL, 3D MARQUESS OF.

Cecil, William: see BURGHLEY, WILLIAM CECIL, 1ST BARON.

Cecilia, Saint, 2nd or 3d cent., Roman virgin martyr, patroness of music, whose name is known in English literature through Chaucer, Dryden, and Pope. Also Cecily. Feast: Nov. 22.

Cecrops (sē′krŏps), in Greek mythology, first king of Athens, half man and half serpent. Established monogamy and first principles of law and religion.

Cedar, river rising in SE Minn., and flowing c.300 mi. SE across Iowa to Iowa R. at Columbus Junction.

cedar, name for certain trees, mostly coniferous evergreens, including northern white cedar and western red cedar (ARBORVITAE); red cedar (JUNIPER); southern white cedar (*Chamaecyparis thyoides*). Cedar of Lebanon (*Cedrus libani*) is native to Asia and Africa. Deodar cedar (*C. deodara*) possibly used in building Temple and house of Solomon (1 Kings 5–7).

Cedar Breaks National Monument: see NATIONAL PARKS AND MONUMENTS (table).

Cedar City, town (pop. 6,106; alt. 5,805 ft.), SW Utah, on Dry Coal Creek near Iron Mts.; founded 1851 by Mormon "iron mission" sent to develop coal and iron deposits. Ranch and tourist center near Zion and Bryce Canyon national parks and Cedar Breaks Natl. Monument.

Cedar Falls, city (pop. 14,334), NE Iowa, on Cedar R. just above Waterloo; settled 1845. Mfg. of farm equipment and pumps.

Cedar Grove. 1 Township (pop. 8,022), NE N.J., in Watchung Mts. N of Montclair. **2** Town (pop. 1,738), S W.Va., on Kanawha R. and SE of Charleston. Site of Booker T. Washington's boyhood home is near by.

Cedarhurst, residential village (pop. 6,051), on SW Long Isl., SE N.Y., SE of Jamaica.

Cedar Rapids, city (pop. 72,296), E Iowa, on Cedar R. and NW of Davenport; settled 1838. Railroad shops. Has cereal mills and mfg. of meat, metal, paper and food products. Seat of Coe Col. (coed.; 1881). Czechs settled here early (1852; now c.30% of pop.).

Cedartown, city (pop. 9,470), NW Ga., WNW of Atlanta near Ala. line. Textile goods and chemicals.

cedar waxwing: see WAXWING.

Cedron (sē′–), same as KIDRON.

Cefalù (chāfälōō′), port (pop. 9,654), N. Sicily, Italy. Cathedral (12th cent.) is splendid example of Norman-Sicilian architecture.

celandine (sĕl′ŭndīn), Old World biennial plant (*Chelidonium majus*), naturalized in E North America. Its small yellow flowers are borne in loose clusters and the compound leaves are rounded or lobed. Alkaloids are found in the yellow juice and other parts of the plant.

Celebes (sĕ′lŭbēz), island (69,277 sq. mi.; pop. 3,781,554), INDONESIA, E of Borneo. Comprises four mountainous peninsulas. Natural resources include gold, silver, coal, nickel, and iron. Coffee, copra, and sago are grown; timber is exported. The Portuguese first came here in 1512 and in 1625 settled in Macassar. They were ousted 1660 by the Dutch. The **Celebes Sea** lies between Celebes and the S Philippines.

celery, biennial plant (*Apium graveolens*) with fleshy stalks, grown largely for use in salads. Celeriac is variety grown for edible, thickened crown.

celesta: see PERCUSSION INSTRUMENTS.

Celestina, La (lä thälästē′nä), Spanish novel in dramatic form attributed to Fernando de ROJAS. Published as *Comedia de Calisto y Melibea* (1499), it came to be called after the principal character, La Celestina, a cunning and kindly old woman.

Celestine I, Saint (sĕ′lŭstīn), d. 432, pope (422–32). Asserted power of the papacy by issuing a judgment against the heresy of Nestorius and instructing his delegates to the Council of Ephesus to judge, not to discuss. Suppressed semi-Pelagianism. Feast: July 27.

Celestine V, Saint, 1215–96, pope (1294), an Italian named Pietro del Murrone. A hermit noted for ascetic holiness, he gathered followers about him (core of the later Celestines). Disagreement among the cardinals led to his being called from his mountain retreat to be made pope. Charles II of Naples took control of affairs, and the impractical pope, realizing that he was a puppet, resigned. Boniface VIII succeeded him. Canonized 1313 at instance of French king Philip IV. Feast: May 19.

Celina (sŭlī′nŭ), resort village (pop. 5,703), W Ohio, SW of Lima, on Grand L. Mfg. of furniture.

Céline, Louis Ferdinand (lwē′ fĕrdēnä′ sälēn′), 1894–, French author, whose real name is Louis Ferdinand Destouches. His misanthropic novels, *Journey to the End of Night* (1932; Eng. tr., 1934) and *Death on the Installment Plan* (1936; Eng. tr., 1938), created a sensation. His misanthropy drove him to fascism.

cell, in biology, unit (usually microscopic) of structure and function of which animals and plants are composed. Protoplasm, the living matter of the cell, consists of the nucleus and cytoplasm; in most cells the nucleus contains a nucleolus (small, round, dense mass); delicate plasma membrane develops on outer boundary of cytoplasm. Both plant and animal nuclei have major role in process of cell division; cytoplasm, controlled by nucleus, performs other cell functions. Cytology is the science of cell study. See also MITOSIS. See *ill.*, p. 813.

cell, in electricity, a source of electric current in which current flow is the result of chemical action. Cell consists of a positive ELECTRODE and a negative electrode, which conduct electricity, and an electrolyte which acts chemically upon one of the electrodes. A simple cell form is glass jar with dilute solution of sulphuric acid holding zinc and copper electrodes which are connected externally by a conductor (such as wire). Chemical action causes electrons to flow through wire from negative (zinc) plate to positive (copper) plate; this is opposite to conventional direction of flow of "electric current." Other cells are the Bunsen, Daniell, and Leclanché cells. Voltage depends on activity of substances used. Common dry cell consists of zinc cylinder enclosed at one end and lined with absorbent material, a central core of carbon, and a paste (serving as the electrolyte) of carbon granules and manganese dioxide saturated with a solution of ammonium chloride.

Celle (tsĕ′lŭ), city (pop. 59,254), Lower Saxony, N Germany, on Aller R. Oil refineries;

machinery and soap mfg. Chartered 1294; residence of dukes of Brunswick-Lüneburg until 1705.

Cellini, Benvenuto (chĕlē'nē, Ital. bānvānōō'tō chāllē'nē), 1500–1571, Italian sculptor, b. Florence. As a metalworker he enjoyed the patronage of Pope Clement VII and later of Francis I of France. Famous for *Perseus with the Head of Medusa* (Florence) and for intricate metalwork, such as the gold and enamel saltcellar of Francis I. Autobiography describes escapades, enmities, and banishments.

cello or **'cello:** see VIOLIN.

Cellophane (sĕ'lŭfān), trade name for thin, transparent, flexible, nonpoisonous, moisture-proof sheeting, a cellulose product made by viscose process.

celluloid, transparent, colorless substance made by treating cellulose nitrates with camphor and alcohol to form paste which can be rolled or molded.

cellulose, carbohydrate produced by cytoplasm of plant cells and forming bulk of cell wall. Absorbent cotton, jute, linen are almost pure cellulose; it forms bulk of paper, wood, wood pulp. Inert, insoluble in water, very absorbent. Used to make guncotton, pyroxylin, celluloid, collodion, cellulose acetate, RAYON, and CELLOPHANE.

Celsius, Anders (än'dûrs sĕl'sēŭs), 1701–44, Swedish astronomer, inventor (1742) of centigrade (of Celsius) thermometer. Made studies of aurora borealis.

Celsus, Aulus Cornelius, fl. A.D. 14?, Latin encyclopedist; his extant work, eight books on medicine.

Celt (sĕlt) or **Kelt** (kĕlt). **1** One who speaks a Celtic language or descends from an area where Celtic is or recently was spoken. **2** Member of a group of peoples known from the early 2d millennium B.C., who advanced to political and cultural leadership in W and Central Europe between 1200 and 400 B.C.

Celtic languages, subfamily of Indo-European languages, spoken in British Isles and in Brittany. See LANGUAGE (table).

Cenci, Beatrice (bäätrē'chä chän'chē), 1577–99, Italian noblewoman. Imprisoned by a vicious father, she procured his murder with complicity of her stepmother, brothers, and lover. Executed after a famous trial. Subject of tragedy by Shelley.

Cenis, Mont (mō' sùnē'), Alpine pass, 6,835 ft. high, on French-Italian border. New road built 1810. Railroad tunnel, 8 mi. long, built 1871, connects Turin with Chambéry.

Cennini, Cennino (chän-nē'nō chän-nē'nē), c.1365–1440, Florentine painter. *Treatise on Painting* describes technical processes of Giotto's followers.

Cenozoic era, fifth grand division of geologic time, covering c.60–75 million years. It has witnessed the shaping of our present landscape. Mammals replaced reptiles as dominant life, and finally man appeared. See also QUATERNARY; TERTIARY; GEOLOGY (table), pp. 474–75.

censorship, official restriction of any public expression believed to threaten the governing authority or the moral order. There are two types, preventive (before material is issued) and punitive (after material is issued). Prac-

tice known in ancient Greece and Rome, was very common in religious troubles of Reformation. Censorship of press, usual in totalitarian countries, is frowned upon in democracies except in wartime. In U.S. most censorship of movies by authorities is on grounds of obscenity.

centaur (sĕn'tôr), in Greek religion, descendant of Ixion, a creature half man and half horse. Centaurs lived in Thessaly. Though generally savage, some, like CHIRON, were friends and teachers of men.

Centennial Exposition, International, held in Philadelphia from May to Nov., 1876, to celebrate 100th anniversary of Declaration of Independence, Fairmount Park was site. First U.S. world's fair, it particularly exhibited U.S. technical advance and industrial growth.

Center Line, residential city (pop. 7,659), SE Mich., near Detroit.

Centerville. 1 City (pop. 7,625), S Iowa, SW of Ottumwa, in coal area. Mfg. of castings and bricks. **2** Borough (pop. 5,845), SW Pa., on Monongahela R., S of Pittsburgh, in agr. and coal area.

centigrade scale: see TEMPERATURE.

centipede (sĕn'tùpēd), flattened, segmented, wormlike, chiefly nocturnal animal of phylum Arthropoda; related to insects. It has numerous jointed legs, the first pair bearing poison claws to paralyze prey (insects, worms). Centipedes are usually 1–8 in. long. Unlike the MILLIPEDE, the centipede does not eat plants.

Central America, term applied to republics of Costa Rica, Guatemala, Honduras, Nicaragua, Salvador, and one colony, British Honduras. Panama is often included. See map, p. 901.

Central American Federation or **Central American Union,** political confederation of republics of Central America (1825–38). Presidents were Manuel José Arce and Francisco Morazán.

Central Australia: see NORTHERN TERRITORY.

Central City, town (pop. 371; alt. 8,560 ft.), N central Colo., in Clear Creek Canyon W of Denver. Boomed with gold discovery 1859. This "ghost town" revives in July with drama, music festival in opera house (1878). Mines reactivated in World War II.

Central Falls, industrial city (pop. 23,550), NE R.I., on Blackstone R. and adjoining Pawtucket. Mfg. of glass, textiles, leather and wood products, plastics, chemicals, and machinery.

Centralia (sĕntrā'lĕù). **1** City (pop. 13,863), S Ill., E of St. Louis; platted 1853. Shipping center of agr., coal, and oil area with railroad shops and metal and food products. Tragic mine explosion of 1947 led to investigations in which certain mines were declared unsafe. **2** City (pop. 8,657), SW Wash., S of Olympia. Grain, dairy, and lumber center.

Central Park, 840 acres, largest park on Manhattan isl., New York city, between 59th and 110th streets and Fifth and Eighth avenues. Land was acquired by city in 1856 and improved after the plans of F. L. Olmstead and Calvert Vaux. Here are Metropolitan Mus. of Art, a formal conservatory garden, a zoo, an Egyptian obelisk known as "Cleopatra's Needle," the Mall, and recreational facilities.

Central Powers, in WORLD WAR I, the coalition of Germany, Austria-Hungary, Bulgaria, and Turkey.

Central Provinces and Berar: see MADHYA PRADESH.

Central Valley, trough c.450 mi. long, 50 mi. wide, central Calif., between the Sierra Nevada (E) and Coast Ranges; composed of Sacramento (N) and San Joaquin valleys. Project for redistribution and use of region's water resources was begun 1935. Abundant Sacramento R. waters are to benefit San Joaquin Valley. Project now includes Shasta Dam (hydroelectric) and Keswick Dam (both in Sacramento R.); Delta Cross Channel, which fights soil salinity in delta and conducts Sacramento R. water to Delta-Mendota Canal, leading to San Joaquin R. (irrigation); and Contra Costa Canal (48 mi.), which supplies Sacramento water to farms and cities in Contra Costa co. From Friant Canal in San Joaquin R., Madera Canal goes 36 mi. N, and Friant-Kern Canal c.150 mi. S. Steam power plant at Antioch. Many other dams, reservoirs, canals, and powerhouses are planned.

Centre College of Kentucky: see DANVILLE.

centrifugal force and **centripetal force:** see FORCE.

centrifuge (sĕn′trừfūj), device using centrifugal force to separate substances of different density, e.g., liquid and solid portions of blood. Has base (or frame), motor, and rotating part which holds mixture. Cream separator is common type.

century plant: see AGAVE.

Ceos, Greek island: see CYCLADES.

cephalic index (sŭfă′lĭk), ratio of breadth of head to its length. Used in anthropological studies.

Cephalonia (sĕfůlō′nyů), Gr. *Kephallenia,* island (289 sq. mi.; pop. 57,384), Greece, largest of IONIAN ISLANDS. Irregular and mountainous, it rises to 5,314 ft. in Mt. Aenos, formerly crowned with a temple to Zeus. Argostoli, port and chief town, exports currants, wine, and olive oil. Sheep raising; fishing. A member of Aetolian League, Cephalonia was ruled by Rome after 189 B.C. and by Byzantium until its occupation by Venice (1126). In 1797 it was ceded to France, and its later history is that of Ionian Isls.

Cephas (sē′fůs), Jesus' nickname for St. PETER.

Cephisodotus (sĕfĭsŏ′důtůs), fl. 4th cent. B.C., two Greek sculptors. The elder was the master of Praxiteles; the younger was probably the son of Praxiteles.

Cephissus (sĭfĭ′sůs), Gr. *Kephisos,* name of Greek rivers. **1** Rising in Parnassus and flowing 75 mi. ESE into N Euboic Gulf. **2** Rising in Mt. Pentelikon and flowing S past Athens into Saronic Gulf.

Ceram (sĕrăm′), island (7,191 sq. mi.; pop. 100,029), one of the Moluccas, Indonesia. Central mountains rise to over 10,000 ft. Copra, resin, sago.

Ceramic Gulf (sửră′mĭk), ancient name of Gulf of Kos or Kerme, SW Turkey, an inlet of the Aegean Sea. On it was Halicarnassus.

Cerberus (sûr′bửrůs), in Greek religion, many-headed dog with a mane and a tail of snakes.

He watched gate of Hades. The honey cake buried by the Greeks with the dead was to quiet him. His capture was one of 12 labors of HERCULES.

cerebellum: see BRAIN.

cerebrospinal meningitis: see MENINGITIS.

cerebrum: see BRAIN.

Ceres (sē′rēz), in Roman religion, goddess of agriculture; daughter of Saturn and Ops. Identified with Greek DEMETER. Her worship included fertility rites and rites for the dead. Her most famous temple was on Aventine Hill; her chief festival was Cerealia.

Cerignola (chārēnyō′lä), town (pop. 37,163), Apulia, S Italy. Scene of major Spanish victory (1503) over French in ITALIAN WARS.

cerium (sēr′ēům), metallic element of RARE EARTHS (symbol = Ce; see also ELEMENT, table). Ductile, malleable, tarnishes in moisture. Forms oxide when heated; alloys. Compounds used to make lamp mantles, and in medicine.

Cernauti: see CHERNOVSTY, Ukraine.

Cerro de Pasco (sĕ′rō dä pä′skō), city (pop. 19,187), central Peru. It is 13,973 ft. high (one of highest cities in world), bleak and barren, but its fabulous silver mines, discovered 1630, have made it world renowned. Copper and vanadium also mined here.

Certosa di Pavia (chärtō′zä dē pävē′ä), former Carthusian abbey in Pavia, Italy; a national monument since 1866. Built between 14th and early 16th cent., it is a masterpiece of the Renaissance, with rich marbles and profuse sculptural decorations.

cerussite (sēr′ůsīt), colorless, white, or gray brittle carbonate of lead, an important ore of lead.

Cervantes (Saavedra), Miguel de (sửrvăn′tēz, Span. mĕgĕl′ dä thĕrvän′täs sä″ävä′dhrä), 1547–1616, Spanish novelist, generally regarded as the greatest figure of Spanish literature, author of DON QUIXOTE DE LA MANCHA. As a soldier Cervantes had a highly adventurous life: a wound at the battle of Lepanto cost him his left arm; five years of captivity as a slave in Algiers ended when he was ransomed by his family. After retiring from the army (1582) he was poor and often in debt. Besides *Don Quixote,* one of the masterpieces of world literature, he wrote other fiction (e.g., *Novelas ejemplares,* 1613), a pastoral romance, and plays.

Cervera y Topete, Pascual (päskwäl′ thĕrvä′rä ē tōpä′tä), 1839–1909, Spanish admiral, commander of Atlantic fleet in SPANISH-AMERICAN WAR. Blockaded (1898) by U.S. fleet at Santiago de Cuba; tried to run blockade but was utterly defeated and captured.

Cesalpino, Andrea: see CAESALPINUS, ANDREAS.

Cesarean section: see CAESAREAN SECTION.

Cesis (tsä′zēz), Ger. *Wenden,* town (pop. 8,-748), N Latvia. Agr. center; paper mills. Former seat of Livonian Knights, who built its ancient castle. Also spelled Tsesis, Zehsis.

cesium (sē′zēům), rare, silver-white, soft, metallic element (symbol = Cs; see also ELEMENT, table). It is the most active metal, a member of ALKALI METALS, never found free in nature; cesium chloride is widely distributed in minute quantities.

Ceske Budejovice, Czechoslovakia: see BUDWEIS.

cesspool, cistern made to receive sewage. Types include watertight (should be 150 ft. from surface water and 60 ft. from cistern or drinking water source), and leaching (built to allow liquid sewage to soak through). Some have drains to carry liquid sewage to adjoining ground.

Cetinje (tsĕ′tĭnyĕ), small town, Montenegro, Yugoslavia, near Adriatic. Grew around monastery, founded 1485; cap. of Montenegro until 1916.

Cette, France: see SÈTE.

Ceuta (syōō′tù), city (pop. c.67,790), Spanish Morocco, a Mediterranean port, opposite Gibraltar. Built on site of a Phoenician colony. Portugal took it in 1415, making the first permanent European conquest in Africa. Under Spanish rule since 1580.

Cévennes (sāvĕn′), mountain range, S France, limiting the Massif Central toward S and E. Mont Lozère (5,584 ft.) is highest peak. Sheep grazing, sericulture, coal mining. Much erosion.

Ceylon (sēlŏn′), Sanskrit *Lanka,* island (25,-332 sq. mi.; pop. 6,657,339), in Indian Ocean, SE of India; since 1948 a dominion of British Commonwealth of Nations; chief port and cap. Colombo. Mainly mountainous with broad coastal plain. Chief crops are rice, coconuts, rubber, and tea. Original inhabitants were conquered in 6th cent. B.C. by Vijaya, Aryan prince of India, who estab. first Singhalese kingdom. Buddhism was introduced in 3d cent. B.C., and ANURADHAPURA became a great Buddhist center. Visited by Arab traders 12th–13th cent. The Portuguese won control over much of the coast in 16th cent. but were ousted by the Dutch in 1658. The British seized Dutch settlements 1795–96 and won control over kingdom of KANDY in 1815.

Cézanne, Paul (pôl′ sāzän′), 1839–1906, French painter, an outstanding figure in modern French art. Studied under Pissarro and exhibited at the impressionist show of 1874. He developed a highly original style which has had a profound influence on later artists. The main characteristics of his paintings are the use of vivid color, but with a striving for depth in shadows and outlines, and an attempt to unite the best elements of impressionism with the art of the past. He worked in oil and water color and excelled in landscapes (esp. of his native Provence) and still lifes.

Cf, chemical symbol of the element CALIFORNIUM.

Chabas, Paul Émile (pôl′ āmēl′ shäbäs′), 1869–1937, French painter. Created sensation with exhibition (1912) of his nude, *September Morn.*

Chablis (shäblē′), village, Yonne dept., N central France, in wine-growing region (white Burgundy).

Chabot, Philippe de (fēlēp′ dù shäbō′), also known as **Admiral du Brion** (brēō′), 1480–1543, admiral of France. Credited with originating project of a French colony in Canada.

Chabrier, Alexis Emmanuel (shäbrēä′), 1841–94, French composer. Among his works are *Joyeuse marche; Bourrée fantasque;* an opera, *Le Roi malgré lui; España.*

Chaco (chä′kō), extensive, sparsely populated lowland plain, central S America, divided among Paraguay, Bolivia, and Argentina. After Chaco War (1932–35), between Paraguay and Bolivia, treaty was signed giving Paraguay three quarters of disputed N area of Chaco and Bolivia a corridor to Paraguay R. and certain port privileges there.

Chaco Canyon National Monument: see NATIONAL PARKS AND MONUMENTS (table).

Chad, Lake (chăd), central Africa. Bordered mainly by French Equatorial Africa and Nigeria. Its area (4,000–8,000 sq. mi.) varies with seasons.

Chadds Ford: see BRANDYWINE, BATTLE OF.

Chadwick, French Ensor, 1844–1919, U.S. naval officer. Cited for conduct at battle of Santiago in Spanish-American War.

Chadwick, George Whitefield, 1854–1931, American composer, director of the New England Conservatory of Music (1897–1931). Composer of overtures, symphonies, chamber music, and operas (e.g., *Judith*).

Chadwick, Sir James, 1891–, English physicist. Won 1935 Nobel Prize for discovery of NEUTRON.

Chaeronea (kĕrùnē′ù), anc. town, Boeotia, Greece. Birthplace of Plutarch. Here Philip of Macedon defeated Athenians and Boeotians (338 B.C.), Sulla defeated Mithridates VI of Pontus (86 B.C.).

Chaffee, Adna Romanza (chăfē′), 1842–1914, U.S. army officer. Led American contingent in Boxer Rebellion. Army chief of staff 1904–6.

Chagall, Marc (märk shǔgäl′), 1889–, Russian painter, b. Vitebsk. Since 1910 he has lived mainly in France. Considered a forerunner of surrealism. He uses flower and animal symbols and draws his main subject matter from Jewish folklore.

Chagres (chä′grās), small river of Panama used for making Gatun Lake for Panama Canal.

Chahar (chä′här′), province (45,000 sq. mi.; pop. 3,500,000), N China; cap. Kalgan. Lies mainly between two sections of Great Wall. One of China's main producers of iron ore. Stock raising is important. Originally formed 1914 as Mongol administrative area. Occupied 1937–45 by Japan.

Chaillé-Long, Charles (shäyä′-lông′), 1842–1917, American soldier and African explorer. Served in Civil War and Egyptian army. Explored Nile area.

Chaillu, Paul Belloni du: see DU CHAILLU.

Chain, Ernst Boris, 1906–, English biochemist. Shared 1945 Nobel Prize in Physiology and Medicine for work on PENICILLIN.

Chalcedon (kăl′sĭdŏn, kălsē′dùn), anc. Greek city of Asia Minor, on Bosporus, facing Byzantium.

Chalcedon, Council of, 451, fourth ecumenical council. It disposed of the heresy of EUTYCHES (which had been advanced by the scandalous Robber Synod) with the final Catholic pronouncement of the nature of Christ in the *Definition.* This, reflecting the *Tome* of Leo I, says that divine nature and human nature of Christ are distinct but inseparably united—Christ is both true man and true God. The decree of the Council that the patriarch of Constantinople should be the single head of the Eastern Church has never been accepted by the Roman Catholic Church.

chalcedony (kălsĕ'dúnē), variety of quartz, transparent to translucent, with minute crystals, waxy luster. Agate, carnelian, jasper, and onyx are forms of chalcedony colored by impurities.

Chalcidice (kălsĭ'dĭsē), Gr. *Chalkidike* or *Khalkidiki*, peninsula, NE Greece, projecting into Aegean Sea from SE Macedonia; chief town Polygyros. S coast forms three peninsulas: Kassandra (anc. Gr. *Pallene*), Sithonia, ATHOS. A dry, mountainous region, it produces olive oil, wine, wheat, tobacco. Anciently famous for its timber. Named for Chalcis, which estab. colonies here (7th–6th cent. B.C.). POTIDAEA was an important city. Region was conquered by Macedon (4th cent. B.C.) and by Rome (2d cent. B.C.). Later history follows that of SALONICA.

Chalcis (kăl'sĭs), Gr. *Khalkis,* city (pop. 26,-097), Greece; a port on EUBOEA. The chief city of ancient Euboea, it estab. colonies in Sicily and Chalcidice (8th–7th cent. B.C.), led revolt of Euboea against Athens (446 B.C.), and was made tributary to her (411). In 338 B.C. it came under Macedon. Aristotle died here. Called Negropont in Middle Ages.

chalcopyrite (kăl″kùpĭ'rīt) or **copper pyrites**, brass-yellow mineral with iridescent and black streaks. A sulphide of iron and copper, it sometimes contains other metals. It is an important and widely distributed copper ore.

Chaldaea or **Chaldea** (both: kăldē'ú), S portion of Tigris-Euphrates valley (Mesopotamia), but sometimes loosely used to include all Babylonia. The restored Babylonian kingdom is frequently called the Chaldaean Empire. Chaldaean or Chaldee came to be loosely used to mean astrologer or magician (e.g., Dan. 1.4) because of the astronomical knowledge in Babylonia.

Chaleur Bay (shùloŏr'), inlet of Gulf of St. Lawrence, c.85 mi. long, 15–25 mi. wide, between N.B. and Gaspé Peninsula, Canada. Is submerged valley of Restigouche R., which enters at its head. Has famous fishing grounds. Discovered and named by Cartier 1534.

Chalfont (chă'fûnt, chăl'fûnt), borough (pop. 828), SE Pa., near Doylestown. Traditional burial place of Delaware Indian chief Tamanend or Tammany.

Chalgrin, Jean François (zhä' fräswä' shälgrē'), 1739–1811, French architect. Chiefly responsible for scheme of Arc de Triomphe de l'Étoile, commissioned by Napoleon.

Chaliapin, Feodor (Ivanovich) (fyô'dúr shŭlyä'pēn), 1873–1938, Russian bass. Appeared at the Metropolitan Opera, New York in 1907 and 1921–29. An excellent actor, he was particularly known for title role in Moussorgsky's *Boris Godunov.*

chalk, a calcium carbonate mineral softer than limestone, consisting of minute marine shells. Chalk cliffs of Dover, England, date from Cretaceous period.

Chalk River, government research establishment, S Ont., Canada, on S shore of Ottawa R., W of Ottawa. Operated by National Research Council of Canada for Atomic Energy

Control Board. Has large heavy-water atomic pile (1947).

Challenger expedition, 1872–76, British scientific expedition which cruised in corvette *Challenger* making physical and biological surveys of Atlantic and Pacific oceans.

Challoner, Richard (chă'lúnúr), 1691–1781, English Roman Catholic bishop. Converted as a boy, he was ordained in 1716 and in 1730 returned to England, where he met many difficulties in trying to win toleration for Catholics. He was beset by anti-Catholic movements culminating in the Gordon riots (1780). A notable scholar, he revised the Douay version of the Bible and wrote and translated devotional works.

Chalmers, Thomas, 1780–1847, Scottish theologian, leader of Free Church of SCOTLAND.

Chalmette National Historical Park: see NATIONAL PARKS AND MONUMENTS (table).

Chalon-sur-Saône (–sõn'), town (pop. 29,851), Saône-et-Loire dept., E central France; inland port on Saône and Canal Central. Ships wine and grain. Cap. of Burgundy in 6th cent.

Châlons-sur-Marne (shälõ'-sür-märn'), town (pop. 28,251), cap. of Marne dept., NE France, on Marne R. Wool mfg., brewing, wine processing.

Cham (käm), pseud. of **Amédée, comte de Noé** (ämädä' kõt dú nõä'), 1819–79, French caricaturist and lithographer. Did sketches of French and Algerian life.

Chamberlain, Sir Austen: see CHAMBERLAIN, JOSEPH.

Chamberlain, Houston Stewart, 1855–1927, Anglo-German writer; son-in-law of Richard Wagner. His *Foundations of the Nineteenth Century* (1899; Eng. tr., 1910) was an important forerunner of National Socialist racist doctrines.

Chamberlain, Joseph, 1836–1914, British imperialist statesman. Resigned from Gladstone government (1886), opposing Irish Home Rule. Became Liberal-Unionist leader in House of Commons in 1891. As colonial secretary (1895–1903) advocated social reforms at home and empire expansion and consolidation. Unjustly blamed for acts leading to South African War (1899–1902); led in reconciling Boers after war. Favored tariff giving preference to empire; resigned to advocate policy. This proposal split Liberal-Unionist-Conservative bloc and caused 1906 fall of government but was adopted in lifetime of his sons. His eldest son, **Sir (Joseph) Austen Chamberlain,** 1863–1937, began 45-year parliamentary career in 1892. Twice chancellor of exchequer (1903–6, 1919–21), he carried out in latter term his father's tariff policy. Became Conservative leader in 1921. Helped negotiate Irish Free State treaty. As foreign secretary (1924–29), his most important post, largely responsible for 1925 LOCARNO PACT. Awarded Nobel Peace Prize. His half-brother, **(Arthur) Neville Chamberlain,** 1869–1940, was chancellor of exchequer (1923, 1931–37) and succeeded Baldwin as prime minister (1937). Became symbol of appeasement of Axis powers; signed MUNICH PACT (1938). Remained in office after outbreak of World War II but increasing opposition forced him to resign after British debacle in Norway (1940).

Chamberlin, Thomas Chrowder, 1843–1928, American geologist, founder of *Journal of Geology*. Formulated PLANETESIMAL HYPOTHESIS with F. R. Moulton.

chamber music, ensemble music for small groups of instruments. Originally performed by amateurs in court or aristocratic circles. With Haydn and Mozart the string quartet became the chief chamber form. In this form Beethoven wrote some of his greatest music.

Chambers, Robert: see CHAMBERS, WILLIAM.

Chambers, Sir William, 1726–96, English architect, foremost in his day. Proponent of Inigo Jones traditions of Palladian design, he published standard work on classic style. Chief work is Somerset House.

Chambers, William, 1800–1883, and **Robert Chambers,** 1802–71, Scottish authors, publishers. Their firm best known for *Chambers's Edinburgh Journal, Chambers's Encyclopaedia*.

Chambersburg, borough (pop. 17,212), S Pa., SW of Harrisburg; settled 1730. Trading center in agr. area with fruit growing and mfg. of metal and paper products. Was hq. of John Brown 1859; burned by Confederates 1864. Seat of Wilson Col. (Presbyterian; for women; 1869).

Chambéry (shäbārē′), city (pop. 26,641), cap. of Savoie dept., E France. Historical cap. of Savoy; archiepiscopal see.

Chambiges (shäbēzh′), family of French architects. **Martin Chambiges** (märtē′), d. 1532, helped design cathedrals of Sens, Troyes, and Beauvais. Assisted by son, **Pierre Chambiges** (pyēr′), d. 1544, who also worked on the Hôtel de Ville, Paris.

Chambly (shäblē′), group of villages, S. Que., Canada, on Richelieu R. and E. of Montreal. Includes Chambly Bassin (pop. 2,160) and Chambly Canton (pop. 1,636). **Fort Chambly,** built 1665, was captured and burned by Americans 1775–76; restored 1880.

Chambord, Henri, comte de (ärē′ kōt′ dù shäbôr′), 1820–83, French pretender, known to legitimists as Henry V; posthumous son duc de Berry. Accompanied his grandfather, Charles X, into exile (1830). Actively claimed throne 1871–73, but lost his prospects through insistence on restoring Bourbon flag. Died childless. Claim passed to Orléans family.

Chambord, village, Loir-et-Cher dept., N central France, between Blois and Orléans. Famous for huge Renaissance château built by Francis I.

chameleon (kùmē′lyùn), small, slow-moving arboreal lizard of Africa and S Asia. Its skin color changes with feelings, varying light intensity, and temperature. The American chameleon is a small lizard of another family.

Chamfort, Sébastien Roch Nicholas (säbästyē′ rōk′ nēkōlä′ shäfôr′), 1740–94, French writer of maxims and epigrams. Though a savage critic of society and a republican, he was favored by the court, persecuted under the Revolution. Committed suicide to escape the guillotine.

Chaminade, Cecile (säsēl′ shämēnäd′), 1857?–1944, French composer and pianist. She

chiefly wrote songs and piano pieces (e.g., the *Scarf Dance*).

Chamisso, Adelbert von (Chamisso de Boncourt) (ä′dùlbĕrt fùn shùmĭ′sō), 1781–1838, German poet, b. France; son of émigré nobles. His lyric cycle *Frauenliebe und Leben* was set to music by Schumann. His tale of the man who sold his shadow, *Peter Schlemihls wunderbare Geschichte* (1814), has virtually passed into legend.

chamois (shä′mē), hollow-horned hoofed mammal (*Rupicapra*) related to antelope, found in Europe and E Mediterranean lands. It is about the size of a goat, light brown with black tail, and has erect hooked horns. It was the original source of chamois leather; other skins now are so named.

chamomile: see CAMOMILE.

Chamonix (shämônē′), Alpine resort, Haute-Savoie dept., E France, base for the ascent of Mont Blanc.

Champagne, Philippe de: see CHAMPAIGNE.

Champagne (shämpän′, Fr. shäpä′nyù), region, NE France, in Aube, Marne, Haute-Marne, Ardennes, and Yonne depts., roughly coextensive with former Champagne prov.; historic cap. Troyes. Mostly an arid plateau; agr., sheep grazing. Small fertile dist. around RHEIMS and Epernay produces nearly all French champagne wine. Acquired by house of BLOIS (11th cent.), Champagne was among most powerful fiefs of medieval France. Its counts also ruled Navarre from 1234. Louis X of France, inheriting Champagne from his mother, incorporated it with the royal domain (1314). The medieval Fairs of Champagne, particularly those of Troyes and Provins, brought together merchants from all Europe and were of immense economic importance. Large parts of Champagne were devastated in World War I.

champagne, celebrated sparkling white wine. The best is made from grapes grown around Rheims, France. After two fermentations and blending, it is again fermented in bottles and has some sugar (and usually cognac) added, according to desired degree of dryness (from *brut* to sweet).

Champaign (shämpän′), city (pop. 39,563), E central Ill., ENE of Springfield and adjoining URBANA; founded 1854. Rail (has repair shops), commercial, and industrial center in agr. area. Univ. of ILLINOIS lies between Champaign and Urbana.

Champaigne or **Champagne, Philippe de** (both: fēlēp′ dù shäpä′nyù), 1602–74, French painter. Did religious paintings for Marie de' Medici and Richelieu.

Champlain, Samuel de (Fr. sämüĕl′ dù shäplē′), 1567–1635, French explorer, chief founder of New France. Estab. colony at Quebec, discovered L. Champlain, extended French claims W to Wis.

Champlain, Lake, 107 mi. long, ½–14 mi. wide, forming N.Y.–Vt. state line for c.100 mi. and extending into Que. Lies in broad valley between the Adirondacks (W) and Green Mts. (E). Connected with the Hudson by part of the Barge Canal, with the St. Lawrence by Richilieu R., with L. George by short channel. Plattsburg, N.Y., Burlington, Vt., and many resorts are on its shores. ISLE LA MOTTE and VALCOUR ISLAND are in it.

Named for Champlain, who discovered it, 1609. Scene of battles in French and Indian War and in Revolution at CROWN POINT and Ticonderoga and of victory of MACDON-OUGH in 1814.

Champollion, Jean François (zhä' fräswä' shäpôlyõ'), 1790–1832, French Egyptologist. Considered the founder of Egyptology, he set (1821) the principles for deciphering Egyptian hieroglyphics by using ROSETTA STONE.

Champs Élysées (shä zālēzā'), avenue of Paris, from Place de la Concorde to Arc de Triomphe, famous for its beauty and elegance.

chance, in mathematics: see PROBABILITY.

Chancellor, Richard, d. 1556, English navigator. Sent out by English group in 1553 to seek Northeast Passage. With Stephen Borough, reached White Sea; traveled overland to Moscow to prepare way for trade. Perished on return voyage.

Chancellorsville, battle of, in Civil War, May 2–4, 1863. R. E. Lee attacked Joseph Hooker's Federals, entrenched near Chancellorsville, Va. In brilliant flank attack, Stonewall Jackson surprised and routed Federals, but was mortally wounded. On May 3–4 J. A. Early and J. E. B. Stuart drove Hooker and John Sedgwick across Rappahannock R. in defeat. This was Lee's last great victory.

chancery: see EQUITY.

Chandernagor (chŭn"dûrnùgôr'), town (pop. 44,786), W Bengal, India; port on Hooghly R. belonged to the French from late 17th cent. to 1949.

Chandler, Raymond (Thornton), 1888–, American writer of "tough" detective fiction (e.g., *The Big Sleep* 1939, *Farewell, My Lovely,* 1940).

Chandler, Zachariah, 1813–79, U.S. Senator from Mich. (1857–75), and Secretary of the Interior (1875–77). A leading advocate of radical Reconstruction. As cabinet member, a typical Grant appointee.

Chandragupta: see SANDRACOTTUS.

Changchun (chäng'-chōōn'), industrial city (pop. 630,049), central Manchuria, on South Manchurian RR. As Hsinking it was cap. of MANCHUKUO.

change of life: see MENOPAUSE.

change ringing: see BELL.

Chang Hsueh-liang (chäng' shüĕ-lyäng'), 1898–, Chinese general, called the Young Marshal. Succeeded his father Chang Tso-lin as military governor of Manchuria. Ousted 1931 by the Japanese. Kidnaped Chiang Kai-shek at Sian in 1936, allegedly to force him to work with the Communists against Japan. Held prisoner by Chiang Kai-shek since 1937.

Changkiakow (jäng'jyä'kō') or **Kalgan** (kälgän'), city (pop. 151,234), cap. Chahar prov., N China. Leading trade center of Inner Mongolia. Under Communist control since 1948. Formerly called Wanchüan.

Changsha (chäng'shä'), city (pop. 421,616), cap. Hunan prov., China; port on Siang R. Major trade and industrial center on Peiping-Canton RR.

Chang Tso-lin (chäng' tsõ'-lĭn', jäng'), 1873–1928, Chinese general. Appointed inspector general of Manchuria in 1918; constantly warred to expand personal control of N China. Killed by bombing of train in which he was retreating before Kuomintang army.

Chankiang (chän'jyäng'), municipality (325 sq. mi.; pop. 268,416), SW Kwangtung prov., China. Until 1945 it was French territory of Kwangchowan, leased by China in 1898 for 99 years.

Channel Islands, Fr. *Îles Normandes,* archipelago (75 sq. mi.; pop. 102,770), off Normandy coast, France, in English Channel. Main isles are Jersey, Guernsey, Alderney, Sark, Jethou; all (but a few French owned) have belonged to Great Britain since Norman Conquest. Divided into two administrative areas: Jersey, with half the total population and chief town, St. Helier; and Guernsey, which includes all other islands. English replacing French as official language. Chiefly agr. and pastoral, isles send quantities of produce to English markets. Famous for cattle. Occupied by Germans in World War II.

Channel Islands National Monument, Calif.: see NATIONAL PARKS AND MONUMENTS (table).

Channing, William Ellery, 1780–1842, American author, Unitarian minister in Boston, great preacher, lucid writer on labor problems, education, slavery, religious tolerance, and humanitarianism. His nephew and biographer, **William Henry Channing,** 1810–84, was an author and Unitarian minister, interested in the Brook Farm experiment. His brother, **William Ellery Channing,** 1818–1901, an author, contributed verse to *Dial.* His son was **Edward Channing,** 1856–1931, historian, Harvard professor. Several lesser works preceded his masterpiece, *A History of the United States* (6 vols., 1905–25).

chansons de geste (shäsõ' dù zhĕst'), epic poems of medieval France (11th–13th cent.), composed by trouvères in cycles grouped around a great central figure, such as Charlemagne. Oldest and most famous is *Chanson de Roland* (c.1098–1100; see ROLAND).

chant, sacred song in which several syllables of text may be sung to one sustained tone. Chant of Roman Catholic and Orthodox Christianity is called PLAIN SONG. Anglican chant, developed during the Reformation, uses harmonized melodies, English texts.

chantey or **shanty,** work song with marked rhythm, particularly one sung by sailors at work. Often has stanzas sung by leader, each followed with chorus sung by group. Similar songs also sung by shore gangs and lumbermen.

Chantilly (shätēyē'), town (pop. 5,105), Oise dept., N France, NE of Paris. Famous lace mfg.; race course. Château contains art museum.

Chantrey, Sir Francis Legatt, 1781–1841, English sculptor, known for portrait statues and busts.

Chanukah: see HANUKKAH.

Chanute, Octave (shùnōōt'), 1832–1910, American civil engineer, pioneer glider experimenter, b. Paris. Noted iron-bridge builder. Retired 1889 to study gliding. Studies and personal help aided Wright brothers.

Chanute, city (pop. 10,109), SE Kansas, on Neosho R. and WNW of Pittsburgh; settled c.1870. Trade center for agr. and oil area, it has railway shops and oil refineries. Site of first mission (1824–29) in state is near.

Chaos (kā'ŏs), in Greek religion, unfathomable space whence arose everything, earthly and divine. From it came Gaea, Tartarus, and Eros.

Chapala (chäpä'lä), lake, c.50 mi. long and 8 mi. wide, W Mexico, in Jalisco and Michoacán; largest in country; popular scenic resort. Fishing is important native occupation.

chaparral (chăpŭrăl'), plant community of shrubs, both evergreen and deciduous, usually in regions with 10 to 20 in. annual rainfall. It is drier than forest regions but less arid than deserts. Chaparral growth exists in W and SW U.S. and may include scrub oaks, squawbush, western serviceberry, mesquite, buckthorn, and manzanita.

Chapel Hill, town (pop. 9,177), N central N.C., SW of Durham. Seat of Univ. of NORTH CAROLINA.

Chaplin, Charles Spencer, 1889–, Anglo-American film actor who writes, directs, and produces his own pictures. Discovered by Mack Sennett c.1913, Charlie Chaplin soon was famous for his baggy trousers and little mustache. Among his many films are *Easy Street, Shoulder Arms, The Kid, The Gold Rush, City Lights, Modern Times, The Great Dictator, Monsieur Verdoux,* and *Limelight.* His art is the most universal yet to appear on film.

Chapman, George, 1559?–1634, English dramatist and poet. Notable for translations of *Iliad* (1612) and *Odyssey* (1614–15). Among best plays, tragedy *Bussy d'Ambois* (1607) and comedy *All Fools* (1605).

Chapman, John, 1774–1847, American pioneer, more familiarly known as Johnny Appleseed. Wandering cultivator and promoter of apple orchards in Ohio, Ind., and Ill.

Chapman, John Jay, 1862–1933, American essayist, author of fiery works such as *Emerson and Other Essays* (1898), *New Horizons in American Life* (1932).

Chapultepec (chäpōōl'tāpĕk") [Aztec,= grasshopper hill], rocky eminence in SW section of Mexico city. Occupied successively by Aztec emperors, Spanish viceroys, and later rulers of Mexico (including Emperor Maximilian). Pres. Cárdenas decreed (1937) that castle become museum and grounds a public park. For Chapultepec Conference see PAN-AMERICANISM.

Charcas (chär'käs), Spanish colonial *audiencia* and presidency in S America, known also as Upper Peru and Chuquisaca; established 1559 and attached to viceroyalty of Peru. Transferred to viceroyalty of La Plata (1776). Roughly same as modern Bolivia.

Charchemish, anc. city: see CARCHEMISH.

charcoal, substance, mostly pure carbon, from destructive DISTILLATION of wood, animal matter (e.g., bone black from bones), or sugar. A smokeless fuel, it yields a large amount of heat. It is an efficient agent in ADSORPTION of solids from solution and is used in making gunpowder, in sugar refining, in purification of water and air, and in gas masks.

Charcot, Jean Martin (zhä' märtĕ' shärkō'), 1825–93, French neurologist, organizer of noted Paris clinic for nervous system dis-

eases. He studied the treatment of hysteria by hypnosis.

Chardin, Jean Baptiste (zhä' bätēst' shärdĕ'), 1699–1779, French painter, famous for still lifes and domestic interiors. One of greatest French colorists.

Charente (shärät'), department (2,306 sq mi.; pop. 311,137), W France; cap. Angoulême. The **Charente** river, 220 mi. long, flows from central France past Augoulême, Cognac, and Rochefort into Atlantic.

Charente-Maritime (märĕtĕm'), department (2,792 sq. mi.; pop. 416,187), W France, on Atlantic coast; cap. La Rochelle. Formerly called Charente-Inférieure.

Chares (kâ'rēz, kā'–), 3d cent. B.C., Greek worker in bronze; sculptor of the COLOSSUS OF RHODES.

chargé d'affaires: see DIPLOMATIC SERVICE.

Charing Cross (chăr'ĭng), open space at W end of Strand, London. One of Eleanor Crosses (see ELEANOR OF CASTILE) erected here. Charing Cross station is busy rail terminal.

chariot (chă'rēŭt). earliest type of carriage. Ancient form had two wheels; car usually consisted of floor and waist-high semicircular guard in front. Wheels of war chariot sometimes mounted with scythes as weapons. In Greece and Rome chariots were used primarily to carry passengers and were featured in races and processions.

Chariton (shă'rĭtŭn), city (pop. 5,320), S Iowa, W of Ottumwa. Center of farm and coal area.

Charlemagne (shär'lûmān) (Charles the Great or Charles I), 742–814, emperor of the West (800–814), king of the Franks (768–814); son of Pepin the Short. Shared kingdom with his younger brother Carloman until Carloman's death (771). Invaded Italy to support pope against DESIDERIUS; crowned king of Lombards at Pavia (774). Conquered NE Spain ("Spanish March") from Moors (778); subjugated and Christianized Saxons after long struggle (772–804); defeated Avars and Wends. In 800 he restored LEO III to papal see and was crowned emperor by him in Rome on Christmas Day, thus laying basis for HOLY ROMAN EMPIRE. To assure his succession he had his son, LOUIS I, crowned joint emperor (813). To defend and control his immense empire, Charlemagne created military frontier marches and an administrative system by which his personal representatives (*missi dominici*) made his power felt in regular inspection tours. His CAPITULARIES testify to his concern with general welfare and justice for the poor. He frequently held consultative assemblies and took personal interest in Church reform. His palace school at Aachen, founded by ALCUIN, became the cradle of the "Carolingian renaissance" of learning. He was beatified by the Church and is locally honored as a saint. Legend soon enhanced and distorted his actual achievements. Surrounded by his 12 legendary peers, he became the central figure of a cycle of medieval romances (see CHANSONS DE GESTE).

Charleroi (shärlûrwä'), town (pop. 26,262), Hainaut prov., S central Belgium, on Sambre R. and on Charleroi-Brussels Canal. Coal-mining and steel-milling center. Important fortress 17th–18th cent.

Charleroi (shär'lûroi), borough (pop. 9,872), SW Pa., S of Pittsburgh and on Monongahela R. Has glass and iron works and coal mines.

Charles, emperors (see HOLY ROMAN EMPIRE). **Charles I:** see CHARLEMAGNE. **Charles II** (the Bald), 823–77, son of Louis, joined with his brother LOUIS THE GERMAN against his brother LOTHAIR I, whom they defeated at Fontenoy (841). Became king of West Franks (France) by Treaty of VERDUN (843); partitioned Lotharingia with Louis in Treaty of MERSEN (870). Crowned emperor 875. **Charles III** (the Fat), 839–88, inherited Swabia from his father, Louis the German. Crowned king of Italy (879), emperor (881), king of France (885). Deposed 887 after he failed to stop Norman inroads in France. **Charles IV,** 1316–78, succeeded his father JOHN OF LUXEMBURG as king of Bohemia (1346), was elected in the same year antiking to Emperor Louis IV, after whose death he made good his claim. Crowned emperor in 1355, he promulgated in 1356 the Golden Bull (see ELECTORS); added Silesia and Lusatia to his family territories; had his son WENCESLAUS elected German king (1376). His chief interest lay in Bohemia. He embellished Prague and founded Charles Univ. (1348). **Charles V,** 1500–1558, emperor (1519–58) and, as Charles I, king of Spain (1516–56); son of PHILIP I and JOANNA of Castile; grandson of Ferdinand V of Aragon, Isabella of Castile, Emperor Maximilian I, and Mary of Burgundy. The greatest of all Hapsburg emperors, he inherited an empire on which "the sun never set"—the Spanish kingdoms, Spanish America, Naples, Sicily, the Low Countries, and the Austrian hereditary lands. Born and raised at Ghent, he at first antagonized his Spanish subjects but later espoused their national traits and religious zeal and burned their rich loyalty. This reign was crucial in every way. A series of social uprisings ended with the victory of central authority in Spain and of the great princes in Germany (1520–25; see Juan de PADILLA; SICKINGEN, FRANZ VON; PEASANTS' WAR). The imperialist struggle with France was a Pyrrhic triumph for Spain (1521–59; see FRANCIS I and HENRY II of France; ITALIAN WARS). In his fight against Protestantism, announced at the Diet of WORMS (1521) but long delayed by war with France and Algiers, Charles seemed triumphant when he defeated the Protestant princes at Mühlberg (1547; see SCHMALKALDIC LEAGUE), but in 1555 he was forced to accept the compromise Peace of AUGSBURG and left Germany forever. He was more successful in his promotion of the Catholic REFORM, and he brought the Spanish empire to its height by the conquest of MEXICO and PERU. After his imperial coronation at Bologna (1530; he was the last German emperor crowned by a pope), Charles increasingly delegated his authority in Germany to his brother Ferdinand. In 1554–58 he abdicated all his titles; his son Philip II received Spain, America, Sicily, Naples, and the Netherlands; his

brother became emperor as FERDINAND I. Charles himself retired in 1556 to the monastery of Yuste. **Charles VI,** 1685–1740, emperor (1711–40), and, as Charles III, king of Hungary. Before his accession he claimed the succession to Charles II of Spain (see SPANISH SUCCESSION, WAR OF THE) and in 1733 he became involved in the War of the POLISH SUCCESSION. These dynastic struggles left him with the Spanish Netherlands and Milan. Without male issue, he had a succession problem of his own. The PRAGMATIC SANCTION, by which he settled the Hapsburg lands on his daughter Maria Theresa, was challenged after his death. In his campaigns against Turkey he secured the favorable Treaty of PASSAROWITZ (1718), largely offset by the Treaty of Belgrade (1739). He was a patron of learning and of music. **Charles VII,** 1697–1745, emperor (1742–45) and, as Charles Albert, elector of Bavaria (1726–45), married a niece of Charles VI. He refused to recognize the Pragmatic Sanction, joined the coalition against Maria Theresa in the War of the AUSTRIAN SUCCESSION, and was elected emperor but lost his own Bavaria to Austrian occupation.

Charles I, 1887–1922, last emperor of Austria and, as Charles IV, king of Hungary (1916–18); grandnephew of Francis Joseph. Married Zita of Bourbon-Parma. Failed in attempt to secure separate peace. Abdicated Nov., 1918, but twice sought, without success, to regain Hungarian throne by coup d'état. Died in exile on Madeira. His son Otto succeeded to his claims.

Charles, kings of England, Scotland, and Ireland, of the Stuart house. **Charles I,** 1600–1649, reigned 1625–49. Took little part in politics while his father, James I, ruled except for trip to Spain in abortive negotiations for his marriage. Upon accession, offended English opinion by his marriage to Catholic Henrietta Maria of France, sister of Louis XIII. Foreign ventures of king's favorite, duke of BUCKINGHAM, were unsuccessful. Bitter struggle between king and Parliament known as PURITAN REVOLUTION soon developed. Parliament, largely Puritan, controlled money. Charles supported bishops under William LAUD. Forced to agree to PETITION OF RIGHT 1628, Charles governed without Parliament 1629–40. Civil and religious liberties were at low point and large emigrations to America took place. Attempt to impose episcopacy in Scotland caused Bishops' Wars and king was forced to call Parliament. Long Parliament of 1640, led by JOHN HAMPDEN, PYM, and VANE, secured itself against dissolution and brought about death of earl of STRAFFORD, abolition of Star Chamber courts, and end of arbitrary taxation. Fear of king and Catholics mounted and civil war broke out. Defeated at Marston Moor (1644) and Naseby (1645), Charles surrendered to Scottish army in 1646 and finally fell into hands of English army. Tried by a high court of justice controlled by enemies, he was convicted of treason and beheaded. His son, **Charles II,** 1630–85, reigned 1660–85. Fled to France 1646. At his father's death, was proclaimed king in Scotland and, accepting terms of Covenanters, was crowned there (1651). After defeat by Cromwell, escaped to Europe and lived in comparative poverty. Issued conciliatory Declaration of Breda. Aided by General MONCK, was restored 1660. Earl of CLARENDON made chief minister. Episcopacy was restored and nonconformity weakened by Clarendon Code although king favored toleration. Great London plague (1665) and fire (1666) took place during second DUTCH WAR (1664–67). CABAL ministry replaced Clarendon (1667). As result of secret Treaty of Dover (1670) with Louis XIV, Charles entered third Dutch War in 1672. It was unpopular and he was forced to approve Test Act (1672) and make peace (1674). Alliance with Louis broken by marriage of king's niece, Mary, to William of Orange. Intervened in Titus OATES affair to protect queen. Dissolved Parliament in 1681 to block passage of Exclusion Act against duke of York and ruled absolutely thereafter. Although father of children by several mistresses (e.g., Nell GWYN), he had no legitimate children and was succeeded by his brother, JAMES II. Reign was marked by gradual increase in power of Parliament, rise of political parties, advance in colonization and trade, and progress of England as a sea power. His pleasure-loving and immoral character set tone of brilliant Restoration period.

Charles, kings of France. Charles I: see CHARLEMAGNE. Charles II and Charles III (the Fat): see CHARLES II and CHARLES III, emperors. Charles III (the Simple), 879–929, son of Louis II, joint king with Eudes from 893, sole king 898–923. Ceded Normandy to ROLLO (911). Deposed and imprisoned by rebellious nobles, who made RAOUL king. Charles IV (the Fair), 1294–1328, succeeded his brother Philip V in 1322; last of direct Capetians. Charles V (the Wise), 1337–80, son of JOHN II, was regent during John's captivity (1356–60), succeeded him in 1364. As regent, dealt with JACQUERIE and reformist movement of Étienne MARCEL. During his reign, DU GUESCLIN drove English out of France (except Guienne). With his ministers, the MARMOUSETS, he strengthened royal power, founded standing army, reformed taxation. Patron of learning. His son, Charles VI (the Mad, or the Well Beloved), 1368–1422, reigned 1380–1422. Intermittently insane after 1392. France was ruled and plundered by his uncles; by his brother, Louis d'ORLÉANS; by his wife, ISABEAU OF BAVARIA. Their rivalries led to civil war between ARMAGNACS AND BURGUNDIANS; laid France open to invasion by HENRY V of England (1415). By Treaty of TROYES (1420) he named Henry his successor. His disinherited son, Charles VII (the Victorious, or the Well Served), 1403–61, repudiated the treaty. Still called dauphin (or, in derision, "king of Bourges"), he ruled indolently over what parts of France remained to him S of the Loire, but in 1429 JOAN OF ARC spurred him to action and had him crowned king at Rheims. In 1435 he won the alliance of Burgundy against England, and in 1453 he ended the HUNDRED YEARS WAR by expelling the last English from France. He reorganized the army and, with the help of Jacques CŒUR,

restored the finances. The PRAGMATIC SANCTION OF BOURGES (1438) and the suppression of the PRAGUERIE (1440) strengthened royal authority against Church and nobles. His last years were troubled by rebellions of his son, Louis XI. Charles VIII, 1470–98, son of Louis XI, reigned 1483–98. His sister, Anne de Beaujeu, regent during his minority, arranged his marriage with ANNE OF BRITTANY. In 1495 Charles began the ITALIAN WARS with the short-lived conquest of Naples. Charles IX, 1550–74, reigned 1560–74, at first under the regency of his mother, CATHERINE DE' MEDICI. Later chose COLIGNY as chief adviser, but was swayed to take part in massacre of SAINT BARTHOLOMEW'S DAY (1572). Charles X, 1757–1836, was known as count of Artois before he succeeded his brother, LOUIS XVIII, in 1824. Led powerful ultraroyalist group before his accession; appointed such reactionaries as VILLÈLE, J. A. de POLIGNAC as premiers. Liberal and capitalist forces joined to bring about JULY REVOLUTION of 1830. Charles abdicated and died in exile.

Charles, kings of Hungary. Charles I (Charles Robert of Anjou), 1288–1342, grandson of Charles II of Naples; son-in-law of Stephen V of Hungary. Elected king 1308; crowned 1310; founder of Hungarian branch of ANGEVIN dynasty. Reorganized army on feudal basis; increased city privileges. Followed dynastic foreign policy, securing succession to Poland for his oldest son, LOUIS I of Hungary. Charles II: see CHARLES III, king of Naples. Charles III: see CHARLES VI, emperor. Charles IV: see CHARLES I, emperor of Austria.

Charles, king of Naples. Charles I, 1226–85, count of Anjou and Provence, youngest brother of Louis IX of France, championed the papal cause against MANFRED, was crowned king of Naples and Sicily by Pope Clement IV in 1266. Had his rival CONRADIN executed (1268). Won hegemony over Italy as leader of Guelphs; conquered Albania from Byzantium. In 1282 Sicily rebelled (see SICILIAN VESPERS) and chose PETER III of Aragon as king. War against Aragonese continued until 1302 under his son, Charles II, 1248–1309, king of Naples and count of Provence (1285–1309). Charles III (Charles of Durazzo), 1345–86, king of Naples (1381–86), was a great-grandson of Charles II. JOANNA I adopted him as heir but later repudiated him in favor of Louis of Anjou (Louis I of Naples). Charles invaded Naples, was crowned by the pope (1381), and imprisoned Joanna (and probably killed her). Elected king of Hungary as Charles II (1385), he was murdered soon afterward.

Charles II or Charles the Bad, 1332–87, king of Navarre (1349–87). Carried on long feud with his father-in-law, John II of France. Helped suppress JACQUERIE (1358). Chosen by Étienne MARCEL to defend Paris against dauphin, he betrayed his trust.

Charles I, 1863–1908, king of Portugal (1889–1908). Yielded to British "ultimatum" (1890) which demanded cessation of Portuguese colonial expansion. His attempt to foster dictatorship under João Franco caused violent reaction. Charles and the heir ap-

parent were shot. Manuel II succeeded him.
Charles, kings of Spain. **Charles I:** see CHARLES V, emperor. **Charles II,** 1661–1700, king of Spain, Naples, and Sicily (1665–1700), last of the Spanish Hapsburgs, saw his country weakened by wars with Louis XIV. Died childless. War of the SPANISH SUCCESSION broke out on his death. **Charles III,** 1716–88, son of Philip V by Elizabeth Farnese, was duke of Parma and Piacenza (1731–35) and king of Naples and Sicily (1735–59) before succeeding his half-brother Ferdinand VI as king of Spain (1759–88). Entered Seven Years War after signing FAMILY COMPACT of 1761 with France; intervened (1779) in American Revolution on American side (for territorial changes, see PARIS, TREATY OF, 1763 and 1783). With his minister FLORIDA-BLANCA he restored some prosperity in Spain. His son, **Charles IV,** 1748–1819, king of Spain (1788–1808) was dominated by Queen MARÍA LUISA and his minister GODOY. Withdrew from French Revolutionary Wars 1795, entered disastrous alliance with France (1796), which led in 1807 to PENINSULA WAR. Palace revolution of 1808 forced him to abdicate in favor of his son, FERDINAND VII, but Napoleon I soon afterward enticed both Charles and Ferdinand to Bayonne, forced both to abdicate, and held them captive until 1814.

Charles, kings of Sweden. **Charles IX,** 1550–1611, youngest son of Gustavus I. Acted as regent from 1592; established Lutheranism as state religion; had his nephew, SIGISMUND III of Poland, deposed as king of Sweden (1599); accepted crown 1604. His expansionist policy involved him in wars with Poland and Denmark, which continued after his death under his son, Gustavus II. **Charles X** (Charles Gustavus), 1622–60, succeeded on the abdication of his cousin Christina (1654). Invaded Poland, took Warsaw and Cracow (1655), but was expelled after miracle of CZESTOCHOWA. Russian and Denmark having declared war, he threatened Copenhagen and forced Denmark to accept Treaty of ROSKILDE (1658), but war was resumed in same year. His son, **Charles XI,** 1655–97, ended the war upon his accession (1660) by the Peace of OLIVA and the Treaty of Copenhagen (confirming that of Roskilde). Siding with France in last of DUTCH WARS, he was defeated at Fehrbellin by Frederick William of Brandenburg (1675) but retained Pomerania at Treaty of Saint-Germain (1679). In 1682 he received absolute powers from the Riksdag. His son and successor, **Charles XII,** 1682–1718, was faced in 1699 by a Russo-Polish-Danish alliance which precipitated the NORTHERN WAR (1700–1721). An extraordinarily brilliant but foolhardy strategist, Charles quickly crushed Denmark, routed Peter the Great, and overran Poland, but his Russian campaign of 1708–9 ended disastrously at Poltava. Charles fled to Turkey and persuaded Sultan Ahmed III to declare war on Russia, but after the Russo-Turkish peace of 1711 he was requested to leave Turkey. Charles, residing at Bender, flatly refused and ultimately defended his house with only a handful of men against a whole Turkish army

(1713). Taken a prisoner to Adrianople, he finally left in 1714. He invaded Norway in 1716 and was killed by stray bullet while besieging the fortress of Fredrikssten. His heroic failure cost Sweden its rank as a great power. **Charles XIII,** 1748–1818, king of Sweden (1809–18) and Norway (1814–18) succeeded his nephew GUSTAVUS IV. He accepted a constitution, made peace with Russia (to which he ceded Finland), France, and Denmark, and adopted as heir the French Napoleonic marshal Jean Baptiste Jules Bernadotte (1764–1844; b. Pau, France), who later succeeded him as king of Sweden and Norway styled **Charles XIV.** With the consent of Napoleon, he had agreed to his adoption by Charles XIII (1810) and actually governed in the name of the infirm king. He joined the allies against Napoleon I, played an important part in the battle of Leipzig (1813), and secured the union of NORWAY with Sweden (1814). His reign was an era of economic progress, but his hostility to the liberals made him unpopular. **Charles XV,** 1826–72, king of Sweden and Norway (1859–72), Bernadotte's grandson, was a liberal and popular ruler. He consented to the creation of a bicameral parliament.

Charles, dukes of Lorraine. **Charles IV,** 1604–75, succeeded to duchy in 1624 but lost it repeatedly to Louis XIV because of his anti-French policy. He fought as a general in the imperial service. His son, **Charles V** (Charles Leopold), 1643–90, fought successfully against the Turks at Vienna and in Hungary but never recovered Lorraine.

Charles, Jacques Alexandre César (zhäk' älěk-sä'drü säzär' shärl'), 1746–1823, French physicist. Worked in electricity and aeronautics; ascended in hydrogen balloon (1783). **Charles's law:** at constant pressure, volume of a gas is directly proportional to temperature.

Charles, river in E Mass., winding past Cambridge and Boston to Boston Bay. Harvard boat races.

Charles, Cape, E Va., S point of Eastern Shore opposite Cape Henry; separates Chesapeake Bay from Atlantic Ocean. Ferries connect to Va. mainland.

Charles, Lake, SW La. Calcasieu R. is its inlet and outlet and connects it with Intracoastal Waterway and Gulf of Mexico. Lake Charles city on shores.

Charles Albert, 1798–1849, king of Sardinia (1831–49). To forestall revolution he granted constitution of 1848 (in force until 1947). Fought two campaigns (1848, 1849) of RISORGIMENTO against Austria. Routed at Novara, he abdicated in favor of his son, Victor Emmanuel II.

Charles Augustus, 1757–1828, duke and, after 1815, grand duke of Saxe-Weimar. Friend and patron of GOETHE. Played influential role in German politics.

Charles Borromeo, Saint (bŏrōmā'ō), 1538–84, Italian churchman; nephew of Pius IV. Made a cardinal and papal secretary of state, he brought about reopening of the Council of Trent and pushed the Catholic Reform. As Bishop of Milan, he rigorously reformed clerical life and education. Feast: Nov. 4.

Charlesbourg, village (pop. 5,734), S Que., Canada, on St. Charles R. just N of Quebec. One of oldest parishes in Que., settled 1659 as Bourg Royal.

Charles City, city (pop. 10,309), NE Iowa, on Cedar R. and NNW of Waterloo; settled 1850. Mfg. of farm machinery.

Charles Edward Stuart: see STUART or STEWART, JAMES FRANCIS EDWARD.

Charles Martel (märtĕl'), 668?–741, Frankish mayor of the palace (714–41). United all Merovingian kingdoms under his rule. Halted Moslem invasion of Europe in battle of Tours or Poitiers (732), one of decisive battles in history. Father of Pepin the Short; grandfather of Charlemagne.

Charles of Blois (blwä), c.1319–1364, French prince; nephew of Philip VI. One of claimants in War of the BRETON SUCCESSION; killed at Auray. Beatified.

Charles of Valois (välwä'), 1270–1325, French prince; third son of Philip III; father of Philip VI. Sought thrones of Sicily, Byzantium, Rome, and Arles—all without success —and campaigned for Pope Boniface VIII in Italy. Took Florence 1301 and exiled Dante, who in *The Divine Comedy* placed him in Purgatory.

Charles of Viana (vēä'nä), 1421–61, Spanish prince; son of Queen Blanche of Navarre (d. 1442) and John II of Aragon. Ruled Navarre after 1442, but became involved in civil war with his father. Died soon after John had recognized him as heir.

Charles Robert of Anjou: see CHARLES I, king of Hungary.

Charles's law: see CHARLES, JACQUES ALEXANDRE CÉSAR.

Charles the Bad: see CHARLES II, king of Navarre.

Charles the Bold, 1433–77, duke of Burgundy (1467–77). Joined League of the Public Weal (1465) against LOUIS XI of France, whose lifelong adversary he remained. Master of Burgundy, Franche-Comté, and Low Countries, he dreamed of restoring kingdom of Lotharingia. His annexation of Lorraine and several Alsatian towns aroused the Swiss, who defeated him at Grandson and Morat (1476) and at Nancy, where he was killed. His empire fell apart after the accession of his daughter, MARY OF BURGUNDY.

Charles the Great, emperor: see CHARLEMAGNE.

Charleston. 1 City (pop. 9,164), E Ill., SE of Decatur. Mfg. of shoes, brooms. Lincoln Log Cabin State Park (site of Thomas Lincoln's farmhouse) is S. **2** City (pop. 5,501), SE Mo., SW of Cairo, Ill. A cotton center, it also has mfg. of shoes and lumber products. **3** City (pop. 70,174), SE S.C., state's oldest (1670) and largest city, on peninsula between Ashley and Cooper rivers at head of bay formed by them. On or in bay are FORT MOULTRIE, James Isl. (U.S. quarantine station), Morris Isl. (lighthouse), FORT SUMTER, and Castle Pinckney. Center for coastwise and foreign shipping and of a truck and seafood area, it has mfg. of fertilizer, wood products, paper and pulp, chemicals, and steel. Hq. of sixth naval district and SE division of U.S. Corps of Engineers. In Revolution, it was in British hands 1780–82. Convention of secession met here 1860.

Fort Sumter was fired on by Confederates April 12, 1861. Charleston, besieged by Union forces, finally fell in 1865. Many old buildings and landmarks remain. Seat of The Citadel (Military Col. of South Carolina; state supported; for men; 1842) and Medical Col. of State of South Carolina. **4** City (pop. 73,501), state cap., W W.Va., on Kanawha R. at mouth of Elk R., E of Huntington. State's second largest city and industrial, shipping, and wholesale-distribution center of Kanawha valley, it has oil refining and mfg. of ordnance, implements, and glass. Large chemical plants are in outskirts. Near by is West Virginia State Col. City chartered as Charles Town 1794; was cap. 1870–75, became permanent cap. 1885. New capitol (1932) designed by Cass Gilbert.

Charles Town, city (pop. 3,035), W.Va., in E Panhandle SW of Harpers Ferry; laid out 1786 by George Washington's brother Charles, whose home still stands. John Brown was tried (1859) and hanged here. Near by is "Harewood," where Dolly Madison was married. Racing meets held here.

Charlestown, part of Boston, Mass., on Charles R.; settled 1629, included in Boston 1874. Scene of battle of Bunker Hill, June 17, 1775.

Charles William Ferdinand, 1735–1806, duke of Brunswick (1780–1806). Prussian field marshal in Seven Years War; commander (1792–94) of Austro-Prussian armies in the FRENCH REVOLUTIONARY WARS. His son was FREDERICK WILLIAM, duke of Brunswick.

Charlet, Nicolas Toussaint (nēkōlä' tōōsē' shärlä'), 1792–1845, French lithographer, best known for scenes of the Napoleonic Wars. Also worked in oil and water color.

Charlevoix, Pierre François Xavier de (pyĕr' fräswä' zävyä' dù shärlùvwä'), 1682–1761, French Jesuit traveler and historian. Traveled in New France 1705–9 and 1720. His *Histoire de la Nouvelle France* (1744; Eng. tr., 6 vols., 1900) is only full account of interior America in early 18th cent.

Charlevoix (shä'lùvoi), resort city (pop. 2,-695), N Mich., between L. Michigan and L. Charlevoix (fishing). Area has Indian remains.

Charlot, Jean (zhä' shärlō'), 1898–, American painter, b. France. A favorite subject is the Mexican Indian. Wrote *Art from the Mayans to Disney* (1939).

Charlotte (Sophia), 1744–1818, queen consort of George III of England. During king's mental illness, she was given charge of his person and household.

Charlotte. 1 (shùrlŏt', shärlŏt') City (pop. 6,-606), S Mich., SW of Lansing, in agr. area. Mfg. of electronic equipment and radios. **2** (shär'lùt) City (pop. 134,042), S N.C., near S.C. line; settled c.1750. State's largest city, it is textile center and rail hub with mfg. of cotton and wool goods, hosiery, and machinery. MECKLENBURG DECLARATION OF INDEPENDENCE signed here May 1775. Occupied by Cornwallis, Sept.–Oct., 1780. Seat of Queens Col. (Presbyterian; for women; 1857) and Johnson C. Smith Univ. (Negro; Presbyterian; coed.; 1867).

Charlotte Amalie (ùmäl'yù), town (pop. 10,-

399), cap. of VIRGIN ISLANDS (U.S.), on St. Thomas, founded 1673.

Charlotte Harbor, SW Fla., inlet of Gulf of Mexico, c.25 mi. long and 5 mi. wide.

Charlottesville, city (pop. 25,969), central Va., on Rivanna R. and NW of Richmond; founded 1762. Mfg. of textiles and machinery. Near by are MONTICELLO, home of Jefferson; "Ash Lawn," home of James Monroe; and birthplaces of Meriwether Lewis and G. R. Clark. Seat of Univ. of VIRGINIA. Burgoyne's captured army quartered here 1799–80; Tarleton raided town in 1781. Taken by Federals in Civil War.

Charlottetown, provincial cap. and only city (pop. 15,887) of Prince Edward Isl., Canada, on S coast. Chief port, with steamship lines and shipbuilding. Seat of Prince of Wales Col. (1860; affiliated with Dalhousie Univ.) and St. Dunstan Univ. (affiliated with Laval Univ.). Founded as French trading post in early 18th cent. Town laid out 1768. Scene of Charlottetown Conference of Maritime Provs. (1864), which began Canadian confederation.

Charnwood, Godfrey Rathbone Benson, 1st **Baron,** 1864–1945. English author of a well-known biography of Abraham Lincoln (1916).

Charolais (shärôlä'), small region and former county, E central France, named for Charolles, a town in Saône-et-Loire dept. Cattle breeding. Under dukes of Burgundy 1390–1477; then under Hapsburg (Spanish) rule until annexation by Louis XIV, who incorporated it into Burgundy prov. after 1674.

Charon (kā'rŏn), in Greek mythology, ferryman of Hades, who bore newly arrived dead across the STYX.

Charpentier, Gustave (güstäv' shärpätyä'), 1860–, French composer. His opera *Louise,* reflecting Parision bourgeois life, has been very popular.

chartered companies, associations for foreign trade or colonization that appeared with expansion of European national states. Chartered by the state, they had trade or settlement monopolies in specific colonial areas. Foreshadowed by English Merchants Adventurers. Notable companies were British and Dutch East India companies (1600) and Hudson's Bay Co. (1670).

Charterhouse (chär'tûrhous) [Fr.,= Chartreuse], in London, founded as Carthusian monastery 1371; became a boys' school 1611. Now a noted public school. Removed 1872 to Godalming, Surrey. Thackeray describes it in *The Newcomes.*

Charter Oak: see HARTFORD, Conn.

Chartier, Alain (älê' shärtyä'), c.1385–c.1433, French poet, secretary to Charles VII. Wrote *Le Quadrilogue invectif* (1422), anti-English prose pamphlet, and the poem *La Belle Dame sans mercy* (1424).

Chartism, workingmen's reform movement in Great Britain, 1838–48. "People's Charter," drafted by William Lovett and Francis Place, advocated universal manhood suffrage and other reforms.

Chartres (shär'trù), city (pop. 23,509), cap. of Eure-et-Loire dept., N France; chief center of BEAUCE. The magnificent Cathedral of Notre Dame epitomizes the spirit of

French Gothic; its stained glass windows and sculpture are particularly famous. City damaged in World War II.

chartreuse (shärtrûz'), a LIQUEUR originated and long made exclusively by Carthusian monks at La Grande Chartreuse, France. Green chartreuse has c.57% alcohol; the sweeter yellow kind, c.43%.

Chartreuse, Grande (gräd' shärtrûz'), mountain group (highest point 6,487 ft.), SE France, in Dauphiné Alps. The monastery, founded 1084 by St. Bruno in a high valley, was main seat of CARTHUSIANS until expulsion of order from France (1903). The monks were allowed to return in 1941. The present monastery was built in the 17th cent.

Charybdis (kûrĭb'dĭs), in Greek legend, whirlpool near rock of SCYLLA; home of a greedy monster.

Chase, Pliny Earle, 1820–86, American scientist and writer on meteorology, mathematics, philosophy.

Chase, Salmon P(ortland), 1803–73, American statesman. U.S. Senator from Ohio (1849–55, 1861); anti-slavery leader. U.S. Secretary of the Treasury (1861–64); responsible for national bank system (estab. 1863). Chief Justice of U.S. Supreme Court after 1864. His dissenting opinion in SLAUGHTERHOUSE CASES subsequently became accepted position of the courts as to restrictive force of Fourteenth Amendment. Presided fairly over impeachment trial of Pres. Johnson. Chase earnestly sought the presidency four times, but was never nominated.

Chase, Samuel, 1741–1811, American Revolutionary patriot, signer of Declaration of Independence, Associate Justice of U.S. Supreme Court (1796–1811). Impeached in 1804 on charge of political partiality, but acquitted.

Chase, Stuart, 1888–, American writer. Investigated meat-packing industry (1917–22), and was long with Labor Bureau, Inc. Among his books are *Men and Machines* (1929), *The Economy of Abundance* (1934), *Rich Land, Poor Land* (1936), and *The Tyranny of Words* (1938).

Chase, William Merritt, 1849–1916, American painter and teacher. Known for portraits and still lifes.

Chassériau, Théodore (taōdôr' shäsäreō'), 1819–56, French painter; a pupil of Ingres. Murals for the Church of St. Méry, Paris, and for the Palais d'Orsay.

Chassidim: see HASIDIM.

chat, largest American warbler. Yellow-breasted chat is shy; nests in E U.S. in thickets and winters in Mexico and Central America. Long-tailed chat is in W North America. In Europe are found the wheatear, the whinchat, and the stonechat.

Chateaubriand, François René, vicomte de (fräswä' rùnä' vēkôt' dù shätōbrēä'), 1768–1848, French author. Visited U.S. 1791; émigré in England until 1800. A royalist, he was foreign minister (1823–24) and active in politics until 1830. Wrote *The Genius of Christianity* (1802; Eng. tr., 1856), including the famous extracts *Atala and René.* Last work was *Mémoires d'outre-tombe* [memoirs from beyond the tomb] (1849–50). A founder of French romanticism, he is noted for his rich, noble, and poetic style.

Château d'If (dēf'), castle on small If isl. off Marseilles, SE France. Built 1524; long a state prison. Scene of Dumas's *Count of Monte Cristo.*

Château Gaillard (gīär'), castle, N France, on the Seine near Les Andelys, SE of Rouen. Built 1196 by Richard I of England to protect Normandy from French; taken 1204 by Philip II. Ruins are splendid example of medieval military architecture.

Chateaugay (shă'tŭgē, shă″tŭgā'), Fr. *Chateauguay,* river rising in Chateaugay L. in the Adirondacks, NE N.Y., and flowing N through Quebec to empty into St. Lawrence R. Strong American troops under Wade Hampton were defeated (1813) by a small Canadian-Indian force on its Quebec shores.

Château-Thierry (shätō-tyĕrē'), town (pop. 7,283), Aisne dept., N France, on Marne R. Focal point in second Marne battle (1918), in which last German offensive was stopped largely by U.S. troops.

Chatham, William Pitt, 1st earl of: see PITT, WILLIAM.

Chatham. 1 Town (pop. 5,223), E N.B., Canada, on Miramichi R. Shipping center with lumber, pulp, and paper mills, shipyards, and fish-processing plants. **2** City (pop. 21,218), S Ont., Canada, E of Detroit, Mich., at head of navigation on Thames R. Industrial center in farming and fruit-raising region. Mfg. of tractors and auto parts.

Chatham, municipal borough (pop. 46,940), Kent, England, on Medway R., a major naval station. First dockyard estab. by Elizabeth 1588.

Chatham. 1 Resort and fishing town (pop. 2,457), SE Mass., on S Cape Cod; settled 1665. **2** Suburban borough (pop. 7,391), NE N.J., on Passaic R. and W of Newark; settled 1749.

Châtillon, Sébastien: see CASTALION, SÉBASTIEN.

Chatrian, Alexandre: see ERCKMANN-CHATRIAN.

Chattahoochee (chătŭhōō'chē), river rising in N Ga. and flowing S 436 mi. to Flint R. at Fla. line, forming Apalachicola R. Navigable to Columbus. Forms part of Ga.-Ala. and Ga.-Fla. lines.

Chattahoochee or **River Junction,** town (pop. 8,473), NW Fla., on Apalachicola R. at Ga. line and NW of Tallahassee, in tobacco area. Lumber and furniture.

Chattanooga (chătŭnōō'gù), city (pop. 131,-041), E Tenn., on Tennessee R. near Ga. line; settled 1815, laid out as Chattanooga 1837. Almost surrounded by mountains, including Missionary Ridge, Signal Mt., and Lookout Mt: First a river port, it grew with coming of railroads in 1840s and 1850s. Strategically important in Civil War (see CHATTANOOGA CAMPAIGN). Near-by Chickamauga and Chattanooga Natl. Military Park, on site of campaign, adjoins Fort Oglethorpe, Ga. Industrial, transportation, market, and resort center for agr. and mining area, and hq. for TVA power system (Chickamauga Dam near), it has mfg. of metal products, farm machinery, textiles, furniture, and hosiery.

Chattanooga campaign, Aug.–Nov., 1863, in Civil War. Chattanooga, as center of com-munications, was important Union objective. In 1863 Federals under W. S. Rosecrans drove Braxton Bragg from area. Bragg attacked at Chickamauga Sept. 19–20, but G. H. Thomas held line until ordered by Rosecrans to Chattanooga. When Bragg besieged town, U. S. Grant opposed him; with Joseph Hooker and Thomas Grant drove Confederates from Lookout Mt. in Battle above the Clouds, and then from Missionary Ridge.

Chatterton, Thomas, 1752–70, English poet. At 12 he was composing his "Rowley Poems," claiming that they were copies of 15th-cent. manuscripts. Came to London in 1770, failed to sell his poems, poisoned himself. His genius was recognized later.

Chaucer, Geoffrey (jĕf'rē), c.1340–1400, English poet. The few facts known of his life based mainly on official records. Page in Prince Lionel's household (1357–58), later probably in service of John of Gaunt. Captured while with Edward III's army in France (1359–60), but ransomed. By 1366 married to Philippa (de Roet?), lady-in-waiting to queen. By 1367 valet in king's household. Among frequent diplomatic missions to Continent (1370–78) were trips to Italy (1372–73, 1378). From 1374 held several official posts; comptroller of customs on wool and hides at London (1374–86) and of petty customs (1382–86), knight of the shire for Kent (1386), clerk of the king's works (1389–91). First important poems, *Book of the Duchess* (1369) and partial translation of the ROMAN DE LA ROSE, draw on French sources. From his visits to Italy until c.1385, strongly influenced by Italian literature, especially by Dante in the *House of Fame* and the *Parliament of Fowls.* At height of powers produced *Troilus and Criseyde* (c.1385–86) based on Boccaccio's *Filostrato* (see TROILUS AND CRESSIDA) and began the *Canterbury Tales* (c.1387), richly varied collection of stories represented as told by pilgrims traveling together from London to shrine of St. Thomas at Canterbury. This narrative frame and the characterization of pilgrims vividly presented in Prologue and links between tales. Chaucer is most important figure in English literature before Shakspere. Helped to reestablish English language as vehicle for literature and introduced iambic PENTAMETER into English verse. Always acknowledged great narrative poet, he has recently been recognized as one of greatest English metrists.

Chaudière (shōdyĕr'), river rising in SE Que., Canada, N of Maine-Que. line, and flowing 120 mi. NW to St. Lawrence R. above Quebec.

Chaudière Falls (shōdyĕr'), 50-ft. drop in Ottawa R., SE Ont., Canada, within city of Ottawa.

Chauliac, Guy de (gē' dù shōlyäk') c.1300–c.1370, French surgeon, author of noted work on surgery.

Chaumette, Pierre Gaspard (pyĕr' gäspär' shōmĕt'), 1763–94, French revolutionist. Leader of Paris commune; extremist member of CORDELIERS, after whose downfall he was guillotined.

Chaumont (shōmō'), town (pop. 15,068), cap. of Haute-Marne dept., NE France. Liner and cutlery mfg. U.S. field hq. in World War I. For treaty signed here 1814, see QUAD-RUPLE ALLIANCE.

Chausson, Ernest (shōsō'), 1855–1899, French composer of chamber, orchestral, and operatic music. His work combines elements of romanticism and impressionism. Best known for his Symphony in B Flat and the *Poème* for violin and orchestra.

Chautauqua (shùtôk'wù), resort village, W N.Y., on W shore of **Chautauqua Lake**, 18 mi. long and 1–3 mi. wide, near L. Erie, in resort and fruit-growing region. Chautauqua Inst. (1874) offers popular summer lectures and concerts.

Chautauqua movement, adult education similar to lyceum movement. First institute estab. 1874 at Chautauqua, N.Y., as development of Methodist Episcopal summer Sunday-school institute. Developed into eight-week program of courses and lectures in arts, science, humanities, and religion. Chautauquas were formed in other communities and continued until c.1924. Assembly at Chautauqua still draws thousands each year.

chauvinism (shō'vùnīzùm) [after Nicolas Chauvin, Napoleonic soldier], aggressive and exaggerated nationalism. Exalts national consciousness and spreads hatred of other peoples.

Chaux-de-Fonds, La (lä shō-dù-fō'), town (pop. 33,154), Neuchâtel canton, W Switzerland; a center for making of watches.

Chavannes, Puvis de: see PUVIS DE CHAVANNES.

Chávez, Carlos (chä'väs), 1899–, Mexican composer and conductor. He has done extensive research in native Indian music, which has influenced his own writing. His works include ballets, symphonies, a piano concerto, and choral works.

Chaykovsky, Nikolai Vasilyevich (nyĭkŭlī' vùsē'lyùvĭch chīkôf'skē), 1850–1926, Russian revolutionist, a leader of People's Socialist party. Headed anti-Bolshevik government at Archangel (1917–19).

Chazars: see KHAZARS.

Cheaha (chē'hô), peak, 2,407 ft. high, in Talladega Mts., E Ala.; highest point in Ala.

Cheapside, street in the City of London, most important market center of medieval London. Tournaments and some excursions were held here. Mermaid Tavern was in district.

Cheb, Czechoslovakia: see EGER.

Cheboygan (shĕboi'gùn), city (pop. 5,687), N Mich., on S channel of Straits of Mackinac at mouth of Cheboygan R. Resort and farm trade center, with mfg. of metal and wood products. Exports fish.

Chechen (chĭchĕn'), Moslem people native to N slopes of central Greater Caucasus, RSFSR. Fought Russian conquest in 19th cent., particularly during SHAMYL rebellion. With closely related Ingush, they formed (1936–44) an autonomous soviet socialist republic (6,100 sq. mi.; pop. 697,408); this was dissolved by USSR government because of their collaboration with Germans in World War II. Population was resettled elsewhere in Russia.

Che-chiang, province, China: see CHEKIANG.

checkers, game for two players, played with 24 counters on board with 64 squares; known in England as draughts. Played in Europe

since 16th cent.; similar game known to ancients.

cheese, known as food since antiquity, is today made mainly from milk of cows, sheep, or goats. The making of all the varied kinds begins with coagulation of casein, the chief milk protein, by enzyme action or by lactic acid, or a combination. Hard cheeses include Cheddar (originally from England), Edam and Gouda (Holland), Emmental or Gruyère (Switzerland), and Parmesan (Italy). Stilton, Roquefort, Gorgonzola, and American brick are semihard. Soft cheeses may be either fresh (unripened), e.g., cream cheese and cottage cheese, or softened by microorganisms (which also develop flavor) in ripening: Camembert, Brie, and Limburger.

cheetah (chē'tù) or **hunting leopard,** member of cat family, native to Asia and Africa. From early times it was trained to hunt game. *Acinonyx jubatus* of Africa is about the size of a leopard and has long legs and a tawny black-spotted coat.

Chefoo (chē'fōō') or **Yentai** (yĕn'tī'), city (pop. 227,000), E China, on Shantung peninsula and on Yellow Sea. Treaty port, opened 1858.

Chehalis (chĭhā'lĭs), city (pop. 5,639), SW Wash., on Chehalis R. Lumber, coal, and food products.

Cheka: see SECRET POLICE.

Chekhov, Anton Pavlovich (chĕ'kôf), 1860–1904, Russian author. His prevailing themes are man's essential loneliness and frustration and the dullness and stagnation of Russian life in his day. Sympathetic yet realistic toward his characters, he varied these themes in hundreds of masterful short stories and in the dramas *The Sea Gull* (1898), *Uncle Vanya* (1899), *The Three Sisters* (1901), and *The Cherry Orchard* (1904). Widely translated, Chekhov had immense influence on contemporary literature.

Chekiang or **Che-chiang** (both: chĕ'kyăng', jû'-jyäng'), province (40,000 sq. mi.; pop. 20,000,000), E China, on East China Sea; cap. Hangchow. Includes many islands, notably Chusan Archipelago. Most fertile area is Yangtze delta where rice, cotton, tobacco, and hemp are grown. Also produces tea and silk.

Chelan, Lake (chĭlăn'), c.50 mi. long and ½–1½ mi. wide, N central Wash., in Cascade Range. Resort area.

Chelmno, Pol. **Chełmno** (khĕ'ōōmnô), Ger. *Kulm,* town (pop. 11,634), W Poland, near the Vistula. Dates from 10th cent. Under Teutonic Knights 1226–1466; under Prussia 1772–1919. Napoleon defeated near by, 1813.

Chelmsford (chĕmz'fùrd), town (pop. 9,407), NE Mass., SW of Lowell; settled 1633. Processes wool.

Chelsea, metropolitan borough (pop. 50,912), W London, England; a literary and artistic quarter. Much damaged by air raids 1940–41.

Chelsea, city (pop. 38,912), E Mass., NE industrial and residential suburb of Boston; settled 1624. Mfg. of rubber goods, shoes, and chemicals.

Cheltenham (chĕlt'nùm), municipal borough (pop. 62,823), Gloucestershire, England. A resort near the Cotswolds, it is a hunting center.

Chelyabinsk (chĭlyä′bĭnsk), city (pop. c.450,-000), RSFSR, in W Siberia, in S Ural foothills and on Trans-Siberian RR. A major metallurgical center of USSR, it nearly doubled in population after World War II, when many industries were transferred here.

Chelyuskin, Cape (chĭlyōō′skĭn), northernmost point (lat. 77°41′N) of Asiatic continent, on Taimyr peninsula, RSFSR. Named after 18th-cent. Russian navigator. Airfield; observation post.

chemical affinity, attractive force between atoms, i.e., tendency of one element to react with another.

chemical reaction, action taking place during change in internal molecular structure of substance, which loses characteristic properties. In some reactions, heat given off (exothermic); in some, heat absorbed (endothermic). When compound substance is broken down into constituents, it is simple decomposition. When two compounds react to form two new compounds, it is double decomposition. In replacement reactions, place of element in compounds is taken by another element. In chemical combination (SYNTHESIS), elements combine to form compounds. OXIDATION and REDUCTION are important reactions. Reaction rate depends on temperature, pressure, concentration, CATALYST, etc. EQUATION represents change.

chemical warfare, in its widest sense, the application of chemical knowledge for offensive or defensive purposes in hostilities. An early example was the use of Greek fire. In World War I poison gas was used extensively. Chlorine was first used April 22, 1915, by the Germans. In World War II preparations for various sorts of chemical warfare were made by all major countries, but little resulted—partly because of mutual fear of retaliation. Chemistry did, however, contribute greatly to the fashioning of new types of airborne bombs and to such implements as flame throwers. It also contributed to the knowledge of nuclear fission that made possible the atomic bomb.

Chemin des Dames (shmē dä däm′), road along crest between Aisne and Ailette rivers, N France. Held by Germans in World War I until they were dislodged in bitter fighting (1917–18).

chemistry, science of nature and composition of matter and changes it undergoes. Appearance and behavior of substances are described in physical and chemical properties; changes during reactions are shown by equations. Two categories of matter are elements, represented by symbols; and compounds, represented by formulas. Composition of compounds determined by analysis: qualitative, for elements present, and quantitative, for their proportion. Organic chemistry is study of carbon compounds, and inorganic is study of other elements and compounds plus simple oxides of carbon and metallic carbonates. See also ALCHEMY; BIOCHEMISTRY.

Chemnitz (kĕm′nĭts), city (pop. 250,188), SAXONY, SE Germany, on Chemnitz R., near one of world's largest open-pit lignite mines.

Leading industrial center, mfg. of machine tools, machinery, chemicals, textiles. Chartered 1143. Suffered greatly in Thirty Years War and World War II.

Chemulpo (chä′mōōl′pô′) or **Inchon** (in′chŏn′), city (pop. 265,767), E central Korea; port on Yellow Sea. UN forces landed here 1950. Mfg. center.

Chemung (shĭmŭng′), river formed near Corning, S N.Y., and flowing c.45 mi. SE, past Elmira, to Susquehanna R. near Sayre, Pa. Valley was scene of fighting in Revolutionary campaign of JOHN SULLIVAN.

chemurgy (kĕ′mûrjē), branch of chemistry applied to preparation of industrial materials from agricultural products.

Chenab, India: see PUNJAB.

Chengteh (chŭng′dŭ′), commercial city (pop. 60,000), cap. Jehol prov., Manchuria. Wool trading and weaving. Was summer cap. of Ch'ing dynasty. Formerly called Jehol.

Chengtu or **Ch'eng-tu** (both: chŭng′dōō), commercial city (pop. 647,877), cap. Szechwan prov., S China; port on Min R. Seat of three universities.

Chénier, André (ädrä′ shänyä′), 1762–94, French poet. His pamphlets against the excesses of the French Revolutionists led to his execution. His poems range from classical lyrics, such as *La Jeune Captive, Élégies,* and *Bucoliques,* to political satires.

Chennault, Claire Lee (shě′nôlt″), 1890–, American general. Formed American Volunteer Group ("Flying Tigers") in China (1941). Headed U.S. air task force in China (1942–45).

Cheops, anc. Egyptian king: see KHUFU.

Chephren: see KHAFRE.

Chequamegon Bay (shĭkwä′mŭgŭn), arm of L. Superior, N Wis. Visited by French explorers in 17th cent. Father Allouez founded mission on its shore 1665. Forms harbor for Ashland.

Cher (shĕr), department (2,820 sq. mi.; pop. 286,070), central France, in Berry; cap. Bourges. It is traversed by the **Cher** river, 200 mi. long, which flows from Massif Central NW to join Loire near Tours.

Cherbourg (shĕrbōōr′), town (pop. 34,034), Manche dept., NW France, on English Channel at tip of Cotentin peninsula. Fortified naval station since 17th cent.; transatlantic port since World War I. Further fortified by Germans in World War II; capitulated to U.S. troops June, 1944.

Cherchel (shĕrshĕl′), town (pop. 7,263), Algeria; a Mediterranean port. As Caesarea it was cap. of Mauretania. Has many relics of Roman period.

Cheremiss, RSFSR: see MARI AUTONOMOUS SOVIET SOCIALIST REPUBLIC.

Cheribon (chĕrĭbŏn′), town (pop. 54,079), N Java, Indonesia; port on Java Sea. Exports sugar, copra, and rice. At near-by village of Linggajati was drafted the agreement mapping eventual formation of United States of Indonesia under Dutch crown.

Cherkess, people of USSR: see CIRCASSIA.

Chernigov (chĭrnyē′gŭf), city (pop. 67,356), N Ukraine; agr. center and port on Desna R. The Spaski Sobor (Byzantine cathedral, built 1024), oldest building in Russia, was destroyed in World War II.

Chernovtsy (chĭrnôf'tsē), Ger. *Czernowitz*, Rumanian *Cernauti*, city (1930 pop. 112,427), W Ukraine, on Pruth R., former cap. of BUKOVINA. Pop. was largely German and Jewish until World War II.

Cherokee (chĕr'ŭkē), city (pop. 7,705), NW Iowa, on Little Sioux R. and ENE of Sioux City. Center for farm, dairy, and livestock area. Near-by Pilot Rock was landmark for early settlers.

Cherokee Indians (chĕr'ŭkē), largest and most important single tribe in SE U.S. Language is of the Iroquoian family. Cherokee Nation (estab. 1827) had a constitution providing for elected chief, senate, and house of representatives. The syllabic alphabet invented by Sequoyah gave them writing, and their material culture was high. In 1838 they were brutally removed from their homes and moved to the Indian Territory. Tribe split by differing sympathies in U.S. Civil War. In 1906 tribe disbanded, and Cherokee became U.S. citizens.

Cherrapunji: see ASSAM.

cherry, name for several trees or shrubs of genus *Prunus* and their fruits, grown in home and commercial orchards. There are many varieties derived from two Old World species —*Prunus avium* (sweet cherry) and *P. cerasus* (sour cherry). Fruit is eaten raw and used in preserves, pies, and liqueurs (see (MARASCHINO). Flowering cherry is derived from other species and there are many varieties with showy single or double flowers. Species of American wild cherry include chokecherry, pin cherry, and wild black cherry.

Cherry Valley, village (pop. 760), E central N.Y., W of Albany. Tories and Indians led by Walter Butler and Joseph Brant burned most of the village and massacred over 40 people on Nov. 11, 1778.

Chersiphron (kûr'sĭfrŭn), Cretan architect. Traditional builder of the original Ionic temple of Artemis at Ephesus in 550 B.C.

Cherso (kĕr'sō), Serbo-Croatian *Cres* (tsûrĕs'), Adriatic island (c.150 sq. mi.), off Croatia, Yugoslavia. Ceded by Italy 1947.

cherub (chĕr'ŭb), plural **cherubim** (-ûbĭm), kind of angel, with seraphim attendant upon God. In old Jewish tradition described as winged creatures with human, or often, animal faces; late Christian art pictures them as plump children. Gen. 3.24; Ex. 25.18–22; 37.6–9; 1 Kings 6.23–28; Pss. 18.10; 80.1; Ezek. 10.

Cherubini, Maria Luigi (märē'ä lwē'jē kārōōbē'nē), 1760–1842, Italian composer; lived in Paris after 1788. Composed operas (e.g., *Les Deux Journées, Anacreon, Médée*) and church music.

Chesapeake, U.S. frigate, famous for her role in *Chesapeake* affair (June 22, 1807) and for her battle with British ship *Shannon* (June 1, 1813). In *Chesapeake* affair ship was fired on by British ship *Leopard* when James BARRON refused demand to search *Chesapeake* for British deserters. During battle with the *Shannon* James Lawrence reportedly issued famous last command, "Don't give up the ship!" She was, however, captured.

Chesapeake and Delaware Canal, 19 mi. long, connecting head of Chesapeake Bay near Chesapeake City, Md., with Delaware R. below Delaware City, Del. Built 1824–29; bought by U.S. 1919 and enlarged 1935–39.

Chesapeake and Ohio Canal, former waterway, c.185 mi. long, from Washington, D.C., to Cumberland, Md., running along left bank of Potomac R. Built 1828–50. Had busiest days in 1860s. Now included in Natl. Capital Parks.

Chesapeake & Ohio Railway, U.S. transportation company, with 5,062 mi. of lines in six states, Washington, D.C., and Ont., Canada. Incorporated 1878. Merged 1947 with Pere Marquette Railway Co.

Chesapeake Bay, inlet of the Atlantic (c.200 mi. long N–S, 3–30 mi. wide), between Delmarva Peninsula (called Eastern Shore of Md. and Va.) and the major parts of Va. and Md. Enters between Cape Charles and Cape Henry, Va. Receives Susquehanna, Patuxent, Potomac, Rappahannock, York, and James rivers. Important ports on shores are Baltimore, Norfolk, and Hampton Roads area. Has well-known fishing grounds. New bridge connects Kent Isl. of Eastern Shore with main part of Md.

Chesapeake City, town (pop 1,154), NE Md., S of Elkton. W end of Chesapeake and Delaware Canal.

Cheselden, William (chĕ'zŭldŭn), 1688–1752, English surgeon who improved the kidney-stone operation and was author of works on bones and on general anatomy.

Cheshire (chĕ'shŭr) or **Chester,** maritime county (1,014 sq. mi.; pop. 1,258,050), W central England, co. town Chester. A low, flat, and fertile region; dairy farming extensive and Cheshire cheese famous. Estuaries of chief rivers, Mersey and Dee, form Wirral peninsula in Irish Sea. Chief industries are salt and coal mining, shipbuilding, and mfg. of railroad cars, textiles, and chemicals. Communications include Manchester Ship Canal.

Cheshire, town (pop. 6,295), S central Conn., N of New Haven; settled before 1700. Metal goods.

Chesney, Francis Rawdon, 1789–1872, British soldier and explorer in Asia. Demonstrated feasibility of Suez Canal route (1829) and surveyed the Tigris and Euphrates (1835), proving their navigability.

chess [from Persian *shah* = king], game for two players each using 16 counters (a king, a queen, two rooks or castles, two bishops, two knights, and 8 pawns) on board of 64 squares. Probably originated in India. By 13th cent. chess was played all over Western Europe. Modern chess dates from 15th cent.

Chester, county borough (pop. 48,229), co. town of Cheshire, England. Site of important Roman camp, it later was last place in England to surrender to William the Conqueror (1070). Many medieval buildings survive, including cathedral with architecture from Norman to Late Perpendicular. Chester Miracle Plays originated here.

Chester. 1 City (pop. 5,389), S Ill., on the Mississippi below St. Louis. Shipping center of agr., coal, and quarry area. Park with site of old KASKASKIA is near by. **2** Village (pop. 1,215), SE N.Y., SW of Newburgh. Trotting horse HAMBLETONIAN was foaled and buried here. **3** City (pop. 66,039), SE Pa., on Delaware R. and SW of Philadelphia; settled c.1644 by Swedes as Uppland. Renamed by William Penn whose house (1683) still stands. One of oldest cities in state, it has shipbuilding and mfg. of steel, paper, and glass products, and chemicals. First provincial assembly met here 1682. **4** City (pop. 6,893), N S.C., NNW of Columbia. Mfg. of textiles, fertilizer, cottonseed oil, and foundry products.

Chesterfield, Philip Dormer Stanhope, 4th earl of, 1694–1773, English statesman, author of worldly-wise *Letters to His Son* (1774; addressed to his natural son). Lort Chesterfield was rebuked in a famous letter by Samuel Johnson for belated tribute to the *Dictionary*.

Chesterton, G(ilbert) K(eith), 1874–1936, English essayist, convert to Roman Catholicism and apologist for Catholicism in many essays and books. His novels include *The Man Who Was Thursday* (1908) and detective fiction, featuring Father Brown. Writings—as in *Tremendous Trifles* (1909)—cover a wide range of literary, social, moral criticism. Associated with Hilaire Belloc. Also wrote poetry (notably narrative *Lepanto*).

Chestertown, town (pop. 3,143), Eastern Shore, Md., on Chester R., NE of Annapolis. Trade center of resort area. Seat of Washington Col.

chestnut, deciduous tree of genus *Castanea* of N Hemisphere and its edible nuts borne in burs. American chestnut (*Castanea dentata*), native E of the Mississippi now nearly extinct because of chestnut blight, a fungus disease. See also CHINQUAPIN. See *ill.*, p. 999.

Chestnut Hill, suburb of Boston, Mass., in Brookline and Newton towns. Main seat of Boston Col. (R.C., Jesuit; partly coed.; 1863).

Chesuncook Lake (chĭsŭn'kook), 22 mi. long and 1–4 mi. wide, N central Maine, in wilderness region noted for hunting and fishing.

Chevalier, Guillaume Sulpice: see GAVARNI.

Chevalier, Michel (mĕshĕl' shŭvälyä'), 1806–79, French economist, an influential advocate of industrialization and free trade.

Cheviot (shĭv'ĕŭt, shĕv'–), city (pop. 9,944), SW Ohio, W of Cincinnati. Mfg. of boxes and clothes.

Cheviot Hills (chĕv'ĕŭt), 35 mi. range on Scotland-England border; once scene of much border strife.

Chevreuse, Marie de Rohan-Montbazon, duchesse de (märē' dù rōä'-mōbäzō' düshĕs' dù shŭvrûz'), 1600–1679, French beauty, intimate of Anne of Austria. Intrigued against Richelieu; twice exiled. During Fronde she first opposed, then supported, Mazarin.

Chewing gum is usually made from chicle, which is melted, sterilized, sweetened, flavored, and shaped into sticks or candy-coated pellets. Insoluble plastics may be mixed with, or substituted for, chicle.

Cheyenne (shīăn'), city (pop. 31,935; alt. c.6,000 ft.), state cap., SE Wyo., near Colo. and Nebr. lines. Selected as Union Pacific RR division point 1867. Became territorial cap. 1869. Cattle ranching and Black Hills gold stimulated growth in 1870s. State's largest city, it is a sheep and cattle market and center for transportation (air, highway, rail)

and shipping. Annual Frontier Days celebration (since 1897).

Cheyenne, river 527 mi. long, rising in E Wyo. and flowing NE to Missouri R. in central S.Dak., above Pierre. Has U.S. projects on river and tributaries (see BELLE FOURCHE R.). River's basin is in MISSOURI RIVER BASIN PROJECT.

Cheyenne Indians, North American tribe of Algonquian linguistic family. Divided (c.1830) at headwaters of Platte river into northern band (now in Mont.) and southern band (now in Okla.); both had typical Plains culture. Southern band had severe war (1861–68) with whites, marked by massacre of Indians by U.S. soldiers at Sandy Creek (1864).

Chiang Kai-shek (chĕăng" kī"-shĕk', jyäng"), 1886–, Chinese generalissimo and statesman. Chief aide of Sun Yat-sen in revolution of 1911. Became prominent in Kuomintang party in 1923; led army N from Canton. Originally worked with the Communists but broke with them in 1927. Held enormous power as Nationalist leader from 1928 to 1948. With his wife Mei-ling SOONG he attended Cairo Conference (1943) with Roosevelt and Churchill. After World War II unsuccessfully opposed Communist drive into S China; by April, 1950, retained only Formosa.

Chianti, Monti (mōn'tē kyän'tē), small range of Apennines, Tuscany, central Italy. Chianti wine comes from vineyards on its slopes.

Chiapas (chĕä'päs), state (28,732 sq. mi.; pop. 903,200), S Mexico, on Pacific, between Isthmus of Tehuantepec and Guatemala; cap. TUXTLA. Exploitation of state's natural resources retarded by its inaccessibility. Recently airlines and Inter-American Highway have been opening country. Notable source of hardwoods.

Chiatura (chĕŭtoo'rŭ), city (pop. c.10,000), W central Georgian SSR. Large manganese production.

Chibcha (chĭb'chù), group of Indian tribes in E Colombian Andes, with a highly developed material culture (agr., mining of emeralds, making of gold- and copperwork, fine textiles). Two chief tribes, headed by Zaque at Tunja and Zipa at Bogotá, were conquered by Jiménez de Quesada (1536–41). Chibchan languages were probably spoken as far N as Nicaragua. Chibchan custom of gilding new rulers probably gave rise to the legend of El Dorado.

Chicago (shĭkä'gō), city (pop. 3,620,962), NE Ill., on L. Michigan. Second U.S. city in size and importance, it is world's greatest rail and meat-packing center and a highway hub and Great Lakes port. Seat of world's largest grain and livestock markets and of Midwest stock exchange, it has mfg. of iron and steel, machinery, electrical equipment, railroad cars and equipment, chemicals, and textiles. Marquette and Joliet came here 1673 and trading post was founded c.100 years later. Fort DEARBORN was estab. 1803. Erie Canal speeded settling of Midwest, and Chicago was platted 1803. Town grew with lake traffic and coming of railroads. From the ashes of the great fire of 1871 grew a city of stone and steel. With growing industries came labor troubles, notably HAYMARKET SQUARE

RIOT of 1886 and Pullman strike of 1894 (see DEBS, E. V., and ALTGELD, J. P.). There was considerable growth in both World Wars. From World War I to 1933, Chicago was known as a resort of gangsters and racketeers. The city's material progress was evidenced in the World's Columbian Exposition of 1893 and Century of Progress Exposition of 1933–34. Notable highlights of this cultural center are Chicago Symphony, ART INSTITUTE OF CHICAGO, CHICAGO NATURAL HISTORY MUSEUM, Hull House, and Chicago Civic Opera. It is the seat of Univ. of CHICAGO, De Paul Univ. (R.C.; coed.; 1898), Illinois Inst. of Technology (nonsectarian; coed.; since 1940 consists of Armour Col. of Engineering, opened 1893 by P. D. Armour as Inst. of Technology, and Lewis Inst. of Arts and Science), LOYOLA UNIVERSITY, Mundelein Col., and parts of Northwestern Univ. and Univ. of Illinois.

Chicago, river, NE Ill., formed in Chicago by junction of two branches. Formerly flowed E to L. Michigan; flow was reversed into South Branch and Sanitary and Ship Canal (1900), carrying Chicago's wastes to Mississippi R. via Illinois Waterway system. Now part of Great Lakes to Gulf of Mexico waterway.

Chicago, Art Institute of: see ART INSTITUTE OF CHICAGO.

Chicago, University of, in Chicago; nonsectarian, private, coed.; chartered 1891 (Baptist), opened 1892 with gifts from J. D. Rockefeller. R. M. HUTCHINS inaugurated "Chicago plan," i.e., a four-year junior college and a liberal arts university divorced from professional schools. University is notable for research and graduate work. Seat of Hutchins' "great books" program. Maintains two observatories (Yerkes, at Williams Bay, Wis., and McDonald, with Univ. of Texas, at Mt. Locke, Texas). Has Oriental Inst. and Inst. for Nuclear Research. Library is rich in Lincolniana and Americana. Includes pioneer Univ. of Chicago Press (1891).

Chicago Heights, industrial city (pop. 24,551), NE Ill., S of Chicago; settled in 1830s. Mfg. of metal products, glass, and chemicals.

Chicago Natural History Museum, founded at Chicago, Ill. 1893, through gifts of Marshall Field and others. Chartered as Columbian Mus. of Chicago, name later became Field Columbian Mus., then Field Mus. of Natural History, and (1943) Chicago Natural History Mus. Known for habitat groups (largely prepared by methods of Carl Akeley), botanical, anthropological, and geological collections, and works of sculpture. Sponsors many expeditions.

Chichagof Island (chĭ'chŭgŏf), off SE Alaska, in ALEXANDER ARCHIPELAGO, N of Baranof Isl. Has fish canning, gold mining, and wolfram deposits.

Chichén Itzá (chēchän' ētsä'), anc. Mayan city, occupied by the Itzá group (according to one system of dating c.514–692 and late 10th cent.–1194). Ruins, showing Old Empire and New Empire architectural styles, have been much studied by archaeologists.

Chicherin, Georgi Vasilyevich (gēôr'gē vŭsē'lyŭvĭch chēchä'rĭn), 1872–1936, Russian foreign commissar (1918–30). Prepared recog-

nition of USSR by Great Powers at Conference of GENOA and through Treaty of RAPALLO (1922).

Chichester (chĭ'chĭstŭr), municipal borough (pop. 19,110), Sussex West, England. Once a Roman town; an amphitheater was discovered here 1935. Cathedral (12th–13th cent.) has detached bell tower.

Chichi-jima: see BONIN ISLANDS.

chickadee (chĭk'ŭdē″), small North American bird related to titmouse. Black-capped chickadee is a permanent resident in much of E North America; several species are in W U.S., one in S U.S.

Chickahominy (chĭkŭhŏ'mĭnē), river of E Va., rising NW of Richmond and flowing SE c.90 mi. to the James. In Civil War there was heavy fighting along its banks (see PENINSULA CAMPAIGN).

Chickamauga (chĭkŭmô'gù), city (pop. 1,747), NW Ga., S of CHATTANOOGA, Tenn. Scene of a Civil War battle in CHATTANOOGA CAMPAIGN. Chickamauga and Chattanooga Natl. Military Park is near.

Chickasaw Indians (chĭk'ŭsô), tribe of Natchez-Muskogean linguistic stock, once occupying N Miss. One of FIVE CIVILIZED TRIBES.

Chickasha (chĭk'ŭshä), city (pop. 15,842), SW central Okla., on Washita R. and SW of Oklahoma City. Market and processing center for agr. and oil area, it has cotton gins, cottonseed-oil mills, and oil refineries.

chicken: see POULTRY.

chicken pox (varicella), contagious, infectious childhood disease caused by a filterable virus. Red spots becoming blisters appear on trunk two to three weeks after exposure.

chick-pea, annual plant (*Cicer arietinum*) grown since antiquity for its edible pealike seeds in Asia, S Europe, Mexico, and South America. It is also called *garbanzo* and gram.

chickweed, low-growing weed (*Stellaria media*) of temperate regions. Mouse-ear chickweeds are rock garden perennials of genus *Cerastium*.

chicle (chĭ'kúl), name for gum obtained from latex of sapodilla tree, a tropical American evergreen (*Achras zapota*) also grown for edible fruit. Chicle exported to U.S. for making chewing gum.

Chico (chē'kō), city (pop. 12,272), N Calif., N of Sacramento, in agr. area (fruit, almonds, alfalfa, grain); laid out 1860. Flour milling, canning, and fruit processing.

Chicopee (chĭ'kúpē), city (pop. 49,211), SW Mass., on Connecticut R. near Springfield; settled 1652. Mfg. of electrical apparatus, tires, firearms, textiles, sporting goods. U.S. air base is here.

chicory or **succory,** blue-flowered herb (*Chicorium intybus*) of Europe, naturalized in North America. Root used as coffee substitute and adulterant. When blanched for winter salads, known as witloof or French endive. True endive is in same genus.

Chicoutimi (shĭkŏō'tĭmē″), city (pop. 23,216), S Que., Canada, on Saguenay R. at mouth of Chicoutimi R. Has pulp, lumber, and woolen mills. Has many Roman Catholic institutions.

Chidambaram (chĭdŭm'bŭrŭm'), town (pop. 26,212), SE Madras, India. Has remains of

Dravidian art, including a statue of the dancing Siva.

Chidon (kī'dŏn): see PEREZ-UZZA.

chief, a leader of a clan or tribe. Hereditary succession is most common, though special qualities may aid in attainment of this status. Functions of chief may be shared by two or more persons.

Chiemsee (kēm'zä), lake, area 31 sq. mi., Bavaria, SE of Munich. An island has palace built by Louis II in imitation of Versailles.

Ch'ien Lung: see CH'ING, dynasty.

chigger, minute, six-legged, reddish larva of harvest mite or red bug commoner in S U.S. than in N U.S. Related to the spider, the adult has eight legs. Attacks warm-blooded mammals, including man, by attaching to the skin and gorging with blood.

Chignecto (shǐgnĕk'tō), isthmus connecting N.S., Canada, with the Canadian mainland.

chigoe (chǐ'gō) or **jigger,** small flea of tropical America and S U.S. Female bores into flesh of humans and animals; flea's abdomen swells forming sack wherein eggs develop; this irritation gives rise to sores and danger of infection.

Chihli, Gulf of (chē'lē', jū'lē'), Chinese *Po Hai,* arm of Yellow Sea, NE China. Bounded on S by Shantung peninsula and on NE by Liaotung peninsula.

Chihuahua (chēwä'wä), state (94,831 sq. mi.; pop. 841,077), N Mexico; cap. Chihuahua (pop. 56,805). Largest Mexican state, it is divided into two regions with mountains in W and desert basin in N and E. Chief occupations: mining (silver, gold, copper, manganese), cattle raising, and agr. (by irrigation). First known to Spanish through Cabeza de Vaca; became state after independence from Spain. JUÁREZ, a border city, is commercial link with U.S.

Chihuahua dog: see TOY DOGS.

Chikamatsu, Monzaemon (mōnzä'ämō chǐkä'mätsoō), 1653–1724, great Japanese dramatist, who wrote primarily for puppet stage. Influenced development of modern Japanese theater.

Child, Francis James, 1825–96, American scholar. Compiled *English and Scottish Popular Ballads* (5 vols., 1883–98).

childbirth: see BIRTH.

Childebert (chǐl'dŭbŭrt), Frankish kings. **Childebert I,** d. 558, king of Paris (511–58). Partitioned his brother Clodomer's kingdom of Orléans with his brothers Clotaire I and Theodoric I (524), and Burgundy and Provence with Clotaire (534). **Childebert II,** 570–96, king of Austrasia (575–96) and Burgundy (593–96). Dominated by his mother, BRUNHILDA.

Childeric I (chǐl'dŭrǐk), c.436–481, Merovingian king of Salian Franks; father of Clovis I.

child labor was recognized as a social problem in late 18th-cent. England, where employment in factories became virtual slavery for the children. Factory acts of 1802 and later bettered conditions. Today almost all European countries limit the working day for children to 6–8 hr. In U.S. problem became acute after the Civil War. All but two states forbid full-time employment of children under 14 in industry; 14 states forbid employment of children under 16 in school hours. Congressional laws against child labor were declared invalid 1918 and 1922; attempts to secure a constitutional amendment have failed.

Children's Crusade: see CRUSADES.

Childress (chǐl'drǐs), city (pop. 7,619), N Texas, SE of Amarillo in Panhandle. Rail hub and center of agr. area in old ranch country.

child welfare. When the effects of the Industrial Revolution in exploiting CHILD LABOR were being recognized in the late 18th and early 19th cent., educators such as Rousseau, Pestalozzi, and Froebel called attention to children's special needs. The 19th cent. saw the organization of charitable institutions for orphaned, destitute, and handicapped children, and the 20th cent. saw the expansion of child welfare agencies and services (private, municipal, state, national, and international). The British Children's Charter Act (1908), the Ohio Children's Code Commission (1911), and the founding of the U.S. Children's Bureau (1912) were early landmarks.

Chile (chǐ'lē, Span. chē'lä), republic (286,396 sq. mi.; pop. 5,760,571), S South America; cap. SANTIAGO. A long (c.2,600 mi.) narrow (never more than 250 mi. wide) strip between the rugged Andes (lofty ACONCAGUA is just over the Argentine border) and the Pacific, Chile also includes outlying EASTER ISLAND and JUAN FERNÁNDEZ isls. The mainland has deserts in the N producing nitrates (see ATACAMA) and copper, exported through ANTOFAGASTA and ARICA. In the center is a long rich valley, the "garden" of Chile, where the population is concentrated (65% mestizo, 30% white, 5% Indian). Here are the cap. and other large cities (notably the port VALPARAISO and near-by VIÑA DEL MAR). Where the Andes approach the sea in the S there is a resort area of alpine lakes near PUERTO MONTT, and further S is a region of wet, wooded islands and the southerly city, PUNTA ARENAS. Chile's S tip is in the frigid TIERRA DEL FUEGO. The predominant language is Spanish, the predominant religion Roman Catholicism—both brought by Spanish conquerors. First of these was Almagro, who in an expedition from Peru (1536) was defeated by the deserts and by fierce Araucanian Indians. Valdivia after 1540 founded Spanish cities, but resistance of the Indians was not really broken until late in the 19th cent. Chile, developed as an area of large pastoral landholdings, was a captaincy general, dependent until 1778 on the viceroyalty of Peru. The first move for independence, led by Juan Martínez de Rosas, Bernardo O'Higgins, and José Miguel Carrera, failed in the battle of Rancagua (1814), but José de San Martín led a force from Argentina through high USPALLATA PASS, and a victory at Maipu (1818) assured Chilean independence. Since the colonial aristocracy and royalist clergy were discredited the revolutionary, the army, the intellectuals, and some creole landholders framed the new government, first crystallized in the constitution of 1830, which gave a base for later emergence of parliamentary government. Longstanding border disputes with Bolivia and Peru were climaxed by the War of the PACIFIC (1879–84), which gave Chile rich nitrate deposits and other minerals but left the TACNA-ARICA CONTROVERSY long unsettled; the end of a border dispute with Argentina was marked by erection of the CHRIST OF THE ANDES. Exploitation of mineral resources brought wealth and growth in commerce and transportation (e.g., the TRANSANDINE RAILWAY) but left Chile vulnerable to changes in world markets and to depressions. This has been met by industrialization (largely with hydroelectric power), mfg., and intensive use of agr. products. Chile, neutral in World War II, is a member of the United Nations.

Chilkoot Pass, c.3,500 ft. high, in Coast Mts. on British Columbia–Alaska boundary. Route through pass between Yukon R. valley and coast was long a monopoly of Chilkoot Indians; first white man passed through 1878. Route to the Klondike from Skagway in gold rush of 1890s with WHITE PASS as alternate.

Chillán (chēyän'), city (pop. 31,280), S central Chile; founded c.1580; agr. and commercial center.

Chillicothe (chǐ"lǐkŏ'thē). **1** City (pop. 8,694), N Mo., NE of Kansas City near Grand R. A grain trade center, it has mfg. of wood, steel, dairy products. **2** City (pop. 20,133), S central Ohio, on Scioto R. and Paint Creek and S of Columbus; settled 1796. Trade and shipping center with mfg. of shoes, paper and food products, and furniture. Cap. of Northwest Territory 1800; cap. of Ohio 1803–10 and 1812–16.

Chillingworth, William, 1602–44, English theologian. Converted to Catholicism, he left that faith and took orders (1638) in the Church of England. Known for *The Religion of Protestants a Safe Way to Salvation* (1638), arguing the right of the individual to personal interpretation of the Bible, the sole source of religion.

Chilliwack (chǐ'lǐwăk), city (pop. 5,663), SW B.C., Canada, on Fraser R. and E of New Westminster, in agr. and lumbering area.

Chillon (shǐlôn', shǐ'lùn, Fr. shēyô'), castle at E end of L. Geneva, Switzerland, built 9th–13th cent. Prison of François BONNIVARD. Now a museum.

Chiloé (chēlōä'), island (3,241 sq. mi.) off S Chile, largest island of Chile.

Chilperic I (chǐl'pûrǐk), d. 584, Frankish king of Neustria (561–84). With his mistress and future wife, FREDEGUNDE, he murdered his wife Galswintha (567), thus precipitating a savage feud with BRUNHILDA (Galswintha's sister) and his brother Sigebert I of Austrasia (Brunhilda's husband). The feud was inherited by his son, CLOTAIRE II.

Chiltern Hills, chalk hill range (width, 15–20 mi.; length, 45 mi.), NW of London, England.

Chiltern Hundreds, administrative districts in Buckinghamshire, England, known for the phrase "applying for the Chiltern Hundreds" (used by member of Parliament in giving up seat, since he may not resign). Reference is to stewardship of districts (now obsolete but still profitable), which no M.P. may hold.

Chimay, princesse de: see TALLIEN, THÉRÉSA.

Chimayó (chǐmīō'), village (pop. c.2,000), N N.Mex., N of Santa Fe. Spanish frontier post 1598–1695. Famous for blanket weaving in early 19th cent. Has El Santuario shrine (1816). Tsimajó pueblo was here or near by.

Chimborazo (chēmbōrä'sō), inactive volcano, 20,577 ft. high, central Ecuador.

chime: see BELL.

Chimera (kǐmēr'ů), in Greek legend, monster, part lion, part goat, and part dragon. It was slain by BELLEROPHON.

Chimkent (chǐmkyĕnt'), city (pop. 74,185), S Kazakh SSR, on Turksib RR. Lead refinery, chemical plant, textile mills. Once important caravan center. Citadel stormed by Russians 1864.

chimpanzee, anthropoid ape (*Pan* or *Anthropopithecus*) of central and W Africa. Like the gorilla it is more manlike than other apes; considered the most intelligent and teachable. Adult is 4–5 ft. tall, 150–200 lb. In captivity sometimes turns savage.

Chimu (chē'mōō), ancient Indian civilization on desert coast of N Peru, flourished probably 500–1500 A.D.

Ch'in (chǐn), dynasty of China, which ruled from 221 to 207 B.C. Founder was Shih Hwang-ti [first emperor]. He devised centralized system of government and decreed use of standard style of writing. Built original Great Wall.

Chin, dynasty of China (265–420): see TSIN.

China, republic (3,800,000 sq. mi.; est. pop. 475,000,000), E Asia. Bounded on NE by USSR and Korea, on N by USSR and Mongolian People's Republic, on SW by India, and on S by Burma and Indo-China. MANCHURIA in N is historically distinctive area. Off shore are HAINAN and FORMOSA. Hsia is traditionally first dynasty, but Shang (c.1523–c.1027 B.C.) is first in documented history. Great cultural and imperialist periods were CHOU, HAN, T'ANG, SUNG, YÜAN, and MING dynasties. Portuguese settled Macao in 1557, but foreign trade was unimportant until 1842, when defeat of CH'ING dynasty by the British in Opium War forced China to make major concessions. Regime was further weakened by Japan's success in First CHINO-JAPANESE WAR (1894–95). U.S. promotion of OPEN DOOR policy failed to prevent BOXER REBELLION, a last effort to expel foreigners. Success of republican revolution, led by SUN YAT-SEN, forced emperor's abdication 1912. Sun's successor Yüan Shih-kai used repressive tactics which led to formation of rival government at Canton. China's entry into World War I on Allied side helped to thwart early expansionist designs of Japan. Washington Conference (1921–22) guaranteed China's territorial integrity. After 1919 civil war raged between Kuomintang and N government (supported by war lords, notably Chang Tso-lin). Winning foreign recognition, Kuomintang government was estab. 1928 at Nanking. The 1927 purge of Communist wing of party had forced Communists, led by Mao Tse-tung and Chu Teh, to retreat to north, which became their center of power. Disunity aided Japan's drive for conquest. Second CHINO-JAPANESE WAR began 1931 with Japanese occupation of Manchuria. Chinese resistance steadily weakened despite Allied aid after Dec., 1941, when Japan's attack on U.S. and British bases merged Chinese war in World War II. At war's end China regained sovereignty over all areas (except Hong Kong and Macao) from foreign powers. Civil war, partly interrupted by World War II, flared anew. In late 1946 natl. assembly (boycotted by Communists) adopted democratic constitution; in 1948 CHIANG KAI-SHEK became first constitutional president. In Sept., 1949, Communists proclaimed rule over all China, setting up Chinese People's Republic, with cap. at Peking (called Peiping by Nationalists) and Chou En-lai as premier. By Jan., 1950, Communist regime was recognized by USSR, Great Britain, and India, but not by U.S. In late April, 1950, Chiang controlled only Formosa. Communists officially entered Korean War in Nov., 1950. Soviet-Chinese pact (Sept., 1952) reaffirmed friendship between two Communist governments. In 1949 the Communists divided China (including Tibet and Inner Mongolia) into six regional districts. These grouped for administrative purposes the existing provinces, which include (besides those in Manchuria) N and S Anhwei, Chahar, Chekiang, Fukien, Honan, Hopeh, Hunan, Hupeh, Kansu, Kiangsi, N and S Kiangsu, Kwangsi, Kwangtung, Kweichow, Ningsia, Pingyuan, Shansi, Shantung, Shensi, Sikang, Sinkiang, Suiyuan, Szechwan, Tsinghai, and Yunnan. For geographical information see under these headings.

China, Great Wall of, fortifications, c.1,500 mi. long, winding across N China, from Kansu prov. to Hopeh prov., mostly along edge of Mongolian plateau. First built in early Ch'in dynasty; present form dates mainly from Ming dynasty.

china clay, a fine-textured, pure clay, consisting chiefly of the mineral kaolinite, and often called kaolin. Easily molded, it turns white when fired and is used in making fine porcelains. Sometimes used in paper making.

China Sea, western part of Pacific Ocean. Divided by Formosa into East China Sea and South China Sea.

chinch bug, small hemipterous insect. *Blissus leucopterus,* feeding on sap of grains and grasses, causes huge U.S. crop losses (esp. in Mississippi, Missouri, Ohio valleys). *Blissus hirtus* is lawn pest in NE U.S.

chinchilla (chĭnchĭ'lû), small rodent (*Chinchilla*) of South America, living in rocky burrows in Andes of Bolivia, Chile, and Peru. Its soft grey pelt is one of costliest furs.

Chincoteague (chĭng'kûtēg), town (pop. 2,724), E Va., on Chincoteague Isl.; connected to Eastern Shore by causeway and bridge. Hunting and fishing resort. Has annual wild pony roundup and auction. Chincoteague Bay, inlet of the Atlantic, extends N from island.

Chindaswinth (chĭn'dûswĭnth), d. 653, Visigothic king of Spain (642–53). Began compilation of *Forum judicum,* completed by his son RECESWINTH.

Chinese architecture. The classical period of Chinese building was T'ang dynasty (A.D. 618–906), but there are few surviving build-

ings dated before the Ming dynasty (1368–1644). Major achievement of Ming period is Forbidden City in Peking with its intricate plan and decorations of exceptional richness. Notable is the Temple of Heaven, circular structure on triple platform. Both religious and secular architecture follow one basic type, involving one-story rectangular chamber on stone platform and covered by single or several superimposed roofs of richly colored glazed tiles. The roof, which projects on brackets in upward curve beyond eaves, is supported by interior columns; walls serve merely as screens. Ancient regulations govern dimensions and number of columns. Typical temple has three parallel buildings approached by monumental steps, gateways, and buildings. A main architectural principle is harmonizing of structure with natural settings. Distinctive Chinese structures are PAGODA and pailou (memorial arch with upturned tile roof).

Chinese art. Founding of Shang dynasty (c.1523 B.C.) possibly marks transition from Stone Age to Bronze Age. Cast bronze ritual vessels (with decoration varying from meager to ornate, from abstract to naturalistic) are clearest extant record of Shang, Chou, and Early Han stylistic development. Advent of Buddhism gave new impetus to sculpture; representation of Buddha and bodhisattvas focused interest on human figure. Buddhist sculpture (marked by precise modeling and linear rhythms) reached its height in early T'ang dynasty (618–906) and flourished for c.300 more years. Ancient Chinese art of painting can be traced clearly only from 4th cent. Painters used basic technique of calligraphy, relying mainly on line and silhouette. Little survives of works of T'ang dynasty, classic period of figure painting. Landscape painting reached peak in Sung dynasty. Masterpieces were done in ink (colors or monochrome) on absorbent silk or paper. Though secular in subject, they were Buddhist or Taoist in spirit. After 12th cent. more intimate subjects appeared. Ming period produced paintings of highly decorative quality. Development of Chinese pottery roughly paralleled that of painting; perfected in Sung dynasty, it became technically elaborate in Ming. Chinese art has deeply influenced Western artists since 18th cent.

Chinese Eastern Railroad: see SOUTH MANCHURIAN RAILROAD.

Chinese exclusion. After U.S. acquired Calif., large inflow of Chinese into state was welcomed at first because of need of cheap labor. Treaty Anson Burlingame signed with China in 1868 guaranteed right of Chinese immigration, but did not guarantee right of naturalization. In following decades much anti-Chinese feeling arose in Calif. and complete ban on Chinese immigration was urged. In a treaty of 1880 China allowed U.S., some right to restrict, but not to prohibit, Chinese immigration. Chinese exclusion act of 1882 did, however, ban immigration of Chinese laborers for ten years. Later acts flatly violated 1880 treaty. In a treaty of 1894 China agreed to exclusion of Chinese laborers for ten years. When that period was up, Congress continued exclusion unilaterally until immigration arrangements of 1924 made control automatic.

Chinese language, most important and most widely spoken of Sino-Tibetan or Indo-Chinese languages. See LANGUAGE (table).

Chinese literature. Oldest records date from Shang dynasty (c.1523–c.1027 B.C.). Oldest surviving literature, probably dating from late CHOU dynasty: *Shih Shu* [four books], containing early statements of Confucianism, notably *Book of Mencius; Wu Ching* [five classics], traditionally attributed to Confucius, including records of ancient traditions, chronology of Lu (Confucius's native state), system of divination, description of ceremonials and utopian state, and a collection of 305 poems in simple rhyming stanzas about peasant life and feudal wars. Other important early books include Lao-tze's *Taoteh-king* (mid-3d cent. B.C.) and works of Chuang-tze. Early Chinese wrote on strips of bamboo and later on silk. Invention of paper (A.D. 105) and wood block printing (8th cent.) stimulated book production. Poetic freedom of Chou period was supplanted by minutely prescribed forms. Prosodic rules of greatest poetic era, T'ang dynasty (618–906), continued to be observed later despite pronunciation changes. Great T'ang poets, notably Li Po, Tu Fu, and Wang Wei, and the later Sung poet Su Tung-po have strongly influenced modern English imagist poets. Chinese poems tend to be brief, suggestive, and nonintellectual. Earliest dynastic history dates from 1st cent. B.C. Popular romances in jingling couplets or easy prose appeared continuously, but few prior to 10th cent. survive. Drama was estab. by Yüan dynasty (1260–1368). Plays have sentimental plots and stylized performances with symbolic props. Trend toward practicality, since 1918 revolution, led to writing in the vernacular, notably by Hu Shih, but use of complex ideographs instead of an alphabet has persisted.

Chinese music can be traced back to very ancient times, but little is known about it, since in 212 B.C., all musical books and instruments were ordered destroyed. However, certain outlines of ancient Chinese music can be ascertained. The single tone was most important and considered an attribute of the substance which produced it. Hence musical instruments were classified according to the material from which they were made—gourd (*sheng,* a free-reed instrument); bamboo (panpipes); wood (*chu,* a kind of percussion instrument); silk (various types of zither with silk strings); clay (flute); metal (bell); stone (sonorous stone); and skin (drum). Music was believed to have power over the elements and had ethical connotations. Scale of Chinese music was five-toned, roughly represented by the black keys on a piano. The various types of notation did not indicate rhythm. Ancient musical practice has given way to folk song, religious music, Western jazz, and classical music in modern China.

Chinese Turkistan: see SINKIANG.

Ch'ing (chǐng) or **Manchu** (măn″chōō), last dynasty of China, which ruled from 1644 to 1912. Estab. by the Manchu, a people

of N. China. Under Emperor Ch'ien Lung (reigned 1736–96) China reached maximum size, extending in N beyond Amur R. and in S through Indo-China. The Ch'ing strongly opposed sea-borne foreign trade but were forced by series of wars in 19th cent. to open China's ports and to give extraterritorial rights to European powers. Efforts of Emperor Kwang Hsü to promote reforms for strengthening China were blocked by dowager empress Tz'u Hsi. Revolution of 1911 forced abdication of HENRY PU YI.

Chinghai, province: see TSINGHAI.

Chin Hills (chĭn), mountain range, W Burma, bordering Assam. Chin Hills division (13,-903 sq. mi.; pop. 220,410) of Upper Burma is semi-autonomous.

Chinnereth or **Chinneroth** (both: kĭn′–; –rōth): see GALILEE, SEA OF.

Chino (chē′nō), city (pop. 5,784), S Calif., E of Los Angeles. Processing center for walnuts, citrus fruits, and truck.

Chino-Japanese War, First, 1894–95. Caused by rivalry for control of Korea. In 1885 Japan had agreed to Chinese overlordship over Korea, but in 1894 induced Korean king to reject it when a revolt broke out. In ensuing war the Japanese won a quick victory over the Chinese. Treaty of Shimonoseki gave Korea nominal independence and provided for cession of Formosa, Pescadores Isls., and Liaotung peninsula by China to Japan. Also called First Sino-Japanese War.

Chino-Japanese War, Second, 1931–45. Caused by long-standing desire of Japan to dominate E Asia. In 1931 Japan reinforced her garrison in Manchuria, ostensibly to protect Japanese property there. After bombing of Japanese troop train near Mukden the Japanese took over all Manchuria. By 1935 much of NE China had been captured. Peking, Shanghai, and Nanking (national cap.) fell 1937; by 1940 the Japanese had taken all major cities on E coast. The Chinese, based at Chungking (temporary cap.) fought on. Japan's attack on Pearl Harbor merged the war in World War II as China declared war on Axis powers. Despite Allied aid and diversion of Japanese armies, China's military position failed to improve until April, 1945. Japan capitulated Aug., 1945, formally surrendered Sept. 9, 1945. Also called Second Sino-Japanese War.

Chinon (shēnō′), town (pop. 4,312), Indre-et-Loire dept., central France, on Vienne R. Its imposing castle (actually a complex of three castles, built 12th–15th cent.) was a royal residence in Middle Ages. Here Joan of Arc first met the dauphin. Rabelais was born near by.

Chinook Indians (shǐnōōk′, chǐ′), tribe in the Columbia valley, of Chinook linguistic stock (as were near-by tribes). Had plank houses in settled villages; were skilled with canoes; traded much; and had the custom of potlatch. **Chinook jargon** was the lingua franca of early trade on the Northwest Coast; had Chinook, Nootka, English, and French words.

chinquapin (chĭng′kŭpĭn), chestnut species (*Castanea pumila*) of E U.S. Golden-leaved chestnut or giant chinquapin (*Castanopsis chrysophylla*) is evergreen tree of W U.S.

Chioggia (kyôd′jä), city (pop. 23,577), Venetia, NE Italy; major fishing port on islet in Adriatic near Venice. Bridge joins it to mainland. Picturesque old houses, canals. Several naval battles were fought here in "Chioggia War" between Venice and Genoa (1378–80), which ended with Venetian victory.

Chios or **Khios** (kī′ŏs), Aegean island (321 sq. mi.; pop. 72,777), Greece, 5 mi. W of Asia Minor; chief town and port Chios (pop. 26,617). Mountainous, it rises to 4,157 ft. in Mt. Elias. Famed for scenic beauty and good climate. Produces wine, fruits, wheat, mastic. Marble, lignite; sulphur springs. Colonized by the Ionians; held by Persia 494–479 B.C.; later under Athenian influence; free city of Roman Empire until Vespasian's reign. From the Byzantines, it passed to the Latin Empire of Constantinople (1204), to Genoa (1261), to Turkey (1566) and to Greece (1912). Anti-Turkish revolt of 1822 ended in massacre of Chian Christians. Chios claims to be Homer's birthplace.

Chipewyan (chĭpŭwī′ŭn), trading post, NE Alta., Canada, on NW shore of L. Athabaska. Old Fort Chipewyan (built 1788), on S shore, was base for Alexander Mackenzie's expeditions in 1789 and 1793. Present post was fur trade center.

chipmunk, rodent of squirrel family. Chipmunk of E U.S. and SE Canada is of genus *Tamias*. Common Eastern chipmunk (*Tamias striatus*) is 5–6 in. long, reddish or grayish brown on top, black and white on sides, with 4–5 in. hairy, flattened tail. It eats nuts, seeds, berries, and insects; carries food in expansible cheek pouches. Winters in underground burrow provided with stores of food. Chipmunks of W North America are of genus *Eutamias*.

Chippawa (chĭ′pŭwô), village (pop. 1,762), S Ont., Canada, just above Niagara Falls. Scene of battle in War of 1812.

Chippendale, Thomas, 1718–79, English cabinetmaker. A whole general category of 18th cent. English furniture is grouped under his name. His style is based on Queen Anne and Georgian design, but with Chinese, Gothic, and French rococo elaborations. His favorite material was dark mahogany, always without inlays. Influenced American cabinetmakers. See *ill.*, p. 456.

Chippewa (chĭ′pŭwù), river rising in lake region of N Wisconsin, and flowing c.200 m. S and SW to the Mississippi at foot of L. Pepin. Has three dams.

Chippewa Falls, city (pop. 11,088), W central Wis., on Chippewa R. just NE of Eau Claire, in lake region; settled 1837. Center of dairy and farm area with mfg. of clothing and meat and wood products. Has important hydroelectric plant.

Chippewa Indians: see OJIBWA INDIANS.

Chiputneticook Lakes (chĭpŏotnē′tēkŏok), chain on Maine-N.B. border, forming international boundary for 28 mi. Source of St. Croix R.

Chiricahua National Monument: see NATIONAL PARKS AND MONUMENTS (table).

Chirico, Giorgio de (jōr′jō dā kē′rēkō), 1888–, Italian painter, b. Greece. Known mainly for his earlier works (characterized by an at-mosphere of mystery) which greatly influenced early surrealist painting. Broke with surrealism in late 1920s.

Chirikov, Aleksey Ilich (ŭlyĭksyä′ ĭlyēch′ chē′rĭkŭf), d. 1748, Russian explorer. Lieutenant of Vitus Bering on voyage leading to discovery of Alaska.

Chiron (kī′rŏn), in Greek religion, CENTAUR; son of Cronus, ancestor of Achilles and Ajax. A famous teacher, he taught Jason, Asclepius, Hercules, and Achilles. He gave his immortality to Prometheus.

chiropractic (kī″rŭpräk′tĭk), system of treatment by manipulation, especially of spinal column. Its purpose is to restore normal nerve function. It was originated 1895 by Daniel D. Palmer.

Chisholm (chĭz′ŭm), city (pop. 6,861), NE Minn., on Mesabi iron range and NE of Hibbing.

Chisholm Trail, route over which vast herds of cattle were driven from Texas to railheads in Kansas after Civil War. Took name from Jesse Chisholm, who, in 1866, drove his wagon, heavily loaded with buffalo hides, through Indian Territory which is now Okla. to his trading post near Wichita, Kansas. Wheels cut deeply into prairie; marked route used for almost two decades by traders and drovers.

Chisinau: see KISHINEV, Moldavian SSR.

Chiswick, England: see BRENTFORD AND CHISWICK.

Chita (chētä′), city (pop. 102,555), RSFSR, in SE Siberia, on Trans-Siberian RR; founded 1653. Center of a region rich in tungsten, molybdenum, gold, tin, iron, coal, lumber, cattle.

Chittagong (chĭ′tŭgŏng), city (pop. 269,000), SE East Bengal, Pakistan, on Bay of Bengal. E. Pakistan's main port, it exports jute, tea, and hides.

Chiusi (kyōō′sē), Latin *Clusium,* Etruscan *Chamars,* town (pop. 2,534), Tuscany, central Italy. Cap. of ancient Etruria under Lars Porsena. Etruscan tombs (5th cent. B.C.); museum.

chivalry: see KNIGHTHOOD AND CHIVALRY.

chive, herb (*Allium schoenoprasum*) with globular lavender flower heads and slender tubular leaves which are used in seasoning.

Chkalov (chkä′lŭf), formerly **Orenburg** (ŏ′rŭnbōorg), city (pop. 172,925), E European RSFSR, on Ural R. Agr. processing. Founded 1735 as fortress; resisted (1773–74) siege by Pugachev. Renamed 1938.

Chloë, Greek shepherdess: see DAPHNIS AND CHLOË.

chloral, oily, colorless liquid from treating absolute ethyl alcohol with chlorine. With water it forms chloral hydrate, used in medicine to produce sleep.

chlorate, salt of chloric acid, compound of metal and chlorate radical. Potassium chlorate is a colorless, crystalline oxidizing agent. Used to make matches, fireworks, and explosives, and as oxygen source. Explosive when mixed with certain chemicals.

chloric acid, compound of hydrogen and chlorate radical ($-ClO_3$), appears only as colorless solution. It is moderately stable and a strong oxidizing agent. Salts are chlorates.

chloride, compound of chlorine and other element or radical. It is a salt formed by direct union of elements or by reaction of hydrochloric acid with base, metal, or oxide. Most form aqueous solution, conduct electricity, and are decomposed (see ELECTROLYSIS). Among uses: calcium chloride as drying agent and in refrigeration; silver chloride in photography; chloride of sulphur in vulcanizing rubber. In aqueous solution hydrogen chloride (colorless, irritating gas) is called HYDROCHLORIC ACID.

chloride of lime, white powder, a disinfectant and bleach, made by treating slaked lime with chlorine.

chlorine (klô'rĭn), active, nonmetallic element (symbol = Cl; see also ELEMENT, table), in HALOGEN family. Greenish-yellow, poisonous gas with suffocating odor, heavier than air. Forms many compounds that occur abundantly in nature. Prepared by electrolysis of sodium chloride. Used in water purification; as disinfectant, antiseptic; to make bleaching powder, dyes, fire extinguishers, explosives; in many poison gases; in medicine.

chloroform (klô'rŭfôrm), volatile liquid, compound of carbon, hydrogen, and chlorine. Discovered 1831, it was first used as anesthetic by Sir J. Y. Simpson (1847). Solvent for fats and other organic compounds.

chlorophyll (klô'rŭfĭl"), substance that gives plants their green color and enables them to carry on PHOTOSYNTHESIS. It is contained in chloroplasts (small, oval bodies in plant cells) and chemically is similar to blood. Sunlight appears to be essential to chlorophyll formation. Certain plants lacking chlorophyll, e.g., yeasts and bacteria, live as parasites or saprophytes. Chlorophyll is used in drugs and as food coloring.

Chmielnicki or Khmelnitsky, Bohdan (bŭkh-dän' khmĕlnĕt'skē), 1593–1657, hetman of the Ukraine. Stirred Cossack revolt against Polish overlordship (1648). United Ukraine with Russia (1654).

Choate, Joseph Hodges (chōt), 1832–1917, American lawyer and diplomat. Handled many famous cases in New York city. Distinguished himself as U.S. ambassador to Great Britain (1899–1905).

Chocano, José Santos (hōsä' sän'tōs chōkä'nō), 1875–1934, Peruvian poet, a leader of *modernismo*.

chocolate is extracted from seeds of CACAO tree by complex process of grinding, heating, and blending, without removal of fat. Chocolate liquor is used in confectionery, powdered or molded chocolate in chocolate beverage, in confectionery, and cookery.

Choctaw Indians (chŏk'tô), tribe of SE U.S., of Natchez-Muskogean linguistic stock. Culture similar to that of Creek Indians. Were removed to the Indian Territory in 1832. One of FIVE CIVILIZED TRIBES.

Choderlos de Laclos: see LACLOS.

choir. 1 See CHORUS. 2 Instruments of any one type in the orchestra, as brass choir, wood wind choir. 3 That part of a church reserved for the singers and officiating clergy.

Choiseul, Étienne François, duc de (ätyĕn' fräswä' dük' dù schwäzül'), 1719–85, French foreign minister (1758–70). Negotiated FAMILY COMPACT; annexed Lorraine, Corsica. Protégé of Mme de Pompadour.

cholera (kŏ'lŭrù), or Asiatic cholera, acute infectious disease caused by bacterium (*Vibrio cholerae* or *V. comma*). Transmitted by polluted food or water. Symptoms include watery diarrhea, vomiting, collapse. Death rate high. Preventable by vaccination.

cholera infantum (ĭnfăn'tŭm), condition in infants probably resulting from severe intestinal infection by various bacteria. Symptoms resemble those of true cholera.

Cholula (chōlōō'lä), town (pop. 8,424), Puebla, E central Mexico. An old Toltec city, it was Aztec sacred city when Spanish came. Cortés destroyed city, built church over pyramid. Has numerous churches and is place of pilgrimage.

Chopin, Frédéric (frädārēk' shôpĕ'), 1810–49, composer and pianist, b. Poland of French and Polish parents, lived in Paris after 1831. Almost all his music is for solo piano. Even in his two piano concertos, the orchestra is dominated by the piano. Polish nationalism is evident in the sets of mazurkas and polonaises, while the nocturnes, waltzes, and preludes are more often elegiac. He also wrote a series of etudes, scherzos, ballades, and sonatas. His music, highly romantic, is important in the development of piano techniques. He had a notable love affair with George Sand.

Chopin, Kate O'Flaherty (shōpăn'), 1851–1904, American author of stories of La., b. St. Louis.

Chorale or choral, term originally used to denote part of the Roman Mass, usually sung in unison; now, more often, a Protestant hymn of stately tempo. During the Reformation, German composers used the traditional tunes of chorales in writing contrapuntal works with organ accompaniment.

chorea (kōrē'ù) or Saint Vitus's dance, nervous disorder accompanied by involuntary jerking and emotional instability. Rarely occurs after puberty.

chorus. 1 In music, group of singers, usually divided into four sections—soprano, alto, tenor, and bass. A chorus performing only sacred music is called a choir. 2 In drama of ancient Greece, the group that speaks to accent the action. They spoke in dithyrambs without action until Thespis in the 6th cent. B.C., introduced the actor, and made it a dramatic chorus. In the 2d cent. B.C. it ceased completely to have anything to do with the action and later disappeared.

Chorzow, Pol. Chorzów (hô'zhōōf), Ger. Königshütte, city (pop. c.142,000), S.W. Poland, in Silesia. Center of KATOWICE mining and industrial region. Passed from Germany to Poland 1921.

Chosroes: see KHOSRU.

Chou (chou), dynasty of China. According to tradition ruled from 1122 to c.256 B.C., but according to some modern scholars from c.1027 to 256 B.C. Confucius, Mencius, and Lao-tze lived in Chou era.

Chouans (shōō'ùnz, shwä), peasants of NW France who rose against French revolutionary government in 1793. Movement merged with royalist risings in VENDÉE, continued sporadically till 1815.

Chou En-lai (jō' ĕn'-lī', chou'), 1898–, Chinese Communist leader. Active Communist since student days in France. Became first premier and foreign minister of People's Republic of China (estab. 1949).

Chouteau, René Auguste (rùnā' ōgüst' shōōtō', shōtō'), 1749–1829, American fur trader and a founder of St. Louis (1763–64) with Pierre LACLEDE. Developed business with brother, **Jean Pierre Chouteau,** 1758–1849, fur trader and U.S. Indian agent. His son, **Auguste Pierre Chouteau,** 1786–1838, aided in the family fur trade. Another son, **Pierre Chouteau,** 1789–1865, bought interest in old American Fur Co. and expanded his business activities.

chow or **chowchow,** dog known from antiquity in the Orient, where it was a hunting dog. It has a massive head, ruffed neck, broad short muzzle, and small pointed ears. The tongue and inside of mouth are blue-black. The dense coat is of solid color, usually reddish brown, black, or slaty blue. The chow, Spitz, and Eskimo or husky dogs probably had a common origin. The Spitz weighs 25–30 lb., is of solid color (usually white or black). The Eskimo dog has long been used in arctic regions for pulling sleds. There are several types, and the colors vary greatly; most Eskimo dogs weigh 70–100 lb. The coat is double with long guard hairs overlying a dense woolly undercoat. Most dogs of this group have tails which curl up over the body.

Chrestien de Troyes or **Chrétien de Troyes** (both: krātyē' dü trwä'), fl. 1164, French poet, author of first great literary treatments of ARTHURIAN LEGEND. Among surviving works are *Érec et Énide; Cligès; Lancelot ou Le Chevalier de la charette; Yvain ou Le Chevalier au lion;* and *Perceval ou Le Conte del Graal* (unfinished; see PARSIFAL). All but the last appear in tr. of W. W. Comfort, *Arthurian Romances* (1913).

Christ: see JESUS.

Christadelphians [Ger.,= brothers of Christ], religious sect in U.S. in 1840s by John Thomas. They show simple, early Christian faith and expect second coming of Christ to set up theocracy in Jerusalem.

Christchurch, city (pop. 112,681; metropolitan pop. 150,047), E South Isl., New Zealand; founded 1850. Canterbury Col. (1873) and School of Arts (1882) are here. Has tanneries and meat-packing plants.

Christ Church College: see OXFORD UNIVERSITY.

Christian, Danish kings. **Christian I,** 1426–81, king of Denmark (1448–81), Norway (1450–81), and Sweden (1457–64), count of Oldenburg; founder of Oldenburg dynasty of Danish kings. Also inherited Schleswig and Holstein (1460). His defeat at Brunkeberg by Sten STURE (the elder) ended his attempt to subdue Sweden (1471; see KALMAR UNION). **Christian II,** 1481–1559, king of Denmark and Norway (1513–23), king of Sweden (1520–23). His wholesale massacre of Swedish nobles at Stockholm (1520) led to rebellion. GUSTAVUS I was raised to the Swedish throne, the Kalmar Union terminated. In Denmark Christian alienated the Church and nobility by his high-handed reforms. Deposed 1523, he died a prisoner. **Christian III,** 1503–59, king of Denmark and Norway (1534–59). Broke power of Hanseatic League; estab-

lished Lutheranism; declared Norway a Danish dependency. **Christian IV,** 1577–1648, king of Denmark and Norway (1588–1648). Playing a major part in THIRTY YEARS WAR, he invaded Germany as champion of Protestants (1625); was defeated by Tilly at Lutter (1626); relieved STRALSUND with Swedish help (1628). He signed a separate peace (1629) but in 1643–45 reentered the war, siding against Sweden, and lost two Norwegian provinces. **Christian V,** 1646–99, king of Denmark and Norway (1670–99). His minister GRIFFENFELD dominated his reign until 1676, made the monarchy absolute. **Christian VII,** 1749–1808, king of Denmark and Norway (1766–1808), was insane. His physician STRUENSEE held power until 1772; A. P. BERNSTORFF was chief minister from 1773. **Christian VIII,** 1786–1848, king of Denmark (1839–48). Proclaimed SCHLESWIG-HOLSTEIN part of Denmark (1846), thus precipitating war of 1848. **Christian IX,** 1818–1906, king of Denmark (1863–1906). Issued from cadet line of Sonderburg-Glücksburg. Annexed Schleswig to Danish crown (1863; see SCHLESWIG-HOLSTEIN). In the resulting war of 1864 with Prussia and Austria he lost Schleswig, Holstein, and Lauenburg. **Christian X,** 1870–1947, king of Denmark (1912–47) and of ICELAND (1912–44). His self-imposed seclusion during the German occupation of Denmark in World War II made him a symbol of national resistance.

Christian Catholic Apostolic Church in Zion, sect founded (1896) by J. A. DOWIE (hq. Zion, Ill.). Members are popularly known as Zionites.

Christian Church: see CHRISTIANS; CHURCHES OF CHRIST; CONGREGATIONALISM; DISCIPLES OF CHRIST.

Christian Endeavor, Protestant interdenominational, international young people's association for encouraging spiritual life and Christian activities; founded 1881 by Dr. F. E. Clark.

Christiania, Norway: see OSLO.

Christianity, all doctrines and religious groups based on the teachings of Jesus Christ. Those who subscribe to any such group are called Christians. Little is definitely known of the years of early spread and nature of the teachings or of the forms of worship, and different interpretations of the known facts give one of the chief bases for the fundamental difference between "traditionalist" churches (e.g., ROMAN CATHOLIC CHURCH, ORTHODOX EASTERN CHURCH), which claim to maintain an elaborated and developed version of early doctrines and rites, and the "reformed" churches (see PROTESTANTISM), which claim to restore pristine doctrines and forms, cleansing them of false additions and developments. From the start Christianity tended to be highly organizational (in contrast to Islam and most other major religions), a tendency that developed in sporadic persecutions by Roman emperors (until toleration was proclaimed by CONSTANTINE I) and in the struggle over differences within the Church. These differences in early times centered on arguments as to the nature of Christ in relationship to the other members of the

Christian Trinity. Councils were called to settle these questions, the accepted answers being deemed orthodox, the rejected ones heretical. Among the early heresies were Arianism, Nestorianism, and Monophysitism. Perhaps the most celebrated of the early councils was First Council of Nicaea (325). In the East the Byzantine emperors exercised much control over the Church, in the West the power of the papacy grew. From both centers Christianity was extended until it embraced all Europe, monks playing a large part in the missionary work of converting pagans. Until the rise of Islam, Christianity was also dominant in Asia Minor and N Africa. The break between the Eastern and Western churches was gradual but was more or less permanent after 1054. A main current of development in both areas was conflict between secular and church authorities. When the REFORMATION came as the most important single movement in Christian history since early days, it added a new element in the diversity of sects. Strife between the various groups, attempts at union, and various struggles to establish sound and enduring relationships between religion and the state have characterized modern Christianity.

Christian Reformed Church. Protestant church formed 1857 by Dutch immigrants dissenting from Reformed Church in America. Name adopted 1890.

Christians, name given followers of evangelical, anti-sectarian preachers on American frontier. Some joined Disciples of Christ; others formed Christian Church, finally merged (1931) with Congregational Churches. See also CHRISTIANITY.

Christian Science, religion based on principles and divine laws formulated from acts and sayings of Jesus Christ by Mary Baker Eddy for Church of Christ, Scientist. Mrs. Eddy's teachings developed after her recovery of health in 1866 through reading in New Testament of healing by Jesus. Her *Science and Health* (1875) is textbook of doctrine. Church founded 1879; Mother Church, the First Church of Christ, Scientist, set up in Boston, 1892.

Christian socialism, movement begun in England in 1848 intended to advance Christian ideals in economic life in opposition to ruthless practices of industrialists. Led by Frederick Denison Maurice and Charles Kingsley, it was very active among workingmen. Its anti-Marxist tradition passed to the Fabian Society, guild socialists, and Catholic groups. In U.S., Society of Christian Socialists (estab. 1889) took up the movement, as did various church groups preaching the "social gospel." On the Continent the term Christian Socialist was given to varied groups, usually connected with particular religious leaders.

Christiansted (krĭs'chŭnstĕd"), town (pop. 4,-126), on St. Croix isl.; port of Virgin Islands (U.S.).

Christie, Agatha, English detective-story writer. Her many volumes, extremely popular, often feature the detective Hercule Poirot. They include *The Murder of Roger Ackroyd* (1926), *Murder in the Calais Coach* (1934), and *And Then There Were None* (1940).

Christie's, English firm of art auctioneers and appraisers, founded 1766. One of world's largest clearinghouses for art objects.

Christina, 1626–89, queen of Sweden (1632–54); daughter and successor of Gustavus II. OXENSTIERNA headed a regency until 1644. She ruled irresponsibly and eccentrically, devoting her time to the study of philosophy. Descartes lived at her court. Her refusal to marry was chiefly responsible for her abdication in favor of her cousin, Charles X (1654). She left Sweden in men's clothes, entered the Catholic Church (1655), and settled at Rome. Later attempts to regain the Swedish throne failed.

Christine de Pisan: see PISAN, CHRISTINE DE.

Christmas [Christ's Mass], feast day celebrating the birth of Jesus Christ (the Nativity), in the Western churches Dec. 25, a date almost certainly chosen for its nearness to the Epiphany (Jan. 6). Not observed earlier than A.D. 200, it grew popular in the Middle Ages, and many customs clustered about the feast, especially in English-speaking countries: the Yule log (the Yule season is simply Christmastide), gathering decorations of holly and mistletoe, the singing of carols, giving of gifts, and sending of greeting cards. The Christmas tree is a German contribution to the season; the American Santa Claus is derived from the Dutch customs in N.Y. (see NICHOLAS, SAINT).

Christmasberry or **toyon** (tō'yŭn), western evergreen shrub (*Photinia arbutifolia*), with red berries.

Christmas Island (60 sq. mi.; pop. 866), of Singapore crown colony, in Indian Ocean. Has large deposits of phosphate of lime. Leased to phosphate company.

Christmas Island, largest atoll in the Pacific, area 95 sq. mi., near equator, one of Line Isls. Discovered 1777 by Capt. James Cook, added 1919 to British colony of Gilbert and Ellice Isls.

Christmas rose: see HELLEBORE.

Christ of the Andes, statue built (1904) in Uspallata Pass on Argentine-Chilean boundary to commemorate peace and boundary treaties. Dispute had arisen because crest of Andes and continental watershed did not coincide.

Christophe, Henri (ärē' krēstôf'), 1767–1820. Negro king of Haiti. A freed slave he aided Toussaint L'Ouverture in liberation of Haiti; was army chief under Dessalines. Elected president of Haiti (1806), he disputed control of island with Pétion. Declared himself king 1811; committed suicide 1820 when revolts broke out.

Christopher, Saint [Gr.,= Christ bearer], 3d cent.?, martyr of Asia Minor. Chief legend is that when he was charitably carrying a child across a river, he felt the weight on his shoulders grow almost too great to bear and discovered that he was carrying Jesus, who carried the world in His hands. He is patron of travelers; hence St. Christopher medals for automobiles. Feast: July 25.

Christophsen, Pieter: see CHRISTUS, PETRUS.

Christ's College: see CAMBRIDGE UNIVERSITY.

Christ's Hospital, once a hospital (founded 1533) in London, it became a school, known as "bluecoat school" from the boys' habit.

Now includes school for girls. Has been at Horsham, Sussex, since 1902.

Christ's-thorn, name for several thorny plants, especially a spiny shrub (*Paliurus spina-christi*) with hat-shaped fruit. Also called Jerusalem thorn.

Christus or **Cristus, Petrus** (both: pē'trus krĭ'stŭs), c.1400–1473, Flemish painter, also called Pieter Christophsen; a follower of the Van Eycks.

Christy, Edwin P., 1815–62, American showman. Estab. c.1842 a company of Negro minstrels known as Christy's Minstrels, which became the typical minstrel show with interlocutor, end men, and performers in blackface.

Christy, Howard Chandler, 1873–1952, American illustrator. Known for the "Christy girl" of posters and magazine illustrations. Also did portraits.

chromatic scale, in music: see SCALE.

chromium (krō'mēŭm), gray-white, crystalline, hard, nontarnishing metallic element (symbol = Cr; see also ELEMENT, table). Forms chromates and dichromates used as paint pigments, in dyeing, in leather tanning. Metal comparatively rare, always occurs in compounds. Used for PLATING and in several alloy steels, e.g., chromium steel, stainless steel.

chromosome (krō'mŭsōm″), form assumed by chromatin material of cell nucleus during stages of MITOSIS and meiosis. The form and number of chromosomes depend upon the species. They contain genes, which determine hereditary characteristics, and are thus important in heredity, evolution, mutation of plants and animals, and determination of SEX. For process of mitosis, see *ill.,* p. 813.

chromosphere (krō'mō–), rarefied layer of gases surrounding sun and lying outside photosphere. It consists chiefly of hydrogen (radiating scarlet light), helium, and calcium and extends 5,000–7,500 mi.; layer 100 to 200 mi. thick at the base is known as reversing layer. Moving gases form projections (prominences) observable during eclipses or through spectroscope. Eruptive prominences burst forth in jets; cloudlike quiescent prominences extend from pole to pole.

Chronicles or **Paralipomenon** (păr″ŭlĭpŏm′ĭnŏn) [Gr.,= things left out], books of Old Testament, called 1 and 2 Chronicles in AV, 1 and 2 Paralipomenon in Greek Bible and Western canon. Books contain: genealogies; history of reigns of David and Solomon; history of kingdom of Judah. Historical material parallels (and supplements) parts of Samuel and Kings.

chrysanthemum (krĭsăn'thŭmŭm), annual or perennial plant of genus *Chrysanthemum.* Late-blooming flowers, of various colors except blue or purple, range from single daisy-like to large, rounded shaggy forms. Cultivated in Orient for at least 2,000 years.

Chryseis (krīsē'ĭs), in the *Iliad,* girl captured by Agamemnon. Forced by Apollo to return Chryseis, Agamemnon took Briseis from Achilles to replace her and thus aroused the wrath of Achilles.

chrysoberyl (krĭ'sŭbĕ″rĭl), a beryllium aluminate used as a gem. It is transparent to translucent and has a vitreous luster. One va-

riety, alexandrite, is green by daylight and red under artificial light. Chrysolite is a yellow-green chrysoberyl.

Chrysoloras, Manuel (krĭsŭlô'rŭs), c.1355–1415, Greek teacher who helped introduce Greek into Italy.

Chrysostom: see JOHN CHRYSOSTOM, SAINT.

Chuang-tze (chŏōäng'-tsä'), fl. 4th cent. B.C., Chinese philosopher, a follower of Lao-tze, whose doctrines he interpreted with great skill and charm.

chuck-will's-widow, bird of S U.S. allied to nighthawk and whippoorwill. Its call has the sound of its name.

Chukchi Peninsula (chŏōk'chē), NE extremity of Asia and Siberia, RSFSR, terminating in EAST CAPE. Population largely Chukchis, of Hyperborean language family; subsist on reindeer raising, fishing, fur trapping. Coal mines on Anadyr Gulf. Chukchi Natl. *Okrug* [area] (274,520 sq. mi.; pop. c.20,000) was formed 1930.

Chula Vista (chŏō'lŭ), city (pop. 21,578), S Calif., S of San Diego, in agr. area. Aircraft mfg.

Chungking (chŏŏng″kĭng′), commercial city (pop. 1,000,101), Szechwan prov., SW China; port at junction of Kialing and Yangtze rivers. Opened 1891 to foreign trade. War-time cap. of China (1937–46).

Chuquisaca: see SUCRE, Bolivia.

Chur (kōōr), Fr. *Coire,* town (pop. 19,256), cap. of Grisons canton, E Switzerland, on Plessur R. Roman settlement; early episcopal see. Temporal power of prince-bishops was ended by Reformation (1524–26). Has 8th-cent. church (restored), cathedral (12th–13th cent.), episcopal palace.

Church, Frederick Edwin, 1826–1900, American landscape painter of the Hudson River School.

Church, aggregation of Christian believers; in its widest sense embracing all believers, living and dead, headed by Jesus Christ, who founded the community through his apostles. An early traditionalist division distinguishes the church militant (living Christians) from the church suffering (the dead in Purgatory) and the church triumphant (the saints in Heaven). In more usual parlance the church is the organized aspect of any sect or group of believers (e.g., the Lutheran Church, the Church of England, the Church of the Brethren, the Roman Catholic Church), but in most cases each group conceives itself to be the one true Christian body. See CHRISTIANITY.

Churches of Christ, conservative body of Protestant Christians, formerly united with Disciples of Christ.

Churchill, Charles, 1731–64, English satirical poet, author of *The Rosciad* (1761), satire on actors.

Churchill, John: see MARLBOROUGH, JOHN CHURCHILL, 1st DUKE OF.

Churchill, Lord Randolph Henry Spencer, 1849–95, British statesman. Sought to create a democratic Tory party. Resigned as chancellor of exchequer 1886 to oppose high military spending. Father of Winston Churchill.

Churchill, Winston, 1871–1947, American author of historical novels (*Richard Carvel,*

1899, *The Crisis*, 1900) and novels on political problems (*The Inside of the Cup*, 1913).

Churchill, Winston (Leonard Spencer), 1874–, British statesman, soldier, and author. Fought in India, the Sudan, and South Africa. Elected to Parliament 1900. First lord of the admiralty in World War I (1911–15) until discredited by failure of Dardanelles campaign. Returned to office in Lloyd George Liberal government 1917–21. Conservative chancellor of exchequer 1924–29; subsequent influence as opponent of "appeasement" of Germany led to his replacing (1940) Neville CHAMBERLAIN as prime minister of coalition government seven months after outbreak of World War II. Became symbol of British resistance. Before the entry of U.S. into war he met President Roosevelt at sea (see ATLANTIC CHARTER). Twice addressed U.S. Congress. Attended series of international conferences—CASABLANCA; QUEBEC; CAIRO; YALTA; TEHERAN; POTSDAM. After Labour Party victory 1945 became leader of the opposition. Conservative victory in 1951 brought him back as prime minister. Author of several histories, biographies, memoirs.

Churchill, river, N Sask. and N Man., Canada, issuing from Methy L. and flowing c.1,000 mi. SE, E, and NE to Hudson Bay at Churchill. Traverses many lakes and was famous fur-trading route. Mouth of river discovered 1619 by Scandinavian Jens Munck. Hudson's Bay Co. estab. trading post (1689) which was later abandoned and then refounded at Fort Churchill (later known as Fort Prince of Wales). Superseded c.1732 when heavy stone fort was built on W side of river's mouth. Remains of this fort now in national park. **Churchill,** port on Hudson Bay at mouth of Churchill R., was selected 1927 as terminus of Hudson Bay RR (completed 1929). Serves N Man. as grain-shipping port from mid-Aug. to mid-Oct.

Churchill Downs: see LOUISVILLE, Ky.

Church of Christ, Scientist: see CHRISTIAN SCIENCE.

Church of England: see ENGLAND, CHURCH OF.

Church of God: see ADVENTISTS.

Church of the Brethren: see DUNKARDS.

Churriguera, José (chŭr″ĭgâr′ŭ; chōōr-rēgä′rä), 1650–1725, Spanish baroque artist and sculptor, b. Salamanca. Went to Madrid 1688 where he designed the catafalque for Queen María Luisa. Works include palace of Don Juan de Goyeneche. Extravagant design and capricious use of Renaissance motives led to the use of the term **Churrigueresque** (chŭr″ēgŭrĕsk′) for Spanish architecture of the late 17th and early 18th cent. The style influenced Spanish colonial work in Mexico and SW U.S.

Churubusco, battle: see CONTRERAS.

Chu Teh (jōō′ dŭ′), 1886?–, Chinese Communist leader. Trained at Yünnan military academy and in Germany. Commander in chief of all Chinese Communist forces in World War II; retained that post after founding of People's Republic of China in 1949.

Chuvash Autonomous Soviet Socialist Republic (chōōväsh′), autonomous state (7,100 sq. mi.; pop. 1,077,614), E European RSFSR, in middle Volga valley; cap. Cheboksary.

Agr., forests. Population 80% Chuvash, a people of Finnic language.

Ciano, Galeazzo (gäläät′tsō chä′nō), 1903–44, Italian Fascist leader, count of Cortellazzo. Married Mussolini's daughter Edda. Foreign minister 1936–43. Helped to bring about Mussolini's fall in 1943. Arrested by Germans; executed by Fascist republic in N Italy. His diaries are a remarkable document.

Cibber, Colley, 1671–1757, English actor and playwright. Successful in comic roles (1692–94), later was a leading actor of eccentric characters (1697–1732). His play, *Love's Last Shift* (1696), regarded as first sentimental comedy. Poet laureate 1730–57, attacked by Pope in *The Dunciad*. His son, **Theophilus Cibber,** 1703–58, acted in Colley's plays. Theophilus's wife, **Susannah Maria (Arne) Cibber,** 1714–66, sang in operas and acted tragic roles (e.g., Lady Macbeth and Desdemona). Handel wrote contralto arias in his *Messiah* for her.

Cibola: see MARCOS DE NIZA; CORONADO, FRANCISCO VÁSQUEZ DE.

cicada (sĭkā′dŭ), name for homopterous insect with wide, blunt head, prominent eyes, two pairs of membranous wings. Periodical or 17-year (13-year in U.S.) cicada is miscalled locust. Shrill song of males caused by vibrating membranes near abdomen. See *ill.*, p. 601.

Cicero, Marcus Tullius (sĭ′sŭrō), or **Tully,** 106–43 B.C., Roman orator, politician, philosopher. Consul from 63 B.C. Prosecuted Cataline. Exiled by Clodius and recalled by Pompey (58–57 B.C.). A republican, he opposed Caesar; attacked Antony in the *Philippics.* Under Augustus he was put to death. His letters reveal Roman life. His philosophical works (*On Ends, On the Nature of the Gods,* etc.) express his mild Stoicism and, together with his rhetorical works, reveal him as the great master of Latin prose.

Cicero, industrial town (pop. 67,544), NE Ill., adjoining Chicago; founded 1857. Electrical equipment, metal products, and building materials.

Cid or Cid Campeador (sĭd′ kăm′pēŭdôr), d. 1099, Spanish national hero; real name Rodrigo (or Ruy) Díaz de Vivar. Served under Castilian kings, emir of Saragossa, fighting both Moors and Christians. Conquered Valencia (1094), where he ruled until death. For his chivalry, generosity, became prototype of noble Castilian warrior. Hero of *The Song of the Cid* (12th-cent. anonymous epic) and dramas by Guillén de Castro and Corneille.

cider, in Europe, is fermented juice of apples, often aged in casks; in U.S., unless qualified as "hard" cider, it is unfermented apple juice, usually pasteurized and often blended to balance the flavor.

Ciego de Ávila (syä′gō dä ä′vēlä), city (pop. 23,802), central Cuba; a commercial center halfway between Santiago de Cuba and Havana.

Cienfuegos (syĕnfwä′gōs), city (pop. 52,910), central Cuba, port on Caribbean. Has large and beautiful harbor. Sugar is chief product.

Cierva, Juan de la (hwän′ dä lä thyĕr′vä),

1895–1936, Spanish aeronautical engineer. Inventor of autogiro, first flown in 1923.

Cieszyn: see TESCHEN.

cigar and cigarette. Habit of smoking rolls of tobacco was acquired by Spanish conquistadors from Indians of W Hemisphere and it spread into Europe. Cigars consist typically of filler leaves held by binder leaves and wrapped spirally with wrapper leaves; largely machine-made after c.1902. Cigarettes consist of shredded tobacco (usually blended and often sprayed with flavorings) rolled in paper.

Cilicia (sĭlĭ'shŭ), anc. region of SE Asia Minor, between the Mediterranean and the Taurus range. Divided into unproductive plateau (Cilicia Trachia) and fertile plain (Cilicia Pedias). Part of the Assyrian Empire and the Persian Empire, it was later Hellenized. The cities of Tarsus and Seleucia throve under Roman and Byzantine rule. Cilicia, invaded by Arabs in the 8th cent., and in 1080 an Armenian state was set up here (later Little Armenia), to last until conquered by the Turks in 1375.

Cilician Gates (sĭlĭ'shŭn), mountain pass, S Turkey, across Taurus mts., known anciently as Pylae Ciliciae, now as Gulek Bogaz. Crossed by an ancient highway from Cappadocia to Cilicia.

Cimabue, Giovanni (jōvän'nē chēmäboo'ä), d. c.1302, Florentine painter, reputedly the teacher of Giotto. Frescoes in Church of St. Francis, Assisi, are attributed to him. His work is a transition from the formalized Byzantine style to the more naturalistic 14th-cent. manner.

Cimarosa, Domenico (dōmā'nēkō chēmärō'zä), 1749–1801, Italian composer. *Il matrimonio segreto* is the best of his *opera buffa*. He also wrote serious operas, church music, and instrumental music.

Cimarron (sĭm"ùrōn'), river, 692 mi. long, rising in NE N.Mex. and flowing E, barely touching Okla. Panhandle and SE Colo., to enter Kansas. Crosses and recrosses Okla. line, then swings SE and E across Okla. to Arkansas R. just W of Tulsa.

Cimarron, Territory of, now the Panhandle of Okla. Settled by cattle ranchers. Efforts to estab. separate territory failed, and in 1890 area became part of Oklahoma Territory.

Cimber, Lucius Tillius, d. after 44 B.C., one of the conspirators against Julius Caesar. On the pretext of presenting a petition he approached Caesar, then held him as Casca stabbed him.

Cimbri: see GERMANS.

Cimmerians (sĭmēr'ēŭnz), anc. people who in 8th cent. B.C. moved from the Crimea to the region of Lake Van. In the early 7th cent. B.C. they swept across Asia Minor. Traditionally considered as fierce barbarians, they are actually little known in history.

Cimon (sī'mŭn), d. 449 B.C., Athenian general and statesman; son of Miltiades. In the Persian Wars he fought at Salamis and commanded in the defeat of the Persians on the Eurymedon (468 B.C.). The leader of the aristocratic party after the death of Aristides, he was exiled but later recalled.

cinchona (sĭngkō'nù), evergreen tree (*Cinchona*), native to Andes of South America.

Its bark is source of QUININE. Before World War II, Java and India grew commercial supply; later South America cultivated wild trees.

Cincinnati (sĭnsĭnă'tē, –nă'tù), city (pop. 503,-998), SW Ohio, port on Ohio R. opposite Covington, Ky., at mouth of Licking R.; laid out 1788. State's second largest city and commercial and cultural center for a large area. Meat packing and mfg. of alcoholic beverages, soap, machine tools, steel products, chemicals, and clothing. A busy shipping point for early settlers, it was aided by opening of Miami and Erie Canal. Received settlers from Germany and Ireland. Was early abolitionist center and Underground Railroad station. Survived disastrous floods, notably in 1884 and 1937. Adoption of city-manager government in 1924 ended long period of political misrule. Seat of Univ. of CINCINNATI and Xavier Univ. Points of interest include Music Hall and Exposition Building (houses Cincinnati Symphony and May Music Festival), Taft House Mus., and Eden Park, with city art museum and art academy.

Cincinnati, Society of the [Latin plural of *Cincinnatus*], formed in 1783 by officers of Continental army after American Revolution. Founded for fraternal, patriotic, and allegedly nonpolitical aims.

Cincinnati, University of, at Cincinnati; municipal, coed.; chartered 1870, opened 1873. Col. of Engineering and Commerce, with Inst. of Scientific Research, pioneered in a work and study plan. School has made archaeological excavations at Troy. Library has collection of Historical and Philosophical Society of Ohio. Col. of Music of Cincinnati and Cincinnati Conservatory of Music are allied.

Cincinnatus (sĭnsĭnā'tùs, –nā'tùs), fl. 5th cent. B.C., semilegendary Roman hero. Consul in 460, he in 458 left his farm to become dictator, defeated the Aequi and the Volsci, and immediately returned to his farm. He repeated this performance to put down a plebeian revolt in 439.

cinema: see MOVING PICTURES.

cineraria (sĭn"ùrâr'–), pot plant of genus *Senecio*, with daisylike flower clusters above big leaves.

Cinna, Lucius Cornelius (sĭ'nù), d. 84 B.C., Roman statesman, leader of the popular party, consul (87 B.C.–84 B.C.). When Sulla left Italy, Cinna undertook anti-Sullan electoral reforms, and the conservatives drove him from power. He gathered an army, recalled MARIUS from Africa and took Rome, where he slaughtered Sulla's followers. Cinna was murdered in a mutiny as the civil war began. His daughter Cornelia was married to Julius Caesar.

cinnabar (sĭ'nùbär), mineral, sulphide of mercury, used chiefly as a source of mercury.

cinnamon, tropical evergreen tree (*Cinnamomum zeylanicum*) of Ceylon, and its aromatic bark. Cut-back plants produce many shoots from which commercial stick cinnamon, a flavoring, is obtained. Bark of another species, cassia bark tree, is considered inferior substitute. *C. camphora* yields camphor.

cinnamon vine: see YAM.

Cinq Mars, Henri Coëffier, marquis de (ärē′ kŏĕfyä′ märkē′ dü sēmär′), 1620–42, French conspirator. Favorite of Louis XIII; plotted with Spain against Richelieu. Was executed.

cinquefoil (sĭngk′–), plant of widely distributed genus *Potentilla*, bearing yellow flowers and foliage with five leaflets. Some species are grown in rock gardens and some are used for home remedies.

Cinque Ports (sĭngk) [Fr.,= five ports], group of maritime towns in Sussex and Kent, England. Originally five, other places later added. Chartered by Edward the Confessor, they provided ships and men against invasion before English navy estab. Walmar Castle, Deal, is official residence of Lord Warden. This post, now honorary, held by Churchill.

Cintra, Port. *Sintra* (sēn′trŭ), town (pop. 6,307), Portugal, near Lisbon. Beautiful situation made it favorite residence of Portuguese kings. Has ruins of Moorish castle, old royal palace and monastery. By Convention of Cintra (1808) French troops under Junot were permitted to leave Portugal.

C.I.O.: see CONGRESS OF INDUSTRIAL ORGANIZATIONS.

cipher: see CRYPTOGRAPHY.

Circassia (sûrkă′shŭ), historic region, SE European RSFSR, between Black Sea, Kuban R., and Greater Caucasus, now in Krasnodar and Stavropol Territories. The Circassians (also known as Cherkess, Adyge, Adighe), a people of the N Caucasian language family, abandoned Christianity for Islam in 17th cent. Circassian women, famed for beauty, were prized as slaves in Turkey. Ceded by Turkey to Russia in 1829, Circassia resisted Russian conquest until 1864. About 400,000 Circassians now live in the Adyge and Cherkess autonomous *oblasts* [regions].

Circe (sûr′sē), in Greek legend, celebrated enchantress; daughter of Helios. She changed companions of Odysseus into swine, but he made her break the spell.

circle, closed plane curve each point of which is equidistant from point within called the center. Also defined as a CONIC SECTION cut by plane perpendicular to cone axis. Surface within curve also called circle; curve itself called circumference; line with each end on circumference called chord; chord through center called diameter; any line joining center with circumference called radius. For formula for area of a circle see AREA.

Circleville, city (pop. 8,723), S central Ohio, on Scioto R., S of Columbus. Laid out 1810 within remains of circular fort erected by mound builders.

circuit, electric: see ELECTRIC CIRCUIT.

circuit rider, itinerant preacher of Methodist denomination, who served "circuit" of 20 to 40 "appointments." System, devised by John Wesley for his scattered English groups and adapted in America by Francis Asbury, greatly aided spread of Methodism.

circulation of the blood, continuous passage of blood through heart and blood vessels. Oxygenated blood is forced into general systemic circulation from left ventricle of heart through arteries into network of capillaries through whose thin walls oxygen and nutriment pass into tissues and carbon dioxide and other wastes enter blood. Deoxygenated blood returns through veins to right auricle of heart, then passes through right ventricle into pulmonary circulation. After interchange of carbon dioxide and oxygen in lungs, oxygenated blood passes through pulmonary veins and left auricle into left ventricle where cycle begins anew. See *ill.,* p. 763.

circus [Latin,= circle], associated historically with horse and chariot races and contests known in anc. Rome as Circensian games. Roman circus was a round or elliptical structure with tiers of spectators′ seats enclosing the space in which races, brutal and bloody games, and gladiatorial combats took place. Modern circus (a tent show with wild animals, acrobats, freaks, and clowns) dates from close of 18th cent. Outstanding American circus was that of P. T. BARNUM.

Cirencester (sĭs′ĭtŭr, sī′rŭnsĕstûr), urban district (pop. 11,188), Gloucestershire, England. Site of Roman settlement Corinium. Royal Agricultural Col. here.

Cirta: see CONSTANTINE, Algeria.

Cisalpine Republic (sĭsăl′pĭn), N Italian state created 1797 by Bonaparte through union of Cispadane and Transpadane republics, which he had set up in 1796 N and S of Po R. In practice a French protectorate. Renamed Italian Republic 1802. Merged with Venetia in Napoleonic kingdom of Italy 1805.

Cisco (sĭs′kō), city (pop. 5,230), N central Texas, E of Abilene. Shipping and processing center of agr. and oil area. Artificial L. Cisco near by.

Cisleithania: see AUSTRO-HUNGARIAN MONARCHY.

Cisneros, Francisco Jiménez de: see JIMÉNEZ DE CISNEROS, FRANCISCO.

Cispadane Republic: see CISALPINE REPUBLIC.

Cistercians (sĭstûr′shŭnz), order of Roman Catholic monks founded (1098) by St. Stephen Harding in Cîteaux, France (hence the name); the white Monks (from their white habit). The greatness of the order came with their second founder, St. Bernard of Clairvaux, under whom it expanded phenomenally. In attempting to restore the early simplicity of the Benedictines, they stressed love of God, cheerful practice of austerities, and practice of manual labor, especially farming. The order became less prominent after 1400. Of later Cistercian reforms most important was that of the TRAPPISTS. The center of Cistercian communal life is the abbey. Cistercian nuns (order founded 12th cent.) lead contemplative lives, secluded from the world; a 17th-cent. reform of this order gave rise to the remarkable development of Port-Royal.

Citadel, The—The Military College of South Carolina: see CHARLESTON.

Cîteaux, Côte-d′Or dept., France: see CISTERCIANS.

Cithaeron (sĭthē′rŭn), Gr. *Kythairon,* mountain ridge, c.10 mi. long, central Greece, between Boeotia (N) and Attica and Megaris (S). Rises to 4,623 ft. Scene of many mythical events; sacred to Dionysus.

citrange, citrus-fruit hybrid from cross between sweet and trifoliate oranges. Hardier than orange.

citric acid (sĭ'trĭk), white, crystalline organic acid with tart taste, found in fruits. With alkaline earths and metals, it forms citrates used as laxatives. Acid used as antalkali, in calico printing, in soft drinks (as lemon juice substitute). May be prepared by fermenting sugar.

citron, small evergreen tree (*Citrus medica*), native to tropical Asia and related to other citrus fruit trees. Rind of its large lemon-shaped fruit, when candied and preserved, is used in confectionery and cookery.

citrus fruits: see CITRANGE; CITRON; GRAPE-FRUIT; KUMQUAT; LEMON; LIME; ORANGE; TANGERINE.

Città Vecchia (chēt-tä' vĕk'kyä), **Città Notabile** (nōtä'bēlä), or **Mdina** (ûmdē'nä), town (pop. 1,384), central Malta. Former cap. of Malta, has old palace of grand masters of Knights Hospitalers.

City College: see NEW YORK, COLLEGE OF THE CITY OF.

city government, political administration of urban areas. In U.S. generally, incorporated urban areas were given freedom in local matters, with a mayor and council as administrators. In 20th cent., complexity increased, efficiency waned, and reform movements (e.g., for commission form or for city manager) developed.

City of David, epithet of BETHLEHEM, the birthplace of David, and of JERUSALEM, his capital.

City Point, Va.: see HOPEWELL.

city-state, autonomous neighborhood as a political and social unity, normally a single city or town with the surrounding countryside. At the dawn of history in Mesopotamia it was the normal type of organized life, and the Babylonian and Assyrian empires grew out of the cities. City-states have been known at various times and in various lands, but the most celebrated were those of ancient Greece, which cradled Western civilization. Though the modern idea of democracy stems from them (particularly from Athens) they were by no means all democracies; more commonly they were monarchies or oligarchies. Other famous examples of the city-state were the free imperial cities of the Holy Roman Empire and many of the Italian states in the Renaissance.

Ciudad (syōōdhädh') [Span.,= city]. For cities beginning thus but not so listed, see under following name; e.g., for Ciudad Juárez, see JUÁREZ.

Ciudad Bolívar (syōōdhädh' bōlē'vär), city (pop. 31,009), E Venezuela, port on Orinoco; founded 1764 as Angostura.

Ciudad Real (thyōōdhädh' rääl'), city (pop. 30,150), cap. of Ciudad Real prov., central Spain, in New Castile. Medieval walls; Gothic cathedral.

civet (sĭ'vĭt) or **civet cat,** mammal of family Viverridae, related to cats. Both sexes have scent pouch (near anus) which yields fatty secretion used in Orient as perfume base; much of commercial supply comes from African civet (*Civettictis*). Oriental civet (*Viverra*) found in India and SE Asia.

Civilian Conservation Corps (CCC), organization (estab. 1933; abolished 1942) to provide useful work and vocational training for unemployed young men. Aided nation by conservation of natural resources.

civil law, the law governing private affairs in contrast to public law and criminal law. In a restricted sense, signifies a modern legal system (see CODE) based on Roman law, especially as formulated in *Corpus Juris Civilis* and revived by law scholars in 11th and 12th cents. Civil law prevails on Continent, Latin America, and Westernized countries of Asia. Contrasts with COMMON LAW, usual in English-speaking countries (only La. and Quebec have civil law).

civil rights, the rights which a state's inhabitants enjoy by law. They have a legal as well as a philosophical basis. All bars to discrimination because of creed, origin, or color go to estab. civil rights. The **Civil Rights Acts** were passed after the U.S. Civil War to give Negroes legal and political status equal to that of whites. The act of 1875 was largely voided by Supreme Court in 1883.

civil service, body of persons employed in the civil administration of a government (not including the military or elected officials). Term first used for British administrators in India, later for British home officials. It became popular in U.S. with rising demand for reforming the system after the Civil War. A Civil Service Commission was set up (1871) but was allowed to lapse and was restored by Pendleton Act (1883) only after Pres. Garfield was killed by a disappointed office seeker. Commission draws up rules to give positions on merit in certain classifications; the number of classified posts has constantly been increased. The British tradition of separation of civil service from politics has been adopted in U.S., notably by the Hatch Act (1940) forbidding officeholders to contribute to political campaigns. Similar reform movements have advanced in state and local service.

civil war, in English history: see PURITAN REVOLUTION; ROSES, WARS OF THE.

civil war, in Roman history: see MARIUS and SULLA; POMPEY and CAESAR, JULIUS.

Civil War, in U.S. history (1861–65), conflict between Northern states (Union) and Southern states in secession (see CONFEDERACY), also called the War between the States or the War of the Rebellion. Many contributing causes included sectional rivalry, moral campaign of ABOLITIONISTS, and especially quarrel concerning Federal control *vs.* STATES' RIGHTS. When compromise failed, conflict loomed. Election of Abraham Lincoln as President, and secession of Southern states (1860–61), precipitated war. When on April 12, 1861, P. G. T. Beauregard ordered Confederates to fire on Fort Sumter, hostilities began. In 1861 opening battles were Confederate victories. Irvin McDowell was defeated by Beauregard at first battle of BULL RUN, July 21. In 1862 G. B. McClellan's PENINSULAR CAMPAIGN was foiled by R. E. Lee. However, Lee's ANTIETAM CAMPAIGN was checked by McClellan in September. Lincoln then issued EMANCIPATION PROCLAMATION. Year closed with Union defeat at Fredericksburg, Dec. 13. The next year saw Confederate victory over Joseph Hooker at Chancellorsville, May 2–4, marred by death of Stonewall Jackson. Then Lee undertook the GETTYSBURG CAMPAIGN, that marked the down turn of Confederate fortunes. Meanwhile Northern navy had successfully blockaded Southern coast, under D. G. Farragut captured New Orleans (April 28, 1862), and ended day of wooden battleships (see MONITOR AND MERRIMAC). CONFEDERATE CRUISERS, built or bought in England, in turn caused great loss to Northern shipping. In West, U. S. Grant won great victory at Fort DONELSON (Feb., 1862), followed by drawn battle at Shiloh on April 6–7. Union gunboats on the Mississippi opened way for Grant's successful VICKSBURG CAMPAIGN. The Confederate general Braxton Bragg, checked by G. H. Thomas at Chickamauga in CHATTANOOGA CAMPAIGN (1863), was driven back to Ga. Grant moved against Lee in WILDERNESS CAMPAIGN (May–June, 1864), forcing him toward Richmond, and laying siege to PETERSBURG. W. T. Sherman won ATLANTA CAMPAIGN (May–Sept., 1864), and made his march to the sea. After victory of P. H. Sheridan at FIVE FORKS, April 1, 1865, Confederates evacuated Richmond on April 3. His retreat blocked, Lee surrendered to Grant at Appomattox Courthouse, April 9, 1865. Victory was marred by assassination of Pres. Lincoln. But seceding states, after trials of RECONSTRUCTION, were readmitted, and Union was saved, with slavery abolished.

Civitavecchia (chē'vētä-vĕk'kēä), city (pop. 24,822), Latium, central Italy, on Tyrrhenian Sea; port of Rome. Arsenal built by Bernini; citadel by Bramante and Michelangelo.

Cl, chemical symbol of the element CHLORINE.

Clackmannanshire (klăkmă'nŭnshĭr), smallest county (55 sq. mi.; pop. 37,528) of Scotland, at head of Firth of Forth; co. town of Clackmannan. Oats are chief crop. Mfg. includes textiles, ale, and whisky.

Claflin, Tennessee, 1845–1923, lecturer on woman suffrage; sister of Victoria WOODHULL.

Clair, René (klâr'), 1898–, French film director. His films, filled with sophisticated wit and fantastic satire, include *Sous les toits de Paris, À nous la liberté, Le Million, The Ghost Goes West,* and *Beauty and the Devil.*

Clairaut, Alexis Claude (älĕksē' klōd' klĕrō'), 1713–65, French mathematician, noted for work on differential equations and curves. He formulated Clairaut's theorem dealing with geodesic lines on ellipsoidal surface.

Clairton, city (pop. 19,652), SW Pa., on Monongahela R. and SE of Pitsburgh. Produces coal and steel and coke by-products.

Clairvaux (klârvô'), former abbey, NE France, SE of Troyes. Founded 1115 by St. BERNARD OF CLAIRVAUX; became center of CISTERCIANS; suppressed in French Revolution.

clam, bivalve mollusk with muscular foot for burrowing in sand or mud. Shell valves are hinged, movable; the mantle, a skin fold of body, secretes shell and with gills carries on respiration; cilia of gills cause water current (bearing food and oxygen) to enter one siphon and exit (with wastes) through other. The hard or round clam (adult of little neck or cherry stone) is widely eaten.

clambake, a form of picnic peculiar to U.S.,

adopted from New England Indians. Clams (and often lobsters, fish, potatoes, corn, etc.) are steamed on bed of hot stones, under layer of wet seaweed.

clan, social grouping based on common, unilateral descent of its members. Includes number of families and is included in larger tribal organization. Unlike family, descent is traced through one parent. Within clan, family relations are extended beyond biological lines, and in some clans marriage to fellow member is prohibited or discouraged.

Clapham, residential district, SW London, England.

Clare or Clara, Saint, 1193?–1253, Italian nun, founder of the Franciscan nuns or Poor Clares. Feast: Aug. 12.

Clare, John, 1793–1864, English bucolic poet, called the English Burns.

Clare, John Fitzgibbon, 1st earl of, 1749–1802, Irish statesman; lord chancellor of Ireland. Hated by the Irish for advocating union with Britain.

Clare, Richard de: see PEMBROKE, RICHARD DE CLARE, 2D EARL OF.

Clare, maritime county (1,231 sq. mi.; pop. 85,064), Munster prov., Ireland; co. town Ennis. Broken, hilly region, with bogs and lakes and rugged coastline. Fishing and farming chief occupations; much of land barren. Pop. has declined in last cent.

Clare College: see CAMBRIDGE UNIVERSITY.

Claremont. 1 City (pop. 6,327), S Calif., E of Los Angeles. Ships citrus fruits. Seat of Claremont Col. (nonsectarian; coed.; chartered 1925 as Claremont Colleges, renamed 1944) and associated colleges: Claremont Men's Col. (1946), Pomona Col. (coed.; opened 1888 by Congregationalists), and Scripps Col. (for women; opened 1927). **2** Town (pop. 12,811), SW N.H., on Sugar R., near its junction with Connecticut R. and S of Lebanon; settled 1762. Machinery, textiles, shoes, and paper. Has oldest churches in state (R.C., begun 1823; Episcopal, begun 1773).

Claremont College: see CLAREMONT, Calif.

Claremore, city (pop. 5,494), NE Okla., NE of Tulsa. Site of Indian battle near by. Has U.S. Indian hospital and memorial to native son Will Rogers.

Clarence, George, duke of, 1449–78, son of Richard, duke of York. Joined Richard, earl of WARWICK, in rebellions against his brother Edward IV, 1469–70. Arrested for treason and thrown into the Tower (1478); allegedly drowned in a butt of malmsey wine. Prominent character in Shakspere's *Richard III.*

Clarence, Lionel, duke of, 1338–68, third son of Edward III of England. Governor of Ireland 1361–67; presided at assembly adopting notorious Statute of Kilkenny, forbidding all dealings between the English in Ireland and the Irish.

Clarendon, Edward Hyde, 1st earl of, 1609–74, English statesman and historian. A monarchist, he aided Charles I and went into exile with Charles II, whose chief adviser he became. At Restoration became lord chancellor. Favored religious toleration. Unsuccessful in diplomacy and disliked at court, he was removed from office (1667), fled England, and died in exile. Wrote *History of the*

Rebellion. His daughter, Anne, married James II.

Clarendon, George William Frederick Villiers, 4th earl of, 1800–1870, English statesman. Three times foreign secretary; in CRIMEAN WAR kept together French alliance with England.

Clarendon, Constitutions of, 16 articles signed in 1164 by Great Council of HENRY II. Important in development of English law; extended jurisdiction of civil over church courts. THOMAS À BECKET later repudiated them, and his quarrel with Henry ended with his murder (1170).

Clarendon Code, English statutes adopted by Cavalier Parliament 1661–65 to strengthen Established Church. Laws, four in number, decreased following of dissenting sects (esp. Presbyterians). Named for Earl of Clarendon who opposed enactment but enforced them. Charles II unsuccessfully tried to interfere by Declaration of Indulgences, 1662 and 1672. They were largely superseded by Test Act (1673).

Clarens (klärä′), resort village, Vaud canton, SW Switzerland, on L. Geneva near Montreux. Residence of Byron. Scene of Rousseau's *Nouvelle Héloïse.*

Clarinda (klûrĭn′dù), city (pop. 5,086), SW Iowa, near Mo. line. Mfg. of dairy products.

clarinet: see WIND INSTRUMENTS.

Clark, Alvan, 1804–87, and his son, **Alvan Graham Clark,** 1832–97, American manufacturers of astronomical lenses, noted also for discoveries of celestial bodies.

Clark, Champ, 1850–1921, American legislator, U.S. Representative from Mo. (1893–95, 1897–1921); speaker of House (1911–19). Led successful fight in 1910 to curtail powers of J. G. CANNON as speaker.

Clark, George Rogers, 1752–1818, American Revolutionary general, conqueror of Old Northwest. Captured Vincennes from British in 1779. Led expeditions against Indians in present Ohio. His brother, **William Clark,** 1770–1838, was a leader of the LEWIS AND CLARK EXPEDITION and later served as governor of Missouri Territory (1813–21).

Clark, John Bates, 1847–1938, American economist, teacher at Columbia (1895–1923). Was chief exponent of theory of marginal utility. His son, **John Maurice Clark,** 1884–, also an economist and Columbia professor, argued for including psychological, sociological, and institutional factors in study of economics.

Clark, Jonas Gilman, 1815–1900, American philanthropist, founder of Clark Univ.

Clark, Mark (Wayne), 1896–, American general. Commanded in N Africa and Italy in World War II. Appointed UN Supreme Commander in Korea (1952).

Clark, Tom (Campbell), 1899–, Associate Justice of U.S. Supreme Court (1949–). He was Attorney General of U.S. 1945–49.

Clark, William: see CLARK, GEORGE ROGERS.

Clark, William Andrews, 1839–1925, U.S. Senator and copper magnate. Struggled with Marcus DALY for control of copper and of political forces in Mont. Elected Senator in 1901 after his election in 1899 had been challenged.

Clark College: see ATLANTA, Ga.

Clarkdale, village (pop. 1,609), central Ariz., on Verde R. and NE of Prescott. Tuzigoot Natl. Monument, with Indian ruins, is near.

Clarke, James Freeman, 1810–88, American religious writer, a Unitarian minister, associated with Transcendentalists. One of his books is *Ten Great Religions* (1871–83).

Clarke, John, 1609–76, one of founders of R.I., b. England. Founded Portsmouth (1638) with Anne HUTCHINSON and William CODDINGTON. Chief figure in obtaining R.I. charter of 1663.

Clark Fork, river, c.360 mi. long, part of Columbia R. system, rising in SW Mont. near Butte and flowing N, NW past Missoula to Pend Oreille L. in Idaho Panhandle. PEND OREILLE R., flowing W from lake, is sometimes called part of Clark Fork.

Clarksburg, city (pop. 32,014), N W.Va., SSE of Wheeling and on West Fork of Monongahela R.; chartered 1785. Trade center of mining area with mfg. of stone, clay, carbon, and glass products. Important Union supply base in Civil War. Birthplace of Stonewall Jackson.

Clarksdale, city (pop. 16,539), NW Miss., on Sunflower R. and SSE of Memphis, Tenn., in rich cotton area; settled 1848 on site of Indian fortification.

Clarkson, Thomas, 1760–1846, English abolitionist. Helped Wilberforce abolish British slave trade (1807).

Clarkson College of Technology: see POTSDAM, N.Y.

Clarkston, city (pop. 5,617), SE Wash., on Snake R. at Idaho line. Ships grain, fruit, livestock.

Clarksville, city (pop. 16,246), N Tenn., on Cumberland R. at mouth of Red R. and NW of Nashville; platted 1784. Produces tobacco, flour, and rubber products. Dunbar Cave near by.

Clark University: see WORCESTER, Mass.

clary: see SAGE.

classicism, in literature and art, attention to traditional and recognized forms, producing clearness, elegance, symmetry, and repose. In music it is objectivity of conception, emphasis on balance of structure, and absence of violent passions. To be contrasted with ROMANTICISM.

classic revival, widely diffused phase of taste (known as neoclassic) which influenced architecture and the arts in Europe and the U.S. during the late 18th and first half of the 19th cent. Interest in antiquity was stimulated by excavations at Pompeii and by *Antiquities of Athens* by James Stuart and Nicholas Revett. Stuart's garden temple at Hagley, England, was first example in Europe of Greek design, and the Madeleine in Paris first of Roman temple reproductions. In France, interest in ancient Rome led to the Empire style sponsored by Napoleon. In the U.S. the Greek revival achieved first expression in 1799 in the Bank of Pennsylvania, Philadelphia, by Benjamin H. Latrobe. Fusion of Greek and Roman forms brought movement to its height in c.1820. It was the dominant influence in the U.S. until it gave way to romanticist styles of Victorian period.

Claudel, Paul (pōl' klōdĕl'), 1868–, French poet, dramatist, diplomat. Ambassador to Japan 1921–26; to U.S. 1927–33. His poetry is influenced by Rimbaud, deeply imbued with Catholic symbolism. Best-known are *Corona Benignitatis Anni Dei* (1914; Eng. tr., *Coronal*) and the plays *Le Partage de midi* (1906), *L'Annonce faite à Marie* (1912; Eng. tr., *Tidings Brought to Mary*) and *Le Soulier de satin* (1928–29; Eng. tr., *The Satin Slipper*).

Claude Lorrain (klōd' lôrē'), 1600–1682, French painter of expansive, luminous landscapes. His real name was Claude Gelée or Gellée. Settled in Rome in 1627 under the patronage of Pope Urban VIII.

Claudian (Claudius Claudianus) (klô'dēŭn), d. 408?, last Latin classic poet. Author of minor poems and epics, including the *Rape of Proserpine.*

Claudius (klô'dēŭs), Roman emperors. **Claudius I**, 10 B.C.–A.D. 54, reigned A.D. 4–54; son of the elder Drusus and thus nephew of TIBERIUS. When Caligula was murdered, the soldiers found Claudius hiding behind a curtain, hauled him out, and made him emperor. His reign was one of consolidation and renewing of the empire. He landed in Britain and made it a Roman province. He brought about the execution of his third wife, Messalina, and his fourth wife, Agrippina II (his niece), after persuading him to name her son Nero as heir instead of his own son Britannicus, is said to have poisoned him. **Claudius II**, d. 270, reigned 268–70. Notable chiefly for defeating the Goths at Naissus (Nis) in 269, he was called Gothicus.

Clausel or **Clauzel, Bertrand** (bĕrträ' klōzĕl'), 1772–1842, marshal of France. Commander in chief in Algeria (1830–31, 1835–37).

Clausewitz, Karl von (klou'zŭvĭts), 1780–1831, Prussian general and writer on military strategy, of Polish descent. Saw much active service before he was appointed (1818) director of the German War School. His masterpiece, *On War*, expounded the doctrine of total war, i.e., war against the citizens, territory, and property of the enemy nation in every possible way. The effect of this theory on military science was enormous.

Clausius, Rudolf Julius Emanuel (rōō'dôlf yōō'lyōōs ämä'nōöĕl klou'zyōōs), 1822–88, German mathematical physicist. Introduced concept of entropy; restated second law of thermodynamics. Developed a kinetic theory of gases and a theory of electrolysis.

Clauzel, Bertrand: see CLAUSEL, BERTRAND.

Claverhouse, John Graham of: see DUNDEE, JOHN GRAHAM OF CLAVERHOUSE, 1st VISCOUNT.

clavichord: see PIANO.

Clavijero, Francisco Javier (fränsē'skō hävyĕr' klävēhä'rō), 1731–87, Mexican scholar and historian, author of *The History of Mexico* (Eng. tr., 1787).

Clavijo y Fajardo, José (hōsä' klävē'hō ē fähär'dhō), 1730?–1806, Spanish journalist. In newspaper *Pensador* forwarded ideas of the Enlightenment. His duel with Beaumarchais inspired a play by Goethe.

Clawson, city (pop. 5,196), SE Mich., near Detroit. Has machine shops.

Clay, Clement Claiborne, 1816–82, U.S. Sena-

tor (1853–61). Member of Confederate diplomatic mission to Canada (1864) in abortive plan for peace negotiations with U.S. government. After war, imprisoned for conspiracy, but freed.

Clay, Henry, 1777–1852, American statesman. U.S. Senator from Ky. (1806–7, 1810–11, 1831–42, 1849–52). U.S. Representative (1811–14, 1815–21, 1823–25). Leader of "war hawks" prior to War of 1812. Formulated national program for internal improvement, tariff protection, and rechartering of Bank of the United States. Pushed MISSOURI COMPROMISE through the House. U.S. Secretary of State (1825–29). Opposed Jackson regime, particularly on the bank issue. NATIONAL REPUBLICAN PARTY candidate for President 1832, WHIG PARTY candidate 1844. Denouncing extremists in both North and South, asserting superior claims of the Union, Clay sponsored the COMPROMISE OF 1850. Called the Great Pacificator and the Great Compromiser.

Clay, Lucius D(uBignon), 1897–, American general. As U.S. military governor of Germany (1947–49), directed operations to overcome Berlin blockade.

clay, fine-grained aluminum silicate mixed with other substances. Classed as residual if left by decay of limestone and shale or rocks containing feldspar (see KAOLINITE), or transported if moved by agent of erosion. Bentonites are very fine clays derived usually from volcanic ash. Clays are plastic when wet (hence easily shaped) and become hard when dry or fired. Important uses: making brick, tile, porcelain, china, earthenware, drainage pipes; for filtering and purifying liquids. Some clay is desirable in soil since it helps retain moisture, but an excess has many disadvantages. See also CHINA CLAY.

Clay, Mount: see PRESIDENTIAL RANGE.

Clayton. 1 Suburban city (pop. 16,035), E Mo., just W of St. Louis. **2** Resort village (pop. 1,981), N N.Y., on the St. Lawrence (sailing races) and NW of Watertown, in Thousand Isls. region.

Clayton Anti-Trust Act, 1914, passed by U.S. Congress as amendment to clarify and supplement SHERMAN ANTI-TRUST ACT of 1890. Drafted by Henry De Lamar Clayton. Prohibited exclusive sales contracts, local price cuttings to freeze out competitors, rebates, interlocking directorates in corporations capitalized at $1,000,000 or more in the same field of business, and intercorporate stock holdings. Labor unions and agricultural cooperatives were excluded from the forbidden combinations. Act restricted use of injunction against labor; legalized peaceful strikes, picketing, boycotts. Act was basis for numerous suits against large corporations.

Clayton-Bulwer Treaty (–bŏŏl'wŭr), concluded at Washington, D.C., on April 19, 1850, between U.S., represented by Secretary of State John M. Clayton, and Great Britain, represented by Sir Henry Bulwer. U.S.–British rivalries in Central America, particularly over a proposed isthmian canal, led to treaty, which checked British expansion in Central America but prevented U.S. from building its own canal and exercising political control over it. Very unpopular, treaty remained effective until 1901 (see HAY-PAUNCEFOTE TREATY).

Clearchus (klēär'kŭs), d. 401 B.C., Spartan officer. Governor of Byzantium, he recruited the Greek troops who supported CYRUS THE YOUNGER and after the defeat at Cunaxa he led the retreat of the Ten Thousand (as told by XENOPHON) until he was treacherously murdered.

Clearfield, borough (pop. 9,357), W central Pa., on W branch of Susquehanna R. and N of Altoona. Has railroad shops, coal mining, and mfg. of leather and clay products.

Clear Lake, c.21 mi. long, W Calif., NNW of San Francisco. Fishing resort in wooded hills.

Clearwater, city (pop. 15,581), W Fla., on Clearwater Bay (causeway to Clearwater Beach resort) and W of Tampa; settled after Fort Harrison estab. here 1841. Fruit packing and canning.

Cleaveland, Moses, 1754–1806, American pioneer. Led party to settlement in Western Reserve region of Ohio (1796), site of present Cleveland.

Cleburne, Patrick Ronayne, 1828–64, Confederate general, b. Ireland. One of ablest division commanders. Distinguished himself at Murfreesboro.

Cleburne, city (pop. 12,905), N Texas, S of Fort Worth, founded 1867. Shipping and processing center of agr. area, it has cotton gins, cottonseed-oil mills, and creameries.

Cleef or Cleve, Joos van (yōs' vän klāf', klā'vŭ), c.1485–1540, Flemish portrait painter. His son **Cornelis van Cleef** (kŏr'nä"lĭs), c.1520–1567?, painted Italianate religious pictures as well as portraits; called Zotte van Cleef because he went mad.

Cleisthenes (klīs'thĭnēz, klĭs'–), fl. 510 B.C., Athenian statesman, head of the family of Alcmaeonidae. Ruler of Athens after the exile of Hippias, he instituted democratic reforms that ended civil strife in Athens.

clematis (klĕm'–), vine or nonclimbing perennial of genus *Clematis*. Flowers are either small and clustered, bell-shaped, or anemonelike; fruits have feathery appendage. Purple-flowered Jackman clematis and white-flowered Japanese clematis are vines widely grown in North America.

Clemenceau, Georges (zhôrzh' klämäsō'), 1841–1929, French premier (1906–9, 1917–19), called "the Tiger." His "Sacred Union" cabinet was instrumental in achieving Allied victory in World War I. Opposed Pres. Wilson at Peace Conference. Though he regarded Versailles Treaty as too lenient, he was defeated in 1919 elections because of his moderate attitude toward Germany.

Clemens, Samuel L(anghorne): see TWAIN, MARK.

Clement I, Saint, pope (A.D. 88?–A.D. 97?). Highly revered in his day, he wrote the *Epistle of St. Clement to the Corinthians* (A.D. 96?), admonishing Corinthians to stop quarreling; the tone of authority indicates the power of the bishop of Rome in the early church. This was in the 4th cent. considered as part of the Scriptures (see NEW TESTAMENT). It and other writings wrongly attributed to him are now classed as PSEUDE-PIGRAPHA. Also known as Clemens Romanus or Clement of Rome. Feast: Nov. 23.

Clement III, antipope: see GUIBERT OF RAVENNA.

Clement V, 1264–1314, pope (1305–14), a Frenchman named Bertrand de Got. Appointed archbishop of Bordeaux by Pope BONIFACE VIII, he gained the favor of the French king Philip IV, who engineered his election as pope. He set up residence in Avignon, thus beginning the long "captivity" of the PAPACY. Completely under the domination of Philip, he did resist attempts to condemn Boniface VIII posthumously but he meekly did the king's bidding in dissolving the Knights Templars on unproved charges. He issued an important collection of canon law.

Clement VI, 1291–1352, pope (1342–52), a Frenchman named Pierre Roger. Kept a splendid court at Avignon. When the Black Death struck Europe he helped sufferers and tried to stem subsequent wave of anti-Semitism. He at first favored then opposed RIENZI.

Clement VII, antipope: see ROBERT OF GENEVA.

Clement VII, 1478–1534, pope (1523–34), originally Giulio de' Medici, a member of the MEDICI family. Was archbishop of Florence and a cardinal before becoming pope. Vacillating and timorous, he seemed unaware of the problems the Reformation posed for the church. He disagreed with Emperor Charles V, who sent troops to sack Rome (1527) and take the pope prisoner. A peace was patched up in 1529, and Clement crowned Charles. The struggle with Henry VIII of England over the king's divorce was vigorously pursued by Clement.

Clement VIII, 1536–1605, pope (1592–1605), an Italian named Ippolito Aldobrandini. He abandoned the traditional papal alliance with Spain and was friendly with Henry IV of France. Clement was noted for piety and charity.

Clement XI, 1649–1721, pope (1700–1721), an Italian named Giovanni Francesco Albani. Known for great learning. As pope, he first favored Philip V as candidate for the Spanish throne, but later was forced to recognize Philip's rival, Charles of Hapsburg. Clement sought to stamp out JANSENISM in the church, and in his bull *Unigenitus* (1713) he condemned several Jansenist doctrines.

Clement XIV, 1705–74, pope (1769–74), an Italian named Lorenzo Ganganelli, a Conventual Franciscan. Much pressure from European monarchies (esp. France and Spain) was being exerted against the Jesuits (see JESUS, SOCIETY OF). In 1773 Clement issued a brief suppressing the order.

Clement, coworker of Paul. Philip. 4.3. Traditionally identified with St. Clement.

Clément, Jacques (zhäk' klämä'), 1567–89, French fanatic, a Dominican monk; assassin of Henry III.

Clementi, Muzio (mōō'tsēō klämĕn'tē, 1752–1832, Italian virtuoso pianist and composer. He was the first to compose in a style for piano rather than harpsichord. His studies, *Gradus ad Parnassum,* and his many sonatas are widely used.

Clement of Alexandria, d. c.215, Greek theologian, b. Athens. After conversion to Christianity he taught at Alexandria and was the first to attempt reconciling Platonic and Christian teachings. Defended orthodoxy against Gnosticism, though he apparently held that intellectual knowledge set the holder of it above other Christians (a Gnostic notion). Fragments of his work survive. Origen was his pupil.

Clemson, town (pop. 1,204), NW S.C., WSW of Greenville. Seat of **Clemson Agricultural College** (land-grant, state supported; for men; chartered 1889, opened 1893 with bequest from T. G. Clemson). Campus formerly J. C. Calhoun's plantation.

Cleomenes (klēŏ'mĭnēz), kings of Sparta, **Cleomenes I,** d. c.489 B.C., helped the Athenians to oust Hippias only to find Cleisthenes an anti-Spartan leader. He is said to have killed 6,000 Argives. **Cleomenes III,** d. 219 B.C., was an energetic ruler who defeated the Achaean League, but was overcome when Antigonus III allied himself with the League (c.222 B.C.).

Cleon (klē'ŏn), d. 422 B.C., Athenian statesman. A relentless enemy of Sparta, he won a victory at Sphacteria, but was killed in the defeat at Amphipolis. He is pictured by his enemies Thucydides and Aristophanes as an unprincipled demagogue.

Cleopatra (klēŭpä'trù, –pä'trù, –pă'trù), 69 B.C.–30 B.C., queen of Egypt, one of the great romantic figures of history; daughter of Ptolemy XI. Married according to family custom to her brother, Ptolemy XII, she led a revolt supported by Julius Caesar. Her husband was accidentally drowned in the Nile, and she was married to her younger brother Ptolemy XIII but was the mistress of Caesar, to whom she bore a son Caesarion (Ptolemy XIV). After Caesar's death she was visited by Marc Antony, who fell in love with her. Their love affair, which for a time threatened the Roman Empire, was ended when Octavian (later Augustus) defeated their forces at Actium (31 B.C.) and later at Alexandria. Antony committed suicide, and Cleopatra, unable to move the cool Octavian, went to her death by having an asp bite her. Apparently not beautiful, she was still a fabulously alluring woman. Shakspere's *Antony and Cleopatra* deals with her later story, G. B. Shaw's *Caesar and Cleopatra* with earlier events.

Cleopatra's Needles, popular name for two Egyptian obelisks, c.69 ft. high, originally erected at Heliopolis in c.1475 B.C. One is now in London, the other in New York.

Clergy Reserves, lands in Upper and Lower Canada set apart under Constitutional Act of 1791 "for the support and maintenance of a Protestant clergy." "Protestant clergy" was interpreted to mean clergy of Church of England. This interpretation, opposed by other Protestant denominations, became an issue in the Rebellion of 1837. In 1854 a law was passed providing for secularization of the reserves, but Anglican and Presbyterian churches retained endowments that had been granted them.

Clerk, Sir Dugald (klärk), 1854–1932, British engineer and inventor of gas engines.

Clerk-Maxwell, James: see MAXWELL, JAMES CLERK.

Clermont-Ferrand (klĕrmō'-fĕrä'), city (pop. 93,695), cap. of Puy-de-Dôme dept., SE France; historic cap. of Auvergne. Formed 1731 by merger of Clermont and Montferrand. Rubber industry (automobile tires). Clermont dates from Roman times. At Church council held here in 1095 Pope Urban II preached First Crusade. Has Gothic cathedral (12th–15th cent.); Romanesque Church of Notre Dame (12th cent.); university (founded 1854).

Cletus (klē'tùs) or **Anacletus, Saint** (ănùklē'tùs), pope (A.D. 76?–A.D. 88?), a martyr. Feast: April 26.

Cleve, Joos van: see CLEEF, JOOS VAN.

Cleve, Germany: see CLEVES.

Cleveland, (Stephen) Grover, 1837–1908, 22d President of the United States (two terms, 1885–89, 1893–97). Mayor of Buffalo (1881–82). Governor of N.Y. (1883–85). Cleveland as President continued his independent, reformist, but conservative course. Argued for lower tariff. Panic of 1893 struck hard blow at his second administration. He secured repeal of SHERMAN SILVER PURCHASE ACT. His tariff measures altered by Senator A. P. GORMAN, he allowed Wilson-Gorman Tariff Act to become law without his signature. Opposed by radical Democrats, especially over gold standard, which he upheld. On grounds that movement of U.S. mail was being halted by the strikers, he sent troops to PULLMAN in 1894. In foreign affairs he took a strong stand on the VENEZUELA BOUNDARY DISPUTE; refused recognition to Hawaiian government set up by Americans.

Cleveland. 1 City (pop. 6,747), NW Miss., NE of Greenville, in cotton-growing area. **2** City (pop. 914,808), NE Ohio, port on L. Erie at mouth of Cuyahoga R. Largest city in state, it was seventh in U.S. in 1950. Great ore port and center of iron and steel production, it has mfg. of chemicals, cement, machinery, and electrical apparatus and oil refineries, lumberyards, and meat-packing plants. Laid out 1796 by Moses CLEAVELAND. Developed rapidly after completion of Ohio and Erie Canal (1832) and arrival of railroad (1851). Iron production began in 1850s and oil refining (including Rockefeller operations) soon became a major industry. Later electrical plants boomed when research hq. of General Electric were located at near-by Nela Park. Seat of Case Inst. of Technology (nonsectarian; for men; chartered 1880; science and engineering school of university grade), WESTERN RESERVE UNIVERSITY, and Fenn Col. (Y.M.C.A.; coed.; 1881). John Carroll Univ. is at near-by UNIVERSITY HEIGHTS. City has Western Reserve Historical Society Mus., Cleveland Mus. of Art, Rockefeller Park, and Cleveland Symphony. **3** City (pop. 12,605), E Tenn., ENE of Chattanooga. Woodworking. Cherokee Natl. Forest hq. **4** City (pop. 5,183), E Texas, near San Jacinto R. and NNE of Houston, in lumber and oil area.

Cleveland Heights, City (pop. 59,141), NE Ohio, E residential suburb of Cleveland.

Cleves (klēvz), Ger. *Kleve* or *Cleve,* former duchy, NW Germany, on both sides of the Rhine; historic cap. Kleve (pop. 28,704), North Rhine-Westphalia. Originally a county; united with county of Mark 1368; raised to duchy 1417. Duke John III inherited JÜLICH, BERG, and RAVENSBURG 1524; his daughter Anne married Henry VIII of England. Extinction of male line (1609) led to complicated dynastic quarrel over succession. Treaties of 1614 and 1666 settled Cleves, Mark, and Ravensburg on Brandenburg; Jülich and Berg on Palatinate branch of Wittelsbachs.

cliff dwellers. Buildings perched on mesas and on ledges of canyon walls in the U.S. Southwest were once thought to be the work of an extinct people, but now it is known that they were built by the ancestors of the Pueblo Indians as defense against nomadic tribes. The cliff dwellers were skilled farmers, employing irrigation. Many of the buildings are now in national parks and monuments.

Clifford of Chudleigh, Thomas Clifford, 1st Baron, 1630–73, English Catholic statesman, member of Cabal ministry of Charles II. Knew of secret passages in Treaty of Dover pledging reestablishment of Catholicism in England. Forced to resign by passage of Test Act (1673) and committed suicide.

Cliffside Park, suburban borough (pop. 17,-116), NE N.J., NE of Jersey City and near the Hudson.

Clifton, industrial city (pop. 64,511), NE N.J., adjoining Passaic. Mfg. of airplane propellers, rubber and metal goods, clothing, and chemicals.

Clifton Forge, city (pop. 5,795), western Va., N of Roanoke, in coal area. Railroad shops.

Clifton Heights, borough (pop. 7,549), SE Pa., W of Philadelphia. Has textile mills.

climacteric: see MENOPAUSE.

climate, sum total of weather elements over long period. Elements include temperature, precipitation (see RAIN), HUMIDITY, WIND, barometric pressure. Latitude is primary factor, modified by secondary influences (e.g., relation to water and land; altitude; topography; prevailing winds; OCEAN CURRENTS; cyclonic-storm prevalence). Climatic zones include equatorial zone (see DOLDRUMS); subtropical (tradewind belts; horse latitudes); intermediate, prevailing-westerlies region; and polar zone. Subtropical-intermediate transition belt (Mediterranean type) found on continental west coasts. Climatic types combining latitude and secondary items: continental (sunny with low humidity, except at equator; temperature extremes); marine (slight temperature changes; much rain on windward side of mountainous islands); coastal or littoral; and mountain or plateau. Climatology is study of climate and its relation to plant and animal life.

climbing perch, spiny-finned, perchlike, freshwater, walking fish (genus *Anabas*), of India and SE Asia. Adult is c.10 in. long, dark brown, with a blunt, hard head, thick skin, and scales. It walks and climbs by using its tail, fins, and spines on fins. It can breathe atmospheric oxygen.

Clinch, river formed by juncture of two forks in SW Va. and flowing c.300 mi. SW across E Tenn. to Tennessee R. Impounded by Norris Dam, it flows into Watts Bar Reservoir. Important in TENNESSEE VALLEY AUTHORITY.

clinic, institution providing medical diagnosis and treatment for ambulatory patients. Clinics are maintained by hospitals, public and private organizations, or groups of physicians. They evolved from dispensaries which supplied free dugs to the poor; in England these date from late 17th cent., in U.S. first estab. 1786 in Philadelphia by Benjamin Rush.

Clink, former district on the Bankside in Southwark, London, England; site of the famous prison.

Clinton, George, 1739–1812, American statesman. First governor of N.Y. (1777–95) under new state constitution; managed trade and public welfare problems ably. Opposed Federal Constitution. Was Vice President of United States 1805–12. His nephew, **De Witt Clinton,** 1769–1828, was mayor of New York city for ten annual terms between 1803 and 1815; promoted public education and city planning. Sponsored Erie Canal. Unsuccessful presidential candidate 1812. Governor of N.Y. (1817–21, 1825–28).

Clinton, Sir Henry, 1738?–1795, British general in American Revolution. In supreme command in America 1778–81. Captured Charleston, S.C., 1780.

Clinton. 1 City (pop. 5,945), central Ill., N of Decatur. Farm trade center. Has railroad shops. **2** City (pop. 6,462), W Ind., on Wabash R. and N of Terre Haute. Bituminous coal is mined. Site of Fort William Henry Harrison near by. **3** City (pop. 30,379), E Iowa, on the Mississippi and NE of Davenport; laid out 1838. Industrial and rail center in agr. area with mfg. of metal, wood, grain, and dairy products. **4** Town (pop. 12,-287), central Mass., near Wachusett Reservoir; settled 1654. Mfg. of steel goods and chemicals. **5** Town (pop. 2,255), W central Miss., W of Jackson. Seat of Mississippi Col. **6** City (pop. 6,075), W Mo., SE of Kansas City, in farm and coal area. **7** Village (pop. 1,630), central N.Y., SW of Utica. Seat of Hamilton Col. (nonsectarian; for men; chartered 1812, originating from an academy founded by Samuel KIRKLAND). **8** City (pop. 7,555), W Okla., on Washita R. Shipping and mfg. center for wheat, cotton, and livestock area. **9** Town (pop. 7,168), NW S.C., S of Spartanburg, in cotton and grain area. **10** Town (pop. 3,712), E Tenn., NW of Knoxville. OAK RIDGE and Norris Dam are near by.

Clio, Muse of history: see MUSES.

clipper, fastest type of sailing ship. Long and narrow, it had the greatest beam aft of center and carried, besides topgallant and royal sails, skysails and moonrakers. Originated in the U.S., the Baltimore clippers were but forerunners of the real clipper begun with the *Ann McKim* (completed Baltimore 1832). This type was perfected by Donald McKAY of Boston who built the *Flying Cloud,* the *Glory of the Seas,* and the *Lightning.* The clippers dominated long-distance commerce, cutting time and vying in famous races. The clipper at first outran the rival steamship, but in the 1860s the improved steamship began to win out over all sailing ships.

Clisson, Olivier de (ōlēvyä′ dü klēsō′), 1336–1407, constable of France. Defeated Ghent insurgents at Roosebeke (1382). One of MARMOUSETS, he used his position to amass a huge fortune.

Clive, Catherine, 1711–85, English singer and actress, of Irish descent. Notable in comedies by Cibber, Gay (*Beggar's Opera*), and Coffey. Kitty Clive also sang in Handel's *Sampson* 1742. Was a friend of Johnson, Fielding, and Horace Walpole.

Clive, Robert, Baron Clive of Plassey, 1725–74, British soldier and statesman. In service of East India Company he won a series of victories (culminating in Plassey, 1757). He destroyed French power in India by his military genius. Twice governor of Bengal, he brought Behar and Orissa under British control as well as CALCUTTA. Fought corruption and promoted reform. On return to England (1767) was charged with acceptance of large gifts in India; finally acquitted but committed suicide. See *Essay on Clive* by T. B. Macaulay.

clock, instrument for measuring and indicating time. First wheel clock is believed to date from 6th cent., first weight-driven clock from 9th cent. Until 17th cent. there were few mechanical clocks except in cathedral towers, monasteries, and public squares. Smaller, lighter types constructed after coiled spring came into use c.1500. Invention of pendulum clock (c.1656) attributed to Christiaan Huygens. Clocks with long cases to conceal pendulums or weights date from mid-17th cent.; forerunners of grandfather clocks. Electric clocks, first made in 19th cent., extensively used after c.1930. Until 19th cent. clockmaking industry centered chiefly in France and England; later Germany and U.S. became leading producers. Among well-known clocks are astronomical clock with elaborate mechanical devices in cathedral of Strasbourg; clock in tower of British Houses of Parliament, with 13½ ton bell known as Big Ben; and clock in Metropolitan Life Insurance Building, New York city, with four dials, each 26½ ft. in diameter.

Clodia (klō'dēǔ), fl. 1st cent. B.C., Roman beauty; sister of Publius Clodius. As notable for her immorality as for her appearance, she is supposed to have murdered her husband. The poet Catullus was one of her many lovers.

Clodius (Publius Clodius Pulcher) (klō'dēǔs), d. 52 B.C., Roman politician. In 62 B.C., disguised as a woman, he took part in the Bona Dea mysteries in the house of Julius Caesar, thus causing Caesar to divorce his wife. Made tribune of the people in 58 B.C., he proved to be a demagogue. His gang of hired ruffians changed the complexion of Roman politics, and he was killed by a rival gang hired by Milo.

Cloisters, the, museum of medieval art, Fort Tryon Park, New York city; a branch of Metropolitan Mus. of Art, opened May, 1938. Five French cloisters, 12th-cent. Romanesque chapel, and chapter house contain 600–700 examples of medieval art. Collection (gathered by George Grey Barnard) was given to the Metropolitan by John D. Rockefeller, Jr.

Clonmacnoise (klŏnmăknoiz'), historic religious center, Co. Offaly, Ireland. Has inter-

esting ruins, including abbey founded by St. Kieran 541.

Cloquet (klōkā'), city (pop. 7,685), NE Minn., on St. Louis R. and W of Duluth, in agr. area. Mfg. of wood products.

closed shop and open shop. A closed shop (or "union shop") is an establishment employing only members of a labor union. An open shop is not restricted to unionized employees. In U.S., since 1840, the closed-shop policy has been adopted by most labor unions. Until 1935, judicial decisions usually went against the closed shop, and many states have banned it. Collective bargaining under the Wagner Act (1935) tended to promote closed-shop policy; the Taft-Hartley (1947) Act, to discourage it.

Clotaire (klōtâr'), Frankish kings. **Clotaire I,** d. 561, became king of Soissons at the death of his father, Clovis I (511). With his brothers THEODORIC I and CHILDEBERT I he conquered Thuringia and Burgundy. Their deaths left him sole king of the Franks by 558. His grandson, **Clotaire II,** 584–629?, succeeded his father CHILPERIC I as king of Neustria (584), his mother FREDEGUNDE acting as regent. In 613 he put BRUNHILDA to death, became king of all Franks.

clothes moth, name for several moths of family Tineidae; adults of commonest ones are yellowish or buff, c.½ in. long. Larvae feed on wool, furs, other animal products. Fumigation, spraying fabrics with chemicals, cleaning, airing, and cold storage of garments help prevent damage.

Clotho, one of the FATES.

cloth of gold has been made since anc. times, esp. in the East; in medieval Euorpe, it was much used ceremonially. Gold thread for weaving and embroidery is prepared either as very fine wire or by wrapping a core yarn with thin metal (lamé).

Clotilda, Saint, Frankish queen: see CLOVIS I.

clotting of blood, process of blood coagulation in which red and white corpuscles and blood platelets are caught in network of fibrils consisting of fibrin. Fibrin forms when skin is broken. Normal clotting time about four minutes; prolonged in HEMOPHILIA.

cloud, dense suspension in air of water droplets or ice particles condensed (from water vapor in air cooled below dew point) around nuclei of microscopic atmospheric dust particles. Usually air is cooled by upward movement and expansion; sometimes by reduced air pressure aloft, or mixing of warmer and cooler air currents. Air may rise by convection (from intense ground heat); by cold-air wedge at ground forcing warm air aloft; or by mountain range deflecting air flow upward. Classification of clouds (based on Luke Howard's work, 1803, and proposed by International Meteorological Commission in 1929): high clouds, 20,000 ft. or over (cirrus, cirrocumulus, cirrostratus); middle clouds, 6,500–20,000 ft. (altocumulus, altostratus); low clouds, 6,500 ft. or below (stratocumulus, stratus, nimbostratus); vertical-development clouds, 1,600–20,000 ft. (cumulus, cumulonimbus).

cloud chamber: see WILSON CLOUD CHAMBER.

Cloud Peak: see BIGHORN MOUNTAINS.

Clouet, Jean (zhä' klōōā'), called **Janet** or

Jehannet, c.1485–c.1541, court painter to Francis I of France. Probably of Flemish origin. His son **François Clouet** (fräswä′), c.1516–c.1572, was court painter to Francis I, Henry II, Francis II, and Charles IX. Both excelled in precision of draughtsmanship.

Clough, Arthur Hugh (klŭf), 1819–61, English poet, friend of literary figures of his day, best remembered for narrative poem *The Bothie of Toper-na-Fuosich* (1848), for lyric "Say not the struggle naught availeth"; and for Matthew Arnold's monody on his death, *Thyrsis*. His sister, **Anne Jemima Clough,** 1820–92, was first principal of Newnham College, Cambridge.

clove, evergreen tree (*Syzygium aromaticum* or *Eugenia aromatica*) of the Moluccas, and its unopened flower bud, an important spice. The dried nail-shaped buds are used whole or ground to flavor confections and ham. They yield a volatile oil used medicinally and in perfumes.

Clover, town (pop. 3,276), N S.C., near N.C. line. Kings Mountain Natl. Military Park near by.

clover, leguminous forage and hay plant and cover crop, of genus *Trifolium,* native to northern regions. Common species are red, crimson, and white or Dutch clovers, and alsike (*Trifolium hybridum*). Characterized by three-lobed leaves, clover was emblem of Ireland from which shamrock was derived. Four-leaved clover is symbol of good luck.

Clovis I (klō′vĭs), c.466–511, Frankish king (481–511), founder of Frankish monarchy (see MEROVINGIANS). Rose from tribal chieftain to sole leadership of Salian Franks by dint of patience and murder; conquered most of Gaul and SW Germany by defeating Romans (486, at Soissons), Alemanni (496), Burgundians (500), Visigoths (507, at Vouillé). His wife, St. Clotilda, a Burgundian princess, encouraged his conversion to Christianity, but he was baptized only after 496, in fulfillment of a vow made in battle against Alemanni.

Clovis, city (pop. 17,318), E N.Mex., on the Llano Estacado near Texas line; settled 1907. Rail division point and trade center in farm and cattle area. Artifacts of Folsom culture found near by.

clown, jester in circus or pantomime: see FOOL.

clubfoot (talipes), foot deformity resulting from changes in joints of ankle and foot which arise from muscle defect. A notable sufferer was Lord Byron.

club moss, low evergreen plant, of the genera *Lycopodium* and *Selaginella,* related to ferns but with small needlelike or scalelike leaves. Species of *Lycopodium,* also called ground pine and ground cedar, grow in moist, shaded places. Yellow spores of running pine, *Lycopodium clavatum,* sold as lycopodium powder or vegetable sulphur for medicinal uses. Most *Selaginella* species are tropical but some are found in temperate regions.

clubroot, slime mold disease of cabbage and other plants of mustard family. Attacks roots, causing malformation and preventing normal plant growth.

Cluj (klōōzh), Ger. *Klausenburg,* Hung. *Kolozsvár,* city (pop. 117,915), W Rumania. Chief commercial and cultural center of Transylvania; metallurgical industry. Univ. founded as Jesuit academy by Stephen Bathory (1581). Dating perhaps from Roman times and a free city from 1405, Cluj has kept many historical buildings of 14th–18th cent. Population over 50% Hungarian.

Cluniac order, medieval group of Benedictines, centering in the abbey of Cluny, France; founded 910. In the 10th, 11th, and early 12th cent. the Cluniac monks were a potent force, greatly forwarding the reforms in the church that were to reach a climax with Gregory VII: working for reforms in general Christian life; and promoting independence of the church from lay control. Their centralized organization increased their power, and they were criticized as rich and arrogant; in the 12th cent. they lost in rivalry with the Cistercians.

Cluny (Fr. klünē′), former abbey, E France, NW of Mâcon. Founded 910; center of Cluniac order. Abbey church dates partly from 10th cent .

Cluny Museum, 14th- and 15th-cent. structure in Paris, housing collection of medieval and Renaissance art objects. State-owned since 1842.

Clusium: see CHIUSI, Italy.

cluster, in astronomy, group of stars, probably of common origin, moving at same rate in same direction. More than 300 open, or galactic, clusters are catalogued. About 100 globular clusters are known, the nearest being over 20,000 light years away; in them the stars, numbering many thousands, appear to be densely massed.

clutch, device for controlling power transmission from the drive shaft to another working part, usually without interrupting the rotation of the drive shaft. Commonly consists of friction plates pushed together by springs. Less common are cone clutch, with cone fitting into end of flywheel; band clutch, with expanding segments; and magnetic fluid clutch.

Clyde, river of SW Scotland rising in S Lanarkshire and flowing N and NW for 106 mi. Near Lanark are four series of falls. Below these is Scotland's greatest industrial area, with Glasgow as head of navigation for large vessels. Shipyards here bombed 1940–41. At Dumbarton, river widens into the **Firth of Clyde** (length, 64 mi.; width, 1–37 mi.) with many commercial and industrial ports on its banks.

Clydebank, shipbuilding burgh (pop. 44,625), Dumbartonshire, Scotland, on the Clyde below Glasgow. *Queen Mary* and *Queen Elizabeth* built here. Suffered severe air raid damage 1940–41.

Clymene (klī′mŭnē), in Greek mythology. **1** Daughter of the Titan Oceanus, wife of Iapetus, and mother of Atlas, Prometheus, and Epimetheus. **2** Nymph, wife of Helios and mother of Phaëthon.

Clytemnestra (klī″tŭmnē′strŭ), in Greek legend, daughter of Leda and Tyndareus, half sister of Helen. Wife of AGAMEMNON, she was mother of Orestes, Electra, and Iphigenia. When she and her lover Aegisthus slew Agamemnon, Orestes in revenge slew both lovers.

Cm, chemical symbol of the element CURIUM.

Cnidus or **Cnidos** (both: nī′dŭs), anc. Greek city of Asia Minor, in present SW Asiatic Turkey. The town had the famous statue by Praxiteles, the Aphrodite of Cnidus.

Cnossus or **Knossos** (both: nŏs′ŭs), anc. city near the N coast of Crete. Occupied long before 3000 B.C., it was center of the MINOAN CIVILIZATION, which is known chiefly through excavations of the Cnossus palace. In legend Cnossus was the home of Minos.

Co, chemical symbol of the element COBALT.

coach: see CARRIAGE; STAGECOACH.

Coachella Valley (kō″ùchĕl′ù), arid region, SE Calif., N of Salton Sea. Irrigated by artesian wells and Coachella Main Canal (123 mi. long; completed 1948), a branch of ALL-AMERICAN CANAL. Produces dates, citrus, truck, alfalfa, and cotton. Indio and Palm Springs resorts are here.

coagulation, collection into a mass and precipitation of minute particles of a substance that was dispersed through another substance. In a colloidal solution it results from neutralization of charges on colloidal particles; they remain together on collision and form a precipitate.

Coahuila (kōä·wē′lä), state (58,067 sq. mi.; pop. 720,145), N Mexico, on N bulge of Rio Grande, S of Texas; cap. SALTILLO. Mountains in E Coahuila have quantities of largely unexploited mineral resources. Lumbering and coal mining are important. Cattle raising is chief occupation in NE. Border city, PIEDRAS NEGRAS, is across Rio Grande from Eagle Pass, Texas. LAGUNA DISTRICT lies in S part with TORREÓN its chief city. Exploration of territory began in middle of 16th cent. Joining of Texas and Coahuila (1830) was contributing factor to Texas Revolution (1835–36). Joined to Nuevo León in 1857, Coahuila became independent state in 1868.

coal, fuel of plant origin composed of carbon with varying amounts of mineral matter. There is a complete series, differing in content of carbon, moisture, and volatile substances: peat is lowest in carbon, and it is followed by lignite or brown coal, bituminous, semibituminous, and anthracite (nearly pure carbon). Coal beds or seams occur in sedimentary rocks, having originated from vegetation growing in slowly submerging swampland. Weight of overlying deposits helped the conversion into coal, the greater the pressure the higher the grade of coal produced. Most coal was formed during the Carboniferous period.

Coaldale, borough (pop. 5,318), E central Pa., NE of Pottsville. Has coal mining and mfg. of clothing.

Coal gas is obtained in destructive distillation of soft coal as by-product from coke preparation. Composition varies. Used as fuel, illuminant.

Coalinga (kōlǐng′gù), city (pop. 5,539), S central Calif., SW of Fresno. Processes oil and dairy products.

coal tar, product of destructive DISTILLATION of coal. Upon distillation it yields coal-tar crudes that form starting point for syntheses of dyes, drugs, explosives, flavoring, perfumes, paints, etc.

coast guard, special U.S. naval force assigned to seaboard duties such as suppressing smuggling, assisting vessels in distress, and providing protection and aid for maritime commerce and air commerce over the sea. Formed in 1915 by the union of the Revenue Cutter Service (estab. 1790) and the Life Saving Service. In 1939 the Lighthouse Service was merged with the coast guard, and the Bureau of Marine Inspection and Navigation was added in 1942. The coast guard is under the Treasury Dept. but comes under the navy in wartime or for such periods as the President directs. The motto is *Semper Paratus* [Latin,= always ready], and the women's reserve created in World War II is called the SPARS.

coast protection, means of protection against encroachment of sea include dikes, levees, sea walls (of masonry, extending below low-water mark, most effective with slanted or concave front, often with front apron to prevent undermining), and groins (low walls, usually of wood, extending at right angles from shore into water, and from low-water to high-water level).

Coast Ranges, mountain belt of W North America extending S along the Pacific from St. Elias Mts. in Alaska, through B.C. and U.S., into Mexico c.800 mi. S of the border. Represented by islands in S Alaska and B.C. where they are separated from Coast Mts. by Inside Passage. In U.S. they include Olympic Mts. in Wash., Coast Range in Oregon, and, in Calif., Diablo, Santa Lucia, and San Rafael ranges, all between narrow coastal strip and Central Valley. Connected on S with Sierra Nevada by transverse belt. Coast Ranges are sometimes considered to include broken ranges of S. Calif.—e.g., San Gabriel Mts., San Bernardino Mts., San Jacinto Mts., and N part of Peninsular Range—and uplands of Lower Calif. They are geologically young (formed by upheaval), rugged, and well wooded.

Coatesville, city (pop. 13,826), SE Pa., W of Philadelphia; settled c.1717. Steel center with mfg. of textiles, paper, and metal products.

Coaticook (kōä′tǐkook), town (pop. 6,341), SE Que., Canada, on Coaticook R. and S of Sherbrooke. Has textile and lumber mills and mfg. of toys.

coaxial cable: see CABLE.

Cobalt, town (pop. 2,230), E Ont., Canada, NE of Sudbury. Center of rich silver district, discovered 1903. Valuable cobalt ores also mined.

cobalt, silvery-white, lustrous, magnetic metallic element (symbol = Co; see also ELEMENT, table). Chemically active, it forms many compounds. Used in pigments. Occurs alone rarely; found in meteoric metal, in ores with other metals. Used in steel alloys and in carboloy.

cobaltite (kō′bôltīt), opaque, silver-white mineral of pyrite group, an important ore of cobalt.

Cobb, Howell, 1815–68, American statesman. U.S. Congressman from Ga. (1843–51, 1855–57); Secretary of the Treasury (1857–60). Chairman of convention in Montgomery which organized Confederacy.

Cobb, Irvin S(hrewsbury), 1876–1944, American humorist, b. Paducah, Ky.

Cobb, Tyrus Raymond (Ty Cobb), 1886–,

American baseball outfielder. Had .367 lifetime batting average, made 4,191 hits, stole 892 bases.

Cobbett, William, 1763?–1835, British journalist and reformer. After resigning from army went to U.S. (1792); in effective pamphlets championed Federalists against pro-French Republicans. On return to England became radical working class leader and apostle of agrarianism. After flight to U.S. due to the Gaging Bills (1817), returned to become central figure in English agitation for parliamentary reform. After Reform Bill of 1832, he was elected to Parliament. *Rural Rides* (1829) most famous of his many books.

Cobden, Richard, 1804–65, English statesman, a major influence in repeal of CORN LAWS. Guided policy of Anti-Corn Law League with John BRIGHT, Sir Robert PEEL, Lord John RUSSELL. Helped keep England out of Schleswig-Holstein affair (1864). Negotiated "Cobden Treaty" for reciprocal tariffs with France (1859–60). Favored Union in U.S. Civil War.

Cobequid: see TRURO, N.S.

Cóbh (kōv) [Irish = cove], seaport (pop. 5,-619), Co. Cork, Ireland, on Great Isl. in Cork Harbour. An important transatlantic port, it is also a resort and home of oldest yacht club in the world. Called Queenstown after Queen Victoria's visit (1849), it was renamed Cóbh 1922.

Coblenz or **Koblenz** (both: kō'blĕnts), city (pop. 64,961), former cap. of Prussian Rhine Prov., W Germany, at confluence of Rhine and Moselle rivers; since 1945 provisional cap. of Rhineland-Palatinate. Important wine trade; mfg. of machinery, furniture, pianos. Founded 1st cent. B.C. by Drusus as Confluentes. Under archbishops of Trier from 11th cent. until capture by French in 1794. Passed to Prussia 1815. Occupied by U.S. troops 1919–23; by French 1923–29; heavily damaged in World War II. Among ancient buildings is Church of St. Castor, founded 9th cent. Ehrenbreitstein fortress, across the Rhine, became part of Coblenz 1937.

Cobleskill, village (pop. 3,208), E central N.Y., W of Albany. Howe Caverns are near by.

Cobourg, town (pop. 7,470), S Ont., Canada, E of Toronto; a port on L. Ontario; summer resort.

cobra, poisonous snake of Africa and Asia. Common cobra of India and Egypt, often used by snake charmers, and Asiatic king cobra or hamadryad (14–18 ft. long) spread their hoods when angered. Some African forms spit poison.

Coburg (kō'bûrg, Ger. kō'bŏŏrk), city (pop. 44,789), Upper Franconia, N Bavaria, on Itz R. Precision instruments, ceramics. First mentioned 1056. For history, see SAXE-COBURG; SAXE-COBURG-GOTHA.

coca, South American shrub, *Erythroxylon* (or *Erythroxylum*) *coca*. Leaves yield COCAINE.

cocaine (kōkān'), alkaloid prepared from leaves of coca shrub. It is a habit-forming drug used as local anesthetic and illegally as narcotic.

Cochabamba (kōchäbäm'bä), city (pop. 80,-300; alt. c.8,400 ft.), cap. of Cochabamba dept., W central Bolivia, in agr. area.

Cochet, Henri (ārē' kôshā'), 1901–, French tennis player. Member French Davis Cup team that defeated U.S. in 1927 and held the cup until 1933.

Cochin (kō'chĭn'), city (pop. 26,320), SW Madras, India; forms enclave within TRAVANCORE-COCHIN state; major port on Malabar Coast. Exports coconut products, tea, and rubber. Visited 1502 by Vasco da Gama. Portuguese post built here by Afonso de Albuquerque in 1503.

Cochin China (kō'chĭn), southernmost state (25,000 sq. mi.; pop. c.5,000,000) of INDO-CHINA; cap. Saigon. Bounded by Cambodia on N, by Annam on NE. One of world's great rice-growing regions. Population is largely Annamese but includes Cambodian, Cham, and Chinese groups. Area was part of ancient Khmer Empire. Conquered by Annam 17th–18th cent., ceded to France mid-19th cent. In 1949 Cochin China joined Annam and Tonkin in state of VIET NAM.

cochineal (kōchĭnēl'), scarlet dye from extract of bodies of female scale insect found on some cacti.

Cochrane, Thomas: see DUNDONALD, THOMAS COCHRANE, 10TH EARL OF.

Cochrane, town (pop. 3,401), NE Ont., Canada, NNE of Timmins. Commercial center in mining and hunting region of NE Ont. and W Que.

Cockaigne or **Cockayne, Land of** (both: kō-kān'), in medieval tales a legendary country where finest food and drink are to be had for the taking.

cockatoo, name for various crested woodland parrots of Australia. Among them are the pink cockatoo, some white birds with yellow or scarlet on crests, and some with dark plumage.

Cockcroft, Sir John Douglas, 1897–, English physicist. He shared the 1951 Nobel Prize in Physics for pioneer work in transmutation of nuclei of atoms by means of atomic particles accelerated artificially and used as projectiles.

Cockerel, Charles Robert (kŏk'ûrŭl), 1788–1863, English architect, exponent of the classic revival.

cockfighting, sport of pitting gamecocks against other. Popular in ancient Persia, Greece, and Rome. Jousts usually held on small circular stage. Gamecocks placed beak to beak, then released. Cock is defeated when he refuses to fight or is unable to fight.

cockle, marine bivalve mollusk. Shell is marked by ridges radiating from the hinge. It lives in sand or mud and eats microscopic sea life. Some species move about in water; others dig into bottom. Majority of species are in tropical and subtropical waters; one (*Cardium edule*) eaten in Europe.

cocklebur, coarse annual plant of genus *Xanthium*, a persistent weed with oval burs, also called clotbur.

cock of the plains: see SAGE GROUSE.

Cockran, W(illiam) Bourke, 1854–1923, American politician, b. Ireland. U.S. Representative from N.Y. (1887–89, 1891–95, 1904–9, 1921–23); supported organized labor, opposed restrictions on immigration.

cockroach, orthopterous insect of world-wide distribution (c.1,200 species), abundant in tropics. Omnivorous and mainly nocturnal, it has a flat, oval, usually brownish body, long antennae, large eyes, unpleasant odor (glandular secretion). Croton bug found in NE U.S., wood cockroach in E U.S.

cockscomb, annual plant (*Celosia argentea cristata*), with showy red or gold, rounded, ruffled, or feathery flower spikes, used as an EVERLASTING.

cocktail, short mixed drink of spirituous liquor blended with vermouth, fruit juices, or other ingredients, chilled and served as appetizer. Name also given to fruit juices, mixture of cut-up fruit, and seafood served at start of meal.

cocoa, cocoa butter, and **cocoa nibs:** see CACAO.

coconut, fruit of coco palm (*Cocos nucifera*), a tree widely scattered through tropical regions. Mature trees may yield 75–200 nuts a year. The nut, encased in a thick fibrous husk, has a hard shell surrounding its white, edible meat, and contains a nutritious milk. Shredded kernels of nuts are used in confectionery. Of world value in commerce is oil extracted from dried fruit kernels (known as copra). A sweet liquid, obtained from flower buds, is distilled to make arrack or boiled down for its sugar. Coir (coarse fibers from nut husks) is made into brushes, matting, and ropes.

Cocteau, Jean (zhä′ kôktō′), 1891–, French author. A versatile spokesman for modernism in all arts, he has written poetry, fiction, dramas, operatic librettos; directed moving pictures; and excelled as draftsman. His best-known works are the novel *Les Enfants terribles* (1929; Eng. tr., 1930) and the drama *La Machine infernale* (1934; Eng. tr., 1936).

cod, food fish abundant in N Pacific and N Atlantic. It lays eggs in mid-ocean, feeds on marine life, and weighs 10–35 (rarely 75) lb. Chief fisheries are in Norway, Newfoundland, and Mass.

Cod, Cape: see CAPE COD.

Coddington, William, 1601–78, one of founders of R.I., b. England. Founded Portsmouth (1638) with Anne HUTCHINSON. Founded Newport (1639) with John CLARKE. Governor of united towns (1640).

code, in communication: see CRYPTOGRAPHY; MORSE CODE.

code, body of legal rules expressed in fixed and written authoritative form as contrasted with customary law (including common law). Corpus Juris Civilis gave term meaning of an entire legal system. *Code Napoléon* outstanding example of such codes. Official collections of statutes also called codes (e.g., the criminal code).

codeine: see OPIUM.

Code Napoléon or **Code Civil,** first modern law CODE, compiled by a commission 1800–1804, promulgated by Napoleon I; a milestone in development of civil law (modern Roman law).

codling moth (kŏd′–) or **codlin moth,** small moth with larva (called apple worm) enormously damaging to apple crop. It also attacks other fruits. Often it has two or three generations a year; eggs are laid on developing fruit. Larva eats into apple and remains there until mature.

Codrington, Sir Edward, 1770–1851, British admiral. Commanded combined British, French, and Russian fleets in victory at Navarino (1827) which made possible the success of Greek war of independence.

Cody, William Frederick: see BUFFALO BILL.

Cody, town (pop. 3,872), NW Wyo., on Shoshone R., in dude-ranch area. Named for W. F. Cody (Buffalo Bill); has museum, statue, birthday fete in his honor. Gateway to Yellowstone Natl. Park (W), Shoshone Cavern Natl. Monument. SHOSHONE PROJECT is NE.

Coe College: see CEDAR RAPIDS, Iowa.

coeducation, teaching of both sexes in same classes; long opposed as distracting factor, now general in public schools of the U.S. Important growth came with expansion of public education in Western states 1830–45. Girls first admitted to scattered elementary schools, after Civil War to secondary schools. Though Oberlin Col. gave degrees to women in 1837, it was rise of state universities that standardized coeducational higher education.

coefficient, in algebra, a number, letter, letter group, or combination of numbers and letters, preceding another letter and by which it is to be multiplied. Thus in $2xy$, 2 is coefficient of x; $2x$ is coefficient of y. For other coefficients see EXPANSION and FRICTION.

Coello, Alonso Sánchez (älōn′thō sän′chäth kōĕl′yō), c.1531–c.1588, Spanish court painter to Philip II.

Coello, Claudio (klou′dyō), c.1630–1693, Spanish baroque painter, famous for the monumental altarpiece for the sacristy of the Escorial.

coercion, unlawful act of compelling a person to do, or to abstain from doing, something by depriving him of the exercise of his free will, particularly by use or threat of physical or moral force. Important in questions of labor-management relations. See also DURESS.

Cœur, Jacques (zhäk′ kûr′), c.1395–1456, French merchant prince. Chief adviser to Charles VII, founder of French trade in Levant. Amassed fabulous fortune; financed final campaigns of Hundred Years War. Imprisoned and fined millions of dollars on concocted charge of poisoning Agnès SOREL (1453). Escaped to Rome; died campaigning against Turks.

Coeur d'Alene, city (pop. 12,198), N Idaho. Founded in late 1870s in region of gold (1860) and silver and lead (1882) discoveries; mining boom in 1884. Center for mining, lumbering, farming, and dairying area. Summer and winter sports near by.

Coeur d'Alene Lake (kûrdúlān′), N Idaho, E of Spokane, Wash.; 24 mi. long and 1–3 mi. wide. Fed by Coeur d'Alene and St. Joe rivers and drained by Spokane R.

Cœur de Lion: see RICHARD I, king of England.

coffee, beverage made from seeds of a small evergreen tree, the Arabian coffee tree (*Coffea arabica*), native to tropical Africa and from certain other species of *Coffea*. After roasting to develop flavor and aroma, the "beans" are ground. Exhilarating effects result from CAFFEINE content. Coffee was known in Ethiopia before A.D. 1000, in Arabia (whence it spread to Egypt and Turkey) by the 15th cent.; it had reached most of Europe by mid-17th cent. In North America coffee became a staple beverage after the Boston Tea Party.

cofferdam, temporary barrier (wood or steel), a protection against water, used in construction of dams, bridges, etc. In water deeper than 30 ft. CAISSON is generally used instead.

Coffeyville, city (pop. 17,113), SE Kansas, on Verdigris R. near Okla. line; settled 1869. Ships cattle, processes food, and refines oil; has railroad shops. Dalton gang was shot down here, 1892.

Cognac (kônyäk′), town (pop. 16,106), Charente dept., W. France, on Charente R. Export center for French brandy (named for town). FRANCIS I of France formed here alliance against Charles V (1526).

Cogswell, Joseph Green, 1786–1871, American librarian and bibliographer. Helped found Astor Library in New York city. Prepared alphabetical and analytic catalogue.

Cohan, George M(ichael), 1878–1942, American playwright, actor. Began in vaudeville with his family. Wrote plays (e.g., *Forty-five Minutes from Broadway,* 1906) and songs (e.g., *Over There; It's a Grand Old Flag*) exemplifying his favorite themes—Broadway and patriotism. Dramatized mystery novel *Seven Keys to Baldpate* (1913). Acted in *Ah, Wilderness!* (1933), *I'd Rather Be Right* (1937).

Cohasset (kōhăs′ĭt), resort town (pop. 3,731), E Mass., on Mass. Bay. Had first U.S. lifeboat service. Lighthouse here since 1850.

Cohn, Ferdinand (fĕr′dēnänt kōn′), 1828–98, German botanist, known as a founder of science of bacteriology.

Cohoes (kŭhōz′), industrial city (pop. 21,272), E N.Y., N of Albany at junction of Mohawk and Hudson rivers and on the Barge Canal. Mfg. of knit goods, clothing, paper, machinery; boatbuilding.

coil: see INDUCTION.

Coimbatore (kwĭmbŭtôr′), city (pop. 130,348), SW Madras, India. Important in 18th-cent. wars between the British and Mysore sultans.

Coimbra (kwēm′brŭ), city (pop. 35,437), Beira Litoral, W central Portugal; historic cap. of Beira. Important in Roman days; continued to flourish through Moorish times and after its conquest by Ferdinand I of Leon (1047). Cap. of Portugal until 13th cent. Has fine 12th-cent. cathedral. Famous univ., founded by King Diniz, was moved from Lisbon to Coimbra in 1306.

coin, a piece of metal stamped by authority of a government as a guaranty of its value and used as money. Coinage probably originated in the West in Lydia or the Aegean Isls. (first known coin is Lydian, c.700 B.C.), and in the East in China before 700 B.C. Early coins, die-struck by hand, show many variations. Standardized coins date from use (17 cent.) of a mill and screw machine.

Coire, Switzerland: see CHUR.

Coke, Sir Edward (kŏŏk), 1552–1634, English jurist, greatest of all English common lawyers. Solicitor general and speaker of House of Commons before becoming attorney general 1593. Was severe prosecutor. Made chief justice of common pleas 1606; became champion of Parliament against king. Upheld supremacy of common law and enunciated

doctrines of personal liberty. Enmity of James I, Baron Ellesmere, and Francis Bacon caused his dismissal in 1616. Elected to Parliament 1620; was leader of popular party and important in drafting Petition of Right (1628). Writings include *Institutes.*

Coke, Richard (kōk), 1829–97, governor of Texas (1874–77), U.S. Senator (1877–95). Coke, as Democratic governor, restored frontier order, generally rehabilitated state after Reconstruction period.

Coke, Thomas William: see LEICESTER OF HOLKAM, THOMAS WILLIAM COKE, EARL OF.

coke, fuel made by destructive DISTILLATION of soft coal. Its by-products are ammonia, coal tar, and illuminating gas. Used in blast furnace and to make WATER GAS.

Colbert, Jean Baptiste (zhä′ bätēst′ kôlbĕr′), 1619–83, French statesman, chief adviser to Louis XIV after 1661. Procured conviction of Nicolas FOUQUET. The greatest exponent of MERCANTILISM, he protected industries by subsidies and tariffs, regulated prices and quality of goods, built modern road and canal network, and developed navy and colonization.

Colby College: see WATERVILLE, Maine.

Colchester (kōl′chĭstûr), municipal borough (pop. 57,436), Essex, England, on Colne R. Once a great pre-Roman city, it has a Norman castle housing Roman antiquities. Colne oyster fisheries important.

colchicine (kŏl′chĭsēn), plant alkaloid used chiefly in genetics experiments. It interferes with the separation of nuclei in cell division, and the resulting cells have chromosome numbers that are multiples of species number.

Colchis (kŏl′kĭs), anc. country on the Black Sea and in the Caucasus, noted for forest products. In Greek legend it was the home of Medea and the land where Jason sought the Golden Fleece.

Colden, Cadwallader (kōl′dŭn), 1688–1776, colonial scholar and political leader of N.Y., b. Ireland, of Scottish parents. Lieutenant governor of N.Y. after 1761. He was botanist of the Linnaean system, which was mastered also by his daughter, **Jane Colden,** 1724–66, who prepared a scientific illustrated work on flora of New York state. In 1759 she married William Farquhar.

cold frame, low, sun-heated structure with transparent cover, sunk into ground. Used for early seed sowing, to propagate cuttings, and to winter nonhardy plants. Hotbed is similar but soil is heated by stable manure, steam, hot air or water, or electricity; used for starting plants early and for growing plants out of season.

colds, infections involving mucous membrane of nose, throat, or larynx. Common cold usually caused by bacteria or virus; lasts 3 to 10 days.

Cold Spring Harbor, resort village, SE N.Y., on N shore of Long Isl., in Huntington town. Former whaling port. Site of a marine biological station and of department of genetics of Carnegie Inst.

Coldstream, burgh (pop. 1,294), Berwickshire, Scotland. Troops raised here (1659–60) to restore Charles II were later called Coldstream Guards, one of guards regiments of the royal household.

Coldwater, city (pop. 8,594), S Mich., SSE of Battle Creek and on Coldwater R. Farm trade center in lake region, it has mfg. of cement, furnaces, and metal products.

Coldwell, Major James, 1888–, Canadian political leader, b. England. Became national leader of CO-OPERATIVE COMMONWEALTH FEDERATION in 1942.

Cole, Charles Woolsey, 1906–, American historian and educator. President of Amherst (1946–). Wrote *Colbert and a Century of French Mercantilism* (1939); *Economic History of Europe* (with S. B. Clough, 1941; rev. ed., 1946).

Cole, G(eorge) D(ouglas) H(oward), 1889–, English economist, a reader at Oxford. Long an exponent of guild socialism, he later returned to his original Fabianism, and headed (1939–46) Fabian Society. Has written books on economic planning. His wife **Margaret (Isabel Postgate) Cole,** 1893–, collaborated with him, notably on many detective stories.

Cole, Thomas, 1801–48, American landscape painter, b. England; a pioneer of the Hudson River school.

Cole, Timothy, 1852–1931, American wood engraver, b. London. Became known for fine reproductions of great European paintings which appeared for many years in *Scribner's* (later the *Century*) magazine.

Coleman, Glenn, 1887–1932, American painter and lithographer of New York street scenes.

Coleman, city (pop. 6,530), W central Texas, NW of Brownwood. Processing and shipping center of agr., livestock, and oil area. Lake Scarborough (city) and Hords Creek (begun 1947) reservoirs are near.

Colepeper: see CULPEPER.

Coleridge, Samuel Taylor, 1772–1834, English poet, critic, and philosopher, a leader of the romantics. With his friend Robert Southey he planned a utopian settlement in America ("pantisocracy"), which failed. His *Poems on Various Occasions* appeared in 1796. In 1798 he and William Wordsworth published *Lyrical Ballads,* the most important single work of the romantic movement; it included Coleridge's "Rime of the Ancient Mariner." Other poems with haunting, musical, fantastic touch are "Christabel," "Kubla Khan," "Dejection: an Ode." Unstable, addicted to drugs, he retained his brilliance in later poetry (*Sybilline Leaves,* 1817), literary criticism, and romantic philosophy (as in *Biographia Literaria,* 1817). Scraps of his conversations and writings, collected later, influenced greatly the writing of next generations. His eldest son, **Hartley Coleridge,** 1796–1849, wrote poetry and critical biographies (*Biographia Borealis,* 1833). S. T. Coleridge's daughter, **Sara Coleridge,** 1802–52, edited some of her father's works, wrote *Phantasmion* (1837; a fairy tale).

Colet, John (kŏ'lĭt), 1467?–1519, English humanist, friend of Erasmus, associate of Sir Thomas More, Grocyn, and Linacre. After years of Oxford was dean of St. Paul's, London (1505–19), and planned St. Paul's school. With Erasmus and William Lily wrote Eton Latin grammar. Urged Church reform but died in the Church before the Reformation.

Colette (kôlĕt'), pen name of Sidonie Gabrielle Claudine Colette de Jouvenel, 1873–, French novelist. Famous for analytical studies of women, such as *Chéri* (1920; Eng. tr., 1929) and *La Chatte* (1933; Eng. tr., 1936). With her first husband, Willy (pseud. of Henri Gauthier-Villars), she collaborated on the famous *Claudine* stories.

Colfax, town (pop. 1,651), central La., on Red R. Had race riot (April, 1873) in Reconstruction era.

Colgate University: see HAMILTON, N. Y.

colic (kŏ'lĭk), intense pain caused by spasmodic contraction of a hollow organ, especially stomach or intestine. In infants it may follow a large or improper feeding or constipation.

Coligny, Gaspard de (gäspär' dü kōlēnyē'), 1519–72, French Protestant leader, admiral of France; nephew of Anne de Montmorency. With Louis I de Condé, commanded Huguenots in Wars of RELIGION; negotiated peace in 1570. Became favorite adviser to Charles IX, thus arousing enmity of Catherine de' Medici. Was first victim in the celebrated massacre of SAINT BARTHOLOMEW'S DAY.

Colima (kōlē'mä), state (2,010 sq. mi.; pop. 112,292), W Mexico, on Pacific; cap. Colima (pop. 22,601; founded 1523). State includes Revilla Gigedo isls.

Coliseum: see COLOSSEUM.

collective bargaining, in labor relations, negotiating procedure between two parties—union and management—for determining working conditions without dealings with individual workers. Employer's refusal to bargain collectively was made illegal by 1935 National Labor Relations Act. Unions were similarly restrained by 1947 TAFT-HARTLEY ACT.

Collège de France (kôlèzh' dü frãs'), founded in Paris c.1530 by Francis I. Has always been independent and free from supervision. Lectures are open to the public without fee, no examinations are given, and no degrees are granted.

College of Physicians and Surgeons: see COLUMBIA UNIVERSITY.

College of the City of New York: see NEW YORK, COLLEGE OF THE CITY OF.

College Park. 1 City (pop. 14,535), NW Ga., S suburb of Atlanta. **2** Town (pop. 11,170), W central Md., NE of Washington, D.C. Seat of main campus of Univ. of MARYLAND.

Colleges of the Seneca, The: see GENEVA, N.Y.

College Station, city (pop. 7,925), E central Texas, near Bryan. Seat of Agricultural and Mechanical Col. of TEXAS.

Colleoni, Bartolomeo (bärtōlōmā'ō kôl-lāō'nē), 1400–1475, Italian condottiere, generalissimo of Venetian forces from 1454. Equestrian statue by VERROCCHIO.

collie: see SHEEP DOGS.

Collier, Jeremy, 1650–1726, English clergyman, nonjuring bishop (1713), best known for his *Short View of the Immorality and Profaneness of the English Stage* (1698).

Collier, John, 1884–, American social worker and author, commissioner of Indian Affairs (1933–45). Wrote on the American Indian.

Collingdale, borough (pop. 8,443), SE Pa., SW suburb of Philadelphia.

Collingswood, residential borough (pop. 15,-800), SW N.J., near Camden; settled 1682.

Collingwood, town (pop. 7,413), S Ont., Canada, at S end of Georgian Bay. Lake port with large shipyards, grain elevators, and dry docks.

Collins, Edward Trowbridge, 1887–1951, American baseball infielder. Had .333 lifetime batting average, made 3,313 base hits, stole more than 740 bases.

Collins, Michael, 1890–1922, Irish leader of the SINN FEIN. Organized guerrilla warfare which forced British to sue for peace. Joined Arthur GRIFFITH in setting up the Free State (1921). He was assassinated.

Collins, (William) Wilkie, 1824–89, English novelist, best known today for two mystery stories, *The Woman in White* (1860) and *The Moonstone* (1868). Friend of Dickens.

Collins, William, 1721–59, English lyric poet, an early romantic. Wrote odes, notably "Ode to Evening," "Ode Written in 1746" (beginning "How sleep the brave").

Collinsville, city (pop. 11,862), SW Ill., NE of St. Louis, in coal and agr. area; settled 1817. Mfg. of chemicals and food products.

Collodi, Carlo (kär′lō kōl-lō′dē), pseud. of **Carlo Lorenzini** (lōräntsē′nē), 1826–90, Italian writer, author of *Pinocchio: the Story of a Puppet* (1880, 1883), a children's classic, widely translated.

collodion (kŭlō′dēŭn), alcohol-ether solution of PYROXYLIN. When exposed to air, liquid evaporates, leaving thin, colorless, elastic film.

colloid (kŏ′loid), substance dispersed in solvent as particles too small to be seen but larger than molecules. It is not a true SOLUTION for the particles are not of molecular size, do not pass through certain membranes, have only slight effects on freezing and boiling points, and are observable with ultramicroscope; not SUSPENSION, for particles are invisible and do not settle on standing. Milk is an example. COAGULATION and ADSORPTION are characteristic of colloids.

collusion, conspiracy to defraud a person of his legal rights or to obtain some objective by misusing the forms of law. Collusion between husband and wife, or between either and a third party, is a bar to DIVORCE.

Colmar or **Kolmar** (kôl′mär), city (pop. 43,-514), cap. of Haut-Rhin dept., E France, in Alsace. Textile mfg. Made free imperial city 13th cent.; annexed by Louis XIV 1673. Old section keeps medieval architecture. St. Martin's Church (13th cent.) contains painting by SCHONGAUER. Museum, in 13th-cent. convent, has Isenheim altarpiece by GRÜNEWALD.

Cologne (kŭlōn′), Ger. *Köln* or *Köln am Rhein,* city (pop. 590,825; 1939 pop. 772,221), North Rhine-Westphalia, NW Germany, on the Rhine. Though largely destroyed in World War II, it remains a major rail junction and river port. Metallurgy; chemical and textile mfg.; EAU DE COLOGNE. Founded A.D. 50 by Romans as Colonia Agrippinensis. Episcopal see from 4th cent.; archbishopric since time of Charlemagne. As princes of Holy Roman Empire, archbishops ruled strip of land on

W bank of the Rhine; ranked third among ELECTORS. Their constant feud with citizens of Cologne led to transfer of electoral residence to near-by Brühl and later (1263) to Bonn. A free imperial city from 1474 and a member of Hanseatic League, Cologne flourished as commercial center until 16th cent. It was seized by the French 1794. Archbishopric was secularized 1801. Annexed to Prussia as part of Rhine Province (1814), Cologne developed into largest transit port and depot of NW Germany. Industrial Deutz, on right river bank, was united with Old Cologne, on left bank. Among buildings that escaped major damage in Allied air raids of World War II are the famous cathedral (begun c.1248; completed 1880, after original plans), containing relics of the WISE MEN OF THE EAST, and the Church of St. URSULA. Cologne is the center of N German Catholicism. The university was founded 1388.

Coloma (kŭlō′mù), town, E Calif., on American R. and NE of Sacramento. Has monument to 1848 gold discovery at Sutter's Mill here.

Colomb or **Colombe, Michel** (both: mēshĕl′ kôlô′), c.1430–1512, French sculptor, a master of the early French Renaissance.

Colombia (kōlōm′byä), republic (439,828 sq. mi.; pop. 11,259,730), NW South America; cap. BOGOTÁ. The only nation on the continent with both Pacific and Atlantic coasts, Colombia is split by ranges of the Andes that fan out N from the S border with Ecuador. More than half of the land is E of the Andes; there in the S are jungle rain forests of the Amazon basin, threaded with tributaries of the Amazon; in the N are vast plains (llanos), crossed by tributaries of the Orinoco and given over mainly to cattle breeding—Colombia's developing frontier. W of the Andes is the relatively small Pacific area, which produces platinum and gold and (in the N) tropical forest products. The chief Pacific port is BUENAVENTURA. It is less important than the Atlantic ports in the extreme N of the country, notably BARRANQUILLA, CARTAGENA, and SANTA MARTA. Petroleum from rich Colombian fields is shipped from the N ports, as are the products (notably coffee) from the valleys and plateaus of the mountain region. In the uplands where two great rivers, the MAGDALENA and the CAUCA, run between the ranges, the population has concentrated since the days of the CHIBCHA. Here are the cap. and other cities: TUNJA, BUCARAMANGA and CÚCUTA in the E; industrial centers MEDELLÍN and MANIZALES in the center; and CALI in the W. Besides growing of coffee, the area has mines and industries (with hydroelectric power). Conquered by JIMÉNEZ DE QUESADA and others, the region was the core of the Spanish colony and viceroyalty of New Granada, which included Panama and most of Venezuela. Revolution against Spain began in 1810 (see NARINO, ANTONIO) and ended with the victory of Bolívar at Boyacá (1819). Bolívar set up the republic of Greater Colombia (including Venezuela and Ecuador), but separatist movements broke it, and after 1830 Colombia (sometimes called New Granada) was a reduced nation. It was subject to political quarrels (particularly between federalists and centralists), and strong men (*caudillos*) arose. In the late 19th and early 20th cent. industries grew. A major political problem was that of the PANAMA CANAL, which resulted in 1903 in the independence of PANAMA from Colombia. In World War II Colombia joined the Allied side in 1943 and became a member of the United Nations. The Quito Charter in 1948 promised cooperation among the nations once joined in Greater Colombia.

Colombo (kŭlŭm′bō), commercial city (pop. 355,374), cap. of Ceylon, on Indian Ocean. Ceylon's main port, it ships tea, rubber, and copra. Successively the center of Portuguese, Dutch, and British rule in Ceylon from 1565 to 1948.

Colón (kōlōn′), city (pop. 52,035), Panama, at Caribbean end of Panama Canal; thriving commercial center exporting tropical fruits and woods. Cristobal, within zone, is American residential district.

colon, in anatomy: see INTESTINE.

Colonia (kōlō′nyä), city (pop. 8,000), cap. of Colonia dept., S Uruguay, on Río de la Plata; resort and small port in agr. district. Founded by Portuguese (1680), it was secured by Spanish after bitter fighting.

Colonial Conference, British: see IMPERIAL CONFERENCE.

Colonial Heights, city (pop. 6,077), SE Va., on Appomattox R.; a suburb of Petersburg.

Colonial National Historical Park: see NATIONAL PARKS AND MONUMENTS (table).

Colonna (kōlôn′nä), noble Roman family, prominent 12th–16th cent. Though traditionally Ghibelline and antipapal, produced one of most successful advocates of papal authority in Pope MARTIN V. **Sciarra Colonna** (shär′rä), d. 1329, helped French capture Pope Boniface VIII, whose face he slapped. **Vittoria Colonna, marchesa di Pescara** (vēt-tō′rēä, dē päskä′rä), 1492–1547, Italian poet, was a friend of Michelangelo. Much of her verse was inspired by the death of her husband (1525) and by religious themes.

color, property of light that depends on wave length. Apparent color of object depends on wave length of light it reflects. Object that reflects all wave lengths appears white; one that reflects none, black. Dispersion occurs when sunlight passes through glass prism, producing solar spectrum. Speed at which color travels depends on wave length. Primary colors of light or spectrum are red, green, and blue; they can produce, in combination, all colors. Primary pigments are red, yellow, and blue. Any two colors that produce white when mixed are complementary colors. Light causes different color cones in human retina to react, making color perception possible. See also, LIGHT; PROTECTIVE COLORATION; SPECTRUM; VISION.

Colorado, state (104,247 sq. mi.; pop. 1,325,-089), W U.S.; admitted 1876 as 38th state; cap. DENVER. PUEBLO, COLORADO SPRINGS, BOULDER other main cities. Mountain state (Rockies), crossed by Continental Divide. Plains in E section. Agr. (sugar beets, potatoes, fruits, feed crops); mining (coal, ura-

nium, radium, molybdenum, vanadium, gold, silver, zinc); livestock. Processes agr., mining products. Tourist trade important (points of interest are PIKES PEAK, Rocky Mountain Natl. Park, Mesa Verde Natl. Park, 14 national monuments, CENTRAL CITY). COLORADO, Platte, ARKANSAS rivers rise in mountains, as does RIO GRANDE. Area N of Arkansas R. and E of Rockies came to U.S. in Louisiana Purchase, remainder from Mexico (1848), Texas (1850). Penetrated by French, Spanish, and mountain men, but became known mainly through explorations of Z. M. PIKE, S. H. LONG, J. C. FRÉMONT. Boomed with discovery of gold (1859), declined, boomed again with silver (1875). Irrigation, power development extended to aid agr., utilize natural resources.

Colorado. 1 River, rising in N Colo. at Continental Divide and flowing SW through Colo., Utah, and Ariz. (including GRAND CANYON), then between Nev. and Ariz., between Ariz. and Calif., thence to Mexico and into Gulf of California. Great river of SW U.S., c.1,400 mi. long, it drains c.8% of U.S. area aided by the rivers Gunnison (in Colo.), Green (Utah), San Juan, Little Colorado, and Gila (Ariz.). Mouth seen by Francisco de Ulloa 1539, lower part explored by Hernando de Alarcón 1540. Sometimes called Grand R. above entrance of the Green. HOOVER DAM, Davis Dam, ALL-AMERICAN CANAL, and PARKER DAM promote power and irrigation. **2** (kŭlŭrä′dù) River rising in NW Texas in Llano Estacado, fed by "draws" in E N.Mex. Flows 970 mi. SE through Austin to Matagorda Bay. Floods caused legislation on flood control, power, and irrigation. Of three boards, Lower Colorado River Authority (1934) is most active, with Buchanan, Roy Inks, Marshall Ford or Mansfield, and Tom Miller dams. Upper and Middle Colorado River Authorities have undertaken reservoir and power plant projects. All uses are coordinated in over-all plan.

Colorado, University of, mainly at Boulder; state supported; coed.; chartered 1861, opened 1877. Has medical school (with hospitals) at Denver.

Colorado Agricultural and Mechanical College: see FORT COLLINS.

Colorado-Big Thompson project, N Colo., planned by U.S. to divert headstreams of Colorado R., W of Continental Divide, to irrigate and provide power for NE Colo. Water blocked by Granby Dam in Colorado R. and by Green Mountain Dam in Blue R. is pumped through Alva B. Adams Tunnel to E slope and Big Thompson R., tributary of South Platte R. Diversion dams near Fort Collins and Estes Park; power plants at Green Mountain Dam and Estes Park.

Colorado City (kŭlŭrä′dù), city (pop. 6,774), W Texas, on Colorado R. and S of Snyder. Center of cattle, agr. (cotton, grains, peanuts), and dairying area. Has refineries.

Colorado College: see COLORADO SPRINGS.

Colorado National Monument: see NATIONAL PARKS AND MONUMENTS (table).

Colorado potato beetle or **potato bug,** black-and-yellow-striped beetle, destructive both as adult and larva chiefly to potato plant. Adults winter underground and emerge in spring to lay orange-yellow eggs on underside of leaves. Discovered in 1824 in E Rocky Mt. region, it later spread eastward. See *ill.*, p. 601.

Colorado School of Mines, at Golden; state supported; mainly for men; chartered 1874. Pioneer mining and engineering school of university grade.

Colorado Springs, city (pop. 45,472; alt. c.-6,000 ft.), central Colo., S of Denver, at foot of Pikes Peak; founded 1871. Residential city and health resort near Manitou Springs (pop. 2,580; alt. c.6,300), with mineral springs. Garden of the Gods, area of curiously eroded rock formations, is just NW; Cave of the Winds and Will Rogers Shrine near. Here are fine arts center, Colorado Col. (nonsectarian; coed.; 1874), and Ent Air Force Base (hq., since 1951, of Air Defense Command).

color blindness (Daltonism), inability to recognize colors, especially red and green. It is usually a congenital defect occurring in 5% to 10% of men, less than 1% of women.

color photography: see PHOTOGRAPHY.

Colosseum or **Coliseum** (both: kŏlŭsē'ŭm), common name of Flavian Amphitheater in Rome, near SE end of Forum. Built A.D. 72–80; largely preserved; most imposing of existing Roman antiquities. Huge four-storied oval held c.50,000 spectators. Arena was scene of gladiatorial combats.

Colossians (-lŏsh'-), epistle of New Testament written to Christians of Colossae and Laodicea by St. Paul. Emphasizes union of all Christians in mystical body of Christ. Among well-known passages are 1.24–29; 2.12–15; 2.20–3.4.

Colossus of Rhodes (kŭlŏ'sŭs), large bronze statue of the sun god, Helios, in Rhodes harbor; one of the seven wonders of the anc. world. Built by Chares, 292–280 B.C., it fell in an earthquake in 224 B.C.

Colt, Samuel, 1814–62, American inventor of a breech-loading pistol (patented 1835), which became so popular that Colt grew to be a generic term.

Colton, city (pop. 14,465), S Calif., SW of San Bernardino. Processes and ships citrus fruit. Has mfg. of cement, furniture, and mattresses.

coltsfoot, Eurasian perennial plant (*Tussilago farfara*), naturalized in North America. Has yellow flowers, later downy fruits and large leaves.

Colum, Padraic (pä'drĭk kŏ'lŭm), 1881–, Irish-American poet, dramatist, b. Ireland; in U.S. after 1914. His wife is Mary (Maguire) Colum, Irish-American critic.

Columba or **Columcille, Saint** (kŏlŭmkĭl'ĕ), 521–97, Irish churchman. Founded monastery schools at Derry (545), Durrow (553), and Kells (c.554). Went with companions in 563 to Iona and later converted N Scots to Christianity. Buried with St. Patrick and St. Bridget at Downpatrick. Feast: June 9.

Columban, Saint (kŭlŭm'bŭn), c.540–615, Irish missionary to the Continent. Founded many notable abbeys, including Luxeuil and Bobbio. His followers founded others, all notable for learning. Feast: Nov. 21 (in Ireland Nov. 24).

Columbia. 1 City (pop. 6,124), S Miss., W of Hattiesburg and on Pearl R., in agr. area. Mfg. of clothing and naval stores. **2** City (pop. 31,974), central Mo., NNW of Jefferson City; laid out 1821. Center of a farm and coal area. Seat of Univ. of MISSOURI and Stephens Col. (Baptist; for women; 1833). **3** Borough (pop. 11,993), SE Pa., on Susquehanna R. and W of Lancaster; settled 1730. Produces textiles, metal products, and tobacco. **4** City (pop. 86,914), state cap. (since 1786), central S.C. at head of navigation on Congaree R. Center of farm area, it has textile, fertilizer, cottonseed-oil, printing, and farm-produce plants. Trading post was near in 18th cent. Burned by Sherman on night of Feb. 17, 1865. Seat of Univ. of South Carolina (state supported; coed.; chartered 1801, opened 1805), Allen Univ., and Benedict Col. Has VA hospital and Woodrow Wilson's boyhood home. Near by are U.S. Fort Jackson and L. Murray. Holds annual music festival. **5** City (pop. 10,911), central Tenn., on Duck R. and SSW of Nashville; settled 1807. Mule market and trade center for agr. and phosphate mining area. Has J. K. Polk home. Race riot and trials of 1946 drew wide interest.

Columbia, river, NW U.S. and SW Canada, c.1,210 mi. long, rising in Rocky Mts. of British Columbia (receives Kootenai R. here). Flows 460 mi. NW and S to enter U.S. in NE Wash.; continues S, W, SE, and W (forming Wash.-Oregon line) to the Pacific near Astoria, Oregon. Cuts through Cascade and Coast ranges, forming beautiful gorges (esp. E of Portland, Oregon, where a scenic highway parallels it). Commands one of the great U.S. drainage basins in Idaho, Oregon, Wash., Mont., Wyo., Nev., Utah). Discovered 1792 by Robert GRAY and named for his ship. LEWIS AND CLARK EXPEDITION reached it by land, 1805. Headwaters discovered and entire course explored by David THOMPSON, 1807–11. River was focus of American settlement that created Oregon. Has long supported extensive fisheries (mainly salmon). Irrigation began early (esp. for orchards) and gained great significance with plans beginning in 1932. Goals are flood control, navigation improvement, irrigation, and power. Among first big dams were BONNEVILLE DAM and GRAND COULEE DAM. Contemplated projects now number 238. Included are those in SNAKE (its greatest tributary), WILLAMETTE, John Day, Deschutes, and Yakima rivers and at Vale, Oregon.

Columbia, District of: see DISTRICT OF COLUMBIA.

Columbia College: see COLUMBIA UNIVERSITY.

Columbia Heights, city (pop. 8,175), E Minn., N suburb of Minneapolis.

Columbia University, in Manhattan borough of New York city; founded 1754 as King's Col. by grant of George II. First president was Samuel JOHNSON; succeeded by Myles COOPER and W. S. JOHNSON. Closed during Revolution and reopened 1784 as Columbia Col. It moved to Morningside Heights under Seth Low, and greatly expanded under Pres. N. M. BUTLER (1902–45). Gen. Eisenhower president 1948–53. Named Columbia Univ. 1896 and Columbia Univ. in the City of

New York 1912. Columbia Col. remains as undergraduate school for men. Other divisions: Faculty of Medicine (estab. 1767; became responsible in 1945 for programs of schools of Dental and Oral Surgery, Public Health, Nursing); schools of Law (1858), Engineering (estab. 1864 as School of Mines); Architecture (separate status, 1914), Library Service (1926), International Affairs (1946), General Studies (1910; present name 1947), Dramatic Arts (1948), and Painting and Sculpture (1948); graduate schools of Journalism (1912; endowed by PULITZER) and Business (1916; reorganized 1949); faculties of Political Science (1880), Philosophy (1890), and Pure Science (1892); and Russian (1946) and East Asian (1948) institutes. Independent corporations, but parts of Columbia educational system, include Barnard Col. (undergrad.; for women; 1889); Teachers Col. (1888); Col. of Pharmacy (1829); and New York School of Social Work (1898; part of Columbia since 1940, but administered by Community Service Society of New York since 1939). Reciprocal relationship with UNION THEOLOGICAL SEMINARY. Columbia maintains "Nevis," estate (with cyclotron) near Irvington; Lamont Geological Observatory at Palisades; and Yale-Columbia Southern Station in Union of South Africa. Columbia Univ. Press was organized 1893.

Columbine, stock PANTOMIME character, forerunner of the soubrette. Usually Harlequin's beloved.

columbine, perennial plant of genus *Aquilegia,* with spurred blossoms and delicate foliage. Wild red and yellow *Aquilegia canadensis* native to E North America; blue and white *A. coerulea* to W U.S. Garden sorts are evolved from European species.

columbium: see NIOBIUM.

Columbus, Christopher, 1451?–1506, discoverer of America, b. (almost certainly) Genoa, Italy. After much supplication he gained royal support and sailed from Spain in three ships, *Santa María, Pinta,* and *Niña. He* landed on San Salvador Isl., Oct. 12, 1492. His reception in Spain was enthusiastic. On a second expedition (1493), his discoveries included Puerto Rico, Virgin Isls., Jamaica. Upon a third voyage (1498), he discovered the mouth of the Orinoco in Venezuela. His administration of a colony in Haiti resulted in his return to Spain in chains. A fourth expedition (1502), an attempt to regain prestige, reached the coast of Honduras but was forced back by hardships. He died in neglect.

Columbus. 1 City (pop. 79,611), W Ga., at head of navigation on Chattahoochee R. and WSW of Macon. Cotton market and shipping center, it has textile mills (since 1838), foundries, and food-processing plants. Founded 1828 as trading post. Busy river port before railroads came in 1850s. Supply point in Indian war of 1836, Mexican War, and Civil War. Taken by Federals in April, 1865. Hydroelectric plants of 20th cent. have stimulated industrial growth. U.S. Fort Benning is near. **2** City (pop. 18,370), SE Ind., on East Fork of White R. and SE of Indianapolis; settled c.1819. Mfg. of wood and metal products. Large prehistoric Indian mound is here. **3** Town (pop. 482), SW Ky., near Mississippi R. SW of Paducah. Early site (now Clinton) was Confederate stronghold early in Civil War. **4** City (pop. 17,172), NE Miss., on Tombigbee R. near Ala. line; settled 1817. Shipping and processing center for cotton, livestock, and timber area. Seat of Mississippi State Col. for Women (first state-supported woman's college; chartered 1884, opened 1885). **5** City (pop. 8,884), E Nebr., in prairie region, at junction of Loup and Platte rivers W of Omaha. Rail and mfg. center for livestock, dairy, and grain area. Hq. for Loup R. power project. **6** City (pop. 375,901), state cap. (since 1816), central Ohio, on Scioto R. at mouth of Olentangy R.; laid out as state cap. 1812. Coming of feeder canal (1831) to Ohio and Erie Canal, National Road (1833), and first railroad (1850) stimulated growth. Transportation and distribution center of rich farm area, its industries include meat packing, printing and publishing, paper milling, and mfg. of foundry products, aircraft, auto parts, electrical equipment, and glass. Here are OHIO STATE UNIVERSITY, Columbus Gall. of Fine Arts, Batelle Memorial Inst. (industrial research), and U.S. Fort Hayes. Has Confederate cemetery adjoining site of Civil War Camp Chase.

Columbus Day, commemoration of discovery of America. Celebrated Oct. 12 in 34 U.S. states and in Puerto Rico. Observed also in some Latin American nations and in certain Spanish and Italian cities.

Columcille, Saint: see COLUMBA, SAINT.

coma (kō′mŭ), deep insensibility from which person cannot be roused. It may be caused by brain injury, toxic conditions, shock, sunstroke, hemorrhage, or epilepsy.

Comanche Indians, tribe in N and W Texas and W Okla. after 17th cent., of Shoshonean group of Uto-Aztecan linguistic stock. Nomads with a typical Plains culture, they were fiercely hostile to whites.

Combaconum, India: see KUMBAKONAM.

Combe, William, 1741–1823, English satirist, author of doggerel verse for "Dr. Syntax" series illustrated by Thomas Rowlandson (1812–21).

Combes, Émile (ämēl′ côb′), 1835–1921, French premier (1902–5). Initiated separation of Church and state; abolished religious education.

combine: see REAPER.

combining weight, of an element, is computed by dividing atomic weight by its valence.

combustion, burning or rapid oxidation of a substance, liberating heat and light. Kindling temperature must be reached before substance will burn. In **spontaneous combustion,** substance bursts into flame without apparent cause; usually because there is slow oxidation, without heat loss, until kindling temperature is reached. **Heat of combustion** of a fuel is total amount of heat evolved from burning a given amount of it.

Comédie Française (kōmädē′ fräsäz′) or **Théâtre Français** (tää′trù fräsä′), state theater of France. Estab. 1680 by royal decree (see BÉJART), company was given an annual grant and a theater. Closed during the Revolution; Napoleon revived it 1803.

Has no stars; roles assigned by agreement.

comedy, a light and amusing play or any literary work so presented as to leave a pleasant or happy impression. European comedy originated in ancient boisterous choruses and dialogue at feasts of fertility rites at feasts of Dionysus in Greece. These celebrations developed into drama. Plays of Aristophanes are greatest examples of Old Comedy in Greece. Menander was writer of New Comedy, imitated by Plautus and Terence. In England the tradition of the interlude blended with that of Latin classic comedies in 16th cent. Romantic comedy of Elizabethans culminated in plays of Shakspere. In France, Molière combined classical influence with COMMEDIA DELL' ARTE. Reaction against English Restoration comedy of Congreve, Wycherley, and others resulted in sentimental comedy. Later 18th cent. produced brilliant satirical character comedies of Goldsmith and Sheridan. Oscar Wilde carried on comedy of manners in 19th cent. Modern social comedy written by Pinero, G. B. Shaw, Maugham, and Noel Coward.

Comenius, John Amos (kōmē′nēŭs), Czech *Jan Amos Komenský,* 1592–1670, Czech educator, a Moravian churchman. Advocated relating education to everyday life, a universal system with equal opportunities for women, and teaching in vernacular.

comet, heavenly body traveling in orbit around sun. Usually consists of head of cloudy brightness within which lie one or more bright nuclei from which materials, driven away from sun by radiation pressure of sun's light, form a sweeping tail, sometimes over 100,000,000 mi. long. Periods for covering known orbits range from 3.3 to several thousand years. Periodic comets are officially designated by year of closest approach to sun, followed by Roman numeral indicating order of passage.

comic strip, combination of caricature with a story line, laid out in a series of pictures across a page and concerning the same character or set of characters. The first advance toward the present form was made by R. F. Outcault in 1896 with a single cartoon *The Yellow Kid* (New York *World*) which became very popular. In 1897 Rudolph Dirks, creator of *The Katzenjammer Kids* (New York *American*), developed a four-panel square describing consequent actions and using balloons as frames for dialogue. Bud Fisher with his *Mutt and Jeff* (1907) was the first to lay out the panels in a line. The comic strip rapidly became a regular syndicated feature of most newspapers.

Comines, Commines, or **Commynes, Philippe de** (fēlēp′ dù kōmēn′), c.1447–c.1511, French historian and diplomat. Served Charles the Bold of Burgundy and, after 1472, Louis XI and Charles VIII of France. His *Mémoires* (many translations) are outstanding for penetrating analysis of men and motives.

Cominform (kŏ′mĭnfôrm), Communist Information Bureau, estab. 1947 by Communist parties of USSR, satellite countries, and Italy. Purpose is exchange of experience. Membership is voluntary, and its decisions are not binding, though influence is great. Hq. at Belgrade until expulsion of Yugo-

slavia in 1948, thereafter at Bucharest, Rumania.

Comintern (kŏ′mĭntûrn) [from Communist International] or **Third International,** estab. 1919 at Moscow to spread Marxian socialism in world. From original core of Russian and German Communists it grew to include Communist parties from many countries. In 1936 Germany and Japan formed Anti-Comintern Pact, renewed 1941 with enlarged membership. In 1943 USSR dissolved Comintern to reassure its allies in World War II.

Commager, Henry Steele (kŏ′mĭjŭr), 1902–, American historian, professor at Columbia Univ. His writings, often in collaboration, are extensive. Probably best-known is *The Growth of the American Republic* (with S. E. Morison).

Commandments, Ten: see TEN COMMANDMENTS.

commando, small military raiding unit organized (1940) by the British in World War II; akin to U.S. army ranger units. First used by Boers in South African War.

commedia dell' arte (kŏm-mä′dēä dĕl-lär′tä), form of comedy in 16th-cent. Italy. Using improvised dialogue and masked characters in satiric song, dance, farce, it gave rise to traditional pantomime characters (e.g., Harlequin, Columbine). Admitted female performers; helped free Italian theater from artificiality.

Commerce, city (pop. 5,889), E Texas, NE of Dallas. Center of cotton shipping and seat of East Texas State Teachers Col.

Commerce, United States Department of, organized 1903 as Dept. of Commerce and Labor; separated from Dept. of Labor in 1913. Includes Bureau of the Census, Coast and Geodetic Survey, Bureau of Foreign and Domestic Commerce, Weather Bureau, Patent Office, and Civil Aeronautics Administration.

commercial law, body of laws governing business transactions. Beginnings of modern commercial law coincide with opening of large-scale commerce in the late Middle Ages. Strongly influenced by Roman law. Estab. in England in the mid-16th cent. as "law merchant" and was administered by special courts; later under royal courts but in the 18th cent. made a part of the common law and in this form adopted in the U.S., while on the Continent commercial law remains separate with special courts.

Commines, Philippe de: see COMINES.

commissar (kŏ′mĭsär), in the USSR, head of an administration or commissariat, similar to a minister in Western Europe.

Committee for Industrial Organization: see CONGRESS OF INDUSTRIAL ORGANIZATIONS.

Commodus (kŏ′mŭdŭs), 161–92, Roman emperor (180–92), son and successor of Marcus Aurelius. Licentious, vulgar, vain, proud of his physique, he was well hated, finally murdered.

common, formerly in agr., unenclosed tract of land used by community. Old common lands are preserved in some parks in England and also in U.S., e.g., Boston Common, village greens.

common law, legal system of England, originally (13th cent.) so called because common to all England, not limited to a locality; more precisely, that part of the English legal system not reduced to statutes and not arising from EQUITY, maritime law, or other special branches. It is law arising from customs and created by judges to meet problems, unlike modern CIVIL LAW (based upon the code and the STATUTE). Common law followed in British Empire (except Quebec) and the U.S. (except La., Puerto Rico, Virgin Isls.).

Commons, House of: see PARLIAMENT.

Commonwealth of Australia, British dominion including continental AUSTRALIA and TASMANIA.

Commune of Paris, March–May, 1871, government set up in Paris at end of FRANCO-PRUSSIAN WAR, in opposition to government of Adolphe THIERS at Versailles. (Paris had had communal government earlier, a notable occasion being in French Revolution.) Original issue was the Parisians' refusal to accept humiliating peace terms from Prussia. When *Versaillais* troops began siege of Paris (while the Prussians stood by as neutrals), the Commune fell under the sway of leftist extremists, who shot hostages (including arch bishop of Paris), burned Tuileries, city hall, palace of justice. On May 28 the *Versaillais* entered Paris. In subsequent reprisals more than 17,000 people, including women and children, were executed.

communicable diseases, diseases caused by microorganisms and transmissible from an infected person or animal to another. They are known also as infectious diseases. Commonly they are called contagious if transmissible by contact with victim of disease or infected objects or secretions. They may be spread also by substances taken into body, e.g., cholera; by bite or sting of infected animal or disease carrier, e.g., rabies, malaria; by contamination of wound, e.g., tetanus. Preventive measures include vaccination, inoculation, quarantine, disinfection. An endemic disease is one always present in a given locality. Disease may become epidemic if many persons lack immunity or if infectious agent is unusually virulent.

communication, transmission and reception of message between two persons or more. Basic forms: signs (sight), sound (hearing; see LANGUAGE). Reduction of message to WRITING was a fundamental step in social evolution, the beginning of recorded history. Save for limited devices (carrier pigeons, smoke signals, heliograph, etc.) speed of early communication was only as fast as man could travel. Invention of TELEGRAPH divorced transportation from communication; RADIO and TELEPHONE extended sphere of nearly instantaneous electrical communication, working profound revolution in society. Made greater centralization in industry and government possible; widened horizon of every community; tends to amalgamate cultures, arts, techniques, languages. FEDERAL COMMUNICATIONS COMMISSION controls radio and television in U.S.; international phases are directed by Office of Transport and Communications, Dept. of State.

communion: see EUCHARIST.

communism, often a vague and misused term, fundamentally is a social system in which property (esp. real property and means of production) is held in common, i.e., by whole group. Communism in this sense is age-old. Many primitive societies, e.g., Mexican, Inca, early German, were communistic. Plato's *Republic* outlined a communal society. Jewish Essenes and some early Christian sects were communal. Medieval feudalism had communal aspects. Peasants' rebellion under Wat Tyler in 14th-cent. England and Peasants' War in 16th-cent. Germany were communistic. Thinkers of the Enlightenment, Jean Jacques Rousseau, and Immanuel Kant attacked institution of private property and prepared the way for the French Revolution, in which BABEUF preached against private property. So-called utopian communism had been advocated in Sir Thomas More's *Utopia,* Tommaso Campanella's *City of the Sun,* and James Harrington's *Oceana.* Cults arose in 19th cent., and communistic settlements were set up, especially in U.S. Leaders of time were Étienne CABET, Charles FOURIER, and Louis BLANC. In same cent. the rise of capitalism and Industrial Revolution produced social and economic conditions that fostered communism. But Communism as we know it today arose in 1848 with *The Communist Manifesto* of Karl MARX and Friedrich ENGELS (see MARXISM). Marxian communism spread with founding of First INTERNATIONAL and rise of Social Democratic parties on Continent. It took more radical form in 1903, in Russia, when Bolsheviks, led by LENIN, urged immediate and violent revolution to crush capitalism and estab. world socialistic state (see BOLSHEVISM AND MENSHEVISM). Triumph of Bolsheviks in RUSSIAN REVOLUTION OF 1917 made them leaders. Leninism was strengthened by World War I and by Third International or COMINTERN, which now became supreme. Leninists urged uniting of all workers for coming world revolution, to be followed by dictatorship of proletariat and state socialism, which would theoretically wither away leaving classless and stateless universal Communism. Antipathy to these ideas has led occasionally in the democracies to "Red hunts" which have sometimes struck against non-Communist liberals as well as actual Reds. Communism now centered in USSR. Death of Lenin (1924) left STALIN and TROTSKY as rivals. Exile and death of Trotsky gave Stalin triumph, and he built up Russia as model and base of world Communism. Victory in World War II added Baltic States to Soviet Union; Stalin later added as satellites Poland, Czechoslovakia, Hungary, Rumania, Bulgaria, and, with reservations, Yugoslavia. Addition of Communist China in 1950 joined two of most heavily populated states. World in 1952 was sharply divided between Communist East and democratic West. See also COMMUNIST PARTY.

communistic settlements, communities practicing common ownership of goods. Existed in ancient and medieval times, and flourished again in 19th-cent. America. Some were religious (e.g., Amana Society, Shaker communities, Oneida Community); others non-religious and utopian (e.g., New Harmony, Brook Farm, several Fourierist communities, and settlements by Cabet).

Communist party, in U.S., part of world-wide political movement of Communism. First organized 1919. With decline of I.W.W., party became leading revolutionary organization in U.S., having as its avowed aim the overthrow of capitalism and establishment of a dictatorship of the proletariat. Communists led many industrial strikes in 1920s and exploited weaknesses of American democracy. In 1935, following Comintern's new line, party began "cooperating" with liberal groups, and, boring from within, gained control of many organizations (e.g., many trade unions). With the Nazi attack on Russia in June, 1941, party turned overnight from condemnation of World War II as "imperialist" to support of war as "democratic." Following the war cooperation with "progressive" capitalism ended. With the onset of the "cold war," Pres. Truman and Congress took steps to keep Communists out of U.S. government employment and to eliminate their influence in union activity. The Alger Hiss trials (1949, 1950) and the trials and convictions of top Communists served more widely to publicize conspiratorial and subversive nature of U.S. Communism. Party membership, always small, has been drawn mainly from groups that are discriminated against in U.S. society, idealists, and direct-action trade unionists. Political influence has extended into AMERICAN LABOR PARTY and into present PROGRESSIVE PARTY.

community chest, cooperative organization of citizens and social welfare agencies in a city for the purpose of raising and allocating funds for charity.

Commynes, Philippe de: see COMINES.

Comnenus (kŏmně′nŭs), dynasty of Byzantine emperors (reigned 1057–59, 1081–1185): ISAAC I, ALEXIUS I, JOHN II, MANUEL I, ALEXIUS II, ANDRONICUS I. Branch of family founded empire of TREBIZOND (1204–1461).

Como (kō′mō), city (pop. 42,569), Lombardy, N Italy, at SW end of Lake Como. Silk mfg. Founded as Roman colony; independent commune by 11th cent.; conquered 1335 by Milan, after long struggle. Cathedral (14th–18th cent.); town hall (1215). **Lake Como,** Ital. *Lago di Como* or *Lario,* c.30 mi. long, ½–2½ mi. wide, is formed by Adda R. in foothills of Alps. Celebrated scenery; many resorts (Bellagio, Cadenabbia, Cernobbio, Menaggio, Tremezzo).

Comodoro Rivadavia (kōmōdhō′rō rēvädhä′vyä), town (pop. 25,651), SE Argentina; important center of oil production.

Comoro Islands (kŏ′mŭrō), French overseas territory (830 sq. mi.; pop. c.152,000), in Indian Ocean, near Mozambique Channel; cap. Dzaoudzi.

Compactata: see UTRAQUISTS.

compass. 1 In mathematics, an instrument for making circles and measuring distances; usually it consists of a pivot leg and a pencil or pen leg or of two pointed legs. **2** In navigation, an instrument for determining direction. Mariner's compass consists of freely suspended magnetic needle which in earth's magnetic field indicates N and S poles. "Boxing the compass" is naming in order the 32 points starting from north (N, N by E, NNE, etc.). Flux-gate or gyro flux-gate compass contains gyroscopic stabilizer and is useful in airplanes.

Compiègne (kōpēä′nyü), town (pop. 15,392), Oise dept., N France, NE of Paris. Château, rebuilt 18th cent., often a royal residence. Joan of Arc was captured (1430) while defending the town. In a railroad car in near-by Forest of Compiègne were signed the armistice of Nov. 11, 1918, which ended World War I, and the French-German armistice of June 22, 1940.

complex, term indicating group or system of ideas originating in a mind as a result of an experience or set of experiences of high emotional content. Although repressed from consciousness, it affects subsequent mental activity and behavior. Undue dominance of a complex over an individual causes psychopathic condition.

composition, in primitive and medieval law, prevention of retribution for acts of violence by payment of money to injured person or his family. Marks transition from vendetta system to system of criminal law where socially dangerous acts are concern of the state rather than of family unit. A well-known instance of composition is the Old English wergild, payment made by a murderer to the victim's family.

compost (kŏm′pōst), decayed organic material, rich in HUMUS, used to improve texture of soil. Made of vegetable wastes (e.g., lawn clippings, leaves), some soil, and sometimes manure, mixed and allowed to decay.

Compostela, Santiago de, Spain: see SANTIAGO DE COMPOSTELA.

compound, homogeneous chemical combination of two or more elements in definite proportion by weight. Has properties distinct from those of its constituents. Can be decomposed by heat and CHEMICAL REACTION. A compound is indicated by a formula showing symbols of constituent elements in proper proportion.

Compromise of 1850. Annexation of Texas to U.S. and addition of new territory at close of Mexican War aggravated North-South tension over extension of SLAVERY into territories. WILMOT PROVISO was source of contention. Compromise measures, largely originating with Stephen A. DOUGLAS, were sponsored in U.S. Senate by Henry CLAY. Measures proposed admission of Calif. as free state; organization of New Mexico and Utah territories without mention of slavery, but with provisions for SQUATTER SOVEREIGNTY; settlement of Texas boundary claims; prohibition of slave trade in D.C.; a more stringent fugitive slave law. Daniel WEBSTER, through speech on March 7, 1850, virtually assured acceptance of proposals. They were passed as separate bills in Sept., 1850. Compromise was hailed as a final solution to slavery question in territories, but issue arose again in 1854 (see KANSAS-NEBRASKA BILL).

Compton, Arthur Holly, 1892–, American physicist. Shared 1927 Nobel Prize for discovering **Compton effect:** increase in wave lengths of X rays on collision with electrons of atoms of low atomic weights. His brother **Karl Taylor Compton,** 1887–, a physicist, is known especially for work on radar, photoelectricity, ionization of gases, ultraviolet spectroscopy, and electric arcs.

Compton, city (pop. 47,991), S Calif., S of Los Angeles, in industrial and farm (truck, dairy) area; settled 1867. Oil refining, with mfg. of oil-well equipment and steel products.

Compton effect: see COMPTON, ARTHUR HOLLY.

compurgation, in medieval law, legal defense by oath of the accused, supported by oaths of other persons that they believed that he swore truthfully. Found in early Germanic law and in English church law.

Comstock, Anthony, 1844–1915, American moral crusader. Secured New York state and Federal legislation against obscene matter. Organized New York Society for the Suppression of Vice.

Comstock Lode, richest known silver deposit, W Nev., on Mt. Davidson in the Virginia Range. Discovered in 1857 by Ethan Allen Grosh and Hosea Ballou Grosh, who died before recording claims. In 1859 Henry Tomkins Paige Comstock laid claim to lode; later disposed of holdings for insignificant sums. Lode became scene of feverish activity, with VIRGINIA CITY its "capital." Great fortunes were made. By 1898 lode was virtually abandoned.

Comtat Venaissin: see VENAISSIN.

Comte, Auguste (ōgüst′ kŏt′), 1798–1857, French philosopher, apostle of positivism, a philosophical system completely rejecting metaphysics and relying instead on the findings of modern positive sciences. This he first began to develop when contributing (1818–24) to the publications of Saint-Simon. His final aim was to so reform society that all men might live in harmony and comfort. He ranked sociology (a term he invented) as greatest of the sciences. His *Course of Positive Philosophy* (1830–42) set forth the system later elaborated in other of his works and developed to a more inclusive scale by followers all over the world in the late 19th cent.

Comus (kō′mŭs), Greek god of mirth, shown as a winged youth bearing torch and drinking cup. Lover of song, dance, and wine, a follower of Dionysus.

Comyn, John (kŭ′mĭn), d. c.1300, Scottish noble. Known as Black Comyn, he became (1286) one of six guardians of realm. Signed treaty by which MARGARET MAID OF NORWAY was to marry eldest son of Edward I of England. On Margaret's death claimed throne, but submitted to Edward. Meanwhile pushed claim of John de BALIOL, who was crowned in 1292. His son, **John Comyn,** d. 1306, aided de Baliol against Edward I. Murdered by Robert Bruce or his followers.

Conanicut Island: see JAMESTOWN, R.I.

Conant, James Bryant, 1893–, American educator, a chemist. Professor of organic chemistry at Harvard (1929–33). President of Harvard after 1933, he encouraged expansion and trend to general education for democracy. In World War II chairman of Na-

tional Defense Research Committee. Made U.S. High Commissioner for Germany 1953.

concentration camp. In 1933 National Socialist Germany set up forced-labor camps where political undesirables (mainly Jews and Communists) were held without legal procedure. In World War II concentration camps existed throughout German-held Europe. Some (e.g., Majdanek and Oswiecim in Poland) had gas chambers where 6,000,-000 (mostly Jews and Poles) were exterminated. Countless others died of mistreatment. Among largest camps in Germany were Buchenwald, Dachau, Belsen.

Concepción (kōnsĕpsēōn′), city (pop. 87,620), cap. of Concepción prov., S central Chile, near mouth of the Bío-Bío. Founded by Valdivia in 1550, it is now one of Chile's largest cities and a major shipping center through its port, Talcahuano. Attacks by Araucanian Indians in first years and recurrent earthquakes (1570, 1730, 1751, 1939) have plagued city.

Concepción del Uruguay (dĕl ōōrōōgwī′), city (pop. 30,939), NE Argentina, on Uruguay R., one of commercial centers of the Argentine Mesopotamia.

concert, the public performance of music. Earliest recorded public concerts were in London in 1672. Concert life developed greatly in the 18th and 19th cent.; solo recitals were popularized by such artists as Liszt, Clara Schumann, and Paganini.

concertina: see ACCORDION.

concerto, musical form dating from early baroque period. The *concerto grosso,* in which a group of solo instruments alternated with a larger ensemble, was standardized by Corelli and Vivaldi. The form of the classical concerto—three movements, for solo instrument and orchestra—was developed by Mozart.

conch (kŏngk), name for certain marine mollusks with spiral univalve shells, especially those of families Strombidae and Cassididae. Some are called cameo or helmet shells. Conches eat live animal food and also scavenge. Shells, ranging from white to red, are often made into ornaments.

Concini, Concino (kōnchē′nō kōnchē′nē), d. 1617, Florentine adventurer, favorite of MARIE DE′ MEDICI, who made him marshal of France and marquis d'Ancre. Succeeded Sully as chief minister (1611). Notorious for his greed and his spy system. Assassinated by order of Louis XIII. His wife, Leonora Galigaï, was beheaded and burned for sorcery (1617).

Concord. 1 (kŏng′kûrd) Town (pop. 6,953), W Calif., NE of San Francisco, in agr. (grapes), dairy, and livestock area. **2** Town (pop. 8,623), E Mass., on Concord R. and NW of Boston; settled 1635. Scene of Revolutionary battle on April 19, 1775 (see LEXINGTON AND CONCORD, BATTLES OF) is marked by D. C. French's *Minuteman.* Houses where Emerson, the Alcotts, Hawthorne, and Thoreau lived are preserved. The Old Manse (1765) is public shrine (since 1939). S of the village is Walden Pond, Thoreau's retreat. **3** City (pop. 27,-988), state cap. (since 1808), S N.H., on Merrimack R. above Manchester; settled

1725-27, inc. as Rumford in 1733 (Count RUMFORD took his title from this name), renamed 1765. Transportation and trade center for agr. area. Has Rumford Press, famous granite quarries, and factories (wood, metal, leather products). State historical society occupies Franklin Pierce home and office (remodeled 1923). Capitol (1819) is made of granite and marble. Seat of St. Paul's school (prep.; Episcopal; for boys; chartered 1855, opened 1856). Mary Baker Eddy was born at near-by Bow. 4 (kŏn'kôrd″) City (pop. 16,486), W central N.C., in piedmont NE of Charlotte; settled 1796. Center of textile mfg.

Concord, short river, E Mass., joining Merrimack R. at Lowell. Setting for Thoreau's first book.

concordat (kŏnkôr'dăt), contractual agreement between pope, in his spiritual capacity, and temporal authority of a state, regulating points of conflict between Church and state. The earliest concordat (see WORMS, CONCORDAT OF) was concluded in 1122. The Concordat of 1516, with France, abolished the PRAGMATIC SANCTION OF BOURGES but was revoked in 1561. Concordats, common since 19th cent., determine method of appointing bishops and define status of religious schools, orders, and property. Best-known are the LATERAN TREATY with Italy (1929) and the **Concordat of 1801** between Pious VII and Bonaparte, which restored the Roman Church in France. In 1905 France repudiated it and separated Church and state.

Concordia (kōngkôr'dhyä), city (pop. 52,213), NE Argentina, port on Uruguay R. opposite Salto, Uruguay. One of chief towns of the Argentine Mesopotamia, it exports meat, mate, quebracho, and grain.

Concordia, city (pop. 7,175), N Kansas, on Republic R. and N of Salina. Trade center for wheat, livestock, and poultry area.

concretion (kŏnkrē'shŭn), rounded mass occurring in sedimentary rock and differing from it in composition (e.g., flint nodules in chalk).

Condé (kōdā'), French princely family, cadet branch of house of BOURBON. It originated with **Louis I de Bourbon, prince de Condé** (lwē' dù bŏŏrbō'), 1530-69, Protestant leader and general. He took part in conspiracy of AMBOISE (1560), commanded Huguenots in Wars of Religion, fell at Jarnac. His great-grandson **Louis II de Bourbon, prince de Condé,** known as **the Great Condé,** 1621-86, won major victories in the Thirty Years War at Rocroi (1643), Freiburg (1644), Nördlingen (1645), Lens (1648). In the FRONDE he turned against his government, taking command of the army of princes in 1651 and of the Spanish army in 1653. Defeated by Turenne, notably in Battle of the Dunes (1658), he was pardoned in 1659 by Louis XIV, for whom he fought successfully in the Dutch War. He was the brother of Armand de CONTI and of Mme de LONGUEVILLE. His great-grandson, **Louis Joseph de Bourbon, prince de Condé** (zhōzĕf'), 1736-1818, formed the "army of Condé" against the French revolutionary forces (dissolved 1801). He was the grandfather of the duc d'ENGHIEN.

condensation, in physics, change in state of substance from gas to liquid. Velocity and distance between molecules of gas are so decreased by heat withdrawal that substance condenses. Dew, fog, and clouds are formed as a result of condensation of water vapor in atmosphere.

condenser, device to increase capacity of conductor for receiving and holding greater electrical charge. LEYDEN JAR is a simple type. Principle is induction. Used in telephone, radio, and ignition system of automobile. Apparatus causing condensation of gas is also called a condenser.

Condillac, Étienne Bonnot de (kŏdēyäk'), 1715-80, French philosopher, a priest. He started from Locke's ideas and stressed that all psychological processes in an individual are derived from sensations, and that general ideas are built by experience through the medium of language. This sensationalism, expounded in his *Traité des sensations* (1754), was much discussed and influenced later psychologists. His attempts to arrive at exact terms for social and economic concepts had a clarifying effect in French thought.

condor (kŏn'dûr), South American vulture which nests on Andean peaks. California condor or vulture (now rare) lives in North American coastal ranges; it is one of largest birds of prey, with wingspread of 9-10 ft.

Condorcet, Antoine Nicolas, marquis de (kōdôrsā'), 1743-94, French philosopher, mathematician, and revolutionist. He was a friend of most of the leading intellectuals of his day. He made valuable contributions to the mathematical theory of probabilities. An enthusiastic supporter of the revolution, he was active politically until he protested the persecution of the Girondists. He was denounced and went into hiding. There he completed his great philosophical work, a historical sketch outlining the progress of man to the French Revolution, which he thought would usher in perfection of human state. Captured by his enemies, he died mysteriously and immediately.

condottiere (kôndôt-tyā'rā), leader of mercenary soldiers in Renaissance Italy. Condottieri hired their own bands, fought for highest bidder, often changed allegiance. Well-known condottieri were Muzio Attendolo Sforza, Colleoni, Sir John de Hawkwood.

conducting, in music, art of unifying the efforts of a number of musicians playing ensemble. Until c.1600 the conductor was primarily a time-beater, using a roll of music as a baton. In the baroque era the group was at first led by the harpsichordist, later by the first violinist, even today called the concertmaster. The nonplaying conductor, using a baton, appeared in the 19th cent. Beethoven, Mendelssohn, and Wagner often conducted; Hans von Bülow was the first of the modern virtuoso conductors.

conduction. 1 Transfer of heat energy from one part of substance to adjoining part, from molecule to molecule. Substances that readily transfer heat are conductors, e.g., metals; those that do so slowly are insulators, e.g., nonmetals, fluids. **2** Transfer of charge of electricity from one point to another. Metals are good conductors; nonmetals are insulators. Electric wires are insulated to prevent escape of charge during conduction.

cone, the fruit of most conifers. Staminate (male) and ovulate (female) cones are borne on same tree, but hard, woody ovulate cones are ones commonly seen. Among largest are the 10–20 in. cones of sugar pine of W U.S.; most are 1–6 in. long.

cone, in mathematics, a surface (called a conical surface), generated by a moving line (generator) which passes through a given point (vertex) and continually intersects a given fixed curve (directrix). A cone is also the solid bounded by such a surface.

Conecuh, river: see ESCAMBIA, river.

Conemaugh (kŏn'ûmô"), river of SW Pa. rising in Alleghenies, and flowing c.70 mi. NW to branch of Allegheny R. Flood control projects are on river.

Conestoga wagon, freight-carrying vehicle originated in Conestoga region of Pennsylvania c.1725. Used by farmers and later in commerce with frontier settlements until c.1850. Large wagons, drawn by six horses, carried up to eight tons. Bottom of the wagon box curved upward at both ends; white hood over wagon was protection against elements.

coney: see CONY.

Coney Island, Atlantic beach resort, N.Y.: see BROOKLYN, New York city.

Confederacy or **Confederate States of America** (1861–65), government estab. by Southern states of U.S. which seceded from Union. When Pres. Lincoln was elected, seven states seceded—S.C., Ga., La., Miss., Fla., Ala., and Texas. Provisional government was set up at Montgomery, Ala., and constitution drafted. After firing on Fort Sumter and Lincoln's call for troops, four more states joined—Ark., N.C., Va., and Tenn. Richmond, Va., became capital, and Jefferson DAVIS and Alexander H. STEPHENS were elected president and vice president. Judah P. BENJAMIN was outstanding member of cabinet. Story of Confederacy was story of loss of CIVIL WAR. Its citizens bore privations and invasion with bravery and courage, loyal to end. Refused recognition by England and France, which did recognize Northern blockade of Southern ports. Volunteers were insufficient; conscription used but opposed. Financial troubles were heavy from start, and paper money became worthless. Mounting Union victories made end inevitable. Confederacy fell after Lee's surrender in April, 1865.

Confederate cruisers. In Civil War, Confederacy set out to destroy North's merchant marine. Of some 18 cruisers *Florida, Alabama,* and *Shenandoah* were outstanding. *Florida* took some 60 prizes before her capture in 1864. *Alabama* took almost 70, causing over $6,000,000 damage as settled in ALABAMA CLAIMS. She was sunk by U.S.S. *Kearsarge,* July, 1864. *Shenandoah* took 38 prizes; she reverted to U.S. Raids caused decline of nation's merchant marine.

Confederate States of America: see CONFEDERACY.

Confederation, Articles of, in U.S. history, ratified in 1781 and superseded by Constitution of U.S. in 1789. Proved unsatisfactory

because of subordinate position occupied by central government; Congress was dependent upon states for funds and execution of its decrees. Government commanded little respect because of its weaknesses. Most significant achievement was Ordinance of 1787.

confederation, Canadian: see BRITISH NORTH AMERICA ACT.

Confederation of the Rhine, league of German princes, formed 1806 under protection of Napoleon I. Members included Bavaria, Württemberg, Saxony, Westphalia, Baden. Confederation broke apart in 1813.

confession, formal admission of criminal guilt, usually made in the course of examination by the police or by the prosecutor or at the trial. To be admissible must be made voluntarily—not induced by torture, threat, or promises. See also PENANCE.

confession, in religion: see PENANCE.

Confession of Augsburg: see CREED.

confirmation: see SACRAMENT.

conflict of laws, situation arising when the law of more than one territorial unit may be applied to a case; also the legal rules governing such conflicts. In Europe this branch of law is frequently called private international law. In the U.S. the variance of laws from state to state makes the subject of conflict of laws urgent. Certain provisions of the U.S. Constitution—notably the "full faith and credit" clause of Article 4, Section 1—limit the freedom of the states in deciding cases and in certain cases compel one state to treat as valid a judgment rendered in another state which had proper jurisdiction.

Confucius (kùnfū'shùs), Chinese *K'ung Futse,* 551–479 B.C., Chinese ethical teacher. Though his life is surrounded by later legend, it is known that he was born in the feudal state of Lu, that he was a public official, and that he and his followers urged social reform. In the midst of warfare, corruption and tyranny, he urged a system of morality and statecraft to bring about peace, justice, and universal order. His teachings became the basis of the moral system of **Confucianism** (kùnfū'shùnīzùm), which was of course based on earlier ideas and was developed in some of the most important works of CHINESE LITERATURE, including the *Analects* (sayings of Confucius and his disciples), classic works supposedly edited by Confucius, and the writings of Mencius. The basic moral principle of the system is the maintenance of *jen* (roughly, sympathy) between men by keeping right relationships: treat those who are subordinate to you as you would be treated by those in positions superior to yours. This is the Confucian Golden Rule. Filial piety is heavily stressed and became more dominant as the system endured, but Confucianism created a universal pattern for government, with emphasis on the middle way, avoidance of extreme. Originally atheistic, Confucianism was later colored by religious elements from earlier beliefs, and the hierarchy of relationships was capped by Shang-Ti [ruler of heaven], the superior of earthly rulers. Confucius was himself deified. Confucianism was triumphant by the 1st cent. A.D. Though it had to contend with TAOISM and BUDDHISM and was often eclipsed by them, the actual system of government continued with Confucian principles. In the Sung dynasty (960–1279), the system was revised as Neo-Confucianism, opposing the meditation and quietism of the other religions by stress on improvement through acquiring knowledge. This remained dominant until the 20th cent. though it gradually rigidified the system of respectful relationship into a conservative approval of the existing social order.

Congaree (kŏng'gûrē), river, central S.C., formed by junction of Broad and Saluda rivers at Columbia. Flows 52 mi. SE to Wateree R., forming Santee R.

Congo (kŏng'gō), river, c.2,900 mi. long, 2d longest in Africa. Drainage basin (c.1,450,-000 sq. mi.) includes Belgian Congo and much of S French Equatorial Africa and N Angola. Its upper course, from its rise in SE Belgian Congo to STANLEY FALLS, is called the Lualaba. Forms border of French Equatorial Africa and broadens into STANLEY POOL, beyond which begin Livingstone Falls in which the river drops 852 ft. in 220 mi. Its estuary forms Angola border. Its mouth was discovered 1482 by the Portuguese navigator Diogo Cão. Livingstone explored area around upper course 1867–73, Sir Henry Stanley made first known descent to the mouth 1874–77.

Congo, Belgian: see BELGIAN CONGO.

Congo Free State: see BELGIAN CONGO.

Congregationalism, type of Protestant organization in which each local church has free control of its own affairs. It has no bishops or presbyteries. Movement arose in 16th and 17th cent. in England in revolt of SEPARATISTS against formalized worship and state control of Established Church. Robert BROWNE published in 1582 first exposition of Congregational principles. Pilgrims brought Congregationalism to America in 1620. Cambridge Platform was adopted (1648), and Congregationalists took leading part in GREAT AWAKENING. Natl. Council of Congregational Churches of the U.S. formed 1871; in 1931 it merged with Christian Church to form General Council of the Congregational and Christian Churches of the U.S.

Congress, Library of: see LIBRARY OF CONGRESS.

Congress of Industrial Organizations (C.I.O.), originally Committee for Industrial Organization, formed 1935 by affiliates of the A.F. of L. to unionize mass-production workers by industries rather than by crafts. First leader was John L. Lewis. The A.F. of L. expelled (1937) the C.I.O. unions. Powerful in C.I.O. are United Steel Workers and the United Automobile Workers. Lewis and his United Mine Workers left C.I.O. in 1942. Philip Murray, president (1940–52), was succeeded by Walter Reuther. C.I.O. noted for vigorous organizational drives and political activity.

Congress of the United States, legislative branch of Federal government, instituted in 1789 by Article I of U.S. Constitution, which prescribes its membership and defines its powers. Congress is composed of two houses, the Senate and the House of Representatives. The Senators, two from each state, have six-year terms and were chosen by the state legislatures until 1913, when the Seventeenth Amendment, providing for their direct popular election, went into force. The terms of one third of the Senators expire every two years. A Senator must be at least 30 years old, not less than nine years a U.S. citizen, and a resident of the state in which he is elected. The Vice President of the United States presides over the Senate, voting only in case of a tie. Representatives are apportioned to the states according to their populations in the Federal census, every state being entitled to at least one Representative. Representatives are chosen for two-year terms, and the entire body comes up for reelection every two years. A Representative must be 25 or older, at least seven years a U.S. citizen, and an inhabitant of the state in which he is elected. The presiding officer of the House, the speaker, is elected by the members of the House. The two houses have an equal voice in legislation, though revenue bills must originate in the House of Representatives. The Senate, regarded as the more powerful body, must ratify all treaties and confirm important presidental appointments.

Congreve, William, 1670–1729, English Restoration dramatist, known for cynical, witty comedies. Among them are *The Old Bachelor* (1693), *The Double Dealer* (1693), *Love for Love* (1695), and his masterpiece *The Way of the World* (1700). His tragedy, *The Mourning Bride* (1697), popular in his day, is now best remembered for lyrics, "Music hath charms" and "Hell hath no fury." Congreve, Vanbrugh, and others attacked for immorality by Jeremy Collier.

conic section (kŏ'nĭk), any curve made by intersection of a right circular conical surface and a plane. These curves are the CIRCLE, ELLIPSE, PARABOLA, HYPERBOLA. If plane passes through vertex, result is a point, straight line, or pair of intersecting lines; these are called degenerate conic sections.

conifer (kŏ'nĭfûr), tree or shrub of order Coniferales, usually evergreen and cone-bearing, e.g., PINE, SPRUCE, CYPRESS, SEQUOIA.

Conjeeveram (kŭnjē'vŭrŭm), city (pop. 74,-635), E Madras, India. Sacred to Hindus; known as Benares of the South. As cap. of Pallava empire (c.300–c.750), it was a Brahmanical and Buddhist center. Officially called Kanchipuram.

conjunctivitis, inflammation of membrane covering eyelids and front of eyeball. Infectious forms caused by microorganisms (see GONORRHEA) gonococcal conjunctivitis (see GONORRHEA) and pinkeye.

Conkling, Roscoe, 1829–88, American politician. U.S. Representative from N.Y. (1859–63, 1865–67); U.S. Senator (1867–81). When Pres. James A. GARFIELD ignored him in appointing a collector of the port of New York, this Old Guard leader and Republican state "boss" resigned from the Senate in protest.

Connaught (kŏ'nôt), province (6,611 sq. mi.; pop. 492,797), W Ireland; comprises counties MAYO, SLIGO, LEITRIM, ROSCOMMON, and GALWAY. Was an ancient kingdom of Ireland. Has some agr., but poor soil.

Conneaut (kŏ'nēŏt"), city (pop. 10,230), NE Ohio, on L. Erie near Pa. line; settled 1799. Lake and rail shipping (iron, coal, steel) center with mfg. of tin cans and communication equipment.

Conneaut Lake, NW Pa., S of L. Erie. Largest natural lake in state.

Connecticut, state (4,899 sq. mi.; pop. 2,007,-280), NE U.S.; one of Thirteen Colonies; cap. HARTFORD. NEW HAVEN, BRIDGEPORT, WATERBURY important cities. Bordered S by Long Isl. Sound. Highlands rise gently from coastal plains of Sound, divided by CONNECTICUT R. and its valley, drained E by THAMES R., W by HOUSATONIC R. Mainly industrial, mfg. of metal products (machinery, firearms, clocks, typewriters, hardware), textiles, rubber products; printing, publishing. Farming yields dairy and poultry products, broadleaf tobacco, truck. Fishing, some mining. Connecticut R. discovered 1614 by Adriaen Block (Dutch). Pilgrims of Plymouth Colony estab. trading post 1633, were joined by Puritans from Mass. Bay. FUNDAMENTAL ORDERS adopted 1639. New Haven colony was included under 1662 royal charter. Had semi-liberal religious system, with Congregationalism as official faith. Contributed men, supplies to American Revolution. Oliver ELLSWORTH helped frame U.S. Constitution; Conn. one of first to ratify it. Settled WYOMING VALLEY dispute 1782. Gave up W land claims (1786), except WESTERN RESERVE. Hurt by Embargo Act of 1807, War of 1812; resentment led to HARTFORD CONVENTION. Congregational church disestablished by new state constitution (1818). Mfg. grew steadily after decline of shipping. Conn. inventors include Eli WHITNEY. Two world wars greatly expanded industries. SW Conn. has suburbs of New York city.

Connecticut, largest river in New England, c.350 mi. long, rising in lakes in extreme N N.H. and flowing S along Vt.-N.H. line, then across Mass. (past Springfield) and Conn. (past Hartford) to Long Isl. Sound at Old Saybrook. Upper course used for power. Lower valley is good farm land. Great damage done by 1936 flood and 1938 hurricane. Congress authorized flood-control project 1936.

Connecticut, University of: see MANSFIELD, Conn.

Connecticut College: see NEW LONDON, Conn.

Connecticut Lakes, three lakes, N N.H.; source of Connecticut R.

Connecticut Reserve: see WESTERN RESERVE.

Connecticut Wits or **Hartford Wits,** literary group (late 18th–early 19th cent.), mostly Yale men. Attacked anti-Federalists. Representative were Joel BARLOW, Timothy DWIGHT, Theodore DWIGHT, John TRUMBULL.

Connellsville, city (pop. 13,293), SW Pa., on Youghiogheny R. and SE of Pittsburgh; settled c.1770. Mfg. of coke, metal products, and glass. H. C. Frick was attacked here during Homestead strike (1892).

Connelly, Marc(us Cook), 1890–, American dramatist. His Pulitzer Prize play, *The Green Pastures* (1930) is based on Roark Bradford's *Ol' Man Adam an' His Chillun.*

Connemara (kŏnümä'rü), wild, mountainous region, W Co. Galway, Ireland. Has many lakes and streams.

Connersville, city (pop. 15,550), E Ind., on Whitewater R. and E of Indianapolis; laid out 1817. Rail center. Mfg. of metal and enamel products.

Connolly, James, 1870–1916, Irish republican leader and socialist. In U.S. (1903–10) helped to organize the I.W.W. but for Ireland believed that the nationalist cause came before socialism.

Conolly, John, 1794–1866, English physician, who introduced humane treatment of insane at Hanwell Asylum, where he abolished mechanical restraints.

Conon (kō'nŏn), d. after 392 B.C., Athenian commander in the Peloponnesian War. The fleet under his command was defeated at Aegospotamos (405 B.C.), but later with Persian help he defeated the Spartans off Cnidus (394 B.C.). When Persian favor turned toward Sparta, Conon's fortune fell.

Conon, 3d cent. B.C., Greek astronomer.

Conowingo Dam, NE Md., on Susquehanna R., 4,648 ft. long and 105 ft. high, completed 1927. Here is Conowingo village. Conowingo L. extends 14 mi. N.

Conrad, rulers of Holy Roman Empire. **Conrad I,** d. 918, duke of Franconia, elected German king 911. Unable to impose his authority on great feudal dukes. Designated his ablest foe, Henry the Fowler (Henry I), as successor. **Conrad II,** c.990–1039, duke of Franconia, elected German king 1024, crowned emperor 1027. Suppressed several revolts of his vassals; annexed kingdom of ARLES or Burgundy (1033); intervened energetically in Italian troubles (1026–27, 1035–37); promoted lesser nobility and officials of low birth to affirm his authority in Germany and Italy. **Conrad III,** c.1093–1152, German king (1138–52); nephew of Henry V and founder of the HOHENSTAUFEN dynasty. Antiking to LOTHAIR II from 1127. Warred against Guelphs (see GUELPHS AND GHIBELLINES). Took part in Second Crusade. **Conrad IV,** 1228–54, German king (1237–54), king of Sicily and Jerusalem (1250–54); son of Emperor FREDERICK II. Several antikings challenged his rule in Germany after 1246 and in Italy after 1251, in both cases at the behest of Pope INNOCENT IV, his implacable enemy, who excommunicated him in 1254. His son CONRADIN was the last of the Hohenstaufen to rule.

Conrad, d. 1192, king of Jerusalem (1192), marquis of Montferrat, leader in Third Crusade. Saved Tyre from the Saracens and became its lord (1187). Sought to displace Guy of LUSIGNAN as king by marrying Isabella, daughter of Amalric I. Acknowledged king, he was mysteriously assassinated. Title passed to two later husbands of Isabella—Henry, count of Champagne (reigned 1192–97), and Amalric II.

Conrad, Joseph, 1857–1924, Polish-born English novelist, originally Teodor Jozef Konrad Korzeniowski. A sailor, he became an officer in the British merchant fleet and a British citizen; after retirement in 1894 wrote novels and short stories in English, with notable, fluid style. Among his novels (laid mostly in South Seas, Malaya, and Indonesia) are *Almayer's Folly* (1895), *An Outcast of the Islands* (1896), *The Nigger of the "Narcissus"* (pub., 1897, as *The Children of the Sea*), *Lord Jim* (1900), *Typhoon* (1903), *Victory* (1915), *The Arrow of Gold* (1919). Most celebrated short story "Youth." His chief theme is demoralizing effect of isolation.

Conradi, Hermann (hĕr'män kônrä'dē), 1862–90, German author, leading exponent of naturalist school. Best known for *Lieder eines Sünders* [songs of a sinner] (1887) and *Adam Mensch* (1889).

Conradin (kŏn'rŭdĭn), 1252–68, duke of Swabia, last legitimate Hohenstaufen; son of Conrad IV. Claimed Sicily after death of his uncle MANFRED. Defeated by Charles of Anjou (Charles I of NAPLES) at Tagliacozzo; beheaded at Naples.

Conrad the Red, d. 955, duke of Lorraine (944–53). Conspired against his father-in-law, Otto I, allied himself with invading Magyars (954), but later submitted and died fighting Magyars on Lechfeld.

Conrad von Hötzendorf, Franz, Graf (fränts' gräf' kôn'rät fŭn hût'sûndôrf), 1852–1925, Austro-Hungarian field marshal. Chief of staff 1906–11, 1912–17. Fanatic promoter of war on Serbia.

Conroe (kŏn'rō), city (pop. 7,298), S Texas, NNW of Houston. Center of oil and timber area, it has recycling and carbon-black plants.

Conscience, Hendrik (kōsēās'), 1812–23, Flemish novelist, a founder of modern Flemish literature. His works include historical novels (e.g., *The Lion of Flanders*, 1838) and stories of village life (e.g., *Ricke ticke tack*, 1851).

conscientious objector, person who, on grounds of membership in a pacific sect or personal ethical views, passively resists military service. Democracies in world wars faced problem concerning them: how to uphold both personal freedom and authority of the state. U.S. and Great Britain allowed objectors of recognized sects to enter noncombat service, but segregated or imprisoned others.

consciousness, in general a person's awareness of the environment; more specifically, the manner in which he is aware. Freudian psychology distinguishes the conscious (actual awareness) from unconscious (store of experience not recognized by individual). Sometimes consciousness is used to mean the sum of self-understood activities that constitute individual personality.

conscription, compulsory enrollment of personnel for service in the armed forces, as opposed to voluntary service. Enforced service was known from the earliest days of history and was customary in Greece and Rome. The first modern national law conscripting soldiers was, however, that adopted in the French Revolution. In the course of the 19th cent. the practice was adopted in most major European nations. Great Britain accepted conscription in World War I. In the U.S., conscription was practiced on a large scale in the Civil War (see SELECTIVE SERVICE; UNIVERSAL MILITARY TRAINING).

conservation of energy: see ENERGY.

conservation of natural resources, prevention of waste of man's physical environment, including wildlife, timber, fertile topsoil, and pasture. Conservation long practiced in Europe, was forwarded in U.S. by creation of a U.S. commissioner of fish and fisheries (1871), a forestry bureau (1891), the National Conservation Commission (1909), and the National Park Service (1916). Theodore Roosevelt and Gifford Pinchot outstanding leaders. New Deal forwarded conservation with CCC, TVA, and water-control programs.

Conservative party, British political party, continuation of TORY group which began at end of 17th cent. Name first popularized in 1830. Tory reformers George Canning and Robert PEEL killed old reactionary Tory party by Reform Bill of 1832. Party split over corn laws issue, 1846. Returned to power 1874–80, revitalized by "Tory democracy" and imperialism program of DISRAELI. In office 1885–1905 (with two brief intervals), it split over tariff reforms of Joseph CHAMBERLAIN, with consequent Liberal ascendancy until World War I coalition. Aside from Labour victories in 1924 and 1929 party maintained leadership (1922–40) despite appeasement policies. World War II brought new coalition under Conservative Winston Churchill. After 1945–51 Labour government, Conservatives returned to power under Churchill.

Conshohocken, borough (pop. 10,922), SE Pa., on Schuylkill R. and NW of Philadelphia; settled 1831. Mfg. of steel, automobile tires, and metal products.

Considérant, Victor Prosper (vēktôr' prōspâr' kōsēdārä'), 1808–93, French social theorist and reformer, follower of Fourier.

conspiracy, agreement of two or more persons to commit a criminal or unlawful act, with some overt words or acts to that end. In medieval England conspiracy was only a combination to abuse judicial procedure; later meaning was broader. Some acts lawful when done by an individual are illegal if the aim of a conspiracy. Under this doctrine labor unions were long prosecuted for strikes but later legislation in Great Britain (1875) and U.S. (Norris-LaGuardia Act, 1932) halted this practice.

Constable, John, 1776–1837, English painter, famous for landscapes. *The Hay Wain* created sensation 1824 at Louvre and is said to have profoundly impressed Delacroix. Used broken color with freedom extraordinary in his day. Admired classical painting but worked directly from nature.

Constance, 1152–98, consort of Emperor HENRY VI; mother of Emperor FREDERICK II. Her nephew, William II of Sicily, named her as his successor, but the Sicilians crowned TANCRED instead. Warfare resulted between Tancred and Henry, who was crowned at Palermo after Tancred's death (1194).

Constance, Ger. *Konstanz*, city (pop. 42,209), S Baden, SW Germany, at W end of L. of Constance. Textile and clothing mfg. Founded as Roman fort 4th cent. A.D.;

episcopal see from c.580; made free imperial city 1192. Here in 1183 Emperor Frederick I recognized LOMBARD LEAGUE. At Council of Constance John Huss was burned (1415). In 1548 Charles V punished Constance for joining SCHMALKALDIC LEAGUE by abrogating its freedom and awarding it to Austria. City passed to Baden 1805; bishopric was secularized 1802–3; diocese was abolished 1827. Among many historical buildings are the 11th-cent. minster and the Dominican convent where the council was held (now a hotel).

Constance, Council of, 1414–18, council of the Roman Catholic Church, in part considered ecumenical. It was called to end the Great SCHISM, which had produced three rival popes: GREGORY XII (since considered canonical, i.e., legal), John XXIII (see COSSA, BALDASSARRE), and Benedict XIII (see LUNA, PEDRO DE). It also was intended to reform the Church and end heresy. The conciliar theory (that councils are superior to the pope) was actively advanced, and the council was organized on national lines. Gregory resigned, John and Benedict were deposed, and MARTIN V was named pope. Measures of reform were adopted but were rather inconsequential. John HUSS, who had come to the council with a safe-conduct of Emperor SIGISMUND, was nevertheless burned at the stake for heresy (1415), as was JEROME OF PRAGUE the next year. The rulings on the power of councils were never effective.

Constance, Lake of, Ger. *Bodensee,* lake, 208 sq. mi., bordered by Switzerland, Germany, and Austria. Formed by the Rhine, it divides near Constance into two arms. Remains of lake dwellings have been found.

Constans (kŏn'stănz), Roman and Byzantine emperors. **Constans I,** b. 320 or 323, d. 350; youngest son of Constantin I. Shared empire with his brothers CONSTANTINE II and CONSTANTIUS II upon his father's death (337). His vices and extortions led to his murder. **Constans II,** 630–68, Byzantine emperor (642–68). Forbade discussion of MONOTHELETISM; arrested and banished Pope Martin I. Fought Moslems successfully; reorganized imperial administration. Was assassinated.

Constant (de Rebecque), Benjamin (bĕzhämē' kŏstä' dù rûbĕk'), 1767–1830. French author and political theorist, b. Switzerland. His liaison with Mme de STAËL (1794–1809) was a tempestuous one. An advocate of constitutional monarchy, he generally opposed but occasionally supported both Napoleon and the Bourbons. His reputation as a writer rests on the introspective and quasi-autobiographical short novel *Adolph* (1816; Eng. tr., 1908). A similar novel, *Cécile,* was first published 1951.

Constant, (Jean Joseph) Benjamin (bĕzhämē' kŏstä'), 1845–1902, French painter. His Oriental scenes, influenced by a journey to Morocco, are remarkable in color, drama, and technique. Did portraits (e.g., Queen Victoria, Queen Alexandra).

Constant, Paul Henri Benjamin, baron d'Estournelles de: see ESTOURNELLES DE CONSTANT.

Constanta (kônstän'tsä), city (pop. 78,586), SE Rumania, in Dobruja; chief Rumanian Black Sea port. Oil pipeline to Ploesti. Founded 4th cent. A.D. by Constantine I.

Constantine (kŏn'stŭntēn, –tīn), Roman and Byzantine emperors. **Constantine I** (the Great), 288?–337, son of CONSTANTIUS I and St. HELENA. Though proclaimed emperor on his father's death at York (306), he was content with the title Caesar until the death of GALERIUS (310), which left four contestants for the imperial office. In the ensuing struggle, Constantine and LICINIUS joined against MAXENTIUS and MAXIMIN, whom they overwhelmed in 312. They then ruled as co-emperors (Constantine in the West, Licinius in the East) until they fell out in 324; Licinius lost his life in the struggle, leaving Constantine sole emperor. Constantine, already attracted by Christianity, had allegedly seen a flaming cross in the sky as the sign by which he would conquer just before his crucial victory at the MILVIAN BRIDGE (312). In 313 he and Licinius established toleration for Christianity by the Edict of Milan. His interest in Christianity continued, though he was baptized only on his deathbed, and in 325 he convened the epoch-making Council of NICAEA. In a reign of peace he rebuilt the empire on a basis of absolutism. He shifted his cap. to CONSTANTINOPLE (330), which he dedicated to the Virgin. At his death he divided the empire among his sons CONSTANS I, CONSTANTIUS II, and **Constantine II,** 316–40, who received Britain, Gaul, and Spain. Feeling cheated in the division, he warred with Constans I, but was killed while invading Italy. **Constantine IV** (Pogonatus), d. 685, Byzantine emperor (668–85). Answered annual naval attacks of Moslems with GREEK FIRE; ceded land S of the Danube to Bulgars after being defeated by them (679); called Third Council of CONSTANTINOPLE (680). **Constantine V** (Copronymus), 718–75, Byzantine emperor (740–75). Able administrator. His rigorous support of ICONOCLASM caused Pope Stephen III to transfer Rome to protection of Pepin the Short. **Constantine VI,** b. c.770, Byzantine emperor (780–97). His mother IRENE was regent, then co-empress (792). In 797 she took advantage of his unpopularity to have him deposed and blinded. **Constantine VII** (Porphyrogenitus), 905–59, Byzantine emperor. His reign (912–59) was interrupted by usurpation of ROMANUS I (919–44). Fostered learning and legal reform. Was a scholar and assiduous writer. **Constantine XI** (Paleologus), d. 1453, last Byzantine emperor (1448–53). Proclaimed union of E and W churches to secure aid from West against Turks (1452). No help came. In 1453 he defended Constantinople for two months against the 20 times superior army of Mohammed II. Died fighting when Turks stormed city.

Constantine, 1868–1923, king of the Hellenes (1913–17, 1920–22). Opposed Premier VENIZELOS in World War I; was forced to abdicate by Allied pressure (1917). Recalled in 1920, he was again deposed after the Turks defeated the Greeks at Smyrna.

Constantine, fortified city (pop. 80,233), E Algeria; a major trade center. Originally a

Carthaginian settlement. As Cirta it was cap. of Numidia and vital shipping point in Roman grain supply. Destroyed A.D. 311 in civil war; rebuilt by Constantine I. Taken 1837 by the French.

Constantine, Donation of, document supposed to be a grant by Constantine I of great temporal authority in Italy to the pope. It actually was forged, presumably to enhance papal claims to territory to build what became the Papal States. In practice it had no great effect, but it was important in giving Lorenzo Valla the chance to demonstrate critical methods in proving it false, and his firm, clear argument is called the beginning of modern textual criticism.

Constantine the African, c.1020–c.1087, translator of Arabic works (esp. on medicine) into Latin.

Constantinople, former capital of the Byzantine and Ottoman empires (for modern city, see ISTANBUL). Founded by and named for CONSTANTINE I at ancient BYZANTIUM as new cap. of Roman Empire (A.D. 330), it shared the glory and vicissitudes of the Byzantine Empire, which was finally nearly identical with the city and environs. Only three of many sieges were successful: by the army of the Fourth Crusade (1204), by MICHAEL VIII (1261), and by Sultan Mohammed II (1453). Built upon seven hills on the Bosporus and surrounded by a triple wall of fortifications, it was the largest city of medieval Europe, a barbed fortress enclosing a sea of magnificent palaces and gilded domes and towers. At its greatest period (10th cent.) it had c.1,000,000 inhabitants. The Church of HAGIA SOPHIA, the sacred palace of the emperors, the huge hippodrome, and the Golden Gate were its best-known monuments. Its artistic and literary wealth before it was sacked (1204; 1453) was almost inconceivable. Nearly depopulated when it fell to the Turks, it soon revived under the Sultans (whose court was called the Sublime Porte) as a great European center. After World War I it was occupied by the Allies (1918–23). Ankara replaced it as Turkish cap. in 1923.

Constantinople, Councils of, 2d, 5th, 6th, and 8th ecumenical councils of the Roman Catholic Church. **1** Convened (381) by Emperor Theodosius I to confirm the acts of the First Council of Nicaea, it is said to have composed the final Nicene Creed. Declared St. Gregory Nazianzen bishop of Constantinople and appointed his successor when he died. On death of St. Meletius made Flavian of Antioch president, thus prolonging Antiochene schism. Declared against various heresies, and made bishop of Constantinople second only to the pope. **2** Convened (553) by Emperor Justinian I and dominated by him, it condemned the Nestorian writings called the Three Chapters and seems also to have declared Pope Vigilius deposed. Its canons are lost. **3** Convened (680) by Emperor Constantine IV, it condemned the heresy of MONOTHELETISM and condemned several churchmen as Monothelites (including HONORIUS I—a point much discussed). The Oriental Council of 692, called by Justinian II, is considered in the East a continu-

ation of this council, but is called in the West the Trullan Synod [from Trullo, the dome of the palace]. It made the Apostolic Constitutions binding. **4** Convened (869) at the suggestion of Emperor Basil I, it confirmed the condemnation of PHOTIUS and the restoration of St. IGNATIUS OF CONSTANTINOPLE. It is not recognized by the Orthodox Church, which recognizes instead the council of 880 that supported Photius. The two councils mark the bitter division of Eastern and Western churches.

Constantinople, Latin Empire of, 1204–61, feudal empire established in S Balkans and Greek archipelago by leaders of Fourth Crusade (see CRUSADES). It was modeled on Latin Kingdom of JERUSALEM. BALDWIN I, HENRY OF FLANDERS, ROBERT OF COURTENAY, JOHN OF BRIENNE, and BALDWIN II were rulers. It deteriorated at once after its creation, beset by Greek rulers of NICAEA and EPIRUS, by the Bulgars under IVAN II, by the Turks, and by internal discord. Constantinople was taken by MICHAEL VIII, who restored the Byzantine Empire (1261), but Venice retained most of Greek isles; ATHENS passed to Catalins; Achaia was kept by VILLEHARDOUIN family.

Constantius (kŭnstăn'shŭs), name of several Roman emperors. **Constantius I,** c.250–306, was a general who put away St. Helena (mother of CONSTANTINE I) to marry the daughter of Maximian and become (293) subemperor under Maximian. He was successful as commander in Gaul and Britain. When Diocletian and Maximian abdicated (305), he and Galerius became emperors, but the next year he died at York. Constantine took up his claim. **Constantius II,** 317–61, was the son of Constantine I. After 337 he shared the empire with his brothers, CONSTANS I and CONSTANTINE II. Constantine was killed in 340, Constans I murdered in 350. Constantius put down revolt and held sole rule. He advocated ARIANISM. Trouble in Gaul and in Persia caused Constantius to rely on his cousin and general Julian (JULIAN THE APOSTATE), but Julian's men revolted against Constantius, who died on the journey to quell them. **Constantius III,** d. 421, was a general of Honorius. After the murder of his rival ATAULF, he married Ataulf's widow and the emperor's sister, GALLA PLACIDIA. In 421 he became joint emperor but died in a few months.

Constellation, U.S. frigate, launched in 1797. Won victories over French frigates *Insurgente* (Feb., 1799) and VENGEANCE (Feb., 1800). Made a stationary ship at Newport, R.I. (1894).

constellation (kŏnstĭlā'shŭn), originally a configuration formed by a group of stars. The meaning was later extended to refer to 88 areas (boundaries officially estab. 1928) filling sky, in terms of which heavenly bodies are located. Brighter stars are designated (according to Bayer's system), usually in order of brightness, by Greek letters and Latin genitive of constellation in which they lie, e.g., Alpha Tauri, brightest star in Taurus. See also ZODIAC.

Constitution, U.S. 44-gun frigate, nicknamed *Old Ironsides,* launched 1797; perhaps the most famous U.S. naval vessel. Won great sea battle with British vessel *Guerrière* on Aug. 19, 1812. Rebuilt by public subscription in 1925; maintained at Boston navy yard.

constitution, the fundamental principles of government in a nation, either implied in its laws, institutions, and customs or embodied in one document or in several. In the first category is the British constitution; it is termed *flexible*, for it may be modified by an ordinary act of Parliament or by judicial decisions. The **Constitution of the United States** is classified as *rigid*—one that has superior sanction to ordinary laws of the land and that is subject to a gradual process of AMENDMENT. Statutory elaboration and judicial construction (see SUPREME COURT, UNITED STATES, and MARSHALL, JOHN) have been erected on the base of the written document drawn up at the FEDERAL CONSTITUTIONAL CONVENTION (1787). The Constitution (see FEDERALIST PAPERS; MADISON, JAMES), signed on Sept. 17, 1787, and ratified by the required number of states (nine) by June 21, 1788, superseded original charter of U.S. in force since 1781 (see CONFEDERATION, ARTICLES OF) and estab. system of Federal government which began to function in 1789. The Constitution's brevity and its general statement of principles have, by accident more than by design, made possible the extension of meaning that has fostered growth. There are but seven articles and a Preamble; 22 amendments have been adopted. The Preamble's first words, "We the People of the United States," have been used against STATES' RIGHTS advocates. Another phrase of the Preamble, "to . . . promote the general Welfare," has been used to uphold much recent social legislation. The articles set up the legislative, executive, and judicial branches of government and provide for their powers; they also handle problems of the relationships of the states to the Federal government. The first nine amendments, which constitute the Bill of Rights (Tenth Amendment generally considered a part), were added within two years as a result of widespread feeling that Constitution insufficiently guaranteed individual liberties. Remaining amendments provide for matters ranging from income tax to woman suffrage.

Constitutional Convention: see FEDERAL CONSTITUTIONAL CONVENTION.

Constitutional Union party, in U.S. history, organized just before election of 1860. Recognized "no political principle but the Constitution of the country, the union of the states and the enforcement of laws." Ticket of John Bell and Edward Everett carried Ky., Tenn., and Va. in the election.

Constitution Island, N.Y.: see WEST POINT.

Constitution of the United States: see CONSTITUTION.

Constitutions, Apostolic, late 4th-cent. compilation of rules for clergy and laity in the Church, supposedly by the Apostles, but actually including apocryphal letters and most of the Didache. Declared binding by the continuation of the Third Council of CONSTANTINOPLE.

consubstantiation: see LORD'S SUPPER.

consul, title of two chief magistrates of anc. Rome. Office supposed to have originated 510 B.C. and was the supreme office in the republic, with control over the army and the treasury as well as civil affairs. Consular elections were the crucial points of political life. At first only patricians could be consuls, but after 367 B.C., plebeians were eligible. Normally a man served as quaestor, aedile, and praetor before running for the consulate. The Roman years were identified by the names of the consuls. Office became nominal under the Roman Empire.

consular service, organized body of agents maintained by a government at foreign ports and trade centers to protect its nationals and their interests, especially in commercial affairs. In U.S., Rogers Act of 1924 united consular and diplomatic services in Foreign Service of Dept. of State. Consuls and consulates enjoy immunity and EXTERRITORIALITY.

Consulate, 1799–1804, French government established after coup d'état of 18 BRUMAIRE. The three consuls were Bonaparte (see NAPOLEON I), Cambacérès, and C. F. Lebrun. Bonaparte, the actual ruler, was made First Consul for life in 1802, emperor in 1804.

Consumers' League, National, estab. in U.S. (1899) to forward movement begun (1890) in England to educate consumers to buy only goods made under good working conditions.

consumption, in economics, use of wealth to satisfy needs or destruction to create new wealth. Production and consumption, closely linked, form the foundation of modern capitalist economy.

consumption, in medicine: see TUBERCULOSIS.

contagious abortion: see BRUCELLOSIS.

contagious diseases: see COMMUNICABLE DISEASES.

contempt of court, in basic meaning interference with the functioning of a court. Criminal contempts are those that lessen the dignity of a court or tend to limit a judge's freedom of action (e.g., defying a judge or creating disorder in courtroom). Indirect criminal contempts are acts prejudicial to justice committed outside court. Civil contempts are primarily injuries to private parties occasioned by disobeying a DECREE or court order.

Conti (kôtē'), French princely family, cadet branch of house of Bourbon. Founded by **Armand de Bourbon, prince de Conti** (ärmä' dù bōōrbō'), 1629–66, brother of the Great CONDÉ, whom he at first assisted during the FRONDE. Reconciled with the court (1653), he married a niece of Mazarin and held a command in war against Spain. A protector of Molière. Later turned to mysticism, lived in retirement. His great-grandson, **Louis François de Bourbon, prince de Conti** (lwē' fräswä'), 1717–76, fought with distinction in War of the Austrian Succession but displeased Mme de Pompadour and lost favor at court. Sided with parlement against Maupeou. Friend of Rousseau.

continent, largest unit of land mass. The continents are Eurasia (Europe and Asia), Africa, North America, South America, Australia, and Antarctica. Including fringe islands, they comprise c.29% of the total surface of the earth. Average land height in all is c.2,700 ft. above sea level, with highest known point Mt. Everest, over 29,000 ft. According to isostatic theory the floor under the oceans and extending under continents is composed of heavy basaltic rock and the continents are of lighter granitic rock; the balance between continent heights and ocean depths is called *isostasy*.

Continental Congress, 1774–89, Federal legislature of Thirteen Colonies and later of U.S. in American Revolution and under Articles of Confederation. First Continental Congress (Sept. 5–Oct. 26, 1774) sent petitions of colonial grievances to the king. Second Continental Congress, meeting May 10, 1775, created Continental Army and adopted Declaration of Independence on July 4, 1776. Though Congress under Articles of Confederation was shackled by weaknesses of Federal structure, it passed Ordinance of 1787.

Continental Divide, "backbone" of a continent. In North America the great ridge of the Rocky Mts. separates streams flowing W from those flowing E. Sometimes called Great Divide, a name occasionally used for the whole Rocky Mt. system.

Continental System, scheme of economic warfare adopted by Napoleon I against England. Began with BERLIN DECREE (1806); intensified by Milan Decree (1807) and other measures. All trade with Britain was forbidden, even to neutrals. Britain replied with ORDERS IN COUNCIL, seizure of neutral Danish fleet, and bombardment of Copenhagen. English naval supremacy made enforcement of system impossible. Russian refusal to abide by system led to Napoleon's disastrous 1812 campaign.

contrabassoon: see WIND INSTRUMENTS.

contract, agreement binding parties to it to perform, or to refrain from, some specific act or acts. Form usually an offer submitted by one party and accepted by the other in a reasonable time or in a stipulated period by word or act, explicitly or implicitly. To make a valid contract the parties must be mentally sound and of legal age and must be acting with free will. It must also comply with the Statute of Frauds; certain classes of contracts must be in writing and signed. In some American states all contracts must involve a consideration (something of value, however slight, even a promise to do something) given by one party to induce the other to perform something. In modern industrial society contract law has been of ever-increasing importance.

contract bridge: see BRIDGE.

contraction, in physics: see EXPANSION.

contraction, in writing: see ABBREVIATION.

Contreras (kōntrā′räs), village, central Mexico, near Mexico city. On Aug. 19–20, 1847, American forces under Gen. Winfield Scott fought Mexican forces under Santa Anna here and at Churubusco in one of most important battles of Mexican War.

convection, form of heat transmission in liquids and gases. It depends on decrease of density with rise in temperature. Hotter parts of fluid move through rest. When liquid is heated in a container, the hotter part rises to the surface and its place is taken by cooler part. Thus convection current is started. Heat is transferred from point to point in fluids by this current. Convection currents that are set up when the earth's atmosphere is heated by warm land areas cause cloud formation and rain.

convulsion, spasmodic muscular contraction. May accompany toxic conditions and nervous disorders. In young children it may result from tetany or sudden high fever. Stimulating mechanism is obscure.

Conway, Sir Martin (Baron Conway of Allington), 1856–1937, English mountain climber, an art critic. Led exploring expeditions to Spitsbergen (1896–97) and the Bolivian Andes (1898).

Conway, Thomas, 1733–c.1800?, Irish soldier of fortune, general in Continental Army in American Revolution. Gave name to Conway Cabal (1777), intrigue to remove Washington as army commander in favor of Horatio Gates. Letter by Conway criticizing Washington was basis of abortive and cloudy scheme.

Conway. 1 City (pop. 8,610), central Ark., NW of Little Rock. Trade center for cotton, livestock, and poultry area. Seat of Hendrix Col. (Methodist; coed.; 1876). **2** Winter resort town (pop. 4,109), E N.H., at junction of Swift and Saco rivers. Includes Conway village (pop. 1,238) and North Conway, resort and art colony. **3** Town (pop. 6,073), E S.C., on Waccamaw R. and SE of Florence, in agr. area. Tourist center with hunting and fishing.

Conway Cabal: see CONWAY, THOMAS.

cony or coney, name for rabbit (*Oryctolagus*) and its fur; for pika (*Ochotona*), small highaltitude rodent of both hemispheres; and for hyrax (*Procavia*), herbivorous, hoofed animal of Arabia, Syria, Africa.

Cooch Behar, India: see BENGAL.

Cook, Frederick Albert, 1865–1940, American explorer. Accompanied various polar expeditions. Claimed scaling of Mt. McKinley (1906) and reaching of North Pole (1908). Accused of fraud by Robert E. Peary, deprived of honors, but remained controversial figure. Later he was involved in oilfield swindle; was imprisoned (1925–30).

Cook, James, 1728–79, English explorer and navigator. Circumnavigated globe (1768–71) while charting transit of Venus; also explored New Zealand and E Australian coasts. On expedition to S Pacific (1772–75), he disproved rumor of great southern continent and prevented scurvy by dietary and hygienic measures. Led futile search for Pacific-Atlantic passage through North America. Rediscovered Sandwich Isls. (1778). Killed by Hawaiian natives.

Cook, Thomas, 1808–92, English founder of travel agency which bears his name. His most spectacular achievement was transport of 18,000 men up the Nile in 1884 for attempted relief of Gen. Gordon.

Cook, Mount, 12,349 ft. high, on W South Isl., New Zealand; highest in New Zealand.

Cooke, Jay, 1821–1905, American financier. Marketed Civil War loans of Federal government. Failure in financing of Northern Pacific Railway helped precipitate panic of 1873.

Cooke, John Esten, 1830–86, American novelist, author of novels on Va. and the Civil War (notably *Surry of Eagle's Nest,* 1866).

cookery, developed at early stage of history; making of bread, butter, cheese, wine came close upon start of agr. and herding. Ancient Greeks made art of gastronomy; Rome under the empire saw epicurean banquets and, later, was influenced by the Goths' simple tastes. Finest cooking in Middle Ages arose from need of monasteries to prepare ingenious dishes for fast days. Modern cookery derives from Renaissance Italy. French cuisine is characterized by finesse and the use of sauces, English by general simplicity; the U.S. cuisine includes borrowings from many lands as well as such native American foods as turkey, clam chowder, corn bread, pumpkin pie, gumbo. The findings obtained by research in chemistry, biology, nutrition, and other sciences contribute to modern cookery.

Cookeville, town (pop. 6,924), central Tenn., E of Nashville. Trade and industrial center in farm, timber, and coal area. Mfg. of clothing.

Cook Islands, formerly **Hervey Islands,** group (84 sq. mi.; pop. 12,380); with MANIHIKI group (pop. 14,519), S Pacific, SE of Samoa. Comprises volcanic islands of Rarotonga and Mangaia and six coral islets. Some were discovered 1773 by Capt. James Cook, others by John Williams in 1823. Made a British protectorate in 1888. Governed since 1901 by New Zealand. Export copra.

Cookworthy, William, 1705–80, English porcelain maker, first to make English porcelain similar to Chinese. In c.1755 discovered Cornish china clay near St. Austell, Cornwall.

Coolidge, Calvin, 1872–1933, 29th President of the United States (1923–29). Governor of Mass. (1919–20). Decision to use militia in a Boston police strike in 1919 brought national prominence. Vice President of U.S. (1921–23); became President after death of Warren G. Harding. Known for his New England simplicity and personal honesty; had strong popular backing. Opposed agr. price-fixing and strongly favored laissez-faire policy toward business, economy in government, and tax cuts.

Coolidge, town (pop. 4,306), E Ariz., near Casa Grande Natl. Monument, SW of Florence, in cotton and alfalfa area. **Coolidge Dam** (built 1927–28) in Gila R., SE of Globe, c.250 ft. high and c.900 ft. long, is used for power. It forms San Carlos Reservoir irrigating 100,000 acres (half are Indian lands) around Florence, Casa Grande, and Coolidge.

coolie labor, unskilled Asiatic laborers. In 1830s and 1840s many Indian and Chinese laborers were taken to British and French colonies on five-year contracts. Practice continued, and coolies were taken to Latin America, U.S., and Canada. Conditions of contract and of work were bad. Chinese labor, much used in building railroads in

U.S., shut out by Chinese Exclusion Act of 1888.

cooling system. Many processes and engines while operating require cooling. Cylinder heat generated by internal-combustion engines damages parts if not counteracted, usually by circulating water or air. Blast furnaces, cupolas, gas generators, casting molds, etc., are cooled by water. Rapidly moving machinery is often cooled and lubricated by oil bath. Radial airplane engines expose maximum cylinder surface to cooling effect of air flow. Air-conditioning systems maintain desirable conditions of temperature, humidity, and cleanliness of the air indoors.

Coomaraswamy, Ananda Kentish (ä″nŭndä′ kĕn′tĭsh kōōmä″rŭswä′mē), 1877–1947, art historian, b. Ceylon. Largely responsible for great Far Eastern collection of Boston Mus. of Fine Arts.

Cooper, (Alfred) Duff, 1890–, British statesman. A Conservative, he served after 1935 as secretary of state for war and then first lord of the admiralty in the coalition cabinet, resigning in 1938 to protest the Munich Pact. Was later minister of information under Churchill and ambassador to France (1944–47). Author of distinguished biographies. Created Viscount Norwich of Aldwick in 1952.

Cooper, Anthony Ashley: see SHAFTESBURY.

Cooper, Sir Astley Paston, 1768–1841, English surgeon, noted for operations on hernia and aneurysms, and for anatomy lectures and surgical treatises.

Cooper, Hugh Lincoln, 1865–1937, American hydraulic engineer for Dneproges power plant, Ukraine, plants at Keokuk, Iowa, and Niagara Falls, and Wilson Dam project.

Cooper, James Fenimore, 1789–1851, American novelist, the first to gain world reputation. Son of a wealthy landowner, who founded Cooperstown on Otsego L. on the N.Y. frontier, he spent five years in naval service, then became a country gentleman. Entering on a literary career when he was 30, he was a highly prolific writer. Of his many novels best known and best loved are his adventurous stories of frontiersmen and Indians, notably the *Leatherstocking Tales* (in order of the narrative: *The Deerslayer,* 1841; *The Last of the Mohicans,* 1826; *The Pathfinder,* 1840; *The Pioneers,* 1823; *The Prairie,* 1827); his sea stories (e.g., *The Pilot,* 1823; *The Red Rover,* 1828); and his historical novels, especially on the American Revolution (e.g., *The Spy,* 1821; his first success). He was an apologist for American democracy, but after several years (1826–33) in Europe he returned to the U.S. and became a mordant critic of the shortcomings of U.S. democracy in action—in satires, polemical works, and novels. His last years were embittered by an excessive number of lawsuits, which he launched to protect himself from his detractors and his lands from invading settlers. Among his works of history is a controversial but excellent history of the U.S. navy (1839).

Cooper, Myles, c.1735–1785, second president of King's College (now Columbia Univ.),

b. England. A Loyalist, he fled to England in 1775.

Cooper, Peter, 1791–1883, American inventor, industrialist, and philanthropist. Built the *Tom Thumb,* first railway locomotive to be used successfully on an American railroad (1830). Helped develop national and international telegraph. Led in securing public school system in New York city. COOPER UNION was built to provide education for working classes. Cooper was GREENBACK PARTY presidential candidate 1876.

Cooper, Thomas, 1759–1839, American scientist, b. London, an associate of Joseph Priestley. Also was a Jeffersonian in politics; convicted of violating Alien and Sedition Acts. Taught at Dickinson Col. and Univ. of Pennsylvania. President of South Carolina Col. 1820–34.

Cooper, river: see CHARLESTON, S.C.

cooperative, voluntary association of people for self-management of economic enterprises. Consumers' cooperatives are organized for distribution of products cheaply, with no or few middlemen and little or no advertising. Cooperatives have operated in many fields—banking, housing, insurance, medicine, and marketing of agr. produce. Producer cooperatives, in which workers own the enterprise, are relatively few. Robert Owen in 19th cent. advocated cooperation, which became a movement in Britain with founding (1844) of the Rochdale Society. Cooperatives are numerous and highly successful in Scandinavian countries. Movement slow in U.S. until after World War I.

Co-operative Commonwealth Federation, Canadian political party, popularly known as CCF. Founded (1932) at Calgary, Alta., by representatives from farmer, labor, and socialist parties (largely of the W provinces) with aim of establishing a planned cooperative commonwealth in Canada. Regina Manifesto, issued at the party's first annual convention, outlines aims which include socialization of finance, social ownership of public utilities, and various welfare measures. J. S. Woodsworth was its first leader. M. J. Coldwell succeeded him. In 1944 the party secured a majority in Saskatchewan legislature and estab. first CCF government in Canada. CCF is represented in other provincial legislatures and in Canadian House.

Cooperstown, village (pop. 2,727), E central N.Y., W of Albany and on Susquehanna R. and Otsego L. James Fenimore Cooper lived here and described the region in *Leatherstocking Tales.* Tradition says that Abner DOUBLEDAY invented baseball here. Has Natl. Baseball Hall of Fame and Mus.

Cooper Union, in Manhattan borough of New York city; nonsectarian, coed.; opened 1859. Founded by Peter Cooper. Pioneered with evening art and engineering schools; day schools added in 1900. Abraham Lincoln made famous speech here in 1860.

Coorg (ko͞org), state (1,593 sq. mi.; pop. 229,-255), SW India, in W Ghats; cap. Macara.

Coos (ko͞os), island, the modern Kos. Acts 21.1.

Coosa (ko͞o'sŭ), navigable river, NW Ga. and E Ala. Formed by headstreams at Rome, Ga.; winds 286 mi. W and S to join Talla-

poosa R. and form Alabama R. above Montgomery. Three power dams in lower course.

Coos Bay (ko͞os), city (pop. 6,223), SW Oregon, on Coos Bay of the Pacific; founded 1854 as Marshfield, renamed 1944. Ships lumber, fish (esp. salmon).

coot, marsh bird of North America and Europe, related to the rail and crane. American coot or mud hen or marsh hen is slaty gray with black head and neck and white-marked wings. It swims and dives well; the feet are partially webbed.

copal (kō'pŭl), resin from certain tropical trees, a source of hard-surfaced lacquers and varnishes.

Copeau, Jacques (zhäk' kôpō'), 1879–1949, French theatrical producer. Director of influential Théâtre du Vieux-Colombier, in Paris, 1913–24.

Copenhagen (kō'pŭnhā"gŭn), Dan. *København,* city (pop. 765,580; with suburbs 1,-166,204), cap. of Denmark, on E Zealand and N Amager isls. and on the Oresund. Major fishing and naval port; commercial, industrial, cultural center. Shipyards; metallurgy; mfg. of COPENHAGEN WARE. First fortified 12th cent. and chartered 1254, Copenhagen became Danish cap. 1443. It resisted a long Swedish siege (1558–59). Treaty of Copenhagen (1660) confirmed Treaty of ROSKILDE. In 1807 the city was bombarded and nearly destroyed by the British, neutral Denmark having refused to surrender its fleet. Occupied 1940–45 by the Germans in World War II, Copenhagen was bombed by the Allies, but only the shipyards suffered damage. One of the handsomest cities of Europe, it has many famous landmarks, including the picturesque houses along the Nyhavn arm of the harbor; Kongens Nytorv, the central square, with the 17th-cent. Charlottenborg palace; Amalienborg Square, enclosed by four palaces—the present royal residence; the Cathedral Church of Our Lady; and Christiansborg palace (18th cent.), housing the Rigsdag, on moated Slotsholm isl. Most of the historic buildings were restored after 1807. University was founded 1479.

Copenhagen, battle of, 1801, naval engagement of the French Revolutionary Wars. Neutral Denmark having refused to comply with British rules on neutral navigation, an English fleet was sent into the Baltic under admirals Sir Hyde PARKER and Horatio NELSON. The Danish fleet, caught at the roadsteads of Copenhagen, was defeated after a hard battle.

Copenhagen ware, underglaze and overglaze pottery produced in Copenhagen since c.-1760. Fine tableware and fluted porcelain of blue Danish pattern (derived from Chinese) are produced by Royal Porcelain works. Animal and figure sculptures (in white underglaze porcelain) are distinctive products.

Copernicus, Nicholas (kōpûr'nĭkŭs), 1473–1543, Polish astronomer, founder of Copernican system on which modern astronomy is based. In his famed treatise *De revolutionibus orbium coelestium* (published 1543), he described the sun as the center of great system, with earth revolving around it.

Cophetua (kŏfĕ'chŏoù), legendary African king who wooed and won a beggar maid. Legend appears in a ballad in Thomas Percy's *Reliques of Ancient English Poetry* (3 vols., 1765).

Copland, Aaron, 1900–, American composer. His music has been influenced by jazz and other American types. He has written concert music in all forms and music for the films and radio. His ballets include *Billy the Kid* (1938), *Rodeo* (1942), and *Appalachian Spring* (1944). Among his important orchestral works are *El Salón México* (1936) and *A Lincoln Portrait* (1942).

Copley, John Singleton (kŏp'lē), 1738?–1815, American portrait painter, b. Boston. Settled c.1774 in London, where he enjoyed many honors. His reputation today rests mainly on his early American portraits, rather than on the more polished works of his English period.

Coppard, A(lfred) E(dgar), 1878–, English short-story writer and lyric poet. Both his stories (as in *Adam and Eve and Pinch Me*, 1921; *Selected Tales*, 1946) and his poems (as in *Collected Poems*, 1928; *Cherry Ripe*, 1935) are distinguished by fantasy, wit, and precise word choice.

Coppée, François (fräswä' kôpä'), 1842–1908, French Parnassian poet, noted for poems of sympathy for the underprivileged, as *Les Humbles* (1872).

Copper, river rising in Wrangell Mts., SE Alaska, and flowing c.300 mi. S through the Chugach Mts. to Gulf of Alaska. Copper taken by Indians from deposits near upper river attracted Russians and Americans. Copper River and Northwestern RR (built 1908–11) from Cordova to great Kennecott mine partly followed lower river; was abandoned 1938.

copper, common, malleable, ductile, relatively soft metallic element (symbol = Cu; see also ELEMENT, table). It is a good conductor, changes slowly in air, and resists dilute acids. Salt water causes it to corrode. Used in roofing; for utensils, coins, metalwork; in making electrical apparatus and wires; in alloys. Occurs free and in combination; refined by electrolysis. It was one of first metals known to man. See also BRONZE AGE.

Copper Age: see BRONZE AGE.

copperas (kŏ'pûrùs) or **green vitriol,** ferrous sulphate, a hydrous compound of iron, sulphur, and oxygen. It is a green, crystalline, water-soluble salt.

Copper Cliff, town (pop. 3,974), S Ont., Canada, SW of Sudbury. Has one of largest copper refineries in British Commonwealth. Adjoins smelters of International Nickel Co.

copperhead, poisonous snake of E U.S. It is 2–3 ft. long; has coppery head; body is brown with hourglass-shaped chestnut markings above, pinkish white with dark spots below. Bite is not often fatal.

Copperheads, in Civil War, reproachful term for Northerners sympathetic to South. Especially active in Ill., Ind., and Ohio. KNIGHTS OF THE GOLDEN CIRCLE was Copperhead secret society.

Coppermine, river, Mackenzie dist., Northwest Territories, Canada. Rises N of Great Slave

L. and flows 525 mi. NW to Coronation Gulf in Arctic Ocean.

copper pyrites: see CHALCOPYRITE.

Coppet (kôpā'), village, Vaud canton, SW Switzerland, on L. Geneva. Château was residence of Mme de Staël.

copra: see COCONUT.

Copt (kŏpt), member of native Christian group in Egypt that resisted conversion to Islam through the centuries. The **Coptic language** (now extinct) was the form of Egyptian spoken in early Christian times (see LANGUAGE, table). The **Coptic Church** officially holds to MONOPHYSITISM, which was declared a heresy by Orthodox and Roman Catholics in 451. It is in communion with the Church of Ethiopia, and its head, the patriarch of Alexandria, names the head of the Ethiopian church (the abuna). The ritual languages are Greek, Coptic, and Arabic. A few "Catholic Copts" are in communion with the pope.

copyright, property right in works of literature, art, and the like, comprising exclusive right of owner to dispose of his property as he wishes and forbid unauthorized use. Specific protection of literary property was very slow in development. The Bern Convention (1887) was adopted by many countries (not including U.S.) for mutual copyright recognition. A conference of 45 nations at Geneva in 1952 adopted a new Universal Copyright Convention, to come in force after 12 nations ratify it. Copyright in U.S. is under an act of 1909, with amendments; requires manufacture in U.S., is valid for 28 years, and may be renewed once.

Coquelin, Benoît Constant (bùnwä' kŏstä' kôklē'), 1841–1909, French actor. Acted for Comédie Française, his greatest role being Cyrano de Bergerac. Played with Bernhardt in *L'Aiglon*.

coquilla nut (kōkē'yù), hard fruit of Brazilian palm (*Attalea funifera*), used in cabinet work, etc. Tree yields stiff fiber used in brooms and ropes.

coral, small marine invertebrate usually living in a colony. The individuals, known as polyps, each consist of a jellylike body surrounded by a skeleton. They live only in warm seas, and exist in great variety. As a colony produces new polyps, the older members die and new layers build up on the dead skeletons. Wave action may pile up the coral material, helping to form **coral reefs.** A fringing reef is separated from the shore by a narrow lagoon; a barrier reef is farther out, enclosing a wide, deep lagoon; an atoll is a ring-shaped reef surrounding a circular lagoon. Coral (many colored) is much used in jewelry and bric-a-brac.

Coral Gables, residential and resort city (pop. 19,837), SE Fla., part of Greater Miami, on Biscayne Bay; planned and built during Fla. land boom of 1920s. Seat of Univ. of Miami (nonsectarian; coed.; chartered 1925, opened 1926), with Hispanic-American Inst. Tropical Park race track is near.

coral reefs: see CORAL.

Coral Sea, SW arm of the Pacific, E of Australia and SE of New Guinea, W of New Hebrides and New Caledonia. Battle of aircraft carriers here in 1942 ended by checking S expansion of the Japanese.

coral snake, poisonous snake of W Hemisphere, related to cobra. Found chiefly in Mexico, Central and South America. Two species in U.S.: coral or harlequin snake (*Micrurus fulvius*) of SE U.S. is c.2½ ft. long, with small blunt head, body ringed with bands of black and of red, with narrow yellow bands on either side of black; Sonoran coral snake (*M. euryxanthus*) found from Arizona to N Mexico.

Coraopolis (kô″rēŏ′pûlĭs), borough (pop. 10,-498), SW Pa., on Ohio R. and NW of Pittsburgh. Mfg. of metal products and glass.

Corbett, Harvey Wiley (kôr′bĭt), 1873–, American architect. With F. J. Helmle he designed the Bush Terminal Building (1920) in New York, one of the first impressive solutions in skyscraper design.

Corbett, James J(ohn), 1866–1933, American boxer. "Gentleman Jim" won heavyweight championship (1892) by knocking out John L. Sullivan, lost title (1897) to Robert Fitzsimmons.

Corbin, city (pop. 7,744), S Ky., NW of Middlesboro on old Wilderness Road. Shipping center of agr., timber, and coal area with mining and mfg. of clothing and food products.

Corbulo (kôr′byōŏlū), d. A.D. 67, Roman general. Under Claudius, Corbulo as legate in Germany built a still-used Meuse-Rhine canal. Later in Asia he defeated the Parthians at Artaxata and Tigranocerta. Still later his successes in Asia caused the jealousy of Nero, who forced him to commit suicide.

Corcoran, William Wilson, 1798–1888, American financier and art collector. Donor of Corcoran Gall. of Art, Washington, D.C., opened 1897.

Corcyra, Greek Ionian island: see CORFU.

Corday, Charlotte (shärlôt′ kôrdä′), 1768–93, French assassin. A sympathizer of GIRONDISTS, she gained admission to MARAT on false pretext, stabbed him in his bath. She was guillotined.

Cordele (kôrdēl′), city (pop. 9,462), S central Ga., SSW of Macon. Market and processing center for farm and timber area.

Cordeliers (kôrdûlyā′), French revolutionary club. Instrumental in destruction of GIRONDISTS (1793). Its early leaders, DANTON and DESMOULINS, were displaced by extreme leftists MARAT and HÉBERT. Suppressed by Robespierre 1794.

Cordilleras (kôrdĭ′lûrŭz), general name for mountain systems of W North America, from N Alaska through Canada, U.S., Mexico, and Panama. In U.S. they include Rocky Mts., ranges of Great Basin, Sierra Nevada, and Coast Ranges. In South America the range from Panama to Cape Horn is known locally as Cordillera de Los Andes.

cordite: see POWDER.

Córdoba, Francisco, Fernández de: see FERNÁNDEZ DE CÓRDOBA, FRANCISCO.

Córdoba, Gonzalo Fernández de: see FERNÁNDEZ DE CÓRDOBA, GONZALO.

Córdoba (kôr′dōvä), city (pop. 369,886), cap. of Córdoba prov., central Argentina; cultural and commercial center on E flank of Sierra de Córdoba at W margin of Pampa;

founded 1573. Dam on Río Primero furnishes hydroelectric power for industries. Popular tourist and health resort. University founded 1613.

Córdoba, city (pop. 17,865), Vera Cruz, E Mexico; founded 1618. Agr. area produces coffee, sugar, cotton, tropical fruits. Treaty establishing independence of Mexico was signed here (1821).

Córdoba or Cordova, city (pop. 351,644), cap. of Córdoba prov., S Spain, in Andalusia, on Guadalquivir R. Flourished under Romans; reached zenith as seat of Moorish emirate (later caliphate) under OMAYYAD dynasty (756–1031). Fell to emir of Seville 1078; to Ferdinand III of Castile 1236. Never regained its former glory but remained famous for its gold, silver, leather crafts. From Omayyad period, when Córdoba was a center of Moslem and Jewish cultures, date the cathedral (built as mosque in 8th cent.) and ruins of alcazar. Birthplace of Seneca, Lucan, Averroës, Maimonides.

Cordova (kôrdō′vû), town (pop. 1,165), S Alaska, port on Prince William Sound. Founded as terminus of Copper River and Northwestern RR to Kennecott copper mine, it declined with closing of mine and railroad (1938). Has fish cannery and cold storage plant.

Cordova, Spain: see CÓRDOBA.

Corelli, Arcangelo (ärkän′jälō kōrĕl′lē), 1653–1713, Italian composer and violinist. He developed the *concerto grosso.* Best known of his many sonatas are his variations on an air, *Folies d'Espagne.*

Corelli, Marie (kūrĕl′ē), 1855–1924, English novelist of Italian-Scottish parentage, educated in France. Her melodramatic novels in lush prose (e.g., *Thelma,* 1887; *Ardath,* 1889; *The Sorrows of Satan,* 1895) suited the popular taste of her day.

coreopsis (–ŏp′–) or **tickseed,** annual or perennial of genus *Coreopsis,* with yellow or yellow-red daisylike flowers. Some forms called calliopsis.

Corfu (kôr′fŏō, –fū), Gr. *Kerkyra,* Latin *Corcyra,* island (229 sq. mi.; pop. 106,593), Greece, second largest of Ionian Islands, separated by a narrow channel from Greek and Albanian coast. Rises to c.3,000 ft. at Mt. Pantokrator, but is largely a fertile agr. lowland. Livestock raising; fishing. Corfu has been identified with Scheria, home of Phaeacians in Homer's *Odyssey.* It was colonized by Corinth (8th cent. B.C.), and with Corinth helped found Epidamnus (see DURAZZO). Rivalry with Corinth over its control led to an alliance with Athens and helped precipitate PELOPONNESIAN WAR (431–404 B.C.). In 229 B.C. Corfu passed to Rome. It was seized repeatedly from the Byzantines by ROBERT GUISCARD and his successors; was held by Venice 1386–1797; shared later history of IONIAN ISLANDS. In 1923 Italy bombarded and occupied Corfu in reprisal for assassination of several Italian officers on Greek soil. Corfu Incident was ended when Italy, at behest of the other Great Powers, evacuated Corfu, and Greece apologized. In World War II, Corfu was again occupied by Italy. The island's cap., **Corfu** (pop. 30,739), is a commercial port.

The near-by Achilleion palace was built for Elizabeth of Austria.

Cori, Carl Ferdinand (kô′rē), 1896–, and his wife, **Gerty Theresa (Radnitz) Cori,** 1896–, American biochemists, who shared (with Houssay) the 1947 Nobel Prize in Physiology and Medicine for research on carbohydrate metabolism and enzymes. Both were associated with Washington Univ. from 1931.

coriander, aromatic herb (*Coriandrum sativum*). Yields oil used as flavoring, in medicine, and in liqueurs.

Corinth, Lovis (lô′vēs kô′rĭnt), 1858–1925, German impressionist painter.

Corinth (kŏ′rĭnth), Gr. *Korinthos,* city (pop. 12,715), Greece, in NE Peloponnesus; a port on Gulf of Corinth. Trades in silk, olive oil, fruits. Founded 1858 after destruction of Old Corinth by earthquake; rebuilt after another quake (1928). Old Corinth, 3 mi. SW of Corinth, is now a village (pop. 1,473). Strategically situated and protected by the ACRO-CORINTHUS, it was a wealthy, powerful, and cultured city of ancient Greece. A Dorian town existing from Homeric times, it became under PERIANDER and his successors a flourishing seapower and colonized Syracuse, Corfu, Potidaea. Rivalry with Athens and alliance with Sparta brought on the PELOPONNESIAN WAR (431–404 B.C.). After the Macedonian occupation Corinth led the ACHAEAN LEAGUE until its conquest and destruction by Rome (146 B.C.). Caesar restored it and reestablished the ISTHMIAN GAMES. Held by VILLEHARDOUIN family in the 13th cent., later by various Italian princes, Corinth fell to Turkey (1458), and to Venice (1687). Turkey recovered it 1714; lost it to Greek insurgents 1822. The **Gulf of Corinth,** an inlet of the Ionian Sea, 80 mi. long, 3–20 mi. wide, lies between central Greece (N) and the Peloponnesus (S), which are connected by the **Isthmus of Corinth,** 20 mi. long, 4–8 mi. wide. The isthmus is crossed by the ancient Isthmian Wall, repeatedly restored by Byzantine emperors to defend the Peloponnesus. Parallel to wall runs the Corinth Canel (built 1881–93; damaged in World War II), which connects Gulf of Corinth with Saronic Gulf.

Corinth, city (pop. 9,785), NE Miss., near Tenn. line. Farm trade and processing center. Strategic rail center in Civil War, captured by H. W. Halleck's Union troops after battle of SHILOH (May, 1862), and defended by Gen. Rosecrans against Confederates under Gens. Van Dorn and Price (Oct. 3–4, 1862).

Corinth, Gulf of: see CORINTH, Greece.
Corinth, Isthmus of: see CORINTH, Greece.
Corinthian order, latest and most ornate of the orders of architecture, reaching full development in the middle of the 4th cent. B.C. Little used by the Greeks, although the temple of Zeus at Athens (begun 2d cent. B.C. and completed by Hadrian 2d cent. A.D.) was the first great Corinthian temple. The Greek Corinthian column is more slender than the Ionic. Its capital, supposedly originated by Callimachus, is decorated with acanthus leaves. The Romans used the order in many works of imperial architecture. See *ill.,* p. 61.

Corinthians (kŭrĭn′thēŭnz), epistles of New Testament written to Christians at Corinth by St. Paul. First Corinthians, written probably early in A.D. 55, is one of longest and most important of epistles. It covers various aspects of Christian conduct, counsels against factionalism, incest, litigation, sensuality, and answers questions on marriage and celibacy. Contains many famous passages, e.g., institution of Eucharist (11.17–34); an eloquent panegyric on Christian love (13). Second Corinthians is shorter, written perhaps within a year of the other. Contains Paul's defense of his mission, citing his authority, and accounting for his actions.

Coriolanus (kŏ′rēŭlā′nŭs), legendary Roman patrician. The story goes that Coriolanus offered to give state grain to the starving people in return for abolition of the tribunate of the people. He was expelled from Rome. Joining the Volscians in an attack on Rome (possibly 491? B.C.), he was moved by the tears of his wife and his mother to spare the city. The frustrated Volscians killed him. The story is used for Shakspere's drama.

Cork, Richard Boyle, 1st earl of: see BOYLE, RICHARD.

Cork [Irish,= swamp], maritime county (2,881 sq. mi.; pop. 343,668), S Ireland, Munster Prov.; largest Irish county. Has rocky coastline with several bays and harbors. Interior has both mountains and fertile valleys. Farming, fishing, and dairying main occupations. Mfg. (textiles, whisky, flour, and leather goods) mostly around county town, **Cork,** county borough (pop. 75,595), on Lee R. near Cork Harbour. Occupied by the Danes (9th cent.), Cromwell (1649), and Marlborough (1690). In 1920 disturbances lord mayor was murdered. Harbor entrance is fortified; Cobh and Passage are important ports, and Haulbowline and Spike Isls. are military and naval depots. Exports mainly farm produce, cloth, and fish. Site of Univ. Col. and two cathedrals.

cork oak, evergreen oak (*Quercus suber*), native to Mediterranean region. Its thick but light bark or cork is used to make many things (e.g., bottle stoppers, life preservers, insulating material).

Corliss, George Henry, 1817–88, American inventor and international authority on steam-engine.

corm, short, thickened underground stem, resembling a bulb. The gladiolus and the crocus form corms. See *ill.,* p. 999.

cormorant (kôr′mŭrŭnt), large aquatic bird, an expert swimmer, related to the gannet and pelican, found in temperate or tropical areas, usually on the sea, but also on inland waters. Plumage is thick, usually dark; the body is 2–3 ft. long; the feet are webbed; the long bill is hooked. Used in Orient to catch fish.

corn, in agr., name given to leading grain crop of a region. In England, it means WHEAT, in Scotland and Ireland, OATS. Grain called corn in America is Indian corn or maize (*Zea mays*), a grass, domesticated and cultivated long before white man's arrival. Indians grew several kinds. In U.S. it is used as foodstuff, for making starch, sugar, etc., as grain feed and fodder.

Cornaro, Caterina (kätāre'nä kôrnä'rō), 1454–1510, queen of Cyprus, a celebrated Venetian beauty. Ruled from death of husband, James II of Cyprus (1473), until 1489, when Venice recalled her and annexed the island. Portrait by Titian (Uffizi, Florence).

Corn Belt, W part of U.S. Midwest with soil and climate best suited to grow corn and corn-fed livestock (esp. hogs). Iowa and Ill. are heart of area.

corn borer or **European corn borer,** small moth, in its larval stage a serious pest to corn. Probably reached U.S. from S Europe c.1910; found near Boston 1917. Has one or two broods a season. Mature larva pinkish, with brown head, and c.1 in. long. Often attacks other plants, such as dahlia.

Corneille, Pierre (pyĕr' kôrnä'yů), 1606–84, French dramatist, master of classical tragedy. *Le Cid* (1637), his masterpiece, is based on Spanish sources (see CID). Among his other plays, the most successful are the tragedies, *Horace* (1640), *Cinna* (1640), and *Polyeucte* (1643), and the comedy *Le Menteur* (1643). In grandiose, dignified style, Corneille exalts the will, subordinating passion to duty. He lived to see Racine replace him in popular favor.

cornel: see BUNCHBERRY; DOGWOOD.

Cornelia, fl. 2d cent. B.C., Roman matron, daughter of Scipio Africanus Major, wife of Ti. Sempronius Gracchus, mother of the Gracchi. Devoted herself to her children after her husband's death, raising them well. When asked by a wealthy lady about her jewels, Cornelia pointed at her sons, saying, "These are my jewels!"

Cornelius, one of first Gentile converts; traditionally first bishop of Caesarea. Acts 10.

Cornelius, Peter von, 1783–1867, German painter who helped revive art of fresco painting. Did fresco decorations in the Glyptothek. Favorite themes were religious or philosophical.

Cornell, Ezra, 1807–74, American capitalist, founder of Cornell Univ. A founder and director of the Western Union Telegraph Co. (formed 1855). His son, **Alonzo B. Cornell,** 1832–1904, was governor of N.Y. (1880–83), associate of Roscoe Conkling.

Cornell, Katharine, 1898–, American actress. Since 1916 has appeared in plays such as *The Green Hat, The Barretts of Wimpole Street,* and *Candida.*

Cornell College: see MOUNT VERNON, Iowa.

Cornell University, mainly at Ithaca, N.Y.; nonsectarian, with land-grant, state, private support; coed.; chartered 1865, opened 1868. Named for EZRA CORNELL. First president was A. D. WHITE. Has colleges of architecture, arts and sciences, engineering, medicine (in New York city); schools of law, nutrition, business administration; N.Y. state colleges of agr. and schools of industrial and labor relations, home economics, veterinary medicine.

corner, the securing of all or nearly all the supply of any commodity so that buyers must pay exorbitant prices. In stock exchanges, corners are made possible by short selling on MARGIN. Corners may be unintentional or deliberately planned. Joseph's corner of Egyptian grain is described in the Bible.

U.S. Supreme Court in 1913 held that a corner in a commodity entering into general use or into interstate commerce is illegal.

Corner Brook, town (pop. 10,276, with Corner Brook West), of W N.F., Canada, on Bay of Islands. Paper mills, iron foundries, and furniture works.

cornet: see WIND INSTRUMENTS.

cornflower, annual plant (*Centaurea cyanus*) with blue, purple, pink, or white flower heads. Also called bachelor's button, ragged sailor, bluebottle.

Corning. 1 City (pop. 2,104), SW Iowa, WSW of Creston. Icarian communistic settlement was near here, 1858–98 (see CABET, ÉTIENNE). 2 City (pop. 17,684), S N.Y., NW of Elmira and on Chemung R.; settled 1788. Famous for glass industry (begun 1868); 200-in. telescope mirror for Mt. Palomar, Calif., Observatory was made here.

Cornish, Vaughan, 1862–1948, English geographer. Dealt with relation of geography to military strategy, action of waves and tides, scenery preservation.

Cornish, town (pop. 989), SW N.H., near Connecticut R. N of Claremont. Resort and art colony. Birthplace of S. P. Chase. "Aspet," summer estate of Augustus Saint-Gaudens, is now a memorial.

Cornish, Brythonic language of Celtic subfamily of Indo-European languages. See LANGUAGE (table).

Corn Islands, two islands off E Nicaragua, opposite Bluefields. Leased to U.S. in 1916 in Nicaragua Canal project.

corn laws, regulations dating from 1361 restricting export or import of grain, especially in England. Laws of 1791 and 1815 forbade import unless prices were high. Food costs rose. Resentment led to Anti-Corn-Law League's campaign and repeal of laws by Robert Peel, 1846.

Corno, Monte, Italy: see GRAN SASSO D'ITALIA.

Cornplanter, c.1740–1836, half-breed chief of the Seneca Indians. Fought for British in New York in American Revolution.

cornucopia (kôr"nůkō'pēů) [Latin,= horn of plenty], in Greek religion, broken-off horn of goat Amalthaea, which became full of whatever owner desired. It is symbol of plenty.

Cornwall, Barry, 1787–1874, English writer of sentimental songs; real name Bryan Waller Procter.

Cornwall (kôrn'wôl), maritime county (1,365 sq. mi.; pop. 345,612), SW England; co. town Bodmin. Peninsula ending in promontory Lands End, region is low-lying plateau with market and dairy farms in fertile valleys. County includes Scilly Isles, famous for flower exports. Cornish tin mines known early to Greek traders. History distinct from rest of England. Cornish tongue did not die out until 18th cent. Great fishing center. Climate and picturesque coast towns make it popular with tourists.

Cornwall, town (pop. 16,899), SE Ont., Canada, on St. Lawrence R. and SE of Ottawa. At NE end of Cornwall Canal (11 mi. long, 6 locks), it is a port with dry dock. Mfg. of textiles, clothing, chemicals, furniture; processing of dairy products from surrounding area.

Cornwallis, Charles Cornwallis, 1st Marquess, 1738–1805, British general. Led fateful CAROLINA CAMPAIGN in American Revolution. Defeat in YORKTOWN CAMPAIGN ended fighting. Later was governor general of India and viceroy to Ireland.

corolla (–rŏl'–), part of FLOWER, usually brightly colored and just within CALYX. May be united as in morning glory or separate petals as in rose. See *ill.,* p. 999.

Coromandel Coast (kŏrōmǎn'dúl), E coast of Madras, India, between Point Calimere and Kistna R. Name probably derives from Cholomandalam, i.e., country of the Cholas, an ancient dynasty.

Corona, city (pop. 10,223), S Calif., ESE of Los Angeles. Ships citrus fruit (esp. lemons). Mfg. of pottery, glass, orchard equipment, chemicals.

corona (kúrō'nù), envelope surrounding sun (outside the chromosphere), believed to consist of fine particles luminous from their own light and reflected sunlight. Pale yellow inner corona is ringed by pearly white halo of outer corona, visible during total eclipse and also by means of coronagraph.

Coronado, Francisco Vásquez de, c.1510–1554, Spanish explorer in America. Unsuccessfully sought fabled wealth of Seven Cities of Cibola and QUIVIRA, but expedition acquainted Spanish with Pueblo Indians and opened Southwest.

Coronado (kŏ"rùnä'dō), residential and resort city (pop. 17,171), S Calif., on peninsula on W side of San Diego Bay.

coronary thrombosis: see THROMBOSIS.

coronation, ceremony of crowning sovereign on accession to throne. Has origins of great antiquity and ritual; usually has some religious as well as political significance (e.g., anointing with oil). In England medieval pageantry retained. English rulers crowned at Westminster Abbey since 1066. **Coronation Stone,** on which Scottish kings were crowned at Scone, was brought to Abbey in 1296 by Edward I and is now part of the coronation chair. Traditionally Jacob's "pillow," it was long Stone of Destiny of Irish kings before removal to Scotland. Stolen 1950 by Scottish nationalists but soon returned.

Coronea (kôr'ùnē'ù), town of anc. Greece, in Boeotia, ENE of Thebes. Here in 447 B.C. Athenians were defeated by Thebans, and in 394 B.C. Spartans won a hollow victory over Thebans.

Corot, Jean Baptiste Camille (zhä' bätēst' kämē'yù kôrō'), 1796–1875, French landscape painter of the Barbizon school. Spent most of his life in Fontainebleau or Ville d'Avray. Depicted the misty hours before dawn, using mainly silvery grays and greens and creating a poetic effect.

corporal punishment, physical chastisement of an offender, as in capital punishment, flogging, mutilating, or branding. Known from the dawn of history, it was opposed by humanitarians in 18th cent., and generally punishments have become less severe in Western countries.

corporation, organization enjoying legal personality for purpose of carrying out certain activities. Though there are many kinds (e.g, ecclesiastic, municipal, cooperative), business corporations organized for profit are commonly meant. Crude forms known in ancient Rome, but modern corporations developed with spread of commerce in Renaissance and growth of industry in 18th and 19th cent. In U.S. most operate under state charters (first general incorporation law in N.Y. 1811). As legal person corporation may hold property, carry on business, and even commit crimes (punishable by fine). Increasing power and narrowing of control to a few owners by holding companies (organized by controlling shares in other corporations) has caused opposition and some restriction by law.

corporative state, governmental economic system, organized with guilds (or corporations) of employers and employees; thus combines capitalism and syndicalism. As exemplified by Fascist Italy, corporative state gives government unlimited control over economic life. Spain and Portugal have modified corporative system.

Corpus Christi (kôr'pùs krĭs'tē) [Latin,= body of Christ], feast of the Roman Catholic Church, celebrated on the Thursday after Trinity Sunday (or on the following Sunday) to commemorate institution of the Eucharist. In many countries the day is marked with great processions and with much show of flowers.

Corpus Christi (krĭs'tē), city (pop. 108,287), S Texas, on Corpus Christi Bay at entrance of Nueces Bay (inlet at mouth of Nueces R.). Bay discovered Corpus Christi Day, 1519. Trading post founded here 1840; land claimed by Texas and Mexico. Boomed in Mexican War; briefly captured (1862) by Federal troops in Civil War. Livestock trade grew in late 18th cent. Recovering from 1919 hurricane, city developed as oil center. A deepwater port, it refines and ships oil, zinc, and other chemicals and processes cotton, milk, sea food, and truck. Seat of great naval air training base. Has resort beaches.

Corpus Christi College: see CAMBRIDGE UNIVERSITY and OXFORD UNIVERSITY.

corpuscles, cells carried in body fluids, especially blood plasma. Red blood corpuscles, yellowish biconcave disks containing hemoglobin (protein combined with iron and carrying oxygen), en masse give blood its red color; 4,500,000 to 5,000,000 are normally found per cu. mm. of human blood. Several types of white cells exist (see WHITE CORPUSCLE), totaling 6,000 to 10,000 per cu. mm. See *ill.,* p. 813.

Corpus Juris Civilis (kôr'pùs jōō'rĭs sĭvĭ'lĭs), most comprehensive code of Roman law, compiled (529–35) under Justinian I, by commission of jurists headed by TRIBONIAN. Four parts are the Codex or Code (collection of imperial constitutions), the Digest of Pandects (selections from classical jurists), the Institutes (textbook of elementary rules), and the Novels or Novellae (constitutions later than the Codex). *Corpus* was main source of modern CIVIL LAW.

Correggio (kúrē'jō), 1494–1534, Italian baroque painter, b. Correggio. His real name was Antonio Allegri. Greatly influenced Italian art of the 16th and 17th cent. by bold use of foreshortening and soft, moving contrasts of color, light, and shade. His most famous work is the grand fresco, *Assumption of the Virgin*, on the cupola of Parma cathedral.

Corregidor (kŭrĕ'gĭdôr"), fortress island, area c.2 sq. mi., off BATAAN peninsula of Luzon, Philippines. First fortified by the Spanish, its defenses were further strengthened by the U.S. after 1898. In World War II U.S. troops under Lt. Gen. Wainwright fought on hopelessly for a month here after fall of Bataan; they surrendered May, 1942.

Corrèze (kôrĕz'), department (2,273 sq. mi.; pop. 254,601), S central France, in Limousin; cap. Tulle.

Corrientes (kôrēĕn'tĕs), city (pop. 56,544), cap. of Corrientes prov., NE Argentina, port on Paraná R. in cattle and agr. district.

corrosion: see RUSTING.

Corry, city (pop. 7,911), NW Pa., SE of Erie. Mfg. of furniture and metal products.

Corsica (kôr'sĭkù), Fr. *Corse,* island (3,367 sq. mi.; pop. 267,873), a department of Metropolitan France, in Mediterranean, SE of France and N or Sardinia. Its cap., Ajaccio, and Bastia are the chief towns and ports. Largely mountainous (Monte Cinto reaches 8,982 ft.). Olive oil, wine, timber are main exports. Poor communications. Large areas are wild, covered by undergrowth (*maquis*), offering ideal hideout to bandits. Blood feuds and banditry were traditional until suppression in 20th cent. Outside chief towns an Italian dialect is spoken. Corsica was seized in turn by the Romans (3d cent. B.C.), Vandals (5th cent. A.D.), Arabs (9th cent.), Pisans (1077), and Genoese (1312). In 1755 Pasquale PAOLI successfully rebelled against Genoa, but French intervention led in 1768 to cession of Corsica to France. The Bonapartes, including Napoleon I, originated here. In 1794 Paoli returned, expelled French, united Corsica with British crown; but in 1796 France recovered it. In World War II German-Italian occupation (1942–43) was ended by local rebellion aided by Free French task force.

Corsicana (kôrsĭkă'nù), city (pop. 19,211), E central Texas, SSE of Dallas, in oil, agr., and cattle region. Processes and ships cotton, food and dairy products, and oil. First important commercial oil well (1895) and first refinery of Texas were here.

Corte Real, Gaspar (gùshpär' kôr'tù rēäl'), c.1450–1501?, Portuguese explorer. Made two voyages seeking Northwest Passage. May have discovered Greenland (1500) and touched North America. Lost on second voyage. His brother, Miguel Corte Real, was lost searching for him.

Cortés, Hernán, or **Hernando Cortez** (ĕrnän' kôrtäs', hĕrnän'dō kôrtĕz'), 1485–1547, Spanish conquistador, conqueror of Mexico. After service in Hispaniola and Cuba, he went (1519) under a commission of the Cuban governor Diego de Velásquez to conquer Mexico. There he was aided by a Spanish survivor of an earlier expedition and by an Indian girl, Malinche (renamed Marina on becoming Christian). He won over some peoples subordinate to the Aztec empire and got the help of Tlaxcalans after defeating them. His march on the Aztec cap., Tenochtitlán, ended triumphantly when Emperor Montezuma received him as a descendant of the god Quetzalcoatl. Cortés made Montezuma hostage and governed through him. He had, however, renounced allegiance to Velásquez and in 1520 had to return to the coast to defeat a force sent by Velásquez under Pánfilo de Narváez. While he was gone the Spanish under Pedro de Alvarado were driven from Tenochtitlán. Cortés rallied his forces and in 1521 besieged and took the city, destroying the Aztec empire. In 1524–26 he led an expedition to Honduras, putting the last puppet Aztec emperor, Cuauhtémoc, to death en route. He returned to find the governing power taken from him and though he was made marqués del Valle de Oaxaca he was not able to reestablish power in long wrangles with other administrators. He died in Spain, neglected by the court.

Cortes (kôr'täs), representative assembly in Spain. Local cortes originated in 12th–13th cent. in Leon, Castile, Aragon, Catalonia, Navarre, Valencia; continued to 19th cent., though much curtailed after Spanish unification (15th cent.). Local cortes were composed of three estates: clergy, nobles, commons. First all-Spanish Cortes met at Cádiz 1812. Since then, its status as parliament has been affected by frequent constitutional changes.

Cortez, Hernando: see CORTÉS, HERNÁN.

Cortez (kôrtĕz'), town (pop. 2,680), SW Colo., near Mesa Verde Natl. Park, Yucca House Natl. Monument, in an agr. and livestock area.

cortin: see ADRENAL GLAND.

Cortina d'Ampezzo (kôrtē'nä dämpĕd'zō), Alpine resort, NE Italy, in heart of Dolomites.

Cortland, city (pop. 18,152), central N.Y., S of Syracuse; settled 1791. Rail center in farm area. Wood, metal (esp. wire), food products.

Cortona, Pietro da (pyä'trō dä kôrtō'nù), 1596–1669, Italian painter and architect; real name Pietro Berrettini. Frescoes in Barberini Palace, Rome.

Cortot, Alfred (kôrtō'), 1877–, French pianist and conductor, authoritative interpreter of Chopin. For many years he played trios with Jacques Thibaud, violinist, and Pablo Casals, cellist.

Coruña, La (kùrù'nù, Span. lä kôrōō'nyä), city (pop. 92,189), cap. of La Coruña prov., NW Spain, in Galicia; Atlantic port. Of pre-Roman origin; flourished as port and textile center in Middle Ages; sacked by Drake 1598. Scene of Peninsular War battle in which Sir John Moore was mortally wounded (1809). Also spelled Corunna in English.

corundum (kùrŭn'dùm), a mineral, aluminum oxide. The finer varieties are used as gems, the coarser as abrasives. Emery is impure corundum. The chief corundum gems are ruby, sapphire, and topaz.

Corunna, Spain: see CORUÑA, LA.

Corvallis (kôrvăl'ĭs), city (pop. 16,207), NW Oregon, on Willamette R. and SSW of Salem, in dairy, fruit, and timber area; settled 1846. Seat of Oregon State Col. (land-grant, state supported; coed.; chartered 1858).

Corvinus, Matthias: see MATTHIAS CORVINUS.

Coryate, Thomas (kŏr'ēāt), 1577?–1617, English traveler. His *Crudities* (1611) reports his journey that covered much of the Continent.

Corybantes (kôr'ǐbăn'tēz), in Greek religion, dancers who accompanied goddess CYBELE on her journeys.

Corydon (kŏr'ĭdŭn), town (pop. 1,944), S Ind., W of Louisville, Ky.; laid out 1808. Territorial cap. 1813–16, state cap. 1816–25. Scene of only Indian battle of Civil War (July 8, 1863).

Cos, island in the Dodecanese: see KOS.

Cosenza (kôzĕn'tsä), city (pop. 30,038), Calabria, S Italy. Chief city of anc. Brutii. Alaric I is said to be buried here under Busento R., which was temporarily diverted from its course. Medieval castle built by Emperor Frederick II. Cathedral.

Cosgrave, William Thomas (kŏz'grāv), 1880–, Irish statesman. After Sinn Fein split (1922) he stood by Free State. Was president of executive council of Ireland, 1922–32. After defeat by De Valera, was opposition leader until his resignation in 1944.

Coshocton (kŭshŏk'tŭn), city (pop. 11,675), E central Ohio, N of Zanesville, at junction of Walhonding and Tuscarawas rivers; laid out 1802. Mfg. of iron and steel products and plastics.

cosmetics to enhance personal appearance have been used since prehistoric times. The ancient Egyptians, Greeks, Romans used them; in Middle Ages, known beauty aids were supplemented by those brought home by Crusaders. Renaissance saw beginning of lavish use, which continued until virtual disappearance of make-up in 19th cent. Revival came at turn of century; manufacture of cosmetics is now huge industry.

cosmic rays, radiation of unknown origin coming to earth from outer space, carrying large amounts of energy and able to penetrate nearly all substances. Primary rays believed to be chiefly protons; many of these collide with air particles. The nuclei of atoms destroyed in collisions break into particles which probably become secondary cosmic rays. Tertiary and quaternary rays said to be formed similarly.

cosmogony (kŏzmŏ'gŭnē), any theory of the origin of the world, of man, and of the universe in a philosophic, scientific setting. See NEBULAR HYPOTHESIS; PLANETESIMAL HYPOTHESIS.

cosmos (kŏz'mŭs), garden annual of genus *Cosmos* with crimson, pink, white, or orange flowers.

Cossa, Baldassarre (bäldäs-sär'rä kôs'sä), c.1370–1419, Neapolitan churchman, antipope as John XXIII in the Great SCHISM. When he was a cardinal he deserted the cause of Gregory XII and supported the Council of PISA, intended to end the schism between Rome and Avignon popes. When antipope Alexander V died, Cossa was elected (1410). He courted the favor of Emperor SIGISMUND and aided Louis II of Anjou against Lancelot (an ally of Gregory) in Naples. He convened the Council of CONSTANCE under pressure from Sigismund and reluctantly promised to abdicate if his rivals would.

They did, but he fled and tried to maintain his position. He was forced to return and was held prisoner until 1418.

Cossa, Francesco, or **Francesco del Cossa** (fränchä'skō dĕl kôs'sä), c.1435–1477?, Italian painter, identified with the schools of Ferrara and Bologna.

Cossacks (kŏ'săks), peasant-soldiers of several regions in Russia who until 1918 held certain privileges of self-government in return for military service. They were descended from fugitive serfs who settled frontier steppes in 16th and 17th cent. and defended them against Turks and Tatars (see DON COSSACKS; ZAPOROZHE COSSACKS). Their prominence in social revolts of 17th–18th cent. cost them many privileges. Cossacks took important part in conquest and colonization of new territories (e.g., SIBERIA, KUBAN). Before 1917 their 11 communities numbered c.4,000,000. Most of them fought against the Bolsheviks in civil war of 1918–20

Costa, Isaäc da (ē'sä-äk dä kôs'tä), 1798–1860, Dutch poet. Of an aristocratic Jewish family, he entered (1822) the Reformed Church, and much of his poetry is fervently Christian.

Costa Mesa (kŏ'stŭ mā'sŭ), village (pop. 11,844), S Calif., S of Santa Ana, in citrus fruit area.

Costa Rica (kŏ'stŭ rē'kŭ) [Span.,= rich coast], republic (19,650 sq. mi.; pop. 800,875), Central America, between the Caribbean (NE) and the Pacific (S and W). The NE area is a broad jungle plain, the NW is jungles and low mountains. The heart of the country is the central plateau, which has on it SAN JOSÉ (the cap.), CARTAGO (founded 1563), Heredia, and Alajuela. The small Indian population made Spanish conquest easy, and colonists had relatively small landholdings. Part of the captaincy general of Guatamela before gaining independence from Spain, Costa Rica was later part of Iturbide's empire (1821–23) and a member of the Central American Federation (1823–38). Coffee, introduced in the 19th cent., became the dominant crop. In 1874 M. C. Keith founded Limón and developed banana plantations on the Caribbean coast (many now abandoned because of leaf blight). The plateau cities are connected by rail and highways and are connected with the Pacific port, Puntarenas. Costa Rica is traditionally democratic and has been active in Pan-American organizations. Took part in World War II on the Allied side and joined the United Nations (1943).

Coster, Charles de: see DE COSTER, CHARLES.

Côte-d'Or (kōt-dôr'), department (3,392 sq. mi.; pop. 335,602), E France, in Burgundy; cap. Dijon. World-famed vineyards.

Cotentin (kôtätē'), peninsular region of Normandy, N France, projecting into English Channel; roughly identical with Manche dept. Historic cap. Coutances; chief towns are Cherbourg, Saint-Lô. Agr., apple orchards. Heavy fighting in World War II (1944).

Côtes-du-Nord (kôt'dü-nôr'), department (2,787 sq. mi.; pop. 526,955), NW France, in Brittany; cap. Saint-Brieuc.

Cöthen, Germany: see KÖTHEN.

Cotman, John Sell, 1782–1842, English landscape painter, best known for water colors and drawings.

Cotopaxi (kōtōpăk′sē), active volcano, 19,-344 ft. high, N central Ecuador.

Cotswold Hills, broken limestone plateau in Gloucestershire, England, extending c.50 mi. NE from Bath. Crest is Thames-Severn watershed. Region famous for Cotswold sheep and picturesque houses.

Cottage Grove, city (pop. 3,536), W central Oregon, on Coast Fork (near dam) of WILLAMETTE R.

cottage holding, in England, agr. tract of three acres or less, producing food for family whose cash income is from some other source. See also SMALL HOLDING.

cotter, cottar, or **crofter,** in Highland Scotland, an agr. tenant who rents a croft (small farm).

Cotton, (Thomas) Henry, 1907–, British golfer. Won British Open (1934, 1937), Professional Golfers' Association of America (1932, 1939, 1946) championships, many others.

Cotton, John, 1584–1652, Puritan clergyman in England and Mass. Bay Colony. Getting into difficulty as Puritan vicar of St. Botolph's, Boston, Lincolnshire, he migrated (1633) to America. The city of Boston renamed to honor him. Responsible for exile of Anne Hutchinson and expulsion of Roger Williams. Helped mold Congregational Church.

Cotton, Sir Robert Bruce, 1571–1631, English antiquarian. His collection of books, manuscripts, coins, and antiquities now is in British Museum.

cotton, most important of vegetable fibers, used from prehistoric times in many lands. The plant, a perennial of genus *Gossypium,* bears capsules (bolls) containing seeds (forming c.⅔ of bulk of boll), each surrounded by downy white or creamy fibers (c.¾ in.–1½ in. long), easily spun into thread. Usually grown as annual; thrives in temperate climate with well-distributed rainfall, as in U.S. COTTON BELT, where upland varieties are mainly grown; sea-island and American-Egyptian cotton are produced in W U.S. U.S., India, China, USSR, Egypt, Brazil are chief producers. Bolls were long hand picked; machine picking, now increasing, is aided by use of chemical to rid plants of leaves before stripping bolls. BOLL WEEVIL is most harmful of many insect pests and diseases. Cotton mfg., a huge industry, esp. in Great Britain and U.S., involves cleaning, ginning, carding, and spinning in order to get thread strong enough for weaving. Innumerable commodities, in addition to textiles, are made from cotton. Linters yield CELLULOSE; seeds, containing c.20% oil, yield **cottonseed oil,** used in refined state in cookery, as ingredient of margarine and cosmetics, and in crude state as industrial raw material.

Cotton Belt, term applied to part of U.S. formerly devoted mainly to cotton. Area included N.C., S.C., Ga., Ala., Miss., La., Ark., Okla., Texas, and sections of Va., Ky., Tenn., Fla., and Mo. Mainly diversified crops now, though cotton still important.

Texas now main cotton grower, and it is also grown in Calif., Ariz., and N.Mex.

cotton gin (jĭn), machine for separating cotton fiber from seeds. Roller gin known from ancient times. Saw gin invented 1793 by Eli Whitney consisted of revolving toothed cylinder which pulled lint through grate. Modern mechanized adaptation has series of circular saws which draw fiber through grid.

cottonmouth: see WATER MOCCASIN.

cottonseed oil: see COTTON.

cottonwood: see POPLAR.

Cottrell, Frederick Gardner (kŏ′trŭl), 1877–1948, American chemist. He was an authority on nitrogen fixation and mineral fertilizers and developed Cottrell method of dust precipitation, using an electric current at high potential.

Cotulla (kŭtŭ′lŭ), city (pop. 4,418), SW Texas, NNE of Laredo. Tourist stop on Pan-American Highway.

Coucy, Robert de (rōbĕr′ dů koōsē′), d. 1311, French architect who helped build Rheims cathedral.

Coué, Émile (koōā′), 1857–1926, French psychotherapist known for formula, "Day by day, in every way, I am getting better and better."

Coughlin, Charles Edward (kŏ′glĭn), 1891–, Roman Catholic priest in U.S., b. Canada. Bitterly opposed New Deal policies through press and radio.

Coulanges, Numa Denis Fustel de: see FUSTEL DE COULANGES, NUMA DENIS.

coulomb (koō′lŏm), quantity of electricity that current of one AMPERE transfers in one second. **Coulomb's law:** force of attraction or repulsion between two charges is inversely proportional to square of distance between them and directly proportional to product. Established by **Charles Augustin de Coulomb,** 1736–1806, French physicist, for whom coulomb named.

Coulter, John Merle, 1851–1928, American botanist, b. China. A pupil of Asa Gray, he edited sixth ed. of Gray's *Manual.* Influential in founding Boyce Thompson Inst. for Plant Research. Founded and edited (for 50 years) the *Botanical Gazette.*

council, ecumenical (ĕ″kūmĕ′nĭkŭl, ē″–) [Gr.,= universal], council of church authorities accepted by the Church as official. Their decrees are called canons if ratified by the pope. Roman Catholics recognize the following ecumenical or general councils: (1) 1 Nicaea, 325; (2) 1 Constantinople, 381; (3) Ephesus, 431; (4) Chalcedon, 451; (5) 2 Constantinople, 553; (6) 3 Constantinople, 680; (7) 2 Nicaea, 787; (8) 4 Constantinople, 869; (9) 1 Lateran, 1123; (10) 2 Lateran, 1139; (11) 3 Lateran, 1179; (12) 4 Lateran, 1215; (13) 1 Lyons, 1245; (14) 2 Lyons, 1274; (15) Vienne, 1311; (16) Constance, 1414; (17) Basel and Ferrara-Florence, 1431, 1438; (18) 5 Lateran, 1512; (19) Trent, 1545; (20) Vatican, 1869. The Orthodox recognize the first seven and also the continuation of 3 Constantinople (the Trullan Synod). At the time of the Great Schism the theory was advanced that the general council, rather than the pope, was supreme in the Church. The chief proponent was John Gerson, and this conciliar theory

GREEK

ROMAN

MEDIEVAL
FRENCH c.1250

EARLY RENAISSANCE
FRENCH c.1430

EARLY TUDOR
ENGLISH c.1540

ELIZABETHAN
ENGLISH c.1600

LOUIS XIV
FRENCH c.1690

LOUIS XVI
FRENCH c.1780

EMPIRE
FRENCH c.1805

TIME OF GEORGE IV
ENGLISH c.1820

EARLY VICTORIAN
AMERICAN c.1850

MID-VICTORIAN
AMERICAN c.1870

flourished at the Councils of Pisa and Constance, later failing.

Council Bluffs, city (pop. 45,429), SW Iowa, on the Missouri opposite Omaha, Nebr.; settled 1846 by Mormons on sites of trading post (1820s) and Indian mission (estab. 1838–40 by Father De Smet). Supply point during 1849–50 gold rush. Grew after being made E terminus of Union Pacific RR 1863. Has railroad shops, grain elevators, and stockyards. Mfg. of metal, wood, and food products. Monument commemorates 1804 meeting of Lewis and Clark with the Indians.

Council Grove, city (pop. 2,722), E central Kansas, SW of Topeka and on Neosho R. Treaty made here with Osage Indians, 1825. Site later became a campground on Santa Fe Trail. Methodist Indian mission (1849) still stands.

Council of Europe, Council of Foreign Ministers, Council of Ten, etc.: see EUROPE, COUNCIL OF; FOREIGN MINISTERS, COUNCIL OF; TEN, COUNCIL OF.

counterpoint, in music, the art of combining melodies, each of which is independent of the others, although together they form a homogeneous whole. Five types of counterpoint have been defined: note against note; two notes against one; four notes against one; syncopation; and florid counterpoint, which combines the other four. See also POLYPHONY.

Counts, George S(ylvester), 1889–, American educator, professor of education at Teachers College, Columbia Univ., after 1927. Advocated teachers' unions and was president (1939–42) of American Federation of Teachers. Has taken part in liberal politics. Wrote many books on history and democracy.

Couperin, François (fräswä' koopŭrē'), 1668–1733, French organist, harpsichordist, and composer, called "le Grand" to distinguish him from other members of his musically prominent family. His four books of harpsichord suites influenced Bach.

Couperus, Louis Marie Anne (koopä'roos), 1863–1923, Dutch novelist. His works, popular at home and abroad, include a collection of four realistic novels, *The Book of the Small Souls* (1901–3).

Courbet, Gustave (güstäv' koorbä'), 1819–77, French painter, b. Ornans. An opponent of vested authority, whether aesthetic or political. Showed his avowed realism in his painting such works as *Funeral at Ornans* and *Painter's Studio;* won prestige but aroused much official criticism. In 1873, after participating in the Commune, he fled to Switzerland where he died in exile and poverty.

coureurs de bois (koorŭr' dübwä') [Fr.,= wood runners], in French regime in Canada unlicensed traders who played active part in fur trade and exploration.

Courier, Paul Louis (pôl' lwē' koorya'), 1772–1825, French author and classical scholar. After the Restoration he wrote political pamphlets which place him among his nation's most brilliant stylists.

Courland, or Kurland (kûr'lŭnd, koor'länt), region and former duchy, W Latvia; historic cap. JELGAVA. Conquered by LIVONIAN KNIGHTS in 13th cent. When the order disbanded (1561), its grand master became first duke of Courland, under Polish overlordship. Under Russian influence from early 18th cent., Courland was annexed by Russia in third Polish partition (1795). Became part of Latvia 1918.

court, in general, official body charged with adjudicating legal cases. In ancient Egypt and Babylonia courts were semi-ecclesiastic; in Greece assemblies had court functions; in Rome emerged secular complex system of courts, staffed with professional jurists. Britain since Judicature Act of 1873 has high court of justice (with divisions of chancery; probate, divorce, and admiralty; Queen's—or King's—Bench) and court of appeal. In U.S. two systems are Federal courts (district courts, circuit courts of appeals, and at head, Supreme Court) and state courts (including many types, e.g., police courts, court of probate).

Courtois, Bernard (bĕrnär' koortwä'), 1777–1838, French chemist. He discovered and isolated iodine.

Courtrai (koorträ'), Flemish *Kortrijk,* town (pop. 40,085), West Flanders, W. Belgium, on Lys R. Textile center since medieval times. Scene of first BATTLE OF THE SPURS (1302). Church of Notre Dame (13th cent.) contains Van Dyck's *Elevation of the Cross.*

court tennis, believed to have been originated about 14th cent. in France, forerunner of most modern racquet games. Played on indoor cement court 110 ft. by 38 ft., surrounded by four walls 30 ft. high.

Cousin, Jean (zhã kooze'), c.1490–c.1560, French painter. His treatise on portraiture and some of his glass paintings are attributed by some to his son and pupil, **Jean Cousin,** c.1522–c.1590.

Cousin, Victor, 1792–1867, French philosopher, minister of education under Louis Philippe. In that period he was practically dictator of education and philosophy. His own philosophy was eclectic in the extreme because Cousin believed that all conflicting doctrines held part of the truth ready for the intuitive eye to discern.

Cousin-Montauban, Charles Guillaume: see PALIKAO.

Cousins, Samuel, 1801–87, English mezzotint engraver.

Coustou (koostoo'), family of French sculptors. **Nicolas Coustou,** 1658–1733, and brother, **Guillaume Coustou,** 1677–1746, worked at Marly and Versailles. Guillaume's son, **Guillaume Coustou,** 1716–77, was also a sculptor.

Couthon, Georges (zhôrzh' kootō'), 1755?–1794, French revolutionist. Fanatic Jacobin. Shared with Robespierre, Saint-Just in triumvirate of Terror. Fell on 9 Thermidor; guillotined.

Couza, Alexander John: see CUZA.

Covadonga (kōvädōn'gä), hamlet, N Spain, in Asturias. Scene (716?) of first Christian victory over Moors.

Covarrubias, Miguel (mēgäl' kōvär-roo'bēäs), 1902–, American artist, b. Mexico. Best known for his caricatures and drawings for *Vanity Fair.*

covenant (kŭ'vŭnŭnt) [O. Fr.,= agreement], in Bible and theology, explicit promise of God to man. In law, contract under seal or agreement by deed. In Scottish history (kŭvŭnănt'), pact by opponents of episcopacy, known as COVENANTERS. Covenants in Bible are not contractual, but free promises of God: e.g., His covenants with Israel culminating in Law of Moses, and known as Old Covenant. In law, covenants follow same rules as other contracts; variously classified, all are characterized by explicit promise of covenantor to covenantee.

Covenanters, in Scottish history, groups of people bound by oath to defend Presbyterianism. Covenant of 1581 sought to combat Catholicism. Covenant of 1638 opposed innovations of Archbishop LAUD, especially use of English Book of Common Prayer. They resisted king's armies in BISHOPS' WARS (1639–40) and supported Parliament in PURITAN REVOLUTION only after acceptance (1643) of Solemn League and Covenant pledging Presbyterian state church in England and Ireland. Their power broken by Cromwell's conquest of Scotland in 1650. After Restoration, Covenanters were alternately coerced and persuaded to accept episcopacy but stubbornly resisted. Troubles ended with Glorious Revolution (1688).

Covent Garden (kŭv'vŭnt), London opera house. Located in produce market district, it is on site of famous theater (opened 1732) associated with Garrick, the Kembles, and others. Present theater built 1858. Patti and Caruso sang here.

Coventry (kŏv'ŭntrē), city (pop. 258,211), Warwickshire, England. Founded 14th cent., has old buildings. Has been important center for airplane and munitions mfg. since 1914. Legend of Lady Godiva and Peeping Tom, celebrated by Tennyson, perpetuated until recently by pageants. City suffered intensely destructive air raid Nov. 14–15, 1940. Hundreds of buildings destroyed, including the 14th-cent. cathedral, and thousands made homeless. Phrase "to send to Coventry" means to ostracize socially.

Coventry, town (pop. 9,869), W R.I., SW of Providence. Mfg. of textiles.

cover crop, temporary crop sown to protect soil (e.g., from erosion), increase nutrients (e.g., nitrogen from legumes), or to improve texture by being plowed under. Valuable in rehabilitating land.

Coverdale, Miles, 1488–1569, English translator of Bible, bishop of Exeter (1551–53). Published translation 1535. Later collaborated in Great Bible (1539), edited "Cranmer's Bible" (1540), and helped on first Book of Common Prayer.

covered wagon: see CONESTOGA WAGON; PRAIRIE SCHOONER.

Coverley, Sir Roger de: see ROGER DE COVERLEY.

Covington (kŭv'-). **1** City (pop. 5,192), N central Ga., SE of Atlanta. Textile and lumber mills. **2** City (pop. 64,452), N Ky., on Ohio R. where Licking R. enters; settled 1812, laid out 1815. Bridges connect with Cincinnati and Newport. Rail focus with breweries, distilleries, meat and tobacco packing plants, and mfg. of X-ray equipment, tools, and wire goods. **3** Town (pop. 5,113), SE La., near L. Pontchartrain, in agr. (strawberries, tung oil) area; settled

1769. Has lumbering and mfg. of wood preservatives. Resort. **4** Town (pop. 5,860), western Va., SW of Staunton, in Jackson R. valley. Paper, pulp, and rayon plants. Iron and coal fields near.

Coward, Noel, 1899–, English playwright, actor, director, composer. His versatile, sophisticated works include dramas (e.g., *Private Lives,* 1930), musicals (e.g., *Bittersweet,* 1929), and films (e.g., *In Which We Serve*).

cowbird, New World bird of oriole and blackbird family. Male eastern, or common, cowbird (cow blackbird) is glossy black and c.8 in. long with brown head and breast. Most species lay eggs in other birds' nests; birds usually incubate the cowbird eggs and feed the young at expense of their own.

Cowdry, Edmund Vincent (kou'drē), 1888–, American biologist, authority on cells and tissues.

Cowell, Henry Dixon (kou'ŭl), 1897–, American composer and pianist. He experimented with new musical resources (e.g., in piano compositions he introduced the tone cluster, played with the arm or fist). In 1927 he founded *New Music,* a quarterly for the publication of music by contemporary composers.

Cowes (kouz), urban district (pop. 17,154), Isle of Wight, England, near Southampton. Seaport, resort, and shipbuilding center, it is headquarters of the Royal Yacht Club and holds annual regattas.

Cowles, Henry Chandler (kōlz), 1869–1939, American botanist, a pioneer in plant ecology.

Cowley, Abraham (kōō'-, kou'-), 1618–67, English poet and essayist. One of the cleverest of the metaphysical poets, he was notable for precociousness and wit. Among volumes of his works are *Poetical Blossoms* (1633), *The Mistress* (1647), *Poems* (1656). Prose essays, simple in style, much praised.

Cowley, Hannah: see DELLA-CRUSCANS.

cowpea or **black-eyed bean,** leguminous plant (*Vigna sinensis*), a forage and cover crop in S U.S.

Cowpens (kou'pĭnz), town (pop. 1,879), NW S.C., ENE of Spartanburg. National battlefield site marks battle (Jan. 17, 1781) of CAROLINA CAMPAIGN near by.

Cowper, William Cowper, 1st Earl (kōō'pŭr), c.1664–1723, English jurist. Took leading part in union of England with Scotland 1706. As first lord chancellor of Great Britain (1707–10) presided at trial of Henry Sacheverell.

Cowper, William (kōō'pŭr, kou'-), 1731–1800, English poet. Subject to melancholia, he was placed with the Unwin family at Huntington and later at Olney. His writings include intensely religious *Olney Hymns* (1779); *The Task* (1785). Pictures of rural life foreshadow romanticism. Also known for shorter poems, "John Gilpin," "To Mrs. Unwin," "To Mary," and longer *The Castaway*. Letters much admired.

cowpox, infectious viral disease of cows, related to SMALLPOX. Similar disease affects horses and sheep.

cowrie or **cowry** (kou'rē), marine gastropod mollusk found in warm waters. Shells of various species used among primitives as money and adornment.

cowslip: see MARSH MARIGOLD; PRIMROSE; SHOOTING STAR; VIRGINIA COWSLIP.

Cox, Jacob Dolson, 1828–1900, Union general in Civil War and American statesman. Served ably in Antietam and Atlanta campaigns. Secretary of Interior (1869–70) under Pres. Grant; advocated civil service reform, opposed spoilsmen in Republican party. Father of **Kenyon Cox,** 1856–1919, painter and art critic.

Cox, Palmer, 1840–1924, American writer-illustrator of the Brownie stories for children.

Coxey, Jacob Sechler, 1854–1951, American social reformer. Interested in unemployment and monetary problems. Farmer-Labor presidential candidate 1932, 1936. Led **Coxey's Army,** band of unemployed men who marched to Washington, D.C., following Panic of 1893, to petition Congress for measures which they hoped would relieve unemployment and distress. Reached Washington with c.500 men instead of the proclaimed 100,000; its leaders were arrested for walking on Capitol lawn.

coyote (kīō′tē, kī′ōt) or **prairie wolf,** small wolf (*Canis*) native to W North America, with thick, long, tawny fur and a bushy black-tipped tail. It hunts small animals and in packs attacks larger mammals. It is a scavenger and a destroyer of rodents. Cry is yelping, doglike.

Coypel (kwä̇pĕl′), family of French painters. **Noël Coypel,** 1628–1707, worked on decorations of royal palaces. His son, **Antoine Coypel,** 1661–1722, painted Aeneid series for Palais-Royal. Antoine's half-brother, **Noël Nicolas Coypel,** 1692–1734, and son, **Charles Antoine Coypel,** 1694–1752, were also well-known painters.

Coysevox, Antoine (kwäzvôks′), 1640–1720, French sculptor who did much of the sculpture at Versailles.

Cr, chemical symbol of the element CHROMIUM.

Crab, the, in astronomy: see ZODIAC.

crab, crustacean with broad, flat outer skeleton, short abdomen bent under body, stalked eyes, five pairs of legs (the first with claws). Crabs are chiefly marine, but some are fresh-water, some land forms. Omnivorous feeders, some are scavengers, others predatory. See also KING CRAB; HERMIT CRAB.

crab apple, type of apple tree and its small, sour fruit used in preserves and jellies. Siberian crab (*Malus baccata*) is widely grown. Other species and varieties, e.g., Bechtel's crab with double flowers, are grown for ornament.

Crabbe, George, 1754–1832, English poet, a physician and clergyman. His strong, drab poetry (as in long poems, *The Village,* 1781; *The Parish Register,* 1807; and *The Borough,* 1810) on the life of the poor illustrates realistic aspect of romanticism.

Crabtree, Lotta, 1847–1924, American actress. A pupil of Lola Montez, she was a popular child actress in Calif. mining camps before a successful career in generally shoddy plays. Retired 1891.

Cracow (krä′kō, krä′cou), Pol. *Kraków,* city (pop. c.347,500), S Poland, on the Vistula;

cap. of Poland from 14th cent. to 1595. Commercial and mfg. center; seat of Jagiellonian Univ. (founded 1364); episcopal see from c.1000. Kings of Poland continued to be crowned and buried at Cracow after fire of 1595 caused transfer of cap. to Warsaw. Cracow passed to Austria in third Polish partition (1795); was made a republic (with surrounding dist.) under protection of Austria, Russia, and Prussia by Congress of Vienna (1815); was annexed by Austria after insurrection of 1846; reverted to Poland 1919. Noted landmarks include royal castle (Wawel), rebuilt 16th cent.; 14th-cent. Gothic cathedral; 13th-cent. Church of Our Lady, with altarpiece by Veit Stoss; 14th-cent. cloth hall.

Craddock, Charles Egbert, pseud. of **Mary Noailles Murfree,** 1850–1922, American novelist, author of novels and stories of Tennessee people.

Crafton, borough (pop. 8,066), SW Pa., W residential suburb of Pittsburgh. Mfg. of stoves.

Craig, (Edward) Gordon, 1872–, English stage designer, producer, and actor; son of Ellen Terry. His poetic, mysterious stage designs and productions for Ibsen's *Vikings* and Shakspere's *Much Ado about Nothing* (1903) and *Hamlet* (Moscow Art Theatre, 1912) greatly contributed to modern theater development.

Craig, James: see CRAIGAVON, JAMES CRAIG, 1st VISCOUNT.

Craig, Sir James Henry, 1748–1812, British soldier, governor in chief of Canada (1807–11), b. Gibraltar. Led English army into Italy (1805–6) and occupied Sicily. As governor in chief of Canada, opposed to representative government and to French Canadians, he dissolved assembly of Lower Canada (1809).

Craigavon, James Craig, 1st Viscount (krāgā′vŭn), 1871–1940, Ulster statesman. Organized resistance against Home Rule. First prime minister of N. Ireland from 1921 until his death.

Craigenputtock, moorland home of the Carlyles (1828–34) near Dumfries, S Scotland.

Craigie, Sir William A., 1867–, British lexicographer. Generally considered the foremost lexicographer of his time, he was joint editor of *New English Dictionary* (commonly called *Oxford Dictionary*) 1901–33 and was chief editor of *A Dictionary of American English on Historical Principles* (issued in parts after 1936; pub. as 4 vols., 1938–43).

Craik, Dinah Maria Mulock: see MULOCK.

Craiova (kräyô′vä), city (pop 84,574), SW Rumania; historic cap. of Oltenia.

Cram, Ralph Adams, 1863–1942, American architect, an exponent of Gothic architecture. Wrote chiefly on medieval architecture and thought.

Cranach or Kranach, Lucas (both: lōō′käs krä′näkh), the elder, 1472–1553, German artist, whose real name was Müller or Sunder. Court painter to three electors of Saxony. A master of piquant line and silhouette in nudes, portraits, and religious paintings. Was a friend and supporter of Luther. His son and pupil **Lucas Cranach,** the younger, 1515–86, continued in his tradition.

cranberry, low creeping evergreen bog plant (*Vaccinium oxycoccus*), with red, tart berries used for sauces and jellies. Cultivated on commercial scale in parts of Mass., N.J., and Wis.

Cranbrook Foundation, school, art academy, and science institute, at Bloomfield Hills, Mich., near Pontiac. Buildings designed by Saarinen.

Crane, Hart, 1899–1932, American poet, author of *The Bridge* (1930) and other poems. Suicide by drowning.

Crane, Stephen, 1871–1900, American novelist, journalist, poet. After *Maggie: a Girl of the Streets* (1893), *The Red Badge of Courage* (1895; a Civil War novel) brought fame and career as war correspondent. Wrote epigrammatic free verse and short stories. Died in Germany of tuberculosis.

Crane, Walter, 1845–1915, English illustrator, painter, and decorator. Founded Arts and Crafts Exhibition Society of London in 1888.

crane, large wading bird of Old World chiefly. Some are in North America, e.g., the whooping crane (nearly extinct), sandhill crane, little brown crane, and Florida crane. Cranes perform rhythmical dance in mating season.

crane, machine using free end of a fixed beam to hoist and transfer heavy loads. Actuated anciently by manual or animal power, modern cranes run by steam, electric, Diesel, and hydraulic, as well as manual power. Cranes used inside include bridge or overhead traveling crane (along steel girder spanning fixed rails). Outside cranes include the gantry (mounted on structure over operating area), the rotary, derrick, and hammerhead (steel tower supports cantilever-type truss with power generator at short end, load-carrying device at other). Locomotor crane revolves on turntable mounted on rail car, caterpillar tread, truck, or pontoons. See *ill.*, page 793.

crane fly: see DADDY LONGLEGS.

Cranford, residential township (pop. 18,602), NE N.J., W of Elizabeth. Printing, mfg. of metal goods.

cranium: see SKULL.

Cranmer, Thomas (krăn′mŭr), 1489–1556, English churchman. Came to attention of HENRY VIII in 1529 by proposing method by which king could divorce Katharine of Aragon without recourse to Rome. Made Archbishop of Canterbury 1533; was subservient to king. As a regent for Edward VI, he largely determined course of English Church. Placed English Bible in churches; revised BOOK OF COMMON PRAYER 1552. Supported claim of Lady Jane Grey to throne. Under Catholic Mary I, was tried for treason, convicted of heresy, and burned at the stake.

Cranston, industrial city (pop. 55,060), central R.I., SW of Providence. Mfg. of textiles, metal and wood products, rubber goods, chemicals, plastics.

crape myrtle (krāp), shrub (*Lagerstroemia indica*), with crinkled flowers, grown in S U.S.

craps: see DICE.

Crapsey, Adelaide, 1878–1914, American poet; originator of the cinquain—a delicate, compressed five-line verse, modeled on Japanese *hokku*.

Crashaw, Richard (kră′shô), 1612–49, English poet, generally considered one of the metaphysical poets, and chief "baroque" poet in English. Son of Puritan clergyman, he turned to the High Church. On the Continent after the Puritans took over Cambridge (1643), he became a Roman Catholic (1646). His intense religious poetry includes richly ornamental poetry on St. Theresa. Chief volumes are *Steps to the Temple and Delights of the Muses* (1646; enlarged 1648) and *Carmen Deo Nostro* (1652).

Crassus (kră′sùs), family of anc. Rome. One well-known member was **Lucius Licinius Crassus** (lĭsĭ′nēùs), d. 91 B.C., orator and political leader. As consul in 95 B.C. he promoted the Licinian Law, intended to banish from Rome all who had gained citizenship by illegal means. This restrictive measure helped to bring on the Social War. Most noted was **Marcus Licinius Crassus,** d. 53 B.C., who managed by personal charm and ambition to become the richest man in Rome. His devices were not always admirable; it is said that as a supporter of Sulla he got property of proscribed persons and also that he had an efficient fire-fighting organization that would not act until the owner of a burning building sold it to Crassus. He earned prestige by helping to defeat the revolt of Spartacus. Politically ambitious, he was consul with POMPEY in 70 B.C., but they disagreed. Julius CAESAR persuaded him to join in the First Triumvirate (Caesar, Pompey, Crassus) and held the organization together. Crassus, assigned the province of Syria, had military ambitions and undertook a campaign against the Parthians. He was routed at Carrhae (53 B.C.) and was murdered by treachery.

crater (krā′tùr), cuplike mouth of the vent of a volcano or geyser. Water sometimes fills the crater of an extinct volcano, as in Crater Lake, Oregon.

Crater Lake National Park: see NATIONAL PARKS AND MONUMENTS (table).

Craters of the Moon National Monument: see NATIONAL PARKS AND MONUMENTS (table).

crawfish: see CRAYFISH.

Crawford, F(rancis) Marion, 1854–1909, American romantic novelist, b. Italy (where he spent much of his life). His popular novels (e.g., *Saracinesca,* 1887; *The White Sister,* 1909) had a remote, exotic air and frequently historical or Oriental backgrounds.

Crawford, Isabella Valancy, 1850–87, Canadian poet, b. Ireland. Her verse was not recognized until after her death.

Crawford, Thomas, 1813–57, American sculptor, best known for his figure *Armed Freedom* on the dome of the Capitol at Washington.

Crawford, William Harris, 1772–1834, American statesman. U.S. Senator from Ga. (1807–13). U.S. Secretary of the Treasury (1816–25). Unsuccessful presidential candidate in 1824.

Crawford Notch, scenic pass, c.5 mi. long, in White Mts., N central N.H., through which Saco R. flows.

Crawfordsville, city (pop. 12,851), W Ind., S of Lafayette; laid out c.1822. Farming and stock-raising center; metal products. Seat of Wabash Col.

crayfish or **crawfish,** fresh-water crustacean smaller than related, similar lobster, and found in most areas except Africa. Usually they live in ponds, streams, or swamps; a few are partially terrestrial. They eat small aquatic animals and carrion. Developing eggs are carried on female's swimming legs.

Crazy Horse, d. 1877, Indian leader, chief of Oglala Sioux. Aided Sitting Bull in defeat of Custer (1876). Surrendered in 1877 but he was accused of planning a revolt and was shot.

cream of tartar, substance obtained from crystalline crust (argol), formed in wine-fermenting tanks. Argol is dissolved, decolorized, and purified and the crystalline product when dried and powdered is cream of tartar. Used in baking and to make ROCHELLE SALT and TARTAR EMETIC.

Creasy, Sir Edward Shepherd (krē′sē), 1812–78, English historian. Best known for *Fifteen Decisive Battles of the World* (1821; see BATTLE).

Crébillon, Prosper (prôspĕr′ krābēyŏ′), 1674–1762, French classical dramatist, author of *Rhadamiste et Zénobie* (1711) and *Catilina* (1748). His son, **Claude Crébillon** (klōd) (Crébillon fils), 1707–77, brought the licentious tale to perfection with *Le Sopha* (1745).

Crécy (krĕ′sē, Fr. krāsē′), in English also spelled Cressy, small town, N France, N of Abbeville. Here in 1346 Edward III of England defeated Philip VI of France in a major battle of Hundred Years War. French nobles were decimated by English longbows, which appeared for first time on Continent. Among combatants were EDWARD THE BLACK PRINCE and the blind king of Bohemia, JOHN OF LUXEMBURG.

Credi, Lorenzo di: see LORENZO DI CREDI.

credit, financial system to facilitate transfer of capital from those who own it to those who can use it in expectation of profit. Credit depends on trust of the person giving money or goods to another in the ability and honesty of the borrower. Modern business relies heavily on use of credit, from simple delivery of goods with later payment of purchase price to gigantic loans for building or expanding a business. Little known in the ancient world, credit developed with commerce. Excess credit in a community brings inflation; too little brings deflation. See DEBT.

Crédit Mobilier of America (krĕ′dĭt mōbĭlyā′), ephemeral construction company, connected with building of Union Pacific RR and with one of the major financial scandals in U.S. history. Led by Oakes AMES and Thomas C. DURANT, inner stockholders of Union Pacific set up Crédit Mobilier and made contracts with themselves, at profits of $7,000,000–$23,000,000. To forestall investigation or interference by Congress, Ames sold or assigned shares of stock to members of Congress at par, though shares were worth twice as much. Scandal broke during 1872 presidential campaign. Congressional investigation resulted in censures, no prosecutions.

creed [Latin *credo* = I believe], summary of basic doctrines of faith. Several have been of fundamental importance in Christianity. **1** The Nicene Creed, usually said to be a revision at the First Council of Constantinople (381) of the creed adopted by the First Council of Nicaea (325) to settle problems raised by Arianism. Actually the original creed was a simple statement including a declaration on the nature of Christ. The Nicene Creed may have been composed by St. Cyril of Jerusalem. In the Roman Catholic Church since the 9th cent. it has said, "the Holy Ghost . . . Who proceedeth from the Father *and the Son (Filioque)*." The Orthodox Church quarrels with the italicized words. **2** See ATHANASIAN CREED. **3** The Apostles' Creed, familiar in most of the more conservative Western churches, probably arose in the 2d or 3d cent. but did not reach its present form before 650. Essentially similar to the Nicene Creed (though simpler), it has two significant differences; it has the statement that Christ descended into Hell, not in the Nicene; it says "resurrection of the body," where the Nicene has "resurrection of the dead." **4** The Augsburg Confession (1530) is the official Lutheran statement, written by Melanchthon, endorsed by Luther. **5** The Thirty-nine Articles is the basic statement of faith for Anglican and Episcopal churches; its present form dates from the reign of Elizabeth I. **6** The Westminster Confession (1645–47) is a pronouncement of Calvinist doctrine in English, basic in the development of Presbyterianism and in Congregationalism.

Cree Indians, tribe, formerly located in Manitoba, of Algonquian linguistic stock. One branch, the Plains Cree, moved SW into buffalo territory. Culture of the Woodland Cree (in N) like that of Ojibwa.

Creek Indians, confederacy of more than 50 Indian towns (or tribes) mostly in Ala. and Ga. and mostly of Natchez-Muskogean linguistic stock. Had advanced agr. In Creek War of 1813–14, they massacred many at Fort Mims but were defeated by Andrew Jackson. Moved to the Indian Territory, they became one of FIVE CIVILIZED TRIBES.

creeper, name for various small birds with long decurved bills and usually inconspicuous plumage. True creepers (Certhiidae) are Old World family related to wrens and nuthatches; represented by one New World species, the brown creeper and its subspecies. Related are the Mexican or Sierra Madre, Rocky Mt., Sierra, and California creepers.

Crefeld, Germany: see KREFELD.

Creighton University: see OMAHA, Nebr.

Crémazie, (Joseph) Octave (krāmāzē′), 1827?–1879, French Canadian poet. Poems were strongly influenced by nationalism and romanticism; of great importance in French Canadian poetry.

crème de menthe, mint-flavored LIQUEUR.

Crémieux, Isaac (or Adolphe) (ēzäk′ krāmyü′), 1796–1880, a French minister of justice. Abolished slavery in colonies and secured full citizen's rights for Jews in Algeria.

Cremona (krāmō′nä), city (pop. 54,564), Lombardy, N Italy, on Po R., in rich agr. dist. Was Roman colony; independent commune in Middle Ages; conquered by Milan 1344. Famous for violins made by Amati, Guarneri, Stradivari. Impressive main square has cathedral (12th–16th cent.), 13th-cent. town hall.

creole [perhaps from Span.,= servant or child], in Latin America, native descendants of French and Spanish conquerors. In S U.S., descendants of French settlers as distinct from "Cajuns," descendants of Acadian exiles. The idea that Creole means part-Negro persons is incorrect though mixed bloods and Negroes may be called Creole.

Creon (krē′ŏn), in Greek legend, uncle of OEDIPUS. Regent of Thebes after banishment of Oedipus, he helped Eteocles, son of Oedipus, wrest kingdom from his brother POLYNICES. Forbade funeral rites for Polynices, and killed Antigone for defying him.

creosote (krē′ŭsōt), volatile, heavy oily liquid, a strong antiseptic, obtained by distillation of wood tar. Active principle is guaiacol. Creosote oil is used as preservative of timber and meat.

crepe (krāp), thin silk fabric with crinkled texture. Hard-finished crepe (crape) is used for mourning; soft crepes include crepe de Chine. Wool, rayon, cotton threads can be given crepe weave.

Crépy, Treaty of (krāpē′), 1544, concluded between Emperor Charles V and FRANCIS I of France at Crépy-en-Laonnois (formerly Crespy), N France. Charles renounced claim to Burgundy; Francis renounced claims to Naples, Flanders, Artois.

Crerar, Henry Duncan Graham (krēr′är), 1888–, Canadian general in World War II. After serving as chief of Canadian general staff, and in several commands, he was given command in 1944 of Canadian Army Overseas.

Crerar, John (krēr′är), 1827–89, American capitalist and philanthropist. Provided for the **John Crerar Library**, Chicago, noted for scientific and technical reference library and many special collections.

Cres, Yugoslavia: see CHERSO.

Cresap, Michael (krē′săp), 1742–75, American frontiersman and soldier. Accused by some of starting Lord Dunmore's War (1774). In American Revolution he marched his company so fast to support patriots at Boston—550 mi. in 22 days—that he died of exhaustion.

Cresilas (krē′sĭlŭs), fl. c.450 B.C., Greek sculptor. His statue of Pericles is the earliest Greek portrait statue that has been identified.

Crespy, Treaty of: see CRÉPY, TREATY OF.

cress: see NASTURTIUM; PEPPERGRASS; WATER CRESS.

Cressent, Charles (krĕsä′), 1685–1768, French cabinetmaker, one of originators of Regence style. Studied under Boulle.

Cressida: see TROILUS AND CRESSIDA.

Cressy, France: see CRÉCY.

Creston, city (pop. 8,317), SW Iowa, SW of Des Moines, in livestock-raising area. Has food-processing plants and railroad shops.

Crestview, town (pop. 5,003), NW Fla., near Choctawhatchee Natl. Forest.

Cretaceous period (krētā′shŭs), third period of the MESOZOIC ERA of geologic time. It was marked by extensive submergence and vast changes in the earth's surface and life. By middle Cretaceous a seaway extended from the Gulf of Mexico to the Arctic. Late Cretaceous saw uplift and withdrawal of the water; conditions resembling the Carboniferous prevailed, and coal deposits accumulated. Near the close of the period came the Laramide revolution, and the first generation of the Rockies was born. Cretaceous marine life included reptiles, some resembling fish and some of huge size. Dinosaurs were still dominant on land, but primitive mammals were beginning to appear. Before the end of the period such modern plant forms as willow, elm, birch, oak, and maple were abundant. See also GEOLOGY, table.

Crete (krēt), Gr. *Krete,* largest island (3,235 sq. mi.; pop. 438,239), of Greece, in the E Mediterranean, c.60 mi. SE of mainland; cap. Canea. Extending c.160 mi. E-W, it is S limit of Aegean Sea. Candia is the largest city. Largely mountainous, it rises to 8,058 ft. in Mt. Ida. Agr. (olive oil, fruit, vegetables); wine growing; stock raising, dairying. There are iron and lignite deposits. Crete's ancient MINOAN CIVILIZATION, named after mythical King MINOS, was one of the world's oldest; it reached its height c.1600 B.C., then ended suddenly and mysteriously. Impressive remains have been found at CNOSSUS. Later Dorian settlers founded many flourishing city-states, including Cnossus and Cydonia (modern Canea). Crete became an important trade center but played no vital political part in the Greek world. Conquered by Rome (68–67 B.C.) it later was held by Byzantium (except during Arab occupation, 826–961), then fell to Venice (1204) and to Turkey (1669; last two Venetian forts were ceded 1715). The Cretan insurrection of 1896–97 led to war between Greece and Turkey. Greece was utterly defeated, but the Great Powers forced Turkey to evacuate Crete (1898) and occupied the island until 1909. Union with Greece, proclaimed 1908, became official in 1913. Antimonarchist uprising by followers of VENIZELOS was suppressed after some fighting (1935). In World War II Anglo-Greek forces were evacuated to Crete (April, 1941); in May they were overwhelmed in a German airborne invasion. Late in 1944 the Germans were isolated by British ships and surrendered to guerrilla forces.

cretinism (krē′tĭnĭzŭm), condition, usually congenital, resulting from lack of thyroid secretion. Cretins are often feeble-minded and dwarfed.

Creusa (krēōō′sŭ), in Greek and Roman legend, princess of Corinth. When Jason wished to marry Creusa, his wife, MEDEA, killed her.

Creuse (krûz), department (2,164 sq. mi.; pop. 188,669), central France, in Marche; cap. Guéret.

Creusot, Le (lù krûzō′), city (pop. 17,133), Saône-et-Loire dept., E central France, in coal-mining region. Seat of large Schneider plants (steel and munitions). Heavily damaged in World War II.

crevasse (krŭvăs′), crack in surface of a glacier caused by stresses developed as ice moves. The word is also applied to a crack in a river levee.

Crèvecœur, J. Hector St. John (krĕvkûr′), 1735–1813, American author and agriculturist, b. France. He introduced culture of European crops in America and wrote *Letters from an American Farmer* (1782).

Creve Coeur (krēv′ kōōr′), village (pop. 5,-499), N central Ill., near Peoria, in agr. and coal area.

Crewe (krōō), municipal borough (pop. 52,-415), Cheshire, England; an important railway junction.

Crichton, James (krī′tŭn), 1560?–1582, Scottish adventurer and scholar, called the Admirable Crichton. Attracted much attention in Italy (1579) by personal charms and scholarship; reputedly spoke 12 languages. Was killed in a street brawl.

cricket, insect of order Orthoptera related to grasshopper and katydid. Typical species have long antennae and powerful hind legs. Some are winged. Most are nocturnal. They often destroy vegetation; some also eat insects. Males "chirp" by rubbing one front wing against other, causing vibration; pitch and rate vary with temperature.

cricket, national sport of England. Played with bats and ball by two opposing teams of 11 men on level, closely cut green turf preferably measuring about 525 ft. by about 550 ft., with two wickets 66 ft. apart. Cricket was played in medieval England. London Cricket Club drew up (1774) first authoritative set of rules. Marylebone Cricket Club, governing body of game, founded 1787.

Crile, George Washington (krīl), 1864–1943, American surgeon. He was an authority on thyroid operations and surgical shock and author of technical and popular scientific works.

crime, legally, act in violation of the law consciously committed by a sane adult. Punishment is meted out by the government. Causes of crime are complex. Former beliefs in hereditary criminality and link of crime with physical characteristics are now generally discarded, and emphasis of study has shifted to environmental and psychological factors —poverty, family background, emotional disorders. With increasing complexity of industrial society came more laws and more crime. Offenses against property (e.g., theft) more common in cities, but crimes of violence (e. g., murder, rape) equally common in urban and rural areas. General attitude toward crime has changed since humanitarian movement began late in 18th cent. Emphasis now is placed on crime prevention and rehabilitation of criminal.

Crimea (krīmē′ù), Rus. *Krim,* anc. *Chersonesus Taurica,* peninsula (c.10,000 sq. mi.; pop. c.1,050,000), S European RSFSR, on N shore of Black Sea, connected with mainland by PEREKOP Isthmus. Cities: Simferopol, Sevastopol, Kerch, Feodosiya, Eupatoria. Consists of wheat and cotton-growing steppe in N; Crimean or Yaila Mts. (highest point 5,062 ft.) in S; and subtropical littoral ("Russian Riviera"), growing fruit, wine, tobacco, with famous resorts such as Yalta. KERCH peninsula (E) has mineral wealth and heavy industries. Early inhabitants, Cimmerians, were followed in 8th cent. B.C. by Scythians. Coast was colonized by Ionian Greeks 7th cent. B.C. Ruled by a Thracian dynasty after 438 B.C., the "kingdom of a Cimmerian

Bosporus" was annexed c.110 B.C. by Mithridates VI of Pontus and soon afterward by Rome. Between 3d and 13th cent. A.D. the Crimea was overrun by Goths, Huns, Khazars, Cumans, Mongols. Coast was controlled by Byzantium 6th–12th cent., then by Genoa, which set up prosperous colonies, notably at FEODOSIYA. In 1475 Crimea fell to the TATARS, whose khans were vassals to Ottoman sultans from 1478. From their cap. at BAKHCHISARAI the khans conquered ports of S Russia, pushed their raids as far as Moscow and Poland. In 1774 Catherine II forced Turkey to declare the khanate independent; in 1783 she annexed it to Russia. Many Russian, Greek, and other settlers came. The Crimea was a battleground in the Crimean War (1854–56), in both world wars, and in the Russian civil war, when in 1920 it became the last refuge of the Whites. Its status as autonomous soviet republic, created 1921, was abolished during World War II; the Tatar pop., charged with aiding the Germans, was deported.

Crimean War (krīmē′ùn), 1853–56, between Russia and allied powers of Turkey, England, France, Sardinia. General causes: see EASTERN QUESTION. Pretext: quarrel between Russia and France over guardianship of Palestinian holy places. Turkey having turned down Russian demands, Russia occupied Moldavia and Walachia, and Turkey declared war (1853). France and England joined Turkey in 1854; Sardinia in 1855. Main campaign, centered on siege of SEVASTOPOL in Crimea, was marked by futile gallantry (e.g., battle of BALAKLAVA) and scandalous condition of hospitals (which prompted the work of Florence NIGHTINGALE). Peace treaty (see PARIS, CONGRESS OF) checked Russian influence in SE Europe.

criminal law, distinct body of legal rules governing the definition and trial of crimes (acts deemed detrimental to the state), a part of public law. The state rather than a private individual seeks out and punishes the offender. In England criminal law developed out of common law; principles brought by settlers to British American colonies. In U.S. some important fundamental rules are: no act is a crime unless defined as such in law; accused is considered innocent until proved guilty; bills of attainder (legislative decrees declaring guilt without trial) and *ex post facto* laws (which define as crimes acts committed before the law was adopted) are forbidden.

crinoid (krī′noid, krī′-), marine animal, an echinoderm of class Crinoidea, related to starfish and sea urchin, and found in deep sea and tropical waters. Crinoids include sea lily and feather star. The body is usually a central disk with plumelike arms; many forms have stalks.

Cripple Creek, city (pop. 853; alt. 9,375 ft.), central Colo., SW of Colorado Springs. Started as mining camp after 1891 gold discovery. Had c.50,000 pop. in 1901. Production declined, but mining continued. New veins found and worked after 1934; old mines reactivated after drainage tunnel built, 1941.

Cripps, Sir Stafford, 1889–1952, British statesman; nephew of Beatrice Webb. Brilliant lawyer, was solicitor general in Labour government 1930–31. Expelled from Labour party 1939 for urging united front with communists; readmitted 1945. Under Churchill was ambassador to USSR (1940), lord privy seal and leader in Commons (1942), and envoy to India (1942) with self-government plan. In Labour government initiated (1945) Britain's austerity program. As minister of economic affairs and chancellor of exchequer (1947–50) virtually controlled British economy until ill health forced his resignation.

Crispi, Francesco (fränchä′skō krē′spē), b. 1818 or 1819, d. 1901, Italian premier (1887–91, 1893–96). Fostered colonial expansion.

Crispin and Crispinian, Saints, 3d cent., missionaries in Gaul martyred under Diocletian. They were brothers, both shoemakers. Feast: Oct. 25. The "Crispin Crispinian" speech in Shakspere's *Henry V,* Act IV, refers to the feast.

Crispus, Christian convert. Acts 18.8; I Cor. 1.14.

Cristobal (kristo′bŭl), Span. *Cristóbal* (krēstō′bäl), town (pop. 417), Panama Canal Zone, near the Atlantic end of Canal; American residential quarter for Colón.

Cristus, Petrus: see CHRISTUS, PETRUS.

criticism, judging or evaluating works of art or literature. Canons have changed with tastes of different periods. In early 20th cent., neo-humanism was rivaled by economic and sociological theories of interpretation. Psychology and semantics have strongly affected recent criticism. Notable in history of criticism have been Aristotle, Horace, Alexander Pope, Lessing, Sainte-Beuve, Matthew Arnold, Saintsbury, Vernon L. Parrington, I. A Richards, and T. S. Eliot.

Critius (krĭ′shŭs) and **Nesiotes** (nēshēō′tēz), 5th cent. B.C., Greek sculptors during the Persian Wars.

Crittenden, John Jordan, 1787–1863, American statesman. U.S. Attorney General (1841, 1850–53). As U.S. Senator (1855–61) from Ky., he attempted to conciliate North and South by **Crittenden Compromise,** proposal to settle slavery issue through constitutional amendments, including restoration of Missouri Compromise line; plan was defeated.

Crivelli, Carlo (krēvĕl′lē), b. c.1430, d. after 1493, Venetian religious painter, active in the Marches. His *Pietà* in Metropolitan Mus.

Crna Gora, Yugoslavia: see MONTENEGRO.

Croaghpatrick (krō′äpä′trĭk), mountain, Co. Mayo, Ireland. Connected by legend with St. Patrick, its summit has long been a place of pilgrimage.

Croatan (krō′ŭtăn′), unexplained word derived incorrectly from letters CROATOAN, which were found carved on tree of ROANOKE ISLAND in 17th cent., claimed by some to indicate that the "lost colony" had joined Indians.

Croatia (krōä′shŭ),Croatian *Hrvatska,* autonomous republic (21,611 sq. mi.; pop. 3,749,-039), NW Yugoslavia; cap. Zagreb. W section is crossed by DINARIC ALPS; E part is agr. plain, drained by Sava and Drava rivers. Republic consists of Croatia proper, SLAVONIA, DALMATIA, and most of ISTRIA. Chief

cities: ZAGREB, FIUME, OSIJEK, SPLIT, ZARA. Part of Pannonia prov. under Rome, region was settled in 7th cent. by Slavic Croats, who accepted Roman Catholicism (9th cent.) and set up a kingdom (10th cent.). From 1091 to 1918 (except during Turkish occupation, 1526–1699; French occupation, 1809–13; and Austrian annexation, 1849–68), Croatia was in personal union with Hungary—i.e., the kings of Hungary were also kings of Croatia, which, however, was governed by native bans and had its own diet. United with Serbia in 1918 (see YUGOSLAVIA), Croatia despite intense nationalist agitation secured autonomy only in 1939. After Germany invaded Yugoslavia (1941), a nationalist and terrorist group—the Ustachi —declared Croatia an independent kingdom under the nominal rule of Aimone, duke of Spoleto (an Italian prince) and under the dictatorship of their leader, Ante Pavelich. In 1943 Croatia passed under German control, but a large part of the people joined the anti-German partisan forces. In 1946 Croatia became one of Yugoslavia's six constituent republics.

Croce, Benedetto (bānädĕt′tō krō′chä), 1866–1952, Italian philosopher and critic. His broad idealistic thought is reflected in his *Philosophy of the Spirit* (1902–17), divided into four parts: *Aesthetic as Science of Expression and General Linguistic; Logic as the Science of Pure Concept; Philosophy of the Practical;* and *History: Its Theory and Practice.* Minister of education 1920–21, he lived in retirement under Fascism.

crochet work (krōshā′), form of knitting in which a hook is used to draw thread into patterns of interconnected loops. Used in making lace, bedspreads, tablecloths, apparel (e.g., hats and bags).

Crocker, William, 1876–1950, American botanist, director of Boyce Thompson Inst. for Plant Research from 1921. Known for research on plant growth.

Crockett, David (Davy), 1786–1836, American frontiersman. U.S. Representative from Tenn. (1827–31, 1833–35), known for backwoods humor. Died at the ALAMO. Supposed author of autobiographical exploits.

Crockett, town (pop. 5,932), E Texas, SSE of Palestine, in lumber and farm area. Replica of first Spanish mission (1690) in E Texas near by.

crocodile (krŏ′kŭdĭl), large carnivorous reptile of order Crocodilia. It has tough scales on top, bony plates underneath, powerful jaws, short legs, and a vertically flattened tail. American species, inhabiting fresh (sometimes salt) water near S Fla., in West Indies, and Central and N South America, is not hostile to humans.

crocus, low plant of genus *Crocus,* with grasslike foliage and purple, yellow, or white flowers (usually goblet shaped) in spring or autumn. See also MEADOW SAFFRON; SAFFRON.

Croesus (krē′sŭs), d. 546? B.C., king of Lydia after 560 B.C. He was to the Greeks a symbol of wealth. Allied himself with Egypt and Babylonia against Cyrus the Great of Persia and was defeated and captured.

crofter: see COTTER.

Croghan, George (krō'gŭn), d. 1782, American Indian agent, b. Ireland. Became deputy superintendent of Indian affairs in 1756 under Sir William Johnson. Responsible for much of Johnson's success.

Croker, Richard, 1841–1922, American politician, boss of Tammany Hall (1886–1902), b. Ireland. Abdicated after Tammany defeat in 1901 election.

Cro-Magnon man: see MAN, PRIMITIVE.

Cromarty, county: see ROSS AND CROMARTY.

Cromarty Firth, deep narrow inlet of Firth of Moray in Ross and Cromarty co., Scotland. An excellent anchorage, it was a naval base in World War I.

Crome, John, 1768–1821, English landscape painter, founder of Norwich School; often called Old Crome. Influenced by Gainsborborough and Dutch masters. His son, **John Bernay Crome,** 1794–1842, painted landscapes in father's style.

Cromer, Evelyn Baring, 1st earl of, 1841–1917, British administrator and diplomat in Egypt. Was virtual ruler 1883–1907, reforming Egyptian finances, administration, and education.

Crommelynck, Fernand (fĕrnä' krômŭlĕk'), 1888–, Belgian poet and dramatist, author of tragic farce *Le Cocu Magnifique* (1921).

Cromwell, Oliver, 1599–1658, lord protector of England. Was strong Puritan in Parliament. Prominent in PURITAN REVOLUTION because of military ability (esp. at Edgehill 1642 and Marston Moor 1644). In struggle between largely Presbyterian Parliament and Puritan army, he proposed army reorganization (1644). Given command with Baron Fairfax; defeated Charles I at Naseby. After flight of Charles in 1645, he lost hope of dealing with king and was leader in demand for his execution. Led cruelly punitive expedition to Ireland (1649) where he continued policy of settling English. Invaded Scotland 1650; defeated Charles II and royalist Scots. Dissolved Rump Parliament 1653; tried to replace it with feeble Barebone's Parliament appointed by himself. PROTECTORATE estab. 1653 with Cromwell as lord protector. Declined the crown 1656. New constitution (1657) strengthened his powers. Tried to build up Protestant league abroad but policy was governed by need for foreign trade. Navigation Act (1651) led to first DUTCH WAR (1652–54). War with Spain (1655–58) was over trade rights. Opinions of him vary widely. Favored religious toleration and democracy, but tolerated only Jews and non-Anglican Protestants and could not work with Parliament. His military genius and force of character are recognized but necessities of governing forced him into cruelty and intolerance. Dependence of Protectorate on him was shown when his son, **Richard Cromwell,** 1626–1712, succeeded him as lord protector, 1658. Army and Parliament struggled for power until Commonwealth was reestab. 1659. He lived abroad, 1660–80, and later in England under assumed name. A man of virtue and dignity, he was forced into a situation beyond his talents.

Cromwell, Thomas, earl of Essex 1485?–1540, English statesman. Legal secretary to Cardinal Wolsey; avoided implication in his fall and attracted attention of Henry VIII. Carried out suppression of monasteries (some of whose wealth he received). Made lord great chamberlain 1539; negotiated Henry's marriage to Anne of Cleves to secure German alliance. This failed and he was convicted of treason and heresy and beheaded.

Cronstadt, RSFSR: see KRONSTADT.

Cronstedt, Axel Fredrik, Baron (äk'sŭl frä'drĭk krōōn'stĕt), 1722–65, Swedish mineralogist. Discovered nickel in niccolite; one of first to recognize importance of chemical constituents of minerals.

Cronus (krō'nŭs), Gr. *Kronos* [time], in Greek legend, the youngest TITAN, son of URANUS [heaven] and GAEA [earth]. He led Titans in revolt against Uranus and ruled the world. Father by RHEA of the great gods—ZEUS, Poseidon, Demeter, Hera, and Hestia. Fated to be overthrown by one of his children, he tried unsuccessfully to destroy them. Zeus later led the Olympian gods against his father in successful revolt called TITANOMACHY. He is equated with Roman Saturn.

Crook, George, 1828–90, U.S. general. An able Indian fighter, especially against Paiute and Snake Indians in Idaho, in Sioux War of 1876, and against Apaches under Geronimo. Noted for patience and integrity in dealing peaceably with Indians.

Crookes, Sir William (krōōks), 1832–1919, English chemist, physicist. He discovered thallium; studied radioactivity, selenium, rare earths, diamonds. He invented a high-vacuum tube, the **Crookes tube:** a glass bulb with air exhausted and anode and cathode set in walls. When high-voltage current is used, electrons come from cathode and cause yellow-green fluorescence of the glass.

Crooks, Ramsay, 1787–1859, American fur trader, b. Scotland. Second in command to John Jacob Astor in American Fur Co.

Crookston, city (pop. 7,352), NW Minn., on Red Lake R. and SE of Grand Forks, N.Dak. Trade center in agr. (grain, sugar beets, potatoes) area.

croquet (krōkā'), lawn game in which players hit wooden balls with wooden mallets through series of wire arches (9 or 10). A favorite game in Ireland in 18th cent., also popular in France, England, U.S.

Crosby, Bing, 1904–, American singer and moving-picture actor, whose real name is Harry Lillis Crosby. A popular singer with dance bands, he gained enormous success on the radio. Popularized many songs (e.g., *White Christmas*). He also won fame as an actor in films (e.g., *Going My Way*).

Cross, Wilbur L(ucius), 1862–1948, American educator and public official. Professor of English at Yale (1902–30), dean of graduate school (1916–30); authority on the English novel. As Democratic governor of Conn. (1931–39), he brought about much reform legislation.

crossbow, medieval military weapon consisting of a bow set on a stock to give it greater strength than an ordinary bow. It was used to fire stones and metal as well as arrows (sometimes flaming, used to ignite buildings under siege). A late form was the arbalest, which worked with a kind of ratchet. The advantage of the crossbow was power. This was in the end outweighed by clumsiness— as evidenced by the victory of English long-bowmen over Genoese crossbowmen (fighting for the French) at Crécy (1346).

cross vine: see BIGNONIA.

Crothers, Rachel (krŭ′dhŭrz), 1878–, American dramatist. Her comedies, notable for craftsmanship and clever dialogue, include *A Man's World* (1909), *Let Us Be Gay* (1929), and *Susan and God* (1937).

Croton, short river, SE N.Y., flowing S and SW to Hudson R. near Ossining. Paralleled by **Croton Aqueduct** (38 mi. long; built 1837–42), which carries water from Croton basin reservoirs to New York city. Aqueduct begins at Croton L. in Croton R.; crosses Harlem R. into New York over High Bridge. Supplemented by a second aqueduct (built (1885–91).

Crotona (krōtō′nŭ), anc. city, S Italy, on E coast of Calabria, a city founded (8th cent.) by Greeks. Reached its height in 6th cent. B.C., when Pythagoras had his school here and the army, led by the athlete Milo, defeated Sybaris (510 B.C.). Declined later. Called Cotrone from Middle Ages to 1928.

Croton Aqueduct: see CROTON, river.

crow, partially migratory black bird of same family as the raven, magpie, jay, rook, and European jackdaw. American or eastern crow is c.19 in. long with wingspread of c.3 ft. It destroys injurious insects and rodents, but also eats some eggs, nestlings, and grain. It is easily tamed.

crowberry, low, alpine evergreen plant (*Empetrum*), with berrylike fruits. It is suited to rockeries.

crowfoot: see BUTTERCUP.

Crow Indians or **Absaroka,** tribe ranging chiefly about Yellowstone R., of Siouan linguistic stock. Had typical Plains culture.

Crowley (krou′lē), city (pop. 12,784), SW La., SW of Baton Rouge; founded 1886. Processes and ships rice, and has rice experiment station.

Crowninshield, Frederic, 1845–1918, American decorative artist. Work includes murals and landscapes.

Crown Point 1 Residential city (pop. 5,839), NW Ind., S of Gary. Mfg. of monuments and signs. **2** Town (1940 pop. 1,661), NE N.Y., on L. Champlain and N of Ticonderoga; a summer resort. French fort, built 1731, was demolished 1759 in French and Indian Wars. British fort, built 1759, was captured by Green Mountain Boys (1775) but abandoned in Saratoga campaign (1777). Crown Point Reservation is here.

Croydon, county borough (pop. 249,592), Surrey, England; a suburb of London. Airport, formerly important, used by military during World War II.

Cruden, Alexander, 1701?–1770, British scholar, a London bookseller and proofreader. His *Complete Concordance to the Holy Scriptures* (1737) is basis of later biblical concordances.

Cruikshank, George (krŏŏk′-), 1792–1878, English caricaturist and illustrator. Etchings include notable illustrations for *Oliver Twist*.

cruiser, large, fast, moderately armed warship, intermediate between battleship and destroyer. Modern cruisers fall in two classes: battle cruisers (in effect small battleships, representing an effort to combine maximum gun caliber, armor protection, and speed); and light cruisers (of moderate tonnage, lightly armed, and very fast).

Crusades, wars undertaken by European Christians between 11th and 14th cent. to recover the Holy Land, particularly JERUSALEM, from Islam. The movement began in France, when Pope URBAN II at the Council of Clermont (1095) exhorted Christendom to war, promising that the journey would count as full penance and that a general truce would protect the homes of the absent ones. From the crosses distributed at this meeting the Crusaders took their name. Religious motives dominated at first, but worldly considerations were never absent, and the conflict between spiritual and material aims grew increasingly serious: the nobles hoped for loot and territorial aggrandizement; the Italian cities expanded trade with the Near East; all were lured by travel and adventure. The **First Crusade,** 1095–99, began with the march of several undisciplined hordes of French and German peasants, led by WALTER THE PENNILESS, PETER THE HERMIT, and others. They started out by massacring the Jews in the Rhineland; incensed the Bulgarians and Hungarians, who attacked and dispersed them; reached Constantinople in shreds; crossed over to Asia Minor; and were promptly defeated by the Turks. The organized host, led by Count RAYMOND IV of Toulouse, GODFREY OF BOUILLON, BOHEMOND, and TANCRED, followed in 1097. All save Raymond and Tancred swore fealty to the Byzantine Emperor, ALEXIUS I, binding themselves to accept him as overlord of their conquests. Their victorious campaign was crowned by the conquest of Jerusalem (1099). The establishment of the Latin Kingdom of JERUSALEM and of the orders of KNIGHTS HOSPITALERS and KNIGHTS TEMPLARS followed. The **Second Crusade,** 1147–99, preached by St. BERNARD OF CLAIRVAUX after the fall of EDESSA (1144) was led by Emperor Conrad III and by Louis VII of France. It ended in dismal failure. In 1187 SALADIN captured Jerusalem. The **Third Crusade,** 1189–92, led by Emperor FREDERICK I, PHILIP II of France, and RICHARD I of England, failed to recapture the city, but Richard I negotiated a truce by which Christians were granted free access to the Holy Sepulchre. The **Fourth Crusade,** 1202–4, began in France but was completely diverted from its purpose by its leader, Enrico Dandolo, for the benefit of Venice. To pay for their passage, the Crusaders assisted the Venetians to recover Zara from Hungary (1202). Despite violent papal condemnation after the sack of that Christian city, the host next turned toward Constantinople, ostensibly to restore ISAAC II on his throne. In 1204 they stormed and sacked the city, divided the spoils with Venice, and set up the Latin Empire of CONSTANTINOPLE. The pathetic **Children's Crusade** of 1212 was preached by a visionary French peasant boy, Stephen of Cloyes. Thousands of children set out for Holy Land but instead were sold into slavery by unscrupulous skippers. Another group, of German children, made their way by land; they perished of hunger and disease. The **Fifth Crusade,** 1217–21, preached by Innocent III, was aimed at Egypt and failed. The **Sixth Crusade,** 1228–29, undertaken by Emperor FREDERICK II, was actually a peaceful visit. Frederick made a truce with the Moslems, securing the surrender of the Holy Places. Sporadic warfare soon broke out again. The Christian rout by the Egyptian MAMELUKES at Gaza (1244) led to the **Seventh Crusade,** 1248–54, led by LOUIS IX of France. Despite Louis's gallantry, the enterprise failed; his death cut short the **Eighth Crusade** (1270). The **Ninth Crusade,** 1271–72, led by Prince Edward (later Edward I of England) was abortive. In 1291 Acre, the last Christian stronghold, fell. The term *crusade* was also applied to other expeditions, sanctioned by the pope, against heretics and heathens (e.g., the WENDS, the ALBIGENSES) and, more loosely, to campaigns of the 15th–16th cent. against the Turks.

crustacean (krŭstā′shùn), animal of class Crustacea of phylum Arthropoda. Examples are CRAB, LOBSTER, SHRIMP, CRAYFISH, BARNACLE, water flea or daphnia, cyclops, pill bug, sow bug. They have jointed appendages and a horny outer skeleton. Breathing organs are gills. Colorless blood usually circulated by a heart. Some are omnivorous, some eat flesh only, some plants only. Many are parasites.

Cruveilhier, Jean (zhä′ krüvěyă′), 1791–1874, French physician, pioneer in descriptive pathology.

Cruz, Juana Inés de la: see JUANA INÉS DE LA CRUZ.

Cruz, Ramón de la (rämōn′ dä lä krōōth′), 1731–94, Spanish dramatist, best known for *sainetes,* short realistic comedies of Madrid lower-class life. Also wrote tragedies and a Spanish version of *Hamlet.*

cryolite or **kryolite** (krī′ûlīt), a mineral, fluoride of sodium and aluminum, used in making lampshades, hard glass, porcelain. Found in Greenland.

cryptography (krĭptŏ′grŭfē) [Gr.,= hidden writing], art of secret writing, employed from anc. times. A cryptogram is a sacred message and also the form in which it is couched. Forms include codes, ciphers, invisible writing, and other devices which make true meaning discernible only to the one holding the proper key. Codes used in business are usually systems of pronounceable words with meanings listed in code books held by firms involved. Ciphers often consist of unpronounceable words made up by transposition of letters within the message or substitution of one letter for another or of a number for a letter. A famous cipher was that devised by Francis Bacon (1605). In modern times official government cryptography, the solution of cryptograms, and even the general methods employed are jealously controlled by governments, since codes and ciphers are used for secret messages in peacetime as well as in war.

crystal, solid having definite internal structure owing to atomic arrangement and definite external form (polyhedron bounded by natural plane surfaces) which is the manifestation of its internal structure. Crystallization is the assumption of crystal form when a substance passes from liquid or gaseous state to solid state or when it goes out of solution. Crystalline species are grouped, according to their type of symmetry, into 32 classes, which in turn are grouped into six systems: cubic or isometric, hexagonal, tetragonal, orthorhombic, monoclinic, triclinic.

Crystal City, city (pop. 7,198), SW Texas, SW of San Antonio, in irrigated winter-garden area. Spinach is main product.

Crystal Palace, building erected in Hyde Park, London, for the Great Exhibition in 1851. Served for a time as a museum. Torn down in 1941 because it served as a guide to enemy air raiders.

Cs, chemical symbol of the element CESIUM.

Csaba, Hungary: see BEKESCSABA.

Csepel (chě′pěl), city (pop. 46,171), central Hungary, on Csepel isl. (30 mi. long) in the Danube, near Budapest. Aluminum and iron mills; mfg. of machinery and munitions.

Ctesibius (tĭsĭ′bēûs), 2d cent. B.C., Alexandrian Greek reputed first to perceive and apply expansive power of air as motive force.

Ctesiphon (tě′sĭfŏn), ruined anc. city, near Baghdad, Iraq, on the Tigris at mouth of the Diyala. Was cap. of Parthian kings and later of Sassanidae.

Cu, chemical symbol of the element COPPER.

Cuauhtémoc (kōō-outä′môk), d. 1525, Aztec emperor. After the Spanish were driven from the Aztec cap., he fought valiantly until the city was taken and he was made captive. Taken along on the march to Honduras, he was hanged by order of Cortés. Also Cuauhtemoctzín, Guatémoc, Quauhtémoc.

Cuba (kū′bù, Span. kōō′vä), republic (44,218 sq. mi.; pop. 4,778,583, incl. Isle of Pines), occupying all the island of Cuba, westernmost and largest of the West Indies; cap. HAVANA (largest city of the West Indies). The island (c.700 mi. long, averaging 50 mi. in breadth) lies at the entrance to the Gulf of Mexico, with the Atlantic on the N, the Caribbean on the S; its W tip is 90 mi. from Key West, Fla. The chief ports besides Havana are SANTIAGO DE CUBA, MATANZAS, CIENFUEGOS, and GUANTÁNAMO. The mountains (in several groups) have deposits of iron, manganese, copper, nickel, chromium, and barite, and the forests of the interior yield timber and naval stores, but Cuba has been mainly dependent for exports on sugar, fine tobacco, and coffee. Other products are tropical fruits, henequen, sponges, hides, and winter vegetables. After discovery by Columbus (1492), Cuba was explored by the Spanish, and by 1511 a colony was firmly planted. Expeditions went out to conquer other territories (notably Mexico), and the island, "the Pearl of the Antilles," was a gathering point for Spanish treasure fleets from the New World. It was much harassed by French and English buccaneers. The native Arawak Indians soon died out, and the sugar plantations were worked with the labor of imported Negroes. The Negro element has contributed much to Cuban life. In the early 19th cent., when most of Latin America won independence from Spain,

Cuba remained in the empire. There were intermittent revolts and filibustering expeditions, rising to a climax in the TEN YEARS WAR (1868–78). Spain retained control until a new revolt precipitated the SPANISH-AMERICAN WAR (1898), in which Cuba gained independence with U.S. help. Its history thereafter was dominated by the question of relationship with the U.S. and with the problem of a one-crop economy. U.S. military occupation of the island lasted until 1902, and the Platt Amendment (see PLATT, ORVILLE H.) giving the U.S. the right to intervene led to new occupations (1906–9, 1912). U.S. citizens owned many plantations and industries, and "Yankee imperialism" in Cuba was much decried in Latin America until a new basis for relationship was estab. in the administration of F. D. Roosevelt. A sugar boom in World War I led to later false prosperity ("the dance of the millions") and then almost total collapse. Diversification of agr. has been forwarded to avoid the ills of one-crop economy. Political life in Cuba has been stormy and intermittently marked by dictatorships (e.g., that of Gerardo Machado). After 1940 the dominant figure was Fulgencio BATISTA, who became president for the second time by a coup d'état in 1952.

Cubberley, Ellwood Patterson, 1868–1941, American educator. At Stanford Univ. after 1898, he was professor of education after 1906, dean of the school of education from 1917 to 1933. Wrote *A History of Education* (1920).

cube, in geometry, a regular solid bounded by six equal squares perpendicular to one another.

cubeb (kū′bĕb), dried, unripe berry of a climbing pepper plant, *Piper cubeba,* native to East and West Indies. Used medicinally and as a condiment.

cube root, see ROOT, in mathematics.

cubism, a movement primarily in painting, originating c.1910 in France. One of the earliest forms of modern abstract art, it tended to reduce painting to design in space based on three-dimensional geometry. While it no longer flourishes, many are indebted to its discipline. Picasso, Braque, and Gris were among the early cubists.

Cuchulain (kōōkǔ′lǐn, kōō′khōōlǐn), [Irish,= the hound of Culan], Irish legendary hero of Ulster. He is central figure of Ulster legends, of which greatest is *Táin Bó Cúalnge* [the cattle raid of Cooley], wherein he defends his province singlehanded against armies of the rest of Ireland.

cuckoo (kōō′kōō), name for certain birds abundant in tropics, widespread in both hemispheres except in colder regions. They are usually insectivorous, arboreal, and have slightly decurved bills, long tails, and usually dull plumage. Many cuckoos make no nests but lay eggs in nests of other birds. Family includes ROAD RUNNER, ani, trogon, and KINGFISHER. Black-billed and yellow-billed cuckoos of U.S. are slender, long-billed, olive-brown birds which eat destructive insects. Maynard's cuckoo and California cuckoo are other related birds. The cuckoo has featured largely in English literature as early herald of spring from Middle English "Sumer Is Icumen In," through Wordsworth, to present day.

cucumber, fruit of *Cucumis sativus,* an annual vine. It is eaten either raw or pickled.

cucumber tree: see MAGNOLIA.

Cúcuta (kōō′kōōtä), city (pop. 37,323), NE Colombia, c.10 mi. from Venezuelan border on E cordillera of Andes, in rich coffee-raising region. Congress of 1821 met here to draft constitution for Greater Colombia.

Cudahy (kǔ′dúhē), city (pop. 12,182), SE Wis., on L. Michigan between Milwaukee and South Milwaukee; city and its meat-packing industry founded 1892.

Cuenca (kwĕn′kä), city (pop. 46,428; alt., c.8,000 ft.), S central Ecuador; founded 1557. In rich agr. basin of Ecuadorian Andes, it produces grains, subsistence crops, and cattle. Panama hats are woven here.

Cuenca, city (pop. 23,038), cap. of Cuenca prov., E central Spain, in New Castile. Medieval castle; 13th-cent. cathedral.

Cuernavaca (kwĕrnävä′kä), city (pop. 14,336), cap. of Morelos, central Mexico; popular tourist and health resort. Palace built here by Cortés now is decorated with murals by Diego Rivera. Maximilian and Carlotta frequently stayed in Cuernavaca.

Cuero (kwâ′rō), city (pop. 7,498), S Texas, on Guadalupe R. and NW of Victoria. Processes poultry, cotton, milk, and farm products. Annual Turkey Trot.

Cueva, Beatriz de la (bäätrēs′ dä lä kwä′vä), d. 1541, governor of Guatemala, only woman to govern major American political division in Spanish times. Succeeded her husband, Pedro de Alvarado, to position but was killed a few weeks later in flood.

Cueva, Juan de la (hwän′ dä lä kwä′vä), 1550?–1610?, Spanish dramatist, precursor of Lope de Vega. Wrote *Los siete infantes de Lara* (presented 1579).

Cui, César (Antonovich) (tsäzär′ küē′), 1835–1918, Russian composer and critic. He proclaimed the ideals of the nationalist composers, especially the Russian Five, of which he was a member. His own works include operas, songs, orchestral and salon music.

Cuiabá (kōōyúbä′), city (pop. 24,119), cap. of Mato Grosso state, W Brazil, at head of navigable Cuiabá R.; founded in gold rush of 18th cent.

Culbertson, Ely (ē′lē kǔl′bǔrtsùn), 1893–, American expert on contract bridge, b. Rumania of American-Russian parentage. Became a leading figure in the playing of bridge. After World War II he wrote and lectured widely on world peace. His writings include *The Contract Bridge Blue Book* (1930) and *Must We Fight Russia?* (1946).

Culiacán (kōōlēäkän′), city (pop. 22,025), cap. of Sinaloa, NW Mexico; founded 1531. It figured prominently in Spanish colonial period as point of departure for expeditions to N, notably that of Coronado (1540). Surrounding area produces tropical fruits, sugar, cotton, some minerals.

Culion (kōōlyôn′), island (150 sq. mi.; pop. 7,328), one of Calamian Isls., Philippines. Has leper colony.

Cullen, Countee, 1903–46, American Negro poet.

Cullman, city (pop. 7,523), N Ala., N of Birmingham. Ships strawberries, cotton, timber.

Culloden Moor (kŭlŏ′dŭn), moorland, Inverness-shire, Scotland. Scene of decisive defeat (1746) of Prince Charles Edward by English troops.

Culpeper or **Colepeper, Thomas Culpeper,** 2d **Baron** (both: kŭl′pĕ″pŭr), 1636–89, British colonial governor of Va. (1675–83).

cultivation, working soil to improve its condition, by means of tools (e.g., hoe, plow) or machinery. Includes mixing, loosening, adding humus, destroying weeds; aided by IRRIGATION and ROTATION OF CROPS.

culture, in anthropology, the way of life of a society, without implication of refinement or advanced knowledge. Culture is historically transmitted, primarily through language, and is the attribute that most distinguishes man from the animals.

Culver City, residential city (pop. 19,720), S Calif., between Los Angeles and the Pacific coast; laid out 1913. Has moving-picture studios. Los Angeles International Airport is here.

Culver-Stockton College, at Canton, Mo.; coed. (probably first W of the Mississippi); chartered 1853, opened 1855 by Disciples of Christ as Christian Univ., renamed 1917.

Cumae (kū′mē), anc. city of Campania, Italy; a Greek colony. A powerful city, it was conquered by Samnites (5th cent. B.C.), later rose and declined under Roman control, disappeared only in 13th cent. A.D.

Cumans (kū′mŭnz), nomadic people of Turkic language; also called Kipchaks and, in Russian, Polovtsi. Conquered S Russia and Walachia (11th cent.); warred with Byzantium, Hungary, Kiev. After defeat by Mongols (c.1245), part of Cumans fled to Hungary, where they merged with Magyars.

Cumberland, Richard, 1732–1811, English dramatist, author of sentimental plays such as *The Brothers* (1769), *The West Indian* (1771), *The Wheel of Fortune* (1795).

Cumberland, county (1,520 sq. mi.; pop. 285,-347), N England, next to Scotland; co. town Carlisle. Low in N, county is mountainous in SW and E. Scafell Pike (3,210 ft.) highest point in England. Pastoral area, with some mining, quarrying, textile mfg., and smelting. Scene of centuries of border strife between England and Scotland. The region, with Westmorland and Lancashire known as LAKE DISTRICT, popular with 19th-cent. literary figures.

Cumberland. 1 City (pop. 37,679), NW Md., on North Branch of Potomac R. and W of Hagerstown; laid out 1785 on site of trading post and around Fort Cumberland (hq. of Gen. Braddock 1755). Railroad shipping point with mfg. of rayon, clothing, and tires. Gateway through Appalachians to Ohio valley, city became E end of Cumberland or NATIONAL ROAD, division point for Baltimore & Ohio RR, and W terminus of Chesapeake and Ohio Canal. **2** Town (pop. 12,-842), NE R.I., between Blackstone R. and Mass. line. Mfg. of textiles and metal goods. Has Ballou Meetinghouse (c.1740).

Cumberland, river formed on Cumberland Plateau in E Ky. by juncture of Poor and Clover forks, and flowing 693 mi. SW then

NW through Ky. and Tenn. to Ohio R. above Paducah, Ky. Locks, dams, levees, and canals improve navigation and irrigation; power projects planned. TVA authorized to market power from three dams.

Cumberland Gap, natural mountain pass, near point where Va., Ky., and Tenn. meet. Discovered 1750; WILDERNESS ROAD ran through it. Gap was held by both sides during Civil War. National historical park authorized.

Cumberland House, Hudson's Bay Co. fur-trading post, W Man., Canada, on Cumberland L., near The Pass. Built 1774 by Samuel Hearne; first permanent settlement on Saskatchewan R. and the company's first interior post. Commanded fur trade and exploration routes to upper Saskatchewan and Churchill rivers.

Cumberland Island: see SEA ISLANDS.

Cumberland Plateau or **Cumberland Mountains,** SW division of Appalachian Mts. Extends NE-SW through S W.Va., SW Va., E Ky., E Tenn., and N Ala. Rises E from Great Valley of E Tenn., and slopes roughly W. Source of Cumberland and other rivers. Has coal and timber resources.

Cumberland Presbyterian Church, branch of Presbyterian Church in U.S. It arose as revival movement in "Cumberland country" of Tenn. and Ky. Its presbytery was dissolved by synod but reorganized (1810) as independent body. Negro organization set apart (1869) as Colored Cumberland Presbyterian Church.

Cumberland Road: see NATIONAL ROAD.

Cumberland Valley, part of great Appalachian valley, N of Shenandoah Valley, extending from Potomac R. in Md. to the Susquehanna in Pa. Had much Civil War action.

cumin (kŭm′ĭn), low annual herb (*cuminum cyminum*) with threadlike foliage; native to Mediterranean region. Seedlike aromatic fruits used in bread, soup, and cheese; oil used in liqueurs.

Cummings, E(dward) E(stlin), 1894–, American poet. His lyrics are marked by imaginative virtuosity, flashing originality, and crisp romanticism. They also have startling typographical effects (e.g., omission of capital letters). Notable also is his prose work, *The Enormous Room* (1922; on his war internment in France).

Cummings, Homer S(tillé), 1870–, U.S. Attorney General (1933–39). Strong supporter of New Deal.

Cummington, town (pop. 620), W Mass., E of Pittsfield. Birthplace of Bryant; his home is memorial.

Cunard, Sir Samuel (kūnärd′), 1787–1865, Canadian pioneer of regular transatlantic steam navigation. With others he formed company which in 1840 initiated first regular mail service between North America and Britain. This was beginning of Cunard Line, which was united with White Star Line in 1934.

Cunaxa (kūnăk′sŭ), town, Babylonia, near the Euphrates; scene of victory (401 B.C.) of Artaxerxes II over Cyrus the Younger—victory only because Cyrus had been killed. The retreat of the Ten Thousand after the battle is told in the ANABASIS.

cuneiform   (kūnē′ĭfôrm)   [Latin,= wedge

shaped], writing developed in lower Tigris and Euphrates valley, probably by Sumerians. Characters consist of arrangements of four kinds of wedge strokes impressed into brick or stone. History of the script is parallel to that of Egyptian HIEROGLYPHIC (see also ALPHABET; INSCRIPTION). Babylonians and Assyrians used cuneiform writing extensively, but it existed outside Mesopotamia, notably among the Hittites. A very late use was in Old Persian, written in the era of the Achaemenidae, whose greatest monument is that of Darius I at BEHISTON. Key finds have been made at Nineveh, Lagash, Erech, Tel-el-Amarna, Susa, and Boghazkeui. The Assyrian king Assur-bani-pal had a huge cuneiform library at Nineveh. Sir Henry C. Rawlinson and G. F. Grotefend were great interpreters of cuneiforms.

Cunha, Euclides da (ā″ōōklĕ′dĭsh dä kōō′nyù), 1866–1909, Brazilian writer. Best-known work is account which he wrote as "on the spot" reporter of revolt in W Bahia: *Os sertões* (1902; Eng. tr., *Rebellion in the Backlands,* 1944), a study of conditions, prospects, and national soul of Brazil.

Cunha, Tristão da (trĕshtä′ŏ), c.1460–c.1540, Portuguese navigator. Led 15 ships to India (1506); took Socotra in hope of controlling Red Sea.

Cunningham, Allan, 1784–1842, Scottish poet, collector of *The Songs of Scotland, Ancient and Modern* (1825), which includes his own "A Wet Sheet and a Flowing Sea." His son, **Sir Alexander Cunningham,** 1814–93, English archaeologist, army engineer, headed archaeological survey of India (1861–65, 1870–85).

Cunninghame-Graham, Robert: see GRAHAM, ROBERT.

Cunninghame Graham, R(obert) B(ontine), 1852–1936, Scottish author, whose sketches and tales reflect his life and travels in Latin America, Morocco, and Spain.

Cunobelinus: see CYMBELINE.

Cupid [Latin, = desire], Roman equivalent of EROS, Greek god of love; also called Amor. Son of Venus and Mars. For his own love story, see PSYCHE.

Curaçao (kōōräsou′), Dutch colony (366 sq. mi.; pop. 95,000), West Indies; cap. WILLEMSTAD. Includes widely separated islands, some off Venezuela (Curaçao, Bonaire or Buen Ayre, Aruba), some in NW Leeward Isls. (St. Martin—S part, St. Eustatius, Saba). Though discovered by Spanish (1499) and occupied briefly by English (1798, 1807–14) the islands have been under Dutch control since 1634. Discovery and exploitation of petroleum in Venezuela greatly increased importance of Curaçao and Aruba.

curaçao (kyōōrùsō′), LIQUEUR distilled from dried orange peel and spirits, flavored with rum. Grand Marnier and Cointreau kinds have a brandy base.

curare (kyōōrä′rē), aqueous poisonous extract of certain South American plants, used by South American Indians as arrow poison. Causes muscle paralysis. It is used in medicine to relax muscles.

curb market, originally, unorganized customary street meetings of brokers; now well organized and state regulated. Primary function is to introduce new securities, but a curb market lists both estab. securities and those which later "graduate" to stock exchange.

curculio (kûrkū′lēō), any typical snout beetle with a beak which is long and decurved in some, short and wide in others. Over 1,800 U.S. species, including serious pests: apple and plum curculios, imbricated snout beetle, many species of WEEVIL.

Curia Regis: see PARLIAMENT.

Curia Romana: see CARDINAL.

Curicó (kūrēkō′), city (pop. 19,165), cap. of Curicó prov., central Chile; founded c.1743; market for cattle and agr. produce. Flour mills and distilleries are main industries.

Curie, Pierre (pyĕr kyōōrē′), 1859–1906, and his wife, **Marie Sklodowska Curie** (märē′ sklôdôf′skä), 1867–1934, b. Poland, French chemists and physicists. Pierre's early work was on crystallography, effects of temperature on magnetism, and piezoelectricity (form of electric polarity) discovered in crystals. Marie studied uranium, radioactive element in pitchblende. In 1898 she reported a probable new element in pitchblende; Pierre joined this research. They discovered polonium and radium (1898), isolated one gm. of radium salts (1902), and determined atomic weights and properties of both elements. They shared with Becquerel the 1903 Nobel Prize in Physics for radioactivity work. Marie Curie won 1911 Nobel Prize for isolation of metallic radium. Their daughter, **Ève (Denise) Curie,** 1904–, author, lecturer, and pianist, is known especially for her biography of Mme Curie. See also JOLIOT-CURIE, IRÈNE.

Curitiba (kōōrētē′bù), city (pop. 141,349), cap. of Paraná state, SE Brazil. Founded in 17-cent. gold rush. Immigration into Paraná hinterland in 20th cent. has made it center of agr. and ranch area with some mfg. Univ. of Paraná is here.

curium (kyōō′rēùm), radioactive element identified in 1944 (symbol = Cm; see also ELEMENT, table). Emits alpha particles, highly active (half life about five months).

curlew (kûr′lū), name for a number of large shore birds of both hemispheres. Among them are the long-billed curlew (rare) of E U.S.; Hudsonian and Eskimo (rare) curlews, which migrate from arctic breeding grounds to South America; bristle-thighed curlew; and some godwits and ibises. See *ill.,* page 135.

curling, winter sport played on ice court by teams of four. Each player hurls squat, circular stone, weighing 44 lbs., at tees or fixed goals, placed 38 yds. apart. Stones nearest tee count for score.

Curran, John Philpot, 1750–1817, Irish statesman, trial lawyer, and orator. Opposed repressive policy of British in Ireland. Defended Wolfe Tone, Lord Edward Fitzgerald, and other anti-British rebels. His daughter was in love with Robert EMMET.

currant, shrub of genus *Ribes,* native to colder climates. Its tart black, red, or white berries are used for jellies and sauces. The shrub is a host of white-pine blister rust but an immune variety has been developed.

current, electric: see ELECTRICITY.

Currie, Sir Arthur William (kŭ′rē), 1875–1933, Canadian commander in World War I.

Currier & Ives, American lithographers and print publishers of scenes and events of 19th-cent. American life. Nathaniel Currier (1813–88), who founded the firm in 1835, was joined in 1850 by J. Merritt Ives, an artist.

Curry, John Steuart, 1897–1946, American painter. Known primarily for scenes of his native Kansas.

curry, pungent Eastern dish based on meat, fish, eggs, or vegetables, usually served with rice, and spiced with curry powder, a compound of turmeric, fenugreek, ginger, black and cayenne pepper, coriander, caraway, and sometimes other ingredients.

cursive: see PALEOGRAPHY.

Curtea-de-Arges (kŏŏr′tä-dā-är′zhĕsh), town (pop. 9,180), S central Rumania; a former cap. of Walachia. Has 16th-cent. Byzantine cathedral (burial place of Rumanian kings).

Curtin, Andrew Gregg, 1817–94, Civil War governor of Pa. Rallied state to cause of Union. Later served as Democrat in U.S. Congress (1881–87).

Curtis, Benjamin Robbins, 1809–74, Associate Justice of U.S. Supreme Court (1851–57). Dissented in DRED SCOTT CASE. Chief counsel to Andrew Johnson at impeachment trial. His brother, **George Ticknor Curtis,** 1812–94, lawyer and writer, was one of the defense counsel in Dred Scott Case. Wrote classic Federalist interpretation of Constitution.

Curtis, Cyrus H(ermann Kotzschmar), 1850–1933, American publisher. In Philadelphia after 1876, he bought a publication which became (1883) the *Ladies' Home Journal.* Founded (1890) Curtis Publishing Co. Bought the *Saturday Evening Post* (1897), the *Country Gentleman* (1911), and several newspapers.

Curtis, George Ticknor: see CURTIS, BENJAMIN ROBBINS.

Curtis, George William, 1824–92, American author, editor, and orator. His most popular book was a series of essays, *Prue and I* (1856). He was long one of the editors of the magazines *Harper's Monthly* and *Harper's Weekly.* Campaigned against slavery and for civil service reform and woman suffrage. Chancellor of New York Univ. after 1890.

Curtis Institute of Music, in Philadelphia; founded 1924. Operates entirely on scholarship basis with faculty made up chiefly of concert artists.

curvature of the spine, abnormal curves of spinal column. Causes include faulty posture, pathological bony changes, and congenital factors. Lateral curvature (scoliosis) is more common than backward (kyphosis) or forward (lordosis).

curve, in mathematics, a line no part of which is straight; sometimes considered to be any one-dimensional group of points (straight line is then included as a special curve). In analytic geometry plane curve is used mainly as graph of equation or function; properties of algebraic curves (i.e., those with algebraic equations) depend largely on degree of the equation; transcendental curves (nonalgebraic) are dependent on the particular func-

tion. Plane curves include CIRCLE; ELLIPSE; HYPERBOLA; PARABOLA. Twisted (skew) curve does not lie all in one plane.

Curzola, Yugoslavia: see KORCULA.

Curzon, George Nathaniel, 1st Marquess Curzon of Kedleston, 1859–1925, British statesman. As viceroy of India (1899–1905) promoted reforms, pacified NW border. As foreign secretary presided at Lausanne Conference 1922–23. Paved way for Dawes Plan.

Cusa, Alexander John: see CUZA.

Cusa, Nicholas of: see NICHOLAS OF CUSA.

Cush (kŭsh), in Bible, eldest son of Ham. Descendants lived in "land of Cush"—usually referring to Ethiopia (roughly modern Anglo-Egyptian Sudan). The Bible also mentions an Asiatic nation called Cush (perhaps same as historical group with similar name which flourished c.1500 B.C. in E Mesopotamia). Gen. 10.6–8; 1 Chron. 1.8–10.

Cushing, Caleb (kŏŏ′shĭng), 1800–1879, American statesman. First U.S. commissioner to China, negotiated opening of Chinese ports to U.S. trade. U.S. Attorney General (1853–57).

Cushing, Harvey Williams, 1869–1939, American neurosurgeon, noted for brain surgery and as teacher and author. He won the 1925 Pulitzer Prize in biography for his life of Sir William Osler.

Cushing, city (pop. 8,414), central Okla., near Cimarron R. and SW of Tulsa. Trade and industrial center of agr., oil, and stock area.

Cushitic (kŭshĭ′tĭk), group of Hamitic languages, spoken S of Egypt. See LANGUAGE (table).

Cushman, Pauline, 1835–93, Union spy in Civil War, known for her services in Tenn. in 1863.

Cushny, Arthur Robertson (kŭsh′nē), 1866–1926, Scottish physician and pharmacologist, noted for study of action of digitalis on heart and for text on pharmacology.

Custer, George Armstrong, 1839–76, American army officer. Youthful general in Civil War; made spectacular record. Custer's last stand, during campaign against the Sioux in 1876, is still much debated: on the Little Bighorn on June 25, he and over 200 men were killed by the Indians. Battlefield is now a national monument in Mont. His wife, **Elizabeth Bacon Custer,** 1842–1933, devoted much of her life to upholding his memory.

Custer, resort city (pop. 2,017), SW S.Dak., SSW of Rapid City. Oldest town in the Black Hills, it was laid out 1875. Wind Cave Natl. Park, Jewel Cave and Fossil Cycad national monuments, and Mt. Rushmore Natl. Memorial are near.

Custer Battlefield National Monument see NATIONAL PARKS AND MONUMENTS (table).

Custine, Adam Philippe, comte de (ädä′ fēlēp′ kŏt′ dü küstēn′), 1740–93, French general in French Revolutionary Wars. Guillotined on charge of treason after failure of 1793 campaign.

customs, government taxes, imposed since early times, on imports or exports. Two common types are specific duty (on quantity of goods) and ad valorem duty (on price). See PROTECTION.

Custozza (kŏŏstôd′zä), village, N Italy, near

Verona. Scene of Austrian victories over Sardinia (1848), and over Italy (1866).

Cutch: see KUTCH.

Cutler, Manasseh (mùnă'sù), 1742–1823, American clergyman, scientist, and colonizer. Wrote first systematic description and classification of New England flora. Aided in forming OHIO COMPANY OF ASSOCIATES. Helped estab. Marietta, Ohio, 1788.

Cutter, Charles A(mmi), 1837–1903, American librarian, a minister. A pioneer in subject cataloguing, he used letters instead of numbers. His classification is basis of Library of Congress sytem.

cutter, small, one-masted sailing vessel, with rig similar to the SLOOP. Notable for speed, cutters used in service between England and France 1800–1830. Also used as revenue cutters to pursue smugglers; the name was retained for later steam-type revenue vessels. Similarly, vessels of the coast guard are called cutters. See *ill.*, p. 1109.

cutting, method of plant propagation in which part of stem, leaf, or root is cut off and produces a new plant by forming buds and roots. Cuttings are made of chrysanthemums, grapes, African violets, and shrubs.

cuttlefish, marine mollusk of warm and temperate coastal waters with shield-shaped body, distinct head, well-developed eyes, and 10 arms. Its internal limy plate, the cuttlebone, is used in abrasives, fertilizers, and as source of lime for cage birds. Artist's sepia is made from a dried glandular secretion.

Cuttyhunk, Mass.: see ELIZABETH ISLANDS.

cutworm, larva of various noctuid or owlet moths. Eggs are laid in midsummer. After hatching, larva eats young shoots and roots, and in autumn goes underground, emerging in spring. Cutworms work by night, destroying more than they eat.

Cuvier, Georges Léopold Chrétien Frédéric Dagobert, Baron (zhôrzh lāôpôld′ krätyĕ′ frädärĕk′ dägôbĕr′ bärô′ küvyä′), 1769–1832, French zoologist and geologist, a founder of comparative anatomy and paleontology. He rejected theories of continuous evolution and supported catastrophism.

Cuxhaven (kōōks′häfùn), city (pop. 47,174), Lower Saxony, N Germany; transatlantic port at mouth of Elbe R., c.60 mi. NW of Hamburg. Chartered 1907; transferred from Hamburg to Hanover prov. 1937. Naval yard was often bombed in World War II.

Cuyahoga (kī′′ùhō′gú), river of NE Ohio, rises near Chardon, flows SW then N to L. Erie at Cleveland.

Cuyahoga Falls, city (pop. 29,195), NE Ohio, near Akron on Cuyahoga R.; laid out 1837. Mfg. of machinery, rubber products, tools, and paper products.

Cuyp or **Kuyp** (koip), family of Dutch painters of Dordrecht. **Jacob Gerritszoon Cuyp** (yä′kōp gĕ′rītzōn) 1594–c.1651, was a portrait and landscape painter. His nephew **Benjamin Cuyp,** 1616–52, did peasant scenes. Jacob's son and pupil **Aelbert Cuyp** (äl′bùrt), 1620–91, was a leading Dutch landscapist.

Cuyuna, iron range in Minn.: see MESABI.

Cuza, Alexander John (kōō′zä), 1820–73, first prince of Rumania; also known as Couza, Cusa, or Alexander John I. Elected prince of both Moldavia and Walachia 1859; recognized by Turkey as prince of united Rumania 1861. Was forced to abdicate 1866 because of his corrupt regime.

Cuzco (kōō′skō), city (pop. 45,158; alt., 11,-207 ft.), cap. of Cuzco dept., S Peru. Site was probably actually occupied by pre-Incan tribes, but legend has city founded by first Incan ruler, Manco Capac. Pizarro entered it in 1533. Today's population is predominantly Indian. Cuzco is center for agr. produce and has woolen textile mills.

cyanide (sī′ùnīd), salt or ester of hydrocyanic (prussic) acid. Both sodium and potassium cyanide are corrosive and systematic water-soluble poisons, giving off prussic acid in presence of moisture. Used in insecticides, casehardening, electroplating. **Cyanide process** for extracting gold and silver from ore: gold or silver dissolved in cyanide solution, then precipitated from solution by another metal.

cyanogen (sīă′nùjĭn), colorless, inflammable, poisonous gas composed of carbon and nitrogen. Chemically active. **Cyanogen chloride:** poisonous liquid with low boiling point, used as poison gas.

Cybele (sī′bùlē), in Phrygian religion, the Great Mother of the Gods. She rode in a chariot drawn by lions and attended by Corybantes and Dactyls. Her worship, involving fertility rites, was imported to Greece, where she was identified with Demeter and Rhea.

Cyclades (sī′klùdēz), Gr. *Kyklades,* Aegean island group (1,023 sq. mi.; pop. 129,015), Greece, stretching SE from Attica and including DELOS, NAXOS, Andros, Tenos, Melos, Paros, Keos, and Syros; chief town Hermopolis (on Syros). Mountainous, with mild, dry climate, islands produce wine, fruit, olive oil, wheat, tobacco. Became Athenian dependency 479 B.C.; later belonged to Rome and Byzantium. After 1204, they formed major part of the duchy of the Archipelago, ruled by Italian nobles and Venice until its fall to the Turks (1566).

cyclamen (sĭk′–), tuberous-rooted pot plant (*Cyclamen indicum*), native to Mediterranean region. It has nodding flowers with reflexed white, purple, or rose petals.

cycle (sī′kùl), in astronomy, time required to bring about recurrence of same relative positions or aspects of heavenly bodies. Important cycles include revolution of earth about sun (365 days 5 hr. 48 min. 46 sec.); revolution of moon about earth (c.29½ days); solar cycle (c.28 years), marking same relative position of earth and sun; solar ECLIPSE cycle (18 or 19 years); PRECESSION OF THE EQUINOXES; SUNSPOT cycle.

cyclone (sī′klōn), low-pressure storm area, almost circular, with wind blowing spirally inward (clockwise in S Hemisphere, counterclockwise in N Hemisphere). Extratropical cyclone a term for large storms of temperate latitudes. See also HURRICANE; TORNADO.

Cyclops (sī′klŏps), plural **Cyclopes** (sīklŏ′pēz), in Greek religion, one of a group of one-eyed giants, descended from Uranus and Gaea. Some were shepherds, others worked in smithy of Hephaestus. In battle called the

TITANOMACHY they forged a thunderbolt which enabled Zeus to vanquish the Titans.

cyclotron (sī'klŭtrŏn), magnetic resonance accelerator invented by E. O. Lawrence. Rapidly oscillating electric current in constant magnetic field makes particles accelerate in curved paths. They move with increasing speeds in widening circles until they reach chamber's edge, where they escape into reteptacle and bombard atoms therein. Cyclotron has made it possible to make ordinary elements radioactive, leading to element transmutation, discovery of new elements, production of radioactive isotopes. See *ill.*, page 989.

Cydonia: see CANEA, Crete.

cymbals: see PERCUSSION INSTRUMENTS.

Cymbeline (sĭm'bûlēn) or **Cunobelinus** (kū"nōbĭlī'nŭs), fl. A.D. 40, British king; wealthy and powerful ruler. Gave his name, but little else, to Shakspere's play.

Cymru and **Cymry:** see WALES.

Cynewulf (kĭn'ûwŏŏlf), fl. early 9th cent.?, Old English religious poet of Northumbria or Mercia. *Elene* best of his four extant poems.

Cynics (sī'nĭks), members of a Greek school of philosophy, founded by Antisthenes. On the principle that "Virtue is the only good," the Cynics viewed all else—riches, honor, freedom, even other beings—as worthy only of contempt. Their criticisms were harsh, their manners uncouth. Among cynics were Diogenes of Sinop, Crates, and Menippus.

Cynoscephalae (sĭnŭse'fûlē), two hills in Thessaly; scene of the victory of Pelopidas in 364 B.C. and of Flamininus over Philip V of Macedon in 197 B.C.

Cynthiana, city (pop. 4,847), N Ky., NE of Lexington. Scene of two raids by Gen. J. H. Morgan in Civil War. Has log house where Henry Clay appeared as lawyer, covered bridge (c.1837), and burying ground (1793).

cypress, coniferous evergreen tree. True cypress (*Cupressus*) is native to S Europe, China, and W U.S. Monterey cypress (*Cupressus macrocarpa*) native to limited region in Calif. Italian cypress of classical literature is *C. sempervirens*. Bald cypress (*Taxodium distichum*), common in swamps of SE U.S., produces upright root projections called knees. Other evergreens called cypress are of genus *Chamaecyparis*.

Cyprian, Saint (sī'prĕún), d. 258, Father of the Church, bishop of Carthage. Though stern in his demands on Christians, he sturdily opposed the teachings of NOVATIAN that Christians who had lapsed under persecution should not be readmitted to the Church. In pleading for unity of the Church he estab. orthodox doctrines. Feast: Sept. 16.

Cyprus (sī'prŭs), Gr. *Kypros*, British colony (3,572 sq. mi.; pop. 450,114), island in E Mediterranean; cap. Nicosia. Pop. mostly Greek, but also Turkish. A wide plain lies between two mountain ranges which rise to Mt. Olympus (6,406 ft.). Island rich in agr. products, mainly wine, wheat, olives, and tobacco. Minerals include copper, name derived from Cyprus. Excavations show neolithic culture existed 4000–3000 B.C. Ancient Cyprus ruled by many countries, including Phoenicia, Egypt, Greece, and Rome. Chris-

tianity introduced by apostles Paul and Barnabas. During Third Crusade, given (1192) to French LUSIGNAN dynasty. Later ruled by Venetians and Turks. Placed under British administration (1878), Cyprus received colonial status 1925. Used by British as detention center for "illegal" Jewish immigrants to Palestine 1945–48.

Cyrano de Bergerac, Savinien (sävēnyē' sĕränō' dù bĕrzhùräk'), 1619–55, French author. His *Voyages to the Moon and Sun* (1657–62; Eng. tr., 1923) are two satirical, utopian romances. A swaggering personality, he was romanticized by Edmond Rostand in the drama *Cyrano de Bergerac* (1897).

Cyrenaica (sīrŭnā'ĭkŭ, sī–), region about anc. CYRENE, N Africa. Became Roman province. Name revived for Italian province.

Cyrenaics (sīrĭnā'ĭks, sĭrĭ–), members of Greek school of philosophy of 5th and 4th cent. B.C., founded by Aristippus. All were hedonistic, i.e., they held pleasure to be the highest good, but they varied in defining pleasure. Some stressed spiritual satisfactions, others advocated mere painlessness.

Cyrene (sīrē'nē), anc. port, center of anc. Cyrenaica. A Greek colony (7th cent. B.C.), it was a kingdom with much commerce (wheat, wool, silphium) and some development of art. Cyrene became powerful over other cities and held nominal independence until the marriage of Berenice (d. 221? B.C.) to Ptolemy III. There were severe Jewish outbreaks in Cyrene against Roman Emperor Trajan, and the city declined after severe punishment.

Cyril (of Jerusalem), Saint (sī'rŭl), 315?–386?, bishop of Jerusalem, Doctor of the Church. He opposed Arianism and may have been the actual author of the Nicene Creed. Feast: March 18.

Cyril (of Alexandria), Saint, d. 444, patriarch of Alexandria, Doctor of the Church. He was stern in attack on heretics and nonbelievers. His fight against NESTORIANISM came to a triumphant conclusion in the Council of EPHESUS (431). He for a time alienated the churchmen of Antioch but reached a compromise with them. His writings on the Trinity, though orthodox, contained seeds of later heresies of EUTYCHES and MONOPHYSITISM. Feast: Feb. 9.

Cyril and Methodius, Saints (–thō'–), d. 869 and 885 respectively, Greek Christian missionaries, brothers. Sent to convert the Moravians (863), they met opposition of the German rulers and were haled back to Rome on charges of heresy. They were cleared, but Cyril died before he could return to the field. Methodius returned, was "deposed" by the Germans from the archbishopric of Moravia, and was restored by the pope. Methodius completed the Slavic translation of religious works begun by Cyril (after whom the Cyrillic alphabet is named, though he did not invent it). Feast: July 7.

Cyrus the Great, d. 529 B.C., king of Persia, who estab. rule of Achaemenidae. Herodotus says he overthrew his grandfather Astyages. He created a firm Persian Empire, including not only Media but all the Near East. Croesus of Lydia, Nabonidus of Babylonia, Amasis II of Egypt—all fell before him. He did not actually conquer Egypt but prepared for later Persian conquest there. He affected the Greek cities of Asia Minor and recreated the power of the Jews in Palestine. His successor was Cambyses.

Cyrus the Younger, d. 401 B.C., Persian prince, son of Darius II, who favored him and gave him large commands. After the death of Darius he was accused of a plot against his brother, ARTAXERXES II. Pardoned, he soon began a rebellion and hired a Greek force (the Ten Thousand) to help him. He won much local help, but in battle with Artaxerxes at CUNAXA (401 B.C.) he was killed and his army defeated. See also ANABASIS; XENOPHON.

Cythera (sĭthēr'ù), Gr. *Kythera,* island (109 sq. mi.; pop. 7,932), Greece, southernmost of IONIAN ISLANDS; chief town Kythera (pop. 1,235), on S shore. Cult of Aphrodite was centered here.

cytoplasm: see PROTOPLASM.

Cyzicus (sĭ'zĭkús), ancient city of Asia Minor, on Cyzicus Peninsula (modern Kapidapi Peninsula), NW Turkey; a port on Sea of Marmara. Colonized by Greeks from Miletus 756 B.C., it was a member of the Delian League and rivaled Byzantium. Alcibiades defeated Spartan fleet off Cyzicus 410 B.C.

Czajkowski, Michael (chīkôf'skē), 1804–86, Polish novelist. Took part in Polish insurrection of 1831, later went to Turkey and fought in Crimean War against Russia. Wrote novels on the life of Cossacks and South Slavs and on Polish history.

Czartoryski, Adam Jerzy, Prince (yĕ'zhĭ chärtôrĭ'skē), 1770–1861, Polish-Russian statesman, a close adviser of Alexander I. Russian foreign minister 1803–6. Created Polish school system; persuaded Alexander to grant Polish constitution of 1815. Opposing later Russian policies, he headed the Polish provisional government of 1830–31; after failure of the insurrection he lived in exile at Paris.

Czech language (chĕk), a Western Slavic language of Indo-European family. See LANGUAGE (table).

Czechoslovakia (chĕk″ōslōvăk′éù), Czech *Československo,* republic (49,354 sq. mi.; pop. 12,196,730), central Europe, bordering on Poland (N), USSR (E), Hungary and Austria (S), and Germany (W and N); cap. PRAGUE. Other large cities: BRNO, BRATISLAVA, MORAVSKA OSTRAVA. (For geography, economy, and history before 1918, see articles on constituent provinces: BOHEMIA; MORAVIA; SILESIA; SLOVAKIA.) Population is largely Slavic (c.8,100,000 Czechs, 3,100,000 Slovaks, 115,000 Ukrainians); of the once large German and Magyar minorities (c.3,-200,000 and 700,000, respectively, before World War II) less than a million remain. Roman Catholicism is the majority religion, but there are large Protestant (notably Hussite) and Eastern Orthodox groups. During World War I Czech units fought on the Allied side, and in 1918 Czechoslovakia emerged as independent republic from the ruins of the Austro-Hungarian Monarchy. Its creation was largely the work of its first and second presidents, T. G. MASARYK and Eduard BENES. The most favored of the Austro-Hungarian "successor states," Czechoslovakia was rich in agr. land, forests, minerals; had well-developed industries; and benefited from a liberal, democratic constitution. Its weakness lay in the disaffection of its German and Magyar minorities and the separation of Slovakia, which were fostered by Germany and Hungary in the hope of obtaining a revision of their frontiers. Against this threat, the government relied on its alliance with France and on the LITTLE ENTENTE. The rise of Hitler and Western appeasement resulted in 1938 in the MUNICH PACT, through which Germany obtained the Bohemian borderlands; Poland and Hungary shared in the spoils. The truncated state, renamed Czecho-Slovakia, was altogether dissolved in March, 1939, when Germany created and occupied the "Protectorate of Bohemia and Moravia," while Slovakia became nominally independent. The destruction of LIDICE was symbolic of the brutality of German occupation during World War II. In 1945 Czechoslovakia was liberated by U.S. and Russian forces. Pre-Munich Czechoslovakia was restored (except for RUTHENIA, ceded to USSR). The expulsion of the German population was authorized by the Potsdam Conference (1945). A coalition government was in power until Feb., 1948, when the Communists (who formed the largest single party, but not an absolute majority) seized the power. Their leader, Klement Gottwald, succeeded Benes as president. Under Russian influence, Czechoslovakia was transformed into a "people's republic." All opposition was suppressed. The constitution of 1949 abolished the provinces and divided the country into two constitutent states—the Czech Lands (Bohemia, Moravia, Silesia) and Slovakia. After Gottwald's death (1953), Antonin Zapotocky was chosen president.

Czernowitz, Bukovina: see CHERNOVTSY.

Czerny, Karl (chĕr'nē), 1791–1857, Austrian pianist. Best known for his technical studies for the piano, which are much used in instruction.

Czestochowa (chĕn″stùkô'vù), city (pop. 101,-255), S Poland, on Warta R. Has iron, textile, chemical, and food industries. Chiefly famed for its monastery on Jasna Gora [mountain of light], with image of Our Lady, a major shrine of pilgrimage. In 1655 the monastery, defended by a handful of soldiers, withstood Swedish siege for 40 days. The Swedes withdrew, and the alleged miracle fired Poland to successful resistance to the invaders. Since then Our Lady of Czestochowa, venerated as the "Queen of Poland," has been a symbol of national survival.

Czolgosz, Leon F. (chŏl'gŏsh), c.1873–1901, American anarchist, assassin of Pres. McKinley.

D

Dabo, Leon (dä′bō), 1868–, American landscape and mural painter.

Dabrowski, Jan Henryk (yän′ hěn′rĭk dämbrôf′-skē), 1755–1818, Polish general. Organized and led Polish legions in Napoleon's campaigns.

Dacca (dă′kû), city (pop. 213,218), cap. of East Bengal, Pakistan. Its glory as 17th-cent. Mogul cap. is reflected in Bara Katra palace. Formerly famous for muslins. Mfg. and trade center of E Pakistan. Seat of Univ. of Dacca.

Dachau (dä′khou), town (pop. 23,567), Upper Bavaria, near Munich. Site of a notorious concentration camp under Hitler regime.

D'Ache, Caran: see CARAN D'ACHE.

dachshund: see HOUND.

Dacia (dā′shû), region of Roman Empire, roughly modern Transylvania and Rumania. Its people were called Getae by the Greeks, Daci by the Romans. With advanced material culture they resisted Domitian, who in A.D. 90 paid them tribute to keep them quiet. Trajan planted colonies in Dacia (A.D. 105), and it became a Roman province until Aurelian had to withdraw the colonists. Their legacy to the area was the Romance language, Rumanian.

Da Costa, Isaäc: see COSTA, ISAÄC DA.

Da Costa, Jacob Mendez (dù kŏ′stû), 1833–1900, American physician, outstanding teacher, and author of works on diagnosis and functional heart disease.

Dada (dä′dä) or **Dadaism** (dä′däĭzm), international and nihilistic movement (1916–21) among European artists and writers. A doctrine of utter formlessness, it attacked all conventional standards of aesthetics and behavior, thus encouraging surrealism and other later radical movements.

daddy longlegs, name for harvestman (a relative of the spider) and for crane fly (an insect related to mosquito). Harvestman has small body, eight slender legs. It sucks fluids from fruits, other vegetable matter, and insects (some say it eats whole insects). Crane fly has a slender body and two pairs of wings.

Dadeville, town (pop. 2,354), E central Ala., near Martin L. At near-by Horseshoe Bend of Tallapoosa R. a state monument marks Andrew Jackson's defeat of Creek Indians in March, 1814.

Daedalus (dĕ′dûlûs), in Greek myth, builder of labyrinth for the Minotaur; father of ICARUS.

daffodil: see NARCISSUS.

Dafydd ap Gwilym (dä′vĭdh äp gwĭ′lĭm), 1340?–1400?, Welsh poet. Introduced new meters and new themes. Most notable are his nature poems.

Dagenham (dä′gùnûm), urban district (pop.

114,588), Essex, England. Huge Ford plant estab. 1929.

Dagestan or **Daghestan** (dägùstän′), autonomous soviet socialist republic (14,750 sq. mi.; pop. c.900,000), SE European RSFSR, between Terek R., Greater Caucasus, and Caspian Sea; cap. Makhachkala. Mostly bare inaccessible mountains. Wine, cotton, corn in irrigated lowlands. Population, mostly Moslems, includes c.30 nationalities. Ceded to Russia by Persia 1813; native revolts until 1877.

Dagobert I (dăg′ōbûrt), d. c.639, Frankish king (629?–639). Last of MEROVINGIANS to exercise personal rule.

Dagon, Philistine god, perhaps a fish god. Probably his was a fertility cult.

Daguerre, Louis Jacques Mandé (lwē′ zhäk′ mädä′ dägâr′), 1789–1851, French scene painter and physicist, inventor of the daguerreotype. With C. M. Bouton he also invented the diorama.

dahlia (däl′–), tuberous-rooted perennial of genus *Dahlia*, native to Mexico. Widely grown for late-blooming colorful, composite flowers of many types (e.g., large double, single, pompon). See *ill.*, p. 999.

Dahlstjerna, Gunno Eurelius (gŭ′nō ā-ōōrā′lěŭs däl′shěr″nä), 1661–1709, Swedish poet, first to use native themes.

Dahomey (dáhō′mē), French overseas territory (c.45,560 sq. mi.; pop. 1,458,000), SE French West Africa, on Slave Coast of Gulf of Guinea; cap. Porto Novo. Cotton, palm oil, and coffee are exported. Under French rule since 1894.

Dáil Éireann (dôl′ ā′rôn, dīl′ â′rûn [Irish,= diet of Ireland], popular representative body of National Parliament of republic of IRELAND. Second chamber, the Senate, has little power; prime minister responsible to Dáil. Members of first Dáil, elected to British Parliament, proclaimed republic 1919.

Daimler, Gottlieb (däm′lûr), 1834–1900, German engineer, inventor, automobile manufacturer. Contributed to development of automobile industry by improving the internal-combustion engine.

daimyo or **daimio** (both: dīm′yō), great feudal barons of Japan. Owned vast tax-free estates (built up after 8th cent.); in 12th cent. held more power than imperial government until Yoritomo established system of centralized feudalism.

Daingerfield, Elliot (dān′jûrfēld), 1859–1932, American religious and landscape painter.

Daingerfield, town (pop. 1,668), E Texas. Metallurgical plant built in World War II near by.

Dairen (dī′rěn′), Chinese *Talien*, Rus. *Dalny*, industrial city (pop. 543,690), S Manchuria, on LIAOTUNG peninsula; port on Korea Bay,

SMALL CAPITALS = cross references.   Pronunciation key: pp. xiv and xv.   Abbreviations: p. 2.

314

S terminus of South Manchurian RR. Included in Kwantung leased territory 1898–1945. Opened 1906 to foreign trade by Japan. After World War II included in Port Arthur naval base under joint Sino-Soviet control.

dairying, industry producing milk and milk products, the largest single source of income of U.S. farmer. Supplies c.20% of average food intake. Butter and market milk account for about two thirds of production; rest goes into cheese, by-products, farm uses. Creameries process and market dairy products; many are farmers' cooperatives, esp. in Denmark.

daisy, name for many plants of composite family with petallike rays. True daisy of literature is English daisy (*Bellis perennis*), a low biennial with white, pink, or red flowers. Common white field or oxeye daisy (*Chrysanthemum leucanthemum*) is naturalized in U.S. from Europe. The Shasta daisy is a species of *Chrysanthemum*. See also MARGUERITE; PYRETHRUM.

Dakar (dŭkär'), city (pop. c.185,400), Senegal, cap. of French West Africa, a major Atlantic port at tip of Cape Verde peninsula. A naval base and stopover point for transoceanic air lines. In World War II held by Vichy forces from 1940 until Dec., 1942, when it peaceably joined the Allies.

Dakin's solution, dilute (0.5%) solution of sodium hypochlorite. It is unstable, liberating chlorine, thus valuable as surgical antiseptic and for wound dressing. It was named for **Henry Drysdale Dakin,** 1880–1952, British-born American chemist.

Dakota Indians: see SIOUX INDIANS.

Daladier, Édouard (ādōōär' dälädyā'), 1884–, French politician. Three times premier (1933, 1933–34, 1938–40); minister of war 1936–40. Signed MUNICH PACT (1938). One of defendants in RIOM trial (1942); interned by Germans until 1945.

Dalai Lama: see LAMAISM.

Dalarna (dä'lärnä'') or **Dalecarlia** (dälŭkär'lĕŭ), historic province of central Sweden, nearly identical with KOPPARBERG co. In 1521 peasants of Dalarna, under GUSTAVUS I, freed Sweden from Danish rule. Old rural customs and home industries have survived.

D'Albert, Eugen Francis Charles: see ALBERT, EUGEN FRANCIS CHARLES D'.

Dalcroze, Émile Jaques: see JAQUES-DALCROZE.

Dale, Sir Henry Hallett, 1875–, English scientist. Shared 1936 Nobel Prize in Physiology and Medicine for study of acetylcholine agent in transmission of nerve impulses.

Dalecarlia, Sweden: see DALARNA.

D'Alembert's principle. Jean le Rond d'Alembert introduced (1742) and estab. (1743) a principle of mechanics which shows that Newton's third law of motion applies to bodies free to move as well as to stationary bodies.

Dalen, Nils Gustaf (nīls' gŭs'täv dälän'), 1869–1937, Swedish scientist. Won 1912 Nobel Prize chiefly for invention of automatic regulator for acetylene-gas lights used for railway signals, beacons, buoys.

Dalhart (dăl'härt), city (pop. 5,918), N Texas, NW of Amarillo in Panhandle. Has railroad shops, stockyards, and grain eleva-

tors. Near by is Rita Blanca Creek, dammed for irrigation.

Dalhousie, James Andrew Broun Ramsay, 1st marquess of (dălhōō'zē), 1812–60, British statesman. As governor general of India (1847–56) annexed Sikh territory of the Punjab 1849, promoted economic and social reforms, and annexed princely states with no natural heirs.

Dalhousie (dălhou'zē), town (pop. 4,939), N N.B., Canada, at mouth of Restigouche R. Fishing port and seaside resort with lumber and paper mills.

Dalhousie University: see HALIFAX, N.S.

Dali, Salvador (sälvädhôr' dä'lē), 1904–, Spanish surrealist painter. Tried futurism and cubism before he turned to surrealism. With fine draughtsmanship he expresses an irrational dream world.

Dalin, Olof von (ōō'lôv fŭn dälēn'), 1708–63, Swedish historian, lyric poet, and journalist, foremost literary figure of his day. Founded periodical, the *Swedish Argus*. Also wrote poetical satires, drama, and popular history.

Dalkeith (dŭlkēth'), burgh (pop. 8,786), Midlothian, Scotland. Important grain center, it also has metal works. Near one of few oil fields in England. Dalkeith House seat of duke of Buccleuch.

Dallas, Alexander James, 1759–1817, U.S. Secretary of the Treasury (1814–16), b. West Indies. Restored confidence in U.S. currency during critical period. His son, **George Mifflin Dallas,** 1792–1864, was Vice President of the United States (1845–49). As minister to Great Britain (1856–61), he signed Dallas-Clarendon Convention (1856), which set basis for settlement of difficulties in Central America.

Dallas, city (pop. 434,462), N Texas, E of Fort Worth at head of Trinity R. Settled 1841; growth augmented 1858 by French from disbanded Fourierist Colony. A cotton center, it makes gin machinery, processes, weaves, and ships cotton; regional style center. Has oil processing and related industries and mfg. of auto and aircraft parts. Expanded in World War II. Financial, industrial, and cultural center of much of Southwest, it is second largest Texas city. Here are SOUTHERN METHODIST UNIVERSITY, symphony orchestra, Little Theatre, and U.S. airfield. Old reservoir, White Rock L., is now in park; new one, L. Dallas (see TRINITY, river), near Denton. Annual state fair held.

Dalles, The, Oregon: see THE DALLES.

Dalmatia (dălmā'shŭ), coastal region of Yugoslavia, extending along Adriatic from Fiume to Kotor. Interior forms part of Dinaric Alps. Coastline, famed for beauty, has many islands, bays, and harbors. ZARA, SPLIT, DUBROVNIK are main ports and cities. From the 10th cent. Dalmatia was divided among Croatia, Serbia, and Venice, which controlled the islands and main ports. Venetian possessions passed to Austria in 1797. In 1919 Yugoslavia received all Dalmatia except Zara and several islands, which were given to Italy but which passed to Yugoslavia in 1947.

Dalmatian dog: see HUNTING DOGS.

Dalrymple, earls of Stair; Viscount Stair: see STAIR, JAMES DALRYMPLE, VISCOUNT.

Dalrymple, Alexander (dăl′rĭmpŭl, dălrĭm′pŭl), 1737–1808, British hydrographer. Traveled in the S Pacific for the East India Co. For the British admiralty he collected charts, memoirs, and records and wrote accounts of the South Seas.

Dalton, John (dôl′tŭn), 1766–1844, English scientist. He revived the ATOMIC THEORY and applied the concept to a table of atomic weights and in formulating **Dalton's law:** total pressure of a mixture of gases equals sum of pressures of gases in the mixture, each gas acting independently.

Dalton, city (pop. 15,968), NW Ga., in Appalachian Valley. Major producer of candlewick bedspreads; mfg. also of yarn, hosiery, and lumber. Confederate hq. in Civil War after CHATTANOOGA CAMPAIGN, it fell to Sherman in ATLANTA CAMPAIGN (1864).

Dalton plan: see PROGRESSIVE EDUCATION.

Dalton's law: see DALTON, JOHN.

Daly, Augustin, 1838–99, American theatrical manager. A playwright and drama critic, made debut as manager with his melodrama *Under the Gaslight.* Opened his first theater 1869. Later started Daly's Theatre where he presented magnificent productions of Shakspere and of French and German adaptations.

Daly, Marcus, 1841–1900, American copper magnate, b. Ireland. Estab. Anaconda Copper Mining Co. in Mont. and became fabulously rich. His fierce and long-lasting rivalry with William A. CLARK dominated Mont. politics and economy.

Daly, Thomas Augustine, 1871–1948, American humorous poet, known for Italian-dialect verse.

Daly City, residential city (pop. 15,191), W Calif., adjoining San Francisco, in truck and dairy area.

Dam, Henrik (hăn′rēk däm′), 1895–, Danish biochemist. For identification and studies of vitamin K he shared 1943 Nobel Prize in Physiology and Medicine. Also worked on role of vitamin E in nutrition.

dam, barrier of rock, earth, masonry, concrete, timber (seldom used), or some combination, which restrains water. Rock or earth dams usually have upstream surface made watertight. Masonry and concrete dams are either gravity type (resist water only with own weight) or single- or multiple-arched type. Single-arched dams are usually constructed in narrow canyon having rock walls to withstand tremendous thrust of horizontal, upstream arch. Multiple-arched dams employ buttresses. Many modern dams serve multiple purposes—provide irrigation, aid flood control, provide power for hydroelectric plants.

Damão (dämä′ō) or **Daman** (dŭmän′), district (176 sq. mi.; pop. 63,521) of Portuguese India; cap. Damão. Consists of three separate enclaves within Bombay state. Acquired 1558 by Portugal.

Damariscotta (dăm″ŭrĭskŏt′ŭ), town (pop. 1,113), S Maine on Damariscotta R. and SE of Augusta. Has St. Patrick's Church (1803), said to be oldest Roman Catholic church in New England. Near the river are seemingly ancient mounds.

Damascene, John: see JOHN OF DAMASCUS, SAINT.

Damascus (dŭmă′skŭs), Arabic *Esh-Sham,* city (pop. 303,952), S Syria, cap. of Syria, on Barada R. Dates from unknown antiquity. Successively held by Assyrians and Persians. Conquered 332 B.C. by Alexander the Great, after whose death it fell prey to other conquerors, notably Armenians. In 64 B.C. it passed to Romans under Pompey, becoming one of cities of Decapolis. On road to Damascus Paul was converted to Christianity. With Arab occupation (begun 635) city became Moslem; great Christian church, built A.D. c.375 under Emperor Theodosius I, became Great Mosque. Seat of Omayyad caliphate 661–750. City prospered and became known for fine metalwork (esp. swords). Fell to Mongols under Hulagu Khan in 1260, sacked by Tamerlane in 14th cent. Was under Ottoman Turks 1516–1918. Captured 1918 by the British, it was under French mandate 1920–1941. Became cap. of independent Syria 1943.

damask (dă′mŭsk), fabric whose ground and pattern are of different weaves: e.g., ground may be in twill with the design in satin. True damasks, unlike brocade, are flat and reversible.

Damian, Peter: see PETER DAMIAN, SAINT.

Damien, Father (dä′mĕŭn, dämyē′), 1840–89, Belgian missionary priest named Damien de Veuster. After working as a missionary among the natives of Hawaii, he was transferred at his own request to the leper colony on Molokai, where he labored among the afflicted until he himself died of leprosy.

Damietta (dămēĕ′tŭ), city (pop. 53,620), NE Egypt; textile center. As Tamiathis it was twice captured by Crusaders in 13th cent. Destroyed 1250, later rebuilt by Egyptians.

Damocles (dă′mŭklēz), in classic legend, Syracusan at court of Dionysius. To demonstrate dangers of high estate, the ruler gave a banquet in his honor; Damocles was happy until, looking up, he saw a sword suspended above his head by a single hair.

Damodar (dä′mōdär), river, c.340 mi. long, India, in Bihar and West Bengal. Major multi-purpose project (8 dams) is in its valley.

Damon and Pythias (dā′mŭn, pĭ′thĕŭs), two faithful Syracusan friends. When Pythias, condemned to death, was freed to arrange his affairs, Damon stayed as pledge. On Pythias' return, tyrant Dionysius, impressed, freed both and asked to be their friend.

Damophon (dă′mŭfŏn), fl. 2d cent. B.C., Greek sculptor. Did colossal heads of Demeter and Artemis.

damp, in mining, any of several gases. Firedamp, found in coal mines, is mostly methane and, mixed with air, is highly combustible. Afterdamp is gaseous mixture remaining after firedamp explosion. Chokedamp, mostly carbon dioxide, is imperceptible and when in quantity is dangerous to life.

Dampier, William (dăm′pēr), 1651?–1715, English explorer and buccaneer. Fought in Dutch War (1673), managed plantation in Jamaica, took part as buccaneer against Spanish America (1679–81). Wrote masterly hydrographic treatise. As commander of expedition in S Pacific, discovered Dampier Archipelago and Dampier Strait, named New Britain as island.

Damrosch (dăm'rŏsh), German-American family of conductors, composers, and educators. **Leopold Damrosch,** 1832–85, came to New York in 1871. He founded the New York Symphony Society in 1878. Many works of Brahms and Wagner received their first American performances under his baton. His compositions include violin concertos, cantatas, and a symphony. His son, **Frank Damrosch,** 1859–1937, supervised music in New York public schools. In 1905, he helped organize the Institute of Musical Art (later a unit of the Juilliard School). Another son of Leopold Damrosch, **Walter Damrosch,** 1862–1950, first conducted at the Metropolitan Opera. Later he conducted both the New York Philharmonic and the New York Symphony. He directed a series of music education programs on the radio for children. His compositions include operas and choral works.

damsel fly: see DRAGONFLY.

Dan [Heb.,= judge]. **1** Son of Jacob, ancestor of one of 12 tribes of Israel. Tribe finally settled in N Palestine. Samson was famous Danite. Many references in Genesis, Exodus, Numbers. **2** City at N extremity of Palestine, hence expression "from Dan to BEERSHEBA." Jeroboam erected golden calf here.

Dan, river rising in SW Va. in piedmont and flowing c.180 mi. E to the Roanoke in S Va., twice crossing N.C. line.

Dana, Charles A(nderson) (dā'nù), 1819–97, American newspaper editor. Was at Brook Farm. Later was associated (1847–62) with Horace Greeley on the New York *Tribune.* Became (1864) Assistant Secretary of War. As editor and part owner of the New York *Sun* (1868–97) he estab. high standards of readability and hired many famous writers.

Dana, Edward Salisbury: see DANA, JAMES DWIGHT.

Dana, Francis, 1743–1811, American diplomat. Accompanied (1779) John Adams to Paris and was sent (1780) to the court of Catherine the Great of Russia. Stayed there 1781–83, although he was never recognized. His son, **Richard Henry Dana,** 1787–1879, was a poet and essayist. His son, **Richard Henry Dana,** 1815–82, was an author and lawyer. Shipped as a common seaman around Cape Horn to Calif. Narrative of this voyage, *Two Years before the Mast* (1840), became a classic.

Dana, James Dwight, 1813–95, American geologist, author of standard works on geology and mineralogy and studies of volcanoes, coral, and crustaceans. He taught at Yale 1850–90. His son, **Edward Salisbury Dana,** 1849–1935, taught physics at Yale (1890–1917) and also wrote on mineralogy.

Dana, John Cotton, 1856–1929, American librarian, long director of Newark Museum. Inaugurated many progressive library projects.

Dana, Richard Henry: see DANA, FRANCIS.

Danaë (dā'nāē), in Greek legend, daughter of Acrisius. Zeus visited her in a shower of gold, and she bore him PERSEUS.

Danaüs (dă'nāŭs), in Greek myth, brother of

Aegyptus; he had 50 daughters, the Danaïds or Danaïdes, Aegyptus had 50 sons. When the sons demanded Danaïds as brides, Danaüs told each one to slay her husband. Only Hypermnestra failed to kill her husband, Lynceus, and their descendants were the Danaï, another name for the Greeks.

Danbury, city (pop. 22,067) in Danbury town (pop. 30,337), SW Conn., NW of Bridgeport; settled 1684. Hat mfg. center since 1780. Noted annual fairs (since early 1800s). Military depot in Revolution.

Danbury Hatters' Case, decided in 1908 by U.S. Supreme Court. The holding that hatters' union, which had boycotted products of a nonunion hat manufacturer in Danbury, Conn., was subject to injunction and treble damages set precedent for Federal Court interference in labor activities.

Danby, Thomas Osborne, earl of, 1631–1712, English statesman. One of chief ministers of Charles II. Impeached and imprisoned 1678–84, later joined Whigs in inviting William of Orange to England. Was virtual premier 1690–95.

dance. Among primitive people, dancing developed as natural expression of united feeling and action, usually of ritualistic, ceremonial nature. In dances of religious ecstasy (esp. in the Orient, Africa) trance-like states are induced. In many Pacific isls. and in the Orient there are dances performed entirely in a sitting posture. Primitive dances survive today in FOLK DANCE. Dance played an important role in developing drama in Greece, India, and Japan (see JAPANESE DRAMA). Dancing as social activity and BALLET are of relatively recent origin. Dancing reached a height in France during Louis XIV's reign—era of the saraband, pavan, MINUET, and gavotte. Later forms include the Spanish bolero, German WALTZ, American fox trot, and S American tango. Early in the 20th cent. dance as an art form was profoundly affected by Isadora DUNCAN, who paved the way for, and Mary WIGMAN, who actually founded, "modern dance"—the somewhat inappropriate name for nonballetic 20th-cent. theater dance. As developed by Martha GRAHAM, Hanya Holm, Doris HUMPHREY, Charles Weidman, and others, modern dance became a medium for expressing complex emotions and abstract ideas. Such media as films and television also are developing and transmuting dance forms.

dandelion, common, milky-juiced perennial plant (*Taraxacum officinale*), with a rosette of toothed leaves and bright yellow flower heads borne on hollow stalks. Young leaves are edible both cooked and in salad; wine made from flowers. See *ill.,* p. 999.

Dandolo, Enrico (ĕnrē'kō dän'dōlō), c.1108–1205, doge of Venice (1192–1205). Led Fourth Crusade to capture Zara and Constantinople (see CRUSADES). Of the same family was **Andrea Dandolo** (ändrā'ä), c.1307–1354, doge of Venice (1343–54). Reformed laws; wrote chronicle of Venetian history.

Danegeld (dān'gĕld"), medieval land tax, originally raised to buy off raiding Danes. First levied in England by Æthelred in 991; collected irregularly until 1163. In France monks of Saint-Denis paid a Danegeld in 845 and several times later.

Danelaw (dān'lô"), originally body of law which prevailed in part of England occupied by Danes after treaty of King ALFRED with Guthrum (886). Soon applied to area in which Danish law prevailed. Had four main regions: Northumbria; shires dependent on boroughs of Lincoln, Nottingham, Derby, Leicester, and Stamford; East Anglia; SE Midlands.

Danforth, Thomas, 1703–86, American pewterer, founder of a family of celebrated pewterers. First shop was in Norwich, Conn.

Dania (dā'nều), city (pop. 4,540), SE Fla., on the Atlantic just S of Fort Lauderdale; settled 1896 by Danes. Seminole Indian Reservation is near.

Daniel [Heb.,= God is my judge], prophet, central figure of book of DANIEL.

Daniel, Samuel, 1562–1619, English poet known chiefly for *Delia* (1592), a collection of sonnets.

Daniel, book of Old Testament. Some parts occur only in Greek and are placed in Apocrypha in AV, but are included in Western canon (see SUSANNA; BEL AND THE DRAGON; THREE HOLY CHILDREN). Book tells story of Daniel, a Jew living in 6th cent. B.C., who was taken in captivity into court of Nebuchadnezzar, where he rose to power and was called Belteshazzar. Proverbial for wisdom, he was hero of many stories, e.g., his interpretation of Nebuchadnezzar's dreams; his reading of handwriting on wall; his escape from lion's den; his apocalyptic visions. Book also tells of his three friends who faced ordeal of fiery furnace. Critics question date of book, its authorship and historical accuracy, but agree on its inspirational value as story of uncompromising faith.

Daniels, Josephus, 1862–1948, American statesman, newspaper editor, and author. Was editor in Raleigh, N.C., after 1884. U.S. Secretary of the Navy (1913–21); ambassador to Mexico (1933–42). Wrote *The Wilson Era* (1944–46). His son **Jonathan Worth Daniels,** 1902–, succeeded to editorship of Raleigh *News and Observer* in 1948.

Danielson, Conn.: see KILLINGLY.

Danilo (dänế'lô), princes of MONTENEGRO. **Danilo I** (Danilo Petrovich of Niegosh), (1677–1735), reigned 1696–1735. Instigated massacre of Moslems (1703; "Montenegrin Vespers"); began traditional alliance with Russia against Turkey. **Danilo II,** 1826–60, reigned 1851–60. Secularized the prince-bishopric by transferring his ecclesiastic functions to an archbishop. Defeated Turks at Ostrog (1853) and Grahovo (1858). Assassinated.

Danish language, North Germanic language of Indo-European family. See LANGUAGE (table).

Danish West Indies: see VIRGIN ISLANDS OF THE U.S.

Dannemora (dă"nŭmô'rŭ), village (pop. 4,122), NE N.Y. Clinton State Prison is here.

D'Annunzio, Gabriele (gäbrēā'lä dän-nōōn'tsyō), 1863–1938, Italian author and adventurer, a leader of the decadents. A strong nationalist, he led an expedition to free

Fiume (1919) and was an early idol of fascism. Poems, novels, and plays include *Canto novo* [new song] (1882) and the play *Il sogno d'un tramonto d'autunno* (1898). His love affair with Eleanora Duse is described in the novel *Il fuoco* (1900).

Dansville, village (pop. 5,253), W central N.Y., S of Geneseo, in agr. area. Here Clara Barton founded (1881) first local chapter of American Red Cross.

Dante (Alighieri) (dän'tā älēgyä'rē), 1265–1321, Italian poet, author of the DIVINE COMEDY, b. Florence. *La vita nuova* [the new life] (1292), a prose narrative with inserted lyrics, told of his love for a beautiful girl, identified by many as Beatrice Portinari. He went into exile with the White Guelphs (1302). He died in exile in Ravenna. Dante also wrote in Italian many fine lyrics and an unfinished encyclopedic work, the *Convivio*. His Latin works include an unfinished treatise (*De vulgari eloquentia*), on Italian language and poetics, and a masterful apology for world government (*Monarchia*).

Danton, Georges Jacques (zhôrzh' zhäk' dätô), 1759–94, French revolutionist. A lawyer, he won immense popularity through his powerful oratory. As a leader of the CORDELIERS he championed the extreme left in the National Assembly and was instrumental in overthrowing the monarchy (1792). As head of the provisional republican government and minister of justice he set up the Revolutionary Tribunal and dominated the first Committee of Public Safety (1793). The rise of the extremists led by ROBESPIERRE led Danton to seek a relatively moderate course. His struggle with Robespierre was, however, personal rather than ideological. Danton gradually lost his influence. Early in 1794 he was arrested on a charge of conspiracy and, after a mock trial, guillotined.

Danube (dă'nŭb), Ger. *Donau,* Hung. *Duna,* Serbo-Croatian *Dunav,* Rumanian *Dunarea,* river, c.1,750 mi. long, Central and SE Europe; largest in Europe after Volga. Draining c.320,000 sq. mi., it rises in the Black Forest (SW Germany) and flows generally SE through S Germany, E Austria, Hungary, NE Yugoslavia, and SE Rumania into the Black Sea. It forms sections of the Czechoslovak-Hungarian border and of the borders of Rumania with Yugoslavia, Bulgaria, and the USSR. After passing the IRON GATE it broadens steadily and at Galati it divides into a swampy delta. Its course passes Ulm (where it becomes navigable), Regensburg, Passau, Linz, Vienna, Bratislava, Esztergom, Budapest, Belgrade, Galati, and Izmail. Among some 300 affluents are the Inn, Drava, Theiss, Sava, and Pruth. A vital traffic artery, the Danube also is a link of many cultures. It was the N border of the Roman Empire; its fertile plains have attracted many invaders. In 1919 it was placed under an international commission, which was dissolved in 1940. The Belgrade convention of 1948, which the U.S., Great Britain, and France refused to sign, created a navigation commission composed of the riparian nations only (excluding Germany and Austria).

Danvers, town (pop. 15,720), NE Mass., NW

of Salem; settled 1636. Mfg. of shoes and metal products.

Danville. 1 City (pop. 37,864), E Ill., on Vermilion R. at Ind. line; plotted 1827. Center of agr. and coal area with railroad shops. Mfg. of brick, food, and zinc products. Abraham Lincoln had law office here for five years. **2** City (pop. 8,686), central Ky., SSW of Lexington; settled 1775. Rail hub with stockyards, flour and lumber mills, and mfg. of clothing and furniture. One of state's oldest settlements, seat of govt. 1784–92. Kentucky constitutional conventions held here (setting preserved). Seat of Centre Col. of Kentucky (Presbyterian; coed.; 1819). **3** Borough (pop. 6,994), NE central Pa., on Susquehanna R. and NE of Harrisburg. Has iron and steel works. **4** City (pop. 35,066), S Va., SE of Roanoke and on Dan R.; founded 1793. One of world's largest brightleaf tobacco markets, it has cotton mills and mfg. of textiles and furniture. Operates Pinnacles of Dan hydroelectric project. Was last cap. of the Confederacy in April, 1865.

Danzig (dăn'sĭg), Pol. *Gdańsk*, city (pop. 117,894; 1941 pop. 267,251), a Baltic seaport on a branch of the Vistula; transferred to Polish administration 1945. The ancient cap. of Pomerelia, it was settled by German merchants; joined the Hanseatic League 13th cent.; passed to the Teutonic Knights 1308; became an autonomous state under Polish overlordship 1466; passed to Prussia 1793; was a free city 1807–14; was restored to Prussia 1814. It was the cap. of West Prussia prov. until 1919, when the Treaty of Versailles again made it a free city, united with Poland by a customs union and supervised by a League of Nations high commissioner. After 1935 the local National Socialist party gained control over the legislature and agitated for reunion with Germany. Hitler's demand for Danzig was the chief direct cause of World War II. Danzig was annexed to Germany Sept. 1, 1939; it fell to the Russian army early in 1945. The construction of the Polish port of GDYNIA after World War I reduced its importance as a port. Virtually destroyed in World War II, Danzig lost all its fine medieval architecture; only the port escaped destruction. Most of the German population was expelled after 1945 and replaced by Poles.

Daphne (dăf'nē), in Greek myth, nymph who attracted love of Apollo. Pursued by him, she prayed for escape and was changed into a laurel tree.

Daphnis (dăf'nĭs), in Greek literary legend, shepherd in love with a Naiad. Made blind for unfaithfulness, he played sad songs upon his shepherd's pipes and thus began pastoral melody.

Daphnis and Chloë (dăf'nĭs, klō'ē), Greek pastoral romance attributed to one Longus of 3d cent. A.D.

Da Ponte, Lorenzo (lôrĕnd'zō dä pōn'tā), 1749–1838, Italian poet and librettist, a pioneer in spreading Italian culture in the U.S. Wrote librettos for Mozart's *Così fan tutte* (1790), *The Marriage of Figaro* (1786), and *Don Giovanni* (1787). Came to U.S. in 1805, was made professor at Columbia Univ. 1830.

D'Arblay, Madame: see BURNEY, FRANCES.

Darby, John Nelson, 1800–1882, a founder of PLYMOUTH BRETHREN. He formed congregations on the Continent and in U.S. and Canada.

Darby, borough (pop. 13,154), SE Pa., SW suburb of Philadelphia; settled 1682. Has colonial landmarks. Mfg. of boats, textiles, and clothing.

Dardanelles (därdůnĕlz'), strait, c.40 mi. long, 1–4 mi. wide, connecting the Aegean with the Sea of Marmara and dividing the Gallipoli peninsula of European Turkey from Asiatic Turkey. Called the Hellespont in antiquity; scene of legend of HERO and Leander. Controlling navigation between the Black Sea and the Mediterranean, the Dardanelles and BOSPORUS straits have been important from the dawn of history. Ancient Troy prospered near W entrance of Hellespont. Xerxes and Alexander the Great crossed it by a bridge of boats (c.481 B.C.; 334 B.C.). Under the Byzantine and Ottoman empires the Straits were essential to defense of Constantinople; with the decay of Turkey (see EASTERN QUESTION), their status became an international problem. In 1841 the Great Powers agreed to close the Straits to all but Turkish warships in peacetime. This was reaffirmed by the Congress of Paris (1856). In World War I the Allied GALLIPOLI CAMPAIGN failed to force the Straits. The Treaty of SÈVRES (1920) internationalized the Straits zone, but the Conference of LAUSANNE (1923) restored it to Turkey on condition of demilitarization. In 1936, by the MONTREUX CONVENTION, Turkey was permitted to refortify it.

Dardanus (där'dŭnŭs), in Greek mythology, founder of Troy; son of Zeus and the Pleiad Electra.

Dare, Virginia, b. 1587, on Roanoke Isl., first white child of English parents born in America.

Dares Phrygius (dâ'rēz frĭ'jēŭs), supposed author of a history of Trojan War. Latin MS of 5th cent. A.D. was popular source for medieval stories.

Dar-es-Salaam (där'-ĕs-sŭläm'), city (pop. 69,227), cap. of Tanganyika; a port on the Indian Ocean.

Dariel, Georgian SSR: see DARYAL.

Darien (dâ"rēĕn', dâ'rēĕn', Span. däryän'), E part of Panama. Properly today Isthmus of Darien is that part of Isthmus of Panama between Gulf of Darien and Gulf of San Miguel, but formerly name was applied to entire isthmus. Visited by Bastidas (1501) and Columbus (1502). Arias de Ávila (Pedrarias) succeeded ENCISO as governor in 1514 and established harsh rule over entire isthmus.

Darien. 1 (dâ"rēĕn') Residential town (pop. 11,767), SW Conn., on Long Isl. Sound E of Stamford. **2** (dā'rēĭn) City (pop. 1,380), SE Ga., N of Brunswick. Founded 1736 by Scotch Highlanders recruited by Oglethorpe to supersede Spanish influence. Site of Fort King George (1721–27), first English settlement in Ga., is near.

Darien Scheme, Scottish colonial project. Scottish Parliament chartered trading company 1695. Efforts made to estab. colony on Isthmus of Panama failed (1698–99) with loss of many lives and great losses to Scottish investors. Showed Scotland's commercial disadvantage outside British "realm."

Darío, Rubén (rōōběn′ därě′ō), 1867–1916, Spanish American poet, b. Nicaragua. Spent many years in diplomatic service. Was leader of MODERNISMO. His poems have elegance and grace strengthened by vigor and power, technical mastery, and achieve poetic universality. First important volume was *Azul* [blue] (1888).

Darius (dûrĭ′ŭs), kings of anc. Persia. **Darius I** (the Great), c.549–485? B.C., reigned 521–485? B.C. Succeeding his cousin Cambyses after the fall of a false claimant, he put down rebellions, then set up the administrative system under satraps (governors responsible only to him, with checks by the army and police). This system lasted even beyond the fall of the empire to Alexander the Great. Darius campaigned against the Scythians but is best remembered as the king against whom the Ionian Greek cities revolted (c.500 B.C.), thus beginning the PERSIAN WARS. His first expedition against Greece was turned back by storms, his second defeated at MARATHON (490 B.C.). Succeeded by XERXES I. **Darius II**, d. 404 B.C., son of Artaxerxes I, succeeded his half brother Xerxes II and reigned 423?–404 B.C. Succeeded by Artaxerxes II, but CYRUS THE YOUNGER claimed the throne. **Darius III**, d. 330 B.C., was raised to the throne (336 B.C.) by the eunuch Bagoas, who had murdered Artaxerxes III and his heir. Darius had Bagoas killed but could not estab. his rule firmly. His empire fell to ALEXANDER THE GREAT, who defeated his armies at Issus (333 B.C.) and Gaugamela (331 B.C.) and pursued Darius into Bactria, where he was murdered by his cousin, the satrap Bessus. Called Darius Codomannus.

Darius the Mede, in Bible, called son of Ahasuerus and king of Chaldeans after defeat of Belshazzar; exact identity unknown. Dan. 5.31; 9.1; 11.1.

Darjeeling (därjē′lĭng), resort town (pop. 25,873), N West Bengal, India, in Himalaya foothills, alt. c.7,000 ft. Tea-growing center.

Dark Ages: see MIDDLE AGES.

dark horse, in U.S. politics, a comparatively unknown man chosen by a major party as candidate for public office, especially the presidency. Usually chosen to break a deadlocked national convention. W. H. Harrison was first important dark horse.

Darlan, Jean François (zhä′ fräswä′ därlä′), 1881–1942, French admiral. Important member of VICHY GOVERNMENT from 1940; received command of armed forces 1942; advocated collaboration with Germany. After Allied landing in N Africa (Nov., 1942) went over to Allies, who made him high commissioner in N Africa. Assassinated by an antifascist.

Darling, river of SE Australia, 1,702 mi. long, mainly in New South Wales; longest tributary of Murray R. Explored by Charles Sturt in 1844.

Darlington, county borough (pop. 84,861), Durham, England; railroad center. Has locomotive works, iron, steel, and woolen mills.

Locomotive which drew first passenger train (1825) preserved here.

Darlington, town (pop. 6,619), NE S.C., NW of Florence. Center of cotton, tobacco, and lumber area.

Darmstadt (därm′stăt, därm′shtät), city (pop. 94,132), former cap. of Hesse-Darmstadt (see HESSE), W Germany. Commercial center; chemical industry. Severely damaged in World War II.

Darnley, Henry Stuart or **Stewart, Lord,** 1545–67, claimant to English throne and second husband of MARY QUEEN OF SCOTS. Son of powerful earl of Lennox, he claimed succession to Elizabeth through his grandmother, Margaret Tudor. Catholic sympathies, claim on throne, and perhaps his handsome appearance induced Mary to marry him (1565). He proved vicious and dissipated, and she did not make him royal consort. Joined in murder of David Rizzio (1566); was soon without friends. Plot formed to murder him, probably under earl of Bothwell. Killed under mysterious circumstances. Father of James I.

Darrow, Clarence (Seward), 1857–1938, American lawyer. After defending (1894) Eugene V. Debs during the Pullman strike, he gave up his lucrative practice to champion the "underdog." Defended many labor leaders (e.g., William J. Haywood) and over 100 persons charged with murder (e.g., Leopold and Loeb). Opposed W. J. Bryan in the SCOPES TRIAL.

Dartford, urban district (pop. 40,544), Kent, England. Wat Tyler's rebellion broke out here. England's first paper mill built here in Elizabeth's time.

Dartmoor, picturesque upland c.25 mi. long, Devonshire, England. Includes ancient Royal Forest of Dartmoor. Has copper, tin, and iron mining, granite quarrying, and grazing. In the middle of Dartmoor, near Princetown, is **Dartmoor Prison,** built 1806–9. Housed French captives in Napoleonic Wars, American captives in War of 1812. Made a convicts' prison 1850. In World War I conscientious objectors were imprisoned here.

Dartmouth (därt′mŭth), industrial town (pop. 15,037), S N.S., Canada, on Halifax Harbour opposite Halifax; settled 1751. Has sugar refineries, shipbuilding, and iron founding.

Dartmouth (därt′mŭth), municipal borough (pop. 5,842), Devonshire, England. Site of Royal Naval Col. Richard I embarked here for the Crusades.

Dartmouth, town (pop. 11,115), SE Mass., on Buzzards Bay SW of New Bedford; settled c.1650. Quaker center with 18th-cent. Friends' meetinghouse.

Dartmouth College, at Hanover, N.H.; nonsectarian, for men, chartered 1769, opened 1770 by Eleazar WHEELOCK. A state college connected (1868–93) with Dartmouth became Univ. of New Hampshire (see DURHAM). Dartmouth stresses liberal arts. Its famous outing club holds a winter carnival.

Dartmouth College Case, decided by the U.S. Supreme Court in 1819. New Hampshire legislature amended (1816) the college charter to make it a public institution. Trustees, represented by Daniel Webster, argued that the state had violated a contract and won the case. The opinion rendered by John Marshall was that a charter is in effect inviolable.

Darwin, Erasmus, 1731–1802, English poet. A physician who cultivated a botanic garden, he wrote *The Botanic Garden* (1789–91) and *Zoonomia* (1794–96), more important as science than literature. His grandson **Charles (Robert) Darwin,** 1809–82, was a naturalist. He studied medicine and ministry before becoming official naturalist on the *Beagle.* His explorations, observations, and investigations led to his formulating a concept of EVOLUTION, known as DARWINISM, set forth in his *Origin of Species* (1859). A. R. WALLACE worked out a similar theory independently. His son, **Francis Darwin,** 1848–1925, a botanist, assisted his father and edited his biography and letters. **Sir George Howard Darwin,** 1845–1912, brother of Francis, was an astronomer and mathematician and an authority on cosmogony. His son, **Sir Charles Galton Darwin,** 1887–, a physicist, served as director of the National Physical Laboratory (1938–49).

Darwin, port (pop. 2,538), cap. of Northern Territory, Australia, on inlet of Timor Sea. Originally called Palmerston, renamed for Charles Darwin. Important for its airport on Singapore-Sydney route. A key Allied base in World War II.

Darwinism, concept of EVOLUTION set forth by Charles Darwin. Observing the tendency of organisms to increase geometrically while numbers of given species remained about stable, he deduced a struggle for survival. He emphasized individual variation within a species and survival of those with most favorable variations, some being transmitted to offspring. This principle of natural selection is, with modifications, almost universally accepted by scientists.

Daryal (däryăl′) or **Dariel** (däreēl′), gorge, c.5,900 ft. deep, Georgian SSR, in central Greater Caucasus, below Mt. Kazbek. Formed by Terek R.; traversed by road linking Dzaudzhikau (Vladikavkaz) with Tiflis. Famed for wild grandeur. Known in antiquity as Caucasian or Iberian Gates.

dasheen: see TARO.

Dass, Petter, 1647–1707, Norwegian poet, author of still-popular *Norway's Trumpet.*

date, long-lived, tall palm (*Phoenix dactylifera*) and its edible, brown fruit (1–3 in. long) borne in heavy, pendent clusters. A principal food in many desert and tropical regions from early times. Trees are now cultivated in SW U.S. and Mexico.

Dathan (dā′–), rebel with KORAH against Moses. Brother of Abiram.

Datia (dŭ′tēä), town (pop. 22,086), Vindhya Pradesh, India. Has superb 17th-cent. Hindu palace. Was cap. of Rajput state of Datia, founded c.1626.

dative: see CASE.

Daubigny, Charles François (shärl′ fräswä′ dōbēnyē′), 1817–78, French landscape painter, best known for his scenes of the banks of the Seine and the Oise. Usually classed with the Barbizon school, although he never lived in Barbizon.

Daudet, Alphonse (älfōs′ dōdä′), 1840–97, French author. He wrote with charm and

gentle satire of his native Provence in *Lettres de mon moulin* (1866) and *Tartarin de Tarascon* (1872), his most enduring works. *Froment jeune et Risler aîné* (1874), *Le Nabab* (1877), *Numa Roumestan* (1881), *Sapho* (1884), and *L'Immortel* (1888) are novels of social criticism and satire. *Le Petit Chose* is autobiographical. His son, **Léon Daudet** (lāō′), 1867–1942, author, edited the royalist, extreme rightist daily *Action française* and wrote valuable memoirs (6 vols., 1914–21; partial Eng. tr., 1925).

Daugherty, Harry M(icajah) (dô′ûrtē), 1860–1941, U.S. Attorney General (1921–24). Accused of taking part in Teapot Dome scandal, but case was dismissed.

Daughters of the American Revolution, patriotic society in U.S., open to women whose ancestors aided patriot cause in Revolution. Organized 1890.

Daulatabad (doulûtûbäd′), village, S Hyderabad, India. The Chand Minar (1294) is a noted moslem minaret.

Daumier, Honoré (ônôrā′ dōmyā′), 1808–79, French lithographer, cartoonist, and painter. Satirized the bourgeois society of his day, producing c.4,000 lithographs, now considered masterpieces of the art. Imprisoned for 6 months in 1832 for his political cartoon *Gargantua.* Painted c.200 small canvases, including *The Good Samaritan* (Metropolitan Mus.).

Daun, Leopold, Graf von (lā′ōpôlt gräf′ fŭn doun′), 1705–66, Austrian field marshal. Drove French from Bohemia (1742) in War of Austrian Succession; defeated Frederick II of Prussia at Kolin (1757), but lost at Torgau (1760) in Seven Years War.

Dauphin (dô′fĭn), town (pop. 6.007), W. Man., Canada, on Vermilion R. and NW of Winnipeg. Agr. and milling center. Riding Mountain Natl. Park is S.

dauphin (dô′fĭn, Fr. dōfē′), title of eldest son (sometimes grandson) of a king of France. See DAUPHINÉ; LOST DAUPHIN.

Dauphiné (dōfēnä′), region and former province, SE France, in Hautes-Alpes, Isère, and Drôme depts.; historic cap. Grenoble. In E, Alps culminate in the BARRE DES ÉCRINS. Vineyards and silkworm raising in lower districts. Cities: Grenoble, Vienne, Valence. As part of kingdom of ARLES, region was ruled by counts of Vienne, who took title "dauphin" (etymology uncertain). Dauphin Humbert II sold it to Philip VI of France (1349). Dauphiné was governed by eldest sons of French kings until accession of Louis XI, who incorporated it with France, although technically it was part of Holy Roman Empire. Title "dauphin" thenceforth was merely honorific.

Dauthendey, Max (doutĕn′dä), 1867–1918, German poet and novelist. Wrote many volumes of exotic, impressionistic verse and a number of novels and plays (e.g., *Caprices of an Empress,* 1910).

Davao (dävou′), city (pop. 111,263), SE Mindanao, Philippines, on Davao Gulf; hemp-producing center.

D'Avenant or **Davenant, Sir William** (dăv′ûnŭnt), 1606–68, English poet, dramatist, theater manager. A royalist, he was imprisoned in 1651, released through efforts of Milton and others.

Davenport, George, 1783–1845, American Indian trader, b. England. Managed fur-trading post at Rock Island, Ill. Davenport, Iowa, named for him.

Davenport, John, 1597–1670, Puritan clergyman, b. England. Founded New Haven, Conn. (1637–38), with Theophilus EATON. Important figure in colony.

Davenport, city (pop. 74,549), E Iowa, on the Mississippi. Forms, with ROCK ISLAND, MOLINE, and EAST MOLINE (all in Ill.), economic unit called Quad Cities. Founded 1836 by George Davenport on site of early trading post, it prospered with coming (1856) of first railroad to bridge the Mississippi and with heavy river traffic of late 19th cent. Rail, commercial, and industrial center, it has mfg. of machinery and other metal products, clothing, beer, and foodstuffs. Credit Isl., a park, is site of War of 1812 battle.

David, Saint, d. 588?, patron saint of Wales, first abbot of Menevia (SAINT DAVID'S). His shrine was an important place of pilgrimage in the Middle Ages. On his feast, March 1, the national Welsh festival is celebrated.

David [Heb.,= beloved], d. c.972 B.C., shepherd boy who became king of Hebrews (c.1012–c.972 B.C.). One of greatest of Hebrew national heroes, celebrated not only for his valor as a warrior but for his ability as a ruler and for his gifts as a poet and musician as well. Among popular stories about him: his victory over Goliath, his friendship with Jonathan, his love for Bath-sheba, the revolt of his son Absalom. Many Psalms ascribed to him. Under David, Hebrews changed from loose confederation of tribes to strong national state. According to Gospels, Jesus was of House of David. 1 Sam. 17.12–1 Kings 2.12; 1 Chron. 11–29.

David, kings of Scotland. **David I,** 1084–1153, was king 1124–53. In struggle for English crown between Matilda (his niece) and Stephen, he fought for Matilda without success; made peace 1141. His rule was wise and momentous. **David II** (David Bruce), 1324–71, was king 1329–71. Edward III and Edward de BALIOL invaded Scotland 1332. David invaded England 1346, was captured, and held until 1357.

David or **Davit, Gerard** (gä'rärt dä'vēt), c.1450–1523, painter of the early Flemish school.

David, Jacques Louis (zhäk' lwē' dävēd'), 1748–1825, French painter. His *Andromache* and *Oath of the Horatii* established him as the leading exponent of the classical reaction. His *Mme. Recamier* and the *Assassination of Marat* are renowned. He was an ardent republican despite his honored position as painter to Louis XVI. Later served Napoleon.

David, Pierre Jean: see DAVID D'ANGERS.

David, Sir Tannatt William Edgeworth (dā'vĭd), 1858–1934, British geologist. As geologist for the Shackleton antarctic expedition, he led the party which first reached the south magnetic pole.

David d'Angers (dävēd' däzhä'), or **Pierre Jean David** (pyĕr' zhä'), 1788–1856, French

sculptor. A typical work is the group on pediment of the Panthéon.

David Harum: see WESTCOTT, EDWARD NOYES.

Davids, (Thomas William) Rhys (rēs), 1843–1922, English Orientalist, a leading authority on Buddhism and on Pali texts.

Davidson, George, 1825–1911, American geographer and astronomer, b. England. Staff member of U.S. Coast and Geodetic Survey (1845–95). Directed charting of Pacific coast for navigation (1850–60). Surveyed Delaware R.; mapped Philadelphia area for fortification (1860–66). Directed Survey's Pacific coast work (1867–87). Built first Pacific coast observatory in San Francisco 1879. Made valuable meteorological and astronomical studies.

Davidson, Jo, 1883–1952, American sculptor, best known for busts of famous contemporaries.

Davies, Arthur Bowen (dā'vēz), 1862–1928, American painter. His romantic work includes symbolic pictures of the female nude in idyllic landscapes. Largely responsible for famous Armory Show of 1913.

Davies, Sir John (dā'vĭs), 1569–1626, English poet, author of *Nosce Teipsum* (1599; a philosophical poem) and *Hymns to Astraea* (1599).

Davies, Joseph E(dward) (dā'vēz), 1876–, American diplomat. Ambassador to USSR (1937–38), ambassador to Belgium (1938–40). His book, *Mission to Moscow* (1945), pictures conditions in USSR.

Dávila, Gil Gonzáles: see GONZÁLES DE ÁVILA, GIL.

Dávila, Pedrarias: see ARIAS DE ÁVILA, PEDRO.

Da Vinci, Leonardo: see LEONARDO DA VINCI.

Davis, Alexander Jackson, 1803–92, American architect, exponent of the Greek-revival style.

Davis, Arthur Powell, 1861–1933, American civil engineer and hydrographic authority on many important irrigation and water-supply projects.

Davis, Benjamin Oliver, 1877–, American general. First Negro general in U.S. army (1940).

Davis, Charles Henry, 1807–77, American naval officer. In Civil War he repulsed Confederate fleet near Fort Pillow (May, 1862); annihilated fleet before Memphis, captured city (June, 1862).

Davis, David, 1815–86, Associate Justice of U.S. Supreme Court (1862–77). His decision in *Ex parte Milligan* (1866), denouncing arbitrary military power, became a bulwark of civil liberty in U.S.

Davis, Elmer (Holmes), 1890–, American author and radio commentator, director (1942–45) of the Office of War Information.

Davis, Henry Winter, 1817–65, American political leader. U.S. Representative from Md. (1855–61, 1863–65). Opposed Reconstruction program of Pres. Lincoln with more radical plan of his own.

Davis, Jefferson, 1808–89, American statesman. President of CONFEDERACY (1861–65). U.S. Senator from Miss. (1847–51). Secretary of War (1853–57). Again Senator (1857–61), he resigned at secession of Miss. Provisional president of Confederacy, then regular president; inaugurated Feb., 1862. Administration stormy as he assumed strong centralized power, thus weakening states' rights policy for which South had seceded. Lee surrendered without his approval. Captured and confined at Fort Monroe for two years; released 1867, never prosecuted.

Davis or **Davys, John,** c.1550–1605, British navigator. In seeking Northwest Passage, clarified much arctic geography N of Labrador. Discovered Falkland Isls. (1592). Lost his life in East Indies fighting Japanese pirates. Invented useful quadrant.

Davis, John William, 1873–, American lawyer, public official. U.S. Congressman (1911–13). Nominated as compromise Democratic presidential candidate in 1924 after two-week convention deadlock; won only 136 electoral votes.

Davis, Richard Harding, 1864–1916, American correspondent for all major wars of his era, author of romantic stories and plays. His mother, **Rebecca Harding Davis,** 1831–1910, was the author of several novels dealing with the effect of social problems on individuals.

Davis, Stuart, 1894–, American painter of abstractions. Studied with Robert Henri.

Davis, William Morris, 1850–1934, American geographer. Global traveler, authority on land forms, prolific contributor to geographical journals, he helped advance science of physiography.

Davis, Mount, peak (3,213 ft.), SW Pa., in the Alleghenies near Md. line. Highest point in state.

Davis Mountains, W Texas, SE of El Paso, rising to 8,382 ft. in Mt. Livermore (or Baldy Peak or Old Baldy). Parks and scenery attract visitors.

Davisson, Clinton Joseph, 1881–, American physicist. He shared the 1937 Nobel Prize for demonstrations confirming Louis de Broglie's theory of wave nature of moving electrons.

Davis Strait, between Greenland and Baffin Isl., connecting Atlantic Ocean and Baffin Sea, 180–400 mi. wide. John Davis sailed through it 1787.

Davit, Gerard: see DAVID, GERARD.

Davos (dävōs'), town (resident pop. 10,332), Grisons canton, E Switzerland. Winter sports; health resort for tuberculosis.

Davout, Louis Nicolas (lwē' nēkôlä' dävōō'), 1770–1823, marshal of France, duke of AUERSTEDT, prince of Eckmühl; one of Napoleon's ablest lieutenants.

Davy, Sir Humphry (dā'vē), 1778–1829, English chemist and physicist. He investigated laughing gas; isolated sodium, potassium, calcium, barium, boron, magnesium, and strontium; did electrochemical research; established elementary nature of chlorine; and advanced theory that hydrogen is characteristic of acids.

Davys, John: see DAVIS, JOHN.

Dawes, Charles G(ates) (dôz), 1865–1951, American statesman and banker. Vice President of United States (1925–29). Forwarded **Dawes Plan** in 1924 to Reparations Commission of the Allied nations. Plan provided for reduction in payment of REPARATIONS and the stabilization of German finances.

Dawes, Henry Laurens, 1816–1903, U.S. Senator from Mass. (1875–93). Sponsored **Dawes Act,** 1887, passed by U.S. Congress to provide for granting of individual landholdings to civilized Indians who would renounce their tribal holdings. Began the absorbing of Indians into body politic. **Dawes Commission,** commission to Five Civilized Tribes, was created by Congress in 1893. It reorganized Indian Territory by getting consent of chiefs to substitute individual for tribal land holding.

Dawes Plan: see DAWES, CHARLES GATES.

Dawson or **Dawson City,** town (pop. 783), territorial cap., W Yukon, Canada, at junction of Yukon and Klondike rivers. Trade center of a mining region, it is usually reached via Skagway, Alaska, the White Pass RR, or by boat from White Horse. In 1898 gold rush Dawson was a boom town.

Dawson Creek, village (pop. 3,589), E B.C., Canada, near Alta. border, NE of Prince George. S terminus of Alaska Highway, connected by railroad and highway to Edmonton.

Day, Benjamin Henry, 1810–89, American journalist. Founded the New York *Sun* (1833) and made it a cheap popular paper before selling it (1838) to Moses Y. Beach. His son, **Benjamin Day,** 1838–1916, invented the Benday process for reproducing maps and illustrations.

Day, Clarence (Shepard), 1874–1935, American humorist, author of *This Simian World* (1920), *God and My Father* (1932), *Life with Father* (1935), *Life with Mother* (1937).

Day, Edmund Ezra, 1883–1951, American educator. Professor of economics, Univ. of Michigan (1923–27) and dean of school of business administration. President of Cornell Univ. (1937–49).

Day, John, 1522–84, English printer. Designed and made type, including musical notes and the first Anglo-Saxon type. Printed (under another title) first English edition of John Foxe's *Book of Martyrs* (1562).

Day, Thomas, 1748–89, English social reformer. His *History of Sandford and Merton* (3 vols., 1783–89), contrasts "natural" and conventional education.

Daye, Stephen, c.1594–1668, British settler in Mass., a locksmith, usually called first printer in English American colonies. Supervised Cambridge Press, first colonial printing plant. Published *Bay Psalm Book* (1640); first book printed in colonies. Actual printing was probably done by his son, **Matthew Daye,** c.1620–1649, a trained printer.

Day Lewis, C(ecil), 1904–, English writer, b. Ireland, author of several volumes of highly praised poetry and (under pseud. Nicholas Blake) of detective stories.

daylight-saving time, time reckoned later (usually one hour) than standard time. Adopted by federal law in U.S. as wartime measure (1918–19) and during World War II, its use was continued as summer time at option of state and local governments by turning clocks ahead in spring and back in autumn.

day lily, Old World perennial of genus *Hemerocallis,* with yellow, orange, or reddish flowers. Species often cultivated include fragrant lemon day lily and widely naturalized tawny day lily.

Dayton. 1 City (pop. 8,977), N Ky., on Ohio R. and near Covington, opposite Cincinnati. **2** City (pop. 243,872), SW Ohio, NW of Cincinnati and on Great Miami R. at influx of Mad and Stillwater rivers; settled 1796. Shipping and industrial center for agr. area, it has mfg. of cash registers, refrigerators and air conditioning equipment, precision tools, lighting equipment, motors, and aircraft and auto parts. Chief U.S. aviation center with many installations, both governmental and private. Wright brothers started experimental air plant here 1911. Here are Univ. of Dayton (R.C.; coed.; 1850), Dayton Art Inst., P. L. Dunbar Mus., Newcom Tavern (1796), and old courthouse (1850). **3** City (pop. 1,870), E Tenn., near Tennessee R. and NNE of Chattanooga. Scene of SCOPES TRIAL.

Daytona Beach (dātō′nù), resort city (pop. 30,187), NE Fla., on Atlantic coast S of St. Augustine and on Halifax R. (lagoon), in citrus-fruit area. Founded 1870 in area where Spanish monks estab. missions in 16th and 17th cent. Present city formed 1926 by consolidation of Seabreeze, Daytona, and Daytona Beach. Beach (c.25 mi. long) is often used for auto races (since 1903). Seat of Bethune-Cookman Col. (Negro; coed.; 1904).

DDT: see INSECTICIDE.

Dead, Book of the: see BOOK OF THE DEAD.

deadly nightshade: see NIGHTSHADE.

Dead Sea, salt lake, on border of Jordan and Israel; 49 mi. long, 3–10 mi. wide, 1,292 ft. below sea level, c.1,300 ft. deep. Lies in the Ghor, a great depression. Far saltier than the ocean, it yields minerals (esp. potash and bromides). It is the biblical Salt Sea, Sea of the Plain, and East Sea.

Deadwood, city (pop. 3,288), W S.Dak., in Deadwood Gulch in the Black Hills, and near Lead; settled 1876 after discovery (1875) of gold here. City's boom-and-bust cycles followed fortunes of near-by gold and silver mines. Tourist center, it has Adams Memorial Mus. and graves of Wild Bill Hickok and Calamity Jane. Grave of Deadwood Dick is near.

Deadwood Dick, American frontiersman, celebrated in many dime novels. Original is supposedly Richard W. Clarke (1845–1930), an Englishman who came to the gold diggings of the Black Hills and became a scout.

deafness, partial or complete loss of hearing. Causes include infections, especially in the head; diseases, e.g., scarlet fever, syphilis; obstructions of auditory canal; and bone formation in ear labyrinth capsule. Electrical aids are commonly employed. School for education of deaf estab. 1755 in Paris by C. M. de l'EPÉE. Other pioneers in teaching deaf include A. M. and A. G. BELL, and T. H. Gallaudet and his sons. Most of the deaf can be taught to speak; others use manual alphabet.

Deak, Francis (dĕ′äk), Hung. *Deák Ferenc,* 1803–76, Hungarian statesman. Opposed extremism of Louis KOSSUTH during revolution of 1848–49; became leader of his nation after defeat of revolutionists. Insisted on recognition of Hungary as separate kingdom, but in union with Austria; negotiated, in co-

operation with Julius ANDRASSY, creation of AUSTRO-HUNGARIAN MONARCHY (1867).

Deakin, Alfred, 1856–1919, Australian statesman. Helped federation of Australian states. Was three times prime minister.

Deal, municipal borough (pop. 24,276), Kent, England. Reputed landing place of Caesar 55 B.C. One of CINQUE PORTS, it has official residence (Walmer Castle) of Lord Warden. Naval station and shipbuilding center.

Deal Island, off Eastern Shore, Md., in Tangier Sound N of Crisfield. Has seafood industry.

De Amicis, Edmondo (ādmōn′dŏ dā ämē′chēs), 1846–1908, Italian author of travel books and novel *Cuore: an Italian Schoolboy's Journal* (1886; Eng. tr., 1887).

Dean, Jerome Herman (Dizzy Dean), 1911–, American baseball pitcher, outstanding right-hander. With St. Louis Cardinals (1932–38). Original name possibly Jay Hanna Dean.

Dean, Forest of, ancient royal forest, Gloucestershire, England.

Deane, Silas, 1737–89, American Revolutionary patriot and diplomat. As diplomatic agent in France, secured commercial and military aid for colonies and recruited foreign officers.

Dearborn, Henry, 1751–1829, American general, U.S. Secretary of War (1801–9). Relieved of command of N frontier in War of 1812 because of his inaction. Fort Dearborn named for him.

Dearborn, city (pop. 94,994), SE Mich., on River Rouge and W of Detroit; settled 1795. Home of Ford Motor Co., it also has mfg. of aircraft parts and metal products. Here are Edison Inst. of Technology, GREENFIELD VILLAGE, and birthplace of Henry Ford.

Dearborn, Fort, U.S. army post on Chicago R., estab. 1803; named for Henry Dearborn. Site of Indian attack in 1812. Chicago grew around rebuilt fort.

death. In man, death is definite if no heartbeat is detectable by stethoscope for some time, if circulation is not backed up by cord around arm or leg, or if rigor mortis has set in. Heart may beat after breathing ceases; nervous system stimulation is possible for short time after heart stops beating, thus resuscitation sometimes possible.

Death Valley, SE Calif., deep and arid basin E of Panamint Range and W of Amargosa Range. Annual average rainfall is 1.4 in. Summer temperatures are among world's highest, but climate is mild from Nov. to May. Has alkali and salt flats, briny pools, and grotesque rocks. Badwater, 280 ft. below sea level, is lowest point in Western Hemisphere. Valley named in 1849 by party of gold seekers. Borax deposits discovered in 1880s. Small animals enliven the solitude; peculiar plants attract scientists. Panamint Indians (valley's only inhabitants for centuries) live in model village here. Here are Scotty's Castle, ostentatious home of Walter Scott (Death Valley Scotty) and resorts. Includes **Death Valley National Monument:** see NATIONAL PARKS AND MONUMENTS (table).

Deauville (dōvēl′), seaside resort (pop. 5,438), Calvados dept., N France, on English Channel.

De Bary, Heinrich Anton (hīn′rĭkh än′tōn dù

bärē'), 1831–88, German botanist, authority on fungi.

Debierne, André Louis (ădrā' lwē důbyĕrn'), 1874–, French chemist. He discovered actinium and worked with the Curies on radioactivity.

Deborah, Israel's only woman judge. Helped Barak defeat Sisera and free Israel from King Jabin. Song of Deborah one of great poems in Bible. Judges 4; 5.

De Bow, J(ames) D(unwoody) B(rownson), 1820–67, American editor. Began publishing monthly *De Bow's Review* 1846. Also a statistician.

Debrecen (dĕ'brĕtsĕn), city (pop. 125,936), E Hungary. Commercial center. Historic stronghold of Hungarian Protestantism. Univ. (chartered 1912) grew out of Calvinist college (founded 1588). Hungarian independence was proclaimed at Debrecen by revolutionary government April 14, 1849. Formerly spelled Debreczen.

Debs, Eugene V(ictor), 1855–1926, American Socialist leader. Advocate of industrial unionism and a pacifist; imprisoned 1895 for violating injunction in strike at Pullman, Ill., and in 1918 under Espionage Act. Presidential candidate five times. Widely revered as martyr for his principles.

debt, obligation in services, money, or goods owed by one party (debtor) to another (creditor). If debtor fails to pay, a court may assign payment out of his property. In ancient times debtors unable to pay were sold into slavery, and imprisonment for debt persisted into 19th cent. Today in the West relief is afforded by BANKRUPTCY.

debt, public, indebtedness of a government expressed in money terms. Such debts typically result from revenue deficiences, wars, and expenses for public works or emergency projects. Modern form of debt is public loan through government bonds, treasury notes, and other instruments. Ultimate security of public debt is willingness of public to pay taxes and ability of government to collect.

Debussy, Claude (klōd' důbüsē'), 1862–1918, outstanding composer of the French impressionist movement. His piano music includes the *Suite bergamasque* (containing *Clair de Lune*); *The Children's Corner;* 24 preludes, including *La Cathédrale engloutie;* and 12 etudes. Among his orchestral works are *L'Après-midi d'un Faun, Nocturnes,* and *La Mer.* He also wrote many songs and an opera, *Pelléas et Mélisande.*

Debye, Peter Joseph Wilhelm (dēbī'), 1884–, American physicist, b. Netherlands. He won the 1936 Nobel Prize for work on structure of molecules.

decadents (dīkā'důntz, dĕ'kůdůntz), name loosely applied to late 19th-cent. artists and writers who strove to express morbid and macabre elements in human emotions; often confused with French SYMBOLISTS, who influenced the movement. They were most evident in England (e.g., Oscar Wilde, Ernest Dowson, Aubrey Beardsley).

Decalogue: see TEN COMMANDMENTS.

Decameron, The (dīkă'mŭrŭn), or II **Decamerone** (ēl dākämärō'nä) [Gr.= 10 parts], collection of 100 charming and often licen-

tious tales by Giovanni BOCCACCIO, written 1348–53.

decathlon (dīkăth'lŏn), composite contest consisting of broad jump, high jump, discus throw, shot put, javelin throw, pole vault, 100-meter, 400-meter, and 1500-meter flat races, 110-meter hurdle race.

Decatur, Stephen (dēkā'tůr), 1779–1820, American naval officer. Became famous in TRIPOLITAN WAR. In Algerine War (1815) he forced dey of Algeria to sign treaty ending American tribute to Algeria. Responsible for toast, ending, "may she always be in the right; but our country, right or wrong."

Decatur. 1 City (pop. 19,974), N Ala., on Tennessee R. and N of Birmingham; founded 1820. Processes and ships iron, steel, textiles, timber, fertilizer, foodstuffs. Has shipyards. Uses TVA power. Almost destroyed in Civil War. **2** City (pop. 21,635), NW Ga., an Atlanta suburb at foot of Stone Mt. Seat of Agnes Scott Col. (for women; founded 1889). **3** City (pop. 66,269), central Ill., E of Springfield and on Sangamon R. (here dammed to form L. Decatur); founded 1829. Distributing point for agr., oil, and coal area, it has railroad shops, mfg. of chemicals, plastics, and metal products, and corn and soybean processing. Has log cabin courthouse where Lincoln practiced and, near by, site of first Lincoln home in Ill. Grand Army of the Republic organized here 1866. Seat of James Millikin Univ. (coed.; 1901). **4** City (pop. 7,271), NE Ind., SSE of Fort Wayne. Food and cement products and motors.

Decazes, Élie (ālē' důkäz'), 1780–1860, French premier (1819–20) under LOUIS XVIII; a moderate.

Deccan (dĕ'kän"), region, S India. Historically defined as all India S of Narbada R., thus including the CARNATIC.

December: see MONTH.

Decembrist Conspiracy, military revolt at St. Petersburg, Russia, at the accession of NICHOLAS I (Dec., 1825). The plotters, belonging to liberal revolutionary societies, hoped to place Nicholas's brother Constantine on the throne and to obtain a constitution. The revolt was crushed by artillery fire; five of the leaders were hanged.

decimal system (dĕ'sĭmůl), notation system for number writing based upon powers of 10. Number is written as row of digits, each standing for a certain power of 10. Each place left of decimal point raises to higher power of 10; each place to right divides by 10 or raises to a negative power of 10. Decimal is name for any number in system; sometimes only for proper fraction in system, not a mixed number. Decimal system of Melvil Dewey is system for classification of library books.

Decius (dē'shůs), 201–51, Roman emperor (249–51). Sent to put down a mutiny against Philip the Arabian, he headed it instead, defeated and killed Philip, and became emperor. Persecuted the Christians vigorously. He was killed trying to repel the Goths in Moesia.

Decker, Thomas: see DEKKER, THOMAS.

Declaration of Independence, adopted July 4, 1776, by delegates of Thirteen Colonies, announcing their separation from Great Britain and making them into the United States. Written almost wholly by Thomas Jefferson. Opening paragraphs state idea of government based on theory of NATURAL RIGHTS.

Declaration of Rights: see BILL OF RIGHTS.

Declaration of the Rights of Man, historic French document, drafted by Sieyès (1789), embodied as preamble of French constitution of 1791. Based on J. J. Rousseau's theories and on American Declaration of Independence, it asserted the equality of all men, the sovereignty of the people, the inalienable rights of the individual to "liberty, property, security."

Decorah (dĭkô'rà), city (pop. 6,060), NE Iowa, NNE of Waterloo. Seat of Luther Col. (Evangelical Lutheran, coed.; opened 1861, chartered 1865), a center of Norwegian-American culture.

Decoration Day: see MEMORIAL DAY.

decorations, civil and military. Practice of rewarding achievements grew from medieval custom of conferring knighthood. In Great Britain this still exists in such orders as Garter, Thistle, and Bath. In Europe such orders have tended to lose feudal connotations. Among best known are Order of Golden Fleece (1429 or 1430, Austria and Spain); Danneborg and Elephant (1219 and 1462, Denmark); Annunciata and SS. Maurice and Lazarus (1362 and 1434, Italy); papal order of Golden Spur (1559); Black Eagle, Red Eagle, and Pour le Mérite (Prussia); White Eagle and Polonia Restituta (Poland); and Legion of Honor (France). Military decorations for heroism include Croix de Guerre (France); Iron Cross (Germany); Distinguished Service Order, Royal Victoria Order, and Order of the British Empire (England); Congressional Medal of Honor (1862), Distinguished Service Cross, Distinguished Service Medal, Distinguished Flying Medal, Purple Heart (1782), and silver and bronze stars (U.S.); and Red Star, Victory, Lenin, Suvarov, and Alexander Nevsky awards (USSR).

De Coster, Charles Théodore Henri (dù kô'stùr, Fr. shärl' tāōdôr' ärē' dù kôstĕr'), 1827–79, Belgian author. His chief work, *La légende et les aventures héroïques, joyeuses et glorieuses d'Ulenspiegel et de Lamme Goedzak* (1867; Eng. trs., 1918, 1921), is written in archaic style and based on the Germanic folk hero Till Eulenspiegel.

decree, in British and U.S. law, final decision of a court of equity or in equitable actions, differing from a judgment (of a court of law) in being less rigid and not limited to the award of money damages. Can be more easily enforced by proceedings for CONTEMPT OF COURT. Familiar are the INJUNCTION and the decree of DIVORCE.

Dedham (dĕ'dùm), town (pop. 18,487), E Mass., SW of Boston; settled 1635. Oldest frame house in U.S., Fairbanks house (1636), is here. Scene of Sacco-Vanzetti trial. Mfg. of paper products.

Dee, John, 1527–1608, British scientist and astrologer. Drew up geographical materials on newly found lands for Queen Elizabeth and urged adoption of Gregorian calendar. His interest in the occult led to accusations of sorcery and fame as a magician.

Dee, rivers in Scotland; 1 Aberdeenshire and Kincardine; famous for its beauty, flows 90 mi. past Balmoral Castle to North Sea; 2 Kirkcudbrightshire.

Dee, river of Wales and England, flowing 70 mi. to Irish Sea. Expanse of sand of shallow estuary at low tide is Kingsley's "Sands of Dee."

Deepwater, village (1940 pop. 798), SW N.J., on Delaware R. below Penns Grove. E terminus of Del. Memorial Bridge; S terminus of N.J. Turnpike.

deer, ruminant mammal of family Cervidae found over most of world except Australia. Males usually have antlers, which are shed annually. If they lack antlers (e.g., the MUSK DEER and Chinese river deer) their upper canines are long and serve as weapons. Deer are polygamous. They eat herbaceous plants, lichens, and mosses. The white-tailed deer, a source of many necessities for American Indians and settlers, was nearly exterminated through years of slaughter, but is restored in parts of the U.S. See also CARIBOU; ELK; MOOSE; REINDEER; WAPITI.

Deere, John, 1804–86, American manufacturer of agr. implements, pioneer maker of steel plows. His factory at Moline, Ill. became world-known.

Deerfield, town (pop. 3,086), NW Mass., on Deerfield R. and N of Northampton. Seat of Deerfield Acad. for boys (chartered 1797, opened 1799).

Deerfield, river, c.70 mi. long, rising in S Vt. and flowing S into NW Mass., then SE to Connecticut R. near Greenfield, Mass. Furnishes power.

Deering, William, 1826–1913, American farm machinery manufacturer. He developed the first successful grain binder.

Deer Park, village (pop. 7,241), SW Ohio, a NE suburb of Cincinnati.

Defense, United States Department of, created 1947; reorganized 1949. James V. Forrestal, who pioneered in its organization, became first Secretary of Defense. Department guards U.S. security and coordinates activities of army, navy, and air force. Its organization has eliminated much overlapping and duplication.

defense mechanism, psychoanalytic expression indicating unconscious mode of behavior designed to ward off anticipated or imagined criticism or condemnation. These "dynamisms" include rationalization—substitution (for ego's sake) of socially acceptable for unsocial motives; repression—barring of distressing ideas from consciousness; regression—to infantile behavior, gratifications; projection—assignment to others of own ego-repudiated urges; identification—reaction to others' desires as if one's own; sublimation—redirection of libido to constructive ends; conversion—transformation of psychological conflict into actual physical symptoms.

Defense Mobilization, Office of, created 1950 by executive order of U.S. Pres. Harry S. Truman to direct and control mobilization activities of executive branch of government, including control over production, procurement, man power, stabilization, and transport activities. Charles Edward Wilson was first director (1950–52).

Deffand, marquise du: see DU DEFFAND.

Defiance, city (pop. 11,265), NW Ohio, at junction of Auglaize and Maumee rivers SW of Toledo; settled 1790. Mfg. of machinery and machine tools. Here was Fort Defiance (1794); near by was Fort Winchester (1812). Seat of Defiance Col.

Defoe or **De Foe, Daniel,** 1660–1731, English writer, author of ROBINSON CRUSOE. A pamphleteer and journalist, he won the favor of William III with his poem, *The True-born Englishman* (1701), but strong anti-Tory sentiment in *The Shortest Way with Dissenters* (1702) brought imprisonment under Anne. His *Review* (1704–13) was an early and influential journal. Besides his *Life and Strange, Surprising Adventures of Robinson Crusoe* (1719), he wrote *Moll Flanders* (1722); *Journal of the Plague Year* (1722; fictitious), *The Fortunate Mistress; . . . or Roxana* (1724) and various other pieces of vigorous, journalistic prose.

De Forest, Lee, 1873–, American inventor. Pioneered in development of wireless telegraphy, sound pictures, television; granted over 300 patents.

De Funiak Springs (dē fū'nēăk), town (pop. 3,077), NW Fla., NW of Panama City. Fresh-water spring here is c.1 mi. in circumference.

Degas, (Hilaire Germain) Edgar (ĕdgär' dügä'), 1834–1917, French impressionist painter. Fanatic in his self-criticism and despairing of attaining perfection in oils, he turned in his middle life to pastels. Ballet dancers, modistes, and women at their toilet were among his favorite subjects. His later works, daring in composition, free in execution, and immensely effective in color, greatly influenced such men as Gauguin and Picasso.

De Gasperi, Alcide (älchĕ'dä dä gä'spärē), 1881–, Italian premier (1945–), leader of Christian Democrats.

De Gaulle, Charles: see GAULLE, CHARLES DE.

degree, academic, bestowed on student fulfilling stated requirements or on eminent person as honor. Usual degrees in U.S.: Bachelor of Arts (B.A. or A.B.), of Science (B.S.), of Laws (LL.B.); Master of Arts (M.A. or A.M.), of Science (M.S.); Doctor of Philosophy (Ph.D.), of Medicine (M.D.), of Laws (LL.D.), of Divinity (D.D.), of Letters (Litt.D.).

De Haven, Edwin Jesse, 1816–65, American arctic explorer. Led fruitless search for Sir John Franklin and party (1850); discovered Grinnell Land.

De Heem, Jan Davidszoon: see HEEM, JAN DAVIDSZOON DE.

Dehmel, Richard (rīkh'ärt dā'mŭl), 1863–1920, German poet. His works, some of which lean toward social themes but away from naturalism, include the collection *Erlösungen* [redemptions] (1891), *Schöne wilde Welt* [fair wide world] (1913), and the novel in verse *Zwei Menschen* [two souls] (1903).

Dehn, Adolf (Arthur) (dān), 1895–, American lithographer and painter. Became known through his satiric figures in black and white.

De Hooch or **De Hoogh, Pieter:** see HOOCH, PIETER DE.

Dehra (dâ'rŭ) or **Dehra Dun** (dōōn), city (pop. 78,228), NW Uttar Pradesh, India.

Site of temple (1699) of Ram Rai, founder of Hindu Udasi sect.

Deira (dē'īrŭ), Anglian kingdom between the Humber and the Tyne, united (late 6th cent.) with Bernicia to form Northumbria.

Deirdre (dēr'drē, –drā, dâr'–), heroine of Irish story. Reared to be wife of King Conchobar of Ulster; she fell in love with Naoise and fled to England with him and his brothers. On their return home Conchobar slew the brothers, and Deirdre died on their grave.

deists (dē'ĭsts), group of rationalists of 17th and 18th cent. who rejected formal religion and supernatural revelation but argued that the course of nature demonstrates the existence of God. There were deistic elements in the thinking of Voltaire, Rousseau, Franklin, and Jefferson. The religious orthodox called them freethinkers.

De Kalb, Johann: see KALB, JOHANN.

De Kalb (dē kălb'), city (pop. 11,708), N Ill., W of Chicago. Center of agr. area. Mfg. of canned food, machinery, and musical instruments.

Deken, Agatha: see WOLFF, ELISABETH.

Dekker or **Decker, Thomas,** 1572?–1632, English dramatist, author of *The Shoemaker's Holiday* (1600), *Old Fortunatus* (1600). Collaborated with Middleton on *The Honest Whore* (1604; Part II, 1630) and *The Roaring Girl* (1611), with Massinger on *The Virgin Martyr* (1622). Also wrote pamphlets and satirical *The Gull's Hornbook* (1609).

de Koven, Reginald, 1859–1920, American composer. He is best known for his operettas, especially *Robin Hood* (1890), which has the song *Oh, Promise Me.*

de Kruif, Paul (dŭ krīf'), 1890–, American writer on scientific subjects. Works include *Microbe Hunters* (1926) and *Hunger Fighters* (1939).

Delaborde, Henri, Comte (ärē' kōt' dŭläbôrd'), 1811–99, French historical painter and art critic, best known for writings on Flandrin and Ingres.

Delacroix, Ferdinand Victor Eugène (fĕrdänā' vēktôr' ûzhĕn dŭläkrwä'), 1798–1863, leading French romantic painter. Studied with Guérin but early revolted against academicism. Aroused controversy by using bright color and dynamic treatment, as in *Dante and Vergil* (c.1822), *Massacre of Scio,* and scenes of Morocco (visited 1832). As a colorist he ranks among the great French painters.

de la Mare, Walter (dĕl'ùmâr"), 1873–, English poet and novelist. His work is marked by rich imagination in poetry and prose. Some of his poetry is primarily for children (e.g., *Peacock Pie,* 1912). Best-known novel *Memoirs of a Midget* (1921).

Delambre, Jean Baptiste Joseph (zhä' bätēst' zhôzĕf' dŭlä'brŭ), 1749–1822, French astronomer and mathematician, noted for astronomical computations and work in spherical geometry.

De Lancey (dŭ lăn'sē), family of political leaders, soldiers, and merchants prominent in colonial N.Y. **Étienne De Lancey** or **Stephen De Lancey,** 1663–1741, b. France, became one of New York city's wealthiest merchants. His son, **James De Lancey,** 1703–60, was chief justice of provincial supreme court

(1733–60) and served as lieutenant governor (1753–55, 1757–60). Later members of family supported the British in American Revolution.

De Land (dē lănd′), resort city (pop. 8,652), NE Fla., N of Orlando and SE of L. George, in citrus-fruit area; founded 1876. Seat of John B. Stetson Univ. (Baptist; coed.; 1883). Near-by Ponce de Leon Springs empty c.94,000 gal, a minute.

Delano (dĕ′lŭnō), city (pop. 8,717), S central Calif., NNW of Bakersfield in San Joaquin Valley. Ships truck, fruits, grain, wine. Cotton gin.

Delany, Martin Robinson (dúlā′nē), 1812–85, American Negro leader. Furthered return of American Negroes to Africa in 1850s.

Delaroche, Hippolyte (ēpôlēt′ dùlärôsh′), 1797–1856, French historical and portrait painter, commonly called Paul Delaroche.

de la Roche, Mazo, 1885–, Canadian novelist, known for her books about Whiteoak family of "Jalna."

De la Rue, Warren (dĕ′lŭrōō), 1815–89, British scientist and inventor, a pioneer in celestial photography and inventor of a photoheliograph.

Delaware, state (1,978 sq. mi.; pop. 318,085), E U.S.; one of Thirteen Colonies; cap. DOVER. WILMINGTON only large city. On NE part of peninsula between Chesapeake Bay and Delaware Bay (joined at Delaware City by canal). Bordered E by the Atlantic, Delaware Bay, Delaware R. Major part of state lies in Atlantic coastal plain, rising to rolling uplands in N. Industrial life dominated by Du Pont Co. Easy laws on business incorporation bring many large corporations to state. Farming (esp. poultry) also important. Region was contested by Dutch and English. First Dutch settlement (1631) was short-lived. NEW SWEDEN founded 1638, captured by Dutch 1655. Seized by British 1644, transferred to William Penn 1682. Became sovereign state 1776. First to ratify Constitution. Remained loyal to Union in Civil War, but pro-Southern feeling grew during war. Industrial growth accelerated by World War II.

Delaware, city (pop. 11,804), central Ohio, on Olentangy R. and N of Columbus; laid out 1808. Trade center in farm area with mfg. of motor vehicles and rubber goods. Birthplace of R. B. Hayes. Seat of Ohio Wesleyan Univ. (coed.; opened 1844 by Methodists; absorbed Ohio Wesleyan Female Col. in 1877).

Delaware, river, 315 mi. long, rising in the Catskills, SE N.Y., and flowing SE between N.Y. and Pa. to Port Jervis, then generally S between N.J. and Pa. to Delaware Bay. Trenton and Camden (N.J.), Philadelphia and DELAWARE WATER GAP (Pa.), and Wilmington and New Castle (Del.) are on its course. Major bridges are at Trenton, Philadelphia, Wilmington, and near Newcastle. Chesapeake and Delaware Canal links river with Chesapeake Bay. Delaware Aqueduct on headstream is part of New York city water supply. Interstate bodies have been formed to plan use of river's water. Washington Crossing villages (N.J. and Pa.) are at point where Washington crossed river (1776) before capture of Trenton.

Delaware, University of: see NEWARK, Del.

Delaware and Raritan Canal, N.J., abandoned canal connecting Delaware and Raritan rivers between Bordentown and New Brunswick; completed 1834.

Delaware Bay, inlet of the Atlantic between N.J. and Del., receiving Delaware R.

Delaware City, town (pop. 1,363), N Del., on Delaware R. and S of Wilmington, near E end of Chesapeake and Delaware Canal. Fort Du Pont is here.

Delaware Indians, members of related Indian tribes, once living in region of Delaware R., later in Susquehanna valley, of Algonquian linguistic stock. Called themselves Lenni-Lenape or Lenape. Friendly with Dutch; made famous treaty (1682) with William Penn. Iroquois drove them W into Ohio (1720). Defeated (1794) by Anthony Wayne. Later they moved to Kansas and Texas and were finally removed to the Indian Territory.

Delaware Water Gap, borough (pop. 734), E Pa. where Delaware R. cuts through Kittatinny Mt., near Stroudsburg. Scenic summer resort.

De la Warr, Thomas West, Baron (dĕ′lŭwŭr), 1577–1618, first governor of Virginia colony, b. England. Delaware was later named for him.

Delcassé, Théophile (tāôfēl′ dĕlkäsä′), 1852–1923, French foreign minister (1898–1905, 1914–15), one of chief architects of Entente Cordiale and Triple Entente (see TRIPLE ALLIANCE and TRIPLE ENTENTE).

Deledda, Grazia (grä′tsēä dālĕd′dä), 1875–1936, Italian novelist, b. Sardinia. Among novels are *Elias Portoliu* (1903), *Cenere* (1904; Eng. tr., *Ashes*, 1908), *La Madre* (1920). Won Nobel Prize for 1926.

De Lee, Joseph Bolivar, 1869–1942, American obstetrician and gynecologist. Improved obstetrical methods through his practice, teaching, and writing.

Delémont (dùlāmō′), Ger. *Delsberg,* town (pop. 6,625), Bern canton, W Switzerland, in Jura. Château was residence of prince-bishops of Basel 1528–1792. Prince-bishopric, which did not include Basel itself, passed to France 1792, to Bern 1815.

De Leon, Daniel (dē lē′ŏn), 1852–1914, American socialist leader, b. Curaçao; came to U.S. 1872. A doctrinaire Marxist, he split the Socialist Labor party. Favored industrial rather than trade unions. Helped found the Industrial Workers of the World.

Delescluze, Charles (shärl′ dùläklüz′), 1809–71, French journalist and radical leader. Often exiled and imprisoned. Led resistance of COMMUNE OF PARIS of 1871. When defeat became inevitable, he threw himself into line of fire and was killed.

Delft, municipality (pop. 62,018) and town South Holland prov., W Netherlands, near The Hague. Famous for ceramics known as delftware. Its aspect has changed little since Jan Vermeer, who was born here, painted his famous *View of Delft.* The Gothic Nieuwe Kerk contains the tomb of William the Silent, who was assassinated at Delft.

delftware. Earliest delftware was a faïence of late 16th cent., brown with opaque white glaze and polychrome decoration in Oriental style. Modern delftware (usually blue and white) is of average quality.

Delhi (dĕ'lē), state (574 sq. mi.; pop. 1,743,-992), N India. Within state are sites of several dynastic seats. Earliest center was 12th-cent. citadel of Chauhan Rajput, containing Lal Kot or Red Fort (built 1052) and famous Kulb Minar and Iron Pillar. Located just SW of Delhi city, it became nucleus of first cap. of DELHI SULTANATE in 1206. Just E of New Delhi, on legendary site of cap. of ancient Pandava dynasty, is Mogul fort Purana Kila. State cap. is **Delhi** (pop. 542,-984), on Jumna R. In 1638 it became Mogul cap. of Shah Jehan, who built beautiful palace within Red Fort. It contained fabulous Peacock Throne, carried off by Nadir Shah in 1739. Occupied 1803 by the British. Became cap. of India in 1912, succeeded 1931 by adjacent city of **New Delhi** (pop. 116,-784), notable for its new government buildings based on Palladian-classic style. Residence of India's president is here. Scene of Gandhi's assassination (Jan. 30, 1948).

Delhi Sultanate, Moslem state, ruling most of India 1206–1526. Founded by Kutb-ud-din, Afghan general, who took Delhi in 1192. His dynasty (called Slave dynasty because of his slave origin) was succeeded by the Kulji (1290–1320) and Tughlak (1321–98). Sultanate was crushed 1398 by Tamerlane.

Delian League, confederation of Greek states under leadership of Athens, with original hq. at temple of Apollo in Delos. The first Delian League, 478–404 B.C., was formed with Ionian cities to oppose the Persian kings. After the successful outcome of the PERSIAN WARS, it was made into an Athenian maritime empire that lasted until Sparta won the long-drawn PELOPONNESIAN WAR (404 B.C.). After Conon reestablished Athenian naval power at Cnidus (394 B.C.), a new league was formed (378 B.C.). This lasted, with Athenian-Theban quarrels, until dissolved by the victory of Philip II of Macedon at Chaeronea (338 B.C.).

Délibes, (Clément) Léo (dālēb'), 1836–91, French composer. He wrote several operas, of which *Lakmé* is best known, and ballets (e.g., *Coppélia*).

Delilah (dĭlī'lŭ), courtesan hired by Philistines to betray SAMSON. Judges 16.4–20.

delirium tremens (trē'mĕnz), disordered mental state, occasional result of continued alcoholic excess. Tremors and hallucinations common.

Delisle, Guillaume (gēyōm' dŭlēl'), 1675–1726, French geographer, founder of modern cartography. Noted for highly accurate world map (1700), first without errors of Ptolemy.

Delius, Frederick (dēl'yŭs), 1862–1934, English composer. His works, which combine elements of romanticism and impressionism, include an opera, *A Village Romeo and Juliet;* a choral work, *Sea Drift;* and orchestral pieces, *Brigg Fair* and *On Hearing the First Cuckoo in Spring.* He also composed chamber music, concertos, and songs.

Dell, Floyd, 1887–, American author of reformist articles, novels (e.g., *Moon-Calf,* 1920), and plays (e.g., *The Angel Intrudes,* 1918).

Della Casa, Giovanni: see CASA.

Della-Cruscans (dĕl'ŭ-krŭs'kŭnz) [from Accademia della Crusca, founded for linguistic purity, Florence, 16th cent.], group of English poets in Italy who published *The Florence Miscellany* (1785). Chief follower in England was Hannah Cowley (1743–1809).

Della Porta: see PORTA.

Della Quercia, Jacopo: see QUERCIA.

Della Robbia (dĕ"lŭ rŏ'bēŭ, Ital. dĕl'lä rôb'-byä), Florentine family of sculptors famous for enameled terra cotta or faïence. The atelier founded by **Luca della Robbia** (lōo'kä), 1400?–1482, was continued by his nephew **Andrea della Robbia** (ändrā'ä), 1435–1525?, and by Andrea's sons, **Luca II della Robbia,** c.1480–c.1550, **Giovanni della Robbia** (jōvän'-nē), 1469–c.1529, and **Girolamo della Robbia** (jĕrō'lämō), 1488–1566. Andrea did the famous medallions on the Foundling Hospital in Florence.

Dells of the Wisconsin or **The Dells,** scenic gorge (c.8 mi. long) of Wisconsin R., central Wis., near city of Wisconsin Dells. Of sandstone carved by river into curious forms, often beautifully colored.

De Long, George Washington, 1844–81, American arctic explorer. Lost with most of his men in attempted dash to North Pole, under auspices of U.S. navy and private backing. Expedition proved essential facts about polar drift and that Wrangel Isl. was not southern tip of a northern continent.

Delorme, Marion (märyō' dŭlôrm'), 1613?–1650, French courtesan, mistress of CINQ MARS, whom she sought to avenge during Fronde.

Delorme or **de l'Orme, Philibert** (dŭlôrm' fēlēbĕr'), c.1515–1570, great French architect of the Renaissance who designed the Tuileries.

Delos (dē'lŏs), island (c.1 sq. mi.), in the Aegean off Greece, one of the Cyclades; in Greek legend the birthplace of Apollo and Artemis. Of great commercial importance in ancient times, it had the treasury of the Delian League until it was removed (454 B.C.) to Athens. Sacked by Mithridates VI of Pontus in 88 B.C., Delos never recovered.

Delphi (dĕl'fī), locality in Phocis, Greece, near foot of Mt. Parnassus, seat of Delphic oracle. Oracle, which answered all questions, public or private, arose from worship of an earth-goddess, possibly Gaea. It passed to Apollo and was his preeminent shrine, with oracle housed in temple built in 6th cent. B.C. Oracles, spoken by priestess Pythia, were interpreted in verse by a priest; answers were revered and had great influence in Greece. Delphi was unifying influence in otherwise fragmented life of Greece, meeting place of Delphic Amphictyony, and seat of Pythian games. Shrine was later despoiled by Romans under Sulla and Nero.

delphinium: see LARKSPUR.

Delphos (dĕl'fŭs), city (pop. 6,220), NW Ohio, NW of Lima. Mfg. of motors and food products.

Delray Beach (dĕlrā'), resort city (pop. 6,312), SE Fla., on Atlantic coast S of Palm Beach. Polo center. Holds annual gladiola festival.

Del Rio, city (pop. 14,211), SW Texas, port of entry on Rio Grande opposite Villa Acuña, Mexico; founded 1868. Makes wine and leather goods and ships wool, mohair, and farm produce.

Deluge, in Bible, overwhelming flood which covered earth and destroyed every living thing except family of NOAH and creatures in ARK. Gen. 6–8; Isa. 54.9; Mat. 24.38; Luke 17.27; Heb. 11.7; 1 Peter 3.20; 2 Peter 2.5. Flood stories resembling biblical one found in folklore of many cultures, e.g., Babylonian, Greek, Indian, aboriginal Australian, American Indian.

delusion, false belief based on misinterpretation of reality. Passing delusions are not abnormal, but fixed delusions (e.g., of persecution, external influence, grandeur) characterize paranoia, schizophrenia. Social psychologists study delusions for their crucial role in development of mass hysteria.

De Mabuse, Jan: see MABUSE, JAN DE.

dementia praecox: see SCHIZOPHRENIA.

Demerara, river, British Guiana: see GUIANA.

Demeter (dĭmē'tŭr), in Greek legend, earth-goddess of corn, harvest, and fruitfulness; daughter of Cronus and Rhea and mother of PERSEPHONE by Zeus. She and her daughter were chief figures in ELEUSINIAN MYSTERIES. Her festival, Thesmophoria, was held in autumn. Identified with Roman Ceres.

Demetrius (dĭmē'trēŭs), kings of Macedon. **Demetrius I** (Poliorcetes), c.337–283 B.C., aided his father ANTIGONUS I in the wars of the DIADOCHI until they were defeated at Ipsus (301 B.C.). Managed to get the throne of Macedon (294 B.C.), but his enemies drove him to take refuge with Seleucus I. He was father of ANTIGONUS II. **Demetrius II,** d. 229 B.C., reigned 239–229 B.C. His heir was young Philip V.

Demetrius, kings of Syria. **Demetrius I** (Soter), c.187–150 B.C., reigned 162–150 B.C.; son of Seleucus IV. A hostage in Rome, Demetrius escaped, killed his cousin Antiochus V, took the throne, but was beset by rebellion, notably that of Alexander Balas and the Maccabees. Demetrius was defeated. **Demetrius II** (Nicator), d. c.125 B.C., got the aid of Ptolemy VI against Alexander Balas, married Cleopatra (already the wife of Alexander), and took the throne in 146 B.C. Captured by Parthians (141 B.C.), he returned, regained the throne (128 B.C.), but again lost it and died fighting the Egyptians.

Demetrius, in Russian history: see DMITRI.

De Mille, Cecil B(lount), 1881–, American film director, noted for "spectacle" films. His niece, **Agnes De Mille,** 1905?–, is a dancer and choreographer. Her ballets include *Three Virgins and a Devil, Rodeo,* and *Fall River Legend.* Her choreography for musical comedies (e.g., *Oklahoma!*) made ballet popular on the Broadway stage.

Deming (dĕm'ĭng), village (pop. 5,672), SW N.Mex., in valley of Mimbres R. (here underground). Trade center for agr., grazing, mining area. Resort.

democracy [Gr.,= power of the people], government under control of the people as a whole rather than that of a class, group, or individual; by extension, in such phrases as social democracy and economic democracy, control of human institutions by and in the interest of the people. Democracy was born in the Greek city-states. The Roman Repub-

lic had principle of representation of people, basic to modern democratic republics. General democracy all but disappeared under the Roman Empire and in the Middle Ages, emerged again in modern times, greatly advanced by the Puritan, American, and French revolutions. Among names influential in growth of democratic theory are J. J. Rousseau, John Locke, Thomas Jefferson, and Abraham Lincoln. U.S. founded on democracy. Democratic forms adopted in most Western countries by 20th cent. Challenged recently by fascism and communism (which has rule by proletarian class, though theoretic aim is complete economic democracy).

Democratic party, in U.S. history. Arose, under Thomas JEFFERSON, in opposition to Alexander Hamilton and Federalist party; emphasized personal liberty and limitation of powers of Federal government. Early party name of Democratic Republican yielded to Democratic by 1828. Election of Jefferson in 1800 had virtual force of a revolution; victory of radical group under Andrew JACKSON in 1828 represented second revolution. Arguments over slavery created or deepened splits within party; Civil War all but destroyed it. Party revived in disputed election of 1876. End of Reconstruction brought emergence of "solid South," a bulwark of Democratic strength thereafter, except for rare instances. With nomination of W. J. BRYAN in 1896 on a "free silver" platform, radicals again gained ascendant. His defeat posed problem of keeping together party's diverse factions—Southern and Western farmers, big-city industrial classes, a few of the wealthy. Leader appeared in idealistic liberal, Woodrow WILSON. Economic depression helped to sweep F. D. ROOSEVELT and Democrats into power in 1932, and party was again identified as reform party with New Deal. Roosevelt died in office in 1945, in fourth term, and Harry S. TRUMAN became President. In 1948, despite disaffection of the South, due to Negro civil-rights issue, and of dissidents under Henry WALLACE, Truman brought Democrats to surprising victory. Republican victory under Dwight D. Eisenhower in 1952 ended 20-year rule of Democratic party and seemed to forecast two-party system in once "solid South."

Democritus (dĭmŏk'rĭtŭs), c.460–c.370 B.C., Greek philosopher. A materialist, he held that the world was made up of tiny particles, imperceptible to the senses but indivisible and indestructible. These are atoms and by constant motion they combine to make the universe. The true nature of things can be discovered only by thought, for sense perceptions are confusing.

Demopolis, city (pop. 5,004), W Ala., SSW of Tuscaloosa at confluence of Black Warrior and Tombigbee rivers; founded 1818 by Bonapartist exiles.

De Morgan, William (Frend), 1839–1917, English novelist. A designer of glass and tiles, he began on retirement to write long leisurely novels such as *Joseph Vance* (1906), *Alice-for-Short* (1907), *Somehow Good* (1908), *An Affair of Dishonour* (1910).

Demosthenes (dĭmŏs'thŭnēz), 384?–322 B.C.,

Greek orator, one of the greatest orators of all time. His fame rests chiefly on his orations against the conquering Philip II of Macedon—three *Philippics* and three *Olynthiacs* (asking aid for the city of Olynthus). Other orations are *On the Peace, On the False Legation* (against his rival, Aeschines), and *On the Crown* (a defense of himself against Aeschines). Even after Philip triumphed, Demosthenes was honored until he was exiled on obscure charges of financial corruption. Returning after the death of Alexander the Great, he failed to rebuild Greek strength and took poison when fleeing before Antipater.

demotic: see HIEROGLYPHIC.

Dempsey, William Harrison (Jack Dempsey), 1895–, American boxer. Won heavyweight championship from Jess Willard (1919), lost title to James J. (Gene) Tunney (1926). Dempsey was again defeated by Tunney (1927) in fight involving controversial "long count" in seventh round.

Demuth, Charles (dā'mooth), 1883–1935, American water-color painter. Shows influence of cubism.

Denain (dùnĕ'), town (pop. 22,299), Nord dept., N France. Coal fields, ironworks. Scene of French victory (1712) in War of Spanish Succession.

Denbighshire (dĕn'bĕshĭr) or **Denbigh,** maritime county (669 sq. mi.; pop. 170,699), N Wales; co. town Denbigh. Largely high pastoral moorland with agr. in valleys. Mineral resources (coal, iron, lead, and slate) around Wrexham.

Denikin, Anton Ivanovich (ùntôn' ēvä'nŭvĭch dyĭnyĕ'kĭn), 1872–1947, Russian general. Commanded anti-Bolshevik forces in S Russia 1918–20.

Denis, Saint (dĕn'ĭs, dùnē'), 3d cent.?, patron saint of France. Said to have been first bishop of Paris and to have been martyred on Montmartre. The name is a form of Dionysius. Feast: Oct. 9.

Denis, Maurice (môrēs' dùnē'), 1870–1943, French muralist and writer on art.

Denison, city (pop. 17,504), N Texas, near Red R. NNE of Dallas. Grew around antebellum stagecoach station. Rail division point and shipping center, it processes cheese, milk, cotton, wheat, peanuts. Mfg. of machinery, metal goods. Birthplace of Pres. Eisenhower. **Denison Dam** is NW, in Red R. between Denison and Durant, Okla.; completed 1943–44, for flood control, power. Main dam is 165 ft. high, 15,200 ft. long. Its reservoir, L. Texoma, is one of largest artificial lakes in U.S. and much used for recreation.

Denison University: see GRANVILLE, Ohio.

Denmark, Dan. *Danmark,* kingdom (16,576 sq. mi.; pop. 4,279,151), NW Europe, southernmost of Scandinavian countries; cap. Copenhagen. Except for JUTLAND peninsula, bordering on Germany, Denmark consists of several Baltic isls., notably ZEALAND, FYN, FALSTER, LAALAND, LANGELAND, BORNHOLM. Overseas possessions are GREENLAND and the FAEROE ISLANDS. A low-lying, highly cultivated country, Denmark specializes in dairying and stock raising and has important commercial and fishing fleets. Form of government is parliamentary democracy (see RIGSDAG). Ruling house: Schleswig-Holstein-Sonderburg-Glucksburg. Reigning king: Frederick IX. Established Church is Lutheran. In the Viking Age (see VIKINGS) Danes took important part in Norse raids of W Europe. Harold Bluetooth (d. c.985) was their first Christian king. His son SWEYN conquered England, and CANUTE united Denmark, England, and Norway from 1018 to 1035. S Sweden was part of Denmark to 1658. Danish hegemony over the N was first estab. under Waldemar I and Waldemar II (12th–13th cent.); WALDEMAR IV restored Danish power but was successfully challenged by the HANSEATIC LEAGUE (14th cent.). His daughter MARGARET created (1397) the KALMAR UNION of Denmark, Sweden, and NORWAY; the union with Norway lasted to 1814, but that with Sweden never was effective and ended in 1523. The house of Oldenburg, from which the present dynasty is descended, acceded in 1448 with CHRISTIAN I, who also united SCHLESWIG and HOLSTEIN with the Danish crown. The Reformation was introduced by Christian III. Danish participation in the Thirty Years War (see CHRISTIAN IV) and the wars of FREDERICK III caused 17th-cent. Denmark to lose its leading position to Sweden. An absolute monarchy was estab. under Christian V, and colonial imperialism resulted in the creation of trade monopolies in ICELAND and the VIRGIN ISLANDS. Important social reforms (e.g., abolition of serfdom, 1788) marked the late 18th cent., especially under the ministries of STRUENSEE and A. P. BERNSTORFF. Denmark sought to maintain neutrality in the French Revolutionary and Napoleonic wars but was attacked by England and joined the French camp. As a result, the Congress of Vienna deprived it of Norway. The complex question of SCHLESWIG-HOLSTEIN led to the German-Danish war of 1848–49 and to war with Prussia and Austria in 1864, in which Denmark lost both duchies. (N Schleswig was restored to Denmark after a plebiscite, 1920.) Of more lasting importance was the internal reform of 19th-cent. Denmark, which transformed its poor peasantry into the most prosperous small farmers in Europe. This achievement was largely due to the educational efforts of Bishop GRUNDTVIG and to the cooperative movement. Neutral in World War I, Denmark was occupied (1940–45) by German forces in World War II. It joined the UN (1945), the European Recovery Program (1948), and the North Atlantic Treaty (1949).

Dennie, Joseph, 1768–1812, American Federalist journalist, editor of anti-Jefferson weekly.

Dennis, resort town (pop. 2,499), SE Mass., on Cape Cod NE of Yarmouth. Has summer theater.

density, measurement of a quantity of matter in a unit volume of a substance. It is usually expressed in grams per cubic centimeter; grams per liter, or pounds per cubic foot and is calculated by dividing the MASS by the volume occupied at standard temperature and pressure. SPECIFIC GRAVITY of solid or liquid is density compared with that of water;

that of gas is compared with hydrogen or air.

Dent du Midi or **Dents du Midi** (both: dä′ dü mēdē′), Alpine mountain group, Vaud canton, SW Switzerland, rising to 10,696 ft. in Haute Cime.

dentistry, science of treatment and care of teeth and associated oral structures. Important contributions to evolution of modern dentistry made by Ambroise Paré, John Hunter, Pierre FAUCHARD, G. V. BLACK, C. A. HARRIS, and many others. Progress aided by development of X ray, local anesthetics, artificial dentures, drilling machine, and methods of preparing fillings and inlays. As dentistry became field separate from medicine, training schools multiplied and educational requirements became stringent. Preventive and corrective treatment and education in care of teeth stressed today.

Denton, city (pop. 21,372), N Texas, NW of Dallas, NE of Fort Worth; founded 1855. Seat of North Texas State Col. and Texas State Col. for Women (1901). Processing and mfg. center in varied farm area. L. Dallas is near.

D'Entrecasteaux Islands (dätrúkästō′), volcanic group, area c.1,200 sq. mi., off SE New Guinea, part of Territory of Papua. Named for the French navigator Entrecasteaux.

Dents du Midi, Switzerland: see DENT DU MIDI.

Denver, city (pop. 415,786; alt. 5,280 ft.), state cap., N central Colo., on South Platte R.; settled 1858, made territorial cap. 1867. Rich gold, silver strikes of '70s and '80s boomed Denver. At this time, H. A. W. TABOR built opera house, and Silver Dollar saloon flourished. As transportation, processing, distributing center for huge agr. and livestock area, growth was steady by 1900. It is now metropolis of the Rockies, largest city in Colo., financial center. Has stockyards, oil refineries, rail shops, fruit and vegetable canneries, flour mills; mfg. of mine and farm machinery, furniture, rubber and cotton goods; motorcar assembly. Large tourist trade. Has fine climate. Here are hq. for many Federal agencies, a U.S. mint, mountain parks, Colorado Mus. of Natural History, zoological gardens, Denver Art Mus., Lowry Air Force Base. Seat of Loretto Heights Col. (R.C.; for women; 1891); Univ. of Colorado medical school; **University of Denver** (Methodist; coed.; chartered and opened 1864 mainly by John Evans).

deodar or **deodar cedar:** see CEDAR.

De Patinir, De Patenier, or **De Patiner, Joachim:** see PATINIR, JOACHIM DE.

De Paul University: see CHICAGO, Ill.

DePauw University: see GREENCASTLE, Ind.

De Pere (dĭ pēr′), city (pop. 8,146), NE Wis., on Fox R. and S of Green Bay. Father Allouez founded mission here 1671. Mfg. of paper, boats, and brick.

Depew, Chauncey (Mitchell) (dĭpū′), 1834–1928, American railroad president and orator. President (1885–99) and chairman of board (1899–1928) of New York Central lines. Noted as after-dinner speaker.

Depew, village (pop. 7,217), W N.Y., near Buffalo. Mfg. of textiles, metal products, cereals.

De profundis (dā prōfōōn′dēs), one of penitential psalms, Ps. 130 (or 129). See PSALMS.

Deptford (dĕt′fûrd), metropolitan borough (pop. 75,694), SE London, England; industrial district. Noted in Elizabethan times for cattle market and royal dockyard. Christopher Marlowe was killed here.

De Quincey, Thomas (dĭ kwĭn′sē), 1785–1859, English essayist. Settled (1816) at Grasmere, near Wordsworth and Coleridge. The opium habit overcame him for a time and inspired "Confessions of an English Opium-Eater" (in *London Magazine,* 1821). Became prolific contributor of essays and critical articles to journals.

Derain, André (āndrä′ dûrē′), 1880–, French painter. Associated with the fauvists, but his art shows an assimilation of various other influences.

Derbent (dyĭrbyĕnt′), city (pop. 23,097), SE Dagestan, SE European RSFSR; Caspian fishing port. Founded 5th or 6th cent. A.D. by Persians at Iron Gates (called Caspian or Albanian Gates by ancients), a defile between Caucasus and Caspian, on a major commercial route. Ceded by Persia to Russia 1813. Remains of 6th-cent. Caucasian Wall (or Alexander's Wall), built by Persians to stem N invaders.

Derby, Edward George Geoffrey Smith Stanley, 14th **earl of** (där′bē), 1799–1869, British statesman. As Whig colonial secretary he pushed through abolition of slavery 1833. Influenced by Robert PEEL he became a Conservative. Was colonial secretary 1841–45. As head of two ministries (1852, 1858–59), he was a great force in liberalizing the Tory party.

Derby, England: see DERBYSHIRE.

Derby (dûr′bē), city (pop. 10,259), SW Conn., at junction of Naugatuck and Housatonic rivers; founded 1642. Metal and rubber products. Yale holds annual spring regatta on the Housatonic here.

Derby (där′bē, dûr′bē), famous horse race held annually since 1780 at Epsom Downs, near London, England. The name derby is also applied to other well-known horse races, notably Kentucky Derby (dûr′bē), held annually since 1875 at Churchill Downs, Louisville, Ky.

Derbyshire (där′bēshĭr) or **Derby,** county (1,002 sq. mi.; pop. 826,336), central England. Area flat in S, rising to Peak district in N. Has rich coal deposits in E section. Heavily cultivated; dairy farming and sheep raising are important. County town, **Derby,** borough (pop. 141,264) on Derwent R., is a rail center. Has mfg. of cars (Rolls-Royce), pottery (Derby ware), textiles, and paper. Birthplace of Herbert Spencer. George Eliot lived here.

Derby ware, delicate, richly decorated English china produced at Derby since c.1750. Became Royal Crown Derby in 1890 by permission of Queen Victoria. Most Derby marks show a crown over a D.

Derg, Lough (lōkh′ dĕrg′), lakes, Ireland. 1 Expansion of Shannon R. (length, 23 mi.; width, 1–5 mi.) on borders of Counties Galway, Tipperary, and Clare. 2 SE Donegal. Station Isl. here, traditional place of St. Patrick's Purgatory, has extensive religious establishments and is noted place of pilgrimage.

De Ridder, city (pop. 5,799), SW La., E of Sabine R. Center of sheep raising, lumbering, and agr. area.

Dermot McMurrough or **Diarmuid mac Murchada** (both: dûr′mŭt mŭkmŭ′rù), d. 1171, Irish king who brought the English into Ireland. Banished 1166. Promised aid by Richard Strongbow and other adventurers, he returned to Ireland in 1168. With the invaders, he had conquered SE Ireland, including Dublin, by 1170.

Derna (dĕ′rnä), town (pop. 20,782), E Cyrenaica, Libya, a Mediterranean port. Occupied 1805 by U.S. in Tripolitan War. In World War II it changed hands several times 1941–42.

Derry, Northern Ireland: see LONDONDERRY.

Derry, town (pop. 5,826), SE N.H., SE of Manchester, in agr. and resort area. Has horse races on ice (since 1928). Robert Frost farmed and taught here.

Derwent (dûr′wŭnt), rivers in England. 1 Cumberland, in the Lake District. 2 Derbyshire, tributary of the Trent. 3 Yorkshire, tributary of the Ouse.

Derwentwater, oval lake, 3 mi. long and 1 mi. wide, Cumberland, England. Formed by widening of Derwent R., it is surrounded by wooded hills. Lodore waterfalls are at upper end.

Derzhavin, Gavril Romanovich (gŭvrēl′ rŭmä′- nŭvĭch dyĭrzhä′vĭn), 1743–1816, Russian classical poet; poet laureate to Catherine II. His fame rests chiefly on his *Ode to God* (Eng. tr., 1861).

De Sanctis, Francesco (fränchäs′kō dā sängk′- tēs), 1818–83, Italian literary critic, notable for *Saggi Critici* [critical essays] (1866) and *History of Italian Literature* (1871).

Desargues, Gérard (zhärär′ dùzärg′), 1593– 1662, French mathematician, engineer, founder of modern geometry. He discovered the involution and transversal theorems named for him and worked on conic sections.

Descartes, René (rùnā′ dākärt′), 1596–1650, French philosopher, mathematician, and scientist. His teachings are called Cartesian from his name in Latin (Renatus Cartesius). Studied at the Jesuit school at La Flèche and the Univ. of Poitiers; served in the army of Maurice of Nassau; retired to Holland for research and reflection (1628); accepted the invitation of Queen Christina (1649), but died soon after reaching Sweden. A mathematical genius, he worked out the treatment of negative roots and a system of notation in algebra; originated Cartesian coordinates and Cartesian curves and is said to have founded analytic geometry. He attempted to apply mathematical methods to philosophy (notably in *Discourse on Method*), and discarding authoritarian scholasticism, he founded his system on universal doubt. One thing, he says, cannot be doubted: doubt itself. The action of the mind proves reality; his motto was *Cogito, ergo sum* [I think, therefore I am]. He refined scholastic arguments for the existence of God and held God to be the link between the mechanical world of the senses and the rational world of the mind. In physical science he rejected tradi-

tion but relied on rationalization, mathematics, and logic rather than experiment. He made numerous advances in optics (notably in reflection and refraction of light), in psychology, and in physiology. His influence on modern thought is incalculable.

Deschanel, Paul (pôl′ dāshänĕl′), 1855–1922, president of France (1920).

Deschutes (dāshōōts′), river rising in W central Oregon in Cascade Range, flowing NNE to Columbia R. near The Dalles. Used for power, irrigation.

desert (dĕz′ûrt), arid region, at least partly covered by sand, with scanty vegetation, limited and specially adapted animal life. High-altitude deserts, often perpetually covered with ice or snow, are not usually considered with deserts of warm regions. One fifth of world's land is desert. Largest desert regions lie between 20° and 30° N and S of equator, where mountains block trade winds or atmospheric high-pressure areas cause descending air currents and lack of precipitation. Other factors: amount of sunshine, water evaporation rate, temperature range, annual rainfall. Europe, only continent without deserts, has semideserts around Black and Caspian Seas, in Ukraine, and in the N Caucasus. The GOBI, in Asia, is desert because of remoteness from water. The SAHARA, in Africa, is largest desert; second largest is central and W Australian desert region. North American deserts include MOJAVE DESERT, IMPERIAL VALLEY, and DEATH VALLEY. Desert plants, widely spaced, have stems and leaves adapted to lessen water loss; roots form spreading network penetrating down to 50 ft. North American desert animals include birds, mice, foxes, deer, snakes, lizards, and spiders.

desertion, in military law, the abandonment of a place of duty without leave and with the intention not to return. It is punishable in wartime by death. In maritime law, the abandonment of a ship by a seaman without leave. In family law, willful abandonment of the spouse or children of a marriage without consent of the other party or parties. In most states, desertion is ground for DIVORCE.

Desiderio da Settignano (dāzēdā′rēō dä sĕt″- tēn-yä′nō), 1428–64, Florentine sculptor, known for church decorations and marble busts of women and children.

Desiderius, d. after 774, last Lombard king in Italy. Attacked Pope ADRIAN I, who appealed to Charlemagne. Charlemagne (who had married and later repudiated Desiderius' daughter) invaded Italy (773) and captured and deposed Desiderius (774).

De Sitter, Willem: see SITTER, WILLEM DE.

De Smet, Pierre Jean (dē smĕt′), 1801–73, missionary in U.S. Pacific Northwest, a Jesuit, b. Belgium. Often mediated between Indians and whites.

Des Moines (dù moin′), city (pop. 177,965), state cap., S central Iowa, largest city of state, at junction of Des Moines and Raccoon rivers, in heart of Corn Belt. Estab. 1843 as Fort Des Moines, it was settled by homesteaders 1845. Transportation, industrial, insurance, and commercial center, it has mfg. of food, metal, rubber, and clay products, and printing and publishing.

Adopted Des Moines (commission) plan of city government 1907. Here are state historical collections, Fort Des Moines, and DRAKE UNIVERSITY. Camp Dodge is near by.

Des Moines, river rising in SW Minn. and flowing c.535 mi. SSE across Iowa to Mississippi R. at Keokuk.

Desmond, ancient division of Munster prov., Ireland, including present Co. Cork and Co. Kerry. The Fitzgeralds became powerful earls of Desmond.

Desmoulins, Camille (kämē′yů dämōōlē′), 1760–94, French revolutionist and journalist, early leader of CORDELIERS. His oratory led to storming of Bastille, July 14, 1789. Executed with Danton.

De Soto, Hernando (Span. dā sō′tō), c.1500–1542, Spanish explorer. Led unsuccessful treasure hunt, on which he died, from Fla. to Okla. (1539–42).

De Soto (dǐ sō′tō), city (pop. 5,357), E Mo., SSW of St. Louis. Railroad shops and apparel factories.

Despenser, Hugh le (hū′ lǔ dǐspěn′sůr), d. 1265, chief justiciar of England. Supported barons against Henry III, fought in Baron's War, and was killed at Evesham 1265. Two best-known members of this family were **Hugh le Despenser,** the elder, 1262–1326, and **Hugh le Despenser,** the younger, d. 1326. The elder Despenser became chief adviser to EDWARD II. The younger Despenser later joined his father and the king. Were banished by barons 1321; returned to England 1322 and became real rulers of the kingdom. Hated by barons; were executed when Isabella returned from France and seized control 1326.

Despiau, Charles (shärl′ dāpēō′), 1874–1946, French sculptor. Studied under Rodin. Best known for his bronze busts and nudes of young women.

Des Plaines (děs plānz′), city (pop. 14,994), NE Ill., on Des Plaines R. and near Chicago; founded in 1830s. Mfg. of electrical equipment. Annual Methodist encampment.

Des Plaines, river rising in SE Wis. and flowing c.110 mi. S and SW to join Kankakee R. near Joliet, Ill. This combined stream is Illinois R.

Des Prés, Josquin: see JOSQUIN DES PRÉS.

Dessalines, Jean Jacques (zhä′ zhäk′ děsälēn′), c.1758–1806, Negro emperor of Haiti (1804–6), born a slave. Served under Toussaint L'Ouverture in wars of liberation. Was named governor (1801), later crowned emperor, Jacques I. Because of his despotic rule, he was murdered.

Dessau (dě′sou), city (pop. 88,139), former cap. of ANHALT, central Germany, at junction of Elbe and Mulde rivers. Produces machinery. Seat of BAUHAUS school 1925–32.

Destaing, Charles Hector: see ESTAING.

destroyer, warship of 1,500 to 2,000 tons, very fast, with powerful torpedo armament, a few medium-caliber guns, and anti-aircraft artillery. Introduced in 1892, much improved in World War I. Equipped with new electronic devices, destroyers proved highly effective against submarines during World War II and were used for convoying larger naval vessels and merchant ships. In battle, they rely on speed and maneuverability.

detective story, popular type of fiction in which solution of a crime is traced step by step. Poe's *Murders in the Rue Morgue* is considered first modern detective story. Mystery story, an allied type in which there is no detective and often no crime, only unexplained situation, is exemplified by Wilkie Collins' *Woman in White.* Famous detective-story writers include Conan Doyle, E. C. Bentley, Agatha Christie, Georges Simenon, Dashiell Hammett, Raymond Chandler, Erle Stanley Gardner, and S. S. Van Dine.

detergent (dětûr′jůnt), substance that aids in dirt removal by reducing surface tension of water. Soap is a good detergent but has the disadvantages of forming insoluble compounds with salts of hard water and of decomposing in acid solutions. Synthetic detergents produced in quantities after 1930.

Detmold (dět′môlt), city (pop. 30,192), former cap. of LIPPE, NW Germany. Near by is monument to victory of ARMINIUS over Romans.

detonator (dě′tůnā″tůr), type of explosive that reacts rapidly and is used to set off more inert explosives. Commonly used are fulminate of mercury mixed with potassium chlorate. Term is also applied to equipment to set off chemical detonator.

Detroit (dǐtroit′) city (pop. 1,849,568), SE Mich., on Detroit R. and between lakes St. Clair and Erie. State's largest city and fifth largest in U.S., it is a great transportation center with mfg. of motor vehicles, aircraft, railroad cars, and rubber and metal products. Its carriage industry helped Henry Ford and others make Detroit the center of world's auto industry. Settled 1701 by French; British took over in 1760 and withstood long siege in PONTIAC'S REBELLION (1763). Has been American since 1796, except for short British occupation in War of 1812. Territorial and state cap. 1805–47. Grew rapidly (esp. in 1830s) with development of land and water transportation. Became important in last half of 19th cent. through shipping, shipbuilding, and manufacturing. Notable sights are Ambassador Bridge, spanning river for 2 mi. to Windsor, Ont., and Belle Isle, a park in the river with symphony shell and yacht basins. Detroit includes independent cities of HAMTRAMCK and HIGHLAND PARK. Seat of Univ. of DETROIT and Wayne Univ. (city, county support; coed.; formed 1933 from five city colleges opened 1868–1927).

Detroit, river, c.28 mi. long, flowing from L. St. St. Clair, between SE Mich. and S Ont., S into L. Erie. Forms part of international boundary.

Detroit, University of, at Detroit; R.C. (Jesuit), coed.; opened 1877, chartered as college 1881, became university 1911.

Detroit Lakes, city (pop. 5,787), NW Minn., E of Moorhead. Lake resort and farm trade center.

Dettifoss (dě′tǐfôs), fall, c.200 ft. high, in Jokulsa R., NE Iceland, the most powerful in the country.

Dettingen (dě′tǐngůn), village, NW Bavaria, on Main R. Here in 1743 allies under George II of England defeated French in War of Austrian Succession.

Deucalion (dūkā′lēůn), in Greek mythology, son of Prometheus and father of Hellen. He and his wife, Pyrrha, only survivors of a great flood, were told to cast behind them bones of their mother, the stones of the earth. These became human beings.

deuterium: see HYDROGEN.

deuterocanonical books: see OLD TESTAMENT.

deuteron: see HYDROGEN.

Deuteronomy (dūtûrŏn′ûmē) [Gr.,= second law], book of Old Testament, last of 5 books of Law (Pentateuch or Torah) ascribed by tradition to Moses. It gives the final words of Moses—his last instructions to his people and his blessing of them. Book ends with death of Moses.

deutzia (dū′tsēū), ornamental shrub of genus *Deutzia*, with abundant white, pink, or purple blooms.

Deux-Sèvres (dû-sĕv′rù), department (2,337 sq. mi.; pop. 312,756), W France, in Poitou; cap. Niort.

De Valera, Eamon (ā′mûn dĕ″ vûlâ′rù), 1882–, Irish statesman, b. New York. Imprisoned (1916) for part in Easter Rebellion. Made president of Sinn Fein 1917. As head of DÁIL ÉIREANN raised funds in U.S. 1919–20. After period of virtual war against British rule, Irish Free State was estab. 1921. Opposing Free State, he left the Dáil in 1922. Nominal leader of republicans, he deplored subsequent civil war. Re-entering Dáil in 1927 with his party, the FIANNA FAIL, he became prime minister in 1938. Kept Ireland neutral in World War II. Defeated 1948, he was returned to office 1951.

developer, in PHOTOGRAPHY, solution used to prepare NEGATIVE after exposure of film. It acts on silver salts that were affected by light.

Deventer (dĕ′vĕntûr), municipality (pop. 44,-089) and town, Overijssel prov., E central Netherlands, on the Ijssel. Produces machinery, textiles, carpets. It was a medieval center of piety and learning (Thomas à Kempis and Erasmus studied here) and member of the Hanseatic League. There are many medieval and Renaissance buildings.

Devereux, Robert: see ESSEX, ROBERT DEVEREUX, EARL OF.

devil: see SATAN.

Devil Postpile National Monument: see NATIONAL PARKS AND MONUMENTS (table).

Devils Island, Fr. *Île du Diable,* tiny island off French Guiana. Until 1946 used as penal colony, largely for political prisoners.

Devils Lake, city (pop. 6,427), NE N.Dak., WNW of Grand Forks, near salty Devils L. (c.30 mi. long; steadily receding). Rail junction, resort, and trade center in livestock and grain area.

Devils Tower National Monument: see NATIONAL PARKS AND MONUMENTS (table).

De Vinne, Theodore L(ow) (dù vĭ′nē), 1828–1914, American printer, most famous of his day. By example and through his writings he advanced the cause of good printing

Devolution, War of, 1667–68, between France and Spain, caused by complicated legal claim of Louis XIV to Spanish Netherlands. The French overran the Spanish Netherlands and Franche-Comté, but made peace when the United Provs. formed anti-French TRIPLE ALLIANCE with England and Sweden (see AIX-LA-CHAPELLE, TREATY OF).

Devon, county, England: see DEVONSHIRE.

Devonian period (dĭvō′nĕûn), fourth period of the PALEOZOIC ERA of geologic time. It began with the continents mainly dry; later large areas were flooded and thick sediments deposited. The OLD RED SANDSTONE was laid down. Fish in great numbers dominated marine life, among them sharks, lungfish, armored fish, and ganoids. Amphibians emerged in this period. Invertebrates included trilobites, corals, starfish, and sponges. On land, forests of giant ferns and fernlike trees appeared. See also GEOLOGY, table.

Devonport, Devonshire, England: see PLYMOUTH.

Devonshire, Spencer Compton Cavendish, 8th duke of, 1833–1908, English statesman. Led Liberal Unionists who broke (1886) with Gladstone over HOME RULE for Ireland.

Devonshire or **Devon,** maritime county (2,612 sq. mi.; pop. 798,283), SW England; co. town Exeter. Surface largely hilly, rises to 2,000 ft. in Dartmoor. Has many rivers and streams. Mainly agr. and pastoral (Devonshire cream famous); there is also fishing, mining, and quarrying. Of great maritime importance in Elizabethan times, county is associated with Ralegh, Drake, Hawkins, and Grenville. Pilgrim Fathers sailed from Plymouth.

De Vos, Cornelis: see VOS, CORNELIS DE.

De Voto, Bernard (Augustine) (dù vō′tō), 1897–, American writer. He was editor (1936–38) of the *Saturday Review of Literature* and attracted attention when writing a column in *Harper's Magazine.* His writings include novels as well as literary criticism and historical works; notable are *Mark Twain's America* (1932) and *Across the Wide Missouri* (1947). Has edited Mark Twain manuscripts.

Devoy, John, 1842–1928, Irish-American journalist and leader of FENIAN MOVEMENT. In U.S. founded *Irish Nation* and (1903) *Gaelic-American.* Secured American support for Irish Land League movement and 1916 rebellion. Backed Irish Free State.

dew, water formed by condensation of atmospheric water vapor as air cools (above freezing point). Dew point is temperature at which condensation begins.

Dewar, Sir James (dū′ûr), 1842–1923, British chemist and physicist. He worked on properties of matter at low temperatures, liquefaction of gases; he liquefied and solidified hydrogen and was co-inventor of cordite. Invented Dewar flask: two flasks, one inside other, with vacuum between, silvered to cause heat reflection; keeps liquid hot or cold.

dewberry, trailing bramble of genus *Rubus,* similar to blackberry, but with earlier and larger fruit.

De Wet, Christian Rudolf (dù vĕt′), 1854–1922, Boer general, prominent in the South African War. Opposed entry of South Africa into World War I and led an unsuccessful revolt.

Dewey, George, 1837–1917, American admiral, hero of battle of Manila in SPANISH-AMERICAN WAR. Briefly boomed for President in resulting enthusiasm.

Dewey, John, 1859–1952, American philosopher and educator, long associated with

Columbia Univ. His philosophy, called instrumentalism, is related to pragmatism. He held truth to be evolutionary, not fixed or eternal, and that the modes and forms of human activity are instruments for solving psychological and social problems—instruments that change with the problems. He recognized democracy as a primary source of ethical value. In education he abandoned belief in authoritarian methods and the use of rote practices, arguing for learning by experience, motivated by a sense of the student's need. This was the basic principle that underlay the 20th-cent. progressive education theory and movement. Among his many works are *Psychology* (1887), *The School and Society* (1899), *Democracy and Education* (1916), *Experience and Nature* (1925), *Art as Experience* (1934), and *Logic: the Theory of Inquiry* (1938).

Dewey, Melvil, 1851–1931, American library pioneer, originator of Dewey decimal system, a scheme of book classification using numbers 000 to 999 to cover the general fields of knowledge and narrowing the system to fit special subjects by the use of decimal points. Librarian of Columbia Col., Dewey estab. first school for training librarians. A founder of American Library Association. Advocated spelling reform. Organized Lake Placid Club.

Dewey, Thomas E(dmund), 1902–, governor of N.Y. (1942–). Unsuccessful Republican presidential candidate (1944, 1948).

De Witt, Jan, and **Cornelius de Witt:** see WITT.

Dexter, Timothy, 1747–1806, American merchant and eccentric. Made a fortune by buying up depreciated Continental Congress currency, which was later reclaimed at full value. Author of *A Pickle for the Knowing Ones* (1802), remarkable for its individual spelling and absence of punctuation.

dextrin, a carbohydrate with same general formula as starch, but with a smaller, less complex molecule. It is an intermediate product in starch hydrolysis. Commercial type is powder that forms adhesive paste when mixed with water; used in adhesives and for sizing cotton cloth.

dextrose: see GLUCOSE.

Dezhnev, Cape, RSFSR: see EAST CAPE.

Dhar (där), town (pop. 22,015), Madhya Bharat, India. Rajput cap. and cultural center 9th–18th cent. Taken by Mahrattas in 1730.

diabase (dī′ūbās), an igneous rock common in intrusive masses. The Hudson Palisades and Connecticut valley trap rock hills are largely diabase.

Diabelli, Antonio (dēäbĕl′ē), 1781–1858, Austrian music publisher. Published works of Beethoven, Schubert.

diabetes (dīübē′tēz, –bē′tĭs), continued excessive secretion of urine. *Diabetes mellitus*, a serious form caused by INSULIN deficiency, results in excess sugar in blood and usually also in urine. Often marked by loss of weight; acidosis and coma may follow. Treated by diet and insulin injections.

Diadochi (dīā′dūkī) [Gr.,= successors], generals and administrators of ALEXANDER THE GREAT who attempted to take over his empire on his death (323 B.C.). Chief among them were Antipater (and his son Cassander), Perdiccas, Antigonus I, Ptolemy I, Seleucus I, and Lysimachus. Rivalry led to dreary succession of wars. The main events were the victory of Antipater over Perdiccas for the regency (321 B.C.); the coalition against Antigonus after Antipater's death (319 B.C.), which brought the defeat of Antigonus and his son, Demetrius I, at Ipsus (301 B.C.); and the victory of Seleucus I over Lysimachus (281 B.C.). The result was the irrevocable splitting of the empire into smaller empires, notably under the descendants of Ptolemy, Seleucus, and Antigonus.

Diaghilev, Sergei Pavlovich (sǐrgā′ päv′lŭvǐch dyä′gǐlyǐf), 1872–1929, Russian ballet impresario. In Paris founded (1909) Diaghilev's Russian Ballet with painter Bakst, choreographer Fokine. Dancers included Pavlova and Nijinsky. Productions include *The Afternoon of a Faun, The Rite of Spring.*

dialect, variety of a language. In 20th-cent. scientific usage, a dialect is language of a person or group considered as it varies from that of other members of same speech community (which includes all speakers whose native language is intelligible to other—but not necessarily all other—members of the group). With increasing isolation differences may accumulate to the point of mutual unintelligibility. An example is Dutch-German speech community, extending from Flanders to Schleswig and to Styria, yet speakers of Flemish and Styrian dialects cannot understand each other. In the area there are standard languages (i.e., official Dutch and German) which are mutually unintelligible because developed from mutually unintelligible dialects.

dialectic, in philosophy, method of logical procedure, originating in the question-answer-resolution method of Socrates, developed by Plato into a method of reducing the many and the contradictory into systematic organized concepts. Kant used the term for his method of demonstrating metaphysics (as opposed to knowledge derived from phenomena). Hegel based his philosophy on the logic of dialectic, moving from thesis (statement) through antithesis (counterstatement) to synthesis (joining of the two in higher truth); he also held that this process underlay movement in history.

dialectical materialism, method of historical analysis developed by Karl Marx and Friedrich Engels, fundamental in the method of Socialists and Communists. Basically derived from Hegel's dialectic, the theory is notable for thorough-going materialism and insistence that history proceeds only from economic drives. Thus, opposing classes are born of economic stress and must inevitably struggle until the working class gains power and a classless and stateless society ultimately emerges. See MARXISM.

dialysis (dīā′lĭsĭs), in chemistry, a method of separating a colloid from a substance in true solution by using a membrane permeable only to one. Molecular particles of solution pass through membrane; particles of colloid are too large.

diamond, crystallized pure carbon, valued as a gem. It is the hardest substance known, and inferior stones are used as abrasives. Earliest sources were stream gravels (see MINING). Most of the world's gem supply comes from the pipes of old volcanoes in South Africa; Brazil is a source of carbonados (black diamonds).

Diamond Head, extinct crater, 761 ft. high, SE Oahu, T.H. Once burial grounds of ancient Hawaiians. U.S. Fort Ruger is on plateau.

Diamond Necklace, Affair of the, scandal which took place in 1784–86 at the French court. An adventuress, calling herself the comtesse de Lamotte, persuaded Cardinal de ROHAN that he could gain Queen Marie Antoinette's favor by buying her a diamond necklace worth nearly $1,000,000. The necklace, assembled by two jewelers, was bought on installment by the cardinal in the queen's name. When he could not meet the payments, the jewelers brought a complaint. It was discovered that Mme de Lamotte's husband had absconded with the necklace to London (where it was broken up and sold). At the trial (1785) the cardinal was acquitted but disgraced; Mme de Lamotte was branded and imprisoned, but escaped. CAGLIOSTRO, at first suspected of complicity, was acquitted. Although the queen had no part in it, the affair revealed a moral laxity at her court which increased her unpopularity.

Diana, in Roman legend, goddess of the moon, of forests, of animals, and of women in childbirth; identified with Greek Artemis. Her temple at Aricia was a shrine of women.

Diane de Poitiers (dyän' dü pwätyä'), 1499–1566, mistress of Henry II of France.

dianthus: see PINK.

Diarmuid mac Murchada: see DERMOT MCMURROUGH.

diarrhea (dīŭrē'ù), frequent discharge of watery feces, resulting from irritation or nervous stimulation of intestines. Tissues and blood lose fluids and minerals which need to be replaced.

diastase (dī'ùstās) or **amylase** (ă'mīlās), an enzyme that converts starch to sugar and thus is important in digestion and fermentation. It is present in some plants and in saliva (as ptyalin) and pancreatic fluid (as amylopsin).

diathermy: see ELECTROTHERAPY.

diatom (dī'ùtŏm''), microscopic plant form of algae group. Diatoms exist as single cells or joined as colonies in fresh or salt water, in moist soil, and on moist surfaces of other plants. They are most abundant in arctic and other cold regions. Diatomaceous earth and the more compact rock, diatomite, are formed from shells of dead diatoms. Diatomite, found in parts of U.S., is used industrially, especially for insulating against both heat and sound. See *ill.,* p. 813.

Diaz, Armando (ärmän'dō dē'äts), 1861–1928, Italian field marshal. Routed Austrians at Vittorio Veneto and accepted their surrender (Nov., 1918).

Díaz, Bartholomew (dē'äz), d. 1500, Portuguese navigator. First European to round Cape of Good Hope (1488), thus opening sea route to India.

Díaz, Porfirio (pôrfē'rēō dē'äs), 1830–1915, Mexican statesman, a mestizo who became president (1876) and remained in power until 1911. His regime saw material prosperity in Mexico grow largely through investment of foreign capital, but oppressed masses were neglected and education stagnated. A revolution led by Madero was successful. Díaz died in exile.

Díaz de la Peña, Narciso Virgilio (dyäz' dù lä pänyä'), 1807?–1876, French landscape and figure painter of the Barbizon school, b. Bordeaux.

Díaz del Castillo, Bernal (bĕrnäl' dē'äth dĕl kästē'lyō), c.1492–1581, Spanish conquistador, author of *The True History of the Conquest of New Spain* (1632; Eng. tr., 5 vols., 1908–16).

Dibon (dī'–) or **Dibon-gad,** anc. city, E of Dead Sea, now a ruin called Dhiban. MOABITE STONE found here.

Dice, one of the HORAE.

dice [plural of *die*], small cubes usually made of ivory, bone, wood, similar materials. The six sides are numbered by dots from 1 to 6, so placed that sum of dots on opposite sides equals 7. Most popular dice game in U.S. is craps. Dice also used in poker dice, backgammon, parcheesi, many other games. Dice known to the ancient Egyptians and the Babylonians and were very popular among the Greeks and Romans.

Dick, George Frederick: see DICK TEST.

Dickens, Charles, 1812–70, English novelist, one of the outstanding writers of fiction in English. His childhood was poverty-stricken, and at 12 he worked in a blacking warehouse. Was a court and parliamentary reporter before he began writing sketches (first collected as *Sketches by Boz,* 1836). He was commissioned to write *Posthumous Papers of the Pickwick Club* (1836–37; connected humorous sketches) and began the long series of major novels: *Oliver Twist* (as book 1838), *Nicholas Nickleby* (1839), *The Old Curiosity Shop* (1841), *Barnaby Rudge* (1841), *Martin Chuzzlewit* (1843), *Dombey and Son* (1848), *David Copperfield* (1850), *Bleak House* (1853), *Hard Times* (1854), *Little Dorrit* (1857), *A Tale of Two Cities* (1859), *Great Expectations* (1860–61), *Our Mutual Friend* (1865), *The Mystery of Edwin Drood* (1870; unfinished). Also wrote Christmas books and stories (e.g., *A Christmas Carol,* 1843) and many short stories. Visit to United States in 1842 brought highly critical *American Notes* (1842) and section of *Martin Chuzzlewit.* Married Catherine Hogarth (1836) and had 10 children; separated from her in 1858, possibly because of interest in an actress, Ellen Ternan. His novels are remarkable for depicting quirks of character, for rich panoramas of social scenes, for sentimentality, for crusades against social evils (e.g., imprisonment for debt, legal delays, bad education). Edited magazines, was interested in drama and amateur theatricals.

Dickinson, Emily, 1830–86, American poet. She spent almost all of her life in Amherst, Mass., mostly in seclusion, seeing only a limited number of persons. Whether or not she had a brief and abortive love affair is hotly argued. Certainly she began c.1862 writing the short, frequently cryptic lyrics that have made her one of America's major poets. Her fame began when Mabel L. Todd and T. W. Higginson edited and published her poems (1890–91). Other volumes were issued later, the publications accompanied by vigorous quarreling among her editors.

Dickinson, G(oldsworthy) Lowes, 1862–1932, British author, internationalist and pacifist. Of his varied work perhaps best known is *The Greek View of Life* (1896).

Dickinson, John, 1732–1808, American patriot and statesman. A conservative, his *Letters from a Farmer in Pennsylvania* (1767–68) criticized Townshend Acts and recommended conciliation.

Dickinson, Jonathan, 1688–1747, American Presbyterian clergyman, founder and first president of Col. of New Jersey (now Princeton Univ.).

Dickinson, city (pop. 7,469), SW N.Dak., on Heart R. Ships livestock and wheat. Lignite mines.

Dickinson College: see CARLISLE, Pa.

Dickson City, borough (pop. 8,948), NE Pa., on Lackawanna R. and NE of Scranton. Has anthracite mining and produces metal products.

Dick test, skin test for determining susceptibility to scarlet fever. American physician, **George Frederick Dick,** 1881–, and wife Gladys Dick developed test and immunity serum and isolated streptococcus causing disease.

dictator, originally, a Roman magistrate appointed to rule the state in time of crisis; now, any absolutist or autocrat. Modern dictators may, as head of party or personal following, seize power or may come to office constitutionally and later create dictatorship. Typically they rely on an official party, secret police, and heavy propaganda. Hitler and Mussolini outstanding examples, and Russia under Communist rule developed a party dictatorship with large elements of personal dictatorship. See also CAUDILLO.

dictionary, published list of forms of a language, with content governed by some specific purpose. Descriptive dictionaries (e.g., foreign-language dictionaries) attempt, ideally, to give objectively exact meaning of all forms of their languages. The modern dictionary of its own standard language is often prescriptive, for it attempts to establish certain forms as preferable (as in dictionary of the French Acad.). In 20th cent. American dictionary makers began to replace notions of purity (esp. based on ETYMOLOGY) by criteria of use. The sound line of English dictionaries may be said to begin with *Universal Etymological English Dictionary* (1721) and *Dictionarium Britannicum* (1730), by Nathan Bailey. Samuel Johnson used Bailey's second work to prepare *A Dictionary of the English Language* (1755). His definitions are basic in later lexicography. The next great lexicographer was an American, Noah Webster, whose *Spelling Book* appeared in 1783. His more advanced *Compendious Dictionary of the English Language* (1806) and his larger work, *An American Dictionary of the English Language* (1828), followed. Authorized publishers have made a series of skillful revisions, which have caused Webster's dictionaries to retain popularity. *The Century Dictionary,* an American work in six volumes, with encyclopedic features, was completed in 1891. In England dictionary work after Johnson progressed with John Walker's dictionary (1791), which gave special care to pronunciation, and later with that of the Philological Society, published 1884–1928 as *New English Dictionary, Oxford English Dictionary,* or *Murray's Dictionary* (for Sir J. A. H. Murray, one of the editors), in which examples of usage were collected and organized, with dates given.

Dictys Cretensis (dĭk′tĭs krētĕn′sĭs), supposed hero of Trojan War. Latin MS of his "diary" (A.D. 4th cent.) was popular source for medieval stories.

Didache (dĭ′dúkē) [Gr.,= teaching], collection of Christian moral precepts, directions for baptism and the Eucharist, and instructions to ministers. It is in Greek, is also called in English *The Teaching of the Twelve Apostles,* and probably dates from before A.D. 100.

Diderot, Denis (dŭnē′ dēdûrō′), 1713–84, French philosopher, a leading figure of the ENLIGHTENMENT and a universal genius of the modern era. His life work was the editorship of the ENCYCLOPÉDIE (1747–72). His philosophy, scattered in numerous writings, combines extreme skepticism with bold materialism. As a playwright, he created the "bourgeois drama" with *Le Père de famille* (1758). *La Religieuse* and *Jacques le fataliste,* novels, and *Le Neveu de Rameau,* a satire in dialogue (all pub. posthumously) are, like all his works, highly individualistic and personal in style. In his *Salons* (1759–71) he pioneered in modern art criticism. Late in life he enjoyed the patronage of Catherine II, whom he visited at St. Petersburg (1773–74).

Dido (dī′dō), in Roman legend, founder and queen of Carthage. Of several versions of her story the most famous is in Vergil's *Aeneid,* which tells how she loved Aeneas and how, when he had to leave her, she destroyed herself on her own funeral pyre.

Didot, François (fräswä′ dēdō′), 1689–1757, Parisian printer. His son, **François Ambroise Didot** (äbrwäz′), 1730–1804, was called by Benjamin Franklin Bache "the best printer of this age and even the best that has ever been seen." Scholarly and typographic excellence of Didot's books is unquestioned. He designed some "modern" type and improved and secured adoption of Pierre Simon Fournier's "point" system of type measurement. His sons, **Pierre Didot,** 1761–1853, and **Firmin Didot** (fĕrmē′), 1764–1836, continued family tradition of printing excellence, choosing and editing texts conscientiously and also producing good inexpensive books for students.

Didrikson, (Mildred) Babe (dĭ′drĭksŭn), 1913–, American athlete. Broke four records at Olympic games of 1932. Has won many golf titles. Married George Zaharias 1938.

Didymus: see THOMAS, SAINT.

Diels, Otto Paul Hermann, 1876–, German chemist. He shared 1950 Nobel Prize for discovering and developing method of producing synthetically certain complex compounds.

Diemen, Anton van (än'tŏn vän dē'mŭn), 1593–1645, Dutch colonial official. Became governor general of Dutch East India Co. in 1636. Sent out Abel TASMAN on exploring voyages. Van Diemen's Land was original name of Tasmania.

Dieppe (dēĕp'), town (pop. 20,877), Seine-Inférieure dept., N France; fishing port and resort on English Channel. Scene (1942) of Allied commando raid in World War II.

Diesel engine (dē'zŭl), internal-combustion type of engine invented by Rudolf Diesel (1858–1913, German engineer). Since patented in 1892, it has developed into competitor of steam engine, steam turbine, and electric motor, particularly for marine work and for driving locomotives, trucks, electric generators, and pumps. Instead of igniting fuel by spark as in gasoline engines, it uses compression of air to raise air temperature to igniting point. Although heavier than gasoline engines, the Diesel uses cheaper fuel (crude oil). See *ill.*, p. 389.

Dies irae (dē'äs ē'rā) [Latin,= day of wrath], hymn of the Roman Catholic Church, part of the Requiem Mass, a description of the Last Judgment. Its plain-song tune has been used in instrumental music, as in Berlioz's *Symphonie fantastique.* Verdi and Mozart composed original music for it.

diet, daily intake of food. For maintenance of physical and mental health it should include adequate daily amounts of proteins (e.g., from meat, fish, eggs, legumes, milk, cheese); carbohydrates, i.e., starches (grain products, potatoes, rice) and sugar (fruits, honey, moderate amount of other sweets); fats; and a sufficient intake of minerals (calcium phosphorus, iron, copper, iodine) and VITAMINS, as well as water. Obesity is caused by a diet with more calorie (i.e., energy) value than the body requires. Special diets are needed in certain diseases and to correct obesity or underweight.

diet, a deliberative or legislative assembly. The diet (Ger. *Reichstag*) of the HOLY ROMAN EMPIRE was summoned irregularly. Emperor Charles IV organized it into three bodies—ELECTORS, princes, and representatives of imperial cities (1356). In 1648 it became a federal body, above the emperor; from 1663 it met at Regensburg. For the federal diet (Ger., *Bundesrat*), of 1815–66, see GERMAN CONFEDERATION. Parliamentary bodies of some other countries have also been called diets. See also WORMS, DIET OF.

Dieulafoy, Marcel Auguste (dyûläfwä'), 1844–1920, French archaeologist. Discovered palaces of Darius and Artaxerxes at Susa while exploring in Persia (1885). Aided by his wife, **Jeanne** (or **Jane**) **Rachel Magre Dieulafoy,** 1851–1916.

differential, in automobile a set of gears used on driving axle (usually the rear) to divide torque of common power source (drive shaft) equally between two rear wheels, at the same time allowing each wheel to revolve at its own speed.

diffraction. Light travels in straight lines through a uniform, transparent medium. When an opaque object partly blocks its

path, the rays that just pass the edges are bent slightly. This is diffraction; it occurs when light waves pass through narrow slits. A **diffraction grating** is used for producing spectra and for direct measurement of wave lengths of lines in certain spectra. Sound waves are also diffracted.

diffusion, uniform distribution of molecules of one substance through those of another in apparent contradiction to laws of gravity. Rate is inversely proportional to square root of density of diffusing gas (Graham's law). It is seen also in liquids and in some solids in contact with others.

Digby, earls of Bristol: see BRISTOL, JOHN DIGBY, 1ST EARL OF.

Digby, Sir Kenelm, 1603–65, English writer, man of affairs. Varied career included brief piracy, loyal support of king in civil war. A Roman Catholic, he tried to convert Cromwell. Promotion of a panacea, the "powder of sympathy," overshadowed real scientific achievements.

Digby, fishing and resort town (pop. 2,047), W N.S., Canada, on Bay of Fundy opposite St. John, N.B.

Digest: see CORPUS JURIS CIVILIS.

digestion, conversion of food in alimentary canal into simple, soluble form which can pass into the circulation and be used by tissues. In man, it occurs chiefly by the action of SALIVA, BILE, and juices of STOMACH, PANCREAS, and INTESTINE.

Diggers, members of small English religio-economic movement (fl. 1649–50), so called because of efforts to cultivate wastelands. Offshoot of LEVELERS; favored egalitarian communism. Leader was Gerrard Winstanley (1609?–1660?). Colonies, estab. in Surrey, were destroyed by mob (James 1600).

Dighton (dī'tŭn), town (pop. 2,950), SE Mass., on Taunton R. and S of Taunton. Origin of inscriptions, probably Indian, on Dighton Rock is uncertain.

digitalis: see FOXGLOVE.

Dijon (dēzhŏ'), city (pop. 92,686), cap. of Côte-d'Or dept., E France; historic cap. of Burgundy. Chief trading center for Burgundy wine. Reached its flower under Duke Philip the Good (15th cent.). Among art treasures are funeral statues of dukes by Claus SLUTER and his disciples in former ducal palace (12th cent.; rebuilt 17th and 18th cent.); several 13th-cent. churches, including cathedral; 16th-cent. palace of justice (once housing parlement). University founded 1722.

dill, Old World annual (*Anethum graveolens*), with aromatic seeds used for pickling and flavoring.

Dillard University: see NEW ORLEANS, La.

Dillinger, John (dĭ'lĭnjûr), 1902–34, American bank robber. In 1933 he terrorized the Midwest with an organization of criminals, killing 16 persons before he was shot by FBI agents.

Dillon, town (pop. 5,171), NE S.C., near N.C. line NE of Florence, in farm (cotton, tobacco) area.

Dilthey, Wilhelm (vĭl'hĕlm dĭl'tī), 1833–1911, German philosopher. Argued for analytic psychology as base for philosophy, a central spiritual science distinct from natural sciences. He stressed history and development of ideas, to the exclusion of metaphysics.

DiMaggio, Joseph Paul (dĭmä'jēō), 1914–, American baseball outfielder. Joe DiMaggio estab. (1941) major league record by hitting safely in 56 consecutive games.

dime novels, swift-moving, thrilling novels, mainly about American Revolution, frontier period, or Civil War. First sold in 1860 for 10 cents. Among most famous were those about DEADWOOD DICK and Nick CARTER. Quality of stories was lowered by imitators after 1880, and dime novels acquired bad name.

Dinah (dī'nú), daughter of Jacob. Gen. 30.21; 34.1–31.

Dinan (dēnä'), town (pop. 11,111), Côtes-du-Nord dept., NW France. Medieval ramparts and 14th-cent. castle of dukes of Brittany still stand.

Dinant (dēnä'), town (pop. 6,925), Namur prov., S Belgium, on Meuse R. Railroad junction; market center. Fortified since Merovingian times, it was noted in Middle Ages for metalware.

Dinard (dēnär'), town (pop. 7,353), Ille-et-Vilaine dept., NW France, facing Saint-Malo across inlet of English Channel. Bathing resort.

Dinaric Alps (dīnâ'rĭk), mountain range, occupying one third of Yugoslavia and part of Albania. Prolongs Alps along E coast of Adriatic; includes KARST in N. Highest peak (8,714 ft.) is in Albania.

D'Indy, Vincent: see INDY, VINCENT D'.

Dinesen, Isak (ē'säk dē'núsùn), pseud. of Karen, Baroness Blixen, 1885–, Danish author. Notable among her works in English are *Seven Gothic Tales* (1934), *Winter's Tales* (1943), autobiographical *Out of Africa* (1937).

dingo (dĭng'gō), wild dog of Australia, similar to the fox but larger, with short legs and a brown coat marked on the back with black. Hunts its prey (rabbits, sheep, poultry) chiefly at night. Genus *Canis.*

Diniz, Port. *Dinis* (dĭnēzh'), 1261–1325, king of Portugal (1279–1325). His reign was generally peaceful. A patron of literature, founder of Coimbra Univ. (originally at Lisbon), he also increased the royal domain (particularly at the expense of the Templars) and greatly encouraged farming. Nicknamed "the farmer." His queen was St. Elizabeth of Portugal.

dinosaur (dī'núsôr), extinct land reptile of the MESOZOIC ERA, ranging in length from 2½ to c.90 ft. Some were herbivorous, others carnivorous. They died out by the end of the Cretaceous period.

Dinosaur National Monument: see NATIONAL PARKS AND MONUMENTS (table).

Dinwiddie, Robert, 1693–1770, colonial governor of Va. (1751–58), b. Scotland. Sent George Washington on unsuccessful mission to forestall French in Ohio valley in 1754. Aided Braddock's campaign.

Dio: see DION.

Diocletian (dīúklē'shùn), 245–313, Roman emperor (284–305), b. Salona, Dalmatia, of humble parents. An army commander, he was chosen to succeed after Numerian was murdered, and he killed the suspected mur-

derer, Arrius Aper. Ruled jointly with Carinus, who had been joint emperor with Numerian, until Carinus was killed. Later to defend the empire with responsible officials he made MAXIMIAN joint emperor (286) and CONSTANTIUS I and GALERIUS Caesars (sub-emperors). This policy succeeded brilliantly: Britain was restored, the Persians were subdued, and some barbarians driven out. The empire throve. There was, however, severe persecution of the Christians; economic measures turned out badly; and the division of the empire formally instituted by Diocletian led to much warfare after he and Maximian abdicated (305). Diocletian retired to a splendid castle at Salona.

Diodorus Siculus (dīùdô'rùs sĭ'kūlùs), d. after 21 B.C., Sicilian historian. Author of world history ending with Gallic Wars; in Greek, in 40 books, of which I–IV and XI–XX are fully preserved.

Diogenes (dīōj'únēz), c.412–323 B.C., Greek Cynic philosopher. Lived in Athens, where he stressed belief in the simple life by living in a tub. When Alexander the Great asked what he might do for Diogenes, the philosopher answered, "Only step out of my sunlight." Diogenes is also said to have gone about in daylight carrying a lantern and looking for a "man" (i.e., someone showing proper human virtues).

Diomed (dī'ōmĕd), **Diomede** (–mēd), or **Diomedes** (dī"ōmē'dēz), in Greek legend. **1** One of the EPIGONI, prominent in the Trojan War. **2** Son of Ares who fed his horses on human flesh. HERCULES killed him.

Diomede Islands (dī'úmēd), group of three islands in Bering Strait between Alaska and Siberia. USSR-U.S. boundary and International Date Line pass between two larger islands.

Dion Cassius (Cassius Dio Cocceianus) (dī'ún kă'shùs), c.155–235?, Roman historian, b. Bithynia. He held high imperial office but is known for his history of Rome, written in Greek and now only partly extant. Also Dio Cassius.

Dion Chrysostom (krī'sùstùm, krīsō'stùm) [Gr.,= golden-mouthed], d. after A.D. 112, Greek sophist and rhetorician. Author of 80 extant orations.

Dionne quintuplets (dēōn'), five daughters (Annette, Émilie, Yvonne, Cécile, and Marie) born to Oliva Dionne and his wife at Callender, Ont., on May 28, 1934. In 1935 the Ontario legislature made them wards of the province. Allan Roy Dafoe was their physician.

Dion of Syracuse (dī'ún), 409?–354? B.C., Greek political leader in Sicily. Brother-in-law of Dionysius the Elder, he knew Plato and philosophically favored moderate government. Led a force from Athens to overthrow Dionysius the Younger (357 B.C.) and commanded Sicily until murdered by an Athenian companion.

Dionysia (dīúnĭ'shēù), in Greek religion, festivals to honor god Dionysus. Resembling the Bacchanalia, they stressed fertility. From them developed the dithyramb, the choral procession, and Greek drama (see COMEDY and TRAGEDY).

Dionysius (dīúnĭ'shēùs), tyrants of Syracuse.

Dionysius the Elder, c.430–367 B.C., rose as representative of the poor to become tyrant (406 B.C.). He kept the people in obedience through fear of the Carthaginians. Led expeditions against Italian cities and the Carthaginians. Patronized literature and the arts. His son, **Dionysius the Younger,** fl. 368–344 B.C., succeeded him, tried to maintain popularity, but lost it to DION OF SYRACUSE (357 B.C.). After Dion's murder he regained power, but was expelled by Timoleon (344 B.C.).

Dionysius of Halicarnassus (hă″lĭkärnă′sŭs), fl. 1st cent. B.C., Greek rhetorician and historian. Author of *Antiquities of Rome.*

Dionysius the Areopagite, Saint (dĭŭnĭ′shĕŭs, ârăŏp′ŭjīt), 1st cent. Athenian Christian, converted by St. Paul; traditionally first bishop of Athens and a martyr. He is sometimes confused with St. Denis (their names are different forms of the same one). In the Middle Ages some letters and treatises important in scholasticism were attributed to him. Actually they were written (in Greek) in 5th- or 6th-cent. Palestine. Their author is now called Pseudo-Dionysius.

Dionysius the Elder. see DIONYSIUS.

Dionysius the Younger: see DIONYSIUS, tyrants.

Dionysus (dĭŭnĭ′sŭs), in Greek legend, god of fertility and wine, patron of choral song and drama; son of Zeus and Semele. His worship (said to have been imported from Thrace) was full of enthusiasm and emotionalism, as in the DIONYSIA. Pan and Silenus were his companions, and he was surrounded by the BACCHAE. His grave was supposedly at Delphi, which was sacred to him in winter; thus he achieved a sort of parity with Apollo. He was chief deity in ORPHIC MYSTERIES and shared in ELEUSINIAN MYSTERIES. As nature god he was confused with Bacchus.

Diophantus (dĭŭfăn′tŭs), 3d cent., Greek algebraist, pioneer in solving a type of indeterminate algebraic equations. This work is now known as Diophantine analysis.

Dioscorides, Pedanius (pĭdā′nēŭs dĭŭskô′rĭdēz), 1st cent. A.D. Greek physician, author of standard work on materia medica.

Dioscuri: see CASTOR AND POLLUX.

dip, in stock raising, antiseptic solution to kill skin parasites. Applied by dipping animals in tank.

diphtheria (dĭfthēr′ēŭ), communicable disease caused by toxin produced by bacterium and characterized by membranous film in air passages. Incubation period is two to five days. Toxoid used for immunization. Antitoxin given after exposure and to treat disease. SCHICK TEST determines susceptibility. See *ill.*, p. 813.

diplomatic service, body of agents maintained by a government to conduct its relations with foreign nations. First ambassadors acted only on specific missions. In early Middle Ages Venice set up first permanent system of resident ambassadors in foreign caps., and permanent legations became general by end of 18th cent. Congress of Vienna (1815) adopted classification of officers now widely accepted: ambassador, minister plenipotentiary, envoy extraordinary, minister, chargé d'affaires. Diplomats enjoy "diplomatic immunity," their residences rights of EXTERRI-

TORIALITY. One function of diplomats is to observe political, economic, and military trends subject to international restrictions barring espionage. A diplomat is responsible usually to his own foreign minister. His business is carried on with foreign minister of country to which he is accredited in form of memorandums, oral and written notes, and formal notes. Diplomatic language has patterns and gradations which may seem meaningless but which often smooth difficult situations. Diplomatic service is distinguished from CONSULAR SERVICE, though often they are combined, as in U.S. under Rogers Act of 1924. Foreign Service Act of 1946 set up merit system for protection of staff.

Dipoenus (dīpē′nŭs) and **Scyllis** (sĭ′lĭs), c.580 B.C., Greek sculptors, mentioned by Pliny the Elder.

Dirac, Paul Adrien Maurice (dĭrăk′), 1902–, English physicist. Shared 1933 Nobel Prize for work in developing Heisenberg's theory of quantum mechanics.

direct current: see ELECTRICITY; GENERATOR.

direction finder, name for various radio, radar, and other electronic devices used to navigate ship, plane, or other craft.

Directoire style (dērĕktwär′), in French interior decoration and costume, the style of the Directory (1795–99); transition between Louis XVI and Empire styles. Departed from ornateness of aristocratic regime and emphasized classic design (esp. Pompeian forms). Furniture was more massive, with painted or waxed wood surfaces. See *ill.*, p. 456. Wallpaper and plain walls replaced tapestries and wainscoting. Women wore tight skirts, low necklines, and high waistlines.

Directory, Fr. *Directoire,* French government from 1795 to 1799. Its executive branch consisted of five directors, chosen by the two legislative chambers. Its history was marked by corruption, coups d'état, inflation, and, in 1799, military disaster. Sieyès and Barras, who were directors in 1799, helped Bonaparte in overthrowing the Directory and establishing the Consulate by the coup d'état of 18 Brumaire.

dirigible balloon: see AIRSHIP.

Dis, Roman name for PLUTO.

Disarmament Conference, 1932–37. In 1926 preparatory commission for general disarmament met under League of Nations auspices at Geneva. First general conference met in Feb., 1932 (including members of League, USSR, and U.S.), and drafted plans for budgetary restrictions of armaments, limitation of armed forces, and permanent committee to advise on execution of treaty. France opposed draft and offered substitute. In resulting deadlock Germany demanded either world disarmament to her level or right to rearm. Germany withdrew from conference and League in Oct., 1933. Sporadic meetings were held until indefinite postponement in April, 1937. UN commission dealing with problem has had little success thus far.

disciple: see APOSTLE.

Disciples of Christ, Protestant religious body in U.S., estab. in early 19th cent. by Thomas and Alexander Campbell in W Pa. With other groups they finally formed the "disciples" and "Christians." Progressive group is called Disciples of Christ. Stress is on the simple gospel and on Bible alone as basis of faith. See CHRISTIANS; CHURCHES OF CHRIST.

Discobolus (dǐskǒ'búlǔs) [Gr.,= discus thrower], statue by Myron. Only copies of it remain.

disease, departure from health resulting from changes in structure or function of tissues. See also COMMUNICABLE DISEASES.

disease carrier, person or animal harboring and capable of distributing to others the causative agent of a disease. Carrier may be immune to, or recovered from the disease. Famous example was cook known as Typhoid Mary. Typhoid fever and diphtheria are spread by human carriers; malaria, by mosquitoes.

disinfectant, agent which destroys organisms causing disease. Contaminated materials are disinfected by burning, boiling, sterilizing by steam under pressure, or by the use of a GERMICIDE.

Disko (dǐ'skǒ), island, area 3,312 sq. mi., off W Greenland. Telluric iron has been found; lignite is mined. Godhavn is on S shore.

Dismal Swamp, SE Va. and NE N.C. Now c.20 mi. long, it was once much larger and almost impenetrable; trees and plants have fallen into it, creating much organic material. Visited by William Byrd (1728) and George Washington (1763; as member of draining commission). Canal (1828) connects Chesapeake Bay and Albemarle Sound. Much subsequent drainage and lumbering has been undertaken. L. Drummond, at center, is c.5 mi. long. Scene of Harriet B. Stowe's novel *Dred*.

Disney, Walt (dǐz'nē), 1901–, producer of animated cartoons. Studied at Acad. of Fine Arts in Chicago. Began making comic films in Hollywood in 1923 and became known through his "Mickey Mouse" series. His *Snow White and the Seven Dwarfs* (1938) was the first full-length animated cartoon.

dispensary: see CLINIC.

dispersion. 1 In chemistry, the dispersal of fine particles of one substance through another. According to size and nature of particles a dispersion is classed as a SOLUTION, COLLOID, SUSPENSION, or emulsion. **2** In physics, the separation of beam of white light by prism into various colors of SPECTRUM because of unequal refraction.

Disraeli, Benjamin, 1st earl of Beaconsfield (dǐzrā'lē), 1804–81, British statesman and author of Jewish descent. His novels (e.g., *Coningsby*, 1844, and *Sybil*, 1845) gave him a place in English literature. Elected to Parliament 1837; became leader of Tory protectionists. Succeeded DERBY as prime minister 1867. His REFORM BILL of 1867 enfranchised c.2,000,000 men; greatly benefited CONSERVATIVE PARTY. His second ministry (1874–80) had an aggressive foreign policy —annexation of Fiji Isls. (1874) and of the Transvaal (1877); war against Afghans and Zulus (1878–79). Purchase of controlling share of Suez Canal stock strengthened Britain in the Mediterranean. After Russo-Turkish War he induced Turkey to cede Cyprus to Great Britain. Through Congress of Berlin he reduced Russia's power in the

Balkans. Favorite of Queen Victoria, he had her crowned Empress of India (1876). His twofold policy of democracy and imperialism revitalized the Tory party. His father, **Isaac D'Israeli,** 1761–1848, was an author. His best-known work is *Curiosities of Literature* (2 ser., 1791; 1823).

dissenters: see NONCONFORMISTS.

dissociation, in chemistry, separation of molecules into simpler parts. It occurs at high temperatures (thermal dissociation) and when a substance dissolves (electrolytic dissociation, see ION).

distemper, in veterinary medicine, any of several infectious diseases of animals, especially canine distemper, a serious contagious catarrhal disease of young dogs.

distillation, process for purifying a substance, for separating substances from one another, and for breaking down a substance into fractional parts. In purifying water, for example, the impure water is heated to its boiling point and steam, the vapor thus formed, is led into condenser tubes where it is cooled and condensed to form liquid called the distillate. Impurities with higher boiling point than the water are left in the original container. "Double distilled" and "triple distilled" products have undergone further distillations. Many alcoholic beverages are distilled. In **fractional distillation** a liquid mixture of substances with different boiling points is repeatedly distilled at different temperatures and the parts or fractions obtained from each distillation are drawn off and condensed separately. This process is used in refining petroleum, yielding such fractions as gasoline, benzine, kerosene, fuel and lubricating oils, paraffin. **Destructive distillation** involves heating, out of free contact with air, materials such as wood, coal, or oil shale, and collecting separately the portions driven off. Wood thus yields acetic acid, methyl or wood alcohol, charcoal, and hydrocarbons. Coal yields coal gas, coal tar, coke, and ammonia. In **steam distillation,** steam is introduced at high temperatures to carry off volatile matter.

Distinguished Service Cross, Distinguished Service Medal, and **Distinguished Service Order:** see DECORATIONS, CIVIL AND MILITARY.

District of Columbia (pop. 802,178), E U.S., Federal district (c.70 sq. mi.) on E bank of Potomac R., coextensive with city of WASHINGTON, cap. of U.S. Estab. by congressional acts of 1790, 1791. Md. and Va. granted land on each side of river, including towns of Alexandria and Georgetown. Alexandria was returned to Va. 1847. Territorial government estab. 1871, present system 1878. Governed by Congress through executive board of presidential appointees. Inhabitants have no voice in local government, no representation in Congress, no vote for President.

dithyramb (dǐ'thǐrǎm), in anc. Greece, choral lyric, a hymn to the god Dionysus. The TRAGEDY seems to have been developed from it.

Ditmars, Raymond L(ee) (dǐt'märz), 1876–1942, American naturalist and author, authority on snakes.

Diu (dē'ōō), district (14 sq. mi.; pop. 19,731), of Portuguese India; consists mainly of Diu isl. off S tip of Kathiawar peninsula, W India. Diu town was acquired 1535 by Portugal.

Dives (dī'vēz), rich man of parable. Luke 16.19–31.

dividend, that part of a corporation's net earnings which is distributed to its stockholders, usually at regular intervals. In U.S. dividends may be paid in bonds, stocks, cash, or scrip. Businesses being terminated may issue liquidation dividends.

Divine, Father, c.1882–, American Negro leader of Peace Mission movement, begun in Harlem section of N. Y. city. Born in Ga. as George Baker, he moved (c.1915) to North as Major M. J. Divine, later Father Divine. Many accept him as personification of God. Movement is nonsectarian and interracial.

Divine Comedy, Italian epic poem in *terza rima* by DANTE. Dante called it *Commedia* because it ended happily; *Divina* was added in the 16th cent. The narrator is led by Vergil through Hell and Purgatory, by Beatrice through Paradise.

divine right, doctrine that sovereigns derive their right to rule by birth alone, inheriting it from their ancestors, according to the law of God and of nature. A ruler claiming divine right rejects responsibility to his subjects. The theory, much argued in 17th-cent. England, ended there with the Revolution of 1688.

diving. Since the early days of his history and in all parts of the world man has developed the skill of plunging into water for pleasure and for profit (e.g., diving for pearls, coral, sponges). Yet deep-water diving was not possible until the early 19th cent. when Augustus Siebe devised diving dress for prolonged stays under water. The "open-type" dress was essentially a helmet with a pipe to supply air and a waterproof jacket. This type required that the diver stay upright, and Siebe therefore designed a less dangerous "closed-type" suit, which covered the diver entirely except for his hands. Later deepwater suits have merely been improvements on this. Waterproofed canvas, rubber, metal, and plastics are usual materials for making them. They have made possible much exploration of the ocean depths as well as recovery of valuable articles in sunken ships. Types of diving bells have also been used for investigating the underwater world—two notable examples being the bathysphere, a windowed steel globe invented by Otis Barton and used by him and William Beebe (who went to a depth of 3,028 ft. off Bermuda in 1934), and the somewhat similar benthoscope, which Barton invented and took to a depth of 4,500 ft. (off Calif., 1949). Shallow-water diving was developed as a sport late in the 19th cent. and fancy diving contests are a usual part of all swimming meets, the divers being rated for precision, grace, and skill. The use of diving helmets (usually with breastplates) became popular for sport, including spear fishing, after the 1930s. Invention of the aqualung allows diving to 100 ft. or more without diving suit.

division, a basic arithmetical operation; the symbol is ÷ or /. The inverse of multiplication, it is the process of finding a number by which to multiply the divisor to get a product equal (with remainder added) to the dividend. Quotient results from dividing one number by another; dividend is number divided; divisor is number by which dividend is divided; remainder is units left over. For division other than of whole numbers, see FRACTION.

divorce, dissolution of a marriage by court judgment. Partial dissolution (divorce "from bed and board") is effected by judicial SEPARATION. Divorce is distinct from nullity of marriage, which is a decree that the marriage was originally illegal. In U.S., divorce powers belong to the individual states, and policies are varied; all attempts to reach some agreement between different laws has failed. Generally in all courts chief grounds are adultery, DESERTION, and cruelty. After decree is final both parties may remarry, and the wife is entitled to ALIMONY at the discretion of the court.

Dix, Dorothea Lynde, 1802–87, American reformer, pioneer in movement for more humane treatment of the insane.

Dix, Fort, U.S. army training center, SE of Trenton, N.J. Built in World War I, it was the largest army training center in U.S. in World War II.

Dixie, song composed by Daniel Emmett in 1859, the patriotic song of the Confederacy during Civil War. Dixie now regarded as those states lying below Mason-Dixon line; originally "Dixie's Land" referred to a Manhattan farm owned by Johaan Dixie.

Dixon, Thomas, 1864–1946, American novelist, a Baptist clergyman. His militantly Southern novel *The Clansman* (1905) was the basis for the film *The Birth of a Nation* (1915).

Dixon, city (pop. 11, 523), N Ill., on Rock R. and SW of Rockford, in agr. area; founded 1830. Wire and dairy products. Statue of Lincoln as captain in Black Hawk War is on Dixon Blockhouse site.

Dixville Notch, 2-mi. pass in White Mts., N N.H.

Diyarbakir (dēyärbĕkēr'), city (pop. 45,495), E central Turkey, on the Tigris. Commercial center. Occupies site of ancient Amida. Also spelled Diarbekr.

Djibouti or **Jibuti** (jĭbōō'tē), town (pop. c.22,000), cap. of French Somaliland, on inlet of Gulf of Aden. Major port on shipping lanes to Suez Canal and chief outlet for Ethiopian exports.

Djokjakarta, Indonesia: see JOGJAKARTA.

Dmitri (dŭmē'trē) or **Demetrius,** d. 1591, son of Ivan IV of Russia. He was murdered, probably by order of Boris GODUNOV. In 1604 an impostor, pretending that he was Dmitri, invaded Russia with Polish aid and claimed the throne from Boris. Crowned tsar in 1605, he married Marina, a Polish noblewoman. In 1606 he was killed in an insurrection. Another false Dmitri appeared in 1607, was recognized by Marina as her husband, received Polish aid, and successfully invaded Russia. He was killed (1610), as were two later impostors who claimed to be Dmitri's son. Michael Romanov's election (1613) ended the confusion, known as the Time of Troubles.

Dneprodzerdzhinsk (dŭnyĕ″prŭdzĭrzhĕnsk′), city (pop. 147,829), S central Ukraine, on the Dnieper, near Dnepropetrovsk. Steel mills, chemical plants.

Dneproges (dŭnyĕprŭgĕs′), suburb of Zaporozhe, Ukraine, on the Dnieper, site of largest dam and hydroelectric power station in Europe (capacity over 500,000 kw per hour). Its construction (1927–32) raised level of Dnieper 123 ft., made river navigable. H. L. Cooper was chief among American consultant engineers. Destroyed in World War II; rebuilt 1947. Originally named Dneprostroi.

Dnepropetrovsk (dŭnyĕ″prŭpĕtrôfsk′), city (pop. 500,662), central Ukraine, on the Dnieper bend. River port, rail center, heavy industries. Growth began late 19th cent. with exploitation of Donets Basin coal, Krivoi Rog iron, and Nikopol manganese. Receives power from Dneproges. Suffered in World War II, when fighting raged in area. Named Ekaterinoslav or Yekaterinoslav until 1926.

Dneprostroi, Ukraine: see DNEPROGES.

Dnieper (nē′pŭr), Rus. *Dnepr,* river, 1,420 mi. long, Belorussia and Ukraine. Anc. name is Borysthenes. Rises in Valdai Hills, flows S past Smolensk, Kiev, Dnepropetrovsk, Zaporozhe (site of DNEPROGES dam), Kherson into Black Sea, describing vast bend between Kremenchung and Nikopol. Navigable in nearly entire length since construction of Dneproges; linked by canals with Bug, Niemen, Western Dvina.

Dniester (nē′stŭr), Rus. *Dnestr,* river, 850 mi. long, SW European USSR. Rises in Carpathians; flows generally SE, partly along border between Ukraine and Moldavian SSR; joins Black Sea SW of Odessa. Navigable below Mogilev-Podolski. Formed Rumanian-USSR border 1918–40.

Doab (dō′ăb), in India, a tract of land between two rivers. The Doab, unqualified by any names, designates tract between Ganges and Jumna rivers.

Doane, George Washington, 1799–1859, Episcopal bishop of N.J. (1832–59). Author of a number of hymns, including *Softly Now the Light of Day.*

Doane College, at Crete, Nebr.; coed.; 1872.

Dobbs Ferry, residential village (pop. 6,268), SE N.Y., on the Hudson above Yonkers. Masters School for girls is here.

Döbereiner, Johann Wolfgang (yō′hän völf′gäng dû′bŭrīnŭr), 1780–1849, German chemist. He discovered similar triads of elements, a step in development of PERIODIC LAW.

Doberman pinscher, sleek, short-haired dog developed originally in Germany. The coat is predominantly black, brown, or blue marked with rust; males stand 24–27 in. at the shoulder, females 23–25 in. The body is well knit and muscular and the dog has a proud bearing. It needs considerable exercise.

Döblin, Alfred (dûblēn′), 1878–, German novelist, best known for *Berlin Alexanderplatz* (1929; Eng. tr., 1931), which shows the influence of James Joyce.

Dobrich, Bulgaria: see TOLBUKHIN.

Dobruja (dō′brōōjŭ), region, SE Rumania and NE Bulgaria. Constanta is the chief city of the Rumanian section (5,998 sq. mi.; pop. 503,217); Tolbukhin, of the Bulgarian section (2,971 sq. mi.; pop. 318,772). Largely agr.; forests inland. Region was part of Roman Moesia, later of Byzantine Empire and of medieval Bulgaria. Under Ottoman rule from 15th cent. to 1878, when Congress of Berlin awarded most of it to Rumania. Bulgaria forced to cede S Dobruja to Rumania in 1913, recovered it in 1940.

Dobson, (Henry) Austin, 1840–1921, English author of light verse in French forms (rondeau, villanelle, ballads) and of essays on 18th-cent. literature.

Docetism (dōsē′tĭzŭm), early Christian heretical movement, holding that Christ was not a man, but a mere phantasm, who only seemed to live and to suffer. Gnostics held a similar belief.

dock, weedy plant of genus *Rumex,* widely distributed. It has small flowers and winged fruits. Common species are large curled dock, spinach dock, and canaigre (a food of Indians of SW U.S.). Species with arrow-head-shaped foliage are called sorrel, e.g., sheep sorrel of pastures.

documentary film: see MOVING PICTURES.

Dodd, William E(dward), 1869–1940, American historian and diplomat, long at the Univ. of Chicago. He was ambassador to Germany (1933–37), and his diary (pub. 1941) records early days of Nazism there. He was an authority on the history of the South.

dodder, leafless parasitic plant of genus *Cuscuta,* with small flowers. Often a pest in fields of alfalfa, clover, and flax.

Dodds, Harold Willis, 1889–, American educator. Authority on economics and politics in Latin America, he has had international posts. A professor of politics at Princeton after 1927, he became president in 1933.

Dodecanese (dōdĕ″kŭnēs′, –nēz, dō″dĕ–), island group (1,044 sq. mi.; pop. 120,000), Greece, in the SE Aegean, between Asia Minor and Crete; chief city Rhodes. Despite its name [12 islands], it consists of c.20 islands and islets, notably RHODES, Karpathos, Kalymnos, Patmos, Astypalaia, Kasos, Telos, Syme, Leros, Nisyros, Chalke, Kastellorizo. Mostly mountainous. Agr., livestock raising, sponge fishing. With fall of Rhodes to Suleiman I (1522), Dodecanese came under Turkish rule. Islands were occupied by Italy 1912; formally ceded to Italy 1922; awarded to Greece 1947.

Dodge, Grenville Mellen, 1831–1916, Union general in Civil War and railroad builder. Greatest achievement was as chief engineer (from 1866) in building of Union Pacific RR.

Dodge, Henry, 1782–1867, American frontiersman, governor of Territory of Wisconsin (1836–41, 1845–48), U.S. Senator (1848–57).

Dodge, Mary Mapes, 1831–1905, American editor of *St. Nicholas* magazine, author of juvenile classic, *Hans Brinker; or, The Silver Skates* (1865).

Dodge City, city (pop. 11,262), SW Kansas, on Arkansas R. and on old Santa Fe Trail; laid out 1872 near Fort Dodge (1864). Called the "cowboy capital" it flourished as cattle town and, after 1872, as railhead. Now a distributing center for wheat and livestock area. City hall is on site of Boot Hill, burial ground of early cowboys.

Dodgson, Charles Lutwidge: see CARROLL, LEWIS.

dodo, flightless forest-dwelling bird of Mauritius, extinct since late 17th cent. Although related to pigeon, it was larger than the turkey.

Dodona (dōdō'nù), in Greek religion, oldest oracle, in inland Epirus, sacred to Zeus and Dione.

Dodsley, Robert, 1703–64, English publisher, compiler of a well-known collection of plays (12 vols., 1744) and projector (with Burke) of *Annual Register* (1758).

Doeg (dō'ĕg), Edomite who massacred priests at Nob at Saul's command. 1 Sam. 21.1–9; 22.6–23.

Doenitz, Karl (dû'nĭts), 1891–, German admiral. Commanded submarine operations in World War II; chief naval commander from 1943. Named by Hitler as his successor, he ordered unconditional surrender of Germany to Allies (May 7, 1945). Sentenced to imprisonment for 10 years at Nuremberg war crimes trial (1946).

dog, domesticated mammal. Evidence that dogs were domesticated in the late Paleolithic period shows them to be the first domestic animals. A theory that only certain kinds of dogs were descended from wolves and that others were descended from jackals, coyotes, and foxes has been largely disproved by comparative studies of the teeth of dogs and those of the other animals. The generally accepted conclusion is that dogs of both hemispheres developed originally in Asia from the wolf. By selective breeding of dogs, man has perpetuated and intensified certain characteristics and eliminated others. For some of the better-known types see CHOW; HOUND; HUNTING DOGS; POODLE; SHEEP DOGS; SPANIELS; TERRIERS; TOY DOGS. See also SEEING-EYE DOGS.

dogfish, name for small sharks of several families of both hemispheres, found chiefly in temperate but also in tropical waters. Commonest is the spiny dogfish (*Squalus acanthias*), of the family Squalidae. It is 3–4 ft. long. In front of each dorsal fin is a stout spine, supplied with poison. It destroys food fish and nets.

Dogger Bank (dô'gŭr, dŏ'–), extensive sand bank, central North Sea, between England and Denmark, covered by shallow water. It has fisheries.

dogtooth violet, adder's tongue, or **trout lily,** wild flower of genus *Erythronium*, with pendent, lilylike spring blossoms and mottled foliage.

dogwood or **cornel,** shrub or tree of genus *Cornus,* chiefly of N Hemisphere. Best known, flowering dogwood (*Cornus florida*), has white or pink flowers (botanically they are bracts), in spring. Its hard wood is used for shuttles, door handles. See also BUNCHBERRY.

dogy or **dogie** (both: dō'gē), cowboys' name for orphan or scrubby calf, sometimes for all cattle.

Dohnanyi, Ernst von (dô'nänyē), 1877–, Hungarian composer, pianist, and conductor. His compositions include four operas, chamber music, concertos, piano pieces, orchestral suites, and the witty *Variations on a Nursery Tune* for piano and orchestra.

Doisy, Edward Adelbert, 1893–, American biochemist. Shared 1943 Nobel Prize in Physiology and Medicine for discovery of the chemical nature of vitamin K.

Dolci, Carlo or **Carlino** (kär'lō, kärlē'nō dōl'chē), 1616–86, Florentine painter. Excelled in sorrowful heads of Christ and the Mater Dolorosa.

doldrums (dŏl'drŭmz), or **equatorial belt of calms,** area just N of equator, circling earth between two tradewind belts. Characterized by low pressure, light variable winds, squalls, thunderstorms.

Dole, Sanford Ballard, 1844–1926, American statesman of Hawaiian Isls., b. Honolulu. Became first president of republic of Hawaii 1894. Was first governor of Territory of Hawaii 1900–1903.

Dôle (dōl), town (pop. 16,340), Jura dept., E France, on Doubs R. Stronghold and cap. of Franche-Comté until conquest (1674) by Louis XIV, who transferred the parlement and university (founded c.1422) to Besançon. Birthplace of Pasteur.

Dolet, Étienne (ātyĕn' dôlā'), 1509–46, French scholar and printer. Wrote treatises on grammar and history and a famous commentary on the Latin language. Printed these and a translation of the Bible. He was finally accused of heresy, imprisoned, and executed.

doll. Small figures were early used as cult objects. In Christian era the Nativity was represented by crèche dolls. From 15th cent. styles were spread by exchange of fashion dolls. Play dolls probably used by children in ancient Egypt, Greece, and Rome; commonly used in Europe by 17th cent. Made of many materials.

Dollfuss, Engelbert (ĕng'ŭlbĕrt dôl'fŏŏs), 1892–1934, chancellor of Austria (1932–34). A Christian Socialist, he opposed both National Socialists and Social Democrats, was driven into alliance with native fascists of E. R. von STARHEMBERG. After ruthlessly suppressing a Socialist rising, he made Austria a one-party, corporative state, under constitution drafted by SCHUSCHNIGG (1934). He was assassinated by Austrian Nazis.

Döllinger, Johann Joseph Ignaz von (yō'hän yō'zĕf ig'näts fŭn dŭ'lĭng-ûr), 1799–1890, German theologian, church historian, leader of OLD CATHOLICS. Ordained (1822) as a Roman Catholic priest, he was long associated with the Univ. of Munich and a leading member (1845–52) of Catholic party in Frankfurt Parliament. Spurned dogma of papal infallibility pronounced by Vatican Council (1870) and was excommunicated in 1871. Although in sympathy with Old Catholics, he never intended a separate church to emerge from the movement and he never was formally a member of the Old Catholic Church.

dolmen (dŏl'mĕn, dōl–), rough stone structure, consisting usually of two uprights and a capstone. Characteristic megalithic monument, probably erected as substitute for cave burial.

dolomite (dō'lŭmīt). **1** A mineral, calcium magnesium carbonate. **2** A carbonate rock composed chiefly of dolomite, similar to limestone but harder.

Dolomites (dŏ'lùmīts), Alpine group, N Italy, famed for striking outline and vivid colors of its DOLOMITE rocks. Marmolada (10,964 ft.) is highest peak. Many resorts, e.g., Cortina d'Ampezzo.

dolphin. 1 Gregarious mammal, a toothed whale found in most oceans, sometimes in rivers. Its length is 4–30 ft., usually 5–14 ft. Pointed muzzle distinguishes dolphin from true porpoise. Common Atlantic and Mediterranean dolphin has bearlike jaws; bottlenosed dolphin inhabits all but polar seas; killer whale or grampus (*Orcinus* or *Orca*) has a large, black and white mottled body, and it attacks seals, porpoises, fish, sea birds, and, in packs, large whales. River dolphins are found in Asia and South America. **2** Name for the coryphene, a small swift, iridescent, spiny-finned fish of warm seas.

Dolton, residential village (pop. 5,558), NE Ill., S suburb of Chicago, in truck-farm area.

Dom (dōm), peak, 14,923 ft. high, Valais canton, S Switzerland; highest in Mischabelhörner group.

Domagk, Gerhard (gär'härt dŏ'mäk), 1895–, German chemist and pathologist. Because of Nazi decree he declined 1939 Nobel Prize in Physiology and Medicine awarded for discovery of use of prontosil, forerunner of SULFA DRUGS.

Domenichino (dōmänēkē'nō) or **Domenico Zampieri** (dōmä'nēkō tsämpyä'rē), 1581–1641, Italian painter of the Carracci school.

Domenico Veneziano (dōmä'nēkō vānätsēä'nō), c.1400–1461, Florentine painter who introduced the technique of finishing tempera works with an oil glaze.

Domesday Book (dōmz'dā, dōōmz'dā), record of general survey of England made at order of William I, 1086. It ascertained economic resources of most of the country for purposes of more accurate taxation. Unsurpassed in medieval history for speed and thoroughness, it is invaluable historical source.

domestication, of plants and animals. All major plant crops and domestic animals (except the dog, tamed earlier) were brought into man's service during Neolithic period. Archaeological evidence has fixed points of origin of many crops. No new animals are known to have been domesticated during recorded history, although BREEDING has produced improved types.

domicile, one's legal residence, the permanent home to which one has the intention of returning after a temporary absence. Question of domicile is especially important in tax laws and in legal matters concerning domestic relations.

Dominic, Saint (dŏ'mùnĭk), 1170?–1221, Castilian churchman, named Dominic Guzmán, founder of the Dominicans. He and his bishop (of Osuna) were sent to preach to the Albigenses in S France, and did so with some success. In 1216 he was given a house at Toulouse for his growing band of preachers, and Pope Honorius III allowed him to form them into an order devoted to study and preaching. Tradition says that the first rosary was given to him by Our Lady in a vision. Feast: Aug. 4.

Dominica (dŏmĭnē'kù), island (304 sq. mi.; pop. 47,624), British West Indies. Discovered by Columbus (1493), it changed hands frequently. Detached from Leeward Isls., it became separate colony in 1940. People, largely Negro, speak a French patois.

Dominican Republic (dùmĭ'nĭkùn), republic (19,129 sq. mi.; pop. 2,121,083), West Indies, occupying the E two thirds of Hispaniola; cap. TRUJILLO. The whole island was first settled as the Spanish colony of SANTO DOMINGO, but later the W part became a French colony (present HAITI). After revolution had broken out in Haiti, Spain ceded all to France (1795), but triumphant Haitians conquered the W section (1801). The Spanish-speaking Dominicans opposed this union and there were numerous changes of domination—French, independent, Spanish, Haitian—before the Dominican Republic was estab. 1844. Even later one president planned reunion with Spain and another negotiated a treaty of annexation to the U.S., but both schemes fell through. The country had political and economic difficulties. Bankruptcy in 1905 brought a U.S. customs receivership (lasting to 1941), and U.S. marines occupied the country (1916–34). Rafael TRUJILLO MOLINA came to power in 1930 and thereafter tried to bring about material advancement, though his rule was widely criticized elsewhere as dictatorial. Sugar is the chief export. Others are cacao and coffee.

Dominicans (dùmĭ'nĭkùnz), Roman Catholic religious order, founded by St. Dominic 1216. More officially the order of Preachers (O.P.). Beginning as a band of preachers in S France, the order spread very rapidly and it is today one of the most important in the Church. Members (friars) are admitted not to specific houses but to the order as a whole. The heads of houses and of provinces are elected for set terms. Dominicans, who wear a white habit with a black mantle (worn while preaching), were formerly called Black Friars. Devoted to study, preaching and teaching, the order has supplied many eminent theologians, notably St. Thomas Aquinas. The Dominicans were prominent in the Inquisition. In the 19th cent. in France and England they forwarded social reform. The order came to the U.S. soon after 1800 (first U.S. province 1805). There is an order of contemplative Dominican nuns and a large third order (including many nuns devoted to teaching and good works).

dominion, territory controlled by a particular government. Commonly refers today to one of autonomous divisions of BRITISH EMPIRE.

Dominion Day, celebrated in Canada, July 1, anniversary of confederation of the provinces (1867).

dominoes, game played with pieces (most often 28) called dominoes—oblong pieces of wood, bone, or ivory, with one face blank, other marked with dots. Game introduced in Europe via Italy in 18th cent.

Domitian (dōmĭ'shùn), A.D. 51–A.D. 96, Roman emperor (A.D. 81–A.D. 96); son of Vespasian and successor of his brother Titus. Obsessed with the idea of law and order, he became a despot. Plots against him ended when his wife had him murdered. Nerva succeeded.

Domrémy-la-Pucelle (dŏrāmē-lä-püsĕl′), village, Vosages dept., E France, in Lorraine. Birthplace of Joan of Arc. Her house still stands, as do church and font where she was baptized.

Don, river of Yorkshire, England, 70 mi. long.

Don, river, 1,222 mi. long, S European RSFSR, rising SE of Tula, flowing SE, then SW, into Sea of Azov. Its eastward bend comes to within 40 mi. of the Volga at Stalingrad (Volga-Don canal here completed 1952). Navigable from Voronezh, accessible to seagoing vessels as far as Rostov, the Don is an important artery for grain, coal, lumber shipments. Chief tributary, the Donets, links it with industrial Donets Basin. The ancient Tanais, the Don has been a trading channel since Scythian times. In 16th cent. COSSACKS founded virtually independent republic of the **Don Cossacks** along its lower course. Stenka RAZIN was their most famous ataman. Gave nominal allegiance to tsar in 1614 but retained self-government until collapse of PUGACHEV rebellion (1775). Famed for their songs and choirs.

Don, river of Aberdeenshire, Scotland; 82 mi. long. Empties into North Sea near Aberdeen.

Donaghadee (dŏn″ŭkhŭdē′), urban district (pop. 3,398), Co. Down, N Ireland. Irish port nearest to Great Britain; connected by cable with Scotland.

Donatello (Donato di Niccolò di Betto Bardi) (dŏnŭtĕ′lō), c.1386–1466, Florentine sculptor of the early Renaissance. In *St. George* he abandoned earlier Gothic style for realism, climaxed in later works such as *David* and *St. John Baptist* (all: Bargello). The equestrian *Gattamalata,* made 1453 for Padua, was first of its kind since antiquity.

Donati, Giovanni Battista (jōvän′nē bät-tē′stä dōnä′tē), 1826–73, Italian astronomer. He pioneered in spectral analysis of comets and discovered six comets including Donati's comet (June 2, 1858).

Donatism (dō′nŭtĭzŭm), heretical movement of the 4th cent. in N Africa, led by Donatus of Casa Nigra and the later Donatus the Great. In the Roman persecutions they took the position that those who lapsed from the faith could not be readmitted fully to the Church. Bishops and priests who had given up sacred books to the government were, they held, traitors and had lost their sacramental powers. Opposed, they seceded from the Church and had a formidable church of their own, but they were condemned by the Synod of Arles (314). Extreme Donatists in Numidia terrorized the orthodox, but the teaching of St. Augustine destroyed the Donatist theology, and by 450 it had lost power in N Africa.

Donatus, fl. 333, Roman grammarian; teacher of St. Jerome. His *Ars grammatica* [elements of grammar] was the standard elementary Latin grammar throughout the Middle Ages.

Donauwörth (dô′nouvûrt″), town (pop. 7,-298), Swabia, W Bavaria, on the Danube. Noted for medieval architecture. In Thirty Years War city fell to Swedes 1632, to imperials 1634.

Donbas, USSR: see DONETS BASIN.

Doncaster (dŏng′kŭstûr), county borough (pop. 81,896), West Riding of Yorkshire, England, on the Don. Has coal mines, railroad shops, and steel mills. Near-by racecourse long estab.

Don Cossacks: see DON, river.

Donders, Franciscus Cornelius (fränsī′skŭs kôrnā′lĭŭs dôn′dûrs), 1818–89, Dutch ophthalmologist, pioneer in study of the eye and its disorders. Wrote treatise on accommodation and refraction (1864).

Donegal (dŏ′nĭgôl), maritime county (1,865 sq. mi.; pop. 136,317), Ulster prov., Ireland; co. town Lifford. Coastline irregular and indented; interior rugged and hilly (Mt. Errigal 2,466 ft.). Mainly agr. and pastoral (no large towns), but boggy soil makes farming hard. Deep-sea fishing important. Was ancient kingdom of Tyrconnell.

Donegan, Horace William Baden, 1902–, American Episcopal bishop, b. England; made bishop of N.Y. in 1950.

Donelson, Andrew Jackson (dŏ′nŭlsŭn), 1799–1871, American diplomat, nephew of and private secretary to Andrew Jackson. Successfully negotiated annexation of Texas.

Donelson, Fort, Confederate fortification on Cumberland R. at Dover, Tenn., commanding river approach to Nashville. Captured Feb. 16, 1862, by U. S. Grant, opening way for Union advance on Nashville.

Donets (dŭnyĕts′), river, 655 mi. long, S European RSFSR and S Ukraine, flowing generally SE into lower Don R. Navigable 140 mi. The **Donets Basin,** abbreviated as **Donbas,** SW of the river, is one of main coal-producing and industrial areas of Russia and Ukraine. Stalino is largest of many industrial cities producing steel, heavy machinery, chemicals. Scene of heavy fighting in World War II.

Doniphan, Alexander William (dŏ′nĭfŭn), 1808–87, American soldier. Led 3,600-mi. march into Mexico during Mexican War, taking Chihuahua and Saltillo.

Donizetti, Gaetano (gäätä′nō dōnēdzĕt′tē), 1797–1848, Italian composer. His melodic operas range from serious to pure *opera buffa.* Best known are: *Lucia di Lammermoor* (1835); *La Fille du regiment* (1840); *L'elisir d'amore* (1832) and *Don Pasquale* (1843).

Don Juan (dŏn jōō′ŭn, Span. dōn hwän′), legendary hero of many literary works, supposedly based on life of Don Juan Tenorio of Seville. Don Juan seduces girl, then kills her father. He invites statue of the father to a feast; it comes, seizes the libertine, and drags him to hell. Subject of Mozart's opera *Don Giovanni;* also used by Molière, Byron, Balzac, Robert Browning, and Shaw.

donkey: see ASS.

Donna, city (pop. 7,171), S Texas, WNW of Brownsville, in irrigated lower Rio Grande valley. Has canneries and dehydrating plants.

Donne, John (dŭn), 1572–1631, English poet, a clergyman; generally considered the greatest of the metaphysical poets. Reared a Roman Catholic, he later became an Anglican divine. Secretary to Sir Thomas Egerton, lord keeper of the great seal, he earned a reputation for his clever, often sensual, lyrics and for essays and verse satires, but his court career was ruined by discovery of his secret marriage to Anne More, Egerton's niece by marriage. Later he earned a reputation as a writer of exalted religious poetry as in *An Anatomy of the World* (1611) and *Of the Progresse of the Soul* (1612)—both written as elegies for the daughter of a patron and called the First and the Second Anniversary —took orders (1615), and became a preacher well-known for eloquence. His poetry is remarkable not only for its deep religious feeling (notably solemn in the *Holy Sonnets*) but for virtuosity, with long-drawn, complicated figures called "conceits," exquisite melody and rhyme, and sharp wit to underline his philosophical utterances. His prose works also have distinction as in *Biathanatos* (1644; a qualified apology for suicide), the *Pseudo-Martyr* (1610), and his sermons.

Donnelly, Ignatius, 1831–1901, American author and political reformer. His *Atlantis: the Antediluvian World* (1882; rev. ed., 1949) argued that ATLANTIS was seat of world's original civilization. He championed underdog; helped found Populist party.

Donner Party (dŏ'nŭr), group of emigrants to Calif. who in winter of 1846–47 met with tragedy. Prominent in group were two families named Donner. In Oct. party was trapped by snow in passes at what is now Donner L. in the Sierra Nevada; survivors were driven to cannibalism before rescue. Only about half of party reached Calif. **Donner Lake** is today a popular mountain resort, near Truckee. Near-by **Donner Pass** has U.S. weather observatory.

Donnybrook, suburb of Dublin, Ireland; site of famous fair suppressed 1855 because of disorderliness.

Donora, borough (pop. 12,186), SW Pa., on Monongahela R. and S of Pittsburgh. Mfg. of wire, steel, and zinc products.

Don Quixote (de la Mancha) (dŏn' kēhō'tä dä lä män'chä, Eng. dŏn kwĭk'sŭt), romance satirizing chivalry, masterpiece of Miguel de CERVANTES SAAVEDRA and one of the great works of world literature (first part pub. 1605, and, after a spurious continuation by Alonso Fernández de Avellaneda, second part pub. 1615). Don Quixote, a country gentleman whose mind is addled by chivalric romances, undertakes absurd adventures, riding his nag Rosinante and aided by a squire, the shrewd and realistic peasant Sancho Panza. His lady is a country girl whom he calls Dulcinea del Toboso. The tone is not sharp but compassionate; humor, pathos, and philosophy are blended.

Dooley, Mr.: see DUNNE, FINLEY PETER.

Doolittle, Hilda, pseud. H. D., 1886–, American poet, abroad after 1911, one of the IMAGISTS.

Doomsday Book: see DOMESDAY BOOK.

Doon (dōōn), river of Ayrshire, Scotland. Robert Burns sang of its beauties.

Door Peninsula, NE Wis., between Green Bay and L. Michigan. Crossed by waterway at Sturgeon Bay. Visited 17th cent. by French. Has cherry growing.

Doppler, Christian Johann (krĭs'tyän yō'hän dŏ'plŭr), 1803–53, Austrian physicist and mathematician. **Doppler's principle:** as distance between source of sound or light and

observer becomes less or greater, frequency of waves received increases or decreases respectively. Effect called **Doppler effect.** Examples: rise in pitch of sound with decreased distance between source and observer; in light, this causes shift of color toward violet end of spectrum.

Dorcas or **Tabitha,** Christian woman raised from dead by St. Peter. She sewed for the poor. Acts 9.36–43.

Dorchester, Guy Carleton, 1st Baron: see CARLETON, GUY.

Dorchester, municipal borough (pop. 11,623), county town of Dorsetshire, England, on Frome R. Birthplace of Thomas Hardy, it is Casterbridge of his novels. Has Roman remains.

Dorchester, district (since 1870) of Boston, Mass. Estab. 1630, it was important in colonial history.

Dordogne (dôrdô'nyù), department (3,561 sq. mi.; pop. 387,643), SW France, in Périgord; cap. Périgeux. It is crossed by the **Dordogne** river, 305 mi. long, rising in Auvergne mts. and joining the Garonne N of Bordeaux to form the Gironde.

Dordrecht (dôr'drĕkht) or **Dort** (dôrt), municipality (pop. 68,217) and town, South Holland prov., SW Netherlands, on Lower Merwede R. Rail junction, river port; mfg. of machinery and chemicals. Chartered 1220, it was the scene of William the Silent's proclamation as stadholder (1572) and of the Synod of Dort (1618–19; see REMONSTRANTS). Has 14th-cent. Gothic church (Groote Kerk).

Doré, (Paul) Gustave (pōl' güstäv' dôrā'), 1833?–1883, French illustrator and engraver. His illustrations for *Don Quixote, Paradise Lost, Divine Comedy,* and other classics are famous.

Dore, Mont, France: see MONT-DORE.

Doria, Andrea (ändrä'ä dō'rēä), 1468–1560, Genoese admiral and statesman. Fought in French service in ITALIAN WARS until 1528, when he suddenly went over to Emperor Charles V. Helped Charles capture Tunis (1535) but failed at Algiers (1541). Virtual dictator of Genoa, yet preserved republican institutions.

Dorians, members of one of the traditional branches of the Greek peoples, supposedly the last comers (just before 1,000 B.C.). Sparta and Crete were Dorian centers. The Dorian dialect was considered harsh by Athenians but gave rise to the choral lyric. Doric style is one of great simplicity.

Doric order, the earliest of Greek architectural orders. Appeared in definite form in 7th cent. B.C., and perfected in 5th cent. B.C., especially in the PARTHENON. The Greek Doric column has no base, a massive, fluted shaft, and a simple capital. The Tuscan order, estab. in 16th-cent. Italy, is a simplified form of Doric. See *ill.,* p. 61.

Dormont, borough (pop. 13,405), SW Pa., SW residential suburb of Pittsburgh; settled c.1790.

dormouse, small, squirrellike nocturnal rodent of the Old World. Lives in bushes and trees, feeding on nuts and acorns and hibernating in winter. The family includes a number of genera, e.g., *Glis, Muscardinus, Dryomys, Eliomys,* and *Glirulus.*

Dorpat, Estonia: see TARTU.

Dorr, Thomas Wilson, 1805–54, leader of Dorr's Rebellion (1842) in R.I. Urging universal manhood suffrage, Dorr's party estab. its own government, resorted to arms. New state constitution of 1843, liberalizing voting requirements, was result.

Dorset, Charles Sackville, 6th **earl of:** see SACKVILLE, CHARLES.

Dorset, Thomas Sackville, 1st **earl of:** see SACKVILLE, THOMAS.

Dorset, town (pop. 1,150), SW Vt., N of Manchester. Artists' and writers' resort. First commercial marble quarry in U.S. opened here 1785. Conventions that led to Vt. independence held here 1775 and 1776.

Dorsetshire or **Dorset,** maritime county (973 sq. mi.; pop. 291,157), S England; co. town Dorchester. Rolling country crossed by chalk ranges, it has fine harbor at Poole and agr. in fertile valleys. Sheep raising and dairy farming chief occupations. Marble quarried. Pre-Roman remains include large earthwork, Maiden Castle. Thomas Hardy wrote of region in "Wessex" novels.

Dort, Netherlands: see DORDRECHT.

Dortmund (dôrt′mŏont), city (pop. 500,150), North Rhine-Westphalia, NW Germany. A major industrial center of the RUHR, on Dortmund-Ems Canal. Heavily damaged in World War II.

Dorval, town (pop. 5,293), S Que., Canada, on S shore of Montreal Isl. Resort and site of Montreal international airport. Offshore is Dorval isl.

Dorylaeum (dŏr′ĭlē′ŭm), city of N Phrygia, now in NW Turkey. An important trade center in Roman times, it later declined. Here (1097) Crusaders defeated the Seljuk Turks.

Dos Passos, John (Roderigo), 1896–, American author of novels with broad social themes. *Manhattan Transfer* (1925) was followed by two trilogies, *U.S.A.* (separate vols., 1930–36; about industrial society) and *District of Columbia* (separate vols., 1939–49; about American politics).

Dosso Dossi (dôs′sō dôs′sē), 1479?–1542, Italian painter of the Ferrarese school. His real name was Giovanni de Luteri.

Dost Mohammed (dōst′), 1793–1863, emir of Afghanistan. Fought against the British in first Afghan War (1839–42). Later tried to play Russian interests against the British.

Dostoyevsky, Feodor Mikhailovich (fyŏ′dùr měkhī′lŭvĭch dŭstûyĕf′skē), 1821–81, Russian novelist, one of the giants of modern literature. He won his first success with *Poor Folk* (1845). Arrested 1849 for membership in a Fourierist circle, he was sentenced to death; while he was waiting for death, his sentence was commuted to hard labor in Siberia. The shock of the experience and the hardship of Siberian life (described in *The House of the Dead,* 1862) aggravated his epilepsy and caused him to turn to religion. He returned to St. Petersburg 1859. His chronic financial difficulties were increased by his passion for gambling. His novels are characterized by deep psychological insight; compassion for all men, even the vilest of whom he thought capable of redemption; and morbid preoccupation with guilt and crime. His greatest novels are *Crime and Punishment* (1866), *The Idiot* (1869), *The Possessed* (1872), *The Brothers Karamazov* (1879–80). *Notes from the Underground* (1864) and other short novels are equally powerful. All his major works are translated by Constance Garnett and others.

Dothan (dō′thăn), ancient city, central Palestine. Near there Joseph was sold into slavery, Syrians were blinded at Elisha's prayer. Gen. 37.17; 2 Kings 6.13. Dothaim: Judith 4.6; 7.3,18; 8.3.

Dothan (dō′thŭn), city (pop. 21,584), extreme SE Ala., near Chattahoochee R. and Fla. line. Farm trade center; processes livestock, cotton, peanuts.

Douai (dōōā′), town (pop. 35,509), Nord dept., N France, in Flanders. Coal mining; machinery. Here Philip II of Spain estab. college (R.C.) where Douay Bible was prepared. Taken by Louis XIV 1667; rebuilt 18th cent. Despite heavy damage in both World Wars, most old buildings still stand.

Douaumont (dōō-ōmō′), fort on VERDUN battlefield, NE France. Lost and retaken by French 1916. Graves of 10,000 unidentified soldiers are near by.

double bass: see VIOLIN.

Doubleday, Abner, 1819–93, alleged originator of BASEBALL, a Union general in Civil War. Said to have created game 1839 at Cooperstown, N.Y.

doublet, in W Europe until late 17th cent., a close-fitting, usually sleeveless upper garment for men. Doublet of defense was body armor.

Doubs (dōō), department (2,031 sq. mi.; pop. 298,255), E France, in Franche-Comté; cap. Besançon. The **Doubs** river, 267 mi. long, rises in the French Jura, flows NE, makes loop into Switzerland, then continues SW to join Saône near Chalon, c.60 mi. W of its source.

Doughty, Charles Montagu (dō′tē, dou′tē), 1843–1926, English traveler, author of *Travels in Arabia Deserta* (1888).

Doughty, Thomas (dou′tē), 1793–1856, American painter of the Hudson River school.

Douglas, Scottish noble family, divided into two branches. **William de Douglas, lord of Douglas,** d. 1298, was first to take title. Joined William Wallace revolt 1297, was captured, and died in Tower of London. His son, **Sir James de Douglas, lord of Douglas,** 1286?–1330, was called Black Douglas or Douglas the Good. Deprived of his estates by Edward I, became terror of border. Joined Robert I, fought at Bannockburn, and was a regent of Scotland. After death of Robert I, started for Palestine to bury king's heart but was killed in Spain. His nephew, **William Douglas, 1st earl of Douglas and Mar,** 1327?–1384, added lands to family holdings. His son, **James Douglas, 2d earl of Douglas and Mar,** 1358?–1388, married daughter of Robert II. Killed at battle of Otterburn. His uncle, **Archibald Douglas, 3rd earl of Douglas,** 1328?–1400?, was illegitimate son of Sir James de Douglas. Acquired large estates. At his death, family most powerful in Scotland. His son, **Archibald Douglas, 4th earl of Douglas,** 1369?–

1424, married daughter of Robert III 1390. Fought against Henry IV and Henry V. Tried and acquitted for murder of heir to Scottish throne. Joined the French and was killed at Verneuil. His son, **Archibald Douglas, 5th earl of Douglas**, 1391?–1439, was twice imprisoned by James I who feared his power. After James's death (1437) he was most powerful man in Scotland. His son, **William Douglas, 6th earl of Douglas**, 1423?–1440, was beheaded (together with his brother) by advisers of James II and family power was temporarily broken. Succeeded by his great-uncle, **James Douglas, 7th earl of Douglas**, 1371?–1443. His son, **William Douglas, 8th earl of Douglas**, 1425?–1452, reunited family estates by marrying his cousin. His brother, **James Douglas, 9th earl of Douglas**, 1426–88, rebelled twice (1452, 1455) against James II, was defeated, and fled to England. Captured 1483, spent rest of his life in prison. With him, power of older or "Black" Douglas branch ended. Younger or "Red" Douglas branch descended from illegitimate son of William Douglas, 1st earl of Douglas and Mar, and Margaret Stuart, countess of Angus. **Archibald Douglas, 5th earl of Angus**, 1449?–1514, was chancellor of Scotland 1493–98. In revolt against James III 1487–88, earned nickname of Bell-the-Cat by capture of king's favorite. Father of Gawin DOUGLAS. His grandson, **Archibald Douglas, 6th earl of Angus**, 1489?–1557, married Margaret Tudor, sister of Henry VIII and widow of James IV, and attempted to gain control of her son, James V. She divorced him 1528 and he fled to England. Returned 1542 and was restored to power. His grandnephew, **Archibald Douglas, 8th earl of Angus**, 1555–88, supported his uncle, the earl of MORTON, and opposed James Stuart, earl of Arran.

Douglas, Clifford Hugh, 1879–1952, English social economist, author of theory of SOCIAL CREDIT.

Douglas, David, 1798–1834, Scottish botanist, one of the first travelers in Oregon country and Calif. The Douglas fir (or spruce) is named for him.

Douglas, Gawin (gä′wĭn) or **Gavin** (găv′ĭn), 1474?–1522, Scottish poet and churchman. Member of the powerful DOUGLAS family, he was involved in political disputes after 1515. A major poet of the Chaucerian tradition, his works include *The Palace of Honour*, *King Hart*, and a translation of the *Aeneid* (one of first classical translations into English).

Douglas, George, pseud. of George Douglas Brown, 1869–1902, Scottish novelist, author of *The House with the Green Shutters* (1901).

Douglas, James, 2d duke of Queensberry: see QUEENSBERRY, JAMES DOUGLAS, 2D DUKE OF.

Douglas, James, 2d earl of Douglas and Mar: see DOUGLAS, family.

Douglas, James, earls of Douglas: see DOUGLAS, family.

Douglas, James (d. 1581): see MORTON, JAMES DOUGLAS, 4TH EARL OF.

Douglas, Sir James, 1803–77, Canadian fur trader and colonial governor, b. Scotland. In 1846 he succeeded to command of Hudson's Bay Co. territory W of the Rockies. Appointed governor of Vancouver Isl. (1851) and also became governor of new colony of British Columbia in 1858. Retired 1864.

Douglas, Sir James de Douglas, lord of: see DOUGLAS, family.

Douglas, (George) Norman, 1868–1952, English writer, best known for novel *South Wind* (1917) and sketches in *Old Calabria* (1915).

Douglas, Paul H(oward), 1892–, American economist and U.S. Senator (1948–) from Ill., b. Salem, Mass.; an authority on wages and social security.

Douglas, Stephen A(rnold), 1813–61, American statesman. U.S. Representative from Ill. (1843–47); U.S. Senator (1847–61). Responsible for SQUATTER SOVEREIGNTY aspects of COMPROMISE OF 1850 and KANSAS-NEBRASKA BILL; championed popular sovereignty as way of settling North-South controversy peacefully. Lincoln-Douglas debates featured his 1858 campaign for reelection; at Freeport, on Aug. 27, 1858, he asserted that people of a territory could exclude slavery. Freeport doctrine made him anathema to Southern Democrats. Democratic national convention of 1860 nominated him for President, but Southern delegates broke away. In election he won only 12 electoral votes, but stood second in popular votes. Douglas, it is now held, was one of few men in his era with truly broad national vision.

Douglas, William: see DOUGLAS, family.

Douglas, William O(rville), 1898–, Associate Justice of U.S. Supreme Court (1939–).

Douglas. 1 City (pop. 9,442), extreme SE Ariz., at Mexican line. Copper-smelting and ranching center, resort. **2** City (pop. 7,428), S central Ga., NW of Waycross. Tobacco market and processing center.

Douglas and Mar, earls of: see DOUGLAS, family.

Douglas fir or **Douglas spruce**, huge coniferous evergreen (*Pseudotsuga taxifolia*) of W North America. Named for David Douglas, it is not a true fir or spruce. Wood valued for construction.

Douglass, Frederick, c.1817–1895, American abolitionist, son of slave mother. Escaping in 1838, he took surname from Scott's *The Lady of the Lake*. At Rochester, N.Y., estab. and edited *North Star* for 17 years in abolitionist cause.

Douglas spruce: see DOUGLAS FIR.

Douhet, Giulio (jōō′lyō dōōā′), 1869–1930, Italian military theorist, a general. Held that command of air could win a war despite land and sea power.

Doukhobors: see DUKHOBORS.

Doulton ware, English pottery produced at Lambeth after 1815, first by John Doulton, then by his descendants. Includes brown stoneware and faïence. Now known as Royal Doulton.

Doumer, Paul (pōl′ dōōmâr′), 1857–1932, president of France (1931–32).

Doumergue, Gaston (gästō′ dōōmĕrg′), 1863–1937, president of France (1924–31). Headed a rightist coalition cabinet in Feb.–Nov. 1934.

Doura: see DURA.

Douro (dō′rōō) or **Duero** (dōōā′rō), river, c.475 mi. long, Spain and Portugal; Douro is Port., Duero Span. name. Rises in N central Spain, flows generally W into Atlantic beyond Oporto. Hydroelectric plants.

Dove (dŭv), river rising in Derbyshire, England, and forming much of Derbyshire-Staffordshire border. Its water-course was a haunt of Izaak Walton. Glen of Dovedale celebrated by artists and poets.

dove, name for certain smaller birds of pigeon family; name often used synonymously with pigeon. European rock dove is probably ancestor of domesticated pigeons. Mourning dove, native to North America, is common.

Dover, municipal borough (pop. 35,217), on a bay beneath chalk cliffs, Kent, England. Chief of CINQUE PORTS, called "key to England." Easternmost English port (21 mi. from France), it was important naval base World War I and constant target of German long-range guns World War II. Subterranean caves and tunnels in the cliffs, once used by smugglers, were shelters 1940–44. Important travel and shipping port to the Continent. Noteworthy are Shakespeare Cliff and Dover Castle.

Dover. 1 City (pop. 6,223), state cap., central Del. on St. Jones R. near Silver L. and S of Smyrna; settled 1683. Shipping and canning center of farm and fruit region. Statehouse (partly built 1722) has been capitol since 1777. **2** City (pop. 15,874), SE N.H., near Piscataqua R. NW of Portsmouth; settled 1623, held 1633–41 by Lord Saye and Sele. Mfg. of leather goods, machinery, and wood products. Woodman Inst. has historical and natural science collections. **3** Town (pop. 11,174), N N.J., NW of Morristown; settled 1722. Former iron center and port on old Morris Canal. Mfg. of metal products, machinery, and rock wool. Picatinny Arsenal and U.S. naval rocket experiment station are near. **4** City (pop. 9,852), E Ohio, on Tuscarawas R. and SSW of Canton. Mfg. of steel, electric light bulbs, clay products, and chemicals.

Dover, Strait of, separates England from France and connects English Channel with North Sea. Width 21 mi. between Dover and Cape Gris-Nez near Calais. Called Pas de Calais by French.

Dovrefjell (dô′vrŭfyĕl), rough plateau of central Norway, culminating in Snohetta (Nor. Snøhetta; 7,498 ft. high) and dividing country in two.

Dow, Lorenzo, 1777–1834, American evangelist, who introduced camp meetings into Ireland and England.

Dowagiac (dōwô′jăk), city (pop. 6,542), SW Mich., SW of Kalamazoo, in farm and lake region. Mfg. of stoves, furnaces, and heaters.

Dowie, John Alexander (dou′ē), 1847–1907, founder of Christian Catholic Apostolic Church in Zion, b. Scotland. In Australia became interested in faith healing. Came to U.S. (1888); founded church in Chicago (1896) and community in Zion, Ill. (1901). Deposed as leader in 1905.

Down, maritime county (952 sq. mi.; pop. 241,-105, excluding Belfast, which is partly within county), Ulster prov., N. Ireland; co. town Downpatrick. Coastline indented by Strangford Lough and Dundrum Bay; beautiful Mourne Mts. rise in south. Area extensively

cultivated (oats, potatoes, wheat, and flax). There are many linen mfg. towns.

Downers Grove, village (pop. 11,886), NE Ill., just W of Chicago; settled 1832. Metal products.

Downing, Andrew Jackson, 1815–52, American horticulturist, rural architect, and landscape gardener, author of many books on gardening and landscaping. He planned the grounds of the Capitol, the White House, and the Smithsonian Institution in Washington, D.C.

Downing, Major Jack: see SMITH, SEBA.

Downing College: see CAMBRIDGE UNIVERSITY.

Downing Street, London. British colonial and foreign offices located here. No. 10 residence of first lord of Treasury, usually prime minister. Figurative use of term means government in power.

Downpatrick (dounpă′trĭk), urban district (pop. 3,878), co. seat of Co. Down, N Ireland. Has long been a religious center and place of pilgrimage as tomb of Ireland's saints—Patrick, Colomba, and Bridget of Kildare. Holy wells of Struell near by.

Downs, the, low chalk hills, SE England. N. Downs range in Surrey and Kent separated by the WEALD from S. Downs in Sussex. Excellent sheep pasturage.

dowry, property a woman brings to her husband at marriage. Institution apparently originated in marriage gift made by family of the bride to the groom, estab. as custom in many peoples from earliest days. Known to Greece, Rome, India, medieval Europe, and modern civil-law countries. Generally on divorce the husband must return dowry.

Dowson, Ernest (Christopher) (dou′–), 1867–1900, English lyric poet, one of the best-known poets of the decadents. Perhaps most familiar of his delicate, highly musical poems is that with the refrain "I have been faithful to thee, Cynara! in my fashion." A Roman Catholic, he also wrote religious poetry. His brief, wretched life was ended by tuberculosis.

doxology, sacred hymn of praise. Best-known doxologies of Christian church are "Gloria in Excelsis," "Gloria Patri," and Thomas Ken's "Praise God from Whom All Blessings Flow," sung to the tune *Old Hundred* from the Genevan Psalter.

Doyle, Sir A(rthur) Conan, 1859–1930, English author, creator of Sherlock Holmes, most celebrated of all fictional detectives. Among detective stories are *A Study in Scarlet* (1887), *The Sign of the Four* (1890), *The Memoirs of Sherlock Holmes* (1894), *The Hound of the Baskervilles* (1902), *The Return of Sherlock Holmes* (1905). Doyle in later life was a spiritualist.

Doylestown, borough (pop. 5,262), SE Pa., N of Philadelphia. Trade center in agr. area. Seat of Natl. Farm School.

Drachenfels (drä′khŭnfĕls), cliff, 1053 ft. high, on the Rhine, S of Bonn, W Germany. Legendary scene of Siegfried's triumph over the dragon. Ruins of Drachenburg castle, on top of cliff, date from 12th cent. Popular excursion point.

Draco or **Dracon,** fl. 621 B.C., Athenian lawgiver, at least semilegendary. Said to have assigned death penalty for many offences; hence Draconian means harsh.

Dracut (drā'kŭt), textile town (pop. 8,666), NE Mass., on Merrimack R. and N of Lowell.

draft riots, in Civil War. Nation-wide opposition to Union conscription act of March 3, 1863, broke into bloody riots in New York city (July 13–16, 1863). Huge mob overpowered police and militia, seized Second Ave. armory, set fires, and assaulted abolitionists and Negroes. Damage over $1,500,000, with est. 1,000 casualties.

Draga, queen of Serbia: see ALEXANDER, king of Serbia.

Drago, Luis María (lōōes' märē'ä drä'gō), 1859–1921, Argentine statesman, jurist, and writer on international law. His protest against coercion of Venezuela by Great Britain, Germany, and Italy (1902) became known as the **Drago Doctrine** (a corollary to Monroe Doctrine). It set forth principle that no public debt should be collected from sovereign American state by armed force or through occupation of American territory by foreign power. Modified form was approved at Hague Conference (1907).

dragon, in mythology, composite winged reptilic beast, generally said to have lion's claws, eagle's wings, and serpent's tail. The conception, dating from Babylonian times, is widespread, and is sometimes used as national symbol. Story of slaying of a dragon by a hero appears frequently in literature.

dragonfly, large insect of order Odonata, which includes also the damsel fly. Found in most parts of world, they are numerous in South America and Japan. Eggs are laid in or near water, and nymphs (the young) are aquatic. Metamorphosis is incomplete. Adults have four membranous wings; some surpass swallow in flying speed and agility. They eat larvae and adult insects. See *ill.,* p. 601.

dragon's blood, red resin obtained from certain plants, including *Dracaena draco.* Used in photoengraving.

drainage, in mining, accomplished by causing surface or subterranean water to flow by gravity into reservoirs or sumps dug at lowest level, whence it is usually pumped out.

drainage basin: see CATCHMENT AREA.

Drake, Daniel, 1785–1852, American physician, author of a study on relation of disease to geography in valley of Mississippi R.

Drake, Edwin Laurentine, 1819–80, American oilwell driller. He sank the first U.S. well to strike oil, Aug. 27, 1859.

Drake, Sir Francis, 1540?–1596, English navigator, admiral, first Englishman to circumnavigate world (1577–80). From 1572 commanded marauding expeditions against Spanish, taking rich booty from treasure ships and Spanish possessions in the Americas for treasury of Queen Elizabeth, who finally knighted him and openly recognized his exploits. Commanded sea forces against rebellious Ireland; destroyed a Spanish fleet at Cádiz (1587) and participated in destruction of the Armada (1588). Died of dysentery during last and unsuccessful expedition against Spanish West Indies.

Drake, Joseph Rodman, 1795–1820, American poet, satirist, physician, author of "The Culprit Fay" and light satirical verse (with Fitz-Greene HALLECK).

Drakensberg (drä'kŭnzbûrg), mountain range, South Africa. Extends c.700 mi., rises to 11,425 ft. at Thabantshonyana.

Drake University, at Des Moines, Iowa; coed.; chartered, opened 1881 by Disciples of Christ; named for F. M. Drake. Includes College of the Bible.

Drammen (drä'mŭn), city (pop. 26,994), SE Norway, on Drammen R. and at head of Drammen Fjord. Wood products. **Drammen** river, c.25 mi. long, SE Norway, empties into Drammen Fjord, a branch of Oslo Fjord. Lumber mills; hydroelectric plants.

Draper, John William, 1811–82, American scientist, philosopher, and historian, b. England. He helped organize medical school of New York Univ., taught chemistry and physiology there, and became its president 1850. Conducted important research on radiant energy. His works include *Human Physiology* (1856), containing the first published microphotographs; *History of the Intellectual Development of Europe* (1863). His son **Henry Draper,** 1837–82, taught physiology at New York Univ. (1870–82) and was a pioneer in astronomical photography and spectroscopy.

draughts: see CHECKERS.

Drava or **Drave** (both: drä'vû), Ger. *Drau,* river, c.450 mi. long, central Europe; tributary of the Danube. Rises in Italian Alps; flows E through Carinthia (Austria), then SE, forming part of Hungarian-Yugoslav border, past Villach, Maribor, and Osijek.

Dravidian (drŭvĭ'dēŭn), name of largest group of inhabitants of India before coming of Aryans. Also name of group in S India today presumably descended from prehistoric Dravidians.

Dravidian languages, family of languages of S India; see LANGUAGE (table). Attempts have been made to connect them with other groups.

drawbridge, movable bridge, usually over stream or river in situation requiring maintenance of waterborne traffic, but prohibiting erection of fixed bridge high enough to allow passage under it. In fortresses surrounded by ditch or moat, it was part of defense system. Common types include the lifting, bascule, and swing bridges. See *ill.,* p. 167.

Drayton, Michael, 1563–1631, English poet. Sonnet beginning "Since there's no help, come let us kiss and part" most famous in *Ideas Mirrour* (1594, 1619) and other volumes. Notable longer poems, panoramic *Poly-Olbion* (1612–22) and charming *Nymphidia* (1627).

dream, mental activity of disputed duration, associated with sleep and commonly made up of visual images. Like hallucinations, dreams are not usually aroused by sense impressions; somatic disturbances (e.g., toothache, indigestion) and external stimuli occasionally affect form but not content. Dream interpretation vigorous among ancient, primitive, and superstitious peoples. Freud, an early exponent of scientific dream study, distinguished manifest content (the experienced dream-image) from latent content (meaning). Dream-images are symbols —universal, cultural, or personal (translatable through free association). Symbolism protects dreamer from recognition of attempted fulfillment of impulses that consciousness forbids. Freud believed dreams insure sleep by draining force of emotional disturbances that would waken sleeper. Jung considered them testing ground for possible future steps. Adler emphasized compensatory function.

Drebbel, Cornelis Jacobszoon (kôrnā'lis yä'-kôp-sōn drě'bŭl), 1572–1634, Dutch inventor, physicist, and mechanician who settled in England. His many inventions include "perpetual motion" machine and a diving boat (first navigable submarine).

dredging, process of underwater excavation to clear or deepen channels and entrances of harbors, docks, rivers, and canals. Modern dredging equipment divisible into four main classes. The **grab dredge,** for small operations, consists of grab buckets operated by cranes. Bucket is similar to clamshell bucket used ashore, as is the **dipper dredge** (known as boom and dipper assembly) used extensively in canal construction. **Ladder-bucket dredge,** operated usually from self-propelling vessel built with well in center open to water, consists of endless succession of buckets operating through the well and discharging, as they rise, into a chute projecting to hopper barge, or to hopper in dredge itself. **Suction dredge** used principally to remove sand and mud through flexible pipe extended to bottom, by means of centrifugal pump.

Dred Scott Case, argued before U.S. Supreme Court in 1856–57. Brought as a test case; concerned status of Dred Scott, a Negro who had lived with his master for several years in free territory. Chief Justice R. B. Taney delivered court's opinion that a Negro "whose ancestors . . . were sold as slaves" was not entitled to rights of a Federal citizen and had no standing in court, and that Missouri Compromise was unconstitutional. John McLean and B. R. Curtis dissented. Verdict further enflamed North-South controversy. Decision later nullified by FOURTEENTH AMENDMENT.

Dreiser, Theodore (drī'sùr), 1871–1945, American author. His first novel (*Sister Carrie,* 1900) was suppressed by the publisher, but his later novels (including *Jennie Gerhardt,* 1911; *The Titan,* 1914; *An American Tragedy,* 2 vols., 1925) won acclaim for their power despite their ponderous style.

Drenthe (drěn'tŭ), province (1,011 sq. mi.; pop. 271,909), NE Netherlands, bordering on Germany; cap. Assen. Stock raising, dairy farming.

Dresden (drěz'dŭn), city (pop. 467,966; 1939 pop. 630,216), cap. of Saxony, E Germany, on the Elbe. Mfg. center (machine tools, optical instruments, glass, chemicals) and large inland port. Originally a Slavic settlement; settled by Germans 13th cent.; residence of electors (later kings) of Saxony 1547–1918. In late 17th and 18th cent. it became a center of the arts, outstanding for baroque and rococo architecture. City was about three quarters destroyed in World War II. Former landmarks include Zwinger palace and museum; Hofkirche [court chapel]; cathedral. Many art treasures, in-

cluding Raphael's *Sistine Madonna,* were removed to Russia. "Dresden china," despite name, was made in Meissen. Napoleon defeated allies near Dresden in 1813. For Treaty of Dresden (1745), see AUSTRIAN SUCCESSION, WAR OF THE.

Drew, Daniel, 1797–1879, American capitalist. Bold and scheming, he helped manipulate Erie RR stock (1866–68) to defeat attempt of Cornelius Vanderbilt to gain control. Drew was bankrupt by 1876.

Drew, Louisa Lane, 1820–97, American actress, b. London. From girlhood appeared in support of era's leading actors until she married (1850) John Drew (1827–62). They costarred at his Arch St. Theater, Philadelphia. On his death she assumed its management. Her children were Sidney, Georgiana (see BARRYMORE), and **John Drew,** 1853–1927, who joined the Daly company in 1875. Acted in Daly's Shaksperian productions. Under Charles Frohman did modern comedies with Maude Adams.

Drewrys Bluff (drōō'rēz), height on S bank of James R., E central Va., S of Richmond, scene of two battles in Civil War. Union gunboats repulsed here (May 15, 1862). B. F. Butler defeated by inferior Confederate force under Beauregard (May 16, 1864). Also called Drewry Bluff, Drury's Bluff.

Drew University: see MADISON, N.J.

Drexel Institute of Technology: see PHILADELPHIA, Pa.

Dreyer, John Louis Emil (drī'ùr), 1852–1926, Danish astronomer in Great Britain, compiler of standard catalogue of nebulae and clusters (1888; supplements, 1895, 1908).

Dreyfus Affair (drā'fûs, drī'-), began 1894 with the discovery of a schedule (the famous *bordereau*) addressed to Maj. Schwartzkoppen, German military attaché in Paris, which listed secret French documents that the writer promised to furnish. A court martial convicted Capt. Alfred Dreyfus (1859–1935) of treason on the slim evidence that the handwriting on the *bordereau* was similar to his. Dreyfus never ceased to protest his innocence, but his being both a Jew and an Alsatian weighed heavily with his bigoted judges. He was sentenced to degradation and to life imprisonment on Devils Isl. (1894). The case flared up again in 1896, when Col. Georges PICQUART discovered evidence pointing to Maj. Ferdinand Walsin ESTERHAZY as the real author of the *bordereau*. Picquart was silenced by the authorities, but in 1897 Dreyfus's brother Mathieu independently made the same discovery and energetically pressed for a new trial. The case now became a major political issue, dividing all France into two violent partisan groups for 10 years. Royalists, militarists, and (with a few notable exceptions) Catholics made up the anti-Dreyfusard camp; republicans, socialists, and anti-clericalists professed faith in Dreyfus's innocence. The anti-Dreyfusards, by dint of patriotic forgeries and pious perjuries, prevailed at first; Esterhazy was acquitted by a court martial and Émile Zola was sentenced for his article "J'accuse" (1898), which had accused the authorities of framing Dreyfus. However, when Maj. Henry, who had forged evidence against

Dreyfus at the Esterhazy trial, committed suicide in 1898, revision of the Dreyfus case became imperative. The court of appeals ordered a new court martial, but surprisingly the military court at Rennes found Dreyfus guilty again (1899). Though Pres. Loubet pardoned him, agitation for complete exoneration continued until 1906, when the supreme court of appeals (a civil court) cleared Dreyfus, who was reinstated as a major. Publication of the Schwartzkoppen papers (1930) conclusively proved his innocence. The Dreyfus Affair discredited the monarchists and clericalists and hastened separation of Church and state in France.

drift, mixture of clay, sand, and boulders left by an ice sheet. Unstratified drift is also called boulder clay. Stratified drift was deposited by glacial streams.

Driftless Area, over 10,000 sq. mi. largely in SW Wis., but also in SE Minn., NE Iowa, NW Ill. Area, untouched by continental glacier which once covered surroundings, has no glacial drifts.

Drin (drēn), largest river of Albania, c.170 mi. long, formed by White and Black Drin, which rise in Yugoslavia and join in NE Albania. Flows W and S through deep gorges into Adriatic.

Drinkwater, John, 1882–1937, English writer, author of many plays (e.g., *Abraham Lincoln,* 1918; *Bird in Hand,* 1927), biographies, poetry.

Drogheda (drô'ùdù, droi'dù), urban district (pop. 15,715), Co. Louth, Ireland, on the Boyne. POYNINGS'S LAW enacted here in 1494. Town taken and inhabitants massacred by Cromwell 1649. Battle of the Boyne fought near here 1690.

Drogobych (drûgô'bĭch), Pol. *Drohobycz,* city (1931 pop. 32,622), W Ukraine, SW of Lvov; center of important petroleum and natural gas fields. Under Austria 1772–1918; ceded by Poland to USSR 1945.

Droitwich (droit'wĭch), municipal borough (pop. 6,453), Worcestershire, England, on Salwarpe R. Has canal to the Severn. Noted for its brine baths and salt trade.

Drôme (drōm), department (2,533 sq. mi.; pop. 268,233), SE France, in Dauphiné; cap. Valence.

Drontheim, Norway: see TRONDHEIM.

Droysen, Johann Gustav (yōhän' gŏŏs'täf droi'zùn), 1808–84, German historian. Known for *Geschichte der preussischen Politik* (14 vols., 1855–86) and biography of Yorck von Wartenburg (3 vols., 1851–52).

drug addiction, craving for drug resulting in need for increasing quantity to produce effect and in nervous disturbances when not under its influence. Chief habit-forming drugs are opium, cocaine, hashish, marijuana, alcohol, and nicotine.

drugs, substances used internally or externally for cure, alleviation, or prevention of disease. They include inorganic substances, alkaloids and other plant derivatives, and hormones, vaccines, serums, and other substances derived from animals. SULFA DRUGS and ANTIBIOTIC SUBSTANCES are valued in treating infections. Many countries list standards and tests in official PHARMACOPOEIA. U.S. legislation to safeguard users began 1906, was superseded by Federal Food, Drug, and Cosmetic Act of 1938; laws enforced by Food and Drug Administration.

druids, priests and medicine men of Celtic peoples, especially in Gaul and Great Britain. Practiced herbal medicine and ruled in ritualistic religion based on sun worship and belief in immortality of soul. They had a confederation which was politically powerful and fostered revolt against Rome. Druidic system finally yielded to Christianity. Many prehistoric ruins such as Stonehenge, once attributed to druids, appear to have other sources.

drum: see PERCUSSION INSTRUMENTS.

drumlin, smooth oval hill of glacial DRIFT, elongated in the direction of ice movement.

Drummond, Thomas, 1797–1840, Scottish engineer, inventor. He took part in trigonometrical survey of United Kingdom 1820; devised Drummond light (using incandescent properties of lime) to aid observations in murky weather.

Drummond (of Hawthornden), William, 1585–1649, Scottish poet. A friend of Ben Jonson, he wrote graceful sonnets, elegies, hymns (as in *Flowers of Sion,* 1623). His prose *Cypresse Grove* (1623) is on death.

Drummond, William Henry, 1854–1907, Canadian poet, b. Ireland. His verse portrays French Canadians, using habitants' own dialect of English.

Drummond, Lake: see DISMAL SWAMP.

Drummond Island: see MANITOULIN ISLANDS.

Drummond light: see DRUMMOND, THOMAS.

Drummondville, city (pop. 14,341), S Que., Canada, on St. Francis R. and ENE of Montreal. Rayon-milling center, with textile mfg. and printing.

Drumright, city (pop. 5,028), central Okla., WSW of Tulsa, in oil region. Oil refineries.

Drury College: see SPRINGFIELD, MO.

Drury Lane, London street and district; site of Drury Lane Theatre. Original 17th-cent. theater was a cockpit. Present theater designed by Benjamin Wyatt 1812.

Druses (drōō'zĭz), people of S Syria and Lebanon who inhabit hills of the Hauran, much of the Lebanon and the Anti-Lebanon. They believe in divinity of 11th-cent. Fatimite caliph, Hakim. Massacred Christians in 19th cent., fought against French control of Syria and Lebanon 1925–26.

Drusus (drōō'sús), Roman family. **Marcus Livius Drusus,** d. 109? B.C., was tribune of the people with C. GRACCHUS (122 B.C.) and led the senatorial attack on Gracchus, succeeding by dubious means. He was consul in 112 B.C. His son **Marcus Livius Drusus,** d. 91 B.C., also led the senatorial party and by generous sums of money and wholesale grant of citizenship he won the allegiance of the Italians. The senate turned against him and by withdrawing the citizenship laws provoked the SOCIAL WAR. A member of family by adoption was LIVIA DRUSILLA, mother of **Nero Claudius Drusus Germanicus** (Drusus Senior), 38 B.C.–9 B.C., who as stepson of Augustus got an army command early and fought against Rhaetians, Gauls, and Germans. His sons were Germanicus Caesar and Claudius I. The son of his brother Tiberius was **Drusus**

Caesar (Drusus Junior), d. A.D. 23, who served against the Germans, awoke the jealousy of Sejanus, and died, supposedly of poison, at the instance of Sejanus.

Dryburgh Abbey (drī′bûrû), Berwickshire, Scotland. Built 1150, now a beautiful ruin. Contains Sir Walter Scott's tomb.

dry cell: see CELL, in electricity.

Dryden, John, 1631–1700, English poet, dramatist, and critic. First came to notice with *Heroick Stanzas* (1659) commemorating Oliver Cromwell, but welcomed Charles II with *Astraea Redux* and rose to prominence in the Restoration. He was made poet laureate in 1668. He was converted to Catholicism and on the accession of William III lost the laureateship and court patronage but continued prominent. Among his long poems are *Annus Mirabilis* (1667), *Absalom and Achitophel* (first part 1681; second part, with Nahun Tate, 1682; on the plot in favor of Monmouth), *MacFlecknoe* (1682; a satirical attack on Thomas Shadwell), *Religio Laici* (1682; a defense of Protestantism), and *The Hind and the Panther* (1687; on his conversion to Catholicism). Two of his best-known shorter pieces are his "Ode to the Memory of Mrs. Anne Killigrew" and "Alexander's Feast." He was also a prolific writer of plays—comedies such as *Marriage-à-la-Mode* as well as tragedies, including *The Conquest of Granada, Aureng-Zebe,* and *All for Love* (his version of the Antony and Cleopatra story). His essays are much admired for their style, and he also wrote brilliant critical prefaces, prologues, and discourses; his *Essay of Dramatick Poesy* (1668) is notable. He also translated and adapted much Latin literature.

dry farming produces crops in low-rainfall areas, without irrigation. Aided by drought-resistant strains, deep soil, crop rotation, and fallowing.

dry ice, solid CARBON DIOXIDE, formed when liquefying pressure is removed and liquid is allowed to evaporate in a confined space. Some liquid becomes gas at once, drawing heat from remaining liquid, which "freezes" to solid.

drying oil, an oil (from either plants or animals), which oxidizes easily and forms resistant film when exposed to air. Used in paints, varnishes, etc.

dry rot, fungus disease that attacks seasoned timber, often causing it to collapse. Certain fungus diseases of fruits and vegetables are also called dry rot.

Dry Tortugas (tôrtōō′gùz), island group off S Fla., W of Key West. On Garden Key (sometimes called Shark Isl.) is Fort Jefferson Natl. Monument (see NATIONAL PARKS AND MONUMENTS, table), a Civil War prison.

Dual Alliance, 1879–82: see TRIPLE ALLIANCE AND TRIPLE ENTENTE.

dualism, any philosophical system that explains the universe in terms of two distinct and exclusive principles—e.g., form and matter, mind and matter, being and nonbeing. In religion, dualism usually means belief in an ultimate evil principle as well as an ultimate good principle. This appeared in striking form in Zoroastrianism, in Gnosticism, and in Manichaeism.

Dual Monarchy: see AUSTRO-HUNGARIAN MONARCHY.

Duane, James (dūān′), 1733–97, American Revolutionary statesman. Member of Continental Congress (1774–83). Helped draft Articles of Confederation.

Duane, William, 1760–1835, American journalist. Editor (1798–1822) of Philadelphia *Aurora,* leading Jeffersonian organ. Arrested under both Alien Act and Sedition Act; vindicated. His son, **William John Duane,** 1780–1865, was U.S. Secretary of Treasury (June–Oct., 1833). Replaced after refusing Pres. Jackson's request to transfer government deposits from Bank of the United States to state banks.

Duarte (dwär′tù), 1391–1438, king of Portugal (1431–1438). Called the "philosopher-king," he was better known for his learning than for his indecisive statesmanship. Brother of Henry the Navigator.

Duban, Jacques Félix (zhäk′ fäleks′ dübä′), 1797–1870, French architect, a leader of the Neo-Greek movement in France, 1830–50. Helped restore the color adornment of Sainte-Chapelle, Paris.

Du Barry, Jeanne Bécu, comtesse (zhän′ bäkü′ kōtĕs′ dü bärē′), 1743–93, last mistress of Louis XV. Of extremely vulgar background, she was notorious for her extravagance but did not seek political influence. Guillotined in Revolution.

Du Bartas, Guillaume de Salluste (gēyôm′ dù sälüst′ dü bärtäs′), 1544–90, French poet and Huguenot soldier. Wrote epic poem on creation (1578).

Dubawnt, river, SE Mackenzie dist. and W Keewatin dist., Northwest Territories, Canada. Rises NE of L. Athabaska and flows 580 mi. NE through Dubawnt L. to Thelon R. W. of Aberdeen L.

Du Bellay, Joachim (zhōäshē′ dü bĕlä′), 1522?–1560, French poet of the PLÉIADE. Wrote its manifesto, *La Deffence et illustration de la langue francoyse* (1549), and sonnet collections such as *Les Regrets* (1558), nostalgic poems of Rome.

Dubinsky, David (dōōbĭn′skē), 1892–, American labor leader, b. Poland. President after 1932 of International Ladies Garment Workers Union, he led it into the C.I.O. in 1936, but broke with C.I.O. in 1938 and later rejoined A.F. of L. He advocated political action; helped to found American Labor Party, Liberal Party, and Americans for Democratic Action.

Dublin, county (327 sq. mi.; pop. 636,193), Leinster prov., Ireland. City area, including Wicklow Mts. and Liffey R., dominated by Dublin. Rural area has farming, cattle, and fishing. Has several large suburban towns.

Dublin, Irish *Baile Átha Cliath* (bä′lē ä klē′), county borough (pop. 506,051), cap. of Ireland and co. seat of Dublin Co., on Dublin Bay at mouth of Liffey R. Harbor with shipyards and docks connected with interior by two canals. Chief industries brewing (Guinness), distilling, linen milling, and mfg. of chemicals, soap, textiles, carpets, lace, and machinery. Site of Univ. of Dublin (or Trinity Col. founded 1591) which has famous book of KELLS, Univ. Col. (R.C.), and Natl. Gallery of Art. Dublin Castle (c.1200) houses government offices. Leinster House seat of Irish Parliament. City became seat of English government and center of Pale 12th cent. Black Monday massacre of English residents occurred 1209. Cromwell landed here 1649 after city's surrender to parliamentarians. Dublin saw much bloodshed 19th and 20th cent.—Robert EMMET's insurrection 1803, FENIAN MOVEMENT uprising 1867, murder of Lord Cavendish 1882, and Easter Rebellion 1916. ABBEY THEATRE world famous, as are many Dublin literary figures (e.g., Swift, Yeats, and Joyce).

Dublin, city (10,232), central Ga., on Oconee R. and SE of Macon. Farm and timber market. Mfg. of cotton products, woolen textiles, and lumber.

Dubois, Guillaume (gēyōm′ dübwä′), 1656–1723, French cardinal, chief adviser (1715–23) to the regent, Philippe d'Orléans. Astute diplomat.

du Bois, Guy Pène (dü bwä′), 1884–, American painter and art critic, b. Brooklyn, N.Y.

Du Bois, W(illiam) E(dward) B(urghardt) (dübois′), 1868–, American Negro author, editor of *Crisis.*

Du Bois (dōō′bois), city (pop. 11,497), central Pa., NE of Pittsburgh; settled 1812. Has railroad shops, coal mining, and metal and textile plants.

Du Bois-Reymond, Emil (ā′mēl dü bwä′-rämō′), 1818–96, German physiologist, authority on muscle and nerve action and accompanying electrical changes.

Dubos, René Jules (rŭnā′ zhül dübō′), 1901–, American bacteriologist, b. France. He isolated gramicidin from soil bacteria.

Dubrovnik (dōō′brôvnĭk), Ital. *Ragusa,* city (pop. 16,060), Croatia, NW Yugoslavia; Adriatic port and resort. Founded by Greek refugees c.7th cent. A.D., it became a powerful, virtually independent merchant republic (under Venetian rule 13th–14th cent.; later tributary to Turkey). Seized by French (1806), it was awarded to Austria at Congress of Vienna (1815). A medieval center of Serbo-Croatian culture, city retains much medieval architecture, including city walls.

Dubuque, Julien (dübūk′), 1762–1810, pioneer settler of Iowa, b. Quebec.

Dubuque (dübūk′), city (pop. 49,671), NE Iowa, on bluffs above the Mississippi; organized 1837 and named for Julien Dubuque. Rail, trade, and industrial center and river port for agr. area, it has railroad shops and shipyards and mfg. of food, metal, and wood products. Seat of Univ. of Dubuque, Clarke Col., and Loras Col. (R.C.; mainly for men; opened as pioneer theological seminary 1839, chartered as college 1894). Grave of Dubuque near by.

Du Cange, Charles du Fresne, sieur (shärl′ dü frēn′ syûr dü käzh′), 1610–88, French medieval scholar, compiler of *Glossarium mediae et infimae Latinitatis,* greatest collection ever made of forms of early medieval Latin and of oldest Romance.

Ducas (dū′kùs), Greek family of Constantinople. Four members were Byzantine emperors—Michael VII, ALEXIUS V, John III, and Constantine I.

Duccio (di Buoninsegna) (dōōt′chēō dē bwōnēnsā′nyä), fl. 1278–1319, Italian painter,

founder of Sienese school. Only authenticated work is double altar in Siena cathedral. Rucellai Madonna (in Santa Maria Novella, Florence) is attributed to him.

Du Cerceau: see ANDROUET.

Du Chaillu, Paul (Belloni) (dü shāyü′), 1831?–1903, French-American explorer in Africa, b. probably in Paris. Backed by Philadelphia Acad. of Natural Sciences, explored Gabun country in Africa (1855–59). Published account upsetting previous ideas of region's geography. Second expedition (1863–65) visited unknown tribes, verified reports of a Pygmy race.

Duchamp, Marcel (märsĕl′ düshā′), 1887–, French painter. Famous work is *Nude Descending a Staircase,* painting depicting continuous action with series of overlapping figures. Was a leader of the Dadaists.

Duchesne, Père: see HÉBERT, JACQUES RENÉ.

duck, waterfowl smaller than related goose and swan. Accurately, duck refers to female and drake to male. Usually divided into three groups: river or fresh-water ducks (mallard, wood duck, black duck, teal), sea ducks (canvasback, scoter, eider, redhead), and mergansers or fish-eating ducks. Domestic meat producers are Pekin or Peking, Aylesbury, and Rouen ducks, all descendants of mallard duck. See *ill.,* p. 135.

Duck Lake, central Sask., Canada, SW of Prince Albert. Saw first encounter of Riel's Rebellion, 1885.

Ducommun, Élie (ālē′ dükômü′), 1883–1906, Swiss journalist and pacifist. Organized Internatl. Peace Bureau at Berne (1891). Shared 1902 Nobel Peace Prize with C. A. Gobat.

ductless gland: see GLAND.

Duddell, William Du Bois (dŭdĕl′), 1872–1917, English consulting electrical engineer. His research on resistance of electric arc led to Poulsen arc.

Du Deffand, Marie de Vichy-Chamrond, marquise (märē′ dù vūohō′ shārō′ märkē′ dü dēfä′), 1697–1780, French woman of letters. Her salon was frequented by the leaders of the Enlightenment. Mme du Deffand's later years were made tragic by blindness and by her attachment to Horace Walpole, one of the chief recipients of her brilliant correspondence.

Dudley, John: see NORTHUMBERLAND, JOHN DUDLEY, DUKE OF.

Dudley, Joseph, 1647–1720, colonial governor of Mass. (1702–15). Unpopular because of earlier connection with rule of Sir Edmund Andros.

Dudley, Plimmon Henry, 1843–1924, American civil and metallurgical engineer, inventor of instruments for testing and ways of improving railroad beds.

Dudley, Robert: see LEICESTER, ROBERT DUDLEY, EARL OF.

Dudley, town (pop. 5,261), S central Mass., near Conn. line SW of Worcester. Mfg. of textiles.

duel, prearranged armed fight between two persons to settle a point of honor. Presumably arose from wager of battle (form of trial in which formal fight between accuser and accused settled the case). Duels popular in 16th-cent. France, later in England. Student duels prominent in 19th-cent. German universities, revived by Nazis. In U.S. most famous duel was that in which Aaron Burr killed Alexander Hamilton. Andrew Jackson was also known as a duelist. Dueling now illegal in all Western countries.

due process of law: see FOURTEENTH AMENDMENT.

Duer, William (dū'ûr), 1747–99, American Revolutionary patriot and capitalist, b. England. One of largest contractors supplying army during Revolution. Became Assistant Secretary of Treasury in 1789; sued by government for irregularities in his work. Imprisoned for debt. His son, **William Alexander Duer,** 1780–1858, American jurist and educator, was president of Columbia Col. (1829–42). There he estab. scientific courses not requiring Latin and increased instruction in modern languages.

Duero, river: see DOURO.

Dufay, Guillaume (gēyŏm' düfä'), c.1400–1474, leading composer of the Burgundian (sometimes called Netherlands) school. His style united Gothic, Italian, and English elements. He wrote three-part vocal chansons, Masses, songs with instrumental accompaniment, and motets.

Dufour, Guillaume Henri (gēyŏm' ärē' düfōōr'), 1787–1875, Swiss general. Led federal forces to victory over SONDERBUND (1847). Wrote military treatises. Helped estab. International Red Cross (1864).

Dufourspitze: see ROSA, MONTE.

Dufy, Raoul (räōōl' düfē'), 1877–1953, French painter and illustrator, with decorative, calligraphic style and subtle use of brilliant color.

Du Gard, Roger Martin: see MARTIN DU GARD.

Dugdale, Richard Louis (dŭg'dāl), 1841–83, American social investigator, author of a study on criminality in the "Jukes" family.

dugong (dōō'gŏng), herbivorous aquatic mammal (*Dugong* or *Halicore*) of Red Sea, Indian Ocean, and Australian waters. Like the manatee of same order (Sirenia) it is called sea cow. Brownish or grayish, 7–9½ ft. long, it has flexible front flippers and a two-lobed, flat tail. Hunted for hide, tusks, oil, and palatable flesh, it is now scarce.

Duguay-Trouin, René (rŭnā' dügā'-trōōē'), 1673–1736, French admiral. Enlisted as privateer 1689. By 1709 he had captured 300 merchantmen, 20 warships. Took Rio de Janeiro 1711.

Du Guesclin, Bertrand (dügĕs'klĭn, bĕrträ' dü gĕklē'), c.1320–1380, constable of France (1370–80), one of most popular heroes of France, particularly in his native Brittany. Most notable achievement was his reconquest of English-held France (1370–74; see HUNDRED YEARS WAR).

Duhamel, Georges (zhôrzh' düämĕl'), 1884–, French author. Best known for novel, *Cycle de Salavin* (1920–32; Eng. tr., 1936), whose "hero," Salavin, is unable to adjust himself to society.

Duisburg (düs'bŏŏrk), city (pop. 408,877), North Rhine-Westphalia, NW Germany, at junction of Ruhr and Rhine rivers. Industrial center of RUHR dist. (steel, machinery, textiles) and large inland port. Armaments industry drew World War II air raids which destroyed three quarters of the city.

Dukas, Paul (dükä'), 1865–1935, French composer of symphonic poem *The Sorcerer's Apprentice* (1897) and opera *Ariane et Barbe-Bleue* (1907).

Duke, James Buchanan, 1856–1925, American processor of tobacco products and benefactor of Duke Univ.

Duke University, at Durham, N.C.; for men and women; opened 1838, chartered 1841 by Friends and Methodists as Union Col. Reorganized as Normal Col. (1852) and again as Trinity Col. (1859; Methodist); moved to Durham 1892. Renamed 1924 for benefactor J. B. Duke. Has two undergraduate colleges, Trinity and Woman's. Tobacco culture and medical research are noted.

Dukhobors or **Doukhobors** (both: dōō'kŭbôrz) [Rus.,= spirit wrestlers], religious sect that arose among Russian peasants in 17th cent.; now more properly Christians of the Universal Brotherhood. They believe in absolute equality of men and resist all authority, civil or ecclesiastic. This attitude brought persecution in Russia. Alexander I allowed them to settle on the Sea of Azov, but later resistance to military conscription caused their removal to a barren section now in Georgian SSR. This they brought to blossom, but in 1887 military conscription again reached them. In the 1890s with the help of Leo Tolstoy and of the Quakers most of them moved to Saskatchewan, Canada. Again they created a thriving community—under the leadership of Peter Veregin after he was allowed to leave Siberia and, after his death, under his son, another Peter Veregin. Trouble with their neighbors and the government led to spectacular demonstrations, notably the "nudist strikes." A small group of more ascetic Dukhobors split from the main body as the Sons of Freedom. Some Dukhobors presumably remain in Russia; a few are in the Paraguayan Chaco.

dulcimer (dŭl'sŭmûr), stringed musical instrument. Consists of wooden box strung with strings which are struck with mallets instead of being plucked. Oriental in origin; appeared in Europe in Middle Ages.

Du Lhut, Daniel Greysolon, sieur: see DULUTH.

Dulles, John Foster (dŭl'lŭs), 1888–, U.S. delegate to the United Nations (1945–48, 1950); grandson of John Watson Foster. Chosen (1952) by Eisenhower to be Secretary of State.

Dulong, Pierre Louis (pyĕr' lwē' dülō'), 1785–1838, French physicist and chemist. Dulong and Petit's law: specific heats of elements are inversely proportional to their atomic weights; specific heat is constant for all solid elements.

Duluth or **Du Lhut, Daniel Greysolon, sieur** (Fr. dülüt'), 1636–1710, French explorer in Canada. He won the L. Superior and upper Mississippi region for France.

Duluth (dŭlōōth'), city (pop. 104,511), NE Minn., at W end (and ahead of navigation) of L. Superior; harbor shared with Superior, Wis. Site visited in 17th cent. by explorers, including sieur Duluth; permanently settled after 1850. Grew as trade and shipping center for lumber area, became one of world's chief ore shipping points after discovery in 1890s of Mesabi and Vermilion iron ranges. Now commercial and industrial center of N Minn. and entrance to resort area, it has foundries, shipyards, flour and lumber mills, canneries, creameries, and mfg. of farm and telephone equipment, metal and wood products, and clothing. Dock facilities for handling ore, grain, and other products are extensive. Here are Aerial Lift Bridge and a branch of state university.

Dulwich (dŭl′ĭj), residential suburb, S London, England. Has a well-known public school, Dulwich Col. (founded 1613).

duma (do͞o′mä), Russian representative body, particularly the Imperial Duma (lower house) estab. 1906 as a result of 1905 Revolution.

Dumas, Alexandre (älĕksä′drü dümä′), known as **Dumas père** (pĕr), 1802–70, French author, partly of African descent. He wrote many historical adventure novels, notably *The Three Musketeers* (1844), *Twenty Years After* (1845), *The Count of Monte Cristo* (1844–45). Among his dramas *La Tour de Nesle* (1832) is best known. He employed many collaborators. His son, **Alexandre Dumas**, known as **Dumas fils** (fēs′), 1824–95, French dramatist and novelist, wrote *La Dame aux camélias* (1852; known in England as *Camille*; basis of Verdi's *La Traviata*, *Le Demi-Monde* (1855), *Le Fils naturel* [the natural son] (1858), mainly plays of moral or social theme. He is also considered a creator of the modern comedy of manners.

Dumas (do͞o′mŭs), city (pop. 6,127), N Texas, N of Amarillo in Panhandle. Oil, gas, and wheat center with chemical plants.

Dumas fils: see DUMAS, ALEXANDRE (1824–95).

Dumas père: see DUMAS, ALEXANDRE (1802–70).

Du Maurier, George (Louis Palmella Busson) (dü môr′ēä), 1834–96, English artist and novelist, b. Paris. His best-known novels are *Peter Ibbetson* (1892) and *Trilby* (1894). Was an illustrator on *Punch* staff. His granddaughter, **Daphne du Maurier**, 1907–, has written popular novels, notably *Rebecca* (1938).

Dumbarton (dŭmbär′tŭn), burgh (pop. 23,-703), co. town of Dumbartonshire, Scotland. Shipbuilding center, it also has mfg. of aircraft, pharmaceuticals, whisky, soap, and hosiery. Chief town of ancient kingdom of Strathclyde.

Dumbarton Oaks, estate, now in Washington, D.C.; scene of a conference (1944) at which the U.S., Great Britain, the USSR, and China reached an agreement to create the United Nations.

Dumbartonshire or **Dunbartonshire** (dŭn–), county (241 sq. mi.; pop. 164,263), central Scotland; co. town Dumbarton. Bordered on E by Loch Lomond, on S by Clyde estuary, and on W by Loch Long. It is mountainous region (up to 3,000 ft.) with little agr. Cattle and sheep raised. Industries include fishing, shipbuilding, and cotton mfg.

Dumdum (dŭm′dŭm), town (pop. 39,434), S West Bengal, India. The deadly soft-nosed (dumdum) bullets, banned in 1899 by Hague Conference, were first made here. Its large airport serves Calcutta.

Dumfriesshire (dŭmfrēs′shĭr) or **Dumfries,** border county (1,073 sq. mi.; pop. 85,656),

SW Scotland. Surface largely hilly with agr. in valleys. Salmon fishing and cattle grazing important; limestone and sandstone quarried. There are many beautiful lochs. Scene of much border warfare until 18th cent. County town, **Dumfries,** burgh (pop. 26,320), includes Maxwelltown across Nith R. Has Burns's mausoleum.

Dummer, Jeremiah, 1645–1718, American silversmith. His mark is ID over a fleur-delis in a heart.

Dumont (do͞o′mŏnt), suburban borough (pop. 13,013), NE N.J., NE of Hackensack; settled 1730.

Dumouriez, Charles François (shärl′ fränswä′ dümo͞orēä′), 1739–1823, French general in French Revolutionary Wars. Victor at Valmy and Jemappes (1792); conquered Belgium, invaded Netherlands, but deserted to Austrians after his defeat at Neerwinden (1793).

Dunant, Jean Henry (zhä′ ērē′ dünä′), 1828–1910, Swiss philanthropist. Brought about founding of Red Cross. Shared 1910 Nobel Peace Prize with Passy.

Dunbar, Paul Laurence, 1872–1906, American Negro poet, b. Dayton, Ohio. Wrote *Lyrics of Lowly Life* (1896).

Dunbar, William, c.1460–c.1520, Scottish poet strongly influenced by Chaucer. Noted for inventiveness and metrical skill. "Dance of the Sevin Deidly Synnis" most characteristic poem.

Dunbar (dŭnbär′), burgh (pop. 4,115), East Lothian, Scotland, at mouth of Firth of Forth; resort and fishing port. Has remains of castle to which Mary Queen of Scots was abducted by Bothwell 1567. Cromwell defeated Covenanters here 1650.

Dunbar, city (pop. 8,032), W W.Va., on Kanawha R. WNW of Charleston. Mfg. of glass and farm tools.

Duncan I, d. 1040?, king of Scotland (1034–1040?). He was murdered by his general Macbeth.

Duncan, Isadora, 1878–1927, American dancer. Early failures preceded triumphs (1903–8) in Budapest, Berlin, London, and finally in U.S. A daring, dynamic innovator, she danced barefoot in flowing robes. Greatly influenced modern dance through her concert tours and schools. She died at Nice, accidentally strangled by her scarf.

Duncan, city (pop. 15,325), S Okla., S of Chickasha; founded 1892. Supply and trade center for oil, cattle, and agr. area, it processes oil and cotton and has mfg. of oil-field equipment.

Duncansbay Head or **Duncansby Head,** 210 ft. high, northeastern extremity of Scotland, in Caithness.

Dundalk (dŭndôk′), urban district (pop. 18,-562), co. seat of Co. Louth, Ireland, on Dundalk Bay of Irish Sea; seaport. Industries include export of farm produce, brewing, shipbuilding, and fishing. Railroad center with large car works.

Dundas, town (pop. 6,846), S Ont., Canada, at head of Burlington Bay and NW of Hamilton. Head of Desjardins Canal. Mfg. of machinery and clothing.

Dundee, John Graham of Claverhouse, 1st Viscount (klä′vŭrŭs), c.1649–1689, Scottish Jacobite chieftain and soldier, known as

Bonnie Dundee. Hated by Covenanters whom he tried to suppress 1678–88. Fought for James II in Glorious Revolution; raised force to restore him but was killed in battle of Killiecrankie. Subject of ballads and novels.

Dundee (dŭndē′), independent burgh (pop. 177,333), Angus, Scotland, on Firth of Tay. Has docks and various industries. Dundee marmalade famous. Site of Univ. Col., part of Univ. of St. Andrews. City early adopted doctrines of Reformation.

Dundonald, Thomas Cochrane, 10th **earl of,** 1775–1860, British naval commander in Napoleonic wars. Commanded Chilean navy in liberation of Chile and Peru and Greek navy in war against Turkey 1827.

Dunedin (dŭnē′dĭn), city (pop. 65,771; metropolitan pop. 83,351), SE South Isl., New Zealand; port at base of Otago Peninsula; founded 1848. Seat of Univ. of Otago (1869). Woolen mills.

Dunellen (dŭnĕ′lŭn), borough (pop. 6,291), N central N.J., SW of Newark; laid out 1868. Mfg. of concrete mixers, adhesives, pumps, printing presses.

Dunes, Battle of the, 1658, victory of French and English under Turenne over Spanish under John of Austria and Louis II de Condé; fought near Dunkirk, France.

Dunfermline (dŭmfûr′lĭn), burgh (pop. 44,-710), Fifeshire, Scotland. Residence of Scottish kings from 11th cent. Abbey is burial place of Robert I and others. Birthplace of Andrew Carnegie, town is hq. of Carnegie Trusts. Has textile mills and metal foundries.

Dunkards, Dunkers, or **Tunkers,** a popular name for a sect of German Baptist brethren, divided into five denominations. Name derived from German "to dip," baptism being by immersion. Having evolved in Germany from Pietism, the sect was brought (1719) to Pa. It bans war, oaths, alcohol, tobacco, worldly amusements. Members wear simple, plain garb.

Dunkirk (dŭn′kûrk), Fr. *Dunkerque,* town (1946 pop. 9,869; 1936 pop. 28,450), Nord dept., N France; fishing port on North Sea. A key city in centuries-long struggle between France and its neighbors, Dunkirk often changed masters, passed permanently to France 1662. In 1940 (May 26–June 4) it was scene of one of most memorable naval actions in history when some 300,000 Allied troops, cut off by German advance on Channel ports, were evacuated to England. Dunkirk was left in ruins. Germans held out here against Allies until May, 1945.

Dunkirk, city (pop. 18,007), W N.Y., on L. Erie. Mfg. (heaters, silk, tool steel, glass) and fisheries.

Dunlap, William, 1766–1839, American playwright, prolific writer of Gothic romances and tragedies. Adapted many French and German works. Was theater manager (1796–1805), a founder of Natl. Academy of Design, and author of books on theater and design.

Dunmore, John Murray, 4th **earl of,** 1732–1809, British colonial governor of Va. Led Indian campaign in 1774, known as Lord Dunmore's War. Opposed colonists until forced to return to England in 1776.

Dunmore, borough (pop. 20,305), NE Pa.,

near Scranton; settled 1783. Produces coal and textiles.

Dunmore's War: see DUNMORE, JOHN MURRAY, 4TH EARL OF.

Dunn, Gano, 1870–1953, American electrical engineer of large-scale projects and designer of electrical equipment for production.

Dunn, town (pop. 6,316), central N.C., S of Raleigh. Farm trade center with lumber and flour mills.

Dunne, Finley Peter, 1867–1936, American humorist, journalist. His Irish-American "Mr. Dooley" excelled in deflating politicians' pretensions.

Dunnet Head, promontory, Caithness, Scotland, forming N extremity of Great Britain proper.

Dunois, Jean, comte de (zhă′ kōt′ dù dünwä′), c.1403–1468, French general, called the Bastard of Orléans; natural son of Louis d'Orléans. In charge of defense of Orléans when Joan of Arc relieved it (1429); joined Joan in subsequent campaign; took part in capture of Paris (1436).

Dunoyer de Segonzac, André: see SEGONZAC.

Dunsany, Edward John Moreton Drax Plunkett, 18th **Baron** (dŭnsăn′ē, -sā′-), 1878–, Anglo-Irish author. Plays (e.g., *A Night at an Inn,* 1916), prose tales (e.g., *The Gods of Pegana,* 1905) of Lord Dunsany are half-satire, half-fantasy.

Dunsinane (dŭn″sĭnān′), one of Sidlaw Hills, Perthshire, Scotland. Has ruins of fort, called Macbeth's Castle, supposedly scene of Macbeth's defeat by earl of Northumbria, as told by Shakspere.

Dunsmuir (dŭnz′mūr), city (pop. 2,256), N Calif., S of Mt. Shasta. Hunting and fishing resort. Lava Beds Natl. Monument is near.

Duns Scotus, John (dŭnz′ skō′tùs), d. 1308, British or Irish scholastic philosopher, a Franciscan, called the Subtle Doctor. There is no authentic list of his works, but some are definitely known. He was the founder of Scotism, opposed to Thomism (i.e., the school of St. Thomas Aquinas) in Roman Catholicism. He denied that individuality comes from matter; said that knowledge of finite truths rests on the ultimate Truth, which is God; argued that God's possible existence, demonstrable from sense experience, involves his necessary existence; and held that the state got its sanction from consent of the people and that private property is not sanctioned by natural law.

Dunstable (dŭn′stŭbŭl), municipal borough (pop. 17,108), Bedfordshire, England. Traces of Stone and Bronze Age exist. Excavations in 1926 produced relics of woman of c.2000 B.C.

Dunstan, Sir Wyndham Rowland, 1861–1949, English chemist, expert on alkaloids, authority on tropical agriculture and mineralogy.

Dunster, Henry, c.1612–1659, first president of Harvard (1640–54), b. England.

duodecimal system, notation system corresponding to decimal system but based on 12 instead of 10. Since 12 has more factors than 10 more fractions can be expressed evenly. System common in British and American measure (e.g., inches, feet) in contrast to metric system, which has a thorough-going decimal base.

Dupleix, Joseph François, marquis (zhōzĕf' fräswä' märkē' düplĕks'), 1697–1763, French governor of Pondichéry, India (1741–54). Captured Madras (1746); held Pondichéry against British (1748); formed plan of establishing French supremacy in India. By armed force and by diplomacy he made himself master of the Carnatic and most of Deccan (1749–51), but British intervention under Robert Clive and fear of war with England induced the French government to recall him. Died in poverty.

Duplessis, Maurice Lenoblet (mōrēs' lŭnôblä' düplĕsē'), 1890–, premier and attorney general of Quebec, Canada (1936–39, 1944–).

Du Pont (dū pŏnt'), French-American family. **Pierre Samuel Du Pont de Nemours** (dù nùmōōr'), 1739–1817, was a French economist, one of the PHYSIOCRATS. Also active in politics. He migrated to U.S. in 1799. His son, **Eleuthère Irénée Du Pont** (ālûtēr' ērānä'), 1771–1834, b. Paris, set up a powder mill near Wilmington, Del., in 1802. He developed an extensive business, which he named E. I. du Pont de Nemours & Company (firm's present name). **Samuel Francis Du Pont,** 1803–65, American naval officer, was grandson of Pierre Samuel du Pont de Nemours. In Civil War he led successful attack on Port Royal, S.C. (1861). Against his own will, he led unsuccessful attack on Charleston (1863). **Pierre Samuel Du Pont,** 1870–, served as president of family business for many years. Under him the company developed scores of chemical manufactures, acquired many other industries.

Dupré, Jules (zhül' düprā'), 1811?–1889, French landscape painter of the Barbizon school.

Dupuy de Lôme, Stanislas (stänēsläs' düpüē' dù lōm'), 1816–85, French naval engineer. Built first French armored ship. Demonstrated (1872) practicability of dirigible balloon.

Dupuytren, Guillaume, Baron (gēyŏm' bärō' düpüëtrē'), 1777–1835, French surgeon, influential as a clinical teacher and through his writings.

Duquesne (dùkān'), city (pop. 17,620), SW Pa., on Monongahela R. and near Pittsburgh; settled 1789. Mfg. of iron, steel, and chemicals.

Duquesne, Fort, on site of PITTSBURGH, Pa. Strategic position at junction of Monongahela and Allegheny rivers made it major objective in last of French and Indian Wars. Abandoned by French to British in 1758 and renamed Fort Pitt.

Duquesne University: see PITTSBURGH, Pa.

Duquesnoy, François (fräswä' dükĕnwä'), 1594–1643?, Flemish sculptor, also called François Flamand. Worked mostly in Italy. Did reliefs of children.

Du Quoin (dōō koin'), city (pop. 7,147), S Ill., N of Cairo. Center of agr. and coal region.

Dura (dōō'rù), anc. city on the Euphrates, E of Palmyra; also called Europos, Doura, and Doura-Europus. A prominent post from the 3d cent. B.C. to the 3d cent. A.D., it fell to ruins. Excavations after 1922 gave much information on Hellenistic and Roman Mesopotamia.

duralumin (dōōrăl'yùmĭn), alloy of aluminum,

copper, magnesium, manganese. Because of lightness and tensile strength, is used in dirigible frameworks.

Duran, Carolus: see CAROLUS-DURAN.

Durance (dürās'), rapid river, c.180 mi. long, SE France, rising in Dauphiné Alps and joining Rhone near Avignon. Fertile valley.

Durand, Asher Brown (dūrănd'), 1796–1886, American painter, a founder of Hudson River school.

Durango (dōōräng'gō), state (47,691 sq. mi.; pop. 629,502), N Mexico; cap. Durango (pop. 33,412). Mountains in W are rich mining area; semiarid plains to E are ranch country; farther E is fertile LAGUNA DISTRICT. Gómez Palacio is chief city. Francisco de Ibarra undertook its exploration and colonization in 1562.

Durango (dōōräng'gō), city (pop. 7,459; alt. c.6,500 ft.), SW Colo., on Animas R., in farm, ranch, mine area. Mining of carnotite for uranium. Processes uranium, vanadium. Mesa Verde Natl. Park is W, Fort Lewis School of Agriculture near by.

Durant, Thomas Clark, 1820–85, American railroad builder, chief figure in construction of Union Pacific RR. Organized CRÉDIT MOBILIER.

Durant, city (pop. 10,541), SE Okla., near Red R. and Denison Dam, settled c.1870. Commercial and processing center for agr. region (esp. cotton).

Durazzo (dōōrät'sō), Albanian *Durrës*, town (pop. 14,031), Albania; Adriatic port. Founded c.625 B.C. as Epidamnus, a joint colony of Corinth and Corcyra, whose quarrel over it precipitated the PELOPONNESIAN WAR (431 B.C.). Renamed Dyrrhacchium c.300 B.C., it passed under Epirus; fell to Rome 229 B.C.; became a major Roman naval and military base. Passing to Byzantine Empire, Durazzo was often seized by foreigners, notably by the Angevin kings of Naples, who made it a duchy in 1267, and by Venice, which held it from 1392 until its fall to the Turks in 1501. Majority of pop. accepted Islam. City has many mosques; three early Byzantine towers; Venetian fortifications.

Durban (dûr'bùn), city (pop. 339,247), Natal, South Africa, a port on Natal Bay and Natal's largest city. Exports coal, manganese, chrome.

Düren (dü'rùn), city (pop. 35,121), North Rhine-Westphalia, NW Germany, on Roer R. between Aachen and Cologne. Most of city was pulverized in World War II bombings and shellings.

Dürer, Albrecht (äl'brĕkht dü'rùr), 1471–1528, German artist, famous for prints and drawings of keen observation and rich detail; b. Nuremberg, where he studied with Michael Wolgemut. In 1494 he estab. own studio in Nuremberg and did woodcuts for the *Apocalypse* and *Great Passion*. Visited Venice 1505–7. During his most fertile period (1507–20) he painted several great altarpieces and created his most celebrated engravings, including *Melancholia, The Knight*, and *St. Jerome in His Study*. Visited the Netherlands 1520. Was a friend of Luther. Wrote on human proportions, perspective, geometry, and fortifications.

duress, actual or threatened violence or imprisonment to force a person, directly or indirectly, to enter into an agreement or perform some other act against his will. To void such a contract, duress must be shown to have been such as to overcome the party's mind and will. See also COERCION.

Durfee, William Franklin (dûr'fē), 1833–99, American engineer and producer of first steel by Bessemer process in America.

Durham, John George Lambton, 1st earl of, 1792–1840, British liberal statesman. Promoted Reform Bill of 1832. As Governor General of Canada he prepared masterly *Report on the Affairs of British North America* (1839), supporting self-government and reforms but opposing French nationalism in Canada.

Durham (dŭr'rŭm), maritime county (1,015 sq. mi.; pop. 1,463,416), N England, one of most densely populated English counties. Has dairy farming and cattle raising, but mainly industrial (rich coal deposits) and iron, steel, chemical, and glass industries. Shipbuilding along Tyne R. Sunderland and Hartlepool are important seaports. County ruled by bishops of Durham until 1836. The county town, **Durham,** municipal borough (pop. 19,283), has 11th-cent. castle occupied by Univ. of Durham. Cathedral, begun 1093 and one of England's finest examples of Norman architecture, contains relics of St. Cuthbert.

Durham. 1 Town (pop. 4,770), SE N.H., SW of Dover. Seat of Univ. of New Hampshire (land-grant, state supported; coed.), which was chartered 1866, opened 1868 as state college of agr. and mechanic arts at DARTMOUTH COLLEGE, moved 1893, and became a university 1923. **2** City (pop. 71,311), central N.C., in piedmont NW of Raleigh; settled c.1852. Great center for marketing and processing tobacco, it also has textile and hosiery mills. Tobacco industry grew after Civil War, with J. B. Duke as leader. Hq. of largest Negro life insurance company in U.S. Seat of DUKE UNIVERSITY.

Durkheim, Émile (āmēl' dürkĕm'), 1858–1917, French sociologist. Influenced by Comte, he held that religion and morality originated in the collective mind of society.

Durkin, Martin P(atrick), 1894–, U.S. Secretary of Labor (1953–). President of plumbers' and steamfitters' union (1943–52).

Durres, Albania: see DURAZZO.

Duryea, Charles Edgar (dŏŏr'yā), 1862–1938, American inventor and automobile manufacturer. With his brother, J. Frank Duryea (1870–), he built one of first practical internal-combustion automobiles.

Duryea, borough (pop. 6,655), NE Pa., on Lackawanna R. SW of Scranton. Has coal mines and silk mills.

Duse, Eleonora (dŏŏ'zŭ, Ital. ālāōnō'rä dŏŏ'zä), 1859–1924, Italian actress. Made debut at 14 as Juliet. Later vehicles included Sardou's *Fédora,* Goldoni's *La Locandiera,* and Ibsen's *Lady from the Sea.* Her acting combined simplicity with emotional power. For some years a romantic attachment existed between Duse and Italian poet D'Annunzio.

Dushan, Stephen: see STEPHEN DUSHAN.

Düsseldorf (dü'sůldôrf), city (pop. 498,347), cap. of North Rhine-Westphalia, NW Germany, at junction of Rhine and Düssel rivers. Industrial and commercial center; steel, machinery, textiles. Cap. of duchy of Berg from 1288; passed to Prussia 1814. Largely ruined by World War II air raids. Birthplace of Heinrich Heine. Has famous art academy (founded 1819).

dust, atmospheric, minute particles of matter (chiefly inorganic) settling from or suspended in air. Sources: city activities, blown dry earth, volcanic eruptions, ocean salt spray, organic matter (e.g., pollen), and meteorite combustion.

Dust Bowl, areas of U.S. prairie states where dust storms carry off topsoil which has lost its natural cover of grass by overgrazing, burning over, or plowing. Remedies include planting of cover crops, trees, and much grass to anchor soil.

Dutch East India Company: see EAST INDIA COMPANY, DUTCH.

Dutch East Indies: see INDONESIA.

Dutch Guiana: see GUIANA.

Dutch Harbor, village on Amaknak isl. in Unalaska Bay, which indents Unalaska, off W Alaska. One of few good harbors in ALEUTIAN ISLANDS, known early to Russian fur traders. Became transshipping point for Nome after 1899 gold strike. U.S. naval base, estab. 1940, was important in World War II. Attacked by Japanese planes 1942.

Dutch language, West Germanic language of Indo-European family. See LANGUAGE (table).

Dutchman's-breeches, North American wild flower (*Dicentra cucullaria*) related to bleeding heart. It has drooping racemes of yellow-tipped white flowers and ferny foliage.

Dutchman's-pipe, twining vine (*Aristolochia durior*) of E U.S. It has pipelike flowers and heart-shaped leaves. Flowers can trap and later release insects.

Dutch New Guinea: see NEW GUINEA.

Dutch Reformed Church: see REFORMED CHURCH IN AMERICA.

Dutch Wars. 1 1652–54, war between English and Dutch. Marked crisis between two nations' rivalry as carriers of world trade; precipitated by English search and seizure of Dutch merchant ships and by English Navigation Act of 1651, directed against Dutch trade with British possessions. Sea fight between Robert Blake and Maarten TROMP, May, 1652, opened hostilities. Tromp's victory over Blake off Dungeness, Nov., 1652, gave Dutch control of Channel; control was broken by British victory at Portland (1653). After victory off Gabbard's Shoal, British blockaded Dutch coast. Tromp attacked blockading fleet, July 31, 1653, and was defeated. Peace signed April, 1654. Dutch agreed to salute British flag in British seas, to pay compensation for English losses, and to submit territorial claims to arbitration. **2** 1664–67, another war between Dutch and English. Dutch had continued to threaten English commercial supremacy. In 1664 British raided Dutch colonies on African coast and took New Netherland in North America. England declared war, March,

1665. Duke of York (later James II) won battle of Lowestoft in June, 1665; in Sept., bishop of Munster, an English ally, overran E province of Netherlands, but was soon expelled. Louis XIV of France declared war on England, Jan., 1666, but took little part in war. British fleet under Monck and Prince Rupert was defeated in Four Days battle or battle of the Downs (June 1–4, 1666) by Michiel de RUYTER and Cornelis Tromp; in Aug. they defeated Dutch and destroyed shipping along Dutch coast. Charles II having let the navy fall into unprepared state, De Ruyter exacted heavy losses in raid in the Thames, 1667. In Treaty of Breda (July, 1667), trade laws were modified to favor Dutch, conquests of war were retained (English received N.Y., N.J., and Del.; Dutch kept Surinam), and English and French made mutual restoration of conquests. 3 1672–78, first of great wars of Louis XIV of France. Aimed at destruction of Dutch rivalry to French trade and expansion of French empire. Having gained allies in CHARLES II of England, in Sweden, and several German states, Louis overran S provinces of Netherlands, May, 1672. His advance on Amsterdam was stopped when Dutch opened the dikes. De Ruyter defeated English and French fleets at Southwold Bay. Dutch peace offers having been spurned, a revolution took place, and William of Orange (later WILLIAM III of England) took over from Jan de WITT, July, 1672. In 1673 Dutch received support of Spain, the emperor, Brandenburg, Denmark, and other powers, and England made peace 1674, but French victories on land (Maastricht, Seneff, Sinzheim, Cassel, Freiburg) under Louis II de CONDÉ and TURENNE and the 1676 naval campaign of Abraham Duquesne gained peace at Nijmegen (1678–79). Maastricht was ceded to Dutch, and French restrictive tariffs were modified in their favor. In subsequent treaty with Spain, France got Franche-Comté and chain of border fortresses in return for evacuating Spanish Netherlands. In treaty with the emperor (1679), France was confirmed in possession of Freiburg and part of Lorraine.

Dutch West India Company, trading and colonizing company, chartered by Dutch republic 1621, organized 1623. Founded NEW NETHERLAND (New York). Given trading rights on African coast between Tropic of Cancer and Cape of Good Hope, on American coast between Newfoundland and Straits of Magellan. Company had almost complete power in its territory.

Dutch West Indies: see WEST INDIES.

Dutton, Clarence Edward, 1841–1912, American geologist. He served in 1875 with John W. Powell on U.S. Geological Survey in the Rocky Mt. region. He introduced the term *isostasy,* and was a pioneer advocate of the isostatic theory (see CONTINENT).

Duun, Olav (ōʹläv dōōnʹ), 1876–1939, Norwegian novelist, author of a monumental series, *The People of Juvik* (6 novels; 1918–23).

Duveen, Joseph, 1st Baron Duveen of Millbank, 1869–1939, English art dealer. Benefactor of many museums and galleries, no-

tably the Natl. Gall. in London. Helped form several American art collections.

Duveneck, Frank (dūʹvŭnĕk), 1848–1919, American portrait and genre painter, an inspired teacher.

Duvergier de Hauranne, Jean (zhäʹ düvĕrzhyäʹ dù ōränʹ), 1581–1643, French theologian, one of the molders of JANSENISM. A friend of Cornelis Jansen and of the ARNAULD family, he helped make Port-Royal a Jansenist stronghold. He had trouble with the Jesuits and with Cardinal Richelieu, who had him imprisoned (1638–42).

du Vigneaud, Vincent (dū vĕnʹyō), 1901–, American biochemist, known for research including chemistry of insulin, protein, sulphur compounds, and biotin.

Duxbury, resort town (pop. 3,167), SE Mass., on Duxbury Bay and SE of Boston. Plymouth colonists including John Alden, Miles Standish, and William Brewster settled here. Alden's house still stands.

dvi-manganese: see RHENIUM.

Dvina (dvēnäʹ) or **Northern Dvina,** Rus. *Severnaya Dvina,* river, 455 mi. long, N European RSFSR, formed near Veliki Ustyug by two affluents. Flows NW, empties into White Sea below Archangel. Navigable May–Nov., it carries much commerce. Connected with MARIINSK SYSTEM.

Dvina or **Western Dvina,** Lettish *Daugava,* Rus. *Zapadnaya Dvina,* river, 620 mi. long, E Europe, rising in Valdai Hills, RSFSR, and flowing W through Belorussia and Latvia into the Gulf of Riga of the Baltic Sea. Navigable from Vitebsk. Connected by canal with Berezina.

Dvorak, Anton (änʹtôn dvôrʹshäk), Czech *Antonín Dvořák,* 1841–1904, Czech composer. Much of his music is nationalistic in spirit and influenced by Brahms and Wagner. He is best known for his symphony in E Minor, *From the New World,* written while he was in the U.S., and for his Slavonic Dances. He wrote nine symphonies, chamber works, a violin concerto, a cello concerto, and overtures.

dwarf, a plant, animal, or person whose size is less than normal; proportions sometimes abnormal. Human dwarfs usually have normal size parents.

dwarf cornel: see BUNCHBERRY.

Dwiggins, W(illiam) A(ddison), 1880–, American type designer, calligrapher, and book designer. Brought to type and book designing fresh boldness of advertising work. Designed clean, spare type faces (notably Electra and Caledonia) for linotype composition.

Dwight, Timothy, 1752–1817, American author and educator; grandson of Jonathan Edwards. An army chaplain in Revolutionary Army, he was later a Congregational pastor at Greenfield Hill, Conn. A famous preacher and writer of verse (one of CONNECTICUT WITS), he is perhaps better known as able president of Yale (1795–1817). His brother, **Theodore Dwight,** 1764–1846, also belonged to Connecticut Wits and was a conservative political leader. Theodore's son, **Theodore Dwight,** 1796–1866, wrote travel books and forwarded antislavery movement.

A grandson of Timothy Dwight (1752–1817), **Theodore William Dwight,** 1822–92, headed Hamilton College law school, then was sole member of Columbia School of Law, later headed it. Another grandson of Timothy Dwight (1752–1817) was **Timothy Dwight,** 1828–1916, who helped to reorganize the Yale Divinity School and, as president of Yale (1886–98), helped change it from college to university.

Dy, chemical symbol of the element DYSPROSIUM.

Dyck, Sir Anthony van: see VAN DYCK, SIR ANTHONY.

dye, substance used to color materials. Natural dyes obtained from plants (e.g., alizarin), animals (e.g., COCHINEAL), minerals (e.g., OCHER) have been largely replaced by synthetic dyes. Most of these are prepared benzene (see also ANILINE) or anthracene. Some materials can be dyed directly, others require use of MORDANT. Dyes may be acid or basic. Vat dye is so named for the method of application. Method of attachment of dye to material it colors may be chemical reaction between dye and fibers or may be absorption of dye by fiber. Dyeing was practiced centuries ago by Chinese, Persians, and Indians.

Dyer, Mary, d. 1660, Quaker martyr in Mass., b. England. Banished, she returned to Boston twice to minister to imprisoned Quakers. Arrested both times, reprieved in 1659, but hanged in 1660.

Dyersburg, city (pop. 10,885), W Tenn., near Mississippi R. NNE of Memphis; laid out 1825. Mfg. of textiles, cotton, grain, timber, and dairy products.

Dying Gaul, statue in Capitoline Mus., Rome. Example of Pergamene school of Greek sculpture (c.200 B.C.). Depicts fallen Galatian warrior.

Dykh-Tau (dĭkh″-tou′), peak, 17,054 ft. high, USSR, in central Greater Caucasus.

Dykstra, Clarence Addison (dĭk′strŭ), 1883–1950, American educator, civic administrator. City manager of Cincinnati 1930–37. President of Univ. of Wisconsin 1937–45. Provost of Univ. of California at Los Angeles 1945–50.

dynamics: see MECHANICS.

dynamite, explosive made from nitroglycerin and a porous substance; charge is set off by DETONATOR. It was discovered 1866 by A. B. NOBEL.

dynamo: see GENERATOR.

dyne (dīn), unit of force in centimeter-gram-second system producing an acceleration in a one-gram mass of one centimeter per second for each second the force acts.

dysentery, intestinal inflammation resulting from swallowing certain microorganisms, parasitic worms, or irritating substances. Amoebic dysentery is caused by a protozoan; bacterial, by bacillus.

dysprosium (dĭsprō′shĕŭm), metallic element (symbol = Dy; see also ELEMENT, table) found in certain minerals with other metals of the RARE EARTHS. It is the most highly magnetic substance.

Dzaudzhikau (dzoujĭkou′), city (pop. 127,172), cap. of North Ossetian ASSR, SE European RSFSR, on Terek R., at foot of Caucasus. Metallurgy (zinc, lead, silver). Founded 1874 as Vladikavkaz; was military, political center of Russian Caucasus.

E

Ea (ā′ä), Sumerian water-god, widely known in Mesopotamia. Eridu was one center of his worship.

Ead-. For some Anglo-Saxon names beginning thus, see ED-; e.g., for Eadward, see EDWARD.

Eads, James Buchanan (ēdz), 1820–87, American engineer. He invented a diving bell (c.1841) to salvage wrecks in Mississippi; built fleet of Civil War ironclads, St. Louis steel-arch bridge, and system of jetties which made New Orleans an ocean port.

Eagels, Jeanne, 1894–1929, American actress, noted especially for her portrayal of Sadie Thompson in *Rain.*

eagle, large predatory bird related to kite, hawk, and falcon, and of world-wide distribution. American or bald or white-headed eagle is U.S. national emblem; other forms are southern and northern bald eagles, and golden or mountain eagle. Eagles eat fish, sometimes carrion.

Eagle Pass, city (pop. 7,276), W Texas, port opposite Piedras Negras, Mex. Ships spinach, has creameries, cotton gins, and food processing plants. Connected by rail and highway to Mexico City.

Eakins, Thomas (ā′kĭnz), 1844–1916, American painter and sculptor. Painted humble types and scenes of everyday world with uncompromising realism.

Eames, Emma (āmz), 1865–1952, American soprano, b. China, of American parentage. Sang at the Metropolitan Opera, New York, 1891–1909. Among her famous roles were Aïda, Juliet, and Micaela.

Eames, Wilberforce (ēmz), 1855–1937, American bibliographer, long at New York Public Library, an expert of Americana and literature on Indians. Edited Vols. XV–XX of Sabin's *Dictionary of Books Relating to America.*

ear, organ of HEARING in mammals. External ear and auditory canal are separated by eardrum from middle ear which contains three bones (malleus, incus, stapes) and opens into EUSTACHIAN TUBE. Internal ear, labyrinth of temporal bone, contains three semicircular canals important for equilibrium.

Earhart, Amelia (âr'härt), 1898–1937, American aviator. First woman to fly Atlantic: as passenger in 1928, solo in 1932. Flew Honolulu to California, 1935. Lost in Pacific during 1937 round-the-world flight attempt. She married George Palmer Putnam in 1931.

Earle or **Earl, Ralph,** 1751–1801, American portrait and landscape painter, pupil of Benjamin West.

Early, Jubal Anderson, 1816–94, Confederate general. Prominent in battle of Chancellorsville and in Gettysburg campaign. In Wilderness campaign (1864), defeated David Hunter and Lew Wallace. Burned Chambersburg, Pa., for refusal of ransom. After defeats by P. H. Sheridan in 1864, and at Waynesboro in 1865, he was removed from command.

early man: see MAN, PRIMITIVE.

Earn, Loch (lŏkh' ûrn'), lake in Perthshire, Scotland. Ardvorlich House, on its shore, is Darlinvarach of Scott's *Legend of Montrose*. Earn R. flows 46 mi. from the lake to estuary of the Tay.

earth, fifth largest PLANET of the SOLAR SYSTEM and third from sun (average distance c.93,-000,000 mi.). The earth rotates on its axis (which is perpendicular to plane of the equator) causing day and night. It revolves in an elliptical orbit about the sun in 365¼ days; this, with the fact that the axis is tipped 23½° to the plane of the orbit, causes change of seasons. The earth is slightly flattened at the poles, its equatorial diameter being c.7,926 mi. and polar diameter c.27 mi. less. Land is said to occupy 57,469,928 sq. mi. of the surface and water to cover 139,480,841 sq. mi. Theory of isostasy postulates that the various segments of the crust are in balance (see CONTINENT). Earth's age is estimated at from two to three billion years. See *ill.,* p. 1187.

earthquake, trembling or shaking of earth's surface, commonly caused when rock masses slip along a FAULT. Other causes are violent volcanic activity and the collapse of roofs of caves. Tremors involve longitudinal, transverse, and surface waves (which produce the most severe shocks). Seismic sea waves (erroneously called tidal waves) are caused by submarine earthquakes. See also SEISMOLOGY.

earthworm, segmented worm (phylum Annelida or Annulata) found over most of world except in deserts and cold regions; valuable to agriculture because it improves condition of soil. *Lumbricus terrestris* (common in Europe and the Americas) has no head but is sensitive to light and vibrations; it goes underground in winter, drought, and on bright days. Moves by circular and longitudinal muscles, aided by rows of bristles along sides; muscular gizzard grinds leaves and other food. Each individual produces both eggs and sperms; two worms exchange sperm cells and each worm secretes a cocoon (placed in ground) in which fertilization occurs and young develop.

earwig, popular name of rather small, mostly nocturnal insect of order Dermaptera, usually black or brown but in tropics some are brightly colored. Pincerlike organs are attached to end of abdomen. Metamorphosis is gradual. In temperate zones, they are often garden or household pests.

easement, in law, right to limited use of another's land. It is either a personal privilege, which cannot be transferred without consent of the landowner (easement in gross) or a right attached to the land (servitude or easement appurtenant), which is transferred with sale or lease. Servitude (derived from Roman law) comes from use of land for prescribed time without protest of owner or from necessity of using another's land (as in drainage).

Easley, cotton-milling city (pop. 6,316), NW S.C., W of Greenville.

East Alton, village (pop. 7,290), SW Ill., on the Mississippi adjoining Alton. Mfg. of ammunition.

East Anglia (ăng'glĕů), kingdom of Anglo-Saxon England, comprising the modern counties of Norfolk and Suffolk. Settled in 5th cent. by Angles, it was one of most powerful kingdoms of late 6th cent. Became an underkingdom of MERCIA against which it later rebelled (825) to submit to Wessex. Danish invading army was quartered (865–66) in East Anglia and later conquered (869) the state entirely. Treaty of 886 made region a part of DANELAW. After 917 East Anglia was an earldom of England.

East Aurora, village (pop. 5,962), W N.Y., SE of Buffalo. Mfg. of metal and leather goods. Site of Roycroft Shops (1895–1939) of Elbert HUBBARD.

East Avon: see AVON 2, river, England.

Eastbourne, county borough (pop. 57,801), Sussex East, England. Popular resort on the coast, the city is backed by the South Downs.

East Cape, northeastern extremity of Asia, RSFSR, on Chukchi Peninsula and on Bering Strait. Official name (since 1898) is Cape Dezhnev, for Russian navigator who first reached it (1648).

Eastchester, village (pop. 3,096), S Alaska, just SE of Anchorage.

Eastchester, town (pop. 27,174), SE N.Y., E of Yonkers; settled 1664. Became a township 1788. Middle section became independent city of Mt. Vernon 1892, S part annexed by New York city 1895. Now includes residential villages of Bronxville (pop. 6,778) and Tuckahoe (pop. 5,991; marble quarrying). Bronxville is seat of Sarah Lawrence Col. (for women; chartered 1926, opened 1928); experimental college without fixed requirements; curriculum based on individual needs and interests of students, who are largely responsible for self-direction.

East Chicago, city (pop. 54,263), NW Ind., on L. Michigan SSE of Chicago; settled 1888. Largest port in state. Produces coke, chemicals, gypsum, petroleum, and metal products. Indiana Harbor, its lake front, is connected with Grand Calumet R.

East China Sea, arm of Pacific Ocean, between China and Japan, connected with South China Sea by Formosa Strait.

East Cleveland, city (pop. 40,047), NE Ohio, suburb of Cleveland. Here are Nela Park, hq. of General Electric laboratories, and

Forest Hill Park, former Rockefeller estate.

East Detroit, residential city (pop. 21,461), SE Mich., suburb of Detroit; settled 1827.

Easter, chief Christian feast, anniversary of resurrection of Jesus Christ. Falls between March 22 and April 25 inclusive (see CALENDAR), following LENT and HOLY WEEK. Roman Catholics must perform "Easter duty" (i.e., they must receive communion at some time between Ash Wednesday and Trinity Sunday).

Easter Island, island (c.46 sq. mi.; pop. 563), in Pacific c.2,350 mi. W of Chile, to which it belongs. Has long been known for indecipherable petroglyphs and monolithic stone heads (30 to 40 ft. tall, average weight, 5 to 8 tons), whose origin is unknown.

Eastern Empire: see ROME; BYZANTINE EMPIRE.

Eastern Question, the European problem presented by the decline and disintegration of the OTTOMAN EMPIRE after c.1700. Western powers, notably England and Prussia, took alarm at Russian expansion in RUSSO-TURKISH WARS of 18th cent. Austro-Russian plan to partition Turkey (with Constantinople and DARDANELLES going to Russia) was thwarted, but Turkish disintegration continued in 19th cent. with rise of independent Balkan states. Russian setbacks in CRIMEAN WAR (1853–56) and at Congress of BERLIN (1878) did not stop Russian influence in Balkans. Russian interference and encouragement of pan-Slavism clashed with Austro-German imperialism in East (*Drang nach Osten*), nearly caused war in crisis over BOSNIA AND HERCEGOVINA, and was a major factor leading to World War I. See also KUCHUK-KAINARJI, TREATY OF; ADRIANOPLE, TREATY OF; SAN STEFANO, TREATY OF; and articles on Balkan countries.

Eastern Rumelia: see RUMELIA.

East Flanders, province (1,147 sq. mi.; pop. 1,223,073), NW Belgium; cap. GHENT. Fertile soil; textile mfg. Population is mostly Flemish-speaking. For history, see FLANDERS.

East Friesland (frēz'lǔnd), region, extreme NW Germany, separated from Netherlands by the Dollart (estuary of Ems R.); chief city Emden. Region includes E FRISIAN ISLANDS, in North Sea. Became county of Holy Roman Empire 1454; duchy 1654; passed to Prussia 1744; to Hanover 1815.

East Galloway, county, Scotland: see KIRKCUDBRIGHTSHIRE.

East Gary, town (pop. 5,635), NW Ind., near L. Michigan. Surgical instruments.

East Grand Forks, city (pop. 5,049), NW Minn., on Red R. opposite Grand Forks, N.Dak., in farm area.

East Greenwich, town (pop. 4,923), central R.I., SW of Providence. Textiles (since c.1790). Northeastern Naval Air Station is at near-by Quonset Point.

East Ham, county borough (pop. 120,873), Essex, England; suburb of London. Has extensive shipyards, docks, chemical factories, and ironworks.

East Hampton, resort and residential village (pop. 1,737), on E Long Isl., SE N.Y., near Southampton. Home of J. H. Payne is here.

Easthampton, town (pop. 10,694), W Mass.,

S of Northampton; settled 1664. Textiles, metal products.

East Hartford, town (pop. 29,933), central Conn., across Connecticut R. from Hartford; settled c.1640. Aircraft mfg.

East Haven, town (pop. 12,212), S Conn., E of New Haven. Metal goods.

East India Company, British, 1600–1858, chartered by Parliament for monopoly of trade with Eastern Hemisphere. Soon limited itself to Indian trade, chiefly textile export. Abolished 1698, restored 1708, it grew virtually supreme in India after Clive's victories over French rivals (1745–61). It acquired territory for military establishments and was placed by Parliament under cabinet control (1773). Warren Hastings was first governor general of the Indian possessions. Monopoly was abolished 1813; activities became purely administrative 1833. Sepoy Rebellion (1857) hastened crown's direct assumption of Indian rule.

East India Company, Dutch, 1602–1798, chartered by States-General to aid war of liberation against Spain and to expand trade. Drove British and Portuguese from Indonesia, Malaya, Ceylon; monopolized trade of Spice Islands; founded colony at Cape of Good Hope (S Africa). Its possessions became part of Dutch colonial empire.

East India Company, French, 1664–1769, chartered by Louis XIV to compete with British trade in India. Briefly merged into Compagnie des Indes, 1719–20 (see MISSISSIPPI SCHEME). Dissolved after British victories over DUPLEIX and LALLY (1745–61).

East Indies, name used primarily for Indonesia (formerly Netherlands East Indies), but also more widely to include SE Asia. It once referred mainly to India.

Eastlake, city (pop. 7,485), NE Ohio, NE of Cleveland. Post office is Willoughby.

East Lansing, residential city (pop. 20,325), S Mich., on Cedar R. adjoining Lansing; settled c.1850. Seat of MICHIGAN STATE COLLEGE OF AGRICULTURE AND APPLIED SCIENCE.

East Liverpool, city (pop. 24,217), NE Ohio, on Ohio R. and N of Steubenville; settled 1798. Mfg. of clay products, machinery, and steel.

East Lothian (lō'dhēǔn), formerly **Haddingtonshire,** county (267 sq. mi.; pop. 52,240), SE Scotland; co. town Haddington. Chief river is the Tyne. Rich lowlands extensively cultivated; sheep raised in highlands. Other occupations are fishing, coal mining, brick making, and distilling.

East Lyme (līm), town (pop. 3,870), SE Conn., W of Niantic Bay. Has Thomas Lee House (1664) and Little Red Schoolhouse (1734?).

Eastmain, river rising in central Que., Canada, and flowing W 375 mi. to James Bay. Near mouth is 1685 Hudson's Bay Co. post.

Eastman, George, 1854–1932, American inventor, industrialist, philanthropist, founder of Eastman Kodak Co. He invented a dry-plate photographic process, devised roll film, Kodak camera, and a process for color photography.

Eastman, Joseph Bartlett, 1882–1944, U.S. government administrator. Appointed (1919) by Pres. Wilson to Interstate Commerce Commission. Director of Office of Defense Transportation (1941–44).

Eastman, Max, 1883–, American author. Edited (1913–17) the *Masses* until it was suppressed in World War I. His works include *Enjoyment of Poetry* (1913), *Enjoyment of Laughter* (1936), and his autobiography, *Enjoyment of Living* (1948).

Eastman School of Music: see ROCHESTER, N.Y.

East Moline (mōlēn′), city (pop. 13,913), NW Ill., on the Mississippi. Industrial suburb of MOLINE.

Easton. 1 Town (pop. 6,244), SE Mass., SW of Brockton. Mfg. of metal products. **2** City (pop. 35,632), E Pa., on Delaware R. near mouth of Lehigh R. and N of Philadelphia; laid out 1752. In canal days was coal-receiving port. Has mfg. of machinery and metal products. Seat of Lafayette Col. (Presbyterian; for men; 1826).

East Orange, city (pop. 79,340), NE N.J., mainly a residential suburb of New York and Newark; settled 1678. Seat of Upsala Col. (Lutheran; coed.; 1893) and Panzer Col. of Physical Education and Hygiene.

East Palestine, city (pop. 5,195), NE Ohio, at Pa. line S of Youngstown, in coal and clay area. Mfg. of clay and steel products.

East Paterson, borough (pop. 15,386), NE N.J., near Paterson. Mfg. of paper, leather, metal products.

East Peoria, city (pop. 8,698), N central Ill., on Illinois R. opposite Peoria.

East Pittsburgh, borough (pop. 5,259), SW Pa., on Monongahela R. and near Pittsburgh. Braddock's army defeated here 1755 by French and Indians. Has mfg. of electrical equipment.

East Point, city (pop. 21,080), NW Ga., an Atlanta suburb. Mfg. of cotton and metal products, fertilizer, and batteries. Has creosoting plants.

Eastport, resort city (pop. 3,123), SE Maine, on Moose Isl. in SE PASSAMAQUODDY BAY. Fishing and sardine canning (since c.1875). Tidal variation averages 18 ft.

East Providence, town (pop. 35,871), E R.I., on Seekonk R. opposite Providence; originally in Mass., inc. as a R.I. town 1862. Mfg. of food, petroleum, and steel products and building materials and chemicals. Narragansett race track near by.

East Prussia, former province (14,283 sq. mi.; 1939 pop. 2,333,301) of Prussia; historic cap. KÖNIGSBERG. On 1938 map it was separated from the rest of Germany by the Polish Corridor and the Free City of Danzig, and bordered on Poland, Lithuania, Memel, and the Baltic Sea. It is a heavily wooded and largely agr. region, dotted by many lakes (as in MASURIA). At the POTSDAM CONFERENCE (1945), East Prussia was partitioned between the USSR (which received c.6,100 sq. mi., incl. Königsberg) and Poland (received the rest, incl. Allenstein, Elbing, Marienburg). Transfers, subect to ratification in final peace treaty with Germany, are not considered final by U.S. For earlier history, see PRUSSIA.

East Ridge, town (pop. 9,645), E Tenn., Chattanooga suburb.

East Riding: see YORKSHIRE, England.

East River, New York city, navigable tidal strait (c.16 mi. long and 600–4,000 ft. wide) connecting Upper New York Bay with Long Isl. Sound and separating Manhattan and the Bronx from Brooklyn and Queens. Hell Gate channel (long dangerous to ships because of strong tidal currents and rocks) connects it with HARLEM RIVER (link to the Hudson). Lined with piers and shipyards. Welfare, Wards, Randalls, and Rikers islands are in it. Crossed by many bridges (e.g., Brooklyn, Queensboro, Triborough, Hell Gate, Bronx-Whitestone) and tunnels (subway, rail, vehicular).

East Rochester, village (pop. 7,022), W N.Y., SE of Rochester. Pianos, farm machinery, chemicals.

East Rockaway, resort and residential village (pop. 7,970), SE N.Y., on SW Long Isl. near Lynbrook.

East Rutherford, borough (pop. 7,438), NE N.J., NE of Newark. Mfg. of clothing, chemicals, and asbestos and metal products.

East Saint Louis (lōō′ĭs), city (pop. 82,295), SW Ill., on the Mississippi (here checked by large levees) opposite site St. Louis (connecting bridges); platted 1816. Large railroad yards and shops, stockyards, meat-packing plants and oil refineries. Mfg. of chemicals, metal products, glass, fertilizer, flour, and feed. Coal mines and rock quarries near by. City had violent race riots 1917. Has Parks Col. of Aeronautical Technology of St. Louis Univ. Cahokia Mounds are NE.

East Stroudsburg, borough (pop. 7,274), E Pa., N of Stroudsburg. Has railroad shops, printing, and mfg. of textiles.

Eastview, NE suburb of Ottawa (pop. 13,799), SE Ont., Canada, on Rideau Canal. Has lumbering, woodworking, and flour milling.

Eaton, John Henry, 1790–1856, U.S. Senator from Tenn. (1818–29), Secretary of War (1829–31). Social snubbing of his second wife (see Margaret O'NEILL) helped disrupt Pres. Jackson's cabinet.

Eaton, Theophilus, 1591–1657, Puritan leader in Conn., b. England. Founded New Haven (1637–38) with John DAVENPORT. Governed colony there.

Eaton, William, 1764–1811, U.S. Army officer, celebrated for exploit in Tripolitan War. Devised plan to win war against Tripoli by supporting claimant to rule of Tripoli. Set off on long overland march with small band to take Tripoli from rear. War ended with truce (1805) before he arrived.

Eau Claire (ō″ klâr′). **1** Town (pop. 9,238), central S.C., suburb of Columbia. **2** City (pop. 36,058), W Wis., on Chippewa R. at mouth of Eau Claire R., in dairy area. Built on site of 18th-cent. trading post, it developed as lumbering center. Farm trade center with mfg. of metal and rubber products.

eau de Cologne (ō″ dù kùlōn′), dilute perfume introduced c.1709 in Cologne, Germany, by Jean Marie Farina. Probably was a modification of formula made before 1700 by Paul Feminis, an Italian in Cologne; it was based on bergamot and other citrus oils.

Ebal, Mount (ē′–), central Palestine. Hebrews were cursed here for violating God's commands. Joshua built altar and monument inscribed with Mosaic law. Deut. 11.29; 27.4,-13; Joshua 8.30–33.

Eber (ē'bŭr), variant of HEBER.

Ebert, Friedrich (frē'drĭkh ā'bŭrt), 1871–1925, first president of the German republic (1919–25); a Social Democrat.

Eberth, Karl (kärl ā'bŭrt), 1835–1926, German bacteriologist and anatomist, authority on pathological anatomy. Bacterial genus *Eberthella* named for him.

Ebner-Eschenbach, Marie, Baronin von (märē' bärō'nĭn fŭn āb'nŭr-ĕsh'ŭnbäkh), 1830–1916, Austrian author. Her *Novellen,* famed for "poetic realism," include *The Two Countesses* (1855; Eng. tr.), *The Child of the Parish* (1887; Eng. tr., 1893), and the dog story *Krambambuli* (1894; Eng. tr., 1913–15).

Éboli, Ana de Mendoza de la Cerda, princesa de (ä'nä dā mändō'thä dä lä thâr'dä, ā'bōlē), 1540–92, Spanish noblewoman. A famous beauty (though she had lost an eye when a girl), she probably was loved by Philip II but lost his favor through her liaison with Antonio PÉREZ. Shared Pérez's disgrace when he was accused of Escobedo's murder. Spent years after 1579 in prison and exile.

ebony, handsome, dark heartwood of several tropical trees, especially of persimmon genus. Used for ornaments, tableware, inlay, piano keys.

Eboracum: see YORK, England.

Ebro (ē'brō, ā'brō), river, c.575 mi. long, NE Spain, flowing from Cantabrian Mts. SE, along foot of Pyrenees, past Sargossa, to Mediterranean. Irrigation canals; hydroelectric plants.

Eça de Queiroz, José Maria (zhōōzā' mŭrē'ŭ ā'sŭ dŭ kārôsh'), 1846?–1900, realistic Portuguese novelist, author of *A ilustre casa de Ramires* (1900), and *A cidade e as serras* (1901).

Ecbatana (ĕkbă'tŭnŭ, –bŭtā'nŭ), cap. of anc. Media, at the foot of Mt. Elvend. Later the summer residence of Persian and Parthian kings. Modern Hamadan is on the site.

eccentric, in mechanics, device by which rotary motion in one part of machine becomes longitudinal motion in another part. Cam is similarly used.

Ecclesiastes (ĕklē"zēăs'tēz), book of Old Testament. In ancient times ascribed to Solomon. A philosophical essay, somewhat cynical in tone, it opens with theme that "all is vanity" and continues with passages in praise of wisdom and mercy. Book is example of wisdom literature (see WISDOM).

Ecclesiasticus, in Western canon, book of Old Testament; placed in Apocrypha in AV. Called also Wisdom of Jesus the Son of Sirach. Theme of book is the excellence of wisdom. Among well-known passages: praise of wisdom and protest against determinism (14.20–15.20); praise of God for works of nature (43); praise of famous men who added to Israel's glory (44–50). Example of wisdom literature (see WISDOM).

Echegaray, José (hōsā' āchägärī'), 1832–1916, Spanish dramatist, a mathematician and economist. A common theme in his romantic realistic dramas is the clash of honor and duty. Well known are *O locura o santidad* (1876), *El hijo de don Juan* (1892), *El gran Galeoto* (1881). Shared with Mistral 1904 Nobel Prize in Literature.

Echeverría, Esteban (āstā'vän ā"chāvĕrē'ä), 1805–51, Argentine romantic poet, prose writer, and revolutionary propagandist against dictator Rosas.

echinoderm (ĭkī'nŭdûrm, ĕ'kĭnŭ–), invertebrate marine animal of phylum Echinodermata, having a calcareous, often spiny, outer skeleton and tube feet controlled by a water-vascular system. Many forms have five or more arms. Examples of the group are STARFISH, SEA URCHIN, CRINOID.

Echmiadzin (ĕchmēädzēn'), town (1926 pop. 8,436), central Armenian SSR, W of Erivan. Dates from 6th cent. B.C.; cap of Armenia 2d–4th cent. A.D. Called Vagarshapat until 1945. The near-by monastery, seat of the catholicus (head) of the Armenian Church, is famous for its gardens and its cathedral (traditionally dated from 4th cent.).

Echo, in Greek mythology, mountain nymph who helped Zeus in a love affair by distracting Hera with her chatter. As penalty, she could only repeat last words of someone else. In unrequited love for Narcissus, she pined away into nothing but her voice.

echo, phenomenon caused by reflection of sound waves. When wave strikes a reflecting surface, it is partly absorbed and partly reflected. When echo is reflected again and again from different surfaces the effect is called reverberation.

Eck, Johann Maier von (yō'hän mī'ûr fŭnĕk'), 1486–1543, German Catholic apologist. Disputed with Martin Luther at Leipzig (1519).

Eckermann, Johann Peter (yō'hän' pā'tûr ĕ'kûrmän), 1792–1854, German scholar and author, long a secretary to Goethe. He wrote *Conversations with Goethe* (1836–48; Eng. tr., 1850), an invaluable key to Goethe's thought.

Eckhart, Meister (mīs'tûr ĕk'härt), c.1260–c.1328, German mystical theologian. A Dominican, he awoke 14th-cent. mystical movement in Germany. He was accused of connection with the Beghards, and Pope John XXII condemned 17 of his propositions as heretical (1329).

Eclectic school, in painting: see CARRACCI.

eclipse (ĕklĭps', ĭ–), in astronomy, partial or complete obscuring of one heavenly body by another. Spherical opaque bodies cast cone-shaped shadows away from sun; when one opaque body shining by reflected light lies in shadow of another, it is eclipsed. Lunar eclipse (entire period lasting c.4 hr. and period of totality c.1 hr. 42 min.) occurs if moon's orbit crosses ecliptic when earth lies between sun and moon (full moon); it is visible from all parts of earth's surface where moon is above horizon. Solar eclipse occurs when sun and moon are on same side of earth (at new moon) if sun is not more than 18°5' from point where moon's orbit crosses ecliptic and if moon and earth are close enough for moon's relatively short shadow to reach earth. Solar eclipse is visible at different moments from different points as moon's shadow moves eastward. Total eclipse visible about once in 400 years from any one place; maximum possible duration 7 min. 30 sec. at equator when sun is directly overhead; duration decreases as latitude increases. In true shadow (umbra), all direct sun rays are cut off; in surrounding partial shadow (penumbra) there is illumination from part of sun's face. If apex of moon's cone-shaped umbra does not reach earth, annular (ring) eclipse is observable from region on earth directly beyond apex of umbra. During total solar eclipse moon appears as dark object moving across face of sun, daylight fades, temperature drops. At totality sun's corona and prominences glow around black disk of moon. Nearly similar solar eclipses occur in cycles of c.18 years. Also important in astronomy are eclipses of Jupiter's satellites. See *ill.*, p. 1187.

ecliptic (ĕklĭp′tĭk, ĭ–), great circle in heavens which marks sun's apparent yearly course, actually the path of earth's revolution about sun. Obliquity of the ecliptic, the cause of changing seasons, is inclination at c.23.5° angle of plane of ecliptic (earth's orbit) to plane of celestial equator (imaginary extension of equator into sky).

Ecnomus, Cape: see LICATA, Sicily.

École des Beaux-Arts (ākôl′ dā bōzär′), French national school of fine arts in Paris, founded 1648 as École académique. Has three departments: painting and graphic arts, sculpture, and architecture. Free to those who pass entrance examination. Prepares students to compete for PRIX DE ROME.

ecology, scientific study of plants and animals in relation to environmental conditions, e.g., temperature, soil, light, wind, and moisture. It is also concerned with interrelations in plant and animal communities, and stages (succession) leading to final development (known as climax community or area) for a particular region. Ecology as a social science (relation of man to natural environment) developed in 20th cent.

Economic and Social Council, constituent organ of the UN. Undertakes investigation of economic and social conditions throughout the world and reports its suggestions for action to the General Assembly and other organs of the UN.

Economic Cooperation Administration: see EUROPEAN RECOVERY PROGRAM.

economic planning, from the budgeting of a family's needs to the control of a nation's business and industry, has a long history. In one form or another it was practiced by governments in Egypt, Greece, and Rome, and, through craft and mercantile guilds, in the Middle Ages. In modern times doctrines such as SOCIALISM, COMMUNISM, and FASCISM propose dominant control, but all governments have some degree of economic planning: public works, taxation, tariff agreements, fair trade laws, immigration laws—all have their origin in economic considerations. Most industrial countries have over-all economic planning.

economics (ē″kŭnŏ′mĭks, ĕ″–), study of the supplying of man's physical needs. Not well developed in ancient and medieval times, economics took form with that growth of commerce which began in the 16th cent. and gave rise to the policy of MERCANTILISM. The 18th-cent. PHYSIOCRATS advocated LAISSEZ FAIRE—allowing business to follow freely the "natural laws" of economics. The effect on economic theory of the INDUSTRIAL REVOLUTION was reflected in Adam SMITH, advocate

(1776) of free trade and the division of labor; MALTHUS, who believed population outruns subsistence; and RICARDO, with his theory of diminishing returns. The early exponents of socialism, such as Saint-Simon, Proudhon, and Fourier, attacked the belief in the necessity of private property and competition, and *Das Kapital*, by Karl MARX, appeared as the major work in socialist economics.

Economy, Pa.: see AMBRIDGE, Pa.; HARMONY SOCIETY.

Ecorse (ĕkôrs′), city (pop. 17,948), SE Mich., on Detroit R. and S of Detroit; settled c.1815. Mfg. of metal products, chemicals, and auto parts.

Écrins, Barre des, France: see BARRE DES ÉCRINS.

Ecuador (ĕ′kwŭdôr) [Span.,= Equator, which traverses the country], republic (108,478 sq. mi.; pop. 3,076,933), W South America, on the Pacific; cap. QUITO. Two ranges of the Andes cross the country. There are many active volcanoes (including Chimborazo and Cotopaxi), and frequent earthquakes cause much damage. The highlands, with fertile intermontane valleys, support the main bulk of the population (in which the percentage of sedentary agr. Indians is high). E of the Andes is a largely unexplored wilderness of plains and rain forest, sparsely populated by "wild" Indians. W of the Andes is the hot, humid Pacific coast. From the port of GUAYAQUIL are exported cacao, petroleum, gold and cyanide precipitates, tagua nuts, and Panama hats. Francisco Pizarro sent Benalcázar into the region in 1533 to forestall Pedro de Alvarado. Unimportant in the colonial region (when it was the presidency of Quito), it was liberated from Spain by Sucre in the victory at Pichincha (1822) and was incorporated into Bolívar's republic of Greater Colombia. On dissolution of that union Ecuador became a separate republic (1830). In 1832 Ecuador gained the Galápagos Isls., but recurrent border disputes with neighboring countries did not bring Ecuador much gain. In 1948 the Quito Charter recommended a customs union and political and cultural cooperation among Colombia, Venezuela, Ecuador, and Panama.

ecumenical council: see COUNCIL, ECUMENICAL.

ecumenical movement (ĕ″kūmĕ′nĭkŭl, ē″–), term for a movement aimed at the unification or reunion of the Protestant churches of the world and ultimately of all Christians. The Evangelical Alliance (1846) was an early attempt in this direction, and the Federal Council of Churches of Christ (U.S.) was estab. 1908. Several world-unity conferences have been held (e.g., first meeting of the WORLD COUNCIL OF CHURCHES, 1948). Some Protestant denominations have been consolidated (e.g., formation in U.S. of the Methodist Church by three Methodist groups, 1939).

Edam (ē′dŭm, Dutch ādäm′), town (pop. 3,741), North Holland prov., NW Netherlands, on the Ijsselmer. Important market for famous Edam cheese.

Edda (ĕ′dŭ), title of two works in old Icelandic. Edda of Snorri Sturluson or *Prose Edda* was intended as a guide to scaldic poetry, has rules of that poetry as well as much mythology. *Poetic Edda,* also called Elder Edda (though compiled later) is a collection of 33 or 34 heroic lays (incomplete).

Eddington, Sir Arthur Stanley, 1882–1944, British astronomer, physicist. Contributed to study of evolution, motion, and internal constitution of stars. He was a leading exponent of the theory of relativity and a prolific author of scientific works.

Eddy, Mary Baker, 1821–1910, discoverer of principles of CHRISTIAN SCIENCE, and founder of the church based on them. In frail health from childhood, she was interested in the problem of health and faith and formulated doctrine and system which became Christian Science, dating from 1866. Her *Science and Health* appeared 1875. In 1877 she married Asa Gilbert Eddy. She planned *Manual* for conduct of church and all details of its upbuilding, and was pastor of Mother Church, Boston.

Eddystone (ĕ'dĭstŭn), lighthouse, on dangerous rocks off coast of Cornwall, England. First light here built 1696. Present structure (built 1878–82) fourth lighthouse at site.

Eddyville, city (pop. 1,840), SW Ky., near Kentucky Dam on Cumberland R. and E of Paducah. Ruins of iron furnace where William KELLY invented steel-making method are near by.

edelweiss (ā'dŭlvīs), low-growing perennial (*Leontopodium alpinum*) of high Alps. Its small yellow flower heads are surrounded by woolly-white bracts.

Eden, (Robert) Anthony, 1897–, British foreign minister. Became noted for support of League of Nations 1934–35. Foreign minister 1935–38, he resigned in opposition to Neville Chamberlain's "appeasement" of Axis. Was foreign minister in Churchill's war cabinet (1940–45) during alliance of Great Britain, USSR, and U.S. and building of UN. On fall of Labour Government (1951) he again became foreign secretary.

Eden, in Bible: see EDEN, GARDEN OF.

Eden, name of several rivers in England and Scotland. Principal one flows 65 mi. NW from Westmorland, England, into Solway Firth.

Eden, Garden of, in Bible, first home of man. God created the garden, with its trees of knowledge and of life, as home for Adam and Eve, until, eating of forbidden fruit, they were banished. Gen. 2; 3. In Babylonia there was legend of a holy place with tree of life inhabited by a god and goddess.

Edenhall, village, Cumberland, England, on Eden R. Family seat of Musgraves, whose luck (according to legend) depended on keeping unbroken an enameled goblet taken from the fairies near St. Cuthbert's Well; basis of Longfellow's "Luck of Edenhall."

Edenton, town (pop. 4,468), NE N.C., SW of Elizabeth City. Townswomen had "Edenton Tea Party," boycotting English goods 1774. Historic buildings include courthouse (1767) and St. Paul's Church (1736).

Edessa (ĭdĕ'sù), anc. city of Mesopotamia, modern URFA, Turkey. Center of a kingdom, later a Roman city, it was under Byzantine Empire a religious center. Fell to Arabs 639; captured by Crusaders 1097. BALDWIN I was

count of Edessa before becoming king. City fell to Moslems in 1144.

Edgar or **Eadgar** (ĕd'gùr), 943?–975, king of England (959–75). With a reign of orderly prosperity he won title of the Peaceful. He initiated widespread monastic reforms and granted practical autonomy to the Danes in England (see DANELAW) in return for their loyalty. Political unity ended with his death.

Edgar Atheling (ä'thûlĭng), 1060?–1125?, English prince. Chosen to succeed to throne on Harold's death, but submitted (1067) to WILLIAM I. Fled to Scotland, and, after unsuccessful uprising (1069), he later settled in France. He led (1097) English expedition which dethroned Donald III and seated Atheling's nephew Edgar on Scottish throne.

Edgartown, resort town (pop. 1,508), SE Mass., on E Martha's Vineyard; main center for the island.

Edge Hill, ridge on border of Warwickshire and Oxfordshire, England. Scene of first great battle of the civil war 1642.

Edgeworth, Maria, 1767–1849, Irish novelist. Wrote realistic novels of Ireland, notably *Castle Rackrent* (1800), *Belinda* (1801), *The Absentee* (1812), *Ormond* (1817). Also wrote children's stories.

Edina (ēdī'nû), village (pop. 9,744), E Minn., SW suburb of Minneapolis.

Edinburg (ĕ'dĭnbûrg), city (pop. 12,383), S Texas, WNW of Brownsville. Processes citrus fruits, truck, and cotton. Oil and gas wells in area.

Edinburgh, Philip Mountbatten, duke of (ĕ'dĭnbûrù), 1921–, husband of ELIZABETH II of Great Britain. Descended from kings of Greece, Denmark, and England, he became a British citizen before his marriage in 1947. Served in British navy in World War II.

Edinburgh (ĕ'dĭnbûrù), independent burgh (pop. 466,770), cap. of Scotland and co. town of Midlothian, near Firth of Forth. Often referred to in literature as Dunedin, it has nickname of "Auld Reekie." City is built on a series of ridges. Became burgh 1329 and capital 1437. Town sacked by English 1544. After Act of Union 1707 Parliament House, now seat of Supreme Law Courts, ceased to be meeting place of national assemblies. Noteworthy are HOLYROOD palace, Norman Chapel of St. Margaret, the cathedral, Royal Botanic Gardens, and Princes St. There are several art museums, and Natl. Library has valuable manuscripts. Univ. of Edinburgh (1583) has noted medical school. City developed as center of learning and literature in 18th and early 19th cent. (*Edinburgh Review* founded 1802) and is associated with many famous men of learning. Industries—engineering, tanning, making of machine tools, chemicals and biscuits— are mostly in suburbs. LEITH is city's port.

Edinburghshire, county, Scotland: see MIDLOTHIAN.

Edirne, Turkey: see ADRIANOPLE.

Edison, Thomas A(lva), 1847–1931, American inventor. His early inventions include a transmitter and receiver for automatic telegraph, a system of transmitting four simultaneous messages, and an improved stock-ticker system. He invented a carbon telephone transmitter and the first successful phonograph. In 1879 he produced the first commercially practical incandescent lamp; developed complete system of electricity distribution for use with it. Later (1881–82) he developed first central electric-light power plant in world. Edison demonstrated synchronization of moving pictures and sound; produced superior storage battery; developed kinetoscope; built and ran experimental electric railroad. He held over 1,300 patents.

Edisto (ĕ′dĭstō), river rising in W central S.C. and flowing 90 mi. SE and S to the Atlantic, separating near ocean to form Edisto Isl.

Edman, Irwin, 1896–, American philosopher; teacher at Columbia after 1918. Achieved wide popularity, particularly in the field of aesthetics. His works include *Philosopher's Holiday* (1938), *Arts and the Man* (1939), and *Philosopher's Quest* (1947).

Edmond, city (pop. 6,086), central Okla., N of Oklahoma City. Farm trade center with oil fields. Wiley Post memorial near by.

Edmonds, Walter L(umaux), 1903–, American author of historical novels, mostly about N.Y. state, such as *Rome Haul* (1929), *Drums Along the Mohawk* (1936), *Chad Hanna* (1940).

Edmonton, city (pop. 159,631), provincial cap. (since 1905), central Alta., Canada, on North Saskatchewan R. Transportation and distribution center for Peace and Athabaska river area and for N Mackenzie region, it is S terminus of Alaska Highway. Has important fur trade, grain elevators, lumber and flour mills, oil refineries, woodworking and meat-packing plants, and major airport. Seat of Univ. of ALBERTA. Fort Edmonton was built 1794, rebuilt 1819 after 1807 destruction by Indians.

Edmonton, urban district (pop. 104,244), Middlesex, England, near London. Associated with Charles Lamb, Keats, and Cowper.

Edmund, Saint (Edmund Rich), 1170?–1240, English churchman; archbishop of Canterbury under HENRY III, with whom he vainly struggled.

Edmund Crouchback: see LANCASTER, HOUSE OF.

Edmund Ironside, d. 1016, king of England (1016). Son of ÆTHELRED, he was prominent in fighting against CANUTE. On Æthelred's death, Edmund was proclaimed king although Canute received support of over half of England. Courage and bravery earned him name of Ironside. After battle of Assandun, he and Canute came to terms and partitioned England.

Edmundston, town (pop. 10,753), NW N.B., Canada, at Maine border, on St. John R. at mouth of Madawaska R. Pulp-milling center, fishing and hunting base. Settled c.1785 by Acadians as Petit Sault.

Edom (ē′dŏm), **Idumaea,** or **Idumea** (both: ĭdūmē′ủ), mountainous country, called also Mt. Seir, given to Esau and his descendants. Extended from Dead Sea to Gulf of Aqaba. Edomites were often in conflict with their neighbors, especially the Hebrews; later they moved to S Judah and were finally subdued by the Maccabees.

Edrisi: see IDRISI.

Education, United States Office of, estab. 1867 as independent governmental agency, trans-

ferred 1869 to Dept. of the Interior, transferred 1939 to Federal Security Agency. Created to collect and disseminate information on education and to promote better U.S. educational standards. Expanded functions now include administering funds appropriated as aids to education, conducting special studies.

Edward, kings of England. **Edward I,** 1239–1307, was king 1272–1307. Son of Henry III, he fought for him in BARONS' WAR (1263–67) and was responsible for triumph. Conquest of Wales was followed by long campaign against Scotland. Made notable efforts to extend English rule to all of Britain. His legal reforms (notably Statutes of WESTMINSTER) earned him name of the English Justinian. Restricted private and church courts and prohibited land grants to church without his permission. His Model Parliament (1295) marked greater representation of barons, merchants, and clergy whose resistance to war taxation forced king to confirm previous charters (e.g., Magna Carta). His promise to collect taxes only with consent of parliament became basis of "no taxation without representation." His son, **Edward II,** 1284–1327, was king 1307–27. The dominant strains of his reign were internal dissension and the loss of Scotland. His insistence on having Piers GAVESTON at court caused rebellion of barons, who later killed Gaveston. Edward's later favorites, the Hugh Despensers, virtually ruled 1322–26. They made a truce with Robert the Bruce and recognized him as king of Scots. Queen Isabella refused to return from France while the Despensers ruled, entered an adulterous alliance with Roger de Mortimer, and invaded England (1326). The Despensers were executed and Edward forced to abdicate. Brutally mistreated, he was finally killed by henchmen of Isabella and Mortimer. His son, **Edward III,** 1312–77, was king 1327–77. Real power was held by Isabella and Mortimer until Edward seized it in 1330. He supported Edward de Baliol against Scottish king David II, but, despite his victory at Halidon Hill in 1333, Scottish question remained unsettled. HUNDRED YEARS WAR, which was to dominate his reign, began in 1337. He and his son, EDWARD THE BLACK PRINCE, took an active part in the war, the first phase of which ended with Treaty of London in 1359. War was renewed after various treaties and truces, but, like the Scottish wars, was inconclusive in Edward's reign. Parliament, which withheld money grants and forced concessions from king, now began to take on form it was to retain. Black Death (see PLAGUE) decimated the population and brought about social changes in demands of lower classes for higher wages and social advancement. Edward quarreled with the Church, and religious unrest found a spokesman in John WYCLIF. There was rivalry between court party headed by JOHN OF GAUNT (supported by Edward's mistress Alice Perrers) and parliamentary party led by Black Prince and Edmund Mortimer. **Edward IV,** 1442–83, son of Richard, duke of York, became king (1461–70) as leader of York party (see ROSES, WARS OF) after his defeat of Lancastrians and capture of HENRY VI. Edward's disaffected cousin, earl of Warwick, fled to France and formed alliance with MARGARET OF ANJOU, queen of deposed Henry VI. They returned to England with troops and replaced Henry on throne. Their final defeat by Edward led to Henry's death in the Tower (1471) and quiet end to Edward's reign. His son, **Edward V,** 1470–83, boy king (1483), was pawn of conflicting ambitions of his uncles, Richard, duke of Gloucester, and Earl Rivers. Gloucester confined the king and his younger brother to the Tower, had them declared illegitimate, and took the throne as RICHARD III. More than 20 years later Sir Thomas More declared the princes had been smothered in their sleep on Gloucester's orders. Shakspere's *Richard III* deals with their fate. **Edward VI,** 1537–53, succeeded his father Henry VIII as king (1547–53) under council of regency controlled by his uncle and protector, Edward SEYMOUR, duke of Somerset. Tudor absolutism was relaxed by liberalizing treason and heresy laws. Government moved slowly towards Protestantism. Somerset's sympathy with yeomen's problems led to overthrow by his rival, John Dudley, duke of NORTHUMBERLAND. He secured ascendancy over the king and persuaded him to settle crown on Lady Jane GREY. Resulting struggle for throne ended in victory of Mary I. **Edward VII,** 1841–1910, was king 1901–10. Eldest son of Queen Victoria, he was prince of Wales for 60 years. Cooperated reluctantly in Herbert Asquith's attempt to limit veto power of House of Lords. Improved international understanding by traveling on continent, by promoting alliance with France, and by arbitration treaties with other powers. Father of George V, whose eldest son, **Edward VIII** (1894–), was king 1936. As prince of Wales he attracted attention by interest in social reform problems. The issue of his marriage to Wallis Warfield Simpson (see duchess of WINDSOR) precipitated a crisis with the cabinet headed by Stanley Baldwin. Their fear of a threat to constitutional procedure forced his abdication in 1936. As duke of Windsor he married Wallis Warfield 1937. Was governor of the Bahamas 1940–45.

Edward Nyanza (nīän'zŭ), lake, area 830 sq. mi., in Great Rift Valley, central Africa, on border of Belgian Congo and Uganda; alt. 3,240 ft. Discovered 1889 by Stanley. Also called L. Edward.

Edwards, Jonathan, 1703–58, American theologian and metaphysician. His strict Calvinist preaching brought GREAT AWAKENING to New England. His masterpiece, *The Freedom of the Will* (1754), sets forth metaphysical and ethical arguments for determinism.

Edwardsville. 1 City (pop. 8,776), SW Ill., NE of St. Louis, in coal area. Metal products. **2** Borough (pop. 6,686), NE Pa., on Susquehanna R. near Wilkes-Barre. Coal mining.

Edward the Black Prince, 1330–76, son of Edward III of England. Was first duke (of Cornwall) ever created in England (1337). He fought in battle of Crécy and siege of Calais. In 1356 he won battle of Poitiers and captured John II of France. Edward III created a principality of his French holdings,

and the Black Prince maintained a brilliant court at Bordeaux after 1363. He aided Peter I (of Castile and Leon) in keeping his throne against rebellious Castilians, but the taxes he was forced to levy in Aquitaine resulted in war with Charles V of France. Bad health forced him to resign his principalities in 1372. Opposed his brother, JOHN OF GAUNT, who had become virtual ruler of England with the aging of Edward III. He died before his father but his son succeeded to the throne as Richard II.

Edward the Confessor, d. 1066, king of England (1042–66). Son of Æthelred, he grew up in France and returned to succeed Harthacanute. Governed well and freed his people from heavy taxes. Strife with powerful noble, Earl GODWIN, was heightened by Edward's favor of the Normans in England. Godwin and his family were exiled (1051) but soon returned. During their absence Edward received William, duke of Normandy, and probably promised him the succession. Since both William and Harold III of Norway had claims to the English throne, Edward recognized Godwin's warlike son, HAROLD, as his heir. Crisis was resolved by the NORMAN CONQUEST. Edward's piety won him name of Confessor.

Edward the Elder, d. 924, king of Wessex (899–924). Son of Alfred and joint king with him, he played an active part in wars with the Danes. Gradually became ruler of all England S of the Humber.

Edward the Martyr, d. 978, king of England (975–78), son of Edgar. Murdered at Corfe, his body was removed to Shaftesbury. Miracles occurred there and he was regarded as a saint and martyr.

Edwin or **Eadwin** (both: ĕ'dwĭn), 585?–632, king of Northumbria (616–32). Kept from the throne by Æthelfrith, he was restored by Rædwald and became overlord of all the Anglo-Saxon kingdoms except Kent.

Eeckhout, Gerbrand van den (gĕr'bränt vän dĕn äk'hout), 1621–74, Dutch painter, a close follower of Rembrandt.

eel, edible fish of family Anguillidae of order Apodes. Common fresh-water eel (*Anguilla*) found in Atlantic waters of North America, Europe, and in Mediterranean. Minute scales embedded in skin cover snakelike body; dorsal and anal fins are continuous around tail. Females grow to c.4 ft. long; males to c.2 ft. American and European species breed in Atlantic Ocean S and SE of Bermuda. They hatch as tiny, flattened, transparent larvae which travel back to ancestral shores, developing as elvers. Females swim up rivers, while males remain near mouth. Sexually mature adults migrate to breeding grounds, reproduce, and die.

Efate: see NEW HEBRIDES.

efficiency: see INDUSTRIAL MANAGEMENT; MACHINE; WORK.

Effingham, city (pop. 6,892), SE central Ill., SE of Decatur, in agr., dairy area. Rail and mfg. (food products) center. L. Kanaga (resort) borders city.

efflorescence: see HYDRATE.

Égalité, Philippe: see ORLÉANS, family.

Egan, Pierce, 1772–1849, English sports writer of the Regency.

Egbert, d. 839, king of Wessex (802–39), son of an underking of Kent. He eventually secured submission of Kent, East Anglia, Mercia, and Northumbria, thus gaining overlordship of all the Anglo-Saxon kingdoms.

Eger (ā'gŭr), Czech *Cheb,* city (pop. 14,533; 1939 pop. 35,507), NW Bohemia, Czechoslovakia. Commercial center. Town hall and castle were scene of assassination of Wallenstein and his officers (1634). German-speaking pop. expelled after World War II.

Eger (ĕ'gĕr), Ger. *Erlau,* city (pop. 32,482), NE Hungary, on Eger R., in wine-growing region. Created bishopric by St. Stephen (now an archiepiscopal see), it is called the "Rome of Hungary" for its many churches. Its fortress withstood Turkish siege in 1552, fell through treachery in 1596, was razed after Francis II Rakoczy used it in his fight against Austria.

Egeria (ējēr'ēŭ), in Roman religion, water goddess. She was invoked as a goddess of childbirth. Because she was adviser to King Numa, her name has been applied to all women of culture who advise writers and artists.

Egerton, Thomas: see ELLESMERE, THOMAS EGERTON, BARON.

egg: see OVUM.

Egge, Peter (pä'tŭr ĕ'gŭ) 1869–, Norwegian novelist, author of *Hansine Solstad* (1925).

Eggleston, Edward, 1837–1902, American author, a Methodist clergyman, circuit rider in Indiana, best known for *The Hoosier Schoolmaster* (1871).

eggnog, beverage of eggs beaten with milk or cream, sweetened and flavored. It often contains spirits or wine. It is a traditional Christmas drink.

eggplant, tropical vegetable (*Solanum melongena*) widely grown for purple or white fruit.

Egham (ĕg'ŭm), urban district (pop. 24,515), Surrey, England, on the Thames. Near by are Virginia Water, an artificial lake, and RUNNYMEDE.

Eginhard, Frankish historian: see EINHARD.

eglantine: see SWEETBRIER.

Eglon (ĕg'–), king of Moab: see EHUD.

Egmont, Lamoral, count of (lä'mōräl), 1522–68, Flemish statesman, governor of Brabant and Artois. Though a devout Catholic and a loyal servant of Philip II of Spain, he intervened in behalf of the persecuted Protestants. Duke of ALBA had him and count of HOORN arbitrarily arrested (1567) and beheaded after an irregular trial. Their death stirred the Netherlanders to open rebellion. Egmont is central figure in tragedy by Goethe, with overture and incidental music by Beethoven.

ego: see PSYCHOANALYSIS.

egret (ēgrĕt'), name for several heron species in both hemispheres. Slaughtered in nesting colonies for white, silky plumage (called aigrettes) used in millinery, they were nearly exterminated before they were protected by law.

Egypt, kingdom (386,198 sq. mi.; pop. 19,-087,304), occupying NE corner of Africa and Sinai peninsula of SW Asia; cap. CAIRO, chief port ALEXANDRIA. Bounded on W by Libya and on S by ANGLO-EGYPTIAN SUDAN. Mainly a plateau, split by the Nile into Western Desert and Eastern Desert. Some 95% of population lives in fertile valley and delta of the Nile. Chief export crop is cotton, and oil, salt, and potash are exploited. Chief industry is cotton spinning and weaving. Some 91% of population is Moslem; 8% is Christian (Coptic); and there is small minority of Jews. Earliest known date in world history is that of adoption of Egyptian calendar in 4241 B.C. A widely accepted dating system divides Egyptian history into 30 dynasties (3400–332 B.C.). In c.3400 B.C. Menes united two earlier kingdoms to create centralized Egyptian state, with cap. at Memphis. Fall of Old Kingdom in 25th cent. B.C. was followed by dark age. Unity restored in 2160 B.C. by IX dynasty, with cap. at Thebes; Middle Kingdom reached its height in 2000 B.C. After its fall (1788 B.C.) Egypt passed under the Hyksos (apparently Semites from east), who were expelled 1580 B.C. by native founder of New Kingdom. Weakened by decline of royal power, Egypt came under rule of the Nubians in 712 B.C. and later, briefly, under the Assyrians. Returned to orderly native rule in c.663 B.C., but again came under foreign rule in 525 B.C. with conquest by Cambyses of Persia. Regained freedom in 405 B.C. by successful revolt. Alexander the Great took Egypt unopposed in 332 B.C. His brief empire faded, and Egypt fell to his general Ptolemy who became king as Ptolemy I, with cap. at Alexandria. Rising power of Rome early overshadowed Egypt, and even the wily efforts of CLEOPATRA failed to regain power for Egypt. Octavian annexed Egypt to Rome and killed Ptolemy XIV (last of the Ptolemies). Christianity was welcomed in Egypt, and several of most famous Doctors of the Church were Egyptians; Coptic Church arose out of MONOPHYSITISM. Arabic conquest (639–42) made Egypt an integral part of Moslem world. In 10th cent. Egypt fell to FATIMITE family, who founded Cairo as their capital. During period of Ayyubite dynasty (founded by Saladin) Egypt came under control of the MAMELUKES (1250–1517). Ottoman Turks conquered Egypt in 1517, but by 18th cent. their rule had become almost nominal. Napoleon's occupation of Egypt (1798–1801) was undertaken ostensibly to restore Turkish rule in region but actually to sever British trade lines with India; his withdrawal was forced by Anglo-Turkish forces. MOHAMMED ALI, who rose to power in 1805 as Egyptian pasha (governor), became founder of present royal line. With growing independence from Ottoman rule the title khedive (viceroy) was granted to ISMAIL PASHA. In World War I the British (who had brought Egypt under their control 1883–1907) made it a British protectorate. Agitation by WAFD party led to granting of independence in 1923, with FUAD I as Egypt's first constitutional monarch. Anglo-Egyptian treaty of 1936 promised eventual withdrawal of all British troops. In World War II Egypt was defended by the British (see NORTH AFRICA, CAMPAIGNS IN); it did not declare war against the Axis until Feb., 1945. Under FAROUK I, Egypt (as member of ARAB LEAGUE) attacked Israel in 1948. In Aug., 1952, an army coup forced Farouk's abdication and estab. reform government under Gen. NAGUIB.

Egyptian architecture reached formulation prior to 3000 B.C. Lack of wood and availability of clay and stone led to development of an architecture of massive and static quality. Immensely thick walls, containing only a few small openings, were covered with colorful pictorial and hieroglyphic carvings. Columns were confined to halls and inner courts, and supported flat stone roofs. Belief in existence after death resulted in sepulchral architecture of impressiveness and permanence. Remains of Old Kingdom (3400–2475 B.C.) are chiefly tombs of monarchs (see PYRAMID). Tombs of Middle Kingdom (2475–1788 B.C.) were tunneled out of rock cliffs. New Empire (1580–1090 B.C.) was great period of temple construction, exemplified by temple at KARNAK.

Egyptian art. Characteristic stylistic conventions appear with beginning of Old Kingdom period (3400–2475 B.C.). Relief sculpture and painting show human figure with eyes and shoulders in front view, head, pelvis, legs, and feet in profile view. Little attempt at plastic or spatial illusionism; color applied in flat tones. Sculpture in the round emphasized symmetry and minimized suggested movement. Painting served primarily as accessory to sculpture. In Middle Kingdom Period (2475–1788 B.C.) painting and sculpture became increasingly formalized. In Empire period (1580–1090 B.C.) they tended toward greater elasticity of line and boldness of design; a masterpiece of period is painted limestone bust of Queen Nefretete. Art of Saite period (8th cent. B.C.) returned to simplicity of Old Kingdom style. Egyptian art began to decline during Ptolemaic dynasty and was eventually stifled by infiltration of Greek and Roman forms.

Egyptian language, chief of the anc. Hamitic languages. See HIEROGLYPHIC and LANGUAGE (table).

Egyptian religion. Although documentary evidence on religion of ancient Egypt is rich and varied, interpretations are difficult because of its complexity and contradictions. Gods are identical and yet coexist, and contradictory myths explaining creation of world and natural phenomena were simultaneously accepted. Gods had relationship to various animals and were represented as part animal and part human—e.g., Ptah and Serapis, the great gods, with the Apis bull; Nut and Hathor, mother goddesses, with the cow; Bast, mother goddess, with the cat; and Horus, sun-god, with the hawk. Sun worship was very important in Egypt. The one attempt to establish monotheism there—the reforms of IKHNATON—was aimed at making sun-god the sole deity. Horus, Ra, and Amon were sun-gods. Great emphasis was placed on cult of the dead; hence building of PYRAMID as tomb of king and preservation of body by embalming and mummification. There was belief in immortality of body and of vital spirit or ka. King as successor to god and himself a god was chief priest. Many Egyptian gods, notably ISIS, Horus, and Serapis, became popular in Greece and Rome.

Egyptians, Gospel of the: see PSEUDEPIGRAPHA.

Ehrenburg, Ilya (Grigoryevich) (ēlyä′ grǐgôr′yǔvǐch ā′rŭnbōork), 1891–, Russian novelist and journalist. Among translated works are *The Love of Jeanne Ney* (1924); *The Tempering of Russia* (1944; reports on World War I and II). Received Stalin Prize twice (1942, 1948).

Ehrlich, Paul (poul′ âr′lǐkh), 1854–1915, German bacteriologist. He shared 1908 Nobel Prize in Physiology and Medicine for work in immunology. Discovered drugs effective against syphilis.

Ehud (ē′hŭd), man who assassinated King Eglon of Moab and freed Israel from Moabite oppression. He later became a judge of Israel. Judges 3.12–30.

Eichendorff, Joseph, Freiherr von (yō′zĕf frī′hĕr fŭn ī′khŭndôrf), 1788–1857, German poet. His lyric nature poems are spontaneously musical and have attracted many composers, notably Schumann. Some have passed into folklore. *Memoirs of a Good-for-Nothing* (1826; Eng. tr., 1866), a delightful short novel, shows German romanticism at its best.

Eichholtz, Jacob (īk′hôlts), 1776–1842, American portrait painter, pupil of Gilbert Stuart.

Eider (ī′dŭr), river, 125 mi. long, N Germany, separating Holstein from Schleswig. Flows W into North Sea.

Eifel (ī′fŭl), plateau, NW Germany, N of Moselle R. and E of the Ardennes. Barren area with deep valleys, extinct volcanoes, crater lakes. Highest point 2,447 ft.

Eiffel, Alexandre Gustave (ī′fŭl, Fr. älĕksä′drŭ güstäv′ āfĕl′), 1832–1923, French engineer, bridge and viaduct builder, authority on aerodynamics. He designed the **Eiffel Tower** (984 ft. high) erected for the Paris exposition of 1889.

Eight, The, group of American artists in New York, formed in 1908 to exhibit paintings. Comprised Arthur B. Davies, Maurice Prendergast, Ernest Lawson, William Glackens, Everett Shinn, Robert Henri, John Sloan, and George Luks. These men of widely different tendencies were bound by common opposition to academism and were stigmatized as "the ashcan school." They organized Armory Show of 1913 which introduced modern European art to a reluctant but curious America.

Eijkman, Christian (krīs′tyän īk′män), 1858–1930, Dutch physician. Shared 1929 Nobel Prize in Physiology and Medicine for work on cause of beriberi.

Eikon Basilike (īkŏn bùsī′lǐkē) [Gr.,= royal image], work generally believed an autobiography by Charles I of England. Later John GAUDEN claimed authorship and started long controversy. Also Icon, Ikon.

Eildon Hills (ēl′dùn), three conical hills, Roxburghshire, Scotland. Associated with legends of Thomas of Erceldoune.

Eilshemius, Louis Michel (īlshē′mèùs), 1864–1941, American painter of numerous landscapes. His work first won notice at Armory Show of 1913.

Eindhoven (īnt′hō″vùn), municipality (pop. 134,527), North Brabant prov., S Netherlands. Mfg. of electrical appliances, radios, plastics, textiles. In World War II Allied airborne troops landed successfully here (Sept., 1944).

Einhard (ēn'härd) or **Eginhard** (ā'gĭnhärd), c.770–840, Frankish historian. Known for biography of Charlemagne, a prime contemporary source book.

Einsiedeln (īn'zē"dùln), town (pop. 8,392), Schwyz canton, central Switzerland. Benedictine abbey (founded 9th cent.) has fountain with statue of Blessed Virgin; noted place of pilgrimage.

Einstein, Albert (īn'stīn), 1879–, American theoretical physicist, b. Germany. He won the 1921 Nobel Prize for contributions to theoretical physics, especially for work on the photoelectric effect. He postulated (1905) light quanta or photons, comparable to energy quanta, and on these based his explanation of the photoelectric effect; he developed the quantum theory of specific heat. In 1905 he set forth his special theory of relativity on electrodynamics of moving bodies and equivalence of mass and mechanical energy. In 1911 he asserted the equivalence of gravitation and inertia and c.1916 completed the mathematical formulation of his general theory of relativity which included gravitation as a determiner of curvature of space-time continuum and represented gravitation as a field rather than a force. His mathematical expression of the theory appeared in 1950. In 1939 he stressed the urgency of investigating the use of atomic energy in bombs.

Einthoven, Willem (vĭ'lùm ĭnt'hōvùn), 1860–1927, Dutch physiologist. Won 1924 Nobel Prize in Physiology and Medicine for development of electrocardiograph which makes graphic records of heart action.

Eire: see IRELAND.

Eisenach (ī'zùnäkh), city (pop. 51,834), Thuringia, central Germany. Mfg. of electrical supplies, chemicals. Birthplace of J. S. Bach; residence of Luther, 1498–1501. German Social Democratic party formed here by Bebel and Liebknecht at Socialist congress of 1869. WARTBURG is near by.

Eisenhower, Dwight D(avid) (ī'zùnhou"ûr), 1890–, American general, 33d President of the United States (1953–), b. Denison, Texas. Commanded Allied forces in North Africa in World War II. Appointed supreme commander of Allied Expeditionary Force in 1943; integrated forces in battle for Europe. Made general of the army ("five-star general") in 1944. U.S. army chief of staff 1945–48. President of Columbia Univ. 1948–53. Appointed supreme commander of Allied forces in Europe (NATO) in 1950; resigned post 1952. Successful Republican presidential candidate in 1952. His nickname is Ike.

Eisenstadt (ī'zùnshtät), town (pop. 7,626), cap. of Burgenland, E Austria. Haydn resided here under patronage of Esterhazy family.

Eisenstein, Sergei Mikhailovich (sīrgā mēkhī'lùvĭch āzùnshtyän'), 1898–1948, Russian film director. Won world wide fame (1925) with *Potemkin.* Other films include *Alexander Nevsky* (1938) and *Ivan the Terrible* (1944; Part II withheld by Soviet Film Trust).

Eisleben (īs'lābùn), city (pop. 29,652), Saxony-Anhalt, central Germany, at foot of Harz mts. Copper-mining center for 750 years. Houses where Martin Luther was born and died still stand.

Eisner, Kurt (kōôrt īs'nùr), 1867–1919, German Socialist. Organized revolution which overthrew Bavarian monarchy (1918); was first republican premier of Bavaria. A separatist, he opposed the reestablishment of a federal Germany. Assassinated by an anti-Semitic nationalist.

eisteddfod (āstĕdh'vōd) [Welsh,= session], Welsh festival. Contests are held in all arts and crafts, with special emphasis on music and poetry. National Eisteddfod held annually in August; local eisteddfods held throughout year. Important in preserving Welsh language and culture.

ejido (āhē'dō) [Span.,= common land], in Mexico, agricultural land expropriated from large private holdings and redistributed to small farmers. Common holding practiced by Aztecs, reinstituted under Cárdenas. First large-scale ejido estab. in LAGUNA DISTRICT (1936).

Ekaterinburg, RSFSR: see SVERDLOVSK.

Ekaterinodar, RSFSR: see KRASNODAR.

Ekkehard (ĕ'kùhärt), name of several monks of St. Gall, Swiss monastery. **Ekkehard I** wrote the *Waltharilied* (c.930), a Latin epic. **Ekkehard II,** fl. 10th cent., appears in Scheffel's novel *Ekkehard.* **Ekkehard IV,** fl. 11th cent., revised *Waltharilied* and contributed to chronicle of St. Gall.

Ekron (ĕ'krŏn), Philistine city, ESE of Jaffa, last foreign city to keep Ark of the Covenant before its return to Israel. Now called Akir.

El. For Arabic and Spanish names beginning thus and not listed here, see second element; e.g., for El Alamein, see ALAMEIN; for El Salvador, see SALVADOR.

Elagabalus: see HELIOGABALUS.

Elah (ē'lù), **1** Died c.885 B.C., king of Israel (c.886–c.885 B.C.), successor of Baasha. He was murdered by Zimri, who succeeded him. 1 Kings 16.8–14. **2** Valley in which David slew Goliath.

El Alamein, Egypt: see ALAMEIN.

Elam (ē'lùm), anc. Asiatic country, N of Persian Gulf, now in W Iran. A civilization began in 5th millennium B.C. Cap. was SUSA, and country is often called Susiana. In 18th cent. B.C. it overthrew Babylonia. Golden age came after 1200 B.C. Fell to ASSUR-BANI-PAL (c.645 B.C.).

eland (ē'lùnd), the largest living African antelope. Bull may be 6 ft. high at shoulder and weigh over 1,200 lb. Spiral horns extend straight upward.

elasticity, ability of matter to return to original shape or volume after distortion. Elasticity is measured in the amount of force a substance can resist without permanent deformity; smallest force that brings this about is elastic limit.

Elath (ē'–), ancient port, on Gulf of Aqaba. Built by King Uzziah of Judah, lost by King Ahaz. Also appears as Eloth. Was on or near site of modern Aqaba.

Elba (ĕl'bù), island (86 sq. mi.; pop. 29,462), off Tuscany, central Italy, in Tyrrhenian Sea; chief town Portoferraio. Iron mines. Principality 1814–15 under exiled Napoleon.

Elbasan (ĕlbäsän'), town (pop. 14,968), central Albania; center of fertile agr. region.

Elbe (ĕl'bù), Czech *Labe,* river, c.700 mi. long, Czechoslovakia and Germany, rising in N Bohemia and flowing NW through Bohemia,

Saxony, and N Germany (past Dresden, Magdeburg, and Hamburg) into North Sea. Connected by canal system with Oder and navigable for 525 mi., it is a major European waterway. Germany repudiated (1938) its internationalization by Versailles Treaty.

Elberfeld, Germany: see WUPPERTAL.

Elbert, Mount: see SAWATCH MOUNTAINS.

Elberton, city (pop. 6,772), NE Ga., ENE of Athens near Savannah \R. State's granite center.

El-beth-el, name given by Jacob to place at BETHEL where God appeared to him. Gen. 35.7.

Elbing (ĕl'bĭng), Pol. *Elbląg,* city (pop. 20,924; 1939 pop. 85,952), former East Prussia, E of Danzig (under Polish administration since 1945); port on Elbing R. near its mouth on Baltic Sea. Was member of Hanseatic League. The city passed to Poland 15th cent., to Prussia 1772.

Elbrus, Mount (ĕl'brōōs), highest mountain of Caucasus and Europe, NW Georgian SSR, formed by two extinct volcanic cones, respectively 18,481 and 18,356 ft. high.

Elburz (ĕlbōōrz'), mountains, N Iran, S of Caspian Sea. Highest is Mt. Demavend (c.18,600 ft. high).

El Cajon (ĕl kähōn'), city (pop. 8,653), S Calif., E of San Diego, in avocado, citrus fruit, and grape region.

El Campo (ĕl kăm'pō), city (pop. 6,237), S Texas, SW of Houston. Market center for oil, cattle, dairy, and agr. area. Mfg. of food and metal products; meat packing plants.

El Centro (ĕl sĕn'trō), city (pop. 12,590), SE Calif., S of Salton Sea; laid out 1905. Shipping center for IMPERIAL VALLEY truck and livestock.

El Cerrito (ĕl sûrē'tō), residential city (pop. 18,011), W Calif., on San Francisco Bay.

elder or **elderberry,** deciduous tree or shrub of genus *Sambucus,* widely distributed. Common elderberry (*Sambucus canadensis*) has purple berries in late summer used to make wine and jelly. Other species, e.g., European elder (*S. nigra*), are sometimes grown for ornament.

Eldon, John Scott, 1st earl of, 1751–1838, English statesman and jurist. As attorney general he drew up repressive laws of 1793–98. Lord chancellor almost continuously 1801–27 and virtual prime minister 1807–12, he was a reactionary Tory. Opposed Catholic Emancipation and liberal reform.

El Dorado (ĕl' dùrä'dō) [Span.,= the gilded man], mythical country sought by adventurers in North and South America. Used figuratively to mean any country of wealth or land of desire.

El Dorado (ĕl dùrā'dù). **1** City (pop. 23,076), S Ark., near La. line; settled 1843. Oil center of the state (after 1921) and a farm trade center, with lumber and cotton mills. **2** City (pop. 11,037), SE Kansas, on Walnut R. and ENE of Wichita; laid out 1868. Refines and ships oil.

Eldorado Mines, Canada: see PORT RADIUM.

Eleanor Crosses: see ELEANOR OF CASTILE.

Eleanor of Aquitaine (ăkwĭtān'), 1122?–1204, queen of HENRY II of England; daughter of William X, duke of Aquitaine. Her marriage to LOUIS VII of France was annulled in 1152. Shortly thereafter she married Henry, then duke of Normandy. Two of her sons became kings of England—RICHARD I and JOHN. Henry's infidelities (see ROSAMOND) caused her to estab. (1170) her own court at Poitiers. Aided her sons in an unsuccessful revolt (1173) against Henry (who confined her for many years) and helped Richard secure the throne. Her court was the scene of much artistic activity.

Eleanor of Castile (kăstēl'), d. 1290, queen consort of EDWARD I of England. After her death Edward supposedly had Eleanor Crosses erected to mark stages of her funeral journey at Lincoln, Grantham, Stamford, Geddington, Northampton, Stony Stratford, Woburn, Dunstable, St. Albans, Waltham, Westcheap, and Charing. Three are extant, though restored.

Eleatic school (ēlēă'tĭk), Greek pre-Socratic school of philosophy at Elea, Italy, including Xenophanes, PARMENIDES, Melissus, and ZENO. Taught that being is ultimate reality and that sense perceptions and change are illusory.

elecampane (ĕ"lùkămpān'), hardy Old World herb (*Inula helenium*) naturalized in U.S. It has yellow-rayed flowers. Its thick root was formerly used as cough remedy and in horse medicine.

election, organized voting to choose candidates for office. Greek officials, though occasionally elected, were more often selected by lot than elected by balloting, and in Rome the popular assemblies elected the tribunes. Popular suffrage and elections, practically abandoned in Middle Ages, have grown principally along with democracy. In England, elections, associated with parliamentary procedures from the 13th cent., were regularized after 1688 and led to the secret ballot in 1872. In the U.S., the Seventeenth Amendment provided for the popular election of Senators, the Fourteenth (1868) and Fifteenth (1870) for the enfranchisement of the Negro, and the Nineteenth (1920) for the enfranchisement of women.

electoral college, in U.S. government, the body of electors in the states which chooses the President and Vice President. The Constitution provides that each state may appoint a number of electors equal to the whole number of the state's U.S. Senators and Representatives. Congress is authorized to count their votes. To win, a presidential candidate must have a majority in the electoral college (not necessarily a majority of popular votes). Twelfth Amendment (1804) enjoins electors to vote for President and Vice President separately and provides that, in case no candidate has a majority of the electoral vote, the House of Representatives (voting by state, with one vote for each state) shall choose the President from among the three candidates highest on electoral list. Present popular election of electors superseded earlier choice by state legislatures; prevailing general-ticket system enables a party to carry whole state if it achieves a plurality vote.

electors. In theory, the head of the HOLY ROMAN EMPIRE was elected by a number of princes called electors; until 1562 his title was king of the Romans unless he was crowned emperor by the pope. In practice, in all elections but one after 1438, a member of the house of HAPSBURG was chosen. The Golden Bull (so called because of its golden seal), issued by Charles IV in 1356, designated as upper house of the DIET the seven prince-electors; archbishops of Mainz, Trier, and Cologne; king of Bohemia; count palatine of the Rhine; duke of Saxony; margrave of Brandenburg. The palatine vote was transferred (1623) to duke of Bavaria, but in 1648 an eighth vote was created for the count palatine. A ninth vote was given to the dukes of Hanover (after 1714 also kings of England). Elections took place amid great pomp at Frankfurt.

Electra (ĭlĕk'trŭ), in Greek mythology. **1** Daughter of Agamemnon and Clytemnestra. She helped her brother ORESTES avenge murder of their father by their mother. Portrayed by Aeschylus, Sophocles, and Euripides. **2** One of the Pleiades; daughter of Atlas and mother by Zeus of Dardanus. **3** Daughter of Oceanus and mother of Iris and the Harpies.

electric circuit, unbroken path along which current of electricity flows. A simple circuit can be set up with electric cell, two conducting wires (one attached to negative and one to positive pole of cell), small lamp and socket to which free ends of wires from cell are attached. When wires are made fast, circuit is "closed," lamp will light. External circuit is part in which current flows from cell along wire to lamp, through lamp, and back along other wire to cell; internal circuit is where current flows from one electrode to another through electrolyte of cell. When wires are disconnected, circuit is "open" or broken. In practice this is done by switches and fuses. Series circuit is one in which current flows through its parts one after another; negative electrode of one cell is connected with positive electrode of another. Resistance to flow of current in series circuit is sum of the separate resistances; voltage is sum of voltages for different parts; current strength is same throughout circuit. In parallel circuit current flows through all parts at same time; like electrodes are connected, i.e., negative with negative, positive with positive. Resistance is less than that of part having least resistance; voltage same for all parts; current strength is sum of current strengths in different parts. Parallel circuit is most commonly used. Devices connected in series must all operate at same time. Series circuit generally used for street lighting, in windings of generators and motors, and transformers when high voltages are needed. See *ill.,* p. 377.

electric eye: see PHOTOELECTRIC CELL.

electric fish, name for various fish with organs (usually from modified muscle tissue) producing electricity to kill or paralyze prey or enemies. Electric eel (*Electrophorus*), a fresh-water fish related to carp, has organs producing 450–600 volts. Others are electric ray or torpedo (species in warm waters of Europe and U.S.); fresh-water electric catfish (*Malapterurus*); and U.S. Atlantic coast marine stargazer (*Astroscopus*).

electricity [from Gr.,= amber; named by Wm. Gilbert]. Modern electron theory views matter as basically electrical and the ATOM, basic unit of matter, as composed of negative charges (electrons), positive charges (protons), and neutral charges (neutrons). Electrons move within atom in orbits around nucleus and sometimes move to another atom. Loss of an electron leaves atom positively charged; gain of an electron charges it negatively. Static electricity is concerned with nature, strength, and effect of charge on bodies; ways of charging a body include bringing it close to a charged body (see INDUCTION), rubbing a glass rod with silk, and rubbing a hard rubber rod with flannel. Capacity to receive and hold charge varies; some metals, called good conductors, pass charge on rapidly; some other materials are poor conductors (see INSULATION). Current is generally said to flow from positive to negative but actually both positive and negative charges move either way in electrolytic and gaseous conductors. Electric current (or electron flow) is set up in a conductor when it connects cell electrodes, forming a closed electric circuit; one-direction flow called direct current; generator current (if no commutator is used) alternates directions. Current can produce magnetism (see ELECTROMAGNET); GALVANOMETER measures force and strength of current; electric MOTOR transforms electrical into mechanical energy. Heat produced in conductor depends on strength of current and resistance of conductor; light-bulb filament is heated to incandescence, as is electric ARC. Passage of current through solutions (see ION; ELECTROLYTE; ELECTROLYSIS) is important to metallurgy in various ways. Among the many who contributed to the knowledge and utilization of electricity are Henry Cavendish, Coulomb, Ohm, Joule, Galvani, Volta, Oersted, Ampère, Joseph Henry, Michael Faraday, J. C. Maxwell, Heinrich Hertz, W. T. Kelvin, T. A. Edison, A. G. Bell, Michael Pupin, and E. H. Armstrong. See *ill.,* p. 377.

electrochemistry, branch of chemistry concerned with relations between chemical reactions and electricity. It deals with production of electric current by chemical means, with conductivity of solutions, ELECTROLYSIS, theory of ION and ionization, and related phenomena.

electrode (ŭlĕk'trōd), a terminal or pole of electric cell or other source of current. It may be positive (anode) or negative (cathode). In any external electric circuit the flow of electrons is from negative to positive electrode.

electrolysis (ŭlĕktrŏ'lŭsĭs), passage of electric current through conducting solution (electrolyte) with decomposition of this compound. One explanation: when a compound dissolves it undergoes DISSOCIATION, i.e., each atom either loses or gains electrons to become a charged ION. When current is introduced, positive ions move to negative pole (cathode) and each gains an electron, negative move to positive (anode) and each loses an electron, and thus they revert to atoms of the new substances formed. Principle applied in metal refining and PLATING; electrotype plates are prepared by electrolysis.

electrolyte (ŭlĕk'trŭlīt), compound which, in

ELECTRICAL AND RADIO SYMBOLS

BATTERIES AND LAMPS IN SERIES

BATTERIES AND LAMPS IN PARALLEL

TRIODE

TRANSISTOR

Triode and transistor used as amplifiers. With different hook-ups they can also be used as detectors, oscillators, and rectifiers.

PHOTOELECTRIC TUBE

Electrons emitted by the light-sensitized curved plate (cathode) pass to the rod (anode), thus converting radiant energy into electric current.

DIAGRAM OF A SIMPLE RADIO CIRCUIT

solution, conducts an electric current and is decomposed by it (see ELECTROLYSIS).

electromagnet, magnet in which magnetism is produced by electric current. If bar of soft iron is placed in coil of wire through which current is flowing, the iron becomes a magnet only so long as current flows. Strength depends on number of turns in coil. Electromagnets are used in electric bell, telephone, telegraph, electric generator, and motor.

electromotive force: see VOLT.

electromotive series: see METAL.

electron (ŭlĕk'trŏn), unit charge of negative electricity or particle with negative (−) charge. Electron and proton (positive or + charge) are considered fundamental units of which all matter is composed. Electrons move in orbits around nucleus of atom; valence of element depends on number and arrangement of extranuclear electrons. Sir J. J. Thomson showed cathode rays made of electrons; R. A. Millikan determined size of charge. See *ill.*, p. 989.

electronics (ĭlĕk"trŏ'nĭks), science that deals with use of electrons emitted from solids or liquids and made to move through a vacuum or a gas. Electrons in outer orbit of an atom of a metal can be liberated by heating the surface (thermionic emission); by allowing light to fall on certain surfaces (as in PHOTOELECTRIC CELL); by bombarding metal surface with electrons or with ions (secondary emission); and by use of intense electric field of high positive potential (high-field emission or cold-cathode effect). Electron emission also occurs in naturally radioactive substances (e.g., radium, thorium, uranium, plutonium) and in cyclotron and other atom-disintegrating machines. Edison observed thermionic emission in lamp bulb (1883). Sir J. A. Fleming utilized thermionic emission in his two-element vacuum tube, or diode; Lee de Forest produced triode (1907) which advanced radio. Radio, television, Loran, radar devices, electron microscope, betatron, cyclotron, X-ray machine and certain other medical tools are products of science of electronics. Light of neon signs and of mercury-vapor, sodium-vapor, and fluorescent lamps is produced by passage of electrons through the gas. See *ill.*, p. 377.

electron microscope: see MICROSCOPE.

electron tube: see TUBE, VACUUM.

electrophorus: see VOLTA, ALESSANDRO, CONTE.

electroplating: see PLATING.

electrotherapy (ĭlĕk"trŏthĕ'rŭpē), use of electricity for medical treatment and diagnosis. Galvanic (direct) current is used to destroy skin tumors and blemishes, to stimulate surface circulation, to introduce charged particles into tissues. Diathermy (use of long- or short-wave high-frequency currents) reaches deeper tissues.

elegy, in poetry, originally a poem written in elegiac verse, i.e., a couplet consisting of a hexameter line followed by a pentameter line, now a short, subjective, reflective poem of lamentation or regret, generally dealing with death or unhappy or unrequited love. Elegiac verse reached height in work of Catullus, Propertius, Callimachus, and Ovid. Famous elegies in English include Spenser's "Astrophel," Milton's "Lycidas," Thomas Gray's

"Elegy Written in a Country Churchyard," Arnold's "Thyrsis," Shelley's "Adonais," and Whitman's "When Lilacs Last in the Dooryard Bloom'd."

element, in chemistry, substance that has not as yet been decomposed into simpler substance by chemical action. Each element is represented by a symbol. Listing elements in order of increasing ATOMIC WEIGHT was important step in formulation of PERIODIC LAW. Elements differ in VALENCE, boiling and melting points, density and specific gravity, hardness, specific heat, spectrum, radioactivity, compressibility, elasticity, thermal expansion, electrical conductivity. Some appear in different forms (see ALLOTROPY; ISOTOPE). Oxygen is most abundant element. Elements may be gas, liquid, or solid, and either metals or nonmetals. Some metallic elements were known to early man and alchemists discovered some. Hennig Brandt probably was first to discover a new element; in 1669 he prepared phosphorus from human urine. With production of transuranium elements with cyclotron, gaps in periodic table were filled and new elements were discovered.

elephant, largest living land mammal, of order Proboscidea, related to extinct mammoth and mastodon. Ancestral home believed to be Egypt, from where it migrated to Asia, Europe, North and South America. Two genera living: Asiatic or Indian (*Elephas*), and African (*Loxodonta*) now found S of Sahara only. African bulls reach 11 ft. shoulder height, Asiatic c.9 ft. African elephant has larger ears and tusks; longer, more wrinkled trunk terminating in two fingerlike protuberances (one in Asiatic). Trunk conveys plant foods to mouth and sucks up water to spray into mouth. Adults mature at 25 yrs.; at 50 are old. Usually one calf born at time; gestation lasts 18–22 months. Pygmy elephant (5–7 ft. high) inhabits W Africa.

Elephanta, island, area c.14 sq. mi., in Bombay harbor, India. Brahmanic cave temples (8th cent.).

Elephant Butte Dam, N.Mex.: see RIO GRANDE.

elephantiasis (ĕ"lŭfăntī'ŭsĭs, -fŭn–), condition resulting from obstruction of lymphatic vessels and marked by enlargement of affected part and thickening of skin. It sometimes accompanies filariasis (disease caused by parasitic roundworms).

elephant's ear: see TARO.

elephant's-foot or **Hottentot bread,** twining S African vine (*Testudinaria elephantipes*), with huge edible roots.

Eleusinian Mysteries (ĕl"ūsĭ'nēŭn), principal religious mysteries of anc. Greece, held at Eleusis. Dealt with legends of Demeter, Persephone, and Dionysus, symbolized yearly decay and renewal of vegetation, and assured a happy afterlife to those who were initiates.

elevator, device for vertical transportation. Term is applied to both enclosed structures and open ones used in buildings, ships, and mines and also to continuous-belt device with buckets for handling bulk material. Power elevators, often run by steam, were used from middle of 19th cent. Elisha Graves Otis in 1853 introduced elevator with safety device in case cable should break. Sir William Armstrong's introduction of hydraulic crane

Element	Symbol	Atomic Number	Atomic Weight	Melting Point	Boiling Point	Valence
actinium	Ac	89				
aluminum	Al	13	26.97	659.7°C.	1800°C.	3
americium	Am	95				
antimony (stibium)	Sb	51	121.76	630.5°C.	1380°C.	3, 5
argon	A	18	39.944	−189.2°C.	−185.7°C.	0
arsenic	As	33	74.91	sublimes at 615°C.		3, 5
astatine	At	85				
barium	Ba	56	137.36	850°C.	1140°C.	2
berkelium	Bk	97				
beryllium	Be	4	9.02	1350°C.	1500°C.	2
bismuth	Bi	83	209	271.3°C.	1450°C.	3, 5
boron	B	5	10.82	2300°C.	2550°C.	3
bromine	Br	35	79.916	−7°C.	58.8°C.	1, 3, 5, 7
cadmium	Cd	48	112.41	320.9°C.	767°C.	2
calcium	Ca	20	40.08	810°C.	1170°C.	2
californium	Cf	98				
carbon	C	6	12.010	3500°C.	4200°C.	2, 4
cerium	Ce	58	140.13	640°C.	1400°C.	3, 4
cesium	Cs	55	132.91	28.5°C.	670°C.	1
chlorine	Cl	17	35.457	−101.6°C.	−34.7°C.	1, 3, 5, 7
chromium	Cr	24	52.01	1615°C.	2200°C.	2, 3, 6
cobalt	Co	27	58.94	1480°C.	3000°C.	2, 3
copper	Cu	29	63.57	1083°C.	2300°C.	1, 2
curium	Cm	96	242			
dysprosium	Dy	66	162.46			3
erbium	Er	68	167.2			3
europium	Eu	63	152.0			2, 3
fluorine	F	9	19	−223°C.	−187°C.	1
francium	Fr	87				
gadolinium	Gd	64	156.9			3
gallium	Ga	31	69.72	29.7°C.	1600°C. (†)	2, 3
germanium	Ge	32	72.6	958.5°C.	2700°C.	4
gold	Au	79	197.2	1063°C.	2600°C.	1, 3
hafnium	Hf	72	178.6	(1700°C.)	3200°C. (†)	4
helium	He	2	4.003	−272°C. (‡)	−268.94°C.	0
holmium	Ho	67	164.94			3
hydrogen	H	1	1.0080	−259.14°C.	−252.7°C.	1
indium	In	49	114.8	155°C.	1450°C. (*)	3
iodine	I	53	126.922	113.5°C.	184.3°C.	1, 3, 5, 7
iridium	Ir	77	193.1	2350°C. (*)	4800°C. (†)	3, 4
iron	Fe	26	55.84	1535°C.	3000°C.	2, 3
krypton	Kr	36	83.7	−169°C.	−151.8°C.	0
lanthanum	La	57	138.92	826°C.	1800°C.	3
lead	Pb	82	207.21	327.4°C.	1620°C.	2, 4
lithium	Li	3	6.940	186°C.	1220°C. (†)	1
lutetium	Lu	71	175			3
magnesium	Mg	12	24.32	651°C.	1107°C. (*)	2
manganese	Mn	25	54.93	1260°C.	1900°C. (*)	2, 3, 7 (4, 6)
mercury	Hg	80	200.61	−38.87°C.	356°C	1, 2
molybdenum	Mo	42	96	2620°C.	3700°C. (*)	3, 4, 6
neodymium	Nd	60	144.27	840°C.		3
neon	Ne	10	20.183	−248.67°C.	−245.9°C.	0
neptunium	Np	93				
nickel	Ni	28	58.69	1455°C.	2900°C.	2, 3
niobium	Nb	41	92.91	1950°C.	3300°C. (†)	3, 4, 5
nitrogen	N	7	14.008	−209.86°C.	−195.81°C.	3, 5
osmium	Os	76	190.2	2700°C. (*)	5300°C. (†)	2, 3, 4, 6, 8
oxygen	O	8	16	−218.4°C.	−183°C.	2
palladium	Pd	46	106.7	1553°C.	2200°C. (*)	2, 4
phosphorus	P	15	30.98	See PHOSPHORUS		3, 5
platinum	Pt	78	195.23	1773.5°C.	4300°C.	2, 4
plutonium	Pu	94				
polonium	Po	84	210			
potassium	K	19	39.096	62.3°C.	760°C.	1
praseodymium	Pr	59	140.92	940°C.		3
promethium	Pm	61				
protactinium	Pa	91	231			
radium	Ra	88	226.05	960°C. (*)	1140°C. (*)	2

(*) Approximately. (†) Over. (‡) Under.

ELEMENTS (continued)

Element	Symbol	Atomic Number	Atomic Weight	Melting Point	Boiling Point	Valence
radon (niton)	Rn	86	222			0
rhenium	Re	75	186.31	3000°C.(*)		
rhodium	Rh	45	102.91	1985°C.	2500°C.(†)	3
rubidium	Rb	37	85.48	38.5°C.	700°C.	1
ruthenium	Ru	44	101.7	2450°C.(*)	2700°C.(†)	3, 4, 6, 8
samarium	Sm	62	150.43	1300°C.(†)		3
scandium	Sc	21	45.10	1200°C.	2400°C.	3
selenium	Se	34	78.96	220°C.	688°C.	2, 4, 6
silicon	Si	14	28.06	1420°C.(*)	2600°C.(*)	4
silver	Ag	47	107.88	960.5°C.	1950°C.(*)	1
sodium	Na	11	22.997	97.5°C.	880°C.	1
strontium	Sr	38	87.63	800°C.(*)	1150°C.(*)	2
sulphur	S	16	32.06	113°–119°C.	444.6°C.	2, 4, 6
tantalum	Ta	73	180.88	2850°C.(*)	4100°C.(†)	5
technetium	Tc	43				
tellurium	Te	52	127.61	452°C.	1390°C.(*)	2, 4, 6
terbium	Tb	65	159.2			3
thallium	Tl	81	204.39	303.5°C.	1650°C.(*)	1, 3
thorium	Th	90	232.12	1845°C.(*)	3000°C.(†)	4
thulium	Tm	69	169.4			3
tin	Sn	50	118.7	231.89°C.	2260°C(*)	2, 4
titanium	Ti	22	47.9	1800°C.(*)	3000°C.(†)	3, 4
uranium	U	92	238.07	1850°C.(‡)		4, 6
vanadium	V	23	50.95	1710°C.(*)	3000°C.	3, 5
wolfram	W	74	183.92	3370°C.	5900°C.(*)	6
xenon	Xe	54	131.3	−140°C.	−109.1°C.	0
ytterbium	Yb	70	173.04	1800°C.		3
yttrium	Y	39	88.92	1490°C.	2500°C.	3
zinc	Zn	30	65.38	419.47°C.	907°C.	2
zirconium	Zr	40	91.22	1900°C.(*)	2900°C.(†)	4

(*) Approximately. (†) Over. (‡) Under.

(1846) led to hydraulic elevators, which began to replace steam elevators in early 1870s. Toward close of 19th cent. electric elevators came into use.

Elfsborg, Sweden: see ALVSBORG.

Elgar, Sir Edward, 1857–1934, English composer. Music composed for Queen Victoria's Diamond Jubilee (1897) brought him recognition; he was knighted in 1904. Perhaps his best-known works are the *Variations on an Original Theme* (called the *Enigma Variations*) and the five marches, *Pomp and Circumstance.*

Elgin, Thomas Bruce, 7th **earl of** (ĕl′gĭn), 1766–1841, British soldier and diplomat. Brought to England the so-called ELGIN MARBLES from Athens. His son, **James Bruce,** 8th **earl of Elgin** (1811–63), governor general of Canada (1847–54), implemented plan for responsible government outlined by his father-in-law, the earl of DURHAM. Negotiated with U.S. the reciprocity treaty of 1854. His son, **Victor Alexander Bruce,** 9th **earl of Elgin,** 1849–1917, was viceroy of India 1894–99 and colonial secretary 1905–8.

Elgin (ĕl′jĭn), city (pop. 44,223), NE Ill., on Fox R. and WNW of Chicago; founded 1835. Rail and trade center with mfg. of dairy products, watches, wood products, and clothing; and publishing.

Elgin Marbles (ĕl′gĭn), ancient sculptures taken from Athens to London in 1806 by Thomas Bruce, 7th earl of Elgin. Consist of PARTHENON frieze and part of the ERECHTHEUM. They are now in British Museum.

Elginshire, county, Scotland: see MORAYSHIRE.

El Greco: see GRECO, EL.

Eli (ē′lī), high priest and judge of Israel, teacher of Samuel. 1 Sam. 1–4.

Elia: see LAMB, CHARLES.

Eliakim (ēlī′ŭkĭm), king of Judah: see JEHOIAKIM.

Elias (ēlī′ŭs), Greek form of ELIJAH.

Eli, Eli, lama sabachthani? (ē′lī, lā′mù sābăk′thùnī; ā′lē, lā′mä säbäkh′thänē) or **Eloi, Eloi, lama sabachthani?** (ē′loi; ā′loi) [*Eli, Eloi:* Heb. or Aramaic,= Lord; *lama sabachthani?:* Aramaic,= why hast thou forsaken me?], cry of Jesus on the cross. Mat. 27.46; Mark 15.34. Seemingly a quotation of Ps. 22.1.

Elihu (ēlī′hū) [Heb.,= he is my God], one of Job's comforters. Job 32.2–37.24.

Elijah (ēlī′jù) or **Elias** (ēlī′ŭs) [Heb.,= God's God], fl. c.875 B.C., Hebrew prophet. His mission was to destroy cults of Baal brought into Israel by Jezebel, wife of King Ahab. He is the hero of many stories (e.g., his raising of widow's son from the dead; his contest of faith with priests of Baal; his being fed by ravens; his experience of the still, small voice on Mt. Horeb). He departed from earth in a chariot of fire, leaving his sacred mantle and the continuation of his work to his disciple Elisha. Elijah appeared in the Transfiguration. He is prominent in the Koran. 1 Kings 17–19; 21.17–29; 2 Kings 1–2; Mal. 4.5; Mat. 11.14; 16.14; 17.3; Luke 4.25; John 1.21; James 5.17.

Elijah ben Solomon, 1720–97, Hebrew scholar, called the Gaon [genius] of Vilna. Fought spread of Hasidic mysticism among Jews of Poland and Lithuania.

Eliot, Charles W(illiam), 1834–1926, American educator, president of Harvard Univ. (1869–1909). Under his guidance many changes were made—e.g., introduction of elective system—the university grew, and standards were raised. Eliot also fostered development of Radcliffe Col. He was later a member of the General Education Board, a trustee of the Carnegie Foundation for the Advancement of Teaching, and an emissary abroad of the Carnegie Endowment for Internatl. Peace. He edited *The Harvard Classics* ("President Eliot's Five-Foot Shelf") to further adult education.

Eliot, George, 1819–80, English novelist, real name Mary Ann or Marian Evans. She defied convention to live a happy life with George Henry LEWES, mentor of her literary career. Her novels picture middle-class life in realistic terms with stern moral interest: in *Adam Bede* (1859), *The Mill on the Floss* (1860), *Silas Marner* (1861), *Middlemarch* (1871–72), *Daniel Deronda* (1876). *Romola* (1862–63) is a historical romance of Savonarola's Italy, and *Felix Holt* (1866) is a political novel. Also wrote poems. After Lewes's death she married John W. Cross (1880).

Eliot, Sir John, 1592?–1632, English statesman. Promoter of Petition of Right (1628), he refused to submit to Charles I and died in prison.

Eliot, John, 1604–90, English missionary in colonial Mass., called the Apostle to the Indians. Estab. villages for Christian natives.

Eliot, T(homas) S(tearns), 1888–, English poet and critic, b. St. Louis, Mo., studied at Harvard, Sorbonne, Oxford. His poetry, highly influential and much imitated, is complex with allusions and references in intellectual, often difficult, language and subtle music. Early poems—in *Prufrock and Other Observations* (1917), *The Waste Land* (1922), "The Hollow Men"—express disillusion and despair over modern life in nervous rhythms. Later he became an Anglo-Catholic, and his poems broadened with religious meaning as in *Ash Wednesday* (1930), *Four Quartets* (1943). His early poetic dramas (e.g., *Sweeney Agonistes,* 1932) were strictly literary, but later (e.g., *Murder in the Cathedral,* 1935; *Family Reunion,* 1939; *The Cocktail Party,* 1950) were successfully produced. His critical essays, stressing classical standards, did much to revive interest in Elizabethan and Jacobean authors. Awarded the 1948 Nobel Prize in Literature.

Elis (ē'lĭs), region of anc. Greece, W Peloponnesus, noted for horses and for games at OLYMPIA.

Elisabethville, city (pop. 67,980), SE Belgian Congo; founded 1910. Chief city of Katanga, a rich mining area. Copper, tin, gold, uranium refineries.

Elisha (ēlī'shŭ) or **Eliseus** (ĕlīsē'ŭs) [both: Heb.,= God is salvation], fl. 875 B.C., Hebrew prophet. He continued the work of ELIJAH under successors of Ahab. His miracles include raising of the dead boy, curing of Naaman's leprosy, and timely aid to widow in debt. 1 Kings 19.16–21; 2 Kings 2.9; 13.14–21; Luke 4.27.

Elizabeth, Saint, mother of St. John the Baptist and cousin of the Virgin MARY. Luke 1. Feast: Nov. 5.

Elizabeth, Saint, 1207–31, daughter of Andrew II of Hungary, wife of Louis II of Thuringia; noted for devotion to the needy.

Elizabeth, 1837–98, empress of Austria and queen of Hungary, consort of Francis Joseph; a Bavarian princess. Her life was marked by tragedy, notably the death of her son, Archduke RUDOLF, and her own assassination by an Italian anarchist at Geneva.

Elizabeth, 1709–62, empress of Russia (1741–62); daughter of Peter I and Catherine I. Gained throne by deposing IVAN VI. Rid Russia of German influence; successfully warred against Prussia in SEVEN YEARS WAR. Founded Moscow Univ. Her nephew, Peter III, succeeded her.

Elizabeth, 1876–, queen of Belgium, consort of ALBERT I; a Bavarian princess. Revered for her hospital work in World War I, interest in improvement of social conditions, and patronage of arts.

Elizabeth, 1596–1662, queen of Bohemia and countess palatine, consort of FREDERICK THE WINTER KING; daughter of James I of England. Nicknamed "Queen of Hearts" for her beauty. After her husband's defeat (1620) she lived in poverty in Holland; returned to England. Among her 13 children were Prince RUPERT and SOPHIA, electress of Hanover.

Elizabeth I, 1533–1603, queen of England (1558–1603). Daughter of HENRY VIII and Anne BOLEYN, she was declared illegitimate after her mother's execution. Parliament reestab. her in succession in 1544. Imprisoned as rallying point for discontented Protestants, she regained freedom by outward conformity to Catholicism. On her succession England's low fortunes included religious strife, a huge government debt, and failure in wars with France. Her reign took England through one of its greatest periods. It produced such men as Shakspere, Spenser, Francis Bacon, and Walter Ralegh. It saw the country united to become a first-rate European power with a great navy. It saw commerce and industry prosper and colonization begin. Her Tudor concept of strong rule and need for popular support helped her select excellent counselors. She reestab. Anglicanism and measures against Catholics grew harsher. Important measures enacted included stabilization of labor conditions, currency reforms, poor laws, and acts to encourage agr., commerce, and mfg. Elizabeth began a policy of peace and her series of diplomatic maneuvers eventually defeated Spain and stalemated France. Treaty of Edinburgh (1560) started policy of supporting Protestant lords against Catholics. After abdication of MARY QUEEN OF SCOTS from Scottish throne, Elizabeth gave her refuge, kept her prisoner, and executed her only after plots to seat Mary on English throne. By marriage negotiations with Francis, duke of Alençon and Anjou, she secured (1572) defence alliance against Spain and, later, French aid for the Dutch against Spain, who now emerged as England's main enemy. Philip II of Spain, whose offer of marriage Elizabeth had refused in 1559, planned Spanish Armada expedition as reprisal against English raids on Spanish shipping. Defeat of Armada broke power of Spain. Vain, fickle in bestowing favors (see 2d earl of ESSEX and earl of LEICESTER), prejudiced, vacillating, and parsimonious, she was also highly aware of responsibility of rule and immensely courageous.

Elizabeth II, 1926–, queen of Great Britain (1952–), eldest daughter of GEORGE VI. She married (1947) Philip Mountbatten, duke of Edinburgh. They have two children: Prince Charles (1948–) and Princess Anne (1950–). Her mother, **Elizabeth,** 1900–, queen consort of George VI, is the daughter of the 14th earl of Strathmore.

Elizabeth, 1843–1916, queen of Rumania, consort of Carol I; a German princess. Wrote extensively, under pseud. Carmen Sylva, in German, French, English, Rumanian. Her works include *Pensées d'une reine* (1882); *The Bard of Dimbowitza* (1891; Rumanian folk tales).

Elizabeth, city (pop. 112,817), NE N.J., S of Newark, on Newark Bay and Arthur Kill (Goethals Bridge to Staten Isl.). English bought site from Indians 1664; called Elizabethtown until 1740. Became first provincial cap. of N.J.; assembly met here 1668–82. School that became Princeton Univ. opened here 1747. Village raided and partly burned by British in Revolution. Industrialization began in late 1800s; Singer sewing-machine factory opened 1873. Mfg. of machinery, printing presses and type, paper containers, chemicals, and radio, auto, and aircraft parts. Also oil refining, bookbinding, and railroad shops. Has Nathaniel Bonnell House (before 1682), Belcher Mansion (before 1750), and Elias Boudinot's home (c. 1750).

Elizabeth City, town (pop. 12,685), NE N.C., port on Pasquotank R. N of Albemarle Sound; founded 1793. Commercial and fishing center with lumber, hosiery, and cotton mills. Resort with U.S. coast guard base.

Elizabeth Farnese (färnā′sā), 1692–1766, queen of Spain, second wife of PHILIP V; niece of duke of Parma. She dominated her weak husband; secured Naples and Parma for her sons Charles and Philip.

Elizabeth Islands, chain forming SE boundary of Buzzards Bay, off SE Mass. Cuttyhunk (discovered 1602, settled 1641) is farthest W; Naushon (nô′shŭn), 7 mi. long, is largest. Penikese Isl. had summer school of marine biology estab. by Louis Agassiz.

Elizabeth of Valois (välwä′), 1545–68, queen of Spain, third wife of Philip II; daughter of Henry II of France. She had been originally promised to Philip's son CARLOS, but the story of a tragic love between her and Carlos is unfounded.

Elizabethton, town (pop, 10,754), NE Tenn., at junction of Watauga and Doe rivers; one of state's earliest settlements. Sycamore Shoals Monument commemorates organization of WATAUGA ASSOCIATION 1772, Richard Henderson's Cherokee treaty 1775, and formation of Revolutionary force. Rayon mills. Unaka Natl. Forest near by.

Elizabethtown. 1 City (pop. 5,807), central Ky., S of Louisville; settled 1780. Trade center for agr. and limestone area. Thomas Lincoln lived here for time. Garrison captured by Gen. J. H. Morgan in Civil War, Dec., 1862. Indian mounds have yielded artifacts. Fort Knox near by. **2** Borough (pop. 5,083), SE Pa., SE of Harrisburg. Trade center for agr. area.

elk, member of deer family, genus *Alces* (or *Alce*), found in reduced numbers in parts of N Europe and Asia. Smaller but similar to American MOOSE.

Elk City, city (pop. 7,962), W Okla., in dairy region. Has cooperative medical center (1929).

Elkhart, city (pop. 35,646), N Ind., at junction of Elkhart and St. Joseph rivers and E of South Bend; settled 1832. Shipping and trading center for agr. area. Rail junction with mfg. of metal, rubber, and clay products.

Elkhorn City or **Praise,** town (pop. 1,349), E Ky., in Cumberlands, SE of Pikeville and near scenic Breaks of Big Sandy R.

Elkhorn Tavern: see PEA RIDGE.

Elkins, Stephen Benton, 1841–1911, American statesman. U.S. Secretary of War (1891–93). As U.S. Senator from W.Va. (1895–1911), he authored Elkins Act of 1903 against REBATE system.

Elkins, city (pop. 9,121), N W.Va., on Tygart R. and SE of Clarksburg. Center for timber and mining area with foundry and lumber products. Seat of Davis and Elkins Col.

Elk Island National Park, central Alta., Canada, E of Edmonton; estab. 1913. Canada's chief fenced preserve of buffalo and other prairie animals.

Elk Mountains, range of Rocky Mts., W central Colo. Its highest point, Mt. Carbon (also called Castle Peak), rises to 14,259 ft.

Elko, city (pop. 5,393), NE Nev., on Humboldt R. and N of Diamond Mts. Shipping point for ranches and mines.

Elkton. 1 City (pop. 1,312), S Ky., E of Hopkinsville near Tenn. line. Birthplace of Jefferson Davis (with memorial park, monument) near by. **2** Town (pop. 5,245), NE Md., NE of Baltimore. Until state changed marriage laws (1938), town was Gretna Green of the East. Mfg. of toys, paper, clothing, and fireworks.

Ellensburg, city (pop. 8,430), central Wash., on Yakima R., in lumber, dairy, agr., mining area. Center of Yakima reclamation project.

Ellesmere, Thomas Egerton, Baron, c.1540–1617, lord chancellor of England. He took part in trial of Mary Queen of Scots (1586) and was a favorite and adviser of Queen Elizabeth. Originally a friend of the 2d earl of Essex, he was a witness against him at the trial which resulted in his execution. Retained by James I, he upheld James's harsh policy toward Puritans and was severe to Catholics. He was a man of learning and an incorruptible judge.

Ellesmere Island, area 77,392 sq. mi., most northerly and second largest of Arctic Archipelago, Franklin dist., Northwest Territories, Canada, in Arctic Ocean. Largely covered by ice cap in SE. Central area called Grinnell Land.

Ellice Islands (ĕl′ĭs), group of atolls (9.5 sq. mi.; pop. 4,487), S Pacific; with Gilbert Isls. constitutes a British colony. Most important of nine islands are Funafuti and Nanumea. Main export is copra. Occupied 1943 by U.S. forces.

Ellicott, Andrew, 1754–1820, American surveyor. As surveyor of capital at Washington (1792), he issued an altered city plan. Surveyed U.S.–Fla. boundary (1796–1800) and Ga.–S.C. boundary (1811–12).

Ellicott City, village (1940 pop. 2,682), N Md., on Patapsco R., W of Baltimore. Near by is Doughoregan Manor (c.1720), home of Charles Carroll.

ellipse (ĭlĭps′), closed plane curve of which sum of distances between point on curve and two fixed points (foci) is same for all points on curve. Center is point halfway between foci; major axis is chord passing through foci; vertices are two points at which major axis intersects curve. Ellipse is also conic section (other than circle) formed by plane cutting all elements of cone in same nappe.

Ellis, Havelock, 1859–1939, English psychologist. A qualified physician, his major work, *Studies in the Psychology of Sex* (1897–1928), greatly influenced the public attitude toward sex problems.

Ellis, William, 1794–1872, English nonconformist missionary. He developed a form of writing for the Hawaiian language and set up at Tahiti first printing press in the South Seas. Also wrote a history of Madagascar.

Ellis Island, SE N.Y., in Upper New York Bay, SW of Manhattan isl.; c.27 acres. Government property since 1808. Nation's chief immigration station 1892–1943. Now a detention center for deportees and immigrants whose entry is questioned.

Ellora (ĕlō′rŭ), village, NW Hyderabad, India. Buddhist, Brahman, and Jain rock-cut temples (3d–13th cent.) extend over a mile. The Kailasa, Dravidian temple carved from a single mass of rock, has some of India's greatest sculptural treasures.

Ellsworth, Henry Leavitt, 1791–1858, American agriculturist who helped bring about establishment of Dept. of Agriculture.

Ellsworth, Lincoln, 1880–1951, American explorer. Financial supporter and associate of Roald Amundsen in arctic aviation ventures. Flew over North Pole in 1926. Accomplished first flight over Antarctica in 1935. Published several accounts of his experiences.

Ellsworth, Oliver, 1745–1807, American statesman. Advanced "Connecticut compromise" at FEDERAL CONSTITUTIONAL CONVENTION. Chief Justice of U.S. Supreme Court (1796–99).

Ellwood City, borough (pop. 12,945), W Pa., NW of Pittsburgh; settled 1890. Mfg. of metal products.

elm, deciduous tree of genus *Ulmus* of wide distribution. Among North American species are American or white elm (*Ulmus americana*), a favorite shade tree, and slippery elm (*U. fulva*). Elm wood is hard and durable. The Dutch elm disease, caused by a fungus carried by beetles, has exterminated many plantings in U.S. of both American and European species.

Elman, Mischa (ĕl′mŭn), 1891–, Russian-American violinist. Since his debut in New York (1908), he has toured widely in Europe and the U.S.

Elmhurst, residential city (pop. 21,273), NE Ill., W of Chicago, in truck-farm area; settled 1843.

Elmira, city (pop. 49,716), S N.Y., on Chemung R. and W of Binghamton; settled 1788. Distributing and mfg. (milk bottles, fire-fighting equipment and chemicals, office equipment, business machines) center. Here are Arnot Art Gall., Elmira State Reformatory (see Z. R. BROCKWAY), Mark Twain's grave, **Elmira College** (nonsectarian; for women; opened 1855), first woman's college to grant degrees (1859) for work equivalent to that offered in men's colleges.

Elmo, Saint: see PETER GONZALEZ, SAINT.

El Monte, city (pop. 8,101), S Calif., E of Los Angeles, in truck and dairy area. A lion farm is near by.

El Morro National Monument: see NATIONAL PARKS AND MONUMENTS (table).

Elmwood, city (pop. 1,613), N central Ill., WNW of Peoria. Birthplace of Lorado Taft, whose statue to his parents, *Pioneers of the Prairies,* is here.

Elmwood Park, village (pop. 18,801), NE Ill., residential suburb W of Chicago.

Elohim (ĕlōhēm′, ēlō′hĭm), common Hebrew name of God.

Eloi, Eloi, lama sabachthani?: see ELI, ELI, LAMA SABACHTHANI?

Eloth (ē′lŏth), the same as ELATH.

El Paso (ĕl pă′sō), city (pop. 130,485), W Texas, port of entry on Rio Grande opposite JUAREZ, Mexico. Largest U.S.–Mex. border city, its past is bound with that of Juarez. Both in El Paso del Norte region to which missionaries, soldiers, and traders came in 17th cent. Missions founded at YSLETA and elsewhere, but main settlement was in Juarez. First El Paso house built 1827. Settlement grew after U.S.–Mex. border was estab. and after railroad came (1881). Has refineries, mfg. of food and wine products, cement, and textiles. International trade most important. Seat of Texas Western Col. Here are Fort Bliss (with guided missiles experiment station), army hospital, and U.S. airfield. Elephant Butte Dam (N.Mex.) irrigates area.

Elphinstone, George Keith, 1746–1823, British admiral. In wars of American and French revolutions, he was noted for the reduction of Charleston (1780) and the capture of Capetown (1795).

El Reno, city (pop. 10,991), central Okla., near North Canadian R. and W of Oklahoma City; settled 1889. Market center with flour mills and railroad shops. U.S. reformatory and Fort Reno are near by.

El Segundo (ĕl sĭgŭn′dō), city (pop. 8,011), S Calif., WSW of Los Angeles; founded 1911. Oil refineries. Mfg. of aircraft and chemicals.

Elsheimer, Adam (ä′däm ĕls′hīmŭr), 1578–1610?, German painter. Biblical and mythological pictures notable for landscape backgrounds and light effects.

Elsinore (ĕl′sĭnôr″), Dan. *Helsingør,* city (pop. 21,010), NE Zealand, Denmark; a port on the Oresund opposite Halsingborg. Flourished until 1857 as toll-collection station for ships passing through Oresund. Kronborg castle (built 1577–85; restored 1635–40) is sometimes used for performances of Shakspere's *Hamlet,* which is laid in Elsinore.

Elssler, Fanny (ĕl′slŭr), 1810–84, Austrian ballet dancer. Made her debut in 1833 and was very popular in London, Paris, and U.S. until her retirement in 1851. Her forte was folk dancing.

Eluard, Paul (pôl′ älwär′), 1895–1952, French

poet. Was long associated with surrealism, later with Communism. Among his volumes of poetry are *Mourir de ne pas mourir* (1924), *Poésie et vérité* (1942), *Au rendez-vous allemand* (1945). Was active in anti-German resistance during World War II.

Elvehjem, Conrad Arnold (ĕlvā'ŭm), 1901–, American biochemist. His research led to use of niacin (part of vitamin B complex) in treating pellagra. He discovered that copper is essential to hemoglobin formation and made many other valuable contributions.

Elvend or **Elwend** (both: ĕlvĕnd'), mountain, c.11,600 ft. high, W Iran, SW of Hamadan. Has rock inscriptions of Darius and Xerxes.

Elwood, city (pop. 11,362), E central Ind., NNE of Indianapolis. Canning center for tomato-growing area, it ships grain and livestock. Mfg. of metal products. W. L. Willkie born here.

Ely. 1 City (pop. 5,474), NE Minn., on Vermilion iron range, in wooded lake region. Resort center with hq. of Superior National Forest. **2** City (pop. 3,558), E Nev., in rich copper area. Lehman Caves Natl. Monument is near.

Ely, City of, urban district (pop. 9,989), Isle of Ely, England, NNE of Cambridge. Ely cathedral (begun 1083), one of largest in England, has architecture of varied periods. Within its grounds are Tudor palace of the bishop, a theological college, and King's Grammar School, founded by Henry VIII.

Ely, Isle of, administrative county (372 sq. mi.; pop. 89,038), E England; administrative center March. Region of extensive fens, now drained for agr. Historically a part of CAMBRIDGESHIRE.

Elymas (ĕ'lĭmăs), the same as BAR-JESUS.

Elyria (ĭlēr'ēŭ), city (pop. 30,307), N Ohio, on Black R., SW of Cleveland; settled 1817. Trade center of agr. area, it has mfg. of aircraft, electrical products, and motor vehicles.

Elysian fields (ĭlĭ'zhŭn) or **Elysium** (ĭlĭ'zhēŭm), in Greek religion, happy otherworld for heroes favored by the gods. Identified with Isles of the Blest or Fortunate Isls., and, in Vergil, part of underworld.

Elzevir, Louis (ĕl'zŭvŭr, –vēr), 1540–1617, Dutch publisher, whose name also appears as Elsevier and Elzevier. The business he founded in 1583 at Leiden was continued by his descendants until 1712, and the name is still used. They owned presses and type and hired good editors and printers to turn out legible inexpensive books. Because of types designed for the house by Christopher van Dyck, the type known in English-speaking countries as "old-style" is called "Elzevir" on the Continent.

Emancipation, Edict of, March 3, 1861 (N.S.), edict by which Alexander II freed all Russian serfs (c.22,000,000—one third of total pop.). Provisions for peasants' purchase of land were complex and cumbersome, made private ownership of land nearly impossible until belated reform of STOLYPIN (1906).

Emancipation Proclamation. Despite insistence of abolitionists, Pres. Lincoln, in early Civil War, did not issue edict freeing slaves lest it alienate loyal border states. But on July 22, 1862, he read a draft to his cabinet. After successful Antietam campaign he issued pre-liminary edict, and on Jan. 1, 1863, the formal Emancipation Proclamation. It did not free all slaves in U.S. but only those in states in rebellion "as a fit and necessary war measure for suppressing said rebellion." Designed to deplete Southern manpower reserve in slaves and to enhance Union cause abroad.

embalming (ĕmbä'mĭng), treatment for preserving a corpse. Practiced by ancient peoples, notably Egyptians. Bodies can now be preserved indefinitely.

Embargo Act of 1807, passed Dec. 22, 1807, by U.S. Congress in answer to British ORDERS IN COUNCIL restricting neutral shipping and to Napoleon's opposing CONTINENTAL SYSTEM. Forbade all international trade to and from American ports in attempt to persuade England and France of the value and rights of a neutral commerce. In Jan., 1809, prohibition was extended to inland waters and land commerce to halt trade with Canada. England and France stood firm, and enforcement of act was difficult, especially in New England. Acts replacing it effectually dissolved whole purpose of embargo.

embezzlement, misappropriation of another's property by a wrongdoer who is in lawful possession. Since common law considered only "felonious taking" as larceny, the misuse of funds by the legal administrator for selfish ends is covered in England and U.S. by statutes making embezzlement a distinct crime or enlarging definition of larceny to include it.

embroidery, ornamental needlework in thread, fiber, or leather thongs, applied to a fabric or to leather. As an art it is probably older than weaving; primitive peoples used embroidered skins. From ancient times, the East has produced rich embroideries; the art came to Europe through Byzantine influence. From 12th to 14th cent., church embroidery (e.g., altarcloths, vestments) flourished; later, secular embroidery, such as that on the rich costumes of Elizabethan England, reached its height. Advent of machinery caused decline of embroidery, but eyelet, cutwork, and other light forms are still done.

embryo (ĕm'brēō), name for developing young of animal and plant. Embryology is the scientific study of development up to hatching or birth. Exact duration of embryo stage is not well defined; in mammals the young in later prenatal stages is called fetus. In all animal reproduction involving union of sperm and egg cells, a series of cell divisions begins soon after fertilization; succeeding stages vary. In many forms, a blastula, a hollow ball consisting of one layer of cells, develops and later becomes two-layered cuplike gastrula; in higher forms, a third cell layer develops. Various body parts develop from each layer.

Emden (ĕm'dŭn), city (pop. 36,762), Lower Saxony, NW Germany, chief city of East Friesland; a North Sea port at mouth of Ems R. and on Dortmund-Ems Canal. Shipyards, herring fisheries. Dates from 10th cent. Heavily damaged in World War II.

emerald, green gem variety of BERYL. The finest come from South America. Oriental emerald is a variety of corundum.

Emerson, Ralph Waldo, 1803–82, American essayist, poet, and philosopher, b. Boston.

Educated at Harvard for the Unitarian ministry, he became pastor of the Old North Church, Boston, in 1829 but retired in 1832 because of doctrinal difficulties. A trip to Europe broadened his acquaintance with the literary world of his day and wide reading in English, Continental, classic, and Oriental literature stimulated his thought. He settled in Concord, Mass., which became a center of American culture. He gained notice as a lecturer, his Phi Beta Kappa address at Harvard, *The American Scholar* (1837), being especially remarkable in its call for American intellectual freedom. He became a spokesman for a group that included his friends Thoreau and Margaret Fuller, and the principles of TRANSCENDENTALISM shone forth in his lectures and writings. His lectures (which were yearly more famous) were based on the *Journal* he had kept since Harvard days, and his essays were closely linked to the lectures. These *Essays* (1st series, 1841; 2d series, 1844), still much read today, generally set forth his sturdy belief that the individual can find redemption only in his own soul; among them are "The Over-Soul," "Compensation," and "Self-Reliance." Though technically he left much to be desired as a poet, some of his short lyrics are familiar to all American readers, such as "Brahma," "The Rhodora," and "The Concord Hymn." Among his many volumes are also *Nature* (1836; new ed., 1849), *English Traits* (1856; lectures after a trip to England in 1847), *Addresses and Lectures* (1849), and *Representative Men* (1850).

emery: see CORUNDUM.

Emesa: see HOMS, Syria.

Emigrant Aid Company, formed 1854 to promote organized antislavery immigration to Kansas from the Northeast. Name associated exclusively with New England Emigrant Aid Co., though other Kansas aid societies were subsequently formed. Founder Eli Thayer received 10% of all money he collected. Amos A. Lawrence was treasurer. Company sent out 1,240 settlers. Natl. Kansas Committee, formed at Buffalo, N.Y., 1856, as joint endeavor of aid societies, divided over problem of how to handle proslavery excesses. Whole movement was virtually ended by 1857. The movement, although it did little toward making Kansas a free state, captured public attention and engendered much bitterness and hate.

emigration: see IMMIGRATION; MIGRATION.

Emilia-Romagna (ämē'lyä-rōmä'nyä), region (8,542 sq. mi.; pop. 3,338,721), N central Italy, extending S from Po R.; cap. BOLOGNA. Other cities: FERRARA, FORLÌ, MODENA, PARMA, PIACENZA, RAVENNA, REGGIO EMILIA, RIMINI. Fertile agr. plain; few industries. Annexed to Sardinia 1860. For earlier history, see articles on individual cities; ROMAGNA.

Eminescu, Mihail (yĕmēnĕ'skŏō), 1850–89, foremost Rumanian poet, whose last name was originally Iminovici. His poetry has been widely translated.

Emmanuel, in Bible: see IMMANUEL.

Emmanuel. For Byzantine and Portuguese rulers thus named, see MANUEL.

Emmanuel College: see CAMBRIDGE UNIVERSITY.

Emmanuel Philibert, 1528–80, duke of Savoy (1553–80), called Ironhead. In Spanish service, he fought the French, who had occupied Savoy; won a brilliant victory at Saint-Quentin (1557); recovered Savoy at Treaty of Cateau-Cambrésis (1559). An energetic reformer, he restored his duchy to prosperity, shifted his cap. to Turin, made Savoy an Italian rather than French state.

Emmaus (ĕm'äŭs), place near Jerusalem where Cleopas and another disciple met the risen Christ. Luke 24.13.

Emmaus (ĕm'äŭs), borough (pop. 7,780), E Pa., S of Allentown; settled c.1740 by Moravians. Mfg. of commercial gases and rubber products.

Emma Willard School: see TROY, N.Y.

Emmental (ĕ'mŭntäl), valley of Emme R., Bern canton, Switzerland. Produces fine cheese.

Emmet, Robert, 1778–1803, Irish patriot. After an unsuccessful attempt at a French-aided uprising in Ireland (1803), he was captured and hanged. He made a stirring speech from the gallows and became a great hero of Irish patriots.

Emmett, city (pop. 3,067), SW Idaho, on Payette R. and SE of Payette, in BOISE PROJECT.

Emmitsburg, town (pop. 1,261), N Md., near Pa. line NE of Hagerstown. Seat of Mt. St. Mary's Col. and St. Joseph's Col.

Emory University, near Atlanta, Ga.; mainly for men; chartered 1836, opened 1838 by Methodists, became a university 1915. Cooperates with Agnes Scott Col. (for women; 1889) at near-by Decatur.

emotion, term loosely used synonymously with feeling. In psychology: a response to stimuli involving physiological changes, tending to stimulate further activity. Fear, love, anger (primary responses) are roused directly by external stimuli, indirectly through memory, and expressed variously according to individual and to culture. Psychosomatic medicine has shown that tension from unrelieved emotions may cause physical disorders.

Empedocles (ĕmpĕ'dŭklēz), c.495–c.435 B.C., Greek philosopher. Taught that two opposing forces—harmony and discord—combine indestructible material particles into varying forms.

Empire State Building, in central Manhattan, New York city, on Fifth Ave. between 33d and 34th streets, built 1930–31. Tallest building in the world; 1,250 ft. high, 102 stories.

Empire style, manner of interior decoration evolved in France from Directoire style and identified with reign of Napoleon I. Roman forms were used to emphasize grandeur of Napoleonic era, and symbols of imperial pomp added to traditional classic motifs. Staple wood was mahogany, but rosewood and ebony also used. Brass and ormolu mounts were chief ornaments. Style fell into disuse c.1840. Simplified form was adopted in England and U.S.; a German bourgeois adaptation is Biedermeier. See *ills.*, pp. 295, 456.

empiricism, philosophical doctrine that all knowledge is derived from experience. Opposed to RATIONALISM, it denies innate ideas and a priori truth and stresses generalizations based only on observation (experience). Basic to scientific method, it dominated British philosophy from Francis Bacon to John Stuart Mill.

employment bureau, establishment for bringing together the employer offering work and the employee seeking it. In England the first employment bureau was opened 1855; a national system was established 1909. France has had public employment agencies since 1916. In the U.S. the first state regulation of private agencies was in Mass. in 1848. Regulations requiring licensing have been enacted in 41 states. The U.S. government has operated employment offices since 1907. In 1918 the Employment Service of Dept. of Labor was estab. The state agencies, brought directly under Federal operation in 1942, were turned back to the states in 1946. In 1948 the U.S. Employment Service was transferred to the Federal Security Agency.

Emporia. 1 City (pop. 15,669), E central Kansas, near Neosho R. and SW of Topeka; founded 1857. Trade and rail center in dairy and grain area. William Allen WHITE made the Emporia *Gazette* famous. **2** Town (pop. 5,664), S Va., on Meherrin R. and S of Petersburg. Shipping and processing center for agr. (cotton) and timber area.

Ems or **Bad Ems** (bät' ĕms'), town (pop. 8,454), Rhineland-Palatinate, W Germany, on Lahn R. It is one of Europe's oldest watering places.

Ems, river, 208 mi. long, NW Germany, rising near Paderborn and flowing NW into North Sea near Emden. Wide mouth is called the Dollart. Much of its course is paralleled by the Dortmund-Ems Canal. Oil and natural gas were discovered after 1940 in the Emsland (region about lower course).

Ems dispatch, July 12, 1870, incident leading to Franco-Prussian War. The Spanish throne had been offered to a Hohenzollern prince. France having protested, the prince refused the offer, but the French ambassador Benedetti, meeting William I of Prussia at Ems, demanded assurance that no Hohenzollern should ever seek the Spanish throne. William turned him down flatly but politely. Seeking to goad France into declaring war, Bismarck published the interview in skillfully altered and insulting language, with complete success.

emu (ē'mū), large flightless bird of Australia, related to cassowary and ostrich. A swift runner, it is 5–6 ft. tall. It is almost extinct.

emulsion: see SUSPENSION.

encephalitis lethargica: see SLEEPING SICKNESS.

Encina or **Enzina, Juan del** (both: hwän' dĕl änthē'nä), 1469?–1530, Spanish dramatist, musician, poet, a priest.

Enciso, Martín Fernández de (märtēn' fĕrnän'däth dā ĕnthē'sō), fl. 1509–19, Spanish conquistador and geographer. Refounded colony in Darien (1509), but was replaced by Pedrarias (1514). Wrote commentary on flora and fauna in New World.

enclosure of land: see INCLOSURE.

encomienda (änkōmyän'dä), system of tributary labor adapted in Spanish America, modeled on that imposed in Spain on conquered Moors. It permitted conquistadors receiving land grants from crown to exact tribute from Indians living thereon. In return Indians received the protection of owner and subsistence rights on the land. See also REPARTIMIENTO.

encyclical: see BULL.

encyclopedia, either a general compendium of knowledge in all fields or a work which aims to be comprehensive in some one field. *Natural History* of Pliny the Elder is often considered the most ancient encyclopedia because it aimed at encompassing all knowledge. Various medieval scholars attempted to make all knowledge available to less informed. Example of modern encyclopedia—including alphabetical arrangement of material and bibliographies—was set by John Harris (c.1667–1719) in his *Lexicon technicum* (1704). *The Encyclopaedia Britannica* was first published in 1771. Famous French ENCYCLOPÉDIE was completed in 1772. The German *Brockhaus' Konversations-Lexikon* was first issued in 1796–1808. On this was based *The Encyclopaedia Americana,* edited by Francis Lieber (13 vols., 1829–33). Among the encyclopedias limited to a single branch of knowledge are the *Encyclopaedia of the Social Sciences* and *The Catholic Encyclopedia.*

Encyclopédie (äsĕklōpädē'), French encyclopedia, in 28 vols., edited by DIDEROT, published 1751–72. D'ALEMBERT, coeditor until 1758, wrote "Preliminary Discourse"; other collaborators included MONTESQUIEU, QUESNAY, J. J. ROUSSEAU, VOLTAIRE. Banned by the government in 1759, it was clandestinely printed with the secret tolerance of the police chief. The emphasis of the *Encyclopédie* is on science, crafts, mechanics; it contains no biographic articles. Its outlook is deliberately rationalist and materialistic. It had great influence on European learning.

Endecott or **Endicott, John,** c.1588–1665, first governor of Mass. Bay colony (1628–30).

endemic disease: see COMMUNICABLE DISEASES.

Enderbury Island, area 4 sq. mi., Phoenix Isls., central Pacific, near CANTON ISLAND; under Anglo-American control since 1939.

Enderby Land, area in Indian Ocean sector of Antarctica. Claimed by British because of John Biscoe's discovery (1831); not visited again until 1929.

Endicott, John: see ENDECOTT, JOHN.

Endicott, village (pop. 20,050), S N.Y., on Susquehanna R and W of Binghamton and Johnson City, with which it forms the Triple Cities; settled c.1795. Shoes, business machines, and foundry products.

endive (ĕn'dīv; Fr. ēdēv'), salad plant (*Cichorium endivia*) with crisp curly or broad leaves; related to chicory. Commonly blanched.

endocrine gland: see GLAND.

endogamy: see MARRIAGE.

En-dor, village, Palestine, S of Mt. Tabor. Here Saul consulted famous witch. 1 Sam. 28.7; Ps. 83.10.

Endymion (ĕndĭ'mēŭn), in Greek legend, shepherd of Mt. Latmos, loved by Selene (the moon). He was given immortality and eternal sleep.

energy, in physics, defined usually as ability to

do work. It includes heat, light, sound, electricity, and chemical energy. **Potential energy** of a body is work capacity because of its position. **Kinetic energy** of a body is work capacity because of its motion. **Law of conservation of energy** states that although its form may change, energy can neither be created nor destroyed. **Chemical energy** is a form involved in chemical reaction. Solar energy, considered ultimate energy source, is utilized in PHOTOSYNTHESIS.

Enesco, Georges (zhôrzh ĕnĕs'kō), 1881–, Rumanian violinist, composer, and conductor. Most popular are his two Rumanian Rhapsodies for orchestra.

Enfield, urban district (pop. 110,458), Middlesex, England, N of London. Site of Royal Small Arms factory which makes Enfield rifles.

Enfield, town (pop. 15,464), N Conn., on Connecticut R. at Mass. line; settled c.1680. Had Shaker settlement c.1780–1915. Town includes mfg. village of Thompsonville (pop. 9,633; textiles, wood products).

Engadine (ĕng'gŭdēn), upper part of Inn R. valley, Grisons canton, E Switzerland. BERNINA group rises at S end. Many tourist and health resorts, e.g., St. Moritz, Pontresina. Pop. largely Romansh-speaking and Protestant.

Engelberg (ĕng'ŭlbĕrk), village, Obwalden half-canton, central Switzerland. Winter and summer resort. Has 12th-cent. Benedictine abbey.

Engels, Friedrich (frē'drĭkh ĕng'ŭls), 1820–95, German socialist, one of the two founders, with Karl MARX, of modern COMMUNISM. After organizing (1845–50) revolutionary movements in Europe, he lived in England, collaborating with Karl Marx on the *Communist Manifesto* (1848); after Marx's death, edited 2d and 3d volumes of *Das Kapital.* He elaborated theories of MARXISM and DIALECTICAL MATERIALISM, fundamental to communism. Basic to communist literature are his *Landmarks of Scientific Socialism* (1878) and *The Origin of the Family, Private Property, and the State* (1848).

Enghien, Louis Antoine Henri de Bourbon-Condé, duc d' (lwē ātwän' ärē' dú bōŏrbō'-kōdä' dük dägē'), 1772–1804, French prince. Emigrated with his father, Louis Henri Joseph de Condé. Unjustly suspected by Napoleon of participation in conspiracy of CADOUDAL, he was kidnaped from Baden, court-martialed, and shot within few hours.

engine: see DIESEL ENGINE; INTERNAL-COMBUSTION ENGINE; STEAM ENGINE; *ill.,* p. 389.

engineering, science dealing with design, construction, and operation of structures, machines, engines, and other devices used in industry and everyday life. Until Industrial Revolution engineering embodied only civil engineering (construction of tools, roads, bridges, etc.) and military engineering (construction of fortifications, engines of war, etc.); afterward mechanical engineering developed separately for design and construction of machinery. Vast field of modern engineering includes aeronautical, agricultural, chemical, civil, electrical, geological, industrial or management, marine, mechanical, and metallurgical engineering.

England, John (ĭng'glŭnd), 1786–1842, Irish-American churchman, b. Ireland. Catholic bishop of Charleston, S.C. after 1820, he was a devoted American, interested especially in the needs of the Negroes.

England, largest political division (all figures without Monmouthshire: 50,327 sq. mi.; pop. 41,147,938) of island of Great Britain in British Isles; core of British Empire. To the W is WALES; to the N is SCOTLAND (above Solway Firth). Cut off from continent of Euorpe by English Channel, Straits of Dover, and North Sea, England's growth was determined by defensibility from attack, mild climate, and geographic accessibility by S ports and E and W river estuaries. The 38 (or 39) political divisions, the counties or shires, are Bedfordshire, Berkshire, Buckinghamshire, Cambridgeshire, Cheshire, Cornwall, Cumberland, Derbyshire, Devonshire, Dorsetshire, Durham, Essex, Gloucestershire, Hampshire, Herefordshire, Hertfordshire, Huntingdonshire, Kent, Lancashire, Lincolnshire, Middlesex, Monmouthshire (often included in Wales), Norfolk, Northamptonshire, Northumberland, Nottinghamshire, Oxfordshire, Rutland, Shropshire, Somerset, Staffordshire, Suffolk, Surrey, Sussex, Warwickshire, Westmorland, Wiltshire, Worcestershire, and Yorkshire. S and SE are low and fertile; marshy NE has been mostly reclaimed. W is rough country, ending in peninsula of Cornwall. N of the Humber the Pennine Chain leads to scenery of Lake District and to Scotland. For the last 200 years England's chief wealth has derived from great industries of the Black country (based on coal and iron fields N of large Midlands plain), from the industrial centers of Lancashire and Yorkshire, and from shipping and mfg. of leading cities—London (capital), Manchester, Liverpool, Leeds, Sheffield, Birmingham, Bristol, Bradford, and Hull. In 19th cent. England led the world in exports of manufactures. A limited monarchy, England is joined with Scotland and N. Ireland in the United Kingdom of Great Britain and N. Ireland. Legislative and actual sovereignty reside in PARLIAMENT. Executive authority, nominally vested in the crown, lies with a cabinet responsible to parliament. The estab. church is the Church of England. Education Act of 1944 attempted coordination of all secondary and public schools, including Eton, Harrow, Rugby, and Winchester. Oxford and Cambridge are oldest and most noted of the 11 universities, the others being Birmingham, Bristol, Durham, Leeds, Liverpool, London, Manchester, Reading, and Sheffield.

Celt and Roman, Saxon and Dane. For history of these early invaders and settlers, see BRITAIN. By 865 the Danes (term for all Norse invaders) had conquered England until resistance by ALFRED and his successors finally ended the DANELAW. New invasions led to CANUTE becoming Danish ruler of all England in 1017. The ANGLO-SAXONS had important effects on English culture—they developed Christianity, stimulated trade and the growth of towns, and brought central government from tribal chieftanships to a monarchy controlling executive and judicial powers. Period was ended by the NORMAN CONQUEST in 1066.

Feudal England. Norman king William I marked a new point in English history. His strong rule and efforts at centralization were typified in DOMESDAY survey. Political and military FEUDALISM were introduced. Under his successors baronial wars produced noted English constitutional document, the MAGNA CARTA (1215). Increased royal holdings in France led to the first Anglo-French struggles and to the HUNDRED YEARS WAR (1337). Subsequent dynastic Wars of the ROSES were ended by accession of Henry VII (1485) of family of Tudor, with whom modern English history begins.

Tudor and Stuart. Tudor period was a glorious one. REFORMATION, introduced by Henry VIII, ran parallel with the flowering of the Renaissance. Trade expanded. Succession to throne was a vital issue in reigns of Edward VI, Mary I, ELIZABETH I. STUART period, introduced by James I, was dominated by PURITAN REVOLUTION, culminating in civil war (1642). Parliamentarian victory led to execution of CHARLES I (1649) and to the Protectorate under Oliver CROMWELL. Reaction against puritanism was shown by the Restoration of CHARLES II. Supremacy of parliament final after overthrow of James II by the Glorious Revolution of 1688 and the accession of WILLIAM III and Mary. WHIG and TORY party government developed under Sir Robert Walpole. Colonial expansion and rivalries led to wars of European alliances, mainly with France. Tudors, Stuarts, and Cromwell continued conquest of Ireland. Under Queen ANNE Scotland was joined to England by Act of Union in 1707. For later history see GREAT BRITAIN and BRITISH EMPIRE.

In a World of Industry. England's leadership in INDUSTRIAL REVOLUTION in 19th cent. was derived from industrial Midlands. Attendant depressions produced CHARTISM. Expanding trade caused enormous growth of cities. World War II brought huge damage from air raids. War was followed by nationalization of industry, loss of England's financial supremacy to U.S., and shrinkage of empire. England reemerged as the center of the British Commonwealth of Nations.

The royal rulers of England since William the Conqueror have been: *Norman*—William I, 1066–87; William II, 1087–1100; Henry I, 1100–1135. *Stephen*—Stephen, 1135–54. *Plantagenet*—Henry II, 1154–89; Richard I, 1189–99; John, 1199–1216; Henry III, 1216–72; Edward I, 1272–1307; Edward II, 1307–27; Edward III, 1327–77; Richard II, 1377–99. *Lancaster*—Henry IV, 1399–1413; Henry V, 1413–22; Henry VI, 1422–61 and 1470–71. *York*—Edward IV, 1461–70 and 1471–83; Edward V, 1483; Richard III, 1483–85. *Tudor*—Henry VII, 1485–1509; Henry VIII, 1509–47; Edward VI, 1547–53; Mary I, 1553–58; Elizabeth I, 1558–1603. *Stuart*—James I, 1603–25; Charles I, 1625–49 (executed 1649; Commonwealth and Protectorate, 1649–60; Charles II in exile); Charles II, 1660–85; James II, 1685–88. *Orange*—William III, 1688–1702, and Mary II, 1688–94. *Stuart*—Anne, 1702–14. *Hanover*—

George I, 1714–27; George II, 1727–60; George III, 1760–1820; George IV, 1820–30; William IV, 1830–37; Victoria, 1837–1901. *Saxe-Coburg-Gotha*—Edward VII, 1901–10. *Windsor*—George V, 1910–36; Edward VIII, 1936; George VI, 1936–52; Elizabeth II, 1952–.

England, Church of, official church of England. Its break with Roman Church came when Henry VIII withdrew from allegiance to pope and announced that the king would be head of English church; this move was confirmed by Act of Supremacy of 1534. Henry suppressed monasteries and authorized Great Bible (1539). First Book of Common Prayer was adopted 1549. Under Mary, England came again under Catholic communion, but Elizabeth restored Protestantism. Act of Supremacy of 1559 defined constitutional position of Church and relation to the crown. Under James I rising tide of Puritanism necessitated Hampton Court Conference (1604), where king upheld estab. doctrine. Under Charles I measures of Archbishop Laud against Calvinists contributed to civil war (1642). The Long Parliament estab. Presbyterianism (1646). With Restoration (1660) episcopacy was restored and the Prayer Book was made the only legal service book by Act of Uniformity (1662), which also required episcopal ordination of all ministers. Thereafter, despite many internal controversies, the Church held firm. In polity, High Church party holds to ritualism and APOSTOLIC SUCCESSION, and is contravened by Low Church party. The archbishop of Canterbury is the chief (primate) of the church; archbishop of York is second to him. Worship is liturgical; creeds used are Nicene, Apostles', and Athanasian. Standards of doctrine are in Thirty-nine Articles, Book of Common Prayer, Catechism, and two books of homilies.

Engleheart, George, 1752–1829, English miniature painter, pupil of Reynolds. His nephew **John Cox Dillman Engleheart,** 1784–1862, was also a noted miniaturist.

Englewood. 1 Residential city (pop. 16,869), N central Colo., S suburb of Denver, in farm and dairy area. **2** Residential suburban city (pop. 23,145), NE N.J., near the Hudson and N of Jersey City.

English Channel, Fr. *La Manche* = the sleeve; arm of the Atlantic, 350 mi. long and 21 mi. to c.150 mi. wide, between France and England, connecting with North Sea at E end. Main islands are Isle of Wight and Channel Isls. Train-ferry service from Paris to London opened 1936. Tunneling Channel has long been discussed. First crossed by balloon 1785; by airplane 1909. First to swim across was Matthew Webb 1875. Channel has important fisheries. Ports include Plymouth, Southampton, Portsmouth, Folkestone, and Dover (England), and Cherbourg, Le Havre, and Calais (France).

English horn: see WIND INSTRUMENTS.

English ivy, Old World woody evergreen vine (*Hedera helix*), a ground or wall cover and house plant.

English language, language prevalent in U.S. and much of Canada, in British Isles, in Australia and New Zealand, in much of South

DIAGRAM OF RECIPROCATING STEAM ENGINE

The slide valve admits steam alternately on either side of the piston. Arrows indicate the direction of force.

PELTON TYPE   PROPELLER TYPE   FRANCIS TYPE

WATER TURBINES

DIAGRAM OF A STEAM TURBINE

INTAKE STROKE   COMPRESSION STROKE   POWER STROKE   EXHAUST STROKE

DIAGRAM OF A FOUR-CYCLE (FOUR-STROKE-CYCLE) INTERNAL-COMBUSTION ENGINE

DIAGRAM OF A FOUR-CYCLE DIESEL ENGINE

No spark is needed, since the heat of the compressed air is so great that spontaneous combustion of the sprayed fuel oil occurs.

Africa, and in a few other places. Today the most widely scattered of great speech communities, English is probably native tongue of more people than any other except North Chinese and is used extensively as an auxiliary language. There are many dialect areas. Today's English is continuation of language of 5th-cent. invaders of Britain (see ANGLO-SAXON LITERATURE). This Old English (to c.1050) was followed by Middle (to c.1450; see MIDDLE ENGLISH LITERATURE) and that by Modern (from a London dialect), with no discontinuity, even during French hegemony. Vocabulary includes words derived from earliest English and words from Latin Christianity, Scandinavian settlers, Norman French, and from classical languages.

Enid (ē'nĭd), city (pop. 36,017), N Okla., NNW of Oklahoma City; settled 1893. Trade and processing center for agr. and livestock area, it has oil refining, dairying, and mfg. of machinery.

Enisei, river, USSR: see YENISEI.

Eniwetok (ĕnĭwē'tŏk), circular atoll of Marshall Isls., central Pacific; comprises 40 islets. Captured 1944 by U.S. forces, became naval base 1945. Installations for atomic tests estab. 1948. Tests made in 1951 and 1952 advanced development of hydrogen bomb.

Enlightenment, the rationalist, liberal, humanitarian, and scientific trend of thought of the 18th cent. Foreshadowed by scientific revolution of 17th cent., it found expression in such works as Diderot's ENCYCLOPÉDIE; in the writings of such men as Diderot, Voltaire, Montesquieu, J. J. Rousseau (France), Hume, Thomas Paine (England, America), Lessing, Kant (Germany), and Beccaria (Italy); in the reforms of such "enlightened despots" as Frederick II of Prussia, Catherine II of Russia, and Emperor Joseph II; and in the American and French revolutions.

Enna (ĕn'nä), city (pop. 21,261), central Sicily, Italy; formerly called Castrogiovanni. Sulphur mines in vicinity. Fell to Syracuse 396 B.C., to Rome 258 B.C.; center of Sicilian slave rebellion 135–132 B.C. Medieval citadel.

Ennis, city (pop. 7,815), N Texas, SSE of Dallas. Center of agr. area, it processes cotton and grain; railroad shops.

Ennius, Quintus (kwĭn'tús ĕ'nēús), 239–169? B.C., father of Latin poetry and a dramatist, author of the epic *Annales*.

Enoch (ē'nŭk), father of Methuselah. Said to have walked with God, and, like Elijah, to have been translated into heaven. Gen. 5.18–24; Luke 3.37; Heb. 11.5; Jude 14. Henoch: 1 Chron. 1.3. For Book of Enoch and Secrets of Enoch, see PSEUDEPIGRAPHA.

Enschede (ĕn'skhúdä), municipality (pop. 80,-346), Overijssel prov., E Netherlands. Textile center.

ensilage (ĕn'sŭlĭj), animal fodder made by fermenting a chopped green crop (e.g., corn, legumes) in a SILO.

Ensor, James Ensor, Baron, 1860–1949, Belgian impressionist painter. A founder of the experimental group *Les XX* and a major influence on 20th-cent. Belgian art.

entail, restriction of inheritance to a limited class of descendants for at least several generations in order to preserve large estates

from disintegration. Similar devices were known in Roman law and in all countries of Europe. In the U.S. entails are for the most part either prohibited or limited to a single generation. See also PRIMOGENITURE.

Entente: see TRIPLE ALLIANCE and TRIPLE ENTENTE; LITTLE ENTENTE.

Entente Cordiale: see TRIPLE ALLIANCE AND TRIPLE ENTENTE.

Enterprise, city (pop. 7,288), SE Ala., WNW of Dothan, in area devoted to diversified agr. since boll weevil destroyed cotton crops (1910–15).

Entrecasteaux, Joseph Antoine Bruni d' (dätrú-kästō'), 1739–93, French navigator. In command of expedition to search for La Pérouse (1791–92), he explored coast of New Caledonia, Tasmania, and New Holland, and located several island groups.

Entrecasteaux Islands, D', Territory of Papua: see D'ENTRECASTEAUX ISLANDS.

Enver Pasha (envâr' päshä'), 1881–1922, Turkish general. Prominent in Young Turk revolution (1908). Led Turkey into World War I, holding virtually dictatorial powers. Was killed while leading anti-Soviet expedition in Bukhara.

envoy: see DIPLOMATIC SERVICE.

Enzina, Juan del: see ENCINA, JUAN DEL.

Enzio (än'tsēō) or **Enzo** (än'tsō), c.1220–72, king of Sardinia; illegitimate son of Emperor Frederick II. Captured by Guelphs 1249; imprisoned at Bologna till his death.

enzyme (ĕn'zīm), organic compound secreted by plant and animal cells which causes chemical change in substance on which it acts. Action believed to be CATALYSIS but differs in that it is more specific, has optimum temperature and acidity, and the effect of changing enzyme concentration or substrate is not always predictable by simple chemical theory. Enzymes catalyze digestion, oxidation, other metabolic processes.

Eocene epoch, first epoch of the TERTIARY PERIOD and Cenozoic era of geologic time. The early part is usually distinguished as the Paleocene. During these epochs North America assumed practically its present outline. The Eocene was marked by submergence of the Atlantic and Gulf coastal plains (as far north as S Ill.), and, in the west, of the Great Valley of California. Paleocene mammals were primitive, but in the Eocene proper ancestors of modern mammals appeared, including Eohippus, the "dawn horse."

Eos (ē'ŏs) [Gr.,= dawn], Greek personification of dawn, daughter of Hyperion and Theia. Mother of the winds and the stars and of MEMNON. She was Aurora to the Romans.

Eotvos, Joseph, Baron (ût'vûsh), Hung. *Eötvös,* 1813–71, Hungarian writer and statesman; minister of public instruction and religious affairs (1848, 1867). His novels and dramas reflect his liberal views.

Epaminondas (ĭpä"mĭnŏn'dús), d. 362 B.C., Greek general of Thebes, who defeated the Spartans at LEUCTRA (371 B.C.). Killed after winning at MANTINEA (362).

Epée, Charles Michel, Abbé de l' (shärl' mēshĕl' äbä' dú läpä'), 1712–89, French Jansenist. Developed manual system of communications for deaf-mutes.

Épernay (āpĕrnä'), town (pop. 18,716), Marne

dept., NE France, in Champagne, on Marne R. A center of champagne industry.

Ephesians (-fē'-), epistle of New Testament, traditionally written by St. Paul to Christians of Ephesus from his captivity at Rome (A.D. c.60). Book contains: doctrine of mystical body of Christ; example of ideal harmony of husbands and wives; famous metaphor of the Christian as a soldier.

Ephesus (ĕ'fŭsŭs), anc. Ionian Greek city of Asia Minor, in modern Turkey; a wealthy seaport. Under Rome became leading city of Asia. Temple of Diana (Artemis) was one of the Seven Wonders of the World. Ephesus was later a center of Christianity.

Ephesus, Council of, 431, third ecumenical council called to deal with NESTORIANISM. St. CYRIL of Alexandria was the leader of the faction that after a struggle succeeded in exiling Nestorius and condemning his doctrines. The council declared Mary might be called the Mother of God, since God and Christ were one person, a doctrine further defined later by the Council of CHALCEDON. For the Robber Synod (Latrocinium) of Ephesus, see EUTYCHES.

ephod (ē'fŏd, ĕ'fŏd), sacred linen garment worn by high priests of Israel; apparently somehow used in divination. Ex. 28; Judges 8.27; 17.5; 18.14; 1 Sam. 2.28; 14.3; 22.18; 23.6,9; 30.7; Hosea 3.4.

Ephraim (ē'frŭm), son of Joseph, ancestor of one of 12 tribes of Israel. Tribe occupied region around Shiloh. Gen. 41.52; 46.20; 48.14–20; Joshua 16; 1 Chron. 7.20. Samuel was of house of Ephraim.

Ephraim, city (pop. 1,987; alt. 5,543 ft.), central Utah, S of Provo. Irrigated by Sanpete project.

Ephrata (ĕ'frŭtŭ), borough (pop. 7,027), SE Pa., NE of Lancaster; settled 1728–33 by Seventh-Day Baptists as communal religious community. Was famous for music; estab. early printing press. Buildings preserved as shrine by state. Center of agr. area with mfg. of clothing, textiles, and furniture.

Ephratah (ĕ'frŭtŭ) or **Ephrath:** see BETHLEHEM.

epic, long narrative poem, elaborate and dignified, in which theme is treated in heroic proportions and in grand style. Story of hero is usually unifying subject. Epics are generally classed as those conceived and composed by one mind (Vergil's *Aeneid*, Milton's *Paradise Lost*) and those by various unknown poets working at different times on popular legends concerning heroes (BEOWULF and ROLAND); Greek epics, the *Iliad* and the *Odyssey*, embrace both groups. Some epics embody ideals of a nation, e.g., Finnish KALEVALA and *The Lusiads* of Camões. Other epics include the *Jerusalem Delivered* of Tasso, *The Faerie Queene* of Spenser, and the Spanish CID.

Epictetus (ĕpĭktē'tŭs), b. c.60 A.D., Roman Stoic philosopher.

Epicurus (ĕpĭkū'rŭs), 341–270 B.C., Greek philosopher. Defined philosophy as the art of making life happy, with intellectual pleasure or serenity the only good. His teaching (Epicureanism) later debased to "eat, drink, and be merry" formula—opposite of his belief. See also LUCRETIUS.

Epidaurus (ĕpĭdô'rŭs), anc. city, NE Peloponnesus, Greece. To the temple of Asclepius here came many health seekers.

epidemic disease: see COMMUNICABLE DISEASES.

Epigoni (ĕpĭg'ŭnī) [Gr.,= the offspring], in Greek legend, sons of the SEVEN AGAINST THEBES. Led by Adrastus, they conquered Thebes and gave the kingdom to THERSANDER.

epigraphy: see INSCRIPTION.

epilepsy, condition marked by attacks usually accompanied by loss of consciousness and convulsions. Most cases begin in youth; seizures vary in frequency and duration. Treatment includes rest.

Epimetheus (ĕpĭmē'thēŭs, -thūs) [Gr.,= afterthought], in Greek religion, Titan. Brother of Prometheus, who warned him against marrying PANDORA—but in vain.

Épinal (āpēnäl'), town (pop. 21,939), cap. of Vosges dept., E France, in Lorraine. Famous for *images d'Épinal*—popular colored portrayals of melodramatic events long printed here.

Épinay, Louise de la Live d' (lwēz' dù lä lēv' dāpēnā'), 1726–83, French patroness of letters, friend of Diderot and Grimm. She was a benefactress of J. J. Rousseau, who broke with her in 1757 and calumnied her in his *Confessions*.

epinephrine: see ADRENALINE.

Epiphania: see HAMA, Syria.

Epiphany (ĭpĭ'fŭnē) [Gr.,= showing], a prime Christian feast, celebrated Jan. 6; called also Twelfth Day, Little Christmas, and Manifestation of Christ to the Gentiles. Its eve is TWELFTH NIGHT. It commemorates three events—baptism of Jesus (Mark 1), visit of Wise Men to Bethlehem (Mat. 2), and miracle at Cana (John 2). Feast is more ancient than Christmas and technically more important, ranking after Easter and Whitsunday. The term *epiphany* (without capital letter) means a manifestation (usually of divine power) or a moment of intuitive perception.

epiphyte: see AIR PLANT.

Epirus (ĕpī'rŭs), anc. country of W Greece, on Ionian Sea. Reached its height in 3d cent. B.C. under PYRRHUS. Sided with Macedon against Rome, was sacked (167 B.C.), and passed under Roman rule. In A.D. 1204, as result of Fourth Crusade, an independent state, the **despotat of Epirus,** was set up here by a branch of Angelus family. It became nominally dependent on the empire of NICAEA (c.1246), passed to Serbs and Albanians (14th cent.) and to Turks (15th cent.).

Episcopal Church, Protestant, in the United States of America, in communion with the Anglican church. Services in America were first held (1607) in Jamestown, Va. In 1689 King's Chapel was opened in Boston, and Trinity Church in N.Y. city. Col. of William and Mary was founded 1693, King's Col. (now Columbia Univ.) 1754. After Revolution American Anglicans organized, with Samuel Seabury first bishop (1784). First General Conference (1789) approved name of church, and adopted constitution and revised Book of Common Prayer. Church spread rapidly in U.S. Standards of doctrine are Apostles' and Nicene creeds and Thirty-nine Articles.

Episcopal Church, Reformed: see REFORMED EPISCOPAL CHURCH.

Episcopius, Simon (ĕpĭskō'pēŭs), 1583–1643, Dutch theologian; originally named Bisschop or Bischop. As leader of Arminians or REMONSTRANTS, he formulated in his *Institutiones theologicae* (1650) the doctrines of Jacob Arminius.

epistemology (ĭpĭ″stŭmŏ'lŭjē), branch of philosophy devoted to theories of knowledge, its origin and nature. Empirical epistemology teaches that all knowledge comes from experience; rationalistic epistemology holds that the mind contributes innate ideas.

epistle, a formal letter. Of books of New Testament, 21 are epistles. Those traditionally ascribed to St. Paul are Romans, 1 and 2 Corinthians, Galatians, Ephesians, Philippians, Colossians, 1 and 2 Thessalonians, 1 and 2 Timothy, Titus, Philemon, Hebrews. Catholic, or General Epistles are James, 1 and 2 Peter, 1, 2, and 3 John, Jude. Use of letters as literary form popular in 18th cent. when the novel was epistolary. Celebrated epistles are those of Petrarch, Pascal, Swift, and (in verse) Pope and Dryden.

Epping Forest, NNE of London, England, the anc. Royal Waltham Forest. Originally included all Essex. Has been a 5,600-acre public park since 1882.

Epsom and Ewell (yōō'ŭl), urban district (pop. 68,049), Surrey, England. DERBY and Oaks horse races are run on Epsom Downs.

Epstein, Jacob (ĕp'stīn), 1880–, sculptor, b. New York city. Studied under Rodin; worked chiefly in England. His massive creations done in startlingly unconventional style have caused much controversy. Some of best work is bronze portraiture.

equal temperament, in music, a system of tuning based on the arbitrary division of the octave into 12 equal semitones. The octave is the only acoustically correct interval; other tones of scale are adjusted or tempered so that, in keyboard instruments, a single key can represent two tones—for example, both F sharp and G flat. Scale thus derived is called a tempered scale. Bach supported this system with his *Well-tempered Clavier,* containing preludes and fugues in all major and minor keys. See also TEMPERAMENT.

equation. 1 in mathematics, a statement of the equality of two quantities or algebraic expressions. If equation contains only numbers, it is called numerical; if it has letters as well as numbers, literal; if literal equation is true for all values of the variable, it is called an identical equation; if not, it is called a conditional equation. To solve equation, obtain value or values of variables which satisfy it. **2** in chemistry, an equation represents a reaction, the first member of the equation consisting of the formulas for the reacting substances and the second member the formulas for the resulting products. An arrow (——→) is used instead of an equals sign and its direction shows the direction in which the reaction is proceeding. In physics, equations are means of expressing fundamental relationships.

equatorial belt of calms: see DOLDRUMS.

equinox (ē'kwĭnŏks), in astronomy, either of two points of intersection of ECLIPTIC and celestial equator. Night and day are of equal length over entire earth on dates when sun's center crosses celestial equator southward (vernal equinox, about March 21) or northward (autumnal equinox, about Sept. 23). See also PRECESSION OF THE EQUINOXES. See *ill.,* p. 1187.

equites (ĕ'kwĭtēz) [Latin,= horsemen, knights], original cavalry of the Roman army, later selected (to number 3,600) on basis of wealth. By the 1st cent. B.C. had become the influential capitalist class.

equity, principles of justice developed by chancellor and court of chancery in England to make up for inadequacies of common law. Equity originally drew many of its principles from Roman and canon law. Contest with common law was important in 16th and 17th cent. In 1875 common law and equity amalgamated by Judicature Acts in England. In U.S. most states have also done away with distinction between equity and common law.

Er, chemical symbol of the element ERBIUM.

era of good feeling, phrase applied to period 1817–23 in U.S. history, when, the Federalist party having declined, there was little open party feeling. Under the surface, however, vast sectional issues and personal rivalries were shaping themselves to break loose in campaign of 1824.

Erasistratus (ĕrŭsĭ'strŭtŭs) 3d cent. B.C., Greek physician, a founder of medical school at Alexandria.

Erasmus (ĭrăz'mŭs) or **Desiderius Erasmus** (dĕsĭdĕr'ēŭs), 1469?–1536, Dutch humanist. A Catholic priest and teacher, he had great influence after 1500. Acquainted with most scholars of the day, he was the broadest of humanists. Edited Greek and Latin works, including those of Church Fathers. Wrote satires (*The Praise of Folly,* 1509; *The Education of a Christian Prince,* 1515). His position with regard to the Reformation caused enmity of Luther.

Erastus, Thomas (ĭră'stŭs), 1524–83, Swiss physician and theologian, b. Lieber or Liebler. Opposed Calvinist doctrine and punitive power of church. Term **Erastianism** represents approval of dominance of civil authority in punitive matters, and, by extension, dominance of state over church.

Erato, muse of the poetry of love: see MUSES.

Eratosthenes (ĕrŭtŏs'thŭnēz), c.275–c.195 B.C., versatile Greek scholar, head of Alexandria library. Especially noted for measuring circumference and tilt of earth and for map of known world.

Erbil (ĕr'bĭl), town (pop. 26,086), NE Iraq. On site of ARBELA, it has an old Turkish fort.

erbium (ûr'bēŭm), rare metallic element (symbol = Er; see also ELEMENT, table; metals of the RARE EARTHS).

Ercilla y Zúñiga, Alonso de (älōn'sō dä ĕrthĭ'lyä ē thōō'nyēgä), 1533–94, Spanish author of epic poem, *La Araucana,* about Araucanians, whom he had fought.

Erckmann-Chatrian (ĕrkmän'-shätrēä'), joint authorship of Émile Erckmann (āmēl'), 1822–99, and Alexandre Chatrian (älĕksä'drŭ), 1826–90. They wrote historical romances and plays set in native Lorraine, e.g., *Madame Thérèse* (1863) and *L'Ami Fritz* (1864; adapted into a play 1876).

Erdelyi, John (ĕr'dālyĭ), Hung. *Erdélyi,* 1814–

68, Hungarian writer and critic, prominent in the Hungarian language reform movement. Edited (1846–48) the first collection of Hungarian folk poetry.

Erebus (ĕr′ĭbŭs) [Gr.,= darkness], in Greek mythology, gloomy part of underworld on way to Hades.

Erebus, Mount, volcanic peak, more than 13,-300 ft. high, on Ross Isl., in the Ross Sea off Antarctica. Discovered 1841 by Sir James C. Ross.

Erech (ē′rĕk) or **Uruk** (ōō′rōōk), anc. Sumerian city of Mesopotamia, on Euphrates, near Ur; long the cap. of Lower Babylonia.

Erechtheum (ĭrĕk′thēŭm), temple in Pentelic marble on the Acropolis, Athens; built c.420–409 B.C., probably designed by Mnesicles. Contains finest examples of Greek IONIC ORDER. On S portico is Porch of the Caryatids, with its six draped female figures which support its entablature. Used as a church in Justinian's reign and as a harem during Turkish rule. Much damaged in Greek revolution of 1827. Part of it is included in ELGIN MARBLES.

Erechtheus (ĕrĕk′thŭs), ancient mythological king of Athens; son of Hephaestus and Gaea. He invented four-wheeled chariot and founded Panathenaea.

Eretria (ĕrē′trĕŭ), anc. city of Greece, on Euboea. Mother-city of colonies in N Aegean, it supported the Ionian revolt against Persia (499 B.C.). Darius I destroyed it (490 B.C.).

Erfurt (âr′fŏŏrt), city (pop. 174,633), cap. of Thuringia, central Germany. Mfg.; center of gardening and truck-farming region. Bishopric of Erfurt, founded 741 by St. Boniface, passed to electors of Mainz 1664, to Prussia 1802. Occupied by French 1806–13, it was scene of Congress of Erfurt (1808), where Napoleon I and Alexander I renewed their alliance of 1807. City was incorporated into Thuringia in 1946, replaced Weimar as cap. 1948. Univ. of Erfurt (1392–1816) had Luther as student. Erfurt Program, adopted by German Social Democrats at party congress of 1891, marked triumph of Marxist doctrines over those of Lassalle. Erfurt's cathedral and Church of St. Severus (both 13th cent.) are notable.

erg, unit of work and energy in centimeter-gram-second system. It is the work done by one DYNE acting through distance of one centimeter. Joule is 10,000,000 ergs.

Eric, kings of Sweden. **Eric IX** (The Saint), d. 1160. Forcibly converted Finland to Christianity. Murdered by a Danish pagan, he became patron saint of Sweden. **Eric XIV,** 1533–77, reigned 1560–68. In conflict with nobility, he had Nils Sture and other powerful nobles assassinated. His unpopularity and soon evident insanity led to his deposition and imprisonment.

Ericsson, John (ĕ′rĭksŭn), 1803–89, Swedish-American inventor and marine engineer, b. Sweden. Chiefly remembered as designer and builder of the *Monitor* (see MONITOR).

Ericsson, Leif: see LEIF ERICSSON.

Eric the Red, fl. 10th cent., Norse chieftain, discoverer and colonizer of Greenland. Vainly resisted the introduction of Christianity there by his son, Leif Ericsson.

Eridu (ā′rĭdōō), anc. Sumerian city of Mesopotamia, near the Euphrates, not far from Ur. It perhaps was in existence in 8th millennium B.C. and was a center of the worship of Ea.

Erie, city (pop. 130,803), NW Pa., on L. Erie SW of Buffalo; laid out 1795. Only Pa. port on Great Lakes, it has mfg. of electrical and metal products. Site fortified by French, then British. In 1843 first all-iron battleship was assembled here. Was station on Underground Railroad.

Erie, Lake, 241 mi. long, 30–57 mi. wide, fourth in size and shallowest of the Great Lakes. Lies c.572 ft. above sea level, maximum depth 210 ft., area 9,950 sq. mi. Bordered N by Ontario, S by N.Y., Pa., and Ohio, W by small portion of Mich. Connected with L. Huron by natural channel, with L. Ontario by Niagara R. and by Welland Canal. N.Y. State Barge Canal and Hudson R. connect it with the Atlantic. Partially icebound and largely closed to navigation from mid-December to April. Principal U.S. ports include Buffalo, N.Y.; Erie, Pa.; Cleveland and Toledo, Ohio; and Detroit, Mich. First white man to see lake was probably Louis Jolliet (1669). Forts and trading posts were built on shores. Great Britain controlled area after French and Indian Wars until War of 1812 when international boundary was set. In War of 1812 at **battle of Lake Erie** (Sept. 10, 1813) British were defeated by U.S. fleet under O. H. PERRY.

Erie Canal, artificial waterway, extending from Albany to Buffalo and connecting the Hudson with L. Erie. Authorized by N.Y. in April, 1817; completed 1825. Later converted into NEW YORK STATE BARGE CANAL. The Erie furthered New York city's financial development, opened Eastern markets to farm products of the Great Lakes region, fostered immigration to Old Northwest, helped create numerous large cities.

Erie Indians, sedimentary tribe of Iroquoian linguistic stock, in region E and S of L. Erie in 17th cent. Enemies of the Iroquois Confederacy, they were almost exterminated after 1656.

Erie Railroad. Incorporated 1832 as New York and Erie Railroad Co. Struggle for control among railroad barons after Civil War, with victory for Jay Gould, was main phase of company's unstable financial history in 19th cent. Beginning as a short N.Y. railroad, it had by 1880 branch lines to Chicago, and E terminus at Jersey City. Reorganized 1895 as Erie Railroad Co. After reorganization of 1941, company yielded a dividend for first time in 69 years.

Erigena, John Scotus (skō′tŭs ĕrĭ′jĭnŭ), c.810–880, scholastic philosopher. Identified philosophy and theology and made a four-fold division of nature, a creative cycle that begins and ends with God.

Erin (ĕr′ĭn, ēr′ĭn), poetic name of IRELAND.

Erinyes (ĕrĭn′ē-ēz), in Greek religion, Furies or goddesses of vengeance, represented as three maidens, winged, with snakes in their hair. Born from blood of Uranus which fell on land. They pursued criminals and tormented them in Hades. Euphemistically, also called Eumenides [favorable ones], their title in the chorus in the *Eumenides* of Aeschylus.

Eris (ē′rĭs) [Gr.,= discord], in Greek legend, female personification of strife. In revenge for not being invited to a wedding, she threw the APPLE OF DISCORD.

Eritrea (ĕrĭtrē′ū), former Italian colony (45,-754 sq. mi.; pop. c.1,087,000), NE Africa, on Red Sea; cap. Asmara; now part of Ethiopia. Bounded on W by Anglo-Egyptian Sudan and on S by Ethiopia. Desert coastal strip adjoins rugged plateau of interior. Fertile valleys in central part. Inhabited by pastoral nomads of Ethiopian stock. Products include citrus fruits, cereal, cotton, and hides. Eritrea was virtual possession of Ethiopia until 16th cent., when it fell to Ottoman Turks. Divided among local chieftains from 17th to mid-19th cent. Became Italian colony in 1890. British troops expelled the Italians in April, 1941. In 1949 the UN awarded most of Eritrea to Ethiopia; all unified under Ethiopia 1952.

Erivan (ĕrĭvän′), Armenian *Yerevan*, city (pop. c.300,000), cap. of Armenian SSR, on Zanga R., beautifully set among orchards and mountains. Founded 7th cent. A.D.; cap of Armenia under Persian rule; after 15th cent. passed back and forth between Persia and Turkey; ceded by Persia to Russia 1828. New machinery, textile, chemical industries quadrupled pop. after 1926.

Erlach, Johann Bernhard Fischer von: see FISCHER VON ERLACH, JOHANN BERNHARD.

Erlangen (ĕr′läng-ŭn), city (pop. 49,886), Middle Franconia, N Bavaria, on Regnitz R. Has important mfg. of medical equipment (X-ray machines, hearing aids). Under margraves of Bayreuth-Kulmbach (house of Hohenzollern) from 1402; to Prussia 1792; to Bavaria 1810. University was founded at Bayreuth 1742, transferred to Erlangen 1743; Schelling and Schleiermacher taught here. City was rebuilt after a fire (1706), has baroque architecture.

Erlanger, Joseph (ûr′lăng-ûr), 1874–, American scientist. Shared 1944 Nobel Prize in Physiology and Medicine for work in physiology, especially nerve action.

Ermak, Cossack leader: see YERMAK.

ermine (ûr′mĭn), name for various species of weasel and their fur. Fur trappers use name weasel for North American skins and stoat for chief species (*Mustela erminea*) of N Europe and Asia. The pelts (the most valuable white with black markings) make wraps, coats, and trimmings; black tails are used in Europe with ermine robes of royalty.

Ermine Street, early Roman road in Britain said to have extended from London to Lincoln.

Erne, river of Ireland and N. Ireland, flowing 72 mi. from Lough Gowna to Donegal Bay in the Atlantic.

Ernest I, 1784–1844, duke of Saxe-Coburg-Gotha; brother of Leopold I of Belgium, uncle of Victoria of England, father of Victoria's consort, Albert. Succeeded to Coburg 1806; acquired Gotha 1826.

Ernst, Max (mäks′ ĕrnst′), 1891–, German surrealist painter. Was a Dadaist in his early period.

Eros (ĭ′rŏs, ĕ′rŏs) [Gr.,= love], in Greek mythology, god of love. He is the force of love in all its manifestations. Pictured by some as one of oldest gods, born from Chaos. Associated with Dionysus in Orphic Mysteries, he was worshiped as Protogonos, first-born. More usually, he was called son of Ares and Aphrodite and pictured as winged youth or child armed with bows and arrows. Identified with Roman Cupid or Amor. For his own love story, see PSYCHE.

erosion, wearing away of the earth's surface by running water, waves, glaciers, wind. Streams transport rock fragments formed by weathering, and these particles serve as cutting tools. Sea coasts are worn back by waves and the rock waste they carry. A glacier erodes by grinding boulders against its bed. In arid regions wind is an important erosive agent, transporting sand as dunes.

Errigal, Mount (ĕrēgôl′), 2,466 ft. high, Co. Donegal, Ireland; highest point in the county.

Erskine, John, 1879–1951, American author and musician, teacher of English at Amherst (1903–9) and Columbia (1909–37). He is best remembered for his tongue-in-cheek satiric novels, notably *The Private Life of Helen of Troy* (1925). He appeared as a concert pianist and was president of the Juilliard School of Music (1928–37).

Erskine, Thomas, 1st **Baron Erskine,** 1750–1823, British jurist. A great trial lawyer, he defended Thomas Paine's *The Rights of Man* against charge of sedition. Caused liberal revision of libel laws.

Ervine, St. John (Greer) (sĭn′ jŭn, ûrvĭn), 1883–, British dramatist, b. Ireland. Among his plays are *John Ferguson, Jane Clegg,* and *The First Mrs. Fraser.* Also wrote novels.

Eryri, Wales: see SNOWDON.

erysipelas (ĕrŭsĭ′pŭlŭs, –lĭs, ĭrŭ–), acute febrile disease attended by inflammation of skin and underlying tissues. Results from invasion of break in skin by hemolytic streptococcus.

Eryx (ĕ′rĭks), ancient city, W Sicily, Italy. Long a bone of contention between Carthage and Syracuse; destroyed by Carthaginians c.260 B.C. Cyclopic walls and Phoenician inscriptions remain.

Erzberger, Matthias (mätē′äs ĕrts′bĕrgûr), 1875–1921, German statesman, leader of Catholic Center party. Headed delegation which signed armistice of Nov., 1918. Assassinated by a nationalist.

Erzerum or **Erzurum** (both: âr′zûrōōm), city (pop. 54,360), NE Turkey, in Armenia. Agr. trading center. Long of strategic and commercial importance.

Erzgebirge (ĕrts′gŭbĭr″gŭ) or **Ore Mountains,** Czech *Krušné Hory,* mountain range of Bohemia (Czechoslovakia) and Saxony (Germany), extending c.100 mi. SE from the Elbe. Highest point, Mt. Klinovec (Ger. *Keilberg*), in Czechoslovakia, is at 4,080 ft. Important silver and iron mines exploited 14th–19th cent., notably at JACHYMOV. Now uranium, wolframite, lead, tin, copper, and sulphur are mined. Among the many spas, CARLSBAD and MARIENBAD are best-known. Intensive mfg. (textiles, machinery). Czech part of Erzgebirge was annexed by Germany in 1938, but was restored in 1945.

Erzsebetfalva, Hungary: see PESTSZENTERZSEBET.

Erzurum, Turkey: see ERZERUM.

Esaias (ēzā'yùs), variant of ISAIAH.

Esar-Haddon (ē"sär-hä'dùn), king of Assyria (681–668 B.C.), son of SENNACHERIB. Put down revolts, defeated the Chaldeans; conquered Egypt (673–670); curbed Elam. Succeeded by Assur-bani-pal.

Esau (ē'sô), [Heb.,= hairy], son of Isaac, tricked out of his inheritance by his twin, Jacob. He settled on Mt. Seir. As ancestor of Israel's enemies, the Edomites, he is called EDOM. Gen. 25–28; 32; 33; 36; Deut. 2.4,5; Joshua 24.4; Jer. 49.7–22; Heb. 12.14–17.

Esbjerg, Dan. *Esbjaerg* (ĕs'byĕr), city (pop. 48,205), SW Jutland, Denmark; a North Sea port.

Escambia (ĕskăm'bēù), river rising in SE Ala. (called Conecuh [kûnē'kû] there). Flows 231 mi. SW, then S through NW Fla. to Escambia Bay, which is an arm of Pensacola Bay.

Escanaba, city (pop. 15,170), W Upper Peninsula, N Mich., on inlet of Green and NE of Menominee; settled 1852. Ships much iron ore, has fishing and mfg. of wood products. Resorts in area.

escarpment or **scarp,** a long cliff, bluff, or steep slope. It is usually the result of erosion or of geologic faulting; often both causes are involved.

Escaut (ĕskō'), French name of SCHELDT river.

Esch, town (pop. 26,851), grand duchy of Luxembourg, on Alzette R. Steel center.

Eschenbach, Wolfram von: see WOLFRAM VON ESCHENBACH.

Eschweiler (ĕsh'vīlùr), city (pop. 35,446), North Rhine-Westphalia, NW Germany, near Aachen. Center of a soft-coal Basin; iron and steel mills.

Escondido (ĕskùndē'dō), city (pop. 6,544), S Calif., N of San Diego, in valley yielding citrus, grapes, poultry, and dairy products; laid out 1885. Mexican War battle at near-by San Pasqual (1846).

Escorial (ĕskô'rēùl, Span. äskōrēäl') or **Escurial,** former royal residence near Madrid, Spain. Built 1563–84, it comprises massive palace, monastery, church; contains royal tombs. Decorated by noted artists; has fine collection of Spanish painting.

Esdraelon (ĕs'drùē'lùn), fertile plain, central Palestine, drained by Kishon R., extending from SE foot of Mt. Carmel to Jordan valley. In ancient times a battleground, especially around MEGIDDO (see also GILBOA). Called also plain of JEZREEL or of Megiddo.

Esdras (ĕz'–) [Gr. from Heb. Ezra], name given in Western canon to four books of Old Testament and PSEUDEPIGRAPHA. Esdras 1 and 2 are same as AV EZRA and Nehemiah; Esdras 3 and 4 are pseudepigrapha, called, in Apocrypha of AV, Esdras 1 and 2. In Greek Bibles, Ezra and Nehemiah together are called 1 Esdras and pseudepigrapha are called 2 and 3 Esdras. Pseudepigrapha are (1) Greek translations of portions of 2 Chron., Ezra, and Nehemiah, and (2) an account of visions of Ezra.

Esenin, Sergei Aleksandrovich: see YESENIN.

Esher (ē'shùr), urban district (pop. 51,217), Surrey, England. Wolsey's Tower, remains of "Esher Place" occupied by Cardinal Wolsey, is here.

Esk, name of several rivers in Scotland. N and S Esk in Midlothian join and enter Firth of Forth; Black and White Esk of Dumfriesshire join and enter Solway Firth; and N and S Esk of Kincardine and Angus flow into the North Sea.

esker (ĕs'kùr), long, narrow, winding ridge of stratified DRIFT. Eskers resemble abandoned railway embankments; probably were deposited by streams flowing beneath a retreating ice sheet.

Eskilstuna (ĕ'skĭlstü"nä), city (pop. 53,577), SE Sweden. Center of Swedish cutlery industry.

Eskimo (ē'skùmō), native inhabitant of the arctic and subarctic regions of North America. Estimated Eskimo pop. c.30,000. Despite their wide dispersal they are highly uniform in language, physical type, and culture; Mongoloid features point to an Asiatic origin. The ingenuity of their material culture is essential to survival in the Arctic.

Eskimo dog: see CHOW.

Eskisehir (ĕskĕ'shĕhĕr), city (pop. 88,459), W central Turkey; probably identical with ancient Dorylaeum. Export center for meerschaum, chromium, magnesite, agr. market, railroad junction; cotton and tile mfg. Mineral springs

espalier (ĕspăl'yùr), tree (usually a fruit such as apple or pear) or vine trained to grow flat against wall or trellis. Plants so trained take up little space and are ornamental (often fan or fork shaped).

Española: see HISPANIOLA.

Espartero, Baldomero (bäldōmä'rō ĕspärtä'rō), 1793–1879, Spanish general. After his victory over the CARLISTS in civil war of 1836–39 he was created duque de la Victoria. As regent he ruled dictatorially (1841–43), was forced to flee by an uprising. Served as premier 1854–56.

Esperanto: see UNIVERSAL LANGUAGE.

Espinel, Vicente Martínez (vēthän'tä märtē'nĕth äspēnĕl'), 1550–1624, Spanish poet, novelist, musician. Added fifth string to guitar. Created 10-line stanza. Wrote picaresque novel, *Vida del escudero Marcos de Obregón* (1618).

Espiritu Santo: see NEW HEBRIDES.

Espronceda, José de (hōsä' dä äsprônthä'dhä), 1808–42, Spanish romantic poet, author of *El estudiante de Salamanca* and *El diablo mundo* (1841).

Espy, James Pollard (ĕ'spē), 1785–1860, American meteorologist. Developed a convection theory of storms. His work in War and Navy departments laid basis for scientific weather forecasting.

Esquimalt (ĕskwī'môlt), W suburb of Victoria, on Vancouver Isl., B.C., Canada. Here is chief naval station and naval dockyard in W Canada.

Essad Pasha (ĕ'sät pä'shä), 1863–1920, Albanian dictator (1914–16). Expelled the king (William, prince of Wied), who had appointed him premier. Defeated by the Austrians (1916); was assassinated.

Esseg, Yugoslavia: see OSIJEK.

Essen (ĕ'sùn), city (pop. 605,125), North Rhine-Westphalia, NW Germany. Center of RUHR dist.; seat of KRUPP steel works. Three quarters destroyed in World War II air raids.

Essenes (ĕ'sēnz), members of a Jewish religious

order (2d cent. A.D.). They believed in immortality, but not in resurrection. Ceremonial purity was rigidly practiced. Property was held communally; trading and slavery were prohibited.

essential oils: see OILS.

Essex, Robert Devereux, 2d earl of (dĕ'vŭrōō), 1567–1601, English nobleman, favorite of Queen Elizabeth. His position involved him in rivalry with Sir Walter RALEGH. He angered (1590) the queen by his secret marriage to Sir Philip Sidney's widow. Advised by Francis Bacon he entered politics, hoping to seize power from the aging Lord Burghley. Elizabeth, wary of his demands, conferred power on Robert Cecil. Made lord lieutenant of Ireland (1599), Essex was sent there to quell rebellion of earl of Tyrone. He failed, was confined on his return to England, and later banned from court. He unsuccessfully tried to oust opposing party and estab. his own party about queen in 1601. He was arrested, Elizabeth signed the death warrant, and he was executed. His son, **Robert Devereux, 3d earl of Essex,** 1591–1646, was restored (1604) to his estates by James I. He fought with royal army in first Bishops' War and later commanded parliamentary forces. After failure and disgrace in 1644, he relinquished his command.

Essex, kingdom of Anglo-Saxon England. Probably settled in early 6th cent., it eventually included modern counties of Essex, London, Middlesex, and most of Hertfordshire. Having early accepted Christianity the kingdom lapsed into heathenism until reconverted by Cedd in 7th cent. Long dominated by MERCIA. Essex joined other kingdoms in 9th cent. in submitting to Wessex and became an earldom. Became part of DANELAW in 886; was later retaken (917) by Edward the Elder of Wessex. Its most famous later earl was Byrhtnoth, defeated (991) at Maldon.

Essex, maritime county (1,528 sq. mi.; pop. 2,043,574), E England, on N bank of Thames estuary; co. town Chelmsford. Chief products are fish, oysters, fruits, and vegetables. SW portion, in Greater London area, has mfg. of chemicals, machinery, textiles, and cement. There are popular coastal resorts. Area near London and coast much bombed in World War II.

Essex Junction, village (pop. 2,741), in Essex town (pop. 3,931), NW Vt., E of Burlington and on Winooski R. Has annual Champlain Valley Exposition.

Essex Junto, group of New England merchants, so called because many of them came from Essex co., Mass. Opposed radicals in Mass. in American Revolution and supported the Federalists. Later encouraged disaffection of Hartford Convention.

Esslingen (ĕs'lĭng-ŭn), city (pop. 70,610), Württemberg-Baden, SW Germany, on Neckar R. Produces machinery, textiles. Free imperial city from 1219; passed to Württemberg 1803. Swabian League was founded here (1488). Has 13th-cent. castle.

Established Church: see ENGLAND, CHURCH OF; SCOTLAND, CHURCH OF; IRELAND, CHURCH OF.

Estaing, Charles Hector, comte d' (shärl' ĕktôr' kōt' dĕstĕ'), 1729–94, French admiral. Commanded French fleet sent to aid American

revolutionists, 1778–80. His planned attack on Newport, R.I., was undone by a storm (1778). Cooperated with Benjamin LINCOLN in unsuccessful attack on Savannah (1779). Was guillotined as a royalist.

estate. 1 In law of property, manner of owning realty and realty itself; more broadly any property held or bequeathed. **2** In constitutional law, one of the classes given a separate voice in government in Middle Ages and later. Three estates were nobility, clergy, commons (townspeople of substance, bourgeoisie, "third estate"). By extension "fourth estate" means newspapers.

Estates-General: see STATES-GENERAL.

Este (ĕ'stä), Italian noble family; branch of the GUELPHS. Derives name from town of Este, near Padua. Ruled FERRARA (1240–1597; from 1471 as dukes) and MODENA (1288–1796; from 1452 as dukes). Court of the Este family at Ferrara in 15th–16th cent. was a major center of literature and art. **Isabella d'Este,** 1474–1539, wife of Francesco GONZAGA, and her sister **Beatrice d'Este,** 1475–97, wife of Ludovico SFORZA, were brilliant ladies of the Renaissance and patronesses of Leonardo and Ariosto. Their brother, **Alfonso d'Este I,** 1476–1534, duke of Ferrara and Modena (1505–34), also was a lavish patron. In the Italian Wars he sided first with France against Pope Julius II (who in 1510 declared him forfeit of his fiefs), later with Emperor Charles V against Pope Clement VII (who had to reinstate him in 1530). He was the second husband of Lucrezia BORGIA. His brother, **Ippolito I, Cardinal d'Este** (ēp-pô'lētō), 1479–1520, was long the patron of Ariosto, who dedicated *Orlando furioso* to him. Alfonso's son, **Ippolito II, Cardinal d'Este,** 1509–72, built the famous Villa d'Este at Tivoli, near Rome. The direct male line of dukes died out 1597; in 1598 Pope Clement VIII incorporated Ferara into Papal States, despite claims of cadet line, which retained Modena. Deposed by Bonaparte 1796, last duke died 1803. His daughter married Archduke Ferdinand of Austria, a son of Emperor Francis II, who founded line of Austria-Este. Their descendants were dukes of Modena, Massa, and Carrara 1815–59.

ester, compound formed by a reaction, esterification, between alcohol and acid. Esters react with water under some conditions to form alcohol and acid; some saponify, i.e., yield soap and glycerin when heated with hydroxide. Common fats and oils are ester mixtures. Esters are used for flavoring; and in making perfumes, paints, explosives.

Esterhazy (ĕ'stŭrhä"zē), Hung. *Esterházy,* Hungarian noble family; princes of Holy Roman Empire since 1712. Best-known are **Paul Anton, Fürst Esterhazy von Galantha** (gä'läntä), d. 1762, and his brother and successor to the title, **Nikolaus Joseph, Fürst Esterhazy von Galantha,** 1714–90, because of their patronage of Haydn, who was in their service 1761–90. Nikolaus Joseph was extremely lavish with his immense wealth, built the famous château of Esterhaz on the Neusiedler Lake, endowed Haydn with handsome pension in his will.

Esterhazy, Ferdinand Walsin (Fr. fĕrdēnä'

välsĕ' ĕstĕräzĕ'), 1847–1923, French army officer, claiming membership in old Hungarian Esterhazy family. His guilt in selling military secrets to Germany was pinned on Captain Dreyfus (see DREYFUS AFFAIR). He was later dismissed from the army.

Estes Park (ĕs'tēz), resort town (pop. 1,617; alt. c.7,500 ft.), N central Colo., in the Rockies NNW of Denver. Hq. for Rocky Mt. Natl. Park. Two power dams of COLORADO–BIG THOMPSON PROJECT are near.

Esther, book of Old Testament. It tells of a Jewish girl, named originally Hadassah, who became queen of Persian king Ahasuerus (Xerxes). A wicked courtier, Haman, tried to incite a massacre of the Jews, but Esther, with aid of her uncle Mordecai, saved her people. The feast of Purim commemorates this. Chapters 10.4–16 are in Apocrypha in AV but are in Western canon.

Estherville, city (pop. 6,719), NW Iowa, on West Fork of Des Moines R. near Minn. line. Center for livestock, farm, and lumber area. Site of Fort Defiance (1862) is preserved near by.

esthetics: see AESTHETICS.

Estienne, Étienne (ātyĕn'), Latin **Stephanus,** family of printers and scholars in Paris and Geneva. **Henri Estienne,** d. 1520, was a printer in Paris by 1502. His son, **Robert Estienne,** b. 1498 or 1503, d. 1559, printed scholarly works, many edited by himself. Specialized in editions of classical authors, dictionaries—his own Latin thesaurus (1541) is a masterpiece—and critical editions of the Bible. Geofroy Tory designed his printer's mark (the Olive Tree) and Claude Garamond designed some of his type faces. A Protestant, he found himself in trouble and moved to Geneva (1550). His brother **Charles Estienne,** c.1504–1564, took over the Paris shop in 1551. Educated in medicine and in the classics, he wrote on many subjects. Got out an early French encyclopedia, a treatise on dissection, and *Praedium rusticum* [country property]. Robert's son, **Henri Estienne,** 1531?–1598, was the greatest scholar of the family. He took over the Geneva business, and though his books were not so good typographically as his father's, he brought out editions of Greek and Latin works notable for accuracy and textual criticism. He compiled a notable *Thesaurus Graecae linguae* (1572). Championed the use of French as a literary language. Trouble with Geneva authorities, begun by his satirical *Apologie pour Herodote* (1566), forced him to leave Geneva and later caused imprisonment. Became wandering scholar.

Estonia, Estonian *Eesti,* republic (17,400 sq. mi.; 1934 pop. 1,126,413), NE Europe, bounded by RSFSR (E), Latvia (S), and Baltic Sea (N and W); cap. Tallinn. Its inclusion (1940) into USSR is not recognized by U.S. A generally flat, dairy-farming country, it also has shale oil, timber, fisheries. Estonians speak a Finnic language, are mostly Lutherans. Country, part of historic LIVONIA, was ruled by Livonian Knights from 13th cent.; passed to Sweden 1561; was conquered by Russia 1710 (formally ceded by Sweden 1721). Descendants of German knights formed ruling class till 1917. Independence from Russia was proclaimed 1918; peace treaty with Russia was signed 1920. Democratic rule ended 1934, when Pres. Konstantin Päts began authoritarian regime. USSR secured military bases 1939 and in 1940 occupied Estonia and made it constituent Soviet republic. Occupied by Germany 1941–44.

Estournelles de Constant, Paul Henri Benjamin, baron d' (pôl' ărĕ' bĕzhämĕ' bärō' dätōōrnĕl' dù kõstä'), 1852–1924, French diplomat and pacifist. Shared 1909 Nobel Peace Prize with Auguste Beernaert.

Estrées, Gabrielle d' (gäbrĕĕl' dĕsträ'), 1573–99, famous beauty, mistress of Henry IV of France.

Estremadura (ĕshtrŭmùdōō'rù), historic province, SW Portugal, now divided among provs. of Estremadura (2,064 sq. mi.; pop. 1,379,-533; cap. Lisbon), Ribatejo, and Beira Litoral. Contains fertile valley of Tagus R. Agr., orchards, vineyards, forests.

Estremadura (ĕstrŭmùdōō'rù), Span. *Extremadura,* region (16,059 sq. mi.; pop. 1,253,924), W central Spain, bordering on Portugal. Cities: Badajoz, Cáceres. Arid tableland except for fertile Tagus and Guadiana valleys. Sheep grazing, hog raising.

Estremoz, Port. *Estremós* (ĕshtrŭmôsh'), city (pop. 6,765), Alentejo, Portugal. Famous for white marble and pottery. Castle was built by King Diniz.

Eszek, Yugoslavia: see OSIJEK.

Esztergom (ĕ'stĕrgôm), Ger. *Gran,* city (pop. 22,171), N Hungary, on the Danube. Birthplace of St. Stephen; seat of archprimates of Hungary since 1198. Has beautiful domed cathedral (built 19th cent.). Primate's palace contains museum and rich library. Also a warm-springs spa.

Eteocles (ētē'ōklēz), in Greek legend, son of Oedipus. He defended kingdom of Thebes, usurped from his brother, POLYNICES, in war of SEVEN AGAINST THEBES.

Ethan [Heb.,= strong], a wise man. 1 Kings 4.31; title of Ps. 89. May be same as Ethan of 1 Chron. 2.6.

ethanol: see ETHYL ALCOHOL.

Ethel–. For some Anglo-Saxon names beginning thus, see ÆTHEL–; e.g., for Ethelbald, see ÆTHELBALD.

ether, in chemistry, term used for ethyl ether, compound of ethyl radical (C_2H_5) and oxygen. Colorless liquid, volatile, inflammable; used as organic solvent and anesthetic. In physics and astronomy, it is hypothetical medium that transmits light and heat and fills all unoccupied space. Invisible, odorless, it does not interfere with motions of bodies through space. Many deny its material existence.

Etherege, Sir George (ĕth'ùrĭj), 1635?–1691, English Restoration dramatist, author of witty, licentious comedies of manners.

Ethical Culture movement, originating in Society for Ethical Culture founded in New York City (1876) by Felix Adler. It stresses ethical factor in life, apart from theological or metaphysical considerations. The society holds religious services; it lays emphasis on education and pioneered in kindergarten and adult education. In England, Stanley Coit founded society (1887). Internatl. Union of Ethical Culture Societies estab. 1896.

ethics, study and evaluation of human conduct in light of moral principles. Historically, various theories have developed as to man's conscience and responsibility for his actions. The intuitionists (e.g., ROUSSEAU) hold that conscience is innate and instigates moral action. Empiricists (e.g., COMTE, LOCKE, John Stuart MILL) instead explain it as a by-product of experience. Some philosophers seek an absolute ethical criterion in religion. Idealists (e.g., PLATO, KANT) see basis of ethics in metaphysics. Some (e.g., HEGEL, MARX) teach that the state is the arbiter of morals, others (e.g., DEWEY, Felix ADLER) that the individual controls.

Ethiopia (ēthēō'pēŭ) or **Abyssinia** (ăbĭsĭ'nēŭ), empire (c.400,000 sq. mi.; pop. c.15,500,-000), E central Africa; cap. Addis Ababa. Comprises low-lying deserts and mountainous plateau rising to 15,158 ft. at Ras Dashan. In NE is Tana L., source of Blue Nile. Exports include coffee, grains, hides, and gold. Ethiopia's main link with outside world is its single railroad, from Addis Ababa to Jibuti. According to tradition, founded in c.1000 B.C. by Solomon's first son, borne by Queen of Sheba (identified with Ethiopia), but records go back only to 1st cent. A.D. In 4th cent. ruler was converted to Coptic Christianity. Judaism probably introduced from Yemen. Rise of Islam (7th cent.) deprived Ethiopia of its coast. Period of chaos followed, but order was restored in 13th cent., when new dynasty was founded. Portuguese embassies and missionaries arrived in 16th cent. Emperor was converted to Roman Catholicism, but Coptic Church was fully restored mid-17th cent. and all foreigners expelled. Civil strife of next two centuries ended 1889, when MENELIK II became dominant with help of Italy. Claiming that Menelik had agreed to establishment of protectorate, Italy invaded Ethiopia 1895. Decisive battle of Aduwa compelled Italy to recognize Ethiopia's independence. HAILE SELASSIE, who ascended throne in 1930, faced renewed Italian threat, culminating in full-scale invasion (1935). Economic sanctions imposed against Italy by League of Nations were soon abandoned. Ethiopia was incorporated into Italian East Africa until 1941, when it was liberated by British troops. Unification with ERITREA was finally achieved in 1952.

Ethiopic (ēthēōp'ĭk), subgroup of Semitic languages. See LANGUAGE (table).

ethnology: see ANTHROPOLOGY.

ethyl (ĕ'thĭl), in chemistry, organic radical of carbon and hydrogen (C_2H_5). Compounds in which it occurs are called ethane derivatives.

ethyl alcohol, ethanol, or **grain alcohol,** colorless liquid alcohol with strong affinity for water. Absolute alcohol, a poison, is ethyl alcohol free of water. It burns in air, reacts with acids and active metals, is prepared by fermentation of sugar or starch. Used as industrial solvent; biological preservative; to make essences, tinctures, medicines; as fuel. It is denatured by addition of poison.

ethylene (ĕ'thĭlēn), colorless gas with faint odor, sweet taste. Forms explosive mixture with oxygen. Used in illuminating gas, as anesthetic, to bring out color of citrus fruit. It is an unsaturated HYDROCARBON with two atoms of carbon joined by double bond, each holding two hydrogen atoms. It is first member of **ethylene series;** each member has twice number of hydrogens as carbons. Lower members, gases; middle, liquids; higher, solids.

Étienne, family of printers: see ESTIENNE.

Etna, borough (pop. 6,750), SW Pa., on Allegheny R. near Pittsburgh. Mfg. of iron and steel products.

Etna or **Aetna** (ĕt'nŭ), active volcano, 10,700 ft. high, on E coast of Sicily, Italy. Shape and height of central cone often changed by eruptions. There are c.260 lesser craters. Its densely populated, fertile base is subtropical; the top has snow most of the year. Observatory at 9,650 ft. First known eruption 475 B.C. Those of 1069 and 1669 were particularly destructive.

Eton (ē'tŭn), urban district (pop. 3,250), Buckinghamshire, England. Chiefly known for **Eton College,** largest of famous English public schools, founded by Henry VI 1440. Unlike other similar schools, Eton is controlled by elected student representatives. Closely allied with King's Col., Cambridge. Many outstanding Englishmen educated here. Since World War II more scholarships granted to poorer students. Has annual cricket match with Harrow.

Etowah, river rising in N Ga. in the Blue Ridge and flowing 141 mi. SW to Rome, where it joins the Oostanaula to form the Coosa. Allatoona Dam (completed 1950; for flood control, power, navigation), near Cartersville, is first project in plan to develop Alabama-Coosa river system.

Etruria (ĭtrōō'rēŭ), anc. land, W Italy, now Tuscany and W Umbria. See ETRUSCAN CIVILIZATION.

Etruscan civilization (ĭtrŭ'skŭn), highest civilization in Italy before rise of Rome. Modern research upholds Herodotus that the Etruscans came (c.800 B.C.) from Asia Minor, possibly Lydia. In language and culture they differed from other Italians. Their wealth was based partly on knowledge of metalworking. They made fine pottery and improved agr. The oligarchical Etruscan cities (e.g., Tarquinii, Caere, Veii, Clusium) formed a loose confederacy. By 500 B.C. their civilization was at its height and included the Umbrian cities and part of Latium. In 5th and early 4th cent. B.C. Rome beat them back, capturing Veii after long struggles (396 B.C.). Invading Gauls in N aided disintegration.

Ettrick Forest, former woodland and royal hunting ground famous in legend, Selkirkshire, Scotland.

Ettrick Water, river of Selkirkshire, Scotland, flowing c.32 mi. from Capel Fell NE to the Tweed.

etymology, historical derivation of linguistic forms, especially words. Study had prestige for centuries because of an accepted theory that knowledge of the history of a word made its meaning clearer. This study revealed the regular relations of sounds in Indo-European languages (as in Grimm's law). In 20th cent.

linguists continued to use etymology to learn how meanings change, but they came to consider that the meaning of a form at a given time must be understood without reference to its history if it is to be understood at all.

Eu, chemical symbol of the element EUROPIUM.

Euboea (ūbē′ú), Gr. *Evvoia,* Aegean island (1,457 sq. mi.; pop. c.162,800), Greece, off Boeotia and Attica; chief city CHALCIS (connected with mainland by drawbridge across EURIPOS). Island is mostly mountainous. Agr., cattle raising. Euboea belonged to Athenian empire from 506 B.C.; passed to Macedon 338 B.C.; to Rome 191 B.C. After the Fourth Crusade it passed to Venice (1209), which lost it to the Turks in 1470. Its Venetian name was Negropont.

eucalyptus (ūkŭlĭp′tŭs) or **gum tree,** large tree or shrub of genus *Eucalyptus,* native to Australia and Asia. Some, e.g., blue gum and red gum, are widely planted on W coast of U.S. Various species yield timber and medicinal oils.

Eucharist (ū′kûrĭst) [Gr.,= thanksgiving], Christian SACRAMENT which repeats Jesus' giving bread and wine at the Last Supper. Catholics believe that in the sacrament bread and wine actually become the body and blood of Christ by transubstantiation. Partaking of the bread and wine is called communion. Performance of the sacrificial ritual is called liturgy, and the Roman liturgy is the MASS. For Protestant communion, see LORD'S SUPPER.

Eucken, Rudolph Christoph (oi′kún), 1846–1926, German philosopher. His "activism" stressed experience as the source of value. Awarded 1908 Nobel Prize in Literature.

Euclid (ū′klĭd), fl. c.300 B.C., Greek mathematician famous for his *Elements,* a collection of theorems and problems forming basis of geometry.

Euclid, city (pop. 41,396), N Ohio, on L. Erie, NE of Cleveland; settled 1798. Mfg. of electrical goods and office machinery. Here is Natl. American Shrine of Our Lady of Lourdes.

Eudes (ūdz, ûd) or **Odo,** c.860–898, French king (888–98); great-uncle of Hugh Capet. As count of Paris he defended his city against the Normans (885–87).

Eudoxus of Cnidus (ūdŏk′sús, nīdús), 408?–355? B.C., Greek astronomer and mathematician, credited with calculating length of solar year and discovering certain parts of Euclidean geometry.

Eufaula (ūfô′lú), city (pop. 6,906), SE Ala., on Chattahoochee R. and SE of Montgomery. Ships cotton; produces textiles, lumber products.

Eugene III, d. 1153, pope (1145–53), a CISTERCIAN, friend of BERNARD OF CLAIRVAUX. His rule was disturbed by Arnold of Brescia. Eugene promoted the disastrous Second Crusade.

Eugene IV, 1383–1447, pope (1431–47). Opposed antipapal acts of Council of BASEL, but was driven by Roman rebellion to exile at Florence (1434). In 1437 he ordered the council to Ferrara, but leaders at Basel refused to obey and declared Eugene deposed. Meanwhile the Council of FERRARA-FLORENCE met.

Eugene, city (pop. 35,879), W Oregon, at head of navigation on Willamette R. and S of Salem; settled 1846. Has creameries, fruit canneries, wool and lumber mills. Main seat of Univ. of Oregon (state supported; coed.; chartered 1872, opened 1876; medical and dental schools at Portland).

Eugene of Savoy, Prince, 1663–1736, French general in imperial service; son of a prince of Savoy-Carignano and of Olympe MANCINI. Louis XIV having refused him a commission, he entered service of Emperor Leopold I (1683). Defeated Turks at Zenta (1697) and Belgrade (1717), making possible victorious Treaty of PASSAROWITZ (1719). In War of the SPANISH SUCCESSION he shared in victory of Blenheim with Marlborough (1704); defeated French at Oudenarde (1708) and Malplaquet (1709); negotiated Peace of Rastatt (1714). His only major defeat was inflicted on him by his cousin Vendôme (Cassano, 1705).

eugenics (ūjĕ′nĭks), study of methods to improve human race physically and mentally. It is directed chiefly toward discouraging propagation by unfit and encouraging it in the fit. Some states have laws relating to sterilization of mental defectives, but many problems are involved in carrying out such laws. Probably the greatest hope lies in education and in euthenics (bettering the environment).

Eugénie (Fr. ûzhänē′) (Eugenia María de Montijo de Guzmán), 1826–1920, empress of the French, consort of Napoleon III; a Spanish noblewoman famed for her beauty. Fled to England when Second Empire was overthrown (1870).

Euhemerus (ūhĕ′mûrŭs), fl. c.300 B.C., Cyrenaic philosopher who developed a theory of mythology holding that gods were deified heroes (euhemerism).

Eulenspiegel, Till (oi′lún-shpē′gúl), N German peasant clown of the 14th or 15th cent., immortalized all over Europe by chapbooks describing his tricks, particularly on upper class persons. Subject of tone poem by Richard Strauss and of literary treatment by De Coster. Also spelled Tyl Ulenspiegel.

Euler, Leonhard (lā′ônhärt oi′lúr), 1707–83, Swiss mathematician. A founder of higher mathematics, known especially for work on calculus of variations, trigonometry, and analytic mathematics and mechanics. His work in astronomy, hydrodynamics, and optics was also notable. Eulerian equation and Euler's formula named after him.

Euler-Chelpin, Hans von (häns fŭn oi′lúr-kĕl′pĭn), 1873–, Swedish chemist, b. Germany. He shared 1929 Nobel Prize for work on sugar fermentation and chemistry of enzymes.

Eumenides: see ERINYES.

Eunice (ūnī′sē, ū′nĭs) [Gr.,= good victory], mother of Timothy; a Christian. 2 Tim. 1.5; Acts 16.1.

Eunice (ū′nĭs), town (pop. 8,184), SW La., W of Baton Rouge. Trade center for oil, cotton, and rice area.

Eunomia, one of the HORAE.

euonymus (ŭŏn′ĭmŭs) or **spindle tree,** shrub or vine of genus *Euonymus.* Some are evergreen and some have winged stems and brilliant autumn foliage and fruits. See also BURNING BUSH.

Eupatoria (ūpủtô'rēŭ), Rus. *Yevpatoriya* or *Evpatoriya,* city (pop. 23,512), RSFSR, in W Crimea; Black Sea port. Founded 1st cent. A.D.; named for Eupator, king of Pontus. Occupied by allies in Crimean War, by Germans in World War II. Old section contains ruins of Tatar fortress, 16th-cent. mosque.

Eupen (oi'pûn), town (pop. 14,462), Liége prov., SE Belgium. Wool mfg. Districts of Eupen and MALMÉDY (c.380 sq. mi.; pop. 60,000) were transferred from Germany to Belgium by Treaty of Versailles (1919). Population is predominantly German-speaking.

Euphranor (ûfrā'nủr), fl. 364 B.C., Greek painter and sculptor. His statues were praised by Pliny.

Euphrates (ūfrā'tēz), river of SW Asia, rising in E Turkey. Flows c.1,675 mi. to Iraq, there joining TIGRIS R. to form the SHATT EL ARAB. Lower course irrigates Iraq's great date plantations. With the Tigris it watered Mesopotamia, birthplace of early civilization.

Euphrosyne, one of the GRACES.

euphuism (ū'fūīzủm), in English literature, a highly artificial style derived from the *Euphues* (1579) of John Lyly. Has come to mean any artificial and high-flown style.

Eupompus (ūpŏm'pủs), fl. 4th cent. B.C., Greek painter, founder of Sicyonic school.

Eurasia (yoͦorā'zhú, –shú), land mass comprising continents of Europe and Asia.

Eure (ûr), department (2,331 sq. mi.; pop. 315,902), N France, in Normandy; cap. Évreux.

Eure-et-Loir (ûr-ā-lwär'), department (2,293 sq. mi.; pop. 285,110), N France, in Beauce; cap. Chartres.

Eureka, city (pop. 23,058), N Calif., on Humboldt Bay, in heart of redwood country; founded 1850. Lumber milling and commercial fishing.

Euric (yoͦo'rĭk), d. c.484, Visigothic king of Spain (466–c.484). Conquered nearly all Iberian peninsula and part of Gaul; made Toulouse his cap.; issued first code of Visigothic law.

Euripides (yoͦorĭ'pĭdēz), b. 480 or 485 B.C., d. 406 B.C., Greek tragic poet. Author of perhaps 92 plays, 19 extant. Most important: *Alcestis, Medea, Hippolytus, Andromache, Trojan Women, Electra, Iphigenia in Tauris, Iphigenia in Aulis,* and *Bacchae.* A realist, with an interest in contemporary people and problems and with an iconoclastic attitude toward the gods. Used the *deus ex machina* [god from a machine] to resolve a play's problem.

Euripos (yoͦorĭ'pủs), strait, 130 ft. to 1 mi. wide, between Euboea and Greek mainland.

Europa (yoͦorō'pủ), in Greek religion, Phoenician princess; daughter of Agenor. Zeus (taking the form of a bull) took her to Crete, where she bore him Minos. She later married king of Crete.

Europe, continent (with adjacent islands c.4,-000,000 sq. mi.; pop. c.550,000,000), a vast peninsula of the Eurasian land mass. Separated from Asia by Ural mts., Ural R., Caspian Sea, Caucasus, Black Sea, Bosporus, and Dardanelles; from Africa by Mediterranean Sea and Strait of Gibraltar. It is washed in the N by the Arctic Ocean (incl. Barents Sea, White Sea), in the W by the Atlantic, with which the Irish, North, Baltic, Mediterranean, and Black Seas are connected. A huge mountain chain (Pyrenees, Alps, Carpathians, Balkans, Caucasus) crosses continent from W to E. Highest points: Mt. Elbrus (18,481 ft.), Mont Blanc (15,772 ft.). Between the mountainous Scandinavian peninsula and this chain extends the great European plain—largely fertile soil, with steppe, forest, lake, and tundra dists. in E and N. S of the mountain chain are the fertile Po and Danubian plains and the mountainous Balkan, Italian, and Iberian peninsulas. Among chief rivers are (from E to W) the Volga, Don, Dnieper, Danube, Oder, Elbe, Rhine, Loire, Garonne, and Tagus. Climate, though greatly varied, is subject to moderating prevailing westerly winds. The states of Europe, grouped here by geographic regions, are: E Europe—USSR (incl. Lithuania, Latvia, Estonia) and Poland; SE Europe—Rumania, Hungary, Yugoslavia, Albania, Bulgaria, Greece, Turkey; Scandinavia—Sweden, Norway, Denmark, Finland; Central Europe—Austria, Czechoslovakia, Germany (now split into E and W Germany), Switzerland, Liechtenstein; W Europe—Belgium, Netherlands, Luxembourg, France, Monaco; S Europe—Italy, Free Territory of Trieste, San Marino, Vatican City, Spain, Portugal, Andorra; British Isles—United Kingdom of Great Britain and Northern Ireland, republic of Ireland; and Iceland. Turkey and USSR lie only partly in Europe. Great Britain, France, Portugal, Spain, Netherlands, Belgium, Denmark, and Norway have overseas possessions.

Europe, Council of, international body created 1949 as first step toward a federation of European states; hq. at Strasbourg, France. Consists of a committee of ministers and a consultative assembly. Members as of 1952: Belgium, Denmark, France, [West] German Federal Republic, Great Britain, Greece, Iceland, Ireland, Italy, Luxembourg, Netherlands, Norway, Saar Territory, Sweden, Turkey.

European Coal and Steel Community: see SCHUMAN PLAN (under SCHUMAN, ROBERT).

European corn borer: see CORN BORER.

European Defense Community, term for nations to be covered by a proposed European army. Includes France, West Germany, Belgium, the Netherlands, Luxembourg, and Italy. If ratified, army will be associated with NORTH ATLANTIC TREATY ORGANIZATION.

European Recovery Program, name popularly given project instituted at Paris Economic Conference (July, 1947) to foster post-war economic recovery in certain European countries. Took form when U.S. Secretary of State George C. Marshall—for whom program was also called Marshall Plan—urged (June, 1947) integration of U.S. economic aid to European countries. The Economic Cooperation Administration (ECA) administered program 1948–51; activities then transferred to Mutual Security Agency.

europium (yoͦorō'pēŭm), rare metallic element of rare earths (symbol = Eu; see also ELEMENT, table).

Europos or **Europus:** see DURA.

CAPITAL CITIES are designated by CAPITAL AND SMALL CAPITAL type

Eurydice, nymph, wife of ORPHEUS.

Eurymedon (yŏŏrī'mŭdŏn), small river of anc. Pamphylia, S Asia Minor. Here in the Persian Wars Cimon defeated the Persians (c.467 B.C.).

eurythmics (yŏŏrĭdh'mĭks) [as if Gr.,= good rhythm], system of musical training through harmonious bodily movements; first advanced by Émile Jaques-Dalcroze. Method begins with a set of gymnastics in response to music. Finally, student is able to improvise an interpretation, through gesture language, of an entire composition. System has influenced ballet and acting.

Eusebius of Caesarea (ūsē'bēŭs sēzŭrē'ŭ) or **Eusebius Pamphili** (păm'fĭlī), c.263–339?, Greek historian. Wrote *Ecclesiastical History,* in 10 books.

Eustace II (ū'stĭs), d. 1093, count of Boulogne, kinsman by marriage of Edward the Confessor. Over his visit to England (1051) Earl Godwin of Wessex broke with Edward. His great-grandson, **Eustace IV,** d. 1153, count of Boulogne, was the son of Stephen of England. Died before his father.

Eustachi, Bartolomeo (bär″tōlōmä'ō ā″ōōstä'kē), d. 1574, Italian anatomist, discoverer of many structures recorded in remarkable drawings (1552, published 1714). Discoveries include **Eustachian tube** (ūstā'kēŭn, –shŭn), the auditory canal equalizing air pressure between throat and middle ear.

Euterpe, Muse of music or of lyric poetry: see MUSES.

Eutyches (ū'tĭkēs), c.378–c.452, archimandrite in Constantinople, sponsor of Eutychianism, the first phase of MONOPHYSITISM, and leader of opponents of NESTORIANISM. His chief doctrine was that Christ's humanity was absorbed in his one divine nature. His teachings were denounced and he was deposed (448), but the so-called Robber Synod at Ephesus (449) reinstated him. At the synod St. Flavian, who opposed Eutyches, was manhandled and died. Theodoret was deposed. The Council of CHALCEDON annulled Robber Synod and ended Eutychianism.

Eutychides (ūtī'kĭdēz), fl. 4th cent. B.C., Greek sculptor of Sicyon; pupil of Lysippus. A marble copy of his *Fortune* is in the Vatican.

Evander (ēvăn'dŭr) [Gr.,= good man], figure taken from Greek mythology by Romans to connect Roman with Grecian legend.

Evangelical Alliance, association of Evangelical Christians, not of churches but of individuals from many denominations and countries. Estab. (1846) in London; in 1923 the largest association became known as the World's Evangelical Alliance.

Evangelical and Reformed Church, Protestant denomination, merger (1934) of Reformed Church in U.S. and Evangelical Synod of North America. Reformed Church, or German Reformed Church, estab. 1747. Evangelical Synod was union (1840) of Reformed and Lutheran Christians. Polity is presbyterian.

Evangelical Church: see EVANGELICAL UNITED BRETHREN CHURCH.

Evangelical United Brethren Church, Protestant denomination, merger (1946) of Evangelical Church and United Brethren in Christ. Both bodies grew from evangelistic efforts. Former

estab. (1807) under Jacob Albright, Lutheran convert to Methodism; latter founded (1800) by P. W. Otterbein and Martin Boehm. Church has episcopal government and Arminian doctrine, and stresses individual responsibility.

evangelist [from Gr.,= Gospel], title first given to SS. Matthew, Mark, Luke, and John. Now used for Protestant preachers who preach personal conversion. See also CAMP MEETING and REVIVAL, RELIGIOUS.

Evans, Herbert McLean, 1882–, American anatomist and embryologist, discoverer of vitamin E.

Evans, Lewis, c.1700–1756, colonial surveyor and geographer, b. Wales. His detailed maps of the middle colonies were used by migrating colonists and by Braddock. He drew attention to Ohio, suggested how to wrest it from French.

Evans, Luther H(arris), 1902–, American librarian and political scientist. Appointed librarian of Congress 1945. Member UNESCO executive board since 1949.

Evans, Maurice, 1901–, Anglo-American actor-manager. Noted for Shakspere productions (esp. *Hamlet*).

Evans, Oliver, 1755–1819, American inventor of grain-handling machinery and pioneer builder of high-pressure steam engines. He built the first steam river dredge in America.

Evans, Mount: see FRONT RANGE.

Evanston, residential city (pop. 73,641), NE Ill., on L. Michigan N of Chicago; settled 1826. Mfg. of radios and metal products. Once home of Frances E. Willard; hq. of Woman's Christian Temperance Union. Seat of NORTHWESTERN UNIVERSITY.

Evansville, city (pop. 128,636), SW Ind., on Ohio R. and SW of Indianapolis; settled 1817. Shipping point for agr. and coal-mining region. In World War II had largest inland shipyards in world. Mfg. of wood and metal products, and flour; packs meat. Evansville Col. is here.

Eva Perón, Argentina: see LA PLATA.

evaporation, conversion of liquid to gas at temperature below boiling point; rate depends on amount of exposed surface and on humidity. Molecules at surface bound into air, are prevented from returning by collision with molecules of air and resulting deflection. Increased energy of molecules depends on heat drawn from surrounding substances, e.g., the skin is cooled when liquid evaporates from it.

Evarts, William Maxwell, 1818–1901, American lawyer and statesman; grandson of Roger Sherman. Counsel for U.S. in several important legal cases. As U.S. Secretary of State (1877–81) he formulated U.S. position that any isthmian canal must remain under American control.

Evatt, Herbert Vere (vēr ē'vŭt), 1894–, Australian statesman. Judge of Australian High Court 1930–40, he became foreign minister (1941–49). President of UN General Assembly 1948–49, he was noted for upholding rights of small nations.

Eve [Heb.,= life], in Bible, first woman, Adam's wife. Led by serpent to eat forbidden fruit from tree of knowledge, she tempted Adam to eat. Both exiled from the Garden of Eden in punishment. Gen. 2–4; 2 Cor. 11.3; 1 Tim. 2.13.

Eveleth (ĕv'ŭlĕth), city (pop. 5,872), NE Minn., on Mesabi iron range and S of Virginia, in wooded lake region.

Evelyn, John (ĕv'ŭlĭn, ĕv'lĭn, ēv'lĭn), 1620–1706, English diarist. A royalist, he took little part in the civil war. After 1652 he lived as a wealthy country gentleman and wrote on many subjects. His diary, first published in 1818, offers much information on late 17th-cent. life.

evening primrose, plant of genus *Oenothera*, native to North America. Yellow flowers open in evening.

Everest, Sir George (ē'vŭrĭst), 1790–1866, British surveyor, b. Wales. Worked on trigonometrical survey of India (1806–43). Mt. Everest named for him.

Everest, Mount, peak, 29,141 ft. high, on Tibet-Nepal border, in the Himalayas; highest point on earth. Named for Sir George Everest. In 1952 a Swiss expedition led by Edouard Wyss-Dunant estab. world's climbing record of 28,210 ft.

Everett, Edward (ĕv'rĭt, ĕ'vŭrĭt), 1794–1865, American orator and statesman. U.S. Representative from Mass. (1825–35); adopted conservative attitude on slavery question. Governor of Mass. (1836–39). U.S. Senator (1853–54). In Civil War he traveled throughout North speaking for Union cause. Delivered principal oration at Gettysburg on same occasion that called forth Pres. Lincoln's address.

Everett. 1 City (pop. 45,982), E Mass., N of Boston. Mfg. of steel, iron goods, petroleum and wood products, chemicals, coke, and shoes. **2** Port city (pop. 33,849), NW Wash., on Puget Sound; settled c.1890. Ships lumber, fish, dairy and paper products.

Everglades, subtropical area, c.100 mi. long and 50–75 mi. wide, covering most of S Fla., S of L. OKEECHOBEE. Bounded on E by coastal strip (beaches), W by Big Cypress Swamp, and S by mangrove forests along Florida Bay and Gulf of Mexico. Consists of saw grass savannas and water dotted by hammocks (island-like clumps of trees). Occupies limestone plain, partly covered by muck and peat deposits. Heavy rainfall. Fringe areas support agr. (truck, sugar cane) and stock raising. Overdrainage, caused by reclamation projects of early 1900s, resulted in great fires in 1939. Most of S portion below Tamiami Trail is now in Everglades Natl. Park (see NATIONAL PARKS AND MONUMENTS, table), only tropical national park within U.S. boundaries. Has great variety of flora (some of it virgin) and fauna (esp. herons, egrets, ibises, pelicans, spoonbills). Reservation of SEMINOLE INDIANS is W of lower Everglades.

Evergreen Park, village (pop. 10,531), NE Ill., S suburb of Chicago.

everlasting or **immortelle,** plant with papery or chaffy flowers which on drying retain their form and color. Often used thus in winter bouquets are COCKSCOMB, GLOBE AMARANTH, SEA PINK, STRAWFLOWER.

Everyman, late 15th-cent. morality play in English, counterpart of Dutch play *Elckerlijc.* Which is the original has been disputed.

Summoned by Death, the hero, Everyman, can persuade none of his friends—Beauty, Kindred, Worldly Goods—to go with him, except Good Deeds.

Evesham (ēv'shŭm, ē'shŭm), municipal borough (pop. 12,066), Worcestershire, England, on Avon R. in productive fruit and vegetable region. Scene of royalists' victory over Simon de Montfort 1265.

Évian (āvyä') or **Évian-les-Bains** (-lä-bē'), resort, Haute-Savoie dept., E France, on L. Geneva. Mineral spa.

evidence, in law, sum of all facts stated in a trial, including documents and testimonial evidence of witnesses under oath. Particular evidence may be excluded by the judge on grounds that it is irrelevant (having no bearing on the case), immaterial (having no direct connection with substance of the case), or incompetent (outside the knowledge of the witness; e.g., hearsay evidence). In civil suits each party must prove its affirmative contentions; in criminal suits, the burden of proof rests on the plaintiff (prosecutor).

evolution, concept that animals and plants developed by gradual, continuous change from earlier forms. This concept, known as organic evolution (in contrast to inorganic evolution or origin of the physical universe) conceives of life as having arisen from simple primordial protoplasmic mass, probably in sea. Evolutionary concepts appeared in early Greece; during 15 centuries of Christian era under Church restraint, none developed until glimpses of later evolutionary theory began to appear after mid-16th cent. Invention of microscope and classification studies contributed to development. Charles Darwin, after 20 years of gathering evidence, formulated evolutionary theory later known as DARWINISM (and similar independent work of Alfred Russel Wallace). Darwin presented his theory in 1859, when first edition of his *Origin of the Species* appeared. Influence of theory upon scientific thought and philosophy incalculable. The concept was later enlarged by the growth of science of genetics, based on Mendel's laws of inheritance and extended through the work of T. H. Morgan, H. J. Muller, and others.

Évora (ē'vôrŭ), city (pop. 21,851), S Portugal, chief city of Alentejo. The Ebora of Roman times, it has impressive ruins ("temple of Diana"). Commercial center under Moors; captured by Portuguese 1166. Cathedral dates from 12th cent. Former Jesuit univ. (1559–1758) now a high school.

Evpatoriya, RSFSR: see EUPATORIA.

Évreux (āvrû'), town (pop. 16,645), cap. of Eure dept., N France, in Normandy. Counts of Évreux were also kings of NAVARRE 1349–1425. Cathedral (14th–17th cent.) damaged in World War II.

Ewald, Georg Heinrich August von (gā'ôrk hīn'rĭkh ou'gŏost fŭn ā'vält), 1803–75, German Orientalist and philologist, an authority on Hebrew and the Bible. He was one of the seven professors of the Univ. of Göttingen who protested the revocation of the Hanoverian constitution (1837).

Ewald, Johannes (ā'väl), 1743–81, Danish romantic poet. Author of dramas *Rolf Krage* (1770; first original Danish tragedy), and

The Fishers (1779; containing the Danish national anthem). Name also spelled Evald.

Ewbank, Thomas (ū'băngk), 1792–1870, American inventor of methods of manufacturing metal tubing, author of works on water-lifting machines and travel. As U.S. patent commissioner he improved patenting methods.

Ewell, Richard Stoddert (ū'ŭl), 1817–72, Confederate general. Suported Stonewall Jackson in Shenandoah Valley (1862). Succeeded Jackson in command (1863) and ably led Lee's advance in Gettysburg campaign. Fought in Wilderness campaign (1864), and defended Richmond (1865).

Ewing, Sir James Alfred, 1855–1935, Scottish engineer and physicist. His research in magnetism disclosed phenomenon of hysteresis, and he advanced the knowledge of crystalline structure of metals. His studies of earthquakes in Japan were significant.

Excalibur: see ARTHURIAN LEGEND.

Excelsior, resort village (pop. 1,763), E Minn., on L. Minnetonka and E of Minneapolis.

Excelsior Springs, city (pop. 5,888), W Mo., NE of Kansas City. Health resort (mineral springs). Frank and Jesse James lived near by.

exchange, mutual transfer of goods, money, or services. Barter, a pure form of exchange, is replaced in modern society by money and price system. The value of exchanged items is set mainly by the market demand. In commerce, an exchange is a place where trading goes on, such as a STOCK EXCHANGE.

Exchequer, Court of (ĕkschĕ'kŭr), British governmental agency. Originated after Norman Conquest as a financial committee of the Curia Regis. By end of 13th cent. the court of appeal was separated from the exchequer or treasury. After 1830 a single Court of Exchequer emerged as court of appeal intermediate between common-law courts and House of Lords. The Judicature Act of 1873 made it the exchequer division of the high court of justice.

excise: see INTERNAL REVENUE.

excommunication, formal expulsion of a person from a religious community, particularly notable in Judaism (e.g., expulsion of Spinoza) and Roman Catholicism. Elaborate Catholic form involves pronouncement of anathema and public exclusion from Church and was important in Middle Ages. In wider sense any "fallen away" Catholic is excommunicate.

excretion, elimination of useless matter by living organism. In man, organs that form excretions include skin, lungs, kidneys, and large intestine.

Exe (ĕks), stream of Somerset and Devonshire, England, flowing from Exmoor to the English Channel.

executors and administrators. An executor is the person designated in a will to carry out its provisions. An administrator is appointed for same purpose by the court, if there is no capable executor named or living or also if a person dies without a will.

Exeter (ĕk'sŭtŭr), county borough (pop. 75,-479), co. town of Devonshire, England, above Exe R. Strategically located, town was besieged by Danes, William the Conqueror,

Yorkists, and religious factions. Great cathedral contains remarkable oak throne of the bishops; chapter house has Exeter Book (Old English MS). Severely bombed in World War II.

Exeter. 1 Town (pop. 5,664), SE N.H., SW of Portsmouth; settled 1638. Cap. of N.H. in Revolution. Birthplace of Lewis Cass and D. C. French. Seat of Phillips Exeter Acad. (nonsectarian; for boys; chartered 1781, opened 1783 by John Phillips). **2** Borough (pop. 5,130), NE Pa., on Susquehanna R. and NE of Wilkes-Barre. Coal mining.

Exeter College: see OXFORD UNIVERSITY.

Exile: see CAPTIVITY.

existentialism (ĕgzĭstĕn'shŭlĭzŭm, ĕksĭ–). Although there are three main developments of this philosophic school, the basic beliefs are commonly held—the problem of human existence is the major one; reason, by itself, is an inadequate method of explanation; anguish is an emotion common to men confronting life's problems; and morality demands participation. Soren Kierkegaard developed a Christian existentialism in which anguish is relieved by transcendent faith in God. Martin Heidegger and Jean Paul Sartre deny existence of God and stress man's absolute freedom to choose, with resulting anguish and despair. Jacques Maritain has approached a Christian existentialism, based upon St. Thomas Aquinas, in which desire to be and fear of nothingness are rendered powerless by faith in God.

Exmoor, high moorland, Somerset and Devonshire, England. Largely a wasteland, with hills, valleys, and wooded glens, underlain by slate and sandstone. Grazing ground for sheep and small Exmoor ponies.

Exmouth (ĕks'mouth), urban district (pop. 17,232), Devonshire, England; port and summer resort.

Exodus (ĕk'sŭdŭs), book of Old Testament, second of books of Law (Pentateuch or Torah), ascribed by tradition to Moses. Some of the most important events of biblical history occur in Exodus, e.g., the deliverance of Hebrews in Egypt from bondage, the institution of Passover, the parting of the Red Sea, and the giving of the Ten Commandments. A most solemn moment is the appearance of God to Moses in the burning bush revealing His name as I Am.

exogamy: see MARRIAGE.

expanding universe: see UNIVERSE.

expansion, in physics, increase in volume resulting from temperature increase; contraction is reverse. When heat is applied, rate of vibration and distance between molecules increases; increased volume results. Degree of expansion is specific property of each liquid and solid; amount per unit volume per onedegree temperature rise is coefficient of cubical expansion. Coefficient of linear expansion is increase per unit of length per degree rise in temperature. Expansion coefficient about same for all common gases at ordinary temperatures; Kelvin scale of temperature is based on this number.

Exploits, largest river of N.F., Canada, rising in Long Range and flowing NE to Exploits Bay. Grand Falls and Bishop's Falls have hydroelectric plants.

exploration was undertaken by primitive peoples in search of supplies, and most regions of the world were discovered by them. Recorded exploration contributing to Western civilization began c.3000 B.C. An Egyptian-sponsored expedition is said to have sailed around Africa c.600 B.C. Ancient Greeks probably sailed beyond Britain c.330 B.C., having previously explored the Mediterranean and Black Sea regions. Romans penetrated well into Europe and traded directly with China. Crusades turned European attention to Eastern riches. Important achievements after 1400 that revealed extent of globe include reaching of India by Vasco da Gama, discovery of America by Columbus, and first circumnavigation of globe under Magellan. The 16th cent. brought Spanish exploration of the Americas. Much of North American interior explored by French in 17th cent. Spanish and Portuguese monopoly of trade routes challenged by English and Dutch voyages in the Pacific. Australian interior was explored by mid-19th cent., and most of Africa by end of century. Arctic, antarctic, and deep-sea exploration begun in 19th cent. was expanded in 20th cent. Scientific interest and desire for natural resources and strategic bases motivate most modern exploration; explorer is aided by vast technological advances.

explosive, substance undergoing decomposition or combustion rapidly with evolution of heat and production of large volume of gas, which exerts enormous sudden pressure causing blasting of rocks, etc. Some explosives are not truly explosive but are mixtures of substances which undergo very rapid combustion; others are compounds which liberate much energy during rapid decomposition. Most high explosives are prepared from nitric acid. Some high explosives are set off by a DETONATOR.

exponent (ĕk′spōnŭnt), in mathematics, a number, letter, or algebraic expression written above and to the right of another number, letter, or expression called the base. Exponent indicates power to which base is to be raised.

export: see BALANCE OF TRADE.

exposition. Word has wider meaning but is applied typically to international exhibitions or fairs, designed to register the state of civilization. Fine and industrial arts lend themselves well to such expositions. Later expositions emphasize scientific and technological progress. They help to raise standards of popular taste, to lessen provincialism, and to promote international understanding. London, Paris, Vienna, Zurich, New York, Chicago, and San Francisco have housed famous expositions (popularly called world's fairs).

expressionism, term for movement in art following impressionism, used generally to describe any art work in which representation of nature is subordinated to expression of emotion. Used more specifically to classify modern art characterized by intuitive, spontaneous distortion for emotional effect. In literature the effort to project spiritual actualities rather than naturalistic records of events was of most importance in the drama and the novel. Outstanding among expressionist playwrights of post-World War I period was the German Ernst Toller. Movement gained much from work of the experimental stage designers of the period.

exterritoriality or **extraterritoriality,** privilege of alien of exemption from local jurisdiction in foreign country. Applies to officials of UN while performing duties; and to a nation's official personnel and residences, public vessels in port, and sometimes armed forces. Nonofficial residents have enjoyed exterritoriality in many foreign countries, custom persisting longest in Egypt and China. It was resented, however, and legal reforms led to abolition. China in World War I abolished rights of Central Powers, in World War II of Italy and Japan. In 1924 USSR abandoned rights, followed by Britain and U.S. in 1943, and France in 1946.

extortion, unlawful obtaining of money or property through wrongful use of fear, force, or authority of office.

extradition (ĕkstrŭdĭ′shŭn), delivery of a person suspected or convicted of a crime by the state where he has taken refuge to the state asserting jurisdiction over him. International extradition is normally governed by special treaties, and it is usual for neighboring countries to grant extradition more readily than countries remote from each other. The first U.S. treaty with an international extradition clause was Jay's Treaty (1794). In the 19th cent. many extradition treaties were concluded by Western nations. Usually extradition for political crimes is excluded, though a nation may refuse asylum to a political fugitive. In the U.S., Congress has established a uniform law for state-to-state extradition; it provides that any person properly charged shall be extradited.

extra-sensory perception: see PSYCHICAL RESEARCH.

extraterritoriality: see EXTERRITORIALITY.

Extremadura, Spain: see ESTREMADURA.

extreme unction: see SACRAMENT.

extroversion and **introversion,** terms introduced by C. G. Jung for opposed psychological types. The extrovert's general activity or drive (libido) is directed toward external world, the introvert's upon himself. Everyone has both tendencies, with one generally dominant as a result of both temperament and environment. Extreme extrovert behavior becomes an irrational flight from self, the acting out of feelings in society, as in hysteria. Extreme introvert retreats into inner world, with fantasies displacing reality. Jung saw schizophrenia as introvert's psychosis.

Eyck, Huybrecht van (hoi′ brĕkht vän īk′) or **Hubert van Eyck,** c.1370–1426, and **Jan van Eyck** (yän) c.1390–1441, founders of Flemish school of painting; brothers. Inaccurately credited with discovery of oil painting, but they were first to use a resin or oil medium in naturalistic painting to achieve greater spacial depth and richness of color. Controversy as to part taken by each in their masterpiece *The Adoration of the Lamb* (Ghent). Attributed to Jan is portrait of Arnolfini and his wife (Natl. Gall., London).

Eyde, Samuel (sä′mō̆ĕl ā′dŭ), 1866–1940, Norwegian engineer, co-developer of Birkeland-Eyde process for nitrogen fixation.

eye, organ of vision consisting of eyeball enclosing refracting media. Outermost fibrous layer of eyeball comprises white, opaque sclera at back and sides and transparent cornea in front. Vascular, pigmented middle lyer consists of chorioid (or choroid) under the sclera; iris, behind cornea and perforated by pupil; and ciliary body connecting chorioid and iris rim. Over inner layer, the retina, lie optic nerve fibers. Refracting media consist of transparent lens behind iris; jellylike vitreous humor between retina and lens; and aqueous humor between lens and cornea. See *ill.,* p. 763.

Eyja Fjord (ā′ù fyôrd″), longest fjord in Iceland (37 mi.), on N coast. At its head is Akureyri.

Eylau (ī′lou), town (pop. 7,485), former East Prussia, near Königsberg; inc. into USSR 1945 and renamed Bagrationovsk. Here in Feb., 1807, Napoleon I fought a bloody but indecisive battle against Russian and Prussian forces (in which Prince Bagration distinguished himself). Also known as Preussisch Eylau.

Eyre, Lake (âr), shallow salt lake, area 3,430 sq. mi., NE South Australia; frequently dry.

Ezechiel: see EZEKIEL.

Ezekias (ĕzùkī′ùs) : see HEZEKIAH.

Ezekiel or **Ezechiel** (both: ēzē′kēĕl) [Heb.,= God strengthens], book of Old Testament, an account of the prophetic career of the priest Ezekiel (fl. 592 B.C.). Central point is the fall of Jerusalem, what goes on before being prophetic of doom, the rest inspired by hope of restoration. Among famous passages are chapters 18, 21, 26–28, 31–32, 37.

Ezra [Heb.,= help] and **Nehemiah** (nēùmī′ù) [Heb.,= consoled by God], in AV, books of Old Testament; called 1 and 2 ESDRAS in Western canon; a single work in Hebrew canon. Ezra (fl. after 460 B.C.) was a priest and scribe; Nehemiah (fl. 444 B.C.) was cupbearer to Artaxerxes I and later governor of Jerusalem. Books tell of return of Jews to Palestine from captivity. Important events are the reading of the Law to the assembled people, the signing of a covenant, and the completion of the wall.

Ezzelino da Romano (ĕt″sālē′nō dä rōmä′nō), 1194–1259, Italian Ghibelline leader, lord of Verona, Vicenza, Padua. A supporter of Emperor Frederick II, he dominated N Italy after 1237; was excommunicated by Pope Innocent IV 1254; suffered defeat shortly before his death. Reputedly a cruel tyrant; mentioned in Dante's *Inferno.*

F, chemical symbol of element FLUORINE.

Faber, Frederick William (fā′bùr), 1814–63, English theologian, adherent of the Oxford movement; friend of J. H. Newman. Founded community at Birmingham which became the Oratory of St. Philip Neri (1848) and an oratory at London (1849).

Fabian Society, influential English socialist society, developed 1884 out of the Fellowship of the True Life (1883). Among its outstanding exponents were G. B. Shaw and Sidney and Beatrice Webb. Fabians repudiated the Marxist class struggle, believing in natural development of socialism. They helped found the British Labour Party in 1900.

Fabius (fā′bèùs), family name of several Romans. **Quintus Fabius Maximus Rullianus** (kwĭn′tùs, măk′sĭmùs rùlēā′nùs) or **Rullus** (rù′lùs), d. c.291 B.C., renowned as a general for his victory over Etruscans, Samnites, and allies at Sentinum (295 B.C.). His descendant, **Quintus Fabius Maximus Verrucosus** (vĕrōōkō′sùs), d. 203 B.C., opponent of HANNIBAL in the Second PUNIC WAR, was called Cunctator (kŭngk′tùtôr) [Latin,= delayer] because of his tactics, which have given the term Fabian to any waiting policy. Tired of his masterly inaction, the Romans replaced him as consul and were defeated at Cannae.

fable, short moral story, often one in which characters are beasts or inanimate objects. One of oldest collections is Indian PANCHATANTRA. Fables of AESOP were earliest to be written down. In medieval times began satirical series about REYNARD THE FOX. Great French fabulist was LA FONTAINE. John Gay and Dryden continued tradition of beast fable in England. Use of fable to mean general narrative with a lesson is demonstrated in J. R. Lowell's *Fable for Critics* (1848).

Fabre, Jean Henri (zhä ärē′ fä′brù), 1823–1915, French entomologist and author, known for observations and studies of insect behavior. Chief work is *Souvenirs entomologiques* (10 vols., 1879–1907); English translations of parts of this work include *The Life of the Spider* (1912); *The Wonders of Instinct* (1918); *The Marvels of the Insect World* (1938).

Fabriano, Gentile da: see GENTILE DA FABRIANO.

Fabricius, Hieronymus (hīùrŏ′nùmùs), 1537–1619, Italian anatomist, teacher of William Harvey at Padua. His discoveries include valves in veins.

Fackenthal, Frank Diehl (fă′kùnthôl), 1883–, American educator and administrator. He served Columbia Univ. 1906–48 as, successively, chief clerk, secretary, provost, and acting president.

facsimile (făksĭ'mŭlē), in communication, a radio or wire transmission system for pictures and other graphic matter. By light-beam and photoelectric-cell arrangement light and dark areas of material are translated into transmittable tones; receiver reproduces them on chemically treated paper.

factor, in arithmetic, any number dividing a given number evenly without any remainder.

Facundo Quiroga, Juan: see QUIROGA, JUAN FACUNDO.

fading, in radio, irregular variation in strength and quality of received signal. Chief cause considered changing altitude and density of Kennelly-Heaviside layer; transmitted wave reflects unevenly, arrives out of phase. Automatic volume control corrects.

Faenza (fään'tsä), city (pop. 23,823), Emilia-Romagna, N central Italy, in Romagna. Renaissance cathedral and palace. Richly colored ceramics, called faïence, made here since 12th cent.

Faerie Queene, The: see SPENSER, EDMUND.

Faeroe Islands or **Faroe Islands** (both: fâ'rō), Dan. *Faerørne*, Faeroese *Føroyar*, group of 21 volcanic islands (c.540 sq. mi.; pop. 29,-178), in N Atlantic Ocean, between Iceland and the Shetlands; Danish crown possession. Stromo (with cap., Thorshavn) and Ostero isls. are largest. Transferred from Norway to Denmark 1814; under British protection in World War II; obtained home rule 1948. Faeroese language is akin to Icelandic. Fish and wool are main exports.

Fages, Pedro (pä'dhrō fä'häs), fl. 1767–96, Spanish governor of Alta Calif. (1782–91). Notable for encouraging colonization, agr., and missionary work.

Fahrenheit, Gabriel Daniel (fä'rŭnhīt, Ger. gä'brēĕl dä'nyĕl fä'rŭnhīt), 1686–1736, German physicist. He devised Fahrenheit TEMPERATURE scale and substituted mercury for alcohol in thermometer.

fair. Before transportation and marketing developments made distribution of goods to all markets easy, marketing opportunities arose from religious observances which brought widely separated people together. Markets or fairs of this kind developed in Greece and Rome. Their advantages multiplied during the Middle Ages in Europe, the greatest period being the 13th-14th cent. Always a business institution for buying, selling, and bartering, they declined under competition with continuous marketing; a few (e.g., at Leipzig) survived. The typical American fair (e.g., at Danbury, Conn.) is dissimilar, being an exhibition of farm and home products ranked by judges for excellence of quality.

Fairbairn, Sir William (fâr'bârn), 1789–1874, Scottish engineer, builder of iron ships and railroad bridges.

Fairbanks, Douglas, 1883–1939, American film actor, whose real name was Douglas Elton Ulman. After 1915 he made such swashbuckling films as *The Mark of Zorro, Robin Hood*, and *The Thief of Bagdad*. He was married (1920–35) to Mary Pickford.

Fairbanks, Thaddeus, 1796–1866, American inventor of the platform scale, patented 1831.

Fairbanks, town (pop. 5,771), central Alaska,

on Chena Slough, where Chena R. enters the Tanana. Transportation, distribution, and financial center for Tanana R. area and all of inland Alaska. Grew as mining camp after 1902 gold discovery; hydraulic mining succeeded placer mining. Building of Alaska RR increased town's importance. Richardson Highway from Valdez on coast reaches Fairbanks, which became terminus of ALASKA HIGHWAY in World War II. Has one of chief airports of territory; army air base near. Near by is Univ. of ALASKA.

Fairborn, city (pop. 7,847), NW Ohio, ENE of Dayton; formed 1950 by consolidation of Fairfield and Osborn. Wright-Patterson Air Force Base near by.

Fairbury, city (pop. 6,395), SE Nebr., near Kansas line. Flour, meat and dairy products.

Fairchild, David Grandison, 1869–, American botanist. He organized and was later in charge of division of plant exploration and introduction in U.S. Dept. of Agriculture. His works include *The World Was My Garden* (1938); *The World Grows Round My Door* (1947).

Fair Employment Practices Committee (FEPC), established (1941) during World War II to eliminate discriminatory employment practices. Suspended (1946) for lack of funds. A few states have established similar bodies. After 1946 efforts were made to establish a permanent U.S. FEPC.

Fairfax, Thomas, 3d Baron, 1612–71, English soldier-statesman. Commanded the New Model Army that crushed Charles I in 1645. Fearing military dictatorship, he opposed Cromwell. Was instrumental in return of Charles II to the throne (1660).

Fairfax, Thomas Fairfax, 6th Baron, 1693–1781, British proprietor of Northern Neck of Va. Claim to land between Rappahannock and Potomac rivers, disputed by Va., confirmed in 1745.

Fairfax, town (pop. 1,946), N Va., W of Washington, D.C. In old courthouse are wills of George and Martha Washington. Mount Vernon, Gunston Hall (1755–58), and Pohick Church (1774) are in county.

Fairfield. 1 City (pop. 13,177), N central Ala., near Birmingham; founded c.1910. Steel goods. **2** Industrial town (pop. 30,489), SW Conn., on Long Isl. Sound SW of Bridgeport; settled 1639. Metal goods, chemicals. Burned by British, 1779. **3** City (pop. 5,576), SE Ill., E of Mount Vernon, in agr. area. Mfg. of auto parts. **4** City (pop. 7,299), SE Iowa, E of Ottumwa. Has mfg. of washing machines and farm equipment. Here are Parsons Col. and Old Settlers Park (with log cabin built 1836). **5** Town (pop. 5,811), S Maine, on Kennebec R. above Waterville. Pulp and woolen mills. **6** See FAIRBORN, Ohio. **7** Town (pop. 1,428), NW Vt., E of St. Albans. C. A. Arthur's birthplace is near.

Fairhaven, resort town (pop. 12,764), SE Mass., Acushnet R. mouth opposite New Bedford; settled 1670. Boatbuilding.

Fairhope, resort town (pop. 3,354), SW Ala., on Mobile Bay. Founded (1894–95) by followers of Henry George, it remained a single-tax town until 1937.

Fair Isle, rocky island (pop. 108), off N Scotland. Known for knitted hosiery of bright, many-colored designs. Also a famous bird migration station.

Fair Lawn, borough (pop. 23,885), NE N.J., near Paterson; includes planned community of Radburn.

Fairmont. 1 City (pop. 8,193), S Minn., near Iowa line. Resort and shipping center of agr. area. **2** City (pop. 29,346), N W.Va., on Monongahela R.; founded 1843. Center of coal area, it has mfg. of glass and sheet aluminum.

Fair Oaks: see PENINSULAR CAMPAIGN.

Fairport, village (pop. 5,267), W N.Y., SE of Rochester and on Erie Canal. Tin cans and chemicals.

fairy, in legend of British Isles, supernatural being similar to humans and usually beautiful but having magical powers and generally ill-disposed toward men. Shakspere led in conventionalizing fairies, which became popular in 16th-cent. English literature and were connected with various classical names and ideas. On the Continent, supernatural beings were linked with pagan gods. **Fairy tales** are characterized by appearance of supernatural beings and magic. Great adapters of popular fairy tales were Charles Perrault, the brothers Grimm, and Hans Christian Andersen.

Faisal: see FEISAL.

Faiyum, Egypt: see FAYUM.

Faizabad, Uttar Pradesh, India: see FYZABAD.

Falange (fä'länj), Spanish political party, founded 1933 as Falange Española Tradicionalista by José Antonio Primo de Rivera. Based on FASCISM; emphasized Spanish national tradition. Sided with Insurgents in civil war of 1936–39; emerged as strongest party but was absorbed by Franco into one-party government (1942).

Falashas (–lä'–) [Ethiopic,= emigrant], group of Abyssinians of Jewish affinity.

falcon (fôl'kŭn, fô'kŭn), name for numerous species of long-winged, swift birds of prey, found throughout the world. They have strong hooked, notched bills and eat birds, small mammals, and insects. Duck hawk (American variety of Old World peregrine), pigeon hawk, sparrow hawk, and prairie falcon are American falcons. The female of some species is trained for **falconry,** hunting birds and small animals for masters. Known to ancient Chinese, Persians, Egyptians.

Falfurrias (fălfŭr'ēŭs), city (pop. 6,712), S Texas, SW of Corpus Christi. Center of agr. and oil area with recycling and gypsum plants and cotton gins.

Falguière, Jean Alexandre Joseph (zhä' ălĕksä'drŭ zhôzĕf' fälgyēr'), 1831–1900, French sculptor, noted for monuments and portrait statues.

Faliero or **Falier, Marino** (märē'nō fälyä'rō, fälēĕr'), 1274–1355, doge of Venice (1354–55). Joined in plot against patricians to overthrow oligarchic government and make him dictator. Plot was discovered, Faliero and accomplices executed.

Falkberget, Johan (yōhän' fälk'bĕrgŭ), 1879–, Norwegian novelist. Wrote of miners in *Lisbeth of Jarnfjeld* (1915), trilogy *Christianus Sextus* (1927–35), and *Night Bread* (1940).

Falkirk (fôl'kŭrk), burgh (pop. 37,528), Stirlingshire, Scotland. In mining and mfg. region, it produces chemicals and leather goods. Has annual stock fairs. English defeated Scots here 1298; Gen. Hawley defeated by Prince Charles Edward's Jacobites 1746.

Falkland, Lucius Cary, 2d Viscount (fôk'lŭnd), 1610?–1643, English statesman and literary figure. Represented Charles I in attempts to make peace with Parliament. He supposedly let himself be killed in battle rather than fight either king or Parliament.

Falkland Islands (fô'klŭnd), islands, S Atlantic, c.300 mi. E of Strait of Magellan. Ownership disputed by Argentina and Great Britain. Group administered as British crown colony (4,618 sq. mi.; pop. 2,268); cap. Stanley. Spanish name *Islas Malvinas.*

Falkner, William: see FAULKNER, WILLIAM.

Fall, Albert Bacon, 1861–1944, U.S. Secretary of the Interior (1921–23). Convicted in 1929 for his part in TEAPOT DOME conspiracy.

Falla, Manuel de (mänwĕl' dä fäl'yä), 1876–1946, Spanish composer. Notable among his compositions are *La vida breve,* an opera; *Nights in the Gardens of Spain,* for piano and orchestra; the ballets *El Amor Brujo* and *The Three-cornered Hat.*

Fallada, Hans (häns' fä'lädä), pseud. of Rudolf Ditzen, 1893–1947, German novelist. Best remembered for *Little Man, What Now?* (1932; Eng. tr., 1933).

fallen arches: see FLAT FOOT.

Fallen Timbers, state park, NW Ohio, on Maumee R., near Maumee. Site of battle where Anthony Wayne's forces decisively defeated hostile Indians 1794.

Fallières, Armand (ärmä' fälyĕr'), 1841–1931, president of France (1906–13). Under him law of separation of Church and state was carried out; Dreyfus Affair was concluded (1906).

falling star: see METEOR.

fall line, boundary between upland region and coastal or tidewater plain. Marks place where rivers drop to plain in falls or rapids. Since falls supply water power for industries, fall-line cities rival ports in economic importance.

Fallon (fäl'ŭn), city (pop. 2,400), W Nev., ENE of Carson City. Trade center for ranches and for Newlands project.

Fallopius (fŭlō'pēŭs), 1523–62, Italian anatomist, noted teacher at Padua. His discoveries include **Fallopian tubes** leading from ovaries to uterus.

fallow land, in agr., land plowed but not seeded, to conserve moisture and check weeds. ROTATION OF CROPS is now often preferred.

Fall River, industrial city (pop. 111,963), SE Mass., at Taunton R. mouth on Mt. Hope Bay; settled 1656. Mfg. of textiles (first cotton mill built 1811), metal, rubber, and paper products.

Falls Church, city (pop. 7,535), N Va., W of Washington, D.C. The Falls Church was built 1767–69 on site of earlier church (1734).

Falls City, city (pop. 6,203), extreme SE Nebr., on Nemaha R., near Kansas line. Railway division point in livestock, grain, and dairy area.

Falmouth (făl'mŭth), municipal borough (pop. 17,036), Cornwall, England; port and fishing town. Has excellent harbor guarded by two castles. Unusually warm climate; subtropical plants thrive.

Falmouth. 1 Town (pop. 4,342), SW Maine, on Casco Bay. One of earliest settlements in Maine (c.1632), it included Portland until 1786. Nearly destroyed by British in 1775. **2** Town (pop. 8,662), SE Mass., on extreme SW Cape Cod; settled 1660. Includes Woods Hole resort (1940 pop. 549). Has U.S. fish and wildlife station, marine biological institute, and Oceanographic Inst. (1930; endowed by Rockefeller Foundation), which maintains research ship *Atlantis.*

False Decretals (dĭkrē'tŭlz), collection of partly spurious documents treating of canon law, published c.847–852 probably in France. Compiler called himself Isidore Mercator (hence term Pseudo-Isidorian Decretals). By incorporation in GRATIAN the False Decretals received authority in medieval canon-law texts. One of the great forgeries of history, they were first exposed by Nicholas of Cusa and Juan de Torquemada (15th cent.).

false imprisonment, complete restraint upon a person's liberty of movement against his will and without legal justification, either by a private person or by an official improperly issuing a warrant for arrest. If the restrainer is an official, release may be had through HABEAS CORPUS.

Falstaff (fôl'stăf), famous jovial companion of Prince Hal (later Henry V) in Shakspere's play *Henry IV.* Also leading character in Shakspere's *Merry Wives of Windsor.* The character was originally called Sir John Oldcastle (as in Shakspere's source on Henry V) but has no resemblance to the real Sir John Oldcastle—nor to the historical Sir John Fastolf, whose name may have suggested the name Falstaff.

Falster (fäl'stŭr), island (198 sq. mi.; pop. 45,665), S Denmark, in the Baltic Sea; cap. Nykobing.

Falun (fä'lŭn"), town (pop. 16,858), central Sweden, co. seat and industrial center of KOPPARBERG CO. Oldest Swedish industrial company was organized in 12th cent. to operate its copper mine, now exhausted.

Famagusta (fämägōō'stä), city (pop. 16,194), on E Cyprus; chief port of island. Seat of Venetian governors (15th-16th cent.); thought to be main scene of Shakspere's *Othello.* Ruins include so-called Tower of Othello, 13th-cent. Gothic cathedral, and Venetian governors' palace. A British naval base, it was bombed in World War II.

family, social group consisting of parents and their children. Other close relatives and even servants and slaves may be added, forming the "large" or "joint" family, an important economic and biological unit. Commonest unit in Western civilization is one male, one female, and their children. Hebrew and Roman law gave the father almost complete control over the family. In modern times the family unit has been affected by the legal equalization of women (beginning in 19th cent.), removal from the family of economic tasks, and state interest in children's education. The changed relationships of the members of the family to each other and to the community are thought to contain the germ

of many psychological and sociological maladjustments.

Family Compact. 1 Name of three agreements (1733, 1743, 1761) between French and Spanish branches of Bourbon family. The last provided for Spanish entry into Seven Years War on French side. **2** Term popularly applied to small, powerful group of men who dominated government of Upper Canada from late 18th cent. to the beginnings of responsible government under the Baldwin-LaFontaine ministry (1848–51). Opposition movement developed into the Reform party. Religious differences embittered the struggle, since the Family Compact (term first appeared c.1828) was composed almost entirely of members of the Church of England. Chateau Clique was name given to similar powerful group in French Lower Canada.

Fanariots: see PHANARIOTS.

Faneuil Hall (făn'l, făn'yŭl), public market and hall given to Boston by merchant Peter Faneuil, 1742. Burned 1761, then rebuilt; enlarged by Bulfinch, 1806. Called "the cradle of liberty" because of Revolutionary meetings held here.

Fannin, James Walker (fă'nĭn), 1804?–1836, hero in Texas Revolution, b. Ga. Distinguished himself in first victories of 1835. Captured after evacuating Goliad, shot at Santa Anna's orders.

Fanning, Edmund, 1769–1841, American trader and explorer. Discovered Fanning Isl., Washington Isl., and other islands (1783). Became agent for group of New York city merchants to promote and organize South Sea trading expeditions.

Fanning Island, atoll, 15 sq. mi., central Pacific, NW of Christmas Isl. Added 1916 to British colony of Gilbert and Ellice Isls. Cable relay station here connects Canada and Suva, Fiji.

Fantin-Latour, Ignace Henri Jean Théodore (fätē-lätōōr'), 1836–1904, French painter and lithographer. Best known for portrait groups of famous contemporaries.

Faraday, Michael (fă'rŭdā"), 1791–1867, English scientist. He developed the first dynamo, the precursor of modern dynamos and generators. From his discovery of electromagnetic induction stemmed the development of electrical machinery for industry. He formulated laws of electrolysis.

Farallon Islands (fă'rŭlŏn), Calif., two groups of small rocky islands in the Pacific W of the Golden Gate; part of San Francisco. Here are bird sanctuary and U.S. radar station.

farce [Latin,= stuffing], light, comic theatrical piece. Form of comedy in which characters and events are greatly exaggerated to produce broad, simple humor. Examples are Latin comedies of Plautus and Terence, but term is derived from *farces* of medieval France. Early English farce is *Ralph Roister Doister* (pub. 1566). Molière and Henry Fielding also wrote farces. In most recent times farce is used in slapstick comedies of American moving pictures.

farcy: see GLANDERS.

Far Eastern Territory, former administrative division, RSFSR, in E and NE Siberia. Its vast area is now divided into KHABAROVSK TERRITORY and MARITIME TERRITORY. Khabarovsk was cap., Vladivostok chief port. Russian colonization began 17th cent.; SE sections ceded by China 1858 and 1860. During civil war and Allied intervention following 1917 Revolution, much of area was occupied by Japanese. In 1920 local Bolsheviks organized Far Eastern Republic, with cap. at Chita, but Japanese held Vladivostok until 1922. Territory was organized 1926, redivided 1938.

Farel, Guillaume (gēyōm' färĕl'), 1489–1565, French reformer, associate of Calvin in Swiss Reformation.

Farewell, Cape, southernmost point of Greenland, on Egger Isl.

Fargo, William George, 1818–81, American pioneer expressman. Helped found American Express Co. (1850). By 1852 he and Henry Wells organized Wells, Fargo & Co. to handle express service between New York and San Francisco.

Fargo, city (pop. 38,256), E N.Dak., largest city in state, on Red R.; settled 1871. Rail center and river port. Chief distributing point in region, it handles agr. machinery and foodstuffs, processes food, has mfg. of fur coats, luggage, and electrical apparatus. Seat of North Dakota Agricultural Col. (state and land-grant supported; coed.; 1890).

Faribault (fä'rĭbō), city (pop. 16,028), SE Minn., S of Minneapolis at confluence of Cannon and Straight rivers, in farm area; platted 1854. Alexander Faribault, French fur trader, built port here 1826. Became Episcopal center with work of J. L. Breck and Bishop H. B. Whipple. Seat of pioneer school for feebleminded and of schools for the deaf and the blind. Mfg. of food products and household equipment.

Faridun: see FERID ED-DIN ATTAR.

Farinelli, Carlo Broschi (brō'skē färēnĕl'lē), 1705–82, Italian male soprano, greatest of the *castrati*, official singer to Philip V of Spain.

Farley, James A(loysius), 1888–, American political leader, U.S. Postmaster General (1933–36, 1937–40). As Democratic Natl. Committee chairman, he managed successful 1932 and 1936 F. D. Roosevelt presidential campaigns.

Farm Credit Administration (FCA), agency of U.S. Dept. of Agriculture supervising loans to farmers and agricultural cooperatives. The Federal Farm Loan Act of 1916 established land banks as a centralized source of farm-mortage credit. In 1933 the FCA took over the land banks, and additional farm-credit measures were taken. By 1940 the FCA held 40 per cent of all outstanding farm mortgages. The original plan that the farm-credit system would be cooperatively owned was not achieved.

Farmer, Fannie Merritt, 1857–1915, American expert on cookery, editor of *The Boston Cooking School Cook Book* (1896; many times reissued and translated).

Farmer-Labor party, in U.S. history, political organization formed 1920 by former members of the older Progressive party together with farm and labor representatives, chiefly from Middle West. Advocated socialistic program. Party particularly strong in Minn. Dissolved 1924, reorganized later, but lost

strength as New Deal incorporated some of its reforms.

farming: see AGRICULTURE.

farming, in taxation, the collection of taxes through private contractors. Tax farmers pay a lump sum; difference between that sum and sum actually collected is their profit or loss. Practiced since ancient times (e.g., by publicans in Rome), the system was most fully applied in 18th-cent. France, where indirect taxes were collected by the farm general (a body consisting of 40 financiers). Notorious for extortion, some 30 farmers general were executed in French Revolution.

Farmingdale, village (pop. 4,492), SE N.Y., on W Long Isl. near Mineola. Large aircraft factories. Long Isl. Agricultural and Technical Inst. is here.

Farmington. 1 Town (pop. 7,026), central Conn., SW of Hartford. Has Miss Porter's School for girls. Includes Unionville village (pop. 2,197; metal goods). **2** Town (pop. 4,677), W central Maine, NW of Augusta. Gateway to Rangeley Lakes and Dead R. resort regions. **3** Town (pop. 3,637), NW N.Mex., on San Juan R. Distributing point for Navajo reservation. Aztec Ruins, Chaco Canyon natl. monuments are near.

Farmville, town (pop. 4,375), S Va., on Appomattox R. and E of Lynchburg. Near by is Hampden-Sydney Col. (at Hampden-Sydney, Va.; for men: opened by Presbyterians as academy 1776, chartered as college 1783).

Farnborough, urban district (pop. 27,702), Hampshire, England. Site of important RAF stations, it includes part of Aldershot military camp. Empress Eugénie lived here (1881–1920) and is buried (with Napoleon III) in crypt of church she built.

Farne Islands, group of islets off Northumberland coast, England. Sheltered St. Cuthbert in 7th cent. Scene of Grace Darling's heroism at wreck of *Forfarshire* in 1838.

Farnese (färnä'zā), Italian noble family, long prominent in Rome, which ruled duchy of PARMA and PIACENZA 1545–1731. Duchy was created out of papal lands by Pope PAUL III (Alessandro Farnese) in favor of his natural son Pierluigi. Pierluigi's son and heir Ottavio married MARGARET OF PARMA. Their son, Alessandro Farnese, 1545–92, duke of Parma and Piacenza (1586–92), fought under his uncle, John of Austria, at Lepanto (1571) and in the Netherlands. Succeeding John as Spanish governor of the Netherlands (1578), he took Tournai, Maastricht, Breda, Bruges, Ghent, and Antwerp from the rebels, thus securing continued possession of S Low Countries for Spain. In 1509 he led an army to support the League against Henry IV of France. He relieved Paris (1590) and Rouen (1592), but died from a wound. After male line of family died out, ELIZABETH FARNESE secured Parma and Piacenza for her son Philip.

Farnese Bull, sculptured group attributed to Apollonius of Tralles and his brother Tauriscus of 1st or 2d cent. B.C. Shows Dirce being tied to an infuriated bull. A copy in Naples national museum was formerly in Farnese Palace.

Farnese Hercules, marble statue by Glycon,

Athenian sculptor of 1st cent. B.C. Once in the Farnese Palace, now in Naples national museum.

Farnese Palace, in Rome, designed by Antonio da Sangallo for Cardinal Alessandro Farnese (Pope Paul III). Begun before 1514 and completed by Giacomo della Porta; Michelangelo also worked on it. Built of huge blocks taken from Colosseum and theater of Marcellus. Halls decorated by Annibale Carracci.

Farnesina (färnäzē'nä), Renaissance villa, Rome, Italy. Built 1508–11 by Peruzzi. Frescoes by Raphael and pupils.

Farnsworth, Philo Taylor, 1906–, American inventor. Demonstrated television system (1927); developed Orthicon or "dissector tube."

Faro (fä'rō), town (pop. 19,695), cap. of Algarve prov., S Portugal; seaport. Exports fish, cork.

faro (fä'rō) [for *Pharaoh,* from old French card design], gambling game played with pack of 52 cards. First played in France and England, especially popular in American gambling houses in 19th cent.

Faroe Islands: see FAEROE ISLANDS.

Farouk I (färōōk'), 1920–, king of Egypt (1937–52), son and successor of Fuad I. Revolt led by Gen. Naguib forced his abdication and his infant son, Fuad II, was proclaimed king.

Farquhar, George (fär'kùr, –kwùr), 1678–1707, British Restoration dramatist, b. Ireland. Best known for his licentious, naturalistic comedies is *Beaux' Stratagem* (1707).

Farragut, David Glasgow, 1801–70, American admiral, hero of New Orleans and Mobile Bay in Civil War. Commanding West Gulf Blockading Squadron (1862), he boldly sailed up the Mississippi past Forts St. Philip and Jackson to defeat Confederate flotilla, enabling B. F. Butler to take New Orleans. In 1864 he moved on Mobile. Forcing defenses in Mobile Bay, he defeated Franklin Buchanan, thus closing last Gulf port of Confederate blockade-running. The outstanding naval commander in war, honored by rank of admiral, created for him in 1866.

Farrar, Geraldine (fùrär'), 1882–, American operatic soprano; pupil of Lilli Lehmann. Sang at the Metropolitan Opera, New York, 1906–22. Her most famous roles were in *La Bohème, Madame Butterfly,* and *Carmen.*

Farrell, James T(homas) (fä'rùl), 1904, American novelist. Wrote realistically of Chicago's Irish population in the *Studs Lonigan* trilogy (1923–35).

Farrell, city (pop. 13,644), W Pa., on Shenango R. at Ohio border and adjoining Sharon. A rail center, it has steel and iron works.

Fars (färs) or **Farsistan** (färsĭstän'), region (75,476 sq. mi.; pop. 1,403,583), SW Iran, corresponding to Seventh Prov. Almost identical with ancient Persis, nucleus of Persian Empire. Chief city is Shiraz, chief port Bushire.

farsightedness, vision defect resulting when light rays focus behind retina. It is caused by shortness of the eyeball from front to back.

Farsistan, Iran: see FARS.

fascism (fä'shĭzùm). In narrower sense, Fascism was political and economic system in Italy under MUSSOLINI; it developed after 1922 and lasted until Italy's defeat in World War II. In wider sense, the term *fascism* has been applied rather loosely to similar ideologies elsewhere; e.g., to NATIONAL SOCIALISM in Germany, and to Franco's regime in Spain. Fascism in general has been negative reaction against socialism and democratic equalitarianism, its roots reaching back to reaction of ruling classes against French Revolution. It plays upon national pride and prejudice and often exploits ANTI-SEMITISM, and sets itself up as champion of law and order against threat of mob rule. In Italy particularly social unrest was mixed with nationalist dissatisfaction over poor fruits of victory after World War I. Governmental paralysis enabled Mussolini to become premier by a show of force. He posed as strongarmed savior of Italy from anarchy and Communism. With strong organization and party militia, Black Shirts, he set up dictatorship. Use of Roman fasces as emblem gave regime name Fascist. Fascism differed from Communism in two respects: it followed Darwinian theory of survival of fittest, making youth and struggle paramount; and its organization was based on representation by classes, making CORPORATIVE STATE. Masses were won by paternalistic methods of works and relief, but real power was in hands of élite.

Fashoda Incident (fùshō'dù), 1898, diplomatic dispute between France and Great Britain caused by rivalry for control of upper Nile region. While British troops under Kitchener were quelling Mahdist revolt in Sudan, a French-Ethiopian party led by J. B. Marchand entered S Sudan and took town of Fashoda (now Kodok). Upon British insistence the French withdrew from area and in March, 1899, yielded their claims to upper Nile region. Peaceful settlement mainly due to efforts of Delcassé.

fat: see FATS AND OILS.

fata morgana, optical illusion: see MIRAGE.

Fatehpur Sikri (fŭtùpŏōr' sĭk'rē), town, W Uttar Pradesh, India. On site of Mogul cap. founded 1569 by Akbar and abandoned 1584. Remains present a nearly intact Mogul city.

Fates, in Greek mythology, three goddesses who controlled lives of men; daughters of Zeus and Themis. Known as Moerae or Moirai; they were Clotho, who spun web of life, Lachesis, who measured its length, and Atropos, who cut it off. Roman Fates were called Parcae (see PARCA) and Germanic, NORNS.

Fathers of the Church, orthodox Christian writers of early times (See PATRISTIC LITERATURE). One of many groupings distinguishes eight Doctors of the Church: (Greek Church) St. Basil the Great, St. Gregory Nazianzen, St. John Chrysostom, St. Athanasius; (Latin Church) St. Ambrose, St. Jerome, St. Augustine, St. Gregory the Great.

fatigue, in physiology, decreased ability or inability of tissue or organ to respond to stimulus because of continual stimulation without adequate rest. Believed to result from accumulation of waste products and using up of nutritive material in cells.

Fatima (fă'tĭmù), 606?–632, daughter of Mohammed by his first wife. Wife of Ali, mother of Husein; reputedly the ancestress of Fatimites.

Fátima (fä'tēmù), hamlet, W Portugal, near Leiria. Near-by shrine of Our Lady of the Rosary became a great Roman Catholic center of pilgrimage after apparitions of Virgin Mary to shepherd children in 1917.

Fatimite (fă'tĭmĭt) or **Fatimide** (fă'tĭmĭd), family claiming to hold the CALIPHATE on basis of alleged descent from FATIMA, a daughter of Mohammed the Prophet. In c.904 Obaidallah, leader of Syrian Shiite group, went to NW Africa, where he was hailed as the long-awaited Mahdi. In 909 he claimed the caliphate in opposition to the Abbasids. Conquered Cyrenaica and Libya. His successors consolidated his empire and conquered Sicily, W Arabia, Palestine, and Syria. Cairo became Fatimite cap. with conquest of Egypt in 969. The sixth Fatimite caliph, Hakim, proclaimed 1020 that he was a reincarnation of God; his claim is still espoused by DRUSES. Fatimite rule officially came to an end when SALADIN entered Cairo in 1171.

fats and oils, simple or mixed glyceryl esters of organic acids of fatty-acid series, important in diet and industry. Fats usually are solid; oils, liquid. They are derived from both plants and animals. Vegetable oils are obtained by cold pressing of cleaned fruits or seeds; this is followed by warm pressing which yields industrial grades. Vegetable fats are usually made by hydrogenation of oils: hydrogen is brought into contact with heated oil in presence of catalyst. Fats and oils in the diet are an energy source; cod-liver oil contains vitamins A and D. See also OILS; PETROLEUM.

Fauchard, Pierre (pyĕr' fōshär'), 1678–1761, French dentist, a founder of modern dentistry.

Faulhaber, Michael von (mĭkh'äël fùn foul'häbùr), 1869–1952, German cardinal, archbishop of Munich, an unflinching opponent of the Nazis.

Faulkner, William (fôk'nùr), 1897–, American novelist, b. Miss. His major novels are studies of family disintegration and of degeneration in an imaginary Miss. county. Though they are explicitly about the Deep South, they deal with universal problems of man and evil. Among them are *The Sound and the Fury* (1929), *As I Lay Dying* (1930), *Sanctuary* (1931), *Light in August* (1932), *Absalom, Absalom!* (1936), and *Intruder in the Dust* (1948). His literary style is often long-drawn and confused to represent the thoughts of his characters, and incidents in the novels are sometimes macabre. Has also written notable short stories. Was awarded the Nobel Prize in Literature for 1949. Earlier used the spelling Falkner.

fault, in geology, a fracture in the earth's surface, with displacement on one side of the fault plane relative to the other. This displacement may be horizontal, vertical, or oblique, or both horizontal and vertical. The immediate cause of faults is stretching and compression of the earth's crust; the remote causes are probably the same as those of folding, since faulting and folding alike are involved in mountain making. Faults are responsible for most earthquakes.

faun (fôn), in Roman religion, creature similar to Greek SATYR, half man and half goat.

Faunus (fô'nùs), in Roman religion, popular god of nature, protector of farmers and herdsmen, identified with Greek PAN. He was attended by many little fauns.

Faure, Élie (ālē' fōr'), 1873–1937, French art historian. Related history of art to progress of human culture.

Faure, Félix (fălēks' fōr'), 1841–99, president of France (1895–99). His term was marked by the Dreyfus Affair.

Fauré, Gabriel (gäbrēēl' fōrā'), 1845–1924, French composer. His works, largely of a refined, intimate quality, include nocturnes and barcaroles for piano, chamber music, operas, a Requiem, and many songs.

Faust (foust) or **Faustus** (fô'stùs), in German legend, a learned doctor who sold his soul to the devil (Mephistopheles) in exchange for youth, knowledge, and magical power. Supposedly based on the life of one Dr. Johann Faust (d. 1541), the subject has been used in literature since 1570. The *Volksbuch* of Johannes Spies (1587), an early version, was the basis of Marlowe's *Dr. Faustus* (1593). GOETHE wrote a masterpiece on Faust (treated also by other authors, including Thomas Mann). Musical treatments of the legend include those by Berlioz, Gounod, Liszt, and Wagner.

Fausta (fô'stù), d. c.326, wife of Constantine I, daughter of Maximian, mother of Constantine II, Constantius II, and Constans I. Constantine I is supposed to have had her murdered after discovering that she had brought about the murder of his son Crispus through false accusations.

Faustina (fôstī'nù), name of two Roman empresses. **Faustina,** the elder, c.104–141, was wife of Antonius Pius. **Faustina,** the younger, c.125–176, was wife and companion of Marcus Aurelius. Called *Mater Castrorum* [mother of camps].

fauvism (fō'vĭzùm) [Fr. *fauve* = wild beast], name adopted by group of French painters including Matisse, Derain, and Braque for short-lived art movement which preceded cubism. Essentially an expressionistic movement, marked by bold distortion and vivid color used for emotive effect.

Favre, Jules (zhül' fä'vrù), 1809–80, French statesman. A republican, he was a leading opponent of the July Monarchy and of Napoleon III. Served in provisional governments of 1848 and 1871.

Fawkes, Guy: see GUNPOWDER PLOT.

Fay, Charles Ernest (fā), 1846–1931, American mountain climber, known as "dean of American mountain climbing." First president (1902–8) American Alpine Club. Mt. Fay in Canadian Rockies named for him.

Fay, Sidney B(radshaw), 1876–, American historian, authority on European diplomatic history, known for *The Origins of the World War* (1928; 2d ed., 1939).

Fayetteville. 1 City (pop. 17,071), NW Ark., in the Ozarks; founded 1828. Farm trade center; has canning and woodworking. Captured by both sides in Civil War. Several battles fought near here (e.g., Pea Ridge). Main seat of Univ. of Arkansas (land-grant, state supported; coed.; chartered 1871, opened 1872, called Arkansas Industrial Univ. until 1899). **2** City (pop. 34,715), S central N.C., at head of navigation on Cape Fear R. and SSW of Raleigh; founded 1739 by Scots. Has textile and lumber mills. State cap. 1789–93; state convention ratified U.S. Constitution 1789. Occupied 1865 by Sherman, who destroyed arsenal. Fort Bragg, U.S. military reservation, near by. **3** Town (pop. 5,447), S Tenn., SSE of Nashville, in farm area. Has old inn (1813). Near by is site of Camp Blount, scene of troop-mustering for Andrew Jackson's campaign against the Creek Indians.

Fayum or **Faiyum** (both: fīyōōm′), fertile region, N Egypt, W of the Nile. Produces cereals, fruits, sugar cane, and cotton. Rich in archaeological remains, it has yielded many 8th-cent. papyri in ancient Egyptian and Arabic. Chief city, Fayum (pop. 72,465), is trade and rail center; cotton spinning.

Fe, chemical symbol of the element IRON.

Fear, Cape, promontory on Smith Isl., off SE N.C., at mouth of Cape Fear R. Lighthouse. Lightship off Frying-Pan Shoals (extend c.20 mi. to sea).

Feather, river rising in N Calif. in the Sierra Nevada and flowing S to Sacramento R. above Sacramento. Rich gold strikes made here. Supports power projects.

feathers, skin outgrowths characteristic only of birds. Considered modified scales, they grow in definite areas called feather tracts or pterylae; each feather develops from papilla of cells of both layers of the skin embedded in a pit; blood supply nourishes it until feather is grown, then discontinues. Contour or body feathers consist of shaft bearing barbs with small barbules that have microscopic interlocking projections. Down feathers lack projections. Bristles are modified feathers.

February: see MONTH.

February Revolution, 1848, French revolution which overthrew LOUIS PHILIPPE (abdicated Feb. 24) and set up Second Republic. Caused by increasingly reactionary policy of king and his chief minister, GUIZOT, and by dissatisfaction of workers, whose condition had deteriorated in Industrial Revolution. Provisional government, which included Lamartine and LEDRU-ROLLIN, was predominantly bourgeois and moderate. At first, concessions were made to the radicals: right to work was guaranteed, national workshops (planned by Louis BLANC) were created. Deliberate sabotage and eventual dissolution of workshops led to JUNE DAYS rebellion, which was bloodily suppressed. After completion of republican constitution Louis Napoleon was elected president (Dec., 1838; see NAPOLEON III). February Revolution set off similar outbreaks in most of Europe; all were eventually suppressed.

Fécamp (fākā′), town (pop. 16,072), Seine-Inférieure dept., N France; fishing port on English Channel. Famous for benedictine liqueur invented here by monks. Abbey church is a splended example of 12th-cent. Norman architecture.

Fechner, Gustav Theodor (fĕkh′nŭr), 1801–87, German philosopher, founder of psychophysics.

Federal Art Project: see WORK PROJECTS ADMINISTRATION.

Federal Bureau of Investigation, division of U.S. Dept. of Justice, created 1908, given present name 1935. J. Edgar HOOVER is director. FBI investigates Federal law violations, including crimes pertaining to internal security.

Federal Capital Territory: see AUSTRALIAN CAPITAL TERRITORY.

Federal Communications Commission, independent executive agency of U.S. government estab. by Federal Communications Act of 1934. Replaced Federal Radio Commission (estab. 1927). FCC has jurisdiction over all radio and television activities.

Federal Constitutional Convention, in U.S. history, held at Philadelphia, May to Sept. 1787. Under Articles of Confederation the central government was too weak to be effective, incapable of enforcing obligations entered into with foreign nations, impotent to quell internal disorder or maintain economic stability among the states. The wealthy and conservative class and the investors in Western territories favored a stronger central government. All states except R.I. sent delegates to convention. George Washington presided. Convention's only real division lay between smaller states, wishing to retain their power, and larger states, wishing to have power fall where population and wealth lay. Disagreement centered on composition of new Congress. A compromise measure proposed by Oliver Ellsworth finally won approval; this provided for Congress as it is now constituted. James Madison was chief drafter of Constitution; Gouverneur Morris also worked on it. Document went to states for ratification. Despite opposition, a sufficient majority to make Constitution binding had ratified it by the end of June, 1788.

federal government, a union of states which delegate some powers to the central government. It is always stronger than a confederation, having power over individuals as well as over the local governments. Federal powers usually include war, coinage, foreign relations, and commerce. Federal government has developed out of confederations, of which there are many examples, from the Greek city-states to such groups as the Hanseatic League (13th cent.), the Swiss Confederation (1291), and the U.S. (1781; superseded by a more centralized federation in 1789).

Federalist Papers, series of 85 essays written by Alexander Hamilton, James Madison, and John Jay in 1788 explaining and urging adoption of the Federal Constitution, then before the states for decision. Widely published in newspapers, they helped greatly to secure the Constitution's adoption.

Federalist party, in U.S. history. When political division appeared in Pres. Washington's cabinet the party that emerged to champion views of Alexander HAMILTON was Federalist party. It was conservative, favoring a strong centralized government, encouragement of industries, attention to needs of great merchants and landowners, and establishment of a well-ordered society. Pro-British in foreign affairs. Geographically, they were concentrated in New England, with strong element in Middle Atlantic states. After Democratic victory of 1800, Federalist party remained powerful locally, but leadership passed to reactionaries, rather than moderates. Federalist opposition to EMBARGO ACT OF 1807 and to War of 1812 resulted in HARTFORD CONVENTION. Successful issue of war ruined party; by election of 1824 it was virtually dead.

Federal Power Commission, independent executive agency of U.S. government estab. by Federal Water Power Act of 1920. Commission controls activities of privately-operated hydroelectric and natural gas projects on navigable rivers and public lands. Also supervises various parts of Federal hydroelectric projects.

Federal Reserve System, central banking system of the U.S., established 1913. Each of 12 reserve banks (at Boston, N.Y., Philadelphia, Cleveland, Richmond, Atlanta, Chicago, St. Louis, Minneapolis, Kansas City, Dallas, San Francisco) serves a national region. All national banks belong to this system and must maintain reserves on deposit with their regional reserve banks. The operation of the reserve system is on a nonprofit basis. System seeks to maintain sound national monetary and credit conditions; it has markedly improved American banking.

Federal Theatre Project: see WORK PROJECTS ADMINISTRATION.

Federal Trade Commission (FTC), U.S. government commission (set up 1914) serving to check monopolies, prevent fraudulent advertising, investigate doubtful business practices, and preserve competition. Its attempts at legal enforcement of its cease-and-desist orders, in cases where violations are observed, have frequently been frustrated by differing court interpretations of the intent and phrasing of antitrust laws. It now seeks to obtain voluntary adoption of its recommendations wherever possible.

Federal Writers' Project: see WORK PROJECTS ADMINISTRATION.

federation: see FEDERAL GOVERNMENT.

Fedor. For Russian rulers thus named, see FEODOR.

feeble-mindedness, state of arrested mental development. In U.S. three degrees are recognized: idiots (I.Q., 0–25) who have mental age up to three years, need constant supervision; imbeciles (I.Q., 26–50), mental age 3–7 years, can learn simple tasks, rarely reading; morons (I.Q., 51–70), mental age 8–12 years, can do manual labor as complex as operation of lathe or sewing machine under supervision. Less than 10 percent show physical defects: cretinism, stunted growth owing to underactive thyroid gland; Mongolism, mongoloid appearance caused by unknown influence on embryo; microcephalia, small skull, receding forehead, resulting from fetal injury; hydrocephalia, large head, protruding forehead, cause unknown, high infant mortality rate. Disease, glandular disturbance, birth injury, as well as heredity cause mental deficiency. In U.S. only 10 percent of feeble-minded are in institutions.

Fehling's solution (fā'lĭngs) is used to test for glucose, fructose, and other reducing agents. Discovered by Hermann von Fehling (1812–85) German chemist. Two solutions, cupric sulphate and alkaline Rochelle salt, are combined just before use; when heated with reducing agent red precipitate forms.

Fehmgericht: see VEHMGERICHT.

Feininger, Lyonel (fī'nĭng-ùr), 1871–, American painter. Until 1907 worked as illustrator and cartoonist. Taught at the Bauhaus in Germany (1919–32) and at colleges in U.S.

Feisal or **Faisal** (both: fī'sûl), kings of Iraq. **Feisal I,** 1885–1933, reigned 1921–33. In 1916 joined T. E. Lawrence in Arab revolt against Turkey. Became king of Syria in 1920 but deposed in same year by the French. Won Iraqi throne with British support. **Feisal II,** 1935–, succeeded his father, Ghazi I, in 1939. State affairs are conducted by a regent. Visited U.S. 1952.

Feke, Robert (fēk), c.1705–c.1750, early American portrait painter, b. Oyster Bay, N.Y. Worked in Newport, New York, Philadelphia, and Boston.

feldspar or **felspar,** mineral of many widely distributed varieties. It has clean cleavage planes in two directions. It is colorless when pure but occurs in pinkish, red, white, gray, and other colors. As constituents of granite and other crystalline rocks the feldspars form part of the earth's crust.

Felix V, antipope: see AMADEUS VIII.

Felixstowe (fē'lĭkstō), urban district (pop. 15,080), Suffolk East, England. It is a fishing port, seaplane base, and summer resort (yachting).

Feller, Robert William Andrew (Bob Feller), 1918–, American baseball pitcher. Right-handed ace of Cleveland Indians (1936–). Holds two major-league records—most strikeouts in one game (18, against Detroit Tigers, 1938), most strikeouts in one season (348, 1946). Pitched 3 no-hitters.

Fellows, Sir Charles, 1799–1860, English archaeologist, who discovered 15 anc. cities in Asia Minor. Brought back group of marbles, now in British Mus.

felony, grave crime, in contrast to a misdemeanor, or petty crime. Felonies in Great Britain and U.S. are usually tried by jury and carry with them as possible consequences imprisonment, loss of citizenship, or (for an alien) deportation.

felspar: see FELDSPAR.

felt, fabric made by matting (felting) together the fibers of wool, hair, or fur. Woven felt is a coarse fabric with nap first raised by teaseling, then ironed flat; true felt, however, is a fiber mass compressed to desired thickness. As an art, feltmaking antedates weaving.

Felton, William Harrell, 1823–1909, American political leader. After Civil War he was leading independent Democrat of Ga., opposing reactionary machine politics. U.S. Representative (1875–81). His second wife, **Rebecca Latimer Felton,** 1835–1930, was first woman to enter U.S. Senate, serving briefly in 1922 by appointment.

Femgericht: see VEHMGERICHT.

feminism, movement for political, social, and educational equality for women and men. Prior to Industrial Revolution women had no personal or property rights. Early leaders in England such as Mary Astell and Mary WOLLSTONECRAFT pleaded in vain. In U.S. active feminist movement dates from 1848 convention at Seneca Falls, N.Y., where Elizabeth Cady STANTON, Lucretia MOTT, and others issued a declaration of independence for women. Sparked by leaders such as Mrs. Stanton and Susan B. ANTHONY, movement spread rapidly. See also WOMAN SUFFRAGE.

fencing, sport of attack and defense with foil, épée, saber, and similar weapons, by two opponents. Held on strip 40 ft. long, about 6 ft. wide. In 1920 the sport was first included in the Olympics.

Fénelon, François de Salignac de la Mothe (fräswä' dù sälēnyäk' dù lä môt' fänùlō'), 1651–1715, French theologian and author, archbishop of Cambrai. Wrote *Télémaque* (1699) for young duke of Burgundy, his pupil. Defended QUIETISM.

Feng Yu-hsiang (fŭng' yü'-shyäng), 1880–1948, Chinese general, called the Christian General. Fought with Chang Tso-lin and Wu P'ei-fu, 1920–26, for control of N China and Manchuria. Later, though an opponent of Chiang Kai-shek, he held high posts in Nationalist government.

Fenian movement (fē'nēun), Irish secret revolutionary society (organized c.1858) for independence from England by force. Under James Stephens (1825–1901), the main appeal in Ireland was to the nonagrarian population and was opposed by the Catholic Church. Risings and terrorism led first to suppression by the British but finally to their attention to Irish problems. In U.S. John O'Mahony was the leader of embittered Irish emigrants whose attempts to invade Canada increased Anglo-American tension at end of Civil War—although Fenian raids fostered Canadian confederation. By 1914 Fenian influence was drawn into the new SINN FEIN organization founded by a former Fenian.

Fenn College: see CLEVELAND, Ohio.

fennel, Old World herb (*Foeniculum vulgare*) with fine, licorice-scented foliage and seeds used to flavor sauces, bread, liqueurs. Finochio or sweet fennel has bulbous-based stalk eaten like celery.

Fens, the, district W and S of the Wash, England. Includes parts of Bedford, Norfolk, Cambridge, Huntingdon, and Lincoln counties. Extending c.70 mi. from N to S and c.35 mi. from E to W, it is traversed by several streams. Originally a swampland; Romans attempted drainage and built roads. First effective drainage developed by Cornelius Vermuyden (Dutch) after 1621. District now has fertile soil and is largely cultivated.

Fenton, Reuben Eaton, 1819–85, U.S. Senator from N.Y. (1869–75). Fought with Sen. Roscoe Conkling over distribution of patronage; Conkling won.

Feodor (fyô'dùr), tsars of Russia. **Feodor I,** 1557–98, son of Ivan the Terrible, reigned 1584–98. Dominated by his brother-in-law and successor, Boris GODUNOV. **Feodor II,** 1589–1605, succeeded his father Boris Godunov; was killed the same year at accession of first false DMITRI. **Feodor III,** 1656–82, succeeded his father Alexis 1676. Crippled; energetic reformer. His brother Ivan V and half-brother Peter I jointly succeeded him. Name sometimes appears as Theodore.

Feodosiya (fä"ŭdô'sēū), city (pop. 28,656), RSFSR, E Crimea, on Black Sea. Grain export center; health resort. Founded 6th cent. B.C. by Greek colonists as Theodosia; known as Caffa or Kaffa in Middle Ages, when Genoese had flourishing colony here, from which they virtually monopolized Black Sea trade. Fell to khan of Crimea 1475, to Russia 1783. Twice occupied by Germans in World War II. Ruins of Genoese fortifications.

Ferber, Edna, 1887–, American novelist, playwright, author of novels (e.g., *So Big,* 1924; *Show Boat,* 1926, later a musical), stories, plays.

fer-de-lance (fâr"dù-läs'), poisonous snake, c.5–6 ft. long, related to bushmaster and rattlesnake and found in tropical America and some of West Indies. It hunts at night.

Ferdinand, emperors, kings of Hungary and Bohemia. **Ferdinand I,** 1503–64, younger brother of Emperor CHARLES V, was brought up in Spain at court of his grandfather Ferdinand the Catholic. Charles gave him Austria (1521), had him crowned German king (1531), put him in charge of German affairs, and abdicated in his favor (1558). Meanwhile, Ferdinand had inherited Hungary and Bohemia from his brother-in-law, LOUIS II of Hungary (1526). In Hungary, he fought against rival claimants JOHN I and JOHN II, whom Sultan SULEIMAN I was supporting. Eventually, Ferdinand kept NW Hungary and the royal title but had to pay tribute to sultan. In Bohemia, Ferdinand vigorously pushed the Catholic Reform and established Hapsburg absolutism by abolishing most of local liberties (1547). In Germany he dealt with the PEASANTS' WAR and other rebellions and negotiated the PEACE OF AUGSBURG (1555). His grandson **Ferdinand II,** 1578–1637, succeeded his cousin MATTHIAS as king of Bohemia (1617) and Hungary (1618) and as emperor (1619). In 1619 the Bohemian nobles rebelled against him (because of his strong anti-Protestant stand) and elected FREDERICK THE WINTER KING. Thus the THIRTY YEARS WAR began. Ferdinand defeated Frederick (1620). His generals won major victories, but Ferdinand's Edict of Restitution (1629) provoked renewed opposition. He almost certainly instigated the murder of WALLENSTEIN (1634). The war reached its conclusion under his son, **Ferdinand III,** 1608–57, who succeeded him as king of Hungary (1626) and Bohemia (1627) and as emperor (1637). Under him the war took a disastrous turn, and he reluctantly accepted the Peace of WESTPHALIA (1648).

Ferdinand, 1793–1875, emperor of Austria (1835–48). Was subject to fits of insanity. A council of state, dominated by METTERNICH, governed in his name. Fled Vienna after outbreak of 1848 revolution; abdicated in favor of nephew Francis Joseph.

Ferdinand, 1861–1948, tsar of Bulgaria (1908–18); a prince of Saxe-Coburg-Gotha. Was chosen to succeed Alexander of Battenberg as prince of Bulgaria (1887); took advantage of Young Turk revolution (1908) to declare full independence of Bulgaria and proclaim himself tsar. First triumphed, then lost, in BALKAN WARS (1912–13). In World War I he joined Central Powers (1915). Was forced to abdicate in favor of his son, Boris III. Died in Germany.

Ferdinand II, king of Aragon: see FERDINAND V, Spanish king of Castile.

Ferdinand, kings of Portugal. **Ferdinand I,** 1345–83, nicknamed "the Handsome" and "the Inconstant"; reigned 1367–83. Leonor Teles, whom he married after securing dubious annulment of earlier marriage, had a baleful influence on his reign. He fought three unsuccessful wars against Henry II and John I of Castile. In 1382 he abandoned his ally, JOHN OF GAUNT, and made peace with John I, to whom he gave his daughter and heiress Beatrice in marriage. Portugal would thus have gone to Castile after his death if a revolution had not given the throne to John of Aviz (see JOHN I of Portugal). **Ferdinand II,** 1816–85, oldest son of Ferdinand, duke of Saxe-Coburg-Gotha, was titular king of Portugal (1837–55) through his marriage with MARIA II.

Ferdinand, 1865–1927, king of Rumania (1914–27). Entered World War I on Allied side (1916); annexed Bessarabia (1918); intervened in Hungary to break up Communist government of Bela Kun (1919); acquired Transylvania and SE Hungary in peace treaties. Agr. reforms and universal suffrage were introduced during his reign. His consort was MARIE of Rumania. Succeeded by grandson MICHAEL.

Ferdinand, Spanish kings. **Ferdinand I** (the Great), d. 1065, king of Castile (1035–65) and Leon (1037–65); son of Sancho III of Navarre. Reduced Moorish emirs of Saragossa, Badajoz, Seville, and Toledo to vassalage. Divided his kingdom among three sons. **Ferdinand III,** 1199–1252, king of Castile (1217–52) and Leon (1230–52). Crusaded successfully against Moors. Canonized a saint of Roman Church (1671). **Ferdinand IV,** 1285–1312, king of Castile and Leon (1295–1312). Conquered Gibraltar. **Ferdinand V** or **Ferdinand the Catholic,** 1452–1516, king of Castile and Leon (1474–1504); king of Aragon (as Ferdinand II, 1479–1516), king of Sicily (1468–1516), king of Naples (1504–16); son of John II of Aragon. Married ISABELLA I of Castile (1469), shared kingship of Castile with her until her death (1504), when he became regent for his daughter JOANNA. The Catholic Kings, as Ferdinand and Isabella are called, completed the reconquest of Spain from the Moors by taking GRANADA (1492); expelled JEWS and Moors from Spain (1492; 1502); instituted Spanish INQUISITION; financed expedition of Christopher COLUMBUS (1492); divided world with Portugal by Treaty of TORDESILLAS (1494). Their reign thus was crucial in the history of the world as well as of Spain. Ferdinand also took a leading part in the ITALIAN WARS and annexed most

of NAVARRE (1512). His grandson, Emperor CHARLES V, inherited the Spanish empire from him. **Ferdinand VI,** b. 1712 or 1713, d. 1759, king of Spain (1746–59); son of Philip V and Marie Louise of Savoy. Sent his stepmother Elizabeth Farnese into retirement. Kept Spain neutral in Seven Years War. **Ferdinand VII,** 1784–1833, king of Spain (1808–33). Deposed his father CHARLES IV, but was lured to Bayonne by Napoleon I, who forced him to renounce throne in favor of Charles IV, who in turn was forced to resign his rights to Napoleon (1808). Imprisoned in France until 1814, when he was restored to Spanish throne. He disappointed his liberal supporters by abolishing constitution of 1812. A revolution in 1820 forced him to reinstate it, but in 1823 French military intervention (sanctioned by Holy Alliance) restored him to full authority, and he revoked the constitution once more. He set aside the Salic law to give the succession to his daughter ISABELLA II; the Carlist Wars resulted (see CARLISTS). During his reign Spain lost its colonies on N and S American mainland.

Ferdinand, kings of the Two Sicilies. **Ferdinand I,** 1751–1825. In 1759 he became king of Naples as Ferdinand IV, of Sicily as Ferdinand III. Succeeding his father, who had become king of Spain as Charles III. Promoted absolutism under influence of Queen MARIE CAROLINE and Sir John ACTON. Suppressed PARTHENOPEAN REPUBLIC (1799), but after joining Third Coalition against Napoleon I (1805) he lost Naples to French (1806–15). After his restoration he styled himself king of the Two Sicilies as Ferdinand I (1816), ruled despotically. **Ferdinand II,** 1810–59, reigned 1830–59. During revolutionary outbreaks of 1848–49, he ordered bombardments of Messina and Palermo, thus earning nickname "King Bomba."

Ferdinand the Catholic: see FERDINAND V.

Fergana Valley or **Ferghana Valley** (fĕrgä'nŭ), region, central Asiatic USSR, in Uzbek SSR, Tadzhik SSR, and Kirghiz SSR. Fergana Range (part of Tien Shan system) rises in NE, Pamir in S. Drained by SYR DARYA R., valley consists partly of desert, partly of densely populated irrigated steppe (cotton, grapes, fruit). Kokand is chief city. One of world's oldest cultivated regions, valley has long been a major silk-producing area, with such ancient trade centers as MARGELAN and OSH. Arabs introduced Islam 8th cent. Valley passed under rule of shahs of KHOREZM (12th–14th cent.), of Jenghiz Khan, of Tamerlane, and of Uzbek khans of KOKAND (16th–19th cent.). Russian conquest completed 1876.

Fergus Falls, city (pop. 12,917), W Minn., SE of Fargo, N.Dak.; settled 1857. Dairy and wood products.

Ferguson, James Edward, 1871–1950, governor of Texas (1915–17). Impeached and removed from office. His wife, **Miriam A. Wallace Ferguson,** 1875–, known as Ma Ferguson, became governor in 1925; served again 1933–35. Ferguson was actual, though not nominal, governor.

Ferguson, suburban city (pop. 11,573), E Mo., NW of St. Louis; settled c.1874.

Fergusson, Robert, 1750–74, Scottish poet, author of "Auld Reekie."

Ferid ed-Din Attar (fĕrēd′ ĕdēn′ ŭtär′), d. c.1229, Persian poet, a Sufi; one of greatest mystic poets of Islam. Also called Faridun.

Fermanagh (fùrmă′nù), inland county (653 sq. mi.; pop. 53,040), N Ireland, in Ulster; co. town Enniskillen. Erne R. divides county almost in half. Hilly land, largely devoted to grazing. Exports include butter, eggs, and oats. Pottery and linen are made, and some limestone and sandstone quarried.

Fermat, Pierre de (pyĕr′ dù fĕrmä′), 1601–65, French mathematician, known as founder of modern theory of numbers and calculus of probabilities.

fermentation, chemical change caused by enzyme action. Formation of lactic acid in milk and production of vinegar are fermentation. Alcoholic fermentation is most important commercially. Pasteur proved it is caused by yeast; later it was found that yeast enzyme system of which zymase is chief component is responsible. Reaction involves production of alcohol and carbon dioxide from simple sugars; it is a source of both industrial alcohol and alcoholic beverages.

Fermi, Enrico (ĕnrē′kō fĕr′mē), 1901–, American physicist, b. Italy. Won 1938 Nobel Prize for work on radioactive substances. He greatly aided atomic bomb project by research (1934–38) and active participation after 1939 when he came to U.S.

fern, flowerless perennial plant of which there are more than 6,000 species, widely distributed, especially in tropics. They range in form from the climbing fern to the TREE FERN. Those of North America usually have green fronds (leaves) rising from a rootstalk. Reproduction is by asexual spores usually found on backs of fronds or on special frond stalks. Valued as ornamental plants for growing in shade and as house plants (e.g., Boston fern).

Fernández or **Hernández, Gregorio** (grägō′rēō fĕrnändäth, ĕrnän′däth), c.1576–1636, Spanish baroque sculptor of religious figures.

Fernández de Córdoba, Francisco (fränthē′skō fĕrnän′däth dä kōr′dhōbä), d. 1518?, Spanish explorer. Died of wounds suffered in battle with Mayas in Yucatan.

Fernández de Córdoba, Francisco, d. 1526?, Spanish conquistador. Sent by Pedrarias (1524) to take Nicaragua from González de Ávila, he tried to seize territory for himself; he was captured and executed.

Fernández de Córdoba, Gonzalo (gōnthä′lō), 1453–1515, Spanish general, called the Great Captain. Took part in conquest of Granada; expelled French from Naples twice (1495, 1503). First Spanish viceroy of Naples.

Fernández de Lizardi, José Joaquín (hōsä′ hwäkēn′ fĕrnän′däs dä lēsär′dē), 1776–1827, Mexican journalist, novelist, and dramatist, author of novel *El Periquillo Sarniento* (1816–30).

Fernández de Moratín, Leandro (lään′drō fĕrnän′däth dä mōrätēn′), 1760–1828, Spanish dramatist, author of comedies after the manner of Molière.

Fernández Navarrete, Juan: see NAVARRETE, JUAN FERNÁNDEZ.

Fernandina (fûrnăndē′nù), city (pop. 4,420), NE Fla., on Amelia Isl. at mouth of St. Marys R. Site of Spanish fort in 1680s. Changed hands many times in 18th cent. Declared free port in 1808, it developed rapidly as base of pirates, slave traders, smugglers. Permanently captured by U.S. 1817. Fort Clinch (built 1847–61) captured by Union troops, 1862.

Fernando da Noronha (fĕrnän′dō dù nùrō′nyä), islands in Atlantic, off NE Brazil. Discovered by Portuguese (1503). Long used as a penal colony by Brazil, it is now military base.

Fernán González (fĕrnän′ gōnthä′läth), d. 970, count of Castile. Won virtual independence from Leon. Hero of 13th-cent. popular epic poem.

Ferndale, city (pop. 29,675), SE Mich., N residential suburb of Detroit. Mfg. of metal products and synthetic resins.

Fernel, Jean François (zhä fräswä′ fĕrnĕl′), 1497–1558, French physician and author of influential works on medicine, mathematics, and astronomy.

Ferney-Voltaire (fĕrnä′-vôltĕr′), village, Ain dept., E France, near Geneva. Voltaire bought seigniory 1758; lived here till 1778; founded still flourishing pottery industry.

Ferrar, Nicholas (fĕ′rùr), 1592–1637, English theologian, founder of religious community at Little Gidding, Huntingdonshire.

Ferrara (fär-rä′rä), city (pop. 58,187), Emilia-Romagna, N central Italy. Agr. center. Its past splendor as princely cap. of the ESTE family is recalled by its palaces and works of art. It declined after passing to Papal States (1598). Notable buildings include Palazzo dei Diamanti, Schifanoia palace, 14th-cent. moated castle, Romanesque cathedral. It was the birthplace of Savonarola.

Ferrara-Florence, Council of, 1438–45, second part of 17th ecumenical council of Roman Church (see BASEL, COUNCIL OF). Chief goal at Ferrara was to end Schism of East and West. Promoted by Byzantine Emperor John VII, who hoped Christian union might save his empire from the Turks. Leading figure was Bessarion, archbishop of Nicaea. In Jan., 1439, the council moved to Florence, and in July the pope issued the bull *Laetentur coeli,* announcing the religious union of E and W churches. After the Eastern delegates went home, the party opposing union gained power. The council moved to the Lateran (1443) and devoted itself to reuniting smaller, non-Orthodox E churches and the Holy See.

Ferrari, Gaudenzio (goudän′tsēō fĕr-rä′rē), c.1480–1546, Italian religious painter, a leading member of Lombard school.

Ferraris, Galileo (gälēlä′ō fär-rä′rēs), 1847–97, Italian physicist and electrical engineer. He discovered the rotary magnetic field and thereby promoted the development of alternating-current motors.

Ferrel, William (fĕ′rùl), 1817–91, American meteorologist. Worked on government coast and geodetic survey (1867–82); did research on tides, currents, winds, storms. Formulated **Ferrel's law:** because of earth's rotation moving bodies on earth's surface are deflected to right in N Hemisphere, to left in S Hemisphere; amount varies with velocity of motion and latitude (zero at equator, greatest near poles).

Ferrer, José (Vicente), 1912–, American actor, director, and producer, b. Puerto Rico. After his debut in 1935 he won acclaim in such varied plays as *Charley's Aunt, Othello* (as Iago), and *Cyrano de Bergerac* and such films as *Joan of Arc, Cyrano de Bergerac,* and *Moulin Rouge.*

Ferrer, Vincent: see VINCENT FERRER, SAINT.

Ferrero, Guglielmo (gōōlyĕl'mō fā-rā'rō), 1871–1942, Italian man of letters and historian. Noted for works on Roman history, notably *The Greatness and Decline of Rome* (Eng. tr., 5 vols., 1907–9).

ferret, American (black-footed) ferret is largest and very rare North American weasel. It inhabits Great Plains; chief prey is prairie dog. It is c.2 ft. long, yellow-buff marked with brown, with black band across eyes, black-tipped tail, and black feet. Old World ferret is domesticated polecat (c.14 in. long) used in hunting.

Ferri, Ciro (chē'rō fĕr'rē), 1634–89, Italian painter, pupil and follower of Pietro da Cortona.

Ferris wheel, huge, revolving wheel for carrying passengers in cars suspended on the wheel, built by George W. Ferris, American engineer, for World's Columbian Exposition (1893).

Ferrol, El (ĕl fĕrôl'), officially El Ferrol del Caudillo (dĕl koudhē'lyō), city (pop. 40,-664), NW Spain, in Galicia, on the Atlantic. Important naval base. Birthplace of Francisco Franco.

Ferry, Jules (zhül' fĕrē'), 1832–93, French statesman. Minister of education (1879–80, 1882); premier (1880–81, 1883–85). Established modern French educational system on secular, anticlerical basis. Built up French colonial empire in Africa, Indo-China.

ferry, a passage across water by boat, provided for the public upon payment of toll. Ferries include rowboats for transport of persons, flat-bottomed barges (carrying vehicles, persons, or animals) propelled by hand or by utilizing water currents, and power-driven ferryboats. Trains can be carried across the English Channel by ferry.

Fersen, Hans Axel, Count (häns' äk'sùl fĕr'-sùn), 1755–1810, Swedish soldier. Served in French army from 1779; became•a favorite of Marie Antoinette; helped to plan flight of royal family (1791) and himself drove their coach out of Paris. Made marshal of Sweden 1801. Killed by a mob after Swedish revolution.

fertility rites, magico-religious rites to insure ample food and birth of children. In primitive cultures natural phenomena, such as cycle of vegetation, were personified and symbolized in mythical marriages of earthgoddess and sun-god and birth and death of their progeny. Myths of death and resurrection of the hero god (e.g., Adonis) were the basis of elaborate fertility rites, frequently phallic in nature. Later MYSTERIES apparently grew out of fertility rites. The sacred drama was developed from them. Survivals in disguised form abound (e.g., Maypole dance and carnivals).

fertilization, in biology, a process in plant and animal reproduction, involving union of two unlike sexual cells, or gametes (SPERM and OVUM). Process occurs in seed-producing plants after POLLINATION. **Cross-fertilization,** in botany, refers to fusion of sperm of one flower with ovum of another, in contrast to self-fertilization (fusion of sperm and ovum in one flower).

fertilizer, material containing nitrogen, phosphorus, potash, and other elements essential to plant growth, applied to soil or other growing medium. Fertilizers may be organic (e.g., animal manures, bone meal), or inorganic or commercial (e.g., nitrate of soda, superphosphate).

fescue, (fĕs'kū), annual or perennial grass (*Festuca*), used for pasture, forage, or lawns.

Fessenden, William Pitt (fĕ'sùndùn), 1806–69, American statesman. U.S. Representative from Maine (1841–43). U.S. Senator (1855–64, 1865–69). U.S. Secretary of the Treasury (1864–65). Made excellent record in public finance.

Festival of Lights, Jewish festival: see HANUK-KAH.

Festus, Sextus Pompeius, fl. at some time between A.D. 100 and 400, Roman lexicographer. His surviving work, *On the Meaning of Words,* an abridgment of the lost glossary of M. Verrius Flaccus, is an important source for Roman antiquities.

Festus, city (pop. 5,199), E Mo., on the Mississippi below St. Louis. Shoes, textiles, grain products.

Fetterman, William Judd, 1833?–1866, American army officer. **Fetterman massacre** occurred when, despite his unfamiliarity with frontier conditions and methods of Indian fighting, he volunteered to lead supply party of 80 men, ignored orders not to leave trail, and was ambushed by Indians under Red Cloud. Entire party was killed.

fetus or foetus (both: fē'tùs), unborn offspring of a viviparous animal, especially in later stages of development. In earlier prenatal life the offspring is called an embryo. Circulatory system is separate from maternal system; nourishment and oxygen are received through placenta.

Feuchtwanger, Lion (le'ōn foikht'väng-ùr), 1884–, German author; in U.S. after 1940. Historical novels include *The Ugly Duchess* (1923), *Jud Süss* (1925; U.S. ed., *Power*), and the *Josephus* trilogy (1923–42). All these have been translated into English.

feudalism, social order in W Europe from end of Charlemagne's empire to rise of absolute monarchies. Basic character was local, agricultural political economy. Usual unit was manor—peasants, VILLEIN and SERF, held land from lord of manor, the seigneur, who gave protection and use of land in return for personal services and dues. This was MANO-RIAL SYSTEM. In ideal feudal society, ownership of all land was vested in king. Under him was hierarchy of nobles, highest holding from him directly, lesser ones from them, and so on to seigneur, holding single manor. Holding was by fief, acquired by formal ceremony of INVESTITURE. Basically system rested upon unsettled conditions of time and a lord's need for armed warriors. The KNIGHT was the typical warrior. Gradations of nobility were based on both land-holding and military service. The Church had great influence in shaping feudalism; it owned much land, and its hierarchy somewhat paralleled feudal system. The system probably had its roots in disruption of decaying Roman institutions by inroads and settlements of Germans. It spread from France to Spain, to Italy, and later to Germany and E Europe. Frankish form was imposed on England by William the Conqueror (1066). System disappeared gradually with rise of monarchies that broke down local systems, but it persisted in France until French Revolution (1789), in Germany and Japan until 19th cent., and in Russia until 1917.

Feuerbach, Ludwig, 1804–72, German philosopher. Abandoned Hegelianism for materialism, asserting religion is but a symbolic "dream."

Feuermann, Emmanuel (foi'ŭrmän), 1902–42, virtuoso cellist, b. Kolomea, Galicia. Taught in Europe and America. Gave concerts in U.S. after 1935.

Feuillants (fûyä'), political club of French Revolution. Formed 1791 by right-wing JACOBINS led by Barnave. Advocated constitutional monarchy, peace policy. Suppressed by Jacobins in 1792.

feverfew, strong-scented perennial herb (*Chrysanthemum parthenium*), with small daisylike flowers.

fever therapy, treatment of disease by artificially produced fever. High temperature can destroy organisms causing disease without injuring patient. Original method of injecting microbes to produce fever, introduced 1917 by Wagner-Jauregg, is largely replaced by use of electric cabinets or blankets, hot baths, radiation, injection of foreign proteins.

Fez, city (pop. 200,946), French Morocco, at central point on routes to Tangier, Rabat, and Marrakesh. Fez was cap. of several dynasties (8th–19th cent.). Consists of old city (founded 808), new city (founded 1276), and European suburb. Has c.100 mosques and ancient Moslem university. Noted for native industries, it gave its name to the brimless felt cap.

Fianna Fail (fē'ŭnŭ fäl'), [Irish,= Fenians of Ireland], Irish political party (organized 1926). Led by Eamon DE VALERA, it opposed Irish Free State. In control of the government after 1932, it advocated complete separation from Great Britain. Defeated (1948) by a coalition, it returned to power in 1951.

fiber, threadlike strand, usually pliable and capable of being spun into yarn. Of about 40 commercially important kinds, those of animal origin (mainly composed of protein) include silk and wool and the hair of the goat (mohair), llama (alpaca), vicuña, camel, horse, rabbit, beaver, hog, badger, sable; vegetable fibers (containing mostly cellulose) include cotton, kapok, flax, hemp, Manila hemp, istle, ramie, sisal hemp, Spanish moss. Rayon and nylon are best-known synthetic fibers. Chief inorganic fiber is asbestos.

Fibiger, Johannes (yôhä'nŭs fē'bēgŭr), 1867–1928, Danish pathologist. Won 1926 Nobel Prize in Physiology and Medicine for his research on cancer.

Fibonacci, Leonardo (lāōnär'dō fēbōnät'chē), late 12th, early 13th cent., Italian mathematician, also called Leonardo da Pisa. Wrote early work on algebra and arithmetic, standard for centuries; organized, extended known geometry and trigonometry.

Fichte, Johann Gottlieb (yō'hän gôt'lēp fīkh'tŭ), 1762–1814, German philosopher and political leader. His ethical idealism was a development of Kantianism. His *Addresses to the German People* (1808) awoke liberal nationalism.

Fichtelgebirge (fīkh'tŭlgŭbēr"gŭ), mountain range, Upper Franconia, NE Bavaria, near Czech border. Highest point 3,447 ft. (Schneeberg). Many resorts.

Ficino, Marsilio (märsē'lyō fēchē'nō), 1433–99, Florentine humanist. He translated Plato into Latin, wrote works of Platonic philosophy, and forwarded humanism as head of Cosimo de' Medici's academy.

Field, Cyrus West, 1819–92, American promoter of first Atlantic cable. Unsuccessful attempts of 1857–58 preceded success of *Great Eastern* in laying a cable in 1866. His brother, **David Dudley Field,** 1805–94, a lawyer, worked in behalf of law reform. His codes of procedure for N.Y. were adopted by several other states; strongly influenced English Judicature Acts of 1873 and 1875. Also worked to establish a code of international law. Another brother, **Stephen Johnson Field,** 1816–99, was U.S. Supreme Court Justice (1863–97). As member of Calif. legislature in 1850s, he estab. legal recognition of mining camp usages and regulations.

Field, Eugene, 1850–95, American poet, journalist. In Chicago *Daily News* (later the *Record*) his column, "Sharps and Flats," helped establish the newspaper columnist. His poems of childhood include "Little Boy Blue" and "Wynken, Blynken, and Nod."

Field, John, 1782–1837, composer and pianist, b. Dublin, settled in Russia. Chopin's nocturnes were modeled after those of Field.

Field, Marshall, 1834–1906, American merchant. As head of Marshall Field and Co. from 1881, he pioneered in modern retailing practices. Benefactor of Art Institute of Chicago, Univ. of Chicago, Chicago Museum of Natural History (formerly Field Museum of Natural History). His grandson, **Marshall Field III,** 1893–, has devoted himself to various social projects. Backed New York city liberla newspaper *PM* (1940–48). Started Chicago *Sun* in 1941; merged it with Chicago *Times* in 1948.

Field, Stephen Johnson: see FIELD, CYRUS WEST.

Fielding, Henry, 1707–54, English novelist. Began career by writing comedies, farces, and parodies, with many attacks on Walpole's government. These helped bring about the censorship of the Licensing Act (1737), and Fielding had to give up drama. His first novel *Joseph Andrews* (1742) was undertaken to burlesque Richardson's *Pamela*. Strong satire laces the vigorous prose of his other fine realistic novels. *Tom Jones* (1749) is generally considered a masterpiece of world literature. Other novels are *Jonathan Wild* (1743), *Amelia* (1752).

Field Museum of Natural History: see CHICAGO NATURAL HISTORY MUSEUM.

Field of the Cloth of Gold, meeting ground of Henry VIII of England and Francis I of France, near Calais, France (1520); so called because of splendor of pageantry. Projected Franco-English alliance did not come off.

Fields, Lewis Maurice: see WEBER, JOSEPH.

Fiene, Ernest (fē′nù), 1894–, American painter, b. Germany. Best known for landscapes of New England and New York. A popular teacher.

Fiesole (fyā′zōlā), town (pop. 2,647), Tuscany, central Italy, on hill above Florence. Once an important Etruscan and Roman town (Faesulae). Has Roman theater, baths; Romanesque cathedral. Near-by Church of San Domenico has Fra Angelico paintings.

Fife or Fifeshire, maritime county (505 sq. mi.; pop. 306,855), Scotland, between Firths of Forth and Tay; co. town Cupar. Part of central Scottish Lowlands, well cultivated terrain rises to Lomond Hills. One of most prosperous Scottish counties, it has coal mining, linen mfg., brewing, and shipbuilding. Once home of the Picts, county has long been called kingdom of Fife. Saint Andrews, famous golfing resort, is seat of oldest Scottish University.

Fifth Avenue, famous street of Manhattan, New York city, from Washington Square to Harlem R. Business and shopping center between 34th and 59th Street; passes Empire State Building, New York Public Library, Rockefeller Center, and St. Patrick's Cathedral. From 59th to 110th streets it borders Central Park. Runs through Harlem N of the park.

Fifth Monarchy Men, religious group during Puritan Revolution in England, millennarians expecting second coming of Christ, who would set up fifth monarchy (earlier four being Assyrian, Persian, Greek, and Roman empires). Opposed church and civil government.

Fifty-four forty or fight, phrase commonly used by extremists in controversy with Great Britain over Oregon country. They held that U.S. rights extended to lat. 54° 40′ N, the recognized S boundary of Russian America. Phrase was used by Democrats as 1844 campaign slogan. Boundary set in 1846 at 49°.

fig, a tree (*Ficus carica*), native to Mediterranean region and long grown for its commercially valuable fruit, now cultivated in California and Gulf states. Some varieties require pollination by fig wasp before setting fruit.

figured bass, in music, a system of notation in which the notes of the bass part have figures written below them to indicate which chords are to be played. Also called thorough bass and *basso continuo*. Used much in harpsichord and organ music of baroque era. Now chiefly used as device for teaching harmony.

Fiji (fē′jē), island group (7,056 sq. mi.; pop. 259,638), S Pacific; most important British colony in the Pacific. Comprises 250 islands, of which 80 are inhabited. Main islands are Viti Levu, with Suva, cap. of colony, and Vanua Levu; gold mines on both islands. Crops include sugar cane, tropical fruits,

rice, and cotton. Discovered 1643 by Tasman, annexed 1874 by Great Britain. Missionaries arriving in 1835 helped abolish cannibalism. Fijians, of Melanesian origin, make up only c.40% of population. Indian laborers, imported 1879–1916 under indenture system, are chiefly engaged in sugar industry. Governor of Fiji is also British high commissioner of Western Pacific.

filament, in incandescent lamp, threadlike wire (usually tungsten) wound in center of bulb, which becomes hot when current runs through it. In vacuum tube an uncoiled filament is used.

filament battery: see BATTERY, ELECTRIC.

Filaret, Vasily Drosdov: see PHILARET, VASILY DROSDOV.

filbert: see HAZEL.

Filene, E(dward) A(lbert) (fīlēn′, fī–), 1860–1937, American merchant. As president of Boston firm of William Filene's Sons he pioneered in scientific methods of retail distribution.

filibuster, in 17th cent., buccaneer who plundered Spanish colonies in New World. In 19th cent., adventurer who led privately organized armed forays into friendly countries; e.g., from U.S. into Cuba and Mexico. Term now denotes obstructionist tactics in legislative bodies.

Filipino: see PHILIPPINE ISLANDS.

Fillmore, Millard, 1800–1874, 13th President of the United States (July, 1850–March, 1853). U.S. Representative from N.Y. (1833–35, 1837–43); promoted high tariff of 1842. Vice President of U.S. (1849–50); succeeded to presidency on death of Zachary Taylor. Signed Compromise of 1850; tried to enforce Fugitive Slave Act. Upheld nonintervention in foreign disputes and approved treaty opening Japan to Western commerce. Unsuccessfully strove to make Whigs a national party to conciliate sectional struggle. Hoping to unite North and South, he joined KNOW-NOTHING MOVEMENT; its presidential candidate in 1856.

Fillmore, city (pop. 1,890), W central Utah. Territorial cap. 1851–56.

film, photographic: see PHOTOGRAPHY.

Filson, John, c.1747–1788, Kentucky pioneer, b. Pa. Author of *Discovery, Settlement, and Present State of Kentucke* (1784), containing alleged autobiography of Daniel Boone. Boone's subsequent high reputation mainly stems from this work.

filtration: see WATER.

fin, locomotive organ of fish consisting of cartilaginous or bony rays covered by thin tissue. In some (e.g., eel) single fin extends from back around tail along ventral surface. Majority have one, two, or three dorsal fins, a tail fin, and an anal fin (called median or unpaired fins). Paired fins are pectoral (behind gills) and pelvic (position varies; sometimes lacking). Some (e.g., salmon, catfish) have adipose fin (fatty tissue without support) behind dorsal fin.

finch, member of largest bird family (Fringillidae). Finches have cone-shaped bills and eat chiefly seeds. Among the finches are SPARROW, GROSBEAK, CANARY, GOLDFINCH, BULLFINCH, chaffinch, INDIGO BUNTING,

JUNCO, purple finch, hawfinch. See *ill.*, p. 135.

finder. The discoverer of lost property is treated differently in the various countries. In some he has the right to retain it against anyone except the owner. In most countries, however, he is obligated to deliver the property to the police, though he is entitled to a legally fixed reward against the owner. In some states (e.g., New York) the finder becomes the owner, if the article after delivery to the police is not claimed within a certain period.

Findlay, city (pop. 23,845), NW Ohio, on Blanchard R. and S of Toledo; laid out 1821. Mfg. of auto tires and tubes and agr. machinery; oil refineries. Findlay Col. is here.

Fingal: see FINN MAC CUMHAIL.

Fingal's Cave, unusually beautiful cavern, on Staffa Isl., Inner Hebrides, Scotland. Associated with many legends. Mendelssohn composed an overture called *The Hebrides* or *Fingal's Cave.*

Finger Lakes, W central N.Y., group of long, narrow glacial lakes in N-S valleys, in scenic resort and agr. (fruits, esp. grapes, vegetables, wheat) region between Geneseo and Syracuse. From W to E lakes are Conesus; Hemlock; Canadice; Honeoye; Canandaigua (kănŭndả'gwŭ) (c.15 mi. long); Keuka (kū'kủ) (c.18 mi. long); Seneca (largest; extends c.35 mi. N from Watkins Glen to Geneva; on E shore is Sampson, where U.S. naval training station, estab. 1942, functioned for a time after 1946 as an emergency college for veterans); Cayuga (kả yōō'gủ) (longest; c.38 mi. long; joined by canal to the Barge Canal, by Seneca R. to Seneca L.; on cliffs near S end are Cornell Univ. and Taughannock Falls, 215 ft. high); Owasco (c.11 mi. long); Skaneateles (skĭnēăt'lŭs) (15 mi. long; Syracuse water supply; at N end is Skaneateles resort village, pop. 2,331); Otisco.

fingerprint, an impression of the inside of the end of a finger or thumb, used for identification because the arrangement of lines is thought to be unique with each person. First practical classifications of fingerprints were those of Sir Francis Galton and Juan Vucetitch in 1891.

Fini, Tommaso di Cristoforo: see MASOLINO DA PANICALE.

Finiguerra, Maso or **Tommaso** (mä'zō, tômmä'zō fēnēgwĕr'rä), 1426–64, Florentine goldsmith and engraver, who probably introduced copperplate engraving process into Italy.

Finistère (fēnēstâr'), department (2,714 sq. mi.; pop. 724,735), NW France, at the tip of Brittany; cap. Quimper.

Finisterre, Cape, rocky promontory, extreme NW Spain, on Atlantic. Here English navy twice defeated French (1747, 1805).

Fink, Albert, 1827–97, American engineer, b. Germany. Designed a truss bridge known by his name. After Civil War he helped regulate Southern railway freight rates.

Fink, Mike, 1770?–1822, American frontier hero, river boatman. A notable shot and fighter, he is said to have ended by shooting one companion and being shot by another.

Finland, Finnish *Suomi,* republic (117,970 sq.

mi., with water surface 130,160 sq. mi.; pop. 4,076,624), N Europe; cap. Helsinki. Bounded in W and S by the Gulf of Bothnia and Gulf of Finland (branches of Baltic Sea); in NW by Sweden and Norway; in N and E by USSR. Central and S Finland is covered by thousands of interconnected lakes. N section (a part of LAPLAND) rises to 2,000–3,000 ft. Half of population is agr., although only 7% of land is arable. Forests cover c.70% of area; timber and timber products form chief exports. Major part of economic life is carried on by cooperatives. Most Finns are Lutherans. There is a small Swedish-speaking minority. Conquered and Christianized by Sweden (12th cent.), Finland was made a grand duchy (16th cent.), and was ceded by Sweden to Russia in 1809. With its own parliamentary constitution, Finland enjoyed semi-independence as Russian grand duchy, though Russian rule was tightened after 1890. Full independence was proclaimed in 1917. Communists were defeated in civil war by Marshal MANNERHEIM; republic was established 1919. Land reforms made 90% of farmers independent. After outbreak of World War II, Russia demanded demilitarization of Finnish fortifications facing Leningrad (the Mannerheim Line) and cession of military bases. Finland refused, and Russian troops invaded Finland (Nov., 1939). Despite heroic and, at first, successful resistance, Russia won the war and by the peace treaty of March, 1940, obtained part of Karelian Isthmus, Vyborg, and other border sections. To recover its territories, Finland joined in the German attack on Russia (1941). Forced to capitulate in Sept., 1944, it kept its promise to expel German troops. N Finland suffered much in resulting German-Finnish warfare. Peace treaty between Finland and principal Allies (except U.S., which had not been at war with Finland) was signed at Paris in 1947. In addition to territories ceded in 1940, Finland ceded Petsamo and leased Porkkala area to USSR. Democratic government continued under Pres. Juho K. Paasikivi (elected 1946), despite recurrent tension with Communist party and USSR. Finland was the only country to honor its debts to U.S. after World War I.

Finlay, Carlos Juan, or **Charles John Finlay,** 1833–1915, Cuban physician of Scotch and French blood. In 1881 he suggested that yellow fever is carried by the mosquito (he specified genus *Stegomyia* as carrier in 1882). Reed Commission of 1900 undertook experiments which proved his theories.

Finlay, river of N B.C., Canada, rising in Stikine Mts. and flowing 210 mi. SE to join Parsnip R. at Finlay Forks and form chief tributary of the Peace.

Finnish language, one of the Finno-Ugric languages. See LANGUAGE (table).

Finn mac Cumhail, Fionn mac Cumhail, or **Finn MacCool** (all: fĭn' mŭkōōl'), a central hero in the Irish legend of OSSIAN and the original of Macpherson's Fingal. Leader of corps of professional fighters, the Fenians, in 3d cent.

Finnmark (fĭn'märk), county (18,799 sq. mi.; pop. 58,790), N Norway, forming northernmost part of Scandinavian peninsula; cap. Vadso. NORTH CAPE is on one of numerous islands off coast. A plateau rising to barren glaciated mountains, Finnmark is largest and least populated county of Norway. Fishing, reindeer raising (mainly by Lapps) are main sources of livelihood.

Finno-Ugric languages: see LANGUAGE (table).

finochio: see FENNEL.

Finsbury, metropolitan borough (pop. 35,347), N London, England. Site of Bunhill Fields (Bunyan, Blake, Defoe, and Isaac Watts buried here), John Wesley's chapel and house, Sadler's Wells Theatre (home of English ballet), and mint of Bank of England.

Finsen, Niels Ryberg (nēls rü'bĕr fīn'sŭn), 1860–1904, Danish physician. Won 1903 Nobel Prize in Physiology and Medicine for method of treating certain diseases by light-ray therapy.

Finsteraarhorn (fĭn"stŭrär'hôrn"), peak 14,032 ft. high, Switzerland; highest of the Bernese Alps.

Fiorenzo di Lorenzo (fyōrän'tsō dē lōrän'tsō), b. c.1440, d. after 1521, Italian painter, b. Perugia. May have been master of Perugino.

fir, tall, coniferous evergreen tree (*Abies*), widely distributed. North American kinds include BALSAM FIR, silver fir, and red and white firs.

Firbank, (Arthur Annesley) Ronald, 1886–1926, English writer. His mannered short novels highly esteemed by some critics.

Firdausi (fŭrdou'sē) (Abul Kasim Mansur), c.940–1020, Persian poet, author of *Shah Namah* (great Persian epic, which set standard for Persian poetry).

fire. For nature of fire, see COMBUSTION and FLAME. There is no record of any human community without use of fire, an exclusively human property. Ideas of indispensability and mysterious force have made fire a sacred object (in Zoroastrianism and other sun-worshiping religions it is a god). In Greece, fire in colony was kindled from that of mother city as tie between them. In Rome, cult of Vesta, goddess of hearth, was strong. Story of Prometheus, the fire bringer, is a great Greek myth. Greek philosophers regarded fire as one of the four elements.

fire apparatus, devices to combat fire or escape from it. Fire-fighting apparatus is designed to remove one or more of the conditions essential to burning: fuel, oxygen, and heat. For ordinary combustible materials (wood, paper, cloth), water is commonly used, serving to cool burning substance and help exclude oxygen. Since water spreads fires of liquid (e.g., gasoline, alcohol, oil, paint) and electrical types, they require chemicals. Soda and acid mixture is commonly used in metal extinguishers indoors. Addition of chemical detergents to water gives it greater penetrating power and this mixture is used for both forest fires and indoor fires (liquid, electrical, or ordinary). Foam-type extinguishers emit carbon dioxide foam from a cylindrical container. Vapor-type extinguishers include those of liquid carbon tetra-chloride, which forms heavy vapor shutting off oxygen; and liquid carbon dioxide under pressure, which flakes upon release, vaporizes, and forms layer of gas over fire. Nu-

merous chemicals are used in dry form. Sprinkler systems, from which excessive heat automatically releases water, are employed in many buildings. Motorized equipment includes pumping engines, hook-and-ladder trucks, searchlight apparatus, rescue wagons, smoke ejectors, water towers, chemical apparatus, and salvage weapons. Fireboats are used at sea and on water fronts.

firebrick, heat-resistant brick used in construction of kilns, furnaces, ovens, and fireplaces, especially in metalworking industries. Firebrick should not fuse below 1600° C. and should resist chemical decomposition. Its composition varies according to intended use.

fire clay, a clay high in percentage of silica and alumina, and offering great resistance to heat. Used in making firebrick and metal-working utensils such. as crucibles and retorts.

firedamp: see DAMP.

fire-eaters, in U.S. history, term applied by Northerners to Southern proslavery extremists before Civil War. Led by R. B. Rhett and W. L. Yancey, they urged secession as early as 1850.

fire extinguisher: see FIRE APPARATUS.

firefly, luminescent carnivorous beetle (often called lightning bug) of family Lampyridae, more numerous in tropical than in temperate regions. Light organs on abdomen are several layers of small cells acting as reflectors and a lower layer of luminescent or photogenic cells, all permeated by nerves and by air tubes permitting oxidizing of luciferin in presence of enzyme called luciferase. Color of light (yellow, greenish, bluish, or reddish) varies with species, as do intensity and intervals between flashes. Light believed to be related to attraction between sexes. Males, females, larvae, and eggs of some forms emit light.

Fire Island, SE N.Y., c.30 mi. long, off S shore of Long Isl., between Great South Bay and the Atlantic. Has several resorts and a lighthouse (1858). Ferries from Bay Shore and Babylon.

fire lands: see WESTERN RESERVE.

Firenze, Italy: see FLORENCE.

fireproofing, method of making combustible materials resistant to fire. Usually it is a treatment with solution or coating which merely retards ignition. Wood can be impregnated with ammonium phosphate solution; paints can be made fire-retardant by using certain pigments (antimony oxide and calcium carbonate) or chlorinated resins, chlorinated oils, chlorinated paraffins. Asbestos and cement are mixed to make fireproof board. Fireproof doors are made of steel or of wood pressed between metal covering sheets; sometimes they are closed by automatic devices to check spread of fire. Hollow clay tile, brickwork, gypsum, plaster, and concrete are fire-resistant building construction materials. Steel fails rapidly above 1000° F. and must be protected when used in construction; very heavy slow-burning timber is sometimes used. Textiles are made flameproof by being dipped in or brushed with certain chemical solutions. Asbestos, which is noncombustible and a nonconductor of heat, is used for insulation, roofing, and many other purposes and the fibers can be woven into flexible cloth used in many products.

Firestone, Harvey Samuel, 1868–1938, American manufacturer of rubber products.

fireworks: see PYROTECHNICS.

Firkins, Oscar W., 1864–1932, American critic, a professor at the Univ. of Minnesota.

first aid. The immediate treatment of a patient in case of emergency while awaiting the arrival of a physician is often a means of saving life and also may result in a better and more rapid recovery. Prevention of further injury is important. Essential knowledge includes that of the proper bandage for a wound; that of the treatment of bleeding, fracture, sprain, dislocation, fainting, bites and stings, burns and scalds, poisoning (in all such cases call doctor), sunstroke, and heat exhaustion; and that of the method of artificial respiration for drowning and asphyxia. See also Red Cross literature.

Asphyxia. Symptoms: blue color; gasping; unconsciousness. Treatment: remove cause, e.g., a foreign body or gas; use artificial respiration.

Bites. Symptoms: wound. Treatment: bandage part on side towards heart. Use antivenin for snake bite. Cauterize with nitric acid for bite of rabid dog and follow with vaccination.

Bleeding. Symptoms: external wound; pallor; weakness if internal. Treatment: local pressure; temporary tourniquet for severe arterial bleeding.

Burns. Symptoms: redness; blistering; charring. Treatment: coat with oily material. If from acid, first use baking soda. If from alkali, first use vinegar. Caution: treat for shock.

Dislocation. Symptoms: pain; swelling; deformity of the joint. Treatment: rest; cold or hot wet applications. Caution: do not move.

Drowning. Treatment: artificial respiration. Caution: patient should be on stomach, with head low and mouth and nose unobstructed.

Fainting. Symptoms: pallor; cold; rapid pulse. Treatment: elevate legs. When conscious, give stimulants.

Foreign body in eye. Symptoms: pain; redness; tears. Treatment: wash out with clean water; remove with clean cloth. Caution: do not touch cornea, the eyeball covering over pupil and iris.

Fracture. Symptoms: pain; deformity of bone. Treatment: splint the whole limb. Caution: do not move until splint is in place. Treat for shock.

Heat exhaustion. Symptoms: pale, clammy skin; weakness; subnormal temperature. Treatment: rest; stimulants. Caution: no cold application to skin.

Poisoning. Symptoms: corrosive stain around mouth from irritants; depression from narcotics. Treatment: emetic; soothing liquids such as eggs, milk, oils.

Shock. Symptoms: pallor; cold; weak breathing; weak pulse. Treatment: head low; warmth; stimulants; treat cause of shock. Caution: do not move; avoid contact if electric shock.

Sprain. Symptoms: pain; swelling. Treatment: rest, cold wet applications.

Sunstroke. Symptoms: headache; unconsciousness; fever; red, dry, hot skin. Treatment: rest; cold applications to skin; cool drinks. Caution: no stimulants.

Wound. Treatment: remove foreign body; apply clean dressing and bandage. Caution: treat for bleeding and shock.

firth or **frith,** name applied to an estuary in Scotland. For Firth of Clyde, see CLYDE.

Firuzabad (firōō′zŭbäd″), ruined city, S Iran, S of Shiraz. Palace built by Artaxerxes.

Fischart, Johann (yōhän′ fĭ′shärt), c.1545–c.1590, German satirist. Wrote an imitation of Rabelais, *Geschichtklitterung* (1575), and religious satires.

Fischer, Emil (ā′mēl fĭ′shŭr), 1852–1919, German organic chemist. Won 1902 Nobel Prize for work on structure and synthesis of sugars, purines, and purine base derivatives, e.g., caffeine.

Fischer, Hans (häns), 1881–1945, German organic chemist. Won 1930 Nobel Prize for studies of chlorophyll and synthesis of hemin (salt of a constituent of hemoglobin).

Fischer von Erlach, Johann Bernhard (yō′hän bĕrn′härt fĭ′shŭr fŭn ĕr′läkh), c.1656–1723, Austrian architect. His baroque buildings, notably the Karlskirche and Schönbrunn palace, give a definite stamp to Vienna.

Fish, Hamilton, 1808–93, American statesman. U.S. Representative from N.Y. (1843–45); U.S. Senator (1851–57). U.S. Secretary of State (1869–77); one of ablest to hold that office. Greatest achievement was bringing about treaty of Washington (see WASHINGTON, TREATY OF), accomplished amid great difficulties. Settled VIRGINIUS affair. Long chairman of board of trustees of Columbia Col. His son, **Hamilton Fish,** 1849–1936, was long a Republican leader in N.Y. His son, **Hamilton Fish,** 1888–, was a U.S. Representative from N.Y. and isolationist leader.

fish, aquatic gill-breathing vertebrate animal with fins, skin with mucous glands and usually scales or plates, and no distinct neck. Lamprey and hagfish (cyclostomes) are primitive, elongated creatures without paired fins, attaching themselves by suctorial mouths to larger fish on whose tissues they feed. Cartilaginous fish (including shark and ray) are more highly developed. Highest in scale are bony fish (those with true bone in skeleton), which includes most fresh-water and marine species. Whale shark (said to reach 50 ft. length) is largest living fish; smallest is goby (c.⅜ in. long) of Philippines. Fish move by contracting body muscles, moving fins, and expelling water through gill slits(giving thrust). They eat plankton, aquatic animals, plants, and refuse. See also CLIMBING PERCH; ELECTRIC FISH; FIN; FLYING FISH; GILL.

Fisher, Dorothy Canfield, 1879–, American novelist, chiefly of Vermont. Among her works are *The Bent Twig* (1915), *The Brimming Cup* (1916), *The Deepening Stream* (1930), *Seasoned Timber* (1939), and children's books.

Fisher, Geoffrey Francis, 1887–, archbishop of Canterbury after 1945, an educator for 21 years, bishop of Chester (1932–39), of London (1939–45).

Fisher, John (Saint John Fisher), 1459–1535, English cardinal, a very learned man. Opposed divorce of Henry VIII and Katharine of Aragon, and was imprisoned (1534). Pope Paul III in defiance made Fisher a cardinal (1534). Bishop Fisher was beheaded. Canonized by Roman Church 1935. Feast: June 22.

fisher, large species of marten (genus *Martes*) of N U.S. and Canada. It is over 3 ft. long and the beautiful fur is brown shading to black. It hunts other mammals and robs traps by night. Also called pekan, black cat, and Pennant's marten.

Fisher, Fort, Confederate outpost on peninsula between the Atlantic and Cape Fear R., defending port of Wilmington, N.C., in Civil War. Taken by Adm. D. D. Porter and Gen. A. T. Terry on Jan. 15, 1865.

fisheries. From earliest times and almost universally fisheries have had industrial and commercial importance. Largest grounds are in N Atlantic off Labrador and Newfoundland, yielding cod, herring, mackerel, haddock, and bluefish. Pacific fisheries of Japan, sardine fisheries of Baltic and North Sea, and inland fisheries of Russia are among largest. Fishing on high seas is subject to international agreements. Treaties covering rights of Americans to fish on entire Atlantic coast date from Treaty of Paris (1783); final agreement was made 1910 by North Atlantic Coast Fisheries Arbitration at The Hague. In 1882 Great Britain, Germany, France, Denmark, and Belgium signed North Sea Fisheries Convention, and other pacts in 1901 and 1904, ending lawlessness in that area. Pacific has been subject of many controversies, e.g., Japanese right to fish in Siberian waters, and celebrated BERING SEA FUR-SEAL CONTROVERSY.

Fishers Island, SE N.Y., c.8 mi. long, off NE tip of Long Isl. and SE of New London, Conn. Summer-resort and residential area, with Long Isl. coast guard hq. Discussions regarding island's annexation to Conn. held in the 1940s.

fish hawk: see OSPREY.

Fishkill Landing: see BEACON, N.Y.

Fisk, James, 1834–72, American financial buccaneer. Manipulation of Erie RR stock by him and Jay Gould wrecked the road. Fisk had a part in BLACK FRIDAY scandal.

Fiske, Bradley Allen (fĭsk), 1854–1942, American naval officer and inventor. Aide for naval operations (1913–17). Invented electric range-finder and other instruments for shipboard use.

Fiske, John, 1842–1901, American philosopher and historian; b. Edmund Fisk Green. In early lectures and books he thought to reconcile orthodox belief with science. Later he lectured and wrote many popular books on American history of years 1000–1865.

Fiske, Minnie Maddern, 1865–1932, American actress, long a leading figure in the theater. On stage at three, she starred at 15. A great interpreter of intellectual drama, she introduced Ibsen to U.S. Also won fame as Becky Sharp, Tess of the D'Urbervilles. Did famous revival of Sheridan's *Rivals*.

Fisk University, at Nashville, Tenn.; Negro; nonsectarian; coed.; opened 1866, chartered 1867 by Congregationalists (American Missionary Assn.), Western Freedmen's Aid Commission of Cincinnati, aided by C. B. Fisk. Fisk Jubilee Singers have toured U.S. and Europe.

Fitch, (William) Clyde, 1865–1909, American playwright. His plays are psychological studies (e.g., *The Girl with The Green Eyes,* 1902; *The Truth,* 1907; and *The City,* 1909), and historical romances (e.g., *Beau Brummel,* 1890).

Fitch, John, 1743–98, American inventor, believed to be first to invent American steamboat. Unable to commercialize his invention and robbed of recognition, he committed suicide.

Fitchburg, city (pop. 42,691), N Mass., N of Worcester; settled c.1730. Mfg. of paper, metal products, electrical machinery, tools, and textiles.

Fitzgerald, Irish noble family. **Maurice Fitzgerald,** d. 1176, Anglo-Norman invader of Ireland, aided Dermot McMurrough and acquired vast Irish landholdings. From his sons descend the two branches of the Fitzgeralds, the earls of Kildare and the earls of Desmond. **Thomas Fitzgerald, 10th earl of Kildare,** 1513–37, rebelled against the pro-English Ormondes in 1534 and was hanged with five of his uncles. To avenge his death **Gerald Fitzgerald, 15th earl of Desmond,** d. 1583, made allies of his relatives in Kildare. Was defeated in life-long fight against pro-English Butlers of Ormonde. **James Fitzgerald, 20th earl of Kildare** and **1st duke of Leinster,** 1722–73, defeated attempts to divert surplus Irish revenues to the Crown. His son, **Lord Edward Fitzgerald,** 1763–98, Irish patriot, fought (1779–81) in American Revolution in British army from which he was later expelled for republicanism. Joined United Irishmen in French-aided rebellion and was captured (1798) by the English.

FitzGerald, Edward, 1809–83, English poet, adapter of the Persian *Rubáiyát* of Omar Khayyam in three well-known English versions (1859, 1868, 1872).

Fitzgerald, F(rancis) Scott (Key), 1896–1940, American novelist. Pictured the jazz age in *This Side of Paradise* (1920), *All the Sad Young Men* (short stories, 1926), *The Great Gatsby* (1925), and *Tender Is the Night* (1934).

Fitzgerald, Gerald, earl of Desmond; James and **Thomas, earls of Kildare;** and **Maurice:** see FITZGERALD, family.

Fitzgerald, city (pop. 8,130), S central Ga., SSE of Macon; founded 1895 by Union veterans. Processing and shipping center for farm area. Jefferson Davis was taken prisoner by Union troops near here in 1865.

Fitzgibbon, John: see CLARE, JOHN FITZGIBBON, 1ST EARL OF.

Fitzherbert, Maria Anne, 1756–1837, wife (1785–95) of George IV. The marriage, illegal under English law, was ignored when the then prince of Wales married Caroline of Brunswick.

Fitzmaurice, Henry Charles Petty: see LANSDOWNE, HENRY CHARLES PETTY, 5TH MARQUESS OF.

Fitzmaurice, William Petty: see SHELBURNE, WILLIAM PETTY FITZMAURICE, 2D EARL OF.

Fitzpatrick, Thomas, c.1799–1854, American trapper, fur trader, and guide, one of greatest of MOUNTAIN MEN, b. Ireland.

Fitzsimmons, Robert, 1862–1917, British boxer. Won heavyweight championship 1897 by defeating James J. Corbett, lost title 1899 to James J. Jeffries.

Fiume (fyōō'mä), Serbo-Croatian *Rijekav,* city (pop. 72,120), Croatia, NW Yugoslavia; Adriatic seaport. Chief port of Hungary until World War I. Contested by Italy and Yugoslavia after 1918, it was seized by Italian free corps under D'ANNUNZIO 1919; made a free state by Treaty of Rapallo of 1920; occupied by Italy 1922. Treaty of Rome (1924) gave Yugoslavia the suburb of Susak, which became its leading port. Fiume was occupied by Yugoslavs 1945, formally ceded by Italy 1947.

Five Civilized Tribes, inclusive term for portions of Cherokee, Chickasaw, Choctaw, Creek, and Seminole tribes settled in E Okla. Were officially recognized as domestic dependent nations, with constitutional governments modeled on those of American states. This status was lost after Civil War because of support rendered to Confederacy.

Five Forks, crossroads near Dinwiddie Courthouse, SW of Petersburg, Va., scene of last important battle of Civil War, April 1, 1865; a Union victory.

Five Nations: see IROQUOIS CONFEDERACY.

Five-Year Plan, Rus. *Pyatiletka,* program adopted 1928 with primary objective of industrializing USSR. Subsequent five-year plans became standard feature of Soviet economic planning (see UNION OF SOVIET SOCIALIST REPUBLICS).

flag. Flags and standards—either a piece of cloth or figure on spear—have been used at least since early Egyptian times. Biblical references to them are many. Early Greeks and Romans used standards. Later Romans used vexillum, square flag on crosspiece suspended from end of a spear. Constantine adopted labarum bearing Christian symbol. Early flags usually had religious significance. In medieval times many flags were used. The Dannebrog of Denmark, red ensign, swallowtailed, bearing a white cross, is no doubt oldest existing flag. An early French flag was oriflamme of abbey of St. Denis. It was replaced by Bourbon white flag sprinkled with fleurs-de-lis, succeeded in turn by the tricolor at time of the Revolution. British flag (Union Jack) is formed by crosses of St. George, St. Andrew, and St. Patrick, national saints, respectively, of England, Scotland, and Ireland. On Jan. 2, 1776, first flag of U.S. was raised by George Washington at Cambridge, Mass. On June 14, 1777, Congress delineated general form of present U.S. flag. This was revised in 1818 to provide that 13 alternate red and white stripes, denoting original 13 colonies, remain fixed and a white star be added to the blue union for each state at its admission to the Union. In armies and navies of the world, flags are used for signaling. Special codes govern display of flags—e.g., flag at half-mast denotes mourning.

Flag Day, anniversary of adoption of American flag in 1777. In 1895, June 14 was set in U.S. as Flag Day. It is not a legal holiday.

flagellants (flă'jûlŭnts, flŭjĕ'lŭnts), groups of Christians who practiced public flagellation as a penance. Appeared as a movement in 12th cent. in N Italy. It was put down by the church, but there were later occasional flare-ups (e.g., at time of Black Death, 1348–49). In 1349 Pope Clement VI prohibited the practice. Most important heretical sects were the Bianchi of Italy and France (1399) and a group led by Karl Schmid or Schmidt in Thuringia (1414). There was a short-lived rebirth of practice within the Church after the Reformation. In Spanish America flagellant orders persisted; in New Mexico the Penitentes still practice secret rites.

flageolet: see WIND INSTRUMENTS.

Flagg, Ernest, 1857–1947, American architect. In 1908 built Singer Building in New York which marked a revolutionary height (612 ft.).

Flagg, James Montgomery, 1877–, American painter and magazine illustrator. Made posters as official artist for New York state during World War I.

Flagler, Henry Morrison, 1830–1913, American capitalist. Early associate of John D. Rockefeller. His backing of Fla. developments was chiefly responsible for state's growth as winter playground.

Flagstad, Kirsten (fläg'stät), 1895–, Norwegian soprano. First appeared at the Metropolitan Opera, New York, in 1935 in Wagner's *Die Walküre.* She is considered the greatest Wagnerian soprano of her time.

Flagstaff, city (pop. 7,663), N Ariz., near San Francisco Peaks, NE of Prescott, in lumbering, ranching area; founded 1881. Tourist center near pueblo ruins, Mormon L., Sunset Crater, Walnut Canyon. Has Lowell Observatory (1894). Indian powwow in July.

Flaherty, Robert J(oseph) (flā'ûrtē), 1884–1951, American moving-picture producer. His *Nanook of the North* (1922) was the first full-length documentary film. His other films include *Tabu* (1931), *Man of Aran* (1934), and *Louisiana Story* (1949).

Flamand, François: see DUQUESNOY, FRANÇOIS.

flame, result of chemical reaction of a gas heated above kindling temperature with another gas, usually oxygen (see COMBUSTION); heat and light are produced. Luminosity is usually caused by foreign matter; shape of flame is commonly a hollow cone. BUNSEN BURNER increases heat by mixing gas with air before igniting. **Flame test** is used to identify metals. Salt of metal introduced into Bunsen burner flame produces a characteristic color: barium, yellow-green; calcium, reddish-orange; copper, bluish-green; potassium, violet; lithium, crimson; sodium, yellow; strontium, red.

flamingo (flŭmĭng'gō), large, gregarious wading bird. Found in marshes and lagoons of both hemispheres; it has vermilion plumage with black-edged wings. Rare American flamingo nests in Bahamas and other islands. See *ill.,* p. 135.

Flaminian Way, principal Roman road to Cisalpine Gaul, 215 mi. long, built by C. Flaminius (220 B.C.).

Flamininus, Titus Quinctius (tī'tŭs kwĭngk'shŭs flămĭnī'nŭs), c.230–175 B.C., Roman general, known as Liberator of Greece. Defeated Philip V of Macedon at Cynoscephalae (197 B.C.). Crushed Sparta (195) and forced king of Bithynia to give up Hannibal.

Flaminius, Caius (kā'ŭs flŭmĭ'nēŭs), d. 217 B.C., Roman statesman, general, constructor of Circus Flaminius and Flaminian Way.

Flamsteed, John (flăm'stēd), 1646–1719, English astronomer, compiler of noted star catalogue. First astronomer royal.

Flanders, former county in the Low Countries, extending W of Scheldt R. along North Sea; now divided between Belgium (see EAST FLANDERS; WEST FLANDERS) and France. In Belgian Flanders, Flemish is spoken by most inhabitants (Flemings). A county from 862, Flanders soon came under overlordship of France (though later acquisitions in the E were held in fief from the Holy Roman Empire). Direct line of counts died out 1191 and was succeeded by counts of HAINAUT. The cities, notably GHENT, BRUGES, YPRES, and COURTRAI, enjoyed virtual independence. Their cloth industry (which is still important) was the largest in Europe (13th cent.), but intense industrialization brought such modern problems as economic crises and class war. In the chronic struggle between the French kings and the counts of Flanders the lower classes generally sided with the *Clauwaerts* (supporters of the counts), the upper classes with the *Leliaerts* (supporters of the kings). Routed at Bouvines (1214), the *Clauwaerts* triumphed in the BATTLE OF THE SPURS (1302). However, despite the efforts of Jacob and Philip van ARTEVELDE, the French party won out eventually at Roosebeke (1382). In 1384 PHILIP THE BOLD became count of Flanders. Under his successors (see BURGUNDY) Flemish commerce and art reached their flower, but industry declined and local liberties were curtailed. The death of MARY OF BURGUNDY (1482) brought Flanders under Hapsburg rule (for subsequent history until 1797, see NETHERLANDS, AUSTRIAN AND SPANISH). Annexed by France in 1797 and awarded to the Netherlands in 1815, Flanders became part of Belgium in 1830 and was divided into two provinces. It has long been a traditional battleground. In World War II, Battle of Flanders began with German invasion of Low Countries (May 10, 1940) and ended with Allied evacuation at Dunkirk (June 4, 1940).

Flanders, French, region and former province, N France, on North Sea, bordering on Belgium; historic cap. Lille. Rich coal fields; industries. Part of county of Flanders until annexed by France (1662–78). Flemish is still widely spoken.

Flandrau, Charles Macomb (flăn'drō), 1871–1938, American author. Wrote pictures of college life in *Harvard Episodes* (1897), *The Diary of a Freshman* (1901), and *Sophomores Abroad* (1935). His best-known work is a travel book, *Viva Mexico!* (1908).

Flandrin, Jean Hippolyte (zhä' ēpôlēt' flädrē'), 1809–64, French painter, a follower of Ingres. Best known for religious paintings.

Flatbush: see BROOKLYN, New York city borough.

flatfish, fish of order Heterosomata with compressed body and, in adult form, both eyes on same side of head. Larvae are bilaterally symmetrical at first; asymmetry of adult involves skeletal and digestive changes, migration of one eye. Includes flounder, halibut, sole, plaice, turbot.

flat foot, condition of human foot in which entire sole rests on ground. This depression of the arches is caused by distorted alignment of bones forming longitudinal arch, which extends from heel to toes on inner side of foot, and transverse arch extending across foot in metatarsal region. Distortion usually results from muscle weakness and consequent straining and stretching of ligaments.

Flathead, river formed by three forks in NW Mont. Flows S through Flathead L. to Clark Fork. In South Fork is Hungry Horse Dam for power, irrigation, and flood control.

Flathead Indians, tribe of Salishan linguistic stock in Bitterroot river valley, W Mont. in 19th cent. After introduction of the horse, adopted Plains area culture. Suffered heavily in wars with Blackfoot.

Flat River, city (pop. 5,308), E Mo., ESE of Potosi. Lead-mining center.

Flattery, Cape: see JUAN DE FUCA STRAIT.

Flaubert, Gustave (güstäv' flōbĕr'), 1821–80, French novelist. An untiring stylist striving for complete objectivity and exactitude of expression, he produced *Madame Bovary* (1857), *Salammbô* (1862), *Éducation sentimentale* (1869), *The Temptation of St. Anthony* (1874), *Three Tales* (1877; including "A Simple Heart" and "St. Julian the Hospitaler"), and *Bouvard et Pécuchet* (1881), his unfinished satire on the French bourgeois and all his works and thoughts.

Flavian (flā'vēŭn), epithet given to three Roman emperors, Vespasian, Titus, and Domitian.

flax, annual plant (*Linum usitatissimum*), grown for its fiber and seed. A plant domesticated in man's early history, it was chief source of textile fiber, but is now largely replaced by other fibers. Still grown in USSR, in Belgium for fine LINEN, and in U.S. and Argentina for flaxseed, the source of linseed oil. Other flax species are grown in gardens.

Flaxman, John, 1755–1826, English artist, known for memorial sculptures, notably those in Westminster Abbey.

flea, wingless, leaping insect. Mouth parts of the adult can pierce skin and suck blood of mammals and birds. Dog flea and cat flea also attack man. Human flea is abundant in warmer parts of Europe and Asia. Flea parasitic on rodents transmits bubonic PLAGUE. CHIGOE is a flea. See *ill.,* p. 601.

Flecker, James Elroy, 1884–1915, English writer of poetry (e.g., *The Golden Journey to Samarkand,* 1913) and plays (e.g., *Hassan*).

Fleet Prison, former London jail. Rebuilt several times, finally demolished 1845–46. Mainly notable for incarceration of debtors. "Fleet marriages," clandestine and irregular, performed here by debtor clergymen. System abolished under George II.

Fleet Street, center of journalism in London. Named for Fleet R., now a sewer under Farringdon St. Many buildings destroyed in bombings 1940–41.

Flémalle, Master of: see CAMPIN, ROBERT.

Fleming, Sir Alexander, 1881–, Scottish bacteriologist. He shared 1945 Nobel Prize in Physiology and Medicine for work on penicillin, which he discovered. He also discovered lysozyme.

Fleming, Sir John Ambrose, 1849–1945, English electrical engineer, a leader in developing the use in England of electric lighting, telephone, and telegraph. He invented a thermionic valve.

Fleming, Sir Sandford, 1827–1915, Canadian civil engineer, b. Scotland. Appointed chief engineer of Canadian Pacific Railway (1871); surveyed route W from Fort William. Introduced idea of 24-hour-a-day standard time and urged its adoption. Was the chief influence in laying of Pacific cable from Canada to Australia.

Flemington, borough (pop. 3,058), W N.J., NNW of Trenton. Scene of Hauptmann's trial for the kidnaping and murder of Charles A. Lindbergh, Jr., 1935.

Flemish [adjective for Flanders], Germanic language (see LANGUAGE, table), very closely allied to Dutch. The distinction is made on a more or less political basis, the Flemings being the Germanic-speaking people of Belgium (in earlier days, those of Flanders). Dutch and Flemish literature have maintained affinity to the present day, with Flemish authors contributing notably. The great period of Flemish painting (1400–1600) began with the brothers Van Eyck. After the 18th cent. Flemish painting, sculpture, and architecture generally showed decided French influence.

Flensburg (flĕns'boōrk), city (pop. 102,045), Schleswig-Holstein, N Germany; a port on Baltic Sea. Shipbuilding; mfg. of machinery, chemicals, foodstuffs.

Fletcher, Giles, the elder, c.1548–1611, English writer and diplomat. An envoy to Russia in 1588, he published *Of the Russe Common Wealth* (1591), which was suppressed. Also wrote a number of Latin poems. His son, **Phineas Fletcher,** 1582–1650, was a poet whose best-known work is *Purple Island* (1633; an involved, somewhat scientific poem on the human body). His brother, **Giles Fletcher,** the younger, b. 1585 or 1586, d. 1623, was also a poet. His best poem is *Christ's Victory and Triumph* (1610), a baroque devotional work.

Fletcher, John, 1579–1625, prolific English dramatist, frequent collaborator with others. Often composed larger part of plays written with Francis BEAUMONT. With Shakspere wrote *The Two Noble Kinsmen* and *Henry VIII* (1613). Extravagant in plot, facile in poetic style, his own best work includes the comedies *The Woman's Prize* and *Rule a Wife and Have a Wife* (1624) and the tragicomedy *The Island Princess.* In later years collaborated with various other dramatists but most frequently with Philip MASSINGER.

Fletcher, John Gould, 1886–1950, American poet. *Preludes and Symphonies* (1922) typifies imagist verse. Later work (e.g., *XXIV Elegies,* 1935) shows more exacting forms.

Fletcher, Phineas: see FLETCHER, GILES.

Flettner, Peter: see FLÖTNER, PETER.

Fleurus (flûrüs'), town (pop. 6,949), Hainaut prov., Belgium. Scene of Protestant victory in Thirty Years War (1622); of French victory in War of the Grand Alliance (1690); and of a decisive French victory in French Revolutionary Wars (1794).

Fleury, André Hercule de (ädrä' ĕrkül' dù flûrē'), 1653–1743, French cardinal, chief minister to Louis XV. Virtually ruled France, 1726–43. Restored finances, strove for peace, but was unwillingly drawn into wars of Polish and Austrian successions.

Flexner, Abraham, 1866–, American educator. His report (1910) to Carnegie Foundation for the Advancement of Teaching hastened reforms in American medical schools. He was first director of Inst. for Advanced Study at Princeton (1930–39). His brother, **Simon Flexner,** 1863–1946, noted pathologist, was director (1920–35) of Rockefeller Institute.

flicker, large North American woodpecker, the only brown woodpecker. Northern or yellowshafted flicker has many local names (e.g., yellowhammer, high hole). Southern form is similar. In flight the white rump patch is prominent. Red-shafted flicker found in W U.S.

Fliegende Holländer: see FLYING DUTCHMAN.

flight, sustained progress through air by aircraft or animal. Science of flight included in study of aerodynamics, the physics of air (and other gases) in motion. Balloons and airships inflated with lighter-than-air gas stay aloft by ARCHIMEDES' PRINCIPLE. Airplanes, autogiros, helicopters, and gliders sustained by forward motion, their airfoils developing lifting air pressure on under surfaces and reduced air resistance on upper surfaces. Engine-driven craft are pulled or pushed by propellers (air screws) or jets. Mechanical flight was first suggested by natural flight of birds. The leading edge of the slightly concave wings of birds is rather sharp and feathers are small and close-fitting, so streamlined surface meets the air. On trailing edge of each wing the interlocking of larger feathers forms surface that simulates action of ailerons of plane. In all of three general types of bird flight—flapping, soaring, gliding—principal flight feathers overlap so that air pressure on underside of wing causes feathers to form airtight surface; on upstroke feathers part enough to allow some air to pass through, thus reducing pressure against which wings must work. Form and size of wings and speed of flight vary; most bird flight ranges from 10 to 60 mi. an hour. See *ill.,* p. 23.

Flinders, Matthew, 1774–1814, English naval captain and hydrographer, noted for his charting and coast surveys of Australia and Tasmania (1795–99, 1801–3). W. M. Flinders Petrie was his grandson.

Flinders Island: see FURNEAUX ISLANDS.

Flinders Petrie, Sir William Matthew: see PETRIE.

Flin Flon (flĭn flŏn), town (pop. 9,899), W Man., Canada, at Sask. border, NNW of The Pas. Important mining and smelting center (copper, zinc, gold, silver, cadmium).

Flint, Timothy, 1780–1840, American author of several works on the West.

Flint, county, Wales: see FLINTSHIRE.

Flint, city (pop. 163,143), S Mich., on Flint R. and NW of Detroit; settled 1819 as fur-trad-

Flint 428 Florida

ing post. One of state's chief automobile centers with mfg. of metal products, cement blocks, and furniture. Has General Motors Inst. of Technology.

Flint, municipal borough (pop. 14,257), Flintshire, Wales. Castle was scene of Richard II's submission to Bolingbroke in 1399.

Flint, river rising S of Atlanta, Ga., and winding 330 mi. generally S, past Albany (head of navigation), to join Chattahoochee R. and form Apalachicola R. in SW corner of Ga. at Fla. line. Power dams.

flint, variety of QUARTZ often found in chalk and limestone. Since it was easy to chip, primitive man made tools and weapons of flint. It was long used with steel for fire making and to discharge flintlock guns.

Flintshire or **Flint,** county (256 sq. mi.; pop. 145,108), NE Wales; co. town Mold. Uplands devoted to pasturage; farming in fertile valleys. Has rich coal, metal, clay, and limestone deposits, and mfg. of pottery, chemicals, and artificial silk.

Flodden, hill, Northumberland, England; scene of battle of Flodden Field (1513) where English defeated Scots under James IV, who was killed. Battle is described in Scott's *Marmion.*

Flood, in the Bible: see DELUGE.

flood plain, level land along lower course of large river formed by deposition of sediment during floods. Often extensive, extremely fertile.

Flor, Roger de, d. c.1306, German soldier of fortune, b. Italy. Led band of Spanish adventurers (Catalan company) in service of Byzantium; defeated Turks but oppressed native population and was assassinated. His followers set up duchy of Athens (1311).

Flora [from Latin,= flower], Roman goddess of flowers. Her temple was near the Circus Maximus.

Flora, city (pop. 5,255), SE Ill., ENE of Centralia. Center of oil and agr. area with mfg. of shoes.

Floral Park, residential village (pop. 14,582), SE N.Y., on W Long Isl. near Mineola.

Florence, Ital. *Firenze,* city (pop. 271,975; with suburbs 321,176), cap. of Tuscany, central Italy, on Arno R. Of Roman origin, it rose to prominence after 1200, when it gained autonomy and grew into a commercial and cultural center of world importance. Despite civil strife between GUELPHS AND GHIBELLINES—later between Black and White Guelphs—Florence waged successful warfare against rival cities, notably PISA, which it absorbed within its growing territories. The silk, wool, and jewelry industries brought enormous wealth. In the 15th cent. the MEDICI family of merchants and bankers took the power, but the republican constitution was ostensibly retained. Twice exiled (1494–1512, 1527–30), the Medici were both times restored through foreign intervention; in the first of these revolutions SAVONAROLA and MACHIAVELLI played leading parts. In 1569 Cosimo I de' Medici was made grand duke of Tuscany (for later history, see TUSCANY). Florence was the cap. of Italy 1865–70. The cradle and chief jewel of the Italian RENAISSANCE, Florence saw an enormous outburst of creativeness in the 14th–16th

cent.: Dante, Boccaccio, Fra Angelico, Brunelleschi, Donatello, Da Vinci, Raphael, Michelangelo, and Cellini are among the best-known of the many geniuses who were born or worked in Florence. Probably the world's greatest repository of art, Florence abounds in famous churches, palaces, museums, and monuments. Among these are the Gothic Cathedral of Santa Maria del Fiore; the near-by baptistery, with doors by Ghiberti; the churches of Santa Croce, Santa Maria Novella, and San Lorenzo; the Palazzo della Signoria (city hall) and the near-by Loggia; the UFFIZI, Strozzi, and Pitti palaces; and the BARGELLO. Each of these contains works by the most famous Renaissance artists. Many historic buildings suffered bomb hits in World War II; all bridges except the famous Ponte Vecchio were blown up.

Florence. 1 City (pop. 23,879), NW Ala., on Tennessee R. near MUSCLE SHOALS and Wilson Dam (provides power); laid out 1818. Region yields minerals, cotton. Mfg. of textiles, heaters; lumber milling; meat packing. Large aluminum plant near by (1941). **2** Resort town (pop. 1,776), S Ariz., on Gila R. and SE of Phoenix near Coolidge Dam (irrigation). **3** City (pop. 22,513), E central S.C., ENE of Columbia; founded in 1850s. Rail focus and mfg. (metal products, fertilizer) and trade center for farm, tobacco, and livestock area. Important point during Civil War. Has national cemetery.

Florence, Council of: see FERRARA-FLORENCE, COUNCIL OF.

Flores, Indonesia: see SUNDA ISLANDS.

Florey, Sir Howard Walter, 1898–, Australian pathologist. He shared 1945 Nobel Prize in Physiology and Medicine for work in penicillin.

Florianópolis (flô″rēŭnä′pŭlĭs), city (pop. 49,-290); cap. and chief port of Santa Catarina state, SE Brazil, on Santa Catarina Isl.; founded 1700.

Florida, state (58,560 sq. mi.; pop. 2,771,305), extreme SE U.S., admitted 1845 as 27th state (slaveholding); cap. TALLAHASSEE. Other cities are TAMPA, JACKSONVILLE, MIAMI, SAINT PETERSBURG. Low peninsula, mostly in coastal plain, washed on E by the Atlantic and W by Gulf of Mexico. Rolling hills in NW, EVERGLADES in S; interior has numerous lakes (e.g., OKEECHOBEE) and extensive swamps. Climate mainly subtropical. State's largest industry is tourism, but agr. (esp. citrus, truck, sugar cane), cattle raising, lumbering (pine, cypress), fishing (esp. shrimp, sponges), mining (e.g., phosphates), food processing, naval stores are important. Region explored by PONCE DE LEÓN 1513; French settlements under René de LAUDONNIÈRE failed (1562–66); settlement begun by Spanish at SAINT AUGUSTINE (1565), oldest city in U.S. Spain ceded colony to England in 1763; returned to Spain 1783 (see WEST FLORIDA CONTROVERSY). Sold to U.S. in 1819. Became a territory (with present boundaries) in 1822. Wars with SEMINOLE INDIANS impeded development. Fla. joined Confederacy 1861, but suffered little in Civil War and Reconstruction. Drainage of the Everglades, growth of railroads and hotels, and land booms have aided development in 20th cent. Fla. prospered in World War II from army, navy, air force installations.

Florida, village, NE central Mo., SW of Hannibal. Birthplace of Mark Twain.

Florida, ship: see CONFEDERATE CRUISERS.

Florida, Straits of, SE and S of Fla., between Florida Keys and Cuba. Here the Gulf Stream passes from Gulf of Mexico to the Atlantic.

Florida, University of, at Gainesville; land-grant and state supported, mainly for men; opened 1853 as seminary at Ocala, moved 1906 after union of state schools. The General Col. (jr.; 1935) pioneered in modern curriculum and guidance plans. Has Inter-American Inst.

Florida Agricultural and Mechanical College, at Tallahassee; Negro, land-grant and state supported; coed.; 1887.

Floridablanca, José Moñino, conde de (hōsā' mōnyē'nō kōn'dä dä flōrē'dhäbläng'kä), 1728–1808, Spanish statesman. As ambassador to Rome he secured suppression of Society of Jesus (1773). As premier (1777–92) he consolidated absolutism, pushed program of economic reform, promoted peace, but was drawn into war with England in American Revolution.

Florida Keys, chain (c.150 mi. long) of small i r a d m a d l a n e s t o n e i s l a n d s o r r o c k s, r u n n i n g S tip of Fla. Separated from mainland by Florida Bay and from Cuba by Straits of Florida. Joined to mainland from Key Largo (the largest, c.30 mi. long) by a highway (opened 1944), which also links the islands from here to KEY WEST. Many are habitable and have commercial fisheries and resorts. Devastated by hurricane in Sept. 1935.

Florida Southern College: see LAKELAND.

Florida State University, at Tallahassee; coed.; chartered and opened 1905 as Florida State Col. for Women, renamed 1947.

Florio, John (flō'rēō), 1553?–1625, English author, best remembered for his translation (1603) of the essays of Montaigne.

Florissant, city (pop. 3,737), E Mo., on the Missouri and near St. Louis. Settled 1785 by French, it was later called St. Ferdinand by Spanish. Has Church of St. Ferdinand (1821) and Jesuit St. Stanislaus Seminary (1823, rebuilt 1840–49). Father De Smet was ordained here, 1827.

Flötner or Flettner, Peter (pä'tûr flût'nûr, flĕt'-nûr), c.1485–1546, German medalist and craftsman, a pioneer of German Renaissance.

Flotow, Friedrich von (flō'tō), 1812–83, German composer of operas, of which *Martha* is best known.

flotsam, jetsam, and ligan (flŏt'sŭm, jĕt'sŭm, lī'gŭn), in maritime law, goods lost at sea, distinguished from wreck, goods which come to shore. Flotsam refers to goods floating on surface, jetsam to those thrown overboard and generally partly submerged. Ligan (or lagan) designates goods which go down with a ship, or sunken goods marked with a buoy. The return of such is obligatory; flotsam and jetsam are returned only upon claim by owner. Rules of salvage apply.

flounder, name used for any FLATFISH (except true sole of Europe) or sometimes only for certain members of family Pleuronectidae.

Many are also called flukes. Flesh is delicate. Flattened body has whitish underside and brown or olive, often mottled, upperside. In many species color and pattern are changeable to blend with background. Found chiefly in salt water, but some swim up rivers. Abundant in North America and parts of Europe.

flour, the finely ground meal of grain or of such plants as the potato, cassava, peas, or beans; it is the chief ingredient of bread. Wheat flour predominates in U.S., Canada, W Europe; millet and durra are used in India and China, while rye, buckwheat, rice, corn, and other grains lead in other areas. Wheat flour is separated into grades by milling. Composition depends upon type of wheat and processing; gluten is chief protein, starch the principal carbohydrate.

Flower, George, 1788–1862, pioneer settler of Ill., b. England. With Morris Birkbeck, undertook settlement scheme which led to founding of Albion, Ill.

flower, specialized part of a seed plant containing organs of reproduction. Outermost parts are usually green sepals of CALYX, within which are the often showy, colored petals of the COROLLA. Innermost are the organs of reproduction: the male organs (or stamens) bear powdery pollen, and the female organ (the pistil or pistils) is enlarged at the base to form the ovary containing eggs. Some flowers have both stamens and pistil, others are unisexual. Fruit and seed develop after POLLINATION, which results in fertilization of the egg. See *ill.*, p. 999.

flowering maple: see ABUTILON.

flowering quince, spiny, Asiatic shrub (*Chaenomeles*), with early spring flowers ranging from white to red. Yellowish fruits, similar to related quince, are sometimes used in preserves. *Chaenomeles japonica* is called Japanese quince or japonica.

Floyd, John Buchanan, 1807–63, U.S. Secretary of War (1857–60) and Confederate general. In quarrel over Fort Sumter, and because of irregularities in War Dept., he resigned by request and became secessionist. Equally incompetent in war, he was removed from command after his defeat at Fort Donelson.

fluke, parasitic flatworm of class Trematoda, phylum Platyhelminthes. In parts of Orient, humans may become infested with liver fluke by eating raw fish, by lung fluke from raw crab. Blood flukes are prevalent in Egypt, parts of tropical America; enter body through drinking water or skin of bather. Intestinal flukes attack man and pigs. Liver fluke *Fasciola hepatica* is cause of liver rot, fatal to sheep and other herbivorous animals. See also FLOUNDER.

fluorescence, emission of light of visible color from substance stimulated by light waves or other means. Light is given off only during stimulation. Rock fluorescence known for many years. Sir George G. Stokes named fluorescence and discovered it can be induced by ultraviolet light. Stokes's law states: wave length of fluorescent light is (with few exceptions) greater than that of the exciting radiation. Visible light, infrared, X rays, radio waves, cathode rays, friction, heat, or pressure can all cause fluorescence. Fluorescent lights are long, sealed, glass tubes with electrode at each end; argon and small amount of mercury are inside tube. Inner surface of tube is coated with fluorescent powders; when electric discharge is maintained through mercury vapor, ultraviolet light so produced causes excitation of coating, producing fluorescent light.

fluorine (floo'ūrēn), most active nonmetallic element (symbol = F; see also ELEMENT, table); yellowish, poisonous, corrosive gas. It is a member of HALOGEN series. Its compounds are used in metallurgy, in etching, and also in making insecticides. It does not occur free in nature.

fluorite (floo'ūrīt) or **fluorspar** (floo'ūrspär), a mineral, calcium fluoride, varied in color. Used as a flux in metallurgy; also in preparation of hydrofluoric acid, opal glass, and enamel.

fluoroscope (floo'rŭskōp), device used in medical diagnosis. Bismuth salts are given to patient, who is placed between screen and X-ray source; since X rays cannot penetrate salts, course of bismuth through alimentary canal is seen.

fluorspar: see FLUORITE.

Flushing (flŭ'shĭng), Dutch *Vlissingen*, municipality (pop. 20,217), Zeeland prov., SW Netherlands; a port on S coast of Walcheren isl. Terminus for boats crossing English Channel; oil refineries, shipyards, machinery and metallurgical plants. One of first Dutch towns to rebel against Spain (1572), Flushing has strategic position at mouth of Scheldt R. British took it from French 1809, from Germans 1944.

Flushing: see QUEENS, New York city borough.

flute: see WIND INSTRUMENTS.

Fly, largest river of New Guinea, 650 mi. long; rises in NE, flows to Gulf of Papua. Forms part of boundary between Netherlands New Guinea and Territory of Papua.

fly, name for many winged insects; accurately only for certain members of order Diptera, including housefly, gnat, midge, and mosquito. One pair of wings is functional; vestiges of second pair, knobbed threadlike structures called halteres, aid in balancing. Many flies are disease carriers and crop destroyers; some parasitize harmful insects. See *ill.*, p. 601.

flycatcher, name for various members of Old World songbird family, Muscicapidae. For some members of New World tyrant flycatcher family (Tyrannidae), see KINGBIRD; PEEWEE; PHOEBE; SCISSOR-TAILED FLYCATCHER.

flying animals. Only large animal group moving chiefly by FLIGHT are birds and insects. Among mammals only BAT is capable of true flight. See also FLYING FISH; FLYING SQUIRREL; LIZARD.

Flying Dutchman, according to sailors, ominous apparition of a ship seen near Cape of Good Hope. The legend of its blasphemous captain, doomed to sail forever, is used in Wagner's *Der fliegende Holländer*.

flying fish, name for various gliding fish of warm seas, usually traveling in schools. In some only the pectoral or anterior paired fins are enlarged and winglike as in members of genus *Exocoetus,* usually c.1 ft. long, seen in N Atlantic. Others (Catalina flying fish,

Cypselurus, c.18 in. long) have enlarged pelvic or hind paired fins. After swimming rapidly in water, then "taxiing" along surface propelled by tail movements, they rise into air, sometimes to 25 ft.

flying squirrel, name chiefly for certain nocturnal tree squirrels of Asia, North America, and Europe. Using furry skin fold around body which spreads parachute-like, they glide, rather than fly, from heights. Tail is used as rudder. North American tree squirrel (*Glaucomys*) is 9–14 in. long.

flywheel, heavy, metal wheel attached to drive shaft of an engine or other machine; its weight is concentrated at the circumference. It is used to equalize energy exerted and work done, thereby regulating velocity.

Foch, Ferdinand (fĕrdēnä' fôsh'), 1851–1929, marshal of France. In World War I he stopped Germans at the Marne (1914); became chief of French general staff (1917); headed Allied supreme command 1918.

focus, in optics, point of convergence of rays after reflection by mirror or refraction by LENS is real focus. Virtual focus is imaginary point from which rays seem to have diverged after reflection by convex mirror or refraction by diverging lens.

foetus: see FETUS.

fog, cloudlike aggregation of water droplets immediately above land or water. If light, usually called mist. Forms when moisture content of air increases above saturation point (e.g., when cold air is in contact with warm body of water or warm rain) or when air cools below dew point, causing radiation fog (earth at night after losing heat by radiation cools adjacent air), advection fog (warm air flows on cold surface), and upslope fog (ascending air expands, cools).

Fogazzaro, Antonio (äntō'nyō fōgät-tsä'rō), 1842–1911, Italian novelist, author of *Piccolo mondo antico* (1896; Eng. tr., *The Patriot,* 1906).

Foggia (fôd'jä), city (pop. 57,234), Apulia, S Italy. Important communications center and wheat market. Damaged in World War II, when it was a German air base. Has cathedral (12th cent., much restored).

foie gras (fwä grä'), livers of specially fattened geese, a delicacy usually prepared as *pâté de foie gras* (containing wine, truffles, other seasonings) in vicinity of Strasbourg and Toulouse, France.

Foix (fwä), town (pop. 6,026), cap. of Ariège dept., S France, on Ariège R. Counts of Foix rose to great power after 11th cent., acquired BÉARN 13th cent., inherited NAVARRE 1479. Their titles and lands passed by marriage to house of ALBRET 1494. Foix was incorporated into French royal domain 1607.

Fokine, Michel (mēshěl' fōkēn', Rus. fô'kyĭn), 1880–1942, Russian ballet dancer and choreographer; a founder of modern ballet. Helped form Diaghilev's Russian Ballet (Paris, 1909). Among his works are *The Dying Swan* (for Pavlova), *Les Sylphides, Petrouchka, Scheherazade,* and *L'Oiseau de feu.*

fold, in geology, a bend in stratified rocks, which normally are horizontal (see STRATIFICATION). Arches are called anticlines; troughs, synclines. Folds are often formed far below the surface and are exposed by erosion. The top of an anticline may be eroded till only the worn-down stumps remain. The cause of folding is related to compression of the earth's crust involved in mountain building.

Folengo, Teofilo (tāô′fēlō fōlĕng′gō), 1491–1544, Italian burlesque poet, author of *Baldus,* a burlesque on chivalric romance.

Foley, John Henry, 1818–74, Irish sculptor; studied in London. Designed seal of the Confederacy.

Folger, Henry Clay, 1857–1930, American capitalist and collector of Shaksperiana. With help of his life, Emily Jordan Folger, acquired one of the largest collections. Endowed **Folger Shakespeare Library,** Washington, D.C., dedicated 1932.

folk dance, primitive, tribal, or racial form of the DANCE. Term also includes characteristic national dances, country dances, and figure dances in costume to folk tunes. Good examples are the Spanish fandango, Bohemian polka, Hungarian czardas, Irish jig, Highland fling, English morris and maypole dances, and the American Virginia reel.

Folkestone (fōk′stǔn), municipal borough (pop. 45,200), Kent, England, on the Channel; summer resort and seaport. Bombed World War II.

folklore, in its widest extent, body of oral traditions, art, and superstitions of any society. It includes folk dances, folk songs, folk tales, and folk medicine. Its study was originally domain of the antiquarian, but rise of European romanticism and of nationalism made this a serious pursuit. Folk tales have been collected, and folk heroes (e.g., Robin Hood in England, the Cid in Spain, and Paul Bunyan in U.S.) have received much attention. Today anthropologists regard folk tales as imaginative expression by a social group of its desires, attitudes, and cultural values. Almost every country now has a folklore society.

folk school, form of adult education originated in Denmark by Bishop Nikolai GRUNDTVIG in mid-19th cent. Idea was to stimulate intellectual life of young adults of rural Denmark, foster patriotism and religion, and provide agricultural and vocational training. First school estab. 1844. Folk-school idea spread through Europe and even to U.S.

folkways, term coined by William Graham Sumner (c.1907) to define more clearly the patterning of behavior usually denoted as custom. Included traditions, laws, manners, usages, mores, and the like, which make up the culture of a group.

Follen, Charles (Karl Theodor Christian Follen) (fŏ′lǔn), 1796–1840, American educator, b. Germany. Appointed to Harvard faculty in 1825, he taught first course in German offered in America. Later became identified with reform movements. His wife, **Eliza Lee (Cabot) Follen,** 1787–1860, influential as a writer in Unitarian movement, led in antislavery and feminist causes.

Folsom culture, early North American culture known through artifacts first found near Folsom, N.Mex. The findings suggest the presence of man in North America c.10,000 or more years ago.

Fond du Lac (fŏn′ dù lăk″), city (pop. 29,-936), E Wis., at S end of L. Winnebago and SSE of Oshkosh; settled c.1835. Has railroad shops, limestone quarries, and metal products plants (tools, machinery). Resort.

Fonseca, Gulf of (fōnsä′kä), inlet of Pacific, c.50 mi. long and 30 mi. wide, Central America. Harbor shared by Nicaragua, Honduras, and Salvador. Rights for Nicaragua Canal given to U.S. by Nicaragua disputed by other nations.

Fontaine, Pierre François Léonard (fōtĕn′), 1762–1853, French architect, associate of CHARLES PERCIER, with whom he fostered Empire style in France.

Fontainebleau (fōtĕnblō′), town (pop. 13,498), Seine-et-Marne dept., N France, SE of Paris. The vast Forest of Fontainebleau was a favorite hunting ground of French kings. In the magnificent Renaissance palace, built by Francis I, Pope Pius VII was imprisoned (1812–14) and Napoleon I abdicated (1814).

Fontana, Domenico (dōmā′nēkō fōntä′nä), 1543–1607, Italian architect, who played leading part in rebuilding of Rome. Designed Lateran palace and parts of the Vatican; helped finish dome of St. Peter's.

Fontana, Prospero (prō′spärō), 1512–97, Italian painter. Worked mainly in Bologna. His daughter **Lavinia Fontana,** 1552–1614?, was a portrait painter in Bologna and Rome.

Fontane, Theodor (tä′ōdōr fôntä′nù), 1819–98, German author. He is best known for his ballads and for the novels *L'Adultera* (1882), *Irrungen, Wirrungen* (1888; Eng. tr., *Trials and Tribulations*), and *Effi Briest* (1895; Eng. tr., 1913–15).

Fontanne, Lynn (fōntän′), 1887?–, American actress. Acts with her husband Alfred LUNT (e.g., in *The Guardsman, Reunion in Vienna, O Mistress Mine*).

Fonte, Jacopo della: see QUERCIA.

Fontenelle, Bernard le Bovier de (bĕrnär′ lù bōvyä′ dù fōtùnĕl′), 1657–1757, French author. His *Entretiens sur le pluralité des mondes* (1686) is a model of scientific popularization.

Fontenoy (fōn′tùnoi, Fr. fōtùnwä′), village, Hainaut prov., Belgium, SE of Tournai. Here in 1745 French under Maurice de Saxe won celebrated victory over British and allies under duke of Cumberland in War of Austrian Succession.

Fontenoy, village, N central France, near Auxerre. Reputed site of a battle in which Charles II of France and Louis the German checked their brother, Emperor LOTHAR I (841). Battle led to Oath of STRASBOURG and Treaty of VERDUN. Also known as Fontenay, Fontanet, or Fontenailles.

Foochow (fōō′chou′), commercial city (pop. 331,273), cap. Fukien prov., China, on Min R. One of treaty ports opened 1842 at end of Opium War. In mid-19th cent. was China's leading tea-exporting center.

food adulteration, the intentional debasement of quality of foods offered for sale, has been dealt with from consumers' standpoint only since mid-19th cent., when new knowledge made close analysis possible. First British food law passed in purchaser's interest came in 1860; in U.S., Pure Food and Drugs Act of 1906, often amended and later superseded, came only after stormy campaign. Federal and local regulations now govern content, handling, labeling, and advertising of food, drugs, and cosmetics, and certain aspects of importation and interstate traffic.

Food and Agriculture Organization (FAO), agency of UN. Estab. in Oct., 1945; under UN in Dec., 1946. FAO contributes to expanding world economy by bettering rural conditions, improving production and distribution, and raising level of nutrition.

food poisoning, any of a number of illnesses marked by gastrointestinal disturbances and caused by eating food contaminated by poisonous substances. The term "ptomaine poisoning" is now generally replaced because ptomaines (produced by action of decay bacteria on proteins) are not known to cause illness. Substances causing food poisoning include inorganic chemicals; organic substances derived from animals and plants (e.g., certain mushrooms); and bacterial toxins, especially toxins produced by species of *Staphylococcus, Salmonella,* and *Clostridium* (see BOTULISM).

food preservation has been practiced since remotest times; early products of experiment were cheese, butter, wine, bacon, parched grain. Advances came with scientific investigation (notably by Pasteur) of causes of putrefaction. Basic preserving processes include drying, heating (as in CANNING and PASTEURIZATION), refrigeration (both freezing and chilling), exclusion of air, and use of such substances as salt, sugar, vinegar, smoke, alcohol, and saltpeter. Use of certain chemicals is generally limited by legislation.

fool, absurdly irresponsible person, often subject to spells of mirth or melancholy. Some fools are benevolent, others cunningly malevolent. In all countries from ancient times to 18th cent., dwarfs, cripples, and idiots provided amusement at court. Court fools were not necessarily deformed or mentally deficient. Keen, witty men often obtained powerful patronage as fools. Clowns and jesters were common in Elizabethan drama.

foot, organ in most higher vertebrates, used chiefly for support and locomotion. In man seven bones form heel; five parallel metatarsals form long arch and their lower ends form transverse arch. Each toe has three phalanges except great toe, which has two. See also FLAT FOOT. See *ill.,* p. 763.

foot and mouth disease or **hoof and mouth disease,** communicable virus disease of cattle and other cloven-footed animals. It causes great losses to cattle industry and is more prevalent in Europe and South America than in U.S. It is characterized by eruption of blisters on mucous membranes, especially of mouth, feet, and udder. Control is by slaughter and deep burial of infected animals, disinfection of area occupied, and strict quarantine.

football, in U.S., game played by two opposing teams of 11 men on level field 100 by 53⅓ yd. Game originally developed from Greek *harpaston.* American football similar to rugby, dating from 1823 in England. Rutgers and Princeton played (1869) first intercollegiate football game in America at New Brunswick, N.J. Organized professional football in U.S. dates from 1920.

Foote, Andrew Hull, 1806–63, American naval officer. In Civil War he gave brilliant support to Union army in victories at Fort Henry, Fort Donelson, and Island No. 10, and was made rear admiral but had to retire.

Foote, Arthur William, 1853–1937, American organist, composer, and teacher. His compositions include sacred choruses, chamber music, and choral settings of Longfellow's poems.

Foote, Henry Stuart, 1804–80, U.S. Senator (1847–52), governor of Miss. (1852–54). Fought states' rights doctrines in the Senate and later opposed Jefferson Davis in Confederate congress; supported Republicans after the war.

Foote, Lucius Harwood, 1826–1913, American minister to Korea (1883–84), first regular diplomat from a Western power to that country.

foot-pound: see WORK.

Foot Resolution, offered 1829 by Samuel A. Foot in U.S. Senate. Instructed committee on public lands to inquire into limiting of public-land sale. Jacksonian Democrats, encouraging migration W, opposed resolution; New England manufacturing interests, demanding a ready labor supply, backed it. Advocates of states' right identified themselves with interests of West. Touched off dramatic debates of 1830 between Robert HAYNE and Daniel WEBSTER.

Foppa, Vincenzo (vēnchän′tsō fôp′pä), c.1427–c.1515, Italian painter, founder of Lombard school. Worked in Pavia and Milan.

Forain, Jean Louis (zhä′ lwē′ fôrě′), 1852–1931, French painter, etcher, and lithographer. Best known for political cartoons in manner of Daumier.

Foraker, Joseph Benson (fôr′ukŭr), 1846–1917, American political leader. U.S. Senator from Ohio (1897–1909). Old Guard Republican; accused of accepting retainers from Standard Oil Co.

foraminifera (fŭră″mŭnĭ′fŭrŭ), members of an order of protozoa most of which have a shell. They inhabit all oceans, and there are a few species in fresh and brackish water. Discarded skeletons of genus *Globigerina* form on ocean bottom a deposit which solidifies into chalk.

Forbes, John, 1710–59, British general in French and Indian Wars. Captured Fort Duquesne 1758.

Forbes, John Murray, 1813–98, American capitalist. Under his direction the Michigan Central and Chicago, Burlington & Quincy railroads were marked by financial stability.

Forbes-Robertson, Sir Johnston, 1853–1937, English actor. On stage from 1874, he had his first great success in 1889. Appeared as Hamlet (1898) and in such plays as *The Passing of the Third Floor Back.*

Forbidden City, China: see CHINESE ARCHITECTURE.

Forbush, Edward Howe (fôr′bŏŏsh), 1858–1929, American ornithologist, state ornithologist of Mass. from 1908 and director of division of ornithology of state board of agr. (1893–1908; 1921–29).

force, in physics, is commonly defined as any

"push" or "pull" acting on a body or as that effort acting to change its state of motion (i.e., its acceleration or direction of movement) or state of rest. Forces are measured in pounds, grams, or kilograms, depending upon system of weights used. For every force there is an equal and opposite force. Both direction and magnitude enter into effect of a force upon a given body. Forces can produce rotation of certain bodies, e.g., of a lever bar free to revolve about its center. A rotating part is acted upon by centrifugal force, i.e., a force acting to make it fly off at a tangent from its path around the center. This force must be balanced, if equilibrium is to be maintained, by a centripetal force, i.e., a force acting in the opposite direction and toward the center, holding the body in its regular path. Forces acting on the various parts of structures and machines are factors determining stress and strain and STRENGTH OF MATERIALS. Certain force measurements are based on velocity imparted to a given mass in a certain unit of time. The DYNE is unit of force in cgs (centimeter-gram-second) system; in English system it is the poundal. See also GRAVITATION; MAGNETISM; PRESSURE; VOLT. See *ill.*, p. 793.

force bill, popular name for several laws in U.S. history, notably act of March 2, 1833, and Reconstruction acts of 1870 and 1871. First force bill, passed in response to ordinance of NULLIFICATION of S.C., empowered Pres. Jackson to use army and navy, if necessary, to enforce laws of Congress, specifically the tariff measures at issue. In second set of force bills, radical Republicans strengthened their Reconstruction program by imposing severe penalties on those Southerners who tried to obstruct it. Act of May 31, 1870, penalized anyone preventing qualified citizens (in this case Negroes) from voting, and placed congressional elections under exclusive Federal control. Act of April 20, 1871, inspired by activities of Ku Klux Klan, declared acts of armed combinations tantamount to rebellion and empowered President to suspend privilege of habeas corpus in lawless areas.

Ford, Edsel Bryant: see FORD, HENRY.

Ford, Ford Madox, 1873–1939, English author. As editor of literary reviews he greatly influenced modern writing. Taught Joseph Conrad English and collaborated with him. Originally Ford Madox Hueffer.

Ford, Henry, 1863–1947, American industrialist, pioneer automobile manufacturer. An inexpensive, standardized car, resulting from mass production, helped make Ford world's largest automobile producer. Had employee profit-sharing plan; opposed union organization until 1941. Estab. FORD FOUNDATION. His son, **Edsel Bryant Ford,** 1893–1943, was president of Ford Motor Co. 1919–43. **Henry Ford II,** 1917–, succeeded his grandfather as president in 1945.

Ford, John, b. 1586, English dramatist, author of verse plays, including *'Tis Pity She's a Whore* (1633). Collaborated with Dekker and Rowley in *The Witch of Edmonton,* 1621.

Ford, Worthington Chauncey, 1858–1941, American historian and editor. He was chief

of the manuscripts division of the Library of Congress (1902–9) and editor of the Mass. Historical Society (1909–29). Works he edited include the writings of George Washington (14 vols., 1889–93) and of John Quincy Adams (7 vols., 1913–17). Joint editor of *Winnowings in American History* (15 vols., 1890–91), together with his brother, **Paul Leicester Ford,** 1865–1902. He edited many early U.S. writings, including those of Thomas Jefferson (10 vols., 1892–99), and wrote biographies (notably *The True George Washington,* 1896) and novels (e.g., *Janice Meredith,* 1899; *The Honorable Peter Stirling,* 1894).

Ford City, borough (pop. 5,352), W Pa., on Allegheny R. NE of Pittsburgh. Mfg. of glass products.

Ford Foundation, incorporated 1936 with funds from Henry Ford and Edsel B. Ford for general purpose of advancing human welfare. Greatly expanded program was inaugurated in 1950 with five main aims: to support activities directed toward world peace; to secure greater allegiance to basic principles of freedom and democracy; to advance economic well-being of people everywhere; to promote educational and cultural activities; and to support scientific study.

Fordham University (fôr'dùm), in the Bronx, New York city; R.C. (Jesuit), partly coed.; opened 1841 as St. John's Col., chartered 1846 as university, renamed 1905. Noted for seismography work.

Fords Island, T.H.: see PEARL HARBOR.

Forefathers' Day, celebrated by New Englanders Dec. 21, to commemorate landing of Pilgrims in 1620 on Plymouth Rock. It was first observed in 1769.

Foreign Legion, French volunteer infantry regiment, created 1831 for pacification of Algeria, where it is normally stationed. Enlisted men are mostly foreigners. Important in French colonial expansion, Legion also fought gallantly in World War I. It was renovated and reorganized 1946.

Foreign Ministers, Council of, informal body set up at Yalta Conference Feb., 1945 by U.S., British, and Russian ministers. France was admitted 1946. After POTSDAM CONFERENCE, group met in London, then in Moscow in late 1945. It decided on certain peace treaties, an 11-power Far Eastern Commission and Council for Japan, and an atomic energy commission within UN. It steered Paris peace conference of 1946 and subsequent decisions; but failed in 1947 to draft peace treaties with Germany and Austria. Revived in June, 1949, it achieved ending of Soviet blockade of Berlin.

foreign missions: see MISSIONS.

foreign service: see DIPLOMATIC SERVICE; CONSULAR SERVICE.

Forel, Auguste or August (ōgüst' fôrĕl'), 1848–1931, Swiss psychiatrist and entomologist. As a boy he began his studies of ants on which he wrote a number of books and which later influenced his approach to psychiatry. He promoted humane treatment of the insane and contributed to study of hypnotism and of sexual problems.

Forel, François Alphonse (fräswä' älfôs'), 1841–1912, Swiss physician and naturalist.

He taught anatomy and physiology at Univ. of Lausanne and studied Swiss glaciers and lakes.

Foreland, North, and **South Foreland;** headlands of Kent, England. Both are chalk cliff formations. Defeat of Dutch in 1666 associated with Forelands.

forest, plant community in which trees are dominant. Three main types of forests: equatorial or tropical rain-belt forests, found especially in basins of Amazon and Congo rivers and marked by luxuriant growth of a variety of trees; and deciduous and coniferous forests, both occurring mainly in temperate latitudes. Some conifers are found in the tropics at high altitudes, and at low altitudes of subarctic regions. Mixed stands of deciduous trees and conifers occur in temperate zones. Generally conifers are the climax growth of regions above about 40° N lat.; below this, deciduous trees usually dominate. Forests are of vital importance in conservation of water and wildlife, prevention of erosion and floods, for timber supply, and for recreation. Great areas of U.S. forest land are now preserved as NATIONAL FORESTS, national parks, and state, county, and municipal parks. Forestry or silviculture is the scientific development and management of forests.

Forester, C(ecil) S(cott), 1899–, British author of superior adventure stories (notably those about naval hero Horatio Hornblower).

Forest Hill, village (pop. 15,305), S Ont., Canada, residential suburb of Toronto.

Forest Hills. 1 See QUEENS, New York city borough. **2** Borough (pop. 6,301), SW Pa., E suburb of Pittsburgh.

Forest Park, village (pop. 14,969), NE Ill., W residential suburb of Chicago. Has greenhouses.

Forfarshire: see ANGUS, county.

forgery, willful fabrication or alteration of a written document (private or public—e.g., birth or marriage certificate) with the intent fraudulently to injure the interests of another. In the U.S. forgery ordinarily is a state crime, but to send forged documents through the mail may constitute Federal crime.

forget-me-not, plant (*Myosotis*) with small flowers, usually blue, used in borders and rock gardens.

forging, working metals by heating, then hammering and rolling. Metal is heated to red or white heat in forge; charcoal and coke are usual fuels. Heated metal is removed with tongs to anvil, hammered to desired shape, and thrust into water for tempering. Like founding, forging was practiced prehistorically, probably first in Asia. Early importance of metals is indicated by names Bronze Age and Iron Age.

Forlì, Melozzo da: see MELOZZA DA FORLÌ.

Forlì (fôrlē´), city (pop. 33,505), Emilia-Romagna, N central Italy, in Romagna. Free commune from 11th cent.; later a principality; passed to Papal States 1504. Citadel (14th cent.); art gallery.

formaldehyde (fôrmǎl´dūhīd), simple gaseous ALDEHYDE with suffocating odor. Used to make dyes, plastics, resins; subject to POLYMERIZATION. **Formalin,** 40% water solution of formaldehyde, used as antiseptic, disinfectant, biological preservative.

formic acid, colorless, corrosive organic acid, lowest member of fatty-acid series. It is a compound of hydrogen, carbon, and oxygen. Found in red ants, sting of bees, and other insects.

Formosa (fôrmō´sù) [Port.,= beautiful], Chinese *Taiwan,* island (13,808 sq. mi.), off SE coast of Chinese mainland; with PESCADORES isls. forms Formosa province (13,886 sq. mi.; pop. 7,617,753) of China; cap. Taipei. Mountainous, rises to c.13,600 ft. at Mt. Morrison. Produces rice, sugar cane, and oolong tea. Lumbering (oak, cypress, camphor), mining (mainly coal, gold, copper). Portuguese came 1590, followed 1624 by the Dutch, who were dominant until 1662, when they were ousted by Koxinga, Chinese general of Southern Ming dynasty. Brought under Ch'ing dynasty in 1683, ceded 1895 to Japan, restored to China after World War II. In 1949 became last refuge of Nationalists under Chiang Kai-shek. In Feb., 1953, the U.S. lifted the 7th Fleet's blockade of Formosa, thus presumably freeing Chiang to attack the Communist-held mainland of China.

formula, in chemistry, a written expression which indicates elements, in proportion by weight, making up one molecule of a chemical COMPOUND. Formula of water is H₂O: symbol H = hydrogen, O = oxygen; subscript 2 shows that there are 2 atoms of hydrogen. Formula also shows that 2 parts of hydrogen by weight (2 × its ATOMIC WEIGHT of 1) and 16 parts of oxygen (1 × 16) are combined to form 18 parts by weight of water. Structural formula shows arrangement of atoms.

formula, in mathematics and physics, a statement in symbols of relationship between certain quantities. Quantities are expressed usually by letters, relationships by algebraic symbols.

Forres (fŏr´rĭs), burgh (pop. 4,462), Morayshire, Scotland; ancient town with many legends. One of possible places where Macbeth murdered Duncan.

Forrest, Edwin, 1806–72, American actor, one of the era's great tragedians. His roles included Othello, Lear, Macbeth, and Hamlet. Married (1837) Catherine Sinclair, an English actress, who brought (1852) sensational divorce suit against him. Violent rivalry with MACREADY and demonstrations instigated by Macready and Forrest adherents culminated in the Astor Place riot (1849), but failed to dim Forrest's reputation as an actor.

Forrest, John Forrest, 1st Baron, 1847–1918, Australian explorer and statesman. Led coastal expedition from Perth to Adelaide (1870). Surveyor general of Western Australia (1883); first premier (1890–1901).

Forrest, Nathan Bedford, 1821–77, Confederate general. Commanded cavalry units in Tenn. (1862–63); in N Miss., where his victories menaced Sherman's communications; and again in Tenn. (1864) under J. B. Hood. Probably greatest Confederate cavalryman, he is the hero of many legends in South. To him is attributed the formula for victory: "Git there fustest with the mostest men."

Forrestal, James V(incent) (fŏr´rĭstäl), 1892–

1949, U.S. Secretary of the Navy (1944–47) and first Secretary of Defense (1947–49). A suicide.

Forrest City, city (pop. 7,607), E Ark., at foot of Crowley's Ridge. Trade center for agr. area.

Forster, E(dward) M(organ), 1879–, English novelist. Lived in Italy, India, Egypt. His novels are noted for crisp style and subtle irony: *Where Angels Fear to Tread* (1905), *The Longest Journey* (1907), *A Room with a View* (1908), *Howards End* (1910), *A Passage to India* (1924). Also wrote short stories, essays, and literary criticism.

Forsyth, John, 1780–1841, American statesman. U.S. Senator from Ga. (1818–19, 1829–34); supported Pres. Jackson in nullification controversy in Ga. U.S. Secretary of State (1834–41).

forsythia (–sĭth'ēu̇), Old World shrub (*Forsythia*) with abundant yellow flowers appearing in spring before the leaves.

Fort, Paul (pōl' fôr'), 1872–, French symbolist poet, noted for use of "rhythmical prose," as in *Ballades françaises* (1897).

Fortaleza (fôrtu̇lä'zu̇), city (pop. 213,605), cap. of Ceará state, NE Brazil; Atlantic port, founded 1609. Long a center of great sugar plantations; today important also for cotton.

Fort Atkinson, city (pop. 6,280), S Wis., SE of Madison. Trade center of dairy region.

Fort Beauséjour National Park: see BEAUSÉJOUR, FORT.

Fort Benton, city (pop. 1,522), N central Mont., at head of navigation on Missouri R. and NE of Great Falls. Grew around fur-trading post (1846). Reached by steamboat in 1859, it became supply point for gold seekers and cattlemen.

Fort Bridger State Park, SW Wyo., E of Evanston and on Blacks Fork of Green R. The supply post, founded 1843 by James BRIDGER, was held by Mormons 1853–57, then leased by U.S. as fort until 1890.

Fort Collins, city (pop. 14,937), N Colo., N of Denver and on Cache la Poudre R.; settled around fort (1864–71). Trade, processing center in irrigated area (grain, sugar beets, livestock). Dams of COLORADO-BIG THOMPSON PROJECT are near. Seat of Colorado Agricultural and Mechanical Col. (land-grant; coed.; 1879); includes Fort Lewis School near Durango.

Fort Davis, village, W Texas, SE of El Paso in Davis Mts. Much visited for mountain scenery. Near by is McDonald Observatory (1932; Univ. of Texas and Univ. of Chicago).

Fort-de-France (fôr-du̇-fräs'), city (pop. 48,-576), cap. of Martinique dept., French West Indies; chief port of island. It exports sugar and rum.

Fort Dodge, city (pop. 25,115), central Iowa, on Des Moines R. and NNW of Des Moines; settled c.1846. Fort Clarke estab. here 1850, renamed Fort Dodge (for Henry Dodge) 1851, abandoned 1853. Rail and industrial center of agr. and mining area with mfg. of gypsum, clay, and food products.

Fort Donelson National Military Park: see NATIONAL PARKS AND MONUMENTS (table).

Fort Erie, town (pop. 7,572), S Ont., Canada, on Niagara R. (bridged) opposite Buffalo,

N.Y. Has steel mills, gold refineries, mfg. of aircraft and auto parts. Some U.S. firms have branch units here. Fort built 1764 by British. Taken by Americans in War of 1812 and successfully defended in 1814. Merged 1934 with Bridgeburg.

Fort Fairfield, town (pop. 5,791), NE Maine, on Aroostook R. at N.B. line. Potato-growing center.

Fort Frances, town (pop. 8,038), W Ont., Canada, on Rainy R. opposite International Falls, Minn. Hunting and camping center with paper, pulp, and lumber mills. Built as Hudson's Bay Co. post.

Fort Frederica National Monument: see NATIONAL PARKS AND MONUMENTS (table).

Fort George, river, central and W Que., Canada, longest river (520 mi.) flowing into Hudson Bay from the East. Formerly called Big R.

Fort Gibson, town (pop. 1,496), E Okla., E of Muskogee. Founded 1824 as army post for coming of Five Civilized Tribes; served until 1857. Natl. cemetery and Fort Gibson Dam near by.

Forth, river of Scotland. Flows c.50 mi. from Stirlingshire to Alloa. **Firth of Forth** extends c.50 mi. from Alloa to North Sea and is 1–18 mi. wide. Crossed at Queensferry by cantilever railroad bridge (5,330 ft. long). Rosyth, on bay, is a naval base. Several other rivers flow into the firth.

fortification. Defense structures appeared with the beginning of organized warfare. By the Middle Ages, the walled city and the castle were the standard fortifications. Masonry walls, however, failed to withstand artillery, which came into use about the 15th cent. Subsequent fortifications featured posts for the defenders' artillery and a far-flung defense perimeter around the main fortress. Extensive systems of intricate fortifications were used in Europe during the recent two great wars. As emphasis fell again on mobile warfare, the accent has returned to temporary, even improvised, fortifications designed primarily to delay an invader until reinforcements arrive.

Fort Jefferson National Monument: see NATIONAL PARKS AND MONUMENTS (table).

Fort Kent, town (pop. 5,343), N Maine, on St. John R. and NNW of Presque Isle. Potato processing.

Fort Laramie National Monument: see NATIONAL PARKS AND MONUMENTS (table).

Fort Lauderdale (lô'du̇rdāl), city (pop. 36,-328), SE Fla., N of Miami, on Atlantic coast and on navigation canal to L. Okeechobee; settled around fort built (1837) in Seminole War. Ships fruits and vegetables. Fishing and yachting resort. Port Everglades and a Seminole Indian reservation are near.

Fort Lee, borough (pop. 11,648), NE N.J., on the Hudson, connected with upper Manhattan by George Washington Bridge. Fort here abandoned Nov. 20, 1776, by Gen. Greene after Fort Washington, across the river, was taken by British. Early center of moving-picture industry.

Fort McHenry National Monument and Historical Shrine: see NATIONAL PARKS AND MONUMENTS (table).

Fort McMurray, village, N Alta., Canada, on

Athabaska R. Chief base for air travel to central Northwest Territories. Built 1790 as fur-trading post.

Fort Madison, city (pop. 14,954), SE Iowa, on the Mississippi below Burlington; settled 1833. Fort Madison, U.S. trading post, here 1808–13. Rail hub with mfg. of food products and writing equipment.

Fort Marion National Monument, renamed (1942) Castillo de San Marcos National Monument: see NATIONAL PARKS AND MONUMENTS (table).

Fort Matanzas National Monument: see NATIONAL PARKS AND MONUMENTS (table).

Fort Morgan, city (pop. 5,315), NE Colo., NE of Denver and on South Platte R. Trade, processing center for rich farm, dairy, livestock region.

Fort Myers, city (pop. 13,195), SW Fla., near Gulf of Mexico. Grew around fort built (1841) in Seminole War, held by Federals in Civil War. Ships citrus fruit, winter vegetables, and fish. T. A. Edison wintered and experimented here.

Fort Necessity National Battlefield Site: see NECESSITY, FORT.

Fort Nelson, village, N B.C., Canada, on Alaska Highway and Fort Nelson R. and N of Dawson Creek. Hudson's Bay Co. post here estab. c.1800.

Fort Payne, city (pop. 6,226), NE Ala., NE of Gadsden, in farm area, with mineral deposits.

Fort Peck Dam, NE Mont., in Missouri R. above mouth of Milk R. Built 1933–40 to control floods and improve navigation, it is used also for irrigation and power. One of world's largest earth-filled dams, it is 21,026 ft. long and 250 ft. high.

Fort Pierce, city (pop. 13,502), SE Fla., port on Indian R. (here connected to the Atlantic by an inlet). Grew around fort built 1838. Ships citrus fruit, vegetables, and lumber.

Fort Pulaski National Monument: see NATIONAL PARKS AND MONUMENTS (table).

Fortress Monroe: see MONROE, FORT.

Fort Scott, city (pop. 10,335), SE Kansas, N of Pittsburg near Mo. line. Grew up around military post (estab. 1842, abandoned 1855, rebuilt in Civil War). Rail and trade center in dairy and farm area.

Fort Smith, city (pop. 47,942), NW Ark., at Okla. line where Arkansas and Poteau rivers join. Founded 1817 as military post; was supply point in gold rush of 1848. State's chief industrial center, it has mfg. of furniture, glass, textiles, and metal and wood products and processing of zinc, oil, and gas. Mule market. Rail and trade center for farm area. Has Civil War cemetery and the Old Fort and other old buildings.

Fort Stockton, city (pop. 4,444), W Texas, on plateau W of Pecos R. Grew around army post (1859). Near Comanche Springs (once camp site for Indians and California overlanders). Tourist center.

Fort Sumner, village (pop. 1,982), E N.Mex., NNE of Roswell. Near by are Alamogordo Dam and cemetery with grave of Billy the Kid.

Fort Sumter National Monument: see SUMTER, FORT.

Fort Thomas, residential city (pop. 10,870),

N Ky., on Ohio R. in Cincinnati metropolitan area. Fort Thomas, U.S. army post, estab. here 1887.

Fortuna (fôrtū'nà) [Latin,= fortune], in Roman religion, popular oracular goddess of chance.

Fortunate Isles or **Isles of the Blest,** in classical and Celtic legend, islands in Western Ocean, eternal home of souls of favored mortals. Long thought to be Canary or Madeira Isls.

Fortunatus (Venantius Honorius Clementianus Fortunatus), d. c.600, last Gallic Latin poet, author of the hymn *Vexilla Regis prodeunt.*

Fortune, Robert, 1813–80, British botanist. He introduced in England the kumquat and many other plants which he collected in the Orient. His experiments led to the growing of tea in India.

Fort Valley, city (pop. 6,820), S central Ga., E of Columbus. Center for peach-growing area.

Fort Wayne, city (pop. 133,607), NE Ind., where St. Joseph's and St. Mary's rivers form Maumee R. Miami Indians, who early resisted taking of site by French (who built Fort Miami here 1704), then by British, were subdued by Anthony Wayne, who built (1794) fort that bore his name. After further Indian fighting in War of 1812 town grew with fur trade. Now state's second largest city, key rail and shipping point of agr. and dairying region. Mfg. of electrical and metal products; food processing.

Fort William, city (pop. 34,947), W Ont. Canada, on NW shore of L. Superior at mouth of Kaministikwia R. With twin city, Port Arthur, is W Canadian lake port and shipping center. Terminus of Canadian National and Canadian Pacific railways. Has grain elevators and paper, pulp, lumber, and flour mills, foundries, machine shops, and shipyards. Fort Kaministiquia built here 1717, and Fort William estab. 1801 as post of North West Co.

Fort William, burgh (pop. 2,661), Invernessshire, Scotland, on Loch Linnhe, near Ben Nevis; tourist center for Highlands. Fort (built by General Monck 1655) was twice besieged by Jacobites, whose relics are in a museum. Has important aluminum industry.

Fort Worth, city (pop. 278,778), N Texas, at junction of Clear and West forks of Trinity R. and W of Dallas; settled 1843. Army Fort Worth estab. 1847. Was cowtown after Civil War. Railroad (1876) aided growth. Industrial and transportation center of cattle and agr. area with stockyards, grain elevators and mills, and meat packing plants; also refineries and aircraft plants. Grew through two World Wars. Here are TEXAS CHRISTIAN UNIVERSITY and U.S. military air base. Served by three reservoirs on West Fork.

Forty Fort, residential borough (pop. 6,173), NE Pa., on Susquehanna R. near Wilkes-Barre. Militia marched from fort here in WYOMING VALLEY massacre 1778.

forum, market and meeting place in anc. Roman towns in Italy; consisted of open square surrounded by public buildings. Old Roman Forum extended SE from Capitoline Hill, later reaching almost to Colosseum. Arch of Augustus was entrance to Forum proper. In NE were Basilica Aemilia and the curia, where the senate met. Temple of Saturn housed the treasury. In imperial times new fora, with marble pavements and grandiose colonnades, were built to NE, from Basilica of Constantine to valley between Capitoline and Quirinal. Decay of Old Forum began in 4th cent.; in Middle Ages the fora were stripped to provide materials for new monuments.

Foscolo, Ugo (ōō'gō fō'skōlō), 1778–1827, Italian poet and patriot. His novel *The Last Letters of Jacopo Ortis* (1796–1802; Eng. tr., 1818), modeled on Goethe's *Werther,* stirred Italian hearts for generations. His "graveyard" poem *Sepolcri* (1807) is notable.

Fosdick, Harry Emerson, 1878–, American clergyman. Pastor Park Ave. Baptist Church (1926) and its successor, Riverside Church, New York (1930–46). Noted for Modernist stand in controversies of 1920s.

Fosse Way (fŏs), Roman road in England, supposed to have linked present Exeter, Bath, Cirencester, Leicester, and Lincoln.

fossil, organic remains or impressions preserved in sedimentary rocks from the geologic past. Favorable conditions included burial in asphalt, mud, or other materials which prevent decay. Fossilization is usually confined to skeletons or hard parts, but entire mammals of the late Pleistocene have been found frozen in ice. Footprints of land animals and tracks of marine invertebrates are regarded as fossils. Petrified wood and other petrified plant and animal remains form when the original structure is slowly replaced by mineral matter.

Fossil Cycad National Monument: see NATIONAL PARKS AND MONUMENTS (table).

Foster, John Watson, 1836–1917, American diplomat. Minister to Mexico (1873–80), Russia (1880–81). Secretary of State (1892–93). Represented U.S. in arbitration of Bering Sea Fur-Seal Controversy.

Foster, Stephen Collins, 1826–64, American composer. His knowledge of the Negro was gained from minstrel shows, for which he wrote many of his songs. He had little business acumen, and despite the popularity of his songs, died in extreme poverty. Among his best-loved songs are *Oh! Susanna* (1848), *Camptown Races* (1850), *Old Folks at Home* (1851), *My Old Kentucky Home* (1853), *Jeanie with the Light Brown Hair* (1854), and *Old Black Joe* (1860).

Foster, William Z(ebulon), 1881–, American Communist leader. Three-time presidential candidate.

Fostoria, city (pop. 14,351), NW Ohio, S of Toledo; estab. 1854. Trade center for farm area with stockyards and mfg. of wood products and auto parts.

Fothergill, John (fŏ'dhûrgĭl), 1712–80, English physician, a Quaker, noted for his London practice, for botanic garden at Upton, Essex, and for work to improve jails and sanitation.

Fotheringhay (fŏdh'ûrĭng-gā), village, Northamptonshire, England. Castle was birthplace of Richard III and scene of Mary Queen of Scots' execution.

Foucault, Jean Bernard Léon (zhä' bĕrnär' lāō' fōōkō'), 1819–68, French physicist. He determined velocity of light in air; found that speed of light in other media is reduced in

proportion to index of refraction. He devised the Foucault PENDULUM.

Fouché, Joseph (zhôzĕf' fōōshā'), 1759–1820, French police minister (1799–1802, 1804–10); created duke of Otranto 1809. A lifelong opportunist, he sided with every party in power from the French Revolution through the Bourbon restoration. Through his private spy system he discovered the CADOUDAL plot (1804), thus earning a return to favor. Sometimes considered the father of the modern police state, he created a ruthlessly efficient system of criminal and political police. After his second dismissal (because of secret dealings with England) he held several high posts but never regained his power.

Foucquet: see FOUQUET.

Fouillée, Alfred (fōōyā'), 1838–1912, French philosopher. Developed motor theory of consciousness, making ideas agents of change and progress.

founding or **casting,** shaping of metals by melting and pouring into molds. Foundry is place where this is done. Sand or loam mold (held to desired form by wooden pattern) used to cast iron or steel. Pattern is made slightly large to allow shrinkage when metal solidifies. Rapid cooling increases hardness of casting. Metal molds are used in type founding and also in die-casting.

Fountains Abbey, ruined 12th-cent. abbey, West Riding of Yorkshire, England, SW of Ripon.

Fouqué, Friedrich, Freiherr de la Motte- (frē'drĭkh frī'hĕr dü lä môt'-fōōkā'), 1777–1843, German Romantic poet, best known for the fairy tale *Undine* (1811; many trs.).

Fouquet or **Foucquet, Jean** or **Jehan** (all: zhä' fōō-kā'), c.1415–c.1480, founder of 15th-cent. school of French painting which shows influence of Van Eycks and early Florentines. Famous for kneeling portrait of Etienne Chevalier (Louvre) and for illuminations in duc de Berry's Book of Hours (Chantilly).

Fouquet or **Foucquet, Nicolas** (nēkōlä'), 1615–80, French statesman, superintendent of finance (1653–61). Mismanaged treasury, accumulated huge private wealth. Denounced by Colbert and resented by Louis XIV for his ostentatious entertainments, he was brought to trial (1661) and sentenced (1664) to banishment. The king "commuted" the sentence to life imprisonment. Fouquet was a patron of La Fontaine and Molière.

Fouquier-Tinville, Antoine Quentin (ätwän' kätē' fōōkyä-tēvēl'), 1746–95, French revolutionist, chief prosecutor in Revolutionary tribunal during REIGN OF TERROR. Guillotined after fall of Robespierre.

Fourcroy, Antoine François, comte de (ätwän' fräswä' kôt dü fōōrkrwä'), 1755–1809, French chemist. Pioneer in animal and plant chemistry; collaborated in reforming chemical nomenclature.

Four Forest Cantons, Ger. *Vier Waldstätten,* cantons of UNTERWALDEN, SCHWYZ, URI, and LUCERNE; first Swiss communities to win freedom. Lake of the Four Forest Cantons is called in English Lake of LUCERNE.

Four Freedoms. In message to Congress (Jan. 6, 1941), Pres. F. D. Roosevelt stated that Four Freedoms should prevail throughout world—freedom of speech and expression, freedom of worship, freedom from want, and freedom from fear. These were substantially incorporated in ATLANTIC CHARTER.

Four-H or **4-H clubs,** organizations under Dept. of Agr. for boys and girls in rural areas. They aim to improve methods of agr. and home economics and to promote good citizenship. Name is derived from fourfold purpose of improving head, heart, hands, health. Groups are very active.

Four Horsemen of the Apocalypse (ŭpŏk'-ŭlĭps), allegorical figures in Bible. Rev. 6.1–8. Rider on white horse has many interpretations—one is that he represents Christ; rider on red horse is war; rider on black horse is famine, and rider on pale horse, death.

Fourier, Charles (shärl' fōōryā'), 1772–1837, French social philosopher. Projected social utopia organized in small economic units (phalanxes) of 1,620 persons. Doctrine of **Fourierism** spread to America under auspices of Prosper Considérant, Albert Brisbane, Horace Greeley. BROOK FARM was for a time Fourierist; most successful community was at Red Bank, N.J.

Fourier, Jean Baptiste Joseph, Baron (fōō'rēä", Fr. zhä' bätēst' zhôzĕf' bärō' fōōryä'), 1768–1830, French mathematician and physicist. Noted for research on heat and numerical equations; he originated Fourier's theorem on vibratory motion and Fourier series which provided method for representing discontinuous functions by trigonometric series.

Four Lakes, S Wis., chain of lakes (Mendota, largest; Monona, Waubesa, Kegonsa). Madison is between first two. Univ. of Wisconsin is on Mendota.

Fournier, Pierre Simon (fōōrnyä'), 1712–68, Parisian type founder. Devised first point system for measuring type. Wrote *Manuel typographique* (1764–66).

Fourteen Points, formulation of a peace program, presented by U.S. Pres. Woodrow Wilson in address before Congress on Jan. 8, 1918. Message was intended to reach people and liberal leaders of Central Powers as a seductive appeal for peace, in which purpose it was successful, and to provide a framework for peace discussions. Message made Wilson moral leader of the Allies, but after the Armistice opposition to the points quickly crystallized, and actual treaty (see VERSAILLES, TREATY OF) represented a compromise or defeat of many of them.

Fourteenth Amendment, to the U.S. Constitution (1868). Section 1 established the basis of U.S. citizenship and forbade states to abridge privileges and immunities of U.S. citizens, to deprive any person of life, liberty, or property without due process of law, or to deny any person equal protection of law. The U.S. Supreme Court used Section 1 extensively to limit restrictive state legislation (e.g., the states were forbidden to favor or suppress any religious establishment). The equal-protection clause became the main weapon of Negroes in their fight for equality. It was also a claim for corporations seeking immunities of citizens.

fourth dimension: see SPACE TIME.

Fourth of July, Independence Day, or **July Fourth,** U.S. patriotic holiday par excellence,

commemorating adoption of Declaration of Independence. Observance began during American Revolution.

Fowke, Gerard (fouk), 1855–1933, American archaeologist. Noted for study of the Ohio valley. Investigated aboriginal remains in E U.S. (1885–88, 1891–93). Explored Vancouver Isl. (1898). Made ethnological studies in Hawaiian Isls. (1920).

Fowler, H(enry) W(atson), 1858–1933, English lexicographer. He and his brother, F. G. Fowler, collaborated on *The King's English* (1906) and on an abridgment of *Oxford English Dictionary* (1911). After F. G. Fowler died in 1918 H. W. Fowler completed alone *A Dictionary of Modern English Usage* (1926).

Fowliang (fōō'lēäng'), town (pop. 86,744), Kiangsi prov., China, on Chang R. Founded 6th cent. Long celebrated as porcelain-making center.

Fox, Charles James, 1749–1806, English Whig statesman and orator. Disliked by George III, he was a friend of the prince of Wales (George IV). Opponent of Lord North, he attacked British policy in the American war. Was foreign secretary for brief periods (1782, 1783, 1806). Supported repeal of Poynings's Law in 1782. Opposed William Pitt by demanding British nonintervention in French Revolution. Urged abolition of slave trade (passed in 1807 after his death) and political freedom for dissenters.

Fox, George, 1624–91, English founder of Society of FRIENDS. He turned from organized religion to direct, personal relationship with God through "inward light" of Christ and began to preach in 1647. Despite persecutions and imprisonments he won many followers. Plan of organization was set up in 1668, with first London Yearly Meeting in 1671. His writings include his noted journal (1694; preface by William Penn).

Fox, John, Jr., 1862–1919, American novelist, b. Ky., author of *The Little Shepherd of Kingdom Come* (1903), *The Trail of the Lonesome Pine* (1908).

Fox or **Foxe, Luke,** 1586–1635, English explorer. Sought Northwest Passage; explored W shore of Hudson Bay, satisfied himself there was no passage through it (1631).

Fox, Margaret, 1836–93, American spiritualist. She claimed connection with spirit world and toured U.S. and Europe with her sisters. In 1888 she admitted that effects were fraudulent.

Fox, river, c.176 mi. long, rising in central Wis. and flowing SW to within c.1½ mi. of Portage, on Wisconsin R., with which it is connected by ship canal. Thence flows NE to Green Bay, at Green Bay city. Drains L. Winnebago. Above lake it is known as Upper Fox R., below lake as Lower Fox. Route of early explorers, missionaries, traders into Wis. and Northwest; forts, missions, and trading posts were estab. along course. Jolliet and Marquette were first white men to reach the Mississippi by way of Fox-Wisconsin portage 1673.

fox, predatory intelligent animal of dog family. Fur is usually long and thick; tail bushy, and longer than the wolf's. It eats small animals, berries, and fruits. Red fox (*Vulpes*) inhabits parts of Europe, Asia, N Africa, most of U.S., and Canada. Usually the coat is reddish, the tail white-tipped, the ears black-tipped. Silver, black, and cross fox (yellowish to pale orange) are color phases which may appear in any red fox litter. Breeders have developed platinum fox. Arctic fox has circumpolar range. Gray fox found over most U.S. and through Mexico to N South America.

Foxboro or **Foxborough,** town (pop. 7,030), SE Mass., W of Brockton. Mfg. of precision instruments.

Foxe, John, 1516–87, English clergyman, author of *Book of Martyrs.* In Strasbourg appeared (1554; in Latin) story of Protestant martyrs to c.1500. At Basel appeared (1559) first complete edition. John Day issued (1563) first complete English edition.

Foxe, Luke: see FOX, LUKE.

foxglove, Old World biennial or perennial plant of genus *Digitalis.* It has handsome, spirelike spikes of purple, pink, or white bell-shaped flowers in early summer. Its leaves yield the drug digitalis.

Fox Indians: see SAC AND FOX INDIANS.

Fox Islands: see ALEUTIAN ISLANDS.

fox terrier: see TERRIER.

Foyle, river of Co. Tyrone, N. Ireland. Its navigable estuary is called Lough Foyle.

F.P.A.: see ADAMS, FRANKLIN PIERCE.

Fra Angelico: see ANGELICO, FRA.

Fracastoro, Girolamo (jĕrōʹlämō fräkästōʹrō), 1483–1553, Italian physician, authority on epidemic diseases. He wrote a poem on syphilis from which the disease takes its name.

Frackville, borough (pop. 6,541), E Pa., NNW of Pottsville. Anthracite mining.

fraction, in arithmetic, expression representing a part, or several equal parts, of a unit. In writing ⅖, number 5 is denominator (total number of parts into which unit is divided); number 2 is numerator (number of equal parts taken of unit). When the numerator is less than the denominator, the fraction is called proper; when the reverse is true it is improper. To add two fractions, denominators must be like, or be made like, after which numerators are added together; or, for subtraction, subtracted. To multiply fractions, multiply numerators together and denominators together. To divide, invert divisor; then multiply. In algebraic fractions procedure is the same.

fracture, a breaking, especially of a bone. Types include simple, in which overlying skin is unbroken; compound, in which broken bone communicates with external wound; and greenstick, in which one side of bone is broken, other side bent.

Fra Diavolo (frä″ dēäʹvōlō) [Ital.,= brother devil], 1771–1806, Neapolitan bandit and soldier whose real name was Michele Pezza. Taking up the cause of the Bourbon rulers of Naples, he fought the French, who captured and hanged him. Auber's opera, *Fra Diavolo,* is in no way historical.

Fragonard, Jean Honoré (zhä önôräʹ frägônärʹ), 1732–1806, French painter. Studied with Chardin and Boucher. Painted scenes of love and gallantry for the French court.

Framingham, town (pop. 28,086), E Mass., WSW of Boston; settled 1650. Mfg. of autos, paper products, shoes, and carpets. Seat of Massachusetts State Teachers Col. (for women; chartered 1838, opened 1839 at Lexington); oldest existing U.S. school for teachers; estab. by Horace MANN.

France, Anatole (änätôlʹ fräsʹ), pseud. of Jacques Anatole Thibault (zhäkʹ tēbōʹ), 1844–1924, French author. The style of his early works is charming and ironic, as in *Le Crime de Sylvestre Bonnard* (1881), *Le Livre de mon ami* (1885), *Thaïs* (1890), *La Rôtisserie de la Reine Pédauque* (1893), *Le Lys rouge* (1894). Following the Dreyfus Affair, in which he supported Zola, he turned to political satire with *Penguin Island* (1908) and *La Révolte des anges* (1914). Awarded 1921 Nobel Prize in Literature.

France, republic (212,700 sq. mi.; pop. 40,502,-513), W Europe, bordering on English Channel (N), Atlantic Ocean (W), Spain (SW), Mediterranean (S), Italy, Switzerland, Germany (E), Luxembourg, and Belgium (NE); cap. Paris. Called Metropolitan France, it is the chief member of the FRENCH UNION and consists of the 89 departments of continental France and the island-department of CORSICA. Its central natural feature is the MASSIF CENTRAL. N of that rugged mountain mass and of the Loire R. extend the fertile Paris basin, drained by the SEINE and MARNE, and the hilly landscapes of NORMANDY and BRITTANY. W and SW of the Massif Central the Aquitanian plain, drained by the GARONNE and DORDOGNE, stretches to the Atlantic and the PYRENEES; S of the Massif is the coastal plain of LANGUEDOC. A chain of mountains parallels the E border —the ARDENNES, VOSGES, and JURA, and the ALPS of SAVOY, DAUPHINÉ, and PROVENCE (highest point MONT BLANC). Despite extreme administrative centralization, the old provinces (abolished 1789) retain striking diversity and are basic cultural, economic, and geographic units—e.g., ALSACE, AUVERGNE, Brittany, CHAMPAGNE, GASCONY, TOURAINE. Nearly self-sufficient in agr., France is a country of small, independent farmers and of many small towns. Only PARIS, MARSEILLES, LYONS, and BORDEAUX have more than 250,000 inhabitants. Wine and luxury articles are among chief exports. Natural resources include coal (NORD dept.), iron (LORRAINE), hydroelectric power (RHONE valley). Lille, Saint-Étienne, Roubaix, Clermont-Ferrand, Le Creusot are important industrial centers. Le Havre, Rouen, Cherbourg, Saint-Nazaire, Nantes, Bordeaux, Marseilles are the chief ports. Though some German, Flemish, and Basque are spoken in border regions, as well as Breton in lower Brittany, Latin culture predominates, as does Roman Catholicism. Separation of Church and state dates from the struggle of 1905–6. *Medieval France.* Roman conquest of GAUL was completed by Caesar 51 B.C. A Christian, Latin, highly civilized, prosperous country by the 5th cent. A.D., Gaul was suddenly reduced by Germanic invaders to chaos and barbarism. The FRANKS, emerging as sole masters under CLOVIS I, ruled Gaul as part of their empire under the dynasties of the MEROVINGIANS (481–751) and CAROLINGIANS (751–987). CHARLES MARTEL saved Gaul from Arabic conquest; CHARLEMAGNE gave it an era of order and cultural rebirth; the treaties of VERDUN (843) and MERSEN (870) made France a separate kingdom; the decline of Carolingian rule hastened the establishment of FEUDALISM and the MANORIAL SYSTEM. Powerful feudal lords easily usurped the authority of the weak kings. In 987 began the dynasty of the direct Capetians (Hugh Capet, Robert II, Henry I, Philip I, Louis VI, Louis VII, Philip II, Louis VIII, Louis IX, Philip III, Philip IV, Louis X, John I, Philip V, Charles IV). Their rule was a patient uphill struggle for control over the nobles and robber barons, extension of the royal domain, and revival of commerce; in this they were aided by the rising urban bourgeoisie. The reform of the CLUNIAC ORDER, the prestige of the SORBONNE, and its leading role in the CRUSADES gave France cultural supremacy in medieval Christendom. These gains were lost in the HUNDRED YEARS WAR with England, which devastated France and nearly ended its national existence (1337–1453). The VALOIS kings, aided by such heroes as DU GUESCLIN and JOAN OF ARC, emerged victorious; LOUIS XI (reigned 1461–83) created a new, unified France under a strong royal authority.

From Renaissance to Revolution. The later Valois kings—CHARLES VIII, LOUIS XII, FRANCIS I—wasted much effort on their imperialist struggle with Spain (see ITALIAN WARS); under the last Valois—Henry II, Francis II, Charles IX, Henry III—France bled in bitter civil strife (see RELIGION, WARS OF). Nevertheless, French culture in the 16th cent., stimulated by the Renaissance, went through a golden age which continued through the 17th cent. HENRY IV, first Bourbon king, ended the civil war and restored prosperity. The reigns of LOUIS XIII (1610–43) and LOUIS XIV (1643–1715), parts of which were dominated by cardinals RICHELIEU and MAZARIN, made France a nearly absolute monarchy and in a series of costly wars raised it to the chief power of Europe. But the quest for glory strained the treasury and drained the people. LOUIS XV's wars were no less ruinous but brought no glory; LOUIS XVI's intervention in the American Revolution made France bankrupt. At the same time the bourgeoisie had risen to prosperity and increasingly resented an antiquated system which restricted its economic activities (see MERCANTILISM), drained it through an iniquitous and inefficient fiscal system, misspent the revenues, and to some extent barred it from the government. This, rather than royal absolutism—which in fact was limited by custom and law—was the chief factor leading to the revolution of 1789. *Modern France.* The upheaval that shook Europe from 1789 to 1815 is covered in the articles FRENCH REVOLUTION; FRENCH REVOLUTIONARY WARS; NAPOLEON I. France emerged from it a uniform, bureaucratic state, dominated by its bourgeoisie, whom the Industrial Revolution brought into its own. The Bourbon Restoration was shortlived (see LOUIS XVIII; CHARLES X). The

July Revolution of 1830 set up the monarchy of LOUIS PHILIPPE, overthrown in turn by the FEBRUARY REVOLUTION of 1848. The Second Republic was changed into the Second Empire by NAPOLEON III (1852), whose rule ended disastrously in the FRANCO-PRUSSIAN WAR (1870). French prosperity and colonial expansion continued under the Third Republic (1871–1940), but political disunity was a constant cause of instability. At tremendous sacrifice, France won in WORLD WAR I, but it was unable to deal with the crises of the post-war period. In WORLD WAR II France had to conclude an ignominious armistice (1940). While Gen. Charles de GAULLE continued to lead the Free French movement from London, France itself was partly under direct German occupation, partly under the subservient VICHY GOVERNMENT of Marshal Pétain; after the Allied invasion of N Africa (1942) all France came under German occupation. Liberated in 1944, France was slow in recovering from the sufferings of occupation, the destruction of war, and the shock to its economy. The Fourth Republic began with the new bicameral constitution of 1946. A member of the UN, France also joined in the European Recovery Program (1948) and the North Atlantic Treaty (1949).

Francesca, Piero della: see PIERO DELLA FRANCESCA.

Francesca da Rimini (fränsĕ′skŭ, Ital. fränchä′skä dä rē′mēnē), 13th-cent. heroine of tragic verse. Her love for Paolo, brother of her crippled husband, was immortalized in Dante's *Divine Comedy.*

Franceschi, Piero de': see PIERO DELLA FRANCESCA.

Franche-Comté (fräsh-kôtā′), region and former province, E France, in Haute-Saône, Doubs, and Jura depts.; historic cap. Dôle (until 1676), later BESANÇON. A mountainous region (JURA in E, VOSGES in N), it has forests, pastures, agr. Mfg. of clocks, machinery, plastics. Free County of Burgundy or Franche-Comté was created 9th cent.; passed with kingdom of Arles to Holy Roman Empire 1034. Philip the Bold of Burgundy acquired it by marriage (15th cent.); through his daughter, Mary of Burgundy, it passed to the Spanish Hapsburgs, but it retained considerable autonomy. A battleground in the Wars of Religion and the Thirty Years War, it was twice laid waste. Louis XIV conquered it twice (1668, 1674) and obtained its cession from Spain in 1678.

franchise, a right specifically conferred by the government, especially that business franchise conferred by a municipality for the use of its streets to furnish public utilities. In politics, franchise is the right to vote.

Francia (frän′chä), c.1450–1517, Italian painter of early Bolognese school.

Francia, José Gaspar Rodríguez (hōsä′ gäspär′ rōdrē′gäs frän′syä), 1760–1840, dictator of Paraguay (1814–40) and creator of national independence, known as El Supremo. By keeping Paraguay from foreign intercourse he stimulated internal growth and strong nationalistic spirit.

Franciabigio (frän″chäbē′jō), 1482–1525, Florentine painter. Collaborated on several works with his master, Andrea del Sarto.

Francis, Saint (Francis of Assisi), 1182?–1226, founder of the Franciscans, one of the greatest of Christian saints, b. Assisi, Italy. His original name was Giovanni di Bernardone, but he was called Francesco [Frenchman] from his father's travels in France. Was briefly a soldier, but at 22 he turned from worldly things and became devout. In 1209 he set out to preach, and from the first he won others by his humility, his joyful poverty, his singular devotion to other men, and his religious fervor. A little group of men gathered about him, and they went to Rome, where they were permitted to form a band of friars. These new Franciscans went about Italy, and soon they were preaching in foreign lands. Francis went abroad too and was in the Holy Land when dissension in the order led to his return. He held an assembly (1221), at which, with typical self-abnegation, he laid down command. He went on preaching and leading an ascetic life, and he wrote the rule for his order. In 1224 in a vision he received the stigmata (painful wounds corresponding to the wounds of the crucified Christ). He was well loved in his time and mourned throughout Italy when he died. Stories clustered about his holy, simple life, some of them later collected in *The Little Flowers of St. Francis;* very familiar are the stories of his preaching to the birds and of his taming a wolf at Gubbio by gentleness. He may have written the joyous appreciation of nature called *Hymn of the Sun.* Feast: Oct. 4.

Francis, emperors of the Holy Roman Empire. **Francis I,** 1708–65. Married MARIA THERESA 1736; elected emperor 1745 (see AUSTRIAN SUCCESSION, WAR OF THE). Earlier, he had been duke of LORRAINE (1729–37) and grand duke of TUSCANY (1737–65). Ruled ably in Tuscany, but left imperial government largely in hands of Maria Theresa. Father of Joseph II, Leopold II, Marie Antoinette. **Francis II,** 1768–1835, succeeded his father Leopold II as emperor and king of Hungary and Bohemia (1792). Was defeated four times in FRENCH REVOLUTIONARY WARS (1797, 1801) and in wars against NAPOLEON I (1805, 1809). Took title emperor of Austria as **Francis I** in 1804; dissolved Holy Roman Empire in 1806. Gave his daughter Marie Louise in marriage to Napoleon (1810). Joined new coalition against Napoleon 1813; presided over Congress of VIENNA (1814–15). With his minister METTERNICH he dominated HOLY ALLIANCE and German Confederation. His son Ferdinand succeeded him.

Francis, kings of France. **Francis I,** 1494–1547, son-in-law of Louis XII, reigned 1515–47. Resuming ITALIAN WARS, he won at MARIGNANO (1515). He lost in imperial election of 1519 to CHARLES V, his life-long rival. Despite failure to win English alliance at FIELD OF CLOTH OF GOLD he attacked Charles (1521), was routed and captured at Pavia (1525). Having, in his words, "lost all save life and honor," he obtained freedom by signing Treaty of Madrid (1526), in which he renounced territorial claims. His creation of

the League of Cognac (with Pope Clement VII, Henry VIII of England, Venice, and Florence) precipitated a second war (1527–29), which ended, unfavorably, with the Treaty of CAMBRAI. A third war (1536–38) was inconclusive. In 1542, in alliance with SULEIMAN I of Turkey, he again attacked Charles (allied with Henry VIII). Peace with Charles (1544; see CRÉPY, TREATY OF) and with Henry (1546) confirmed his previous failures. A typical Renaissance monarch, unscrupulous, spendthrift, and dissolute, Francis also was a patron of arts and letters. Da Vinci, Cellini, and Rabelais were among his protégés. His grandson **Francis II,** 1544–60, son of Henry II, reigned 1559–60. Married Mary Queen of Scots (1558). Government was in hands of Charles and François de GUISE. Reprisals against Conspiracy of AMBOISE antagonized Protestants.

Francis, kings of the Two Sicilies. **Francis I,** 1777–1830, reigned 1825–30. His rule was reactionary and corrupt. **Francis II,** 1836–94, reigned 1859–61. Fought against RISORGIMENTO. His capitulation at Gaeta to Victor Emmanuel II (1861) led to proclamation of united Italy.

Francis, c.1554–1584, French prince, duke of Alençon and Anjou; youngest son of Henry II of France. One of suitors for hand of Elizabeth of England. In 1580 William the Silent offered him the rule of Netherlands (then in rebellion against Spain). He accepted, set sail from England in 1582, but was expelled by his subjects and lost Elizabeth's support when he tried to obtain absolute power (1583). His death opened French succession to Henry of Navarre (Henry IV).

Francis II, 1453–88, duke of Brittany (1458–88). Sought to preserve Breton independence from France. Joined League of Public Weal against LOUIS XI, who forced him to sign Peace of Ancenis (1468). Died shortly after his rout by Charles VIII (1488), who eventually married his daughter ANNE OF BRITTANY.

Francis Borgia, Saint (bôr'jù), 1510–72, Spanish Jesuit, third general of his order (1565–72). A member of the Borgia family, he was great-grandson of Pope Alexander VI and was duke of Gandia and a wealthy courtier of Emperor Charles V. After his wife's death (1546) he went to join St. Ignatius Loyola in Rome to become a Jesuit. Gave money to build the Roman College. After ordination in 1551, he built up the order and took charge of foreign missions (including those to America). As general of the Society of Jesus, he sent missionaries to N and E Europe and did much to promote the Catholic Reform. Edited the Jesuit rule and the *Spiritual Exercises.* Feast: Oct. 10.

Franciscans (frăn'sĭ'skŭnz), members of the religious orders following the rule of St. FRANCIS (approved by the pope 1223). They include three organizations of friars: the Friars Minor (formerly called Observants; they use the abbreviation O.F.M.), the Friars Minor Capuchin (see CAPUCHINS), and the Friars Minor Conventual. The Franciscans began as friars living in absolute poverty without property, but later generations relaxed this custom, and there were recurrent moves within the order to return to "pure" poverty. These caused some dissension, particularly that led by zealots called Spirituals; briefly they were very powerful in Italy, and one of their heroes was pope as CELESTINE V, but had to abdicate. In 1322 the pope settled the matter by putting Franciscans on the same basis as other orders as to property holding. Later another move toward primitive practice produced the Observants, who were made independent in 1517. Friars wishing still more strict observance of the rule became the Capuchins in 1525. The Franciscans were prominent at the medieval universities and contributed to scholasticism. They also were vigorous missionaries and did much work in many parts of the New World. St. CLARE, a follower of St. Francis, founded an order of Franciscan nuns (also called Poor Clares). There are also many members of the third order, both men and women, some living as laymen in the world, others in religious communities. Formerly the Franciscans were called the Gray Friars, but their habit now is typically brown.

Francis Ferdinand, 1863–1914, Austrian archduke, heir apparent of his great-uncle, Emperor Francis Joseph. Was assassinated, with his wife, by a Serbian nationalist at Sarajevo (June 28). Serbia's partial rejection of stiff Austrian ultimatum (July 23) led to WORLD WAR I.

Francis Joseph, 1830–1916, emperor of Austria (1848–1916), king of Hungary (1867–1916); nephew of FERDINAND, who abdicated in his favor. Subdued Hungary and defeated Sardinia (1849), but lost Lombardy in Italian War of 1859, Venetia in AUSTRO-PRUSSIAN WAR of 1866. Reorganized in 1867, his empire became the AUSTRO-HUNGARIAN MONARCHY. His private life was beset by the tragedies of his wife, ELIZABETH; his brother, MAXIMILIAN of Mexico; his son, Archduke RUDOLF. Charles I succeeded him.

Francis of Sales, Saint, 1567–1622, Savoyard Roman Catholic preacher, Doctor of the Church. Of an aristocratic family, he joined the priesthood contrary to his father's wishes and rose to become bishop coadjutor (1599) and bishop (1602) of Geneva. With St. Jane Francis de Chantal he founded the Order of the Visitation for women. His eloquent sermons moved to religion and converted many Protestants. Their burden was love of God and love of man. Two treatises *L'Introduction à la vie dévote* and *Treatise on the Love of God* are masterpieces of religious writing. Feast: Jan. 29.

Francis Xavier, Saint (zā'vyŭr), 1506–52, Basque Jesuit missionary, called the Apostle to the Indies. Friend of St. IGNATIUS OF LOYOLA, with whom he and five others formed the Society of JESUS; he was ordained with Ignatius (1537). After 1540 he spent the last 11 years of his life as a missionary in India and the Far East.

Franck, César (sāzär' frăk'), 1822–90, Belgian-French composer and organist. Much of his finest music was for organ. Among his most significant works are the Symphony in D Minor; *Variations symphoniques* for piano and orchestra; *Les Béatitudes*, oratorio; a violin sonata; *Trois Chorals* for organ; *Prélude, choral et fugue,* for piano.

Franck, Hans: see LÜTZELBURGER, HANS.

Franck, James, 1882–, German physicist. He shared 1925 Nobel Prize for discovery of laws governing effect of impact of electron on atom.

Franco, Francisco (fränthē'skō frän'kō), 1892–, Spanish generalissimo and dictator. Joined Insurgents in civil war of 1936–39 (see SPAIN); became chief of government in 1936, Caudillo [leader] in 1937, premier in 1939, regent (pending installment of a king) in 1947. Dissolved all parties except FALANGE (1937); dissolved Falange 1942. Kept Spain out of World War II despite commitments to Mussolini and Hitler.

Franco-German War: see FRANCO-PRUSSIAN WAR.

Franconia (frăngkō'nēů), Ger. *Franken,* duchy of medieval Germany. Created 9th cent., it extended from W bank of the Rhine eastward along Main R. Emperor Otto I broke it up into two nominal duchies—W or Rhenish Franconia (incl. archbishoprics of Mainz and Speyer, free cities of Frankfurt and Worms, Rhenish Palatinate, landgraviate of Hesse) and E Franconia (incl. bishoprics of Würzburg and Bamberg, margraviates of Ansbach and Bayreuth, free city of Nuremberg). Titular dukes of W Franconia furnished Franconian or Salian dynasty of emperors (1024–1125; see HOLY ROMAN EMPIRE). In E Franconia the ducal title, long in disuse, was revived by bishops of Würzburg (15th cent.). E Franconia passed to Bavaria in 1806–15 and was later divided into the provinces of **Lower Franconia** (cap. Würzburg), in the Main valley, NW Bavaria; **Middle Franconia** (cap. Ansbach), in hilly region of N Bavaria, with Nuremberg, Fürth, and Erlangen; and **Upper Franconia** (cap. Bayreuth), which includes the wooded Frankenwald plateau and the Fichtelgebirge, in NE Bavaria.

Franconia Mountains, range in White Mts., NW N.H., rising to 5,249 ft. in Mt. Lafayette. To W is **Franconia Notch,** c.6-mi. pass, with Old Man of the Mountain or the Profile ("Great Stone Face" of Hawthorne's story) and the Flume. Tramway (1938) mounts Profile Mt. near Echo L. **Franconia** town (pop. 549), NW of notch, is ski resort.

Franco-Prussian War or **Franco-German War,** July 19, 1870–Jan. 28, 1871. By his publication of EMS DISPATCH, Bismarck deliberately goaded the aggressive French government into declaring war on Prussia, which was joined by the other German states. A brilliant campaign, led by H. K. B. von Moltke, resulted in French rout at Sedan, where NAPOLEON III was captured (Sept. 1). French resistance continued under a provisional government but became useless after surrender of BAZAINE at Metz (Oct. 27). Paris, however, resisted Prussian siege until Jan., 1871, despite growing famine, and refused to accept preliminary peace signed at Versailles (see VERSAILLES, TREATY OF, 1871) until May, when COMMUNE OF PARIS was suppressed by regular French forces. Chief results of war were creation of German Empire under William I of Prussia (proclaimed at Versailles on Jan. 18, 1871); cession of Alsace-Lorraine to Germany; establishment of Third Republic in France.

Frankenstein: see SHELLEY, MARY WOLLSTONE-CRAFT.

Frankfort. 1 City (pop. 15,028), W central Ind., NW of Indianapolis; laid out 1830. Trade center for apple region. Food and metal products. **2** City (pop. 11,916), state cap. (since 1792), N Ky., on Kentucky R. and E of Louisville; settled 1779, organized by Gen. James Wilkinson 1786. Trade and shipping center for farm and limestone area with mfg. of whisky, shoes, and twine. Here are present capitol (1909), old capitol (1827–30), Liberty Hall (1796, perhaps designed by Thomas Jefferson), cemetery with graves of Daniel and Rebecca Boone, and Kentucky State Col. for Negroes (land grant; coed.; 1886).

Frankfurt (frängk'fûrt, Ger. frängk'fōōrt) or **Frankfurt-am-Main** (äm-mīn'), city (pop. 523,923), Hesse, W Germany, on Main R. Historic, cultural, industrial, commercial, financial, and publishing center; river port. Produces chemicals, pharmaceutic articles, machinery, electrical equipment, clothing. Seat of university (opened 1914). Founded on site of Roman settlement; a royal residence under Carolingians, free imperial city from 1372; site of imperial elections from 1356 (see ELECTORS). Emperors-elect were crowned at Church of St. Bartholomew, then proceeded amid medieval pageantry to banquet at city hall, the Römer. Semiannual fairs, first mentioned 1240, brought city prosperity. Jews played important part until Nazi regime; Rothschild family originated here. Frankfurt accepted Reformation (1530), belonged to Schmalkaldic League (1536–47), was seat of diet of GERMAN CONFEDERATION (1815–66). In 1848–49 the Frankfurt Parliament met here at Church of St. Paul to plan unification of Germany; it adopted a federal constitution (excluding Austria) and offered imperial crown to FREDERICK WILLIAM IV of Prussia, whose refusal caused the failure of the whole scheme. Having sided with Austria in Austro-Prussian War, Frankfurt was annexed by Prussia (1866) and incorporated into Hesse-Nassau prov. After World War II, when it was in great part destroyed, Frankfurt became hq. of U.S. occupation forces. Its historic landmarks, including the Römer, the Catholic Church of St. Bartholomew, the Protestant Church of St. Paul, and the house where Goethe was born, have been largely rebuilt.

Frankfurt, Treaty of, 1871: see VERSAILLES, TREATY OF, 1871.

Frankfurt-an-der-Oder (-än-dĕr-ō'dŭr), city (pop. 51,577), Brandenburg, E Germany, on Oder R. Mfg. of machinery, textiles, frankfurter sausages.

Frankfurter, Felix, 1882–, Associate Justice of U.S. Supreme Court (1939–), b. Austria. Has long public record in support of liberal tradition.

frankincense, resin of E African and Arabian tree of genus *Boswellia*. It is gathered in lumps for use in incense for religious cere-monies—a use it has had since Old Testament times (Ex. 30.34).

Frankland, Sir Edward, 1825–99, English chemist. He evolved the theory of valence; made studies of flame, luminosity, and gases; discovered helium.

Franklin, Ann Smith, 1696–1763, American printer. Succeeded her husband, James Franklin, Benjamin Franklin's brother, in commercial printing business. Published Newport, R.I., *Mercury*, and printed legal documents, paper money of R.I., and almanac series.

Franklin, Benjamin, 1706–90, American statesman, printer, scientist, and writer, b. Boston. Went to Philadelphia as printer (1723). His common-sense philosophy and wit won attention, especially in his *Poor Richard's Almanack*, published 1732–57. Helped estab. (1751) present Univ. of Pennsylvania. Experiment with kite in a thunderstorm proved identity of lightning and electricity. Deputy postmaster general of colonies (1753–74). Proposed plan of union for colonies at ALBANY CONGRESS (1754). Agent for several colonies in England before American Revolution. Helped draft Declaration of Independence, which he signed. Successful diplomatic agent to France for new republic. Chosen commissioner (1781) to negotiate peace with Great Britain. Popular figure in France and England. Took part in Federal Constitutional Convention (1787). His autobiography is well known. His natural son, **William Franklin,** c.1730–1813, last royal governor of N.J., sided with Loyalists in American Revolution.

Franklin, Sir John, 1786–1847, British explorer in N Canada. Led two expeditions into arctic regions (1819–22, 1825–27). Set out in 1845 to seek Northwest Passage. Entire expedition of 129 men lost. More than 40 rescue parties subsequently sought traces of expedition, gaining immense geographical knowledge. Evidence of expedition's tragic fate finally discovered in 1850s.

Franklin, William: see FRANKLIN, BENJAMIN.

Franklin, provisional district: see NORTHWEST TERRITORIES, Canada.

Franklin. 1 Village, SE Idaho, at Utah line; founded 1860 by Mormons. Idaho's first permanent settlement. **2** City (pop. 7,316), S central Ind., S of Indianapolis. Trade center of agr. area. Mfg. of automobile parts and rayon. **3** Town (pop. 6,144), S La., on Bayou Teche. Processing center of sugar area. **4** Town (pop. 8,037), including Franklin village (pop. 5,348), SE Mass., near R.I. line, SW of Boston. Mfg. of woolens and foundry products. Birthplace of Horace Mann. **5** City (pop. 6,552), S central N.H., N of Concord. Merrimack R. is formed here. Mfg. of paper, textiles, and metal products. Birthplace of Daniel Webster. **6** City (pop. 5,388), SW Ohio, S of Dayton. Mfg. of paper products and clothing. **7** City (pop. 10,006), NW Pa., on Allegheny R.; laid out 1795. Has oil wells and refineries and mfg. of machinery and metal products. **8** Town (pop. 5,475), central Tenn., on Harpeth R. and S of Nashville, in farm area. Has phosphate mines and lumber mills. Scene of Civil War fighting 1864.

Franklin, State of, government (1784–88) formed by inhabitants of Washington, Sullivan, and Greene counties in present E Tenn. after N.C. ceded (June, 1784) its western lands to U.S. The government under John Sevier passed out of existence when terms of its officers expired.

Franklin and Marshall College: see LANCASTER, Pa.

Franklin Institute, in Philadelphia; for the promotion of mechanic arts; chartered and opened 1824, first of its kind in U.S. Named for Benjamin Franklin. An important research center, it includes Fels Planetarium, applied-science museum, technical library, Bartol Research Foundation (physics, now housed at Swarthmore Col.), and Biochemical Research Foundation. Has published journal since 1825; makes awards for work in physical sciences.

Franklin Park, village (pop. 8,899), NE Ill., W suburb of Chicago.

Franks, group of Germanic tribes which by the 3d cent. A.D. had settled along the Rhine (Salian Franks in N, Ripuarian Franks in S). Salian Franks moved into Gaul in 4th cent. A.D. as Roman allies. Their leader CLOVIS I united all Franks under his kingship (481), accepted Christianity, founded dynasty of MEROVINGIANS. He and his successors conquered most of W and central Europe, but the Frankish empire was usually divided into several kingdoms, notably NEUSTRIA, AUSTRASIA, and BURGUNDY. In 8th cent. began rule of CAROLINGIANS, which culminated under CHARLEMAGNE. After Treaty of MERSEN (870), kingdom of W Franks became France; that of E Franks, Germany.

Franz, Robert (fränts'), 1815–92, German composer of about 350 lieder, intimate songs, which have some of the feeling of folk song.

Franzen, Frans Michael (fränsän'), 1772–1847, early Swedish romantic poet, a bishop, b. Finland.

Franz Josef Land (fräns' jō'zúf, fränts' yō'zĕf), archipelago, c.8,000 sq. mi., in the Arctic Ocean, N of Novaya Zemlya. Claimed by USSR 1926. Its 85 islands include settlements and government observation stations, but are 90% covered by ice interspersed with poor lichen vegetation. Discovered by Karl Weyprecht and Julius van Payer (1873); explored by Fridtjof Nansen (1895–96) and others.

Franz Joseph: see FRANCIS JOSEPH.

Frascati (fräskä'tē), town (pop. 10,660), Latium, central Italy, in Alban Hills near site of anc. Tusculum. Noted for its wine and its fine Renaissance villas (e.g., Villa Aldobrandini, Villa Torlonia). Damaged in World War II.

Frasch process extracts sulphur from deposits. Three concentric pipes are sunk in bed; water heated above melting point of sulphur is sent down outer pipe, air under pressure down inner and sulphur is forced to surface through middle pipe. Process was named for Herman Frasch, 1851–1914, German-born American chemist.

Fraser, James Earle, 1876–, American sculptor. Best known for monuments and statues of the American Indian, notably *The End of the Trail.* Designed Indian head and buffalo for five-cent piece. His wife, **Laura Gardin Fraser,** 1889–, is also a sculptor.

Fraser, Simon, 1776?–1862, Canadian explorer and fur trader. Explored Fraser R. to its mouth while establishing trading posts for North West Co.

Fraser, chief river of B.C., Canada. Rises on W slope of the Rockies and flows c.350 mi. NW to Prince George, then c.500 mi. S and W to the Strait of Georgia S of Vancouver. Chief tributaries are Nechako, Quesnal, Thompson, Chilcotin, Blackwater and Lillooet rivers. Navigable to Yale, c.80 mi. from the mouth. Above this is scenic Fraser R. canyon. Discovered 1793 by Alexander Mackenzie and named for fur trader Simon Fraser. Gold discovered on upper reaches 1859, after which Cariboo Road opened area to settlement.

Fraserburgh (frä'zúrbúrú), burgh (pop. 10,-444), Aberdeenshire, Scotland. Has a fine harbor and is one of chief herring fishing centers in Scotland.

fraternal orders, social organizations offering members a fellowship reminiscent of code and spirit of medieval guild. Local "lodges," in such orders as FREEMASONRY (oldest in the U.S.) and the Odd Fellows, use symbolic rituals. Orders may be restricted to one sex only, or may be mixed.

fraud, willful misrepresentation intended to deprive another person of some right. It may also constitute the crime of false pretenses. Fraud may be interposed as defense in a suit based on a contract to which the defendant was fraudulently induced.

Frauenfeld (frou'únfĕlt), town (pop. 11,026), cap. of Thurgau canton, N Switzerland. Aluminum and food industries. Has 11th-cent. castle.

Fray Bentos (frī bān'tōs), city (pop. 9,500), SW Uruguay, port on Uruguay R.; founded 1859 as Independencia. Has large meat-packing plants.

Frayser's Farm: see SEVEN DAYS BATTLES.

Frazee, John, 1790–1852, American pioneer sculptor. Did busts of Daniel Webster and John Marshall.

Frazer, Sir James George, 1854–1941, Scottish classicist and anthropologist, known especially for *The Golden Bough,* a study of magic and religion.

Fréchette, Louis Honoré (fräshĕt'), 1839–1908, French Canadian poet. First Canadian poet whose works were crowned by French Academy. His verse shows genuine feeling for nature and for heroic history of French Canada.

Fredegunde (frĕ"dúgŭn'dù), c.545–597, Frankish queen. Married CHILPERIC I of Neustria after inducing him to murder his wife Galswintha (567). Resulting feud with BRUNHILDA of Austrasia continued until 613 under her son CLOTAIRE II.

Frederic, Harold, 1856–98, American novelist. A newspaperman, he was after 1884 a foreign correspondent for the New York *Times.* Of his novels, his masterpiece was *The Damnation of Theron Ware* (1896; a study of moral degeneration).

Frederica, town, S central Del., S of Dover. At near-by Barratt's Chapel annual services commemorate formation of Methodist Episcopal Church.

Frederick, emperors and German kings. **Frederick I** or **Frederick Barbarossa** [Ital.,= red beard], c.1122–1190, of the house of HOHENSTAUFEN, succeeded his uncle Conrad III as German king (1152), pacified Germany by proclaiming a general land peace (1152), and was crowned emperor by Pope ADRIAN IV (1155). In four subsequent campaigns in Italy he struggled against the papacy (notably ALEXANDER III) and the cities of Lombardy (see LOMBARD LEAGUE). Though victorious at first, he was excommunicated by Alexander, defeated at Legnano (1176), and forced to accept the Lombard League's demands in the Peace of Constance (1183). He succeeded, however, in breaking the power of his Guelphic rival, HENRY THE LION, in 1180–81. In 1189 he set out on the Third Crusade. He drowned in Cilicia. Legend has him still alive, awaiting German unification in the KYFFHÄUSER. His grandson, **Frederick II,** 1194–1250, was the son of Emperor HENRY VI and of Empress CONSTANCE. Pope Innocent III invested him with Sicily (1197) and promoted his election as antiking to OTTO IV (1212). He was crowned king at Aachen after Otto's formal deposition (1215) and emperor at Rome (1220). His long-delayed crusade (1228–29), actually a state visit, resulted in the peaceful cession of Jerusalem, Nazareth, and Bethlehem to the Christians and his own coronation as king of Jerusalem. This treaty was denounced by Pope GREGORY IX and soon broken by the Moslems. Sporadic warfare between emperor and pope flared into a life-and-death struggle in 1239 and reached its culmination under INNOCENT IV, who declared Frederick deposed and excommunicated (1245). Frederick died of dysentery while the war was turning in his favor. It was left for his son CONRAD IV and his grandson CONRADIN to see the final downfall of their house and the triumph of the papacy. An Italian by birth and temperament, Frederick left German affairs largely to his sons Henry (whom he had imprisoned in 1235 after a rebellion) and Conrad IV. Henry made sweeping concessions to the German princes, and under Conrad Germany fell into anarchy. In Sicily, Frederick promoted far-seeing legal and fiscal reform and expanded commerce and industry. His universal gifts made him a patron and student of medicine, mathematics, astronomy, and poetry. His court at Palermo was of oriental splendor. **Frederick III,** 1415–93, duke of Styria (1435–93) and of Austria (1457–93), became head of the house of HAPSBURG at the death of his cousin Albert II. Elected German king (1440) and crowned emperor (1452), he overcame his many rivals and enemies by dint of sheer indolence and longevity. Through his marriage policy he came near to realizing his motto, AEIOU (*Austriae est imperare orbi universo:* "it is Austria's destiny to rule the whole world"). The marriage of his son MAXIMILIAN I with MARY OF BURGUNDY was indeed the cornerstone of Hapsburg world power.

Frederick III, 1831–88, emperor of Germany,

king of Prussia (March–June, 1888); son of William I, father of William II. He was a liberal and a patron of art and learning. His consort, Victoria, daughter of Queen Victoria of England, was known after his death as Empress Victoria.

Frederick, Danish kings. **Frederick III,** 1609–70, king of Denmark and Norway (1648–70). Lost Skane, Halland, and Blekinge to Sweden in Treaties of Roskilde (1658) and Copenhagen (1660). His minister GRIFFENFELD drew up "King's Law" (*Kongelov*), which made Denmark an absolute hereditary monarchy (1665). **Frederick IV,** 1671–1730, king of Denmark and Norway (1699–1730). Joined alliance with Poland and Russia against Charles XII of Sweden in NORTHERN WAR. In peace treaties of 1720–21 he renounced claims to S Sweden but obtained ducal Schleswig. Consolidated absolutism; abolished serfdom. **Frederick V,** 1723–66, king of Denmark and Norway (1746–66). His reign was period of commercial prosperity. **Frederick VI,** 1769–1839, king of Denmark (1808–39) and of Norway (1808–14). After English attack on Copenhagen (1807) he allied himself with Napoleon I and was punished at Congress of Vienna by transfer of Norway to Sweden. **Frederick VII,** 1808–63, king of Denmark (1848–63). The vexed SCHLESWIG-HOLSTEIN question caused trouble throughout his reign. **Frederick VIII,** 1843–1912, king of Denmark (1906–12) was the father of Christian X of Denmark and Haakon VII of Norway. **Frederick IX,** 1899–, king of Denmark (1947–), succeeded his father Christian X.

Frederick, kings of Prussia. **Frederick I,** 1657–1713, elector of Brandenburg (1688–1713), was crowned first king of PRUSSIA in 1701. **Frederick II** or **Frederick the Great,** 1712–86, succeeded his father FREDERICK WILLIAM I in 1740. Despised by his father as effeminate esthete (he cultivated music, philosophy, and poetry), he spent a miserable youth. In 1730 he planned to flee abroad and barely escaped execution as a deserter. As soon as he became king, Frederick showed unexpected qualities of leadership and decision. With a spurious claim on parts of SILESIA, he opened the War of the AUSTRIAN SUCCESSION with a surprise attack on Maria Theresa (1740); having secured Silesia, he abandoned his allies and made peace (1745). This war and the SEVEN YEARS WAR (1756–63) made Prussia the foremost military power of Europe and established Frederick as one of the great military geniuses of all time. Frederick also was the prime mover for the first partition of POLAND (1772), which vastly increased his kingdom. The War of the BAVARIAN SUCCESSION (1778–79) and his creation of the Fürstenbund [league of princes] (1785), thwarted the schemes of Emperor JOSEPH II. A "benevolent despot," he promoted important legal and social reforms. His stormy friendship with VOLTAIRE is well known, as are his philosophical midnight suppers at SANS SOUCI. His writings, mostly in French, are collected in *Œuvres de Frédéric le Grand* (33 vols., 1846–57). His poetry is mediocre, his prose excellent. Though idolized by

German nationalists, he despised German cultural aspirations. His philosophy was skeptical and materialistic. A champion of religious tolerance, he disliked all religions. He composed passable flute concertos and other music. Childless, he was succeeded by his nephew, Frederick William II. **Frederick III**: see FREDERICK III, emperor of Germany.

Frederick I, c.1372–1440, elector of Brandenburg (1415–40); as Frederick VI, burgrave of Nuremberg. Emperor Sigismund rewarded his good services by investing him with Brandenburg, of which he was the first Hohenzollern ruler.

Frederick, electors palatine. **Frederick III** (the Pious), 1515–76, reigned 1559–76. Inclining toward Calvinism, he caused HEIDELBERG CATECHISM to be drawn up (1563). **Frederick IV**, 1574–1610, reigned 1592–1610. Promoted and headed PROTESTANT UNION. **Frederick V**: see FREDERICK THE WINTER KING.

Frederick III (the Wise), 1463–1525, elector of Saxony (1486–1525). Founded Univ. of Wittenberg (1502). A protector of Luther, he gave him asylum at the Wartburg but himself remained a Catholic.

Frederick. 1 City (pop. 18,142), NW Md., near Monocacy R.; settled 1746. Trade and mfg. (clothing, brushes, electrical apparatus) center in farm area. Seat of Hood Col. (Evangelical and Reformed; for women; 1893). Here are homes of R. B. Taney and Barbara Frietchie, and Francis Scott Key Monument. Confederate victory near by in Civil War. **2** City (pop. 5,467), SW Okla., near Red R., in farm area. Processes cotton.

Frederick Augustus, rulers of Saxony. **Frederick Augustus I** and **Frederick Augustus II**, electors: see AUGUSTUS II and AUGUSTUS III, kings of Poland. **Frederick Augustus III**, 1750–1827, elector (1763–1806), became king of Saxony as **Frederick Augustus I** in 1806 after concluding a separate peace with Napoleon I. Napoleon also made him titular duke of Warsaw (1807–14). He abandoned his alliance with Napoleon a little later than everybody else and as a result lost half his kingdom to Prussia at the Congress of Vienna (1815).

Frederick Barbarossa: see FREDERICK I, emperor.

Frederick Henry, 1584–1647, prince of Orange; son of William the Silent. As stadholder of the Netherlands (1625–47) he secured (1635) French and Swedish alliance in Thirty Years War; captured 's Hertogenbosch (1629), Maastricht (1632), and Breda (1637) from Spaniards. In 1631 stadholderate of United Provs. was made hereditary in his family. His rule is known as "The Golden Age of Frederick Henry" because of its great artists (Rembrandt, Frans Hals) and scientists, and the commerce, prosperity, and prestige of the Netherlands.

Frederick Louis, 1707–51, prince of Wales, eldest son of George II of England. His opposition to the king was furthered by Bolingbroke and William Pitt. Father of George III.

Fredericksburg. 1 Town (pop. 3,854), S central Texas, W of Austin; founded 1846 by Germans whose customs, architecture, and speech persist. **2** City (pop. 12,158), N Va., on Rappahannock R. and N of Richmond; settled 1671. Trade center in agr. area with mfg. of apparel and food products. Tourist center. Points of interest include Mary Washington's home (1774–89); "Kenmore," home of Washington's sister; Rising Sun Tavern (c.1760); James Monroe's law office; and home of J. P. Jones. Near by are George Washington Birthplace Natl. Monument and Fredericksburg and Spotsylvania County Battlefields Memorial, commemorating battles of Fredericksburg, CHANCELLORSVILLE, Wilderness, and Spotsylvania Courthouse (see WILDERNESS CAMPAIGN). Seat of Mary Washington Col. (now affiliated with Univ. of Virginia).

Fredericksburg, battle of, in Civil War, fought Dec. 13, 1862, at Fredericksburg, Va. A. E. Burnside, aiming for Richmond, sent his Union troops across Rappahannock R. in frontal assault on James Longstreet's impregnable position. A severe Union defeat, with losses of over 12,000.

Frederick the Fair, c.1286–1330, German anti-king (1314–26), duke of Austria. Elected by Hapsburg party as rival king to Emperor LOUIS IV. Renounced his rights in 1326.

Frederick the Great: see FREDERICK II, king of Prussia.

Frederick the Winter King, 1596–1632, king of Bohemia (1619–20), as Frederick V elector palatine (1610–20). The Protestant diet of Bohemia chose him king after deposing FERDINAND II. The expected help from his father-in-law, James I of England, did not materialize, and he was disastrously defeated at the White Mountain (1620). Nicknamed the Winter King for his short tenure, he was stripped of all his territories. Through his daughter Sophia he was grandfather of George I of England.

Frederick William, kings of Prussia. **Frederick William I**, 1688–1740, reigned 1713–40; known as the soldier-king. Laid foundation for Prussian greatness by creating efficient army and administration. Notoriously avaricious, he left surplus in treasury, avoided warfare. His tastes were coarse, and he despised his gifted heir, FREDERICK II. **Frederick William II**, 1744–97, nephew of Frederick II, reigned 1786–97. Defeated in French Revolutionary Wars, he made separate peace in 1795. Shared in Polish partitions of 1793, 1795. An amateur cellist, he was a patron of Mozart. His son, **Frederick William III**, 1770–1840, reigned 1797–1840. He accepted the harsh Treaty of TILSIT (1807) after his defeat at Jena by Napoleon I. Though weak and vacillating, he had the aid of such men as Karl vom und zum STEIN, K. A. von HARDENBERG, and SCHARNHORST, who reformed the Prussian state and prepared the way for the Prussian "War of Liberation" against Napoleon (1813–14). Joining the Holy Alliance in 1815, he became increasingly reactionary. His elder son, **Frederick William IV**, 1795–1861, reigned 1840–61. A romanticist, mystic, and half-hearted liberal, he crushed the revolution of March, 1848, and turned down the imperial crown offered him by the FRANKFURT Parliament (1849), arguing that a monarch by divine right could not receive authority from an elected assembly. His scheme for a German union was prevented by Austria in the Treaty of OLMÜTZ (1850). In 1857 his mental unbalance necessitated the regency of his brother and successor William I.

Frederick William, known as **the Great Elector,** 1620–88, elector of Brandenburg (1640–88). Secured E Pomerania and other territories at Peace of Westphalia (1648); rebuilt his devastated state after Thirty Years War; obtained full sovereignty over Prussia at Peace of OLIVA (1660). His victory over Charles XI of Sweden at Fehrbellin (1675) in third Dutch War increased his prestige. His son became king of Prussia as Frederick I (1701).

Frederick William, 1771–1815, duke of Brunswick; son and successor of CHARLES WILLIAM FERDINAND. Dispossessed of his duchy by Napoleon (1806), he seized it in a dashing raid of his free corps, the "Black Brunswickers" (1809), but soon had to flee to England. Was killed in the Waterloo campaign.

Frederickton, city (pop. 16,018), provincial cap. (since 1788), S central N.B., on St. John R. and NW of St. John; founded 1785 by United Empire Loyalists. Seat of Univ. of New Brunswick (provincially supported; coed.; opened 1800). Hunting and fishing center with lumbering and mfg. of wood and leather products.

Frederikshaab (frĭdh'rĭks-hôp), district (pop. 1,432) and settlement (pop. 634), SW Greenland. District has important cryolite mines at Ivigtut.

Fredonia, village (pop. 7,095), W N.Y., near L. Erie and S of Dunkirk. Makes wine and grape juice.

free association: see ASSOCIATION; PSYCHOANALYSIS.

Free Church of Scotland: see SCOTLAND, FREE CHURCH OF.

Freedmen's Bureau, U.S. government agency, estab. by act of March 3, 1865, under name "bureau of refugees, freedmen, and abandoned lands," to aid and protect newly freed Negroes in South after Civil War. Organized under War Dept., bureau provided relief work for both blacks and whites in war-stricken areas, regulated Negro labor, managed abandoned and confiscated property, and supported education for Negroes. In its relief and educational activities bureau compiled an excellent record, often marred, however, by excesses of its local agents. Ultimately, bureau became little more than a political machine, organizing the black vote for Republican party. Work of bureau was discontinued in 1869, but its educational activities were carried on for another three years.

freedom: see LIBERTY.

freedom of speech, of the press, of the seas: see SPEECH, FREEDOM OF, etc.

Freehold, borough (pop. 7,550), E central N.J., E of Trenton; settled before 1700, called Monmouth Courthouse 1715–1801. Farm trade center with rug works and liquor distilleries. Monument (1884) commemorates Revolutionary battle (see MONMOUTH, BATTLE OF). Has race track and 18th-cent. buildings.

Freeland, borough (pop. 5,909), NE Pa., NE of Hazleton. Coal-mining center with mfg. of clothing.

Freeman, Douglas Southall, 1886–, American editor and historian, biographer of R. E. Lee and George Washington.

Freeman, Edward Augustus, 1823–92, English historian. Major work was *History of the Norman Conquest* (6 vols., 1867–79). Others included history of Sicily and Byzantine history in Middle Ages.

Freeman, Mary (Eleanor) Wilkins, 1852–1930, American author. Wrote on New England life as in *A New England Nun and Other Stories* (1891).

Freeman's Farm, battle of: see SARATOGA CAMPAIGN.

Freemasonry, teachings and practices of the secret fraternal order of Free and Accepted Masons. Not restricted to stoneworkers, it retains much of the spirit and code of the medieval masons' guild. Charity is enjoined on Masons and practiced by them. Custom is the supreme authority in the order, and its teachings include obedience to the law of the land. There has been strong opposition to such secret societies (see ANTI-MASONIC PARTY). The order—always an independent national group—has had adherents in many parts of the world, George Washington and Goethe among them.

Freeport. 1 City (pop. 22,467), N Ill., W of Rockford; settled 1835. Center of agr. and dairy area producing cheese, toys, and batteries. Douglas expounded famous "Freeport doctrine" in Lincoln-Douglas debate here 1858. Near by occurred battle with Black Hawk's Indian forces. **2** Town (pop. 3,280), SW Maine, on Casco Bay. Papers preliminary to admission of Maine into Union as a state signed here, 1820. Desert of Maine, sandy region, is near by. **3** Residential and resort village (pop. 24,680), SE N.Y., on S shore of Long Isl.; settled c.1650. Deep sea fishing. Clothing and machinery. **4** City (pop. 6,012), S Texas, at mouth of Brazos R. SSW of Houston. Port with chemical (esp. sulphur) plants. Center of Brazosport area. Intracoastal Waterway crosses Brazos R. here.

Freer, Charles Lang (frēr), 1856–1919, American art collector and industrial capitalist. Gave his collection and the building which houses it to Smithsonian Institution of Washington, D.C. Freer Gallery of Art is best known for its collection of works of Whistler and of Oriental masters.

freesia, fragrant flower (*Freesia*) native to S Africa. Grown from corms, largely in greenhouses, for winter and spring cutting. Five to seven white or yellow tubular blossoms are borne near tip of stem.

free silver. Free coinage of silver became a popular proposal in U.S. soon after panic of 1873 and a major political issue in the next quarter century. Hard times of 1873–78 stimulated advocacy of cheap money; GREENBACK PARTY flourished in local elections. Inflationists, not getting paper-money expansion, turned to silver. Silver-mining interests also wanted silver coinage. BLAND-ALLISON ACT of 1878 and SHERMAN SILVER PURCHASE ACT of 1890 represented compromises. POPULIST PARTY demanded free silver. Nomination of W. J. BRYAN in 1896 made free silver major issue of presidential campaign. McKinley's victories of 1896 and 1900, coupled with increasing gold supplies and returning prosperity, minimized free silver as a political issue.

Free-Soil party, in U.S. history, a political party born 1847–48 out of rising opposition to extension of slavery into territories newly acquired from Mexico. In 1848, vote for its ticket gave N.Y. to the Whigs, made Zachary Taylor President. Following Compromise of 1850 party's Barnburner element returned to Democratic party, but radical antislavery men kept organization alive until 1854, when new Republican party absorbed it.

freethinkers, those who reach religious conclusions by reasoning, rejecting supernatural authority and ecclesiastical tradition. Name used in England c.1713 to denote esp. deists. In France it was associated with time of Revolution. In U.S. chief groups founded were American Rationalist Association, American Secular Union, Freethinkers of America.

Freetown, city (pop. 64,576), cap. of Sierra Leone; port on the Atlantic. Founded 1788 by the British as settlement for freed slaves.

free trade, commerce without restrictive duties. Domestic free trade is customary, but international commerce is frequently subjected to taxation. Theoretical basis for free trade is territorial division of labor: each region producing what it can most cheaply and best. France has generally followed an anti-free-trade policy, as have other European nations. The U.S. has generally followed a high-tariff policy. In England, Adam Smith endorsed free trade, the repeal of the corn laws in 1846 furthered it, and Gladstone reestablished it in 1869. (After the First World War England reintroduced an empire protection system.) Trade barriers have been increasingly viewed as promoting international discord, and in Europe attempts are being made to further free trade. See CUSTOMS; PROTECTION.

free verse or **vers libre** (vĕr' lē'brù), term loosely used for rhymed or unrhymed verse made free of conventional and traditional limitations and restrictions in regard to metrical structure. Cadence, especially cadence of common speech, is often substituted for rhythmical meter. Term applied to irregular poetry of Whitman and to some of the poetry of such writers as Ezra Pound, Amy Lowell, H. D., John Gould Fletcher, and T. S. Eliot.

freezing: see MELTING POINT; REFRIGERATION.

Freiberg (frī'bĕrk), city (pop. 42,303), Saxony, E Germany. Mfg. of precision instruments. Was long a lead and silver-mining center; has mining academy (founded 1765).

Freiburg, Switzerland: see FRIBOURG.

Freiburg im Breisgau (Ger. frībōŏrk ĭm brīs'-gou), city (pop. 109,822), S Baden, W Germany, at the edge of Black Forest. Archiepiscopal see; seat of famous university (founded 1457); since 1945 cap. of French-occupied Baden. Founded 1120; passed to Hapsburgs, with rest of BREISGAU, 1368. Scene of French victory over imperials in

Thirty Years War (1644). Held by France 1677–97 and 1744–48; passed to Baden 1805. Has splendid 13th-cent. cathedral and other historic buildings.

Freising (frī'zĭng), city (pop. 25,326), Upper Bavaria, on Isar R. Mfg. of agr. machinery, brewery implements, textiles. Founded 724. Prince-bishopric until 1803; diocese was united with that of Munich 1817. Cathedral was started in 8th cent.

Frelinghuysen, Frederick Theodore (frĕ'lĭng-hī''zùn), 1817–85, U.S. Secretary of State (1881–85). Urged reciprocity agreements with Latin America; generally carried on a patient, pacifistic policy.

Fremantle, principal port (pop. 18,791) of Western Australia, SW of Perth, at mouth of Swan R. and at terminus of Trans-Australian RR; founded 1829. Exports are wheat, wool, and fruit.

Frémiet, Emmanuel (ĕmänüĕl' frāmyā'), 1824–1910, French sculptor, noted for studies of animals and portrait statues.

Frémont, John Charles (frē'mŏnt), 1813–90, American explorer, soldier, and political leader. His enthusiastic reports of explorations in West did much to publicize that region. Prominent in liberating Calif. from Mexico; governor there in 1847 until his quarrel with S. W. Kearny. U.S. Senator (1850–51). Republican candidate for President in 1856. Removed from command of Western Dept. in Civil War. Lost fortune in railroad venture (1870). Governor of Arizona Territory (1878–82). The Pathfinder, as he was called, is one of most controversial figures of Western history. His wife, **Jessie Benton Frémont,** 1824–1902, daughter of Thomas H. Benton, encouraged and aided her husband. Wrote accounts of her experiences to support household when their fortune was lost.

Fremont (frē'mŏnt). **1** City (pop. 14,762), E Nebr., on Platte R. and WNW of Omaha; founded 1856. Trade center in prairie region, it produces grain, livestock, and dairy products. Seat of Midland Col. **2** City (pop. 16,-537), N Ohio, on Sandusky R. and SE of Toledo. Trade center of agr. area with mfg. of auto parts and clothing. Two post-War of 1812 towns united 1829, named Fremont 1849. Has home and tomb of Pres. R. B. Hayes.

Fremstad, Olive (Nayan) (frĕm'städ), 1870?–1951, Swedish-American soprano; pupil of Lilli Lehmann. Sang at the Metropolitan Opera, New York, 1903–14. Best known for Wagnerian roles.

French, Daniel Chester, 1850–1931, American sculptor. Executed first commission *The Minuteman* (Concord, Mass.) at age of 23. Among other works is the heroic Lincoln in Lincoln Memorial, Washington, D.C.

French Academy, first and chief constituent of the INSTITUT DE FRANCE. Founded 1635 by Cardinal Richelieu; suppressed 1793; reinstated 1803. Its chief aim was the governance of French literary effort, grammar, orthography, and rhetoric. Its dictionary (1694; 8th ed., 1932–35) and grammar (1932) are noted for conservatism. Another function is the awarding of prizes. Its 40 members (often called "the forty immortals") are self-perpetuating; elections may be vetoed by head of state. Members include mostly literary men but also other eminent Frenchmen, such as ecclesiastics and military men. Among prominent authors who failed to be admitted were Molière, Rousseau, Balzac, Stendhal, Flaubert.

French and Indian Wars, 1689–1763, name given to North American colonial wars between England and France in late 17th and 18th cent., roughly linked to wars of European coalitions. Ultimate aim was domination of eastern part of continent; wars were marked by capture of seaboard strongholds and Western forts and attacks on frontier settlements, including Indian border warfare. First war was King William's War, corresponding to European War of the GRAND ALLIANCE (1688–97), marked principally by frontier attacks on British colonies. Queen Anne's War (1701–13) corresponded to War of the SPANISH SUCCESSION. King George's War (1745–48) was connected with War of the AUSTRIAN SUCCESSION. Last and most important conflict, called simply French and Indian War (1754–60), was linked to SEVEN YEARS WAR. British captured French forts in the West, Lord AMHERST captured Louisburg (1758), and Quebec fell to the British (see ABRAHAM, PLAINS OF). Treaty of Paris (1763) ended French control in Canada and the West.

French Broad River, rising in W N.C. in the Blue Ridge and flowing 204 mi. NE, NNW past Asheville into Tenn., joining Holston R. near Knoxville to form Tennessee R.

French Cameroons: see CAMEROONS.

French Congo: see FRENCH EQUATORIAL AFRICA.

French East India Company: see EAST INDIA COMPANY, FRENCH.

French Equatorial Africa, group of four French overseas territories (c.970,000 sq. mi.; pop. c.4,131,000), W Africa; cap. Brazzaville. Called French Congo until 1910. Border with Belgian Congo on E is partly marked by Congo R. Constituent territories are Gabon, Middle Congo, Ubangi-Shari, and Chad. Products include hardwood, cotton, coffee, and peanuts. As members of French Union the territories are represented in French parliament.

French Establishments in Oceania, colony (1,554 sq. mi.; pop. 55,734) formed 1903 to embrace 105 islands constituting French possessions in S Pacific; cap. Papeete on Tahiti, Society Isls. Popularly called French Oceania. Includes SOCIETY ISLANDS, MARQUESAS ISLANDS, TUBUAI ISLANDS, TUAMOTU ISLANDS, GAMBIER ISLANDS.

French Guiana: see GUIANA.

French Guinea (gĭ'nē), overseas territory (c.95,000 sq. mi.; pop. c.2,125,000), French West Africa, on the Atlantic; cap. Conakry. Has swampy coastal zone and mountainous interior. Produces rubber, lumber, coffee, palm oil, and hides. Represented in French parliament.

French horn: see WIND INSTRUMENTS; also ill., p. 857.

French India, overseas territory (193 sq. mi.; pop. 317,259) of France, in India; cap. Pondichéry. Comprises four settlements, Karikal, Mahé, Pondichéry, and Yanaon. Formerly included Chandernagor.

French Indo-China: see INDO-CHINA.

French language, Romance language. See LANGUAGE (table).

French Lick, resort town (pop. 1,946), S Ind., NW of Louisville, Ky. Mineral water is obtained from sulphur springs here. Was a French trading post in colonial times.

Frenchman Bay, inlet of the Atlantic, S Maine, extending c.20 mi. inland between Mt. Desert Isl. and the mainland.

French Oceania: see FRENCH ESTABLISHMENTS IN OCEANIA.

French Revolution, political upheaval which began in France in 1789 and which affected the whole world. Historians differ widely as to its "causes"—some see it as an intellectual movement, born from the liberal ENLIGHTENMENT of the 18th cent.; some, as a rebellion of the underprivileged classes against feudal oppression; some, as the assertion of the new capitalist bourgeoisie against an outdated and restrictive social and economic system. It is now generally held that the oppressive features of the ancien régime have been much exaggerated. The immediate cause of the revolution was without doubt the bankrupt state of the public treasury. The wars of the 17th and 18th cent., an iniquitous and inefficient system of taxation, waste, and intervention in the American Revolution had resulted in a gigantic public debt, which neither NECKER, nor CALONNE, nor LOMÉNIE DE BRIENNE was able to reduce. As last resort, LOUIS XVI called the STATES-GENERAL, which, it was hoped, would pass the necessary fiscal reforms. It convened at Versailles on May 5, 1789. From the start, the deputies of the third estate, joined by many members of the lower clergy and by a few nobles, pressed for sweeping political and social reforms that far exceeded the assembly's powers. Defying the king, they proclaimed themselves the National Assembly (June 17) and took an oath not to separate until a constitution had been made. The king yielded, but his dismissal of Necker led to the storming of the BASTILLE by an excited mob (July 14). Louis XVI, ever anxious to avoid bloodshed, gave in once more: Necker was recalled; the commune was estab. as city government of Paris; the National Guard was organized. On Aug. 4 the Assembly abolished all feudal privileges. Rumors of counterrevolutionary court intrigues were exploited by extremist demagogues, and on Oct. 5 a mob marched on Versailles and forcibly moved the royal family and the Assembly to Paris. Honoré de MIRABEAU, foreseeing the uncontrolled revolution that the king's weakness was about to unleash, tried to restore strength to the executive branch, but the Constituent Assembly (as the National Assembly was now called) drafted a constitution which reduced the executive to impotence (1791; its preamble was the famous DECLARATION OF THE RIGHTS OF MAN). Anticlerical legislation was capped when the clergy was required to take oaths to civil authority (1790), a measure which alienated many pious rural districts from the Revolution. The king decided to join those nobles who had already fled abroad (émigrés), but his flight (June 20–21, 1791) was arrested at Varennes. Brought back to Paris, Louis accepted the new constitution. In the Legislative Assembly the republican GIRONDISTS and the extreme JACOBINS and CORDELIERS gained the upper hand. "Liberty, Equality, Fraternity" became the watchword. Meanwhile, the émigrés were inciting other European courts to intervene. The Declaration of PILLNITZ played into the hands of the Girondists, who hoped that a foreign war would rally the nation to the republican cause. With the declaration of war on Austria (April 20, 1792) the FRENCH REVOLUTIONARY WARS began. Early reverses led to rumors of treason by the king and, particularly, Queen MARIE ANTOINETTE. A mob stormed the Tuileries palaces and massacred the SWISS GUARDS (Aug. 10, 1792); all police power was seized by the Paris commune (dominated by DANTON and MARAT); the Assembly suspended the king and ordered elections for a new body, the National Convention; and hundreds of royalist prisoners were killed by "spontaneous" mobs in the September Massacres. The Convention on Sept. 21 abolished the monarchy, set up the First Republic, and proceeded to try the king for treason. Louis's execution (Jan., 1793) led to royalist uprisings, notably in the VENDÉE, and was followed by the REIGN OF TERROR, in which ROBESPIERRE and his associates triumphed in turn over the more moderate Girondists and over his rivals Danton and HÉBERT. The republican constitution never became active; the Committee of Public Safety and the Revolutionary Tribunal reigned supreme. Robespierre's final excesses frightened the Convention into the coup d'état of 9 THERMIDOR (July 27, 1794), which resulted in his execution and in a period of relative reaction. Under the new constitution of 1795 the DIRECTORY came into existence. Its rule, which was marked by corruption, intrigues, run-away inflation, and bankruptcy, was ended by Bonaparte's coup d'état of 18 BRUMAIRE (Nov. 19, 1799). With the establishment of the CONSULATE (followed 1804 by Napoleon's empire), the victory of the moneyed bourgeoisie became final. Together with the French Revolutionary and Napoleonic wars, the French Revolution tore down the ancient structure of Europe, opened the path for 19th-cent. lilberalism, and hastened the advent of nationalism and the era of modern, total warfare.

French Revolutionary calendar, official calendar of France, 1793–1805. It was computed as from Sept. 22, 1792. Year was divided into 12 months of 30 days—Vendémiaire, Brumaire, Frimaire, Nivôse, Pluviôse, Ventôse, Germinal, Floréal, Prairial, Messidor, Thermidor, Fructidor; the 5 remaining days, called sansculottides, were feast days; in leap years the extra day (last of year) was Revolution Day. Months were divided into three decades; every 10th day (décadi) was day of rest. Example: 18 Brumaire of year VIII = Nov. 9, 1799.

French Revolutionary Wars, 1792–1802, general European war precipitated by the FRENCH REVOLUTION. The Declaration of PILLNITZ was used by the revolutionists as pretext for declaring war on Austria (April, 1792). Meeting little resistance at first, allied Austrian and Prussian armies invaded France, but the cannonade of VALMY proved a turning point. Late in 1792 the French overran the Austrian Netherlands, crossed the Rhine into Germany, and seized Savoy and Nice from Sardinia, while the National Convention proclaimed its determination to carry the revolution to all Europe. This and the execution of Louis XVI led to the formation of the First Coalition (Austria, Prussia, England, Holland, Spain). In the emergency, the Committee of Public Safety was created in France (see REIGN OF TERROR) and a *levée en masse* (universal conscription) was ordered. Guided by Lazare CARNOT, the committee raised new armies which, by the end of 1793, had driven the allies from France. The French again took the offensive in the Low Countries (1794). Holland, transformed into the BATAVIAN REPUBLIC, made peace in 1795, as did Prussia and Spain (Treaties of Basel, 1795). Against Austria and Sardinia, Carnot now evolved a plan of three-pronged attack: Jourdan was to advance SE from the Low Countries; Moreau was to strike at S Germany; Bonaparte was to strike at Piedmont and Lombardy, cross the Alps, and join Jourdan and Moreau. Only the Italian campaign, where one victory followed another (see NAPOLEON I) was completely successful and ended with the Treaty of CAMPO FORMIO (1797). England alone stayed in the war. Bonaparte's hope to strike at England by way of Egypt and India failed utterly and resulted in the destruction of the French fleet at Aboukir (1798). French interference in Italy, Switzerland, and Egypt led to the Second Coalition (England, Russia, Austria, Turkey, Portugal, Naples). Hastening back to France from Egypt, Bonaparte estab. himself as First Consul and set about to repair French losses in Italy and Switzerland. Faulty cooperation between the Austrians and Russians facilitated the victory of Masséna over the Russians at Zurich (Sept., 1799), followed by Suvarov's epic retreat across the Alps and the defection of Russia from the coalition. In 1800 Bonaparte crossed the St. Bernard and routed the Austrians at Marengo. Moreau's victory at Hohenlinden (Dec., 1800) demolished Austrian resistance. Austria consented to the Peace of LUNÉVILLE (1801) and the Second Coalition collapsed. England continued the war alone, expelling the French from Egypt and destroying the neutral Danish fleet (see COPENHAGEN, BATTLE OF), but after Pitt's retirement it also made peace with France and its allies (Spain and Batavian Republic) in the Treaty of AMIENS (1802). Peace was shortlived, for in 1803 began the Wars of NAPOLEON I.

French Sudan (sōōdăn′), French overseas territory (c.448,200 sq. mi.; pop. c.3,080,000), French West Africa; cap. Bamako. Drained by Senegal and Niger rivers in fertile S part. Much of country is arid. Under French control since 1896, it is represented in French parliament.

French Union, according to French constitution of 1946, the French republic and associated states. French republic consists of: Metropolitan France (France proper and Corsica); Algeria; the overseas departments and territories of Martinique, Guadeloupe, Réunion, French Guiana, French West Africa, French Equatorial Africa, Madagascar, Comoro Isls., French Somaliland, French India, New Caledonia, French Establishments in Oceania, Saint-Pierre, and Miquelon; the UN trusteeships of Togoland and the Cameroons; the Anglo-French condominium of New Hebrides. The associated states are Morocco, Tunisia, and Indo-China. President of France is also president of French Union. Parliamentary body of French Union consists of a high council and an assembly; these are distinct from the council and national assembly of the French republic.

French West Africa, group of eight French overseas territories (c.1,800,000 sq. mi.; pop. c.15,996,000); cap. Dakar. Comprises DAHOMEY, FRENCH GUINEA, FRENCH SUDAN, IVORY COAST, MAURITANIA, NIGER, SENEGAL, and UPPER VOLTA.

French West Indies: see WEST INDIES.

Freneau, Philip (frēnō'), 1752–1832, American poet. A Revolutionary prisoner on brig *Aurora,* he wrote "The Prison Ship." Was a Jeffersonian journalist, but his fame rests on lyrics ("The Wild Honeysuckle," "The Indian Burying Ground," "Eutaw Springs.")

frequency: see RADIO FREQUENCY; SOUND; VIBRATION; WAVE.

frequency modulation, radio transmitting and receiving system, called FM in contrast to older AM system (amplitude modulation). FM reduces static; improves fidelity. Amplitude of carrier wave is constant; its frequency varies.

Frescobaldi, Girolamo (jěrō'lämō frăskōbäl'dē), 1583–1644, Italian organist and composer, organist at St. Peter's in Rome between 1608 and 1643. He wrote toccatas, fugues, and other works for organ.

Fresno (frěz'nō), city (pop. 91,669), central Calif., SE of San Francisco; founded 1872. Railroad, processing, and shipping center in San Joaquin Valley (raisins, figs, sweet wine). Lumbering and mfg. of machinery, clothing, cottonseed and olive oil.

Freud, Sigmund (froid, Ger. zēk'mŏont froit'), 1856–1939, Austrian psychiatrist, founder of PSYCHOANALYSIS. His collaboration with Josef Breuer on use of hypnosis to treat hysteria marked beginning of psychoanalysis, revealed that symptoms of hysteria, traceable to early psychic trauma, represent undischarged emotional energy (conversion). He and Breuer separated over Freud's growing conviction that undefined energy causing conversion was sexual. Freud replaced hypnosis with free ASSOCIATION. His theories roused bitter antagonism. He was joined in 1906 by Eugen Bleuler, Jung, and Adler, but later Jung and Adler formed their own schools (1911–13) in protest against Freud's emphasis on infantile sexuality and the Oedipus complex. Basic structure of analysis is still Freudian and disagreement is in emphasis on concepts largely originated by Freud. After 1923 he used psychoanalytic theory in cultural studies. He greatly influenced anthropology, education, art, and literature.

Frey and Freyja (frī, frī'yu̇), Scandinavian god and goddess, brother and sister, deities of fertility, love, and matrimony and of light and peace. Frey's chief shrine was at Uppsala, Sweden.

Freycinet, Louis Claude Desaulses de (du̇sōls' dü fräsēnā'), 1779–1842, French marine officer. Commanded, and edited findings of, scientific expedition to South Pacific on the *Uranie* (1817–20).

Freyre, Gilberto (jělběr'tō frā'rü), 1900–, Brazilian sociologist and anthropologist, known for social history of plantation system in NE Brazil.

Freytag, Gustav (gŏo'stäf frī'täk), 1816–95, German author. His most lasting works include the comedy *The Journalists* (1852; Eng. tr., 1888) and the novels *Debit and Credit* (1855; Eng. tr., 1856) and *The Lost Manuscript* (1861; Eng. tr., 1865).

Friant Dam, central Calif., in San Joaquin R., E of Fresno; completed 1944. It is one of world's largest dams (320 ft. high, 3,430 ft. long) and a key unit of CENTRAL VALLEY project. Forms Millerton L.

friar's balsam, alcoholic solution of benzoin, storax, aloes, tolu balsam. Used for wounds, ulcers.

Fribourg (Fr. frēbŏor'), Ger. *Freiburg,* canton (645 sq. mi.; pop. 157,919), W Switzerland, on N slopes of Bernese Alps. Agr., cattle raising, cheese production (Gruyère). City of Fribourg (pop. 28,767), its cap., on Sarine R., was founded 1157, joined Swiss Confederation 1481. Largely Catholic, it is an episcopal see and has a Catholic university and a cathedral (14th–15th cent.).

Frick, Henry Clay, 1849–1919, American capitalist. Key figure in coke industry. Engineered expansion of Carnegie Steel Co. Largely responsible for antiunion policy of steel industry. His New York city mansion, together with art collection and large endowment, was willed to public as a museum.

friction, resistance between surfaces moving against one another. Factors on which it depends include nature of surfaces in contact, magnitude of force holding them together (including gravity), their weight, their chemical natures, and the attractive force between different materials. So-called **coefficient of friction:** quotient obtained by dividing the value of force necessary to move one body over another at constant speed by the weight of the body. Coefficient varies with type of surface even though weight of body is constant, but it is constant for any two given kinds of materials. **Fluid friction** is observed in flow of liquids and gases. It is affected by increased velocities and streamlining is attempt to minimize it.

Friday: see WEEK.

Friedel, Charles (shärl frēdĕl'), 1832–99, French chemist, mineralogist, co-developer of Friedel-Crafts reaction for production of hydrocarbons and ketones.

Friedland (frēt'länt), Czech *Frýdtlant,* town (pop. 4,308), N Bohemia, Czechoslovakia.

Castle was seat of duchy awarded to Wallenstein in 1625.

Friedland, small town, former E Prussia, near Königsberg; renamed Pravdinsk after transfer to USSR (1945). Napoleon's victory at Friedland over Russians led to Treaty of Tilsit (1807).

Friedlander, Leo (frēd'ländŭr), 1890–, American sculptor. His many decorative works include groups for R.C.A. Building in New York.

Friedrichshafen (frē'drĭkshä"fŭn), town, (pop. 20,477), S Württemberg, SW Germany, on L. of Constance. Mfg. of machine parts. Zeppelin works here were destroyed by World War II air raids.

Friends, Society of, religious body originating in England in 17th cent. under George Fox. He believed that a person needed no spiritual intermediary but could find understanding and guidance through "inward light" supplied by Holy Spirit. Fox's followers were known as Religious Society of Friends, popularly called Quakers because they trembled with emotion in meetings. They refused to worship in estab. churches, to take oaths, and to bear arms in war. They rejected social and official titles and used "plain" forms of address (notably "thee" and "thou"). Mission effort took them to Asia, Africa, and America. Persecuted in New England, they found refuge in R.I. and in colony estab. (1682) for them by William Penn in Pa. In 1827 they split into "Hicksites" under Elias Hicks, who stressed inner guidance, and "Orthodox" group, with guidance by church elders. Meetings of Friends are periods of silent meditation, only those urged by "Inner Light" offering prayer or exhortation. Friends are noted for activity in education and social welfare. The American Friends Service Committee and the Service Council of the British Society of Friends were jointly awarded the 1947 Nobel Peace Prize.

Fries, John, c.1750–1818, American rebel. Stirred Pennsylvania Germans into uprising (called Fries's Rebellion) against assessors and collectors of Federal property taxes (1799). Arrested, sentenced to death, but pardoned by Pres. John Adams.

Frieseke, Frederick Carl (frē'zĭkŭ), 1874–1939, American painter. Developed a highly popular style influenced by French impressionism.

Friesland (frēz'lŭnd) or **Frisia** (frĭ'zhŭ), province (1,249 sq. mi.; pop. 459,361), N Netherlands; cap. Leeuwarden. Comprises several of W FRISIAN ISLANDS. Intensive dairying and cattle raising. Frisians, a Germanic people, were conquered by Franks in 8th cent.; they have preserved their language. Medieval Frisia, under counts of HOLLAND, extended from Scheldt R. in W to Weser R. in E. After 1433 Frisians defied authority of their successive new masters—the dukes of Burgundy, Duke Albert of Saxony, and the Hapsburgs—until they were subdued by Emperor Charles V (1523). Friesland joined the United Provs. 1579. It appointed its own stadholders until 1748, when its stadholder, Prince William IV of Orange, became sole and hereditary stadholder of the Netherlands. EAST FRIESLAND, in Germany, had a separate history after 1454.

Friesz, Othon (ôtō' frēĕs'), 1879–1949, French painter. Calligraphic style was influenced by impressionism.

frigate (frĭ'gĭt), originally a long, narrow type of vessel propelled by oars or sails in the Mediterranean. Now denotes a warship, with raised quarterdeck and forecastle, of about the same tonnage as the destroyer.

Frigg or **Frigga,** in Germanic mythology, wife of Woden. Originally an earth-goddess, she became confused with Scandinavian Freyja and thus was worshiped as goddess of fertility and love. From her likeness to Venus, the Latin day of Venus became in Germanic-speaking countries *Frigg's day* or *Friday.*

frijole (frēhō'lē), used mostly in plural **frijoles,** in Mexico and Spanish American countries, any cultivated bean of genus *Phaseolus;* in particular, small black bean second only to maize as article of diet.

Frioul (frēōōl'), Romance language. See LANGUAGE (table).

Frisia: see FRIESLAND.

Frisian Islands (frĭ'zhŭn), chain of islands off North Sea coast of Netherlands, Germany and Denmark. W Frisian Isls., belonging to Netherlands, include Texel, Vlieland, Tershelling, Ameland. E Frisian Isls., in Germany, include Norderney, Borkum. N Frisian Isls., off Schleswig-Holstein, Germany, and S Jutland, Denmark, include Sylt, Föhr, Romo. Fishing, cattle raising are important on all the islands. Many bathing resorts.

Frisian language, Germanic language of Frisian Isls. and near-by coasts, the language most like English. See LANGUAGE (table).

Frithjof (frēt'yôf), hero of Icelandic saga (late 13th or early 14th cent.). Swedish poet Esaias Tegner used legends of him in *Frithjof's Saga* (1825).

Friuli (frēōō'lē), historic region, NE Italy and NW Yugoslavia, between E Alps and Adriatic. Includes a fertile plain and part of KARST region. Chief cities: Udine, Gorizia (both in Italy). Once a Lombard duchy (6th–8th cent.), Friuli was later divided into county of Gorizia (E) and county of Friuli (W). W Friuli (with Udine) passed to patriarchs of Aquileia (11th cent.), to Venice (1420), and to Austria (1797). Gorizia passed to Austria in 1500. Italy received W Friuli in 1866 and the rest in 1919, but by the Italian peace treaty of 1947 E Friuli (except Gorizia) was ceded to Yugoslavia, where it forms part of Slovenia. The remaining Italian part of Friuli was merged with what is left of VENEZIA GIULIA to form the autonomous province of **Friuli-Venezia Giulia** (vänä'tsyä jōō'lyä) (2,948 sq. mi.; pop. 837,000); cap. Udine.

Frobenius, Leo (lā'ō frōbā'nēŏos), 1873–1938, German archaeologist and anthropologist, authority on prehistoric art and culture (esp. African).

Frobisher, Sir Martin (frō'bĭshŭr), 1535?–1594, English mariner. Licensed by Queen Elizabeth, backed by merchants, he made three fruitless voyages (1576, 1577, 1578) to arctic regions seeking Northwest Passage. Commanded a ship in Sir Francis Drake's West Indies expedition (1585). Knighted for role in defeat of Spanish Armada (1588). Discovered (1576) **Frobisher Bay,** arm of the Atlantic, 150 mi. long, 20–40 mi. wide, cutting into SE Baffin Isl., Northwest Territories, Canada. There is a trading post and an air base at its head.

Froding, Gustaf, Swed. *Fröding* (frü′ding), 1860–1911, Swedish lyric poet.

Froebel, Friedrich Wilhelm August (frä′bŭl, frö–, Ger. frē′drĭkh vĭl′hĕlm ou′gŏŏst frü′bŭl), 1782–1852, German educator and founder of KINDERGARTEN system. In 1837 he founded first kindergarten and in 1849 first kindergarten training school. His educational system, based on unity of nature, or God, reflects influence of Fichte and Schelling. He stressed importance of pleasant surroundings, self-activity, and physical training in child development. Most important work is *Menschenerziehung* (1826; Eng. tr., *The Education of Man,* 1877).

frog, amphibian living usually in quiet fresh water or woods. Skin is smooth, usually green or brown, often spotted; in some species produces irritating or poisonous secretions. Most frogs hibernate underwater in mud over winter and lay eggs (which are fertilized as they are laid) in early spring. Gelatinous covering secreted by female causes eggs to adhere in mass, giving buoyancy, protection. In 3–10 days, small tadpole hatches; by summer's end metamorphosis from fishlike form to lung-breathing, tailless, carnivorous adult is completed (except in BULLFROG). Growth to adult size takes several years. Edible U.S. frogs include leopard, pickerel, and green frogs, common and southern bullfrogs, and Oregon red-legged frog. See also TREE FROG.

Frohman, Charles, 1860–1915, American theatrical manager and producer. Bronson Howard's *Shenandoah* (1889) made him a successful producer. Known for ability to develop talent, he launched stars (e.g., Julia Marlowe, Maude Adams, Ethel Barrymore) and playwrights (e.g., Clyde Fitch, Barrie, Rostand). His brother, **Daniel Frohman,** 1851–1940, managed small theatrical companies c.1871; settled in N.Y. 1879. Augustin Daly's business manager for a time, he later was manager and part owner of Lyceum theater.

Froissart, Jean (zhä′ früwäsär′), c.1337–1410?, French chronicler, poet, and courtier. His chronicle covers history of W Europe from early 14th cent. to 1400, i.e., first half of Hundred Years War. Historically it suffers from inaccuracy and unobjectiveness, but in literary merit ranks high and brings whole era to life. Standard English translation is by John Bourchier, Lord Berners.

Fronde (frŏd), 1648–53, series of outbreaks in France during minority of Louis XIV. Caused by rivalry between Parlement of Paris and royal authority (as championed by MAZARIN); by the discontent of the great nobles; by the excessive fiscal burden of the people. The **Fronde of the Parlement,** 1648–49, began with the Parlement's refusal to register a fiscal edict. The court retired to Rueil; government forces under Louis II de CONDÉ blockaded Paris until a compromise peace was arranged. The arrest of the overbearing Condé, by Mazarin's orders, precipitated the much more serious **Fronde of**

the Princes, 1650–53. Although Condé was released and Mazarin left for voluntary exile (1651), Condé with the support of several powerful nobles and the provincial parlements of S France waged open warfare on the government and even concluded an alliance with Spain, then at war with France. Defeated at the Faubourg Saint-Antoine (1652), he was given shelter in Paris through the intervention of Mlle de MONTPENSIER. His arrogance soon alienated the Parisians, and the Fronde disintegrated. In 1653 Mazarin returned to Paris, but Condé continued to wage war at the head of a Spanish army until the Peace of the PYRENEES (1659).

Frontenac, Louis de Buade, comte de (frôn′tĭnăk), 1620–98, French governor of New France (1672–82, 1689–98). Dealt successfully with Indians, encouraged explorations, and aided in establishment of forts. Sought to restrain British in French and Indian Wars. Reestab. **Fort Frontenac,** on site of Kingston, Ont., Canada, in 1696. La Salle was made commandant of original fort (1673). Its capture by British in 1758 gave them control of L. Ontario.

frontier, borderland, in various senses. May be used to mean actual border between two countries or region about an international boundary. In U.S. history, however, it means border area of white settlement, vital in conquest of land between Atlantic and Pacific. Theory that frontier was a governing factor (if not the governing factor) in developing U.S. civilization as distinct from that of other nations was announced by F. J. Turner in 1893. Thesis is that American democracy was shaped by the frontier, by the contest of settler with wilderness. In the contest man learned self-reliance; he became assured of equality with other men and resentful of class distinctions and any attempt at civic and social coercion. Belief that the frontier shaped American thought and character is now almost universally accepted. It has been pointed out, however, that other factors (e.g., industrialization) were of telling weight, that individualism on the frontier has been perhaps overemphasized, and that the frontier farming community was possibly not as classless as has been pictured.

Front Range, part of Rocky Mts., extending c.300 mi. SE and S from E central Wyo. to S central Colo. and rising to 14,274 ft. in Grays Peak. Forms part of Continental Divide in Colo. Includes Laramie and Medicine Bow mts. and most of Rocky Mt. Natl. Park, where highest peak is Longs Peak (14,255 ft.). Range also includes PIKES PEAK; Mt. Evans (14,260 ft.), with Inter-Univ. High Altitude Laboratory at summit; Arapahoe Peak (13,506 ft.), with glacier on E face; and James Peak (13,260 ft.), cut by Moffat Tunnel, railroad tube (6.4 mi. long; built 1923–27).

Front Royal, town (pop. 8,115), N Va., on S Fork of Shenandoah R. and S of Winchester, at N end of Skyline Drive near Shenandoah Natl. Park and George Washington Natl. Forest. Mfg. of chemicals and rayon. In Shenandoah Valley campaign Stonewall Jackson routed Union troops here (1862).

Frost, Arthur Burdett, 1851–1928, American

illustrator and cartoonist, best known for illustrations for "Uncle Remus" stories.

Frost, Edwin Brant, 1866–1935, American astronomer, authority on astrophysics. Director of Yerkes Observatory (1905–32).

Frost, Robert, 1875–, American poet, b. San Francisco; in New England after 1885. Won recognition while in England, where *A Boy's Will* (1913) and *North of Boston* (1914) appeared; was famous after return to U.S. Later volumes of lyrical, dramatic, and reflective poetry include *West-running Brook* (1928) and *A Further Range* (1936). Four times awarded Pulitzer Prize.

frost or **hoarfrost,** feathery ice deposit caused by direct condensation of water vapor in crystalline form on surfaces at below-freezing temperatures. Frost-occurrence factors: topography, altitude, latitude, relation to land and water. Killing (to vegetation) frosts occur variously (Sept. 1–June 1 in Rocky Mt. region; Dec. 1–Mar. 1 along Gulf coast, parts of Calif., Ariz.).

Frostburg, resort and trading town (pop. 6,876), NW Maryland, W of Cumberland in coal area.

Froude, James Anthony (frōōd), 1818–94, English historian. Wrote voluminously on many historical and biographical topics. Major work is *The History of England from the Fall of Wolsey to the Defeat of the Spanish Armada* (12 vols., 1856–70).

fructose (frōōk′tōs), **levulose** (lĕ′vūlōs), or **fruit sugar,** found in honey and fruits; sweeter than cane sugar. It is a CARBOHYDRATE with same chemical formula as GLUCOSE.

fruit, fully developed seed-producing organ of a FLOWER. Botanically it is the ripened ovary. Seedlike fruit (see GRAIN) of grasses is commonly called seed, and many food fruits are popularly called vegetables (e.g., beans, tomatoes). Fleshy fruits include the pome (e.g., apple, pear), berry (raspberry), and drupe (cherry, peach). See also NUT. See *ill.*, p. 999.

Fruita (frōō′tù), town (pop. 1,463), W Colo., NW of Grand Junction. Colorado Natl. Monument is near.

fruit fly, name for certain insects of family Trypetidae whose larvae bore through fruits and other plant parts. Damagers of North American fruit include apple or blueberry maggot, currant and gooseberry fruit fly, cherry fruit fly. Mexican, West Indian, and papaya fruit flies are serious pests farther south. Mediterranean fruit fly is a pest in many areas. Fruit (or vinegar) flies of genus *Drosophila* are much used in genetic research.

fruit sugar: see FRUCTOSE.

Frunze, city (pop. c.140,000), cap. of Kirghiz SSR, on branch of Turksib RR; center of rich agr. area. Founded 1873 as Pishpek; renamed 1927.

Fry, Christopher, 1907–, English dramatist. His verse plays, often compared in style to those of the Elizabethans, include *The Lady's Not for Burning* (1948), *Venus Observed* (1950), and *A Sleep of Prisoners* (1951).

Fry, Roger (Elliott), 1866–1934, English art critic and painter. Helped to introduce postimpressionists to England.

Fuad I (fōōäd′), 1868–1936, first king of modern Egypt (1917–36), son of deposed khedive, Ismail Pasha. Became sultan in 1917, acquired title of king in 1922. Autocratic rule opposed by Wafd party. Succeeded by his son Farouk I.

fuchsia (fū′shù), tropical American shrub (*Fuchsia*), with graceful, pendulous flowers in various shades of red and purple. Grown outdoors in mild climates and as pot or summer bedding plant elsewhere.

fuchsine (fōōk′sĭn) or **magenta,** bright red biological dye composed of aniline derivatives.

fuel, material combustible in presence of air to produce usable heat. Chemical principle of COMBUSTION is essentially same for all fuel forms: rapid oxidation involving union of carbon and hydrogen (important fuel constituents) with oxygen, and liberation of heat energy (exothermic reaction). Fuels are valued in terms of heat (in calories or in B.T.U.) that a unit weight can produce.

Fuertes, Louis Agassiz (fūĕr′tēs), 1874–1927, American artist and naturalist. He is known for his paintings of birds which appeared in leading American ornithological works and for murals and habitat groups in the American Mus. of Natural History.

Fuessli, Johann Heinrich: see FUSELI, HENRY.

Fugger (fōō′gùr), German family of merchant princes at Augsburg. Its fortune reached its zenith with Jacob Fugger II (1459–1525), who held a virtual monopoly in the mining and trading of silver, copper, and mercury. He lent immense sums to Emperor Maximilian I and financed the election of Charles V, who ennobled the family and granted them sovereign rights over their vast land holdings. Owning merchant fleets and palatial establishments throughout Europe, the Fuggers were also noted patrons of art and learning. Their fortunes declined with the Hapsburgs, whose wars they financed.

fugitive slave laws, in U.S. history, Federal acts of 1793 and 1850 providing for return between states of escaped Negro slaves. As Northern states abolished slavery they relaxed enforcement of 1793 law; abolitionism brought the UNDERGROUND RAILROAD. Many Northern states passed personal liberty laws allowing fugitives jury trial; others forbade state officials to help capture alleged fugitive slaves or to lodge them in state jails. As a concession to the South, COMPROMISE of 1850 incorporated a more rigorous fugitive slave law. Required "all good citizens" to help execute it; heavily penalized anyone aiding fugitive slaves; denied fugitive jury trial and right to give testimony. New personal-liberty laws of Northern states contradicted 1850 legislation; abolitionists fearlessly defied it. Trials of fugitive slave cases increased sectional hostility. Both acts were repealed by Congress on June 28, 1864.

fugue (fūg), [Fr., from Ital.,= flight], in music, a polyphonic composition of several parts or voices, wherein a melody, phrase, or motive is used in more than one voice. The melody (called the subject) makes its entry in each voice successively. The various devices of COUNTERPOINT may, or may not, be used. Fugue writing reached its peak in the music of Bach; declined after Beethoven; has attracted much interest in 20th cent.

Fujiyama (fōō"jēyä'mä) or **Mount Fuji**, sacred mountain, 12,389 ft. high, central Honshu, Japan; highest point in Honshu. Symmetrical cone with dormant volcanic crater at summit.

Fukien (fōō'kyĕn'), province (46,376 sq. mi.; pop. 11,053,860), SE China, on Formosa Strait; cap. Foochow. Largely mountainous. Chief rivers are Min and Lung. Leading ports (Foochow, Amoy) export sugar cane and tobacco. Rice crop is large but inadequate for population's needs. Declined as great tea center but still known for fine tea. Lumbering and fishing are important. Mining (coal, manganese) is minor industry.

Fukuoka (fōōkōō'ôkä), city (pop. 328,548), N Kyushu, Japan; port on Hakata Bay. Textile mfg. Seat of Kyushu Imperial Univ.

Fulda, Ludwig (lōōt'vĭkh fōōl'dä), 1862–1939, German playwright. His works include *Der Talisman* (1893) and *The Pirate* (1911; adapted by S. N. Behrman 1942). Also translated Ibsen, Molière, Shakspere, and Spanish dramatists.

Fulda (fōōl'dä), city (pop. 42,238), Hesse, W Germany, on Fulda R. Grew around Benedictine abbey founded 744 by St. Boniface. From this abbey Christianity spread through central Germany. Abbots held temporal power under Holy Roman Empire; became prince-bishops 1752. Secularized 1802, Fulda passed to Electoral Hesse in 1815. Still an episcopal see, Fulda is meeting place of annual conference of Catholic bishops of Germany. Buildings, restored after World War II, include baroque cathedral, where St. Boniface is buried; Church of St. Michael (9th cent.); baroque château.

Fulham (fōōl'ŭm), metropolitan borough (pop. 122,047), London. Has a palace of the bishops of London.

Fulk (fŭlk), 1092–1143, king of Jerusalem (1131–43), count of Anjou (1109–29). Journeyed to Holy Land 1120 and again 1129, when he made over Anjou to his son Geoffrey IV (Geoffrey Plantagenet). Married daughter of Baldwin II of Jerusalem, whom he succeeded as king.

Fuller, George, 1822–84, American portrait, figure, and landscape painter.

Fuller, Henry Blake, 1857–1929, American author. His novels are divided into romantic novels laid in Europe (e.g., *The Chevalier of Pensieri-Vani*, 1890) and realistic works about the Chicago scene (e.g., *The Cliff-Dwellers*, 1893), Also wrote short stories and newspaper editorials and book reviews.

Fuller, (Sarah) Margaret, 1810–50, American writer, lecturer, b. Mass. Translated Eckermann's *Conversations with Goethe* (1839), was a feminist (*Woman in the Nineteenth Century*, 1845), a transcendentalist, and a literary critic. In Rome, she married Marchese Ossoli; in 1850, en route to U.S., they drowned in a shipwreck.

Fuller, Melville Weston, 1833–1910, Chief Justice of U.S. Supreme Court (1888–1910). Leaned toward strict construction of Constitution.

Fuller, Thomas, 1608–61, English writer, a moderate Anglican clergyman, compiler of antiquary *Worthies of England* (1662), author of *History of the Holy Warre* (1639) and *The Holy State and the Profane State* (1642).

fuller's earth, a sedimentary clay which has the property of absorbing basic colors. Chiefly used in clarifying petroleum and refining edible oils.

Fullerton, city (pop. 19,050), S Calif., SE of Los Angeles. Processes citrus fruits, vegetables, and walnuts. Oil-field center.

fulminate (fŭl'mĭnāt), commonly a name for explosive, crystalline mercury salt of fulminic acid, used as detonator when mixed with potassium chlorate.

Fulton, Robert, 1765–1815, American inventor, engineer, painter. His *Clermont*, launched in 1807, though not first steamboat in America, was first to be commercially successful in American waters.

Fulton. 1 City (pop. 10,052), central Mo., NE of Jefferson City, in farm area. Mfg. of firebrick and shoes. Seat of Westminster Col. (Presbyterian; for men; 1851). **2** City (pop. 13,922), N N.Y., on Oswego R. and the Barge Canal and NW of Syracuse. Mfg. of candy, textiles, paper, and aluminum products.

Fulvia (fŭl'vĕŭ), d. 40 B.C., Roman woman. Her third husband was Marc Antony. She led an unsuccessful revolt against Augustus (40 B.C.).

fumitory, Old World herb (*Fumaria officinalis*) with red-tipped purplish flowers. It is naturalized in North America. Climbing fumitory or Allegheny vine (*Adlumia fungosa*) is a North American vine.

Funafuti: see Ellice Islands.

Funchal (fōōnshäl'), city (pop. 58,856), chief city of Madeira isl., Portugal. Port and resort. Cathedral built 15th cent.

function, in mathematics, quantity having numerical value (a variable) which varies with value of one or more other such quantities (independent variables). For example, the distance a body falls is a function of the time it is allowed to fall.

fundamentalism, conservative religious movement in Protestant denominations early in 20th cent. Aim was to maintain traditional interpretations of Bible and fundamental doctrines of faith against what they considered threat of scientific discoveries. There were bitter controversies. In 1925, William Jennings Bryan, a fundamentalist leader, won state's case in famous Scopes trial.

Fundamental Orders, in U.S. history, basic law of Conn. colony, 1639–62. Contained preamble and 11 orders, including voting restrictions. Placed welfare of community over that of individual.

Fundy, Bay of, inlet of the Atlantic (100 mi. long, 60 mi. wide at entrance), between N.B. and SW N.S., Canada. In its upper arms, Chignecto Bay and Minas Basin, its tides or bore rise to 70 ft. Some flatlands have been diked off and reclaimed. Annapolis Royal, on N.S. shore, is oldest settlement in Canada. St. John, N.B., its chief port.

Fundy National Park, 79.5 sq. mi., S N.B., Canada, on Bay of Fundy and ENE of St. John; estab. 1949.

Fünfkirchen, Hungary: see Pecs.

fungicide, chemical used for spraying or dust-

EGYPTIAN
Seat of plaited string
15th Century B.C.

GREEK

ETRUSCAN
Marble honorary chair
c. 5th Century B.C.

ROMAN
Marble

CENTRAL EUROPEAN
c. 10th Century

ITALIAN
Savonarola chair
15th Century

FLORENTINE
Strozzi chair
15th Century

SPANISH
15th-century Gothic

SPANISH
16th Century

CHINESE
18th Century

ENGLISH – Tudor
Late 16th Century

ENGLISH
Queen Anne
Early 18th Century

ENGLISH
Hepplewhite
Late 18th Century

ENGLISH
Adam
Late 18th Century

ENGLISH
Chippendale
Late 18th Century

ENGLISH
Sheraton
Late 18th Century

FRENCH
Louis XV
18th Century

FRENCH
Louis XVI
Late 18th Century

FRENCH
Directoire
Late 18th Century

FRENCH
Empire
Early 19th Century

AMERICAN
Pennsylvania
Early 18th Century

AMERICAN
New England Windsor
Late 18th Century

AMERICAN
Duncan Phyfe
Early 19th Century

AMERICAN
Hitchcock
19th Century

AMERICAN
c. 1950

ing on plants, or applied to seeds, soils, woods, or fabrics to destroy fungi. Sulphur, copper (BORDEAUX MIXTURE), and organic mercury compounds are used to destroy or prevent fungus diseases of plants.

fungus (fŭn'gŭs), plural **fungi** (fŭn'jī), simple plant lacking true roots, stems, and leaves and belonging like algae to lowest division of plant kingdom. Unlike algae the fungi have no chlorophyll and must get food from living or dead organic matter. Examples are BACTERIA, MUSHROOM, YEAST. See *ill.*, p. 813.

Funk, Casimir (kä'zĭmēr fŏŏngk'), 1884–, American biochemist, credited with discovery of vitamins.

Funston, Frederick, 1865–1917, U.S. general. Captured Emilio AGUINALDO in 1901. Commanded occupying troops at Veracruz in 1914.

fur, hairy covering of an animal, especially the skins of such animals as have thick, soft, close-growing hair next to the skin itself and coarser protective hair above it. Term *fur* extends to dressed sheep and lamb skins prepared for wearing with hair kept on and (usually) curled (persian lamb, karakul, astrakhan, and mouton). Since prehistoric days man has used furs for clothing. Some of the more prized furs are sable, marten, mink, ermine, and chinchilla. Staple fur of great fur-trading days in North America was beaver. Fur trade reached its peak in wilderness of North America and Asia from 17th to early 19th cent. Effect in opening wilderness was even more striking in Canada. Important fur-trading companies were HUDSON'S BAY COMPANY, and AMERICAN FUR COMPANY. Advance of settlement, depletion of beaver and other fur-bearing animals, and decline in importance of beaver hat ended day of fur trader in 1840s in U.S. and S Canada. Later threat of extinction of fur seal led to BERING SEA FUR-SEAL CONTROVERSY. Preparation and sale of furs remains, however, a very considerable business; fur farming has become in U.S. and Canada a major industry in 20th cent.

furfural (fûr'fŭrăl") or **furfuraldehyde,** ALDEHYDE of pyromucic acid. It is a colorless, oily liquid with aromatic odor. Used as solvent and in making deodorants, disinfectants, preservatives, etc.

Furies, goddesses of vengeance: see ERINYES.

Furka (fŏŏr'kä), road, central Switzerland, linking Uri and Valais cantons. Built 1864–66, it crosses Furka Pass, 7,971 ft. high. A rail line goes through Furka Tunnel.

Furman University: see GREENVILLE, S.C.

Furneaux Islands (fûr'nō), group in Bass Strait between Tasmania, to which it belongs, and Australia; discovered 1773. Largest is Flinders Isl. Sheep, dairy products, tin.

Furness, hilly district of Lancashire, England. In SW are rich iron mines and great engineering works which center at Barrow-in-Furness.

Furniss, Harry, 1854–1925, British caricaturist and illustrator of many books, including works of Dickens, Thackeray, and Lewis Carroll.

Fürth (fürt), city (pop. 99,503), Middle Franconia, Bavaria, on Regnitz R., near Nuremberg. Produces machinery, precision instruments, textiles.

furze, spiny Old World shrub (*Ulex europaeus*), also called gorse. It has scalelike leaves and fragrant yellow pealike flowers. Often used as sand binder in the U.S.

fuse, electric, safety device in electric circuit; when current exceeds safe amount, fuse breaks circuit, stopping flow of electricity.

Fuseli, Henry (fū'zĭlē), 1741–1825, Anglo-Swiss artist, b. Zurich; also called Johann Heinrich Fuessli or Füssli. Famous for dramatic drawings. Was a friend of William Blake.

fusel oil (fū'zŭl), oily colorless liquid with disagreeable odor and taste. It is a mixture of alcohols and fatty acids used as a solvent.

Fushun (fŏŏ'shŏŏn), city (pop. 279,604) in, but independent of, Liaotung prov., Manchuria, in important coal-mining area.

fusion, in physics: see MELTING POINT; HEAT.

Füssli, Johann Heinrich: see FUSELI, HENRY.

Fust, Johann, d. 1466, printer at Mainz. Johann Gutenberg, unable to repay Fust's loans, had to give Fust his press and types. Fust and his partner, Peter Schöffer, were first to print in colors and among the first to use Greek type (1465). Issued first dated book (1457).

Fustel de Coulanges, Numa Denis (nümä' dünē' füstĕl' dù kŏŏlāzh'), 1830–89, French historian. His *Histoire des institutions politiques de l'ancienne France* (6 vols., 1882–92) opened way for new thought on early medieval history.

futurism, Italian school of painting, sculpture, and literature which flourished 1909–c.1915. Futurists strove to portray dynamic character of 20th-cent. life. They glorified danger, war, and machine age, and in theory favored growth of fascism.

Fyn (fün), island (1,149 sq. mi.; pop. 338,013), Denmark, in Baltic Sea, between Little Belt (W) and Great Belt (E); chief city Odense. Second largest Danish island. Fertile lowland; it has dairy farming and cattle breeding.

Fyne, Loch (lŏkh fīn'), arm of Firth of Clyde, Argyllshire, Scotland. Famous for its herring fisheries. Leading city on Loch is Inverary.

Fyt, Jan (yän' fīt'), 1611–61, Flemish animal painter and etcher. Collaborated with Rubens and Jordaens.

Fyzabad or **Faizabad** (fī'zùbăd), city (pop. 57,632), E central Uttar Pradesh, India. Cap of kingdom of Oudh (1724–75). Its suburb, Ajodhya or Ayodhya, is sacred to Hindus; mentioned in Ramayana.

G

Ga, chemical symbol of the element GALLIUM.

Gabirol: see IBN GABIROL, SOLOMON BEN JUDAH.

Gablonz, Czechoslovakia: see JABLONEC NAD NISOU.

Gabriel (gā–) [Heb.,= man of God], archangel, the divine herald. In Bible he appears to Daniel, to Zacharias, and to the Virgin Mary in the Annunciation. Dan. 8.16; 9.21; Luke 1.19,26,27. Christian tradition makes Gabriel the archangel trumpeter of the Last Judgment. 1 Thes. 4.16. In Islam, Gabriel revealed the Koran to Mohammed. Feast: March 24.

Gabriel, Jacques Ange (zhäk′ äzh′ gäbrēĕl′) c.1698–1782, French architect, who designed Place de la Concorde (Paris) and finished Petit Trianon (Versailles).

Gabrieli, Giovanni (gäbrēä′lē), 1557–1612, Italian organist and composer. His music shows the beginnings of baroque techniques; thus, his *Sonata pian′ e forte* employs the baroque use of contrasts in dynamics and contains elements of modern orchestration.

Gabrilowitsch, Ossip (ô′sĭp gäbrĭlô′vĭch), 1878–1936, Russian-American pianist and conductor. Conductor of the Detroit Symphony Orchestra, 1918–36.

Gad, son of Jacob, ancestor of one of 12 tribes of Israel. Tribe settled in GILEAD. Gen 30.11; 35.26; 49.19; Num. 2.14; 13.15; 32.1,2,34; Deut. 3.12; 33.20; Joshua 13.24; 1 Chron. 5.18,26; 12.8,14.

Gadara (gă′–), anc. city, SE of Sea of Galilee, in the Decapolis. The "country of the Gadarenes"—or Gergesenes or Gerasenes—given in Bible as scene of miracle of the possessed swine probably refers not to this city but to obscure town on E shore of Sea of Galilee. Mat 8.28; Mark 5.1; Luke 8.26.

Gaddi (gäd′ de), family of Florentine artists. **Gaddo Gaddi** (gäd′dō), c.1260–c.1333, painter and mosaicist, was probably an associate of Cimabue and Giotto. His son, **Taddeo Gaddi,** c.1300–c.1366, was godson and pupil of Giotto, whom he assisted for 24 years. Also painters were Taddeo's sons, **Agnolo Gaddi,** c.1350–96, and **Giovanni Gaddi,** d. 1383.

gadolinium (gădŭlĭ′nēŭm), rare metallic element of RARE EARTHS (symbol = Gd; see also ELEMENT, table).

Gadsden, James, 1788–1858, American railroad promoter and diplomat. Urged construction of railroad from South to the Pacific. Minister to Mexico (1853–56); negotiated GADSDEN PURCHASE. Recalled for exceeding instructions.

Gadsden, industrial city (pop. 55,725), NE Ala., on Coosa R. and NE of Birmingham, in mining area; founded c.1845. Alabama City annexed 1932. Metalworking (iron, steel). Rubber tires, textiles.

Gadsden Purchase, strip of land purchased (1853) by U.S. from Mexico. Pres. Franklin Pierce wanted to insure U.S. possession of Mesilla Valley near the Rio Grande—most practicable route for southern railroad to the Pacific. James GADSDEN negotiated purchase. Area of 45,535 sq. mi., purchased for $10,000,000, now forms extreme S N.Mex. and Ariz. S of the Gila.

Gadshill (gădz′hĭl), low hill, Kent, England. Scene of Falstaff's robberies in Shakspere's *Henry IV*.

Gaea (jē′ů) [Gr.,= earth], Greek earth-goddess; daughter of Chaos, mother of Uranus and Pontus. Mother by Uranus of Cyclopes and Titans, by Pontus of five sea-deities. Worshiped as mother of all things, a counselor of gods and men. Oracles of Delphi and Olympia traced their origin to her.

Gaelic (gā′lĭk), Celtic languages spoken in Ireland (Irish) and Highland Scotland (Scottish or Scottish Gaelic). It may include Manx. Erse is sometimes a synonym for Gaelic. See LANGUAGE (table).

Gaelic literature, literature of Gaelic-speaking Ireland and Scotland. Irish literature is divided into Old Irish (before 900), Middle Irish (until 1350), Late Middle or Early Modern Irish (until 1650), and Modern Irish (from 1650). Old Irish works survive in Middle Irish copies (e.g., Book of Leinster). Middle Irish literature consists of two groups of romances or sagas—the Red Branch of Ulster cycle and the Fenian cycle. Red Branch deals with pagan heroes (e.g., *Cuchulain*). Fenian cycle, later in origin, is gentler, and Christianity is introduced during time of *Ossian*. Form of sagas is prose with interspersed verse dialogue. Poetic revival and rise of modern Irish prose (16th–17th cent.) culminated in work of Geoffrey Keating. Poetry after time of Cromwell (1649) was in hands of wandering poets. Depopulation of Ireland after potato famine of 1847 brought great decrease in number of those who spoke Gaelic. Late 19th cent. brought Gaelic revival, led by the Gaelic League and Douglas Hyde. Scottish Gaelic literature has been separate since 16th cent. Rebellion (1745) of Charles Edward Stuart led to great outburst of poetry by such men as Alexander Macdonald. Controversy over *Ossian* of James MACPHERSON renewed interest in Gaelic. Some Highland writers have used Gaelic in 19th–20th cent.

Gaeta (gää′tä), city (pop. 4,967), S Latium, central Italy; Mediterranean port on Gulf of Gaeta. Long a stronghold of kingdom of Naples. On its fall to Victor Emmanuel II of Sardinia after long siege (1860–61), the kingdom of Italy was proclaimed.

Gaffney, city (pop. 8,123), NW S.C., NE of Spartanburg near N.C. line. Has textile mills.

SMALL CAPITALS = cross references.　　Pronunciation key: pp. xiv and xv.　　Abbreviations: p. 2.

458

Seat of Limestone Col. (for women; 1845).

Gafsa (găf′sù), anc. *Capsa,* town (pop. 11,-320), S central Tunisia, in an oasis. Exports phosphates, dates, and olives. Surrounding region has yielded artifacts of an upper Paleolithic culture (Capsian) of N Africa and S Europe.

Gág, Wanda (gäg), 1893–1946, American artist and writer for children; noted for her lithographs.

Gage, Thomas, d. 1656, English traveler. Lived and traveled among Indians of Central America (1625–37). Wrote *The English-American: His Travail by Sea and Land* (1648).

Gage, Thomas, 1721–87, British general. Commanded British forces in North America (1763–73). As governor of Mass. (1774–75) he enforced coercive measures on eve of American Revolution.

gag rules, procedural rules in force in U.S. House of Representatives from 1836 to 1844. Southerners, aided by Northern Democrats, secured their passage to prevent discussion of antislavery proposals in the House. Repealed following John Quincy Adams's successful fight to secure right of petition. Their effect was to strengthen cause of abolitionists.

Gaillard, David DuBose (gā′lùrd), 1859–1913, American army engineer. Directed construction of central division of Panama Canal, including excavation of Culebra (now Gaillard) Cut, most difficult portion of undertaking.

gaillardia (gälär′–), annual or perennial plant (*Gaillardia*) of W U.S. It has showy red or yellow daisylike flower heads, used for cutting.

Gaines's Mill: see SEVEN DAYS BATTLES.

Gainesville. 1 City (pop. 26,861), N central Fla., SW of Jacksonville; founded c.1854 on site of trading post (1830). Resort. Industrial and shipping center for tung oil, naval stores, lumber, citrus fruit, and vegetables. Seat of Univ. of FLORIDA. Paynes Prairie, a marsh, is near. **2** City (11,936), N Ga., near Chattahoochee R. NE of Atlanta, in Blue Ridge foothills. Textile mfg. and poultry processing. Brenau Col. (for women; 1878) is here. **3** City (pop. 11,246), N Texas, on Elm Fork of Trinity R. NNW of Dallas; founded 1850 on Calif. trail. Center of oil and agr. area processing cotton, grains, and oil. Railroad shops. Has annual community circus.

Gainsborough, Thomas (gänz′bùrù), 1727–88, English portrait and landscape painter. Began as apprentice to a London silversmith. At peak of career his popularity rivaled that of Reynolds. Famous for elegance of his portraits (esp. of women), which have a light and airy quality. Greens and blues predominate in his work. Among famous paintings is *The Blue Boy* (Huntington Art Gall., San Marino, Calif.).

Gainsborough, urban district (pop. 17,509), Lincolnshire, England, on Trent R. It is St. Ogg's of George Eliot's *Mill on the Floss.* Town estab. very early; Old Hall supposedly built by John of Gaunt.

Gaiseric (gī′sùrĭk) or **Genseric** (gĕn′sùrĭk, jĕn′–), c.390–477, king of the VANDALS (428–77). Invaded Roman Africa from Spain (429); took Carthage 439; won control of Mediterranean through his pirate fleets; sacked Rome 455. When he made peace with Zeno (476), he held N Africa, Sicily, Sardinia, Corsica, Balearic Isls.

Gaithersburg, town (pop. 1,755), W central Md., NW of Washington, D.C. U.S. Coast and Geodetic Survey runs international latitude observatory here.

Gaius (gā′ùs, gī′–), 2d cent. A.D., Roman jurist, known for his *Institutes,* a legal textbook used in the compilation of the Corpus Juris Civilis.

galactose: see LACTOSE.

Galahad, Sir: see ARTHURIAN LEGEND.

Galápagos Islands (gülä′pùgōs) [Span.,= tortoise]. Pacific archipelago (2,966 sq. mi.; pop. 1,346), c.650 mi. W of Ecuador, to which they belong. Discovered in 1535, the islands have biological interest. Visited by Charles Darwin (1835).

Galatea (gălùtē′ù), in Greek mythology, beautiful statue made by the sculptor PYGMALION. Aphrodite granted his prayer that it might come to life.

Galati or **Galatz** (gäläts′), city (pop. 80,411), E Rumania, in Moldavia; a major port on the lower Danube. It was the seat of Danube Navigation Commission from 1856 to 1939.

Galatia (gülä′shù), anc. territory of central Asia Minor, in the present Turkey (around Ankara). So called from its inhabitants, the Gauls, who conquered it in 3d cent. B.C. and increased territory to extend from Bithynia and Pontus on N to Pamphylia on S. Their advance was checked c.230 B.C. by Attalus I of Pergamum. Fell to Romans 189 B.C., became Roman province 25 B.C. Chief city was Ancyra (present Ankara).

Galatians (gülä′shùnz), epistle of New Testament, written by St. Paul to Christians of central Asia Minor. The Galatians had acquired the belief that rigid obedience to the Law of Moses was the means of salvation. This, Paul thought, would vitiate the whole of Christian freedom won for men on the Cross. He states that man is justified in the sight of God by faith, rather than by adherence to the Law. This doctrine is of great importance in Christian theology.

Galatz, Rumania: see GALATI.

Galax (gā′läks), town (pop. 5,248), SW Va., SW of Roanoke. Mfg. of furniture, caskets, and glass products. Galax plant gathered and shipped.

galax (gā′läks″), low-growing evergreen plant (*Galax aphylla*), native to mountain woods from Va. to Ga. Its spikes of white flowers and heart-shaped leaves are used by florists.

Galaxy: see MILKY WAY SYSTEM.

Galba (Servius Sulpicius Galba) (găl′bù), 3 B.C.–A.D. 69, Roman emperor. An able soldier, he was proclaimed emperor on Nero's death (68) but soon was killed in a rebellion. Otho became emperor.

Galdhoppigen: see JOTUNHEIM.

Galdós, Benito Pérez: see PÉREZ GALDÓS, BENITO.

Gale, Zona, 1874–1938, American novelist, b. Portage, Wis. Won notice for her idealized stories of small-town life (e.g., *Friendship*

Village, 1908). Her later novels were realistic and her best-known work, *Miss Lulu Bett* (1920), was satiric.

Galeed (gă'lēĕd) or **Mizpah** (mĭz'pủ), cairn, raised by Jacob and Laban to mark their covenant. So-called "Mizpah benediction" given here was mutual warning, not a blessing. Gen. 31.44–55. Also called Jegarsahudutha.

Galen (gā'lŭn), c.130–c.200, physician of Greek parentage, systematizer of contemporary medical learning. His authority was almost undisputed until the 16th cent. He wrote many treatises; about 83 of his medical works are extant.

Galena, city (pop. 4,648), extreme NW Ill., on Galena R. near the Mississippi. Lead mined here since early 18th cent. From 1807, when U.S. took mines under its protection, to 1860's, busy steamboat port and center of NW Ill. and SW Wis. lead area. Home of U. S. Grant is state museum.

galena (gủlē'nủ) or **lead glance,** lustrous, blue-gray crystalline mineral, an important ore of lead and in some areas of silver. It is chiefly lead sulphide, but often contains silver and sometimes copper, zinc, or other elements.

Galena Park, city (pop. 7,186), S Texas, E suburb of Houston, absorbed 1948 by Houston.

Galerius (gủlēr'ẻủs), d. 310, Roman emperor (305–10). Appointed Caesar by Diocletian in 293, he succeeded (305) to empire in the East when Constantius I succeeded in the West. After Constantius' death, Galerius recognized Severus as coemperor, but after they were defeated by the troops of Maxentius, he supported Licinius. A confused fight for power was still going on when Galerius died.

Galesburg, city (pop. 31,425), W Ill., WNW of Peoria; founded 1836. Rail center (with shops) and livestock market. Mfg. of bricks and metal products. Seat of KNOX COLLEGE. Town and college founded by N.Y. Presbyterians under G. W. Gale. Birthplace of Carl Sandburg.

Galiani, Ferdinando (fārdēnän'dō gälyä'nē), 1728–87, Italian economist. His *Della moneta* [on money] (1750), and *Dialogues sur le commerce des blés* (1770), set forth modern theory of value and historical approach to economics.

Galich (gä'lĭch), Pol. *Halicz,* city (pop. 4,386), NW Ukraine, on the Dniester. The seat of the dukes of Przemysl from c.1134, it later became the cap. of the duchy of Galich, which in 1188 was united with Vladimir (see VLADIMIR-VOLYNSKI). In 13th cent. Galich-Vladimir (which then included GALICIA and VOLHYNIA), extended E to Kiev. Under Tatar overlordship from 1245, duchy was partitioned in 1366 between Poland and Lithuania. City, now insignificant, has medieval remains.

Galicia (gủlĭ'shủ), former Austrian crownland, now in NW Ukraine; chief city Lvov (Lemberg). The W section of old duchy of GALICH and Vladimir, it passed to Poland 1366, to Austria 1772. Polish population enjoyed limited autonomy 1861–1918. A battleground during World War I, Galicia was contested by Poland and Ukrainian republic in 1918–20. Poland secured all Galicia and

was confirmed in possession by Treaty of Riga with USSR (1921). By Polish-Soviet Treaty most of Galicia (incl. Lvov and Drogobych oil fields) passed to USSR.

Galicia, region (10,984 sq. mi.; pop. 2,495,860), NW Spain, bordering on Atlantic Ocean and on Portugal. Largely mountainous. Fishing, cattle raising, agr. Chief cities: Santiago de Compostela, La Coruña, Vigo, El Ferrol, Pontevedra. Galician dialect, akin to Portuguese, has a great literary past. Region was conquered from Moors by kings of Asturias 8th–9th cent.

Galigaï, Leonora: see CONCINI, CONCINO.

Galilee (gă'lĭlē), agr. region, N Palestine, chief scene of ministry of Jesus. The lake, countryside, and towns—Cana, Capernaum, Tiberias, Nazareth—are repeatedly referred to in the Gospels. Jesus was called the Galilean. Joshua 20.7; 21.32; 1 Kings 9.11; 2 Kings 15.29; Isa. 9.1; Mat. 26.69–75; John 7.52.

Galilee, Sea of, fresh-water lake, 13 mi. long, 3–7 mi. wide, NE Palestine. It has fisheries. In Old Testament called Chinnereth or Chinneroth; in New Testament called Galilee, Gennesaret, or Tiberias. Modern Arabic name is Bahr Tabariyeh. In Jesus' time there were nine flourishing towns on its shores.

Galilei, Vincenzo (vēnchän'tsō gälēlā'ē), d. 1591, Italian lutanist, singer, writer, and composer; father of Galileo. A pioneer of the baroque era, he was one of the first to compose recitatives.

Galileo (gă''lĭlē'ō), It. *Galileo Galilei,* 1564–1642, Italian astronomer, mathematician, and physicist whose investigation of natural laws laid the foundations of modern experimental science. He formulated mathematically many physical laws and is credited with conclusions foreshadowing Newton's laws of motion. Constructed the first complete astronomical telescope (1609). His astronomical discoveries confirmed Copernican theory of solar system which he supported in his dialogue on the two chief systems of the world (published 1632). He was forced by the Inquisition, however, to abjure belief that earth moved about sun.

Galion, city (pop. 9,952), N central Ohio, SW of Mansfield. Mfg. of road machinery and vehicles.

Galitzin or **Galitsin:** see GALLITZIN.

Gall (gôl), c.1840–1894, war chief of Sioux Indians. Refused to accept treaty of 1868 confining him to reservation. Joined Sitting Bull in defeat of Custer (1876). Surrendered at Poplar, Mont., and became farmer on reservation.

gall (gôl), abnormal growth of plant tissue produced by stimulus of external agent. Commonest agents are gall insects (certain aphids, wasps, midges, beetles, thrips, moths) and mites. Usually gall maker produces same type of gall even on different hosts. Galls are source of tannin and of good quality permanent ink.

Gallait, Louis (lwē' gälä'), 1810–87, Belgian historical painter. Headed a school of historical painting in Brussels.

Galla Placidia (gă'lủ plủsĭ'dẻủ), d. 450, West Roman empress; daughter of Theodosius I. Long a hostage among the Visigoths, she married ATAULF (414) but was returned to her brother HONORIUS after Ataulf's death. Her second husband through her influence was made coemperor as CONSTANTIUS III. After 425 she was regent for her son VALENTINIAN III.

Gallas, Matthias, Graf von (mä'tē'äs gräf' fŏn gä'läs), 1584–1647, Austrian field marshal in Thirty Years War. Sided with emperor against his superior, WALLENSTEIN; succeeded to Wallenstein's command and led most of his duchy of Friedland. Won major victory at NÖRDLINGEN (1634).

Gallatin, Albert (gǎ'lŭtĭn), 1761–1849, American statesman and financier, b. Switzerland. Member, U.S. Congress (1795–1801). As U.S. Secretary of the Treasury (1802–14), he reshaped country's financial policy from Federalist to Jeffersonian principles. Key figure in negotiating Treaty of Ghent. Authority on banking and finance.

Gallatin, town (pop. 5,107), N Tenn., NE of Nashville near Cumberland R. Tobacco, farm, and livestock center with mfg. of shoes. Town, with Union garrison, captured Aug., 1862 by Gen. J. H. Morgan.

Gallatin, river, 120 mi. long, SW Mont., rising in NW Yellowstone Natl. Park and flowing N between Madison and Gallatin ranges, then NW to join Madison and Jefferson Rivers to form the Missouri.

gall bladder: see BILE.

Galle, Johann Gottfried (yō'hän gôt'frēt gä'lŭ), 1812–1910, German astronomer. He discovered the planet Neptune from calculations of Leverrier.

Galle (gäl), city (pop. 49,038), SW Ceylon, port on Indian Ocean. Flourished under Portuguese rule (1507–1640).

Gallegos, Rómulo (rō'mōōlō gäyä'gōs), 1884–, Venezuelan novelist, president of Venezuela (Feb.–Nov., 1948). Best-known novel is *Doña Bárbara* (1929; Eng. tr., 1931).

galleon (gǎ'lēŭn), type of ocean-going sailing vessels used by Spanish in 15th and 16th cent. They were cumbersome three-masted, square-rigged ships with high bow and stern, the latter ornamented with carvings. Though they were much used to bring goods from the Americas, their service in Spanish Armada brought defeat by smaller, swifter English ships (1588).

galley, type of long, narrow vessels of anc. and medieval times, propelled usually by oars, sometimes by sails. Earliest type was sometimes 150 ft. long with 50 oars, decked at bow and stern but otherwise open. Benches along sides were for chained rowers (slaves, prisoners), while center was for cargo. Usual number of banks of oars was three (triremes); smaller biremes had two banks. Galleys allegedly grew to as many as 40 banks; these were abandoned for smaller vessels by 1st cent. B.C. When used for war, sides were raised to protect rowers. Romans used hooks for grappling and carried bridges for boarding other vessels. French and Venetians used galleys in the Mediterranean until 17th cent.

gallic acid, colorless, crystalline solid organic acid usually obtained from tannins. Used as astringent and disinfectant.

Gallicanism (gǎ'lĭkŭnĭzŭm), theory that the French monarch had special rights in the Roman Catholic Church in France. It was put forward with the doctrine that the pope was subordinate to the ecumenical council (the conciliar theory), which emerged from the Univ. of Paris during the Great SCHISM and was confirmed by Charles VII in the Pragmatic Sanction of Bourges (1438). Francis I repealed the act after the Concordat of 1516 in which the papacy surrendered rights of appointment. The concordat was revoked in 1561, and the struggle resumed. LOUIS XIV in his trouble with INNOCENT XI had an assembly of bishops pass the "Four Gallican Articles of 1682," putting both councils and kings above the pope. Innocent XII managed to quiet the trouble in 1693, and Louis abandoned Gallican theory. Its effect was felt later in Jansenism, in the Revolutionary Civil Constitution of the Clergy, and in clauses added by Napoleon to the Concordat of 1801. Gallicanism has been impossible since the enunciation of papal infallibility of the Vatican Council (1869).

Galli-Curci, Amelita (gäl'lē-kōōr'chē), 1889–, Italian-American coloratura soprano. She made her American debut (Chicago, 1916) as Gilda in *Rigoletto;* she sang with the Chicago Opera Co. until 1926 and with the Metropolitan, New York, 1921–30.

Gallic Wars (gǎ'lǐk), campaigns of Caesar as proconsul of GAUL (58–51 B.C.). His first task was to prevent the Helvetii from entering SW Gaul. Next the Aedui asked his help against the German ARIOVISTUS. In 57 he pacified Belgica. In 56 he attacked the Veneti. In 55 he went to the Low Countries and crossed the Rhine. In 54 he invaded Britain. Next, some Belgian tribes led by AMBIORIX raised a revolt which Caesar dispersed. In 53 all central, E, and N Gaul revolted under VERCINGETORIX. With incredible speed and brilliant tactics Caesar crossed the Alps and stifled the uprising. The prime source is his own commentary, *The Gallic Wars.*

Galli da Bibiena: see BIBIENA, GALLI DA.

Gallieni, Joseph Simon (zhōzěf' sēmō' gälyänē'), 1849–1916, French general. As military governor of Paris early in World War I, he vitally contributed to the victory of the Marne (Sept., 1914), sped troops from Paris to front in commandeered taxicabs. Made marshal posthumously (1921).

Gallienus (gǎ'lĭē'nŭs), d. 268, Roman emperor, colleague of his father, VALERIAN (253–60), and alone (260–68). Dissolution of the empire started in his reign.

Gallipoli (gŭlī'pŭlē), Turkish *Gelibolu,* city (pop. 16,496), European Turkey; a port near the neck of the Gallipoli Peninsula, which extends c.60 mi. to the SW between the Aegean Sea and the Dardanelles. Peninsula was scene of **Gallipoli campaign,** April, 1915–Jan., 1916, an Allied expedition in World War I to gain the Dardanelles, capture Constantinople, and make contact with Russia through the Black Sea. Idea of forcing Straits was originally Winston Churchill's. A naval expedition having failed (March), British troops landed on peninsula, French on Asiatic shore. Allies, whose cooperation was poor, were prevented from joining by stubborn Turkish resistance (directed by Liman von Sanders) and had to withdraw. Sir Ian Hamilton and, after Oct., Sir Charles Munro were the Allied commanders.

Gallipolis (găʺlĭpŭlēsʹ), city (pop. 7,871), SE Ohio, on Ohio R. Mfg. of furniture and food products.

Gallitzin (gŭlĭtʹsĭn), Rus. *Golytsin*, Russian princely family; also spelled Galitzin, Galytzin. **Vasily Vasilyevich Gallitzin** (vĕsēʹlyē vŭsēʹlyŭvĭch), d. 1619, helped to enthrone first false Dmitri. **Vasily Vasilyevich Gallitzin**, 1643–1714, lover and adviser of SOPHIA ALEKSEYEVNA, was banished to Siberia by Peter I (1689). **Boris Alekseyevich Gallitzin** (bŭrēsʹ ŭlyĭksyāʹĭvĭch), 1654–1714, tutor of Peter I, helped him to depose Sophia. **Dmitri Mikhailovich Gallitzin** (dŭmēʹtrē mēkhĭʹlŭvĭch), 1665–1737, diplomat and general, was exiled by Empress Anna for seeking to limit her power (1730). **Dmitri Alekseyevich Gallitzin**, 1735–1803, Russian ambassador to Paris (1765–73), was a friend of Diderot and Voltaire. His son, **Demetrius Augustine Gallitzin**, 1770–1840, became a Roman Catholic, went to America. Ordained 1795; worked in SW Pennsylvania as frontier missionary; was known as Father Smith. Founded Catholic colony of Loretto near Gallitzin, Pa. **Aleksandr Nikolayevich Gallitzin** (ŭlyĭksänʹdŭr nyĭkŭlîʹŭvĭch), 1773?–1844, was minister of education under Alexander I; a liberal.

gallium (gălʹlēŭm), silver-gray metallic element (symbol = Ga; see also ELEMENT, table), widely distributed in small quantities. Since it is liquid over a wide temperature range it is sometimes used in high-temperature thermometers.

Galloway, Joseph, c.1731–1803, American colonial leader. Urged conciliation and written constitution as means of avoiding conflict prior to American Revolution and later remained loyal to the king.

Galloway, district of SW Scotland, comprising Wigtownshire and Kirkcudbrightshire. Black, hornless Galloway cattle bred here.

gallstone: see CALCULUS, in medicine.

Gallup, George Horace, 1901–, American public opinion statistician, originator of the Gallup poll. Founded (1935) American Institute of Public Opinion.

Gallup, town (pop. 9,133; alt. 6,503 ft.), NW N.Mex., on Puerco R. and near Ariz. line; founded c.1879. Rail and trade center in coal, wool, and livestock area, and in heart of Indian country. Scene of annual intertribal rites.

Galois, Évariste (ävärēstʹ gälwäʹ), 1811–32, French mathematician. He contributed to theories of equations, numbers, and functions and was a pioneer in establishing theory of groups in algebraic solutions.

Galswintha (gălswĭnʹthŭ), d. 567, Frankish queen, sister of BRUNHILDA and wife of CHILPERIC I, by whom she was murdered.

Galsworthy, John, 1867–1933, English novelist and dramatist. Many plays concern social problems (e.g., *Strife*, 1909). Novels portray the limited social consciousness and viewpoint of upper-middle-class families of Victorian era. Many are grouped in three trilo-

gies, *The Forsyte Saga* (1922), *A Modern Comedy* (1928), *The End of the Chapter* (1935). He also wrote short stories, *Caravan* (1925), and poems (in a collected edition, 1934). Received 1932 Nobel Prize in Literature.

Galt, John, 1779–1839, Scottish novelist, founder of CANADA COMPANY (1826). Novels and stories portray Scottish country life. His son, **Sir Alexander Tilloch Galt,** 1817–93, was a Canadian statesman, b. England. A leader for confederation of Canadian provinces. As minister of finance (1858–62, 1864–66) he defended protective tariff. Dominant member of Halifax Fisheries Commission. First Canadian high commissioner in London (1880–83).

Galt, city (pop. 19,207), S Ont., Canada, on Grand R. and WNW of Hamilton. Has textile and lumber mills and mfg. of clothing, shoes, and machinery.

Galton, Sir Francis (gôlʹtŭn), 1822–1911, English scientist, founder of eugenics (term coined by him); cousin of Charles Darwin.

Galuppi, Baldassare (bäldäs-säʹrä gälo͞opʹpē), 1706–85, Italian composer of oratorios, chamber music, and operas. Immortalized in Browning's poem "A Toccata of Galuppi's."

Galvani, Luigi (lwēʹjē gälväʹnē), 1737–98, Italian physician. After observing contraction of frog's leg when touched with metal, he made an arc of two different metals and used it to cause muscle contractions. He held that tissue was the electricity source; Volta said the arc was. This controversy stimulated research.

galvanizing, term commonly used for process of coating a metal (usually iron or steel) with zinc, which resists oxidation and moisture. Methods include dipping, electroplating, and baking.

galvanometer, instrument for determining presence of a current in a conductor, the direction of flow, and strength of current. It is based on Hans C. Oersted's discovery that magnetic needle is deflected by passage of electric current along a conductor; magnetic needle tends to turn at right angles, the extent of turn being, in general, dependent upon strength of current. Modern galvanometers have fixed magnet and movable coil. Ammeter is a form of galvanometer with scale to indicate number of amperes. Voltmeter is moving-coil galvanometer which has high-resistance coil and which indicates number of volts of current—the greater the electromotive force of the current, the greater the deflection of the needle.

Galveston (gălʹvŭstŭn), port city (pop. 66,568), on Galveston Isl., S Texas. Island lies across Galveston Bay (inlet of Gulf of Mexico) entrance. Spanish knew it early; probable scene of Cabeza de Vaca's shipwreck (1528). Explored late 18th cent., later outlaw country (esp. for pirates of Jean Lafitte). Settled in 1830s, city progressed despite yellow fever, hurricanes, and Union blockade and brief occupation 1862. Sea wall built after 1900 hurricane. Two causeways connect with mainland. Stores, processes, and ships cotton, sulphur and other chemicals, foodstuffs, and metals. Has fishing and shrimping. Beach resort. Fort Travis (1898) and Fort Crockett (1897–99) were active in World War II. Seat of Univ. of Texas medical school.

Gálvez, José de (hōsā' dā gäl'věth), 1720–87, Spanish colonial administrator, visitor general to New Spain (1765–71). Upon return to Spain was responsible for two important changes in Spanish colonial policy: more liberal trade policy to replace earlier narrow mercantilism; system of intendancies. His brother, **Matías de Gálvez** (mätē'äs), 1717–84, was Spanish colonial administrator; viceroy of New Spain (1783–84). Matías's son, **Bernardo de Gálvez,** c.1746–1786, became Spanish governor of Louisiana in 1777. Aided patriot cause in American Revolution. After Spain declared war on England (1779), he captured Baton Rouge and Natchez (1779), Mobile (1780), and Pensacola (1781). Succeeded his father as viceroy.

Galway (gôl'wā), maritime county (2,293 sq. mi.; pop. 165,201), W Ireland, in Connaught. Lough Corrib divides the county; W is Connemara, with picturesque mountains, and E a rolling plain. The Shannon is chief river, and Aran Isls. chief islands. Industries mainly agr. and fishing. The county town is Galway, urban district (pop. 20,-370), on Galway Bay. A fort for men of Connaught (1124), it saw later fighting. Has good harbor and exports agr. produce, salmon, herring, marble, woolen goods. Site of University Col.

Galway Bay, inlet of the Atlantic, 30 mi. long and 23 mi. wide at entrance on W Ireland coast, in counties Galway and Clare. Aran Isls. at entrance.

Gama, Vasco da (vă'skō dù gă'mù), c.1460–1524, Portuguese navigator, first European to reach India by sea (1497–99). Voyage around Africa made wealth of Indies accessible to Europe and made possible growth of Portuguese wealth and empire. On second voyage (1502) he estab. Portuguese power in Indian waters and on African coast by harsh methods.

Gamaliel of Jabneh, fl. A.D. 100, Hebrew leader. He added the 18 benedictions to the daily prayers in an attempt to retain the spirit of Judaism after the destruction of Jerusalem.

Gambetta, Léon (lāō' gäbětä'), 1838–82, French statesman. In FRANCO-PRUSSIAN WAR (1870–71) organized French resistance in provinces. Played important part in creation of Third Republic, was premier 1881–82. Republican and anticlerical, he steered mid-course between radicals and royalists, advocated revenge against Germany.

Gambia (găm'bēù), British colony and protectorate (4,033 sq. mi.; pop. c.250,000), W Africa, on the Atlantic; cap. Bathurst. A narrow enclave in Senegal, it borders both banks of Gambia R., the chief trade artery of region. The colony (69 sq. mi.) comprises St. Mary's Isl. (site of Bathurst) and several inland areas. Largely inhabited by Moslem Negro tribes. Exports peanuts. The Portuguese, who estab. settlements here in mid-15th cent., were succeeded by the British in early 17th cent. Present boundaries estab. 1888.

Gambier (găm'bēr), village (pop. 1,037), central Ohio, E of Mt. Vernon. Here is Kenyon Col. (for men; chartered 1824 as Episcopal theological seminary); publishes literary quarterly *Kenyon Review.*

Gambier Islands (găm'bēr) or **Mangareva** (män"gärä'vä), coral group, S Pacific; part of FRENCH ESTABLISHMENTS IN OCEANIA. Mangareva (pop. 553) is largest island. Discovered 1797 by the British, annexed 1881 by France. Produces copra and coffee.

gamboge (gămbōj'), reddish yellow gum RESIN (from tree sap) used as paint pigment and as a purgative.

Gambrinus (gămbrī'nùs), mythical Flemish king, to whom is attributed invention of beer.

gamma ray: see RADIOACTIVITY.

Gammer Gurton's Needle, second extant English comedy, acted 1566 at Christ's College, Cambridge. Once attributed to John Still (later bishop of Bath and Wells), but more probably by William Stevenson, fellow of the college.

Gander, town (pop. including airport personnel, c.3,000), E N.F., Canada. Main North American terminal for air service to Europe. Was a major Allied base in World War II.

Gandhi, Mohandas Karamchand (mō"hùndäs' kù"rùmchùnd gän'dē), 1869–1948, great Indian leader. Educated in India and London; admitted to the bar in 1889. While in South Africa he fought for rights of Indians in that country. Returned 1915 to India and began working for India's independence. Gave up Western ways to lead life of abstinence in accordance with Hindu ethics; advocated revival of home industries (esp. cloth weaving). Asserting man's unity under one God, he preached Christian and Moslem scriptures along with the Hindu; vigorously espoused abolition of untouchability. Several times leader of INDIAN NATIONAL CONGRESS he opposed British policy with *Satyagraha* [Sanskrit = truth force] or, in English, nonviolent resistance. Imprisoned 1930 for violating state salt monopoly by publicly extracting salt from sea water, but released 1931 to attend London conference on India. Called the Mahatma [great souled], he was so widely revered that he could exact political concessions by threatening "fasts unto death." Called for *Satyagraha* in 1942, when the British rejected offer to cooperate in war if India were freed at once; interned until 1944. A major figure in conferences leading to India's freedom (1947), he was deeply disappointed by partition of India. Shot fatally on Jan. 30, 1948, by a Hindu who blamed him for the partition.

Gandzha, Azerbaijan SSR: see KIROVABAD.

Ganges (găn'jēz), river, c.1,560 mi. long, in N India and E Pakistan, rising in Himalayas in N Uttar Pradesh and flowing to Bay of Bengal; most sacred Hindu river. Especially holy bathing sites at Allahabad and at Benares.

gannet (găn'ĭt) or **solan goose** (sō'lùn), large white sea bird related to pelican. Common gannet of N Atlantic dives for fish from high in air to deep in water. Boobies are related tropical sea birds.

Gannett, Henry, 1846–1914, American geographer. Chief geographer of U.S. Geological

Survey after 1882; improved system of census taking. His efforts led to establishment of U.S. Board of Geographical Names (1890); its chairman until 1910.

Gannett Peak, Wyo.: see WIND RIVER RANGE.

Ganso, Emil, 1895–1941, American painter and etcher, b. Germany.

Ganymede (gă′nĭmēd), in Greek mythology, beautiful boy seized by Zeus to be his cup-bearer.

Garamond, Claude (gă′rŭmŏnd; Fr., klōd′ gärämō′), d. 1561, Parisian designer and maker of printing types. His designs were used by the Estiennes and Bodoni and were used as a base for designs used by the Elzevir family. His roman and italic types were the first to be primarily designed for metal type, not imitated after handwriting. His roman also helped make roman standard rather than black letter. Modern Garamond types do not closely resemble his.

Garand, John C(antius) (gă′rŭnd), 1888–, American inventor of the Garand semiautomatic rifle (on principle of expanding gas), b. Canada.

Garay, Juan de (hwän′ dü gärī′), c.1528–83, Spanish conquistador in South America. Refounded Buenos Aires (1580) from Asunción.

Garbo, Greta, 1905–, American film actress, whose real name is Gustafsson, b. Sweden. Her beauty and restrained acting won fame in such films as *Anna Christie, Queen Christina, Camille,* and *Ninotchka.*

Garborg, Arne Evensen, 1851–1924, Norwegian poet and novelist. Championed use of Landsmaal, the language of the peasants.

García (y Iñigues), Calixto (kälēk′stō gärse′ä ē ēnyē′gĕs), 1836–98, Cuban revolutionist, leader in Ten Years War and Spanish-American War. Elbert Hubbard's essay *A Message to Garcia* has made his name famous.

García, Manuel del Popolo (mänwĕl′ dĕl pōpō′lō gärthē′ä), 1775–1832, Spanish tenor, teacher, impresario, and composer. His opera company included his wife, his son, and his daughter, Maria MALIBRAN. He was first to produce opera in Italian in New York. His son, **Manuel Patricio García** (pätrē′thyō), 1805–1906, inventor of the laryngoscope, taught in Paris and London. Jenny Lind was his pupil.

García Calderón, Francisco (fränse′skō gärse′ä käldärōn′), Peruvian writer. Lived in France many years. Wrote (in French) *Latin America: Its Rise and Progress* (Eng. tr., 1913).

García Lorca, Federico (fädhärē′kö gärthē′ä lôr′kä), 1899–1936, Spanish poet and dramatist, steeped in the folklore of his native Andalusia. With *Romancero gitano* [gypsy balladeer] became his generation's most popular poet. Also wrote farces and tragedies. Shot by the Franco forces in the civil war.

Garcilaso de la Vega (gärthēlä′sō dä lä vä′gä), 1503?–1536, Spanish lyric poet of the Renaissance, a courtier and soldier. Wrote sonnets, odes, eclogues; adapted 11-syllable Italian verse to Spanish.

Garcilaso de la Vega (gärsēlä′sō dä lä vä′gä), 1539?–1616, Peruvian historian; son of Spanish conquistador and Incan princess; called the Inca. Writings (notably *Royal Commentaries of Peru*) tell of conquest of Peru and legends of the Inca.

Gard (gär), department (2,271 sq. mi.; pop. 393,279), S France, in Languedoc; cap. Nîmes. The Gard R., a tributary of the Rhone, is crossed at Remoulins by PONT DU GARD aqueduct.

Garda, Lake (gär′dä), Ital. *Lago di Garda* or *Benaco,* lake (143 sq. mi.; 32 mi. long), N Italy, between Lombardy and Venetia. Fed by Saraca R., drained by the Mincio. N tip, with Riva di Trento, is Alpine resort. Shores are dotted with vineyards, resorts.

Garden, Mary, 1877–, American operatic soprano, b. Scotland. She made her U.S. debut (New York, 1907) with the Manhattan Opera Co. as Thaïs. Other famous roles were Louise, Mélisande, Salomé.

Gardena (gärde′nŭ), city (pop. 14,405), S Calif., S of Los Angeles. Fruit, truck, and poultry farms.

Garden City. 1 City (pop. 10,905), SW Kansas, on Arkansas R.; founded 1878. Center of an irrigated farm and dairy area, it refines beet sugar. **2** Residential city (pop. 9,012), SE Mich., near Dearborn, in farm area. **3** Village (pop. 14,486), SE N.Y., on W Long Isl. near Hempstead; founded c.1869. Has large publishing business; mfg. of greases and aerial and marine instruments. Seat of Adelphi Col. (coed.; 1896). Mitchel Air Force Base is near.

garden city, community surrounded by a rural belt, owned by inhabitants, with predetermined maximum population and area. Scheme originated as preventative of urban crowding following Industrial Revolution. Original proponents were Robert Owen, James Silk Buckingham, and Charles Fourier. A number of such cities have been built since 1851 in England and America, but outside of England most such cities have become simply satellite suburbs of a larger industrial city, rather than communities whose industries have a self-sufficient labor force.

gardenia, subtropical shrub (*Gardenia jasminoides*), also known as Cape jasmine. It has fragrant white flowers and glossy evergreen leaves. Grown outdoors in mild regions, as house plant in cold areas.

Garden of the Gods: see COLORADO SPRINGS.

Gardiner, Sir Christopher, fl. 1630–32, personage in early history of Mass. Bay colony. When Puritans arrived at Mass. Bay to found colony (1630), they found him and a young woman. Later discovered to be agent of Sir Ferdinando Gorges, whose claims to Mass. he aided.

Gardiner, Samuel Rawson, 1829–1902, English historian. Wrote a thorough, careful history of Puritan Revolution in England, covering years 1603–60. Also edited constitutional documents of Revolution. Editor (1891–1901) *English Historical Review.*

Gardiner (gärd′nŭr), city (pop. 6,649), SW Maine, on Kennebec R. below Augusta. First technical school in U.S. estab. here (1823) by Benjamin Hale. E. A. Robinson grew up here. Mfg. of shoes and textiles.

Gardiners Island, 3,000 acres, SE N.Y., between flukes of E Long Isl.; settled 1639 by

Lion Gardiner. Site of first permanent English settlement in present N.Y.

Gardner, Erle Stanley, 1889–, American writer of detective stories featuring fictional lawyer, Perry Mason.

Gardner, Ernest Arthur: see GARDNER, PERCY.

Gardner, Isabella Stewart, 1840–1924, American art collector. Her collection and Fenway Court, which houses it, were willed to Boston as a museum.

Gardner, Percy, 1846–1937, English classical archaeologist and author of works on Greek art, history, and coins. While professor of archaeology at Oxford (1887–1925) he built up the archaeology department and its library and collections. His brother **Ernest Arthur Gardner,** 1862–1939, was director of British School of Archaeology at Athens (1887–95), professor of archaeology (1896–1929) and vice chancellor at Univ. of London, and author of works on Greek art and history.

Gardner, city (pop. 19,581), N central Mass., NNW of Worcester; settled 1764. Mfg. of furniture (from c.1805), metal products, stoves, and machinery.

Garfield, James A(bram), 1831–81, 20th President of the United States. U.S. Representative from Ohio (1863–80). Elected President in 1880 after being chosen by Republicans as compromise candidate. By appointing J. G. Blaine, political foe of Roscoe CONKLING, as Secretary of State, Garfield declared war with most important faction of his party. He won first battle by getting his appointee for New York port collectorship approved. Began prosecution of STAR ROUTE frauds. Constantly harassed by office seekers, he was shot by one of them, Charles J. Guiteau, on July 2, 1881; on Sept. 19 he died. Chester A. Arthur succeeded to presidency).

Garfield, city (pop. 27,550), NE N.J., on Passaic R. and ENE of Passaic. Mfg. of machinery, mechanical equipment, pharmaceuticals, rubber goods, textiles.

Garfield Heights, city (pop. 21,662), NE Ohio, SE suburb of Cleveland; founded 1904.

garfish, marine fish with long, slender body and long, pointed, toothed beak. It is found in most temperate and warm waters. Sometimes it enters rivers. Some of the 50 known species reach length of 5–6 ft. Swift and predatory, they swim near surface.

Garibaldi, Giuseppe (jōōzĕp'pä gärēbäl'dē), 1807–82, Italian patriot and soldier, hero of the RISORGIMENTO; b. Nice. Fled abroad after taking part in an unsuccessful republican plot (1835); fought in civil wars of Brazil and Uruguay (1835–46); returned to Italy and fought with Sardinian forces against Austria (1848–49) and with Mazzini's Roman republic against French interventionists (1849). Renouncing his republican ideal, he gave support to the policy of CAVOUR and VICTOR EMMANUEL II. In 1860, with Victor Emmanuel's connivance, he led 1,000 volunteer "Red Shirts" in spectacular conquest of Sicily and Naples. After handing his conquests over to Victor Emmanuel, who thus became king of Italy, Garibaldi retired to his home on Caprera isl. He twice attempted to conquer the Papal states, but was stopped by Italian troops at Aspromonte

(1862) and by French and papal troops at Mentana (1867).

Garigliano (gärēlyä'nō), name of LIRI R., S central Italy, below junction with Rapido R.; empties into Tyrrhenian Sea. Scene of bitter fighting (1943–44) during battle for CASSINO.

Garland, Augustus Hill, 1832–99, American lawyer, U.S. Attorney General (1885–89). In *Ex parte Garland* (1867), Garland, a former Confederate, won plea to resume practice before U.S. Supreme Court.

Garland, Hamlin, 1860–1940, American writer of stories of the Middle Western prairie country. Wrote *Main-travelled Roads* (1891; stories), novels, and autobiographical classic, *A Son of the Middle Border* (1917).

Garland, town (pop. 10,571), N Texas, NE of Dallas. Industrial suburb producing aircraft and seismic instruments.

garlic, perennial herb (*Allium sativum*), native to Europe and closely related to onion. The bulb is used as food flavoring.

Garmisch-Partenkirchen (gär'mĭsh-pär"tŭnkĭr'khŭn), town (pop. 25,022), Upper Bavaria. Winter resort at foot of ZUGSPITZE.

Garmo Peak, USSR: see STALIN PEAK.

Garneau, François Xavier (gärnō'), 1809–66, French Canadian historian. His *Histoire du Canada* (3 vols., 1845–48; 2d ed., with added material, 1852) covers Canadian history to union of two Canadas. Later editions by author's grandson brought work up to date. History has influenced and stimulated French Canadian literature, especially poetry.

Garner, John Nance, 1869–, Vice President of the United States (1933–41).

garnet, name given to a group of widely distributed crystalline minerals some of which are gems. They are commonly red and are double silicates. Garnets are rather soft, hence not highly valued.

Garnett, Richard (gär'nĭt), 1835–1906, English librarian and author. Served at the British Mus. with distinction. Wrote biographies (of Carlyle, Emerson, Milton, Coleridge, and others), essays, and critical works. His son, **Edward Garnett,** 1868–1937, was a critic who encouraged many great writers. His wife, **Constance (Beach) Garnett,** 1862–1946, made widely read translations from the Russian. Their son, **David Garnett,** 1892–, was a partner in the Nonesuch Press and wrote the fantastic short novel, *Lady into Fox* (1923), and other works.

Garnett (gär'nĕt), city (pop. 2,693), E Kansas, S of Lawrence. Birthplace of Edgar Lee Masters.

Garnier, Jean Louis Charles (gärnyä'), 1825–98, French architect, who built the Paris OPÉRA.

Garnier, Marie Joseph François, 1839–73, French explorer and naval officer usually known as Francis Garnier. Accompanied Doudart de Lagrée's expedition through Indo-Chinese area unfamiliar to Europeans (1866–68). Captured Hanoi on Tonkin expedition (1873). Wrote accounts of experiences.

Garofalo, Il (ēl gärō'fälō), 1481–1559, Italian painter of Ferrarese school. Real name was Benvenuto Tisi or Tisio.

Garonne (gärôn'), river, 402 mi. long, SW France, rising in Pyrenees. It flows NE to

Toulouse, then swings NW, and below Bordeaux joins the Dordogne to form the GIRONDE.

Garonne, Haute, France: see HAUTE-GARONNE.

gar pike, fresh-water fish of E and S U.S., Central America, Mexico, West Indies. It has a cylindrical body, platelike scales, snoutlike jaws, sharp teeth. Flesh is unpalatable. Gars eat more useful fish. Garfish is name for salt-water gar.

Garrett, João Batista de Almeida: see ALMEIDA.

Garrick, David, 1717–79, English actor and manager. Accompanied Dr. Johnson to London and set up a wine shop. Launched theatrical career by acting in his own *Lethe* (1740) and by association with Peg Woffington. Was London's idol after playing Richard III in 1741. Other roles included Hamlet, Lear, and Abel Drugger (in Jonson's *Alchemist*). His simple diction and manner swept declamatory actors from the stage. As manager of the Drury Lane after 1747, he made important stage reforms. Appeared last in 1776. He was a member of Dr. Johnson's circle.

Garrison, William Lloyd, 1805–79, American abolitionist. Founded the *Liberator* (1831), in which paper he waged uncompromising antislavery campaign for 35 years. Although a nonresistant and a believer in moral persuasion, his militant style antagonized many. His opposition to political action divided abolitionists. A founder of American Anti-Slavery Society (1833), its president 1843–65. Opposed Civil War until Emancipation Proclamation.

Garry, Fort, early trading post on site of present city of Winnipeg, Man. Founded 1821. Until city was founded (1860s), it was seat of authority in Manitoba region. Louis Riel captured it in rebellion of 1869. Sold in 1882, it was torn down except for the gate. Lower Fort Garry, on Red R., 19 mi. below Fort Garry, was built 1831 and still stands.

Garter, Order of the, oldest and most important order of knighthood in England. Instituted c.1346 by Edward III, it was originally limited to 25 members. Motto is *Honi soit qui mal y pense* [evil be to him who evil thinks]. Title is abbreviated K.G.

garter snake, common harmless North American snake, usually c.2 ft. long. Common form of NE U.S. varies, but usually is blackish or brownish with three yellow stripes. Young born alive in litters of 30 to 65. Ribbon snake is a garter snake found in wet places.

Garvey, Marcus, 1887–1940, American Negro leader, b. Jamaica. Plans for an African settlement ended when he was charged with fraud.

Gary, Elbert H(enry), 1846–1927, American industrialist, a lawyer. Chairman of board of directors of U.S. Steel Corp. (1903–27). Helped found GARY, Ind. Promoted employee benefits, but refused labor union recognition and insisted on the open shop.

Gary, city (pop. 133,911), NW Ind., at end of L. Michigan SE of Chicago. On U.S. Steel Corp. land, city was chartered and named for E. H. Gary, 1906. Great world steel center, midway between iron-ore beds of NW U.S. and coal of E and SE, it also has oil refining and mfg. of chemicals and cement. Calumet rivers have been made into lake harbors. The **Gary plan** was developed 1908–15 in the school system here by W. A. Wirt. It increases utilization of school plant by alternating classes between regular and special teachers, by running two schools simultaneously, and by coordinating various levels of schooling. Also called platoon system.

gas. 1 In general usage, any substance appearing in gaseous state at ordinary temperature and pressure; may be compound, element, or mixture. POISON GAS is used in chemical warfare, in insecticides, fumigation; LAUGHING GAS in anesthesia. Illuminating gases include air gas, natural gas. **2** In physics, one of the three states of matter, i.e., that state in which a substance is without definite shape or volume. Gases are classed with liquids as fluid. Molecules of gas move faster and are farther apart than those of liquids or solids. Cohesion between molecules is small; when not confined gas is capable of unlimited DIFFUSION. Volume can be reduced by compression; gases undergo liquefaction after being cooled below critical temperature. At constant temperature volume of gas decreases in direct proportion to increase in pressure (Boyle's law). At fixed volume, increase in pressure and in temperature are directly proportional. Dalton's law deals with mixtures of gases. At constant pressure, volume of gas is directly proportional to temperature. Kelvin temperature scale is used in calculating changes in volume and pressure on gases when temperature change is involved. Avogadro discovered that there are same number of molecules in equal volumes of gases under standard conditions. Each molecule of an elemental gas has two atoms; molecular weight is twice the atomic weight. If molecular weight of any gas is measured at standard conditions, the volume (gram-molecular volume) is 22.4 liters. When gas diffuses into a liquid and is held there it is said to have undergone absorption.

Gasca, Pedro de la (pä′drō dā lä gä′skä), c.1485–1567?, Spanish colonial administrator. A priest and lawyer, he was sent to Peru (1547), where he restored order. Repealed New Laws of Las Casas.

Gascoigne, George (gäskoin′), c.1539–1577, English poet. He was the first to write an essay on prosody (in *The Posies of George Gascoigne,* 1575). Also wrote first prose comedy in English (*Supposes,* 1566), introduced nondramatic blank verse (in *The Steel Glass,* 1576).

Gasconade (gäskúnäd′), river rising in S Mo. in the Ozarks and flowing c.265 mi. NE to the Missouri near Gasconade, E of Jefferson City.

Gascony (gä′skúnē), Fr. *Gascogne,* region and former province, SW France, in Landes, Gers, Hautes-Pyrénées, Basses-Pyrénées, Lot-et-Garonne, Tarn-et-Garonne, and Haute-Garonne depts.; historic cap. Auch. Agr., fishing (along Atlantic coast), cattle raising, winegrowing, brandy mfg. (in Armagnac dist.) are main occupations. Basque is still spoken in old Basque provs., notably in and around Bayonne. Part of Roman Aquitania, region was inhabited by BASQUES, who created duchy of Vasconia or Gascony in 7th cent. A.D. Duchy fell into anarchy in 9th cent.; was united in 11th cent. with AQUITAINE, whose later history it shared. Reconquered by France at end of Hundred Years War, Gascony consisted of several fiefs, held mainly by the counts of ARMAGNAC and of FOIX and the lords of ALBRET; all these passed, through marriage and inheritance, to Henry of Navarre, who after becoming king of France as Henry IV incorporated them with the royal domain (1607).

gas engine: see INTERNAL-COMBUSTION ENGINE.

Gaskell, Elizabeth (Cleghorn Stevenson), 1810–65, English novelist. Known especially for *Mary Barton* (1848) and *Cranford* (1853; a charming tale of British village life). She also wrote a controversial biography of Charlotte Brontë (1857).

gasoline, volatile fuel oil obtained by fractional distillation of petroleum and also from natural gas. Chief uses are as gas-engine fuel and organic solvent.

Gaspar: see WISE MEN OF THE EAST.

Gasparri, Pietro (pyä′trō gäspär′rē), 1852–1934, Italian cardinal. Directed great codification of canon law and received cardinal's hat from Pius X (1907); as papal secretary of state in World War I, worked for peace; under Pius XI concluded the LATERAN TREATY (1929).

Gaspee (gă′spē″, găspē′), British revenue cutter, burned (June 10, 1772) at Gaspee Point in Narragansett Bay, R.I. Ship sent to enforce revenue laws; burning was act of defiance by colonists.

Gaspé Peninsula (găspā′), tongue of land (150 mi. long, 60–90 mi. wide), E Que., Canada, extending E into the Gulf of St. Lawrence between St. Lawrence R. (N) and Chaleur Bay (S). **Gaspé Bay** is a deep inlet at E end of the peninsula. The resort and market village of **Gaspé** (pop. 1,692) is near the head of the bay. **Cape Gaspé** is at the E end of the peninsula. Population (chiefly French Canadian) is scattered in villages along coast. Fishing, the major industry, is supplemented by lumbering, pulp milling, and some agr. Excellent hunting and fishing is found in the heavily forested and mountainous interior. Since a highway has been completed (1928) encircling the peninsula, tourists have been attracted by the charm of picturesque villages and fine scenery.

Gasperi, Alcide de: see DE GASPERI, ALCIDE.

Gassendi, Pierre (gäsädē′), 1592–1655, French materialist philosopher and scientist. Opposed Aristotelian authority; as vigorous rival of Cartesian school, revived atomic theory; sought to reconcile mechanism and theology.

Gasser, Herbert Spencer (gă′sŭr), 1888–, American physiologist. Shared 1944 Nobel Prize in Physiology and Medicine for work on electrophysiology of nerves. Became director of Rockefeller Institute in 1935.

Gasset, José Ortega: see ORTEGA Y GASSET, JOSÉ.

Gastein (gä′stīn), valley and resort area in Salzburg, W central Austria. Bad Gastein, a fashionable bathing place, has radium thermal springs; its water is also piped to Bad Hofgastein. By Gastein Convention (1865) Austria assumed administration of Holstein, Prussia that of Schleswig.

Gastonia (găstō′nĕŭ), city (pop. 23,069), W central N.C., in piedmont. Mfg. of textiles and tire fabric. Near by is Kings Mountain battlefield.

gastric juice: see STOMACH.

Gatchina (gä′chĕnŭ), city (pop. 18,589), RSFSR, SSW of Leningrad. Developed around imperial summer residence (built 1766–70). Palace (now museum) looted by Germans in World War II.

Gate City, town (pop. 2,126), SW Va., near Tenn. line. Near by is Natural Tunnel (75–100 ft. high, c.900 ft. long).

Gates, Horatio, 1727–1806, American Revolutionary general, b. England. National hero after success of SARATOGA CAMPAIGN. Commanded Carolina campaign until disgraceful defeat at Camden, S.C. (1780).

Gates, Sir Thomas, fl. 1585–1621, British colonial governor of Va. (1611–14). One of grantees in original charter to found colony.

Gateshead (găts′hĕd), county borough (pop. 115,017), Durham, England, on Tyne R. opposite Newcastle. Has locomotive works, railroad shops, shipbuilding, and mfg. of glass, iron goods, cables and chemicals. Near by are coal mines and grindstone quarries.

Gath, Philistine city, on borders of Judah; birthplace of Goliath; refuge of David during years when he was outlawed.

Gatineau (gä′tĭnō″), village (pop. 5,771), SW Que., Canada, on N shore of Ottawa R. and E of Hull.

Gatineau, river of SW Que., Canada, flowing from the Laurentians 230 mi. S to Ottawa R. at Hull.

Gatlinburg, resort city (pop. 1,301), E Tenn., SE of Knoxville near foot of Mt. Le Conte. Near hq. of Great Smoky Mts. Natl. Park.

Gatling, Richard Jordan, 1818–1903, American inventor of Gatling multiple-firing gun, precursor of machine gun. His name gave rise to slang word *gat.*

Gatti-Casazza, Giulio (jōō′lyō gät′tē-käzät′sä), 1869–1940, Italian operatic manager. Director of La Scala Opera Co., Milan, 1898–1908; director of Metropolitan Opera, New York, 1908–35.

Gatun Lake, artificial lake (alt. 85 ft.; area 163.38 sq. mi.), Panama Canal Zone, formed by impounding of Chagres R. Used as part of canal route. Gatun Dam, 1½ mi. long, 115 ft. high, controls level of lake.

gaucho (gou′chō), cowboy of Argentine pampa, typically a mestizo, a skillful horseman, lover of adventure. Played important part in national life of Argentina (also Uruguay and Paraguay) 18th–19th cent. Glorified in José Hernández' *Martín Fierro.*

Gaudeamus igitur (gou″dää′mōōs ĭ′gĭtōōr″) [Latin,= let us rejoice therefore], student song; based on songs dating back to at least 13th cent. Present variant forms did not appear in print until 18th cent. Probably originated in parodies of, and borrowings from, religious songs. Brahms used its tune in his *Academic Festival Overture.*

Gauden, John (gô′dŭn), 1605–62, English bishop, who claimed authorship of the EIKON BASILIKE (1649).

Gaudier-Brzeska, Henri (äre′ gōdyä′-bùr-zĕskä′), 1891–1915. French sculptor, the chief exponent of vorticism in sculpture.

Gauguin, Paul (pôl′ gōgē′), 1848–1903, French painter, b. Paris. At 35 he gave up a successful banking career to devote himself to art. Allied himself with impressionists and contributed to their last exhibition (1886). During next five years spent some time in Martinique, Brittany, and Arles (with Van Gogh). In 1891 went to Tahiti where he painted some of his finest pictures; except for one brief trip to France spent rest of his life in South Seas. Died in Marquesas Isls. His paintings, neglected in his time, are now highly prized. His figure compositions, gorgeous in color, place him among the great postimpressionists.

Gaul (gôl), Latin *Gallia*, anc. name for the land S and W of the Rhine, W of the Alps, and N of the Pyrenees. The name was extended by the Romans to include N Italy. The name is derived from its settlers of the 4th–3d cent. B.C.—invading Celts, called Gauls by the Romans. Julius CAESAR conquered Gaul in the GALLIC WARS (58–51 B.C.). He is the best ancient source and has immortalized its three ethnic divisions, Aquitania, Gaul proper (central France), and Belgica. It was rapidly Romanized.

Gauley Bridge, unincorporated village (pop. 1,134), S central W.Va. The death from silicosis of a number of workers building a tunnel near here (1930–32) led to a congressional investigation.

Gaulle, Charles de (shärl dù gōl′), 1890–, French general and politician. In World War II he opposed armistice of 1940; fled to England; organized "Free French" forces, which fought successfully in Syria, Madagascar, N Africa; was sentenced to death *in absentia* by a French military court. In 1943 he became co-president with Gen. GIRAUD of the French Committee of Natl. Liberation at Algiers. Despite coolness of U.S. government, he succeeded in ousting his rival Giraud from the committee, which in June, 1944, proclaimed itself the provisional government of France. Elected president of France in 1945, he resigned 1946 when he lost leftist support. In 1947 he became head of the Reunion of the French People, a generally rightist movement which became a major factor in French politics. In his book *The Army of the Future* (1934; Eng. tr., 1941), De Gaulle correctly predicted the strategy and tactics of motorized warfare.

Gaunt, John of: see JOHN OF GAUNT.

Gaur (gour), anc. city of West Bengal, India. Center of Moslem culture (1198–1575). Has fine Golden Mosque. A stone in Kadam Rasul Mosque supposedly bears imprint of Mohammed's foot.

Gauss, Christian (gous), 1878–1951, American educator, dean of Princeton Univ. from 1925 to 1945.

Gauss, Karl Friedrich (kärl frē′drĭkh gous′), 1777–1855, German mathematician and astronomer. He made important contributions to theory of numbers, solving of binomial equations, geometry of curved surfaces, and method of least squares, and also in geodesy. He pioneered in applying mathe-matical theory to electricity and magnetism. Unit of intensity of magnetic field was called gauss until 1932 when gauss was applied to unit of magnetic induction.

Gautama: see BUDDHA.

Gautier, Théophile (tāôfēl′ gōtyä′), 1811–72, French poet, novelist, and critic. His aesthetic creed, illustrated in the carefully tooled poems of *Émaux et camées* [enamels and cameos] (1852), influenced the Parnassians. His best-known novels are *Mademoiselle de Maupin* (1835) and *Le Capitaine Fracasse* (1863), all translated into English.

Gavarni (gävärnē′), 1804–66, French caricaturist and lithographer, whose real name was Guillaume Sulpice Chevalier. His work appeared in the periodicals *Charivari* and *Illustration*.

Gavarnie, Cirque de (sērk′ dù gävärnē′), gigantic natural amphitheater in central Pyrenees, SW France. From its bottom, at c.5,740 ft., it rises in concentric circles and is enclosed by crests over 9,000 ft. high. The famous Brèche de Roland is a cleft in one of crests. Near by is a waterfall 1,385 ft. high.

Gaveston, Piers (pērz′ gă′vùstùn), d. 1312, favorite of EDWARD II of England. Had great influence with Edward and in his absence acted as regent. His greed and arrogance aroused the barons' hostility; they twice banished him and then put him to death.

Gavle, Swed. *Gävle* (yĕv′lù), city (pop. 46,-834), co. seat of Gavleborg co., E Sweden; a Baltic Sea port. Produces wood pulp, textiles, tobacco, chemicals. Chartered 1446; oldest and largest city of Norrland.

gavotte, originally a peasant dance of the Gavots, inhabitants of the Gap region, France; introduced at court of Louis XIV; used by Lully in ballets and operas, by Bach and Couperin in keyboard suites.

Gawain, Sir: see ARTHURIAN LEGEND; PARSIFAL.

Gay, John, 1685–1732, English playwright and poet. Friend of wits and courtiers of his day, he is famous for realistic, satiric *Beggar's Opera* (1728), a ballad opera still revived. Also wrote verse, *The Shepherd's Week* (1714), and essays, *Trivia* (1716).

Gay, Walter, 1856–1937, American painter. Studied and lived mostly in Paris. Noted for paintings of elegant 18th-cent. interiors.

Gaya (gī′ù), commercial city (pop. 105,223), central Bihar, India. Has noted Vishnuite temple.

gay-feather: see BLAZING STAR.

Gay Head, W tip of Martha's Vineyard, in Gay Head town (pop. 88), SE Mass. Has lighthouse (1799) on high clay cliffs.

Gay-Lussac, Joseph Louis (zhôzĕf′ lwē gä′lüsäk′), 1778–1850, French chemist and physicist. Discovered cyanogen; made advances in industrial chemistry; collaborated in isolating boron; invented alcoholometer, hydrometer; discovered Charles's law independently. **Gay-Lussac's law** of combining volumes: volumes of gases that interact to give gaseous product are in ratio of small whole numbers to each other and each has similar relation to volume of product.

Gayoso de Lemos, Manuel (mänwĕl′ gīō′sō dä lä′mōs), c.1752–1799, Spanish governor of Louisiana (1797–99). Intrigued to separate American West from U.S.

Gaza, Theodore (gä′zù, gä′zù), c.1398–c.1478, Greek scholar and humanist of the Renaissance. When Turks attacked Constantinople, he went to Italy. His Greek grammar was printed (1495) by Aldus Manutius.

Gaza (gä′–), or **Ghuzzeh** (gŭ′–), town (pop. c.18,000), SW Palestine, near the Mediterranean; in anc. times a chief city of the Philistines. Here Samson brought down temple on his captors and himself. Town has long been meeting place of caravans between Egypt and Syria.

gazelle (gŭzĕl′), graceful antelope of genus *Gazella*. Number of species are found chiefly in Africa, also in central and SW Asia and India. They are small (2–3 ft. high) and fleet, usually fawn color, but some are marked with black and white.

gazetteer, originally one who wrote gazettes; now a dictionary of geographical names (of a region, of certain classes, or of the world). First used in its modern sense after publication of Lawrence Echard's geographical index, *Gazetteer's or Newsman's Interpreter* (1703). Such lists have been made since the 6th cent., but general gazetteers date only from the 19th cent. Well-known gazetteers include Johnston's (Scotland, 1850), Blackie's (Scotland, 1850), Bouillet's (France, 1857), Ritter's (Germany, 1874), Longman's (England, 1895), Garollo's (Italy, 1898), Lippincott's (U.S., 1865; latest revised issue *The Columbia Lippincott Gazetteer of the World*, 1952).

Gaziantep (gä″zēäntĕp′), formerly **Aintab** (īntäb′), city (pop. 72,743), S Turkey. Textile mfg. Taken by Saladin 1183. Fell after six-month siege (1920–21) to the French in occupation of Syria, but it was returned to Turkey 1921.

Gd, chemical symbol of the element GADOLINIUM.

Gdansk: see DANZIG.

Gdynia (gùdĭn′yù), city (pop. c.117,700), NW Poland; a Baltic seaport on gulf of Danzig. Constructed after 1921 to end Poland's dependence on Danzig. Damaged in World War II.

Ge, chemical symbol of the element GERMANIUM.

gearing, in a machine, device for transmitting motion by means of teeth or friction wheels. **Spur gearing** utilizes wheels with teeth at right angles to their shafts. **Bevel gearing**, accomplished by inclined tooth edges, transmits motion to shafts intersecting drive shaft. **Screw** or **worm gearing** transmits by screwlike action. **Friction gearing** transmits motion, without use of teeth, by friction of two surfaces in contact.

Geary, John White (gēr′ē), 1819–73, American politician, Union general in Civil War. As governor of "bleeding" Kansas (1856–57), he helped bring peace to territory. Governor of Pa. 1866–73.

Gebal (gē′–), biblical name of BYBLOS.

Gedaliah (gĕdûlī′ù), governor of Jews not carried off in Captivity. He was treacherously murdered. Day of death still observed as Jewish fast. Jer. 40–41.

Geddes, Norman Bel, 1893–, American scenic designer. Originated modernistic style in shop-window displays. *The Miracle* is perhaps his most popular work.

Geddes, Sir Patrick, 1854–1932, Scottish biologist and sociologist. Interested in the evolution of sex, he sought to relate biological knowledge with civic welfare and to city planning.

Gedeon (gē′dēùn), same as GIDEON.

Gegenbaur, Karl (kärl gä′gùnbou″ùr), 1826–1903, German comparative anatomist, influential as a teacher and through his writings.

Gehenna: see HELL.

Gehrig, (Henry) Lou(is) (loō gâ′rĭg), 1903–41, American baseball infielder. As first baseman (1925–39) of N.Y. Yankees, estab. major-league record of playing 2,130 consecutive league games. Had lifetime batting average of .341, batted .361 in seven world series. Four times won American League most-valuable-player award.

Geiger, Abraham (ä′brähäm gī′gùr), 1810–74, German rabbi, Semitic scholar, foremost exponent of the reform movement, a chief rabbi of Berlin.

Geiger counter (gī′gùr), instrument for detection and quantitative determination of ionizing particles, such as beta rays and cosmic rays. Variously designed, it usually consists of a thin metal cylinder (forming one electrode) and a needle (or a thin wire as the other electrode) enclosed by glass tube in which a gas is also sealed. Current passes from electrode to electrode when the counter is near radioactive substances. Emanations, however faint, ionize the gas, allowing current to jump gap and close circuit, activating audible indicator. Instrument named for Hans Geiger (1882–1945), German physicist.

Geijerstam, Gustaf af (äv yā′yùrstäm), 1858–1909, Swedish novelist, author of realistic studies of peasant life and of "problem novels."

geisha (gā′shù), trained Japanese professional entertainer, skilled in dancing and in repartee. Her status varies; she may or may not be a courtesan. Many live luxuriously and influence state policies. She may marry, but always bears a certain stigma.

Geissler tube (gīs′lùr), a gas discharge tube in which light is produced when electricity is passed through gas in the tube. It is used in spectroscopy. It was named for **Heinrich Geissler,** 1814–79, German mechanic and inventor.

Gela (jē′lù), city (pop. 31,918), SW Sicily, Italy, on Mediterranean; founded c.690 B.C. by Greek colonists. Reached its height under tyrants Gelon and Hippocrates (5th cent. B.C.). Modern Gela (known as Terranova di Sicilia until 1927) was founded by Emperor Frederick II in 1230.

Gelasius II (jĭlä′shēùs), d. 1119, pope (1118–19), elected in protest against weakness of PASCHAL II in struggle with Emperor Henry V over INVESTITURE. Thrown in prison by emperor's party, he was delivered by the people. but advance of Henry with an army forced Gelasius to flee to Gaeta, then to France. Henry set up Gregory VIII as antipope.

gelatin, glutinous material, an animal jelly, obtained from supporting structures of vertebrates. Pure product is brittle, transparent, colorless, odorless, tasteless; it dissolves in hot water, congeals when cold. It swells to an elastic mass in cold water. Some of its many uses are: in making confectionery, jellied soups, and molded meats and salads, in preserving meat and fruit, in electrotyping, photography, waterproofing, dyeing, as bacteriologic culture medium, coating for pills and capsules, and emulsifying agent. Glue and size are impure forms. AGAR is vegetable gelatin.

Gelderland, Guelderland, or **Guelders** (gĕl′dûr-lund, gĕl′dûrz), province (1,922 sq. mi., pop. 1,028,127), E and central Netherlands; cap. Arnheim. Drained by Ijssel, Lower Rhine, and Waal rivers, which enclose fertile agr. lowland in SW. Duchy of Gelderland was conquered by Charles the Bold of Burgundy 1473; passed to Hapsburgs after his death; joined United Provs. of Netherlands 1579. Part of province, including ducal cap., Geldern, was ceded to Prussia 1715.

Gelibolu, Turkey: see GALLIPOLI.

Gellius, Aulus (jĕl′yûs), fl. 2d cent., Latin writer, a lawyer; author of *Noctes Atticae,* a collection valuable for its quotations from lost works.

Gelon (jē′lŏn), d. 478 B.C., Greek Sicilian ruler. Tyrant of Gela, he ruled Syracuse (485–478 B.C.), dominating Greek Sicily. In 480 he crushed the Carthaginians under Hamilcar. He was succeeded by HIERO I.

Gelsenkirchen (gĕl″zŭnkĭr′khŭn), city (pop. 310,108), North Rhine–Westphalia, NW Germany, adjoining Essen; a major industrial and coal-mining center of RUHR dist. Heavily damaged in World War II.

gem, substance of mineral or organic origin used for adornment. Beauty, rarity, and durability determine value. Beauty depends mainly on optical properties, which impart luster, color, and fire; durability on HARDNESS. Other properties include form of crystal, index of refraction, cleavage, type of fracture. Gems most prized are DIAMOND, RUBY, SAPPHIRE, EMERALD, PEARL (organic); some semiprecious stones are AQUAMARINE, AMETHYST, GARNET, TOURMALINE, TOPAZ, TURQUOISE, MOONSTONE, JADE, CHRYSOBERYL.

Gemara: see TALMUD.

Gemini [Latin,= twins] (jĕ′mĭnē), third sign of ZODIAC. The twins were Castor and Pollux.

Geminiani, Francesco (fränchä′skō jämĕny-ä′nē), d. 1762. Italian violinist and composer of music for strings. He wrote on methods of playing stringed instruments (e.g., *The Art of Playing the Violin*).

Gemniczer, Wenzel: see JAMNITZER.

gender, in grammar, subclassification of a form class (or part of speech) in which members of the subclass have characteristic features of agreement with other words. The term *gender* is usually restricted to such a classification of nouns or nounlike words and is not usually considered to include NUMBER. In French *la viande* [the meat] and *le vin* [the wine] are distinguished by *la* and *le* as different genders, *la* being feminine, *le* masculine (because most French nouns referring to females are feminine, most referring to males are masculine). German, Russian, and Latin have three genders—masculine, feminine, and neuter. A two-gender distinction between animate and inanimate is widespread (as in Algonquian languages). English nouns may be divided into gender classes according to personal pronoun used to refer to them; these do not match sex classes (e.g., *she* for *ship*). The grammatical device of concord or agreement is bound up with gender distinctions; thus in Romance languages adjectives "agree" with the corresponding nouns in being masculine or feminine.

gene (jēn), ultimate unit in transmission of hereditary characters in plants and animals. Genes are believed to be contained within chromosomes and to control development of specific morphological characters by control of biochemical reactions. See also GENETICS.

General Land Office, estab. 1812 in U.S. Treasury Dept. and transferred in 1849 to U.S. Dept. of the Interior. Managed and disposed of public domain. Emphasized conservation of remaining public land after 1900. Consolidated in 1946 with Grazing Service into Bureau of Land Management.

general strike, cessation of work by all or a majority of workers in a region. The motive is economic if the strike is directed against employers, political if it seeks to eventuate in governmental concessions or governmental overthrow. It has been advocated by syndicalists and anarchists, and has been a powerful weapon of European labor.

generator, machine for changing mechanical into electrical energy, using principle of electromagnetic INDUCTION. Simple generator consists of coil of wire rotating between two magnetic poles; as turning coil cuts magnetic lines of force, electric current is generated in coil, from which metal strips (brushes) lead current into closed circuit. Turning coil cuts lines of force first in one direction then another, so current flows first in one then another direction (AC or alternating current). One-direction current (DC or direct current) obtained by using device called commutator, but current remains pulsating. Commercial generators avoid pulsation by use of more complicated structure involving so-called ARMATURE. In dynamo, the ELECTROMAGNET is commonly used.

Genesee, river, c.158 mi. long, rising in N Pa. in the Alleghenies and flowing N through N.Y. to L. Ontario at Rochester. In beautiful, fertile valley.

Genesis (jĕ′nŭsĭs) [Gr.,= origin], first book of Old Testament, first of the five books of Law (the Pentateuch or Torah), ascribed by tradition to Moses. It is a religious account of the creation of the world and of man, of man's first fall from grace, of the great Deluge. It tells the stories of the great religious patriarchs: Noah, Abraham, Isaac, and Jacob—who later became Israel. Book ends with story of Joseph and the migration of Jacob's family to Egypt. For religious conceptions derived from opening chapters, see SIN and GRACE. Importance of Genesis in Jewish and Christian thought is inestimable.

Genesis, Little: see PSEUDEPIGRAPHA.

Genêt, Edmond Charles Édouard (zhûnā′), 1763–1834, French minister to U.S. (1793–94), known as Citizen Genêt. Welcomed by pro-French Jeffersonians, his efforts to raise troops against Spanish Florida and to commission privateers against British commerce were not approved by Pres. Washington. His recall was demanded.

genetics (jŭnĕ'tĭks), scientific study of heredity. The basis of the science was the work of Gregor MENDEL rediscovered in 1900 independently by Hugo De Vries, K. E. Correns, and Erich Tschermak-Seysenegg. Mendel's principles were modified and extended by discovery of CHROMOSOME and GENE as physical basis of transmission of hereditary characters; by discoveries such as those related to tendency of certain characters to be inherited together, of some characters to be sex-linked, and of interaction of different genes to determine presence of characters. Work of T. H. Morgan and his followers on *Drosophila melanogaster* (fruit fly) was important to progress of genetics in U.S. See also HEREDITY; MUTATION.

Geneva (jŭnĕ'vù), Fr. *Genève,* canton (109 sq. mi.; pop. 201,505), SW Switzerland, at SW tip of L. of Geneva, almost entirely surrounded by French territory. Rural section produces fruits, vegetables, wine. Its cap., **Geneva** (pop. 144,422), lies on both sides of the Rhone, which emerges here from the lake. It is a cultural and financial center, mfg. machinery and watches. Included in Roman Gaul, Geneva early became an episcopal see, shared history of first and second kingdoms of BURGUNDY and passed to Holy Roman Empire 1033. Though citizens won extensive rights of self-rule (1387), these rights were increasingly encroached on by the dukes of Savoy, whose representatives shared the authority with the bishops. In alliance with Swiss cantons of Fribourg and Bern, the citizens expelled the bishops in 1533 and accepted the Reformation, preached by Guillaume Farel, in 1536. Under CALVIN Geneva became the focal point of the Reformation. An attempt by Charles Emmanuel I of Savoy to recapture the city was repulsed (1602). Huguenot refugees contributed to growing prosperity of Geneva, which was a cosmopolitan intellectual center by the 18th cent. Under French occupation 1798–1814, Geneva joined Switzerland as a canton 1815. It is the seat of the Internatl. Red Cross, the Internatl. Labor Organization, and several UN bodies. The huge Palais des Nations housed the League of Nations until it was taken over by the UN. Univ. of Geneva originated with academy founded by Calvin. Historic monuments include cathedral, city hall. Its fine parks and splendid situation make Geneva a cosmopolitan resort. It is the birthplace of J. J. Rousseau. The **Lake of Geneva** or **Lake Leman,** between Switzerland and France, is 45 mi. long, 2–9 mi. wide. The Rhone is its main feeder and only outlet. N (Swiss) shore is bounded by vineyards and orchards and dotted with resorts. From S (French) shore rise the French Alps. Scenery has been celebrated by many writers.

Geneva (jŭnĕ'vù). **1** City (pop. 5,139), NE Ill., W of Chicago and on Fox R. **2** City (pop. 17,144), W central N.Y., at N end of Seneca L. and SE of Rochester; settled 1788. Farm trade center with mfg. of canned goods, machinery, heaters, and optical goods. Seat of The Colleges of the Seneca, corporate title since 1943 of Hobart Col. (affiliated Episcopalian; for men; chartered 1822) and William Smith Col. (nonsectarian; for women; opened 1908). **3** See PROVO, Utah.

Geneva, Lake, c.8 mi. long, SE Wis., near Ill. line. Shores have summer homes. Yerkes Observatory is at Williams Bay near W end.

Geneva, Lake of: see GENEVA, Switzerland.

Geneva Arbitration: see ALABAMA CLAIMS.

Geneva Convention: see RED CROSS.

Geneva Protocol: see PROTOCOL.

Genevieve, Saint, d. 512, patron saint of Paris, a nun said to have averted an attack of Attila on Paris. Feast: Jan. 3.

Genghis Khan: see JENGHIZ KHAN.

genie, an older name for JINNI.

Génissiat Dam, France: see RHONE.

genista: see BROOM.

genitive: see CASE.

Gennesaret (gĕnĕ'sûrĕt): see GALILEE, SEA OF.

Genoa (jĕ'nùwù), Ital. *Genova,* city (pop. 512,313; with suburbs 634,646), cap. of Liguria, NW Italy, on the Mediterranean. Chief Italian port; industrial center (shipyards, automobiles, airplanes). City flourished under Romans; became free commune, governed by consuls, c.10th. cent. Its growth as a commercial and Mediterranean power brought wars with Pisa and Venice (13th–14th cent.). Genoa acquired colonies and trading privileges in wars from Spain to the CRIMEA; its expansion was largely financed by a group of merchants who in 1408 founded a powerful bank, the Banco San Giorgio. After 1339 the republic (which came to include most of Liguria) was governed by doges elected for life. The foreign possessions were gradually lost, and internal strife made possible intervention by France and Milan. Genoese power was briefly revived by Andrea DORIA (16th cent.), but his rule was followed by periods of Spanish, French, and Austrian control. Austrians were expelled 1746, but in 1768 Genoa lost Corsica to France. Annexed to France in 1805, Genoa and Liguria were united in 1815 with the kingdom of Sardinia. City was heavily damaged in World War II. Notable buildings include Cathedral of San Lorenzo (rebuilt 1100) and the doges' palace. The harbor section is very picturesque. Univ. of Genoa was founded 1812. Birthplace of Christopher Columbus, Mazzini, Paganini.

Genoa. 1 Village (pop. 1,026), E central Nebr., W of Columbus and on Loup R. Pawnee village has been excavated near by. **2** Town, W Nev., SW of Carson City; founded c.1849. First permanent settlement in the state.

Genoa, Conference of, 1922, international conference held at Genoa, Italy, to discuss economic reconstruction of Europe after World War I. Main item was Russian debt, which the Soviets had repudiated. Some progress was made, but announcement of German-Soviet Treaty of RAPALLO cut negotiations short.

genocide, attempt to destroy a national, ethnic, racial, religious, or political group. Genocide was made an international crime by a UN convention, unanimously adopted in 1948. The convention took effect in 1950 after ratification by 20 nations. It had not been ratified in April, 1953, by either the U.S. or USSR. See also WAR CRIMES.

gens (jĕnz), ancient Roman family group, counterpart of clan or sib in other societies. Descent was traced in male line only, from common ancestor worshiped by all. Marriage within gens was discouraged.

Genseric: see GAISERIC.

gentian (jĕn'shŭn), perennial or annual plant of widely distributed genus *Gentiana*, bearing predominantly blue flowers, usually in autumn. Two species native to E North America are fringed gentian (*Gentiana crinita*), a biennial and difficult to grow, and bottle, or closed, gentian (*G. saponaria*). Others are prized for rock gardens.

Gentile da Fabriano (dä fäbrēä'nō), c.1370–1427?, Italian painter, first great representative of Umbrian school. Retained gilt ornament and glowing color of early Umbrian painters. Influenced Venetians. Masterpiece is *The Adoration of the Magi.*

Gentileschi, Orazio (ōrä'tsēō jäntēlä'skē), c.1562–1647, Florentine mural and portrait painter. In 1626 settled in England at invitation of Charles I. His daughter **Artemisia Gentileschi** (ärtämē'zyä), 1590–c.1642, was a renowned portraitist.

gentlemen's agreement, in business, an informal, private, usually verbal agreement among rivals as to prices charged, goods handled, or areas served. They are outlawed in the U.S. by antitrust legislation. In U.S. and Japanese history the gentlemen's agreement was the understanding arrived at (1907) in the administration of Theodore Roosevelt, with Ishii the Japanese negotiator. It provided that Japan should stop emigration of Japanese workers to the U.S. and the U.S. should halt discrimination against Japanese. The U.S. immigration laws of 1924 automatically ended this agreement.

Gentz, Friedrich von (frē'drĭkh fŭn gĕnts'), 1764–1832, German publicist. Conducted polemics against Napoleon; became Metternich's secretary 1812. The brain of the Holy Alliance, he was secretary at congresses of Vienna, Aachen, Troppau, Laibach, Verona.

geodesy (jēŏ'dŭsē) or **geodetic surveying,** theory and practice of determining points on the earth's surface and dimensions of areas so large that the curvature of the earth must be taken into account.

Geoffrey IV, known as **Geoffrey Plantagenet** (plăntăj'ŭnĕt) [O.Fr.,= sprig of broom; he usually wore a sprig in his helmet], 1113–51, count of Anjou (1129–51); son of FULK. Married MATILDA, daughter of Henry I of England (1128?); claimed Normandy in her name and completed its conquest 1144. Went on crusade with Louis VII (1147). His son became Henry II of England.

Geoffrey of Monmouth, c.1100–1154, English author, bishop of St. Asaph after 1152. His largely fictional *Historiae regum Britanniae* is a source for Arthurian legend.

Geoffroy Saint-Hilaire, Étienne (ätyĕn' zhôfroͦä' sētēlĕr'), 1772–1844, French zoologist, member of Napoleon's scientific staff in Egypt. His theory that all animals conform to single structural plan was opposed by Cuvier. His son, **Isidore Geoffroy Saint-**

Hilaire (ēzēdôr'), 1805–61, also a zoologist, was an authority on deviations from normal structure.

geography, science that observes, catalogues, analyzes, correlates facts of area differentiation on earth's surface. First systematic study was Greek: Aristotle demonstrated world's sphericity, delimited its habitable parts; Strabo's interest in human adaptation to physical setting enlarged scope of study beyond mathematical relationships; study culminated in Ptolemy. Arabs carried learning through Middle Ages. Marco Polo's travels, growing Eastern trade, and exploration voyages revived geographic interest beyond Moslem world. The 16th and 17th cent. textbooks (Varenius) and maps (Mercator) formulated sound theoretical geography. Modern era began late 18th cent. with Alexander von Humboldt and Karl Ritter. Two basic methods of approach are systematic and regional. Systematic approach was spurred by growth of physical and social sciences; regional approach integrates results of systematic method, focuses them on specific place or area—meeting demand for inventory of resources of newly discovered regions. These approaches are actually interdependent. Two branches of geography are physical and human (or cultural). First, based on physical sciences, studies features of world's surface in relation to cosmic influences; climate, land form, soil are examined as to origin, classified as to distribution; flora and fauna are brought into areal pattern. Human (economic, social, political) geography studies man's relation to environment, also his conscious adaptation of himself to it and it to his needs. Geography integrates data of other sciences in terms of areal differentiation. Cartographers, gazetteer compilers, scientific expeditions, university studies, Federal agencies, and geographic institutes promote modern geographic knowledge.

Geological Survey, United States, bureau organized under Dept. of the Interior (1879) to explore surface and geological structure of country, investigate natural resources, classify public lands, and issue papers, bulletins, and maps based on surveys.

geology (jēŏ'lŭjē), the science of the earth with respect to its structure, rocks, surface features. Its branches include petrology, structural geology, geomorphology, physiography, cosmology, and economic and historical geology. Geologic history includes five grand divisions or eras: ARCHEOZOIC, PROTEROZOIC, PALEOZOIC, MESOZOIC, CENOZOIC. Each is supposed to have marked a new stage in life development, and to have ended with profound structural changes. The geologic cycle, repeated again and again, consists of a period of mountain building, followed by one of erosion and, in turn, by renewed uplift. Time elapsed since deposition of oldest known rocks is probably at least a billion and a half years. See table, pp. 474–75.

geometry, branch of mathematics dealing with space properties and relations of figures in space. Elementary, Euclidean, axiomatic geometry includes plane (study of figures lying entirely in one plane), solid (three-dimensional figures), and spherical (figures drawn on spherical surface). More advanced geometries have a less formally stressed axiomatic basis. Analytical geometry includes geometric relations between curves, using algebraic relations between equations corresponding (by coordinate system) to curves; descriptive includes study of reproducing solid figures on a plane; differential includes theory of properties of figures describable in terms of calculus. Modern geometry includes study of non-Euclidean spaces, Riemannian geometry, spaces of abstract elements, and topology.

geomorphology, study of origin and evolution of earth's topographic features. Developed after 1890 as a result of William M. Davis's concept of the geomorphic cycle, theory that land forms pass through a series of well-organized stages in an inorganic evolution.

geopolitics, geographical principles applied to world politics. Chief exponent was Karl Haushofer, adviser to Hitler. He held growing nations must gain *Lebensraum* [living space], specifically Germany at expense of Great Britain (one of the "oceanic nations") and Russia (which is the "heart land" of Eurasia, the "world island").

George, Saint, 4th cent.?, patron of England, perhaps a soldier in the imperial army who died for the faith in Asia Minor. Ancient patron of soldiers, he was adopted in medieval England. In old plays and art St. George is the slayer of the dragon (the tale was popularized in *The Golden Legend*). His red cross appears on the Union Jack.

George, kings of Great Britain and Ireland. **George I** (George Louis), 1660–1727, was king 1714–27. Great-grandson of James I, he was the first British sovereign of house of HANOVER under Act of SETTLEMENT. His indifference to government led to first real cabinet and rise of the Whigs to power. Quadruple Alliance guaranteed Hanoverian succession in 1718. His son, **George II** (George Augustus), 1683–1760, was king 1727–60. More active in government, in War of AUSTRIAN SUCCESSION he was last British king to lead troops in person. His wife, CAROLINE OF ANSPACH, furthered long dominancy (1721–42) of Robert WALPOLE. Whigs united behind policy of William PITT (the elder) in SEVEN YEARS WAR (1756–63). King's grandson, **George III** (George William Frederick), 1738–1820, was king 1760–1820. Ended long Whig control by securing Pitt's resignation in 1761. Wanting to rule personally, he found amenable minister (1770–82) in Lord North whose policy of coercion led to AMERICAN REVOLUTION. Notable Tory ministry of the younger William Pitt (1783–1801) saw the end of royal attempts to control the ministry. His reign saw changes effected by Industrial Revolution; a flowering of arts and letters. King's insanity led to regency (1811) of his son, **George IV** (George Augustus Frederick), 1762–1830, who was king 1820–30. Ruling through Tory ministers, he was the leader of a profligate society and was personally hated. Succeeded by William IV. **George V** (George Frederick Ernest Albert), 1865–1936, king 1910–36, was the second son of Edward VII.

Interested in empire affairs, he visited India in 1911. In 1916 he gave up all German titles and changed the name of the royal house from Saxe-Coburg-Gotha to Windsor. His second son, **George VI**, 1895–1952, became king of Great Britain (Ireland being then independent) in 1936 when his brother, Edward VIII, abdicated. With his consort, Elizabeth, he made royal visits to France (1938), Canada and U.S. (1939), and South Africa (1947). In World War II he visited bombed areas and toured theatres of war. His eldest daughter, Elizabeth II, succeeded him.

George V, 1819–78, last king of Hanover (1851–66). Sided against Prussia in Austro-Prussian War; lost Hanover to Prussia. He was blind.

George, kings of the Hellenes. **George I,** 1845–1913, second son of Christian IX of Denmark, was elected 1862 to succeed Otto I on Greek throne. Introduced democratic constitution (1863); acquired Thessaly and part of Epirus (1881) and Crete (1908). Was assassinated. His grandson was **George II,** 1890–1947. Reigned 1922–23; exiled 1923–35; restored 1935. Countenanced dictatorship of METAXAS. In exile during Axis occupation of Greece in World War II, he returned 1946 after plebiscite had decided in favor of monarchy. Civil war with Communists continued under his brother Paul, who succeeded him.

George, David Lloyd: see LLOYD GEORGE, DAVID.

George, Henry, 1839–97, American economist, founder of the single-tax movement. He believed a single tax on land would meet all costs of government and even leave a surplus. In 1879 he wrote *Progress and Poverty,* the Bible of the movement.

George, Stefan (shtā'fän gāôr'gù), 1868–1933, German poet. Influenced by the French symbolists, he perfected a style of classic, polished beauty and hardness which raised him to the position of major poet and had tremendous influence on the younger generation. His lyric cycles include *Hymnen* (1890), *Algabal* (1892), *Die Bücher der Hirten* [book of the shepherds] (1895), *Das Jahr der Seele* [the soul's year] (1897), *Der Teppich des Lebens* [tapestry of life] (1899), *Das neue Reich* [the new kingdom] (1928).

George, river of N Que., Canada, flows N 365 mi. into Ungava Bay on Hudson Strait.

George, Fort, B.C., Canada: see PRINCE GEORGE.

George, Lake, 33 mi. long and 1–3 mi. wide, NE N.Y., in foothills of the Adirondacks and S of L. Champlain, into which it drains. Center of resort area. Discovered and named Lac du Saint Sacrement by Isaac Jogues, 1646; renamed by Sir William Johnson, 1755. At S end is Lake George village (pop. 1,005), year-round sports center. Has ruins of Fort William Henry (1755) and Fort George (1759; in near-by L. George Battleground Park), battle scenes in French and Indian and Revolutionary wars.

George Junior Republic, community at Freeville, N.Y., founded 1895 by W. R. George, and similar communities elsewhere, for neglected and maladjusted adolescents. Commu-

Time	Geologic Development	Life Forms
AZOIC TIME		
3000–5000 million years ago.*	Formation of the earth; lands and seas developed.	No life forms.
PRE-CAMBIAN TIME. Lasted c.1000–1500 million years. Includes two eras.		
1. ARCHEOZOIC ERA	Much volcanic activity. Mountain ranges formed, then eroded to hills. Minerals deposited.	Rudimentary life forms probably existed.
2. PROTEROZOIC ERA	Iron, copper, and other metallic ores deposited. Glacial periods at least twice. At end of period, volcanic disturbances in North America, followed by erosion of mountains.	Simple marine life: probably soft-bodied wormlike animals; algae.
PALEOZOIC ERA. Age of invertebrates and marine forms; lasted c.300 million years.*		
Cambrian period Began c.505 million years ago, lasted c.80 million years.*	Seas covered much of world; conditions unstable, with many periods of uplifts. Highlands mostly leveled. Climate generally mild.	Marine invertebrates: trilobites dominant; primitive snails; first shells. Calcareous marine algae. Lichens in some regions.
Ordovician period Began c.425 million years ago, lasted c.65 million years.	Fully half of North America covered by seas periodically. Greatest deposition of limestones, marbles, and slates. Great disturbances at end of period; Taconics (N.Y.) thrust up. No sharp geological gradations in climate.	Great numbers of marine animals; some corals, gastropods, clams. Continued dominance of marine invertebrates. First primitive, fish-like vertebrates.
Silurian period Began c.360 million years ago, lasted c.35 million years.	Seas flooded inland basin of North America; great salt beds deposited in E U.S. Mountains eroded, but Appalachians continued high and volcanic. In late period, lands emerged almost completely; arid deserts formed in E U.S.	Sea scorpions most distinctive; also mollusks, corals (reefs), primitive vertebrate fish. Animals similar to scorpions, possibly the first air-breathing forms. Beginnings of land plants.
Devonian period Began c.325 million years ago, lasted c.45 million years.	About 40% of U.S. under water at times, but emerged gradually and completely. North America connected with Europe by land bridge. Volcanic activity. Second upthrusting of Appalachian chain. At close of period E coast rose while W sank. Climate mild.	Age of fishes: marine and armored; also lungfish. Primitive land vertebrates (amphibians); wingless insects and spiders. Ferns, mosses, horsetails; forests of tree ferns. Primitive evergreens.
Carboniferous period (in North America, Mississippian and Pennsylvanian) Began c.280 million years ago, lasted c.50 million years.	Lands flooded several times. Almost 80% of world's coal beds formed from marshy vegetation—in U.S., especially in Pa. Mountains formed in North America, Europe, and Asia. At end of era E North America largely dry. Air warm and moist.	Fish abundant. First land vertebrates (reptiles). Insects larger than at any other period: giant dragonflies, c.800 species cockroaches. Tree ferns, scale trees, primitive conifers; first seed plants.
Permian period Began c.230 million years ago, lasted c.25 million years.	Lands rose, swamps dried up, and some deserts formed. Widespread aridity. Salt beds formed in Kansas, Germany, and USSR. At end of period, world-wide mountain making. Ice over parts of world.	Reptiles (four-legged, not large, and mostly sprawling) developed in number and variety. Some insects (beetle, dragonfly) survived ice age. Spore-bearing ferns and conifers survived aridity.
MESOZOIC ERA. Age of reptiles; lasted c.130 million years.		
Triassic period Began c.205 million years ago, lasted c.40 million years.	Marked erosion of mountains in E North America; at close of period, complex faulting and tilting known as Palisade disturbance. Parts of W U.S. invaded by sea; waters retreated late in period. Climate mild; aridity and semiaridity widespread but some areas were moist.	Vertebrate animals included freshwater fishes, aquatic reptiles (e.g., ichthyosaur), and dinosaurs (many bipedal) which became dominant life by mid-period. Forests chiefly conifers and cycads; also ferns, tree ferns, scouring rushes.

* All figures vary widely among authoritative sources.

Time	Geologic Development	Life Forms
Jurassic period Began c.165 million years ago, lasted c.30 million years.*	Pacific coastal region of North America submerged during most of period; deposition of sediments (esp. red beds) and volcanic matter. At close of period vast disturbances formed Sierra Nevada, Cascade, and coastal ranges. Gold-quartz veins formed in Sierras. In E North America land continuously elevated and eroded. Period best defined in Europe; rich fossil beds.	Reptiles dominated land, sea, air (winged reptile, pterosaur). Chief land animals dinosaurs. First bird (archaeopteryx). Chief insects: bees, moths, flies. Cycads dominant plant life; also conifers, ginkgos, tree ferns.
Cretaceous period or Chalk age Began c.135 million years ago, lasted c.60 million years.	Greatest submergence of continents: 50% of North America submerged. Most of world chalk supply formed, chiefly from limy skeletons of foraminifera. Coal and oil in W U.S. At end of era, Rockies elevated, Appalachians rose again, Andes formed, seas retreated. Climate generally mild but a cold age late in period.	Dinosaurs included Tyrannosaurus and armored, horned, and duck-billed forms. At close of period dinosaurs became extinct. Marsupials and primitive placental mammals evolved. Flowering plants appeared; deciduous trees became dominant. Sequoias widely distributed.

CENOZOIC ERA. Age of mammals and modern seed plants. Period variously estimated from c.60–75 million years; 75 million used here.

Time	Geologic Development	Life Forms
Paleocene and Eocene epochs** Began c.75 million years ago, lasted c.36 million years.	Mountain building continued in early period, followed by erosion. Atlantic and Gulf coasts partly submerged. Climate mild in most of world.	Modern birds. Primitive mammals: Eohippus (early horse, c.1 ft. high), ancestors of cat, dog, elephant, camel; small primates. Vegetation fairly modern: seed-bearing plants.
Oligocene epoch Began c.39 million years ago, lasted c.11 million years.	Erosion continued; volcanoes on Pacific coast and in parts of Europe. North America increasingly emergent; N Atlantic coast and most of Pacific coast dry land.	Mammals dominant: cat and dog families supreme; three-toed horse; mastodon; true carnivores. Primates walked erect; primitive anthropoid ape.
Miocene epoch **Began c.28 million years ago, lasted c.16 million years.**	In mid-era, great mountain making: Sierras and Rockies rose again, as well as Himalayas, Andes, and Alps. Volcanic activity in W U.S. Climate cooler and drier.	Modern birds. Horse further developed; varied. Great ape in Europe. Cooler climate reduced forests and resulted in more plains. More modern trees.
Pliocene epoch Began c.12 million years ago, lasted c.11 million years.	Land still rose; volcanoes on Pacific coast and inland. At end of era, Sierras, Cascades, Rockies, Appalachians lifted. Climate increasingly cooler and drier.	Horse evolved almost to modern form; mastodons migrated from Old World to W North America. Manlike apes: gibbon, gorilla. Beginning of Old Stone Age: earliest implements of man, antedating any skeleton of man himself thus far discovered.
Pleistocene epoch or Ice age Began c.1 million years ago.	Glaciers covered parts of Americas, Europe, and Asia four or five times; disappeared from N.Y. c.38,000 years ago and from Sweden c.12,000 years ago. Great Lakes formed when ice last disappeared. Erosion in nonglacial regions; volcanoes on Pacific coast.	Four species elephants in North America, including mastodon and mammoth; also camels, sabretooth tiger. Camels and horse survived glacial eras but died out in U.S. before advent of man. Beginning extinction of mammals and rise of man: Piltdown, Java, Peking, Heidelberg, Neanderthal, Cro-Magnon (known for cave paintings).
Recent Began c.25,000 years ago.	Most glaciers melted and lands became warm. Deserts formed in parts of world.	Neolithic man developed after last glacial age, at least 20,000 B.C. Beginnings of civilization: pottery, community life, agriculture, domestication of animals. Copper and Bronze Ages began 5000–2000 B.C. and Iron Age 3000–800 B.C.

* All figures vary widely among authoritative sources.

** The epochs Paleocene through Pliocene are sometimes classed as Tertiary period, and the subsequent time as Quaternary period.

nity is self-governing, but all must work. Schooling is provided.

George of Podebrad (pô'dyĕbrät), 1420–71, administrator (1448–58) and king (1458–71) of Bohemia. Came to power as leader of UTRAQUISTS. Was excommunicated by Pope Paul II (1466); expelled MATTHIAS CORVINUS, whom Catholic nobles had proclaimed king in 1469. Restored peace and prosperity to Bohemia.

George Pepperdine College: see LOS ANGELES, Calif.

Georgetown, city (pop. 73,509), cap. and largest city of British Guiana; port on Demerara R.

Georgetown. 1 Part (since 1895) of Washington, D.C., on Potomac R. near confluence of Rock Creek; settled c.1665. It was part of land granted by Md. in 1790 to U.S. government for national cap. Has fine old houses, e.g., DUMBARTON OAKS. Here is Georgetown Univ. (Jesuit; for men; opened 1791, chartered 1815; oldest R.C. college in U.S.). **2** City (pop. 5,516), N Ky., N of Lexington. Processing center in bluegrass agr. area. Seat of Georgetown Col. **3** Village (pop. 2,200), SW Ohio, SE of Cincinnati. Has boyhood home of U. S. Grant, whose birthplace is at near-by Point Pleasant. **4** City (pop. 6,004), E S.C., at head of Wynah Bay, c.15 mi. from ocean, where Pee Dee, Waccamaw, Black, and Sampit rivers enter bay. Port, resort, and shipping center with lumber and paper mills. Has Church of Prince George (1740s). **5** City (pop. 4,951), central Texas, N of Austin at head of San Gabriel R. Seat of Southwestern Univ. (Methodist; coed.; 1873).

Georgetown University: see GEORGETOWN, D.C.

George Washington Birthplace National Monument: see NATIONAL PARKS AND MONUMENTS (table).

George Washington Bridge, vehicular suspension bridge over Hudson R. between Manhattan borough of New York city and Fort Lee, N.J.; main span is 3,500 ft. long; constructed 1927–31.

George Washington University, at Washington, D.C.; nonsectarian, coed.; chartered 1821 as Columbian Col., became a university 1873, renamed 1904.

Georgia, USSR: see GEORGIAN SOVIET SOCIALIST REPUBLIC.

Georgia, state (58,876 sq. mi.; pop. 3,444,578), SE U.S.; one of Thirteen Colonies; cap. ATLANTA. Other cities are SAVANNAH, AUGUSTA, MACON, ROME, ATHENS. Chief rivers are the SAVANNAH, forming boundary with S.C., the OCMULGEE, the CHATTAHOOCHEE, and the SAINT MARYS. Coastal plains rise to piedmont plateau and to mountains in N. Agr. (cotton, tobacco, peanuts, corn, peaches, pecans, truck); mfg. of cotton textiles, wood products; food processing. Leading producer of kaolin, fuller's earth, naval stores. Hernando De Soto crossed Ga. 1540; Spanish later estab. SEA ISLANDS missions. English-Spanish struggle for possession resulted in English ownership. James E. OGLETHORPE founded Savannah 1733. Tory and patriot sentiment divided in Revolution; British held most of state. First Southern state to ratify Constitution, but early took strong states' rights stand. Seceded from Union 1861; suffered in Civil War from ATLANTA CAMPAIGN of W. T. SHERMAN, especially in his march to the sea. Industry rose after war. Recent progressive force was liberal governorship of Ellis G. Arnall (1943–47).

Georgia, Strait of, channel, c.150 mi. long, between mainland of B.C. and Vancouver Isl., Canada, connecting Puget Sound and Queen Charlotte Sound. Forms part of inland waterway to Alaska.

Georgia, University of, at Athens; land-grant and state supported, for men and women. Had the first state university charter (1785). Its first college (Franklin) opened 1801. Abraham Baldwin and Lyman Hall were instrumental in its founding.

Georgia Institute of Technology, at Atlanta; state supported, for men; chartered 1885, opened 1888.

Georgian Bay, NE arm of L. Huron, S Ont., Canada (120 mi. long, 65 mi. wide), separated from main part of lake by Saugeen Peninsula and Manitoulin Isl. Connects with L. Ontario via Severn R., L. Simcoe, and Trent Canal. The **Georgian Bay Islands National Park** (3,458 acres; estab. 1929) includes 30 islands in the bay.

Georgian Soviet Socialist Republic or **Georgia,** constituent republic (c.29,400 sq. mi.; pop. c.3,600,000), USSR, in W Transcaucasia; cap. TIFLIS. Extending S from crest of Greater Caucasus, it borders on Black Sea in W, on Turkey in S. KURA and RION are chief rivers. Climate and vegetation vary from subtropical coastal region of MINGRELIA in W to high mountain crest and dry Kura steppe in E. Fruit, tea, tobacco, silk, wine are grown in warmer districts. Manganese at Chiatura. Batum, Poti, Sukhum are chief ports. Main political subdivisions are ABKHAZ ASSR, ADZHAR ASSR, S OSSETIA. About two thirds of pop. are Georgians, speaking a S Caucasian language. Minorities include Russians, Armenians, Greeks, various Moslem peoples. Georgian church is one of oldest Orthodox Eastern foundations. Known in antiquity as COLCHIS (in W) and Iberia (in E), Georgia became a kingdom c.4th cent. B.C., with cap. at MTSKHET. Persian Sassanidae ruled it 3d–4th cent. A.D.; branch of Armenian Bagratid dynasty 6–19th cent., with interruptions caused by numerous invasions. Greatest flowering under Queen Thamar (12th–13th cent.). Pressed by its Moslem neighbors, Georgia accepted Russian overlordship in 18th cent. Last king abdicated 1801. Additional territories ceded by Turkey between 1803 and 1829. Briefly independent after 1917, Georgia became soviet republic 1921.

Georgian style, in English architecture of the reigns (1714–1820) of George I, George II, and George III. Based on principles of Andrea Palladio introduced into England by Inigo Jones and Sir Christopher Wren. Emphasized classic correctness, which made symmetry the essential feature. Typical Georgian house was brick structure with courses and cornices of white stone and trimmings of white painted woodwork. Corridors in interiors were an innovation. Notable examples of public architecture of the period include St. James's Club, by Robert Adam; Somerset House, by Sir William Chambers; Bank of England, by Sir John Soane; and St. Martin's-in-the-Fields, by James Gibbs. American buildings of the period, closely resembling their English prototypes, are usually called Colonial.

Georgia State College for Women: see MILLEDGEVILLE.

Georgia State Womans College: see VALDOSTA.

Gera (gā'rä), city (pop. 89,212), Thuringia, E central Germany; until 1918 cap. of principality of REUSS (younger line). Textile center.

geranium, name for widely grown house and bedding plant of genus *Pelargonium,* native to S Africa. Many varieties have showy flowers; others are grown for their scented leaves. Native American wild geranium or crane's-bill belongs to the genus *Geranium.*

Gérard, François Pascal Simon, Baron, 1770–1837, French portrait and historical painter, a favorite pupil of David.

Gerard, James Watson (jŭrärd'), 1867–1951, U.S. ambassador to Germany (1913–17).

Gerbert: see SYLVESTER II, pope.

Géricaut, Jean Louis André Théodore (zhā' lwĕ' ädrä' täödôr' zhärēkō'), 1791–1824, French painter, who helped to introduce romanticism into France. In 1819 he exhibited his famous *Raft of the Medusa* (Louvre), which brought violent protests from those of classical school. Acclaimed in London, where he produced many fine paintings of horses. Exerted great influence on French painting.

Gérin-Lajoie, Antoine (zhārĕ'-läzhwä'), 1824–82, French Canadian author. Most popular works are two novels which idealize simple life of French Canadian habitants.

Gerizim (gĕ'rŭzĭm), mountain, central Palestine. Samaritans considered it the only proper place of worship; 300-year-old Samaritan temple was destroyed by Maccabean leader, John Hyrcanus, c.130 B.C.

Gerlachovka, Czechoslovakia: see TATRA.

germ, term applied to any minute disease-causing organism, including certain bacteria, viruses, protozoa, molds, and rickettsia. Theory that disease is caused by introduction of germs into another living organism was accepted following Pasteur's experiments and Lister's use of antiseptics to reduce infection. Germ plasm is living material inherited through sex cells. A seed or portion of seed is often called germ.

German, Sir Edward, 1862–1936, English composer. Known for incidental music to plays, e.g., *Henry VIII, Nell Gwynn,* and for light operas. Knighted 1928.

German Baptist Brethren: see DUNKARDS.

German Confederation, 1815–66, estab. by Congress of Vienna. Membership consisted of the sovereign states and free cities of Germany; the emperor of Austria; the king of Denmark (as duke of Holstein and Lauenburg); the king of Hanover; and the king of the Netherlands (as duke of Luxembourg). The federal diet, which met at Frankfurt under presidency of Austria, was reduced to impotence through unanimity rule; suspended 1848–50, when the FRANKFURT Parliament was meeting, it resumed under Austrian leadership after Treaty of OLMÜTZ. AUSTRO-PRUSSIAN WAR led to dissolution of the confederation and establishment of NORTH GERMAN CONFEDERATION.

German East Africa, former German colony, area c.370,000 sq. mi., E Africa. Divided into three parts after World War I. Kionga was annexed to Mozambique, and TANGANYIKA and RUANDA-URUNDI became mandated territories held by Great Britain and Belgium, respectively.

Germanic languages, subfamily of Indo-European, of which English and German, standard language of Germany, are members. See LANGUAGE (table).

Germanic laws, codes adopted (5th–9th cent.) after the Germanic invaders of the Roman Empire had created governments. Since law then applied to the person rather than the territory or governmental unit, there were codes for the Germans themselves (called *leges barbarorum*) and, in S Europe, other codes for Romans under German rule *(leges Romanorum).* Although all except the Anglo-Saxon were in Latin and all imitated the form of the Roman law code, the *leges barbarorum* are now accepted as incorporating much of the older Germanic customary law. They are largely concerned with penal law and particularly with COMPOSITION for personal injuries. Some of the more important codes, however, show strong Roman influence. The Visigoths in Spain had a series of notable codes: that of King Euric (5th cent.), the *Breviary of Alaric* (or *Lex Romana Visigothorum*) in 506, and the *Lex Visigothorum* or *Liber iudiciorum* (later translated as the *Fuero juzgo* and applying to Goths and Romans alike) of c.654. Notable also was the *Edictum Rotharis* (643), which with a collection of Italian legislation of the Holy Roman Empire became the basis for the later renaissance of Roman law in Italy.

Germanic religion. Tacitus' *Germania* and *Beowulf* are our best sources on it. It was polytheistic, with "Olympian" and underworld gods. Its principal gods were Woden, Tiw, Frey and Freyja, and an earth-goddess. Sacrifices, oracles, and fertility rites were practiced. Mythology was not highly developed, but there was much story-telling, and from later works (such as NIBELUNGENLIED) mythical ideas can be gained. Ideas of death and afterworld were similar to those of the Greeks. In Iceland, sources of its mythology are the Eddas, the oldest direct material on Germanic myth. Norse mythology differs from that of other Germanic peoples because of Christian influence, isolation of Old Norse, and longer development of the system.

Germanicus Caesar (jŭrmă'nĭkŭs), 15 B.C.–A.D. 19, Roman general; son of Drusus Senior, nephew of TIBERIUS. Fought well against the Germans, but was replaced by his brother Drusus. He was later poisoned at Tiberius' request. CLAUDIUS I was his brother. AGRIPPINA II and CALIGULA were his children.

germanium (jŭrmā'nēŭm), rare, gray, brittle metallic element (symbol = Ge; see also ELE-

MENT, table). It resembles tin and lead and occurs in a few minerals.

German language, a Germanic language. See LANGUAGE (table).

German measles: see MEASLES.

German New Guinea: see NEW GUINEA, TERRITORY OF.

German Order: see TEUTONIC KNIGHTS.

German Reformed Church: see EVANGELICAL AND REFORMED CHURCH.

Germans, great ethnic complex of Europe, a basic stock in the composition of the peoples of Scandinavia, Germany, Austria, Switzerland, N Italy, the Low Countries, France, and England. They lived in N Germany and along the Baltic Sea before their great expansion S, SE, and W in the early Christian era. Prime sources for their culture and distribution are works of Caesar and Tacitus. The Teutons and Cimbri whom Marius defeated in 102–101 B.C. may have been Germans. Germans became increasingly troublesome to the Roman Empire; attacks were made by the VANDALS in the W and by the OSTROGOTHS in the E. The Germans probably retained a certain ethnic solidarity until the 2d or 3d cent., but later broke up into many peoples. Chief among these were the ALEMANNI, the FRANKS, the ANGLO-SAXONS, the Burgundii (see BURGUNDY), the LOMBARDS, the SAXONS, and the VISIGOTHS. The Scandinavians, a large group, included the Icelanders, who produced the first Germanic literature (see OLD NORSE LITERATURE).

German silver or **nickel silver,** silver-white alloy of copper, zinc, nickel in varying proportions. Hard, tough, and resistant to corrosion, it is used in tableware and in heating coils.

German Southwest Africa: see SOUTH-WEST AFRICA.

Germantown, residential section of Philadelphia, Pa.; settled by Germans c.1683. Early American center of printing and publishing. Annexed to Philadelphia 1854. In Revolution British were quartered here; Washington defeated here 1777. Howe House and other colonial buildings stand.

Germany, Ger. **Deutschland** or **Deutsches Reich,** largest country of Central Europe, stretching from the Baltic Sea and the North Sea on the N to the Alps on the S. Lacking a peace treaty with its enemies of World War II, it remains in 1953 without settled boundaries, unified government, or well-defined status. In 1949 two separate republics came into existence: (1) Federal Republic of [West] Germany (c.94,900 sq. mi.; 1950 pop. 47,585,872; temporary cap. Bonn), under U.S., British, and French occupation, consisting of the states of BAVARIA, WÜRTTEMBERG-BADEN, HESSE, and BREMEN (U.S. zone); NORTH RHINE-WESTPHALIA, LOWER SAXONY, SCHLESWIG-HOLSTEIN, and HAMBURG (British zone); RHINELAND-PALATINATE, WÜRTTEMBERG-HOHENZOLLERN, and BADEN (French zone); and W BERLIN. (2) [East] German Democratic Republic (c.41,400 sq. mi.; 1946 pop. 18,489,713; cap. E Berlin), under Russian occupation, consisting of the states of BRANDENBURG, MECKLENBERG, THURINGIA, SAXONY, and SAXONY-ANHALT. N Germany is generally level and low lying.

Central Germany, with the HARZ mts. and Thuringian Forest, and S Germany, with the mountains of SWABIA and FRANCONIA and the Bavarian Alps (highest peak, ZUGSPITZE) are generally mountainous and forest-covered. The RHINE, WESER, ELBE, ODER, and DANUBE are the principal rivers. The heaviest industrial concentrations are in the NW (N Rhineland and RUHR dist., with Cologne, Düsseldorf, and Essen); at Berlin; and in Saxony (with Leipzig, Dresden, and Chemnitz). Other major commercial and industrial centers: Munich, Stuttgart, Nuremberg (S); Frankfurt, Mannheim (W); Dortmund, Duisburg (NW); Hanover, Magdeburg (N); and the port cities of Hamburg, Bremen, Kiel, and Lübeck. For its huge metallurgical industry Germany depends largely on Ruhr coal and on imported ores. Other major industrial products are textiles, chemicals, electrical machinery. In 1945 the SAAR TERRITORY and the E provinces of SILESIA, POMERANIA, and EAST PRUSSIA were detached from Germany, which thus lost some of its chief industrial, mining, and agr. districts. About 25% of the population is engaged in agr. In the Federal Republic of [West] Germany, Protestants have a slight majority over Catholics, with Catholicism prevailing in the S and W. E Germany is predominantly Lutheran.

Germany before 1871. In antiquity, Germany was inhabited by a number of Germanic tribes (see GERMANS). Rome conquered (1st cent. B.C.–1st cent. A.D.) the regions along the Rhine and parts of S Germany, but further conquest was stopped at the battle of TEUTOBURG FOREST (A.D. 9). In the 4th–5th cent. German tribes invaded the Roman Empire, while the Slavs occupied the lands E of the Elbe. The FRANKS soon subjugated other German tribes and created a vast empire in Germany and Gaul (see also MEROVINGIANS; CAROLINGIANS; CHARLEMAGNE). Christianization of Germany, begun by St. BONIFACE, was completed in the 12th–13th cent. with the German colonization of the lands E of the Elbe (see WENDS; TEUTONIC KNIGHTS). From divisions of the Frankish empire (9th cent.) came a separate kingdom under LOUIS THE GERMAN. Weakened by foreign invaders (Norsemen, Slavs, Magyars) and by the rise of powerful feudal princes (the dukes of FRANCONIA, SWABIA, BAVARIA, SAXONY, and LOTHARINGIA), the kingship recovered authority under HENRY I and OTTO I (crowned as emperor, 962). German history then overlapped with that of the HOLY ROMAN EMPIRE. The feudal structure of Germany proved persistent. The great "stem duchies" were broken up by the emperors in the 10th–12th cent., but still lesser principalities and free cities made Germany a loose federation over which the emperors presided with varying degrees of effectiveness. After the Thirty Years War (1618–48) imperial control was nominal, and within the federal structure arose two powerful rival states—AUSTRIA (i.e., the far-flung, multinational Hapsburg empire) and the modern, centralized kingdom of PRUSSIA. Austro-Prussian rivalry was temporarily interrupted by Napoleon I, who swept aside the Holy Roman Empire (1806) and created the CONFEDERATION OF THE RHINE. The Congress of Vienna (1814–15) reduced the number of sovereign German states but retained the federal structure by creating the GERMAN CONFEDERATION. The liberal-nationalist revolution of 1848 was easily suppressed and the FRANKFURT Parliament vainly sought to create a unified Germany. However, under the leadership of BISMARCK, Prussia eliminated Austria from German affairs (see AUSTRO-PRUSSIAN WAR, 1866), and at the end of the FRANCO-PRUSSIAN WAR William I of Prussia was proclaimed emperor of Germany (1871). The new empire, increased by ALSACE and LORRAINE, was united by a common ruler, a federal diet (Reichstag), and a customs union (see ZOLLVEREIN), but it remained a confederation of kingdoms (Prussia, Bavaria, Württemberg, Saxony), grand duchies (Baden, Hesse, Saxe-Weimar, Mecklenburg), lesser principalities, and Hanseatic cities (Hamburg, Bremen, Lübeck).

From Bismarck to Hitler. In half a century, Germany had evolved from a feudal, disunited, socially and industrially retarded area into the chief military and economic power of the Continent. The phenomenal speed of industrial and commercial expansion continued after 1871 and, combined with the program of colonial and naval expansion under WILLIAM II, became a serious threat to England. As long as Bismarck held power (i.e., until 1890) the government sought peaceful relations with its neighbors, but William II's aggressive diplomacy helped to bring about WORLD WAR I (1914–18). Germany in 1914 was at the peak of its prosperity. By 1918, it was exhausted by the war. A Social Democratic revolution forced the abdication of William II and the conclusion of an armistice. In 1919 Germany accepted the harsh Treaty of VERSAILLES and adopted the republican constitution drafted at Weimar. The "Weimar Republic" retained the federal structure of the empire, with some minor territorial adjustments. It was beset from the beginning by extremist agitation (both nationalist and Communist), mass unemployment, and a currency inflation that wiped out the nation's savings. Pres. Ebert, who steered a middle course, was succeeded by HINDENBURG. After 1925 came economic recovery, while the foreign policy of STRESEMANN restored Germany as a great power. However, the world economic crisis that began in 1929 again plunged Germany into near-bankruptcy. Both Communism and NATIONAL SOCIALISM made great electoral gains. By 1932 Hitler's party was the largest single party in the Reichstag; in Jan., 1933, disunion among his opponents made possible the appointment of HITLER as chancellor. *Third Reich and Collapse.* Within a year, Hitler estab. absolute dictatorship, virtually abolished the powers of the state governments, and reduced all German life to Nazi control. Repudiating the Treaty of Versailles, he began a program of intensive rearmament, remilitarized the Rhineland (1936), and annexed Austria (March, 1938). Allied with Fascist Italy from 1936 (see AXIS), Germany interfered in the Spanish

civil war of 1936–39, and was allowed by the Western Powers to seize part of Czechoslovakia in Sept., 1938 (see MUNICH PACT). Bohemia and Moravia were annexed altogether in April, 1939, along with the Memel dist., and Germany began to demand DANZIG and part of the POLISH CORRIDOR. After concluding a nonaggression pact with the USSR (Aug., 1939), Germany invaded Poland and began WORLD WAR II. Despite spectacular victories up to 1942, the war ended with Germany's unconditional surrender in May, 1945, and left the German cities in ruin. According to decisions made at the YALTA and POTSDAM conferences, Germany was divided into four occupation zones; Berlin, under four-power occupation, received special status. Dissension between the USSR and the West paralyzed the Allied control council, from which the USSR withdrew in 1948. The REPARATIONS question was a major factor in the failure to arrive at a general peace treaty. The Soviet blockade of W BERLIN (1948–49) widened the rift between E and W Germany, which in 1949 became two separate republics. While E Germany underwent increasing sovietization, W Germany, under supervision of a three-power Allied High Commission, became a federal, parliamentary democracy. Its chancellor, Conrad Adenauer, headed (as of 1953) a coalition cabinet of Christian Democrats and other conservatives. Economic recovery was remarkably speedy, but many problems remained: aside from the influx of millions of Germans who had been expelled (or had fled) from Poland, Czechoslovakia, and other countries, and aside from the danger of a Nazi revival, there was the constant threat of aggression from the E and the unwillingness of all Germans to accept a permanent division of their country. In 1951 W Germany and the Western Powers signed a peace contract by which W Germany was to obtain nearly complete jurisdiction over internal affairs and foreign trade, but which gave the Allies the right to maintain security forces in Germany. The contract was made contingent on W Germany's joining the SCHUMAN PLAN (which it did) and furnishing troops for a projected European army; it was ratified (1952) by the U.S. and Great Britain but not (as of March, 1953) by Germany and France. Chief factors in the delay of ratification were French-German differences over the Saar Territory and the opposition of German Social Democrats (and many others) to the army plan.

germicide (jûr'mŭsīd), chemical capable of killing germs. It may be ineffective against resistant spores formed by some germs. Many are injurious to living tissue. Some body secretions act as germicides toward certain disease-causing organisms.

germination, in a seed, the growth of the embryo (after period of dormancy) and emergence of young plant from seed. Suitable conditions of temperature, moisture, and oxygen are necessary. Seed viability ranges from a few days to (rarely) 50 years or more. Use of germination tested seed prevents planting of old or inferior seed. For parts of a seedling, see *ill.*, p. 999.

Gérôme, Jean Léon (zhä′ lãõ′ zhärōm′), 1824–1904, French historical and genre painter.

Gerona (hārō′nä), city (pop. 28,752), cap. of Gerona prov., NE Spain, in Catalonia. Textile mfg. Heroically resisted French in Peninsular War 1808–9. Notable Gothic cathedral.

Geronimo (jûrō′nŭmō), c.1829–1909, chief of a Chiricahua band of the Apache Indians. Terrorized Ariz. by brutal raids in 1880s.

Gerry, Elbridge (gĕ′rē), 1744–1814, American statesman. Supported patriot activities before and during American Revolution. Opponent of strong central government. Had a part in XYZ AFFAIR. Governor of Mass. (1810, 1811); Vice President of U.S. (1813–14). Name used by opponents in political practice called **gerrymander** (jĕ′rēmăn″dûr), rearrangement of voting districts so as to favor party in power. Origin of term, though not origin of practice, was in such an arrangement made in Mass. when Elbridge Gerry was governor.

Gers (zhĕr), department (2,429 sq. mi.; pop. 190,431), SW France, at foot of Pyrenees, in Armagnac region of Gascony; cap. Auch.

Gershon, Levi ben: see GERSONIDES.

Gershwin, George, 1898–1937, American composer. Songs from his musical comedy scores (e.g., *Embraceable You* and *The Man I Love*) are masterpieces of their kind. His principal larger compositions are *Rhapsody in Blue* (1923), the classic example of symphonic jazz; Piano Concerto in F (1925); *An American in Paris* (1928); and *Porgy and Bess* (1935), a folk opera from which comes the well-known *Summertime.*

Gerson, John (Jean Charlier de Gerson) (gûr′sùn), 1363–1429, French ecclesiastical statesman. With Pierre d′AILLY (his teacher at Paris), he sought to end the Great SCHISM by advancing the conciliar theory (basically, doctrine that councils are superior to the pope; later declared heretical) for Council of Pisa. Attended Council of CONSTANCE, and helped to end the schism and condemn John Huss. Wrote much and, as chancellor of the Univ. of Paris, opposed teaching of Occam and began change to realism.

Gersonides (gûrsō′nĭdēz) or **Levi ben Gershon** (lē′vī bĕn gûr′shùn), 1288–1344, Jewish philosopher, author of *Milchamoth Adonai* [the wars of the Lord], a criticism of the philosophy of Maimonides.

Gersoppa Falls (gùrsō′pù) cataract of Sharavati R., on Mysore-Bombay border, India. Highest of four cascades is c.830 ft.

Gesenius, Wilhelm (vĭl′hĕlm gāzā′nyōōs), 1786–1842, German Orientalist, known for his *Hebrew Grammar;* one of first to open Semitic to scientific study.

Gessner, Salomon (zä′lōmôn gĕs′nùr), 1730–88, Swiss poet, landscape painter, and etcher. His poems and "idyllic prose pastorals" (e.g., *The Death of Abel,* 1758) were very popular and had great influence on European literature.

Gestalt (gùshtält′), school of psychology interpreting phenomena as organized wholes greater than the sums of their parts. The term was coined in Germany by Charles von Ehrenfels (1890). Early experimentation led to the laws of membership character (i.e., each element of a pattern through its dy-namic participation in that pattern alters its individuality), and of *Prägnanz,* the dynamic attribute of self-fulfillment in all structured wholes. Structural correspondence between sensory and extrasensory mental processes was postulated.

Gestapo: see SECRET POLICE.

Gesta Romanorum (jĕ′stù rō″mùnô′rùm) [Latin,= deeds of the Romans], medieval collection of Latin stories, each tale characterized by a moral.

gestation: see PREGNANCY.

Gethsemane (gĕthsĕ′mùnē), olive grove or garden, near foot of Mt. of Olives, E of Jerusalem, scene of the agony and betrayal of Jesus. Mark 14.32; Mat. 26.36.

Gettysburg, borough (pop. 7,046), S Pa., near Md. border; named for James Gettys, grantee of land from William Penn. Seat of Gettysburg Col. (Lutheran; coed.; 1832) and Lutheran Theological Seminary. Gettysburg Natl. Military Park is shrine of Civil War battle (see GETTYSBURG CAMPAIGN). At dedication of national cemetery here Abraham Lincoln delivered the **Gettysburg Address** Nov. 19, 1863.

Gettysburg campaign, June–July, 1863, of Civil War. After victory at Chancellorsville, R. E. Lee undertook second invasion of North via Shenandoah Valley into S Pa. At Chambersburg he learned Army of Potomac under G. G. Meade was concentrating N of Potomac. Two armies met just W of Gettysburg. On July 1 Federals were driven to Cemetery Hill, S of town. Meade, in strong position, consolidated forces. On July 2 Confederates failed in assaults both on Union left at Round Top and Little Round Top and on its right at Cemetery Hill. On July 3 Lee sent Longstreet with G. E. Pickett's division in famous charge against Union center; briefly successful, it was beaten back. On July 4 Lee withdrew. Confederate defeat, turning point of war.

geyser (gī′zûr), a hot spring that intermittently erupts steam and hot water. Geysers occur only in New Zealand, Iceland, Yellowstone Park. Some build up cones of mineral matter about their vents.

Geysir (gā′sĭr), hot spring, SW Iceland, W of Reykjavik. Eruptions (at intervals of several weeks) last c.20 minutes. Max. height of jet is 200 ft.; max. temperature 180°F. Neighborhood has many hot springs. English name *geyser* derives from Geysir.

Gezelle, Guido (gē′dō khûzĕ′lù), 1830–99, Flemish lyric poet, a Roman Catholic priest, b. Bruges; forerunner of the Flemish literary revival.

Gezer (gē′–), natural fortress, Palestine, on ridge overlooking the road between Jerusalem and Jaffa. In Bible, important in the wars of Joshua, David, and the Maccabees; several times a scene of battle in the Crusades.

Ghats (gôts, gäts), two mountain ranges of S India. Eastern Ghats extend c.875 mi. along E coast and merge in S with Western Ghats, which parallel W coast for c.1,000 mi., with Palghat Gap as only major break. Anai Mudi Peak (8,841 ft.) in SW is highest point.

Ghazali, Al-: see AL-GAZEL.

Ghazipur (gä′zēpōōr″), town (pop. 31,326),

SE Uttar Pradesh, India, on Ganges R.; opium mfg. Tomb of Lord Cornwallis.

Ghazni (gŭz'nē), town (pop. 25,000), E Afghanistan. Flourished under Turkish Ghaznivid dynasty (962–c.1152), founded by Mahmud of Ghazni, whose domain reached from Persia to the Punjab. Held by British in Afghan wars (1839–42).

ghee: see BUTTER.

Ghent (gĕnt), Flemish *Gent*, Fr. *Gand*, city (pop. 166,797; with suburbs 228,798), cap. of East Flanders prov. and historic cap. of Flanders, N Belgium, at confluence of Scheldt and Lys rivers and at focus of a canal network. Second largest port and chief textile center of Belgium; episcopal see; seat of university (founded 1816); art center. City grew around fortress built by first count of Flanders on a small island (9th cent.). A major cloth-mfg. center by the 13th cent., it witnessed bitter social strife between the "lesser folk" and the rich bourgeoisie. Under Jacob and Philip van ARTEVELDE Ghent led Flanders in struggle against the French. Ghent's liberties were curtailed by Philip the Good after an insurrection (1453); Mary of Burgundy restored them through the Great Privilege, signed at Ghent (1477). Emperor Charles V, who was born and reared at Ghent, abrogated its liberties after another rebellion (1540). By the Pacification of Ghent, signed here 1576, the provinces of the Netherlands allied themselves with William the Silent to drive out the Spanish. Capture of Ghent by Alessandro Farnese (1584) completed Spanish reconquest of Flanders. Among landmarks of Ghent are ruins of Abbey of St. Bavon (10th cent.) and of castle of counts (12th cent.); Cathedral of St. Bavon (13th–16th cent.); cloth hall (16th cent.); and 14th-cent. belfry, with famous carillon. Flemish painting flourished here in 15th cent. with Hugo van der Goes and the brothers Van Eyck. The Treaty of Ghent, signed here Dec. 24, 1814, ended War of 1812 between U.S. and Great Britain. Provision for restoring territories and places taken by either party represented diplomatic victory for U.S.

Gherardesca, Ugolino della: see UGOLINO DELLA GHERARDESCA.

ghetto (gĕ'tō), section of a city (usually walled) in which Jews were obliged to live after 4th cent. In 1870 the last ghetto (in Rome) was abolished.

Ghibellines: see GUELPHS AND GHIBELLINES.

Ghiberti, Lorenzo (lōrän'tsō gēbĕr'tē), c.1378–1455, Florentine sculptor. In 1401 he won competition for bronze doors of Florence baptistery. His superb panels on N and S doors show scenes from life of Christ and Old Testament.

Ghilan, Iran: see GILAN.

Ghirlandaio or **Ghirlandajo, Domenico** (both dōmä'nēkō gērländä'yō), 1449–94, Florentine painter. Studied with Baldovinetti and later taught Michelangelo. Magnificent frescoes in Santa Trinità and Santa Maria Novella (both in Florence) are famous for contemporary portraits and settings. His son **Ridolfo Ghirlandaio** (rēdôl'fō), 1483–1561, was also a painter.

Ghor (gôr) or **Ghur** (gōōr), mountainous region, W central Afghanistan. Powerful Moslem dynasty was estab. here in 12th cent.

ghost dance, central ritual of messianic religion instituted by Paiute Indian, Wovoka. It included dancing, shaking, and hypnotic trances. After 1887 spread among Western tribes.

Ghur, Afghanistan: see GHOR.

Ghuzzeh: see GAZA.

Giacosa, Giuseppe (jōōzĕp'pä jäkō'zä), 1847–1906, Italian dramatic poet. His plays include *Tristi amori* (1888) and *La Dame de Challant* (1891; written for Bernhardt). With Luigi Illica, he wrote librettos for Puccini's *La Bohème, Tosca,* and *Madame Butterfly.*

giant, manlike being of great size and strength. Giants appear in mythology of various peoples (Greeks, Germans, Celts). No evidence of such beings is known. Gigantism in humans results from over-secretion in childhood of growth hormone of anterior lobe of pituitary gland.

Giant Mountains: see RIESENGEBIRGE.

Giant's Causeway, headland on N coast of Co. Antrim, N. Ireland, extending 3 mi. along coast. Thousands of basaltic columns form three natural platforms. Built, according to legend, for giants to cross to Scotland.

Giauque, William Francis (jēōk'), 1895–, American chemist. Won 1949 Nobel Prize in Chemistry for studies of properties of substances at extremely low temperatures. He is codiscoverer of the second and third isotopes of oxygen.

Gibbon, Edward, 1737–94, English historian, author of monumental *Decline and Fall of the Roman Empire.* It was conceived on a visit to Rome. Appearing in six volumes (1776–83), it met wide acclaim. Standard edition is J. B. Bury's (7 vols., 1896–1900). Gibbon also wrote an autobiography.

gibbon (gĭ'bŭn), smallest of anthropoid apes (genera *Hylobates* and *Symphalanga*) found in SE Asia and East Indies. Gibbons have slender bodies and very long arms; they travel through trees with speed and agility and on ground often walk erect. They live in family groups and are monogamous.

Gibbons, Grinling, 1648–1721, English wood carver and sculptor. Employed by Sir Christopher Wren to do architectural decorations for his buildings, notably St. Paul's.

Gibbons, James, 1834–1921, American cardinal. Became bishop of Baltimore (1877), cardinal (1886). Notable for praising the blessings of American democracy for the Church. He persuaded the pope to lift the ban on the Knights of Labor.

Gibbons, Orlando, 1583–1625, English composer and organist, the last of the great Elizabethans. His works include madrigals, English anthems and services, and music for strings and for virginal.

Gibbs, James, 1682–1754, English architect, distinguished exponent of Georgian style. His finest works are St. Martin's-in-the-Fields (1722–26) and St. Mary-le-Strand (1714–17).

Gibbs, Josiah Willard, 1839–1903, American mathematical physicist, known especially for contributions in field of thermodynamics.

Gibraltar (jĭbrôl'tùr), town (pop. 28,460, including garrison), constituting a British crown colony. Located at NW end of Rock of Gibraltar (one of PILLARS OF HERCULES), a peninsula of S Spain at E end of Strait of Gibraltar. Strait connects the Atlantic and the Mediterranean. Gibraltar Bay, an inlet of the Strait, has safe enclosed harbor of c.450 acres. Rock, 2¾ mi. long and ¾ mi. wide, rises to height of 1,408 ft. Of Jurassic limestone, its caves have produced valuable archaeological finds. Has been an English possession since 1704. Town, a free port, serves as coaling station and port of call. Naval station and fortress, its population is kept small. Underground tunnels built in World War II. Since the war, Spain has renewed its claims on Gibraltar.

Gibson, Charles Dana, 1867–1944, American illustrator, a leading exponent of black-and-white art in America. Creator of Gibson Girl.

Gibson, W(ilfrid) W(ilson), 1878–, English poet of Georgian group, writing on the obscure and lowly.

Giddings, Franklin Henry, 1855–1931, American sociologist. Based explanation of social phenomena on principle of "consciousness of kind."

Gide, André (ädrä' zhēd'), 1869–1951, French author and intellectual leader. Of Calvinist background, he projected the conflict between the wish for self-fulfillment and the barriers of convention into semi-autobiographical fiction, such as *L'Immoraliste* (1902; Eng. tr., 1930), *Strait Is the Gate* (1909; Eng. tr., 1924), and *The Counterfeiters* (1925; Eng. tr., 1927). His lucid, gemlike style also illuminates his journals (1939; Eng. tr., 4 vols., 1947–51) and translations. Awarded Nobel Prize in Literature in 1947.

Gide, Charles (shärl), 1847–1932, French economist, expert on monetary problems. Played important role in cooperative movement.

Gideon (gĭ'dēŭn) or **Gedeon** (gĕ'–), judge of Israel. Called by an angel of the Lord to free Israel from Midianite oppressors, he won a spectacular victory with only 300 men. An interesting event is his oracle of the fleece. Judges 6–8; Heb. 11.32. Jerubbaal: Judges 6.30–32; 7.1. Jerubbesheth: 2 Sam. 11.21.

Gideons, givers of Bibles: see BIBLE SOCIETIES.

Gideonse, Harry D(avid) (gĭ'dēŭnz), 1901–, American educator, president of Brooklyn Col. after 1939.

Gielgud, John (gĭl'go͝od), 1904–, English actor. Made his stage debut in 1921. Has played Hamlet (his greatest role) many times in U.S. and England.

Giers, Nikolai Karlovich (nyĭkŭlī' kär'lŭvĭch gēyĕrs'), 1820–95, Russian foreign minister (1882–95). Promoted peace policy.

Giessen (gē'sŭn), city (pop. 46,701), Hesse, W Germany, in Upper Hesse, on Lahn R. Seat of well-known Protestant university 1607–1945. Heavily damaged in World War II.

Giffard (zhē'fär), town (pop. 8,097), S Que., Canada, on the St. Lawrence and NE of Quebec city.

Gijón (hēhōn'), city (pop. 72,053), N Spain, in Asturias; Atlantic port on Bay of Biscay.

Exports minerals. Fishing; mfg. Dates from pre-Roman times.

Gila (hē'lù), river, rising in mountains of W N.Mex. and flowing W across all of Ariz., to Colorado R. at Yuma, Ariz. Early peoples in "Valley of the Sun" farmed by irrigation. Near head is U.S. "unimproved" Gila Wilderness Area (entered via Silver City, N.Mex., but not by auto). Has irrigation dams in N.Mex., COOLIDGE DAM in Ariz. Other projects are on lower Gila and its tributaries, notably in SALT RIVER VALLEY.

Gila Cliff Dwellings National Monument: see NATIONAL PARKS AND MONUMENTS (table).

gila monster (hē'lù), a species of *Heloderma*, only genus of poisonous lizards. Found in deserts of SW U.S. It averages c.18 in. long. Tuberclelike scales cover the skin and the stout, clumsy body is black with a marbled pattern of orange or pink, yellow, or dull white. The tail is a food reservoir. Poison glands are in lower jaw; grooved teeth (carrying venom) are far back in mouth. Mexican gila monster is black and yellow.

Gilan or **Ghilan** (both: gēlän'), region, NW Iran, between Elburz Mts. and Caspian Sea; formerly a province. Held by Russia 1723–32. Was Soviet republic (1920–21). Produces rice, fruit, and silk.

Gilberd, William: see GILBERT, WILLIAM.

Gilbert, Cass, 1859–1934, American architect. Built the 60-story Woolworth Building, New York, and Supreme Court Building, Washington, D.C.

Gilbert, Charles Kendall, 1878–, American Episcopal bishop. Editor of the *Churchman* (1912–18); suffragan bishop of N.Y. (1930–46); bishop (1947–50).

Gilbert, Grove Karl, 1843–1918, American geologist. He was appointed senior geologist when the U.S. Survey was created in 1879 and published many reports, including a notable one on extinct Lake Bonneville.

Gilbert, Sir Humphrey, 1539?–1583, English soldier, navigator, and explorer; half brother of Sir Walter Ralegh. Knighted (1570) for Irish campaign services. His *Discourse* (1576), arguing existence of Northwest Passage, long motivated English exploration. Claimed Newfoundland for Queen Elizabeth and assumed authority over fishermen's colony already there (1583). Lost on return voyage.

Gilbert or **Gilberd, William,** c.1540–1603, English scientist and physician, noted for pioneer studies of magnetism described in his *De magnete* (1600; Eng. tr., 1893, 1900).

Gilbert, Sir W(illiam) S(chwenck), 1836–1911, English playwright and poet. Wrote amusing, cynical *Bab Ballads* (1869). In 1871 he began his long collaboration with composer Arthur Sullivan, resulting in popular satiric operettas: *Trial by Jury* (1875), *H.M.S. Pinafore* (1878), *The Pirates of Penzance* (1879), *Patience* (1881), *Iolanthe* (1882), *Princess Ida* (1884), *The Mikado* (1885), *Ruddigore* (1887), *The Yeomen of the Guard* (1888), *The Gondoliers* (1889).

Gilbert and Ellice Islands (ĕl'ĭs), British colony (375 sq. mi.; pop. 36,000), central and S Pacific, estab. 1915 and placed under Western Pacific High Commission at Suva, Fiji; cap. Tarawa. Includes GILBERT ISLANDS, EL-

LICE ISLANDS, OCEAN ISLAND, FANNING ISLAND, WASHINGTON ISLAND, CHRISTMAS ISLAND, and part of PHOENIX ISLANDS. Chief exports of colony are copra and phosphate.

Gilbert Islands, group of atolls (144 sq. mi.; pop. 27,824), central Pacific, belonging to Great Britain. Discovered 1764 by Capt. Byron, group became a British protectorate 1892; included in Gilbert and Ellice Isls. colony 1915. Occupied 1941 by the Japanese. After fierce fighting Tarawa and Makin isls. were regained 1943 by U.S. forces.

Gilboa (–bō′–), ridge, Palestine, on E edge of plain of Esdraelon. Here Saul and Jonathan were defeated and killed. 1 Sam. 28.4; 31; 2 Sam. 1.21.

Gilder, Richard Watson (gĭl′–), 1844–1909, American editor, poet, editor of *Century* magazine.

Gildersleeve, Virginia (Crocheron), 1877–, American educator. She was dean of Barnard Col. (1911–47) and only woman member of U.S. delegation to the San Francisco Conference (1945).

gilds: see GUILDS.

Gilead (gĭl′ēăd), mountainous region, NE of Dead Sea; allotted to Reuben, Gad, and Manasseh. Noted for spices, myrrh, and balm. Also called Mt. Gilead and Land of Gilead.

Giles, William Branch (jīlz), 1762–1830, American statesman. Anti-Federalist U.S. Representative from Va. (1790–98, 1801–03); U.S. Senator (1804–15). Opposed Albert Gallatin and James Monroe.

Gilgamesh (gĭl′gŭmĕsh), hero of a Babylonian epic of c.3,000 lines written on 12 tablets. Tells of adventures of Gilgamesh, how he spurned Ishtar, how he wandered with his friend Enkidu (half bull and half man), and how he sought key to immortality possessed by Ut-napishtim, his ancestor.

Gill, Sir David (gĭl), 1843–1914, Scottish astronomer, astronomer royal of Cape of Good Hope (1879–1907); a leader in use of photography in star cataloguing.

Gill, Eric (Rowland), 1882–1940, English sculptor and wood engraver. Some of best work is religious sculpture. His books give his views on art and life.

gill (gĭl), respiratory organ of many aquatic animals. In fish, gill is chief respiratory organ throughout life. Blood in tiny vessels permeating gill filaments absorbs oxygen, releases carbon dioxide; filaments are attached to the outer edge of cartilaginous or bony branchial (or gill) arch. Projections from inner edge of arch are gill rakers; these are present except in fish eating whole fish or other large food and serve to strain food from water which enters mouth and leaves through gill clefts. Gills differing in structure are found in developing amphibians (also in adult of some forms), in mollusks, echinoderms, crustaceans, and aquatic insect larvae.

Gillette, William, 1853–1937, American actor and playwright. Permanently associated with *Sherlock Holmes*—play and stage character he created after Conan Doyle. Appeared also in Barrie plays.

Gillmore, Quincy Adams, 1825–88, Union general in Civil War. Known especially for serv-

ice as commander of Dept. of the South (1863–64, 1865).

gillyflower: see STOCK; WALLFLOWER.

Gilman, Charlotte Perkins, 1860–1935, American feminist, reformer, and writer; great-granddaughter of Lyman Beecher. Edited *Forerunner.*

Gilman, Daniel Coit, 1831–1908, American educator. He helped to found Sheffield Scientific School at Yale. After serving 1872–75 as president of Univ. of California, he became first president (1875–1901) of Johns Hopkins Univ. He was president of Carnegie Inst. of Washington, 1902–4.

Gilmer, Thomas Walker, 1802–44, U.S. Secretary of the Navy (Feb., 1844). His death from gun explosion while on the *Princeton* with other government officials raised question of succession to presidency in event of wholesale death of public officials.

Gil Vicente: see VICENTE, GIL.

Gimbel, Adam, 1817–96, American merchant, founder of a family of merchants and philanthropists, b. Bavaria. His sons furthered the Gimbel department store business in Philadelphia, New York city, and many other cities.

gin, spirituous liquor distilled chiefly from fermented cereals and flavored with juniper berries. Types include London, sloe (flavored with sloes instead of juniper), dry (distilled several times).

ginger, tropical perennial plant (*Zingiber officinale*) and its rootstalk, a commercially important spice. It is marketed as preserved or green ginger, mostly in China, or as dried or cured ginger. It is used in cookery and medicine; the oil flavors ginger ale.

ginger ale, sweetened carbonated beverage flavored with ginger. Ginger beer is unrelated fermented drink brewed from ginger and bitter vegetables.

Ginkel, Godart van, 1st earl of Athlone (văn gĭng′kŭl, ăthlōn′), 1630–1703, Dutch general in service of WILLIAM III of England. In War of Grand Alliance he was commander in chief in Ireland (1690–91); captured Ballymore and Athlone, defeated forces of James II at Aughrim, and took Limerick.

ginkgo (gĭngk′gō) or **maidenhair tree,** deciduous tree (*Ginkgo biloba*), with fan-shaped leaves. It is native to China but widely planted elsewhere for shade and ornament. It is a survivor of group of trees that existed in geologic times.

ginseng (jĭn′sĕng″), perennial herb (*Panax*) of North America and Asia. Asiatic ginseng (*Panax schinseng*) has long been prized by Chinese as a panacea. Demand for ginseng led to cultivation of a substitute for export, the American *P. quinquefolium*.

Gioberti, Vincenzo (vēnchän′tsō jōbĕr′tē), 1801–52, Italian statesman; a priest and philosopher. Premier of Sardinia 1848–49. Advocated at first a federation of Italian states under papal arbitration; later a unified, constitutional monarchy.

Gioia or **Gioja, Melchiorre** (both: mälkyôr′rä jō′yä), 1767–1829, Italian economist, an early advocate of unification of Italy. An opponent of Adam Smith, he insisted on economic duty of the state.

Giolitti, Giovanni (jōvän′nē jōlēt′tē), 1842–

1928, Italian premier (1892–93, 1903–5, 1906–9, 1911–14, 1920–21). A leftist but no Socialist, he favored labor unions, promoted social reform, opposed participation in World War I and Fascism.

Giono, Jean (zhä′ jônō′), 1895–, French novelist. His novels, mostly laid in his native Provence, exalt the soil. They include *Colline* (1920; Eng. tr., *Hill of Destiny*, 1929) and *Regain* (1930; Eng. tr., *Harvest*, 1939). A short story, *The Baker's Wife*, was successfully filmed in 1938.

Giordano, Luca (lōō′kä jōrdä′nō), 1632–1705, Neapolitan painter, pupil of Ribera and Cortona. Executed frescoes in Naples, in Florence, and in Madrid and in Toledo.

Giordano, Umberto, 1867–1948, Italian composer of operas (e.g., *Andrea Chénier, Madame Sans-Gêne*).

Giorgio, Francesco di (fränchä′skō dē jōr′jō), 1439–1502, Italian artist, b. Siena. Paintings show influence of Filippo Lippi. Did sculpture for choir of Siena cathedral. Was also an engineer.

Giorgione (jōrjō′nä), c.1478–1510, Venetian painter, fellow student of Titian under Giovanni Bellini. A great innovator, he initiated fusion of forms and subordination of local color to the pervading tone. His works have luminous color and poetic sensibility. Extant works include *Concert champêtre* (Louvre) and *Venus and Cupid in a Landscape* (Natl. Gall., Washington, D.C.).

Giotto (jôt′tō), c.1266–c.1337, Florentine artist. Tremendously influenced course of European painting. Turned from Italo-Byzantine conventionalism to study of nature, achieving lifelike, expressive faces and illusion of movement. Tradition says he was a pupil of Cimabue. Undoubtedly influenced by naturalistic trend in sculpture begun by the Pisani and by Franciscan movement in religion. Earliest extant works are probably frescoes in Church of St. Francis, Assisi. Most famous works are the 38 biblical frescoes in Scrovegni (Arena) Chapel, Padua. Among many works attributed to him are frescoes in Church of Santa Croce, Florence. Succeeded Arnolfo di Cambio as chief architect of Santa Maria del Fiore, Florence; designed its richly decorated campanile.

Giovanni da Bologna: see BOLOGNA, GIOVANNI DA.

Giovanni delle Bande Nere: see MEDICI, GIOVANNI DE′ (under MEDICI, *Younger line*).

giraffe (jĭrĕf′), ruminant mammal (genus *Giraffa*) of Africa living in open country S of Sahara. The tallest animal, it may be 18 ft. from hoof to crown and can outrun most enemies. Its short horns are covered with skin and hair. It is protectively colored with large sandy to chestnut angular spots, closely spaced. It eats chiefly acacia and mimosa leaves, using extensible tongue and mobile lips; can live without water for long intervals.

Giralda (jĭräl′dù, Span. hēräl′dä), tower adjoining cathedral of Seville, Spain. Built 1163–84 as minaret for mosque which originally stood on cathedral's site. Converted 1568 into bell tower by addition of Renaissance superstructure (123 ft. high). Original Moorish section is 197 ft. high.

Girard, Stephen (jĭrärd′), 1750–1831, American merchant, banker, and philanthropist, b. France. A merchant in Philadelphia, he set up a bank, and helped finance U.S. in War of 1812. Bequeathed money to found Girard College, free educational institution for poor white orphan boys.

Girard, city (pop. 10,113), NE Ohio, on Mahoning R. and NW of Youngstown; settled c.1800. Mfg. of steel, leather goods, and metal products.

Girard College: see GIRARD, STEPHEN.

Giraud, Henri Honoré (ärē′ ōnôrä′ zhērō′), 1879–1949, French general. Captured by Germans in both world wars, he escaped both times. After his second and more dramatic escape (1942), he landed with the Allies in N Africa, succeeded Darlan as high commissioner of French N and W Africa, and briefly was co-president, with his rival DE GAULLE, of the French Committee of Natl. Liberation (1943). He was commander in chief of the Free French armed forces until April, 1944.

Giraudoux, Jean (zhä′ zhērōdōō′), 1882–1944, French novelist and dramatist. Among his novels are *Suzanne et le Pacifique* (1921) and *Siegfried et le Limousin* (1922; adapted into a play 1928). His plays include *Amphitryon 38* (1929) and *The Madwoman of Chaillot* (1945).

Girgenti, Italy: see AGRIGENTO.

Girl Scouts, organization founded 1912 at Savannah, Ga., by Mrs. Juliette Gordon Low (who had been a leader of Girl Guide troops in England), to promote good citizenship, sociability, and outdoor life among girls from 7 to 16.

Gironde (zhērōd′), department (4,141 sq. mi.; pop. 858,381), SW France, in Guienne; cap. Bordeaux. Includes Bordeaux wine region. Crossed by the **Gironde,** an estuary 40 mi. long and 3–7 mi. wide, formed by junction of Garonne and Dordogne rivers 12 mi. N of Bordeaux; great artery of wine trade.

Girondists (jĭrōn′dĭsts), Fr. *Girondins,* group of moderate republicans in French Revolution; so called because early members were mostly deputies from Gironde dept. (1791). Among leaders were Brissot de Warville, Vergniaud, Condorcet, Dumouriez. In June, 1793, the Jacobin and Cordelier extremists expelled the Girondists from the Convention and had their leaders executed. The assassination of Marat by Charlotte Corday brought further persecution. Joined by the royalists, the Girondists rose in revolt in the provinces, but their efforts were drowned in blood.

Girtin, Thomas, 1775–1802, English watercolorist. He was among first to abandon the tinted drawing and to paint directly in water color.

Girton College (gûr′tùn), English college for women, founded (1869) at Hitchin, Hertfordshire, by Emily Davies. Moved (1873) to Cambridge. Recognized as a college of CAMBRIDGE UNIVERSITY in 1948.

Girty, Simon (gûr′tē), 1741–1818, American frontiersman, known as the white renegade. Joined British in 1778. Led or participated in many savage Indian raids; known for his cruelty.

Gissing, George, 1857–1903, English author. His novels (best known is *New Grub Street,* 1891) were influenced by Dickens and the French naturalists. Wrote semiautobiographical *Private Papers of Henry Ryecroft* (1903).

Gist, Christopher (gĭst), c.1706–1759, American frontiersman. Explored Ohio valley region for Ohio Co. (1750). Served as guide on Braddock's expedition (1755).

Giulio Romano (jōō'lyō rōmä'nō), c.1492–1546, Italian artist, whose real name was Giulio Pippi. Favorite pupil of Raphael, some of whose Vatican frescoes he completed. Architect to duke of Mantua (1524) and briefly of St. Peter's. Sometimes called the first academic painter.

Giusti, Giuseppe (jōōzěp'pä jōō'stē), 1809–50, Italian poet and patriot. His satires (notably the lyrical "Saint Ambrose") were generally nationalistic.

Gizeh or **Giza** (both: gē'zŭ), market town (pop. 68,520), Egypt, on the Nile opposite Cairo. Pyramid of Khufu (Cheops) and Great Sphinx are near by.

Gjellerup, Karl Adolf (yě'lŭrōōp), 1857–1919, Danish poet and novelist. Early novels are largely autobiographical; later writings show influence of Buddhism. Shared with Henrik Pontoppidan the 1917 Nobel Prize in Literature.

Glace Bay (glās), coal-mining town (pop. 25,-586), Cape Breton Isl., N.S., Canada, on NE coast. Good harbor and large fishing fleet.

glacial periods (glā'shŭl), times in past geologic history when owing to excessively cold climate great ice sheets extended over the land. Most recent ice invasion occurred in PLEISTOCENE. See table, pp. 474–75.

glacier, slowly moving ice mass formed from accumulated snow. Chief types are valley, piedmont, and continental. Valley glaciers are ice tongues which start in mountain snow fields and follow stream valleys. A piedmont glacier forms when valley glaciers unite. Greenland and Antarctica now have the only continental ice sheets (see PLEISTOCENE EPOCH). Ice is an important agent of erosion and transportation, having shaped the present topography of Canada and much of N U.S.

Glacier Bay National Monument: see NATIONAL PARKS AND MONUMENTS (table).

Glacier National Park: see NATIONAL PARKS AND MONUMENTS (table).

Glackens, William (James), 1870–1938, American landscape and genre painter and illustrator. First exhibited with The EIGHT. His work shows influence of French impressionists.

Gladewater, city (pop. 5,305), E Texas, W of Shreveport, La. and near Sabine R. Boomed after 1930 discovery of East Texas oil field.

gladiolus (glădēō'lŭs), tender cormous-rooted plant (*Gladiolus*), native to Africa. It has sword-shaped leaves and long stalks of flowers of many pastel as well as vivid colors.

Gladkov, Feodor Vasilyevich (fyŏ'dŭr vŭsē'lyŭvĭch glŭtkôf'), 1883–, Russian author. Won fame with novel *Cement* (1926; Eng. tr., 1929), describing post-revolution reconstruction.

Gladstone, William Ewart, 1809–98, British statesman, dominant personality of the Liberal Party 1868–94. As chancellor of exchequer (1852–55, 1859–66), he promoted free trade and fairer tax distribution. Was prime minister four times—1868–74, 1880–85, 1886, 1892–94. A man of no fixed political principles, he achieved notable reforms—Irish land act, changes in civil service, vote by ballot, abolition of the sale of army commissions, parliamentary reform, and educational expansion. Constant advocacy of Irish HOME RULE ended his last ministry. He was a great orator and a master of finance.

Glamis (glämz; in Shakspere glä'mĭs), parish and village, Angus, Scotland. Macbeth was thane of Glamis; castle here wrongly claimed as scene of Duncan's murder. Birthplace of Elizabeth, queen consort of George VI.

Glamorganshire (glŭmôr'gŭnshĭr) or **Glamorgan,** maritime county (813 sq. mi.; pop. 1,201,989), S Wales, on Bristol Channel; co. seat Cardiff. Has rich coal deposits in N, dairy farming and cattle grazing on coastal plain. Great mineral wealth (iron and copper) make it one of chief industrial areas of British Isles. Severe industrial depression struck area in 1920s; conditions now improved. Cardiff and Swansea important ports.

gland, organ which forms a SECRETION from material extracted by its cells from body fluids. Varies from single cell to many cells, or system of tubes uniting into a duct (e.g., salivary glands, breast, liver). Hormones, secretions of endocrine or ductless glands (e.g., thyroid, adrenals), are taken up directly by blood. Some glands (e.g., liver, testis) produce both a hormone and a secretion which flows from a duct.

glanders, chronic bacterial disease (*Pfeifferella mallei*) of horses and other animals, which also attacks man. There are various forms but all cause lesions in the lungs. When the disease infects skin tissue, it is known as farcy.

Glarus (glä'rŭs), canton (264 sq. mi.; pop. 37,674), central Switzerland, S of the Wallensee; cap. Glarus (pop. 5,695). Mountainous and pastoral; hydroelectrical and textile industries. Glarus joined Swiss Confederation 1352. Inhabitants are mainly German-speaking Protestants.

Glasgow, Ellen (gläs'gō), 1874–1945, American novelist, b. Va. Among her realistic novels are *Barren Ground* (1925), *The Romantic Comedians* (1926), and *Vein of Iron* (1935). *A Certain Measure* (1943) contains her critical prefaces.

Glasgow (gläs'gō, –kō), independent burgh (pop. 1,089,555), Scotland, on the Clyde. Largest city in Scotland, it is mostly in Lanarkshire but partly in Renfrewshire and Dumbartonshire. Most important seaport of Scotland, it has huge shipyards. Other industries include tanning, weaving, brass casting, and many manufactures. Has art museums and Univ. of Glasgow, founded 1451, whose undergraduates wear short red gowns.

Glasgow. 1 City (pop. 7,025), S Ky., E of Bowling Green. Trade center for agr., timber, and oil area with mfg. of clothing and food products. **2** City (pop. 3,821), NE Mont., on Milk R. and near Fort Peck Dam, in Milk R. project.

Glaspell, Susan (glăs'pĕl), 1882–1948, American writer. A novelist, she became interested in the Provincetown Players (after her marriage to George Cram Cook) and wrote plays (e.g., *Alison's House*, 1930).

Glass, Carter, 1858–1946, U.S. Secretary of the Treasury (1918–20), U.S. Senator from Va. (1920–46). Active in framing of Federal Reserve System.

Glass, Hugh, fl. 1822–33, trapper in American West. Experience while on expedition in Missouri river country of being mauled by a grizzly bear, left for dead, and dragging himself 100 mi. to Fort Kiowa is told in John G. Neihardt's *Song of Hugh Glass.*

glass, hard substance, usually brittle and transparent. Its composition varies but it is commonly made chiefly of silicates, an alkali (usually soda or potash), and lime (as stabilizer), fused at high temperatures. Materials are boiled down, skimmed, and cooled; then molten glass (called metal) is ladled or poured into molds and pressed, or is blown (sometimes into molds), or is drawn. Shaped glass is annealed—usually by carrying it on rollers through annealing ovens (lehrs). Most common hollow vessels (e.g., light bulbs) are machine blown but much fine ware is still made by glass blowers using blowpipes. Methods of decoration include cutting, copper-wheel engraving, etching with hydrofluoric acid, enameling, gilding, and painting. Sheet glass is drawn into sheets by a continuous process; plate glass is rolled, ground, and polished; safety glass is made of plate glass so tempered that it crumbles when broken or it is laminated (two or more sheets are cemented by a plastic that prevents it from scattering if broken). Glass can be drawn into continuous filaments (fiber glass) or produced in short staple fibers (glass wool). Other forms include foam glass, glass blocks, and polaroid glass. Glass is used in architecture, illumination, electrical transmission, and for making instruments, spectacles, utensils, and containers. Many art treasures are fashioned in glass. First glass objects made by man were of natural glass such as obsidian and rock crystal. Manufactured glass dates from prehistoric times in Far East, India, and Egypt, but its place and date of origin are unknown. The art spread to Europe and the Romans were especially skilled in it. After the time of the Crusades Venice, Bohemia, France, and England, in turn, became noted for special kinds of glass. In America Sandwich glass (made 1825–88) became widely known. The glass-pressing machine (invented c.1827) brought about great changes in the industry. See also STAINED GLASS.

Glassboro, borough (pop. 5,867), SW N.J., S of Camden. Farm trade center with glassworks.

Glassport, borough (pop. 8,707), SW Pa., on Monongahela R. and SSE of Pittsburgh. Produces glass, steel, and refined oil.

glass snake, legless burrowing lizard of genus *Ophisaurus* of S and central U.S. It averages c.2 ft. long; shiny body is gray or greenish brown, sometimes striped, above; the sides are darker with light lines; ventral surface is whitish. Its long tail breaks easily from body;

new, usually shorter, tail without real backbone grows to replace it. The glass snake has eyelids, ear openings, broad tongue; eats insects, worms, and small snakes.

Glastonbury, municipal borough (pop. 5,081), Somersetshire, England. Place of many legends. One tells that Joseph of Arimathea founded England's first Christian church here. He rested his staff, which rooted and grew into Glastonbury thorn. Another says Glastonbury is Isle of Avalon of Arthurian legend. Abbey dates from 8th cent.

Glastonbury, town (pop. 8,818), central Conn., on Connecticut R. below Hartford. Textiles, metals.

Glatz (gläts), Pol. *Kłodzko,* city (pop. 22,814), Lower Silesia, on Glatzer Neisse R., transferred to Polish administration 1945. Was cap. of a county created 1462. The **Glatzer Gebirge** (glä'tsŭr gŭbĭrgŭ), a range of the Sudetes, rises to 4,672 ft. at Czech border. For **Glatzer Neisse R.,** see NEISSE.

Glauber's salt, hydrated sodium sulphate, a compound of sodium, sulphur, and oxygen, with 10 molecules of water. On exposure to air it effloresces (gives up water of crystallization). It is used as a mild laxative. It was named for Johann Rudolf Glauber (1604–68), German alchemist.

glaucoma (glôkō'mŭ), eye disease marked by increased pressure within eyeball and often resulting in impaired vision or blindness.

Glaucus (glô'kŭs), in Greek legend, sea-god who loved SCYLLA.

Glazunov, Aleksandr (Konstantinovich) (ŭlyĭk-sändr' gläzōō'nôf), 1865–1936, Russian composer. He wrote eight symphonies, a piano and a violin concerto, ballets (e.g., *Raymonda, The Seasons*), and chamber music.

Gleiwitz (glī'vĭts) Pol. *Gliwice,* city (pop. c.128,200), Upper Silesia, transferred to Polish administration 1945. It is a center of the KATOWICE mining region.

Gleizes, Albert Léon (älbĕr' lāō' glēz'), 1881–, French cubist painter and illustrator.

Glencoe (glĕn'kō), residential village (pop. 6,980), NE Ill., N suburb of Chicago.

Glencoe (glĕnkō'), valley of Coe R., Argyllshire, Scotland, overhung by lofty mountains. Macdonald clan massacred here by the Campbells in 1692.

Glen Cove, city (pop. 15,130), SE N.Y., on N shore of Long Isl., in summer resort area; settled 1668. Mfg. of office supplies, clothing, and radios.

Glendale. 1 City (pop. 8,179), S central Ariz., NW of Phoenix. Agr. trade point in SALT RIVER VALLEY. **2** Suburban city (pop. 95,-702), S Calif., N of Los Angeles; laid out 1886 on site of first Spanish land grant in Calif. Mfg. of petroleum products, aircraft, and glass. Has Forest Lawn Memorial Park, cemetery containing reproductions of great works of art.

Glendale, battle of: see SEVEN DAYS BATTLES.

Glendive (glĕn'dīv), city (pop. 5,254), E Mont., on Yellowstone R. and NE of Miles City. Center of farm, stock, and poultry area. Has railroad shops.

Glendower: see OWEN GLENDOWER.

Glen Echo, resort town (pop. 356), W central Md., near Potomac R. Clara Barton had house near by.

Glen Ellyn, residential village (pop. 9,524), NE Ill., W suburb of Chicago.

Glenolden, borough (pop. 6,450), SE Pa., SW suburb of Philadelphia. Mfg. of pharmaceuticals.

Glen Ridge, suburban residential borough (pop. 7,620), NE N.J., NW of Newark.

Glen Rock, borough (pop. 7,145), NE N.J., SW of Ridgewood.

Glens Falls, city (pop. 19,610), E N.Y., on Hudson R. (water power) and N of Saratoga Springs; settled 1763. Has paper and lumber mills, makes clothing and food and metal products. Birthplace of C. E. Hughes.

Glenview, residential village (pop. 6,142), NE Ill., N suburb of Chicago.

Glenwood Springs, city (pop. 2,412), NW Colo., on Colorado R. Mineral springs resort.

glider, engineless aircraft similar to airplane, using gravity and natural air currents to obtain forward motion. Otto Lilienthal demonstrated (1890–96) superiority of curved over flat surfaces. Other pioneers: Percy Pilcher, England; Henri Farman, France; Octave Chanute and John J. Montgomery, U.S. Chanute first used movable plane parts to obtain stable flight. Wright brothers added landing skids. Troop-transport gliders towed by airplane were used for World War II invasions.

Glière, Reinhold (Moritzovich) (rīn'hŏlt glēĕr'), 1875–, Russian composer. His music is nationalistic. Most popular of his many works are the ballet *The Red Poppy* and the Third Symphony, *Ilya Mourometz.*

Glinka, Mikhail (Ivanovich) (mēkhŭyĕl glĭn'kä), 1804–57, first of the Russian nationalist composers. Known for his operas, *A Life for the Tsar* and *Russlan and Ludmilla.*

Glittertind, mountain of Norway: see JOTUNHEIM.

Gliwice, Upper Silesia: see GLEIWITZ.

Globe, city (pop. 6,419), E Ariz., near Pinal Mts., in mining, ranching area; settled 1876. Built by silver boom, it then became big copper center, later (c.1918) superseded by Miami, Ariz.

globe, spherical body used to illustrate the earth (terrestrial globe) or sky (celestial globe). Terrestrial globe represents sizes and shapes of continents without distortion of shape, mistakes in relative area, or inaccuracy of angles and direction, except that while globes are spheres, earth's equatorial diameter exceeds the polar one by c.27 mi. Probably oldest globe was made by Crates, Greek geographer, 2d cent. B.C. First modern globes made by Martin Behaim (1492), by Leonardo da Vinci soon after. On celestial globes star positions correspond to actual ones on sky; if globe is in correct position a line drawn from its center to any star on surface, if extended, focuses actual star.

globe amaranth, annual plant (*Gomphrena globosa*) with chaffy dome-shaped flowers in various colors. Used as an EVERLASTING.

globeflower, perennial (*Trollius*) of N temperate regions with white, yellow, orange, or purple blooms, similar to buttercups but larger.

Globe Theatre, London playhouse, built 1598. Most of Shakspere's plays were first pre-

sented there. Puritans destroyed it in 1644.

glockenspiel: see PERCUSSION INSTRUMENTS.

Glogau (glō'gou), Pol. *Głogów*, town (1939 pop. 33,500; 1946 pop. 1,681), Lower Silesia, on the Oder; transferred to Polish administration 1945. Cap. of principality of Glogau under Piast dynasty (1249–1506); under Bohemian suzerainty from 1331; passed to Prussia 1745. Destroyed in World War II.

Glomma (glô'mä), chief river of Norway, rising in highlands S of Trondheim Fjord and flowing c.375 mi. S into the Skagerrak. Large falls at Sarpsborg furnish power for industrial concentration.

Gloria in excelsis (ĕksĕl'sĭs) [Latin,= glory in the highest], the *Angelic Hymn* or greater doxology, anc. Christian hymn; an amplification of Luke 2.14. In the Roman Mass it follows the *Kyrie;* in Anglican communion it is just before the benediction. Omitted from both services at certain seasons.

Glorious Revolution, in English history, the events of the years 1688–89 resulting in deposition of JAMES II. His overt Catholicism and the birth of a Catholic heir united Tories and Whigs in opposition. Seven nobles invited William of Orange and his consort Mary, Protestant daughter of James, to come to England's aid. After Bloodless Revolution they ruled jointly as WILLIAM III and Mary II. Their acceptance of the BILL OF RIGHTS showed final ascendancy of parliament over "divine right of kings."

glory lily, tropical tuberous-rooted climbing plant (*Gloriosa*), with lilylike yellow and red flowers.

Gloucester, Gilbert de Clare, earl of: see GLOUCESTER, RICHARD DE CLARE, 7TH EARL OF.

Gloucester, Humphrey, duke of (glô'stŭr), 1391–1447, English nobleman; son of Henry IV. Fought for his brother (Henry V) in France and served (1420–21) as regent of England during Henry's absence. After the accession of the infant Henry VI, he was powerful in the regency and (after 1435) heir to the throne. His influence waned and in 1447 he was arrested on charges of plotting Henry's death. He died in custody. A patron of Oxford Univ., his gift of books formed nucleus of the Bodleian Library.

Gloucester, Richard de Clare, 7th earl of, 1222–62, English nobleman. He vacillated between support of Henry III and baronial party. Gloucester and his rival, Simon de MONTFORT, were most powerful political figures of the time. His son, **Gilbert de Clare, 8th earl of Gloucester,** 1243–95, was first a leader of the barons under Simon de Montfort. Henry III surrendered to him (1264) after the battle of Lewes. He later aided the accession of Edward I (1272) and married (1290) Edward's daughter. His son, **Gilbert de Clare, 9th earl of Gloucester,** 1291–1314, was several times regent of England and was killed at Bannockburn.

Gloucester, Robert, earl of, d. 1147, English nobleman; illegitimate son of Henry I. Earldom created c.1121 for him. Refused to claim throne at his father's death (1135) and supported STEPHEN. Later quarreled with him, declared for MATILDA (Robert's half-sister), and was leader of the Angevin party.

Gloucester, Thomas of Woodstock, duke of, 1355–97, English nobleman; seventh son of Edward III. Was a leader (1388) of baronial opposition to his nephew, RICHARD II. Made peace with the king (1389), but later intrigues caused his arrest and conviction for treason. Richard probably had him killed.

Gloucester, England: see GLOUCESTERSHIRE.

Gloucester (glŏ′stûr), city (pop. 25,167), NE Mass., on Cape Ann, at head of Gloucester Harbor; settled 1623. Fishing (for over three cent.) and fish-processing center. Summer resort and artists' colony since late 19th cent. Hammond Mus. has art collections. Bronze *Fisherman* is memorial to Gloucestermen lost at sea.

Gloucester City, city (pop. 14,357), SW N.J., on Delaware R.; settled 1682 by Friends. Mfg. of asbestos, cork and paper products, and chemicals.

Gloucestershire or **Gloucester** (glŏ′stûrshĭr), county (1,255 sq. mi.; pop. 938,618), W England. Includes Cotswold Hills (sheep grazing) in E; fertile Severn valley (dairy farming) in center; and Forest of Dean in W. Mfg. centered around Bristol. Rich in ecclesiastical remains. County seat is **Gloucester,** county borough (pop. 67,268), on Severn R., an industrial city and site of a cathedral.

Gloversville, city (pop. 23,634), E central N.Y., N of Johnstown. Glove-mfg. center since early 19th century; other leather goods, and textiles.

glowworm, name for luminescent larva and wingless female of certain beetles or fireflies chiefly of families Lampyridae and Phengodidae. Common European glowworm is wingless female of beetle *Lampyris noctiluca;* cells of abdominal segments emit greenish light.

gloxinia, tuberous-rooted Brazilian plant (*Sinningia speciosa*), with richly colored bell-shaped flowers and velvety foliage. It is grown as a summer pot plant.

glucinum: see BERYLLIUM.

Gluck, Alma (glŏok), 1884–1938, American soprano, b. Rumania. Sang at Metropolitan Opera, New York, 1909–1912, and afterwards in concerts. One of the first singers to make phonograph records.

Gluck, Christoph Willibald von (krĭs′tôf vĭl′lē-bält), 1714–87, operatic composer, b. Bavaria, studied in Prague and Italy. His early operas were in Italian tradition. With *Orfeo ed Euridice* (1762) he began his reform of opera, giving greater unity to text and music and eliminating meaningless coloratura in arias. To Ranieri Calzabigi, librettist of *Orfeo* and of *Alceste* (1767) he credited much of his new operatic style. *Iphigénie en Tauride* (1779) is considered his masterpiece.

glucose, dextrose, or **grape sugar.** Commonly *glucose* is term for sweet sirupy liquid (called corn sirup), really a mixture. Chemically *glucose* indicates d-glucose, dextroglucose, or dextrose, a white, crystalline solid carbohydrate found in fruit juices. There are a number of forms with the same formula (6 carbon atoms; 12 hydrogen; 6, oxygen), differing in arrangement or optical properties. Presence of glucose is shown by FEHLING'S SOLUTION.

glue: see ADHESIVE.

gluten (glōō′tŭn), albuminous substance, tough, elastic, almost tasteless, found in northern wheat.

glycerin, glycerine, or **glycerol,** colorless, odorless liquid ALCOHOL, used in perfume, cosmetics, some inks, explosives, antifreeze mixtures, and in medicine. It is a by-product of soapmaking.

glycogen (glī′kŭjĕn), form of carbohydrate stored in animal cells; also called animal starch. It is made of d-glucose molecules. Some animal cells convert glucose into glycogen for storage. It resembles plant starch in physical properties.

Glycon: see FARNESE HERCULES.

Glyndebourne Festivals (glīn′bôrn), operatic festivals, begun 1934 in Sussex, England. First few devoted to Mozart; later other composers included. Became a second Salzburg during World War II.

Glyptothek (glüp″tōtäk′), museum in Munich, founded by Louis I of Bavaria. Designed by Leo von Klenze, built 1816–30. Destroyed in World War II, but collection (ancient and modern sculptures) was saved.

Gnadenhutten (jǐnä′dŭnhǔ″tŭn), village (pop. 895), E central Ohio, on Tuscarawas R. and W of Steubenville. State park marks site of Gnadenhutten massacre (1782) of 96 Christian Indians by white men.

gnat (năt), name for various small flies of order Diptera. BLACK FLY is pest to humans and most other warm-blooded animals. Several fungus gnat species injure mushrooms and various greenhouse plants. Potato scab gnat bores through tubers; gall gnats and midges damage plants.

Gneisenau, August, Graf Neithardt von (ou′gŏost gräf′ nīt′härt fŭn gŭnī′zünou), 1760–1831, Prussian field marshal. Won fame in Napoleonic Wars for his defense of Kolberg (1807); was Blücher's chief of staff 1813–15.

gneiss (nīs), rock which shows alternating light and dark bands. Usually it is metamorphosed granite.

Gneist, Rudolf von (rōō′dŏlf fŭn gŭnīst′), 1816–95, German jurist. Tried to reform the Prussian constitution and to make administration a cooperative function of citizens, local officials, and central administration.

Gnesen, Poland: see GNIEZNO.

Gniezno (gŭnyĕz′nô), Ger. *Gnesen,* town (pop. 30,292), Poland, NE of Poznan. Legendary cradle and first cap. of Polish nation; metropolitan see of Poland from 1000 (transferred to Poznan 1821). Under Prussian rule 1793–1919.

Gnosticism (nŏ′stĭsĭzûm) [from Greek *gnosis* = knowledge], religious and philosophical movement, arising in the Hellenistic era. Its fundamental doctrine was that salvation is to be obtained through knowledge rather than through faith or good works. Gnostics generally accepted a strong dualism of good and evil and adopted many magical practices. Some Jewish sects (the Essenes and Therapeutae), affected by Gnosticism, rejected the Old Testament idea of God as Righteousness and substituted that of Divine Wisdom. Early Christian Gnostics rejected the Jewish foundations of Christianity and the Old Testament. Redemption through Wisdom

(Sophia) was the basis of the complex doctrines of Valentinus and other 2d-cent. Gnostics. They divided men into three classes: the Gnostics, sure of salvation; non-Gnostic Christians who might be saved through faith in Christ; and all others, who are incapable of salvation. Gnosticism merged with MANICHAEISM. The MANDAEANS are the only surviving Gnostic sect. The movement had a great effect on early Christianity by forcing the new religion to define doctrines in declaring Gnosticism heretical. Present knowledge of the movement is based on Coptic texts and wisdom literature of the PSEUDEPIGRAPHA.

gnu (noo), S African antelope resembling the ox. White-tailed gnu (genus *Connochaetes*) or black wildebeest is believed extinct in wild state. It is dark brown or blackish; long hair tufts stand erect on muzzle, and hang from throat and between forelegs; the broad head has horns and an upright mane. Males stand c.4 ft. high at the shoulder. Brindled gnu (genus *Gorgon* or *Connochaetes*) or blue wildebeest exists in small herds; it is bluish gray with brown on the sides, larger than the white-tailed gnu and with a narrower head.

Goa (gō′ù), district (1,348 sq. mi.; pop. 540,-925) of Portuguese India, on coast of Bombay. Founded by Afonso de Albuquerque. Its original cap., Old Goa, is site of St. Francis Xavier's tomb. Present cap., Pangim or New Goa (pop. 14,213), is also cap. of Portuguese India (which includes Damão and Diu).

goat, ruminant animal with hollow horns, related to sheep. Probably it was domesticated in Persia from wild bezoar goat or pasan. True goats belong to genus *Capra*, family Bovidae; they are raised for milk, wool, flesh. Milk goats are common in Old World and are increasing in U.S.

Goat Island, N.Y.: see NIAGARA FALLS.

goatsbeard, tall perennial plant (*Arcanus sylvester*), with handsome spikes of small white flowers. The unrelated purple goatsbeard, better known as salsify or oyster plant (*Tragopogon porrifolius*), is grown as a vegetable for its edible roots.

Gobelins, Manufacture nationale des (gōbūlě′), state-controlled tapestry manufactory in Paris. Founded as dye works in mid-15th cent. by brothers, Gilles and Jehan Gobelin. Purchased 1662 by Louis XIV. Famous Gobelin tapestries include the set based on Raphael's frescoes in Vatican.

Gobi (gō′bē), Mandarin *Sha-mo*, sandy desert, area 500,000 sq. mi., in China and Mongolia; average alt. c.3,000 ft. Winds have stripped off most of its soil. Small number of pastoral Mongols inhabit scanty grasslands. Many paleontological finds have been made here.

Gobineau, Joseph Arthur, comte de (zhōzěf′ ärtür′ kŏt′ dù gōbēnō′), 1816–82, French author and diplomat. *The Inequality of Human Races* (1853–55; Eng. tr., 1915) was an early and influential attempt at proving the supremacy of the "Nordic race."

God, the divinity of the great monotheistic religions, Judaism, Christianity, and Islam. In the Old Testament the most celebrated form of his name was the ineffable (not to be spoken) name represented by the four letters transcribed as YHWH (the tetragrammaton). The origin of this is unknown; the reconstruction *Jehovah* is mistaken, and the form *Yahweh* is not now widely accepted. Because the name was ineffable the Hebrews used substitutes such as *Adonai* [my Lord] and *Elohim* (a plural form). *El* is not related to *Elohim* but is connected with *Allah*, used by Arabs (Moslem and Christian) as the name for God. The general conception of God in all three religions is that of a Being infinite, all powerful, all good, all creating, all knowing, loving but judging mankind, transcendent over and immanent in the world. He is often treated as a personality, though not necessarily in an anthropomorphic sense. The 19th-cent. rationalists argued that the Hebrew God was originally simply the chief of many gods and that He absorbed the attributes of His fellow divinities. Gradually He was considered as more and more powerful until He became the one God (though still preferring the Hebrews). In recent times in the Western world the term God has come to be applied to any overriding universal concept (such as the world soul or the Absolute). Scholasticism produced several demonstrations of the existence of God that are still current. One is the argument from First Cause: every effect in the world has its cause but this chain must lead back to the primary cause of the whole existing universe, which must have been itself both cause and effect (i.e., God). The cosmological argument is that the relations extant in the world must have their base in some independent, absolute existence (God), since all that is in the world is relative. The teleological argument is that the world operates on a great plan and toward set ends; therefore a master planner (God) must exist. The ontological argument is that since the human mind can reach the highest conception, which is God, that conception must have existence, for if not there could be a higher conception—one including existence. In the Western world the word god written without a capital letter is used for all the gods of polytheism (see MYTH).

Goddard, Henry Herbert, 1866–, American psychologist, director of research (1906–18), Training School for Feeble-Minded Children, Vineland, N.J. He is noted for systematic hereditary studies, especially for *The Kallikak Family* (1912).

Goderich (gŏd′rĭch), town (pop. 4,934), S Ont., Canada, on L. Huron, NW of London. Farming and fishing center and lake port with grain elevators, saltworks, flour and lumber mills.

Godesberg, Germany: see BAD GODESBERG.

Godey, Louis Antoine (gō′dē), 1804–78, American publisher of *Godey's Lady's Book*.

Godfrey of Bouillon (booyō′), c.1058–1100, duke of Lower Lorraine, leader of First Crusade. Elected king of Jerusalem, which he helped capture, but took title "protector of the Holy Sepulchre." His brother Baldwin succeeded him.

Godhavn (gôdh′houn), settlement (pop. 319), W Greenland on S shore of Disko isl. Administrative center of N Greenland. Fishing base.

Godiva, Lady (gōdī'vû), fl. c.1040–1080, wife of Leofric, earl of Mercia and lord of Coventry. Legends claim she rode naked through the town to get her husband to lower heavy taxes of the people. The only man who looked became known as Peeping Tom.

Godkin, E(dwin) L(awrence), 1831–1902, American editor, b. Ireland. His fearless and perceptive criticism made the *Nation* and the New York *Evening Post*, which he edited, influential in reform.

Godolphin, Sidney Godolphin, 1st earl of, 1645–1712, English statesman. By financial ability as lord treasurer aided victories of Marlborough (with whom he was politically associated after marriage of their children). Queen Anne dismissed him in 1710.

Godoy, Manuel de (mänwäl' dā gōdoi'), 1767–1851, Spanish statesman. Favorite of Queen MARÍA LUISA; chief minister to CHARLES IV after 1793. Favored war on revolutionary France, but made peace 1795. *Principe de la Paz* [prince of the peace] was one of many titles showered on him. The corruption of his regime and his increasing subservience to France led to his overthrow by Ferdinand VII (1808).

God Save the King (or **Queen**), English national anthem. Both words and music of uncertain origin. Tune probably evolved from folk and plain song elements; present tune (often ascribed to Henry Carey) and words appeared in 1745. See also AMERICA.

Godthaab (gŏt'hôp), town (pop. 970), cap. of S Greenland and of Godthaab dist. (pop. 1,962); a port on Godthaab Fjord of SW Greenland. Founded 1721 by Hans Egede, it was first Danish colony in Greenland. Has U.S. and Canadian consulates.

Godunov, Boris (būres' gūdōōnôf'), c.1551–1605, tsar of Russia (1598–1605). A favorite of Ivan IV, he ruled Russia as regent during reign of Feodor I (1584–98). He probably had Feodor's brother DMITRI murdered (1591). Chosen successor to Feodor, Boris ruled capably but lost popular support. He died during the false Dmitri's invasion of Russia. His son, Feodor II, lost his throne to the impostor. Boris's life is the subject of a drama by Pushkin, basis of Moussorgsky's opera.

Godwin or **Godwine** (both: gŏd'wĭn), d. 1053, English statesman. Earl of Wessex, he was chief adviser to Canute and most powerful earl in England. After king's death he supported claims to throne of Harthacanute. Opposed the French favorites of Harthacanute's successor, Edward the Confessor, and was exiled (1051). Invaded England (1052) and regained his former importance.

Godwin, Mary: see WOLLSTONECRAFT, MARY.

Godwin, William, 1756–1836, English author and political philosopher. His materialism pervaded his anarchistic tract, *An Enquiry concerning the Principles of Political Justice and Its Influence on General Virtue and Happiness* (1793) and also his novel *The Adventures of Caleb Williams* (1794). In 1797 he married Mary Wollstonecraft. Their daughter, Mary, became wife of SHELLEY.

Godwin-Austen, Mount, or **K2**, peak, 28,250 ft. high, Kashmir, in Karakorum range; second highest in world.

Godwine: see GODWIN (d. 1053).

Goebbels, (Paul) Joseph (poul' yō'zĕf gû'búls), 1897–1945, German National Socialist (Nazi) propaganda minister (1933–45), an able orator and writer. Worked on principles of self-justification of power and inculcating "the big lie" by varied repetition. Died by suicide when Berlin was being conquered.

Goering or **Göring, Hermann Wilhelm** (hĕr'män vĭl'hĕlm gû'rĭng), 1893–1946, German National Socialist (Nazi) leader. An air force hero of World War I, he joined the party early. President of the Reichstag from 1932, he became in 1933 air minister for Germany and Prussian premier. He founded the Gestapo (secret police), which he headed until 1936; directed German economy with dictatorial powers, 1937–43 (invented slogan "guns instead of butter"); was designated by Hitler as successor (1939). Also boasted such unique titles as "imperial marshal" and "imperial master of the hunt." In World War II he was responsible for initiating total air war. Excessively fond of pomp and pageantry, he amassed fabulous wealth and art collection. Surrendered to U.S. troops 1945. Chief defendant at Nuremberg war crimes trial (1945–46); sentenced to death but took poison before scheduled hanging.

Goes, Hugo van der (hōō'gō vän dĕr gōōs'), d. 1482, Flemish painter. Realism and rich detail mark portraits and Portinari altarpiece (Uffizi).

Goethals, George Washington (gō'dhŭlz), 1858–1928, U.S. army engineer. Chief engineer of Panama Canal (1907–14). Governor of Canal Zone (1914–16).

Goethe, Johann Wolfgang von (yō'hän vôlf'gäng fŭn gû'tû), 1749–1832, German poet, dramatist, novelist. His universal genius also embraced other fields, notably science. After a happy childhood in Frankfurt, he studied the law at Leipzig and later at Strasbourg, where he came under the spell of the STURM UND DRANG movement. In 1773 he won recognition with his drama *Götz von Berlichingen* (see BERLICHINGEN, GÖTZ VON). While a lawyer at Wetzlar (1772), he fell unhappily in love with Charlotte Buff; he overcame his despair by writing *The Sorrows of Young Werther* (1774), an epistolary novel of morbid sensitiveness. It made him famous overnight. In 1775 he accepted an invitation to the court of Charles Augustus, duke of Saxe-Weimar, where he remained for the rest of his life. For 10 years he served the duke as chief minister. Goethe's first trip to Italy (1786–88), fired his enthusiasm for the classical ideal. His drama *Egmont* (1788) still shows traces of *Sturm und Drang*, but the drama *Iphigenie auf Tauris* (1779, rewritten 1787), *Römische Elegien* (1788), and the domestic epic *Hermann und Dorothea* (1797) are pure products of classicism. His two great novels, *Wilhelm Meisters Lehrjahre* (1796) and *Die Wahlverwandtschaften* [elective affinities] (1809), aside from their intrinsic merit, showed the way for the German novel of character development and the German psychological novel. His friendship with Schiller, begun in 1794, had a stimulating effect on both men. In 1808 he published the first part of his life work, FAUST, completed shortly before his death. Increasingly aloof in his old age, Goethe became more and more the Olympian divinity, to whose shrine at Weimar all Europe flocked. Literary products of his later years include *Dichtung und Wahrheit* (1811–33), his charming autobiography, and *Westöstlicher Diwan* (1819), a collection of exquisite lyrics inspired by readings of Persian poets. Goethe attached equal importance to his scientific and his poetic work. His discovery of the intermaxillary bone in man (1784) was important to the theory of evolution; his work in botany showed great intuitive insight; his *Zur Farbenlehre* (1810) was a stubborn attack on Newton's theory of light. His philosophy, greatly influenced by Spinoza, was a mystic pantheism. Most of his best-known works have been translated into English, as have been many of his lyrics and ballads.

Gog, leader who, according to prophecy, will come from land of Magog, attack Israel, and be defeated. Ezek. 38–39. Rev. 20.8 warns of Gog and Magog.

Gogarty, Oliver St. John (gō'gùrtē), 1878–, Irish poet, a surgeon. In youth a friend of James Joyce, he has since written much criticism of him.

Gogebic (gōgē'bĭk), range, c.80 mi. long, extending W from W Upper Peninsula, N Mich., into N Wis. Known for its iron content.

Gogh, Vincent van (văn gō', Dutch, vĭnsĕnt' vän khôkh'), 1853–90, postimpressionist painter, b. Netherlands. Decided to become a painter only 10 years before his death. His early pictures were dark, but after moving in 1886 to Paris, where he met Pissarro, Degas, and Gauguin, he began to paint the brilliantly colored and dynamic pictures that later made him famous. Despite periodic fits of insanity he succeeded in producing numerous, now popular works.

Gogmagog (gŏg'māgŏg), low chalk hills, Cambridgeshire, England.

Gogol, Nikolai Vasilyevich (nyĭkûlī' vŭsē'lyùvĭch gô'gôl), 1809–52, Russian author. Won his first success with romantic tales of Cossack life, as in *Evenings on a Farm near Dikanka* (1831) and "Taras Bulba" (1835). With his later short stories, notably "The Overcoat," and with his satiric novel and masterpiece, *Dead Souls* (1842), he founded the great school of Russian realism. In a religious and moral crisis, Gogol destroyed the second part of *Dead Souls.* His fame as a dramatist rests on *Revizor* (*The Inspector-General,* 1836), a satire of provincial officialdom. All his major works are available in English.

Goiás (goï'ash'), state (240,333 sq. mi.; pop. 1,234,740), central Brazil; cap. Goiânia (pop. 41,584). On landlocked plateau, it has some rivers in Amazon system, some in Paraná system.

goiter: see THYROID GLAND.

Golan (gō–), one of the cities of refuge, E of the Jordan. Deut. 4.43; Joshua 20.8; 21.7; 1 Chron. 6.71.

Golconda (gŏlkŏn'dù), deserted city, Hyderabad, India. Was cap. of Moslem kingdom of Golconda (1512–89). Declined after conquest by Aurangzeb in 1687. Famed diamond

trade made Golconda a byword for wealth.

gold, metallic element (symbol = Au [Latin *aurum*]; see also ELEMENT, table). Very ductile and malleable, it can be beaten into gold leaf. It is a good conductor of electricity and is chemically inactive. Usually it is hardened by being alloyed with other metals. The gold content of an alloy is stated in carats (a carat being 1/24 by weight of the total mass; because of this "pure" gold is 24 carats fine). Gold is a favored metal for the backing of currency. The quest for gold has had an important and colorful place in history. Chief producers are Union of South Africa, USSR, Canada, and U.S.

Goldberg, Rube, 1883–, American cartoonist. Known for his panels showing fabulously involved machinery for simple operations.

Goldberger, Joseph, 1874–1929, American medical research worker, discoverer of cause of pellagra.

Gold Coast, British colony and protectorates (91,690 sq. mi.; pop. 4,095,276), W. Africa, on Gulf of Guinea; cap. Accra. Bordered on N by French West Africa. Comprises crown colony of Gold Coast (80,190 sq. mi.; pop. 2,194,466) with cap. at Cape Coast, British TOGOLAND, and inland protectorates of NORTHERN TERRITORIES and ASHANTI. Has swampy coast and forested interior. Gold is produced in NW area. Other products are manganese, bauxite, diamonds, hardwoods, and cacao. In 1482 the Portuguese estab. first European settlement in area. British crown colony was created 1874. Since 1951 the natives have enjoyed considerable self-rule.

Golden, resort city (pop. 5,238), N central Colo., just W of Denver, in area yielding coal, gold, clay, farm produce; founded 1859. Territorial cap. 1862–67. Seat of COLORADO SCHOOL OF MINES. Grave of Buffalo Bill is on near by Lookout Mtn.

Golden Ass, The, Latin novel: see APULEIUS, LUCIUS.

Golden Bough, The: see FRAZER, SIR JAMES GEORGE.

golden bull. 1 In history of Holy Roman Empire: see ELECTORS. **2** In Hungarian history: see ANDREW II.

Golden Fleece, in Greek mythology, magic fleece of a ram. Fleece was hung in a wood guarded by a dragon in Colchis. JASON and Argonauts sought this fleece, which they took after fulfilling tasks assigned by Aeëtes, king of Colchis.

Golden Gate, strait, 5 mi. long and 1–2 mi. wide, W Calif., between San Francisco Bay and the Pacific. **Golden Gate Bridge** (built 1933–37) crosses strait from San Francisco to Marin co. Longest single-span suspension bridge in world (4,200 ft. between towers; over-all length 9,266 ft.). See *ill.,* p. 167.

golden glow, double-flowered yellow variety of a North American coneflower (*Rudbeckia laciniata*).

Golden Horde, Mongol host, so called because of magnificence of the camp of its leader BATU KHAN. Their empire (see TATARS) was founded in mid-13th cent. and comprised most of Russia, with cap. at Sarai (near modern Stalingrad). At first tributary to Great Khan at Karakorum, Golden Horde took part in Kublai Khan's conquest of S China. Islam became official religion after 1314. Ascendancy of grand duke of Moscow after 1380 brought decline; after 1405 empire broke up into independent khanates of Astrakhan, Kazan, Crimea, Sibir.

Golden Horn: see ISTANBUL.

Golden Legend, The, popular collection of saints' lives written in the 13th cent. by JACOBUS DE VORAGINE; originally entitled *Legenda sanctorum.*

goldenrod, perennial plants of large North American genus *Solidago.* Their spikes or panicles of fluffy yellow (rarely white) flowers brighten fields and roadsides in late summer. Goldenrod pollen now rarely considered a cause of hay fever.

Golden Rule, a saying of Jesus, "As ye would that men should do to you, do ye also to them likewise." Luke 6.31; Mat. 7.12.

Golden Valley, village (pop. 5,551), E Minn., W suburb of Minneapolis.

Goldfield, town (pop. of district 336), SW Nev., S of Tonopah. Gold discovery here of 1902 brought a rush in 1903. Peak production was reached 1910, then fell off rapidly.

goldfinch, name for several finches of Europe and America. North American eastern goldfinch (thistle bird or wild canary) is olive yellow, but in spring the male becomes vivid yellow and black. There are several forms in W U.S. See *ill.,* p. 135.

goldfish, fresh-water fish of carp and minnow family, used in aquariums and ponds. It was domesticated from wild form in China centuries ago; reverts to type upon escape. Bizarre varieties are bred.

Goldman, Edwin Franko, 1878–, American bandmaster. Organized the Goldman Band (1918), for which he wrote many marches. Author of books on band techniques.

Goldman, Emma, 1869–1940, American anarchist, b. Russia. Her speeches attracted wide attention, she was imprisoned for advocating birth control (1916) and for obstructing the draft (1917). She was deported (1917) to Russia, which she left in 1921.

Goldoni, Carlo (kär'lō gōldō'nē), 1707–93, Italian dramatist. He wrote real and witty comedy to replace *commedia dell' arte* on Italian stage. His plays include *La bottega del caffè* (1751) and *La locandiera* (1753). His memoirs (1787) are in French.

Goldsboro, city (pop. 21,454), E central N.C., near Neuse R. and SE of Raleigh; settled c.1840. Trades and ships tobacco, cotton, and truck.

Goldsborough, Louis Malesherbes, 1805–77, American naval officer. In Civil War, commanded North Atlantic Blockading Squadron in support of successful expedition against N.C. coast (1862).

Goldsmith, Oliver, 1730?–1774, English poet, dramatist, and novelist, b. Ireland. Unsuccessful as physician, he turned to writing. Fame, won with "Chinese letters" of *The Citizen of the World* (1762), grew with poems *The Traveller* (1764) and *The Deserted Village* (1770). He wrote one novel, *The Vicar of Wakefield* (1766; a masterpiece of domestic literature), and popular comedies (notably *She Stoops to Conquer,* 1773). The anonymous children's classic

Little Goody Two-Shoes (1765) is sometimes attributed to him. Eccentric but lovable, he was a close friend of Reynolds, Burke, Garrick, and Samuel Johnson.

gold standard: see BIMETALLISM and MONEY.

golem (gō'lŭm) [Heb.,= embryo], in medieval Jewish legend, an automaton given life through the invocation of religious symbols.

golf, game played with specially made clubs and balls on outdoor course called links. Game identified with Scotland, where it has been popular since 15th cent. Royal and Ancient Golf Club of St. Andrews, Scotland, founded 1774, became international shrine of golf; its basic rules accepted throughout the world. U.S. Golf Association, founded 1894, governing body of game in U.S. Standard golf course, usually more than 6,000 yd. around, is divided into 18 holes of varying length.

Golgi, Camillo (kämēl'lō gōl'jē), 1844–1926, Italian physician, noted as neurologist and histologist. Shared 1906 Nobel Prize in Physiology and Medicine for work on structure of nervous system.

Golgotha (gŏl'gŭthù), the same as CALVARY.

Goliad (gō'lēăd), city (pop. 1,584) S. Texas, on San Antonio R. SE of San Antonio. Spanish mission moved here 1749 from Lavaca Bay (Goliad then La Bahia). Captured twice (1812, 1821) by filibusters from U.S. Texans regained it in Texas Revolution. Mexicans defeated and massacred Col. J. W. FANNIN and troops, March 19–27, 1836. Restored mission and presidio ruins now in state park.

Goliardic songs (gōlēär'dĭk), Late Latin poetry written by "wandering scholars." The origin of the name is uncertain. Songs, resembling medieval hymns in form but not in content, were usually licentious and attacked the church. Number of vagabond scholars grew so great as to become a plague in the 13th cent., but it is no longer thought that they actually organized a burlesque religious order. Church began (c.1230) to take strong measures against them, and they gradually declined.

Goliath (gōlī'ùth), Philistine giant, killed by young David. 1 Sam. 17; 21.9; 22.10; 2 Sam. 21.19.

Gombos, Julius, Hung. *Gömbös Gyula* (gûm'bûsh dyōō'lō), 1886–1936, Hungarian premier (1932–36); a nationalist and revisionist leader.

Gomel (gô'mĭl), city (pop. 144,169), SE Belorussia. Varied light industries. Dates from 12th cent.; to Russia in first Polish partition (1772). Pre-World War II Jewish pop. (c.40%) was largely exterminated by the Germans.

Gómez, Juan Vicente (hwän' vēsän'tä gō'měs), 1857–1935, ruler of Venezuela (1908–35), a *caudillo.* Of Indian and white parentage, he grew up as nearly illiterate cattle herdsman. Supported Cipriano CASTRO (1899), then replaced Castro as president (1908). Ruled Venezuela—not always as president—until his death. Though tyrannical, he was honest and industrious and improved his country economically, largely through encouraging foreign investments.

Gomorrah or **Gomorrha,** city, destroyed with SODOM.

Gompers, Samuel (gŏm'pŭrz), 1850–1924, American labor leader, b. London. Helped found (1881) the Federation of Organized Trades and Labor Unions, which became (1886) the American Federation of Labor, of which he was president, except for 1895, until his death. He rejected cooperative business plans and socialist or radical programs, maintaining that the just aims of labor were simply shorter hours, more wages, and greater freedom.

Gonaïves (gônäëv'), city (pop. 13,534), NW Haiti, a port on Gulf of Gonaïves. In 1804 Haitian independence was proclaimed here, and DESSALINES, first of the Negro emperors, was crowned.

Gonçalves Dias, Antonio (äntô'nyō gônsäl'vĭsh dē'ùsh), 1823–64, Brazilian romantic poet.

Goncharov, Ivan Aleksandrovich (ēvän' ûlyĭk-sän'drùvĭch gŭnchŭrôf'), 1812–91, Russian novelist; author of *Oblomov* (1858; Eng. tr., 1915), a minute portrayal of the indolent Russian gentleman.

Goncourt, Edmond (Huot) de (ĕdmō' üō' dù gōkōōr'), 1822–96, and **Jules (Huot) de Goncourt** (zhül), 1830–70, French authors, brothers. Together, in their own nervous, telegraphic style, they wrote art criticism (much promoting Japanese art), naturalistic novels, as *Renée Mauperin* (1864) and *Germinie Lacerteux* (1865), and the famous *Journal des Goncourt* (9 vols., 1887–96), an intimate picture of Parisian society. Edmond founded the Goncourt Academy to award annual prizes for fiction.

Gondola, Giovanni: see GUNDULIC, IVAN.

gondola (gŏn'dùlù), boat used on canals of Venice since 11th cent. Long, narrow, and flat-bottomed, with high tapering prows and sterns, gondolas average 30 by 4 ft. The gondolier propels the boat with one oar from stern. Curtained cabin in center holds four to eight persons. Once gaily colored, law now requires that gondolas be black.

gong: see PERCUSSION INSTRUMENTS.

Góngora y Argote, Luis de (lwēs' dä gōn'gōrä ē ärgō'tä), 1571–1627, last great Spanish poet of the Golden Age, a priest. Stylistic refinement and somewhat exaggerated elegance gave rise to Gongorism, equivalent to euphuism in England.

gonorrhea (gŏnùrē'ù), an infectious venereal disease caused by gonococcus. It is commonly transmitted to genital organs by direct contact; may spread to adjacent structures or be carried to other parts of body by lymphatic system. Gonococcus, transmitted to infant at birth from genital tract of mother, sometimes causes conjunctivitis and blindness (preventable by silver-nitrate treatment).

Gonville and Caius College: see CAMBRIDGE UNIVERSITY.

Gonzaga (gōntsä'gä), Italian princely family. Senior line ruled MANTUA 1328–1627 (first as captains general, from 1433 as marquesses, from 1530 as dukes) and acquired MONTFERRAT in 1536. After its extinction (1627) it was succeeded by a younger line, which by marriage had acquired the French duchies of NEVERS and RETHEL; this in turn became

extinct 1708. Another branch ruled GUASTALLA (1539–1746). Many rulers of Mantua were lavish patrons of art and letters, notably **Francesco Gonzaga,** d. 1519, who married Isabella d'ESTE. In the Italian Wars he preserved Mantuan independence with difficulty, siding first with Venice, then with France, then with Pope Julius II.

Gonzaga University: see SPOKANE, Wash.

Gonzales (gŭnzä'lĭs), city (pop. 5,659), S central Texas, near Guadalupe R. and ENE of San Antonio. First battle of Texas Revolution fought near by, Oct. 2, 1835. Park marks battlefield. Region yields cotton and poultry.

González de Ávila, Gil (hēl' gōnthä'lĕth dä ä'vēlä), d. 1543, Spanish conquistador. Conquered Nicaragua (1522); his claims usurped by Francisco Fernández de Córdoba (1524).

González de Ávila, Gil, 1578?–1658, Spanish historian. Royal chronicler of Castile and Indies, he wrote history of the Church in Spanish colonies.

Gooch, George Peabody, 1873–, English historian. An editor of *Cambridge History of British Foreign Policy, 1783–1919* (3 vols., 1922–23). His *History and Historians in the Nineteenth Century* (1913; 2d ed., 1946) is among best in modern historiography.

Good Hope, Cape of: see CAPE PROVINCE.

Goodhue, Bertram Grosvenor, 1869–1924, American architect. Evolved a distinctive style for his ecclesiastical work, which was Gothic in form yet permeated with a modern spirit.

Gooding, city (pop. 3,099), S Idaho, W of Shoshone, in MINIDOKA PROJECT.

Goodman, Benny (Benjamin David Goodman), 1909–, American clarinetist and dance band leader. In 1934 he organized his own orchestra, which became nationally famous. His contributions to the development of swing music earned him the title "king of swing." He also appeared as solo clarinetist with many symphony orchestras and in chamber ensembles.

Goodnews Bay, inlet of Kuskokwim Bay, SW Alaska. Platinum and osmiridium are found here.

Goodnight, Charles, 1836–1929, Texas cattleman, a pioneer in improving cattle breeds. He laid out Goodnight cattle trail to Wyoming in 1866.

Goodrich, Samuel Griswold, pseud. **Peter Parley,** 1793–1860, American editor and writer of juvenile stories. His *Peter Parley Tales* were sugar-coated moralistic stories of instruction. Edited periodicals, including *The Token* and juvenile *Robert Merry's Museum.*

Goodspeed, Edgar Johnson, 1871–, American Greek scholar. He is principally known for his new translation of the Bible: *The New Testament—an American Translation* (1923) and *The Complete Bible—an American Translation* (with J. M. P. Smith, 1939).

Good Thief or **Penitent Thief,** the thief crucified with Jesus who did not mock Him but accepted Him; Jesus promised him Paradise that day. Luke 23.39–43. His feast is March 25. Tradition names him Dismas or Desmas, the other thief Gesmas.

Goodwin Sands, 10 mi. stretch of shoals and

shifting sands, off E coast of Kent, England. Formerly scene of many shipwrecks, Sands were supposedly once a fertile isle, property of Earl Godwin.

Goodyear, Charles, 1800–1860, American inventor, originator of rubber vulcanization (1839; patent 1844). His son **Charles Goodyear,** 1833–96, was pioneer in use of sewing machine for shoe manufacturing.

Goole, urban district (pop. 19,227), W Riding of Yorkshire, England; a port. Has shipbuilding and passenger lines to several continental ports.

goose, wild and domesticated bird related to duck and swan. Accurately, goose is the female, gander the male. Common Canada or wild goose of North America migrates in V-shaped flocks in spring and autumn. Other wild geese are BRANT, the blue, the snow, and the white-fronted or laughing geese. Domestic are Toulouse or gray goose, African and Embden geese, and oriental breeds (from wild Chinese goose).

Goose Bay, village of SE Labrador on Goose Bay. Has large air base and radio station built in World War II for transatlantic transport.

gooseberry, shrub (*Ribes*) of temperate regions and its fruit, a berry used in preserves. It is related to the currant and is a host to white pine blister rust.

Goose Creek, Texas: see BAYTOWN.

Goosport, village (pop. 8,318), SW La., near Lake Charles.

gopher (gō'fŭr) or **pocket gopher,** burrowing rodent of North American and Central America. In U.S. chief genera are western (*Thomomys*) and eastern (*Geomys*) gophers. Gophers are gray, buff, or dark brown and 7–14 in. long. They have fur-lined pouches opening on outside of cheeks for carrying food and nesting material. They live and forage mostly underground, feeding on roots and tubers.

Gorboduc (gôr'bŭdŭk), legendary early British king who created murderous strife by dividing his realm between two sons. The story is treated in early English tragedy (1562) by Thomas Norton and Thomas SACKVILLE.

Gorchakov, Aleksandr Mikhailovich, Prince (ŭlyĭksän'dŭr mēkhī'lŭvĭch gŭrchŭkôf'), 1798–1883, Russian foreign minister (1856–82). Sought to nullify Treaty of Paris which closed Crimean War. Though friendly to Prussia and hostile to Austria, kept Russia neutral in Austro-Prussian and Franco-Prussian wars and helped form THREE EMPERORS' LEAGUE. Opposed Russo-Turkish War of 1877–78; represented Russia at Congress of BERLIN.

Gordian I (Marcus Antonius Gordianus Africanus) (gôr'dĕŭn), d. 238, Roman emperor. Ruled (238) with his son, **Gordian II,** 192–238, who was killed in Carthage. The father committed suicide. Gordian II's son, **Gordian III,** c.223–244, was emperor (238–44).

Gordian knot: see GORDIUS.

Gordin, Jacob Mikhailovich, 1853–1919, American writer of Yiddish plays, b. Russia.

Gordius (gôr'dĕŭs), legendary king of Phrygia and founder of Gordium. Pole of his wagon was tied to yoke with intricate knot. Oracle said that he who untied it would rule all Asia.

Alexander the Great severed it with his sword. Hence the figure "to cut the Gordian knot," meaning to solve a perplexing problem with one bold stroke.

Gordon, Charles George (Chinese Gordon), 1833–85, British soldier and administrator. Commander of Chinese army that suppressed the Taiping Rebellion. Was governor of Egyptian Sudan 1877–80. Trying to crush power of the Mahdi, he was killed in the siege of Khartoum. Popular indignation at his death was partial cause of fall of Gladstone government in 1885.

Gordon, Lord George, 1751–93, English agitator, responsible for the tragic Gordon riots in London (June 2–7, 1780). Protestant demonstration against removal of civil restrictions from Catholics; became an orgy of destruction and plunder.

Gordon, John Brown, 1832–1904, Confederate general and Ga. statesman. Served brilliantly in Wilderness campaign and Shenandoah Valley (1864). A leader in Ga. politics after war; governor 1886–90.

Gordon, Sir John Watson-, 1788–1864, Scottish portrait painter. Succeeded Raeburn as leading portraitist in Scotland.

Gordon, Leon, 1830–92, Russian-Hebrew novelist and poet, leader in renaissance of Hebrew culture.

Gordon riots: see GORDON, LORD GEORGE.

Gore Range: see PARK RANGE.

Gorgan, Iran: see GURGAN.

Gorgas, William Crawford (gôr'gŭs), 1854–1920, American disease and sanitation expert, surgeon general of U.S. (1914–19). Cleansed Havana and the Canal Zone of yellow fever.

Gorges, Sir Ferdinando (gôr'jĭz), c.1566–1647, British colonizer, proprietor of Maine. A leading figure in Plymouth Co. Conducted long struggle with Mass. Bay and Salem colonies over patent rights.

Gorgons (gôr'gŭnz), in Greek myth, female monsters. Winged and snake-haired, the three hideous creatures turned to stone all men who looked on them. Chief Gorgon was MEDUSA (killed by Hercules).

Gorham, town (pop. 2,639), NE N.H., on Androscoggin R. below Berlin, within sight of Presidential Range. Resort and lumber center, it has paper mills and holds winter carnival.

gorilla, anthropoid ape (genus *Gorilla*) native to W equatorial Africa. Largest of the great apes, males reach 5–6 ft. in height, and weigh 300–600 lb. Usually terrestrial, they walk on all fours, hands doubled under. They are chiefly vegetarian. Females and young sleep in tree platform nests; males sleep at base. Threatened by extinction, they are now protected.

Göring, Hermann Wilhelm: see GOERING.

Gorizia (gôrē'tsēä), Ger. *Görz,* city (pop. 30,-265), Friuli-Venezia Giulia, NE Italy, in FRIULI, on Isonzo R. Under Austria 1500–1918. Bitterly contested in World War I.

Gorki, Maxim (mŭksyĕm gôr'kē), pseud. of Aleksey Maximovich Pyeshkov, 1868–1936, Russian author. After years of vagabondage, he began writing in 1892. Among his early short stories, "Twenty-six Men and a Girl," "Chelkash," and "Malva" are well known in

English, as are his novels *Foma Gordeyev*
(1899) and *Mother* (1907) and his drama
The Lower Depths (1902). A Marxist from
his youth, he sought social realism in his
descriptions of the outcasts of society, in
whom he saw the hope of the future. Living
abroad after 1905, he returned to Russia in
1928, where he was given the highest honors.
Late novels include *The Artamanov Affair*
(1925; Eng. tr., *Decadence*, 1927) and *The
Life of Klim Samgin* (1927–36; Eng. tr., in
four separate vols., 1930–38), covering the
whole revolutionary period from 1880 to
1934. He also wrote *My Childhood* (1913;
Eng. tr., 1915) and *Reminiscences* (Eng. tr.,
1946).

Gorki or **Gorky,** formerly **Nizhni Novgorod**
(nyēzh′nyē nôv′gŭrŭt), city (pop. c.900,000),
central European RSFSR, on right bank of
the Volga and at mouth of the Oka. Major
transportation and industrial center (rolling
stock, heavy machinery, electric equipment,
chemicals). Univ., technical schools.
Founded 1221 as outpost by prince of Vladimir; became seat of a principality 1350; fell
to Moscow 1393. Site of famous annual fairs
1817–1930. Renamed 1932 for Maxim Gorki,
who was born here. Old section contains
13th-cent. kremlin, with palace and two cathedrals.

Görlitz (gûr′lĭts), city (pop. 85,686), Saxony,
E Germany, on Görlitzer Neisse R.; chief
city of Lusatia. Mfg. of textiles, machinery,
glass, beer. A flourishing medieval duchy
under Bohemian overlordship, it passed to
Saxony 1635, to Prussia 1815, again to Saxony 1945. Jakob Boehme lived here. For
Görlitzer Neisse river, see NEISSE.

Gorman, Arthur Pue, 1839–1906, U.S. Senator
from Md. (1881–99, 1903–6). Led in making Wilson-Gorman Tariff Act of 1894 a
high-tariff act.

Gorno-Badakhshan, Tadzhik SSR: see MOUN-
TAIN-BADAKHSHAN.

gorse: see FURZE.

Gorton, Samuel, c.1592–1677, one of founders
of R.I., b. England. He settled Warwick
(1642), where he preached unorthodox religious views.

Görz: see GORIZIA, Italy.

Gosforth (gŏz′fûrth). **1** Village, Cumberland,
England; site of famous Viking cross. **2** Urban district (pop. 24,424), Northumberland,
England; coal-mining center. George Stephenson built his first locomotive here in
1814.

goshawk (gŏs′hôk), fearless, relentless hawk of
Old World and North America. Eastern goshawk male is c.22 in. long, female c.24 in. As
adults both have black crown, white stripe
over red eye, blue-gray upper parts, and
white, gray-barred lower parts. Western goshawk has darker plumage. Goshawks destroy poultry and game birds. See *ill.*, p. 135.

Goshen (gō′–), fertile part of Egypt occupied
by Israelites during bondage. Gen. 47.6; Ex.
8.22; 9.26.

Goshen. 1 City (pop. 13,003), N Ind., on Elkhart R. and SE of South Bend; settled c.1830.
Agr. distribution center. Metal and wood
products. Large Mennonite population. **2**
Village (pop. 3,311), SE N.Y., SE of Mid-
dletown. Good Time (scene of the Hamble-

tonian) and Historic or Harriman harness-
racing tracks are here.

Goslar (gôs′lär), city (pop. 40,735), Lower
Saxony, central Germany, at N foot of Harz
mts. Mining center since its foundation in
10th cent. (formerly silver; now copper,
lead, zinc, iron, sulphur). A favorite residence of early German emperors. A free imperial city until 1802, it was awarded to
Hanover 1815, transferred to Brunswick
1941. City has preserved its medieval character. Much Romanesque and Gothic architecture (notably the 11th-cent Kaiserhaus,
built for Henry III).

Gosnold, Bartholomew (gŏz′nōld), fl. 1572–
1602, English explorer and colonizer. Explored coast from Maine to Narragansett
Bay (1602). Commanded *God Speed* in first
settlement of Va. (1606).

Gospel [M.E.,= good news; cf. *evangel* from
Gr.,= good news], one of the four biographies of Jesus in New Testament. The gospels are named MATTHEW, MARK, LUKE, and
JOHN. First three called SYNOPTIC GOSPELS
because of apparent relationship. Solemn
reading of the Gospel of the day is special
feature of liturgy of many churches. Formerly a book of the Gospels was used instead of Bible for the oath in courts in
Christian countries. Illumination of the Gospels became an art (e.g., the Lindisfarne
Gospels, the Book of Kells). For apocryphal
Gospels, see PSEUDEPIGRAPHA.

Gosport (gŏs′–), municipal borough (pop. 58,-
246), Hampshire, England; port on Portsmouth Harbour.

Gosse, Sir Edmund W(illiam), 1849–1928, English poet, critic, and literary biographer.

Gossen, Herman Heinrich (hĕr′män hīn′rĭkh
gô′sŭn), 1810–58, German economist, anticipated (1854) theory of marginal utility of
Jevons and others.

Gota, Swed. *Göta älv,* river, 56 mi. long, SW
Sweden, draining Vänern lake into the Kattegat. Forms part of **Gota Canal,** 240-mile
system of rivers, lakes, and canals, from
Goteborg to Stockholm.

Gotaland or **Gotarike:** see SWEDEN.

Goteborg (Swed. yûtûbôr′yŭ) or **Gothenburg**
(gŏ′thŭnbûrg), Swed. *Göteborg,* city (pop.
353,991), SW Sweden, co. seat of Goteborg
and Bohus co.; a seaport at mouth of Gota
R. on Kattegat. Second largest city of Sweden; shipyards, machinery mfg. Seat of Lutheran bishop. Founded 1619, city was
planned by Dutch architects and retains
many stately old buildings. University was
founded 1887.

Goteborg licensing system: see LIQUOR LAWS.

Gotha (gō′thŭ, Ger. gō′tä), city (pop. 57,639),
Thuringia, central Germany. Mfg. center
(railroad cars, machinery); printing (mainly
cartography). *Almanach de Gotha,* reference work on European royalty and nobility,
was published here from 1764 to World War
II. Passed to Ernestine line of Wettin
dynasty 1485; cap. of Saxe-Gotha 1640–
1826; cap. of Saxe-Coburg-Gotha 1826–
1918. Historic buildings include ducal palaces (17th and 18th cent.). City was damaged in World War II.

Gotham (gō′tŭm), village, Nottinghamshire,
England. Inhabitants reputed to do ridicu-

lous things (e.g., trying to drown an eel). Stories may stem from efforts to prevent King John from living there. Hence, Gotham (gŏ′thŭm), name for New York city, first used by Washington Irving and others in *Salmagundi Papers*.

Gothenburg: see GOTEBORG.

Gothic architecture, style of building practiced in Europe, 13th–15th cent.; sometimes called pointed style because of use of pointed arch and vault. Style is found in its most consistent form in France. Evolving from ROMANESQUE ARCHITECTURE, the Gothic structure consisted basically of open skeleton of stone supporting stone vaulting. Diagonal ribs were introduced to support and strengthen groined vaults, and advent of pointed arch in early 12th cent. made possible a structure of greater height. Flying buttresses (arches of masonry leaning on parts of outer walls to counteract pressure of the vaults) gave greater stability to the structure. Earliest complete expression of skeleton method of construction was Notre Dame, Paris (1163–c.1230); loftiest and most fully evolved French church is Amiens cathedral (1220–88). In England the transition from Norman style to Gothic was made in latter half of 12th cent. Building of Westminster Abbey was directly influenced by the French, but distinctive national styles were evolved. German architecture (e.g., Cologne cathedral) borrowed from France in 13th cent. In Spain and Italy decorative elements tended to overshadow purely structural aspects of Gothic architecture. Medieval artists everywhere produced magnificent sculptures and stained glass as architectural decorations. See *ill.*, p. 61.

Gothic language, East Germanic language. Earliest literary remains in any Germanic tongue are in Gothic Bible of Ulfilas. See LANGUAGE (table).

Gothic revival, a 19th-cent. style of architecture and decoration imitating arts of Middle Ages. Reached its peak in c.1850. In England it gained support of the Church and many medieval structures were restored. Came into conflict with classic revival, with respective exponents taking sides in "battle of the styles." A triumph for Gothicists was building of Houses of Parliament in Perpendicular Gothic in 1840. Revival of interest in arts and crafts, with medieval work as inspiration, was led by William Morris. Movement spread to France, where Viollet-le-Duc became its chief exponent, and to U.S., where it was influenced by Victorian taste and, despite some masterpieces, tended to become trivial and ugly.

Gothic romance, a type of novel which flourished in late 18th and early 19th cent. in England. Mystery of each tale is heavily tinged with horror derived from gloomy background of medieval architecture and with terror of the supernatural. *Castle of Otranto* by Horace Walpole was forerunner of type which flourished in works of Mrs. Ann Radcliffe, M. G. Lewis, and C. R. Maturin.

gothic type: see TYPE.

Goths: see OSTROGOTHS; VISIGOTHS.

Gotland (gôt′lŭnd), Baltic island, SE Sweden,

off coast of Kalmar co. With several smaller islands it forms a county (1,224 sq. mi.; pop. 59,505). Agr., fishing. For its colorful history, see article on its cap., WISBY.

Gottfried von Strassburg (gôt′frēt fŭn shträs′-bŏŏrk), fl. 13th cent., German poet. Ranks among greatest medieval writers for his epic *Tristan* (c.1210), which brings the story to the point where Tristan meets Isolt (see TRISTRAM AND ISOLDE). The poem was concluded by Ulrich von Türheim and Heinrich von Freiberg.

Gottheil, Gustav (gŏt′hīl), 1827–1903, American reform rabbi, b. Prussia, a leader of reform Judaism.

Gotthelf, Jeremias (yārämē′äs gôt′hĕlf), 1797–1854, Swiss author whose real name was Albert Bitzius; a Protestant clergyman. A forerunner of German naturalism, he crusaded against the materialism of his time in the novels *Uli der Knecht* [Ulric the farmhand] (1840) and *Uli der Pächter* [Ulric the tenant] (1849), written partly in Swiss-German idiom.

Göttingen (gû′tĭng-ùn), city (pop. 78,438), Lower Saxony, W central Germany, in Hanover, on Leine R. Mfg. of optical and precision instruments. Its famous university was founded 1737 by Elector George Augustus (later George II of England). When King Ernest Augustus revoked Hanoverian constitution (1837), seven professors (incl. Jakob and Wilhelm Grimm) protested and were summarily dismissed. In late 19th cent. university became a world center for study of mathematics and physics.

Gottsched, Johann Christoph (yō′hän krĭs′tôf gôt′shät), 1700–1766, German poet and critic. He married the famous actress Karoline Neuber. As professor at Leipzig Univ., he dominated the literary scene of the German Enlightenment, advocated classical drama on French model. His influence waned after the attacks of Bodmer and Lessing.

Götz von Berlichingen: see BERLICHINGEN, GÖTZ VON.

Goucher College: see TOWSON, Md.

Gouda (gou′dù, Dutch khou′dä), municipality (pop. 37,283), South Holland prov., W Netherlands. Pottery mfg.; cheese trade. Has Gothic city hall.

Goudy, Frederic William, 1865–1947, American type designer. The most prolific type designer in history (Kennerley, Deepdene, and Garamond are among more than 100 faces), he also wrote about his craft.

Goujon, Jean (gōōzhō′), c.1510–c.1566, French Renaissance sculptor, known for decorations in low relief for buildings. Associated with Pierre Lescot, architect of the Louvre.

Gould, Jay, 1836–92, American capitalist. Helped defeat Cornelius Vanderbilt for control of ERIE RAILROAD. He and James FISK caused BLACK FRIDAY panic. Later, Gould controlled four Western railroads. His son, **George Jay Gould,** 1864–1923, inherited all his father's holdings and, through daring policies, seemed to have a transcontinental system in his grasp. By 1918, however, he lost all his roads.

Gould, Thomas Ridgeway, 1818–81, American sculptor of portrait busts and statues.

Gounod, Charles (shärl′ gōōnō′), 1818–93, French composer. He wrote church music, e.g., *La Rédemption* and *Messe à Sainte Cécile,* but his fame rests chiefly on his operas *Faust* and *Romeo and Juliet.*

gourd (gōrd), fruit of vinelike tender annual plants of several genera related to cucumber, melon, and pumpkin. The dried cleaned fruit shells have been used from ancient times as drinking cups, dippers, bowls, etc., in tropical and Asiatic countries. In U.S. they are mostly grown for decoration.

Gourgues, Dominique de (gōōrg′), c.1530–1593, French soldier and adventurer. Avenged massacre of Huguenot colony of Jean RIBAUT by slaughtering Spanish garrison on Fla. coast (1568).

Gourlay, Robert Fleming (gōōr′lē), 1778–1863, Scottish writer and agitator. Came to Upper Canada in 1817. Led agitation against control of land grants by Family Compact. Banished from province (1819). Sentence was nullified in 1842. Wrote account of Upper Canada (1822) and autobiographical work (1843).

Gourmont, Rémy de (rāmē′ dù gōōrmō′), 1858 1915, French critic. Chief apologist for SYMBOLISTS.

gout, disease characterized by joint inflammation, much uric acid in blood, and deposits of sodium urate crystals about joints. It tends to recur.

Gouthière, Pierre (pyēr′ gōōtyār′), 1740–1806, French metalworker, foremost artist of ornamental bronzes of period of Louis XVI.

Gouverneur (gŭ″vûrnōōr′), resort village (pop. 4,916), N N.Y., S of Ogdensburg. Named for Gouverneur Morris, whose mansion still stands.

Govan (gŭ′vûn), parish (pop. 364,801) of SW Glasgow, Scotland. Has extensive shipbuilding yards and mfg. of chemicals, asbestos, and machine tools.

government ownership: see PUBLIC OWNERSHIP.

Government Printing Office, United States, authorized by joint Congressional resolution (1860), purchased for $135,000 (1861). Its activities, defined by the Printing Act of 1895, include executing orders of Congress and the various Federal offices for printing and binding, distributing government publications, and reprinting documents for public purchase.

Governors Island, 173 acres, SE N.Y., in Upper New York Bay, S of Manhattan isl. (ferry connections). Bought from Indians in 1637 by Dutch governor of New Netherland. Present name adopted in 1784 because colonial governors lived here. Historic landmarks include Fort Jay (early 19th cent.) and Castle Williams (military prison; built 1807–11). Became hq. of 2d Corps Area 1878, of 1st Army 1933.

Gower, John (gou′ûr, gôr), d. 1408, English poet, contemporary and friend of Chaucer. Author of *Confessio Amantis* (c.1393; collection of tales in English verse illustrating Seven Deadly Sins) and of other poems in English, French, and Latin.

Gower (gou′ûr), peninsula, c.15 mi. long and 5 mi. wide, Glamorganshire, Wales, SW of Swansea.

Gowrie, earls of: see RUTHVEN, family.

Goya (y Lucientes), Francisco José de (fränthē′skō hōsā′ dā gō′yä ē lōōthēān′tĕs), 1746–1828, Spanish artist, b. near Saragossa. Gained royal notice with his witty scenes of popular life for tapestry designs. As court painter to Charles III and Charles IV, he did candidly realistic portraits. Most Madrid notables, including the duchess of Alba, posed for him. Mordant social satire fills the three series of etchings: *Caprichos, Proverbios,* and *Tauromaquía* [bullfight]. The great *Desastres de la guerra* [disasters of war] is a terrifying series of etchings, suggested by Peninsular War. At 70 he retired to his villa, which he decorated with macabre paintings, such as *Saturn Devouring his Children* (Prado). Spent last years in Bordeaux. Generally conceded to be greatest painter of his time.

Goyen, Jan Josephszoon van (yän′ yō′zŭfsōn vän gō′yùn), 1596–1656, Dutch landscape painter, one of first to subordinate detail to atmospheric effect.

Gozzi, Carlo, Conte (kär′lō kōn′tä gôt′tsē), 1720–1806, Italian dramatist. He defended the *commedia dell' arte* against Goldoni. His *Fiaba dell' amore delle tre melarance* (1761) inspired Prokofiev's *The Love for the Three Oranges,* and his *Re Turandot* (1762) was made into an opera by Puccini. His brother **Gasparro Gozzi** (gä′spärō), 1713–86, stimulated critical interest in Dante.

Gozzoli, Benozzo (bänōt′tsō gôt′tsōlē), 1420–97, Florentine painter, whose real name was Benozzo di Lese. Assisted Fra Angelico, whose influence is seen in his decorative style. Famous for frescoes in San Gimignano and in Campo Santo, Pisa.

GPU: see SECRET POLICE.

Graaf, Reinier de (rīnēr dù gräf′), 1641–73, Dutch physician, noted for studies on pancreatic juice and generative organs. He discovered the follicles of the ovary known as Graafian follicles.

Grabbe, Christian Dietrich (krĭs′tyän dē′trĭkh grä′bù), 1801–36, German dramatist. His powerful dramas are marked by genius and bizarreness—e.g., *Don Juan und Faust* (1829), *Napoleon* (1831).

Graça Aranha, José Pereira da (zhōōzā′ pĕrā′rù dù grä′sù ärä′nyù), 1868–1931, Brazilian novelist.

Gracchi (grä′kī), two Roman statesmen and reformers; brothers, sons of CORNELIA. **Tiberius Sempronius Gracchus,** d. 133 B.C., the elder, alarmed by the growth of wealth of the few, stood for tribunate in 133 B.C. as an avowed reformer. He passed the Sempronian Law (see AGRARIAN LAWS), to redistribute public lands. At the next election he renominated himself, and the senate postponed the election. In a great riot the following day he was murdered. **Caius Sempronius Graachus** (kā′ŭs), d. 121 B.C., publicly committed himself to avenging his brother and completing his work. Elected tribune (123 B.C.), he initiated a series of remarkable social reforms. He was reelected (122) and proceeded with further schemes, checking the power of consuls and senate. In 121 he was defeated. When repeal of his measures was proposed, riots ensued and he was killed.

grace, in Christian theology, free favor of God towards men necessary for their salvation. Natural graces (e.g., gift of life) are distinguished from supernatural graces, by which God makes man (depraved through original sin) capable of enjoying eternal life. Supernatural grace, keystone of the whole Christian theological system, is usually defined as actual grace, which turns the soul to God, or sanctifying grace, which perpetuates this conversion. Most theologies, except CALVINISM, distinguish prevenient grace, which makes man's will free, from cooperating grace, by which God assists to salvation the free man who seeks it. Grace may be so powerful that a man cannot escape conversion (efficacious grace), or it may be of lesser strength so that a man can reject it though always sufficient for conversion if he accepts it (sufficient grace). As to the means of grace, there is serious cleavage regarding the SACRAMENT. Catholics hold the sacrament actually confers grace; Protestants that it is the sign, not the means, of grace. Certain Christian systems have developed other ideas of grace (e.g., the Society of FRIENDS, who deny original sin). A blessing or benediction is sometimes called grace (notably in grace before and after meals, universally advocated by Christians).

Graces, three Greek goddesses, daughters of Zeus and Eurynome—Aglaia (ăglā'ủ), Thalia (thălĩ'ủ), and Euphrosyne (ūfrŏs'-ínē). They were personifications of beauty and charm. Called Charities by Greeks and Gratiae by Romans.

Gracián, Baltasar (bältäsär' gräthyän'), 1601–58, Spanish philosopher, scholar, satirist, a Jesuit, notable for epigrams. Among his works is *El criticón,* 1651–57.

grackle, name for some members of family of New World orioles and blackbirds. Purple or common grackle of Atlantic coast is black with metallic hues, iridescent in sun. It eats grain and insects and is a cannibalistic nest robber. Bronze grackle found inland, W to Rocky Mts., Florida and boat-tailed grackles in S U.S.; great-tailed or jackdaws in Texas and Mexico.

Graecia Magna: see MAGNA GRAECIA.

Graefe or **Gräfe, Albrecht von** (both: äl'-brěkht fủn grä'fủ), 1828–70, German ophthalmologist, noted for eye surgery and as a teacher. His father, **Karl Ferdinand von Graefe** (kärl fěr'děnänt), 1787–1840, was a pioneer in plastic surgery.

Graetz, Heinrich: see GRÄTZ, HEINRICH.

grafting, method of propagation in which two parts of closely related plants are united so that they grow as one. The scion (a bud or shoot) united with the stock retains its own characteristics. Either seedlings or mature trees may be grafted. The method is particularly important in growing fruit, notably in orange and grapefruit groves.

Grafton. 1 Town (pop. 8,281), S central Mass., SE of Worcester. Mfg. of textiles, leather, and abrasives. **2** City (pop. 7,365), N W.Va., near Fairmont. Rail junction with mfg. of glass products.

Graham, James: see MONTROSE, JAMES GRAHAM, 5TH EARL and 1ST MARQUESS OF.

Graham, Martha, American dancer and teacher of the dance; a leading figure in modern dance. With Denishawn company 1919–23; she made independent debut 1926. Her compositions include *Frontier, Every Soul Is a Circus, Letter to the World* and *Judith.*

Graham, Robert, later **Robert Cunninghame-Graham,** d. 1797? Scottish poet, author of lyric, "If Doughty Deeds My Lady Please."

Graham, Robert Bontine Cunninghame: see CUNNINGHAME GRAHAM, ROBERT BONTINE.

Graham, Thomas, 1805–69, Scottish chemist. He distinguished between colloids and crystalloids, and discovered DIALYSIS. His research on diffusion led to **Graham's law:** rate of diffusion of gas is inversely proportional to square root of density.

Graham. 1 Textile-mill town (pop. 5,026), central N.C., E of Greensboro. **2** City (pop. 6,742), N Texas, S of Wichita Falls. Has cottonseed and flour mills, meat packing and carbon-black plants, and oil refineries. Possum Kingdom L. is near.

Graham Coast: see PALMER PENINSULA.

Grahame, Kenneth, 1859–1931, English writer of children's books, author of *The Wind in the Willows* (1908), a classic.

Graham Island, largest of the Queen Charlotte Isls., W B.C., Canada, in the Pacific Ocean.

Graham Land: see PALMER PENINSULA.

Graham of Claverhouse: see DUNDEE, JOHN GRAHAM OF CLAVERHOUSE, 1ST VISCOUNT.

Grail, Holy, a feature of medieval legend and literature. Appears variously as a chalice, cup, or dish and sometimes as a stone or caldron into which a bleeding lance drips blood. Identified by Christians as chalice of the Last Supper. It would be revealed only to a pure knight; Grail Quest appears in different stories. In Arthurian legend purest knight is variously Parsifal or Galahad. Legend has features of Christian story, Celtic myth, and ancient fertility cults.

grain, name for cereal grasses, certain other plants (e.g., buckwheat), and their edible fruits, which whole or ground supply the main food of man and some domestic animals. Principal grain crops are wheat, Indian corn, oats, barley, rye, and rice; all staple grain crops were domesticated in Neolithic period. In preparing the seedlike fruits of these plants for many uses the husk, outer coat, or bran is removed. To make whole-wheat flour part of the bran is removed; for graham flour whole grain is used.

grain alcohol: see ETHYL ALCOHOL.

Grainger, Percy (Aldridge), 1882–, Australian-American pianist and composer; friend and disciple of Grieg, whose music he often played. Known for his adaptations of folk music, e.g., *Molly on the Shore, Shepherd's Hey, Mock Morris,* and *Country Gardens.*

Gram, Hans Christian Joachim (gräm, Dan. häns krĩs'tyän yō'äkĩm gräm'), 1853–1938, Danish physician. He developed a differential staining method useful in identification and classification of bacteria. Bacteria that retain the dye after immersion in decolorizer are Gram positive; others, Gram negative.

Gramont or **Grammont, Philibert, comte de** (fēlēbĕr' kŏt' dủ grämŏ'), 1621–1707, French courtier. Exiled by Louis XIV, he was prominent at court of Charles II of England

(1663–64). His brother-in-law, Anthony HAMILTON, wrote the celebrated *Mémoires du comte de Grammont,* a racy and thoroughly amoral account of his time.

Grampians, mountain system, cutting NE–SW across central Scotland, separating Highlands from Lowlands. Highest peak is Ben Nevis (4,406 ft.). Wild, magnificent scenery on N side; deer forests on more gently sloping S side.

Gran, Hungary: see ESZTERGOM.

Granada (gränä'dhä), city (pop. 21,743), W Nicaragua, on L. Nicaragua; founded 1524. Was long stronghold of landed aristocracy. Controls extensive commerce on lake.

Granada, city (pop. 140,941), cap. of Granada prov., S Spain, in Andalusia, picturesquely situated in view of the Sierra Nevada. It became in 1238 the cap. of the kingdom of Granada, the last Moorish foothold in Spain, and flourished as a center of Moslem art and culture. Long torn by feuds among the noble families, notably the Zegris and Abencerrages, the kingdom fell to Ferdinand and Isabella of Castile during the reign of Boabdil. The city itself fell in 1492 after a long siege. Its Moorish fortress, the ALHAMBRA, is its most famous monument. Near by is the imposing palace of Emperor Charles V. The late Gothic and plateresque cathedral (16th cent.) is adjoined by a chapel containing the tombs of Ferdinand and Isabella.

Granados (y Campiña), Enrique (ĕnrē'kä gränä'dōs ē kämpē'nyä), 1867–1916, Spanish composer. *Goyescas,* a set of piano pieces which later formed the basis for an opera of the same name, is his best-known work.

Granby, city (pop. 21,989), S Que., Canada, on North Yamaska R. and E of Montreal. Has textile mills and mfg. of furniture and rubber products.

Grand Alliance, War of the, 1688–97, war between France and the powers of the League of AUGSBURG, known as Grand Alliance after 1689. Louis XIV had been promised the support of James II of England, who however was overthrown by William III. French support of counterrevolution in Ireland was frustrated by William's victory at the Boyne (1690). On the sea, also, England was victorious at La Hogue (1692), but on land the French defeated the allies at Fleurus (1690), Namur (1692), Neerwinden (1693), and Marsaglia (1693). The Treaty of RYSWICK ended the war, which in America was known as King William's War (see FRENCH AND INDIAN WARS).

Grand Army of the Republic, organization estab. by Union veterans of Civil War. First post formed at Decatur, Ill., April 6, 1866; first national encampment at Indianapolis, Nov. 20, 1866. Aims were to preserve friendships, honor fallen comrades, aid widows and handicapped, and increase pensions. Members were mostly Republicans; added to that party's strength until 1900. Parallel Southern group, United Confederate Veterans, was founded in 1889. The 83d and last G.A.R. encampment met Aug. 28–31, 1949, at Indianapolis, with 6 of 16 surviving members present.

Grand Bank, town (pop. 2,148), S N.F., Can-

ada, on SE shore of Fortune Bay. Important base for Grand Banks fisheries.

Grand Banks, submarine plateau off SE N.F., Canada, extends 420 mi. E–W and 350 mi. N–S, with depths of 22–100 fathoms. Mostly in the Labrador Current, with E edge in Gulf Stream. Meeting of warm and cold air results in persistent fogs. Probably most important cod-fishing region in world. Fishing endangered by icebergs.

Grand Canal. 1 Chinese *Yun-ho* [transit river], largest canal of China, c.1,000 mi. long, extending from Hangchow to Tientsin. Oldest portion (connecting Yellow and Yangtze rivers) was completed in 7th cent.; remainder built 13th–14th cent. Silting has reduced canal's former economic importance. **2** See VENICE.

Grand Canyon, gorge, c.1 mi. deep, 4–18 mi. wide, and 217 mi. long, of Colorado R., NW Ariz. Visible strata show still-continuing record of geologic change beginning with Archeozoic era. Varicolored layers, steep and embayed rims, and eroded rock forms in chasm catch the light of sun and shadow and glow with changing hues of intense beauty. Discovered by G. L. de Cardenas (1540); boat party taken through by J. W. Powell (1869). Much of canyon now included in Grand Canyon Natl. Park and Grand Canyon Natl. Monument (see NATIONAL PARKS AND MONUMENTS, table).

Grand Coulee, city (pop. 2,741), NE central Wash., on Columbia R. and WNW of Spokane. Work base for **Grand Coulee Dam,** built 1933–41 for power, irrigation, flood control. One of world's largest dams (4,300 ft. long; 550 ft. high). Impounds Roosevelt L. (151 mi. long), a recreational area.

Grand Detour, unincorporated village, N Ill., SW of Rockford and on Rock R. Leonard ANDRUS and John DEERE associated in building first Grand Detour steel plow here 1837.

Grand Falls. 1 Town (pop. 2,365), W N.B., Canada, on St. John R. Falls here attract many visitors. Has large hydroelectric development. **2** Town (pop. c.4,508), central N.F., Canada, on Exploits R. and NW of St. John's. Has large paper mills and hydroelectric plant.

Grand Falls, spectacular waterfalls of upper Hamilton R., S Labrador. River drops 245 ft., then flows 12 mi. through canyon over series of rapids in a total fall of 1,038 ft. Discovered 1839 by John McLean of Hudson's Bay Co., but forgotten and rediscovered 1891.

Grand Forks, city (pop. 26,836), E N.Dak., at junction of Red and Red Lake rivers, N of Fargo; settled 1871. Second largest city in state. Distributing center for spring-wheat region, it has grain elevators, flour mills, creameries, and meat-packing plants. Seat of Univ. of North Dakota (state supported; coed; chartered 1883, opened 1884).

Grandgent, Charles Hall (grän'jŭnt), 1862–1939, American philologist and distinguished student of Italian language and Italian literature.

Grand Haven, city (pop. 9,536), S Mich., on L. Michigan at mouth of Grand R. and NW of Grand Rapids. Port, fishing and mfg. center. Ships grapes and celery. Resort.

Grand Island. 1 City (pop. 22,682), S Nebr., near Platte R., W of Lincoln; settled 1857 by Germans. Rail and processing center for livestock (horses, mules, cattle), dairy, and agr. (grain, fruit, beet sugar) area. U.S. Central Monitoring Station, radio-broadcasting checking point, is near. 2 See NIAGARA, river.

Grand Island, N Mich., in L. Superior N of Munising; one of largest Mich. islands (c.13,000 acres). Wooded area, it is a resort with game refuge.

Grand Junction, city (pop. 14,504), W Colo., at junction of Gunnison and Colorado rivers near Utah line; founded 1881. Resort. Ships and processes livestock, farm produce. Colorado Natl. Monument is near.

Grand Lake. 1 Lake c.2 mi. long, N central Colo., at W edge of Rocky Mt. Natl. Park and in Colorado-Big Thompson project. Resort; has annual yacht race. 2 See GRAND RIVER DAM.

Grand Manan, island (pop. c.2,457), c.16 mi. long and c.7 mi. wide, S N.B., Canada, in Bay of Fundy near entrance to Passamaquoddy Bay. Summer resort and fishing center. Settled after Revolution by Loyalists; claims disputed by U.S. until 1817.

Grand'Mère (grä'mĕr″), city (pop. 11,089), S Que., Canada, on St. Maurice R. and NNW of Trois Rivières. Here are hydroelectric station, paper and woolen mills, and lumbering.

Grand Portage (pôr'tĭj), nine-mile carrying place, famous in American fur trade, in extreme NE corner of present Minn. Led from L. Superior N to widening of Pigeon R.

Grand Prairie, city (pop. 14,594), N Texas, WSW of Dallas. Industrial suburb with aircraft mfg.

Grand Pré (grän′ prā, Fr. grä prā′), agr. village, N N.S., Canada, on Minas Basin. Old village, founded near by c.1675, was early home of Acadians and of Evangeline, heroine of Longfellow's poem.

Grand Rapids. 1 City (pop. 176,515), S Mich., on Grand R. and NW of Lansing. State's second largest city and most famous furniture mfg. and market center in U.S., it also has mfg. of railroad equipment, metal products, chemicals, paint, and food products. Here are furniture museum and Calvin Col. 2 Village (pop. 6,019), N central Minn., on the Mississippi and NW of Duluth. Mfg. of paper and dairy products.

Grand River. 1 River, 165 mi. long, S Ont., Canada, flows into L. Erie at Port Maitland. Navigable for 70 mi. from mouth. 2 Former name of the OTTAWA river, E Ont. and W Que., Canada.

Grand River. 1 See COLORADO, river. 2 River rising in S Michigan and flowing c.260 mi. N, NW and W past Lansing and Grand Rapids (head of navigation) to L. Michigan at Grand Haven. 3 River rising in SW N.Dak. and flowing c.209 mi. ESE through S.Dak. to Missouri R. near Mobridge. 4 River in Okla.: see NEOSHO, river, and GRAND RIVER DAM.

Grand River Dam, NE Okla., in Grand R. (local name of NEOSHO R.) and SE of Vinita. Built for flood control and power (completed 1940). It is 6,565 ft. long, also called Pensacola Dam. Created Grand L.

Grandson (gräsō′), town (pop. 1,726), Vaud canton, Switzerland, on L. of Neuchâtel. Here Swiss defeated Charles the Bold 1476. Also spelled Granson.

Grand Teton National Park: see NATIONAL PARKS AND MONUMENTS (table).

Grandview Heights, city (pop. 7,659), central Ohio, W suburb of Columbus.

Grangemouth, burgh (pop. 15,305), Stirlingshire, Scotland, on the Forth estuary. Has extensive docks and shipyards.

Granger, Francis (grän'jŭr), 1792–1868, American political leader. Defeated as Anti-Masonic party nominee in 1830 and 1832. Later became a leader of conservative Whigs.

Granger movement, American agrarian movement taking its name from the Natl. Grange of the Patrons of Husbandry, organization founded in 1867 by Oliver H. Kelley and others. Local units were called granges and the members grangers. Expanded rapidly after Panic of 1873. Though originally estab. for social and educational purposes, local granges became political forums, channels of protest against economic abuses; sought correction partly through cooperative enterprises. Their political activity secured passage in Ill., Wis., Minn., and Iowa of so-called Granger laws, dealing with railroad and storage rates. So-called Granger Cases challenged constitutionality of these laws (see MUNN VS. ILLINOIS). Inadequacy of state regulation led to demands for national legislation. After 1876 other groups led agrarian protest and granges returned to being social organizations.

Grangesberg, Sweden: see KOPPARBERG.

Grangeville, city (pop. 2,544), N central Idaho, in wheat section of the Camas Prairie and old Nez Percé country. Outfitting point in 1898 gold rush.

Granicus (grŭnī'kŭs), anc. name of small river of Mysia, Asia Minor; now the Turkish Kocabas. Here Alexander the Great defeated Persians in 334 B.C., and Lucullus defeated Mithridates VI in 73 B.C.

granite, hard igneous rock of coarse structure, commonly containing quartz, feldspar, mica. It takes a high polish, and is used for buildings, monuments.

Granite City, industrial city (pop. 29,465), SW Ill., on the Mississippi above St. Louis. Rail center producing metal products and chemicals.

Graniteville, village (pop. 3,362), W S.C., near Aiken. Founded 1846 as state's first mill town by William GREGG.

Granjon, Robert (grän'jŭn, Fr. rōbĕr′ grä zhō′), fl. 1545–88, French designer of type. Worked in Paris, Lyons, Antwerp, and Rome. Created *caractères de civilité,* intended as a French equivalent of italic; though beautiful, they lost out in competition with more legible italic. He is honored by having a later type face named for him.

Gran Paradiso (grän″ pärädē′zō), mountain, 13,323 ft. high, NW Italy, in Alps S of Aosta. It is the highest peak entirely in Italian territory.

Gran Quivira National Monument: see NATIONAL PARKS AND MONUMENTS (table).

Gran Sasso d'Italia (grän säs′sō dētä′lyä),

mountain group, Abruzzi, S central Italy, highest of the Apennines. Culminates at 9,557 ft. in Monte Corno or Corno Grande.

Granson, Switzerland: see GRANDSON.

Grant, Ulysses S(impson), 1822–85, commander in chief of Union army in Civil War, 18th President of the United States (1869–77); originally named Hiram Ulysses Grant. Captured Fort Henry and Fort Donelson in 1862, then fought controversial battle of Shiloh. VICKSBURG CAMPAIGN (1862–63) was great success. Became supreme commander in the West, Oct., 1863. After CHATTANOOGA CAMPAIGN, became commander in chief, March, 1864. Directed WILDERNESS CAMPAIGN (1864) against Lee. Accepted Lee's surrender at APPOMATTOX COURTHOUSE (1865). His campaigns were successful largely because he practiced elementary military doctrine that destruction of enemy's main armies was principal objective in warfare. Made a full general in 1866, first U.S. citizen after Washington to hold that rank. Successful Republican candidate for presidency in 1868; possibly most ill-fitted man for that office nation ever had. Punitive radical reconstruction program was pushed with new vigor; monetary legislation favorable to commercial and industrial interests was passed (see GREENBACK). Grant, though honest himself, associated with disreputable politicians and financiers. In foreign affairs, however, much was accomplished by Secretary of State Hamilton Fish. Grant's *Personal Memoirs* (2 vols., 1885–86) are among the great military narratives of history.

Granta, river, England: see CAM.

Grantham (grăn'tŭm, grăn'thŭm), municipal borough (pop. 23,405), Lincolnshire, England. Here Richard III condemned duke of Buckingham to death (1483) and Cromwell won first victory over royalists (1643). Site of George Hotel described in Dickens's *Nicholas Nickleby.*

Grants Pass, city (pop. 8,116), SW Oregon, W of Medford and on Rogue R. Trade center of farm and lumber area. Oregon Caves Natl. Monument is S.

Granvelle, Antoine Perrenot de (ätwän' pĕrŭnō' dü grävĕl'), 1517–86, cardinal, statesman in service of Emperor Charles V and King Philip II of Spain; b. Besançon, France. As chief adviser to MARGARET OF PARMA (1556–64), he brought Spanish troops and Inquisition into Netherlands. His unpopularity stirred up rebellion and necessitated his recall.

Granville, John Carteret, 1st Earl, 1690–1763, British statesman. Ambassador to Sweden (1719–21), he mediated treaties ending the Northern War. Secretary of state 1721–24, he clashed with Robert Walpole and became (1730–42) leader of the opposition which brought about Walpole's downfall. Became unpopular for favoring George II's Hanoverian policies. Was president of the privy council 1751–63.

Granville, village (pop. 2,653), central Ohio, NE of Columbus. Seat of Denison Univ. (Baptist; coed.; 1831).

Granville-Barker, Harley Granville, 1877–1946, dramatist, actor, producer of G. B.

Shaw's plays. Wrote plays (e.g., *Madras House*), translated others.

grape, woody vine of genus *Vitis,* widely cultivated in N Hemisphere, and its fruit. Varieties of *Vitis vinifera* are native to Mediterranean region and have been cultivated there from ancient times (now also grown in Calif.). They are used for making most WINE and are source of the RAISIN. In U.S. grapes grown E of the Rockies are hybrids or are derived from native species.

grapefruit or **pomelo,** citrus fruit (*Citrus paradisi*), related to orange and lemon, and originally native to SE Asia. The large globular fruit grows in bunches and weighs up to 4–5 lb. Fla., Texas, and Calif. lead in U.S. production.

grape hyacinth, bulbous plant of genus *Muscari,* bearing clusters of dainty blue or white flowers in spring.

grape sugar: see GLUCOSE.

graphite (grǎ'fīt), allotropic form of CARBON, also called plumbago and black lead, soft and greasy with metallic luster. It is used in "lead" of pencils, stove polish, some paints, as a lubricant, etc.

Grasmere, village, Westmorland, England. Dove Cottage, Wordsworth's home 1799–1808, now a museum. De Quincey and Coleridge also lived here. Grave of Wordsworth, his family, and Hartley Coleridge.

grass, any plant of important and widely distributed family Gramineae. Grasses, which have hollow, jointed stems and bladelike leaves, include hay and pasture grasses, the cereals (see GRAIN), sugar cane, and bamboo. See also LAWN.

Grasse, François Joseph Paul, comte de (kŏt' dü gräs'), 1723–88, French admiral. Played crucial part in YORKTOWN CAMPAIGN of American Revolution by blockading York and James rivers, thus bottling up Cornwallis at Yorktown.

Grasse (gräs), town (pop. 13,731), Alpes-Maritimes dept., SE France, in hills above Cannes, in a flower-growing dist. Center of French perfumery industry.

grasshopper, name for leaping insect of order Orthoptera. Common grasshoppers and locusts belong to short-horned grasshopper family. Long-horned family includes katy-did, meadow grasshopper, Mormon, sand, and cave or camel crickets. Most grasshoppers have firm but flexible forewings, membranous underwings, powerful jumping legs, and strong jaws. Many are herbivorous, some carnivorous. See *ill.,* p. 601.

grass-of-Parnassus, perennial plant (*Parnassia*) with green-veined white flowers. Grows in damp places.

Grass Valley, city (pop. 5,283), N central Calif., NE of Sacramento, in gold-mining area. Homes of Lola Montez and Lotta Crabtree preserved here.

Gratian (grā'shŭn), 359–83, West Roman emperor (375–83). Ruled with his brother, VALENTINIAN II. In 378 he made Theodosius I emperor of the East. He took St. Ambrose as adviser and attacked paganism. In 383 he was assassinated by MAXIMUS.

Gratian, fl. 1140, Italian founder of the science of CANON LAW, a monk who taught at Bologna. His great work, the *Decretum,* or

Concordia discordantium canonum, appeared c.1140. A private synthesis, it was used by later popes and became the kernel of the *Corpus juris canonici*.

Grattan, Henry, 1746–1820, Irish patriot statesman. Through his fight to repeal Poynings's Law (1782) the Irish Parliament became free from the English government. Gained Catholics the right to vote in Ireland (1792) and consent for them to sit in Parliament. This latter right was overruled by George III, thus encouraging the Rising of '98.

Gratz, Barnard (gräts), 1738–1801, American merchant, b. Upper Silesia. With his brother Michael Gratz (1740–1811) he estab. firm that acquired land in Ohio, Ky., Ind., and Ill. for pioneer settlement and ran boats on Ohio R. Michael's daughter, **Rebecca Gratz,** 1781–1869, known for her philanthropies in Philadelphia, is remembered chiefly as probable prototype of Rebecca in Scott's *Ivanhoe*.

Grätz or **Graetz, Heinrich** (both: hīn'rĭkh grĕts'), 1817–91, German-Jewish historian, champion of orthodox Judaism, author of *History of the Jews* (1853–75).

Gratz, Rebecca: see GRATZ, BARNARD.

Graubünden, Switzerland: see GRISONS.

Grau San Martín, Ramón (rämōn' grou' sän märtēn'), 1887–, president of Cuba (Sept., 1933–Jan., 1934, 1944–48), a physician, professor of Univ. of Havana.

gravel, rock fragments rounded by water, coarser than sand and classed according to size as pebble, cobble, or boulder gravel. Quartz is commonest constituent. Used in road building and in concrete.

Gravelines (grävlēn'), small Channel port, Nord dept., N France. Scene of Spanish victory over French (1558).

Gravenhage, 's, Netherlands: see HAGUE, THE.

Graves, Frank Pierrepont, 1869–, American educator, commissioner of education and president of Univ. of the State of New York from 1921 to 1940.

Graves, Robert (Ranke), 1895–, English poet, critic, and novelist, best known for historical novels, such as *I, Claudius* (1934). Interested in myth (both in fiction and socioreligious history).

Gravesend (grāv'zĕnd'), municipal borough (pop. 45,043), Kent, England, on S bank of the Thames. Has long been official reception place of London's distinguished visitors and starting place of expeditions. Station of pilots and customhouse officers. Has shipbuilding and mfg. Hq. of Royal Thames Yacht Club. Grave of Pocahontas.

Graves's disease: see THYROID GLAND.

gravitation. Law of gravitation states that all bodies in universe have a mutual attraction for one another. This attractive force is in direct proportion to product of masses of bodies concerned and varies inversely as square of distance between them. Gravitation constant is force exerted by a body with mass of 1 gm. upon another body with same mass at a distance of 1 cm. Law of gravitation was first stated by Isaac Newton but work of Johannes Kepler contributed to it, and experiments of Cavendish helped to establish its universality. **Gravity,** although commonly used synonymously with gravita-

tion, is more accurately defined as that force operating between other bodies and the earth. This force is the cause of a body's having weight; the force is considered to act upon the whole body at a definite point (the center of gravity) within the body. The force of gravity varies slightly in different places, therefore the weight also varies accordingly. Gravity gives to a falling body a uniform acceleration; the value for this acceleration generally used as a standard is 32 ft. per second per second at sea level.

Gray, Asa, 1810–88, American botanist and taxonomist. As Harvard professor and through his writing, he helped popularize study of botany. He was author of *Manual of the Botany of Northern United States* (1848) known in numerous revisions.

Gray, Robert, 1755–1806, American sea captain, discoverer of Columbia R. (1792). First American to circumnavigate globe (1787–90).

Gray, Thomas, 1716–71, English poet; friend of Horace Walpole. His early poems were classical (e.g., odes "To Spring," "On a Distant Prospect of Eton College," both 1742). Most familiar of his works is "An Elegy Written in a Country Churchyard" (1750). "The Progress of Poesy" (1754) is a critical poem. Later verse was near-romantic (e.g., "The Descent of Odin," 1761). He refused the laureateship in 1757 and was made professor of ancient history at Cambridge in 1768.

Gray Eminence: see JOSEPH, FATHER.

grayling, game fish related to salmon, found chiefly in clear, cold, fresh waters of N Hemisphere. It has a high dorsal fin, is usually vivid with mixed purples and blues, sometimes marked with other colors. Its flesh is delicious. Generic name *Thymallus* refers to wild thyme odor. Common grayling (*Thymallus thymallus*) found in European rivers.

Grays Harbor, a Pacific inlet, W Wash., at mouth of Chehalis R. Aberdeen and Hoquiam are on N shore.

Gray's Inn: see INNES OF COURT.

Grayson, David: see BAKER, RAY STANNARD.

Grays Peak: see FRONT RANGE.

Graz (gräts), city (pop. 226,271), cap. of Styria, SE Austria, on Mur R. Second largest city of Austria. Metallurgy; mfg. of machinery. Has Gothic cathedral, several medieval churches (13th–15th cent.), 16th-cent. Landhaus [provincial parliament], museum. Kepler taught at Graz univ. (founded 1585).

Graziani, Rodolfo (rōdōl'fō grätsēä'nē), 1882–, Italian marshal. Viceroy of Ethiopia (1936–37); governor of Libya (1940–41). Resigned after rout by British. Trial for high treason suspended 1949.

greasewood, spiny shrub (*Sarcobatus vermiculatus*) native to alkali soils of W U.S. Leaves are eaten by cattle and hard yellow wood is used as fuel.

Great Australian Bight, wide bay of Indian Ocean, indenting S coast of Australia.

Great Awakening, wave of religious revivals in American colonies in later half of 18th cent. It began in N.J. under the evangelical preaching of Gilbert Tennent. In New England, where the Congregationalists played a leading role, it was stirred by Jonathan Edwards. It was spread by the tour (1739–41) of George Whitefield and by the preaching of Samuel Davies among the Presbyterians of Va. It led to missionary work among Indians by Samuel Kirkland and others. It also caused bitter disputes that resulted in doctrinal changes; swayed social and political thought; and served to build up intercolonial relations and to create a democratic spirit in religion.

Great Barrier Reef, 1,250 mi. long, largest coral reef in world, in Coral Sea, forming natural breakwater for coast of Queensland, Australia. Contains islets with coral gardens and unusual marine life.

Great Barrington, town (pop. 6,712), SW Mass., on Housatonic R., in the Berkshires near N.Y. line. Summer resort and ski center.

Great Basin, interior region of W U.S., E of Sierra Nevada, W of Rocky Mts., NW of Colorado Plateau, NE of Sonoran Desert. Its more than 200,000 sq. mi. comprise most of Nev., W half of Utah, parts of Idaho, Oregon, and SE Calif. Its rugged N–S ranges are divided by deep, flat valleys. Altitude varies from c.10,000 ft. above sea level to 280 ft. below in Death Valley. Little rain falls, streams do not reach ocean (e.g., Humboldt R., Carson R.), most lakes are saline. In ancient era, N part was covered by Bonneville (Great Salt L. is a remnant) and Lahontan Lakes. Basin is scene of silver, gold, other mining, and some irrigated farming.

Great Bear Lake, 200 mi. long and 25–110 mi. wide, N central Mackenzie dist., Northwest Territories, Canada. Drained W by Great Bear R. (flows c.100 mi. to Mackenzie R.). Port Radium on E shore. Waters open about four months of year. Discovered by North West Co. traders c.1800. Fort Franklin built on SW shore by Sir John Franklin 1825.

Great Belt: see BELT, GREAT.

Great Bend, city (pop. 12,665), central Kansas, on Arkansas R. and on old Santa Fe and Chisholm trails; settled 1871. Trade center for wheat and oil region.

Great Berkhampstead, Berkhampstead, or **Berkhamstead** (all: bûrk'ŭmstĕd, bärk'–), urban district (pop. 10,777), Hertfordshire, England. Site of 11th-cent. royal castle associated with many historical figures. Birthplace of William Cowper.

Great Britain, largest of the British Isles. Politically the name is given to England, Scotland, and Wales since Act of Union of 1707. With NORTHERN IRELAND they form the United Kingdom (which earlier included all of IRELAND). Island was originally called BRITAIN. For history, see ENGLAND, SCOTLAND (until 1707), and WALES (until 1284). *The Growth of Empire.* After 1707 Union the government remained as described under England. Founding of BANK OF ENGLAND (1694) showed growing English dominance of world trade and finance. After victories over Holland and France, the empire was expanded in late 18th cent. under the Georges and party leaders Sir Robert WALPOLE, William PITT, Charles James FOX, and

Edmund BURKE. After victories of War of the AUSTRIAN SUCCESSION and SEVEN YEARS WAR Britain's predominance was confirmed in India by Robert Clive and Warren Hastings; in North America by the conquests of James Wolfe. Loss to empire through the AMERICAN REVOLUTION was soon made up by settlements in Australia and New Zealand and by victories in FRENCH REVOLUTIONARY WARS and over NAPOLEON I. Rapid internal changes were caused by the INDUSTRIAL REVOLUTION. Irish grievances were only intensified by union with England (1800). *Commercial Leadership of the World.* In the reign of VICTORIA (1837–1901) prosperity reached a peak. REFORM BILLS brought political reforms, and economic legislation removed the worst social abuses. Pressure from the new LIBERAL PARTY ended slavery (1832). The CORN LAWS were repealed in 1846. Robert Peel's advocacy of free trade split the CONSERVATIVE PARTY. A policy of colonial representative self-government contrasted with further conquests in INDIA. Britain's commercial interests led to OPIUM WAR with China (1840); its European diplomacy to participation in CRIMEAN WAR. Dominating statesmen of late 19th cent. were Liberal William GLADSTONE and Conservative Benjamin DISRAELI. Problems of empire expansion (see BRITISH EMPIRE) led to SOUTH AFRICAN WAR. Creation of the civil service improved government administration. The growth of trade unions increased the power of labor. *Before the Second World War.* The reigns of Edward VII and George V saw tariff and social reforms, reduction of the power of the House of Lords by LLOYD GEORGE, the TRIPLE ALLIANCE and TRIPLE ENTENTE, WORLD WAR I, and the Treaty of VERSAILLES (1918). Problems mounted—reparations, WAR DEBTS, and new relation with Irish Free State. The LABOUR PARTY won its first victory (1924). 1931 saw a government crisis and a world-wide depression from which Britain recovered only slowly. Premiership of Neville CHAMBERLAIN (1937–40) saw policy of preferential tariffs maintained, decline of LEAGUE OF NATIONS, appeasement of Axis by MUNICH PACT (1938), delayed rearmament, pact with Poland, Soviet-German accord, and outbreak of World War II. *The Second World War and Social Change.* After British defeat in Norway, Winston CHURCHILL became war-time coalition prime minister. DUNKIRK was followed by widely destructive air bombings of Britain. Outstanding military leaders were Bernard Montgomery, Archibald Wavell, and Lord Louis Mountbatten. After increasing aid from U.S. the ATLANTIC CHARTER was proclaimed in 1941. Britain took part in international conferences of CASABLANCA, CAIRO, MOSCOW, TEHERAN, and YALTA. Living standards were lowered drastically. German surrender (1945) was followed by a Labour government headed by Clement Attlee. Britain withdrew from India (1948), turned over problem of PALESTINE to UN, and signed a 50-year pact with France, Belgium, Luxembourg, and the Netherlands. Programs of nationalization of industry, socialized medicine, and housing and educational reforms were started. After termination of LEND-LEASE large U.S. loans (see EUROPEAN RECOVERY PROGRAM) failed to stop depletion of Britain's dollar reserve and devaluation of the pound. Conservatives returned to office (1951) under Churchill. For list of British kings see ENGLAND.

Great Chebeague Island (shĭbēg'), SW Maine, in Casco Bay. Resort and residential island.

great Dane: see HOUND.

Great Divide: see CONTINENTAL DIVIDE.

Great Dividing Range, general name for mountains and plateaus roughly paralleling E and SE coasts of Australia. Includes Australian Alps.

Great Falls, city (pop. 39,214), N central Mont., on Missouri R. opposite mouth of Sun R. (irrigation) and near falls for which city is named; founded 1883. Largest city in state. Industrial and commercial center for a power development and for an agr. and mining area. Processes zinc, copper, oil, flour, and livestock. A U.S. Air Force base is near.

Great Fish, river: see BACK, SIR GEORGE.

Great Glen, depression extending NE–SW across Scotland. Traversed by CALEDONIAN CANAL.

Great Lakes, five fresh-water lakes, central North America, between Canada and U.S. Stretching 1,610 mi., they are L. SUPERIOR, L. MICHIGAN (entirely in U.S.), L. HURON, L. ERIE, and L. ONTARIO, out of which flows SAINT LAWRENCE R. French traders first saw lakes in c.1612. War of 1812 ended long English-French struggle for region, and settlement was fast. Erie Canal opening in 1825 accelerated commerce. Huge quantities of iron ore, grain, coal, oil, steel, and manufactured products are shipped out from April until Dec. when winter closes most ports. Shipbuilding and fishing are major industries. The lakes are linked to Mississippi R. and Gulf of Mexico by Illinois R. waterway, to Hudson R. and the Atlantic by N.Y. State Barge Canal.

Great Lakes-Saint Lawrence Seaway and Power Project, proposal by U.S. and Canada to deepen the waterway from W end of L. Superior to the Atlantic via Saint Lawrence R., for passage of ocean-going vessels and creation of water-power sites. Most attention would be given to river between Montreal and L. Ontario, where canals by-passing rapids are too shallow. Bills for joint development failed to pass U.S. Congress in 1932, 1941, 1952.

Great Meadows: see NECESSITY, FORT.

Great Miami (mĭä'mŭ), or **Miami,** river rising in W Ohio and flowing generally SW c.160 mi., past Dayton, to Ohio R. at Ind. line. Little Miami R., to E, enters Ohio R. at Cincinnati.

Great Mother of the Gods, in ancient religions, Mother Earth, goddess of motherhood and of wild things, the symbol of fertility. She was worshiped under many names—Gaea, Rhea, Demeter, Artemis, and Aphrodite in Greece; Magna Mater and Bona Dea in Rome; Cybele in Phrygia; Isis in Egypt; Astarte in Phoenicia; and Ishtar in Babylonia and Assyria. See FERTILITY RITES.

Great Neck, village (pop. 7,759), SE N.Y., on N shore of Long Isl., in summer-estate area.

Great Northern Peninsula or **Petit Nord Peninsula,** NW part of N.F., Canada, extending 170 mi. NNE from Bonne Bay (SW) and White Bay (E) to Cape Bauld (N). Long Range lies along W coast.

Great Ouse, river, England: see OUSE 1.

Great Plains, high, extensive grasslands of W U.S. and Canada; generally level, treeless, semiarid. Bounded W by Rocky Mts., S by Llano Estacado and South Plains of Texas Panhandle, E by level prairies of Mississippi valley. In U.S. they include W parts of N.Dak., S.Dak., Nebr., Kansas, Okla.; E parts of Mont., Wyo., Colo., N.Mex.; and NW Texas. Plateau's elevation slopes gently from 6,000 ft. on W to the 2,000 ft. of prairies on E. Flowing E are the rivers Platte, Republican, Kansas, Arkansas, Cimarron, and Canadian rivers. Wheat raising on this natural grazing land has caused some drought.

Great Rift Valley, geological FAULT system of E Africa and SW Asia, marked by chain of lakes. Ranges in elevation from 1,300 ft. below sea level (Dead Sea) to 6,000 ft. above in S Kenya.

Great Salt Lake, N Utah, W of Wasatch Range. Largest lake W of Mississippi R. (75 mi. long, 50 mi. wide, averages 13 ft. deep, but dimensions fluctuate greatly). Crossed by railroad. A remnant of anc. L. Bonneville fed by Weber, Jordan, Bear rivers; has no outlet. Only brine shrimp survive in extreme salinity. Some islands become peninsulas in low water. Long promontory extends from N shore. Salt wastelands to W now used for auto racing. Lake yields commercial salt. Explored 1825 by James Bridger.

Great Salt Plains Dam, NW Okla., in Salt Fork (Arkansas R. tributary); 5,700 ft. long, 68½ ft. high, completed 1948. Built for flood control and wildlife refuge.

Great Sand Dunes National Monument: see NATIONAL PARKS AND MONUMENTS (table).

Great Schism: see SCHISM, GREAT.

Great Slave Lake, 11,170 sq. mi., S Mackenzie dist., Northwest Territories, Canada, 300 mi. long and 30–140 mi. wide. Drained at W end by Mackenzie R. Discovered 1771 by Samuel Hearne. Gold found in 1930s on N shore and town of Yellowknife estab. as mining center. Receives the Hay (SW) and the Mackenzie (S), which is called **Great Slave** or **Slave River** between L. Athabaska and Great Slave L.

Great Smoky Mountains, part of Appalachian system, W N.C. and E Tenn., between Asheville and Knoxville, and between French Broad and Little Tennessee rivers. Part set aside for national park (estab. 1930). Rise to 6,642 ft. in Clingman's Dome. Folk and Indian museums and trails for hikers are to be found.

Great South Bay, SE N.Y., Atlantic arm between S shore of Long Isl. and barrier beach. Extends c.45 mi. from inlet near Rockaway Beach (W) to Moriches Bay. Both shores are rimmed with resorts and residential communities.

Great Stone Face: see FRANCONIA MOUNTAINS.

Great Wall of China: see CHINA, GREAT WALL OF.

Great Whale, river, rising in N central Que., Canada, and flowing 365 mi. W to Hudson Bay.

Great Yarmouth, Norfolk, England: see YARMOUTH.

grebe (grēb), diving bird related to loon and found on lakes and oceans over most of world. It has short wings, a vestigial tail, smooth plumage, and long, individually webbed toes. Grebes swim and fly well, but walk clumsily. Nests are on floating vegetation or fastened to water plants. Pied-billed grebe is well known in W Hemisphere. See *ill.,* p. 135.

Greco, El (ĕl grĕ′kō), c.1541–1614, Greek painter in Spain, b. Candia, Crete; real name was Domenicos Theotocopoulos. Studied in Venice. Settled 1577 in Toledo, where he painted the famous *View of Toledo* (Metropolitan Mus.). In his own day he enjoyed little popularity, but modern criticism ranks him among the great baroque artists. His typical paintings have elongated, distorted figures and vibrant color contrasted with subtle grays; pervading tone is one of religious ecstasy. Works are best seen in Toledo, Madrid, and the Escorial.

Greece, Gr. *Hellas* or *Ellas,* kingdom (50,147 sq. mi.; pop. 7,460,203), SE Europe, in S Balkan Peninsula and on islands in surrounding Ionian and Aegean Seas (largest EUBOEA and CRETE; islands variously grouped; see CYCLADES, DODECANESE, IONIAN ISLANDS, SPORADES). Continental Greece is cut sharply into two sections at the Isthmus of Corinth. S portion is the Peloponnesus, with Patras as its largest center. More populous and prosperous N has most of the cities, notably the cap., ATHENS, and the ports, PIRAEUS (part of Greater Athens), SALONICA, and KAVALLA. The country is hilly to mountainous, cut by short rivers, some with very fertile valleys. Though predominantly agr., Greece does not grow enough food for its population, and the land has been much eroded because of centuries of goat and sheep raising. The chief exports are tobacco, olive oil, raisins, currants, dried figs, and wine. Some minerals (iron ore, magnesite, chromite, and emery) and sponges are also shipped out. The prevailing religion is the Greek Orthodox.

Ancient Greece. The region had seen the rise and fall of splendid civilizations (see MINOAN CIVILIZATION, MYCENAEAN CIVILIZATION) before Greek-speaking peoples migrated in waves and thoroughly entrenched themselves. Traditional branches of the Greeks are Aeolians, Ionians, and Dorians, who supposedly arrived at different times, the last coming before 1000 B.C. In the mountain-divided lands they developed many independent CITY-STATES, which engaged in a constant succession of wars and alliances. Most important of these were to be Athens, SPARTA, THEBES, and CORINTH. Even before the era celebrated in the poems of Homer the Greeks had looked to the sea and had begun to spread colonies across the Mediterranean that were ultimately to create a net of city-states from the Ionian shores of Asia Minor to Sicily, S Italy, and even to S France and Spain (see MAGNA GRAECIA). All the cities were united by a feeling of being Hellenes; they had common shrines (as at DELPHI) and common celebrations (as the OLYMPIC GAMES). Nevertheless, political disunity was so strong that even when the Persians threatened the Ionian cities there was only a half-hearted union to oppose them in the PERSIAN WARS (500–449 B.C.). When the war was successful the greatest period of Greek history was begun. The city-states, and Athens in particular, felt a surge of cultural development scarcely equaled in world history. Prosperity came to Athens with the aid of the DELIAN LEAGUE, and the age of Pericles was one of glory. Drama and poetry, art, architecture, and philosophy flourished, and Greece became the fountainhead of later Western civilization. The list of great men whose words still echo is astonishing, and the list continued to grow after political misfortune set in; Aeschylus, Sophocles, Euripides, Aristophanes, Phidias, Socrates, Plato, and Aristotle are all well known to all the West. Though Athens lost to Sparta in the PELOPONNESIAN WAR (431–404 B.C.), Athenian thought prevailed. Even in politics, though the city-states varied from monarchy to aristocracy, oligarchy, and tyranny, the idea of democracy was born in Greece. Sparta's short-lived triumph was followed by the hegemony of Corinth and of Thebes, but all soon yielded to the conquest of PHILIP II of Macedon at Chaeronea (338 B.C.). Ironically, this defeat made it possible for Philip's son, ALEXANDER THE GREAT, to carry Greek civilization across the known world. While Greece itself fell prey to wars and conquest (despite the efforts of the Achaean League and the Aetolian League), HELLENISTIC CIVILIZATION spread, and though the Romans by 146 B.C. had reduced Greece to a political cipher, they looked up to the Greeks as bearers of civilization. When the Roman Empire was split (A.D. 395), the E portion, the BYZANTINE EMPIRE, was thoroughly Greek in tradition.

Medieval and Modern Greece. Greece was not an important factor in Byzantine history, and was frequently overrun by barbarians. In the 11th cent. began the Turkish inroads and Norman attacks. The Fourth Crusade led (1204) to disintegration of the empire and creation of the Latin Empire of Constantinople. When the Byzantine Empire was restored (1261–1453), only parts of Greece were recovered, European rulers holding the rest until all fell to the Turks (by 1456). Greece was unimportant in the Ottoman Empire. With the awakening of nationalism in the early 19th cent. the Greeks dreamed of independence and in 1821 commenced a rebellion that, with the leadership of the Ypsilantis and the aid of European liberals, succeeded. In 1827 CAPO D'ISTRIA became president of a Greece whose independence was assured by the battle of Navarino (1827), the Russo-Turkish Treaty of Adrianople (1829), and wide recognition (1832). Civil struggles continued, and the Bavarian king imposed on the Greeks, OTTO I, was finally deposed (1862) and succeeded by GEORGE I. A war with Turkey (1896–97) to obtain Crete was unsuccessful, but later international pressure forced incorporation of Crete into Greek territory (1913). In the Balkan Wars Greece got SE Macedonia and W Thrace. When in World War I King CONSTANTINE insisted on neutrality and resisted joining the Allies even after the Salonica campaigns, the political leader Venizelos led a movement that forced Constantine's abdication (1917) in favor of his son, ALEXANDER. After the war the Greeks were given most of European Turkey and the Bulgarian coast. An attempt to invade Asia Minor led to defeat by the Turks (1922). Under a League of Nations commission Greece and Turkey then exchanged nationals to make their boundary an ethnic as well as a political one. Constantine, who had returned as ruler after the death of Alexander (1920), was deposed again (1922) and succeeded by GEORGE II, who was in turn deposed in 1923 but was restored in 1935 after Greece suffered many warring years as a republic. Shortly Greece was under the dictatorship of METAXAS. In World War II Greece was neutral until invaded by the Italians from Albania (1940). The Greeks gave a good account of themselves, but in 1941 the Germans attacked and were shortly triumphant over resistance of the Greeks and British allies. There resulted organized guerrilla warfare that was successful though there was strife between leftist (ELAS) and rightest (EDES) guerrillas. After the Germans were expelled with some British help (1944), attempts were made to restore the war-ridden country, but bad conditions were made worse by internal strife. Though George II was recalled by plebiscite (1946), Communist-led leftists opposed him and set up a rival government. In 1947 Truman announced U.S. support to anti-Communists, and U.S. aid was poured into Greece. The Communist forces were defeated and some headway made in clearing up the appalling economic conditions left by the war. In 1947 George II died and was succeeded by his brother PAUL. Admission of Greece into the North Atlantic Treaty Organization was made final early in 1952. A new constitution was adopted in 1951.

Greek Anthology, collection of Greek epigrams or short poems, including poetry down to the decay of Byzantium. Edited and added to successively by ancient and medieval scholars; versions of 10th and 14th cent. most used.

Greek architecture began with advent of the Dorians in Greece (before 1000 B.C.) and was evolved between 10th and 6th cent. B.C. The Heræum at Olympia, most ancient temple yet discovered, illustrates beginning of Doric style. Chief Greek works were produced between 700 B.C. and Roman occupation (146 B.C.). Great age was reign of Pericles, in which the architects Callicrates, Mnesicles, and Ictinus flourished and in which the perfected DORIC ORDER appeared in PARTHENON and PROPYLAEA. The Greeks laid masonry without mortar but with joints cut to great exactness. Colors and gilding were used to emphasize decorative sculpture. The IONIC ORDER, evolved in Greek colonies of Asia Minor, was used extensively at Miletus. It appeared after 500 B.C. in Greece proper, where its only great example is the ERECHTHEUM. Latest and most ornate Greek style, CORINTHIAN ORDER, was little used. After shift of power from Greece proper to Asia Minor, Hellenistic architecture arose (4th–3d cent. B.C.) with florid elements, more complicated design, and a new emphasis on city planning. See *ill.*, p. 61.

Greek art may be said to have begun with pottery making (c.900–700 B.C.), marked by abstract, mathematical systems of design. New interest in representation arose between 700 and 600 B.C. Sculpture emerged as dominant artistic form in archaic period (c.625–480 B.C.) with statues of nude walking youths, *kouroi*, which suggest Egyptian prototypes, and draped female figures, which suggest Near Eastern influence. Painters of archaic period depicted many mythological and contemporary scenes as decoration for vases; outstanding masters were Euthymides and Euphronius. Early classical or transitional period (c.480–450 B.C.) tried to find balance between naturalism and abstraction. Classical period or Golden Age (c.450–400 B.C.) aimed to represent the ideal human being, both in form and in character. Significant sculptures of the period are from Athenian Acropolis. In late classical period (400–300 B.C.) emphasis on emotion was increased (esp. in sculptures of Scopas). Among great sculptors who flourished 500–300 B.C. were Praxiteles, Lysippus, Myron, Cresilas, Timotheus, and Bryaxis; the painters included Apollodorus, Zeuxis, Parrhasius, and Apelles. Hellenistic period was last phase of Greek art; its best-known masterpiece is *Victory of Samothrace.*

Greek Church: see ORTHODOX EASTERN CHURCH.

Greek fire, inflammable substance, a "liquid" fire, said to have been invented by Callinicus of Heliopolis who, at Constantinople in reign of Constantine Pogonatus, used it to set fire to enemy ships. Byzantine Greeks used it in early Middle Ages. Chemical nature not known, but probably contained sulphur, various easily inflammable materials, and a substance (e.g., lime) which reacts with water to produce heat.

Greek language, Indo-European language. Modern Greek is derived from the standard Greek (or Koine) of Hellenistic world. The New Testament is written in a form of this. See LANGUAGE (table).

Greek music. Music in ancient Greece was evidently a highly developed art. Few examples are extant, but something about it can be learned from secondary sources, e.g., the third book of Plato's *Republic* and writings on musical theory by Aristoxenus of Tarentum (fl. 4th cent. B.C.). Early Greek music was inseparable from poetry and dancing. Its melodic system was based on the MODE. Music was believed to have an emotional and moral influence. Chief instruments were the oboe-like aulos (used in festivals of Dionysus) and a kind of lyre called the kithara (sacred to Apollo). Notation was indicated by letters. There were two such systems, one vocal and one instrumental. Early in Greek music's history, its relation to physics was recognized. See *ill.*, p. 857.

Greek religion. Sources and history of Greek myth are subject of much argument and conjecture. Religious beliefs in ancient Greece were complex and often contradictory. There was a basic animism, but it was complicated by confusion with local deities. Even in Homer's time, when gods were pictured anthropomorphically, no code of ethics or morals was connected with them. Cults of mortal heroes were common from earliest times. Later, heroes and gods became inextricably mixed in legends. Characteristics and stories of the great gods were drawn from many sources: some stemmed from early worship of the Greeks outside the peninsula, some came from Minoan and Mycenaean civilizations, and some were brought in from Asia and Egypt. ZEUS was ruler of OLYMPIAN gods, whose home was Mt. Olympus but who wandered freely about the world. There were also underworld gods. These dwelt in Hades, ruled by Pluto and PERSEPHONE. The underworld and the cycle of vegetation were the base for ELEUSINIAN MYSTERIES. Other MYSTERIES such as ORPHIC MYSTERIES were connected with worship of DIONYSUS. Mysteries were important for their strong ethical and moral teachings, and their priests were exalted, as were those of the great oracles (see ORACLE; DELPHI). By 5th cent. B.C. literal belief in gods was fading in minds of the educated, and dematerialization of gods into great forces enabled poets and philosophers to picture a cosmos in which moral struggle was paramount.

Greek revival: see CLASSIC REVIVAL.

Greeley, Horace, 1811–72, American newspaper editor, founder of New York *Tribune* (1841). Sought to provide for laboring classes a cheap paper that would be both clean and intelligent. Staff included distinguished talent; his editorials made paper widely known. Supported protective tariff; other causes he advocated included many social reforms. The *Tribune* was popular in the West; many had acted upon Greeley's advice, "Go West, young man, go West." One of first editors to join Republican party. His humanitarian hatred of war often embarrassed Lincoln's administration; at end of Civil War he advocated amnesty for all Southerners. Though an early supporter of U. S. Grant, Greeley encouraged growth of LIBERAL REPUBLICAN PARTY. Party's unsuccessful candidate for President in 1872.

Greeley, city (pop. 20,354), N Colo., NNE of Denver near South Platte R. Rail, trade, processing center for irrigated farms (grain, sugar beets). Cooperative Union Colony was founded here in 1870 by an agent of Horace Greeley.

Greely, Adolphus Washington, 1844–1935, American army officer and arctic explorer. Commanded U.S. expedition to establish one of chain of international circumpolar meteorological stations (1881). Rescued with few survivors (1884). Noted builder of army telegraphic communications. Directed relief operations after San Francisco earthquake. Awarded Congressional Medal of Honor (1935).

Green, Anna Katharine, 1846–1935, American detective-story writer. Her thrillers (e.g., *The Leavenworth Case*, 1878) popularized the master detective.

Green, Duff, 1791–1875, American journalist and politician. His paper, the *United States Telegraph*, supported Pres. Jackson until Green turned to support of J. C. Calhoun and to defense of South on slavery and tariff issues. Later was diplomatic agent to Texas and Mexico.

Green, George, 1793–1841, English mathematician. He worked on equilibrium of fluids and was first to introduce potential as applied to theories of magnetic and electric fields.

Green, Henry, pseud. of Henry Vincent Yorke, 1905–, English novelist, an industrialist. His novels, somewhat experimental in style, combine the comic spirit with a sympathetic detachment. They include *Living* (1929), *Loving* (1945), *Back* (1946), *Nothing* (1950), *Doting* (1952).

Green, Hetty (Howland Robinson), 1835–1916, American financier. Managed inherited fortune so shrewdly that she was considered greatest woman financier in the world.

Green, John Richard, 1837–83, English historian. His *A Short History of the English People* (1874) stressed social rather than political change.

Green, Julian, 1900–, French writer, of American origin. Studied in U.S. Author of somber psychological tales (*The Closed Garden*, 1927; Eng. tr., 1928), journals (1938–39; Eng. tr., *Personal Record*), and reminiscences (*Memories of Happy Days*, 1942).

Green, Paul, 1894–, American author, b. N.C. His works include plays (e.g., *In Abraham's Bosom*, 1926), short stories, and a novel (*Laughing Pioneer*, 1932). Has also written symphonic dramas (*The Lost Colony*, 1937; *The Common Glory*, 1948) dealing with American history.

Green, Samuel Swett, 1837–1918, American librarian. One of the founders and president (1891) of American Library Association; author of *The Public Library Movement in the United States, 1853–1893* (1913).

Green, Seth, 1817–88, pioneer American pisciculturist, credited with making large-scale fish breeding practical. He transplanted Atlantic shad to Pacific.

Green, Thomas Hill, 1836–82, English neo-Hegelian philosopher. Asserted that consciousness made knowledge possible, thus setting idealism against prevailing empiricism and sensationalism. His *Prolegomena to Ethics* (1883) was an influential book.

Green, William, 1873–1952, American labor leader, president of American Federation of Labor (1924–52). Built up A.F. of L.; led fight with C.I.O.

Greenaway, Kate, 1846–1901, English illustrator of children's books and water-color painter.

greenback. In 1862 U.S. government first issued, on a temporary basis, legal tender notes (popularly called greenbacks) which were placed on a par with notes backed by specie. By end of Civil War such notes were outstanding to amount over $400,000,000. In accordance with Funding Act of 1866 Secretary of State Hugh McCulloch began retiring them. Hard times in 1867 led to demand that currency should be inflated rather than contracted; Congress suspended retirement. In 1868 a compromise left greenbacks to amount of $356,000,000 in circulation. Law creating them was declared constitutional in later LEGAL TENDER CASES. Following Panic of 1873 agrarians wanted currency inflated with more greenbacks. Conservatives triumphed with Resumption Act of 1875, which fixed Jan. 1, 1879, as date for redeeming greenbacks in specie. Congress provided in 1878 that greenbacks then outstanding ($346,681,000) remain permanent part of currency.

Greenback party, in U.S. history, political organization formed in years 1874–76 to promote currency expansion. Members were principally Western and Southern farmers; stricken by Panic of 1873, they wanted inflated currency because it would wipe out farm debts contracted in times of high prices. Failing to capture the Democratic party in 1874, Greenback party nominated Peter Cooper for President in 1876; got only 81,737 votes. In 1878, however, the Greenback-Labor party, representing a union of labor and greenback supporters, polled over 1,000,000 votes and elected 14 Representatives to Congress. Party dissolved after 1884 election. Many members later became Populists.

Green Bay, city (pop. 52,735), NE Wis., at mouth of Fox R. and on Green Bay. Here Jean Nicolet estab. trading post 1634, and Father Allouez a mission 1669. Oldest permanent settlement in Wis., estab. 1701. Augustin LANGLODE chief early fur trader. French had fort here from 1717, which British held from 1761 until PONTIAC'S REBELLION. U.S. Fort Howard built 1816. Furs lost importance after opening of Erie Canal and expansion of lumbering and farming. Shipping, wholesale, and jobbing trade center; processing paper and cheese. Has professional football team, Green Bay Packers.

Green Bay, W arm of L. Michigan, c.100 mi. long, indenting NE Wis. and along Mich. Upper Peninsula.

Greenbelt, town (pop. 7,074), W central Md., near Washington, D.C.; chartered 1937. Garden city constructed by the Federal Resettlement Administration as model community (others are Greenhills, Ohio, and Greendale, Wis.). Businesses are cooperatively owned.

greenbrier: see SMILAX.

Greencastle, city (pop. 6,888), W central Ind., WSW of Indianapolis. Rail and trade center for agr. and livestock area. Produces zinc and lumber. Seat of DePauw Univ. (Methodist; coed.; 1837).

Greendale, village (pop. 2,752), SE Wis., near Milwaukee. A Federal Resettlement Association garden city (see GREENBELT, Md.).

Greene, Graham, 1904–, English writer. Earlier novels gave literary merit to "shockers" (e.g., *Brighton Rock*, 1938); later deal with Catholic themes (e.g., *The Heart of the Mat-*

ter, 1948; *The End of the Affair*, 1951). Also powerful short stories.

Greene, Nathanael, 1742–86, American Revolutionary general. Commander in CAROLINA CAMPAIGN.

Greene, Robert, 1558?–92, English dramatist, poet, miscellaneous writer. His short romantic "novels" (e.g. *Pandosto*, 1588) were popular. His plays, pseudo-historical in tone, include *Friar Bacon and Friar Bungay* (1594) and *James IV* (1598). Among his many didactic tracts, those on cony-catching show sordid London underworld.

Greeneville, town (pop. 8,721), NE Tenn., SW of Johnson City, in tobacco and farm area. Cap. of State of FRANKLIN 1785–88. Has Andrew Johnson Natl. Monument (his home, tailor shop, grave), monument to Gen. J. H. Morgan (killed here in Civil War). Tobacco experiment station and Tusculum Col. (coed.; 1794) are near by.

Greenfield. 1 City (pop. 6,159), central Ind., E of Indianapolis. Birthplace of J. W. Riley. **2** Town (pop. 17,349), including Greenfield village (pop. 15,075), NW Mass., near junction of Deerfield R. with Connecticut R.; settled 1686. Mfg. of metal products. E terminus of Mohawk Trail.

Greenfield Village, reproduction of early American village, estab. 1933 by Henry Ford at Dearborn, Mich., as part of Edison Inst. About a typical New England village green are grouped public buildings and other structures, including Edison's Menlo Park workshop, Noah Webster's birthplace, Stephen Foster's home. Mills and craft shops illustrate early methods.

Greenhills, village (pop. 3,005), SW Ohio, near Cincinnati; estab. 1938 by Federal Resettlement Administration. See GREENBELT, Md.

greenhouse, enclosed glass house used for growing plants in regulated temperatures and humidity. In size range from lean-to type attached to home to large commercial buildings or hothouses for growing flowers and vegetables out of season.

Greenland, Dan. *Grønland,* Danish colony (c.840,000 sq. mi.; pop. 21,412), island, largely within Arctic Circle, between Canada (W) and Iceland (E); max. length 1,660 mi., max. width 750 mi. Geologically part of Canadian shield, Greenland is covered by an ice sheet (over 8,000 ft. thick in some places) ringed with mountains, except for c.132,000 sq. mi. of coastland. Numerous glaciers (Humboldt is largest), which "calve" icebergs, debouch into coastal fjords. Over 90% of pop. lives on warmer W coast. Natives are mostly of mixed Danish and ESKIMO ancestry. Greenland is administered by board of governors at Copenhagen. Important settlements are Godthaab and Godhavn. Chief resources are minerals (esp. cryolite at Ivigtut; also lignite and graphite). Agr. and sheep grazing are limited to SW, but Peary Land supports musk oxen. There are cod and halibut fisheries, and seals and walruses are hunted. Entire trade of Greenland is a state monopoly. Island was discovered and colonized (c.982) by ERIC THE RED, but it fell into neglect in 14th and 15th cent. and was not rediscovered until 16th cent. Then coast was charted by seekers of Northwest Passage. Modern colonization was begun (1721) by a Norwegian missionary, Hans Egede. Greenland was explored and mapped by many arctic explorers in 19th and 20th cent. In World War II, U.S. estab. (1940) a consulate at Godthaab and received permission to set up military bases. In late 1952 a huge strategic air base was under construction at THULE. A plan for raising Greenlanders' economic, educational, and hygienic standards was drafted in 1946.

Greenland Sea, arm of Arctic Ocean, off NE coast of Greenland. Main outlet of Arctic Ocean to Atlantic. Due to ice it is rarely open to navigation.

Green Mountain Boys, popular name of partisan armed bands in present Vt. Defended region against New York control in NEW HAMPSHIRE GRANTS controversy. Chief leader was Ethan ALLEN. In American Revolution they captured Ticonderoga in 1775 and won victory at Bennington in 1777.

Green Mountains, range of the Appalachians extending from Que. (N) to Mass. (S); generally low (2–3,000 ft.), but rising to 4,393 ft. in Mt. Mansfield, NW of Montpelier. This peak, highest in Vt., has pre-1860 hotel at summit and deep gorge, Smugglers Notch, at foot. There are many streams (water power) and fertile valleys. Noted for scenic beauty; many resorts. Yield marble and granite.

Greenock (grē'nŭk, grĭ-), burgh (pop. 76,-299), Renfrewshire, Scotland, on S shore of Firth of Clyde. A port, it has shipbuilding and varied mfg. Has unusually heavy rainfall. Birthplace of James Watt.

Greenough, Horatio (grē'nō), 1805–52, American sculptor, b. Boston. Worked in Florence 1829–51. His colossal statue of Washington is in Smithsonian Institution building, Washington, D.C.

Green River. 1 River rising in central Ky. and flowing 370 mi. WNW to Ohio R. near Evansville, Ind. **2** River, 730 mi. long, rising in W Wyo. in Wind River Range and flowing through W Wyo. and E Utah, with loop in NW Colo., to Colorado R. in SE Utah. Largest tributary of the Colorado, it receives Yampa, White, Black Fork, Duchesne, Price, and San Rafael rivers. Large U.S. reclamation project planned.

Greensboro, city (pop. 74,389), central N.C., E of Winston-Salem in piedmont; settled 1749. Rail junction and textile center. Seat of Bennett Col. (Negro; Methodist; for women; 1873); Woman's Col. of Univ. of NORTH CAROLINA; Agricultural and Technical Col. of North Carolina (Negro; land-grant, state supported; coed; chartered 1891, opened 1893); and Guilford Col. (Friends; coed; 1834). Birthplace of O. Henry. Battle of Guilford Courthouse was near.

Greensburg. 1 City (pop. 6,619), SE Ind., SE of Indianapolis. Trade center for agr., oil, and gas area. Ships tobacco. **2** City (pop. 16,923), SW Pa., SE of Pittsburgh; settled 1782. Mfg. of plumbing supplies and metal products. Seat of Seton Hill Col. (R.C.; for women; 1883).

Greenville. 1 City (pop. 6,781), S Ala., SSW of Montgomery, in cotton, truck, pecan area. **2** City (pop. 6,668), S Mich., NE of Grand Rapids. Potato market; mfg. of refrigerators. **3** City (pop. 29,936), W Miss., on Mississippi R. and NW of Jackson. Trade, processing, and shipping center of Mississippi-Yazoo delta (cotton). Flood of 1927 caused building of higher levees and creation of L. Ferguson. **4** Town (pop. 16,724), E N.C., on Tar R. and ESE of Raleigh; founded 1786. Tobacco market. **5** City (pop. 8,859), W Ohio, NW of Dayton. Trade center of agr. area. Gen. Anthony Wayne built Fort Greenville 1793, and negotiated Treaty of Greenville 1795 with Indians, who ceded large part of Old Northwest to U.S. **6** Borough (pop. 9,210), W Pa., near Ohio border NNE of Sharon. Trade center in agr. area. **7** City (pop. 58,161), NW S.C., in piedmont near Blue Ridge on Reedy R., laid out 1797. A main SE U.S. industrial and commercial center, it processes textiles and farm produce, and has packing plants and other industries. Center of mill-town region. Has biennial Southern Textile Exposition. Seat of Furman Univ. (Baptist; 1825; coordinated with Greenville Woman's Col. 1933). **8** City (pop. 14,727), E Texas, NE of Dallas; settled 1846. Cotton growing, processing, and shipping center with oil refineries.

green vitriol: see COPPERAS.

Greenwich (grĭ'nĭj), metropolitan borough (pop. 91,492) of SE London, England, on the Thames. Located here are the Royal Naval Col., Greenwich Hospital (on the site of a former palace where Henry VII, Mary I, and Elizabeth were born), and the Natl. Maritime Mus. The Royal Observatory was located until 1946 on a hill in Greenwich Park selected by Sir Christopher Wren. Geographic longitude is still figured from the prime meridian here.

Greenwich. 1 (grē'nĭch) Residential and resort town (pop. 40,835), extreme SW Conn., on Long Isl. Sound at N.Y. state line. Purchased from Indians 1640; raided by British 1779. Includes villages, e.g., Riverside, Old Greenwich, Cos Cob. Printing and publishing. Has Edgewood and Rosemary Hall schools. Audubon Nature Center (1943) is near. **2** (grĕn'wĭch) Village, SW N.J., SW of Bridgeton. Scene of a tea-burning "party" 1774.

Greenwich Village (grĕ'nĭch), district of lower Manhattan borough of New York city, lying roughly between 14th St. (N) and Houston St. (S), Washington Square (E) and Hudson R. (W). Separate village in colonial times, it became, successively, exclusive residential area, tenement area, and (c.1910) home and workshop of nonconformist artists, writers, and theater people. Many artists still live here. Visitors are attracted by lingering aura of bohemianism which surrounds picturesque streets and buildings. Holds semi-annual outdoor art exhibits.

Greenwood. 1 City (pop. 18,061), W central Miss., on Yazoo R. and N of Jackson; settled 1834. Processing, marketing, and shipping center of cotton area. **2** City (pop. 13,-806), W S.C., WNW of Columbia; settled 1824. Has textile and lumber mills, foundries, and machine shops. Buzzard Roost hydroelectric development near by.

Greenwood Lake, c.7 mi. long, SE N.Y. and N N.J., in mountain resort area.

Greer, town (pop. 5,050), NW S.C., NE of Greenville. Has textile mills.

~eet, (Sir Philip) Ben, 1857–1936, English ~tor and theatrical manager. Noted for pro-~ions of Shakspere and of morality play, *~yman.*

Gre~~, Josiah, 1806–50, American trader, historian of Santa Fe Trail. Wrote *Commerce of the Prairies* (1844), classic of American frontier history.

Gregg, William, 1800–1867, "father of Southern cotton manufacture." Estab. Graniteville, S.C. (1846), first Southern mill town.

Gregorian chant: see PLAIN SONG.

Gregory I, Saint (the Great), c.540–604, pope (590–604), Doctor of the Church. A Roman prefect, he gave his property to the Church and became a monk. Though he resisted each promotion, his abilities carried him finally to the papacy. His rule was notable for the firmness with which he defended his office and Rome, attacking Donatism in Africa, refusing to recognize the patriarch of Constantinople as ecumenical (an act that helped split East and West), treating with attacking Lombards (592) after the imperial exarch failed to act. Gregory did much to shape the history of the Church for centuries; he encouraged the spread of monasticism, made laws for the lives of the clergy, and sent missionaries to England. He wrote much and well (commentaries on Job; saints' lives; *Pastoral Care*) and contributed to development of Gregorian chant or PLAIN SONG.

Gregory VII, Saint, d. 1085, pope (1073–85) (Hildebrand; Ital., *Ildebrando*). A Benedictine, he became a notable figure under Pope Gregory VI, and under Leo IX launched the Hildebrandine reform, aimed at correcting chief Church abuses of simony, lay INVESTITURE, and violation of clerical celibacy. As chief figure in the curia under Leo's successors, he transferred papal election from the Romans to the college of cardinals and formed an alliance with the Normans of S Italy. A powerful antireform party grew among laymen who feared church domination; with this ambitious German King HENRY IV sided. Hildebrand, made pope (1073) as Gregory VII, pressed his reform and sent papal legates throughout Europe enforcing his decrees. The quarrel between Henry and Gregory came to an open break in 1076. The pope excommunicated Henry, who, losing his support, humbled himself before Gregory at Canossa. In 1080 the two again fell out. Henry, again excommunicated, set up GUIBERT OF RAVENNA (Clement III) as antipope. Gregory's appeal to the Christian world failed, and when the German civil war ended Henry marched into Italy. He took Rome (1083) and Gregory retired into the Castel Sant' Angelo. The Normans under ROBERT GUISCARD rescued him but were quickly expelled from Rome. Gregory went with them; he died in Salerno after a year of exile. His last words were said to be, "I have loved justice and hated iniquity, therefore I die in exile." His extreme assertion of papal prerogative

and devotion to reform made him one of the most powerful and greatest of the popes. He was canonized in 1728. Feast: May 25.

Gregory IX, 1145–1241, pope (1227–41); nephew of Innocent III. He excommunicated Emperor FREDERICK II for delaying to fulfill his vow to go on crusade (1227). Imperialists in Rome then revolted, and the pope fled to Viterbo and Perugia. Later, in a struggle over Italian liberties Gregory again excommunicated Frederick and ordered his dethronement. Frederick prevented German publication of the bulls and blocked a general council. Gregory died as Frederick was about to attack Rome.

Gregory XI, 1330–78, pope (1370–78), a Frenchman (Pierre Roger de Beaufort). He received prophetic warnings from St. Bridget of Sweden and St. CATHERINE OF SIENA to remove papacy from Avignon to Rome, but Avignon court was opposed and Italy inhospitable. He defeated Bernabò Visconti of Milan with hired aid of Sir John de Hawkwood (1374). A struggle with Milan and Florence ensued, ending with the interdict on Florence. Gregory finally consented to Catherine's pleas and moved to Rome (1376–77). Gregory first condemned Wyclif. Elections after his death began the Great SCHISM.

Gregory XII, c.1327–1417, pope (1406–15). He agreed before his election during course of Great SCHISM to resign if Avignon antipope Benedict XIII (Pedro de LUNA) would also resign. The agreement failed, and Gregory created four new cardinals despite agreement against new creations. But the cardinals united in convoking the Council of Pisa (1409), which declared pope and antipope deposed, and elected a new antipope, Alexander V. After years of confusion the Council of CONSTANCE recognized Gregory as canonical pope, after which he resigned.

Gregory XIII, 1502–85, pope (1572–85), best known for his reformed Gregorian CALENDAR. He was prominent in the Catholic Reform and at Council of TRENT (1545, 1559–63). As pope, he proposed deposition of Queen Elizabeth, refused to compromise with German Protestants, and held public thanksgiving at Rome for the massacre of St. Bartholomew's Day (having been told it was suppression of a rebellion). Issued new edition of the canon law. His government of Papal States was execrable.

Gregory XVI, 1765–1846, pope (1831–46); a conservative, much denounced by European liberals. His most famous act was condemnation of LAMENNAIS (1832).

Gregory, Augusta (Persse) Gregory, Lady, 1859–1932, Irish author and playwright. A founder of the ABBEY THEATRE, she devoted many years to managing and directing it and writing for it. Her journals are a vivid source of Irish literary history.

Gregory, Horace, 1898–, American poet and critic.

Gregory, James, 1638–75, Scottish mathematician. He invented a reflecting telescope and a photometric mode of measuring the distance of stars.

Gregory Nazianzen, Saint (nāzēăn′zĭn), c.330–390, Cappadocian theologian, Doctor of the

Church. An intimate of St. Basil the Great, he was chosen bishop of Constantinople (379), but on the failure of the First Council of Constantinople, he retired. Feast: May 9.

Gregory of Nyssa, Saint (nĭs′ū), d. 394, bishop of Nyssa, Cappadocia (after 371); brother of St. BASIL THE GREAT; one of great orthodox Catholic writers on Trinity, redemption, grace. Feast: March 9.

Gregory of Tours, Saint, 538–94, French historian, bishop of Tours (from 573), author of *History of the Franks.* Feast: Nov. 17.

Greiz (grīts), city (pop. 45,410), Thuringia, central Germany; until 1918 cap. of principality of REUSS (older line). Textile, paper, chemical mfg.

Grenada (grĭnā′dū), island (c.119 sq. mi.), British West Indies. Part of Grenada colony (133 sq. mi., pop. 72,387), in Windward Isls.; cap. Saint George's.

Grenada (grĭnā′dū), city (pop. 7,388), N central Miss., on Yalobusha R. and NW of Greenwood, in cotton and timber area.

grenadine: see POMEGRANATE.

Grenfell, Sir Wilfred (Thomason), 1865–1940, English Protestant medical missionary. Served 40 years in Labrador and Newfoundland among fishermen and Eskimos.

Grenoble (grŭnō′blŭ), city (pop. 97,287), cap. of Isère dept., SE France, on Isère R.; historic cap. of Dauphiné. Mfg. (paper, cement); electrical industries. Famous university estab. 1339. Among notable buildings are cathedral (12th–13th cent.), Church of St. André (13th–14th cent., with tomb of Bayard), and Renaissance palace of dauphins. Birthplace of Stendhal. Grande CHARTREUSE is near by.

Grenville, George, 1712–70, British prime minister (1763–65). Initiated unpopular prosecution of John Wilkes and caused unrest in America by ill-advised STAMP ACT (1765). His son, **George Nugent Temple Grenville, 1st marquess of Buckingham,** 1753–1813, Whig member of Parliament (1774–79), opposed Lord North's policy of coercion of the American colonies. His brother, **William Wyndham Grenville, Baron Grenville,** 1759–1834, was William Pitt's foreign secretary 1791–1801. In 1806 he formed the "ministry of all the talents" which abolished the slave trade.

Grenville, Sir Richard, 1542–91, English naval hero. Commanded fleet carrying first colonists to ROANOKE ISLAND in 1585. On an expedition to capture Spanish treasure ships in 1591, his ship *Revenge* became separated from the rest of the fleet. He tried to break through the Spanish line, fought 15 ships, and was mortally wounded.

Grenville, William Wyndham Grenville, Baron: see GRENVILLE, GEORGE.

Gresham's law (grĕ′shŭmz), economic principle that "bad money drives out good," i.e., when debased money is in concurrent circulation with money of high value in terms of precious metals, the good money disappears. Named for Sir Thomas Gresham (1519?–1579), English merchant and financier, though it has now been shown that he did not originate it.

Gretchaninov, Aleksandr (Tichonovich) (ŭlyĭk-săn′dùr grĕchänē′nöf), 1864–, Russian composer. Although he wrote symphonies and operas, he is best known for his many songs and sacred choral works. Settled in the U.S. 1939.

Gretna, city (pop. 13,813), SE La., S of New Orleans. Industrial and residential suburb.

Gretna Green or **Gretna,** parish (pop. 2,857), Dumfriesshire, Scotland. Famous as a place of runaway marriages 1754–1856.

Grétry, André Ernest (ädrā′ ĕrnĕst′ grātrē′), 1741?–1813, French composer, master of the *opéra comique.* His masterpiece is *Richard Cœur-de-Lion.*

Greuze, Jean Baptiste (zhä′ bäptĕst′ grûz′), 1725–1805, French genre and portrait painter. Tried to paint according to Diderot's aesthetic theories.

Greville, Fulke: see BROOKE, FULKE GREVILLE, 1ST BARON.

Grévy, Jules (zhül grāvē′), 1807–91, president of France (1879–87); a moderate republican.

Grew, Joseph C(lark), 1880–, American diplomat. U.S. ambassador to Japan from 1932 until Pearl Harbor, he was earlier ambassador to Turkey (1927–32) and twice served as Undersecretary of State (1924–27, 1944–45).

Grew, Nehemiah, 1641–1712, English botanist, physician. He practiced medicine in London and made important microscopic studies of plants. His observations of sex in plants were probably the first.

Grey, Charles Grey, 2d Earl, 1764–1845, British prime minister (1830–34). Put through Wilberforce's act to abolish African slave trade (1807). Secured passage of Reform Bill of 1832 by forcing William IV to threaten to create enough Whig peers to carry it in the House of Lords. His grandson, **Albert Henry George Grey, 4th Earl Grey,** 1851–1917, English statesman, was liberal member, House of Commons (1880–86); opposed Home Rule Bill of 1886. Governor general of Canada (1904–11).

Grey, Lady Jane, 1537–54, candidate for the throne of England; greatniece of Henry VIII. Married to the son of duke of Northumberland who persuaded Edward VI to name her as his successor. Unwillingly proclaimed queen (1553), she was imprisoned after nine days and Mary I became queen. Her father joined Wyatt's rebellion and she was beheaded.

Grey, Zane, 1875–1939, American writer of many Wild West tales (e.g., *Riders of the Purple Sage,* 1912).

greyhound: see HOUND.

Greylock, peak, Mass.: see BERKSHIRE HILLS.

Grey of Fallodon, Edward Grey, 1st Viscount (fä′lŏdŭn), 1862–1933, British statesman. Foreign secretary (1905–16), he worked long but fruitlessly to avert war in Europe.

Griboyedov, Aleksandr Sergeyevich (ŭlyĭksän′dùr sĭrgā′ŭvĭch grĕbŭyĕ′dŭf), 1795–1829, Russian playwright, author of *The Misfortune of Being Clever* (1825; Eng. tr., 1914), a satire on Moscow society.

Gridley, Charles Vernon, 1844–98, U.S. naval officer. To him Adm. Dewey said, "You may fire when you are ready, Gridley," at Manila in 1898.

Grieg, Edvard (ĕd'vär grēg'), 1843–1907, Norwegian composer. He often used Norwegian folk themes in his music. Apart from the Piano Concerto in A Minor, his most successful work was in the small forms—songs and piano and chamber music. His suites for Ibsen's *Peer Gynt* are very popular.

Grien, Hans Baldung: see BALDUNG, HANS.

Grierson, Sir George Abraham, 1851–1941, Irish philologist. He directed compilation of the great *Linguistic Survey of India* (19 vols., 1894–1927).

Griffenfeld, Peder Schumacher, Count (pā'dhŭr shoō'mäkhŭr, grĭ'fünfĕlt), 1635–99, Danish statesman; created count 1673. Secretary to Frederick III, 1665–70; chief minister to Christian V, 1671–76. Introduced absolute monarchy; centralized administration; promoted trade, industry, peace. Opposition of nobles and army led to his fall and trial on trumped-up treason charges. Death sentence was commuted to life imprisonment.

Griffes, Charles Tomlinson (grĭ'fĭs), 1884–1920, American composer. His best-known works combine elements of romanticism and impressionism (e.g., *The Pleasure Dome of Kubla Khan* and *The White Peacock*).

Griffin, city (pop. 13,982), W central Ga., S of Atlanta, in cotton, truck, and fruit area; laid out 1840. Textile mfg. and food processing.

griffin, in anc. and medieval mythology, animal represented as a cross between lion and eagle. Conspicuous in Assyrian and Persian sculpture. In heraldry it symbolizes vigilance. Origin traced to Hittites.

Griffith, Arthur, 1872–1922, Irish statesman, founder of SINN FEIN. Served cause by propaganda in his newspapers. Commanded revolution in De Valera's absence. First president (1922) of Free State.

Griffith, David Wark, 1875–1948, American film director and producer. Began (1908) association with Biograph Company as scenarist and actor, then as director. Evolved many film techniques (e.g., cross-cutting, flashback, fade-in, fade-out). His experiments were summed up in first notable long American film, *Birth of a Nation* (1915). Among his other films are *Intolerance* (1915), *Broken Blossoms* (1919), and *Orphans of the Storm* (1921).

Grignard, Victor (vēktôr' grēnyär'), 1871–1935, French chemist. He shared 1912 Nobel Prize for work in organic synthesis based on discovery of **Grignard reagent:** halogen compound used with other substances to synthesize organic compounds.

Grijalva, Juan de (hwän' dä grēhäl'vä), d. 1527, Spanish explorer. Led expedition to Yucatan (1518).

Grillparzer, Franz (fränts' grĭl'pärtsŭr), 1791–1872, Austrian dramatist. His plays, notable for power and poetic beauty, include *Der Traum: ein Leben* (1817–34); *Des Meeres und der Liebe Wellen* (1819); the posthumous *Die Jüdin von Toledo.*

Grimaldi, Giovanni Francesco (jōvän'nē fränchä'skō grēmäl'dē), 1606–80, Italian painter and architect, called Il Bolognese.

Grimaldi, Joseph (grĭmäl'dē), 1779–1837, English pantomime actor and clown. A master of grimace and of stagecraft, he was so popular that his songs were demanded long after his death.

Grimké, Angelina Emily (grĭm'kē), 1805–79, American abolitionist and feminist, b. Charleston, S.C. She and her sister, **Sarah Moore Grimké,** 1792–1873, settled in North and worked for freedom of slaves and woman's rights. Their nephew, **Archibald Henry Grimké,** 1849–1930, son of slave mother, was a lawyer, author, and crusader for Negro advancement.

Grimm, Friedrich Melchior, Baron (frē'drĭkh mĕl'khēôr grĭm'), 1723–1807, French author, b. Germany. His *Correspondence littéraire* (1st complete ed., 1829–30) was a private newsletter service which throws a unique light on intellectual life of 18th-cent. Paris. He was a friend of Diderot.

Grimm, Jakob (yä'kôp), 1785–1863, German philologist; a founder of comparative philology. His chief contributions were formulation of GRIMM'S LAW; German grammar (1819–37); *German Mythology* (1835; Eng. tr., 1880–88). With his brother **Wilhelm Grimm** (vĭl'hĕlm), 1786–1859, he collected and published German folktales, world-famous as *Grimm's Fairy Tales* (1812–15).

Grimmelshausen, Hans Jakob Christoffel von (häns' yä'kôp krĭs'tôfŭl fŭn grĭ'mŭlshou''zŭn), 1625?–1676, German author. His satirical *The Adventuresome Simplicius Simplicissimus* (1669) is a picaresque, partly autobiographical novel of the Thirty Years War.

Grimm's law, principle of relationships in Indo-European languages, first observed by Jakob Grimm in 1822. It shows that primitive tenues (k, t, p) become aspirates in Low German (e.g., English) and mediae in High German (German); that primitive aspirates (gh, dh, bh) become mediae in Low German, tenues in High German; and that primitive mediae (g, d, b) become tenues in Low German, aspirates in High German. In English, aspirates are h, th, f; mediae, g, d, b; tenues, k, t, p. In German, mediae are h, d, f; tenues, k, t, p; aspirates, ch, z, f.

Grimsby, county borough (pop. 94,527), Lincolnshire, England, at mouth of Humber R.; largest fishing port in Great Britain. Has over 100 acres of docks.

Grindelwald (grĭn'dŭlvält), resort in Bernese Alps, Switzerland, at foot of the Eiger. Celebrated for grandeur of scenery.

grindstone, abrasive stone mounted so that it rotates and can sharpen edges of tools and other instruments.

Grinnell, Josiah Bushnell, 1821–91, American pioneer, clergyman, and abolitionist. Lost pastorate in Washington, D.C., after antislavery sermon. Went West following Horace Greeley's advice to him, "Go West, young man, go West!" Founded Grinnell, Iowa.

Grinnell, city (pop. 6,828), central Iowa, between Des Moines and Iowa City; founded 1854 by J. B. Grinnell. **Grinnell College** (nonsectarian; coed.) chartered 1847 as Iowa Col., opened 1848 at Davenport by pioneer Congregational missionaries. Moved

1859 when Grinnell donated land and building; college named for him 1909.

Gris, Juan (hwän' grēs'), 1887–1927, Spanish cubist painter. Settled in Paris 1906. Produced mostly still lifes in oil and collage.

Griselda (grĭzĕl'dù), in medieval story, heroine who patiently endures many trials imposed by her husband to test her devotion.

Gris-Nez, Cape (grē-nā'), cliff near Calais, N France, projecting into Strait of Dover, 21 mi. from English coast. Lighthouse.

Grisons (grēsônz', Fr. grēsō'), Ger. *Graubünden*, canton (2,746 sq. mi.; pop. 136,-050), E Switzerland; cap. Chur. Largest but least populated of Swiss cantons. Pastures, forests, hydroelectric stations; some agr. in valleys. ENGADINE valley and other resorts attract many tourists. German, Romansh (a Rhaetic dialect), and Italian are official languages. Part of ancient Rhaetia, region passed to Ostrogoths 493, to Franks 537. Bishops of Chur exercised considerable temporal power after 9th cent., but their control was broken after 1367 by three local leagues of towns; the Gray League gave the canton its name. Joining Swiss Confederation as allies, the leagues conquered Valtellina from Milan in 1512 (lost 1797). In the Thirty Years War the country was torn by civil war between Protestants and Catholics and by French and Spanish intervention. Forced by Napoleon to enter the Helvetic Republic (1799), Grisons became a Swiss canton (1803) after Napoleon's mediation.

Griswold, town (pop. 5,728), SE Conn., NE of Norwich. Includes Jewett City borough (pop. 3,702; textiles).

Grocyn, William (grō'sĭn), 1446?–1519, English humanist. An associate of John Colet and Linacre, he reputedly introduced teaching of Greek at Oxford.

Grodno (grôd'nô), city (pop. 49,818), Belorussia, on the Niemen. Mfg. of agr. machinery, textiles, tobacco. Seat of Polish diets 1673–1793. Passed to Russia 1795; to Poland 1921; to Russia 1945.

grog, name given to unsweetened mixture of spirits and water, hot or cold; formerly, rum and water.

Grolier de Servières, Jean, vicomte d'Aguisy (grōl'yùr, Fr. grôlyā'), 1479–1565, French collector of fine books.

Gromyko, Andrei Andreyevich (ŭndrā' ŭndrā'ŭvĭch grŭmī'kŭ), 1909–, Russian diplomat. Soviet ambassador at Washington 1943–46, chief permanent delegate to UN 1946–48, chief deputy foreign minister 1949–52, and ambassador to England 1952–.

Grongar Hill, Caermarthenshire, Wales. It is celebrated in a poem by John Dyer.

Groningen (khrō'nĭng-ùn), province (867 sq. mi.; pop. 449,862), N Netherlands, on North Sea coast. Cattle raising, dairying, agr. History is that of its cap., the municipality of **Groningen** (pop. 132,021), an agr. trading center. Nominally under bishops of Utrecht from 11th cent., city joined Hanseatic League 1284; gained control over central Friesland (i.e., modern Groningen prov.); joined United Provs. 1579. University was founded 1614.

Gronlund, Laurence (grōn'lùnd), 1846–99, American socialist, b. Denmark. Wrote the

Cooperative Commonwealth (1884), the first adequate exposition of German socialism in English.

Groote, Gerard or **Geert** (khä'rärt, khärt', khrō'tù), 1340–84, Dutch Roman Catholic reformer. A Carthusian deacon, he preached in Netherlands, founded Brothers of the Common Life (later joined with Augustinian canons), urged monastic reform. *The Following of Christ* is attributed to him by some.

Groote Eylandt (grōōt ī'lùnd), area 950 sq. mi., off N Australia, largest island in Gulf of Carpentaria. Aboriginal reservation.

Gropius, Walter (väl'tùr grō'pēōōs), 1883–, German architect, one of leaders of modern "functional" architecture. Headed the famous BAUHAUS, 1919–28. Set of buildings he designed for it at Dessau in 1926 is one of his finest achievements. Worked in London 1934–37, came to U.S. 1937.

Gropper, William, 1897–, American painter. Contributed radical cartoons to periodicals, notably the *New Masses*. Won recognition as a painter when he first exhibited his oils in 1936.

grosbeak (grōs'bēk), name used (generally in combination) for various birds, especially of finch family. They have large, conical bills and bright summer plumage, and are 8–9 in. long. Rose-breasted grosbeak, pine grosbeak, western or black-headed grosbeak, and common European grosbeak (hawfinch) are well known.

Groseilliers, Médard Chouart, sieur des (mädär' shwär' syûr dù grôsāyā'), 1618?–c.1690, French trader and explorer in North America. Brother-in-law of Pierre E. RADISSON; his companion on journeys.

Gros Morne (grō' môrn'), mountain, 2,666 ft. high w N.F., Canada, in Long Range. Highest point in Newfoundland.

Gross, Samuel David, 1805–84, American surgeon, influential as teacher and writer. He invented surgical instruments and techniques.

Grosse Pointe (grōs point'), residential city (pop. 6,283), SE Mich., suburb of Detroit, on L. St. Clair. Also near Detroit are residential villages, **Grosse Pointe Farms** (pop. 9,410), **Grosse Pointe Park** (pop. 13,075), and **Grosse Pointe Woods** (pop. 10,381).

Grosseteste, Robert (grōs'tĕst), c.1170–1253, English prelate; chief founder of Oxford Franciscan school. As bishop of Lincoln after 1235, he fought efforts of HENRY III to control appointments and supported reforms of Simon de Montfort; upheld papal prerogative but censured INNOCENT IV for exactions. His studies of Aristotle were the basis for scholastic thought of THOMAS AQUINAS. Very learned, he wrote hundreds of works.

Grossglockner (grōs'glôknùr), highest peak of Austria, 12,460 ft. high, in the Hohe Tauern. First ascended 1800. The Grossglocknerstrasse, a highway rising to 8,215 ft., now crosses near peak.

Grossgörschen, Germany: see LÜTZEN.

Grosswardein, Rumania: see ORADEA.

Grosvenor Square (grōv'nùr), fashionable residential square, W London. Site of American Embassy; hq. American troops in London World War II. Statue of F. D. Roosevelt erected here 1949.

Gros Ventre Indians (grō vä'trù) [Fr.,= big belly], name for two quite distinct North American Indian tribes. One was the Atsina, a detached band of the Arapaho, of Algonquian linguistic stock. The other was the Hidatsa Indians, of Siouan stock.

Grosz, George (grōs), 1893–, German painter and caricaturist in America. Famous in postwar Germany for his vitriolic, satirical drawings of bourgeois society. Came to U.S. 1933.

Grote, George, 1794–1871, English historian of ancient Greece. His *History of Greece* (12 vols., 1846–56) is a classic of historical writing.

Grotefend, Georg Friedrich (gä'ôrk frē'drĭkh grō'tüfĕnt), 1775–1853, German archaeologist and philologist. Deciphered cuneiform inscriptions of Persia.

Grotius, Hugo (grō'shùs), 1583–1645, Dutch jurist, author of *De jure belli ac pacis* (1625) [concerning the law of war and peace]. The book is on natural law and is generally considered the first definitive text on international law.

Groton (grŏ'tùn). **1** Town (pop. 21,896), including Groton borough (pop. 7,036), SE Conn., on Thames R. (bridged to New London, 1943); settled c.1650. Has U.S. submarine base. **2** Town (pop. 2,889), N Mass., NW of Boston. Seat of Groton School for boys (1884). Among famous graduates was F. D. Roosevelt.

Grouchy, Emmanuel, marquis de (ĕmänüĕl' märkē' dù grōōshē'), 1766–1847, marshal of France. Was largely responsible for Napoleon's disaster in WATERLOO CAMPAIGN by letting Prussians join English.

ground bass (bās), short musical phrase constantly reiterated in the bass of a composition, with variations in the upper parts. Popular during baroque era; used by Purcell, Bach, and Buxtehude.

ground hog: see WOODCHUCK.

ground ivy, creeping perennial plant (*Glecoma,* or *Nepeta, hederacea*) also called gill-over-the-ground, naturalized in North America. It has small purple flowers and rounded leaves.

ground pine: see CLUB MOSS.

groundsel, common name for large, varied, widely distributed plant genus *Senecio* of daisy family. Includes such plants as golden groundsel, purple ragwort, CINERARIA, dusty miller, and german ivy. Groundsel bush (*Baccharis halimifolia*) native to U.S. coastal regions, has downy white seed heads.

ground squirrel, rodent of squirrel family. The name is used chiefly for those of genus *Citellus* (or *Spermophilus*) of North America, Europe, and Asia, and also for the African ground squirrel *Xerus,* and for the chipmunk.

group insurance: see INSURANCE.

grouse (grous), game bird of colder parts of N Hemisphere (c.25 species). It is henlike and terrestrial, and has red, brown, and gray plumage. American grouse include eastern ruffed grouse (called also partridge or pheasant), SAGE GROUSE, PTARMIGAN, and PRAIRIE CHICKEN.

Grove, Sir George, 1820–1900, English musicographer, whose *Dictionary of Music and Musicians* (1879–89) is a standard reference work. First director of the Royal Col. of Music, 1883–94.

Grove, Robert Moses (Lefty Grove), 1900–, American baseball pitcher. In 1931 he won 31, lost 4, equaled American League record of 16 consecutive victories. In 17 years in major leagues, he won 300, lost 141, struck out more than 2,000 batters.

Grove City, borough (pop. 7,411), W Pa., NNW of Pittsburgh. Mfg. of engines.

growth, in biology, development of plant or animal from early stages. Involves increase in size, cell division (see *ill.,* p. 813), differentiation of tissues; often called growth by intussusception (from within), in contrast to growth by accretion (addition of materials externally, as in crystal growth).

Grozny (grôz'nē), city (pop. 172,468), RSFSR, at N foot of Greater Caucasus. Center of rich oil dist., linked by pipe lines with Caspian, Black Sea, Donets Basin. Major German objective in World War II, but Germans were stopped c.50 mi. to W (1942).

Grub Street, in London, since 1830 named Milton St. Once famous as home of poor authors, it was used as symbol of hack work by Dr. Johnson and others.

Grün, Hans Baldung: see BALDUNG, HANS.

Grundtvig, Nikolai Frederik Severin, 1783–1872, Danish writer and educator, founder of the Danish folk school.

Grünewald, Mathias (mätē'äs grü'nùvält), c.1480–c.1530, German religious painter. Famous for *Isenheim Altarpiece* (Colmar) which portrays passion of Christ with dramatic realism.

Grünwald, battle of, 1410: see TANNENBERG.

Grütli, Switzerland: see RÜTLI.

Gruyère (grüyěr'), Ger. *Greierz,* area in Fribourg canton, Switzerland. Known for its cattle and for Gruyère cheese. Town of Gruyères has well-preserved medieval architecture.

Guadalajara (gwä"dhälähä'rä), city (pop. 229,235), cap. of Jalisco, W Mexico, second largest city of Mexico; modern commercial city with picturesque survivals of colonial period. Permanently settled (1542), it was later seat of *audiencia* of Nueva Galicia and center of reformists in war against Spain (1810–21) and War of Reform (1858–61). Famous for handmade glassware and pottery.

Guadalajara, city (pop. 21,466), cap. of Guadalajara prov., central Spain, in New Castile, on Henares R. Near by is battlefield where Loyalists defeated Insurgents, mostly Italian "volunteers," March, 1937.

Guadalcanal (gwädùlkùnäl'), volcanic island (2,500 sq. mi.; pop. c.14,000), S Pacific, one of SOLOMON ISLANDS. Largely jungle, rises to c.8,000 ft. Occupied 1942 by the Japanese, regained 1943 by U.S. forces. Battles of Cape Esperance and Lunga Point were important U.S. victories.

Guadalquivir (gwä"dhälkĕvēr'), river, c.350 mi. long, S Spain, in Andalusia, flowing from Sierra de Cazorla SW through fertile region, past Córdoba and Seville (head of navigation), into Atlantic.

Guadalupe (Span. gwädhälōō′pä), village, W central Spain, in Estremadura. Noted for shrine of Our Lady of Guadalupe, whose cult was transferred (16th cent.) to Guadalupe Hidalgo, Mexico.

Guadalupe Hidalgo (gwähdälōō′pä ēdäl′gō) shrine, central Mexico, suburb of Mexico city; one of principal shrines in Christendom. In 1531, an Indian, Juan Diego, had vision of Virgin at place renamed Guadalupe in honor of shrine in Spain; Hidalgo was added in 1810 to honor revolutionary priest, Hidalgo y Costilla. **Treaty of Guadalupe Hidalgo,** signed and ratified in 1848, ended Mexican War. In it Mexico recognized Texas as U.S. possession and ceded most of present SW U.S.; U.S. agreed to pay Mexico $15,000,000 and assumed American claims against Mexico.

Guadalupe Mountains (gwä′dulōōp), SE N.Mex. and W Texas. In Texas are El Capitan (8,078 ft.) and Guadalupe Peak (8,751 ft.), state's highest point, W of which are salt lakes and flats.

Guadalupe Victoria (gwädhälōō′pä vēktōr′yä), 1786?–1843, Mexican general, president of Mexico (1824–29). Active in revolution against Spain from 1811, he adopted the name of the revolutionary standard (his real name, Manuel Félix Fernández).

Guadarrama, Sierra de (sēē′rä dä gwädhärä′mä), mountain range, central Spain, N of Madrid, culminating in Peñalara peak (7,972 ft.).

Guadeloupe (gôdulōōp′, gwä–), overseas department of the French Republic (687 sq. mi.; pop. 278,864), in Leeward Isls., West Indies; cap. BASSE-TERRE. Discovered by Columbus, 1493, it was abandoned by Spain 1604. French settled it 1635, but English contended for its ownership until 1815.

Guadiana (gwädhyä′nä), river, c.500 mi. long, central Spain and S Portugal. Flows W past Ciudad Real and Badajoz, then S, forming Spanish-Portuguese border till it empties in Gulf of Cádiz.

Guaira, La (lä gwī′rä), town (pop. 10,103), N Venezuela, port on Caribbean.

Guam (gwäm), island (203 sq. mi.; pop. 58,754), W Pacific, belonging to U.S.; largest, most populous, and southernmost of MARIANAS ISLANDS. AGANA is seat of government. Inhabited mainly by Chamorros. Discovered 1521 by Magellan, it came under Spanish rule in late 17th cent. Taken 1898 by U.S., under Dept. of Navy since 1917. Fell Dec. 9, 1941, to the Japanese invaders. Regained July, 1944, by U.S. and became major air and naval base.

guanaco (gwänä′kō) or **huanaco** (hwänä′kō), wild South American mammal (genus *Lama*) of camel family of Andes. Llama and alpaca were probably domesticated from it. Its shoulder height is c.3½ ft. and it has a dark face, brown back and sides, and light under parts. Indians use its flesh, hide, bones.

Guanajuato (gwänähwä′tō), state (11,805 sq. mi.; pop. 1,317,629; average alt. c.6,000 ft.), central Mexico, on central plateau. Leading mining state of Mexico, it produces silver, gold, mercury, lead, tin, copper, opals. Principal cities are Celaya (pop. 22,766), LEÓN, Irapuato (pop. 32,377), Guanajuato (cap.; pop. 23,521).

guano (gwä′nō), fertilizer of dried excrement of sea birds collected from equatorial coasts.

Guantánamo (gwäntä′nämō), city (pop. 42,423), SE Cuba. Large sugar center on Guantánamo Bay (with U.S. naval station).

Guaraní Indians (gwäränē′), people of Tupi-Guaraní linguistic stock in S Brazil and Paraguay. Lived in patrilineal communities, practiced seminomadic agr. Called Tupí in Brazil.

Guardi, Francesco (fränchä′skō gwär′dē), 1712–93, Venetian landscape painter. Developed more brilliant style than that of his master Canaletto.

guardian and ward, relationship, in which a ward—an infant, insane person, or spendthrift—and (in most cases) his property are placed under the management and control of a guardian. Generally the guardian is appointed by the court; in some countries appointed by one of the parents (in others by the father only).

Guarini, Giovanni Battista (jōvän′nē bät-tē′stä gwärē′nē), 1537–1612, Italian poet, author of the pastoral drama *Pastor Fido* (1590), rival of Tasso.

Guarneri (gwärnä′rē) or **Guarnerius,** family of violinmakers of Cremona, Italy, beginning with **Andrea Guarneri** (ändrä′ä), c.1626–1698, a pupil of Niccolò Amati. His grandnephew, **Giuseppi Guarneri** (jōōzĕp′pä), 1687?–1745, called "del Gesù" because he signed his labels with a cross and the letters IHS, was the greatest craftsman of the family.

Guastalla (gwästäl′lä), town (pop. 3,934) and former duchy, Emilia-Romagna, N Italy. Bought by Gonzaga family 1539; duchy from 1621; passed to Parma 1748. Napoleon I gave it to his sister Pauline (1806); it reverted to Parma on his downfall, was transferred to Modena 1847.

Guatemala (gwätämä′lä), republic (42,042 sq. mi.; pop. 2,786,403), Central America, just S of Mexico, most populous of Central American countries; cap. GUATEMALA. Tropic areas on Pacific and Caribbean coasts and jungles of Petén yield produce, but cool highlands from border of Mexico to borders of Salvador and Honduras have most of the population. Except in urban areas—notably Guatemala and Quetzaltenango—the Indian patterns of life persist. The chief ports are San José and Puerto Barrios; chief exports are bananas and coffee. Near W coast is a chain of volcanoes. The Maya-Quiché had a notable civilization before the Spanish conquest under Pedro de Alvarado. The first capital was Ciudad Vieja, the second Antigua, the third Guatemala. Though a captaincy general, it was of little importance in the Spanish Empire. Gained independence in 1821 and was briefly part of Iturbide's Mexican Empire. Guatemala was the nucleus of the Central American Federation (1825–38) and since that time, under such leaders as Rafael Carrero, Manuel Estrada Cabrera, and Justo Rufino Barrios, has tried to gain hegemony in Central America. Border disputes have been numerous. In World

War II Guatemala declared war against the Axis countries (1941), and in 1945 became a member of the United Nations.

Guatemala, city (pop. 283,100), S central Guatemala, cap. and largest city of republic, in highland valley. Founded 1776 as cap. after Antigua was abandoned; rebuilt after destruction by earthquake (1917–18).

Guatémoc: see CUAUHTÉMOC.

guava (gwä′vù), small tree (*Psidium*) native to tropical America, and its fruit, a fleshy berry with many hard seeds. Guava jelly is made from the fruit. Both strawberry guava (*Psidium littorale*) with round red fruit, and common guava (*P. guajava*) are grown in Fla. and Calif.

Guayaquil (gwīūkēl′), city (pop. 262,624), W Ecuador, on Guayas R.; Pacific port and largest city of Ecuador; founded by Benalcázar 1535. Historic meeting between Bolívar and San Martín occurred here 1822.

Guaymas (gwī′mäs) city (pop. 8,796), Sonora, NW Mexico, a port on Gulf of California; a popular resort for gulf fishing. Exports agr. and fish products of area.

Gubbio (gōōb′byō), town (pop. 7,432), Umbria, central Italy. Was anc. town of Umbrians (IGUVINE TABLES found here). Flourished in Middle Ages, first as free commune, later under dukes of Urbino. Fine ceramics made here in 16th cent. City retains much medieval architecture.

Gudbrandsdal (gōōd′bränsdäl″), valley, central Norway, extending from Mjosa L. NW to Dovrefjell. Rich agr. and timber district; horse breeding. Many valley farmers trace ancestry to saga times; population preserves own dialect, customs.

Guden (gōō′dùn), Dan. *Gudenaa*, river, 98 mi. long. Jutland, Denmark. Only important Danish river; partly navigable. Flows N and NE to the Kattegat.

Gudmundsson, Kristmann, 1902–, Icelandic writer of Norwegian novels.

Gudrun or **Kudrun,** name of principal female character of the Icelandic *Laxdaelasaga*, a stalwart heroine; also of a character in the *Volsungasaga* (corresponding to Kriemhild in the *Nibelungenlied*).

Guelderland or **Guelders,** Netherlands: see GELDERLAND.

Guelph (gwĕlf), city (pop. 27,386), S Ont., Canada, on Speed R. and NW of Hamilton; founded 1827 by John Galt. Has knitting and paper mills, meat packing, woodworking, and varied mfg. Site of Ontario Agricultural Col.

Guelphs (gwĕlfs), European dynasty, tracing descent from Guelph I or Welf I (9th cent.), father-in-law of Emperor Louis I. Guelph d'Este IV (d. 1101), duke of Carinthia from 1055 and duke of Bavaria from 1070, was common ancestor of Italian house of ESTE and of the German Guelphs, who ruled Bavaria and Saxony to 1180 (see HENRY THE PROUD; HENRY THE LION). In feud with house of HOHENSTAUFEN, German Guelphs lost all but the duchy of BRUNSWICK. The line of Brunswick-Lüneburg or HANOVER ascended the British throne in the person of George I (1714). Because of Salic law of succession, Hanover was separated from British crown when Victoria became queen of England (1837). After the deposition of GEORGE V of Hanover (1866), the so-called Guelphic party sought to restore the kingdom, but with no success.

Guelphs and Ghibellines (gĭ′bùlēnz, –lĭnz), opposing political factions in later Middle Ages. They originated 12th cent. In the rivalry between the German Guelphs or Welfs and the Hohenstaufen emperors. (See HENRY THE PROUD; HENRY THE LION.) The name Ghibelline probably derives from the Hohenstaufen castle of Waiblingen. The struggle continued in Italy, where the Guelphs at first were the papal party in the struggle between emperors and popes. The Guelphs included many important cities (e.g., LOMBARD LEAGUE, Bologna, Florence, Genoa) and the Angevin kings of Naples. The Ghibellines included several noble families and petty tyrants, such as Ezzelino da Romano, the Della Scala of Verona, the Visconti of Milan, and several cities (e.g., Pisa, Arezzo). The cities themselves were often divided, and bloody strife resulted. The party names soon lost their original connotations, and local feuds disturbed party alignments— as in Florence, where the Guelphs split into Blacks and Whites. The names fell into disuse by the 15th cent.

Guercino (gwĕrchē′nō), 1591?–1666, Italian eclectic painter; real name was Giovanni Francesco Barbieri. Work shows influence of Caravaggio and Guido.

Guericke, Otto von (ô′tō fūn gā′rĭkù), 1602–86, German physicist. Made first air pump; devised Magdeburg hemispheres for demonstrating air pressure.

Guérin, Pierre Narcisse, Baron, 1774–1833, French painter, exponent of the classicism of David.

Guernica (gĕrnē′kä), historic town, Vizcaya prov., N Spain. Oak of Guernica, former meeting place of Vizcayan diet, symbolizes lost liberties of Basques. In 1937 German planes, in aid of Insurgent forces, bombed the defenseless town. The action, which provoked widespread indignation, inspired Picasso's famous painting.

Guernsey, one of the CHANNEL ISLANDS.

Guernsey cattle: see CATTLE.

Guerra Junqueiro, Abílio (äbē′lyō gĕ′rù zhōōnkā′rō), 1850–1923, Portuguese poet, author of violent satiric poems and also of touching lyrics.

Guerrero (gĕrā′rō) [for Vicente Guerrero, revolutionary leader], state, SW Mexico, on Pacific; cap. Chilpancingo (pop. 8,834). Extremely mountainous except for narrow coastal strip around ACAPULCO. Silver works at TAXCO are famous. Prominent in war against Spain (1810–21), it was not a state until 1849.

Guerrière: see CONSTITUTION, ship.

Guesclin, Bertrand du: see DU GUESCLIN, BERTRAND.

Guess, George: see SEQUOYAH.

Guest, Lady Charlotte (Bertie), 1812–95, English author, translator of MABINOGION.

Gueux (gû) [Fr.,= beggars], nickname given to the Dutch and Flemish noblemen and burghers (both Protestant and Catholic) who in 1566 signed a petition protesting against Spanish encroachments on their traditional liberties. The petition was a toned-down version of the Compromise of Breda (1566), which pledged the signers to resist Spanish oppression. The nickname was taken up by the patriots in the ensuing struggle. Patriotic privateers chartered in 1569 by William the Silent were called Beggars of the Sea; their chief success was the raising of the siege of LEIDEN (1574).

Guevara, Antonio de (äntō′nyō dā gävä′rä), 1480?–1545, Spanish novelist, author of didactic *Libro llamado Relox de príncipes* (1529).

Guevara, Luis Vélez de: see VÉLEZ DE GUEVARA.

Guggenheim (gōō′gŭnhīm), family of American industrialists and philanthropists. **Meyer Guggenheim,** 1828–1905, b. Switzerland, made fortune from metal smelting and refining. His son, **Daniel Guggenheim,** 1856–1930, was largely responsible for combining Guggenheim interests with the American Smelting and Refining Co. in 1901. The Daniel and Florence Guggenheim Foundation is his principal philanthropy. His brother, **Simon Guggenheim,** 1867–1941, estab. (1925), with his wife, the John Simon Guggenheim Memorial Foundation, which grants fellowships to scholars, writers, and artists. Another brother, **Solomon Robert Guggenheim,** 1861–1949, estab. foundation to increase appreciation of non-objective art.

Guiana (gēä′nä), region, NE South America, roughly bounded by the Orinoco basin, the Casiquiare channel (connecting the Orinoco with the Río Negro), the Amazon basin, and the Atlantic. The narrow coastal region is rainy and hot. The vast, unexploited interior includes the Guiana Highlands as well as broad savannas and vast rain forests. The region includes SE Venezuela and part of N Brazil as well as the three colonies called Guiana. The westernmost of these is **British Guiana** (83,000 sq. mi.; pop. 375,701), a crown colony; cap. GEORGETOWN on the Demerara R. (colony still sometimes called Demerara). The population is polyglot—a few whites and Indians, many East Indians, and many Negroes. Sugar, rum, rice, hardwoods, gold, diamonds (the Mazaruni fields are rich), and bauxite are exported. British settlement in Guiana began in present Dutch Guiana by 1630, and the Dutch settled Essequibo, Berbice, and Pomeroon in present British Guiana. In the course of continental and colonial wars involving the Dutch, the British, and the French, the areas changed hands often and it was not until the Congress of Vienna that the present division of the three colonies was more or less fixed. Discovery of gold in British Guiana led to British expansion and to the VENEZUELA BOUNDARY DISPUTE. **Dutch Guiana** (55,143 sq. mi.; pop. 211,804) is between British and French Guiana; cap. PARAMARIBO. Colony called also Netherlands Guiana, Surinam, and Suriname. The population includes Javanese, East Indians, and Jewish refugees, as well as Dutch and Negroes (many of them bush Negroes or maroons, descended from escaped slaves). Rum, timber, coffee, and bauxite are exported. The Dutch first

estab. colonies (beginning 1616) in present British Guiana, and the Dutch West India Co. encouraged settlement. Ultimate settlement in 1815 gave Dutch their present territory. The easternmost of the three, **French Guiana** (c.34,740 sq. mi.; pop. 28,537), a department of Metropolitan France, comprises the colony proper and the interior Territory of Inini; cap. CAYENNE. The name —and even more the name of Devil's Isl. in the colony—was made notorious as a penal colony until 1946.

Guiana Highlands, mountainous tableland, mostly in Venezuela, bounded by Orinoco and Amazon basins and coastal lowlands of British Guiana. Tablelands rise in escarpments and create magnificent waterfalls in rivers which pour over edges. Gold and some diamonds have been mined.

Guibert of Ravenna (gwī′bŭrt, gēbĕr′), d. 1100, antipope as Clement III (1080–1100). Led antireform party which repudiated Pope Alexander II. HENRY IV made him archbishop of Ravenna (1072). Henry, excommunicated in 1080 by GREGORY VII, declared Gregory deposed and enthroned (1084) Guibert, who then crowned Henry emperor.

Guicciardini, Francesco (fränchä′skō gwĕtchärdē′nē), 1483–1540, Italian historian and statesman. Served Florentine government and Pope Leo X. His history of Italy during 1492–1534 (period of the Italian Wars) is masterwork of Italian historical literature of Renaissance.

Guido d'Arezzo (gwē′dō därĕt′tsō) or **Guido Aretinus** (ârŭtī′nŭs), c.990–1050, Italian Benedictine monk, important in the history of musical notation. He added two lines to the two already serving as a staff, using the spaces as well as the lines. His chief contribution was the solmization syllables (a system to denote tones by syllables), called the Aretinian syllables or Guido's scale. He had observed that each line of a certain hymn began a note higher than the previous line, so, as an aid to memorizing, he named each of the tones of the hexachord (a group of six consecutive notes) after the first syllable of each line of the hymn: *Ut* queant laxis; *Re*sonare fibris; *Mi*ra gestorum; *Fa*muli tuorum; *Sol*ve polluti; and so on. As the octave superseded the hexachord, an additional *si* or *ti* was added; *ut* was replaced by the more singable *do.* These syllables became the basis of various systems of MUSICAL NOTATION (see also SOLFEGE) used today.

Guido Reni (rä′nē), 1575–1642, Italian painter, b. near Bologna. Studied briefly with the Carracci. In 1600 made first of many trips to Rome, where he became rival of Caravaggio. Later he estab. own academy in Bologna. Eclecticism and voluptuous sentimentality of such baroque paintings as *Aurora* (Rospigliosi Palace, Rome) made him one of favorite artists of 17th and 18th cent.

Guienne (gēĕn′, gwēĕn′), Fr. *Guyenne,* region and former province, SW France; historic cap. Bordeaux. Synonymous with AQUITAINE until Hundred Years War. Largely under English rule 1152–1453. Guyenne prov. in 17th–18th cent. consisted of present Gironde, Dordogne, Lot, Lot-et-Garonne, and Aveyron depts.—i.e., the regions of BORDEAUX, AGEN, PÉRIGORD, QUERCY, and ROUERGUE.

Guildford, municipal borough (pop. 47,484), co. town of Surrey, England. Identified with Astolat of Arthurian Legend. Grave of Lewis Carroll.

guilds or **gilds,** economic and social groups of people in same business or craft, typical of W Europe in Middle Ages. Membership was never by class but by profession or trade. Primary functions were to control profession or trade in a locality, to set standards of workmanship and price, to protect business from capricious exactions, to prevent encroachment from other localities, and to establish status for guild members in society. Similar groups both of merchants and of craftsmen were known from early Greek times, some of them extremely powerful. Merchant guilds had vast effect on what is known as Commercial Revolution. No less important were craft guilds, which grew rapidly in 12th cent. Generally members were masters, apprentices, and journeymen. Masters owned shops and trained apprentices, bound to them. Journeymen were men who had finished training but could not attain status of masters, limited in number. Guilds reflected medieval desire for orderly society, and often dominated municipal government, e.g., LIVERY COMPANIES of London. Increasing power of nations in 15th and 16th cent. reduced power of guilds, which, by 17th cent., had withered in England, but persisted on Continent until French Revolution.

guild socialism, type of socialism developed in England, advocating industrial self-government through worker-controlled guilds; originated by A. J. Penty in 1906. Aspects of Marxism and SYNDICALISM were adopted. Control of industry was emphasized, rather than political reform. Movement eventually waned, although it influenced British trade unions.

Guilford, town (pop. 5,092), S Conn., on Long Isl. Sound E of New Haven. Has some of state's oldest houses, e.g., Whitfield House (1639–40, restored 1936). Dairy products, truck, metal goods, sea food.

Guilford College: see GREENSBORO, N.C.

Guillaume, Charles Édouard (shärl' ādwär' gēyōm'), 1861–1938, French physicist. Won 1920 Nobel Prize for discovery of several alloys, among them invar and platinite.

Guillaume de Lorris (dü lōrēs'), c.1215–c.1278, French poet, author of first part of ROMAN DE LA ROSE.

Guillén, Jorge (hôr'hā gēlyän'), 1893–, Spanish intellectual lyric poet.

Guimarãis or **Guimarães** (both: gē"mùrä'ēsh), city (pop. 12,568), NW Portugal, SE of Braga. Seat of Henry of Burgundy and his son, Alfonso I of Portugal. Favorite royal residence; noted old castle.

Guimerà, Angel (än'zhĕl gēmärä'), 1845–1924, Catalan romantic poet and dramatist.

Guinea, Gulf of, inlet of the Atlantic, W Africa. Extends from W Gold Coast to mouth of Congo R.

guinea fowl, breed of domestic poultry related to the pheasant and developed from wild species of Africa. It is in demand for its delicate, but gamelike flesh.

guinea pig, domesticated form of the cavy (genus *Cavia*), descended from wild South American species. In North America it is chiefly a laboratory animal used for testing serums, antitoxins, and for experiments in genetics and nutrition.

Guinegate (gēngät'), village, Pas-de-Calais dept., N France, near Saint-Omer. Scene of two French defeats: 1479, by Archduke Maximilian, in war over Burgundian succession; 1513, by English and imperialists, in second BATTLE OF THE SPURS.

Guinevere: see ARTHURIAN LEGEND; also spelled Guenever or Guenevere.

Guiney, Louise Imogen (gī'nē), 1861–1920, American Catholic poet and essayist; in England after 1901.

Guipúzcoa, Spain: see BASQUE PROVINCES.

Guiscard, Norman rulers of Sicily: see ROBERT GUISCARD and ROGER I.

Guise (gēz, gwēz), French ducal family, founded as cadet branch of house of LORRAINE by **Claude de Lorraine, 1st duc de Guise** (klōd' dü lōrĕn'), 1496–1550, whom Francis I made duke and peer. His daughter MARY OF GUISE married James V of Scotland and was the mother of Mary Queen of Scots. His sons **François de Lorraine, 2d duc de Guise** (fräswä'), 1519–63, and **Charles de Guise, Cardinal de Lorraine,** c.1525–1574, controlled French politics in the reign of Francis II, first husband of Mary Queen of Scots. Championing the Catholic cause against the Huguenots, they cruelly suppressed the conspiracy of AMBOISE (1560). After Francis's death they opposed the tolerant policy of CATHERINE DE' MEDICI and provoked the outbreak of the Wars of RELIGION (1562). François defeated the Huguenots at Dreux, but was assassinated shortly afterward. Charles negotiated for Spanish help and held power at court in 1567–70. **Henri de Lorraine, 3d duc de Guise** (ärē'), 1550–88, son of François, helped to plan the massacre of SAINT BARTHOLOMEW'S DAY and after 1576 formed the Catholic LEAGUE. Immensely ambitious and popular, he instigated the revolt of Paris against King HENRY III (1588) and took control of the city. After an ostensible reconciliation the king had him murdered. His brother, **Louis de Lorraine, Cardinal de Guise,** 1555–88, was killed at the same time. Leadership of the League devolved upon their brother, Charles, duc de MAYENNE. **Henri de Lorraine, 5th duc de Guise,** 1614–64, conspired against Richelieu (1641); fought in Naples against Spain (1647–48, 1654); later was grand chamberlain at court of Louis XIV.

guitar: see STRINGED INSTRUMENTS.

Guitry, Lucien Germain (gētrē'), 1860–1925, French actor. Was among first exponents of realistic drama in plays by Zola, France, and Bernstein. His actor son, **Sacha Guitry** (säshä'), 1885–, is also a prolific, witty dramatist and film director.

Guizot, François (fräswä' gēzō'), 1787–1874, French statesman and historian; leading intellectual exponent of the bourgeois monarchy of LOUIS PHILIPPE. He dominated the cabinet from 1840, was premier 1847–48. His complacency led to FEBRUARY REVOLUTION of 1848. Ranking high as historian, he wrote *Histoire de la révolution d'Angleterre* (2 vols., 1826–27); *General History of Civilization in Modern Europe* (1829–32; Eng. tr., 3 vols., 1846).

Gulf. For names beginning thus, see second part; e.g., for Gulf of Mexico, see MEXICO, GULF OF.

Gulfport, city (pop. 22,659), SE Miss., on Mississippi Sound W of Biloxi; settled 1891. Resort and sea port (fine artificial harbor) processing sea-food, naval stores, lumber, tung oil, and cotton. Has large VA hospital.

Gulf Stream, ocean current found (1513) by Ponce de León. It originates in Gulf of Mexico, passes through Straits of Florida, flows NE parallel to U.S. coast, separated from it by narrow "cold wall" of water. Temperature is 80°F. at beginning, drops as stream moves N. Stream slows up and spreads out, finally merges with North Atlantic Drift (lat. 40°N, long. 60°W). Stream results from general vertical circulation of ocean; cold water from N sinks down, warm water of equatorial region rises and flows N above cold current.

gulfweed, a SEAWEED of genus *Sargassum,* a brown alga of tropical waters, which commonly floats in large patches in Sargasso Sea and Gulf Stream.

Gulick, Luther Halsey (gū'lĭk), 1865–1918, American pioneer in physical education. He helped to originate game of basketball and in 1910 helped found Camp Fire Girls.

Gulistan, Treaty of, 1813, between Russia and Iran, ended Russo-Persian War begun in 1804. Persia ceded khanates forming present Azerbaijan SSR, renounced claims to Georgia, Dagestan.

gull, aquatic bird of tern family found near all oceans and many inland waters. Sea gull is a common name for herring gull (a subspecies of common European gull) found on Atlantic and Pacific coasts of Canada and U.S., as well as inland. Larger and heavier than terns, gulls have webbed feet and hooked bills. They are useful as scavengers.

Gullah, dialect spoken by Negroes of the Sea Isls., SE U.S. Originally a mixture of W African words with English, it is now a very corrupt form of English.

Gulliver's Travels (1726), political, social satire by Jonathan SWIFT. Despite the satire, its fairy-tale quality has made it a children's classic.

Gullstrand, Allvar (äl'vär gŭl'stränd), 1862–1930, Swedish ophthalmologist. Won 1911 Nobel Prize in Physiology and Medicine for study of optical images and of light refraction in eye.

gum, term for a variety of plant substances, many not true gums. True gums are complex organic materials; some are soluble in water, others are insoluble but absorb large amounts of water. Gum arabic is typical; it is used in making inks, adhesives, confections; as fabric filler; as emollient.

gumbo, a name for OKRA. In W U.S. it is name for rich, black alluvial soil, sticky or soapy when wet.

Gumplowicz, Ludwig (lōōt'vĭkh gōōm'plō-

vĭch), 1838–1909, Austrian sociologist. Held that social development rose out of conflict, first among races, then among states, then among other social groups.

gum tree: see EUCALYPTUS; BLACK GUM; SWEET GUM.

guncotton, explosive formed by action of cold nitric and sulphuric acids on cotton. Burns when ignited; explodes with detonator. Used in torpedoes, in blasting (mixed with nitroglycerin), in underwater blasting and mines; in making smokeless powder.

Gundulic, Ivan (ē'vän gōōndōō'lĭch), Ital. *Giovanni Gondola,* 1588–1638, Croatian poet. Held high office in his native Dubrovnik (Ragusa). His chief work, *Osman* (1626), is an epic of the Polish-Turkish wars.

gun metal, a BRONZE, an alloy of copper, tin, and zinc in varying proportions. Originally used for making guns; now used for casting machine parts.

Gunnarsson, Gunnar, 1889–, Icelandic novelist. Early works in Danish, later in Icelandic.

Gunnison, town (pop. 2,770; alt. c.7,680 ft.), W central Colo., on Gunnison R., in resort, mining, irrigated-farm area.

Gunnison, river formed in W central Colo. and flowing c.180 mi. W and NW to Colorado R. at Grand Junction. Courses through Black Canyon of the Gunnison (a national monument). Some water diverted for irrigation by Gunnison Tunnel (1905–9), 30,582 ft. in length.

gunpowder, explosive mixture of potassium nitrate (75%), sulphur (10%), and carbon (15%). Formerly much used in blasting and in weapons. In guns, because of the large residue of solid matter, it has been superseded by smokeless powder. Though some have called Roger Bacon or Berthold Schwarz the inventor, it is now agreed that gunpowder was invented in Asia (probably 9th-cent. China). Introduction to Europe in 14th cent. revolutionized warfare.

Gunpowder Plot, frustrated plan to blow up the British houses of Parliament and King James I on Nov. 5, 1605, the opening day of Parliament. A rising of English Catholics was to follow. Plot was exposed by a warning to a relation of one of the plotters not to attend Parliament on that day. Guy Fawkes, a conspirator, was arrested as he entered the cellar of the House of Lords. Nov. 5 is still celebrated as Guy Fawkes Day and effigies of him are burned.

Gunsaulus, Frank Wakeley (gŭnsô'lùs), 1856–1921, American Congregational clergyman and lecturer, president of Armour Inst., of Technology (now Illinois Inst. of Technology) after 1893.

Gunter, Edmund, 1581–1626, English mathematician and astronomer. He invented a portable quadrant, Gunter's surveyor's chain, Gunter's sector or scale; discovered variation of magnetic compass. Probably was first to use terms *cosine* and *cotangent.*

Guntersville, city (pop. 5,253), NE Ala., port on Tennessee R. near Guntersville Dam (TVA), and in farm and resort area. Textile mills.

guppy or **rainbow fish,** small fish (*Lebistes reticulatus*) abundant in parts of South America. It is a popular aquarium fish. It can survive temperatures of 65°–100° F. Rainbow-colored, inch-long male has black bars and spots. Female is greenish gray, c.1½ in. long. Adults are cannabalistic. They produce 12–25 living young every few weeks.

Gupta (gŏŏp'tù), dynasty, 320?–544?, of N India, founded by Chandragupta I. It saw a golden age of Hindu culture.

Gurgan (gŏŏrgän') or **Gorgan** (gŏr–), town (pop. 21,376), NE Iran, c.25 mi. E of the Caspian in area known as Hyrcania in anc. times. Flourished c.1800 during rise of Kajar dynasty, which originated here. Formerly called Asterabad.

Gurkha (gŏŏr'kù), ethnic group of Nepal, of mixed Mongol-Rajput extraction and predominantly Hindu in religion. The British formerly recruited large military contingents from this group.

Gustavus (gŭstä'vùs), kings of Sweden. **Gustavus I** (Gustavus Vasa), 1496–1560. His father, Erik Johansson, was a Swedish senator murdered in the Stockholm massacre (1520). Gustavus led the peasants of Dalarna in the rebellion against CHRISTIAN II of Denmark, defeated the Danes, and was elected king by the Riksdag in 1523. Thus the KALMAR UNION of Denmark, Norway, and Sweden was dissolved. Gustavus's reign was marked by the establishment of a national Protestant Church (1527) and by the Swedish-Danish victory over Lübeck (1537), which freed Sweden from economic subjection to the Hanseatic League. He reigned firmly, made the crown hereditary in the Vasa family, transformed Sweden into a modern, national state. **Gustavus II** (Gustavus Adolphus), 1594–1632, reigned 1611–32. Helped by his chancellor, Axel OXENSTIERNA, he insured internal stability by granting concessions to the nobles and ended the KALMAR WAR by buying off the Danes (1613). His resumption in 1621 of intermittent warfare with Poland gained him a large part of Livonia when a truce was made at Altmark (1629). Meanwhile, however, he had been drawn into an alliance with Christian IV of Denmark (1628) and with France (1629); to both powers he promised to intervene on the Protestant side in the THIRTY YEARS WAR. Gustavus landed in Pomerania (1630) and in a spectacular sweep through Germany defeated the imperials at Breitenfeld (1631), at the Lech (April, 1632), and at Lützen (Nov., 1632). In that last battle, he was killed. His daughter Christina succeeded him. **Gustavus III**, 1746–92, reigned 1771–92. By a coup d'état (1772) he restored the royal prerogatives lost by his predecessors. He waged successful war on Russia (1788–90). His reform policies and his autocratic tendencies earned him the hatred of the nobles, one of whom murdered him. His son and successor, **Gustavus IV** (Gustavus Adolphus), 1778–1837, joined the third coalition against Napoleon I (1805). He lost Swedish Pomerania to French occupation and Finland to Russia (1808). His despotism and mental unbalance led to his enforced abdication (1809). He died in Switzerland. **Gustavus V**, 1858–1950, reigned 1907–50. Sweden evolved toward advanced democracy and economic prosperity; kept

neutral in both world wars. His son **Gustavus VI** (Gustavus Adolphus), 1882–, succeeded him in 1950.

Gustavus Adolphus: see GUSTAVUS II, GUSTAVUS IV, and GUSTAVUS VI, kings of Sweden.

Gustavus Adolphus College: see SAINT PETER, Minn.

Gutenberg, Johann (gŏŏ'tùnbûrg; Ger. gŏŏ'tùnbĕrk), c.1397–1468, German printer, generally considered the first European to print from movable type, though some claim that honor for Laurens Janszoon Koster, for Pamfilo Castaldi, or for some unknown. Little is known of his life. His father's name was Gensfleisch, and the name Gutenberg was derived from his mother. He is believed to have lived in Strasbourg, where he may have made his great invention in 1436 or 1437. He founded a print shop in Mainz (apparently his birthplace), where he issued the MAZARIN BIBLE. Mainz became the center of the new printing trade, but Gutenberg had to give up his press and types to Johann FUST for debt. See PRINTING and TYPE.

Guthrie, city (pop. 10,113), central Okla., near Cimarron R. N of Oklahoma City, in farm and dairy area; founded 1889. Territorial, state cap. until 1910. Langston Univ. (Negro; land-grant, state supported; coed.; 1897) is near.

Gutiérrez Nájera, Manuel (mänwĕl' gŏŏtyĕ'rĕs nä'härä), 1859–95, Mexican poet, showing transition from romanticism to modernism.

gutta-percha, solidified milky juice or latex of various Malayan evergreen trees (esp. *Palaquium gutta*). It is nonelastic and insoluble in water; pliable when heated in water. Of great value as insulation for submarine cables; also used in golf balls, telephone receivers, adhesives, waterproofing materials, etc.

Guttenberg (gŭ'tùnbûrg), town (pop. 5,566), NE N.J. near the Hudson and NE of Jersey City. Textiles.

Gutzkow, Karl (kärl gŏŏts'kō), 1811–78, German author; a leader of the Young Germany group. His drama *Uriel Acosta* (1847; Eng. tr., 1913–15) is considered his best work, but he is known chiefly as a radical polemicist.

Guyenne: see GUIENNE.

Guy of Chauliac: see CHAULIAC, GUY DE.

Guy of Lusignan: see LUSIGNAN.

Guyon, Jeanne Marie Bouvier de la Motte (zhän' märē' bŏŏvyä' dù lä môt' güĕyō'), 1648–1717, French mystic, author of works on QUIETISM. Confined by government to convent because of heretical opinions and correspondence with Miguel de MOLINOS, she was released through aid of Mme de Maintenon but was later imprisoned in Bastille (1695–1702).

Guys, Constantin (gois), 1805?–1892, French draughtsman, b. Holland. Did superb drawings in line and wash, first reproduced in *Illustrated London News*.

Guzmán, Nuño de (nŏŏ'nyō dā gŏŏthmän'), d. 1544, Spanish conquistador. As head of first *audiencia* of New Spain (1529), he ruled so notoriously that he was forced to leave Mexico city. Conquered Nueva Galicia; founded Culiacán and Guadalajara.

Guzmán Blanco, Antonio (äntō'nyō gŏŏsmän'

blän′kõ), 1829–99, president of Venezuela. A *caudillo*, he dominated the nation 1870–88 as a benevolent despot. After overthrow of his regime, he lived in Paris until his death.

Guzmán de Alfarache: see ALEMÁN, MATEO.

Gwalior (gwä′lēôr), former princely state, Madhya Bharat, India. Founded in 18th cent. by Ranoji Sindhia, a Mahratta chief. Town of **Gwalior** (pop. 34,488) is near Lashkar and lies at foot of a hill fort containing ornate palaces and shrines.

Gwilt, Joseph (gwĭlt), 1784–1863, British architect, known chiefly for his encyclopedia of architecture (8 vols., 1842).

Gwin, William McKendree, 1805–85, American politician. U.S. Senator from Calif. (1850–55, 1857–61). Spokesman for Calif. slavery interests. Involved in political battles with antislavery rival, David C. BRODERICK.

Gwinnett, Button, c.1735–1777, American Revolutionary patriot, signer of Declaration of Independence, b. England. His signature, one of the rarest of American holographs, is very valuable.

Gwyn or **Gwynn, Nell** (Eleanor), 1650–87, English actress, notable in comic roles. Charles II's mistress after 1669, she bore him two sons.

gymnastics, exercises for balanced development of body. In Greece the gymnasium was originally the place of training for the Olympic games. Modern gymnastics date from early 19th cent., when Ludwig Jahn estab. *Turnplätze* in Berlin. In U.S., principal gymnastics events are side and long horse, parallel and horizontal bars, Indian club swinging, rope climbing, flying rings, tumbling.

Gyor (dyûr), Hung. *Györ*, Ger. *Raab*, city (pop. 57,192), NW Hungary, on Raab R. Chief textile center of Hungary; mfg. of machinery. Episcopal see since 1001; cathedral was built 12th cent., rebuilt 17th cent. Scene of decisive Austrian victory over Hungarian revolutionists (1849).

gypsum (jĭp′sùm), name for hydrated calcium sulphate. Alabaster and satin spar are varieties. Plaster of Paris is obtained from gypsum.

gypsy or **gipsy,** nomadic people numbering roughly 1,000,000, found on every continent. They are probably part of East Indian origin and speak an Indo-Iranian language called Romany. Disinclined to assimilate, they hold to own customs. Usually depend on trading for living.

gypsy moth, European insect with larva destructive to forest and fruit trees. It appeared in U.S. c.1869 and is confined to NE portion. Adult male is yellowish brown; female whitish; dark lines mark forewings of each. Larva is c.2 in. long, dark brown or black with yellow markings and rows of blue and red tubercles bearing hairs. Air sacs on hairs make the larva buoyant; it can be carried by wind.

gyroscope (jī′rùskõp), rotating wheel movable about a second axis. This secondary motion, called "precession," is the azimuthal motion of the spin axis of the top. Gyroscope was invented in 1852 by Foucault and was used to demonstrate earth's rotation. With later invention of electric rotor its uses grew to include giant gyroscopic ship stabilizers, directional instruments such as gyrocompass (unaffected by magnetic variations), automatic pilot for guiding aircraft, and other devices.

H, chemical symbol of element hydrogen.

Haag, Den, Netherlands: see HAGUE, THE.

Haakon (hä′kùn, Nor. hô′kõõn), kings of Norway. **Haakon I** (the Good), c.915–961, son of Harold I, was brought up as Christian at court of King Athelstan in England. Displaced his brother Eric as king c.935. Strengthened national army and fleet; sought unsuccessfully to introduce Christianity. **Haakon IV** (Haakon Haakonsson), 1204–63, a grandson of Sverre, was formally recognized as king in 1223 after overcoming rival claimants. Under him medieval Norway reached its zenith. He acquired Greenland and Iceland, carried out legal reforms, held a splendid court. He died during an expedition in the Orkney Isls. **Haakon VII,** 1872–, second son of Frederick VIII of Denmark,

was elected to Norwegian throne 1905. Married Maud, daughter of Edward VII of England. Headed government in exile in England during World War II.

Haarlem (här′lùm), municipality (pop. 156,856), cap. of North Holland prov., W Netherlands, near North Sea. World center of tulip breeding and bulb exporting since 17th cent. Mfg. of machinery, textiles. Chartered 1245; sacked 1573 by Spanish. Center of 17th-cent. Dutch painting: Frans Hals, Ruisdael worked here. Landmarks include Church of St. Bavo (Groote Kerk, 15th cent.) and city hall (begun 1250; former palace of counts of Holland). Formerly also spelled Harlem.

Habakkuk or **Habacuc** (both: hùbă′kùk, hă′–), book of Old Testament, a set of poems on the triumph of justice and divine mercy over evil. Identity and time of prophet unknown. A prophet of this name appears in story of Bel and the Dragon. Also Habbacuc.

Habana, Cuba: see HAVANA.

habeas corpus (hā'bēŭs kôr'pŭs) [Latin,= you may have the body], writ directed by a judge to some person who is detaining another; it commands that the person in custody shall be brought at a specified time to a specified place for a specified purpose. It was known in England as early as the 14th cent. and came to be in England and later in the U.S. the prime remedy for false imprisonment and illegal detention without a judicial hearing. The U.S. Constitution provides that the privilege of the writ shall not be suspended unless, when in cases of rebellion or invasion, public safety may require suspension.

Haber, Fritz (hä'bŭr), 1868–1934, German chemist. He won the 1918 Nobel Prize. The **Haber process** for commercial synthesis of ammonia by direct combination of hydrogen and nitrogen was his invention.

Habsburg, family: see HAPSBURG.

hackberry, deciduous tree of genus *Celtis,* widely distributed, and often grown for ornament. It has warty bark, elmlike leaves, small edible fruit.

Hackensack, city (29,219), NE N.J., on Hackensack R. and NW of New York city; settled 1639 by Dutch. Has mfg. of pumps, metal products, glass, and furniture. Several Revolutionary engagements fought here. Has Dutch Reformed church (1696).

Hackensack, river rising in SE N.Y., W of Haverstraw, and flowing c.50 mi. S into N.J., past Hackensack and through Hackensack Meadows to Newark Bay.

Hackney, metropolitan borough (pop. 171,-337), NE London, England; once exclusive residential area.

Hadassah (hŭdă'sŭ), Hebrew name of ESTHER.

Hadassah (hŭdă'sŭ), the women's Zionist organization of America; founded 1912 by Henrietta Szold. Maintains medical and child welfare services in Israel, educational services in U.S.

Haddington, burgh (pop. 4,497), co. seat of East Lothian, Scotland, on the Tyne. Cruciform parish church is called "Lamp of the Lothians."

Haddingtonshire: see EAST LOTHIAN, Scotland.

haddock, food fish of N Atlantic similar to cod. Black lateral line runs from gill to tail. It averages 2–4 lb., with maximum of c.17 lb. Flesh is tender, white, flaky. Smoked haddock is finnan haddie.

Haddonfield, borough (pop. 10,495), SW N.J., suburb of Camden; settled 1682. Has Indian King Tavern (1750), where first state legislature met, 1777.

Haden, Sir Francis Seymour (hā'dŭn), 1818–1910, English etcher. His writings did much to familiarize the public with Rembrandt's etchings.

Hades, Greek underworld: see HELL and PLUTO.

Hadhramaut, Arabia: see HADRAMAUT.

Hadley, Henry Kimball, 1871–1937, American composer and conductor. Typical of his well-constructed and facile music are the opera *Cleopatra's Night* and the orchestral works *Salome* and *The Culprit Fay.*

Hadramaut or **Hadhramaut** (both: hädrŭmout'), region, Arabia, on Gulf of Aden and Arabian Sea, occupying roughly the central portion of Aden protectorate. Called Hazarmaveth in Bible.

Hadrian: see also ADRIAN.

Hadrian (hā'drēŭn), A.D. 76–138, Roman emperor (117–38), b. Spain. A ward of TRAJAN, he distinguished himself as commander and administrator and was named to succeed to the throne. His rule was vigorous, and he traveled about the empire, stabilizing government and beautifying cities with new architecture. He abandoned Trajan's aggressive policy in Asia, fixing the Euphrates as a boundary; had great walls built in Germany and Hadrian's Wall in Britain. In Palestine he put down the uprising under Bar Kochba and built a temple of Jupiter Capitolinus on the ruined Temple, renaming Jerusalem as Aelia Capitolina. Patronized the arts, and his regard for his favorite Antinoüs is recorded in many statues. Chose ANTONINUS PIUS as his successor. Name also appears as Adrian.

Hadrian's Mole: see CASTEL SANT' ANGELO.

Hadrian's Wall, anc. Roman wall, 73½ mi. long, across narrow part of Great Britain from Wallsend on Tyne R. to Bowness at head of Solway Firth. Built A.D. c.121–127 by Emperor Hadrian. Fragments remain of wall (6 ft. high and 8 ft. thick) and stone forts along it. British government preserves wall, one of largest Roman remains.

Haeckel, Ernst Heinrich (ěrnst' hīn'rĭkh hě'kŭl), 1834–1919, German biologist and philosopher. He evolved a mechanistic form of monism based on Darwin's theories. His studies of invertebrate marine organisms are well known. Although often erroneous, his theories stimulated research.

haemo-, for words beginning thus: see HEMO-.

Hafiz (häfēz'), d. 1389?, Persian poet, known for lyrics and drinking songs. Was a teacher of the Koran. Moslem critics interpret his poems allegorically.

hafnium (häf'nēŭm), widely distributed metallic element (symbol = Hf; see also ELEMENT, table).

Hafrs Fjord or **Hafs Fjord** (both: häfs'fyôrd), inlet of North Sea, SW Norway, near Stavanger. HAROLD I won decisive victory here, 872.

Hagar (hā'gŭr) [Heb.,= flight], handmaid of Sarah and mother of Ishmael by Abraham. Sent into desert because of Sarah's jealousy, she was comforted by an angel. Gen. 16: 21.9–21. St. Paul used Hagar as symbol for bondage of the Old Law. Gal. 4.2. Also Agar.

Hagen, Walter (hā'gŭn), 1892–, American golfer. Won U.S. Natl. Open (1914, 1919), British Open (1922, 1924, 1928, 1929), U.S. Professional Golfers Association championships (1921, 1924–27), many other titles.

Hagen (hä'gŭn), city (pop. 146,099), North Rhine-Westphalia, NW Germany. Industrial center of Ruhr dist. Heavily damaged in World War II.

Hagerstown, city (pop. 36,260), NW Md., NW of Frederick; settled c.1740. Trade center of agr. area with mfg. of organs and aircraft. Has Confederate cemetery.

haggada: see HALAKAH.

Haggai (hă'gāī), book of Old Testament, written in Jerusalem after the return from captivity. It urges renewal of work on restoring the Temple and contains a Messianic prophecy (2.7). In Vulgate: Aggeus.

Haggard, Sir H(enry) Rider, 1856–1925, English novelist, author of romantic adventure stories (e.g., *King Solomon's Mines,* 1885; *She,* 1887).

Hagia Sophia (hä'jù sōfē'ù, hä'jù, hă'gyù) [Gr., = Holy Wisdom] or **Santa Sophia,** originally a Christian church at Constantinople, now a museum of Byzantine art; supreme masterpiece of Byzantine architecture. On site of earlier churches (destroyed by fire) built in 360 by Constantine II and in 415 by Theodosius II. Present fireproof structure was built 532–37 by Justinian on designs of Anthemius of Tralles and Isidorus of Miletus. With Turkish conquest of city in 1453, it became a mosque. Nave is covered by lofty central dome (102 ft. in diameter, 184 ft. high) in which opens a luminous corona of 40 arched windows. All interior surfaces are sheathed with polychrome marbles and gold mosaic. Four slender minarets rise at outer corners of building. A cross surmounts the dome.

Hague, Frank, 1876–, Democratic political boss, mayor of Jersey City, N.J. 1917–47).

Hague, The (hāg), Dutch *'s Gravenhage* or *Den Haag,* municipality (pop. 532,998), cap. of South Holland prov. and *de facto* cap. of Netherlands, near the North Sea. Seat of royal court, legislature, supreme court of justice, and foreign embassies. City is almost entirely residential. It grew around palace begun 1250 by William, count of Holland, the Binnenhof, which now houses the legislature. As residence of stadholders of United Provs. in 17th–18th cent. it grew into a major diplomatic and intellectual center. Since First Hague Conference (1899) it also has been the center for promotion of internatl. justice and arbitration; Peace Palace (completed 1913) has housed Permanent Court of Arbitration, Permanent Court of Internatl. Justice, and, since 1945, Internatl. Court of Justice. Other landmarks include royal palace; Gevangenenpoort (14th-cent. prison, where brothers De Witt were murdered 1672); Mauritshuis (residence of John Maurice of Nassau, now a museum containing outstanding paintings by Rembrandt); 16th-cent. city hall; and Nieuwe Kerk [new church], with Spinoza's tomb.

Hague Conferences (hāg), term for the Internatl. Peace Conference of 1899 and the Second Internatl. Peace Conference of 1907, both proposed by Russia and held at The Hague. Failed to effect an arms reduction, but modified some of the rules of war. First conference estab. (1899) the Permanent Court of Arbitration, known popularly as the **Hague Tribunal.** Each member nation may appoint up to four members of a panel of judges from which arbitrators are picked when two or more nations submit a dispute for arbitration. More than 20 international disputes have been arbitrated. After World War I the Tribunal lost most of its importance to the World Court.

Hahn, Otto (ô'tō hän), 1879–, German chemist and physicist. Won 1944 Nobel Prize for splitting uranium atom and discovering possibility of chain reactions. Atom bomb was based on this work.

Hahnemann, Samuel (hä'nùmùn), 1755–1843, German physician, founder of homeopathy.

Hahnemann Medical College and Hospital, in Philadelphia; chartered 1848 as Homeopathic Medical Col. of Pennsylvania. United 1869 with Hahnemann Medical Col. of Philadelphia (1866–67); assumed present name 1885.

Haida Indians (hī'dù), North American Indian tribe, on Queen Charlotte Isls. and Prince of Wales Isl. Language is only one of Haida family. They belong to Pacific Northwest culture area.

Haidar Ali: see HYDER ALI.

Haifa (hī'fä), seaport (pop. c.130,000), NW Israel, on the Mediterranean, at foot of Mt. Carmel; chief port of Israel. Terminus of pipe line from Iraq.

Haig, Douglas Haig, 1st Earl, 1861–1928, British soldier. In World War I he was British commander in chief after 1915. Maintained confidence of the public despite antagonism of Lloyd George.

hail, pellets or lumps of ice, snow, or rime, falling usually over small areas in hot weather at onset of thunderstorm. The freezing nuclei of hailstones are carried by turbulent winds and grow between wetting and freezing until heavy enough to fall.

Haile Selassie (hī'lē sùlä'sē), 1891–, emperor of Ethiopia, originally named Tafari Makonnen; grandson of Menelik II. Was governor of several provinces during reign of Lij Yusu. When emperor became a Mohammedan, Haile Selassie (a Coptic Christian and then known as Ras Tafari) forced his deposition and put Menelik's daughter Judith on the throne, with himself as regent. Crowned emperor in 1930. During Italian invasion (1935–36) he personally led troops against the enemy. Fled to England 1936, returned in early 1941 to regain his throne.

Hailey, resort city (pop. 1,464), S central Idaho, E of Boise. Has hot springs.

Haileybury, town (pop. 2,346), E Ont., Canada, N of North Bay, on L. Timiskaming. Center of mining region. Popular ski resort.

Hainan (hī'nän'), island (13,000 sq. mi.; pop. 2,500,000), off Kwantung prov., China, in South China Sea. Separated from mainland by Hainan Strait (10–15 mi. wide). Agr., lumbering, and iron mining. Occupied 1939–45 by the Japanese, fell 1950 to Communists.

Hainaut (ĕnō'), province (1,437 sq. mi.; pop. 1,247,299), SW Belgium, bordering on France; cap. Mons. Formerly spelled Hainault. Drained by Scheldt, Sambre, and Dender rivers. Agr.; cattle raising and dairying in S. Important coal mines (Borinage dist.); metallurgy (at Charleroi); textile mfg. (at Tournai). Population is mainly French-speaking. Hainaut became a county in 9th cent., was part of Lotharingia. In 1191 Flanders passed to counts of Hainaut by marriage. Baldwin VI (as Baldwin IX, count of Flanders) became emperor of Constantinople as BALDWIN I (1204). In 1278 the two counties were separated: Flanders passed to Guy of Dampierre, a great-grandson of Baldwin; Hainaut passed to John of Avesnes, another great-grandson, who also became count of Holland. With HOLLAND, Hainaut passed to the houses of Burgundy (1433) and Hapsburg (1482). (For later history, see NETHERLANDS, AUSTRIAN AND SPANISH). Parts of Hainaut were annexed to France 1659, 1678.

Haines, village (pop. 338), SE Alaska, on Chilkoot Inlet of Lynn Canal, SSW of Skagway. Fur-trading post estab. 1867, U.S. army post later. Has good harbor, fishing, and fur farming. Haines Cutoff built in World War II to connect with Alaska Highway at Haines Junction, Yukon territory, provides short route from Panhandle to interior.

Haines City, city (pop. 5,630), central Fla., ENE of Tampa and NNW of L. Kissimmee. Ships citrus.

Haiphong (hī'fŏng'), city (pop. 142,956), Indo-China, on arm of Thaibinh R. delta near Gulf of Tonkin; main port and naval base of Tonkin.

hair, modified skin structure, consisting of a shaft and a root which is expanded into hair bulb embedded in dermis of skin. Life cycle of scalp hair is about four years.

hairworm or **horsehair worm,** long, slender, unsegmented roundworm usually included in phylum Nemathelminthes. Larvae are parasitic, usually in body of an aquatic insect larva, later in another insect. Once mature they escape from second host into water, where they live as adults.

Haiti (hā'tē), Fr. *Haïti* (äētē'), republic (c.10,700 sq. mi.; pop. 3,111,373), West Indies, on W third of Hispaniola (rest occupied by DOMINICAN REPUBLIC); cap. PORT-AU-PRINCE. The island (called also Haiti and SANTO DOMINGO) belonged to the Spanish, but English and French buccaneers used Haiti region as a base, and French colonists developed sugar plantations with Negro slaves in 17th cent. Spain ceded Haiti (then Saint-Domingue) to France in 1697. French Revolution caused uprising of slaves, which was successful under TOUSSAINT L'OUVERTURE. Spain ceded all the island to France in 1795, but Toussaint conquered it all, and the Haitians resisted Napoleon's punitive force under Gen. Leclerc and even kept up resistance after Toussaint was captured by trickery. Independence, proclaimed in 1804, was achieved. Jacques DESSALINES and Henri CHRISTOPHE became emperors, then Alexandre Pétion, J. P. Boyer, and Faustin SOULOUQUE ruled. Political trouble continued, and financial trouble followed. The U.S. exercised customs receivership (1905–41), and U.S. naval control was strong until 1934. Haiti produces coffee, cotton, sugar, sisal, bananas, and cacao, diversification being enforced by law since the collapse of the sugar market in 1926. Mulattoes dominate the political scene, and most of the population (95% Negro) lives on bare subsistence from farms. Practice of *vodun* (voodoo) rites has been much studied. Border clashes with the Dominican Republic continue and are sometimes violent.

Hakluyt, Richard (hă'klōōt), 1552?–1616, English geographer. Noted for *The Principal Navigations, Voyages, Traffics, and Discoveries of the English Nation* (3 vols., 1598–

1600), called by J. A. Froude "the prose epic of the English nation."

Hakodate (häkō'dätä), city (pop. 211,441), extreme SW Hokkaido, Japan; port on Tsugaru Strait. Shipbuilding center and chief port of island.

Hakone (hä"kō'nä), resort region of mountains, lakes, and hot springs, central Honshu, Japan.

halakah or **halacha** (both: hälä'khä, häläkhä'), the part of the MIDRASH and the TALMUD which embraces the legal statutes of the unwritten commentaries based upon the teachings of the Old Testament. Contrasting is the haggada, the literary element of the Oral Law, which illustrates application of the law by parables.

Halbe, Max (mäks' häl'bû), 1865–1945, German naturalist dramatist. Best known for *Jugend* (1893; Eng. tr., *When Love Is Young,* 1904).

Halberstadt (häl'bûrshtät), city (pop. 47,652), Saxony-Anhalt, central Germany. Has many fine medieval buildings, notably Liebfrauenkirche (12th cent.) and cathedral (13th–17th cent.; heavily damaged in World War II).

Halcyone (hälsī'ûnē) [Gr.,= kingfisher], in Greek mythology, daughter of Aeolus. At death of her husband she leaped into the sea. The gods, from compassion, changed the pair into kingfishers, and Zeus forbade the winds to blow for 14 days at the winter solstice, the time when halcyons breed. Hence the expression "halcyon days," a time of tranquillity.

Haldane, John Scott (hôl'dān), 1860–1936, English scientist, known for studies in respiration and gasometry of blood, industrial hygiene, safety and health in mines. His son, **J(ohn) B(urdon) S(anderson) Haldane,** 1892–, is known for application of mathematics to biology and for expositions of science for layman.

Haldimand, Sir Frederick (hôl'dĭmûnd), 1718–91, British general and colonial governor of Quebec (1778–84), b. Switzerland.

Hale, Edward Everett, 1822–1909, American author of *The Man without a Country* (1863). A Unitarian clergyman, he was famous as a preacher. His sister, **Lucretia Peabody Hale,** 1820–1900, is best remembered for amusing stories for children, *The Peterkin Papers* (1880).

Hale, George Ellery, 1868–1938, American astronomer, authority on solar vortices and magnetic fields, inventor of spectroheliograph. He organized the Mt. Palomar, Yerkes, and Mt. Wilson observatories.

Hale, Lucretia Peabody: see HALE, EDWARD EVERETT.

Hale, Sir Matthew, 1609–76, English jurist, author of scholarly works on criminal law (*Pleas of the Crown,* 1678; *History of the Pleas of the Crown,* 1685).

Hale, Nathan, 1755–76, American patriot in American Revolution. Hanged by British as spy. Remembered for reputed last words, "I only regret that I have but one life to lose for my country."

Hale, Sarah Josepha (Buell), 1788–1879, American author, long editor of *Godey's Lady's*

Book. "Mary Had a Little Lamb" is attributed to her.

Haleakala (hä″lää″kälä′), mountain, 10,032 ft. high, on E Maui, T.H. World's largest extinct crater, 20 mi. in circumference, 2,000 ft. deep.

Haledon (hāl′dŭn), borough (pop. 6,204), NE N.J., NW of Paterson. Textiles, labels, pharmaceuticals.

Hales, Alexander of: see ALEXANDER OF HALES.

Hales, John, 1584–1656, English clergyman and scholar, often called the Ever-Memorable. His lectures on Greek at Oxford, his preaching, and his writings won him renown.

Hales, Stephen, 1677–1761, English physiologist, a clergyman (curate of Teddington), noted for experimental studies in plant and animal physiology.

Halévy, Jacques Fromental (zhäk′ frômätäl′ älävē′), 1799–1862, French operatic composer. His one successful opera was *La Juive* (1835). Father-in-law and teacher of Bizet, he was the uncle of **Ludovic Halévy** (lü-dôvēk′), 1834–1908, author of the librettos of Offenbach's most successful operettas and, with Henri Meilhac, of the libretto of Bizet's *Carmen* (1875).

Halévy, Joseph (zhôzěf′ älävē′), 1827–1908, Jewish French Orientalist. Deciphered Sabean and Himyaritic inscriptions and argued that Sumerian literature was merely Babylonian literature in secret writing.

Halevy, Judah: see JUDAH HA-LEVI.

Halévy, Ludovic: see HALÉVY, JACQUES FROMENTAL.

Half-Way Covenant, doctrinal decision of Congregational churches in New England regarding membership in 1662. Original rule had permitted children of "converted" adults to share in covenant. New rule included also grandchildren even though their parents had not been converted. Decision, nicknamed Half-Way Covenant, caused dissension and secession.

Haliburton, Thomas Chandler, pseud. **Sam Slick,** 1796–1865, Canadian author, a jurist. His popular series of the sayings and doings of Sam Slick, Yankee peddler, were collected in *The Clockmaker* (1836) and in later volumes.

halibut, important food fish, largest of flatfish, of genus *Hippoglossus.* Two species are known, one in N Atlantic and one in N Pacific. Females sometimes weigh 500 lb., males rarely over 50 lb.

Halicarnassus (hă″lĭkärnă′sŭs), anc. city of Caria, SW Asia Minor. Widow of ruler MAUSOLUS (4th cent. B.C.) built him a great tomb (see MAUSOLEUM).

Halicz, Ukrainian SSR: see GALICH.

Halifax, Charles Montagu, earl of (hă′lĭfăks, hă′lŭ-), 1661–1715, British statesman. Wrote (with Matthew Prior) *The City Mouse and the Country Mouse* (1687). Persuaded Commons to estab. (1692) national debt. Adopted plan to found Bank of England and was made (1694) chancellor of the exchequer. Prime minister 1697–99.

Halifax, Edward Frederick Lindley Wood, 1st earl of, 1881–, British statesman. Governor general of India 1926–31. As foreign secretary (1938–40) he played a large part in negotiating the MUNICH PACT. Ambassador to U.S. 1941–46.

Halifax, city (pop. 85,589), provincial cap., S N.S., Canada, on Halifax Harbour on the Atlantic. Largest city and chief port of N.S. All-year port is main Canadian winter terminal for transatlantic shipping. Industries include oil and sugar refining, shipbuilding, and meat packing. Has large fishing fleet. Founded 1749, it became a naval base in 1758 expedition against Louisburg, in American Revolution, and in War of 1812. Important naval and air base in both World Wars. The Citadel, fortress built 1794–97, overlooks town and harbor. Seat of Dalhousie Univ. (nonsectarian; coed.; 1838) and associated or affiliated Univ. of King's Col. (opened 1790, became first Canadian university by royal charter in 1802, moved from Windsor, N.S., 1923), Nova Scotia Technical Col., and St. Mary's Col. The Halifax *Gazette* (1752), first Canadian newspaper, continues as the *Nova Scotia Royal Gazette.*

Halifax, county borough (pop. 98,376), West Riding of Yorkshire, England. Noteworthy are Akroyd museum and art gallery. Defoe supposedly wrote part of *Robinson Crusoe* here. Industries include mfg. of carpets, cotton, wool, and worsteds.

Halifax, town (pop. 346), N N.C., on Roanoke R. and NE of Raleigh. Had state's first constitutional convention 1776. Some 18th-cent. buildings.

Hall, Basil, 1788–1844, British naval officer and traveler. Commanded vessels on voyages of exploration. His *Travels in North America* (3 vols., 1829) form valuable description of America.

Hall, Charles Francis, 1821–71, American arctic explorer. Made two expeditions (1860–62, 1864–69) seeking Sir John Franklin's party. Added much to geographical knowledge of area. Led government North Pole expedition (1871).

Hall, Charles Martin, 1863–1914, American chemist, a founder of Aluminum Company of America. He discovered electrolytic process that made large-scale aluminum production possible.

Hall, Granville Stanley, 1846–1924, American psychologist, educator. He was the first president of Clark Univ. (1889–1920). His work *The Contents of Children's Minds on Entering School* (1894) initiated the child-study movement in U.S.

Hall, James, 1793–1868, American author of works on the West, a magazine editor.

Hall, James, 1811–98, American geologist and paleontologist. His work served as a basis for later geological histories of North America.

Hall, Marshall, 1790–1857, English physician and physiologist, pioneer in study of reflex action.

Hall, Fort, trading post, SE Idaho, on Snake R. and near present Pocatello. Built 1834. Important stopping point on Oregon Trail.

Hallam, Arthur Henry (hăl′ŭm), 1811–33, English poet. Tennyson's *In Memoriam* is an elegy for him.

Halland (hä′länd), Swed. *Hallands län,* county (1,901 sq. mi.; pop. 163,363), SW Sweden, on the Kattegat; co. seat Halmstad. This area was conquered from Denmark by Charles X of Sweden, 1658.

Halle (hä′lŭ), city (pop. 222,505), cap. of Saxony-Anhalt, E central Germany, on Saale R. Center of an important salt-mining dist.; chemical and machine-building industries. Ruled in Middle Ages by archbishops of Magdeburg; accepted Reformation 1544; was awarded to Brandenburg (i.e., the later Prussia) 1648. Famous university was founded 1694; it absorbed Wittenberg Univ. 1817. First Bible Society was founded here 1710. Among many fine buildings are Gothic Red Tower and Marienkirche, on medieval market place. Birthplace of Handel.

Halleck, Fitz-Greene, 1790–1867, American poet. With Joseph Rodman Drake wrote satirical verse in "Croaker" papers. Also known for "Marco Bozzaris" and elegy on Drake.

Halleck, Henry Wager, 1815–72, Union general in Civil War. Commanded Dept. of the Missouri (1861–62). Gained unwarranted prestige from victories under his command. General in chief at Washington (1862–64); exerted little influence as military adviser to President and Secretary of War.

Hallelujah (hă″lŭlōō′yŭ) or **Alleluia** (ă″lŭlū′-yŭ) [Heb.,= praise the Lord], expression of joy in Hebrew worship; cf. Pss. 104–6, 111–13; 115–17; 135; 146–50. Used in Christian liturgy, especially at Easter.

Haller, Albrecht von (äl′brĕkht fŭn hä′lŭr), 1708–77, Swiss scientist and author. Especially noted for researches in experimental physiology, he was distinguished also as botanist, writer on bibliography and medical history, poet, and novelist.

Hallet, Étienne Sulpice (ātyĕn′ sülpēs′ älā′), 1755–1825, French architect, known in U.S. as Stephen Hallet. Became supervisor of execution of William Thornton's design for the Capitol, Washington, D.C., but was dismissed for attempted alterations.

Halley, Edmund (hă′lē), 1656–1742, English astronomer, astronomer royal from 1720. First to predict (1682) return of a comet (Halley's comet).

hallmark, plate mark or impress on silver or gold work officially approving purity of metal. Introduced by statute in England in 1300 and enforced by Goldsmiths' Hall, London. Other marks include date mark (usually a letter) and maker's initials.

Hall of Fame, national shrine estab. 1900 at New York Univ. with aid of $250,000 donation by Mrs. Finley J. Shepard. Names of 50 outstanding Americans were inscribed on bronze tablets in 1900. Other names were added later.

Halloween, Oct. 31, evening before feast of All Saints. Tales and customs concerned with witches and ghosts on Halloween are Celtic in origin.

hallucination, false sensory perception lacking external stimulus. Most psychiatrists consider hallucinations symbolic of repressed wishes; they help reveal emotional conflicts, especially in schizophrenic patients. Some hallucinations are caused by emotional stress or great fatigue, e.g., the fata morgana or imagined oasis of desert travelers.

Halmahera (hälmähä′rä) or **Jailolo** (jīlô′lô), island (c.6,870 sq. mi.; pop. including near-by Morotai 83,743), E Indonesia; largest of the Moluccas. Mountainous, volcanic. Products include nutmeg, resin, sago, and rice. In World War II it was major Japanese air base, neutralized by Sept., 1944.

Halmstad (hälm′städ″), industrial town (pop. 35,276), co. seat of Halland co., SW Sweden, seaport on the Kattegat. Mineral baths are near.

halo, in physics, circle of light around sun or moon, produced when light from either is refracted and reflected by atmospheric ice crystals. Most complex and brilliant near poles. Corona is similar.

halogen (hă′lŭjŭn), member of a family of very active elements. FLUORINE is lightest, most active; CHLORINE, BROMINE, and IODINE are least active. All are monovalent, nonmetallic, and form negative ions.

Hals, Frans (fräns′ häls′), c.1580–1666, Dutch painter, b. Antwerp. Spent most of his life in Haarlem. Painted both single and group portraits as well as studies of low-life types. His bold brushwork gives his work an air of vivacity and informality. Used heavy browns in early period; later alternated blacks and grays with brilliant color. His *Laughing Cavalier* is among widely known works. Also painters were his son **Frans Hals,** c.1620–c.1669, and his brother **Dirk Hals,** c.1591–1656, noted for festivals and drinking scenes.

Halsey, William F(rederick) (hôl′sē), 1882–, American admiral. Commanded naval action in South Pacific area and in Philippines in World War II. Admiral of the fleet 1945–47.

Halsingborg (hĕlsĭng′bôryŭ), Swed. *Hälsingborg,* city (pop. 71,718), Malmohus co., S Sweden, seaport on the Oresund opposite Elsinore, Denmark. Trade center and stronghold from 9th cent., it was ceded 1658 by Denmark to Sweden, seized and plundered 1676 by Danes, and regained 1710 by Sweden. Its products include copper, sugar, beer, and superphosphates. To NE is only coal field in Sweden. Formerly also spelled Helsingborg.

Halsted, William Stewart (hôl′stĕd), 1852–1922, American surgeon, professor at Johns Hopkins. His many surgical innovations include use of rubber gloves.

Halys, river of Asia Minor: see KIZIL IRMAK.

Ham [Heb.,= swarthy], son of Noah and father of Cush, Mizraim, Phut, and Canaan. Gen. 9; 10. Hamitic languages named after him; see LANGUAGE (table).

Hama (hä′mä), city (pop. c.70,000), N Syria, on Orontes R. Was Hittite center in ancient times. Called Hamath in Bible, it was renamed Epiphania by Antiochus IV. Once famed for fine textiles, now a trade center for grain-producing area.

Hamadan (hä′mŭdăn), city (pop. 103,874; alt. 6,280 ft.), W Iran, at foot of Mt. Elvend; market center. On site of Ecbatana, cap. of Media. Traditional tomb of Esther is here.

Haman (hä′–), courtier of Ahasuerus. He ordered the massacre of the Jews but was thwarted by Esther and Mordecai and was hanged. Esther 3–7. Also Aman.

Hamar (hä′mär), city (pop. 10,183), SE Norway, on Mjosa L. It is center of rich agr. area, with mfg. of machinery and leather goods. Founded 1152 as an episcopal see by Nicholas Breakspear (later Pope Adrian IV), it is now a Lutheran see. Remains of 12th-cent. cathedral survive, but modern city dates only from 19th cent.

Hamasa (hämä′sä), anthology of beautiful early Arabic poems, gathered by Abu Tammam (c.805–c.845).

Hamath, Syria: see HAMA.

Hambidge, Jay (hăm′bīj), 1867–1924, American writer and artist. His measurements of classical works of art led to his discovery of mathematical principles which he believed had been consciously used by ancient Egyptian and Greek designers. These principles, called dynamic symmetry, were developed into an extensive system of application.

Hambletonian (hămbŭltō′nēŭn), 1849–76, American trotting horse, foundation sire of trotting horses bearing his name. Hambletonian Stake Race for three-year-old trotters held annually at Goshen, N.Y.

Hamburg (hăm′bûrg, Ger. häm′bŏŏrk), state (288 sq. mi.; pop. 1,604,600), N Germany. It consists mainly of the free Hansa city of **Hamburg,** on the Elbe near its mouth on the North Sea. Largest German seaport; shipyards; mfg. (machinery, chemicals); fishing fleet. A cultural center, it has a university (founded 1919) and several technical and medical institutes. Founded by Charlemagne, Hamburg soon grew to commercial importance and became a free imperial city. Its alliance with Lübeck (1241) was the basis of the HANSEATIC LEAGUE. Hamburg joined the German Confederation (1815), the German Empire (1871), the Weimar Republic (1919), and the Federal Republic of [Western] Germany (1949). In 1938 its outlying port, CUXHAVEN, was ceded to Prussia in exchange for ALTONA. Half the city and many lives were destroyed by air raids in World War II. Postwar reconstruction was rapid. The state has been under British occupation since 1945.

Hamburg. 1 Borough (pop. 1,305), NW N.J., N of Dover. "Gingerbread Castle" here has fairy-tale scenes. **2** Village (pop. 6,938), W N.Y., S of Buffalo.

Hamden, town (pop. 29,715), S Conn., N of New Haven; settled c.1664. Site of Eli Whitney's arms factory is marked, his model barn (1816) preserved. Metals.

Hameln (hä′mŭln) or **Hamelin** (hă′mŭlĭn), city (pop. 48,086), Lower Saxony, NW Germany, in Hanover, on Weser R. Scene of legend of PIED PIPER OF HAMELIN.

Hamhung (häm′hŏong′), Jap. *Kanko,* city (1944 pop. 112,184), N Korea; industrial center.

Hamilcar Barca (hă′mĭlkär, hŭmĭl′kär), d. 228 B.C., Carthaginian commander. Gave a good account of himself in Sicily in the First Punic War. When the peace settlement surrendered Sicily, he withdrew without submission. He ruthlessly put down an insurrection of the mercenaries (238 B.C.) and became practically dictator of Carthage. Set out (237 B.C.) to conquer Spain and was successful until he fell in battle. Father of HANNIBAL.

Hamilton, Scottish noble family. **James Hamilton, 2d Baron Hamilton** and **1st earl of Arran,** 1477?–1529, grandson of King James II, was regent (1522–26) for boy king, James V, whom he helped to keep prisoner. His son, **James Hamilton, 2d earl of Arran,** d. 1575,

joined English party as a Protestant, then French party as a Catholic. Again Protestant, he fled Scotland when Mary Queen of Scots married Darnley. Tried unsuccessfully to marry Mary to his son, **James Hamilton, 3d earl of Arran,** 1530–1609, who later became insane. Succeeded as head of the family by his brother, **John Hamilton, 1st marquess of Hamilton,** 1532–1604, nearest heir to Scottish throne after James VI. Banished after his part in murder of earl of Murray, he later enjoyed the king's favor. His grandson, **James Hamilton, 3d marquess** and **1st duke of Hamilton,** 1606–49, was Charles I's chief adviser for Scottish affairs. Tried to pacify the Covenanters. Fought for the king at Preston in 1642 and was found guilty of treason by same court which condemned Charles. His brother, **William Hamilton, 2d duke of Hamilton,** 1616–51, was also favored by Charles I. Signed for the Scots the treaty known as the engagement with Charles in 1647.

Hamilton, Alexander, 1757–1804, American statesman, b. West Indies. Supported patriot cause and fought in American Revolution. Through FEDERALIST PAPERS he did much to get Constitution ratified. Strong exponent of centralized government. A leader of FEDERALIST PARTY. As first Secretary of the Treasury, he estab. Bank of the United States. Favored strengthening Federal government at expense of the states, tying administration more or less tightly to moneyed interests, and following a pro-British foreign policy. Though Jeffersonianism was more popular, Hamilton's vision of the future America as a wealthy, industrial land proved more accurate than Jefferson's agrarian dream. Hamilton was killed in a duel by Aaron Burr, whom he had kept from the presidency in 1800 and from the governorship of N.Y. in 1804.

Hamilton, Andrew Jackson, 1815–75, provisional governor of Texas (1865–66). Pursued wise and courageous course, but much of his work was undone by radical Republican plan of Reconstruction.

Hamilton, Anthony, c.1645–1719, Scottish author of the French *Mémoires du comte de Grammont* (1713?), based on the reminiscences of his brother-in-law, Philibert de GRAMONT. It is a thoroughly amoral but vastly entertaining account of the times.

Hamilton, Emma, Lady, c.1765–1815, English beauty. Mistress (and later wife) of Sir William Hamilton, ambassador to Naples, she had great influence with the queen of Naples. After 1798 she was the mistress of Horatio NELSON whose daughter she bore in 1801. There are many portraits of her by Romney.

Hamilton, Henry, d. 1796, British army officer. In American Revolution, accused of being a "hair buyer"—i.e., one who paid bounties to Indians for scalps taken in frontier raids. Captured by George Rogers Clark at Vincennes (1779).

Hamilton, James, earls of Arran, and **James, 3d marquess** and **1st duke of Hamilton:** see HAMILTON, family.

Hamilton, James, 1786–1857, U.S. Representative (1822–29), governor of S.C. (1830–32). Presided over convention which passed nullification ordinance. Diplomatic agent in Europe for Texas (1839).

Hamilton, John, 1st marquess, and William, 2d duke, of Hamilton: see HAMILTON, family.

Hamilton Sir William, 1788–1856, Scottish philosopher. Revived Scottish "common sense" school of metaphysics.

Hamilton, city (pop. c.3,000) and cap. of Bermuda; chief port and center of governmental, commercial, and social life.

Hamilton, city (pop. 208,321), S Ont., Canada, on Hamilton Harbour at head of L. Ontario, SW of Toronto; laid out 1813. Lake port, rail and air center. Has steel, cotton, and knitting mills, automobile plants, and railroad shops. In fruitgrowing region. Seat of McMaster Univ. (Baptist; coed.; 1887).

Hamilton, burgh (pop. 40,173), Lanarkshire, Scotland. Rudolf Hess landed on near-by Hamilton estate after his flight from Germany in May, 1941.

Hamilton. 1 Village (pop. 3,507), central N.Y., SW of Utica. Seat of Colgate Univ. (nonsectarian; for men; opened as Baptist seminary 1820. Named for William Colgate, a benefactor, 1890). **2** City (pop. 57,951), SW Ohio, on Great Miami R. and N of Cincinnati; settled on site of Fort Hamilton (1791). Trade center for agr. area with mfg. of paper products, machinery, and steel and iron products. Boyhood home of W. D. Howells.

Hamilton, river, 600 mi. long, S Labrador. Rises as Ashuanipi R. from Ashuanipi L. and flows in arc N then SE through series of lakes to the GRAND FALLS where it becomes the Hamilton. Below it flows SE to Lake Melville.

Hamilton, Mount, 4,372 ft. high, W Calif., in Diablo Range near San Jose. Lick Observatory (built 1876–88) of Univ. of California is here.

Hamilton College: see CLINTON, N.Y.

Hamilton Inlet, large bay on SE Labrador coast. Rigolet, Hudson's Bay Co. post, is at its narrows.

Hamitic languages: see LANGUAGE (table).

Hamlet, town (pop. 5,061), S N.C., near S.C. line. Trade and shipping center for fruit area.

Hamlin, Alfred Dwight Foster, 1855–1926, American architect and teacher. Taught architecture at Columbia Univ. His son, Talbot Faulkner Hamlin, 1889–, is author of several books on architecture.

Hamlin, Hannibal, 1809–91, Vice President of the United States (1861–65). U.S. Senator from Maine (1848–57, 1869–81). Minister to Spain (1881–82).

Hamline University: see SAINT PAUL, Minn.

Hamm (häm), city (pop. 59,372), North Rhine-Westphalia, NW Germany, on Lippe R. Railroad and industrial center in Ruhr dist.

Hamm, village, grand duchy of Luxembourg. Has large American military cemetery.

Hammarskjold, Dag (däg´ häm´ärshŭld´), 1905–, Swedish statesman, secretary general of the United Nations (1953–). Was Swedish deputy minister of finance 1936–45, assistant foreign minister 1949–51, and deputy foreign minister 1951–53.

hammer, tool known since Neolithic period. It evolved from club weighted at striking end by hammerstone. Stone hammer is emblem of Thor. Power hammer came into use c.1840. See also PNEUMATIC APPLIANCES AND TOOLS.

Hammerfest (hä´mŭrfĕst), city (pop. 3,538), Finnmark co., N Norway, port on Kval isl.; inc. 1789. Though it is northernmost city of Europe, harbor is always ice free. It is fishing, whaling, and sealing center. Germans, who used it as naval base in World War II, demolished it upon retreating.

Hammersmith, metropolitan borough (pop. 119,317), W London, England. Has St. Paul's School for boys (founded 1509), attended by Milton and Pepys. Site of Kelmscott Press and Doves Press.

Hammerstein, Oscar (hä´mŭrstīn), 1847–1919, German-American operatic impresario. He brought many famous singers to the U.S. and introduced such operas as *Louise, Pelléas et Mélisande,* and *Elektra.* His grandson, **Oscar Hammerstein, 2d,** 1895–, is a lyricist and librettist. His musicals (e.g., *Oklahoma!, South Pacific*) with the composer Richard Rodgers have made theatrical history by running for great lengths of time and by using serious plots.

Hammett, Dashiell, 1894–, American writer of "tough" detective stories (e.g., *The Maltese Falcon,* 1930).

Hammond, James Henry, 1807–64, governor of S.C. (1842–44). Early advocate of secession. Elected to U.S. Senate in 1857, he made famous "Cotton is King" speech there.

Hammond, John Hays, 1855–1936, American mining engineer. Employed by Cecil Rhodes in South Africa. Involved in Jameson raid (1895–96), captured and sentenced to death, released on payment of fine. Promoted many mining and hydroelectric projects. His son, **John Hays Hammond, Jr.,** 1888–, gained note as inventor and electrical engineer. His inventions include torpedoes for coastal defense, incendiary projectiles, telegraphic apparatus.

Hammond. 1 City (pop. 87,594), NW Ind., near L. Michigan between Gary and Chicago, on Grand Calumet R.; settled 1851. Mfg. of railroad cars, metal, petroleum and wood products, and surgical supplies. **2** City (pop. 8,010), SE La., E of Baton Rouge. Rail and trade center of strawberry-growing area.

Hammonton, town (pop. 8,411), S central N.J., SE of Camden. Farm trade center with canneries.

Hammurabi (hämoŏrä´bē), fl. 2100 B.C., king of BABYLONIA and founder of its greatness. His code of laws is one of the most famous of ancient documents.

Hampden, John, 1594–1643, English statesman; cousin of Oliver Cromwell. Popular hero of the parliamentarians after his attempted arrest (1642) by Charles I helped to precipitate the civil war.

Hampden, Walter (hăm´dŭn), 1879–, American actor. Has acted in classical repertory (London, 1901), Ibsen, and Shakspere. With his own company after 1923 did such plays as Rostand's *Cyrano de Bergerac.*

Hampden-Sydney College: see FARMVILLE, Va.

Hampshire (hămp´shĭr) or **Hants** (hănts), maritime county (1,649 sq. mi.; pop. 1,292,211), S England; co. town WINCHESTER. Officially Southampton since 1888, county no longer includes Isle of WIGHT. Undulating region devoted to sheep raising and dairy farming, it also has shipbuilding and large martime trade. SOUTHAMPTON and Portsmouth major ports. Has many literary and historical associations.

Hampshire sheep: see SHEEP.

Hampstead (hămp'stĭd), metropolitan borough (pop. 95,073), NW London, England. Associated with artists and writers. On a hill above is **Hampstead Heath**, a public park of 869 acres.

Hampton, Wade, 1818–1902, Confederate general. Succeeded J. E. B. Stuart as cavalry corps commander (1864). Restored home rule as governor of S.C. (1876–79). Until 1890 he was dominant in S.C. politics.

Hampton, former urban district, now part of Twickenham, Middlesex, England. Site of David Garrick's house. **Hampton Court Palace** was built by Cardinal Wolsey in 1515 as his private residence. After his downfall, it was a royal residence until time of George II. Has an art gallery and public gardens. **Hampton Court Conference** was held (1604) to find agreement between Puritans and Established Church, with results most unsatisfactory to Puritans.

Hampton. 1 Town (pop. 2,847), SE N.H., S of Portsmouth. Hampton Beach is a resort. **2** City (pop. 5,966), SE Va., port on HAMPTON ROADS opposite Norfolk; settled 1610. One of oldest continuous English settlements in U.S. Sacked by British 1813; burned by Confederates 1861. Processes and ships seafood. Near by is Langley Field, U.S. Army air base. Seat of **Hampton Institute** (Negro; nonsectarian; coed.; opened 1868, founded by American Missionary Assn. through efforts of S. C. Armstrong). B. T. Washington studied here. Indians attended 1878–1923. Best-endowed school for Negroes in country.

Hampton Court Conference and **Hampton Court Palace:** see HAMPTON, England.

Hampton Institute: see HAMPTON, Va.

Hampton Roads, roadstead, SE Va., outlet of James, Nansemond, and Elizabeth rivers into Chesapeake Bay. One of finest natural harbors and one of busiest U.S. seaports; port of Newport News, Hampton, Portsmouth, and Norfolk. In Civil War, scene of fight between ironclads MONITOR AND MERRIMAC. The **Hampton Roads Peace Conference** was a meeting to end Civil War, held Feb. 3, 1865, on board Union transport *River Queen* here. Lincoln presented Union terms. They were unacceptable to South, and meeting failed.

hamster, small rodent of temperate parts of Europe and W Asia. It has a thickset body c.6 in. long and a hairy tail ½ in. long. Usually it is brown or gray (sometimes black or marked with black) above with white under parts. It has a rather broad head, round ears, and large internal cheek pouches. In the wild state it eats small animals in summer and grain stored underground in winter.

Hamsun, Knut (kŭnōōt häm'sōōn), 1859–1952, Norwegian novelist. His wandering life brought him twice to U.S., where he had many jobs. His best-known novels—*Hunger* (1890), *Pan* (1894), and *The Growth of the Soil* (1917)—are uncompromisingly realistic. Awarded 1920 Nobel Prize in literature. In World War II sympathized with Germans in Norway.

Hamtramck (hămtră'mĭk), city (pop. 43,355), SE Mich., within confines of Detroit. Mfg. of automobiles, metal products and machinery. Public schools here undertook notable plan for education for democracy 1923.

Hamun-i-Helmand (hämōōn'ē-hĕl'mŭnd), lake, area 5,000 sq. mi., on border of Iran and Afghanistan.

Han (hän), dynasty of China, which ruled 202 B.C.–A.D. 220. Ruled 400 years with only one break, caused by Hsin dynasty (A.D. c.9–c.25) which divided Early or Western Han period from Later or Eastern Han. Era of expansion and cultural growth. First Chinese dictionary and encyclopedic history compiled; Buddhism introduced. Collapse of Han was followed by c.350 years of petty states.

Han, river, c.750 mi. long, in Shensi and Hupeh provs., China. At junction with Yangtze R. are Hankow, Wuchang, and Hanyang.

Hananiah (hănŭnī'ŭ), one of the THREE HOLY CHILDREN.

Hancock, John, 1737–93, American Revolutionary patriot, signer of Declaration of Independence. Advocated resistance to British. President of Continental Congress (1775–77).

Hancock, Winfield Scott, 1824–86, Union general in Civil War. Conspicuous as leader of 2d Corps at Gettysburg; foremost in repulsing Confederate attacks, notably Pickett's charge on July 3, 1863.

Hancock, city (pop. 5,223), extreme N Mich., on Portage L. On Keweenaw Waterway ship canal, in copper region. Mfg. of metal products.

Hand, Learned, 1872–, American jurist; judge of Federal District Court 1909–24, of U.S. Court of Appeals 1924–51. *The Spirit of Liberty,* a collection of his papers and addresses, was published in 1952.

hand, terminal portion of arm. Human hand has eight bones in wrist, five parallel metacarpals, and three phalanges in each finger and two in thumb. Actions of small hand muscles and arm tendons permit intricate motions. See *ill.*, p. 763.

handball, indoor and outdoor game played on one-wall or four-wall court. In one-wall game, court is 20 ft. by 34 ft. In four-wall game, court is 23 ft. by 46 ft., surrounded by three walls 23 ft. high and back wall 12 ft. high. Four-wall handball, played in England and Ireland for many centuries, was introduced in U.S. in 1870s.

Handel, George Frideric, 1685–1759, German-English composer, b. Halle. After traveling through Germany and Italy, presenting his early operas, he finally settled in England in 1712. Much of his finest music is to be found in his operas, e.g., *Atalanta, Berenice,* and *Serse* (containing the tenor aria now known as *Largo*). His great oratorio, *The Messiah,* was presented in Dublin in 1742. Among other oratorios are *Samson, Judas Maccabeus,* and *Esther*. His orchestral suites, *Fireworks Music* and *Water Music,* are popular today. He also wrote many songs, sonatas, and concertos for various solo instruments and instrumental combinations, and an anthem for the coronation of George II, still used at coronations today. He was buried in Westminster Abbey.

Handy, W(illiam) C(hristopher), 1873–, American Negro composer. First to set down the blues. His songs, such as *Memphis Blues, St. Louis Blues,* and *Beale Street Blues,* are classic examples of their type.

Hanford, city (pop. 10,028), S central Calif., S of Fresno. Trade and processing center in San Joaquin Valley.

Hangchow or **Hang-chou** (both: hăng'chou'), city (pop. 517,559), cap. Chekiang prov., China; port on Tsientang R. at head of Hangchow Bay. Commercial and cultural center on scenic West Lake; S terminus of Grand Canal. Exports silk, tea, and paper fans. Founded A.D. 606. Cap. of Southern Sung dynasty in 12th cent. Occupied 1937–45 by the Japanese.

Hanko (häng'kō), Swed. *Hangö,* city (pop. 6,836), SW Finland, icefree port on small peninsula in Baltic Sea; summer resort. Following Finnish-Russian War (1939–40) Hanko peninsula was leased to USSR as naval base. Returned to Finland 1944 in exchange for lease on Porkkala dist.

Hankow (häng'kou"), commercial city (pop. 749,952) in, but independent of, Hupeh prov., China, at junction of Han and Yangtze rivers. Port (accessible to ocean-going ships) opened to foreign trade 1858.

Hanna, Marcus Alonzo (Mark Hanna), 1837–1904, American capitalist and politician. Handled 1896 campaign of William McKinley for presidency. U.S. Senator from Ohio (1897–1904). A great party boss who exemplified union between business and politics for purposes of economic policy.

Hannah [Heb.,= grace], mother of Samuel. 1 Sam. 1; 2.1–26. Anna and Ann are variants of Hannah.

Hannibal [Punic,= grace of Baal], 247–182? B.C., Carthaginian general, one of the great military geniuses of all time; son of Hamilcar Barca, of the great Barca family. In the Punic Wars he succeeded his brother-in-law, Hasdrubal, as commander in Spain (221 B.C.). With a small force of picked troops he set out to invade Italy, crossed the Alps with full baggage train and elephants, and with his cavalry overran the Po valley. He wiped out a Roman force and in 217 set out toward Rome. After defeating the Romans again at L. Trasimeno, he went to S Italy and gained many allies. At Cannae (216 B.C.) he won one of the most brilliant victories of history, but he failed to get proper support from Carthage and could not take Rome. In 207 B.C. his brother Hasdrubal was defeated on the Metaurus, and Hannibal had to draw back. Recalled (203) to defend Carthage against Scipio, he was decisively beaten in the battle of Zana (202). After peace was concluded (201 B.C.), he was chief ruler in Carthage, governing well, but Rome demanded him as a prisoner, and he went into exile, finally poisoning himself to avoid being given to the Romans.

Hannibal, city (pop. 20,444), NE Mo., on the Mississippi and S of Quincy, Ill.; founded 1819. A river port and rail center, it has mfg. of shoes and wood and metal products. Birth-

place of MARK TWAIN, who is commemorated by various structures here.

Hanno, fl. c.470? B.C., Carthaginian navigator. Supposedly explored NE coast of Africa.

Hannover, Germany: see HANOVER.

Hanoi (hă'noi), city (pop. 237,146), Indo-China; cap. of Tonkin, port on Red River. Shipping center for agr. and industrial products, mainly rice and leather. Consists of old Annamese town and modern European-style quarter. Seat of Chinese rulers of Annam, 7th–15th cent. Continued as chief government center after French occupation in late 19th cent. Was cap. of Viet Nam government 1945–46.

Hanover (hă'nōvùr), Ger. *Hannover,* former province (14,960 sq. mi.; 1939 pop. 3,457,-477) of Prussia, NW Germany, stretching from Dutch border and N Sea (NW) to Harz mts. (SE); since 1946 part of LOWER SAXONY. Cities include Hanover, Osnabrück, Hildesheim, Emden, Lüneburg, Celle, Göttingen. Mostly agr. lowland (grain, potatoes, sugar beets). Part of old duchy of BRUNS-WICK, the region constituted the duchy of Brunswick-Lüneburg until 1692, when Duke Ernest Augustus was raised to rank of elector and his duchy became the electorate of Hanover. Personal union of England and Hanover under Hanoverian dynasty began 1714 with George I (see HANOVER, HOUSE OF). Hanover formed part of Jérôme Bonaparte's kingdom of Westphalia (1807–13). After restoration of its dynasty, it was raised to a kingdom (1815) and became member of GERMAN CONFEDERATION. Because of Salic law of succession it was separated from British crown when Victoria became queen of England (1837). Ernest Augustus, son of George III, who became king of Hanover, began his reactionary reign by rescinding the constitution but was forced to restore it in 1848. His son, George V, succeeded in 1851. As a result of his pro-Austrian stand in the Austro-Prussian War (1866) he lost his kingdom, which became a Prussian province.

Hanover city (pop. 441,615), on Leine R., is a commercial center and has varied and important industries. The cap. of the former kingdom and province of Hanover, it became the cap. of Lower Saxony in 1946. It was more than half destroyed in World War II.

Hanover. 1 Town (pop. 6,259), W N.H., NW of Lebanon near Connecticut R. Seat of DARTMOUTH COLLEGE. 2 Borough (pop. 14,048), SE Pa., SW of York. Harness-racing horses bred in area. First Civil War battle N of Mason-Dixon line fought here 1863. 3 Village, E Va., N of Richmond. Patrick Henry lived here for many years.

Hanover, house of, royal family, of Guelphic origin (see HANOVER, province). Succeeded to English throne by Act of Settlement (1701) through a claim based on descent from James I. The first of five Hanoverian kings of Great Britain was (1714) George I, elector of Hanover. With Victoria (1837) the crowns of Hanover and Great Britain were separated.

Hanseatic League (hăn"sēā'tĭk, hăn"zē–), mercantile league of medieval German towns. It came into existence gradually. Originally a *hansa* seems to have been a company of individual traders to foreign lands. The principal establishments of Hansa companies were at WISBY, NOVGOROD, BERGEN, BRUGES, and London (see STEELYARD, MERCHANTS OF THE). To protect themselves against piracy and to overcome foreign competition and trade restrictions, the mercantile cities drew closer. In 1241 LÜBECK and HAMBURG signed a treaty of mutual protection. Some 70 other cities joined. The League was formally organized in 1358. In 1370 it forced on WALDEMAR IV of Denmark the Treaty of Stralsund, which gave it trade monopoly in Scandinavia for more than a century. After a steady decline, the league dissolved in the 17th cent., but the name "Hansa city" has lived on in Bremen, Hamburg, and Lübeck.

Hanson, Howard, 1896–, American composer; director, after 1924, of the Eastman School of Music, Rochester, N.Y., where he estab. American Composers Concerts. His Second, or Romantic, Symphony and an opera, *Merry Mount,* are among his most popular works.

Hanson, John, 1715–83, first "President of the United States in Congress Assembled." First President (1781–82) to serve one-year term under Articles of Confederation, but his duties were merely those of a presiding officer.

Hants: see HAMPSHIRE.

Hanukkah (hä'nookä), Jewish holiday, the Festival of Lights or the Feast of the Maccabees (also transliterated Chanukah). It celebrates the rededication of the Temple of Jerusalem in 165 B.C. The festival usually occurs in December and lasts eight days.

Hanyang (hän'yäng'), city (pop. 69,483), E Hupeh prov., China, at junction of Han and Yangtze rivers, near Hankow and Wuchang. Steel mills.

Hapeville, residential city (pop. 8,560), NW Ga., S suburb of Atlanta.

Hapsburg or Habsburg (both; hăps'bûrg, Ger. haps'boork), ruling house of AUSTRIA from 1292 to 1918. Original holdings of family, which can be traced to 10th cent., were in NW Switzerland and Alsace. Name is taken from Habsburg castle, now in ruins, in Aargau, Switzerland. By 13th cent. family held most of Upper Alsace, Switzerland, and Baden. Count Rudolf IV of Hapsburg was elected (1273) German king as RUDOLF I. He confiscated Austria, Styria, Carinthia, Carniola from Ottocar II of Bohemia (1276) and in 1282 made these duchies hereditary family possessions. SWITZERLAND was soon lost, but Tyrol was added in 1363. All Hapsburg possessions as a whole were held together by a family law and could not be alienated from family nor inherited by females. With the election of Albert II as German king (1438), the imperial office, though theoretically still elective, became vested in the house of Hapsburg (for list of Hapsburg emperors, see HOLY ROMAN EMPIRE). Three marriages made the Hapsburgs a world power: (1) that of Maximilian I with MARY OF BURGUNDY, which brought the Low Countries; (2) that of their son, Philip I, to Joanna of Castile, which gave their elder son, Emperor CHARLES V, Spain

and the Spanish empire; (3) that of Philip and Joanna's younger son, Ferdinand, with Anna, sister of Louis II of Hungary and Bohemia, which in 1526 brought these two crowns to the Hapsburgs. Thus the Hapsburg empire, "where the sun never set," stretched from the Carpathians to the Philippines. In the division made by Charles V, his son Philip II received the Spanish empire, including Sicily, Naples, Milan, and the Netherlands (see NETHERLANDS, AUSTRIAN AND SPANISH); Ferdinand, as FERDINAND I, became emperor and retained Austria, Bohemia, Hungary, and various German territories. Imperial wars of the 17th cent. weakened authority and cost them Alsace, Franche-Comté, Artois, and parts of Flanders and Hainaut, but at the same time they recovered Hungary from Turkey. The Spanish branch ended in 1700 with Charles II; the resulting War of the SPANISH SUCCESSION (1701–14) forced Austria to give up its claim to Spain but gave it the Austrian Netherlands and Milan. The PRAGMATIC SANCTION made it possible for a woman, MARIA THERESA, to inherit the Hapsburg lands; in the War of the AUSTRIAN SUCCESSION (1740–48) she defended her inheritance against a coalition, losing only SILESIA. Her husband, the grand duke of Tuscany, became emperor as FRANCIS I (1745). With their son, JOSEPH II, one of the greatest Hapsburg monarchs, began the line of **Hapsburg-Lorraine.** TUSCANY was ruled by a separate branch 1790–1860; Modena, acquired by marriage, was ruled by branch of Austria-Este (see ESTE) until 1859. The main branch was continued by Leopold II and by Francis II, who in 1804 took title "Emperor of Austria" as Francis I. From this point, the history of the Hapsburgs became that of Austria and, after 1867, of the AUSTRO-HUNGARIAN MONARCHY. After the death of Emperor Charles I (abdicated 1918), the claims of the dynasty passed to his son, Archduke OTTO.

hara-kiri (hä'rŭ-kĭr'ē, hä'rŭ-) Japanese form of honorable suicide. Before 1868 was obligatory for disobedience or disloyalty to emperor. Still occasionally performed voluntarily after misfortune.

Harald: see HAROLD.

Haran (hā'răn) or **Harran** (hä'rän), anc. city of Mesopotamia, now in SE Asiatic Turkey, SE of Urfa. A trade center, seat of the temple of the Assyrian moongod, it was also the home of Abraham's family after the migration from Ur. As Carrhae in Roman times it was the scene of a disastrous defeat of Romans by Parthians (53 B.C.).

Harbin (här'bĭn), city (pop. 760,000), cap. Sungkiang prov., Manchuria; port on Sungari R. Transportation hub of N Manchuria. Founded 1897 by Russia as construction settlement on Chinese Eastern RR. Soybean products are main export.

Hardanger Fjord (härdäng'ûr fyôrd'), second largest fjord of Norway, penetrating 114 mi. from the Atlantic into SW Norway. At head of a S branch is Skjeggedalsfoss (waterfall, 525 ft. high); Voringfoss (535 ft. high) is near head of an E branch. The Hardangerfjell, mountain mass extending inland from fjord, rises to 6,153 ft. in the Hardangerjokel.

Picturesque villages and scenery make region a favorite of tourists.

Hardee, William Joseph, 1815–73, Confederate general. An able leader in Army of Tennessee. Surrendered to W. T. Sherman in N.C. in April, 1865.

Harden, Sir Arthur (här'dŭn), 1865–1940, English biochemist. Shared 1929 Nobel Prize for research in alcoholic fermentation; he established the character of zymase and discovered that other yeast enzymes are also concerned with fermentation.

Harden, Maximilian (mäk"sēmē'lyän här'dŭn), 1861–1927, German journalist whose real name was Witkowski. An admirer of Bismarck, he attacked the regime of William II in his weekly, *Die Zukunft.*

Hardenberg, Friedrich von: see NOVALIS.

Hardenberg, Karl August, Fürst von (kärl' ou'gŏŏst fürst' fŭn här'dŭnbĕrk), 1750–1822, Prussian minister of foreign affairs (1804–6) and chancellor (1810–22). Continued reform program begun by Karl vom und zum STEIN; abolished trade monopolies; turned feudal land into freeholds; emancipated Jews. Persuaded Frederick William III to join coalition against Napoleon (1813). After 1815 he came increasingly under the conservative sway of Metternich.

hardening of the arteries: see ARTERIOSCLEROSIS.

hardhack or **steeplebush,** a North American spirea (*Spiraea tomentosa*) with clusters of rose or white flowers.

Harding, Chester, 1792–1866, American portrait painter. Worked in London and Boston.

Harding, Stephen: see STEPHEN HARDING, SAINT.

Harding, Warren G(amaliel) (gŭmā'lēŭl), 1865–1923, 28th President of the United States (1921–23). U.S. Senator (Republican) from Ohio (1915–21). His noncommittal utterances in presidential campaign of 1920 (he coined the word *normalcy* to express social and economic conditions he promised the nation) helped win him election. One achievement of his administration was calling of the Washington Conference (see NAVAL CONFERENCES). He died suddenly in San Francisco, Aug. 1923. Exposure of TEAPOT DOME scandal and lesser scandals came later; as a result, his administration has been stigmatized as one of most corrupt in U.S. history.

hardness, the resistance a substance offers to being scratched. Mohs's scale (named for Friedrich Mohs) ranges from softest to hardest: talc, 1; gypsum, 2; calcite, 3; fluorite, 4; apatite, 5; feldspar, 6; quartz, 7; topaz, 8; corundum, 9; diamond, 10. The hardness of many minerals falls between those listed; e.g., barite is 3.3.

hardpan, condition of soil or subsoil in which particles become bound together in an impervious mass. It is a serious handicap to farming.

Hardy, Thomas, 1840–1928, English novelist and poet, b. Dorsetshire. Fame came in 1874 with novel *Far from the Madding Crowd.* Novels laid in his native region (which he called Wessex) include *The Return of the Native* (1878), *The Mayor of Casterbridge* (1886), *The Woodlanders* (1887), *Tess of the D'Urbervilles* (1891), *Jude the Obscure*

(1896). They are generally gloomy and naturalistic studies of character and environment. Adverse criticism led him to turn to poetry. His pessimism was expressed in such books as *Wessex Poems* (1898); a poetic drama, *The Dynasts* (1904–8); and *Moments of Vision* (1917; lyrics). He also wrote distinguished short stories, such as *Wessex Tales* (1888).

hare, mammal of North America, Europe, Asia, and Africa, formerly considered a rodent, now usually placed in order Lagomorpha. True hares (genus *Lepus*) have longer ears and hind legs than rabbits. At birth they are covered with hair and the eyes are open. Varying hare or snowshoe rabbit and jack rabbit (with ears sometimes c.⅓ body length) are native to North America; arctic hare has circumpolar distribution; European hare native to central and W Europe is introduced in North America.

harebell, bluebell, or **bluebells-of-Scotland,** slender wiry-stemmed perennial bellflower (*Campanula rotundifolia*), with dainty blue bell-shaped blossoms.

Harfleur (ärflûr'), town (pop. 5,052), Seine-Inférieure dept., N France; a Channel port at mouth of the Seine. Captured 1415 by Henry V of England.

Hargreaves, James, d. 1778, Englishman credited with invention of spinning jenny (see SPINNING).

Hari, Mata: see MATA HARI.

Hariri (härē'rē), 1054–1122, Arabian writer of Basra. Chief work is the popular *Makamat,* a kind of picaresque novel, consisting of 50 episodes.

Hari Rud (hä'rē rŏŏd'), anc. *Arius,* river, 650 mi. long, rising in central Afghanistan. Forms part of Iran-Afghanistan and Iran-USSR boundaries. Called Tedzhen in USSR.

Harkness, E(dward) S(tephen), 1874–1940, American philanthropist. Extended philanthropies especially to colleges, hospitals, and museums.

Harlan, John Marshall, 1833–1911, Associate Justice of U.S. Supreme Court (1877–1911). On the whole, a strict constructionist; known as a "dissenter."

Harlan, city (pop. 4,786), E Ky., in the Cumberlands near Va. line. Shipping center for coal mines of Harlan co., where only after 20 years of bitter strife between coal operators and miners were the mines unionized (1941).

Harlech (här'lĕkh), village, Merionethshire, Wales. Its heroic defense against Yorkists (1468) is theme of Welsh battle song, *The March of the Men of Harlech.* Has best golf course in Wales.

Harleian Library (här'lēŭn), collection of manuscripts and legal documents, formed by Robert Harley, 1st earl of Oxford, and his son Edward Harley, 2d earl of Oxford. Purchased by British government in 1753; now in British Museum library.

Harlem, congested residential and business section of upper Manhattan borough of New York city, bounded roughly by Central Park and 110th St. (S), East R. (E), Harlem R. (NE), 168th St. (N), Amsterdam Ave. and Morningside Park (W). Estab. 1658 as Dutch settlement of Nieuw Haarlem. In

Revolutionary battle of Harlem Heights, the Continentals stopped British advance up Manhattan isl. (Sept. 16, 1776). Largely rural until modern transportation linked it to lower Manhattan in 19th cent. Largest Negro community (pop. over 400,000) in U.S. grew up here after 1910.

Harlem River, navigable tidal channel 7 mi. long, in New York city, separating Manhattan from the Bronx. With Spuyten Duyvil Creek (spī'tùn dī'vùl) (1-mi. ship canal) on W, it connects Hudson R. with Hell Gate channel of EAST RIVER. Bridges.

Harlequin (här'lùkwĭn), stock PANTOMIME character. A nimble, witty, grotesque rogue, he plays opposite Columbine, sometimes as her father.

Harley, Robert, 1st earl of Oxford and **Earl Mortimer,** 1661–1724, English statesman. Had great influence on Queen Anne through his cousin, Lady Masham, and was virtual prime minister 1711–14. Began SOUTH SEA BUBBLE scheme. Secretly negotiated end of War of Spanish Succession in 1713. Struggled for power with Henry ST. JOHN and was forced out of office. His library was basis of HARLEIAN LIBRARY.

Harlingen (här'lĭnjùn), city (pop. 23,229), S Texas, NW of Brownsville, founded c.1901. Processes and ships cotton, truck, and citrus fruit.

Harmhab (härm'hăb), fl. 1350 B.C., king of anc. Egypt. Powerful under Ikhnaton and Tut-ankh-amen, he himself became king and founder of the XIX dynasty. He suppressed corruption in government and restored prosperity. RAMSES I succeeded him. Also appears as Horemheb.

Harmodius and Aristogiton (härmō'dēùs, ä″rĭstōjī'tùn), d. c.514 B.C., Athenian patriots. Hipparchus the tyrant tried to win the affection of Aristogiton away from Harmodius and, spurned, insulted Harmodius' sister. The two friends planned to kill Hipparchus and his brother Hippias. They did kill Hipparchus but not Hippias. Harmodius was killed on the spot, Aristogiton executed. The two were regarded as heroes by liberty-loving Athenians.

harmonica. 1 in music, the simplest of the free-reed instruments; also called the mouth organ. The reeds, set in a narrow wooden or metal case, are supplied with holes through which air is drawn or blown. Most harmonicas have only a diatonic scale. **2** Musical glasses, introduced 1743, improved by Benjamin Franklin. Franklin's instrument consisted of a graduated series of glass bowls fitting inside one another and supported by a spindle which revolved the edges of the bowls through a water trough. Fingertips touching the moistened edges produced the sound. Both Mozart and Beethoven composed for it.

Harmony, borough (pop. 912), W Pa., WSW of Butler. First settlement (1805) of HARMONY SOCIETY.

harmony, in music, the simultaneous sounding of two or more tones, which produces chords. The study of harmony examines chords and their relation to each other. The idea of chords was definitely estab. about the 16th cent. Before then, music was polyphonal, and

although sounds resembling chords did occur, horizontal and melodic considerations took precedence over vertical or harmonic ones. In 1722, Rameau presented theories that form the basis for the highly complicated rules of harmony. During the 18th cent., the concept of TONALITY became general. Freer uses of tonality developed in the 19th cent., and the 20th cent. saw the evolution of ATONALITY and some breakdown of the old laws of harmony.

Harmony Society, religious society founded by German Separatists led by George Rapp. Harmonists held property in common and subscribed to celibacy. Several communities (Harmony, Pa., in 1805; New Harmony, Ind., in 1814; and Economy, Pa., in 1825) were created in the U.S.

Harmsworth, Alfred Charles William: see NORTHCLIFFE.

Harnack, Adolph von (ädôlf fün här'näk), 1851–1930, German theologian and church historian, noted for *Lehrbuch der Dogmengeschichte* (4 vols., 1886–1900).

Harney, William Selby, 1800–1889, American general. Ranking cavalry officer in Mexican War, he fought brilliantly at Cerro Gordo (1847). In early Civil War he commanded Dept. of the West; his conciliatory policy lost him his command in 1861.

Harney Peak: see BLACK HILLS.

Harnosand (härnûsänd'), Swed. *Härnösand,* city (pop. 15,263), co. seat of Vasternorrland co., NE Sweden, seaport (ice-bound in winter) at mouth of Angerman R. Exports timber, tar, cellulose, and wood pulp. It is a Lutheran episcopal see. Settled in 14th cent. and inc. 1585. It was sacked 1721 by Russians.

Harold, 1022?–1066, king of England (1066), rival of WILLIAM I. Son of GODWIN, he belonged to most powerful noble family in reign of Edward the Confessor. Exiled in 1051, family returned and recovered power in 1053. Driven by wind to French coast, he was seized and forced to take oath to support William's claim to English throne. Returning home he renounced oath. In a revolt of the Northumbrians, Harold sided against his brother Tostig. Family was thus divided at death of Edward, who named Harold his heir. William at once invaded in S and Tostig, with Harold III of Norway, invaded from N. Harold defeated and killed Tostig and Harold III. Opposed William at Hastings and was killed.

Harold, kings of Norway. **Harold I** (Harold Fairhair), Norse *Harald Haarfagre,* c.850–c.933, became first king of Norway after victory at Hafrs Fjord over several petty kings (872). Many Viking rulers fled to Iceland as a result; others (e.g., ROLLO) conquered and settled Normandy. **Harold III,** Norse *Harald Hardhrádhi* [stern council], d. 1066, half-brother of OLAF II, entered Byzantine service after Olaf's defeat (1030). He returned in 1042, joined revolt against MAGNUS I, became joint ruler with Magnus 1046, sole ruler 1047. In 1066 he took part with TOSTIG in invasion of England; fell at STAMFORD BRIDGE.

Harold Bluetooth, d. c.985, first Christian king of Denmark (935–85).

Harold Harefoot, d. 1040, king of England (1037–40). Illegitimate son of Canute, he struggled with his half-brother Harthacanute for control of England.

Haroun-al-Rashid: see HARUN-AL-RASHID.

harp, stringed musical instrument of anc. origin, whose strings are plucked with the fingers. Modern harp consists of three parts—sound box, neck, and pillar. Strings are stretched from sound box to neck, where tuning pegs are fastened. The harp was originally diatonic. More strings were added to make it chromatic, but its capabilities were still limited. Introduction of double-action pedals (c.1810) made it possible to raise the pitch of a string either a tone or a semitone, thus increasing the possibilities of the instrument and making it popular in the orchestra.

Harper, William Rainey, 1856–1906, American educator and Hebrew scholar. He became professor of Semitic languages at Yale in 1886. In 1891 he was appointed first president of Univ. of Chicago.

Harpers Ferry, town (pop. 822), E W.Va., on bluffs at confluence of Potomac and Shenandoah rivers, c.55 mi. NW of Washington, D.C. Scene of John Brown's raid on U.S. arsenal, Oct. 16, 1859. Key to Shenandoah Valley in Civil War, it changed hands several times, being finally taken by Union forces in 1863.

harpsichord: see PIANO.

Harpy, in Greek religion, predatory monster with head of a woman and body, wings, and claws of a bird.

harpy, large bird of prey found from S Mexico to Brazil. It is 38–40 in. long.

Harran, anc. city of Mesopotamia: see HARAN.

Harriman, E(dward) H(enry), 1848–1909, American railroad executive. Gained control of several Western railroads. Attempt to control Chicago, Burlington & Quincy RR was blocked by James J. HILL. His son, **W(illiam) Averell Harriman,** 1891–, was ambassador to the USSR (1943–46), U.S. Secretary of Commerce (1946–48), and director of the Mutual Security Agency (1951–53).

Harriman, city (pop. 6,389), E Tenn., W of Knoxville and near Tennessee R. Rail and trade center in farm area. Mfg. of wood products and blankets.

Harrington, James, 1611–77, English political writer. His utopian *Commonwealth of Oceana* (1656) influenced democratic thought in America and elsewhere.

Harris, Chapin Aaron, 1806–60, American dentist, pioneer in modern dentistry, noted for writings and as founder of *American Journal of Dental Science* and of first school of dentistry.

Harris, Frank, 1856–1931, British-American author, b. Ireland; educ. in U.S.; a magazine editor in London and New York. Created scandal with partly fictional memoirs, *My Life and Loves* (3 vols., 1923–27).

Harris, Joel Chandler, 1848–1908, American Southern author, a newspaper editor, famous for "Uncle Remus" stories in Negro dialect.

Harris, Roy, 1898–, American composer; pupil of Nadia Boulanger. Among his works are *When Johnny Comes Marching Home,* an "American Overture"; Symphony for Voices, to poems by Whitman; Folk-song Symphony; and a piano quintet. While he is not a strict modernist, he occasionally uses such devices as polytonality and irregular metrical patterns.

Harris, Thomas Lake, 1823–1906, American Christian mystic, founder of Brotherhood of the New Life, b. England. Estab. at Wassaic, N.Y. (1861), the community was moved to Amenia, N.Y. (1863), and to Brocton, near Buffalo (1867), where it was known as Salem-on-Erie. In 1875 Harris and part of the group settled in Calif.

Harris, Townsend, 1804–78, American diplomat. Appointed first U.S. consul general to Japan in 1855, raised to minister in 1859. Negotiated commercial treaty (1858).

Harris, Hebrides, Scotland: see LEWIS WITH HARRIS.

Harrisburg. 1 City (pop. 10,999), S Ill., N of Paducah, Ky., in coal, grain, and timber area; platted in 1850s. Produces wood products, flour, and brick. **2** City (pop. 89,544), state cap. (since 1812), SE Pa., on Susquehanna R.; laid out 1785. Settled by German religious sects and Scotch-Irish, it grew as canal and rail center. Has mfg. of steel, clothing, and lumber products.

Harrison, William Henry, 1773–1841, 9th President of the United States (1841). Governor of Indiana Territory (1800–1812); primarily responsible for opening Ohio and Indiana to white settlement. Won battle of Tippecanoe against Indians, Nov. 6–7, 1811. In War of 1812, as commander in Northwest, he won battle of the Thames (see THAMES, BATTLE OF THE). U.S. Representative (1816–19) and Senator from Ohio (1825–28). The Whigs, presenting Harrison as a rugged Westerner and using "Tippecanoe and Tyler too" as a slogan, waged first "rip-roaring" campaign in U.S. history to elect him President. He died a month after taking office. His grandson, **Benjamin Harrison,** 1833–1901, was 23rd President of the United States (1889–93). Served in Civil War. U.S. Senator (Republican) from Ind. (1881–87). As President he approved all regular Republican measures, including highly protective McKinley Tariff Act. His moderate stand on civil service reform displeased both reformers and spoilsmen. First Pan-American Conference was held in his administration (1889).

Harrison. 1 City (pop. 5,542), NW Ark., in the Ozarks. Commercial center for agr. area. Wood products, cheese, and flour. Diamond Cave is near. **2** Town (pop. 13,490), NE N.J., industrial suburb of Newark. Mfg. of steel, elevators, pumps, machine parts, gases, and ink. **3** Town (pop. 13,577), including residential Harrison village (1940 pop. 6,307), SE N.Y., between Mamaroneck and Rye.

Harrisonburg, city (pop. 10,810), N Va., in Shenandoah Valley, NNE of Staunton; settled 1739. Trade center in agr. area. Mfg. of textiles, shoes, and furniture. Hq. of George Washington Natl. Forest.

Harrod, James, 1742–93, American frontiersman. In 1774 he founded first settlement in Ky., later named Harrodsburg in his honor.

Harrodsburg, city (pop. 5,262), central Ky., S of Frankfort; founded 1774 by James Harrod. Oldest settlement in state; G. R. Clark was early leader. Trades in livestock, grain, and cattle. Resort. Near by are replica of Fort Harrod and cabin where Nancy Hanks and Thomas Lincoln were married.

Harrow or **Harrow-on-the-Hill,** urban district (pop. 219,463), Middlesex, England. Seat of Harrow (founded 1571), one of England's great public schools.

Harsha (hûr′shǔ), d. 647, Indian emperor. Conquered all N India 606–12. His cap. at Kanauj was artistic and literary center. Turned from Hinduism to Buddhism.

Hart, Albert Bushnell, 1854–1943, American historian. Harvard professor (1883–1926) and prodigious worker, responsible for over 100 volumes written or edited by him. Editor of and contributor to "American Nation" series (28 vols., 1904–18) and *Epochs of American History* (4 vols., 1891–1926). Editor or coeditor of many series, notably *Guide to the Study and Reading of American History* (1896; revised ed., 1912), an important bibliography.

Hart, Charles Henry, 1847–1918, American writer and art expert. Director of Pennsylvania Academy of Fine Arts (1882–1902).

Hart, George Overbury, 1868–1933, American water-color painter. Traveled widely to paint scenes depicting everyday life of people everywhere.

Hart, William S., 1870–1946, American stage and film actor. After a long stage career (1895–1914), he entered films and became the model of the strong, silent man of the West.

Harte, (Francis) Bret, 1836–1902, American writer. A gold seeker, teacher, and journalist, he wrote stories (e.g., "The Luck of Roaring Camp," "The Outcasts of Poker Flat"), novels, and humorous poems of the West. Last years spent in England.

hartebeest (här′tĭbēst″), name for certain African antelopes. Usually it refers to genus *Alcelaphus* (or *Bubalis*); sometimes to *Damaliscus,* the bontebok and blesbok. The bubal hartebeest (*Alcelaphus buselaphus*) is believed by some to be extinct. It is reddish or fawn, stands c.3½ ft. at the shoulder, and has ringed, pointed, curved horns. The larger red hartebeest (*A. caama*) is native to S Africa.

Hartford. 1 City (pop. 177,397), state cap., central Conn., on Connecticut R.; settled 1635–36 on site of Dutch trading post (1633). State's largest city and financial, industrial, and commercial center. It is internationally famous for insurance business (since 1794). Mfg. of firearms, typewriters, airplane parts, tools, and brushes. Hartford *Courant,* founded 1764, is one of oldest U.S. newspapers. Was home of Connecticut Wits. Birthplace of Noah Webster, John Fiske, and elder J. P. Morgan. Harriet Beecher Stowe and Mark Twain lived here. Has old statehouse (1796; designed by Bulfinch), capitol (1872), state library and supreme court building (1910; with Stuart's full-length *Washington*), Trinity Col. (for men; 1823), and parts of Univ. of Connecticut. Charter Oak stood here until 1856. Tradition says that Conn. charter was hidden in this tree when Sir Edmond Andros demanded it (1687). **2** Town (pop. 5,827), E Vt., on Connecticut R. Includes White River Junc-

tion, industrial and rail center (pop. 2,365).

Hartford City, city (pop. 7,253), E Ind., N of Muncie. In agr., gas and oil area. Jute board, hardware mfg.

Hartford Convention, Dec. 15, 1814–Jan. 4, 1815, meeting of 26 delegates to consider the problems of New England in the War of 1812, held at Hartford, Conn. Grew out of opposition to embargo acts and to war. It recommended that New England secession, which extremists had urged, if it came at all, should be gradual and should be executed in peaceful times. Importance of meeting is twofold: it continued the view of states' rights that was the refuge of minority groups; it virtually destroyed the Federalist party politically, since the Federalists, who had sponsored the convention, were unable to regain lost prestige.

Hartford Wits: see CONNECTICUT WITS.

Harthacanute (här′thǎkŭnūt), d. 1042, king of Denmark (1035–42) and of England (1040–42), son of Canute. Ruled in Denmark until the death of Harold Harefoot, then in England. Left throne to Edward the Confessor.

Hartlepool (härt′lē-, härt′ŭl–), municipal borough (pop. 17,217), Durham, England; a seaport. Has extensive docks and trade in coal and timber.

Hartley, Marsden, 1878–1943, American landscape and still-life painter. Early paintings were abstract; later work largely representational. Also wrote poetry.

Hartmann, Eduard von (härt′män), 1842–1906, German philosopher. His philosophy of the "unconscious" (meaning forces of nature) stressed struggle in man between impulse and reason.

Hartmann von Aue (härt′män fŭn ou′ŭ), c.1170–c.1220, German poet. He wrote lyrics, chivalric romances (*Erec, Iwain*), a religious legend (*Gregorius,* which inspired Thomas Mann's *The Holy Sinner*), and the idyl *Der arme Heinrich* (used by Longfellow for his *Golden Legend*).

Hartsville, town (pop. 5,658), NE S.C., ENE of Columbia. Mfg. of textiles, bricks, furniture, and paper.

Harun-al-Rashid (härōōn-äl-räshēd′, hǎ′rōōn-äl-rä′shĭd), c.764–809, 5th ABBASID caliph (786–809). Imprisoned the Barmecides, a powerful Persian family who had helped him become caliph. Under him Baghdad was at its height as a cultural center. Figures prominently in *Thousand and One Nights*.

Harunobu (Harunobu Suzuki) (hä′rōō′nō′bōō), c.1725–1770, Japanese artist. Introduced multiple color printing with wood blocks.

Harvard, John, 1607–38, chief founder of Harvard Col. He bequeathed half his estate and his library toward the college, which was named for him.

Harvard, town (pop. 3,983), E central Mass., NW of Boston. In town is "Fruitlands," once scene of cooperative community of Bronson ALCOTT.

Harvard, Mount: see SAWATCH MOUNTAINS.

Harvard University, first New England college, mainly at Cambridge, Mass.; nonsectarian, mainly for men; founded 1636 by Mass. Bay colony, opened 1638, chartered 1650. Named after John HARVARD, 1639. Closely allied with

Congregational Church, later with the Unitarian until 1851. In Pres. Charles W. Eliot's administration (1869–1909), Harvard Col. became great university. He introduced elective system. Under A. Lawrence Lowell tutorial system and general examinations were begun. J. B. Conant was president 1933–53. Includes Harvard Col. and, among others, graduate schools of divinity (1816), law (1817), arts and sciences (1872; with journalism), and some professional schools at Boston. Radcliffe Col. (nonsectarian; for women) is associated but not corporately connected with Harvard. Classes began 1879; Society for the Collegiate Instruction of Women (known as Harvard Annex) chartered 1882; rechartered and renamed 1894. Elizabeth C. Agassiz was president, 1879–1903. Instruction is given by Harvard faculty. Harvard has one of largest libraries in America. Maintains several astronomical observatories in U.S. and one near Bloemfontein, Union of South Africa. Has Fogg Mus. of Art (1894), Univ. Mus. containing Peabody Mus. of Archaeology and Ethnology (1866) and Mus. of Comparative Zoology (1859), several botanical collections. Harvard-Yenching Inst. (for aid in China) founded 1928. Has traditional sports rivalry with Yale Univ. Harvard Univ. Press founded 1913.

harvestman: see DADDY LONGLEGS.

Harvey, Gabriel, 1545?–1630, English poet and miscellaneous writer; friend of Spenser, bitter opponent (in pamphlets) of Thomas Nashe.

Harvey, William, 1578–1657, English physiologist, discoverer of circulation of blood and function of heart as pump. His theory was stated in 1616, published 1628. Known also for research in embryology.

Harvey, city (pop. 20,683), NE Ill., just S of Chicago. Mfg. of engines and machinery.

Harwich (här′ĭj), municipal borough (pop. 13,-488), Essex, England; port and chief naval station on E coast. Frequently bombed 1940–41.

Harz (härts), densely forested mountain range, central Germany, extending c.60 mi. between Elbe and Weser rivers and occupying parts of Lower Saxony and Saxony-Anhalt. Upper Harz, in NW, is rich in silver, iron, lead, copper; culminates in the BROCKEN. There are many resorts.

Hasa, El (ĕl hä′sù), region, NE Saudi Arabia, on Persian Gulf. Extensive oil drilling.

Hasan (hä′sùn), c.625–c.669, 5th caliph; son of Ali and Fatima (Mohammed's daughter). Succeeded Ali as caliph, 661; abdicated under Omayyad pressure. His brother, HUSEIN, took up the family cause. He is a saint of the Shiites.

Hasbrouck Heights (hăz′brŏŏk), residential borough (pop. 9,181), NE N.J., S of Hackensack; settled c.1685. Teterboro airport is near.

Hasdrubal (hăz′drŏŏbùl), name of two Carthaginian generals. **Hasdrubal,** d. 221 B.C., succeeded his father-in-law, Hamilcar Barca, as commander in Spain, increased the Carthaginian empire, founded Cartagena. He was succeeded by his brother-in-law HANNIBAL. Another brother-in-law, **Hasdrubal,** d. 207 B.C., took command in Spain when Hannibal left for Italy. He fought against the Scipios

and, to avoid a disaster, crossed the Alps to Italy. There on the Metaurus he was killed in battle (207 B.C.), and his head was thrown into Hannibal's camp. The defeat marked the beginning of Carthaginian decline.

hashish (hă′shĭsh), name used chiefly in Asia for narcotic and intoxicating substance prepared from hemp plant and sometimes limited to extract of leaves. It is chewed, smoked, or taken as liquid.

Hasidim (häse′dĭm) or **Assideans** (ăsĭdē′ùnz) [Heb.,= pious], originally the most rigid adherents of Judaism. The sect developed between 300 B.C. and 175 B.C. When Antiochus IV decreed that the Jews must offer sacrifices to the Greek gods, the Hasidim led the resistance. The modern sect of Hasidim was founded in Europe in the 18th cent. by BAAL-SCHEM-TOV. It opposed the inflexible rationalism of the Talmud and is characterized by a belief in the immediate coming of the Messiah and emotional exaltation in prayer. The Talmudists in 1781 pronounced the Hasidim heretics. The sect still has adherents. The name is also transliterated as Chassidim.

Hasmoneans: see MACCABEES.

Hassam, Childe (chĭld′ hă′sùm), 1859–1935, American painter and etcher. His landscapes and interiors show strong influence of impressionism.

Hasse, Johann Adolph (hä′sù), 1699–1783, German composer. Although he wrote in all forms, he was chiefly known for operas written in the Italian tradition, e.g., *Allesandro nell' Indie* and *Arminio.*

Hasselt (hä′sùlt), city (pop. 29,369), cap. of Limburg prov., E Belgium.

Hassler, Ferdinand Rudolph, 1770–1843, American geodesist, b. Switzerland. Helped organize U.S. Coast and Geodetic Survey. His original survey of Atlantic seacoast has not had to be repeated.

Hastings, Warren, 1732–1818, first governor general of British India (1774–84). Began as clerk for East India Company (1750). His aggressive policy of judicial and financial reform rebuilt British prestige in India but met with opposition. When he returned to England after resigning he was charged with high crimes by Edmund BURKE and was impeached (1787). Was finally acquitted in 1795.

Hastings, county borough (pop. 65,506), Sussex East, England, on S coast. One of the CINQUE PORTS. Famous as scene of battle of Hastings (Oct. 14, 1066) between Normans under William the Conqueror and Saxons under HAROLD. One of history's most celebrated battles, it was won by William's smaller but better trained and equipped force after a whole day's fighting. It was first and most decisive victory of NORMAN CONQUEST.

Hastings. 1 City (pop. 6,096), S Mich., WSW of Lansing and on tributary of Grand R. Mfg. of metal products. Indian mounds near by. **2** City (pop. 6,560), E Minn., SE of St. Paul and on the Mississippi at mouth of St. Croix R.; farm trade center. **3** City (pop. 20,211), S Nebr., S of Grand Island; founded 1872. Rail and trade center for wheat region. Mfg. of farm equipment, wheat and corn products. Seat of Hastings Col. (Presbyterian; coed; 1882).

Hastings-on-Hudson, residential village (pop. 7,565), SE N.Y., on E bank of the Hudson N of Yonkers. Mfg. of chemicals, copper wire, and cables.

Hatay, Turkey: see ALEXANDRETTA, SANJAK OF.

Hathaway, Anne: see SHAKSPERE, WILLIAM.

Hatshepsut, Egyptian queen: see THUTMOSE I.

Hatteras, Cape (hătˈtŭrŭs), promontory on low sandy island, off E N.C., E of Pimlico Sound. Dangerous because of frequent storms; marked by lighthouses since 1798. Has recreational area.

Hattiesburg, city (pop. 29,474), SE Miss., on Leaf R. and SE of Jackson; settled early 1880s. Rail, trade, and industrial center of farm and timber area, it has mfg. of explosives, chemicals, naval stores, and silk. U.S. Camp Shelby near by.

Hauff, Wilhelm (vĭlˈhĕlm houfˈ), 1802–27, German author. *Lichtenstein* (1826) was a popular historical novel. English translations of his tales are *Fairy Tales* (1910) and *Caravan Tales* (1912).

Haugesund (houˈgŭsōōn), city (pop. 18,407), Rogaland co., SW Norway, fishing port and fish-processing center on North Sea. Near-by Viking monuments include grave of Harold I.

Hauptmann, Bruno Richard, 1899–1936, convicted kidnaper and murderer of infant son of Charles A. Lindbergh, b. Germany. Electrocuted after sensational trial at Flemington, N.J.

Hauptmann, Gerhart (gĕrˈhärt houptˈmän), 1862–1946, German poet, dramatist, novelist. After his naturalistic plays *Before Dawn* (1889) and *The Weavers* (1892), he turned to a romantic medium in the dream play *Hannele* (1893) and in *The Sunken Bell* (1897). The tragedies *Drayman Henschel* (1899) and *Rose Bernd* (1903) mark a return to realism. His novels, notably *The Fool in Christ, Emanuel Quint* (1910) and *The Heretic of Soana* (1918), show his mastery of prose. Awarded the 1912 Nobel Prize in Literature; ranks among foremost modern German writers.

Hauran (hourän'), district, SW Syria, E of Jordan R. Many caverns (once inhabited) are in mountainous NE. Region has volcanic peaks and rich lava soil. Inhabited mainly by Druses. At least part of Hauran belonged to biblical kingdom of BASHAN; it marked NE boundary of the Promised Land. Some 300 ancient towns, with buildings and furniture made of lava, have been located.

Hausa or **Haussa** (both: hou'sú, –sä), Negro people, largely Moslem, numbering over 5,000,000 of N Nigeria and Niger territory. They practice agr. and trading. Their language is a lingua franca in much of W Africa.

Hauser, Kaspar (käs'pär hou'zùr), 1812?–1833, German foundling; possibly an impostor. Appeared in Nuremberg as a "wild boy" (1828), claiming to have spent years in a dark prison hole. Rehabilitated, he wrote his autobiography (1829); was adopted by earl of Stanhope (1832); died of a knife wound, possibly self-inflicted. The theory that he was a son of the grand duke of Baden has not been substantiated. Subject of a novel by Jakob Wassermann.

Haushofer, Karl (kärl' hous'hōfùr), 1869–1946, German geographer, chief exponent of GEOPOLITICS. A professor at Munich, he became one of Hitler's advisers on foreign affairs. Died by suicide.

Haussmann, Georges Eugène, Baron (ōsmän'), 1809–91, French city planner, largely responsible for layout of present-day Paris. Boulevard Haussmann named in his honor.

Haute-Garonne (ōt"-gärôn'), department (2,-458 sq. mi.; pop. 512,260), S France; cap. Toulouse. S part lies in Pyrenees.

Haute-Loire (–lwär'), department (1,931 sq. mi.; pop. 228,076), S central France, in Auvergne; cap. Le Puy.

Haute-Marne (–märn'), department (2,416 sq. mi.; pop. 181,840), NE France, in Champagne; cap. Chaumont.

Hautes-Alpes (ōt"zälp'), department (2,178 sq. mi.; pop. 84,932), SE France, in Dauphiné; cap. Gap.

Haute-Saône (ōt"-sōn'), department (2,075 sq. mi.; pop. 202,573), E France, in Franche-Comté; cap. Vesoul.

Haute-Savoie (–sävwä'), department (1,775 sq. mi.; pop. 270,468), E France, in Savoy; cap. Annecy.

Hautes-Pyrénées (–pērānä'), department (1,751 sq. mi.; pop. 201,954), SW France, bordering on Spain; cap. Tarbes.

Haute-Vienne (–vyĕn'), department (2,145 sq. mi.; pop. 336,313), W central France; cap. Limoges.

Haut-Rhin (ō"-rē'), department (1,354 sq. mi.; pop. 471,705), E France, in Alsace; cap. Colmar.

Havana (hùvă'nù), Span. *La Habana,* city (pop. 659,883), W Cuba, cap. of Havana prov. and Cuba; largest city and chief port of the West Indies; founded c.1515. Its position has been strategic historically and commercially. After Cuban independence (1898), U.S. forces improved sanitary conditions in Havana, now popular winter resort. Principal exports: sugar, fruits, tobacco. MORRO CASTLE is at harbor entrance.

Havelok the Dane, English 14th-cent. metrical romance, telling the story of a prince brought up as a peasant who comes into his own.

Haverford, village (pop. 2,529), SE Pa., W of Philadelphia. Seat of Haverford Col. (Friends; for men; opened 1833), with notable Quakeriana collection.

Haverhill (hā'vùrĭl), city (pop. 47,280), NE Mass., on Merrimack R. and NE of Lawrence; settled 1640. A leading U.S. shoe producer. Whittier's birthplace preserved.

Haverstraw, industrial village (pop. 5,818), SE N.Y., on W bank of the Hudson opposite Ossining.

Havre (hă'vùr), city (pop. 8,086), N Mont., NE of Great Falls and on Mill R. (irrigation); founded 1887. Ships livestock. Has railroad shops.

Havre, Le (lù ä'vrù), city (pop. 105,491), Seine-Inférieure dept. N France, at mouth of the Seine. Chief French transatlantic port. Founded 1517. Heavily damaged in World War II.

Havre de Grace (hăv'ùr dù grās'), city (pop. 7,809), NE Md., on Chesapeake Bay at mouth of Susquehanna R. (bridged 1940), NE of Baltimore. Trade and resort center in agr. area with canneries and commercial fisheries. Has famous race track.

Hawaii (hŭwī′ē, hävä′ē), island (4,921 sq. mi.; pop. 68,350), largest and southernmost of Hawaiian Isls. Dominated by mountain masses of MAUNA LOA, MAUNA KEA, and Hualalai. Climate ranges from tropical heat of S coastal areas to icy chill of mountain summits. Major Hawaiian producer of sugar cane; coffee and sisal also grown. Large cattle ranch at foot of Mauna Kea. Hilo on NE coast is chief port.

Hawaii, University of, at Honolulu; land grant and territorial, coeducational. Chartered 1907, opened 1908 as Col. of Agr. and Mechanic Arts; known as Col. of Hawaii 1911–20. Colleges of arts and sciences, agr., applied science, and education.

Hawaiian Islands, group of 20 islands (6,420 sq. mi.; pop. 499,794), central Pacific, c.2,400 mi. from San Francisco. A territory of U.S. since 1900, officially known as Territory of Hawaii; governor is appointed by U.S. President and Congress. Cap. HONOLULU. Islands, formerly called Sandwich Isls., are of volcanic origin and are fringed with coral reefs. Climate is notably fine. OAHU, HAWAII, MAUI, KAUAI, and MOLOKAI are main islands. Sugar cane and pineapples are chief products and basis of principal industries; coffee, rice, sisal, and cotton also grown. Many ethnic and cultural groups are represented in population. Islands discovered by Capt. James Cook 1778. KAMEHAMEHA I became sole sovereign 1810. Missionaries arrived 1820. Queen LILIUOKALANI was deposed 1893; S. B. DOLE was president of republic before annexation to U.S. in 1898. Tourist trade grew in 1930s. Plebiscite of 1940 showed Hawaiians in favor of statehood. U.S. entrance into World War II came with Japanese attack on Pearl Harbor, and the islands became an armed base for Pacific fighting.

Hawaii National Park: see NATIONAL PARKS AND MONUMENTS (table).

Hawick (hô′ĭk), burgh (pop. 16,718), Roxburghshire, Scotland. Castle at near-by Branksome is Branksome Hall of Scott's *Lay of the Last Minstrel.* Woolen and hosiery mfg. center.

hawk, bird of prey of same family as eagle, kite, osprey. It is short winged and swift flying and has sharp claws and a hooked bill. Completely harmful North American hawks are sharp-shinned hawk, Cooper's or chicken hawk, GOSHAWK. Largely beneficial are American, rough-legged, broad-winged, red-tailed, and red-shouldered hawks which eat insects and rodents. Marsh hawk sometimes kills game. Name hawk is applied to some birds of FALCON family. See *ill.,* p. 135.

Hawkesbury, town (pop. 7,194), SE Ont., Canada, on Ottawa R. and W of Montreal. Has paper and lumber mills.

Hawkins or **Hawkyns, Sir John,** 1532–95, English mariner. In profitable slave trading expeditions he sold African Negroes in Spanish ports. As treasurer and comptroller of the navy he improved ship construction. Fought against the Spanish Armada (1588) as did his son, **Sir Richard Hawkins,** 1562?–1622. Served under his father and Drake. Captured by Spanish while raiding South America, he was imprisoned 1597–1602. Later served in Parliament.

Hawksmoor, Nicholas, 1661–1736, English architect. Known chiefly for work done under Sir Christopher Wren and Sir John Vanbrugh. His own designs show influence of Italian baroque.

hawkweed, perennial plant of genus *Hieracium,* widely distributed, generally considered a weed but sometimes cultivated in rocky soil. It has small dandelionlike flower heads of yellow, orange, or red.

Hawley-Smoot Tariff Act, enacted 1930 by U.S. Congress. Highest protective tariff act in U.S. history. Retaliatory foreign tariffs caused sharp decline in U.S. foreign trade.

Haworth, Sir Walter Norman (härth), 1883–1950, English biochemist. Shared 1937 Nobel Prize in Chemistry for work on carbohydrates and vitamin C.

Haworth (hô′ŭth, hou′–), part of Keighley, West Riding of Yorkshire, England. Has home of Brontë family, now a museum and library. All the Brontës but Anne are buried here.

hawthorn, thorny shrubs or small trees of genus *Crataegus,* particularly prevalent in E North America. Clusters of white or red flowers in spring are followed by showy, variously colored fruits sometimes used in jelly. Much used in landscaping in U.S. and England.

Hawthorne, Charles Webster, 1872–1930, American portrait and genre painter, a noted teacher.

Hawthorne, Nathaniel, 1804–64, American novelist and short-story writer, b. Salem, Mass. After graduation from Bowdoin Col. (1825) he spent years in seclusion in his home doing literary hack work and winning notice with his short stories (collected in *Twice-told Tales,* 1837; 2d series 1842). He secured a job as measurer at the Boston customhouse, then tried (1841) life at Brook Farm. He married Sophia Peabody in 1842 and through her grew to know well Emerson, Thoreau, Margaret Fuller, and other transcendentalists. His *Mosses from an Old Manse* (1846) was written in Concord. He was a surveyor of the port at Salem (1846–49) and was made consul to Liverpool by his friend Franklin Pierce. His novels, like many of his short stories, deal with the gloomy, brooding spirit of Puritanism: *The Scarlet Letter* (1850), *The House of the Seven Gables* (1851), *The Blithedale Romance* (1852; based on the Brook Farm experience), and *The Marble Faun* (1860; laid in Italy). His *Wonder-Book* (1852) and *Tanglewood Tales* (1853; named for an estate near Lenox, Mass., where he lived) are children's classics. His notebooks have been subjected to much scholarly study. Hawthorne, with his superb creation of dark-hued atmosphere, his symbolism, and his blend of realistic detail and romantic—even melodramatic—theme, stands as a major American novelist.

Hawthorne. 1 City (pop. 16,316), S Calif., SW of Los Angeles, in oil and truck area. Mfg. of aircraft. **2** Borough (pop. 14,816), NE N.J., NNE of Paterson; settled 1850. Mfg. of chemicals, clothing, and metal goods.

Hay, John, 1838–1905, American author and diplomat. Assistant private secretary to Pres. Lincoln. Wrote *Pike County Ballads* (1871) and, with J. G. Nicolay, *Abraham Lincoln: a*

History (10 vols., 1890). As U.S. Secretary of State (1898–1905), Hay was responsible for Open Door policy in China (1899) and for the HAY-PAUNCEFOTE TREATY.

Hay, river, rising in NE B.C., Canada, and flowing c.350 mi. across NW Alta. into Great Slave L.

hay, wild or cultivated plants (e.g., timothy, alfalfa, clover), dried and cured for livestock feed.

Haya de la Torre, Víctor Raúl (vĕk'tôr räōōl' ä'yä dā lä tô'rĕ), 1895–, Peruvian leader, founder of APRA (Alianza Popular Revolutionario Americana) party, which advocates overthrow of Peruvian oligarchy.

Haydn, Franz Joseph (hī'dŭn), 1732–1809, Austrian composer. Most of his music was written in the 29 years he was musical director for the Princes Esterhazy. The number of his symphonies is usually set at 104. Many bear nicknames, e.g., Toy, London, Surprise, and Clock. Outstanding also are symphonies No. 88 in G and No. 99 in E Flat. His early string quartets influenced Mozart. Haydn also wrote sonatas, songs, Masses, chamber music, and *The Seven Last Words*, originally written for orchestra, but later arranged as a choral work. His last great works were the oratorios, *The Creation* and *The Seasons*.

Haydon, Benjamin Robert, 1786–1846, English painter, whose admirers included the great literary figures of his day. His *Lazarus* is in Natl. Gall., London.

Hayes, Carlton J(oseph) H(untley), 1882–, American historian and diplomat. Noted especially for studies in nationalism, *Essays on Nationalism* (1926) and *The Historical Evolution of Modern Nationalism* (1931). Ambassador to Spain (1942–45), he was influential in keeping Spain neutral in World War II.

Hayes, Helen, 1900–, American stage and film actress. One of her well-known roles was the queen in Laurence Housman's *Victoria Regina* (1935–39).

Hayes, Isaac Israel, 1832–81, American arctic explorer. Led expedition in search of open seaway to North Pole (1860–61). Wrote several books on his experiences.

Hayes, Patrick Joseph, 1867–1938, American cardinal (created 1924), archbishop of New York (1919–38). Organized the Catholic Charities of New York; sponsored social reform.

Hayes, Roland, 1887–, American Negro tenor. He is recognized in Europe and the U.S. as a great singer of both Negro spirituals and of art songs.

Hayes, Rutherford B(irchard), 1822–93, 19th President of the United States (1877–81). Served in Civil War. U.S. Representative (1865–67). Governor of Ohio (1868–72, 1876–77). In 1876 an electoral commission appointed by Congress decided disputed presidential elections in S.C., Fla., La., and Oregon in his favor and against Samuel J. TILDEN. His administration was generally conservative and efficient. Reconstruction era was ended. His conciliatory policy toward the South and his interest in civil service reform alienated important Republican party groups. An advocate of hard money, he pro-vided for resumption of specie payments in gold.

Hayes, river of NE Man., Canada, rising NE of L. Winnipeg and flowing generally NE c.300 mi. to Hudson Bay. Chief route of Hudson's Bay Co. traders from Hudson Bay to L. Winnipeg.

hay fever, inflammation of mucous membrane of nose and eyes resulting from specific sensitivity to foreign substance, usually pollen of plants.

Hay-Herrán Treaty (hā''-ĕrän'), concerning Panama Canal, signed by U.S. Secretary of State John Hay and Foreign Minister Tomás Herrán of Colombia on Jan. 22, 1903. Provided that New Panama Canal Co. might sell its properties to U.S.; Colombia was to lease a strip of land across the Isthmus of Panama to U.S. for canal construction; U.S. was to pay Colombia $10,000,000 and, after nine years, an annuity of $250,000. U.S. Senate ratified treaty, but Colombian congress declined ratification.

Haymarket Square riot, outbreak of violence in Chicago on May 4, 1886. Demonstration for an eight-hour working day, largely staged by anarchists, caused a crowd of some 1,500 to gather at Haymarket Square. Policemen attempted to disperse the meeting; a bomb exploded and rioting ensued. Eleven persons were killed, over 100 were wounded. A trial convicted eight anarchist leaders of inciting violence; four of them were hanged. Incident was frequently used by adversaries of organized labor to discredit the waning Knights of Labor movement and oppose organization.

Hayne, Paul Hamilton, 1830–86, Southern lyric poet of the Charleston group, called "the last literary cavalier." Wrote of the South and the Civil War. Friend of Henry Timrod.

Hayne, Robert Young, 1791–1839, American statesman. U.S. Senator from S.C. (1823–32); in famous debate of Jan., 1830, with Daniel WEBSTER, he upheld doctrines of states' rights and nullification. Governor of S.C. (1832–34).

Haynes, Elwood, 1857–1925, American automobile manufacturer and inventor, designer of one of earliest gasoline automobiles (tested 1894).

Hay-Pauncefote Treaty (hā''-pôns'fŏŏt), negotiated in 1901 by U.S. Secretary of State John Hay and Julian Pauncefote, 1st Baron Pauncefote of Preston, British ambassador to U.S. Replaced CLAYTON-BULWER TREATY. Estab. supremacy of U.S. in the Caribbean. Original treaty, signed Feb. 5, 1900, was ratified, with amendments, by U.S. Senate; Great Britain refused ratification. Revised treaty represented a compromise. It provided that U.S. might construct a transisthmian canal and have full control of it, retained nominally the principle of neutrality under sole guarantee of U.S., and provided that the canal be open to ships of all nations on equal terms. Panama Canal Act (1912), exempting from tolls U.S. ships engaged in coastwise trade, was protested by Great Britain as a treaty violation; Pres. Wilson secured repeal of act in 1914.

Hays, Arthur Garfield, 1881–, American lawyer, long director of the American Civil Liberties Union.

Hays, Will(iam) H(arrison), 1879–, president of the Motion Picture Producers and Distributors of America (1922–45). Headed voluntary censorship of moving-picture moral code (the "Hays Code").

Hays, city (pop. 8,625), W central Kansas, W of Salina; founded 1867 near Fort Hays (estab. 1865, abandoned 1889). Center of a wheat and oil area.

Hayward, city (pop. 24,292), W Calif., SE of Oakland; founded 1854. Poultry center. Fruit canning.

Haywood, William Dudley (Big Bill Haywood), 1869–1928, American labor leader. Helped found INDUSTRIAL WORKERS OF THE WORLD. Joined Socialist party, but was ejected for advocating violence. Imprisoned for sedition in World War I, he escaped (while awaiting a new trial) in 1921 to Russia.

Hazael (hă′zāĕl, hūzā′ŭl), fl. 840 B.C., king of Damascus; murderer and successor of Benhadad 2. In Bible, he is designated by Elijah and Elisha as God's scourge to punish Baalworshipers. He ravaged Judah and Israel. 1 Kings 19.15; 2 Kings 8–10.

Hazard, Paul (pôl′ äzär′), 1878–1944, French scholar, one of the outstanding authorities on comparative literature. He taught at the Sorbonne, Collège de France, and Columbia Univ. In 1939 he was elected to French Acad. Though made president of Univ. of Paris in 1941, he was rejected by Germans.

Hazard, city (pop. 6,985), E Ky., on North Fork of Kentucky R., in Cumberland foothills. Trading and shipping center of coal area (also oil, gas, timber). Frontier Nursing Service near by.

haze, diminished transparency of air owing to suspension in it of dust or salt particles, or water droplets. Optical haze or "shimmer" caused when unequally heated air, varying in density, refracts light unequally.

hazel, hazelnut, or **filbert,** shrub or small tree of genus *Corylus.* It is often grown for ornament but European species (*Corylus maxima*) is grown commercially for its nut crop.

Hazel Park, city (pop. 17,770), SE Mich., N residential suburb of Detroit.

Hazleton, city (pop. 35,491), E Pa., S of Wilkes-Barre; settled 1780. Coal-mining center with mfg. of textiles, clothing, and paper goods.

Hazlitt, William, 1778–1830, English essayist, literary and dramatic critic. Works include *Characters of Shakespear's Plays* (1817), *Lectures on the English Poets* (1818), *Lectures on the English Comic Writers* (1819), *Table Talk* (1821–22), and *The Spirit of the Age* (1825). With Coleridge he led in reinterpreting Shakspere and Elizabethan drama. His perceptive essays, such as "On Going a Journey" and "My First Acquaintance with Poets," are noted for their lucid style.

H.D.: see DOOLITTLE, HILDA.

He, chemical symbol of the element HELIUM.

Head, Sir Francis Bond, 1793–1875, British administrator in Canada. Lieutenant governor (1835–37). His reactionary policy and alliance with Family Compact estranged moderate reformers and drove W. L. Mackenzie and other radical reformers to open rebellion in 1837.

head-hunting, taking the head of a slain enemy.

It occurs in many parts of the world and often is associated with attempt of the taker to gain status.

health: see HYGIENE; PUBLIC HEALTH.

health insurance, plan for prepayment of medical care, effected by compulsory national insurance. Initiated (1883) by Bismarck, it was adopted in other countries after World War I. Fear of government "regimentation" of medicine has restricted its spread, particularly in the U.S., where voluntary plans were begun as early as 1850. In 1947 there were in the U.S. 24,000,000 subscribers to voluntary health plans, which, although helpful, fail to cover many people and must limit benefits to avoid prohibitive rates.

Healy, George Peter Alexander, 1813–94, American painter. Did portraits of eminent Americans and Europeans, including Guizot and Lincoln.

hearing, sense by which sound is appreciated. Vibrations are collected by outer EAR, transmitted by eardrum to bones of middle ear, and pass to spiral tube (cochlea) of inner ear where fluid-filled sacs convey them to specialized cells in organ of Corti which generate nerve impulses reaching brain.

Hearn, Lafcadio (lăfkä′dēō hûrn′), 1850–1904, multinational author of works in English, b. Ionian Isls. of Irish-Maltese parents; in U.S. 1869–90. In Japan after 1890, he became a Japanese citizen. Representative works are *Chita* (1889), a Louisiana romance; *Japan: An Attempt at an Interpretation* (1904).

Hearne, Samuel (hûrn), 1745–92, British fur trader, explorer in N Canada. His expedition to mouth of Coppermine R. opened unknown territory.

Hearst, George (hûrst), 1820–91, American mining magnate, U.S. Senator from Calif. (1886–91). His wife, Phoebe Apperson Hearst (1842–1919), became a prominent philanthropist and donated freely to Univ. of California. Their son, **William Randolph Hearst,** 1863–1951, was a journalist and publisher. After managing the San Francisco *Examiner* for his father, he bought (1895) the N.Y. *Morning Journal* and demanded (1897) war with Spain. Outdoing other "yellow" journalists, he founded a news empire including 30 big dailies (also magazines, moving-picture interests). Influential in N.Y. politics, he opposed U.S. entry in World War I, all internationalism.

Heart, river rising in SW N.Dak. and flowing E to Missouri R. at Mandan. Part of MISSOURI RIVER BASIN PROJECT.

heart, cone-shaped, muscular organ which maintains CIRCULATION OF THE BLOOD. In man and other mammals it lies in the chest and is enclosed in a sac (pericardium). The mammalian heart consists of four chambers, two auricles lying above two ventricles; right and left sides are separated by septum which in prenatal life has opening between auricles. Diseases of the heart have attracted much medical attention in the 20th cent. (see ANGINA; THROMBOSIS). See also BLOOD; PULSE. See *ill.,* p. 763.

heat, form of ENERGY into which others are convertible. It is also described as the energy of motion that the molecule possesses. Sun is the most important source of heat. Heat results from friction, chemical reactions, compression of substances, impact, passage of electric current over a high resistance. It is measured qualitatively by THERMOMETER; CALORIE and BRITISH THERMAL UNIT indicate amount of heat. Specific heat of substance is amount of heat needed to raise temperature of 1 gm. of the substance 1°C. Heat needed to change unit mass of substance from solid to liquid at melting point is latent heat of fusion; amount needed to change substance from liquid to gas at boiling point is heat of vaporization. Heat is transmitted by CONDUCTION, CONVECTION, and RADIATION. Relationship between mechanical energy and heat was first determined by Sir James P. Joule.

heath, level or rolling wasteland covered with dry-land shrubs, such as heather in Great Britain. Heath land is sometimes cultivated, as in Denmark.

heather, low evergreen shrub (*Calluna vulgaris*) of Old World, with scalelike foliage and red, rose, purple, or white nodding flowers in late summer. Also known as heather, but more properly called heath, are shrubs of closely related genus *Erica*. They have needlelike leaves and bell-shaped white, rose, or yellow flowers in winter and early spring.

heating. Methods began with open fire, progressed to fireplace with chimney, stove, and to modern hot-air, hot-water, steam-heating, and radiant-heat systems. VENTILATION must be considered when designing heating equipment. Open grate system is inefficient. Stove is more efficient but does not create natural ventilation. Heating by hot-air or hot-water system has many advantages over older methods. Use of solar energy for heating buildings is being studied.

heatstroke: see SUNSTROKE.

heaven, in Christian theology, the state of bliss in which God is seen face to face; abode of souls of the good, reunited to their glorified bodies after the RESURRECTION. Roman Church teaches that many must prepare for heaven by suffering in purgatory. Popular notion of heaven is of place full of material delights. Islamic heaven often thought to contain fleshly pleasures, but passages of Koran describing it may be allegorical. See ELYSIAN FIELDS; FORTUNATE ISLES; VALHALLA.

heaves, respiratory disease of horses causing chronic cough, wheezing, difficulty in exhaling, and indigestion. It is relieved by low-roughage diet, feeding only clean hay, and rest after feeding.

Heaviside, Oliver (hĕ′vēsīd), 1850–1925, English physicist. He contributed to development of telephony and predicted existence of conducting layer in upper atmosphere known as Kennelly-Heaviside layer and also as Heaviside layer.

heavy hydrogen: see HYDROGEN.

heavy spar: see BARITE.

heavy water: see WATER.

Hebbel, Friedrich (frē′drĭkh hĕ′bŭl), 1813–63, German dramatist. Ranking him as a leading tragic poet, his plays include *Maria Magdalena* (1844), *Herod and Mariamne* (1850), *Agnes Bernauer* (1852), and the trilogy *The Nibelungs* (1855–60).

Hebe (hē′bē), in Greek mythology, goddess of youth; daughter of Zeus and Hera. She had power to make old people young again, and is said to have rejuvenated HERCULES after his ascent to Olympus.

Heber (hē′bŭr), man's name from which Hebrews is supposedly taken. Luke 3.35. Eber: Gen. 10.21.

Heber (hē′bŭr), city (pop. 2,936; alt. 5,595 ft.), N central Utah, NE of Provo. Hot-water pools of extinct geysers near by.

Hébert, Jacques René (zhäk′ rŭnā′ ābĕr′), 1757–94, French revolutionist. Edited a virulent paper, *Père Duchesne;* led CORDELIERS after Marat's death; promoted worship of Reason. Largely responsible, during Reign of Terror, for tightening maximum price laws and Law of Suspects. His power over Paris commune threatened position of Robespierre, who had him and his followers guillotined on a concocted charge of conspiracy. Hébert's fall marked triumph of propertied middle classes.

Hébert, Louis (ābĕr′), d. 1627, French pioneer, known as first Canadian farmer. Settled in Quebec in 1617.

Hébert, Louis Philippe, 1850–1917, most noted Canadian sculptor and monument designer of his time. His son, Henri Hébert, was also a sculptor.

Hebrew language, Semitic language of the Canaanite group. See LANGUAGE (table).

Hebrew literature. The earliest great work is the OLD TESTAMENT. From the 2d cent. until the 6th, the TALMUD, the great anonymous encyclopedic work, and the MIDRASH were compiled. In the 4th cent. the TARGUM to the Pentateuch and to the Prophets was finished. The 6th and 7th cent. saw the development of the MASORA in Palestine, while in Babylonia commentaries on the Talmud were written until the suppression of the academies (11th cent.). Jewish literary activity then shifted to Spain, where fine poetry and philosophy were written. In the 14th cent. the great work of CABALA, the *Zohar,* appeared. Famous scholars and authors of Hebrew literature in the Middle Ages were Solomon ben Judah IBN GABIROL, RASHI, MAIMONIDES, and Joseph ben Ephraim CARO. After the 14th cent., the Jews, driven from country to country, clung to their existing literature, especially the Old Testament. Modern Hebrew literature began with Moses MENDELSSOHN. Important names of the more recent period are the novelist Solomon Yakob Abramovich, whose pen name was MENDELE MOCHER SFORIM, and the poet Hayyim Nahman BIALIK. The rise of Zionism made Palestine the Hebrew publication center. Outside of Israel, Jews usually write in the vernacular or in YIDDISH, the literary use of which developed rapidly in the 19th cent.

Hebrew music: see JEWISH MUSIC.

Hebrews. For history, see JEWS; for religion, see JUDAISM.

Hebrews, epistle of New Testament. Tradition ascribes it to St. Paul, but few critics agree. It is treatise on the superiority of the new religion over the old and proclaims the ascendancy of Christ over the angels and Moses. It describes the new priesthood under Christ replacing that of Aaron and speaks of the sacrifice by Christ of himself as taking away sin. Hebrews is a call to faith, urging dynamic action in following Christ—even unto martyrdom. Its teachings are very important in history of theology.

Hebrews, Gospel according to the: see PSEUDE-PIGRAPHA.

Hebrew University, at Jerusalem. First proposed 1882, formally opened 1925. Originally comprised institutes of chemistry, microbiology, and Jewish studies (all opened 1924). Includes school of agr. (1940), Hebrew Univ.-Hadassah Medical School (1949), and Weizmann Inst. of Science (merged 1950 with the university).

Hebrides (hĕ′brĭdēz) or **Western Islands,** group of more than 500 islands, off W and NW Scotland. Less than a fifth inhabited. Outer Hebrides, extending 130 mi., separated from mainland and from Inner Hebrides by straits of Minch and Little Minch and Sea of the Hebrides. Mild, humid climate and beautiful scenery draw tourists. Chief occupations fishing, farming, sheep grazing, quarrying, and mfg. of tweeds. Tales of Scott and William Black helped familiarize islands. There has been much emigration, particularly to Canada in 20th cent.

Hebrides, New: see NEW HEBRIDES.

Hebron (hē′–), city (1946 est. pop. 26,390), Israel, SW of Jerusalem. Modern Arabic name; El-Khalil. Bible first mentions it as site where Abraham estab. family tomb. Was David's capital before Jerusalem. Hebron figured in every Palestinian war—Maccabean, Roman, and Crusaders'. Also appears in Bible as Kirjath-arba and Mamre. Hebron is a shrine of Moslems and Jews.

Hecate (hĕ′kŭtē, hĕ′kĭt), in Greek mythology, mysterious moon-goddess. Attendant of Persephone in underworld where she had power to conjure up spirits of dead and hence was goddess of ghosts. In upper world she haunted graveyards and crossroads.

Hecht, Selig (hĕkt), 1892–1947, American biophysicist, pioneer in applying physiochemical principles to sensory physiology. He determined minimal quantal requirements at threshold of vision. Wrote scientific works for laymen (e.g., *Explaining the Atom,* 1947).

Hecker, Isaac Thomas, 1819–88, American Roman Catholic priest, founder (1858) of Paulist Fathers. Associated with New England transcendentalists, was converted to Catholicism (1844) and ordained priest (1849). Worked among immigrants. Founded Paulist organ, *Catholic World.*

Hector, in the *Iliad,* leader of Trojan forces in Trojan War, greatest Trojan hero; son of Priam and Hecuba, brother of Paris, husband of Andromache, and father of Astyanax. Slain by Achilles in revenge for death of PATROCLUS.

Hecuba (hĕ′kyōōbù), in Greek legend, queen of Troy, wife of PRIAM. After Trojan War she was taken as slave by Odysseus. She is a prominent character in two plays by Euripides.

hedge, ornamental or protective barrier of shrubs, e.g., box, privet, barberry, or yew. Formal hedges were once pruned to resemble statuary.

hedgehog, insectivorous, nocturnal, hibernating Old World mammal with spines among its hairs. American porcupine is incorrectly called hedgehog. European hedgehog is of genus *Erinaceus;* related forms are in Africa and Asia.

Hedin, Sven (Anders) (hĕdēn′), 1865–1952, Swedish explorer in central Asia. Wrote scientific and popular accounts of travels in Kunlun and Trans-Himalaya ranges, Tibet, and Sinkiang prov., China.

Hedjaz, Saudi Arabia: see HEJAZ.

hedonism, philosophy that holds pleasure to be the chief goal of man. Pleasure may be variously defined—from the mere satisfaction of sensual desires (as with the Cyrenaics) to a lofty belief in rationally ascetic control of desires (as in the school of Epicurus). All materialistic philosophies contain elements of hedonism (thus utilitarianism stresses the chief ethical and social aim of life as the greatest good for the greatest number).

Hedrick, Ulysses Prentiss, 1870–1951, American horticulturist, authority on fruit cultivation, and author of many works including *History of Horticulture in America to 1860* (1950).

Heem, Jan Davidszoon de (yän′ dä′vētsōōn dù häm′), 1606–c.1683, celebrated Dutch still-life painter, known for fruit and flower pieces.

Hegel, Georg Wilhelm Friedrich (gā′ôrk vĭl′hĕlm frē′drĭkh hā′gùl), 1770–1831, German philosopher, formulator of an idealistic philosophy that has had enormous influence since his day. He taught at various universities, being a professor at Jena, Heidelberg, and Berlin. His idealism, set forth in a series of books (*Phenomenology of Mind,* 1807; *Science of Logic,* 1812–16; *Encyclopedia of the Philosophical Sciences,* 1817; *Philosophy of Right,* 1821), is all-embracing and highly unified, welding together a world view with theories of ethics, aesthetics, history, politics, and religion. The system is complicated, and no brief statement does justice to it. Fundamentally he believed in an enveloping Absolute. The world soul is seen through contemplation of dialectical knowledge. In this dialectic, one concept (thesis) inevitably evokes its opposite (antithesis), and the two interact to form a new concept (synthesis), which in turn becomes a new thesis. Thus the idea of being evokes the idea of not being, and the two necessarily produce the synthesis, becoming. The universe is thus in a state of perpetual self-creation. The absolute is the active principle in this process. History also shows the progress from lower to higher manifestations of the principle. Thus cultures conflict, and the higher is triumphant. In art also different periods succeed each other. In religion Christianity was considered as succeeding to nature religions, and Christ is the union of God and man, of spirit and matter. Various later philosophers developed differing aspects of this system. Hegelian dialectic appealed strongly to the Socialists and was developed into Marxian dialectical materialism.

hegira or **hejira** (hējî′rù, hĕ′jîrù), flight of the prophet MOHAMMED from Mecca, June, 622, to Yathrib (Medina). Since the foundation of Islam was laid in Medina, Mohammedan era dates from the hegira. Abbreviation A.H. is used in West with year number to mean After the Hegira.

Heiberg, Johan Ludvig (hī′bâr), 1791–1860,

Danish poet, dramatist, critic, and director of the Natl. Theater. His play, *The Hill of the Elves* (1828), very popular.

Heidegger, Martin (hī′dĕgŭr), 1889–, German philosopher. Professor at Marburg (1923–28) and Berlin (1928–33), he became rector at Berlin in 1933. He considered and adapted ideas put forward by Kierkegaard and Husserl and created a system of thought which has been labeled atheistic existentialism. Viewing man as oppressed by anguish and forlornness in his brief existence in the finite world, Heidegger rejected the conventional religious answers to man's problem and argued that by questioning man may learn the nature of eixstence and, accepting it, may assert his essence and destiny by "resolute decision." One of his best-known works is *Sein und Zeit* (1927). Jean Paul Sartre became his disciple.

Heidelberg (hī′dŭlbĕrk), city (pop. 115,750), Württemberg-Baden, W Germany, on Neckar R., beautifully situated in a region of orchards and vineyards. It is best known for its university, founded 1386. The cap. of the Rhenish PALATINATE until 1720, it was devastated by the imperials in 1622, by the French in 1689 and 1693. There was only minor damage in World War II. The famous castle dates from the 15th–17th cent. The **Heidelberg Catechism**, a profession of faith of German Reformed (Calvinistic) Church, was drawn up at the request of Elector Frederick III and was published 1563.

Heidelberg College: see TIFFIN, Ohio.

Heidenstam, Verner von (hā′dŭnstäm), 1859–1940, Swedish lyric poet, novelist, and essayist. Opposed naturalism and in his novels evoked a patriotic sense of the continuing unity of Sweden's history. Awarded 1916 Nobel Prize in Literature.

Heifetz, Jascha (yä′shū hī′fĭts), 1901–, Russian-American violinist, known for his virtuosity. Studied at St. Petersburg Conservatory with Leopold Auer. Came to the U.S. 1917.

Heilbronn (hīlbrôn′), city (pop. 64,544), Württemberg-Baden, W Germany, in Württemberg, on Neckar R. Mfg. of machinery, tools. Free imperial city 1281–1803. In World War II old city was largely destroyed. Götz von Berlichingen was imprisoned (1522) in the Götzenturm, a tower built in 1392.

Heilungkiang: see MANCHURIA.

Heine, Heinrich (hīn′rĭkh hī′nŭ), 1797–1856, German author, of Jewish parentage. His *Buch der Lieder* [book of songs] (1827) placed him among the greatest German poets. Lyrics have musical, folklike quality (as in "Lorelei"), often spiced with subtle irony or dissonant endings, have attracted many composers, notably Schubert, Schumann, Mendelssohn, Brahms. His prose travel sketches, beginning with *Die Harzreise* (1826), show the same mixture of lyric emotion and corrosive wit. In 1831, drawn by his revolutionary sympathies, he left Germany for Paris, where he died after eight years of tragic sickness, confined to his "mattress grave." There he wrote the verse satires *Atta Troll* and *Deutschland; Neue Gedichte* (1847) and *Letzte Gedichte* (1853), in which his verse takes on an increasingly bitter and tragic tone; prose essays on German literature and

philosophy (in French); and political reports for a German newspaper. Nearly all his work has been translated into English, although his verse often defies translation.

Heisenberg, Werner (vĕr′nŭr hī′zŭnbĕrk), 1901–, German physicist. Won 1932 Nobel Prize for theory of quantum mechanics and discovery of allotropic forms of hydrogen.

Heiser, Victor George (hī′zŭr), 1873–, American physician, authority on public health, associated with Rockefeller Foundation (1915–34). His works include *An American Doctor's Odyssey* (1936); *Toughen Up, America* (1941).

Hejaz or **Hedjaz** (both: hĕjäz′) region, NW Saudi Arabia, on Gulf of Aqaba and Red Sea. Mainly a mountain range and plateau, lying between coastal strip and interior desert. Holy cities of Mecca and Medina are here. Husein ibn Ali overthrew Turkish rule in 1916, but was ousted 1924 by Ibn Saud.

hejira: see HEGIRA.

Hekla (hĕk′lä), volcano, 4,746 ft. high, SW Iceland. Since 1004 many eruptions have been recorded.

Held, Anna, 1873?–1918, American musical comedy actress, b. Paris. Famed for her beauty and for her temperamental private life.

Helen, in Greek legend, daughter of Leda and Zeus. From many suitors she chose MENELAUS. When PARIS awarded APPLE OF DISCORD to Aphrodite, she, in return, gave him the fairest of women, Helen, whom he carried off to Troy, thus causing TROJAN WAR. After the war Helen returned with Menelaus to Sparta. She bore him only one child, Hermione.

Helena, Saint (hĕ′lŭnŭ), c.248–328?, mother of Constantine the Great. Converted to Christianity in 313, she is said to have gone to Jerusalem, where she found the True Cross and the Holy Sepulcher.

Helena (hĕ′lŭnŭ). **1** City (pop. 11,236), E Ark., on Mississippi R. and SW of Memphis, Tenn. A rail center and river port, it ships cotton, lumber, and farm products. Canning, woodworking, and mfg. of cottonseed oil and hosiery. **2** City (pop. 17,581), state cap., W central Mont., NNE of Butte near Missouri R.; founded in Last Chance Gulch after 1864 gold discovery. Became territorial cap. 1874, replacing Virginia City. Also had silver strikes. Center of mining, ranching, and agr. (Prickly Pear valley) area. Seat of Carroll Col. (R.C.; for men; 1910) and Fort Harrison army post (now a VA hospital).

Helgoland (hĕl′gölänt) or **Heligoland,** island, area less than 150 acres, Germany, in North Sea off the Elbe estuary. Consisting of red sandstone, it rises c.160 ft. above sea and is covered by grazing land. Once a Danish possession, it was ceded to England 1814; traded to Germany for Zanzibar 1890. It served as German naval base in World War II; fortifications were blown up by British 1947.

Helicon (hĕ′lĭkŏn), Gr. *Elikon*, mountain group, Boeotia, Greece. In Greek legend, abode of the MUSES.

helicopter (hĕ′lĭkŏptŭr), rotor aircraft obtaining lift and propulsion from engine-driven rotors. It differs from the autogiro, the rotor of which is moved by aerodynamic forces resulting from propulsion in the conventional manner by engine-driven propeller. Helicopter is valuable for air-sea rescue and aeromagnetic surveying; it can maneuver and hover at nearly zero ground speed. See *ill.*, p. 23.

Heligoland, German island: see HELGOLAND.

Heliodorus (hē″lēŏdō′rùs), fl. 175 B.C., Syrian political leader. Murdered Seleucus IV in vain hope of getting the throne. In 2 Mac. 3 he is said to have been prevented by three angels from taking the treasure from the Temple at Jerusalem.

Heliogabalus (hē″lēōgă′bùlùs), c.205–222, Roman emperor (218–22). He was Varius Avitus Bassianus, a priest of the sun-god of Emesa, cousin and, according to his mother, son of CARACALLA. The troops in Syria chose him as emperor on the defeat of Macrinus, the legitimate heir. He had a reign notorious for the indecency of the rites of his sun-god and of his own life. He and his mother were killed in an uprising of Praetorian guards. His cousin, Alexander Severus, succeeded. Also Elagabalus.

heliograph (hē′lēùgrăf), signaling device consisting of a mirror reflecting sunlight and shuttered to permit interruption of light beam for long and short signal flashes. Heliostat similarly reflects light beam on distant spot. Spectroheliograph, combining heliostat and spectroscope, is used by scientists to photograph sun.

Hélion, Jean (ālyō′), 1904–, French abstractionist painter. Settled in U.S. in 1932.

Heliopolis (hēlēŏ′pùlĭs) [Gr.,= city of the sun], anc. city, N Egypt, near Cairo, center of the worship of Ra (or Re), who was long the state deity. It was under the New Empire (c.1580–c.1090 B.C.) seat of the viceroy of N Egypt. Obelisks called Cleopatra's Needles were erected here. Its school of philosophy was said to have been visited by Plato. Egyptian name was On.

Heliopolis, anc. Syrian city: see BAALBEK.

Helios (hē′lēŏs) [Gr.,= sun], in Greek religion, sun-god; son of Hyperion and Theia, husband of nymph Clymene, and father of PHAËTHON. Each day he drove a golden chariot from his palace in the E to his palace in the W. In Rhodes he was national god, and Colossus represented him. He symbolized material aspects of the sun, Apollo its spiritual aspects. In the *Odyssey* Helios shipwrecked Odysseus for eating his sacred cattle. He was called Sol by Romans.

heliotrope (hē′–), tender perennial plant (*Heliotropium arborescens*) with fragrant purple flower clusters. Commonly called garden heliotrope is a valerian (*Valeriana officinalis*).

helium (hē′lēùm), colorless, odorless, tasteless, inert gaeous element (symbol = He; see also ELEMENT, table). Because of its lightness (only hydrogen is lighter) and non inflammability it is used in balloons and airships. Used in pressure chambers for divers and caisson workers because of low solubility in human blood. U.S. controls production. Alpha rays from radium are helium nuclei. See *ill.*, p. 989.

hell, in Christian theology, eternal abode of those damned by God's judgment and forever denied sight of Him. It is ruled by Satan (Lucifer, the devil). Tradition and legend have made of it a place of fire and brimstone, with the damned souls undergoing physical torment. The vivid description of hell (Inferno) by Dante is known over the Western world. The Islamic idea of hell is similar to the Christian. The Sheol or Tophet of the ancient Jews was a gloomy place where the souls of the dead wander about unhappy; the name Gehenna (from Hinnom) is used in the New Testament. The Greeks believed that the souls of the dead (good and evil) went to an underworld, Hades, ruled by the god Hades (also called Pluto) and his wife Persephone. Its entrance was guarded by Cerberus, and Hades was surrounded by the river Styx, across which Charon ferried the dead. Tartarus below Hades was a place of torment for the very wicked. The Romans also called the underworld Hades and Orcus, Dis (also a name for Pluto) and Avernus. The Hel of the Icelandic *Edda* is probably a borrowing from Christianity.

Hellas, name for GREECE.

hellebore (hĕl′ù–), name for winter- or spring-blooming Eurasian perennial plants of genus *Helleborus*. The Christmas rose (*Helleborus niger*) has evergreen leaves and its flowers (usually white) resemble wild roses and often bloom in winter. Roots of North American false hellebores (*Veratrum*) yield veratrine used in insecticides.

Hellen, in Greek mythology, ancestor of Hellenes or Greeks.

Hellenism, culture, ideals, and pattern of life of Greece, as represented in Athens at the time of Pericles; frequently contrasted with Hebraic seriousness in the Old Testament. Hellenism gave way to Hellenistic civilization in 4th cent. B.C., but any modern attempt to revive Greek ideals is called Hellenism.

Hellenistic civilization, widespread, Greek-tinctured culture that grew out of the efforts of ALEXANDER THE GREAT to spread Hellenism with his conquests across the known world. After his death (323 B.C.) the DIADOCHI estab. dynasties that helped to give that world political disunity but at the same time Greek unity of trade and learning. A new culture in art, letters, and science developed. Alexandria and Pergamum were notable centers. Physical comfort increased for the well-to-do, education was general among the wealthy. Literature grew to vast proportions and learning (as distinct from knowledge and philosophy) came into being. Though accused of being derivative and ponderous, literature had great richness. Libraries were built, anthologies compiled. Sculpture developed, and some of the most familiar statues of the present day (e.g., the Venus of Milo, the Dying Gaul) are Hellenistic. Philosophy became the field of all the educated. The triumph of Rome meant the Roman absorption of Hellenistic culture, not its extinction.

Hellertown, borough (pop. 5,435), SE Pa., near Delaware R. and S of Bethlehem. Mfg. of electrical products and commercial gases.

Hellespont: see DARDANELLES.

Hell Gate, N.Y.: see EAST RIVER.

Helmand (hĕl′mùnd), river, c.700 mi. long, rising in central Afghanistan. Flows to Hamun-i-Helmand on Iranian border. Vital irrigation works.

Helmholtz, Hermann Ludwig Ferdinand von (hĕr′män lōōt′vĭkh fĕr′dĕnänt fŭn hĕlm′hôlts), 1821–94, German scientist. He extended the application of law of conservation of energy and formulated it mathematically; contributed to thermo- and electrodynamics. He extended Young's theory of color vision; explained lens accommodation in eye; invented ophthalmoscope. He was an authority on acoustics.

Helmont, Jan Baptista van (yän bäptĭ′stä vän hĕl′mônt), 1577–1644, Flemish scientist. He discovered carbon dioxide, distinguished gases from solids and liquids, and is credited with introducing the term *gas* in present scientific sense.

Heloise: see ABELARD, PETER.

Helper, Hinton Rowan, 1829–1909, American author. A Southerner, he wrote *The Impending Crisis of the South* (1857), an attack on slavery as an economic evil that delighted Republicans. Later wrote anti-Negro books.

Helsingborg: see HALSINGBORG.

Helsingfors, Finland: see HELSINKI.

Helsingør, Denmark: see ELSINORE.

Helsinki (hĕl′sĭngkē), Swed. *Helsingfors,* city (pop. 375,981), cap. of Finland; a Baltic seaport on Gulf of Finland. Intellectual, commercial, administrative center of Finland. Mfg. of paper, tobacco, sugar, liquor, textiles, machinery. Called White City of the North for its cleanliness and buildings of native granite. Founded 1550, it grew rapidly after cap. was moved here from Turku (1812). Oustanding sites include university (moved here from Turku 1828), railway station (designed by Saarinen), national archives, opera house, Church of St. Nicholas. Slightly damaged in World War II. Olympic games were held here 1952.

Helst, Bartholomeus van der (hĕlst′), c.1613–1670, Dutch portrait painter. *Banquet of the Civic Guard* (Rijks Mus.) is considered his masterpiece.

Helvellyn (hĕlvĕl′ĭn), mountain, 3,118 ft. high, Cumberland and Westmorland, England.

Helvetia (hĕlvē′shù). **1** Latin name of Switzerland; short for *Confoederatio Helvetica.* **2** Roman administrative district of Upper Germany, 1st cent. B.C.–5th cent. A.D. It occupied W part of modern Switzerland. The Helvetii, a predominantly Celtic people, tried to conquer S Gaul in 58 B.C., were defeated by Julius Caesar at Bibracte.

Helvetic Republic, 1798–1803: see SWITZERLAND.

Helvétius, Claude Adrien (hĕlvē′shùs; Fr. ĕlvāsyüs′), 1715–71, French philosopher, one of the Encyclopedists. After serving as farmer-general and as chamberlain to the queen he retired in 1751. His philosophy as set forth in *Essays on the Mind* (1758) held that all men are born with equal ability and that educational influences create distinctions. He argued that all intellectual activity arises from sensation, even the soul being at first a capacity for sensation. He regarded self-interest as the sole motive for action and influenced the utilitarians. In France he was condemned by the Sorbonne.

Hemans, Felicia (Dorothea Browne), 1793–1835, English poet, noted for sentimental poems, such as "Casabianca" and "The Landing of the Pilgrims."

hematite (hĕ′mŭtīt), a mineral, an oxide of iron, important as an ore. It occurs in red earthy masses and gray to black crystals.

Hemingway, Ernest, 1898–, American writer, notable for terse, direct style and realistic tone. Among his novels are *The Sun Also Rises* (1926), *A Farewell to Arms* (1929), *For Whom the Bell Tolls* (1940). Favorite theme, also expressed in vigorous short stories (as in *Men without Women,* 1927) is struggle of man mutilated by environment. Nonfictional *Death in the Afternoon* (1932) concerns bullfighting.

Hemling, Hans: see MEMLING, HANS.

hemlock, name for several plants, especially coniferous evergreen trees of genus *Tsuga,* native to North America and Asia. They are popular ornamentals with small cones and flattened leaves on horizontal branches. The poison hemlock (*Conium maculatum*) by which Socrates died, a perennial meadow plant with flattened clusters of white flowers, is naturalized in North America. Similar to it is the North American water hemlock (*Cicuta maculata*), sometimes grown in bog gardens.

hemoglobin: see CORPUSCLES.

Hémon, Louis (lwē′ āmō′), 1880–1913, French Canadian novelist, b. France. Wrote *Maria Chapdelaine* (1913), story of pioneer life in Quebec.

hemophilia (hē″mŭfĭ′lēù, hē″–), rare disease marked by delayed CLOTTING OF BLOOD. Death sometimes results from bleeding after even minor injuries. Inherited by males only, it is transmitted as a sex-linked character only through females.

hemorrhage (hĕ′mŭrĭj), escape of blood from heart or blood vessels. Bleeding from arteries is red and of rhythmic flow; from veins, it is dark and of constant flow. See also HEMOPHILIA.

hemorrhoids (hĕ′mŭroidz) or **piles,** dilated veins at anus. They often result from constipation, poor circulation, and pressure on rectum.

hemp, tall annual plant (*Cannabis sativa*), native to Asia but cultivated elsewhere for its bast fiber, also called hemp, and as a source of the narcotic drug marijuana. It has large, digitately divided narrow leaves and inconspicuous male and female flower spikes on separate plants. Cordage, paper, canvas, etc., are made from the bast fiber. Dried plant parts, especially female flowers, are the source of marijuana and hashish; the U.S. government restricts its cultivation.

Hempstead. 1 Residential village (pop. 29,135), SE N.Y., on W Long Isl. and E of Jamaica; settled 1644. Hofstra Col. (coed.; 1935) is here. **2** Town (pop. 1,395), S Texas, NW of Houston. Near-by "Liendo" was plantation home of Elizabeth Ney.

Hems, Syria: see HOMS.

henbane, weedy annual Old World plant of nightshade family. Black henbane (*Hyoscyamus niger*) is naturalized in E North America. It has yellow flowers and is poisonous, especially to poultry.

Hench, Philip Showalter, 1896–, American

Henderson, Alexander 546 Henry (Germany)

physician. An authority on rheumatic diseases, he has long been associated with Mayo Clinic and Mayo Foundation (of Univ. of Minnesota). He shared 1950 Nobel Prize in Physiology and Medicine for work on hormones of the cortex of adrenal glands.

Henderson, Alexander, 1583–1646, Scottish churchman. Opposed English domination of Church of Scotland. As moderator of general assembly he conferred with Charles I on Presbyterian aims of Covenanters.

Henderson, Leon, 1895–, American economist, head of Office of Price Administration (1941–42).

Henderson, Richard, 1735–85, American colonizer in Ky. Chief promoter of TRANSYLVANIA COMPANY. Important figure in early frontier expansion.

Henderson. 1 City (pop. 16,837), W Ky., on Ohio R. and S of Evansville, Ind.; founded 1797. Mfg. and shipping of tobacco, wood, food, and cotton products. J. J. Audubon lived here (1810–19); Audubon Memorial Park near by. **2** City (pop. 10,996), N N.C., NNE of Raleigh; settled 1814. Tobacco market with cotton and flour mills. **3** City (pop. 6,833), E Texas, WSW of Shreveport, La. First gusher of rich East Texas oil field struck near by, 1930. Shawnee Indian village site near.

Hendersonville, city (pop. 6,103), W N.C., in Blue Ridge SSE of Asheville. Resort with farm trade and textile mills.

Hendon, urban district (pop. 155,835), Middlesex, England. Has RAF airfield, scene of June Display.

Hendrix College: see CONWAY, Ark.

Hengist and Horsa (hĕng′gĭst, hôr′sŭ), traditional names of two leaders of 5th-cent. Germanic invasion of Britain. Supposedly invited to help Britons against Picts and Scots, they settled in Kent.

Henie, Sonja (sō′nyŭ hĕ′nē), 1913–, Norwegian-American skater. Won Olympic figure-skating championship (1928, 1932, 1936).

Henle, Jacob (yä′kôp hĕn′lŭ), 1809–85, German anatomist and pathologist, noted for work on microscopic structure of tissues.

Henley, William Ernest, 1849–1903, English lyric poet, critic, and editor. Best known of his poems "England, My England" and "Invictus." He wrote plays with Stevenson and edited literary reviews.

Henley-on-Thames (-tĕmz), municipal borough (pop. 7,970), Oxfordshire, England, at base of the Chilterns, on the Thames. Scene of annual Henley rowing regatta (begun 1839) in which several English and some American crews take part.

Henlopen, Cape (hĕnlō′pŭn), SE Del., at mouth of Delaware Bay opposite Cape May, N.J. Lightship.

henna, Old World tropical shrub (*Lawsonia inermis*) with small fragrant flowers. From its dried leaves henna dye is made.

Hennepin, Louis, 1640–1701?, Franciscan Recollect friar, explorer in North America. With Michel Aco he explored the upper Mississippi valley.

Henri, Robert (hĕn′rī), 1865–1929, American painter and teacher, b. Cincinnati. His teachings helped to destroy tradition of academicism and to inspire development of living art for America. One of The EIGHT, he sponsored first exhibit in America without a jury. Excelled in dramatic portraits.

Henrietta Maria, 1609–66, queen consort of Charles I of England, daughter of Henry IV of France. Her dealings with the pope, foreign powers, and army officers increased suspicion of Charles and fear of a Catholic uprising which partly led to civil war.

Henrietta of England (Henrietta Anne), 1644–70, duchess of Orléans, called Madame; sister of Charles II of England and wife of Philippe I d'ORLÉANS. Negotiated Treaty of Dover with Charles II in behalf of Louis XIV. An unfounded rumor ascribed her sudden death to poison.

Henry, emperors and German kings. Henry I or **Henry the Fowler,** 876?–936, duke of Saxony, was elected king 919 to succeed Conrad I. He won Lotharingia from allegiance to France (925), defeated the Magyars (933), built many walled towns in E border regions. His queen, St. Matilda (d. 968) founded many monasteries. His son Otto I succeeded him. **Henry II,** 973–1024, duke of Bavaria, was elected German king 1002; crowned king of the Lombards 1004; crowned emperor at Rome 1014. He and his empress, Kunigunde, were canonized saints of the Roman Church. **Henry III,** 1017–56, was crowned joint king with his father Conrad II in 1028; became sole king 1039; was crowned emperor 1046. Under him the medieval empire reached its greatest power. He supported the reforms of the CLUNIAC ORDER. In 1046 he deposed three rival claimants to the papacy at the Synod of Sutri and caused the election of a reform-minded German (Clement II). Popes Leo IX and Victor II were also his candidates (1048, 1055). His son, **Henry IV,** 1050–1106, succeeded him as king (1056). During his minority archbishops Anno of Cologne and ADALBERT of Bremen held the power. Beginning his personal rule in 1065, Henry restored his authority in the duchies, notably Saxony. His appointments of bishops in 1075 met the condemnation of Pope GREGORY VII (see INVESTITURE), whom Henry declared deposed (1076). Gregory in turn declared Henry excommunicated and deposed, and Henry, threatened with revolt, made his humiliating journey to CANOSSA, where the pope gave him absolution (Jan. 1077). Nevertheless, the German nobles elected Rudolf of Swabia antiking. Civil war resulted, and in 1080 Gregory renewed his excommunication of Henry. But Henry was now supported by a large party. Invading Italy (1081), he drove Gregory from Rome in 1084 and was crowned emperor by GUIBERT OF RAVENNA. He was forced to abdicate in 1105 by his rebellious son, **Henry V,** 1081–1125, who had the support of Pope Paschal II. The new king soon fell out with the pope over the question of lay investiture. In 1111, at Rome, he took the pope and cardinals prisoners. To obtain his release, Paschal conceded to Henry the right to invest at will and crowned him emperor. The struggle was continued with popes Gelasius II and Calixtus II until a final compromise was reached in 1122 (see WORMS, CONCORDAT OF). Henry's widow,

Matilda, married Geoffrey Plantagenet. **Henry VI**, 1165-97, succeeded his father Frederick I as German king (1190) and was crowned emperor in 1191. As husband of CONSTANCE, heiress of Sicily, he took possession of that kingdom in 1194, after the death of TANCRED of Lecce. In the same year good fortune delivered RICHARD I of England into his power, whom he forced to swear fealty as vassal. He died on his way to lead a crusade to Holy Land. His son, who later became Emperor Frederick II, succeeded him in Sicily; his brother Philip of Swabia, succeeded him as German king. **Henry VII**, c.1275-1313, count of Luxemburg, was elected German king to succeed Albert I (1308). He vainly sought to restore imperial authority in Italy by ending the strife between Guelphs and Ghibellines. Crowned king of the Lombards (1311) and emperor (1312), he died in the middle of a campaign in S Italy. He was the father of John of Luxemburg.

Henry, kings of England. **Henry I**, 1068-1135, king 1100-1135, was the youngest son of William I. On death of his brother William II he obtained crown by a coup d'état which excluded his brother Robert II, duke of Normandy, who was on crusade. Robert invaded England (1101) but was bought off by Henry. Henry invaded Normandy (1105) and imprisoned his brother for life. Was involved in a struggle with ANSELM over investiture. His attempts to secure succession for his daughter MATILDA later led to long civil war between STEPHEN and Matilda. **Henry II**, 1133-89, king 1154-89, was son of Matilda and Geoffrey IV. Duke of Normandy, he married ELEANOR OF AQUITAINE, thus gaining vast territories in France. Invaded England and forced Stephen to acknowledge him as heir. He restored order to war-ravaged England, subdued barons, centralized power of government in royal authority, and strengthened royal courts. His long controversy with THOMAS À BECKET concerned sole jurisdiction of ecclesiastical courts over clergymen accused of crimes. Henry adopted Constitutions of Clarendon (1164) which brought such men into lay courts; Becket protested and fled to France. Soon after his return and continued insistence on ecclesiastical prerogative, Thomas was murdered by four knights in Canterbury Cathedral. Henry was forced by public indignation to do penance. During his reign he gained N counties of England from Scotland and subdued N Wales. He was also involved in family struggles—revolt of his son Henry, and intrigues of sons Geoffrey, RICHARD I, and JOHN. Richard, with Philip II of France, defeated the aged king, who died. He was the founder of ANGEVIN or Plantagenet line. **Henry III**, 1207-72, king 1216-72, was the son of John. Became king under a regency; was granted full powers in 1227. Against advice of HUBERT DE BURGH, chief justiciar and greatest power in government, he led unsuccessful expedition to Gascony and Brittany. Dismissed De Burgh in 1232 and began a reign of extravagance, absolutism, and general incapacity. Spent vast sums on futile wars in Gascony. Henry's absolutism, and

his attempt to put his son Edmund, earl of Lancaster, on Sicilian throne eventually led to outbreak of BARONS' WAR (1263). Simon de MONTFORT, leader of barons, won at Lewes and summoned (1265) a famous Parliament. Another son, Edward (later EDWARD I) led royal troops to victory at Evesham where Montfort was killed. From 1267 Edward was actually ruler and Henry king in name only. **Henry IV**, 1367-1413, king 1399-1413, was son of JOHN OF GAUNT. Opposed RICHARD II in 1387 and was one of lords appellant who ruled England for a year. After accusing duke of Norfolk of treason against Richard he was banished for six years. In the absence of Richard (whose rule was unpopular) he landed in England in 1399 and claimed throne, thus founding Lancastrian dynasty. Put down rebellions by Richard's followers, by the Scots and the Welsh, and by the Percies. Maintained prerogatives of the crown against Parliament, but he left crown enormously in debt. His son, **Henry V**, 1387-1422, king 1413-22, presided over privy council during his father's illness. As prince (Shakspere's Prince Hal) he had led armies against Welsh Owen Glendower and been active in royal victory over the Percies. Rebellion by the Lollards continued after his accession until 1417. Determined to regain lands which he sincerely but mistakenly believed to be his, he invaded France in 1415, thus reopening HUNDRED YEARS WAR. Announced his claim to French throne and defeated the French at Agincourt. Henry conquered Normandy (1417-19) and in 1420 married CATHERINE OF VALOIS. Fell ill and died in 1422. Despite early recklessness he ruled with justice and industry and restored civil order and nationalism. His charm, military genius, and care for less fortunate subjects made him a popular hero even though his wars left the crown heavily in debt. His son, **Henry VI**, 1421-71, king 1422-61 and 1470-71, became king when less than a year old. During his early years England was under protectorate of his uncles, John of Lancaster and Humphrey, duke of Gloucester. The English, after their defeat by Joan of Arc, attempted to protect their French interests by crowning Henry king of France at Paris (1431) but their cause became hopeless. Rebellion of Jack Cade was one of many riots showing dissatisfaction with government. Struggle between factions headed by Queen, MARGARET OF ANJOU, and Edmund Beaufort, duke of SOMERSET, and by Richard, duke of YORK, developed into dynastic battle between Lancasters and Yorkists called Wars of the ROSES. In battle of St. Albans (1455) Somerset was killed and Henry captured. York, who had been made protector and named successor to Henry (whose mind had given way), was killed in 1460 but his son Edward defeated Lancastrians and was proclaimed king as EDWARD IV in 1461. He later fled to Holland and Henry was restored briefly. Edward retook crown and Henry died in the Tower in 1471. **Henry VII**, 1457-1509, king 1485-1509, became head of house of Lancaster at Henry VI's death. Invaded England from Brittany (1485) and at battle of Bosworth Field defeated forces of RICHARD III. Married Elizabeth, daughter of Edward IV, uniting houses of York and Lancaster and founding Tudor dynasty. Sent Edward POYNINGS to Ireland in 1494 to consolidate British rule there. Peace treaty (1499) between Scotland and England was followed by marriage of Henry's daughter, Margaret, to James IV of Scotland. Henry estab. Tudor tradition of autocratic rule tempered by justice and brought order out of chaos. Estab. (1487) court of Star Chamber. His reign saw end of Wars of the Roses and is generally considered beginning of modern English history. His son, Henry VIII, 1491–1547, king 1509–47, married his brother's widow, KATHARINE OF ARAGON, who bore him a daughter, Mary. His chief minister, Thomas WOLSEY, concluded an alliance with France but Henry (despite FIELD OF THE CLOTH OF GOLD) joined (1522) Emperor Charles V in war against France. England prospered internally under Wolsey (who had almost complete control). Court was a center of learning and the pope gave Henry title of "Defender of the Faith" for treatise against Luther. Henry now wished to marry Anne BOLEYN but Pope Clement VII resisted his demands for a divorce from Katharine. Wolsey's failure in the affair caused his downfall and Thomas Cromwell became chief minister. An anti-ecclesiastical policy was begun and subservient Thomas Cranmer became archbishop of Canterbury. Henry married Anne (1533) and was excommunicated. Papal powers were now transferred to king who became supreme head of English church. Break with Rome was complete and Church of ENGLAND was estab. Anne had one daughter, Elizabeth. The marriage ended when Anne was convicted of adultery and beheaded. Ten days later Henry married Jane Seymour who died in 1537 giving birth to Edward VI. Dealt harshly with such rebellions as the Pilgrimage of Grace. Licensed (1537) publication of Bible in English. His marriage (1540) to ANNE OF CLEVES (whom he disliked and divorced) led to execution of Cromwell. He then married Catherine HOWARD who suffered (1542) Anne Boleyn's fate. In 1543 Catherine Parr became his sixth queen. War with Scotland began again (1542) and Henry made unsuccessful attempts to unite the two kingdoms. Wales was officially incorporated into England (1536) but conquest of Ireland proved too expensive. End of his reign saw gradual move toward Protestantism. He remained immensely popular despite his advancement of personal desires under guise of public policy or moral right. His political insight, however, steadily grew better; he gave England a comparatively peaceful reign.

Henry, kings of France. Henry I, c.1008–1060, reigned 1031–60. He was a powerless tool of the great feudal lords. Henry II, 1519–59, son of Francis I, reigned 1547–59. Was dominated by Anne de Montmorency, by his mistress Diane de Poitiers, and by François and Charles de Guise. He continued his father's struggle against Emperor Charles V; recovered Calais from England (1558). Treaty of CATEAU-CAMBRÉSIS ended French pretensions to Italy (1559). He was accidentally killed in a tournament. His queen was Catherine de' Medici. His third son, Henry III, 1551–89, was elected king of Poland in 1573 but returned to France in 1574 to succeed his brother Charles IX. His reign was almost continually disturbed by the Wars of RELIGION. The death in 1584 of his brother Francis made him the last male member of the house of Valois. His recognition of Henry of Navarre (later Henry IV) as heir presumptive was opposed by Henri, 3d duc de GUISE, head of the Catholic LEAGUE (the "War of the Three Henrys" resulted). Having procured the murder of Guise (1588), the king was faced with a revolt of League and was expelled from Paris. Henry of Navarre came to his aid, but Henry III was assassinated in the siege by Jacques Clément, a fanatic monk. Henry III was notorious for his vices. Henry IV (Henry of Navarre), 1553–1610, first BOURBON king of France, was the son of Antoine de Bourbon and JEANNE D'ALBRET. On her death he succeeded to the kingdom of Navarre (1572). He took leadership of the Huguenot (Protestant) party in 1569. His marriage in 1572 with MARGARET OF VALOIS was the occasion for the massacre of SAINT BARTHOLOMEW'S DAY. Henry saved his life by abjuring Protestantism, but in 1576 he escaped from his virtual imprisonment at court and returned to Protestantism. When in 1584 HENRY III named him heir presumptive, the Catholic LEAGUE, headed by Henri, 3d duc de GUISE, refused to recognize him as heir and persuaded Henry III to send an army to force his conversion. In the resulting "War of the Three Henrys," Henry of Navarre defeated Henry III at Coutras (1587) but came to the king's support in the troubles of 1588, and after Henry III's death (1589) defeated the League forces at Arques (1589) and Ivry (1590); he was unable to enter Paris until 1594, after he had abjured Protestantism— allegedly with the remark, "Paris is worth a Mass." His war with Spain, the ally of the League, ended in 1598 with the Treaty of VERVINS. In 1598 also he established religious toleration through the Edict of NANTES. With his minister SULLY he spent the rest of his reign restoring order, industry, and trade. His slogan, "A chicken in every peasant's pot every Sunday," has remained famous. In 1600 he married Marie de' Medici, having had his earlier marriage annulled. He was stabbed to death by RAVAILLAC. His gallantry and wit, his concern for the common people, and his exploits with the ladies have become legendary. Henry V: see CHAMBORD, HENRI, COMTE DE.

Henry II or Henry of Trastamara (trästù-mä′rù), 1333?–1379, Spanish king of Castile and Leon (1369–79); natural son of Alfonso XI. In his struggle against his half-brother PETER THE CRUEL he was aided by Du Guesclin, Peter by Henry the Black Prince. Though defeated at Najéra (1367), he routed and killed Peter in 1369. His son JOHN I succeeded him.

Henry, Joseph, 1797–1878, American physicist, first secretary and director of Smithsonian Institution (estab. 1846). He improved the electromagnet, discovered self-inductance, and independently of Michael Faraday he discovered principle of the induced current (basic to dynamo, transformer, and many other devices).

Henry, O., pseud. of **William Sydney Porter,** 1862–1910, American short-story writer, notable for unexpected twist at end of stories. Charged with fraud in an Austin, Texas, bank, he fled to Central America, later returned to imprisonment, then lived as a writer in New York. Many stories (as in *The Four Million,* 1906) picture great-city life.

Henry, Patrick, 1736–99, American patriot and orator. Spurred colonial revolt in the South by oratory; he was responsible for the phrase, "Give me liberty or give me death." Later fought to add Bill of Rights to the Constitution.

Henry, William: see HENRY'S LAW.

Henry, Cape, SE Va., at entrance to Chesapeake Bay E of Norfolk. Jamestown settlers landed here April 26, 1607. Site included in Colonial Natl. Historical Park, 1939.

Henry, Fort, fortification, SE Ont., Canada, on St. Lawrence R. overlooking Kingston harbor. Built 1812, demolished 1832, rebuilt 1000 06. Poineered ramp in 1 th World Wars.

Henry Clay, suburb (pop. 6,104) of Lexington, Ky.

Henry E. Huntington Library and Art Gallery: See HUNTINGTON, COLLIS POTTER.

Henryetta, city (pop. 7,987), E central Okla., S of Tulsa. Has coal mines and processes zinc, oil, and glass.

Henry of Burgundy, d. 1112 or 1114, count of Portugal. A brother of Eudes, duke of Burgundy, he was called by Alfonso VI of Leon to help in the fight against the Moors and was assigned a portion of land which under his son, Alfonso I, became the independent kingdom of Portugal.

Henry of Flanders, c.1174–1216, Latin emperor of Constantinople (1206–16); brother of Baldwin I. Fought successfully against Bulgarians.

Henry of Navarre: see HENRY IV, king of France.

Henry of Trastamara: see HENRY II, Spanish king.

Henry's law states that amount of gas that dissolves in liquid is proportional to pressure of gas above liquid. Named for William Henry (1774–1836), English chemist and physician.

Henryson, Robert, c.1425–c.1506, Scottish poet, imitator of Chaucer. His *Testament of Cresseid* is a sequel to *Troilus and Criseyde.* Also wrote the lively *Moral Fables of Aesop* and *Robene and Makyne.*

Henry Street Settlement: see WALD, LILLIAN D.

Henry the Fowler, German king: see HENRY I.

Henry the Lion, 1129–95, Guelphic duke of Saxony (1142–80) and Bavaria (1156–80); Son of HENRY THE PROUD. Emperor Frederick I restored the two duchies to him in the hope of restoring peace between the Guelphs and the Hohenstaufen. Henry took part in Frederick's early Italian campaigns; was a leader in the Wendish Crusade of 1147; and extended his power over the Wendish lands of NE Germany, where he introduced Christianity. The growth of his power resulted in friction with Frederick, who in 1180 seized

upon a pretext for confiscating Henry's fiefs. Bavaria and Saxony, last of the great German duchies, thus were subdivided into a patchwork of small principalities. Henry went into exile in England but returned 1189, recovered parts of Saxony (Brunswick and Lüneburg), and was left in possession of them by the Peace of Fulda (1190). His younger son became emperor as Otto IV.

Henry the Navigator, 1394–1460, Portuguese prince, patron of exploration; son of John I of Portugal. Founded naval arsenal, observatory, school for study of geography and navigation. His navigators explored W coast of Africa, penetrated into Sudan and Senegal, estab. slave and gold trade (but Henry in 1455 forbade kidnaping of Negroes). He also fought in Moroccan campaigns and exerted considerable political influence, but his chief importance was his contribution to art of navigation and progress of exploration.

Henry the Proud, c.1108–1139, Guelphic duke of Bavaria (1126–39) and Saxony (1137–39). He helped his father-in-law, Emperor LOTHAIR II, against the HOHENSTAUFEN. CONRAD III of Hohenstaufen defeated him in the imperial elections of 1138 and deprived him of his duchies. Henry was in the process of reconquering them when he died, leaving HENRY THE LION as his heir.

Henson, Josiah, 1789–1883, reputed original of Uncle Tom in *Uncle Tom's Cabin.* Escaped from slavery and became leader of community of escaped Negroes in Canada. Autobiography published 1849.

Henty, G(eorge) A(lfred), 1832–1902, English journalist and writer of boys' books. Wrote 80 tales of adventure as popular in America as in England.

hepatica or **liverwort,** low woodland wild flower (genus *Hepatica*) of the temperate zone. It has three-lobed leaves and white or lilac blooms in spring.

Hephaestus (hēfē'stŭs), in Greek religion, Olympian god of fire and metalwork; son of Zeus and Hera and father of Erechtheus. He was usually represented as a bearded man, with mighty shoulders and arms, but lame. A comic figure on Olympus, he was butt of many jokes. Once he split Zeus' aching head, and the goddess Athena sprang forth. His favorite abodes on earth were volcanic islands where he had workshops manned by the Cyclopes. As the craftsman's god he was worshiped at industrial centers such as Athens. In Trojan War he supported the Greeks. Romans called him Vulcan.

Hepplewhite, George (hĕp'əlhwīt), d. 1786, English cabinetmaker and furniture designer. His style is marked by such details as slight tapering legs with spade feet, chair backs in shield, oval, hoop, and interlaced heart forms. Used mahogany, satinwood, and beechwood, with painted or inlaid decoration (esp. of classical motifs). See *ill.,* p. 456.

Heptameron: see MARGARET OF NAVARRE.

Hera (hēr'ù), in Greek religion, queen of Olympian gods, protectress of women; daughter of Cronus and Rhea, sister and wife of Zeus, and mother of Hephaestus and Ares. A jealous wife, she persecuted Zeus, his earthly mistresses, and their progeny. The Trojan Prince Paris did not award to her

APPLE OF DISCORD, and she in revenge supported Greeks in Trojan War. She had especially fine temples at Argos and Samos. Romans called her JUNO.

Heraclea (hĕrŭklē'ŭ), anc. Greek city, S Italy, not far from the Gulf of Taranto. Here Pyrrhus defeated the Romans 280 B.C.

Heraclea Pontica (pŏn'tĭkŭ), anc. Greek city, on S shore of the Black Sea, site of modern Eregli, Turkey; large commercial center (5th–6th cent. B.C.).

Heracles, another name for HERCULES.

Heraclitus (hĕrŭklī'tŭs), c.535–c.475 B.C., Greek philosopher of Ephesus. He held that the only reality is change and that permanence is an illusion. All things carry with them their opposites, and therefore being and not being are in everything and the only real state is one of transition. Heraclitus believed that fire was the underlying substance of the universe.

Heraclius I (hĕrŭklī'ŭs, hĭrŭ'klēŭs), c.575–641, Byzantine emperor (610–41). Recovered Syria, Palestine, and Egypt from Persia (622–28), only to see them fall to the Moslem Arabs (629–41). Favored MONOTHELETISM.

Herakleion, Crete: see CANDIA.

Heralds' College, body first chartered in 1484 by Richard III of England. Purpose is to assign coats of arms and trace lineages. Officials are called Garter king-of-arms, other kings-of-arms, heralds, and pursuivants. Officials also proclaim accession of king and attend at state occasions.

Herat (hĕrät'), anc. *Aria,* city (pop. c.80,000), cap. of Herat prov., NW Afghanistan, on Hari Rud R. On trade route from Persia to India, it was taken by various conquerors, notably Alexander the Great and Tamerlane. Disputed by Persians and Afghans until mid-19th cent.

Hérault (ārō'), department (2,403 sq. mi.; pop. 461,100), S France, in Languedoc; cap. Montpellier.

herb (ûrb, hûrb), botanically any plant lacking woody tissue as distinguished from shrubs or trees. More specifically, it is a plant used either medicinally or for its flavor or scent.

herbarium, collection of dried plant specimens used in study of botany. They are mounted on heavy paper and arranged according to genera. Notable herbariums in U.S. include Gray Herbarium at Harvard Univ. and those at the National Museum and the New York and Missouri botanical gardens.

Herbart, Johann Friedrich (yō'hän frē'drĭkh hĕr'bärt), 1776–1841, German philosopher, professor at Königsberg and Göttingen. He made important contributions to psychology and education. To Herbart the universe was made up of simple independent "reals" and change came from shifting relationships of these "reals" in their efforts at self-preservation. In education he emphasized the conscious effort to relate learning to the learner's former experience and stressed moral education.

Herbert, A(lan) P(atrick), 1890–, English humorist. One of his many books is novel *The Water Gipsies* (1930).

Herbert, George, 1593–1633, English religious poet. His poems (posthumously pub. as *The Temple: Sacred Poems and Private Ejacula-* *tions,* 1633) are some of the finest of metaphysical poetry, marked by deep feeling, precise language, and metrical versatility. His brother, **Edward Herbert, 1st Baron Herbert of Cherbury,** 1583–1648, was a philosopher and poet. Precursor of deism, he wrote *De religione laici* (1645). In *Poems* (1665) he published secular metaphysical verse.

Herbert, Mary: see PEMBROKE, MARY HERBERT, COUNTESS OF.

Herbert, Victor, 1859–1924, Irish-American composer and conductor. He began his career playing cello; was conductor of the Pittsburgh Symphony Orchestra, 1898–1904. His operettas (e.g., *Babes in Toyland,* 1903; *Mlle Modiste,* 1905; *The Red Mill,* 1906; *Naughty Marietta,* 1910; and *Sweethearts,* 1913) have been much revived.

Herbert, William: see PEMBROKE, WILLIAM HERBERT, 3D EARL OF.

Herbert of Cherbury: see HERBERT, GEORGE.

Hercegovina: see BOSNIA AND HERCEGOVINA.

Herculaneum (hûrkyōōlā'nēŭm), anc. city, S Italy, on the Gulf of Naples, at the foot of Mt. Vesuvius, notable chiefly because it was buried (along with Pompeii) by the eruption of Vesuvius in A.D. 79. Excavations have uncovered walls, statues, books, and the like in fine preservation.

Hercules (hûr'kyōōlēz) or **Heracles** (hĕ'rŭklēz), most popular hero in Greek and Roman legends, famous for his extraordinary strength and courage. Son of Zeus and Alcmene, he was hated by Hera, who sought to kill him by sending two serpents to his cradle, but these he strangled; later she sent madness upon him, so that he slew his wife and children. As advised by Delphic oracle, he sought (and achieved) purification at court of King Eurystheus, who demanded of him 12 labors: killing Nemean lion, nine-headed Hydra, and man-eating Stymphalian birds; cleaning stables of Augeas; procuring golden apples of Hesperides and girdle of Hippolyte; and capturing fleet-footed Cerynean hind, mad Cretan bull, flesh-eating mares of Diomed, Erymanthian boar, cattle of Geryon, and three-headed watchdog of Hades, Cerberus. Later he joined Calydonian hunt and expedition of Argonauts. At his death he ascended to Olympus, where he married Hebe. He was widely worshiped. Hero of plays by Sophocles, Euripides, and Seneca. Most famous statue of him is *Farnese Hercules* in Naples.

Hercules, Pillars of: see PILLARS OF HERCULES.

Hercules'-club, small North American tree (*Aralia spinosa*) with a stout thorny trunk, huge compound leaves, and a large flower cluster at the top of the tree.

Herczeg, Francis (hĕr'tsĕg), Hung. *Herczeg Ferenc,* 1863–, Hungarian dramatist, novelist, short story writer.

Herder, Johann Gottfried von (yō'hän gôt'frĕt fün hĕr'dŭr), 1744–1803, German philosopher, poet, and critic. Studied theology and after winning attention by literary criticism he became (1776) court preacher at Weimar at the instance of Goethe, whom he influenced. He was a leader in the *Sturm und Drang* movement in German literature, a passionate opponent of the cool rationalism of 18th-cent. Enlightenment and a precursor of the romantics. Herder sought to develop a philosophy of history showing the march of man's progress. His most ambitious work was *Outlines of the Philosophy of Man* (1784–91). He did much to introduce foreign literature (notably Shakspere, Ossian, and English and Romance folk songs) to German intellectuals and stirred interest in the science of language.

Heredia, José María (hōsā′ märē′ä ārä′dhēä), 1803–39, Cuban journalist and poet. Though his poetry is classic in form, he was in temperament a romantic.

Heredia, José María de, 1842–1905, French poet, b. Cuba. *Les Trophées* (1893), a collection of sonnets of classic inspiration, brings to perfection the ideals of the PARNASSIANS.

heredity (hŭrĕ′dĭtē), transmission, through reproductive process, of factors in plants and animals which cause offspring to resemble parents. First scientifically founded concepts, those of Gregor J. MENDEL, indicated that characters are inherited as units independently of each other. Studies of chromosomes, genes, MITOSIS, meiosis, and sex-linked characters shed light on mechanism of heredity. Constancy of transmission of hereditary characters from generation to generation does not preclude changes required by evolutionary concept since MUTATION can occur. See also GENETICS.

Hereford, England: see HEREFORDSHIRE.

Hereford (hûr′fŭrd), city (pop. 5,207), N Texas, SW of Amarillo in Panhandle. Center of cattle and agr. area. Noted for low rate of dental decay attributed to fluorine in soil.

Hereford cattle: see CATTLE.

Herefordshire or Hereford (hĕ′rŭfŭrd), county (842 sq. mi.; pop. 127,092), W England, on Welsh border. Has undulating terrain, rising to Black Mts. and Malvern Hills. Mainly agr. and pastoral region famous for orchards and cattle. Scene of border warfare with Welsh. The county town is Hereford, municipal borough (pop. 32,490), on the Wye. Has cathedral dating from 11th cent., scene every third year of Festival of the Three Choirs, held other years at Gloucester and Worcester. White Cross near town marks end of great plague, 1347. Birthplace of Nell Gwyn and David Garrick.

Hereward the Wake (hĕ′rĭwŭrd), fl. 1070, thane of Lincolnshire. A leader of resistance against William I, he was folk hero of conquered Anglo-Saxons.

Herford, Oliver (hûr′fŭrd), 1863–1935, American humorist, b. England; author and illustrator of many popular volumes of light verse (e.g., *Rubáiyát of a Persian Kitten*, 1904).

Herford (hĕr′fôrt), city (pop. 50,431), North Rhine-Westphalia, NW Germany. Varied mfg. (furniture, chocolate, textiles). An old Westphalian city, it was founded 823.

Herisau (hā′rīzou), town (pop. 13,464), cap. of Ausser-Rhoden half canton, Appenzell, Switzerland. Embroideries, cotton textiles, machinery.

Héristal, Belgium: see HERSTAL.

Herkimer (hûr′kĭmŭr), village (pop. 9,400), central N.Y., on Mohawk R. and SE of Utica; settled c.1725 by Palatines. Farm trade center with mfg. of clothing and furniture.

hermandad (ĕrmändädh′) [Span.,= brotherhood], league of towns in medieval Spain. *Hermandades* were formed as protection against lawless nobles. Ferdinand and Isabella founded the Holy Hermandad for all Spain to act as permanent police force. Local *hermandades,* greatly modified, continued to 1835. Mexican Acordada was similar organization.

Hermann, d. A.D. 21: see ARMINIUS.

Hermannstadt, Rumania: see SIBIU.

Hermaphroditus (hŭrmă″frŭdī′tŭs), beautiful son of Hermes and Aphrodite. He and his consort became one body, with characteristics of both the male and the female.

Hermes (hûr′mēz), in Greek religion, Olympian god; son of Zeus and Maia. He had great variety of functions: god of commerce, of cheats and thieves, of luck (and hence gamblers), of athletic contests, and of eloquence; messenger of the gods; and conductor of souls to Hades. Lyre and flute were his inventions. He was thought of as a merry youth with much cunning, and he inspired riotous festivals. In art he is usually shown wearing a winged hat and winged sandals and carrying the CADUCEUS. His Roman equivalent is Mercury.

Hermes Trismegistus (trĭsmŭjĭ′stŭs), name given to reputed author of books of occult wisdom. Hermes here means Thoth, Egyptian god of learning. *Hermetic Books* encompassed wisdom of ancient Egypt. Hermetical philosophy was popular in 17th cent. and is still used by believers in the occult.

Hermione (hŭrmī′ŭnē), in Greek legend, only child of Helen and Menelaus and wife of Orestes.

Hermitage, museum in Leningrad. Rebuilt in 19th cent. as a museum in Neo-Greek style from Catherine II's pavilion palace. Fine collection includes Spanish and French paintings and rare Greek jewelry.

Hermitage, home of Andrew Jackson, central Tenn., near Nashville. House built 1819–31, rebuilt 1835. Jackson and wife buried here. Has church (1823) built by him.

hermit crab, crustacean with soft, asymmetrical, usually coiled abdomen. It is chiefly a marine animal but in the tropics some are largely land forms. Most hermit crabs occupy shells of snails or other gastropod mollusks, thus protecting the abdomen with a portable shelter.

Hermite, Charles (shärl ĕrmēt′), 1822–1901, French mathematician. He made valuable contributions to theory of numbers, theory of elliptic functions, and theory of equations.

Hermite, Tristan l': see TRISTAN L'HERMITE.

Hermon, Mount, on Syria-Lebanon boundary, near Palestine. Highest of its three peaks rises to c.9,000 ft. Snow-capped in winter and spring, it was sacred landmark in ancient Palestine. Mentioned in Bible as Hermon, Sion, Senir, and Shenir.

Hermopolis (hŭrmŏ′pŭlĭs), city (pop. 18,925), Syros Isl., Greece, chief city and port of the CYCLADES.

Hermosa Beach (hŭrmō′sŭ), resort and residential city (pop. 11,826), S Calif., on Santa Monica Bay.

Hermosillo (ĕrmōsē′yō), city (pop. 18,601), cap. of Sonora, NW Mexico, on Sonora R.;

trading and manufacturing center in tropical-fruit district.

Hernandarias: see ARIAS DE SAAVEDRA, HERNANDO.

Hernández. For some Spaniards thus named, see FERNÁNDEZ.

Hernández, José (hōsā′ ĕrnän′dĕs), 1834–86, Argentine poet, author of classic of gaucho literature, *Martín Fierro* (1872).

Herndon, Angelo, 1913–, American Negro labor organizer. A Communist, he led a demonstration against the Ga. relief administration and was the subject of a celebrated civil liberties case.

Herndon, William Henry, 1818–91, law partner and biographer of Abraham Lincoln. Much of *Herndon's Lincoln: the True Story of a Great Life* (3 vols., 1889) ran counter to established legend.

Herne (hĕr′nŭ), city (pop. 111,249), North Rhine-Westphalia, NW Germany; a center of Ruhr dist.

hernia or **rupture,** protrusion of any internal organ from cavity in which it is normally located. Common form is protrusion of a loop of intestine through weak point in wall of abdomen or groin.

Hero, in late Greek legend, priestess of Aphrodite in Sestos. Her lover, Leander, swam the Hellespont nightly to see her. He drowned one night, and she threw herself into sea.

Hero, mathematician: see HERON OF ALEXANDRIA.

hero, in Greek religion, dead person of note who was given reverence and worship as quasi-divine. Heroes were regarded as ghosts to be appeased, and rites were like those for underworld gods. Heroes might be actual dead men, real or imaginary ancestors, or "faded gods," those demoted to human status.

Herod, dynasty reigning in Palestine at time of Christ. Founder of family fortune was Antipater (ăntĭp′ŭtŭr), d. 43 B.C., who was in favor with Caesar after defeat of Pompey and who had gained power in Palestine by aiding Hyrcanus II (see MACCABEES). His son, Herod the Great, d. 4 B.C., gave family its name. Through Marc Antony, Herod secured title of King of Judaea (37 B.C.–4 B.C.); after battle of Actium he made peace with Octavian (Augustus). Herod married 10 times, and the various families intrigued against each other. In his last years Herod was subject to insanity and executed his sons Aristobulus (ăr″ĭstōbū′lŭs), Alexander, and Antipater. It was this Herod who was ruling at time of Jesus' birth and who ordered massacre of the Innocents. Mat. 2; Luke 5. He divided his kingdom among his sons Archelaus, Herod Antipas, and Philip. Archelaus (är″kēlā′ŭs), d. after A.D. 6, ruled Judaea and Idumaea (4 B.C.–A.D. 6). Mat. 2.22. Herod Antipas (ăn′tĭpăs), d. after A.D. 39, tetrarch of Galilee and Peraea, was the Herod who executed John the Baptist and who was ruling at Jesus' death. He repudiated his wife to marry Herodias (hĕrō′dēŭs), daughter of his half brother Aristobulus, divorced wife of his half brother Herod Philip, and mother of Salome. Her vaulting ambition caused his ruin, and Caligula banished him (A.D. 39). Mat. 14; Mark 6; Luke 3; 23;

Acts 13. Herod the Great's son Philip, d. A.D. 34, was made tetrarch of region E of Galilee. The eldest son of Aristobulus became Herod Agrippa I, d. A.D. 44. Caligula made him king (A.D. 39) of Philip's tetrarchy and of region W of Damascus. On Claudius' accession he was made ruler of S Syria and of Palestine E and W of Jordan R. His son, Herod Agrippa II, d. c.100, was a poor ruler who alienated his subjects. St. Paul spoke before him. Acts 25; 26. After fall of Jerusalem he went to Rome. As a dynasty the Herods were neither good nor capable rulers; they depended largely on power of Rome and are usually blamed for state of virtual anarchy in Palestine as Christian era began.

Herodotus (hĕrŏ′dŭtŭs), 484?–425? B.C., Greek historian, called father of history. His work, the first comprehensive attempt at secular narrative history, marks start of Western history writing. It deals primarily with Persian Wars, but its rich diversity of contemporary information makes it an important source book on ancient Greece.

heroic couplet, a verse form: see PENTAMETER.

heroin: see OPIUM.

heron (hĕ′rŭn), large wading bird of most temperate parts of world, abundant in the tropics and subtropics. It has a long, sharp bill, long neck and legs, and large wings. Many nest in large colonies. Among American species are great and little blue herons, little green heron, black-crowned and yellow-crowned night herons, and Louisiana heron.

Heron of Alexandria (hēr′ŏn) or **Hero,** mathematician, inventor; birth and death dates probably between 2d cent. B.C. and 3d cent. A.D. He wrote on measurement of geometric figures, studied mechanics and pneumatics, and invented many devices operated by water, steam, and compressed air.

Herophilus (hĭrŏ′fŭlŭs), fl. 300 B.C. Greek anatomist, a leader of Alexandria school of medicine.

Herrera, Fernando de (fĕrnän′dō dā′ ĕrā′rä), 1534–97, Spanish poet, notable for graceful sonnets and love lyrics, heroic odes.

Herrera, Francisco de (fränthē′skō), the elder, 1576–1656, Spanish religious painter, a founder of naturalistic school of Seville. A teacher of Velazquez. His son, **Francisco de Herrera,** the younger, 1622–85, studied in Rome, where he painted still lifes. Designed baroque Saragossa cathedral.

Herreshoff, John Brown (hĕ′rŭs-hŏf), 1841–1915, American yacht and speedboat builder. He and his brother, **Nathaniel Greene Herreshoff,** 1848–1938, introduced radical features of design in sailing yachts after 1891. The *Gloriana* won them a reputation, and they subsequently produced five successful defenders of the *America's* Cup.

Herrick, Robert, 1591–1674, English poet, usually called greatest of CAVALIER POETS. Took orders c.1627 and lived at Dean Prior in Devon. The volume *Hesperides* (1648) contains his *Noble Numbers* (sacred songs) and bucolic love lyrics (e.g., "Night-Piece: To Julia," song opening "Gather ye rosebuds," and "Cherry-ripe") and epigrams. Among sacred poems is the touching "Litany to the Holy Spirit." Herrick's poetry is notable for its simple naïveté, melody, and perfectly chosen words.

Herrick, Robert, 1868–1938, American novelist. His realistic novels include *The Web of Life* (1900), *Clark's Field* (1914), and *The End of Desire* (1932).

Herrin, city (pop. 9,331), S Ill., N of Cairo. Trade center of coal area. Site of "Herrin Massacre" (1922), local clash in country-wide coal strike, which resulted in death of about 25 persons.

herring, common food fish in N Atlantic waters of North America and Europe. There are many species; common herring is *Clupea harengus*, which travels in huge schools. It is c.1 ft. long, blue above and silver on the sides. In spring or autumn it lays c.30,000 eggs, which sink to bottom and develop; young mature in three years.

Herrings, battle of the, 1429, episode in siege of Orléans. An English wagon train, led by Sir John Fastolf, repulsed a French attack at Rouvray by using wagons with herring barrels as barricade.

Herriot, Édouard (ādwär' ĕryō'), 1872–, French politician. As leader of Radical Socialists, who dominated French politics 1899–1940, he played a prominent part in the chamber of deputies, in several cabinets, and as premier (notably 1924–25, 1932). Favored conciliatory foreign policy, payment of war debts to U.S. Imprisoned by Germans 1942–45. Has been mayor of Lyons since 1904 (except 1941–45). Has strongly advocated a United States of Europe. Also known as scholar and author (notably of a biography of Beethoven, Eng. tr., 1935).

Herrnhut (hĕrn'hōōt'), town (pop. 2,024), Saxony, E Germany. Founded 1722 by ZINZENDORF as colony of MORAVIAN CHURCH.

Herron, George Davis, 1862–1925, American clergyman. Became Christian Socialist, helped organize RAND SCHOOL OF SOCIAL SCIENCE. Aided President Wilson in peace negotiations after World War I.

Herschel, Sir William, 1738–1822, English astronomer, b. Germany, originally named Friedrich Wilhelm Herschel; pioneer systematizer of sky exploration and cataloguing of heavenly bodies. His many discoveries with reflecting telescopes which he constructed include the planet Uranus (1781). He concluded that solar system as a whole moves through space. His sister Caroline (1750–1848) worked with him. His son **Sir John Frederick William Herschel,** 1792–1871, confirmed and extended his observations and cataloguing of nebulae and double stars.

Hersey, John (hûr'sē), 1914–, American author and journalist. A former war correspondent, he wrote works on events of World War II. They include *Hiroshima* (1946) and the novels *A Bell for Adano* (1944) and *The Wall* (1950).

Hershey, uninc. village, S central Pa., E of Harrisburg. Owned by the Hershey company, it makes chocolate confectionery.

Herstal (hĕr'stäl), town (pop. 27,092), Liége prov., E Belgium; suburb of Liége. Also known as Héristal. Mfg. of arms. Residence of early Carolingian mayors of the palace and of Charlemagne.

Hertford, England: see HERTFORDSHIRE.

Hertford College: see OXFORD UNIVERSITY.

Hertfordshire (här'fûrdshĭr, härt–), **Hertford,** or **Herts** (härts, hûrts), inland county (632 sq. mi.; pop. 609,735), S England. Agr. county with level terrain, it produces wheat, hay, vegetables, and flowers. St. Albans an important urban center. County prominent in military history, particularly during Wars of the Roses. The county town, **Hertford,** municipal borough (pop. 13,890), was important in Saxon times. First national church council held here 673. Haileybury col., important English public school, near here.

Hertogenbosch, s': see 's HERTOGENBOSCH.

Herts: see HERTFORDSHIRE.

Hertwig, Oscar (ôs'kär hĕrt'vĭkh), 1849–1922, German embryologist. He discovered that fertilization consists of union of male and female germ cells.

Hertz, Gustav (gōōs'täf hĕrts'), 1887–, German physicist. Shared 1925 Nobel Prize for work on effect of impact of electrons on atoms.

Hertz, Heinrich Rudolf (hûrts, Ger. hīn'rĭkh rōō'dôlf hĕrts'), 1857–94, German physicist. In the course of his experiments confirming J. C. Maxwell's electromagnetic theory, he produced and studied electromagnetic waves (known also as hertzian waves or radio waves).

Hertzog, James Barry Munnik, 1866–1942, South African military and political leader. Commanded a division of Boer forces in South African War 1899–1902. Organized (1913) nationalist party for independence from British Empire. Prime minister (1924–39) in coalition government with Labour party.

Hervey Islands: see COOK ISLANDS.

Hervey of Ickworth, John, Baron (här'vē, hûr'vē), 1693–1743, English statesman and memoir writer. Vice chancellor and privy councilor, Lord Hervey influenced Queen Caroline. Bitterly attacked by Pope. Author of *Memoirs of the Reign of George II.*

Herzen, Aleksandr Ivanovich (ŭlyĭksän'dŭr ēvä'nŭvĭch hâr'tsĭn), 1812–70, Russian revolutionary leader and writer. Lived abroad after 1847, attacking tsarist autocracy in various writings and in the influential periodical, *Kolokol* (1857–62).

Herzl, Theodor (tā'ōdōr hĕr'tsŭl), 1860–1904, Hungarian journalist, founder of modern Zionism. Aroused by the Dreyfus Affair, he devoted his life to the creation of a Jewish state, which he advocated in his booklet *Der Judenstaat.*

Hesiod (hē'sēŭd, hĕ'–), fl. 8th cent.? B.C., Greek poet. Little-known, self-styled Boeotian farmer; author of the didactic *Works and Days* (advice to farmers) and of the *Theogony.*

Hesperides (hĕspĕ'rĭdēz) [Gr.,= in the west], in Greek religion, nymphs; daughters of Atlas. On an enchanted island in the western sea they guarded tree bearing golden apples, which HERCULES took.

Hess, Germain Henri (hĕs, Fr. zhĕrmĕ' ärē ĕs'), 1802–50, Swiss-Russian chemist, a founder of thermochemistry. Hess's law: amount of heat liberated or absorbed in chemical reaction is constant regardless of number of stages occurring, if same original substances and end products are involved.

Hess, Dame Myra, 1890–, English pianist. Made her London debut, 1907; first appeared in the U.S., 1922.

Hess, Rudolf (rōō′dôlf hĕs′), 1894–, German National Socialist leader. Hitler made him deputy Führer and minister without portfolio (1933). Hess created world-wide sensation by his secret airplane flight to Scotland (1941), where he was imprisoned. Of doubtful sanity, he was sentenced to life imprisonment at Nuremberg war-crimes trial (1946).

Hess, Victor Francis, 1883–, American physicist. Shared 1936 Nobel Prize for discovering cosmic rays.

Hess, Walter Rudolf, 1881–, Swiss physiologist. Shared 1949 Nobel Prize in Physiology and Medicine for work on control of organs by certain areas of the brain.

Hesse, Hermann (hĕr′män hĕ′sù), 1877–, German novelist and poet, son of missionaries in India. Concerned with man's spiritual loneliness, his novels include *Peter Camenzind* (1904), *Demian* (1919; Eng. tr., 1923), *Der Steppenwolf* (1927; Eng. tr., 1929), *Narziss und Goldmund* (1930; Eng. tr., *Death and the Lover,* 1932), and *Das Glasperlenspiel* (1943; complete ed., 1945; Eng. tr., *Magister Ludi,* 1949). Awarded 1946 Nobel Prize in Literature.

Hesse, Philip of: see PHILIP OF HESSE.

Hesse (hĕ′sĕ, hĕs), Ger. *Hessen,* state (8,153 sq. mi.; pop. 4,303,920), Federal Republic of [W] Germany, between Thuringia and the Rhine; cap. Wiesbaden. It is a generally hilly, agr., and forested region, with famous vineyards along the Rhine. Industries are concentrated at Frankfurt (chemicals), Kassel (machinery), and Darmstadt. The Taunus area is famed for its resorts. Hesse has no historical unity. Its name is derived from the landgraviate of Hesse, which in 1247 became an immediate fief of the Holy Roman Empire. After the death (1567) of PHILIP OF HESSE, who introduced the Reformation, Hesse underwent several subdivisions among branches of the ruling family: Hesse-Kassel and Hesse-Darmstadt were the chief divisions. The rulers of the 18th-cent. Hesse improved their finances by letting mercenaries for hire (notably to the English in the American Revolution). In 1803 the landgrave of Hesse-Kassel was raised to the rank of elector; Hesse-Kassel henceforth was known as Electoral Hesse (Ger. *Kurhessen*). Napoleon I in 1806 raised the landgraviate of Hesse-Darmstadt to a grand duchy and in 1807 annexed Electoral Hesse to the kingdom of Westphalia under his brother Jérôme. The Congress of Vienna (1814–15) restored Electoral Hesse and awarded it and Hesse-Darmstadt substantial territorial gains. In 1866 Electoral Hesse, NASSAU, and the free city of Frankfurt, having all three sided with Austria in the Austro-Prussian War, were annexed by Prussia and merged in Hesse-Nassau prov., with its cap. at Kassel. Hesse-Darmstadt continued under its grand dukes until 1918 (after 1871 as a member of the German Empire) and joined the Weimar Republic in 1919. After World War II all of former Prussian Hesse-Nassau and all of Hesse-Darm-

stadt E of the Rhine were consolidated into the single state of Hesse under U.S. occupation. The section W of the Rhine (called Rhenish Hesse and containing MAINZ and WORMS) was incorporated into French-occupied Rhineland-Palatinate.

Hesse-Nassau, Germany: see HESSE; NASSAU.

Hessian fly, widely distributed wheat pest, a gall gnat, said to have been carried across the Atlantic from its native Europe by Hessian troops. The larvae injure plants by removing sap from stem; control methods include late planting of seed and plowing under infected wheat.

Hestia (hĕ′stĕù), in Greek mythology, old and honored virgin goddess of the hearth and domestic life and guardian of state's welfare; daughter of Cronus and Rhea. Identified with Roman Vesta.

Heston and Isleworth (īz′ùlwûrth), urban district (pop. 106,636), Middlesex, England; residential suburb of London. Site of a large airport.

Hetch Hetchy Valley, in Yosemite Natl. Park, central Calif., on Tuolumne R. O'Shaunessy Dam (built 1923, enlarged 1938) turned valley into lake 7 mi. long, supplying San Francisco with water and power.

Hevelius, Johannes (hĭvĕ′lĕùs, Ger. yōhä′nùs hävä′lēōōs), 1611–87, astronomer, b. Danzig. He was a pioneer in the study of the moon's surface.

Hevesy, Georg von (gā′ôrk fùn hĕ′vĕshē), 1885–, Hungarian physicist and chemist. Won 1943 Nobel Prize for work on use of isotopes as indicators in studying chemical processes.

Hewitt, Abram Stevens (hū′ĭt), 1822–1903, American industrialist and political leader; son-in-law of Peter Cooper. Promoted advanced methods of ironmaking and steelmaking. U.S. Representative from N.Y. (1875–79, 1881–86).

hexameter (hĕksă′mùtûr) [Gr.,= measure of six], in prosody, a line to be scanned in six feet. In dactylic hexameter, most celebrated hexameter measure, each foot may have a long syllable followed by two shorts, except last, which has only two syllables, the first being long; any of first four feet may have two long syllables. Dactylic hexameter appears in first, and purest, form in Homer. Stress accent in modern languages substitutes for quantitative differences of classical meters; hence English dactylic hexameter has singsong effect when read aloud. The alexandrine is most common modern hexameter.

Hexapla (hĕk′sùplù) [Gr.,= sixfold], polyglot version of Old Testament made by Origen. Mainly in six columns—Hebrew text. Greek transliteration of it, and four Greek versions. Fragments survive.

Heymans, Corneille (kôrnä′yù hī′mäns), 1892–, Belgian physiologist. Won 1938 Nobel Prize in Physiology and Medicine for study of regulation of respiratory center.

Heyse, Paul (poul′ hī′zù), 1830–1914, German realistic author. His voluminous work includes novels (*Children of the World,* 1872; Eng. tr., 1882), dramas, and *Novellen* (notably *L'Arrabbiata,* 1855; Eng. tr., *The Fury*). Was awarded 1910 Nobel Prize in Literature.

Heyward, DuBose (dùbōz′), 1885–1940, American author, b. Charleston, S.C., author of

Porgy (1925)—a story of Negro life, later made into a play and an opera (*Porgy and Bess;* score by George Gershwin).

Heywood, John, c.1497–c.1578, English dramatist, most famous writer of the interlude, short comic dialogue (e.g., *The Play of the Weather,* 1533; *The Four P's*).

Heywood, Thomas, 1574?–1641, English playwright and actor. Of his numerous plays *A Woman Killed with Kindness* (pub. 1607) is notable.

Hezekiah (hĕzŭkī'ŭ), d. c.698 B.C., king of Judah (c.727–c.698 B.C.), successor of Ahaz. Resisted two invasions of Sennacherib of Assyria; the second was ended by plague in Assyrian army. Hezekiah, one of best of Judah's kings, abolished idolatry and listened to Isaiah and Micah. 2 Kings 18–20; 2 Chron. 29–32; Isa. 36–39; Prov. 25.1. Ezekias: Mat. 1.10.

Hf, chemical symbol of the element HAFNIUM.

Hg, chemical symbol of the element MERCURY.

Hialeah (hīŭlē'ŭ), residential city (pop. 19,-676), SE Fla., part of Greater Miami; settled 1921. Hialeah Park race track is here.

Hibbing, village (pop. 16,276), NE Minn., on Mesabi iron range and NW of Duluth; laid out 1893. Moved to present site after 1917 to make way for world's largest open-pit iron mine.

hibernation (hī"bûrnā'shŭn), practice among certain animals of passing part of cold season in more or less dormant state. It is believed that the habit arose as protection against cold when food was scarce, or as an alternative to migration (like migration, probably is connected with reproductive life). Hibernation is possible only for those animals able to store enough food in their bodies to carry them over until food is again available. In hibernation bodily activity is at a low ebb. Deepness of sleep varies; on warmer winter days, some emerge. Aestivation (dormant period of escape from heat when water is scarce) occurs chiefly among amphibians, reptiles, fishes.

Hibernia: see IRELAND.

hibiscus (hĭbĭs'kŭs), annual or perennial shrub or small tree of widely distributed genus *Hibiscus,* many of which are known as rose mallow. Variously colored flowers are large and showy (esp. in tropical forms). See also ROSE OF SHARON.

hiccup or hiccough, sharp sound associated with spasm of larynx and diaphragm and produced when inhaled air strikes closed glottis.

Hickam Field (hĭ'kŭm), U.S. Air Force base, on Oahu, T.H., near Pearl Harbor. Bombed Dec. 7, 1941, by the Japanese.

Hickok, Wild Bill, 1837–76, American frontier marshal in Kansas. Real name was James Butler Hickok. Known as a marksman in encounters with outlaws. Murdered in Deadwood, S.Dak.

Hickory, city (pop. 14,755), W central N.C., NW of Charlotte in piedmont; founded 1874. Annexed Highland and West Hickory 1931. Mfg. of textiles, cordage, wagons, and metal products. Seat of Lenoir Rhyne Col. (Lutheran; coed.; 1891).

hickory, deciduous nut-bearing tree of genus *Carya,* chiefly native to North America. One species, the PECAN, is an important nut tree of U.S. Others include shagbark hickory (*Carya ovata*), shellbark hickory (*C. laciniosa*), and mockernut (*C. tomentosa*), all found in E and SE U.S. The pignut (*C. glabra*) has small bitter nuts. Hickory wood, hard and strong, is valued commercially for tool handles, furniture, etc.

Hicks, Edward, 1780–1849, American painter, best known for *The Peaceable Kingdom,* of which c.25 versions are extant.

Hicks, Elias, 1748–1830, American preacher of Society of FRIENDS. In schism of 1827 he led liberal separatist party called Hicksites.

Hicksville, residential village (1940 pop. 6,835), SE N.Y., on W Long Isl.

Hidalgo (ēdhäl'gō), state (8,058 sq. mi.; pop. 840,760), central Mexico. Largely mountainous, Hidalgo has plains in S and W and fertile valleys within central plateau. Mining, the main industry, has centered at PACHUCA (cap.). Conquered 1530 by Spanish, territory was not made separate state until 1869.

Hidalgo y Costilla, Miguel (mĕgĕl' ēdhäl'gō ē kōstē'yä), 1753–1811, Mexican revolutionist and a national hero, a priest. Hidalgo was among the creoles who met at Querétaro to plan revolution against Spain. On Sept. 16, 1810, he issued the *grito de Dolores* which precipitated the revolt. The banner of Our Lady of Guadalupe was his standard. Initially successful in encounters with Spanish forces, he was finally defeated at Calderón Bridge, betrayed, degraded by Inquisition, and shot.

Hidari Jingoro (hēdä'rē jēn'gōrō), c.1594–1633, Japanese sculptor, famous for delicate wooden friezes of birds and flowers.

Hidatsa Indians (hēdät'sä), North American tribe, also known as the Minitari and the Gros Ventre of the River, of Siouan linguistic stock. In 18th cent. they lived on upper Missouri, in N.Dak. Were typical of "village Indians" of Plains area, cultivating corn and organizing annual buffalo hunt.

Hideyoshi (Hideyoshi toyotomi) (hēdä'yōshē), 1536?–1598, Japanese dictator. Succeeded NOBUNAGA and completed unification of Japan by defeating powerful feudal barons. In 1592 began fruitless campaign to conquer China by way of Korea. As civil ruler he encouraged foreign trade and froze class structure by banning change of occupation. First tolerated but later persecuted Christian missionaries.

hieratic: see HIEROGLYPHIC.

Hiero (hī'ŭrō), Greek tyrants of Syracuse. Also Hieron. **Hiero I** was tyrant 478–467 B.C., succeeding his brother Gelon. He was a patron of literature and was victor over the Etruscans in a naval battle at Cumae (474 B.C.). **Hiero II,** d. c.215 B.C., because of his ability, chosen tyrant (c.270 B.C.). At first an ally of the Carthaginians, he saw the rising power of Rome and as an ally aided the Romans in the Punic Wars. He encouraged his relative, Archimedes, who made him great engines for warfare.

hieroglyphic (hī"rŭglī'fĭk, hī"ŭrŭ–) [Gr.,= priestly carving], pictographic writings of anc. Egypt (by extension also those of Crete, Asia Minor, and Central America and Mexico). Interpretation of Egyptian hieroglyphics, begun by CHAMPOLLION, is quite complete. Hieroglyphics are conventionalized pictures used chiefly to represent meanings that seem arbitrary and are seldom obvious. Egyptian hieroglyphics were already perfected in the I dynasty. They began to go out of use in Middle Kingdom; in New Empire they were no longer well understood, and from 500 B.C. their use was a *tour de force*. A given hieroglyphic might be put to three uses (though very few were used for all three), i.e., as an ideogram, as a phonogram, or as a determinative. Phonograms, controlling factor in progress of hieroglyphic writing, became basis of an alphabet. A developed cursive (the hieratic) was used in the Middle Kingdom. This was later supplanted by the demotic, so conventionalized that its hieroglyphic origin was not discernible.

Hieron, tyrants of Syracuse: see HIERO.

Higginson, Thomas Wentworth, 1823–1911, American author, a Unitarian minister. An abolitionist, he headed the first regiment of Negroes in the Civil War. After being wounded, he devoted himself to writing essays on reforms, popular history, biography. Edited poems of Emily Dickinson.

high bush cranberry or cranberry bush, name for two tall viburnum shrubs, *Viburnum opulus,* native to Europe, and the North American *V. trilobum.* Both have flat-topped white clusters and red berries.

High Church: see ENGLAND, CHURCH OF.

Highgate, residential suburb of London, England. Dick Whittington supposedly was resting at foot of Highgate Hill when he heard Bow Bells recalling him to London.

Highland, residential town (pop. 5,878), NW Ind., SW of Gary. Truck farming.

Highland Park. 1 City (pop. 16,808), NE Ill., Chicago suburb on L. Michigan; settled 1834. Ravinia Park here is Chicago summer music center. U.S. Fort Sheridan is near. 2 City (pop. 46,393), SE Mich., within confines of Detroit; laid out 1818. Mfg. of automobiles, trucks, and steel tubing. 3 Residential borough (pop. 9,721), E N.J., on Raritan R. opposite New Brunswick. 4 Town (pop. 11,-405), N Texas, N suburb of Dallas.

Highlands, mountainous country in Scotland, N of line running from Moray Firth to Dumbarton. Late Middle Ages produced clan system and dress (kilt, tartan, sporran, tam, dirk) outlawed by British in drastic suppression of Highland support of Jacobites in 18th cent. With decline of Scottish Gaelic language in 19th cent., revival of dress and use of bagpipes were allowed. Rugged beauty and persisting old customs are depicted in romantic literature.

High Point, city (pop. 39,973), central N.C., SW of Greensboro in piedmont; laid out 1853. Mfg. of furniture, hosiery, and textiles.

High Point: see KITTATINNY MOUNTAIN.

Hightstown, borough (pop. 3,712), central N.J., ENE of Trenton. Seat of Peddie School for boys.

Hildebrand: see GREGORY VII, SAINT.

Hildesheim (hĭl′dŭs-hīm), city (pop. 71,821), Lower Saxony, SE of Hanover. Was seat of a prince-bishopric until 1803; passed to Hanover 1815. Its wealth of medieval architecture was largely destroyed in World War II— e.g., the 11th-cent. Romanesque cathedral

and the Knochenhaueramtshaus [butchers' guildhouse], built in 1529.

Hildreth, Richard, 1807–65, American historian. Chief work *The History of the United States* (6 vols., 1849–52), written from Federalist viewpoint.

Hill, Ambrose Powell, 1825–65, Confederate general. His 3d Corps initiated fighting at Gettysburg, and he directed battle on July 1, 1863. Led corps in Wilderness campaign (1864). Killed in action at Petersburg (1865).

Hill, Archibald Vivian, 1886–, English physiologist. Shared 1922 Nobel Prize in Physiology and Medicine for work on thermodynamics of muscular activity.

Hill, Daniel Harvey, 1821–89, Confederate general. Served with distinction in Peninsular campaign and Antietam campaign (1862). Protesting Braxton Bragg's command in Chattanooga campaign, he was himself removed by Jefferson Davis.

Hill, James J(erome), 1838–1916, American railroad builder, b. Canada. His extension of St. Paul and Pacific RR to Seattle, completed 1893, was probably greatest feat of railroad building in U.S. Formed Great Northern Railway Co. in 1890. With J. P. Morgan, in 1901, he defeated E. H. Harriman in struggle for the Chicago, Burlington & Quincy.

Hillah or Hilla (both: hĭl′lŭ), town (pop. 51,361), Iraq, on branch of Euphrates R. Largely built of materials taken from ruins of near-by Babylon.

Hillel (hĭl′ĕl), fl. 30 B.C.–A.D. 10, Jewish scholar, b. Babylon. Laid the foundation of a systematic interpretation of the Midrash. Many of his teachings approximate those of Christ.

Hilliard, Henry Washington (hĭl′yŭrd), 1808–92, U.S. Representative from Ala. (1845–51). A Whig, chief opponent of secession in Ala.

Hilliard, Nicholas, 1537–1619, first true miniaturist in England; court painter to Elizabeth and James I.

Hillman, Sidney, 1887–1946, American labor leader, b. Lithuania. Became (1915) president Amalgamated Clothing Workers, helped found C.I.O., American Labor Party, and World Federation of Trade Unions. A moderate, he promoted labor-management cooperation and sought labor support for political platforms favored by labor, especially the New Deal. Headed (1943–46) C.I.O. Political Action Committee.

Hillquit, Morris, 1869–1933, American lawyer and Socialist leader, b. Latvia, entered U.S. 1886. Led rightwing Socialists against radical leadership of Daniel De Leon in 1897 and founded the Social Democratic party, which evolved into the present Socialist party. Was a prominent pacifist.

Hillsboro. 1 Town (pop. 2,179), S N.H., WSW of Concord. Here is Franklin Pierce home (1804; restored 1925). 2 Town (pop. 1,329), central N.C., NW of Durham. Early cap. of N.C. province; scene of disturbances in REGULATOR MOVEMENT. Birthplace of T. H. Benton. 3 City (pop. 5,126), SW Ohio, E of Cincinnati. Trade center in agr. area. Woman's Temperance Crusade founded here 1873. 4 City (pop. 5,142), NW Oregon, W of Portland. Quick freezes fruits and vegetables. 5 City (pop. 8,363), N central Texas,

SSW of Dallas. Processes cotton, textiles, and dairy products.

Hillsdale, city (pop. 7,297), S Mich., on St. Joseph R. and SW of Jackson. Mfg. of machinery. Has an arboretum.

Hillside, township (pop. 21,007), NE N.J., SW suburb of Newark. Mfg. of metal, rubber, asbestos, cork, paper goods, hydrogen, pharmaceuticals, plastics.

Hilo (hē'lō), city (pop. 27,198), co. seat of Hawaii co., on NE Hawaii, T.H.; port on Hilo Bay. Commercial center of island. Main export is sugar.

Hilprecht, Hermann Volrath (hĕr'män fôl'rät hĭl'prĕkht), 1859–1925, American Assyriologist, noted authority on cuneiform writing. He was scientific director of four expeditions (1895–1914) to Nippur.

Himachal Pradesh (hĭmä'chŭl prä'dĕsh), state (10,600 sq. mi.; pop. 989,437), NW India, in Himalayas; cap. Simla. Produces timber, wheat, rice, and corn. Formed 1948 by merger of 21 former Punjab states.

Himalayas (hĭmä'lŭyŭz, hĭmŭlä'ŭz) [Sanskrit,= abode of snow], Asiatic mountain system, c.1,500 mi. long, in Pakistan, Kashmir, India, Tibet, China, Nepal, Sikkim, and Bhutan. Comprises three nearly parallel ranges: Greater Himalayas, which include Mt. EVEREST (world's highest peak) and Kanchenjunga; Lesser Himalayas, enclosing noted Vale of Kashmir; and Outer Himalayas. A range N of Brahmaputra R. is sometimes called Trans-Himalayas. The ranges form almost insuperable barrier between Tibet and India and give rise to many great rivers, notably the Indus, Ganges, and Brahmaputra.

Himeji (hēmä'jē), city (pop. 197,299), S Honshu, Japan; railroad and mfg. center.

Himera (hĭ'mŭrŭ), anc. Greek city, N Sicily. Here according to tradition Gelon of Syracuse defeated the Carthaginians (480 B.C.), but in 408 B.C. Carthaginians destroyed the city.

Himmler, Heinrich (hĭn'rĭkh hĭm'lŭr), 1900–1945, German National Socialist leader. Headed SS (see NATIONAL SOCIALISM) from 1929; became head of entire German police system in 1936 (see SECRET POLICE) and minister of the interior in 1943. After putting down a conspiracy against Hitler in July, 1944, he acted as virtual dictator of Germany. The most ruthless of Nazi leaders, he was responsible for the death of millions in forced-labor and extermination camps and ended up by terrorizing his own party hierarchy. He died by taking poison shortly after his arrest by the British.

Himyaritic, Semitic language. See LANGUAGE (table).

Hincks, Sir Francis, 1807–85, Canadian journalist and statesman, b. Ireland. Became editor in 1838 of Toronto *Examiner,* a Reform party newspaper. As premier in joint Hincks-Morin administration (1851–54) he sought a reciprocal trade treaty with U.S. and promoted railroad construction. Minister of finance (1869–73).

Hindemith, Paul (hĭn'dŭmĭth), 1895–, German-American composer and violist; became U.S. citizen 1946. Early compositions were often atonal; later works display a return to tonality. Among his works are the symphony (1934) drawn from his own opera *Mathis der Maler;* a song cycle, *Das Marienleben* (1924; revised 1949); the viola concerto *Der Schwanendreher* (1935); the ballet *Nobilissima Visione* (1938); and *Ludus Tonalis* (1943) for piano.

Hindenburg, Paul von (Paul von Hindenburg und Beneckendorff) (hĭn'dŭnbûrg, Ger. –bōōrk), 1847–1934, German field marshal and president, b. Poznan (then in Prussia). In World War I he and his chief of staff, LUDENDORFF, routed the Russians at TANNENBERG (1914) and occupied Poland. In 1916 Hindenburg became chief commander of the Central Powers. After the armistice of 1918, he led his troops back in sufficiently good order to prevent a radical revolution. Though a monarchist, he was elected president of the Reich in 1925. He was a tool in the hands of the reactionary Junker class. With Socialist help, he defeated Hitler in the presidential elections of 1932, but in Jan., 1933, largely through the intrigues of PAPEN, he was persuaded to appoint Hitler as chancellor. He continued as a figurehead till his death.

Hindenburg, Pol. *Zabrze,* (pop. 104,184), Upper Silesia; transferred to Polish administration 1945. A center of Katowice mining and industrial region.

Hindi (hĭn'dē), Indo-European languages of N India. See LANGUAGE (table).

Hinduism, Western term for religious beliefs and practices of most of the people of India. Corresponding Indian term is *dharma* [law]. It has no fixed scriptural canon, but VEDA, *Brahmanas,* and *Bhagavad-Gita* have elaborate theological commentary. Brahmanism substituted (c.550 B.C.) for Vedic religion a complex system of ritual and theosophy expounded in *Brahmanas* and *Upanishads. Brahmanas* regulate sacrifices to gods and personify moral qualities. *Upanishads,* foundation of modern Hindu philosophy, develop doctrine of a universal soul or being to which individual souls will be reunited after *maya* (illusion of time and space) is conquered. Buddhism and Jainism, which flourished from c.300 B.C. to A.D. c.400 in India, attacked this complex ritual and theology. However, Brahmanism adopted features of those religions and codified its own ritual in *Laws of Manu.* Several schools of interpretation of *Upanishads* appeared (see VEDANTA) and YOGA was developed. A later stage of Hinduism is represented by *Tantras* and *Puranas. Tantras* are mainly prescriptions for securing divine favor; *Puranas* comprise poems addressed mainly to Siva (or Shiva) the Destroyer and Vishnu the Preserver. These and Brahma, a remote deity who created the universe and is equated with it, form triad at center of modern Hinduism. Many cults, with widely variant practices, exist side by side. Modern Hinduism, always more than a religion, is a complete way of life. Conditions have forced much modification (e.g., child marriage, rite of suttee, and untouchability are now illegal). Still widely observed is sacredness of animals (esp. cow and snake). Pilgrimages to sacred shrines are a marked feature of Hinduism.

Hindu Kush (hĭn'dōō kōōsh'), mountain sys-

tem, central Asia, lying mainly in NE Afghanistan and extending E to Pakistan. Culminates in Tirich Mir (25,263 ft.). Crossed by passes (10,000–17,000 ft.), which were used by conquerors of India.

Hindu music. In the music of India, only one voice part carries the melody. The tonal system divides the octave into 22 segments, each roughly equivalent to one quarter of the whole tone of Western music. The most important scale, called *sa-grama,* closely resembles our C major scale. Melody is based on the system of *ragas* or melody types which are used as the basis of an improvisation. There are 60-odd *ragas,* each having its own rules for improvising in that *raga.* Each has its own musical and emotional properties; each is associated with a certain season or time of day. Traditionally, a night *raga,* sung by a skilled performer at noon, could produce darkness. *Gamakas,* the ornaments or graces of *ragas,* are very important. The accompanying rhythm is based on certain constantly repeated rhythm patterns called *talas.* Among instruments used are various types of drums, the vina (in modern times, a kind of zither), and kinds of bagpipes, lutes, fiddles, oboes, trumpets, flutes, cymbals, and gongs.

Hindustan (hǐn″dŏōstăn′) [Persian,= Hindu land], a term applied to various areas of India and Pakistan. Sometimes refers to region between Narbada R. and the Himalayas, but sometimes limited to mean N central India. Since partition of Indian subcontinent (1947) it has sometimes been applied to the largely Hindu state of India as opposed to Moslem Pakistan.

Hindustani (hǐndŏōstän′ē), standard Indo-European language of Hindus. See LANGUAGE (table).

Hingham (hǐng′ùm), town (pop. 10,665), E Mass., on Boston Bay arm. Shipbuilding during World War II.

Hinkle, Beatrice M(ores Van Geisen), 1874–1953, American psychiatrist. Opened first U.S. psychotherapeutic clinic (1908) at Cornell Medical Col. She wrote *The Re-Creating of the Individual* (1923).

Hinnom, valley, near Jerusalem. Despised as place of Moloch worship and dump for Jerusalem's refuse. Tophet was in the valley. In New Testament, Gehenna, a form of Hinnom, meant HELL, perhaps because of fires of Moloch or dump fires always burning there.

Hinsdale, residential village (pop. 8,676), NE Ill., just W of Chicago.

Hinsley, Arthur, 1865–1943, English cardinal, Roman Catholic archbishop of Westminster (after 1935).

Hinton, city (pop. 5,780), S W.Va., SE of Beckley. Agr. shipping point with railroad shops.

Hipparchus, tyrant of Athens: see HIPPIAS.

Hipparchus (hǐpär′kùs), 2d cent. B.C., Greek astronomer. Ptolemy based his geocentric theory of the universe largely on conclusions of Hipparchus whose researches are recorded in Ptolemy's *Almagest.*

Hippias (hǐp′ēùs), 6th–5th cent. B.C., tyrant of Athens. He and his brother Hipparchus governed jointly after the death of their father PISISTRATUS until Hipparchus was

killed by Harmodius and Aristogiton (c.514 B.C.). Hippias then reigned alone until overthrown by the Alcmaeonidae and the Spartans. He advised the Persians in the campaign ending at Marathon.

Hippocrates (hǐpŏ′krùtēz), c.460–c.370 B.C., Greek physician, recognized as father of medicine. Placed medicine on scientific basis through practice of bedside observation of disease. Hippocratic writings (including those of disputed authorship) appeared in many translations; some are in Loeb Library. Hippocratic oath, administered to many graduates in medicine, is said to represent his ideals of ethical professional conduct.

Hippodamus (hǐpŏ′dùmùs), fl. 5th cent. B.C., Greek architect, earliest known planner of cities. Designed Piraeus (port of Athens) and Rhodes.

Hippolyte (hǐpŏ′lītē), in Greek mythology, queen of the Amazons; daughter of Ares. HERCULES captured her girdle.

Hippolytus, Saint (hǐpŏ′lītùs), c.160–235, anti-pope (217–35), a theologian. Urging a Neoplatonic theology rejected by the popes, he left the Church to become the first antipope. Later officially reconciled, he died a martyr in Maximin's persecution. Feast: Aug. 13.

Hippolytus, in Greek myth, son of Theseus and Antiope or Hippolyte. His stepmother, Phaedra, loved him, but, rebuffed by him, she accused him of dishonoring her. Poseidon then caused his death.

Hippomenes, in Greek legend, winner of ATALANTA.

hippopotamus (hǐpùpŏ′tùmùs), herbivorous mammal (genus *Hippopotamus*) of Africa, related to pig. It has short legs, a broad body, tough gray or brown hide, and a wide mouth. Its incisors and lower canines are large tusks, a source of "ivory." Frequents water and eats aquatic plants. Pygmy hippopotamus (genus *Choeropsis*) is in W Africa.

Hippo Regius: see BÔNE, Algeria.

Hiram (hī′-). **1** Fl. 1000 B.C., king of Tyre, friend of David and Solomon. Sent magnificent gifts for Temple. 2 Sam. 5.11; 1 Kings 5; 9; 10. Huram: 2 Chron. 2; 8; 9. **2** Artisan in metals, sent to Solomon by King Hiram to work on ornamentation of Temple. 1 Kings 7.13–45. Huram: 2 Chron. 4.11–22.

Hiram College, at Hiram, Ohio, SE of Cleveland; coed.; opened 1850. Has well-known plan for intensive study of one subject for nine weeks.

Hirohito (hērŏ′hētō), 1901–, emperor of Japan. Became regent 1921. Under reign name of Showa succeeded his father Yoshihito in 1926. Publicly rejected concept of imperial divinity in 1946. Constitution of 1947 deprived him of all real power.

Hiroshige (Hiroshige Ando), 1797–1858, Japanese landscape painter and color-print artist. *Mishima in Morning Fog* and *Rain at Shono* are typical.

Hiroshima, city (pop. 224,100), SW Honshu, Japan; port on Inland Sea. Mfg. of textiles and rubber goods. Founded 16th cent. as castle city on delta of Ota R. In World War II was target (Aug. 6, 1945) of first atomic bomb.

Hishigawa, Moronobu: see MORONOBU.

Hispaniola (hǐ″spänyō′lù), island (c.30,000 sq.

mi.), West Indies, between Cuba and Puerto Rico. Haiti occupies W third and Dominican Republic the remainder. Discovered by Columbus 1492. In Spanish the name is Española.

Hiss, Alger, 1904–, American public official. In Aug., 1948, Whittaker Chambers charged that Hiss, while in the Dept. of State, helped to transmit confidential government documents to the Russians. After denying the charges, Hiss stood trial twice and was finally convicted of perjury (Jan., 1950) and sentenced to a five-year prison term.

Hitchcock, Alfred (Joseph), 1899–, English film director. Brilliant creator of suspense in such films as *The Lady Vanishes, Rebecca,* and *Spellbound.*

Hitchcock, Frank Harris, 1869–1935, U.S. Postmaster General (1909–13). Estab. parcel post and postal savings banks; promoted founding of air mail.

Hitchcock, Lambert, 1795–1852, American chairmaker. Village erected by his factory in Conn. was called Hitchcockville (now Riverton). The **Hitchcock chair,** now sought by collectors, is a factory product of good wood, painted black over red and often having designs stenciled in colors or bronze. Seats are of wood, cane, or rush. See *ill.,* p. 456.

Hitchcock, Thomas, Jr., 1900–1944, American polo player. Probably greatest polo player of all time, he received highest polo rating from U.S. Polo Association, a 10-goal handicap, 1922–40 (except in 1935, when he had 9-goal rating).

Hitchcock chair: see HITCHCOCK, LAMBERT.

Hitler, Adolf, 1889–1945?, German dictator, founder and leader (Ger. *Führer*) of NATIONAL SOCIALISM; b. Braunau, Upper Austria, the son of an Austrian customs official. Studied at Munich; moved to Vienna 1907, where he was refused admission to art academy and spent years of utmost poverty. His violent anti-Semitism began in that period. In 1913 he moved to Munich. He enlisted in the Bavarian army in World War I; became a corporal, received Iron Cross for bravery, and was gassed. After the war he and a few malcontents founded at Munich the National Socialist German Workers' party (NSDAP). Still small but well-disciplined and backed by such men as LUDENDORFF, the NSDAP sought to gain control over Bavaria by a coup d'état, the so-called "beer-hall putsch" of Nov. 8–9, 1923. The plot was put down by the army, on whose support Hitler had counted; 14 Nazis were killed. Hitler was sentenced to five years at Landsberg fortress, where he wrote *Mein Kampf* [my battle], the bible of Nazism, but he was released after 13 months. The depression after 1929 helped in the spectacular growth of the NSDAP. Hitler and his propaganda chief GOEBBELS blamed all ills on Jewish capitalism, Communism, the Treaty of Versailles, and the Social Democrats and promised a millennium for pure-blooded Germans. Secretly backed by a few great industrialists (who hoped to use him as a tool for their own ends), he controlled a powerful press and a private militia. Though he lost the 1932 presidential election to Hindenburg, his party became the largest in the Reichstag.

In Jan., 1933, Hindenburg appointed him chancellor. Even with his allies, the monarchist German National party, Hitler had no absolute majority in the Reichstag. To estab. his dictatorship, he outlawed the Communists, whom he accused of setting the REICHSTAG fire, and in March, 1933, an obedient Reichstag voted him dictatorial powers. Hitler placed Germany under the absolute rule of the NSDAP, which took control not only of the state but of all German life, including youth activities (through the Hitler Jugend). Within his party, he crushed opposition in the "blood purge" of 1934. Anti-Semitism was enacted into law. Concentration camps were set up to take care of all suspected enemies of the regime. Only in the churches was some opposition left alive. In 1934, 88% of the voters favored the union of the presidency and the chancellorship in the person of the Führer. Hitler's aggressive foreign policy, though long abetted by English and French appeasement (see MUNICH PACT) led GERMANY on the road to WORLD WAR II (1939–45). Late in 1941 Hitler personally took over the conduct of the war in Russia, with disastrous results. To save Germany from total defeat, a group of high military and civil officials resolved upon assassinating Hitler. The bomb placed under his chair failed to kill him, and the conspiracy was put down ruthlessly by the police chief, HIMMLER. On April 30, 1945, with the Allies closing in from all sides, Hitler committed suicide at Berlin, together with Eva Braun, his mistress, whom he had just married. No trace of their burned bodies was found, and there are persistent though dubious rumors that Hitler actually escaped into hiding. His appointed successor, Adm. DOENITZ, arranged for the unconditional surrender of Germany a few days later. The ruin and misery that Hitler's folly and cruelty brought upon the world and his own people is beyond computation.

Hittites (hǐ′tīts), anc. people of Asia Minor and Syria, who had a culture that is still imperfectly known despite many inscriptions that have been uncovered (notably at Boghazkeui). Most inscriptions in cuneiform are in Hittite or Kanesian and in Babylonian, with some in Luish, Khattish, and Khurrish (the last two not related to Hittite). One reconstruction has it that the Hittites created a powerful federation of cities in Cappadocia by c.1800 B.C., then moved S, and finally came into conflict with Ramses II of Egypt. Supposedly their state was destroyed in late 12th cent. B.C. by Thracians, Phrygians, and Assyrians. Lydia was one of the successor states.

Hittorff, Jacques Ignace (hǐ′tôrf, Fr. zhäk′ ēnyäs′ ētôrf′), 1792–1867, French architect, a leader of classic revival in France. Chief work is church of St. Vincent de Paul, Paris. Designed fountains for Place de la Concorde and the column in Place Vendôme (both in Paris).

hives (uticaria), skin eruption, marked by raised areas (wheals) which burn and itch, thought to be an allergic reaction. Causative agents include foods, drugs, infections, insect bites, tapeworm.

Hjalmaren (yĕl′märŭn), Swed. *Hjälmaren,* lake,

area 190 sq. mi., central Sweden. It is connected with Malaren L. and Abroga R.

Hjort, Johan (yōhän' yōōrt'), 1869–1948, Norwegian oceanographer and biologist, authority on fisheries.

Ho, chemical symbol of the element HOLMIUM.

Hoadly, Benjamin, 1676–1761, bishop of Bangor, Wales, center of BANGORIAN CONTROVERSY.

Hoar, Ebenezer Rockwood, 1816–95, American lawyer, U.S. Attorney General (1869–70). One of Grant's few excellent appointments. U.S. Senate rejected his nomination to U.S. Supreme Court in 1870.

hoarfrost: see FROST.

Hoban, James (hō'bùn), c.1762–1831, American architect, b. Ireland. Designed and built the White House (1792–99); rebuilt it after its burning in 1814 by the British.

Hobart (hō'bùrt), city (pop. 56,640; metropolitan pop. 76,534), cap. and principal port of Tasmania, Australia, on Derwent estuary; founded 1804. Seat of Univ. of Tasmania. Woolen mills.

Hobart. 1 City (pop. 10,244), NW Ind., SE of Gary; settled c.1849. Mfg. of clay products. **2** City (pop. 5,380), SW Okla., N of Wichita Mts., in a farming and oil producing area.

Hobart College: see GENEVA, N.Y.

Hobbema, Meindert (mīn'dùrt hô'bùmä), 1638–1709, great Dutch landscapist; probably studied with Jacob van Ruisdael. His woodland and village scenes are luminous and full of life. Much of work is in England, where it influenced later English landscapists.

Hobbes, Thomas, 1588–1679, English philosopher. In his works, both in Latin and in English, he set forth a rationalist materialism, which offended the religious. His view was strongly mechanistic. His best-known work, the *Leviathan* (1651), made him the first of the great English political theorists. This argues that men in their natural existence are self-seeking, brutish, and constantly at war with one another. To escape the dangers of this anarchy groups of men agree to set up an artificial body for maintaining peace. They submit absolutely to the sovereign, who is, however, obliged to protect the people and to promote truth. Hobbes implies that if the sovereign failed in this duty the citizens would have a right to revolt. In his psychology he was a strict sensationalist.

hobblebush or **wayfaring tree,** a viburnum (*Viburnum alnifolium*) of E North America. It has long straggling branches which often root at the tips.

Hobbs, city (pop. 13,875), SE N.Mex., on Llano Estacado, near Texas line. Trade center for livestock and farm region. Hq. for rich oil fields found in 1927.

Hobby, Oveta Culp, 1905–, American public official and journalist. Organized and directed WAC in World War II. Executive vice president of Houston *Post*. Became Secretary of Health, Education, and Welfare in 1953.

Hoboken (hō'bōkùn), town (pop. 31,941), Antwerp prov., N. Belgium, on Scheldt R.; part of greater Antwerp. Shipyards; copper, tin, and silver refineries; wool-processing plants.

Hoboken (hō'bōkùn), city (pop. 50,676), NE NJ., on the Hudson opposite lower Manhat-

tan (ferry, Lincoln Tunnel, subway connections). Commercial and industrial center (since mid-19th cent.) and ocean port (marine and rail terminals) with shipbuilding and mfg. of food products, electrical equipment, machinery, furniture, chemicals, and scientific instruments. Seat of STEVENS INSTITUTE OF TECHNOLOGY. Dutch trading and farming began c.1630. Indians deeded land to Stuyvesant 1658. John STEVENS bought site 1784, and laid out town 1804. He operated (1811) first steam ferry between New York and Hoboken, built (c.1825) and ran first locomotive to pull a train on tracks in U.S. Noted early 19th-cent. authors gathered at John Jacob Astor home (1828).

Hobson, John Atkinson (hŏb'sùn), 1858–1940, English economist. Criticized classical economics, holding that economic theory should be a guide to resolution of problems of social welfare.

Hobson, Richmond Pearson, 1870–1937, American naval officer. Gained notice by his effort to sink collier *Merrimac* to block harbor of Santiago in Spanish-American War.

Hoche, Lazare (läzär' ōsh'), 1768–97, French general. Pacified VENDÉE (1794–96); failed in invasion of Ireland (1796); defeated Austrians at Neuwied (1797).

Hochelaga (hō"shŭlä'gù, –lä'gù), former Indian village, Canada, discovered by Jacques Cartier in 1535. At foot of Mt. Royal in what is now central part of Montreal. Capital of Hochelagan people, chief inhabitants of St. Lawrence valley. Recent excavations have unearthed early cultural remains.

Ho Chi-minh (hō' chē-mĭn'), 1890?-, Indo-Chinese revolutionary leader. Visited Moscow 1925–27. Leader of Viet Minh (League for Independence of Viet Nam), he headed VIET NAM provisional government in 1945. Warfare begun 1946 between the French and Ho's regime was still raging in 1953.

Höchstädt (hûkh'shtĕt), village, W. Bavaria, on Danube R., near battlefield of BLENHEIM. Scene of French victory over Austrians (1800).

hockey, game played on field or ice. Field hockey, played in England for several centuries, has been popular in U.S., since 1901, especially among college girls. Played on level field measuring 50 to 60 yd. by 90 to 100 yd. by two teams of 11 players. Ice hockey, played exclusively by men, originated in Canada and was probably standardized by McGill Univ. students in 1870s. Game is played on regulation ice rink 200 ft. by 85 ft. by teams of six players.

Hodgenville (hŏj'ĭnvĭl), town (pop. 1,695), central Ky., S of Louisville. Abraham Lincoln Natl. Historical Park, with cabin said to be his birthplace, is near by.

Hodmezovasarhely (hôd'mĕzŭvä"shärhä) Hung. *Hódmezővásárhely*, city (pop. 61,776), S Hungary. A typical "peasant city," it occupies 294 sq. mi.

Hoe, Richard March, 1812–86, American inventor, manufacturer of first U.S. flat bed and cylinder press and designer (1846–47), of the first Hoe rotary press.

hoe, usually a flat blade set in long handle and used for loosening soil and weeding; probably the first exclusively agricultural implement. Forerunner was forked stick or antler; from it adz and plow were evolved.

Hoek van Holland: see HOOK OF HOLLAND.

Hofer, Andreas (ändrä′äs hō′fŭr), 1767–1810, Austrian patriot; a Tyrolean innkeeper. Led peasants of TYROL in revolt against Bavaria (1809) and was made governor of Tyrol by the Austrians. Betrayed to the French, he was shot at Mantua.

Hoffman, Charles Fenno, 1806–84, American author. Associated with many periodicals. His works, which were widely popular, include a travel book (*A Winter in the West, 1935*), a novel (*Greyslaer: a Romance of the Mohawk,* 1840), and lyrics.

Hoffman, Malvina, 1887–, American sculptor. Studied under Rodin. Best known for portrait busts; did 100 bronzes of racial types for Field Mus., Chicago.

Hoffmann, E(rnst) T(heodor) A(madeus) (ĕrnst′ tä′ōdōr ämädä′ōōs hôf′män), 1776–1822, German author, composer, and artist. Was active as conductor and as jurist. Himself an eccentric personality, he was a master of fantastic fiction, which his poetry and flashes of psychological insight raised to the highest level. His works include *The Serapion Brethren* (1819–22), *The Devil's Elixir* (1815–16), *Kater Murr, the Educated Cat* (1820–21). These and many selected tales have been translated into English. *The Nutcracker and the Mouse-King* served as basis for Tchaikovsky's ballet; three other tales were used for Offenbach's opera *Tales of Hoffmann.*

Hoffmann-Donner, Heinrich (hīn′rĭkh hôf′män-dô′nŭr), 1809–94, German author of *Struwwelpeter* [slovenly Peter] (1845), widely known children's book.

Hofmann, August Wilhelm von (ou′gŏŏst vĭl′hĕlm fŭn hôf′män), 1818–92, German organic chemist. He was first to prepare rosaniline and its derivatives, thereby laying basis for aniline dye industry.

Hofmann, Joseph (hôf′mŭn), 1876–, Polish-American pianist. Made his American debut (1887) at the Metropolitan Opera House. Director (1924–38) of the Curtis Inst. of Music, Philadelphia.

Hofmannsthal, Hugo von (hōō′gō fŭn hôf′mänstäl), 1874–1929, Austrian dramatist and poet. His *Electra* (1903), *Der Rosenkavalier* (1911), *Ariadne auf Naxos* (1912), *Die Frau ohne Schatten* [the woman without a shadow] (1919), and *Die ägyptische Helena* (1928) were set to music by Richard Strauss. Also famous is his adaptation of *Everyman* (*Jedermann,* 1911).

Hofstra College: see HEMPSTEAD, N.Y.

hog: see SWINE.

Hogan, Ben (hō′gŭn), 1912–, American golfer. Won many tournaments, including P.G.A. championship (1946, 1948) and U.S. open (1948).

Hogarth, William (hō′gärth), 1697–1764, English painter and engraver. Won fame and financial security with his engravings, notably the three series *The Harlot's Progress, The Rake's Progress,* and *Marriage à la Mode,* which reveal his power as a satirist. Also made didactic prints (e.g., *Gin Lane*) to spur social reform. In his own time he won little recognition as a serious painter, although he produced some magnificent canvases, including the famous *Shrimp Girl* (Natl. Gall., London).

Hogben, Lancelot (Thomas) (hŏg′bĕn), 1895–, English scientist and author. Known for work in genetics and endocrinology and for popular science books.

hog cholera, infectious, very contagious, often fatal virus disease of hogs. It can be prevented by vaccination.

Hogg, James, 1770–1835, Scottish poet, the "Ettrick Shepherd." Known for his rustic verse, such as *The Mountain Bard* (1807) and *The Queen's Wake* (1813).

Hog Island, in Delaware R., SE Pa. Government shipyard in World War I. Acquired by Philadelphia 1930 as airport and shipping and mfg. area.

Hogue, La (lä ôg′) or **La Hougue** (lä ōōg′), harbor on English Channel, NW France, on NE coast of Cotentin peninsula. Scene of English-Dutch naval victory over French (1692).

Hohenfriedberg (hōŭnfrēt′bĕrk), village, Silesia, near Breslau. Scene of decisive victory of Frederick II of Prussia over Austro-Saxon forces (1745).

Hohenlinden (hōŭnlĭn′dŭn), village, Upper Bavaria. Scene of French victory over Austrians (1800).

Hohenlohe-Schillingsfürst, Chlodwig, Fürst zu (klōt′vĭkh fürst′ tsōō hō′ŭnlōū-shĭ′lĭngsfürst′), 1819–1901, chancellor of Germany (1894–1900).

Hohenstaufen (hō″ŭnshtou′fŭn), German dynasty; dukes of Swabia from 1079; emperors and German kings 1138–1254; kings of Sicily 1194–1266 (see CONRAD III; FREDERICK I; HENRY VI; PHILIP OF SWABIA; FREDERICK II; CONRAD IV; MANFRED; CONRADIN). Their chief rivals were the Guelphs (see GUELPHS AND GHIBELLINES), who sided with the popes in their struggle with the Hohenstaufen emperors.

Hohenwald (hō′ŭnwôld), town (pop. 1,703), central Tenn., SW of Nashville. Near by is Meriwether Lewis Natl. Monument.

Hohenzollern (hō″ŭntsō′lŭrn), German dynasty, named for its ancestral castle in Swabia. Frederick of Hohenzollern (d. c.1200) became burgrave of Nuremberg 1192. His sons founded the two main lines of the house—the Swabian line (see HOHENZOLLERN, former province) and the Franconian line, which received the margraviates of ANSBACH and BAYREUTH (which later passed to separate branches) and, in 1415, the electorate of BRANDENBURG. In 1525 ALBERT OF BRANDENBURG created the duchy of Prussia, which passed to the main line of Brandenburg in 1618. Elector FREDERICK WILLIAM (reigned 1640–88) vastly increased his territories, which his son Frederick I transformed in 1701 into the kingdom of PRUSSIA. From 1871 to 1918 the Hohenzollern kings of Prussia were also emperors of Germany (William I, Frederick III, William II).

Hohenzollern, former province (441 sq. mi.; pop. 85,863), of Prussia, SW Germany, in Swabia, between Württemberg and Baden; cap. Sigmaringen. After World War II it became part of WÜRTTEMBERG-HOHENZOLLERN. Mountainous; agr., forestry. Zollern or Hohenzollern castle, in N, gave name to

Prussia's ruling house. About 1600 territory split into two counties, later principalities, ruled by two branches of the Swabian Hohenzollern line—**Hohenzollern-Hechingen** and **Hohenzollern-Sigmaringen**. Both houses yielded their rights to Prussia 1849. Charles of Hohenzollern-Sigmaringen became king of Rumania as Carol I.

Hohe Tauern (hō′ṳ tou′ṳrn), range of E Alps, S Austria, in Salzburg, Carinthia, and E Tyrol. Rises to 12,460 ft. in GROSSGLOCKNER.

Hokan, hypothetical linguistic family of North America deriving from unproven unification of a number of Western and Eastern stocks.

Hokkaido (hōkī′dō), island (c.30,000 sq. mi.; pop. 3,852,821), N Japan; cap. Sapporo. Northernmost, second largest, and most sparsely populated of the four major islands of Japan. Rugged interior with many volcanic peaks; c.60% of area is forested. Ishikari R. in W is second largest in Japan. Has severe winters. Chief products: coal, lumber, paper, iron. One of world's major fishing centers. Until 1800 Ainus outnumbered the Japanese. Formerly called Yezo.

Hokusai (hō′kōōsī), 1760–1849, Japanese artist, the foremost figure of ukiyoye school. Accurately depicted Japanese scenes and contemporary life. A famous color-print series is *Hundred Views of Fuji.* His landscapes had much influence on Western art.

Holbach, Paul Henri Thiry, baron d' (ôlbäk′; also German hôl′bäkh), 1723–89, French philosopher, b. the Palatinate. A friend of Diderot, Condorcet, and Rousseau, he was an Encyclopedist. He is remembered chiefly as a stalwart opponent of all positive religion. Man, he held, was innately moral but perverted by education.

Holbein, Hans (hôl′bīn), the elder, c.1460–1524, German painter, designer of stained glass, and silverpoint portraitist. His son **Ambrosius Holbein,** c.1494–1519, is best known for book illustrations and portraits. The other son, **Hans Holbein,** the younger, 1497–1543, was an outstanding artist of German Renaissance. Spent early half of life in Basel, where he enjoyed friendship of Erasmus, whose *Praise of Folly* he illustrated and of whom he painted many portraits. In 1526 he visited England, where he painted Sir Thomas More and other eminent persons. Settled in England after brief return to Basel. Became painter to Henry VIII in 1536 and made many portraits of the king and his wives. As impressive as his paintings are numerous preliminary portrait drawings, remarkable for sensitivity of line and characterization. Among other famous works are his woodcuts, which include *Dance of Death* series and illustrations for Luther's Bible.

Holberg, Ludvig, Baron (lōōdh′vē, hōl′bĕr), 1684–1754, Danish dramatist and historian, b. Norway. One of the great figures of Danish literature, he was first to use Danish as a literary medium. *The Danish Stage* (1731) is a collection of 15 comedies.

Holborn (hō′bûrn), metropolitan borough (pop. 24,806), central London, England. Has British Mus., Univ. of London, Gray's Inn and Lincoln's Inn, Royal Col. of Surgeons, and Hatton Garden, all damaged by bombing

in World War II. Known for its diamond trade.

Holbrook, Josiah (hōl′brōōk), 1788–1854, American educator. He founded the LYCEUM movement at Millbury, Mass., in 1826.

Holbrook (hōl′brōōk), town (pop. 2,336), E central Ariz., on Little Colorado R. and SE of Winslow. To E is Petrified Forest Natl. Monument.

Holden, city (pop. 1,765), W Mo., SE of Kansas City. Carry Nation lived here.

Holdenville, city (pop. 6,192), SE central Okla., SE of Shawnee. Trade center for farm and oil region. Site of Fort Holmes near by.

Hölderlin, Friedrich (frē′drĭkh hûl′dûrlĭn), 1770–1843, German poet. Before he became insane at 36 he wrote lyric poetry of deep and intensely personal content, in classic meter and in free rhythms, which place him among the foremost German poets. Equally notable for its blending of classical and romantic elements is the epistolary novel *Hyperion* (1797–99).

holding company: see CORPORATION.

Holinshed, Raphael, d. c.1580, English chronicler. His *Chronicles of England, Scotland, and Ireland* (1577) was source for many English history plays.

Holland, former county of the Holy Roman Empire and, from 1579 to 1795, chief member of the United Provs. of the Netherlands; historic cap. The Hague. The name is popularly applied to the entire Netherlands. Created a county in 10th cent., Holland originally also controlled ZEELAND and FRIESLAND. It was seized in 1299 by John of Avesnes, count of HAINAUT, and was ruled by his successors till 1433, when Duke Philip the Good of Burgundy wrested it from Jaqueline, countess of Hainaut, Holland, Zeeland, and Friesland. After the death of Mary of Burgundy (1482) Holland was taken over by Maximilian of Austria (later Emperor Maximilian I), who suppressed a Dutch rebellion in 1490. The ports and cities of Holland—e.g., Amsterdam, Rotterdam, The Hague, Leiden, Delft—rose to prosperity in the 15th and 16th cent., and Holland led in the struggle for Dutch independence from Spain (16th–17th cent.). Its history became virtually identical with that of the NETHERLANDS. In 1840 Holland was divided into NORTH HOLLAND and SOUTH HOLLAND provs.

Holland, resort city (pop. 15,858), S Mich., SW of Grand Rapids and on Black R. and Black L.; founded 1847 by Dutch. Mfg. of metal and rubber products. Has tulip growing and annual tulip festival. Here are Hope Col. and Netherlands Mus.

Holland, Parts of: see LINCOLNSHIRE, England.

Holland House, residence of the Holland family in Kensington, London, made famous in first half of 19th cent. by hospitality of Henry Richard Vassall Fox, 3d Baron Holland. Did much for English liberalism by providing an intellectual center for scientists, writers, and statesmen.

Hollandia (hŏlăn′dēὺ), trading post (district pop. 6,228), cap. of Netherlands New Guinea, on Humboldt Bay, N New Guinea. In World War II it was Japanese air base, taken 1944 by U.S. troops.

Holland Land Company, a Dutch venture active

in the settlement of much of W N.Y. and some of NW Pa. Organized 1796. Company developed its holdings, planned town sites, and sold lands directly to settlers on liberal terms.

Hollar, Wenzel or **Wenceslaus** (hŏ'lûr, –lär), 1607–77, Bohemian etcher. Works included portraits, architectural studies, still lifes, and religious scenes. Worked mainly in England.

Hollidaysburg, borough (pop. 6,483), S Pa., S of Altoona and on Juniata R. Has railroad shops and plants for metal products and explosives.

Hollidays Cove, W.Va.: see WEIRTON.

Hollingworth, Leta Stetter, 1886–1939, American educator and psychologist. From 1916 until her death she taught at Teachers Col., Columbia Univ. She was noted for her studies in child psychology.

Hollins College: see ROANOKE, Va.

Hollister, city (pop. 4,903), W Calif., E of Monterey Bay. Pinnacles Natl. Monument is near.

holly, handsome evergreen or deciduous tree or shrub of widely distributed genus *Ilex* with berrylike fruits of various colors. Male and female flowers are often on different plants. English holly (*Ilex aquifolium*), with glossy spiny evergreen leaves and bright red berries, is closely associated with Christmas tradition. The similar American holly (*I. opaca*) may reach 50 ft. in the South. Other hollies include inkberry, winterberry, and commercially important MATE.

hollyhock, a tall biennial or perennial plant (*Althaea rosea*), with large leaves and showy single or double flowers of various colors.

Hollywood. 1 Part (pop. c.185,000) of Los Angeles (since 1910), S Calif.; founded in late 1880s. Center of moving-picture industry, though many of the studios are now outside. Hollywood's first picture was made in 1911. The word Hollywood now means American film industry in general—its morals, manners, and characteristics. Community is also a Western broadcasting center for radio and television. Hollywood Bowl, Griffith Park, and estates of many cinema stars are here. **2** City (pop. 14,351), SE Fla., on Atlantic coast N of Miami; founded 1921 as planned resort.

Holmes, John Haynes, 1879–, American clergyman (undenominational), minister (1907–49) of the Community Church, New York city; founder of Natl. Association for the Advancement of Colored People and of American Civil Liberties Union.

Holmes, Oliver Wendell, 1809–94, American author and physician, b. Cambridge, Mass.; grad. Harvard. He brought out a volume of *Poems* in 1836, and verse written throughout his life was to provide familiar poems for Americans (e.g., "Old Ironsides," "The Chambered Nautilus," "The Deacon's Masterpiece; or, The Wonderful One-Hoss Shay," and "Lord of all being, Throned afar"). He also wrote medical pamphlets of considerable importance. Sketches, contributed to the *Atlantic Monthly,* gave rise to several collections (e.g., *The Autocrat of the Breakfast-Table,* 1858; *The Professor at the Breakfast-Table,* 1860). These and his poems made him a sort of apostle of good humor, but his un-

successful novels (*Elsie Venner,* 1861; *The Guardian Angel,* 1867; *A Mortal Antipathy,* 1885) were anti-Calvinist and "medical" and have been recently called the first American psychological novels. His son, **Oliver Wendell Holmes,** 1841–1935, was Associate Justice of U.S. Supreme Court (1902–32). Known as the "great dissenter," he by his clear, forceful opinions gained the notice of the nation's liberals. He believed in respecting human rights more than property rights. His writings (e.g., *The Common Law,* 1881) are much admired.

Holmes, William Henry, 1846–1933, American geologist and anthropologist. He served with U.S. Geological Survey, contributing pioneer reports on Yellowstone, Grand Canyon, and other areas. His interest in cliff dwellings of the Southwest turned him to archaeology. From 1910 to 1920 he was curator of anthropology at U.S. National Museum.

holmium (hŏl'mēŭm), metallic element of rare earths (symbol = Ho; see also ELEMENT, table).

Holofernes (hŏlûfûr'nēz, hōlō'–), invading general killed by JUDITH to save her city. Judith 2–13.

Holst, Gustav (hŏlst), 1874–1934, English composer. Among his compositions are *The Mystic Trumpeter* (1904), for voice and orchestra; *The Planets* (1914–16), a suite for orchestra; and *The Perfect Fool* (1920–22), an opera.

Holst, Hermann Eduard von (fŭn hôlst'), 1841–1904, American historian. Main work, *The Constitutional and Political History of the United States* (7 vols., 1876–92), studies struggle to preserve Union.

Holstein (hōl'stīn, Ger. hôl'shtīn), former duchy, N Germany; the part of Schleswig-Holstein S of the Eider R.; cap. Kiel. Created a county of the Holy Roman Empire in 1111, Holstein was ruled until 1459 by the house of Schauenburg, which in 1386 also received SCHLESWIG. In 1459 it passed by inheritance to Christian I of Denmark, of the house of OLDENBURG, who in 1460 estab. the relationship of Denmark, Schleswig, and Holstein as a personal union. Holstein was raised to a duchy in 1474. For subsequent history, see SCHLESWIG-HOLSTEIN.

Holstein, Friedrich von (frē'drĭkh fŭn hôl'-shtīn), 1837–1909, German civil servant, the "Gray Eminence" of the German foreign office. Holding a relatively obscure post, he was a powerful influence in shaping German foreign policy after the fall of his enemy, Bismarck. Resigned 1906.

Holstein-Friesian cattle: see CATTLE.

Holt, Henry, 1840–1926, American publisher and author. Joined (1866) the publishing firm which became (1873) Henry Holt & Co. Founded (1913) the *Unpopular Review.* Wrote novels and an autobiography.

Holt, Joseph, 1807–94, judge advocate general of U.S. army (1862–75). Followed Pres. Lincoln's desires in extending military jurisdiction over civil affairs.

Holt, Luther Emmett, 1855–1924, American physician, specialist in children's diseases, author of *Care and Feeding of Children* (1894).

Holtby, Winifred, 1898–1935, English novelist

and journalist. Director of *Time and Tide* after 1926. Her novel *South Riding* (1936) widely known.

Holtsville, city (pop. 2,472), SE Calif., SE of Salton Sea in IMPERIAL VALLEY. Ships truck.

Holy Alliance, formed 1815, agreement among Alexander I of Russia (its sponsor) and the rulers of Austria and Prussia. Its wording, which reflects Alexander's confused mysticism, bound the sovereigns to conduct themselves according to Christian principles and was later interpreted to mean that the political status of Europe as of 1815 was divinely inspired and should remain unchanged forever. All sovereigns of Europe adhered to the alliance save three—George IV of England (who could not for constitutional reasons) and the pope and the sultan (who could not for religious reasons). The QUADRUPLE ALLIANCE of 1814, though distinct from the Holy Alliance, became soon confused with it and under the leadership of Metternich acted as its instrument. The defection of England from the Quadruple Alliance (1822) did not prevent the survival of the Holy Alliance as a spiritual climate until the Revolution of 1848.

Holy City: see ALLAHABAD; BENARES; JERUSALEM; MECCA; ROME.

Holy Cross, College of the: see WORCESTER, Mass.

Holy Cross National Monument: see NATIONAL PARKS AND MONUMENTS (table).

Holy Ghost or **Holy Spirit,** in Christian doctrine, third Person of the Trinity, often defined as the aspect of God immanent in the world; the giver of faith, the Paraclete (Comforter or Strengthener). Descended upon the apostles at first Pentecost, giving them the gift of tongues (Acts 2). The dove is symbol of the Holy Ghost.

Holy Grail: see GRAIL, HOLY.

Holyhead (hŏ'lēhĕd), urban district (pop. 10,-569), on Holyhead Isl., Wales, small island off W coast of Anglesey. Chief port for mail and passenger service to Dublin. Also a fishing port and resort.

Holy Island, England: see LINDISFARNE.

Holy Land: see PALESTINE.

Holy League. 1 In French history: see LEAGUE. **2** In Italian history, alliance formed 1510 by Pope Julius II with Venice, Swiss Confederation, Spain, England, Emperor Maximilian I, and others to expel LOUIS XII of France from Italy. Swiss routed French at Novara (1513), but league broke up when Julius died.

Holyoke, city (pop. 54,661), SW Mass., on Connecticut R. (water power) above Springfield; settled 1745. Mfg. of paper and metal products and textiles.

holy orders: see ORDERS, HOLY.

Holy Roman Empire, political body embracing most of central Europe from 962 to 1806; "Roman" because it claimed succession to imperial Rome; "holy" because it originally claimed supremacy over Christendom. Its universality was never recognized in the E by the Byzantine emperors and only briefly in the W, where England, France, and Spain developed into separate states. A constantly evolving organism, the Holy Roman Empire was a mixture of conflicting theories and realities. CHARLEMAGNE in 800 recreated a Western Empire and sought to restore the order and unity Europe had known under Rome; this empire broke up under his successors (LOUIS I, LOTHAIR I, LOUIS II, CHARLES II, CHARLES III, ARNULF). The union of GERMANY and ITALY under OTTO I and his imperial coronation (962) created a new empire, based on FEUDALISM. Its rulers were chosen by the princes of Germany (after 1356, by a fixed number of ELECTORS); unless crowned emperor by the pope, they bore the title German king or king of the Romans. Customarily, after being crowned king at Aachen, the emperor-elect proceeded to Rome to be crowned emperor there. To keep the succession in his family, he normally had his heir elected king of the Romans in his lifetime. After 1562 the emperors-elect dispensed with coronations by the pope and were crowned at Frankfurt. The emperors exercised direct rule only over their hereditary family domains (e.g., the Saxon dynasty, over Saxony; the Hapsburg dynasty, over Austria); they also held immediate jurisdiction over the free imperial cities (e.g., Frankfurt, Regensburg, Augsburg), which they chartered in the 12th–13th cent. The rest of the empire they controlled only to the extent to which they controlled the DIET, which might even depose them. They succeeded, in the 10th–12th cent., in breaking up the powerful "stem duchies" (see GERMANY) and raised a multitude of lesser temporal and ecclesiastic princes to the rank of immediate vassals. This process was completed by FREDERICK I, who also brought to a head the long-standing rivalry between emperors and popes. One factor in that bitter struggle was that both popes and emperors claimed supremacy over Christendom—the popes in spiritual matters, the emperors in temporal matters, but with no agreement as to ultimate rights in administration and authority. From this arose the quarrel over INVESTITURE (settled 1122 by the Concordat of WORMS). Another factor was the dual role of the emperors as kings of both Germany and Italy and the dual role of the popes as both spiritual and temporal rulers. If the emperors stayed N of the Alps, they lost effective control over Italy; if they invaded Italy (as they did at irregular intervals) to reassert their authority, the popes as a rule managed to stir up trouble in Germany, thus forcing the invader to hasten back. Frederick I lost out in his struggle against the LOMBARD LEAGUE, which had papal backing; FREDERICK II, who was also king of Sicily, shifted his center of interest to Italy, which he temporarily subdued, but after his death (1250) the papacy emerged triumphant and imperial rule over Italy was lost. After an interregnum which put Germany at the mercy of robber barons, feuding nobles, and rival kings, a new phase began with the election of RUDOLF I of Hapsburg (1273). The HAPSBURG dynasty, which became permanently entrenched after 1438, directed its primary attention to its own aggrandizement and to its hereditary domains, which under CHARLES V stretched around the entire globe, far beyond the boundaries of the Holy Roman Empire. The victory of the princes and the towns in the PEASANTS' WAR (1524–26) prolonged serfdom and feudalism for another three centuries; the REFORMATION destroyed even the religious unity of the empire and offered the German princes a pretext for rebelling against Hapsburg supremacy in the THIRTY YEARS WAR (1618–48). The Peace of WESTPHALIA dissolved the empire in all but its name. Some 300 princes obtained virtual sovereignty, limited only by vague provisions forbidding alliances directed against the emperor. Hapsburg power was further weakened by France in the wars of Louis XIV (17th cent.) and by PRUSSIA in the War of the AUSTRIAN SUCCESSION and the SEVEN YEARS WAR (18th cent.). The FRENCH REVOLUTIONARY WARS and Napoleon I swept away the empire. In 1803 the diet deposed and indemnified the majority of princes, creating a smaller number of larger states; in 1804 Francis II took the title Francis I, emperor of Austria; in 1806 the empire was dissolved. The following is a list of German kings and emperors from 919.

Saxon dynasty (919–1024): Henry I, Otto I, Otto II, Otto III, Henry II.

Salian or Franconian dynasty (1024–1125): Conrad II, Henry III, Henry IV, Henry V.

Lothair II (reigned 1125–37; duke of Saxony).

Hohenstaufen dynasty (1138–1254): Conrad III, Frederick I, Henry VI, Philip of Swabia (antiking: Otto IV), Frederick II, Conrad IV (antiking: William, count of Holland).

Interregnum (1254–73): Richard, earl of Cornwall and Alfonso X of Castile, rivals.

Hapsburg, Luxemburg, and other dynasties: Rudolf I (1273–91; Hapsburg); Adolf of Nassau (1292–98); Albert I (1298–1308; Hapsburg); Henry VII (1308–13; Luxemburg); Louis IV (1314–46; Wittelsbach); Charles IV (1346–78; Luxemburg); Wenceslaus (1378–1400; Luxemburg); Rupert (1400–1410; Wittelsbach); Sigismund (1410–37; Luxemburg).

Hapsburg dynasty (1438–1740); Albert II, Frederick III, Maximilian I, Charles V, Ferdinand I, Maximilian II, Rudolf II, Matthias, Ferdinand II, Ferdinand III, Leopold I, Joseph I, Charles VI.

Interregnum (1740–42).

Charles VII (emperor, 1742–45; elector of Bavaria).

Francis I (emperor, 1745–65; ex-duke of Lorraine; husband of Maria Theresa).

Hapsburg-Lorraine dynasty (1765–1806): Joseph II, Leopold II, Francis II.

Holyrood (hŏ'lērōōd) [i.e., holy cross], former residence of Scottish kings, in Edinburgh. David I founded abbey here in 1128. Its Chapel Royal contains remains of several kings. Present building begun 1501; rebuilt after fire of 1650. Scene of murder of David Rizzio (1566).

Holy Sepulcher, church in Jerusalem on the supposed site of Jesus' tomb, officially the Church of the Resurrection. St. HELENA is said to have pointed out the site. Most of the church is controlled by the Orthodox, though other Christian groups have sections.

Holy Spirit: see HOLY GHOST.

Holy Week, week before Easter marked by commemoration of Jesus' passion and death.

Chief days are Palm Sunday, Maundy Thursday, Good Friday, and Holy Saturday (Lent ends Saturday at noon).

Holywell (hŏ'lēwĕl), urban district (pop. 8,196), Flintshire, Wales. Gothic chapel (place of pilgrimage for Roman Catholics) covers St. Winifred's Well, which, legend says, sprang up on the spot where St. Winifred was beheaded.

Holywood, urban district (pop. 6,316), Co. Down, N. Ireland. Has ruins of 13th-cent. monastery on the site of one founded in the 7th cent.

Holz, Arno (är'nō hôlts'), 1863–1929, German poet; an influential critic and a founder of the naturalistic school.

Homburg (hôm'bŏŏrk), town (pop. 27,670), Hesse, W Germany; officially called Bad Homburg. Famous spa and fashionable resort. Until 1866 cap. of landgraviate of Hesse-Homburg.

Home, Daniel Dunglas, 1833–86, American spiritualist medium. He claimed to have discovered his gifts at 13 and from 1850 on had triumphant career in U.S. and Europe. His séances produced highly physical manifestations of spirits. Many efforts were made to expose him but none was successful.

Home, John, 1722–1808, Scottish dramatist, author of successful tragedy *Douglas* (1756), which has speech beginning, "My name is Norval."

Homedale, village (pop. 1,411), SW Idaho, on Snake R. near Oregon line, in OWYHEE project.

home economics deals with homemaking and the relation of the home to the community. Formerly (called domestic science) it was limited to problems of food (nutrition and cookery), clothing, sewing, textiles, home equipment and maintenance, and hygiene; today it includes also aspects of family relations, parental education, consumer education, institutional management. Scientific aspects preceded the social, economic, and aesthetic phases. In U.S., home economics on college level dates from the '70s; teaching of cooking and sewing in public schools began in the '80s.

home missions: see MISSIONS.

homeopathy (hōmēŏ'pŭthē), system of medicine based on principle that disorders are cured by small doses of drugs producing effects similar to the disorder. It was originated by Samuel Hahnemann and gained great popularity (now somewhat dwindled).

Home Owners' Loan Corporation, established (1933) to refinance urban mortgage debt and stabilize depreciated real estate. HOLC lent $3,000,000,000, of which 90 per cent had been liquidated by 1949.

Homer, first Greek poet. His actual existence much debated in 19th cent., but most recent scholars say that such a poet lived before 700 B.C. Legend says that he was blind and that seven cities claimed him. Narrative poems, the ILIAD and the ODYSSEY, are masterpieces of world literature and models for all later epics. The HOMERIC HYMNS, a comic poem (MARGITES), and a mock epic (*The Battle of the Frogs and the Mice*) anciently attributed to him.

Homer, Louise, 1871?–1947, American operatic

contralto. Sang at the Metropolitan Opera, New York, 1900–19); at the Chicago Opera until 1924. She sang the principal contralto roles in *Aïda, Il Trovatore,* and *Hansel and Gretel,* but considered Orpheus, in Gluck's opera, her greatest role.

Homer, Winslow, 1836–1910, American landscape, marine, and genre painter. Many of his studies of everyday life date from Civil War period when he was a popular magazine illustrator. Best known for his dramatic interpretations of the sea in water color.

Homeric Hymns (hōmĕ'rĭk), hexameter poems, complimentary to the gods, composed c.800–400 B.C., anciently attributed to Homer.

Home Rule. Economic conditions in Ireland gave rise to demand for autonomy. Home Rule movement began in 1870 and was strengthened by rise of Charles Stewart PARNELL who unified Irish party in British Parliament. Accompanied by a campaign of violence in Ireland. First Home Rule Bill introduced by Gladstone (1886) failed to pass. Second Home Rule Bill (1893) was passed by House of Commons but defeated by House of Lords. Third Home Rule Bill passed by Commons (1912) led to threats of civil war and House of Lords excluded Ulster. Bill never took effect because 1916 rebellion led to recognition of the Irish Free State with dominion status in 1921. Since 1949 Republic of Ireland has had no legal ties to Britain. N. Ireland is governed under the Fourth Home Rule Bill of 1920.

home rule, municipal, system permitting cities to draft and amend their own charters without state interference. Adopted first (1875) in Missouri and now also used in other states, it has not—because of great variation from state to state and court strictures—accomplished all that was expected of it.

Homestead, borough (pop. 10,046), SW Pa., on Monongahela R. adjoining Pittsburgh. Iron and steel works (now largely in Munhall borough) were scene of bitter **Homestead strike** (1892). Pinkerton men, hired by Carnegie company, and strikers met in armed battle in which a number of men were killed or wounded. Strike broken when governor called out Natl. Guard.

Homestead Act, 1862, passed by U.S. Congress. It gave a quarter section of unoccupied public land to homesteader for nominal fee after five years' residence. It replaced earlier government practice of selling land for purposes of revenue.

Homestead National Monument of America: see NATIONAL PARKS AND MONUMENTS (table).

Homestead strike: see HOMESTEAD, Pa.

homicide (hŏ'mĭsĭd), taking of human life. A homicide is considered excusable if it results from an accident not amounting to culpable negligence. Justifiable homicide is defined variously but generally includes legal execution of criminals, killing committed to prevent a felony or arrest a felon, and killing in self-defense (i.e., committed by someone reasonably fearing death or serious injury at the hands of the person slain). Other homicides are criminal; if committed with malice aforethought the homicide is murder, otherwise manslaughter—though statutes in various states use different terminology.

hominy, hulled corn, coarsely broken or ground. As a pioneer food it was prepared by soaking grains in weak wood lye. Now marketed as hominy grits.

Homma, Masaharu (mäsä'härōō hōmä'), 1888?–1946, Japanese general. Led invasion of Philippines 1941; ordered Bataan "death march." Hanged 1946 as war criminal.

Homs (hôms), anc. *Emesa,* city (pop. c.100,000), W Syria, on Orontes R. and S of Hama. The Roman emperor Heliogabalus was originally a priest of Homs temple to Baal. Here Aurelian defeated Zenobia's forces in 272. Name also written as Hems.

Honan (hō'nän', hŭnän'), province (55,000 sq. mi.; pop. 25,000,000), N central China; cap. Kaifeng. Mountainous with fertile valleys in SW and N. Main products: rice, silk, cotton, peanuts. Some coal and iron mined. Earliest region of Chinese settlement.

Honduras (hŏndōō'rŭs), republic (59,160 sq. mi.; pop. 1,533,625), Central America, bordering on Nicaragua, Salvador, and Guatemala, with Caribbean and Pacific coasts; cap. TEGUCIGALPA. The N (Caribbean coast) has on its W half vast banana plantations owned by U.S. companies; principal ports are Trujillo, La Ceiba, Tela, and Puerto Cortés. S (Pacific) coast largely semiarid and unproductive; has small port of Amapala. Between the coasts are mountain ranges, ending in the E in jungles and swamps of MOSQUITO COAST. Silver mining developed Comayagua and Tegucigalpa, and silver is still exported. First visited by Columbus (1502), it was reached by Cortés (1524) and conquered and settled by Pedro de Alvarado. Gained independence from Spain (1821) then was part of Iturbide's Mexican Empire and a member of the CENTRAL AMERICAN FEDERATION (1825–38). Great Britain long controlled all the Mosquito Coast and the BAY ISLANDS, and Honduras has been involved in long border struggles with neighbors. The country is generally self-sufficient in foodstuffs, but foreign capital is the basic factor in the economy.

Hone, Philip, 1780–1851, American diarist. A successful businessman, he was (1825) mayor of New York. His diary (1828–51) is an invaluable historical record.

Honegger, Arthur (hŭ'nĕgŭr), 1892–, Swiss-French composer. His music, often polytonal, ranges from satire to the intensely religious. Besides *Pacific 231,* his best-known works are largely theatrical, such as ballets, the operas *Judith* and *Antigone,* and the oratorio *King David.*

Honesdale, borough (pop. 5,662), NE Pa., on Lackawaxen R. and NE of Scranton. Mfg. of shoes and textiles. First regular trial run of a locomotive in U.S. made here 1829. Was NW terminus of Delaware and Hudson Canal.

honey, sweet, viscid fluid produced by the bee from nectar of flowers. Taken into worker bee's honey sack, nectar is converted by enzymes there into glucose and fructose sugars. The bees put the fluid in open wax cells of the honeycomb; after evaporation to proper consistency, it is sealed in. Average bee colony requires for its own use 400–500 lb. of honey a year; at least 20,000 trips to field are needed to make 1 lb. Production on commercial scale is in apiaries. Color and flavor of honey depend upon the kind of flower nectar used.

honey locust, thorny leguminous deciduous tree (*Gleditsia triacanthos*) native to E U.S. and widely planted as a shade tree. It has fragrant flowers and the fruits are long pods often used as cattle feed.

honeysuckle, ornamental shrub or vine of genus *Lonicera,* widely distributed in N Hemisphere. White, red, or purple flowers, usually fragrant, are followed by variously colored berries.

Hong Kong (hŏng' kŏng'), Chinese *Hsiang-chiang,* British crown colony (391 sq. mi.; pop. 1,850,000), S China, adjoining Kwantung prov.; cap. Hong Kong (Victoria). Comprises Hong Kong isl. (32 sq. mi.) ceded by China in 1842; Kowloon peninsula (c.3 sq. mi.), ceded 1860; and the New Territories (359 sq. mi.), on adjoining mainland area with Mirs Bay, leased in 1898 for 99 years. Hong Kong city is chief port and distributing center for S China; also an international air hub. Surrendered Dec. 25, 1941, to Japan; restored to the British after World War II. Refugees from Communist-held area of China swelled colony's population 1948–49.

Honolulu (hŏnůlōō'lōō), city (pop. 248,034), cap. Territory of Hawaii, on SE shore of Oahu. With Palmyra it constitutes Honolulu co. (pop. 353,020). Chief port of Hawaiian Isls. and vital stopover point for air service between U.S. mainland and Orient. Lies on narrow plain between the sea and Koolau Range. Famous bathing beach at Waikiki. Notable institutions are Univ. of HAWAII, Bishop Mus. (1889), and Acad. of Arts (1926). Iolani Palace (former home of Hawaiian kings) is territorial capitol. Succeeded Lahaina, Maui, as Hawaiian cap. in 1845. Has sugar refineries, pineapple canneries. Pearl Harbor naval base near by.

Honorius I (hŏnô'rēŭs), pope (625–38). Wrote a letter apparently supporting the heresy of MONOTHELETISM. He and the letter were condemned by the Third Council of Constantinople, but this condemnation is held not to affect the doctrine of papal infallibility because Honorius was not speaking *ex cathedra.*

Honorius II, d. 1130, pope (1124–30). As adviser to Paschal II, he concluded the Concordat of Worms (1122) with German King Henry V. Supported Lothair II, who yielded to church demands on episcopal election. Quarreled with Henry I of England.

Honorius III, d. 1227, pope (1216–27), an Italian, successor of Innocent III. He had been tutor to Frederick II, crowned him, and tried in vain to get the emperor to go on crusade.

Honorius, 384–423, West Roman emperor (395–423); son of Theodosius I. His brother Arcadius inherited the East. Honorius had his guardian STILICHO murdered in 408. He held out at Ravenna against ALARIC I (409–10) but made peace with the Visigoths in 412. In 421 he had to make his brother-in-law joint emperor as CONSTANTIUS III. His reign marked important stage in decline of Western Empire.

Honshu (hōn'shōō), island (c.88,000 sq. mi.; pop. 58,769,968), central Japan, between Sea of Japan and the Pacific; largest and most important island of Japan. Largely mountainous, rises to 12,389 ft. at Fujiyama; Mt. Asama highest of active volcanoes. Chief lowland area is Kanto Plain in central part. Climate ranges from extreme cold of N to subtropical warmth of S. Frequent earthquakes. Agr. and raw-silk production are widespread. Heavy industry at Yokohama, Tokyo, Nagoya, Osaka, Kobe.

Honthorst, Gerard van (gĕr'ärt vän hŏnt'hôrst), 1590–1656, Dutch painter, called Gerardo dalle Notti for his preference for nocturnal scenes.

Hooch or **Hoogh, Pieter de** (both: pē'tŭr dů hōkh), b. c.1629, d. after 1677, noted Dutch genre painter. Typical themes are quiet domestic interiors, often with housewives and children.

Hood, John Bell, 1831–79, Confederate general. Commanded in ATLANTA CAMPAIGN. Advanced to Nashville, Tenn., where forces were virtually annihilated by G. H. Thomas. Resigned command Jan., 1865.

Hood, Raymond M(athewson), 1881–1934, American architect. Designed Daily News Building (New York).

Hood, Thomas, 1799–1845, English poet, known today especially for poems of sentiment and social protest ("The Bridge of Sighs" and "The Song of the Shirt"). Also wrote humorous verse and prose.

Hood, Mount: see CASCADE RANGE.

Hood College: see FREDERICK, Md.

Hood River, city (pop. 3,701), N Oregon, on Columbia R., E of Portland, and near Mt. Hood. Area noted for fruits (esp. apples). Annual music fete.

hoof, horny epidermal casing at end of digits of an ungulate mammal. In some animals (pig, sheep, cattle) hoof is cloven, in others (horse, zebra) solid.

hoof and mouth disease: see FOOT AND MOUTH DISEASE.

Hooft, Pieter Corneliszoon (hôft), 1581–1647, Dutch historian and poet, author of a classic history (1642, incomplete) of the Netherlands from 1555 to 1584. A fine lyric poet, he introduced into Dutch the tones of French and Italian Renaissance love poetry.

Hoogh, Pieter de: see HOOCH, PIETER DE.

Hooghly (hōō'glē), river, c.200 mi. long, West Bengal, India; arm of Ganges R. Shipping artery to major industrial area around Calcutta. On it is town of Hooghly, founded 1537 by the Portuguese.

Hooke, Robert, 1635–1703, English scientist. He was first to formulate the theory of planetary movements as a mechanical problem. He improved astronomical instruments; devised practical system of telegraphy; invented spiral watch spring; constructed first arithmetical machine and Gregorian telescope. He described cells in plant tissues. **Hooke's Law:** within the limit of elasticity, the stress on a body is in direct proportion to strain.

Hooker, Joseph, 1814–79, Union general in Civil War. Known as "Fighting Joe." Commanded Army of the Potomac; defeated at Chancellorsville (1863). Commanded ably in Chattanooga campaign.

Hooker, Richard, 1554?–1600, noted English theologian. His *Of the Laws of Ecclesiastical Polity* formulated concepts of Anglicanism and influenced civil as well as ecclesiastical government.

Hooker, Thomas, 1586–1647, Puritan clergyman in American colonies, chief founder of Hartford, Conn. (1635–36), b. England.

Hooke's law: see HOOKE, ROBERT.

Hook of Holland, Dutch *Hoek van Holland,* port (pop. 2,536), South Holland prov., SW Netherlands, on North Sea; an outer port of Rotterdam. Terminus for Channel crossings from Harwich, England.

hookworm (ancylostomiasis), disease in man caused by certain parasitic nematode worms lodged in intestine. Anemia results from blood sucking and bleeding. Worm egg passed from intestine of victim develop into larva stage in warm, moist soil, then burrow into skin of persons in contact with infected soil and travel by way of body fluids to lungs and thence to pharynx where they are swallowed.

Hoopeston (hoōp'stŭn), city (pop. 5,992), E Ill., N of Danville. Canning (corn, beans) center.

Hoorn or **Horn, Philip de Montmorency, count of** (both: hôrn), 1518?–1568, Netherlands nobleman. Joined EGMONT in protesting Spanish abuses in the Netherlands. Was beheaded after an irregular trial. He is a national hero.

Hoosac Range (hoō'sŭk), S continuation of Green Mts. in SW Vt. and NW Mass., E of the Berkshires. Pierced by 5-mi. railroad tunnel (built 1852–73).

Hooton, Earnest Albert (hoō'tŭn), 1887–, American anthropologist, specialist on early man and primates.

Hoover, Herbert (Clark), 1874–, 30th President of the United States (1929–33), b. Iowa. Before 1915 he engaged in world-wide mining and engineering activities. Headed food administration and war relief bureaus during and after World War I. As U.S. Secretary of Commerce (1921–29), he reorganized and expanded department. Stock market crash of 1929 ushered in an economic depression which continued throughout his administration as president. Hoover recommended extensive public works, appointed commissions to study urgent problems. Destitute farmers were aided by Federal Farm Board. RECONSTRUCTION FINANCE CORPORATION was created. Congress, which had a Democratic majority after 1930 election, passed Emergency Relief Act and created Federal home loan banks. Veterans seeking a bonus marched on Washington; Hoover ordered Federal troops to oust them from Federal property. Disarmament conferences were ineffective (see NAVAL CONFERENCES); debt moratorium which Hoover proposed in 1931 to alleviate Germany's financial situation had no practical results. Hoover left office in 1933 during serious banking crisis. Handled world food problems in 1946. Headed "Hoover Commission" (1947–49), which studied and advised on organization of the executive branch of government.

Hoover, J(ohn) Edgar, 1895–, American administrator, director of the FEDERAL BUREAU OF INVESTIGATION (1924–).

Hoover Dam, in Black Canyon, at Nev.-Ariz. line, in Colorado R.; built 1931–36. One of world's largest, 727 ft. high, 1,282 ft. long. Key unit of projects on Colorado R., it provides water power (mainly to Calif.), flood control, and irrigation. Formerly called Boulder Dam (1933–47). L. Mead, reservoir, 115 mi. long, is resort center.

Hoover Library on War, Revolution, and Peace, at Stanford Univ., Palo Alto, Calif.; estab. 1919 by Herbert Hoover. Contains mostly materials on period of World War I and afterward. Housed in Hoover Tower since 1941.

hop, perennial twining vine (*Humulus lupulus*) grown from early times for brewing purposes. The conelike female flowers, "hops," contain lupulin, a bitter-tasting yellow powder added to beer.

Hopatcong, Lake (hōpăt'kŏn), c.7 mi. long and 3 mi. wide, N N.J., NW of Dover. Summer resort.

Hope, Anthony, pseud. of Sir Anthony Hope Hawkins, 1863–1933, English novelist, known for his romantic *Prisoner of Zenda* (1894).

Hope, city (pop. 8,605), SW Ark., ENE of Texarkana. Shipping center for farm products (esp. watermelons), it has cotton processing, woodworking.

Hopeh or **Ho-pei** (both: hō'pā, hŭ'bā'), province (50,000 sq. mi.; pop. 27,000,000), N China, on Gulf of Chihli of Yellow Sea; cap. Paoting. Bounded in N along Great Wall by Manchuria. Lies entirely on alluvial plain. Crops include wheat, millet, kaoliang, and soybeans. Major coal mines here. Chief centers are Peking and Tientsin. Held 1937–45 by the Japanese; under Chinese Communists since 1949. Formerly called Chihli.

Hope Island: see SPITSBERGEN.

Hopewell. 1 Borough (pop. 1,869), W N.J., N of Trenton. John Hart lived here. Has historical museum. Home for juvenile delinquents near here is former Lindbergh estate (deeded to state 1941). **2** City (pop. 10,219), E Va., at junction of James and Appomattox rivers; founded 1913 as munitions center. Mfg. of rayon, chemicals, and cans. City Point (annexed 1926) was Grant's base of operations in 1864–65.

Hopewell Village, national historic site, SE Pa., SE of Birdsboro. Restored iron-making village of 18th and 19th cent.

Hophni (hŏf'nī), wicked son of Eli. See PHINEHAS.

Hopi Indians (hō'pē), tribe of Pueblo Indians, formerly called Moki, or Moqui. Almost all speak Hopi language (Uto-Aztecan family). They live in pueblos, practice sedentary farming (corn, beans, squash), with irrigation. The highly developed Hopi culture is typical of Southwest Indians.

Hopkins, Sir Frederick Gowland, 1861–1947, English biochemist. Shared 1929 Nobel Prize in Physiology and Medicine for pioneer work on vitamins. Authority on carbohydrate metabolism and muscular activity.

Hopkins, Gerard Manley, 1844–89, English poet. Followed Newman into Roman Catholicism, and became a Jesuit. Wrote best poetry after shipwreck called forth "Wreck of the

Deutschland." His *Poems*, edited by Robert Bridges, appeared in 1918, and have had much influence on 20th-cent. poets.

Hopkins, Harry (Lloyd), 1890–1946, American public official. Intimate friend of Pres. F. D. Roosevelt, held high posts as his special assistant.

Hopkins, Johns, 1795–1873, American financier and philanthropist. In 1867 he founded a free hospital and Johns Hopkins Univ. at Baltimore.

Hopkins, Mark, 1802–87, American educator. He was professor of philosophy at Williams until his death and president of the college from 1836 to 1872. He was also president of American Board of Commissioners for Foreign Missions, 1857–87.

Hopkins, Samuel, 1721–1803, New England clergyman and theologian. He adopted doctrine of Jonathan Edwards as basis of his own, called Hopkinsianism.

Hopkins, Stephen, 1707–85, colonial governor of R.I., American Revolutionary patriot, signer of Declaration of Independence. Governor for nine years between 1755 and 1768.

Hopkins, village (pop. 7,595), E Minn., SW suburb of Minneapolis, in truck-farm area. Mfg. of farm machinery.

Hopkinson, Francis, 1737–91, American writer and musician, signer of Declaration of Independence. Considered first native American composer. Wrote political satires.

Hopkinsville, city (pop. 12,526), S Ky., WSW of Bowling Green. Tobacco and livestock market with mfg. of clothing. Jefferson Davis Memorial Park near by.

Hopkinton, town (pop. 1,831), S N.H., W of Concord. Long Memorial Library holds New Hampshire Antiquarian Society collection. Congregational Church (1789) has a Paul Revere bell.

Hoppe, William Frederick (Willie Hoppe) (hŏ′pē), 1887–, American billiards champion. Generally acknowledged world's billiard champion since 1906.

Hopper, DeWolf, 1858–1935, American singer and comedian. Associated (1895–1904) with Weber and Fields, he later sang in Gilbert and Sullivan operettas (e.g., Bunthorne in *Patience*). Made recitation "Casey at the Bat" famous.

Hopper, Edward, 1882–, American painter. Excels in realistic pictures of sunlit streets and houses.

Hoppner, John, 1758–1810, English portrait painter, known for idealized portraits of women and children. Was a protégé of George III.

hops: see HOP.

Hoquiam (hŏ′kwēŭm), city (pop. 11,123), W Wash., on Grays Harbor adjoining ABERDEEN; settled 1859.

Hor, mountain (4,383 ft.), SW Jordan, overlooking ruins of Petra. Peak was scene of Aaron's death. Num. 20. Called Jebel Nebi Harun in Arabic. The Hor of Num. 34.7 is probably Mt. Hermon.

Horace (Quintus Horatius Flaccus), 65 B.C.–8 B.C., Latin lyric poet. Vergil introduced him to MAECENAS, who became his patron. His *Satires* and *Epodes* (35–29 B.C.) established him as leading lyric poet in Rome. The *Odes*, *Epistles*, and *Ars Poetica*, products of

his mature years at Sabine farm, display his mastery of phrase and poetic form. His verse, though it owes something to the Greek Archilochus, reflects an emancipated Roman cultivation of the arts and the true spirit of the Augustan Age. He was an urbane Epicurean, and the pungency, beauty, and descriptive power of his verse influenced greatly English poetry.

Horae (hō′rē), three Greek symbolic personages, controlling order of nature and recurrence of seasons; daughters of Zeus and Themis. They were Irene (īrē′nē), i.e., Peace, Dice (dī′sē), i.e., Justice, and Eunomia (ūnō′mēŭ), i.e., Order.

Horatius (hōrā′shŭs), legendary Roman hero. He and two companions held Lars Porsena's Etruscan army at bay while the Romans cut down the Sublician Bridge to protect the city. He then swam the Tiber safely and was given as much land as he could plow around in a day.

Horeb, mountain where God appeared to Moses in burning bush. Ex. 3–4.17. May be same as Mt. SINAI.

horehound, aromatic Old World perennial herb (*Marrubium vulgare*) with woolly-white foliage. Used to make horehound candy and cough and cold remedies.

Horemheb: see HARMHAB.

hormone: see GLAND and SECRETION.

Hormuz (hôr′mŭz″) or **Ormuz,** island, off S Iran, in Strait of Hormuz between Persian Gulf and Gulf of Oman. Town of Hormuz was chief trade center for Persian Gulf area, 16th–17th cent. Portuguese under Afonso de Albuquerque took the island (1507–14), but lost it (1622) to Persian-English forces.

Horn, Philip de Montmorency, count of: see HOORN.

horn, in biology, organ projecting from head of animal and used chiefly in offense and defense. Three main types among mammals: hollow, permanent, unbranched horns, each horn overlying a bony core growing on skull (as in cattle, sheep, buffalo, musk oxen, Old World antelopes, related animals); branched horns or antlers of DEER family composed of true bone, usually shed annually; and that of the PRONGHORN, with characteristics of both bovine and deer types. Rhinoceros horns derive entirely from epidermis of skin of snout; probably are modified hairs.

horn, in music: see WIND INSTRUMENTS.

Horn, Cape, headland, 1,391 ft. high, S Chile, most southerly point of South America, in archipelago of Tierra del Fuego. Discovered and first rounded by Willem Schouten in 1616.

Hornaday, William Temple (hôr′nŭdā), 1854–1937, American naturalist, leader in wildlife conservation.

hornbeam, deciduous tree of genus *Carpinus* native to N Hemisphere. American hornbeam, blue beech, or ironwood (*Carpinus caroliniana*) has strong wood used for tool handles, etc. The hop hornbeam (*Ostrya virginiana*), also called ironwood, and of same family, has wood of similar strength and value.

horned toad, lizard, several species of which live in deserts of SW U.S. and Mexico. Body (3–5 in. long) is broad and flattened, the tail short and thin, and the legs short. Spines are on the head; some scales on sides and back are sharp. It is protectively colored, usually dull grays and browns.

Hornell, city (pop. 15,049), S N.Y., S of Rochester. Mfg. of textiles, clothing, and furniture.

hornet: see WASP.

Horney, Karen, 1885–1952, American psychiatrist, b. Germany. She was founder (1941) and dean of American Inst. of Psychoanalysis. She modified orthodox Freudian analysis by emphasis on social factors, holding that environmental disturbances cause "basic anxiety" that forces one to meet problems in new ways (neurotic because rigid and compulsive).

Hornsby, Rogers, 1896–, American baseball player and manager. Had lifetime batting average of .358 in 19 major-league seasons, hit (1924) .424, a 20th-cent. major-league record, was Natl. League batting champion seven times.

horoscope: see ASTROLOGY.

Horowitz, Vladimir (hŏ′rōwĭts), 1904–, Russian-American pianist, known for his technical virtuosity; son-in-law of Toscanini. Made his American debut in 1928 with the New York Philharmonic.

Horsa: see HENGIST AND HORSA.

horse. The horse family (Equidae) is now represented by only one genus (Equus) which includes the horse, the ASS, the ZEBRA, and the QUAGGA (extinct from 1872). Evolution of the horse from its tiny primitive ancestor (Eohippus) occurred in North America, whence it reached the Old World over a now vanished land bridge. Horses became extinct in America about the time the Indians arrived. One of the last animals to be domesticated, the horse was probably first tamed by central Asian nomads. First used in hunting and war, it did not supersede the ox for farm work until the 19th cent. Modern draft horses owe much of their quality to the breeding of heavy chargers in the Middle Ages. The Percheron, of French origin, is the chief draft breed in America. The Arabian breed has the longest history; it and the thoroughbred are primarily saddle horses. All wild horses now living, except the TARPAN, are descended from tame horses. See also MUSTANG.

Horse Cave, town (pop. 1,545), S Ky., E of Mammoth Cave Natl. Park. Resort of cave area. Hidden River Cave underlies part of town.

horse chestnut, deciduous tree (Aesculus hippocastanum) of Mediterranean region, widely planted for ornament and shade. It has pyramidal clusters of white or salmon flowers and nonedible chestnutlike fruits.

horsefly, large, swift, hairy fly of family Tabanidae, a common pest of stock and sometimes of humans. Male sucks flower nectar; female sucks blood as well. Some transmit disease. In North America are nearly 200 species of genus Tabanus. Genus Chrysops includes smaller horseflies; some attack man. Eggs are laid on plants or stones close to water.

horsehair worm: see HAIRWORM.

horse latitudes, two belts of calms (with generally fair weather) between trade winds and

prevailing westerlies; about 30° or 35°N and S.

horsepower, unit of power (rate of doing work) originated by James Watt. He determined experimentally that a horse can do work equal to 33,000 foot-pounds per minute; this unit is now standard in computing power generated by an engine.

horse-radish, perennial herb (Armoracia lapathifolia) native to S and central Europe and naturalized in North America. The grated roots are mixed with vinegar to make a sharp sauce for meats and sea food.

horsetail, perennial rushlike plants of genus Equisetum, related to ferns and club mosses. They have jointed hollow stems and small scaly leaves.

Horsley, Samuel, 1733–1806, English bishop and scientist, particularly remembered for controversy (c.1783–1790) with Joseph Priestley concerning doctrine of Christ's incarnation.

Horsley, Sir Victor, 1857–1916, English surgeon, a specialist in surgery of the ductless glands and the nervous system.

Horta (hôr′tủ), city (pop. 8,184), cap. of Horta dist., Portugal, on Fayal isl., one of Azores.

Horthy (de Nagybanya), Nicholas (hôr′tē dủ nŏ′dyủbä′nyŏ), Hung. Nagybányai Horthy Miklós, 1868–, Hungarian admiral and statesman. Headed counterrevolutionary government during Communist dictatorship of Bela Kun (1919); was regent of HUNGARY 1920–44. Forced to resign by German pressure after his attempt to make an armistice with Russia, he fled to Bavaria, where he later was briefly held a prisoner by the U.S. army (1945).

horticulture, a branch of agr.; includes cultivation of ornamental plants, market gardening, fruit growing, landscape gardening. Known to prehistoric peoples and in civilizations of both East and West. Formal gardening developed first in irrigated regions of Orient. Crusaders disseminated in Europe many ideas gathered from Eastern gardens. Horticulture has become a complex science; the Dept. of Agr., state experiment stations, agr. colleges, and horticultural societies in the U.S. provide information.

Horus (hō′rủs), sun-god, one of great gods of EGYPTIAN RELIGION, often identified with Amon. A popular myth tells how he avenged death of father, Osiris, aided by his mother, Isis, and the god Thoth.

Hosanna [perhaps Heb.,= save now; cf. Ps. 118.25,26], word shouted in greeting to Jesus as He entered Jerusalem. Mat. 21.9,15; Mark 11.9,10; John 12.13. Mistaken by early Christians as a joyous salutation; in this sense widely used in Christian worship today.

Hosea (hōzē′ủ) or **Osee** (ōsē′), book of Old Testament, written by prophet of 8th cent. B.C. Book contains allegory comparing the idolatrous Israel to a faithless woman; sermons against moral decadence; promise that after punishment will come redemption.

Hoshea (hōshē′ủ). **1** See JOSHUA. **2** Died after 722 B.C., last king of Israel (c.730–722 B.C.). A vassal of king of Assyria, he rebelled. Israel was invaded, Hoshea taken prisoner. 2 Kings 15.30; 17.

Hospitalers: see KNIGHTS HOSPITALERS.

Host, in Roman Catholic communion: see EUCHARIST.

hostage (hŏ'stǐj), person delivered by a constituted authority to another as guarantee that some stated promise will be executed or some stated loyalty upheld. In the Middle Ages the practice of giving hostages for fulfillment of treaty obligations was common and was governed by a strict code of feudal honor; this practice was generally abandoned in the 18th cent. The fundamental idea was that the hostage might be killed if the obligation was not fulfilled. By extension the seizure of civilians in an occupied country is called taking of hostages. The practice has been known since early times. In World War II the Germans used it ruthlessly in an attempt to put down resistance movements. Germans responsible for the massacre of such hostages were tried as war criminals.

Hostos, Eugenio María de (ā͞o͞ohā'nyō märē'ä dā ō'stōs), 1839–1903, Latin American philosopher, sociologist, writer, and political and educational reformer, b. Puerto Rico.

hothouse: see GREENHOUSE.

Hotin, Ukraine: see KHOTIN.

Hot Springs. 1 Resort city (pop. 29,307), SW central Ark., in Ouachita Mts. SW of Little Rock; settled 1807. It is in Hot Springs Natl. Park. **2** See TRUTH OR CONSEQUENCES, N.Mex. **3** City (pop. 5,030), SW S.Dak., SSW of Rapid City, near Cheyenne R. and the Black Hills. Health resort with hot sulphur springs. Fossil Cycad and Jewel Cave national monuments and Wind Cave Natl. Park are near. **4** Famous resort, western Va., WSW of Staunton, in a valley of the Allegheny Mts.

Hot Springs National Park: see NATIONAL PARKS AND MONUMENTS, table.

Hotspur: see PERCY, SIR HENRY.

Hottentots (hŏ'tŭntŏts″), people of S and SW Africa numbering c.20,000 and resembling the Bushmen in language and physical type. They were forced into the interior by Dutch. Economy based on herding with some farming and metallurgy.

Hötzendorf, Franz Conrad von: see CONRAD VON HÖTZENDORF, FRANZ.

Houdin, Jean Eugène Robert (zhä' ûzhĕn' rōbĕr' ōōdē'), 1805–71, French conjurer and magician. He was noted for his optical illusions and for fact that he made no claim that his devices were supernatural.

Houdini, Harry (hōōdē'nē), 1874–1926, American magician and writer. Born Erich Weiss, he took his stage name after the French magician Houdin. He was world famed for escapes from bonds and noted for his exposure of fraudulent mediums and their phenomena.

Houdon, Jean Antoine (zhä' ätwän' ōōdō'), 1741–1828, French sculptor. His portrait sculpture has hardly been surpassed (esp. his *Voltaire* in Comédie Française). Bronze copy of his *Washington* and his *Bathers* are in Metropolitan Mus.

Houghton, Richard Monckton Milnes, 1st **Baron** (hô'tǔn, hou'–), 1809–85, English author, philanthropist, and patron of letters.

Houghton (hô'tǔn), village (pop. 3,829), extreme N Mich., opposite Hancock on Keweenaw Waterway. Here are Michigan Col. of Mining and Technology and mainland hq. of Isle Royale Natl. Park.

Hougue, La, France: see HOGUE, LA.

Houlton (hōl'tǔn), town (pop. 8,377), including Houlton village (pop. 6,029), E Maine, NNE of Bangor, near N.B. line. Potato-growing and resort center.

Houma (hō'mù), city (pop. 11,505), SE La., on Bayou Terrebonne and SW of New Orleans; founded 1834. On Intercoastal Waterway, it processes and ships seafood, fur, oil, and sugar cane.

hound. Certain hunting dogs of various breeds are known as hounds. Usually hounds are classified as to whether they follow the prey chiefly by scent (e.g., dachshund, beagle, foxhound, bloodhound, and great Dane) or by sight (e.g., greyhound, Afghan hound, Irish wolfhound, and borzoi or Russian wolfhound). The dachshund is distinguished by its long body and short legs—a body three times as long as the dog is high at the shoulder being considered a good proportion. It has an elongated, tapered head, forefeet that turn outward, and ears of medium length. Its coat may be smooth, wiry, or long-haired. The beagle is a small (not over 15 in. high), smooth-haired dog with ears of medium length. The larger foxhound is bred for speed and used in packs. Like the beagle, it has the typical hound markings—black saddle, tan on legs, hips, and shoulder, with a varying amount of white. The bloodhound has very long soft ears and thin, loose skin falling in folds around head and neck. It combines the hound colors of black or red with tan or tawny, stands 25–27 in. high, and weighs c.90 lb. Its remarkable sense of smell makes it valuable in following a trail in police work. It has a gentle disposition. The great Dane (c.30 in. at shoulder) is a sleek, short-haired dog of obscure origin. In color it varies from brindle, fawn, or black, to white with black spots. It is powerful and fast and makes an excellent watch dog. The greyhound is a tall (28–31 in. at shoulder), slender dog with narrow pointed nose and short hair; it is usually gray in color. Graceful and very swift, it is trained for racing and sometimes achieves speeds of 35 mi. per hour or more. Related to the greyhound is the Afghan hound. Its coat is thick and silky; its head has a topknot; and its legs and ears are feathered. The term *wolfhound* is applied to several breeds of dogs but especially to the Irish wolfhound and the borzoi or Russian wolfhound. The Irish wolfhound is more robust than the greyhound but less massive than the great Dane. Tallest of dogs, it may reach 36 in. at the shoulder, weighs at least 120 lb., and is cream, brindle, or gray to black in color. The borzoi is 30 in. high, weighs 75–105 lb., and has a long narrow head. It is usually white marked with lemon, tan, black, or gray.

Hounslow, suburb in Heston and Isleworth urban district, Middlesex, England, W of London; once an important coach stop. Hounslow Heath, near here, was noted as a resort for highwaymen.

hours of labor: see LABOR, HOURS OF.

Housatonic (hōōsùtŏn'ĭk), river rising in the Berkshires, W Mass., and flowing c.130 mi.

S through Conn. to Long Isl. Sound at Milford.

House, E(dward) M(andell), 1858–1938, American statesman. Col. House (a Texas state title) was a confidant of Pres. Woodrow Wilson. Helped to draft Treaty of Versailles, particularly concerned with drawing up of Covenant of the League of Nations.

housefly, common name of *Musca domestica*, found over most of world. It visits excrement and other filth and transports bacteria, protozoa of many diseases (typhoid fever, cholera, dysentery) in its digestive system, on hairy body, and sticky foot pads. Breeds in manure and other decaying organic matter; larvae are white maggots. It ejects a liquefying material on food before eating it. See *ill.*, p. 601.

House of Commons: see PARLIAMENT; WESTMINSTER PALACE.

House of David: see BENTON HARBOR, Mich.

House of Lords: see PARLIAMENT; WESTMINSTER PALACE.

House of Representatives: see CONGRESS OF THE UNITED STATES.

housing, the living accommodations provided for people in a community. Housing for workers during Industrial Revolution was constructed by employers on a profit basis. First housing legislation in U.S. was N.Y. tenement house law of 1867. Government housing began in World War I. Housing shortages in Europe in the '20s resulted in government construction of workers' apartments. In England the GARDEN CITY was developed. In 1934, the U.S. set up the Federal Housing Administration to insure private loans and mortgages; in 1937 the U.S. Housing Authority was established; and in 1942 the Federal Public Housing Authority was formed. Mass production methods, such as prefabrication, are now widely used.

Housman, A(lfred) E(dward), 1859–1936, English poet. A classical scholar, he edited Manlius, Juvenal, and Lucian. He is best known for his lyrics, such as "Bredon Hill" and "Loveliest of Trees." Volumes include *A Shropshire Lad* (1896), *Last Poems* (1922), and *Collected Poems* (1940). His brother **Laurence Housman**, 1865–, author and artist, is best known for *Victoria Regina* (1934), a dramatic biography compiled from his play cycle *Palace Plays* (1930–33).

Houssay, Bernardo Alberto (bĕrnär'dhō älbĕr'tō ou'sī), 1887–, Argentine physiologist. Shared 1947 Nobel Prize in Physiology and Medicine for demonstrating role of pituitary secretion in inhibiting body's use of insulin.

Houston, Sam(uel) (hū'stŭn), 1793–1863, American frontier hero and statesman of Texas. Commanding Texas revolutionary troops, he captured Santa Anna at battle of SAN JACINTO (April 21, 1836). First president of Texas republic 1836–38; again president 1841–44. U.S. Senator 1846–59. Governor of Texas 1859–61; his refusal to join the Confederacy brought about his removal.

Houston (hū'stŭn) [for Gen. Samuel Houston], city (pop. 596,163), S Texas, on Gulf Coast plain NW of Galveston Bay. Harrisburg (now part of Houston) settled 1823; Houston settled 1836. Cap. of Texas republic 1837–39. Grew in 19th cent. as railroad and shipping center. Great expansion came with ship canal (1912–14; making it deepwater port), and development of Gulf Coast oil fields. One of main U.S. ports and Texas' largest city, it has mfg. of metals, chemicals, food products, and paper; also oil refineries. World War II brought many industries, including shipbuilding. Seat of RICE INSTITUTE and Texas Medical Center. Battlefield of SAN JACINTO is near by.

Hovenden, Thomas, 1840–95, American genre painter, b. Ireland; studied in New York and Paris.

Hovenweep National Monument: see NATIONAL PARKS AND MONUMENTS (table).

Hovey, Richard (hŭ'vē), 1864–1900, American poet; author of *Songs from Vagabondia* (1894; with Bliss Carman).

Howard, British noble family. First called Hereward, their career in England goes back to 10th cent. A Hereward fought against William I. His descendants were created earls of Arundel (1139), Barons Maltravers (1330), earls of Surrey and dukes of Norfolk (1483), Barons Fitzalan (1627), earls of Norfolk (1644), and Barons Herries (1884). **John Howard, 1st duke of Norfolk**, 1430–85, adherent of the house of York in the Wars of the Roses, was killed at Bosworth fighting for Richard III. His son, **Thomas Howard, 2d duke of Norfolk**, 1443–1524, was imprisoned after Bosworth but released by Henry VII. Arranged the marriage of Margaret Tudor and James IV of Scotland. Became leading general of England and defeated (1513) the Scots at Flodden. He is the ancestor of all the living Howards in the main line. His son, **Thomas Howard, 3d duke of Norfolk**, 1473–1554, bitterly opposed Cardinal Wolsey. Supported the marriage of his niece, Anne Boleyn, to Henry VIII but later presided at her trial and execution. Remained Catholic although he conducted campaign against Pilgrimage of Grace in 1536. Accused of treason (1546), he was saved by death of Henry. Mary I released him (1553) and he led campaign against Wyatt's rebellion. His power had waned since the execution of his niece, **Catherine Howard**, 1521?–1542, queen of England, fifth wife of Henry VIII. Married in 1540, she was accused (1541) of immoral conduct and confessed. Beheaded largely to rid Henry of Howard family influence. **Henry Howard, earl of Surrey**, c.1517–1547, was the son of the 3d duke of Norfolk. A poet, he introduced new forms (chiefly blank verse) into English poetry. Arrested with his father on questionable treason charges, he was beheaded. His son, **Thomas Howard, 4th duke of Norfolk**, 1536–72, was favored by Elizabeth but jealous of the earl of Leicester. Became a candidate for the hand of Mary Queen of Scots and aroused Elizabeth's suspicions. Imprisoned (1569–70), he became involved in a Spanish plot on his release and was beheaded. His brother, **Henry Howard, earl of Northampton**, 1540–1614, was a courtier known for his great learning and lack of principle in public life. His cousin, **Charles Howard, 1st earl of Nottingham**, 1536–1624, was lord high admiral of England and commanded (1588) the forces against the Spanish Ar-

DIAGRAM OF STAIRS

Ramp · Corner post · Baluster · Handrail · Tread · Nosing · Drop · Landing · Riser · Newel post

Shingles · Building paper · Sheathing · Ridgepole · Rafter · Lath · Plaster · Subflooring · Partition cap · Stud · Window frame · Second-floor joist · Bridging · Diagonal brace · Girder · Door lintel · Ribband or ribbon board · First-floor joist · Stud · Sheathing · Sill · Girder post · Tar paper · Stone or concrete foundation · Clapboard · Corner post

SKELETON DIAGRAM OF HOUSE CONSTRUCTION
(BALLOON FRAMING)

SQUARE BUTT · RABBET · OBLIQUE · HOUSED · MITER · DOVETAIL · MORTISE AND TENON

TYPES OF JOINTS

Head casing · Side casing · Apron · Stool

DOUBLE-HUNG · CASEMENT · SLIDING · DORMER

TYPES OF WINDOWS

Overhang · Ridge · Pitch

SHED OR LEAN-TO · GABLE · HIP · GAMBREL · MANSARD

TYPES OF ROOFS

mada. **Thomas Howard, 1st earl of Suffolk,** 1561–1626, was son of the 4th duke of Norfolk. Commanded squadron that attacked Spanish treasure fleet in 1591. Became lord high treasurer in 1614. His daughter, Frances, and her husband, the earl of Somerset, were tried (1615) and convicted of the murder of Sir Thomas Overbury. Convicted (1619) of fraud and embezzlement as treasurer, Suffolk never regained power. **William Howard, 1st Viscount Stafford,** 1614–80, was the son of Thomas Howard, 2d earl of ARUNDEL. Falsely accused at the time of Popish Plot, he was convicted on false testimony of Titus Oates and others and beheaded. Other prominent Howards have included **Charles Howard, 1st earl of Carlisle,** 1629–85; **Frederick Howard, 5th earl of Carlisle,** 1748–1825, viceroy of Ireland and guardian of Lord Byron; and **Esme William Howard, 1st Baron Howard of Penrith,** 1863–1939, ambassador to U.S. 1924–30. Present head of the family is **Bernard Marmaduke Fitzalan-Howard,** 1908–, 16th **duke of Norfolk,** premier duke of the kingdom and hereditary earl marshal of England.

Howard, Bronson, 1842–1908, American dramatist. Among his plays are *Young Mrs. Winthrop* (1882; drama of social criticism), *The Henrietta* (1887; satire on American business), *Shenandoah* (1888; a Civil War play), and *Aristocracy* (1892).

Howard, Catherine; Charles, 1st earl of Carlisle; and Charles, 1st earl of Nottingham: see HOWARD, family.

Howard, Sir Ebenezer, 1850–1928, English town planner, chief founder of English garden-city movement.

Howard, Frederick, 5th earl of Carlisle: see HOWARD, family.

Howard, Henry, earl of Northampton; Henry, earl of Surrey; and John, 1st duke of Norfolk: see HOWARD, family.

Howard, Leland Ossian, 1857–1950, American entomologist. He profoundly influenced development of economic and medical entomology in America. Author of *The Insect Menace* (1931) and other works.

Howard, Leslie, 1893–1943, British actor. After his first appearance (in *Peg o' My Heart,* 1917) his air of gentle cynicism made him popular in U.S. and England in such plays as *Berkeley Square* and such films as *Of Human Bondage* and *Pygmalion.*

Howard, Oliver Otis, 1830–1909, Union general in Civil War. Fought in East from Bull Run through Gettysburg campaign. Commanded Army of the Tennessee in W. T. Sherman's march to sea. Advocate of Negro betterment, a founder of Howard Univ. and its president (1869–73).

Howard, Sidney (Coe), 1891–1939, American dramatist, author of *They Knew What They Wanted* (1924), *The Silver Cord* (1926), *Yellow Jack* (1934).

Howard, Thomas, dukes of Norfolk; Thomas, 1st earl of Suffolk; and William, 1st Viscount Stafford: see HOWARD, family.

Howard College: see BIRMINGHAM, Ala.

Howard of Penrith, Esme William Howard, 1st Baron: see HOWARD, family.

Howard University, at Washington, D.C.; predominantly Negro, nonsectarian, with congressional support, coed. Chartered and opened 1867 by Freedmen's Bureau under Gen. O. O. HOWARD and others.

Howe, Ed(gar Watson), 1853–1937, American editor and author. Known for pithy editorial paragraphs in Atchison, Kansas, *Daily Globe* and *E. W. Howe's Monthly.* Wrote realistic novel, *The Story of a Country Town* (1883).

Howe, Elias, 1819–67, American inventor. He obtained (1846) first patent on a lock-stitch sewing machine.

Howe, Joseph, 1804–73, Canadian journalist and statesman. In 1828 he became editor of the *Novascotian,* which became leading journal of the province. Campaigned for responsible government, but opposed confederation. Premier of N.S. (1860–63).

Howe, Julia Ward, 1819–1910, American author. Espoused reforms—abolition, woman suffrage, and world peace. Wrote *The Battle Hymn of the Republic.* Also aided her husband, **Samuel Gridley Howe,** 1801–76, reformer and philanthropist. He organized New England Asylum for the Blind (now Perkins Institution and Massachusetts School for the Blind) and headed it for 44 years.

Howe, Richard Howe, Earl, 1726–99, British admiral. Defended English Channel in Seven Years War. Commanded (1776–78) British fleet in American Revolution. Best known for victory over the French in 1794. His brother, **William Howe, 5th Viscount Howe,** 1729–1814, was a British general in American Revolution. Succeeded Gen. Thomas Gage as commander in chief (Oct., 1775). Commanded in successful battle of Long Island; defeated Washington at BRANDYWINE. Resigned 1778.

Howe, Samuel Gridley: see HOWE, JULIA WARD.

Howe, William Howe, 5th Viscount: see HOWE, RICHARD HOWE, EARL.

Howell, William Henry, 1860–1945, American physiologist, authority on blood clotting and nerve fibers, author of standard physiology textbook.

Howells, William Dean, 1837–1920, American novelist and literary critic. Trained as a printer, he later began to write, and after five years as American consul in Venice he wrote the first of many travel books, *Venetian Life* (1866). Later as editor of the *Atlantic Monthly* and an editor of *Harper's Magazine,* he set forth his critical ideas. His own novels were realistic (e.g., *Their Wedding Journey,* 1872; *A Modern Instance,* 1882; *The Rise of Silas Lapham,* 1885). He was a friend and an editor of Mark Twain. Howells also wrote light comedies and farces. In *Criticism and Fiction* (1891) he defended realism. He was interested in social reform and friendly to Socialism.

howitzer (hou'ĭtsŭr), artillery piece longer than mortar, differing from a gun especially in the very high trajectory of its fire.

Howland Island, area 1 sq. mi., central Pacific near the equator. Discovered 1842 by U.S. traders, claimed 1857 by U.S. with Jarvis Isl. and Baker Isl. Became important with development of Pacific air commerce. Settled 1935 by Americans, placed 1936 under Dept. of Interior. Its airfield is on direct route between Honolulu and Australia.

Howrah (hou'rä), industrial city (pop. 379,292),

S West Bengal, India, on Hooghly R. Produces cotton cloth, jute products, and steel.

Hoy, second largest of the ORKNEY ISLANDS.

hoya, tropical climbing shrub (*Hoya carnosa*) with thick leaves and fragrant white or pink flowers.

Hoyle, Edmond (hoil), 1672–1769, English writer on games. Codified rules of whist, quadrille, backgammon, piquet, others. "According to Hoyle" has come to mean the definitive word on games. Editions of his work are kept up to date.

Hradec Kralove (hrä′dĕts krä′lôvĕ), Czech *Hradec Králové,* Ger. *Königgrätz,* city (pop. 19,242), E Bohemia, Czechoslovakia, on the Elbe. Battle of SADOWA or Königgrätz was fought near by (1866).

Hrdlicka, Ales (ä′lĕsh hŭrd′lĭchkä), 1869–1943, American anthropologist, b. Bohemia. He organized division of physical anthropology at U.S. Natl. Mus. His investigations of supposed migration tracks in Siberia and Alaska were significant.

Hroswitha or **Roswitha** (rōswī′thù, rôsvē′tä), c.940–c.1002, German Latin poet, a Benedictine nun at Gandersheim. Wrote lyrics; six saints' lives, notable for naïve charm and piety; and six morality plays, intended as antidote to Terence.

Hsia (shyä), earliest and semilegendary dynasty of China. Said to have ruled either from c.2205 to c.1766 B.C. or from c.1994 to c.1523 B.C.

huanaco: see GUANACO.

Huancayo (wän-kī′ō), city (pop. 28,680; alt. c.11,000 ft.), S central Peru; agr. center.

Huáscar (wäs′kär), d. 1533, Inca of Peru; son of Huayna Capac. Shared empire with half brother, Atahualpa, who had him drowned.

Huayna Capac (wī′nä kä′päk), d. 1525, Inca of Peru, last of great emperors. His decision to divide his empire by leaving recently conquered kingdom of Quito to his favorite son, Atahualpa, and the rest to his legitimate heir, Huascar, and the resultant war between them, weakened the Inca empire and made Francisco Pizarro's conquest easier.

Hubbard, Bernard Rosecrans, 1888–, American priest, scientist, and explorer. Has headed Univ. of Santa Clara geology department since 1926. Made annual scientific expeditions to Alaska (1926–43). Known as the "glacier priest." Noted for lectures, films, and books.

Hubbard, Elbert, 1856–1915, American author. His Roycroft Shops and Press promoted handicrafts and bookmaking. Wrote *Little Journeys* to homes of the great and the inspirational *Message to Garcia* (1899).

Hubbardton, town (pop. 332), W Vt., NW of Rutland, near L. Bomoseen. Near here, troops under Seth WARNER, covering St. Clair's retreat from Ticonderoga, were routed by British, July 7, 1777.

Hubbell, Carl (Owen), 1903–, American baseball pitcher. Left-handed N.Y. Giant ace won 24 consecutive games in 1936–37 seasons, won 253 major-league games.

Hubble, Edwin Powell, 1889–, American astronomer, noted for systematic investigation of nebulae outside of Milky Way system.

Hubert de Burgh (dù bûrg′), d. 1243, chief justiciar of England (1215–32) under John and Henry III. After Henry assumed power in 1227 trouble increased between Hubert and king whose foreign favorites opposed him. Tried to prevent (1230) expedition to France and resisted drain of money to papacy. In 1232 he was accused of disloyalty to crown and imprisoned. Was later reconciled with the king.

Hubertusburg, Peace of (hōōbĕr′tōōsbōōrk), 1763, treaty between Austria and Prussia, at end of Seven Years War, signed at Hubertusburg castle in Saxony. Prussia retained Silesia; Saxony was restored to prewar boundaries.

Huch, Ricarda (rēkär′dä hōōkh′), 1864–1947, German novelist. Her historical novel of the Thirty Years War, *Der grosse Krieg in Deutschland* (1912–14), ranks among the best of its kind.

huckleberry, North American shrub of genus *Gaylussacia* of heath family. Common huckleberry (*Gaylussacia baccata*) is valued for its black edible fruit, usually picked from wild plants. Evergreen box huckleberry (*G. brachycera*) is often cultivated.

Huddersfield, county borough (pop. 129,021), West Riding of Yorkshire, England. An important textile-milling center, it also has other mfg.

Hudibras: see BUTLER, SAMUEL (1612–80).

Hudson, Henry, fl. 1607–11, English navigator and explorer. Ascended Hudson R., establishing Dutch claims to region, later explored Hudson Bay for English, both while seeking Northwest Passage.

Hudson, Manley O(ttmer), 1886–, American jurist. Specialist in international law, he was a justice on the Permanent Court of Arbitration (1933–45) and also served on the Permanent Court of Internatl. Justice (1936–46).

Hudson, W(illiam) H(enry), 1841–1922, English author and naturalist, b. Buenos Aires of American parents. Wrote romances laid in South America—*The Purple Land* (1855) and classic *Green Mansions* (1904). *Far Away and Long Ago* (1918) is autobiographic.

Hudson. 1 Town (pop. 8,211), E Mass., NE of Worcester; settled 1699. Mfg. of shoes and textiles. **2** City (pop. 11,629), E N.Y., on E bank of Hudson R. (bridged to Catskill); settled 1662. Mfg. of matches, cement, and food and leather products.

Hudson, river, c.315 mi. long, rising in NE N.Y. in L. Tear of the Clouds near Mt. Marcy in the Adirondacks and flowing generally S, forming N.Y.-N.J. line for c.17 mi. near its mouth in Upper New York Bay. Port region is called North R. Chief tributary is Mohawk R. One of the world's important highways, the Hudson is linked to the Great Lakes, L. Champlain, and St. Lawrence R. by N.Y. State Barge Canal. Tidal to Albany, head of channel for ocean-going vessels; Troy is at head of 12-ft. channel. At New York city (max. width here 4,400 ft.) Holland and Lincoln tunnels, railroad tunnel, subways, ferries, and George Washington Bridge link N.Y. and N.J. Above New York city river widens at Tappan Zee. First explored by Henry Hudson 1609. Major highway for Indians and early settlers. Has many historic, literary, and artistic associations.

Hudson Bay, great inland sea, 850 mi. long and

650 mi. wide, area c.475,000 sq. mi., E central Canada. Lies generally SE of Northwest Territories, to which bay and islands belong. Has important cod and salmon fisheries. CHURCHILL is chief port on bay, connected to interior by Hudson Bay RR. Among rivers draining into bay are the CHURCHILL, NELSON, ALBANY, Abitibi, and SEVERN. Hudson's Bay Co. posts estab. at the rivers' mouths. Bay open to navigation from mid-July to Oct. Discovered 1610 by Henry Hudson and named for him.

Hudson Bay Railway, part of Canadian Natl. Railways system, 510 mi. long, extending from The Pas, Man., to Churchill, Man., on W coast of Hudson Bay. Built 1910–29; designed to reduce rail and sea rates from grain-producing provinces to Liverpool.

Hudson Falls, village (pop. 7,236), E N.Y., on Hudson R.; settled 1761. Mfg. of paper.

Hudson River school, 1825–75, in American landscape painting. Influenced by European romanticism. So called because the artists classified with the school were attracted to scenic beauty of Hudson R. valley. Group included Thomas Doughty and Thomas Cole.

Hudson's Bay Company. Organized 1668 by English merchants and courtiers to open fur trade with Indians in Hudson's Bay region of North America and to discover Northwest Passage to Orient. Permanent charter issued 1670. French contested claim to region; warfare ended with British in control. Company was harshly criticized in middle of 18th cent. for failure to discover Northwest Passage. NORTH WEST COMPANY became chief rival. RED RIVER SETTLEMENT scheme under earl of SELKIRK brought disaster to company. Amalgamation with North West Co. in 1821 marked beginning of period of true monopoly. Governorship (1821–60) of Sir George Simpson marked peak of company's fortune. Company territory transferred to Canada (1869) by governmental order for £300,000. In 20th cent. company expanded into retail trade and mfg. of all sorts. In 1930 Canadian stores were segregated in separate organization and London portion again turned to fur trade.

Hué (hwä), city (pop. c.40,000), Indo-China; cap. of Annam, on Hué R. near South China Sea. Probably founded by Chinese in 3d cent.

Huelva (wĕl'vä), city (pop. 50,837), cap. of Huelva prov., SW Spain, in Andalusia, on Odiel R. near Atlantic. Exports copper and sulphur from near-by Río Tinto mines.

Huerta, Victoriano (vĕktōryä'nō hwĕr'tä), 1854–1916, Mexican general and president (1913–14). Served under Porfirio Díaz. After successful revolution of Madero (1911), Huerta supported him until 1913, then opposed him and was made president. His reactionary rule brought trouble with U.S. and revolutions led by Carranza, Villa, and Zapata, and he was forced to resign. Died in U.S.

Huesca (wä'skä), city (pop. 16,943), cap. of Huesca prov., NE Spain, in Aragon. Dates from Roman times. Residence of kings of Aragon 1096–1118. Has Gothic cathedral.

Hügel, Friedrich, Baron von (frē'drĭkh bärōn' fŭn hü'gŭl), 1852–1925, British Catholic philosopher, b. Florence. The independent

thought in his writings, stressing inner security and moral responsibility, profoundly influenced modern Catholicism.

Huggins, Sir William, 1824–1910, English astronomer, pioneer in spectroscopic analysis of stars and in spectroscopic celestial photography.

Hugh Capet (kā'pĭt, kă'pĭt), c.938–996, king of France (987–96); son of HUGH THE GREAT and first of the CAPETIANS.

Hughes, Charles Evans, 1862–1948, U.S. Secretary of State (1921–25), Chief Justice of Supreme Court (1930–41). Lost presidential election to Woodrow Wilson in 1916 in very close contest.

Hughes, David Edward, 1831–1900, American inventor of an improved type-printing telegraph and of a microphone.

Hughes, Howard Robard, 1869–1924, American inventor of the widely used cone-shaped oil drill.

Hughes, John Joseph, 1797–1864, American Roman Catholic clergyman; bishop coadjutor (after 1838), bishop (after 1842), and first archbishop (after 1850) of New York.

Hughes, (James) Langston, 1902–, American Negro poet. His lyrics and songs (e.g., *The Weary Blues,* 1926), dramas, and fiction deal with Negro problems.

Hughes, Thomas, 1822–96, English author of the classic of school life, *Tom Brown's School Days* (1857), which idealizes Dr. Thomas Arnold of Rugby.

Hugh le Despenser: see DESPENSER, HUGH LE.

Hugh of Lincoln, Saint, d. 1200, bishop of Lincoln (1186–1200), b. Burgundy. Spokesman of the barons (1198) in their refusal of money to Richard I, he was also in conflict with John. Noted for charity, love of the poor, and holiness. Partially rebuilt Lincoln Cathedral. Feast: Nov. 17.

Hugh of Lincoln, Christian boy supposed to have been murdered by Jews in the 13th cent.

Hugh of Saint Victor, d. 1141, French or German scholastic philosopher. Headed the school of the monastery of St. Victor, Paris, after 1133 and made it a center of learning and of opposition to the teachings of Abelard. Hugh himself wrote learned theological works (notably one on the sacraments) and also works on mysticism. Also Hugo.

Hugh the Great, d. 956, French duke; son of King Robert I, father of HUGH CAPET. Waived succession in favor of RAOUL; placed LOUIS IV on French throne (936), later quarreled with him; virtually ruled France after 954.

Hugo, Victor (Fr. vēktôr' ügō'), 1802–85, French poet, dramatist, and novelist. The preface to his drama *Cromwell* (1827) and the production of the tragedy *Hernani* (1830), which caused a riot, placed him at the head of the romanticists. Other plays include *Le Roi s'amuse* (1832; basis of Verdi's *Rigoletto*) and *Ruy Blas* (1838). After the tragic death of his daughter (1843), his poetry turned from the lush romanticism of earlier collections such as *Les Orientales* (1829) to the philosophic content of *Les Contemplations* (1856). Though created peer and viscount under Louis Philippe, Hugo soon turned to republicanism and ardently advocated reform. He opposed Napoleon III, fled abroad in 1851, and took residence in Jersey (till 1855), then in Guernsey till Napoleon's fall in 1870, when he returned to Paris in triumph. In the poems of *Les Châtiments* (1853) he vituperated Napoleon III. *La Légende des siècles* (1859) is an epic evocation of history. Hugo's great novels are *Notre Dame de Paris* (1831), *Les Misérables* (1862), and *Toilers of the Sea* (1866), on which his popularity in the English-speaking world is founded.

Hugo, city (pop. 5,984), SE Okla., near Red R. Rail and farm center processing peanuts and creosote.

Huguenots (hū'gŭnŏts), the Calvinist Protestants of France. Presbyterian church was founded in France at synod of 1559 and gained many followers among all classes. After the Wars of RELIGION (1562–98), Henry IV promulgated the Edict of NANTES, which gave the Huguenots complete toleration and estab. Protestantism in 200 towns. Cardinal RICHELIEU used an uprising (1621–22) against the introduction of Catholicism into Béarn as a pretext for depriving the Huguenots of all their strongholds save La Rochelle and Montauban. Another Protestant uprising (1625) led to the capture of La Rochelle by Richelieu (1628) and to the peace of Alais (1629), which stripped the Huguenots of all political power. Mounting persecution of Protestants under Louis XIV culminated in 1685 with the revocation of the Edict of Nantes. Countless Huguenots fled to England, Holland, Germany, Switzerland, and America, where they contributed substantially to civic and industrial life. In the Cévennes, the Protestant CAMISARDS long fought Louis XIV's troops (1702–10).

Huitzilopochtli (wē″tsēlōpŏcht'lē), Aztec god of war. Human beings, especially prisoners of war, were sacrificed to him at the splendid temple of Tenochtitlán.

Hulagu Khan (hōōlä'gōō khän'), 1217–65, Mongol conqueror; grandson of Jenghiz Khan. Sacked Baghdad 1258, but westward move was checked 1260 by Mamelukes of Egypt. His Persian khanate lasted until 1335.

Hull, Cordell, 1871–, U.S. Secretary of State (1933–44). Consistently pursued a course making for sound international economic relations and constructive good will toward nonaggressor nations.

Hull, William, 1753–1825, American general. In command of Detroit in War of 1812, he lost it to British on Aug. 16, 1812. Courtmartialed, he was saved only by his Revolutionary War record.

Hull, city (pop. 43,483), SW Que., Canada, on Ottawa R. at mouth of Gatineau R., opposite Ottawa. Paper and lumbering center with iron and steel foundries and hydroelectric station.

Hull, officially **Kingston-upon-Hull,** county borough (pop. 299,068), East Riding of Yorkshire, England, on the Humber. One of chief ports for Yorkshire and Lancashire, it also has extensive mfg. There are steamship lines to the Continent. It is an ocean fishing base. Town has several museums, grammar school (founded 1486), University Col., and Trinity

House (estab. 1369, for sailors). Heavily bombed 1941.

Hull House: see ADDAMS, JANE.

humanism, movement in thought in the Renaissance, characterized chiefly by a revolt against medieval religious authority and attitudes and a great spread of classical learning. The rediscovery of Greek and Latin works was a main preoccupation of scholars, and the classic secular (humanistic) attitudes were generally adopted. The new learning more or less coincided with the religious upheaval of the Reformation, and many humanists became Protestants, though others clung to the old religion. The humanists formed a sort of intellectual community, which continued from the 14th cent. until shattered by the religious struggle in the late 16th cent.; numbered among them were such men as Boccaccio, Petrarch, Pico della Mirandola, Budé, the Scaligers, Reuchlin, Ulrich von Hutten, Erasmus, John Colet, and Sir Thomas More. The term *humanism* has been used for other later movements, most particularly in the 20th cent. by F. C. S. Schiller, Irving Babbitt, and C. F. Potter.

Human Rights, Commission on, division of the Economic and Social Council of the United Nations. Drew up Universal Declaration of Human Rights, adopted by UN on Dec. 10, 1948. A proposed Covenant on Human Rights received a setback when U.S. announced (1953) that it would not sign such a covenant.

Humber, navigable estuary of Trent R. and Ouse R., on E coast of England. It is 40 mi. long and 1–8 mi. wide. Encroachment of sea has destroyed former ports. Hull and Grimsby are chief cities.

Humberstone, village (pop. 3,895), S Ont., Canada, on L. Erie at S end of Welland Ship Canal. Humberstone Lock is one of world's largest lift locks.

Humbert, kings of Italy. **Humbert I,** 1844–1900, reigned 1878–1900. Was assassinated. **Humbert II,** 1904–, was made lieutenant general of the realm 1944, succeeded his father Victor Emmanuel III on his abdication (1946). Referendum of 1946 estab. republic, and Humbert went into exile.

Humboldt, Alexander, Freiherr von (äĕ́ksän'-dŭr frī'hĕr fŭn hōōm'bôlt), 1769–1859, German explorer, scientist, and natural philosopher. His expedition to Cuba, Central and South America (1779–1804), noted for systematic observations, initiated era of scientific exploration. Estab. use of isotherms. In his great work on natural science, *Cosmos* (5 vols., 1845–62), he sought to formulate known facts about universe into uniform conception of nature. His brother **Wilhelm, Freiherr von Humboldt** (vĭl'hĕlm), 1767–1835, was Prussian minister of education (1809–10), reformed school system, founded Univ. of Berlin. In 1819 he left government service in protest against reactionary regime. A friend of Goethe and Schiller, he also wrote a work on Kavi, the ancient language of Java, important in history of philology.

Humboldt, city (pop. 7,426), W Tenn., NNW of Jackson. Rail, mfg., and trade center for farm area.

Humboldt, river rising in NE Nev. and flowing

W and S c.300 mi. into Humboldt Sink near Humboldt Range. Named by J. C. Frémont, it was followed by Utah emigrants bound for Calif. Rye Patch Dam, built 1935–36, serves Humboldt project around Lovelock.

Humboldt Glacier, NW Greenland, largest known glacier. It debouches into Kane Basin. E. K. Kane discovered it on his expedition of 1853–55.

Hume, David (hūm), 1711–76, Scottish philosopher and historian. He pressed the analyses of Locke and Berkeley into a determined, thorough-going skepticism. He found in the mind nothing but a series of sensations and the cause-effect relation in the natural world as apparent only because two sensations were customarily joined. Rejecting the possibility of knowledge that is certain, he fell back on common sense and faith. His essays (e.g., *Treatise of Human Nature,* 1739–40; *Essays Moral and Political,* 1741–42; *Philosophical Essays,* 1748; *An Enquiry Concerning the Principles of Morals,* 1750; *Political Discourses,* 1752) are marked by the purity of literary style that made his *History of England* (1754–62) long standard despite errors in fact. He was patron of Rousseau in his English exile, but later the two quarreled bitterly.

humidity, primary climatic element, atmospheric state regarding moisture content. Measured as absolute humidity (moisture per unit volume of natural air); relative humidity (ratio of moisture content to moisture-holding capacity of air at given temperature); specific humidity (moisture per unit mass of natural air); and mixing ratio (moisture per dry-air unit mass). Hygrometer used to measure humidity.

hummingbird, small perching bird of New World. Most of c.750 species and subspecies are native to Central and South America. They have brilliant plumage with a metallic sheen and long, slender, sometimes curved bills. In seeking insects and nectar of flowers they carry on cross pollination. Giant hummer of Andes (c.8½ in. long) is largest; smallest, Helena's hummingbird or fairy hummer of Cuba (c.2¼ in. long). Ruby-throated hummingbird is only species in N U.S.

Humperdinck, Engelbert (hŭm'pûrdĭngk), 1854–1921, German composer and teacher. Apart from the opera *Die Königskinder,* he is known chiefly for his first opera, *Hansel and Gretel* (1893).

Humphrey, Doris, American dancer and choreographer. Long associated with Charles Weidman. Her outstanding works include *New Dance; With My Red Fires.*

Humphrey, George M(agoffin), 1890–, U.S. Secretary of the Treasury (1953–). President of M. A. Hanna Co., steel mfg. firm, Cleveland (1929–52).

Humphreys, Andrew Atkinson, 1810–83, American army engineer, Union general in Civil War. Known for topographic and hydrographic survey of Mississippi delta (1850–61).

Humphreys, David, 1752–1818, American diplomat and poet. Active in U.S. service abroad. One of the CONNECTICUT WITS. His poetry is largely patriotic and didactic.

Humphreys, Joshua, 1751–1838, American ship designer, responsible in 1790s for successful frigates (*United States, Constitution,* and others).

Humphrey's Peak: see SAN FRANCISCO PEAKS.

humus, decayed vegetable and animal matter, essential to productive soil. It aids plant growth by conserving moisture, loosening soil particles to admit air and water, and by releasing mineral nutrients. Sandy and clay soils lack humus to varying degrees.

Hunan (hōō'nän'), province (80,000 sq. mi.; pop. 28,000,000), S central China; cap. Changsha. Largely hilly. Watered by Siang, Yuan, and Tzu rivers which drain through Tungting L. into the Yangtze. Major producer of tea, rice, and minerals (lead, zinc, coal, antimony, tin, tungsten).

Hundred Days, March 20–June 28, 1815, period of attempt by NAPOLEON I to rebuild empire after return from Elba. See also WATERLOO CAMPAIGN.

Hundred Years War, 1337–1453, between England and France. Basic cause: the kings of England, who as dukes of GUIENNE were vassals of the French kings, opposed the centralizing policies of the French crown and showed increasing reluctance to do homage to France for their continental possessions. Contributing causes: claim of EDWARD III to the French crown as a grandson of Philip IV; territorial disputes between Edward and PHILIP VI of France; English-French rivalry in Flanders; Philip's support of Scotland against England. First phase of war (1337–60) began when Edward proclaimed himself king of France. Allied with the Flemings under Jacob van ARTEVELDE, he defeated the French navy at Sluis (1340); routed the French at CRÉCY (1346); took CALAIS (1347); and routed and captured JOHN II of France at Poitiers (1356). The Treaty of BRÉTIGNY (1360) gave England Calais and W and SW France. Second phase of war (1369–73) was brought on by the oppressive taxation of EDWARD THE BLACK PRINCE and resulted in the reconquest by DU GUESCLIN of most of the lost French territories. After a period of quiescence, HENRY V of England renewed the war in 1415. Victorious at AGINCOURT, he later won the alliance of PHILIP THE GOOD of Burgundy (1419) and in 1420, by the Treaty of TROYES, was recognized by Charles VI as regent and heir of France. The dauphin (later CHARLES VII) refused to accept his disinheritance, and desultory warfare recommenced after Charles VI's death (1422). By 1429 the English and Burgundians were masters of nearly all France N of the Loire, but in that year JOAN OF ARC appeared, relieved besieged ORLÉANS, defeated the English at Patay, and saw Charles VII crowned at Rheims. The tide turned, and in 1435, when by the Treaty of ARRAS Burgundy passed over to the French camp, the final phase of the war began. The French reconquered Paris (1436), Normandy (1449–50), and all Guienne but Bordeaux (1449–51). The capture of Bordeaux (1453) left only Calais in English hands. England, torn by the Wars of the Roses, made no attempt at reconquest and henceforth turned its interest to sea power rather than to expansion on the Continent. France, laid waste and reduced to anarchy by the war, recovered under Charles VII and Louis XI, who took advantage of the virtual destruction of the feudal class to rebuild a centralized monarchy. The Hundred Years War saw the transition from medieval to modern warfare (artillery) and from feudalism to the first awakening of national consciousness.

Huneker, James Gibbons (hŭ'nĭkŭr), 1860–1921, American essayist, critic of music, art, and drama.

Hungarian language, Finno-Ugric language. See LANGUAGE (table).

Hungary, Hung. *Magyarország*, republic (33,-935 sq. mi.; pop. c.9,205,000), SE Europe, in the Danubian plain; cap. Budapest. E of the Danube the Great Hungarian Plain (Hung. *Alföld*) extends beyond the border to the Carpathians; W of the Danube are the Little Alfold, with L. BALATON, and the Bakony, Vertes, and Mecsek mts. Present frontiers, except for minor changes in 1947, were estab. by Treaty of TRIANON (1920), which stripped Hungary of two thirds of former area (incl. its Adriatic coast). Though it has mineral resources (coal, manganese, bauxite, petroleum) and industrial concentrations (esp. at Budapest, Gyor, Miskolc), Hungary is predominantly agr. (wheat, maize, livestock, poultry, wine). Irrigation has reduced the former PUSZTA to a small area around Debrecen. Chief industrial products: textiles, machinery, processed foods, chemicals. Population is c.66% Catholic, 25% Protestant (mainly Calvinist). Part of the Roman provinces of Pannonia and Dacia, Hungary was later conquered by the Huns, Ostrogoths, Avars, and (9th cent.) MAGYARS. Magyar expansion in W was halted by Emperor Otto I at the Lechfeld (955). St. STEPHEN, first king of Hungary, completed the Magyars' Christianization. A feudal society came into being. The power of the magnates (great nobles), who were to play a major role until 1918, was only temporarily curbed by the Golden Bull of ANDREW II (1222). Hungary was occupied by the Mongols in 1241–42. In 1301 the ARPAD dynasty died out. The kingship was elective, but dynastic ties influenced the royal elections. Hungary was ruled after 1308 by the ANGEVIN dynasty and after 1386 by other foreign houses (mostly in personal union with Bohemia and Poland; see esp. JAGIELLO dynasty). The double marriage treaty of 1515 (see ULADISLAUS II) prepared the advent of HAPSBURG rule in 1526. Medieval Hungary reached its zenith under LOUIS I (14th cent.) and under MATTHIAS CORVINUS (15th cent.), whose reign interrupted that of the Jagiellos. John HUNYADI successfully led the resistance against Turkish conquest, but the defeat and death of Louis II at MOHACS (1526) plunged Hungary into chaos. Ferdinand of Austria (see FERDINAND I, emperor) contested the succession with the Zapolya family (see JOHN, kings of Hungary), and in 1541 Turkey annexed most of the country. The resulting threefold partition of Hungary (confirmed by treaty, 1606) lasted until the reconquest of Turkish Hungary by the Hapsburgs after 1683: W Hungary remained under the Hapsburgs, who

kept the royal title; central Hungary was a Turkish province; TRANSYLVANIA, ruled by its own princes, shifted its allegiance back and forth between the sultans and the emperors. By 1711, the rebellion of Francis II RAKOCZY having failed, all Hungary and Transylvania was firmly under Hapsburg control. Religious freedom had been guaranteed by the treaty of 1606 between BOCSKAY and the emperor. The peasantry, subjected to serfdom after its rebellion of 1514, was freed in 1781 by Emperor Joseph II. Magyar opposition to Hapsburg rule remained strong and flared up in the Revolution of 1848. The short-lived Hungarian republic (April–Aug., 1849) under KOSSUTH was put down by Austrian and Russian troops. Hungarian self-rule was abolished until 1867, when Hungary became a constitutional kingdom in personal union with Austria (see AUSTRO-HUNGARIAN MONARCHY). Except in CROATIA, which enjoyed some autonomy, the Slavic and Rumanian minorities (in SLOVAKIA, RUTHENIA, DALMATIA, and the BANAT OF TEMESVAR) were held in virtual subjection by Magyar nationalism. After the collapse of the Dual Monarchy in World War I, Hungary was proclaimed an independent republic (1918) and reduced by the Treaty of Trianon to its predominantly Magyar core. (Large Magyar minorities passed to Czechoslovakia, Rumania, and Yugoslavia.) The Communist dictatorship of BELA KUN (1919) was put down by Rumanian intervention, and in 1920 Hungary became a kingdom without a king, with Adm. HORTHY DE NAGYBANYA as regent. The authoritarian and reactionary regimes of premiers Bethlen and Gombos were tempered by the parliament but blocked a much-needed agrarian reform. Hungarian agitation for treaty revision met the hostility of the LITTLE ENTENTE and eventually caused Hungary to join the AXIS powers in World War II (1941). Invaded by Russian troops in 1944, Hungary made an armistice in Jan., 1945; heavy fighting between Germans and Russians continued. Peace was signed in Paris in 1947. It confirmed the restoration of territories ceded to Hungary by Slovakia in 1938 and by Rumania in 1940, and it provided for $300,000,000 in reparations to the USSR. Hungary became a republic in 1946. Land reforms were introduced by a coalition government of moderates and leftists. In 1948 a coup d'état imposed Communist totalitarianism on the country, which in 1949 became a People's Republic under virtual economic and political control of the USSR.

Hunkers, conservative faction of the Democratic party in N.Y. in the 1840s, so named because they were supposed to "hanker" or "hunker" after office. Opposed the BARNBURNERS. Generally controlling party machinery and patronage, they favored internal improvements and liberal chartering of state banks; opposed antislavery agitation.

Huns, nomadic people from N central Asia. Organized into hordes, they were indomitable horsemen living off the countries they ravaged. They first appeared 3d cent. B.C., when the Great Wall of China was built to contain them. They occupied China from 3d cent. A.D. to 581. About 372 A.D. they invaded the Volga valley and advanced W, pushing the OSTROGOTHS and VISIGOTHS before them, thus starting the waves of migrations that destroyed the Roman Empire. In 432 they forced Emperor Theodosius II to pay tribute. ATTILA, from his hq. in Hungary, levied tribute in nearly all central and E Europe but was defeated in Gaul (451). The Huns withdrew after his death, and little is known of their later movements.

Hunt, Holman, 1827–1910, English painter, a founder of the Pre-Raphaelite brotherhood.

Hunt, (James Henry) Leigh, 1784–1859, English poet, critic, and essayist. Edited weeklies *Examiner* and *Liberal;* contributed to many others. A friend of contemporary writers, he strongly influenced Keats. Some lyrics (e.g., "Abou Ben Adhem," "Jenny Kissed Me"), essays, and autobiography still much read.

Hunt, Richard Morris, 1828–95, American architect, brother of William Morris Hunt; an exponent of 19th-cent. eclecticism. His Tribune Building, New York, was one of first elevator buildings. His son, **Richard Howland Hunt,** 1862–1931, also an architect, led movement against unrestricted skyscraper building.

Hunt, William Morris, 1824–79, American painter, a follower of Barbizon School. As teacher and painter in Boston he exerted wide influence on American art.

Hunt, Wilson Price, 1782?–1842, American explorer, leader of the overland expedition (1810–12) to Astoria, Oregon.

Hunter, John, 1728–93, Scottish pioneer in comparative anatomy and in surgery. His noted anatomical collection was acquired by the Royal College of Surgeons. His brother, **William Hunter,** 1718–83, was famed as obstretician and as head of influential school of anatomy.

Hunter, Robert Mercer Taliaferro (tŏ'lŭvûr), 1809–87, American statesman. U.S. Representative from Va. (1837–43, 1845–47); a leading states' rights Democrat. U.S. Senator (1847–61). Participated in Confederate government.

Hunter, William: see HUNTER, JOHN.

Hunter College: see NEW YORK, COLLEGE OF THE CITY OF.

hunting dogs. Many breeds of dogs used in hunting are not expected to kill the game which they track down, but rather to flush game or to fetch game after it has been shot. Among these are the pointer and the several kinds of retrievers and setters. The pointer is a large, lean, smooth-coated dog weighing c.60 lb. When it comes upon game birds, it points them with its nose, remaining motionless until the bird attempts to fly. It is usually white marked with liver, orange, or yellow. The retriever has a thick coat and generally stands 22–25 in. at shoulder and weighs 65–80 lb. It is bred for fetching game already shot by the hunter, especially game that has fallen in water. In addition to a keen sense of smell, it must have a soft mouth for carrying game without damage. Breeds of retrievers include the Labrador retriever, a hardy dog whose short straight coat is usually black; the Chesapeake Bay retriever, varying from dark brown to faded tan; the golden retriever; and the curly-coated retriever, usually black or

liver in color. Generally setters have silky coats with feathered legs and tail. The English setter is white marked with tan, black, lemon, or liver; the Gordon setter has a very glossy coat of black or tan; the Irish setter is a golden chestnut or mahogany red. The Dalmatian or coach dog was sometimes used in hunting, but was specially trained and long used to trot along beside a carriage. It is short-haired, stands 19–23 in. at shoulder, and is white spangled with round, clearly defined, black or dark brown spots.

Huntingdon, England: see HUNTINGDONSHIRE.

Huntingdon, borough (pop. 7,330), S Pa., E of Altoona. Mfg. of paper, boilers, and radiators. Seat of Juniata Col. (Church of the Brethren; coed.; 1876).

Huntingdonshire or **Huntingdon,** inland county (365 sq. mi.; pop. 69,273), E central England. Mainly agr., it has some paper mfg. and brewing. County town is **Huntingdon,** municipal borough (pop. 5,282), birthplace and home of Oliver Cromwell.

hunting leopard: see CHEETAH.

Huntington, Anna Hyatt: see HYATT, ANNA VAUGHN.

Huntington, Collis P(otter), 1821–1900, American railroad builder. Helped organize Central Pacific RR. Gained for himself and partners practical control of transportation in West. President of Southern Pacific after 1890. Left most of fortune to his nephew, **Henry E(dwards) Huntington,** 1850–1927. Endowed his estate at San Marino, near Pasadena, Calif., for public use. Has fine gardens and the **Henry E. Huntington Library and Art Gallery** with largest collection of incunabula in America; many rare documents, manuscripts and books, with accent on American and British past. Special art treasures are Gainsborough's *Blue Boy,* Reynolds's *Mrs. Siddons as the Tragic Muse,* and Thomas Lawrence's *Pinkie.* The library gives research fellowships and scholarships.

Huntington, Ellsworth, 1876–1947, American geographer. Accompanied expeditions to central Asia (1903, 1905–6). Taught at Yale (1907–15); as research associate (1917–47) he made notable climatic and anthropogeographic studies.

Huntington, Henry Edwards: see HUNTINGTON, COLLIS POTTER.

Huntington, William Reed, 1838–1909, American Episcopal clergyman. Noted pastor (from 1883) of Grace Church, New York city.

Huntington. 1 City (pop. 15,079), NE Ind., on Little R. and SW of Fort Wayne. Farm trade center producing rubber goods, furniture, and metal products. **2** Residential and resort town (pop. 47,506), including Huntington village (pop. 9,324), SE N.Y., on NW Long Isl. near Oyster Bay. Site of Nathan Hale's capture marked in Huntington Bay village. Birthplace of Walt Whitman is in West Hills. **3** City (pop. 86,353), W W.Va. on Ohio R. and WNW of Charleston; founded 1871 as W terminus of Chesapeake & Ohio RR. Largest city in state and commercial center for wide area. Mfg. of monel metal, railroad equipment, steel rails, and glass. Here is Marshall Col. (coed.; 1837).

Huntington Beach, coastal city (pop. 5,237),

S Calif., SE of Long Beach. Oil wells and re-fineries.

Huntington Library and Art Gallery: see HUN-TINGTON, COLLIS POTTER.

Huntington Park, city (pop. 29,450), S Calif., residential and industrial suburb of Los Angeles. Mfg. of iron and steel products and oil-field equipment.

Huntsville. 1 City (pop. 16,437), N Ala., between Tennessee R. and Tenn. line; settled 1807. Textiles, shoes, farm implements. Site of constitutional convention (1819); briefly, state cap. **2** City (pop. 9,820), E central Texas, N of Houston. Home of Sam Houston, it has memorials to him (grave, restored home). Processes cotton, lumber, and dairy produce.

Hunyadi, John (hŏōn'yŏdĭ), c.1385–1456, Hungarian national hero, leader of resistance against the Turks. Was voivode of Transylvania 1441–46; regent of Hungary 1446–53 (for Ladislaus V). His chief victory (together with St. John Capistran) was that of Belgrade (1456), which staved off Turkish conquest of Hungary for 70 years. Matthias Corvinus was his son.

Hupeh or **Hupei** (both: hŏō'pä', hŏō'bä'), province (70,000 sq. mi.; pop. 25,000,000), central China; cap. Wuchang. Largely an alluvial plain; drained by Yangtze and Han rivers. Major iron mines in SE. Produces rice, cotton, and wheat. Trade centered at urban hub comprising Hankow, Wuchang, Hanyang.

Hur, man who upheld hand of weary Moses during battle, thus insuring Hebrew victory. Ex. 17.12; 24.14.

Hurd, Peter, 1904–, American painter of Western scenes and types. Uses realistic style.

hurling, game popular in Ireland, played on field 80 yd. by 140 yd. by two teams of 15 players each with a cork-centered ball and a wooden stick (the hurley).

Huron, city (pop. 12,788), E central S.Dak., on James R. and E of Pierre; laid out 1879. Shipping and trade center for agr. area. Has meat-packing plants and creameries. Seat of Huron Col. (Presbyterian; coed.; 1883).

Huron, river rising in S Mich. and flowing c.97 mi. SE to L. Erie S of Detroit.

Huron, Lake, 206 mi. long, 183 mi. wide, second largest of Great Lakes. Lying 579.79 ft. above sea level, it has maximum depth of 750 ft., area of 23,010 sq. mi. Bounded N and E by Ontario, W by Mich. Drains L. Superior and L. Michigan and empties into L. Erie. Its large Georgian Bay indents Ont.; Saginaw Bay is in Mich. Islands include Mackinac and the Manitoulins. Iron ore, grain, coal, limestone, other articles are shipped. Ports include Bay City, Alpena, and Cheboygan in Mich., and Goderich, Collingwood, and Midland in Canada. L. Huron has violent storms, and is icebound from about mid-Dec. until early April. Probably first of Great Lakes visited by white men, possibly by Étienne Brulé c.1612.

Huronian: see PROTEROZOIC ERA.

Huron Indians, confederation of four North American Indian tribes, who spoke Wyandot language (Iroquoian family). Their culture was of the Eastern Woodlands area. In early 17th cent. occupied region around L. Simcoe and near Georgian Bay, Ontario. The Hurons were friendly to the French, and the confederacy was destroyed by the Dutch-supported Iroquois (1649).

hurricane, tropical cyclone originating in doldrums, on W side of oceans, probably from convective heating. Most frequent in late summer or autumn in N Hemisphere, late winter or spring in S Hemisphere. Called typhoon in India and China.

Hurtado de Mendoza, Diego (dyä'gō ōōrtä'dhō dä mändō'thä), 1503–75, Spanish writer, a diplomat under Charles V. Banished by Philip II to Granada, he wrote an unbiased account of the Moorish rebellion. Also wrote poetry. Picaresque novel *Lazarillo de Tormes* sometimes attributed to him.

Husein (hŏōsīn'), c.626–680, Moslem saint of the Shiites; second son of ALI and FATIMA. On death of his brother Hasan he unsuccessfully claimed caliphate. Tomb at KERBELA is holy place for Shiites. Name also spelled Hussein.

Husein ibn Ali (ī'bŭn ä'lē), 1856–1931, Arabian leader; father of Abdullah of Jordan and Feisal I of Iraq. Led revolt against Turkish rule and made himself king of the HEJAZ in 1916. Overthrown 1924 by Ibn Saud.

Hu Shih (hŏō' shŭ'), 1891–, Chinese writer and diplomat. Educated in China and U.S. (Cornell and Columbia univs.). Leader in Chinese literary renaissance; advocated simplification of written language. Ambassador to U.S. (1938–1942).

husky: see CHOW.

Huss, John, Czech *Jan Hus* (yän' hŏōs'), 1369?–1415, religious reformer. He attacked abuses of clergy, earning their hostility, but was supported by Queen Sophia and Emperor Wenceslaus, who made him rector of Univ. of Prague. He was involved in controversy of rival popes Gregory XII and Benedict XIII, and he won enmity of John XXIII, who excommunicated him. At castle near Tabor, Huss wrote chief works, including *De ecclesia.* Emperor Sigismund invited him to defend views at Council of Constance (1414); but by unfair means he was condemned as heretic and burned. See HUSSITES.

Hussein: see HUSEIN.

Hussein I (hŏōsīn'), 1935–, king of Jordan (1952–), son and successor of Talal; grandson of Abdullah.

Husseini (Amin el Husseini) (hŏōsä'nē; ämēn' ĕl), 1896?–, Arab political leader. Appointed mufti of Jerusalem in 1921. Arrested 1937 for instigation of anti-Semitic riots but escaped to Lebanon and later to Iraq. Broadcast Nazi propaganda from Berlin in World War II. Listed as war criminal, he found asylum in Egypt in 1946.

Husserl, Edmund (hŏōs'ûrl), 1859–1938, German philosopher. His theories on the relationship of the conscious mind and objects—the basis of the system of *phenomenology* —have had great influence.

Hussites, followers of John Huss in Bohemia and Moravia. In 1420 they drew up Four Articles of Prague, demanding freedom of preaching, communion in both kinds for laymen and priests, limited property holding by Church, and civil punishment of mortal sin. In Hussite Wars movement divided into moderate UTRAQUISTS (some of whom in 16th cent. fused with Lutherans and were called Evangelicals) and radical TABORITES (from whom stemmed Moravian Church).

Hussite Wars, 1419–36, conflict caused by the rise of the HUSSITES in Bohemia and Moravia. Its nature was religious and national (Hussite Czechs vs. Catholic Germans) as well as social (radical TABORITES, largely recruited among peasantry, vs. moderate UTRAQUISTS, backed by Czech nobility). The Hussites took up arms in 1419 to prevent the succession of Emperor SIGISMUND to the Bohemian crown. Under the leadership of ZIZKA and, after 1425, of PROCOPIUS THE GREAT, the Hussites defeated Sigismund (1420, 1422), invaded Silesia (1425–26) and Franconia (1429–30), and repulsed several anti-Hussite crusades. Hussite delegates at the Council of BASEL accepted the so-called Compactata, by which the Utraquists were taken back into the Catholic Church (1433), but the Taborites refused to compromise. In the resulting civil war, the Taborites were routed at Lipany (1434); the Compactata were ratified and Sigismund was recognized as king of Bohemia in 1436. The later wars against GEORGE OF PODEBRAD were of primarily political nature, though Hussitism was the ostensible issue.

Hutchins, Robert Maynard, 1899–, American educator. He was dean of Yale Law School, 1927–29, and helped organize Inst. of Human Relations at Yale. In 1929 he became president of Univ. of CHICAGO, where his title was chancellor after 1945. He instituted "Chicago plan" there. In 1946 he was on leave to promote "great books" program. He resigned in 1950 to become associate director of Ford Foundation.

Hutchinson, Anne, c.1591–1643, religious leader in New England, b. England. Banished from Mass. Bay colony as antinomian heretic, she and followers founded Portsmouth, R.I. (1638).

Hutchinson, Thomas, 1711–80, colonial governor of Mass. (1771–74) and historian. Unpopular with colonists because he upheld British measures. Wrote history of Mass. Bay colony.

Hutchinson, city (pop. 33,575), S central Kansas, on Arkansas R. and NW of Wichita; laid out 1871. Rail, trade, and mfg. center of area yielding salt, oil, wheat, and livestock.

Hutten, Ulrich von (ŏŏl′rĭkh fŭn hŏŏ′tŭn), 1488–1523, German humanist, poet, and political reformer. Wrote in Latin, later in German. Was poet laureate of Maximilian I (1517). Supported Johann REUCHLIN; joined with Franz von SICKINGEN (1519); supported Luther. Sickingen's defeat forced him into exile in Switzerland (1522).

Hutterische Community (hŏŏ′tĕ′rĭshŭ) or **Hutterian Brethren** (hŭtĕr′ēŭn), religious communistic group founded (1874) at Tabor, S.Dak., by immigrant descendants of followers of Jacob Hutter. Closely allied with Mennonites in matters of doctrine and principles.

Hutton, James, 1726–97, Scottish geologist. He formulated the theory of UNIFORMISM as opposed to long accepted belief known as CATASTROPHISM.

Huxley, T(homas) H(enry), 1825–95, English

biologist. While assistant surgeon on H.M.S. *Rattlesnake* he collected marine life in Pacific areas (1846–50). A supporter of Darwin, he wrote on evolution, and also on anatomy, physiology, and other fields of science. His son **Leonard Huxley,** 1860–1933, was a poet, general writer, and editor of *Cornhill Magazine.* Leonard's son **Julian S(orell) Huxley,** 1887–, biologist and author, was director general of UNESCO (1946–48). His works include *The Living Thoughts of Darwin* (1939) and *Heredity East and West* (1949). Another son of Leonard, **Aldous (Leonard) Huxley,** 1894–, gained early fame by satirical novels and short stories (*Crome Yellow,* 1921; *Antic Hay,* 1923; *Point Counter Point,* 1928; *Brave New World,* 1932, depicting a repulsive Utopia). Later novels reflect his interest in Eastern mysticism, though mordant criticism of the modern world continued in such works as *Eyeless in Gaza* (1936). Has also written popular history as in *Grey Eminence* (1941) and *The Devils of Loudun* (1952).

Huygens, Constantijn (kōnstäntīn′ hoi′gŭns), 1596–1687, Dutch poet. Noted for descriptive and satirical poems, he wrote in French, Italian, Latin, Dutch. His son, **Christiaan Huygens** (krīs′tyän), 1629–95, was a mathematician and physicist. He improved telescopic lenses and discovered a satellite and the rings of Saturn. He was first to use pendulum in clocks. **Huygens's principle:** every point on wave front of light is source of new waves.

Huysmans, Cornelis (hois′mäns), 1648–1727, Flemish painter of landscapes and religious subjects. His brother and pupil, **Jan Baptist Huysmans,** 1654–1716, also painted landscapes.

Huysmans, Joris Karl (zhōrēs′ kärl′ üēsmäs′), 1848–1907, French novelist. First a naturalist, he became a Catholic convert. His novel, *À rebours* (1884; Eng. tr., *Against the Grain,* 1922), is a self-portrait. *La Cathédrale* (1898; Eng. tr., 1898) shows his magnificent prose and mystic symbolism.

Hvar (khvär), Gr. *Pharos,* Ital. *Lesina,* Adriatic island, 120 sq. mi., Yugoslavia, off Dalmatia. Chief town, Hvar, has 12th-cent. Byzantine cathedral.

Hwaining, China: see ANKING.

Hwang Ho: see YELLOW RIVER.

Hwangpoo, China: see WHANGPOO.

Hyacinth, in Greek myth, beautiful youth loved by Apollo, who accidentally killed him with a discus. Flower named for him sprang up from his blood.

hyacinth, bulbous plant of genus *Hyacinthus* native to Mediterranean region and S Africa. Common or Dutch hyacinth became so popular in 18th cent. that 2,000 kinds were said to be grown in Holland. It has a single dense spike of fragrant flowers in the spring but can be made to bloom earlier indoors.

Hyannis, Mass.: see BARNSTABLE.

Hyatt, Anna Vaughn, 1876–, American sculptor, noted for studies of animals. A well-known statue is *St. Joan of Arc.* Married Archer M. Huntington.

Hyatt, John Wesley, 1837–1920, American inventor of CELLULOID and of Hyatt filter for chemical purification of water while it is in motion.

Hyattsville, town (pop. 12,308), W central Md., NE residential suburb of Washington, D.C.

hybrid (hī′brĭd), term of plant and animal breeders for offspring of two different species or genera. In genetics it is usually a term for offspring of two parents differing in any genetic character.

Hyde, Edward: see CLARENDON, EDWARD HYDE, 1ST EARL OF.

Hyde Park, 363 acres, in W London. Was once a deer park where races were held. Duke of Hamilton and Lord Mohun fought their fatal duel here. The Serpentine, artificial lake, was constructed 1733. Distinctive features of the park are Marble Arch, meeting place of soapbox orators; Rotten Row, famous bridle path; and the Albert Memorial.

Hyde Park, town (pop. 6,136), E N.Y., on E bank of Hudson R. N of Poughkeepsie; settled c.1740. Here are Franklin D. Roosevelt and Vanderbilt Mansion national historic sites.

Hyderabad (hī′dŭrŭbăd″), state (82,313 sq. mi.; pop. 18,652,964), S central India, almost entirely within Deccan plateau. Produces cotton, wheat, rice, and tobacco. Chief industry is cotton spinning and weaving. Conquered in late 17th cent. by Mogul empire. In 1724 the Mogul viceroy, Asaf Jah, won Hyderabad's independence and founded present dynasty, whose ruling head is called the Nizam. Predominantly Hindu state was formally joined to Indian republic in 1950. **Hyderabad,** city (pop. 739,159), the cap., was founded 1589 as cap. of Golconda kingdom; major commercial center.

Hyderabad, city (pop. 134,693), central Sind prov., W Pakistan; trade center. In 1950 succeeded Karachi as cap. of province.

Hyder Ali or **Haidar Ali** (both: hī′dŭr ä′lē), d. 1792, Indian maharaja. Though illiterate and a Moslem, he rose to become highest military leader in Hindu state of Mysore. Seized power in 1761, made himself maharaja in 1766. Defeated the British in 1767, but he and his son Tippoo Sahib were defeated 1781 by Warren Hastings.

Hydra (hī′drŭ) [Gr.,= watery (snake)], in Greek mythology, water serpent with nine heads. When one head was cut off, two new ones grew. HERCULES conquered monster by burning neck after severing each head.

hydrangea (hīdrăn′jŭ), ornamental deciduous shrub of genus *Hydrangea,* native to Asia and the Americas. It has flat-topped or rounded clusters of blue, white, or pink flowers. Used in landscaping and as potted plant.

hydrate (hī′drāt), substance formed by chemical combination of a compound and one or more molecules of water (number of molecules is specific for substance). This water is called water of crystallization; it is given off on heating or in some hydrates at ordinary temperatures (efflorescence).

hydraulic brake: see BRAKE.

hydraulic machine, machine actuated by motion or pressure of fluid (liquid or gas). Water under pressure is used as power agent for presses, riveters, winches, and other machines. Power derived from falling water drives TURBINE and the water wheel. Hydraulic elevator, jack, and press are based on PASCAL'S LAW. Certain machines are driven by accumulator (consisting chiefly of cylinder enclosing weighted ram) which keeps liquid at fixed pressure.

hydraulic press, hydraulic machine (also called hydrostatic press), invented by Joseph Bramah. Consists essentially of two liquid-filled cylinders of very unequal diameter, connected by pipe and each fitted with piston. Pressure exerted on smaller piston is transmitted through liquid and forces up larger piston.

hydraulics: see HYDRAULIC MACHINE; MECHANICS.

hydrocarbon (hī″drōkär′bŭn), organic compound of carbon and hydrogen in varying proportions. Hydrocarbons are divided into series in which each member has definite relation to one preceding and following (a difference of one carbon and two hydrogen atoms); examples are methane series, ethylene series, acetylene series, benzene series, anthracene series. Many common natural substances are complex mixtures of these compounds, e.g., petroleum, asphalt, methane. They vary in chemical activity, resist ordinary reagents, burn in air. Many important compounds are derivatives of hydrocarbons.

hydrochloric acid, aqueous solution of hydrogen chloride, a strong acid of great commercial importance. It reacts with most metals, and with their oxides and hydroxides, forming chlorides. It is used for cleaning metal; in producing chlorides, glue, dyes, glucose; and in medicine. Muriatic acid is a solution of 30–35% by weight.

hydrocyanic (–sī′ā′nĭk) or **prussic** (prŭ′sĭk) **acid,** colorless, volatile, very poisonous liquid with almond odor. Water solution is a weak acid; salts are cyanides. It is used in the laboratory, as poison gas in war, and as a fumigant.

hydrodynamics: see MECHANICS.

hydroelectric power: see POWER.

hydrogen (hī′drŭjŭn), colorless, odorless, tasteless gaseous element (symbol = H; see also ELEMENT, table). It is the lightest known gas, explosive when mixed with air or oxygen, and burns with a hot blue flame. It is slightly soluble in water; can be liquefied under pressure; is active at high temperatures; is a powerful reducing agent; forms many important compounds. Discovered in 1766 by Henry Cavendish, it was named in 1783 by Lavoisier. Heavy hydrogen, deuterium, is isotope with atomic weight 2; it and its atomic nuclei (deuterons) are important in research. Tritium is radioactive isotope, atomic weight 3. See *ill.,* p. 989.

hydrogenation of oils (hī″drŭjŭnā′shŭn), treatment of vegetable oils with hydrogen, in presence of catalyst, at high temperature under pressure. It forms a product resembling solid animal fats.

hydrogen bomb derives energy from union of nuclei of low atomic weight. Atomic bomb probably would have to be used as detonator to get needed amount of heat for this fusion. Most likely ingredients are hydrogen isotopes.

The thermonuclear reactions involved are believed to be same as those producing heat of sun. Energy yield of bomb has no foreseeable peacetime applications; potentially more harmful than atomic bomb. Tests which advanced its development made at Eniwetok (1951, 1952). See *ill.*, p. 989.

hydrogen-ion concentration: see ION.

hydrogen peroxide (pŭrŏk′sīd), colorless, unstable liquid with metallic taste; has two atoms of both hydrogen and oxygen. Used as bleaching agent and in cleansing wounds (germicidal value disputed).

hydrolysis (hīdrŏ′lŭsĭs), type of chemical reaction in which water (dissociated into hydrogen and hydroxyl ions) is involved. It is common in many life processes, e.g., in digestion, food substances (carbohydrates, fats and oils, and proteins) are decomposed by action of water in presence of enzymes. Final product of hydrolysis of starch is glucose; of fats and oils, products are glycerin and fatty acids; and of proteins, amino acids. Some salts undergo hydrolysis in water solution, others do not. Some reactions involving water are not hydrolysis, e.g., when a metal or water reacts to form a base and liberate hydrogen.

hydrometer (hīdrŏ′mŭtŭr), device to determine directly the SPECIFIC GRAVITY of a liquid. Usually it is a thin glass tube closed at both ends, with a bulb at one end filled with mercury or fine shot so that it will float upright in liquid being tested. Scale is so calibrated that reading at level of surface of liquid gives specific gravity. Density can be calculated from specific-gravity readings. Commercial hydrometers usually are calibrated for 20°C.

hydrophobia [from Greek,= hatred of water] (hī″drŭfō′bēŭ) or **rabies** (rā′bēz), acute infectious disease caused by virus which affects nervous system. It is transmitted by bite of rabid animal. Spasm of pharynx on swallowing results in fear of drinking water. Pasteur developed method of preventing disease by inoculation 1884 and first used it on human patient 1885.

hydroponics: see SOILLESS GARDENING.

hydrostatics: see MECHANICS.

hydroxide (hīdrŏk′sīd), term commonly used for a BASE, although some compounds with hydroxyl (OH) radical show acid properties. Others have both acidic and basic characteristics (i.e., are amphoteric); still others are neutral.

hydroxyl radical: see HYDROXIDE; RADICAL.

hyena (hīē′nŭ), nocturnal Old World mammal. Its front legs are longer than hind ones. It eats mostly carrion. Striped hyena of Asia Minor, Persia, India, and N Africa and brown hyena or strand wolf of S Africa both belong to genus *Hyaena*. Spotted hyena (*Crocuta*) in Africa S of Sahara is largest form (2½ ft. high at shoulder). It has a maniacal cry and is said to rob graves and steal children.

hygiene (hī′jēn), science of health and its preservation. Community aspects are handled by PUBLIC HEALTH and SOCIAL HYGIENE programs. Field of MENTAL HYGIENE developed after recognition of health role of mental and emotional factors.

hygrometer (hīgrŏ′mŭtŭr), instrument for measuring moisture content of air. In the condensing, or dew-point hygrometer, fluid in a tube is evaporated, thereby drawing heat from surrounding air; since air holds less moisture as temperature decreases, excess moisture condenses on tube. From temperatures recorded, when condensation begins, by thermometers within tube and outside it, moisture content is calculated. Other hygrometers are based on use of substance that expands or contracts as moisture varies or of substance that absorbs moisture from air with consequent weight increase. In the psychrometer moisture content is determined by difference in temperatures recorded by two thermometers, the bulb of one kept moist, the other dry.

Hyksos (hĭk′sŏs), invaders of anc. Egypt, probably Semitic people. They took the kingship (c.1675 B.C., according to one date) from decadent rulers and kept it a century or more (XV–XVII dynasties) until driven out by Amasis I. By false etymology they are called the Shepherd Kings. Little is known of them.

Hymen or **Hymenaeus** (hīmŭnē′ŭs), Greek personification of marriage, represented as beautiful youth carrying bridal torch and wearing veil.

Hymettus (hīmě′tŭs), Gr. *Hymettos*, mountain group, Attica, Greece. Mt. Hymettus (3,367 ft.) famed since antiquity for its honey. Marble quarries.

hymn, song of praise, devotion, or thanksgiving, especially of a religious nature. Early Christian hymnody consisted mainly of the Psalms and other biblical texts chanted in unison. Metrical Latin hymns developed in 4th cent. Great medieval hymns include *Dies irae*, *Stabat Mater Dolorosa*, and *Pange lingua*. In the Reformation, the Lutheran chorale developed; Luther wrote several (e.g., *A Mighty Fortress*, which has a famous setting by J. S. Bach). Calvinism contributed the Genevan Psalter, containing the tune *Old Hundred*. The English hymn developed largely in the 18th cent. with the sacred texts of Cowper, Watts, and Wesley. An early collection of hymns in America was the *Bay Psalm Book* (pub. 1640).

hyoscine: see SCOPOLAMINE.

Hypatia (hīpā′shŭ), d. 415, Alexandrian Neoplatonic philosopher, a woman renowned for beauty, learning, and eloquence; said to have been murdered by monks at the instigation of St. Cyril of Alexandria, an enemy of the prefect who was Hypatia's lover.

hyperbola (hīpûr′bŭlŭ), a plane curve such that difference between distances from any point on it to two fixed points (*foci*) is same for all points on curve. It is also a conic section formed by a plane cutting both nappes of the cone. Center is halfway between foci; principal axis is straight line through foci; vertices are intersections of axis with curve. *Latus rectum* is chord through either focus perpendicular to principal axis. Asymptotes are lines in same plane which curve approaches as it approaches infinity. Equilateral hyperbola is one whose asymptotes are perpendicular.

Hyperboreans (hī″pûrbô′rēŭnz, –bôrē′ŭnz), in

Greek legend, people dwelling in bliss in the Far North.

Hyperion (hīpēr'ēŭn), in Greek religion, Titan; son of Uranus and Gaea and father of Helios, Selene, and Eos by Theia.

hypertension: see BLOOD PRESSURE.

hypnotism, Braid's term (1842) for animal magnetism or mesmerism (see MESMER). It is induced in a relaxed subject by monotonous repetition of words and gestures—some people are not affected. In slight hypnosis consciousness remains, actions are remembered; in deep hypnosis, sensory system and muscles are affected, supernormal feats cause no fatigue, are forgotten. Hypnosis heightens suggestibility, was used to treat and study hysteria. Briefly used by Freud in psychoanalysis, it is still used in some therapy and in study of mental actitivies.

hypochondria (hī"pŭkŏn'drēŭ), the neurotic reaction marked by habitual preoccupation

with health and with imagined or negligible physical defect.

Hyrcania: see GURGAN.

Hyrcanus, John (hŭrkā'nŭs), name of two of the MACCABEES.

hyssop (hĭs'ŭp), aromatic perennial herb (*Hyssopus officinalis*) native to Old World. It has small violet-blue, white, or pink flowers. Once used as flavoring, it is now grown chiefly for ornament.

hysteria, in general usage, highly emotional and irrational conduct, reflected in bodily disturbance. Psychologists define it as a conversion NEUROSIS. Occasionally hysteria creates organic sickness (see PSYCHOSOMATIC MEDICINE). In late 19th cent., the psychological origin of hysteria was recognized, and hypnosis was used for its cure.

Hythe (hīdh), municipal borough (pop. 9,218), Kent, England; summer resort and one of CINQUE PORTS. School of Small Arms is here.

I, chemical symbol of element IODINE.

iambic pentameter: see PENTAMETER.

Iamblichus (ĭăm'blĭkŭs), d. c.330, Syrian Neoplatonic philosopher; pupil of Porphyry.

Iapetus (ĭă'pĭtŭs), in Greek mythology, Titan; son of Uranus and Gaea and husband of CLYMENE.

Iasi, Rumania: see JASSY.

Ibadan (ēbä'dän), city (pop. 387,133), SW Nigeria, inhabited by the Yoruba. Consists mainly of mud huts. Cacao, cotton, and palm oil are exported.

Ibagué (ēbägä'), city (pop. 27,448), W central Colombia; founded 1550; a commercial center.

Ibáñez, Vicente Blasco: see BLASCO IBÁÑEZ.

Iberia (ībēr'ēŭ), anc. name of a country in Transcaucasia, roughly E part of Georgian SSR.

Iberian Gates, Georgian SSR: see DARYAL.

Iberian Peninsula, SW Europe, comprising SPAIN and PORTUGAL, between Atlantic and Mediterranean. Separated from main continent by Pyrenees, from N Africa by Strait of Gibraltar. Named for the **Iberians,** anc. people believed to have migrated from Africa in Neolithic period. They merged with the Celts (who came later) into "Celtiberian" nation.

Iberville, Pierre le Moyne, sieur d' (pyĕr' lŭ mwän' syûr' dēbērvēl'), 1661–1706, French Canadian naval officer and colonizer. Led attacks on British settlements in North America. Estab. colony in lower Mississippi valley with brother, sieur de BIENVILLE.

Iberville (ē'bûrvĭl), town (pop. 5,185), S Que.,

Canada, on Richelieu R. and SE of Montreal. Trade center in dairy region.

ibex (ī'bĕks), gregarious, sturdy, agile wild goat (*Capra*) living at snow line of mountains of Asia, Europe. It is brown or gray, 2½–3½ ft. high at the shoulder, and has long ridged horns curving backward.

ibis (ī'bĭs), wading bird of warm parts of both hemispheres. Usually it nests in colonies. Its body is c.2 ft. long; the bill is long, slender, decurved, and grooved from nostril to tip. In North America are white ibis, white-faced and eastern glossy ibises, and wood ibis (really a stork).

Ibiza, island, Spain: see IVIZA.

Ibn Batuta (ī'bŭn bätōō'tä), 1304?–1378?, Moslem traveler, b. Tangier. More widely traveled than any known medieval man, he wrote valuable accounts of the Near and Far East.

Ibn Ezra, Abraham ben Meir (mâr' ī'bŭn), 1092?–1167, Jewish poet, biblical critic, astronomer; inspiration of Robert Browning's "Rabbi Ben Ezra."

Ibn Gabirol, Solomon ben Judah (ī'bŭn gäbē'rōl), c.1021–1058, Jewish poet and philosopher, known also as Avicebron. Wrote *The Well of Life,* an attempt to explain man's purpose in life.

Ibn Khaldun (ī'bŭn khäldōōn'), 1332–1406, Arab historian. In *Kitab al-Ibar* [universal history] he treats history as science and outlines philosophy of history. Deemed greatest of Arab historians.

Ibn Saud (Abdu-l-Aziz ibn Saud) (ī'bŭn säōōd'), c.1880–, founder of SAUDI ARABIA. Triumphed over his rival, HUSEIN IBN ALI, in 1924 and declared himself king of the HEJAZ and NEJD. Remained neutral during World War II. A leader in anti-Zionist movement among Arab states.

Ibn Tufail (ĭ'bŭn tōōfēl'), 12th-cent. Spanish-Arabian philosopher and physician. Wrote *Hayy ibn Yaqzan*, a philosophical romance.

Ibn Zohr: see AVENZOAR.

Ibrahim Pasha (ĭbrähēm' pä'shä), 1789–1848, Egyptian general; son of MOHAMMED ALI. Led Turkish forces against Wahabis in Arabia (1816–19) and rebel Greeks (1825–28). Conquered Turkish-held Syria (1832–33), but European troops forced his withdrawal 1838.

Ibsen, Henrik, 1828–1906, Norwegian dramatist, one of the outstanding figures in modern world theater. A satirical verse play, *Love's Comedy* (1862) was followed by dramatic poems *Brand* (1866) and *Peer Gynt* (1867) and a series of powerful, realistic social plays in prose (*The Pillars of Society*, 1877; *A Doll's House*, 1879; *Ghosts*, 1881; *An Enemy of the People*, 1882; *The Wild Duck*, 1884; *Rosmersholm*, 1886; *The Lady from the Sea*, 1888; *Hedda Gabler*, 1890; *The Master Builder*, 1892; *Little Eyolf*, 1894; *John Gabriel Borkman*, 1896; *When We Dead Awaken*, 1899). His uncompromising insistence in presenting natural characters in conflict with social custom and environment brought a fresh breath into the theater. G. B. Shaw was one of his disciples.

Ica (ē'kä), city (pop. 21,437), SW Peru; commercial center for irrigated valley of Ica R.

Icaria: see CABET, ÉTIENNE.

Icarus, in Greek myth. He flew too near the sun with wings made by his father, Daedalus. Wax joints of the wings melted, and he fell into the sea.

ice action, an agent of erosion. Freezing (and expansion) of water in cracks breaks up rocks; glaciers and shore ice wear away land by friction.

Ice Age: see PLEISTOCENE EPOCH.

iceberg, ice mass detached from glacier or ice sheet and floating on ocean. About one ninth of mass projects above water.

ice cream, frozen confection made from milk fat and solids, sugar, and flavoring, and often containing a stabilizer (e.g., starch, gelatine), eggs, fruits, or nuts. Agitation during freezing produces light, smooth texture. Similar desserts include parfaits, mousses, frozen custards, ices, sherbets. Probably originated as a frozen ice in 17th-cent. Italy.

Iceland, Icelandic *Island,* republic (c.40,000 sq. mi.; pop. 141,042), westernmost state of Europe, occupying Iceland isl. and several smaller islands in the Atlantic just S of Arctic Circle, c.600 mi. W of Norway; cap. REYKJAVIK. Iceland is a plateau, averaging 2,000 ft. high and culminating in vast icefields, of which VATNAJÖKULL is largest. Deep fjords indent the coast. Many of the more than 100 volcanoes are still active (highest is Mt. HEKLA). Hot springs such as the GEYSIR abound. Climate is mild and humid because of North Atlantic Drift. Iceland is only c.25% habitable, and most cities are on the coast. Island lacks timber, but has extensive grazing (sheep, horses, cattle). Agr.

(hay, potatoes, turnips) is limited. Fishing is most important industry, codfish and herring constituting chief export. Iceland is governed by parliamentary democracy. Here social-security legislation is very advanced. Most citizens are Lutherans. High educational level is due to ancient tradition and ingrained civilization rather than to formal schooling. Irish monks visited Iceland before 9th cent., but abandoned it on arrival of Norse settlers (c.850–870). In 930 a general assembly, the ALTHING, was estab., and c.1000 Christianity was introduced. However, memory of paganism was preserved in literature of 13th-cent. Iceland, where OLD NORSE LITERATURE reached its greatest flowering (modern Icelandic is virtually same language as that of the sagas). Attempt of SNORRI STURLUSON to establish full control of King Haakon IV of Norway over Iceland failed, but in 1261–64 king obtained acknowledgment of his sovereignty by the Icelanders. With Norway, Iceland passed under the Danish crown (1380). In 17th and 18th cent. pirates ruined trade; epidemics and a general volcanic eruption (1783) killed many; and creation (1602) of a private trading company at Copenhagen, with exclusive rights to Iceland trade, caused economic ruin. Foreign traders were not admitted until 1854. Home rule was finally granted in 1874, and in 1918 Iceland was declared a sovereign state in personal union with Denmark. During World War II, when British and U.S. forces were based in Iceland, the Althing assumed king's prerogatives, and on June 17, 1944, after popular referendum, kingdom of Iceland became an independent republic. Iceland was admitted to the UN in 1946, and joined in European Recovery Program and North Atlantic Treaty.

Icelandic language, North Germanic language. See LANGUAGE (table).

Icelandic literature. The Eddas and sagas of early Icelandic literature (see OLD NORSE LITERATURE) had a lasting effect on later writing. Literature declined after the loss of Iceland's independence (1261–64), but in the 14th cent. arose the *rímur,* a type of narrative poem. After the Protestant Reformation, religion dominated literature until the period of enlightenment (1750–1835). The romantic revival, begun in the 1830s, stressed nationalism as well as romantic elements. The classic Iceland style was developed in 19th and 20th cent. by such men as the short-story writer Jonas Hallgrimsson; the novelist Jon Thoroddsen; the poets Grimur Thomsen, Benedikt Grondal, and Steingrimur Thorsteinsson; and the dramatist Matthias Jochumsson. The historian Jon Sigurdsson helped to promote Icelandic language and literature. Realism appeared to challenge romanticism with attacks on the Church and social institutions; important in the movement were short-story writer Gestur Palsson; the Icelandic Canadian poet Stephen G. Stephansson. A more introspective type of literature also developed. Various strains enriched Icelandic literature, as in the neoromantic movement and "proletarian" writing. Among 20th-cent. figures have been Jon Trausti (pseud. of Gudmundur

Magnusson), Sigurdur Nordal, Kristmann Gudmundson, and Halldor K. LAXNESS.

Iceland moss, a grayish paper-thin lichen (*Cetraria islandica*) of northern countries and found as far south as N U.S. It has long been used in Scandinavian countries for human food and for fodder.

Iceland spar, transparent calcite characterized by double refraction. Used for prisms of polarizing microscopes and other optical instruments.

ice plant, low fleshy plant (*Mesembryanthemum,* or *Cryophytum, crystallinum*) of warm, dry, barren regions. It is a useful ground cover or pot plant.

Ichabod (ĭ'kŭbŏd) [Heb.,= inglorious], grandson of Eli. 1 Sam. 4.21; 14.3. Name given disparagingly to Daniel Webster in poem by John Greenleaf Whittier.

Ichang or **I-ch'ang** (both: ē'chäng), city (pop. 80,979), SW Hupeh prov., China, on Yangtze R.; terminus for ocean-going vessels from Shanghai.

Ickes, Harold L(eClaire) (ĭ'kŭs), 1874–1952, U.S. Secretary of the Interior (1933–46). Long a progressive known for his bluntness in action, he called himself a "curmudgeon."

Icknield Street (ĭk'nēld), Saxon name for an early road in Britain from Berkshire Downs to the Chilterns.

Icolmkill, Inner Hebrides, Scotland: see IONA.

Icon Basilike: see EIKON BASILIKE.

Iconium (īkō'nēŭm), anc. city of Asia Minor, included in various regions as boundaries shifted. In Galatia when Paul visited it as a missionary. Modern Konya, Turkey is here.

iconoclasm (īkŏ'nŏklăzŭm) [Gr.,= image-breaking], opposition to religious use of images. Use of religious pictures and statues was an early feature of Christian worship (see ICONOGRAPHY and CATACOMBS). After the 5th cent., however, images came to be associated with superstitions, and iconoclasm flourished in Monophysite center of Asia Minor and was perhaps influenced by iconoclasm of Islam, Judaism, Manichaeism, and the Paulicians. Emperors Leo III, Constantine V, Leo IV, and Leo V favored iconoclasm, but Empress IRENE restored the images. Iconoclasm was rejected at the Second Council of NICAEA. The controversy gave Byzantine art a spiritual bent, away from naturalism.

iconography (ī"kŏnŏg'-), broadly, act of representation by pictures and images, which may or may not have a symbolic as well as a literal meaning; also the study of such figural representations. Systematic investigation of the history of art has shown that each major phase or epoch has developed an iconography of its own, and the term is necessarily qualified (e.g., iconography of Egyptian deities, iconography of Napoleon, Byzantine iconography). The aim of iconographic research is to recover and express the thought behind a certain type, particularly if the type became a symbol. Christian iconography is extremely rich and varied. It began with the catacombs and developed a complex language of symbols. Every medieval artist had to learn the characters of this sacred "writing" and also the sacred "mathematics" that dictated position, group, sym-

metry, and number of figures in representation. The symbolic code (as in representing the Holy Ghost as a dove) has invited men to look at one thing and see the figure of another. The essence of Christian iconography lies in the expression and reading of the spiritual meaning intended in the art.

Ictinus (ĭktī'nŭs), 2d half of 5th cent. B.C., one of greatest architects of Greece. Designed PARTHENON with Callicrates as associate.

id: see PSYCHOANALYSIS.

Ida, Mount, 8,058 ft. high, central Crete; island's highest mountain. Also known as Psiloriti.

Ida, Mount, range in Phrygia, Asia Minor. Here in legend Paris was reared and fell in love with Oenone.

Idaho, state (82,808 sq. mi.; pop. 588,637), NW U.S.; admitted 1890 as 43d state; cap. BOISE. Other cities are POCATELLO and IDAHO FALLS. SNAKE R. forms part of W boundary. Along Mont. boundary is BITTERROOT RANGE of Rockies. Farming (wheat, oats, alfalfa, potatoes, sugar beets, fruits, livestock, dairy products); mining (lead, silver, zinc, copper, gold, phosphate); lumbering. New atomic energy processing plant was begun at Arco in 1949. Lewis and Clark expedition of 1805 preceded activities of Canadian and American fur traders in region. Franklin was first permanent settlement (1860). Discovery of gold that year led to rapid settlement. Idaho Territory set up in 1863. Indian troubles occurred until late 1870s. Boomed in late 19th cent. through silver and lead mines and growth of railroads. Now has irrigation and power projects (see BOISE PROJECT, MINIDOKA PROJECT). State has increasing tourism (e.g., at the popular resort of Sun Valley).

Idaho, University of: see Moscow.

Idaho Falls, city (pop. 19,218), SE Idaho, on Snake R. and NNE of Pocatello. Settled in 1860s; named Idaho Falls in 1890–91. Chief city of upper Snake valley; trade and processing center for irrigated farms (esp. potatoes), stock ranches, dairies.

Idaho Springs, resort city (pop. 1,769; alt. c.7,500 ft.), N central Colo., just W of Denver. Had first major gold strike in Colo., 1859. Hot mineral springs.

Ida Mountains (ī'dù), range, NW Turkey, SE of site of anc. Troy. Its modern name is Kazdagi. Rises to c.5,800 ft. at Mt. Gargarus.

idealism, in metaphysics, belief that the underlying reality of the universe resides in ideas, ideal forms, or an absolute. It is opposed by all types of materialism and relativistic beliefs. The classic statement of idealism was that of Plato. In modern times Hegel was the most thorough-going philosopher in his doctrines of the Absolute and the unchanging laws by which change takes place. Among later idealists Bernard Bosanquet and A. N. Whitehead may be named. Subjective idealism, represented by Bishop Berkeley, is the belief that all reality exists only in personal consciousness. Outside metaphysics the term is used in several wide senses (e.g., in art, tendency to represent things as artist thinks they should be rather than as they are).

idiocy: see FEEBLE-MINDEDNESS.

Idlewild: see QUEENS, New York city borough.

idol [Gr.], image believed to possess supernatural power because it is dwelling place of supernatural being. Represents fixation of a spiritual force in a material object. Whereas fetish or charm has inherent power, idol must be consecrated before it can be worshiped. It is animal or human in form, and is treated as though alive. Idolatry has inspired many great works of art. Ritual use of idols dates from late Paleolithic times and still prevails in large sections of today's world.

Idomeneus (ĭdŏ'mĭnūs, –mĭnēŭs), in Greek legend, aged Cretan king who led Cretan troops in the Trojan War. Caught in a storm at sea when returning home, he vowed that if the ship was saved he would sacrifice to Poseidon the first living thing he met after landing. This was his son, whom he sacrificed.

Idrisi or **Edrisi** (ĭdrē'sē, ĕ–), b. 1099?, d. after 1154, Arabian geographer. He compiled a description of the earth (1154), most important geographic work of the period.

Idumaea or **Idumea**: see EDOM.

idyl (ī'dŭl), short poem. Ancient idyls, especially those of Bion and Moschus, were intended as little selections in style of longer poems, such as elegies or epics. Since some of the ten famous idyls by Theocritus dealt with pastoral or rural scenes term *idyl* came to be restricted to gently flowing, artistic pieces on rural subjects. Tennyson in his *Idylls of the King* used term in looser original sense.

Ie-jima: see OKINAWA.

Ieyasu (Ieyasu Tokugawa) (ēä'äsōō), 1542–1616, Japanese dictator, founder of TOKUGAWA shogunate. Victory over rival barons in battle of Sekigahara (1601) made him successor to Hideyoshi as supreme leader of Japan. Secured title of shogun 1603, set up cap. at Yedo (Tokyo). First tolerated, then persecuted Christian missions, but encouraged foreign trade. Name also spelled Iyeyasu.

If, Château d', France: see CHÂTEAU D'IF.

Ifni (ĭf'nē), Spanish possession (676 sq. mi.; pop. 45,852), NW Africa, enclave on Atlantic coast of SW Morocco. Ceded by Morocco in 1860.

Iggdrasill, another spelling for YGGDRASILL.

igloo (ĭg'lōō), dome-shaped dwelling of the Eastern Eskimo constructed from snow blocks. It is usually a temporary shelter only.

Ignatius of Antioch, Saint (ĭgnā'shŭs, ăn'tēŏk), d. c.110, bishop of Antioch, Christian martyr. Wrote epistles to Christian communities to combat heresy. First to use word *Catholic;* he enjoined obedience to bishop, deacons, and presbyters. Feast: Feb. 1.

Ignatius of Constantinople, Saint, c.800–877, Greek patriarch of Constantinople. A son of Emperor MICHAEL I, he was castrated and imprisoned by LEO V (813) to prevent his accession. In 846 or 847 he was made patriarch by Empress Theodora, who approved his zeal against iconoclasm. After her banishment St. Ignatius was asked to resign, and MICHAEL III made PHOTIUS patriarch. Under BASIL I, St. Ignatius was restored and was declared legal patriarch by Fourth Council of Constantinople.

Ignatius of Loyola, Saint (loiyō'lủ), 1491–1556,

Spanish founder of the Jesuits (see JESUS, SOCIETY OF). A courtier and then a soldier, he was converted to the religion in 1521 when recovering from wounds. At Monserrat, at Manresa, and at various other places he studied and prepared himself. In 1534 he and six companions took together vows of chastity and poverty and agreed to go to the Holy Land. War prevented their journey, but they were ordained (1537), received by the pope (1538) and kept at Rome. In 1539 Pope Paul III accepted Ignatius' *Formula,* which (called in revised form the *Constitutions*) is still the charter of the Jesuits. Ignatius was general of the order until his death. He was a leader in the Catholic REFORM, but his chief interests were foreign missions and education of boys rather than reconversion of Protestants. He was a mystic as well as a practical leader, and his *Spiritual Exercises* (begun just after his conversion) is a contemplative devotional work. His idea of the Jesuit as a "soldier of Christ" is based on St. Paul (Eph. 6.10–17). Feast: July 31.

igneous rock: see ROCK.

ignis fatuus: see WILL-O'-THE-WISP.

ignition, device for igniting an explosive mixture. Ignition system in automobiles uses electric spark which ignites compressed mixture of air and gasoline vapor in the cylinders. Necessary high-voltage current is obtained from magneto or by battery-ignition system (with engine-driven generator) and is used directly, or indirectly through storage battery. System consists of storage battery, circuit breaker, induction coil (condenser), distributor, and wiring. Low voltage from battery is increased to high voltage by flowing into primary winding of coil and setting up magnetic flux. When circuit breaker is opened low-voltage current ceases and magnetic field collapses; this induces in secondary winding of coil a high voltage which then goes to distributor for relay to spark plugs; these are "fired" in definite order to insure even movement of pistons in cylinder and smooth running of engine.

Igor (ē'gŭr), 1150–1202, Russian prince. Led unsuccessful expedition against Cumans 1185. Hero of Russian epic, *The Lay of the Host of Igor,* discovered in 1795 and attributed to 12th cent.; used by Borodin for opera, *Prince Igor.*

Igorot (ĭgŭrŏt'), proto-Malayan people of N central Luzon isl. They live under village-state form of organization and practice rice-terrace agr. Were formerly head-hunters.

Iguala (ēgwä'lä), city (pop. 12,756), Guerrero, SW Mexico. Famous as place where Iturbide proclaimed **Plan de Iguala,** Feb. 24, 1821, providing that Roman Catholicism should be only religion; Mexico should be independent of Spain; all races in Mexico should be equal.

iguana (ĭgwä'nủ), large lizard of tropical America, West Indies, some Pacific isls. Common tropical American species is greenish (blending with the tree branches which it frequents), 3–6 ft. long, and has a crest of spiny scales from neck to tail. It eats leaves, fruit, sometimes small animals.

Iguassú Falls (ēgwủsōō'), in Iguassú R., South America. Higher and wider than Niagara, they belong partly to Argentina, partly to Brazil. Also Iguazú.

Iguvine Tables (ī'gyŏ̄ovĭn), several inscribed bronze tablets discovered in 1444 at Gubbio, where most of them are still preserved. They proved helpful in understanding ancient Umbrian language and supplied information on ancient Italian religious rites.

Ij or **Y**, Dutch *IJ* (all: ī), inlet of the Ijsselmeer, NW Netherlands, on which Amsterdam is located. Receives Amstel R. and is connected by canals with North Sea and with Lek and Waal rivers.

Ijssel, Dutch *IJssel* (both: ī'sùl), river, 72 mi. long, E and central Netherlands. Branches from the Lower Rhine near Arnhem and flows N into the Ijsselmeer near Kampen. The Hollandsche Ijssel, in W Netherlands, branches from Lek R. and flows WSW to the Meuse just E of Rotterdam. Also Yssel.

Ijsselmeer, Dutch *IJsselmeer* (both: ī'sûlmār″), shallow fresh-water lake, N and central Netherlands. It was formed from old ZUIDER ZEE by construction of a dam (completed 1932) extending 19 mi. between North Holland and Friesland provinces. Ijssel R. is chief feeder. Large areas (293 sq. mi. in all) have been reclaimed from the former Zuider Zee since 1932. Largest is Northeast Polder (185 sq. mi.). Parts of the polders flooded in World War II have since been salvaged. Former Zuider Zee was an important fishing ground.

Ikhnaton (ĭknä'tùn) or **Akhenaton** (ä″kùnä'- tùn) [Egyptian,= Aton is satisfied], d. c.1358 B.C., king of Egypt (c.1375–c.1358 B.C.) of the XVIII dynasty, son of Amenhotep III. Beginning reign as Amenhotep IV, he changed his name on undertaking a complete reform in an attempt to unify political, social, and artistic life under a monotheism, centered about the sun-god Aton. The priests opposed him and domestic and foreign affairs brought ruin, but his period was one of the greatest of Egyptian art. A statue bust of his queen Nefretete (also Nofretete, Nepretiti, Nephretiti) is a familiar treasure of world art.

Ikon Basilike: see EIKON BASILIKE.

Île-aux-Noix, Fort (ēl-ō-nwä'), French fort in Canada, on Île aux Noix, an island in Richelieu R., c.30 mi. SE of Montreal. Built 1759. Fort surrendered to British in 1760. Named Fort Lennox, it fell to Americans in 1775 and became base of operations against Quebec until it was evacuated in 1776. Present fortifications (now included in Fort Lennox Natl. Historic Park; 210 acres) were started in 1782 and maintained as a military post until 1870.

Île-de-France (ēl-dù-fräs'), region and former province, N France, in Seine, Seine-et-Oise, Oise, and Aisne depts.; historic cap. Paris. Other cities: Beauvais, Compiègne, Fontainebleau, Soissons, Versailles. The center of the Paris basin, a fertile depression watered by the Seine, Marne, and Oise rivers, it is a vast agr. area, supplying Paris and its suburbs with fruit, vegetables, dairy products. There are many large and beautiful forests (e.g., at Fontainebleau, Compiègne, Rambouillet). The cradle of the French monarchy, the region grew out of the county

of Paris, whose count, Hugh Capet, became king in 987. The crown enlarged its domains, acquiring parts of Beauce, Brie, the Vexin, and other neighboring areas, and in the 15th cent. the region was made a province.

Île Jésus (ēl zhäzü') or **Jesus Island**, island (93 sq. mi.; pop. 37,843), S Que., Canada, between Mille Îles R. and Rivière des Prairies. Market gardening and dairy center.

Îles du Salut (ēl dü sälü'), small archipelago, off French Guiana, including Devil's Island. Also Safety Islands.

Ilf, Ilya (Arnoldovich) (ēlyä' ŭrnôl'dùvĭch ēlf'), pseud. of I. A. Fainzilber, 1879–1937, Russian humorist. With Y. P. Petrov (pseud. of Y. P. Katayev, 1903–42), he wrote *Little Golden Calf* (1933), a satire of capitalist survivals in Soviet society, and *Little Golden America* (1937), after a tour in the U.S.

Iliad (ĭl'lēùd) [from Gr. *Ilion* = Troy], Greek epic in 24 books by HOMER, telling of the wrath of ACHILLES and its consequences in the Trojan War.

Ilion: see TROY, anc. city of Asia Minor.

Ilion (ĭl'lēùn), village (pop. 9,363), E central N.Y., on Mohawk R. and the Barge Canal and SE of Utica. Mfg. of firearms (see REMINGTON, ELIPHALET) and typewriters.

Ilium: see TROY, anc. city of Asia Minor.

Illampú (ēyämpōō'), peak, 21,275 ft. high, E Bolivia, in Andes near L. Titicaca.

Ille-et-Vilaine (ēl″-ā-vēlĕn'), department (2,697 sq. mi.; pop. 578,246), NW France, in Brittany; cap. Rennes.

Illimani (ēyēmä'nē), mountain (21,184 ft. high), E Bolivia, in Andes.

illinium: see PROMETHIUM.

Illinois, state (55,947 sq. mi.; pop. 8,712,176), N central U.S.; admitted 1818 as 21st state (free); cap. SPRINGFIELD. CHICAGO largest city; other cities are PEORIA, ROCKFORD, EAST SAINT LOUIS, DECATUR, JOLIET, ELGIN. Bounded W by Mississippi R., S by Ohio R., NE by L. Michigan. Region of well-watered plains. Farming (livestock, corn, oats, hay, soybeans, truck, fruit); mining (coal, oil, fluorspar, silica sand). Proccesses meat, food, oil; mfg. of steel, farm machinery; printing, publishing. Transportation center of Midwest. Explored by Marquette and Jolliet (1673), La Salle (1679). Region went to British after last French and Indian War (1763). Won by U.S. in American Revolution after capture by G. R. CLARK of CAHOKIA and KASKASKIA (1778). Became separate territory 1809. Land speculation, factory of Cyrus H. McCORMICK (1847) and rail development of 1850s marked state's rise. Abraham LINCOLN and Stephen DOUGLAS won national attention by their debates on slavery issue in senatorial race (1858). Industry expanded greatly after Civil War. Farmers joined GRANGER MOVEMENT and resisted dominance of railroads. Labor-management tension reflected in HAYMARKET SQUARE RIOT (1886) and strike at PULLMAN (1894). Industrial position in nation was strengthened in World War II.

Illinois, river formed in NE Ill. by junction of Des Plaines and Kankakee rivers. Flows 273 mi. SW past Peoria to the Mississippi at Grafton. Link in shipping route between

Great Lakes and Gulf of Mexico; part of Illinois Waterway system.

Illinois, University of, at Urbana, Champaign, and Chicago; land-grant, state-supported, coed.; chartered 1867, opened 1868 as Illinois Industrial Univ., renamed 1885. Has institute of labor and industrial relations. Rush Medical College in Chicago (chartered 1837, affiliated with Univ. of Chicago 1898–1941) is affiliated. Pioneered in vocational education. Has betatron. Also has an Alma Mater group by alumnus Lorado Taft.

Illinois College: see JACKSONVILLE.

Illinois Indians, group of North American Indian tribes of Algonquian linguistic stock. In 17th cent. were scattered over S Wis., N Ill., and parts of Iowa and Mo. They were of Eastern Woodlands area culture, but also hunted buffalo. Wars with Iroquois and with Lake tribes (provoked by assassination of Pontiac) reduced Illinois Indians almost to nothing.

Illinois Institute of Technology: see CHICAGO.

Illuminati (ĭlōō″mĭnā′tī, –nä′tē) [Latin,= the enlightened], members of a rationalist society founded by Adam Weishaupt (after 1776) and flourishing briefly. It was connected with Freemasonry, was condemned by the Roman Catholic Church, and dissolved (1785) in Bavaria by the government. Later groups have also used the name, and the Rosicrucians call themselves Illuminati.

illuminating gas: see GAS; METHANE; NATURAL GAS.

illumination, in art, the decoration of manuscripts and books with colored and metal pictures, especially initial-letter and marginal decorations. Used in many medieval writings copied in monasteries and cathedral schools. A beautiful example is the Irish Book of Kells (8th cent.), at Trinity Col., Dublin.

illumination of streets and buildings: see LIGHTING; PHOTOMETRY.

Illyria (ĭlī′rēŭ) and **Illyricum** (ĭlī′rĭkŭm). In prehistoric times Indo-European tribes (Dalmatians and Pannonians) migrated to the N and E shores of the Adriatic in region later known as Illyria. Warlike and given to piracy, they withstood Greek influence and defeated Macedon. The Romans conquered the Illyrian kingdom and created the province of Illyricum (167 B.C.) from part of it. Later the region was Dalmatia and Pannonia. Today Illyria means the Adriatic coast N of central Albania.

Ilmen (ĭl′mŭn), lake (c.400 sq. mi.), NW European RSFSR. Empties through Volkhov R. into L. Ladoga. Novgorod and Staraya Russa are near its shores.

Iloilo (ē″lōē′lō), commercial city (pop. 110,-122), on SE Panay, Philippines; port on Iloilo Strait. Seat of Central Philippine Col. of Jaro.

image, in optics, likeness of object produced when light rays from object are reflected from mirror or refracted by lens. A real image, one formed by light rays coming from an object and converging before producing an image, can be thrown on a screen. A virtual image formed by prolongations of rays (not by rays themselves) cannot be thrown on screen, e.g., image from plane mirror. Size of image and whether it is erect or inverted, real or virtual, depend on distance from lens and type of lens or mirror used.

imagists, Anglo-American school of poetry, stressing concentration, hard clear images, new rhythms, and use of common speech. Founded by Ezra Pound, taken over by Amy Lowell. Richard Aldington, Hilda Doolittle, and John Gould Fletcher were imagists.

imam (ĭmäm′), in Islam, leader, especially in Friday prayer at mosque. As synonym for caliph, applied by Shiites to caliphs descended from ALI. After OMAYYAD family had held caliphate for centuries, the believers in Ali's supremacy (esp. Fatimites) adopted theory that Alid caliphs were really carrying on their rule secretly and that one Alid caliph (the MAHDI) would be restored to public rule before the end of the world. The fervor of Alid followers has led to rebellions in some Moslem countries.

imbecility: see FEEBLE-MINDEDNESS.

Immanuel or **Emmanuel** [Heb.,= God with us], Isaiah's name for child who was to be a sign of Judah's deliverance. A name of Jesus. Isa. 7.14; 8.8; Mat. 1.23.

Immermann, Karl (kärl′ ĭ′mûrmän), 1796–1840, German author. Successful as playwright in his lifetime, he survives chiefly through his novel *Die Epigonen* (1836), a satire on his contemporaries, and through short novels, e.g., *Der Oberhof.*

immigration, entrance of a person into a new country where he intends to establish permanent residence. There was a great influx of Europeans into the U.S. in the 19th cent., c.38,000,000 immigrants entering the U.S. between 1820 and 1920; Chinese and Japanese also began to immigrate. But restrictions were imposed (against Chinese) in 1882—the first against any group—and in 1917, 1921, and 1924 there were further restrictions, the last establishing the quota system whereby entrants were limited to 3% annually of the number of natives residing in the U.S. in 1910. In 1924, Asiatics were almost wholly excluded; a "national origins" plan made for more restrictions. The Chinese Exclusion Act was repealed in 1943, and a small quota set up. In 1952 Congress passed, over President Truman's veto, a new immigration law (the so-called McCarran Act) that, though it removed racial barriers to allow a small number of Asians to enter annually, reaffirmed the "national origin" feature of the 1921 and 1924 laws.

immunity, resistance to disease. Natural immunity arises from body's inherent ability to destroy invading organisms by action of certain white blood corpuscles and antibodies in blood. Immunity is acquired by surviving the disease or by inoculation or vaccination. Active immunity arises from antibodies produced in tissues; passive immunity results from introducing defense factors (e.g., antitoxin) into body and lasts for shorter time than active.

impala or **pallah,** antelope (*Aepyceros*) of E and S African bush country. It is reddish brown shading to whitish on under parts; shoulder height c.3 ft. Only male has horns (long, curved, lyre-shaped).

impatiens, touch-me-not, or **balsam,** annual or perennial plant of genus *Impatiens* with seed pods that burst at a touch when ripe. Annual garden balsams (*Impatiens balsamina*) have camellialike flowers. Wild jewelweed (*I. biflora*), native to moist soil in North America, has orange spurred flowers.

impeachment, formal accusation made by a legislature against a public official charging crime or serious misconduct. Also loosely used to describe the ensuing trial. In England, House of Commons presented articles of impeachment of House of Lords, who rendered judgment. Impeachment of Warren Hastings (1788–95) was one of last English cases. U.S. Constitution gives House of Representatives right to impeach U.S. officials (but not members of Congress). Senate tries cases; vote of two thirds of those present necessary to convict. Famous case was that of Pres. Andrew Johnson (impeached, but not convicted).

Impellitteri, Vincent R. (ĭmpĕl″ĭtĕ′rē), 1900–, American public official, mayor of New York city (1950–), b. Italy. Refused the Democratic nomination, he was elected as an independent, a political upset.

Imperial, city (pop. 1,759), SE Calif., oldest community in IMPERIAL VALLEY; founded 1902.

Imperial Conference, assembly of representatives of self-governing members of British Empire, held about every four years. First called Colonial Conferences (1887–1906) and dealt with defense problems. Since 1907 economic problems have been discussed. Dominion premiers now attempt to unify Empire policy. Decisions have no legal power, but are influential.

imperialism, broadly, extension of rule or influence by one people over another. Empires have existed since dawn of history, as in Egypt, Mesopotamia, Assyria, and Persian Empire. Ancient imperialism reached climax in Roman Empire and Byzantine Empire and later Ottoman Empire. In West imperialism emerged with rise of modern national states and age of exploration and discovery; and term is normally restricted to this modern type of empire building. Through colonies European hegemony was introduced by force, with an assumed superiority over native people. Spanish and Portuguese built "trading" empires, British and French true "settlement" empires, all motivated by MERCANTILISM. U.S. spread westward with idea of manifest destiny, but was not an empire until Spanish-American War. Anti-imperialism has grown steadily since American Revolution, and has led U.S. to grant independence to Philippines, and anti-imperialist sentiment following World War II. British and French empires have gradually loosed their hold upon dependent nations as agitation for nationalism has spread.

Imperial Valley, below-sea-level area of old Colorado Desert in SE Calif. and N Lower California, Mexico. Occupies Salton Sink S of SALTON SEA. Rainfall is scanty, and there are sudden, extreme changes in temperature (32°F.–115°F.). Colorado R. irrigation of its rich soils (begun c.1900, hindered by floods) succeeded by 1907. Irrigation now supplied to c.1,000,000 acres (mainly via ALL-AMERICAN CANAL), which produce truck, fruit, dates, grain, alfalfa, cotton, and dairy products. Centers include Brawley, Calexico, El Centro, Holtville, and Imperial in Calif., and Mexicali, Mexico.

import: see BALANCE OF TRADE.

impressionism, in painting, a late 19th-cent. French school. Its adherents attempted to depict quick visual impressions, often painted directly from nature. By using broken color they produced a luminous effect and were particularly successful with sunlight. Movement originated in 1870s and became popular in 90s, when most of its exponents had already left it. Most consistent impressionists were Monet, Sisley, and Pissarro. Others associated with school were Renoir and Degas. The term is used also in music for a late 19th-cent. French movement, typified in works of DEBUSSY. Characterized by breakdown of tonality and attempt to convey vague impression of mood.

impressment, enforcement of conscription. May be applied either to property or to persons in peace or war by virtue of a state's sovereign authority, except that constitutional limitations and legal regulations must be respected. In most modern democracies impressment in the historic sense of a "press gang" actually seizing and carrying an individual into service has been abandoned. Impressment of American sailors by the British was a cause of the War of 1812.

In, chemical symbol of the element INDIUM.

inbreeding, mating of closely related living things. Chief use is to insure preserving of desirable characters among purebred animal offspring. Inbreeding through too many generations reduces chances of diversity of characters and sometimes lessens vigor and reproductive ability.

Inca (ĭng′kû), pre-Colombian Indian empire (c.650,000 sq. mi.; pop. c.6,000,000), centered at Cuzco, Peru. The name Inca specifically refers to emperor and is used loosely to mean his people. Founded c.1200, empire reached its greatest extent under Huayna Capac (1493–1527), who was succeeded by his sons Huascar and Atahualpa. Atahualpa won in ensuing civil war, but Spanish, under Francisco Pizarro, conquered empire in 1553. Through a genius for organization, the Inca had welded together many peoples speaking different languages and exercised close control. The state was responsible for welfare of subjects, and owned everything except houses and movable household goods. Taxes were collected in labor. Populations were shifted at government's discretion for economic and control purposes. The Inca were skilled in engineering and agriculture, their activities in those fields running to road, bridge, drainage, and irrigation construction, and use of fertilizer. Highly developed arts and crafts included textiles, metallurgy, and ceramics.

incest (ĭn′sĕst), sexual relations between persons to whom marriage is prohibited because of blood relationship. Degree of proscribed relationship varies from group to group; in some societies marriage between clan members is taboo; in others even brother-sister marriage is accepted (e.g., among Egyptian and Inca royalty).

Inchcolm (ĭnch'kŭm), small island in Firth of Forth, Fifeshire, Scotland. Has ruins of Abbey of St. Columba (founded 1123).

Inchon, Korea: see CHEMULPO.

incinerator (ĭnsī'nŭrātŭr), furnace for burning combustible refuse. Usually it consists of a brick-lined combustion chamber fitted with stationary or mechanically-operated grates, charging holes, stoking and removal openings, ducts, and valves; often there are forced-draft blowers supplying air for combustion and a flue conducted through tall chimney.

inclined plane, a simple machine, of ancient origin, using a slanted plane up which the load or resistance is moved. Work put into the machine equals the effort multiplied by length of the plane; work output is product of the load and the height of the plane. Applications include the screw, wedge, chisel, carpenter's plane, and ax. See *ill.,* p. 793.

inclosure or **enclosure,** in agr., the practice of setting apart land formerly subject to common rights. Followed shift from the manorial system to free cultivation. In England it began in 12th cent., grew after development of Flemish wool trade in 14th cent., and reached its peak in late 17th cent. Caused shift of the poor to urban centers. Also helped efficient tillage and reclamation of wasteland.

income tax. Experiments on taxation of income were tried in medieval Italy and 19th-cent. England. A permanent income tax was adopted in England 1874, and a temporary one in U.S. 1862–72. The U.S. income-tax law of 1894 was declared unconstitutional, but the 16th Amendment legalized the income tax in 1913. The various states have levied income taxes since 1789; since 1919 most states have adopted them.

incorporation: see CORPORATION.

incubator, artificially heated apparatus for hatching eggs. Crude incubators were devised in ancient times; the Chinese have long used baskets heated by layers of wheat. Modern incubators are usually operated by electricity with automatic controls for heat, air, and moisture, and devices for turning eggs. Small models are used for premature babies.

incunabula (ĭn"kyōōnă'byōōlù), books of the "cradle" days of printing (15th cent.) by such printers as Gutenberg, Jensen, Caxton, and Aldus Manutius. There are many well-known European collections. Notable American collections are in Washington (Library of Congress), New York (Pierpont Morgan Library and others), Providence (John Carter Brown Library and Annmary Brown Memorial), and San Marino, Calif. (Henry E. Huntington Library).

Independence. 1 City (pop. 11,335), SE Kansas, on Verdigris R. near Okla. line; founded 1869. Oil refining and grain processing. Site of Rebel Creek battle (1863) is near. **2** City (pop. 36,963), W Mo., near Kansas City; settled 1825. Produces farm machinery and stoves. Was starting point in mid-19th cent. for SANTA FE TRAIL, OREGON TRAIL, and California Trail travelers. Hq. of Reorganized Church of Jesus Christ of Latter-Day Saints. Home of Harry S. Truman.

Independence, Declaration of: see DECLARATION OF INDEPENDENCE.

Independence Day: see FOURTH OF JULY.

Independence Hall, building in Philadelphia on Independence Square. Houses Liberty Bell and historical museum. Scene of proclamation of Declaration of Independence, Continental Congress, and Constitutional Convention.

Independents, in religion, name given to Christion congregations claiming freedom from ecclesiastical and civil authority. In England called Brownists (see BROWNE, ROBERT) or SEPARATISTS until in 17th cent. name Independents became popular.

Independent Treasury System. Pres. Andrew Jackson secured transfer of government funds from BANK OF THE UNITED STATES to state banks, but Panic of 1837, at least partially brought on by transfer of government surplus to states, showed evils of that arrangement. Pres. Van Buren proposed an independent treasury isolated from all banks. A law to this end was passed in 1840, but the Whigs, victorious in national election, repealed it. Objections of Pres. John Tyler on constitutional grounds prevented establishment of another Bank of the United States. Following Democratic return to power, an act of Aug., 1846, ordered public revenues retained in the Treasury building and in subtreasuries (see SUBTREASURY) in various cities. Treasury was to pay out its own funds and be completely independent of banking and financial system of the nation. In practice, however, specie tended to accumulate in the Treasury to detriment of business. Civil War put strain on Treasury and proved interdependence of Treasury and banks; NATIONAL BANK was created. Old theory of absolute independence was in practice abandoned by 1898. Federal Reserve Act of 1913 marked true end of Independent Treasury.

Index, in full *Index librorum prohibitorum,* list of books forbidden to its members by the Roman Catholic Church. It includes only works that have been brought before the Holy See for judgment and have been officially declared inimical to faith or morals. Catholics are obliged also to avoid any other works that are injurious but are not on the Index, and for critical and scholarly purposes are allowed to read those that are.

index, of a book or periodical, a list, nearly always alphabetical, of the topics treated. Seeks to direct reader to every subject and proper name about which any information is given in book. Index to periodical is less specific. In 16th cent. term *index* began to be commonly applied to such a list. In 1848 in U.S., William F. Poole issued index to most widely circulated periodicals of the time. *Poole's Index* was superseded in 1907 by *Readers' Guide to Periodical Literature.* Various fields of knowledge have special indexes. Newspaper indexes include that to the New York *Times* (from 1913).

index number, figure showing change in price or quantity in ratio to a number taken as norm, or base, often expressed in percentage. Index of wages divided by index of cost of living is index of purchasing power, or real wages.

India, subcontinent, S Asia, cut off from most of the continent by lofty Himalayas. In it are PAKISTAN and republic of **India,** officially also called *Bharat* (1,138,814 sq. mi.; pop. 356,891,624); member of British Commonwealth of Nations; cap. New Delhi. Comprises 27 states, including Bombay, Delhi, Hyderabad, Madras, Mysore, and Punjab. SIKKIM and BHUTAN are protectorates. Republic is bounded NE by Burma and China, N by Tibet and Nepal, and NW by W Pakistan, with E Pakistan forming an enclave in NE India. Small enclaves on E and W coasts constitute FRENCH INDIA and PORTUGUESE INDIA. S half is huge peninsula jutting between Arabian Sea and Bay of Bengal. Great Indian rivers are Ganges, Brahmaputra, and Indus. Agr. output is inadequate for feeding vast population. Crops include rice, cotton, jute, and tea. Among natural resources are valuable forests (esp. teak and ebony) and deposits of mica, manganese, coal, copper, and iron. Heavy industry is centered at Jamshedpur (iron and steel), Bombay (textiles), and Calcutta (jute products). Largest cities and main ports are Bombay, Calcutta, and Madras. Much of Indian life is still largely based on CASTE system, despite official disapproval. Relief from life of poverty is found in religious rites (mainly Hindu and Moslem) and in pilgrimages to holy cities, notably Benares. Earliest known civilization on subcontinent is that of MOHENJO-DARO (fl. 4000-2000 B.C.). Aryans first entered India from NW in c.1500 B.C. and developed a Brahmanic civilization, in which basic tenets of HINDUISM were formulated. BUDDHISM and JAINISM emerged in 6th cent. B.C. Hinduism was at first the religion of MAURYA empire (325-184 B.C.), founded after Alexander the Great's invasion of N India (c.326 B.C.); but in 3d cent. B.C. ASOKA estab. Buddhism as state religion. During Gupta dynasty (A.D. 320?-c.544?) and reign of Harsha (606-47), Hindu culture enjoyed a golden age. After 8th cent., Rajputs dominated NW. Moslem power began with raids of Mahmud of Ghazni in 11th cent. and establishment (1206) of DELHI SULTANATE. MOGUL empire, founded 1526 by BABER, flourished under AKBAR, SHAH JEHAN, and AURANGZEB. Meanwhile the Portuguese had taken Goa in 1510; in 18th cent., while MAHRATTAS and SIKHS were weakening the empire, the British and French carved out colonial domains. Victories of Robert CLIVE over DUPLEIX ended all European threats to power of British East India Co. Warren HASTINGS as governor general did much to solidify Clive's gains. SEPOY REBELLION (1857) led to abolition of East India Co. and transfer of Indian rule to the crown. Movement for independence became important when Gandhi assumed leadership of INDIAN NATIONAL CONGRESS. Desire of Congress to form united front against Britain was balked by MOSLEM LEAGUE (led by Mahomed Ali Jinnah), which agitated for a separate Moslem state. When India became free in 1947, Congress agreed reluctantly to the partition. Dominion of India became a sovereign republic on Jan. 26, 1950. In 1951 she launched a five-year plan (aided in 1952

by Point Four grants from U.S.) to develop her resources. Rival claims to control over KASHMIR strained her relations with Pakistan.

Indiana, state (36,291 sq. mi.; pop. 3,934,224), N central U.S.; admitted 1816 as 19th state (free); cap. INDIANAPOLIS. Other cities are FORT WAYNE, GARY, SOUTH BEND, EVANSVILLE, TERRE HAUTE. Bounded S by Ohio R., SW by Wabash R., NW by L. Michigan. Farming (corn, wheat, livestock, grains, fruit, truck, poultry, dairying); mining (coal, limestone, oil). Mfg. of steel, motor vehicles, machinery, chemicals; food processing, rail and machine shops. French estab. first permanent settlement at VINCENNES c.1735. British took over region in 1763. G. R. CLARK took Vincennes in American Revolution. Process of subduing Indians continued through indecisive battle of TIPPECANOE (1811). Indiana Territory created 1800. State hurt by Panic of 1837. Supported Union in Civil War despite activities of KNIGHTS OF THE GOLDEN CIRCLE. Farmers and laborers fought for rights against rising industry in late 19th cent. Present economy is aided by mfg., but farmers' problems remain.

Indiana, borough (pop. 11,743), W Pa., NE of Pittsburgh; settled c.1772. Coal mining center with mfg. of tires, food products, and clay products.

Indian Affairs, Bureau of, created (1824) in U.S. War Dept. and transferred (1849) by act of Congress to U.S. Dept. of the Interior. Had jurisdiction over Indian trade and removal of Indians to reservations in the West. Developed primarily into land-administering agency. Now also provides educational facilities and other services.

Indiana Harbor, Ind: see EAST CHICAGO.

Indianapolis, city (pop. 427,173), state cap. (since 1825), central Ind., on White R. and SE of Chicago; settled 1819. State's largest city, it is a banking, transportation, and farm trade center with large stockyards. Mfg. of building materials, metal products, pharmaceuticals, and packed meat. Has home and burial place of J. W. Riley, American Legion national hq., and annual motor races on near-by speedway. Seat of Butler Univ. (Disciples of Christ; coed.; chartered 1850, opened 1855; John Herron Art Institute affiliated), and Indiana Univ. units.

Indian art and architecture is essentially decorative and often highly symbolic. Historical period began c.250 B.C. with Buddhist shrines, temples, and stupas (memorial mounds), which show Persian and Greek influence. Paintings were mainly frescoes. Jain work (100 B.C.-A.D. 1300) flourished as Buddhism waned (from 3d cent.), resulting in impressive temples with pointed domes. Hindu style, which borrowed much from the Jains, is marked by pyramidal roof and great richness of detail. Finest example of late Indian Moslem style, characterized by graceful dome, arch, and minarets, is the TAJ MAHAL. As architectural decoration sculpture was more important than painting. Decorative arts (e.g., damascening and jewelry making) have been carried to perfection.

Indiana University, mainly at Bloomington; state supported, coed.; chartered as seminary 1820, opened 1824; became college 1828; university 1838. Has institute of criminal law and criminology.

Indian breadroot: see BREADROOT.

Indian literature. An extensive written literature in vernacular languages of the subcontinent of India did not appear until 16th cent. Its development was spurred by emergence of Hindu pietistic movements which encouraged popularizing of SANSKRIT LITERATURE. Great classics, e.g., *Ramayana*, were put into popular verse form. Classical Persian poetry was basis for Urdu verse written for Mogul court. In early 19th cent. popular prose began to flourish with introduction of printing presses and establishment of vernacular schools. Literature today includes works in English and major languages of India and Pakistan. Best-known writers of modern India include Tagore, Iqbal, R. K. Narayan, Sudhin N. Ghose, and Sarojini Naidu. See PALI LITERATURE and PRAKRIT LITERATURE.

Indian mallow: see VELVETWEED.

Indian millet: see PEARL MILLET.

Indian music of North America is primarily a vocal art. It is entirely melodic, having no harmony or polyphony. Intonation is uncertain, resulting from the use of forced muscular tension in the vocal chords. Drums and rattles are the chief percussion instruments; wind instruments are mainly flutes and whistles. A song is considered a means of communication with supernatural powers; definite result (e.g., victory, rain, or health) are expected. There is no system of notation; songs are handed down from generation to generation. Certain ceremonial and medicinal songs are believed to be owned by the singer and to have been received by him in a dream. Only the owner of such a song may sing it, unless he chooses to sell it and share the mystical properties that accompany it. Most love songs associated with Indians actually show strong European influence.

Indian Mutiny: see SEPOY REBELLION.

Indian National Congress, political organization of India, founded 1885. Original purpose was to make India a British dominion by constitutional means. In 1917 the militants, led by GANDHI, forced resignation of moderates and began call for *Swaraj* [complete independence]. Their chief weapon, nonviolent disobedience campaign, was first used on large scale in 1919. Party's refusal to cooperate with the British in World War II led to arrest of its leaders. Outlawed 1942–45. In conferences leading to India's independence (1947), party was forced to bow to demand of MOSLEM LEAGUE for separate state of Pakistan. With NEHRU as leader the Congress kept its dominant position in Republic of India (estab. 1950).

Indian nut: see PINE.

Indian Ocean, third largest ocean of world, extending from India to Antarctica and from E Africa to Tasmania; stretches c.4,000 mi. along equator and c.6,000 mi. N to S. Greatest known depth, c.24,000 ft., is near Java. Its great seasonal winds (monsoon) bring rain to SE Asia. Only northern part is important for shipping.

Indianola (ĭn"dēŭnō'lŭ), city (pop. 5,145), S Iowa, S of Des Moines. Seat of Simpson Col. (Methodist; coed.; 1860).

Indian paintbrush or **painted cup,** parasitic annual or perennial plant (*Castilleja*), with many species native to W U.S. They bear flowerlike red bracts.

Indian pipe, low funguslike saprophytic woodland plant, waxy white or salmon, of genus *Monotropa,* found in North America and Asia. It has scalelike leaves and pipe-shaped flowers which form seeds.

Indian River, lagoon, c.120 mi. long, E Fla., paralleling coast and extending S from N of Titusville to Stuart. Resorts border its shores. Its fertile valley produces citrus fruit.

Indians, American, peoples who occupied North America, Middle America, and South America before the coming of the Europeans. Most authorities today believe that the Indians came into the W Hemisphere from Asia via the Bering Strait in a series of migrations (the waves accounting for many linguistic families). Common origin is taken to explain the common physical features—coarse, straight black hair, dark eyes, sparse body hair, and brownish skin color. They supposedly brought with them their Neolithic culture; most Indians made fire with a drill, had domesticated dogs, made baskets, and used stone tools. In Middle America and South America high material cultures were built up before the coming of the white man: MAYA, TOLTEC, AZTEC, INCA, and CHIBCHA. The development of powerful city-states and, in the case of the Inca, a true empire, was accompanied by a rich architectural and artistic development. Some tribes, however (e.g., those of Tierra del Fuego) had very sparse material culture. Other groups had intermediate culture, some agricultural, and some dependent on gathering, hunting, and fishing. Among the agricultural societies, maize was generally the basic crop. Anthropologists distinguish so-called culture areas (as Eastern Woodlands, Plains). In 1492 Indians N of Mexico numbered 900,000, but by 1870 they had dwindled to 300,000. In 1945, there were 400,000. In most Central and South American countries, the Indian strain predominates, and in the 20th cent. a movement for reviving and preserving Indian culture (*indianismo*) has been strong.

Indian Territory, in U.S. history, name generally applied to country set aside for Indians by Indian Intercourse Act (1834) and more particularly applied to territory to which Cherokee, Creek, Seminole, Choctaw, and Chickasaw tribes were removed between 1820 and 1845. E part of present Okla., N of Red R., became known as Indian Territory as Indians were gradually forced into settlement there. Tribes other than original five also moved there. Extinction of Territory came in 1907 with entrance of Okla. into the Union.

Indian turnip: see JACK-IN-THE-PULPIT.

India-rubber tree: see RUBBER PLANT.

Indic languages, group of Indo-Iranian subfamily of Indo-European languages. See LANGUAGE (table).

indiction (ĭndĭk′shŭn), a period of 15 years or a year in such a period. Probably suggested by an Egyptian fiscal period, dating by indiction was adopted by the Roman Empire in 4th cent., was practiced by the Byzantine Empire and throughout Europe, and is still occasionally used by the Roman Church.

indictment (ĭndīt′mŭnt) formal written charge of a crime made by a public prosecutor before a grand jury. The grand jury in turn may offer the charge against the accused. A person suspected of crime may also be brought to trial by presentment (accusation issued by the grand jury though the prosecutor has not offered a formal bill of indictment) or by information (accusation made directly by prosecutor without consideration by grand jury; not permissible in capital or otherwise infamous crime). When an indictment or a presentment is approved, the foreman of the grand jury marks it "true bill."

indigo, the most important blue dye. Known in ancient India and Egypt, it was introduced into Europe in 16th cent. It is obtained from leguminous plants of genus *Indigofera* by fermentation of macerated plants; these liberate colorless indican which oxidizes to blue indigo when stirred. Adolf von Baeyer first synthesized it.

indigo bunting or **indigo bird,** small bird of FINCH family. Male summer plumage is metallic blue; female and young have brown sparrowlike plumage. Breeds from N.B. to Ga., W to N.Dak. and central Texas; winters from S Mexico to Panama.

Indio, city (pop. 6,450), SE Calif., ESE of Redlands. Trade center in COACHELLA VALLEY. Joshua Tree Natl. Monument is near.

indium, silver-white, metallic element (symbol = In; see also ELEMENT, table) resembling aluminum. It is relatively soft, malleable, and ductile.

Indo-Aryan, group of the Indo-Iranian subfamily of Indo-European languages. Broader uses on a racial basis are now obsolete. See LANGUAGE (table).

Indo-China (ĭn′dōchī′nŭ), group (272,200 sq. mi.; pop. 27,000,000) of three states (VIET NAM, comprising Cochin China, Annam, and Tonkin; LAOS; and CAMBODIA) in SE Asia, on E Indo-Chinese peninsula. Borders on Burma, Thailand, and China. Associated with France within French Union, which the three states joined in 1950.

Indo-European, family of languages to which English belongs. It includes more speakers than any other family. See LANGUAGE (table).

Indo-Iranian, subfamily of Indo-European languages. See LANGUAGE (table).

Indonesia, republic (575,893 sq. mi.; pop. c.80,-000,000), Malay archipelago, SE Asia; cap. Jakarta. Comprises Sunda Isls. (including JAVA and SUMATRA), Lesser Sundas (including BALI), CELEBES, the MOLUCCAS, part of BORNEO and TIMOR, and thousands of smaller islands. A major producer of tin and oil, with rich deposits of manganese, gold, silver, copper, and zinc. Agr. and forest products include rice, rubber, quinine, tobacco, sugar, coffee, tea, and pepper. Early in Christian era, area came under influence of Indian civilization through influx of Buddhist and Hindu monks; great native empires that emerged after 7th cent. were strongly linked to Hinduism and Buddhism. Islam, introduced by Arab traders in 13th cent., eventually became dominant religion. By 16th cent., when Portuguese traders appeared, Indonesia had disintegrated into many small weak states. The Portuguese were soon ousted by Dutch East India Co., which succeeded also in removing rivalry of British East India Co. (1610–23). After liquidation of company (1798), area came under direct rule of Dutch government; known thereafter as Netherlands East Indies. Dutch rule was broken 1811–15 when islands were occupied by the British under Raffles. In World War II, nationalists were active throughout Japanese occupation (begun early 1942); in Aug., 1945, they estab. Republic of Indonesia, which claimed rule over Java, Madura, and Sumatra. Dutch opposition led to warfare, which did not subside even after Dutch recognition of republic by Cheribon agreement (1947). Finally, after Hague conference (mediated by UN), Indonesia became a sovereign country on Dec. 28, 1949. Called the United States of Indonesia, it comprised the nationalist-sponsored republic of Indonesia and 15 Dutch-supported states. Federation gave way in Aug., 1950, to unified republic (headed by SUKARNO), linked to Netherlands only through loose union under Dutch Crown. In 1952 Indonesians were still disputing Dutch claim to W New Guinea.

Indore (ĭndôr′), former princely state, W central India; since 1948 part of Madhya Bharat. Indore, city (pop. 203,695), was its cap., founded early 18th cent. It is now summer cap. of Madhya Bharat. Major cotton-milling center.

Indra (ĭn′drŭ), in Vedic religion and in Hinduism, god of sky and storms, a beneficent deity of Aryan invaders of India. With rise of Brahmanism, he was displaced by trinity of Brahma, Vishnu, and Siva. See also VEDA.

Indre (ē′drŭ), department (2,666 sq. mi.; pop. 252,075), central France, in Berry, crossed by Indre R.; cap. Châteauroux.

Indre-et-Loire (ēdrālwär′), department (2,378 sq. mi.; 349,685), N central France, in Touraine; cap. Tours.

induction. Electrostatic induction is the production of an electric charge on a body by bringing it near a charged body. This "charging by induction" can be done, for example, by bringing a negatively charged body near an uncharged body; negative charges in the uncharged body are repelled and some will leave the uncharged body if there is a conductor through which they can run off into the ground. If ground connection is removed before charged body is withdrawn, the originally uncharged body will be positively charged since negative charges have become less than number of positive charges. Electromagnetic induction is accomplished by movement of conductor across field of a magnet or movement of magnetic field over the conductor. Self-induction (or inductance), also called electromagnetic inertia, is the setting up of an electromotive force in a conductor which opposes the change of a current, i.e., it retards both an increase and a decrease, so current cannot be instantaneously started or stopped.

indulgence (ĭndŭl'jŭns). The Roman Catholic Church teaches that a sinner, forgiven through the sacrament of penance, must yet make satisfaction for his sins here or in purgatory. But Christ and his saints have by their good works earned a superfluity of satisfaction to God for human sins, and this accumulated grace is called doctrinally the Infinite Treasury of Merits. From this satisfaction the Church as God's ministry remits punishment the sinner would otherwise have to undergo. Official statement of this remission is an indulgence, which may be gained by Catholics in many ways (e.g., prayers, visiting churches). Until the Council of TRENT, there were many abuses in granting indulgences (esp. their purchase for money), and it was these abuses that LUTHER first denounced.

Indus (ĭn'dŭs), river, c.1,900 mi. long, rising in Himalayas in W Tibet. Flows through Kashmir and W Pakistan (where it is joined by Panjinad R.) to Arabian Sea. An ancient civilization (see MOHENJO-DARO) flourished on its banks.

Indus Civilization: see MOHENJO-DARO.

industrial diseases: see OCCUPATIONAL DISEASES.

industrial management, the highly organized modern method of carrying on industrial operations. Growth of manufacturing required special supervision of machinery and elimination of inefficiency. The first sustained effort in this direction was made in the 1880s by F. W. Taylor of the Midvale Steel Co. The motions of workers were studied to speed up production by cutting out excess movements. Such time and motion studies of the flow of materials through the plant became a major item of inquiry, as did product design. Relations with workers became the subject of industrial psychology. Soon after 1910 U.S. firms estab. the first personnel departments, and much attention was given to improving worker morale by providing better facilities and new incentives, such as chance for advancement and, occasionally, a voice in management. Other items that have come to be the concern of management include safety devices, better sanitation, rest, eating, and recreation facilities, health insurance, and pensions.

Industrial Revolution. The term refers primarily to the period in English history, roughly 1750–1850, in which striking changes in economic structure were produced by transition from stable agr. and commercial society to modern industrialism. Voyages of 15th and 16th cent. opened the way for world-wide commerce. Capitalism appeared in 17th cent. Machines were made of wood and driven by water and wind power. In 18th cent. the change to steam power was made by James Watt. England became world textile center and there were such inventions as Arkwright's spinning frame (1769) and Edmund Cartwright's power loom (1785). Coke was used in iron production; coal mines and the use of steel became of paramount importance. Factories and industrial towns sprang up. In 19th cent. railroads and steamboats wrought new changes. Electricity and the gasoline engine have produced further changes. Spread has been world wide. Germany (after 1850), U.S. (after Civil War), and Japan (in 20th cent.) have been transformed by industrialism. Accompanying economic philosophy was laissez faire doctrine of Adam Smith. Later interpretations have been attempted by Karl Marx, Socialism, and the Manchester school. Industrialism has divided society into opposing classes of capital and labor, brought about world economic interdependence, and introduced many economic problems as well as causing a world-wide rise in the level of material goods.

industrial union, one composed of all the workers in a given industry, regardless of skill, craft, or occupation. All American unions were craft unions until the 1870s. Knights of Labor, Industrial Workers of the World, and the C.I.O. have advocated organizations cutting across craft lines. An industrial union is called a vertical union (including workers of all levels of skills), as opposed to horizontal or craft unions.

Industrial Workers of the World (I.W.W.), revolutionary industrial union, organized in Chicago in 1905. Among its leaders were Eugene V. Debs, William D. Haywood, and Daniel De Leon. Members were nicknamed the Wobblies. Aimed to unite all skilled and unskilled workers for purpose of overthrowing capitalism and achieving socialist society. Its methods were direct action, propaganda, the boycott, and the strike; it opposed sabotage, arbitration, collective bargaining, and political affiliation. About 150 strikes were carried out, but from a probable strength of 100,000 in 1912 it had dropped to less than 10,000 by 1930. Its contributions include the temporary organization of migrant and Negro workers, union of skilled and unskilled labor, and influence on later unions.

Indy, Vincent d' (vĕsă' dĕdē'), 1851–1931, French composer; pupil of Franck. His compositions include *Symphony on a French Mountain Air* for piano and orchestra; symphonic variations, *Istar;* songs, chamber music, piano works, and three symphonies.

inertia (ĭnûr'shŭ), in physics, resistance of body at rest to being set in motion and that of body in motion to being accelerated, retarded, or changed in direction. Force must be applied to overcome it.

Inez de Castro: see CASTRO, INÉS DE.

infallibility (ĭnfăl″ûbĭ'lŭtē), in Christian thought, inability of Church to err as a teaching authority. The idea is widely rejected by Protestants. There is disagreement as to which organ of Church is protected by God from teaching error. Orthodox hold ecumenical councils infallible; Roman Catholics agree but do not accept conciliar acts unratified by the pope. The dogma that the pope's pronouncements made ex cathedra on faith and morals are infallible was enounced by the Vatican Council (1870).

infant, human baby from birth to about two years. Development and characteristics vary greatly. Average birth weight 6½–7½ lb; height, 20–21 in. Weight usually is doubled at 5–6 months, trebled at one year. Height increases c.5 in. in first 6 months, 8 to 10 in. by end of year. Skull bones, sutures, and posterior of two fontanels (called "soft spots") close in several weeks; larger, front fontanel at about one year. Teeth usually begin to erupt at 5–8 months; first dentition (20 teeth) complete at 24–30 months. At first human milk or substitute formula provides essential nutrients except vitamins C and D. Cereals and strained foods are added gradually. Injections immunizing against diphtheria, smallpox, and other diseases are advisable during first year. Affectionate care is needed for healthy development.

infantile paralysis: see POLIOMYELITIS.

infectious diseases: see COMMUNICABLE DISEASES.

inferiority complex, Adler's term for a COMPLEX of emotionally toned ideas centered on real or imaginary handicaps. The attempt to compensate for feelings of inferiority leads to behavior aimed at proving them unjustified. Failure to compensate successfully ends in NEUROSIS. Successful compensation is directed to valuable social or personal ends.

infinity, in mathematics, term for quantity larger than any number; indicated by symbol ∞. In geometry, a position an infinite distance from the portion of space considered.

inflection, in grammar. In most languages words can be arranged in formally similar sets, such that members of each set have a common feature (stem, root, or base), and members of different sets have features in common not included in the stem; these features are often called inflections. Examples of languages with extensive inflections are Latin, Eskimo, and Arabic; of those with few inflections, Chinese. Typical Latin noun or adjective is inflected for CASE and NUMBER; adjectives are inflected for gender. Latin verbs have overlapping categories of inflection, MOOD, VOICE, TENSE, person, and number. Some linguists distinguish between inflection and agglutination, which is inflection with relative looseness of fusion between stem and inflectional feature. In 19th cent. theory was widely held that agglutination was more primitive than inflection. This theory is now abandoned.

influenza (ĭn″flōŏĕn′zŭ), contagious, infectious disease characteristically occurring in epidemic and pandemic outbreaks. Cause is thought to be a virus. It is attended by rapid progressive inflammation of mucous membranes of respiratory tract.

infrared rays (ĭn″frŭrĕd′), invisible rays of wave length longer than visible light and having a heating effect.

infusorial earth (ĭn″fyŏōsô′rĕŭl), name sometimes used for diatomaceous deposits built up from remains of microscopic plant life. It is not generally approved as a term.

Inge, William Ralph (ĭng), 1860–, Anglican prelate and author, dean of St. Paul's Cathedral (1911–34). His pessimism earned him name of "gloomy dean."

Ingelow, Jean (ĭn′jŭlō), 1820–97, English author of verse (e.g., "High Tide on the Coast of Lincolnshire, 1571"), novels (e.g., Off the

Skelligs, 1872), children's books (e.g., *Mopsa the Fairy,* 1869).

Ingemann, Bernhard Severin (ĭng′ŭmän), 1789–1862, Danish poet. Poems in *Holger Danske* (1837) became popular national songs. Also wrote religious lyrics in *Morning and Evening Songs* (1839) and historical novels.

Ingermanland (ĭng′gŭrmŭnländ), historic region, RSFSR, S of Gulf of Finland, between L. Peipus and L. Onega; also called Ingria. Subject to Great Novgorod, later to Moscow, in Middle Ages; conquered by Sweden 1617; restored to Russia 1721. Peter I built St. Petersburg (Leningrad) in Ingermanland.

Ingersoll, Charles Jared (ĭng′gŭrsôl), 1782–1862, American political leader and author. U.S. Representative from Pa. (1813–15, 1841–49). Some of his publications urge more intellectual independence and national self-sufficiency.

Ingersoll, Robert Green, 1833–99, American orator, a lawyer. Nominated James G. Blaine for President in famous "plumed knight" speech (1876). Known as "the great agnostic"; his lectures on religion won wide attention. Called Bob Ingersoll.

Ingersoll, town (pop. 6,524), S Ont., Canada, on Thames R. and ENE of London. Mfg. of furniture, hardware and tools.

Ingham, Charles Cromwell (ĭng′ŭm), 1796–1863, American painter, b. Ireland. Achieved fame in New York as painter of beautiful and fashionable women.

Inglewood, city (pop. 46,185), S Calif., industrial and residential suburb of Los Angeles; laid out 1887. Oil refining and mfg. of aircraft. Has race track.

Ingoldsby, Thomas: see BARHAM, RICHARD HARRIS.

Ingolstadt (ĭng′gôlshtät), city (pop. 40,270), Upper Bavaria, on the Danube. Produces textiles, automobiles. Dates from 8th cent. Unsuccessfully besieged by Gustavus II of Sweden 1632. The university, founded 1472, was transferred to Landshut in 1800, to Munich in 1826. The Gothic minster (15th cent.) and other medieval buildings survived damage in World War II.

Ingres, Jean Auguste Dominique (zhä′ ōgüst′ dômēnēk′ ĕ′grŭ), 1780–1867, French painter, a master draughtsman and portraitist; b. Montauban. Studied with J. L. David and became bulwark of classicism in a romantic era. Lived mainly in Rome, where he spent his later years as director of French Acad.

Ingush, people of Caucasus: see CHECHEN.

Inisfail (ĭ″nĭsfāl′), [Irish,= island of destiny], literary name for Ireland.

initiative and referendum, the initiating of a law by popular petition (initiative) and the referring to popular vote a law passed by the legislature (referendum). In the U.S., individual states require signatures of from 5 to 8 percent of the electorate for an initiative. The referendum is required in most states for constitutional amendments.

injection, introduction of liquid into body. Types include intradermal, into skin tissue; intramuscular, into muscle; intravenous, into vein; spinal, beneath outer membrane of spinal cord. Usually administered by means of a needle and syringe or a container which introduces fine spray into tissues.

injunction 598 Innocent VIII

injunction, formal written order of a court (decree) commanding or prohibiting a certain act, usually granted by a judge without a jury. Originally only prohibitive (negative) injunctions were granted, but later courts broadened the practice to include positive commands. Interlocutory injunctions are those issued while an action is pending and tend to protect a plaintiff's interests so that the final judgment may be of use to him. A final injunction is the judgment of the court after all the evidence has been heard. In case of disobedience of an injunction, the defendant is tried for contempt of court. In labor disputes injunctions were formerly very widely used (see CONSPIRACY).

ink, India or China ink, a permanent black ink, made of lampblack or ivory black mixed with glue or gum, probably known in China from c.1200 B.C. Standard black ink containing tannic acid, probably known from 2d cent., is much used because it flows freely. Aniline dyes generally used in colored inks.

Inkerman (ĭng′kŭrmŭn, Rus. ēn-kĭrmän′), E suburb of Sevastopol, RSFSR, scene of costly allied victory (1854) in Crimean War.

Inkster, village (pop. 16,728), SE Mich., residential suburb of Detroit; settled 1825.

Inland Sea, scenic body of water in Japan, between Honshu on N and Kyushu and Shikoku on S. Many pine-covered islets.

Inman, Henry, 1801–46, American portrait, genre, and landscape painter.

Inn, river, 320 mi. long, rising in Engadine valley, Switzerland, and flowing NE through Austria and Bavaria, joining the Danube at Passau.

inn, in Great Britain, means a hotel, public house, tavern, or coffeehouse where lodging is provided. A tavern, in usual sense, provides only food and drink. In U.S., inns usually are small rural houses for transients, or, occasionally, resort establishments. The hotel has emerged since late 17th cent.

Inner Hebrides, Scotland: see HEBRIDES.

Inner Mongolia: see MONGOLIA.

Inner Temple: see INNS OF COURT; TEMPLE, THE.

Inness, George (ĭ′nĭs), 1825–94, American landscape painter. Early work was in Hudson River school tradition. Later influenced by Barbizon school, but achieved free and colorful personal style. A Swedenborgian, he sought the mystical in nature. His son, **George Inness, Jr.,** 1854–1926, was a landscape and animal painter.

Innisfree, small island, Co. Sligo, Ireland, in Lough Gill. Celebrated by W. B. Yeats in his poem "Lake Isle of Innisfree."

Innocent I, Saint, d. 417, pope (401–17). Upheld supremacy of the papacy; supported St. John Chrysostom and condemned Pelagius; tried vainly to prevent Alaric's sack of Rome (410). Feast: July 28.

Innocent II, d. 1143, pope (1130–43), a Roman. Opposed by Antipope Anacletus II, Innocent won the support of Bernard of Clairvaux and Emperor Lothair II and prevailed over Anacletus' successor, Victor IV. Convened Second Lateran Council and condemned some teachings of Abelard and Arnold of Brescia.

Innocent III, b. 1160 or 1161, d. 1216, pope

(1198–1216), an Italian named Lotario di Segni; one of the most prominent figures of medieval history. A learned theologian and jurist, he held the theory that supremacy of the spirit over the flesh meant that the Church ruler (the pope) should have superiority over lay rulers of states—a theory later carried to an extreme by Boniface VIII but not held in present Roman Catholic doctrine. To establish papal supremacy Innocent was active in political affairs. In the Holy Roman Empire he arbitrated the dispute of PHILIP OF SWABIA and OTTO IV in Otto's favor (1201); later favored Philip (1207–8); crowned Otto (1209) after Philip's murder, only to excommunicate him (1210) and bring about the election of FREDERICK II, who was his ward. In England, Innocent by setting aside two claimants for the archbishopric of Canterbury and naming Stephen Langton infuriated King John; in the quarrel Innocent put England under the interdict and formally deposed the king (1212). John submitted and received England and Ireland as a fief from the pope. Later he declared that the Magna Carta was not binding on John because extorted by force and without the knowledge of his overlord (Innocent). In France, the pope could not establish political power over Philip II but did force him to bow to canon law in the matter of a divorce. In Italy he reclaimed and reorganized papal territories and was recognized as overlord of Tuscany, but he failed to subdue N Italian cities. Thus in all Europe he went far to put his theory of papal supremacy into effect, though history was to make his victories hollow. He promoted the Fourth Crusade and protested when the Crusaders instead of going to the Holy Land attacked the Byzantine Empire; nevertheless he recognized the Latin Kingdom of Constantinople which they set up, and by efforts to spread the Latin rite in that kingdom embittered relations between the Eastern and Western churches. Similarly he protested when the crusade he had started against the Albigenses was turned to political and economic ends by Simon de Montfort, but his protests were vain; he later urged St. Dominic's mission. Innocent was vigorous in internal Church affairs and dominated the Fourth LATERAN COUNCIL (1215). He wrote extensively and his De contemptu mundi [on contempt of this world] was popular in the Middle Ages.

Innocent IV, d. 1254, pope (1243–54), a Genoese. His reign was occupied chiefly in a contest with the Hohenstaufen rulers. He opposed Emperor FREDERICK II and had to flee to Lyons, where he convened a council (1245) that declared Frederick deposed. Innocent supported counterclaimants to the throne against Frederick, CONRAD IV, and MANFRED. Just before his death he supported young CONRADIN as claimant to the Sicilian throne. Heavy taxes to support these contests brought criticism on Innocent (from Robert Grosseteste among others).

Innocent VIII, 1432–92, pope (1484–92), a Genoese. Papal affairs were largely directed by his friend Giuliano della Rovere (later Julius II). He originally planned a crusade against the Turks, but later he obtained Djem, the brother of the sultan, from Pierre d'Aubusson (who became a cardinal) and the French king, Charles VIII. Innocent threatened BAJAZET II with recognizing the captive Djem as sultan.

Innocent XI, 1611–89, pope (1676–89), an Italian, noted for his saintliness and desire for reform. Engaged in a quarrel with LOUIS XIV, who actively promoted GALLICANISM. He denounced not only Louis's Gallican statement (1682) but also revocation of the Edict of Nantes (1685).

Innsbruck (ĭnz'brŏŏk, Ger. ĭns'-), city (pop. 94,599), cap. of Tyrol, W Austria, on the Inn. Its beautiful situation, in the Alps, and its architectural treasures make it a favorite tourist resort. Landmarks include 16th-cent. Hofkirche, a Franciscan church, with a monument to Emperor Maximilian I by Peter Vischer; 15th-cent. Fürstenburg palace. The university was founded 1677.

Inns of Court, collective name of the four legal societies in London which have exclusive right of admission to the bar. They are Lincoln's Inn, Gray's Inn, the Inner Temple, and the Middle Temple (see also TEMPLE, THE); all date from before the 14th cent. Names come from the buildings in which masters taught law to "apprentice" lawyers.

inoculation, in strict sense, insertion of virus into a wound to immunize by producing mild form of a disease or to produce disease for experimental purposes. Value in preventing smallpox proved by Edward JENNER.

Inonu, Ismet (ĭsmĕt' ēnŭnŭ'), 1884–, Turkish general. Premier under Ataturk 1923–24, 1925–37; president of Turkey 1938–50.

inquest, inquiry by a coroner's jury into the cause of a death. Procedure is generally like that of a grand jury. Among verdicts returnable are natural death, accidental death, suicide, and murder.

Inquisition. 1 The medieval Inquisition began c.1233 when the pope commissioned certain Dominicans to investigate the ALBIGENSES in S France. As it evolved in France, N Italy, Germany, and the Papal States (where it continued to the 19th cent.), the Inquisition soon resorted to judicial torture, but it rarely condemned accused heretics to burning; imprisonment was the usual punishment. The medieval clerical inquisitors were eager to receive abjurations of heresy and to avoid trials; sentences could be enforced only by the local authorities ("secular arm"). **2** The Spanish Inquisition, estab. 1478 by Ferdinand and Isabella, and first headed by Tomás de TORQUEMADA, was independent of the medieval Inquisition and was controlled by the Spanish kings. Originally supposed to spy out converted Jews and Moors who were insincere, it soon evolved into a form of thought police from which no Spaniard was safe. It was far better organized, harsher, and freer with the death sentence than the medieval Inquisition. Its attempted introduction into the Netherlands led to rebellion. It was driven from Naples in 1510 and was abolished in Spain in 1820. **3** In 1512 Paul III assigned the medieval Inquisition to the Congregation of the Inquisition or Holy Office. The modern Congregation of the Holy Office has the decision as to questions of faith, morals, heresy, and some matrimonial cases, and also has the duties of censorship (the Index).

insanity or **lunacy,** in law, mental aberration or defect which may relieve a person from certain legal consequences of his acts. Criminal and civil insanity differ from concepts of psychopathology (see NEUROSIS; PSYCHOSIS). There is much medical criticism of legal categories. Strictest U.S. jurisdictions limit insanity to ignorance of the nature of one's acts, inability to distinguish right from wrong, i.e., crimes committed in frenzy or by idiots, but paranoiacs may be judged sane. Less strict jurisdictions include PARANOIA and sudden irresistible impulse (temporary insanity). Less mental aberration is required for civil insanity; extreme deficiency of intelligence or marked defect in reason may suffice. Harmless lunatics may be placed under guardianship on application to court. Dangerous lunatics may be committed to institutions on application of close relatives or public authorities; court approval, and sometimes a jury verdict of insanity, must be given. Asylum detention may be reviewed by habeas corpus proceedings.

inscription, writing on durable material. The art is called epigraphy. Modern inscriptions are made for permanent, monumental record, as on gravestones, cornerstones, and building fronts. First writing was probably everywhere done on hard materials, mainly stones, clay, metal, bone, and ivory. When light materials were developed, it was possible to distinguish between temporary writing and permanent recording. Outside Western history epigraphy was important in New World (MAYA, TOLTEC, AZTEC) and in China. Earliest Chinese inscriptions are on bronze (c.1800 B.C.). First Sanskrit inscriptions date from some centuries later than Prakrit inscriptions of ASOKA (3d cent. B.C.). Western epigraphy began in Mesopotamia (CUNEIFORM inscriptions, probably Sumerian, c.4000 B.C.; a similar Eastern instance is epigraphy at MOHENJO-DARO, c.3000 B.C.) and in Egypt (HIEROGLYPHIC inscriptions from 4th millennium B.C.). Influences of Egyptian epigraphy are found everywhere in Arabian peninsula in inscriptions of 1st millennium B.C. In the Mediterranean earliest epigraphy of Greek culture appears in AEGEAN CIVILIZATION and MINOAN CIVILIZATION. From expansion of Greece through career of Rome epigraphy flourished everywhere, and inscriptions are literally innumerable. Greek influence was decisive in Italy, first in inscriptions of ETRUSCAN CIVILIZATION. There are also many inscriptions in Italic languages, notably the IGUVINE TABLES. Latin epigraphy began with religious documents, but by end of the republic it was touching every phase of life. Germanic RUNES and Celtic OGHAM writings are European alphabets used in inscriptions of the early Christian era. Modern monumental inscription is in the same tradition as Latin epigraphy.

insect, air-breathing arthropod of class Insecta, with distinct head, thorax, and abdomen, three pairs of legs, one pair of antennae.

The adult usually has one or two pairs of wings. Many (e.g., BUTTERFLY, MOTH, MOSQUITO, BEE, HOUSEFLY) undergo complete metamorphosis, passing through egg, larva, pupa, and adult stages. Grasshopper and some others undergo gradual metamorphosis (the young resembles the adult). Some primitive wingless ones hatch in adult form and grow in size only. Fossil records indicate that insects are earth's oldest inhabitants; c.%10 of all animals are insects; a few hundred of 500,000 known species are harmful. Many are useful for cross-pollination (see POLLINATION); some are enemies of harmful insects and some form chief food of some fish, reptiles, birds, mammals. Men eat white ants in Brazil; grasshoppers in China. Silk, honey, cochineal, and lac are insect products. See *ill.*, p. 601.

insecticide (ĭnsĕk'tŭsīd), substance used to destroy insect pests. Some insecticides are effective only against specific insects, some are toxic, some can be used only under certain conditions. They are applied by dusting, spraying, fumigating (release of a gas), or by aerosol method (insecticide and liquefied gas are packed in container and released as fine mist under gas pressure). Stomach poisons are used against chewing insects; arsenical poisons (e.g., PARIS GREEN) are the oldest widely applied stomach poisons. Others are fluorine compounds, copper salts, organic poisons, synthetics. Contact poisons (those that penetrate body covering or enter breathing pores) include compounds of sulphur and nicotine, petroleum oils, coal-tar derivatives, pyrethrum (from flowers), rotenone (from derris and other plants), and DDT (dichloro-diphenyl-trichloro-ethane), which has a long-lasting residual effect.

insectivorous plants: see BLADDERWORT; PITCHER PLANT; VENUS'S-FLYTRAP.

Inside Passage, natural, protected waterway, c.950 mi. long, off coast of British Columbia and SE Alaska. Threads through ALEXANDER ARCHIPELAGO. From Seattle, Wash., to Skagway, Alaska, route uses channels and straits between islands and mainland giving protection from storms and open waters of ocean. Known to early explorers. Of great scenic beauty, it is route generally used by steamers between U.S. and Alaska.

installment buying and selling, payment at specified intervals in set amounts for goods taken on credit. Goods belong legally to seller until fulfillment of payment. Practice originated in Paris in 19th cent. and now is applied to purchase of goods of all kinds. It is usually state regulated, and was severely curbed by the Federal government during World War II to reduce inflation.

instinct, controversial term generally indicating an innate tendency, disposition, or drive to action rising from vital needs of an organism, expressed in activity not based on past experience. It is seen in adult insects which emerge from pupa stage after complete bodily changes but with immediate command over food-getting and reproductive structures. In mammals gregariousness is ascribed to herd instinct and maternal activities of suckling and caring for young, to paternal instinct. In man instinctive action, with spe-

cific goals but no specific means of reaching them, is distinguished from reflex action with its specific response to a stimulus. However, some psychologists claim that adult human behavior is too complex, too much modified by civilization and individual intelligence to be explained adequately on the basis of instinct.

Institut de France (ĕstētü' dü fräs'), cultural institution of the French state, founded 1795 to replace five royal academies suppressed in 1793. Subsequent reorganizations restored, within the framework of the Institut, the earlier academies, though the names of several were changed. They are: FRENCH ACADEMY; Académie des Inscriptions et Belles-Lettres (history and archaeology; originally founded 1663); Académie des Sciences (1666); Académie des Beaux-Arts (1648); Académie des Sciences morales et politiques (1795).

Institute for Advanced Study, at Princeton, N.J.; chartered 1930, opened 1933; founded by Louis Bamberger and Mrs. Felix Fuld as research and experimental center beyond the graduate level. Abraham Flexner was first director; succeeded by Frank Aydelotte (1939–47); Einstein is faculty member. Owns Gest Oriental Library; shares many resources with Princeton Univ.

Institutes: see CORPUS JURIS CIVILIS.

instrumental: see CASE.

instrumentalism: see DEWEY, JOHN.

insulation (ĭn"sùlā'shùn), use of materials to prevent passage of heat or electricity. Common heat insulators are asbestos, glass, stone, wood, wool; all are poor conductors. They prevent flow of heat in either direction. Air spaces and vacuums are effective insulators. In conduction of electricity, the conductor acts as a guide for the current and must be insulated at every point of contact to prevent leakage. Ordinary wires are usually insulated by thin rubber coating wrapped with cotton.

insulin (ĭn'sùlĭn), active principle of hormone secreted by groups of cells (islands of Langerhans) in pancreas. It regulates sugar metabolism in body and glycogen storage in liver. Banting and Best first prepared it in a form effective in treatment of diabetes.

Insull, Samuel, 1859–1938, American public-utilities financier, b. England. Vindicated of charges of embezzlement and using mails to defraud following collapse (1932) of his public-utilities empire.

insurance or **assurance,** device for indemnifying or guaranteeing an individual against loss out of a fund to which many individuals exposed to the same risk have contributed certain specified amounts, called premiums. The amount of the premium is determined by the law of averages as calculated by actuaries. Anticipations of modern insurance were to be found in ancient times, among the Babylonians. By the middle of the 14th cent., as evidenced by the earliest known insurance contract (Genoa, 1347), marine insurance was practically universal in Europe. Life insurance began in England in 1583. Fire, burglary, and other forms of insurance were gradually added, so that insurance may now be obtained against any conceivable risk. Since the late 19th cent., the state has

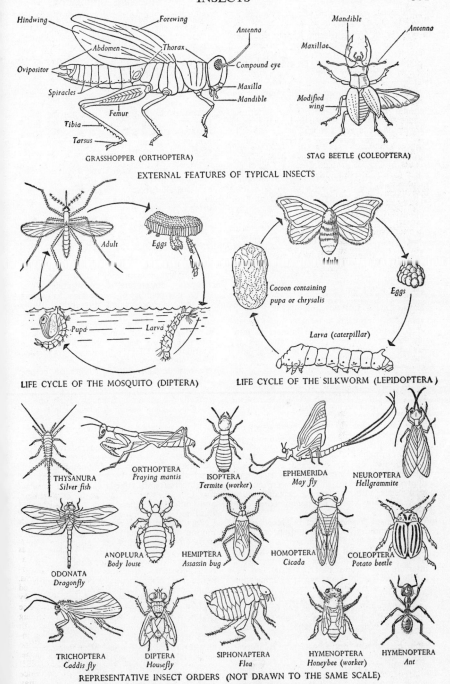

GRASSHOPPER (ORTHOPTERA)

STAG BEETLE (COLEOPTERA)

EXTERNAL FEATURES OF TYPICAL INSECTS

LIFE CYCLE OF THE MOSQUITO (DIPTERA)

LIFE CYCLE OF THE SILKWORM (LEPIDOPTERA)

THYSANURA
Silver fish

ORTHOPTERA
Praying mantis

ISOPTERA
Termite (worker)

EPHEMERIDA
May fly

NEUROPTERA
Hellgrammite

ODONATA
Dragonfly

ANOPLURA
Body louse

HEMIPTERA
Assassin bug

HOMOPTERA
Cicada

COLEOPTERA
Potato beetle

TRICHOPTERA
Caddis fly

DIPTERA
Housefly

SIPHONAPTERA
Flea

HYMENOPTERA
Honeybee (worker)

HYMENOPTERA
Ant

REPRESENTATIVE INSECT ORDERS (NOT DRAWN TO THE SAME SCALE)

entered the field of social insurance (see SO-CIAL SECURITY and HEALTH INSURANCE).

Insurgents, in U. S. history, Republican Senators and Representatives who in 1909–10 revolted against conservative party policies of N. W. Aldrich and J. G. Cannon. Many joined PROGRESSIVE PARTY.

intelligence is usually defined as the general ability of the organism to utilize understanding gained in past experience to deal with similar or new situations. Potential intelligence is somewhat related to heredity, while environment largely determines the extent of its realization. **Intelligence tests** help determine individual ability to learn. Alfred Binet's first scale of tests (1905) inaugurated testing movement. Some psychologists doubt that such tests actually measure intelligence, but they have been valuable in education (to assign class groups and judge aptitude for high school or college) and in industry (to determine suitability for particular positions). Tests are a heterogeneous series of questions, problems, tasks, of varying difficulty to complete within a specified time. Tests are administered to a maximum of people of all ages and standardized by determining average number of questions, problems, tasks, done by any age group. Mental age is determined by those averages. **Intelligence quotient** (I.Q.) is a comparison between mental and chronological age (M.A. and C.A.) multiplied by 100 to eliminate decimal point. Since 1920s interest in pure intelligence tests has declined and has increased in tests that measure special aptitudes and personality factors.

Inter-American Conferences: see PAN-AMERICANISM.

Inter-American Highway, section, 3,349 mi. long, of PAN AMERICAN HIGHWAY system from Nuevo Laredo, Mexico, to Panama city, Panama.

interest, charge for the use of money, usually figured as a percentage of the principal, computed annually. Simple interest is computed on the principal alone; compound interest is computed on the principal plus unpaid interest. In 1545, England fixed a legal max. interest; higher rates than this were considered usury, although among certain groups interest of any kind was condemned as usurious.

interference, in physics, effect produced under certain conditions by combination or superposition of two trains or systems of waves, especially of sound or light, in which these waves reinforce, neutralize, or in other ways interfere with each other. When, for example, two sound waves occur at same time and are in same phase, i.e., when condensations of the two coincide and hence their rarefactions, also, the waves reinforce each other; if the rarefactions of one coincide with condensations of the other (i.e., if they are of opposite phase) they neutralize each other and silence results. Alternate reinforcement and neutralization (or weakening) occur when two sound waves differing slightly in frequency are superimposed; audible result is series of pulsations or beats. Light waves reinforce or neutralize each other in much the same way. Experiments of Thomas Young first illustrated interference and led to wave theory of light. Work of A. J. Fresnel showed that interference phenomena could be adequately explained only on basis of wave theory. A. A. Michelson's determinations of velocity of light are based on interference of light waves. Iridescence results from interference. **Interferometer** is instrument for measuring thickness of very thin films; when the wave length of the light used is known, the instrument indicates the thickness of the film by the nature of the interference patterns it forms. It can also measure length of an unknown light wave. Another type is used in measuring diameters of stars.

Interior, United States Department of the, organized in 1849 by act of U.S. Congress. Responsible for advancing domestic interests in U.S. Includes Indian affairs bureau (see INDIAN AFFAIRS, BUREAU OF), the GEOLOGICAL SURVEY, Bureau of Reclamation, National Park Service, Bureau of Mines, Bureau of Land Management.

Interlaken (ĭn'tûrläkŭn), town (pop. 4,059), Bern canton, Switzerland, between L. of Brienz and L. of Thun. With a fine view of the Jungfrau, it is a major tourist resort.

interlocking directorate, a corporation directorate, one or more of whose members serves on another corporation directorate. While this increases cooperation between the involved corporations, it may also raise prices in order to mulct consumers. Interlocking directorates are legally prohibited (by the Sherman and Clayton antitrust acts) when they lessen competition.

internal-combustion engine, type of engine operating by combustion of fuel within the cylinder of the engine. Heat energy is transformed into mechanical energy. First practical gas engine (using a combustible gas) was invented by Étienne Lenoir of France (c.1860), although earlier attempts date from the 17th cent. The gasoline engine developed later was more compact and relatively light, and its use soon became widespread. In typical automobile gasoline engine, fuel is fed from storage tank by gravity or pump to CARBURETOR and mixed with air; the mixture then goes to cylinder to be compressed and ignited by electric spark (see IGNITION). Resultant explosion forces piston down, transmitting through connecting rod a rotary motion to crankshaft. This activates camshaft attached to cam controlling the cylinder intake and exhaust valves. Typical four-stroke cycle (more common than two-stroke type) consists of: piston downstroke sucking in fuel; piston upstroke compressing fuel vapor, which is ignited as piston reaches top; piston downstroke transmitting force of exploding fuel vapor, leaving burned gases in chamber; and piston upstroke, expelling gases through exhaust valve, for cycle to begin again. (In single-cylinder engine, momentum of heavy flywheel after firing stroke carries through the cycle of intake, compression, and firing.) Besides carburetor, automobile engine accessories usually include water pump, timing gear, oil pump, and generator. Some types are air cooled. Many types of gasoline engines have been developed for use in aircraft. Marine engines are essentially the same as automobile engines but are more ruggedly constructed and are water cooled, and usually have force-feed lubrication and an oil-cooling device. Oil-burning engines are similarly designed but the heavier grade fuel requires different ignition, usually by maintenance of high temperature in chamber to vaporize and ignite the oil jet. This type is being replaced by gasoline engine for small powers; by DIESEL ENGINE for larger powers. See *ill.*, p. 389.

internal revenue, taxes on goods produced and consumed inside a country, also called excise taxes. First developed (17th cent.) by Holland; estab. (1643) by law in England. First use by U.S. in 1791; repealed 1802; alternately increased and all but abandoned until the two world wars. Nearly all the states regularly levy taxes on such items as tobacco, gasoline, liquor, and amusements.

International. International Workingmen's Association, called International or First International, estab. 1864 in London by Karl Marx. Purpose was to unite workers of world for aims of *Communist Manifesto* (1848). Dissension caused dissolution 1874. In 1889 Second or Socialist International estab. hq. at Brussels. Comprised most Socialist parties, with leaders such as Friedrich Engels. It also suffered from dissension and was torn apart by World War I. Bolshevik Revolution (1917) created Third International or COMINTERN at Moscow, dissolved in 1943. Efforts to revive Second International, and Trotsky's Fourth International in Mexico (1937), were of little practical importance.

International Bank for Reconstruction and Development, autonomous body affiliated with UN. Estab. 1945, hq. Washington, D.C. Fund of $10,000,000,000 (provided by UN member states) used for loans to member nations and private investors, to facilitate productive investment, encourage foreign trade, discharge international debts. Called World Bank.

International Civil Aviation Organization (ICAO), affiliate of UN. Estab. 1947, hq. Montreal. Fosters international air trade, and safety and economy.

International Court of Justice, principal judicial organ of the United Nations. Replaced the World Court. Consists of 15 judges named by the Hague Tribunal and ordinarily sits at The Hague. Renders judgment between states on matters of international law. Gives advisory opinions when requested to do so by the UN General Assembly.

International Falls, city (pop. 6,269), N Minn., on Rainy R. near Rainy L. and opposite Fort Francis, Ont. Lumber and summer excursion center.

International Labor Organization (ILO), autonomous institution created in 1919 by Versailles Treaty to standardize and improve working conditions among laborers in member nations. First affiliated with League of Nations, it became affiliated with the UN in 1946. Hq. at Geneva, though its working quarters were moved to Montreal in 1940.

International Monetary Fund, autonomous body affiliated 1947 with UN; hq. Washington, D.C. Fund of $8,000,000,000 used, on application of member nations, to buy foreign currencies to discharge international indebtedness.

International Red Cross: see RED CROSS.

International Refugee Organization: see UNITED NATIONS RELIEF AND REHABILITATION ADMINISTRATION.

International Telecommunication Union (ITU), UN agency, estab. 1934 by merging two existing organizations, hq. Geneva. Operates under Internatl. Telecommunication Convention (adopted 1947, effective 1949). Allots radio frequencies, furthers low rates, and perfects communications in rescue work.

International Trade Organization (ITO), proposed specialized agency of UN to administer and implement a code of principles or rules of fair dealing in international trade. Code is contained in Havana Charter, drawn up at Havana Conference, Nov. 21, 1947–March 24, 1948. Interim Commission was estab. to prepare ground for ITO. Tariff concessions reached in a series of three tariff conferences between 1947 and 1950 were incorporated in the schedules of the General Agreement on Tariffs and Trade (GATT).

Interstate Commerce Commission, estab. 1887 by U.S. Congress as a result of mounting indignation over railroad malpractices. Board was to regulate common carriers in interstate commerce and in foreign commerce within U.S. ICC was designed chiefly to prevent railroads from charging exorbitant rates and from engaging in discriminatory practices (e.g., the REBATE), but its activities were limited by numerous Supreme Court decisions won by railroads. Hepburn Act of 1906, however, extended commission's jurisdiction to include intraterritorial commerce and express, sleeping-car, and pipe-line (exclusive of those carrying water or gas) companies; empowered ICC upon complaint and after a full hearing to reduce rates adjudged unreasonable. Later extensions of board's jurisdiction included power to regulate communications, motor carriers engaged in interstate commerce, and water-borne carriers operating coastwise, intercoastally, and upon inland U.S. waters; power to fix rates without previous complaint; power to evaluate property of common carrier companies; power to deal with labor disputes in interstate commerce.

intertype, trade name of machine that makes slugs, each doing work of a line of hand-set type. Similar to LINOTYPE, they have interchangeable matrices. Developed and produced by Internatl. Typesetting Machine Co. (organized 1912). See MONOTYPE.

intestine or **bowel,** tubular portion of alimentary canal extending from stomach to anus. Food mass is carried along within the intestine by contractions of muscular walls. In small intestine (tube c.23 ft. long), bile, pancreatic juice, and secretion from glands in its lining complete digestion of proteins, fats, carbohydrates; digested nutrients pass through lining into blood and lymph. Large intestine (c.5 ft. long) continues from cecum (blind portion forming right angle with small intestine) as the ascending, transverse, and descending colon, the rectum, anal canal, anus. See *ill.*, p. 763.

Intolerable Acts, name given by American patriots to five laws (including QUEBEC ACT) adopted by Parliament in 1774, limiting political and geographical freedom of colonists. Four of laws punished Mass. for Boston Tea Party.

Intracoastal Waterway, route, c.3,100 mi. long, part natural, part artificial, providing protected water passage from Boston, Mass., to Brownsville, Texas, along Atlantic and Gulf of Mexico coasts. Authorized by Congress, maintained toll free by U.S. Corps of Engineers. Minimum depth 7 ft. Important works are Cape Cod Canal, Chesapeake and Delaware Canal, Okeechobee Waterway, cut from Pensacola Bay to Mobile Bay, New Orleans–Rigolets Cut, and channel from Port Arthur to Corpus Christi, Texas. Final section (Corpus Christi–Brownsville) completed 1949.

introversion: see EXTROVERSION AND INTROVERSION.

intuitionism, philosophic theory that man may have or obtain knowledge (and truth) directly and immediately, quite apart from his experience or his reasoning. A distinction is made between intellect and intuition, between rational argument and suprarational comprehension (e.g., a mystic's knowledge of God). Intuitionists in ethics argue that a human being has an inborn moral sense.

Inverness-shire (ĭn″vûrnĕs′shĭr) or **Inverness,** maritime county (4,211 sq. mi.; pop. 84,924), NW Scotland. Largest Scottish county, it includes many of the HEBRIDES. Caledonian Canal follows Great Glen diagonally across county through several lochs. Mountainous region, it has highest peak in Great Britain (Ben Nevis, 4,406 ft.). Chief occupation is sheep grazing; quarrying and fishing are also important. The county town is **Inverness,** burgh (pop. 28,115), called "Capital of Highlands." Scene of Great Highland Gathering in September, it has museums of Highland lore. Castle is on site of Macbeth's Castle, said to be scene of Duncan's murder.

invertebrate (ĭnvûr′tŭbrāt), any animal without a backbone. Invertebrates are divided into phyla including protozoa, sponges, coelenterates (jellyfish, sea anemone, coral), echinoderms (starfish and related forms), flatworms, roundworms, segmented worms, mollusks, arthropods. In size they range from microscopic protozoans to giant SQUID.

investiture, in FEUDALISM, ceremony by which an overlord transferred a fief to his vassal. After oath of fealty, lord "invested" him with fief, usually by giving a clod or stick or stone, or other token of land or office given. Ceremony imposed on lord duties of suzerain, chiefly protection of vassal's interests. Clerical investiture was of great importance as dispute about it was phase of struggle between Church and state in Middle Ages. Fundamental trouble lay in dual role of bishops and abbots as both spiritual and temporal lords. Always both king and pope were interested in election and installation of bishops. Quarrel was touched off by divergence between Emperor Henry IV and Pope Gregory VII. After long conflict agreement was reached by Henry V and Pope Calixtus II in Concordat of WORMS (1122), a victory for Church. In England William the Conqueror had trouble with the Church. Agreement (1107) by Henry I and Anselm gave investiture to Church, with homage to king.

Io (ī′ō), in Greek religion, princess of Argos, who was transformed into heifer by either Zeus or Hera. Hera persecuted her, but Argus guarded her. A gadfly drove her to Egypt, where she became a woman again. Sometimes ideintified with Egyptian Isis.

Ioannina (yôä′nēnä), city (pop. 32,268), NW Greece, in Epirus; also spelled Janina, Yannina. Agr. center; silk and textile mfg. Was under Turkish rule 1438–1913. Scene of severe fighting in World War II. Famous as residence of ALI PASHA.

iodine (ī′ŭdīn), the least active HALOGEN, it is a dark gray to purple-black, lustrous, crystalline solid element (symbol = I; see also ELEMENT, table). Undergoes SUBLIMATION when heated; its vapor is violet. It forms many compounds; is found in salt deposits and in some seaweed. Used in treating goiter, as antiseptic (in alcoholic solution and as iodoform), and in making certain drugs and dyes.

Iola (ī-ō′lù), city (pop. 7,094), SE Kansas, W of Fort Scott. Center of dairy, grain, and livestock area.

Iolo Marganwg (yō′lō môrgä′nōog), bardic name of Edward Williams, 1746–1825, Welsh poet, who led in Welsh revival.

Ion (ī′ŭn, ī′ŏn), in Greek mythology, son of Apollo and Creusa, who became ancestor of the Ionians.

ion (ī′ŏn). To explain the fact that some substances conduct current only in aqueous solution, S. A. Arrhenius advanced the theory (1887) that molecules dissociate and parts conduct. According to theory of ion, some of the molecules break up into two parts—one with positive (+) charge, one with negative (−). Particles are called ions. Each particle with + charge is an atom that has lost an electron; each with − charge has gained an electron. When electric current is introduced (see ELECTROLYSIS), particles with + charge are attracted to cathode (− pole); those with − charge to anode (+ pole). At the poles, the particles gain or lose electrons to become neutral, combine with other atoms to form molecules. Substances that conduct electricity are called electrolytes (e.g., sodium chloride); those that do not, nonelectrolytes (e.g., sugar). Acids, bases, and salts are, in general, electrolytes. Some substances ionize when melted; important industrial processes are based on this. Acidity or alkalinity of substance in solution depends on concentration of hydrogen ions (H⁺) or hydroxyl ions (OH⁻). Indicators show which ions are present in greater concentration. Litmus is an indicator that turns red in acid solution (excess of H⁺); blue in basic solution (excess of OH⁻ ions). Hydrogen-ion concentration is indicated by pH.

Iona (ī-ō′nù) or **Icolmkill** (ī′kŏmkĭl′), island of Inner Hebrides, in Argyllshire, off W Scotland. It is c.3½ mi. long and 1½ mi. wide. At this early center of Celtic Christianity St.

Columba landed in 563. It has many ancient remains. Cathedral dates from 12th or 13th cent. Cemetery reputed to be burial place of kings from several countries.

Ionia (īō'nēù), anc. Greek region of Asia Minor occupying a narrow coastal strip of what is today W Turkey and the neighboring Aegean Isls. Here Ionian Greek settlers founded colonies, presumably before 1000 B.C. Athens claimed to be mother city of them all. There came to be 12 important cities, among them Miletus, Ephesus, and Samos. After conquest by several empires came under Persian power. In 500 B.C. they revolted against Darius. Athens supported them, and the PERSIAN WARS ensued. Continued rich and important under Roman and Byzantine Empires. After the Turkish conquest their culture was destroyed.

Ionia, city (pop. 6,412), S Mich., on Grand R. and E of Grand Rapids, in agr. area. Mfg. of furniture and auto parts.

Ionian Sea (īō'nēùn), part of Mediterranean Sea, between SE Italy and Greece. Connected with Adriatic Sea by Strait of Otranto. In it are the **Ionian Islands,** chain (752 sq. mi.; pop. 219,562), off W Greece. They include CORFU, CEPHALONIA, ZANTE, CYTHERA, Ithaca, Paxo, Leucas. Largely mountainous. Agr., fruit growing, cattle raising, fishing, soapmaking. Islands passed from Byzantine Empire to Venice in 14th–15th cent. Though ceded by Venice to France in 1797, they were under Russo-Turkish occupation 1799–1807 and under English occupation from 1809. Treaty of Paris made them a British protectorate (1815). England ceded them to Greece 1864.

Ionic order, in architecture. Distinctive feature is spreading, scroll-shaped capital. Originated in Asia Minor in 6th cent. B.C. In 5th cent. appeared in Greece, where its only complete example is ERECHTHEUM. Greek Ionic columns are fluted and slender; Roman versions are heavier. A variant, called Scamozzi Ionic order, is named after Vincenzo Scamozzi, Italian Renaissance architect who standardized it. See *ill.,* p. 61.

ionization: see ION.

ionosphere (īō'nùsfēr), a series of concentric ionized layers in upper atmosphere. It makes possible long-distance wireless communication by reflecting radio waves back to earth. Independently discovered by Oliver Heaviside and A. E. Kennelly; both entire ionosphere and highly ionized layer are known also as Kennelly-Heaviside layer. See *ill.,* p. 23.

Iowa, state (56,280 sq. mi.; pop. 2,621,073); N central U.S., in Middle West; admitted 1846 as 29th state (free); cap. DES MOINES. Other cities are SIOUX CITY, DUBUQUE, CEDAR RAPIDS. Bounded E by Mississippi R., W by Missouri and Big Sioux rivers. State is largely a gently rolling plain. Farming includes grains (esp. corn), livestock, dairying. Has bituminous coal and gypsum deposits. Mfg. of food, meat, dairy products, machinery (agr. and industrial), railroad equipment, buttons. Region explored by French and fur traders. Indians leased land to Julien DUBUQUE in late 18th cent. Part of Louisiana Purchase; most Indian claims abandoned

after BLACK HAWK WAR (1832). Iowa Territory organized by 1838. Supported Union in Civil War. Farmers joined GRANGER MOVEMENT, GREENBACK PARTY, and POPULIST PARTY in hard times of late 19th cent. An agr. commonwealth, Iowa tends toward stable, conservative norm.

Iowa, river, 329 mi. long, rising in N central Iowa and flowing SE across state. Joined by Cedar R. at Columbus Junction, it enters the Mississippi between Muscatine and Burlington.

Iowa, State University of, at Iowa City; state supported, coed.; chartered 1847, opened 1855. Has child-welfare research station and state historical society. Campus, on both sides of Iowa R., includes old capitol, begun 1840.

Iowa City, city (pop. 27,212), E Iowa, on both sides of Iowa R. and S of Cedar Rapids; founded 1839 as cap. of Iowa Territory. Was cap. 1841–57. Became supply center for western trails with opening of railroad 1855. Mfg. of dairy, food, wood, and paper products. Seat of State Univ. of IOWA. Near by are villages of AMANA SOCIETY and birthplace of Herbert Hoover.

Iowa Indians, tribe of Siouan linguistic stock, formerly on the Platte R. Were presumably once part of the Winnebago people and shared culture of Eastern Woodlands and Plains areas.

Iowa State College of Agriculture and Mechanic Arts, at Ames; land-grant and state supported, coed.; chartered 1858, opened 1868. Has atomic, industrial science, and veterinary research institutes, and Guatemala Tropical Research Center.

ipecac (ĭ'pĭkăk″), drug obtained from dried roots and rhizomes of a tropical creeping shrub. Contains toxic, emetic alkaloids capable of destroying amoebae and occasionally used in treatment of certain parasitic diseases.

Iphigenia (ĭ″fùjùnī'ù), in Greek legend, daughter of Clytemnestra and Agamemnon. His ships becalmed at Aulis en route to Trojan War, Agamemnon sacrificed her to Artemis, but goddess rescued her and took her to Tauris as a priestess for her temple. Here she saved Orestes from sacrifice and fled with him to Greece.

Ipiranga or **Ypiranga** (both: ē″pēräng'gù), stream, São Paulo, SE Brazil, where Pedro issued Grito de Ypiranga, declaring independence of Brazil from Portugal, Sept. 7, 1822.

Ippolitov-Ivanov, Mikhail (Mikhailovich) (mēkhŭyēl' ēpŭlyē'tùf-ēvä'nùf), 1859–1935, Russian composer; pupil of Rimsky-Korsakov. His music is nationalistic. His best-known work is his orchestral *Caucasian Sketches.* He also composed operas, choral works, and chamber music.

Ipsus (ĭp'sùs), town, anc. Phrygia, Asia Minor, the modern Ipsili Hissar. Here ANTIGONUS I was defeated and slain by other Diadochi (301 B.C.).

Ipswich, county borough (pop. 104,788), Suffolk East, England. Town is very old and has many historical houses and buildings. Industries include shipping and mfg. of agr. machinery.

Ipswich, town (pop. 6,895), NE Mass., NNE of Salem and on Ipswich R. (crossed by bridge built 1764); area, called Agawam, settled 1633. Hosiery.

Iquitos (ēkē'tōs), city (pop. 34,231), NE Peru, on Amazon, c.2,300 mi. up the river; founded 1863. Was important port in wild-rubber boom of early 20th cent.

Ir, chemical symbol of the element IRIDIUM.

Ira (ī'rù), chief officer of David. 2 Sam. 20.26.

Irak: see IRAQ.

Irala, Domingo Martínez de (dōmēng'gō märtē'näs dā ērä'lä), d. 1556 or 1557, first governor of Paraguay elected by free vote of colonists. Moved inhabitants of Buenos Aires to Asunción (1539).

Iran (ērän', īrän'), kingdom (630,000 sq. mi.; pop. c.18,387,000), SW Asia, widely known in English as Persia; cap. TEHERAN. Bounded on N by USSR and Caspian Sea, on S by Gulf of Oman and Persian Gulf, on W by Iraq, and on E by Afghanistan and Pakistan. On great plateau surrounded by Elburz and Zagros ranges. Great salt deserts are in interior. Trans-Iranian RR links Caspian Sea with Persian Gulf. People are predominantly SHIITES in religion. Wheat and rice are grown; opium and tobacco are state monopolies. Main industrial products are carpets and rugs, but supreme source of wealth is oil. In ancient times the area was the heart of a great empire (see PERSIA). Safavid dynasty (1499–1736) reached its peak under Shah Abbas I. After brief period of Afghan rule, NADIR SHAH estab. Afshar dynasty in 1736. It was succeeded by Zand dynasty (1750–94) and by Kajar or Qajar dynasty (1794–1925), founded by Aga Mohammed Khan. In 19th cent. Iran fell under increasing pressure of European nations. Lost Caucasian lands to Russia by treaties of 1813 and 1828. Divided into British and Russian spheres of influence 1907–19. Agreement with Great Britain in 1919 ambiguously affirmed Iran's independence, while Russians withdrew in 1921. New dynasty was founded 1925 by REZA SHAH PAHLEVI, whose abdication in favor of his son MOHAMMED REZA SHAH PAHLEVI was forced by the British and Russians who in World War II had again occupied Iran. Teheran Conference in 1943 guaranteed independence of Iran. Foreign troops were withdrawn 1946 after a short-lived, Soviet-supported autonomous movement in Azerbaijan had been suppressed under UN direction. Intense nationalism, spurred by Communist Tudeh party, resulted in nationalization of British-owned oil industry in 1951 by Premier MOSSADEGH. Ousting of Anglo-Iranian Oil Co. and subsequent British blockade against Iran led to virtual collapse of the vital industry, which severely strained the national economy. Iran broke off diplomatic ties with Britain in 1952, and despite U.S. mediation the oil dispute remained unsettled in early 1953. Iran is a constitutional monarchy with a legislature consisting of an upper house (senate) and a lower house (Majlis).

Iranian languages, group of Indo-Iranian subfamily of Indo-European languages. See LANGUAGE (table).

Iraq or **Irak** (both: ēräk'), kingdom (c.168,000 sq. mi.; pop. 4,799,500), SW Asia; cap. Baghdad. Bordered on E by Iran, on S by Saudi Arabia, and on N by Turkey. Roughly co-extensive with ancient MESOPOTAMIA. Population concentrated on banks of TIGRIS and EUPHRATES rivers. In dry SE area, dates and cotton are grown with aid of irrigation. In mountainous north oil is exploited by British companies. Chief port is Basra. Most Iraqi are Arabic-speaking Moslems. Fiercely resisted subjugation by Ottoman Turks in 16th cent. Supported Allies in World War I and welcomed British occupation (begun 1915). Treaty of Sèvres (1920) made it a League of Nations mandate under the British. Country became a kingdom under FEISAL I in 1921, but British mandate continued until 1932. Pro-British elements controlled Iraq at outset of World War II but nationalist opposition strengthened as British lost Middle East territory in early phase of war. In 1941 the British defeated pro-Axis usurper Rashid Ali al Gailani and recalled Emir Abdul Illah, regent for FEISAL II. Declared war on Axis powers in 1943. Anti-British sentiment, fed mainly by British control of oil industry, reappeared after the war. In 1948 Iraq joined other ARAB LEAGUE nations in unsuccessful war against Israel.

Ireland, John, 1838–1918, American Catholic prelate, first archbishop of St. Paul (1888–1918), b. Ireland, came to St. Paul as a child. A well-known public figure, he stirred controversy by advocating state support and inspection of Catholic schools and by opposing foreign-language church schools.

Ireland, William Henry, 1777–1835, English forger of Shakspterian documents and manuscripts. Exposed, he admitted hoax in *Authentic Account* (1796).

Ireland [Irish *Eire* (â'rù); to it are related the poetic *Erin* and, perhaps, the Latin *Hibernia*], island (31,839 sq. mi.; pop. 4,329,587), second largest of British Isles. Lies W of Great Britain, from which it is separated by the North Channel, the Irish Sea, and St. George's Channel. At present divided into political regions—NORTHERN IRELAND (cap. Belfast) and the republic of Ireland (26,601 sq. mi.; pop. 2,958,878; cap. Dublin). Island has 32 counties and, historically, four provinces. ULSTER is divided between N. Ireland (counties Antrim, Down, Armagh, Fermanagh, Tyrone, and Londonderry) and republic (counties Monaghan, Cavan, and Donegal). Other three provinces are in republic—LEINSTER has counties Louth, Meath, Dublin, Kildare, Wicklow, Carlow, Wexford, Kilkenny, Laoighis, Offaly, Westmeath, and Longford; MUNSTER has Tipperary, Waterford, Cork, Kerry, Limerick, and Clare; CONNAUGHT has Leitrim, Roscommon, Galway, Mayo, and Sligo. Island has a large central plain, extremely fertile, roughly enclosed by a highland rim. In N are Mourne Mts., Sperrin Mts. and those of Antrim; in W are mountains of Connemara and Mayo; and in S are mountains of Galty, Knockmealdown, and Kerry. Heavy rains (over 80 in. annually in S) account for brilliant green grass of "emerald isle." Off W coast are many islands (including Aran and Blasket Isls.) and in interior are many lakes and

wide stretches of rivers called loughs. SHAN-
NON R., 250 mi. long, provides electric
power for much of the republic. Lagan,
Foyle, Liffey, and Lee are among other
rivers. Economy is mainly agr., chief products being dairy goods and flax. Fine linen
and laces are world famous. Industrial activity is concentrated in Belfast area and
adjoining area in the republic. Population of
republic is overwhelmingly Catholic. Protestants outnumber Catholics in N. Ireland,
but number of Catholics has increased in
recent years, and the traditional religious
difference between sections seems about to
upset.

Ireland to 1169. Ireland was invaded before
the Christian era by several Celtic tribes
who left their culture. Anglo-Saxons and Romans did not affect the island. Ireland enjoyed the golden age of its culture until 8th
cent. when Norsemen began their raids. People were organized into clans owing allegiance to one of five provincial kings (of
Ulster, Munster, Leinster, Connaught, and
Meath) who in turn served high king of all
Ireland at Tara. Despite constant clan fighting, literary and artistic culture flourished
(see GAELIC LITERATURE). In 5th cent. St.
PATRICK completed the island's conversion
to Christianity. Later Irish religious leaders
included St. Columba, St. Columban, and
St. Bridget. In 1014 Brian Boru broke the
hold of Norse invaders. There followed 150
years of freedom from foreign interference.
Overlordship of Ireland was granted in 12th
cent. to Henry II of England by Pope Adrian
IV. English in 1169 began conquest. Anglo-
Irish struggle was to continue intermittently
for nearly 800 years.

Ireland to Union of 1800. Anglo-Norman
rapacity in Ireland led to landlord-tenant
problem. Irish were denied benefit of English
law and their own law was split apart. English control lessened, however, until Henry
VIII became first monarch to bring all Ireland under English control. POYNINGS'S LAW
(1495) gave legislative initiative to English
Parliament. By 16th cent. Irish people were
sunk in desperate poverty which was to last
for centuries. The Protestant English imposed the PENAL LAWS upon the Catholic
Irish. In Elizabeth's reign three serious rebellions were crushed. Scotch settlers were
planted in Ulster. A rebellion began in 1641
which lasted ten years, cost 600,000 lives,
and was brutally crushed by Cromwell (who
massacred Irish at Drogheda). Irish support
of James II led to new Penal Laws and economic exploitation after battle of the Boyne
(1690). In 1782 GRATTAN obtained an independent Parliament which proved ineffective.
After rebellion under Wolfe TONE, England
and Ireland were united (1800), and Irish
were unwillingly represented in English
Parliament.

Ireland under the Union, 1800–1921. Agitation led by Daniel O'Connell caused Catholic Emancipation Act to be passed in 1829.
Other causes for Irish discontent persisted.
Church of Ireland was not disestab. until
1869. Evils of absentee landlordism grew
more serious (see IRISH LAND QUESTION).
Potato blight struck Ireland in 1840s. In five

years ending 1851 c.1,000,000 Irish died of
starvation and disease and some 1,600,000
emigrated, mostly to U.S. FENIAN MOVEMENT
was organized. By 1870 PARNELL had arisen
as a leader. HOME RULE movement was
gradually superseded by SINN FEIN. Easter
Rebellion of 1916 led to guerilla warfare in
1918. English tried to suppress it with auxil-
iaries known as Black and Tans, who ter-
orized country (1920) and met increasing
resistance. Irish cause was strengthened by
literary and cultural revival of late 19th
cent.; by such writers as G. B. Shaw, W. B.
Yeats, and James Joyce; and by Abbey
Theatre.

Irish Free State and the Republic. Irish Free
State was estab. (1921) as result of negotiations between British and Eamon DE VALERA.
Six N Protestant counties accepted dominion status as N. Ireland. Split of Sinn Fein
into right- and left-wing groups led to a
period of civil war. William Cosgrave was
president 1922–32. Succeeded by De Valera
who estab. (1937) sovereign country of Ireland (officially Eire) associated in foreign
policy with British Commonwealth of Nations. Trade war between England and Ireland ended. During World War II Ireland
remained neutral and protested Allied military activity in N. Ireland. Outlawed Irish
Republican Army continued to agitate for
end of separation of N. Ireland from Eire.
In 1948 De Valera was voted out of power
and a coalition chose John Costello new
premier. Republic of Ireland Bill of 1949
estab. independent nation. Executive power
is vested in prime minister and legislative
power in the DÁIL ÉIREANN. De Valera was
again returned to office in 1951.

Ireland, Church of, principal Anglican church
in Ireland. Unlike Church of England, it has
been disestablished since 1869. Represents
minority of population.

Irenaeus, Saint (īrĭnē′ús), c.125–c.202, bishop
of Lyons, Gaul, b. Asia Minor, author of
Against the Heresies (against GNOSTICISM).

Irene (īrēn′, īrē′nē), 752–803, Byzantine empress (797–802). As regent for her son
Constantine VI after 780, she bent all her
efforts on suppression of ICONOCLASM. Constantine's misconduct led to his deposition
(797); Irene had him blinded and ascended
the throne. She was deposed and exiled by
Nicephorus I (802).

Irene, one of the HORAE.

Ireton, Henry (ī′úrtún), 1611–51, English parliamentarian general in Puritan Revolution;
husband of Oliver Cromwell's daughter. As
lord deputy of Ireland (1650) he carried on
Cromwell's policy of dispossessing the Irish
in favor of Englishmen.

Iriarte, Ignacio (ēgnä′thyō ēryär′tä), 1620–85,
Spanish landscape painter, who often collaborated with Murillo.

Iriarte, Tómas de (tōmäs′ dā ēryär′tä), 1750–
91, Spanish poet and critic. Wrote *Fabulas
literárias* (1782).

iridescence (ĭ″rĭdĕ′súns), exhibition of changing, shifting color bands by certain surfaces
(e.g., in mother-of-pearl). It results from
breaking up of white light and INTERFERENCE
of light rays caused by irregularities in the
surface.

iridium (ĭrĭ'dēŭm), rare, silver-white metallic element (symbol = Ir; see also ELEMENT, table). It resembles platinum, is very hard, and one of the heaviest elements known. Alloys are used for making standard weights and other apparatus resistant to action of atmosphere, contact points of electrical apparatus, and fountain pen points.

Irigoyen, Hipólito (ēpō'lētō ērēgō'yän), 1850?–1933, Argentine political leader, president of the republic (1916–22, 1928–30).

Iris, in Greek religion, goddess of the rainbow; daughter of Electra and attendant of Zeus and Hera.

iris, stately perennial plant of genus *Iris* from which the fleur-de-lis is thought to have been derived. Native American irises are called blue flags. Violet-scented rootstalks of some Old World irises, especially *Iris florentina,* are sold commercially as orrisroot, which is powdered and used in perfume, sachet, etc. The bearded irises of June gardens include several thousand varieties; beardless kinds include Japanese and Siberian irises. These all have creeping rootstalks. Spanish, Dutch, and English irises are grown from bulbs. See *ill.,* p. 999.

Irish Free State: see IRELAND.

Irish Land Question. The problem of Irish land ownership, which came to a crisis in 19th cent., goes back many centuries. Feudal landholding system was imposed on Ireland in 12th cent. The Tudors, Cromwell, and William III continued land confiscations. 18th-cent. Penal Laws increased difficulty of landowning by Catholics. CATHOLIC EMANCIPATION did not materially help. Hatred for England grew through great famine of 1840s and influx of speculators after Encumbered Estates Act of 1849. The violent Fenian movement, the Reform Act of 1867, and support by Gladstone led to first land act (1870). Agitation of Michael Davitt and Charles Stewart Parnell led to Land Act (1881) giving the farmer the "three F's"—fair rent, fixity of tenure, and freedom from sale. Main issue then became land purchase by the tenant. Agitation of William O'Brien led to Wyndham Act (1903) and Amended Land Purchase Act (1909). By 1921 Irish tenants owned two thirds of the land; the rest was confiscated by law and given to the tenants. Issue of land annuity payments to England led to trade war with settlement in favor of Ireland in 1938.

Irish language, one of the Goidelic group of the Celtic subfamily of Indo-Iranian languages. It is also called Gaelic and Erse. See LANGUAGE (table).

Irish literature: see GAELIC LITERATURE.

Irish moss, reddish or purplish seaweed (*Chondrus crispus*), found off coasts of Ireland and E U.S. When cooked it yields gelatine used as pudding or as textile sizing.

Irish Sea, part of the Atlantic, 130 mi. long, up to c.130 mi. wide, between Ireland and Great Britain. Connected with the Atlantic by North Channel and (on S) St. George's Channel.

Irish terrier: see TERRIER.

Irish wolfhound: see HOUND.

Irkutsk (ĭrko͞otsk'), city (pop. 243,380), RSFSR, in S central Siberia, W of L. Baikal, on Angara and Irkut rivers and on Trans-Siberian RR. River port; mfg. of aircraft, cars, mining equipment; educational center. Chartered 1683.

Irnerius (ûrnēr'ēŭs), c.1055–c.1130, Italian teacher and commentator on Roman law, founder of the school at Bologna.

iron, silver-white metallic element (symbol = Fe; see also ELEMENT, table), lustrous, ductile, malleable, attracted by magnet. It rusts easily. Chemically active, it forms ferrous (divalent), and ferric (trivalent) compounds. The fourth most abundant element, it comprises about 5% of earth's crust. Its compounds occur in soil, sand, plants, animals. Deficiency causes anemia in humans and some animals. Three forms of commercial iron: cast iron, wrought iron, STEEL. **Cast iron** is made when pig iron, prepared in BLAST FURNACE, is remelted and poured into molds to make castings. Usually has 92–94% iron, 2–6% carbon, small amounts of silicon, sulphur, manganese, phosphorus. Used in making machine parts, ranges, stoves, pipes, radiators. **Wrought iron** is made by purifying melted pig iron in puddling furnace; relatively pure, with 0.1–0.2% carbon. Used for rivets, bolts, water pipes, chains, anchors, fire bars, ornamental ironwork.

Iron Age, period of industrial development that begins with the general use of iron and continues in the present. Beads of meteoric iron shaped by rubbing were worn in Egypt c.4000 B.C., but the oldest known hammered object is a dagger made there before 1350 B.C. Casting of iron was known in ancient Greece, where the Iron Age began c.1000 B.C. From previous times the Iron Age inherited staple farm crops, animals, wheeled vehicles, and a variety of tools and implements. Glass and pottery making, spinning, weaving, and writing developed.

Iron Cross: see DECORATIONS, CIVIL AND MILITARY.

Irondequoit (ûrŏn'dĭkwoit"), town (pop. 34,417), W N.Y., N of Rochester and on L. Ontario; settled 1791.

Iron Gate, narrow, mountainous gorge of the Danube, between Orsova and Turnu-Severin, on the Rumanian-Yugoslav border.

Iron Guard, Rumanian nationalistic, anti-Semitic, terrorist organization, founded 1924 by Corneliu Zelea Codreanu. Banned 1933, it carried on under different name. It helped Ion Antonescu into power (1940), but he suppressed it after a rebellion (1941).

Iron Mask, Man with the, mysterious French prisoner of state, brought to Bastille in 1698, buried 1703 under name Marchioly. Wore black velvet (not iron) mask to prevent identification. Wild speculation as to his identity was started by Voltaire's *Age of Louis XIV,* reached fantastic proportions in Dumas Père's *Le Vicomte de Bragelonne.* Actually, most modern students agree that the Iron Mask was one Count Mattioli, secretary to the duke of Mantua, whom Louis XIV had kidnaped for political reasons; but other theories still flourish.

Iron Mountain, city (pop. 9,679), W Upper Peninsula, N Mich., near Wis. line. Distributing point for iron ore of Menominee range. Winter sports center.

Iron Mountain, elevation, 325 ft. high, central Fla., near L. Wales. Singing Tower, with carillon of 71 bells, and bird sanctuary estab. here by Edward Bok and opened 1929.

Ironton. 1 Resort city (pop. 1,148), SE Mo., SW of St. Louis, in the Ozarks. Union troops under Thomas Ewing defeated Sterling Price's Confederates at near-by battle of Pilot Knob (Sept. 27, 1864). **2** City (pop. 16,333), S Ohio, on Ohio R. opposite Ashland, Ky.; laid out 1848. Mfg. of iron and steel goods and cement; limestone quarries.

Ironwood, city (pop. 11,466), extreme W Upper Peninsula, N Mich., on Montreal R. at Wis. line; founded 1885. Trade center for Gogebic iron range; has some of world's deepest mines.

ironwood: see HORNBEAM.

Iroquoian (ĭrŭkwoi′yŭn), North American Indian linguistic stock, in N.Y., Pa., E Canada, and in S U.S. (Tuscarora, Cherokee). See LANGUAGE, table.

Iroquois Confederacy or **Iroquois League** (ĭ′rŭkwoi), Indian confederation consisting of Mohawk, Oneida, Onondaga, Cayuga, and Seneca tribes; founded c.1570 by prophet Deganawidah and disciple Hiawatha; also called Five Nations. Gave name to Iroquoian linguistic family. Despite some intertribal warfare, the confederacy was tight knit, the main Onondaga village serving as meeting place of the council. Material culture, based on hunting and agr., was most advanced of Eastern Woodlands area, exhibiting also traits of SE area. Iroquois were second to no other Indians N of Mexico in political organization, statecraft, and military prowess. In second half of 17th cent. they conquered neighboring tribes and dominated area bounded by Kennebec, Ottawa, Illinois, and Tennessee rivers. Were allies of British against the French in French and Indian Wars and (excepting the Oneida) American Revolution. Sir William Johnson held their loyalty. In the Revolution Cornplanter, Red Jacket, and Joseph Brant were Iroquois leaders against the patriots. The Cherry Valley and Wyoming Valley massacres incensed Americans, and John Sullivan led a punitive expedition (1779) against them and Walter Butler, the Tory leader, defeating them near Elmira.

Irrawaddy (ĭrŭwŏ′dē), chief river of Burma, c.1,300 mi. long, rising in NW and flowing to Bay of Bengal. Chief tributary is Chindwin R.

irredentism (ĭrĭdĕn′tĭzŭm), Italian nationalist movement for annexation of *Italia irredenta* [unredeemed Italy]—the ethnically Italian territories left to Austria after 1866 (e.g., Trentino, Trieste, part of Dalmatia). Chief motive for Italian entry into World War I.

irrigation, artificial watering of arable lands. It is used chiefly in regions with an annual rainfall under 20 in., but also in areas of greater rainfall to supply the high water requirements of certain crops, e.g., rice. Irrigation has been practiced from ancient times. Methods include free-flooding of entire areas from canals and ditches; check-flooding, in which water is guided over strips of land between levees; furrow method in which water is run between crop rows; and surface-pipe and sprinkler systems. Large-scale irrigation is commonly a part of multiple-purpose water projects combining irrigation, water supply, hydroelectric power production, and flood control.

Irtysh (ĭrtŭsh′), river, 1,844 mi. long, China and USSR, chief tributary of Ob. Rises in Sinkiang, flows generally NW through W Siberia past Semipalatinsk, Pavlodar, Omsk, Tobolsk. Navigable April–Nov. Reached by Russians 1594.

Irving, Edward, 1792–1834, Scottish preacher, a founder of CATHOLIC APOSTOLIC CHURCH, whose members are often called Irvingites. His emphasis on the supernatural and on the second coming of Christ and his other teachings caused expulsion (1833) from Church of Scotland.

Irving, Sir Henry, 1838–1905, English actor and manager, originally named Brodribb. Had acting successes in such dramas as *Eugene Aram* and *Hamlet.* Became (1878) manager of London's Lyceum Theatre where he reigned (with leading lady Ellen Terry) until 1903, presenting spectacular Shakspere productions. He was the first English actor knighted.

Irving, Washington, 1783–1859, American author, b. New York city. Began early contributing essays to periodicals, styled *Letters of Jonathan Oldstyle, Gent.* (1802–3) and after a tour in Europe joined William Irving and James K. Paulding in a series called *Salmagundi* (1807–8), and under the pseudonym Diedrich Knickerbocker he produced the comic *History of New York* (1809). Sent (1815) to England to manage the Liverpool branch of the family hardware business, he saw that fail and turned definitely to literature. Essays and stories, appearing serially and collected as *The Sketch Book of Geoffrey Crayon, Gent.* (1820) made his reputation. This was followed by others in *Bracebridge Hall* (1822) and *Tales of a Traveller* (1824). He was attached to the embassy at Madrid after 1826 and turned to writing of things Spanish: a biography of Columbus (1828), *The Conquest of Granada* (1829), and *The Alhambra* (1832). After returning to the U.S., he wrote several works on the American West: *A Tour of the Prairies* (1835); *Astoria* (1836; written with his nephew, Pierre Irving, for John Jacob Astor); and *The Adventures of Captain Bonneville, U.S.A.* (1837). Except for service as minister to Madrid (1842–46), he lived most of his later years at "Sunnyside," near Tarrytown, N.Y. (and in Irvington, now a sort of shrine to him). Completed biography of Washington (5 vols., 1855–59). One of the first American writers to receive wide recognition abroad, Irving has been held in affectionate regard by Americans ever since his own time. Some essays and tales (e.g., "Rip Van Winkle" and "The Legend of Sleepy Hollow") are known to most Americans. He was notable for effortlessly smooth style, good humor, and playful satire.

Irvington. 1 Town (pop. 59,201), NE N.J., W suburb of Newark; settled 1692 as Camptown, renamed 1852. Mfg. of metal and rubber goods and leather. **2** Residential village (pop. 3,657), SE N.Y., on E bank of Hudson R. S of Tarrytown; settled c.1655. Renamed 1854 for Washington Irving, who bought "Sunnyside" estate in 1835. Columbia Univ. maintains "Nevis," once estate of Alexander Hamilton's son.

Irwell, river of Lancashire, England.

Isaac, Byzantine emperors. **Isaac I,** 1005–1061, first of Comnenus dynasty, was proclaimed emperor by the army in 1057 but abdicated, ostensibly because of bad health, in 1059. Uncle of Alexius I. **Isaac II** (Isaac Angelus), d. 1204, proclaimed emperor by the people in 1185, was deposed and blinded in 1195 by his brother ALEXIUS III. His son, ALEXIUS IV, appealed to the host of the Fourth Crusade (see CRUSADES), which restored father and son as joint emperors in 1203. Their overthrow by ALEXIUS V (1204) led to the sack of Constantinople by the Crusaders.

Isaac [Heb.,= laughter], only son of Abraham and Sarah, father of Jacob and Esau. Offered as sacrifice to God by Abraham in act of supreme faith; saved by divine intervention. Tricked into blessing Jacob instead of Esau. Lived longest and most peaceful life of all the patriarchs. Gen. 21–27; 35.29; 49.31; Amos 7.9,16; Mat. 8.11; Heb. 11.17; James 2.21.

Isaacs, Jorge (hôr'hä ē'säks), 1837–95, Colombian novelist, author of idyllic romance, *María* (1867).

Isabeau of Bavaria (ēzäbō'), 1371–1435, consort of CHARLES VI of France. In league with Burgundy, she helped bring about the Treaty of TROYES (1420), which disinherited her own son, Charles VII.

Isabel, 1846–1921, princess imperial of Brazil; daughter of Pedro II, wife of comte d'Eu. As regent, during father's absence, she signed law abolishing slavery (1889). After downfall of empire, lived in Paris.

Isabella, 1292?–1358, queen consort of EDWARD II of England; daughter of Philip IV of France. Mistreated by her husband, she hated royal favorites, the Despensers. Visited France (1325), formed a liaison with Roger MORTIMER, and invaded England. King abdicated and was murdered. Isabella and Mortimer ruled until Edward III seized power in 1330.

Isabella, Spanish queens. **Isabella I** or **Isabella the Catholic,** 1451–1504, queen of Castile and Leon (1474–1504), consort of Ferdinand II of Aragon, who became Ferdinand V of Castile. Her claim to Castile was contested in civil war by JUANA LA BELTRANEJA until 1479. For the crucial reign of Ferdinand and Isabella, called the Catholic monarchs, see FERDINAND V. **Isabella II,** 1830–1904, queen of Spain (1833–68), succeeded her father Ferdinand VII under the regency of her mother MARIA CHRISTINA. Her accession was challenged by her uncle Don Carlos; the Carlist Wars resulted (see CARLISTS). She married her cousin, Francisco de Asís (1846). Her rule was troubled by continuous party conflicts and frequent rebellions. Deposed in 1868, she went into exile in France. In 1870 she abdicated her rights in favor of her son Alfonso XII.

Isabey, Jean Baptiste (zhä bäptēst' ēzäbā'), 1767–1855, French portrait painter and miniaturist. Portrayed, among others, Marie Antoinette and Napoleon III. His son, **Eugène Louis Gabriel Isabey,** 1804–86, was a marine and genre painter.

Isaiah (īzā'yú) [Heb.,= salvation of God] or **Isaias** (īsā'yús), book of Old Testament. A collection of prophecies attributed to Isaiah (fl. 710 B.C.), one of major prophets. Message partly political, urging recognition of Assyrian power and opposing Egyptian alliance. Book falls into two major sections of prophecies (1–35 and 40–66) concerning the fate of Israel and Judah, with a prose section (36–39) that mainly parallels 2 Kings 18.13–20.19. Has Messianic allusions (8–12; 40–42; 53). Later biblical mention includes Mat. 1.23; 4.15; 13.14. Esaias: Mat. 3.13.

Isaiah, Ascension of: see PSEUDEPIGRAPHA.

Isaias: see ISAIAH.

Isauria (īsô'rēú), anc. district of Asia Minor, N of the Taurus range, in present S central Turkey. A wild region, it was inhabited by bands who lived by depredations on land and sea traffic. They were only partially checked by the Romans and not subdued until the arrival of the Seljuk Turks.

Iscariot: see JUDAS ISCARIOT.

Ischia (ēs'kyä), rocky island (18 sq. mi.; pop. 30,418), S Italy, at entrance of Bay of Naples. Health resort, celebrated for warm mineral springs. Wine.

Ischl or **Bad Ischl** (bät' ĭ'shúl), town (pop. 14,-004), Upper Austria, in the SALZKAMMERGUT. Famous spa; after 1822 summer residence of imperial family.

Isère (ēzēr'), department (3,180 sq. mi.; pop. 574,019), SE France, in Dauphiné; cap. Grenoble. Named for Isère R., tributary of the Rhone.

Iseult: see TRISTRAM AND ISOLDE.

Isfahan (ĭsfúhän'), anc. *Aspadana,* city (pop. 204,598), central Iran, midway between Teheran and Shiraz. Cap. of Persia 1051–63, 1072–92, 1590–1722. Here are Abbas I's palace and the superb imperial mosque (built 1585–1612). The Julfa quarter, originally Armenian, was founded 1605 by Shah Abbas. City endured massacres by Tamerlane (1387) and by Ghalzai Afghans (1723). Occupied by Russian troops 1916. Traditionally known for metalwork, it is now a textile center.

Ish-bosheth (ĭsh-bō'shĕth, ĭsh'bŏshĕth), son of Saul. Contested throne with David for 7 years. 2 Sam. 2; 3; 4. Esh-baal: 1 Chron. 8.33; 9.39.

Isherwood, Christopher (ĭ'-), 1904–, English writer. Collaborated with Auden on plays (e.g., *The Dog beneath the Skin,* 1935; *The Ascent of the F6,* 1936). Among his novels are two on Berlin (1935, 1939; reissued as *The Berlin Stories,* 1946) and *Prater Violet* (1945). Other works on travels and interest in Eastern mysticism.

Ishii, Kikujiro, Viscount (kē"kōō"jerō', ĭshē'), 1867?–1945, Japanese diplomat. In 1907–8 aided in negotiating GENTLEMEN'S AGREEMENT with U.S. Negotiated Lansing-Ishii agreement (1917) with U.S., reaffirming Open Door policy in China.

Ishmael [Heb.,= God hears], son of Abraham and Hagar, half brother of Isaac. Sent, with Hagar, into desert because of family quarrel.

Settled in wilderness; became noted archer. Gen. 16.4–16; 17.18–26; 21.8–21; 25.9,12–17; 28.9; 1 Chron. 1.29–30. Honored as forefather of the Arabs by Moslems who esteem him as the Hebrews do Isaac; thus, use of name Ishmael for a social outcast is unknown in Islam though common in Judaism and Christianity.

Ishpeming (ĭsh'pŭmĭng), city (pop. 8,962), W Upper Peninsula, N Mich., W of Marquette. Center of Marquette iron range. Mining, quarrying, and dynamite mfg. Ski tournaments held since 1888.

Ishtar (ĭsh'tär), in Babylonian and Assyrian religion, goddess of fertility. She corresponds to Phoenician Astarte, Greek Aphrodite, and Roman Venus. As her cult grew, it absorbed others, and Ishtar became common name for goddess. She was a form of the ancient GREAT MOTHER OF THE GODS.

Isidore of Seville, Saint, c.560–636, Spanish encyclopedist, bishop of Seville, best known for his voluminous *Etymologiae* or *Origines*, a compendium of knowledge.

Isidorus of Miletus (ĭzĭdô'rŭs, mīlē'tŭs), name of two architects who helped rebuild Hagia Sophia, one in A.D. 532–37, the other in A.D. 553.

Isis (ī'sĭs), in Egyptian religion, nature goddess, whose worship, originating c.1700–1100 B.C., expanded throughout Egypt and Mediterranean world. She became prototype of all goddesses, and her cult was one of most antagonistic forces met by early Christians. In mythology of Egypt she was faithful wife and sister of OSIRIS and mother of Horus. After Osiris was slain by their brother, Set, and his body scattered in pieces, Isis gathered these together; Osiris was then restored and became ruler of dead. The legend symbolizes the sun (Osiris) overwhelmed by night (Set), followed by birth of the sun of a new day (Horus) from the eastern sky (Isis). Isis was universal mother and mistress of all magic. Centers of her worship were at Memphis, Abydos, and Philae, where her cult prevailed until A.D. 560.

Isis: see THAMES, river, England.

Iskander Beg, Albanian hero: see SCANDERBEG.

Iskenderun (ĭskĕn'dūrōōn), formerly **Alexandretta** (ă″lĭgzăndrĕ'tŭ), city (pop. 22,946), SW Turkey, on inlet of the Mediterranean. Was port for Alep until 1937. See ALEXANDRETTA, SANJAK OF.

Isla, José Francisco de (hōsā' fränthē'skō dā ē'slä), 1703–81, "el Padre Isla," Spanish Jesuit preacher, author of the satirical novel *Historia del famoso predicador Fray Gerundio de Campazas* (1758).

Islam (ĭs'lŭm, ĭsläm') [Arabic,= submission to God], religion of which MOHAMMED was the prophet; adherents are called Moslems or Muslims (popularly also Mohammedans). The latest of the three great monotheisms, it drew upon the other two (Judaism and Christianity); Abraham and Jesus are in the list of prophets preceding Mohammed. It is generally held that Jesus will return as the MAHDI at the end of the world. Islam is based on the sacred book, the Koran, revealed by God (called Allah in Arabic) to Mohammed. The concepts of God and of

heaven and hell are akin to those in Judaism and Christianity. Five duties are prescribed for every Moslem: (1) At least once in his life the believer must say with full acceptance, "There is no god but God and Mohammed is his prophet." (2) He must pray five times daily, facing toward Mecca, and he must say Friday noonday prayers in the mosque. (3) He must give alms generously —above the amount absolutely prescribed by law. (4) He must keep the fast of Ramadan. (5) He must, if he can, once in his life make the pilgrimage (Hajj) to Mecca. This last provision has made the pilgrimage the greatest in the world and a great unifying force in Islam. In addition to the Koran, Islam accepts the Sunna, collections of Traditions (moral sayings and anecdotes) of Mohammed. These were collected as early as the 9th cent. by BUKHARI and others. There are contradictions in the Sunna, but they are resolved by the doctrine of Ijma, which expresses the agreement of Islam; every Moslem holds that a belief held by the greater part of Islam is infallibly true; the principle has made the religion flexible. There was early a great split in Islam between SUNNITES and SHIITES, and this has persisted. The WAHABI defection was the only important later sectarian movement among Sunnites, but many groups developed among the Shiites (e.g., Assassins, Fatimites, Karmathians). The original split was over the CALIPHATE, which was the crowning institution of the theocratic structure of Islam. Though secularism has modified the unity somewhat, in theory the civil law in Mohammedan countries is not separate from religious law; religion governs all aspects of life. There have developed some four different systems of interpretation of the law in Sunnite Islam, all regarded as orthodox. Islamic philosophy is in effect part of theology; the greatest philosopher was Al-Gazel. Rationalism and mysticism (see SUFISM) both grew up in Islam, but were equally absorbed. The spread of the religion after its founding by Mohammed was phenomenally rapid in the 7th and 8th cent., and it soon was dominant from Spain (see MOORS) to India. It is today spread across Asia to the S Pacific, prevails in N Africa (with its intellectual center at Cairo), and is still gaining converts in the rest of Africa. There are also Mohammedan groups in Europe (Albania, Bosnia, and sections of Russia), but only scattered communities in the New World.

island, relatively small body of land surrounded entirely by water. As oceans form continuous water mass, continents are, strictly speaking, islands. Largest island is Greenland, followed by New Guinea, Borneo, Madagascar, Baffin Isl., Sumatra, Honshu, Great Britain. Islands are continental if created by submergence of coastal highlands with only summits left above water, or by sea's breaking through an isthmus or peninsula. Great Britain, Japanese archipelago, Sicily are continental; submarine banks show former coherence of each with mainland. Islands are oceanic if created by ascent of ocean floor, as through volcanic action, or by coral growth (atoll). In rare cases coastal island reunites with mainland.

Island No. 10, formerly a Tenn. island (not now extant) in Mississippi R. near New Madrid, Mo. Scene of Civil War campaign (March 3–April 7, 1862). A Union victory.

Islay (ī'lā, ī'lŭ), island (pop. 4,970) of the Inner Hebrides, off W Scotland, in Argyllshire. It is 25 mi. long and 19 mi. wide. A tower commemorates American soldiers and sailors drowned in torpedoing of the *Tuscania* in 1918. Industries include farming, dairying, distilling, and fishing.

Isle La Motte (īl" lŭ mŏt'), island, 6 mi. long and 2 mi. wide, NW Vt., in L. Champlain and W of St. Albans. Comprises Isle La Motte town (pop. 295), settled permanently c.1788 on site of French Fort Ste Anne (1665), first European settlement in Vt. Black marble quarries.

Isle of. For names beginning thus, see second element; e.g., for Isle of Ely, see ELY, ISLE OF.

Isle Royale National Park: see NATIONAL PARKS AND MONUMENTS (table).

Isles of Shoals, group of seven islands off SW Maine and SE N.H., SE of Portsmouth, N.H. Appledore (Maine) and Star (N.H.) islands have resort hotels; White Isl. (N.H.) has lighthouse.

Isles of the Blest: see FORTUNATE ISLES.

Isleta (īslĕ'tù), Indian pueblo village (1948 pop. 1,462), W central N.Mex., on Rio Grande and S of Albuquerque; discovered 1540. Seat of a Franciscan mission from c.1621 until Pueblo revolt of 1680. Captured by Spanish 1681. Mission revitalized as San Augustín de Isleta in early 1700s. Holds annual feast of St. Augustine. PUEBLO INDIANS here are mainly prosperous farmers. Language Tanoan.

Islington (īz'–), metropolitan borough (pop. 235,645), N London, England; industrial district. Site of Pentonville Prison and Holloway Gaol for Women.

Islip (ī'slĭp), residential and resort town (pop. 71,465), including Islip village (pop. 5,254), SE N.Y., on S shore (Great South Bay) of Long Isl.

Ismail (īsmäēl'), 1499–1524, shah of Persia (1502–24), founder of Safavid dynasty. Made Shiism the official religion of Persia.

Ismail, Ukraine: see IZMAIL.

Ismailia (ēs"mäīlē'ä), city (pop. 68,338), Egypt, at midpoint of Suez Canal. Founded 1863 by Lesseps as operational base for construction of canal.

Ismail Pasha (īsmäēl' pä'shä), 1830–95, ruler of Egypt (1863–79), son of Ibrahim Pasha; first to bear the title khedive (viceroy). His schemes, such as building of Suez Canal, put Egypt seriously in debt, forcing him to sell his stock (c.44%) in Suez Canal to Great Britain, and to submit in 1876 to joint Anglo-French management of Egyptian government. Deposed 1879 in favor of his son Tewfik Pasha.

isobars (ī'sùbärz") or **isobaric lines** (ī"sùbä'rĭk), weather-map lines connecting points of equal barometric pressure to define cyclones, anticyclones.

Isocrates (īsŏ'krùtēz), 436–338 B.C., Greek orator, a pupil of Socrates and perhaps the

greatest teacher in Greek history. *Panegyricus* was considered his most celebrated oration.

Isolde: see TRISTRAM AND ISOLDE.

isomerism (īsŏ'mùrĭzùm), in chemistry, condition in which two or more compounds have same molecular formula but different atomic arrangement. Structural isomers have different structural formulas and properties. Sterioisomerism depends on arrangement of atoms in space. Optical isomerism depends on difference in effect of compounds on polarized light; optical isomers have same structural formulas and same general properties.

isomorphism (ī"sōmôr'fīzùm), similarity of crystal form and chemical composition between two substances.

Isonzo (ēzōn'tsō), river, 86 mi. long, Yugoslavia and Italy. Fiercely contested in World War I.

isotope (ī'sùtōp), in chemistry, one of two or more elements identical in chemical activity but differing in ATOMIC WEIGHT. Weight difference probably caused by difference in number of neutrons in nucleus; identical properties result from atoms having same number and arrangement of electrons outside nucleus. Radioactive isotopes are used as tracers in research.

Israel (īz'rēùl) [as understood by Hebrews,= prevailing with God], in Bible, name given to Jacob as ancestor of the Hebrews, God's chosen people. The 12 tribes of Israel—Reuben, Simeon, Judah, Zebulum, Issachar, Dan, Gad, Asher, Naphtali, Benjamin, Ephraim, Manasseh—were named for 10 sons and 2 grandsons (sons of Joseph) of Jacob. For 13th tribe, see LEVI. When Hebrew kingdom was divided under REHOBOAM, N part called Israel, S part Judah.

Israel (īz'rēùl), republic (8,050 sq. mi.; pop. c.1,414,500), W Asia, on the Mediterranean; cap. JERUSALEM. Boundaries are not permanently fixed; at present Lebanon is N, Syria and Jordan E, and Egypt SW. Grains are grown mainly in Galilee in N, citrus fruits in coastal area. Irrigation and dry-farming methods used in the NEGEV. Agr. cooperatives are widespread. Industrialization is being advanced, mainly at HAIFA and TEL-AVIV. Haifa and Jaffa are chief ports. For early history see PALESTINE. The nearly all-Jewish state of Israel grew out of ZIONISM. After World War II many backed an independent state for Palestinian Jews (1945 pop. c.500,000) which would also be a homeland for surviving European Jews and Jews in Arab countries. Palestinian Arabs (1945 pop. c.1,000,000) and Arab states opposed a Jewish state and demanded independence for all Palestine, with Jews a protected minority. British decision to admit only 2,000 displaced European Jews a month, until 100,000 had been admitted, led to attacks on British military installations by Jewish terrorist groups. In 1947 the UN divided Palestine into a Jewish state, an Arab state, and a small international zone, including Jerusalem. Despite Arab opposition the state of Israel was proclaimed at Tel-Aviv on May 14, 1948. Ensuing war between ARAB LEAGUE countries and Israel was ended Jan.,

1949, by UN mediation supervised first by Count Folke BERNADOTTE and later by Ralph Bunche. The war had increased Israel's holdings about one half. In Jan., 1949, Chaim Weizmann was elected president; Ben Gurion became prime minister as leader of dominant party in *Knesset* (parliament). Itzhak Ben-Zvi succeeded Weizmann in 1952.

Israëls, Jozef (yō'zŭf ēs'rä̈ls), 1824–1911, outstanding Dutch genre painter of 19th cent. Realistically depicted pathetic scenes from life of peasants and fishermen.

Issachar (ĭs'ŭkŭr), son of Jacob, ancestor of one of 12 tribes of Israel. Tribe allotted land W of Jordan R. Gen. 30.18; 46.13; 49.14; Num. 1.29; 2.5; Deut. 27.12; 33.18; Joshua 19.17; 1 Chron. 7.1–5.

Issus (ĭs'ŭs), anc. town, SE Asia Minor. Here in 333 B.C. Alexander the Great defeated DARIUS III.

Istanbul (ĭs'tänbōōl', Turkish ĭstäm'bōōl), city (pop. 1,000,022) Turkey, on both sides of the BOSPORUS; name was officially changed from Constantinople 1930. (For history, see CONSTANTINOPLE.) The cap. of Turkey until 1922 and still its chief commercial center and seaport, Istanbul also is the seat of a university (founded 1453; reorganized 1933) and is the see of three patriarchs (Greek Orthodox, Latin-rite Roman Catholic, Armenian). Only the European side of Istanbul corresponds to historic Constantinople. Rising on both sides of the Golden Horn, an inlet of the Bosporus, it is built on seven hills. Several miles of medieval city walls and forts still stand. The commercial quarter of Galata and the quarters of Pera (formerly reserved for foreigners) and Haskoy (Jewish quarter) are outside the walls. A famous bridge crosses the Golden Horn into Stambul, the core of the city, abutting on the Bosporus and the Sea of Marmara. In the NW are the former Greek quarter of Phanar and the Byzantine imperial palace of Blachernae. The Asiatic part of Istanbul includes Kadikoy (anc. Chalcedon) and Uskudar (also known as Scutari). The chief monument from Byzantine times is the HAGIA SOPHIA. Masterpieces of Turkish architecture include the 16th-cent. mosques of Bajazet II, Suleiman I, and Ahmed I; the Seraglio (former palace of sultans); and the Dolma Bagtche and Yildiz Kiosk (sultans' residences in 19th and 20th cent.). Istanbul is also famed for its polyglot population and its beautiful environs.

Isthmian games (ĭs'mēŭn), athletic events organized c.581 B.C. Held at Corinth in spring of first and third years of Olympiad. Contests generally like OLYMPIC GAMES, but conducted on smaller scale.

Istria (ĭs'trēŭ), Serbo-Croatian *Istra,* mountainous peninsula, c.2,000 sq. mi., projecting into N Adriatic and bounded in N by Karst plateau; chief city Pola. Population is Yugoslav and Italian. Nominal Byzantine rule ceased in 8th cent. A.D., and area was partitioned by Venice, Carinthia, the patriarchs of Aquileia, and the counts of Gorizia. By the 15th cent. Venice held the SW, Austria the NE, and in 1797 all passed to Austria. Awarded to Italy in 1919, Istria was again partitioned in 1947, the major part going to

Yugoslavia, the remainder to the Free Territory of Trieste.

Italian East Africa, former Italian colony, comprising ERITREA, Italian SOMALILAND, and ETHIOPIA.

Italian language, one of the Romance or Romanic group of the Italic subfamily of Indo-European languages. See LANGUAGE (table).

Italian Somaliland: see SOMALILAND, ITALIAN.

Italian Wars, 1494–1529. Rivalry among the states of Renaissance ITALY invited imperialist intervention of the rising national states, especially France and Spain. Alignments of Italian and foreign powers shifted constantly. In the first phase (1494–95) CHARLES VIII of France conquered Naples but was forced to abandon it by a coalition of Spain, the emperor, the pope, Venice, and Milan. In the second phase (1499–1504) LOUIS XII of France occupied Milan, Genoa, and (jointly with Spain) Naples. French-Spanish disagreement flared into warfare (1502); Louis lost at Cerignola and at the Garigliano; the Treaties of Blois (1504–5) gave Milan and Genoa to France but pledged Naples to Spain. The third phase (1508–16) consisted of three subphases: the victorious campaign of the League of CAMBRAI against Venice (1509); the formation of the HOLY LEAGUE and the expulsion of the French from Lombardy by the Swiss (1510–13); the victory of Francis I at Marignano (1515), followed by the Peace of Noyon, which restored Milan to France. The wars between FRANCIS I and Emperor Charles V opened 1521. Defeated and captured at Pavia (1525), Francis bought his freedom by the Treaty of Madrid (1526), in which he renounced all claims in Italy. He promptly repudiated the treaty and formed the League of Cognac with Pope Clement VII, Henry VIII of England, Venice, and Florence, thus beginning a fifth war. Charles's troops sacked Rome (1527), while the French seized Genoa and with the help of Andrea DORIA laid siege to Naples. Doria's defection (1528) forced Francis to accept the Treaty of CAMBRAI (1529). After three more wars, fought largely outside Italy, Spain retained supremacy in Italy by the Treaty of CATEAU-CAMBRÉSIS.

Italic languages, subfamily of Indo-European languages. Latin superseded the other two important groups (Oscan and Umbrian) and was the only one to survive antiquity; from it the Romanic languages are derived. See LANGUAGE (table).

Italy, Latin and Ital. *Italia,* republic (116,235 sq. mi.; pop. 47,021,000), S Europe; cap. Rome. N Italy is separated by the ALPS from France, Switzerland, Austria, Yugoslavia. Central and S Italy, traversed by the APENNINES, form a boot-shaped peninsula between the Tyrrhenian and Adriatic seas and contain VATICAN CITY and SAN MARINO. Of the 19 regions making up Italy, five enjoy autonomous rights—the islands of SICILY and SARDINIA and the border regions of Val d'AOSTA, TRENTINO-ALTO ADIGE, and FRIULI-VENEZIA GIULIA. The other regions are: LIGURIA, PIEDMONT, LOMBARDY, VENETIA, EMILIA-ROMAGNA, MARCHES, TUSCANY, UMBRIA, LATIUM, CAMPANIA, BASILICATA, ABRUZZI E MOLISE, CALABRIA, APULIA. N

Italy, with the fertile Po plain and the commercial and industrial centers of MILAN, GENOA, and TURIN, is the richest part of the country. Central Italy contains such historic and cultural centers as FLORENCE, PISA, BOLOGNA, RAVENNA, ROME. S Italy, with NAPLES as chief city, is scarred by poverty. The varied beauty of the Italian landscape conceals the harshness of its rocky, eroded soil, intensely and patiently worked by a frugal population. Fruit, wine, olive oil, cheese are among the exports; food staples and basic raw materials are largely imported. Industries (silk, textiles, automobiles, machinery, chemicals, luxury goods) depend largely on export markets and imported raw materials; hydroelectric power, sulphur, mercury, and marble are the only important natural resources. Roman Catholicism is the official religion of this overwhelmingly Catholic country, but freedom of worship is guaranteed.

Ancient and Medieval Italy. About the 8th cent. B.C. the Etruscans settled in N Italy, the Greeks along the S coasts (see ETRUSCAN CIVILIZATION; MAGNA GRAECIA). A Celtic invasion (5th cent. B.C.) drove the Etruscans S, until they were stopped by the SAMNITES. Italian history from the 5th cent. B.C. to the 5th cent. A.D. is largely that of rising ROME and of the Roman Empire. The barbarian invasions (5th cent.; see VISIGOTHS, HUNS, ODOACER, OSTROGOTHS) destroyed the Western Empire and Italian unity. THEODORIC THE GREAT preserved Roman institutions, but after his death the papacy alone remained a stable element. JUSTINIAN I reconquered Italy (535–54), but his successors were defeated by the LOMBARDS. Byzantine rule persisted for some time in Ravenna, the PENTAPOLIS, and along the S coast. In Rome, Pope GREGORY I resisted Lombard conquest and laid the foundation for the PAPAL STATES. The persisting Lombard threat to Rome brought the intervention of PEPIN THE SHORT (751) and CHARLEMAGNE (800), who enlarged the papal domain and estab. Frankish hegemony over Italy. After the divisions of the Carolingian empire (9th cent.), Italy gradually slipped from imperial control and fell into anarchy. The coronation of OTTO I as king of Italy (961) and Roman emperor (962) created the HOLY ROMAN EMPIRE, but despite their frequent incursions the German emperors could never establish control over Italy. S Italy, conquered by the Normans (11th cent.), passed, after a period of HOHENSTAUFEN rule, to the Angevins of Naples and the Aragonese kings of Sicily. The cities in the N (where the LOMBARD LEAGUE had defied imperial authority) and in central Italy became separate and warring states, some under princes (the VISCONTI, the SFORZA, the GONZAGA, the ESTE, the MALATESTA), some as republics. VENICE and GENOA built huge commercial empires, while merchants of FLORENCE, SIENA, and LUCCA gained power and wealth. Despite constant struggles between and within cities (see GUELPHS AND GHIBELLINES), the city-states had great prosperity, dominated European finances through their great bankers (e.g., the MEDICI), and produced the miraculous cultural flowering known as the RENAISSANCE.

Disintegration and Rebirth. With the ITALIAN WARS, beginning 1494, Italy became the battleground of French and Hapsburg imperialism. The Treaty of CATEAU-CAMBRÉSIS (1559) gave Sicily, Naples, and Milan to Spain. The Wars of the 17th and 18th cent. completed Italian subjection to foreign rule. By 1748 Naples, Sicily, Parma, and Piacenza were ruled by branches of the Spanish Bourbons; Milan, Mantua, Tuscany, and Modena were under Austrian rule. Venice, Genoa, Lucca, still independent, were declining. The Papal States and the kingdom of SARDINIA, under the rising house of SAVOY, made up the rest. All this was swept away by the FRENCH REVOLUTIONARY WARS and the rise of NAPOLEON I, who remade the Italian map several times. The Congress of Vienna (1814–15) more or less restored the pre-Napoleonic status quo. Austria, receiving Lombardy and Venetia, held a paramount position, but could not for long suppress the nationalist movement for unification (see RISORGIMENTO). The Italy of which VICTOR EMMANUEL II became king in 1861 still lacked Venetia (acquired in AUSTRO-PRUSSIAN WAR of 1866) and Rome. Florence was the cap. In 1870 Italian troops annexed Rome; the resulting conflict with the papacy was resolved only in 1929 (see LATERAN TREATY).

Modern Italy. From 1861 to 1922 Italy was ruled under the relatively liberal Sardinian constitution of 1848 by Victor Emmanuel II, Humbert I, and Victor Emmanuel III. Italy acquired colonies (Somaliland, Eritrea, Libya), expanded industrially, and found an outlet for overpopulation in mass emigration to the Americas. Though a member of Triple Alliance with Germany and Austria, it entered World War I on Allied side (1915). At the Paris Peace Conference of 1919 it obtained S Tyrol, Trieste, Istria, part of Carniola, several Dalmatian isls., and the Dodecanese, but not all the territory it had been secretly promised. Italian seizure of FIUME (1921) was symptomatic of nationalist discontent. Political and social unrest furthered the growth of FASCISM, and in 1922 MUSSOLINI seized the power. He gradually created a totalitarian corporative state and sought to solve the problem of overpopulation through "dynamic expansion." His conquest of ETHIOPIA (1935–36), his intervention in Spain (1936–39), and his seizure of ALBANIA (1939) were followed by formal alliance with Germany (1939; see AXIS). In 1940 Italy entered World War II; by 1943 it had lost Africa and Sicily to the Allies. The king dismissed Mussolini, appointed BADOGLIO as premier, and surrendered Italy to the Allies, who eventually recognized Italy as "cobelligerent" against Germany. The Italian campaign was slow, arduous, and destructive. Rome fell in 1944; in May, 1945, the German troops surrendered. The Italian peace treaty of 1947 deprived Italy of most of VENEZIA GIULIA (including TRIESTE), of its colonies, and some lesser territories. Its economic sufferings were only partially relieved by UNRRA aid and, later, by the European Recovery Program. King Humbert II was deposed by a popular referendum (1946) which made Italy a republic. Premier De Gasperi, a Christian Democrat, headed a series of anti-Communist coalition cabinets after 1945. Though barred by Russian opposition from the UN, Italy became an important partner in the North Atlantic Treaty (1949).

Itasca, Lake (ītăskŭ), small shallow lake in NW central Minn., SSW of Bemidji. Identified by H. R. Schoolcraft as source of the Mississippi, but later geographers consider source to be above lake.

itch: see SCABIES.

Ithaca (ĭ'thĭkŭ, ĭ'thŭkŭ), Gr. *Ithake*, mountainous island (37 sq. mi.; pop. 7,083), W Greece, one of the IONIAN ISLANDS; chief town Ithaca (pop. 3,120). Famed as home of ODYSSEUS.

Ithaca, city (pop. 29,257), W central N.Y., at S end of Cayuga L. and SW of Syracuse in FINGER LAKES region; settled c.1790. Seat of CORNELL UNIVERSITY and Ithaca Col. Mfg. of guns, machines, salt, fertilizers, and cement.

Ito, Hirobumi, Prince (hērō'bōōmē, ē'tō), 1841–1909, Japanese statesman, the outstanding figure in modernization of Japan. Sent abroad 1882 to study foreign governments. Drafted constitution of 1889, largely on Prussian model. Was twice premier 1892–96, 1899–1901; first president of Seiyukai party. Responsible for agreement (1905) which made Korea a virtual protectorate.

Itsuku-shima (ētsōōkōō'shĭmä), sacred islet in Inland Sea, Japan. Has a 9th-cent. Buddhist temple and ancient Shinto shrine with huge torii. Known also as Miya-jima.

Iturbide, Augustín de (ägōōstēn' dä ētōōrbē'dä), 1783–1824, Mexican revolutionist, emperor of Mexico (1822–23). Commander of royalist troops, he united with the insurgents and proclaimed the Plan of IGUALA. Instead of liberal state that separatists had planned, Iturbide had himself made emperor (1822). Forced to abdicate (1823), he fled to Europe. Returning to Mexico (1824), he was tried and shot.

Ituzaingó, battle of (ē''tōōsīn-gō'), fought in S Uruguay, Feb. 20, 1827. Argentine-Uruguayan forces defeated Brazil. Argentina and Brazil both claimed Uruguay but in peace treaty (1828), an independent Uruguay emerged as buffer state.

Itzá (ētsä'), Maya Indians of Yucatán and Petén (Guatemala), probable founders of Chichén Itzá (c.514). Moved c.1450 to L. Petén, remained there until driven from their capital, Tayasal (1697).

Iuka (īū'kŭ), town (pop. 1,527), NE Miss., near Tennessee R. Has ante-bellum houses and mineral springs. In Civil War battle (Sept. 19, 1862), Federal troops defeated Confederates here.

Ivan II (Ivan Asen), d. 1241, tsar of Bulgaria (1218–41). Bulgaria reached its zenith under his rule. He made it the strongest Balkan power but was essentially a man of peace.

Ivan (ī'văn, ĭ'vŭn, Rus. ēvän'), rulers of Russia. **Ivan III** (the Great), 1440–1505, grand duke of Moscow (1462–1505), expanded Muscovite state, freed Muscovy from allegiance to

Golden Horde (1480). Married niece of last Byzantine emperor, claimed successorship of Moscow to East Roman Empire. His grandson, **Ivan IV** (the Terrible), 1530–84, acceded as grand duke of Moscow 1533, had himself crowned tsar 1547. Conquered Kazan (1552) and Astrakhan (1557) from Tatars, thus beginning Russia's eastward expansion, which was carried into Siberia by the Cossack YERMAK. Warfare with Poland and Sweden over Baltic Coast ended to his disadvantage (1558–82). He began and encouraged trade relations with England. At home, Ivan crushed power of boyars (high nobles), favored common people, strengthened tsarist autocracy, and estab. special corps (*Oprichnina*) to fight rebellion. The death of his first wife (1560; six others followed her) apparently affected his mental balance. He was given to alternate fits of cruel rage (in one of which he killed his eldest son) and of prayerful repentance. Two sons survived him—FEODOR I and DMITRI —but his favorite, Boris GODUNOV, inherited the actual power. **Ivan V**, 1666–96, tsar (1682–96), succeeded his brother Feodor III jointly with PETER I under regency of SOPHIA ALEKSEYEVNA. Feeble-minded, he was excluded from affairs of state. He was the father of Empress Anna, who was succeeded in 1740 by her infant grand-nephew, **Ivan VI**, 1740–64, a German by birth. In 1741 he was deposed by Empress Elizabeth, and in 1764 he was murdered in Schlüsselburg fortress on orders of Catherine II.

Ivanovo (ēvä'nŭvŭ), city (pop. 285,069), RSFSR, 155 mi. NE of Moscow. Major textile center. Chartered 1328. First textile mill 1751. Called Ivanovo-Voznesensk until c.1930.

Ives, Charles, 1874–, American composer. In the insurance business for 32 years, he was at the same time composing music in a modern idiom. Most of his works were unknown until 1939. Among his works are symphonies, suites (including *Three Places in New England*), sonatas, chamber music, and songs. His Third Symphony won the Pulitzer Prize in 1947.

Ivigtut (ē'vĭgtōōt), town (pop. 141), SW Greenland, port SE of Frederikshaab. Here is world's largest cryolite mine. Site of a U.S. base in World War II.

Iviza, Span. *Ibiza* (ēvē'thä), island (221 sq. mi.; pop. 33,961), one of the Balearic Isls., Spain; chief town Iviza (pop. 9,644).

ivory, type of dentine present only in the tusks (prolongations of the upper pair of second incisors) of the elephant. Africa, the principal source of supply, furnishes the best and largest tusks. The chief commercial uses are for piano keys, billiard balls, handles, and decorative objects. In art, ivory is an excellent material for miniature painting and has been used through the ages for inlay work and intricate carvings. The civilizations of Egypt, Mesopotamia, Assyria, Babylon, Greece, Rome, India, China, and Japan are represented by works in ivory. Imitations and substitutes for ivory include celluloid and vegetable ivory (tagua).

Ivory Coast, French overseas territory (c.127,800 sq. mi.; pop. c.2,031,000), French West

Africa, on Atlantic coast, between Liberia and Gold Coast; chief port and cap. Abidjan. Has coastal lowland, forested plateau, and high savannas. Exports include cotton, cacao, palm oil, and hardwoods. Portuguese traders settled here in 16th cent. Became French protectorate 1891, incorporated 1904 into French West Africa. Represented in French parliament.

ivory nut: see TAGUA.

Ivrea (ēvrā′ä), town (pop. 8,737), Piedmont, NW Italy, on Dora Baltea R. Medieval marquisate of Ivrea passed to Savoy in 14th cent.

Ivry-la-Bataille (ēvrē′-lä-bätä′yù), village near Évreux, N France, where Henry IV of France won a major victory over the League (1590).

ivy, name referring usually to English ivy but also to other climbing plants, e.g., poison ivy, Boston ivy, ground ivy. Kenilworth ivy (*Cymbalaria muralis*) is a house or garden plant often seen on old ruins in Europe; grape ivy (*Cissus rhombifolia*) is a house plant. See *ill.*, p. 999.

Iwasa Matabei (ēwä′sä mätäbä′), c.1578–1650, Japanese landscape and genre artist, a founder of ukiyoye school of painting, characterized by popular color prints of topical interest.

Iwo Jima (ē′wō jē′mù), volcanic island (c.8 sq. mi.; pop. 1,051), most important and largest of Volcano Isls., W Pacific. In S is Mt. Suribachi (extinct volcano). Sulphur mining. In World War II the site of Japanese

air base, taken in early 1945 by U.S. forces.

I.W.W.: see INDUSTRIAL WORKERS OF THE WORLD.

Ixion (ĭk′sēùn), in Greek mythology. He was chained to revolving, fiery wheel in Hades as punishment for fathering centaur monsters by Hera.

Ixtacihuatl (ēs″täsē′wätùl) [Aztec,= white woman], dormant volcano, 17,342 ft. high, central Mexico, near POPOCATEPETL. Known also as Sleeping Woman.

Iyeyasu: see IEYASU.

Izhevsk (ē′zhĭfsk), city (pop. 175,740), cap. of Udmurt ASSR, E European RSFSR. Metal industry includes machinery and arms mfg.

Izmail (ēzmǖēl′), Rumanian *Ismail,* city (pop. 17,569), SW Ukraine, on the Danube delta and on Rumanian border. Commercial center; naval base. A Turkish fortress from 16th cent., it was captured by the Russians in 1770 and 1790. Ceded to Russia 1812, it shared later history of BESSARABIA.

Izmir, Turkey: see SMYRNA.

Izu-shichito (ē′zōōshĭchĭtō), volcanic island group, extending c.300 mi. S of Tokyo Bay, Japan. O-shima is largest island.

Izvolsky, Aleksandr Petrovich (ŭlyĭksän′dùr pētrō′vĭch ēzvôl′skē), 1856–1919, Russian foreign minister (1906–10). Ended Russo-English rivalry in Middle East by establishing zones of influence (1907). After Austria annexed Bosnia and Hercegovina (1908), he prepared for war by strengthening Triple Entente.

Jabbok, river of Jordan, the modern Wadi Zerka, which enters Jordan R. N of Jericho. On its S bank Jacob wrestled with angel. Gen. 32.22.

Jabesh-gilead (jä′bĕsh-gĭ′lēād), city of Gilead. Saul saved its people from atrocities at the hands of the Ammonites. At his death the grateful city buried him.

Jablonec nad Nisou (yä′blônĕts näd nē′sō), Ger. *Gablonz,* city (pop. 23,112), NE Bohemia, Czechoslovakia. Mfg. center for Bohemian glass.

jaborandi (jäb″ùrän′dē), tropical American shrub (*Pilocarpus*), yielding poisonous drug jaborandi which contains pilocarpine used in medicine.

Jachymov, Czech *Jáchymov* (yä′khĭmôf), Ger. *Joachimsthal,* town (pop. 6,806), NW Bohemia, Czechoslovakia. A major mining center for radium, uranium, and lead, it also has radioactive springs. Its former rich silver mines are now little exploited. From the Joachimsthaler, a coin struck here in the

16th cent., came the words *Thaler* and *dollar.*

jackal (jä′kôl), nocturnal wild mammal (genus *Canis*) of dog family, found in SE Europe, Asia, Africa. It eats carrion, plant food, and animals. It resembles the wolf but is smaller.

jack-in-the-pulpit or **Indian turnip,** American woodland perennial (*Arisaema triphyllum*). Small flowers are borne on club-shaped spadix enveloped by purplish-striped hooded spathe and are followed by cluster of red berries. Cooked roots were eaten by Indians.

jackscrew: see SCREW.

Jackson, Andrew, 1767–1845, 7th President of the United States (1829–37). Decisive victory as U.S. commander in battle of New Orleans made him the military hero of War of 1812. His popularity almost elected him President in 1824. Idol of the democratic West, an expansionist, man of action, he led what later came to be called Jacksonian democracy—government for the good of the small man, of the frontier farmer and the backwoodsman, the laborer and the mechanic of Eastern cities. His sweeping victory of 1828 led to conflict between reformers and settled proponents of order. KITCHEN CABINET was powerful; party was paramount and SPOILS SYSTEM was born. Social slights offered Margaret O'NEILL helped break up the cabinet; John C. CALHOUN provoked further estrangement through his NULLIFICATION doctrine and his resignation from the vice presidency. Jackson's fight against the BANK OF THE UNITED STATES was an important factor in election of 1832, in which he defeated Henry CLAY. Second administration was dominated by bank issue. Jackson sponsored Specie Circular in 1836; stipulating that all public lands must be paid for in specie, it helped hasten Panic of 1837. After presidency he retired to his estate, the Hermitage, in Tenn.

Jackson, Claiborne Fox, 1806–62, governor of Mo. (1860–61). Opponent of Union cause, called by him "unholy crusade." After conflict with Union troops Jackson was deposed.

Jackson, Helen (Fiske) Hunt, 1830–85, American writer, pseud. H. H. Notable for historical account of the Indian problem, *A Century of Dishonor* (1881), and novel on the theme, *Ramona* (1884).

Jackson, Robert H(oughwout) (hou'ŭt), 1892–, Associate Justice of U.S. Supreme Court (1941–). On leave (1945–46) as U.S. chief counsel at Nuremberg war-crimes trial.

Jackson, Thomas Jonathan known as **Stonewall Jackson,** 1824–63, Confederate general. At first battle of Bull Run, he and his brigade won sobriquet by standing "like a stone wall." He won renown by his Shenandoah Valley campaign (1862). Supported Lee in Seven Days battles, and was largely responsible for victory in second battle of Bull Run. Ably led Confederate right at Fredericksburg (Dec., 1862). Mortally wounded at battle of CHANCELLORSVILLE. Next to Lee he was Confederacy's greatest general.

Jackson. 1 Town (pop. 6,772), SE La., N of Baton Rouge. **2** City (pop. 51,088), S Mich., on Grand R. and W of Detroit; settled 1829. Industrial and commercial center of agr. area, it has mfg. of auto and aircraft parts. Founding of Republican party here (July 6, 1854) marked by tablet. **3** City (pop. 98,271), state cap., W central Miss., on Pearl R. State's largest city and railroad and shipping center. Processes cotton, lumber, textiles, and natural gas. Laid out as state cap. 1821; named for Andrew Jackson. Center of military activity in VICKSBURG CAMPAIGN; largely destroyed by Sherman 1863. Points of interest include old capitol (1839) and Confederate monument. **4** Resort town (pop. 344), E N.H., NNW of Conway; winter sports center. **5** City (pop. 6,504), S Ohio, SE of Chillicothe. Has steel mills, foundries, and coal mines. **6** City (pop. 30,-207), W Tenn., NE of Memphis; settled 1819. Rail and trade center of agr. area, it has mfg. of wood, steel, and meat products. Seat of Lane Col. (Negro; Methodist Episcopal; coed.; 1882). Has Indian mounds and "Casey" Jones monument. **7** Resort town (pop. 1,244; alt. c.6,200 ft.), NW Wyo. Gateway to Grand Teton and Yellowstone

national parks. Trade center for hunting, dude-ranch, and livestock area in **Jackson Hole,** fertile valley, 48 mi. long and 6–8 mi. wide, partly in Grand Teton Natl. Park. Abundant game (esp. elk). Snake R. waters valley and flows through Jackson L. (18 mi. long, 4 mi. wide).

Jackson, Port, or **Sydney Harbour,** inlet of the Pacific, E New South Wales, Australia, forming Australia's finest harbor. Sydney on S shore connected with N suburbs by Sydney Harbour Bridge (1932) with arch span of 1,650 ft. Shipyards on Cockatoo Isl. Port was Allied naval base in World War II.

Jacksonville. 1 City (pop. 204,517), NE Fla., second largest city in state and deepwater port on St. Johns R. near its mouth on the Atlantic. One of chief coastal commercial centers of the South, it is a rail, air, and highway focus. City has many wood- and metal-processing industries; also food processing, boatbuilding, and fishing. Lewis Hogan settled here in 1816. City laid out 1822 and named for Andrew Jackson. Growth interrupted by Seminole and Civil wars. Commerce developed in late 1800s with building of good harbor and railroads. Points of interest are municipal docks and yards, war-memorial fountain, and Confederate monument. Has naval air training station (1940). **2** City (pop. 20,387), W central Ill., W of Springfield; laid out 1825. Rail and trade center in grain area with mfg. of apparel and metal products. S. A. Douglas and W. J. Bryan lived here. Was Underground Railroad station. Seat of Illinois Col. (coed.; 1830) and MacMurray Col. for Women (Methodist; 1847). **3** City (pop. 8,607), E Texas, NE of Palestine. Shipping, packing, and processing truck (esp. tomatoes).

Jacksonville Beach, resort city (pop. 6,430), NE Fla., on Atlantic coast ESE of Jacksonville.

Jacob [Heb.,= supplanter]. **1** Son of Isaac, brother of Esau. As ISRAEL, ancestor of the Hebrews. By bargaining and trickery he gained the inheritance and blessing that Isaac intended for Esau. Jacob's life was filled with cruel disappointments (his discovery that after his years of labor to obtain Rachel, Leah was his first bride; the conduct of his wayward older sons), with spiritual revelations (his vision of the ladder to heaven; his wrestling with the angel), and with great joy (his reunion with Joseph in Egypt). Gen. 25–50; Hosea 12.2–4, 12; Mal. 1.2; Acts 7.12–16; Heb. 11.20,21. **2** Father of St. Joseph. Mat. 1.15,16.

Jacob, Max (mäks' zhäkôb'), 1876–1944, French writer and painter. His poems, plays, novels, and short stories, and paintings in their extreme symbolism to some extent anticipated surrealism. He was a Catholic convert and a mystic. Died in a concentration camp.

Jacobi, Abraham (jükō'bē), 1830–1919, American physician, a pioneer in pediatrics. His wife **Mary Putnam Jacobi,** 1842–1906, also a physician, taught at medical schools in New York city and was the first woman member of several medical societies.

Jacobi, Friedrich Heinrich (yäkō'bē), 1743–

1819, German philosopher. Argued that philosophy cannot maintain distinct realms of experience and that unity is based on faith, knowledge on intuition and reason.

Jacobi, Karl Gustav Jakob (kärl gōōs'täf yä'kôp yäkō'bē), 1804–51, German mathematician, noted for his work on elliptical functions, differential determinants, and theory of numbers.

Jacobi, Mary Putnam: see JACOBI, ABRAHAM.

Jacobins (jăk'ŭbĭnz), political club of French Revolution; so called for original meeting place, a monastery of the Jacobins (Parisian name of Dominicans). Founded 1789, it first was led by such moderates as Mirabeau, Sieyès, Lafayette. Jacobins and FEUILLANTS dominated Legislative Assembly (1791–92). Split of Jacobins and GIRONDISTS occurred when Girondist majority advocated war as a means to discredit monarchy; Jacobins (mainly Parisian deputies) opposed war, advocated direct reform, became increasingly radical and republican. In the Convention the Jacobins and CORDELIERS were called the MOUNTAIN. Among their new leaders were DANTON, ROBESPIERRE. After the fall of the Girondists (June, 1793), Jacobins began REIGN OF TERROR, liquidated the extremist Cordeliers and the moderate Danton (1794), and governed dictatorially till Robespierre's fall on 9 THERMIDOR.

Jacobite Church (jă'kŭbīt), Christian church of Syria, Iraq, and India, founded (6th cent.) as part of the Monophysite heresy by Jacob Baradaeus, aided by Empress Theodora. Church is out of communion with both Roman Catholics and Orthodox. Its head is the patriarch of Antioch (at Homs), its rite is the Antiochene, its liturgical language Syriac. One group (the "Syrian Catholics") since 17th cent. has resumed relations with the pope, but keeps its practices and rite (head is another patriarch of Antioch, at Beirut). On the other hand in the 17th cent. most Malabar Christians left communion with the pope and became "Malabar Jacobites" with Antiochene rite; later a group became "Reformed Jacobites," and in 20th cent. another portion returned to communion with Rome (the "Malankarese Catholics"). The Malabar Christians who did not become Jacobites at all are "Syro-Malabar Catholics" (Chaldean rite).

Jacobites (jă'kŭbīts), adherents of exiled branch of the house of STUART after Revolution of 1688. Sought restoration of JAMES II; later advanced claims of his descendants until 1807 when direct Stuart line ended. Included many Catholics, high churchmen, extreme Tories, and the NONJURORS. Two major risings in 18th cent. are known as "the '15" and "the '45." After the death of Queen Anne (1714) Henry St. John and the 6th earl of MAR attempted intrigue and revolt to crown James Edward Stuart; he was defeated at Preston (1715). The abortive invasion of Charles Edward Stuart (Bonnie Prince Charlie), which was crushed at Culloden Moor in 1745, was the last serious action of Jacobitism as an important political force.

Jacobs, Helen (Hull), 1908–, American tennis player. Won U.S. women's singles title 1932–35, British women's singles crown 1936.

Jacobs, W(illiam) W(ymark), 1863–1943, English author, known for humorous short stories of London docks (as in *Many Cargoes,* 1896; *Snug Harbour,* 1931) and for horror tale, "The Monkey's Paw."

Jacobsen, Jens Peter, 1847–85, Danish novelist, creator of a prose style. His *Marie Grubbe* (1876) is a historical novel. Also wrote poetry.

Jacobus de Voragine (vŭră'jĭnē), c.1230–1298, Italian hagiographer. Chiefly remembered as compiler of the GOLDEN LEGEND, he was archbishop of Genoa (1292–98) and was beatified in 1816.

Jacopone da Todi (yäkōpō'nä dä tō'dē), 1230?–1306, Italian religious poet, a Franciscan tertiary, probable author of the hymn *Stabat Mater Dolorosa.*

Jacquard loom: see LOOM.

Jacque, Charles Émile (shärl āmēl' zhäk'), 1813–94, French painter of Barbizon school.

Jacquerie (zhäk"ŭrē'), 1358, revolt of French peasants (nicknamed *Jacques*) against nobles and pillaging soldiers. Put down by Charles II of Navarre. Thousands were massacred in retaliation.

jade, name for two silicate minerals, jadeite and nephrite, used as gems, ranging in color from white to green. Jade is especially prized by Chinese and Japanese, who attribute to it magical properties.

Jadwiga (yädvē'gä), 1371–99, Polish queen (1383–99); daughter of Louis I of Hungary and Poland. Married Ladislaus Jagiello, grand duke of Lithuania (see LADISLAUS II of Poland), who accepted Christianity. She is nationally venerated as a saint.

Jael (jāl), heroine in time of Deborah. She murdered the Canaanite general, Sisera. Judges 4; 5.

Jaén (hään'), city (pop. 48,003), cap. of Jaén prov., S Spain, in Andalusia. The seat of a small Moorish kingdom, it was conquered by Castile 1246. Has imposing cathedral (16th–18th cent.), palaces, ruins of Moorish castle.

Jaffa (jä'fù), city (est. pop. 101,580), W Israel, on the Mediterranean; chief port for Jerusalem. Mentioned in Old Testament in connection with Jonah. City often changed hands in fighting between Maccabees and Syrians. Destroyed by Vespasian A.D. 68. Held by Crusaders in 12th cent. Fell to Napoleon in 1799 and to the British in 1917. Largely inhabited by Arabs until 1948, when Israel captured it. Jaffa is the Japho of Joshua 19.46; elsewhere in Bible it appears as Joppa.

Jaffna (jäf'nù), peninsula, N Ceylon, separated from India by Palk Strait. Chief city is Jaffna (pop. 62,922). Occupied in 17th cent. by the Portuguese and Dutch.

Jaffrey, resort town (pop. 2,911), SW N.H., near Mt. Monadnock.

Jagannath, India: see PURI.

Jagiello (yägyĕ'lō) or **Jagello** (yägĕ'lō), Pol. *Jagiełło,* ruling dynasty of Poland and Lithuania (1386–1572), Hungary (1440–44, 1490–1526), and Bohemia (1471–1526). Founded by Ladislaus Jagiello, grand duke of Lithuania, who became king of Poland as LADISLAUS II. His successors were Ladislaus III, Casimir IV, John I, Alexander I,

Sigismund I, and Sigismund II. See also ULADISLAUS II and LOUIS II, kings of Hungary and Bohemia.

jaguar (jă'gwär), largest New World predatory cat (*Panthera*) ranging from SW U.S. to S central Argentina. Black spots and rosettes mark its yellow fur; occasionally an all black jaguar occurs. Males reach 6–7 ft. body length.

Jahn, Friedrich Ludwig (frē'drĭkh lōōt'vĭkh yän'), 1778–1852, German patriot; a high school teacher in Berlin. Hoped to promote national revival by organizing gymnastic associations (Ger. *Turnvereine*); became known as *Turnvater*. Imprisoned as political agitator 1819–25.

Jahve, Jahveh, Jahweh (jä'vĕ, –wĕ), modern reconstructions of anc. Hebrew name of God (which could be neither spoken nor written). Other forms are Jehovah and Yahweh.

jai alai: see PELOTA.

jail: see PRISON.

Jailolo: see HALMAHERA.

Jainism (jī'nĭzŭm), Indian religion held by c.1,500,000 people. Rose with Buddhism in 6th cent. B.C. as protest against Hinduism. Tradition teaches a succession of 24 Tirthankaras (saints) originated the religion; last was prophet Vardhamana, called Mahavira [the great hero] and Jina ["the victor"]. Basis of Jain doctrine is belief that everything in universe, even matter, is eternal. Spirits retain consciousness of identity through successive incarnations which are determined by cumulative effect of conduct. Nirvana—release from body and matter—may be attained after nine incarnations. For the yati [ascetic] 12 years of self-denial earn Nirvana. For salvation all must be guided by three gems: right faith, cognition, conduct. For Jainist writings, see PRAKRIT LITERATURE.

Jaipur (jī'pōōr'), former princely state in Rajputana, India; since 1949 part of Rajasthan. Estab. in 12th cent. **Jaipur,** city (pop. 175,810), cap. of Rajasthan, was cap. of Jaijur state; financial center. Famed for jewelry, enamels, and muslins. Maharaja's palace and a university. Rajput palace is at near-by deserted city of Amber.

Jairus (jāī'–), man whose daughter Jesus raised from the dead. Mat. 9.18–26; Mark 5.22–43; Luke 8.41–56.

Jakarta, formerly **Batavia,** city (pop. 533,015), cap. of Indonesia, on NW Java. Its port, Tanjungpriok (5 mi. NE), is country's largest. Seat of a university. Produces textiles, rubber goods, machinery, and chemicals. Exports minerals, rubber, tea, and spices. The Dutch founded a fort here in 1619. Seat of British rule in Java, 1811–15. In World War II it was briefly hq. of Allied Far East Command.

Jalalabad (jŭlä″läbäd'), town (pop. c.20,000), E Afghanistan, on Kabul R. near Khyber Pass. Held by British in First Afghan War (1839–42). Trade center.

Jalapa (hälä'pä), city (pop. 6,605), cap. of Veracruz, E Mexico; agr. center and health resort.

Jalisco (hälē'skō), state (31,152 sq. mi.; pop. 1,744,700), W Mexico, on Pacific; cap. Guadalajara. Has coastal plains in W, volcanic mountains in center (L. Chapala is here), and productive plateau in E. Products are maize, wheat, fruits, minerals, timber. Explored 1522, settled 1529, Jalisco led in the liberal reform movement of 1858.

jam: see JELLY AND JAM.

Jamaica (jûmā'kû), island (4,411 sq. mi.; pop. 1,297,900), British West Indies, S of Cuba and W of Haiti. Comprising crown colony of Jamaica are the island itself, Turks and Caicos Isls., and Cayman Isls.; cap. Kingston. Discovered by Christopher Columbus 1494; settled by Diego Columbus 1509. Attacked by English (1596, 1643), Jamaica was formally ceded to Great Britain 1670. Population, largely Negro, is overcrowded and unemployment is high. Agr. products include fruits, spices, coffee, tobacco, cacao.

Jamaica: see QUEENS, New York city borough.

Jamaica Bay, SE N.Y., shallow inlet, c.18½ sq. mi., indenting SW Long Isl. in Brooklyn and Queens boroughs and opening SW into the Atlantic via Rockaway Inlet (bridged). Part of Port of New York.

Jambres: see JANNES AND JAMBRES.

James, Saint [ultimately from Jacob]. **1** One of the Twelve Apostles, called St. James the Greater, son of Zebedee, brother of St. John. Killed by Herod Agrippa. Mark 3.17; 5.37; 9.2; 10.35–45; 14.33; Mat. 20.20–29; Acts 12.1–2. Patron saint of Spain, where he is called Santiago. Feast: July 25. **2** One of the Twelve Apostles, called St. James the Less, son of Alphaeus. Mat. 10.3; Mark 15.50; Acts 1.13. Bible tells of a James who was kinsman of Jesus and head of church at Jerusalem (Acts 15; 21.18; Gal. 1.19; 2.8). One tradition says he is same as James the Less; another claims he is a different person. Epistle of James is commonly ascribed to him. Feast: May 1.

James I (the Conqueror), 1208–76, king of Aragon and count of Barcelona (1213–76). Conquered Balearic Isls. and Valencia from Moors; brought Murcia under Castilian control. In Treaty of Corbeil (1258) he and Louis IX of France renounced their respective claims to territories in S France and Spain. Wrote chronicle of his reign.

James, kings of England. **James I,** 1566–1625, king 1603–25, was the son of Lord Darnley and MARY QUEEN OF SCOTS. Became James VI of Scotland on his mother's abdication (1567). During his minority Scotland was ruled by regents and saw complicated struggle between pro-French Catholic party and pro-English Protestant faction. Began personal rule in 1583. Allied himself (1586) with Elizabeth and accepted calmly his mother's execution in 1587. Succeeded Elizabeth in 1603. From Hampton Court Conference (1604) grew movement which produced Authorized (King James) version of the BIBLE. Inconsistent policy toward English Catholics angered them and Protestants alike. Despite GUNPOWDER PLOT of 1605, James was suspected of favoring Catholics. His reliance on incompetent favorites (Robert Carr, earl of SOMERSET, and George Villiers, 1st duke of BUCKINGHAM) and his extravagance furthered discontent. House of Commons became rallying point of opposition to crown. In 1611 James dissolved Parliament and (except for Addled Parliament) ruled without it until 1621. James acceded (1624) to wish of Commons for war with Spain. His reign saw beginnings of English colonization in North America. **James II,** 1633–1701, king 1685–88, was son of Charles I and brother and successor of Charles II. Escaped to France (1648) in Puritan Revolution. Returned to England as lord high admiral in 1660, but resigned after Test Act (1673). His marriage (1673) to MARY OF MODENA brought close ties to Catholic and imperial policies of Louis XIV and increased Whig hatred of him. His daughter Mary married Protestant prince of Orange (later WILLIAM III). Exiled after accusations of Titus Oates about the Popish plot, he was recalled in 1680. After failure of Parliament to exclude him from succession and the abortive RYE HOUSE PLOT, Charles's death brought him to throne in 1685. His unpopularity was increased by Bloody Assizes of Baron Jeffreys of Wem; by the trial of seven bishops (1688) who opposed his declaration of indulgences giving religious toleration; and by his autocratic methods with a hostile parliament. Birth of James Edward Stuart as possible Catholic heir led to Glorious Revolution of 1688. James fled to France. In 1689 he attempted to restore himself in Ireland but was defeated at battle of the Boyne (1690). Died in exile.

James, kings of Scotland. James I, 1394–1437, king 1424–37, was the son of Robert III. Fearful for his safety because of king's brother, Robert STUART, duke of Albany, Robert sent James to France in 1406. Captured by the English and held prisoner until 1424, he was treated as a royal guest and well educated. Before his return to Scotland he married Joan Beaufort. He brought peace to Scotland by ruthless methods, but his popularity was lessened by his vindictiveness, cupidity, and quick temper. He was assassinated by a group of nobles. Thought to be the author of a number of fine poems. His son, **James II,** 1430–60, king 1437–60, had successive earls of Douglas as regents during his minority. Allied himself with the 8th earl of Douglas (whom he later slew) and from 1449 ruled in his own right. Invaded England in Wars of the Roses and was accidentally killed. His son, **James III,** 1451–88, king 1460–88, was seized at his mother's death by Boyd family who ruled until 1469. He reigned in a turbulent period, and was murdered by nobles at Sauchieburn. His son, **James IV,** 1473–1513, king 1488–1513, was popular, and his reign was a profitable one for Scotland. Married (1502) Margaret Tudor, daughter of Henry VII of England. Relations with England deteriorated with accession of Henry VIII. James invaded England and was killed at battle of Flodden in 1513. His son, **James V,** 1512–42, king 1513–42, was the object of a struggle between his regents. Held captive, he escaped (1528) and allied himself with France against Henry VIII. Married MARY OF GUISE in 1538. War broke out with England (1542). He died shortly thereafter. **James**

VI, king of Scotland: see JAMES I, king of England.

James, kinsman of St. Jude. Luke 6.16.

James, Henry, 1811–82, American student of religious and social problems, b. Albany, N.Y. He rejected the Calvinism taught at Princeton Theological Seminary and was much influenced by Swedenborgian teachings. He became a member of Fourierist circles and a friend of literary men. He spent much time in Europe and, following his own theories of education, had his sons spend much time there. One son, **William James,** 1842–1910, became one of the most eminent of American philosophers and psychologists. He was a teacher at Harvard (1872–1907), at first of physiology and anatomy, later of psychology and philosophy. He considered consciousness as active and purposeful. Will and interest are primary, and knowledge is an instrument. The true is "only the expedient in our way of thinking." Ideas only lead the way to the objective world. For this basic theory of knowledge he borrowed from C. S. Peirce the word PRAGMATISM. In his "radical empiricism" James rejected all transcendent principles and argued that all experience is organized by "conjunctive relations," which are themselves direct experience. His works, notable for lucid and trenchant literary style, include *Principles of Psychology* (1890), *The Will to Believe* (1897), *The Varieties of Religious Experience* (1902), and *Pragmatism* (1907). His brother, **Henry James,** 1843–1916, was one of the most celebrated of American novelists. When studying law at Harvard he determined to devote himself to literature. He decided to settle in Europe and made his home in England after 1876, becoming a British citizen in 1915 as a gesture of his sympathies in World War I. A recurrent theme in his fiction is the contrast between ingenuous, though often charming, Americans and cultured, sophisticated Europeans and between the raw American scene and the centuries-laden, rich civilization of Europe, all on a level of wealth and social position. Among his novels and novellas are *A Passionate Pilgrim, and Other Tales* (1875), *Daisy Miller* (1879), *Washington Square* (1881), *The Portrait of a Lady* (1881), *The Bostonians* (1886), *The Awkward Age* (1899), *The Wings of the Dove* (1902), *The Ambassadors* (1903), and *The Golden Bowl* (1904). Among his short stories, all of high quality, "The Turn of the Screw" is perhaps most familiar. All his fiction is remarkable for conscious refinement of art. He frequently uses the device of the "detached observer" to study the minute reactions in speech and action that limn the psychological variations in character. He also wrote dramas, largely unsuccessful on the stage; travel books that are urbane and deep; literary criticism (including prefaces to later editions of his own work) that has had great influence; and autobiographical works including *A Small Boy and Others* (1913).

James, Jesse (Woodson), 1847–82, American outlaw. In 1866 he and his brother Frank (Alexander Franklin James, 1843–1915) became leaders of gang which robbed and murdered through most of central states.

James, Thomas, 1593?-1635?, English navigator and explorer. In 1631 he explored James Bay (named for him) while seeking Northwest Passage.

James, William: see JAMES, HENRY.

James. 1 River rising in central N.Dak. and flowing 710 mi. SSE across the Dakotas to Missouri R. near Yankton, S.Dak. Often called the Dakota. **2** River formed in western Va. and flowing 340 mi. E to Chesapeake Bay through Hampton Roads. Bridged just N of Newport News. River's lower course rich in historical association. Jamestown founded here 1607. In Civil War river was avenue of Union attempts to take Richmond.

James, epistle of New Testament, ascribed by one tradition to St. James the Less. Book gives various admonitions applying mostly to everyday aspects of Christian behavior; urges Christians to "be doers of the word, not hearers only" (1.22). Scriptural source cited for extreme unction is here (5.14–15). One of later books to be accepted as canonical.

James, Protevangelium of: see PSEUDEPIGRAPHA.

James Bay, S arm of Hudson Bay, 275 mi. long, 135 mi. wide, E central Canada, between Ont. and Que. Posts on bay include Rupert's House, Fort Albany, Moose Factory, Fort George, and Eastman. Discovered 1610 by Hudson and named for Capt. Thomas James, who explored it 1631.

James Island: see CHARLESTON, S.C.

Jameson, Sir Leander Starr, 1853–1917, British colonial administrator and statesman in South Africa. Made famous unauthorized Jameson Raid from Rhodesia into Boer colony of Transvaal (1895).

James Peak: see FRONT RANGE.

Jamestown. 1 City (pop. 43,354), W N.Y., on Chautauqua L. and SW of Buffalo; founded c.1806. Mfg. of furniture, textiles, toys, tools, and machines. Known for cooperative community services. **2** City (pop. 10,697), SE N.Dak., on James R. and E of Bismarck; settled 1872, when army post was estab. to protect railroad workers. Rail and trade center of wheat and livestock area. **3** Resort town (pop. 2,068), S R.I., coextensive with Conanicut Isl. (kŭnăn′ĭkŭt), c.9 mi. long and 1–2 mi. wide, in Narragansett Bay (bridged 1940 to North Kingston). Beavertail Light, on S tip of island, was estab. before 1750. **4** First permanent English settlement in America founded here (May 13, 1607) on peninsula (now island) in James R., SE Va., NW of Norfolk. Early hardships diminished as new settlers and supplies arrived and tobacco culture was introduced. As seat of Virginia government, saw first representative assembly in New World meet here 1619. Village restored after being largely destroyed in Bacon's Rebellion, but declined when cap. was moved to Williamsburg 1699. Few relics remaining include church tower (c.1639), old cemetery, utensils, and building foundations. Included in Colonial Natl. Park except for 22 acres owned by a state society.

Jamestown weed: see JIMSON WEED.

Jami (jä′mē), 1414–92, Persian poet, whose works include the collections *Haft Aurang* (poems) and *Baharistan* (short stories).

Jamitzer, Wenzel: see JAMNITZER, WENZEL.

Jammes, Francis (fräsēs′ zhäm′), 1868–1938, French poet. Influenced by symbolists, but distinctive in his optimism and rustic simplicity, as in *De l'angélus de l'aube a l'angélus du soir* (1898). Later wrote religious verse in classical style.

Jammu and Kashmir: see KASHMIR.

Jamnia (jăm′nēŭ), biblical *Jabneel* and *Jabneh,* anc. town, W Israel. A Philistine center, it was sacked by Judas Maccabeus and later rebuilt. After fall of Jerusalem, Vespasian allowed the rabbi Johanan ben Zaccai to settle here as leader of the Jews. Except for short period, city remained center of Judaism until revolt of Bar Kokba in 130. Fortified by Crusaders in Middle Ages. Near site of ancient city is modern settlement, Yavne (pop. 350).

Jamnitzer, Jamitzer or **Gemniczer, Wenzel** (věn′tsŭl yäm′nĭtsûr, –mĭtsûr, gěm′nĭtsûr), 1508–85, leading member of a German family of goldsmiths and engravers.

Jamshedpur (jŭm″shĕdpōōr′), city (pop. 148,-711), SE Bihar, India; major steel center.

Jamtland (yĕmt′länd), Swed. *Jämtlands län,* county (19,966 sq. mi.; pop. 144,137), NW Sweden, bordering on Norway; co. seat Ostersund. It consists, roughly, of historical provinces of Jamtland in N and Harjedalen in S, both conquered 1645 by Sweden from Norway. There are health and winter resorts, dairy farms, and lumber camps. Formerly spelled Jemtland.

Jamuna: see BRAHMAPUTRA.

Janacek, Leos (lā′ôsh yä′nächĕk), Czech *Janáček,* 1854–1928, Czech composer and collector of Slav folk music. Among his works are an orchestral rhapsody, *Taras Bulba;* and an opera, *Jenufa.*

Janesville, city (pop. 24,899), S Wis., SE of Madison and on Rock R.; settled 1835. Industrial and commercial center in dairy and tobacco area with mfg. of autos and fountain pens.

Janet: see CLOUET, JEAN.

Janet, Pierre (pyěr′ zhänā′), 1859–1947, French physician and psychologist. He contributed greatly to knowledge of mental pathology and origins of hysteria, chiefly by use of hypnosis. He founded automatic psychology and first described psychasthenia.

Janina, Greece: see IOANNINA.

Janizaries (jă′nĭzĕ″rēz) or **Janissaries** (–sě″rēz), élite corps of old Ottoman army, recruited from forced levies of Christian youths and trained in strict discipline. Janizaries later gained enormous power and often made and unmade sultans. In 17th cent. membership became largely hereditary; conscription of Christians gradually ceased. Mahmud II liquidated them in a massacre (1826).

Jan Mayen (yän′ mī′ŭn), island (144 sq. mi.; pop. 8), Norwegian possession (since 1929) in Arctic Ocean, c.300 mi. E of Greenland. It is narrow strip of tundra, rising to 8,347 ft. in Mt. Beerenberg, an extinct volcano. Has meteorological and wireless station. Discovered 1607 by Henry Hudson.

Jannes and Jambres (jă'nēz, jăm'brēz), opponents of Moses. 2 Tim. 3.8. By tradition, names of Pharaoh's magicians. Ex. 7.11. See PSEUDEPIGRAPHA.

Jansen, Cornelis (kôrnā'lĭs yän'sŭn), 1585–1638, Dutch Roman Catholic theologian, professor at Louvain and bishop of Ypres. He and DUVERGIER DE HAURANNE sought to reform Christian life by returning to teachings of St. Augustine. From his posthumously published *Augustinus* (1642) grew up the movement called **Jansenism** (jănsŭnī'zŭm), which stressed greater personal holiness and austerity and made much of the necessity of divine grace for conversion and of predestination. The Jansenists were called "Calvinists" by their opponents, but actually they were bitter opponents of Calvinism and held that the Catholic Church was necessary to salvation. Members of the ARNAULD family became leaders in the movement, and PORT-ROYAL was its center. The Jansenists' teachings of predestination, discouragement of frequent communion for the faithful, and attacks on the Jesuits raised a storm in the Church. In 1653 some Jansenist doctrines were condemned, and in 1656 Antoine Arnauld was expelled from the Sorbonne. The able Blaise PASCAL came to Arnauld's defense. Trouble continued, complicated by the relationship of Jansenism with GALLICANISM, the use Louis XIV made of it to combat the pope. Clement XI condemned a vernacular New Testament with Jansenist notes by Pasquier Quesnel. A Jansenist declaration in 1702 that the pope's infallibility is limited to declaring propositions (and not particular statements) heretical brought matters to a head. The bulls *Vineam Domini* (1705) and *Unigenitus* (1713) practically put the Jansenists out of the Church. Port-Royal was closed, and most Jansenists fled from France. Some submitted; others founded an independent church in the Netherlands. There are Jansenist bishops of Utrecht, Haarlem, and Deventer. The first bishop of the OLD CATHOLICS was consecrated by Jansenists.

Janson, Nicolas: see JENSON, NICOLAS.

Janssen or **Jansen, Zacharias** (zäkhärē'äs yän'sŭn), late 16th–early 17th cent., Dutch spectaclemaker credited with making first compound microscope.

January: see MONTH.

Janus (jā'nŭs), in Roman religion, god of "beginnings" both temporal and spatial. As spatial god he presided over gates and doors; as temporal god, over first hour of day, first day of month, and first month of year (named for him). He was represented with two bearded heads set back to back.

Japan, Japanese *Nippon,* empire (140,681 sq. mi.; 1950 pop. 83,199,637), occupying an archipelago off E coast of Asia; cap. Tokyo. Its four main islands are HONSHU, KYUSHU, SHIKOKU, HOKKAIDO. Before World War II it included KOREA, S half of SAKHALIN, KURILE ISLANDS, FORMOSA, PESCADORES isls., BONIN ISLANDS, Kwantung leased territory (see LIAOTUNG), Caroline Islands, Marshall Islands, Marianas Islands. According to tradition empire was founded 660 B.C. by Emperor Jimmu, descendant of sun goddess.

Foundation for Japanese state was laid in 5th cent. by Yamato clan whose priest-chief later assumed role of emperor. Japan borrowed heavily from Chinese culture, 6th–8th cent.; Buddhism was introduced and influenced in native religion, SHINTO. By 9th cent. authority of imperial government was reduced by rising power of Fujiwara family and Buddhist priesthood. In 12th cent. YORITOMO Minamoto became master of Japan and the first to bear title of SHOGUN. First European contact made by Portuguese 1542; Christianity introduced by St. Francis Xavier 1549. The 16th-cent. dictators NOBUNAGA and HIDEYOSHI were succeeded by IEYASU, founder of TOKUGAWA shogunate (1603–1867). Opening of Japan to the West by Commodore PERRY in 1854 was a factor in overthrow of shogunate and subsequent MEIJI restoration (1868). With policy of Westernization Japan rapidly became a modern industrial state and military power. New constitution of 1889 created a diet consisting of house of peers and elected house of representatives. Victory in FIRST CHINO-JAPANESE WAR (1894–95) and RUSSO-JAPANESE WAR (1904–5) established Japan as world power. Annexed Korea 1910; after World War I won mandate over former German islands in the Pacific. Manchuria occupied in 1931 and puppet state of MANCHUKUO estab. After 1937 SECOND CHINO-JAPANESE WAR was intensified. In 1940 pact signed with Germany and Italy. Rise of Gen. Tojo to premiership in Oct., 1941 marked height of militarist power over Japan; on Dec. 7 Japan struck at Pearl Harbor, Singapore, and other possessions of U.S. and Great Britain. Rapidly made sweeping gains in Pacific and Asia (see WORLD WAR II), but by end of 1942 tide had begun to turn. With explosion of atomic bombs in Hiroshima and Nagasaki, Japan capitulated and surrendered unconditionally Sept. 2, 1945. Allied occupation (following terms laid down by POTSDAM CONFERENCE) began under command of Gen. MacArthur (replaced 1951 by Gen. Ridgway). New democratic constitution, making lower house dominant and enfranchising women, was adopted 1946. Peace treaty was signed Sept., 1951 at San Francisco by all major Allied powers except USSR. It ended Allied occupation, but some U.S. troops remained in areas specified by defense pact (Sept., 1951).

Japan, Sea of, part of Pacific Ocean between Japan and Korea.

Japan Current or **Kuroshio** (kōŏrōshē'ō) warm ocean current of the Pacific. A northward flowing branch of North Equatorial Current, it runs E of Formosa and Japanese archipelago. Near lat. 35° N it divides: E branch nears Hawaiian Isls.; N branch skirts Asia coast, merges with cold Oyashio current.

Japanese architecture. Building art of China came to Japan with introduction of Buddhism in 6th cent. The temple Horyu-ji (near Nara) was completed c.650; it is oldest known example of wood architecture extant and is basis of all later Japanese design. Wood has always been favored material. Chief features of traditional Japanese design are interior columns, thin exterior walls of woodwork, plaster, and rice paper, and curved overhanging roofs. Pavilion called Phoenix Hall in temple at Uji represents peak of native design. Emphasis on ornamentation began in 14th cent. and became increasingly important during Tokugawa shogunate (1603–1867). Striking example of late style is group of lavishly decorated temples at Nikko. All Buddhist temples have courtyards approached by terraces and wide flights of stairs. Accessory structures include square PAGODA (often omitted) and drum tower. Shinto temple (still in pre-Buddhist form) is severely simple and roofed with bark thatch. At approach to it is gateway called *torii.* Typical native dwelling, as developed in Tokugawa era, is elegantly simple. Interior is subdivided by sliding screens; main spaces have *tokonoma* (alcoves for display of flower arrangement or a painting). For public and commercial buildings Western methods are now used.

Japanese art is based on Chinese art, which was introduced in 6th cent. with Buddhism by way of Korea. Kose no Kanoaka (9th cent.), first notable native master, adopted T'ang traditions of Chinese painting. In 11th cent. Motomitsu estab. the Yamato, or native, school, which still leaned heavily on Chinese style. Painters of Tosa school (13th–14th cent.) were aristocrats, who confined their work to the court. Toba Sojo (late 12th cent.) satirically represented various personages as animals in amusing poses; he and later caricaturists expressed the people's incisive humor. Next era produced painters who worked in classic Chinese tradition, with SESSHU and JOSETSU among leading exponents. Emerging in same period was KANO school. Linked with original movements in Japanese art are KORIN and IWASA MATABEI, founder of ukiyoye school of color prints, whose exponents included HOKUSAI, HIROSHIGE, and HARUNOBU. The 18th cent. produced the Shijo naturalistic school and the Ganku school of Chinese traditions. Mid-19th-cent. contact with European culture had negative effect on native art. Traditional method of painting requires Chinese ink and water colors, applied on paper or silk placed flat on the floor. Mounted on silk brocade or paper, pictures are of two types: *kakemono* (hanging picture) and *makimono* (scroll portraying series of scenes). Early sculptors (Chinese and Koreans) made spirited wooden images and small bronzes of Buddhist deities, which show Greco-Indian influences (7th–8th cent.). Stone sculptures are few; but exquisite ivory carvings are numerous. Among highly developed minor arts are porcelain and lacquer work, arms and armor, enamels, cloisonné, and damascening.

Japanese beetle, name for destructive insect related to June bug. Discovered (1916) in New Jersey, it spread so widely that extermination was impossible. Adult is c.½ in. long, has a metallic green head and thorax, and brown wing covers. It skeletonizes leaves and destroys fruits and flowers. Eggs are laid in summer on ground; larvae feed on roots, winter underground, and emerge in June or July.

Japanese drama. The lyric drama, *no* or *noh,* originated in pantomimic dance performed at ancient Shinto and Buddhist festivals. Most of c.250 extant *no* plays were written in 15th cent. Restraint and symbolism characterize both acting and staging of *no;* vocal recitative is indispensable, and wooden masks are used. Farcical interlude, *kyogen* (dialogue or monologue, without music), developed along with *no* to provide comic relief. *No* appealed mainly to intellectual tastes; by 17th cent. need for popular fare had been filled by *kabuki,* a form utilizing bizarre make-up and exaggerated stylized acting. Dramatic ballad, *joruri,* used in *kabuki,* was adapted also to the puppet show (introduced early 16th cent.). In late 19th cent. translations of European plays were successfully introduced.

Japanese ivy: see BOSTON IVY.

Japanese literature. Japan had no written language until late 3d cent. A.D., when Chinese was introduced by Korean scholars. Early in 8th cent. a method of writing Japanese was evolved by adapting Chinese ideographs to spoken Japanese. This system was used in writing of *Kojiki* (712), sacred book of Shinto, which gives basis for myth of emperor's divine origin, but other principal works of the period were written in pure Chinese. In 9th cent. simplification of written language by use of two syllabaries opened golden age of letters. By early 11th cent. such writers as Lady MURASAKI were adding luster to literature in native language (as opposed to classical Chinese). Basic forms of JAPANESE DRAMA were evolved, 12th–17th cent. Under Tokugawa shogunate (17th–19th cent.) written language was standardized and freer verse forms (e.g., *haikai* or *hokku*) began to replace the *tanka,* the classical form. After 1868 Japanese writing was deeply influenced by Western literature.

Japanese music. Much of Japanese music was borrowed from other countries, especially China. Forms of sacred music include: the *gagaku,* ancient ceremonial music, brought from China, 5th cent. A.D.; Buddhist hymns dating from the 6th cent.; the *bugaku,* ceremonial dance music, imported from China in the 7th cent.; and the *kagura,* native to Japan, principally vocal, and used for the most solemn religious rites. Historically midway between sacred and secular music is the music for *no* drama (see JAPANESE DRAMA). Secular music dates from the 16th cent. with the importation of the *samisen* (a type of lute). Other instruments include the *koto* (a zither) and many kinds of flutes, oboes, drums, and gongs. Japanese scales are all five-toned. Those borrowed from China are without semitones; native scales have semitones. There is no harmony as we understand the term. Rhythm background provided by drums forms no pattern recognizable to Western ears. Western music was introduced into Japan in the late 19th cent. and is now an integral part of Japanese culture.

Japanese quince: see FLOWERING QUINCE.

Japheth (jā′fĕth), son of Noah, ancestor of those who were to occupy the isles of the Gentiles. This was taken to mean the Medi-

terranean lands of Europe and Asia Minor.
Gen. 5.32; 6.10; 9.27; 10.1–5.
Japho: see JAFFA.
japonica: see FLOWERING QUINCE.
Japurá (zhŭ″pōōrä′), river, over 1,000 mi.
long, rising in Colombia as Caquetá and
flowing SE across Brazil into Amazon.
Jaques-Dalcroze, Émile (zhäk″-dälkrōz′),
1865–1950, Swiss educator and composer.
Developed the Dalcroze system of EURYTH-
MICS.
Jarnac (zhärnäk′), town (pop. 3,624), Cha-
rente dept., W France. Scene of Catholic
victory over Huguenots, where Louis I de
Condé was killed (1569).
Jarrow, municipal borough (pop. 28,541), Dur-
ham, England, on the Tyne estuary. Industries include iron foundries and shipbuilding.
Scene of labors of the Venerable Bede, who
died here.
Jarves, James Jackson (jär′vĭs), 1818–88,
American art critic and collector of Italian
works of art.
Jarvis, John Wesley, 1781?–1839, American
portrait painter, b. England.
Jarvis Island, area 1 sq. mi., central Pacific
near equator, 1,100 mi. E of Howland Isl.
Claimed 1857 by U.S., placed 1936 under
Dept. of Interior. On Hawaii–New Zealand
air route.
jasmine or **jessamine,** shrub or climbing plant
of genus *Jasminum* of tropical or semitropi-
cal regions. The scented flowers, mostly
white or yellow, are often used in tea; the
oil is used in perfumery. For Cape jasmine,
see GARDENIA.
Jason, in Greek mythology, hero who claimed
kingdom of Ioclus, which his uncle, Pelias,
had stolen from his father, Aeson. Pelias
would return it only in exchange for GOLDEN
FLEECE, owned by Aeëtes, king of Colchis,
where Jason led the Argonauts in ship *Argo.*
He secured the fleece with aid of MEDEA,
who loved him and who returned with him
to Ioclus. He was also a hero of Calydonian
hunt. In one legend Jason committed suicide;
in another he was crushed by beam of the
Argo.
Jasper. 1 City (pop. 8,589), NW central Ala.,
NW of Birmingham, in coal area. Processes
cotton, timber. **2** City (pop. 5,215), SW
Ind., NE of Evansville. Mfg. of desks; coal
mining.
Jasper National Park, 4,200 sq. mi., W Alta.,
in Canadian Rocky Mts.; estab. 1907. Game
reserve and recreation center, noted for spectacular mountain scenery. Jasper is park hq.
and station on Canadian National RR.
Jaspers, Karl (kärl yäs′pûrs), 1883–, German
philosopher, associated with existential
school developed by KIERKEGAARD, and
Heidegger. His philosophy is subjective and
nonrational.
Jassy (yä′sē) or **Iasi** (yäsh), city (pop. 94,075),
E Rumania; historic cap. of Moldavia. Tex-
tile mfg.; food industries. See of Orthodox
archbishop. Former large Jewish population
was massacred in World War II at German
instigation (1941). Has a university
(founded 1860) and several fine churches in
Byzantine style (15th–17th cent.). For Treaty
of Jassy (1792), see RUSSO-TURKISH WARS.
Játiva (hä′tēvä), city (pop. 17,496), Valencia

prov., E Spain. Noted for its Spanish-Moor-
ish castle and several fine churches and
palaces. Was residence of Borgia or Borja
family.
jaundice (jôn′dĭs), condition attended by yellowish discoloration of tissues and excretions
resulting from bile pigments in blood. Causes
include obstruction of bile duct and virus
infections.
Jauregg, Julius Wagner: see WAGNER-JAUREGG.
Jaurès, Jean (zhä′ jōrĕs′), 1859–1914, French
Socialist leader and historian. An idealist
and pacifist, he advocated a peaceful revolution to obtain economic equality. Was killed
by a fanatic nationalist on eve of World War
I, which he desperately sought to avert. His
Histoire socialiste de la Révolution française
is an economic interpretation.
Java (jä′vù), island (48,842 sq. mi.; pop. 39,-
755,902, including offshore islands), INDO-
NESIA, S of Borneo, from which it is separated by Java Sea, and SE of Sumatra. Cultural, political, and economic center of Indonesia. Chain of volcanic mountains rises
to 12,060 ft. Climate is warm and humid,
soil highly fertile. Exports quinine, rubber,
sugar, and teak. Oil fields are in NE. Native
arts include silver craft and batik work. A
home of early man (see MAN, PRIMITIVE);
remains of Java man or *Pithecanthropus
erectus* found here 1891. Religion is predominantly Moslem, but Hinduism and Buddhism have strongly affected native culture.
Highly developed arts include the *wayang*
or shadow play employing puppets and musical accompaniment. Largest city is JAKARTA
(cap. of Indonesia). Other centers include
JOGJAKARTA and SURAKARTA. Hindus colonized central and E Java in 7th cent. Rise of
Hindu-Javanese state of Majapahit (founded
1293) marked peak of Javanese history; it
ruled over much of Indonesia and Malay
Peninsula. Islam, introduced in 13th cent.,
produced Moslem state of Mataram. Following the Portuguese, the Dutch arrived 1596;
after 1619 Dutch East India Co. gradually
absorbed remnants of Javanese empire.
Early in World War II Java was exposed to
Japanese invasion by Allied defeat in battle
of Java Sea (Feb., 1942).
Javanese music, of uncertain origin, is remarkable in its orchestral development. It is
based on two pentatonic systems—*pelog,*
which has semitones, and *slendro* (or *salen-
dro*), which is composed of whole tones.
Slendro is considered masculine, *pelog* feminine. The *gamelan,* an orchestra of tuned
percussion instruments, originated in Java,
but is only rarely heard there today. See
BALINESE MUSIC.
Jaxartes: see SYR DARYA.
Jay, John, 1745–1829, American statesman.
Urged moderate policy as delegate to Continental Congress. As the Secretary of Foreign Affairs (1784–89) he recognized need
of a more powerful central government;
wrote five of the FEDERALIST PAPERS. First
Chief Justice of U.S. Supreme Court (1789–
95). American signer of JAY'S TREATY. His
son, **William Jay,** 1789–1858, a jurist, was an
active abolitionist. His son, **John Jay,** 1817–
94, a lawyer, served as minister to Austria
(1869–74).

jay, common name for certain birds of the crow family, found in Europe, Asia, and the Americas. Well known in America are BLUE JAY and Canada jay (often called camp robber) which is gray, with a white throat and black cap.

Jay's Treaty, concluded in 1794 between U.S. and Great Britain to settle difficulties arising mainly out of violations of Treaty of Paris of 1783 and to regulate commerce and navigation. Treaty, signed in England by John Jay and Baron Grenville, provided for British evacuation of Northwestern posts, unrestricted navigation of the Mississippi, and equal privileges to vessels in Great Britain and the East Indies, but placed severe restrictions on American trade in the West Indies. It did not allow indemnity for those Americans whose Negro slaves were carried off by Britain's evacuating armies, guarantee protection to American seamen against impressment, or secure recognition of principles of international maritime law. Therefore, it aroused indignation in America, and appropriations to carry it into effect were delayed until May, 1796.

jazz, style of music regarded as one of the most distinctive of American contributions to the art of music, characterized by its highly emotional melodic line and its strongly marked, syncopated rhythms. Originated in the late 19th cent. among Negro musicians of New Orleans but not fully developed until c.1910. The word itself is of uncertain origin. The original jazz ensemble was small and composed principally of the trumpet, cornet, trombone, clarinet, various percussion instruments, and sometimes saxophone and piano. Emphasis was on the ability of the individual player to improvise. As the size of the ensemble grew, more formal arrangements became necessary. Jazz was not seriously or critically studied until the 1930s. Outstanding names in its history have been Jellyroll Morton, Louis Armstrong, and Bix Beiderbecke.

Jean Baptiste de la Salle, Saint: see JOHN BAPTIST DE LA SALLE, SAINT.

Jean de Meun (zhä′ dü mü′), d. 1305, French poet, author of second part of the ROMAN DE LA ROSE.

Jeanne d'Albret (zhän′ dälbrā′), 1528–72, queen of Navarre (1555–72); daughter of Henri d'Albret and Margaret of Navarre; mother of Henry IV of France. Unlike her turncoat husband, Antoine de Bourbon, she was a staunch Protestant.

Jeanne d'Arc: see JOAN OF ARC.

Jeannette (jŭnĕt′), city (pop. 16,172), SW Pa., ESE of Pittsburgh; laid out 1888. Mfg. of glass, rubber, and metal products.

Jean Paul: see RICHTER, JOHANN PAUL FRIEDRICH.

Jeans, Sir James (Hopwood), 1877–1946, English astronomer, mathematician, physicist. With H. A. Jeffreys he developed the tidal theory of origin of solar system. His works include *The Universe Around Us* (1931), *Through Space and Time* (1934), *Science and Music* (1937), *Physics and Philosophy* (1942).

Jeball: see BYBLOS.

Jebb, Sir Richard (Claverhouse), 1841–1905,

British classical scholar. He was noted for his standard editions and translations of Greek writers and for his *Growth and Influence of Greek Poetry* (1893).

Jebus (jē′–), **Jebusi,** or **Jebusite,** name of tribe occupying Jerusalem before the Hebrews.

Jedburgh (jĕd′bûrû), burgh (pop. 4,083), co. town of Roxburghshire, Scotland. Border town, it suffered from Scottish-English strife; "Jedburgh Justice" (hanging first, trying after) became an unpleasant byword.

Jedda, Saudi Arabia: see JIDDA.

Jedidiah (jĕdĭdī′ù) [Heb.,= beloved of God], name given by Nathan to baby Solomon. 2 Sam. 12.24,25.

Jeffers, Robinson (jĕ′fûrs), 1887–, American poet. His works, stressing civilized man's divorce from nature, include *Tamar and Other Poems* (1924), *Roan Stallion* (1925), and *The Double Axe & Other Poems* (1948). Several of his plays (esp. his free translation of *Medea*, 1947) have been produced.

Jefferson, Joseph, 1829–1905, American actor. After 20 years as strolling player, he joined (1857) Laura Keene's company. Was famous as Asa Trenchard in *Our American Cousin* and as Bob Acres in Sheridan's *Rivals*. Seeking an original play, he and Dion Boucicault adapted (1865) Washington Irving's *Rip Van Winkle,* a long-time stage favorite.

Jefferson, Thomas, 1743–1826, 3d President of the United States (1801–9), author of DECLARATION OF INDEPENDENCE, and apostle of agrarian democracy. In Va. legislature (1776–79) he laid groundwork for abolition of entail and primogeniture, for establishment of religious freedom, and for a public school system. Served as minister to France (1785–89), U.S. Secretary of State (1790–93). Growing opposition to Alexander Hamilton and his policies associated Jefferson with group called Republicans, forerunners of present DEMOCRATIC PARTY. While serving as Vice President (1797–1801), he drafted Kentucky Resolutions (see KENTUCKY AND VIRGINIA RESOLUTIONS). He was elected President following a long deadlock with Aaron Burr in the House of Representatives, largely because Hamilton considered Burr the more dangerous man and gave support to Jefferson. First President inaugurated in Washington, which he had helped to plan, he instituted a republican simplicity there. Notable achievements of his first administration were LOUISIANA PURCHASE and LEWIS AND CLARK EXPEDITION. In his second administration attempts to enforce measures such as EMBARGO ACT of 1807 brought strong opposition. In retirement at his beloved MONTICELLO, Jefferson secured the founding of Univ. of Virginia and continued his activities as scientist, architect, and philosopher-statesman. He had complete faith that a people enlightened by free education could under democratic-republican institutions govern themselves better than under any other system.

Jefferson, river, 207 mi. long, rising in SW Mont., W of Yellowstone Natl. Park, and flowing W and NW (as Red Rock R.), then NE (as Beaverhead R.). Becomes Jefferson R. at entrance of Ruby and Big Hole rivers, then flows E to join Madison and Gallatin rivers at Three Forks. Main headstream of Missouri R.

Jefferson, Fort: see DRY TORTUGAS.

Jefferson, Mount: see PRESIDENTIAL RANGE.

Jefferson City. 1 City (pop. 25,099), state cap., central Mo., on the Missouri; laid out 1822. Trade and mfg. center of agr. area, it has railroad shops, printing plants, and mfg. of shoes, clothing, wood and grain products. Here are Lincoln Univ. (Negro; land grant; coed.; 1866) and a national cemetery. **2** Town (pop. 3,633), E Tenn., ENE of Knoxville. Seat of Carson-Newman Col. (Baptist; coed.; 1851). Cherokee Dam near by.

Jefferson Medical College (for men; 1825), in Philadelphia.

Jefferson Memorial: see THOMAS JEFFERSON MEMORIAL.

Jeffersonville, city (pop. 14,685), S Ind., on Ohio R. (bridged to Louisville, Ky.); settled 1802. Port with many shipyards. Mfg. of wood and foundry products.

Jeffreys of Wem, George Jeffreys, 1st Baron, 1648–89, English lord chancellor. In the Bloody Assizes after the duke of Monmouth's rebellion (1685) he caused c.300 to be hanged, c.800 transported, and many imprisoned or whipped.

Jeffries, James J., 1875–1953, American boxer. Won (1899) heavyweight championship from Bob Fitzsimmons, retired undefeated 1905. Returned to ring, lost title to Jack Johnson (1910).

Jegar-sahadutha: see GALEED.

Jehannet: see CLOUET, JEAN.

Jehoahaz (jēhō'ŭhăz) or **Joahaz** (jō'-). 1 Died c.804 B.C., king of Israel (c.820–c.804 B.C.), son of Jehu. 2 Kings 13.1–9; 14.1. **2** Fl. 609 B.C., king of Judah (c.609 B.C.), son of Josiah. Deposed and taken to Egypt by Pharaoh Necho, who made Jehoiakim king instead. 2 Kings 38.30–35; 2 Chron. 36. Shallum: 1 Chron. 3.15; Jer. 22.11. **3** See AHAZIAH **2.**

Jehoash (jēhō'ăsh) or **Joash** (jō'-). 1 Died c.789 B.C., king of Israel (c.804–c.798 B.C.). Successful in wars against Damascus and Judah. 2 Kings 13; 14. **2** Died c.802 B.C., king of Judah (c.841–c.802 B.C.), son of Ahaziah **2.** When his father was murdered and Athaliah seized the throne and massacred the royal family, Jehoash, a baby, was saved by his uncle and aunt, Jehoida and Jehosheba. He was placed on throne 6 years later in coup d'état. 2 Kings 11.

Jehoiachin (jēhoi'ŭkĭn, fl. c.598 B.C., king of Judah (c.598 B.C.). Captured by Nebuchadnezzar; imprisoned in Babylon. Later freed and honorably treated. 2 Kings 24.6–16; 25.27–30. Also variously called Jeconiah, Jechonias, and Coniah.

Jehoiada (jēhoi'ŭdŭ), high priest. With his wife, Jehosheba, he saved the baby Jehoash and led conspiracy against Athaliah that put Jehoash **2** on the throne. 2 Kings 11;12; 2 Chron. 22–24.

Jehoiakim (jēhoi'ŭkĭm), d. c.598 B.C., king of Judah (c.609–c.598 B.C.), successor of JEHOAHAZ **2.** Restored idol worship; burned book of Jeremiah's prophecies. Died just before Nebuchadnezzar took Jerusalem. Originally called Eliakim, took name of Jehoi-akim on becoming king. 2 Kings 23.24–24.6. Jer. 36.

Jehol (jŭhōl'), Chinese *Jeho,* province (40,000 sq. mi.; pop. 5,000,000), SW Manchuria; cap. Chengteh. Bounded in S by Hopeh along Great Wall. Largely rugged and rocky. Agr. (wheat, barley, kaoliang, corn, soybeans) limited by meager rainfall. Large coal mines. Originally inhabited by Mongolian leagues; Chinese control dates from Ming dynasty.

Jehoram (jēhō'rŭm) or **Joram** (jō'-). 1 Died c.846 B.C., king of Israel (c.852–c.846 B.C.), successor of Ahaziah **1.** Killed in Jehu's coup d'état; last of house of Ahab in Israel. 2 Kings 1.17,18; 3; 4. **2** Died c.846 B.C., king of Judah (c.851–c.846 B.C.), son of Jehoshaphat. His wife was ATHALIAH. Succeeded by Ahaziah **2.** 2 Kings 8.16–24; 2 Chron. 21.

Jehoshaphat (jēhō'shŭfăt) or **Josaphat** (jŏs'-). 1 Died c.851 B.C., king of Judah (c.870–c.851 B.C.), son of Asa. A "good" king, he made many religious reforms. Often allied with kings of Israel. 1 Kings 22; 2 Kings 3; 2 Chron. 12–20. **2** Recorder under David and Solomon. 2 Sam. 8.16; 1 Kings 4.3. **3** Father of Jehu. 2 Kings 9.2,14. Also Joshaphat.

Jehosheba (jēhō'shēbŭ), princess of Judah; daughter of Jehoram **2,** aunt of Jehoash **2.** See JEHOIADA.

Jehovah (jŭhō'vŭ, jē-), modern reconstruction of the anc. Hebrew ineffable (to be neither spoken nor written) name of God.

Jehovah's Witnesses, sect founded in U.S. in 1872 by Charles Taze Russell, also called Russellites. Doctrine centers on second coming of Christ. Sect has no churches or ministers, but circulates views by *The Watch Tower Announcing Jehovah's Kingdom.*

Jehu (jē'hū), d. c.820 B.C., king of Israel (c.846–c.820 B.C.). Anointed king by Elisha. Jehu murdered Jehoram **1** and Ahaziah **2** and massacred the royal family. His skill as a charioteer is proverbial. 2 Kings 9.

Jekyll, Gertrude (jē'kĭl), 1843–1932, English horticulturist and author of many works on gardening.

Jekyll Island: see SEA ISLANDS.

Jelgava (yĕl'gävä), Ger. *Mitau,* city (pop. 34,-099), Latvia, SW of Riga. Agr. center; varied mfg. Founded by Livonian Knights 1266; cap. of Courland 1561–1795. Notable buildings include Trinity Church (16th cent.) and ducal palace (18th cent.).

Jellicoe, John Rushworth Jellicoe, 1st Earl, 1859–1935, British admiral. In World War I he was commander in chief of the Grand Fleet (1914–16) and first sea lord (1916–17). Commanded at battle of JUTLAND. Governor general of New Zealand 1920–24.

jelly and jam, both preparations of fruit and sugar. Jelly is produced by cooking the juice of fresh fruit with sugar to the concentration at which jelly is formed. Good jelly depends upon proper balance of sugar, acid, and PECTIN. Jam is made from crushed or sliced fruit cooked with sugar until thick or until somewhat jelled. In preserves, unlike jam, the fruit retains its form.

jellyfish, popular name for the medusa, the gelatinous, umbrella-shaped, free-swimming form of marine invertebrate related to coral polyp and sea anemone. Most species pass through both medusa and polyp or hydroid stage. Jellyfish capture small animals by means of tentacles with stinging cells.

Jemappes (zhŭmäp'), town (pop. 12,812), Hainaut prov., SW Belgium, near Mons; coalmining center. Here in 1792 French defeated Austrians in one of first important battles of French Revolutionary Wars.

Jemez (hā'mäs), Indian peublo village (1948 pop. 892), NW central N.Mex., W of Santa Fe. Diminished from several peublos in 1500s to one by 1680, when PUEBLO INDIANS revolted against Spanish. Captured by Spanish in 1691. Jemez Indians once again in 1696, killed the missionary, and fled to Navajo lands. Some finally returned and built present village c.1700. Language Tanoan. Annual feast to San Diego.

Jemima (jēmī'–) [Heb.,= dove], first daughter of Job after his misfortune. Job 42.14.

Jemtland, Sweden: see JAMTLAND.

Jena (yā'nä), city (pop. 82,722), Thuringia, central Germany, on Saale R. Industrial and cultural center. Great Zeiss plant (optical and precision instruments) was partially removed by Russians after World War II. Chartered 13th cent., Jena later passed to Saxe-Weimar-Eisenach; was incorporated with Thuringia 1920. Napoleon I decisively defeated Prussians here 1806. Univ. of Jena (founded 1558) reached height in late 18th-early 19th cent., when Schiller, Hegel, Fichte, and A. W. von Schlegel taught here.

Jenghiz Khan or **Genghis Khan** (both: jĕng'gĭs kän'), 1167?–1227, Mongol conqueror. Succeeded his father, Yekusai, as chieftain of Mongolian confederacy. In 1206 completed conquest of Mongolia and made Karakorum his capital. Began conquest of N China in 1213; by 1215 held most of Ch'in empire. Conquered Turkistan, Transoxania, and Afghanistan (1218–24). Kublai Khan was his grandson.

Jenkins, town (pop. 6,921), E Ky., in Cumberlands on Va. line near Pound Gap. Has coal mining.

Jenkins's Ear, War of, 1739–41, struggle between England and Spain. Based on commercial rivalry, it led into the larger War of the Austrian Succession. Propaganda effect of claim by shipmaster Robert Jenkins that Spanish coast guards cut off his ear forced Sir Robert Walpole to declare war.

Jenkintown, residential borough (pop. 5,130), SE Pa., N of Philadelphia. Seat of Beaver Col. (Presbyterian; for women; 1853).

Jenner, Edward, 1749–1823, English physician, originator of inoculation with cowpox virus to immunize against smallpox. He first demonstrated his method in 1796 on James Phipps.

Jenner, Sir William, 1815–98, English physician, known especially for distinguishing between typhus and typhoid fever.

Jennewein, Carl Paul (jĕ'nŭwīn), 1890–, American architectural sculptor, b. Germany.

Jenney, William Le Baron, 1832–1907, American architect and engineer. In 1883 built the 10-story Home Insurance Building (Chicago), generally known as first skyscraper.

Jennings, Sarah, duchess of Marlborough: see MARLBOROUGH, JOHN CHURCHILL, 1ST DUKE OF.

Jennings. 1 City (pop. 9,663), SW La., E of Lake Charles. Agr. center with rice mills and cotton gins. **2** Town (pop. 15,282), E Mo., just N of St. Louis near the Mississippi.

Jensen, Johannes V(ilhelm), 1873–1950, Danish author. Interest in biological science shown in the epic *The Long Journey* (1909–20). Created a distinctive literary form in short essays (called "myths"). Awarded the 1944 Nobel Prize in Literature.

Jenson or **Janson, Nicolas,** d. c.1480, Venetian printer, b. France. Excellence of designs of roman type inspired many of his successors. He produced many beautiful works after 1470. The Aldine Press used his types from 1480.

jeopardy (jĕ'pŭrdē), danger of punishment involved in trial for crime. In U.S. interesting chiefly for double jeopardy, prohibited by U.S. constitution, which would make a man liable for trial for the same offense more than once. If the trial was abortive (e.g., if it ended with the jury unable to reach a verdict) or if a new trial is ordered after review by a court of appeal, a new trial does not constitute double jeopardy.

Jephthah (jĕf'thù), judge of Israel. Because of rash vow, he had to sacrifice his daughter, an only child. Judges 11.1–12.7. Jephthae: Heb. 11.32.

Jeremiah (jĕrĭmī'ù) or **Jeremias,** book of Old Testament. Tells story of Jeremiah (fl. 600 B.C.), one of the major prophets, who preached in Jerusalem under Josiah and his successors. He foresaw nothing but doom in Judah's foreign policy and urged the people to turn from futile resistance to Babylon and concern themselves with domestic reform and their own religious welfare. For such unpopular advice, he was imprisoned. Released after fall of Jerusalem (586 B.C.). Among Messianic passages in book: 14.8–9; 23.5–6; 30.9–24; 32.37–44. Other references to Jeremiah in Bible: 2 Chron. 35.25; Dan. 9.2; Mat. 2.18; Heb. 8.8. See also LAMENTATIONS; BARUCH.

Jeremy, Epistle of [Eng. form of Jeremiah] (jĕ'rĭmē), name given to sixth chapter of BARUCH.

Jerez de la Frontera ((härāth' dä lä frŏntā'rä), city (pop. 65,166), SW Spain, in Andalusia, near Cádiz. Export center for sherry (named after town).

Jericho (jĕ'rĭkō), anc. city, Palestine, N of Dead Sea. Its spectacular capture by Joshua marked Hebrew entry into Canaan, the Promised Land; its fall to Babylonia centuries later marked end of kingdom of Judah. Sacked and rebuilt by many conquerors —among them Herod the Great, who made it his winter residence. Recent excavations reveal walls said to be those of original Jericho.

Jeroboam I (jĕrŭbō'ŭm), d. c.910 B.C., first king of N kingdom of Israel after it broke away from Rehoboam. Notorious for fostering idolatry and restoring worship of golden calf. 1 Kings 11.26–14.20; 2 Chron. 10; 13.
Jeroboam II, d. c.749 B.C., king of Israel

(c.789–c.749 B.C.), son of Jehoash 1. Amos and Hosea prophesied under him. 2 Kings 14.16,23–29.

Jerome, Saint (jâr'ûm, jŭrōm'), c.347–419?, Christian scholar, Doctor of the Church, one of the Latin Fathers; full name in Latin Sophronius Eusebius Hieronymus. Studies (partly at Rome) made him proficient in pagan learning, but after a vision at Antioch (375) he renounced this scholarship and fled to the desert, where he devoted himself to scriptural studies. These, after he was ordained in 378, he continued under St. Gregory Nazianzen in Constantinople. Went (382) to Rome, where he became secretary to Damasus I and at the pope's request began work on a new version of the Bible. He was spiritual adviser to a number of Roman ladies, including St. Paula, who founded a monastery for him in Bethlehem. There Jerome lived from 386 to his death. His scholarly editing of Latin translations of the Bible together with some of his own translations of some portions from the Hebrew were the basis of the VULGATE. Also wrote exegetical works, tracts (often attacking the opinions of others with some violence), lives of Christian writers, and brilliant letters. Feast: Sept. 30.

Jerome, Jerome K(lapka), 1859–1927, English humorist and playwright, best known for play *The Passing of the Third Floor Back* (1907; still revived).

Jerome, William Travers, 1859–1934, American lawyer. Prominent in cause of reform in New York city. Led campaign against crime and political corruption.

Jerome of Prague, d. 1416, Bohemian religious reformer. With Huss (1407) he urged Bohemian control of Univ. of Prague. Defended Huss (1415) before Council of Constance, but was himself imprisoned and burned (1416) as a heretic.

Jersey, largest of the CHANNEL ISLANDS.

Jersey cattle: see CATTLE.

Jersey City, commercial and industrial city (pop. 299,017), NE N.J., opposite lower Manhattan (ferry, Holland Tunnel, subway connections) on peninsula bounded on W by Hackensack R. and Newark Bay, E by Hudson R. and New York Bay. Part of Port of New York, second largest N.J. city, important rail and steamship terminal. Produces packed meat, ink, chemicals, cans, and metal, petroleum, and graphite products. Area acquired by Michiel Pauw as Pavonia patroonship 1630. Paulus Hook (connected with Manhattan by ferry c.1764), Communipaw, and Harsimus (first permanent N.J. settlement) set up as trading posts. Near-by Dutch village of Bergen (settled before 1620) had first municipal government in N.J. (1661), first church (1660; Dutch reformed), first school (1662). Jersey town, Bergen, Hudson City, and Greenville formed Jersey City 1836. Has medical center. Home and hq. of Frank HAGUE, long-time Democratic boss of N.J. U.S. Supreme Court voided city's laws curbing civil liberties 1939.

Jersey Shore, borough (pop. 5,595), N central Pa., on Susquehanna R. and W of Williamsport, in farm area. Mfg. of metal products.

Jerseyville, city (pop. 5,792), W Ill., NNW of Alton. Trade and shipping center of agr. area.

Jerusalem, Arabic *El Kuds,* city (est. 1946 pop. 164,440), central Palestine, on rocky ridge of Judaean Hills, SE of Tel Aviv. The New City was in 1949 made cap. of Israel; the Old City is in Jordan. Jerusalem is the Holy City of Jews and Christians and one of the chief shrines of Islam. Often called Zion in Jewish and Christian literature, it is the symbol of the City of God (Rev. 21.2). Almost all holy sites of the three faiths are in the Old City. Moslems visit the Haram esh-Sherif, a sacred enclosure, with the Dome of the Rock or Mosque of Omar (built on the old Mt. Moriah) and the Mosque of Aksa. Part of the wall of the Haram is believed to be made from stones from Solomon's Temple; this, the Wailing Wall, is sacred to Jews. Christians revere especially the Church of the Holy Sepulcher which stands on the traditional site of Calvary. The Old City is surrounded by a wall built by Suleiman I (1542). E of the Old City is the valley of Kidron, across which lie the Garden of Gethsemane and the Mt. of Olives; N is Mt. Scopus, with Hadassah Medical Center, the Natl. Library, and Hebrew Univ. New City (W) is political and economic center, with government buildings, schools, Palestine Archaeological Museum, monasteries, and synagogues. Jerusalem is rich in both Old and New Testament associations. Churches and shrines marking sites connected with biblical and other holy persons are innumerable. City dates back to at least 15th cent. B.C. It may be the Salem mentioned in Gen. 14.18. David made it his capital after taking it from the Jebusites; Solomon glorified it with his Temple; here Judah's kings clung to their waning power; many of the great Hebrew prophets spoke in its streets. It fell in 586 B.C. to Babylonia; was rebuilt by Ezra and Nehemiah after return from exile. It was city of the Maccabees and of the Herods. Early Roman emperors were enemies of the Holy City; Titus razed its buildings and destroyed its Temple (A.D. 70). After the revolt of Bar Kokba the Romans made Jerusalem a pagan shrine called Aelia Capitolina (134). With the conversion of Constantine to Christianity, Jerusalem underwent a revival. His mother, St. Helena, is said to have discovered and restored many of its holy places. Moslems believe city was visited by Mohammed, treated it well when it fell into their hands in 637, made it their chief shrine after Mecca; but the molesting of Christian pilgrims and destruction of the Church of the Holy Sepulcher by fanatics led to the Crusades. Jerusalem fell to Crusaders in 1099 (see JERUSALEM, LATIN KINGDOM OF). In 1187, Moslems, led by Saladin, again took the city, and it was to remain almost constantly under Moslem control until it was taken by the British in World War I; it was later the center of British mandate of Palestine. When the mandate ended, both Arabs and Jews were determined to control Jerusalem. After considerable fighting, the Jews surrendered the Old City but held the New.

Jerusalem, Latin Kingdom of, state created in Syria and Palestine by leaders of First Crusade after conquest of Jerusalem (1099; see CRUSADES). Organized along lines of feudal theory, it consisted of the royal domain of Jerusalem (incl. subfiefs, e.g., counties of Jaffa and Ashkelon, lordships of Krak and Montreal), and of the fiefs of Antioch, Edessa, and Tripoli, over which the kings held only nominal overlordship. Kingship was elective (in theory); Assizes of Jerusalem (the law of the country) reflected ideal feudal law. In practice, royal authority was weakened by independence of feudal lords and by rise of great military orders— KNIGHTS TEMPLARS and KNIGHTS HOSPITALERS. Internal dissensions facilitated advance of neighboring Moslems. Edessa fell 1144; Jerusalem 1187; Acre, last stronghold, 1291. Reigning kings of Jerusalem were Baldwin I, Baldwin II (house of Bouillon); Fulk, Baldwin III, Amalric I, Baldwin IV, Baldwin V (Angevin dynasty). Titular kingship passed to various princes, notably Emperor Frederick II, and later was borne by kings of Cyprus.

Jerusalem artichoke: see ARTICHOKE.

Jerusalem cherry: see NIGHTSHADE.

Jervis, John, earl of St. Vincent (jär′vĭs, jŭr–), 1735–1823, British admiral. His victory over a much larger Spanish fleet off Cape St. Vincent (1797) was largely due to an unauthorized attack by Horatio Nelson. First lord of the admiralty 1801–6.

Jervis Bay (jär′vĭs), inlet of the Pacific, E New South Wales, Australia. Harbor and 28 sq. mi. of peninsula sheltering it were transferred 1915 to commonwealth for a port to be linked by rail with Canberra, 85 mi. inland.

Jessamine: see JASMINE.

Jesse, father of David. Name came to symbolize the royal line and Messianic hopes involving it. Ruth 4.17–22; 1 Sam. 16.1–18; 17.12,58; 1 Chron. 2.12,13; Isa. 11.1,10; Mat. 1.5,6; Luke 3.32. Jesus has been called Jesse's Rod and the Virgin Mary Jesse's Root. Jesus' family tree, depicted with Jesse as source, was popular subject of medieval art.

jester: see FOOL.

Jesuit: see JESUS, SOCIETY OF.

Jesuit Estates Act, adopted 1888 by Quebec legislature, partly to indemnify the Society of Jesus for Jesuit property confiscated after Pope Clement XIV had suppressed the society. It caused a violent controversy and was vetoed by the Canadian House of Commons.

Jesuit Martyrs of North America, designation for six Jesuit missionaries and two assistants who were beatified in 1925 and canonized in 1930 for having suffered martyrdom in 1648–49 at the hands of the Iroquois.

Jesuit Relations, reports by French Jesuit missionaries in New France. Important historical sources of French exploration and Indian conditions.

Jesus or **Jesus Christ.** The name *Jesus* is Greek for the Hebrew *Joshua* [savior]; Christ is Greek translation of the Hebrew *Messiah* [anointed]. Primary sources for life of Jesus are the four Gospels of MATTHEW, MARK, LUKE, and JOHN, and the epistles of the New Testament. The apocryphal gospels (see PSEUDEPIGRAPHA) and traditional sayings ascribed to Jesus (see AGRAPHA OF JESUS) are unreliable. Scholarly analysis of life of Jesus was not extensively begun until end of 19th cent. The facts of his career are subject to question (a small group even denying his historicity). In Christian teaching, Jesus was born of Mary, wife of Joseph, a carpenter of Nazareth, who had brought his wife to Bethlehem for the Roman tax-census. The Christian era is computed (according to a 6th-cent. reckoning) to begin with Jesus' birth, A.D. 1. Date is placed several years too late; Jesus was probably born between 8 B.C. and 4 B.C. According to the Gospels, wonderful events surrounded the birth of Jesus (e.g., the Annunciation to Mary, the appearance of the heavenly host, the adoration of the shepherds and the Wise Men). Jesus lived at a critical time in Jewish history. The Jews were restive under Roman rule as administered by the corrupt house of HEROD; Judaism was under control of the Pharisees and scribes who upheld the letter of Mosaic law. The simple people of Galilee and Judaea were eager for the promised Messiah and deliverance from Roman domination. Shortly before A.D. 30, an ascetic preacher, John the Baptist, made a stir in the Jordan valley, urging people to repent and prepare for the Messiah. Among those he baptized was his cousin Jesus. Jesus went from his baptism to solitude and meditation, thence to emerge on his three-year mission. He went about as a wandering teacher, accompanied by a small band of disciples (see APOSTLE). His extraordinary powers (see MIRACLE) and his PARABLES, spoken in the language of the people instead of the pedantries of the priestly scholars, attracted great crowds. His living of the principles he taught, his denunciation of the hypocrisy of Pharisees and scribes, his preference for the company of the miserable and the oppressed, reached the hearts of the people. At the end of three years, he went with his disciples to Jerusalem for the Passover. Jerusalem was seething with unrest at this feast of Jewish independence. Jesus' arrival was marked by an outburst of Messianic enthusiasm, alarming to those in power. After Jesus had created a scene in the Temple by beating the usuring money-changers, the ruling clique decided to destroy this man whom they could see only as a revolutionary leader and violent reformer. They bribed one of his companions, JUDAS ISCARIOT, to betray him. Jesus ate a farewell supper with his disciples and went out of the city to pray in the Garden of Gethsemane. There he was arrested. He was rushed to trial before the ecclesiastical court of the Sanhedrin. His claims to be the Messiah and the Son of God convicted him of blasphemy, a crime carrying the death penalty in Jewish law. Since only the Roman governor (at this time Pontius Pilate) could order a man's death, the court, in turning Jesus over to Pilate, emphasized Jesus' claims of kingship, thus charging him with treason against Rome. Pilate tried to evade action, but he dared not brave popular opinion, which was now aroused against

Jesus. He yielded and delivered Jesus to be crucified. Jesus died and was buried, deserted by all but his mother and a few friends. About three days later, some of the women visiting the tomb found it open and the body of Jesus gone. An angel told them that he had risen from the dead. Later they saw him and spoke with him; his disciples met with him, and many others as well. Here the Gospels end, but the book of Acts tells how, 40 days after the Resurrection, Jesus ascended into heaven in sight of his disciples. In orthodox theology, Jesus is God made man, the second person of the Trinity, born of Mary, a virgin; he was crucified to make atonement to God for man; he rose from the dead and ascended into heaven, and he shall come again with glory to judge the living and the dead; he founded, through his disciples, the Church to continue his work on earth. The Christian calendar revolves around Christmas (Dec. 25), the day set aside to celebrate the birth of Jesus; and Easter, with its movable feasts and fasts, commemorating the Resurrection. In Christianity, split as it is into many parts, two vital facts may be observed: the inspiring nature of the Gospels, and the consciousness of the reality of Jesus. Incidents of his life have long been the inspiration of artists in every medium of art.

Jesus. 1 Son of Sirach, author of ECCLESIASTICUS. **2** *or* **Jesus Justus**, Jewish convert in Rome. Col. 4.11. **3** Greek form of JOSHUA.

Jesus, Society of, religious order of the Roman Catholic Church. Its members are called Jesuits (jĕz'wĭts, jĕzh'ūĭts) and sign the initials S.J. after the names. Originally called *Compañia de Jésus* [Span.,= (military) company of Jesus], when founded (1534–39) by St. IGNATIUS OF LOYOLA (for founding, see article on him) and six companions. Ignatius drafted the rules which still govern the society. Training of those who enter the order is long and rigorous, involving much study. Jesuits have been particularly active as missionaries, as educators, and as scientists. Though not (as frequently asserted) founded to combat the Reformation, Jesuits were active leaders in the Catholic REFORM, laboring with some success to convert Protestants in S and W Germany, France, Hungary, and Poland in 16th and 17th cent. They also made daring attempt to reconvert England. From their beginning Jesuits have always been active in foreign missions. One of the original band, St. FRANCIS XAVIER, went as far afield as the Far East. In India, China, and Japan, Jesuit missions flourished long, and though many were washed away in blood, the Jesuits did estab. Catholicism in the Orient. They were also active in the New World, not only creating the much-discussed reductions (Indian settlements) in Paraguay but also working in all parts of Latin America and in New France (Canada). From Quebec the "black robes" went out into the wilderness of present Canada and N U.S. to convert the Indians, even penetrating as far as Oregon. Six Jesuits and two of their lay helpers, murdered by the Indians in the 1640s, became the Jesuit Martyrs of North America (most celebrated are Isaac Jogues

and Jean Brébeuf). Their zeal and solidarity and their peculiar devotion to the Holy See aroused the jealousy of some other orders and the hatred and fear of some ecclesiastical vested interests and especially of the absolute monarchs of Catholic Europe, who wanted to be free of all papal influence. The pope's power was weakened, and by 1700 the Jesuits were his chief support. They were the object of violent and concerted abuse. Some color was lent to charges of commercialism by a notable scandal. The accusations that they were given to intrigue and were lax in receiving penitents back into the Church have been hotly debated. Some of the claims against them were scurrilously false and were perhaps the basis for ridiculous statements repeated even today (e.g., that they have a secret constitution; that there are secret male and female affiliates; that they have special privileges; that they accept the doctrine that "the end justifies the means"; that they have revolutionary intentions). The princes had their way. The order was suppressed in Portugal 1759, in France 1764, in Spanish dominions 1767, and Clement XIV was compelled to dissolve the order in 1773. Frederick the Great and Catherine the Great refused to publish the papal brief, so the order continued in Russia and Prussia. It was reestablished as a world order on general demand in 1814 and has since resumed and expanded its missionary and educational work. There are notable Jesuit schools and colleges in the U.S. (e.g., Georgetown, Fordham, St. Louis universities).

Jesus College: see CAMBRIDGE UNIVERSITY; OXFORD UNIVERSITY.

Jesus Island: see ÎLE JÉSUS, Que.

jet, black variety of lignite coal. Compact, takes good polish, and is easily worked into beads and other ornaments. Yorkshire, England, is chief source.

Jethou: see CHANNEL ISLANDS.

Jethro (jĕth'rō), Midianite priest of Sinai; father-in-law of Moses. Ex. 2.21; 3.1; 4.18; 18. Reuel: Ex. 2.18; Raguel: Num. 10.29. Hobab: Judges 4.11.

jet propulsion, forward "thrust" resulting from rearward expulsion of mass of gas under high pressure generated by combustion in jet engine. Any apparatus using jet propulsion is essentially a reaction motor based on Newton's law that every action has an equal and contrary reaction. Two general types of reaction machines are rocket or chemical-fuel motor and air-stream or turbojet engine, based on gas turbine engine. First flight entirely by rocket power was made in Germany (1929). R. H. Goddard, an American, developed liquid fuels for rockets. A jet engine for powering full-size airplane was developed (1939) by Frank Whittle, an Englishman. Various types of engines and augmentation devices later used and supersonic speeds were reached. See *ill.,* p. 23.

jetsam: see FLOTSAM, JETSAM, AND LIGAN.

Jevons, William Stanley (jĕv'ŭnz), 1835–82, English economist and logician. He developed the theory, mathematically demonstrated, that value is determined by utility.

Wrote *The Theory of Political Economy* (1871), *The Principles of Science* (1874).

Jewel Cave National Monument: see NATIONAL PARKS AND MONUMENTS (table).

jewelweed: see IMPATIENS.

Jewett, Charles Coffin, 1816–68, American librarian. Worked out catalogue rules internationally used.

Jewett, Sarah Orne, 1849–1909, American novelist, b. Maine. Her stories and sketches of the Maine coast (as in *The Country of the Pointed Firs,* 1896) are delicate local-color pieces.

Jewett City, Conn.: see GRISWOLD.

Jewish Autonomous Oblast, RSFSR: see BIROBIDZHAN.

Jewish literature: see HEBREW LITERATURE; YIDDISH.

Jewish music. According to the Bible, music making was common among the ancient Jews on all important occasions. Instruments mentioned include the *kinnor* (a lyre), the *ugab* (a flute?), and the *shofar* (a ram's horn; still used today). With the formation of the kingdom of Israel, music was systematized with a professional group of musicians in the Temple. New instruments, apparently including varieties of harp, oboe, and organ appeared. Biblical passages were chanted on set modal patterns. After the destruction of the Temple (A.D. 70), instrumental music disappeared, but some of the chants survive today. Jewish music influenced early Christian plain song. With the growing importance of the synagogue came the rise of the cantor, a singer who performed the solo chants in the service. Among North European Jews in the Middle Ages, traditional melodies were corrupted under the influence of German folk song. During the Renaissance, there was a reintroduction of ancient elements by Oriental Jews. Cantors returned to improvisation in the Oriental modes and developed a very distinct type of coloratura. In the 17th cent., this art was found all over Europe. Instruments, especially the organ, were reintroduced into the synagogue. In the early 19th cent., an extreme reform movement eliminated the cantor and set traditional Jewish hymns to the tunes of Protestant chorales. A more moderate reform restored the cantor, returned to traditional chants, but at the same time made use of new music written by Jewish composers for the synagogue. Ernest BLOCH is the leading figure in the attempt to create a Jewish national music.

Jews [from Judah], descendants of the tribes of ISRAEL, adherents of the religion of JUDAISM. Before the Second World War they numbered c.16,000,000; between 5,000,000 and 6,000,000 were massacred during the war. More than half the Jews speak YIDDISH. According to the OLD TESTAMENT, their ancestor was Terah of Ur of the Chaldees, from whom descended the patriarchs Abraham, Isaac, and Jacob. Ancient Jewish history begins with their settlement in Egypt, as farmers, many centuries before Christ. Moses led the persecuted group out of Egypt; at Mt. Sinai he gave them the Decalogue. The Jews then conquered Canaan and united under Saul, their first king, who was defeated by the Philistines. The next king, David, conquered the enemies of the Jews. His son, King Solomon, built the first temple (see TEMPLE). Disruption followed, and the two kingdoms then formed, Israel and Judah, warred during much of the following two centuries (935 B.C.–725 B.C.). In 722 the Israelites (the LOST TRIBES) were exiled. The Temple, destroyed in 586 B.C. by the Babylonians, was rebuilt in 516 B.C. The Jews regained their independence under the MACCABEES, but in 70 A.D. Jerusalem was destroyed by the Romans. With the fall of the Roman Empire, Jews appeared in Western Europe, where from the 9th to the 12th cent. they enjoyed a golden age of literary activity (notably in Spain). From the time of the Crusades until the 19th cent. the Jews were persecuted and driven from many countries. The rise of capitalism improved the conditions of the Jews throughout Europe, as did the revolutionary movements of the 19th cent. The emancipation of the Jews brought forth two opposed movements: cultural assimilation, begun by Moses MENDELSSOHN, and ZIONISM, founded by Theodor HERZL in 1896. A wave of persecution starting in Russia (1881) and moving westward to France slowly abated until 1933, when with the rise to power in Germany of the Nazis, persecution of the Jews became violent. After the massacres of the Second World War, many sought refuge in Palestine, where a Jewish state (see ISRAEL) was established in 1948.

Jex-Blake, Sophia, 1840–1912, English physician, active in opening medical profession to women.

Jezebel (jĕ′–), d. c.846 B.C., wife of AHAB, mother of Ahaziah **1,** Jehoram **1,** and Athaliah. Willful and cruel, she led Israel into idolatry and persecuted the prophets. Killed in Jehu's coup d'état; her body thrown to the dogs. 1 Kings 16.31; 18; 21; 2 Kings 9.1–10,30–37. Reference in Rev. 2.20 obscure.

Jezreel (jĕz′rēĕl), anc. city, Palestine, in plain of Esdraelon, between Megiddo and Jordan R.; residence of King Ahab, whose family is often called the house of Jezreel.

Jhansi (jän′sē), city (pop. 103,254), S Uttar Pradesh, India. Founded 1613 by Bundela Rajputs. Trade center. Mfg. of brassware and silk cloth.

Jhelum (jā′lŭm), anc. *Hydaspes,* river, c.500 mi. long, in Kashmir and W Pakistan; westernmost of five rivers of Punjab.

Jibuti, French Somaliland: see DJIBOUTI.

Jidda (jĭ′dù) or **Jedda** (jĕ′dù), city (pop. 60,000), Hejaz, Saudi Arabia, on Red Sea; port of Mecca. Handles huge influx of pilgrims. Just outside is reputed tomb of Eve.

jigger: see CHIGOE.

Jiménez, Juan Ramón (hwän′ rämōn′ hēmā′-näth), 1881–, Spanish lyric poet. Simplicity of style and obscure depths of meaning make his poems (as in *Diario de un poeta recien casado,* 1917) among the most admired in Spanish literature.

Jiménez de Cisneros, Francisco (fränthē′skō hēmā′näth dä thēsnä′rōs), 1436–1517, Spanish cardinal and statesman. Archbishop of Toledo from 1495; inquisitor general from

1507. Led expedition which captured Oran (1509); founded Univ. of Alcalá; had Polyglot Bible compiled. Became regent on death of Ferdinand V (1516) but was summarily dismissed by Charles I (Emperor Charles V). Formerly spelled Ximenes.

Jiménez de Quesada, Gonzalo (gōnthä'lō hēmä'näth dā käsä'dhä), c.1499–1579, Spanish conquistador in Colombia. Setting out 1536 to explore Magdalena R. in search of El Dorado, he defeated Chibchas; founded Bogotá 1538. His claims, disputed by Federmann and Benalcázar, were verified by Spain 1550. A later expedition (to Orinoco R., 1569) was disastrous.

Jimson weed or **Jamestown weed**, coarse tropical annual plant (*Datura stramonium*) naturalized in North America. It has rank smelling foliage, trumpet-shaped white or purple flowers, and spiny fruits. Contains a narcotic poison similar to belladonna.

Jinnah, Mahomed Ali (mühō'mĭd ä'lē jĭ'nŭ), 1876–1948, founder of Pakistan. Admitted to the bar in England 1896, returned to India to practice law. First supported INDIAN NATIONAL CONGRESS and advocated Hindu-Moslem unity, but after 1934 (when he won control of MOSLEM LEAGUE) he agitated for separate state of Pakistan. Gained power during World War II by supporting the British; forced Congress to accept partition of India (1947). Became first governor general of dominion.

jinni (jĭnē'), plural **jinn** (jĭn), in Arabic folklore and in Moslem literature, creature like man but having certain supernatural powers, especially those of changing size and shape. Jinn may be good or evil. They appear constantly in the *Thousand and One Nights.* Also spelled genie.

jiujitsu or **jiujutsu:** see JUJUTSU.

Joab (jō'ăb), David's nephew, commander of his armies. An able administrator but often cruel, as in his killing of Abner, Absalom, and Amasa. Executed by Solomon for supporting Adonijah. 2 Sam. 2.12–32; 3.22–31; 8.16; 10.7–14; 11; 12.26; 14; 18; 19.1,5–7; 20.7–23; 24.1–9; 1 Kings 1; 2.5,6,28–34.

Joachim, Saint (jō'ŭkĭm), in tradition, father of the Virgin, husband of St. ANNE.

Joachim, Joseph (yō'äkĕm), 1831–1907, Hungarian violinist; friend of Mendelssohn, Brahms, and Schumann. Considered a master interpreter of great violin works, he composed cadenzas for violin concertos of Beethoven and Brahms.

Joachimsthal, Czechoslovakia: see JACHYMOV.

Joad, C(yril) E(dwin) M(itchinson) (jōd), 1891–1953, English rationalist philosopher.

Joahaz: see JEHOAHAZ.

Joanes, Vicente: see MACIP, VICENTE JUAN.

Joanna (jōä'nŭ), queens of Naples. **Joanna I,** 1326–82 (reigned 1343–81), was also countess of Provence. The murder of her husband, Andrew of Hungary (probably with her complicity) in 1345 brought recurrent warfare with Andrew's brother, Louis I of Hungary. She successively adopted Charles of Durazzo (see CHARLES III of Naples) and Louis of Anjou (see LOUIS I of Naples) as heirs. Charles imprisoned her and probably had her murdered. **Joanna II,** 1371–1435, succeeded her brother Lancelot in 1414. Her reign was beset by court intrigues and by rival claims of LOUIS III of Naples. Her successive adoptions as heirs of ALFONSO V of Aragon, Louis, and RENÉ of Anjou plunged Naples into warfare from which Alfonso emerged victorious after her death.

Joanna (the Mad), 1479–1555, Spanish queen of Castile and Leon (1504–5); daughter of Ferdinand V and Isabella I. Married PHILIP I, after whose death her insanity became apparent. She never ruled, her father being regent 1504–6; Philip I, 1506–7; her father again, 1507–16. Her son, Emperor Charles V, governed as joint ruler 1516–55.

Joanna, in Bible, wife of Herod's steward, follower of Jesus. One of those who visited Jesus' tomb and found it empty. Luke 8.3; 24.10.

Joan of Arc, 1412?–1431, French saint and national heroine, called the Maid of Orléans; daughter of a farmer of Domrémy, in Lorraine. She early began to hear "voices"—of St. Michael, St. Catherine, and St. Margaret —exhorting her to bear aid to the dauphin, CHARLES VII, then kept from his throne by the English. After many rebuffs, she was authorized by Robert de Baudricourt, military governor of Vaucouleurs, to journey to the dauphin (1429). She adopted male attire, which she was to keep till her last days. Meeting the dauphin at Chinon, she convinced him of her mission. After some more delays she was given troops, succeeded in lifting the siege of ORLÉANS, took other places along the Loire, routed the English at PATAY, and persuaded Charles to march on Rheims, where he was crowned, with Joan standing beside him (1429). She was eager to push her victories, which had turned the tide of the Hundred Years War, but the king's advisers and his indolence inclined him to negotiations with Burgundy, England's ally. After besieging Paris without success (1429), Joan in 1430 went to relieve Compiègne but was captured by the Burgundians who later sold her to the English. An irregular trial before an ecclesiastic court at Rouen, headed by Pierre CAUCHON, ended with her condemnation for heresy and sorcery (1431). She was burned at the stake. Rehabilitated in a new trial (1456), she was canonized in 1920. Feast: May 30.

João de Deus: see RAMOS, JOÃO DE DEUS.

João Pessoa (zhwä'ō pŭsō'ù), city (pop. 90,-853), cap. of Paraíba state, NE Brazil; Atlantic port founded 1589. Exports cotton, sugar, minerals.

Joash: see JEHOASH.

Job (jōb), book of Old Testament. A dramatic dialogue concerned with problem of good and evil in the world. In prologue in heaven, plan is laid to test Job, a truly good man. Property, family, and health are taken from him. Some friends who come to "comfort" him accuse Job of some great sin; Job protests his innocence. He learns that God's judgment is beyond man's understanding. In epilogue, all that Job lost is restored to him. Ethical problem not explicitly resolved. Parts of original text may be lost, new parts added at later date.

Job's-tears, tall tropical grass (*Coix lacryma-*

jobi) with bony, white or gray beadlike fruits.

Jocasta, mother of OEDIPUS.

Jocelin de Brakelond (jŏs'lĭn dù brāk'lŏnd), fl. 1200, English monk whose chronicle of Bury St. Edmunds (1173–1202) is simple, vigorous, vivid.

Jodhpur (jŏd'poŏr) or **Marwar** (mär'wär), former princely state, part of Rajasthan, India, since 1949. Estab. in early 13th cent. by Rathor Rajputs. Placed under British protection 1818. Jodhpur, city (pop. 126,842), cap. of former state, was founded 1459. Site of several palaces. Trade center with light mfg.

Joel, book of Old Testament. Joel, an otherwise unknown prophet, vividly describes plague of locusts, urges people to repent. Has Messianic prophecy (2.28–32; 3). Peter used Joel as text. Acts 2.

joe-pye weed, tall North American perennial (*Eupatorium purpureum*) bearing pinkish or purple flower clusters in the autumn.

Joffre, Joseph Jacques Césaire (zhôzĕf' zhäk' säzĕr' zhô'frù), 1852–1931, marshal of France. French commander in chief in World War I until 1916; chairman of Allied War Council 1916–18. Won first battle of the Marne (1914); nearly lost Verdun (1916).

Jogjakarta (jŏg"yäkär'tä) or **Djokjakarta** (jŏk"–), town (pop. 136,646), S Java, Indonesia, at foot of Mt. Merapi. Cultural center, known for artistic life and handicrafts. After World War II it was cap. of original republic of INDONESIA (1945–50).

Jogues, Isaac (ēzäk' zhôg'), 1607–46, Jesuit missionary and martyr in New World, b. France. Discovered L. George (1646). Murdered by hostile Mohawks. Canonized in 1930.

Johanan ben Zaccai (jōhă'nùn bĕn ză'kāĭ), Palestinian rabbi, contemporary of the apostles. Preserved Jewish law and the ritual of temple worship.

Johannesburg (jōhă'nĭsbûrg), city (pop. 603,-470), S Transvaal, South Africa; founded 1886. Largest city of South Africa, industrial center of the WITWATERSRAND. Textile milling, metalworking. Seat of a university.

John, Saint, one of the Twelve Apostles; brother of James, son of Zebedee. Accepted since ancient times as author of the fourth Gospel, three epistles, and Revelation. Was apparently the disciple "whom Jesus loved" (John 13.24; 19.26). As Jesus was dying, He committed His mother to John's care. According to 2d-cent. authorities John was exiled for a time on Patmos (Rev. 1.9), died at Ephesus c.100. Variously called St. John the Evangelist, St. John the Divine (i.e., theologian), and the Beloved Disciple. Feast: Dec. 27.

John VIII, d. 882, pope (872–82). Opposed St. Ignatius of Constantinople and recognized Photius as patriarch, thus temporarily reconciling E and W churches. Crowned Charles II (the Bald) and helped Charles III (the Fat) to the imperial throne.

John XII, c.937–964, pope (955–64), a Roman. Called in Otto I to help him against Berengarius, king of Italy, and was confirmed in the Patrimony of St. Peter, but shortly turned against Otto. Otto conquered Rome and called a synod to depose John and elect an antipope, Leo VIII. John retook Rome (964) but was soon murdered. His life was immoral, his pontificate a disgrace.

John XXI, d. 1277, pope (1276–77), a Portuguese, called Petrus Hispanus and reputed to be the author of a textbook on logic. Actually 19th canonical pope named John but called himself John XXI.

John XXII, 1244–1334, pope (1316–34), a Frenchman, chosen after a delay as successor to Clement V. He quarreled with Emperor Louis IV (who was assisted by Marsilius of Padua and William of Occam). Louis invaded Italy and set up as antipope Pietro Rainalducci, who shortly had to submit to John, but the pope's claims to authority over the empire came to nothing. Because of confused numbering also called John XXI.

John XXIII, antipope: see COSSA, BALDASSARRE.

John, Byzantine emperors. **John I** (Tzimisces), c.925–976, gained the throne by murdering Nicephorus II (969), whose anticlerical legislation he revoked. Extended Byzantine power against Russians and Arabs. **John II** (Comnenus), 1088–1143, succeeded his father Alexius I in 1118, despite the intrigues of his sister Anna Comnena to put her husband on the throne. He unsuccessfully tried to cancel Venetian commercial privileges. **John III** (John Ducas Vatatzes), d. 1254, emperor of Nicaea (1222–54), took Salonica from Latin Empire of Constantinople (1246), thus nearly completing reunion of dismembered Byzantine Empire. **John V** (Palaeologus), 1332–91, reigned 1341–76 and 1379–91. His throne was usurped during his minority by John VI and from 1376 to 1379 by his son Andronicus IV. **John VI** (Cantacuzene), c.1292–1383, usurped throne of John V (1341–55). Called Ottoman Turks to his aid and allowed Stephen Dushan to build up Serbian empire. Retired to a monastery. **John VIII** (Palaeologus), 1390–1448, reigned 1425–48. Sought to secure Western aid against Turks by agreeing to union of Eastern and Western churches at Council of Florence (1439).

John, kings of Aragon and counts of Barcelona. **John I,** 1350–95, reigned 1387–95. Patron of learning; held brilliant court. **John II,** 1397–1479, reigned 1458–79. Also inherited Sicily (1458). Married Blanche, heiress of Navarre (1425). After her death (1442) conflict broke out between John and his son, CHARLES OF VIANA, whose death in 1461 was followed by further troubles in Catalonia until 1472. John's son Ferdinand II (Ferdinand V of Castile) inherited Aragon, Catalonia, Sicily; his son-in-law, the count of Foix, inherited Navarre.

John, 1167?–1216, king of England (1199–1216), youngest son of Henry II. Supported his brother, Richard I, against his father in 1189. While Richard was on the Third Crusade, he had himself declared heir and conspired to keep Richard in captivity. Succeeded Richard to exclusion of his nephew, Arthur I of Brittany. Arthur's supporters, aided by PHILIP II of France, revolted and

John was finally forced to surrender most of his French possessions. Excommunicated and deposed by INNOCENT III, he surrendered England to the pope and received it back as fief (1213). Barons, intensely opposed to John, united and forced him to sign (1215) the MAGNA CARTA. Tyrannical, treacherous, and cruel, he is the subject of one of Shakspere's chronicle plays.

John, kings of France. **John I** (the Posthumous), 1316, son of Louis X, lived only a few days. **John II** (the Good), 1319–64. His reign (1350–64) was troubled by HUNDRED YEARS WAR and internal disturbances, notably his quarrels with CHARLES II of Navarre and the JACQUERIE. Captured by English at Poitiers (1356), he was released by Treaty of BRÉTIGNY (1360). In 1364 one of hostages who had taken his place in England escaped; John, to save his honor, returned to England, where he died. During his absences, his son (later CHARLES V) was regent.

John, kings of Hungary. **John I** (John Zapolya), 1487–1540; son of Stephen ZAPOLYA. Voivode of Transylvania (1511–26), he was chosen king by the Hungarian nobles after Louis II's death at MOHACS (1526). Louis's brother-in-law, Ferdinand of Austria (later Emperor FERDINAND I) challenged the succession in a series of campaigns, but in 1529 Sultan Suleiman I intervened and set up John as puppet king. John was succeeded by son **John II** (John Sigismund Zapolya), 1540–71. Suleiman, on pretext of protecting the infant's interests, invaded Hungary in 1541 (thus beginning 150 years of Turkish rule) and made John prince of Transylvania. Deposed by the pro-Austrian party in Transylvania (1551), John was recalled in 1556 on Turkish pressure. Austro-Turkish peace of 1562 left him in possession of Transylvania, with the rest of Hungary divided between Austria and Turkey. In 1664 the Transylvanian diet estab. Calvinism as state religion.

John, kings of Poland. **John II** (John Casimir), 1609–72. His reign (1648–68) is known in Polish history as the Deluge. Cossack rebellion under CHMIELNICKI led to war with Russia (1654–67) and cession of E Ukraine. Invasion by CHARLES X of Sweden (1655) was checked by miracle of CZESTOCHOWA, but in Peace of OLIVA John had to cede N Livonia to Sweden and to grant Elector Frederick William of Brandenburg full sovereignty over Prussia, in exchange for aid against Sweden. Abdicated in 1668; retired to a French monastery. **John III** (John Sobieski), 1624–96, reigned 1674–96. He briefly restored Polish prestige when, in 1683, he led his forces to relieve Vienna from Turkish siege. Pursuing the Turks into Hungary, he formed a Holy League with the pope, Emperor Leopold I, and Venice (1684), but he failed to wrest Moldavia and Walachia from Turkey. His death marked virtual end of Polish independence.

John, kings of Portugal. **John I** (the Great), 1357?–1433, illegitimate son of Pedro I, grand master of the Knights of Aviz. When his half-brother Ferdinand I died (1383), Portugal was ruled by a regency for Ferdi-

nand's daughter Beatrice, wife of John I of Castile. John of Aviz cooperated with Nun' Álvares Pereira in the national revolt against Spanish hegemony and in 1385 was elected king. The great victory of Aljubarrota (1385) assured Portuguese independence. John's reign, one of the most glorious in Portuguese history, was marked by an alliance with England, the beginnings of Portuguese colonial and maritime expansion, the capture of Ceuta from the Moors (1415), and the flowering of Portuguese literature. **John II** (the Perfect), 1455–95, reigned 1481–95. Asserted royal supremacy over nobles; fostered exploration (but refused to aid Columbus); signed Treaty of TORDESILLAS with Spain. Patron of Renaissance art and learning. **John III** (the Fortunate), 1502–57. His reign (1521–57) marked the height of the Portuguese empire but saw the beginning of decadence in Portugal itself. He introduced the Inquisition; imported African slaves. **John IV,** d. 1656, duke of Braganza, descended from Manuel I and in illegitimate line from John I, became king in 1640 when Portugal cast off Spanish rule. Founder of Braganza dynasty. **John V** (the Magnanimous), 1689–1750, reigned 1706–50. **John VI,** 1769–1826, became regent for his insane mother, Maria I, in 1799. Joined second coalition against France; defeated, he accepted humiliating Treaty of Badajoz (1801). Fled to Brazil when French attacked Portugal (1807); succeeded to throne 1816; returned to Portugal 1820. In 1824, after a turbulent reign, he retired to Brazil, which had become an independent empire under his son PEDRO I, leaving Portugal under regency of his daughter Isabella.

John, Spanish kings of Castile and Leon. **John I,** 1358–90, reigned 1379–90; son of HENRY II. Sought to unite Portugal and Castile; defeated by Portuguese at Aljubarrota (1385). JOHN OF GAUNT challenged his succession, but made peace 1388 and married his daughter to John's heir. **John II,** 1405–54, reigned 1406–54. Left government to Alvaro de LUNA. Notable as a patron of literature.

John, in Bible. **1** See JOHN, SAINT. **2** See JOHN THE BAPTIST. **3** See MARK, SAINT. **4** See MACCABEES.

John, Augustus (Edwin), 1879–, British painter and etcher, b. Wales. A leading portrait painter.

John, epistles of New Testament, called First, Second, and Third John; ascribed to St. John the Apostle. **1** John is homily on blending of mystical and practical religion. Discusses God as light (1.5–2.28), God as righteousness (2.29–4.6), God as love (4.7–5.12). **2** John, shortest book of Bible, warns against false teachers who deny historical reality of Jesus. **3** John is protest against a certain church leader's failure to receive teaching missionaries.

John, Gospel according to Saint, book of New Testament, traditionally ascribed to John the Apostle. A biography of Jesus in essay form, its aim is to show that Jesus is a vital force in the world now and forever and that He lived on earth in order to reveal Himself to men in the flesh. The acts of Jesus as a human being introduce discourses on His mystical nature. Thus, the feeding of the multitude is told, and following is sermon on the Bread of Life. Book begins with the famous philosophical passage identifying Jesus as the Word (see LOGOS). There follow two main sections, the ministry of Jesus (1.19–12.50) and the Passion and Resurrection (13–21). Unique position of Jesus Christ in Christian theology as God and man, which involves dogmas of the Trinity, the Incarnation, and the Atonement, is first enunciated in this Gospel.

John Baptist de la Salle, Saint (săl), 1651–1719, French educator. At Rheims he formed the first order devoted solely to Christian education, Brothers of the Christian Schools (Christian Brothers; 1684). In 1685 he founded first normal school at Rheims to train his teachers. Name in French: Jean Baptiste de la Salle. Feast: May 15.

John Bosco, Saint, 1815–88, Italian priest at Turin, founder (1841) of the Salesian order for work with boys and in foreign missions, and of Daughters of Mary Auxiliatrix, for work with girls.

John B. Stetson University: see DE LAND, Fla.

John Capistran, Saint (kŭpĭ'strŭn), 1385?–1456, Italian preacher, a Franciscan. Preached against the Hussites (1451) and led a wing of Hunyadi's army in great victory of Belgrade (1456).

John Carter Brown Library: see BROWN, JOHN CARTER.

John Chrysostom, Saint (krĭ'sŭstŭm, krĭsŏ'stŭm) [Gr.,= golden-mouth], c.347–407, Doctor of the Church, greatest Greek Father. Made patriarch of Constantinople (398), he undertook reforms and defied the imperial powers. Illegally deposed by Empress Eudoxia and Theophilus, bishop of Alexandria (403), he was recalled when people rioted. Later he was exiled by Arcadius. St. John's many authoritative homilies and commentaries, in excellent Greek style, had great influence.

John Crerar Library: see CRERAR, JOHN.

John Damascene, Saint: see JOHN OF DAMASCUS, SAINT.

John Day, river, NE Oregon, rising in Blue Mts. and flowing 281 mi. W and N to Columbia R. near The Dalles. Used for power and irrigation.

John Fisher, Saint: see FISHER, JOHN.

John Frederick I (the Magnanimous), 1503–54, elector of Saxony (1532–47). Divided his lands with his brother Ernest (1542). A member of Schmalkaldic League, he was captured by Emperor Charles V at Mühlberg (1547) and had to renounce electorate in favor of his cousin MAURICE of Saxony.

John Henry, legendary Negro strong man, celebrated in Southern American Negro ballads and "tall tales."

John Mark: see MARK, SAINT.

John Maurice of Nassau, 1604–79, Dutch general; grandnephew of William the Silent. As governor of Brazil (1636–43), for the Dutch West India Company, he conquered NE Brazil from Portuguese, built up state of Pernambuco, made broad plans for development. Subsequently held commands in Thirty Years War and Dutch Wars. His residence

at the Hague is the celebrated Mauritshuis.

Johnny Appleseed: see CHAPMAN, JOHN.

John of Austria, 1547?–1578, Spanish admiral and general; natural son of Emperor Charles V. Won decisive naval victory against Turks at LEPANTO. As governor general of Netherlands (1576–78) Don John fought rebels with inconclusive success.

John of Austria, 1629–79, natural son of Philip IV of Spain. While governor of the Netherlands, he was defeated by French in battle of the Dunes (1658). Took over regency for Charles II in 1677.

John of Brienne (brēĕn'), c.1148–1237, French crusader. Became, through marriage, titular king of Jerusalem (1210); captured Damietta in Fifth Crusade (1219); became regent for the Latin emperor, Baldwin II (1228); defended Constantinople against Greeks and Bulgars (1236). Father-in-law of Frederick II.

John of Damascus, Saint, or **Saint John Damascene** (dă'mŭsĕn), c.675–749, Syrian theologian, Doctor of the Church. Reared at court of the caliph in Damascus, he entered a Palestinian monastery (c.726) and spent most of his life in writing against iconoclasm and defending orthodoxy. *The Fountain of Wisdom* is his theological masterpiece.

John of Gaunt, 1340–99, duke of Lancaster; fourth son of Edward III of England. By his first marriage (see LANCASTER, HOUSE OF) he became one of most influential nobles in England. Served under his brother, Edward the Black Prince, in Hundred Years War. Aided Peter the Cruel of Castile and married his daughter. As viceroy for senile Edward III he espoused cause of court party and, for a time, ruled England. Fought (1386–88) for his claim to throne of Castile against John I. Helped keep peace between Richard II and hostile barons. His eldest son became Henry IV. By his third marriage, he was ancestor of the house of Tudor. Patron of Chaucer.

John of Lancaster, 1389–1435, duke of Bedford; son of Henry IV of England and brother of Henry V. Made protector of Henry VI (1422), he devoted himself to English affairs in France.

John of Leiden, c.1509–1536, Dutch Anabaptist leader. In revolt in Münster (1534) he set up theocracy and was leader of a communistic, chaotic state until in 1535 Anabaptists were ousted and their leaders tortured and executed.

John of Luxemburg, 1296–1346, king of Bohemia (1310–46); son of Emperor Henry VII. Was elected king after marriage with Elizabeth, daughter of Wenceslaus II of Bohemia. The blind king is best remembered for his gallant death at Crécy, where he fought as ally of Philip VI of France; he commanded that his charger be led into the thick of the fight. His son was Emperor Charles IV.

John of Procida (prō'chēdä), c.1210–c.1298, Italian Ghibelline conspirator. Prepared uprising of SICILIAN VESPERS (1282).

John of Salisbury (sôlz–), c.1115–1180, English scholastic philosopher. Studied at Paris and traveled much. Was secretary to St. Thomas à Becket, and later bishop of Chartres (1176–80). His *Metalogicus* sums up the scholastic knowledge of his time; his *Polycraticus* urged independence of church and state.

John of the Cross, Saint, Span. *Juan de la Cruz,* 1542–91, Spanish mystic, founder of the Discalced Carmelites, friend of St. Theresa of Ávila. His mystical poetry and treatises have had great influence on modern Catholicism. Feast: Nov. 24.

John o' Groats House, locality in Caithness, Scotland; often erroneously named as N point of Scotland. House, now gone, was supposedly built by a Dutchman in the 16th cent.

John Scotus: see DUNS SCOTUS; ERIGENA.

Johns Hopkins University, at Baltimore, Md.; nonsectarian, partly coed.; chartered 1867, opened 1876 with bequest from Johns Hopkins. Its medical school, connected with the noted hospital, is one of world's largest. Has continually excelled in laboratory and research work; institute for cooperative research estab. 1946. Had first university press in U.S.

Johnson, Andrew, 1808–75, 17th President of the United States (1865–69). Completely self-educated. A tailor in Greenville, Tenn. U.S. Representative (1843–53); governor of Tenn. (1853–57); U.S. Senator (1857–62). Interested in securing legislation providing Western land for laboring class; as a war Democrat he vigorously supported Lincoln. U.S. Vice President (1865). As President he was denounced by radical Republicans for his RECONSTRUCTION program. After passage over his veto of bill extending life of FREEDMEN'S BUREAU, his administration was the record of one humiliation after another. His efforts to remove from office E. M. STANTON, whom he rightly suspected of conspiring with congressional leaders, led to impeachment proceedings. On Feb. 24, 1868, the House passed a resolution of impeachment against him even before it adopted 11 articles detailing the reasons for it. Most important of the charges, which were purely political, was that he had violated the TENURE OF OFFICE ACT in the Stanton affair. By a narrow margin the Senate failed to convict. Important achievement of his administration in foreign affairs was purchase of Alaska (1867), negotiated by W. H. Seward. Again U.S. Senator in 1875.

Johnson, Eastman, 1824–1906, American portrait and genre painter. Influenced by Dutch masters.

Johnson, Edward, 1884–, Canadian operatic tenor. He sang at the Metropolitan Opera, New York, after 1922, and was its general manager 1935–50.

Johnson, E(mily) Pauline, 1862–1913, Canadian poet. Her poems of Indian life were highly popular.

Johnson, Guy: see JOHNSON, SIR WILLIAM.

Johnson, Herschel Vespasian, 1812–80, American statesman. U.S. Senator from Ga. (1848–49). Nominated by National Democrats as Vice President (1860). Opposed secession of Ga. in 1861, but in Confederate senate he upheld states' rights policies.

Johnson, Hiram (Warren), 1866–1945, American political leader, U.S. Senator from Calif. (1917–45). A founder of Progressive party; its candidate for Vice President in 1912. A Republican supporter of F. D. Roosevelt in 1932. He was a consistent isolationist and opponent of the League of Nations.

Johnson, Hugh (Samuel), 1882–1942, American army officer, government administrator. Supervised World War I draft. Head of National Recovery Administration (1933–34).

Johnson, Jack (John Arthur Johnson), 1876–1946, American boxer. Defeated Tommy Burns (1908), claimed world's heavyweight championship. Johnson definitely won title by knocking out James J. Jeffries (1910), lost championship to Jess Willard (1915).

Johnson, James Weldon, 1871–1938, American author, founder of the National Association for the Advancement of Colored People. Among his works are *Autobiography of an Ex-Colored Man* (fictional, 1912) and *God's Trombones* (Negro sermons in verse, 1927); *Along This Way* (autobiography, 1933). His brother, **(John) Rosamond Johnson,** 1873–, is the composer of several hundred songs, including *Lift Every Voice and Sing* (for which J. W. Johnson wrote the words). His *Rolling Along in Song* (1937) is an anthology of American Negro songs.

Johnson, Sir John: see JOHNSON, SIR WILLIAM.

Johnson, Martin Elmer, 1884–1937, American explorer and author. Photographed wildlife and native tribes on expeditions to South Sea Isls., Borneo, and particularly Africa. His wife, **Osa Helen (Leighty) Johnson,** 1894–1953, was his companion on all expeditions and co-author of accounts of their adventures.

Johnson, Reverdy, 1796–1876, American lawyer and statesman. One of ablest constitutional lawyers of his day. U.S. Senator from Md. (1845–49, 1863–68). U.S. Attorney General (1849–50). Opposed secession. Minister to Great Britain (1868–69).

Johnson, Richard Mentor, 1781–1850, Vice President of the United States (1837–41). U.S. Representative from Ky. (1807–19, 1829–37); U.S. Senator (1819–29). Elected Vice President by U.S. Senate.

Johnson, Rosamond: see JOHNSON, JAMES WELDON.

Johnson, Samuel, 1696–1772, American clergyman, educator, and philosopher. He was first president (1756–63) of King's Col. (now Columbia Univ.). His son, **William Samuel Johnson,** 1727–1819, was a statesman and also president of Columbia Col. (1787–1800). Active in political affairs in Conn.; representative at Continental Congress (1784–87). U.S. Senator (1789–91).

Johnson, Samuel, 1709–84, English author. His first major work was in satiric verse, *London* (1738) and *The Vanity of Human Wishes* (1749). His *Rambler* essays appeared 1750–52. Despite extreme difficulties he published in 1755 *A Dictionary of the English Language,* which won immediate fame. His "Idler" essays appeared 1758–60, and his moralizing fable *Rasselas* in 1759. In 1763 he met James BOSWELL, his future biographer, and in 1764, with Reynolds, Goldsmith, Burke, and others he formed his famous "Club." In 1765 began his long friendship with Mr. and Mrs. Henry Thrale. He published in 1765 an edition of Shakspere (with preface and notes still highly valued). After a tour of Hebrides appeared *A Journey to the Western Islands of Scotland* (1775). Last major work was *Lives of the Poets* (1779–81), full of personal but illuminating criticism. His prose is ponderous, but often incisive and always distinguished; his critical judgments were often prejudiced, but always shrewd and interesting. Johnson was dictator of literary taste in London and, because of his literary judgment and his integrity, the dominating literary figure of his age.

Johnson, Walter (Perry), 1887–1946, American baseball pitcher. Right handed Washington Senator ace, acknowledged fastest hurler in baseball history, he won 414, lost 276 in 21 major-league seasons. His major-league records include most shutouts (113), most strikeouts (3,497), most consecutive scoreless innings pitched (56).

Johnson, Sir William, 1715–74, British colonial leader in America, b. Ireland. Influence over Indians made him a key figure in French and Indian Wars and in control of land afterwards. Founded Johnstown, N.Y. (1762). His son, **Sir John Johnson**, 1742–1830, was a Loyalist leader in American Revolution. Failed in plan to organize settlers and Indians of Mohawk region against patriots. Served in Saratoga campaign. **Guy Johnson**, c.1740–1788, Loyalist leader in colonial N.Y., b. Ireland, was son-in-law of Sir William Johnson. Superintendent of Indian affairs (1774–82). Directed raids against patriot frontier settlements in American Revolution.

Johnson, William Samuel: see JOHNSON, SAMUEL (1696–1772).

Johnson City. 1 Village (pop. 19,249), S N.Y., near Binghamton. With Binghamton and Endicott, forms the Triple Cities, noted for shoes. **2** City (pop. 27,864), NE Tenn., ENE of Knoxville; settled before 1800. Tobacco market and rail center (with shops), has mfg. of wood products, textiles, bricks, foundry and limestone products. VA hospital here.

Johnson C. Smith University: see CHARLOTTE, N.C.

Johnston, Albert Sidney, 1803–62, Confederate general. Commanded operations in West. Death at Shiloh (April 6, 1862) was severe loss to South.

Johnston, Joseph Eggleston, 1807–1901, Confederate general. For vital part played in first victory at Bull Run, made commander of Army of Northern Virginia. Opposed McClellan in PENINSULAR CAMPAIGN. Lost Vicksburg campaign (1863). Commanded Army of Tennessee in ATLANTA CAMPAIGN. Probably peer of R. E. Lee as defensive general.

Johnston, Mary, 1870–1936, American novelist. Among her 30-odd works, combining romance with historical accuracy, are *To Have and to Hold* (1900) and *Audrey* (1902).

Johnston, town (pop. 12,725), NE R.I., just W of Providence. Mfg. of textiles.

Johnston Island (pop. 69), central Pacific, c.715 mi. SW of Honolulu. Discovered 1807 by British, claimed 1858 by U.S. Became naval air station 1941.

Johnstown. 1 City (pop. 10,923), E central N.Y., near Mohawk R., NW of Albany. Founded 1762 by Sir William JOHNSON, whose home, Johnson Hall, remains. Glove center with mfg. of other leather goods and knitted goods. Last Revolutionary battle in N.Y. fought near by, Oct. 25, 1781. **2** City (pop. 63,232), SW Pa., on Conemaugh R. and ESE of Pittsburgh; settled 1794. Industrial area with coal mining and mfg. of iron and steel and machinery. Johnstown flood (May 31, 1889) resulted in great loss of life and property damage.

John the Baptist, Saint, fl. A.D. c.29, prophet, cousin of Jesus, son of Zacharias and Elizabeth. An ascetic, he urged people to repent and prepare for the Messiah. Venerated by Christians as forerunner of Jesus, whose coming he heralded. Jesus was baptized by him before beginning His mission. At instigation of Herodias (see HEROD) and SALOME, John was beheaded. Mat. 11.1–19; 17.11–13; Mark 6.16–19; Luke 1; 3; John 1. Birthday observed June 24; feast of his beheading, Aug. 29.

John the Fearless, 1371–1419, duke of Burgundy (1404–19); son of PHILIP THE BOLD. Captured by Turks at Nikopol (1396), but ransomed. Inherited his father's feud with Louis d'ORLÈANS, whom he had murdered (1407). During the resulting struggle between ARMAGNACS AND BURGUNDIANS he controlled Paris 1411–13 and again from 1418. Connived with English in Hundred Years War but continued to negotiate with Armagnacs. Assassinated during interview with the dauphin (later Charles VII).

Johore (jōhôr'), state (7,321 sq. mi.; pop. 738,-251), S MALAYA, at S tip of Malay Peninsula opposite Singapore; cap. Johore Bahru. Largely jungle, with great rubber plantations. Iron is mined. Accepted British protectorate 1914. Ruled by a sultan, it was one of Unfederated Malay States until 1948, when it joined Federation of Malaya.

joint, in anatomy, articulation between bones. Types of joints allowing free movement are ball-and-socket (hip), hinge (knee), gliding (wrist). Joints may be immovable as in skull or permit limited movement as in spinal column.

Joinville, Jean, sire de (zhä' sēr' dù zhwēvēl'), 1224?–1317?, French chronicler, biographer of Louis IX (St. Louis). Went on Seventh Crusade 1248–54. His memoirs of St. Louis are invaluable record of the king, of feudal France, and of the Crusade.

Jokai, Maurice (yō'koi), 1825–1904, Hungarian novelist, a prolific, popular writer. Many novels have been translated into English (e.g., *An Hungarian Nabob*; *Black Diamonds*).

Jokulsa (yû'külsou), Icelandic *Jökulsá*, river, c.125 mi. long, rising in central Iceland and flowing N into Axar Fjord. DETTIFOSS waterfall is on it.

Joliet, Louis: see JOLLIET, LOUIS.

Joliet (jō'lēĕt"), city (pop. 51,601), NE Ill., SW of Chicago and on Des Plaines R.; settled 1831. Rail center near limestone quarries and coal mines. Mfg. of wallpaper, chemicals, steel, food, and oil products.

Joliette (zhôlyĕt′), city (pop. 16,064), S Que., Canada, on L'Assumption R. and NNE of Montreal. Has steel and paper mills, mica mining, and quarrying. Seat of Seminaire de Joliette.

Joliot-Curie, Frederic (frādärēk′ zhôlyō′-kürē′), 1900–, and **Irène Joliot-Curie** (ērĕn′), 1897–, French scientists. They shared 1935 Nobel Prize in Chemistry for artificial production of radioactive substances by bombarding certain elements with alpha particles.

Jolliet or Joliet, Louis (both: jō′lēĕt″, jō″lēĕt′, Fr. lwē′ zhôlyā′), 1645–1700, French explorer, b. Canada; joint discoverer with Jacques MARQUETTE of upper Mississippi R.

Jonah (jō′–), **Jonas,** or **Jona,** book of Old Testament. Tells of Jonah, a prophet, who tried to avoid his mission by sailing away. His presence on ship was a curse; a violent storm arose. Jonah agreed to be thrown overboard. He was swallowed by a fish and after three days left on shore, alive and now ready to preach. Jonah's escape from fish regarded as foreshadowing resurrection of Jesus. Story alluded to later in Bible: Mat. 12.39–41; 16.4; Luke 11.29–30.

Jonas, Greek form of Hebrew JONAH.

Jonathan (jŏn′–). **1** Oldest son of Saul, brave and gallant hero. Killed at battle of Mt. Gilboa. His close friendship with David is proverbial. 1 Sam. 13; 14.18–20; 20.16–18; 31.1,2. **2** One of the MACCABEES.

Jones, Anson, 1798–1858, last president of the Texas republic (1844–46).

Jones, Casey, 1864–1900, American locomotive engineer famous in ballad and song. Real name was John Luther Jones. His application of brakes saved passengers in crash of *Cannon Ball* express on April 30, 1900, at Vaughan, Miss.; Jones was killed.

Jones, Sir Edward Burne-: see BURNE-JONES.

Jones, Henry Arthur, 1851–1929, English playwright. His plays (e.g., *Wealth,* 1889; *The Liars,* 1897) dealt with social problems.

Jones, Inigo, 1573–1652, earliest of England's great architects. Traveled in Italy, where he closely studied Renaissance buildings of Palladio. In 1619 began his finest work, the royal banquet hall in Whitehall, London, which marked starting point for classic architecture of late Renaissance and Georgian periods in England. Designed settings for masques performed at court of James I and Charles I.

Jones, Jesse (Holman), 1874–, U.S. Secretary of Commerce (1940–45). A director of RFC 1932–39; chairman of board 1933–39.

Jones, John Paul, 1747–92, American naval hero, b. near Kirkcudbright, Scotland. Raided shores of British Isles in command of *Ranger* (1778). Captured frigate *Serapis* (1779) but his own ship, *Bon Homme Richard,* sank; this memorable victory was little noticed at the time. Later served in Russian navy.

Jones, Mary (Harris), 1830–1930, American labor agitator, called Mother Jones.

Jones, Owen, 1809–74, English architect, best known for writings on decorative arts.

Jones, Robert Edmond, 1887–, American stage

designer. Studied with G. P. Baker and Max Reinhardt. His designs include those for *Desire under the Elms, The Green Pastures,* and *The Iceman Cometh.*

Jones, Robert Tyre, Jr. (Bobby Jones), 1902–, American golfer. Won Natl. Open (1923, 1926, 1929), Natl. Amateur (1924–25, 1927–28), British Open (1926–27). First golfer to win (1926) Natl. and British Open tournaments same year. Only golfer ever to score "grand slam"—winning (1930) Natl. Open, Natl. Amateur, British Open, and British Amateur.

Jones, Rufus M(atthew), 1863–1948, American writer on mysticism of Society of Friends. A teacher at Haverford Col. (1893–1934) and a founder of American Friends Service Committee (1917).

Jones, Sir William, 1746–94, English philologist and jurist, one of greatest scholars of England. He was famous in jurisprudence and for translations from Greek (a speech of Isaeus) and Oriental languages (e.g., Laws of Manu, the *Sakuntala* and *Hitopadesa,* all Sanskrit). Wrote a Persian grammar.

Jones Beach, state park, 2,413 acres, on sandy island off S shore of Long Isl., SE N.Y.; estab. 1929. Noted outing resort with 2½ mi. of beaches and boardwalk and a marine stadium.

Jonesboro. 1 City (pop. 16,310), NE Ark., NW of Memphis, Tenn.; founded 1859. Distributing center for area producing cattle, poultry, corn, fruit, truck, cotton, and rice. Seat of Arkansas State Col. (coed.; chartered 1909, opened 1910). **2** Town (pop. 1,126), NE Tenn., near Johnson City; laid out 1779. State's oldest town, first cap. of State of FRANKLIN. Andrew Jackson entered law practice, fought duel here (1788).

Jongkind, Johann Barthold (yōhän′ bär′tôlt yông′kĭnt), 1819–91, Dutch landscape painter and etcher. Worked mainly in France. Paintings have elements of both naturalism and impressionism.

Jonkoping, Swed. *Jönköping* (yûn′chû″pĭng), city (pop. 44,685), co. seat of Jonkoping co., S central Sweden, on Vattern L.; chartered 1284. Has some of world's largest match factories (founded 1844). In 1620 Gustavus Adolphus gave it special privileges after citizens had burned it to avoid sack by Danes.

Jonquière (zhŏkyĕr′), town (pop. 21,618), S Que., Canada, on Sable R. and WSW of Chicoutimi. Has railroad workshops and pulp mills.

jonquil: see NARCISSUS.

Jonson, Ben, 1572–1637, English dramatist and lyric poet, an actor. His life and works bridge the Elizabethan and Jacobean periods. His comedies, such as *Every Man in His Humour* (1598), *Every Man Out of His Humour* (1599), were capped by *Volpone* (1606), *Epicoene* (1609), *The Alchemist* (1610), and *Bartholomew Fair* (1614). His tragedies *Sejanus* and *Catiline* were much praised in his time. His nondramatic poems showed the same neoclassic influence as his plays. Of his graceful lyrics the most familiar today is "Song to Celia" ("Drink to me only witth thine eyes"). He had much influence on a group of younger poets called "the tribe of Ben." He was a friend of Shakspere, Donne, and the other great of his age. His tomb in Westminster Abbey has the inscription, "O rare Ben Jonson."

Jonsson, Einar (ā'när yŏn'sôn), 1874–, Icelandic sculptor and painter. His work is housed in a special museum in Reykjavik, Iceland.

Joplin, city (pop. 38,711), SW Mo., at edge of the Ozarks and W of Springfield; settled c.1840. Rail center in important lead and zinc area, it ships and processes food, metal, and leather products.

Joppa, Palestine: see JAFFA.

Joram (jō'–), kings of Israel and Judah: see JEHORAM.

Jordaens, Jacob (ya'kŏp yŏr'däns), 1593–1678, Flemish painter. Like his master Rubens he excelled in large allegorical paintings and portraits. Ranks among great masters of Flemish school.

Jordan, David Starr, 1851–1931, American scientist and educator. From 1891 to 1913 he was first president of Stanford Univ. and afterwards chancellor, 1913–16. He was director (1910–14) of World Peace Foundation and president (1915) of World Peace Congress. A leading ichthyologist, he served on U.S. and international commissions for fisheries.

Jordan, Dorothea or **Dorothy,** 1762–1816, British actress, whose real name was Bland. Exuberant and charming, she excelled in such roles as Lady Teazle and Rosalind. Mistress of the duke of Clarence (later William IV), she bore him many children.

Jordan, kingdom (c.37,000 sq. mi.; 1948 pop. c.450,000), SW Asia; cap. Amman. Formerly called Transjordan or Transjordania. Bordered by Saudi Arabia on E and S and by Israel on W. Only outlet to the sea is Aqaba, port on Gulf of Aqaba. Mainly arid and mountainous. Wheat, barley, and grapes are grown. Roughly corresponds to biblical lands of Edom, Gilead, and Moab, and to lordships of Montreal and Krak in Latin Kingdom of Jerusalem. Under Turkish rule from 16th cent. to 1918. In 1920 it was part of short-lived kingdom of Syria. Originally part of British mandate of PALESTINE, it was estab. as semi-independent emirate under ABDULLAH in 1923. Agreement of 1928 made Britain suzerain, with right to maintain garrisons. In 1946 mandate was ended and kingdom proclaimed. Treaty in 1948 provided for annual British subsidy for its famed Arab Legion. After partition of Palestine (1948) it joined other members of ARAB LEAGUE in armed attack against Israel. When truce was made in 1949 its forces held most of the Palestinian area that had been designated Arab territory by UN. Annexation in 1950 of occupied area (c.2,500 sq. mi.) was strongly resented by other Arab countries.

Jordan, the great river of Palestine, rising in Anti-Lebanon mts. and flowing c.200 mi. S to Dead Sea. Jordan contains S half of river; N half marks part of Israel-Jordan and Israel-Syria borders. Jordan valley is called the Ghor and is northernmost part of Great Rift Valley. Often mentioned in the Bible; it was scene of baptism of Christ.

Jordan, river, N central Utah, flowing c.60 mi.

N, from Utah L., past Salt Lake City, to Great Salt L.

Josaphat (jŏ'sŭfăt), in Bible: see JEHOSHAPHAT.

Joseph, Saint, husband of Mary, a carpenter of Nazareth, descended from royal line of David. Mat. 1; Luke 2; John 1; Mat. 13.55. Highly honored by Orthodox and Roman Catholics as foster father of Jesus and chaste spouse of Mary the Virgin. Feast: March 19.

Joseph, emperors (also kings of Hungary and Bohemia). **Joseph I,** 1678–1711. His reign (1705–11) was taken up with the War of the SPANISH SUCCESSION and the rebellion of Hungary under Francis II RAKOCZY. **Joseph II,** 1741–90, son of Francis I and MARIA THERESA. Ruled Hungary, Bohemia, and hereditary Hapsburg lands jointly with his mother from 1765 till her death (1780). Succeeded Francis I as emperor 1765. A revolutionary reformer and "benevolent despot," he sought to raise the miserable condition of his people and to centralize his administration by a series of radical decrees, but his impatience undid much of his work in his own lifetime. Falling far short of his aim of abolishing hereditary and ecclesiastic privileges, he nevertheless abolished serfdom and feudal dues (1781); enabled peasants to buy land cheaply; granted wide religious tolerance (1781); abolished judicial torture; humanized the penal code; created two degrees of appeal. He took anticlerical measures, forbidding religious orders to obey foreign generals and suppressing all contemplative orders, and was unmoved by a personal visit of Pope PIUS VI. His schemes for a single land tax and for providing free food and medical care for the indigent were failures. His bullying attempts to centralize all administration provoked revolts in the Austrian Netherlands and in Hungary. His plan to annex Bavaria was frustrated by the War of the BAVARIAN SUCCESSION; his project to exchange his part of the Netherlands for Bavaria was thwarted by Frederick II of Prussia, who formed the *Fürstenbund* [princes' league] for the purpose (1785). His anti-Turkish alliance with Catherine II of Russia brought Austria no advantage.

Joseph, 1715–77, king of Portugal (1750–77). His reign was dominated by his minister POMBAL.

Joseph, in Bible. **1** Favored son of Jacob. Sold into slavery by his jealous brothers, he was taken to Egypt. Imprisoned because of false accusation by the wife of his master (Potiphar), but released after he interpreted Pharaoh's dream. He became governor of Egypt and was reunited with his father and brothers when he helped them during a famine. Gen. 30; 37; 39–50. Story has been expanded in Joseph and Asenath (see PSEUDEPIGRAPHA) and in works of Thomas Mann. **2** See JOSEPH, SAINT.

Joseph (Chief Joseph), c.1840–1904, American Indian leader, chief of the Nez Percé Indians. Since his tribe refused to recognize land cessions made to U.S. in 1863, he undertook to lead them to Canada (1877). Forced to surrender to U.S. troops.

Joseph, Father, 1577–1638, French Capuchin

monk, confidant and agent of Cardinal Richelieu; called "Gray Eminence"; lay name François Leclerc du Tremblay. He dreamed of restoring Catholicism throughout Europe but advanced a policy of supporting Protestant states and the Turks against the house of Hapsburg. Rumor made him the cardinal's evil genius, but actually he was probably simply a tool.

Joseph Barsabas, competitor of Matthias for place among the disciples left vacant by Judas Iscariot. Matthias was chosen. Acts. 1.23.

Josephine (Marie Josèphe Rose Tascher de la Pagerie), 1763–1814, empress of the French, b. Martinique. Her first husband, Alexandre de BEAUHARNAIS, was guillotined 1794, but she escaped persecution through friendship with Barras. Married Napoleon Bonaparte 1796. He ignored her many indiscretions but had marriage annulled (1809) because of her alleged sterility. Died in retirement at Malmaison.

Joseph of Arimathea, Saint (ăr'ĭmŭthē'ù), man who gave body of Jesus decent burial. Mat. 27.57–61; Mark 15.42–47; Luke 23.50–56; John 19.38–42. Grateful Christendom has always honored him.

Josephus, Flavius (flā'vēùs jōsē'fùs), A.D. 37–A.D. 95?, Jewish historian and soldier. Thoroughly Romanized, he won the favor of Vespasian. Wrote *The Jewish War; Antiquities of the Jews; Against Apion* (a defense of the Jews); and an autobiography.

Joses (jō'–) [Gr.= Heb. Joseph]. **1** Kinsman of Jesus. Mark 6.3; Mat. 13.55. **2** Brother of James the Less; may be same as **1.** Mat. 27.56; Mark 15.40,47.

Josetsu (jō"sä'tsōō), fl. 1425, Japanese landscape painter, a priest. His work has characteristics of Ming painting.

Joshua (jŏ'–) or **Josue** (jō'sūē), book of Old Testament. Its hero is Joshua, successor of Moses as leader of the Hebrews. Moses had brought the people to edge of Canaan, the Promised Land; it was Joshua's task to lead them into the country, conquer it, and divide the land among the tribes. Well-known events of book: fall of Jericho; battle in Ajalon valley where the sun stood still. Other forms of Joshua are Jehoshua, Jehoshuah, Jeshua, and Jesus.

Joshua tree: see YUCCA.

Joshua Tree National Monument: see NATIONAL PARKS AND MONUMENTS (table).

Josiah (jōsī'ù) or **Josias** (jōsī'ùs), d. c.610 B.C., king of Judah (c.641–c.610 B.C.). Chief event of his reign was discovery of old book of the law, apparently Deuteronomy, in the Temple. Josiah had it read publicly and led a reform movement to concentrate worship at Jerusalem. He later fell in battle against Egypt. 2 Kings 22–23; 2 Chron. 34–35.

Josika, Baron Nicholas (yō'shĭkŏ), 1794?–1865, Hungarian novelist, first to write Hungarian historical novel.

Josquin des Prés (zhōs'kĕn dĕprā'), c.1450–1521, Flemish composer, considered by his contemporaries as the greatest of his age. Wrote masses and motets.

Jostedalsbreen (yô'stùdälsbrā"ùn), glacier, area 340 sq. mi., Sogn og Fjordane co., W Norway, W of Jotunheim mts. Largest icefield on European mainland, it rises to 6,700 ft.

Josue, variant of JOSHUA.

Jotham (jō'–). **1** Only son of Gideon not killed by Abimelech. Told parable of the trees electing bramble as king. Judges 9.5–21. **2** Died c.731 B.C., king of Judah (c.535 B.C. –c.731 B.C.); contemporary of Isaiah, Hosea, Micah. 2 Kings 15.5,32–38.

Jotunheim (yō'tōōnhäm), mountain group, central Norway, highest of Scandinavia, rising to 8,098 ft. in Galdhoppigen and to 8,048 ft. in Glittertind. JOSTEDALSBREEN glacier is W. Supports summer grazing. In Norse mythology, it was home of the giants.

Jouett, Matthew Harris, 1783–1827, American portrait painter, b. Ky. Studied with Gilbert Stuart.

Jouhaux, Léon (lāō' zhōō-ō'), 1879–, French Socialist labor leader. Headed Confédération Générale du Travail from 1909 but left it in 1947 to found anti-Communist Internatl. Confederation of Free Trade Unions. Played prominent role at Internatl. Labor Organization. Was awarded 1951 Nobel Peace Prize.

Joule, James Prescott (jōōl), 1818–89, English physicist. Made studies in electricity, thermodynamics, and was first to determine equivalent of heat. Electrical unit the **joule** (joul) is named for him. It is work done in one second in maintaining current of one ampere in resistance of one ohm.

Jourdan, Jean Baptiste (zhä' bäptēst' zhōōrdä'), 1762–1833, marshal of France. Fought in American Revolution and in FRENCH REVOLUTIONARY WARS.

journalism, collection and periodical publication of news. Includes writing for, editing, and managing such media as the NEWSPAPER and the PERIODICAL. Journalism had real beginnings at end of 18th cent. Until freedom of speech was instituted, journalism served as handmaiden of politics or a means of business. Growth of individualistic leadership in newspaper field in U.S. in 19th cent. (see GREELEY, HORACE; BOWLES, SAMUEL; DANA, CHARLES) in turn influenced other journalistic media. In 20th cent. power of individualistic journalist declined in face of technological advances, growth of news agency, vast strides in reporting techniques, broadening of education and reform, and growth of advertising. Earliest school of journalism in U.S. was estab. at Univ. of Missouri in 1908.

Jouvenet, Jean (zhä' zhōōvùnä'), 1644–1717, French painter, known for religious pictures. Worked in Paris studio of Charles Le Brun.

Jove, another name for JUPITER.

Jovellanos, Gaspar Melchor de (gäspär' mĕlchôr' dä hōvĕlyä'nōs), 1744–1811, Spanish philosophical poet (as in *Epístola de Fabio a Anfriso*), a statesman and economist.

Jovian (jō'vēùn), c.331–364, Roman Emperor (363–64). Returned Christianity to privileged position it had enjoyed before Julian the Apostate.

Jowett, Benjamin (jou'ĕt), 1817–93, English Greek scholar, an Anglican clergyman, master of Balliol College, Oxford, and vice chancellor of Oxford, one of greatest educators England has had. His translations of dialogues of Plato are famous.

Joyce, James, 1882–1941, Irish novelist, b. Dublin; spent almost all adult life in "exile" on Continent. First published works were poems in *Chamber Music* (1907; later included with *Pomes Penyeach* and *Ecce Puer* in *Poems,* 1937). His *Dubliners* (1914) was a linked collection of stories, his *Portrait of the Artist As a Young Man* (1916) a novel that foreshadowed the two great novels that made Joyce a major figure of world literature—*Ulysses* (1922; banned in U.S. for indecency until 1933) and *Finnegans Wake* (1939). His labyrinthine prose explores many levels of meaning, both conscious and unconscious, and employs many linguistic devices, including many-faceted puns. His influence on writing has been great, though he has few direct imitators.

Juana Inés de la Cruz (hwä'nä ēnäs' dä lä krōōs'), 1651–95, Mexican poet, generally considered greatest lyric poet of colonial Spanish America. Became a nun in Mexico at 16 or 17, devoting her life to pursuit of knowledge. Her poems are marked by spontaneity and sincerity. Family name Asbaje.

Juana la Beltraneja (hwä'nä lä běltränä'hä), 1462–1530, Castilian princess. Her legal father was Henry IV of Castile; her presumed actual father, Beltrán de la Cueva, a courtier. Henry designated first his sister (later ISABELLA I), then Juana as successor. His death brought war between the two (1474–79). Juana, though aided by her husband Alfonso V of Portugal, lost and retired to a convent.

Juan de Fuca Strait (jōō'ùn dē fū'kù), inlet, c.100 mi. long, 15–20 mi. wide, connects Pacific Ocean with Puget Sound and Strait of Ga., between Vancouver Isl. (N) and Wash. state (S). Cape Flattery (Wash.), discovered 1778 by Capt. Cook, is at its entrance.

Juanes, Juan de: see MACIP, VICENTE JUAN.

Juan Fernández (hwän' fěrnän'däs), group of small islands (pop. 434), c.400 mi. W of Valparaiso, Chile, belonging to Chile. Thought to be locale of Daniel Defoe's *Robinson Crusoe.*

Juan-les-Pins (zhüä'-lä-pē'), town (pop. 2,764), Alpes-Maritimes dept., S France, on the Cap d'Antibes; a resort of French Riviera.

Juárez, Benito (bānē'tō hwä'räs), 1806–72, Mexican liberal statesman and national hero, an Indian. Led liberal opposition to conservative government of Santa Anna and was acting president during War of the Reform (1858–61). During French attempt at establishment of Mexican empire under Maximilian (1864–67), Juárez moved his capital to El Paso del Norte (now Juárez). His sturdy resistance defeated the French and destroyed the empire. Reelected president 1871, he died while suppressing a revolution led by Porfirio Díaz.

Juárez (hwä'räs), city (pop. 48,881), Chihuahua, N Mexico, on Rio Grande opposite El Paso, Texas. Originally El Paso del Norte, it included settlements on both sides of river until close of Mexican War (1848). Name of Mexican town changed (1888) to honor Benito Juárez.

Juba (jōō'bù), c.85 B.C.–46 B.C., king of Numidia. Fought for Pompey and ended his life after Caesar won at Thapsus. His young son, **Juba II,** d. A.D. c.20, was educated in Rome and was given rule, probably in Numidia, then in Mauretania, by Augustus. Was very learned.

Jubal, originator of musical instruments. Gen. 4.21.

Jubbulpore (jŭbŭlpôr'), city (pop. 178,339), N Madhya Pradesh, India. Ordnance-mfg. center.

jubilee, in Bible, a year when slaves were freed and debts forgiven. It occurred once in 50 years. Lev. 25.8–55. Name now used to mean celebration of a 50-year or longer period (e.g., Diamond Jubilee of Queen Victoria, 1897). In Roman Catholic Church name is applied to a holy year when special privileges are given by the Church for pilgrimages to Rome. Recent such jubilee years were 1929 and 1950.

Jubilees, Book of: see PSEUDEPIGRAPHA.

Juda. 1 See JUDAH. **2** See JUDE, SAINT.

Judaea or **Judea** (both: jōōdē'ù), Greco-Roman name (from Judah) for S Palestine, southernmost of Roman divisions of Palestine. At time of Christ it was part of province of Syria and a kingdom ruled by the Herods.

Judah I, 135?–220?, Jewish leader, called *ha-Nassi* [prince], editor of the Mishna (see TALMUD), president of Sanhedrin.

Judah, son of Jacob and ancestor of one of 12 tribes of Israel; a leader in family counsels, spokesman for his brothers before Joseph in Egypt. Tribe of Judah settled in S Palestine; gave its name to kingdom. Royal and Messianic line of David was of this tribe. Gen. 29.35; 35.23; 37.26; 38; 43.3; 44.14; 46.12,-28; 49.8; Num. 2.3; 10.14; 13.6; 26.22; 34; Joshua 15.1; 1 Chron. 2–5. Juda: Luke 3.33; Heb. 7.14; Rev. 5.5; 7.5. Judas: Mat. 1.2.

Judah, Theodore Dehone, 1826–63, American railroad builder. Promoted idea of railroad across mountains E from Central Valley of Calif. Central Pacific RR Co. was formed, with Judah as chief engineer.

Judah, southern of the two kingdoms after division of Hebrew nation under REHOBOAM (N kingdom was Israel); cap. Jerusalem; dynasty, the house of David.

Judah ha-Levi or **Judah ha-Levy** (both: hä"lē'vī), 1085?–1140?, Spanish rabbi, Hebrew poet, philosopher, author of *Sefer ha-Kuzari,* which argues for superiority of religious truths arrived at through intuition over those formulated through logic.

Judaism (jōō'dùĭzùm, –dē–) [from Judah; cf. Jews], religion of the Jews, oldest of the great monotheistic religions. It is the complex of law, tradition and doctrine consisting of the OLD TESTAMENT and the TALMUD. Its outstanding feature is its belief in an omnipotent God, and in his law, the TORAH, given by him to Moses, the leader of Israel, whom God had chosen as his people in the time of Abraham, the father of Israel. The great text of Judaism, the Shema, begins "Hear, O Israel: the Lord our God is one Lord" (Deut. 6.4–9). Circumcision of males is practiced as a sign of God's covenant with his people. The synagogue is primarily a place of meeting; the most elaborate feast of Judaism, the PASSOVER, is celebrated in the home. The rabbi is primarily a teacher. The principal Jewish sects of ancient times were the ESSENES, SADDUCEES, and the PHARISEES. In more modern times, the cabalists (see CABALA) and the HASIDIM are notable. In the 18th cent. appeared a new movement, Reformed Judaism. Unlike orthodox Jews, the reformed reject many of the restrictions of the Law, use the vernacular in religious ceremonies, and reduce much of the ritual. One group, the "conservatives," retains some orthodox customs. Judaism demands the recognition of God and the observance of the Law. The importance of the Law is seen in the development and preservation of the exalted ethical standards of Judaism.

Judas [Gr.,= Judah], in Bible. 1 See JUDE, SAINT. 2 See MACCABEES. 3 See JUDAS ISCARIOT.

Judas Iscariot (ĭskă′rēŭt), disciple who for 30 pieces of silver betrayed Jesus, identifying him for capture by kissing him. Judas hanged himself. Blood money went to buy potter's field, thenceforth called Aceldama. Mat. 26. 20–25,47–49; 27.3–10; Acts 1.16–20.

Judas Maccabeus: see MACCABEES.

Judas of Galilee (gă′lĭlē), fl. A.D. 7, a leader of the ZEALOTS, a revolutionary Jewish sect.

Judas tree: see REDBUD.

Jude, Saint, or **Saint Judas** [Jude an Eng. form to distinguish him from Judas Iscariot], one of the Twelve Apostles. Also called Thaddeus and Lebaeus. Epistle of Jude ascribed to him. Mat. 10.3; 13.55; Mark 3.18; Luke 6.16. Juda: Mark 6.3. Feast: Oct. 28.

Jude, epistle of New Testament. Traditionally ascribed to St. Jude the Apostle, but many critics disagree. Book shows the danger of heresy in the church by citing examples from Old Testament.

Judea: see JUDAEA.

Judges, book of Old Testament; sequel to Joshua in biblical history, telling of the Hebrews in Canaan from death of Joshua up to time of Samuel. There are many well-known stories about these violent times when men took the law into their own hands. Leaders, mostly heroes of war, were called judges; among them were Samson, Gideon, Jephthah, Ehud, and Deborah.

judgment, final decision of a court of law. It can be altered by a court of appeal, which rectifies error, but cannot be reconsidered from the beginning like a decree. In criminal cases the judge gives a sentence in accord with the verdict of a jury. In civil cases, a judge normally awards damages (including legal costs). When a debtor fails to pay, the sheriff may seize his property.

Judith [Heb.,= the Jewess], book of Old Testament, placed in Apocrypha in AV, before Esther in Western canon. Tells of time when Palestine was occupied by foreign army led by Holofernes. Judith, a Jewish widow of great beauty, entered the enemy camp, gained the favor of Holofernes, and murdered him. The invaders, without a leader, were easily routed by the Jews. Story repeated in an Anglo-Saxon epic.

judo: see JUJUTSU.

Judson, Adoniram (ădŭnĭ′rŭm), 1788–1850, American Baptist missionary. After two years in India as Congregational worker, he

became a Baptist and transferred to Burma, where he spent most of his life as pioneer in Protestant mission work. Judson's first wife, Ann (Hasseltine) Judson (1789–1826), founded a girls' school at Rangoon. His second wife, Sarah (Hall) Boardman Judson (1803–45), translated Pilgrim's Progress into Burmese. His third wife, Emily (Chubbuck) Judson (1817–54), was an author, whose pseudonym was Fanny Forester.

Judson, Edward Zane Carroll: see BUNTLINE, NED.

Juggernaut, India: see PURI.

Jugoslavia: see YUGOSLAVIA.

Jugurtha (jŏŏgûr′thȧ), c.156–104 B.C., king of Numidia, grandson of Masinissa. He was finally defeated after long warfare with the Romans through treachery of his father-in-law, Bocchus of Mauretania.

Juilliard School of Music (jŏŏl′yärd), in Manhattan borough of New York city; coed.; chartered 1926. In 1946, its two units, Juilliard Graduate School (1924) and Inst. of Musical Art (1905; founded by Frank Damrosch and James Loeb), were amalgamated.

Juiz de Fora (zhwēzh′ dŭ fô′rȧ), city (pop. 86,819), S Minas Gerais state, E Brazil; industrial city.

jujube (jŏŏ′jŏŏb), deciduous or evergreen spiny shrub or tree of genus Zizyphus of tropics and subtropics of both hemispheres. Long grown by Chinese for fruit used fresh, dried, or preserved.

jujutsu (jŏŏjŏŏt′sŏŏ, -jĭt′- or **jiujitsu** (jŏŏjĭt′-sŏŏ), Japanese method of defense and offense without weapons in personal encounter. Requires extensive training and detailed knowledge of anatomy. Probably imported from China, jujutsu was long exclusive property of Japanese nobility. By 20th cent. jujutsu had attracted attention in Europe, America. Judo, outgrowth of jujutsu, was taught in U.S. Army in World War II.

Jujuy (hŏŏhwē′), city (pop. 41,955), cap. of Jujuy prov., NW Argentina, on Jujuy R.; founded 1593; center of cattle and agr. area. Minerals and timber exploited near by.

juke box: see PHONOGRAPH.

Jukes: see DUGDALE, RICHARD LOUIS.

julep or **mint julep,** alcoholic beverage, traditional in the S U.S. containing bourbon whisky, crushed mint leaves, crushed ice, sugar.

Julia, feminine name in the family of the Caesars. 1 Died 54 B.C., daughter of Julius Caesar and wife of Pompey. It was only after her death that warfare broke out between the two. 2 39 B.C.–A.D. 14, daughter of Augustus, wife of M. Claudius Marcellus, M. Vipsanius Agrippa, and Tiberius. Banished for gross immorality to the island of Pandataria, she died of starvation. 3 18 B.C.–A.D. 28, daughter of Julia 2 and Agrippa, also banished for immorality.

Julian, George Washington, 1817–99, American abolitionist, U.S. Representative from Ind. (1849–51, 1861–71). In later life a Liberal Republican and then a Democrat.

Juliana, 1909–, queen of Netherlands (1948–); daughter of Wilhelmina. Married (1937) Prince Bernhard of Lippe-Biesterfeld.

Julianehaab (yŏŏlyä′nŭhôp″), town (pop. 936), SW Greenland; cap. of Julianehaab colony (pop. 4,186), most populous part of Greenland. It is chief trade center in S Greenland and port in cattle-raising area.

Julian the Apostate, 331?–363, Roman emperor (361–63); nephew of Constantine I. Both a scholar and an able general, he unsuccessfully tried to restore paganism, which to him meant the glory of antiquity. He did not institute systematic persecution of Christians and ruled justly and humanely.

Jülich (yü'lĭkh), former duchy, NW Germany, between Cologne and Aachen; historic cap. Jülich (pop. c.8,000). At first a county, Jülich was united with county of BERG (1348) and made a duchy (1356). After extinction of Jülich line both Jülich and Berg passed to dukes of CLEVES (1524); to Palatinate-Neuburg branch of Wittelsbach dynasty (1666); to France (1806); to Prussia (1815).

Julier (yōol'yûr), pass, 7,507 ft. high, Grisons canton, Switzerland; a link between Engadine and Italy. Modern road was built 1820–40.

Julius I, Saint, pope (337–52). When called upon for his opinion in the Arian controversy, he summoned a council at Rome (340). The Arians did not come, and Julius wrote them a letter, chiding them for lack of sincerity and asserting the papal claim to jurisdiction over the whole church. Feast: April 12.

Julius II, 1443–1513, pope (1503–13). As Giuliano della Rovere, created cardinal by his uncle Sixtus IV. As pope he completed work of Cesare Borgia (his enemy) of restoring Papal States to the Church. A warrior, he took a vigorous part in the Italian Wars. In 1512 Julius assembled the Fifth LATERAN COUNCIL, which condemned Gallicanism in France, abolished simony in the college of cardinals. A patron of art, he favored Raphael (for whom he sat), Michelangelo, and Bramante. He laid the cornerstone of St. Peter's.

Julius Caesar: see CAESAR, JULIUS.

Jullundur (jŭ'lŭndûr), city (pop. 135,283), central Punjab, India. Taken by Ranjit Singh 1811. Trade center with mfg. of silk fabrics.

July: see MONTH.

July Revolution, 1830, French revolution which deposed CHARLES X and created the bourgeois July Monarchy under LOUIS PHILIPPE. It resulted from the opposition of the propertied middle class, led by such men as THIERS, and of the radical workers in Paris to Charles's reactionary policies. The repressive, ultra-royalist July Ordinances under ministry of J. A. de POLIGNAC brought matters to a head. Revolution was over in two days.

Jumna (jŭm'nŭ), river, c.850 mi. long, rising in N Uttar Pradesh, India. Its junction with the Ganges at Allahabad forms one of bathing sites most sacred to Hindus.

Junagarh (jōo'nŭgär") or **Junagadh** (jōo'nŭgäd"), former princely state, India, on Kathiawar peninsula; since 1949 part of Saurashtra. Junagarh, town (pop. 58,111), formerly cap. of state, was Rajput stronghold until 15th cent.

junco or **snowbird,** bird of FINCH family. Slate-colored junco is a winter resident in E North America. About the size of a sparrow, it is dark gray with white abdomen. Other juncoes are in W and S U.S.

Junction City, city (pop. 13,462), NE Kansas, at head of Kansas R. and W of Topeka; founded 1858. Rail and trade center in agr. and dairy area. Fort RILEY is near by.

June: see MONTH.

Juneau, Solomon Laurent (jōonō', jōo'nō), 1793–1856, French Canadian fur trader and founder of Milwaukee, Wis. Moved to fur post at Milwaukee in 1818; surveyed town site, built first store, became first mayor (1846).

Juneau (jōo'nō), city (pop. 5,956), territorial cap. (since 1900), SE Alaska, at foot of Mt. Juneau and Mt. Roberts, on Gastineau Channel; settled 1881 following 1880 gold discovery. Bridge connects with Douglas town on Douglas Isl., across channel. Has gold mining, salmon fishing, fur farming, and lumbering. Port with ice-free harbor, seaplane base, and airport. Has U.S. and territorial offices and Alaska Historical Library and Mus.

June beetle, June bug, or **May beetle,** nocturnal blackish or mahogany-colored beetle of scarab family. Larvae (white grubs) eat underground roots.

Juneberry: see SHADBUSH.

June bug: see JUNE BEETLE.

June Days, 1848, in French history, insurrection of Parisian workers, brought on by government sabotage of national workshops established by Louis BLANC. Workers had played major part in FEBRUARY REVOLUTION, felt cheated of its fruits. Rebellion was ruthlessly put down by military in four days' fighting.

Jung, Carl Gustav (kärl gōos'täf yōong'), 1875–, Swiss psychiatrist, founder of school of analytical psychology. As first president of International Psychoanalytic Association he was second only to Freud in the movement; they worked together until differences of approach caused a formal break (1913). Jung conceived of libido as primal, nonsexual energy and postulated two systems in the unconscious: the personal (repressed events of personal life) and the collective unconscious (archetypes of inherited tendencies). He introduced terms EXTROVERSION AND INTROVERSION.

Jünger, Ernst (yüng'ûr), 1895–, German writer. Wrote novels of World War I—e.g., *Storm of Steel* (1919; Eng. tr., 1929); diaries of World War II.

Jungfrau (yōong'frou) [Ger.,= Virgin], peak, 13,653 ft. high, Switzerland, in Bernese Alps. First ascended 1811. The **Jungfraujoch** (-yôkh") is a mountain saddle 11,342 ft. high, highest point in Europe reached by rail. Has scientific institute and weather station.

Juniata (jōonēä'tù), river of Pa., rising in Alleghenies and flowing 150 mi. E to Susquehanna R. above Harrisburg.

Junín (hōonēn'), small town, W central Peru. Near here Bolívar aided by Sucre won first important battle (1824) in liberation of Peru from Spain.

juniper, evergreen tree or shrub of genus *Juniperus,* with berrylike fruits and needle- or scale-shaped leaves. Dwarf or pyramidal forms of the common juniper (*Juniperus communis*) of N Hemisphere are used in landscaping. Their fruits flavor gin. Wood of red cedar, a juniper (*J. virginiana*) native to E U.S., is much used for chests and closets; its oil is used in medicine and perfumery.

Junius, English political controversialist, anonymous writer of letters to London *Public Advertiser* (notably Jan., 1769–Jan., 1772) attacking the king's party and George III himself. Mystery of identity added interest to letters. Authorship ascribed to Sir Philip Francis, to Lord Shelburne, or to Laughlin Macleane, secretary to Shelburne.

Juno (jōō'nō), in Roman religion, queen of gods; sister and wife of Jupiter. Like Greek goddess HERA, she was protector of women.

Junot, Andoche (ädōsh' zhünō'), 1771–1813, French general. Commanded French invasion of Portugal (1807); was driven out by Wellington (1808). Created duke of Abrantès by Napoleon. His wife, Laure Junot, duchesse d'Abrantès (1784–1838) was socially prominent during Restoration and left lively memoirs.

Jupiter [Latin,= God, the father], in Roman religion, supreme god, also called Jove; son of Saturn and Ops and brother and husband of Juno. Identified with Olympian god Zeus.

Jupiter, in astronomy, largest PLANET (mean diameter c.86,728 mi.) of solar system. It revolves around the sun in 11 years 314.8 days at mean distance of 483,310,000 mi. in an orbit between Mars and Saturn. Mean rotation period is 9 hr. 55 min. It is enveloped by atmosphere and has 12 satellites. See *ill.*, p. 1187.

Jura (zhürä'), department (1,952 sq. mi.; pop. 216,386), E France, in Franche-Comté; cap. Lons-le-Saunier.

Jura (jōō'rù), mountain range, E France (Jura and Doubs depts.) and W Switzerland (Vaud, Neuchâtel, and Bern cantons). Extends in parallel ridges from the Rhine R. at Basel to Rhone R. at Geneva; rises above 5,500 ft. Pine forests, pastures, agr. Watch industry in many towns (e.g., Le Locle, La Chaux-de-Fonds). Many resorts. Formed of sandstone and limestone rich in fossils, Jura gives name to Jurassic period. Mountains of S Württemberg are called the Swabian Jura.

Jurassic period (jōōrä'sĭk), second period of the MESOZOIC ERA of geologic time. As in Triassic period E North America was continuously elevated and subject to erosion which reduced the Appalachians to a peneplain. Deserts at first prevailed in SW U.S., but this region was later flooded from the N, and sediments were deposited. The period's close was marked by mountain making and lava instrusions in the W; to the E, by upwarping of the Appalachian peneplain. Reptiles dominated sea, land, air. Plant life included cycads, conifers, tree ferns. See also GEOLOGY, table.

Jurieu, Pierre (pyĕr' zhüryû'), 1637–1713, French Protestant theologian and Calvinist controversialist. Took refuge in Rotterdam after publication (1681) of *La Politique du clergé de France,* an attempt to preserve Huguenot liberties. Attacked Arnauld, Bossuet, and others in controversial works.

jurisprudence, study of the nature, origin, and development of law. Prevailing concept from 13th to 19th cent. was that of natural law—that laws took their sanction from a law of nature estab. by divine ordinance. In 19th cent. there grew up theories that law depends only on sovereign decree or custom of the culture, divorced from theology or morality. Other schools of thought are the historical (that law is the product of development) and the sociological (that law expresses the dominant social pattern in a nation or the community).

Juruá (zhōōrwä'), river, c.1,200 mi. long, rising in E Peru, flowing generally NE through Brazil to Amazon. Important during wild-rubber boom.

jury, in Anglo-Norman times, body of men brought together to decide from personal knowledge in an inquest what the facts were. Institution gradually developed until it became before the 18th cent. the symbolic and actual protection against tyranny for all Englishmen. It was incorporated into the U.S. constitution. Judgment of a man's "peers" as to facts of a case are considered to be binding, above the decision of a judge. A group of prospective jurors (panel) is called the venire. In choosing a petit jury (for trial), counsel may challenge the whole group or any individuals as unfit according to counsel's opinion. A grand jury usually has 12 to 23 members, a petit jury 12 (or less, according to state law). A petit jury takes an oath to reach a fair decision on evidence (the VERDICT). On the Continent jury trials are restricted to criminal cases of great importance.

Jusserand, Jean Jules (zhä' zhül' zhüsürä'), 1855–1932, French diplomat and scholar. As ambassador to Washington (1902–15) he was extremely popular. Among his works are *English Wayfaring Life in the Middle Ages* (1889) and an incomplete autobiography (1933).

Jussieu (zhüsyû'), name of a French family of botanists. **Antoine de Jussieu** (ätwän' dü), 1686–1758, was director of the Jardin des Plantes, Paris, and editor of botanical works. His brother **Bernard de Jussieu** (bĕrnär'), 1699–1777?, was director of gardens at Trianon, Versailles, and developer of a classification system. Another brother, **Joseph de Jussieu** (zhôsĕf'), 1704–79, traveled in South America and introduced into Europe many plants (e.g., heliotrope) from there. A nephew, **Antoine Laurent de Jussieu** (lōrä'), 1748–1836, elaborated Bernard's system of classification in his *Genera plantarum* (1789). He was professor at the Museum of Natural History, Paris, and organized its botanical collection. His son, **Adrien de Jussieu** (ädrēē'), 1797–1853, was also professor of botany at the museum.

Justice, United States Department of, created by act of Congress in 1870. Office of U.S. Attorney General became nucleus of department. Act of 1870 also set up office of Solicitor General to represent government in Supreme Court cases and empowered creation of assistants to aid Attorney General in administering department. Department furnishes legal counsel in Federal cases, provides means for enforcing Federal laws, and officially construes laws—subject to court decisions—under which government officials act. Department consists of seven specialized divisions (e.g., Antitrust Division), three bureaus (e.g., FEDERAL BUREAU OF INVESTIGATION), and two boards.

Justin I, c.450–527, Byzantine emperor (518–27). Chief of imperial guard, he seized power on death of Anastasius I. He was illiterate and entrusted the government to his nephew, Justinian I.

Justinian I, 483–565, Byzantine emperor (527–65); nephew of JUSTIN I. His reign was a rebirth of imperial greatness. His generals BELISARIUS and NARSES recovered Africa from the Vandals and Italy from the Ostrogoths. The *Nika* riot, caused by discontent with heavy taxation and his hostility to Monophysitism, was crushed by the firm stand of Empress THEODORA (532). Justinian advocated caesaro-papism—the supremacy of the emperor over the Church—and in 553 called the Second Council of Constantinople in an attempt to reconcile the Monophysites. His chief accomplishment was the codification of Roman law (see CORPUS JURIS CIVILIS). He also had the Church of HAGIA SOPHIA built.

Justin Martyr, Saint, A.D. c.100–c.165, Christian apologist, b. Palestine. Converted to Christianity at 30, he was finally martyred with disciples at Rome. Two undisputed works (in Greek) remain, both philosophic defenses of Christian doctrine—the *Apology* and the *Dialogue.*

Justin Morgan, 1792–1821, American horse, foundation sire of Justin Morgan breed, which preceded Hambletonian strain as favored type of trotting horse in U.S.

jute (jōot), annual tropical plant (*Corchorus capsularis*) grown for fiber which lies between outer bark and central wood. The fiber, widely used, is cheap, easily spun and dyed. Burlap, webbing, twines, backing yarns for carpets and linoleum, oakum, paper, etc., are made from jute. Calcutta is leading manufacturer and exporter, but the plant can be grown in any hot humid country.

Jutes: see ANGLO-SAXONS; KENT, KINGDOM OF.

Jutland, Dan. *Jylland,* Ger. *Jütland,* peninsula, N Europe, comprising continental Denmark and German SCHLESWIG N of Eider R.; bounded on N by the Skagerrak and W by North Sea. Danish Jutland, including adjacent islands, has area of 11,411 sq. mi. and pop. of 1,826,056. Dairying and cattle raising are chief occupations on fertile and densely populated E coast. Aarhus, Aalborg, and Frederickshavn are main ports here. Jut-

land has many lakes and is crossed by Guden R. South Jutland is name applied in Denmark to N part of former duchy of Schleswig. The **battle of Jutland,** May 31, 1916, chief naval engagement of World War I, was fought c.60 mi. W of Jutland coast; also known as battle of the Skagerrak. Although the German fleet, brilliantly commanded by admirals Hipper and Scheer, suffered lighter losses than the British (under Beatty and Jellicoe), it was forced to return to its bases, where it remained bottled up.

Juvenal (Decimus Junius Juvenalis) (jōo′vŭnŭl), 1st–2d cent. A.D., Roman satirical poet. His 16 savage satires, in denouncing the criminal excesses, immorality, and tyranny of the Romans, give a vivid picture of the society.

juvenile delinquency, behavior of children and adolescents which in adults would be judged criminal (see CRIME). Maximum age of juveniles is variously defined, from 14 to 21 years. Delinquency frequently arises from bad family situations, and it persists in slum neighborhoods. Though juvenile corrective institutions have been separated from regular prisons since early 19th cent., the separate judgment of youth was developed only after 1899 in the juvenile court, and the rehabilitation of delinquents, though benefiting from improved psychiatric and sociological programs, is still recognizably inadequate.

juvenile literature. First books for children were Latin texts of 7th cent., school texts of Venerable Bede, and colloquy of Ælfric in 10th cent. William Caxton printed for children Aesop's fables in 1484. Invention of hornbook in 15th cent. made books readily available. Chapbooks were sold in 17th and 18th cent. John Newbery (1713–67), publisher and author, made small attractive volumes expressly for children. The 18th cent. produced school of writers of didactic literature. The 19th cent. produced such works as fairy tales of brothers Grimm in Germany, tales of Hans Christian Andersen, Edward Lear's *Book of Nonsense* (1846), Lewis Carroll's *Alice in Wonderland* (1865), Stevenson's *Treasure Island* (1883), and Kipling's *Jungle Book* (1894). Series were popular in America; the didactic *Rollo* series of Jacob Abbott and the *Elsie Dinsmore* series were followed by the Horatio Alger books and the Oliver Optic books. From the 19th cent. came works by James Fenimore Cooper, Mark Twain, Howard Pyle, Louisa May Alcott, and Joel Chandler Harris. Recent children's books of note have been written by Kenneth Grahame, Selma Lagerlof, Hugh Lofting, P. L. Travers, and A. A. Milne.

Jylland: see JUTLAND.

K

K, chemical symbol of the element POTASSIUM.

K2: see GODWIN-AUSTEN, MOUNT.

Kaaba or **Caaba** (both: kä′bŭ, kä′ŭbŭ), most sacred building, housing the sacred Black Stone; goal of the pilgrimage to Mecca, center of Islam. Its sanctity is earlier than Islam.

Kabardian Autonomous Soviet Socialist Republic (kŭbär′dĕŭn), autonomous republic (4,550 sq. mi.; pop. c.300,000), S European RSFSR, on N slopes of Greater Caucasus; cap. Nalchik. Includes peaks of Mt. Elbrus, Koshtan-Tau, Dykh-Tau. Kabardians (c.60% of pop.), a Moslem Circassian group, support themselves by agr., stock raising.

kabuki: see JAPANESE DRAMA.

Kabul (kä′bŏŏl), city (pop. 300,000), cap. of Afghanistan, on Kabul R., in fruit-growing region. Early cap. of Baber (1504–19). Succeeded Kandahar as cap. of Afghanistan in 1773. Figured prominently in First Afghan War (1839–42).

Kachin State (kŭchĭn′), constituent unit (33,-871 sq. mi.; pop. 427,625) of Union of Burma, N Upper Burma; cap. Myitkyina; largely autonomous. Many of inhabitants are Kachins or Jinghpaws.

Kaffa, RSFSR: see FEODOSIYA.

kaffir or **kaffir corn:** see SORGHUM.

Kaffraria, South Africa: see KAFIRS.

Kafirs or **Kaffirs** (both: kä′fŭrz), Bantu-speaking Negro people (c.500,000) of South Africa. Chiefly in Kaffraria, region in E Cape Prov., Union of South Africa.

Kafka, Franz (fränts′ käf′kä), 1883–1924, German novelist and essayist, b. Prague, Czechoslovakia, of a Jewish family. Among his works are *The Trial* (1925), *The Castle* (1926), and *Amerika* (1927), all translated into English. In prose remarkable for clarity and precision, Kafka presents a world at once real and dreamlike in which modern man, burdened with guilt, isolation, and anxiety, makes a futile search for personal salvation.

Kagawa, Toyohiko (tōyō′hēkō kä″gä′wä), 1888–, Japanese Christian social worker. Influential in organizing cooperatives and in labor problems. Arrested in World War II for pacifism. Author of poetry, novels, essays, and religious studies.

Kagera, river: see NILE.

Kagoshima (kä″gō′shĭmä), city (pop. 170,416), S Kyushu, Japan; port on inlet of East China Sea. Mfg. of porcelain ware, clothing, and tinware. St. Francis Xavier landed here in 1549. Was seat of powerful lords of Satsuma.

Kahlenberg (kä′lŭnbĕrk), mountain, 1,585 ft. high, Lower Austria, near Vienna, of which it commands a beautiful view. A favorite excursion point.

Kahn, Albert, 1869–1942, American architect, b. Germany. His firm in Detroit applied technique of mass production to architecture; designed many factories and war plants.

Kahn, Otto (Hermann), 1867–1934, American banker and patron of the arts, b. Germany. In U.S. after 1893, he joined Kuhn, Loeb, & Co. Took part in many international finance organizations. Helped finance many theatrical and musical groups. A director of the Metropolitan Opera Co. 1903–31.

Kahoolawe (kähō′ōlävä), uninhabited island (45 sq. mi.), Hawaiian Isls. Leased to a private citizen.

Kailas (kīläs′), peak, 22,028 ft. high, SW Tibet, in Himalayas. Home of Hindu god Siva, it is goal of pilgrimages.

Kairouan (kīrwän′), city (pop. 32,299), Tunisia; sacred city of Islam. Founded 670, it was seat of Arab governors in W Africa until 800. First cap. of Fatimites was estab. here in 909. Has famous 9th-cent. mosque. Noted for carpet industry.

Kaisaria, Turkey: see KAYSERI.

Kaiser, Georg (gä′ôrk kī′zŭr), 1878–1945, German playwright. His plays, which he called thought dramas, have social themes. *From Morn to Midnight* (1916; produced in New York 1922), *The Corals* (1917; a trilogy), and *Gas* (1918) are translated into English.

Kaiserslautern (kī″zŭrslou′tŭrn), city (pop. 62,395), Rhineland-Palatinate, W Germany. Machine and textile mfg.

Kaiser Wilhelm Canal: see KIEL CANAL.

Kalamata (kälŭmä′tŭ), Gr. *Kalamai,* city (pop. 38,363) S Greece, in SW Peloponnesus; a port on the Gulf of Messenia. Fisheries, silk and cigarette mfg., distilleries.

Kalamazoo (kăl′ŭmŭzōō′), city (pop. 57,704), SW Mich., on Kalamazoo R. at junction with Portage Creek; settled 1829. Industrial and commercial center in agr. area, it has mfg. of paper, metal products, and pharmaceuticals. Seat of Kalamazoo Col.

Kalamazoo, river rising in S Mich. and flowing c.138 mi. NW past Battle Creek and Kalamazoo to L. Michigan.

Kalaupapa, T.H.: see MOLOKAI.

Kalb, Johann (Ger. yō′hän kälp′), 1721–80, general in American Revolution, known as "Baron de Kalb" (dĕ kälb), b. Germany. Mortally wounded in battle of Camden, S.C. (1780).

Kalckreuth, Leopold Karl Walter, Graf von (kälk′roit), 1855–1928, German genre painter, one of the Secessionists, who emphasized realism in subject matter. Pictured peasant life.

kale, nonheading cabbage variety (*Brassica oleracea acephala*) with curly leaves, grown for greens and, in Europe, for fodder. Sea kale (*Crambe maritima*) is N European coastal plant sometimes used as a potherb.

SMALL CAPITALS = cross references.   Pronunciation key: pp. xiv and xv.   Abbreviations: p. 2.

kaleidoscope (kŭlĭ'dŭskōp), cylindrical tube, one end containing two mirrors set at angle of 60° and many particles of varicolored glass which can move between two glass disks. Other end has eyepiece. When tube is rotated, glass forms many patterns, always symmetrical because of reflection in mirrors.

Kalevala (kä'lĕvä″lä), Finnish national epic, a compilation of folk verses dealing with the deeds of three semidivine brothers of gigantic stature. Known to scholars as early as 1733, verses were collected in 19th cent. by Zakarias Topelius and Elias LÖNNROT. Effect on Finnish art has been great.

Kalgan, China: see CHANGKIAKOW.

Kali (kŭ'lē), in Hinduism, primarily the black goddess of death and evil, though she has other and more attractive aspects. As consort of Siva, she represents the female principle. The name was also given earlier to one of the tongues of the fire-god Agni.

Kalidasa (kä″lĭdä'sù), fl. 5th cent.?, Indian poet and dramatist, often regarded as greatest figure in classical Sanskrit literature. Three surviving verse dramas (including *Sakuntala*) relate fanciful or mythological tales of lovers separated by adversity but reunited by happy chance. Two epics mingle delicate descriptions of nature with battle scenes. Also wrote shorter lyrical poems.

Kalinin, Mikhail Ivanovich (mēkhŭyēl' ēvä'-nùvĭch kŭlyē'nyĭn), 1875–1946, Russian revolutionist, first president of USSR (officially: chairman of presidium of supreme council of USSR) 1922–46.

Kalinin, formerly Tver, city (pop. 216,131), RSFSR, NW of Moscow and on the Volga. It is an industrial center (railway cars, machinery, textiles). The seat of a powerful principality in 14th–15th cent., it was annexed to Moscow c.1486. Renamed 1933 for M. I. Kalinin. It was briefly held by the Germans in 1941 and was heavily damaged.

Kaliningrad, Russian name of KÖNIGSBERG.

Kalisch, Poland: see KALISZ.

Kalispel Indians: see PEND D'OREILLE INDIANS.

Kalispell (kä'lĭspĕl″), city (pop. 9,737), NW Mont., on Flathead R. and near Glacier Natl. Park. Trade center of agr., mining, and lumbering region.

Kalisz (kä'lēsh), Ger. *Kalisch,* city (pop. 48,-092), W Poland. Mfg. of clothing, food, machinery. By Convention of Kalisz (1813) Prussia promised Russia to declare war on Napoleon I.

Kalm, Peter (pä'tùr kälm'), 1716–79, Swedish scientist. His *Travels in North America,* recording his observations of natural history, plantations, and agriculture, was the first account of its kind by a trained scientist. It was published between 1753 and 1761; was republished in 1937. Genus *Kalmia* (mountain laurel) is named for Kalm.

Kalmar (käl'mär), city (pop. 27,049), co. seat of Kalmar co., SE Sweden, Baltic port opposite Öland isl. across Kalmar Sound. Its medieval castle, the Kalmarnahus, has withstood 24 sieges. Here in 1397 was effected the **Kalmar Union** of Denmark, Sweden, and Norway under Queen MARGARET. Since kingship was elective in all three countries, a lasting union under the Danish crown proved impossible. Sweden definitely left the union in 1523 (see GUSTAVUS I). The **Kalmar War,** 1611–13, between Denmark and Sweden, took its name from the fall of Kalmar to the Danes early in the conflict. Gustavus II bought off the Danish claims at the Peace of Knared.

Kalmucks (käl'mŭks), or **Kalmycks** (käl'-mĭks), Asiatic people, a branch of Oirat Mongols. They migrated from Altai region to lower Volga basin c.1636 and became vassals of Russia. To avoid Russian colonization, a large part of Kalmucks E of the Volga migrated to China in 1771, but were decimated along their arduous route. The others stayed on, clinging to their Lamaist Buddhist faith and to their traditional ways. During the Russian civil war of 1917–20 many migrated to Central and W Europe. The Kalmuck Autonomous Soviet Socialist Republic (28,650 sq. mi.; pop. 220,723; cap. Elista) was estab. 1935 and dissolved 1943, the Kalmucks having allegedly collaborated with the German invaders. Many fled to Germany and became "displaced persons"; those who remained were "resettled" elsewhere in USSR.

Kaluga (kùlōō'gù), city (pop. 89,484), W European RSFSR, on Oka R. Machinery mfg. It was scene of murder of second false Dmitri (1610). Center of action in World War II, 1941.

Kalymnos (kä'lēmnôs), Greek island (41 sq. mi.; pop. 11,864); part of DODECANESE. Sponge-fishing center.

Kama (kä'mŭ), river, 1,262 mi. long, E European RSFSR; chief tributary of the Volga, which it joins below Kazan. Navigable about half the year, it is an important transportation route.

Kamakura (kämä'kōōrä), city (pop. 55,168), central Honshu, Japan. Known for *daibutsu,* 42-ft.-high bronze figure of Buddha, cast in 1252. Was eastern cap. of Ashikaga shogunate (1333–1573).

Kamchatka (kämchät'kù), peninsula (104,200 sq. mi.), Khabarovsk Territory, RSFSR, in NE Siberia. It separates Sea of Okhotsk (W) from Bering Sea and Pacific Ocean. Beyond Cape Lopatka (S tip) lie Kurile Isls. Petropavlovsk is main center. Two volcanic ranges, which rise to 15,666 ft. in Klyuchevskaya Sopka, enclose central valley (N–S), drained by Kamchatka R. (335 mi. long). There are hot springs, peat marshes, forests, petroleum, and coal deposits. Fishing, fur trapping, lumbering, and reindeer raising are chief occupations. The sparse population is mainly Russian, but in N part dwell native Kamchatkans and Koryaks. It was discovered 1697, and its conquest by Russia was completed 1732.

Kamehameha I (Kamehameha the Great) (kämä'hämä'hä), 1758–1819, Hawaiian monarch. United the islands in 1810, estab. law and order.

Kamehameha, Fort, at Pearl Harbor, Oahu, T.H.; hq. of coast defenses of Oahu; estab. 1909.

Kamenev, Lev Borisovich (lyĕf' bùrē'sùvĭch kä'mĭnyĭf), 1883–1936, Russian Communist leader whose real name was Rosenfeld; brother-in-law of Trotsky. One of triumvirate (with Stalin and Zinoviev) which succeeded Lenin in 1924. Joined Trotsky's opposition 1925; twice expelled from party (1927, 1932); executed after 1936 treason trials.

Kamerlingh Onnes, Heike (hī'kŭ kä'mûrlĭng ô'nŭs), 1853–1926, Dutch physicist. Won 1913 Nobel Prize chiefly for study of properties of helium.

Kamet (kä'mĕt), peak, 25,447 ft. high, on Tibet-India border, in Himalayas. Ascended 1931 by British expedition under F. S. Smythe.

kamikaze (kä"mēkä'zä) [Jap.,= divine wind], typhoon that destroyed Kublai Khan's fleet, foiling his invasion of Japan in 1281. In World War II, term used for Japanese suicide pilots (esp. active at Okinawa) who crashed their planes into enemy ships.

Kaministikwia or **Kaministiquia** (both: kŭmĭ"-nĭstĭ'kwēŭ), river, c.60 mi. long, rising in W Ont., Canada, and flowing S, then E to L. Superior at Fort William. Was alternate route to the GRAND PORTAGE.

Kamloops (kăm'lōops), town (pop. 8,099), S B.C., Canada, on Thompson R. Trading post estab. here 1812. Growth spurred by Cariboo gold rush. Canadian Pacific RR reached here 1885. Center of agr., mining, and lumbering area.

Kamperduin, Netherlands: see CAMPERDOWN.

Kanab (kŭnăb'), resort city (pop. 1,287), S Utah, near Ariz. line. Vivid countryside provides location for much film making (esp. "westerns"). Zion and Grand Canyon national parks are near.

Kanaoka (känä'ōkä), c.850–c.931, Japanese landscape and figure painter, founder of Kose school.

Kanawha (kŭnô'wŭ), river formed in SW W.Va. and flowing 97 mi. NW past Charleston to Ohio R. at Point Pleasant. Valley has chemical mfg. and mining.

Kanazawa (kä"nä'zäwä), city (pop. 231,441), central Honshu, Japan, on Sea of Japan. Mfg. of silk textiles, porcelain, and lacquer ware. Park has noted gardens.

Kanchenjunga (kän"chŭnjŏong'gŭ), mountain, 28,146 ft. high, on Sikkim-Nepal border, in Himalayas; third highest in world. German expedition in 1931 climbed 26,220 ft. Also spelled Kinchinjunga.

Kanchipuram, India: see CONJEEVERAM.

Kandahar (kăn"dŭhär'), city (pop. c.60,000) S Afghanistan. Cap. of Afghanistan, 1747–73. Held by the British in 19th-cent. Afghan Wars. Trade center in fruit-growing area.

Kandinsky, Vasily (vŭsē'lyē kŭndyēn'skē), 1866–1944, Russian abstract painter in Germany. With Klee he initiated German expressionism.

Kandy or **Candy** (kăn'dē), city (pop. 50,767), central Ceylon. Was cap. of independent kingdom of Ceylon, 1592–1815. Site of temple supposedly containing one of Buddha's teeth. Surrounding area has tea and rubber plantations.

Kane, Elisha Kent, 1820–57, American arctic explorer. Accompanied first Grinnell expedition (1850) seeking lost Franklin party. Interest in his published account made possible second expedition (1853–55), which discovered Kane Basin.

Kane, borough (pop. 5,706), NW Pa., NW of Ridgeway. Oil wells and refineries; health resort.

Kaneohe Bay (kä'näōhä), E Oahu, Hawaiian Isls. U.S. naval air station here.

kangaroo, vegetarian MARSUPIAL of Australia and Tasmania. The front limbs are small and the long, powerful hind limbs enable the animal to leap swiftly over the ground; the long muscular tail aids balance while leaping and is a prop when standing or moving slowly. In the large kangaroos and wallaroos (genus *Macropus*) the hind foot of adults is more than 10 in. long; in the smaller kangaroos or wallabies (members of several genera) the hind foot is 6–10 in. long. Tree kangaroos (genus *Dendrolagus*) are partially arboreal; rat kangaroos are smallest forms.

Kaniapiskau (kănyŭpĭ'skô"), river, NE Que., Canada, issues from **Kaniapiskau Lake**, on St. Lawrence-Hudson Bay watershed. Flows 450 mi. generally NNW to form Koksoak R. with Larch R.

Kankakee (kăngkŭkē'), city (pop. 25,856), E Ill., on Kankakee R. and SW of Chicago. Industrial and shipping center in agr. area. Mfg. of brick, tile, clothing, furniture, and paint; limestone quarries.

Kankakee, river, c.135 m. long, rising near South Bend, N. Ind., and flowing SW to Kankakee, Ill., then NW to Des Plaines R. below Joliet to form the Illinois.

Kannapolis (kŭnăp'ŭlĭs), cotton-mill "company town" (pop. 28,448), W central N.C., NNE of Charlotte; founded 1906.

Kano (kä'nō), family or school of Japanese painters. Its forerunner, Kano Masanobu (mäsä'nōbōō), c.1453–c.1550, painted landscapes, birds, and figure pieces, chiefly in ink, with touches of palest tints. His son, **Kano Motonobu** (mōtō'nōbōō), c.1476–1559, actual founder of school, gave it its character —the subordination of color to design. The painting of **Kano Eitoku** (ā'tōkō), 1543–90, grandson of Motonobu, is characterized by energy, ease, and inventiveness. His grandson, **Kano Tanyu** (tänyōō'), 1602–74, was so original and versatile that he really created a school of his own.

Kano (kä'nō), city (pop. 89,162), N Nigeria. Built in 16th cent. on site of 9th-cent. settlement. Flourished as caravan center in 19th cent. Now an important transport center, with international airport. Chief town of Nigeria's peanut industry.

Kanpur: see CAWNPORE.

Kansa Indians, North American tribe of Siouan linguistic stock, known also as Kansas and Kaw Indians. They were at the mouth of the Kansas R. in the 18th cent., later moved farther W, were settled on a reservation at Council Grove until 1873, then were moved to present Okla., near the related Osage Indians. Had a typical Plains culture.

Kansas, state (82,276 sq. mi.; pop. 1,905,299), central U.S. (has geographical center of U.S.); admitted 1861 as 34th state (free); cap. TOPEKA. Other cities are KANSAS CITY, WICHITA. Bounded NE by Missouri R. Major rivers are the KANSAS, ARKANSAS. Rises from Mississippi valley plains of E to GREAT PLAINS in W. Agr. of grain (esp. wheat, corn); cattle, hogs, dairy products, poultry.

Mfg. of cement, agr. implements, airplanes, food and dairy products, metal goods, lumber products; meat packing, oil refining. Mining (oil, natural gas, coal, lead, zinc). Part of Louisiana Purchase except for SE corner (ceded by Texas in 1850). Part of INDIAN TERRITORY until made separate territory under KANSAS-NEBRASKA BILL (1854). Violence between proslavery and antislavery factions filled years before Civil War (see BROWN, JOHN). Agr. developed after war. Grasshopper plague (1874), droughts, depression of 1880s caused hardship. Farmers supported POPULIST PARTY until conditions improved, then returned to allegiance to Republican party. State marked by conservative, moral tone. Government subsidies, storage elevators for grain, and conservation measures have been introduced to stabilize the basically agr. economy of the state.

Kansas, sometimes called the Kaw, river formed by junction of Smoky Hill and Republican rivers in NE Kansas. Flows c.170 mi. E to the Missouri at Kansas City. Drains Kansas and parts of Nebr. and Colo.

Kansas, University of, mainly at Lawrence; state supported, coed.; chartered 1864, opened 1866 with aid from A. A. Lawrence.

Kansas City, two adjacent cities of same name, one (pop. 129,553) in Kansas, the other (pop. 456,622) in Mo., at junction of Missouri and Kansas (or Kaw) rivers, almost in geographical center of U.S. Each is second largest city of its state. They are a great commercial, industrial, transportation, and cultural center, with stockyards, grain elevators, oil refineries, and railroad shops, and foodprocessing, soap, and metal products plants. Surrounding area was starting point of many westward expeditions; Santa Fe and Oregon trails passed through here. Several early 19th-cent. settlements were foundations for these present-day cities. One was Westport (in Mo.) where Confederate forces were decisively defeated on Oct. 21–23, 1864, thus ending last Confederate invasion of Far West. Kansas City, Kansas, has Univ. of Kansas Hospitals. Kansas City, Mo., has Nelson Gall. of Art and Univ. of Kansas City (coed.; 1929). Kansas City *Star* was founded by W. R. Nelson, 1880. Political reform move in 1937 led to deposing of T. J. PENDERGAST.

Kansas-Nebraska Bill, legislation by which U.S. Congress estab. territories of Kansas and Nebraska, more properly Kansas-Nebraska Act, since it became law on May 30, 1854. Sectional conflict over slavery and over location of transcontinental railroad made territorial organization a serious problem. Southerners, wanting no free territory W of Mo., had already defeated four attempts to organize a single territory for the area. Bill, presented by Stephen A. Douglas, provided for "popular sovereignty" (see SQUATTER SOVEREIGNTY) and creation of two territories instead of one. An amendment specifically repealed Missouri Compromise. Bill caused sectional division to grow beyond reconciliation. Proslavery and antislavery forces exerted pressure to determine "popular" decision in Kansas in their own favor (see EMIGRANT AID COMPANY); result was "bleeding" Kansas. Opponents of bill founded new Republican party.

Kansas State College of Agriculture and Applied Science, at Manhattan; land-grant, state supported, coed.; chartered and opened 1863.

Kansu (gän'sōō'), province (150,000 sq. mi.; pop. 7,000,000), NW China; cap. Lanchow. Climate conditioned by nearness of Gobi Desert. Agri. (opium, cotton, tobacco), stock raising. Leading Chinese producer of petroleum; coal also mined.

Kant, Immanuel (känt), 1724–1804, German philosopher, one of the greatest figures in the history of philosophy. He lived a quiet life at Königsberg, becoming professor of logic and metaphysics at the university and quietly evolving a system of thought that influenced all succeeding philosophers in one way or another. His great works are *Critique of Pure Reason* (1781), *Foundations of the Metaphysics of Ethics* (1785), *Critique of Practical Reason* (1788), *Critique of Judgment* (1790), and *Religion within the Boundaries of Pure Reason* (1793–94). In them he set forth intricate and well-knit arguments that defy brief summary. He distinguished sharply between the things of our experience (phenomena), which can be fitted into categories of our understanding (including causality and substantiality) and things-in-themselves (noumena), which the intellect cannot actually fathom. To illustrate the failure of the intellect to deal with things-in-themselves, he set up the antinomies, logical contradictions of principles which cannot be resolved; thus, he demonstrated that space and time are infinite and that they are finite, that God exists and that he does not exist. Yet though we cannot *know* the noumenal realm, we can know that it exists. Ethics and aesthetics are grounded in it. Moral conduct rests upon the categorical imperative, which may be expressed as, "Act as if the maxim from which you act were to become through your will a universal law of nature" and also as "So act as to treat humanity, whether in your own person or that of another, in every case as an end in itself, never as a means." Faith, not knowledge, justifies belief in freedom of the will, immortality, and God.

kaolin: see CHINA CLAY.

kaolinite (kā'ŭlĭnīt), crystallized clay mineral forming main constituent of kaolin and china clay. It is a hydrous aluminum silicate resulting chiefly from weathering of feldspar.

Kapilavastu (kä″pīlŭvä'stōō), town, S Nepal. A pillar marks birthplace of Buddha.

kapok (kā'pŏk, kă'–), tropical tree of Bombacaceae family and the fiber (floss) obtained from its ripe pods. Light, resilient, and resistant to water and decay, the fiber has been of commercial value since 1890s for filling and insulation. Oil from seed kernels is used for soap and as edible oil.

Kappel or **Cappel** (kä'pŭl), village, Switzerland, S of Zurich. Here ZWINGLI fell in battle (1531).

Kapteyn, Jacobus Cornelius (yäkō'bùs kôr-nä'lĭŭs käptīn'), 1851–1922, Dutch astronomer, authority on Milky Way system. Computed positions of many stars of S Hemisphere.

Kapuas (kä'pōōäs), longest river of Borneo, rising on Sarawak border, flowing 710 mi. to South China Sea.

Karabakh, USSR; see MOUNTAIN-KARABAKH.

Karachi (kŭrä'chē), city (pop. 1,005,000), W Pakistan, on Arabian Sea. After it passed to the British in 1843 it became main port for NW India. Became cap. of Pakistan in 1947 and grew phenomenally (1941 pop. 386,655). Country's chief port, it ships grains, salt, hides, and wool.

Karafuto, former Japanese possession: see SAKHALIN.

Karaganda (kä"rùgŭndä'), city (pop. c.220,-000), Kazakh SSR, in Kazakh Hills. Center of one of largest coal basins in USSR, developed after 1928.

Karageorge (kä"rùjôrj', kä"räjôr'jä) [Turkish, = Black George], Serbo-Croatian *Czerny George,* 1752?–1817, Serbian patriot. An illiterate peasant, he led Serbian insurrection against Turks (1804), took Belgrade (1806), was proclaimed hereditary chief of Serbia (1808). Abandoned by his Russian allies in 1812, he fled to Austria. On his return to Serbia he was murdered at instigation of MILOSH Obrenovich. From him is descended the **Karageorgevich** (kä"rùjôr'jùvĭch) dynasty of Serbia and Yugoslavia—Prince ALEXANDER, and Kings PETER I, ALEXANDER, and PETER II. The family was long in feud with the OBRENOVICH dynasty.

Karaites (kâ'rùīts), Jewish anti-Talmudic sect, founded c.765 in Persia, which proclaimed freedom of individual to interpret Bible according to his own conception. At present has some adherents in Crimea.

Karajich, Vuk Stefanovich (vōōk' stĕfä'nôvĭch kä'räyĭch), 1787–1864, Serbian philologist and folklorist. He adopted Serbian vernacular as his literary language, introduced phonetic spelling, and invented new letters to complete the Cyrillic alphabet. In 1847 he translated the New Testament into Serbian.

Karakalpak Autonomous Soviet Socialist Republic (kä"rùkŭlpäk'), autonomous republic (61,600 sq. mi.; pop. c.600,000), NW Uzbek SSR, comprising part of Ust-Urt plateau, Kizil Kum desert, and Amu Darya delta on Aral Sea; cap. Nukus. Produces cotton and alfalfa. Population consists mostly of Turkic Karakalpaks, Uzbeks, Kazakhs—all Moslems.

Karakoram (kä"rùkō'rùm), mountain system, N Kashmir, extending c.300 mi. Main range (sometimes called Mustagh) has large glaciers and includes Mt. GODWIN-AUSTEN, second highest peak in world.

Karakorum (kä"rùkō'rùm), ruined city, Mongolian People's Republic. Was cap. of Jenghiz Khan.

Kara Kul (kä'rù kōōl'), mountain lake, area 140 sq. mi., Tadzhik SSR, in the Pamir, near Chinese border; alt. 12,980 ft. and depth 775 ft.

karakul sheep: see SHEEP.

Kara Kum (kä"rù kōōm'), large desert, Turkmen SSR, S of Amu Darya R. Crossed by Trans-Caspian RR. Here is MERV oasis. Seminomadic population raises goats, camels, karakul sheep. Sulphur mines.

Karaman (kärämän') or **Caraman,** town (pop. 13,605), S Turkey, N of Taurus mts. Taken by a Turkic tribe c.1250, it became the cap. of the emirate of Karamania, a successor state of the Seljuk empire. Karamania, which once comprised most of Asia Minor, fell to the Ottoman Turks in the mid-15th cent. There are ruins of a castle and two fine college-mosques.

Karamzin, Nikolai Mikhailovich (nyĭkŭlī' mēkhi'lùvĭch kŭrùmzēn'), 1766–1826, Russian historian and novelist. Wrote *Letters of a Russian Traveler* (1792) and an 11-volume history of Russia (1818–24).

Kara Sea, section of Arctic Ocean, between W Siberia and Novaya Zemlya. Receives Ob, Yenisei, Pyasina, and Taimyra rivers. Navigable Aug.–Sept.

Karbala, Iraq: see KERBELA.

Karelo-Finnish Soviet Socialist Republic or **Karelia** (kŭrēl'yù), constituent republic (68,900 sq. mi.; pop. c.600,000), USSR, in NE Europe, between Finland and the White Sea; cap. Petrozavodsk. A glaciated plateau stretching from Kola Peninsula in N to L. Ladoga and L. Onega in S, it is covered by thousands of lakes and by dense coniferous forests. Karelia has important lumber industries (paper, furniture, prefabricated houses); marble, quartzite, and porphyry quarries; iron, magnetite, and lead-zinc ores. Majority of population is Russian; the rest are Karelians and Finns, whose written languages are identical. W Karelia, conquered by Swedes in 12th cent., shared history of Finland till 1940. E Karelia, conquered by Novgorod in 13th cent., became an autonomous republic of RSFSR in 1923; in 1940 it was made a constituent republic, enlarged by most of the territory ceded by Finland after the Finnish-Russian War. The **Karelian Isthmus** is a land bridge 90 mi. long and 25–70 mi. wide, connecting Russia and Finland, between the Gulf of Finland and L. Ladoga. It contains the cities of Leningrad and Vyborg. Until 1940 all except its S end belonged to Finland, which built the MANNERHEIM LINE across it. The Russo-Finnish peace treaty of 1940 and the Finnish peace treaty of 1947 gave the whole isthmus to the USSR; N part went to Karelo-Finnish SSR; S part to RSFSR.

Karenni State (kŭrĕ'nē), constituent unit (4,-506 sq. mi.; pop. 70,493) of Union of Burma, in Upper Burma; cap. Loikaw. Largely autonomous. Produces tungsten and teak. People are mainly Karens.

Karens (kŭrēnz'), members of Thai-Chinese cultural group, one of most important minorities in Burma (esp. in Karenni State). Some are pagan, but many are Christian and Buddhist.

Karfiol, Bernard (kär'fēōl'), 1886–1952, American painter, known for nudes, landscapes, portraits.

Karikal: see FRENCH INDIA.

Karkonosze, Polish name of RIESENGEBIRGE.

Karlfeldt, Erik Axel, 1864–1931, Swedish lyric poet. He was posthumously awarded the 1931 Nobel Prize in Literature, which he had refused in his lifetime.

Karlovy Vary, Czechoslovakia: see CARLSBAD.

Karlowitz, Treaty of (kär'lōvĭts), 1699, between Turkey and the Holy League (the emperor, Venice, Poland). Turkey ceded Hungary, Croatia, Slavonia to Emperor Leopold I; Podolia to Poland; Peloponnesus to Venice.

Karlsbad, Czechoslovakia: see CARLSBAD.

Karlsburg, Rumania: see ALBA-IULIA.

Karlsefni, Thorfinn: see THORFINN KARLSEFNI.

Karlskrona (kärlskrōō'nä), city (pop. 30,997), co. seat of Blekinge co., S Sweden. A Baltic port built on islands and on mainland, it is hq. of Swedish navy (since 1680). Fortifications and docks are cut out of granite. Sometimes spelled Carlskrona.

Karlsruhe (kärls'rōōü), city (pop. 198,014), Württemberg-Baden, W Germany, near the Rhine, with which it is linked by canal. Industrial center (metallurgy, food mfg.). Has several institutes of higher learning; well-known theaters and art galleries. Founded 1715, it was laid out in a semicircle, with streets converging radially upon ducal palace (heavily damaged in World War II). Was cap. of Baden-Durlach 1715–71; of Baden 1771–1945. Formerly spelled Carlsruhe.

Karlstad (kärl'städ), city (pop. 35,651), co. seat of Varmland co., W central Sweden, port on Vanern L. and on Thingvalla isl. It is a Lutheran episcopal see. It has lumber, pulp, and textile mills and shipyards. Union of Norway and Sweden was severed by treaty signed here, 1905.

Karlstadt, Reformation leader: see CARLSTADT.

Karmathians or **Carmathians,** crypto-Moslem sect, similar to ASSASSIN sect. An independent political force, they conquered Arabia early in the 10th cent., defied Abbasid caliph, and rocked Islam (c.930) by taking the black stone from the Kaaba, keeping it 10 years. They declined after 1000.

Karnak (kär'näk), town (pop. 10,865) central Egypt, on the Nile. Near LUXOR, it occupies part of the site of THEBES. Most notable of ancient ruins here is temple of Amon (XVIII dynasty), with its impressive Great Hall of Columns.

Karo, Joseph ben Ephraim: see CARO.

Karolyi, Count Julius, Hung. *Károlyi Gyula* (kä'rôlyï dyōō'lŏ), 1871–, Hungarian premier (1931–32). Though a nationalist, he abandoned Hungarian agitation for a revision of Treaty of Trianon in an effort to obtain foreign loans. His brother, **Count Michael Karolyi,** Hung. *Károlyi Mihály* (mï'hï), 1875–, a socialistic liberal, became premier of Hungary after abdication of Charles IV (1918). Elected president of the provisional republic (1919), he reluctantly surrendered the government to the Communists. He was Hungarian ambassador in Paris 1947–49.

Karpathos (kär'päthôs), Ital. *Scarpanto,* Greek island (111 sq. mi.; pop. 7,396); part of DODECANESE.

Karrer, Paul (kä'rür), 1889–, Swiss chemist. Shared 1937 Nobel Prize for work on vitamins, flavins, and carotinoids.

Kars (kärs), city (pop. 20,524), NE Turkey, in Armenia. Long an important fortress, it was taken by the Russians in 1828, 1855, and 1878. Kars dist. was formally ceded to Russia at Congress of Berlin (1878) but was returned to Turkey in 1921.

Karst (kärst), Ital. *Carso,* Serbo-Croatian *Kras,* barren limestone plateau, NW Yugo-slavia. Characterized by deep fissures, caves (see POSTOJNA), underground channels. The name karst applies also to similar geological formations elsewhere.

Karun (kärōōn'), biblical *Ulai,* anc. *Euloeus,* river, 500 mi. long, rising in SW Iran and flowing to Shatt el Arab on Iraq border.

Kaschau, Czechoslovakia: see KOSICE.

Kashmir (käshmēr'), officially **Jammu and Kashmir** (jŭ'mōō), state (82,258 sq. mi.; pop. 4,370,000), N Indian subcontinent; summer cap. Srinagar, winter cap. Jammu. Mainly mountainous. Vale of Kashmir (valley of Jhelum R.) is most populous area; produces wheat and rice. Formerly renowned for cashmere shawls. Was under Hindu rulers until 14th cent., when it fell to Moslems who converted most of the people to Islam. Moslem rule was overthrown 1819 by Ranjit Singh, aided by the Rajput Gulab Singh (a Hindu), who became raja and his heirs the maharajas of Kashmir. After partition of India (1947) Moslem tribesmen, aided in 1948 by Pakistan forces, sought control of state; opposed by Hindu maharaja (who acceded to India) and by Indian troops which occupied most of area. Dispute was brought 1948 before UN, which effected a ceasefire early in 1949. Both sides agreed to plebiscite, but no agreement had been reached in late 1952 on how it should be held.

Kashmiri language (käshmē'rē), language of Indic or Indo-Aryan group of Indo-Iranian subfamily of Indo-European languages. See LANGUAGE (table).

Kasimir: see CASIMIR.

Kaskaskia (käskä'skēü), village (pop. 112), Ill., on Kaskaskia Isl. in the Mississippi at junction with Kaskaskia R. Settled by Jesuits 1703. French had fort here 1733–55; destroyed by British 1763. George Rogers Clark took possession for U.S. in 1778. Cap. of Illinois Territory 1809–18. Fort Kaskaskia State Park is near by.

Kaskaskia, river rising in E central Ill., near Urbana, and flowing c.320 mi. SW to the Mississippi NW of Kaskaskia.

Kasner, Edward (kä'snúr), 1878–, American mathematician, known especially for studies of relativity, horn angles, invariants, polygonic functions.

Kassa, Czechoslovakia: see KOSICE.

Kassaba or **Cassaba** (käsä'bä), city (pop. 25,139), W Turkey, NE of Smyrna; modern Turgutlu. Famed for type of melon named after it.

Kassel (kä'sùl), city (1939 pop. 216,141; 1950 pop. 161,322), Hesse, W Germany, on Fulda R.; also spelled Cassel. Center of locomotive and machinery industries; during World War II a center of armaments production. Virtually obliterated by Allied bombings. Paintings of celebrated gallery (itself destroyed) were saved. Kassel was after 1567 the cap. of the landgraviate of Hesse-Kassel (raised to electorate 1803); cap. of kingdom of Westphalia 1807–13; cap. of Hesse-Nassau prov. 1866–1945.

Kasserine Pass, gap, 2 mi. wide, W Tunisia, in an extension of Atlas Mts. Here in World War II German attack was contained by Allies in decisive battle (Feb., 1943) of Tunisian campaign.

Kasson, John Adam (kă′sŭn), 1822–1910, American political leader and diplomat. U.S. Representative from Iowa (1863–67, 1873–77, 1881–84). U.S. minister to Austria-Hungary (1877–81), to Germany (1884–85).

Katahdin (kŭtä′dĭn), mountain, 5,268 ft. high, between branches of Penobscot R. in N central Maine. Highest point in Maine.

Katayama, Tetsu (tĕtsōō kätäyä′mä), 1887–, Japanese statesman. Leader of Social Democratic party, prime minister of coalition cabinet (1947–48).

Katayev, Valentin Petrovich (vŭlyĭntyēn′ pētrô′vĭch kŭtī′ŭf), 1897–, Russian author. His novels *The Embezzlers* (1926), *Time, Forward!* (1932), and *The Wife* (1944), all translated into English, portray Soviet life. Also wrote popular comedies.

Katharine or **Katherine.** For some persons thus named, see CATHERINE.

Katharine of Aragon, 1485–1536, queen of England, daughter of Ferdinand and Isabella of Spain and first wife of HENRY VIII. She did not produce a male heir and her political importance waned after the collapse (1525) of the Spanish alliance. Henry, infatuated with Anne Boleyn, tried to have the marriage annulled. Pope denied the divorce, and Henry married Anne secretly. Led to English Reformation. Katharine never accepted the decision that her marriage was invalid. She was confined and died after a prolonged illness.

Katkov, Mikhail Nikiforovich (mēkhŭyēl′ nyĭkē′fŭrŭvĭch kŭtkôf′), 1818–87, Russian journalist. Became a reactionary and Slavophile adviser of Alexander III.

Katmai National Monument: see NATIONAL PARKS AND MONUMENTS (table).

Kato, Takaakira, Viscount (tä′′kä-ä′kērä kä′tō), 1859–1926, Japanese statesman. Largely responsible for Twenty-one Demands presented to China. As prime minister (1924–25) he cut budget and army strength, sponsored manhood-suffrage law.

Katowice (kätôvē′tsĕ), Ger. *Kattowitz,* city (pop. 128,290), cap. of Silesia prov., SW Poland. It is the center of an important mining district (coal, iron, zinc, lead) which also contains the industrial centers of Beuthen, Chorzow, Gleiwitz, Hindenburg. Katowice has metallurgical, chemical, electrical, and other industries. Inc. 1867, it passed from Prussia to Poland in 1921.

Katrine, Loch (lŏkh kăt′rĭn), lake, c.8 mi. long and 1 mi. wide, Perthshire and Stirlingshire, Scotland. Outlet flows to Teith R. In 1859 Loch became source of water supply for Glasgow.

Kattegat (kă′tĭgăt″), strait, 137 mi. long and 37–c.100 mi. wide, between Sweden and Jutland, Denmark. It connects with North Sea through the Skagerrak, with Baltic Sea through the Oresund, Great Belt, and Little Belt. Goteborg (Sweden) and Aarhus (Denmark) are chief ports. Also spelled Cattegat.

Kattowitz, Poland: see KATOWICE.

katydid, insect of long-horned grasshopper family. Most of c.7,000 species are green and eat plants. Produce sound by rubbing forewings together.

Katyn (kŭtĭn′), village, RSFSR, W of Smolensk. Mass grave of some 10,000 Polish of-ficers, imprisoned after Poland's defeat in 1939, was found in a near-by forest by German occupation forces in 1943. Russians, though they denied having committed the massacre, refused international investigation. They later accused Germans of the crime.

Kauai (kou″wī′), island (551 sq. mi.; pop. 29,-683), one of the Hawaiian Isls. In central mountain mass are Kawaikini (5,170 ft.), the highest peak, and scenic WAIALEALE. Produces sugar, rice, and pineapples. Lihue is principal town.

Kauffman, Angelica, 1741–1807, Swiss historical and portrait painter. As protégée of Sir Joshua Reynolds she enjoyed great success in England and Italy.

Kaufman, George S. (kôf′mŭn, kouf′-), 1889–, American playwright. Sole author of only one play (*The Butter and Egg Man,* 1925), he has collaborated on many, including *Of Thee I Sing* (with Morrie Ryskind, 1931, score by George Gershwin), *You Can't Take It with You* (with Moss Hart, 1936), and *Stage Door* (with Edna Ferber, 1936).

Kaukauna (kôkô′nŭ), city (pop. 8,337), E Wis., on Fox R. and E of Appleton. Railroad shops, creameries, stone quarries, and paper mills.

Kaulbach, Wilhelm von (vĭl′hĕlm fŭn koul′-bäkh), 1805–74, German historical painter.

Kaunas (kou′näs), Rus. *Kovno,* city (pop. 154,-109), central Lithuania. It is an active port on the Niemen, with food and textile mfg. A Lithuanian stronghold against the Teutonic Knights in medieval times, Kaunas passed to Russia in third Polish partition (1795). It was the provisional cap. of Lithuania 1918–40, VILNA being held by Poland. The Germans, who occupied Kaunas 1941–44, massacred nearly all the Jews (c.30% of prewar population) and destroyed most of city before withdrawing. The university was founded 1922.

Kaunitz, Wenzel Anton, Fürst von (vĕn′tsŭl än′tŏn fürst′ fŭn kou′nĭts), 1711–94, Austrian chancellor and foreign minister under Maria Theresa, Joseph II, and Leopold II. His astute diplomacy created the anti-Prussian coalition that led to the SEVEN YEARS WAR and secured a share for Austria in the Polish partition of 1772.

Kautsky, Karl Johann (kärl yō′hän kout′skē), 1854–1938, German-Austrian socialist, cofounder of the Independent Social Democratic party in Germany, and a dominant figure in Second International. He opposed Lenin and Bolshevism as well as those who advocated revision of Marxist doctrines.

Kavalla or **Kavala** (both: kävä′lä), city (pop. 49,667), E Macedonia, Greece; an Aegean port on the Gulf of Kavalla. Chief Greek tobacco center. Taken by Bulgaria from Turkey in first Balkan War; ceded to Greece after second Balkan War (1913).

Kaveri: see CAUVERY.

Kaw, river: see KANSAS, river.

Kawartha Lakes (kŭwôr′thŭ), group of 14 lakes in Lindsay-Peterborough area, S Ont., Canada. Popular resort region.

Kawasaki (käwä′sä′kē), city (pop. 252,923), central Honshu, Japan, on Tokyo Bay. Steel mills, shipyards.

Kaw Indians: see KANSA INDIANS.

Kay, John, 1704–64, English inventor of fly shuttle, patented 1733, important in mechanical weaving.

kayak: see CANOE.

Kayseri (kī'sĕrē), anc. *Caesarea Mazaca,* city (pop. 65,489), central Turkey. Agr. center; cotton and tile mfg. Was important in Byzantine and Seljuk empires. Also known as Kaisaria.

Kazakh Soviet Socialist Republic (käzäk') or **Kazakhstan** (kä"zäkstän'), second largest constituent republic (1,063,200 sq. mi.; pop. c.6,000,000) of USSR, in central Asia, bordering on Caspian Sea (W) and China (E); cap. Alma-Ata. It consists of the dry Caspian and Turan lowlands, the arid Ust Urt plateau, and the Kazakh hills, and it contains the Aral Sea and L. Balkash. In the E and S rise the Altai and Ala-Tau ranges. The Irtysh, Ural, Ili, and Syr Darya are the chief rivers. Wheat is grown in blackearth steppes of N; camels and sheep are raised in arid central section; irrigated S plains grow rubber-bearing plants, cotton, rice, fruit, and other crops. Industry is based on rich mineral resources (copper, coal, lead, zinc, iron). The Kazakhs (57% of pop.) are a Turkic-speaking Moslem group of warlike ancestry. Area came under Russian rule in 19th cent.

Kazan (kûzän'), city (pop. c.500,000), cap. Tatar ASSR, E European RSFSR, near the Volga, where its port and shipyards are. A major industrial and commercial center, it has mfg. of locomotives, aircraft, agr. machinery, synthetic rubber, gunpowder, and textiles. There are various cultural institutions including a university (founded 1804). Founded 1401, Kazan was cap. of a powerful khanate, which was conquered 1552 by Ivan IV. In 18th cent. it became an E outpost of Russian colonization. Of the Moslem period of Kazan little remains except the Suyumbeka tower in the 16th-cent. kremlin.

Kazanlik (kä"zänlĭk'), town (pop. 19,386), central Bulgaria, in a valley famous for its rose fields. Long a mfg. center for attar of roses.

Kazbek, Mount (kŏzbĕk'), peak, 16,541 ft. high, N Georgian SSR, in central greater Caucasus, above DARYAL gorge. Its glaciers give rise to Terek R. First scaled 1868.

Kazvin or **Qazvin** (both: käzvēn'), city (pop. 60,013), NW Iran. Was cap. of Persia, 1514–90. A mosque of Harun-al-Rashid is here. Trades in silk, fruit, and rice. Carpet making.

Kea or **Keos,** Greek island of the CYCLADES.

Kealakekua Bay (kā'úläkäkōō'ú), W Hawaii, T.H., in Kona district. On shore is British monument to Capt. James Cook, killed here by natives in 1779.

Kean, Edmund, 1787?–1833, English actor. His triumph (1814) as Shylock is a landmark in theatrical history. Other great roles of his brief career include Iago, Lear, and Richard III. Kean's intensity and insight made him one of England's greatest actors. His son, **Charles John Kean,** 1811?–1868, was an actor whose forte was melodrama. Played opposite his wife, **Ellen Tree Kean,** 1808–80. Her first appearance (1829) estab. her as

a comedienne. Retired after her husband's death.

Keansburg, resort borough (pop. 5,559), E N.J., on Raritan Bay and ESE of Perth Amboy.

Kearney, Denis (kär'nē), 1847–1907, American political agitator, b. Ireland. In 1870s he inflamed Californians against Chinese labor. Formed a workingmen's party which achieved reform measures.

Kearney (kär'nē), city (pop. 12,115), S Nebr., on Platte R. and SW of Grand Island; founded 1871. Trade, processing, and rail center in Great Plains grain and livestock area. Site of Fort Kearney (1848–71), estab. to protect Oregon Trail, is near.

Kearny, Stephen Watts (kär'nē), 1794–1848, American general in Mexican War. Commanded Army of the West. Took Santa Fe and Los Angeles; served as military governor of California territory until May, 1847. His cousin, **Lawrence Kearny,** 1789–1868, was an American naval officer. Commanding East India squadron (1840–43), he opened negotiations which led to a U.S.–China commercial treaty, signed 1844. **Philip Kearny,** 1814–62, nephew of S. W. Kearny, was a Union general in Civil War. Led 1st N.J. Brigade in Peninsular campaign and second battle of Bull Run. Killed at Chantilly. Noted for courage and dash, idolized by his men.

Kearny (kär'nē), town (pop. 39,952), NE N.J., E of Newark on tidal wastelands (under reclamation) between Passaic and Hackensack rivers. Shipyards, drydocks; mfg. of linoleum, aluminum ware, chemicals, electrical products, and paint.

Kearsarge (kēr'särj"), Union ship in the Civil War. See CONFEDERATE CRUISERS.

Keats, John, 1795–1821, English lyric poet. Educated for surgery, he turned to poetry under influence of Charles Cowden Clarke. *Poems* (1817) included "Sleep and Poetry" and "I stood tip-toe upon a little hill." His long poem *Endymion* (1818) was cruelly attacked by critics. In that year he developed tuberculosis, and began his passionate, hopeless love for Fanny Brawne. His *Lamia, Isabella, The Eve of St. Agnes, and Other Poems* appeared in 1820. He sailed soon after to Italy in search of health with his friend Joseph Severn, but died in Rome. Despite a tragically brief life, Keats is one of greatest English poets. Among the poems that are masterpieces of romanticism are "Ode to a Nightingale," "Ode on a Grecian Urn," "To Autumn," "Ode to Melancholy," and the unfinished narrative "Hyperion." "The Eve of St. Agnes" and "La Belle Dame sans Merci" show romantic medievalism at its best. His most familiar sonnets are "On First Looking into Chapman's Homer," "When I have fears that I may cease to be," and "Bright star! would I were steadfast as thou art."

Keble, John (kē'bûl), 1792–1866, English clergyman and poet. His devotional poems in *The Christian Year* (1827), based on Book of Common Prayer, won him a professorship of poetry at Oxford. His sermon "National Apostasy," given in 1833, Newman called the beginning of OXFORD MOVEMENT. Wrote many hymns.

Keble College: see OXFORD UNIVERSITY.

Kebnekaise (kĕb′nŭkī″sû), glaciated peak, 6,965 ft. high, Norrbotten co., N Sweden; highest in Sweden.

Kecskemet, Hung. *Kecskemét* (kĕch′kĕmāt), city (pop. 87,269), central Hungary; center of fruit export.

Kedah (kĕ′dû), state (3,660 sq. mi.; pop. 554,-581), NW MALAYA, on Strait of Malacca; cap. Alor Star. Ruled by a sultan. Siam transferred sovereignty over Kedah to Great Britain in 1909.

Kedesh (kē′-), one of the cities of refuge, N Palestine. It is frequently mentioned in the Bible. Also Kedeshnaphtali.

Keeler, James Edward, 1857–1900, American astronomer. Discovered many nebulae and confirmed theory that Saturn's rings are composed of meteoric particles.

Keelung (kē′lōong′) or **Kilung,** Jap. *Kirun,* city (pop. 145,240), Formosa, China; also Chilung (jē′lōong′). Naval base on East China Sea. Shipbuilding, food processing. In 17th cent. occupied first by the Spaniards, later by the Dutch. Came under Chinese control in 1683; held by Japan 1895–1945.

Keene, Laura, c.1826–1873, Anglo-American actress and manager. Her most famous production was Taylor's *Our American Cousin,* given (Ford's Theater, Washington, 1865) when Lincoln was shot.

Keene, city (pop. 15,638), SW N.H., W of Manchester, in resort area; settled 1736. Mfg. of wood products, textiles, machinery, and shoes. Has railroad shops. A summer theater is here.

Keewatin (kēwä′tĭn), provisional district: see NORTHWEST TERRITORIES, Canada.

Keewatin: see ARCHEOZOIC ERA.

Kefauver, (Carey) Estes (kē′fävûr), 1903–, U.S. Senator from Tenn. (1949–). Headed Senate crime investigating committee.

Keighley (kēth′lē), municipal borough (pop. 56,938), West Riding of Yorkshire, England. Products include textiles, leather, and paper.

Keitel, Wilhelm (vĭl′hĕlm kī′tûl), 1882–1946, German field marshal. Chief of combined German general staff in World War II. Was hanged after Nuremberg war-crimes trial.

Keith, Sir Arthur (kēth), 1866–, British anthropologist and anatomist, authority on human evolution.

Keith, George, 1638–1716, Scottish preacher. At first a Friend, he estab. (1684) in America Christian Quakers, separatists denounced by William Penn 1692. Ordained priest (1700) in Church of England.

Keith, George, 1693?–1778, 10th earl marischal of Scotland. A leader in the Jacobite rebellion of 1715 and the Spanish expedition to Scotland (1719), he fled to the Continent. Held various high offices under Frederick the Great. His brother, **James Francis Edward Keith,** 1696–1758, also took part in the Jacobite rebellion and fled abroad. After service in Spain and Russia he was made (1747) a Prussian field marshal and rendered great service in the Seven Years War. Killed in the battle of Hochkrich.

Keith, George Keith Elphinstone, Viscount: see ELPHINSTONE, GEORGE KEITH.

Keith, James Francis Edward: see KEITH, GEORGE (1693?–1778).

Keith, Minor Cooper, 1848–1929, American

magnate, founder of United Fruit Co. Dominated banana trade, greatly altered economic life of Central America.

Kekulé von Stradonitz, Friedrich August (frē′-drĭkh ou′gŏost kā′kŏolā fŭn shträ′dōnĭts), 1829–96, German chemist. Worked in organic chemistry, especially on benzene, for molecular structure of which he developed ring theory.

Kelantan: see MALAYA.

Keller, Gottfried (gôt′frēt), 1819–90, Swiss novelist, one of the major German prose writers. Among his chief works are the autobiographical novel *Der grüne Heinrich* (1854–55) and a collection of short novels, *People of Seldwyla* (1856–74; Eng. tr., 1929).

Keller, Helen (Adams), 1880–, American author and lecturer, blind and deaf from the age of two, grad. Radcliffe 1904. Her teacher and companion was Anne Sullivan Macy. Helen Keller gained world fame for her aid to the handicapped.

Kellermann, François Christophe (fräswä′ krēstôf′ kĕlĕrmän′), 1735–1820, marshal of France; created duke of Valmy 1808. He and Dumouriez stopped Prussians at Valmy (1792).

Kelley, Hall Jackson, 1790–1874, American propagandist who urged settlement of Oregon.

Kelley, Oliver Hudson, 1826–1913, American agriculturist, a founder of the Natl. Grange of the Patrons of Husbandry, the central influence in the GRANGER MOVEMENT of the 1870s.

Kelley, William Darrah (dă′rû), 1814–90, U.S. Representative from Pa. (1861–90). Called "Pig Iron" Kelley for his protectionism and his allusions to iron industry of Pa. Humanitarian in his views.

Kellogg, Edward, 1790–1858, American economist. His scheme of government loans at low interest rates was backed by many radical political parties in U.S.

Kellogg, Frank B(illings), 1856–1937, American statesman. As U.S. Secretary of State (1925–29) he promoted KELLOGG-BRIAND PACT. Judge of Permanent Court of International. Justice (1930–35).

Kellogg, city (pop. 4,913), N Idaho, between Coeur d'Alene and Wallace. Grew around Bunker Hill and Sullivan mines (discovered 1885), now combined as one of world's largest lead producers. Sunshine Mine is a leading U.S. silver producer.

Kellogg-Briand Pact (–brēä′), agreement, signed Aug. 27, 1928, condemning war and agreeing to peaceful settlement of international differences. More properly known as the Pact of Paris. Primary moving forces were Aristide BRIAND of France and F. B. KELLOGG of U.S. Effectiveness of pact vitiated by its failure to provide for enforcement.

Kells, town, Co. Meath, Ireland. Has relic of an ancient monastery founded by St. Columba. Here was found the **Book of Kells,** beautifully illuminated manuscript of the Latin Gospels, written probably 8th cent. Now in Trinity Col. library in Dublin.

Kelly, George, 1887–, American dramatist. Wrote satirical comedies (e.g., *The Torch-*

bearers, 1922; *The Show-off,* 1924) and drama *Craig's Wife* (1925).

Kelly, Howard Atwood, 1858–1943, American surgeon, influential professor of gynecology and obstetrics at Johns Hopkins (1889–1919). He was also an authority on American medical history.

Kelly, James Edward, 1855–1933, American sculptor of war memorials and historical subjects.

Kelly, William, 1811–88, American inventor. He independently discovered basic principle of Bessemer process and estab. his priority right. Conflict between Bessemer and Kelly interests was settled by consolidation of the rival companies.

Kelowna (kĭlō'nŭ), city (pop. 8,517), S B.C., Canada, ENE of Vancouver. Center of agr. area.

kelp, name for various species of brown algae, or seaweeds, found in waters along Atlantic and Pacific coasts. Some, e.g., *Macrocystis,* have fronds up to 200 ft. long; others are small. They are a source of potassium and iodine.

Kelso, lumber city (pop. 7,345), SW Wash., near Columbia R. and adjoining Longview. Timber, fish, fruit, and dairy industries.

Kelt: see CELT.

Kelvin, William Thomson, 1st Baron, 1824–1907, British mathematician and physicist. Inventor of many improvements in transmission of messages by submarine cables, of the reflecting galvanometer, and a siphon recorder for telegraphic messages; he also contributed to thermodynamics. He coordinated the various theories of heat, established on a firm basis Joule's law of conservation of energy, and introduced the Kelvin or absolute scale of TEMPERATURE.

Kemal Pasha, Mustafa: see ATATURK, KEMAL.

Kemble, Roger, 1721–1802, English actor and manager. Father of 12 children, he founded one of England's most distinguished acting families. His eldest son, **John Philip Kemble,** 1757–1823, was educated for the priesthood, but turned to the stage. Managed Drury Lane 1783–1802 (gaining fame in Shaksperian roles opposite his sister, Sarah Kemble SIDDONS) and Covent Garden, 1803–8. His brother, **George Stephen Kemble,** 1758–1822, played at Covent Garden and Haymarket. Managed Edinburgh Theater, 1792–1800. His youngest brother, **Charles Kemble,** 1757–1854, excelled in comic roles. Toured U.S. (1832–34) with his elder daughter, **Fanny Kemble** (Frances Ann Kemble), 1809–93. Her debut (1829) at Covent Garden as Juliet brought her fame, which she increased in such roles as Lady Macbeth, Portia, and Beatrice. In England she wrote against slavery during U.S. Civil War. Her sister, **Adelaide Kemble,** 1814–79, was a singer, notable in Italian operatic roles.

Kemerovo (kĕ'mŭrō''vō), city (pop. 132,978), RSFSR, in S central Siberia, on Tom R. and on a branch of Trans-Siberian RR. Coalmining center of Kuznetsk Basin, with chemical industries.

Kemi (kĕ'mē), city (pop. 23,959), NW Finland, on Gulf of Bothnia and at mouth of Kemi R. Lumber and cellulose industry.

Kemp, Will(iam), fl. 1579–1600, English comic actor and dancer, known as a player in Shakspere's company and for his morris dance from London to Norwich (1599).

Kempe, Margery (kĕmp), d. 1438 or after, English religious enthusiast. Her autobiography, perhaps the earliest in English, was known only in part until 1934.

Kempener, Pieter de (kĕm'pŭnŭr), c.1503–1580, Flemish religious painter. Worked in Italy and Spain.

Kempis, Thomas à: see THOMAS À KEMPIS.

Ken, Thomas, 1637–1711, English prelate and hymn writer. Bishop of Bath and Wells, he was deprived of his see in 1691 for refusing oath of allegiance to William III. His best-known hymn is the doxology, *Praise God from Whom All Blessings Flow.*

Kenai Peninsula (kē'nī), S Alaska, jutting into Gulf of Alaska, between Prince William Sound and Cook Inlet. Kenai Mts. cross it from NE to SW. Coastal climate mild, with abundant rainfall; growing season adequate for many crops. Forest, mineral, fishing resources; good farmland in W section. Alaska RR crosses peninsula from Seward. Kenai Natl. Moose Range (1941) is in N.

Kendal, Dame Madge, 1849–1935, English actress, whose maiden name was Margaret Robertson. Made her debut as Ophelia in 1865. Co-starred often with her husband, William Kendal (1843–1917), e.g., in Shakspere's *As You Like It* and in Sheridan's *Rivals.*

Kendall, Amos (kĕn'dŭl), 1789–1869, American journalist and statesman. Leading member of Pres. Jackson's KITCHEN CABINET; defended Jackson's policies in Washington *Globe.* U.S. Postmaster General (1835–40); thoroughly reorganized department.

Kendall, Edward Calvin, 1886–, American biochemist. Shared 1950 Nobel Prize in Physiology and Medicine for work on hormones of the cortex of adrenal glands. Other contributions include isolation of thyroxin, preparation (with others) of cortisone by partial synthesis, and investigations (with coworkers) of effects of cortisone and ACTH (adrenocorticotropic hormone from the pituitary gland) on rheumatoid arthritis and rheumatic fever. Associated with Mayo Clinic from 1914 and with Mayo Foundation (of Univ. of Minnesota) from 1921.

Kendall, George Wilkins, 1809–67, American journalist. Cofounder of New Orleans *Picayune* (1837). His articles during Mexican War made him first modern war correspondent.

Kendall, William Sergeant, 1869–1938, American painter, best known for portraits of children.

Kendallville, city (pop. 6,119), NE Ind., NNW of Fort Wayne. Ships onions. Mfg. of metal products. Mulholland Mus. has Indian and pioneer relics.

Kenilworth (kĕn'ŭl–), urban district (pop. 10,-738), Warwickshire, England. Has ruins of noted castle celebrated in Scott's *Kenilworth.* Built c.1120, it was later the property of Simon de Montfort and of John of Gaunt. Earl of Leicester entertained Queen Elizabeth here lavishly in 1575.

Kenilworth ivy: see IVY.

Kenites, wilderness tribe, friendly to the Hebrews, with whom they came into Palestine.

Kenmore, residential village (pop. 20,066), W N.Y., near Buffalo; settled 1889. Mfg. of chemicals, machinery, and wood, metal, and rubber products.

Kennan, George, 1845–1924, American authority on Siberia. Explored Siberia and other parts of Russia. His articles were for many years only reliable source of information on the area. His grandnephew, **George F(rost) Kennan,** 1904–, became a diplomat. Originated (1947) U.S. policy of "containment" of Russia. He was made ambassador to USSR (1952), but his recall was demanded by Russian government. Retired 1953.

Kennebec (kĕn'ūbĕk), river, c.150 mi. long, flowing S from Moosehead L., NW Maine, to the Atlantic, receiving Dead and Androscoggin rivers. Furnishes power at Skowhegan, Waterville, and Augusta. Champlain explored it, 1604 and 1605.

Kennebunk (kĕ'nĭbŭngk), town (pop. 4,273), SW Maine, SW of Portland, in resort area; settled c.1650. Has Revolutionary church, with Paul Revere bell (1803).

Kennebunkport or **Kennebunk Port** (both: kĕn''ĭbŭngkpôrt'), town (pop. 1,522), SW Maine, on coast SE of Kennebunk; renamed from Arundel, 1821. Summer resort, especially for authors, artists, and actors.

Kennedy, John Pendleton, 1795–1870, American novelist, author of *Horse-Shoe Robinson* (1835). Was a member of Congress (1838–44) and Secretary of the Navy (1852–53).

Kennelly, Arthur Edwin (kĕ'nŭlē), 1861–1939, American electrical engineer, b. India. His theory (advanced 1902, independently of Oliver Heaviside) that layer of ionized air in upper atmosphere deflects electromagnetic waves toward earth was later verified; the deflecting layer is called Heaviside layer, Kennelly-Heaviside layer, and ionosphere.

Kenner, farm trade and industrial town (pop. 5,535), SE La., near New Orleans.

Kennesaw Mountain (kĕn'ŭsô): see NATIONAL PARKS AND MONUMENTS (table).

Kenneth I (Kenneth mac Alpin), d. 858, traditional founder of the kingdom of Scotland.

Kennett (kĕn'ĭt), city (pop. 8,685), SE Mo., near St. Francis R. and Ark. line, in cotton area. Has cotton gins and compresses.

Kennewick, city (pop. 10,106), SE Wash., on Columbia R. opposite Pasco, near influx of Snake R. Fruit and dairy products and wheat. Boomed in World War II by atomic-energy plant near Richland (NW).

Kenny, Elizabeth, 1886–1952, Australian nurse, originator of a system of treating infantile paralysis patients. Her method was based on use of hot, moist applications and passive exercise.

Kénogami (kānŏ'gùmē), town (pop. 9,895), S Que., Canada, on Sable R. and W of Chicoutimi. Here are hydroelectric station, paper and pulp mills.

Kenora (kùnô'rù), town (pop. 8,695), W Ont., Canada, at N end of L. of the Woods. Fishing, hunting, and canoeing base. Here are paper, pulp, lumber, and flour mills, boat-building, and fur trading.

Kenosha (kĭnō'shù), industrial city (pop. 54,-368), SE Wis., on L. Michigan and S of Milwaukee; settled 1835. Mfg. of autos, mat-

tresses, and metal products. Liberal German refugees came in 1850s.

Kensett, John Frederick, 1818–72, American landscape painter of Hudson River school.

Kensico Reservoir, N.Y.: see CATSKILL AQUE-DUCT.

Kensington, metropolitan borough (pop. 168,-054), W London, England; largely a residential district. Kensington Gardens, adjoining Hyde Park, includes Long Water (the Serpentine of Hyde Park), Round Pond, and Flower and Broad Walks. Kensington Palace former royal residence, is W of gardens. South Kensington is site of part of British Mus., Victoria and Albert Mus., Imperial Inst., Science Mus., Royal Col. of Art, Royal Col. of Science, and Albert Hall.

Kensington Rune Stone, found near Kensington, Minn., in 1898. Contains account of Norse exploration party. Authenticity of stone much disputed.

Kent, James, 1763–1847, American jurist, first professor of law at Columbia College. Chancellor Kent had great influence on law in New York and U.S., principally through his *Commentaries on the American Law* (1826–30).

Kent, Rockwell, 1882–, American painter, wood engraver, and lithographer.

Kent, maritime county (1,525 sq. mi.; pop. 1,-563,286), SE England; co. town Maidstone. North Downs cross county E to W. Largely agr. and pastoral, the region has growing industry as London urban area encroaches in W. Strategic location on path to the Continent has always made Kent important. Many religious houses were estab. in Middle Ages; Canterbury was goal of many pilgrimages (Chaucer's *Canterbury Tales*). Coast was heavily fortified in World Wars I and II against possible invasion.

Kent. 1 Resort town (pop. 1,392), W Conn., on Housatonic R. in hills at N.Y. line. Has Kent School for boys (prep.; Episcopal; 1906). **2** City (pop. 12,418), NE Ohio, NE of Akron. Mfg. of motor vehicles and electrical apparatus. Seat of Kent State Univ.

Kent, kingdom of, one of the states of the Anglo-Saxon heptarchy in England. Settled in mid-5th cent. by the Jutes, perhaps under Hengist and Horsa. St. Augustine of Canterbury led first Catholic mission to England here in 597. Became a province of Mercia, then of Wessex. Was one of the most advanced areas in pre-Conquest England.

Kent, Maid of: see BARTON, ELIZABETH.

Kenton, Simon, 1755–1836, American frontiersman. Joined Daniel Boone in settlement at Boonesboro. Took part in expeditions of G. R. Clark. Participated in many Indian raids.

Kenton, city (pop. 8,475), W central Ohio, on Scioto R. and NW of Marion. Mfg. of candy, machinery, and tools. Has limestone quarries.

Kentucky, state (40,395 sq. mi.; pop. 2,944,-806); admitted 1792 as 15th state (slave-holding); cap. FRANKFORT. Other cities are LOUISVILLE, COVINGTON, LEXINGTON. Hilly in E and W (coal areas); gently rolling in center, with bluegrass region in N and Pennyroyal plateau in S. Bordered N by Ohio R., SW by the Mississippi, E by Big Sandy R. and the Tug Fork. Chief rivers are the TEN-

NESSEE, CUMBERLAND, LICKING, KENTUCKY. Processes whisky (esp. bourbon), tobacco, meat, food; farms tobacco, corn, hay, rye, soybeans, potatoes. Mines coal, oil, natural gas, fluorspar. Horse breeding and training are important. First permanent settlement, HARRODSBURG, founded 1774. Daniel BOONE founded BOONESBORO 1775. Early settlers menaced by Indian raids. Resolutions (see KENTUCKY AND VIRGINIA RESOLUTIONS) passed in objection to Alien and Sedition Acts (1798). Remained in Union during Civil War but supplied men to both sides. Industrial development came after war, but farmers met hard times. Marked by turbulent political and economic life (feud between tobacco growers and buyers; industrial strife in mines in 1930s). Agr. has progressed from one-crop (tobacco) system. Internal improvements and extension of education effected in 20th cent.

Kentucky, river formed in central Ky., and flowing 259 mi. NW to the Ohio at Carrollton.

Kentucky, University of, mainly at Lexington; land-grant, state supported, coed.; opened 1865 as part of Kentucky Univ. (now Transylvania College), became state college 1878, and university 1908. College of pharmacy is at Louisville.

Kentucky and Virginia Resolutions, passed 1798 and 1799 in opposition to ALIEN AND SEDITION ACTS. Kentucky Resolutions, written by Thomas Jefferson, with advice of John Breckinridge, stated that Federal government had no right to exercise powers not specifically delegated to it by the Constitution. If it did assume such powers, states had right to judge constitutionality of acts. Virginia Resolutions, written by James Madison, were somewhat milder. Resolutions were later considered first notable statement of STATES' RIGHTS theory.

Kentucky State College for Negroes: see FRANKFORT.

Kentucky University: see KENTUCKY, UNIVERSITY OF; LEXINGTON, Ky.

Kenya (kĕn'yù), British colony and protectorate (224,960 sq. mi.; pop. 5,377,393), E Africa, on Indian Ocean; cap. Nairobi. Lies across equator. Protectorate (within colony) is coastal strip, leased from sultan of Zanzibar. Arid in N, but more fertile in S, where wheat, peanuts, coffee, tea, sisal, and cotton are grown. Coastal area was settled in 7th cent. by Arab and Persian traders in slaves and ivory. Under Portuguese control, 16th–17th cent. The British expanded their influence in mid-19th cent. through British East Africa Co. and made Kenya a protectorate in 1895. In 1920 the leased coastal strip was named Kenya Protectorate, while rest of region became crown colony. Ruled by an appointed governor with advice and consent of legislative council, composed mainly of white representatives. In late 1952 the British began taking measures to suppress the terroristic Mau Mau secret society, which aimed to oust the whites from Kenya.

Kenyon College: see GAMBIER, Ohio.

Keokuk (kē'ùkŭk), c.1780–1848, American Indian, chief of Sac and Fox tribes. Refused to aid British in War of 1812. Keokuk, Iowa, named for him.

Keokuk, city (pop. 16,144), SE Iowa, on the Mississippi at foot of Des Moines R. rapids; platted 1837 on 1829 trading post site. U.S. ship canal (1877) around rapids superseded 1913 by Keokuk Dam (power; impounds L. Keokuk). U.S. dry docks and locks here are among largest ever built. Center of farm area with mfg. of food, metal, and wood products. Has Natl. Cemetery. Mark Twain worked here.

Keos or **Kea,** Greek island of the CYCLADES.

Kepler, Johannes (yōhä'nùs kĕplŭr), 1571–1630, German astronomer, evolver of laws of planetary motion. **Kepler's laws,** summarized, are: (1) Orbit of each planet is an ellipse, of which sun's center is one of the foci; (2) Radius vector of each planet (line joining its center with that of sun) moves over equal areas in equal times; (3) Square of period of each planet's revolution around sun is proportional to cube of its mean distance from sun.

Keppler, Joseph, 1838–94, American cartoonist and founder of *Puck,* b. Vienna.

Kerak, El, Jordan: see KRAK.

Kerbela (kûr'bùlù) or **Karbala** (kär–), city (pop. 122,719), central Iraq, at edge of Syrian Desert. Here is tomb of HUSEIN, a great shrine of pilgrims of Moslem Shiite sect.

Kerch (kyĕrch), city (pop. 104,471), S European RSFSR, in E Crimea; a fortified Black Sea port on Kerch Peninsula. Has iron and steel mills, coking plant, shipyards, fisheries, and canneries. Founded by Greek colonists in 6th cent. B.C., it became a Genoese colony in 13th cent. Conquered by Crimean Tatars in 1475, by Russians in 1771. German-held in World War II. A museum contains Greco-Scythian antiquities. Church of St. John the Baptist dates from 8th cent. Kerch is on **Kerch Strait,** shallow channel, 25 mi. long, connecting Sea of Azov (N) and Black Sea and separating the Crimea (N) from Taman peninsula. Known to ancients as Cimmerian Bosporus.

Kerensky, Aleksandr Feodorovich (kûrĕn'skē, Rus. ŭlyīksän'dùr fyô'dùrŭvĭch kâ'rīnskē), 1881–, Russian revolutionist. A moderate Socialist, he succeeded Prince Lvov as provisional premier in July, 1917. His vacillation enabled Lenin to overthrow his government in November (see RUSSIAN REVOLUTION). Settled in U.S. (1940).

Kerguelen (kûr'gùlĕn), subantarctic island of volcanic origin, in S Indian Ocean, belonging to the French since 1893.

Kerman (kĕrmän'), anc. *Carmana,* city (pop. 50,048), SE Iran. A walled city with citadel and 11th-cent. mosque. Ravaged in 1794 by Aga Mohamad Khan. Noted for fine rugs.

Kermanshah (kĕrmän"shä'), city (pop. 88,-622), W Iran. Dating from 4th cent. it was royal summer residence of Medes and Sassanians. Trade center in grain-producing area. Oil refinery.

kermes (kûr'mēz), natural red dye from bodies of females of scale insects parasitic on oak trees.

Kermit, town (pop. 6,912), W Texas, S of N.

Mex. line and N of Pecos R. Oil and cattle center near carbon-black plants.

Kern, Jerome, 1885–1945, American composer of musical comedies. He wrote *Sally* (1920), containing the song *Look for the Silver Lining; Sunny* (1925); *Roberta* (1933), containing *Smoke Gets in Your Eyes;* and, perhaps his greatest work, *Show Boat* (1929), containing *Ol' Man River.*

Kern, river rising in the S Sierra Nevada, E Calif., and flowing 155 mi. S and SW past Bakersfield to a reservoir in what was Buena Vista L. Irrigates S San Joaquin Valley with the aid of Friant-Kern Canal (see CENTRAL VALLEY). Upper gorge (in Sequoia Natl. Park) is spectacular canyon.

kerosene, colorless, oily mixture of hydrocarbons, obtained from fractional distillation of PETROLEUM. It is also prepared from coal, oil shale, wood. It is used as fuel, illuminant, insecticide.

Kerrville, city (pop. 7,691), S central Texas, on Guadalupe R. and NW of San Antonio. Resort town shipping wool, mohair, dairy products, and poultry.

Kerry, maritime county (1,815 sq. mi.; pop. 133,893), W Ireland, in Munster; co. town Tralee. Consists of mountainous peninsulas extending into the Atlantic. Carrantuohill (3,414 ft.) is highest point in Ireland. Lakes of Killarney attract tourists. Farming, dairying, and fishing chief occupations.

Kesselring, Albert (äl'bĕrt kĕ'sŭlrĭng), 1887–, German field marshal in World War II. Commanded in Italy 1943–45. Was sentenced to life imprisonment after war-crimes trial (1946–47).

Kesteven, Parts of: see LINCOLNSHIRE, England.

Keswick (kĕs'ĭk), urban district (pop. 4,868), Cumberland, England, in Lake District. Southey and Coleridge lived here, and Southey's tomb is here. Has ancient Druids' Circle near by. **Keswick Convention** is interdenominational religious gathering held annually since 1875.

Ketchikan (kĕ'chĭkän"), town (pop. 5,305), on Revillagigedo Isl., in Alexander Archipelago, SE Alaska. Supply point for miners in 1890s gold rush; now salmon industry center. With good port on Inside Passage, it is distribution center for lumbering, furfarming, and mining area. Has U.S. coast guard and lighthouse service stations.

kettledrum: see PERCUSSION INSTRUMENTS.

Keuka College: see PENN YAN, N.Y.

Keuka Lake: see FINGER LAKES.

Kewanee (kĭwä'nē), city (pop. 16,821), NW Ill., SE of Rock Island, in coal and farm area. Mfg. of metal products; oil refining.

Keweenaw (kē'wĭnô), peninsula, extreme N Mich., jutting NE from W Upper Peninsula into L. Superior. Portage L. and ship canal cut across it, making upper portion an island and creating important waterway. Known for copper and as resort. Towns include Houghton, Hancock, and Calumet.

Kew Gardens (kū), Surrey, England, on the Thames, W of London. Royal Botanic Gardens is official name. They cover 288 acres and contain thousands of species of plants, four museums, and laboratories and hothouses. Rare plants destroyed in 1940 bomb-

ing. Near by is Kew Palace, once home of George III.

Key, Ellen (kā), 1849–1926, Swedish author and feminist; advocate of education for motherhood.

Key, Francis Scott (kē), 1779–1843, American poet, author of STAR-SPANGLED BANNER. Was U.S. attorney for the District of Columbia (1833–41).

Keyes, Sir Roger John Brownlow (kēz), 1872–1945, British admiral. In World War I he commanded the Dover patrol that raided Zeebrugge and Ostend. In World War II he was director of combined operations (1940–41) and organizer of the commando forces.

Key Largo: see FLORIDA KEYS.

Keynes, John Maynard, 1st baron of Tilton (kānz), 1883–1946, English economist and monetary expert, studied at Cambridge. Until 1929 a classical economist believing in free economy, Keynes came to support both government large-scale economic planning and spending to promote employment. He profoundly influenced economic policy in democratic nations. Wrote *Economic Consequences of the Peace* (1919), *The General Theory of Employment, Interest, and Money* (1936).

Keyport, borough (pop. 5,888), E N.J.; resort and fishing center on Raritan Bay SE of South Amboy.

Keyser, Cassius Jackson (kī'zùr), 1862–1947, American mathematician, author of works in mathematics, logic, and mathematical philosophy.

Keyser, Thomas de (kī'zùr), c.1596–1667, Dutch portrait and figure painter.

Keyser (kī'zùr), city (pop. 6,347), in E Panhandle of W.Va., on North Branch of Potomac R. and SW of Cumberland, Md. Lumber mills and railroad shops. Important supply base in Civil War.

Keyserling, Hermann, Count (kī'sùrlĭng), 1880–1946, German philosopher and man of letters, b. Estonia. Traveled widely and was influenced by Oriental mysticism. His most popular work was *The Travel Diary of a Philosopher* (1925).

Key West, city (pop. 26,433), occupying Key West island, westernmost of FLORIDA KEYS, S. Fla. Southernmost city of U.S. Granted to Juan Pablo Salas in 1815, it was sold to an American, 1822. Formerly a ship-salvage point and next a cigar-mfg. center. Now a resort and sponge-fishing center. Here are U.S. naval station, naval air station, and coast guard base (Fort Taylor, built 1844–46). Terminus of highway spanning the keys from the mainland. Has lighthouse (1846) and two Civil War forts.

Khabarovsk (khŭbùrôfsk'), city (pop. c.300,-000), RSFSR, in E Siberia, on Amur R. and on Trans-Siberian RR. Has oil refinery and auto, aircraft, and agr. machinery plants. It is cap. of Khabarovsk **Territory,** administrative division (965,400 sq. mi.; pop. c.1,250,-000), a part of former FAR EASTERN TERRITORY. Extends from Okhotsk and Bering seas to Arctic Ocean; separated (SW) from Manchuria by Amur R. It includes KAMCHATKA peninsula and CHUKCHI PENINSULA. Stanovoi, Kolyma, and Anadyr ranges traverse it SW–NE. Rich in gold, iron, coal, petroleum, and nonferrous metals. In N there is reindeer raising, seal hunting, and fur trapping.

Khachaturian, Aram (Ilich) ŭräm′ khä″chŭto͞oryän′), 1904?–, Russian composer, of Armenian parentage. His music contains many themes from Russian folk music. Among his works are a piano concerto, a violin concerto, and the ballets *Gayne* and *Masquerade.*

Khafre (khä′frä), or **Chephren** (kĕf′rĕn), fl. 2869? B.C., king of IV dynasty of Egypt, builder of the second pyramid at Gizeh.

Khania, Crete: see CANEA.

Kharga (khär′gŭ), large oasis (pop. 11,155), S central Egypt; accessible by railroad. Produces dates, cotton, grain. Ruins of ancient temples.

Kharkov (kär′kŏf), city (pop. 833,432), SE Ukraine. Major industrial and engineering center at junction of six railroad lines, with mfg. of machinery, electrical goods, locomotives, precision instruments, and machine tools. Seat of a university (founded 1804). Founded by Cossacks in early 17th cent., it grew rapidly after industrialization of S Ukraine in late 19th cent. Thoroughly modernized and a showpiece of Soviet accomplishment, it was more than half destroyed in World War II.

Khartoum (kärto͞om′), city (pop. 71,400), cap. of Anglo-Egyptian Sudan, on the Blue Nile. Founded in 1820s by Mohammed Ali. Razed 1885 by Mahdists, who besieged and killed Gen. Charles GORDON. Recovered 1898 by Lord Kitchener. Mainly a commercial and educational center.

Khayyam, Omar: see OMAR KHAYYAM.

Khazars (käzärz′), anc. Turkic people partly nomadic, who appeared in Transcaucasia in 2d cent. A.D. and subsequently settled in S Russia between the Volga and the Don (cap. at Itil). In 7th cent. they conquered the Crimea and levied tribute from E Slavs. They embraced Judaism c.740, but kept complete religious tolerance. Khazar empire fell when Sviatoslav, duke of Kiev, defeated its army, 969. Some say Khazars were ancestors of many Russian Jews. Also spelled Chazars.

Kherson (khĕrsôn′), city (pop. 97,186), SW Ukraine, on the Dnieper, 15 mi. above its mouth on Black Sea. Founded 1778 by Potemkin as port and shipbuilding center. Population was 25% Jewish until World War II, when city was German-held, 1941–43.

Khingan, Great (khĭng-gän′), mountain range, W Manchuria; rises to 5,670 ft. Its offshoot, the **Lesser Khingan,** forms watershed between Amur and Sungari rivers; rises to 4,665 ft.

Khios, Greek island: see CHIOS.

Khiva (kē′vŭ), city (1932 pop. c.23,700), Uzbek SSR, near Kara-Kum desert. Carpet mfg. Its medieval Moslem splendor is preserved. In late 16th cent. it became cap. of **khanate of Khiva,** the successor of KHOREZM Empire, S of Aral Sea and of Amu Darya R. Independent until 1873 when it became Russian protectorate. In 1920 it was fully annexed to USSR.

Khmelnitsky, Bohdan: see CHMIELNICKI, BOHDAN.

Khmer Empire (kŭmâr′), Indo-Chinese kingdom (6th-15th cent.) roughly corresponding to modern Laos and Cambodia. Declined after series of wars with the Annamese, Chams, and Siamese. Khmer civilization was largely formed by Hindu influences. Its great achievement in architecture and sculpture is revealed by ruins at ANGKOR THOM.

Khokand, Uzbek SSR: see KOKAND.

Khorezm (khŭrĕ′zŭm), medieval empire, the predecessor of khanate of KHIVA, central Asia, contained by Caspian and Aral seas, Amu Darya R., and Persia; cap. URGENCH. Converted to Islam by Arab conquerors in 18th cent. Under Seljuk Turks it subdued Bukhara, Samarkand, and most of Persia, 12th–13th cent. Conquered by Jenghiz Khan, 1218–24.

Khorramshahr, Iran: see KHURRAMSHAHR.

Khorsabad (khôrsäbäd′), village, NE Iraq, near Tigris R. Built on site of Assyrian city, founded 8th cent. B.C. by Sargon. Its mounds were excavated by P. E. Botta in 1842 and 1851. Cuneiform tablets in Elamite language were discovered in 1932.

Khosru (khôsro͞o′), Sassanid kings of Persia. **Khosru I** (Noshirwan), d. 579, reigned 531–79. Extended rule over Bactria, Arabia, and parts of Armenia and Caucasia. Fought the Byzantine emperors. His grandson, **Khosru II** (Parvis), d. 628, was aided by Emperor Maurice in ousting usurper Bahram. Avenged murder of Maurice by taking Byzantine territory until defeated by Heraclius. Name also appears as Chosroes.

Khotin (khŭtyēn′), city (pop. 7,579), W Ukraine, on Dniester R. Agr. market center. It was a leading town of Moldavia in 17th–18th cent. From 1812 it shared history of BESSARABIA. Also spelled Hotin.

Khufu (kho͞o′fo͞o) or **Cheops** (kē′ŏps), fl. 2900? B.C., king of anc. Egypt, founder of the IV dynasty; builder of greatest pyramid at Gizeh.

Khurramshahr or **Khorramshahr** (khôram″shä′hŭr), town (pop. 20,000), SW Iran, on Shatt el Arab, 10 mi. NW of Abadan; chief overseas trade port of Iran. Handled lend lease to USSR in World War II.

Khyber Pass (kī′bŭr), on border of W Pakistan and Afghanistan; c.28 mi. long and rising to c.3,500 ft. Trade route between Kabul and Peshawar, it has road and railway. One of main routes in ancient times for invasion of India. Was vitally important to the British in 19th-cent. Afghan Wars.

Kiangsi (kyäng′sē), province (65,000 sq. mi.; pop. 14,000,000), SE China; cap. Nanchang. Wide Kan R. valley, bordered by hills, extends N to Poyang L. Major producer of rice, tungsten. Coal mining, lumbering, porcelain mfg. Communists estab. control here after 1927 split with Kuomintang.

Kiangsu (kyäng′so͞o′), province (35,000 sq. mi.; pop. 40,000,000), E China, on Yellow Sea. Since 1949 divided into North Kiangsu (cap. Yangchow) and South Kiangsu (cap. Wusih). Consists of alluvial plain and much of delta of Yangtze R. Many large lakes linked by Grand Canal. Major crops are cotton, grain, soybeans, and rice. Industry limited largely to textile mfg. in urban centers (esp. Shanghai, Soochow, and Wusih).

Held 1937–45 by the Japanese; fell to Chinese Communists 1949.

Kiangtu, China: see YANGCHOW.

Kiaochow (kyou'chou'), former German territory, area c.400 sq. mi., S Shantung prov., China; cap. Tsingtao. Leased by Germany 1898, held 1914–22 by Japan.

Kickapoo Indians, Indian tribe of Algonquian linguistic stock, in SW Wis. in late 17th cent. Were of Eastern Woodlands culture, but also hunted buffalo. Joined in war against Illinois Indians (c.1769); fought against the Americans in the Revolution and the War of 1812, and supported the Sac and Fox in the Black Hawk War. Some went to Mexico (c.1852) but were later induced to return to present Okla.

Kicking Horse, river of SE B.C., Canada, rising on W slopes of the Rockies and flowing SW and NW to the Columbia. **Kicking Horse Pass,** 5,339 ft. high, NW of L. Louise, is highest point of Canadian Pacific route. Connects Bow and Kicking Horse rivers.

Kid, Thomas: see KYD, THOMAS.

Kidd, William, c.1645–1701, British privateer. Commissioned as a privateer (1696), he was arrested (1699) on charges of piracy. Hanged after a probably unfair trial. Has become semilegendary as cruel Captain Kidd with huge hidden treasure.

Kidderminster, municipal borough (pop. 37,-423), Worcestershire, England. Kidderminster carpets have been made here since 1735.

Kiddush (kǐ'dǔsh) [Heb.,= sanctification], a prayer of benediction said at the beginning (and sometimes the end) of the Sabbath and other Hebrew festivals.

kidnaping, the unlawful and willful taking away of a person by force, threat or deceit with intent to cause him to be detained against his will. The object is usually ransom, and the victim is usually a child—though neither condition need be true. Kidnaping differs from abduction (which requires intent of sexual intercourse) and from false imprisonment which does not involve "taking away." Strong public sentiment over such cases as the kidnaping of the Lindbergh child (1932) led to very severe Federal and state legislation.

kidneys, in the human body two reddish, bean-shaped organs c.4 in. long, lying below ribs near spine. Urine is secreted in outer zone, collects in tubules of inner part, and passes through ureter to bladder.

Kidron (kǐd'-) or **Cedron** (sē'-), deep valley between Jerusalem and Mount of Olives.

Kiel (kēl), city (pop. 253,857), cap. of Schleswig-Holstein, N Germany. A major Baltic seaport, it was the chief German naval station until 1945, when its installations were dismantled. Kiel was chartered 1242, was the seat of the dukes of Holstein, and with Holstein passed to Prussia in 1866. Its university was founded 1665. A sailors' mutiny at Kiel touched off the German revolution of 1918. Kiel is connected with the North Sea by the **Kiel Canal** (also known as Kaiser Wilhelm Canal), an artificial waterway 61 mi. long, opened 1895. Its E terminus is on the Elbe estuary opposite Cuxhaven.

Kielce (kyĕl'tsĕ), city (pop. 49,960), S Poland.

Trade center; metal- and woodworking industries.

Kielland, Alexander Lange (khĕ'län), 1849–1906, Norwegian author of novels dealing with social reform (e.g., *Skipper Worse,* 1882).

Kierkegaard, Soren, Dan. *Søren* (sû'rûn kyĕr'-kŭgôr), 1813–55, Danish philosopher, writer on religion, a minister whose unorthodox teaching plunged him in trouble with the national church. He believed that man must find truth within himself and that the religious person suffers greatly because of the opposition of temporal existence and eternal truth. Religion for him is intensely personal and mystical. His ideas influenced later existentialism, and his books (among them *Either/Or,* 1843; *Stages on Life's Way,* 1845) have been read all over the world. His aesthetic teachings have influenced several literatures.

Kiev (kēĕf'), city (pop. 846,293), cap. of Ukrainai SSR, on Dnieper R. One of largest cities of USSR, it is a leading industrial (machinery, rolling stock, radio equipment, textiles), cultural, and commercial center; see of a metropolitan of Russian Orthodox Church. Its university was estab. here 1833. A Slavic settlement on trade route between Scandinavia and Constantinople, it passed from Khazars to Varangians under Oleg in 882. It was cap. of medieval RUSSIA, but declined and became tributary to Mongols in 1240. Passed in 14th cent. to Lithuania, which was united with Poland in 1569. In 1654 Cossacks voted union of UKRAINE with Russia. Kiev changed hands several times in Russian civil war (1917–20), and was devastated in World War II by Germans, who also decimated the inhabitants. Cathedral of St. Sophia and Lavra monastery (formerly a pilgrim's shrine), both dating from 11th cent., indicate Kiev's close link with Byzantium and its role as cradle of Christianity in Russia.

Kilauea (kē'läwā'ū), crater, 4,000 ft. high, on Hawaii, T.H., on SE slope of MAUNA LOA; one of world's largest active craters. Has circumference of c.8 mi.; surrounded by rocky wall 200–500 ft. high. In its floor is fiery pit called Halemaumau.

Kildare (kǐldâr'), inland county (654 sq. mi.; pop. 64,849), S Ireland, in Leinster; co. town Kildare. Flat agr. region, it has the Bog of Allen and the fertile plain of Curragh. History associated with St. Bridget and legendary Finn mac Cumhail.

Kilgore, city (pop. 9,638), E Texas, E of Tyler. Enriched by 1930 discovery of East Texas oil field, it has many wells even amongst houses.

Kilimanjaro (kǐ''lǐmùnjä'rō), mountain, NE Tanganyika; highest in Africa. Extinct volcanic cone. Its two main peaks are Mt. Kibo (19,565 ft.) and Mt. Mawenzi (17,300 ft.)

Kilkenny (kǐlkĕ'nē), inland county (796 sq. mi.; pop. 66,712), SE Ireland, in Leinster. Flat agr. region, it has a coal field around Castlecomer. Area is roughly same as ancient kingdom of Ossory. The county town is **Kilkenny,** urban district (pop. 10,291), on Nore R. Strife between two sections (Englishtown and Irishtown) may account for stories of

Kilkenny cats, who ate each other up. Swift, Berkeley, and Congreve went to school here. Has 12th-cent. castle and two cathedrals.

Killarney, urban district (pop. 5,947), Co. Kerry, Ireland. Tourist center for three Lakes of Killarney. Lough Leane has Ross Isl. and "sweet Innisfallen" of Thomas Moore's poem.

killdeer, a North American upland PLOVER.

Kill Devil Hill National Memorial: see KITTY HAWK, N.C.

Killeen (kĭlēn'), city (pop. 7,045), central Texas, SW of Waco. Farm market near Camp Hood.

Killiecrankie, Pass of (kĭlĭkrăng'kē), Perthshire, Scotland, through which flows Garry R. Battle of Killiecrankie (1689) was fought at N end of pass.

Killigrew, Thomas, 1612–83, English dramatist, a theater manager in the time of Charles II.

Killingly, town (pop. 10,015), NE Conn., NE of Willimantic at R.I. line; settled c.1700. Includes Danielson borough (pop. 4,554; textiles, metal goods).

Kill Van Kull: see NEW YORK BAY.

Kilmainham (kĭlmā'ùm), suburb of Dublin, Co. Dublin, Ireland. Parnell was imprisoned here when he signed (1882) "Treaty of Kilmainham" with Gladstone.

Kilmer, Joyce, 1886–1918, American poet, a journalist. Wrote popular verse, the most familiar example being "Trees." Killed in World War I.

kilowatt: see WATT.

Kilpatrick, William Heard, 1871–, American philosopher. He was professor of the philosophy of education at Teachers Col., Columbia Univ., 1918–38.

Kilpatrick, Old or **West,** parish (pop. 55,641), Dumbartonshire, Scotland; one of the places claiming to be St. Patrick's birthplace.

Kilung, Formosa: see KEELUNG.

Kilwinning (kĭlwĭ'nĭng), burgh (pop. 6,553), Ayrshire, Scotland. Traditional birthplace of Freemasonry in Scotland. Has celebrated archery meets.

Kimball, (Sidney) Fiske, 1888–, American architect and writer. Specialized in restoration of old houses, notably Monticello, Va.

Kimberley, mining town and district (pop. 5,933), SE B.C., Canada, NW of Cranbrook. Has large silver, lead, and zinc mines. Here is Sullivan Mine.

Kimberley, city (pop. 52,576), Cape Prov., South Africa; founded 1871; diamond-cutting center. Its great diamond mines are controlled by a trust organized 1888 by Cecil Rhodes. In South African War it was besieged by Boer forces, Oct., 1899–Feb., 1900.

Kimhi (kĭm'hē) or **Kimchi** (kĭm'khē), family of Hebrew scholars and grammarians. **Joseph ben Isaac Kimhi,** 1105?–1170, introduced the long and short divisions of vowels. **Moses Kimhi,** d. 1190, son of Joseph, wrote *The Paths of Knowledge,* a grammatical textbook. **David Kimhi,** 1160?–1235, another son, wrote *Book of Completeness,* a Hebrew grammar.

Kimpton, Lawrence A(lpheus), 1910–, American educator, chancellor of Univ. of Chicago (1951–).

kin, group of people who have, or believe they have, a common ancestry, which is traced through either the male or female line or through both (see CLAN; GENS).

Kinabalu or **Kinibalu, Mount** (both: kĭ''nùbùlōō'), peak, 13,455 ft. high, British North Borneo; highest peak of Borneo.

Kincardineshire (kĭngkär'dĭnshĭr) or **Kincardine,** maritime county (379 sq. mi.; pop. 47,341), E Scotland; co. town Stonehaven. Has rocky coast and mountainous interior. Sheep grazing, fishing, and quarrying are main occupations; oats and barley chief crops. County sometimes called the Mearns (mârns). Dunnottar Castle located near Stonehaven.

Kinchinjunga: see KANCHENJUNGA.

kindergarten [Ger.,= garden of children], system of preschool education. FROEBEL designed (1837) system less formal than that of elementary schools. Children's creative play instincts are used to develop cooperation and application and to prepare them for school. In U.S. many public school systems include kindergartens.

Kinderhook (kĭn'–), village (pop. 853), SE N.Y., NE of Hudson; has House of History of Columbia Co. Historical Society. Martin Van Buren born and buried here; to S is Van Buren home, "Lindenwald."

Kindi or **Al-Kindi** (Abu Yusuf Yakub ibn Ishak Al-Kindi) (älkĭn'dē), 9th cent. Arabian philosopher. Sought to show harmony of views of Plato and Aristotle. Not accepted by orthodox Moslems, his ideas influenced medieval Christian scholars.

Kineo, Mount (kĭn'ēō), 1,806 ft. high, central Maine, on peninsula in Moosehead L. Summer resort.

King, Charles: see KING, RUFUS.

King, Clarence, 1842–1901, American geologist. He persuaded Congress to authorize 40th Parallel Survey (1867–72), of which he was chief geologist. He organized and served as first director of the U.S. Geological Survey (1879). His publications in geology were significant.

King, Ernest Joseph, 1878–, American admiral, commander in chief of U.S. fleet (1941–45). Made admiral of fleet ("five-star admiral") in 1944.

King, Grace Elizabeth, 1852–1932, American author. Her sketches of New Orleans life include *Monsieur Motte* (1888) and *Balcony Stories* (new ed., 1925).

King, Rufus, 1755–1827, American statesman. Delegate to Federal Constitutional Convention (1787). U.S. Senator from N.Y. (1789–96, 1813–25); minister to Great Britain (1796–1803, 1825–26). Supported Federalists. His son, **Charles King,** 1789–1867, was an editor and educator. During his presidency of Columbia Col., 1849–64, the school moved from Park Place to Madison Ave. and 49th St.

King, Thomas Starr, 1824–64, American Unitarian clergyman, lecturer, and author. Influential in keeping Calif. loyal to Union in Civil War. Wrote *The White Hills* (1860).

King, William Lyon Mackenzie, 1874–1950, Canadian statesman, prime minister for over 21 years; grandson of W. L. Mackenzie. Chosen leader of Liberal party in 1919. Served as prime minister 1921–30, except for brief interval in 1926, and again 1935–48.

Concluded with Pres. Roosevelt the Ogdensburg Agreement (1940) and Hyde Park Declaration (1941) by which Canada and U.S. agreed to create a permanent joint board of defense and to cooperate in production of defense materials.

kingbird, North American flycatcher. Eastern species, also called tyrant flycatcher and bee martin, eats some bees but chiefly noxious insects. It is dark gray above, light gray and white below with a white-banded black tail and an orange crest.

King Charles Land: see SPITSBERGEN.

king crab or **horseshoe crab,** marine athropod (*Limulus*) having a cephalothorax (fused head and thorax) covered by domed, horseshoe-shaped carapace, a triangular abdomen with carapace, and spinelike tail or telson. It has one pair of simple eyes, one of compound eyes, and six pairs of legs.

King Edward VII Land, peninsula, Antarctica, extending NW from Marie Byrd Land into Ross Sea. Discovered and named by Robert F. Scott 1902. Now generally called Edward VII Peninsula.

kingfisher, member of family of birds most abundant in Malayan region and on Pacific isls. but found on all continents. American kingfishers, chiefly fisheaters, live near lakes, ponds, or coast; usually they have large, crested heads, long, heavy bills, and short bodies and tails.

King George's War: see FRENCH AND INDIAN WARS.

Kinglake, Alexander William, 1809–91, English traveler and historian. *Eöthen* (1844), an account of his journey to the Far East, is a classic travel book.

Kingman, town (pop. 3,342), NW Ariz., SE of Hoover Dam and SW of Grand Canyon. Stock raising, mining.

King Philip's War: see PHILIP (King Philip).

King Ranch, S Texas, S and W of Corpus Christi, hq. at Kingsville. Covers c.1,000,000 acres in several divisions (Santa Gertrudis is home ranch). Has Santa Gertrudis cattle, a new breed; race horses; oil wells; and farming. Founded c.1853 by Richard King, ex-Rio Grande steamboat captain. Now managed by grandson Robert Kleberg. Divisions made 1935, but ranch still one of world's largest.

Kings, county, N.Y.: see BROOKLYN, borough.

Kings, river rising in the Sierra Nevada, E Calif., and flowing W and SW until it almost disappears in sands of San Joaquin Valley. Some of its waters reach Tulare L. Traverses Kings Canyon Natl. Park.

Kings, books of Old Testament, called 1 and 2 Kings in AV, 3 and 4 Kings in Western canon (1 and 2 SAMUEL called 1 and 2 Kings in Western canon). They narrate the history of the Hebrews from the death of David to the fall of Judah. Among notable events are the golden reign of Solomon and the building of the Temple; the division of the kingdom under Rehoboam into Israel (N) and Judah (S); the end of the notorious house of Ahab; and the inspiring careers of the prophets Elijah and Elisha.

Kings Bay, inlet, 16 mi. long, in NW coast of West Spitsbergen. It was base (1926) of successful polar flights by R. E. BYRD and AMUNDSEN.

Kings Canyon National Park: see NATIONAL PARKS AND MONUMENTS (table).

King's College: see CAMBRIDGE UNIVERSITY; COLUMBIA UNIVERSITY.

King's College, University of: see HALIFAX, N.S.

King's County, Ireland: see OFFALY.

Kingsford, city (pop. 5,038), W Upper Peninsula, N Mich., on Menominee R. and near Iron Mountain. Large Ford Motor Co. holdings here.

Kingsley, Charles, 1819–75, English clergyman and novelist. His views on Christian socialism were embodied in *Alton Locke* (1850). A controversy with J. H. NEWMAN led to Newman's *Apologia*. Kingsley is best known for *Westward Ho!* (1855), *Hereward the Wake* (1866), and *The Water-Babies* (1873).

King's Lynn, Lynn Regis (rē′jĭs), or **Lynn,** municipal borough (pop. 26,173), Norfolk, England. Once a major port, it dates from Saxon times.

Kings Mountain, town (pop. 7,206), SW N.C., near S.C. line; textile center. On ridge, just S of state line, British force was defeated (1780) in CAROLINA CAMPAIGN of American Revolution. Site marked by national military park (estab. 1931).

king snake, nonvenomous, egg-laying constrictor snake of North America. Common form of E U.S. is 3–5 ft. long, black or brown with yellow or white rings or bands forming chainlike pattern. It and related milk snake are useful destroyers of rodents.

Kings Park, village (pop. 10,960), SE N.Y., near N shore of Long Isl., E of Huntington, in agr. area.

Kings Peak: see UINTA MOUNTAINS.

Kings Point, residential village (pop. 2,445), SE N.Y., on NW Long Isl. near Great Neck. A U.S. merchant marine academy was estab. here in 1942.

Kingsport, city (pop. 19,571), NE Tenn., on Holston R. and NNW of Johnson City near Va. line. On site of old Wilderness Road fort (1761). Book printing; mfg. of book cloth, paper, chemicals, cement, and cellulose acetate yarn.

Kingston, city (pop. 33,459), S Ont., Canada, on N shore of L. Ontario, near head of St. Lawrence R. and at S end of Rideau Canal. Mfg. of locomotives, machinery, chemicals, and aluminum; grain elevators. Seat of Queen's Univ. (coed.; 1841) and Royal Military Col. Fort Frontenac (1673) important in French and Indian Wars. City founded 1784 by United Empire Loyalists. Used as naval base in War of 1812. Cap. of United Canada 1841–44.

Kingston, port (pop. 109,056), cap. and largest city of Jamaica, British West Indies; founded 1693; made cap., 1872.

Kingston. 1 City (pop. 28,817), SE N.Y., on W bank of the Hudson S of Albany; settled 1652 by Dutch. Grew as E terminus of Delaware and Hudson Canal. Clothing, textiles, refrigerators, and brick. Has senate house (1676; meeting place of first N.Y. state legislature) and museum. Ashokan Reservoir near. **2** Borough (pop. 21,096), NE Pa., on Susquehanna R. opposite Wilkes-Barre; settled 1769. Coal mining and mfg. of cigars, rayon, and nylon. Victory of British and Indians here 1788 prefaced the Wyoming Valley massacre. **3** See SOUTH KINGSTOWN, R.I.

Kingston-on-Thames (-tĕms), municipal borough (pop. 40,168), Surrey, England; residential suburb of London. Site of Saxon coronations and of last battle of civil war (1648). Has metalworking and mfg.

Kingston-upon-Hull, Yorkshire, England: see HULL.

Kingstown, port (pop. 14,766), cap. of SAINT VINCENT, British West Indies.

Kingsville, city (pop. 16,898), S Texas, S of Corpus Christi; settled 1902. Hq. of KING RANCH. Processes oil, farm produce, and chemicals. Seat of Texas Col. of Arts and Industries.

King William Island, S Franklin dist., Northwest Territories, Canada, in Arctic Ocean, an island of the ARCTIC ARCHIPELAGO. Discovered 1831 by Sir John Ross. Sir John Franklin and party were lost here 1847–48. Roald Amundsen's winter hq. 1903–4.

King William's War: see FRENCH AND INDIAN WARS.

Kinibalu, Mount: see KINABALU, MOUNT.

Kinnarodden: see NORTH CAPE, Norway.

Kino, Eusebio Francisco (ā-ōōsā′vyō fränsē′skō kē′nō), c.1644–1711, Jesuit missionary explorer in American Southwest, b. Segno, in the Tyrol.

Kinross-shire (kĭnrŏs′-shĭr), inland county (81 sq. mi.; pop. 7,418), Scotland; co. town Kinross. Level plain surrounded by hills. Agr. is chief occupation; there is some mfg. of woolens and linen.

Kinston, city (pop. 18,336), E N.C., on Neuse R. and NW of New Bern; founded 1762. Processes, trades, and markets tobacco, lumber, and cotton.

Kintyre (kĭntīr′) or **Cantire** (kăntīr′), peninsula, 42 mi. long and 10 mi. wide, Argyllshire, Scotland. S extremity is 13 mi. from N. Ireland.

Kioto, Japan: see KYOTO.

Kiowa (kī′ủwủ), city (pop. 1,561), S Kansas, SW of Wichita near Okla. line. Here in 1900 Carry Nation gained notoriety by wrecking a saloon.

Kiowa Indians (kī′ủwủ), North American tribe, occupying W Mont. in 17th cent., later ranging through the West. Language only one of Kiowan stock. Shared Plains area culture, but had several distinctive traits, including a pictographic calendar and the worship of a stone image. Allied with the Comanche, they waged many bloody wars against whites and Cheyenne, Sioux, Navaho, and Osage.

Kipchaks, Turkic people: see CUMANS.

Kipling, Rudyard, 1865–1936, English poet, novelist, and story writer, b. India. His many popular works include poems in *Departmental Ditties* (1886) and *Barrack-Room Ballads* (1892); stories in *Plain Tales from the Hills* and *Soldiers Three* (both 1888); novel *The Light That Failed* (1890); children's stories such as *The Jungle Book* (1894), *Captains Courageous* (1897), *Kim* (1901), and *Just So Stories* (1902). Familiar poems are "Mandalay," "Gunga Din," and *Recessional* (1897). He interpreted India,

the army, and British imperialism, and was England's first Nobel Prize winner in literature (1907).

Kirby, William, 1817–1906, Canadian author, b. England. His *Le Chien d'Or,* also published as *The Golden Dog* (1877), helped popularize historical novel in Canadian fiction.

Kirby-Smith, Edmund: see SMITH, EDMUND KIRBY.

Kircher, Athanasius (ätänä′zyōōs, kĭr′khŭr), 1601?–1680, German Jesuit archaeologist, mathematician, biologist, and physicist. He was possibly first to hold that disease and putrefaction were caused by presence of invisible living bodies. He also perfected the aeolian harp.

Kirchhoff, Gustav Robert (gōōs′täf rō′bĕrt kĭrkh′hôf), 1824–87, German physicist. With Bunsen he worked on spectroscope, discovered cesium and rubidium. He explained Fraunhofer lines in solar SPECTRUM.

Kirghiz Soviet Socialist Republic (kĭrgēz′) or **Kirghizia** (kĭrgē′zhŭ) or **Kirghizstan** (kĭrgē-stän′), constituent republic (c.76,000 sq. mi.; pop. c.1,500,000) of USSR, in central Asia, bordering on China (SE); cap. Frunze. Mountainous country in Tien Shan and Pamir systems, rising to 24,406 ft. in Pobeda Peak, with grazing in highland valleys. Crop production concentrated mainly in FERGANA VALLEY and Issyk Kul basin. Industry is based on mineral resources (e.g., mercury, antimony, uranium). The Kirghiz, a Moslem, Turko-Mongolian pastoral people, migrated here in 16th cent. They were formerly known as Kara Kirghiz to distinguish them from the Kazakhs (formerly called Kirghiz). With khanate of Kokand they passed to Russia in 1876.

Kirin: see MANCHURIA.

Kirjath-arba: see HEBRON.

Kirk, Grayson L(ouis), 1903–, American educator, president of Columbia Univ. (1953–). Was professor of government and of international relations.

Kirkaldy of Grange, Sir William (kûrkôl′dē), c.1520–1573, Scottish soldier and politician. Associated with brutal murder of Cardinal Beaton, he later became prominent Protestant leader to whom Mary Queen of Scots surrendered at Carberry in 1557.

Kirkcudbrightshire (kûrkōō′brēshĭr), maritime county (899 sq. mi.; pop. 30,742), SW Scotland; co. town Kirkcudbright. NW part is wild and hilly. Agr. is chief occupation; cattle grazing is important. Region is sometimes called East Galloway.

Kirke, Sir David, 1596–1654, French-born English merchant adventurer. Attacked the French in Canada and Nova Scotia; forced surrender of Quebec (1629). Became governor and colonizer (1638) of Newfoundland which the Commonwealth later took away from him because he was royalist.

Kirkland, Samuel, 1741–1808, American missionary to the Oneida Indians. Founded an academy which developed into Hamilton Col.

Kirkland Lake, town (pop. c.19,734), E Ont., Canada, N of Sudbury. Center of gold-mining region.

Kirksville, city (pop. 11,110), N Mo., N of

Moberly; founded c.1841. In a dairy, live-stock, poultry, and coal area, it also has mfg. of shoes.

Kirkuk (kĭrkōōk'), town (pop. 69,035), NE Iraq. Its great oil fields are linked by pipe line to Mediterranean ports of Tripoli and Haifa.

Kirkwall (kûrk'wôl, –wûl), burgh (pop. 4,376), cap. of Orkney Isls., Scotland. Has a good harbor and carries on trading, fishing, and boatbuilding.

Kirkwood, city (pop. 18,640), E Mo., W suburb of St. Louis; laid out 1852.

Kirov, Sergei Mironovich (sĭrgā' myĭrô'nûvĭch kē'rŭf), 1888–1934, Russian Communist leader, one of Stalin's closest aides. His assassination was officially laid to a Trotskyist conspiracy and led to treason trials and party purge of 1930s.

Kirov, formerly **Vyatka** (vyät'kŭ), city (pop. 143,181), E European RSFSR, on Vyatka R. Rail junction. Mfg. of machine tools; saw-milling, food processing. Used as place of political exile in 19th cent.

Kirovabad (kē"rùvŭbät'), city (pop. 98,743), W central Azerbaijan SSR. Formerly named Gandzha or Ganja, it was cap. of a khanate under Persian suzerainty until Russian conquest in 1804. Renamed 1935. Produces copper sulphate, cotton textiles, wine.

Kirsehir (kĕrshĕ'hĕr), town (pop. 14,168), central Turkey. Noted for carpet mfg.

Kiruna (kē'rünä), village (pop. 19,023), Norrbotten co., N Sweden. It is center of Lappland iron-mining dist. Ore, c.70% pure, is shipped to Baltic port of Lulea and Atlantic port of Narvik (Norway). Founded as model town after opening of mines. (c.1900).

Kisfaludy, Charles (kĭsh'fōlōōdē), 1788–1830, Hungarian dramatist, founder of the Hungarian national drama. *Tatars in Hungary* (1819), first of his many successes, was first genuinely dramatic Hungarian play. His brother, **Alexander Kisfaludy,** 1772–1844, founded the Hungarian school of lyric poetry.

Kish. 1 Father of Saul. 1 Sam. 9.1; 10.21. Cis: Acts 13.21. **2** Uncle of Saul. 1 Chron. 8.30; 9.36.

Kish, anc. city in the Euphrates valley, E of Babylon. Occupied from early times, it was in the 4th millennium B.C. a powerful Sumerian city.

Kishinev (kĭshēnyôf), Rumanian *Chisinau,* city (pop. c.102,000), cap. of Moldavian SSR. First mentioned c.1420, it was the cultural, spiritual, commercial and (after annexation by Russia, 1812) political center of BESSARABIA. Population was 40% Jewish until World War II.

Kishon, river of central Palestine, flowing NW through Esdraelon to the Mediterranean. On its banks Barak defeated Sisera, Elijah slew the prophets of Baal.

Kiska, island, c.20 mi. long, off W Alaska, in Rat Isls. group of ALEUTIAN ISLANDS, between Adak and Attu. Mountainous, rising to nearly 4,000 ft. in Kiska Volcano. Occupied and garrisoned 1942 by Japanese, it was cut off 1943 by recapture of Attu, and abandoned by Japanese, Aug., 1943. U.S. forces made it an air and naval base.

Kislovodsk (kēslùvôtsk'), city (pop. 51,289), S Stavropol Territory, RSFSR, in central Greater Caucasus; health resort.

Kissimmee, Lake, fresh-water lake, c.15 mi. long and 5 mi. wide, central Fla., N of L. Okeechobee.

Kitasato, Shibasaburo (shĭbä'säbōōrō kē'tä-sä'tō), 1852–1931, Japanese physician, authority on infectious diseases. Discovered, simultaneously with Yersin in 1894, bacterium causing PLAGUE.

Kit-Cat Club, London social and political club, active c.1700–1720. Organized by Whig supporters of the Hanoverian dynasty.

Kitchen Cabinet, popular name for group of intimate, unofficial advisers of Pres. Andrew Jackson. Administration policies were formed in its meetings. Members, all able journalists, included the elder Francis P. BLAIR, Duff GREEN, and Amos KENDALL. John H. Eaton of regular cabinet met with group; Martin Van Buren enjoyed its confidence.

Kitchener, Horatio Herbert Kitchener, 1st Earl, 1850–1916, British field marshal and statesman. As commander in chief of Egyptian army, he reconquered (1896–98) the Sudan and became its governor general. In SOUTH AFRICAN WAR he used fortified blockhouses and systematic denudation of farm lands to conquer the Boers (1900–1902). As secretary for war in World War I he expanded army from 20 to 70 divisions (1914–16). On voyage to confer with the tsar, he was drowned when his ship was sunk under mysterious circumstances.

Kitchener, city (pop. 44,867), S. Ont., Canada, in Grand R. valley W of Toronto. Important mfg. center with tanning and meat packing. Settled 1806 by Germans from Pa. Called Berlin to 1916.

kitchen midden, refuse heap left by a prehistoric community. Valuable in archaeological study.

kite, bird of prey allied to hawk and eagle and noted for flying grace. It eats mainly small reptiles and insects. In U.S. are found the swallow-tailed, white-tailed, Everglade, and Mississippi kites.

Kittanning (kĭtä'nĭng), borough (pop. 7,731), W Pa., on Allegheny R. and N of Pittsburgh. Coal mining and mfg. of clay and metal products.

Kittatinny Mountain (kĭtûtĭn'ē), ridge of Appalachian system, chiefly in extreme NW N.J. Extends SW from Shawangunk Mt., SE N.Y., to Blue Mt., E Pa. Rises to 1,801 ft. in High Point, highest summit in N.J., affording view of three states and surrounded by state park (c.10,900 acres), year-round forest recreational area. Delaware R. cuts ridge forming DELAWARE WATER GAP.

Kittery, town (pop. 8,380), including Kittery village (pop. 6,692), extreme SW Maine, at mouth of Piscataqua R. (bridged here) opposite PORTSMOUTH, N.H.; settled 1622; inc. 1647 as first town in Maine. John Paul Jones's *Ranger* (1777) and the Civil War vessel *Kearsarge* built here. U.S. Naval Base is on islands in river.

Kittredge, George Lyman, 1860–1941, American scholar; professor of English at Harvard 1896–1936. He was an authority on Chaucer,

Shakspere, the English language, balladry, and witchcraft.

Kitty Hawk, peninsula, NE N.C., E of Albemarle Sound. Scene of Wright brothers' glider and aircraft experiments (1900–1903). Kill Devil Hill Natl. Memorial commemorates first successful flight.

Kitzbühel (kĭts′bü″hŭl), town (pop. 7,282), Tyrol, W Austria. Winter resort and skiing center.

Kiushu, Japan: see KYUSHU.

kiva (kē′vŭ), underground ceremonial chamber of Pueblo Indians. Used, by men only, for secret ceremonies, lounging, and as a workshop for weaving.

Kiwanis International (kĭwä′nĭs), organization of business and professional men, founded 1915. Local clubs are active in business and civic affairs.

kiwi (kē′wē), flightless bird (*Apteryx*) of New Zealand. Its wings are vestigial and it walks with back hunched. Nocturnal in habit, it hunts worms, insects, and grubs largely by scent.

Kiyonaga (kyō′nägä), 1752?–1815, Japanese designer of woodcuts of Torii school, best known for cuts of beautiful women and of warriors.

Kizil Irmak (kĭ′zĭl ĭrmäk′), anc. *Halys*, river, 715 mi. long, rising in N central Turkey and flowing in a wide arc to the Black Sea.

Kizil Kum or **Kyzyl-Kum** (both: kēzēl′ kōōm′), desert, USSR, in central Asia, E of Aral Sea between Amu Darya and Syr Darya rivers.

Kladno (kläd′nô), city (pop. 19,166), central Bohemia, Czechoslovakia, in coal-mining dist. Iron and steel plants.

Klagenfurt (klä′gŭnfŏŏrt), city (pop. 62,792), cap. of Carinthia, S Austria, on Glan R., in mountain lake area. Episcopal see. Winter sports center.

Klaipeda: see MEMEL.

Klamath, river, c.270 mi. long, rising in Upper Klamath L., SW Oregon, and flowing SW into NW Calif. and across to the Pacific.

Klamath Falls (klă′mŭth), city (pop. 15,875), SW Oregon, on Upper Klamath L. near Calif. line; settled c.1866. Irrigation project (1900) and railroad (1909) aided growth. Lumbering, farming (potatoes, grain, alfalfa), and livestock center.

Klamath Indians, North American tribe, of Lutuamian linguistic stock, living in 19th cent. in SW Oregon. Got food by hunting, fishing, and root digging. They were friendly to the whites but hostile towards Indians of N Calif.

Klausenburg, Rumania: see CLUJ.

Klaypeda: see MEMEL.

Kléber, Jean Baptiste (zhä′ bäptēst′ klābĕr′), 1753–1800, French general. Left in command in Egypt after Bonaparte's return to France, he defeated the Turks at Heliopolis (1800). Was assassinated by Moslem fanatic.

Klebs, Edwin (klāps), 1834–1913, German-American pathologist, pioneer in study of infectious diseases.

Klee, Paul (poul′ klä′), 1879–1940, German expressionist painter, b. Switzerland. Taught at the Bauhaus. Works are notable for piquancy of design.

Klein, Felix (fä′lĭks klīn), 1849–1925, German mathematician, noted for work in geometry,

theory of functions, and program for unifying geometry by study of equivalence in transformation groups.

Kleist, Heinrich von (hīn′rīkh fŭn klīst′), 1777–1811, German poet. His unhappy life ended in suicide. His plays *Der zerbrochene Krug* [the broken jug] (1806), *Das Käthchen von Heilbronn* (1807), *Penthesilea* (1808), and *Der Prinz von Homburg* (1821) rank among the finest of the German theater, for their dramatic skill, emotional power, and bold poetry. He also wrote a remarkable short novel, *Michael Kohlhaas* (1808; Eng. tr., 1949).

Klenze, Leo von (lā′ō fŭn klĕn′tsŭ), 1784–1864, German architect. Built Glyptothek (Munich) and part of Hermitage (Leningrad).

Kleve, Germany: see CLEVES.

Klinger, Friedrich Maximilian von (frē′drīkh mäk″sēmē′lyän fŭn klĭng′ûr), 1752–1831, German dramatist. His play *Wirrwarr; oder, Sturm und Drang* [confusion; or, storm and stress] (1776) gave the *Sturm und Drang* period its name.

Klinger, Max (mäks′), 1857–1920, German sculptor, painter, and etcher.

Klondike (klŏn′dīk), region of Yukon territory, NW Canada, just E of Alaska border. Gold strike on Klondike Creek led to Klondike stampede of 1897–98. Thousands of prospectors rushed into area, numbering c.18,000 in 1898. Since that time gold production has declined.

Klopstock, Friedrich Gottlieb (frē′drīkh gôt′lēp klôp′shtôk), 1724–1803, German poet. His greatest work is the epic *Messias* (1748–83).

Klosterneuburg (klōs″tûrnoi′bŏŏrk), city (pop. 13,710), Lower Austria, on the Danube near Vienna. Its Augustinian monastery (consecrated 1163) has a noted library with many incunabula.

Kloster-Zeven, Convention of (klō′stûr-tsā′fŭn), 1757. Early in Seven Years War duke of Cumberland, defeated by French at Hastenbeck, capitulated at the former Benedictine abbey near Zeven (a small town NE of Bremen, Germany) and allowed the French to occupy Hanover. English government disavowed convention and dismissed Cumberland.

Knaus, Ludwig (lŏŏd′vĭkh knous′), 1829–1910, German genre painter, who used coloring in manner of Dutch masters. His paintings were often anecdotal.

Kneller, Sir Godfrey (nĕl′ûr), 1646–1723, English portrait painter, b. Germany. Succeeded Lely as court painter to Charles II. Many portraits are in Hampton Court.

Knickerbocker (nĭ′kûrbŏ″kûr), family name, which came to be used as a term for all early N.Y. Dutch and was immortalized by Washington Irving's pseudonym Diedrich Knickerbocker.

knight. 1 In ancient history, a noble of second class who in military service furnished own mount and equipment. In Rome knights (*equites*) ranked between senatorial class and citizens. **2** In medieval history, armed and mounted warrior belonging to nobility. With growth of FEUDALISM term applied to landholders as well as to nobility. Knighthood, in true meaning, was never hereditary but had to be earned. In late Middle Ages son of a noble served as page and as squire before being knighted. Knighthood was conferred by overlord with accolade (blow, usually with flat of sword, on neck or shoulder). Military tenure was subject to law of PRIMOGENITURE, leading to a class of landless knights. In Crusades these formed great military orders such as KNIGHTS TEMPLARS, KNIGHTS HOSPITALERS, and TEUTONIC KNIGHTS. Secular orders also grew up, e.g., orders of Garter and of Thistle in England, Order of the Golden Fleece in Burgundy. Title knight (Ger. *Ritter*, Fr. *chevalier*) was later used as noble title. In modern England knighthood is not title of nobility, but is conferred by king on commoners or nobles for civil or military achievements. Knight is addressed as Sir; a woman knighted, as Dame.

knighthood and chivalry. Ethical ideals of FEUDALISM found highest expression in 12th and 13th cent. They originated in France and Spain and spread over Continent and England. They were fusion of Christian and military ideals, with piety, bravery, loyalty, and honor as virtues. Chivalrous love glorified womanhood (finding supreme expression in cult of the Virgin) and rendered homage in noblest sense. Virtues were proved in battle and tournament. Medieval secular literature dealt primarily with knighthood and chivalry, with ARTHURIAN LEGEND and CHANSONS DE GESTE as patterns. ROMAN DE LA ROSE and work of CHRESTIEN DE TROYES also were influential. For lyric poetry of age of chivalry, see TROUBADOUR; TROUVÈRE; MINNESINGER.

Knights Hospitalers (hŏ'spĭtŭlŭrz), members of the military religious Order of the Hospital of St. John of Jerusalem, called also Knights of St. John and Knights of Jerusalem. The order grew out of a hospital estab. 11th cent. to care for pilgrims in Holy Land. Reconstituted as a military order, it soon grew in wealth and power, with subsidiary establishments (preceptories) all over Europe. Its knights, with their colleagues and rivals, the Templars, took part in all the military ventures of the Latin Kingdom and of the Crusaders. After the Saracens took Jerusalem (1187) the order moved to Acre, then (1291) to Cyprus. Their conquest of Rhodes (1310) and the material benefits derived from the dissolution of the Knights Templars marked the beginning of a period of increasing power. Dominating the Mediterranean, the Knights of Rhodes, as they were called, checked Moslem piracy but often turned to piracy themselves. Under Pierre d'Aubusson they heroically defended Rhodes against Mohammed II (1480), but they had to capitulate to Suleiman I in 1522. In 1530 Emperor Charles V gave them the island of MALTA, which became their fixed home. Under Jean de la Valette they defended Malta against the Turks, whose menace remained acute until the battle of Lepanto (1571). Thereafter the Knights of Malta carried on their charitable hospital work in relative peace until Napoleon seized Malta in 1798. Remnants of the order survived in Europe, and in 1879 the pope restored the office of grand master;

but, as reconstituted, the order bears little relation to the old Knights of Malta. The Hospitalers were called also Knights of the White Cross for the white cross worn on their black robes.

Knights of Columbus (K.C. or K. of C.), American Roman Catholic society for men, founded 1882, at New Haven, Conn.

Knights of Jerusalem: see KNIGHTS HOSPITALERS.

Knights of Labor, American labor organization, started 1869. Organized on an industrial basis, with women, colored workers, and employers welcomed. With the motto "an injury to one is the concern of all," it championed the 8-hour day and abolition of child labor. Reached its apex in 1886, under Terence V. Powderly, with a membership of 702,000. It collapsed from financial and factional difficulties.

Knights of Malta and **Knights of Rhodes:** see KNIGHTS HOSPITALERS.

Knights of Saint Crispin, union of shoemakers organized in 1867. At one time it was the largest trade union in the U.S. By 1878 it was defunct, many of its members having joined the Knights of Labor.

Knights of Saint John of Jerusalem: see KNIGHTS HOSPITALERS.

Knights of the Golden Circle, secret order of Southern sympathizers in North in Civil War. First "castle" estab. 1854 in Cincinnati. Active in Ky., Ind., Ohio, Ill., and Mo. Membership mostly Peace Democrats, opposed to war and increasing Federal power. In 1863 named Order of American Knights, in 1864 organized as Order of the Sons of Liberty; C. L. Vallandigham, leading Copperhead, was commander. Numbered over 200,000 in 1864; with mounting Union victories order soon dissolved.

Knights of the White Camellia: see KU KLUX KLAN.

Knights Templars, in medieval history, members of military religious order of Poor Knights of Christ, called also Knights of the Temple of Solomon. Like their rivals, KNIGHTS HOSPITALERS and TEUTONIC KNIGHTS, Templars formed in period of CRUSADES. Nucleus was band of nine knights headed by Hugh de Payens who united c.1118 for protection of pilgrims. Group increased, adopted Benedictine rule, and had quarters beside Solomon's Temple. They rapidly became one of most powerful bodies in Europe, and their dashing military exploits won great fame throughout Crusades. They held Acre till citadel fell in 1291, then retired to Cyprus. Through receipts of many gifts and lands they became wealthy, and were bankers of Europe. Their financial control aroused jealousy of Philip IV of France, who accused order of many crimes and abuses and persecuted it 1308–14. Last grand master, Jacques de Molay, was burned 1314, and order came to an end.

knitting, construction of fabric by using needles to interlock loops of yarn. In hand knitting, two needles are used to produce flat work; tubular shapes (e.g., hose) are made with several double-pointed needles or a single circular needle. Knitting machines produce fabric either in horizontal courses, as in hand knitting, or in vertical chains interlocked so as to produce run-resistant qualities.

Knobelsdorff, Georg Wenzeslaus von (knō′-būlsdôrf), 1699–1753, German architect, who designed Sans Souci (Potsdam) and State Opera House (Berlin).

Knossos: see CNOSSUS.

Know-Nothing movement, in U.S. history. During 1840s in Eastern cities where Roman Catholic immigrants especially had concentrated and been welcomed by Democrats, local nativistic societies formed to combat "foreign" influences and uphold "American" view. Native American party, stemming from American Republican party (formed in N.Y. in 1843), became a national party in 1845. In 1850s many secret orders grew up. All inquiries of supposed members were met with a statement to the effect that they knew nothing; hence members were called Know-Nothings. They sought to elect only native Americans to office and to estab. a 25-year residence qualification for citizenship. Allied with a Whig faction, Know-Nothings in 1854 swept Mass. and Del. polls. In 1855 they adopted name American party, yielded much of their secrecy. Slavery issue split them apart; Millard Fillmore, party candidate for President in 1856, polled small vote. Movement continued until 1860, mainly in Eastern cities and in border states among Southern Unionists.

Knox, Frank, 1874–1944, U.S. Secretary of the Navy (1940–44). Opposed to New Deal, he was appointed by Pres. F. D. Roosevelt to help create national unity in defense preparations.

Knox, Henry, 1750–1806, patriot general in American Revolution. Directed artillery in many battles. U.S. Secretary of War (1785–94).

Knox, John, 1505?–1572, Scottish religious reformer, founder of Scottish Presbyterianism. Originally a Catholic priest, he attached himself to George Wishart and became a Protestant. Preached (1549–54) in England, was a royal chaplain briefly, and helped revise second Book of Common Prayer. After accession of Mary I he went into exile on the Continent, chiefly at Geneva where he consulted with Calvin. Scottish Protestant nobles made their first covenant in 1557 (see SCOTLAND, CHURCH OF) and invited Knox's help against Mary of Guise. After a civil war (1559–60) the reformers forced withdrawal of the French and won their freedom and dominance of the new religion. Knox, as minister of Edinburgh, tried to abolish pope's authority and condemn creeds and practices of old church. He attacked the religion of Mary Queen of Scots. Her abdication led to estab. of Church of Scotland. His single-minded zeal made him the outstanding leader of the Scottish Reformation but closed his mind to tolerance.

Knox, Philander Chase, 1853–1921, U.S. cabinet officer. Attorney General (1901–4). Secretary of State (1909–13); protected financial interests abroad, policy attacked as "dollar diplomacy."

Knox, Fort [for Henry Knox], U.S. military reservation, 33,000 acres, N Ky., c.30 mi. SW of Louisville; estab. 1917 as training camp; used since 1936 to store bulk of nation's gold bullion.

Knox College, at Galesburg, Ill.; nonsectarian, coed.; chartered 1837, opened 1841 by Congregationalists and Presbyterians under G. W. Gale. Manual-labor college until 1857. In 1930 absorbed Lombard Col. (chartered 1851, opened 1852). Old Main Hall, where Lincoln debated with Douglas, was made national historic shrine 1936.

Knoxville. 1 City (pop. 7,625), S Iowa, SE of Des Moines, in farm and mine area. **2** City (pop. 124,769), E Tenn., on Tennessee R.; settled c.1786. Cap. of Territory South of the River Ohio (1792–96), twice state cap. (1796–1812, 1817–19). Loyal to Union in Civil War, held by Confederates until abandoned to Gen. A. E. Burnside's Federals, Sept., 1863. Subsequent siege by Longstreet (Nov.–Dec., 1863) failed. Livestock and tobacco market and industrial and commercial center for farm, marble, and mine area, it has mfg. of textiles, clothing, marble and wood products. Seat of Univ. of TENNESSEE. Near Norris Dam and Great Smoky Mts. Natl. Park. Has graves of John Sevier and William Blount, Blount Mansion (1792), and Chisholm Tavern (1791).

Knut: see CANUTE.

Knutson, Paul: see PAUL KNUTSON.

koala (kōä′lù), aboreal marsupial animal (genus *Phascolarctos*) of Australia. It is grayish, thickly furred, tailless, usually 2–2½ ft. high, and has a protuberant, curved, black nose, and large furry ears. Each foot has five toes with claws fitted for climbing and grasping. It often sleeps by day, and at night it eats leaves and shoots of certain eucalyptus trees. Mother carries single cub (c.¾ in. long at birth) in pouch for first six months; cub emerges, uses pouch two months more, and is carried in arms or on back until it is a year old. The koala is harmless and defenseless.

Kobe (kō′bä), city (pop. 607,079), S Honshu, Japan; major port on Osaka Bay. Industrial center (shipbuilding, sugar refining, mfg. of chemicals). Includes ancient port of Hyogo, opened 1868 to foreign trade. Seat of two universities, a nautical college, and several ancient Buddhist temples.

Koblenz, Germany: see COBLENZ.

Koch, Robert (rō′bĕrt kôkh′), 1843–1910, German bacteriologist. He developed techniques of bacteriological culture and discovered causative organisms of many infectious diseases including anthrax (1876), tuberculosis (1882), cholera (1884). Won 1905 Nobel Prize in Physiology and Medicine for developing tuberculin test for tuberculosis.

Kochanowski, Jan (yän kôkhänôf′skē), 1530–84, greatest Polish Renaissance poet. Of especial note is his Polish version of Psalms of David.

Kocher, Emil Theodor (ā′mēl tā′ōdōr kô′khùr), 1841–1917, Swiss surgeon. Won 1909 Nobel Prize in Physiology and Medicine for work on thyroid gland.

Kodaly, Zoltan (zôl′tän kô′dälē), 1882–, Hungarian composer. Worked with Bartok in collecting folk tunes and, like Bartok, has used them in his own compositions. Among his works are an opera, *Hary Janos;* the

Psalmus Hungaricus for chorus and orchestra; and the *Dances of Galanta* for orchestra.

Kodiak Island (kō'dēăk), 100 mi. long, 10–60 mi. wide, off S Alaska, on Shelikof Strait. Mountainous, heavily wooded in N and E; good pasturage in S for cattle, sheep. Kodiak bear is native here. Discovered 1764 by Stepan Glotov, it had first permanent Russian settlement in Alaska, planted by Grigori Shelekhov on Three Saints Bay 1784, moved to Kodiak village 1792. Center of fur trade until Aleksandr Baranov moved hq. to Sitka. Salmon fishing now chief occupation; Karluk R. famous for salmon run. U.S. navy estab. base at Womens Bay 1940.

Koestler, Arthur (kĕst'lŭr), 1905–, Hungarian-born author. Led adventurous life as newspaper correspondent; in England since 1941. An ex-radical, he found his chief theme in anti-Communism. Among his works are *Spanish Testament* (1937), *The Yogi and the Commissar* (1945), and novels *Darkness at Noon* (1941), *Thieves in the Night* (1946), and *The Age of Longing* (1951).

Koffka, Kurt, 1886–1941, American psychologist, b. Germany. A founder of GESTALT psychology, he taught at Cornell, Univ. of Wisconsin, Smith College (after 1928).

Koh-i-noor, name of a diamond associated through centuries of India's history with deeds of violence. In 1849 came into possession of the British and after being recut was placed among crown jewels.

kohlrabi (kōl'rä'bē), vegetable (*Brassica oleracea gongylodes* or *B. caulorapa*) with turnip-like edible swollen stems, closely allied to cabbage.

Kokand or **Khokand** (both: kōkänd'), city (pop. 84,665), Uzbek SSR, in Fergana Valley. Important city since 10th cent., it was cap. of Kokand khanate from 16th cent. until Russian conquest, 1876. Textile mfg. (silk and cotton).

Kokomo (kō'kůmō), city (pop. 38,672), N central Ind., N of Indianapolis; founded c.1843. Farm trade center. Elwood Haynes, inventor, tested first practical automobile here, 1894. Metal, glass, and food products.

Koko Nor (kōkō nōr'), Chinese *Tsing Hai,* salt lake (2,300 sq. mi.), NE Tsinghai prov., China.

Kokoschka, Oskar (ôs'kär kōkôsh'kä), 1886–, Austrian expressionistic painter and playwright, now living in England.

Koksoak, river, NE Que., Canada, formed by Kaniapiskau and Larch rivers SW of Fort Chimo. Flows 90 mi. NE and N to Ungava Bay.

Kokura (kōkōō'rä), city (pop. 168,119), N Kyushu, Japan; port on Inland Sea. Industrial center (steel, cotton textiles, porcelain, chemicals).

kola, tropical tree (*Cola acuminata*) native to Africa and grown in warm regions for seeds known as kola (or cola) nuts. They contain caffeine, oil, and a glucoside (kolanin). Native peoples chew the fresh nuts. Some nuts are exported for use in beverages and medicine.

Kola Peninsula (kō'lů), area c.50,000 sq. mi., N European RSFSR, an E extension of Scandinavian peninsula between Barents (N) and White seas. Rich mineral deposits. Rus-

sians live along coasts, Lapps inland. MUR-MANSK is chief city.

Kolar Gold Fields (kōlär'), city (pop. 133,-859), E Mysore, India; India's chief gold-mining center.

Kolbe, Georg (gā'ôrk kôl'bů), 1877–1947, German sculptor. Worked in Paris under Rodin.

Kolchak, Aleksandr Vasilyevich (ŭlyĭksän'dŭr vŭsē'lyŭvĭch kŭlchäk'), 1874–1920, Russian admiral and counterrevolutionist. Commanded Black Sea fleet in World War I. After October Revolution of 1917 he organized anti-Bolshevik government in Siberia, was recognized by Allies, and assumed dictatorship 1918. Successful at first; defeated 1919; retreated to Irkutsk and was captured and shot.

Kolding (kôl'dĭng), city (pop. 31,017), E Jutland, Denmark; a port on Kolding Fjord (inlet of Little Belt). Shipbuilding; machinery and dairy mfg.

Kolhapur (kōlůpōōr'), city (pop. 95,918), S Bombay, India. Was cap. of former princely state of Kolhapur, which merged 1949 with Bombay. Textile mfg.

Kolin, Czech *Kolín* (kô'lēn), city (pop. 19,-820), central Bohemia, Czechoslovakia, on the Elbe. Varied mfg. Scene of victory of Austrians under Daun over Frederick II of Prussia (1757).

Kollar, Jan, Czech *Kollár* (yän' kô'lär), 1793–1852, Slovak poet who wrote in Czech. His ardent pan-Slavism is reflected in his best-known poem, *The Daughter of Slava* (1821–24).

Kölliker, Albert von (äl'bĕrt fŭn kŭ'lĭkŭr), 1817–1905, Swiss anatomist and physiologist. His microscopic studies of animal tissues advanced development of embryology and histology.

Kollwitz, Käthe (Schmidt) (kä'tů shmĭt' kôl'-vĭts), 1867–1945, German lithographer, best known for her superb studies of poor people. Was ardent socialist and pacifist.

Kolmar, France: see COLMAR.

Köln, Germany: see COLOGNE.

Kolomna (kŭlôm'nů), city (pop. 75,139), central European RSFSR, on Moskva R., SE of Moscow. Mfg. of locomotives and rolling stock. Founded 1177, it passed 1301 to Moscow. It was important in defense of Moscow against Tatars until 16th cent.

Kolomyya (kŭlůmĭ'yů), Ger. *Kolomea,* Pol. *Kołomyja,* city (1931 pop. 33,385), W Ukraine, in Galicia, on Pruth R. Petroleum refining. Was important as Polish frontier city 15th–16th cent.; ruled by Austria 1772–1918; ceded by Poland to USSR 1945.

Kolozsvar, Rumania: see CLUJ.

Kolyma (kōlē'mů), river, c.1,500 mi. long, RSFSR, in NE Siberia. Flows N into Arctic Ocean. It is partially navigable June–Oct. There are rich gold mines along upper course. **Kolyma Range** (c.6,000 ft. high) parallels E shore.

Komandorski Islands (kŏmůndôr'skē), group (including Bering Island) off Kamchatka Peninsula, RSFSR, in SW Bering Sea. Foggy, composed of volcanic rock, and subject to frequent earthquakes, they are whaling and sealing base, populated mainly by Aleuts.

Komarno, Slovak *Komárno* (kô'märnô) or **Komarom,** Hung. *Komárom* (kô'märôm), city of Czechoslovakia and Hungary. Komarno (pop. 15,461), on left bank of the Danube, belongs to Slovakia; has machinery and textile mfg., flour mills. Komarom (pop. 8,876), on right (Hungarian) bank, has lumber and textile industries. There are port installations on both banks. Entire city belonged to Hungary until partition after World War I.

Komi Autonomous Soviet Socialist Republic (kō′mē), autonomous republic (156,200 sq. mi.; pop. c.450,000), NE European RSFSR, extending W from the N Urals; cap. Syktyvkar. Nearly half the area is permanently frozen. The sparse population is concentrated in S, where there is farming, lumbering, and stock raising. Coal mines in Pechora Basin. Inhabitants are mostly Komi, a Finnic people, closely related to Permyaks and formerly known as Zyrians.

Komsomolsk (kŭmsûmôlsk′), or **Komsomolsk-on-Amur**, city (pop. c.150,000), S Khabarovsk Territory, RSFSR, in E Siberia. Industrial center of Soviet Far East; steel and lumber mills, shipyards, aircraft plants, petroleum refineries. Founded 1932.

Kona (kō′nù), district, W Hawaii, T.H.; coffee belt of Hawaiian Isls. Among relics of ancient Hawaii is City of Refuge at Honaunau. First American missionaries landed at Kailua Bay in 1820.

Konev, Ivan Stepanovich (ēvän′ styĭpä′nùvĭch kô′nyĭf), 1897–, Russian field marshal in World War II. Took part in capture of Berlin.

Konia, Turkey: see KONYA.

Königgrätz: see HRADEC KRALOVE; SADOWA.

Königsberg (kû′nĭkhsbĕrk), since 1945 **Kaliningrad** (kŭlyē″nyĭngrät′), city (1939 pop. 372,-164), historic cap. of East Prussia; transferred to USSR in 1945 and inc. into RSFSR. It is an ice-free Baltic seaport and produces freight cars, machinery, processed foods. Founded 1255 as fortress of Teutonic Knights, it joined Hanseatic League 1340. Residence of dukes of Prussia 1525–1618; coronation city of kings of Prussia from 1701. Its university, founded 1544, reached greatest fame when Kant taught there; the building, like most of the city, was destroyed in World War II during a two-month siege by the Russians (1945). Kaliningrad, built up after war in NW section of Königsberg, has a Russian population.

Königshütte, Poland: see CHORZOW.

Königsmark, Countess Maria Aurora (märē′ä ourō′rä kû′nĭksmärk), 1666?–1728, Swedish noblewoman, mistress of Augustus II of Poland and Saxony. Their son Maurice became known as Marshal de SAXE.

Konoye, Fumimaro, Prince (fōō″mēmärō′ kōnoi′), 1891–1945, Japanese statesman. Of ancient Fujiwara family. Premier 1937–39, 1940–41. Forsook liberalism to advance Japanese aggression in China. Resigned 1941 when talks with U.S. failed; succeeded by Gen. Tojo. Suicide prevented trial as war criminal.

Konstanz, Germany: see CONSTANCE.

Konya or **Konia** (kôn′yä), city (pop. 64,509), S central Turkey. Center of rich agr. area; mfg. of carpets, textiles, leather goods. The ancient ICONIUM, it reached its peak after

becoming the seat of the powerful Seljuk sultanate of Iconium or Rum, in Asia Minor (11th cent.). After the Seljuks' defeat by allied Mongols and Armenians (late 13th cent.), the territory passed to the emirs of Karaman, then to the Ottoman Turks (15th cent.). Konya remained important as religious center of the whirling dervishes, whose order was founded here in 13th cent. It has kept several medieval mosques and its old city walls. In 1832 Egyptians under Ibrahim Pasha routed Turks at Konya.

Koo, (Vi Kuiyuin) Wellington (kōō′), 1887–, Chinese diplomat; educated at Columbia Univ. At various times minister of foreign affairs and prime minister. Ambassador to France (1932–41) and to Great Britain (1941–46). Chief Chinese delegate to San Francisco conference (1945) which founded UN. Ambassador to U.S. since 1946.

Koolau Range (kō′ùlou′), mountain chain, Oahu, T.H., rising to 3,105 ft. Cut by two scenic passes, Nuuanu Pali (c.1,200 ft. high) and Waimanalo Pali.

Kootenai (kōō′tĭnä), (in Canada, Kootenay), river, rising in SE B.C., Canada, and flowing into NW Mont., W into N Idaho, then N to Kootenay L. in B.C. Part of Columbia R. system.

Kootenai Indians, North American tribes, of distinct linguistic stock (the Kootenai), living in 18th cent. in N Mont., N Idaho, and SE British Columbia. Culture was essentially that of Plateau area till coming of horse changed their culture to that of the Plains.

Kootenay Lake, SE B.C., Canada, E of the Selkirk range, an expansion of Kootenay (in U.S., Kootenai) R. To E, on Alta. line, is **Kootenay National Park,** estab. 1920.

Kooweskoowe: see ROSS, JOHN.

Kopparberg, Swed. *Kopparbergs län* (kô′-pärbĕrùs lĕn′), county (11,648 sq. mi.; pop. 267,019), central Sweden, virtually identical with historical DALARNA prov.; cap. FALUN. Copper mines, from which name derives, are now exhausted, but rich iron mines are worked in Grangesberg dist. In S. There are iron, steel, and lumber mills. It includes Domnarvet metalworks.

Köprülü, family of grand viziers: see KUPRILI.

Korah (kō′rù), Levite leader (with Abiram and his brother Dathan) of revolt against Moses. Rebels ended by being consumed by fire and earthquake. Num. 16; 26.9–11; Deut. 11.6. Core: Jude 11.

Koran or **Quran** (kōrän′, –rän′) [Arabic,= reading], sacred book of Islam; after the Bible, the world's most influential book. Moslems consider it a series of revelations by God to Mohammed. Canonical text (in classical Arabic) estab. A.H. 30 (A.D. 651–52) under the Caliph Othman according to the 114 suras [chapters] of Zaid ibn Thabit, the Prophet's secretary. All variant texts were destroyed. Moslems memorize the Koran, consider all science a commentary on it.

Korbel, Mario (kôr′bùl), 1882–, American sculptor, b. Bohemia. Did fountains and dancing figures.

Korça or **Korçë,** Albania: see KORITSA.

Korcula (kôr′chōōlä), Ital. *Curzola*, Serbo-Croatian *Korčula,* Adriatic island, area 107 sq. mi., off Dalmatia, Yugoslavia. Chief town, Korcula (pop. 2,012), has fine medieval cathedral and fortifications.

Korea (kôrē′ů, ků–), Korean *Choson,* Jap. *Chosen,* country (85,228 sq. mi.; 1944 pop. 25,900,142), E Asia. Occupies a mountainous peninsula bounded on N by Yalu and Tumen rivers (forming borders of Manchuria and USSR), on W by Korea Bay, on S by Korea Strait and Yellow Sea, and on E by Sea of Japan. Has c.3,400 offshore islands. Principal mountain range extends along E coast, rising to 8,337 ft. at Mt. Kwanmo. Gold, iron, tungsten, and coal are chief mineral resources. There is valuable timberland. N Korea is largely industrial, while S Korea is predominantly agr. (crops include rice, barley, soybeans, and tobacco). Long coast line provides extensive fishing grounds. Religion of most Koreans is a mixture of Buddhism, Confucianism, and native shamanism; Christians are a small minority. Recorded history begins in 12th cent. B.C., when a Chinese scholar Ki-tze founded a colony at Pyongyang. In 7th cent. A.D. the native Silla kingdom, aided by China, estab. rule over all Korea. Country was occupied 1592–96 by the Japanese dictator HIDEYOSHI in his campaign to conquer China. It became a vassal state of China in early 17th cent. Long known as the Hermit Kingdom, Korea was forced to abandon isolationism by accepting a commercial treaty with Japan in 1876. Japan's victories in First CHINO-JAPANESE WAR (1894–95) and RUSSO-JAPANESE WAR (1904–5) led to annexation of Korea in 1910. In World War II, Korea was promised independence by U.S., Britain, and China at Cairo Conference (1943). At war's end, the country was divided into occupation zones—the Russians N and Americans S of 38th parallel. When cooperation between the two proved impossible, the division was formalized by establishment of two regimes, Republic of Korea in S (cap. Seoul) and People's Republic of Korea in N (cap. Pyongyang). After the election held in S Korea under UN supervision (1948), Syngman RHEE was elected first president by the parliament. By mid-1949 all occupation troops had been withdrawn. On June 25, 1950, N Korea invaded S Korea and was promptly declared an aggressor by UN Security Council (from which USSR was voluntarily absent). The swift advance of the invaders was stopped in Aug. by UN forces (under supreme command of Gen. MACARTHUR) who held a perimeter defense 50 mi. from Pusan on SE coast. A counterattack, featuring invasion of Inchon on Sept. 15, carried UN forces to Manchurian border, but entrance of Chinese Communists into the war in Nov. again turned the tide; UN troops were forced to retreat far below 38th parallel until early 1951 when UN forces began a counterattack, driving the enemy back of the 38th parallel. Truce talks, begun July, 1951, at Kaesong and continued in the fall at Panmunjom, were deadlocked by July, 1952, on the issue of prisoner exchange (the Communists rejecting UN proposal for voluntary repatriation). After Oct., 1952, when truce talks were indefinitely

postponed, fighting became heavier, with each side vying for control of strategic hills in central Korea. In 1953 the Communists abruptly agreed to Allied proposal for exchange of sick and wounded prisoners, which was begun on April 20, with the Allies returning 5,800 and the Communists 600; at the same time truce talks were resumed.

Korin (Korin Ogata) (kō′rēn), c.1655–1716, Japanese artist, renowned for his lacquer work.

Koritsa (kôrĭt′sů), Albanian *Korçë* or *Korça,* city (pop. 24,035), SE Albania. Commercial and agr. center of a fertile plain. Long claimed by Greeks, who occupied it in Balkan Wars and both world wars.

Kornilov, Lavr Georgyevich (lä′vůr gēyôr′-gyĭvĭch kůrnyē′lůf), 1870–1918, Russian general. Kerensky made him commander in chief after February Revolution of 1917 but dismissed him in Sept. He refused to accept his dismissal, was arrested, escaped after the Bolshevik Revolution, and led an army of counterrevolutionary volunteers in S Russia. Forced to fall back on the Kuban, he was killed in action and was succeeded by Denikin.

Korolenko, Vladimir Galaktionovich (vlŭdyē′-mĭr gŭlŭktyô′nůvĭch kůrůlyĕn′ků), 1853–1921, Russian author and liberal publicist. Best known for his short stories (many tr. into Eng.).

Koros, Hung. *Körös* (kû′rûsh), river of E Hungary, formed by three headstreams rising in Transylvania (Rumania) and flowing c.50 mi. W into the Theiss.

Kortrijk, Belgium: see COURTRAI.

Korzybski, Alfred (Habdank) (kôrzĭb′skē), 1879–1950, Polish-American scientist, b. Warsaw. Founded system of General Semantics. Wrote (1933) *Science and Sanity,* on distinction between words and objects.

Kos (kŏs, kôs), Latin *Cos,* Aegean island (111 sq. mi.; pop. 18,545), Greece, second largest of the DODECANESE, 2½ mi. off Asia Minor; chief city Kos (pop. 7,955). Important cultural center in Roman times; home of Hippocrates.

Kosciusko, Thaddeus (kŏ″sēů′skō), 1746–1817, Polish general. Fought for patriot cause in American Revolution. Champion of Polish independence, he led an unsuccessful rebellion against Russian and Prussian control (1794) and became one of the great heroes of Poland.

Kosciusko (kŏ″sēů′skō), city (pop. 6,753), central Miss., NE of Jackson, in dairy area.

Kosciusko, Mount (kŏzēŭ′skō), 7,305 ft. high, SE New South Wales, in Australian Alps; highest peak of Australia.

kosher [Heb.,= proper, i.e., fit for use], term applied to food which complies with the Jewish dietary laws. Kosher meat is the flesh of animals which chew the cud and have cloven hoofs; both meat and fowl must be slaughtered by a specially trained pious Jew and must be salted and soaked to remove all traces of blood. Kosher fish are those which have scales (mollusks and eels are forbidden). The laws forbid cooking and eating of milk with meat and also the use of the same kitchen or table utensil for handling both meat and milk. It is widely held that many of these laws stem from the health preservation measures of ancient Palestine.

Koshtan-Tau (kŭshtän″-tou′), peak, 16,880 ft. high, USSR, in central Greater Caucasus.

Kosice (kô′shĭtsä), Ger. *Kaschau*, Hung. *Kassa*, Slovak *Košice*, city (pop. 51,689), SE Slovakia, Czechoslovakia. Textile, machinery, food, and tobacco mfg. Episcopal see. Belonged to Hungary until 1918 and reverted to it 1938–45. Has fine residences of former Magyar nobility and 14th-cent. Gothic Cathedral of St. Elizabeth.

Kosovo, Yugoslavia: see Kossovo.

Kossak, Sophia (kô′säk), Pol. *Zofja Kossak-Szczucka*, 1890–, Polish author. Among her works in English translation are the historical novels *The Blaze* (1922), *The Leper King* (1937), and *Blessed Are the Meek* (1938).

Kossel, Albrecht (äl′brĕkht kô′sŭl), 1853–1927, German physiological chemist. Won 1910 Nobel Prize in Physiology and Medicine for work on proteins, cells, and cell nuclei.

Kossovo, Serbo-Croatian *Kosovo* (kô′sôvô), plain in SW Serbia, Yugoslavia. Scene of decisive Turkish victory over Serbs, Bulgarians, and allies (1389) and of another Turkish victory over Hungarians under Hunyadi (1448). Just before first battle of Kossovo, Sultan Murad I was stabbed to death by a Serb posing as deserter.

Kossuth, Louis (kŏsōōth′, Hung. kôsh′ōōt), Hung. *Kossuth Lajos*, 1802–94, Hungarian revolutionary hero. One of the principal figures in the Hungarian revolution of March, 1848, he was a liberal and an extreme nationalist. When Austria prepared to move against Hungary, Kossuth became head of the government of national defense; in April, 1849, he became president of the newly proclaimed Hungarian republic. He resigned in August, when Russian troops came to aid the Austrians, and spent the rest of his life in exile.

Koster, Laurens Janszoon (lou′rŭns yän′sōn kô′stŭr), c.1370–c.1440, Dutch sexton [*koster*], to whom some have attributed the use of movable type in printing prior to Gutenberg.

Kostroma (kŭstrŭmä′), city (pop. 121,205), central European RSFSR, on the Volga. Linen-milling center. Annexed to Moscow 1364. Michael Romanov was elected tsar here in 1613. Has Uspenski Cathedral (c.1250).

Kotelny Island or **Kotelnyy Island** (both: kōtĕl′nē), 100 mi. long, 60 mi. wide, largest of Anjou group of New Siberian Islands. Arctic observation post on NW coast.

Köthen (kû′tŭn), city (pop. 42,588), Saxony-Anhalt, E central Germany. Lignite mines; sugar mills; textile mfg. Until 1847 residence of dukes of Anhalt-Köthen. Formerly spelled Cöthen.

Kotka (kôt′kä), city (pop. 24,528), S Finland; a seaport on Gulf of Finland and at southern end of *Päijänne* waterway. Main Finnish paper, pulp, and timber export center.

Kotor (kô′tôr), Ital. *Cattaro*, town (pop. 5,402), Montenegro, SW Yugoslavia, on the bay of Kotor (Serbo-Croatian *Boka Kotorska*, Ital. *Bocche di Cattaro*), an inlet of the Adriatic. Was held by Venice from 15th cent. till 1797, when it passed to Aus-

tria. An important Austrian naval base, it passed to Yugoslavia in 1918. Has medieval fortifications; cathedral (built 9th cent., rebuilt 17th cent.).

Kotzebue, August von (ou′gŏ̄ost fŭn kôt′sŭbŏ̄o), 1761–1819, German playwright, author of many popular melodramas. After a stay in Russia he returned to Germany as paid agent of Alexander I. His assassination by a student led to suppression of German student organizations by Carlsbad Decrees. His son, **Otto von Kotzebue**, 1787–1846, Russian naval officer and explorer, commanded two voyages around world (1815–17, 1823–26). Discovered and explored Kotzebue Sound (1816).

Koussevitzky, Serge (sĕrzh′ kŏ̄osŭvĭt′skē), 1874–1951, Russian-American conductor. Began his career playing the double bass. Made his conducting debut in Berlin, 1908. Was conductor of the Boston Symphony Orchestra (1924–49); director of the Berkshire Symphonic Festivals after 1936.

Kovel (kō′vŭl), Pol. *Kowel*, city (1931 pop. 27,650), W Ukraine, in Volhynia. Agr. processing center. Passed to Russia from Poland 1795; reverted to Poland 1921; was ceded to USSR 1945.

Kovno, Lithuania: see Kaunas.

Kowel, Ukraine: see Kovel.

Kowloon: see Hong Kong.

Koyukuk (kûyŏ̄o′kŏ̄ok), river rising on S slope of Brooks Range, N Alaska, and flowing c.450 mi. SW to the Yukon near Koyukuk village. Partially explored by H. T. Allen 1855. Gold is mined at headwaters.

Kr, chemical symbol of the element Krypton.

Krafft-Ebing, Richard von (rĭkh′ärt fŭn kräft-ā′bĭng), 1840–1902, German physician and neurologist, authority on psychological aspect of mental disorders and their medicolegal relations.

Kraft or **Krafft, Adam** (both: ä′däm kräft′), c.1455–1509, German sculptor of Nuremberg. Most famous work was Tabernacle for Church of St. Lawrence, Nuremberg.

Krak (kräk) or **El Kerak** (ĕl kĕ′räk), town (pop. c.10,000), S central Jordan; trade center. As the ancient Kir Moab it was walled citadel of Moabites. Lordship of Krak and Montreal was one of chief baronies of Latin Kingdom of Jerusalem. In 1131 Knights Hospitalers built castle (called Krak des Chevaliers), which still stands. Taken 1188 by Saladin. Krak was seat of an archbishop from early Christian era until 1910, when Christians were expelled by Turks.

Krakatoa (kräkŭtō′ú), volcanic island, Indonesia, in Sunda Strait between Java and Sumatra. Its explosion in 1883 caused great destruction in surrounding area and scattered debris across Indian Ocean as far as Madagascar.

Krakow, Poland: see Cracow.

Kramer, Jack (John Albert Kramer), 1921–, American tennis player. Won (1946–47) national singles, British singles. As professional he won U.S. singles (1948), world singles (1949).

Kranach, Lucas: see Cranach, Lucas.

Krasicki, Ignacy (ĕgnä′tsĕ kräsĕts′kē), 1735–1801, Polish writer and archbishop. Noted for prose and verse satires (including

Monachomania, on monastic life), fables, and novels.

Krasinski, Sigismund (kräsē'nyúskē), Pol. *Zygmunt Krasiński*, 1812–59, Polish poet, an ardent Slavophile. His works include the dramatic poems *The Undivine Comedy* (1835; Eng. tr., 1875) and *Irodon* (1836; Eng. tr., 1927).

Krasnodar (krŭs"nŭdär'), city (pop. 203,946), SE European RSFSR, port on lower Kuban R. Rail hub and industrial center (oil refineries, machinery plants, steel foundries). Founded 1794 as Ekaterinodar (after Catherine II), it became hq. of Kuban Cossacks. Renamed 1920. German-held in World War II. It is cap. of **Krasnodar Territory,** administrative division (32,800 sq. mi.; pop. c.3,000,000), RSFSR, extending E from Sea of Azov and Black Sea into KUBAN Steppe, its main agr. region. Subtropical Black Sea littoral, with health resorts, produces citrus fruits, essential oils, tea, and wine. Rich oil fields at Maikop. N section was annexed to Russia 1783; Black Sea littoral ceded by Turkey 1829; the rest, CIRCASSIA, was annexed 1864.

Krasnoyarsk (krŭsnùyärsk'), city (pop. c.300,-000), RSFSR, in S central Siberia, on Yenisei R. and on Trans-Siberian RR. Transportation center, with machinery, lumber, and textile mills. Founded 1628. It is cap. of **Krasnoyarsk Territory,** administrative division (928,000 sq. mi.; pop. c.2,100,000), RSFSR, extending across Siberian steppe, forest, and tundra to Arctic Ocean. Includes TAIMYR PENINSULA. In arable S section dwells 94% of population (Russian, Turkic, Mongol peoples). Farther N are gold, coal, and graphite deposits. Organized 1934.

Krasnoye Selo (kräs'nŭyù syǐlô'), city (pop. over 10,000), RSFSR, SW of Leningrad. Peter III was murdered in a near-by palace in 1762. City was a summer resort for St. Petersburg society before 1917.

Kraszewski, Joseph Ignatius (kräshēf'skē), Pol. *Józef Ignacy Kraszewski*, 1812–87, Polish writer. Translated works include the historical romances *Memories of the Countess Cosel* and *Count Bruehl*, the romance *Iermola*, and the comedy *The Jew*.

Kravchinski, Sergei Mikhailovich: see STEPNIAK, S.

Krefeld (krä'fĕlt), city (pop. 170,482), North Rhine-Westphalia, NW Germany, on the Rhine and NW of Düsseldorf. Silk and rayon mfg. (estab. 18th cent. by Frederick II); mfg. of quality steel, machinery, dyes. About 70% destroyed in World War II. Formerly spelled Crefeld.

Kreisler, Fritz (krī'slûr), 1875–, Austrian-American violinist. Made his debut as a child prodigy. After studying medicine, then art, he returned to the violin and became world famous. His compositions include numerous short works for violin (e.g., *Liebesleid* and *Caprice Viennois*), and a few works that he originally played as being by old masters and later revealed to be his own.

Kremenchug (krĕmĭnchóōk'), city (pop. 89,-553), central Ukraine, on the Dnieper. Riverrail center, with machinery mfg. German-held in World War II.

Kremer, Gerhard: see MERCATOR, GERARDUS.

kremlin, Rus. *kreml,* citadel of several Russian cities, which served as administrative and religious center and offered protection against military attacks in Middle Ages. Among most famous kremlins are those of Astrakhan, Kazan, Moscow, Nizhni Novgorod, Novgorod, and Pskov. That of Moscow, known simply as the **Kremlin,** occupies historic core of the city. Triangular in shape, it contains such structures as Uspenski Cathedral (late 15th cent.), where tsars were crowned; Arkhangelski Cathedral (14th–17th cent.), with tsars' tombs; and 300-ft. bell tower of Ivan the Great, with golden cupola. The Grand Palace, built in 19th cent., was rebuilt under Soviet regime to house supreme council (parliament) of USSR. Other buildings are used as government offices and residences for some high officials.

Kremsier (krĕm'zēr), Czech *Kroměříž,* town (pop. 17,626), Moravia, Czechoslovakia, on Morava R. Here the Austrian constituent assembly or Reichstag, transferred from Vienna, wrote a federal constitution for the Hapsburg empire in 1848–49. Felix zu Schwarzenberg rejected the constitution and dissolved the assembly.

Krenek, Ernst (krĕ'nĕk), Czech *Křenek,* 1900–, Austrian-American composer. Well schooled in the traditions of the past, he is at the same time an innovator (e.g., he wrote a jazz opera, *Jonny spielt auf,* 1926). He adopted (1928) the 12-tone technique (see ATONALITY) originated by Arnold Schönberg and wrote an opera *Karl V* (1933) in it. He has also composed chamber, orchestral and choral music, and a piano concerto.

Kreuger, Ivar (ē'vär kroō'gùr), 1880–1932, Swedish financier. In 1913 he formed a match trust, which became an international financial agency. Speculation and fraud brought Kreuger some $500,000,000 (about half from U.S. creditors) but wrecked the trust. He died by suicide.

Kreutzer, Rodolphe (kroi'tsùr), 1766–1831, French composer and violinist. A prolific composer, he is best remembered for his 40 etudes for violin. Beethoven's Kreutzer Sonata is dedicated to him.

Kreymborg, Alfred (krām'bôrg), 1883–, American poet and anthologist, originally one of the imagists.

Krishna (krĭsh'nù), eighth avatar of the god Vishnu, very popular in Hinduism; one of the more joyful expressions of deity.

Krishnamurti, Jiddu (jī'dōō krĭsh"nùmōōr'tē), 1895–, Hindu religious leader. Mrs. Annie Besant met him in 1907, proclaimed him the incarnation of Maitreya, the world teacher. Toured England and America with her (1926–27), later repudiated her claims.

Kristiania, Norway: see OSLO.

Krivoi Rog (krēvoi' rôk'), city (pop. 197,621), S central Ukraine, on Ingulets R. Industrial center of iron-mining region with ore reserves of over 1,000,000,000 tons. In World War II Germans held city and destroyed most industrial installations.

Krk (kŭrk), Ital. *Veglia,* Adriatic island, area 165 sq. mi., Croatia, NW Yugoslavia, off Dalmatian coast. Chief town, Krk, has medieval walls, castle, and cathedral.

Krkonose: see RIESENGEBIRGE.

Krochmal, Nachman Kohen (näkh'män kō'hĕn krôkh'mäl), 1785–1840, Jewish historian, b. Galicia; a founder of modern Jewish scholarship and a leader of the Jewish enlightenment.

Kroeber, Alfred Louis, 1876–, American anthropologist. He taught at Univ. of Calif. (1901–1946) and is author of many works on cultural anthropology.

Krogh, August (ou'gōŏst krôkh), 1874–1949, Danish physiologist. Won 1920 Nobel Prize in Physiology and Medicine for work on regulation of capillary blood supply in muscle.

Kroll, Leon (krōl), 1884–, American painter, perhaps best known for his studies of women.

Kromeriz, Czechoslovakia: see KREMSIER.

Kronecker, Leopold (lā'ŏpôlt krō'nĕ"kŭr), 1823–91, German mathematician. He was a pioneer in the field of algebraic numbers and in formulating relationship between theory of numbers, theory of equations, and elliptic functions.

Kronstadt, Rumania: see BRASOV.

Kronstadt (krōn'stät), city (pop. c.50,000), RSFSR, on island of Gulf of Finland, near Leningrad; also spelled Cronstadt. Founded 1703 by Peter I as port and fortress; now base of Soviet Baltic fleet. Port lost commercial value after dredging of deep-sea canal to St. Petersburg (1875–93). Mutinies of naval garrison played a part in revolutions of 1905 and 1917. City defended Leningrad in World War II.

Kropotkin, Peter (krŏpŏt'kĭn), 1842–1921, Russian anarchist, a prince who became interested in the peasants and renounced his title. Escaped prison in Russia and, after a three-year imprisonment in France, lived thereafter in England. Returned to Russia after Revolution, despite his opposition to Bolshevism.

Krout, John Allen, 1896–, American historian, long a professor and dean at Columbia Univ. He has written texts and scholarly works. Became vice president and provost of Columbia in 1953.

Krüdener, Julie de (dù krü'dúnúr), 1764–1824, Russian pietist. Before her conversion she wrote a sentimental novel, *Valérie* (1804), which caused some scandal. Later she preached her mystic faith throughout Europe. Under her spell, Alexander I of Russia created the Holy Alliance (1815).

Kruger, Stephanus Johannes Paulus (krōō'gúr), 1825–1904, South African statesman, known as Paul Kruger or Oom Paul. Played important role in history of TRANSVAAL as pioneer, soldier, farmer, and politician. With Joubert and Pretorius he negotiated Pretoria agreement with the British (1881) restoring independence to the Boer state. As president (1883–1900) he implacably opposed the policies of Cecil Rhodes. After outbreak of SOUTH AFRICAN WAR he went to Europe on futile mission to win support for the Boers. Died in Switzerland.

Krugersdorp (krōō'gúrzdôrp), town (pop. 71,-885), S Transvaal prov., South Africa. Named for Paul Kruger. Gold-mining center.

Krupp (krōŏp), family of German armament manufacturers, settled in Essen since 16th cent. **Friedrich Krupp**, 1787–1826, began the modern concern with a steel plant; his son, **Alfred Krupp**, 1812–87, the "cannon king," specialized in armaments. Great financial expansion took place under his son, **Friedrich Albert (Fritz) Krupp**, 1854–1902; under the latter's son-in-law, **Gustav Krupp von Bohlen und Halbach**, 1870–1950, the Krupp works became the center for German rearmament after 1933. His son, **Alfred Krupp von Bohlen und Halbach**, 1907–, was sentenced to imprisonment for 12 years as a war criminal (1948).

Krusevac, Serbo-Croatian *Kruševac* (krōō'-shĕväts), town (pop. 14,104), Serbia, Yugoslavia, SE of Belgrade. Was a cap. of medieval Serbia.

Krusne Hory: see ERZGEBIRGE.

Krutch, Joseph Wood (krōōch), 1893–, American author, long a professor at Columbia Univ. Among his works are *The Modern Temper* (philosophical, 1929) and many books on drama and literature (e.g., *The American Drama since 1918*, 1939; *Samuel Johnson*, 1944).

Krylov, Ivan Andreyevich (ēvän' úndrā'úvĭch krĭlôf'), 1768–1844, Russian poet, celebrated for his fables.

kryolite: see CRYOLITE.

krypton (krĭp'tŏn), inert, colorless, odorless, tasteless, gaseous element (symbol = Kr; see also ELEMENT, table). It forms no known compounds.

Kuala Lumpur (kwä'lù lōŏm'pōŏr), town (pop. 175,961), SW Malaya; cap. of Selangor and of Federation of Malaya. Trade center.

Kuban (kōŏbän'), river, 584 mi. long, Georgian SSR and RSFSR, rising in the Greater Caucasus and flowing N, then W into Sea of Azov and Black Sea via two arms. Kuban Steppe, a major grain region, is on lower course. After Russian annexation of the khanate of Crimea (1783), of which the area was a part, Cossacks were settled here to protect it from Circassian mountaineers. Cossacks fought against Bolsheviks in 1917. Scene of heavy fighting in World War II.

Kubelik, Jan (kōō'bùlĭk), 1880–1940, Czech violin virtuoso. Made his debut in Vienna in 1898; first appeared in the U.S. in 1901.

Kublai Khan (kōō'blī kän'), 1215?–1294, Mongol emperor, founder of Yüan dynasty of China. In 1260 became khan of empire founded by his grandfather Jenghiz Khan. Defeated Sung dynasty of China in 1279. Failed in campaign to conquer Japan, SE Asia, and Indonesia. Fostered Chinese scholarship and arts; favored Buddhism but tolerated other religions. His cap. at Cambuluc was visited by Marco Polo.

Kuching (kōō'chĭng), city (pop. 37,949), on W Borneo; cap. of Sarawak. Ships sago flour and pepper.

Kuchuk Kainarji, Treaty of (kōŏchōŏk' kĭnär'jē), 1774, peace treaty between Russia and Turkey. Khanate of Crimea was declared independent, except for Kerch, which passed to Russia. Russia also gained right to intervene on behalf of the Moldavian and Walachian principalities (which, however, were restored to Turkish overlordship) and certain rights of representation on behalf of the sultan's Greek Orthodox subjects. The treaty prepared Russia's annexation of the

Crimea (1783) and marked Russian ascendancy over Turkey (see EASTERN QUESTION). It was signed at village of Kainardzha, now in Bulgaria; other spellings include Kutchuk and Kainardji.

Kudrun, Germanic heroine; see GUDRUN.

kudzu (kŏŏd′zŏō), perennial leguminous vine (*Pueraria thunbergiana*), native to Japan, with broad leaves and purple flowers. Of rapid growth, it is used in S U.S. as a ground cover and forage or cover crop.

Kuhn, Richard (rīkh′ärt kŏŏn′), 1900–, Austrian chemist. Won 1938 Nobel Prize for work on carotinoids, vitamins, isolation of riboflavin; Nazi decree prevented his acceptance of the award.

Kuhn, Walt (kūn), 1880–1949, American painter. Known for portrait studies of circus and back-stage types. Helped assemble the famed Armory Show.

Kuibyshev (kwē′bĭshĕf), formerly **Samara** (sŭmä′rä), city (pop. c.600,000), E European RSFSR, river port and rail center on the Volga. Mfg. of aircraft, locomotives, machinery, ball bearings, synthetic rubber, textiles; oil refining. Founded 1586 as Muscovite stronghold, it was attacked by Nogai Tatars in 1615 and Kalmucks in 1644; gates opened to Cossack rebels in 1670. Became chief grain center of the Volga. Seat of anti-Bolshevik government in 1918. Renamed 1935. In World War II central government was here.

Ku Klux Klan (kū klŭks″ klăn′, kŏŏ′), name of two distinct secret societies in U.S. history. **1** Original Ku Klux Klan was organized by ex-Confederates at Pulaski Tenn., in Dec., 1865, to oppose radical Republican RECONSTRUCTION, maintain "white supremacy." Absorbed many smaller groups as it spread. Its practices played upon fears and superstitions of the blacks. General organization of local Klans was effected in April, 1867; Gen. N. B. Forrest was made leader. Disbandment ordered in Jan., 1869; local organizations continued. Success in keeping Negroes from polls enabled ex-Confederates to gain political control in many states. Congressional legislation attempted to combat Klan (see FORCE BILL). In Lower South dominant group was more conservative Knights of the White Camellia. **2** Second Ku Klux Klan was founded in 1915; first meeting was held on Stone Mt., Ga. Added to "white supremacy" an intense nativism, anti-Catholicism, anti-Semitism. After 1920 it spread throughout North and South. Controlled politics in many communities. Texas, Okla., Ind., Oregon, Maine were particularly under its influence. Klan frequently took extra-legal measures, some of them extreme. Large membership of mid-1920s declined to estimated 30,000 by 1930. After World War II attempt at revival failed when state after state specifically barred the order. It still exists in incipient form in several Southern states, notably Ga.

Kulikovo, battle of (kŏŏlyĭkô′vŭ), 1380, fought near Don R., SE of Tula, with victory for Grand Duke Dmitri Donskoi of Moscow over the Golden Horde. It made Moscow the center of strengthened resistance to Mongol domination.

Kulm, Poland: see CHELMNO.

Kulmbach, Hans von (kŏŏm′bäkh), c.1476–1522, German painter and engraver; follower of Dürer.

Kulpmont, borough (pop. 5,199), E Pa., SE of Sunbury. Anthracite mining and mfg. of clothing.

Kulturkampf (kŏŏltŏŏr′kämpf″) [Ger.,= conflict of cultures], 1873–87, the conflict between the German government under Bismarck and the Roman Catholic Church. Bismarck saw in political Catholicism, as represented by the Center party (founded 1870), a threat to the unified German state. With a series of drastic laws he sought to intimidate the clergy and to break down the Catholic school system. His measures merely strengthened the Catholic party. In 1887, fearing the rise of socialism, Bismarck rescinded his anti-Catholic measures and reached a *modus vivendi* with Pope LEO XIII.

Kum, Qum, or **Qom** (all: kŏŏm), city (pop. 52,637), N central Iran, on Trans-Iranian RR; Shiite pilgrimage center.

Kumamoto (kŏŏmä′mōtō), city (pop. 245,841), W Kyushu, Japan; mfg. center. Seat of Kumamoto Medical Univ. Was important castle town in 16th cent.

Kumasi (kŏŏmä′sē), city (pop. 70,705), cap. of Ashanti, W Africa; second city of Gold Coast. Center of cacao trade.

Kumbakonam (kŏŏmbŭkô′nŭm), city (pop. 67,008), S Madras, India, on Cauvery R.; Brahmanic cultural center. Silk and cotton weaving, jewelry making. Name formerly spelled Combaconum.

kumquat (kŭm′kwŏt), ornamental evergreen shrub of genus *Fortunella,* native to China and closely related to the orange. It has sweet-scented white flowers and small, orange fruits which can be eaten fresh or in preserves.

Kun, Bela (bä′lŏ kŏŏn′), 1886–?, Hungarian communist. As head of coalition government of Communists and Social Democrats (1919) he set up dictatorship of the proletariat, raised Red Army, overran Slovakia. Forced out of Slovakia by Allies and defeated by Rumanian army of intervention, Kun fled abroad. According to unconfirmed rumor he died in a Russian prison after Communist party purges of 1930s.

Kunersdorf (kŏŏ′nŭrsdôrf″), village in E Brandenburg, where Frederick II of Prussia suffered a critical defeat by Austrians and Russians (1759).

Kungalv (kŭng′ĕlv″), Swed. *Kungälv,* city (pop. 3,632), SW Sweden, N of Goteborg and on the Kattegat. One of chief cities of medieval Norway, it was plundered 1135 by Wends, seized 1368 by Hansa merchants, and ceded 1612 to Sweden.

Kung Hsiang-hsi (kŏŏng shyäng′shē′), better known as **H. H. Kung,** 1881–, Chinese banker and political leader. Educated at Oberlin Col. and Yale Univ. Important in Kuomintang government since 1927. Married SOONG Ai-ling.

Kuniyoshi, Yasuo (yäsŏō-ō′ kŏŏn″ēyō′shē), 1892–, American painter, b. Japan. His decorative work is Oriental in spirit, Western in technique.

Kunlun (kŏŏn′lŏŏn′), mountain system of central Asia, between Himalayas and Tien Shan. Forms N boundary of Tibet, rises to 25,340 ft. on Tibet-Sinkiang border.

Kunming (koon′ming′), commercial city (pop. 300,297), cap. Yunnan prov., S China. In World War II it was vital supply point at E end of Burma Road.

Kuomintang (kwō′mĭntäng′), [Chinese,= national people's party]. Organized 1912 by SUN YAT-SEN with program calling for independent republic and moderate socialism. Suppressed 1913 by Yüan Shih-kai; set up unrecognized governments at Canton in 1918 and 1921. Reorganized 1922 with Russia's help. At party congress (1924) coalition including Communists adopted Sun's political principles. Its army under CHIANG KAI-SHEK advanced N from Canton to gain military control of country. Government established at Nanking received diplomatic recognition 1928; by 1930 all China under its control except for N regions held by Communists (purged in 1927). Until 1947 Kuomintang barred participation of minority parties in official Chinese government. Civil war (begun after World War II) forced Nationalists to take refuge on Formosa in 1950.

Kuopio (koo′ôpē̄o), city (pop. 33,305), central Finland, on L. Kallavesi, in principal forest region of Finland and at head of Saima lake system. Timber industries.

Kuprili (kūprē′lē), Turkish-Albanian family, many members of which served as grand viziers; also spelled Köprülü. It rose into prominence with **Mohammed Kuprili**, 1583–1661, grand vizier of Mohammed IV from 1656. Though an upstart and illiterate, he restored some of its former prestige to the Ottoman Empire, notably by reorganizing the fleet and by his conquest of Transylvania (1658). The power of the family ended with Abdullah Kuprili (d. 1735), acting vizier from 1723.

Kuprin, Aleksandr Ivanovich (ŭlyĭksän′dŭr ēvä′nŭvĭch koo′prĭn), 1870–1938, Russian author. His novels *The Duel* (1905) and *Yama: the Pit* (1909) are well known. The volumes *The River of Life* (1916) and *Sasha* (1920) include some of his best short stories.

Kura (koorä′), anc. *Cyrus*, river, 940 mi. long, chief river of Georgian and Azerbaijan republics, in Transcaucasia. From Turkish Armenia it flows NE, then SE to Caspian Sea. Lower course irrigates cotton-growing plain.

Kurdistan (kûr′dĭstän″, koordĭstän′), extensive plateau and mountainous region, c.74,000 sq. mi., inhabited by Kurds or Carduchis, and occupying parts of E Turkey, Soviet Armenia, NE Iraq, and NW Iran. Ethnically related to the Persians, the Kurds are a nomadic pastoral people of c.2,500,000; their leading industry is carpet mfg. Majority are fanatic Sunnite Moslems. A warlike people, the Kurds have struggled for centuries for autonomy from Ottoman rule, and at the Paris Peace Conference (1919) reaffirmed claims to independence. The Treaty of Sèvres (1921) provided for a free Kurdish state, but the amending Treaty of Lausanne (1923) failed to mention Kurdistan. Kurdish revolts in Turkey (1925, 1930) and in Iran (1946) were suppressed.

Kurds: see KURDISTAN.

Kure (koo′rä), city (pop. 185,740), SW Honshu, Japan, on Hiroshima Bay. Major naval base and port.

Kure Island (koo′rä), formerly **Ocean Island**, atoll in NW part of Hawaiian group. Annexed 1886 by Hawaii; under U.S. navy since 1936.

Kurhessen, Germany: see HESSE.

Kurile Islands (koo′rĭl), island chain (5,700 sq. mi.; pop. 17,549), RSFSR, in N Pacific, between Kamchatka and Hokkaido. Comprises 50 islands, mainly volcanic. Sulphur mining, hunting, and fishing. Became Japanese possession 1875; annexed 1945 by USSR in accordance with Yalta agreement.

Kurisches Haff (koo′rĭshús häf′), coastal lagoon, 56 mi. long, Lithuania and former East Prussia. Separated from Baltic Sea by Kurische Nehrung, a thin sandspit which leaves only a narrow opening at the Memel channel in the N. The Niemen empties into the Kurisches Haff.

Kurland: see COURLAND.

Kuropatkin, Aleksey Nikolayevich (ŭlyĭksyä′ nyĭkûlī′ŭvĭch koorŭpät′kĭn), 1848–1925, Russian general. Took part in Skobelev's 500-mile march from Tashkent to Geok-Tepe (1881). As minister of war from 1898 he opposed the policy leading to Russo-Japanese War of 1904–5, but after its outbreak he took command in Manchuria. Though blameless in the Russian defeat at Mukden, he resigned.

Kuroshio: see JAPAN CURRENT.

Kursk (koorsk), city (pop. 119,972), S central European RSFSR. Rail junction and mfg. center (esp. machinery). Seat of a principality in 11th cent., it was destroyed 1238 by Mongols and not rebuilt until 1586. Scene of heavy fighting in World War II.

Kurusu, Saburo (sä″boorō′ koorōō′sù), 1888–, Japanese diplomat. Signed Berlin Pact Sept., 1940. Special envoy to U.S. in 1941 for negotiations cut short by Japanese attack on Pearl Harbor.

Kuskokwim (kŭs′kōkwĭm), river rising on NW slopes of Alaska Range, W Alaska, and flowing SW to Kuskokwim Bay of Bering Sea. Mining in upper reaches.

Küssnacht (küs′näkht), village, Schwyz canton, Switzerland, on L. of Lucerne. A chapel commemorates legendary shooting of Gessler by William Tell.

Kutais (kootū̃es′) or **Kutaisi**, city (pop. 81,-479), W Georgian SSR, on Rion R. Mfg. of machinery, chemicals, textiles. Founded in 6th cent. B.C., it was cap. of ancient Imeritia. Taken by Russia in 1804.

Kutch or **Cutch** (kŭch), state (exclusive of the Rann 8,461 sq. mi.; pop. 567,825), W India; cap. Bhuj. Mostly barren. Rann of Kutch is salt waste (9,000 sq. mi.), mainly in N, bounded W by Arabian Sea.

Kutchuk Kainardji or **Kutchuk Kainarji, Treaty of:** see KUCHUK KAINARJI, TREATY OF.

Kut-el-Amara (koot′-ĕl″-ŭmä′rù), town, Iraq, on the Tigris and c.100 mi. S of Baghdad; scene of bitter fighting in World War I. It was taken 1915 by the British under Gen. Charles Townshend, who after his failure to take Baghdad retreated to his base and withstood a five-month siege by superior

Turkish forces before surrendering (1915–16). British recovered town in 1917. Construction of a dam across Tigris was completed 1939.

Kutna Hora, Czech *Kutná Hora* (kōōt'nä hô'rä), city (pop. 12,119), central Bohemia, Czechoslovakia. Its silver mines largely created power of medieval kings of Bohemia. After its capture by Zizka in Hussite Wars, city was for two centuries the center of Bohemian Protestantism. Its rich medieval architecture includes two Gothic churches (14th cent.) and "Italian Court," a castle once used both as a mint and as a royal residence (begun 12th cent.).

Kutuzov, Mikhail Ilarionovich (mēkhŭyēl' ēlŭryôn'ŭvĭch kōōtōō'zŭf), 1745–1813, Russian field marshal. Fought brilliantly in Russo-Turkish Wars, replaced Barclay de Tolly as commander in chief against Napoleon (1812), and fought bloody battle of BORODINO but then resumed Barclay's Fabian tactics. Pursued *Grande Armée* into Germany and was created prince of Smolensk shortly before his death.

Kuwait (kōōwīt', –wät'), independent state (c.6,000 sq. mi.; pop. c.170,000), Arabia, near head of Persian Gulf; British protectorate. Mainly desert. Major producer of oil.

Kuyp, family of Dutch painters: see CUYP.

Kuznetsk Basin (kōōznyĕtsk'), abbreviation **Kuzbas,** richest coal basin of USSR, area c.10,000 sq. mi., RSFSR, in S central Siberia, between Kuznetsk Ala-Tau (E) and Salair Ridge. Vast reserves are of high quality and great variety. Mining centers are Anzhero-Sudzhensk, Kemerovo, and Leninsk-Kuznetski. New metallurgical industry is centered at Stalinsk.

Kwajalein (kwä'jûlān), atoll (pop. 832), central Pacific, largest of Marshall Isls. District headquarters of U.S. Trust Territory of the Pacific Isls. Captured 1944 by U.S. forces.

Kwakiutl Indians (kwä'kēōō''tŭl), Indian tribes of Wakashan linguistic stock, on N Vancouver Isl. and adjacent mainland of Canada. Their culture was typical of Pacific Northwest Coast.

Kwangchowan, China: see CHANKIANG.

Kwang Hsü (gwäng' shü'), 1872–1908, emperor of China (1875–98). Enthroned by his aunt, dowager empress and regent Tz'u Hsi; began personal rule 1889. Forced by her to abdicate because he favored reforms.

Kwangsi (gwäng'shē'), province (85,000 sq. mi.; pop. 15,000,000), S China; cap. Kweilin. Bounded SW by Viet Nam. Mainly a tableland, dissected by headstreams of West R. Exports cassia and camphor.

Kwangtung (gwäng'dōōng'), province (85,000 sq. mi.; pop. 32,000,000), S China, on South China Sea; cap. Canton. Includes HAINAN isl. On its coast are foreign enclaves of MACAO and HONG KONG. Mainland Kwangtung touches in extreme W on Viet Nam. Has tropical monsoon climate with high humidity. Largely mountainous; agr. restricted to river valleys and delta lowlands, notably Canton R. delta. Silk is leading export. Mineral resources include tungsten, manganese, coal, and iron. Bulk of population formed by Cantonese. Kwangtung was scene of early activity of Kuomintang party.

Kwantung Territory, China: see LIAOTUNG.

Kweichow (gwā'jō'), province (65,000 sq. mi.; pop. 11,000,000), SW China; cap. Kweiyang. Mainly a high plateau with many deep river valleys, notably that of the Wu. Produces grains, beans, lacquer, and timber.

Kweilin (gwā'lĭn'), commercial city (pop. 130,-790), cap. Kwangsi prov., S China, on Kwei R. Cotton mills. Seat of a university.

Kyd or **Kid, Thomas,** 1558–94, English dramatist, exponent of "tragedy of blood." His best-known work is *Spanish Tragedy* (1592).

Kyffhäuser (kĭf'hoizŭr), forested mountain, c.1,550 ft. high, N Thuringia, central Germany. It is crowned by the ruined castles of Rothenburg and Kyffhausen and by a huge, atrocious monument to Emperor William I. A legend, originally applied to Emperor Frederick II, has been later transferred to Emperor Frederick I (Barbarossa), who is said to be waiting in a cave of the mountain for the right time to return and restore German greatness.

Kyosai, Shofu (shô'fōō kyō'sī), 1831–89, Japanese painter, illustrator, and cartoonist.

Kyoto or **Kioto** (kyō'tō), city (pop. 999,660), S Honshu, Japan; chief cultural center of Japan. Seat of Kyoto Imperial Univ., Doshisha Univ., and many ancient Buddhist temples. Long known for hand-crafted products (cloisonné, bronzes; damascene work, porcelain, lacquer ware, fabrics). Founded 8th cent. Was cap. of Japan from 794 to 1868, when it was succeeded by Tokyo. In World War II it was the only major Japanese city to escape bombing.

Kyrie eleison (kē'rēā älā'ēsōn) [Gr.,= Lord, have mercy], in Roman Catholic Church, prayer of the Mass, following introit, the only part of the ordinary (section that does not change with the day) said in Greek. There are many notable musical settings.

Kyushu or **Kiushiu** (kyōō'shōō), island (c.13,-770 sq. mi.; pop. 11,398,976), S Japan; third largest, southernmost, and most densely populated of four major islands of Japan. Connected with Honshu (just N) by tunnel under Shimonoseki Strait. Mountainous with many hot springs. In N is Japan's chief coal field. Mild climate favors agr. (rice, tobacco, oranges). Chief ports are Nagasaki, Moji, Kagoshima, and Sasebo.

Kyzyl-Kum, Uzbek SSR: see KIZIL KUM.

THE
PACIFIC WORLD
orthographic projection
centered at 170° East and 35° North

SCALE at center, along the circumference, and on any concentric circle:

830 miles or 1340 kilometers.
Drawn for the Columbia-Viking Desk
Encyclopedia by Richard Edes Harrison
1953

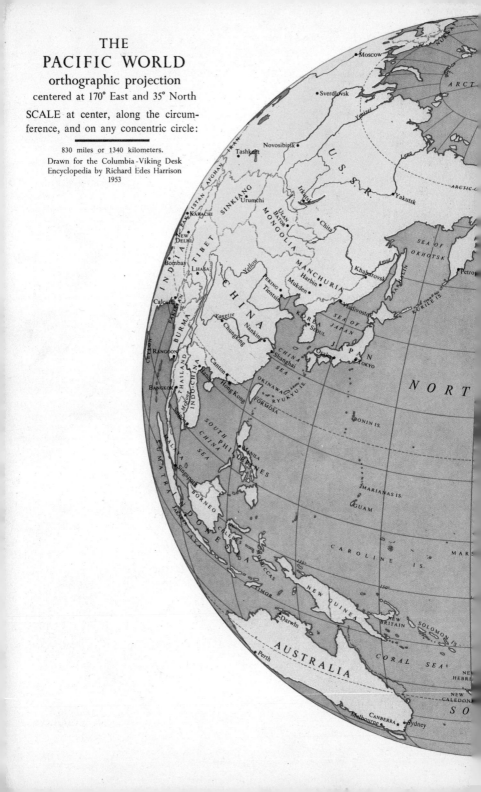